Table of Contents

locates rapidly specific topics within each subject area.

Comprehensive Index

gives ready references to the information in Volumes 1 through 4.

For Further Reference

identifies useful books for those who wish to read more about a subject.

For further reference

Adams, W. Royce
 Increasing Reading Speed
 Macmillan
Agardy, Franklin J.
 How to Read Faster and Better
 Simon & Schuster
Berger, Gilda
 Learning Disabilities and Handicaps
 Watts
Cohn, Marvin
 Helping Your Teen-age Student: What Parents Can Do to Improve Reading and Study Skills
 Dutton & Co.

Ervin, Jane
 Your Child Can Read and You Can Help
 Doubleday
Lewis, Norman
 How to Read Better and Faster
 Harper & Row
Miller, William M.
 Reading Faster and Understanding More
 Little, Brown
Osman, Betty B.
 Learning Disabilities: A Family Affair
 Random House

Student Handbook

with

Roget's University Thesaurus

Volume **3**

Student Handbook

with

Roget's University Thesaurus

Volume **3**

THE SOUTHWESTERN COMPANY
Nashville, Tennessee

Preface

This volume of the *Student Handbook with Roget's University Thesaurus* is the most practical reference book ever designed for use by the American family. All members of the family—students looking ahead to advanced schooling or that important first job, those out of school and wanting to advance their careers, parents concerned with the organization and management of their lives, senior citizens wishing to remain active—will discover essential information about increasing their enjoyment from life by becoming healthier, wealthier, and wiser. *Student Handbook,* Volume 3, covers in a single volume subjects that ordinarily require an entire shelf of books. Thus, it is an indispensable home reference book to be kept next to the other, more specialized books you may already have: cookbooks, telephone books, the Bible, etc.

Though this *Student Handbook* is completely independent and can be consulted separately, it is expressly designed to be the third volume in the well-known and popular *Student Handbook* set. The *Student Handbooks* are intended to help students improve at school. They assemble in an easy-to-learn way the many subjects taught in elementary, junior high, and high schools.

Volume 3, on the other hand, offers help to the whole family in its everyday activities. It is especially useful for those who are looking for a job or who want to move ahead in their careers, and for those who are retired and want new ways to make life more interesting and productive. Thus, Volume 3 is a lifelong resource. It will be as useful to you decades from now as it will be the first time you consult it.

This volume is in two major parts: PART ONE covers all practical aspects of home management, such as finances, health, and the law; and all aspects of career advancement, such as computers, letter writing, memory improvement, speaking, and writing. If published separately, each of these topics would be a book in itself.

PART TWO is a world-famous thesaurus, a treasury of words that will help you find exactly the right one to express your every thought.

The 15 sections of PART ONE are:

1. *Understanding Computers*—You too can be knowledgeable about computers.
2. *Advancing Your Career*—How to get a job, get along in your job, change careers, or start your own business.
3. *Health and Fitness*—How to eat well and stay healthy, with good advice for every family member, even senior citizens.
4. *You and Modern Medicine*—What to do when you are sick; how to choose a doctor; generic drugs; your hospital stay; medical payments.
5. *Managing the Family's Money*—Credit, banking, investment, shopping, vacationing, retirement, money-saving ideas.
6. *You and the Law*—Wills and estates, consumers' rights, criminal law, finding a lawyer.
7. *Improving Your Memory*—A tested and successful way to learn how to remember anything: names, numbers, essential facts, school subjects, on-the-job information.
8. *Building Your Vocabulary*—How to learn new words and their meanings; 15 days to a more forceful vocabulary; vocabulary tests; words you should know.
9. *Improving Your Speech*—How to say what you want clearly and effectively; public speaking made easy; Robert's Rules of Order.
10. *Writing Effective Letters*—Social letters, business letters, hard-to-write letters, postal information, scores of examples for every need.
11. *Improving Your Reading*—How to read better and faster; learning to read special kinds of texts; reading lists.

12. *Taking Major Tests*—How to prepare for such tests as the Scholastic Assessment Tests (SAT's), American College Testing (ACT's), and Graduate Record Examinations (GRE's); and sample questions from those all-important General Educational Development Tests (GED's).

13. *Review of French Grammar*—Parts of speech, rules governing their use, verb tables, sample sentences, important expressions and useful information for travelers, as well as a concise French-English dictionary and English-French dictionary.

14. *Review of German Grammar*—Parts of speech, rules governing their use, verb tables, sample sentences, important expressions and useful information for travelers, as well as a concise German-English dictionary and English-German dictionary.

15. *Review of Spanish Grammar*—Parts of speech, rules governing their use, verb tables, sample sentences, important expressions and useful information for travelers, as well as a concise Spanish-English dictionary and English-Spanish dictionary.

PART TWO is the complete, newly revised publication of the famous *Roget's University Thesaurus*, printed here for the first time in two colors to make it easier and quicker to use. This thesaurus, though it has been modernized, is based on the family word book devised over a hundred years ago by Peter Mark Roget. It has proven so useful that it has been in print continuously ever since. Your family will find it helpful in writing letters, student papers, and reports.

Note that each section of this volume begins with its own table of contents, including page numbers, so that you can turn immediately to the particular subject that interests you most. Each section offers charts, checklists, and boxes of special information that you will use again and again. Learn how the famous *Roget's University Thesaurus* will help you find the word you need and assist you in building your vocabulary, simply and quickly. Are you intimidated by the world of computers? Have a look at the very first section for an introduction to these marvelous machines that every member of your family can use with ease. Learn about the Internet, the World Wide Web, information utilities, and E-mail. Are you interested in brushing up on your French, German, or Spanish language skills? The sections on these languages have been revised to include the latest information for travelers to countries using those languages. Note, finally, that there is a general index that gives you quick access to every topic in the book.

We are certain you will find the *Student Handbook*, Volume 3, of lasting value for the whole family.

—*Gorton Carruth, Editor-in-Chief*

Part I
Student Handbook

Health and fitness 58

You and Modern Medicine 78

Part 2
Roget's
University
Thesaurus

Editorial development of the Student Handbook was directed by
The Hudson Group, Inc., Pleasantville, New York 10570

Administrative editor:	Eugene Ehrlich
Editor-in-chief:	Gorton Carruth
Managing editor:	Hayden Carruth
Administrative assistant:	Nicole Grandjean
Copy-editing and indexing:	Felice Levy/AEIOU, Inc.
Contributors:	Renni Browne/The Editorial Department
	Frances E. Barth, Else Behrendt, Marietta Burrowes,
	Delia Bye, Gisele Carruth, Karl Friese,
	John Harrington, Sylvia Helm, Lawrence Heyl, Jr.,
	Helene Isaac, Naomi Katz, Seymour Levine,
	John Maloney, Antje L. Munroe, Elizabeth Rich,
	Jenny Tesar, Bruce Wetterau
Special advisor:	"Improving Your Memory," Harry Lorayne
Design and art direction:	Pam Forde Graphics
Production:	Rachelle Engelman
Illustration and maps:	Ric Del Rossi/Mulvey Associates
	Leslie Dunlap/Publishers' Graphics, Inc.
	Kathie Kelleher/Publishers' Graphics, Inc.
	Joel Snyder/Publishers' Graphics, Inc.
Photo researchers:	Carousel Research

Student Handbook

with

Roget's University Thesaurus

Volume **3**

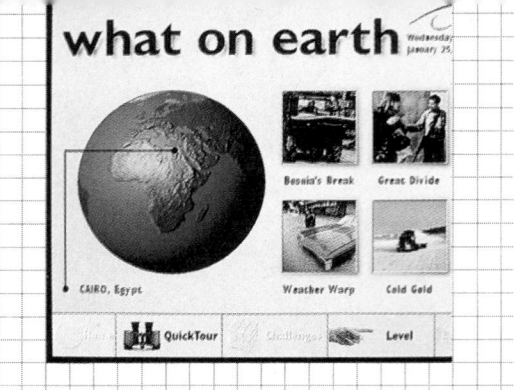

Understanding Computers

Today, computers are everywhere you look, even in places where you might be surprised to find them. Nearly all of us use computers every day, whether we realize it or not.

Computers process your checks at the bank by reading the computer-scannable numbers on your check. Computers in automated cash or teller machines let you withdraw and deposit money regardless of banking hours. Airline ticketing and reservation agents book you on a flight by using a computerized system that keeps track of routes, fares, and seats.

Computers scan the Universal Product Code on your groceries, tally your bill, and adjust the store's inventory. Computers tune the radio, pump gas, set thermostats, and control or monitor engine emissions and fuel economy.

Computers are on your wrist (digital watches) and in your pocket (calculators). Microwave ovens have computers. When you press the "redial" button on a telephone, a computer dials the number you last called.

Computers have had an enormous impact on the job market. Almost every job soon may require some level of computer use. In addition, there are computer-related careers that did not even exist a generation ago. These careers are found not only in the computer industry itself, but in government, banking, manufacturing, publishing—in fact, in every sector of the economy.

The computer age is *your* age. You have the right to live in it comfortably, without feeling threatened by this pervasive new technology. A computer is just another tool for you to use.

Numerous tasks at home can be performed by a computer. You can bank at home, shop at home, and read newspapers on the computer; you can even use your computer as a library. You can also monitor your health and advance your education by means of a computer.

The computer also makes it possible to bring work home. Some companies allow employees to work on company-owned computers placed in employees' homes and connected via telephone lines to the office.

In our schools, the push is on to make children "computer-literate." This means learning more about computers themselves, and being able to use a computer to learn about other subjects. Many parents and teachers fear that those students who are not familiar with computers will be left behind. They know that long after youngsters leave school, computers will remain a powerful tool in their lives.

For young people and adults alike, the computer offers enormous new opportunities for learning and communication. With a computer, you can gain access to enormous amounts of information stored in other computers around the world, through the Internet, the World Wide Web, and information utilities. And you can converse "on-line" with other computer users, or send and receive electronic messages—e-mail—with speed and ease.

This chapter will explain what a computer is, and what it can and cannot do. It will tell you how you can use one in your home to improve your job skills, earn extra income, and enjoy more leisure time.

What is a computer?

Historically, a computer, broadly defined, was a device that helped in computation—counting, calculating, adding, subtracting, multiplying, dividing, etc.—as you might guess from the root of the word *computer*. Today the word computer is used to describe an electronic device that stores, manipulates, and analyzes information. Computers no longer simply perform mathematical calculations; they can perform a much wider range of tasks, as described in the second half of this chapter.

The first computers.
Stonehenge, the prehistoric circular stone monument in Great Britain, and the abacus are two examples of early computers. Stonehenge is a man-made device used to *calculate* the movement of the stars and planets in order to *measure* the seasons and *predict* seasonal change. The abacus, although it is associated almost exclusively with the Chinese, was also used in some version by early Romans, Greeks, and Egyptians to *count* and *calculate*.

Gottfried Leibniz (b. 1646) and Blaise Pascal (b. 1623) each invented calculating machines in the 17th century. Leibniz also developed the system of using the base-two (binary) number system that computers use today.

How computers work

The computing process has four steps:
1. **Input:** A program or data are entered into the computer.
2. **Processing:** The computer executes the program or processes the data.
3. **Output:** The computer delivers the results of its operations to the user on a monitor, and on paper via a printer.
4. **Storage:** The computer saves programs and data for further use.

The shrinking computer.
Although Pascal's simple calculator (which could add and subtract) came before that of Charles Babbage, Babbage is considered the father of the modern computer. An early 19th-century Englishman, Babbage developed the principles on which modern computers are based.

The Difference Engine. Babbage started by inventing a small machine, the Difference Engine, in 1822. The machine computed algebraic expressions with many terms (polynomials), but it did only that. Babbage decided to build a machine that could solve virtually any mathematical problem and perform any kind of mathematical calculation.

The Analytical Engine. Babbage's design—a general-purpose computing machine—encompassed the main elements of a modern computer: It had input, storage, control, and output mechanisms. It was controlled by punched cards and was digital. (Think of a digital computer as a machine that counts on its fingers, or digits.)

Babbage planned for his Analytical Engine to be capable of storing thousands of figures, but as with many modern computer designs, his plans and his machine were never fully realized.

Hollerith's tabulating machine. Across the Atlantic Ocean, about 50 years after Babbage's work, the U.S. Census Bureau was having trouble tabulating the 1880 census, even though the next one was fast approaching. Herman Hollerith, a census agent, was asked to invent a mechanized tabulating system for the 1890 census.

Hollerith's system used paper tape initially, but punched cards worked better. Census takers punched holes in census cards to record data. The cards were fed into Hollerith's device, which had pins that stuck through the punched holes to form a closed electrical circuit, causing the information in each census category to be recorded.

The machine was a success. Hollerith went on to form his own concern, the Tabulating Machine Company, which became the International Business Machines Corporation (IBM) in 1924.

Mark I. The next major advance was the development of Mark I. It was assembled at Harvard University in 1943, under the direction of mathematician Howard Aiken and with funding from IBM. Mark I used electric relay switches instead of punched cards, and punched paper tape for input. Mark I was used by the U.S. Army during World War II to compute ballistic data.

ENIAC. The world's first *electronic* digital computer was ENIAC—or *E*lectronic *N*umerical *I*ntegrator *and C*alculator. Until ENIAC was developed, computers were mechanical.

ENIAC was room-sized, taking up 15,000 square feet. It was built of 18,000 vacuum tubes, and it weighed 30 tons. Developed by a U.S. government team and completed in 1946, it was 17 times faster than Mark I, performing 5000 additions per second. It was used to design the hydrogen bomb.

UNIVAC. Business first computerized with UNIVAC, the *Uni*versal *A*utomatic *C*omputer, which was smaller than its predecessors in size. UNIVAC, introduced in 1951, correctly tabulated the results of the 1952 presidential election.

Transistors. The invention of the transistor at Bell Laboratories in 1947 quickly made possible a miniature world of transistor radios, hearing aids, and electronic equipment of all kinds. The transistor was smaller than a thimble. The first transistorized computers were introduced in 1957 and 1958. They were smaller, faster, more reliable, and much more powerful than vacuum-tube computers. They also cost much less.

Integrated circuits. The next step in the evolution of computers was the development in 1958 of integrated circuits. An integrated circuit consists of a number of transistors, switches, connecting wires, and other components of circuits—all engraved onto a small flat silicon surface called a chip. A single integrated circuit can do the same work as thousands of transistors.

Commercial computers with integrated circuits began appearing in the mid-1960's. Computers that once took up an entire floor of a building could now fit in the corner of an office. The next major development in computer technology, the *microchip*, would make possible computers small enough to sit on a desk or rest on your lap.

Common questions about computers	Why do you want a computer?

Common questions about computers

Q: Do I need to know a lot about computers in order to use one?

A: No. Here is what you *do not need* to know. You do not need to know how to program a computer, nor do you need to know programming languages. You do not have to possess scientific or mathetical aptitude. In fact, you do not have to know any math at all. You do not even know how the computer works. Most users do not.

Q: What should I know about my computer's disk operating system (DOS)?

A: All you have to know about a computer's DOS is which kind it is: Common types include Apple DOS, MS-DOS, OS/2, and UNIX. The operating system manages and controls everything the computer does. All the software and hardware you buy has to run on your operating system, or you cannot use it. Think of your operating system as speaking French—unable to "read" German or Russian.

Q: Do I have to be computer-literate in order to use a computer?

A: You may be intimidated by what is called computer literacy. There is no need to be. Other than the experience of using a computer and a software program or two, nothing is required to join the ranks of the computer qualified.

Why do you want a computer?

How do you translate the things a computer does well into the kinds of things *you* might want a computer to do?

Some common reasons for wanting a compute are listed here to get you started. Look at this list and check off the things you want your computer to do.

____ Balance the checkbook
____ Chat with other computer users
____ Do calculations in class, at meetings, on trips
____ Do taxes
____ Draw pictures/graphs/charts
____ Help to start or run a small business
____ Improve job skills
____ Keep addresses
____ Keep Christmas mailing lists
____ Keep personal records
____ Keep recipes
____ Keep the family budget
____ Organize records and tapes
____ Play games
____ Teach more about computers
____ Teach programming languages
____ Teach spelling, math, or other subjects
____ Tie into computer data banks
____ Track the stock market
____ Write music
____ Write term papers or reports

Understanding Computers

The microcomputer

A *microcomputer* is a computer that is very much smaller in size than other computers. Microcomputers are also commonly called *micros* and *personal computers.* Some inexpensive models, such as the type people use to play games, are called *home computers.* Lightweight models that operate on batteries and can be carried from one place to another are called *portables, laptops,* and *notebook computers* (or simply notebooks).

The microchip. The core of the microcomputer is the *microprocessor,* sometimes called a computer on a chip. Although no larger than a baby's thumbnail, a microprocessor contains all the electronic circuits that make up the central processing unit of a computer. It serves the same function as did the relay switches and vacuum tubes of the older, larger computers.

The first microprocessor, introduced by Intel in late 1970, had 2250 transistors. It could process four bits of data at a time and carry out about 60,000 operations a second—more than ten times the speed of ENIAC at a fraction of the cost. By 1990 microprocessors holding 1 million transistors and able to process 64 bits of data at a time were on the market.

In order to examine the circuitry on a chip, you would have to use a microscope. To "remember" 16K (store in memory 16 kilobytes, or about 16,000 pieces of data), a computer memory bank of the 1950's had to be taller and larger than an average adult standing up. With modern technology that same amount of memory can now be stored on a tiny 16K memory chip.

The technology that put so many transistors on a chip has also reduced drastically the price of computers. Today, personal computers with power and capabilities that rival those once available only to government and big business can be purchased by private individuals and families.

Improvements in electronics made possible ever smaller and more powerful computers. The first electronic computer, ENIAC, occupied an entire room. Today's notebook-size portable computers use integrated circuit chips and have hundreds of times the computing power of ENIAC.

output: monitor

output: printer

laptop computer: CPU, monitor, keyboard, trackball, hard drive, floppy disks, all in one unit

output: speaker

storage: drives

input: keyboard

application: software

input: mouse

mouse pad

storage: CD-ROM, floppy disk

Parts of a computer

The main part of the computer is the central processing unit (CPU). Though the CPU is the "brains" of the computer, you cannot do anything with a CPU by itself. You need some way to communicate with it.

The computer's ears. The computer has to "hear" what you say. This is accomplished with *input devices*, such as game controls, a keyboard, or a mouse.

You use *game controls* to communicate with your computer. These controls, sometimes called joy sticks, come with or without a number pad. The stick moves up, down, right, and left in a two-dimensional axis and controls the movements of the game (your spaceship, your hero, etc.) on the screen. On the stick is a trigger that fires a weapon or, perhaps, a Ping-Pong ball at your command.

A more advanced way of communicating with your computer is to use a typewriterlike *keyboard*. The keys may include a number pad similar to that on a calculator.

A mouse is a hand-operated device that can be used to select data or commands. You use the mouse to "point" to an object on the screen and then press one of its buttons to execute a command. It is faster than a keyboard and easier to master since it does not require that you know how to type.

The computer's mouth. The computer tells you what it has done and is doing through *output devices*.

A *monitor*, or video screen similar to that on a television set, is one form of output device. It enables you to see instantaneously what is occurring inside the computer in response to your input (from the keyboard, game control, mouse, etc.). A *printer* is an output device that records what the computer has done on paper. *Multimedia speakers* add a new dimension to computing—stereophonic sound.

Storage devices, such as floppy disk drives and hard disk drives, enable you to store, or save, what you did on a computer. Another type of storage device, the CD-ROM drive, enables you to gain access to programs and files that already have been stored on *compact discs,* or CDs. You cannot store new information on the discs, however, which is what the "ROM" tells you—the disc is read only memory.

Understanding Computers

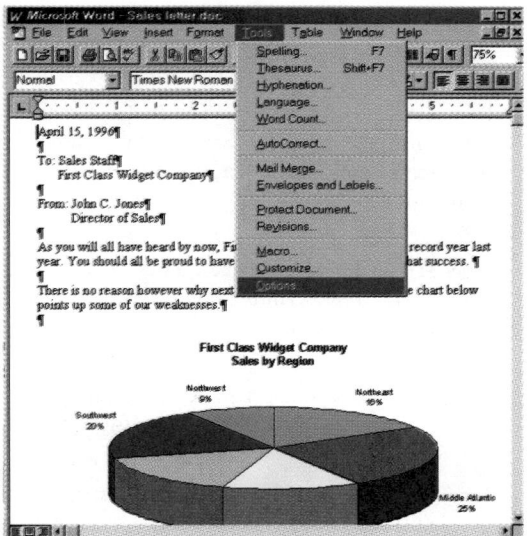

Many modern computer programs offer powerful features and relative ease of use. Drop-down menus, which can be opened by keyboard or mouse, and the ability to produce graphs and charts from numerical data, are two features included in top word processing programs.

Bit/Byte

How does a bit differ from a byte?

Bit is a contraction of "*b*inary dig*it*" and refers to the smallest unit of information a computer can process. Everything a computer does is done with electric circuitry, and electric current has two states: on and off. These two states are represented by the base two, or binary, number system, which has two symbols (0 and 1) to represent all numbers.

A byte is a group of bits, usually eight, forming a character, letter, number, punctuation mark, etc.

Here are some examples:

letter: *byte:*

The letter A is 01000001

The letter B is 01000010

The letter C is 01000011

It is never too late to learn!

Many people feel intimidated by computers or believe they are too old to learn how to use one. However, for those out of work or seeking a new job, experience in using a computer will provide new opportunities. Even if you have been out of school for a long time, it is not too late to learn about computers. There are many training programs aimed at reluctant computer users. Adult education programs and community colleges frequently offer classes in basic computer skills.

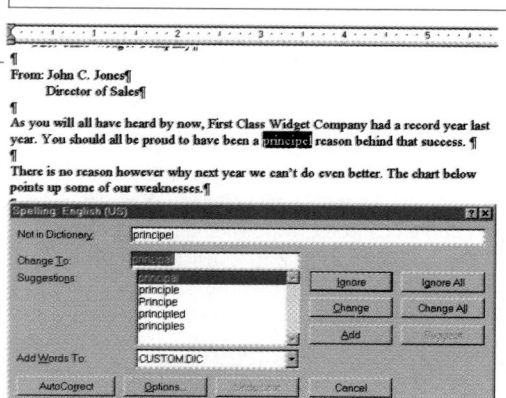

Courses on computers and the software they run (below) give you valuable skills you can use at home and at work, such as how to get a word processing program to check your spelling (above right) or how to conduct a job search on the Internet (below right).

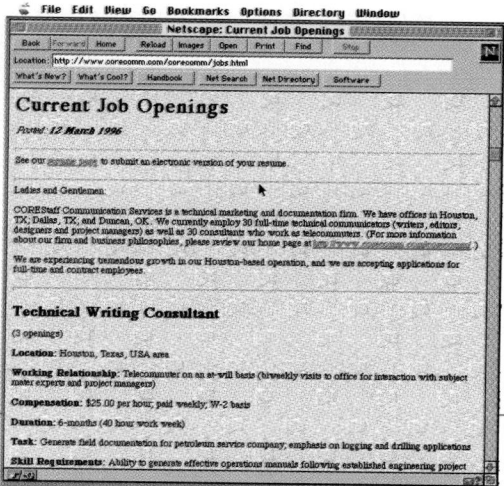

Computer programs.
The computer that you use to play video games on your television set is dedicated to one task: playing games. You tell your computer what to do (play a game) by inserting a game cartridge. More expensive, sophisticated computers also need instructions to tell them what to do. These instructions are called programs, or *software*.

You can write a program yourself, but you certainly do not have to. Some computer owners hire someone to write a program for them. Businesses and some professionals (doctors, accountants, etc.) tailor programming to the exact requirements of their offices. Although you, too, could hire someone to write a program for your computer, the cost would probably exceed the price of the computer itself.

Most likely, you will buy programs the same way you buy books or tape cassettes: in a store or by mail. These are programs designed for use by many people, although they may allow you to make modifications for personal preferences. A set of instructions, called documentation, comes with each program. It explains what the program does and how to use it.

There are two broad categories of software: *system* and *applications*.

System software. This category includes operating systems, utilities (software programs of a specific type), and languages.

A *disk operating system* (DOS) is what the computer uses to run itself. It directs the transfer of information from one part of the computer to another, and controls its storage in memory and on disk. It consists of a supervisory core and a collection of utility programs.

Utilities give the operating system additional features. The programmers of operating systems cannot foresee all user needs so utilities are added to perform functions not included in the operating system. Two of the most common utilities include one that copies files from one disk drive to another and one that lets you specify exactly how you want something to be printed. Some of the more exotic utilities can examine and change specific bytes or groups of bytes in memory.

Languages let you program the computer. Computers are machines that work with electrical impulses; computer languages let you "speak" to the computer without knowing anything about the machine's internal processes. The language is your interpreter.

Applications software. This term describes the task-oriented software programs that your computer uses to run your business, play games, type term papers, teach you or your family how to program, etc.

Applications software uses the operating system to interact with the computer. Although basic understanding of the operating system is necessary when using a computer, much applications software today is written to

"hide" the operating system from the user. Detailed knowledge of the operating system's capabilities is becoming less needed.

The applications software (other than games) that you are most likely to use are programs in the fields of
- business/finance
- education
- health
- word processing

Later in this chapter you will learn more about software categories and how to use them.

Compatibility.
The computer's disk operating system (DOS) determines the kinds of software that will or will not work on your computer. Applications software is run (made to work) by the computer's operating system. For example, if the operating system of a computer is PC-DOS, then the computer can only run PC-DOS software. If the operating system is Apple-DOS, it can only run Apple-DOS software. This is similar to the situation with automobile parts: You cannot put a Cadillac or Ford fuel pump in the engine of a Honda Civic.

When different types of computers use the same operating system, the computers are said to be *compatible*. Many companies manufacture computers that are compatible with either the IBM PC or the IBM PS/2 series.

Software manufacturers often make different versions of their programs for different operating systems. For example, a certain game or accounting program may be available in both Apple-DOS and PC-DOS versions. But this is not always the case. Some operating systems have had much more software written for them than have other operating systems. Therefore, it is important to know what you want your computer to do before you make any purchases. Pick out the software first, before you buy hardware (the computer, printer, etc.). Then choose hardware that works well with the software.

Buying software.

Take your list to a computer store—or to any large retail store that sells computers—and ask to see a demonstration of software that will perform the tasks you want. In addition, look through computer magazines for the names of software programs that do the tasks you have selected. Ask the advice of people who are using their computers to do the kinds of tasks you plan to do. Teachers may be helpful in suggesting educational programs for your children.

While you are trying out software, you will also get a chance to see different types of computers. The best way to begin selecting a computer is to actually try it out, watching it do what you want it to.

Shop around for the best price for both software and hardware.

Selecting hardware.

To select the right computer for you—the hardware—go back to the list of things you want your computer to do.

Once you have a list of applications, make a list of computers that run the software you will be using. Next, consider the following:

Price range. How much money are you able and willing to spend on your computer system?

Necessary features. How much memory is needed to run the programs you plan to use? What peripherals are needed? If you want a computer only for games, you do not need a printer. But a printer is essential if you plan to do word processing. On the other hand, games may require a graphics card, which is not needed for word processing.

Space requirements. How much space do you have for the computer? Will you need special furniture for it? Will you want to move the computer between your home and your office? If space is limited or if you expect to move the computer frequently, you may wish to consider a portable model.

Expandability. Perhaps at the present time you want a computer just for games and simple educational programs. But soon your children may be old enough to use word-processing programs. You may decide to computerize your taxes and other financial data. Being able to communicate with other computers via telephone may also sound appealing, though you probably

Video game or personal computer?

My First Incredible, Amazing Dictionary

a b c d e f g h i j k l m n o p q r s t u v w x y z

rain forest

A rain forest is a hot, steamy forest where the trees grow tall and close together. Rain forests can be called jungles.

Natural habitats

Surprise me   Backtrack   Games   Quick search   Options   Quit

Today's personal computers and video games have powerful microprocessors. Most of them offer dazzling graphics, but the personal computer is the more versatile of the two types of machine because it can run more different types of software. With CD-ROM, modem, and multimedia capabilities, a personal computer can be used for work and play, and for communicating with other computer users. No video game can do all that!

aren't ready to try that right now. Expandability means that a computer system can be upgraded or improved. New features can be added at a fraction of the cost it would take to replace the entire system. Some inexpensive computers cannot be expanded, thus limiting their versatility.

Quality, maintenance, and service. Check the terms of the warranty. Does the retailer provide training and maintenance services? How easy is it to fix the computer—or a peripheral—if it breaks down? How much will repairs cost? Where—and how quickly—will this work be done? Do you have to ship the computer somewhere at your own expense?

Storing your data.

One fact of computer life that people often forget (with sometimes tragic results) is that when you turn off the computer, or the power fails, you lose any information that was stored only in the internal electronic memory of the computer. If you want to keep records, balance the checkbook, plan the budget, keep recipe files, or organize your record collection, then you want your computer to remember what you did the last time you used it. This requires a *storage device*.

Some inexpensive computers, particularly handheld game machines, use programs stored on cartridges that are easily inserted into the computers. Some portable or laptop computers use credit card-size storage cards. Some large business computers use reels of tape. Videodisks and CD-ROM (*Compact Disk-Read Only Memory*) are also used. But the most commonly used storage devices are disks.

Disks and disk drives. There are two main types of disks: floppy and hard. A device called a disk drive is needed to store information on a disk and to read, or retrieve, that information.

The floppy disk—a flexible, flat platter that is enclosed in a protective jacket—is the standard external storage device that is used for most personal computers. Almost all computers today come with hard disk drives that store the operating system, applications, and data files.

Usually both floppy disk drives and hard disk drives are a physical part of the main computer housing.

The essential difference between them is that a floppy disk can always be removed from its drive, while a hard disk is almost always permanently fixed in its drive.

Floppy disks come in a standard 3.5- inch size. Most floppies can hold up to 1.44MB (megabytes or millions of bytes) of data. Some 3.5-inch disks can hold 2.88MB, but they require a special disk drive. Both types are encased in the same size rigid plastic case, making them quite durable. Hard disks generally have storage capacities of between 9GB (gigabytes or billions of bytes) and 20GB, although hard disks with even higher capacities are available.

The storage capacity that you need will be determined for the most part by the applications you intend using the computer for. Most applications programs are very large and can only be stored on and run from a hard disk. The more programs you intend to use, the larger the hard drive you will need. When buying a personal computer, it is best to get the largest hard drive you can afford.

Features—what's necessary and what's not?

The following are some features that can be bought as add-on, peripheral (side) devices or can be built into the computer. Some are useful to have, but others are must-haves.

CD-ROM	CD-ROM is the result of a marriage between the compact disk (CD) and the personal computer. Huge amounts of data can be stored on a CD-ROM, and virtually all software now comes on CD-ROM disks, making a CD-ROM drive a requirement on today's computers. There are several different types of CD-ROM drive, including optical, magneto-optical, and CD-R (CD-Rewritable, meaning the drive can write data to special CD disks). Most users require only a standard optical CD-ROM drive.
Modems	These devices enable a computer to talk over telephone lines to other computers. Most modems are built-in, but sometimes they are external, attached by a cable to the computer. You need a modem to connect with Internet service providers such as America Online, CompuServe, and Prodigy.
Zip and tape drives	It's a good idea to make backup copies of the program and data files on your computer's hard drive as protection against hard drive failure or damage from a computer virus, and floppy disks simply don't have the storage capacity to do the job. Zip drives use a disk that is a cross between a floppy and a hard disk, and tape drives use magnetic tapes similar to cassette tapes. Both formats can store from 100MB to 1GB or more.
Sound cards	These are circuit boards that plug into your computer internally and connect to external speakers, providing the computer user with full stereo sound. Many interactive programs, encyclopedias and other references on CD-ROM, and virtually all computer games include sound.
Voice	Special software and hardware can enable your computer to recognize speech. This is an important feature for those who cannot use a keyboard.

Printers

Certain uses you may have for your computer—writing letters or research papers, keeping your budget, running a business from your home—will require putting the output of your computer on paper. This is called hard copy and it requires a printer.

There are several kinds of printers. Three popular choices are the laser, inkjet, and dot matrix printers. Their names describe the kind of printing element that produces their distinctive type of character. Each has advantages (+) and disadvantages (-).

Laser printers. These printers use a highly focused beam of light to form an image on a charged cylinder that then transfers a powder called toner onto the paper, in much the same way that a copier machine does. Laser printers
+ come in a wide range of prices.
+ are extremely quiet.
+ print high-quality text suitable for professional-looking documents.

+ can produce graphics (bar graphs, charts, pictures, tables, etc.). Some higher priced models can print in color.
+ are able to print thousands of pages on a single toner cartridge.
+ are very fast.
- cost more per page to operate than inkjet or dot matrix printers.
- cannot be used to print multiple-copy forms.

Inkjet printers. These printers spray ink through nozzles in the print head onto the paper, depositing an extremely fine pattern of dots to produce characters and graphics. Most color inkjets use three colored inks—red (magenta), yellow, and blue (cyan)—as well as the black ink used by monochrome inkjets, but some use just the three colors to produce black. Inkjet printers

+ are relatively inexpensive.
+ are extremely quiet.
+ are small and take up little desk (or shelf) space.
+ are fast, but not as fast as laser printers.
- cost more per page to operate than dot matrix printers.
- cannot be used to print multiple-copy forms.

Dot matrix printers. These printers have a printing element that produces letters, numbers, and punctuation, plus graphs and pictures, by "drawing" them with a series of tiny dots at a speed of 80 to 350 characters per second. The print head may contain a total of 9 printing "pins," or 24 pins. A 24-pin dot matrix printer is considered close to laser print quality. Dot matrix printers

+ are relatively inexpensive.
+ are lowest in cost to operate of the three types of printers.
+ can be used to print multiple-copy forms.
- are much noisier than laser or inkjet printers.
- do not print as fast as laser or inkjet printers.
- do not produce characters as sharp or well formed as those produced by laser or inkjet printers.

Which printer is for you? Quality is in the eye of the beholder. You have to look at the print and decide if it is what you want.

Laser printers offer high-quality printing and are generally extremely sturdy and reliable. Most laser printers print only in black. Until recently, color laser printers were so expensive that only businesses or wealthy individuals could afford to buy them. They are still quite expensive, but now cost only a bit more than the average black-only laser printer cost a few years ago.

Most inkjet printers are very close to laser printers in quality. A high-quality, black-only inkjet printer can be purchased for less than $100, and a color inkjet printer can be bought for less than $200.

When shopping for an inkjet printer, check the print quality for both text and graphics to see if the printer will provide the quality you are looking for. Also, if you are looking for a color printer, see if there are separate ink cartridges for each of the colors used. Some less expensive inkjet printers use three color cartridges or a single cartridge containing three color inks. Other inkjets use three color ink cartridges plus a black ink cartridge, or a single cartridge containing all four inks. It is less expensive in the long run to buy a printer with four separate ink cartridges, as you can replace each one as needed.

The most compelling reason to buy a dot matrix printer is to print on multipart forms, or forms with one or more duplicate sheets beneath the main sheet. Most people do not need a dot matrix printer, but they are useful and cost-effective for small business applications.

Computers and education

The computer is a powerful learning and communication tool for young people. KidNews (left) is just one of many Internet sites providing information and entertainment for children. Educational computer programs are often as much fun as they are instructive. They complement learning from books.

Why are computers good for learning new things? Computers can entertain as they educate, with engaging graphics, colors, sounds, movement, and simulations. Computer learning can be fun.

Computers can force one-to-one attention (one person, teacher, or computer to one student), which is known to speed learning.

Unlike a textbook, computers can encourage you when you have grasped the material. By making a sound or by flashing a message on the screen ("GREAT WORK!"), they can congratulate you on a job well done.

Computers are endlessly patient when you are wrong, going over and over the material until you get it right. No harsh words, no lost tempers.

Young children are especially good candidates for computer education because they are fascinated with how a computer works. Early education software takes advantage of a child's natural delight with games, and combines games with learning to produce a painless teaching environment.

Educational software.
A wide variety of educational software is now available for use on home computers. They range in difficulty from the very basic educational software for preschool children to complex math or problem-solving programs for older children.

Some inexpensive game computers that use plug-in cartridges instead of floppy disks to load programs have educational titles. This is an especially attractive option for those with very young children who have no need for an expensive personal computer. It has the added advantage of enabling children to plug in and run programs themselves.

Evaluating the software.
Some educational software consists of nothing more than expensive flash cards, such as those you used in school to learn multiplication and addition. Such software does not take advantage of the full potential of your computer.

How can you tell a good educational software program from a bad one? How do you go about finding a good one?

1. **For children, start in the school.** If your child's school has computers, ask the teacher what kind of software they use. You may wish to duplicate or complement the software your child is already using. Or you may want to use the next, more advanced program in a series.

2. **Next, go to a computer store and try out some programs.** If you are buying the software for children, take them into the store to try it out with you. The software should be labeled with suggested age levels, but a test run will ensure that the software is appropriate for your children. Let them use it.

3. **Read the manual** (the documentation, or instructions that go with the program). Are the instructions easy to read? Good instructions are written in plain English. There is a clear explanation of how to use the program, and all of the program's options are described. Often, manuals contain suggestions for follow-up activities that reinforce the skills taught by the software. In some software, the documentation is actually part of the program. If this is true, can the instructions be skipped once your child is familiar with the program?

4. **When you test-run the program,** look for these features:

Two educational software examples

Speed reading. Speed-reading courses outside the home are often quite expensive, and they require you to spend hours in a classroom that may be far from home. With a computer, you can learn to increase your reading speed, at home, much more economically. You can buy a speed-reading software program for about $70. More than one member of your family can take the same "course," which brings the cost down even further.

The computer is an especially effective tool for learning speed reading. It can train your eye movements to extend your peripheral (side) vision, so that you read larger groups of words at a time instead of one or two at a time. It can flash individual words on the screen at faster and faster rates, enabling you to build up your comprehension. It can also roll text across the screen at increasingly faster rates to train you to read actual running text more and more quickly.

Some of these techniques are the same ones used in speed-reading courses given outside the home. But when you are working on your own computer, you can insert your own reading material so that the selections you use for practice are the kinds of material you enjoy reading.

History. How does history take shape? Instead of memorizing names and dates of famous people and wars, you can use the computer to study factors that influence the way history unfolds. Some history programs trace the interplay of economic, political, religious, and other influences. The programs use the software to present a "model" that allows for the random selection of events within the established limits (historical period, countries, etc.).

Instead of reading the names of kings and generals and the locations of the major wars, for example, you could put yourself in tenth-century Spain or the American Civil War. Then, you could manipulate the historical, economic, and human factors as variables on the computer. The result is a model of theoretical history.

The program is unique each time it runs, although it preserves the broad historical overview. Color displays are used to show maps and graphic detail for the time period, as well as political or religious areas of influence.

The models offer information you might also get from books or a course, but learning through models allows you to make choices and participate in the process.

- *Friendliness.* Is the structure of the program non-threatening and easy to use? It should be. This does not mean that the course content of the program should be something your child can breeze through, thereby learning nothing. It means that the program itself should be something you and your child can use on the computer without major prolems.

  In addition, the content of the program, the actual material to be learned, should be neither above nor below your child's ability. Just because the package says "Ages 5-8" does not mean that your seven-year-old will find the program useful. Your child may not be ready, or may be too advanced, for that particular program.

- *Usefulness.* What does this program purport to do? Read the claims on the package or brochure. It should clearly state what the program will teach your child. Is this what your child wants or needs? Do not waste money on programs that your child cannot, or will not, benefit from.

- *Encouragement.* The software should assess your child's progress. If an answer is incorrect, does the program just move on, or does it offer help, and review the material for your child? Better yet, does it rephrase the original explanation, presenting the

material in a new way for those who did not understand it the first time? A program that simply indicates wrong answers is not as good as one that offers feedback and encouragement.

- *Flexibility.* A good program has the flexibility to adjust to progress. If the child grasps the material with no difficulty (three answers right in a row, for example), the program should adjust accordingly: It should become progressively more challenging. Some programs are flexible enough to let you add new material—for example, extra passages for reading comprehension, additional vocabulary, or a whole new text with questions. When the original content has been mastered, such programs remain useful so long as you continue making additions to them.

- *Entertainment.* Finally, the sotware should take full advantage of the computer's ability to enhance the learning experience with movement, color, sound, interesting displays, simulations, etc. If the program simply presents screen after screen of straight text, followed by multiple choice questions, it offers no advantages over a textbook. Do not buy it. You do not need a computer to read a book, unless you are learning how to speed read.

Word processing

If you want to use your computer for running a home-based business, improving your job skills, or writing long research papers, word processing is the applications software for you. In fact, word processing has become the most important use for most people who have computers in the home.

Word processing: how it works.

Word processing is typing by computer, with a big plus. Word processing software can turn your computer into a typewriter, a typesetter, a printer, a dictionary, a thesaurus, an editor, and a secretary.

Instead of using paper to try out your ideas, you use the computer's memory. Instead of typing and retyping on paper, you type a first draft of a document into the computer. The computer lets you correct or revise it without retyping the whole document.

What can word processing do? If
you can type, you can do word processing. Using a computer instead of a typewriter for reports, memos, letters, etc., has important advantages:

1. **It can justify margins** automatically. That means that everything on the right and left side of the page or column will be lined up evenly.
2. **It can rearrange the order** of anything you have typed. You can move sentences, words, and paragraphs up or down on the page without retyping them.

Related software

A spelling checker. A spelling checker automatically looks through your typed document for spelling errors. Any word that is misspelled will be highlighted for you to correct.

An electronic thesaurus. Do you keep using the same words over and over? With this software, you can be creative instead of repetitive in your word choice. At the stroke of a key, synonyms for the word you want to replace appear on the computer screen.

Mailing lists. You can coordinate word processing software with programs that can handle any mailing list—your Christmas cards, your business clients. Each letter will carry an individual salutation with its own address.

---

3. **It can copy automatically** any part of the document, or even another document, and deposit it at another location using one key.
4. **It can change the format** of material. You can make the margins much wider, or you can make them much narrower if you prefer.
   Without any retyping.
   > You can center material
   > with one keystroke.

   You can underline, highlight, number and renumber the pages, insert footnotes automatically, type ^{above} or $_{below}$ the line, or **use bold type for emphasis.**
5. **It can help you save time** because you do not have to retype. Also, because you do not have to retype the whole document, you reduce the possibility of introducing new errors while correcting old ones. If you are sending one letter, manuscript, or document to several people, the computer saves you even more time.

What equipment do you need?

A keyboard. If you intend to do a lot of typing (whether of words or numbers), you should have a computer with a typewriterlike keyboard to make your typing easier. Instead of such a keyboard, some computers have a membrane with the letters and symbols painted on; some have thin little keys somewhat like those on pocket calculators. Neither is adequate for heavy word processing.

A printer. You will need some kind of printer for the output of your typing.

A word processing program. Many different programs are available, ranging in price from a few dollars to hundreds of dollars. Most home and small business users will find that programs costing less than $100 will meet their needs. There is no reason to pay for features that you will never use. However, if you are planning to bring home work from the office, your word processor should be compatible with the program used in the office. Either buy the same program or have a program that can convert the files from your home word processor into files that can be read by the word processor you use at work.

A monitor, or video display screen. Although some early home computers were designed so that a television set could be used to view copy, the quality and detail of the picture left much to be desired. You will want to buy a monitor with your home computer. If you are going to use it for long periods, it is important to choose a monitor that provides a bright, clear, sharp picture.

14   **Understanding Computers**

Communications

The transmission of information between computers has become one of the major applications of computer technology. People are using computers to access reference libraries, participate in group conferences, play games with others thousands of miles away, download free software, read stock exchange tickers, send mail, buy toys, and carry out other activities quickly, conveniently, and often at a significant savings in cost. There is even a new term to describe this worldwide "virtual community" where people communicate and gather information electronically: cyberspace.

To "go on-line" means to use a computer to communicate with another computer via telephone—and for long-distance communications via wireless services such as microwave towers and communications satellites. To do this a person needs a modem, which converts computer signals into a form that can be handled by the telephone system. The person also needs communications software. Features commonly found in such software include automated dialing, auto-answering, data capture (saving on disk or in RAM the information received from another computer), printing of data as it comes in from another computer, and text file transmission (the ability to send data previously typed).

The best-known components of cyberspace are the Internet, bulletin board systems, and various information utilities that can be accessed by people all over the world. Networks, whether consisting of computers linked together within a single building or over a wide area, are also part of cyberspace.

Information utilities. An information utility is an organization that offers, usually for a fee, both information and services. The most widely used information utilities in the United States are America Online, CompuServe, and Prodigy. All are broad, consumer-oriented utilities that also include extensive business information. They use graphical software, with menus and icons that make it easy for users to find their way to specific services. The main menu lists the major services available; submenus help zero in on the user's interests and needs. Alternatively, a person can use a specified command to go directly to a particular option. For example, to access America Online's travel section, a person clicks on the Travel icon on the main menu or types the keyword Travel. This takes the person to the Travel Forum, which contains information on destinations, travel books that can be ordered, travel discounts, airline schedules and reservations, and much more.

Bulletin board systems. An electronic bulletin board system, or BBS, serves the same function as a traditional bulletin board: It is a place where people may leave messages to be read by anyone looking at that particular board. To access a BBS, a person may dial its telephone number, and upon hearing the electronic carrier tone that indicates that the computer has answered, press the RETURN key twice. The board then may send instructions on what to do next.

The Internet. The Internet, often called the Net, is a worldwide matrix of thousands of computer networks. Some of the networks are large and complex, and are run by major corporations, universities, and government agencies. At the other end of the scale are networks operated by elementary schools, small businesses, and

Information utilities provide access to the Internet and the information contained in computer sites around the world. For example, you can obtain the weather forecast for Biarritz, France (left), or learn about an Egyptian archaeological excavation with a class of students in Michigan (right).

Computers are rapidly changing the way people shop and make purchases, even of expensive items. This screen shows negotiations for an automobile sale in progress. The auto salesperson and prospective buyer see each other on screen and hear one another through multimedia speakers.

even individuals. No one owns the Internet; there is no central location or hierarchy. This is considered one of its major attributes, for it has created a democratic community where an inexpensive PC can communicate with a multimillion-dollar supercomputer, and average citizens can communicate with heads of state, corporate leaders, and famous actors.

There are two ways to get onto the Internet. Information utilities include Internet access among the services they provide for subscribers. Then there are local and national service providers, which provide Internet access only. These service providers typically charge a monthly fee for unlimited usage; for people who spend a lot of time on the Internet, this tends to be cheaper than going through an information utility, which generally charges by the hour.

Every computer on the Internet has a unique address, which follows a scheme known as the domain name system. Individuals whose computers are connected indirectly to the Internet, for instance, through schools or information services, receive their addresses from those organizations. Businesses, groups, and individuals who register domain names directly do so through a federally backed company, Network Solutions Inc. This firm ensures that no two names are alike; it also handles disputes that develop when more than one person or company requests use of the same name.

A domain address consists of a sequence of domains separated by dots (.). Read from left to right, the address goes from the most specific to the most general information. For example, here is an address for a hypothetical Cindy Smith, who works for the Blip Company:

csmith@blip.com

The address begins with the first initial of Cindy's given name and her entire surname. This is followed by the "at" symbol (@). Everything after @ indicates Cindy's domain. This consists of the company name, a dot, and *com*. "Com" indicates that Cindy is at a commercial institution. Abbreviations for other types of institutions include:

edu	educational
gov	governmental
int	international
mil	military
net	networking
org	organizations such as professional associations

World Wide Web.

The Web, or WWW, is a system that organizes information on the Internet in such a manner that users can easily and rapidly move from one document to another, either in the same computer or in another computer. The Web became the fastest growing and most popular part of the Internet. Today, there are tens of thousands of Web sites. They hold millions of documents; enable people to order products and services, including the downloading of software; and offer the possibility of enjoying dialogues with other Web visitors.

Three critical aspects of the Web are HTTP, URLs, and HTML.

HTTP, or hypertext transfer protocol, is the standard that defines how data are transferred on the Web.

A URL, or Uniform Resource Locator, is the address for a site on the Web. For example, the address for the White House site is:

http://www.whitehouse.gov

In this address, *"http://"* stands for hypertext transfer protocol, and indicates that this is a World Wide Web address; *"www"* stands for World Wide Web; *"whitehouse"* indicates the location of the site; and *"gov"* indicates that the site is in a governmental organization. Note that the address is written in lowercase letters, and that it does not include any spaces. This is true for all Web addresses.

Documents on the Web are written in HTML, or Hypertext Markup Language. A critical aspect of HTML is coding "hyperlinks" to other documents on the Web. Each link is highlighted in some manner, usually by underlining it or printing it in a special color. Point and click with your computer mouse on one of these hyperlinks and you move immediately to another document at the Web site or, as is often the case, to another Web site entirely.

To navigate the WWW, a user needs a program known as "a web browser"; Mosaic and Netscape Navigator are popular examples. As the Web has expanded, it has become increasingly difficult for users to conduct data searches. Directory services, most of them free of cost, allow people to do keyword searches for specific subjects. Among the best known of such services are Yahoo! and Lycos. Their addresses are:

http://www.yahoo.com
http://lycos.cs.cmu.edu

Anyone can launch a personal Web site, either by paying a Web designer to create the site or by doing it yourself. You can put anything on your Web pages: photos of your pet, favorite jokes, colorful graphics, links to other Web pages, and so on. Most people and organizations with Web sites regularly update their Web pages in order to keep the pages exciting and help ensure that visitors return again and again.

You can download clip art to add to your reports, letters, and other documents from the Internet and on-line services.

Network and information utility software lets you know at the time you log on, or go on-line, if someone has sent E-mail to you.

E-mail.
With an on-line connection, a person can send messages electronically to anyone else who has an on-line connection. This electronic mail, or E-mail, is placed in the recipient's electronic mailbox, a storage area in the system's computer. For example, a person who uses CompuServe has a mailbox in a CompuServe computer. When the person signs onto CompuServe, he or she is alerted that mail is waiting in the mailbox.

Let's say that John writes a letter to Pat. He types it on his computer but instead of printing it and putting it in a stamped envelope, he connects to his service provider and, at the prompt, types in Pat's E-mail address. If John desires, he can keep a record of the letter on a disk. He also can send the same letter to several people at once, by instructing the software to forward copies to a designated list. Also, once Pat's address is in John's electronic address book, John does not have to type it when he wants to send another letter. He simply selects Pat's name, types the letter, and clicks the send button.

Within seconds, John's letter has reached its destination. It remains in Pat's mailbox until Pat opens the mailbox. Pat may reply to the letter immediately, download it to his own computer, save it on disk for future reference, print it out, forward it to someone else, or simply read it and then delete it.

E-mail software enables a person to compose a message before going on-line. This helps cut on-line time and charges, especially if one sends many, or long, messages.

E-mail is extremely fast, faster and more efficient than writing letters and posting them in traditional mailboxes. Typically, the only cost is telephone time (if the mailboxes are part of the Internet, an information utility, or a bulletin board system, access time fees may also be incurred). And an E-mail message can include anything digital, including graphics and sound.

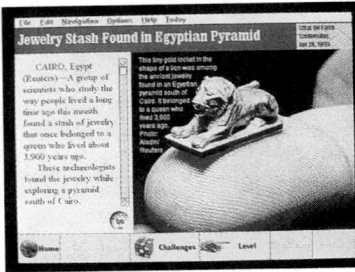
telecommunications

Glossary of computer terms

Some standard keyboard characters with their ASCII equivalents

033 !	063 ?	093]
034 "	064 @	094 ∧
035 #	065 A	095 —
036 $	066 B	096 '
037 %	067 C	097 a
038 &	068 D	098 b
039 '	069 E	099 c
040 (	070 F	100 d
041)	071 G	101 e
042 *	072 H	102 f
043 +	073 I	103 g
044 ,	074 J	104 h
045 -	075 K	105 i
046 .	076 L	106 j
047 /	077 M	107 k
048 0	078 N	108 l
049 1	079 O	109 m
050 2	080 P	110 n
051 3	081 Q	111 o
052 4	082 R	112 p
053 5	083 S	113 q
054 6	084 T	114 r
055 7	085 U	115 s
056 8	086 V	116 t
057 9	087 W	117 u
058 :	088 X	118 v
059 ;	089 Y	119 w
060 <	090 Z	120 x
061 =	091 [	121 y
062 >	092 \	122 z

AI (artificial intelligence). The field or study of computer use to reproduce human intelligence. Also describes the ability of computers to simulate human intelligence and reasoning, as well as attempts to make computers "think."

algorithm. The mathematical or logical steps needed to solve a problem.

applications software. Computer programs that enable a computer to do specific tasks, such as accounting, graphics, and word processing.

ASCII (the *A*merican *S*tandard *C*ode for *I*nformation *I*nterchange). An internationally used coding scheme for representing character information. With ASCII, any two computers—regardless of operating system or brand—can communicate. ASCII uses 128 numbers to represent the letters of the alphabet, the numbers 0 through 9, and punctuation marks. For example, the lower-case letter "a" is represented by the ASCII code 97.

BASIC (*B*eginner's *A*ll-purpose *S*ymbolic *I*nstruction *C*ode). A widely used, easy-to-learn programming language that uses familiar words, such as *print, read,* and *let. See also* language.

baud. A unit of measurement that indicates the speed at which data are transferred via a modem from one computer to another. Usually calculated in bits per second (bps). Thus 1200 bps means that data are sent at a rate of about 120 characters per second.

binary, binary system. The base-two number system used by computers. The two digits used in base two, and in the binary system, are 0 and 1. Each successive digit to the left is a progressive power of two.

Base two is used in computers because it represents the basis of computer operations: on-off or high-low electric current.

bit, binary digit. The basic unit of encoded computer data. A bit is one unit of storage space in a computer. Each electric pulse is one bit. Generally, eight bits form one byte.

boot. Start up a computer by loading essential information, such as an operating system, usually from a disk. Boot can also mean loading a program into computer memory.

Bps. Bits per second. A way of measuring the speed at which a computer sends information. *See also* baud.

buffer. A section of memory used for the temporary storage of information.

bug. An error in the computer or its programming software. The origin of "bug" is interesting. Legend has it that an early large mainframe computer malfunctioned because of an insect trapped somewhere in the computer's tubes. The insect was discovered and removed. Since then, the word "bug" has come to describe general computer problems. Getting rid of the problems is called debugging.

byte. Eight bits, the number required to encode one letter or number or symbol.

character. Any information that can be stored in one byte. Examples are letters of the alphabet.

chip. A tiny piece of silicon or other semiconductor material that contains thousands of transistors joined by microscopic circuits. A computer has one or more chips.

clone. A computer that is compatible with an IBM computer. It can run the same software as the IBM computer.

command. Any instruction given to a computer. Commands are frequently preset by the software program you use.

computer piracy. The unauthorized copying of software.

CPU (central processing unit). The part of the computer that interprets and carries out instructions and sends the results to the user, the computer's memory, or both.

cursor. A spot of light on a computer screen that indicates the place to enter data or give commands to the computer.

database. An organized collection of related information, such as a mailing list, a hospital's medical records, or a library's card catalog.

disk/diskette. The magnetic-coated flexible disk on which software programs are stored, and on which you can store your own data. Disks come in various types and sizes. *See also* hard disk.

disk drive. A device that records data on and retrieves data from a spinning disk (see above).

documentation. The instructions for using a computer or software.

expansion slot. The place in a computer where a circuit board with additional memory or other capabilities can be inserted.

floppy disk. *See* disk/diskette.

hard disk. A rigid magnetic disk sealed in a hard disk drive, used for storing computer programs and data.

hardware. The computer and related machine equipment, such as the printer.

home computer. *See* personal computer.

information utility. An organization that offers access to computerized databases and other information services.

Computer communicating

Your computer can communicate. You can use it like a telephone, to call and chat, using the keyboard and monitor, with other computer users. You can program it to send calls to other computer owners late at night, when rates are cheap.

You can also use your computer to gain access to libraries of books, newspapers, and magazines through computer information services and bibliographic databases.

How it works. Your computer can talk to another computer any distance away over telephone lines. To use normal phone lines, you have to convert the binary or digital signals your computer makes into the voice-frequency signals telephone lines carry.

Modems do that, among other things. They translate digital signals produced by your computer into oscillating signals, and vice versa (when in the receiving mode). That process is one of *mo*dulation and *dem*odulation, hence the name modem.

Equipment. There are two popular types of modems that are used with microcomputers.

Internal modems consist of a board inside the computer that connects to a phone line directly.

External modems connect to the computer with a cable.

Many modems can also send documents directly to fax machines. These devices, known as *faxmodems*, have become extremely popular with microcomputer users.

What must you buy? Some computers are sold with built-in telecommunications ability. But many microcomputers do not have this capability, which means you will need additional hardware and peripheral equipment:

- an asynchronous board with RS-232C port and cable for an external modem, and the modem itself, or
- an internal modem,
- and a telephone line to connect the modem (external or internal) to a telephone wall jack.

You also will need *communications software:* programming on a disk telling your computer how to interact with other computers. You may find modem hardware and communications software sold together.

You can buy good programs for under $200—sometimes well under. Procomm is a shareware program that is highly regarded, with good features and documentation. You can find shareware and public domain software in magazines, through computer clubs, etc.

On-line services. Once you have installed your modem and have become familiar with your communications software, you will probably want to become a subscriber to one or more of the computer information utilities. These provide access to numerous databases and electronic bulletin board systems (bbs's), enable you to send E-mail to other subscribers, and even provide entry to the Internet and World Wide Web (see page 15). A growing number of companies offer direct access to the Internet for a flat monthly fee, so you can "surf the Net" even if you choose not to subscribe to an information utility.

To tap into it, you need a computer, communications software, a modem, and a telephone line.

input/output (I/O). What goes in and what comes out of the computer.

Internet. A worldwide linkup of computer networks, electronic databases, and on-line services.

K (kilobyte). A unit of computer memory equal to approximately 1000 bytes.

language. A special set of vocabulary and rules used to write programs. It allows communication within and between computers or between computers and their users. Examples include BASIC, C, LOGO, and PASCAL.

laptop. A small, portable computer. It is battery powered and has a built-in keyboard and display screen.

load. To enter data or programs into the computer.

LOGO. An easy-to-learn and easy-to-use computer language. Popular in schools, especially with young children.

mainframe. A large, powerful computer that can store huge amounts of data and do many tasks at the same time. It can be connected to and used by smaller computers.

MB (megabyte). A unit of computer memory equal to about 1 million bytes.

memory. Holds the program or data to be worked on. *See also* RAM *and* ROM.

menu. A list of functions or commands for a program. They are displayed on the computer screen for you to indicate the option you want.

merge. Combine data from two or more computer files.

microcomputer. A computer that uses a microprocessor as its central processing unit. A personal computer.

> ### Cybertalk
>
> The term *cyberspace* was coined by science fiction writer William Gibson, and first appeared in his novel *Neuromancer* (1984). Gibson sensed that people who worked with computers came to believe that there was an actual place, or world, behind the screen—a place they couldn't see but knew was there. He called that place cyberspace, describing it as a place of "unthinkable complexity." Gibson's new word has spawned a variety of additional terms, including *cybercafe*, a low-cost eating place where customers can drink a cup of coffee and plug into the Internet; *cybermall*, on-line "stores" where people can gather information on products and make purchases; and *cybertheft*, the use of computers to steal.

---

microprocessor. A chip that contains the "brains," or CPU, of a microcomputer.

modem. A device that lets computers communicate with each other by telephone. It changes computer signals into audio signals that can be carried over telephone lines. It also changes audio signals back into computer signals. The word is derived from the term *mo*dulator-*dem*odulator.

monitor. A unit that looks like a television screen. It has a video screen to display information produced by the computer.

mouse. A hand-held pointer used with a computer for word processing, graphics, etc. It is used as a means of telling the computer what to do.

network. A system for connecting computers. A network can be within a limited area, such as a building, or over a wide area or long distances.

on-line. Connected to another computer through the use of a modem and a telephone line.

operating system. A program that controls the operation of a computer system. It handles such tasks as loading programs and storing data. Common operating systems include MS-DOS, OS/2, and UNIX.

Pascal. A programming language named after the French philosopher, mathematician, and inventor Blaise Pascal.

peripheral. Any hardware connected to a computer, such as printers, modems, and joysticks.

personal computer. A microcomputer, designed for personal use by an individual at home or in a business.

pixel. One of the tiny dots of light on a computer screen. The greater the number of pixels per square inch, the higher the picture resolution.

port. The place on a computer or peripheral where connecting cables can be attached.

program. Any instructions telling the computer what to do. *See also* software.

public domain software. Software that is uncopyrighted and available free of charge.

RAM (*r*andom *a*ccess *m*emory). Temporary computer memory used to hold software and data. It "forgets" whatever is in it when you turn off the computer.

ROM (*r*ead *o*nly *m*emory). Permanent memory built into the computer during manufacture.

RS-232, 232C. A standard interface for computers and peripheral devices, such as a modems.

save. To store a program or data on a storage device, such as a disk, so it can be used again.

scroll. To move text on a screen vertically or horizontally.

semiconductor. A material that transmits electricity better than a resistor or an insulator but not as well as a true conductor.

Understanding Computers

The ability of a semiconductor to conduct electricity can be changed by temperature variation or by adding impurities. Used to make memory chips and other computer circuits.

shareware. Software that is made available on a try-before-you-buy basis. You agree to pay only after you have made a firm decision to continue using the program.

software. The instructions telling a computer what to do. Also called programs. There are two main types of software: system and applications.

spreadsheet program. A tool used for budgeting, accounting, and other financial tasks. Like a paper spreadsheet, an electronic spreadsheet consists of rows and columns.

supercomputer. The fastest type of computer. Used to design bridges and airplanes, do basic research in science, forecast weather, etc.

telecommunications. The transmission of data from one computer to another via telephone lines and other communications links.

user friendly. A term that indicates that a computer or piece of software is easy to use.

user groups. Clubs of computer owners, usually organized around one particular type of computer or software. Some user groups have software libraries—programs members can try out, copy, and use.

virus. A computer program or part of a program made to reproduce itself, like a biological virus, and spread from one program or computer to another. The virus may destroy data and programs or damage equipment.

word processing software. A program that enables you to write and edit text.

For further reference

General
Blasko, Larry
  *ABCs of Computers: A Plain-English
    Guide*
  Computing
Bradbeer, Robin, De Bono, Peter, and
  Laurie, Peter
  The Beginner's Guide to Computers
  Addison-Wesley
Holtz, Herman
  *How to Make Money with Your
    Micro*
  John Wiley

Makower, Ernest
  Personal Computers A–Z
  Doubleday
Roberts, Ralph
  Computer Viruses
  Compute!
Wang, Wally
  101 Computer Business Ideas
  Computer Publishing Enterprises
Weintraub, Joseph
  *Exploring Careers in the Computer
    Field*
  Rosen Publishing Group

How to buy a computer
Consumer Guide
  Computer Buying Guide
  Publications International

Gookin, Dan
  *How to Understand and Buy
    Computers*
  Computer Publishing Enterprises

Children and computers
Gebhart-Seele, Peter A.
  *Computers and the Child:
    A Montessori Approach*
  Computer Science

Pagnoni, Mario
  Computers and Small Fries
  Avery Publishing Group

Computer history
Augarten, Stan
  *Bit by Bit: An Illustrated History
    of Computers*
  Ticknor & Fields
Kidder, Tracy
  The Soul of a New Machine
  Little, Brown

Ritchie, David
  *The Computer Pioneers: The Making
    of a Modern Computer*
  Simon & Schuster
Slater, Robert
  Portraits in Silicon
  MIT Press

Computer programming
Crookall, Philip
  *Computer Programming for Real
    Beginners*
  Arco
Downing, Douglas
  *Computer Programming in Basic the
    Easy Way*
  Barron's Educational Series

Hartnell, Tim
  *Creating Adventure Games on Your
    Computer*
  Ballantine
Lammers, Susan
  Programmers at Work
  Microsoft
Lampton, Christopher
  Basic for Beginners
  Franklin Watts

Special applications
Brand, Stewart
  *The Whole Earth Computer
    Catalogue*
  Doubleday
Hsu, Jeffrey
  *Guide to Commercial
    Telecommunications Services*
  Prentice-Hall
McWilliams, Peter
  Computers and the Disabled
  Doubleday

Noble, David F. and Noble, Virginia
  *Improve Your writing with Word
    Processing*
  Que
Parker, Roger C.
  *Looking Good in Print: A Guide to
    Basic Design for Desktop
    Publishing*
  Ventana
Townsend, Carl
  Electronic Mail and Beyond
  Wadsworth

Advancing Your Career

Whether you are interested in part-time work or a lifetime career commitment, careful reading of this chapter will inform you of the many possibilities before you. If you have already chosen your career, the information will help prepare you for promotion. It will also help those who simply want to ensure that they keep their jobs. Starting a new career in mid-life or after retirement calls for special advice and encouragement.

Here are some of the forecasts worth considering before making any new career decisions:

- About 151 million men and women are expected to comprise the labor force in the year 2006—some 18 million more than the figure for 1996.
- Nearly two-thirds of the increase will be among women. Already, two-income families are the norm rather than the exception in today's economy.
- Job growth in the service industries (such as health services, transportation, communications, public utilities, trade, finance, insurance, real estate, fast food, and government) is expected to account for about 95 percent of all new jobs between 1996 and 2006.
- By 1996, almost 27 million workers had retired and begun collecting Social Security benefits. Many of them have taken advantage of Social Security amendments that allow them to earn additional income without losing any benefits.
- High-school graduates are quickly entering the job market, often foregoing college in favor of computer schools and vocational training institutions.
- A shortage of college graduates is starting to show up in such fields as computer engineering and telecommunications.
- The demand for typists will decrease as the use of word processors creates openings for computer operators and programmers.
- Among the fastest growing occupations will be personal and home health care aide, computer systems analyst, and computer engineer.
- Employment of teachers for preschool and kindergarten children is expected to increase about 30 percent between 1996 and 2006. Employment of special education teachers is expected to grow by almost 60 percent. Specific, practical advice follows in each of the following sections.

Job opportunities in rapidly growing fields

Industry	Fastest growing occupation	Job growth 1996-2006	Percent increase
Health services	Personal and home care aides	171,000	85
	Physical and corrective therapy aides and assistants	66,000	79
	Home health aides	378,000	76
	Medical assistants	166,000	74
	Physical therapists	81,000	71
	Registered nurses	411,000	21
Business services	Paralegals	76,000	68
	Human services workers	98,000	55
	Adjustment clerks	183,000	46
	Receptionists and information clerks	318,000	30
	Guards	221,000	23
	Clerical supervisors and managers	262,000	19
	Cashiers	530,000	17
	General managers and top executives	467,000	15
Education services	Special education teachers	241,000	59
	Adult and vocational education teachers	123,000	41
	Teacher aides and educational assistants	370,000	38
	Secondary school teachers	312,000	22
	Preschool and kindergarten teachers	98,000	20
	College and university faculty	162,000	19
Food services	Bread and pastry bakers	48,000	26
	Short order and fast food cooks	174,000	22
	Food preparation workers	234,000	19
	Restaurant cooks	106,000	15
Computers and electronics	Computer engineers	235,000	109
	Systems analysts	520,000	103

Preparing for the job search

Assessing your abilities.

When preparing for a job search, take the time to sit quietly and assess what you have done with your life. In addition to any work experience, what abilities do you have that qualify you for the job market? If you look closely at your past experiences, you may be surprised at the possibilities they point to for your future.

Take a pencil and paper and list all the skills and talents you have taken for granted all your life. What abilities do you use in your nonpaid activities? Can you cook, drive a car, write letters, sing in the church choir? See how you might apply the skills that you enjoy using most to a job situation.

How to start.

To draw up your success chart, start as far back in your life as you wish. For instance, you may have had to recite a soliloquy from Shakespeare in tenth grade, or a poem in Sunday school when you were even younger. Whatever your age at the time, recitation in front of a group indicates poise, some public speaking ability, commitment—and courage.

Divide your life into five-year intervals. List each success or accomplishment in the first column, the skills or experience gained in a second column. It is also a good idea to consider negative experiences. Perhaps you hated selling Girl Scout cookies. You should ask yourself if this typifies your attitude toward selling

Matching yourself with the World of Work

	1. Leadership/Persuasion	2. Helping/Instructing others	3. Problem-solving/Creativity	4. Initiative	5. Work as part of team	6. Frequent public contacts	7. Manual dexterity	8. Physical stamina	9. Hazardous	10. Outdoors	11. Confined
Automobile mechanics			•		•	•	•	•			•
Bank clerks				•							•
Bank tellers				•	•						•
Blue-collar supervisors		•	•	•	•		•		•		
Dental hygienists		•			•	•	•	•			
Dieticians	•	•	•	•	•	•					
Drafters					•		•			•	
Employment counselors	•	•	•	•	•	•				•	
Firefighters		•	•		•	•	•	•	•		
Landscape architects			•	•	•	•					
Librarians	•	•	•	•	•	•					
Mail carriers						•	•	•		•	
Market research analysts	•		•	•	•						
Police officers	•	•	•	•	•	•	•	•	•		
Photographic process workers						•					•
Secondary school teachers	•	•	•	•	•	•					
Secretaries					•	•	•				
Waiters, waitresses				•		•	•	•			

and, if so, remind yourself to stay out of that field.

Stick to your positive experiences when making an entry on the success chart. Consider what satisfactions and rewards came out of each experience. List these in a third column.

Matching your skills with work. Your success chart will give you the information about your marketable skills that you will need to apply to the Department of Labor *World of Work* chart. A sample from this chart is shown on page 24; you will find the entire chart on page 52.

The average person's length of time at the same job is 4.8 years. Although your career decisions are important, they are not necessarily meant to last forever. Once you have developed some experience at self-assessment, you will be able to go through the process more efficiently five years hence if need be. It would be wise to keep all you paperwork filed away for future reference.

The two examples shown on this page and on page 26 show the success charts of Julie Parsons, a homemaker who wants to reenter the work force, and Edward Stubbs, a hospital administrator who wants to start his own business (with his wife, Alice) after he retires. The amount of your work experience will determine where you start your success chart.

Julie Parsons started her chart back in childhood, which increased her confidence for job-hunting because she saw the range of her own experience. Edward and Alice Stubbs started with adult work experience. Though the Stubbses had tested most of their abilities, they wanted to develop a full profile of themselves because going into business on their own was a big and somewhat risky step for them.

Broad experience is useful in business

Edward and Alice Stubbs's catering business is a perfect example of a business formed from skills that are most enjoyed. Their access to advertising in their community theater program enabled them to reach exactly the right market at a low cost. Their big old house was well suited to their business needs and activities.

Past social and volunteer participation gave them the opportunity to show off their talents to the community and to gain experience and a good reputation.

CATERING SERVICE	Finance/ budgeting	Public Relations	Organizational ability	Communication	Working with people	Leadership	Cooperation	Dexterity	Creativity, cooking	Risk	
Edward Stubbs age 65	•	•	•	•	•	•	•	•	•		Alice Stubbs age 63
Hospital Administrator 35 yrs.	•	•	•	•	•	•			•		
Gourmet cook 40 yrs.							•	•			Gourmet Club Secretary 10 yrs.
Budget chairman 15 yrs. Finance committee	•	•	•								
Board of Directors community theater 7 yrs	•	•	•	•	•	•			•	•	Board of Directors community theater 15 yrs
Co-chairman social committee 8 yrs.				•	•	•	•	•			Co-chairman social committee 14 yrs.
Member of Chamber of commerce 30 yrs.		•		•	•						
Church Deacon 30 yrs			•	•	•	•					Deaconess of Church 30 yrs.
		•	•	•	•			•			Publicity chairman community theater 14 yrs.
		•	•	•	•						Subscription Drive 8 yrs.
	•	•	•	•	•						Secretary of Church choir 13 yrs.
		•	•	•	•	•	•				Volunteer at hospital cafeteria 25 yrs.

JULIE PARSONS' SUCCESS CHART

Age	Successes	Skills used/acquired	Enjoyment/rewards
5-10	Recited poem at school assembly	Courage, poise, following directions, public speaking	Public acclaim, applause, approval
	Learned to swim	Physical fitness, athletic dexterity	Feeling of fitness, prize for diving
	Won spelling contest	Competition, self-motivation	Prize, public acclaim
11-15	Sold most Scout cookies	Salesmanship, competition, teamwork, self-motivation	Prize, personal satisfaction, helped troop
	Babysitting	Dependability, trust, child care	Approval, earning money
16-19	Editor of yearbook	Typing, design, layout, organization, photography, public relations, dependability, leadership	Concrete proof of accomplishment: book, name in print; problem-solving
	Lead in school musical	Teamwork, poise, following directions, dependability	Public acclaim, approval, using talent
	Class treasurer for 3 years	Mathematical ability, leadership, dependability	Problem-solving, public approval, trust, popularity
	Graduation	Intelligence, public relations, leadership	Diploma, feeling of accomplishment
20-25	Job as library assistant	Public relations, mathematical ability	Feeling of independence, earning money
	Church choir	Musical talent, teamwork, dependability	Public approval, using talent
	Marriage	Economics, math, sewing, teamwork, budget management, public relations	Personal acceptance, independence, trust, love
	Mother	Nursing, laundress, instructor, chef, counselor, public relations, arbitrator, flexibility	Trust, approval, love, problem-solving
26-30	Cub Scout leader and Sunday school teacher	Organization, leadership, fund-raising, trust, commitment	Public approval, teamwork, problem-solving
	Treasurer of church fair and fund-raising drive	Mathematical ability, trust, popularity	Teamwork, public approval, leadership
	Treasurer of reading club, member of library board of directors	Mathematical ability, trust, leadership, knowledge of books	Working with books and math again

Advancing Your Career

Career goals

Ultimate goals. Carefully consider your success chart and see what patterns show up. On Julie Parsons' chart, two interests keep reappearing: math/accounting and books/publishing. These patterns caused Julie to list "comptroller of her local newspaper" as her ultimate goal.

Edward Stubbs found the confidence to begin his own catering business after reviewing his success chart. He saw that throughout their 40 years of marriage, he and his wife had gained great satisfaction and given great pleasure to others through cooking, a joint hobby.

Now is the time to let yourself think about your ideal job. Refer to your success chart and ask yourself what you would most like to do with the remainder of your working years. Consider what contribution your work could make to society and make sure that your goal fits your values. A sample goal statement is shown at the top of this page.

Intermediate goals. With your goal statement in front of you, consider what intermediate goals you can set for yourself that will logically lead to your ideal job. If you want to be a teacher, education courses would be one of your intermediate goals. An even shorter range intermediate goal would be finding out about available courses. The point is to break your tasks down into manageable steps so that you can embark enthusiastically on taking the first one.

GOAL STATEMENT	PAUL CARTER
1. Career goal:	Chief computer programmer in medical diagnostics
2. Preparation:	B.S. electrical engineering and computer programming
3. Company:	High-tech industries
4. Social value:	Contributing to medical research

If you find yourself procrastinating, you may have made your intermediate goals too general. Rework them until you have made them so specific that at least one of them can be accomplished immediately. Making a list is an important visual aid, and you have the added pleasure of checking off each step that you complete. Below you will find an intermediate goal scoreboard used by a young man preparing for a job interview.

Paul Carter's scoreboard illustrates one way of setting down intermediate steps. Set up your own scoreboard any way that works for you, as long as it is

Paul Carter's monthly plan

SUN	MON	TUES	WED	THUR	FRI	SAT
	1 SEND FOR HI-TECH ANNUAL REPORT	2 CHECK LIBRARY FOR RECENT ARTICLES ABOUT HI-TECH; LOOK FOR NAMES	3 Call Friends who might know someone in HI-TECH field	4	5	6
7	8 See College Placement Officer Ask For References	9	10 FIND NAME TO WRITE TO IN ANNUAL REPORT	11 Talk with Professors in Related courses; Ask For References	12 CHECK COLLEGE DIRECTORY FOR ALUMNAE IN HI-TECH JOBS; TELL THEM OF PLANNED VISIT	13 CHECK ALL MATERIAL FOR JOB DESCRIPTIONS
14	15 Begin work on résumé	16	17	18 FINISH RÉSUMÉ	19 HAVE RÉSUMÉ PRINTED PROFESSIONALLY	20
21	22 VISIT HI-TECH FIRMS; SPEAK WITH CONTACTS; TAKE NOTES FOR INTERVIEW	23 PICK UP RÉSUMÉ	24 WRITE FOR INTERVIEW; SEND RÉSUMÉ AND COVER LETTER OF INTRODUCTION	25 SEND THANK YOU NOTES TO ALL CONTACTS	26 Plan questions For interview	27
28	29	30 Follow up Letter with call for appointment GET APPOINTMENT!!	31			

specific. Some useful questions to ask yourself are:

- Keeping in mind your ultimate goal, what skills must you develop? How?
- What are the available jobs in your area and how do your qualifications fit their needs? How do *your* needs fit their requirements?
- What are the priorities among the steps you must take to qualify for your ideal job?
- What resources are necessary—money, education, equipment, uniforms, etc.?
- What reasonable time limits can you set for accomplishing each intermediate goal?

If the intermediate goal is a course, when can the course be completed? If it is an interview, when will you set that up? Be realistic, write everything down, and then do your best to stick to your timetable.

If unexpected delays occur, rewrite your scoreboard so that it is once more realistic and manageable. If you face long-term career preparation, such as completing a course, serving an apprenticeship, or getting an advanced degree, divide your goals into yearly steps until they can be broken down into monthly or weekly tasks, as Paul Carter has done.

What schooling do you need?

To school or not to school? If you have been out of the job market for a while, you may immediately think of additional schooling as a solution to your dilemma. Often it is the appropriate first step to embarking on a new or different career. Nevertheless, make sure you do not rush to the registrar's office before taking an inventory of your skills. Lack of confidence rather than lack of education may be your problem.

The essential diploma. There is only one diploma that should not be questioned—your high school diploma. If your high school career was interrupted, there is a basic exam you may take to earn your General Equivalency Diploma (GED). This certificate will make you eligible for jobs requiring the completion of high school.

Your local high school guidance office will refer you to the nearest adult learning center where you can find out what steps are necessary to obtain your GED. Often you can study independently at home and pass your exam without having to go back into the classroom. You may take the exam as many times as necessary to earn your GED.

Going back to school?

Pros and cons. If you are undecided about the necessity of additional schooling, consider these arguments for and against. Applying such arguments to your own situation can help you make the right decision.

PROS

- An additional degree may advance your career in a specific way.
- A particular course of study may guarantee you a job.
- A master's degree may guarantee you a higher salary in your field.
- You may need more education to break into the field of your choice.
- All education is useful and may be applied in unexpected ways in the future.

CONS

- A liberal arts degree does not guarantee a job.
- Most people do not end up working in their field of study.
- Approximately 80 percent of the new jobs (see chart on next page) do not require a degree, though they may require vocational training.
- Many companies prefer to do their own training.
- You may price yourself out of the job market with more degrees, especially in the field of education.

Checklist: Getting the most out of additional training

Recall your previous educational experience. Consider each of the following and check one.

1. You prefer:
   ( ) Studying by yourself
   ( ) Studying with others

2. What suits you best is:
   ( ) Learning at your own speed
   ( ) Learning at the speed of a group

3. You learn best:
   ( ) In a lecture course taking notes
   ( ) In a course where you learn by doing

4. You prefer having material presented:
   ( ) By using words and ideas
   ( ) By sounds, pictures, and objects

Try to tailor any courses you take to fit the choices checked above. You will learn more easily in a situation that suits your educational preferences.

Advancing Your Career

Weekly earnings: VH = very high, H = high, L = low, VL = very low

Degree jobs

Administration and management
Administrative services managers	VH
Construction managers	VH
Education administrators	VH
Industrial production managers	VH
Personnel managers	VH
Purchasing managers	VH

Business services
Accountants and auditors	VH
Claims examiners	H
Purchasing agents	VH

Education
College and university teachers	VH
Elementary schoolteachers	VH
Librarians	VH
Secondary schoolteachers	VH
Special education teachers	VH

Engineering
Chemical engineers	VH
Civil engineers	VH
Electrical and electronic engineers	VH
Mechanical engineers	VH

Physical science
Chemists	VH
Oceanographers	VH
Physicists	VH

Professional
Dentists	VH
Lawyers	VH
Physicians	VH
Registered nurses	VH

Social science
Economists	VH
Psychologists	VH
Social workers	H

Nondegree jobs

Building trades
Carpenters	H
Electricians	H
Plumbers	H

Business services
Bank tellers	L
Bill and account collectors	L
Cashiers	VL
Insurance claims clerks	H
Mail clerks	VL
Postal clerks and mail carriers	VH
Receptionists	L
Sales order fillers	H
Secretaries	L
Retail salespersons	L

Education
Teachers' aides and educational assistants	VL

Food services
Bakers	VL
Cooks	VL
Waiters and waitresses	VL

Health and personal services
Child care workers	VL
Dental and medical assistants	VL
Home health aides	VL
Occupational therapy assistants	L

Manufacturing and transportation
Assemblers, fabricators, and handworkers	L
Bus drivers	L
Electrical and electronic assemblers	L
Heavy equipment operators	VH
Truck drivers	H
Welders and cutters	H

Higher education is a requirement for many professional workers, such as oceanographers and registered nurses. Other workers, such as heavy equipment operators and bakers, may require special or on-the-job training.

Weighing the alternatives. Julie

Parsons, the homemaker who filled out one of the success charts shown earlier, wants to reenter the job market now that her children are in high school. As is the case with many families, the Parsons will find an additional salary more than welcome when the time comes to put two children through college.

How should Julie Parsons go about qualifying for a job in the field of her choice? Although she has had very little paid job experience, the skills she discovered from her success chart affirm her enjoyment of and talent for math and her interest in the field of publishing. Matching her skills to the Department of Labor occupational charts, Julie has decided on a career in public accounting and publishing. Her ultimate goal— her ideal job—is to be the comptroller of her town newspaper. Does Julie need to go back to school?

Julie Parsons has many responsibilities to juggle while preparing herself for a career. She cannot abandon her role of homemaker to become a full-time student. She still wants to participate in activities with her children, and knows she must find a way to advance her knowledge and expertise in the field of public accounting. Can she do all of these?

Educational alternatives. Getting a

Bachelor of Arts or Bachelor of Science (B.A. or B.S.) degree usually involves a four-year commitment, a luxury many people cannot afford. Fortunately, there are other options that still will allow you to advance your career. Listed on the next page are a series of alternatives to a four-year degree. Evaluate each one in the light of your particular career situation and needs.

Going for the college degree

Deciding on the institution. Colleges and universities will send catalogs on request, but your local library may have copies of the ones you are interested in.

SHOULD JULIE PARSONS GO TO COLLEGE?

ULTIMATE GOAL: Treasurer of town paper

JOB DESCRIPTION: Position requires excellent bookkeeping and accounting
                  skills, ability to deal directly with the public, and the
                  leadership qualities necessary to supervise a business
                  office.

QUALIFICATIONS   JULIE'S EXPERIENCE

Knowledge of newspaper business—Editor of yearbook
                                   organizational skills
Experience   leadership
  bookkeeping   initiative
  budgeting
  accounting   Treasurer—various organizations
                                     problem-solving
                                     bookkeeping
                                     budgeting
Skills
  problem-solving
  leadership
  initiative   History of public relations
  administrative   dependability

LACKING: accounting; administrative

JULIE'S CHOICE: Community College

In a community college Julie could take her courses while the children were
in school during the day. Vacations would coincide with their school
vacations.

In two years she completed a course in business administration in a classroom
situation that allowed her to learn and experience leadership roles again in
a setting best suited to her.

Make an appointment with your local high school guidance counselor, who has all the information you need—and, probably, some helpful advice. These guidance services are available to any taxpayer, no matter how long ago or where you received your high school diploma. The counselor will help you choose a college and make out the application.

How do you pay for college? When Paul Carter, the graduating high school student interested in a job in computer programming, decided to go to the state university, his family could not afford to support him throughout his college career. Paul was an exceptionally bright student and he earned a scholarship. This helped but did not entirely solve his financial problems. His guidance counselor referred him to *College Financial Aid*, a book edited by John Schwartz (College Research Group, Prentice-Hall, NY). Another good book prepared by the College Research Group is the *College Financial Aid Annual.*

"How to Get Credit for What You Know"
(alternative routes to educational credit)
This pamphlet is intended for
both men and women.

Contact: Women's Bureau
Department of Labor
200 Constitution Avenue, NW
Washington, DC 20210

For veterans:

Read *The Guide to the Evaluation of Educational Experiences in the Armed Services*, published by the American Council on Education, which is available in some libraries and at many Veterans' Affairs offices.

Alternatives to a four-year degree

Community colleges: Most of these colleges vary their courses to fit the needs of the community where they are located. Usually, courses in both vocational training and management are offered. Specific training courses (hotel and restaurant management, accounting, nursing, hairstyling, dental hygiene, etc.) generally take two years to complete. Associate degrees in applied arts and sciences are often awarded for the completion of a two-year course of study. The academic courses are similar to those given at four-year colleges, and credits are transferable for those who wish to continue their education.

Vocational training schools: Courses are offered full- or part-time to prepare you for a particular occupation. The placement rate for these schools is high, and the costs are reasonable.

Correspondence and evening courses: These courses may take longer to complete than those in which attendance is required, but they make the exploration of new fields available to everyone, no matter where they live. People who cannot attend classes regularly may continue their education or job advancement at their own pace without putting a strain on their financial resources.

Apprenticeship programs: These are offered by many companies or, in some instances, by master craftsmen. Usually the company or craftsman will pay the apprentice and guarantee a job if the program is successfully completed.

Employee training programs: Many companies prefer to train their own personnel (airlines, for example). The training may be considered part of the job in that it requires a full-time commitment and is paid at the same rate as the base salary of the job itself. Often it is regarded as on-the-job training.

Armed services: The U.S. government offers training in marketable skills applicable to civilian life in return for an armed-service career commitment of two to four years.

Temporary services: There are many temporary services throughout the country that offer part-time work, mainly in clerical jobs. Working for one or more of them can be a productive way for a person who has been out of the job market a long time to become familiar with office procedures, earn a salary, and get an idea of what work is available. Getting some experience in a field unfamiliar to you may reveal talents you did not know you had. In addition, working for a company as a temporary employee may lead to a permanent job offer.

Going after the job

Résumés. Résumés are a useful if overrated tool in a job search. Sending out résumés is not an effective way of seeking job interviews. In fact, statistics show that you will receive a response on the average of one out of every 40 to 50 résumés; depending on the competition in the field you want to enter, the response could be as low as one out of every thousand. You could end up very discouraged if you depend on your résumé to launch you. You will, however, need a résumé at some point before being employed.

An important function of your résumé is to serve as a reminder to a prospective employer of your suitability for the job available. A résumé can also serve to notify the company that you have skills or abilities they may wish to call upon in the future. The wisest course is to carry your résumé with you to interviews rather than send it on ahead to be thrown away, or to be filed away, with dozens of other résumés.

Some experts advise writing the résumé *after* the interview, tailoring it to the job. You would then send the résumé along with a thank-you letter. Some people use a heavy beige or cream-colored paper for their résumé so that it will stand out from all the rest. Those sending out a great many résumés should use a professional copying machine or service.

The short form. Anyone faced with writing a résumé knows the frustration of trying to stretch the relevant information to a full page—or to cut it down to fit just one page. The most important thing to remember is that the résumé must point out a special talent or interest you have that matches the job desired. Although the rule is to make your résumé precise and concise, keeping it to one page if possible, you should never crowd the information so that it is hard to read. Special circumstances may necessitate a two- or even three-page résumé. Just make sure that it is neatly typed, correctly spelled, and attractively arranged on the paper. If your typing is inadequate or nonexistent, professional résumé services are available at a small cost. Since a messy, badly typed résumé will represent you very poorly indeed, this expenditure is well worth the investment.

Job search detective work. Once you have prepared yourself for a career in the field of your choice, you need to become a detective dedicated to finding the best job for you. Unless you are lucky enough to have the right job offered to you early in your job search, finding it in the shortest possible time is—and should be—a full-time occupation in itself.

```
JEROME DAY
56 Cash Street
Catersville, Kansas 09376
(814)773-5791

JOB OBJECTIVE
Electrician

WORK EXPERIENCE   Tom's Small Engines
1986-Present      Catersville, Kansas
                  Repaired electrical equipment
                  and parts of engines,
                  hand-crafted parts for
                  obsolete machines.

1981-1985         Jansen Tool and Electrical Parts
                  56 Center Street
                  Evansville, Kansas
                  Apprenticed and worked up
                  to position of foreman of ten men
                  doing industrial wiring.
EDUCATION
1981-1984         Electrician's Apprenticeship
                  Completed all courses
                  including blueprint reading.

1979              General Equivalency Diploma

ARMED SERVICES    U.S. Army. Private to Sergeant.
1979-1981         Served in California and Alaska.
                  Inventoried electrical parts.

PERSONAL          Excellent health. Free to travel.

REFERENCES        Furnished upon request.
```

```
JULIE PARSONS
Halfbend Road
Turnston, Indiana 32557
(702) 560-1422

JOB OBJECTIVE
Accountant, Administrative Assistant

WORK EXPERIENCE   Turnston Standard Journal
1980-Present      45 Main Street
                  Turnston, Indiana
                  Sold classified advertising.
1965-1980         Retired to raise family.
1964-1966         Assistant in Turnston Library.
EDUCATION
1980-1985         Part-time courses in Accounting
                  and Business Administration
                  Turnston Community College
                  Certificate of Completion
                  with distinction.

VOLUNTEER WORK    Served as treasurer of community
Accounting        organizations for 15 years
and               (Parent-Teachers Assn., Reading Club,
Budgeting         church fund-raising campaign and fairs).
Public Relations  Appeared on local radio and TV
and               during fund-raising campaigns,
Communications    promoting church fair and shows.
Publishing        Editor of high school yearbook;
                  in charge of layout, editing,
                  financing, printing, and bookkeeping.

PERSONAL          Mature, in good health,
                  own and drive a car.
REFERENCES        Furnished upon request.
```

Your future is worth your concentrated attention to the details that could make the difference between earning your salary in a boring, dead-end job or advancing over the years in a satisfying and rewarding career.

Looking for valuable clues. You have chosen your field and identified geographically where you are likely to be most successful in your job search. The next step is to target the companies or institutions that could actually offer you the job you want. Your local library and magazine stand are logical places to begin your research.

Magazines covering business generally or concentrating on the particular field you hope to enter will give you an idea about the successful companies, the future trends, and even the openings in new areas. A search through the periodical (newspaper and magazine) catalogs in your library can provide valuable information about any company you are interested in working for.

When you have narrowed down your choice of places to apply, your detective work should focus on learning everything you can about those companies. Ask people in the field for information about the company's future, its problems, its new products, its expansion plans, and, of course, any expected layoffs. Sending for the company's newsletter and promotional material will add bits and pieces to the overall picture of your potential employer. No clue you find to a possible job should be overlooked.

Organizing the job search

Networking. Much has been written on the "old boy network"—a seemingly closed club of powerful men making executive decisions among themselves. Though most of us do not qualify for chairperson of the board, we can thank the "old boys" for a good idea. Realize the power of networking, and create your own network. Enlist the help of people you know or meet in your job search. Tell them what your goals are and ask them to help you in any way they can.

You will be surprised at the way useful bits of information turn up if you keep asking friends and acquaintances what they know about your field or company of choice.

Your butcher, your minister, your car mechanic—do not hesitate to let everyone with whom you are on friendly terms know that you are job hunting. Your mechanic may service a manager in the company where you want to work and may have overheard him mention a problem or an opening. You never know.

Another way to create your own network is to go to conventions or civic interest groups frequented by the personnel of a company you have targeted as a prospect. Make yourself known to these people and listen to any advice they have. There is, of course, a fine line between showing enthusiasm for your job search and making a nuisance of yourself. Watch people's faces, listen to their tone of voice, and politely withdraw if you feel a chill.

Checklist for writing your résumé

1. **Your name, address, and phone number** should be typed at the top of the page.

2. **Your job objective** comes next. Be as specific as you can. Your research should have informed you of the job that the company has available or the area that you want to pursue for your career.

3. **List your work experience and education**, along with any special experience (volunteer work, avocations) that enhances your qualifications for the job. There is no need to list jobs or bosses that were a career mistake for you.

4. **Add personal information** if you wish. Personal information should never be negative (such as "Divorced"). In fact, all the information on your résumé should be positive. Do not lie, but do omit any negative information, such as being fired, or negative preferences, such as "Hate to type."

5. **References** need only be furnished on request; however, you should have your references readily available should they be called upon. Everyone (friends and past employers alike) appreciates advance notice that a stranger may be calling to ask questions about you. This consideration will keep your source from being embarrassed and caught off-guard, and will probably result in a better recommendation for you.

Suggested reading

Résumés that get jobs
Résumé Service
Jane Reed, Editor
Arco Publishing Co., N.Y.

What Color Is Your Parachute: A Practical Manual for Job and Career Changers
Richard Nelson Bolles
Ten Speed Press

Introduction to the Job Hunt Success Kit
Center for Career Development
Phyllis Martin
11385 Landon Lane
Cincinnati, Ohio 45246

Resources for researching careers

For information about particular fields:
Subject Collections: A Guide to Special Book Collections
Lee Ash and William G. Miller, editors
New York: Bowker

For information about organizations:
Annual reports, house organs, stock reports,
public relations offices, newspapers,
historical societies

For information about occupations:
Directory of Professional and Trade Organizations
(check local societies)

For information about people:
Who's Who in America;
Who's Who in the East;
Who's Who in the West
Professional directories

Let Uncle Sam help you in your search

The federal government has agencies engaged in continuous research on careers. This work is funded by your tax dollars.
Let them work for you. Here are a few places to write for assistance:

Director, Office of Plans, Policies, and Design
U.S. Employment Service
Employment and Training Administration
Department of Labor
200 Constitution Avenue NW
Washington, DC 20210
Job seekers and employers will be sent a list of place-
ment related services funded by the government.

Division of Applicant Services
Office of Program Services
U.S. Employment Service
Employment and Training Administration
Department of Labor
200 Constitution Avenue NW
Washington, DC 20210
This job information service is located within local em-
ployment centers. The office provides a *Job Bank Book*
that enables the applicant to conduct his or her own job
search.

Department of Labor
200 Constitution Avenue NW
Washington, DC 20210
For any questions regarding the job possibilities in your
area or forecasts with respect to employment, an inquiry
to this agency will prove useful.
Your letter will be directed to the proper office, which
will send you the information you have requested.

Computerized Placement System
Automated Matching System Division
Office of Program Services
U.S. Employment Service
Employment and Training Administration
200 Constitution Avenue NW
Washington, DC 20210
This office provides a daily printout of all jobs listed
with the employment service in your area and distrib-
utes it to local employment service offices. Automated
Matching system uses computers to identify registered
jobs for which a particular applicant is qualified.

Where to look for job openings

- Local Chamber of Commerce
- Local Better Business Bureau
- *Career Guide to Professional Associations*
  Sulzburger and Graham, Publishers
  169 West 91st Street
  New York, NY 10024
- *National Trade and Professional Associations*
  Columbia Books
  1212 New York Avenue NW
  Washington, DC 20005
- Job listings on the Internet and World Wide Web.
  Perhaps the best-known Web site for job hunters is
  America's Job Bank, which lists some 750,000
  job openings across the country.
  Use the Internet address http://www.ajb.dni.us
  to access this service.

- *The Best Companies for Minorities:*
  Employers Across America Who Recruit, Train,
  and Promote Minorities
  by Lawrence O. Graham
  NAL/Dutton Division of Penguin U.S.A.
  375 Hudson Street
  New York, NY 10014
- *What Color Is Your Parachute? A Practical Manual*
  for Job-Hunters & Career-Changers
  by Richard Nelson Bolles
  Ten Speed Press
  P.O. Box 7123
  Berkeley, CA 94707
  Published annually, this book is an invaluable
  source for job hunters.

Reading want ads

Quite a bit of time may be required to go through want ad columns. You must read enough of each ad to discover whether it interest you, whether you are qualified for the job offered, and—most important—whether you should apply. This is time well spent. With experience, you will be able to read the ads faster because the wording used will become familiar. You will learn, for example, that EOE means equal opportunity employer, a term indicating that the firm offering the job does not discriminate against women or minority groups. FEE PAID or F/PD means that the firm offering the job will pay the employment agency's fee. EXPD F/T means experienced, full-time.

Most important, however, is the caution you develop in deciding whether a job offered in an ad is realistic. Can one really believe a claim that an untrained person can make $35,000 a year at a job? Incidentally, ads that make such claims often do not mention what the job is. Other ads offer work at home for unrealistically high rates of pay. It is wise to be careful.

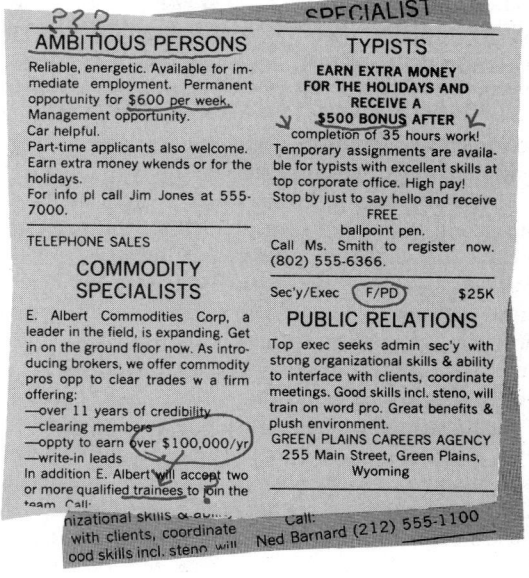

Know your salary range

Before you go to an interview, you should know the salary range for the job you want. Money is always an intimidating subject, so prepare yourself with as much knowledge as possible. Here are some sources to consult for information.

- **Visit your library.** You will find a number of books listed in the card catalogs under "salaries" and under the occupations you are interested in.

- **Write to the Department of Labor,** Bureau of Labor Statistics, Washington, DC 20212. Ask for Area Wage Surveys and the Bureau of Labor Statistics News Releases.

- **Consult the professional organization that serves your chosen field.** The Encyclopedia of Associations (at your local library) will tell you where to write.

- **Call the personnel office of the company you want to interview.** Tell them you are doing research on various careers and ask about their salary range for the job or jobs you are interested in. Such a call should, of course, be made well before any interview letter is sent or appointment made.

- **Inquire at your college placement office.** Here you can find up-to-date material on professional and higher level careers.

- **Check the want ads.** These newspaper advertisements are good for learning about salaries offered for entry-level jobs.

Know the value of fringe benefits

Find out whether the salary includes such fringe benefits as insurance, health plans, vacation, education, and retirement programs. *These benefits can add as much as 25 percent to the value of a salary.* A salary of $1600 a month with maximum benefits is really $2000.

The job interview

Writing for an interview. Consult the letter-writing section of this volume for samples of interview letters. What you want to say about yourself in the letter will be more important than the form. You should know specifically to whom you are writing and be clear about what you have to offer in the job you want. You should conclude the letter by informing the employer that you will phone the following week for an appointment.

If you have briefly referred to experience, education, or training that qualify you for a job, you need not include a résumé with your request for an interview. Even if you have no friend or acquaintance to recommend you, it helps to refer to some reputable person of whom the interviewer may have heard: "Professor Johnson of State University Biology Department suggested that I write to you" is a reasonable approach.

Your letter must make the interviewer want to see you. Think of ways you can contribute to the company even though there may not be a job opening at the time. Your letter may even suggest ways to increase sales or solve a problem or meet a challenge that your research has uncovered. If you are inventive, enthusiastic, and organized in your presentation, you may convince the interviewer to create a job for you. This happens more often than you might imagine, but it takes research, confidence, and imagination to prepare yourself with a solid proposal. On the other hand, you have nothing to lose if the company you want to work for has no openings. Making a good impression on interviewers may serve you well at some future time, when jobs you are suited for do fall open.

How to avoid preinterview jitters. The day of the interview, make sure you allow enough time to make your appearance impeccable. Get up an hour earlier or cancel other appointments. Make sure your appearance matches the appropriate points on the checklist and the drawings on the next page. For instance, if you have a heavy beard growth and your interview is scheduled for late afternoon, allow time for a fresh shave. Confronting your five o'clock shadow in the revolving door as you go into a building for an interview can throw you off balance and ruin your composure. These checkpoints are only guidelines, of course. Showing a clean appearance is obvious to most of us. Yet every one of us has forgotten the obvious under stress, and job interviews may certainly qualify as stressful situations. You should check every detail before you leave for your appointment.

Conservative dress is the recommendation of all experts in the employment field. Loud colors and flamboyant styles are not appropriate when interviewing for most jobs. Nevertheless, the ultimate judge of appropriate dress is you. If you are interviewing for a job as a construction worker, you may decide that clean

Preinterview checklist

Once your research and detective work are completed, check off these next steps:

1. Make sure you have used *all* your contacts and resources to inform yourself thoroughly about the company. Have you been able to identify the person who is in a position to hire you?

2. Ask yourself if you have done everything you can to have an interview arranged by someone in your network. All it takes is one sentence—"A good friend of mine asked me to recommend that you see a young journalism graduate"—and there you have an interview, thanks to the intervention of a stranger. But *you* have to set the process in motion and follow up.

3. Deal with personnel departments when you must. They are useful for entry-level jobs and are sometimes a necessary channel in setting up interviews with the department head you want to see. You may walk into most personnel departments without telephoning in advance. Have with you (in your head or on paper) a list of questions you wish to have answered, and leave with copies of any informational material (annual reports, benefit plan pamphlets, etc.) that may be useful to you.

4. Make use of employment agencies. They can sometimes be the fastest route to a job for which you are qualified. Use them if you feel you are bogging down in your own efforts. Every interview is a learning experience, and your ideal job can turn up through any channel.

5. If none of these approaches is successful, write a letter asking for an interview.

work clothes would be most appropriate. Surveys have shown, however, that even in occupations where a certain type of clothing is necessary on the job, taking the care to dress up instead of down for the interview impresses the employer and may even lead to an offer of a job at a higher level than the one you seek.

It never hurts to present yourself properly dressed. It is the first signal to the interviewer that you are concerned with detail. He will certainly see it as a sign of respect for him and your serious intent about the job.

Finally, write down and memorize the name of the person who will be interviewing you. If possible, find out and write down the names of any company personnel you will be dealing with before or after the interview.

Checklist for night before interview

1. **Hair** trimmed. Check supplies of shampoo, deodorant, toothpaste, etc., for morning shower.

2. **Fingernails** filed conservatively and cleaned. For women, polish should be neutral or coordinated to blend with your clothes and makeup.

3. **Clothes** freshly cleaned and pressed.

4. **Two pairs of hose** ready (one pair for your handbag) is a good idea for women. A sudden unsightly run need not be the cause for panic.

5. **A clean handkerchief** or a packet of tissues. Nervousness often makes the nose run; snuffling your way through an interview is likely to make both you and the interviewer uncomfortable.

6. **A small notebook and pen** for taking notes, such as names of secretaries, assistants, and receptionists. Make sure the notebook already contains the list of questions you want to ask, and the names of the people you will be seeing.

Looking good

The night before your job interview, choose what you will wear. Select clothes that are appropriate for the interview and that will help you feel at ease.

Checklist for arrival at interview

1. **Arrive early enough** to visit the rest room and check your appearance.

2. **Consult your notebook** to refresh your memory on the questions and names you have written down.

3. **Focus your attention** on what is happening around you. Be alert to people's expressions, the atmosphere of the office, and any clues as to how smoothly things are functioning. If what you notice is positive, say so in the interview: "The atmosphere here is electric. It must be an exciting place to work. . . . I find I do my best work in a calm environment like this one. . . . I like the way everything is neat and organized. . . . Your employees seem so cheerful and friendly. . . . I work best in a busy, fast-paced office like this one."

4. **Comment only on what is true and positive.** Negative thoughts should be kept to yourself and noted for your private consideration in accepting or rejecting the job. If noisy, chaotic work areas disturb you, do not think you are going to change the atmosphere. A better decision would be to turn down the job if it is offered.

Tips for the interview

1. **Always knock** on doors before entering.

2. **Use the interviewer's name** when acknowledging the introduction *and* when saying goodby. Introduce yourself by name if there is no one to perform the introduction. Be prepared to shake hands but do not initiate the gesture.

3. **Speak clearly and slowly.**

4. **Do not smoke or chew gum.**

5. **Listen well:**
   - Face the person squarely.
   - Establish eye contact.
   - Sit upright with straight but relaxed posture.
   - Keep hands away from face, preferably resting in your lap.
   - Lean forward to show interest.

6. **Do not use slang** or questionable language.

7. **Be prepared for leading questions:** "Tell me about yourself."
   Have clear, brief answers rehearsed.   "What do you think you could do for this job?"
   "Why are you interested in us?"

8. **Ask open questions** as much as possible:
   "I would like to know more about the qualifications for the job."
   "What do you think Hi Tech's future [production, sales] will hold in the next few years?"
   This sort of question leads to more information and a chance for you to participate by pointing out ways in which your qualifications fit the job description or the company's goals.

9. **When appropriate, ask questions or make comments that reveal your knowledge of the company:** "Hi Tech chose one of my favorite architects to design their executive offices. . . . I am very impressed with SeaLinks' support of the Olympics (or involvement in the community)."

10. **Do not interrupt;** always let the interviewer be the guide. Eye contact will enable you to tell if the interviewer expects you to fill in a silence. If he looks down at something on his desk, he may be thinking a point over. Wait until he looks up again before continuing the conversation.

11. **Do not get flustered** when asked a question you have no answer for. This is an opportunity to show your presence of mind and composure. Simply say, "I don't have the answer right now, but I will get back to you tomorrow." Make an entry on your note pad and follow through.

12. **Do not volunteer negative information.** If you left a previous job because you hated it, a positive but truthful comment might be that you wanted to move on to something more challenging. If you were fired, do not lie about it if asked, but do not volunteer the information. "My previous job was terminated," is just as truthful and less negative-sounding than "I was fired."

13. **Describe yourself by your skills** ("I have good secretarial skills") instead of letting your skills describe you ("I am a secretary"). The message thus conveyed is that you are not limited to a certain job category but can apply your skills to different jobs.

14. **Be alert to signs that the interview is over.** If the interviewer does not seem to know how to conclude, you might say, "I know your time is valuable. Thank you for seeing me. Is there anything more you would like to know about me?"

15. **Say goodby and thank you** (when appropriate) **to assistants, secretaries, and receptionists.** Use their names whenever possible.

16. **Always write a thank-you note.** Include any new information you think relevant, or any responses to unanswered questions. Attach your résumé (tailored to fit the job and preferably on beige or cream-colored paper).

A job search may begin (left) *with a visit to an employment agency or job placement service, state employment office, or a company's human resources office. A warm handshake* (right) *may signal successful conclusion of the search and the start of a promising career.*

Interviewers are people too. Most people who conduct interviews do not think they are very good at it. It is unlikely to be their main occupation. In fact, they may dread the interviewing process more than you do.

Interviewers fear they will fail to screen out applicants who are:

1. Chronic abusers of sick time.
2. Too passive to take any initiative or too headstrong to take instruction.
3. Abrasive or disruptive around coworkers.
4. Dishonest, incompetent, or irresponsible.

Any of these defects showing up in an employee would reflect badly on the interviewer's judgment and represent an expensive mistake for the company. In other words, hiring you could end up costing the interviewer his or her job.

It is up to you to address these silent questions and real fears by conveying the message that you will not turn out to be a problem. Here are some possible ways to do this:

Character: The interviewer is looking for signs that you are honest, trustworthy, and responsible. A mention of charitable activities, volunteer work, personal recommendations, or awards you have received may be appropriate.

Competence: How to handle this subject depends on your previous experience and the type of work you are seeking. The hardest situation is when you want to convey your ability to perform effectively in a job where you have no experience. Your enthusiasm and confidence will have to convince the interviewer. "I'm a quick learner and know I have abilities in this area from [mention avocational experience]. . . . I particularly enjoy mastering new skills. . . . I have always taken pride in my work. . . . I have always had a knack for detail work. . . . I'm good at working with people."

Health: "I never used up my sick time in my previous job," or simply, "I keep myself fit by regular exercise." Or, "My feeling is that if I'm home sick, I'm not doing the job I'm being paid to do."

Your interview rights

Federal law prohibits a hiring decision based on race, color, national origin, religion, sex, pregnancy, marital status, parenthood, age, height, weight, or criminal record.

There are rare exceptions in which an employer is entitled to demand a certain race or sex as a bona fide occupational qualification, as in a job for an actress.

Finally, the law prohibits asking personal questions or questions irrelevant to the position for which you are applying.

How to handle illegal questions

1. Answer politely with a question: "Is this relevant to the requirements of the job?"

2. Answer the question and ignore the fact that it is illegal if the job is important enough to you, or if you think the question is actually innocent of discriminatory intent.

3. Contact the nearest Equal Employment Opportunity Commission Office and file a complaint if you believe you have been discriminated against.

Advancing Your Career

Getting the job

The job offer. Finally your search comes to a successful conclusion. You are offered a job, or perhaps several jobs. At this point, take time to consider before accepting a job.

Show your appreciation for the job offer and ask when your decision is expected. If the employer says immediately, then you must give an answer unless you can use your negotiating skills to convince him or her that you need some time to reflect. You certainly can indicate that you are very interested while postponing your decision for a few days to allow consideration.

Evaluating the job offer. Often a series of interviews is necessary before a job is offered. This gives your prospective employers the opportunity to find out more about you and to observe you at different times; it also gives you the same opportunity. Take the time to consider these questions:

Challenge: Will the work keep you motivated and enthusiastic?

Personalities: Do you like what you have seen of your coworkers? Do you think you can work well with them?

Environment: Is the work space acceptable to you; for example, if you are allergic to smoke, will you be surrounded by chain smokers? Have you observed any safety violation?

Job security: Have you investigated the future of this company? What is the long-range economic outlook for the industry?

Reputation: Do the values of this company come up to your standards? Will you be asked to do anything that would compromise your integrity? (One job applicant thought she had found a job selling by phone until the employer informed her she must lie and say that her husband is a paraplegic.) Save yourself embarrassment by finding these things out ahead of time.

Never sell yourself short. Your research will have given you an idea of the salary range for the job offered. Where you fall in that range will depend on your negotiating ability. There can be as much as a $2000 to $3000 difference in your salary. Your employer wants to save the company that dollar difference as much as you want to earn it.

One negotiating expert has suggested the following tactic for securing the highest salary. Suppose the salary range is $22,000 to $25,000. When the employer asks you what salary you are thinking about, say that you are thinking about $26,000 as fairly representing your abilities, but that you cannot consider an offer under $23,500. Your lowest salary consideration falls

---

What is your bottom line?	Can you afford *this* job?

To arrive at a salary figure you can live with, list all your necessary **monthly** expenses:
 	
rent _____
food _____
gas/electricity _____
transportation _____
clothes _____
miscellaneous _____
    subtotal _____
__% of city, state, and federal taxes* _____
add another 15% for emergencies and _____
    inflation
monthly salary _____
multiply subtotal by 12 for yearly salary _____
divide by 52 for weekly _____
 	
This is your bottom line—weekly, monthly, and yearly. You cannot accept a job paying less without changing your lifestyle.
 	
*Find the approximate percentage of taxes on the income you have arrived at by calling your local tax office.
	1. **Are there hidden expenses,** such as transportation, day care/babysitting, or nursing for elderly members of your family? Are you required to buy equipment or uniforms?
	
	2. **What is the travel time** to and from the work place? Is employee parking provided?
	
	3. **How much overtime is expected?** Is it reimbursed? At what rate? If you are required to work late hours, will you be safe returning home?
	
	4. **Do you need flexible hours** occasionally if children or elderly relations living at home become sick? Will your employer agree to them?
	
	5. **Is it possible to do some of your work at home?**
	
	6. **Are the fringe benefits** (medical, insurance, retirement, vacation, sick days) acceptable to you? If not provided, how much additional salary will you need in order to assume the cost of these benefits?

Advancing Your Career

within their range but is well above the bottom. And if you have impressed them with your abilities enough to make them stretch their salary offer above their range limit, you are on your way to a resounding success.

This is also the time to clarify the company's policy on raises, fringe benefits, and vacations. Often these items are negotiable. It is up to you to put the highest value on yourself. If you know what is possible, your employer can only respect you for wanting to secure the best offer possible. He may even envision your using your negotiating skill on behalf of the company.

Once terms are agreed upon, you should get them in writing. A good way to protect yourself is to write a letter to your boss immediately after these face-to-face negotiations, formally accepting the job. Include a rundown of your verbal agreements and ask him to inform you if you have misunderstood any point. Keep a copy of the letter and of any response to it in case a misunderstanding develops in the future.

Job descriptions

Unless your duties are self-evident or absolutely cut and dried, you should ask for a written copy of your job description when you accept the position. It will save both you and your boss a lot of time in the long run, and it serves as a protection for both of you.

Remember, your job description is a guideline, not a law written in stone. When you see things that need to be done that do not come under your job description, you have a choice. If you choose to take on additional work, your job description will verify your initiative. If you refuse (because of overwork or distaste for the extra work), the job description is your proof that these tasks were not to be expected of you.

Moving up the ladder

Work rules. Every organization has work rules. It is a great mistake to assume that they do not apply to you. Find out from the start what the basic rules are and show your cooperation. Remember, there is usually a good reason for every rule. Employers expect that their employees will live up to work rules.

Common rules of employment

Attendance: You are expected to work a certain number of days or hours for your salary. Most businesses allow you sick leave; some give you days for personal leave, such as funerals; nearly all grant vacation time. Find out *exactly* what is allowed and stick to the rules.

Punctuality: You will be told what time you are expected to be at work each day. Plan accordingly, taking traffic and weather into account. There is seldom a good excuse for being late. Coffee breaks and lunches have set time frames: observe them.

Dress: If you have any questions about what the dress codes are for your job, do not hesitate to ask. Some jobs require dress rules to meet safety standards, such as hard hats, safety glasses, long-sleeved shirts, etc. Do not wear strong perfume or after-shave lotion. Your chewing gum should be left at home.

Safety: Many companies have weekly safety meetings. For instance, public service companies have standards dealing with the parking of their trucks, wearing apparel, the handling of equipment in private homes, the backing out of driveways, etc. Safety rules will be prominently posted. It is your responsibility to observe them for the protection of everyone.

Protocol: Leave your personal business at home. Make personal phone calls *only* in emergencies. Give the respect due a superior. Bypassing the next in line or going over someone's head could cost you your job. Take the time to find out who is in charge and take the care to go through proper channels. These practices are good job insurance.

Communicating on the job.

As a new employee, you will be busy mastering your job. Establishing good relations with your coworkers can provide you with much-needed advice and support.

Avoid the pitfalls of participating in office gossip and taking sides in disputes. Your early communications should be especially friendly and courteous. Your curiosity should be focused on ways to perform your job as efficiently and thoroughly as possible.

Be helpful to your fellow workers but not at the expense of your own job performance. If you have any complaints, direct them to the proper person to solve the problem. Be observant of what is going on around you, but avoid jumping to conclusions. If you are patient and stay uninvolved in any potentially explosive situation, your options will eventually become clear to you. Your long-range assessment of the situation will probably be quite different from your immediate reactions during the first few weeks on the job.

Making suggestions

Suggestion box. As a relatively new employee, you may bring a fresh approach to solving company problems. Many companies have a suggestion box. Unless you have been hired specifically as a troubleshooter, the suggestion box is the best place to direct your ideas. Such initiative often pays off in the form of a bonus or even a promotion.

Direct suggestions. You may soon develop a close enough relationship with your superior to make a written memo to him an appropriate way to make a suggestion. If you can relate the inspiration of the suggestion to your superior ("something you mentioned made me think of the possibility of . . ." or "in keeping with your work philosophy, I would like to suggest . . ."), you have expressed support for your superior and created a positive atmosphere for your suggestion.

Suggesting changes can be risky without the support and enthusiasm of the decision-makers. Sharing the credit by allowing them to feel that they were in part the source of the idea allows them to join you in carrying out a constructive suggestion. Learning to communicate diplomatically is a major key to success.

How to be supportive to your employer

1. **Have a positive attitude:** Take note of your superior's contributions, acknowledge the good ones, and keep quiet about the bad ones.

2. **Know your boss:** Learn his or her working methods and adjust your own to harmonize with them. Be clear on your boss's priorities.

3. **Be informed:** Do your homework by keeping up to date in your field. Read carefully all memos and annual reports.

4. **Become a team worker:** Cooperate with coworkers; contribute whatever you can to a pleasant working environment.

5. **Be honest:** The best way to be supportive to your boss is to be honest, responsible, and trustworthy.

The art of listening.

One of the more satisfying rewards of teaching is the profound silence of someone listening. If you can give this attention to your boss, he will not fail to notice.

Most new employees want to impress everyone with how much they know, their speed in catching on, and their enthusiasm. They are much more concerned with feedback ("How am I doing?") than with giving appreciation to their boss or mentor.

Remember, it may be lonely at the top. Your boss needs appreciation for his contributions as much as you do. In fact, directing your attention to listening and acknowledging him can open blocked channels of communication for everyone.

Yearly job assessments. Many companies now make it a practice to require their employees to turn in statements of their yearly goals and assessments of their past job performances. This exercise can be very helpful. Even though your company may not require it, you

---

Tips for getting along on the job	Checklist for making suggestions
1. Make your job performance your top priority.	1. Examine your suggestion carefully before you submit it.
2. Become a team worker.	2. Make sure you do not imply criticism of a superior or jeopardize anyone's job.
3. Be willing to accept more responsibility.	3. Phrase you suggestion positively.
4. Be loyal to your boss or keep quiet if you are not.	4. Check it from all angles for clarity and detail.
5. Treat everyone with courtesy.	5. Leave no chance for misinterpretation.
6. Avoid office gossip.	
7. Avoid making personal phone calls.	

could celebrate your yearly anniversary by reflecting on your progress. Experience can change your direction. Yearly assessments will clarify your focus on future progress and serve as a useful guide for making changes if you are dissatisfied. And reviewing your progress can be an enormous help when you are asking for a raise.

Shifts in responsibility

Asking for a lighter load. Sometimes your success on the job can create a situation in which it is wise to request a decrease in responsibility. For example, maybe your workload has increased to the point where you cannot possibly keep up with your work or perform it to your (or anyone else's) satisfaction. Or perhaps a classroom teacher has been promoted to assistant principal, a logical next step up the ladder of success. But that promotion may have robbed her of her greatest pleasure, teaching her students, and may have put her in an administrative position where she has no particular skills.

Awareness of your strengths, preferences, and limitations when a well-intentioned promotion is offered is important. If you are competent and enthusiastic in a job, think twice before accepting a promotion that does not feel right to you. More money and prestige are seldom worth the giving up of duties you love for those you dislike or cannot perform well.

If union membership is mandatory

1. Become familiar with union rules on payment of dues, work, and behavior.

2. Use your union's services responsibly. It exists to improve your working conditions and salary, and to protect you.

3. Do not discuss union business with nonunion employees or with members of other unions.

4. Work for changes if you are dissatisfied with your union leadership. Complaining without constructive suggestions is counterproductive. On the other hand, constructive suggestions may be welcomed and result in improved organizational procedures.

5. Look for a job in another field if you cannot support your union and are unwilling to change it.

Increasing responsibilities. As you become more experienced in your job, responsibilities may be assigned to you that are not in your job description. If you are ambitious and like the challenge, you may

---

Asking for a promotion

1. Do you have the necessary qualifications, including experience, to do your present job well?
2. Have you been on your present job long enough to warrant a promotion?
3. Where do you stand in line for a promotion?
4. Do you have a clear understanding of the new position and all it involves?
5. Are you willing to make the necessary commitment to the new job?
6. Does your employer know what your expectations are?
7. Are you on good terms with fellow workers?

Steps in asking for a raise

1. **Check company policy:** Some companies have automatic raises that go into effect at scheduled intervals; some use a merit system. Others will grant increases for merit in addition to regularly scheduled increases.

2. **Use good judgment:** Check salaries for jobs in companies similar to yours. Make sure your own company is in a financial position to grant an increase at this time.

3. **Review your record:** Read over your yearly assessments if you have made them. Have firmly in mind your contributions as an employee—from good attendance and/or productivity to increasing the efficiency of your department.

4. **Be assertive:** Tie your request for a raise to the specific factors most appropriate in your case: your time on the job, comparable salaries in the field, your career goals, your contributions to the company, etc. Asking for a raise is difficult for all of us; taking the first three steps will make this one easier for you—and make you more likely to succeed.

---

welcome the extra work. After proving yourself sufficiently, you should take the opportunity to review your job description with your superior.

It is a good idea to bring two copies of your old job description with you, plus a new description of your present job as you see it. If you have been assigned more work than you can handle efficiently, make constructive suggestions for dealing with the problem. If you think additional training is necessary, present your request for it along with a specific plan. If you need to hire an assistant, back up your request with facts about productivity and costs.

This is a good time to ask for a raise. It is certainly reasonable to ask for confirmation of your new job description and to inquire what increase in salary accompanies the increase in your responsibilities.

Changing careers

Case history. Paul Carter's mother, Carol, has taught English at the local high school for 15 years. Although she enjoys her work, she has always dreamed of becoming a travel agent: she loves travel, and has a real aptitude for learning foreign languages. For the past four years, while Paul has been at college, Carol has been researching her dream job. She has worked part-time in a friend's travel agency every summer, and is now ready to resign from teaching and take a full-time job with the agency.

One of the reasons Carol Carter can afford to give up the superior fringe benefits and security of teaching is that her husband, Jeffrey, has been promoted from his job as sports equipment buyer for a local department store.

It was Jeffrey Carter who came up with the idea of expanding the sports department into a separate facility to include a health club and restaurant. He presented his expansion plan so convincingly that he was made a vice president of the store and put in charge of the entire new operation.

When to make a change. Unlike Carol Carter, who considered her career change for a number of years before she came to a decision, some people wake up one morning and experience a moment

---

Carol Carter consulted this list from the *Department of Labor Occupational Outlook Quarterly* and was pleased to find her background in English related to skills needed in her new career choice.

Occupations related to English

High school graduate

Actor or actress	Insurance agent	Secretary
Claims adjuster	Printer	Service representative
Court clerk	Proofreader	Telephone operator
Court reporter	Receptionist	Travel guide or agent
Flight attendant	Reservation/ticket passenger agent	Typesetter
	Salesperson	Typist

Two years of college

Computer operator	Library technician and assistant	Medical secretary
Film editor	Licensed practical nurse	Paralegal
Legal secretary	Maitre d'hotel	Police officer

College graduate +

Administrator	Employment counselor	Psychologist
Advertising executive	Executive	Public relations worker
Advertising writer	Job analyst	Publisher
Announcer–radio, TV	Journalist	Registrar–college and university
Archivist	Librarian	School counselor
Buyer	Market research analyst	Script writer–radio, TV, movies
Criminologist	Missionary/minister/rabbi/priest	Social worker
Drama coach	Personnel and labor relations worker	Speech pathologist/clinician
Editor	Physician	Teacher
Editorial assistant	Political scientist	Translator
Education and public affairs director	Producer–TV, films, plays	Tutor
Educator	Program director–radio/TV	Writer

Advancing Your Career

of truth: their job is no longer challenging or satisfying, and they fell that no money or benefits are worth so much dissatisfaction.

If this happens to you, do not quit your present job or even start discreetly exploring other possibilities immediately. First, make yourself a plan.

Jeffrey Carter was bored with his job when he got an inspiration from observing the health-club boom spreading across the country. Having always been a fitness addict, Jeffrey now dreamed of opening a health club. He had to restrain himself from putting in his resignation so that he could work full-time on financing his dream.

Instead, he used his spare time to work out a plan, researching it thoroughly and devising a presentation that was practical and specific. Jeffrey was prepared to resign and launch the venture on his own if his proposal met with a negative response. As it was, he got his health club, a big raise and promotion.

Every employee experiences some job dissatisfaction some of the time. If yours is serious and pervasive, however, a change may be indicated. Before you do anything, look at your situation from every possible angle. Sometimes a well-thought-out plan or even a single good idea can make it possible for you to change jobs within your organization.

Changing jobs: what to consider

1. Can you make a job change within your present company?
2. Would you increase your chances of getting a job you like better by staying where you are?
3. Have you done everything you can to increase the rewards in your present job?
4. Are you using the abilities you enjoy most? Are you learning skills important to your career advancement?
5. Are you fulfilling a need for yourself or the community in your present job?
6. Are you willing to risk the loss of security and/or your present benefits if you make a change?
7. Is your family supportive of your desire to change?
8. Can you financially afford to make a change?
9. Would a change involve a geographic move?
10. Is it possible to work part-time in another job to see how well it suits you before leaving your present job?

If you decide to quit

If you are certain that there will be no openings for advancement at your present job, give the boss the proper notice when you decide to leave. He or she should honor your good record with a letter of recommendation. The usual required notice is two weeks, but check your work rules.

Where the jobs are

American workers have always shown an enthusiasm for going after the job if the job will not come to them. If your occupation is threatened with extinction, or if jobs are scarce in your area, you may choose to make a geographic as well as a career move. Consult these charts before you decide.

10 Best Areas	Nonfarm employees in thousands 1980	1998	Percent change
Nevada	400	925	+131
Arizona	1,014	2,078	+105
Florida	3,576	6,677	+87
Utah	551	1,024	+86
Georgia	2,159	3,740	+68
Colorado	1,251	2,051	+64
Alaska	169	275	+63
Washington	1,608	2,596	+61
North Carolina	2,380	3,773	+59
Idaho	330	522	+58

10 Worst Areas	Nonfarm employees in thousands 1980	1998	Percent change
Washington, D.C.	616	615	0
Wyoming	210	228	+9
West Virginia	646	719	+11
New York	7,207	8,229	+14
Rhode Island	398	458	+15
Connecticut	1,427	1,645	+15
Pennsylvania	4,753	5,496	+16
Massachusetts	2,654	3,177	+20
Louisiana	1,579	1,897	+20
Illinois	4,850	5,894	+22

If you lose your job.
If you have been fired, ask questions if you do not know why. The truth may be difficult to face; but only if you know the truth, can you make constructive use of your experience. If you were fired for unreliability, you can try to avoid making the same mistakes next time. If you were dismissed because your company or field is in trouble, you can try to avoid putting yourself in a similar situation next time. Ask for a letter of recommendation.

There is no need to panic, or to rush into a new job you do not want. If you were fired or laid off, you automatically qualify for unemployment insurance to assist you in your search for another job (your local unemployment office will give you all the information you need).

Your time between jobs offers an opportunity to consider carefully where you were, what you have learned, where you are now, and where you want to go.

Warning signs!

1. The company is suffering unusual losses.
2. People are getting laid off.
3. You are not invited to the usual meetings.
4. You feel uninformed.
5. People seem to be avoiding you.
6. You were passed over for a promotion.
7. Your boss shows continued dissatisfaction and impatience with your performance.
8. Your boss leaves.
9. The new boss starts bringing in his own people.
10. Little by little, your responsibilities are being assigned to other people.

You are fired. Why?

1. Were you qualified for the job? Did you honestly represent your skills before you were hired?
2. Were you truly suited for the job?
3. Should you have taken additional courses to keep you up to date?
4. Did you make costly mistakes?
5. Did you get along with your fellow workers?
6. Did you participate in office gossip and politics?
7. Were you given warnings before being fired? Did you make constructive use of criticism from superiors?
8. Did you often find yourself making excuses for work not finished, getting to work late, leaving early, taking excessive sick leave?
9. Have you been fired before? If so, why?
10. Do you see a pattern forming? For example, do you always become bored in your jobs?

Taking an unflinching look at what went wrong can be invaluable for finding the right job in the future and for recognizing how you can perform that job more effectively.

Applying for unemployment insurance

Go *immediately* to your nearest office of unemployment with two forms of identification (driver's license, birth certificate, passport, etc.) and your Social Security number (your Social Security card does not qualify as identification). Pride is *not* a factor: get in line and sign up.

How to survive until the first unemployment check comes

1. Call or visit your local office of Human Services for information about:
   a. food stamps   b. rent allowances   c. fuel assistance

2. An employee laid off or fired will normally receive at least two weeks' severance pay.

3. Look in the first few pages of your telephone book for a special section commonly called Community Service Numbers. There you will find the local telephone number for job services, unemployment, food stamps, and other social services that can help you.

Getting back into the work force

Opportunities for retirees.

Many companies have a mandatory retirement age, as do certain occupations (pilots must retire at age 60, for example). Some retirees are surprised to find that they do not adjust well to so much leisure time and are not happy unless they are in a work-related environment. For others, continuing to work for pay is not a matter of choice but of simple economics: Social Security and pension checks are often inadequate to provide a comfortable or even a reasonable standard of living.

There are many opportunities for older people to get back into the work force or work-related activities. For those who are not concerned with more income, programs such as the Retired and Senior Volunteer Program (RSVP), Foster Grandparent Program, Senior Companion Program, and Peace Corps urgently need older Americans who are willing to share their concern and expertise. See pages 296-297 for more information.

If you discover that your retirement income will be inadequate before you have actually retired, you may be able to arrange with your employer for part-time work as a consultant or during vacation or peak periods. You may even find that full- or part-time work in an entirely different capacity from your present job can be arranged. The fact that you still work for the company gives you more leverage than you would have as a former employee in the months after retirement.

Retirement often allows people the security to take the risk of trying to make money out of a new activity or one formerly considered recreational. America is the home of success stories like those of Ray Kroc and Colonel Harland Sanders, who came out of retirement to start McDonald's and Kentucky Fried Chicken. It is also the home of thousands of cottage industries started all over the country by retirees who turned their hobbies into profit-making ventures.

If you cannot find any work in your field, the JTPA (Job Training Partnership Act) is a program administered mainly by state and local governments that helps workers who need job training, placement, or relocation assistance.

Other areas to investigate are local churches, YMCA and YWCA occupational services, professional or trade associations, and labor union, local, and state employment services. Ample help and counseling are available if you know where to look.

Another avenue to explore is the office of your state representative or senator. Their local offices have workers who collect information in all problem areas, especially unemployment. Upon request they will provide this information and assist you in any other way they can.

Odd jobs can solve problems

For retirees, there are many ways to make money without actually working at a regular job. Here are some ideas to start you thinking:

1. Retired teachers or anyone with expertise in a particular area (in a foreign language, for example) can tutor at home. An ad in your local paper, a call or visit to a school or college in your area, even a notice on a supermarket or shopping-mall bulletin board can help attract this kind of business.

2. In most communities, those qualified to supply music, art, or drama coaching can attract willing students.

3. Anyone who can sew or tailor is likely to find a ready supply of customers.

4. Those who have no specific area of expertise can make money running errands, chauffering, house-sitting, babysitting, or assisting the elderly.

5. Gardening can be profitable to those who sell their own vegetables, flowers, or fruits. Tending other people's gardens while they are traveling can be enjoyable and profitable. Landscaping can supplement your income even more.

6. There is a market in most communities for hand-crafted items, from dolls and pillows to furniture. Homemade baked goods are easy to sell, and can be the start of a home catering business.

7. For more ideas write for the "Consumer Information Catalog," which lists a number of low-cost booklets on employment:
   Consumer Information Center
   P.O. Box 100
   Pueblo, Colorado 81002

Women who work.

Approximately 132.3 million people made up the 1995 labor force—several million more than originally projected. Job growth for women is expected to continue. For example, according to the Department of Labor, the employment of pre-school teachers (nearly all of them women) is expected to increase at least 50 percent between 1992 and 2005.

The majority of people reentering the work force are also women. In 1960, slightly more than 23 million women held paying jobs. Today, the number is more than twice that, and rising every year. Women comprise over 45 percent of the work force in America today. Many of these women are supplementing the family income or working their way up in a chosen career. The majority of them are in the work force because of economic necessity. Over 50 percent of women reentering the work force are single parents.

Far-reaching social changes have contributed to the surge of women workers. Many women have chosen to defer marriage and/or motherhood. Equal pay and anti-discrimination laws, along with new tax allowances for child-care expenses, have opened up the job choices available to women. It is still true that many more women are employed in service rather than goods-producing industries; but it is also true that the service industries are expanding while manufacturing is on the decrease. Service-related industries (public relations, transportation, communications, finance, insurance, real estate, etc.) are projected to account for nearly 75 percent of all jobs in 2005.

Over half of women with children under six are now in the work force. Lack of adequate child care remains the most significant problem for working mothers, although the picture is considerably brighter than it was a few years ago. Federally funded day-care centers, where tuition is scaled to income, are still on the increase. Many corporations, and some local schools, are now providing day-care centers.

About three out of four employed adult American women work full time. Forty-five percent of American mothers with infants are employed outside the home. About 64 percent of American mothers with children under the age of six are members of the American labor force.

Alternative work patterns

For information on part-time work, flexible work schedules, and shared jobs, write to:

New Ways to Work Newsletter
New Ways to Work
985 Market Street
San Francisco, CA 94103

Alternative Work Patterns: Changing Approaches to Work Scheduling, by David Robinson
Work in America Institute, Inc.
700 White Plains Road
Scarsdale, NY 10583

Many companies now offer flexible hours in certain jobs. This trend is a great boon to working mothers, who can arrange their assigned number of hours per week to accommodate their children's schedules. For example, a parent need not miss a child's graduation or school play: the hours can be made up before or after the normal working day, or on the weekend.

Job-sharing is another trend in meeting the special needs of working women. Two people can share the same job, working out their hours and finances between them along whatever lines seem fair to both parties. So long as they get the job done satisfactorily, it does not matter to the employer which worker does what. This arrangement can allow each employee to hold a more challenging or better paying job than part-time work could offer either of them.

Help is as near as your mailbox

The U.S. government spends millions of dollars each year printing information invaluable to women in—or entering—the work force. Write to:

> Information Office
> Women's Bureau
> Department of Labor
> 200 Constitution Ave. NW
> Washington, DC 20210

Ask for a list of their publications. There is likely to be one pertaining to any problem you may have or supplying any information you seek.

Advancing Your Career

Starting your own business

Starting your own *successful* business can be best described as turning your passion into your profession. The secret ingredient in the formula for a successful small business is likely to be an obsessed owner—one willing to put in the time needed to get the job done (often well over eight hours a day) and full of unflagging enthusiasm.

It is likely that running your own business will be harder than working at a regular job. Studies have demonstrated that most entrepreneurs are not motivated primarily by the desire to make money. The satisfactions lie more in the areas of independence, power over the future, and the pleasure of doing a good job.

Whether a business succeeds or fails most often depends on a simple thing called "cash flow." If there is not enough cash coming in or reserved to pay the expenses of running the business, the business will soon fail. It does not matter how much money is owed to you (debtors may also be suffering a cash flow problem); what counts is *cash in hand*.

Smart entrepreneurs reserve every bit of cash they can for unexpected expenses or dry periods. Giving in to the temptation to expand too quickly or display the fruits of sudden profits can turn an apparent success into a sudden failure.

Here are some questions to ask yourself before you embark on any business venture of your own. Answering them thoughtfully will help you decide whether starting your own business is right for you.

Starting your own business

1. Do you have a clear idea of the business you would like to start in terms of the product or service?
2. Do you have (or can you acquire) the necessary knowhow to run that type of business?
3. Have you gained experience in that field or in a related field?
4. Do you have any necessary equipment, or the money to acquire it?
5. Do you have the kind of contacts you will need to launch your business—bankers, accountants, potential customers, promoters, etc.?
6. Do you have the time and energy necessary to commit to a new business? (Remember, this may mean 18-hour work days and seven-day work weeks.)
7. Does your family support your endeavor?
8. Do you have the temperament for taking risks?
9. Are you practical enough to implement your ideas?
10. Are you capable of picking the right people to help you?
11. Do you have a good supply of self-confidence?
12. Are you willing to admit your mistakes and learn from them?
13. Can you tolerate the uncertainty that characterizes any new business?
14. Do you have a plan to provide for you and your family if the business fails?
15. Do you have plans to expand where necessary if the business succeeds?

Advantages and disadvantages of starting your own business

ADVANTAGES
- You are totally responsible for any success.
- You can work at your own speed.
- Your schedule will be flexible.
- You will reap the profits of your hard work and have many tax advantages.
- Your business may provide security and even jobs for your family.
- You will not face forced retirement.

DISADVANTAGES
- You are totally responsible for any failure.
- You may work during all your waking hours.
- You will have no paid vacation; you may have no vacation at all.
- You will have no weekly paycheck or fringe benefits.
- You may go deeply into debt; you may have almost no time to spend with your family.
- If the business fails, your savings and property can be eaten up by debts, leaving nothing for your retirement.

The birth of a small business.

Edward and Alice Stubbs, whose success chart appears on page 25, want to start a catering business now that Edward is retired. They have had many years of volunteer catering experience at their church and community theater. More important, they both love to cook and have ample kitchen facilities in a large house with plenty of storage space.

If you want to start your own business, make an analysis similar to the Stubbs's. Think of every contingency for success and failure. Write everything down. Consult anyone who might have valuable advice or experience, including people operating a similar business far enough out of your area to be noncompetitive. Visit or write to the Small Business Administration, whose retired business people are available for free consultation. Inform yourself about your proposed business from all sources mentioned in this section. It is particularly important to get help in arriving at the right profit margin for your product or services (many businesses fail because they are priced too low). If you are thinking about opening a retail shop, for example, you will probably find that doubling the cost to you of items for sale will not be adequate. Finally, make sure you have enough cash to carry you until the business can carry itself.

Stubbs's catering service: An analysis

Market: Their initial market already existed, since their reputation as splendid cooks was well established in the community.

Pricing: After doing research at the library and drawing from their own knowledge about the actual cost of preparing dishes, they marked up the price of their ingredients three times in order to ensure a profit. Dishes or meals especially time-consuming to prepare were marked up five times.

Competition: The only catering service in their community was a firm that catered for guest lists of 50 or more. The Stubbses were interested in providing a small, personal service.

Goods and overhead: Because they operated out of their own large kitchen, relatively little initial investment was required. They needed trays and some large pots and platters, but their expenditures were minimal. They used their own station wagon for deliveries, making it a company car and a tax deduction.

Regulations: The Stubbses worked out of their home, so there was no need for health department inspections (although theoretically there could have been).

Risk: Relatively little risk was involved. The Stubbs's policy was to ask for one-third to one-half of their fee in advance, which covered their costs. They either sent a bill for the remainder or collected upon delivery, depending on the customer. After consulting a lawyer, they had a legal form drawn up that each customer signed upon ordering. They consulted their insurance agent and took out a liability policy that covered them in the event of a lawsuit from a customer. These precautions protected the Stubbses from unanticipated threats to their business and personal investment and property, and, more important to their everyday business, ensured their cash flow.

Time commitment: At first, the Stubbses were capable of handling all of the business themselves. They worked long hours to keep overhead to a minimum, not minding because theirs was a labor of love. Eventually, the volume of business became too much for them and they hired an assistant.

Start-up expenses checklist

1. Do you need printed business cards, stationery, invoices, wrapping paper, shopping bags, etc.?

2. Do you need to buy a mailing list or lists?

3. Do you need to rent work space, furniture, typewriters, cash registers, etc.?

4. Do you need a separate phone line for the business?

5. What are the advertising rates in the local newspapers? Can you arrange to have a promotional article written about your new business?

6. Will you need a telephone answering service or machine?

7. Do you need to file the name of your business in your state? Do you need to incorporate?

Think of every hidden expense and write it down. Talk with people in similar businesses and ask them what expenses, including unexpected ones, are likely to come up. Then draw up a budget and compare it with your cash on hand to estimate how much money you will have to raise.

     Advancing Your Career

How your government can help

Some of the best information is supported by your tax dollars. It is your for the asking. Write to:

> Office of Small Business Development Centers
> Management Assistance
> Small Business Administration
> 409 Third Street SW
> Washington, DC 20416

Ask for their complete kit of information. There are some 950 Small Business Development Centers located throughout the United States working with state governments to assist small businesses.

Special help for women. Helping women become successful entrepreneurs is a special goal of the Small Business Administration. Write to:

> Office of Women's Business Ownership
> Small Business Administration
> 409 Third Street SW
> Washington, DC 20416

If you want to start a business out of your home, write to: National Alliance of Homebased Businesswomen
P.O. Box 95
Norwood, New Jersey 07648

Publications

The Small Business Administration offers a number of publications and videotapes for entrepreneurs. For the free catalog "Resource Directory for Small Business Management," call the Small Business Administration at their toll-free number 1-800-8-ASK-SBA (1-800-827-5722). The publications range in price from $2.00 to $4.00. Here is a partial listing of available titles:

EB02	Marketing Strategies for Growing Businesses	MP11	Business Plan for Small Service Firms
EB03	Management Issues for Growing Businesses	MP12	Checklist for Going Into Business
EB04	Human Resource Management for Growing Businesses	MP14	How To Get Started with a Small Business Computer
EB06	Strategic Planning for Growing Businesses	MP15	Business Plan for Home-Based Business
EB07	Financial Management for Growing Businesses	MP21	Developing a Strategic Business Plan
FM01	ABCs of Borrowing	MP22	Inventory Management
FM04	Understanding Cash Flow	MP26	Evaluating Franchise Opportunities
FM08	Budgeting in a Small Service Firm	MP28	Small Business Risk Management Guide
FM10	Record Keeping in a Small Business	MP31	Handbook for Small Business
FM14	Financing for Small Business	MP32	How To Write a Business Plan
MP03	Problems in Managing a Family-Owned Business	MT01	Creative Selling: The Competitive Edge
MP04	Business Plan for Small Manufacturers	MT02	Marketing for Small Business: An Overview
MP05	Business Plan for Small Construction Firms	MT08	Researching Your Market
MP06	Planning and Goal Setting for Small Business	MT09	Selling by Mail Order
MP09	Business Plan for Retailers	MT11	Advertising

A hobby developed into a marketable skill and eventually a promising small business (left) for an ambitious couple. Another innovative entrepreneur (right) saw a secure future in a franchise with a well-established fast food company.

Matching yourself to the World of Work

L = lowest level
M = middle level
H = highest level

[1]Estimates not available.
[2]Vary, depending on job.

Column headings — **Job requirements:** 1. Leadership/persuasion · 2. Helping/instructing others · 3. Problem-solving/creativity · 4. Initiative · 5. Work as part of a team · 6. Frequent public contacts · 7. Manual dexterity · 8. Physical stamina · 9. Hazardous · 10. Outdoors. **Work environs:** 11. Confined · 12. Jobs concentrated geographically · 13. Part-time. **Occupational characteristics:** 14. Earnings · 15. Employment growth · 16. Entry requirements.

Occupation	1	2	3	4	5	6	7	8	9	10	11	12	13	14	15	16
Administrative and Managerial Occupations																
Accountants and auditors		•	•		•	•						•		M	M	H
Bank officers and managers	•	•	•	•	•	•						•		H	M	H
Buyers	•		•	•	•									M	M	H
College student personnel workers	•	•	•	•	•	•								1	1	H
Construction inspectors (government)		•	•	•	•		•			•				M	H	M
Credit managers	•	•	•		•	•						•		M	L	H
Health services administrators	•		•	•	•	•								H	H	H
Hotel managers and assistants	•	•	•	•	•	•								1	H	M
Medical record administrators	•		•	•	•									H	H	H
Occupational safety and health workers		•	•	•	•		•			•				H	1	H
Personnel and labor relations specialists	•	•	•		•	•								M	L	H
Purchasing agents	•		•		•									1	L	H
School administrators	•	•	•	•	•	•								H	L	H
Engineers, Surveyors, and Architects																
Architects			•	•	•	•								H	H	H
Landscape architects			•	•		•	•							1	H	H
Surveyors and surveying technicians				•		•	•	•		•				L	M	M
Engineers																
Agricultural engineers		•	•	•										H	H	H
Chemical engineers			•	•	•									H	M	H
Civil engineers and electrical engineers			•	•	•									H	H	H
Electrical engineers			•	•	•									H	H	H
Industrial and mechanical engineers			•	•	•									H	H	H
Metallurgical and mining engineers			•	•	•									H	H	H
Natural Scientists and Mathematicians																
Mathematical scientists and systems analysts																
Mathematicians			•	•										H	L	H
Statisticians			•	•										M	M	H
Systems analysts	•		•	•	•							•		H	H	H
Physical scientists																
Astronomers			•	•										H	L	H
Chemists			•	•										H	M	H
Geographers			•	•	•									H	M	H
Geologists and geophysicists			•	•	•					•				H	H	H
Meteorologists			•	•	•									H	L	H
Oceanographers			•	•	•					•		•		H	M	H
Physicists			•	•										H	L	H

Advancing Your Career

Job requirements / Work environs / Occupational characteristics

Column key:
1. Leadership/persuasion
2. Helping/instructing others
3. Problem-solving/creativity
4. Initiative
5. Work as part of a team
6. Frequent public contacts
7. Manual dexterity
8. Physical stamina
9. Hazardous
10. Outdoors
11. Confined
12. Jobs concentrated geographically
13. Part-time
14. Earnings
15. Employment growth
16. Entry requirements

	1	2	3	4	5	6	7	8	9	10	11	12	13	14	15	16
Life scientists																
Agricultural and biological scientists			•	•										1	M	H
Biochemists			•	•										H	M	H
Food technologists			•	•										H	L	H
Foresters			•	•	•			•	•	•				M	L	H
Soil conservationists		•	•	•					•					H	L	H
Social Scientists, Social Workers, Religious Workers, and Lawyers																
Lawyers	•	•	•	•	•	•								H	M	H
Social scientists																
Anthropologists			•	•	•									H	M	H
Economists			•	•										H	H	H
Historians			•	•										H	L	H
Political scientists			•	•	•	•								H	L	H
Psychologists		•	•	•		•								H	M	H
Sociologists			•	•		•								H	L	H
Social and recreation workers																
Recreation workers	•	•	•	•	•	•	•	•		•			•	L	M	M
Social workers	•	•	•	•	•	•								L	M	H
Religious workers																
Ministers and priests	•	•	•	•	•	•								L	1	H
Rabbis	•	•	•	•	•	•								H	1	H
Teachers, Librarians, and Counselors																
College career counselors	•	•	•	•	•	•								M	1	H
College and university faculty	•	•	•	•	•	•							•	H	L	H
Employment counselors	•	•	•	•	•	•						•		1	1	H
Kindergarten, school teachers	•	•	•	•	•	•	•	•					•	M	M	H
Librarians	•	•	•	•	•	•							•	M	L	H
Rehabilitation counselors	•	•	•	•	•	•								1	1	H
School counselors	•	•	•	•	•	•								M	L	H
Secondary school teachers	•	•	•	•	•	•								M	L	H
Health Diagnosing and Treating Practitioners																
Chiropractors	•	•	•	•	•	•	•	•					•	H	M	H
Dentists	•	•	•	•	•	•	•	•						H	M	H
Optometrists	•	•	•	•	•	•	•	•					•	H	M	H
Physicians	•	•	•	•	•	•	•	•	•					H	H	H
Veterinarians	•	•	•	•	•	•	•	•	•					H	H	H
Registered Nurses, Pharmacists, Dietitians, etc.																
Dietitians	•	•	•	•	•	•							•	L	H	H
Occupational therapists	•	•	•	•	•	•	•	•						1	H	H
Pharmacists	•	•	•	•	•	•						•	•	H	L	H
Physical therapists	•	•	•	•	•	•	•	•						M	H	H
Physician assistants	•	•	•	•	•	•	•	•						M	1	H
Registered nurses	•	•	•	•	•	•	•	•					•	M	H	M

	Job requirements										Work environs			Occupational characteristics		
	1. Leadership/persuasion	2. Helping/instructing others	3. Problem-solving/creativity	4. Initiative	5. Work as part of a team	6. Frequent public contacts	7. Manual dexterity	8. Physical stamina	9. Hazardous	10. Outdoors	11. Confined	12. Jobs concentrated geographically	13. Part-time	14. Earnings	15. Employment growth	16. Entry requirements

Health Technologists and Technicians

	1	2	3	4	5	6	7	8	9	10	11	12	13	14	15	16
Dental hygienists		•		•	•	•	•			•			•	L	H	M
Electrocardiograph technicians		•		•	•	•							•	1	H	M
Emergency medical technicians	•	•		•	•	•	•	•	•					L	M	M
Licensed practical nurses		•		•	•	•	•						•	L	H	M
Medical laboratory workers				•		•		•		•				L	H	2
Radiologic (x-ray) technicians		•			•	•		•					•	L	H	M
Surgical technicians		•		•	•	•								L	H	M

Writers, Artists, and Entertainers

Communications occupations

	1	2	3	4	5	6	7	8	9	10	11	12	13	14	15	16
Public relations workers	•		•	•	•	•								M	M	H
Radio and television announcers and newscasters	•	•		•	•	•					•			L	H	H
Reporters and correspondents	•		•	•	•	•								1	M	H
Writers and editors	•		•	•	•						•		•	1	M	H

Design occupations

	1	2	3	4	5	6	7	8	9	10	11	12	13	14	15	16
Commercial, graphic designers			•	•	•		•						•	1	L	M
Display workers	•		•	•			•		•					L	M	L
Floral designers			•			•	•				•			1	L	L
Industrial designers			•	•	•		•							1	L	H
Interior designers			•	•	•		•							1	M	M
Photographers			•	•			•						•	L	L	M

Performing artists

	1	2	3	4	5	6	7	8	9	10	11	12	13	14	15	16
Actors and actresses			•	•	•	•	•	•			•		•	L	M	M
Dancers and musicians			•	•	•	•	•	•			•		•	L	M	M
Singers			•	•	•	•	•	•			•		•	1	L	M

Technologists and Technicians, Except Health

	1	2	3	4	5	6	7	8	9	10	11	12	13	14	15	16
Air-traffic controllers		•	•	•	•		•				•			H	L	H
Broadcast technicians			•		•		•				•			L	L	M
Drafters				•			•				•			M	H	M
Forestry technicians							•	•	•	•				1	H	M
Engineering, science technicians		•		•			•	2	2	2				M	M	M
Legal assistants			2	•	2									M	H	L
Programmers			•		•						•			M	H	H
Technical writers			•	•	•						•			1	H	M

Marketing and Sales Occupations

	1	2	3	4	5	6	7	8	9	10	11	12	13	14	15	16
Advertising workers	•		•	•	•									1	1	H
Automobile parts counter workers		•				•		•						L	M	M
Automobile salesworkers	•			•		•								M	H	L
Cashiers					•	•					•		•	L	H	L
Insurance agents and brokers	•	•	•	•		•							•	M	M	M
Models					•	•		•				•	•	1	1	L
Real estate agents and brokers	•	•	•	•		•				•			•	M	H	M
Retail trade salesworkers	•					•		•					•	L	M	L
Travel agents	•	•	•	•		•								1	H	M

Advancing Your Career

Job requirements / Work environs / Occupational characteristics

Legend for columns:
1. Leadership/persuasion
2. Helping/instructing others
3. Problem-solving/creativity
4. Initiative
5. Work as part of a team
6. Frequent public contacts
7. Manual dexterity
8. Physical stamina
9. Hazardous
10. Outdoors
11. Confined
12. Jobs concentrated geographically
13. Part-time
14. Earnings
15. Employment growth
16. Entry requirements

Administrative Support Occupations, Including Clerical

Occupation	1	2	3	4	5	6	7	8	9	10	11	12	13	14	15	16
Airline reservation, ticket agents		•	•		•	•					•			M	L	L
Bank clerks			•								•		•	L	H	L
Bank tellers			•		•						•		•	L	M	L
Bookkeepers and accounting clerks			•								•		•	L	L	L
Collection workers	•			•	•	•					•			L	M	L
Computer operating personnel			•		•			•			•			L	M	M
Mail carriers					•	•	•			•				M	L	L
Postal clerks					•	•	•	•			•	•		M	L	L
Receptionists		•			•	•					•		•	L	M	L
Secretaries and stenographers				•	•	•	•							L	H	L
Teacher aides	•	•			•	•	•						•	L	M	L
Telephone operators		•				•					•			L	L	L
Typists							•						•	L	M	L

Service Occupations

Protective service occupations

Occupation	1	2	3	4	5	6	7	8	9	10	11	12	13	14	15	16
Correction officers	•	•			•			•	•		•			1	H	L
Firefighters		•	•		•	•	•	•	•	•			•	M	M	L
Guards					•	•	•	•			•		•	L	M	L
Police officers	•	•	•	•	•	•	•	•	•	•				M	M	L

Food and beverage preparation and service occupations

Occupation	1	2	3	4	5	6	7	8	9	10	11	12	13	14	15	16
Bartenders			•		•	•	•				•		•	L	M	M
Cooks and chefs			•			•	•				•		•	L	M	M
Food and counterworkers			•		•	•	•						•	L	H	L
Waiters and waitresses			•		•	•	•						•	L	M	L
Kitchen helpers			•		•	•	•						•	L	H	L

Health service occupations

Occupation	1	2	3	4	5	6	7	8	9	10	11	12	13	14	15	16
Dental assistants				•	•	•	•						•	L	H	L
Medical assistants				•	•	•								L	H	L
Occupational and physical therapy assistants	•			•	•	•	•						•	1	H	M

Cleaning and building service occupations

Occupation	1	2	3	4	5	6	7	8	9	10	11	12	13	14	15	16
Hotel housekeepers and assistants						•	•	•						L	M	L

Personal service occupations

Occupation	1	2	3	4	5	6	7	8	9	10	11	12	13	14	15	16
Barbers					•	•	•				•		•	L	L	M
Bellhops and bell captains				•	•	•	•						•	L	L	L
Cosmetologists					•	•	•				•		•	L	L	M
Flight attendants		•			•	•	•	•						M	L	L

Mechanics and Repairers

Vehicle and mobile equipment mechanics and repairers

Occupation	1	2	3	4	5	6	7	8	9	10	11	12	13	14	15	16
Aircraft mechanics		•		•		•	•	•	•					H	L	M
Automobile body repairers		•				•	•	•			•			M	M	M
Automobile mechanics		•			•	•	•	•			•			L	M	M
Farm equipment mechanics		•				•	•	•	•					L	M	M
Truck and bus mechanics		•				•	•	•			•			M	M	M

Groups across the top:

	Job requirements			Work environs	Occupational characteristics

Column headers (1–16):
1. Leadership/persuasion
2. Helping/instructing others
3. Problem-solving/creativity
4. Initiative
5. Work as part of a team
6. Frequent public contacts
7. Manual dexterity
8. Physical stamina
9. Hazardous
10. Outdoors
11. Confined
12. Jobs concentrated geographically
13. Part-time
14. Earnings
15. Employment growth
16. Entry requirements

Occupation	1	2	3	4	5	6	7	8	9	10	11	12	13	14	15	16
Electrical and electronic equipment repairers																
Appliance repairers			•	•		•	•							L	M	M
Central office craft occupations			•		•	•	•	•						1	L	L
Computer service technicians			•	•		•	•							M	H	M
Line installers and cable splicers			•		•	•	•	•	•					M	L	L
Maintenance electricians			•	•		•	•	•	•					M	M	M
Telephone installers, repairers			•		•	•	•	•	•					M	L	L
Television, radio technicians			•	•		•	•					•		M	H	M
Other mechanics and repairers																
Air-conditioning, refrigeration, and heating mechanics			•			•		•						M	M	M
Business machine repairers			•	•	•		•							M	H	M
Industrial machinery repairers			•			•	•	•						M	M	M
Piano and organ tuners and repairers						•								L	L	M
Watch repairers			•	•	•		•				•		•	L	L	M
Construction and Extractive Occupations																
Construction occupations																
Bricklayers and stonemasons		•					•	•	•	•				M	H	M
Carpenters		•					•	•	•	•				M	M	M
Electricians (construction)		•					•	•	•	•				H	M	M
Floorcovering installers					•	•	•							L	M	M
Glaziers		•		•			•	•	•	•				L	M	M
Insulation workers							•	•	•	•				M	H	M
Ironworkers				•			•	•	•	•				H	M	M
Painters and paperhangers					•		•	•	•	•				L	L	M
Plasterers							•	•						M	L	M
Plumbers and pipefitters		•			•		•	•	•	•				H	M	M
Roofers				•			•	•	•	•				L	L	M
Sheet-metal workers		•					•	•	•					M	M	M
Extractive occupations																
Coal mining operatives							•	•	•		•	•		M	H	L
Production Occupations																
Blue-collar worker supervisors	•	•	•	•		•		•						M	L	M
Precision production occupations																
Bookbinders and bindery workers		2					•	•	•	•			2	L	L	M
Dental and laboratory technicians							•							L	H	M
Furniture upholsterers							•	•			•		•	L	L	M
Instrument makers (mechanical)			•	•	•		•				•		•	M	M	M
Jewelers			•	•	•		•				•	•		L	M	M
Lithographers							•							H	H	M
Machinists			•				•	•	•		•			M	M	M
Molders (foundry)							•	•	•		•			M	L	M
Patternmakers (foundry)							•	•			•			H	L	M
Photoengravers							•				•			1	L	M
Tool-and-die makers			•				•	•	•		•			H	L	M

	Job requirements											Work environs		Occupational characteristics		
	1. Leadership/persuasion	2. Helping/instructing others	3. Problem-solving/creativity	4. Initiative	5. Work as part of a team	6. Frequent public contacts	7. Manual dexterity	8. Physical stamina	9. Hazardous	10. Outdoors	11. Confined	12. Jobs concentrated geographically	13. Part-time	14. Earnings	15. Employment growth	16. Entry requirements
Plant and system operators																
Stationary engineers		•				•	•	•						M	L	M
Water treatment operators		•	•			•		•	•					L	L	M
Machine operators, tenders, and setup workers																
Boiler tenders						•	•	•						M	L	M
Forge shop occupations						•	•	•		•				M	L	M
Machine tool operators			•			•	•	•		•				M	M	M
Machine tool setup workers			•			•		•		•				M	M	M
Printing press operators						•	•	•		•				M	L	M
Fabricators, assemblers, and hand-working occupations																
Assemblers				•		•				•				L	M	L
Automotive painters						•	•	•		•				H	H	M
Welders and flamecutters						•	•	•	•					M	M	M
Transportation and Material Moving Occupations																
Motor vehicle operators																
Bus drivers			•		•	•	•			•		•		H	L	M
Truck drivers			•			•	•			•				M	M	L
Other transportation and material moving occupations																
Airplane pilots			•	•	•	•				•				H	L	M
Merchant marine sailors				•		•	•	•	•	•	•			M	L	M
Operating engineers						•		•	•					M	L	M

For further reference

Beatty, Richard H.
  The Complete Job Search Book
  John Wiley & Sons
Bolles, Richard Nelson
  What Color Is Your Parachute: A Practical Manual for Job and Career Changers
  Ten Speed Press
Figler, Howard
  The Complete Job-Search Handbook
  Henry Holt & Co.
Fry, Ronald W.
  Your First Job
  Career Press
Gonyea, James C. and Gonyea, Wayne M.
  Electronic Résumés: A Complete Guide to Putting Your Résumé On-Line
Helfland, David P.
  Career Change: Everything You Need to Know to Meet New Challenges and Take Control of Your Career
  VGM Career Horizons

King, Julie Adair and Sheldon, Betsy
  The Smart Woman's Guide to Résumés and Job Hunting
  Career Press
Krannich, Ronald L. and Krannich, Caryl Rae
  The Best Jobs for the 1990's and Into the 21st Century
  Impact Publications
LaFevre, John L.
  How You Really Get Hired: The Inside Story from a College Recruiter
  Prentice-Hall
Lieberoff, Allen
  Climb Your Own Ladder
  Simon & Schuster
Reed, Jean
  Résumés That Get Jobs
  Arco
Stolze, William J.
  Start Up: An Entrepreneur's Guide to Launching and Managing a New Business
  Career Press

Health and Fitness

During the past few decades, a great change has taken place in the attitude of the general public and professionals toward the maintenance of good health. A growing number of individuals are concerned about their own health care and that of members of their family. Doctors, as well as other medical and health professionals, are placing greater emphasis on *preventive medicine:* the use of appropriate measures to help prevent illness.

A century ago, human effort accounted for one-third of all the energy needed to run the factories, farms, businesses, and homes in the United States. However, in the late 20th century, human effort provides only one-half of one percent of the energy needed. We lead softer lives physically, but the pace of life has been stepped up to the point where unbridled stress has become a common problem. The harmful effects of stress contribute to our foremost health concerns: heart disease, stroke, cancer, and high blood pressure.

These degenerative diseases can be controlled and to some extent prevented by your habits and lifestyle. If these diseases were wiped out, the average current life expectancy of 74.5 years would be raised to 90.5 years. This statistical projection, made by the U.S. Public Health Service, is not unrealistic. It can be attained with changes in lifestyle, nutrition and diet, the handling of stress, weight control, and physical activity. Preventive medicine can not only add years to your life, it can put more life into those years.

In this chapter, you will find useful information on nutrition, stress, exercise, and other essentials that can provide preventive health care for your entire family. The highlighted *Health Care Alert* boxes, listing signals of major diseases, are intended to help you in recognizing early symptoms of disease and in reporting them in detail to your doctor. Because there are still so many myths and misconceptions about various health issues, we have included another feature, *Fact or Fiction,* which separates false notions from factual information.

Many such notions are obtained from articles appearing in popular magazines and from product advertising that is misleading in the presentation, or lacks factual information. The Food and Drug Administration advises everyone to review carefully all advertisements, especially those making claims for medical remedies. Bogus medical products include certain weight reduction pills or diets, arthritis and cancer cures, and panaceas for whatever ails you.

Answers to specific medical questions, or medical treatment, should be sought from a reputable doctor. While a majority of medical professionals are trustworthy, there are still many quack doctors who make promises of quick cures to unsuspecting victims of such serious diseases as cancer and arthritis. Choose your doctor carefully and know the drugs you use. For helpful suggestions, see You and Modern Medicine on page 78. See also the section on Health and Safety in volume 1.

Fatigue

Fatigue is a common complaint, one for which you yourself can often pinpoint the reason quite readily: a sleepless night, on-the-job frustration, frazzled nerves from trying to run a busy household.

There are many other less obvious, but equally plausible, explanations for a feeling of tiredness. All too often, people fail to see the connection between poor nutrition and fatigue. A lack of B vitamins or an inadequate intake of carbohydrates may interfere with the production of body energy. Too little activity may result in too little oxygen reaching the tissues.

Unless your tired feeling is related to a specific disease or medical problem, you can fight it with some simple changes in your daily routine. However, before you decide how to deal with fatigue, it is important for you to know what is causing it. Under any circumstances, if tiredness continues for more than a few weeks, you should check with a doctor. Such fatigue may be due to an illness that needs medical treatment.

Basically, fatigue may be placed into three major categories: physical (of the body), pathological (from a disease), psychological (of the mind).

Physical.
This fatigue may be brought on by strenuous activity such as jogging or heavy housework. It may also be caused by such factors as poor muscle tone or bad posture.

Pathological.
A tired feeling is often one symptom present in such conditions as iron-deficiency anemia, heart disease, cancer, arthritis, and diabetes; however, other and even more specific symptoms are also usually in evidence.

Certain prescription drugs (for example, tranquilizers and allergy remedies) may induce fatigue. If medication you are taking seems to rob you of vital energy, ask your doctor to prescribe an alternate drug. Excessive use of alcohol or caffeine, cigarette smoking, and poor eating habits are other factors that may result in fatigue.

Psychological.
Severe emotional stress, tension, anxiety, and other psychogenic factors are predominant in causing a feeling of constant tiredness. The person who feels trapped in a job situation or a marriage, for example, is bound to suffer from a persistent fatigue and lack of energy.

There are any number of ways in which you can fight that tired feeling. Take stock of your lifestyle, and see what you can do to take out the monotony, the frustration, or the stress in your day-to-day routines.

A working couple may need to share household responsibilities more equally; a "workaholic" may need to fit in some time for relaxation; and a weary housewife may need to hire a babysitter and join an exercise or art group. Make certain, too, that you include the essential nutrients in your daily diet; they are all needed for top performance by your body. Get enough exercise and rest, and try not to undertake too many demanding activities at one time.

Fact or fiction?

Exercise will make you feel more tired.
Fiction. Exercise releases tensions, improves sleep patterns, and promotes fitness. Those who exercise regularly get more done with less effort.

A sweet snack will *not* give you energy.
Fact. You will probably feel even more tired an hour or so after a sweet snack between meals. Have some fresh fruit instead.

Coffee or colas will give you energy.
Fiction. Caffeinated drinks may keep you awake, but too much can interfere with sleep and simply add to that tired feeling.

A light supper helps you sleep.
Fact. A high protein meal induces wakefulness; supper should be a low-protein, high-carbohydrate meal.

- **Eat three well-balanced meals a day.** Include the four basic food groups (milk, meat, vegetables and fruits, breads and cereals).

- **Choose a conditioning exercise that you enjoy.** Aerobic exercises (increasing the heart rate and flow of oxygen to the blood) are especially beneficial. Jogging, bicycling, aerobic dancing, and brisk walking fall into this category.

- **Be certain to get as many hours of sleep as *you* need.** Different people require different amounts of sleep.

- **Plan activities according to your natural body rhythms.** If you have more energy in the morning, do your most demanding work at that time, and keep lesser tasks for another time of day.

- **Pace yourself, balancing out your work demands and social activities.** Take revitalizing breaks throughout the day.

- **Cut down, or avoid, the use of caffeine, alcoholic substances, and tobacco.**

- **Do not use over-the-counter drugs to pep you up;** do not become dependent upon sleeping pills (they have a bad effect upon the quality of sleep).

Stress

Stress is an essential part of our lives, and we would not want to be without it. Many types of stress provide the impetus that makes us excel at a chosen task, or at reaching a desired personal goal. Other kinds of stress, however, particularly that arising from the complexities of modern life, can have a disturbing effect upon those who do not know how to handle it.

Simply defined, stress is the total response of your body (physical, mental, and chemical) to events that irritate, frighten, endanger, confuse, or excite you. Some stress is of your own making, as when you enter college, embark on a new career, or get married. Other pressures are forced upon you, such as nerve-wracking job or home situations, or sudden injury or illness. Whatever the nature of the stress, the important thing is how you come to grips with it.

There is no one foolproof way of dealing with stress, but learning to identify the "stressor," or stressful event, can be the first step in turning your stress into positive energy. Stressful situations can help you to be receptive to changes and challenges, and to think and act clearly. On the other hand, if not handled right, stress can thwart clear thinking and decisive action and become a threat to good health. It can add to the likelihood of developing such high stress conditions as anxiety, chronic headaches, ulcers, arthritis, high blood pressure, asthma, and heart disorders.

Remember: Experiencing stress is normal. But sometimes stress can be a real problem. The trick is to turn it from a destructive to a positive force.

Body protection against stress.

The father of modern research on stress, Hans Selye, described stress in terms of a syndrome—the adaptive energy syndrome. Dr. Selye believed that each one of us is born with an individualized amount of adaptive energy and that we use up some of this supply every time we draw upon it.

There are three stages to the adaptive energy syndrome: 1) the alarm reaction, 2) the resistance stage, and 3) the exhaustion stage.

In the alarm reaction, the body is subjected to stress and it responds with a significant drop in its level of resistance. Adrenalin (the stress hormone) is pumped into the bloodstream, the pulse races, and breathing speeds up. The blood supply is promptly redirected from the internal organs to other parts of the body, particularly the muscles, where it is needed to respond during the emergency.

The resistance stage represents the continuing attempt of the body to develop defenses in combatting the stressor. During this period, the body works hard to raise its level of resistance well above normal. Gradually, the distinctive indicators of the alarm reaction disappear and the body seemingly returns to normal. However, if the body remains mobilized for an over-long period of time, the above normal level of resistance will not continue and will drop below normal. At this point, the exhaustion stage sets in, making the body increasingly vulnerable to disease related to stress, organic dysfunction, and even death.

Health and Fitness

Taking time out with a pet or walking through a park are among many ways to change the work scene and relieve daily stress. Mild physical activity is often a welcome change of pace.

STRESS

Signals of badly channeled stress

Many commonly experienced stress reactions signal potential stress damage to the body. These reactions may include heart palpitations or a pounding pulse, nagging headaches, irritability, and a feeling of tightness in the chest, neck, or shoulders. Other symptoms may be difficulty in falling asleep, back pain, upset stomach, loss of appetite, lack of concentration, and fatigue.

With increased stress, the stress reactions intensify and signal possible greater damage to the body. A person may find it impossible to unwind or enjoy physical relaxation, become impatient or depressed, do more drinking or smoking than usual, spend sleepless nights, or have frequent headaches and stomach disturbances.

Eventually, if negatively channeled stress continues for a long time, the accumulated effects can contribute to such serious ailments as asthma, heart disease, migraine headaches, high blood pressure, stomach ulcers, alcoholism, and drug addiction.

Some common stressors

Stressors mean different things to different people. What is high stress to one person may cause no reaction in another.

Day-to-day living: being stuck in traffic; standing on long supermarket or bank lines; a rough day at home or at work; marital discord.

Emotional: negative feelings such as anger, fear, or worry; positive feelings such as profound joy, love, or excitement.

Environmental: intense noise or air pollution; bright blinking lights; exposure to extremes of heat or cold.

Health: allergies or chemotherapy; serious illness; accidents or physical injury; excesses of drugs, alcohol, caffeine, or nicotine.

Life cycle: adolescent's struggle for independence and identity; pregnancy and motherhood; oldsters adjusting to physical limitations of aging.

Life milestones: start of formal education; graduating from school; getting married; embarking on a new career.

Social: overcrowding or unpleasant surroundings; unsuccessful interpersonal relationships at work or at home.

Some ways to beat stress

Basically, a good stress skill is anything that can help *you* deal with the stress you feel. There is little help to be found in the use of alcohol or drugs, or "stress-formula" products bought at the drugstore. If a situation becomes too difficult for you to handle, see a doctor or therapist.

- **Change your attitude.** Either decide to work out or get out of a stressful situation.
- **Give yourself a break.** Get away from yourself and your problems. Take 10-minute breaks during the day; get away for a day, a week, or longer if possible.
- **Eat sensibly.** Eat plenty of high-energy foods each day. Avoid, or greatly limit, the use of sugar, salt, coffee, and alcohol.
- **Exercise regularly.** Keep physically active: walk, run, swim, bicycle to keep trim and strong, and to relieve pent-up feelings.
- **Get moral support.** At times, talking over a problem with family or friends can be of help in deciding how best to deal with it.
- **Learn to relax.** Take up a hobby: art or music, vegetable gardening or flower arranging, handicrafts or photography.

Eye care

It has been estimated that no less than 50,000 Americans become blind each year. *This number could be reduced by one-half if people took proper measures to guard against accident and disease.* By taking simple common-sense precautions, you can help to preserve your sight.

Proper lighting

Reading or close work. A room should have at least 200 watts of general lighting or 100 watts of general lighting and 75 to 100 watts of direct lighting.

Glare. Arrange lighting so that it is not reflected by a book or other reading material. Make certain, too, that no shadows fall upon the reading material.

Television. To avoid eyestrain, a child should sit at least 6 feet from the TV set and at about the same level as the screen. Some other light in the room is necessary, but the TV set should be located where it cannot reflect light from a lamp. Video games are especially tiring for the eyes as children tend to stay closer to the screen and watch it more steadily than when watching TV. Home computers may cause similar problems.

Eye changes in children.
Vision problems occur in 5 percent of all preschool children and 25 percent of all school-age youngsters. Ophthalmologists advise a first test when the child is six months, and again at three or four years of age.

Parents can help their children maintain healthy eyes by being alert to various changes in the eye, and by having their children's eyes examined periodically.
Appearance: an eye that turns in, out, up, or down. Red-rimmed, encrusted, or swollen lids. Inflamed or watery eyes, recurring sties, an enlarged eye, an eye that appears cloudy, or a white spot in the pupil.
Behavior: excessive rubbing of the eyes, shutting or covering of one eye. Tilting or thrusting the head forward. Difficulty in reading or doing close work. Blinking more than usual or irritability when doing close work. Inability to see distant objects clearly, squinting, or frowning.
Complaints: itching, burning, or scratchy feeling. Inability to see well, dizziness, headaches, or nausea following close work. Blurred or double vision.

Health hints on eye care

Rubbing and poking

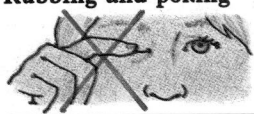

Children especially need to be reminded not to put their fingers into their eyes, particularly if their hands are soiled or if they have touched an open infectious cold sore or wound. Spread of a virus infection to the eye can ulcerate and scar the cornea, a primary cause of blindness.

Safety goggles

These should be worn to protect the eyes from accident or injury. For example, wear goggles when using electric tools such as saws and drills, lawn mowers, and hedge clippers; chemicals such as pesticidal or herbicidal sprays and household cleaning products; and in sports, particularly squash and racketball. An optician can help you choose proper goggles.

Sunglasses

Use sunglasses in reflected sunlight (on the water or the beach). Do not wear sunglasses indoors or for night driving. When selecting sunglasses, check the label to see that they filter out ultraviolet rays. Ask an optician for help, if necessary.

Drugs

At times, prescription drugs may cause complications. If you are taking a medication to control a condition such as high blood pressure, ask your doctor if the drug you are taking can affect the eye in any way.

Visits to the eye doctor

See your eye doctor (ophthalmologist) about any injury to the eye so that he or she can make sure that there is no damage. Check out any eye symptoms such as sudden pain or extreme sensitivity to light. After age 40, eyes should be checked for glaucoma (increased pressure in the eye) every two or three years. Begin checking after age 30 if there is a family history of glaucoma.

Ear care

Together with your eyes, your ears are the most vital sense organs. They are the lines of communication with the world around you.

Wax in the ear. Sometimes wax accumulates in the outer auditory canal; this can impede hearing. Do not remove the wax by using a hairpin, matchstick, or other sharp object. You may cause damage by scratching or perforating the eardrum. If you have a wax plug, an insect, or any foreign body in your ear, keep in mind the advice not to put anything in your ear smaller than your elbow. See your doctor for proper treatment.

Hearing problems. Some people are born deaf. Many others suffer hearing loss as a result of an accident or an infection. When the delicate inner ear structure has been damaged by meningitis or scarlet fever, "nerve deafness" occurs, and very little, if anything, can be done to relieve the condition.

Children who seem to be inattentive at school and who have learning disabilities are often afflicted with hearing problems. To avoid such difficulties, a child's hearing should be checked regularly. The value of good hearing can hardly be overestimated, and any change in hearing ability calls for prompt examination by an ear doctor.

Foot care

Foot problems afflict at least 75 percent of the American adult population. The most common problems are corns and bunions. Proper care of the feet will help keep feet strong and healthy. The most important protective measure is to keep your feet clean and dry. Take soothing foot baths as needed to relieve soreness. Allow toenails to grow to the tip of the toe; then cut straight across, not on a curve. Exercise your feet to keep them flexible and to strengthen the arches.

A large number of foot problems (flat feet, corns, bunions, calluses, and ingrown toenails) are caused by poorly fitted shoes. Select shoes with sensible heels and plenty of toe room. Always try on *both* shoes of a pair for size (one foot is usually larger than the other). Make certain that the back of the shoe fits snugly, and that the shoe has an inner or outer cushioning sole.

Simple care for minor foot problems

Bunions (hallux valgus)	Some people, such as diabetics, need special foot care. Any foot problems that are troublesome should be checked with your doctor or podiatrist (foot specialist). To avoid bunion pain, pressure on the prominent joint must be eliminated. Chiefly, this is a matter of wearing sensible shoes with plenty of toe room.
Calluses and corns (clavus)	After your bath or shower, gently rub your feet with a piece of pumice smeared with soap to remove excess calluses. Use of an emery board a few times a week will help reduce a hard corn. Medicated corn drops must be used very carefully so that there is no damage to good skin. The use of doughnut-shaped corn pads may also afford some relief.
Ingrown toenail (onyxia)	Try to wedge a small piece of cotton (soaked in castor oil) under the edge of the embedded nail. Apply a clean gauze pad to protect the nail from pressure. Soak the foot in water daily.
Athlete's foot (tinea pedis)	To help avoid this infection, keep feet clean and thoroughly dry, especially between the toes. Dusting with a medicated or other foot powder can help keep feet free of moisture.

Important nutrients

There are about 50 different nutrients that your body needs to stay healthy, including vitamins, minerals, carbohydrates, proteins, and fats. In this section, you will find out more about fiber, trace minerals, vitamins, and water.

On the whole, the American diet is thought to be relatively low in fiber. Most experts agree that the average person could probably double the amount of dietary fiber consumed, increasing intake to about 30 to 40 grams a day.

Mainly, there are two forms of minerals: macrominerals (needed in comparatively large amounts by the body) and microminerals (needed by the body in only very small amounts). There are some additional minerals, such as cobalt and nickel, which may take on greater nutritional importance as research determines the full extent of their usefulness in the human body.

Vitamins, organic substances derived from plants and animals, are required in the diet in very small amounts for normal health and growth. Although vitamins do not supply energy, they do help to trigger biochemical reactions that convert food into usable substances by the body.

In a listing of important nutrients, water is not always mentioned, yet the entire body mechanism needs water to function properly. Active people often fail to drink enough fluids; this may result in muscle fatigue, even upon moderate exertion. During strenuous exertion, as when running a marathon, an inadequate amount of water may be scarcely tolerable and even life-threatening.

Eat more high in fiber foods. To
get enough fiber in your diet, eat whole-grain breads and cereals, nuts, fruits, and vegetables. Some good

You should eat some foods high in fiber each day, but beware of high-fiber diets. Eating too much fiber may interfere with the body's absorption of essential nutrients. Regular servings of whole wheat bread, vegetables, and fruit should provide enough fiber for most people.

sources are found in dried figs and apricots, avocados, and apples with their skins, green beans and peas, broccoli, Brussels sprouts, turnips, lentils, black beans, whole-wheat breads, and crackers. Adding fiber to foods that contain fiber is of no value.

All fibers are not the same, which is why you must include some of the various available types in your daily diet. Most fibers prove beneficial in weight control, and whole grains may help tighten a flabby stomach. But pectins and gums are needed for the proper body use of fats, cholesterol, and carbohydrates. A *high-fiber* diet, compared with one that is *adequate* in fiber, can interfere with intestinal absorption, which may result in the loss of essential nutrients. You will probably get enough fiber in your diet by eating two servings of vegetables and two servings of whole grains (whole-wheat bread, for instance) each day.

How to add fiber to your diet

DO'S

- **Make certain** to eat a wide variety of foods in reasonable amounts.
- **Be sure** to drink adequate liquids when you eat fiber to avoid constipation.
- **Look for** the words "whole grain," "whole wheat," or "whole oats" on breads and cereals. Generally, coarse fiber is more effective than the same fiber ground fine.
- **Include** fresh fruits and raw vegetables in your diet. Their fiber content is more useful than peeled, cooked, or puréed fruits and vegetables.

DON'TS

- **Do not** depend upon fiber pills or tablets. You would have to take a whole bottle to get any benefit.
- **Do not** use fiber as a food additive. Change the kinds of foods you eat *gradually* to avoid a bloated feeling, diarrhea, or gas.
- **Do not** cut out all refined carbohydrates at one time. Replace them slowly with natural, whole-grain foods.
- **Do not** concentrate on one or another type of fiber; consider them all.

Trace minerals. Mineral elements account for only about four percent of total body weight. However, the body holds enough iron to make a good size nail, and enough sodium to fill a small salt shaker.

More needs to be learned about the exact daily requirements of trace minerals, but a diet with a sufficient amount of natural foods should be adequate to maintain good health.

Food sources and body functions

Trace mineral	Chief food sources	Chief body functions
Chromium	Liver, beef, dried beans, cheese, whole-grain breads and cereals, peanuts, brewer's yeast, molasses, and beets.	Aids the body, together with insulin, in deriving energy from glucose (blood sugar). Plays an important role in the synthesis of fatty acids and cholesterol in the liver.
Copper	Oysters, fish, nuts, dried peas, beans, beef and pork liver, organ meats, eggs, spinach, asparagus, and corn-oil margarine.	Aids in the manufacture of red blood cells, and helps the body store iron. A component of several respiratory enzymes, copper is also part of the enzyme that helps make melanin (the pigment in the skin).
Fluorine (Fluoride)	Fish, tea, most animal foods, fluoridated water, and foods grown with or cooked in fluoridated water.	Helps form strong teeth and resistance to decay. Aids in maintenance of bone strength.
Iodine	Seafood, saltwater fish, seaweed, sea salt, and iodized salt.	A component of thyroid hormones that control the body's metabolism. Aids in the development and functioning of the thyroid gland, and in the prevention of goiter.
Iron	Liver (especially pork, followed by calf, beef, and chicken), kidneys, red meat, egg yolks, green leafy vegetables, dried raisins, apricots, prunes, dried beans, peas, potatoes, blackstrap molasses; enriched, whole-grain cereals.	Helps form red blood cells and myoglobin in muscles that supply oxygen in cells. Found in enzyme systems, including one that works to produce energy in the body.
Manganese	Nuts, whole grains, fruits, vegetables, tea, instant coffee, and cocoa powder.	Aids in proper function of the nervous system, normal bone structure, and reproduction. Extremely important in many vital enzyme systems in the body. Needed for utilization of iron.
Molybdenum	Legumes, cereal grains, liver, kidney, some dark green vegetables.	Required by three important enzymes. May aid in prevention of tooth decay. Associated with carbohydrate metabolism.
Selenium	Seafood, whole-grain cereals, meat, egg yolks, chicken, and milk.	Antioxidant, preventing breakdown of fats and other body chemicals. Interacts with Vitamin E in protecting cell membranes.
Zinc	Beef, liver, eggs, poultry, seafood, especially oysters, peas, carrots, whole grains, and pure maple syrup.	A component of as many as 100 enzymes in the body. Involved in normal wound healing. Needed for growth and development.

Know your vitamins. There are 13 compounds considered to be vitamins. Four—A, D, E, and K—are soluble in fat. The eight B vitamins and C are soluble in water. The fat-soluble vitamins, stored in body fat, are not readily excreted and therefore do not need to be replaced as often as the water-soluble

How vitamins can keep you healthy

Vitamin	Food sources	How they help you
Vitamin A Retinol (discovered 1913)	Yellow, orange, and dark green vegetables, liver, cheese, milk, eggs, and butter.	Known as the growth vitamin, Vitamin A is essential in maintaining healthy skin, hair, mucous membranes, and bone. It provides visual pigments that allow you to see.
Vitamin B₁ Thiamin (discovered 1936)	Whole-wheat grains, wheat germ, liver and kidney, pork, peas, beans, peanuts, oranges, and many other fruits and vegetables.	All B vitamins play a similar role in the body: they help enzymes to do their job. B_1 acts as a cofactor for 24 enzymes, aiding cells to utilize carbohydrates. It assists in the proper functioning of the nervous system and digestive tract.
Vitamin B₂ Riboflavin (discovered 1935)	Liver, kidney, lamb, beef, veal, eggs, whole-wheat products, yeast, asparagus, beets, peas, and dark green vegetables.	A cofactor in enzymes helping cells to use carbohydrates, proteins, and fats, and producing energy. Promotes growth, healthy skin, and mucous membranes.
Vitamin B₃ Niacin Nicotinamide Nicotinic acid (discovered 1867)	Lean meat, fish, liver, yeast, eggs, whole-grain breads and cereals, peas, beans, and nuts.	An essential component of enzymes that contribute to the production of energy in cells. Also assists in the breakdown of fats.
Vitamin B₆ Pyridoxine Pyridoxal (discovered 1934)	Poultry, fish, liver, whole grains, cereals, breads, tomatoes, yellow corn, spinach, green beans, bananas, and yogurt.	An essential activator of many enzymes, pyridoxine aids in breaking down protein, carbohydrates, and fat, and in forming hormones such as adrenalin and insulin. It also helps to regenerate red blood cells and produce antibodies.
Folic acid Folicin (discovered 1946)	Liver, kidneys, green leafy vegetables, and dried legumes.	Necessary for formation of red and white cells. Aids in protein metabolism and in creating some components of the DNA molecule.
Vitamin C Ascorbic acid (discovered 1919)	Abundant in most fruits and vegetables, especially citrus fruits, tomatoes, potatoes, green peppers, and dark green vegetables.	Enhances the activity of certain enzymes. Aids body use of iron and blood clotting as needed. Helps formation of teeth, gums, and bones; aids in healing of bone fractures and wounds.
Vitamin D Calciferol (discovered 1925)	Egg yolks, butter, fortified milk, liver, fish liver oils, tuna, salmon, herring, sardines, and oysters.	Known as the "sunshine vitamin." Aids in the normal growth and development of bones and teeth. Important in the intestinal absorption of calcium and phosphorus. Affords antirachitic activity.
Vitamin E Alpha tocopherol (discovered 1936)	Lettuce and other leafy green vegetables, seed oils, whole grains, dried beans, and liver.	Helps in the production of red blood cells and in the strengthening of muscles and other tissues. An antioxidant, it protects Vitamin A and fats from reacting with oxygen.

Health and Fitness

vitamins. These must be included in your daily diet in adequate amounts. On the whole, vitamins can be used and reused by the body, which explains why you need only small amounts to replace those lost in the urine or feces. Studying this table will help you choose the right foods for a balanced diet.

Research indications

In animal tests, some researchers found that a lack of Vitamin A can increase the toxicity of aflatoxin (a natural poison produced by a fungus living in peanuts and grains), and with it the chance of getting cancer of the colon. It is also becoming more evident that Vitamin A may play an important part in preventing epithelial cancers, such as are produced by smoking cigarettes.

Vitamin B_1 deficiency is implicated in all stages of alcoholism; a diet rich in B_1 will help prevent polyneuritis in alcoholics. There has been some success in treating children suffering repeated episodes of fever and gland swellings (unresponsive to conventional therapy) with B_1 supplementation.

Vitamin B_2 helps the body obtain energy from food. One study has shown that women who exercise vigorously and regularly may need almost twice as much riboflavin as those who are less active. This may be owed to the part Vitamin B_2 has in producing energy.

Niacin has been used effectively to lower high cholesterol levels associated with familial hypercholesterolemia, which cannot be controlled by diet alone and which quintuples the risk of heart disease.

In test animals, a diet lacking pyridoxine and other B vitamins, and with exposure to aflatoxin, increased the likelihood of cancer of the liver. Pyridoxine has been used medically to treat the toxic effects of carbon disulfide. A diet rich in pyridoxine may help prevent cirrhosis in alcoholics.

Preliminary British studies with pregnant women indicate that a large dose (4 mg daily) of this vitamin may help prevent such congenital defects as spina bifida (a defect in the wall of the spinal canal) and encephalocele (a defect involving the brain). An American study indicates that a megadose (10 mg daily) may lower the risk of cervical cancer in women on the pill who show cervical cell abnormalities.

In animal studies, Vitamin C has shown a possible activity against gum disease. Research shows that large doses of Vitamin C may be able to help the body detoxify such poisonous substances as malathion, lead, and cancer-causing nitrosamines.

Rickets and osteomalacia due to a lack of Vitamin D can be effectively treated with a form of Vitamin D known as 25-hydroxy-cholecalciferol. It has been found that Vitamin D breaks down in the body into compounds that may act as hormones. A synthetic compound, 1-25 Vitamin D, has been approved for use as an agent to promote bone growth.

Animal tests have shown that Vitamin E can lessen the damage that two air pollutants, ozone and nitrogen dioxide, can have on the lungs. Vitamin E, together with Vitamin C and zinc, may reduce toxicity to cadmium. Reportedly, Vitamin E may relieve chronic cystic mastitis in many cases; also, nighttime leg cramps.

SUPPLEMENTS

To be used with caution

The past decade has seen a flowering in the availability, promotion, and use of dietary supplements to promote health and prevent disease. But the Food and Drug Administration (FDA) and other health-related organizations offer stern warnings about the potential dangers of misuse, or overuse, of dietary supplements.

The FDA notes that just because a supplement is naturally produced does not mean it is safe for all users. Some supplements, particularly those targeted at boosting the user's energy level or helping weight loss, may contain ephedrine, which has been linked to high blood pressure, heart attack, stroke, and death.

Dietary supplements were exempted from FDA regulation in 1994. Since then, thousands of cases of side effects, and scores of deaths, have been associated with the use of supplements. Even excessively large doses, or megadoses, of vitamins and minerals can cause serious, and possibly fatal, medical problems.

It is recommended that persons wishing to take one or more dietary supplements check with a physician to learn of any potential risks or side effects associated with them. This is especially important for those with medical conditions such as kidney or liver problems, high blood pressure, neurological problems, or respiratory ailments. Use of any supplement should be discontinued at the first sign of side effects.

OSTEOPOROSIS

Signs of brittle bones

In the United States, women over 45 suffer a million fractures each year. Most are associated with a condition in which there is a degenerative thinning of the bones.

Detection in the early stages is difficult. X-rays, for example, will not show bone loss until there is a loss of 30 to 50 percent. There are a few simple signs that may alert a person to the presence of osteoporosis.

Decrease in height may give the earliest detectable sign, and it is one that often goes unnoticed. It is suggested that people at high risk of osteoporosis (such as menopausal women, alcoholics, and the elderly) keep a record of their height and check it every six to twelve months. Any height loss should be reported to a doctor.

Another sign is tooth loss brought on by periodontal (gum) disease. Gum inflammation, attributed to the formation of plaque on teeth, can also be due to bone degeneration. Regular visits to the dentist will prevent the development of gum disease.

To help avoid brittle bones, women over 35 should get an adequate amount of calcium, magnesium, and vitamins C and D in their diet. Regular exercise, such as walking and stretching, is most important, as it improves calcium absorption and stimulates bone formation. Excessive intake of coffee and alcohol, and smoking, add to bone loss and should be avoided.

Water is a vital nutrient. Your body is about two-thirds water, and contains about 40 to 50 quarts of water. In women, water content averages 55 to 65 percent, while it is around 65 to 75 percent in men.

Every living body cell needs water to perform its vital function. Water aids in the digestion and absorption of nutrients, such as vitamins. It transports oxygen to the cells and removes both liquid and solid wastes. It helps the body maintain a normal temperature, and lubricates the joints. It provides a protective cushion for the tissues, and keeps skin from drying out.

How much water should you drink? Most people drink far less water than the six to eight 8-ounce glasses considered nutritionally adequate even though the fluid requirement includes fruit juices, soft drinks, milk, coffee, and tea as well as plain water. Even greater amounts of liquid are needed during periods of increased water loss in hot weather, strenuous exercise, and illness accompanied by fever. Infants and childbearing women also require extra fluids.

Water forms the larger part of most solid foods. Fruits and vegetables are about 80 percent water, green beans 89 percent, and lettuce 95 percent. Even milk is 87 percent water, and fish foods around 75 percent. Meat is half water, while bread is about one-third water by weight.

The body excretes about 2 quarts of water a day, most of it as urine. Water may also be lost in sizeable amounts through the skin by sweating, through the lungs in the process of breathing, and upon extreme exertion in strenuous exercise.

Good nutrition

Cutting down on fatty foods and eating more fruits and vegetables will reduce deaths by heart disease, the leading cause of death in the United States.

Most Americans eat too much. There is too much fat, refined sugar, and salt in our diets. On the whole, our diets consist of about 50 percent nonessential foods. You can, however, easily improve your eating habits for the better. Start by cutting down on fats and using polyunsaturated for saturated fats. Eat more lean meats and poultry, and fewer dairy products. Instead of overloading your diet with foods high in sugar, substitute fresh fruits and vegetables. Use low-calorie for high-calorie foods whenever possible. Limit your salt intake, using herbs to flavor food.

Types of fats

Saturated *Avoid use of* (tend to raise blood cholesterol)	butter cheese coconut, coconut oil egg yolks lard	meat milk chocolate palm oil vegetable shortening whole milk
Polyunsaturated *Use occasionally* (have no effect on blood cholesterol)	avocados cashews olives, olive oil	peanuts peanut butter peanut oil
Monounsaturated *Good to use* (tend to lower blood cholesterol)	almonds corn oil cottonseed oil filberts fish margarine	pecans safflower oil salad dressing soybean oil sunflower oil walnuts

Heart attacks. The average American, eating a diet high in saturated fats and cholesterol, is at greater risk of having a heart attack than other populations consuming diets low in fat and cholesterol. In the opinion of the American Heart Association, reduction of fat intake is one of the most important steps a person can take to lower the risk of heart disease. Most people obtain their total daily calories from fat. It is recommended that fat intake be cut to 30 percent, and that fats in the diet be equally divided among saturated, polyunsaturated, and monounsaturated fats.

HEALTH CARE ALERT

HEART ATTACK

A key signal: chest pain

In a heart attack, pain may range from a feeling of slight pressure in the chest to a crushing sensation.
- Generally, pain lasts for hours.
- Pain does not respond to rest, or the use of nitroglycerin.
- The face turns ashen gray, and a cold sweat appears.
- Retching, belching, or vomiting may occur, which can easily be confused with an attack of indigestion.
- Pain responds only to use of a narcotic drug.
- *Act promptly:* call for medical help at once, or take victim to the nearest hospital emergency room.

Chest pain may be due to a number of different causes, some of a minor nature, such as gum chewing, drinking too much carbonated water, and excessive smoking. Chest pain may also be caused by such conditions as bruised or fractured ribs or angina pectoris. Angina is similar to a heart attack in that it usually comes on with exertion (for example, running to catch a bus or train), but the type, extent, and duration of pain are quite dissimilar.

Cancer. *Faulty diets, according to a report from the National Academy of Sciences, account for 30 to 40 percent of all cancers in men and as high as 60 percent in women.* The cancers most exclusively linked to diet are cancers of the stomach, colon, breast, and, to a lesser extent, the lung and prostate.

Eat more fruits, vegetables, fiber. Fresh dark green, orange, and yellow vegetables (broccoli, carrots, and others) are rich in a substance called beta-carotene, which the body converts into Vitamin A. Cabbage-family vegetables (Brussels sprouts, cabbages, and others) contain several chemicals that have been found to inhibit cancer in animals. Their plentiful use is associated with a reduced risk of certain cancers, especially of the colon.

Get plenty of foods rich in Vitamin C, especially citrus and red fruits and dark green vegetables. Laboratory studies have shown that Vitamin C stops the formation of certain chemicals causing cancer. In studies of persons at high risk of cancer, Vitamin C reduced the incidence of stomach or esophageal cancer.

When dietary fiber (whole grains, fresh fruits, and vegetables) intake amounts to 20 to 40 grams a day, there is possible protection against colon and rectal cancer.

Eat less fats, smoked foods. Avoid or limit intake of dietary fats. Both saturated (for example, animal fats, butter fat, palm oil, coconut oil) and unsaturated fats (mostly vegetable oils) have been linked with increased cancer, in particular, of the breast and colon. A 25 percent reduction in *all* dietary fats is recommended.

Fact or fiction?

Cow's milk is a perfect food.
Fiction. Cow's milk may be a relatively good food for young children, but most infants fare better on mother's milk. Milk is a good food but does not contain enough of some important nutrients, especially iron, copper, and Vitamin C.

Enriched breads are nutritious.
Fact. Important vitamins and minerals (thiamin, riboflavin, niacin, and iron) are partially removed in the milling of flour. By enrichment, these substances are replaced to a level equivalent to those in whole-wheat flour or bread.

Vegetarians often develop severe nutritional deficiencies.
Fact. Strict vegetarians do not get enough Vitamin D or Vitamin B_{12} (the only B vitamin not found in any vegetable). For good sources of these vitamins, as well as calcium and protein, we must depend upon foods of animal origin.

Eating out . . . healthily and enjoyably

Be in control of your diet, no matter where you eat or what the occasion.

- **Ask that dishes be prepared as you wish:** with reduced salt or no salt at all; with margarine instead of butter; with entrees broiled, roasted, or baked.
- **Avoid rich sauces,** or ask that sauces be served on the side. Spoon off as much sauce as you can when you are served a precooked dish with a rich sauce. Also, pass up such salads as shrimp and tuna.
- **Trim off all fat and skin** from served meats.
- **If high sodium seasonings,** such as soy sauce, monosodium glutamate (MSG), and salt are used, ask that they be used sparingly, or not at all.
- **Snack on nonfattening foods** at a buffet party and leave the patés, dips, smoked fish, and the like.

Smoked, salt-cured, or pickled foods should be used sparingly. In smoking and curing, foods are exposed to certain compounds, such as the nitrosamines. These compounds cause cancer in animals and are suspect in humans.

The consumption of alcohol should be limited to one or two drinks a day, or eliminated. More than a few drinks a day has been linked to cancer of the mouth, larynx, esophagus, and respiratory tract, and beer drinking has been linked to cancer of the colon and rectum. The risk is increased with cigarette smoking.

HEALTH CARE ALERT

CANCER

Seven signals

1. Change in bowel or bladder habits.
2. A sore that does not heal.
3. Unusual bleeding or discharge.
4. Thickening or lump in the breast or any other part of the body.
5. Indigestion or difficulty in swallowing.
6. Obvious change in wart or mole.
7. Nagging cough or hoarseness.

If you have any of these signals, it does not necessarily mean that you have cancer. It does mean that something is wrong in your body, and you need to check with your doctor.

Cigarette smoking is a major cause of lung cancer. For more than a decade, the number of women smokers has been increasing steadily. Today, lung cancer will kill more women than breast cancer.

Health and Fitness

Fast foods. Probably nothing has changed the eating habits of millions of Americans more than the fast-food eateries found nearly everywhere and the introduction of convenience foods, which are steadily increasing in number and variety.

Many of these foods are labeled junk foods. They provide few or no nutrients other than sugar calories. These are rightly called empty calories because they are mostly carbohydrate and contain no proteins, minerals, or vitamins. Most popular soft drinks, pastries, candies, and ice creams contain as much as 100 percent of sugar calories.

While fast foods do not fall into the junk food category, they supply either too little or too much of one or more essential nutrients. Even pizza, which contains more protein and less fat than most other fast foods, has a rather high calorie and salt content. *The average American consumes nearly 10 grams of salt a day, which is more than three times the recommended daily allowance.* This excessive use of salt has led health authorities to suggest that salt intake be restricted to 5 grams a day.

It pays to read food labels. You can readily check packaged foods for their sugar, sodium, or fat content by reading the labels. In general, the ingredient with the highest amount of a given substance is listed first, followed by others in descending order of content.

Familiarize yourself with other names for sugar, sodium, or fat content in packaged foods. Sugar may be listed as sucrose, glucose, zylose, fructose, mannose, and disaccharides or monosaccharides. Sodium is the main ingredient in monosodium glutamate (MSG), phosphates, nitrites, and baking soda as well as in table salt. Some manufacturers give the milligram content of sodium per serving. A product is considered high in sodium if it contains more than 350 to 500 milligrams per serving.

In general, the term "shortening," either animal or vegetable, implies that the fat is saturated, and the term "liquid vegetable oil" suggests a polyunsaturated fat. If the label lists "vegetable oil" as a main ingredient but does not specify the kind, or if it lists coconut or palm oil (high in saturated fat), it is best to avoid use of the product.

Food values of fast foods

Fast food	Calories	Protein (grams)	Carbohydrates (grams)	Fats (grams)	Sodium (mg)
Burger King Hamburger	260	14	28	10	500
Burger King French Fries (medium)	400	5	43	20	240
Burger King Vanilla Shake (medium)	310	9	53	7	230
Burger King Big Fish Sandwich	720	25	59	43	1090
Burger King Whopper	630	27	45	39	850
Dairy Queen Banana Split	610	9	93	11	250
Dairy Queen Cheese Dog	330	12	24	21	920
Dairy Queen Onion Rings	240	4	29	12	135
Kentucky Fried Chicken Extra Tasty Crispy Chicken (breast)	470	31	25	28	930
Kentucky Fried Chicken Original Recipe (breast)	360	33	12	20	870
Long John Silver's Fish (2 pieces)	318	19	19	19	N.A.*
McDonald's Apple Pie	290	3	37	15	220
McDonald's Big Mac	510	25	46	26	930
McDonald's Chocolate Shake (small)	350	13	62	6	240
McDonald's Egg McMuffin	290	17	27	13	730
McDonald's Filet-o-Fish	360	14	41	16	710
Pizza Hut Chunky Meat Pizza (hand tossed crust, 1 medium slice)	325	17	28	16	970
Pizza Hut Personal Pan Pizza (pepperoni)	675	29	76	30	1335
Taco Bell Taco	180	10	N.A.*	11	276
Arthur Treacher's Coleslaw	123	1	11	8	266
Arthur Treacher's Fish Sandwich	440	16	39	24	836

Source: Data supplied by Burger King Corporation; International Dairy Queen, Inc.; KFC Corporation; McDonalds' Corporation; Pizza Hut, Inc.; Taco Bell Corporation. Other companies' data supplied by the companies to the Senate Select Committee on Nutrition and Human Needs.
*N.A.—not available.

Watch your weight

As a nation we are becoming more obese, with the typical American adult male averaging 20 to 30 pounds of excess weight, and the typical female carrying 15 to 30 extra pounds. Overweight people are more likely to run the risk of high blood pressure, diabetes, high blood cholesterol, and heart disease.

To maintain ideal weight, it is necessary to keep your body energy needs in balance. Take in *more* energy than is needed and your body will store it as excess fat and you will gain weight. Take in *less* energy than is used up, and your body will withdraw some from the stored fat and you will lose weight. For the average person, it takes about 3500 extra calories to produce a pound of fat and, conversely, about 3500 fewer calories to use up a pound of stored fat. The easiest way to keep your weight constant is to lose any weight gain promptly, even if it is only 1 pound.

Ideal body weight may be determined by checking a table of suggested body weights. Such tables give no absolute answers on what constitutes ideal weight, but they can be helpful in determining your weight range.

Cut calories, not nutrients. There are almost as many diet plans as there are dieters. They embrace a variety of weight-loss theories: crash diets, liquid protein diets, cleansing and no-food diets, fruit juice, vegetable, or meat diets, high-fat and low-carbohydrate diets, low-fat and high-carbohydrate diets, to mention a few. To this list must be added the numerous reducing drugs that can be bought at the drugstore.

Many diet plans are nutritionally unbalanced. Most are disappointing as they seldom result in permanent weight loss. The repeated gaining, losing, and regaining of weight is considered by some health professionals to have a more damaging effect upon health than being consistently and moderately overweight. In sensible weight loss, you reduce your calorie intake without depriving your body of the nutrients needed for good health.

In the long run, the only diet that can do you real good is one that changes your bad eating habits for the better. The need is not for a 7-, or 10- or 21-day reducing plan, but a lifetime diet that includes all the

Metropolitan Life height and weight tables

Compared with figures as revised in 1959, this latest update on height and weight tables issued by the Metropolitan Life Insurance Company shows that adults can now weigh more than previously. There is an average increase in weight of 13 pounds for short men and 10 pounds for short women; 7 pounds for men of medium height, and 3 pounds for women of medium height; and 2 pounds for tall men, and 3 pounds for tall women. These tables apply to people from ages 25 to 59. The weight is stated in pounds, according to body frame size and the wearing of indoor clothing (5 pounds for men and 3 pounds for women in shoes with 1-inch heels).

Men Height	Small frame	Medium frame	Large frame
5' 2"	128–134	131–141	138–150
5' 3"	130–136	133–143	140–153
5' 4"	132–138	135–145	142–156
5' 5"	134–140	137–148	144–160
5' 6"	136–142	139–151	146–164
5' 7"	138–145	142–154	149–168
5' 8"	140–148	145–157	152–172
5' 9"	142–151	148–160	155–176
5' 10"	144–154	151–163	158–180
5' 11"	146–157	154–166	161–184
6' 0"	149–160	157–170	164–188
6' 1"	152–164	160–174	168–192
6' 2"	155–168	164–178	172–197
6' 3"	158–172	167–182	176–202
6' 4"	162–176	171–187	181–207

Women Height	Small frame	Medium frame	Large frame
4' 10"	102–111	109–121	118–131
4' 11"	103–113	111–123	120–134
5' 0"	104–115	113–126	122–137
5' 1"	106–118	115–129	125–140
5' 2"	108–121	118–132	128–143
5' 3"	111–124	121–135	131–147
5' 4"	114–127	124–138	134–151
5' 5"	117–130	127–141	137–155
5' 6"	120–133	130–144	140–159
5' 7"	123–136	133–147	143–163
5' 8"	126–139	136–150	146–167
5' 9"	129–142	139–153	149–170
5' 10"	132–145	142–156	152–173
5' 11"	135–148	145–159	155–176
6' 0"	138–151	148–162	158–179

© 1983 Metropolitan Life Insurance Company/Source of basic data 1979 Build Study, Society of Actuaries and Association of Life Insurance Medical Directors of America, 1980.

essential nutrients obtained from a variety of foods. It is never too late to correct faulty eating habits, and by doing so you can help children learn good eating habits as they grow up.

To gain weight, add calories.

To those who are forever fighting the battle of the midriff bulge, putting on extra pounds may seem to be an easy task. Such, however, is not always the case. Some people are naturally thin because of their inherited body build; others cannot put on weight no matter how much food rich in calories they consume. In some cases, medical problems such as hyperthyroidism or diabetes must be corrected before considering a program to gain weight.

If you are underweight, it may be due to faulty eating habits, or just eating too little food. You may not have a good appetite, which in itself may signal an underlying illness, and you may also suffer from poor digestion and absorption of food. A physical checkup may be needed to determine the cause of being underweight, or having continued weight loss, before deciding on the measures necessary to assure weight gain.

In general, a person who desires to gain weight needs to eat more nutritious food and to increase the total number of calories in the daily diet. Proper living habits are important, too: eat regular meals, take mild exercise, get sufficient sleep, and avoid tension.

Fact or fiction?

You can shed pounds by skipping breakfast.
Fiction. Breakfast should be your first meal of the day, providing essential nutrients to assure body function at a high level of energy. Without breakfast, you may be tempted to snack between meals, or eat too much at the next meal.

The more exercise, the bigger the appetite.
Fiction. You will not only use up calories with regular moderate exercise, but you will keep physically fit. In many cases, inactivity is a main reason for obesity in children as well as adults.

You can lose ten pounds in ten days.
Fact. This is possible, but it will probably be mostly a water loss, which will be quickly replaced once you go off the crash diet. A sound weight loss program recommends a slow, sure loss of 1 or 2 pounds a week.

With determination, everyone can reduce.
Fact. People who claim they cannot lose weight are usually themselves at fault. Many persons do not eat to appease hunger, but to satisfy a craving. Hunger signals the body's need for food; appetite, based on remembered eating pleasures, is a desire for certain types of food.

Food for thought

If you eat . . .	you add on . . .	to lose, you must walk
2 strips of bacon	100 calories	20 minutes
10 potato chips	100 calories	20 minutes
1 doughnut	150 calories	29 minutes
1 piece cake	358 calories	68 minutes
1 slice apple pie	375 calories	73 minutes
1 malted milk shake	500 calories	97 minutes

Substitute . . . burn off more calories. By substituting one ingredient for another in the preparation of food, and eating one type of food for another, you can reduce your total calorie intake. An ounce of pure protein or carbohydrate will produce 110 calories; an ounce of fat will supply 250 calories. These figures may help you calculate your own calorie intake from a meal or dietary plan.

Food preparation

Instead of . . .	Substitute
whole milk	skim milk
cream	evaporated milk
sour cream	yogurt
cream cheese	low-fat cottage cheese
whole milk cheese	skim-milk or low-fat cheese

Food consumption

Instead of . . .	Substitute . . .	Saved calories
2 tbsp. regular mayonnaise	2 tbsp. diet mayonnaise	about 150
1 cup ice cream	1 cup ice milk	about 90
1 regular hamburger	1 lean hamburger	about 76
1 serving French fries	1 baked potato	about 200
1 can (6½ oz.) tuna, oil-packed, drained	1 can (6½ oz.) tuna water-packed, drained	about 100

Get back into shape

Moderate and regular exercise, which is good for you at any time of life, is doubly important when losing weight. It can help your body burn up unwanted fat faster while firming up muscles and flattening out bulges. Physical activity can also keep your body flexible, and help maintain muscle tone, stimulate body functions, especially the circulatory and respiratory systems, and help relieve tension.

To keep physically fit, you need not take up strenuous exercise or a demanding sport. If you make a conscious effort, you can even find plenty of opportunity to stretch and bend while you are doing some everyday task—dusting, sweeping, making the beds, weeding the garden, doing small repair jobs around the house.

Choose an exercise that you enjoy, and one suited to your physical condition, body build, age, and lifestyle. While you will benefit little from doing exercise in a lax manner, you should not overexercise to the point of physical pain or injury.

Exercise works. Walking is an excellent form of exercise, considered by health authorities to be the best overall nonstrenuous activity for the heart and legs. All you need is a comfortable pair of walking shoes. *A brisk 20- to 30-minute walk each day can help you take weight off and keep it off.*

Swimming, jogging, or bicycling are exercises that develop a strong heart, while calisthenics and gymnastics improve strength, agility, and muscle tone. Whatever your choice of activity, it is important to remember that it will only be beneficial and improve your state of health if you stick with it.

Energy expenditures

This table gives approximate energy expenditures by a 150-pound person in various activities.

Activity	Calories per hour
Bicycling, 5½ mph	210
Bicycling, 13 mph	660
Bowling	270
Domestic work	180
Driving an automobile	120
Gardening	220
Golf	250
Lawn mowing (power mower)	250
Lying down or sleeping	80
Roller skating	350
Running, 10 mph	900
Sitting	100
Skiing, 10 mph	600
Square dancing	350
Squash and handball	600
Standing	140
Swimming, ¼ mph	300
Tennis	420
Volleyball	350
Walking, 2½ mph	210
Walking, 3¾ mph	300
Wood chopping or sawing	400

Source: Based on material prepared by Robert E. Johnson, M.D., Ph.D., and colleagues, University of Illinois.

HEALTH CARE ALERT

ARTHRITIS

There are many forms of arthritis but, in general, sufferers are afflicted with either osteoarthritis or rheumatoid arthritis. Osteoarthritis takes a decade or longer to develop, so most sufferers are at least middle-aged. In this condition, the protective cartilage normally cushioning a joint begins to break down, causing pain and stiffness, and inflammation in some cases.

Rheumatoid arthritis (RA), unlike osteoarthritis, strikes children and young adults as well as older adults. In this arthritic disorder, the body's immune system (defense network) goes haywire and turns on the body itself. There is pain and recurrent inflammation. RA can be severely crippling.

Do not ignore these signals.
Medical care in the early stages of arthritis can often lessen the permanent damage to diseased joints. If you experience any of the symptoms listed below for more than two weeks, check with your physician.
- Swelling in one or more joints.
- Recurring pain or tenderness in any body joint.
- Inability to move a joint properly, or to perform normal activities.
- Obvious redness and warmth in one of the joints.
- Persistent early morning pain and stiffness in joints. Unexplained weight loss, fever, weakness, or fatigue combined with joint pain.

Health and Fitness

Home medical testing

Medical tests help to determine the cause of pain or disease, and in themselves become meaningful only after your physician has studied them in the light of your complete medical history. There are any number of medical tests that can be performed at home. Some require nothing more than close observation, while others, such as various urine tests, require certain medical supplies (which can be purchased at a local pharmacy), and a knowledge of how the tests should be performed. Still others, such as taking your blood pressure, call for the purchase of special equipment and must be carefully performed to be useful. Before buying medical supplies or equipment, it is advisable to check with your doctor to see if there is any drawback to home testing and to obtain detailed instructions on performing a test correctly.

Home medical testing should not be regarded as a means of making a self-diagnosis, or instituting self-treatment. Any body signals, such as persistent pain, unexplained bleeding, skin or other growths, difficulties in breathing, seeing, or hearing, or uncoordinated movements, should be promptly brought to the attention of your physician.

The tests included in this discussion do not call for the purchase of special supplies or equipment. They are intended to help you learn more about your own or your family's health, and to communicate more effectively with your doctor if a medical problem arises.

Two important tests

Taking your pulse. Pulse measurements generally consist of rate, rhythm, and character. The most frequently used location is the wrist. With the palm up, place two or three fingers of the examining hand on the thumb side of the wrist being examined. Do *not* use the thumb, and be careful not to apply too much pressure.

Rest for ten minutes before taking your pulse, and then take it in a sitting position. To begin with, you may want to count the pulse beats for a full minute, timing them by the second hand of a watch. As you become more experienced, you can shorten the time to half a minute, and then 15 seconds, multiplying the result by four. Normal pulse rates may range from 60 to 70 beats per minute for men and from 70 to 80 beats per minute for women. Wide variations in pulse rate, or a weak or irregular pulse, should be checked out with your doctor. Pulse rhythm may be observed at the same time that the pulse rate is being counted. It should be regular without pauses; that is, there should be no skipped beats or extra beats between normal beats. Pulse character is determined by the smoothness of the beat: no beat should be any stronger or weaker than any of the others.

Testing your sense of smell. This type of test is more useful than it may seem at first. There are many people who live in danger of serious harm because they are unable to detect the odor that accompanies spoiled or contaminated foods, smoke from fire, escaping gas from a heating apparatus, and lethal chemical fumes.

Gather together at least three items with familiar odors, such as an onion or garlic, milk chocolate, turpentine, fresh flowers with a distinctive scent (roses, lilacs), and a burning paper match, or burning paper in an ashtray. With the exception of the burning match and paper, the items are best tested by being enclosed in a tightly closed container, and then opened for a few seconds when the test is being made.

Before starting, make certain that your nasal passages are clear. Then, begin the test by closing one nostril (apply pressure to it with a finger). Close your eyes, and smell the odor being tested through the open nostril; repeat with the other nostril. Both sides of the nose should be able to smell the tested odors with equal efficiency.

Glossary

carbohydrates

For definitions of additional medical terms, see Glossary on page 96.

angina pectoris. Painful oppression about the heart which is usually severe and radiates from the heart to the shoulder and down the left arm.

antioxidant. An agent inhibiting oxidation and thereby preventing oils or fats from becoming rancid through the process of oxidation.

aromatic. The series of carbon compounds in which the carbon atoms form closed rings, such as benzene.

arthritis. An inflammatory condition of the joints in which there is usually pain and changes in structure.

asthma. A term generally used to mean bronchial asthma, which is a condition of the lungs having serious narrowing of the airways.

calorie. The energy value of foods, calculated by the amount of heat needed to raise one kilogram of water through 1° C, a kilocalorie.

carbohydrates. Sugar; saccharides. A class of organic compounds in which hydrogen and oxygen are in the same ratio as they are in water.

cells. Minute structures that are the physical basis of all plant and animal life processes.

cellulose. A plant fiber, or fibrous form of carbohydrate, which aids peristaltic stimulation and intestinal elimination.

cholesterol. A sterol (fatlike substance) widely distributed in animal tissues, and occurring in egg yolk, various oils, fats, and nerve tissue (brain and spinal cord).

cornea. A transparent membrane that is part of the outer coat of the eyeball.

degenerative. The state in which a body part or organ becomes impaired or deteriorates.

disaccharides. One of a group of carbohydrates, dissacharose is a complex sugar that may be split into two molecules of monosaccharides.

DNA (deoxyribonucleic acid). A nucleic acid that is found in chromosomes of the nuclei of cells. It is considered to be the carrier of genetic information and the chemical basis of heredity.

enzymes. Complex proteins that are capable of inducing chemical changes in other substances without themselves becoming altered in the process.

fructose. Levulose; a fruit sugar found in corn syrup, honey, and fruit juices. Produces glycogen and maintains normal glucose content in the blood.

glaucoma. Eye disease marked by increased pressure in the eye that results in atrophy of the optic nerve and blindness.

glucose. A sugar that is formed during digestion. It is the most important carbohydrate in body metabolism.

glycogen. A polysaccharide, it is the main carbohydrate reserve in the body that is readily converted into sugar.

goiter. An enlargement of the thyroid gland.

hydrocarbon. A compound made up only of hydrogen and carbon.

hydrogenation. Adding hydrogen to a compound, especially to an unsaturated fat. In this way, soft fats or oils are solidified or "hardened."

hypertension. Condition in which a person has higher blood pressure than is considered to be normal.

mannose. An aldohexose (sugar) obtained from various plant sources: mannons (various legumes).

monosaccharide. A simple sugar (fructose, galactose, glucose) that is absorbed directly. It maintains the glucose content of the blood and aids in the production of glycogen.

monosodium glutamate. Sodium salt of glutamic acid; a white crystalline substance with a meatlike taste. It is used to flavor foods.

myoglobin. Muscle protein that transports oxygen, similar in function to blood hemoglobin.

nitrosamines. A combination of nitrites with a type of organic chemical in food known as amines. Nitrosamines are potent cancer-causing substances.

nutrient. A food supplying the body with essential elements. Carbohydrates, proteins, and alcohol provide energy. Water, electrolytes (acids, bases, salts), minerals, and vitamins are needed for metabolism.

nutrition. The taking in and utilization of food substances for body growth, repair, and maintenance. Successive stages are known as digestion, absorption, metabolism (assimilation), and excretion.

osteomalacia. A disease that is marked by increased softening of the bone. This makes bone flexible and brittle, resulting in deformities.

pectin. Plant carbohydrate that forms a gelatinous mass in the cooking of fruits and vegetables, causing them to jell.

polysaccharide. One of a group of carbohydrates that, upon hydrolysis, yields more than two molecules of simple sugars.

polyunsaturated. Refers to long-chain carbon compounds, especially fats that have many carbon atoms joined by double or triple bonds.

saccharides. A group of carbohydrates (including sugars) that is divided into these classifications: monosaccharides,

HEALTH CARE ALERT

DIABETES

In this disorder, the body does not make proper use of sugar. Sugar, derived from the food we eat, is an important fuel needed by the body to supply energy. Normally, insulin (a substance made in the pancreas) allows sugar to reach the muscles, fat, and other tissues and be burned to produce energy. In diabetes, there is not enough insulin; consequently, the sugar cannot enter the tissues.

Diabetes is found most often in persons who have a relative with diabetes, are overweight, or elderly. In some cases, adults become diabetic without developing any symptoms.

Signals of diabetes
Check with your doctor if you notice any of the following symptoms:
1. Excessive thirst
2. Increased appetite
3. Frequent urination
4. Itching of the skin, especially the genital area
5. Weakness and tiredness
6. Weight loss
7. Pain, numbness, or tingling in the hands and feet
8. Disturbances of vision
9. Irritability, nervousness, or nausea

disaccharides, trisaccharides, and polysaccharides.

saturated. Carbon compounds in which all the atoms are linked by single bonds.

sodium. Sodium salts are found in body fluids, serum, blood, lymph, and tissues. These salts are needed to maintain a balance between calcium and potassium for normal heart function, and for equilibrium of the body.

synthesis. In general, this is the process involved in the formation of a complex substance from simpler elements or compounds; for example, the synthesis of proteins from amino acids.

For further reference

Brody, Jane
  Jane Brody's Nutrition Book
  W.W. Norton
Calabrese, E.J. and Dorsey, Michael W.
  Healthy Living in an Unhealthy World
  Simon & Schuster
Davis, Adelle
  Let's Stay Healthy: A Guide to Lifelong Nutrition
  Harcourt Brace Jovanovitch
Goliszek, Andrew
  Breaking the Stress Habit: A Modern Guide to One-Minute Stress Management
  Carolina Press

Sapolsky, Robert M.
  Why Zebras Don't Get Ulcers: A Guide to Stress, Stress-Related Diseases, and Coping
  W.H. Freeman
Schroeder, Henry A.
  The Trace Elements and Man
  Devin-Adair Publishers
Somer, Elizabeth
  The Essential Guide to Vitamins and Minerals
  HarperCollins
Tubesing, D.A.
  Kicking Your Stress Habits
  Whole Person Associates

You and
Modern
Medicine

There are doctors practicing today who have never seen a case of polio, smallpox, typhoid, childbed fever, or any number of other diseases that devastated human society in the past. As a generation, our life expectancy is longer than that of any other generation in history. Organ transplants and miraculous surgical techniques seem to promise an even brighter future.

We also live in a time when technology has outrun man's ability to absorb its implications or to use it safely and wisely. Life-saving devices are frequently perverted into death-prolonging machinery. Drugs proliferate at a rate beyond the ordinary doctor's capability to use them. Medical costs have skyrocketed, giving us the most expensive system in the world, with many of us living in dread of a catastrophic illness that could bankrupt us.

The average American is caught in the middle. This chapter is a guide for those consumers of medical services who wish to take better control of their lives and to use the medical system to their advantage.

You and the doctor

A doctor is an ordinary human being, highly and expensively trained to treat disease. He sees himself as a saver of lives. All of his training has led him to expect unquestioning obedience from his own staff, hospital personnel, and his patients.

In the past, most patients agreed that "doctor knows best," but as specialization and technology have eroded the patient-doctor relationship, many have begun to ask questions.

Recent court decisions have affirmed patients' right to know and right to informed consent. Informed consent means that the doctor must not only tell his patient what he proposes as treatment, but must make sure that the patient truly understands. A consent form, read and signed, is not enough.

Not all doctors are comfortable with this arrangement, and not all patients are ready to give up a dependent relationship.

When to look for a doctor. The key to good medical care is having a competent, knowledgeable, well-trained primary care physician. Many people postpone finding such a doctor for years. They use an orthopedist if they break a bone, or consult a dermatologist for skin problems. It is only when they become seriously ill that they begin the search. This is the very worst time to look.

A primary care physician has the opportunity to know his patients, their families, and their lifestyles. He is the logical keeper of medical records, an invaluable go-between in the mystifying world of specialists, an important member of the hospital treatment team, and more likely to treat the whole person than just the disease.

The hole left by the disappearing general practitioner is being filled by a growing number of young doctors who choose "family practice" as their specialty. The general internist also serves as a primary care physician. Pediatricians are primary care doctors for children.

How to find a doctor. Talking to as
many people as possible is a good beginning in finding the right doctor. Since other doctors and medical associations are rarely frank about their fellow professionals, the most reliable source of information about doctors are friends, neighbors, storekeepers, pharmacists, and nurses.

Once a tentative list of names is compiled, *The American Medical Directory* (available in libraries) and your local medical association can be consulted about medical schools, medical degrees, board certification, and hospital affiliations.

Particular attention should be paid to the hospital affiliations of doctors under consideration. You should be sure that the doctor you choose is entitled to admit patients to the hospital you determine to be the best in your community.

When the list of doctors has been narrowed to one or two, it is time to make an appointment with the doctor who sounds most promising.

A good strategy is to make a list of things you wish to observe and learn. Time and extent of office hours, who takes over when the doctor is not available, and how he can be reached in an emergency should be among the items on the list. You will want to inquire about fees, and how and when they are payable. Women will ask whether the doctor handles routine gynecological matters, and people with children will ask at what age their children will be accepted as patients.

How a doctor's office is run can affect the quality of medical care. A crowded waiting room may mean poor scheduling. The amount of time you are kept waiting on your first visit probably will not change. Only you can decide what your limits are.

A concerned, courteous, and helpful office staff is an important link between patient and doctor. An arrogant, disinterested, or rude staff can put a real stumbling block in the way of your getting the most for your medical dollar.

Getting the most from a doctor.
A successful patient is one who has reasonable expectations from his doctor; who learns as much as he can

---

Do not lie to the doctor

Many people have things in their lives that they do not want anyone to know about. These things should not be kept from the doctor. Drinking more than just occasionally is a habit he needs to know about—not only because of its possible effect on physical health, but because it can influence the kinds of medications he may safely prescribe. A three-pack-a-day smoker should own up, as should users of drugs, even recreationally. Venereal diseases are treatable but not if you are too embarrassed to describe your symptoms. If you are not comfortable discussing such things with your doctor, you should not hesitate to change to someone you are comfortable with.

It is not uncommon for a patient to accept a prescription and then, for some reason, not use it. The doctor should know about this, too. Consulting another doctor when not satisfied is a mistake only when you fail to tell your own doctor in advance.

You and your doctor are partners in the enterprise of recovering your health. Like all successful partnerships, it requires mutual trust.

about his own illness and treatment; and who follows instructions or informs his doctor when he is not doing so and why. He gets to know the office nurse and talks frankly and openly to her about why he is calling and what he expects from the phone call. He learns to be explicit and insistent with the answering service, and he also learns the value of an early call when he is feeling ill (perhaps making it easier for him to place a call in the middle of the night). A combination of assertiveness and consideration is as effective in dealing with a doctor as it is in dealing with the rest of the world.

When to change doctors.
A continuing feeling of dissatisfaction is a valid reason for changing doctors. The frequent changing of doctors is deplored by the medical profession, and may be an indication that the patient has unrealistic expectations;

When to call the doctor

People are often reluctant to call the doctor for fear of being either a nuisance or an alarmist. There are symptoms that call for an immediate call to the doctor and an immediate response from him.

Symptoms to take seriously
- Chest pain; sudden rapid or irregular pulse
- Difficulty in breathing
- Sudden coughing up of blood
- Severe nosebleed
- Inability to urinate or defecate
- Sudden and profuse vaginal bleeding
- Severe abdominal pain
- Blood in the stool
- Uncontrollable vomiting or diarrhea
- Inability to swallow
- Sudden loss of vision
- Eye pain or double vision
- Loss of balance, hearing, or sudden weakness
- Mental confusion, fainting, or vertigo
- Headache accompanied by stiff neck
- Very high or very low temperature

GET A SECOND OPINION!

Surgery is not always the only effective treatment. Check with another qualified surgeon before agreeing to even minor surgery.

however, when needs are not being met, it is time for a change.

In the case of doctor error, each case should be decided on its own merits. A mistake that is freely acknowledged and does not represent a pattern of carelessness is not necessarily a reason for change. An error that is life-threatening may permanently shake our confidence, however, and make a change advisable.

Do you need a specialist? The decision to consult a specialist should always be made after consultation with your primary care doctor. A referral from him will insure that you are seeing someone whose competence he trusts, and that your care will continue in the hands of someone *you* trust.

A consultation with a specialist does not mean that you will continue to see him on an extended basis. Although your internist may wish you to see a cardiologist for diagnosis of a heart problem, he is quite capable of monitoring and managing heart conditions himself. Not only will this make you more comfortable; it will save you money as well because internists' fees are usually lower than those of specialists.

What about surgery? Surgeons not only save lives but improve the quality of life for many people. They also are rather single-minded in that they are inclined to think only in terms of surgical procedures, frequently rejecting alternative methods of treatment. Since even minor surgery can be hazardous, the patient and his primary care doctor must be on guard against unnecessary surgery.

Many insurance companies now require and pay for a second opinion when surgery is recommended. There are certain operations that are widely considered to be overperformed. If any of the operations listed below are advised, it is wise to ask for a second opinion.

Overused surgical procedures. These operations, which used to be considered more or less routine, are often thought to be unnecessary today. As with any operation, be sure you get the very best advice before proceeding with:

Hysterectomy	Gallbladder removal
Oophorectomy	Radical mastectomy
(removal of ovaries)	Dilation and curettage
Tonsillectomy	Caesarean section

You and Modern Medicine

Doctors: Who they are and what they do

Primary care

Family Practitioner. Receives additional training in family medicine. Replaces old general practitioner. Provides care from birth to death.

Internist. Not to be confused with intern, a recent medical school graduate. Practices "internal medicine." Training qualifies him to care for adult patients in all matters that do not require surgery.

Pediatrician. Trained to deliver primary care to children from infancy to adolescence.

Specialists

Allergist. Treats such diseases as asthma, hay fever, or skin allergy.

Anesthesiologist. Administers anesthetics, or pain killers, during an operation.

Cardiologist. Highly trained to treat complicated diseases of the heart and blood vessels.

Dermatologist. Specializes in diseases of the skin.

Endocrinologist. Deals with disorders of the glandular system.

Gastroenterologist. Treats diseases of the digestive organs—esophagus, stomach, bowels, liver, and pancreas.

Gerontologist. Deals with aging and the problems of old people.

Hematologist. Expert in diseases of the blood.

Infectious Disease Specialist. Helps treat patients with serious or baffling diseases.

Nephrologist. Specializes in diseases of the kidney.

Neurologist. Qualified to treat illnesses of the nervous system.

Obstetrician/Gynecologist. Manages pregnancies, delivers babies, and handles problems concerning the reproductive organs of women.

Oculist. Deals with diseases of the eye.

Oncologist. Treats malignancies; decides on appropriate treatment and administers it.

Pulmonary Specialist. Treats diseases of the lungs; performs pulmonary function tests and bronchoscopy.

Radiologist. Gives and interprets x-ray photographs.

Rheumatologist. Cares for patients with diseases of the joints, and treats diseases such as rheumatoid arthritis, systemic lupus erythematosus, and scleroderma.

Nonmedical Specialists

Osteopath. Licensed to practice medicine and perform surgery, specializes in musculoskeletal manipulation.

Chiropractor. Licensed in most states to practice a system of manipulation of the spine.

Optometrist. Tests the eye for defective vision in order to prescribe corrective lenses.

Podiatrist. Trained in a four-year program as a specialist in disorders of the feet. Admitted to practice in many hospitals, but usually treat and operate on an outpatient basis.

Surgeons

General. Trained to perform abdominal, gynecological, and vascular surgery. In most urban areas, removes gallbladders, appendixes, moles, and cysts. Performs hysterectomies and repairs hernias.

Cardiac. Performs heart surgery such as coronary bypass and grafts. Removes aortic aneurysms.

Neurosurgeon. Operates on brain and spinal tumors, performs back surgery, repairs carotid arteries.

Obstetric/Gynecologic. Performs surgery related to the female reproductive system.

Ophthalmologic. Eye surgeons. Will also treat diseases of the eye.

Orthopedic. Sets bones, replaces joints, pins hips, and cares for traumatic injuries.

Otolaryngologic. Ear, nose, and throat.

Plastic. Performs both cosmetic and reconstructive surgery.

Urologic. Operates on the prostate, scrotum, bladder, and kidneys.

You and the hospital

The modern hospital is a remarkable place. It is a scene of human drama, where lives are saved, pain is eased, babies are born, and people die. The hospital is also a place where serious errors in treatment may be made, where unnecessary surgery may be performed, where technology may prolong life when there is no hope for survival, and where even strong-minded individuals are reduced to childlike dependency.

Increasingly, doctors and insurance companies recognize the advantages of limiting hospital stays, not only to save money for the patient and his insurer, but to assure the ultimate well-being of the individual.

Before you go.
When the doctor recommends putting you in the hospital, it is time to ask serious questions and to make sure they are answered satisfactorily. Are there alternatives? What are the benefits? What are the risks? Is it an emergency? Can it be postponed? Is a second opinion advisable? How long will I be there?

Frequently, hospitalization is suggested by a specialist, and it may be wise to postpone decisions until you have discussed the situation with your primary care doctor.

Which hospital to choose.
Factors such as what is available in the community, where your doctor has admission privileges, or where an ambulance takes you after an accident often limit your choices. Large and famous is not always better. Open heart surgery is probably best performed in a large medical center where there is a concentration of specific skills and experience; the gallbladder patient, however, may actually receive better care in a small community hospital.

Although differences may be blurred in specific cases, the kinds of hospitals can be categorized:

Teaching hospitals are connected with medical schools, are usually large, and are staffed by students, residents, and doctors who both teach and attend patients.

Public hospitals are the large institutions funded by local, county, state, or federal governments. They also have interns, residents, and a permanent medical staff.

Private and community hospitals are usually operated on a not-for-profit basis. They may or may not have a house staff, and they are operated for the convenience of the doctors who admit patients.

Nursing and convalescent homes are designed for patients who no longer need full medical facilities and who cannot be cared for at home.

There are no simple guidelines, but a little research into available facilities, before they are needed, will help a great deal. Nursing homes, particularly, should be investigated in advance. When you visit, talk with patients and their families. Ask your own doctor if a particular home is a place he recommends.

Your decision is made.
Before packing a bag and finding your health insurance card, choose a member of your family or a close friend to act as your personal advocate during your stay in the hospital. When the person in the admitting office asks for "next of kin," give the name of the person you wish to serve as advocate. If the hospital requires further authorization, you will be informed at that time. Your advocate will be able to keep track of your treatment, ask questions on your behalf, register legitimate complaints, and stand between you and hospital bureaucracy.

Defend against hospital error.
Most people emerge from the hospital in better health than when they went in. Usually, their most serious complaints deal with the food or difficulty in sleeping.

Can you stay out of the hospital?	How to help yourself in the hospital
1. Not all surgery requires hospitalization.	*Ask questions!* *Do not remain ignorant of what is being done for you.*
2. Many tests and procedures can be performed on an outpatient basis.	1. Make sure you get the right medication.
3. Many kinds of medical care can be delivered at home through the use of community services.	2. Make sure you get your medication on time.
4. Families of the terminally ill have more options as a result of the hospice movement and changing attitudes toward care of the dying.	3. Make sure you get the right tests—not someone else's tests.
	4. Make sure you get the food your doctor ordered for you.

However, wrong medications, wrong tests, and needless exposure to invasive procedures are all hazards.

Patients are not helpless. The person who constantly asks questions or has his personal advocate ask them in his behalf is putting up a good defense against error. No procedure, test, or medication should come as a surprise—it could be meant for someone else. Make a point of knowing your medication schedule; if medication does not come on time, ask for it. If it is new or unfamiliar, make sure that it is intended for you.

If you have been told to take nothing by mouth prior to surgery or a diagnostic test, do not assume that the arrival of your breakfast tray means that someone has changed his mind.

Be sure to take some of your personal belongings to the hospital. Do not forget your eye glasses so that you can read or watch television.

What to pack for your stay. As an
antidote to the loss of identity that usually occurs when you walk through hospital doors, take part of your home with you: snapshots, a favorite bathrobe, even if it is old, your own cosmetics, deodorant, shaving cream, and toothpaste. Leave valuables at home, but you may want to take a small battery-run radio with earphones. Arrange to have your favorite newspaper delivered. Maintaining a sense of your own personality will help you to stand up for yourself and to make the best use of the facilities that exist to restore you to health.

When you get there. Checking into a
hospital used to be an interminable ordeal. Today, many hospitals arrange for blood tests, x-rays, urine analyses, and many diagnostic tests to be done well in advance of admission. The vast amount of preadmission paperwork is handled by the admitting office before you arrive. This has worked to shorten hospital stays and has nearly eliminated those weekend admissions that once resulted in a patient's being tucked into a very expensive hospital bed days in advance of his need for it.

The Patient's Bill of Rights

The patient has a right to:

- **Complete, current information** concerning his diagnosis, treatment, and prognosis in terms he can understand.

- **Information necessary to give informed consent** prior to any medical procedures, except in emergencies, including knowledge of significant risks, duration of incapacitation, alternatives for care or treatment, and the names of persons who will perform the procedures.

- **Refuse treatment** to the extent permitted by law, and to be informed of the medical consequences of refusal.

- **Privacy** concerning medical care, diagnosis, and records.

- **Reasonable response** to requests for services.

- **Not be transferred** to another facility without his permission.

- **Be advised** if treatment involves human experimentation.

- **Refuse** such experimentation.

- **Continuity** of care following discharge.

- **Examine** and receive an explanation of charges regardless of source of payment.

—excerpted from a document prepared by the American Hospital Association

---

What about all those tests?

Diagnostic techniques have improved and expanded, and words like "CAT scan" and "sonogram" have entered ordinary language. Doctors have an increasingly difficult time knowing when to stop testing and hospitals seek maximun use of these expensive machines in order to pay for them.

Another factor in overtesting is doctors' real fear of malpractice suits. This seems to be a byproduct of over-specialization on the part of the medical profession. However, a patient who has developed a comfortable and trusting relationship with his or her doctor rarely sues, even when things go wrong.

You and your primary doctor can work together to ensure that you get only those tests that are absolutely necessary. High-risk, invasive procedures, such as arteriograms and surgical biopsies, require especially careful consideration. They will not be performed without your consent, but before giving that consent be sure to ask about benefits, risks, and alternatives.

Computer-aided imaging has increased the reliability of medical diagnosis. This ultrasound image shows the head of a fetus.

What they mean when they say...

CAT scan	(Computerized tomography) An x-ray technique that photographs cross-sections of the body. Normal x-rays produce pictures that are flat, like a photograph; the CAT scan sends rays through the body that are picked up by a scanner, fed into a computer, and visualized on a screen. This procedure has eliminated many complicated tests.
MRI	(Magnetic resonance imaging) This procedure uses radio waves and a strong magnetic field to produce highly detailed two- and three-dimensional images of body tissues.
Sonogram	(Ultrasound examination) High-frequency sound waves are directed at the body; the echoes are viewed on a TV screen and photographed. This procedure is often performed in the last trimester of pregnancy to determine the position and health of the fetus.
EEG	(Electroencephalogram) Electrodes are glued to the scalp, and the electrical activity of the brain is painlessly recorded.
EKG	(Electrocardiogram) A machine records the electrical activity of the heart. It gives infor mation about heartbeat, the strength of the heart, and the location of any injury. A stress test is an EKG given while the patient is exercising.
Spinal tap	(Lumbar puncture) A small amount of fluid is drawn from the spinal column to test the internal pressure or to provide a sample for laboratory testing.
Biopsy	A surgical procedure, often performed under a local anesthetic, in which a small amount of tissue is obtained for laboratory study.
GI series	(Upper and lower) X-ray pictures are taken of the digestive tract after the introduction of barium, by mouth or by enema, to make the tract visible.
Amniocentesis	Fluid is drawn from the amniotic sac surrounding the fetus during the end of the first trimester of pregnancy. Cells grown in the laboratory provide information about such genetic defects as Down syndrome.

You and emergency rooms

Some emergency rooms are little more than first-aid stations with a nurse on duty and a doctor on call; others are full-scale trauma centers attached to major medical centers. The average emergency room falls somewhere in between. Locating and evaluating emergency rooms in your immediate area could save a life. The closest place to go is not always the best place to go in a true emergency.

What to look for. A well-run emergency room is staffed around the clock by doctors trained in emergency medicine. If there is not a permanent house staff, specialists are on call. Emergency rooms attached to good hospitals have access to cardiac and intensive care units; these can assume great importance for patients needing such care.

A talk with your doctor about nearby facilities should prove helpful; your choice will be governed by his hospital affiliations whenever possible.

Before you go. No matter how serious the emergency, a cool head is essential. A call to your own doctor for his help in evaluating the seriousness of the emergency is wise. His call to the emergency room—warning them that you are on the way and ordering whatever tests or treatments he thinks necessary—will cut a lot of red tape and assure fast attention. If you cannot reach your doctor before leaving, have the hospital call him on arrival.

In the face of an emergency, calling an ambulance is almost a reflex action. When there is a suspected heart attack, poisoning, severe pain, impaired breathing, or any condition in which rapid medical help is

---

True emergencies

- Severe and uncontrolled bleeding
- Serious difficulty in breathing
- Choking
- Poisoning
- Severe chest pain
- Convulsions
- Heat stroke
- Unconsciousness
- Severe injuries
- Stabbing or bullet wounds, severe burns
- Diabetic acidosis or shock from hypoglycemia
- Hypothermia

DO NOT BE TIMID!

Remember to leave tact and good manners at home. An emergency room is no place to assume automatically that somebody else knows best or to let consideration of other people sway your judgment. If you know that the condition is serious, do whatever is necessary to make sure that the doctor and nurses know it too.

---

essential, it is best to use whatever transportation is available—personal car, taxi, or police car. Many police departments have trained their officers in basic first aid and equipped their cars with life-saving apparatuses.

If there is time, locate insurance cards, regular medication, and, in the case of poisoning or drug overdose, the original container the substance came in. If there is not enough time, a neighbor or a friend can follow soon after with the appropriate information.

When you get there. At a glance, the average emergency room looks like a scene of total chaos. Despite appearances, there *is* a system functioning called "triage." This means that a nurse, a doctor, or other emergency room personnel will determine who will have first call on limited facilities and personnel. Top priority is assigned to patients with suspected heart attacks, seriously injured accident victims, cases of poisoning or drug overdose, or those in need of immediate attention.

Although many people tell horror stories about interminable hours spent waiting for attention, as a rule those who need help the most get it the quickest. To the parent of an hysterical child who has suffered a non-life-threatening injury, the system may seem unfair and insensitive. But remember, the person in charge must balance urgent need against discomfort and inconvenience.

Children and emergencies. Mothers of large families may, when the children are grown up, swear that they spent most of their children's younger years in one emergency room or another. The most common reasons for these trips are accidents, poisoning, and difficulties in breathing.

Often there seems to be a conflict of interest between medical personnel and parents. No child should be left unattended by a familiar adult or made to go through any procedure alone. Parents are often asked to leave the room in the interest of the child's welfare. The answer to that request is an emphatic "No!" Keep quiet and calm, but stay. Your leaving may be better for the doctors and nurses, but it is not better for the child.

The elderly and emergencies.
Fractures are the most common reason for trips by the elderly to emergency rooms. Pseudo-dementia is a close second. If an elderly person becomes suddenly disoriented, hallucinates, or shows signs of paranoia, he may be suffering from a drug reaction. If the attending doctor has a list of all the prescription and nonprescription drugs that the patient is taking, it may save time, money, and discomfort. The tests to determine organic causes, such as those in Alzheimer's disease, stroke, etc., are complicated, upsetting, and expensive.

The emergency room doctor. If
the emergency room does not have a permanent medical staff, it does have a list of doctors who are on call. Make clear to the admitting desk, and to the doctor you see, that you do have your own doctor and that you do wish to have him informed as soon as possible. Although you may receive excellent care from the available doctor, if hospital admission is indicated, you may not welcome the discovery that you have inadvertently changed doctors. It is better to be clear in the beginning than to try to sort things out later.

Misusing the emergency room.
The hospital emergency room has become a substitute for a personal doctor in many people's lives. Families often postpone finding a doctor when they move to a new community and fall into the habit of going to the nearest emergency room whenever anyone in the family needs medical care. Tetanus shots, medication for sore throats, or examination of a sick child are very expensive when delivered by an emergency room.

Other people have a very low tolerance for suffering, their own as well as that of other people. A bump on the head when there is no loss of consciousness, a minor cut that bleeds profusely, mild muscle sprains or strains, and vomiting when there is no indication of poisoning are not reasons for taking up valuable time and space in a busy emergency room. A course in first aid at the local Red Cross—and a greater use of your doctor's telephone number—will save money.

Should you be admitted? Admission
to the hospital is not necessarily the outcome of a visit to an emergency room. If your own doctor is on hand or on the other end of a telephone, this decision should be made under his guidance.

If your own doctor is not available, the discussion will need to be carried on with the attending physician. No one would think of taking a suspected heart attack victim home until his condition has been verified, but a bump on the head may be a different matter. Careful questioning, followed by the use of your own common sense, should resolve the matter.

Unless you are far from home or have been taken by an ambulance to a hospital where your doctor does not have admitting privileges, try to make sure that the hospital has the name of your primary care doctor. If your doctor is not available, you are entitled to be admitted by a private doctor of your choice.

If you are not admitted to the hospital, you should inquire about follow-up care. For example, who will remove the stitches?

Post a note by the telephone

Display prominently the telephone number of your local police and your own street address. Emergency police cars can arrive at your house in minutes. Also, households with young children or elderly parents should place a notice near the telephone for use by babysitters or caretakers.

POLICE • FIRE
AMBULANCE
555-7000
Compliments of
Your Volunteer Fire Department

- If you have found a primary care doctor, investigated local hospitals and emergency rooms, and located a pharmacist you can rely on, this information should be readily available when you are out of the house.

- Current medications, how they are taken, and for what conditions should be noted.

- If children are likely to have croup or experience allergic reactions, the measures to take in case of an attack should be described.

- Working mothers with regular, reliable babysitters or housekeepers should make certain that the doctor knows their names and whether or not they are empowered to act in your behalf.

You and drugs

Most drugs simply alleviate symptoms, modify the course of an illness, or assist the body to achieve normal functioning. Our own bodies fight most illnesses better than most drugs. Given time, many conditions improve without any treatment. For example, early diabetes can often be controlled by diet alone. And drugs used to control high blood pressure need assistance from a modified diet and appropriate exercise.

Otherwise sensible people cling to the notion that all they need to recover from any illness, from a cold to cancer, are the right words written on a prescription blank, or the right bottle of nonprescription medicine brought home from the drugstore.

Any drug powerful enough to have a significant effect on a disease also has the potential to cause harm. The risks range from slight to major, and it is the job of the patient and his doctor to weigh risks against benefits. Powerful drugs are to be reserved for serious illnesses.

No one should refuse medication that is thoughtfully and knowledgeably prescribed, but the wise person guards against misuse and overuse of medication by assuming personal responsibility for knowing as much as possible and for following directions.

Doctors are human.
Most of us have nagged our doctors for a prescription that we think we need to make us feel better, and most doctors have written unnecessary prescriptions for the same reason. In the past, doctors had a very limited number of effective drugs they could use, so they sometimes offered their patients "sugar pills" to make them feel better.

Today, however, modern pharmacology has made a bewildering number of drugs available to doctors, making it difficult for them to keep up with their names, much less their efficacy and side effects. When today's physician reaches for his copy of the *Physician's Desk Reference* to look up a drug he is about to prescribe, he is demonstrating sound medical sense and taking care to prescribe the right drug for the right condition.

The smart patient should not hesitate to use the same reference book, which is available in libraries and pharmacies, before starting a new medicine. Although the information may seem too extensive and too technical, it will provide a basis for asking further questions of your doctor. Understanding all you can about your medication should make it easier to follow instructions and to make the most effective use of it.

Doctors complain that their patients accept prescriptions that they never fill, fill prescriptions that

> ### Warning signs when taking medication
> - Rash, nausea, swelling, muscle cramps
> - Trouble with urination, heart, breathing, circulation, headaches, vision
> - Yellowing of skin or eyes
> - Depression or exhilaration
> - Weight gain or loss
> - Stomach upset, constipation, or diarrhea
> - Feeling worse or showing no sign of improvement

they never take, and take medication only until they feel better. If the goal is to form a full partnership with a doctor, thus ensuring better care, such quirks on the part of a patient get in the way. A doctor needs to know about the course of a disease—what worked and what did not, why a patient seemed to recover and then had a relapse, etc. Good information is one way to ensure good care.

How to use your pharmacist.
Pharmacists are highly trained professionals who are well informed on the use, composition, and effects of drugs. They are qualified not only to advise the consumer, but the doctor as well. They are not allowed to prescribe medications, make a diagnosis, or refuse to fill a prescription. They can offer advice about nonprescription medicines and are usually willing to take the time to answer questions about prescription drugs.

Many good pharmacists keep a complete drug record on each customer; as more and more stores are computerized, this information is stored for instant retrieval.

In an effort to save money, many people use the discount drug stores and chain stores. The pharmacists in these large operations are inaccessible to customers and do not keep personal drug profiles. It is advisable to balance the advantages and disadvantages in making a choice between a well-stocked neighborhood pharmacy and a large commercial operation.

Over-the-counter drugs.
After this category of drugs was studied by the Food and Drug Administration (FDA), many over-the-counter drugs were taken off the market because they were judged to be ineffective.

Some drugs do not mix safely

(see drug chart on pages 90-91)

Do not take even an aspirin without consulting your doctor or pharmacist if you are taking prescription medication. Aspirin, for example, taken with anticoagulants, increases the anticoagulant effect of the aspirin and internal bleeding can result.

Alcohol, even in small quantities, can have fatal effects when combined with barbituates.

It is reasonably safe to use nonprescription drugs for such conditions as a bad cold, headache, mild allergic reaction, constipation, mild diarrhea, or any condition that is self-limiting—so long as you receive some guidance from a doctor or pharmacist.

Elderly people, young children, pregnant women, or people who are taking prescription medication should exercise particular care.

Make sure to read the label, avoiding medications that contain more than two active ingredients. Make sure *not* to use these preparations to put off a visit to the doctor for a condition that might be serious.

Brand name vs. generic. Achromycin
is a brand name antibiotic that costs just under $10. Tetracycline is its generic equivalent; it costs about half that amount. The drugs are equally effective and pharmacists in all states are permitted to fill a prescription with either drug, providing the doctor has not specifically forbidden it.

Unfortunately for the consumer, not all brand-name drugs have a generic equivalent available. Some are still protected by patent. Until recently, the Food and Drug Administration (FDA) made approval of generic copies so complicated and expensive that there was no

Darvon is one of a half-dozen brands, all relatively expensive, for the common generic analgesic Propoxyphene Hydrochloride, which costs much less.

real incentive for other drug companies to manufacture copies, even when the patent expired.

But now, under a recent FDA ruling, drug companies will be able to issue generic copies so long as they demonstrate that the generic drugs are chemically the same and that they perform in the same way as the brand-name drugs. Any FDA-approved generic drug is as safe and effective as any brand-name drug. The saving to the consumer should be enormous.

Medicine and high-risk groups.
These three groups are at particular risk, and extra precautions must be taken to ensure that medications are effective and do no harm.

Children. Children not only require smaller doses of drugs than adults, but they frequently react in opposite ways. Sedatives may stimulate, and stimulants may sedate. Children should be given only those medicines prescribed for them by their own doctor.

Adults should make their own medicine-taking a very private affair. Many doctors and psychologists feel that children who observe their parents taking drugs for any discomfort are getting a message that could pave the way for drug abuse at a later age.

Pregnant women. Extraordinary care must be exercised when taking medication during pregnancy. Nursing mothers should practice the same restraint. The fetus was once considered totally secure while in the womb. The tragic thalidomide babies were a testament to the fallacy of that perception.

Not all pregnant women can forego all medication, but they must cooperate closely with an obstetrician who is sensitive to the possible dangers.

The elderly. This group can present their doctors, their caretakers, and even themselves with troublesome medication problems. They complain of lack of sleep, lose their appetites, develop aches and pains, break bones, lose their sharpness of sight and hearing, and find that their vital organs have slowed in their functioning. As a result, many of them become doctor shoppers and enthusiastic consumers of vast quantities of prescription and over-the-counter drugs. To add to their problems, many old people swap drugs with each other. The result may be a drug-induced nightmare for those who love the elderly and care for them.

A single primary care physician—a gerontologist or an internist—can act as a deterrent to freewheeling drug use. Not only will one doctor have a record of all the drugs taken, but the patient can be encouraged to substitute exercise, relaxation, and good nutrition for some of the medication. An introduction to commonly prescribed drugs, their generic names, and a guide to possible problems appears on the next page.

The home medicine cabinet

The bathroom medicine cabinet is often a disorderly jumble of deodorants, toothpaste, expired prescriptions, cosmetics, dried-up cough syrups, and empty Band-Aid boxes. This may lead to a small child's being rushed to the emergency room after eating a bottle of aspirin.

The smart thing to do is to clean up and lock up. Medications belong in a locked cabinet, preferably located in a cool, dry place. All out-of-date medications should be discarded. The pharmacist will usually be willing to make recommendations about what to keep and what to flush down the toilet.

Home remedies should be confined to a few reliable kinds, and first-aid supplies should be kept organized and ready to use.

A well-ordered medicine cabinet will reduce the temptation to self-medicate with leftover prescription drugs.

Suggestions for the home pharmacy

Keep	For	Keep	For
Aspirin or nonaspirin pain reliever	Pain or fever	Hydrocortisone ointment	Poison ivy, other rashes
Antacid	Upset stomach	Syrup of ipecac	Induction of vomiting
Adhesive tape and bandages	Covering minor wounds	Milk of magnesia	Constipation
Hydrogen peroxide	Antiseptic uses	Kaopectate	Diarrhea
Sodium bicarbonate	Soaking	Eyedrops	Simple irritation

Home remedies and first-aid supplies should be kept in one place. Teach children not to open medicine cabinet doors, which should be kept locked. Do not give old medicines to friends. Destroy them by flushing them down the toilet.

A sample listing of frequently prescribed drugs

Brand name	Generic	Possible problems
Pain killers		
Darvon	Propoxyphene hydrochloride	Habit forming; avoid alcohol, muscle relaxants, tranquilizers, nervous system depressants
Percodan	Oxycodone, aspirin, phenacetin, caffeine	Avoid alcohol, sedatives, antihistamines, oral diabetes drugs, muscle relaxants
Antibiotics		
Achromycin V, SK-Tetracycline, Sumycin	Tetracycline	Avoid milk, dairy products, exposure to sun; oral anticoagulants may have increased effects
Amcill, Omnipen, SK-Ampicillin	Ampicillin	Avoid other antibiotics and antacids
E. E. S., E-Mycin, Erypar, Erythrocin, Ethril	Erythromycin	Avoid other antibiotics and alcohol
Penicillin, SK-Penicillin VK, Pen-Vee K	Penicillin	Avoid if you have a past history of allergy to any penicillin; to be taken for full treatment on empty stomach; do not take with fruit juice; avoid antacids
Anticoagulants		
Coumadin, Panwarfin	Warfarin	Avoid if pregnant or a nursing mother
Antihypertensives		
Aldactatone	Spirionolactone plus hydrochlorothiazide	This group of drugs, used to control high blood pressure, must be taken under regular supervision of the doctor with attention to high or low potassium levels; before any surgical procedure, the surgeon and anesthetist must know about the medication (this includes dental surgery); Regroton can cause sensitivity to sunlight
Apresoline	Hydralazine plus hydrochloride	
Inderal	Propranolol plus hydrochloride	
Lopressor	Metoprolol plus tartrate	
Regroton	Resperine plus chlorthalidone	
Oral antidiabetics		
Diabinese	Chlorpropamide	Avoid taking anticoagulants, aspirin, diuretics, or any other medication without consulting a doctor
Ulcer medication		
Tagamet	Cimetidine	Avoid anticoagulants, some penicillins, Valium, Librium etc., and alcohol and caffeine
Zantac	Ranitidine	Cease using and consult physician if headache, joint pain, or allergic reactions occur

Psychiatric medications

Major tranquilizers and antipsychotic medications

Brand name	Generic	Possible problems
Thorazine	Chlorpromazine	These are important drugs used in controlling serious mental illness; they have many possible side effects when taken over an extended period of time; many patients discontinue medication when they feel better or because of side effects; taking these drugs can mean the difference between being hospitalized or being able to live in the community; cooperation on the part of the patient and careful management on the part of the doctor are essential
Prolixin	Fluphenazine	
Mellaril	Thioridazine hydrochloride	
Stelazine	Trifluoperazine	
Haldol	Haloperidol	
Navane	Thiothixene	
Clozaril	Clozapine	
Seroquel	Quetiapine	
Zybrexa	Olanzapine	
Risperdal	Risperidone	

Other tranquilizers, antidepressants, and stimulants

Brand name	Generic	Possible problems
Librium	Chlordiazepoxide	No other medication should be taken without consulting a doctor; alcohol can be highly dangerous
Valium	Diazepam	
Equanil	Meprobamate	
Serax	Oxazepam	
Tranxene	Clorazepate	
Xanax	Alprazolam	
Prozac	Fluoxetine hydrochloride	
Paxil	Paroxetine hydrochloride	
Wellbutrin	Bupropion hydrochloride	
Ritalin	Methylphenidate hydrochloride	

MAO inhibitor antidepressants

Brand name	Generic	Possible problems
Marplan	Isocarboxazid	Aged cheese, aged meat, pods of broad beans, beer, wine, pickled herring, yogurt, liver, yeast extract, heavy amounts of caffeine, bananas, soy sauce, anchovies, avocados, and sour cream (all with high tramine content) must be avoided; can cause dangerous rise in blood pressure
Nardil	Phenelezine	
Parnate	Transylcypromine sulfate	

Tricyclic antidepressants

Brand name	Generic	Possible problems
Tofranil	Imipramine	Take two to six weeks to become effective; do not combine with other medication except on doctor's specific instruction; avoid alcohol; may have side effects like dry mouth or constipation; people over 60 years of age should have heart and blood pressure checked before beginning medication and regularly thereafter
Norpramin	Desipramine	
Elavil	Amitriptyline	

Sleeping pills

Brand name	Generic	Possible problems
Seconal	Secobarbital	Tolerance develops very quickly and physical addiction can occur from extended use; withdrawal can be dangerous if not undergone slowly; absolutely avoid combining with alcohol
Nembutal	Phenobarbital	
Sodium Amytal	Amobarbital	

You and your mental health

Many people are uncomfortable with discussions of mental illness. A persistent stomach ache sends us to the doctor at once, yet the pain from a deep depression may be endured for months or years out of fear or shame. We talk freely of triple bypass heart surgery or kidney dialysis, but speak of schizophrenia in whispers. Alcoholism or drug addiction may be fervently denied in the face of incontrovertible evidence.

What is mental illness? Mental illnesses fall roughly into two categories: neuroses and psychoses. Neurotic symptoms may become disabling, but they respond well to psychotherapy. Psychosis is a term for serious organic mental illness often thought to be caused by a disruption in the brain's chemistry. These illnesses, such as schizophrenia and manic-depression, are treated by a combination of hospitalization, medication, and supportive therapy for both the patient and his family.

When to go for help. Few people escape periodic feelings of depression. Death, job loss, broken marriages or relationships, and major illness all make normal people feel sad, angry, or unhappy. But when those feelings persist over an extended period of time, even when the situation changes, or when there seems to be no rational explanation for the feelings, it is time to look for outside help. Researchers have found that therapy helps most people to some extent, no matter who delivers it.

Depression is the most common reason for people to seek help. Anxiety attacks, eating disorders, marital conflict, phobias, and some psychosomatic illnesses are all responsive to psychotherapy.

Depression checklist

- Sad moods and crying spells
- Feelings of despair
- Recurring guilt feelings
- Loss of pleasure
- Forgetfulness and lack of concentration
- Insomnia or abnormal amounts of sleep
- Loss of appetite or abnormal hunger
- Loss of interest in sex
- Suicidal thoughts
- Vague or actual physical complaints
- Irritability

Other mental illnesses, such as psychoses, alcoholism, and drug addition, are rarely helped by psychotherapy alone.

How to get help. The phone book is a good place to begin for mental health centers, Alcoholics Anonymous, and drug and alcohol treatment centers, but it is probably the very worst way to locate a psychotherapist.

Although proper credentials are important, they are not as vital as a sense of caring and warmth. A recommendation from a primary care doctor is useful, but word of mouth is also valuable. Talking to people who have been in therapy and who have been helped can put you on the right track.

Many clergymen are trained as counselors. For some people, this help is the most accessible and the least expensive.

Who are the mentally ill?

One out of ten American families has a member who is seriously mentally ill. If you do not have a family member coping with mental illness, a family down the block probably does. It is particularly important not to dismiss a "blue Monday" teenager as just going through an adolescent stage. Seek professional advice if your daughter or son seems persistently depressed.

Understanding alcoholism.

Alcoholism is defined by the American Medical Association as a disease that, if not checked, leads to death. Yet the image of the alcoholic as the town drunk sleeping it off on a park bench fades slowly. Since most people in our society drink safely, it is easy to view alcoholism as the result of moral weakness and poor self-control.

Alcoholism is a leading cause of death and is implicated in 90 percent of physical assaults, 50 percent of murders, and 25 percent of suicides. Drunken drivers account for 25,000 deaths on the highway each year.

The causes of alcoholism are still obscure, although recent research points toward a genetic predisposition in many cases. Young people who combine alcohol with drugs account for a new phenomenon—17- and 18-year-olds who are as physically and mentally ill as older alcoholics who have been drinking for 30 or 40 years.

Who are the alcoholics? Despite the popular stereotype, alcoholics are found in corporate board rooms, on the police force, in the classroom, in the medical profession, among priests, ministers, and rabbis, and in suburban homes. Alcoholism permeates our entire society.

Because the progress of the disease is often slow, many people cross the line into alcoholism without being aware of it. Any wife who has tried to convince her husband that he is drinking too much knows how difficult it is for someone else to make an alcoholic recognize his own problem.

Can an alcoholic be helped? Very real help is available to the alcoholic who is able to recognize his need for it. Lifelong abstinence sounds like a grim sentence in a society that celebrates all occasions with alcohol. However, many people considered "hopeless" by their families, employers, and doctors have recovered through participation in Alcoholics Anonymous (A.A.), the self-help group with the best track record. Many people combine A.A. with alcohol counseling.

Many large corporations now have outreach programs for their employees, often financing extended treatment. Local governments are establishing alcohol treatment centers, and in many states, insurance companies are required by state law to provide coverage for both in-hospital and outpatient treatment.

Are you in trouble with alcohol?

Alcohol can impair judgment and affect behavior, causing people to take dangerous risks or to act impulsively in ways they will later regret.

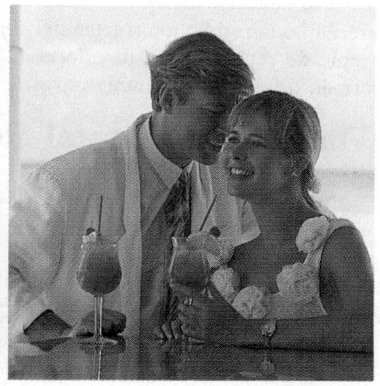

- Do you need a drink to make you feel relaxed? Self-confident? To have a good time?
- Do you drink every day?
- Do you look forward all day to your first drink?
- Are you drinking more than you used to? More than you want to?
- Do you have a drink before going to a party?
- Have you changed your favorite drink lately to help you cut down?
- Have friends, family, or your employer mentioned your drinking?
- Do you frequently plan to stop drinking?
- Do you ever hide bottles or lie about the amount you drink?
- Do you drink in the morning, alone, or at work?
- Do you ever carry liquor in your breast pocket or pocketbook?
- Do you have blackouts, severe hangovers, or guilt feelings?
- Are you proud of being able to hold your liquor?
- Are most of your friends heavy drinkers?

There is no passing grade for this quiz. If you answer "yes" to more than one question, it is probably time to take a hard look at your "social" drinking.

Understanding drug addiction.

The drug addict is as poorly understood as the alcoholic. Although alcohol is available at the corner liquor store, drugs are available only from illegal sources—which puts the drug user at odds with the law.

Some drugs, such as heroin and morphine, are truly addictive. Others are considered to be "habituating." The effect is frequently the same. It is not uncommon for someone to try "recreational" drugs as an experiment at a party, to like the effect, and in time to become as addicted as the heroin user.

Prescription drug abusers are a hidden element in the drug addiction picture. Many people start taking tranquilizers or sleeping pills as recommended by their doctor and find themselves not only addicted but forced to seek illegal sources if they do not have a compliant doctor.

Can the drug addict be helped? The same conditions prevail for the drug addict as for the alcoholic. He must want to stop and be willing to turn to appropriate channels for assistance. Detoxification is almost always essential in the case of such drugs as heroin, amphetamines, barbiturates, and some tranquilizers. "Cold turkey" withdrawal from heroin is merely painful, but with some other drugs, it can cause convulsions and even death.

Chapters of Narcotics Anonymous are appearing all over the country, as are fine drug rehabilitation centers. Although addiction is seemingly intractable, many people do recover from its effects and go on to lead normal, drug-free, productive lives.

What about mental illness? The

discovery of major tranquilizers promised a new era in the treatment of the mentally ill. The hospitals were emptied of long-term patients, and promises were made to support their existence in the community. Those promises were not kept, and many communities find heavily medicated former patients wandering the streets, frequently with no place to live. Some are leading sad and dreary lives, with no supervision, as residents of shamefully inadequate rooming houses.

If serious mental illness strikes someone in your family, becoming informed about treatment, medication, and management is vital for your family's survival and for the well-being of your sick family member. Joining advocacy groups, support groups, and becoming active in your community mental health center will provide a focus.

Schizophrenics who learn to manage their illness, who are properly medicated, and who receive family and community support are often able to lead nearly normal lives, spending most of their time outside a hospital setting.

What are psychiatric medications? Psychotropic (psychiatric) medicines are tools used by psychiatrists in treating many kinds of mental illnesses. These medicines do not cure; they ease symptoms or, in the case of psychotic illnesses, control the disease.

As with any other medication, these drugs carry risks that have to be balanced against benefits. The major tranquilizers, for example, carry the potential for serious, permanent side effects; yet they can make the difference between long-term hospitalization and the possibility of living independently.

Managing medication—whether it involves an antidepressant or a major tranquilizer—should be a joint effort on the part of the therapist, the patient, and the patient's family. See page 91 for a chart of psychiatric drugs, their uses and side effects.

Community substance abuse centers like this one help give people the self-confidence and encouragement they need to avoid using drugs.

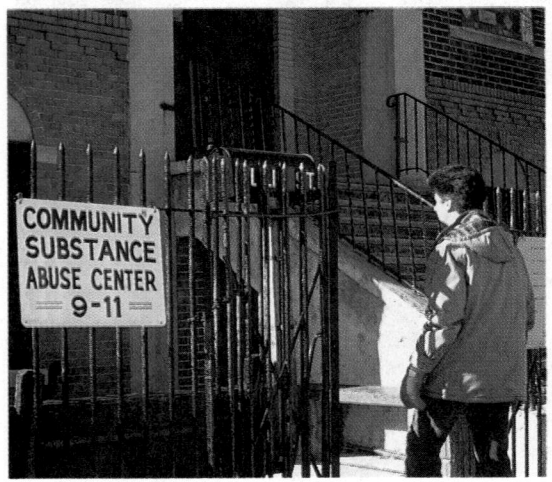

Alateen meetings such as this one provide support for young people coping with family members or friends who are alcohol abusers.

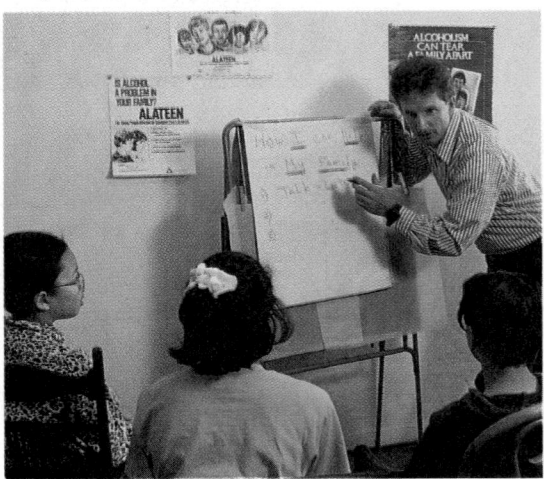

You and Modern Medicine

Who are the therapists?

Psychiatrist (M.D.)
A medical doctor who is trained in diagnosis and therapy. He or she is the only choice when medication is necessary as an adjunct to therapy.

Psychologist (Ph.D.)
A nonmedical doctor trained in therapeutic techniques, skilled at helping people who do not suffer from psychosis. Cannot prescribe medication. Fees are generally lower than those of a psychiatrist.

Psychiatric Social Worker (M.S.W.)
Trained in counseling and particularly effective in family therapy.

Medical payments

Health insurance is a major element in a family's economic security. Many people are insured through their employers and have only a vague idea of their coverage until a sudden, major illness strikes. Sometimes the extent of that coverage comes as a painful and expensive surprise. It is also not uncommon to forget that health coverage stops unless converted to a personal policy when an employee is dismissed.

Get to know your health policy.
If your policy is difficult to understand, consult the person in your company who handles the coverage.

Here are some important things to know: Is there coverage for office visits? What about prescription drugs? Out-of-hospital tests? Pregnancy? Newborns? Premature births? What are the dollar limits and when does the insurance company begin to pay? Do you pay in advance and get reimbursed later? Are doctors and surgeons fees paid in full or according to an established fee schedule? When does coverage run out?

Major medical insurance.
Many people who are self-employed or who have minimal coverage turn to major medical insurance. Basically, this insurance either picks up when primary insurance stops or provides full coverage when medical expenses pass a predetermined amount, the deductible.

How does your doctor get paid?
The day of doctors' bills being sent to the home seems to be passing. It is quite common, today, to be expected to pay as you go. If this is not possible, discuss it with the doctor. Price is often negotiable.

Specialists' fees.
Specialists and surgeons set their own fees, sometimes at a scale that has made many patients gasp upon hearing them. This is a very sound reason for using specialists only when your primary care doctor thinks it absolutely necessary. If a surgeon's fee is beyond your ability to pay immediately, make arrangements in advance to pay it over an extended period of time.

Managed care.
This fast-growing sector of the health care industry attempts to control medical costs by emphasizing preventive care, eliminating unnecessary tests and procedures, and reducing the number of doctor referrals to specialists or hospital care. Subscribers to a managed care plan pay a standard premium, which covers almost all of their medical costs. Their choice of doctors, however, is limited to those physicians participating in the plan.

Medicaid and Medicare.
The simplest thing to remember about these two government-subsidized health benefits is this: Medicaid is linked to income and/or disability; Medicare is linked to age and/or permanent disability.

A doctor must accept the standard of fees set by Medicaid. He or she is not bound to a fee schedule for Medicare, under which patients pay part of their bills.

Many retired persons choose to supplement their Medicare coverage with additional private coverage.

Further information is contained in the chapter *Managing the Family's Money* on page 110, or in the government pamphlet on the subject listed at the end of this chapter.

allergy

Glossary

CAT scan

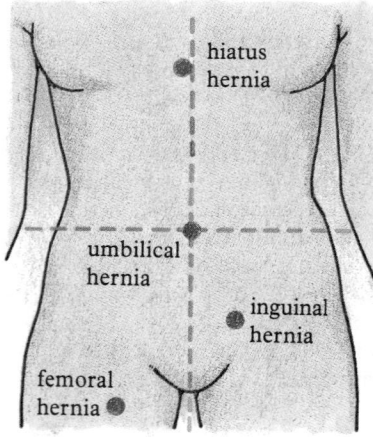

hiatus hernia

umbilical hernia

inguinal hernia

femoral hernia

hernia

pacemaker

abdominal distention. Condition that may be due to overeating or to gross enlargement of any abdominal organ. Other causes include fluid in the abdomen and gas in the bowels.

abscess. A localized collection of pus (dead cell debris) that can develop in any part of the body. Commonly, abscesses are caused by bacteria, but fungi, yeasts, and amoebae may also be involved.

acromegaly. Slowly progressive disease that produces a characteristic appearance: enlarged bones, a protruding jaw, and a coarsening and thickening of all features.

addiction. Medically, the habitual use of alcohol or drugs.

Addison's disease. Condition caused by inadequate secretion of the adrenal glands. Early symptoms include weakness, loss of energy, and muscular aches.

aerophagia. The habitual swallowing of air as while eating fast, drinking large amounts of carbonated beverages, or chewing gum. In severe cases, there may be abdominal distention, difficult breathing, and palpitations.

alcoholism. The compulsive abuse of alcohol, with resultant extreme nervousness, loss of appetite, vitamin deficiencies, nausea, and vomiting. When chronic, there is liver and kidney dysfunction, and DTs (delirium tremens).

allergy. An unusual reaction in an individual to a substance that usually does not affect other people. Most often, dust, feathers, animal hair, cosmetics, some foods and drugs, and fabrics are involved.

Alzheimer's disease. Generally noted between the ages of 40 and 60. It is associated with gradual memory loss, disorientation, and apathy, and is caused by a disorder of the cells of the brain.

amenorrhea. The absence of menstrual flow. Occurs most commonly during pregnancy and the menopause. Menstruation not started by age 18 is termed primary amenorrhea, while cessation of periods after they have begun is called secondary amenorrhea.

amniocentesis. Diagnostic procedure used to assess various genetic defects and some hereditary disorders of the fetus.

anaphylaxis. A potentially life-threatening type of allergic reaction that can result from the injection of some drugs or diagnostic agents. It may also be caused by wasp stings or such foods as shellfish and strawberries.

anemia. A variety of conditions marked by excessive loss, destruction, or faulty production of red blood cells. Iron-deficiency anemia, the most common form, is often due to a lack of dietary iron.

aneurysm. A swelling or localized bulging of a weakened arterial wall, particularly dangerous when it involves the aorta or arteries in the brain. If ruptured, it can lead to massive internal bleeding that may prove fatal.

angina pectoris. A condition marked by sudden pain in the chest. Generally occurs during strenuous exertion, such as shoveling snow or climbing stairs, which makes the heart work harder.

angiography. X-ray technique in which blood vessels are made visible by injection of a radiopaque substance. The test is useful in detecting the presence of tumors, atherosclerosis, and aneurysms.

You and Modern Medicine

anorexia nervosa. A condition that mainly affects adolescent girls and younger women who eat less and less food. As food intake and weight continue to drop, severe nutritional deficiencies and even death by starvation may occur.

antibiotics. Various natural and synthetic substances widely used to treat infectious diseases. If bactericidal, an antibiotic kills organisms; if bacteriostatic, it prevents their growth.

anticoagulant. Term used to describe the prevention of blood coagulation, or an agent that prevents coagulation.

appendicitis. An inflammation of the worm-shaped (vermiform) appendix, which is located at the tip of the cecum (part of the large bowel). A perforated appendix is a serious complication with the potential of peritonitis.

arrhythmia. An alteration in the regular rhythm of the heart, either in the formation or conduction of heart impulses. Such disturbances may be functional or due to disease.

arteriogram. An x-ray picture of an artery after it has been injected with a contrast medium.

arteriosclerosis. Commonly referred to as hardening of the arteries. Involves thickening, hardening, and loss of elasticity of the artery walls.

arthritis. An inflammation of the joints. Rheumatoid arthritis is a chronic and generally progressive inflammatory disease marked by pain and swelling of the joints. Osteoarthritis is a chronic degenerative disease mainly of weight-bearing joints. See also *Still's disease.*

asthma. A condition marked by difficult breathing and wheezing, chronic or episodic. Three major contributory factors are allergy, respiratory infection, and emotional stress.

atherosclerosis. A form of arteriosclerosis in which fatty substances are deposited in the arteries and their inner layers become tough and sinewy.

athlete's foot (tinea pedis). An infection caused by a fungus that thrives on dead skin cells between the toes. It is commonly found in locker rooms, public showers, and swimming pool walkways.

beta blockers. Drugs that reduce the workload of the heart and thereby lower the demand of the coronary arteries for blood. Beta-blocking agents are prescribed for the treatment of angina pectoris, hypertension, and cardiac arrhythmias.

biopsy. The excision and microscopic examination of tissue samples and cells to determine abnormalities. Indicated when cancer, or certain liver or kidney diseases, are suspected.

bone marrow. The soft red (in spongy bones) or yellow (in long bones) tissue filling the interior cavities of bones. Red marrow is the site of production of the red and white blood cells and the platelets.

brain death. Condition in which there is irreversible coma and evidence of irreparable brain damage. There is lack of electrical activity for a prolonged period, no response to external stimuli, fixed pupils, and absence of spontaneous breathing.

brain scan. Diagnostic technique in which a radioactive isotope or tracer is injected into a vein, usually the arm. A scintillation scanner is used to detect the tiny radioactive emissions as the tracer flows through the blood vessels in the brain.

bronchitis. An acute inflammatory condition usually due to exposure to cold and dampness. When chronic and uncontrolled, bronchitis can create serious lung problems.

bronchoscopy. A diagnostic procedure that permits inspection of the interior of the tracheobronchial tree through a bronchoscope. The technique is helpful in obtaining biopsy specimens and removing obstructions.

bursitis. A painful inflammation of the bursa, which are small fluid-filled sacs that facilitate movement of body joints. Most commonly, the shoulder, elbow, hip, and knee are involved.

Caesarean section. A technique in which the fetus is removed by means of an incision into the uterus, usually via the abdominal wall. Generally, it is employed when there is an overly large fetus or an abnormally small pelvis.

cancer. Many diseases, all characterized by an irregular and uncontrolled growth of body cells. These malignant cells may remain in the area where they formed or may spread via the blood and lymph to other parts of the body.

candidiasis. A yeastlike fungus. *Candida albicans* is responsible for this infection, called thrush when it is localized in the mouth or throat, vaginitis when it affects the vaginal walls.

cardiac arrest. A sudden cessation of heartbeat and breathing. This is a medical emergency calling for immediate attention. Cardiopulmonary resuscitation (CPR) is potentially life-saving, but can only be performed by a person trained in the technique.

CAT scan. See *computerized axial tomography.*

chemotherapy. The use of drugs or chemical agents that have a specific and toxic effect upon disease-causing microorganisms. The term is often applied to potent drugs that destroy cancer cells.

chicken pox (varicella). A highly contagious infectious disease that occurs mostly in children. Symptoms include fever, headache, malaise, and at times a sore throat. A red rash that crusts develops.

childbed fever (puerpural fever). Occurs after a prolonged or difficult childbirth and is marked by septicemia. There is absorption of septic products into blood and tissues, or disease-causing organisms that may multiply in these areas.

cholecystitis. Inflammation of the gallbladder, either acute or chronic, often due to obstruction of the bile duct by gallstones. Symptoms include pain, nausea, vomiting, and fever.

cholecystography. The examination of the gallbladder by x-ray study. Useful in detecting gallstones or gallbladder dysfunction.

cholesterol. A sterol, this fatlike substance is found in animal fats and oils, nerve tissue, bile, blood, and egg yolk. A normal constituent of bile, cholesterol can also be manufactured in the liver.

chromosome. A microscopic J- or V-shaped body present in all living cells. Chromosomes contain genes, the particles responsible for determining hereditary characteristics. The normal number of chromosomes in each human cell is 46, arranged in 23 pairs.

cirrhosis. Chronic condition in which there are degenerative changes in the liver cells and thickening of surrounding tissue; interferes with normal liver function. Often associated with advanced alcoholism.

collagen. An insoluble protein that represents about 30 percent of total body protein. Found in the white fibers of connective tissue, cartilage, and bone.

collagen diseases. Various conditions causing cellular changes affecting the body's connective tissue. Diseases include lupus erythematosus, rheumatoid arthritis, and scleroderma.

colonoscopy. Permits examination of the upper portion of the rectum with an elongated speculum. May also be useful in removing polyps and obtaining tissue samples for biopsy.

colostomy. Temporary or permanent surgical opening made from the colon through the abdominal wall. Creates an artificial passage for the elimination of solid wastes to the outside of the body.

computerized axial tomography (CAT scan). A computer-aided x-ray system that can be used with safety and effectiveness, exposing a person to about the same amount of radiation as obtained from a chest x-ray. Provides highly detailed imaging of internal structures of the brain, lungs, pancreas, and kidneys.

concussion. Commonly the result of a severe blow to the head. Brain concussion may be accompanied by temporary or prolonged unconsciousness. Recovery may be gradual, depending upon age, damage, and care given.

congestive heart failure. Impaired circulation when the heart cannot pump sufficient blood to supply the body's needs. Congestion, or fluid accumulation, may develop in the lungs, legs, or abdomen.

conjunctivitis. Refers to inflammation of the conjunctiva, the mucous membrane lining the eyelids and white of the eye. Causative factors include allergy, bacterial and viral infections, smoke, dust, or wind.

convulsions. Condition marked by involuntary jerking movements, often with momentary unconsciousness. Some possible causes may be epilepsy, stroke, meningitis, hypoglycemia, skull fracture, brain tumor, and drug reactions.

coronary bypass. A major operative procedure in which a blocked coronary artery is bypassed with a section of vein taken from the leg and grafted into position. Double, triple, and quadruple bypass can be performed.

coronary occlusion. Blockage of vessels supplying blood to the myocardium (heart muscle). May be produced by growth of plaque (fatty materials), or by growth of a thrombus (blood clot) plugging the artery.

corpus luteum. Ovarian follicle after it has released its ovum. Produces the hormone progesterone, which prepares the uterine lining for possible implantation of the ovum.

crib death. See *sudden infant death.*

cross-eye. See *strabismus.*

croup. An acute viral infection that occurs most often in infants and young children. Marked by difficult breathing and a hoarse cough.

cryosurgery. Surgical procedure in which cells are destroyed by the application of extreme cold (the tissue is usually cooled to below 0° F (−20° C). Used in the treatment of malignant tumors and certain precancerous conditions.

culdoscopy. Examination of the female internal organs and pelvic cavity with an endoscope. Used in cases of

You and Modern Medicine

suspected abnormal uterine tissue growth, infertility, and pelvic disorders.

curettage. Scraping of a cavity with a curette. In uterine curettage, scraping is done to remove contents of the uterus, obtain diagnostic specimens, or remove growths.

cyst. An abnormal sac or swelling filled with fluid or a semisolid material; may occur anywhere in the body. Sebaceous cysts, often forming on the scalp, consist of a small sac containing a yellowish-white caseous matter.

cystocele. A hernia sometimes associated with childbirth, where part of the bladder protrudes into the vagina. The condition may be accompanied by bladder incontinence or infection.

cystoscopy. An examination of the inside of the bladder and urethra with a cystoscope. Indicated when there is a suspicion of bladder or urinary tract cancer or polyps.

D&C (dilation and curettage). Procedure in which the cervix is enlarged (dilated) to facilitate scraping of the uterine walls. Undertaken to remove unwanted tissue from the uterus, remove growths, or obtain tissue for examination.

decubitus ulcers. Bedsores caused by poor circulation in the area under pressure. Common in bedridden patients who must lie in one position. Buttocks, shoulders, elbows, and heels are often involved.

dermatitis. An inflammation of the skin which, in extremely sensitive persons, may be due to contact with such skin irritants as acids and alkalis, cosmetics, fabrics, and animal hair. Marked by itching, redness, and skin lesions.

diabetes insipidus. Form of diabetes in which there is a chronic excretion of very large amounts of urine, accompanied by extreme thirst. Ordinarily results from an insufficient production of the antidiuretic hormone by the pituitary gland.

diabetes mellitus. A metabolic disorder in which the body is unable to utilize carbohydrates, primarily due to the inadequate production of insulin by the pancreas. It is detected by the presence of sugar in the blood and urine.

diagnosis. The use of various methods to determine the cause and nature of a disease. Among the methods are study of the signs and symptoms of a disease, laboratory data, and special tests.

dialysis. A process employed to separate or extract certain substances in solution by diffusion through a porous membrane. Used to purify the blood (hemodialysis) in persons with one or both kidneys defective or absent.

diarrhea. A condition that is marked by the frequent passage of loose, watery stools. May be caused by infection, food poisoning, overeating, or certain drugs.

diverticular disease. Condition marked by diarrhea, colic, and abdominal pain. Diverticula are pouches or pockets that form on the large bowel. In diverticulosis, the colon contains dozens of these pouches.

DNA (deoxyribonucleic acid). A nucleic acid present in chromosomes of the nuclei of cells. Considered the chemical basis of heredity, and the carrier of genetic information.

Down syndrome. Congenital abnormality, formerly known as mongolism, marked by moderate to severe mental retardation. Children born with Down syndrome have a sloping forehead, low-set ears, slanted eyes, and a generally dwarfed physique.

dysmenorrhea. Painful or difficult menstruation. Discomfort is usually felt in the lower abdomen and sometimes the lower back. Often the condition improves with age and may disappear after childbirth.

dysplasia. Abnormal tissue development that can occur in the cervix, lungs, and other parts of the body. Women with cervical dysplasia must be examined regularly as it may become cancerous.

electrocardiogram (ECG or EKG). A graphic record of the electrical activity of the heart. Can indicate whether electrical conduction is normal and whether there is dead tissue due to a previous heart attack.

electroencephalogram (EEG). Graphic recording of the electric activity of the brain. May be used for a number of different purposes, such as diagnosing epilepsy and for research into sleep and dream patterns.

embolism. An obstruction of a blood vessel by a transported solid (an embolus): a blood clot, bacterial mass, or other foreign material. The severity of the condition is in direct relationship to the size and location of the blocked vessel.

emphysema. A chronic lung disease. The alveoli (air sacs) become greatly distended, bronchioles become thinned, and, eventually, the architecture of the lungs is destroyed. Chronic bronchitis or bronchial asthma, smoking, and air pollution may be implicated.

endocardiography. Method used to record the size, motion, and composition of various cardiac structures. Indicated in heart valve problems that are difficult to diagnose.

endocarditis. An inflammation of the heart lining (endocardium). Persons with damaged heart valves are most vulnerable. The condition is often observed in young adults and the middle-aged.

endometriosis. A nonmalignant condition in which tissue normally located in the lining of the uterus (endometrium) begins to grow elsewhere. Often seen in the ovaries, the Fallopian tubes, the bladder, or between the rectum and vagina.

enzyme. One of various complex proteins produced by living cells. Enzymes alter the chemical reactions in other substances while remaining unchanged in the process, and help break down food particles into simple, more readily absorbed compounds.

epilepsy. Includes a group of nervous disorders characterized by either convulsive or nonconvulsive seizures and, generally, a temporary loss of consciousness. Seizures are associated with a sudden unruly pattern of brain waves.

epistaxis (nosebleed). Included among the causes are high blood pressure, injury, infection, foreign bodies, and a direct blow to the nose. If severe or uncontrolled, nosebleed requires medical attention.

erythrocyte sedimentation rate. A laboratory test that determines how fast red blood cells (erythrocytes) in a blood specimen settle to the bottom of a long narrow tube. The speed of settling is increased in various infections, pregnancy, and cancer.

fever (pyrexia). A body temperature above the normal, which, taken orally, is 98.6° F (37° C). Generally, a fever of 101° F (39° C) calls for medical attention.

fibroma. A benign tumor derived from fibrous tissue. May vary in size from a millet seed to large enough to fill the entire abdominal cavity. May be single or multiple in number.

fistula. An abnormal tubelike passage that leads from a normal cavity or tube to the free surface, or to another cavity. Fistulae may be congenital or result from abscesses, injuries, or inflammatory processes.

flatulence. An excessive amount of gas in the stomach and intestine. May be due to habitual air swallowing or indigestion. If it is worse after eating fatty foods, there may be gallstones.

flu. See *influenza*.

fluoroscopy. A technique that permits examination of inner parts of the body by means of the fluoroscope. In the upper body, there is x-ray visualization of the esophagus, stomach, and duodenum; in the lower body, the large intestine is visualized.

gallstones. Concretions or stonelike masses that form in the gallbladder or bile ducts. May not cause much distress or may be associated with painful attacks.

gamma globulin. Various proteins found in the lymphatic system, bone marrow, and spleen, associated with the production of antibodies. They circulate in the blood and help the body to resist infection.

gastritis. Inflammation of the mucous membrane of the stomach. May be due to viral infection, hot spicy food, food poisoning, or overindulgence in alcoholic beverages.

gastroscopy. Inspection of the inner surface of the stomach by the use of an endoscope.

Useful in confirming stomach ulcers, unexplained bleeding, or other abnormalities.

genetics. The branch of science that is concerned with heredity.

German measles (rubella). An acute contagious disease similar to measles and scarlet fever. Women who have not had rubella in childhood should be protected against this disease before considering pregnancy.

glandular. Relates to the nature of a gland, a secreting organ or structure. There are many types of glands, and they serve different purposes throughout the body.

glaucoma. A disease of the eye marked by an unaccountable rise in fluid pressure within the eyeball. If unrelieved, it can cause permanent damage to the eye and result in partial or total blindness.

glossitis. Inflammation of the tongue, which may be associated with stomatitis (inflammation of the mouth). The tongue becomes tender and painful; thick saliva makes swallowing difficult.

goiter. An enlarged thyroid. Due to overactivity of the gland in secreting an excessive amount of hormones. In severe cases, the thyroid gland may swell to several times its normal size and be observable as a large growth on the front of the throat.

gonorrhea. A sexually transmitted disease that, if untreated, can lead to serious damage. In the male, it can cause epididymitis; in women, it may result in painful infection of the Fallopian tubes, often causing sterility.

graft. Insertion of skin or other living substance into similar substance for the purpose of overcoming a defect. In skin graft, a piece of skin is removed from one part of the body to another to cover a large superficial burn.

gynecology. A branch of medicine that deals with diseases of women, in particular, the genital tract and the female endocrine and reproductive systems.

habituation. The act of becoming accustomed to something by frequent use. In general, it refers to the psychological dependence that develops with the continued use of a drug, eventually resulting in drug addiction.

Hashimoto's disease. A chronic form of thyroiditis (inflammation of the thyroid gland) manifested by a particular type of goiter.

headache (cephalalgia). A symptom that is associated with a great many diseases and emotional states. Infection and tension are among the causes.

heart attack. See *myocardial infarction.*

heartburn. An abnormal return of acid liquid from the stomach into the esophagus. Produces a burning sensation deep in the chest together with an oppressive tightening sensation.

hematoma. A localized mass of blood that has escaped from a vessel into the tissues, occurring at the site of an injury where the blood vessels have broken.

hemodialysis. A procedure that is used to purify the blood in persons with kidney failure; usually requires 20 hours a week; 10 hours twice a week; or 6½ hours three times a week.

hemophilia. An hereditary blood disease in which the blood fails to clot and there is an abnormal tendency to bleed from a cut or other injury. Transmitted from mother to son as a sex-linked recessive condition.

hemorrhoids (piles). Varicose (enlarged or swollen) veins of the anal and rectal area. External hemorrhoids occur on the outside of the anal sphincter; internal hemorrhoids develop within the anal canal.

hepatitis (infectious). Acute disease of the liver. Viral hepatitis type A is transmitted by the oral-fecal route. It is spread from person to person by infected food handlers or contaminated food, water, feces, or bedpans.

hepatitis (serum). Viral hepatitis type B. Transmitted by injection of infected blood or by the use of contaminated needles or instruments. Similar to type A, it is caused by a virus found in blood and tissues rather than in the feces.

hepatitis (toxic). An inflammation of the liver caused by exposure to certain chemicals (carbon tetrachloride, insecticides, solvents). In those overly sensitive to such drugs as ioniazid and bromates, liver damage may result.

hernia. A weak point in the abdominal wall through which a part of the intestine can protrude. Commonly seen types are inguinal (groin), umbilical (navel), and femoral (thigh).

hernia (hiatus). Protrusion of the upper part of the stomach into the chest cavity. This condition is associated with weakness in the area where the esophagus opens up into the diaphragm. This impairment permits leakage of acid stomach contents into the esophagus.

herpes smplex. A virus infection that causes painful fluid-filled blisters, called cold sores or fever blisters. Other forms of herpes simplex are denoted according to site; for example, herpes genitalis.

herpes zoster (shingles). A completely different disease from herpes simplex, this painful vesicular eruption occurs along the course of a nerve. It is due to the same virus, herpes varicella, as that causing chicken pox.

Hodgkin's disease. A malignant disease that mostly afflicts men. It is marked by painless and progressive swelling of the lymph glands with enlargement of the spleen. Some symptoms are anemia, fever, and fatigue.

hydrocephalus. An increased accumulation of cerebrospinal fluid within the hollow spaces (ventricles) of the brain. It may result from a malformation, infection, injury, or a brain tumor.

hypertension. High blood pressure denoting arterial pressure that is consistently elevated. Added pressure on the blood vessel walls makes the heart work harder; untreated, it can cause organ damage.

hyperthyroidism (Graves' disease). The result of an overproduction of hormones by the thyroid gland. Besides exophthalmos goiter, symptoms include increased nervousness and heart rate, weight loss, and heat intolerance.

hypoglycemia. An abnormally low concentration of sugar in circulating blood. May be due to an insulin overdose or a missed meal by a diabetic. In nondiabetics, poor diet may be a cause.

hypothermia. A technique used to lower body temperature and so reduce the need for oxygen during surgery. It is especially useful when the heart and the nerves are involved.

hypothyroidism (myxedema). Condition in which the thyroid gland is underactive, failing to secrete an adequate amount of hormones. As the condition progresses, there is slowed pulse rate, sluggish movement, facial puffiness, and muscle weakness.

hysterectomy. An operative procedure that involves removal of the uterus. It is usually indicated when tumors are present, whether benign or malignant.

immunosuppressive agent. Belonging to a group of drugs that interfere with the body's natural immune system. Used before surgical transplant of a foreign organ, such as a kidney, to avert body rejection.

indigestion. Often caused by eating too much too fast, not chewing food well, eating when emotionally upset, or swallowing large amounts of air. Symptoms may be heartburn, gas, and belching.

infarction (infarct). Condition in which there is death of tissue and consequent scarring in an organ deprived of an adequate supply of blood. Myocardial infarction describes such an occurrence in the heart.

influenza (flu). A respiratory infection caused by one of several related, yet distinct, viruses. It strikes suddenly with chills, fever, headache, muscle aches, and a dry cough, most of which subside after a few days.

insomnia. Inability to sleep. In itself, not a disease, but it may be a symptom of disease, either of a slight or serious nature. Most often due to pain or anxiety.

insulin shock. A low blood sugar reaction that can be caused by an insulin overdose. Often the result of lowered blood sugar brought on by a break in normal routine or emotional upset.

irritable bowel syndrome. A common gastric disorder marked by abdominal pain, diarrhea, and/or constipation.

In general, the problem is not organic but stems from the nature of a person's personality, particularly an inability to deal with stress.

jaundice. An excessive amount of bile pigment in the blood and a yellowish discoloration of the skin. Associated with diseases of the liver, gallbladder, bile ducts, and certain blood diseases.

laryngitis. An inflammation of the larynx. May be due to improper use or overuse of the voice. May also be caused by upper respiratory infections, the inhalation of irritating vapors or dust, or tobacco smoke.

lead poisoning. Results from the ingestion of lead, as during prolonged exposure to lead dust in the workplace, when using lead vessels for eating or drinking, or when chewing on lead toys.

legionnaires' disease. Applies to a severe pneumonialike disease that felled 249 American Legion conventioneers in Philadelphia (July, 1976). Marked by fever, cough, and bloody sputum. Additional symptoms may not be distinguishable from other types of pneumonia.

leukemia. A form of cancer in which there is a rapid increase of white blood cells in the bloodstream. The cells infiltrate body tissues and, in particular, bone marrow. This condition leads to anemia, hemorrhaging, and infection.

lumpectomy. Surgical procedure in which only a primary tumor and a varying amount of surrounding breast tissue is removed. Radiation therapy is used postoperatively.

lupus erythematoses. Systemic, and possibly chronic, disease in which a skin rash spreads across the bridge of the nose

and face in a butterfly pattern. The disease affects the blood vessels.

lymphatic vessels. Vessels that transport lymph (the clear fluid bathing all body tissues), lymphocytes (a type of white blood cell), and other substances needed for the body's immune system. These vessels are part of the lymph system along with the lacteals, lymph capillaries, ducts, and nodes.

malignancy. Term that describes a condition occurring in severe form, growing worse, and resisting treatment. In cancer, it denotes uncontrollable growth and dissemination, or recurrence after removal of a tumor, or both.

mammography. Specialized x-ray technique for detecting breast abnormalities, especially early cancers. Recent improvements assure more accurate information and smaller amounts of radiation.

manic-depressive psychoses. A major mental disorder in which a person displays severe changes of mood: overelation and excessive activity during the manic state; depression and anxiety while in the depressed state.

mastectomy. A surgical procedure that involves removal of the breast. If simple, only breast tissue is excised; if major, the underlying chest muscles and the lymph nodes in the armpit are also removed.

mastoiditis. Infection that spreads through the ear to the mastoid process (part of the temporal bone). When acute, symptoms include chills, fever, malaise, and headache. When chronic, mastoid tissue is destroyed and there is loss of hearing.

measles. A highly communicable viral disease that usually occurs in early childhood. Marked by nasal discharge, fever, cough, and reddening of the eyes; also, a blotchy rash and fine white spots inside the mouth.

medication. A medicinal substance that is a medicine or remedy. Also refers to treatment with a remedy. (See pages 90-91 for a list of prescription drugs.)

Ménierè's disease. An impairment of the balancing mechanism of the inner ear. Attacks often come on with alarming suddenness. Symptoms include vertigo, ringing or other disturbing noises in the ear, and progressive loss of hearing.

meningitis. An inflammation of the meninges, the delicate membranes covering the layers of the brain. A local infection of the ears, sinuses, or tonsils may spread the infection to the meninges, or be carried into the bloodstream.

menopause. The cessation of menstruation that brings to a close the reproductive life of a woman. Natural menopause may occur as early as age 35, and as late as 58. Usually, it takes place between the ages of 47 and 52.

metabolism. The sum of chemical changes affecting the function of nutrition. Two fundamental processes are involved: anabolism—converting small molecules into large; and catabolism—converting large molecules into small.

microorganisms. Living organisms too small to be seen with the naked eye. Only a relatively small number are pathogenic (capable of causing disease). Protozoa, bacteria, fungi, rickettsiae, and viruses are all microorganisms.

migraine. A severe, periodic, vascular type of headache, usually one-sided. It may be preceded or accompanied by various symptoms: visual disturbances, extreme sensitivity to light, and nausea.

mole. A congenital discolored spot raised above the skin surface. Generally, moles are harmless unless there is irritation in the area.

mongolism. See *Down's syndrome.*

mononucleosis (infectious). An acute infection, also called glandular fever, believed to be due to a virus. It is manifested by a sore throat, fever, swollen lymph nodes, headache, and a faintly red eruption.

multiple sclerosis (MS). A chronic disease of the central nervous system in which there is degeneration of the myelin (a fatlike substance) sheath in the brain and spinal cord. Symptoms may come and go for years, but incapacitation worsens with progress of the disease.

mumps (epidemic parotitis). An acute febrile disease marked by inflammation of the parotid salivary glands (just below the ears). Although not as communicable as chicken pox or measles, mumps are quite contagious.

muscular dystrophy (Duchenne's disease). A hereditary disorder that primarily affects boys. There is progressive weakness and wasting of muscles, first affecting the abdomen and buttocks, then the chest and other body parts.

musculoskeletal. Relates to the muscles and the skeleton.

myasthenia gravis. A chronic neuromuscular disorder caused by a defective transmission of nerve impulse to the muscles. Marked by extreme muscular weakness, but no wasting of muscles.

myelitis. An inflammation of the spinal cord or of bone marrow. A potentially serious condition that calls for prompt diagnosis and treatment. If the spinal nerves are involved, there may be partial or total paralysis.

myocardial infarction (heart attack). Condition in which part of the heart muscle is deprived of blood and dies, being gradually replaced by a fibrous scar (infarct).

nephritis. Inflammation of the kidneys. Denotes a group of noninfectious diseases involving widespread kidney damage. The glomeruli (filtering units of the kidney) or the tubules may be affected.

nephrolithiasis. Condition in which calculi, or stones, are formed in the kidney and urinary bladder. Many kidney stones eventually pass out; others must be removed surgically.

neuritis. May be inflammation of a nerve (mononeuritis) or nerves (polyneuritis), usually characterized by pain. May be caused by injury, infection, metallic poisoning, or a metabolic disturbance.

neurosis. A psychological or behavioral disorder with the chief underlying factor being anxiety. In contrast with psychosis, persons with neurosis maintain contact with reality and undergo no major personality changes.

nonspecific urethritis. Condition in which the specific organism causing inflammation of the urethra is unknown. May be due to Chlamydia trachomatis, the same microbe that causes the eye disease trachoma.

nosebleed. See *epistaxis.*

oophorectomy. Surgical procedure in which an ovary or a portion of it is removed; also called ovariectomy.

osteoarthritis. Form of arthritis in which there is chronic degeneration of the joints, especially the weight-bearing (spinal column, hip, and knee) joints. Swelling may appear at the sides of each finger joint (Heberden's nodes).

osteomalacia. Disease in which bones gradually become soft due to bonelike tissue that fails to calcify. Bones become flexible and brittle, resulting in pain and deformation.

osteomyelitis. An inflammation of bone marrow and adjacent bone involving sudden pain, fever, and bone tenderness. Movement is painful and restricted, with subsequent swelling over the bone and often the nearby joint.

osteoporosis. A disorder characterized by the loss of bone mass. Increases the potential for fractures, particularly of the weight-bearing vertebrae. With compression of vertebrae, there is loss of height and, at times, kyphosis (humpback).

otitis. Inflammation of the ear differentiated by the part of the ear affected: otitis externa, the outer ear; otitis media, the middle ear; and otitis interna, the inner ear.

otosclerosis. Formation of spongy bone around the stapes (a small bone in the middle ear) that results in progressively worsening deafness. This hearing loss can be corrected surgically or with a hearing aid.

ovarian cyst. An abnormal fluid-filled sac that develops within an ovary. It afflicts many women between the ages of 30 and 60. Enlarged, painful cysts are removed surgically.

pacemaker. Defines any rhythmic center that controls heart rhythm; normally, the sinus node. An artificial pacemaker is a device that substitutes for the normal pacemaker and controls heart rhythm.

Paget's disease (osteitis deformans). Generalized skeletal disease seen mainly in older persons. It is marked by an increased breakdown and reforming of bone that leads to abnormal thickening and softening of the bones.

pancreatitis. Condition in which there is inflammation of the pancreas. In the acute form, may lead to areas of tissue destruction and scattered hemorrhages. Complaints include abdominal pain, nausea, vomiting, and fever.

paralysis. A temporary or permanent loss of voluntary muscular movement in a part of the body. There are many different causes, including injury, infection, and stroke.

paraplegia. Paralysis caused by injury to the spinal cord. Paraplegics suffer paralysis in both legs and, usually, the lower trunk. Quadriplegics have paralysis in all four limbs.

paratyphoid fever. Similar to but less severe than typhoid fever. Caused by an infection of Salmonella bacteria. The infection is transmitted by contaminated food, milk, or water.

Parkinson's disease (paralysis agitans). A chronic, progressive disease involving the brain. Symptoms include a masklike face, muscular tremor of the head and extremities, and muscular stiffness with slowed voluntary movement.

pediculosis. An infestation of the body with lice. The infection is spread by direct contact with an infected person, or by the use of infected clothing or objects. There are three kinds of lice: head, body, and pubic.

pellagra. Chiefly a B vitamin deficiency (nicotinic acid). May also be caused by intestinal diseases or alcoholism. In severe cases, there is inflamed mouth and tongue, skin rash, diarrhea, and anemia.

peptic ulcer. May be a stomach ulcer (gastric) or of the duodenum (duodenal). It is associated with a decreased ability of the organ to withstand bathing by the acid gastric juices (pepsin and hydrochloric acid).

pericarditis. Condition in which there is inflammation of the pericardium, the membranous sac enveloping the heart. It is often accompanied by shortness of breath and chest pains that may be aggravated on coughing or deep breathing.

peritonitis. Inflammation of the peritoneum, the membrane lining the abdominal cavity. Acute peritonitis is caused by infection, such as that caused by a ruptured appendix, which requires immediate hospitalization and treatment.

pheochromocytoma. A disorder caused by a tumor of the adrenal gland. Usually manifested by sustained high blood pressure. Symptoms, varying widely from person to person, include nausea, headache, palpitations, and weakness.

phlebitis. Inflammation of a vein, most often noted in a leg. May involve injury to the vein, obesity, infection, or a problem related to blood circulation.

pleurisy (pleuritis). Inflammation of the membrane covering the lungs. Usually due to a bacterial or viral infection. In acute cases, there is stabbing pain in the affected side, high fever, and a dry cough.

pneumonia. An inflammatory condition of the lungs, marked by cough, chest pains, and fever. Causative agents are bacteria or viruses, but mostly the pneumococcus— *Diplococcus pneumoniae* —is involved.

pneumothorax. A condition in which air or gas escapes into the pleural cavity. It usually results from a penetrating chest wound, or may be due to various lung diseases. In either case, the lung or parts of the lung collapse.

poliomyelitis (infantile paralysis). A viral infection that attacks the gray matter of the spinal cord. This can lead to muscular paralysis, especially of the limbs and of the muscles involved with breathing.

polyarteritis. Condition marked by widespread inflammation of the smaller arteries. Often leads to complications, such as kidney disease and high blood pressure.

polyp. An abnormal, often benign, stalklike growth. Usually occurs in vascular organs, such as the nose, uterus, and rectum. If there is any sign of malignancy, polyps should be removed surgically.

Pontiac fever. A pneumonialike disease first noted in Pontiac, Michigan (1968). The bacteria are believed to be slightly different strains of the same bacteria as those causing legionnaires' disease.

positron emission tomography (PET). A scanner that makes images of the body from radioactive isotopes; the images are deciphered by computers. It is an invasive means of visualizing brain sites to detect neuropsychiatric disorders.

Pott's disease. Spinal tuberculosis. The condition may also affect the hips and knees. It occurs mainly in children and adults up to 40 years of age.

preeclampsia and eclampsia. Conditions commonly referred to as toxemias of pregnancy. Preeclampsia is often marked by fluid retention and high blood pressure. In eclampsia, convulsions occur and pregnancy must be terminated.

pregnancy tests.
Slide test. Simple test that involves mixing urine with a solution on a slide and examining results. It is most accurate when done at least seven weeks after the last menstrual period.
Tube (hemagglutination inhibition) test. Typical of home pregnancy tests, urine is mixed with a testing solution in a tube. It is slightly more accurate and can be done about a week earlier than the slide test.
Radioreceptor assay (RRA) blood test; beta-HCG (human chorionic gonadotropin) test; monoclonal antibodies test. The newest of available tests with which accurate positive results can be obtained as early as the time of the first missed period.

prognosis. Foretelling of the probable course and outcome of a disease.

prolapse. Downward or forward displacement of a part of the body. Most often used in denoting a displaced or "fallen" uterus.

prostaglandins. A group of fatty acid derivatives present in many body tissues. They can lower blood pressure, stimulate uterine contractions, and regulate body temperatures.

prostatitis. Inflammation of the prostate. In the acute bacterial form, marked by fever, chills, and back pain. There is usually accompanying difficulty in urination, as well as pain in muscles and joints.

prothrombin time (PT). Test that measures the time needed for a fibrin (a protein formed by the action of thrombin on fibrinogen) clot to form in a treated blood sample.

pseudodementia. Condition in which a person experiences an exaggerated indifference to his surroundings. However, there is no actual impairment of mental capacity.

psittacosis. A viral disease that may be transmitted to humans by infected birds, especially parrots, parakeets, love birds, and canaries. It is generally acquired by breathing in the dust from the cage contents or feathers of the infected birds.

psoriasis. A skin condition marked by formation of unsightly reddish, silvery-scaled patches. In general, the elbows, knees, legs, lower back, chest, and scalp are affected.

psychiatry. A medical specialty that deals with the diagnosis and treatment of mental illness. Psychotherapy employs mental rather than physical means.

psychosis. Mental disorders in which there is disturbed thought, disintegration of personality, and lack of touch with reality. Schizophrenia is the most common psychosis.

psychosomatic. The influence of the mind (emotions, fears, desires) upon the body functions, especially as it pertains to disease.

psychotropic. All that affects the mind and its processes. Also refers to psychotropic drugs, which have an effect on psychic function, behavior, and experience.

pulmonary embolism. A clot in an artery of the lungs, often due to a detached clot from a leg vein. Those most vulnerable are the bedridden or those with heart or lung disease, cancer, or hip fractures.

purpura. A group of bleeding disorders due to various causes. Characterized by bleeding into the skin and other tissues, mucous membranes, and internal organs.

pyelography. X-ray examination of the renal pelvis and ureter.

It is indicated in cases of recurrent kidney or bladder infection, or severe symptoms of prostate enlargement.

pyelonephritis. Inflammation of the kidney as well as the renal pelvis, commonly caused by an ascending bacterial infection. When chronic, the kidney suffers irreversible changes.

Q fever (query fever, Balkan grippe). An acute infective disease. When first noted, its cause was unknown and the Q stood for "query." The organism is carried by livestock and transmitted to humans by inhalation of infected dusts, or by drinking of contaminated milk of infected animals.

radiation sickness. An illness resulting from chronic exposure to or excessive amounts of high-energy radiation. Symptoms may be mild or may result in serious disturbances in blood cell formation, leukemia, and other changes.

radioisotope scanning. The study of the function and condition of internal organs, vessels, or body fluids with radioactive forms of chemicals, such as iodine.

radiotherapy (radiation, roentgenography). Treatment of disease by the use of roentgen rays (x-rays), radium, ultraviolet, and other radiations. It may be used alone or in combination with surgery or drugs.

Raynaud's disease. Condition in which there is spasm in the blood vessels of the extremities, especially in response to cold temperatures that would not normally affect a person. Most often, the fingers are affected.

reticular activating system (RAS). A complex system of nerve cells and fibers in the brain stem, hypothalamus, and adjacent areas. It plays an important part in maintaining alertness or wakefulness.

retinitis pigmentosa. Chronic and progressive disease that usually starts in childhood. It is marked by retinal degeneration, widespread changes in retinal pigmentation, wasting of the optic nerve, and defective night vision.

Reye's syndrome. Potentially fatal disorder that usually afflicts children under 18 following a viral infection such as chicken pox. It is marked by increased pressure on the brain and fatty degeneration of the liver.

Rh blood factor (Rhesus factor). A factor discovered in red blood cells of the rhesus monkey. It is present in about 85 percent of the human population who are said to be Rh positive (Rh+). Those not having this substance in the blood are Rh negative (Rh−).

rheumatic fever. A disease of childhood and adolescence that often follows symptoms of throat infection. If untreated, it can lead to heart damage.

rheumatoid arthritis. A chronic and usually progressive inflammatory disease of the joints that affects women more than men. Pain and swelling of the joints result in restricted movement.

rickets. A childhood disease primarily due to a lack of dietary Vitamin D, or inadequate exposure to sunlight, or both. Rickets interferes with the normal deposition of calcium.

RNA (ribonucleic acid). The "message" molecule that carries information from the nucleus (the vital body in cell protoplasm) to cytoplasma (cell protoplasm outside the nucleus) sites.

Rocky Mountain spotted fever. An infectious disease caused by a species of rickettsia. Usually acquired in man from the bite of infected ticks. Marked by high fever, muscle and bone pain, and rash.

Salmonellosis. The most common form of food poisoning, caused by ingestion of food contaminated with bacteria of the genus Salmonella. There is severe inflammation of the stomach lining and intestines.

salpingitis. Inflammatory condition of a Fallopian tube usually caused by a bacterial infection spreading upward from the uterus, cervix, or vagina.

sarcoma. A general term for cancer. Composed of cells from connective tissues of the body, such as bone or muscle. The bladder, kidneys, lungs, liver, spleen, and nearby tissues may be involved.

scabies. Highly infectious skin disease caused by the itch mite, *Sarcoptes scabiei*, and spread by close contact with infected persons. Most often, the hands, wrists, armpits, breasts, and thighs are affected.

scarlet fever. Acute contagious disease caused by a bacterial infection. Marked by sore throat, fever, and a scarlet rash. The infection is spread by the breath or cough of an infected person, or by handling contaminated objects.

schistosomiasis (snail fever). Parasitic infestation due to blood flukes (a type of worm) belonging to a species of Schistosoma. Man becomes infected by bathing in water containing parasitic worms issued from snails.

schizophrenia. A group of mental disorders in which there are disturbances in thinking, mood, and behavior. In some cases, there is an altered sense of reality, delusions, and hallucinations.

sciatica. A severe pain involving the sciatic nerve, which extends from the back of the thigh down through the inside of the leg. The pain is sharp, usually more intense when standing, and often accompanied by tingling, numbness, and tenderness.

scleroderma. Progressive skin disease involving collagen tissue. There is widespread hardening of the skin due to swelling and thickening of fibrous tissue. This may be followed by skin atrophy and pigmentation.

scoliosis. An abnormal sideways curvature of the spine. There may be just one curve or a compensatory curve in the opposite direction. It may be due to a congenital defect, injury, disease, or poor posture.

senile dementia (senility, senile psychosis). A wide variety of mental and emotional changes affecting the elderly. Symptoms of this condition include loss of recent memory, short attention span, and irritability.

shingles. See *herpes zoster.*

shock. A state of deep mental and physical depression after receiving severe physical injury or undergoing emotional stress. Some causes are heart failure, hemorrhage, drug reaction, or poisoning.

sickle-cell anemia. An inherited blood disorder marked by a genetic abnormality of the red blood cells in which the cells become crescent or sickle-shaped.

sigmoidoscopy. A technique that permits inspection, through a tubular speculum called a sigmoidscope, of the interior of the sigmoid colon. It is indicated for detection of polyps, cancer, and bowel abnormalities.

sinusitis. Inflammation of the lining membrane of any sinus, but especially the nasal sinus. Most often, the condition occurs as an extension of nasal infections.

sleeping sickness. See *trypanosomiasis.*

slipped disk (prolapsed disk). Herniation or rupture of part of the intervertebral disk, which is normally held in place by fibrous tissues. When fibers weaken, protrusion from between the vertebrae occurs.

smallpox (variola). An acute, contagious, febrile disease that begins with chills, high fever, backache, and headache. Symptoms subside within five days and a skin eruption appears, ending up in dry scabs that fall off and mark the skin.

snail fever. See *schistosomiasis.*

specialist. A physician who, on completion of specialized postgraduate training, is able to practice a particular branch of medicine, such as surgery or obstetrics. (See page 81 for a description of various specialists.)

spinal tap. Involves lumbar puncture, which is used in cases of suspected meningitis and in certain types of spinal cord or brain damage.

Still's disease (juvenile rheumatoid arthritis). Similar to rheumatoid arthritis found in adults; however, children are affected much more severely during the development of the disease and less so in the later stages.

Stokes-Adams syndrome. Characterized by light-headedness or sudden loss of consciousness. Condition is associated with various disorders of the heart that disrupt its normal pumping action and consequent output of blood.

strabismus (cross-eye, squint). Condition in which the eyes fail to point in the same direction. Involves one or more muscles controlling eyeball movement.

stroke (apoplexy). Sudden loss of consciousness and paralysis on one side due to blockage of a cerebral artery by an embolus or thrombus or rupture of a blood vessel in the brain.

sudden infant death (SIDS; crib death). Unexplained death of an apparently well infant occurring most often between the second week and the first year of life. About 10 percent of cases are associated with cardiovascular or central nervous systems.

symptom. Any noticeable change in the body or its functions that indicates the presence of an illness or disease. May be of a general nature or pertain to the part of the body affected.

syphilis. A venereal disease caused by bacterial infection of the species *Treponema pallidum.* Spread almost exclusively by sexual intercourse with an infected partner.

tachycardia. Condition in which there is an abnormally fast heartbeat, especially over 100 beats per minute. May result from an overactive thyroid gland or some form of heart disease.

tapes dorsalis (locomotor ataxia). A late manifestation of syphilis involving the spinal cord. Occurs in persons having had inadequate or no treatment during early stages of syphilis.

Tay-Sachs disease. An hereditary disease caused by transmission of an abnormal gene. It results in a specific enzyme deficiency and is marked by progressive mental and physical retardation, paralysis, spasticity, and blindness.

telangiectasia. Dilation of capillaries, or a group of small blood vessels, which causes a small dark red elevation on the skin. May appear as a birthmark or become noticeable in young children.

temporal arteritis. Inflammation of the arteries that supply the sides of the scalp. Of unknown origin, it is becoming increasingly recognized in the elderly.

tetanus. An acute infection caused by the bacteria *Clostridium tetani*. These bacteria enter the body through a scratch or wound, where they release their poison (toxin) by growth and multiplication.

tetany. Nervous disorder in which there are intermittent tonic spasms involving the extremities. It can occur after a critical drop in the amount of calcium circulating in the blood.

thalassemia. An hereditary form of anemia characterized by the development of abnormally thin and fragile red blood cells. There are several variants of the disease, but no specific treatment is obtainable.

thalidomide. A hypnotic drug widely used in European countries as a sleeping pill in the early 1960's. Use of the drug was discontinued when it was found to cause severe limb deformities in developing fetuses.

therapeutic. The treatment of disease, or the results obtained from treatment. It may also pertain to a healing agent, or having healing properties.

thermography. A technique used to detect, record by a sensitive scanner, and interpret the significance of radiant heat thrown off by tissues affected by disease. It is used to study blood flow in limbs and to detect cancer.

thrombocytopenia. An abnormal decrease in the number of platelets (thrombocytes) in the circulating blood. It results in an inability of the blood to clot efficiently.

tinnitus. Condition in which a person experiences in one or both ears the sensation of noises that are not caused by external sound vibrations. It may be nothing more serious than impacted wax, or it may be an early sign of inner ear disease.

tonsillitis. An inflammation of tonsillar tissue. Tonsils appear enlarged and red, and are painful on swallowing. There may also be high fever, chills, and headache. It is more frequent in children than in adults.

toxic. A poisonous substance, a condition caused by a poison, or pertaining to a toxin. A toxin is a poisonous substance of animal or plant origin.

toxic shock syndrome. A fast-spreading, often deadly form of toxic reaction that sometimes kills or permanently disables a person within hours. About 80 percent of the cases occur in menstruating women using tampons.

toxoplasmosis. An infection caused by a parasite. Usually transmitted to humans through cat litter or from raw or uncooked meat. In pregnant women, the infectious organism can be transmitted to the fetus and cause jaundice, anemia, or nerve damage.

tranquilizer. Drug that acts to reduce mental tension and anxiety without causing depression in the user. Such drugs have facilitated treatment of certain severely disturbed psychiatric patients.

trichinosis. A parasitic disease caused by eating raw or inadequately cooked or processed pork or pork products infected with *Trichinella spiralis*. Symptoms may be absent or there may be pain, nausea, and diarrhea.

trichomoniasis vaginitis. One of the most common vaginal diseases, it is caused by a single-celled organism. Sometimes, it produces no symptoms, but often there is discharge and itching. Untreated, it can cause urinary problems.

trypanosomiasis (sleeping sickness). May be one of several diseases occurring in man and domestic animals caused by a trypanosome. The infection is marked by drowsiness, lethargy, muscular weakness, and cerebral symptoms.

tuberculosis. Three types of tubercle bacillus cause this infection: human, bovine, and avian. The human type is most responsible for the infection in man. Generally, contact is with an infected person or with contaminated milk from an infected cow.

typhoid fever. A bacterial infection caused by ingesting contaminated food, milk, or water. The bacteria responsible, *Salmonella typhosa*, are excreted in the feces and sometimes the urine of infected persons or carriers of the disease.

ulcerative colitis. Inflammation combined with ulceration of the mucous membrane lining the large intestine. Marked by acute abdominal pain, tenderness, and watery stools.

ultrasonography. The use of sound waves to produce an image or photograph of an organ or tissue. It is indicated where there is a suspicion of thyroid or gallbladder dysfunction, in certain heart problems, and in the last trimester of

You and Modern Medicine

pregnancy to determine size and position of fetus.

ultrasound (sonogram). Procedure that produces velocities in tissues that differ in density and elasticity from others. Outlines the shape of various body tissues and organs.

uremia. A toxic condition in which the kidneys fail to filter out various nitrogen-containing waste products in the blood, especially urea.

urticaria. An allergic skin reaction, more commonly called hives or nettle rash. Produces an eruption of wheals (red or white raised patches on the skin) that is accompanied by intense itching.

vaginitis. An inflammation of the vagina that may be caused by a bacterial, fungal, or protozoan infection. May also be due to irritation from chemical douches or foreign bodies, or poor hygiene of the vulval area.

varicose veins. Enlarged, twisted veins, usually in the leg, caused by damage to their one-way valves (which normally prevent a backward flow of blood); stretching of their relatively thin walls results.

vascular. The blood vessels. Collectively, the blood vessels together with the heart and lymph vessels constitute the vascular system.

vertigo. A sensation of whirling about, either of oneself or external objects, associated with difficulty in keeping one's balance. May be due to drug reactions, middle ear disease, or infection.

volvulus. A twisting upon itself of a section of intestine, causing a serious obstruction. Signs and symptoms include severe, sudden abdominal pain followed by vomiting and distention.

wart (verruca). A small skin tumor caused by papilloma viruses. They are usually benign, and may disappear spontaneously. Warts may form on fingers, elbows, face, soles of feet, or genitalia.

whooping cough (pertussis). An acute infectious disease caused by *Bordetella pertussis* and spread in the air by the cough of an infected person. Highly contagious, it is a serious childhood disease.

xanthema. Condition in which a yellow pigment, carotene, is present in the blood. Marked by yellowing of the skin and a pseudo, rather than a true, jaundice, as there is no yellow discoloration of eye whites.

x-rays. Electromagnetic radiation of a wavelength shorter than visible light or ultraviolet radiation. X-rays have the ability to penetrate the body and most other solids, and to act on photographic film, making them valuable in diagnosing diseases.

yeast infection. A popular term for several fungal infections: candidiasis, thrush, and some forms of vaginitis. Yeasts, which reproduce by budding, are unicellar fungi of the genus *Saccharomyces*.

Zollinger-Ellison syndrome. A condition characterized by tumors of the pancreas, about 60 percent of which are malignant. With the secretion of too much hydrochloric acid and pepsin, there is eventual ulceration of the intestinal lining and the stomach.

For further reference

The American Medical Directory
    American Medical Association
Angel, Jack E.
    Physician's Desk Reference
    Medical Economics Company
Belsky, Marvin S., M.D.
    How to Choose Your Doctor
    Arbor House
Berkow, Robert, M.D.
    The Merck Manual (Diagnosis and
    Therapy)
    Merck & Company
Directory of Medical Specialists
    A.N. Marquis Company
It's Good to Know About
    Mental Health
U.S. Government Printing Office
    1724-0037

Medicaid-Medicare, Which Is Which?
    U.S. Government Printing Office
Mindell, Earl
    Earl Mindell's Pill Bible
    Bantam Books
Sehnert, Keith W., M.D.
    How to Be Your Own Doctor
    Grosset & Dunlap
Someone Close to You Drinks Too Much
    U.S. Government Printing Office
Vickery, Donald, M.D. and
Fries, James F., M.D.
    Take Care of Yourself: A Consumer's
    Guide to Medical Care
    Addison-Wesley Publishing
    Company
Wolfe, Sidney and Coley, Christopher
    Pills That Don't Work
    Farrar Strauss & Giroux

Information resources:

American Hospital Association
    1 North Franklin
    Chicago, IL 60606
Joint Commission on Accreditation
    of Healthcare Organizations
    1 Renaissance Blvd.
    Oakdale Terrace, IL 60181
The National Cancer Institute
    9000 Rockville Pike
    Bethesda, MD 20892

The American Heart Association
    7272 Greenville Avenue
    Dallas, TX 75231
The U.S. Government Printing Office
    732 N. Capitol Street NW
    Washington, D.C. 20402

Managing the Family's Money

When most of us think about money, it is either about how it comes in or how it goes out. This section will not tell you how to make more money come in—except through prudent investing. It will tell you some of the ways you can control the way money goes out. Managing the family's money means keeping track of it and making sure you put it to the best use in the ways you spend and save it.

In this age of inflation, changing interest rates, and wide-ranging opportunities for saving and investing, money management has captured the interest of people everywhere. People who never spent much time thinking about the subject before are now paying for the advice of professional financial planners.

There are many paths on the financial landscape, and not all of them lead where we might hope. But there are some basic facts that can help us make sensible choices. This section sets many of them forth.

The information here is generally correct for the entire United States, but state laws do vary in some cases. If you think your state requirements might differ, ask your elected representative to check them for you.

The seven ages of your economic life

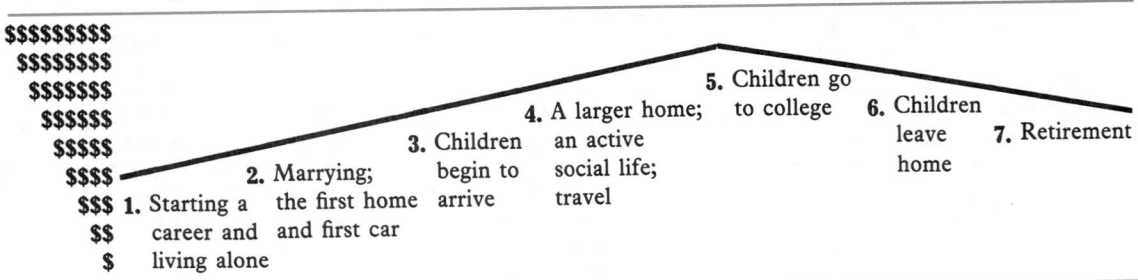

\$\$\$\$\$\$\$\$\$
\$\$\$\$\$\$\$\$
\$\$\$\$\$\$\$
\$\$\$\$\$\$
\$\$\$\$\$
\$\$\$\$
\$\$\$
\$\$
\$

1. Starting a career and living alone
2. Marrying; the first home and first car
3. Children begin to arrive
4. A larger home; an active social life; travel
5. Children go to college
6. Children leave home
7. Retirement

Planning and record-keeping

Dwight D. Eisenhower is said to have remarked when he was a general, "It's not the plan that counts, it's the planning." What he meant, of course, was that the very act of planning—setting goals, gathering facts, deciding what is important, figuring out how to get where you want to go—is worthwhile in itself. It helps you to understand what you are doing and why you are doing it. The particular plan you come up with may have to be changed or discarded in favor of a better one, but the discipline and knowledge that come from working up a plan will always be to your advantage.

Managing the family's money begins with planning. You set your goals for the kind of life you want to lead and the things you want your family to have. You get all the facts you can about how much you will need to save, to spend, and to invest. You also need to know how to make the best use of credit, the services that are available, and the potential pitfalls.

Good record-keeping is essential. You must keep receipts for important items and make note of important cash outlays. To do this, you must find a way to keep records that suits you. For one person, it might be a ledger book with neatly written entries. For another, a shoebox would be just right for keeping records on separate pieces of paper. There is nothing wrong with a shoebox provided you use it consistently and start a new one at regular intervals—every six months or a year—putting each important sales slip or receipt into it and making sure that each item is identified on the slip. Include gifts to charity, interest expense items, sales tax, and all other items you would not find recorded in your checkbook.

Planning also means keeping permanent records of basic information (such as that suggested on the next page). This information can be useful to you and your family at various times throughout the year and is absolutely essential when a family member dies. The mere act of filling out the form may suggest ideas to you. Perhaps you have partly overlapping insurance policies, or not enough coverage. As you review the

record at least once a year, changing conditions will suggest other revisions.

Your financial plan should start with your estimate of how much you are worth. Use the chart on page 112 as your guide.

Your net worth at any one time does not mean very much by itself. But if you go through the exercise of figuring out your net worth every year and you find that it is going down, this is a clear signal that something is wrong.

Next it is time to work up a budget, based on how much you earn and how much you should reasonably

Paying for college

Some schools offer tuition budget plans. You make monthly payments while your son or daughter is in college.

The Stafford Loan Program enables eligible freshmen to borrow up to $2625 a year, sophomores up to $3500, and juniors and seniors up to $5500 at low interest rates. Repayment begins on completion of studies. Parent Loans for Undergraduate Students (PLUS) are available as well. These loans have a variable interest rate, which by law cannot exceed 9 percent.

The Federal Work-Study Program (FWSP) provides part-time jobs for students who need financial aid and want to work.

Students who show exceptional need can get Federal Supplemental Educational Opportunity Grants (FSEOG) up to $4000 a year.

Students with exceptional financial need can also borrow up to $3000 at 5 percent interest from the Federal Perkins Loan program. The Pell Grant program provides grants based on need up to $3000 a year (1998-1999).

spend. Before you draw up a budget, have your family keep an informal record of expenses for a month. Then estimate how much you spend on once-a-year events like a vacation and Christmas, dividing such expenses by twelve. Make sure you take into account all other outlays that come up during the year, such as quarterly tax payments. Then summarize all your income during the year, including interest payments from the bank and dividends on life insurance. With this information on inflow and outgo, you have the basis for your budget.

If the figures show that there is not much left over for savings, review your expense items with your family and decide on what can be cut back or eliminated. Be sure to make some provision for unexpected expenses. A budget will soon fail if it is too tightly drawn up.

$1 × 10 years = 50¢

The problem of our time

Underlying all your planning, there should be an awareness of the recurring problem of our time—inflation. Remember this rule of thumb: a 7 percent increase each year would mean a doubling in ten years, which means that you would need $1 ten years from now to buy what 50 cents buys today.

When you see an advertisement for an investment that claims, for example, that $2000 a year may grow to a million dollars at your time of retirement, remember that a million dollars in the 2030's would be worth $125,000 in today's dollars, assuming 6 percent inflation.

How much are you worth?

Like a business, a family that manages its money effectively starts with a balance sheet. The difference between the assets and the liabilities is what cost accountants call *net worth*.

Assets
Cash and marketable securities
Cash in checking and
  savings accounts   _____
Certificates of deposit   _____
Mutual fund shares   _____
U.S. Savings Bonds   _____
Life insurance cash value
  (obtainable from your
  insurance agent)   _____

Other assets
Real estate (including
  your home)   _____
Pension value   _____
IRA and Keogh accounts   _____
* Automobiles   _____
* Furniture and appliances   _____
* Personal possessions   _____
      Total assets   _____

Liabilities
Current liabilities
Bills payable   _____
Installment loans   _____

Long-term liabilities
Mortgage   _____
Bank loans   _____
    Total liabilities   _____
*Depreciated   **Net worth**   _____

The family budget

No budget format would be right for all families, but here are typical items that should be included in an annual budget.

Income
Salaries   _____
Interest   _____
Dividends   _____
Sale of securities or property
  (these should be recognized
  as unusual items unless you
  sell securities every year)   _____
Bonuses
  (also to be treated as
  unusual items)   _____
      Total income   _____

Outgo
Food   _____
Clothing   _____
Automobile operating costs   _____
Shelter costs, including
  mortgage payments   _____
Miscellaneous purchases   _____
Health care   _____
Entertainment   _____
Vacation   _____
Education   _____
Interest expense   _____
Insurance premiums   _____
Charitable contributions   _____
Taxes   _____
      Total outgo   _____
    **Balance available for
    saving and investing**   _____

Managing the Family's Money

The family record

Information related to money management that should be available to everyone in your family.

Your name:
Your Social Security number: Date and place of birth:

Your spouse's name:
Spouse's Social Security number: Date and place of birth:

First child's name:
Social Security number: Date and place of birth:

Same information for each additional child:

Your employer's name and address:
Name and telephone number of your supervisor:

Spouse's employer's name and address:
Name and telephone number of supervisor:

Your attorney's name and telephone number:

Your accountant's, or tax advisor's, name and telephone number:

Your insurance agent's name and telephone number:

Your bank or savings institution officer:

Date and location of your will:
Your executor:

Numbers of bank checking and savings accounts and certificates of deposit:

Interest income:

Location of check recordbooks, passbooks, and certificates:

Your safe deposit box location and number:
Location of keys:

Description of valuable possessions and serial numbers (of such items as cameras):

Description of real estate you own:
Date and cost of purchase:
Name and address of mortgage holder:

Descriptions of investments, such as mutual fund shares:
Income from investments: Dates investments were made:
Name of investment company, bank or broker,
and numbers of the accounts:

Name of life insurance company:
Numbers and face values of the policies on your life: Loans against the policies:
Same information for policies on your spouse's life: Premium due dates:

Name of automobile insurance company:
Number and amount of the policy: Premium due date:

Name of health and disability insurance company:
Number and amount of the policy: Premium due date:

Name of home-owner's insurance company:
Number and amount of the policy:

Loans outstanding: Interest payment dates:
Repayment dates:
Mortgage balance and monthly payment:
Installment loans: Payments due:

Credit card account numbers:
Address of issuer to be notified:

Your Social Security benefit (if applicable):

Using credit wisely

Like fire and water, credit is a good servant but a poor master. The nation's economy runs on credit, and most of us have come to depend on it every day of our lives.

For most people, credit is not difficult to obtain, whether in the form of a charge account or installment credit at a store, a credit card from a bank, or a loan from a credit union.

Applying for credit. When you apply for credit, you will be asked questions about your stability in society and your ability to pay off loans. How long have you been with your present employer? Do you own your own home? If not, how long have you rented the space where you now live? Do you have checking and savings accounts? Do you have a history of paying your bills on time?

There is no fixed credit rating that follows you wherever you go. Lenders judge you by their own standards. **Credit at a store.** When you open a charge account at a department store, you may be offered a revolving account. This has a set limit on how much you can owe the store at one time, with interest to be paid every month on the unpaid balance.

If you want to buy something on the installment plan, ask yourself these two questions first: Would I pay cash for this if I had the cash available? Is what I am buying going to last longer than it will take me to pay off this loan?

Before you sign the installment contract, ask the seller for the annual percentage rate (APR). The APR, which is the total finance charge expressed as a percentage of the amount you are borrowing, is the true interest cost, and it may be higher than you realize. For example, if you paid off a loan of $100 with twelve equal monthly installments totaling $110, your true interest was not 10 percent; it was 18 percent. The amount you owed kept declining while you continued to pay interest on the total loan.

Also ask the seller for the total cost of the loan, including payments and principal, the cost of late charges, and the penalties, if any, for paying off early.

Credit unions. If you live in an area where there are few banks or savings institutions competing with each other, an economical source of credit is a local credit union. Members purchase shares in the association, and loan applications are reviewed by a committee of members. Since members do much of the administrative work with the help of a small paid staff, a credit union can give its members better value.

Credit card tips

- Be sure to sign your credit card promptly.
- Do not carry more cards than you absolutely need.
- Do not give your card to a salesperson without making sure that you get your own card back.
- When your card expires and a new one is issued, cut the old card in half before you discard it.
- When you get your credit card receipt, ask for and then destroy both of the little pieces of carbon paper. Wastebaskets are searched by credit card defrauders, who can copy your number and signature from the carbon paper, or even manufacture a fake card with your name and number.
- Do not give your credit card number to strangers who telephone you.
- Keep the numbers and issue dates of your cards with your personal records.
- Report the loss of your card immediately, even if someone telephones you to say he has found it and will return it. He may be stalling for time in which to run up charges in your name. You are not liable for any charges if you report the loss promptly.

"Plastic" from the bank. Credit cards issued by banks, such as Visa and MasterCard, are the most widely used form of credit. If you have "plastic," the best rule is to think of it not as a *credit* card but as a *charge* card—a convenience that enables you to take advantage of unexpected sales and bargains, cover emergency expenses, and shop by telephone or on the World Wide Web.

With many bank cards, it is possible to obtain free credit by paying the bill in full before the monthly due date. But if you let your balance accumulate, you may pay interest at the rate of 18 to 21 percent a year. With such a high return, your bank will not object if you take your time paying off the balance. By reducing or eliminating the balance you owe, you significantly reduce your interest costs.

Another type of bank card, called a *check card*, debits your bank account automatically when you make a purchase or withdraw money at an automated teller machine (ATM). Conventional ATM card transactions require the user to provide a personal identification number (PIN), but check card transactions do not. If your check card is lost or stolen, anyone can use it to raid your bank account. Check cards are convenient for making purchases, but they are far from risk-free.

Dealing with your bank

A bank borrows at wholesale and lends at retail. Besides paying you interest on money you deposit and charging you higher interest on money you borrow, a commercial—or full-service—bank offers a wide range of services.

In addition to checking and savings accounts, banks offer money market accounts, Individual Retirement Accounts (IRA's), Keogh accounts, certificates of deposit (CD's), home improvement loans, home mortgages, automobile loans, personal loans, and credit cards. They also provide such services as automatic teller machines (ATM's), safe deposit boxes, purchasing government bonds on your behalf, paying utility bills out of your account, and automatically depositing your paychecks or Social Security checks. Savings institutions offer some of these services, including negotiable orders of withdrawal (NOW) accounts, which are interest-bearing checking accounts.

Choosing your bank.
In selecting your bank or savings institution, remember that no service is truly free. Compare the rates and service charges with those of their competitor institutions and look at the details of the various savings plans, including certificates of deposit and money market accounts.

Ask about savings plans. Among the questions you should ask about savings plans are these: How frequently is interest compounded? What is the effective annual yield, not just the interest rate? Is interest compounded from day of deposit to day of withdrawal? Is there an interest penalty for early or frequent withdrawal? Are deposits insured? How quickly do funds become available?

You should have no difficulty obtaining the answers to such questions. A law passed in 1991 requires financial institutions to provide a great deal more information to depositors than they did in the past.

The checking account.
The greatest convenience a bank or savings institution offers is the checking account. A check is essentially theftproof and, once it has been paid and returned to you, indisputable proof that payment was made. Your check recordbook gives you a dependable and up-to-the-minute record of your cash inflow and outgo.

Banks typically offer several kinds of checking accounts. Find out if the checking services in the bank you are considering are competitive on interest paid (if any), number of checks allowed, service charges, and minimum balance required.

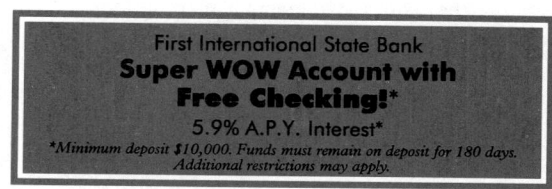

Do not choose a bank until you have read thoroughly the fine print in its brochures and agreements about interest rates and service charges.

Special checking usually involves a fee but no minimum balance; it is best suited to someone who writes less than half a dozen checks a month. *Regular checking,* for people who write more checks, is likely to require a minimum balance or service charge. A *NOW account,* at either a bank or savings institution, pays interest close to savings account rates. A *Super NOW account* pays higher rates, but it may require a minimum balance of $1000 or more, and it imposes relatively high service charges. Instead of separate NOW and Super NOW accounts, many banks simply have interest-paying checking accounts.

A *joint checking account* is a convenience for a couple, provided they both enter all their transactions in the same recordbook, which the bank provides along with the blank checks. A couple should be aware that any money in a joint account belongs legally to either person and can be completely withdrawn without the other's knowledge. Since some states freeze a joint account when one of the co-owners dies, it is essential for the survivor to have access to other funds at such a time.

Do not make out a check to "cash" unless you immediately give it to the recipient, because you have thereby turned your check into cash. If your checkbook is stolen, notify the bank immediately so that your account can be frozen. The bank will honor only those checks that you have written.

If you write a check and then decide you do not want it honored, call the bank's stop-payment department. It will stop payment for a fee, provided there would have been enough in your account to pay the check anyway. Notify the person to whom you issued the check.

When you make a deposit into your checking account, your bank is required by law to credit the account with at least $100 on the next business day; the full amount of a local bank check on the second business day; and the full amount of any out-of-town check by the fifth business day. Always deposit a check as soon as you receive it.

Balancing your checkbook.

After you receive your checking account statement from the bank, balance your check recordbook against the statement within a few days. If you wait longer and find an error in the bank's statement, it may be too late for them to locate their error speedily.

Although it should be a simple matter to balance your check recordbook, some people find it confusing because not all of the checks that have been written clear the bank by the time a statement is completed.

The figure on the last line of your table should equal the balance on the bank statement. If it is off by a significant amount, check your arithmetic, making sure you did not add when you should have subtracted, or vice versa. If your balance is off by an insignificant amount, assume the bank statement to be correct and make a compensating entry on the first open line of your check recordbook.

How to balance your checkbook

1. Arrange the canceled checks in numerical order.
2. Check them off in pencil against the debit column of the bank's statement.
3. Go through the canceled checks again, this time checking them off in pencil against the entries in your check recordbook. The lowest-numbered checks will probably include a few that did not clear before the previous statement.
4. When you come to a check in your recordbook that has not yet cleared the bank, draw a circle in red around the number of that check in the recordbook.
5. Go through the same two procedures with your deposit slips. If you have entered a deposit in your check recordbook that does not show up on the bank statement, draw a red circle around it in the recordbook.
6. Draw a red line underneath the last check in your recordbook that is also shown on the bank statement. This is the cutoff point.
7. Enter in your recordbook the bank's debit for charges and credit for interest (if any), so that these amounts will be reflected in your own balance before the next statement comes from the bank.
8. Draw up a simple table on a piece of paper like this:

Your recordbook balance
    (the last balance above the
    red line you drew)   ———

Plus Total of outstanding checks
    (those you circled in red)   + ———

Plus Any interest credited to your
    statement (if it is an
    interest-bearing account)   + ———
               Total   ———

Minus Recent deposits entered by you
    but not yet credited by the
    bank (circled in red)   − ———
          Difference   ———

Minus Service charges shown on the
    bank statement   − ———
       Difference: Your balance   ———

Do's and don'ts of writing a check

Face of check
1. Name and address printed on check make it easier to cash.
2. Number your checks if they are not already numbered.
3. Date properly; never postdate. It *is* legal to date a check on a Sunday or holiday.
4. Do not use Mr., Mrs., Ms., or Miss.
5. Do not leave a space between $ and the first digit.
6. Start writing at the end of the line. The written figure with the fraction is the amount the bank pays.
7. Draw a line between the fraction and "dollars."
8. The memo entry is for your convenience only.
9. Sign the same way every time. Do not write in pencil, even though it is legal. If you make a mistake, tear up the check and cross out the check number in your check recordbook.

Back of check
10. Endorse on back of left end.
11. Endorse exactly as your name appears on the face of the check as payee. Write your regular name underneath in parentheses.
12. Writing "for deposit only" will prevent the check from being cashed by someone else.

Other kinds of checks. For an unusual transaction, you may be asked to pay with a certified check. In this case, you write your own check for a specific amount to a specific payee and take it to your bank, where it will be signed and stamped by a bank officer. At the same time, the officer will reserve that amount from your account so that there will be enough to pay the check when it comes in, regardless of what other checks you write. At this point, your certified check is as good as cash and should be given directly to the payee. Avoid sending it by mail or messenger.

A cashier's check has similar uses. It is made out and signed by an officer of the bank in return for a payment by you to the bank. It is best to have it made out to your name so that there is a record that the payment is going through your hands. You can then endorse it, photocopy it, hand it over to the payee, and ask for a receipt.

Most banks provide traveler's checks, which are issued by a few large banks or other financial institutions known around the world. Traveler's checks are useful when you are traveling or moving because they are usually accepted everywhere while personal checks are not. If lost, traveler's checks can be replaced and the money returned. But they should not be held for a long time. When you buy one, you are in effect lending the bank your money at no interest, and at a small charge to you. Always carry one or two traveler's checks for emergencies.

A place for your savings.

Banks compete vigorously for your savings. In addition to the traditional passbook savings account, many banks and savings institutions now offer time deposit accounts with fixed interest. Usually referred to as CD's, these insured accounts have minimum periods of deposit ranging from thirty days to as long as ten years, with penalties for early withdrawal.

Banks also offer money market deposit accounts, which pay interest that is adjusted periodically in line with interest rates in the money market. This is the market where short-term debt securities are traded. Some banks require a minimum deposit in a money market account.

A place to borrow.

On the other side of the banking business, there is at least as much competition to lend you money.

One of the simplest and most economical ways to borrow at a bank or savings institution is to borrow against your own passbook. The interest rate is lower than on a regular loan, and you continue to earn interest on your entire deposit. Some banks, however, have discontinued passbook accounts.

Many banks also offer overdraft checking accounts under various names. You activate your account sim-

Do not carry your ATM number

- Be sure *not* to write your ATM identification number on anything you carry or keep at your place of work. Keep the only record of the number in a safe place at home.
- Always check your receipt before leaving.
- Make sure the machine is back to its original setting.
- As soon as you get home, enter your ATM transaction in your recordbook.
- If you lose your ATM access card, call the bank immediately. If the card is used by someone who has found out your ATM identification number, you will have to file a report with the police.

ply by writing one of the special checks for that account given to you by the bank. Each month you receive a statement specifying the part of the loan to be paid back that month and the high interest rate charges you have to pay.

You can obtain loans at banks for a variety of specific needs. In applying for such a loan, be sure to ask the annual percentage rate. This is the total finance charge—more than simple interest—expressed as a percentage of the amount borrowed.

Some banks also offer debt consolidation loans, for people who are unable to keep up with their bills. The idea sounds appealing because your monthly payment for the loan can be less than the monthly total for all your bills. The bank achieves this sleight-of-hand by stretching out the payments over a long period of time; thus, the total interest you pay is very high.

Other bank services.

Automatic teller machines (ATM's) enable you to make deposits or withdrawals at any hour of the day, including weekends and holidays. This means you can make a deposit without carrying cash or checks around, and you can begin earning interest immediately. It also means you can obtain cash whenever you need it.

Safe deposit boxes are useful for storing items difficult to replace. These include securities; the deed to your house; the title to your automobile; birth and marriage certificates; your home-owner's insurance policy; an inventory of possessions in your house; and a copy—not the original—of your will. Since some states seal safe deposit boxes on the death of the owner, do not store any items that would be needed right after your death. Keep a list at home of the contents of your box. The bank is not responsible for the loss of the contents.

Saving and investing

Everyone knows it is wise to put something aside regularly. Everyone also knows of good uses for the money saved.

Clearly, some ways of saving are easier than others, and some investments are safer than others. U.S. Savings Bonds purchased through the payroll savings plan and mutual fund shares acquired with regular monthly payments offer good investment and good savings.

Savings bonds.
U.S. Savings Bonds, Series EE, once considered an unappealing investment choice in a time of high interest rates, are now more attractive. The most secure of all savings or investments, because they are backed by the U.S. government, they now offer—when held for five years or more—an interest rate that equals 85 percent of the average yield on U.S. Treasury five-year notes. The rate changes twice a year, on May 1 and November 1. The bonds are purchased for half of their face value, which ranges from $25 to $10,000, and can be redeemed at any time after the fifth year. After ten years, an EE bond purchased for $25 can be worth its face value of $50 or more, depending on how much interest has been accumulated; it will continue to earn interest until 40 years after the issue date if issued before December, 1965; 30 years if issued after November, 1965. Federal income taxes do not have to be paid on any of the interest until the bonds are redeemed. The interest may be tax free if used to pay college tuition for you or your dependents. EE bonds are not subject to state and local income tax.

Great American tax shelters.
In recent years, three forms of investment have been introduced through changes in the tax laws. They have made it highly attractive for employed and self-employed people to save for their retirement.

Individual Retirement Accounts (IRAs). The Taxpayer Relief Act of 1997 made important changes in the regulations regarding IRAs. Now there are three different IRAs from which to choose.

A traditional IRA offers any person earning at least $2000 a year who is not covered by an employer pension plan or, if covered, has a modified adjusted gross income of less than $32,000 (single person) or $52,000 (joint return) an opportunity to make a tax-deductible contribution of $2000 to an IRA account. In addition, married couples filing a joint return can contribute up to $4000, even if one spouse has little or no additional income.

You can take an IRA deduction even if you do not itemize deductions on your tax return. More important in the long run, any income earned in the IRA account is sheltered from income tax until you withdraw it.

Withdrawals may begin at age 59½ without a tax penalty. You *must* begin withdrawing funds at age 70½, according to a schedule based on your life expectancy.

Your deposit can be made as late as April 15 in the year following the year for which you want to take the deduction on your income tax. The sooner you make the deposit, however, the sooner it will begin earning tax-sheltered income.

The new Roth IRA allows taxpayers to contribute up to $2000, minus any amount contributed to a traditional IRA. The $2000 limit is eliminated in steps for individuals earning between $95,000 and $110,000 and couples earning between $150,000 and $160,000. Unlike the traditional IRA, the contribution is not tax deductible but the earnings from the account are tax free if the account has been funded for five years.

The new Education IRA allows taxpayers to contribute up to $500 per year per child under the age of 18 to pay for postsecondary educational expenses such as tuition, supplies, room and board, and books. Like the Roth IRA, contributions to an Education IRA are not tax deductible but the earnings are tax free. Funds deposited or earned in an Education IRA must be used or transferred to another qualifying Education IRA before the student reaches age 30.

Keogh accounts. Self-employed people can invest not only in IRAs but also in Keogh accounts, which work in a similar way.

Managing the Family's Money

If you are self-employed, you can invest in a profit-sharing Keogh plan and claim a deduction each year for as much as 13.04 percent of your net earnings up to a maximum of $30,000. This would be in addition to the $2000 that you can invest in an IRA if your adjusted gross income is below $25,000 (single person) or $40,000 (joint return). The deposit can be made as late as the due date of your tax return. You can begin withdrawals as early as age 59½ without a tax penalty, and you must begin withdrawing by age 70½.

401 (k) savings plans. Following the reduction of tax benefits from IRAs for middle- and upper-income earners, employees planning for retirement have been attracted to tax-deferred savings plans, principally the 401 (k). Available from many large employers and some smaller ones, a 401 (k) shelters part of your current income from tax by permitting you to defer part of your salary. The limit on how much you can defer, which was $10,000 in 1998, increases with inflation.

Your employer may match at least part of every dollar you set aside, and this addition to your income is also exempt from current tax. Income earned by your investment builds up—also free of tax—until you withdraw your funds. Payroll deduction makes saving attractive.

Your investment choices.
Many people look for opportunities for investment, but few have the expert knowledge to select from the many choices offered by the financial markets. Except for the wealthy person who can pay for expert advice, it is nearly impossible for an investor to obtain professional, unbiased recommendations on which stocks or bonds to buy and, sometimes more important, when to sell.

Mutual funds. Many investors meet the problem of obtaining expert advice by purchasing shares in mutual funds. Owning large, diversified portfolios of stocks or bonds selected and continuously reviewed by professional managers, mutual funds spread the risk, and they can be bought and sold easily.

Many mutual funds have a sales charge as high as 8.5 percent of the investment. These are called "load" funds. "No-load" funds, so called because they have no sales commission and charge only a management fee of typically no more than 1 percent a year, perform in many cases as well as the load funds or better.

In either case, you can select a fund according to its investment objective—income (from high-dividend stocks and corporate or government bonds); growth (with investments in stocks that involve more than average risk); or balance (offering both income and growth). Funds are rated according to their performance every year in magazines that you will find at your library, including *Forbes* and *Money*.

Mutual funds can be purchased under various plans. If you do not have a large sum to invest at once, you might consider the contractual plan, under which you pay a fixed amount each month.

Dividends are paid every quarter from the income on the fund's portfolio of investments. Once a year, the fund makes a capital gain distribution based on any increase in the value of the shares of the stocks it owns.

Money market funds. Many investment companies that manage mutual funds also offer money market funds. These funds are directly competitive with banks' money market accounts, and tend to have somewhat higher returns on investment. Unlike the banks' accounts, money market funds are not insured by the government; but you can, if you wish, select a fund that invests only in U.S. Treasury securities, which is as good as insurance.

A family of funds. If you have not invested in mutual funds before, you could pick an investment company with a family of funds and start in their money market fund until you build up a substantial amount of cash. Then you could switch all or part of that money to one or more of the other funds in the same group.

Real estate.
A completely different kind of investment—and, in the view of many, a hedge against inflation—is real estate. Before the Tax Reform Act of 1986 took effect, real estate investments offered significant tax advantages to people in higher income brackets. But tax considerations aside, there are some disadvantages to real estate for investors to keep in mind.

If the neighborhood deteriorates, you may have to sell at a sacrifice. In a time of depression, any real estate value is likely to suffer. If your property stays undeveloped, it produces no income but still gets taxed. Values are no longer rising as they did in the early 1980's, and in many areas they have fallen.

If you are, nevertheless, persuaded by the argument that the supply of land is fixed while the number of people keeps growing, limit your real estate investing to opportunities in your own area. Then you can see for yourself what is happening to values. Experts say the best residential real estate investment, whether you live in it or not, is a medium-priced house in a neighborhood that is desirable or improving. Typical buyers consider three bedrooms and two baths essential.

An investment that's sure to pay off

Looking for a risk-free investment with a good return? If your credit card debt is piling up, think about paying it all off at once. The return will be equivalent to the interest charge you no longer have to pay—as high as 20 percent.

Looking ahead to tax time

Income tax instructions have been simplified in recent years, and several inexpensive books are available to help you prepare your return. Whether you do your own return or have it done for you, it is essential to keep good records throughout the year. These include

- property tax receipts;
- canceled checks for gifts to charity, tax payments, and other deductible items;
- receipted bills for moving expenses;
- medical bills;
- bills for expenses in connection with your job, such as safety equipment, for which you have not been reimbursed.

The Internal Revenue Service (IRS) urges you to continue keeping such records three years after a return is filed, after which the statute of limitations runs out for IRS action on that particular return.

The IRS also suggests that you read the tax form when you receive it at the beginning of the year and make sure that you understand it; collect all your records early; begin to work on the sample sheets; and call the nearest IRS office if you have any questions. The earlier in the year you do this, the easier it will be to get their attention.

After you have filled out your return, wait until just before April 15 to mail it. The funds that you have to provide with the return can be earning money for you at the bank until the filing date. More important, you are likely to pick up an error you may have made if you give yourself plenty of time to review the figures. The IRS says that people who prepare their returns just before the deadline make the most errors.

Income you do not have to report

- Accident and health insurance benefits
- Benefits from disability insurance you purchased yourself
- Federal income tax refunds
- Gifts to you
- Life insurance dividends (unless they include interest on reinvested dividends)
- Life insurance proceeds
- Sick pay (if permanently and totally disabled)
- Social Security benefits (unless your adjusted gross income [1999]—including half of Social Security retirement benefits—is more than $25,000 for you alone or $32,000 for you and your spouse filing jointly)
- Veterans' benefits
- Welfare payments
- Workmen's compensation

Start work on completing your tax return early, but wait until the last minute before returning it with your check.

Confusing income tax terms

exemption: gives every taxpayer and dependent (except those with high incomes) a deduction ($2800 for 2000).

deduction: an amount that you are allowed to subtract from your income *before* computing your tax.

credit: an amount that you subtract from your tax *after* computing it; thus it is worth more than a deduction.

deferral: a tax obligation that you do not have to pay as long as the income is sheltered.

exclusion: an option to avoid a tax—such as on profits from selling a house or on income earned abroad.

Do you like to get a big refund?

If you like to get a big refund on your income tax, you are not managing your money the best way.

Getting a refund means you have given the government the use of your money for nothing, because a refund comes to you with absolutely no interest.

If you got a big refund last year, try doing an estimate of what your tax is going to be for the current year. If you find that too much of your income is being withheld, ask your employer for a W-4 form. Using the formula on the form, figure out how many allowances to request in order to bring your total withholding for the year close to your estimated tax.

You will not have a nice refund to look forward to, but you will have the use of funds to invest yourself.

Tax facts

Loss on sale. You cannot deduct a loss on a sale of property or goods to close relatives—grandparents, parents, children, brothers, sisters, spouse.

Working at home. If you are unable to set aside a whole room as an office for a business that you carry on at home, you can meet the IRS test for a home office by setting up a partition to separate the office area from the rest of the room.

Selling your house. If you sell your primary residence after May 6, 1997, you can exclude up to $250,000 of the profit on the sale from your income tax if you file as a single taxpayer, or up to $500,000 if you are married and file a joint return and certain conditions are met (see page 150). On home sales prior to May 7, 1997, you can postpone tax on the capital gain if you buy another home within a two-year replacement period or, if you are age 55 or older and meet certain conditions, exclude up to $125,000 from your taxes.

Job deductions. You can deduct the cost of looking for a new job *in the same line of work* as you are currently in, along with the cost of courses to maintain or improve your job skills.

Marriage penalty. A working married couple is penalized in comparison with two single people with the same income, and the couple can no longer take a deduction to minimize the penalty.

Itemizing deductions. Nearly all home owners save taxes by itemizing deductions instead of taking the standard deduction, chiefly because of interest costs on the mortgage.

State tax deduction. Your deduction for state income taxes should be the actual cash outlay for the tax year, not the amount shown on your latest state tax return.

Moving costs. Moving costs and unreimbursed employee business expenses can be subtracted from your income as an itemized deduction. The moving deduction is allowed only if a change in your work place has added at least 35 miles to the distance from your previous home to the new work place.

Travel expenses. Although daily travel expenses from home to work are definitely not deductible, you can deduct travel expenses from one regular job to another.

Child care credit. If you work full- or part-time, you may qualify for a tax credit for the expenses of caring for children—or other dependents—while you are at work. The credit is 20 to 30 percent of as much as $2400 of care expenses for one dependent or $4800 for two or more dependents.

Baby exemption. A baby born on December 31 counts as an exemption for the whole year.

Deceased spouse. If your spouse dies during the year, you may file a joint return for that year and continue to do so for two more years, provided you have at least one dependent child and do not remarry during that time.

Estate taxes. Not to be confused with income taxes, these are paid out of the estate of a deceased person. In no case do heirs pay *income* taxes on money they inherit. (Income tax, however, is paid out of the estate if the deceased had taxable income in the final year.

"Quarterly" intervals. If you file an estimated return, remember that payments are not due at regular three-month intervals. Starting with the April 15 filing, succeeding intervals are two, three, four, and three months.

Buying insurance

When you take out an insurance policy, you are betting that something unfortunate will happen to you at some time. The insurance company is betting it will not happen, at least for quite a while. If nothing happens to you for many years, you and the insurance company both win—in different ways. If something does happen to you, nobody wins, but the insurance coverage helps protect you or your family from financial disaster.

The rates you pay for insurance reflect to some degree the odds of something happening to you. But there is clearly more to buying insurance than knowing the odds. In each field—life, health, home owners, and automobile—you have to make your choice from many types of policies offered by many companies at different prices. Some kinds of coverage are far more economical and effective than others.

Life insurance.
The first rule about life insurance is not to buy it until someone is dependent on the earning power of the insured person. That is why it makes no sense to buy it when you are just out of college, or to insure the life of a child, as some do.

A rule of thumb many people follow is to buy enough life insurance to make up for five years of the breadwinner's take-home pay. You should also find out how much your family would receive in Social Security survivors' benefits if the breadwinner died now. Your local Social Security office will figure this out for you if you make it clear that you are not asking them to estimate how much you will get in retirement benefits at a future date.

After you have decided how much coverage you need, it is time to select an insurance company. Do not wait for an agent to call on you; he or she will come primed with all the reasons why you should buy from a particular company. If you have a good library nearby, ask to see a copy of *Best's Insurance Reports*, which rates the quality of companies from A++ to C−, the lowest passing grade. No matter where you live, make sure the company is licensed to write insurance in New York State, which has unusually strict standards.

There are two basic kinds of life insurance policy—whole life (also called straight, ordinary, or permanent) and term insurance.

Whole life. This is a combination of insurance and savings, since it eventually builds up a cash value that you can borrow against or cash in. Insurance companies will not tell you how much of your whole life premium is going for savings. Purely from a savings point of view, you would probably do almost as well to

---

Insurance-buying strategy

Whether you are buying major medical, homeowner's, or automobile liability insurance, a simple strategy can give you the most effective coverage and help protect you from being financially wiped out.

The strategy is to *accept the highest deductible you think you can handle.* Then, using the money you save, buy the highest coverage you can afford. In exchange for the temporary hardship that a high deductible may cause, you will be buying protection against a financial disaster that could impoverish you and your family for life.

For example, if you increased the deductible on your automobile collision insurance from $200 to $500, you would save up to a quarter of your premium. It would cost you only a small part of that savings to increase your automobile liability insurance from maximum coverage of $300,000 for all the people in one accident to $1,000,000 coverage.

---

save money in a passbook loan account. In fact, the return on your investment in a whole life policy is negative for about the first ten years.

When you take out a whole life policy, the premiums are fixed for life. Since the cost of one company's coverage is hard to compare with that of another, ask your agent to show you the interest adjusted cost index for the policy. This takes into account dividends, cash value, and interest you would have earned if you had invested elsewhere. The lower the index figure, the more favorable the comparison.

Some companies also offer whole life without dividends, which means lower premiums. In any case, ask whether the policy has a waiver of premium in the event of your total and permanent disability, and double indemnity in the event of your accidental death. Also ask about discounts for nonsmokers and people who exercise regularly.

The head of a family needs the most insurance when he or she is young and with dependents. Thus, there may come a time when it no longer seems necessary to continue paying premiums on whole life insurance. At that time, take the cash value, which is roughly two-thirds of the face value after 25 to 30 years, or accept reduced coverage without further premiums. Or con-

Managing the Family's Money

vert to term insurance, with the same coverage for a limited time.

When you have built up cash value in a whole life policy, it is the most accessible source of funds for borrowing, short of a passbook loan. Insurance companies charge in the range of 6 to 8 percent annual interest for loans against whole life policies. If you choose not to pay the interest, the insurance company simply adds the unpaid interest to your outstanding loan. Because there is no time limit on a policy loan—it is really your own money you are borrowing—there is a great temptation not to pay it back. Some investors deliberately do not pay it back because they do so much better by putting the funds elsewhere. If you do this, of course, there would be less coverage for your heirs, or less value for you if you decided to cash in the policy. The interest on a life insurance loan is not tax-deductible in most cases.

Term insurance. This is life insurance pure and simple, without any savings feature. It starts off in the early years with premiums as low as one-fifth of whole life. That is why insurance agents make lower commissions selling term and thus have far less enthusiasm for it than they do for whole life. Like whole life, term insurance can be bought without dividends, which makes the premiums even lower.

The early years of marriage, when you have children and your spouse may be dependent on you, are not only the years when you need a lot of coverage. They are also the years during which you are less able to pay high premiums, hence, the great appeal of term insurance. The most popular way to buy term is called "annual, renewable, and convertible." This means that the rates go up every year on a fixed schedule; you have the right to renew at the end of each term (generally five years) until you are in your sixties or older; you can convert without a physical examination to whole life whenever you choose. Future premiums are stated in the contract and cannot be changed. But term insurance has no cash value and coverage lasts only as long as you pay premiums.

Since term premiums rise sharply as you get older, you may wish to convert to whole life, with its fixed rates. The time to make this conversion is before one's late forties, after which rates go up significantly.

Universal life. A third basic type of life insurance, universal life, combines term insurance with savings that earn bond-market rates. You are told, moreover, how much of your premiums are going into savings, which is not the case with whole life. Because of administrative fees, universal life is not economical in policies of less than about $50,000.

Mail order life insurance. Some life insurance is sold by mail to members of associations or such groups as users of an oil company credit card. This is generally

an economical way to buy insurance, provided the company is well rated by Best's and licensed in New York State, and you cannot be turned down when you apply. Bear in mind, however, that premium rates are not guaranteed and you lose the coverage if you happen to leave the group.

Health insurance.
Every one needs three kinds of health insurance, and a wage-earner needs a fourth as well.

The three kinds are for hospitalization; other basic medical expenses, including surgery and doctors' fees; and major medical fees, in the event of a lengthy or catastrophic illness. The fourth kind, which most wage-earners tend to skimp on, is for disability coverage, to make up for loss of income if a breadwinner is disabled for a long time.

Some private companies offer comprehensive insurance, which combines the first three types. Such a policy is not necessarily the most economical. Compared with private companies, Blue Cross and Blue Shield, which are not-for-profit organizations with great economies of scale, pay out a very high proportion of each dollar they take in. Blue Cross is available through group plans at places of employment or on an individual basis and covers hospitalization. Blue Shield covers the other basic medical expenses. Both provide major medical coverage, mainly to groups.

The Blues have different plans for different areas of the country, with rates based on where you live and how many people are covered, rather than on age, sex,

---

Life insurance over 55?

Advertisements on TV may sound appealing: life insurance for people over 55 with no medical examination and a monthly premium of a few dollars. But the premium is likely to be for $1000 of coverage. Multiply that by twelve months and the number of thousands you want, and the annual premium may not seem a bargain. Finally, it makes no sense to buy life insurance unless someone is dependent on your earning power.

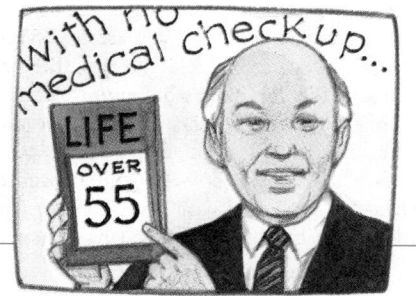

Is an HMO best for you and your family?

If your company offers health benefits, you probably have the option of joining a Health Maintenance Organization (HMO). You can also join one if you are not employed by such a company.

Bringing the physician, the laboratory, and the clinic together, an HMO provides—for a flat fee paid in advance—virtually all the medical services you might need, except dental and long-term psychiatric care.

The largest HMOs include programs run in some states by Blue Cross/Blue Shield in addition to their other operations.

Although HMOs save you money, the services and choices they offer may be less than you want. A variation on the HMO that you might consider includes the IPA (independent practice arrangement), which pays doctors set fees for treating you in their own offices.

or health. The family rate covers a family of any size, a particular attraction for large families. The hospital and the other providers of service are paid directly, saving you the need to have cash available. The policies are guaranteed renewable, and any one may sign up during the annual open enrollment period. The Blues may, however, exclude coverage for a preexisting condition for a certain period. As economical and dependable as Blue Cross/Blue Shield coverage is, you may want to consider purchasing additional major medical coverage from a private company to supplement your coverage from the Blues.

When you purchase major medical coverage, accept a high deductible and buy maximum coverage. Ask whether the maximum applies to each illness or injury, or whether it is merely a lifetime total. The latter is clearly less desirable. Also find out whether the "internal limits" of coverage are adequate—the hospital day rate, for example.

When you purchase disability insurance, the amount of income it would pay should be enough to make up for your loss of wages until you are, say, 65. Make sure the policy is not cancelable and that there is no question about the company's definition of disability: you are unable to work at the occupation for which you have been trained. Premiums will be cheaper if you buy coverage that does not begin until a certain period, such as 90 days after you are disabled. Many wage-earners who buy life insurance have never seriously considered disability insurance, not realizing how much of a burden to a family a disabled person would be.

Home-owner's insurance. This is the insurance that covers damage to your home and belongings, and provides liability coverage for injury to others on your property. It also covers damage to other people's property *accidentally* caused by you or your family, or by accidents originating on your property, such as falling trees.

Two particular points to remember about this insurance are that it does not include damage from floods or earthquakes and that the coverage you buy should be at least 80 percent of the replacement cost—not the market value—of your house. Again, accept a high deductible and use the savings to buy liability coverage that will keep you from being wiped out. Awards by juries of a million dollars are not uncommon. "Umbrella liability" insurance to cover you up to that amount can be purchased as a wrap-around for adequate home-owner's and automobile policies for not much more than $100.

Home-owner's insurance comes in various packages. The most popular, called Home-Owner's 3 (HO-3), includes all-risk coverage on your dwelling—for everything except floods, earthquakes, wars, nuclear accidents, and anything else specified—plus limited risk coverage on your personal belongings.

When you insure your house for 80 percent or more of its replacement cost, damage to any part of the house, such as a bathroom, will be covered at full replacement cost. If the entire house is destroyed, you will receive only 80 percent of the total replacement cost. If you can afford it, you should consider 100 percent coverage on the house.

Your belongings are generally covered for 50 percent of the insured value of the house, which you may want to increase if you have unusually valuable possessions. Your home-owner's policy will also pay your additional temporary living expenses if your house is too damaged to live in, and it will cover losses away from home of belongings up to certain limits for various items. Home-owner's will also pay *up to* $500 if you lose your credit card. The standard personal liability coverage for a home-owner's policy is $100,000, making it highly desirable to purchase additional coverage at a small cost.

Because replacement costs increase every year although the market value of a house may not, it is essential to keep your coverage in step with inflation. You can have an "inflation-guard" provision added to a new or existing policy. This will provide for automatic increases in coverage and save you from having to review your policy each year.

Flood and earthquake coverage

Flood and earthquake coverage, not included in home-owner's policies, can be obtained under separate policies.

For information about flood coverage, which is written by local insurance agents and guaranteed by the federal government, call the National Flood Insurance Program, 800-638-6620.

Automobile insurance. As with health and home-owner's insurance, accept a high deductible and buy extra liability coverage. A rule of thumb for a deductible on automobile insurance is slightly more than a week's take-home pay.

Automobile insurance includes five different kinds: **Liability.** Typical coverage is called 100/300/50: $100,000 for injury to one person; $300,000 maximum for all the people in one accident; $50,000 for property damage. If you own a house and other assets and even have umbrella coverage, consider increasing your liability coverage to 250/500/100 or more. The additional coverage costs little more.

Insurance planning worksheet: a checklist

To find out if you have enough insurance—or more than you need—it pays to look through your policies.

Life insurance
What is the total coverage you have (including group coverage by your employer)?

What is the value of each policy and what is the annual premium and dividend?

Do the policies have double indemnity (double payment in case of death by accident)?

What do you estimate to be the cash value? (Your agent can help you.)

What loans have you made against any of the policies?

What assets would your heirs receive in addition to Social Security survivors' benefits?

How long would you expect your survivors to need to adjust to the loss of your income?

Health and disability insurance
How much coverage do your various policies provide?

What is the cost to you?

How much could you afford to pay yourself in case of an extended illness?

How much disability insurance coverage do you have from your employer?

Home-owner's insurance
What do you estimate is the replacement cost of your home?

How much of that cost could you assume in the event the house was totally destroyed?

What is the value of your personal possessions?

If a valuable possession were lost, how much of the replacement cost would you be able to assume?

Automobile insurance
How much coverage does your policy provide for injury to one person?

What is the maximum for all the people in one accident?

How much coverage do you have for collision insurance? Could you afford a larger deductible?

When will your car be five years old and thus no longer worth covering with collision insurance?

Would your uninsured driver coverage be adequate if the breadwinner in your family were seriously injured?

Umbrella insurance
Do you have umbrella insurance to increase your protection against damage awards not adequately covered by home-owner's or automobile insurance? Is your umbrella coverage adequate in light of the million-dollar-or-more awards frequently granted?

Collision. The most expensive automobile insurance, this covers damage you yourself cause to your car. It should be dropped when a car is four to five years old.
Comprehensive. Also expensive, this covers damage other than that caused by collisions.
Uninsured driver. Cheap and highly desirable, this insurance covers injuries caused by an uninsured or insufficiently insured driver, or a hit-and-run driver.

Medical. This automobile insurance covers treatment for you and your passengers. It is included in your basic coverage except in certain states that have no-fault insurance.

It is worth shopping around for automobile insurance, since rates and quality of service vary widely. Some companies have lower rates for people over 65 no longer driving to work.

Putting your affairs in order

Your estate is what you leave when you die. It consists of all your property, including real estate, investments, bank accounts, life insurance proceeds, personal possessions, and any interests you might have in business ventures. From the total value of your estate are deducted funeral expenses, fees for executors and lawyers, state inheritance taxes, and any outstanding debts.

What is left is subject to federal *estate* taxes—not income taxes. As a result of changes in the tax laws in recent years, few estates are subject to federal taxes. No tax return has to be filed for a gross estate (before deductions) of less than $600,000. Moreover, you can leave any amount in any year to your spouse without incurring a federal estate tax. If your estate will be large enough to be subject to federal tax, you should consult your lawyer or accountant on the best way to

keep your tax to a minimum.

After a person dies, his or her will is probated. Probate is the process of filing a will with the appropriate court and having it declared valid; this process can take several months. Certain property, however, passes directly to the beneficiaries without their having to wait for probate. This includes life insurance proceeds (which are paid directly by the insurance company when notified by your agent); pension benefits to a beneficiary named by the pensioner (although not all pension arrangements call for the survivor to receive benefits); U.S. Savings Bonds (if jointly held or if solely held with a designated beneficiary named on the face of the bond); property held in joint tenancy (that is, with the survivor having the right to receive the property); and joint bank accounts.

Your heirs do not have to pay any *income* taxes on life insurance proceeds or anything else they receive from your estate, whether written into the will or not.

In some states, joint bank accounts may be frozen and safe deposit vaults sealed until the state is satisfied that state taxes have been paid for the year in which the person died. That is why it is important for your survivors to have access to funds outside of joint bank accounts—and why your vault should not contain any document, such as a life insurance policy, that would be needed right after your death.

Funeral arrangements should be made clear in the instructions you leave for survivors. A federal law requires funeral directors to break down the costs of the various services they provide when quoting a price for a funeral.

There are certain facts a funeral director might not mention unless asked. No state requires embalming unless a body is to be shipped, but funeral directors do it routinely. Burial vaults required for caskets by certain cemeteries can be simpler and far less costly than the ones recommended by many funeral directors. Caskets usually are not required for cremation. Cremation costs far less than burial.

**What to do
when the head of the family dies**

- Notify employer.
- Notify lawyer who drew up the will.
- Notify life insurance agent.
- Cancel all credit cards, or convert them to the name of the surviving spouse.
- Notify the local Social Security office, which will arrange for a funeral benefit of $255 and advise on possible benefits for survivors.
- Notify the nearest Veterans Administration (VA) office if the deceased was in the armed services. The VA will provide for a wartime veteran or any veteran who suffered a disability a $300 funeral allowance, a $150 allowance if the burial is not in a national cemetery, and a flag for the casket. (Burial in a national cemetery is free for any veteran and for his or her spouse and children in the same grave.)

Managing the Family's Money

Planning for retirement

The time to start planning for retirement is when you still have many paychecks ahead of you.

Social Security and, for those who have them, pensions are only a base on which to build a satisfactory retirement income. To achieve an income at the desirable level of two-thirds of your preretirement income, you clearly need your own savings and investments. The sooner you start setting aside a certain amount for retirement out of every paycheck, the smaller the monthly amount will have to be.

In planning your retirement income, consider a variety of investments because your Social Security and pension benefits may not be adequate.

Your retirement needs. Allowing for continued inflation, you can project how much income you are likely to need after you retire. Some of your needs, such as transportation, may end. Taxes will be lower. Some of your costs, such as your mortgage, will remain fixed and thus insulated from inflation. Your savings are likely to earn higher interest as inflation continues, and your Social Security benefits will be indexed for inflation.

On this page is a table that suggests how you can go about estimating your retirement living costs. If you are still many years away from retirement, it is too early to work out a close estimate of your income from Social Security; in addition, your local Social Security office will be reluctant to help you until you get much closer to retirement. Your pension would also be difficult to estimate many years ahead. But it is still worth trying to get some idea of your retirement needs so that you can plan your savings and investment program wisely.

How much retirement income will you need?

Item	What each item costs you now per month*	What it would cost you in retirement today (current dollars)	What it would cost you in future retirement (inflated dollars)
Food	_____	_____	_____
Shelter (including mortgage, maintenance, fuel, and utilities)	_____	_____	_____
Transportation	_____	_____	_____
Clothing	_____	_____	_____
Medical	_____	_____	_____
Insurance	_____	_____	_____
Vacation	_____	_____	_____
Entertainment	_____	_____	_____
Savings and investments	_____	_____	_____
Total	_____	_____	_____

To calculate for inflation, use a compound interest table from your local library to see how much one dollar of expense would increase over the number of years until you retire. For example, at 5 percent annual inflation for ten years, it would increase to $1.63. Multiply the current figure by that amount to get an inflation-adjusted total.

*For items that do not come up every month, such as a vacation, divide the total yearly cost by 12.

Social Security.

Your Social Security benefits are based on the number of years you have been paying Social Security taxes and your earnings over certain of those years. No one has to work more than the equivalent of ten years, or 40 quarters, to qualify for retirement benefits. Earnings are credited regardless of how much of the year you actually worked. (For 2000 each $780 earned at any time in the year counted as credit for one quarter, up to a maximum of four quarters.) The amount of your Social Security check will depend not on your quarterly credits but on how much you earn over the years (see table below).

Inequities in the system. Families with similar incomes often receive different benefits. For example, a family in which only the husband was a wage-earner will receive higher benefits than a family in which both husband and wife worked with a combined income equal to the husband's income in the first family.

This is one of various inequities embedded in a system that originated half a century ago, when attitudes and social conditions were different. With all the problems Social Security now faces, such inequities are unlikely to be removed. Social Security is not a fund into which people make "contributions" that they withdraw after retirement. It is a pay-as-you-go system under which working people and their employers are taxed in order to provide benefits for retired people, survivors, and the disabled.

Although you are eligible for full retirement benefits when you reach 65 if you were born before 1938 (67 if born after 1959), you can, if you choose, begin receiving benefits as early as 62. Monthly benefits in that case will be 80 percent of regular benefits (or a prorated percentage for any age between 62 and full retirement age) and will be fixed at that percentage for the rest of your life.

If you delay starting benefits until after full retirement, your monthly benefits will be higher than the basic full rate by 3 percent for each year you delay if you were born before 1925, rising to 8 percent a year for people born after 1942.

When a married man is receiving Social Security benefits, his wife can begin receiving *her* benefits at 50 percent of his rate when she reaches full retirement age. She never receives more than 50 percent of his benefits while he is alive. If she chooses to begin receiving benefits at any age between 62 and full retirement age, she will get between 37½ percent and 50 percent of her husband's retirement check. This lower rate will continue until her husband dies, after which she would receive a survivor's benefit, explained below.

If the wife has been working and paying Social Security taxes herself, she can receive either a spouse's benefit or a benefit based on her own Social Security taxes, but she cannot receive both.

If the husband dies first, the wife can receive 100 percent of his benefit beginning at full retirement age, or 71 percent beginning at age 60.

How big will your Social Security check be?

If you would like an estimate of what your Social Security payments will be when you retire, call the toll-free number 1-800-772-1213 and ask for a "Request for Earnings and Benefit Estimate" form. After you fill out this simple form and mail it in, Social Security will send you your complete earnings history; estimates of your retirement benefits at three ages—age 62, full retirement age (65 until the year 2000, after which it gradually increases to 67), and age 70; and estimates of disability or survivors' benefits that might be payable. To get a general idea of the range of individual retirement benefits, check the table below.

You can obtain a wealth of information on-line at the Social Security Administration's World Wide Web site. Its address is http://www.ssa.gov. If you order your earnings and benefit estimate on-line, it will be delivered to you by mail. You can also download a computer program that you can use to make a general calculation of your retirement benefits.

Approximate monthly benefits if you retire at full retirement age and had steady lifetime earnings

Your age in 2000	Receiver of benefits	Your earnings in 1999				$72,600 or more
		$20,000	$30,000	$40,000	$50,000	
45	You	$ 841	$1,107	$1,352	$1,477	$1,774
	or You and your spouse	$1,261	$1,660	$2,028	$2,215	$2,661
55	You	$ 841	$1,107	$1,352	$1,475	$1,713
	or You and your spouse	$1,261	$1,660	$2,028	$2,212	$2,569
65	You	$ 769	$1,014	$1,224	$1,307	$1,433
	or You and your spouse	$1,153	$1,521	$1,836	$1,960	$2,149

If the husband dies before the wife reaches 60, and after the youngest child reaches 16, the wife receives no benefits as a survivor until age 60. The child receives benefits until age 18.

All of these examples assume that the husband is the principal wage earner. If the wife is, the figures would be the same in reverse.

Applying for benefits. To apply for benefits, you must visit your Social Security office three months before the date that you will become eligible, or the date when you choose to begin receiving your retirement checks, if that is later.

When the husband applies for his Social Security benefits, it is not necessary for the wife to be there, unless she is also applying for her benefits. Take the following documents with you: Social Security card and proof of age (birth certificate or baptismal papers); marriage certificate (if applying as a spouse); copy of W-2 form showing the latest year's earnings, or a copy of the latest income tax return.

Medicare coverage. Apply for Medicare at the same time that you apply for retirement benefits. If you have already begun receiving Social Security payments before 65, you will automatically get your Medicare card in the mail by your 65th birthday, which is when Medicare coverage begins.

If you plan to delay the start of retirement checks past age 65, you and your spouse must each remember to apply for Medicare three months before each of you is 65.

Medicare consists of two parts—A and B. Part A, which costs you nothing, pays for your hospital bills. Part B, medical insurance, pays doctors' bills and a number of other items not covered by Part A. For Part B, you pay a monthly premium that covers your spouse and eligible dependents. This premium, which is deducted from your retirement check, is the same for everybody and increases every year.

Part B is optional. If you do not enroll when you become eligible, you have another chance to sign up in the first quarter of each year, but your monthly premium for medical insurance will be 10 percent higher for each twelve-month period that you could have been enrolled but were not.

Part A helps pay for up to 90 days in each benefit period at any participating hospital. A benefit period runs from the first day of hospital treatment to the 60th day after release from a hospital or nursing home. After that, if you have to go in again, a new 90-day benefit period starts. (In 2000 the deductible for the first 60 days in the hospital was a total of $776 and for the 61st through 90th days, *$194 a day*.)

Part B generally pays 80 percent of approved medical charges after a deductible that you pay once a year.

You can buy Medicare Supplement policies and Major Medical Expense policies to cover costs not

Questions about your pension

If your company has a pension plan, your employer is obligated to give you a description of it once a year. You should know the answers to these questions:

- Is your particular job covered by the plan?
- How long do you have to work before you are vested (before the pension is guaranteed)?
- How old do you have to be for regular or early retirement benefits?
- Is the pension federally insured?
- Is there a benefit for your spouse?

covered by Medicare. If you decide to buy such a policy, make sure it does not duplicate any part of Medicare.

(Medicaid, not to be confused with Medicare, is completely separate. It is a program run by your state government primarily to help people with low incomes and little or no resources.)

Your pension. For many employed people, a pension offers additional retirement income. Most pensions are based, to some extent, on Social Security benefits. The employer usually takes your Social Security benefits into account in deciding how much of a pension to provide for you.

If you die before early retirement age, benefits for your spouse are not likely unless you have contributed to the pension plan yourself.

When you retire, you can choose to have your pension cover your spouse in the event that you die first. In that case, your own monthly payments are reduced while you are living. Depending on your spouse's age, benefits after your death could be as little as 50 percent of your own benefits.

Some pension plans give you a choice of receiving your benefits in monthly payments or in a lump sum. Monthly payments are guaranteed for life but are not adjusted for inflation, unless your employer volunteers to do so. A lump sum can be invested by you, most likely in a rollover Individual Retirement Account, into which you can deposit the entire sum without paying taxes at the time. Unlike a conventional IRA, there is no tax deduction for making the investment, but there are very large tax savings because the income from the investment is sheltered from tax until you make withdrawals, which must begin at age 70½. Assuming that you or your spouse do not draw out all the funds in the account, there would still be money left for your heirs, in contrast to a pension.

Social Security Benefits ☐
(approximately $8000 maximum in this example)

Earned Income ☐
Thousands
of dollars
a year

1. $17,000, which is adjusted annually for inflation, is the most a person 65-69 can earn in 2000 without losing part of Social Security benefits.

Working for yourself. In these inflationary times, many people augment their retirement income by continuing to work.

If you are self-employed and use part of your home as a business, you are allowed significant deductions on your income tax. Check with your local Internal Revenue Service office.

But as long as you work, you will be required to pay self-employment tax to help support the Social Security system, even though you may already be drawing Social Security benefits. Regardless of age, you must pay the tax if you have net income of $400 or more from your own business or profession. The tax also applies if you have income from providing services such as babysitting, nursing, selling door to door, or working as a real estate agent.

The self-employment tax rate is over 15 percent of a "taxable base" equal to almost all your net self-employment income, if that figure is no more than $76,200, in 2000. (If it is over that limit, the tax rate is a little under 3 percent on the part of the taxable base over $76,200.)

When self-employed people receive Social Security payments, any amount they earn over a certain level reduces their Social Security benefits by one dollar for every three earned. The deduction is made from Social Security benefits at the beginning of the calendar year. In 2000, a retired person age 65 to 69 could earn up to $17,000 a year without losing any Social Security retirement benefits. This limit has been increasing every year. From age 70 on, under present regulations, you can earn as much as you want without losing any Social Security benefits.

Managing your shopping

Shopping is where management of the family's money begins. Planning what you are going to buy and following simple rules when you shop can mean the difference between just making ends meet and having money to save.

Going to the supermarket. At least once a week or so, someone in the family has to shop for food and other household needs. Here are some guidelines that can bring considerable savings.

- Do not shop more than once a week. Read the newspaper ads on Wednesdays and Thursdays and plan where you will shop and what you will buy each week. Jot down several menus featuring the specials advertised and note the staples on sale—unperishable items you can stock up on for weeks ahead. Make a shopping list to take with you.
- Go to the supermarket shortly after you have eaten so that you will not have an appetite for expensive

treats. Try to shop early in the morning, when stocks of produce and fresh meats and fish offer the greatest choice. Just before a long weekend, you might try shopping late in the day to take advantage of last-minute markdowns. Schedule your shopping trip without your children. Their impulses can wipe out your economies.

- Do not overstock on produce, the most profitable line for most supermarkets. Do not buy the first of a new crop of fruit or vegetables; prices should come down later. Remember that frozen food prices also go up and down with the season, so try stocking up on a frozen vegetable when the same vegetable is as good a buy as fresh produce. Buy canned fruits and vegetables at the end of summer, when many prices are reduced before the fresh packs come in.
- Keep portions in mind when you are buying meat. Steaks and chops will serve for only one meal; a roast can last for several days.

- Read labels and note how much you are paying per ounce. The large size is not always the economy size.
- Try buying day-old bakery products. After you freeze and thaw them, most people cannot tell them from fresh.
- Remember that junk food is costly, apart from its lack of nourishment.
- Think hard about convenience foods. Instant coffee can be more economical than regular, but does it make sense to pay someone to make your iced tea for you?
- Soft drinks in cans and bottles are an expensive way to buy water—with tiny percentages of artificial flavor. For about the same cost as two 12-ounce cans of soft drink, you can make a sparkling genuine fruit drink by adding store-brand carbonated water to a 6-ounce can of frozen concentrated fruit juice.

Shopping in other stores.

In your other shopping, it is important to time certain purchases according to the seasons and to take advantage of sales. Not all sales, however, are what they appear to be. Some, such as department store white sales, feature items that may have been especially manufactured for the sale. Certain goods ordered by mail are not manufactured until after your order has been received. When a sale is announced, look for words that mean the goods have been marked down from a quoted figure. If the ad uses terms like "special purchase" or "comparable value," the prices may not be genuine reductions.

When you purchase a big-ticket item such as a refrigerator or a television set, you will probably be urged to buy a service contract, which provides that repairs will be made at no additional cost for the life of the contract. What some stores do not tell you is that the service contract may partly duplicate the coverage already offered in the warranty, such as parts and repairs at no cost for a full year. Service contracts, moreover, are usually sold for the early years of the life of your purchase, when a problem is less likely to develop. A study at Cornell University concluded that most service contracts are not good buys.

Those glossy catalogs.

Unsolicited catalogs that come in the mail have become a popular way to shop for clothes, gifts, and a broad range of unusual items. Catalogs offer convenience and, for people away from large cities, a wide choice of high-priced items. But shipping costs can be high.

Some catalogs do offer sales from time to time, but most catalog prices are not competitive, not even with other catalogs. If an item in a catalog catches your eye, watch for it in other catalogs and in your local stores, since prices vary widely. If you do order an item, be prepared to wait a few weeks. According to federal regulations, you have the right to receive any mail-order item within 30 days unless the seller has specified a longer delivery time. If the deadline is not met, you have the right to cancel and get all your money back.

Returns may be a problem unless your catalog is from a nearby department store.

Clubs, outlets, and co-ops

Two recent entries in the retailing business—membership warehouse clubs and factory outlet stores—are offering shoppers in heavily populated areas opportunities to buy quality merchandise at significant savings. A third kind of money-saving institution, the co-op, has been around since the Great Depression of the 1930's.

With prices as much as 40 percent below retail prices elsewhere, the warehouse clubs may charge a membership fee of $25. If you have a chance to join one, spend some time visiting it before you sign up.

Outlet stores, often located in shopping centers of their own, may offer top-of-the-line products at discounts of about half of retail prices.

If there is a co-op in your area, you might try it for dairy products, meat, produce, and various staples, on which big savings are possible. If you would like to start a co-op, write for information to:

National Cooperative Business Association
1401 New York Avenue NW
Washington DC, 20005.

A shopper's calendar

As retailing becomes increasingly competitive, sales on various items are being held more frequently throughout the year. But this calendar of traditional sales periods for department stores may be useful.

January–February	White sales (and other household goods)
After Easter	Storewide clearance sales
Late June	Men's clothing
After July 4	Storewide clearance sales
August	Children's clothing Camping equipment
Autumn	China, glassware, silver
October–November	Women's coats
After Christmas	Women's dressy clothes Men's clothing Storewide clearance sales

---

Your shelter dollar

The American ideal of owning a one-family home has become difficult for many to achieve. Young families seeking a home for the first time find that they have to settle for far less space than they wanted at a cost that takes a disproportionate share of their income.

The principal question to be answered is how much home can you afford. As the table below indicates, your gross annual income needs to be at least a third of the price of the house, assuming you can get a mortgage as low as 8 percent. With a 12 percent mortgage, it should be half the price of the house.

The figures that are shown here do not include closing costs, which are identified in the adjoining table. Closing costs can vary from as low as 2 percent of the amount of the loan to around 7 percent.

Although a 30-year loan has long been the typical mortgage, people who want to save money over the life of the loan have been signing up for 15-year mortgages, when their near-term income permits. On a 10 percent mortgage, they pay back less than twice the price of a $100,000 house over 15 years instead of more than three times the price over 30 years. They are also likely to get a more attractive interest rate.

Partly offsetting the high cost of interest payments is the tax advantage of owning your home, since interest as well as property taxes are deductible from federal income tax.

Lenders' smorgasbord. Lending institutions have come up with a smorgasbord of alternatives to the traditional fixed mortgage. When you select a lender—a bank, savings institution, mortgage banker, or credit union—find out first if mortgages are fairly easy to obtain at that institution. Do they charge a fee for originating the mortgage? (This consists of a one-time charge called "points," explained in the glossary.) Do they offer a choice of mortgage plans? Is there a prepayment penalty?

Traditional fixed rate. This type of mortgage, on which the figures in the table are based, appears at first glance to be the most expensive. That is because the interest rate is higher than starting rates for other kinds of mortgage now being offered. But this appearance is deceptive. The fixed rate mortgage is not only the most certain, it is likely to be the most economical in a time of rising interest rates.

Adjustable rate. The most common of the other types of mortgage available is the adjustable rate mortgage (ARM). Starting at a lower rate than the fixed rate mortgage, the ARM can be adjusted at any time, with 30 days' notice, to reflect changes in interest rates. The change could affect your monthly payment, or the outstanding principal, or the length of the mortgage. There is, however, no penalty for prepayment.

If the terms of an ARM include a cap on the

What can you afford to buy?

Here are some approximate figures that should give you some idea of how much house you can afford. They are based on a down payment of 15 percent, with property taxes and insurance coming to just under a third of your monthly payment.

Following the general rule of thumb, monthly payments assumed here are no more than 28 percent of gross income—essentially the regular income your family has had for at least a year.

House price	$100,000	$150,000	$200,000
Mortgage rate	*Annual gross income you need*		
8 percent	$33,000	$52,000	$70,000
10 percent	$41,000	$62,000	$83,000
12 percent	$48,000	$73,000	$98,000

(Figures in between those shown can be prorated.)

Checklist of closing costs

When you buy the house, you will encounter a whole battery of additional costs, called closing costs. Buyers can expect to pay most or all of these charges, in addition to the purchase price of the house. Actual costs vary from locality to locality; get an estimate from your lawyer or a local real estate man.

- Appraisal
- Title search fees
- Judgment search fees
- Title insurance policy fee
- Survey costs
- Attorney's fee
- Loan origination fee for mortgage
- Mortgage insurance
- Credit report fee
- Fee for bank's lawyer
- Home-owner's insurance premium
- Taxes, recording fees
- Adjustment for costs paid by seller (fuel, water, etc.)

Borrowing on your house

To home owners who have paid a large part or all of their mortgages, lending institutions are actively offering equity conversion. This is a loan with your equity in your house as collateral. Another form is a line of credit, on which you can draw by writing checks.

Unlike other kinds of interest payments, mortgage interest is deductible under the 1986 Tax Reform Act; the interest on home equity loans of up to $100,000 is also deductible.

But equity conversion advertising does not always make it clear that your monthly payments may be for interest only, with the original amount of the loan to be paid off in a "balloon" at the end of the

term. Nor do the ads always tell you that you have to pay closing costs as well as interest.

monthly amount you pay, a rise in interest rates could result in negative amortization. When your payments are not sufficient to cover interest charges at current rates, the lender can make up the difference by increasing the principal—the amount of your loan. This is the opposite of building up equity under a conventional mortgage. To avoid negative amortization, the term of an ARM could be extended, but to no more than 40 years.

Graduated payment. In the Graduated Payment Mortgage (GPM), the rates begin low and build up on a fixed schedule, ending at a higher level than rates on a conventional fixed mortgage.

Buy-down. Still another choice is the buy-down, offered as an incentive to the buyer by house builders. The builder turns over to the lending institution part of the money he receives for the house. This money is used to reduce your interest payments for a limited number of years.

Reverse. This type of mortgage enables senior citizens or others on a fixed income to receive a monthly payment using the equity of their home as security. The mortgage is paid off when the homeowner sells the home, or when the homeowner dies and the property is sold in settlement of the homeowner's estate.

For any kind of mortgage, the lender is likely to urge you to take out mortgage insurance. Like other life insurance on credit purchases, this is more for the convenience and protection of the lender than for yours, since you could probably purchase term insurance more economically on your own. If you do find it convenient to take out mortgage insurance, make sure the policy is *not* made out to the lender; your family might prefer to keep the mortgage and invest the insurance proceeds.

Ways to save energy in your home

Everyone knows that you can save energy by insulating a home and turning off the lights, but here are some points you may not have thought about:

- In cold weather, use the sun's heat by opening blinds or curtains; in summer keep them closed as much as possible.
- When the outside temperature is 78° or cooler, turn off the air conditioner and open the windows.
- Run the dishwasher and clothes washer only with full loads. In the clothes washer, use warm or cold water cycles when you can.
- A shower uses about half as much hot water as a tub bath.
- Clean the condenser coils on the back or bottom of your refrigerator with a vacuum or brush at least once a year.
- Check the gasket on the refrigerator door by seeing if it will resist letting you pull out a slip of paper. Replace it if necessary.
- Do not open the refrigerator or oven doors more than necessary. Opening the oven door lowers the temperature about 25°.
- Check the refrigerator temperature to make sure the settings are correct. The refrigerator compartment should be about 40° and the freezer should be 0°.
- The refrigerator should have enough space around food to let air circulate, but the freezer should be solidly packed, even if it means filling a milk carton with water and freezing it to take up space.
- One 100-watt incandescent bulb gives more light with less energy than two 60-watt bulbs.

Managing your car

The most economical way to own a car, according to a study made by the U.S. Department of Transportation, is to keep driving it until it cannot go anymore.

Most drivers would prefer not to put that proposition to the test, but there is no question that it is less expensive to keep running an old car that is in tolerably good condition than to buy a new one.

Nearly half the depreciation of a new car occurs in the first two years of ownership. In fact, a new car depreciates by as much as a third as soon as you drive it out of the showroom. Repairs and maintenance tend to be at their highest level in the fourth to seventh years, when the original parts begin to fail. That is why many people who could afford new cars used to trade them in after three years. More recently, as car prices have soared, drivers keep their new cars longer, which means fewer choices for used-car buyers.

Buying a new car. Before you go to the showroom, you can find out what the dealer paid for the car you have your eye on. The figure is shown as the base price in one of the guidebooks to new automobile prices available in paperback or at your public library. The sticker on a showroom model will tell you the charges for optional equipment, freight, and dealer preparation. Add those to the base price in the book and you will know how much leeway you have for bargaining on the dealer's price to you.

Buy or lease?

When does it make sense to lease rather than buy a car? Generally, leasing is an option to consider if you plan to drive a car for four years or less, drive only about 15,000 miles per year, and prefer to pay only for that part of the vehicle's value that you actually use. It makes sense to buy a car if you plan to keep it longer than four years, expect to drive more than 15,000 miles per year, and want to own the vehicle.

Before leasing an automobile, read the lease contract thoroughly. Leasing contracts under $25,000 to individual consumers must show all charges and fees associated with the lease and include the total amount to be paid over the leasing period.

For more information, send for the free booklet "Keys to Vehicle Leasing," which is available from Publications Services, Federal Reserve Board, Mail Stop 127, Washington DC 20551.

You should also know the value of the old car you are trading in. Ask your bank lending officer, to whom you will be returning after you buy the car, to let you see his Red Book of Official Used Car Market Values. Knowing the old-car value will alert you to a fairly common practice among dealers—"highballing," or offering a high trade-in to attract the customer while making the price of the new car correspondingly higher.

When the dealer offers you a package of options, remember that his profit margin on them is higher than on the car itself. The most expensive option is factory-installed air conditioning.

Your dealer will be more than happy to arrange financing for your car, because that is likely to be another source of profit for him. In many cases, you can probably get a better deal by financing through your bank.

Buying a used car. A used car is estimated, on the average, to be about 40 percent less expensive than a comparable new one. In selecting a dealer, it is usually wise to go to a well-regarded new car dealer; he has a reputation to protect and hopes to sell you a new car someday. Insist on being allowed to give the car a road test—more than just around the block. You might take it to an automobile mechanic you trust, or an automobile diagnostic service listed in the yellow pages under that heading.

Tips for economical driving

- Do not leave the motor idling if you are stopping for more than a minute. It is more economical to turn off the engine and restart it later than to let it run.
- Speed kills economy. Remember that wind-resistance cuts mileage above 50 mph, and the most economical speed is about 45 to 50. Tire treads wear twice as fast at 70 as they do at 45.
- Switch wheels every 5000 miles so that tires wear evenly.
- Maintain tire pressure, and check it only when the tires are cool.
- Check wheel alignment regularly.
- Avoid sudden stops as well as sudden starts. If you have to brake hard at a traffic light or a toll booth, you were using too much gasoline to get to that point.
- Do not try to maintain speed going up a long grade. Moderate deceleration saves fuel.

An economical vacation

Camping. Certainly the most economical way to vacation and, in many ways, the most rewarding, is to take the family camping.

You have many camping areas to choose from. If you write to the National Park Service, 1849 C Street NW, Washington, DC 20240, you will receive, free of charge, a 50-state map of national parks, with addresses and telephone numbers for each area; a brochure describing special passes available for families, senior citizens, and the disabled; and admission prices for each area. Admission for a single visit ranges from $1 to $10 per person or $4 to $20 per carload.

If you plan to visit in one year several places maintained by the federal government, send $50 to the address above for a Golden Eagle Passport, or buy it in person at any National Park Service (NPS) area. This will entitle you and your family to visit, in your private vehicle, any federal outdoor recreation area that charges an entrance fee, as well as historical houses and museums in federal areas. It does not cover additional park fees, such as those charged for camping, and it is good for one year from the date of purchase.

For senior citizens

People 62 and older may obtain from the National Park Service, for a one time $10 processing fee, a lifetime permit that admits them, and anyone accompanying them in a private vehicle, to federal recreation areas that charge fees. It also provides a 50 percent discount on use fees in park areas, but not on prices charged by concessionaires.

The Golden Age Passport must be obtained in person with suitable identification (not a Medicare card) and is available at most federally operated recreation areas where an entrance fee is charged.

Persons who are blind or permanently disabled can obtain, in person at any NPS entry area, a Golden Access Passport, which provides free admission to the national parks. Proof of medically determined disability is required to obtain this passport.

The National Park Service also recommends to prospective visitors the booklet "The National Parks: Lesser-Known Areas," available for $2.50 from the Superintendent of Documents, U.S. Government Printing Office, P.O. Box 371954, Pittsburgh, PA 15250-7954 (stock number 024-005-01152-8).

You can also obtain information by calling (202) 208-4747, weekdays from 9 a.m. to 3 p.m., or going on-line at the Internet address *http://www.nps.gov.*

Sleeping indoors. If you prefer to sleep indoors on your vacation, there are still ways to hold down costs.

Two people traveling a considerable distance may find that a fly-and-drive trip can be more economical than driving the whole way. To take advantage of airfare bargains, however, you may not be able to leave and return at the times most convenient to you. Moreover, the economical car rental services are not as conveniently located at airports as the well-known ones. But the savings on gasoline and en route motel costs could make this kind of trip worthwhile.

Finally, plan your route carefully. Do not try to cover too many miles in one day; this would necessitate wasteful and tiring high-speed driving. Try also to avoid urban and resort areas, where prices are higher.

Trimming vacation expenses

- Schedule your trip just before or just after the busy season, generally from Memorial Day to Labor Day, when rates are likely to be lower in vacation areas.
- If you are in a hot climate, start driving quite early in the morning and stop around mid-afternoon. This will save on use of the air conditioner and give you a better choice of economical accommodations.
- Do not carry a container on the roof, where it will increase wind resistance.
- Take along a small heating coil so that you can make your own coffee or tea. With fruit juice and pastry picked up the day before, you can have breakfast in your room. Save on lunch as well by taking along a simple picnic kit. Buy fruit, cold cuts, and other easy-to-eat items in small quantities along the way.

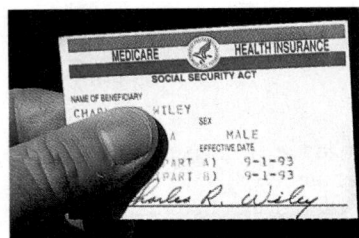
Medicare identification card

Glossary

common stock

amortize. To reduce the principal of a loan by regular payments.

annual percentage rate (APR). The true interest cost of an installment payment, as distinct from simple interest; true interest takes into account the fact that the debt is being paid off during the time the interest is paid.

balance. The difference in an account between debits and credits.

balloon payment. The unpaid part of a mortgage that is due at one time (not typical of most mortgage arrangements).

bankruptcy. The condition of being insolvent and thus unable to meet one's obligations.

binder. A temporary contract issued by an insurance agent that covers the insured until the policy is prepared and executed; it is customary for fire insurance and other insurance protecting property.

blue chip stocks. Stocks issued by leading companies known for a continuing record of good earnings and dividend payments.

bond. An IOU or promissory note of a corporation or government, with a promise to pay a specified amount of interest for a specified length of time, and to repay the face value of the bond when it matures.

bottom line. The net income, which is the last line on an income statement.

bracket creep. A slang term referring to the way inflation pushes salaries and wages into higher tax brackets.

buy-down. Money offered by a builder as an inducement, which reduces monthly mortgage payments.

cash surrender value. Amount for which you can cash in your whole life insurance policy.

certificate of deposit (CD). A savings certificate with a fixed interest rate and a fixed maturity from 30 days to 10 years.

closing. The conclusion of a real estate transaction when all documents are signed and the deed is transferred to the new owner.

co-insurance. Condition, usually in major medical, in which you and the insurance company share costs; typically, the insurer pays 80 percent and you pay the rest.

collateral. Anything you own of value against which you can borrow money.

common stock. Securities that represent an ownership interest in a corporation.

compound interest. Interest that is computed on both the principal and the previously earned interest; in a savings account, interest left on deposit will itself earn interest.

condominium. Individually owned real estate consisting of a dwelling unit and an undivided interest in joint facilities and areas that serve the multi-unit complex.

consumer price index. A measure of the relative change in prices paid for a "market basket" of consumer goods by a typical wage-earner.

contractual plan. In mutual funds, a plan under which the total amount you intend to invest is stated, with a commitment to invest regular amounts monthly.

convertibles. Securities, such as bonds, that can be converted into other securities, such as stocks, at a certain price.

co-operative. Real estate ownership in which each person owns stock in a corporation, which owns and administers the residential units.

debenture. A debt certificate issued by a company that is not

    Managing the Family's Money

secured by a specific asset but by the company's credit in general.

deductible. In insurance, the sum you must pay before insurance coverage begins.

defined benefit pension. A type of pension in which a worker is guaranteed a certain amount of retirement income.

demand deposit. A bank deposit, such as in a passbook or checking account, that is payable to the depositor on demand (unlike a certificate of deposit).

discretionary income. The part of an individual's income that is left after paying taxes and buying necessities.

disposable income. The part of an individual's income that is left after paying taxes.

dividend. A payment made from earnings to the stockholders of a corporation; a payment made by an insurance company to holders of ordinary life or term insurance (if they choose a dividend-paying policy).

double indemnity. A policy rider that provides for double the face amount of the policy in the event of death by accident.

earnings per share. The after-tax earnings of a company divided by the number of shares outstanding.

effective annual interest rate. The total amount, expressed as a percentage, that one dollar will earn in one year; it is higher than the nominal rate when interest is compounded during the year.

equity. The residual value of a business or property beyond any remaining debt.

equity conversion. A loan for which your equity in your house serves as collateral.

escrow. Deposit of money with a neutral third party, as during the sale of a home.

estate tax. A tax imposed by the federal government and some state governments on the value of property transferred at death.

extended coverage. In insurance, extension of a policy to provide coverage against hazards not covered by the basic policy.

face value. In investing, the principal of a debt instrument, such as a bond or certificate of deposit, on which interest is computed and which is payable at maturity; in life insurance, the amount of the death benefit (as opposed to the cash value, which is less).

fee simple. Comprehensive ownership of real estate, with the right to pass it on to one's heirs.

float. In banking, the value of checks that have been written by you but not yet paid by the bank; in credit cards, the value of charges made to the account but not yet paid by the card-holder; in travelers' checks, the value of checks purchased but not yet cashed (in the second case, the cardholder benefits; in the third case, the bank benefits).

government bonds. Obligations of the U.S. government, considered the highest-grade bonds anywhere.

guaranty. A promise that merchandise will perform as claimed; differs from a warranty in that the latter is absolute assurance and failure to perform may void the basic contract; a guaranty merely provides that the guarantor will be liable (the two terms are often used interchangeably).

head of family. A person who maintains a family unit (not necessarily a father or husband).

Individual Retirement Account (IRA). A retirement program for anyone with earned income under which they may benefit from tax deferrals and in some cases from tax deductions while investing for retirement.

insufficient funds. A statement stamped on a check by a bank when the account does not have enough funds to cover that check.

interest. Money paid for the use of borrowed money.

investment company. A company that invests in stocks or bonds of other companies and sells shares to the public.

joint tenancy. The holding of property by two or more persons in such a manner that, upon the death of one, the survivor or survivors take the entire property.

Keogh plan. A retirement program for self-employed people under which they may benefit from tax deferrals and in some cases tax deductions while investing for retirement.

lien. A claim against a person's property.

liquid assets. Cash, or assets that can readily be converted into cash without any serious loss.

major medical. Protection against the expenses of a catastrophic illness.

market value. The value in a free market transaction agreed to by a willing seller and a willing buyer.

Medicaid. Combined federal-state program that pays for many medical expenses of the poor.

Medicare. The comprehensive federal health and medical insurance program that covers almost all people over 65.

money market account. An account offered by a bank with funds invested in short-term securities in the money market; the deposit is federally insured.

money market funds. Mutual funds that trade in short-term securities in the money market.

money markets. Financial markets where short-term debt securities are traded.

mutual fund. An investment managed by a company that pools the money of individual investors and buys a diversity of securities, such as stocks and bonds, to reduce risk.

net income. Also called net earnings or net profit, it is the difference between a company's sales and its expenses, before payment of dividends.

over the counter. Trading in securities that are not listed on major exchanges such as the New York Stock Exchange or the American Exchange.

payroll tax. The tax that an employee and employer each pay to support the Social Security program.

points. A one-time charge by a lending institution for originating a mortgage; one point equals 1 percent of the value of the loan.

price-earnings ratio. The market price of a company's common stock divided by its earnings per share.

prime rate. The interest rate that commercial banks charge their most creditworthy customers (lower than rates charged for loans to most individuals).

promissory note. A written promise to pay a debt.

rate of return. The annual percentage of an investment that is returned to the investor.

recipient. A person who receives public assistance or welfare payments, as distinguished from a "beneficiary," who works in covered employment and pays Social Security taxes.

rollover IRA. A special kind of Individual Retirement Account in which an employee deposits a lump-sum pension, paying no taxes on the lump sum or on the income it earns until starting to withdraw the money after age 59½.

simple interest. The interest earned by the principal only, and thus not compounded.

term life insurance. Insurance without any cash value that provides coverage for a limited term; it can be renewed at specified increasing rates; it is considerably cheaper than ordinary life in the early years but more expensive in later years.

treasury bill. A short-term obligation of the U.S. Treasury that is issued at a discount without interest.

treasury bond. A U.S. Treasury obligation that pays interest and matures in more than seven years.

treasury note. A U.S. Treasury obligation that pays interest, with a maturity of from one to seven years.

vesting. The acquisition by an employee of an interest in the contributions made by the employer to the pension fund, or to other employee-benefit funds.

warranty. A statement that merchandise is as represented; a false warranty is cause for legal action.

yield. Dividends on a stock or interest on a bond expressed as a percentage of current price.

For further reference

Abromovitz, Les
Family Insurance Handbook: The Complete Guide for the 1990's
Liberty Hall Press

Bamford, Janet, et al.
Complete Guide to Managing Your Money
Consumers Union

Cheeks, James E.
The Dow Jones-Irwin Guide to Keoghs
Dow Jones-Irwin

Consumer Reports Buying Guide
Annual issue of *Consumer Reports* magazine, usually issued in December

Garner, Robert J., et al.
Ernst & Young's Personal Financial Planning Guide
John Wiley & Sons

J.K. Lasser Tax Institute
J.K. Lasser's Your Income Tax
Prentice-Hall

Klott, Gary L.
The Complete Financial Guide to the 1990's
Times Books

Kunes, Ellen
Living Well—or Even Better—on Less
Perigee

Leonard, Frances
Money and the Mature Woman
Addison-Wesley

Lieberman, Trudy
Life Insurance
Consumers Union

Loeb, Marshall
Marshall Loeb's Lifetime Financial Strategies
Little, Brown

Miller, Theodore J.
Kiplinger's Make Your Money Grow
Kiplinger Books

Mobil Travel Guide
(seven area editions)
Prentice-Hall

Passell, Peter
How to Read the Financial Pages
Warner Books

Quinn, Jane Bryant
Making the Most of Your Money
Simon & Schuster

Savage, Terry
Terry Savage's New Money Strategies for the '90's
HarperCollins

Sloane, Leonard
The New York Times Personal Finance Handbook
Times Books

Tobias, Andrew
The Only Investment Guide You'll Ever Need
Harcourt Brace & Co.

Managing the Family's Money

Booklets on request (free unless otherwise noted)

College

"The Student Guide"
Student Financial Assistance Programs
U.S. Department of Education
Washington, DC 20202

Investing

"The Investor's Guide to Low-Cost
Mutual Funds" (about 500 funds)
Mutual Fund Education Alliance
1900 Erie Street, Suite 120
Kansas City, MO 64116 ($7 postpaid)

Income tax

"Your Federal Income Tax"
(I.R.S. publication 17)
"Tax Benefits for Older Americans"
(I.R.S. Publication 554)
Write the I.R.S. Forms Distribution
Center for your area (address is in the
Federal Income Tax Forms and
Instructions), or call 1-800-829-3676

Tax information publications and forms are available for reference and photocopying at your public library. They may also be obtained from the IRS on-line at the Internet address http:/www.irs.ustreas.gov and viewed and printed using the Adobe Acrobat file viewer (available free from Adobe on-line at *http://www.adobe.com)*.

Insurance

"Buyers' Guide to Insurance"
Consumer Federation of America's Insurance Group
414 A Street SE
Washington, DC 20003

(send self-addressed business-size envelope with $3)

Vacation

Subject bibliography "Travel and Tourism"
Superintendent of Documents
U.S. Government Printing Office
Washington, DC 20402

Retirement

"Understanding Social Security"
"Retirement"
"Survivors"
"Disability"
"Supplemental Security Income"
"Medicare"

From your Social Security office.

Catalog of Publications (C-48)
American Association of Retired Persons
601 E Street NW
Washington, DC 20049

"Guide to Health Insurance for
     People with Medicare"
Consumer Information Center
P.O. Box 100
Pueblo, CO 81002

Shopping

Subject bibliography
"Consumer Information"
     of booklets
Superintendent of Documents
U.S. Government Printing Office
Washington, DC 20402

(includes guides to buying food and
managing personal finances)

"Consumer Information Catalog"
Consumer Information Center
P.O. Box 100
Pueblo, CO 81002

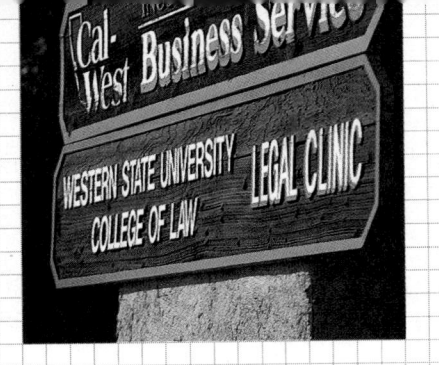

You and the Law

What is the law? Basically, the law is the set of rules that enables the members of a society to live and work together in reasonable harmony and to settle their disputes without violence. Some laws are in the form of written constitutions or statutes; others are legal principles that have arisen over the years from custom, experience, and common acceptance. Law is not confined to courts and legislatures. It pervades our day-to-day relationships with our families, our neighbors, the people we deal with on our jobs, and the members of our community.

When you pick up the phone and order something from a store, you make a contract governed by the law of sales. When you drive your car, you are subject to traffic laws and the laws of negligence and liability. Your wages and working conditions depend on your contract with your employer, perhaps a union contract, and federal and state labor laws. When a couple marries or a child is born, the law establishes the rights and duties of family members. When a person dies, the law determines who gets his or her property and who will care for the children. Even as you sleep at night, you are protected by laws against burglary and trespass— and perhaps by zoning laws that prevent a boiler factory from being built next door.

Most of the time we attend to our everyday affairs without running into any legal problems. Inevitably, though, conflicts arise. The goods we order fail to arrive, or they are unsatisfactory. Accidents happen and people are injured. Disputes arise between employers and employees, or between landlords and tenants. Families break up, or fight among themselves about inheritance or other rights. The person with no knowledge of the law may find that he has put himself in a weak legal position or incurred legal obligations that he never intended. Unscrupulous persons may take advantage of him, or he may simply not know what his rights are or what to do about them.

The purpose of this chapter is to help you deal with legal situations and, if possible, prepare for them. Reading the chapter will not make you a legal expert, but it may help you to recognize the problems most likely to arise in everyday situations, the pitfalls to look out for and errors to avoid, and the means by which you can protect and enforce your legal rights.

This chapter deals with general legal principles; but each state has its own special rules, which may differ from other states. Always check your own state and local law before making any important decisions.

The *Glossary* at the end of this chapter defines some technical terms you may come across in the newspaper or in other reading. *For further reference* lists a number of nontechnical books on law. Many more can be found at your local library, always a good source of information. For more technical information, try the courthouse library. If you are not familiar with using a law library, do not be afraid to ask the librarian for help.

Your family and the law

Marriage. Marriage is a contract, but not an ordinary one. Because of the importance of the family, society sets rules and imposes duties and obligations that usually do not apply to purely private agreements.

A marriage is valid everywhere if valid in the state where it takes place. *Each state sets its own rules,* which usually include a license, a blood test, a waiting period, and a ceremony performed by a clergyman or judge. Some marriages are prohibited because of blood relationship, age, prior marriage, or physical or mental incapacity.

Annulments. Marriages that do not conform to the rules are not automatically void. Unless incestuous or bigamous, a marriage will be valid unless one or both parties takes legal action and has it annulled within a reasonable time. (If an underage person marries, the child's parents can have the marriage annulled.) Annulments may also be obtained on grounds of fraud if, for example, one party expressed a desire for children knowing that he or she could not or would not have any.

Each state sets its own rules.

Common law marriage. Newspapers often use the term "common law marriage" to refer to the state of any couple living together; such use of the phrase is not accurate. A common law marriage is an agreement to marry and live together as man and wife without going through a ceremony. In states where they are permitted, common law marriages are exactly the same, legally, as any other marriage. The difficulty lies in proving the agreement and the intention of the parties, especially if one or both is dead and there is a dispute over inheritance.

Most states no longer recognize common law marriages. However, they will recognize a common law marriage that was valid at the time it was entered into, or one made in a state that does recognize them.

Changing your name

A married woman often wants to continue using her maiden name; she may, for example, have established a useful professional reputation under that name. Using a maiden name is perfectly legal. In fact, anyone can use any name he or she wants, so long as there is no intent to defraud. (You could not, for example, use the name of a well-known person in order to borrow money.) Getting a court order to change your name makes it official; but it is not necessary.

State laws. Some states do require women to use their married names on drivers' licenses or other documents. The state can do this, as it is responsible for public records. In these states, a woman must either comply or go to court and have her name officially changed.

Updating records. Most women do take their husbands' names. Those women should immediately notify the Social Security Administration to avoid any possible confusion in the records, as well as employers, insurance companies, department stores where they have charge accounts, and anyone else whose records should be changed.

Children. A child born to a married woman is presumed to be legitimate, even if the marriage turns out to be invalid. Illegitimate children become legitimate if their parents later marry each other.

Scientific developments, such as artificial insemination and "test-tube babies," pose new legal problems. Many states have passed laws requiring the consent of both husband and wife to these methods of conception or birth. If the law is complied with, the children are legitimate.

Illegitimate children. With respect to their mother, illegitimate children have full legal rights. They also have the right to support from their father; it may, however, take a lawsuit and a court order to establish paternity. Inheritance rights of illegitimate children from their fathers vary from state to state. Many states allow illegitimate children to inherit if the father has acknowledged the child in writing.

Abortion. The U.S. Supreme Court has ruled it unconstitutional to forbid abortion during the first three months of pregnancy. In other situations, each state can set its own abortion laws, and they vary widely.

Adopted children. Adopted children have the same legal relationship to their parents as natural children. In some states, an adopted child may also inherit from his or her natural parents, but in no state can natural parents inherit from the child. The right of adopted children to inherit from the adopting parents' relatives (where there is no will) varies widely from state to state. The trend is toward allowing inheritance rights.

How to adopt a child

Learn your state's law and follow it to the letter. Consent must be obtained from the natural parents unless they have been legally deprived of custody. Consent may also be required from the child, if above a certain age.

The rules vary. Some states allow adoptions by single persons, but singles usually find it hard to get approval. Religious requirements are not absolute but the state may give preference to adoptive parents of the same religion as the child's natural parents.

The essential point. You must satisfy a court, at a hearing, that you are of good moral character, able to provide a good home, and financially responsible. The court usually accepts the recommendation of the social agency in charge, but if it is unfavorable, you can introduce evidence to overturn it. A deaf couple, for instance, overcame an unfavorable report by showing that they had successfully raised their own children, who had normal hearing.

Adults may be adopted. The practice is uncommon, but it has sometimes been done to establish inheritance rights.

Legal status of minors

Contracts	Minors cannot be held to a contract or agreement while underage. Moreover, they can repudiate and cancel a contract at any time. (*Exception:* Real estate contracts cannot be repudiated while the minor is underage.) If the minor does not repudiate and cancel the contract before coming of age or within a reasonable time afterward, the contract will be valid. A minor can cancel a sale and get his money back. This rule does not apply to food, clothing, medical care, or other necessities. However, a minor who bought a car was able to get his money back, even though he had cracked it up. As a general rule, anyone who deals with a minor acts at his own risk, even if he does not know that the person is underage.
Liability for damages	Minors are responsible for injuries they cause to other people or to their property. They can be sued for damages; the damages can be paid from property owned or later acquired by the minor. Parents are usually not liable for the acts of their children, but some states have changed this rule.
Crimes	Under traditional law, a minor over seven could be tried as an adult. Today, children under 16 are charged with juvenile delinquency, not crime, to keep them from being encumbered by a criminal record. (The age may vary in some states.) Minors charged with juvenile delinquency have the right to a trial, a lawyer, and all constitutional safeguards.

Since an underage teenager can not be held to a contract, her parent must cosign a car loan and become legally responsible for making the payments. But the teen can be held responsible for the damage she does with her car.

Legal capacity

Children. Children do not have full legal rights and duties until they reach the *age of majority*. Traditionally, this age was 21, but many states have lowered it to 18, along with the voting age. Most states also have age limits for specific privileges, such as buying alcoholic beverages or obtaining a driver's license.

Incompetent adults. Adults are presumed to have full legal rights and capacities unless declared incompetent by a court after a full hearing. This proce-

dure has severe drawbacks:

- It stigmatizes the person as mentally unsound.
- It is not appropriate for physical disabilities or mental difficulties, such as forgetfulness, that fall far short of mental unsoundness.
- The incompetent loses most of his or her legal rights, including the right to vote, make contracts, buy or sell, lend or borrow money, make gifts, marry, travel, or choose a place of residence. The incompetent may even be committed to a mental hospital.

Property	Minors can own property of all types, but it must be managed by a parent or guardian. A child's earnings legally belong to his father (or mother), unless the child is "emancipated"—no longer dependent upon his parents for support. Examples of emancipated minors are those in the armed forces, those who have married, and those whose parents will not support them.
Right to sue	Lawsuits may be brought on a child's behalf by a parent, guardian, or person appointed by a court. Children can sue parents for intentional injuries, but not for negligence (auto accidents, for example). Some states allow negligence suits against a parent who does not have custody.
School rights	Although every state has adopted compulsory schooling laws, children cannot be compelled to attend public schools. Parents may choose to send their children to private schools or to have them schooled at home. Developmentally disabled children may need special classes or attention that public schools are not able to provide.
	Schools have the right to maintain reasonable discipline, but a child cannot be expelled or suspended without a hearing, except in emergencies. Parents have the right to review their children's school records and correct any misinformation contained therein. The records cannot be shown to others without the parents' consent (except to school officials or to protect a child's health or safety).

A gift belongs legally to the person who receives it. But household furnishings usually belong to the husband, except in those states that have community property laws. A paycheck belongs to the person who earned it.

In some states it is possible to appoint a conservator to manage a person's property simply by showing that he is unable to handle it himself due to mental or physical disability. The usual proof is a doctor's statement. The person has the right to contest the proceeding, but is less likely to do so because he is not declared incompetent and does not lose his other legal rights.

Aliens. Resident aliens have the same rights as citizens, except that they cannot vote or hold elective office. They must register and must get a permit to work in the United States. In some states, they are ineligible for public employment. Illegal aliens may be deported.

Legal rights and duties.

At one time, married women could not manage their own property; in fact, their legal status was almost that of children. These laws are a thing of the past. Husbands and wives have equal legal rights and powers.

Property. Except in community property states, wages and salaries belong to the person who earns them. Income from property belongs to the person who owns it. Property belongs to the person who bought it or in whose name it is placed. Household furnishings belong to the husband unless proven otherwise.

Gifts, including gifts between husband and wife, belong to the person who receives them. However, a man

Planning for old age, illness, or incapacity

Old age is not necessarily incapacity. Elderly people lose none of their legal rights, but the infirmities of age may make it difficult for some to handle their legal affairs. There are ways to plan against possible incapacity without the need for court proceedings; the same methods can be used by persons who simply want to be relieved of business responsibilities, and by people who wish to have someone else take care of their affairs.

Power of attorney	A power of attorney, which must be in writing, gives someone else the power to act on your behalf. It can be a *general* power to handle your affairs, or a *special* power, limited as you see fit. It can be revoked at any time and ends at your death. In some states, you may provide that the power of attorney is to take effect only if your physician certifies you are no longer able to handle your own affairs.
Trusts	You can put your money or property in a trust (see *Glossary*), and appoint a trustee to manage it for your benefit. The trust can be set up to take effect only on your doctor's certification that you are incapacitated; another way is to appoint yourself as trustee and name a co-trustee to take over automatically if you are incapacitated. You can put whatever you want into the trust, impose any limitations you want on the trustee, and reserve the right to cancel the trust at any time and take back the property.
Married couples	Do not keep everything in one spouse's name. If that spouse becomes incapacitated, the other will be in a financial bind. Legal proceedings to straighten things out may be time consuming. Each spouse should have at least enough money or separate property to provide for emergency situations.

who "gave" his wife money to save for his old age was able to get it back by proving no gift was intended. Contrary to popular belief, wedding gifts do not belong to the bride; they belong to both partners, unless clearly intended for just one (a necklace, for example).

Joint bank accounts and other joint property are owned equally by husband and wife; if one dies, the other gets the property. Some states recognize a special form of real estate ownership called "tenancy by the entireties." It is similar to joint ownership, but neither party can sell or mortgage his or her share without consent of the other. Also, creditors cannot get at the property except for debts owed jointly by husband and wife. This form of ownership ends if the parties are divorced; they become ordinary co-owners. See also "Community property laws," page 146.

Antenuptial agreements. Husband and wife can make a property agreement before marriage; each can give up any right to inherit from the other. Agreements are common among people with children from prior marriages; they assure that the children get their property free of any claims from a second spouse. These agreements are enforced by the courts unless grossly unfair. One was set aside because the husband, who had only a moderate income when he married, later became rich.

Husband and wife. Despite the trend toward equality, the husband is still "head of the family" in most states. He can decide where the family is to live. If his wife refuses to accompany him, she cannot charge him with desertion or abandonment. The husband also has the right to direct the children's education and religious upbringing.

Duty to support. A husband has a duty to support his wife and children, even if they have money of their own. If the husband is unable to support the family, the duty passes to the wife.

Support means the provision of "necessaries," but this includes more than the bare necessities of life. It means providing a standard of living in keeping with the father's financial condition. Some courts have held that a father must give his children a college education if he is financially able.

Purchases. A wife can buy necessities for the family and charge them to her husband; she is acting as his agent. A merchant can assume she is acting for the family unless the husband has notified him not to extend credit. A newspaper announcement, such as "I will not be responsible for debts incurred by my wife," is sufficient, but *only if the merchant knows of it.*

There are limits to the rule. It applies to purchases that are reasonable—not to sable coats or Rolls-Royces. If, however, the couple has a joint charge account or credit card, either is entitled to make purchases on it.

Indigent parents. Some states require adult children to support their parents if the parents cannot support themselves and would otherwise have to apply for public assistance.

Divorce and separation.
Traditionally, a divorce could be granted only for an offense committed by one spouse against the other. The "guilty party" was often barred from remarrying and from receiving alimony, which is why most divorce actions were brought by the wife.

Grounds for divorce include adultery, desertion, cruelty, conviction of crime, and habitual drunkenness or drug addiction. Defenses to a lawsuit for divorce include "condonation" (forgiveness of the offense), collusion, and justification (for instance, abandonment by the wife might be justified by the cruelty of the husband).

No-fault divorce. Most states now permit divorces for incompatibility, irreconcilable differences, or separation for a long period of time. No one need be at fault.

"Quickie" divorces. Most divorces, even those granted from foreign countries, will be recognized if both parties have appeared in court, either personally or through an attorney. But "mail-order" divorces and divorces where the defendant was not notified will be set aside if challenged.

Separation. A separated couple can make an agreement between themselves or go to court for a legal separation. The rules are similar to the rules in divorce cases, but a separation does not dissolve the marriage or change the parties' legal status as married persons.

A newspaper ad may not always protect a person from a spouse's debts. Consult a lawyer before placing an ad.

I, CHRISTOPHER SMARTS, also known professionally and publicly as CHRIS MILLS, do hereby declare that I am not responsible for any debts incurred by MISS BETTY WHITE or BETTY SMARTS as of January 15, 2000. I am in the process of challenging the legality of this marriage in Nevada and at no time did Miss White or I establish residence in Boston or any other city in the United States.

Alimony and property settlements. Courts today base their decisions on equity and fairness, not on set rules or formulas. For instance, wives have been awarded alimony for a period of time while attending college or taking training courses to enable them to support themselves. In a few cases, alimony has been awarded to the husband. If the parties can agree to a settlement between themselves, the court will usually accept it and make it a part of the court order.

Property settlements are permanent, but alimony or child support orders can be modified. Alimony normally ends if the wife remarries, but a father's duty to support his children is not ended by the remarriage. A support order may continue even after the child comes of age. For example, the court may find that the father is financially able to help the child through college or to help support a child who is incompetent. The amount, however, can always be modified to reflect changes in the parents' financial status.

Enforcement. A husband who fails to pay is guilty of contempt of court and can be punished by being sent to jail. This is done rarely, but the threat is always there.

Child custody. The welfare of the child is the primary consideration; but, in practice, the mother is almost always awarded custody (unless clearly unfit), with visitation rights for the husband. Recently, there has been a trend toward shared custody.

Custody fights are the bitterest of all lawsuits. One study showed that, even in uncontested divorces, over half the couples with children wound up in court later in custody battles. Couples would be well advised to settle their differences, perhaps with the help of a clergyman or social worker, before engaging in never-ending court battles. Such custody suits can do great harm to children.

Divorce and taxes

While uncontested divorces can be handled by a legal clinic at low fees—or even with a do-it-yourself divorce kit—you should be sure to talk with your tax adviser. There are some tricky income tax points that may depend on the wording of the divorce decree.

Alimony is deductible. Alimony payments are deductible from the husband's income; they are taxable income to the wife. Child support payments are not deductible, and are not income to the wife. Payments are considered alimony if they meet the following rules:

- They are made under a written agreement or court order.
- They are scheduled to continue for at least six years.
- They are to terminate at the death of the wife.
- They are not specifically designated as something other than alimony (such as child support).
- They do not depend on the status of a child (for example, if payments are scheduled to end when a child reaches 18, they are considered child support, not alimony).

Other payments. Property settlements are not taxable to either spouse, but later sales may be taxable. Payments under oral agreements are considered gifts and are not tax deductible.

Fees. Legal fees for getting a divorce are not deductible. Fees for tax advice are. Get separate bills.

Community property laws

Nine states—Arizona, California, Idaho, Louisiana, Nevada, New Mexico, Texas, Washington, and Wisconsin—have community property laws for married couples. The laws vary, but the basic features of community property are these:

Anything owned before marriage remains the property of the person who owns it.

Gifts and inheritances, before or after marriage, are the property of the person who receives them.

All other property acquired after marriage (including wages, salaries, and other earnings) is community property shared equally by husband and wife, no matter how the property was acquired or whose name it is in.

If the couple is divorced, the property is split between them. If one dies, community property does *not* automatically go to the survivor. It goes to the person named in the deceased spouse's will, or to the next of kin if there is no will.

If you are moving into or out of a community property state, talk to a lawyer in the community property state; lawyers in other states often know little about community property law.

Your home and the law

Buying a home. This may be the biggest financial deal of your life, and the one most important to the happiness of your family. Do not let yourself be rushed or pressured. You should probably consult a lawyer as early as possible, before you commit yourself to anything.

Land and buildings are called *real property*. All contracts for the sale of real property *must* be in writing, and cannot be changed except in writing. Never sign anything on the assurance that "It doesn't really mean anything" or "We'll change that later if you don't like it." *You are legally bound by anything you sign, and an oral agreement to change it is worthless.*

You are bound by anything you sign.

If you buy through a real estate broker, he or she may ask you to leave a deposit and sign a binder agreement to hold the property until you can get together with the seller. Do not sign unless you have spoken to a lawyer. And get a receipt for any deposit.

Downpayments. When you sign the sales contract, or before, you will have to put down a deposit. Make sure

Questions to ask *before* signing a contract

About the property	Exactly what is included in the sale? Stoves, refrigerators, ovens? Carpets, shelves, Venetian blinds, storm windows, screens? Awnings? TV antennas? Is a survey needed? Who pays for it? Are there any old mortgages on the house, judgments against the seller, or payments due to contractors or repairmen?
About the sale	When will the sale be completed? When can I take possession? Are any delays likely? Are there penalties for delays? Who is to pay escrow fees, taxes, insurance, etc.? Are there any hidden fees?
About the mortgage	Can I cancel the contract if I cannot get the kind of mortgage I want? Under what conditions? How much time do I have?
About inspection	Do I have the right to inspect? What if the inspection shows damage from termites or other causes? Suppose the house needs repair? Who pays for it? Can I cancel the contract if the inspection shows the house is unsatisfactory?
About restrictions	Are there any restrictions on building or on the use of the property? What are the zoning regulations? Does the town have a building code? Can I build a tennis court? Put in a swimming pool? Keep a horse? Other pets? Store my old car in the backyard? Practice with my band? Can I run a business out of my home? What kind?
About the neighborhood	What kind of neighborhood is the house in? Who are my neighbors? What school will my children go to? Where can I do my shopping? Is the neighborhood entirely residential, or are there some businesses? What kind? Are there any plans to build a factory in the neighborhood, or run a highway through it?

the contract states when you are entitled to get it back. For example, the contract may take effect only if you can get a "satisfactory" mortgage. The bank offers a mortgage, but the interest rate is too high. The seller might argue that the mortgage was "satisfactory," in which case you would have to go to court to get your money back. You might not succeed. The contract should have defined exactly what, in this particular case, is meant by "satisfactory."

The sales contract. To be valid, the contract must contain all essential terms of the agreement, including enough information to identify the property, the buyer, the seller, the date of sale, the price, and how the money is to be paid.

Some tips to the buyer

- **Make sure of the identity of the seller.** Swindlers usually pass themselves off as someone else.

- **Insist that the seller's spouse sign,** in case he or she has any claim on the property.

- **Beware of printed forms.** They favor the seller.

- **Do not sign without having the house and property inspected,** unless the contract gives you the right to cancel if an inspection shows the place to be unsatisfactory.

Contract clauses of importance to buyers. Make sure your lawyer covers them.

Type of deed	A *quitclaim* deed simply releases all right, title, and interest that the seller has in the property. A *warranty* deed also guarantees that he actually does have the right, title, and interest that he claims to have. Buyers should insist on a warranty deed. If the contract does not specify, the seller only has to give a quitclaim deed.
Date of sale	If it is absolutely imperative that you have the house by a certain date (for example, you have to move from your old house), you can request a clause saying "time is of the essence." This makes the seller responsible for any financial loss you suffer from delay. If such a clause is too strict to be accepted, the seller may at least agree to a clause imposing monetary penalties for each day's delay.
Encumbrances	Property may be "encumbered" by unpaid taxes, old mortgages, court judgments against the seller, claims of third parties, etc. Such encumbrances are what the title insurance company looks for when searching the records. Until the search is made, do not sign any agreement to buy "subject to all encumbrances" unless they are listed specifically. (Title insurance protects you against any unknown or undiscovered encumbrances that turn up in the future.)
Fixtures	Items permanently affixed to the property, such as furnaces or plumbing, are part of the real property. Movables, such as tables or chairs, are not. Many other items, such as storm windows, are borderline. The contract should state exactly what goes with the house and what does not.
Risk of loss	Be sure to include a clause canceling the sale if the house is lost by fire or other disaster before the sale is completed.

You and the Law

How the contract is enforced. What if the seller refuses to go through with the deal? The buyer can sue for any damages and can also sue for "specific performance," which is a court order directing the seller to complete the sale. The seller has the same remedies if the buyer backs out. Most likely, though, he will just keep the down payment and sell the house to someone else.

Title closing. The sale is completed and the deed transferred at the closing. Usually, the buyer, the seller, their lawyers, a representative of the bank or other mortgage lender, and a lawyer from the title insurance company are present. Costs and fees are settled, including the buyer's share of costs already paid by the seller, such as taxes, insurance, fuel, etc.

Escrow. If there are encumbrances on the land, such as judgments or unpaid taxes, part of the purchase price may be put in escrow. This means that a neutral third party will hold the money until the seller removes the encumbrances.

When the sale is complete. Finally, the seller gets his money and the buyer gets his home. Besides the deed, the buyer should receive all insurance policies, tax receipts, and a bill of sale for any personal property, such as furniture, that has been purchased along with the house. The buyer will also receive a title insurance policy and a mortgage statement from the bank.

It is important to have the deed recorded immediately to protect your title. Dishonest persons sometimes sell property to more than one buyer. If the first buyer has not recorded his deed, a person who buys later but is first to record his deed may have a valid claim to the property.

Get it in writing.

Building a home. Contracts to build should be in writing, though it is not legally required. The best way to avoid legal disputes with contractors is to make the contract and specifications as exact and detailed as possible, including types and quality of materials and equipment, colors, and brand names. Any changes should require your written approval.

Method of payment. Partial payments are usually made at various stages of construction, with final payment due when the house is completed. If an architect drew the plans, you might hire him to supervise construction and make payment to the contractor subject to his approval. At the very least, you should have periodic inspections by someone who knows the construction business.

The contract may provide for penalties if the contractor does not finish on time, except in the case of causes beyond his control.

Liens. Serious problems can arise if the contractor does not pay his workmen, suppliers, or subcontractors. Even though you did not deal with them directly, they can file liens, or claims, against the property for the amount owed them. The legal status of these liens depends on your state's law, but they are encumbrances on the property and have roughly the same effect as unpaid mortgages. The contractor is liable for

The home owner should always exercise caution when coming to terms with a contractor. The slip shown below is an estimate, not a contract. It does not bind the contractor to do the work for the stated price.

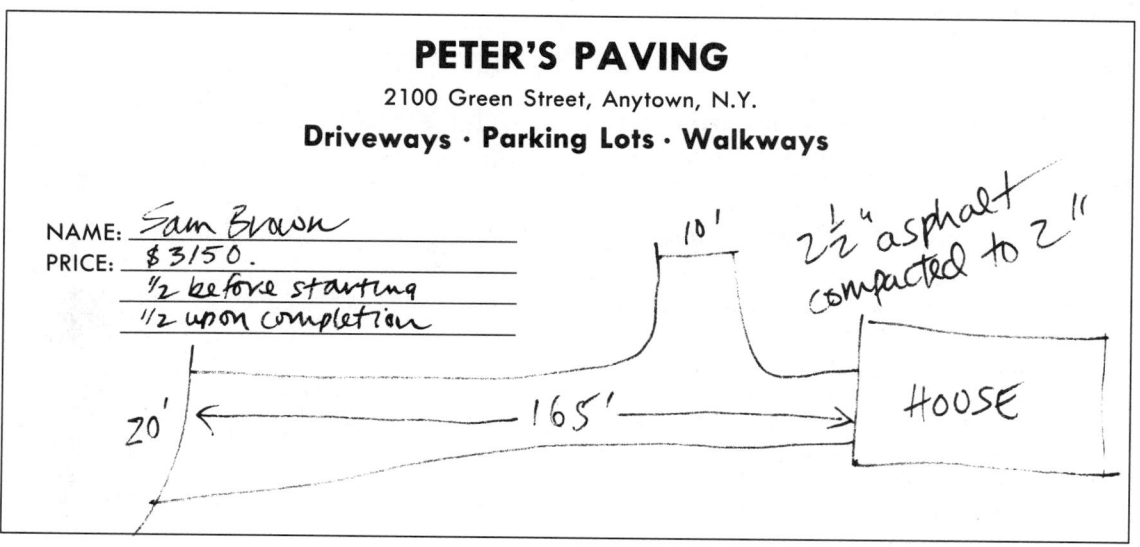

satisfying these claims, but that will not help if he becomes bankrupt or cannot pay.

If you get notice of a lien, do not make any further payments to the contractor until he removes the lien by paying the claim.

One way to protect yourself. You might require the contractor to post a bond to guarantee payment of any claims. Bonds can be obtained from insurance companies; they are common in big commercial projects. There are drawbacks. The premium charged by the insurance company will probably add significantly to the cost of the house, and the insurance company will have a voice in any changes you subsequently want to make in the plans or specifications.

Selling your home.
Sellers have the same legal problems as buyers—but in reverse. If a sales contract is conditional on the buyer's obtaining a mortgage or having an inspection made, be sure to set a time limit, or the sale may be held up indefinitely. Also, stipulate that the buyer relies *solely* on the inspection, not on any promises or statements made by you.

If the buyer cannot get a mortgage, you may be willing to finance all or part of the price by a *purchase money mortgage*. This means you agree to be paid in installments and you retain a mortgage on the property, just like a bank, in case the buyer does not pay.

Real estate brokers. If you sell through a real estate broker, the broker is entitled to his or her commission if he or she produces a buyer who is "ready, willing, and able" to buy at your price. Even if the buyer backs out or cannot get a mortgage, the broker may be entitled to a commission unless you protect yourself by a clause in the contract with the broker.

How to save on taxes when you sell

The Taxpayer Relief Act of 1997 made some 800 amendments to the Internal Revenue Tax Code, including the regulations regarding capital gain from the sale of a home.

If you sell your house after May 6, 1997, you may be able to exclude up to $250,000 of the gains from the sale ($500,000 if filing jointly and certain conditions are met) from your income.

You can qualify for the exclusion if you owned the home for at least two years within a five-year period ending on the date of the home sale *and* if you lived in the home and made it your main residence for at least two years during that period. The ownership and use criteria may be met at different times within the five-year period.

If you sold your house before May 6, 1997, you may exclude up to $125,000 of the gains on the sale of your principal residence if on the date of the sale you

- were 55 years of age or older, *and*
- owned your home for at least three years of the five-year period ending on the date of the sale *and* lived in it for at least three years during the same period, *and*
- neither you nor your spouse excluded gain on the sale of a home after July 26, 1978.

For more detailed information on the regulations regarding capital gains from the sale of a home, see IRS Publication 17, "Your Federal Income Tax (For Individuals)."

Types of real estate brokers' listings

Exclusive right to sell. The broker gets his commission, even if you sell the house yourself.

Exclusive listing. You list with one broker only, but you reserve the right to find a buyer on your own.

Open listing. You list with more than one broker but the one who makes the sale gets the commission. You also reserve the right to find your own buyer.

Which is best? At first glance, an open listing looks best for the seller, but that is not always the case. A broker will work much harder to sell your house if he is sure of getting a commission. Some brokers will not accept open listings. Some of those who do may not exert themselves very much because they would prefer to sell one of their exclusive listings. Your decision may depend on the state of the real estate market and the custom in your community.

Brokers' contracts. Contracts are normally in writing, and should have a time limit, such as six months. When the contract expires, get a list of persons to whom the broker has shown the property. Otherwise, one of those persons may come back later and buy the property. You would then owe the broker a commission because he first produced the buyer.

Look out for the fine print. As always, beware of printed contracts. They favor the broker.

Owners' rights and duties.

Your use of your property may be subject to restrictions for the benefit of other persons or the public in general. Here are some of the most common restrictions.

Covenants and conditions. Deeds often contain restrictions on property, such as a ban on commercial use or rules on the type and size of buildings. Developers often put these rules in deeds to maintain the character of the development. The restrictions are binding on future buyers. If the property has passed through several hands, a thorough search of the records may be needed to discover the restrictions.

If a restriction is made a *condition* of ownership, a violation could cost the owner the title to the property. Most restrictions, however, are *covenants* (promises); if they are violated, nothing happens automatically, but persons who are affected, such as neighbors, can get a court order (injunction) requiring the owner to comply with the covenant. Courts may refuse to enforce covenants if they make no sense because the neighborhood has changed. If in doubt, a landowner can ask for a court ruling in advance. Some covenants are illegal, such as restrictions based on race or religion.

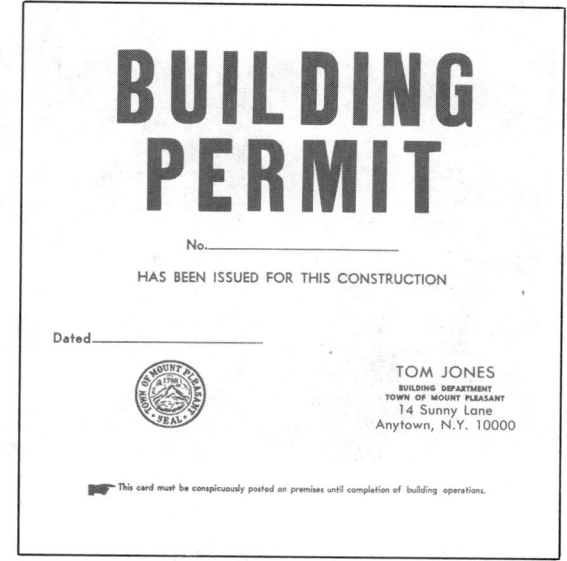

An "Application for Zoning & Building Permit" must be filed with the building department of your local government. The application usually requires specifications about the proposed renovation or new building and may require a survey or architectural drawings.

Public laws. Most communities have zoning laws restricting land use, but they normally do not apply to land or buildings already constructed or in use when the law is passed. Most towns also have building codes and require a permit before building. If you want an *exception* or *variance* from the zoning laws, you have to apply to the zoning board and show good cause. It is very important to show that your neighbors have no objection to the proposed use or construction.

Co-ownership of property

Ownership of property of any kind may be shared by two or more persons. Co-owners are either *tenants in common* or *joint tenants*. (Married couples may also be "tenants by the entirety" or share "community property"—see pages 144–145.)

Do not be confused by the word "tenants." It usually refers to renters of property, but here it means owners.

Tenants in common. Each owns a *fractional* share in the entire property; no one owns any specific part. Each may sell or mortgage his share; creditors may reach it for payment of debt. When a tenant in common dies, his share does not go to the co-owners, but to the person named in his will, or to his next of kin.

Joint tenants. Each owns an *equal* share in the property. Each can sell or mortgage his share, and creditors can reach it. When a joint tenant dies, his share goes to the survivor or survivors. If a joint tenant sells his share, the survivorship feature ends, and the new owner is a tenant in common.

Is co-ownership desirable? Except possibly for married couples or business partners, co-ownership is usually not a good idea. The owners may disagree on what to do with the property. A sale may be missed if one co-owner holds out, as the buyer may be unwilling to take less than full ownership. Even if owners agree on managing the property, one may die or sell out, in which case there would be a new owner to deal with. If the new owner is a minor, the property can be tied up for years.

If the owners are deadlocked, the only solution may be a court order of "partition," which will physically divide the property among the owners.

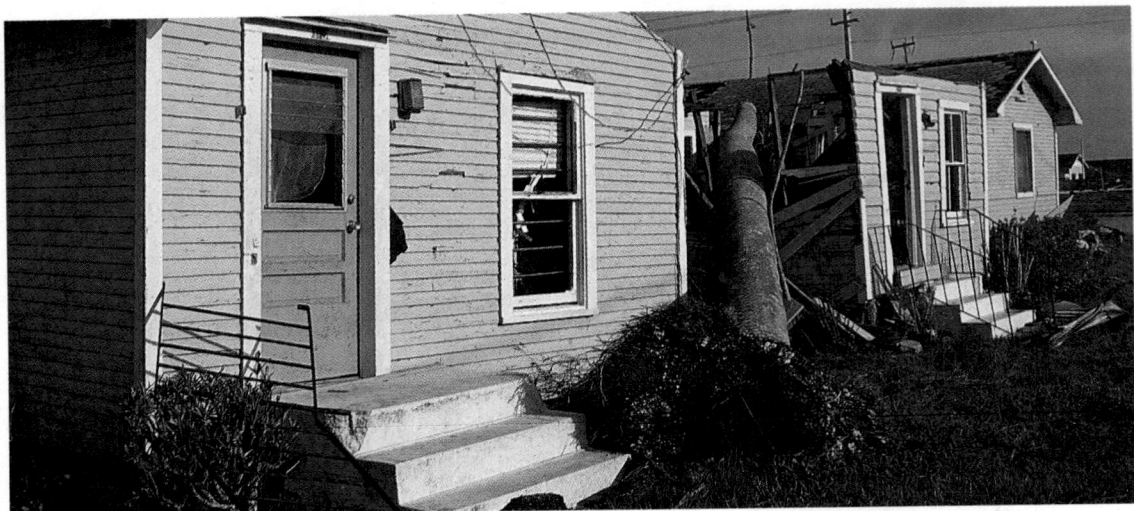
Neighbors have responsibilities toward one another, such as the duty to pay for damage caused by unsupervised children or fallen trees.

Easements. Other persons may have the right to use your property or pass through it. Such easements and rights of way may be purchased, or they may arise from continuous use over a long period of time. If one neighbor has an easement or right of way in the property of another, it will continue even if either or both properties are sold.

Condemnation. The government has the power (eminent domain) to take all or part of your property for public purposes, such as for highways or schools. The power may also be exercised on behalf of public utilities; for example, an electric company may need to run power lines over the land. Landowners are entitled to reasonable compensation, which is decided at a condemnation proceeding, where there is presented evidence from appraisers and experts. You may also be entitled to compensation if the use of your land is interfered with, even if it is not actually taken; for example, low-flying planes from a nearby airport may lessen the value of the property.

Mortgages. If you fail to make mortgage payments, the bank cannot just take your home; it must go to court in a *foreclosure* proceeding. In every state, you are given a period of time (usually a year or more) to make the payments and *redeem* your house—or else work out a new arrangement with the bank, such as smaller payments over a longer period of time.

If you are unable to pay and the mortgage is foreclosed, the property will be sold at auction. If the price does not cover the mortgage, you still owe the balance. If the price is higher than the mortgage, you are entitled to the difference.

Air, water, and mineral rights. You own the air over your land (subject to reasonable use by airplanes) and the minerals beneath it. Air and mineral rights can be sold separately from the land itself, and can be ex-tremely valuable; if you get an offer, see a lawyer.

You own any body of water entirely on your property, such as a pond. But rivers and streams flowing through your land or next to it are subject to the rights of downstream owners. You may not pollute the river, dam it up, or divert it from its course. (Navigable bodies of water are under the jurisdiction of the federal government.)

Neighbors' rights. Neighbors owe each other a duty of *lateral support;* this means they cannot make excavations that would weaken the other's land. If their buildings share a *party wall,* neither can weaken the wall.

Neighbors may not use their land in such a way as to create a *nuisance,* such as loud noise or foul odors. The remedy is to get an injunction banning the nuisance. Overhanging branches from a neighbor's tree may constitute a nuisance, and a landowner has the right to cut them down, but check local laws first.

Insurance. If you have a mortgage, the bank will insist you have fire insurance, but the bank only requires enough insurance to cover the mortgage. You may want to buy more. The cost of replacing a home is likely to be more than the original price because of inflation.

Homeowners should also have liability insurance, in case anyone is injured on the premises. Property owners' liability for injuries is a complicated subject. If you buy insurance, the insurance company will take care of all claims. Some companies sell *comprehensive* policies, which cover most or all kinds of insurance a homeowner wants.

Renting a home.

A contract to rent is a *lease.* Most leases are in a writing, but an oral lease is valid. If no period of time is specified, either the landlord or the tenant can cancel at any time, usually by

You and the Law

one giving a month's notice to the other.

Most written leases specify how long they are to last, usually a year or more. A tenant who stays on after the lease has run out is called a holdover tenant. The landlord has the choice of evicting him, or of regarding the lease as renewed for another term.

Unless the lease states otherwise, the tenant can sublet or assign (transfer) the lease. Most leases, however, ban or restrict the right to assign or sublet, except with the owner's consent.

Landlord's duties. The landlord is responsible for keeping the building structurally sound. The old rule held the tenant responsible for ordinary repairs, but in many states, the landlord is now considered responsible for repairs in residential property, unless otherwise provided in the lease. (In commercial property, the tenant usually makes repairs.) In apartment buildings, the landlord is responsible for maintaining hallways, staircases, driveways, laundry rooms, and other areas used by all the tenants.

A *constructive eviction* occurs if the landlord lets the building run down to the point where it is not fit for use. The tenant can move out, does not have to pay any more rent, and can sue the landlord.

Tenant's duties. The tenant's main obligation is to pay rent. If he moves before the lease expires, he must continue to pay rent until the end of the lease or until the landlord rents the property to someone else. Under traditional law, the tenant had to pay the rent even if the landlord violated his part of the agreement—or even if the house burned down. This rule has been modified in many states.

Some states recognize an "implied warranty of habitability," which means the landlord is regarded as promising that the property is fit for the tenant to live in, even if the lease contains no actual promise or guarantee. Tenants can sue for violation of the implied promise or withhold payment of the rent. How serious does a violation have to be to justify not paying the rent? That depends on the rules of the state. Check with a lawyer or with a tenants' group before trying it.

Tenants are liable for any damage they do to the property. Landlords usually require a security deposit when the lease is signed. The tenant gets the deposit back when he leaves, if he has not damaged the property and does not owe any rent. Sometimes the deposit serves in place of the final month's rent. Some states require the landlord to pay interest on the security deposit.

Government regulations. Many state and local governments have passed laws that extensively regulate the relationship between landlords and tenants, especially in communities with housing shortages; some have rent control. Landlords' associations and tenants' groups will provide members with information and, sometimes, legal counsel.

Co-operatives and condominiums

"Co-ops" and "condos" are the fastest growing type of housing in the United States.

Co-ops. A co-operative apartment house is owned by a corporation. The residents are the stockholders; they own shares in proportion to the value of their apartments. Each has the exclusive use of his own apartment and the right to use common areas: stairways, halls, basement, grounds, driveways. The mortgage covers the entire building; stockholders are not personally liable for payment, but must make up the difference if any stockholder defaults, or risk foreclosure of the mortgage. Anyone who wants to sell must get approval from the other stockholders, who rule on the desirability of the proposed new resident.

Condos. Each condominium resident actually *owns* his apartment and shares ownership of the common areas. Each separate apartment can be mortgaged. This sometimes makes condos easier to buy and sell than co-ops, as banks are more willing to lend money if they can get a mortgage on the owner's apartment. (Co-op owners have only their shares of stock to pledge as security for a loan; the primary mortgage is on the whole building.) Condos are also easier to sell because approval of the other owners is not required (though owners may reserve the right to buy the condo themselves if they do not like a proposed owner).

Both co-ops and condos are run by a committee of residents; often, they hire a professional manager. Residents pay a monthly fee, which often includes maintenance, taxes, mortgage payments, etc. The ground floor is sometimes rented to commercial tenants, but there are legal limitations on how much of the building can be rented.

Advantages of co-ops and condos over renting:
• The residents actually own property. They can sell it or raise money on it. Tenants own nothing.
• Owners usually take better care of property than tenants do.
• Property owners get valuable tax breaks that renters do not, including tax deductions for mortgage interest and real estate taxes.

Wills and estates

What is a will? A will is a way for a person (the testator) to direct who will get his property (estate) after his death. The will has no effect before death and can be changed or revoked at any time. A will is valid even if it does not dispose of *all* the testator's property; anything not mentioned in the will goes to the next of kin under state law. Normally, a will contains a "residuary clause" naming a person or persons to get everything not specifically left to someone else.

Why do you need a will? If you have no will, your property will be distributed according to state law, regardless of your wishes or your family's needs. The court will appoint an administrator (and a guardian if you leave children). They will have to post bond, which will be payable from your estate, along with their fees. If any money or property goes to minors, it will be tied up until they come of age. The guardian will not be able to touch it, even for education or medical costs, without getting a special court order.

If you have a will, you can be sure your property will go to the persons of your choice. You can appoint an executor to handle the estate, and guardians or trustees for the property of children. You can give the persons you appoint any powers that you see fit, or impose any limitations. You can direct what is to happen if you and your spouse (or other heirs) should die at the same time —in an auto accident, for example.

You can also appoint a personal guardian for your minor children; the appointment is not binding, but the court will usually follow your wishes.

How to make a will. The testator must be at least 18 years old and of sound mind. The will must be in writing and signed in the presence of two witnesses (three, in some states); the witnesses should also sign. Witnesses cannot inherit under a will, so do not pick as a witness anyone you are leaving anything to.

If you die without a will . . .

- **If you leave a spouse and children,** they get your estate. In some states, it is divided half and half; in others the children take two-thirds and the spouse one-third. If you leave no spouse, the children get it all. If any of your children die before you, their children take what would have been their share. If you leave no children, the spouse either gets everything or, in some states, divides the estate with your parents, brothers, and sisters.

- **If you leave no wife or descendants,** your parents take the estate; if they are not alive, your brothers and sisters (or their children, if they are deceased) divide the estate.

- **If you leave no close relatives,** you can figure out who is your next of kin by counting generations to and from a common ancestor. For example, you and your first cousins have a common grandparent; so you count back two generations to the grandparent, and two generations down to your cousins. They are of the fourth degree of relationship. Their children would be of the fifth degree. Your estate will be split equally among all those of the nearest degree of relationship. Some states do not allow relatives beyond a specified degree to inherit.

- **If you leave no next of kin,** everything goes to the state.

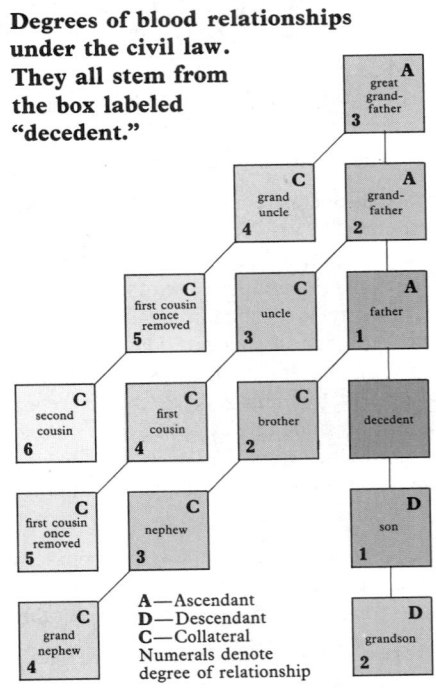

Degrees of blood relationships under the civil law. They all stem from the box labeled "decedent."

A—Ascendant
D—Descendant
C—Collateral
Numerals denote degree of relationship

There are exceptions. Some states require no witnesses to a *holographic* will, one entirely in the testator's handwriting. Some states allow *oral* wills in special circumstances, such as on a deathbed or when a serviceman is going overseas. Holographic or oral wills should be used only in emergencies, and replaced by a regular will as soon as possible.

Changes to a will (codicils) must also be in writing, signed, and witnessed.

A will may be declared invalid if the testator was of such unsound mind that he did not understand what he was doing, or if the will was made because of force, duress, fraud, mistake, or undue influence.

Revoking a will. A will can be revoked by another will or written document, signed and witnessed. It can also be revoked by physical destruction, such as tearing it up or burning it; but this is *not* a good idea. If you die and your will is not found, no one will know whether it was destroyed or just lost. A lost will, however, can be given effect if there is a copy, or some other proof of what was in it.

A will may be revoked by a later marriage or the birth or adoption of a child. In some states, the revocation is only partial. The wife or child gets what he or she would have inherited if there were no will; the balance, if any, is distributed according to the will.

Your rights to your body

UNIFORM DONOR CARD

You do not have an absolute right to decide where you will be buried or what service will be performed. The right belongs to the next of kin. Normally, however, your wishes will be respected.

You do have the right to leave your body to a hospital, college, or medical school for scientific purposes, or to donate any parts of your body for organ transplants. You can do this in your will or by using a special form; one common form is called a "Universal Donor Card." (Using a will may be too slow, especially in the case of transplants.)

Make your decision known. If you are donating your body, be sure to notify your family, your doctor, and any hospital you are in. You should also keep a copy of the donor card with you, in your wallet or purse, in case you die in an accident or away from home.

Sample will clauses

Specific bequests	I bequeath to my niece Jane Roberts, now residing at 4 Main Street, Centerville, IL, the sum of three thousand dollars ($3,000.00). I bequeath to my son John Jones, now residing at 2 Main Street, Centerville, IL, all my jewelry and any other personal effects and mementos which he may desire.
Residuary clause	I give, devise, and bequeath all of the rest, residue, and remainder of my estate to my wife Mary Jones if she survives me. If she fails to survive me, then I give the remainder of my estate to my friend William Brown, now residing at 10 Elm Street, Centerville, IL.
Common disaster clause	In the event that my wife Mary Jones and I die under circumstances where it cannot be established who died first, it shall be presumed that I survived my wife and this will and all dispositions contained herein shall be interpreted on the basis of that presumption.
Appointment of executor	I nominate my son John Jones as executor of my estate, to serve without bond. If my son predeceases me or is for any reason unable or unwilling to serve, then I appoint the First National Bank of Centerville, IL, as executor.
Appointment of guardian	Should my son John Jones be under the age of 18 years when I die, then I nominate my brother Thomas Jones and his wife Ann Jones, now residing at 12 Elm Street, Centerville, IL, to be guardians of his person. I appoint the First National Bank of Centerville to be guardian of all my son's property, subject to the following rules (enumerate powers and limitations on guardian).

Limitations on wills. You can disinherit any relative, including children, but you cannot totally disinherit a spouse. All states require that a certain minimum be left to the spouse. If it is not, the spouse can elect to get the share he or she would have received had the testator died without a will.

Some states limit the amount you can leave to charity if you are survived by a spouse, children, or other close relatives.

Mutual wills. Contracts to make wills or leave property to specific persons are enforceable. Sometimes, husbands and wives make mutual wills. Each leaves his or her property to the other, with the entire property to go to named beneficiaries (such as children) upon the death of the survivor. If the wills are made by agreement, the surviving spouse cannot change his or her will. But the agreement should be stated clearly in the will or in a separate written document. The mere fact that the two wills are the same does not prove that they were made by contractual agreement.

Probate and how to avoid it.

Court proceedings to establish your will and settle the estate (probate) are usually necessary, even if you die without a will. The court will appoint an administrator, usually your next of kin. Some property, however, need not go through court. Joint property goes directly to the joint owner. Insurance proceeds are paid directly to the beneficiary.

Some people want to avoid court proceedings to save costs and delay, and to maintain privacy (court records are open to the public). The best way is to put all your property in a trust (see *Glossary*), naming yourself as beneficiary for life and designating the persons you want to receive the property at your death, just as in a will. You should still have a will, however, as you may own property at your death without realizing it. For example, if you die in an accident, your estate may have a claim against the person responsible. Or you may have inherited property that has not yet been distributed.

Consumers' rights

You may have heard of the old legal rule Caveat emptor, Latin for "Let the buyer beware." If a buyer purchased shoddy goods, paid exorbitant prices, or failed to read the fine print in a contract, any problem was considered to be his own fault. This is still the law in the case of some business deals, but state and federal laws protect consumers in most transactions.

A consumer loan or transaction is for the purchase of goods or services for personal, family, or household purposes, and sometimes for agricultural purposes.

Getting out of bad deals. Federal and

state laws ban false, fraudulent, and deceptive advertising. Not only outright falsehoods are banned, but also deceptive practices such as "bait and switch" advertising, in which a merchant advertises a bargain to get you into his store (the bait), then tells you the bargain item is sold out and talks you into buying something more expensive (the switch).

You may be able to cancel a sale or a contract on grounds of fraudulent advertising, but it is hard to

prove. Mere sales talk or exaggeration about a product is not enough; and if a salesman does tell an outright lie, he will probably deny it. The best course is not to be taken in by tricky advertising in the first place. Many agencies have published pamphlets and booklets telling consumers what to look out for. Write your state consumer agency, or the Consumer Information Center, Pueblo, CO 81009.

Mail-order sales. If you buy something by mail, you can cancel the order and get your money back if the goods are not shipped within 30 days.

You absolutely do not have to pay for unsolicited goods sent through the mail. You do not have to send them back either. Just treat them as a gift.

Door-to-door sales. If you sign a contract with a door-to-door salesman, you have three business days to think it over. Within this period, you can cancel the sale and get back any payments just by giving written notice to the seller. However, if you request immediate delivery, you lose this right.

Warranties. A warranty is a guarantee or

promise about the quality or condition of goods and products; sometimes it includes a promise to repair. An express warranty is one actually made by the manufacturer or seller. Whether or not he makes an express warranty, the law regards him as making an implied warranty that the goods are fit for the purpose they are

"Caveat emptor."
Let the buyer beware.

LIMITED ONE-YEAR WARRANTY

Name _____

Address _____

City _____ State _____ Zip code _____

Date purchased _____ Store name _____

Product name _____ Model number _____

A warranty gives you specific legal rights, but you may also have other rights that vary from state to state. Consult your lawyer.

being purchased for. The seller can avoid this, however, by specifically stating that he makes no warranties whatsoever; this statement is called a disclaimer.

If the goods do not live up to the warranty, the buyer can sue for damages or get his money back.

Federal law. A seller who makes a written warranty must designate the warranty as *full* or *limited*. Under a full warranty, if repeated attempts to repair a product fail, the consumer must be given the choice of a replacement or his money back.

Defective products. What redress is available if someone is injured by an exploding bottle, contaminated food, or an appliance that catches fire? The buyer can sue under the product warranty. But suppose someone else is hurt, or the seller has specifically disclaimed any warranties?

In the past, it was necessary to prove the injury was caused by negligent or improper manufacture or handling of the product. Sometimes negligence is obvious (a dead mouse is found in a bottle of soda). But in many cases it may be difficult to prove negligence in manufacture, or to determine just who was at fault.

The modern trend. Today, many states impose *strict liability* on anyone who sells a consumer product, from the manufacturer to the retailer. The injured person need only prove that the product was defective and caused the injury. The rule of strict liability is applied in most cases involving food, drugs and medicines, clothing, cosmetics, and other products intended for bodily use, and products inherently dangerous, such as automobiles. In other cases, it may still be necessary to prove negligence in manufacturing. It depends on state law.

Credit.

Anyone who makes a loan or extends credit for consumer purposes must disclose all terms and conditions in clear, understandable language, including the annual interest rate, any other charges, and what happens if there is a dispute or if the consumer fails to pay. Credit may not be denied because of race, religion, national origin, age, sex, marital status, or receipt of public assistance. If you are denied credit (a loan, a charge account, a credit card) you must be told why—in writing.

Protecting your credit rating. If you are turned down because of an unfavorable report from a credit rating bureau or agency, you must be told which agency. Upon request, the agency must tell you the nature and source of the unfavorable information (but it does not have to show you its file). It must also disclose the names and addresses of all persons who have been given the information within the past six months (two years if the information was given for employment purposes).

If you disagree, you may insist that the agency reinvestigate. If you still disagree, you may put a brief statement of your own in the file (up to 100 words) telling your side of the story.

Small claims court

All states have small claims courts to handle cases involving less than a maximum amount set by state law. The federal Tax Court has a Small Case Division to handle tax disputes up to $10,000. Small claims courts provide a speedy, inexpensive way for people to assert their legal rights without the time, trouble, and cost of a major lawsuit.

Bringing a lawsuit. The court clerk will help you fill out the forms to start the case. There is a small fee, which the other side will pay if you win. The other party will be notified. Often, this will be enough to get him to settle. If not, you will be notified of the time and place of trial.

Caution: If the other party pays up, you can just drop the case. But if he only *promises* to pay, be sure to show up on the trial date and tell the judge. The case will then be held open, to make sure that you get paid.

Trials are informal. You can have a lawyer, but you do not need one. Here are some tips on how to behave:

- Dress well, but do not dress up.
- Stand when you talk to the judge. Call him or her "Your Honor."
- Describe your case in a general way before going into detail. Be sure to bring with you all documentary evidence, such as bills, canceled checks, letters, forms, etc.
- Testify yourself and call any witnesses.
- Do not fight or argue with the other party. Do not act like a lawyer. Do not ever argue with the judge.
- Do what the judge says. If he or she asks you a question, answer it. If he or she tells you not to say anything, be silent.

Credit cards. If your card is lost or stolen, you should notify the credit card company at once. But even if someone has used the card before you notify the company, you can be held liable for no more than $50.

If you find an error on your monthly statement, you must notify the company within 60 days, in writing, stating your name, address, card number, and the nature and amount of the mistake. *A phone call is not sufficient, nor is a note written on the monthly bill.* Write a separate letter. The company must investigate and give you a written answer within two billing periods, but not longer than 90 days.

Until then, the company may not try to collect the disputed amount; it may not revoke your card; and it may not report you as a delinquent payer to anyone, such as a credit rating bureau.

If the company, after investigation, still insists that you owe the money, it must furnish you with documentary evidence upon your request. If you still disagree, you should protect your credit rating by writing to the company again. If the company then reports you to anyone as delinquent, it must also report that the matter is in dispute and must notify you of the report.

Defective goods. If you buy merchandise that turns out to be defective or worthless, you do not have to pay the credit card company, provided:
- The transaction was for more than $50.
- It was made in your home state or within 100 miles of your home.
- You made an honest attempt to settle the dispute with the merchant.

The rule applies only to the unpaid balance. You cannot get back payments already made. Of course, you can try to get your money back from the merchant.

Bill collectors. Bill collection agencies operate under federal restrictions. The law does not apply, however, to persons or companies trying to collect their own debts. The following practices by collection agencies are forbidden:
- Telling anyone, including your employer, that you owe a debt (but they may ask for your address).
- Contacting you at unreasonable times or places (no middle-of-the-night phone calls).
- Using forms or envelopes that look official.
- Sending collection notices on postcards that other people might read.
- Using any abusive, deceptive, or unfair methods.

Moreover, the agency must stop *all* bill collection efforts if you notify them in writing to stop, or tell them you dispute the debt, or hire a lawyer.

If the agency violates the law, you can sue for actual damages, plus up to $1000 additional damages (if the court so decides), plus costs and attorneys' fees.

Are your debts too big?

Although you should always exercise care not to accumulate too many debts, it may happen that you become overwhelmed by the amount of money you owe. Declaring bankruptcy is the solution of last resort. Prudent management of your money will not only help you avoid bankruptcy, it can often get you out of your overwhelming debt. Read carefully "Managing the Family's Money," pages 110-139, for good advice on how not to overextend yourself. Sometimes it makes sense to consolidate your debts in order to avoid high monthly payments (see page 117 for more information). In order to get a fresh start, however, you may have to file for personal bankruptcy in a federal court.

How it works. You give the court a list of everything you own, the debts you owe, and any debts owed to you. The court appoints a trustee to collect your assets and distribute them to creditors. Mortgaged property or property pledged as security (collateral) goes to the particular creditor involved; the rest is distributed proportionately to all. If you have not misrepresented or concealed anything, your debts will be canceled (discharged) except for taxes, alimony, and child support.

Caution: Judges have the power to deny discharges if they find that the debtor *can* pay his debts and is improperly trying to take advantage of the bankruptcy law.

What you keep. Not everything you own can be taken. You can keep personal belongings, most household goods, your car (up to $1200 in value), the tools of your trade, and a certain amount of cash. But if you own a home, you could be in danger of losing it. There is a "homestead exemption" of $7500, but if your house is worth more, it will be sold, and you will receive only the $7500.

Wage earner plans. The bankruptcy law provides another alternative, under which you submit to the court a plan to pay a specified amount each month, depending on your income, how much you owe, and the needs of your family. If the court approves the plan and you make the monthly payments, your creditors are not allowed to demand more. Eventually, you will be free of debt.

Personal property

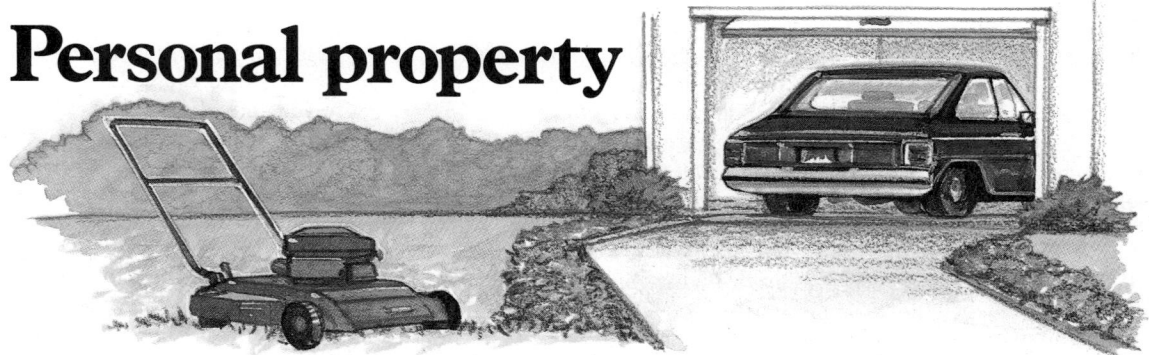

Your neighbor is responsible for your lawnmower if he borrows it for his own use, but you are not responsible for his car if you let him park in your garage.

Land and buildings are *real* property. All other property is *personal* property, including cash, movable goods, stocks, bonds, and intangible legal rights.

Abandoned property belongs to the finder. *Lost* property belongs to the finder only if the real owner cannot be found. Many states require that anything over a certain value be turned over to the police; the finder gets it if the owner fails to turn up within a specified period. *Stolen* property continues to belong to the owner; he can get it back, even from people who bought it without knowing that it was stolen. The exception is *cash*. If cash is stolen, you can recover it only if it is still in the possession of the thief.

Owners and possessors

Bailments. Temporary transfers of possession, but not ownership, of property are called bailments. If someone borrows property for his own use (your neighbor borrows your lawnmower), he is normally required to return it or pay for any loss or damage. If the bailment is for the benefit of the owner (you let someone keep his car in your garage), you, the possessor, are responsible only for intentional damage or gross negligence.

Most bailments are business transactions for mutual benefit (you take your TV set to the repair shop, or leave your jewelry as security for a loan). The possessor must use reasonable care, and is responsible for loss or damage that results from his negligence.

Some special cases. Hotels and motels are usually protected by state laws limiting liability to a small amount—and then only if the property is put in the hotel safe. Common carriers, such as railroads or trucking companies, are held to a high standard of care. They are generally liable for all loss or damage, unless caused by improper packing or an act of God, such as lightning, a flood, or a hurricane.

Liens. Repairmen, hotelkeepers, and others have a lien on goods in their possession; they can keep them until their bill is paid. If you want your property back, you have no choice but to pay—or go to court. (If you are

overcharged, consider suing in small claims court—see page 157.)

Ideas as property. You cannot "own" an idea. If you have a business idea you think is worth money, do not divulge it to anyone unless you get an agreement to pay for its use, or to keep it confidential. **Copyrights** protect writing, music, works of art, and computer programs. What is protected is not the idea, but the form in which it is expressed. The copyright belongs to the producer of the work (or to his employer, if the work was done for hire). Copyrights can be registered, but need not be.

Patents are issued by the U.S. Patent Office to protect inventors. No one else may copy or manufacture the invention for a period of years. There is an exception, however. The inventor's employer may own the invention or have rights in it if it was invented during the course of employment.

Trademarks are names, designs, or slogans associated with a company or product; they may not be copied by competing companies. Trademarks may be registered or may simply arise from long use and association.

Installment sales. Sales of autos, furniture, and the like are often *conditional sales.* The buyer takes possession, but the seller remains legal owner until the goods are paid for. He can repossess the goods (if this can be accomplished without violence) or get them back from third parties if the buyer has sold or transferred them.

Watch out for this trap. An installment buyer usually signs a *promissory note* for the amount due. If a merchant sells the note to a finance company, the buyer will find himself in debt to the finance company even if the goods are defective or worthless. The finance company is a "holder in due course," not responsible for the condition of the goods. Many states have modified this rule. If you find yourself in this spot, talk to a lawyer or consumers' rights agency.

Your car. Legally, buying a car is no different from buying any other consumer product, but mistakes can be more costly. (For the law of conditional sales, see page 159; for the law of warranty, see page 156.) Be sure to read the warranty you get with your car. It tells you what rights you have if anything goes wrong.

"Lemon" laws. Many states have laws, stronger than the federal law, protecting consumers who buy cars that turn sour. The laws vary, but most work like this: If, within a year (or the warranty period, if less than a year), the dealer or manufacturer has been unable to repair a defect after four tries, or if the car has been out of commission for 30 days or more, the buyer is entitled to a new car or his money back.

Used cars. If you buy from a used car dealer, you are probably buying at your own risk, except for whatever warranty the dealer may give you. This holds even more so when you buy from a private party, unless you can show that you were defrauded.

Registration. A dealer will probably handle the registration of the car. If you buy privately, you may have to handle it yourself, and you may have to pay a sales tax to get the car registered. Contact your local motor vehicle bureau.

Insurance. Most states require car owners to carry liability insurance to cover any claims arising from auto accidents. Other types of insurance, such as fire, theft, or collision, are not required. You can buy them or not, as you choose.

Used car buyers do not have as much legal protection as new car buyers should the car prove to be a disappointment.

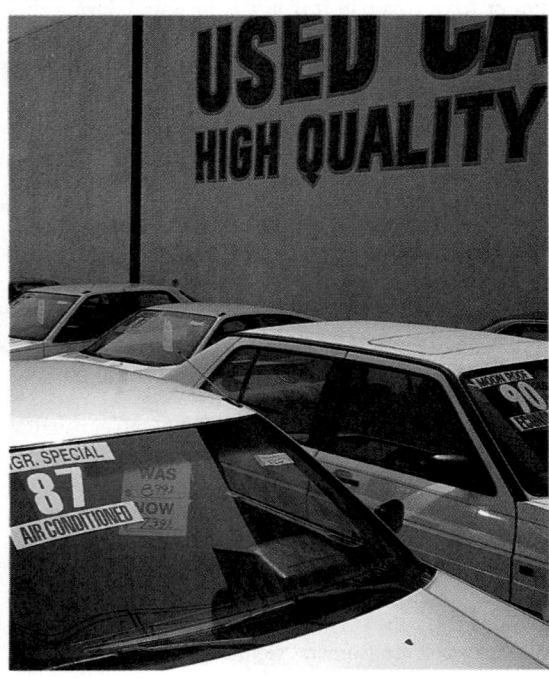

Accidents. More lawsuits arise from auto accidents than from any other single cause. If you are involved in one, notify your insurance company immediately. The company will handle any claim against you, provide a lawyer if you are sued, and pay any judgment. If the judgment is for more than your insurance coverage, you are liable for the balance. You are required to cooperate with the insurance company in the defense of the case.

If you are injured. You may wish to make a claim for personal injuries or property damage. Write to the owner or driver of the other car, stating that you are making a claim, and asking him to turn it over to his insurance company, which will probably contact you. *Do not give the opposing insurance company any written statement about the accident;* it can be used against you. If you do not have a lawyer, you will have to communicate the nature of your claim and provide evidence, such as doctors' reports and repair bills. Do not give more evidence than is necessary, and never make any admissions. (If you have a lawyer, he will handle all this; it would be improper for the other side to contact you personally.)

Should you get a lawyer? A lawyer can probably get more than you can from the insurance company, but he will take part of it for his fee. Most accident cases are on a *contingent fee* basis. The lawyer gets nothing if you lose; but if you win he gets a percentage, which may run from a third to a half. It may even be more for small claims, as the lawyer may have to do as much paperwork in a small case as a large one. If the percentage seems too high, you might try to settle the claim yourself. You can call in a lawyer later, if necessary.

Evaluating a claim. You are entitled to be paid for actual losses, such as lost wages, repair bills, and medical costs (even if paid by insurance). These are called special damages. You are also entitled to damages for pain and suffering. As a general rule, a settlement should run from two to four times the amount of special damages. If there is doubt as to who was at fault in the accident, the settlement may be less. If there are permanent injuries, it will be much more, since future losses, expenses, and pain and suffering must be taken into account.

The law of negligence. Except in states with no-fault insurance, you can recover damages only from a person who has caused an accident through negligence (carelessness). Negligence means the failure to use the ordinary care that could be expected of a reasonable person. Violation of the traffic laws is evidence of negligence, but a driver may be negligent without violating any law.

Who may recover? In some states, the injured person may not recover damages if he has also been guilty of negligence, even in the slightest degree. This is called contributory negligence. Other states follow a rule of comparative negligence. The injured party can recover, but the amount he gets will be reduced in proportion to the extent he was at fault for the accident. A jury, for example, might find that the injured party was 20 percent responsible, and reduce his damages by that percentage.

Owner's liability. The driver is liable for his negligence. Under traditional law, the owner of the vehicle was liable only if the driver was his employee or was acting on the owner's behalf. In some states, it was presumed that any member of the owner's family was acting on his behalf (family purpose rule).

Many states now hold the owner responsible whenever the car is being driven with his consent.

Uninsured motorist laws. Many states have passed laws and established funds to pay persons injured by stolen cars, cars that do not carry insurance, and hit-and-run drivers who cannot be identified.

Who can sue? In most states, one spouse cannot sue the other for negligence, nor can a minor child sue a parent for negligence. Some states allow a child to sue if the parent does not have custody.

Some states have "guest statutes" that ban a guest in an automobile from suing the owner. The guest can, of course, sue the driver of the other car.

No-fault insurance

A growing number of states are adopting no-fault insurance laws, under which persons injured in auto accidents are paid for their economic losses no matter who was at fault, including lost wages and out-of-pocket medical expenses (not covered by medical insurance). Under this system, you apply to your own insurance company for payment instead of suing the other driver. Passengers in your car also apply to your company. Injured pedestrians apply to the company carrying insurance on the car that hit them.

Lawsuits are still possible. In serious cases, you can also sue the other driver for damages, including pain and suffering. A serious case is one involving death or permanent injury, or medical expenses above a threshold amount, which is set by state law.

A good idea? Advocates of no-fault insurance claim that it speeds payments, avoids lawsuits, and cuts the cost of insurance. Some claimants receive smaller amounts than under the old system, but they save the cost of a lawyer.

What to do if you are involved in an accident

1. Get help

First of all, get medical help for anyone who is injured. If the accident is at all serious, call the police.

2. Exchange information

Exchange information with the other driver. Get his name, address, phone number, license number, and the make and license number of his car. If the driver does not own the car, get the owner's name, address, and phone number.

Do not admit you were at fault. Do not get into any argument about who was at fault. Stay calm and simply exchange information.

3. Get evidence

Get names, addresses, and phone numbers of passengers and witnesses. If the police come to the scene, get the officers' names and badge numbers, and the address and phone number of their station.

If you have a camera with you, take pictures of the scene. Otherwise, get photographs as soon after the accident as possible. Write down the details of the accident as soon as you get the chance, while you still remember them clearly. Include all details, such as the weather, time of day, and visibility.

4. Give notice

All states require a report to the police if anyone was injured. It is also required for property damage beyond a certain amount, set by state law. If in doubt, play it safe and file a report.

Notify your insurance company as soon as you possibly can. Failure to report, or unnecessary delay, could jeopardize your insurance coverage.

Injuries and damages

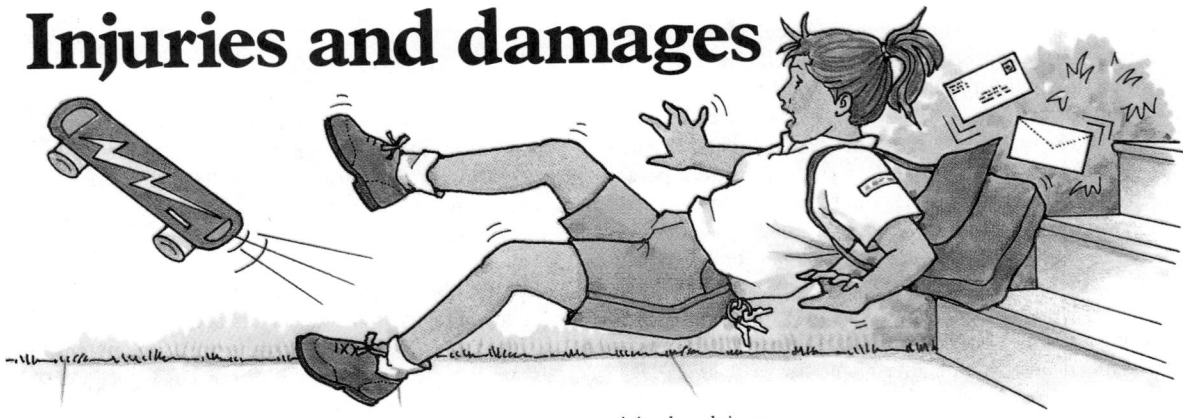

Property owners must exercise reasonable care that customers or guests are not injured on their property.

A wrongful act that injures another person or his property is called a tort. Torts are classified as intentional or negligent. Auto accidents are the most common examples of negligent tort; another is malpractice by doctors, lawyers, or other professionals.

Property owners' liability.
Many lawsuits arise over injuries on someone else's property; for example, someone trips and falls. Whether the property owner is liable may depend on who is injured. Here are the rules:

- **Invitees** are invited on the premises for business purposes; an example is customers in a store. The owner owes them a duty of reasonable care and is liable for any negligence.
- **Licensees** are persons allowed on the premises who are not business invitees. Social guests generally fall into this category. Licensees are on the premises at their own risk, but owners are under a duty to warn of hidden dangers, such as a loose floorboard.
- **Trespassers** have no right on the premises, and owners owe them no duty except to refrain from intentional harm. However, if the trespassers are children, and the owner knows that some building, structure, condition, or object on the property is likely to attract children, he may be held liable for any failure to exercise reasonable care.

Intentional torts.
The word "intentional" does not necessarily imply an intention to hurt anyone. For example, if you slap someone on the back, thinking he is an old friend, and he turns out to be a stranger with a heart condition, you are liable for any damage.

Intention to harm (malice) is necessary to recover *punitive damages*. Punitive damages, over and above any actual damages, may be awarded to punish the wrongdoer and deter him (and others) from repeating the wrongful act.

Assault and battery. Assault is a threat of violence that puts someone in fear of bodily harm. Battery is the actual physical contact. Either (or both) is grounds for a lawsuit.

Self-defense is the only legal excuse. Insults or provocative language do not excuse assault and battery; but the jury may consider them in awarding damages.

Illegal confinement. This term includes any interference with personal liberty, including false arrest, false imprisonment, or any detention by physical barriers, force, or the threat of force. Normally, no one may be detained against his will. But most states permit shopkeepers and others to detain persons suspected of theft, provided they have reasonable grounds for suspicion and do not use excessive force or make unnecessary false public accusations.

Private citizens who make citizen's arrests do so at their own risk. If the arrested person is released or acquitted, he may sue. (For police arrests, see pages 167-168.)

Defamation of character. Defamation is the communication of false statements that injure the reputation of a living person. False statements about the dead, or about groups in general, are not defamation, no matter how offensive.

Libel is written defamation; slander is spoken defamation. Traditionally, libel was more serious, as the written word can be more widely circulated. Radio and TV have made the distinction less important. Pictures or other communications may be defamatory, as well as words.

A statement is automatically defamatory if it accuses a person of crime, immoral or unethical conduct, loathsome disease, unfitness for one's trade or profession, or unchastity (if female). Even if there is no financial damage, a person may sue to vindicate his reputation. For other statements, a person must show in what way they were defamatory and what damages were suffered.

You and the Law

Publication. To be defamatory, a statement must be communicated to a third person; private insults do not count. But communication to even one other person is enough to constitute publication. Anyone who repeats or republishes a defamation also commits defamation.

Defenses. If you are sued for defamation, there are several ways to defend yourself.

• By showing the statement was *true*.

• By proving the person gave *consent* to the statement.

• By showing the statement was *fair comment* on a matter of public interest. (A fair comment is one based on fact, or an honest expression of belief or opinion, and not made from malicioua or dishonorable motives.)

• By showing you had a *privilege* to make the statement. Any statement is absolutely privileged if made between husband and wife, or if made in court, legislative, or other government proceedings.

There is also a *qualified privilege* for statements by an employer who is asked about an employee, and for statements by newspapers or other media about public figures. But the privilege is lost if the statement was made with malice and with either a knowledge of its falsity or a reckless disregard for the truth.

Invasion of privacy. No one may use your name or picture for commercial or advertising purposes without your consent. You can sue for damages and can also get a court order stopping such use.

There has been much discussion of the right of privacy and the danger of computerized data banks that hold information about private lives and personal affairs. So far, however, there are few laws on the subject.

Trespass. Anybody who goes on someone else's land (or enters their buildings) without permission, or places or throws anything on the property, is a trespasser and can be sued for any damage to the property. Even if no damage is done, the owner may want to sue to establish his right to keep the person off the property.

Conversion. Trespass applies to real property; the term "conversion" applies to personal property. Anyone who takes another's personal property or uses it without permission, or obtains it by fraud or trickery, or destroys or damages it, or disposes of it without permission by sale, gift, lease, or other means, has committed a conversion (meaning he "converted" the property to his own purposes). Even if someone has legal possession of another's property, he commits conversion if he damages it, loses it, gives it away, or refuses to return it. The owner can sue for any damage to the property, or the full value, if it is lost or destroyed.

A lawsuit for conversion is a lawsuit for money. If the owner wants the actual property back, he may file a lawsuit known as replevin.

Rights to privacy extend to public settings. Your name and picture may not be used for commercial purposes without your consent.

Emotional damages

Courts are reluctant to award damages when the only injury is emotional. There is too much chance of fraud or of exaggerated claims for hurt feelings. But where there has been actual physical injury, the court or jury may award additional damages for emotional harm. The physical injury proves the claim is not a fraud and that it involves more than hurt feelings.

Recent trends. Recently, there has been a trend toward allowing damages solely for emotional harm where it is obvious that the harm is real. For instance, a mother who watched her child run down by a car recovered emotional damages from the driver. Damages will also be awarded if they result from some illegal act.

There has also been a trend toward allowing damages for intentional infliction of emotional harm. Examples would include vicious harassment by bill collectors and obscene phone calls.

A special case. Common carriers, such as railroads and bus lines, are obligated to provide passengers with courteous service. Therefore, they can be sued for insulting behavior on the part of their employees.

Earning a living

Your job. At one time, employers could hire, fire, and set the terms and conditions of work almost at will. About all an employee could do was quit or accept the conditions. Today, employees' rights are protected by federal and state laws, enforced by government agencies. Some laws give employees the right to sue on their own, but it is usually better to go to an agency and take advantage of its services. Some important laws and agencies are in the chart below.

Who are employees? If your boss has the right to control the manner and means by which you do your job, you are an employee. If not, you are an independent contractor. A good example of an independent contractor is your doctor; you hire him to cure your illness, but you do not tell him how to examine you or

PLACEMENT SUPERVISOR: (Work-site) to provide vocational training to handicapped adults for job placement in area business & industry. Community work-site position working with handicapped people. Related Bachelor's Degree required. Prior experience in rehabilitation desirable. Reply Box 204. EOE, M/F.

An Equal Opportunity Employer will not discriminate when hiring on the grounds of race, age, sex, religion, or national origin.

what medicine to prescribe. Some occupations are borderline cases; some commission salesmen are employees, some are not.

Persons working at home may be employees: an example would be women hired by clothing manufacturers to do sewing. Some office workers now work at home, with a computer tie-in to the office.

Officers of a corporation are employees, but partners are not employees of the partnership.

Laws protecting employees rights and the agencies that enforce them

Union activity	Protected and regulated for nonsupervisory employees by National Labor Relations Act. *Contact:* National Labor Relations Board.
Racial, ethnic, or religious discrimination	Banned by Civil Rights Act of 1964. *Contact:* Equal Employment Opportunity Commission (EEOC).
Sex discrimination	Banned by Civil Rights Act of 1964. *Contact:* EEOC. Wage discrimination banned by Equal Pay Act. *Contact:* U.S. Labor Department, Wage and Hour Division.
Age discrimination	Banned, for persons aged 40 to 69, by the Age Discrimination in Employment Act. *Contact:* U.S. Labor Department, Wage and Hour Division.
Safety and health	Occupational Safety and Health Administration sets workplace and industry standards and conducts inspections. Special laws apply for coal miners and other hazardous occupations.
Wages and salaries	Fair Labor Standards Act guarantees a minimum wage and time and a half for hours worked over 40 a week to most nonsupervisory employees. *Contact:* U.S. Labor Department, Wage and Hour Division. Consumer Credit Protection Act limits the amount of wages and salaries a creditor can seize for payment of a debt.
Veterans	Right to reemployment at previous job. *Contact:* Department of Veterans Affairs.
Child labor	Limited and restricted by Fair Labor Standards Act. *Contact:* U.S. Department of Labor, Wage and Hour Division.
Disability	The Americans with Disabilities Act of 1990 prohibits employers from discriminating against any qualified person with a disability and requires most employers to make existing facilities accessible to the disabled. *Contact:* EEOC.

Employment is a contract.
Except in union plants, the contract is usually oral, and either employer or employee can end it at will, with or without notice. But as long as the contract lasts, both parties must comply with its terms. Your employer, for example, cannot cut your salary for work already done.

Some courts have ruled that company manuals, employee handbooks, and the like are to be considered part of the contract; employees are entitled to all benefits described in them. Many companies, however, now put a specific statement in company publications reserving the right to make changes at any time.

Unlawful discharge. Traditionally, employers had an absolute right to fire at will, subject only to antidiscrimination laws and union contracts. Recent court decisions cast doubt on the old rule. Courts have awarded damages to employees dismissed for refusing to give false testimony at a hearing, and to employees dismissed for filing workers' compensation claims. Employees have sued when fired for opposing company practices or products they considered unethical or against public policy—such as products harmful to the environment. Some won, some lost. The law is changing in the direction of greater employee rights; but no one knows how far the change will go.

Union contracts. Employers must deal with unions representing a majority of workers in a bargaining unit, which may be the whole company, a division, or some group of employees. The National Labor Relations Board (or a state board) decides the proper bargaining unit and holds elections, if necessary. In a union shop, you must join the union or, at least, pay dues (except in a minority of states, which have right-to-work laws).

Wages and conditions of employment are set by a written collective bargaining agreement between company and union. Most contain grievance or arbitration procedures for resolving disputes. If you have a grievance or dispute with your employer, you must go through the union; if it decides not to press your claim, you have no remedy. There is an exception. The union owes a "duty of fair representation" to its members and cannot discriminate against any of them. If the union violates this duty, a member may be able to sue.

Union members have the right to run for union office, vote in union elections, and express their opinions on union matters—subject to reasonable regulations.

Employee benefits.
Some benefits are required by law:

Social Security pays benefits to retired or disabled workers and their families, and families of deceased workers. It includes Medicare. (For details, see pages 95 and 128-130.)

Unemployment insurance pays benefits to workers laid off or unemployed through no fault of their own. They must be ready, willing, and able to work.

Disability insurance is required by a few states (including California, New York, and New Jersey). It is similar to unemployment insurance, but applies to those unable to work because of illness, not unemployment. Some companies carry disability insurance even when not required.

Workers' compensation pays medical bills and sick benefits to workers injured on the job.

Pensions are *not* required by law. But if an employer does have a pension system, it must comply with federal pension law, which sets minimum standards for eligibility, length of service, etc. It also requires that participants be given a summary of the plan, written in language the average man can understand, explaining all the rules and provisions of the plan. It is important to read the summary; if you have any questions, ask the company personnel people for an explanation.

Other benefits. Many companies and union contracts provide other fringe benefits, including highly important ones, such as life insurance and medical insurance. Be sure to learn your rights to these benefits, and find out what will happen if you leave the company or are laid off. How long will the insurance continue? Can you renew it on your own? How much will it cost?

Starting your own business.
If you have the money to set up or buy a full-scale business, you undoubtedly have a lawyer. Many people, though, start out on a small scale, often working from their homes, sometimes as a sideline to their regular jobs. Many housewives do typing at home or run small telephone answering services. Here are some legal problems that may arise with a new business.

How to save on taxes. If you operate from your home, reserve part of the home *exclusively* for business. You can take a percentage of household costs as a home office business deduction, including heat, repairs, maintenance, utilities, depreciation, and rent.

Hobbies, such as photography or woodworking, can often be turned into profitable businesses. But the Internal Revenue Service will be suspicious, especially if you show a loss (as many new business do, at first). If you are just pursuing a hobby, you cannot deduct any losses or home office expenses. To prove you are really in business, you should operate in a businesslike fashion. Keep records of income and expenses. Get business cards. Put out a sign, or advertise. Comply with any licensing or registration laws. You do not have to be making a profit, but you must show that you are trying to. (*Note:* If you make a profit in two years out of five, the law presumes you are in business for profit.)

There may be tax advantages in hiring your spouse and children. Check with your accountant.

Hiring employees. You must comply with all labor laws. You must also withhold taxes and send them in to the government, including Social Security and unemployment. You must buy workers' compensation insurance.

If you need only part-time or occasional help, you can avoid these problems by using free-lance workers or independent contractors, such as public stenographers who do clerical work. Another way is to get your help from a temporary agency. The agency is the legal employer of the employees. You pay a fee to the agency, and the agency pays the employees.

Government regulations. You need a license for some occupations, especially those affecting public health or safety. If your business has anything to do with food or drink, you will certainly be subject to regulation and inspection. If you use a business name (Acme Plumbing Co.), you may have to register it somewhere. For information, contact local authorities or any business group.

Partnerships. Each partner acts as agent for the others. Each is personally liable for all debts of the business; this means that creditors can get at a partner's home, bank account, or other property—not just the property of the partnership. Partners share profits (or losses) in any way they agree on. It is best to have a written agreement, specifying what each partner is entitled to, how much money he is to invest, how much time he is to put in, and any other agreements between the partners.

Every partnership must have at least one *general* partner. It may also have *limited* partners, who put money in the partnership and are entitled to share in the profits, but who have no say in running the business. Limited partners are personally liable for partnership debts only to the extent of their investment.

Buying a franchise. A franchise is the right to use a name or trademark, or to manufacture or sell a product. Fast food chains like McDonald's are well-known examples. Local people own and operate the restau-

---

Should you form a corporation?

A corporation is a legal "person," separate and distinct from the stockholders who own it. Its great advantage is *limited liability.* Stockholders are not personally liable for corporate debts; they may lose their investment, but no more. (Small businesses, however, may find it difficult to get bank loans or credit unless officers or stockholders agree to be personally liable.)

Other advantages:

- Corporations can raise money by issuing stock; it is a lot easier to sell shares of stock than a percentage interest in a business.
- Corporations go on, even if individual stockholders die.
- Family corporations can be used to split income among family members to save on taxes.

A disadvantage is double taxation. Corporations pay income tax; then stockholders pay personal income tax when profits are distributed to them. On the other hand, if the corporation grows in value, so does the stock. And if a stockholder sells, he is taxed on only 40 percent of the profit.

Small corporations can avoid double taxation by electing to be taxed as if they were partnerships.

Forming a corporation is simple, legally. What you need more than a lawyer is a good accountant or businessman to advise you.

Doing business with relatives

Your brother has a great idea for a new business, so you stake him to the money to get started. A few months later, he dies in an auto accident. What happens now?

- *If the money was a loan,* you can get it back.
- *If the money was a gift,* you cannot get it back; you may even owe a gift tax.
- *If the money was an investment,* you might be considered your brother's partner, entitled to a share of any business profit. On the other hand, you might be liable for business debts.

You probably have nothing in writing, and you cannot remember exactly what was said. In fact, neither you nor your brother may even have thought about the possibilities. As a result, you may be faced with the trouble of a lawsuit, with no assurance of getting your money.

The moral is, when making a loan to a friend or relative, setting up a partnership, or doing anything with legal consequences, *put it in writing,* just as you would with a stranger. Aside from the possibility of a death, you never know when there may be a falling out in the family. Any lawyer can tell you that family disputes are more bitter than any other.

In addition, the Internal Revenue Service is always suspicious of family deals. If your taxes are ever audited, you may need proof of exactly what transpired.

GARDNER & GARDNER TREE WORK

rants, using the companies' names. Other common franchises are gas stations and automobile dealerships. The owner gets the benefit of the name, the advertising, and a lot of management and financial help. There is a drawback. The franchising company will retain a great deal of control.

Before signing any agreement, have it read by your lawyer. These are important questions to ask: How long will the franchise last? Is it permanent? Can I sell it? Can I lose it? If so, under what circumstances? Do I have to buy only from certain suppliers? What are the restrictions on my right to run the business?

Getting help. The U.S. Small Business Administration gives information, counseling, financial aid, and help in getting bank loans and government contracts. A special division aids minority businesses.

Criminal law and procedure

What is a crime? A *felony* is a serious crime, such as murder, manslaughter, rape, robbery, arson, burglary, or assault with a weapon. Lesser crimes are *misdemeanors*. Traffic violations or violations of local ordinances are not crimes. An attempt to commit a crime is itself a crime. An *accessory* (one who aids in a crime though not present when it is committed) is guilty of a crime.

No law may make an act a crime, if the act was not a crime when it was performed. Nor may penalties be increased retroactively.

Who can commit a crime? An insane person cannot commit a crime. Insane means "unable to understand the nature of his act, or unable to know right from wrong." Drunkenness or voluntary use of drugs is not insanity and is not a defense to crime; but a person whose mind is affected by drugs prescribed as medicine may be excused. Children under a specified age set by state law (usually 15 or 16) cannot commit a crime (juvenile delinquency is not a crime). Young people over that age may be treated as "youthful offenders," and their crime later expunged from the record if not repeated.

Defenses. Ignorance of the law is not a defense, but ignorance of the fact may be. For example, a person may take another's property believing it to be his own.

If a person reasonably believes himself to be in danger of death or bodily harm, he may use force and even kill another person in self-defense.

Arrests. A policeman may arrest a person who commits *any* crime in his presence. He may arrest on reasonable suspicion in cases of *felony*. Otherwise, he needs a warrant.

Searches. An officer may make a search in the course of a lawful arrest. He may search a person for weapons if he thinks it is necessary to ensure his own safety. He may search a vehicle if he has reasonable grounds to believe that it contains evidence of a crime and that it may be driven away before he can get a search warrant.

If your child is arrested

If you are ever unlucky enough to get a phone call informing you that your son or daughter has been arrested, *what you do next can affect your child's whole future.* So do not panic, however you may feel. Here is what to do:

- **Get all the information you can,** including the address of the police station, the names and badge numbers of the arresting officers and the desk sergeant, the district attorney's man in charge of the case, and when and where your child will be taken for arraignment (a court hearing to advise the defendant of the charges and set bail).

- **Ask to talk to the desk sergeant and tell him you do not want your child questioned until you or your lawyer get there.** Ask him to write this request down. If your child has medical or emotional problems requiring any special treatment, tell the desk sergeant. (As soon as you can, have the child's doctor call the police.)

- **When you talk to the child, try to calm him down.** If possible, one parent should keep the child on the phone while the other goes to the station. Tell the child to be courteous and polite to the police and not to antagonize them, but not to answer any questions.

- **Do not argue or fight with the child at the station,** no matter how you feel. It is important to show the police a good family relationship. Get the child out on bail; if there is any delay, try to have him held at the station house, not the county jail. Jails are not safe, and can be a harrowing experience for young people.

- **Get a lawyer who is experienced at criminal law,** and do what he says.

In other cases, he must get a warrant. If a search is unlawful, nothing that is discovered can be admitted as evidence against the person searched.

Rights of accused persons. Anyone

charged with a crime has the right to remain silent. He has the right to a lawyer and a speedy trial before a jury. He has the right to confront and cross-examine his accusers, and he is entitled to be considered innocent until proven guilty "beyond a reasonable doubt." Even if convicted, he may not be subjected to "cruel or unusual punishment."

When a person is arrested, he must be informed of his rights, including the right to a lawyer and the right to remain silent. Otherwise, any admission or confession may not be used as evidence against him. This rule applies only to arrests.

When the police are questioning witnesses or persons at the scene of a crime, they are not required to give any warning, and anything a person says at that time may be used against him.

What to do if you are arrested. There are two basic rules: (1) Do not answer questions, and (2) Get a lawyer. The more serious the charge, the more important these rules are. Most non-criminals have a strong urge to explain themselves. Resist the urge. You can always make a statement later after you have talked to your lawyer.

If you do say anything, tell the truth. Any lies will probably be found out, and no one will believe anything you say after that.

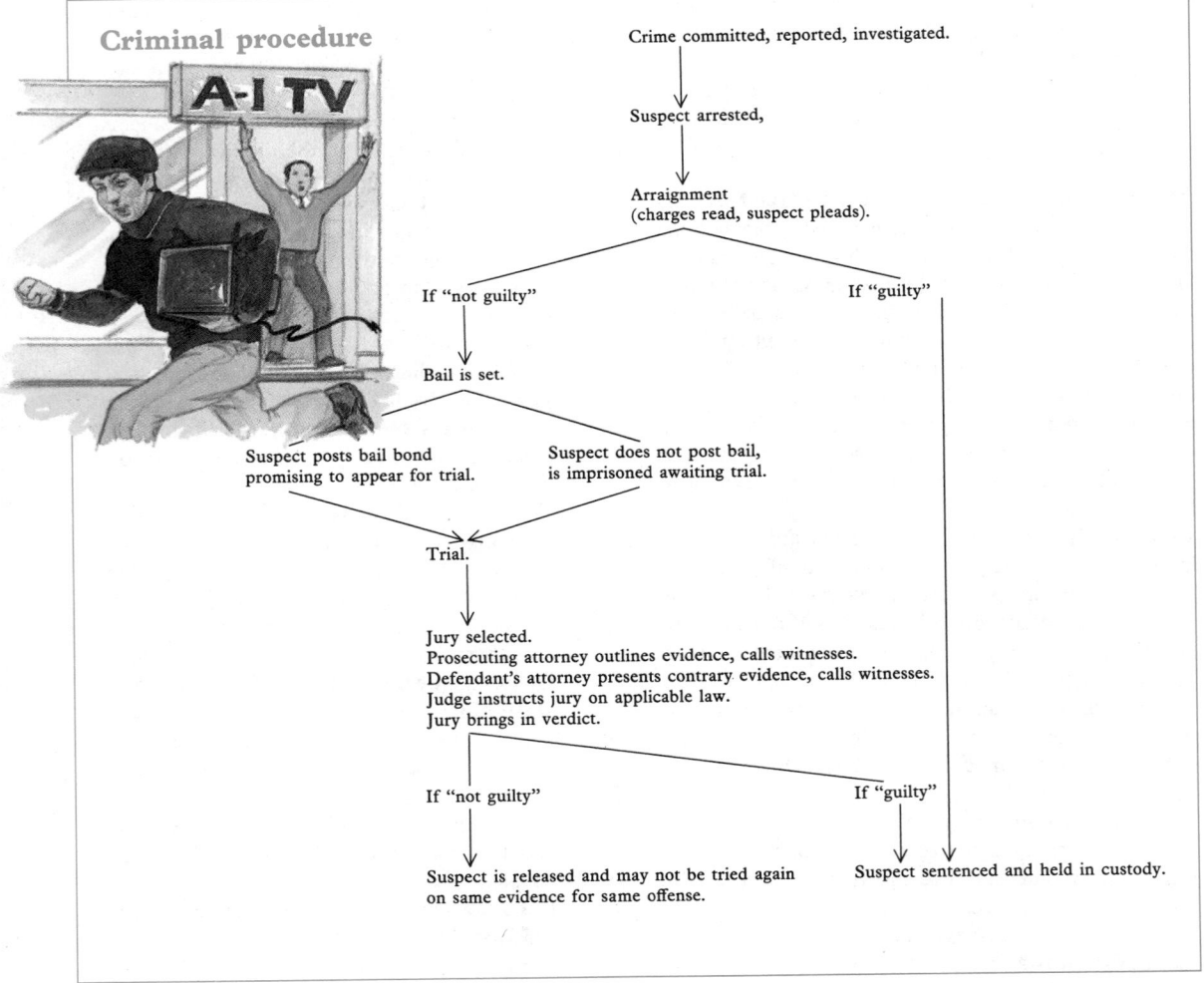

Criminal procedure

A-1 TV

Crime committed, reported, investigated.

Suspect arrested,

Arraignment
(charges read, suspect pleads).

If "not guilty"   If "guilty"

Bail is set.

Suspect posts bail bond
promising to appear for trial.   Suspect does not post bail,
is imprisoned awaiting trial.

Trial.

Jury selected.
Prosecuting attorney outlines evidence, calls witnesses.
Defendant's attorney presents contrary evidence, calls witnesses.
Judge instructs jury on applicable law.
Jury brings in verdict.

If "not guilty"   If "guilty"

Suspect is released and may not be tried again
on same evidence for same offense.   Suspect sentenced and held in custody.

How to find a lawyer

Do you need one? Many simple legal matters can be handled without a lawyer. Simple wills, uncontested divorces with no property or custody complications, personal bankruptcies, even settling simple estates often involve nothing more than filling out standard forms available at legal supply stores or from the courts. But be careful not to take legal advice from anyone who is not a lawyer.

Many books contain sample clauses for wills, contracts, leases, etc. You can find them at your library or the law library at the courthouse. Ask the librarian for help.

Here are other inexpensive ways to handle legal matters:

- **Legal clinics** handle routine matters for a small fee. Often the work is done by *paralegals*—nonlawyers trained in specific areas—under a lawyer's supervision.
- **Prepaid legal services,** a form of insurance like medical insurance, are provided by many employers and union contracts. If you need legal help, use a participating lawyer and the insurance pays the fee.
- **Arbitration** is used extensively in labor and commercial disputes, and now in consumer and housing disputes. Arbitration is like an informal court hearing, and the arbitrator's decision is binding. Usually, both sides must agree, in advance, to arbitrate the dispute.

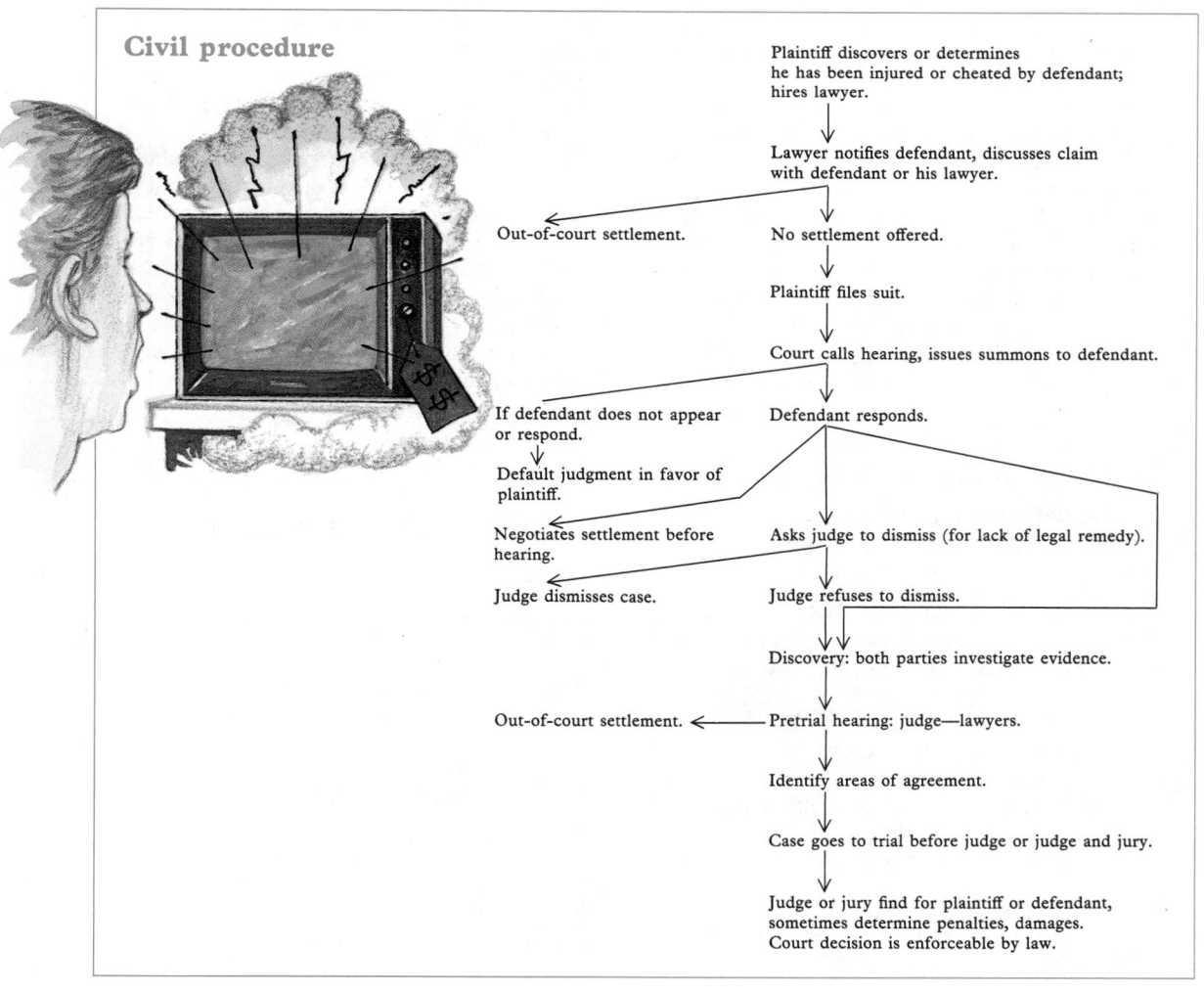

Civil procedure

Plaintiff discovers or determines he has been injured or cheated by defendant; hires lawyer.

Lawyer notifies defendant, discusses claim with defendant or his lawyer.

Out-of-court settlement. ← No settlement offered.

Plaintiff files suit.

Court calls hearing, issues summons to defendant.

If defendant does not appear or respond.

Defendant responds.

Default judgment in favor of plaintiff.

Negotiates settlement before hearing.

Asks judge to dismiss (for lack of legal remedy).

Judge dismisses case.

Judge refuses to dismiss.

Discovery: both parties investigate evidence.

Out-of-court settlement. ← Pretrial hearing: judge—lawyers.

Identify areas of agreement.

Case goes to trial before judge or judge and jury.

Judge or jury find for plaintiff or defendant, sometimes determine penalties, damages. Court decision is enforceable by law.

If you do need a lawyer, look for someone with experience in your type of case. Many lawyers specialize, particularly in the fields of criminal law, accident and negligence law, domestic relations law, real estate law, tax law, and various kinds of business law. If you do not know any lawyers, here are some people to ask:

- *Friends* who have had a similar legal problem.
- *Your boss,* on business matters.
- *Your union,* on employment matters or questions of your entitlement to benefits.
- *Your clergyman,* or a social worker, on family matters, divorce, child custody, and so on.
- *Your accountant or banker* on financial, tax, or inheritance matters.
- *Your doctor* on injury cases. He has probably been called to testify, and may know a good lawyer.
- *People who work at the courthouse.* They see the lawyers in action.
- *Civic or community groups,* or groups like the American Association of Retired People, the National Association for the Advancement of Colored People, or women's groups.

Interviewing a lawyer. You do not have to hire the first lawyer you talk to; you can shop around. Never be reluctant to talk about fees; you are the one who pays them. There are various ways to set fees:

- *Contingent fees,* in accident cases (see page 160).
- *Statutory fees* may be set by law. For instance, workers' compensation laws may limit the lawyer's fee.
- *Flat fees* are suitable for cases where it is known in advance just what has to be done. The drawback is that the lawyer is not likely to put in extra time.
- *Hourly fees* depend on how much time the lawyer

puts in. That sounds fair, but there is a danger: the longer the case drags on, the higher the fee, so your lawyer may be in no hurry to get anything done. Put a limit, in advance, on how much you can afford to pay.

Other factors affecting fees are the difficulty of the case, the amount of money involved, the skill and experience of the lawyer, and the customary fee charged in your community. (Local bar associations used to set minimum fee schedules. No lawyer who was a member could charge less. The practice has been banned by the U.S. Supreme Court as illegal price-fixing. Unfortunately, it still goes on, though not openly.)

What is a retainer? When you hire a lawyer, you make a down payment on the fee, called a retainer, which binds the lawyer to act in your interests and to accept no business that conflicts with your interests. You should have a written payment schedule, and insist that all bills show just what services were performed, especially if you are paying by the hour.

Working with your lawyer. You are the boss. You make all final decisions, such as whether to settle, how much to offer or to accept, whether to appeal, etc. But it would be foolish to try to dictate strategy or day-to-day handling of the case. Your lawyer knows more about it than you do, and the best course, almost always, is to follow his advice. You should, however, insist on being kept informed on a regular basis. Lawyers, like everybody else, tend to put things off, and sometimes need prodding. Legal matters take a long time anyway; you do not want any additional unnecessary delays.

You can dismiss your lawyer at any time. Usually, it is not a good idea unless he totally mishandles the case.

Do some basic research before choosing a lawyer. Some lawyers or law firms specialize in a particular field of law. Others offer a broad range of services. Ask about legal fees for the services you require. If you cannot afford a lawyer, consult a Legal Aid attorney.

You have to pay him for work already done, and you will have to pay a new lawyer as well. If a case is already on trial, changing lawyers can make a bad impression on a judge or jury.

Cooperate with your lawyer. Do not lie or conceal anything from him. The more damaging the information, the more the lawyer needs to know it. Anything you tell your lawyer is *absolutely confidential.* He is not allowed to tell anyone else, even if he wants to; the same rule applies to his employees.

Do not try to decide what is important and what is not. That is what you hire a lawyer for. There is no way that he can win a case if the other side comes up with evidence he knows nothing about. This advice is not limited to lawsuits. A lawyer who is drawing a will or a contract has to understand the entire situation. Most lawsuits about the meaning of legal documents arise because something has been left out, or some aspect of the situation has not been covered.

How to complain.
You can file a complaint with the bar committee, which can take disciplinary action or even recommend disbarment. If your lawyer has actually stolen or misappropriated your money, you can file a criminal complaint. (Lawyers are supposed to keep clients' money separate from their own; it is entirely improper to mingle the funds.)

You can also sue for malpractice, which means failure to exercise the reasonable care expected of a professional. Making an error of judgment would not be malpractice; but failure to know the elementary principles of law would. So would a failure to file a lawsuit on time, thereby costing the client the right to sue.

Where to go if you cannot afford a lawyer

The Legal Aid Society gives free legal help to those who cannot afford to pay. It does not handle divorces or criminal cases.

Lawyers referral services of local bar associations do not offer free aid, but they may refer you to a lawyer who bases his charges on what the client can afford.

The Legal Services Corporation, federally funded, provides legal help to poor people. Neighborhood Justice Centers try to settle disputes without lawyers.

Government agencies, such as consumer agencies, human rights commissions, and labor departments, will bring legal actions on behalf of people who file complaints.

Law schools sometimes run legal clinics staffed by law students. If not, the school can give you information.

Civil rights groups, such as the NAACP Legal Defense Fund and the American Civil Liberties Union, may handle a case or refer you to someone who can help.

Private organizations, such as landlords' and tenants' groups, trade associations, business groups, and labor unions, may provide legal services for their members.

Questions to ask before hiring a lawyer

Do you handle cases like mine? Ask the lawyer about some of them. How did they come out? How long did they take? What were the costs? Were there any special problems?

Will you actually do the work? If the lawyer's secretary or staff does the work, will the bill be reduced? You do not want to pay high professional rates for a clerk filling out a standard form.

What are your fee arrangements and billing practices? Some lawyers, for instance, bill by the quarter-hour. If they make a two-minute phone call, they bill for the full quarter hour. A few phone calls and your bill starts to mount. You should also check on other costs that may be incurred: Xeroxing of documents, filing fees and other court costs, and the cost of taking depositions from witnesses.

About how long will the whole thing take? You want to know, first, what the total period of time will be, and second, how much time the lawyer will actually put in.

How closely do you work with clients? You want to be kept informed and have some say in what is being done.

What happens if something goes wrong or we disagree? Suppose you have a dispute over fees? If your lawyer mismanages, will he still expect to be paid? Will he agree to submit disputes to an impartial arbitrator other than the bar association? (Bar associations are notorious for favoring lawyers over clients.)

chattel

Glossary

circumstantial evidence

felony

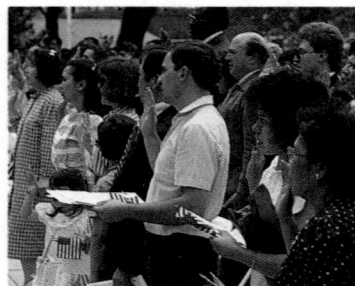
naturalization

ab initio. From the beginning.

abatement. Reduction or decrease.

accord and satisfaction. An agreement between two persons that settles a claim or lawsuit.

administrative law. The law regulating the procedure to be followed by government agencies.

adverse possession. Acquisition of ownership of land by continuous use for a long period of time, usually 20 years.

affidavit. A written statement made under oath.

agent. One who has authority to act for another (the principal). Acts or promises of the agent are binding on the principal.

alibi. Latin for "elsewhere." Alibi does not mean excuse. It means a person was somewhere else when a crime was committed.

alienate. To transfer ownership of property.

amicus curiae. Friend of the court. A person not a party in a case, but allowed to participate because of some indirect interest.

amortization. Payment of a debt over a period of time, usually a mortgage or bond.

appellant. A person who requests a higher court to review the decision of a lower court. The other party is called the *appellee* or *respondent.*

arraignment. Bringing a person charged with crime before a court to be advised of the charges against him.

assign. Transfer one's right or interest in something to another.

attachment. Seizure of property for payment of debt.

attestation. Witnessing the signature of a will or document.

attorney. One who has power to act for another.

bail. Money or property deposited in court to guarantee the appearance of a criminal defendant at his trial.

bailee. One in legal possession of another's property (has nothing to do with criminal bail; see page 159).

bench warrant. A court order for someone's arrest.

bequest. A gift of personal property in a will.

bill of exchange. A written order directing one person to pay a sum of money to another. The most common bill of exchange is a check, which directs a bank to pay a sum of money to the person named on the check.

bill of lading. A written contract for delivery of goods by freight.

bill of particulars. A written statement of the details of a claim in a lawsuit.

bill of sale. Written transfer of rights for personal property.

bona fide. In good faith; genuine.

breach of the peace. Disturbance of public order, usually by fighting.

brief. Written statement by a lawyer in support of his legal position in a case.

burden of proof. The obligation to produce evidence in support of allegations in a lawsuit. Whoever alleges a fact has the burden of proving it if it is disputed.

burglary. The crime of breaking into and entering property with intention to commit a felony.

capital. The money invested in a business, adjusted each year for the business's profits or losses.

capital crime. A crime punishable by death.

capital stock. The stock issued by a corporation.

causa mortis. "In contemplation of approaching death." Gifts made causa mortis are subject to special legal rules.

You and the Law

cause of action. The legal basis of a lawsuit, such as negligence, debt, breach of contract, or libel.

certiorari. A legal procedure by which a higher court reviews the decision of a lower one.

challenge. An objection to a juror. A juror may be challenged "for cause," if, for example, he is biased in favor of one side. In addition, each side has a certain number of peremptory challenges, for which no reason need be given.

chattel. An item or article of personal property.

chattel mortgage. A loan on which personal property is put up as security; for example, an auto loan or a loan on jewelry.

circumstantial evidence. Evidence from which a fact can be inferred; for example, a person's fingerprint is evidence of his presence at the place the fingerprint was found.

C.O.D. Cash on delivery. A type of sale in which the buyer pays when the goods are delivered to him.

codicil. An amendment to a will (see page 155).

collateral. Property pledged as security for a debt.

collateral relatives. Relatives other than direct ancestors or descendants.

common carrier. A transportation facility, such as a railroad or trucking company, in the business of transporting passengers or goods for a price.

common law. The body of law that has grown up over the centuries from custom and from the decisions of the courts—as opposed to statutory law, which is law passed by legislatures.

common law marriage. Marriage without a formal ceremony (see page 141).

commutation. Reduction in punishment, ordered by the governor or another authority.

complaint. A document in a lawsuit setting forth the claim that is being made.

condemnation. Taking of property by the government (see page 152).

condition. A provision in a contract which *must* be performed, or the contract loses its validity.

condonation. Forgiveness (see page 145).

consanguinity. Blood relationship.

consideration. See *contract*.

consortium. A person's right to the sex, services, and society of his or her spouse. Traditionally, a husband could sue for loss of consortium if his wife were injured. In many states today, a wife can sue for loss of consortium if her husband is injured.

conversion. Misappropriation or misuse of personal property.

convey. To transfer property in writing.

corpus delicti. Latin for "body of the crime." Proof that a crime was committed; it does *not* mean the body of the victim.

co-signer or co-maker. One who signs a note or other

Contract

contract. An agreement by which one person promises to do something in return for the act or promise of another. Contracts usually arise from an *offer* by one person and *acceptance* by the other. An *executory* contract is one consisting of promises that have not yet been *executed*.

Consideration is the legal term for the act or promise of one side that induces the act or promise of the other. For example, I agree to sell you my watch for $100. My promise to sell the watch is the consideration for your promise to pay the $100, and vice versa.

A mere promise, without consideration, is not a contract and cannot be enforced. But a promise given for consideration is binding, even if the consideration is of no benefit to the promisor. *Example:* You promise to give your nephew $1000 if he does not smoke or drink until he is 21. If he performs his side of the bargain, you must give him the $1000 even though his act (not smoking or drinking) is of no material benefit to you.

Contracts may be written or oral, and may be *implied* from conduct or even silence. For example, if you go into a restaurant and eat a meal, you have to pay for it. If you let someone perform services for you knowing that he expects to be paid, you have to pay him. Implied contracts are sometimes called quasicontracts (*quasi* is Latin for "as if"). You accepted the benefit of another's action, so you must pay for it *as if* you had made a contract.

Some contracts, because of their importance, are required to be in writing or they will not be enforced by the courts. The most common are:

• Contracts for the sale of real property.
• Contracts which, by their terms, cannot be performed within one year.
• Contracts holding one responsible for the debt of another.
• Contracts to sell goods for more than a specified amount of money (the amount varies from state to state).

document and makes himself liable to pay if the original signer does not.

counterclaim. A claim made by the defendant in a lawsuit against the plaintiff.

covenant. A promise in a deed (see page 151).

curtesy. A widower's legal right to a share of the lands owned by his wife.

damages. Money awarded to compensate for injury to person or property.

decedent. A person who has died and whose estate is being settled.

decree. Written judgment of a court.

deed. A document transferring ownership of land.

defamation. A false statement that injures a person's reputation (see page 162).

default. Failure to appear for trial. The defaulting party loses unless he can show good reason for not appearing. Also refers to failure to perform a contract or failure to make payments when due—for example, defaulting on a mortgage.

defendant. The person who is being sued. In criminal cases, the person being tried for a crime.

demurrer. A denial by the defendant that there are any legal grounds for the lawsuit.

deposition. A written statement made under oath, generally for use in a lawsuit.

descent and distribution. The law governing the disposition of property of someone who dies without a will.

devise. To transfer real property by will.

dictum. A statement of law made by a judge, but not necessary to decide the case, and therefore not binding.

discovery. See *pretrial procedure.*

dishonor. To refuse to accept an obligation; for example, a bank dishonors a check, if it refuses to pay it.

dispossess. To evict a tenant from the premises he rents.

dividend. Money paid to stockholders of a corporation from the profits of the corporation.

domicile. A person's permanent place of residence.

donee. A person to whom a gift is made.

donor. A person who makes a gift.

double indemnity. A provision in an insurance policy under which the company must pay double the face amount if a person dies by accidental means.

double jeopardy. Trying a person more than once for the same crime; prohibited by the U.S. Constitution.

dower. The right of a widow to a share of her husband's lands.

draft. A written order directing one person to pay a sum of money to another. For example, a person may direct his bank to pay a sum of money to someone.

due process. The constitutional right not to be deprived of life, liberty, or property, except after fair legal proceedings.

duress. Force or threat of force to compel someone to do something against his will.

earnest money. A down payment to make a contract binding.

easement. A right to use the land of another (see page 152).

ejectment. A legal action to remove a person who is wrongfully occupying land.

embezzlement. The crime of misappropriating money by a person to whom it has been entrusted.

eminent domain. The right of the government to take private property for public purposes (see page 152).

encroachment. Something that extends on the land of another, such as part of a building or fence.

encumbrance. Any claim against property that diminishes its value, such as an unpaid mortgage or a lien.

endorsement. Writing one's name on the back of a check or promissory note to cash or transfer it. An endorser normally guarantees the check or note, and is liable if the original signer cannot pay.

enjoin. To direct someone to do something or refrain from doing something.

equity. Court action in a case where money damages are not enough. Examples of equity include a court order directing a person to stop the commission of a nuisance; and an order of specific performance directing a seller to go through with a contract to sell land.

equity of redemption. The right of a landowner to redeem his land by paying the mortgage at any time before it is foreclosed.

escheat. Return of property to the state when there is no one to inherit it.

escrow. Delivery of money or property to a neutral party, to be held until certain conditions are fulfilled.

estate. The property left by a person who has died. (The term may also refer to property in general or any interest in property.)

estoppel. Refusal to allow a person to change his statement or legal position if he has induced people to act on the basis of his previous statement or position.

ex parte. A legal action taken by one side without notice to the other.

ex post facto law. A law making an act a crime, although it was not a crime when it was done;

prohibited by the U.S. Constitution.

executor. The person named in a will to handle and distribute an estate.

exemplary damages. Punitive damages.

extortion. The crime of obtaining money by threats.

extradition. Return of a fugitive from justice to the state in which he is wanted.

false arrest. Unlawful arrest (see page 162).

false imprisonment. Unlawful restraint (see page 162).

fee simple. Absolute ownership.

felony. A serious crime, usually one punishable by imprisonment in the state penitentiary.

fiduciary. One who holds or manages property for another and is held to a high standard of conduct because of his position of trust.

fixture. An item of personal property that becomes real property by being "affixed" to the realty, for example, a furnace.

F.O.B. Free on board. A type of sale in which the seller agrees to deliver the goods to a carrier, such as a railroad, for shipment to the buyer.

foreclosure. Court proceedings to take over property for failure to pay a mortgage.

forgery. The crime of fraudulently making or changing writing or a signature, with intent to deceive.

franchise. The right to vote. A form of business arrangement (see pages 166-167).

fraud. False statement or misrepresentation made to deceive someone into taking an action he would not have taken had he known the truth.

garnishment. Taking all or part of a person's salary in payment of a debt. The amount that can be taken is limited by law.

guaranty. A promise to perform some act or pay some debt on behalf of another if the other fails to perform or pay.

guardian. One legally entrusted with the duty of caring for the person or property of a minor or incompetent adult.

habeas corpus. Latin for "you have the body." A legal proceeding (called a "writ") commanding that a prisoner be brought before a court to decide whether he is legally being held.

hearsay evidence. Evidence of what someone else said, rather than what the witness knows.

heir. One who inherits the property of a person who dies.

holder in due course. A purchaser of a negotiable instrument in good faith without knowledge of any defect (see page 159).

holdover tenant. One who remains on the property after the lease has expired (see page 153).

holographic will. A will entirely in a person's own handwriting (see page 155).

homicide. The killing of one human being by another. "Justifiable" homicide is in self-defense.

impeach. Challenge the truthfulness of a witness. Bring charges against a public official to remove him from office.

implied. Understood from the circumstances, although not directly stated, as an implied promise or an implied contract.

indemnity. An insurance or other agreement guaranteeing payment if a person suffers a loss.

indenture. A formal written contract.

indictment. An accusation of crime made by a grand jury.

infant. A minor. In law, the term refers to any minor, not just a small child.

information. A written accusation of crime by a district attorney or prosecuting officer without a grand jury.

injunction. A court order directing a person to do something or to refrain from doing something.

inquest. Any inquiry by a court to determine a disputed fact. Most commonly, it refers to a coroner's inquest to discover the cause of death.

insolvency. Inability to meet one's debts as they come due.

interest. Any legal right or claim. The amount charged for the use of money.

interlocutory decree. A preliminary decree that does not become final until some further action is taken.

interrogatories. A set of written questions to be proposed to a witness in a pending lawsuit, or to the opposing party.

intestate. Without a will.

joint tenancy. A form of co-ownership (see page 151).

judgment. The decision of a court.

judicial notice. Recognition of certain facts by a court without the need for proof, such as historical events, scientific laws, or geographic facts.

jurisdiction. The authority of a court to decide a case. The jurisdiction of a court is generally set out in the law establishing the court.

jurisprudence. The study of law in general.

kidnapping. The crime of stealing and carrying away a human being.

laches. Excessive delay in asserting a legal right.

larceny. The crime of taking another's property.

leading question. A question that suggests the answer, such as, "Were you walking past Mr. Johnson's house at noon on January 12th?" The proper question would be, "Where were you at noon on January 12th?"

lease. A contract to rent.

legacy. A gift made in a will.

lessee. The tenant under a lease.

lessor. The owner or landlord under a lease.

letters of administration. A court document appointing someone to handle the estate of a person who died without a will.

letters testamentary. A court document authorizing the executor named in a will to take charge of the estate.

levy. A tax. A seizure of property by order of court to pay a judgment.

libel. Written defamation (see page 162).

lien. A claim or charge against property, such as an unpaid mortgage or other debt.

life estate. An interest in property during a person's lifetime ending upon the person's death. For example, a husband's will leaves his house to his wife for her lifetime, and then to his children.

life tenant. A person who owns a life estate in property.

liquidated damages. A specified sum of money agreed on beforehand as damages in case one party to a contract fails to perform.

lis pendens. A notice filed in a county office stating that a lawsuit is pending over a designated piece of real property. Anyone who purchases the property is bound by the result of the lawsuit.

living will. A document by which a person directs whether or not he is to be kept alive by artificial devices if he should fall into an irreversible coma. Living wills are not legally binding in most states, but people often prepare them to inform the family of their wishes.

majority. The age at which a person is considered an adult, with full legal rights and capacities.

malfeasance. Performing an act that is wrong; see also *misfeasance.*

malice. Intention to harm.

malicious mischief. Intentional destruction of property.

malicious prosecution. Knowingly bringing criminal charges that are false.

mandamus. A court order directing a public official to perform his official duty.

manslaughter. The crime of killing a human being without premeditation or malice aforethought.

mayhem. The crime of violently depriving a person of the use of a member, such as an arm, leg, or eye.

mechanic's lien. A claim against property by someone who has done work on it, as a repairman or a workman on a house.

misdemeanor. A crime less serious than a felony.

misfeasance. An act that is not wrong but is improperly performed; see also *malfeasance.*

mistrial. A trial that ends because of some procedural error, or because the jury cannot agree on a verdict.

moot question. A question that is undecided and subject to argument, but is not directly related to a case.

motion. An application to a court for a ruling, decision, or order, usually in connection with some pending case.

murder. The crime of killing a human being, with premeditation or malice aforethought.

naturalization. The process of becoming a citizen. Normally, an alien must reside in the United States for at least five years before he can apply for citizenship; but the period is shortened for aliens married to

or adopted by American citizens. The alien must show that he is mentally and morally fit to become a citizen. Minor children of naturalized citizens also become citizens.

negligence. Failure to use reasonable care, thereby causing an injury to person or property (see pages 160-161).

negotiable instrument. A document, such as a check or promissory note, that can be endorsed and transferred from person to person, almost like cash. Whether an instrument is negotiable depends entirely on how it is worded.

nisi. Latin for "unless." A decree nisi is a court order to take effect on a specified date unless some action is taken in the meantime.

nolle pros. Short for *nolle prosequi,* a decision not to proceed with a prosecution or lawsuit.

nolo contendere. Latin for "I will not contest it." In criminal cases, a plea with the same effect as a plea of guilty, but without actually admitting guilt.

non compos mentis. Latin for "not of sound mind."

nonage. Underage; the period during which a person is a minor.

nonfeasance. Failure to perform an act required by law; for example, nonperformance of duties by a public official.

notary public. An official authorized to administer oaths, witness signatures, and certify to affidavits or other documents.

note. A written promise to pay.

novation. The making of a new contract or agreement to replace one that now exists.

nuncupative will. An oral will (see page 155).

oath. A promise to tell the truth, sworn on one's belief in a

Supreme Being. An *affirmation* is a similar promise by those who have religious or other scruples against taking oaths.

obligee. A person to whom some contractual obligation is owed.

obligor. The person who owes an obligation.

option. The right to buy or sell property at a specified time for a specified price.

palimony. A term applied to lawsuits for payments similar to alimony, brought when an unmarried couple separates after living together. Courts have not recognized any right to such payments, but they have sometimes recognized a contractual right to payment for services rendered, as when a woman gives up her career and provides companionship, assistance, and business help to her male partner. (Note, however, that a contract to pay for sexual relations is against public policy and will not be enforced by a court.)

parol evidence. Oral evidence. The parol evidence rule is that a written document may not be changed or amended by oral testimony.

partition. A court order physically dividing property owned by co-owners who cannot agree on the use to be made of the property. Sometimes the property is sold and the proceeds divided among the owners.

party wall. A common wall shared by two adjoining buildings, providing support to both.

patent. The exclusive right to manufacture and sell an invention.

per capita. In the law of wills, equal division of property among all persons with the same relationship to the deceased. For example, if a will leaves property to grand-children per capita, each grandchild gets an equal share.

per curiam. An opinion by the entire court, rather than an opinion written by one judge.

per stirpes. In the law of wills, division of property by groups rather than individuals. For example, if the deceased had a son who had two children, and a daughter who had three, the two children of the son would get half the property, and the three children of the daughter would get the other half.

perjury. The crime of making false statements under oath.

personal property. Any movable property; anything but land and buildings (see page 159).

petit jury. A jury that decides cases. A *grand jury* decides whether a person should be charged with a crime.

plaintiff. The person who brings a lawsuit.

plea bargaining. An agreement between a prosecutor and a criminal defendant by which the charge is reduced, or a lesser sentence agreed on, in return for the defendant's plea of guilty. Most plea bargaining is unavoidable, as it would be impossible to hold all the trials that would be necessary if most defendants did not plead guilty.

pleadings. The written documents in a lawsuit that state the position of the parties. The usual pleadings are a complaint by the plaintiff and an answer by the defendant. In some cases, further pleadings may be submitted by both sides.

pledge. Delivery of property to a creditor, as security for a debt.

polling the jury. Asking each juror individually for his verdict.

postmortem. Latin for "after death." Usually applied to the medical examination of a dead body to determine the cause of death.

power of attorney. A written authorization giving one person the power to act for another.

precedent. A previous court decision on a case similar to the one being tried.

prescription. A way of acquiring an interest in property by long and continuous use.

presumption. A rule requiring a judge or jury to draw certain conclusions from certain facts. For example, from the fact that a child is born to a married woman, the conclusion must be drawn that the child is legitimate. A *conclusive* presumption is one that cannot be disproven. Other presumptions can be overcome by evidence to the contrary.

pretrial procedure. The process, before a lawsuit comes to trial, of taking depositions, producing documents, conferring with the judge, etc. It is intended to help settle cases or, at least, to make sure that each party is aware of the issues.

prima facie case. Sufficient evidence to win a lawsuit, provided the other side cannot contradict or explain it.

privileged communication. A statement, made in private, which the other party is not allowed to divulge in court, and which cannot be used in evidence. The most common examples are communications between husband and wife, attorney and client, doctor and patient, priest and penitent.

probate. Proving a will. In a wider sense, all the proceedings relating to an estate (see page 156).

probation. In criminal law, a suspended sentence on condition of continued good behavior.

promissory note. A negotiable instrument consisting of a written, unconditional promise to pay a sum of money.

proof. Evidence that is believed by the judge or jury.

protest. A formal notice that a negotiable instrument, such as a check or promissory note, was presented for payment, and that payment was refused.

proximate cause. In the law of torts, an act that directly leads to and results in an injury.

proxy. One entitled to vote on behalf of another; usually applied to meetings of stock-holders of a corporation. Proxy marriages were once recognized, but no longer.

public defender. A lawyer hired by the state to defend persons accused of crime who cannot afford their own lawyers.

publication. Making a statement public. In the law of defamation, telling one person constitutes publication.

punitive damages. Damages over and above actual damages, awarded to punish a wrongdoer and deter him from repeating the wrong (see page 162).

quantum meruit. Latin for "amount deserved." A sum of money awarded for services rendered when no specific sum is provided by contract.

quash. To annul or set aside.

quitclaim. A type of deed (see page 148).

quorum. The number of people who must be present at a meeting of a group in order to legally transact business.

rape. The crime of having sexual intercourse with a woman against her will. Statutory rape is the crime of having sexual intercourse with a minor below the age of consent.

ratification. Approval or confirmation of an act already done.

real property. Land and buildings.

rebuttal. Introduction of evidence to contradict a claim made in a lawsuit.

receiver. A person appointed by a court, in a lawsuit about property, to hold and manage the property at the court's direction.

recidivist. A repeater; an habitual criminal.

referee. A person appointed by a court to hear testimony, receive evidence, and report back to the court on his findings.

release. A document giving up a legal claim or right, usually when a case is settled. When an insurance company pays a claim, for example, it will require the claimant to sign a release.

remand. Send back a case from a higher court to a lower one for additional or corrective action.

replevin. A legal action for the return of property (see page 163).

reply. In a lawsuit, the plaintiff's written answer to a counter-claim by the defendant.

res ipsa loquitur. Latin for "the thing speaks for itself." A presumption of negligence, applied when there is no direct proof, but no other explanation makes sense. For example, if something falls from a window sill and injures a passerby, negligence will be presumed, even if it is impossible to prove what caused the accident.

res judicata. A legal or factual dispute that has already been decided by the judgment of a court, and that cannot be disputed any further.

respondent. See *appellant.*

restrictive endorsement. An endorsement when a check or other negotiable instrument is transferred for a specific purpose; for example, "for collection only," or "for deposit only."

retainer. A down payment to a lawyer to retain his services (see page 170).

retroactive. Relating backward in time, as a retroactive pay increase.

reversion. The return of property to its original owner after a trust or a gift for a period of years.

robbery. The crime of taking property by force or threat of force.

royalties. Payments (often a share of profits) to inventors, authors, songwriters, etc., or to owners of mineral or oil rights.

satisfaction piece. A document stating that a recorded mortgage has been paid.

seisin or seizin. The right to possession of real property.

service. Delivery of a summons to a defendant, informing him of a lawsuit against him.

setoff. A claim by the defendant against the plaintiff that reduces or eliminates the plaintiff's claim.

slander. Spoken defamation (see page 162).

specific performance. A court order to perform a contract for the sale of land (see page 149).

statute. A law passed by a legislative body, such as Congress.

statute of limitations. The time limit for bringing a lawsuit (or criminal prosecution). Different types of lawsuits have different limitation periods, but once the particular time limit has passed, no legal action may be taken.

stipulation. An agreement between parties to a lawsuit.

subornation of perjury. Persuading or bribing another to give false testimony.

subpoena. A document com-manding a person to appear in court, either as a witness or as a party to a lawsuit.

subpoena duces tecum. A subpoena directing someone to produce documents or records in court.

substantive law. That part of the law that deals with legal rights rather than with legal procedures.

summary judgment. A court decision, made without a trial, when there are no facts in dispute.

summons. The first document in a lawsuit, advising the defendant that the lawsuit is being filed.

surety. One who promises to pay a debt if the original debtor fails to pay.

surrogate's court. A court that handles wills and estates.

tenancy by the entireties. A form of ownership by husband and wife (see pages 145, 151).

tenancy in common. A form of co-ownership (see page 151).

testament. A will.

testator. A person who has made a will or testament.

title. Evidence of one's right to property.

title search. A search of public records to trace the history of ownership of land.

tort. A wrongful act that injures another person (see page 162).

treason. The crime of waging war against the United States or aiding its enemies (treason is the only crime defined in the U.S. Constitution).

trespass. Any wrongful act affecting real property.

true bill. An indictment by a grand jury charging someone with a crime.

usury. Charging more than the legal rate of interest on a loan.

vendee. A purchaser.

vendor. A seller.

venue. The place where a trial is to be held.

verdict. The decision of a jury.

verification. An affidavit swearing that a writing or document is true.

voidable. Anything that can be made void; for example, a contract made by a minor is voidable at the option of the minor.

warrant. A legal document, signed by a judge, authorizing an arrest or a search.

Trust

trust. Money or property legally owned by one person (the trustee) for the benefit of another. The person who establishes the trust, and sets out its terms, conditions, and purposes, is called the *grantor* or *settlor.* The person entitled to the income is the *income beneficiary.* The person who gets the property when the trust comes to an end is the *remainderman,* except when the property is to be returned to the grantor.

A trust may be set up during the grantor's life (living trust) or by his will (testamentary trust). It may be *revocable* or *irrevocable;* in a revocable trust, the grantor reserves the right to cancel the trust and take back the property. In an irrevocable trust, the grantor may not cancel the trust.

The trustee must manage the trust for the sole benefit of the beneficiaries. He may not make any profit for himself, directly or indirectly. He may, however, charge a fee for his services. Many financial institutions, such as banks, have special departments set up for the management of trusts.

Trusts may be set up for many purposes; here are some of the most common:

- To provide an income for children who are minors until they come of age.
- To provide for people who are not good at handling business or financial affairs.
- To provide a lifetime income for someone (such as yourself or your spouse) with the property eventually to revert to someone else (such as your children).
- To provide income to someone for a temporary period.
- To make gifts for charitable purposes.

For further reference

Ashley, Paul P.
  You and Your Will
  McGraw-Hill
Belli, Melvin M. and Wilkinson, Allen P.
  Everybody's Guide to the Law
  HarperCollins
Brown, Robert N.
  The Rights of Older Persons
  Southern Illinois University Press
Burnett, Barbara A.
  Everywoman's Legal Guide
  Doubleday
Carrel, Annette
  It's the Law: A Young Person's Guide to Our Legal System
  Volcano Press
Coughlin, George G., Jr.
  Your Handbook of Everyday Law
  HarperCollins
Koff, Gail J.
  The New Jacoby & Meyers Practical Guide to Everyday Law
  Simon & Schuster
Lasson, Kenneth
  Representing Yourself
  Farrar Straus Giroux
Ross, Martin J. and Steven, Jeffrey
  Handbook of Everyday Law
  Fawcett
Schimmel, David and Fischer, Louis
  Parents, Schools, and the Law
  The National Committee for Citizens in Education

Improving Your Memory

When you learn something, you practice three skills: *finding* what you need to know, *remembering* what you find, and *applying* that information usefully and effectively. Everyone who attends school, from first grade through college, is drilled over and over in the skills of finding and applying useful information. But without the middle skill—remembering—the other two are short-lived at best. However, most schools do not teach memory skills; they teach you to learn by rote memory—by routine drill—without your necessarily understanding or thinking about the text material. And so, very soon, you tend to forget.

Good memory is not a trick, nor does it require great intellectual resources. It does require systematic mental organization, that is, concentration on what you need to remember. The rest is practice, and the rewards—remembering people, places, and things that you always used to forget—are self-sustaining.

Through the centuries, some of the world's greatest thinkers and philosophers have tried to promote systems of memory improvement. No one system ever caught on; each one turned out to be too personal for general application. In this century mnemonists—memory experts—have shied away from complicated personal systems in favor of simpler methods with everyday applications. You will learn such step-by-step methods in this chapter. "There is memory without learning," writes memory expert Harry Lorayne, "but there is no learning without memory."

Think about that for a moment. How can one say that he has learned something effectively if he cannot recall it when it is needed. This is true whether we are talking about a particular skill or a bit of knowledge or an entire procedure or a religion or a philosophy. True learning puts information, ideas, or systems of thought at one's fingertips, ready for immediate use when needed, ready for direct application, ready for explanation to others, in short, for whatever application is generally called for.

As a result, the process of learning can only be considered complete when you have stored in your memory the subject to be learned. It is for this reason that so much emphasis must be placed on training the memory, especially for those who customarily find difficulty in recalling things they think they have learned, in recalling tasks they must perform, in bringing to mind thoughts they seek to explain to others. The objective of memory training is to make complete the process of learning: *finding, remembering,* and *applying* knowledge.

Self-training. No one is born with a poor memory. As you grow up, you develop highly personal habits of awareness and observation. You choose to see and hear, touch and taste certain things, and you choose to ignore most others. Quite likely, you began as a child to organize your daily life around those things you needed most, or were pleased by, or had an interest in. Those meaningful things constitute your earliest memories. Happy childhoods tend to be remembered longer and more fully.

Normally, you pay attention to those things around you that are important, potentially rewarding, and potentially pleasurable, and you teach yourself to remember them. As a child, for instance, your mother may have given you a dime and made you memorize your own phone number ("Always call home if you get lost somewhere"). Now, as an adult, you probably have immediate recall of at least one phone number—your own—even though you may seldom use it. But the memory seed was planted long ago, and you trained yourself to always know your own phone number. It was a start.

Think of how effective your memory is. Besides recalling your telephone number whenever you wish—even though you may hardly ever use it—you also have stored within your memory an enormous number of other bits of information. But you cannot always remember everything you are sure you know. This chapter will help you overcome that problem and greatly improve your recall.

Because your memory is yours alone, you can profitably train yourself to improve what needs improvement. Check your memory out with this list of facts and numbers:

Wait a minute . . . it's on the tip of my tongue

(No peeking, please.
Answer everything from memory.)

1. What is your home phone number?
2. Your license plate number?
3. Your Social Security number?
4. Whose face is on the $20 bill?
5. What is your mother's birthday?
6. How many days are there in June?
7. How many pints are in a gallon?
8. Name the Great Lakes.
9. Name your U.S. congressman.
10. What is your father's birthday?
11. Name your first-grade teacher.
12. Diamond-shaped road signs always indicate what?
13. Top to bottom, name the three colors on a stop light.

A high-school diploma or a college degree cannot help you answer any of these questions. But the succeeding pages will help you remember all of them.

Observation

How observant are you? How observant do you think you are? Most people assume they are competent eyewitnesses. The fact is, nearly everyone sees the same sequence of events differently.

Testing observation.
TV talk show hosts once were fond of a stunt that included the studio audience in addition to the viewers at home. While the host chatted with his guest onstage, a scuffle would break out in the audience. Angry voices would be raised, stopping the onstage conversation. Members of the audience would look on. Suddenly, one of the combatants would whip out a handgun and shoot one or both of the other participants. Then all the troublemakers would scurry for the exits. Total elapsed time: about one minute.

Of course, the whole drama was staged, and there were no bullets. But the studio audience was taken by surprise. At this point, the TV host would choose four members of the audience and bring them onstage to describe what happened, who was involved, and what the perpetrators looked like. These eyewitness accounts turned out to be at odds. The audience members rarely agreed about anything—who started it, who shot whom, what they wore, what they said, even their sexes. Finally, the perpetrators—two or three actors—would reappear onstage and reenact the "crime," and the studio audience would see it all clearly for the first time.

The point of this exercise is to show that eyewitness testimony is too often distorted by shock and surprise. Every viewer at home, untouched by the heat of the moment, was a better witness to the crime than the studio audience that was part of it.

How well do we observe?
For the most part, you see what you are accustomed to seeing. You glimpse something, and you have immediate recall of whatever you have trained yourself to expect to see. Your powers of observation, over the years, are restricted to self-imposed limits, to a field of vision that is relevant to your personal or professional life. The television audience was prepared to be entertained. When the unexpected happened, it was a blur.

Whenever there is a dramatic story on the TV news—a violent crime, a fire, or a natural disaster—you are likely to see an interview with a witness or a victim. "How do you feel?" the reporter asks. "Can you tell us what happened?" The answer rarely makes any sense. The distraught victim may be in shock and is usually too confused to say anything coherent.

Observation is subjective. Often, eyewitnesses do not agree on the details of an event they have just seen.

Then the same reporter interviews a fireman or a policeman who, with sirens wailing in the background, supplies a precise reconstruction of the tragedy without tears or emotion. The uniformed man is not hard-hearted or all-knowing. He is trained to make sense out of what seem to be chaotic events. You, too, can train yourself to observe with detachment what others might recoil from in horror or disgust. Better yet, you can learn to remember anything.

For a moment, think of something completely familiar—your wristwatch. Try to remember: Does it have a six on it? A Roman numeral VI? A dot? An empty space? If yours is a digital watch, how many lines are there in the number eight? Even if you answered correctly, chances are you had to double-check to make sure.

The tests and drills in these pages are designed to get you in the habit of memorizing by stages: observing, paying attention, organizing, forming images, and applying the methods of memory training. All these steps are part of the memory habit and, like most habits, this one can be maintained only through exercise.

Untrained memory is haphazard and unreliable. Trained memory brings all recollections to the surface.

Try this. The following three exercises are designed to test your native, untrained memory. You may not do well at all, but take heart: In the pages that follow you will learn the techniques for memorizing lists, names, and numbers. And you can gauge your training progress. The tests will be repeated on pages 198-199.

Quick-recall tests

1. Study this 15-digit number for two minutes. Then try to duplicate it exactly on a piece of paper— without looking at the number here

   238158649376914

2. Here are seven phone numbers, each corresponding to a local tradesman or professional. Study the list for six minutes, then copy the seven titles in any order. Finally, without looking, match the memorized numbers to the titles.

Doctor	762-5881	Lawyer	681-9558
Grocer	616-2053	Dentist	386-9156
Plumber	358-0854	Electrician	872-9647
Florist	784-3579		

3. This is an apparently random list of twelve objects found in the home. Study it for just two minutes, then reconstruct the list from memory, in order.

   couch, refrigerator, newspaper, clock, television, mirror, toaster, lamp, toilet, stove, carpet, window

Paying attention

There is nothing wrong with this story, but read it carefully:

You are driving a bus that contains 50 passengers. At 57th Street, ten people get off and three get on. At 55th, seven get off and two get on. At 53rd and at 51st, four passengers get off each time; three get on at 53rd, no one at 51st. The bus breaks down at 51st, and eight passengers get crosstown transfers and leave. The bus starts up again and proceeds to 49th, where it breaks down once again. The remaining passengers ask for transfers and leave the bus.

Most of us, by paying strict attention, can probably answer several anticipated questions about this bus story (answers below). How many passengers finally got off? How many got transfers? How many stops did the bus make?

But hardly anyone can answer the most obvious question of all: *What is the bus driver's name?*

(Answers in order: 26, 34, 5)

Remember the very first word in the story? *You.* You drove the bus; your own name is the answer. Of course, this was a trick. By misdirection you were led to overlook that critical first word, and to pay close attention to everything else. More important, you tried hard to figure out that story; you were interested in all those bus riders, and you probably had a moving picture in your mind of that bus on its route. The building blocks of memory were all there: concentration plus attention plus image formation—minus misdirection.

Memory needs no notes.

One early step in memory improvement is difficult: *no more note-taking.* If your interest is genuine, part of the drill is to throw away your pencil and paper. As you come to know new memory techniques, you must trust your ability to employ them. Constant list-making, note-taking, and memo-writing betray a lack of self-confidence in your memory and a lack of commitment to memory training. But once you start to remember names and numbers that you never remembered before, you will no longer need to stuff your wallet or pocketbook with little scraps of paper—half of whose messages and numbers make no sense to you when you finally read them.

Memory and high intelligence are not necessarily related. The absent-minded professor knows all there is to know about his academic specialty, but cannot remember to wear two socks of the same color. The professor focuses so hard on one thing that he forgets nearly everything else. At the other end of the spectrum, medical literature contains intriguing case histories of idiots savants—mentally defective people who can play classical piano instinctively, or immediately name the day of the week for any date in history. Like the professor, the idiot savant has a one-track mind: his concentration is perfectly focused and his interest is single-minded. And his memory is pure.

Most of us, in fact, possess a store of useless information that has come to be known as trivia. Boys often have a knack for memorizing the batting averages of hundreds of baseball players. Many women have an astonishing recall of what other women wore, or looked like, when last met. Gamblers stake huge sums on their memory of a single deck of cards. Whatever you are most interested in, you tend to remember best. Memory building, in large part, is a matter of broadening your interests.

Names and faces.

What do you *want* to remember better? Names and faces top the list for most people. Study the faces on the next page for a few minutes, then match them to the names. Cover up the names and see if you can put the right name to the right face. This is rote memorization; even if you can do the match-ups successfully, chances are that the achievement will be short-lived. As you learn better name/face memorization techniques, you may want to refer back to these names and faces and match the memorized names to the anonymous faces on page 195.

In a later section you will learn precise methods for memorizing names and faces. For now, as you study the page, try to isolate a single outstanding feature from each face. These are strangers, after all; trying to memorize an entire new countenance—plus eleven others—is too great a task. Focusing your attention on just one feature (nose, mouth, eyebrows, etc.) will serve your purpose best.

Some of the names may defy rote memorization. They may sound like nothing else you have ever heard, nor look like any word in English. But everyone's name —if you study it hard enough—can be manipulated in sound into *something* else that sticks in your mind. And the mental effort of that transformation has value in itself. When you take the time and trouble to turn O'Bradovich into Over the Bridge, you are not likely to forget that name soon.

For the time being, first names are less important than last names. Concentrate on a distinguishing facial feature, plus a last-name word association, and try to knit them together in your mind. (You can use the same technique later to remember first names, which usually are easier.) This exercise is really just a warm-up to test your capacity to memorize by rote. When you next come across these same names and faces on page 195, you will be much better equipped to remember them. No matter how good your rote memory powers may be, the gains from using them are fleeting. *Trained memory lasts and lasts.*

Paper slips—and our recollection of what they mean—are rapidly lost.

Improving Your Memory

Sarah Chambers

Steve Wallace

Alice Moore

John Lee

Angela Vargas

Philip Sanchez

Sue Miller

Gordon Green

Sheila Rice-Taylor

Michael Young

Eileen Murray

Tobey Christiansen

Getting organized

Everyone has immediate memory, and almost anyone can get by with a functional short-term memory. But a good long-term memory requires conscious and systematic organizational skills. Foremost among these skills is a technique called *chunking*. Several items (or numbers) worth remembering are grouped together—chunked—for longer and easier recall. A list of nine seems unmanageable unless written down. But three chunks of three, properly organized, can be retained in your head.

Take a grocery shopping list, for instance. Say you need milk, cereal, coffee, lettuce, cheese, sugar, tomatoes, eggs, and celery. Now try to organize your list: three of the items are dairy products (milk, eggs, and cheese); three are dry foods (cereal, coffee, and sugar); and three are vegetables (lettuce, celery, and tomatoes).

Once in the supermarket, you really need only remember dairy (3), dry goods (3), and vegetables (3). Those cues will likely call to mind your specific items. (Similarly, the quantities you need do not have to clutter your mental list.) Of course, if you are thoroughly familiar with the store, you can chunk your purchases according to sections or aisles.

Chunking.
Try the chunking principle on your next shopping expedition. Plan ahead in your mind. Group your purchases into categories, colors, things beginning with the same letter, or goods located in the same part of the store. Put them in chunks of three or four and they become infinitely more memorable—and manageable—than they were in one huge lump. Your list is organized, and so is your brain.

Chunking is made to order for numbers. Many numbers are too big to remember, and no wonder. Memory specialists say that the upper limit for long-term number retention is seven digits—and it is no coincidence that phone numbers are just that long. Nor is it coincidence that, when area codes came into everyday use, the extra three digits were traditionally separated from the original seven by parentheses. Three digits in parentheses happens to be a perfect example of a chunk, set neatly apart from the already memorized number.

Graphically, the memory advantage of chunking is quickly apparent. Consider a twelve-digit number:

4 9 2 3 5 7 1 6 8 2 4 7

Even in mathematical order—492 billion, and so on—it is too big to grasp, much less hold on to. But now try chunking it:

(492) (357) (168) (247).

> ## Using acronyms
>
> Suppose you are going to the store to buy *peas, mustard, soda, artichokes,* and *tea.* Reorder to *s*oda, *t*ea, *a*rtichokes, *m*ustard, and *p*eas:
>
> **STAMP**
>
> You have created a mnemonic.

Suddenly it becomes comprehensible: you may think of it as four area codes. If you need to know an absurdly long number—a charge account or bank account code, for instance—try using the chunking method. If the number does not break down into neat multiples of three, tack on a one- or two-digit prefix. With practice, and habit, chunking works.

Some useful facts have been imprinted on your memory bank in a peculiarly childish way, through rhymes and ditties that you learned in school or at home. They may be childish, but they save everyone a lot of time and trouble. You probably know these:

(calendar)	Thirty days hath September, April, June, and November . . .
(time change)	Spring forward, fall back
(spelling)	*I* before *E*, except after *C,* Or when sounded like *A* . . .
(treble clef)	*E*very *G*ood *B*oy *D*eserves *F*udge

Mnemonics.
Each of these is an example of a *mnemonic* (nee-MON-ik): a learning aid, often a rhyme, that cues your conscious mind to recall some fact in your long-term memory bank. Some mnemonics are best left to serious memory experts, but many others (supplied in succeeding pages) are accessible to all learners. Each new technique represents a mnemonic progression from some previous level of memory training, and none involves parlor tricks or special intellectual gifts.

Every level of memory building will involve a sustained effort on your part: close *observation*, concentrated *attention*, and mental *organization*. Your progress may be shaky at first, slower than you like, but there will be nothing painful about it, and no one will grade your performance. Best of all, the reward will be considerable: never forgetting names and faces again, no more list-making and note-taking, and the sure self-knowledge that you are more fully aware of everything happening around you.

Image formation

Ridiculous associations can be an aid to memory. For example, you may visualize a dog-food sandwich to help remember dog food and bread.

Image formation, or imaging, is a cornerstone of memory building. You probably do it already, nearly every night, when you dream. Every time you dream, you indulge your natural capacity for forming images. In memory training you teach yourself to dream consciously, on purpose, with your eyes open, in order to make forgettable things memorable.

Any common object can be made memorable by mentally assigning three qualities to it: *detail, color,* and *movement.* Consider something you may frequently misplace. A key is a good example. It is small, dull and much like any other key. Now make your key special in your mind: gleaming, flashing gold in the light, with sharp teeth that might cut you if you are not careful. Next, imagine that this thing is alive and has a mind of its own—if you do not keep track of it, it is likely to jump up and lock you up. You might even give it a name. Once you see this key as somehow distinctive or dangerous, you will be unlikely to lose it again.

Paired images. Remembering two different things is much easier if you pair them in your mind, however improbably. Unpaired, they are readily forgotten. "Oh, and on the way back would you please pick up some dog food and some bread?" On your way home you may vaguely recall something—two things —you were supposed to get at the store, but you are unlikely to recall what they were. But if you had drawn this picture in your mind, you would not soon forget it: a dog-food sandwich, two slices of white bread enclosing three inches of golden brown canine chunks.

In making paired images, it is important to remember that logic, reality, even propriety must be discarded. The idea is to imprint on your mind a truly outrageous and colorful picture, one that takes imagination to come up with. At first this process, like learning to paint, will require time and thought, but soon enough the process will seem easy. In fact, most people find it fun. Image formation is a conscious investment

in remembering. Having made that investment, you will be unlikely to give it up easily.

Most lists of things to remember contain more than two or three items. However, your mind picture can accommodate an extensive list, this one, for example:

1. culottes
2. tennis racket
3. rain hat
4. fur-topped boots
5. knee pads
6. bib overalls
7. swim goggles
8. windbreaker
9. ski gloves
10. duck-hunting whistle

Imagine yourself wearing or using all this gear at once, from top to bottom, from the inside out. Silly? Certainly, but not nearly as silly as it could have been— if half your list had been grocery items, for instance.

The primary trick in image formation is to *gather everything together in one room,* or *hang everything on one person.* Construct a situation in which each item belongs with another one, in which unrelated objects become related through the medium of your imagination. By seeing yourself equipped with all ten items in the list, you will be able to remember all ten. Imaging is a useful memory tool.

When trying to remember a long list of items, you might relate each to yourself. Find a way to wear or hold each item on your list.

Peg words

To prepare for the use of peg words in building memory, try to imagine that every number, 0 through 9, *looks like* a certain letter of the alphabet. Here is the version that memory experts use and memory students find most useful. It is sometimes called the number/consonant system or the letter-number alphabet:

Number	Letter/sound	Reason
0	z (*or* s)	zero begins with *z*
1	t (*or* d)	vertical stroke of a *t* looks like number *1*
2	n	printed *n* has *2* downstrokes
3	m	printed *m* has *3* downstrokes
4	r	written-out *4* ends in *r*
5	l	your *5*-fingered left hand, thumb out, forms an *L*
6	ch (j *or* g *or* sh)	turned-around *j* looks like a *6*
7	k (*or* c)	European *7* looks like a *k*
8	f (*or* v)	written *f* looks like a skinny *8*
9	p (*or* b)	mirror-image of *p* is a *9*

Remember one phrase—TeN MoRe LoGiC FiBS—minus the vowels—and you will know 1 through 10. Now you are ready to work with peg words.

The letter-number alphabet, with its single-letter equivalent numbers, is not suitable for all numerical combinations, especially the long ones. The true *memory pegs* for all numbers are pictorial equivalents: 1 = t = a picture (in your mind) of a tie. Tie, of course, begins with t and can be tacked on to almost any word picture you can think up. Each effective pictorial equivalent, or peg, must be short, must begin with the correct letter, and must be readily transferable into picture form. You might think of 1 to 10 this way:

Tie (1) should be a loud necktie or bow tie.
Noah (2) is usually thought of as an old man in robes, with a flowing white beard.
Ma (3) can be your mind's-eye view of your own mother, or any other motherly person.
Rye (4) works well as a loaf of bread.
Law (5) is John Law, a policeman or sheriff.
Shoe (6) stands for a single shoe, preferably a large one.
Cow (7) is the dairy animal. (The hard *c* in cow is the same as phonetic *k*.)
Ivy (8) is the climbing vine, capable of growing on anything. (This is the only exception to the rule that peg words should begin with the correct letter, but ivy is easy to see in your mind and so is remembered easily.)
Bee (9) is the noisy insect.
Toes (10) combine 1 and 0—the *t* sound plus the *z* sound. They stand for your toes.

Peg words for 1–10: TeN MoRe LoGiC FiBS

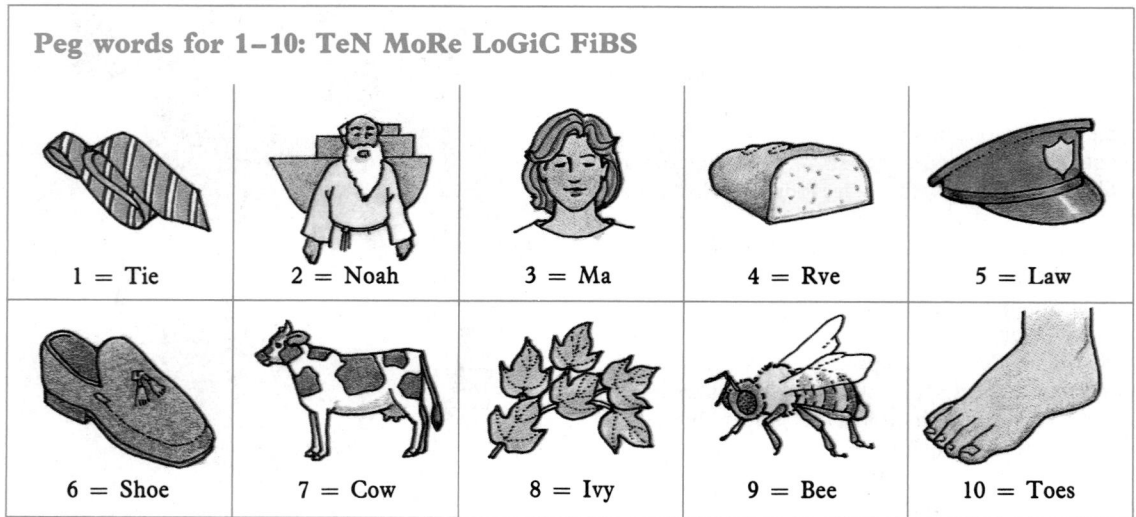

| 1 = Tie | 2 = Noah | 3 = Ma | 4 = Rve | 5 = Law |
| 6 = Shoe | 7 = Cow | 8 = Ivy | 9 = Bee | 10 = Toes |

Improving Your Memory

246-3579

It takes some doing to construct a picture such as this for a telephone number. But once it's done, you'll never forget the number.

The numbers 1 to 10 are enough to learn for now; they include all the basic peg sounds, peg words, and peg pictures. With them alone you can memorize any phone number and itemize any short list in your head. But first you need practice. At every reasonable opportunity, practice using these pegs with phone numbers and street addresses until every number you hear immediately sparks a picture in your mind. Then you can start stringing numbers together in multiples. Your word pictures will become murals. With them, you can start trying to memorize almost any complicated combination. But start modestly.

Peg words are *substitutes* for numbers. Because they are based on the letter-number alphabet, and because they are backed by pictorial equivalents, they are clearly superior to plain numbers as memory builders. (There are peg words for 11 to 100 also, listed in the Appendix, pages 198-199.) By using letter *and* picture substitutes for numbers, every new number takes on two- or three-dimensional significance in your mind's eye.

When you attempt to memorize a phone number, for example, 246-3579, using one-dimensional rote memory, you will usually forget it by the next day. This is because there is nothing memorable about that number. Its letter-number equivalent is a different story. The number 246-3579 becomes *NoRwiCH MiLKuP,* a country scene one can easily remember. Now consider one more version—the pictorial equivalent—of the same phone number:

(246)   Picture old Noah (2), arms outstretched, with a ham on Rye (4) sandwich in one hand and a huge Shoe (6) in the other.

(3579)   There goes your Ma (3) riding double with an Officer of the Law (5) on a Cow (7), galloping away from a swarm of Bees (9) in hot pursuit.

That is a picture. More importantly, it is a phone number you will not soon forget. Take your own phone number, fill in the right peg sounds and peg pictures, and see what you come up with. You will soon become good at using letter-number equivalents and peg words.

Link method

The hardest things to remember are those that lack logical association between the items. By contrast, for example, it is easy to remember the multiplication tables—the logic of 1 times 2, 1 times 3, etc. is apparent to all of us. When it comes to remembering to buy shoes, shirts, and soap, the association is missing.

Links are the mortar that holds individual memories together. Links make mental connections between unrelated objects, numbers, or items. Names of objects can be linked in two ways: by placing them one after another in a narrative, or by constructing new words from the first letters of those objects (using the initial method plus connecting vowels, as in *NoRwiCH MiLKuP*).

Initial method. For example, suppose you want to remember the sites of the last six Olympic Games. Beginning in 1964, they are Tokyo, Mexico City, Munich, Montreal, Moscow, and Los Angeles. You could invent a narrative—a travelogue—that took you to all those cities in order, but you need not do so. It would be better, because there are only six of them, to try the first-initial method. Here is how it might work:

Too	MuCh	M&MMs	LAnguage
(Tokyo)	(Mexico City)	(Munich, Montreal, Moscow)	(Los Angeles)

Many of us enjoy M & M candy, so now we can link together Too MuCh M&MMs LAnguage, not the greatest of thoughts but surely a fine story of someone enjoying candy. When you invent your own link phrase, you become the author of your own memory aid. The phrases are yours alone, and you will remember them.

Narrative method. The other kind of link association, the narrative method, requires all the imagination you can come up with. Nothing is too outrageous, *if it helps you remember*. As an example, take the nine-item grocery list used earlier (page 186):

> milk, cheese, eggs, cereal, coffee,
> sugar, lettuce, tomatoes, celery

For the sake of demonstration, this is a short and easy list. With practice, the link narrative method will work equally well even for a much longer and more varied shopping list. First, put yourself in the center of the picture: everything that happens will be made to happen by you.

A trip to the supermarket

You are going—in your mind, of course—to the supermarket. You are on a mission of mercy. Some people, you have decided, need groceries more than you do. You commandeer nine shopping carts, tucked into one another, and make your way down the first aisle: Dairy. A young mother is trying to corral her two small youngsters who are sampling everything on the shelves.

"Need some *milk?*" you ask her. She nods. You hand each child a gallon jug of milk—nearly as big as they are—and lift the boys and the milk into the first of your shopping carts. The mother smiles and heads for the check-out counter.

Just then a burly young man comes by with about 15 packages of hamburger buns under each arm. "*Cheese*burgers?" you ask. He nods, and you heap the second of your carts with dozens of prewrapped packages of assorted cheeses; the young man dumps his hamburger meat on top of it and is on his way, with thanks.

Across the aisle an old lady is painstakingly opening every cardboard *egg* carton in the display to check for breakage. "It would be easier to do that at home," you say pleasantly, and soon the old lady is pushing your third cart filled with 45 dozen eggs. You have made her day.

You come across a little girl in tears, vainly trying to rip open the bottom of a box of *cereal* to get at the prize. No problem: the young lady is packed off in your fourth cart with 24 boxes of cereal, calling out to her mother, "Mommy, I won!"

Improving Your Memory

Hidden in a corner is an enormous aluminum *coffee* urn, steaming from the top, with no sign attached. "The coffee must be free," you conclude. You unplug the coffee-maker and wrestle it into your fifth shopping cart—a perfect fit, with just enough room for three dozen styrofoam cups.

"Take a break, shoppers!" you announce. "Hot coffee. On me." You lead a growing procession to the middle aisle of the store and start dispensing coffee from your cart. More than one shopper remarks that the brew is too bitter.

Not for long: you empty two 5-pound bags of *sugar* into the urn and load your sixth cart with five more bags. Your fellow shoppers are enjoying themselves. But not the store manager, who has been watching you from the moment the coffee urn disappeared. (The coffee was free, but it tasted so bad that the store wanted it hidden.) He is right behind you as you approach your last stop: Produce.

"Pardon me," the manager says, "could I have a word with you in my office?"

"Just a minute," you say. "I'm mixing a salad." You have three shopping carts left. You fill the first with heads of *lettuce,* the second with dozens of *tomatoes,* and the third with every bunch of *celery* in the bin. The shoppers raid each cart and buy out the entire supply, which brings a smile to the store manager's face at last.

"Now, my good man, I believe I owe you for two bags of sugar," you say on your way out, peeling off a five-dollar bill. "Charge the coffee to good customer relations."

Now that is a shopping excursion you will remember —which means, of course, that will also remember your nine-item shopping list. Most shopping lists, however, leave little to the imagination. They are colorless and lifeless. The storytelling method, on the other hand, contains everything a list does not: detail, color, and movement. In addition, of course, you are the star performer in your own story. Like an actor, you have only to remember to follow through the sequence of events. Imagination and the patience to concoct a scenario are the only requirements. After you practice a few times, it will take far less effort to make up a story than it does to write down a list.

Always try to paint your mind pictures in the broadest possible strokes, freely using disproportion, movement, exaggeration, and even substitution. Substitution means using one object in place of another—a potato, say, in place of a prizefighter's broad lumpy nose—because the resemblance is clearly there or because the image is so memorable. Using linked mind pictures, you can learn to memorize lists of 20 or more items that have no apparent relation to one another.

Everyday applications

Even as a beginner in the use of memory systems, you can go a long way with the link method and your ten peg words. Links are used to memorize anything in sequence; pegs help you remember any kind of number, in or out of sequence. Pegs and links can be combined to memorize schedules and appointments.

Using links.
Suppose one morning you have eight things to do: (1) phone the vet about your cat; (2) get the car washed; (3) make a deposit at the bank; (4) mail a package at the post office; (5) buy four items at the hardware store (light bulbs, extension cord, duplicate key, and catnip); (6) buy a watchband at the jeweler's; (7) pick up three food items at the convenience store; and (8) stop by a friend's house, where you left your umbrella.

Now for your links. Your movie for the day begins at breakfast, where you imagine yourself milking cows —one cow is sick, call the vet (1). As you get in your car, imagine that it is dripping wet and clean (2). See yourself driving up to the bank teller's drive-in window (3). Your bank deposit slip could be considered postage for your package, which it is time to mail (4). While you are at the post office, study the "Wanted" posters and imagine that you are pictured there as a burglar. You will need tools from the hardware store (5): light bulbs for bright ideas, an extension cord for second-story

work, a skeleton key, and catnip. Right down the street from the hardware store is the jeweler's where you treat yourself to a new watchband (6). The rest is easy. You always pass the convenience store on your way home and you nearly always stop for something. Milk, bread, and eggs (7) are needed this time. So is your umbrella. It always rains when you do not have it. It is raining now—in your mental movie—so you stop at your friend's house to retrieve it (8). Eight errands and eight links, combining to fashion a chain of actions.

Using pegs.
The other way to memorize this schedule/list is to peg each stop to its pictorial symbol. You might wear a Tie (1) to talk to the vet. Imagine your car being washed by Noah himself (2). Your Ma (3), wearing an eyeshade, might be the bank teller. Your parcel for mailing might be a loaf of Rye (4) bread. Your imaginary burglar's foray at the hardware store would be thwarted by the Law (5). Your Shoe (6) might be held together by a watchband. Your milk is custom-dispensed by a Cow (7). Finally, your umbrella is found to be upholstered with Ivy (8).

For a short list, the peg method permits a briefer scenario and seems to make more sense. But good sense and good memorability are not always the same. For most students of memory, the link method seems to yield more satisfaction.

Links and pegs

Two surefire ways to memorize the otherwise forgettable:

Link

Peg

     Improving Your Memory

Links and pegs in action

Phone numbers Your task is, of course, very much simplified if you only want to memorize local numbers. You already know the prefix; just deal with the last four numbers. For simplicity, try to make a peg word from those final four numbers; 3819, for example, might become MuFf-Top, which prompts a picture of a fur-topped boot. Link the peg word to the face (or figure) of the person you want to call.

Historical dates First get rid of the extraneous factors. Replace the names of months with their sequential numbers, 1 to 12. As for years, eliminate the first two century numbers; you already know what century you are dealing with. Thus Lincoln's Gettysburg Address, November 19, 1863, becomes 11 19 63, whose first (peg) initials form TaTTeD SHaM. Picture Mr. Lincoln tatting a sham—that is, stitching a pillowcase—while he tries to memorize the Gettysburg Address.

Playing cards Think up your own peg words to represent all the cards in the deck, with 13 *s* words in the spade suit, 13 *h* words in hearts, 13 *d* words in diamonds, and 13 *c* words in clubs. Your own one-syllable pegs will be better than a ready-made set, because you will have to memorize them perfectly and practice thoroughly before applying your knowledge of unplayed cards in a game of chance.

Foreign words This advice is limited to individual words, short expressions, and proper names. Memorization is no substitute for learning a foreign language, but it is a great help in learning useful words. Whatever word gives you trouble can be manipulated, somehow, to approximate an English substitute—a word or name that sounds like the foreign one. Whenever you see or hear the foreign version, a mind picture of your version will give you an instant translation. Pronunciation is not important in this aspect of the work involved in learning a foreign language.

Birthdays Use the same method as for historical dates, but make a special birthday link between the peg date and the person. If one of your nephews was born on August 2, 1965, for instance, streamline the date—8 2 65—and make a first-letter peg substitution: INSoLe, your nephew's bare foot. The same principle applies to anniversaries, except that you have two people to keep in your mind picture.

Aging and absent-mindedness

Resistance to change is most noticeable when a grandparent or great-grandparent simply stops paying attention; the suspicion sets in that our beloved seniors are finally just too old to function, that senility is taking its toll.

Senility can easily be a misdiagnosis. Old-age mental infirmity, usually called senility, may be the natural product of two maladies of old age: inattention and inactivity. Usually, both are easily reversible, and neither is indicative of true memory loss, which is a clinical condition accompanying physical deterioration. Memory loss rarely shows itself as an isolated symptom.

A leading authority on adult education, Edward L. Thorndike, once stated that "age is no handicap to learning a new trade, profession, or anything you want to do at any time of life." Remember: *anything you want to do.* Your brain can always use exercise. A sedentary brain means a sedentary memory. Absent-mindedness may simply mean not caring.

By practicing the memory-building exercises in this chapter, older people are likely to tap reserves of vitality they thought they had outlived. Memory experts agree: the best memory students are often the oldest. The alertness and involvement you use in practicing a memory system not only sharpen memory but sharpen all your mental faculties as well. Every flex of a memory muscle strengthens it.

Names and faces

If you are like most people, you wish you could remember names and faces better. After all, any man or woman who remembers *your* name is likely to win your respect and attention; it is almost disrespectful if you fail to reply in kind. And when someone knows your name, and assumes you remember his, there is rarely a graceful way out if you do not. First a word of reassurance: do not assume that you are cursed with the inability to remember names. You simply have never gone about it in a systematic way.

Getting a name right. To begin with, you may have never listened to an introduction properly. On meeting someone—a perfect stranger—at some social function, attend to these ground rules:

- Hear his or her whole name clearly.
- If unclear, ask for the spelling.
- If odd, comment on it.
- Repeat the name during conversation.
- Say the name once more on parting.

Surnames fall into three categories for the purpose of memorization. The first two are easy:

1. Self-descriptive names (Baker, Cook, White, Day, Knight, Brown, Foote, Post, and so on) that in themselves have meaning or spark images.

2. Same-as or sound-like names that duplicate or approximate those of famous people, historical figures, or well-known brand names.

You should have no trouble associating these names with a pictorial equivalent, whether it be a celebrity, an occupation, or a color.

But the third category—meaning 90 percent of all surnames—will require some work. Except to linguists, most names mean nothing by themselves; they defy visualization or definition, perhaps even pronunciation, and they are meaningless as words. The solution: a substitute word or words to stand for the difficult name and to make a picture for deposit in your memory bank. Each syllable in a name will likely add a picture, and then the pictures must be linked. Below are some names, along with suggested pictorial equivalents, to get you started.

After you have practiced this substitution technique, no one's name should be meaningless anymore. But that is only half the battle. It is essential, of course, to memorize someone's name, but it is equally important to match that name to its owner's face. So there is one last association technique to learn. Match your outlandish mind picture (from the name) to *one* outstanding feature of that person's face.

Just as you take pains to get his or her name right, so you must look the other person straight in the face to get it right, too. Almost certainly something will strike you as distinctive—a scar, a hairline (or lack of it), a wide (or pursed) mouth, high cheekbones, a disproportionate nose, a drooping eyelid, a five o'clock shadow, a long chin, squinty eyes or prominent eyeglasses, a long (or dimpled) chin. Then take that one facial feature and combine (link) it with your mind picture of the person's last name. Never mind the ridiculousness of your finished portrait; its lack of logic is what makes it memorable.

Knowing what you have just read, try once more to truly memorize the names and faces on page 185. Then turn back to this page and note your improvement.

Making pictures of names

Name	Phrase	Picture
Cohen	ice cream *cone*	
Olzcewski	*old* + *chef* + *ski*ing	
Gordon	vegetable *garden*	

Name	Phrase	Picture
Kassebaum	*castle* + *bomb*	
Pottinger	*pot* + *injure*	
Pfeiffer	*fife* player	

Suggestions for students

Too many people go through high school and college and adult education courses stuffing themselves with information one day only to disgorge it all the next. They cram for an exam, take it, and emerge with little or no permanent knowledge. Why is all that information forgotten so quickly?

The scholastic method of memory building is rote repetition without regard for meaning. Thus, such students will read something over and over again until it sinks in—for a little while. To memorize something by rote is not really to learn it, and certainly not to understand it. Learning is not a one-shot recital of facts or ideas; it is the informed application of information and ideas. When you build true memory, you absorb facts and ideas in such a way that you store them away, ready to be employed profitably for the rest of your life.

So far you have learned the fundamentals of the peg and link methods of memory, both unsurpassed for the recollection of tangible objects and numbers, and both suitable for translation into mind pictures.

Pegs and links will not work, however, in certain fields of academic study. There is no practical way to conjure up a picture of a French verb, a mathematical equation, or a scientific term. Something else is needed to aid the memory.

Memory techniques for students

English vocabulary

Some words do not look at all like what they mean. In such cases, break the word into separate syllables and give each part a new meaning in a new linkage.

Execrate—to hate, detest. Imagine having to put *eggs* in a *crate* all the time. You would *detest* such a chore.

Hirsute—hairy. Look at that woman in the woolen suit—*her suit* is all covered with *hair*.

Litany—a kind of prayer. Think of yourself *praying* on one knee—praying for mercy because you just *lit* your other *knee* with the votive candle.

English spelling

There is no magical way to become a better speller. The most practical solution is to seize on a habitually misspelled word like "calendar" and write it down five times wrong— c-a-l-e-n-d-e-r—and then cross out the second *e*. Then write it five times correctly and circle the second *a*. Or you might make associations between words you know already and troublesome words you want to know. See *all* lines as para*ll*el, *iron* as part of the envir*on*ment, a *guar*d as *guar*anteeing safety, and *loss* as being co*loss*al.

Mathematics

Your knowledge of peg sounds 1 to 10 (and 1 to 100, on pages 198-199) can be put to good use for learning fractions, formulas, equations, measurements, ratios, and theorems. Use the first-initial link method for individual numbers, then tie them together in a mind picture. The pictures thus formed may be ridiculous in the extreme, but they are intended only to make you familiar with a mathematical concept. When you truly learn it, you will have memorized the concept, not the funny picture.

Biology

Unlike most sciences, biology is well adapted to memory building because most of its terms have direct application to something you can visualize—a human body, an animal, a neural network. Take what you need to know, shorten it to pegs and links, and picture it right on or in the body part to which it belongs.

Chemistry

The language of chemistry is made up of symbols, and symbols are made to order for changing into pegs and links. You can, for instance, treat a subscript—the 2 in H_2O, for example—as its peg sound equivalent. The task is to make something from a chemical formula that illustrates the substance.

H_2SO_4 is sulfuric acid. Using pegs, H_2SO_4 might become HeN SORe. Why is the hen sore? Because it was doused in sulfuric acid.

Improving Your Memory

Substitution.

The something else is the *substitution* method. If you are faced with an intangible or abstract nugget of information, find a sound-alike English substitute for it, something you can *picture* in your mind. Here is how substitution works with two French words:

Pont means bridge. In pronunciation it is similar to the English word *pawn*. You might remember both the word and its pronunciation if you make a mind picture of yourself dragging a bridge—the Brooklyn Bridge or the Golden Gate—to a pawnshop.

Pamplemousse means grapefruit. Imagine a big *moose* head on the wall with an enormous *dimple* on its cheek. The dimple is so large that you are able to balance a grapefruit in it.

To help remember that the French word pont *means bridge, picture yourself dragging a bridge into a pawnshop.*

Lectures	Your goal is to *stop taking lecture notes* altogether. In lectures you are supposed to be listening and understanding. Remember the memory virtues: close *observation*, strict *attention*, and systematic *organization*. Practice doing these in your head, not your notebook. Lecturers are as eager to make sense to you as you are to make sense of them, so pay attention. In their opening remarks, lecturers will tell you what they will talk about. The lecturers then will talk about their subjects at length. Finally they will usually summarize what they have just said. The middle part—the mental note-taking part—is the most difficult part of a lecture for the audience. The opening remarks and the conclusion, which may last a combined total of five minutes, contain most of what must be retained. Most people, however, are not listening at those times. They are still settling in with note-taking paraphernalia at the start, and they are packing up to leave at the conclusion. A practiced listener should know in advance what the lecture subject is, and write that down. At first, you may need to take minimal notes on paper, as if they were chapter headings. Eventually, with practice, you will be able to take mental notes only.

| **Reading** | As you become more fluent in the construction and use of word pictures, using substitute word pegs, you are likely to find yourself visualizing peculiar mind's-eye views of things you read. Do not be alarmed. This is a sign that pegs, links, and substitutes are becoming part of your conscious memorization process. Without those mind pictures, the reading material might never be recalled at all.

The substitution method is most useful for memorizing quotations and lines of poetry. If the line or passage is a philosophical thought, or simply beautiful language, then make sound-alike substitutions to fix it in your mind. Never forget that it is difficult to memorize anything unless you invest it with *detail, color,* and *movement.* Your aim should be to simplify whatever you read to its memorable essence, and then, through substitutions, to fix it in your mind. |
| --- | --- |

Maps	First consult a map of the United States. From the western border, draw approximately vertical lines southward from the borders of the northernmost states. The West Coast grid, or zone, will take in Washington, Oregon, and California plus Alaska and Hawaii. The East Coast grid, by far the largest, may encompass as many as 17 states under Maine. Try to place all the states within six or eight zones. Then figure out your own substitute word for each state, form a link word picture for each zone, and you will have a six- or eight-chapter mind picture of the map of America.

Appendix

For those readers who had little or no success the first time (page 183), try this test again.

1. Study this 15-digit number for two minutes. Then try to duplicate it exactly on a piece of paper.

238158649376914

Peg words 1–100

1. tie	11. tot	21. net	31. mat	41. rod
2. Noah	12. tin	22. nun	32. moon	42. rain
3. Ma	13. tomb	23. name	33. mummy	43. ram
4. rye	14. tire	24. Nero	34. mower	44. rower
5. law	15. towel	25. nail	35. mule	45. roll
6. shoe	16. dish	26. notch	36. match	46. roach
7. cow	17. tack	27. neck	37. mug	47. rock
8. ivy	18. dove	28. knife	38. movie	48. roof
9. bee	19. tub	29. knob	39. mop	49. rope
10. toes	20. nose	30. mouse	40. rose	50. lace

2. Here are seven phone numbers, each corresponding to a local tradesman or professional. Study the list for six minutes, then copy the seven titles in any order. Finally, without looking, match the memorized numbers to the titles.

Doctor	762-5881	Lawyer	681-9558
Grocer	616-2053	Dentist	386-3579
Plumber	358-0864	Florist	784-3579
Electrician	872-9647		

3. This is a list of twelve objects found in the home. Study it for just two minutes, then reconstruct the list from memory, in order.

couch, refrigerator, newspaper, clock, mirror, toaster, lamp, toilet, stove, television, carpet, window

51. lot
52. lion
53. limb
54. lure
55. lily
56. leech
57. log
58. lava
59. lip
60. cheese

61. sheet
62. chain
63. jam
64. cherry
65. jail
66. choo choo
67. chalk
68. chef
69. ship
70. case

71. cot
72. coin
73. comb
74. car
75. coal
76. cage
77. coke
78. cave
79. cob
80. fez

81. fat
82. phone
83. foam
84. fur
85. file
86. fish
87. fog
88. fife
89. fob (or fib)
90. bus

91. bat
92. bone
93. bum
94. bear
95. bell
96. beach
97. book
98. puff
99. pipe
100. disease (or dozes)

Names and their pictorial equivalents

Feminine

Abby: abbey, a bee
Abigail: a big ale
Ada: aid her
Addy: add E
Adelaide: a dell aid, addle aid
Adele: a dell
Adeline: add a line
Agatha: agate tore
Agnes: egg nest
Alberta: Al bought her
Alexandra: lick sand raw
Alexis: all ex's, all legs
Alice: blue gown
Alicia: a leash
Aline: lean
Alvira: I'll wire her
Amanda: a man there, amend, a mender
Amelia: a meal yeah
Amy: aim me, hey me
Andrea: hand dryer, angrier
Angela: angel, and Jell-o
Angelina: angel leaner
Anita: anteater, an eater
Annabel: a new bell
Annette: a net
Antoinette: ant turn net
Arlene: I lean
Audrey: all dry, aw dry
Augusta: gust her
Avis: a whiz
Babette: bad bet
Babs: bobs, blabs
Barbara: barber
Becky: bad key, peck E
Bernadette: burn a debt
Bernice: burn niece, burnoose
Bess: best, bass
Beth: bet bath
Beverly: beef early
Bobbie: pin, bob E
Bonnie: bony, bone knee, bonnet
Brenda: bran there
Candace: canned ace, candy
Candy: candy
Carla: car law
Carmen: car men
Caroline: carry line
Carrie: carry
Cecile: says seal
Cecilia: steal ya
Celeste: see less, see last
Celia: seal ya
Charlene: char lean
Cheryl: chair ill
Chrissie: cross E
Christine: pristine, grist in
Cicely: Sicily, sees a lea

Cindy: cinder, sin D
Clara: clearer, clarify
Clarissa: clear as air
Claudia: claw D, clawed ya
Clementine: clam on time
Colleen: call in, coal lean
Conchita: conch eater
Constance: con stands, cons dance
Consuelo: con swallow
Cora: core, corer
Cordelia: core deal ya
Corinne: chlorine, core in
Cornelia: corn kneel
Crystal: crystal, cross tall
Cynthia: send to ya, sin tear
Daphne: deaf knee
Darleen: darling, door lean
Deborah: the borer
Deirdre: deer draw
Delia: deal ya
Denise: the niece, dentist
Diana: piano, die on her, dye Anna
Dinah: diner
Dixie: south, dig sea
Dolly: doll
Dolores: the law is
Dora: door, adore her
Doreen: tureen, door in
Dorothy: adore a tea, door tea
Dot: dot
Eden: eatin', E den
Edith: edict
Edwina: head winner
Eileen: I lean, eye lean
Eleanor: a lean oar
Elena: a loner, a leaner
Elise: a lease, release
Eliza: L icer, he lies t'her
Elizabeth: he lifts a bed
Ellie: alley, a lea
Eloise: hello ease, yellow E's
Elsa: L saw, else
Elsie: L sea, el see
Elva: elf, L where?
Elvira: elf higher, L wirer
Emily: a mill E, M in lea
Emma: hey Ma, hemmer
Enid: he knit, in it
Erica: error car
Ernestine: earnest in, a nest in
Essie: ess sea, S see, I see, icy
Estelle: S tell
Esther: yester(day), yes dear, ess tear
Etta: eater, editor
Eugenia: ewe genius, ewe jeans

Evangeline: evangelist
Eve: eve, heave
Evelyn: evil in, a violin
Faith: faith
Fay: fade, fail
Felicia: full leash
Flo: flow
Flora: flower, floor
Florence: floor ants
Flossie: floor see
Frances: France is
Francesca: France's car
Francine: France seen, ran scene
Freda: freed her
Fritzie: ritzy, frisky
Gabrielle: horn, gabby L
Gail: gale
Genevieve: gem verve
Georgia: gorga ya, gorgeous, gorge
Geraldine: chair old dine
Germaine: German, germane
Gertrude: protrude, go through
Gilda: gill there, gild, guild
Gina: china, gee no
Ginny: gin knee
Gisele: gazelle
Glenda: lender, glen deer
Grace: grace, race
Greta: get her, (re)gretter
Gretchen: retchin', great chin
Griselda: grows older
Gussie: gassy, gust sea
Gwen: when, goin'
Gwendolyn: mandolin, wend all in
Hannah: hand her
Harriet: hurry it, harried
Hattie: had tea, hat tea
Hazel: nut, haze, hassle
Heather: heather, feather
Hedda: header, head her
Hedy: heady
Heidi: hide E, hide
Helen: hellin', hailin'
Helena: hill leaner
Helga: held car
Henrietta: hen reader
Hermione: her my own knee
Hester: S tore, has tear
Hettie: heady
Hilary: hilarious, hill airy
Hilda: builder, hill there
Hildegarde: hill the guard
Holly: holly, holy
Honey: honey
Hope: hope
Hortense: horse sense
Ida: cider

Ilka: ilk, elk, ill car
Ilse: ills, else
Imogene: emergin', in motion
Ina: iron, eye no, I know
Inez: iron S, inn Ess
Ingrid: in grid, ink rid
Irene: eye ran, iron in
Irma: I'm a, her Ma
Isabel: is a bell
Isadora: is a door, adorer
Jackie: jack key
Jacqueline: jackal in, jack line
Jane: jay hen, chain
Janet: chain it, chain net
Janice: chain ice, chain ease
Jean: jeans
Jeannette: gem net, shine it
Jeannie: jean knee, chain knee
Jennifer: chain off her, gem fur
Jenny: jay knee, chain knee
Jessica: sick car, chase a car
Jessie: chase E
Jewel: jewel, chew L
Jill: chill, jail
Jo: show, (G.I.) Joe
Joan: showin', own
Joanna: show Anna, showin' her
Jocelyn: jostlin'
Jody: show D, show tea
Josephine: show sip fine
Joyce: juice, (re)joice, choice
Juanita: one eater, war neater
Judith: showed it, chewed it
Judy: chew D
Julia: jewel, jewel yeah
Juliana: shoe lea Anna
Julie: jewel E
Juliet: balcony, jewel ye
June: chewin'
Justine(ina): just in, just tea
Karen: carryin', carin'
Kate: gate
Katherine: cat run, cat tore in
Kathleen: cat lean
Kathy: cat see
Katie: katydid, K tea
Katrina: cat runner
Kay: K, cake, key
Kim: come, grim
Kirsten: curse tin
Kit: kit, cat
Kitty: kitty, kit E
Laura: lurer
Lauren: lurin', lowerin'
Laurette: lower it, lorgnette
Laurie: lower E, lorry

Laverne: love urn
Lavinia: love in here
Leah: lea ah, leader
Lee: lea, lee (shelter)
Lena: leaner
Leonora: lea and aura,
 lee and oar
Leslie: less lea
Letitia: the teacher
Letty: let E
Lila: lie low
Lillian: lily in
Linda: lender, lint
Lisa: leaser, lease her
Liza: lies here
Lois: loose
Lola: loller, low lair
Lolita: low lighter,
 low leader
Loretta: lure a tire, lower it
Lorna: law no, (for)lorn,
 lawn
Lorraine: low rain
Lottie: lottery, lot tea
Louisa: low icer
Louise: low ice, low ease
Lucia: lose ya'
Lucille: loose sail, low sill
Lucinda: lose cinder,
 loose in there
Lucy: loose E, low sea
Lulu: tutu, (that's a) lulu,
 lullaby
Lydia: lid here, lady, lid ya'
Lynne: lin(iment), lean
Mabel: may bell, may bull
Madeleine: mad lean
Madge: mad G, badge
Mae: may(pole)
Magda: make door,
 nagged her
Magdalena: make door
 leaner
Maggie: magpie, my key
Maisie: maize, maze E,
 may see
Malvina: mail wiener
Mamie: maim me
Mandy: mandolin, man D,
 man handy
Marcella: Ma cellar
Marcy: Ma see
Margie: march E
Margot: Ma go
Marguerite(ta): Ma car eat
Maria: mare here
Marian: marryin'
Marie: marry, mare E
Marietta: marry Etta
Marilyn: merrily,
 marry lin(iment)
Marion: marryin', carry on
Marjorie: Ma jury

Marsha: marsh, marcher
Mary: marry
Mathilda: mat ill there
Mattie: mat E
Maureen: more in, tureen
Mavis: may whiz
Maxine: Macks(trucks) in
Mehitabel: me hit a bell
Melanie: melody, melon knee
Melissa: me listen,
 mail a saw
Mercedes: Benz, me say D's,
 mercy
Meredith: married it,
 merry dish
Mildred: mill dread
Millicent: mill sent,
 mini cent
Millie: mill, mill E
Mimi: me me, mime me
Minerva: my nerve
Minnie: my knee
Miranda: veranda,
 mirror and door
Miriam: mirror him,
 merry ham
Mitzi: mitt sea
Molly: tropical fish, Ma lea
Mona: moaner
Monica: money car, Monaco
Morna: more no, mourner
Muriel: mural
Myra: my rah, mirer
Myrtle: me tell, more till
Nadine: neigh dine
Nan: nun
Nancy: nun see
Nanette: nun net, no net
Naomi: neigh owe me
Natalie: not tell E,
 gnat toll E, naturally
Nell: knell, kneel
Nellie: knell E
Nettie: net E, net eel
Nicole: nickel, nick hole
Nicolette: nickel let
Nina: knee no
Nita: neater
Noel: Christmas, no el
Nona: no no
Nora: gnaw her
Noreen: gnaw in, no rain
Norma: no Ma, normal
Octavia: hocked a view
Odette: owed debt
Olga: old car, ogre
Olive: olive
Olivia: oh liver
Opal: opal, old pal
Pam: bam, P ham
Pamela: pummel her
Pandora: box, pan door,
 panda

Pansy: pansy, pan sea
Pat: pat
Patricia: pat richer
Patty: (meat)patty, pat E
Paula: pull her
Pauline: pull in, poor line
Pearl: pearl
Peg: peg
Peggy: peg E, piggy
Penelope: pen elope
Penny: penny
Philippa: full lip
Philomena: fill meaner
Phoebe: fee bee
Phyllis: fill us
Polly: parrot, pulley
Priscilla: press cellar
Prudence: prude ants
Prue: true, rue, rude
Rachel: ray chill
Ramona: ray moaner,
 ram owner
Rebecca: ray
Regina: reach in,
 reachin' her
Rena: rain her
Renee: run hay, grenade
Renni: wren E, runny
Rhoda: road
Rita: reader
Roberta: robe hurt her
Robin: robbin',
 robin (red breast)
Rochelle: row shell
Rosa: rose
Rosalie: rose lea
Rosaline: rose land
Rosalyn: rose lin(iment)
Rosamund: rose mount
Rose: rose
Rosemarie: rose marry
Rosita: rose eater
Rowena: row wiener
Roxanne: rocks in
Ruby: ruby, rude bee
Ruth: Babe(Ruth), ruth(less)
Sabina: soapin' her,
 sap eye now
Sadie: say D, lady
Sally: sail E, sally
Salome: veil, salami
Samantha: saw man there
Sandra: sander, sand draw
Sandy: sandy
Sarah: say rah, sharer
Sasha: sash
Saundra: sauna, sundry
Selma: sell Ma
Shari: share E, chair ease
Sharon: chair on
Shawn: shorn
Sheila: shield
Sherry: sherry, cherry

Sheryl: chair ill, share ill
Shirley: surely, surly
Sibyl: see bill
Sidney: sit knee
Sigrid: sea grid, secret
Simone: sea moan
Sonia: sewin' ya', sun ya',
 sun
Sophia: sew fire, sew fee
Sophie: sew fee
Stacy: stay see
Stella: stellar, cella
Stephanie: staff a knee
Sue: sue
Sue Ann: sue ant
Susan: sues Ann, snoozin',
 (lazy) Susan
Susannah: sues Anna
Susie: sue sea
Sylvia: silver
Tammy: tan me
Terry: terry(cloth) towel
Tess: toss, test
Tessie: toss E, dressy
Thelma: tell Ma
Theodora: see a door
Theresa: tear easy, terrace
Tilda: tell door
Tillie: till E, dilly
Tina: teeny
Toby: toe bee
Toni: toe knee
Tracey: trace E
Tricia: tree share
Trixie: trick see
Trudy: true D, threw D
Una: owner
Ursula: ice cellar
Valerie: valet read
Vanessa: van a saw
Velma: well Ma
Vera: veer, fear
Verna: firmer
Vicky: icky, V key
Victoria: victory
Vida: feed her
Viola: viola
Violet: violet, file it,
 violent
Vivian: we win, vivid inn
Wanda: wander
Wendy: wend windy
Wilhelmina: will helm inn
Wilma: will Ma
Winifred: when if red,
 win if red
Winnie: whinny, win knee
Yetta: yeah tar
Yolanda: you launder
Yvette: he wet, E vet
Yvonne: he won, heave on
Zelda: sell there, seldom
Zoe: sew E

Names and their pictorial equivalents

Masculine

Aaron: air run
Abe: hey bee, ape
Abel: able, a bell
Abner: abnor(mal), nab knee
Abraham: ape ram, a bear ham
Abram: ape ram, a broom, bram(ble)
Adam: atom, at 'em
Adolph: a dolph(in)
Adrian: aid dream, a dream
Alan: a lens, a land
Albert: Prince (Albert)
Alden: all den
Alec: a lick
Alex: all eggs, legs
Alexander: leg sander
Alfred: half red
Algernon: all jaw nun
Alonzo: alone sew
Aloysius: all wishes
Alvin: all win
Ambrose: ham browse
Amos: hey miss
André: hand ray
Andrew: hand drew
Andy: handy
Angelo: angel low
Archibald: arch bald
Archie: archer
Armand: almond
Arnold: arm old
Arthur: author
Ashley: ash lea
Aubrey: orb ray
August: gust
Augustine: gustin'
Augustus: gust us
Austin: awes tin, oars tin
Avery: aviary
Axel: axle
Baldwin: bald one
Barnaby: barn a bee
Barney: bar knee, barn E
Barry: bury
Bart: bought, bart(er)
Bartholomew: bottle anew
Basil: bay sill
Bayard: bay yard
Benedict: benedict(ion)
Benjamin: bend a man
Bennett: bend net
Benny: bend E
Bentley: bent lea
Bernard: burn hard
Bernie: burn knee
Bert: bird
Bertram: bought ram
Bertrand: bird ran
Bobby: bob E
Boris: bore us

Boyd: bird
Bradford: bread ford
Bradley: bread lea
Brandon: brandin'
Brian: brine, buyin'
Bruce: bruise
Bruno: burn O
Burton: buy ton
Byron: buy run
Calvin: cave in
Cameron: camera on
Carlos: car loose
Carter: carter, car tear, cart her
Cary: carry
Casper: cast pear
Cecil: cease ill, see sill
Chad: charred, chat
Charles: quarrels, chars
Charlie: char lea
Charlton: quarrel ton, char ton
Chester: chest, jester
Chet: jet
Chris: cross, kiss, grist
Christian: cross tin
Christopher: grist fur, kissed a fur
Clarence: clearance
Clark: clock
Claude: clawed
Clayton: clay ton
Clement: cement, (in)clement
Clifford: cliff oared, cliff awed
Clifton: cliff ton
Clint: lint
Clinton: clean ton
Clive: alive
Clyde: slide, lied, clod
Cole: coal
Colin: coal in, callin'
Connie: con D, con knee
Conrad: con rat, comrade
Corey: core E
Craig: crack
Curtis: caught us, curt
Cyril: see reel, cereal
Cyrus: sires
Damon: demon
Dana: deign, day, dinner
Daniel: den yell
Danny: den knee
Darren: darin'
Darryl: barrel, dare ill
Dave: dive, gave
David: gave it, save it, slingshot
Davy: day V
Dennis: tennis
Derek: derrick
De Witt: the wit, do it

Dexter: deck stir
Dick: tick, detective
Dirk: dark, dirk, Turk
Dominick: down my neck
Donald: duck, darn old
Douglas: dug glass
Duane: D wane
Dudley: dud lea, deadly
Duke: duke, duck
Duncan: dunkin'
Dustin: dustin'
Dwight: white, D white
Earl: oil
Eddie: eddy, a D, heady
Edgar: headgear
Edmund: head mount
Edward: head ward
Edwin: head win, head wind
Egbert: egg butt
Elbert: el butt
Eldred: el dread
Eli: eel eye
Elias: eel highest
Eliot: L E yacht, eel yacht
Ellery: celery
Elmer: el Ma, el more
Emanuel: manual, he man
Emil: a mill, hem ill
Emmett: hem met, aim it
Enoch: he knock
Ephraim: half ram, F rim
Erasmus: erase most
Erastus: erased us, he razzed us
Eric: a rick(shaw), air egg
Ernest: earnest, her nest, honest
Ernie: earn knee
Errol: error
Ervin: I win, urban
Erwin: her win
Eugene: you jean, ewe jean, huge E
Eustace: used us
Evan: a van, heaven
Everett: ever et (ate), over it
Ezekiel: a Z kill L, seek L
Ezra: S roar, ess raw
Felix: feel eggs
Ferdinand: bull, fur in hand
Fletcher: lecher, fetcher
Floyd: flood
Foster: forced her
Francis: fan sis
Frank: frank(furter)
Franklin: Benjamin (Franklin)
Fred: red, fret
Freddy: ready
Frederick: red rick(shaw)
Fritz: freeze
Gabriel: horn, gave reel
Garrett: garret, carry it

Gary: carry, gory
Gaston: gas ton
Gavin: gave in
Gaylord: gay lord
Gene: jean
George: gorge, judge
Gerald: chair old
Gerard: chair hard
Gideon: Bible, giddy on
Gifford: give Ford
Gil: gill, kill
Gilbert: gill butt
Giles: guiles
Gino: gee no
Godfrey: got free
Godwin: God win, good win
Gordie: gaudy
Graham: cracker, gray ham
Grant: grant, granite
Greg: grog, crack, dreg
Gregory: grog airy, crack gory
Griff: gruff, grip
Griffin: grippin', grip fin
Grover: grove
Gunther: gun tore
Gus: gas, gust
Gustave: gas stove
Hadley: head lea, heady
Hal: hall, hail
Hank: hanky, yank
Hans: hands, hens
Harold: hair old
Harry: hairy
Harvey: hard V
Hector: hick tore
Henry: hen, hen ray
Herb: herb
Herbert: her boot
Herman: her man, ermine
Hilary: hilarious, hill airy
Hiram: hire 'im, eye ram
Homer: homer
Horace: her ace
Horatio: ratio, her ratio
Howard: how ward, coward
Hoyt: hurt
Hubert: you bet, ewe bet
Hugh: you, ewe, hue
Hugo: ewe go, you go
Humphrey: home free
Hy: high
Hyman: high man
Ian: eon, ion
Ignace: egg nice, egg nuts
Ignatius: egg nauseous
Ingram: ink ram
Ira: eye rah, irate
Irving: nerve ink, serving
Irwin: I win
Isaac: eye sack, I sick
Isadore: is a door
Israel: his rail, is real

Ivan: eye van
Ivor: I wore, ivy ore
Jacob: Jacob('s ladder), shake up
Jake: shake
James: aims
Jamie: aim me
Jarvis: jar whiz
Jason: jay son
Jasper: just pair, gasp pear
Jay: jay(bird), jail
Jed: shed
Jeff: shave, shove, chaff, chef
Jeffrey: shove free, chef free
Jeremiah: chair mire
Jeremy: chair on me
Jerome: d'ya' roam?, chair room
Jerry: cherry
Jess: jazz
Jesse: James, d'ya see?, let's see
Jim: gym
Jimmy: jimmy (a door), gimme
Joel: jewel, jowl
Joey: showy, chewy
Johnny: on knee, john
Jonah: whale, show new
Jonas: showin' us
Jonathan: john thin
Jordan: Jordan (River), jaw down
José: oh say, hose
Joseph: shows off
Joshua: josh shoe, josh shower
Juan: one, won, wan
Jud: jut
Jude: chewed
Judson: jut son
Jules: jewels
Julian: jewel in
Julie: jewel, July
Justin: just in, justice
Keith: keys
Kenneth: can it
Kent: can't, canned
Kevin: cave in
Kimball: come bull
Kirk: kick
Lance: lance, lands
Lancelot: lance a lot
Larry: lair E, leery
Lawrence: lower ants
Lemuel: lamb mule
Lenny: lend knee
Leo: lion, lea O
Leon: lean on, lea on
Leonard: lean hard
Leopold: leap old, leap pole
Leroy: lea roil
Leslie: less lea

Lester: less tear
Lionel: lion el, lion L
Lloyd: lewd
Lonny: low knee
Louis: loose
Lowell: low el, lower, loll
Lucas: luke kiss
Ludwig: load wig
Luther: looser
Malcolm: mail come
Manny: many, man E, manly
Marcus: mark us
Mario: marry O
Marmaduke: Mom a duke
Marshall: marshal, marsh ill
Marty: Ma tea
Marvin: Ma win, move in
Mason: mason, my son
Matthew: mat ewe
Maurice: more rice
Maury: more E
Maximilian: makes a million
Maxwell: mix well
Maynard: main yard
Melvin: melt win, delve in
Meredith: married it
Mervin: movin'
Meyer: mire
Michael: my call, mike ill
Mickey: my key
Milton: melt on
Mitchell: mitt shell
Monroe: man row
Montague: mount glue
Montgomery: mount gum airy
Monty: mount tea, mountie
Morgan: more can
Mortimer: morti(fy) Ma, more tea Ma
Morton: more ton
Morty: more tea
Moses: Moseys, Ma says
Murray: more ray
Myron: my run, mire on
Nathan: nay sun
Nathaniel: neigh tan yell
Neil: kneel
Nelson: half nelson
Nero: fiddler, knee row
Neville: never, never ill
Nicholas: nick alas
Niles: miles, Niles (rivers)
Noah: ark, no air
Noel: Christmas, no el
Norbert: no berth
Norman: no man, Norseman
Norton: no ton
Ogden: egg den
Olaf: oh laugh, O laugh
Oliver: olive
Orson: oar sun

Oscar: Academy Award
Otis: elevator
Owen: owin'
Ozzie: ah see, I see
Patrick: pat rick(shaw)
Pattie: (meat) patty
Pedro: pet row
Percy: per se, purse see
Perry: bury, pear E, pair eel
Peter: eater, pea eater
Philip: full lip, fill up
Pierce: pierce
Pierre: pea air
Prescott: press cot
Preston: press ton
Quentin: went in
Quincy: win sea
Ralph: rough
Randall: ran doll
Randolph: ran dolph(in)
Randy: ran D
Raoul: rah oil, roll
Raphael: rah fail
Raymond: ray mount
Reggie: red G
Reginald: red G old
Reuben: ruby in
Rex: king (Latin), wrecks
Reynold: ran old
Richard: rich hard
Richie: rich E
Robbie: rob bee
Robert: robber
Robin: robin (red breast), robbin'
Roddy: ruddy, ready
Roderick: ruddy rick(shaw)
Rodney: rod knee
Roland: row land, rollin'
Rolph: roll off
Ronald: run old
Ronnie: run knee, runny
Rory: roar E
Roscoe: rescue
Ross: roars
Rudolph: rude dolph(in), rude doll off
Rufus: roof us
Rupert: rude pat
Russell: rustle
Sammy: ham me, hammy
Samson: biblical strong man
Samuel: some mule
Sandy: sandy
Schuyler: scholar
Scott: Scott(ish kilt)
Sean: shorn, sh yawn
Sebastian: sea bashed in
Seymour: see more
Shelley: shell E, shell ease
Sherman: sure man, German
Sidney: sit knee

Silas: silence, silo
Silvester: silver vest, investor
Simeon: see me on
Simon: says, sigh man
Sinclair: sin clear, sink lair
Solomon: wise man, solo man
Spence: dispense, pens
Spencer: spend sore
Stanley: stand lea
Stephen: steep hen
Stewart: steward
Teddy: ready, dead E
Terence: tear ants
Terry: terry(-cloth towel)
Theo: see O
Theodore: see a door
Thomas: tom-tom, the miss
Timmy: tinny, dim E
Timothy: dim tea
Titus: tied us
Tobias: toe buy us, bias
Toby: toe bee
Tod: toddy, toward
Tommy: tummy
Tonio: tone E O
Tony: toe knee
Tracy: trace E
Tristan: twistin'
Tyrone: throne, tie rowin'
Upton: uptown
Uriah: you're higher
Valentine: heart, valley dine
Vance: vans
Vergil: verge L
Verne: V earn, fern
Vernon: fur nun
Victor: victor
Vince: wince
Vincent: win cent
Vinnie: fini, V knee
Wade: wade
Waldo: wall dough
Wallace: wall lace, walrus
Wally: wall E
Walter: wall tear
Wayne: wane
Wendell: wend L
Wesley: west lea
Whitney: white knee
Wilbur: will burr, will bear
Wilfred: wolf red
Willard: will lard
William: will yam
Willis: will lace
Willy: willy(-nilly), will E
Winston: wins ton
Winthrop: win troop
Wyatt: Y hat, white
Zachary: sack airy, sack hairy
Zeke: seek

Names and their pictorial equivalents

Surnames

Abbott: abbott, I bought
Abelson: a bell son
Abrams: rams, ape rams
Acheson: hatch a son
Ackerman: hacker man
Addison: add a son
Adler: add law, paddler
Alcott: old cot
Alexander: lick sand, lick sander
Altman: old man
Ambrose: ham browse
Anderson: hand and son
Andrews: Ann draws
Arnold: arm old, darn old
Ashburn: ash burn
Atkins: hat kin
Atkinson: hat kin son
Atwater: at water
Austin: awes tin
Bailey: bale E, bay leaf
Baldwin: bald one, bald win
Ballinger: ball injure
Bankhead: bank head
Barnett: bar net, barn hat
Bartlett: bottle it
Baxter: back stir, backs tear
Begley: beg lea
Benham: bend ham
Benson: bend son
Bentley: band lay, English car
Bergman: (ice)berg man
Bernstein: burn stein
Blum: plum
Borden: milk, boarding
Braddock: bad dock
Bradley: brad lay
Bradshaw: bad shore
Brandt: brand
Brennan: burnin', bran nun
Brent: rent, bent
Brewster: brew stir, rooster
Brock: rock, broke
Brody: broad E
Brophy: trophy
Bryant: buy ant, buoyant
Buchanan: blue cannon
Buckley: buckle
Burgess: purchase
Burke: (ice)berg, perk
Byron: buy run
Cabot: cab butt
Cahill: gay hill
Caldwell: cold well, called well
Callahan: call a hand
Cameron: camera on
Campbell: soup, camp bell
Carlson: call son
Carmichael: car mike call

Carson: car son
Carter: car tear, cart her
Cassidy: cast tea
Cates: gates
Cavanaugh: cave in oar
Chamberlain: chamber lain
Chandler: chandelier
Channing: chaining
Chester: chest tear, jester
Chilton: chill ton
Christenson: Christian son
Clark: clock, clerk
Clinton: clean ton
Colby: cold bee
Coleman: cold man, coal man
Collins: collie, (Tom) Collins
Compton: camped on
Cooper: (chicken) coop, coo pair, barrel maker
Cosgrove: cost grove
Costello: cost hello
Coughlin: coughin'
Cowen: cow in
Crandall: ran doll
Crawford: crawl Ford
Crosby: Bing Crosby
Cunningham: cunning ham
Curtis: curt, caught us
Cushing: cushion
Custer: custard
Dalton: dull ton
Davenport: havin' port
Davis: Davis Cup
Dawson: door son
Delaney: delay knee
Denham: den ham
Denton: dent ton
Devlin: devil in
Diaz: dais
Dillon: tillin', dill on
Dixon: ticks on
Dodson: dud son
Donahue: don a hue (color)
Donaldson: darn old son
Donovan: don a van
Dooley: duel lea
Dougherty: dough in tea
Douglas: dug glass, dug less
Dowling: dowel ink, toweling
Driscoll: drizzle
Drummond: drummin'
Duffy: the fee, toughy
Dugan: do again, due again
Duncan: dunkin'
Dunlap: down lap, down lip
Durant: the rent, tour ant
Durham: door ham
Dutton: button, the ton
Dwyer: wire, dryer
Easley: easy, ease lea, easily

Eastman: yeast man
Eberhardt: ever hard
Eldridge: held ridge
Elliott: yacht, lot, L E hot
Ellsworth: el's worth
Endicott: end a cot
Ericson: a rig son
Ettinger: head injure
Everett: ever et (ate), over it
Farley: far lea
Farrell: far rail, barrel
Faulkner: fork near
Ferguson: fur go son
Findlay: find lea, finned lee
Finney: fishy, fini
Fitzgerald: fits chair old
Fitzpatrick: fits pat rick(shaw)
Flanagan: fan again
Fletcher: fetch her, lecher
Foley: fall E, foal
Forrester: forest, forest tear
Foster: forced her
Fowler: foul law, fouler
Frazer: freezer, raise her
Frederick: red rick(shaw)
Freund: friend, frond
Fuller: full, brush
Fulton: full ton
Galbraith: gal breath
Gaynor: gain her
Geller: gala, gal law, kill her
Gibbons: ribbons
Gilbert: kill bed, gill butt
Gillespie: kills pea
Giordano: jawed an O
Gladstone: glad stone
Gleason: glee son, grease on
Gonzales: guns are less
Gordon: garden
Gorman: gore man
Gould: gold, cooled
Graham: cracker, gray ham
Granger: ranger
Gregory: grog airy
Gulliver: giant, gull over
Gunther: gun tore
Haber: hay bear
Haggerty: haggard tea
Halpern: help urn
Hamilton: hammer ton
Hammond: ham mount
Hanrahan: hen ran
Hansen: hansom (cab), handsome
Harrington: herring ton
Harrison: hairy son
Hartley: heart lea, hardly
Hastings: haste inks
Hathaway: hat away
Hawkins: hawk inns
Hayden: hay den
Haynes: hay nose

Hecht: hacked
Hellman: held man
Henderson: hen son
Hendricks: hen tricks
Herbert: her boot
Hernandez: hurryin' ant is
Higgins: he gains
Hobart: whole bar, hope bard
Hobbs: hops
Hodges: hedges
Hoffman: huff man, half man
Hogan: hoe can, whole can
Holden: hold in, hold den
Hooper: hoop
Hopkins: hop kin
Horton: her ton, hurtin'
Houlihan: hold a hand
Houston: house ton, use ton
Howard: how hard, coward
Hubbard: cupboard
Humphrey: home free
Hutchinson: hutch in son
Hyatt: high hat
Hyman: high man
Ingersoll: anger soul
Ingram: ink ram
Irving: serving
Isaacs: eye sacks, ice axe
Jackson: jack son
Jacobs: cobs, Jacob's (ladder)
Jacobson: shake off son
Jacoby: jack cold bee
Jamison: aim at son
Jarrett: jar it
Jeffers: chef airs
Jeffries: chef freeze
Jenkins: chain cans
Johanson: show hand son
Jonas: showin' us
Jordan: jaw down
Joseph: shows off
Josephson: hose off son
Joyce: juice, choice, joyous
Kaiser: geyser, guy sore
Kaufman: cough man
Kearns: coins
Keenan: keen nun
Keith: keys
Kelleher: killer her
Kelly: call E, kill E
Kemp: camp
Kenny: can knee, penny
Keogh: keyhole
Kessler: cast law, wrestler
Kimball: gamble, come ball
Kingsley: kings lea
Knapp: nap, knap(sack)
Knowles: Noels, knolls
Koenig: king, coin nick
Krakauer: crack hour
Kramer: creamer, gray Ma

204

Improving Your Memory

Kroger: crow gore
Kruger: crew gore, cruder
Lafferty: laugh tea
Lambert: lamb butt
Landau: land dough
Langer: longer, linger
Larson: larceny, arson
Lawrence: law ants, lower ants
Lawson: law son
Lazarus: lather us
Lederman: leader man, letter man
Lehman: layman
Leonard: lean hard
Leopold: leap old, leap pole
Lester: less tear, jester
Leventhal: lovin' tall
Levinson: level son
Levitt: love it, leave it
Lewis: lose, loose, who is
Lieberman: labor man
Lindsey: lint sea, lindy (hop)
Lindstrom: lint strum
Livingston: living stone
Logan: low again
Loring: low ring, lowering
Loughran: lock ran
Lovell: love el
Lovett: love it
Lowell: low el
Lowenthal: low and tall
Lubin: low bin
McCarthy: Mack cart tea
McCormick: Mack core mike
McDonald: Mack darn old
McGraw: Mack raw
MacGregor: Mack rigor
McKay: Mack hay, my key
McMann: Mack man
Mahoney: Ma hold knee
Maloney: alone knee, baloney
Manning: man ink, manning
Marcus: mark us
Marshall: marshal, Ma shall
Martin: Ma tin, mar tin
Martinez: martinets
Martinson: Ma tin son
Matheson: matter son
Matthew(s): mat ewe(s)
Maxwell: makes well, mix well
Maynard: mane hard
Mercer: mercy
Meredith: married it
Metcalf: met calf
Michaelson: mike call son
Middleton: middle ton
Mitchell: shell, mitt shell
Montgomery: mount gum airy

Morales: morals, more or less
Morgan: more can
Morrison: marry son
Morse: moss
Morton: mutton, more ton
Moynihan: mind a hand
Murray: more ray
Nash: gnash
Nathanson: no tan son
Nichols: nickels
Nicholson: nickel son
Noonan: new nun
Norman: no man, Norseman
Norris: no risk
Norton: no ton, gnaw ton
Nugent: new gent
O'Brien: oh burn, brine
O'Connor: O con her
O'Donnell: ode down hill
Ogden: egg den, egged on
O'Malley: home alley
Oppenheim: open home
O'Reilly: oar oily
O'Rourke: O roar
Ortiz: oared ease
Osborne: is born
Osgood: is good
Otis: elevator
Owen: owin'
Padgett: patch it, page it
Palmer: palm, palm Ma
Papadopoulos: Papa topple us
Patterson: pat a son
Pawley: pulley
Pearce: pierce
Pearson: pierce son
Pendleton: peddle ton
Perlman: pearl man
Peterson: eater son
Phelps: helps
Phillips: full lips
Platt: plate
Poindexter: point egg stir
Pollock: pole lock
Prentiss: parent is, parenthesis

Proctor: doctor
Quentin: went in
Quinn: win
Raleigh: roll lea, raw lea, roll E
Ramirez: ram ear ess (curve)
Randall: ran doll
Randolph: ran dolph(in)
Raymond: ray mount
Reeves: reefs
Reinhard: rain hard
Richardson: rich son, rich yard son
Rigney: rig knee
Riley: rye lea, rile E
Riordan: rear down, reared on
Rivera: river
Robeson: robe son
Robinson: robbin' son
Romero: roam arrow
Rooney: ruin knee
Rossiter: rose sitter
Rudolph: rude dolph(in)
Rutherford: rode a Ford
Ryan: cryin', rind, Rhine (River)
Samuelson: some mules on
Sanchez: send chest
Sanders: sand, senders
Saunders: sanders, sun doors
Saxon: sacks on
Schultz: shields, shoots
Seaton: see ton, sit on
Sedgwick: search wick
Seiden: side in, sigh den
Seward: steward, seaward
Seymour: see more
Schaeffer: shave four
Shannon: shine on, chainin'
Sheehan: sheen
Shelton: shell ton, shelter
Sheridan: share a den
Sherman: show man, sure man

Simpson: simple son, simper son
Sinclair: sin clear
Slater: slayed her
Sommers: summers
Spaulding: sprawled ink
Spenser: expense her
Stafford: staff ford
Stoddard: stood hard
Sutherland: other land
Sweeney: sweet knee, sweety
Tate: tight, tea ate
Thatcher: that chair, thatcher
Thompson: tom-tom son
Thorpe: tore up
Tompkins: thump kin
Travers: traverse
Tucker: tuck'er
Ullmann: old man
Unger: hunger, hung her
Vance: vans
Vaughn: warn
Vincent: win cent
Wallace: wall lace, wall is, wall ace
Walsh: waltz
Warner: warn her
Warrington: warring ton
Watson: what son
Waverly: wave early, waver lea
Welch: grape juice, welsh
Wesley: west lea
Whalen: whalin', whale, wailing
Whitney: white knee
Whittaker: wit taker, with a car
Wilkinson: milkin' son
Williamson: will yam son
Winston: Churchill
Winthrop: win troop
Woolsey: wool see
Wrightson: write son
York: cork
Young: baby
Zachary: sack airy

For further reference

Cermak, Laird S.
Improving Your Memory
McGraw-Hill
Gallant, Roy A.
Memory: How It Works and How to Improve It
Four Winds Press
Lorayne, Harry
How to Develop a Super-Power Memory
Frederick Fell

Lorayne, Harry
Remembering People
Stein and Day
Lorayne, Harry, and Lucas, Jerry
The Memory Book
Stein and Day

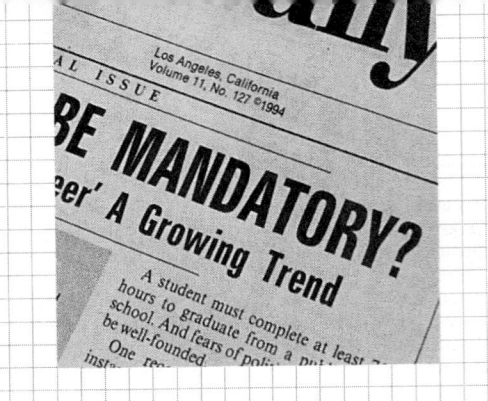

Building Your Vocabulary

"There is a weird power in a spoken word . . . And a word carries far—very far—deals destruction through time as the bullets go flying through space."
Joseph Conrad, 1857–1924

The world recognizes Joseph Conrad as one of the great English novelists. Yet he knew little of the language before he was twenty. A Polish orphan, the teenage Conrad sailed on British ships, where he learned English from his fellow seamen. Conrad was awed by the power of words, and set about becoming a writer. The quotation above is from his masterpiece, *Lord Jim.*

"A powerful agent is the right word. Whenever we come upon one of those intensely right words in a book or a newspaper the resulting effect is physical as well as spiritual, and electrically prompt."
Mark Twain, 1835–1910

Starting his career as a twelve-year-old apprentice newspaper printer, Mark Twain never lost his ambition to be a Mississippi riverboat pilot. Twain, whose real name was Samuel Clemens, used life along the river as background for *The Adventures of Tom Sawyer* and *Adventures of Huckleberry Finn.* Like Joseph Conrad, he was self-taught. Both writers respected the power of words and used them with extreme precision.

A key to success. Those women and men who possess a large vocabulary usually advance more rapidly in their careers and ultimately attain more responsible positions than those whose vocabularies are limited. The Human Engineering Laboratory has studied thousands of successful executives pursuing a wide variety of careers. It found that the only trait the executives held in common was their command of large vocabularies.

What does "to command a large vocabulary" mean? Knowing the meanings of words is part of it; but another part is knowing how to use those words effectively. Other sections in this volume help you learn how to write and speak well. See "Writing Effective Letters," pages 266-301, "Improving Your Reading," pages 302-327, and "Improving Your Speech," pages 244-265. You will also want to consult volume 1, pages 4-77, and volume 2, pages 318-347.

Do not assume that because you know the jargon of your own field, as in accounting, say, or nursing, law, or medicine, that you can communicate successfully. Just think of your own doctor, whom you, as a lay person, may not understand because he uses only incomprehensible medical words. For most people, a vocabulary rich in depth and wide in scope is more useful than one limited to the confines of a particular field. A famous professor at Columbia University once said that graduates from the English department generally ended their careers earning more money and having more responsible positions than graduates from any other field.

So you will gain considerably from the mastery of a large vocabulary. When you are interviewed for a job, or are talking to a manager at your current place of employment, the words you use are an important part of the impression you make.

Even before you are interviewed for a job or a promotion, you may be asked to take a vocabulary test. A passing grade is a necessity. To gain that passing grade, you will want to know the meanings of hundreds of new words. You will learn, and remember, 300 to 400 interesting new words as you read the next three dozen pages. But more than that, you will find three full pages of hints and techniques for passing verbal/vocabulary tests, together with questions similar to the ones you can expect to find in examination booklets.

Memorizing lists of new words and their definitions is not a recommended method for improving your vocabulary. There are several more effective ways to acquire a larger stock of words and the ability to use them correctly.

Those paths to a more powerful vocabulary are explored on the pages of this section. Whichever method you choose to follow, it will work best when you have begun building your own *Word Power* file.

Your Word Power file.
Keep a file card or small notebook in your pocket or handbag. During the day, jot down unknown or puzzling words that you read in newspapers, magazines, or on signs, or hear in conversations or on radio broadcasts. You might even overhear an unknown term as two strangers are talking together near you on a crowded bus.

Wherever you come across it, write the word on your card. If possible, try to include a portion of the way it was used in conversation or a portion of the sentence in which you read it. A typical day's entries might look like the cards at the right.

Using one of the new techniques you have mastered, there is a good chance you will have an approximate idea of the meanings of these new words. But your aim is to use more words with greater accuracy, so approximate meanings are not good enough.

The solution: At the end of each day, write each word on a separate 3×5 card. Put into your own words a dictionary's definition of the word, and enter that on the card. Also add a synonym or two if the dictionary lists them. (A **synonym** is a word that has the *same meaning* as the original word. *Grand* and *magnificent* are synonyms, as are *punish* and *discipline*.)

Keep the cards in alphabetical order. When you add new entries in your *Word Power* file, select a handful of the existing cards at random. Glance at the words but not their meanings. Test yourself. Reinforce the power of your burgeoning vocabulary. (There's a good one to start with: **burgeoning.**)

Keep a notebook in your pocket or purse so you can jot down immediately those new, unknown words you meet in your daily activities.

Building Your Vocabulary

How do you rate?

How much larger will your vocabulary be when you have mastered most of the techniques in this section? That depends on the effort you expend, beginning today. The percentage of your gain can be measured by taking this simple test, recording your score, and a month from now comparing it with your score on the test that appears on page 237.

For each of the questions, select the one term that *most nearly defines* the meaning of the word in dark print. Other readers will be using this book, so please do not write in it; mark your selections on a separate sheet of paper.

1. **acrimony** a) agility; b) court-ordered payments; c) bitterness; d) dryness

2. **adulation** a) growing up; b) adding water; c) hero worship; d) mixture

3. **appellation** a) name; b) maintain; c) small bullet; d) country

4. **capillary** a) form of butterfly; b) slender tube; c) large quantity; d) head, or top

5. **cobalt** a) metallic element; b) African antelope; c) partner; d) garden tool

6. **covert** a) secret; b) ditch, or gutter; c) lid; d) quarrelsome

7. **destitute** a) illegal; b) wicked; c) poverty-stricken; d) enhanced

8. **diffident** a) unlike; b) shy; c) argumentative; d) shining

9. **diurnal** a) under water; b) easily fooled; c) selfish; d) daily

10. **effigy** a) easy task; b) image; c) degree; d) ratio of output to input

11. **exude** a) put away; b) clear out; c) investigate; d) ooze

12. **famished** a) done, completed; b) starved; c) mixed up; d) related, as a cousin or aunt

13. **florid** a) warm; b) ornate; c) damp; d) southern

14. **glean** a) gather bit by bit; b) tilt dangerously; c) flash of light; d) smooth

15. **grotesque** a) bizarre; b) cavelike; c) comical; d) hyacinth

16. **martial** a) art; b) judo; c) general; d) warlike

17. **mendicant** a) remedy; b) ointment; c) beggar; d) prescription

18. **migrant** a) traveler; b) move to another country; c) severe headache; d) worker

19. **natal** a) Asian; b) living under water; c) birth; d) federal

20. **phobia** a) small bird; b) fear; c) drowning; d) falling

21. **pinnacle** a) peak; b) card game; c) evergreen tree; d) sail

22. **sallow** a) empty; b) yellow; c) not deep; d) filled with salt water

23. **tactile** a) crawling; b) touchable; c) pointy; d) cottonlike material

24. **troll** a) streetcar; b) mischievous dwarf; c) drumbeat; d) three of a kind

25. **usury** a) putting on makeup; b) illegal interest rate; c) impersonation; d) counterfeiting

Answers. Score one point for each correct answer. 1, c; 2, c; 3, a; 4, b; 5, a; 6, a; 7, c; 8, b; 9, d; 10, b; 11, d; 12, b; 13, b; 14, a; 15, a; 16, d; 17, c; 18, a; 19, c; 20, b; 21, a; 22, b; 23, b; 24, b; 25, b.

Analyze your score. A score of 25 is perfect (and quite rare), 22 to 24 very good, 18 to 21 above average, and 15 to 18 the score that most adults achieve. With *Word Power* you will gain during the next few weeks. It should be interesting to see how much better you do when you test yourself again.

A permanent memory system

Suppose you are reading a news magazine and come across this sentence: "She attributed the superiority of her tomatoes to the **humus** in which she grew them." You think humus has something to do with the amount of moisture in the gardener's backyard, but you are not sure. You look up the word in your dictionary and learn that it means "organic matter; decayed plants that provide nutriments to soil."

If you merely read a definition in a dictionary, make a mental note of it, and go on with your reading, your chances of retaining the meaning are slim. If you write the new word down, however, you greatly increase the probability that you will remember the meaning of **humus.** Experts in educational psychology say that the act of writing increases a person's ability to remember by as much as 100 percent.

But you are not an ordinary reader who wants to learn the meaning of an occasional new word. You are actively engaged in a campaign to radically increase your *Word Power.* To reinforce your learning process, you require additional techniques to make the new words you encounter every day a part of your working vocabulary.

Review the four-step system that follows.

Four steps to a larger vocabulary

1. **Understand what the word means, in your own terms.** If the dictionary tells you that **perfidy** means "a calculated breach of faith," do not try to add the word and that meaning to your active vocabulary in that form. Instead, read the entire dictionary entry and rephrase it, perhaps as "acts of a traitor; deliberate breaking of trust; spies engage in *perfidious* activities."

2. **Write the meaning on a card.** It requires some discipline to make a habit of the daily transference of words from your pocket notes to a permanent file card. You may be tempted to let it go for the weekend, but weekends often are more crammed with activities than we thought they would be, and file-building may be postponed yet again. The way to guarantee success is to establish a routine: fill out your file cards before you settle down for an evening's television watching or magazine reading. And keep your pocket card with you during those two activities so that any new words you hear or read will be included in the next day's entries.

   If a newspaper or magazine is the source of a word, you may want to clip the sentence from the page; then you can tape the printed sentence right on your *Word Power* card.

3. **Add the new card to your file.** An empty box, any shoebox-sized container, makes a fine storage space for your *Word Power* cards. If you have a special interest or two, you may want to color-code the cards that pertain to it for extra review. Words from the world of law and order, for example, could have green dots in the cards' upper right corners.

   Do you own a home computer? If you do, it will be easy to program a cumulative list of words, definitions, and examples of their use. Prepared software packages for vocabulary building are available, but you will find them less effective than the *Word Power* file you build for yourself.

4. **Systematically use your file.** During your first week of file-building, you may accumulate 20 or more *Word Power* cards. Once you have that many, you are ready to establish a routine that will reinforce your familiarity with the words' meanings.

   All that is required is to take out a handful of cards. Do not shuffle them, or they will have to be repositioned in alphabetical order later. Just lift one card from the pack, glance at the main word, and define it without looking at the printed definition. Then read the definition to see if you remember it correctly. If you do, replace the card and select another word. If you get it wrong, jot down the word on a list you keep for this purpose. A day or two later, look at the list and try to recall the word's meaning. If you remember a new word correctly for several days, in all probability you will remember it for many years.

   By reaching into the box and randomly choosing eight or ten words to test yourself on each day, you are certain to repeat many of the cards. Do not abandon the system. Repetitive practice, as with an athlete's training, brings superior performance.

How words are used

Words, like bricks or shingles, do not have much value when standing alone—a single brick on a patch of bare ground, or a solitary word on a page, is not of much use. But when a number are arranged in a purposeful pattern, both words and bricks are extremely useful.

When you read a newspaper and notice an unfamiliar word, you are seeing it in **context.** That is, you are seeing it in use, among other words. Context can give you clues to an unknown word's meaning. Often, the clues are so strong that you will be able to define the word without **recourse** to a dictionary.

The sense of a sentence. The way in which *recourse* was used in the previous sentence gives you a strong clue as to its meaning. "Without recourse to a dictionary" might mean without returning to a dictionary, or perhaps, without the heaviness of a dictionary. But neither of those possibilities makes much sense. What does make sense is being able to understand the word's meaning without turning to or consulting a dictionary. And that is exactly what *recourse* means in the context of that sentence.

Echo words. At times, the context of an unfamiliar word includes another word that closely duplicates its meaning. "She had never before seen on a tray so many beautiful glasses as she saw on Mrs. March's large **salver.**" In this sentence, it is easily understood that the glasses are, at the same time, on a tray and on a *salver.* The two words have the same meaning; they are *synonyms.*

Easy opposites. Just as echo words, or *synonyms,* are strong context clues, so are opposites, or *antonyms.* "Carl's blueprint specified rigid sheets of plastic, but the ones he brought were **malleable.**" The key clues here are "rigid" and "but." In the context, **malleable** refers to a kind of plastic that is the opposite of rigid. It is correct to assume that the target word means pliable or easily bent.

Read on a bit further. The last of the more common contextual techniques takes you beyond the sentence in which the unknown word appears. If there is no clue to the word's meaning in that sentence—read on. The definition may become clear a sentence or two later. Here is an example: "We recognized those sagging **jowls.** No one else ever had such baggy *jaws.*" There you have a clear definition of the wanted word, right in the next sentence.

On this page and the following pages are paragraphs, each containing several unfamiliar words. Examine those words in the context of their sentences and paragraphs. Then check your conclusions against the explanations printed right below the paragraphs. Of course, you will want to add to your *Word Power* file all words that are new or that you never have used in conversation.

The six-story **edifice** symbolized the values of **bourgeois, bustling** prewar Chicago. The building's solid **facade,** though granite and limestone, had a certain warmth. Built as the **abode** of bankers, it still was **accessible** by trolley car and other public transportation.

In the first two sentences, we learn that the paragraph describes a six-story building. *Edifice,* therefore, means building. *Bourgeois* and *bustling* are harder; you might guess the pair of words refers to busy or businesslike values of prewar Chicago. The precise definition of *bourgeois* is respectable, middle-class, property-owning. *Bustling* means busy, hurrying, or active.

Facade, a form of the word "face," refers to the front of a building. "The *abode* of bankers" can be understood to mean, loosely, their home. And if the building is *accessible* by public transportation, those trolleys have access to it; they can reach it easily.

Though the reason can't be pinned down, Mackey strikes some viewers as a **vaguely** unprofessional anchorman. It might be his slight speech **impediment** (trouble with "r's") or his **wry,** dry sense of humor. Yet, among each night's **welter** of disturbing facts and new worries, Mackey brings comfort to a large audience.

Vaguely tells us something about how or why some viewers think Mackey is unprofessional. Studying the sentence, we see that *vaguely* echoes the "can't be pinned down" quality of their feelings. *Vaguely* means indistinct, or no definite reason. If Mackey has trouble pronouncing "r's," something is standing in the way of clear speech; that is exactly what *impediment* means: an obstacle.

Wry and *dry,* when applied to sense of humor, are synonyms. The two words have the same meaning. *Welter* is not surrounded by enough clues to provide an accurate definition, but it clearly refers to a number of "facts and worries." Later, when you look it up, you will find it means a miscellaneous, hodge-podge grouping; a jumble.

Building Your Vocabulary

Try to visualize the situation, or context, in which new words appear and you may be able to guess their meanings and remember them better.

Her friends at work **twitted** Elaine about her **obsession** with her new grandchild. She was a **caricature** of an adoring grandma, **incessantly recounting** examples of the baby's brilliance. And, of course, she carried **myriad** photographs of the infant.

Her friends probably would not be mean or cruel to Elaine, but they would tease her and make fun of her constant bragging about her granddaughter. *Twitted* means teased. Elaine's mind is occupied with thoughts of the infant: she is *obsessed* with those thoughts. Drawings or actors' portrayals of easily recognizable characters, done in an exaggerated manner, are *caricatures*.

To *recount* a story is to tell it over again, and to do it continually, or without ceasing, is to do it *incessantly*. (Sometimes a story or anecdote is called an "account." Telling it again is to *recount* it.) If you did not know the meaning of *myriad*, you might guess that Elaine would carry very many photographs of the baby. *Myriad* does mean a very large number.

I wondered about Joanne's interest in **exotic** Peruvian shawls. The ancient woolens were harsh and too rough for comfort. The designs were childlike and **rudimentary**, almost primitive. Later, when her husband **confided** that Joanne was a **curator** at the Field Museum, I understood.

It would be difficult, from the context in which it is used, to know exactly what is meant by *exotic*. But the flavor, the general sense, of "exotic Peruvian shawls" indicates that the shawls are strange or foreign in appearance. And that is very close to the exact meaning of *exotic*: unusual, from another part of the world.

Rudimentary designs are described as "childlike" and "primitive." It is clear that the word means basic, elementary, or an early form. You may recognize *confided* as a form of the word *confidential* (secret). When "Joanne's husband *confided*," he made a private, almost secret, statement.

We can associate Joanne's interest in Peruvian weavings, and also the word *curator*, with her work at the museum. Actually, a *curator* is a person who is in charge of a department in a museum, library, or art gallery.

A soccer superstar for a dozen years, Ivor remained an **enigma** to his fans. They could not understand his childlike, stubborn **petulance** and his sudden temper **tantrums**. At the same time, they puzzled over his equally sudden bursts of **altruism**. Within moments, Ivor could be as generous as he had been **irascible** and mean.

If Ivor's fans could not understand his behavior, even after twelve years, *enigma* must refer to his puzzling habits. An *enigma* is a puzzle. Clues to the meaning of *petulance* are the echo words "childlike, stubborn." Ivor is grumpy, with flashes of quick, unreasonable anger. You can assume that his *tantrums* are fits of bad temper. He might kick the ball up into the stands, or shout rude remarks to the fans.

If Ivor has all those unpleasant traits, and *altruism* is strangely different, it might be related to "generous," mentioned in the last sentence. That is exactly right; *altruism* means unselfish help to others. Now, with all we know about Ivor, *irascible* becomes quite clear. It is a form of *irate*, and it means easily angered.

Now that you have seen how the *context method* works when **assessing** the meanings of words, you may be ready to use it with some harder examples. (Did *assessing* stump you? Or did you recognize that it means estimating; forming an opinion of something?) The sample sentences on this page use less of the echo words technique, described on page 210, than the sentences you have worked on so far. But the other techniques for using context clues still **obtain**. (Note the unusual use of *obtain*. Very likely you are familiar only with the meaning to get, or gain possession of. In this instance, *obtain* completes the thought that other techniques exist or are accepted.)

meticulous
Very careful about small details.
Almost too concerned. "Precise."
    experience entering her kitchen. The spices
    were lined up *meticulously* on a shelf
    carefully lined with heavy white paper.
    Every pot, every pan, was
Syn: fussy ; super-careful

Make sure your Word Power *file grows every day. In a short time you will learn many new words. Use them in your conversation and writing.*

Anyone who owns a cat knows that domestic **felines** have certain behavior patterns. They are **unremitting** in their care of their fur. All cats' tails **undulate** gently when cats hunt. And they are **discriminating** eaters, refusing new or suspicious kinds of food.

This short article is about *felines,* the family of animals that includes lions, tigers, and "domestic *felines*" —the ones that live with people. Cats. *Unremitting* has few context clues. You may have guessed, though, that it means unstopping or ceaseless.

If you have ever seen a cat creeping toward an unsuspecting bird, you know its tail waves gently. It *undulates. Discrimination,* as we most commonly use it, means to select or choose certain people, for unfair reasons. But *discriminating* can refer to the careful selection of certain objects. Cats are quite particular— or *discriminating*—about the food they will accept.

The Milwaukee-based sporting goods company is known for its **innovation**. It was the first to develop a safe, **incombustible** tent, and it pioneered an unsinkable, one-hulled **catamaran.** The company's sales are the **cynosure** of the industry.

If the company is first to develop one product and "pioneered" another, it is known for its new ideas. That is what *innovative* means: creative. A safe tent might be one of several kinds, including one that will not blow over. But an *incombustible* tent is one that cannot burn. *Catamarans* almost always are boats with two bottoms, or hulls, so a reference to an *innovative,* unsinkable item of sporting goods with one hull provides a strong context clue to *catamaran's* meaning. *Cynosure* refers to sales that are the envy of the industry; other companies admire and look up to that company's record.

Denizens of towns and cities never **encounter** deer in their natural **habitats.** The **visualize** Bambi or Rudolph, lovable big-eyed creatures. Farmers and **exurbanites,** often **plagued** by deer, see them as **voracious** animals that devour crops and shrubbery. Moreover, the **marauders** never travel alone, but in herds.

Reading all four sentences of the paragraph and then coming back to the target words will make the words' meanings clearer. *Denizens* must be people who are in towns and cities; actually, it means residents or inhabitants—people who live there. *Encounter,* in this context, obviously means to meet or see deer. The exact meaning is to meet unexpectedly. What could be a deer's natural *habitat?* Not towns or cities, but the woods and fields where deer live. (Their *habitation* is their home, or where they are most likely to be found.) You know that *audiovisual* is something you hear and see, and that *invisible* means cannot be seen. *Visualize* is related to those words; it means to see in your mind, or to imagine. City people imagine that deer are big-eyed, lovable creatures.

Urbanites are people who live in cities. *Exurbanites,* together with farmers, live far out from cities. You know that a *plague* is a disaster, generally an epidemic of serious sickness or disease. The word has come to mean any severe annoyance or nuisance. "Animals that devour crops and shrubbery" is a strong clue to the meaning of *voracious*—a huge appetite; greedy; eats great amounts of food.

Marauders is more difficult; you may have seen an athletic team with that name, and recall them using a pirate as their symbol. Like pirates, *marauders* roam around, raiding and stealing others' property. They never travel alone, but in bands.

Test questions. There are two kinds of test questions that often appear in civil service, employment, and college entrance examinations. Both kinds ask you to define words in the context of a sentence.

Supply a synonym.

Their lawyer, unfortunately, avoided the **salient** issues.

scrupulous   prominent   foreign   childish

You are asked to select the word among the four choices that most closely duplicates the meaning of *salient*.

Starting with *scrupulous,* which means conscientious, or very careful, we see it makes no sense in that sentence. *Prominent,* if we recognize it as meaning standing out or important, does make sense. *Foreign?* Not likely that it would be unfortunate if the lawyer avoided the *foreign* issues. And the last choice, *childish,* makes no sense in the context of the sentence.

In most questions of this kind, the possibilities narrow down to two choices, as the other two words are unlikely or obviously unsuitable. When all four, or three of the four, choices are difficult new words, selecting the right answer becomes considerably harder. You will find some of those difficult questions in the samples on this page. All the words you do not know should be added to your *Word Power* file.

Learning synonyms

1. The Red Cross set up emergency tents in the **devastated** areas of the valley.
   remote   wasted   elevated   largest

   1. *Devastated* means *wasted*. Think about the Red Cross's mission. Few people live in *remote,* or far away, sections of the valley. There is no obvious reason to set up tents in *elevated,* high regions, nor in the *largest* areas of the valley.

2. After failing two inspections, the diner's license was **revoked.**
   revised   released   reissued   recalled

   2. *Revoked* means *recalled.* It is clear that the diner lost its license, so *revised* is inappropriate; it means fixed, or made over. *Released,* a commonly used word, does not fit either. And the license would not be *reissued,* or given out again, if the diner failed to pass inspections.

3. Sharks were seen in the **vicinity**, but all three divers continued their work.
   nearby area   deeper water   emptiness   undersea wreck

   3. *Vicinity* means *nearby area. Deeper water* and *undersea wreck* might make sense, but *vicinity* is used in everyday language, and should be recognized. *Emptiness* is totally out of place in the context of the sentence.

4. Outraged parents and dog lovers sent **irate** letters to the school board.
   legal   lengthy   angry   questioning

   4. *Irate* means *angry.* "Outraged" is the clue to the tone of the parents' letters. The letters might have been *legal, lengthy,* or *questioning,* but *angry* is the word called for by the context of the sentence.

5. Is the association a **vestige** of times past, when streets were dusty and unpaved?
   trace   memory   religion   raiment

   5. *Vestige* means *trace,* or remnant, of something that has disappeared over the years. *Religion* and *raiment* (clothing) do not make sense. *Memory* comes close, but it would be awkward referring to an association as a *memory* of times past.

6. $700,000 was granted to a **consortium** of four states, to form a defense against tax evaders.
   legislatures   association   treasury   police

   6. A *consortium* is an *association* or grouping together of people or organizations, for a specific purpose. Several churches might form a *consortium* calling for stricter laws against drunk drivers. *Legislatures,* a plural word, should not follow the singular article 'a.' One *treasury* cannot belong to four states. It would be unusual for *police* to deal with tax evaders.

Fill in the blank. The second type of context-based examination question is like the first kind in that you are offered a choice of four words. But it has a slightly different format. Instead of supplying a synonym for the target word as it is used in a sentence, you are asked to fill in the word—from among the four choices—that best completes the sentence.

Your procedure will be much like the one you followed in answering type 1 questions. Try each of the four words. Think how it relates to the central thought of the sentence. Eliminate the one or two impossible selections. Does either of the remaining words conflict with any of the **adjectives** (describing words)? Even if you are unfamiliar with a new word's meaning, does it give you a feeling of belonging—of not destroying the sentence's logic?

Choose the right word

1. It was the same _____ whose advice Julius Caesar had ignored.
criminal   gesture   soothsayer   cravat

1. A *soothsayer* reads such signs as cloud formation or tea leaves, and gives advice. He is a fortune teller. (An old term for truth was *sooth;* a soothsayer 'says the truth.') Julius Caesar ignored a fortune teller's advice, not a *criminal* or a *gesture.* A *cravat* is a kind of necktie or scarf.

2. We hear about adolescent _____, yet most teenagers in this town are pleasant and likable.
translucence   alienation   allegory   viability

2. *Alienation* is the right word. *Aliens* are foreign; they do not belong to the society in which they find themselves. Adolescents sometimes feel out of place, or isolated: *alienated.* The clue here is knowing that this town's adolescents behave in a manner opposite to *alienation;* they are pleasant and likable.

3. Imagine Joan's _____ after she prepared that marvelous barbecue and only three guests showed up.
frustration   cuisine   perception   hallucination

3. *Frustration* is what Joan felt. It means discouragement; a sense of being unable to accomplish one's goal. *Cuisine* is the French word for kitchen; it is an awkward, improper fit. *Perception* means vision or seeing. *Hallucinations* are imaginary sights, nightmares, or the visions of unstable persons.

4. Maria's family was _____, in their sorrow, by a visit from the bishop.
rewarded   cosseted   controlled   consoled

4. Maria's family was comforted in their sorrow; they were *consoled* by the bishop's visit. He brought them *consolation,* or sympathy, as well as comfort. There is no reason he would try to *reward* or *control* the family. The fourth choice, *cosseted,* means pampered, petted, or made a great fuss of.

5. When a modern shopping mall opened, the downtown merchants were forced to use strong _____ against it.
textiles   tactics   statutes   covenants

5. The merchants used strong *tactics* against their competitor, the shopping mall. Those were maneuvers or actions. Two others of the four choices, *statutes* and *covenants,* are on the right track. They refer to laws. *Textiles* is entirely wrong; it means fabrics or materials, like woven cotton in a dress.

6. Secrecy surrounded the ambassador's plans, and his _____ chef was transferred to another post.
rustic   perceptive   garrulous   esteemed

6. The ambassador's chef was *garrulous,* or talkative. *Rustic* refers to country life; rough and simple furniture is called *rustic* furniture. One who sees meanings is called *perceptive.* And though the chef might have been *esteemed*—thought well of, or honored— that would have been no reason for the ambassador to transfer him to another post.

Natural settings for words

A powerful aid to remembering the meanings of new words is to discover them in settings that hold interest for you: in the pages of a magazine or book, or on a television or radio broadcast. Here, where your aim is to come into contact with as many new words as possible, the grouping of target words serves as an effective substitute for those "natural" settings.

On the next few pages you will find such headings as *Health and medicine, Films and theater,* and *Sports.* For each category, there will be a list of six words, followed by six sentences, each containing one blank space. Select the one word from the list that best completes the thought expressed in each sentence. Below the sentences you will find the correct solutions; often, there also will be a brief explanation for the choice.

Note that you will not be able to use the context method for defining all the words in this section, but it can be applied to many of them. Every word here, though, is a perfect one to add to your growing *Word Power* file. Make out a card for each and you will add more than six dozen new words to your vocabulary.

Try creating natural settings of your own and provide new words to fit them. Be sure to make your *Word Power* file grow every day.

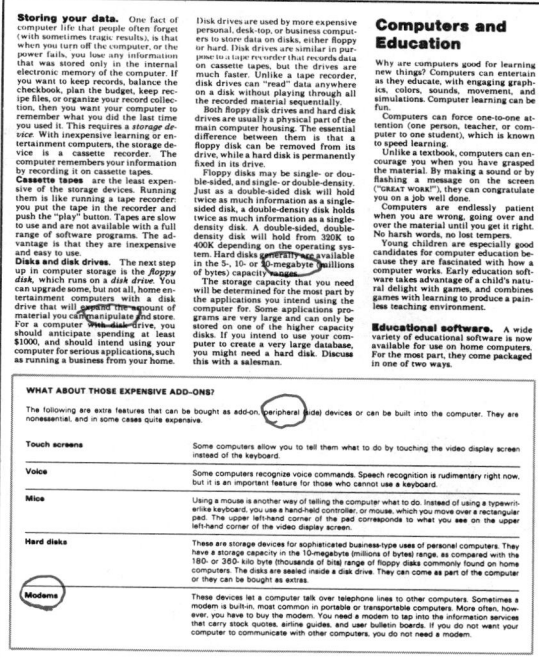

New words in natural settings

Health and medicine

insomnia
intermittently
epidemiology
anatomical
chronic
sedentary

insomnia

1. _____ liver disease is diagnosed without much difficulty using techniques easily available to most doctors.
2. A _____ person has much lower resistance to muscular strains than one who is active.
3. The symptoms were not present constantly, but appeared _____.
4. Determining rates of disease in population groups, and studying the causes, is what _____ is all about.
5. The amount of sleep necessary for good health varies from person to person, and _____ can cause serious discomfort.
6. Through endless study of the body, Galen, who died in 203 A.D., became known as the father of _____ research.

1. *chronic:* lasting for a long time; continual. It refers to time, as in *chronometer,* a precise clock or watch. **2.** *sedentary:* too much sitting; too little exercise. An active person is exactly the opposite of one who is *sedentary.* **3.** *intermittently:* stopped and started. The symptoms appeared and disappeared, or were *intermittent,* which is why they were not present constantly. **4.** *epidemiology:* the sentence itself is a definition of the word. It is related to *epidemic,* a widespread incidence of disease in a community or territory. **5.** *insomnia:* inability to sleep; unhealthy wakefulness. A *somnolent* person is a sleepy one; *insomnia* is the opposite condition. **6.** *anatomical:* the structure of the body, or any of its parts. *Anatomy* sometimes is used in its wider sense, meaning a general structure: She understood the *anatomy* of company management, and was well paid for her knowledge.

New words in natural settings

Buying a home

prospectus
amortize
condominium
panorama
amenities
modular

modular

1. We decided to buy the house when we stood on the front steps and saw the _____ of autumn leaves.
2. Did you know that your neighbors were musicians before you bought the _____?
3. The description in the _____ was far different from the building we saw when we drove out to the lake.
4. "Are you prepared to _____ this debt in 20 years?" asked the banker.
5. It was a wonderful day for the Kroeger family, for their _____ home was finally delivered from the factory.
6. The _____, including the carpeting, were attractive, but they brought the price up beyond our reach.

1. *panorama:* unlimited view over a wide area. 2. *condominium:* apartment or portion of a building owned by its occupants, while the rest of the building, and the grounds around it, are owned in common with other owners. 3. *prospectus:* a brochure (booklet) that describes a property offered for sale. A *prospect* is an expectation; a *prospectus* tells what you can expect from your purchase of this property. 4. *amortize:* to pay off a debt in a specified amount of time—in this instance, 20 years. 5. *modular:* made in parts that are later assembled. A child's building blocks are *modular* toys. A *modular* home, like a block construction, is composed of separate parts that fit together. 6. *amenities:* things that increase an object's value or comfort. A swimming pool, sun deck, and wall-to-wall carpeting are *amenities*. Another use of the word refers to social courtesies or pleasantries: Charlie overlooked the *amenities,* and Martha never forgave him for his rudeness.

Design and fashion

nonchalant
pretentious
beguiling
intricately
repertoire
hybrid

nonchalant

pretentious

1. The furniture seemed a _____ of two styles, French provincial and early American.
2. We admired Robert's _____ appearance as he strolled along the boulevard with his fiancée.
3. Doris selected a _____ version of a modern classic, the coatdress.
4. Above the mantel was a mirror with an _____ carved wooden frame.
5. Kate decided not to buy the bracelet, calling it "_____ and showy."
6. After she had attended four sessions of the sewing class, Beverly's _____ of techniques had tripled.

1. *hybrid:* mixture. The word's origin is in the natural sciences, where selected strains of plants and animals are bred to produce *hybrids* with mixed characteristics. 2. *nonchalant:* a word borrowed from the French, meaning casual, cool, unworried. Robert's carefree appearance could also be described as *debonair.* 3. *beguiling:* demanding attention, or distracting. At the same time, it means charming or delightful. *Bewitching* is sometimes used as a synonym for *beguiling.* 4. *intricately:* the frame has many carefully carved details; *intricate* means elaborate, or done with a great deal of skill and effort. 5. *pretentious:* demanding attention that is not justified. *Showy* is an echo word with almost the same meaning and tone; so is *ostentatious,* which can be added to your *Word Power* file. 6. *repertoire:* a person's, or group's, range of skills and accomplishments. This word, like *nonchalant* and many others in the world of fashion and design, is borrowed from the French. It originally referred to the songs, plays, or compositions that dramatic or musical groups were able to perform. An English version of the word, used in that theatrical sense, is *repertory.*

Sports

foiled
caliber
interim
regimen
grimaced
spate

grimaced

1. No smoking.
2. No beer.
3. No junk food.
4. Regular practice.
5. In bed by 10.

regimen

1. When Dr. Newbold retired, Chris Stanley was named as _____ head coach of the Blue Devils.
2. Josephine had unusual natural ability, but was unwilling to stick to the training _____ demanded of professional athletes.
3. He fell on the field and _____ in intense pain after colliding with Parrish.
4. A _____ of matches against weak opponents gave Miss Yerby a strong boost in the tournament standings.
5. An eighth-inning triple by Hunt _____ pitcher Ken Leslie's attempt at a no-hitter.
6. Reporters agreed Miss Bryant was a superior player, but not quite Olympic _____.

1. *interim:* temporary, or the time between. Chris Stanley's appointment is not permanent. He will act as head coach only between the time that Dr. Newbold resigned and a new coach is appointed. **2.** *regimen:* a system or process; routine procedures. Governments, or *regimes,* control the way many things are done, and *regimen* is formed from that word. **3.** *grimaced:* made a distorted or "scrunched-up" facial expression. A *grimace* usually indicates pain, though sometimes it expresses anger or displeasure. **4.** *spate:* a sudden rush. Miss Yerby had a flood of tennis matches, all during a short time. *Spate's* original meaning was a sudden downpour of heavy rain. **5.** *foiled:* upset, or prevented from being successful. A synonym is *thwarted.* **6.** *caliber:* a measure of worth or quality. The inside of a gun barrel is measured as .22, .38, or some other specific *caliber.* From that single meaning, the measure of a bullet's size, the word has come to mean a measure of any kind.

More sports

climactic
peripheral
disparity
conceded
soared
snared

soared

1. "Most of my shots from mid-court are lucky to hit the rim," Anna _____.
2. Jerry Lloyd caught a seemingly impossible pass and trotted away with the _____ six points.
3. The crowd rose to its feet when Thompson _____ a line drive in the third inning.
4. A split second after the ball met her bat, it _____ into the left-field stands.
5. Crowley was paid a star's salary, but was kept in a _____ position all season.
6. Marge acknowledged the _____ in their national rankings, but insisted on first-class travel accommodations.

1. *conceded:* gave, admitted, yielded; acknowledged as true. Anna admitted that most of her shots from mid-court fell short. **2.** *climactic:* refers to a *climax,* the final and most important part of an action. **3.** *snared:* trapped, or caught. A *snare* is a trap for catching animals or birds, but the word has come to have a broader meaning. **4.** *soared:* flew through the air. Hawks *soar* above valleys, and baseballs *soar* when a batter hits a high fly. **5.** *peripheral:* off to one side; not in the center of things. **6.** *disparity:* inequality. Marge may have ranked 34th, but she insisted on the same accommodations (airplane seats and hotel rooms) as the top-ranking players.

New words in natural settings

Films and theater

antagonist
documentary
choreographer
improvise
interlude
genre

choreographer

1. The city council budgeted $500,000 to make a _____ film about its new mental health center.
2. After a brief musical _____, the curtain rose on the second act of Shakespeare's comedy.
3. "I'm particularly proud to be awarded this Oscar," she said, "because romances are my favorite _____ of film."
4. In those early James Cagney movies, it was usually a G-man or detective who was Jimmy's _____.
5. The brilliant young team of comics rarely work from a script; they _____ nearly every sketch they perform.
6. By the time she had grown too old for an active career as a dancer, she had begun to win notice as a _____.

1. *documentary:* factual. Most *documentary* films explain a social, historical, or natural event as accurately as possible, using a narrator's (announcer's) voice rather than actors' speeches. 2. *interlude:* something that comes between the acts of a theatrical entertainment. The word's meaning extends beyond the theater to indicate any in-between period or activity, such as an *interlude* between wars. 3. *genre:* type, class, or style. The actress may have felt comfortable acting in comedies and mysteries, too, but romances were her favorite type of movie. 4. *antagonist:* a person who is opposed to another one; an *adversary.* The opposite of *antagonist* is *protagonist,* a person who is friendly—a hero. 5. *improvise:* invent, or make up as one goes along. 6. *choreographer:* a person who creates dances or ballets.

Food

piquant
cholesterol
mandatory
ramekin
complement
entails

ramekin

1. Excess amounts of _____, a substance present in dairy products and animal fats, should be avoided.
2. More and more consumers are taking time to read the _____ information printed on food package labels.
3. Following her aunt's recipes, Molly made some of the most _____ sauces we ever had tasted.
4. Ron has become a popular host ever since he has learned that barbecuing _____ constant, extremely high heat.
5. They ended the meal with a _____ of custard for each guest.
6. In some Near Eastern recipes, raisins are used as a tasty _____ to rice.

1. *cholesterol* is defined in the sentence. A doctor or nurse can advise you about diets that contain normal and excessive amounts of *cholesterol.* 2. *mandatory:* required by regulations. Laws require food manufacturers to list the ingredients of their products on the packages. *Mandates* are regulations that must be obeyed. 3. *piquant:* spicy; pleasantly sharp taste. The word is an uncommon one, but would make a fine addition to anyone's vocabulary. 4. *entails:* is a necessary part of an action or thing. Cooking over extremely high heat is a necessary part of barbecuing. In legal matters, to *entail* has a totally different meaning—to prevent the transfer of property or real estate: The building's title was *entailed,* so the owner was not allowed to sell it. 5. *ramekin:* a small dish, used for both baking and serving individual portions. 6. *complement:* something that *completes* a whole, or goes with another thing. To avoid confusing this word with *compliment* (making pleasant or flattering comments), remember that *complement* and *complete* both begin with *comple.*

Building Your Vocabulary

Law and courtroom procedure

ordinance
warrant
jeopardy
precedent
jurisdiction
arraignment

arraignment

1. The court issued a search _____, and Sgt. Mellon made the arrest.
2. Within a week, he appeared at his _____ and entered a plea of "not guilty."
3. Mary had never heard of the antinoise _____, but still was ordered to pay the fine.
4. "This court has no _____ over matters in Jefferson County," the judge explained.
5. The Constitution prohibits trials that would put a defendant in double _____.
6. "This may set a _____ for families with similar problems," she told the judge.

1. *warrant:* a certificate authorizing an officer to make an arrest or search or seize property. 2. *arraignment:* a time at which an accused person is called before a court. *Arraignments* take place before trials are scheduled. 3. *ordinance:* a law or regulation. A similar word, lacking an "i," is *ordnance;* it has an entirely different meaning—military weapons and ammunition. 4. *jurisdiction:* the right and power to apply the law; or the territory in which a law is applied. Words that begin with *jur* refer to law—among them are *juror, jury,* and *jurisprudence* (formal study of the law). 5. *jeopardy:* risk or danger. In courtrooms, *jeopardy* refers to the danger of being found guilty and convicted. The Constitution states that a person can be tried only once for any crime; he cannot be put at risk twice for the same crime. 6. *precedent:* an action or legal decision that sets an example for similar cases that follow.

Books and reading

creed
squibs
narrative
paraphrase
appendix
prose

HOW MANY ARTIFICIAL ONES?
There were 535,000 natural scientists working in the United States in 1994.

squib

1. "To _____ Gertrude Stein," he wrote, "a dog is a dog is a dog."
2. Berryman had gained his reputation as a poet, but _____ seemed beyond his reach.
3. We looked carefully through the _____, but could not find the source of the statistics in chapter 4.
4. The author said that this is her _____: "Never take your writing too seriously—or too lightly."
5. It was a lively _____, but far too long to finish reading in one evening.
6. Young E. B. White got his start writing _____ that were published in newspapers of the day.

1. *paraphrase:* put someone else's writings or thoughts in your own language, or change them somewhat. Gertrude Stein, a noted author of the 1920's, had written "...a rose is a rose is a rose." 2. *prose:* ordinary speech or writing, not poetry. Novels and newspapers are written in *prose.* 3. *appendix:* additional material that "hangs" at the end of a book. 4. *creed:* a statement of belief or opinion. 5. *narrative:* story. A reporter might *narrate* a true story, while a comedian might *narrate* a series of jokes that he made up on his way to the studio. 6. *squibs:* short, usually humorous, items in a newspaper or magazine. *Squibs* are used by editors to fill the space at the bottom of a column of print.

creed

> "I believe in the supreme worth of the individual and in his right to life, liberty and the pursuit of happiness."
> —JOHN D. ROCKEFELLER, JR.

New words in natural settings

Music

libretto
uninhibited
syncopated
searing
idiom
ovation

ovation

1. Until we got to New Orleans, we had never heard the wonderful tones of rhythmic, _____ riverboat music.
2. Her _____ high notes won Miss Larcher a Golden Recording award.
3. The audience rose to its feet in a wild, frenzied _____.
4. Ray Charles's vocal style was strongly influenced by a modern gospel _____.
5. Once he had the idea for an opera's music, Mozart searched for a poet who could write a suitable _____.
6. Her boisterous, _____ approach to country music made her a great favorite on the West Coast.

1. *syncopated:* music played with a strong beat where it might normally be expected to have a weaker beat. Dixieland music has a toe-tapping, *syncopated* quality. 2. *searing:* literally means scorching or burning. In music, *searing* refers to extremely high notes, sung or played on an instrument. 3. *ovation:* continued, enthusiastic applause. We often hear the phrase standing *ovation* to describe a wildly cheering audience that has risen to its feet in tribute to a performer. (Are you sure about the meaning of "frenzied" in sentence 3? Check it in the dictionary if you have any doubt.) 4. *idiom:* a special style of artistic expression. Singers might be influenced by a gospel *idiom,* an operatic *idiom,* or any of many other schools of singing. The word more often refers to spoken or written language that is not easily understood by anyone who is a foreigner to that language. "Up to snuff" is an *idiomatic* expression. 5. *libretto:* the words that are sung in an opera. 6. *uninhibited:* unrestrained; not held back. A singer who lets herself go is *uninhibited.*

Personalities

contagious
tenacity
affability
skylarking
boisterous
sarcastic

contagious

boisterous

1. Marc's reputation for _____ helped when the vice president was deciding whom to make sales manager.
2. Not everyone appreciated Linda's _____ laughter, but her husband never failed to enjoy it.
3. When Linda laughed, Harry found it _____; it broke him up and left him gasping.
4. "I've had enough of his _____ comments," Hope complained. "He can't say a word without cutting my friends to ribbons."
5. His supervisor made Jess understand that a supermarket was no place for _____ and clowning around.
6. "With all the long faces you see around here," Mr. Watkins said, "Helen's _____ makes her a standout—she's a delight."

1. *tenacity:* holding fast to one's views; persistent. Probably, the aspect of Marc's *tenacity* that appealed most to his boss was Marc's habit of not giving up, even when the competition seemed likely to win. 2. *boisterous:* loud, noisy, uncontrolled. 3. *contagious:* spreading from one person to another; catching. Measles is a *contagious* disease; to Linda's husband, her laughter was a *contagious* emotion. 4. *sarcastic:* remarks intended to be biting, cutting, belittling. *Sarcasm* is usually expressed as humor—but humor that is intended to ridicule someone or something. 5. *skylarking:* frolicking and fooling around. 6. *affability:* friendliness, gentleness.

Building Your Vocabulary

Gardening

herbicide
lobes
defoliate
prostrate
dormant
variegated

defoliate

1. It was an uncommon type of ivy, with a streaked, _____ leaf.
2. Don paid no attention to the warning on the _____ label, so he killed all the grass in his front yard.
3. "Don't worry," she told me, "these bushes aren't dead. They are _____ in the winter."
4. The rounded _____ of the leaf were the size of half dollars.
5. It resembled a moss, lying low along the soil, but we learned it was a healthy _____ shrub.
6. It took the beetles only four days to completely _____ our entire crop of peas.

1. *variegated:* patches of different color. *Streaked* is an echo word that gives a strong clue to the meaning of *variegated.* 2. *herbicide:* a substance that kills plants. Words ending in *icide* refer to *death*—*suicide,* killing oneself; *matricide,* killing one's mother; *fungicide,* killing fungi (mushroomlike plants). 3. *dormant:* inactive, resting, seemingly asleep. *Dormant* plants grow leaves and become active in the spring. A related word, *dormitory,* means place where people sleep. 4. *lobes:* rounded parts. You will recall that the rounded, lower part of your ear is called an *earlobe.* 5. *prostrate:* in plants, growing flat along the ground. People who *prostrate* themselves bow or kneel down before a superior person; sometimes they throw themselves flat on the ground. 6. *defoliate:* to remove all the leaves from a plant or tree. Leaves are referred to as *foliage;* to remove them is to *defoliate* them, as to remove frost from frozen food is to *defrost* it.

Television

indispensable
vernacular
ennui
eclipsed
absorbed
chide

It's out of this world!

That's pretty heavy!

Far out!

vernacular

Give me a break!

1. In surveys among American families, television has _____ radio in listener-hours per household.
2. It is the one medium _____ by all ages: small children, adolescents, young adults, and the elderly.
3. Politicians find television _____ for getting their messages into voters' households.
4. On newscasts, political candidates gain the opportunity to _____ their opponents and be seen by huge audiences.
5. "We ran my comedy series for five years, and then dropped it before _____ set in," she explained.
6. The newscaster's popularity was due, in part, to his use of the _____.

1. *eclipsed:* we know that as television has become more important over the years, radio has become less so. *Eclipse* originally referred to one star or planet being hidden behind another. It now means any person's or thing's giving way to a more popular one. 2. *absorbed:* taken up. All ages are totally interested in watching television. A synonym is *engrossed.* 3. *indispensable:* cannot do without; necessary. 4. *chide:* scold, reprimand, or express disapproval. 5. *ennui:* boredom, general dissatisfaction. (A French word, pronounced *ahn-we'.*) 6. *vernacular:* commonly used language, as opposed to the more formal, literary language used in some books and newspapers.

Pairs, pears

Our language is laced with sets of words that sound alike—or enough alike to confuse many people—yet have entirely different meanings. On these pages we offer some of the most confusing of those pairs of words and their definitions. Be on the lookout, as you read and listen during the coming months, for additional pairs of "confusers." Adding these pairs to your *Word Power* file is a **diverting** way to build your vocabulary.

A military colonel *and a seed or grain called a* kernel *are pronounced the same but spelled very differently.*

annal, annual. An *annal* is a written chronicle or record of events. *The annals of baseball. Annual* means yearly. *We payed our annual taxes.*

arc, ark. An *arc* is a curved or arched shape resembling a rainbow. An *ark* is a boat. In the Old Testament, the *ark* was Noah's boat during the Flood.

ardorous, arduous. A person who is *ardorous* has strong emotions, enthusiasms, or love. An *arduous* task is a difficult one, filled with hardship.

bazaar, bizarre. *Bazaar* refers to one shop, or a street of shops, selling various items. *Bizarre* means odd or extraordinary. *A bizarre costume.*

carat, carrot. A *carat* (also spelled *karat*) is a unit of weight for gems and jewels. *A half-carat diamond. Carrots* are common, orange-colored vegetables.

cite, site. To *cite* is to mention or quote as proof. *Their record was cited in the* World Almanac. A *site* is a place, or the location of a building or group of buildings. *The mayor conducted an on-site inspection.*

colonel, kernel. A military *colonel* (ker´-nell) is an officer ranking above a lieutenant colonel and below a brigadier general. A *kernel* is a grain or seed, usually one that can be eaten.

deceased, diseased. A *deceased* person is a dead person. One who is *diseased* is sick, infected, cannot function normally.

decent, descent. A *decent* appearance or person is modest, not shocking, meeting accepted standards. *A decent rate of pay. Descent* is the act of moving downward. Sometimes it means following from. *She traced the descent of jazz from early 20th-century New Orleans to today.*

demean, demeanor. To *demean* oneself is to act in a way that causes a loss of dignity and respect. *Demeanor* is the manner in which a person conducts himself; a synonym is *deportment.*

flounder, founder. A *flounder* is a flat saltwater fish. To *flounder* means to flop around clumsily, like a fish out of water; to be off balance. To *founder* is to sink. *John quit the foundering company* means that John quit because the company was going under.

flout, flaunt. To *flout* means to disobey openly and scornfully. *He flouted the law.* To *flaunt,* on the other hand, means to display proudly or in a showy way. *She flaunted her new red dress.* A man who *flaunts* his disrespect for women *flouts* the common courtesies of civilization.

gauge, gouge. A *gauge* (gayj) is a meter or dial for measuring an activity or amount. It is also the act of measuring or estimating. A *gouge* (gowj) is a chisel-like tool, or the scooping-out action of such a tool.

hawk, hock. A *hawk* is a falcon, or eaglelike, bird. To *hawk* is slang for to sell by calling out. *He hawked programs in the theater lobby.* To *hock* is slang for to pawn—to pledge personal property in return for a cash loan.

impromptu, improper. An *impromptu* speech is one given without preparation or rehearsal. An *improper* action is one that is irregular, not suitable, offensive.

language, languish. *Language* is the spoken words and written symbols that humans use to communicate thoughts. To *languish* is to lose strength, to become feeble and weak; to lie around doing nothing; to be neglected.

lop, lope. To cut off, or trim, part of a bush or tree is to *lop* it off. To *lope* is to run, or to ride a horse, at a steady, even rate.

lucid, ludicrous. *Lucid* writing is easily understood; its meaning is clear. A person who is *lucid* is sane and can make himself understood. *Ludicrous* statements or actions are laughable, ridiculous, or absurd.

lumbar, lumber. *Lumbar* refers to the lower back. *She had a pinched nerve in her lumbar vertebrae. Lumber* is wood in the form of boards or planks.

miller, milliner. A *miller* mills, or grinds, grain into flour or meal. A *milliner* makes or sells women's hats.

morning, mourning. *Morning* is the early part of the day, from sunrise to noon. *Mourning* is grieving for the dead. *Bereavement* is a synonym for *mourning.*

noisome, noisy. A *noisome* odor is one that is foul or disgusting, or giving off dangerous fumes. *Noisy* means making sounds, usually loud and unwanted.

occult, oculist. *Occult* happenings are supernatural, unexplained, ghostly. An *oculist* is an eye doctor—sometimes called an *optometrist*.

pampas, pamper. The *pampas* is a huge grassy area of South America, principally in Argentina, much like our Western prairies. To *pamper* is to pay too much attention to one's own, or another's, desires. *Indulge* and *spoil* are synonyms for *pamper*.

pitfall, pitiful. *Pitfalls* are traps made by digging deep holes, then covering them over lightly. *Pitfall* also means a danger that is not easily seen. *Pitiful* means pathetic; arousing sorrow. Less charitably, it can mean inferior.

quarry. *Quarry* has two entirely different meanings: 1) an open mine or pit, as a gravel *quarry;* 2) a hunted animal, or a person who is pursued.

quota, quote. A *quota* is a number of persons or things. The number is calculated to make the *quota* become a certain share of the whole. To *quote* is to repeat or copy another's words. It also means to state a price.

rouse, ruse. To *rouse* (rhymes with *how's*) someone is to wake him from sleep, or excite him into activity. A *ruse* is a trick, or ploy, meant to mislead someone.

scarce, scares. A *scarce* item is one that is seldom seen or found; it is rare. A dog that *scares* the neighbors is one that frightens them.

several, severance. *Several* means more than two or three, but not many. *She drew several flowers in a bowl.* *Severance* is the act of cutting off or separating. *The company gave Ruth a large amount of severance pay.*

sheik, chic. A *sheik* is the leader of an Arab family or tribe. *Chic* (sheek) is a French word meaning stylish; sophisticated and classy.

slew. *Slew* has two entirely different meanings: 1) killed (the past form of *slay*); 2) a large amount of things or people. *We watched a whole slew of actors perform.*

stake, steak. A wooden or metal *stake* is sharp at one end, which is hammered into the ground. A *steak* is the familiar cut of beef or other meat.

tracked, tract. *Tracked* is the past form of to *track*, to follow footprints or other traces or also to observe. *The police tracked her on their radar.* *Tract* has two meanings: 1) a piece of property or land; 2) a booklet or paper stating a special point of view, such as a political *tract*.

vanish, varnish. To *vanish* is to disappear; to be no longer able to be seen. *Varnish* is a paintlike coating for surfaces, usually wooden. It leaves a hard, smooth finish.

Groups of word parts

In classrooms and textbooks, it has long been the custom to teach vocabulary lessons through *word parts*. This method is also called *derivations*, because many of our English words are *derived* from (came from, or arrived from) Latin and Greek terms.

In all likelihood, you are not a student of Latin or Greek, so you will **benefit** from the more practical nonderivative techniques for building *Word Power* in this section of your handbook. Yet, you should still know just a few word-source facts.

ben, the first part of *benefit,* is called a *prefix. Ben* means good, and the whole word means good deed or advantage. Other words starting with *ben* are *benediction*, good speech or blessing; and *benevolent*, kindly, or one who is charitable.

Here are four of the hundreds of word parts that form our modern English language.

aud—hear
  audience—people gathered to hear an event
  audition—hear actors or musicians demonstrate their skills
  audiophile—person extremely interested in hearing sounds, particularly electronic reproduction

locut, loqu—to talk, speak
  loquacious—talkative; garrulous
  colloquy—conversation; talking together
  ventriloquist—person who makes his voice "come from his stomach"
  interlocutor—person who speaks between, or interrupts.
  soliloquy—one person's thoughts; a speech by one person in a play

nav—ship
  naval—pertaining to ships or a navy
  navigable—water deep enough to sail on
  navigate—to control the course of a ship or an airplane

pend—to hang, or be inclined toward
  pendulum—hangs from a clock's works
  depend—to hang on, or need, someone or something
  impending—hanging on, or waiting, for an event to take place
  appendage—a connected part, perhaps hanging from the main part

15 days to a forceful vocabulary

Studies have shown that the average American uses relatively few words—about 2000—for normal conversation. That same person may recognize another 12,000 to 13,000 words when he hears or sees them. But he hesitates to try them; he feels uncomfortable because he is not certain of the meanings of the words.

If you have been adding 40 or more words a week to your working vocabulary, you are moving far ahead of the average. Here is a way to boost your rate even higher. In just 15 days, you can add approximately 125 new terms to your working stock. Spend only 15 min-

utes a day beyond your regular *Word Power* activities and you will have accomplished that gain in less than three weeks!

Each day's activity is designed to be stimulating and enjoyable. Yet, before you start, keep in mind that there is nothing magical about the number "15." If an unexpected drain on your time prevents you from working the plan suggested for day six on the day following day five, do not be concerned. As long as you eventually get back to the routine, and maintain your *Word Power* file at the same time, the plan will work.

DAY 1: A few cents' worth

A daily newspaper is the easiest and least expensive source of new words. For variety and added challenge, get a copy of an out-of-town paper: one from the largest city in your state or a neighboring state. Or get a Washington, D.C., Houston, or New York daily, or *The Wall Street Journal*.

Make a list of eight or ten words that you are not sure about, and the sentences in which you find them. Using your dictionary, add them to your *Word Power* file.

Here are eight sentences, slightly paraphrased, from papers published on the same day in Illinois, Florida, and California.

1. Hungary was the first Soviet **bloc** nation to question the agricultural policy.
2. As he has during much of his **tenure,** Mr. Richards took issue with the district attorney.
3. "We cannot continue to operate on this level, at only half of our full sales **potential**."
4. All except one commander agreed to a **phased** withdrawal of the land forces.
5. Eight more terrorists were seen on the **outskirts** of the city.
6. His manager demanded an aplogy, saying, "They cannot call Sam a **demagogue** and get away with it."
7. The state of Colorado argued that it had not **delegated** that authority to Boulder.
8. "They never actually said we lied, but I do believe the word **prevaricate** was heard."

1. *bloc:* a group of organizations, nations, or persons united for a common purpose. **2.** *tenure:* the time during which a person holds an office or a job. **3.** *potential:* capability for growth that has not yet been realized. **4.** *phased:* done in stages. In *phase* one they pulled out the tanks, in *phase* two the artillery. **5.** *outskirts:* parts away from the central area; the *periphery.* **6.** *demagogue:* an unprincipled political leader who appeals to the emotions of citizens. **7.** *delegated:* a person or organization authorized to act for, or represent, another. **8.** *prevaricate:* to avoid the truth, or twist it to one's purposes.

Russians deploy tanks, artillery in Chechnya

Chechen rebels   CAMPAIGN 2000

Double victory vindicates Walsh, Washington High

NEW YORK — George Washington High's football team defeat-
·d host Stevenson 14-6 Friday, the
·d major win for the team this

that had to be met before the team could resume play.
• A large measure of pride. Friday's triumphant return served as vindication for Walsh and his play-ers.

Building Your Vocabulary

DAY 2: Upping the price slightly

Move upward, in price and degree of specialization, from newspapers to magazines. The periodicals that are most widely read—*People, Time, Cosmopolitan,* and *Reader's Digest,* among others—are good sources of vocabulary-stretching words.

Any single issue is almost sure to provide several useful additions to your *Word Power* file. The sentences to the right were gathered from just three magazines.

1. Reservation services often are **biased** in an airline's favor.
2. Pain caused by bursitis can become **excruciating** with the slightest movement.
3. A mix of traditional English and American styles produced the rich **patina** of years.
4. It was a **premise** stated with authority, but one we had great difficulty accepting.
5. I had become **adept** at using the smaller keyboard.
6. Pat's high school ring had something resembling an **amethyst** at the center.
7. **Trend**-conscious designers abandoned the "layered look."

1. *biased:* prefers one person or thing; prejudiced. **2.** *excruciating:* intensely, agonizingly painful. **3.** *patina:* appearance of aging. Originally, a thin coating of brown or green on bronze or other metals. **4.** *premise:* an underlying or basic statement that can be assumed to be true. **5.** *adept:* skillful. **6.** *amethyst:* a purple semiprecious stone. **7.** *trend:* movement toward a new fashion or style.

DAY 3: Name-words

Late in the 19th century, all across the United States people watched for news of the completion of the Brooklyn Bridge. Knowing it was the focus of so much attention, a publicity-seeking young man called the newspapers, climbed one of the towers, and dived into the East River. He survived the dive, and his name survives in the language as a synonym for "high dive" or "publicity stunt." He was Steve Brody, the originator of "taking a Brody."

Once you know the stories behind some of the names that have become often-used words in our language, it becomes easier to remember their meanings and how they are used. Here is a group of such words—some of them derived from names, others from places.

gerrymander

Annie Oakley: a free pass to a show or concert is called an *Annie Oakley.* Annie was a star of Buffalo Bill Cody's Wild West Show in the 1890's; she shot holes in playing cards and other small targets. A free ticket, punched full of holes, reminded people of her act.

bowdlerize: to take out from, or change, portions of a book that are thought to be offensive. In 1818 an Englishman, Thomas Bowdler, published an edition of Shakespeare's plays "suitable for reading aloud to a family." Bowdlerized versions of stories or plays often are weaker and less effective than the originals.

boycott: to refuse to have anything to do with a person or thing. Captain Boycott was a land agent in Ireland who was shunned by everyone because he bought up the property of evicted farmers.

billingsgate: rude, abusive, often foul language. A fishmarket has been located for centuries near the ancient London tower of Billingsgate. The language used there by fish merchants gave rise to the word.

donnybrook: a brawl or free-for-all commotion. Yearly, in Donnybrook, Ireland, a fair was held. Every year there were said to be blackened eyes, bloodied noses, and many arrests.

Draconian: extremely harsh. Draco was a Greek lawmaker who ruled that death must be the punishment for all crimes, even small ones. A *Draconian* measure is a severe ruling.

gerrymander: to divide a voting district into parts that give an unfair advantage to one party. Elbridge Gerry, 1744–1814, was a governor of Massachusetts who created an odd-shaped election district that looked like a salamander.

malapropism: a comical confusion of words, especially those that sound alike ("a shrewed (for rude) awakening"). The word comes from Mrs. Malaprop in a famous comedy, *The Rivals,* by Richard Sheridan.

DAY 4: Time-words

Hundreds of words in our language have *prefixes,* or parts placed in front of a main stem, that give a special meaning to the word. Some of the most commonly used prefixes indicate *time;* that is, one action's occurrence in relation to another's. Looking at a few examples of the way these prefixes work is the easiest way to understand prefixes that indicate time.

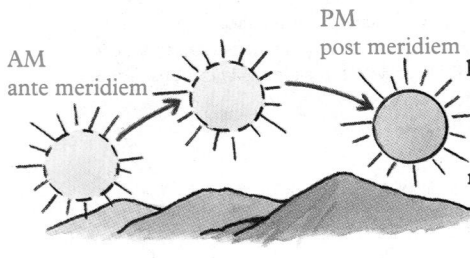

AM
ante meridiem

PM
post meridiem

ante (Latin): before
  antebellum before the Civil War (*bellum* = war).
  antedate at a time before the time mentioned.
archa (Greek): old
  archaeology the study of old (ancient) life and culture.
  archaic belonging to a much earlier time.
neo (Greek): new
  neoclassicism revival of classical form in arts.
  neologism a recently invented word or phrase.
  neonate a newborn infant.
post (Latin): after
  postdate to use a date, as on a check, later than the actual date.
  postmeridian afternoon (*meridian* is the highest part of the sun's course across the sky).
pre (Latin): before
  preadolescence a child's age, ten to twelve, before adolescence.
  predict to say, or make known, before an act happens.
  premature growing or existing before the customary time.
re (Latin): again
  rebound bounce back again.
  recognize know something or someone again.
  rehearse practice in preparation for a performance (originally, hear again).

DAY 5: Your lucky number

As a change from yesterday's word-gathering based on formations and derivations from classical languages, try this relaxer. Write down any seven numbers from one to one thousand—roughly, the number of pages in your dictionary. Then turn to each of those numbered pages. Select any unknown words on those pages that come to your notice. Make a *Word Power* card for them, and put the cards in your file.

Here are ten "lucky number" words" chosen by one word-collector on a recent evening.

deride *(p. 204 in his dictionary):* to speak with scorn, laughter, or contempt; to ridicule.
astral *(p. 45):* of or about the stars; star-shaped.
nectar *(p. 501):* the drink of the mythic gods; any sweet or delicious drink.
polyp *(p. 579):* a growth in the lining of the stomach, nose, or other body part.
extort *(p. 267):* to gain something by forcing it from another person, often by threats or intimidation.
compunction *(p. 155):* a sense of guilt; uneasiness.
legume *(p. 428):* a plant, eaten as a vegetable, that bears seeds in a pod (as peas or beans).
sobriquet *(p. 709):* a nickname; an alias or assumed name.
triturate *(p. 800):* to grind or crush into a very fine powder; to chew thoroughly.
quadruped *(p. 609):* any animal with four feet.

---

legroom 428 **leprechaun**

of mutton: said of a sleeve that puffs out toward the shoulder, etc.
leg·room (leg′rōōm′) *n.* adequate space for the legs while seated, as in a car
leg·ume (leg′yōōm, li gyōōm′) *n.* [< Fr. < L. *legumen* < *legere,* to gather] **1.** any of a large family of plants, including the peas, beans, clovers, etc., with fruit that is a pod splitting along two sutures: many legumes are nitrogen-fixing **2.** the pod or seed of some members of this family, used for food
le·gu·mi·nous (li gyōō′min əs) *adj.* **1.** of, having the nature of, or bearing legumes **2.** of the family of plants to

length·en (-'n) *vt., vi.* to make or become longer —**length′-en·er** *n.*
length·wise (-wiz′) *adv., adj.* in the direction of the length: also **length′ways'** (-wāz′)
length·y (-ē) *adj.* **length′i·er, length′i·est** long; esp., too long —**length′i·ly** *adv.* —**length′i·ness** *n.*
le·ni·ent (lē′ni ənt, lēn′yənt) *adj.* [< L. prp. of *lenire,* to soften < *lenis,* soft] not harsh or severe in disciplining, judging, etc.; mild; merciful —**le′ni·en·cy,** *pl.* **-cies, le′ni·ence** *n.* —**le′ni·ent·ly** *adv.*
Len·in (len′in; *Russ.* lye′nyin), **V(ladimir) I(lyich)** (orig. surname *Ulyanov:* also called *Nikolai Lenin*) 1870–1924; Russ. Communist revolutionary leader; premier of the

DAY 6: The study of studies

Any word that ends in *ology* refers to the study of, or the science of, the subject named in the first part of the word. Since that hard-to-know first part is sometimes a Greek or Latin word, your job is not easy. **Dermatology,** for example, is the study of the skin—and a **dermatologist** is a doctor who specializes in that study.

As your working vocabulary widens, you will find many basic word parts appearing again and again. You will recognize *derm* as part of *hypodermic*—under the skin—and the meaning of *dermatologist* will be reinforced.

For now, here are 14 *study of* words. They will form the **nucleus** (core; center) of this part of your vocabulary.

anthropology: the study of the biologic history and habits of mankind.
archaeology: the study of ancient civilizations through buildings, pottery, and other traces that remain.
biology: the study of life processes and living organisms.
chronology: time-connected studies. The word has come to mean a sequence of events, as they took place in time.
entomology: the study of insects.
etymology: the study of words—how they originated and how they took their present form. (Do not confuse this word with the previous one. There is an "n" in *insect*—and none in *etymology*.)
geology: the study of the structure and development of Earth's crust and its strata.
ichthyology: the study of fish.
meteorology: the study of the atmosphere.
oenology: the study of wine making.
ornithology: the study of birds.
philology: the study of languages and their development.
psychology: the study of the mind, mental processes, and the way humans respond to events around them.
theology: the study of religion.

DAY 7: Words that are *before*

We have already seen two word parts that mean *before* in the sense of time, or when an event happened. One is *ante;* the other is *pre.* Both come to us from Latin and are in common use. Another Latin word part that we use frequently also means before, but in the sense of in front of, concerned with space rather than time. It is *pro,* the first syllable of the following nine words.

proboscis: a long, flexible nose, as of an elephant. Also, an insect's noselike feeding tube. A human nose, if large, is sometimes called a *proboscis.*
proceed: to go before.
prodigal: wasteful, reckless, extravagant. The word's origin is not easily recognized in English, but in Latin it means driving recklessly ahead.
produce: to bring forth, make, or give rise to. Its roots are in *to lead forward.*
profile: the outline of a human head or other object. Also, an essay, graph, or table summarizing an idea or thing; it goes before a full, extended description.
program: a listing of events. It is writing that comes before the event.
progress: movement forward, or toward a goal.
prologue: a short speech or dramatic action presented before a play begins.
promontory: a high ridge of land extending out into the sea.

proboscis

DAY 8: Words that are *against,* and some that are *with*

It is possible that this sudden **immersion** (dunking; a teabag is *immersed* in hot water) into the ancient roots of words has proved confusing. So day eight will be used to clarify a few of the ideas that may have bewildered you.

connect

Take **ante,** for example. We saw that it is Latin and that it means before, or earlier, as in *antedate.* But how about **antifreeze?** The answer lies in the spelling. *Ante* with an "e" means before—*anti* with an "i" means against, or opposing. Some of the *opposing* words are **antibacterial, antibody, anticlimax, anticlockwise, antidepressant, antimagnetic, antipoverty,** and **antitrust.**

You may have wondered where, among all those **pro** words, was **con**—as in "they argued *pro and con* the new rent laws." *Con* is short for the Latin *contra,* meaning against. The full *contra* is used in such English words as *contrary, contraband,* and *contravene.*

When you do see *con* at the beginning an English word, it nearly always means together, or with. These are some typical uses of *con* as the first syllable of a word:

concentrate: to direct or bring together toward a common center.
concert: to work (or produce music) together.
conclave: a secret meeting.
concrete: real, existing things. *A table is a concrete object.* Also, a construction material of mortar or cement mixed together with pebbles or stones.
confabulate: to talk informally, or chat, together.
confederate: an ally, accomplice, or fellow member in a *conspiracy.*
congest: to overfill; bring together too many.
connect: to unite, join, or fasten together.

DAY 9: Culling the classroom

Does a neighbor, or a friend, have a son who is in junior high school? Or does your cousin's daughter go to high school or college not far from where you live? If you know someone who regularly attends school, enlist his or her help in your *Word Power* campaign.

Just ask your helping student to be on the lookout, in the books he reads and the assignments he does, for words he does not recognize. Instead of passing them by, ask him to note them on a piece of paper.

You will notice that the heading for day nine reads "**Culling** the classroom." Is *culling* an unfamiliar term? To *cull* is to select, or gather, from a place; here, to collect new words from the classroom. Here is a typical day's catch.

savant: one who knows many answers; a wise person. (A French word that means knowing.)
perfunctory: done in a routine, uninspired manner; careless; merely getting the job done.
levity: a joking, light manner; frivolity.
matrix: the surrounding environment in which an object is found. *Her ambition must be viewed within the matrix of her family's poverty.*
exacting: making severe demands. *Joan objected to her employer's exacting requirements.*
corpulent: fat; obese.
grapple: to hold or seize something or someone; to struggle, wrestle. A *grappling iron* is a large hook, dragged along a river bottom to seize submerged objects or drowned persons.
jetty: a large pier or wharf that protects a harbor or coastline from damage by the tide.
correlate: to compare or connect in a systematic way.
riposte: a quick retort or counterattack.
fatuous: foolish, silly.
propitious: favorable.
marauding: going in search of plunder or prey.
perverse: obstinately doing something different from what is reasonable or expected.
recondite: refers to an obscure subject, or to writing about an obscure subject.

DAY 10: Largeness

Think about those times when you have tried to describe to someone something you have seen earlier in the day. It was a big accident, or a big crowd, or something else much larger than ordinary. You probably had to hesitate to find exactly the right word—and settled for "huge" or "very big."

That need not happen again. There are dozens of easily used words for expressing *bigness,* and each of them has a distinct, separate meaning. Learn most of them on this list, and you will have made an **imposing** gain in your *Word Power.*

vast: very great area, space, or number of things. *A vast acreage of forest.*

immense: extremely large; so vast it cannot be measured.

substantial: a large number or size; large enough to be worthy of notice.

expansive: open and wide; capable of growing larger or stretching. *We saw an expansive stretch of beach.*

mammoth: huge. *Mammoths* were prehistoric forms of elephants; the word often describes giant animals or people.

monster: actually means "a frightening creature." Has come to mean an abnormally large person or object.

massive: bulky; a very large organism or undertaking. *The Girl Scouts undertook a massive charity drive.*

monumental: outstanding; enduring; remembered; amazing. *She displayed monumental ability to overcome disease.*

towering: higher than all surrounding objects; outstanding in its group or class.

tremendous: extremely large; enormous. Actually means "so large it makes one tremble."

enormous: immense; tremendous. Actually means "so large it is abnormal."

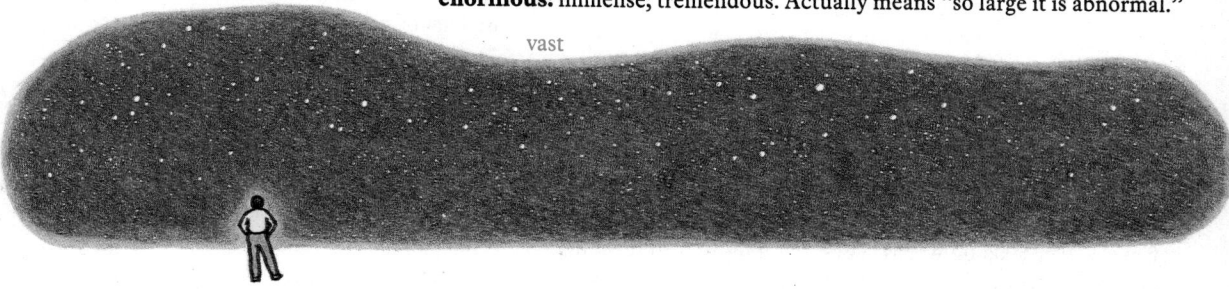

vast

DAY 11: Smallness

When it is not the idea of largeness that makes us pause and search for just the right word, it is often the very opposite **concept** (idea)—smallness.

It is not hard to come up with, say, *tiny* when we want to express extreme smallness: The doll's house contained the *tiniest* table and chair I've ever seen.

Sometimes, though, *tiny* and *very small* do not seem exactly right. For those times, here is a collection of words expressing smallness. Some may be ones you know, others may be unfamiliar. All will add strength to your *Word Power* abilities.

diminutive: of very small size. Also, a name that indicates smallness, as *booklet* for "a small book."

minute (min-oot'): exceptionally small; too small for ordinary notice. The Latin *min* in a word almost always indicates smallness, as in *miniature* and *diminish.*

pygmy: an individual or object of unusually small stature (height). Called after a race of African or Asian people who are about 4 feet tall.

infinitesimal: an amount or thing so small it cannot be measured.

insignificant: an amount or thing too small to matter; easily ignored or overlooked.

trace: a barely visible amount.

speck: a very small bit, or spot, or mark.

petite (peh-teet'): dainty, fragile. From the French word for *little.*

bantam: diminuitive, miniature. From a small, domestic fowl.

microscopic: too small to be seen.

midget: extremely small. From midge, a very small, gnatlike insect.

grain: a small particle, such as a *grain of sand.*

mite: a very small quantity, such as *a mite of sympathy.*

DAY 12: Words about words

As you learn more words, you will find it interesting to learn more *about* words. There is, in fact, a whole body of terms that describes specific aspects of word study. Some of those terms you already have added to your *Word Power* file: *etymology* and *neologism* are two. You will rediscover two more in this list.

acronym (MADD = Mothers Against Drunk Driving)

lexicography: the work of putting together a dictionary. A person who does this work is a **lexicographer,** and the dictionary itself is a **lexicon.** *Lexicon* also refers to the special terms used in a trade or profession. *The word "quit" was not in the ballplayers' lexicon.*

linguistic: relating to language, or a person who speaks several languages.

locution: a style of speaking; words and phrases used in a style of speaking.

acronym: a word formed by the initial letters of an organization or name, as EPA for Environmental Protection Agency.

provincial: an unsophisticated, heavily rustic word or term, as *taters* instead of *potatoes.*

homonym: a word that sounds like another word: *pail* and *pale,* or *shear* and *sheer.* (You already know the other two terms of the *nym* trio—*antonym* and *synonym.*)

interjection: a word that stands alone and expresses sudden thoughts or emotions. *Darn!* and *Oops!* are interjections. They often come between *(inter)* other thoughts.

usage: the way that a word expresses a thought in a language. See volume 2, pages 336-347 for explanations of correct modern English *usage.*

DAY 13: Free—on the shelves

The fullest, most "official" dictionary—the *Oxford English Dictionary* (O.E.D.)—gives the meanings of more than 500,000 words. Several million words are devoted to those definitions; the complete, multivolume O.E.D. is too heavy for an average man or woman to lift.

Yet right on the nearest shelf of your local library is nearly as good a source of *Word Power*—and easily lifted, too. It is any book that you pick out, skim through—or read fully, if the subject interests you—and from which you select unknown words. Why nearly as good as the OED? Because you see the words in context, actually being used by a writer.

Here, from a book about a scandal in New York City's Department of Water Supply, Gas and Electricity (*A Percentage of the Take,* by Walter Goodman) are a handful of words as they appear, together with their meanings. (The sentences have been shortened for inclusion here.)

That story was **diligently** *reported in the city's newspapers.* Carefully; conscientiously; done with unsparing effort.

What is striking is the **passivity** *of the press.* Accepting without argument, inquiry, or objection.

Marcus's comments about toughness **comprised** *a great deal of the conversation.* Filled.

He was a man whose profession required that a grudge not be lightly **relinquished.** Given up; abandoned; put aside.

This version contains an **inherent implausibility.** *Inherent:* an essential part; without it, the whole could not exist. *Implausibility:* difficulty in believing. (An important part of this version is difficult to believe, so it is difficult to believe the entire story.)

The newspaper commented on Albano's **"adroit** *footwork."* Nimble, agile.

The lawyer had appeals of his own for the **neophyte** *politician, whose hold was* **faltering.** *Neophyte:* beginner or novice. *Faltering:* slipping, missing one's step; beginning to make mistakes.

His stock began a **precipitous** *drop.* Steep; dropping sharply, as when falling off a *precipice* (cliff).

Observers regarded the electric company as highly **paternal** *to its employees.* Like a father. (Providing many of the needs of the employees beyond their salaries.)

DAY 14: Sending out scouts

Your campaign to improve your vocabulary need not be a **solitary** one (done by one person only —you). It will make your project considerably more interesting if you let others participate in it.

If you have a neighbor who works in an auto showroom, for example, have him or her bring you ten words that are used in the trade. Or your cousin may work for the phone company. What are some new words that he has heard? Here is a sampling of what you might expect from two kinds of "word scouts."

Sheriff's assistant

deterrent: something that prevents or discourages an action. *Increasing the police force would be a deterrent to crime.*

larceny: theft or robbery.

recidivism: slipping back into criminal behavior after being released from prison.

subpoena (suh-peen'-a): an order requiring the receiver to appear in court.

Carpenter/housing contractor

ferrule: a metal ring near the end of a wooden pole or tool handle, to prevent splitting.

shim: a thin wedge of wood or metal, used to level parts or fill spaces.

miter: cutting each of two surfaces at a 45° angle, to form a right angle when they are joined.

rabbet: a groove cut into a piece of wood, in which another piece of wood will be glued or screwed.

DAY 15: Tripling your list

During the past 14 days you have added more than 125 new words to your working vocabulary. No need for you to be modest about it—that is an extraordinary leap beyond the average person's rate of word **accretion** (gradual growth by adding or including new material) and you deserve congratulations.

Better yet, you can triple—or at least double—your number of new words by going back over the 14 formulas and reworking them. Use them to produce two or three sets of all-new words.

Be flexible. If you are not too sure about day six techniques, or if you feel uncomfortable with day eight, skip them. Try to concentrate on those days' plans that interest you the most.

You probably will find a thesaurus extremely helpful, if not essential. Turn now to the *Roget's University Thesaurus* at the back of this book. Study it carefully. Look up some general subjects and add the words you do not know to your *Word Power* file.

Or working at a library—at least in the planning stage of your tripling-up project—may give you just the help you need. You will find the librarian, who works with words all day, a knowledgeable, helpful collaborator.

accord

abutter 199	*additive* 37
aby *remain* 141	*adjunct* 39
endure 821, 826	*accompanying* 88
abysm 198	*aid* 707
abysmal *deep* 208	*auxiliary* 711
abyss *space* 180	**acciaccatura** 413
interval 198	**accidence** 567
depth 208	**accident** *event* 151
pitfall 667	*chance* 156
hell 982	*disaster* 619
acacia 367	*misfortune* 735
academic *theory* 514	—of an accident 156
teaching 537, 542	*fatal*–361
academical *style* 578	**accidental** *extrinsic* 6
academician 492	*irrelative* 10
Royal–559	*occasional* 134
academy 542	*fortuitous* 156
acanaceous 253	*undesigned* 621
acanthophorous 253	**accidentalism** 156
acanthus 847	**Accipitres** 739
acariâtre 901	**acclamation**
acarpous 169	*assent* 488
acatalectic 597	*approbation* 931
acatastasia 139	acclaim
acaudal 38	**acclimat**
acaudate 38	*domest*
accede *assent* 488	*inure*
submit 725	**acclivit**
consent 762	**accloy**
accelerate *early* 132	**accolad**
stimulate 173	**accom**
velocity 274	*adjus*
hasten 684	*aid*
accelerometer 490a	*reco*
accension 384	*give*
accent *sound* 402	*lend*
tone of voice 580	—on
rhythm 597	*con*
accentuate 642	**acco**
accentuated 581	*ki*
accentuation 580	**acc**
accept *assent* 488	(s
consent 762	s
receive 785	—t

5. Intrinsicality

[*L.*] etc. (*luminary*) 423; "such stuff as dreams are made on" [*Tempest*]; air, thin air; bubble etc. 353; mockery.

blank; void etc. (*absence*) 187; hollowness.

inanity, fatuity, fool's paradise.

v. **vanish**, evaporate, fade, fleet, sink, fly, dissolve, melt away; die, die away, die out; disappear etc. 449.

adj. **unsubstantial**; baseless, groundless; ungrounded; without foundation, having no foundation.

visionary etc. (*imaginary*) 515; immaterial etc. 317; spectral etc. 980; dreamy; shadowy; ethereal, airy, gaseous, imponderable, tenuous, vague, vaporous, dreamlike, mushroom; cloud

8. Circumstance

characteristic etc. (*special*) 79, (*indicative*) 550; invariable, incurable, ineradicable, fixed.

adv. **intrinsically** etc. *adj.*; at bottom, in the main, in effect, practically, virtually, substantially, *au fond* [*F.*]; fairly.

6. Extrinsicality

n. **extrinsicality**, objectiveness, *non ego* [*L.*]; extraneousness etc. 57; accident.

adj. **extrinsic**, extrinsical; derived from without; objective; extraneous etc. (*foreign*) 57; modal, adventitious; ascititious, adscititious; incidental, **accidental**, nonessential, unessential, accessory; contingent, fortuitous, casual, subsidiary.

Preparing for vocabulary tests

Any time you are applying for some step upward—admission to college, or a new job, or a promotion—there seems to be a vocabulary test involved.

That is because a broad vocabulary is recognized as a reliable indicator of intelligence (and, often, education). Also, vocabulary tests are easy to administer and to score: they are right or wrong, pass or fail, with no maybes or gray areas.

Now that you have a significantly improved vocabulary, be sure you know the ins and outs of testing.

Confidence. For most of us, an attitude of *I'm going to win* goes a long way toward making us actually win.

Salesmen who know they are going to make that sale, even before they walk in the door, are much more likely to get the order.

This will hold true for you when you are faced with a vocabulary test. You have worked on the plans and strategies and projects in these pages. You have built an impressive *Word Power* file. So be confident.

Samples. Know beforehand, as exactly as possible, the kinds of questions you will be asked to answer. There are four commonly used forms of vocabulary questions. They are explained on these pages, and samples are provided for extra practice; see also pages

Four forms of questions

1. Select the appropriate word or term that is most nearly the same in meaning as the capitalized word.

Sample: **ignite**   a) look away   b) put out   c) set fire   d) sleep

There are no context clues, so it is necessary to know or recognize the words themselves in this type of test. Be aware that one or two wrong answers are designed to mislead you. *Look away* might make you think of *ignore,* which could be confused with *ignite;* and *sleep* might relate to the *nite* (night) sound in *ignite.* The right answer is c) *set fire.* Here are some practice questions.

joggle	a) shake slightly	b) run slowly	c) ankle	d) turn a corner
seance	a) after	b) rabbit	c) sofa	d) meeting
buzzard	a) saw	b) fox	c) intestines	d) vulture
evict	a) send to jail	b) put out	c) raise up	d) saying
align	a) line up	b) marker	c) insult	d) press down

answers: joggle, a; seance, d; buzzard, d; evict, b; align, a.

2. For each statement, select the choice that best completes it or answers the question.

Sample: To be **profuse** with compliments means to
                    a) be obscene   b) give them freely   c) withhold them   d) be vague

Your only clue is the prefix *pro,* which we have seen means *forward* or *in front of.* Among the four choices, all have a negative or backward implication, except b). To be *profuse* means to give freely, even extravagantly. There is no easy way to answer type 2 questions; the more words you know, the better you will do. Practice with these typical questions.

Farmland that is **parched** is			
a) elevated	b) dry	c) flooded	d) posted
A **turquoise** would most likely be found in a			
a) zoo	b) tunnel	c) bracelet	d) restaurant
A **seamy** neighborhood is			
a) sordid	b) morbid	c) elegant	d) hot
The **barrage** consisted of			
a) wooden sheds	b) gunfire	c) tiles	d) clear plastic
Who gave the **compress** to Jason?			
a) a barber	b) a carpenter	c) a nurse	d) a teacher

answers: parched, b; turquoise, c; seamy, a; barrage, b; compress, c.

328-331 for more help on taking tests.

Usually, you can obtain copies of last year's test, or special review copies of tests similar to the one you will be taking. They are in review books and easily obtainable from a guidance counselor, library, or the testing organization itself.

Learn the rules. Should you guess at answers you are not quite sure of? Or are points taken off your score for wrong answers? And what about time? How many minutes will you be allowed?

When you practice for a particular vocabulary test, you will want to do it under conditions that are much like those under which the real test is administered. You should become accustomed to working within a time frame similar to the actual one. If there is no penalty for wrong answers, and there usually is not, you should practice guessing at every question.

The school, government office, or employer that will be testing you will answer your questions well in advance of test day. Phone or drop by in person. Make sure you are talking to someone who really knows the procedures, not a clerk who is only guessing.

Relax. Do not put unnecessary pressure on yourself as you prepare for the test. Cramming until late the night before the test guarantees that you will be groggy on the big day. There is no need for last-minute panic if you have been building *Word Power* day by day, week by week.

Know exactly how you will get to the test place, and plan to arrive ten or fifteen minutes early, with a pocket full of extra pens and pencils. Then relax and let your *Word Power* take over.

---

3. Each question consists of four pairs of words. In one pair among the four, both words have the same meaning: they are synonyms. Select that pair.

Sample: a) magnify-diminish   b) section-partition   c) capitulate-defy   d) encrust-salvage

By looking closely at all four pairs, you may recall that *diminish* means "to make smaller," and is the opposite of *magnify*. *Capitulate* and *defy* are opposites, too; and though you may not be sure about d), you probably will recognize that in b) a *section* and a *part* are the same thing. Your answer is b). See how well you do with these practice questions.

1. a) simile-quote   b) monastery-monograph   c) bisect-divide   d) create-basket
2. a) deprecate-belittle   b) crass-cliff   c) ominous-many   d) biology-oculist
3. a) captain-demagogue   b) curator-bishop   c) fiasco-failure   d) flagrant-tramp
4. a) familiar-intimate   b) recognize-venal   c) proximity-distance   d) thermal-sunshine
5. a) tripod-oyster   b) confide-trust   c) reveal-conceal   d) unite-sever

answers: 1 c; 2 a; 3 c; 4 a; 5 b.

4. For each of the following statements, select T if the statement is *true,* F if it is *false.*

Sample: A **parable** is a type of umbrella.   T   F

The question was designed to mislead you slightly. A sunshade, very much like an umbrella, is called a *parasol*. But a *parable* is a story illustrating a religious or moral lesson, so the correct answer is F. Decide if each of these examples is true or false.

1. A **saga** is a long story or report.   T   F
2. A **terminal** is the last car of a railroad train.   T   F
3. To **mediate** is to apply bandages to a wound or a rash.   T   F
4. **Archives** are written records.   T   F
5. **Largesse** is a large, generous gift.   T   F

answers: 1. T; 2. F (a *caboose* is the last car; a *terminal* is a station at the end of the line, or the final portion of a thing); 3. F (to *mediate* is to come between two opposing parties, to resolve their differences); 4. T; 5. T.

American English

American English is made up, to a large extent, of borrowings from the many immigrants who arrived on U.S. shores, each speaking his native tongue. Even the American Indians were immigrants, arriving across a land bridge to Alaska from Asia that no longer exists. And they brought their language with them, too.

American Indian. Among the words that Indians have given to modern American English are **tomahawk; moccasin; wigwam; tepee;** and **cayuse** (horse). Probably, the Indians' most lasting contribution is place names. Consider the following states:

Arkansas: land of south wind people.

Idaho: light on the mountains.

Illinois: warriors (**Chicago,** for some reason, meant place that smells bad).

Iowa: the sleepy people, referring to a local tribe of the Dakota nation.

Kentucky: meadowland.

Minnesota: sky-blue water.

Mississippi: big river.

Spanish. The Indians of the Southwest mingled closely with the Spanish settlers of that territory. The area attracted pioneers from the settled eastern colonies, and the mingled westerners put their own stamp on the language. These cowboy terms are Spanish in origin: **buffalo** (explorer DeSoto's word for our native bison); **chaps** (short for *chaparejos,* a cowboy's leather leg protectors); **cinch; corral; buckaroo** (derived from Spanish *vaquero*); **lariat; lasso; pinto** (spotted horse); **rodeo; pronto; canyon; loco; cabana; fiesta; hombre; siesta; tequila; tortilla; vamoose.** We call a low island a **key** and a common insect pest a **cockroach;** both terms are based on similar Spanish words. If we want someone to leave in a hurry, we tell him to **vamoose**—one more Spanish borrowing.

African. When slaves were shipped to America in chains, they brought with them African words that were converted to the nation's growing language. Among them are **banana; banjo; goober** (peanut); **juke** (to misbehave, much later adapted to mean a tavern music player, or *jukebox*); **tote** (carry).

The various waves of settlers brought with them customs and words they used in their new homes. Dutch, French, English, German, Scandinavian, Italian, and many, many other ethnic groups contributed to the growing language. Here are a few borrowings.

Dutch

bedspread	cookie	sauerkraut
boss	hex	sleigh
bush	landscape	waffle
cole slaw	Santa Claus	Yankee

French

barrage	depot	music
castle	(railroad station)	pantry
chowder	détente	parlor
crime	(easing of tensions)	prairie
dance	manor	procession

Among French place names are **Baton Rouge** (LA), red stick; **Des Moines** (IA), the monks; **Terre Haute** (IN), high ground; **Vermont,** green mountain; and **Louisiana,** for King Louis XIV.

German

and how	dumb	klutz
bub	ecology	(clumsy person)
bum	frankfurter,	phooey
(loafer, tramp)	hamburger	pumpernickel
check	(styles of meat	vampire
(restaurant bill)	served in	("to vamp,"
dachshund	Frankfurt and	bewitch)
delicatessen	Hamburg)	

Italian. A nation of brilliant cooks and dedicated eaters, Italians changed forever the composition of American menus. Among the additions:

espresso	macaroni	spaghetti
lasagna	ravioli	tortoni

And, of course, **pizza.** Contrary to legend, the word does not mean pie. It refers to pinching or plucking the dough, as in the musical term *pizzicato*—to pluck a violin string.

Yiddish. The first large waves of Jewish immigrants from Central and Eastern Europe arrived in the late 1800's. By 1910, 3 million had settled in the United States, mostly in the North Atlantic states. Jews had been colonists in New York, Rhode Island, and Massachusetts since 1654, but their contributions to American English became most significant in the period before and after World War I.

Most American Jews do not speak Hebrew. Their original tongue was Yiddish, a German-based language used by Jews in Central and Eastern Europe. These Yiddish words are common in our language.

bagel: doughnut-shaped hard roll.

chutzpah: audacity; nerve; impudence.

ghetto: living area in which a minority is confined by the majority.

kibitz: give unwanted advice (kibitz at a card game).

kosher: proper, legitimate (derived from special dietary laws observed by Orthodox Jews).

lox: smoked salmon.

mavin: an expert, an authority.

schlemiel: a foolish, clumsy person.

schlep: to drag or carry.

Our evolving language.

Words you might overhear spoken in Springfield, Massachusetts, or any other American town or city, would be widely different from those you might hear in Peterborough or any other English city or town. We lift the *hood* on our car; they lift the *bonnet*. We might see a *cop* on his *vacation;* an Englishman would see a *bobby* on *holiday.*

Our two languages, of course, started as one. Over a 300-year span, the division has encompassed more than variations in common terms and their usages. Americans have coined their own words and phrases. These are some from various periods in American history:

The Revolutionary War
militia: a reserve force; a citizen army.
redcoats: British soldiers.
rifle: a musket with a spiraled inner barrel.
stockade: a fort protected by a wall of pointed stakes.

The Civil War
carpetbagger: an unscrupulous northerner who went south in 1868 for cheap land; an opportunist.
scalawag: southerner who accepted Reconstruction.

World War I
doughboy: infantry soldier; also used, to a lesser extent, in the Civil War.
goldbrick: to loaf or avoid work (Army term).
rookie: new recruit.

Prohibition
flapper: a "modern," unconventional young woman.
gang wars: battles for supremacy among rival groups of gangsters.
public enemy: notorious criminal, high on the FBI's most-wanted list.
scram: get out of here; leave.
speakeasy: illegal tavern or barroom.
teetotaler: one pledged to total abstinence from intoxicating beverages.

World War II
black market: trafficking in rationed, scarce goods.
Dear John: a letter to a soldier from his sweetheart, calling off their relationship.
GI: an ordinary soldier; based on the term *government issue,* applied to all military materials.
wild blue yonder: the sky, as it applied to the site of aerial battles.

The '50's, '60's, and '70's
dove: one who advocates peaceful overtures, particularly to the Soviets.
game plan: strategy; used in business and politics.
hawk: one who advocates a hard line, particularly against the Soviets; the term was first used, in another context, in Jefferson's era.
leak: disclosure of government papers and plans.
stonewall: resist investigation, as during the Watergate episode of the Nixon Presidency

The '80's
burnout: exhaustion caused by intensive work over an extended period.
computerese: terms used by computer users; examples are byte (unit of information stored in the computer's memory); glitch (error); user-friendly (program that is easy to operate).

The '90's
e-commerce, e-trade, e-biz: business conducted by computer, particularly on the Internet and World Wide Web.
net surfing, web surfing: looking for information, etc., on the Internet and World Wide Web.

Stud, draw, or deuces wild

Poker is the most American of card games. (Only basketball and baseball have stronger claims to being "the Great American game"—they were invented by Yankees. Poker is an old European card game, its name derived from the French name for the game, *poque.*)

Today, people who do not know a full house from a royal flush use poker terms. Some that have become engrained in popular speech follow.
poker face: a wooden, nonrevealing expression.
penny ante: insignificant, petty action or game.
bluff: behavior intended to make an opponent think your position is stronger than it really is.
wild card: an unexpected factor, one that could change the anticipated outcome.
dead man's hand: two aces and two eights, said to have been in the hand Wild Bill Hickok was holding when he was murdered.
stand pat: stay with what you have; do not budge.

poker face

Puzzles and word games

What is good for us is often bad tasting—but there are exceptions. You can enjoy yourself as you progress on several of the paths to a more powerful vocabulary. Word games and puzzles, whether played alone or in competition, are effective learning devices. They really do reinforce your knowledge of new words' meanings, and build considerably your ability to recall those words.

Crossword puzzles. Americans seem to be a nation of crossword puzzlers. Newspapers print daily puzzles; paperback and hardcover books of puzzle collections fill several shelves in most bookstores; crossword puzzle dictionaries and other specialized aids are widely available.

If you are new to the world of crosswords, consider these tips:

1. Search around, while you are still getting the hang of it, for a source of *easy* puzzles. Ones that are difficult are likely to discourage you.
2. Use pencil, write lightly, and do not hesitate to erase guesses that might be wrong.
3. For your first move, skim through the puzzle and insert words you are sure about: names of people or movies; places; facts about games, crafts, or instruments. Then you will have enough letters in place to give you hints for words you are less sure about.

Packaged word games

Any bookstore or toy store should be a good source for a half-dozen or more different word games, packaged and ready for spreading out on your table.

Examine the game; read the rules before purchasing it. You may decide it is too specialized or requires too extensive a vocabulary for the people who will be playing it.

Anagrams: the granddaddy of all "take-a-card" or "take-a-tile" word games. Players form their own words, capture opponents' words, and the whole family joins in.

Scrabble:® each player forms a word with any number of his seven randomly selected tiles. He lays the letters on the board's marked spaces. Some letters and spaces are good for bonus points. Players add on to, or branch out from, previously laid-down words.

Boggle:® 25 letters appear in a square. Players compose hidden lists of all possible words, using only letters that are touching one another. After three minutes, lists are compared and a winner declared.

Ghosts

This age-old game requires two or more players. Each player in turn calls out a letter. If, from the fourth letter on, a player completes a word, he loses that round, and must "carry" letter G.

A new round is begun. If there is a new loser, he too carries letter G. Losers of subsequent rounds must carry G, then H, then O, S, T, and S. When one player has all six letters, he loses. The others play on until one winner remains.

If it is Mary's turn and the letters VAL, for example, have been named, she might call letter I. If she had called E, the word VALE would have been spelled, and she would have lost that round. If the next player cannot think of a word starting VALI, he can challenge Mary, who will say VALISE or VALID. Mary proves she has a word in mind, so the challenger loses that round.

Hangman

This word game requires at least two players. One of the players, the leader, has a word in mind. He tells the other players the number of letters in the word. The other players try to guess the word by calling out letters. When a letter is guessed correctly, the leader tells the others at what position or positions in the word the letter falls.

However, for every letter that is called out that is not in the word, the leader draws a portion of a stick figure. Usually, the figure is made up of a head, eyes, nose, mouth, torso, arms, hands, legs, and feet. If the figure is completed before the word is guessed, then the figure is considered hanged, and the leader has won the game. If someone guesses the word, then that person becomes the next leader.

Building Your Vocabulary

Rate yourself again

Some time ago, when you were setting out to build your *Word Power,* you tested yourself. ("How do you rate?" on page 208.) Now that you nearly have completed the program, it will be interesting to measure your gain over your earlier effort.

To make the comparison valid, you should test your facility with difficult words—ones that you have examined and added to your vocabulary. All of the target words in this self-exam appear and are defined in the preceding pages.

For each of the questions, select the one term that *most nearly defines* the meaning of the word in dark print. Score one point for each correct answer.

If you are determined to improve your vocabulary, but score 17 or under, start over. Work on your *Word Power* file daily. Be certain that you understand the meaning of each word before progressing to the next one. Go back over your new vocabulary. A daily review can go a long way toward cementing new words in your memory.

1. **dubious** a) twin; b) prejudiced; c) doubtful; d) double

2. **humus** a) amateur comedian; b) good feelings; c) bad reputation; d) decayed plants

3. **perfidy** a) smells good; b) large taxes; c) traitor's actions; d) risk

4. **meticulous** a) precise; b) fingernails; c) angry; d) foolish

5. **impediment** a) fooling; b) showing; c) statue; d) blocking

6. **facade** a) front; b) mimic; c) framework; d) mobility

7. **accessible** a) can be captured; b) must leave; c) can be reached; d) too much

8. **curator** a) doctor's assistant; b) museum director; c) bullfighter's sword; d) church official

9. **enigma** a) puzzle; b) birthmark; c) pride; d) energetic

10. **petulance** a) birdlike; b) grumpiness; c) shyness; d) holiday

11. **altruism** a) honesty; b) generosity; c) completion; d) conservatism

12. **irascible** a) held up; b) easily angered; c) ready for action; d) green

13. **felines** a) fish; b) snakes; c) criminals; d) cats

14. **undulate** a) wave; b) chew; c) blink; d) shout

15. **cynosure** a) show; b) deterrent; c) detergent; d) swan

16. **habitat** a) farmyard; b) home; c) unpleasant; d) nun

17. **voracious** a) gets in front; b) eats huge amounts; c) frightening; d) never wins

18. **incombustible** a) untidy; b) unburnable; c) unbreakable; d) can't be equaled

19. **marauders** a) raiders; b) jumpers; c) winners; d) swimmers

20. **gregarious** a) religious; b) young; c) frightened; d) sociable

21. **devastated** a) exasperated; b) humbled; c) wasted; d) enlarged

22. **vestige** a) clothing; b) appropriate; c) persuasion; d) remnant

23. **consoled** a) comforted; b) entertained; c) controlled; d) welcomed

24. **garrulous** a) talkative; b) plump; c) foolish; d) proud

25. **antagonist** a) sufferer; b) opponent; c) follower; d) merchant

Answers. 1, c; 2, d; 3, c; 4, a; 5, d; 6, a; 7, c; 8, b; 9, a; 10, b; 11, b; 12, b; 13, d; 14, a; 15, a; 16, b; 17, b; 18, b; 19, a; 20, d; 21, c; 22, d; 23, a; 24, a; 25, b. A score of 25 is perfect, 22–24 very good, 18–21 above average.

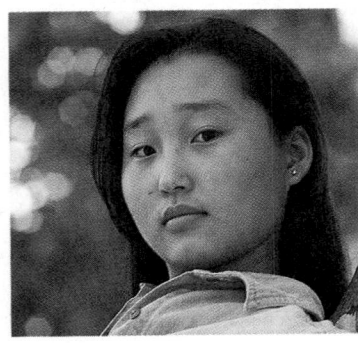

askance

Words you should know

badinage

genial

seethe

absolve. To clear or pardon; to pronounce that no blame exists.

abstract. 1. Not concrete or definite (an *abstract* thought). 2. A portion reprinted from a larger book or article.

acerate. Sharpened; pointed at one end.

acquiesce. To agree; consent; to go along with a suggestion.

acrylic. A resin-based synthetic fiber.

acute. 1. Sharp, pointed. 2. Important. 3. Sensitive (an *acute* sense of hearing).

agitate. 1. To move suddenly or violently; to shake up. 2. To disturb. 3. To interest in a cause (*agitated* for higher pay).

albatross. 1. Large sea bird. 2. A burden, handicap, or curse (this meaning is derived from a poem, *The Rime of the Ancient Mariner,* by Coleridge).

alewife. Small, herringlike fish.

anemic. A disease in which too few red blood cells results in weakness and fatigue.

aorta. The largest of the arteries carrying blood from the heart.

apothecary. Druggist; pharmacist.

appalling. Frightening; upsetting (the filth was *appalling*).

askance (a-skans'). Disapproval or distrust; a sidewise glance indicating doubt.

aspect. 1. Appearance. 2. The direction something faces.

assert. To state positively or forcefully.

assuage (a-swaje'). To remedy; make easier, less painful.

badinage (bad-n-ahj'). Playful, joking talk; chitchat.

baste. 1. To sew loosely, temporarily. 2. To keep moist (as with sauce or melted butter) while cooking.

bastion. Fort or strongly held position (the league was a *bastion* of patriotism).

behoove. Necessary or proper (*behooves* us to pay attention).

bellow. To roar or shout; the roar of a large animal, as a buffalo.

benign. Harmless, kindly, mild.

bequeath. To pass on, or leave, as in a will.

bequest. That which has been *bequeathed* (Mary's aunt left her a *bequest* of $50,000).

bigamy. Being married to two persons at one time, a criminal offense.

blackguard (blag'-erd). An unprincipled rascal; a scoundrel.

blanch. To bleach or whiten; to remove the color from an object.

blather. Nonsensical or foolish talk.

blemish. A flaw or spot that spoils the appearance of an object or a person.

blunder. A mistake caused by stupidity or confusion.

bob. To move up and down (Jim *bobbed* alongside the boat).

bolster. 1. A pillow or cushion. 2. To support or prop up (contributions *bolstered* her campaign funds).

bountiful. Plentiful; generous.

Brahmin. Descendant of old, exclusive family (a New England *Brahmin*); derived from Hindu term for *highest rank.*

bravado. A show of false, swaggering bravery.

calligraphy. Handwriting; penmanship.

camber. 1. An arched surface. 2. The way in which automobile wheels are set slanting inward toward their tops.

caster. A small, swiveled wheel under furniture or another heavy object.

cherish. To treat with love and tenderness; to hold dear.

circa. Approximately, about (first used *circa* 1900).

cistern. A tank for holding rainwater.

constrict. To squeeze, compress, make smaller.

Building Your Vocabulary

consummate. 1. To conclude or bring to perfection. 2. Perfect; highly skilled (a *consummate* baker of pastries).

cougar. A mountain lion.

covenant. An agreement or contract that binds two or more persons.

cringe. To move back in fear (synonym: *cower*).

croissant (kwoss-sahn′). A crescent-shaped roll of light, sweet dough.

damsel. A girl or maiden (used in ancient times, but rarely heard today).

decimate. To kill or destroy a large part of something; to kill one-tenth.

desecrate. To disturb something sacred; to profane.

detonate. To explode.

dire. Dreadful, terrible, extreme; having horrible consequences (a *dire* threat).

discord. Tension, strife, lack of agreement.

divan. A backless couch.

dominant. The highest; the one in control, with the most authority.

dominate. To rule or control; to be higher than others.

dub. To apply a nickname (they *dubbed* him "Mr. Careful").

dynasty. A group or family that keeps power for several generations.

edgy. Tense; nervous; anxious.

eject. To throw out; to evict (the noisy couple was *ejected* from the theater).

ember. A dying coal in a fire that is partially out.

embroil. To involve in an argument or contest; to entangle.

empirical. Believing ideas, actions, or things that one has observed for oneself (*empirical* evidence).

epicure. One who has uncommon, highly refined preferences in food and wine.

evince. To demonstrate clearly.

expire. 1. To end; to die; a last breath. 2. To breathe out.

expostulate. To present one's reasons; to argue intelligently.

extol. To praise highly.

extricate. To free or release from an entanglement.

farce. Far-fetched, humorous show; broad, exaggerated comedy.

fastidious. 1. Careful, exacting attention to detail. 2. Overly attentive to good manners.

fervent. Showing great emotional depth; highly enthusiastic.

fetish. 1. Something that is said to have mystic powers. 2. An excessively strong habit or attitude (Tim made a *fetish* of washing his hands).

fickle. Unpredictably changeable in regard to attitudes and affections.

figment. Something made up or invented (the whole story was a *figment* of his imagination).

forage. 1. To look for food. 2. Hay, grain, or other food for domestic animals.

forfeit (for′-fit). Something given up, in punishment for a crime or offense; that which is forfeited.

forlorn. Extreme sadness or loneliness; the appearance of a sad, lonely person.

furl. To roll up a flag.

gabardine. Cotton twill fabric.

gaggle. 1. A flock of geese. 2. A group of silly or cackling people.

gape. To stare, with mouth opened wide in wonderment.

garret. An attic.

genial. Friendly; pleasant; a kindly manner.

gird. 1. To prepare for action. 2. To put on a belt or band.

gist. The main point of a topic; the core, or essence, of a subject.

gnash (nash). To grind one's teeth together.

graphic. Relating to writing, drawing, painting, typesetting, and other representations on paper or a similarly flat surface (*graphic* arts).

grave. 1. Serious, important, dangerous (declaring war was a *grave* decision). 2. A burial place.

guffaw. Coarse, noisy laughter.

gustatory. Relating to the sense of taste (eating at Joe's was a *gustatory* experience).

gyrate. To circle or revolve around a point or axis.

hack. To chop, cut, or break up.

hagiology. Study of the lives of saints.

hale. To drag or pull; to compel someone to go somewhere (*haled* into court). 2. Healthy; not sickly.

hark. To listen carefully.

harridan. Unpleasant, complaining woman.

hearth. The floor of a fireplace, and that part of it extending into a room.

hepatitis (hep′-a-tie-tiss). A serious disease of the liver.

heretic. A person who disagrees with generally accepted opinions, or dissents from religious views.

hexagonal. Six-sided.

hindsight. Noticing the importance and cause of an event after it has happened.

hormone. A chemical substance formed in the body and carried in the bloodstream.

horticulture. The growing of fruits, vegetables, or plants; gardening.

hospice. 1. A place or program that cares for patients who are incurably ill. 2. A shelter for needy travelers.

huckster. 1. A peddler; one who sells merchandise in the street. 2. A writer of advertisements.

hydraulic. Related to water pressure (*hydraulic* pump; *hydraulic* engineer).

iconoclast. One who attacks and destroys popularly held, or traditional, values. (Ancient

Greeks called religious statues *icons. Iconoclasts* were "breakers of statues," or breakers of ideas.)

ignominious. Disgraceful; shameful.

immune. Not affected; excepted from a general condition.

immutable. Unchangeable.

imperial. 1. Relating to an empire or emperor. 2. A nation that maintains control over colonies.

imperturbable. Calm; cannot be shaken or disturbed.

implicit (im-plis′-it). Understood, though stated only indirectly (an *implicit* understanding).

impunity. Will not be punished or harmed (state your opinions with *impunity*).

inception. The beginning; start.

incumbent. Currently holding an office or position (the *incumbent* governor).

inept. Clumsy; foolish; incompetent; not suitable.

influx. Flowing in (an *influx* of immigrants).

inordinate. More than could be expected; an unreasonable amount.

insouciant (in-soo′-see-ont). Carefree, nonchalant, untroubled.

interrogate. Ask questions.

iota. An extremely small amount (we did not care one *iota* what their opinion might be).

itinerant. One who travels from place to place, as part of his work; traveling in such a way.

jamb (jam). The vertical framework of a door or window.

jibe. To agree (your information *jibes* with ours).

jubilant. Joyful; happy enough to sing or laugh aloud.

juxtapose. To put one thing or idea next to another in order to compare them.

kamikaze (ka-me-kah′-zee). A suicidal crash attack (a tactic used by Japanese pilots in World War II).

keynote. Main theme (President Kennedy gave the *keynote* speech at the convention).

koala. An Australian animal, the model for teddy bears.

labyrinth (lab′-a-rinth). Mazelike series of connecting passages and tunnels.

lacerate. To tear, wound, rip, or cut.

laconic (la-kon′-ick). Using few words; short-spoken (Coolidge, who was *laconic,* was called "Silent Cal").

lacuna (la-koo′-nah). An empty space; missing part; gap.

laggard. Straggler; one who falls behind the others.

laity (lay′-ih-tee). People who are not members of a given profession; in churches, those who are not members of the clergy.

lament. To mourn or grieve; to express sorrow; a spoken or written expression of grief.

lapse. 1. To slip or drift backward; to neglect or overlook. 2. A missed opportunity or privilege; the amount of time during which the privilege expired.

late. In addition to the common meaning of coming after the expected time, late also means dead, or recently died (the *late* Mrs. Patterson).

lax. Not strict. Unfirm.

LED. The display of letters or numerals, as on a calculator, furnished by a semiconductor; *LED* is an acronym for Light Emitting Diode.

lenient (lee′-ne-yent). Not inclined to punish; forgiving.

levitate. To rise into the air with no apparent support; a mystical act or illusion that defies gravity.

libation. An alcoholic drink; a drink offered to a god.

limber. Moving easily; supple; working without effort (he sent a more *limber* player into the game).

linear. (linn′-ee-er). Relating to a straight line (a *linear* descendant of the Adams family).

locus. A place or location.

lozenge. A medicated tablet for relief from coughs and colds.

macadam. A type of road made of stone and asphalt or tar.

machination (mack-in-ayshun). 1. The act of plotting or scheming, usually for an evil purpose; the plot itself.

maculate. Spotted or soiled; to spot or stain (*immaculate* means "without spots," or pure, clean, unstained).

magnate. Powerful person, usually a businessman or industrialist (a lumber *magnate*).

malcontent. Unhappy or discontented; also, a person in that condition (*mal* means bad, or generally negative, as in *malformed* and *malodorous*).

manacle. Handcuff.

mangle. 1. To ruin through clumsiness (Howard *mangled* his speech). 2. To cut, hack, or otherwise physically ruin.

mare's nest. 1. A tangled, complicated situation. 2. A fraud.

marginal. 1. Near the edge or border. 2. Of barely passable quality.

maroon. 1. A color, ranging from reddish brown to reddish purple. 2. To abandon a person; to put him off a boat with little hope of rescue.

martinet. A rigid military leader or taskmaster; one who demands total obedience.

mediate. To settle disputes by acting as a neutral party.

melange (may-lahnj′). A mixture.

menial (mean′-ee-al). 1. A servant. 2. Relating to a job or task that a servant might do.

metamorphosis. A change in shape, appearance, or function (a tadpole's *metamorphosis* into a frog).

Building Your Vocabulary

metropolis. A large city.

microcomputer. A very small computer (*micro* means small or greatly reduced in size).

mien (mean). Facial expression or the way one carries oneself; appearance.

mildew. A fungus, similar to a mold, that grows on leather, plants, cloth, or paper under damp conditions.

minatory. Threatening; fearsome.

minutia (mi-noo'-sha). A very small, unimportant item (we cannot bother with the *minutia* of their complaints).

mode. A way of doing something; a style of action (an unusual *mode* of dress, or of speech).

molest. To harass, bother, or physically disturb.

monarch. A king, emperor, or ruler.

monogram. The initials of a person's name formed into a design.

moot. A matter that can be argued in any of several ways; not easily decided.

mucilage (myoo'-si-laj). Glue.

murky. Dark, gloomy; heavy mist or fog; thick, unclear waters (a *murky* atmosphere).

nape. The back of the neck.

nether. Lower or below (the *nether* regions).

niggling. Fussy; petty; too concerned with unimportant detail.

novel. 1. New, different (Bill's wagon had a *novel* design). 2. A book of fiction; prose narrative.

obfuscate. To hide slightly, or make obscure (he deliberately *obfuscated* the facts about the accident).

Occident. Europe and the western hemisphere (Asia and the Pacific islands are the *Orient*).

offing. Soon, or the near future (a large gift is in the *offing*).

oratory. The skill of public speaking; rhetorical style.

ossify. 1. To become bony. 2. To become set in an unchanging pattern.

ostracize. To shut out or exclude from a group; to banish.

palate. The roof of the mouth.

palette. 1. A hand-held board on which an artist mixes colors. 2. The range of colors used by an artist.

panacea (pan-a-see-a). A cure for all diseases or difficulties, the value of which is doubtful.

paradox. A statement, difficult to believe, that is true (*paradoxically*, the two opponents were brothers).

paragon. A model of excellence.

peccadillo. A small fault; a prank.

pewter. Silver-gray metal used for kitchen and cooking utensils.

pillage. To rob or plunder, as by invading armies in wartime.

poise. 1. To balance, or the state of being balanced. 2. Bearing oneself with dignity and composure (she exhibited *poise* and maturity).

ponder. To think carefully; to consider.

predator. One who preys on others for his own profit, as an animal preys on (kills and eats) weaker animals.

propinquity (pro-pin'-kwi-tee). Nearness (*propinquity* is at the root of most friendships).

quagmire. 1. Swampy, boggy land into which a walker might sink. 2. A predicament or difficult situation that might entrap a person.

quail. 1. To move backward in fear. 2. A small, chickenlike bird; a bobwhite.

quash. To put down; suppress; set aside (the judge *quashed* the motion for appeal).

quiver. 1. To tremble or shake. 2. A case in which an archer's arrows are carried.

radiate. 1. To spread out from a central point (spokes of a wheel *radiate* from the hub). 2. To issue energy—heat, light, or sound.

radical. Carried to an extreme; not moderate.

rail. To speak strongly against; to verbally abuse (Ken *railed* against the new tax collector).

rampart. A fort or defensive position higher than the surrounding ground.

rant. To shout in a violent manner; to rave.

rapport (ra-pour'). A good relationship, marked by mutual trust and admiration.

rationale (rash-a-nal'). A reason (sometimes used as an excuse) for doing something.

redundant. Unnecessarily repeated; not needed.

refute. To disprove; to argue against.

regress. To move backward, usually to a worsened condition (the opposite of *progress*).

reiterate. To say again; repeat.

relent. To soften an attitude; to give up a previously held, harder position.

remonstrate. To protest; object; argue.

repartee (re-par-tay'). Witty, clever conversation, particularly a witty reply.

replete. Plenty, or an oversupply. (a party *replete* with butlers and waitresses).

rife. Appears frequently; often occurs (his work was *rife* with errors).

rook. 1. A crow. 2. To cheat or swindle.

ruminate. 1. To think about something for a long time; to reflect on it. 2. For cattle, to chew and rechew.

Rx. A prescription for medicine or pharmaceutical drugs.

saccharine (sack'-a-rin). Too sweet (*saccharin* is the white, powdery substitute for sugar).

salutation. A greeting, especially at the start of a letter ("Dear Mr. Brenner," for example).

sanctum. A holy place; sacred part of a church or temple.

sarcophagus (sar-kof'-a-gus). A stone coffin.

savvy. (*Slang*) To understand; knowhow (he is *savvy* enough to make a good deal).

scale. Thin, flaky substance on the skins of animals, fishes, or plants. 2. Rate of pay, determined by union schedules, for musicians and other skilled technicians. 3. A device for weighing; a measure.

scant. Meager; a small degree less than a specified amount (a *scant* four miles).

scenario. 1. An outline of a play or book. 2. The probable way in which events will take place, if certain unpredictable circumstances govern the action (here is the *scenario* for our rescue operation, if all the bridges flood out).

scow. A large flat-bottomed boat.

scrawny. Skinny; bony.

scuffle. To grapple or fight with someone in an indeterminate, confused manner.

sealing wax. A soft substance when heated, it hardens to seal bottles and packages.

secondary school. High school.

seethe. 1. To be extremely excited; agitated. 2. To have a motion like that of boiling water.

semantics. The study of the meaning of language.

seminary. 1. A school for the training of religious persons— ministers, priests, rabbis. 2. A school of higher education for young women.

sensor. A machine that receives or sends impulses, like light or heat, not otherwise detected by humans.

sentient. Conscious; able to experience thought and feelings.

sequester. To move away; set apart; place in seclusion (they chose to *sequester* themselves in a far valley).

serrated. Having an edge that is notched or saw-toothed.

servile. Subordinate or submissive in attitude, like a servant.

sham. False, fraudulent; a trick intended to pass off someone or something as other than as it really is.

shear. To remove hair or fleece from an animal (the farmer *sheared* his sheep; the barber *sheared* Don's hair too short).

shoal. Shallow water, sometimes unexpectedly so and a threat to navigators.

shoddy. Inferior; made of poor quality materials.

shortfall. A shortage; an amount below the expected, usually referring to money.

showboating. Showing off; attempting to attract attention.

showdown. An act that forces the outcome of an issue or event (the feud had gone on long enough, so the families arranged a *showdown*).

shrew. 1. A woman who nags and scolds; an unpleasant, constantly criticizing woman. 2. A small, mouselike animal with poor vision.

shrewd. Clever, sharp, cunning; quick-witted.

shrivel. To shrink and dry up, remaining in a wrinkled condition.

shun. To deliberately avoid (Carol walked across the street, *shunning* her nephew).

sickle. A tool with a long, curved blade used for cutting grain, grass, or other tall plants (the Communist flag is known as the hammer and sickle because those two tools are depicted on it).

sidereal. About, or relating to, the stars; stellar.

sidle. To step or move sideways; usually done when trying to avoid another person, or to remain unnoticed.

significant. Having a valuable or important meaning.

silent treatment. To totally ignore an unliked person, as a means of expressing contempt (everyone in the class gave Kim the *silent treatment*).

simper. A silly, childish smile.

simulate. 1. To imitate, or take on the manner and appearance of another person or thing. 2. To pretend (Carl *simulated* interest in Rose's career).

sketchy. Slight; incomplete; leaving out many of the details and finer points.

skimpy. Not enough; too small an amount for the purpose, often due to insufficient money having been spent.

slake. To satisfy; to lessen a condition that had existed (the announcement *slaked* Dan's rage; the water *slaked* Ann's thirst).

snide. Sarcastic; offensive in a rude, superior manner.

solar. Having to do with the sun. (*solar* heat; *solar* rays; *solar* blindness).

sonar. A technique of using sound waves, reflected off objects under water.

sordid. 1. Extremely dirty; filthy; vile. 2. Motivated solely by greed.

souvenir (soo'-va-neer). A memento; something that helps one remember a place or an event (we were given key rings as *souvenirs* of the party).

spectrum. A range of ideas, thoughts, or activities (the whole *spectrum* of medical science).

stalwart. Strong, determined.

stance. One's attitude or position; the way one stands; also, one's thoughts on a controversial issue.

stifle. 1. To smother; suffocate. 2. To cut off opposition.

stunt. To slow or stop the growth of a person or thing.

taboo. A strict rule or custom against an action, imposed by social or religious beliefs.

Building Your Vocabulary

tactful. Sensitive, considerate; taking care not to offend.

taint. To infect; to stain someone's reputation (the *taint* of his dishonorable discharge).

tension. 1. The act of stretching or being stretched. 2. A condition of nervous strain.

thwart. To frustrate; to prevent an action or event desired by another person from taking place.

tirade. A long, angry speech, aimed at an enemy or an enemy's position.

topsy-turvy. Totally confused; upside-down.

torrid. 1. Very hot and dry, parched. 2. Passionate, intense.

touchy. 1. Quick to take offense; too sensitive. 2. A situation that requires delicate handling.

tranquil. Calm and undisturbed.

transitory. Existing only for a brief time; short-lived; an in-between period.

traverse. To move across or through; to travel up or down, or backward and forward, through a place or region.

trounce. To beat, as in a fight.

tumult. Noise and commotion caused by an unruly crowd.

tyrant. A harsh, cruel ruler.

unvailing. Useless.

uncouth. Clumsy, crude, impolite.

unflappable. Calm and unexcited.

ungainly. Awkward; lacking grace; moving clumsily.

unpalatable. Not easily swallowed or accepted; unpleasing; unpleasant.

valor. Bravery; courage (a *valiant* person is one who exhibits *valor*).

vandalism. Meaningless, criminal destruction of property.

veer. To turn in another direction; to move off one's course.

venerable. Honored and respected because of age, position, or reputation.

vicissitudes (vi-siss'-i-toods). Unexpected shifts and changes in one's life; commonly used to mean hardships (the *vicissitudes* of widowhood).

vivid. Bright; strongly experienced; distinct; described in a lifelike manner.

wane. To decline, come to an end, decrease.

wary. Watchful; cautious; on one's guard.

wistful. Vaguely, or sadly, wishful.

word processing. Producing reports, books, and other documents via the use of computers.

wrest. To forcefully pull or grab an object from another person.

For further reference

American language

Boatner, Maxine T. and Gates, J. E.
A Dictionary of American Idioms
Barron's. Four thousand commonly used expressions, including slang, proverbs, and clichés. For each entry, definitions and examples of use in sentences.

Mathews, Mitford M.
Americanisms
Phoenix. A dictionary of words that first came into use in the United States. Includes the earliest recorded use of each word.

Mencken, H. L.
The American Language
(one-volume abridged edition)
Knopf. The enduring classic study of our language: how it evolved and how it is used today. Still as fascinating as when written more than 60 years ago.

Vocabulary building

Davidson, Jessica
How to Improve Your Spelling and Vocabulary
Franklin Watts. Rules, tips, procedures, exercises, and games for students and young adults.

Evans, Bergen
Comfortable Words
Random House. Witty, brief analyses of the origins and accurate meanings of commonly used words and phrases.

Specialized interests

Barnhart, Clarence L., Steinmetz, Sol, and Barnhart, R.
The Second Barnhart Dictionary of New English
Harper & Row. Definitions of new words that appeared in print during the years 1973 to 1979.

Bernstein, Theodore M.
Reverse Dictionary
Quadrangle. Meanings are arranged alphabetically; the word that is defined follows its meaning (for example: "Rope or cable for mooring or towing: HAWSER").

Partridge, Eric
Origins
Macmillan. An etymological dictionary, providing information about the evolution of 12,000 commonly used words.

Pei, Mario
Language of the Specialists
Funk & Wagnalls. Specialists in 20 categories—astronomy, literature, and medicine are typical—each select and define a hundred or more terms.

Webster's New Dictionary of Synonyms
G. & C. Merriam Company. Helpful for finding the right word with precisely the meaning you require.

Games and puzzles

Brandreth, Gyles
The World's Best Indoor Games
Pantheon. Complete rules and explanations for dozens of word games from "Ghosts" to "Guggenheim."

Hill, Norman
How to Solve Crossword Puzzles
Funk & Wagnalls.

Kurzban, Stan and Rosen, Mel
The Compleat Cruciverbalist
Van Nostrand Reinhold. Subtitled "How to solve and compose crossword puzzles for fun and profit." (*Cruciverbalist* is a made-up word meaning "crossword.")

Improving Your Speech

It is said that man is instinctively afraid of only two things: falling and speaking in public. Just a clever remark, you may think, and not one that applies to you. But think a moment longer. Do any of the following cause you anxiety?
- Making an important phone call.
- Being introduced to an important person.
- Trying to convince someone.

Many people are uneasy in such everyday situations, and they betray their anxiety by the way they speak. On the phone, an anxious person may stumble or mumble, and the other party may quickly stop listening. Meeting an influential stranger, an anxious person may launch into a self-promoting one-way conversation—and forget to introduce himself. During a good-natured exchange involving a difference of opinion, an anxious person may undermine his argument by unintentionally bullying or ridiculing his opponent.

What do these situations have to do with public speaking? Most phone calls, many two-way discussions, and all introductions take place between you and a stranger, between you and your "public." Whatever you say is going to leave an indelible first impression; how you speak to a stranger is as memorable to him as your face. For this reason, your private conversation may need improvement before you are ready to go public.

Broadly interpreted, public speaking is the art of communicating effectively. It is a learned skill, always starting at the level of one-to-one communication. By understanding the way people exchange information verbally and symbolically, you can learn to improve the way you speak—to friends, co-workers, and even strangers.

Formal speechmaking is, of course, the highest form of public speaking. But there are virtually no natural public speakers, born to the podium. The great spellbinders in history—politicians, preachers, and actors—were polished and well-rehearsed performers who knew precisely what they were doing. All of them practiced hundreds of times before hundreds of audiences. In fact, every great speaker is likely to remember at least one time when he was terrified: his first time.

Until the basics of speaking are mastered, the best-written speech on Earth will not be truly heard. On the next pages you will find the five keys to effective speech:

1. Pronunciation; 2. Pace; 3. Attention; 4. Eye contact; and 5. Pauses.

Take each key in order, then apply it to your own mannerisms. (Here as elsewhere in this chapter, access to a tape recorder will be highly useful.) The five keys might be called the tools of your private communications trade; all of them together, in order and ready to use, make up your public speaking tool kit. Each of the five is essential if you expect to be a fully effective speaker.

The five keys

Pronunciation. Beginning now, imagine that everything you say is for someone else's consumption. First, ask yourself if you are usually understood when you talk to anyone outside of your immediate family (families sometimes speak in code). Do you make an effort to enunciate each word? Or do you run the words together as if in a hurry to get the sentence over with? Among friends, face to face, you may get by with careless pronunciation. But do you notice any problem in being understood by people who do not know you? By older people? By people with different regional accents?

Your own regional accent or dialect need not concern you; it is part of your personality and may well be part of your charm. Three of the last six U.S. Presidents had pronounced regional accents, and they made no attempt to change them.

Many English words sound similar, but the slightest adjustment between tongue and lips can make the difference between one sound (or word) and another—between *far* and *fire*, for example. One self-test for pronunciation addresses itself to words beginning with *d, t,* and *th.* Try saying *din, tin, thin,* and *then.* Can you hear the difference clearly? If you cannot, perhaps a friend can. Ask other friends if they have any trouble understanding the way you pronounce words. When you read or hear a difficult word or name, write it down and practice saying it. Soon you will develop a highly desirable pronunciation habit: *wanting* to say things right.

Reading from a prepared text, you will have the time to look up the pronunciation of any word about which you feel uncertain—and the time will be well spent. Proper names, too, can be found phonetically notated in large dictionaries. A correctly pronounced proper name or place is always well received by an audience. A mispronounced name is, at best, unnecessary; at worst, it is insulting. Most common mispronunciations arise through constant misuse.

For best results with the following list, cover up the *wrong* and *right* columns and read the words aloud, using a tape recorder if possible. Some of the words on the list are routinely mispronounced by some of the most prominent people in the United States. But no matter who says *new-*cue-ler at a press conference, it is wrong.

Test your pronunciation

	Wrong	*Right*
accidentally	ak-si-*dent*-ly	ak-si-*den*-tal-ly
across	a-*krost*	a-*kross*
anyway	*en*-ee-wayz	*en*-ee-way
anywhere	*en*-ee-wayrze	*en*-ee-ware
asked	axed	asked
burst	bust	burst
drowned	drown-did	drownd
escape	ek-*scape*	es-*cape*
film	*fill*-um	film
government	*guv*-mint	*guh*-vern-ment
heartrending	*hart*-ren-der-ing	*hart*-ren-ding
height	*hite*-th	hite
hold	a-hold	hold
hundred	*hun*-nert	*hun*-drid
incidentally	in-si-*dent*-ly	in-si-*den*-tal-ly
interesting	*in*-nur-es-ting	*in*-tur-es-ting
judgment	*judg*-uh-ment	*judg*-ment
nowhere	*no*-wayrze	*no*-ware
nuclear	*new*-cue-ler	*new*-clee-ur
often	*off*-ten	*off*-en
police	*poh*-leece	poh-*leece*
recur	re-o-*cur*	re-*cur*
regardless	ir-ri-*gard*-liss	ri-*gard*-liss
scared	uh-*scared*	scared
toward	tuh-*ward*	tawrd
unaware	un-uh-*wayrze*	un-uh-*ware*
undoubtedly	un-*dow*-tuh-blee	un-*dow*-tid-lee

Pace. The initial requirement for effective speech is intelligibility. If you are not understood, your thoughts are not conveyed, and if you are to be understood, then you must speak at a pace that enables your listeners to get your message. Rapid-fire speech may be acceptable for comic effect, but it is unacceptable for the purpose of communication.

Most Americans harbor the prejudice that people who speak a foreign language talk too fast. Whatever is unfamiliar, in your own language or another, nearly always seems to be spoken too fast.

Perhaps you have been told that you speak too fast, or too slowly; or perhaps you suspect that your conversational speed is not quite right for public speaking. To test your speaking rate, choose a page from a favorite book and read it aloud, at your normal speed, for three minutes. Then count the number of words you have just read. Fewer than 400 is considered too slow; 450 is the comfortable spoken average; and 500 words or more is too fast.

Most people find after taking this test that they read faster than they thought. Reading aloud takes longer, of course, than normal conversation; your own words are spoken more easily than someone else's. As a starting point, assume that you should try to speak slower in public than in private.

An aid to slower speaking is louder speaking. Trying to talk louder will cause you to slow your pace. Think for a moment about how people respond to fast, soft speech. In a classroom, for example, a student who rattles off an answer in a whispery voice will neither be heard nor understood—even if his answer is correct. The student who speaks deliberately and clearly makes a better impression—even if his facts are not quite right. In terms of public speaking, slower and louder are usually better.

To be sure, you cannot learn effective speaking pace from a book. There are far too many variables in a speech: points of emphasis, pauses for effect, audience responses and interruptions, and catches of breath. Some novices are fearful that they will not have enough to say, or that what they *do* have to say will take up no more than five minutes. (They are often surprised to discover, once they have finished, that they have held forth for ten, even fifteen minutes.) Others are fearful that they will not cover all their points in the time allotted, and speak at a disconcertingly fast pace.

You will find that just a few prepared remarks, or notes for reference, can go a long way in your actual presentation. It is better to have a few well-chosen things to say, and to say them slowly and with conviction, than to overstay your welcome. Remember, once you get started, time goes by much faster for the speaker than for the audience.

For the present, try to get to know the sound of your own voice. Use a tape recorder if possible. Listen to your normal talking speed. Ask yourself if the pace seems unhurried, or slightly frantic. Practice will enable you to speak at a rate that is comfortable for you.

Attention. When speaking to others, your task is to get them to pay attention to *you.* Presumably, standing in front of an audience will give you their attention to begin with. Now you must keep it.

First you must cope with the fear of speaking in public. The best defense against stage fright is an offense. In public speaking, offense usually means loudness. Assuming that you will not use a microphone, you will need to speak louder in performance than you ever did in practice. Most speakers find the process helpful; by concentrating on talking louder than usual, you become less preoccupied with your fear of talking in the first place. Loudness, in its best sense, becomes outspokenness; outspokenness quickly breeds confidence.

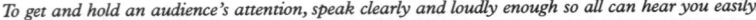

To get and hold an audience's attention, speak clearly and loudly enough so all can hear you easily.

Improving Your Speech

Overcoming problems. The most common failing of inexperienced speakers is mumbling—talking too low, not saying things clearly, and sounding apologetic. Consider the way mumblers look when they talk: slouched shoulders, shuffling feet, downward head, eyes darting in every direction except that of the audience. This type of body language will undermine the effectiveness of any spoken language that accompanies it. Clearly the mumbler has no confidence in what he is saying; that message is plain to anyone who sees or hears him. The speaker who mumbles gets sympathy, not attention.

Attention is gotten by a speaker who talks loudly, who stands up straight and leans slightly forward, and who looks as though he believes what he is saying. A loud and forceful delivery also requires more time and energy, thus slowing you down. The extra effort makes you pay more attention to each word, improving your enunciation. If you are too loud, your audience will signal you quickly by the expressions on their faces. It is far easier to tone down your voice than to raise it.

Before you speak in front of an audience, consider how effective you are—or are not—at holding attention when you speak. Among friends, for instance, do you find it difficult to make yourself heard? Are you accused of making short stories long? Do you have trouble remembering the punch line of a joke or the windup of a story? These are common shortcomings of inexperienced speakers; all are overcome through practice and preparation. When you are thoroughly familiar with what you want to say and how you are going to say it, you will stop worrying about making mistakes. You will speak up. An audience will feel your confidence. You will get—and hold—their attention.

Speech improvement tools. A tape recorder is an invaluable tool for getting to know your best voice level. Most people are surprised and dismayed when they hear themselves for the first time on tape. Both the tone and the volume of your voice sound like someone else's. "I hate the way I sound" is a common reaction. But take heart: the very playback that has dismayed you can help you make truly dramatic improvements. Listen to yourself again and again. Then rerecord your voice, making any adjustments in loudness that seem indicated. You may, for example, find that too many words are being emphasized with volume, creating a strident effect, such as the effect a writer creates who constantly uses italics. Whatever the problem, with loudness or any other aspect of your delivery, a few sessions with a tape recorder can be very revealing.

Another useful aid to self-improvement is the radio. Nearly all radio announcers are chosen for their quality of voice: tone, precise enunciation, and smoothness of delivery. It took years of practice for them to achieve a level of consistency and professionalism that sounds effortless and natural to the listener. Parrot the words of a newscaster as he reads his copy, using his pauses to supply your own version a split second after his. Compare your sound with the newscaster's. Make adjustments and repeat the process. If you do this exercise often enough, improvement will take place on a subconscious as well as a conscious level.

Going a step further, try this experiment. Turn on a baseball game, a football game, or a tennis match, and turn off the sound on the TV. "Broadcast" the whole game, using a tape recorder. Most top sportscasters have used just such radio/TV exercises to learn their trade. They also started out just like you: unsure of themselves (and their voices) and quite anxious about speaking in public. They conquered their uncertainty and anxiety, and so can you.

How your voice comes across

Many people make value judgments based on the way your voice comes across to them. Using a tape of your normal, conversational speaking voice, monitor yourself for the following:

- **Crispness.** If you slur your words, even unintentionally, your listener is likely to think you are in no condition to talk.

- **Rapidity.** Talking too fast in a conversation gives the listener—particularly a stranger—the idea that he or she will be given no chance to speak at all.

- **Harshness.** A listener or an audience will be put off by harsh, strident tones, which are the verbal equivalent of shaking someone by the arm.

- **Rising inflection.** The habit of ending phrases and sentences on an upward note makes declarations sound like questions. Listeners will question your self-assurance.

- **Falling inflection.** Phrases or sentences that trail off make you sound as if you changed your mind (or lost your conviction) in mid-sentence.

- **Shrillness.** Speaking at too high and sharp a pitch will alienate most listeners. It comes across as over-emotionalism, immaturity, or poor argument.

- **Tenseness.** A slight amount of tension showing up in the voice of a public speaker is quite common and need not concern you. The best cure for a noticeably tense voice, which makes a speaker sound nervous, is practice.

- **Whispering.** Low, "sexy," or whispery tones should be avoided. A whispery voice is hard to hear, and will keep listeners from taking you seriously.

How to get attention and control of an audience

We all admire speakers who can hold an audience from the time they begin to speak until the moment they finish. No one is born with this talent; experience and the following good practices can build it.

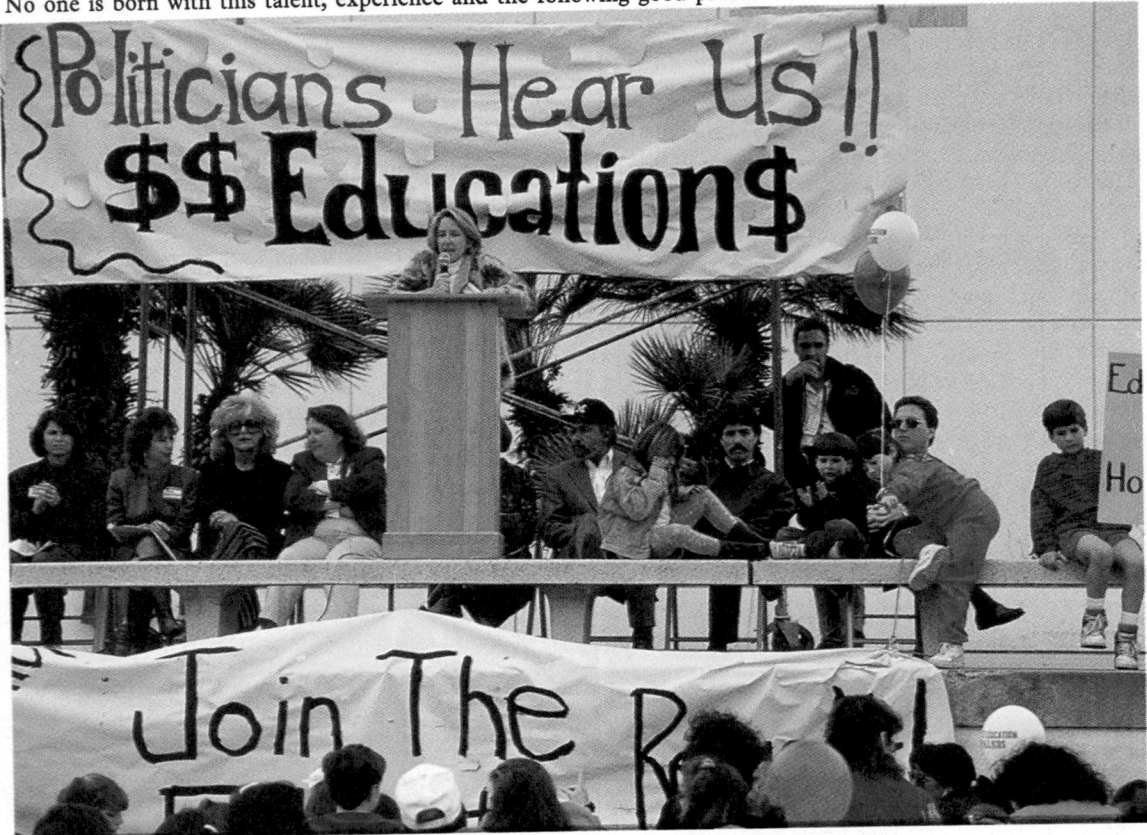

1. Find out how many people will be in your audience. (You can speak less formally in front of a small group.)

2. Determine how many are friends and how many are strangers. (Strangers warrant a different approach than friends.)

3. Decide on what sort of message the audience is likely to appreciate. (Never offend the audience's self-interest.)

4. Keep your ideas and remarks to the intellectual level of the audience.

5. Learn the age level of the audience. (Young people may be unfamiliar with historical references.)

6. Learn how many men and how many women will be in attendance. (Avoid language and examples that are sex-biased.)

7. Find out, approximately, the racial and ethnic composition of the audience. (Giving offense to part of an audience usually affects the whole audience.)

8. Determine beforehand the probable reaction of your audience to your subject. (If you invite controversy, be ready to defend your position.)

9. Eliminate *all* irrelevant material. (A knowledgeable audience will be uninterested in hearing what it knows already, and not at all impressed that you know it, too.)

10. Find out beforehand how well the audience knows *you*. If not at all, take some time at the beginning to introduce yourself, personally and professionally.

Improving Your Speech

Tips for using a microphone

A microphone can frighten even an experienced speaker who has never used one. These tips will help:

- Remember that the microphone will make it possible for your normal speaking voice to be heard easily by everyone in the room—even a large room. Think of it as a friend.

- If possible, arrive early when you know you will be using a microphone. This will give you time to make sure it is in working order and to test your voice level without an audience.

- Check the height of a stationary microphone before you say anything. If it is uncomfortably high or low, you can adjust the height.

- When you reach the podium, stand at a comfortable speaking distance from the microphone and ask, "Can you hear me?" If your voice is underamplified, the audience will let you know. If it is overamplified, *you* will know. Someone in charge will adjust the mike, or you can take care of the problem yourself by taking a step or two backward or forward.

- Do not lean forward over the microphone. It will be able to pick up your voice from a close but comfortable distance without your bending over.

- Do not touch a stationary microphone, or the head of a hand-held microphone. Your lightest touch can produce a resounding thump or piercing whine.

- If you are given a hand-held microphone, hold it about 6 inches from your mouth and ask, "Can you hear me?" Make any adjustments necessary, moving the mike farther away from or closer to your mouth.

- Stay put behind a podium with a microphone. If you move, you will be moving away from the mike, and you will no longer be heard at the same voice level.

Eye contact. If you use your voice to get attention, you use your eyes to hold attention. People tend to believe you, trust you, and listen to what you say if you are looking at them. "Shifty-eyed" and "cross-eyed" are not negative adjectives by chance. Direct eye contact is not just preferable; it is essential to effective private conversations and public addresses.

As a tool for public speaking, your eyes are second only to your voice. While you are speaking, you judge your audience to determine how they are reacting to your words. Their eyes, mirrored by the expressions on their faces, tell the story. Even at a distance you can gauge whether your listeners are attentive.

Never forget for a moment that your listeners watch your eyes just as intently. How you look at them will determine to a great extent how faithfully they will listen to you. If your eyes never stray from your prepared text, never acknowledge the presence of your live audience, then you might as well hand out copies of your speech instead of delivering it. Without eye contact, you seem to dismiss your audience. Why should they listen if you do not seem to care whether or not you are heard? But when you take pains to establish eye contact with your listeners, they know you mean what you say.

There are three basic ways to use eye contact to your advantage:

Look your listener straight in the eye. Looking someone in the eye while you speak has a similar effect to that of shining your car headlights on a deer: he is transfixed, your captive audience so long as you maintain the beam. The eyes are the meaningful target—

Making eye contact puts the person to whom you are speaking at ease and adds force and conviction to your words.

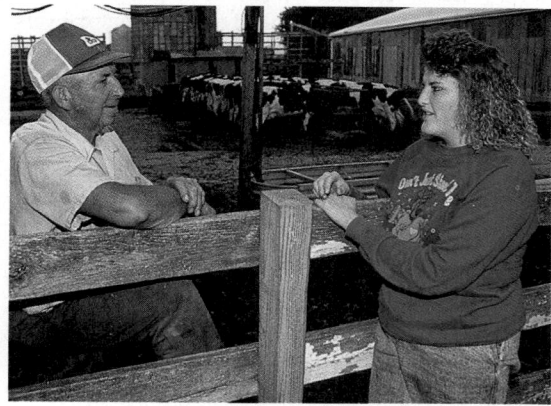

foreheads, lips, and chins are not good enough—and the other person's eyes can tell the difference. Direct eye contact assures your listener that you are sincere, that you care about what you are saying. Direct eye contact enables direct communication to take place.

For contrast, imagine the consequences of these examples of indirect eye contact:

- At a party, you follow the progress of other guests with your eyes while you chat with a friend.
- Standing with a shorter friend, you direct your remarks to the top of his head.
- Making a deal with a business acquaintance, you shake on it—while staring at his shoes.

Look the whole audience straight in the eye. Maintaining eye contact is a simple enough matter when you are face to face with one other person. But what if you are addressing two people? Ten people? Scores of people in a large room?

The answer lies in the target method. For each sentence you speak, zero in on the eyes of a different (target) member of the audience. Use an orderly right-left-center pattern, fixing your gaze on one particular man or woman for each phrase or sentence. The method may sound simplistic, but professional speakers adhere to it with excellent results. The whole audience feels included, cared for, spoken to. Targeting takes some effort to master, but it is worth the effort. **Let your eyes talk for you.** Your eyes are the best indicator of your emotions. If you talk about courage and perseverance while your eyes show fear and indecision, your listeners will probably stop listening, and will certainly stop believing you.

Pauses.
Everyone pauses from time to time in the course of giving a talk. There are good pauses, for an intended effect, and there are bad ones. The bad ones leave you sounding unprepared. There are constructive ways to fill speaking space. First, however, learn to avoid the destructive ways.

An almost universal space filler is hemming and hawing: the all-purpose *uh* and its cousin *um*. These syllables find their way into nearly every phone conversation, where they are simply an irritant if noticed at all by either party. But they can destroy the effectiveness of anyone speaking in public.

Listen again to yourself speaking (not reading) on tape. Just as you may not have realized that you talk too fast, you may be surprised at how many ums and uhs show up in your speech. You do not hear yourself using them, and it is unlikely that anyone else will point them out. Fortunately, the habit is easily broken.

The best cure for such space fillers is the simplest: breathing space. If you find yourself bogging down in mid-sentence, just stop. Pause for a few seconds and collect your thoughts. Once you resume your sentence,

it is likely to end up better than it started out. It will certainly *sound* better, uncluttered by uhs or ums—which tend to make your audience forget what preceded them. Best of all, mid-sentence pauses lend any speaker an aura of thoughtfulness, gravity, and maturity that a space-filling hem or haw cannot match. So take your time. You, the speaker, have the floor.

A particularly irksome space filler is "y'know?" It is not even logical. If your audience already knows, there is no point in telling them. If *you* already know, then "y'know?" cues the audience that you lack the verbal equipment to say what you know. In either case, "y'know?" has no place in good speaking. It may not bother you, and it may not bother your friends, but the average audience reacts to this space filler very poorly indeed. Avoid it.

Grammar counts too. Proper grammar is an essential part of correct speech, particularly since an audience is likely to judge you as much on how you say things as on what you say. The following list consists of common errors in American diction. Do any of them apply to you?

25 words and phrases to watch for

Incorrect	Correct
a criteria	a criterion
a phenomena	a phenomenon
Can I go now?	May I go now? (if asking permission)
finalize	complete; finish up
for free	free; for nothing
hardly nothing	hardly anything; almost nothing
hisself	himself
I ain't; it ain't	I am not; it is not
I been	I have been
I can't help but feel	I can't help feeling
I can't hardly	I cannot; I can hardly
I done	I did; I have done
it don't	it does not
off of	off
out loud	aloud
over with	over; finished; done with
quote (as noun)	quotation
reason is because	reason is
snuck	sneaked
supposing I am	suppose I am
theirselves	themselves
the media	the press; a medium
this here	this
this point in time	now; then
thusly	thus

Help yourself

Pronunciation, pace, attention, eye contact, pauses; each of the five keys is an integral part of successful speechmaking; none can be overlooked. To check your progress, try these three self-help exercises:

- Talk to yourself in front of a mirror, with strict emphasis on making eye contact.

- Tape-record yourself—reading from a text and talking extemporaneously—to check your pronunciation, pace, and voice level.

- Listen carefully to the tape playbacks to see how poised you are during pauses.

Tape recorder checklist

You are your own worst judge of your own voice. You simply do not hear yourself accurately. Your ears are misplaced for the purpose, and you need an outside, objective opinion. A tape recorder is the obvious solution, and it makes no judgments at all.

With a tape recorder, you have plenty of time to make adjustments and refinements. Start simply. Talk conversationally into the machine, merely recounting what is on your mind or what you might like to say to somebody else if he were present. Sessions like these teach you what your "normal" voice level is.

As you get more comfortable with self-recording, you can record emotional flare-ups, perhaps, or tiny tantrums. With diligence and patience, you can learn from your tapes just how you sound to everyone else at your best and your worst. Then you can begin to change what you do not like. Remember, this vocal self-improvement is a strictly private matter, between you and your machine.

Here are some tape-playback questions to ask yourself:

1. Do you pronounce each word clearly?
2. Does any of the pronunciation sound uncertain?
3. Do you sometimes run two or more words together?
4. Do you talk too fast to be understood easily?
5. Do you sound tired or bored?
6. Do you speak loudly enough for each word to be heard clearly?
7. Does your speech sound too soft to reach a large audience?
8. Do you sound timid or uncertain?
9. Do you sound angry or belligerent?
10. Is your tone monotonous?
11. Within sentences, do you emphasize certain words?
12. Do you put emphasis on the wrong words?
13. Do you start sentences with the word "well"?
14. Does "y'know?" creep into your speech?
15. Do you handle pauses silently, without hemming or hawing?
16. Are there any grammatical mistakes? Incorrect words?
17. Is your speech marred by slang or profanity?
18. If you were in the audience, would you trust this speaker?
19. Do you sound as if you mean what you are saying?
20. Could you say what you have said on tape to an audience?
21. Do you sound better now than you did when you began taping?

Usually, it is best to listen for one or two speech habits at a time. If you prefer, listen to the tape several times in a row, making notes about whatever you observe. Make adjustments and rerecord. In a surprisingly short time, your answer to Number 21 will be "yes."

Correct speech

Speaking correctly means using the English language correctly. That, necessarily, means paying attention to grammar and word usage. You may have a great deal to say, but if you do not say it right—according to the rules—your listeners will not take you seriously. Sloppy grammar and mispronunciation often go together; the speaker who uses words incorrectly will often mispronounce them as well.

Your basic diction—the way you use and apply words—is probably well grounded as the result of reading, writing, and hearing others talk. But you may be unaware of some common misuses and misapplications of everyday speech. Check your own diction against the following examples. Some of these words are used mistakenly all the time in informal speech.

You may wonder why you should be so careful about your diction. Your friends understand you anyway, and you want to sound like your normal self when you speak in public. But your friends have learned to read between the lines of what you say; you do the same thing when you listen to them. Sometimes, among friends and spouses, almost no words are needed.

This is not so in public speaking. In public, among strangers, the rules of grammar and correct speech are universal. A public speaker wants and needs to be understood the first time—which may be his only time. By learning and using proper diction, you increase your chances of expressing yourself clearly, whoever your audience. However unsophisticated an audience may be, it will understand and respect good diction.

Words commonly confused

affect, effect. *Affect* is a verb meaning to influence. *Effect,* though it can be a verb, usually is a noun meaning result.

compare, contrast. Use *compare* for pointing out similarities *and* differences between things. Use *contrast* only to show differences.

compare to, compare with. Use *compare to* when drawing a comparison between two things that are not really similar: "*Compared to* a glacier, you move quickly." Use *compare with* when drawing a comparison between two things that are similar: "*Compared with* her, you are a fast runner."

each. In formal prose and speech, treat each as meaning *each one* (singular): "*Each* of the soldiers did *his* duty."

either. Always a singular pronoun, meaning *either one:* "*Either* of the teams *is* capable of winning."

exhausting, exhaustive. Use *exhausting* to mean using up completely, especially using up energy, that is, becoming fatigued: "*Exhausting* exercise is not recommended for me." Use *exhaustive* to mean thorough: "My physician gave me an *exhaustive* examination and declared me fit as a fiddle."

farther, further. *Farther* means measurable distance; *further* means intangible distance: "There is no point in talking any *further* if you keep moving *farther* away."

flaunt, flout. Use *flaunt* to mean display conspicuously: "She *flaunted* her new car before all of us." Use *flout* to mean treat with contempt. "Some people *flout* traffic laws."

imply, infer. *Imply* is what the speaker does; *infer* is what the listener does: "The professor *implied* that he was not through yet. I *inferred* that he had yet to conclude his lecture."

it is I, it is me. In strictly formal speech, "It is *I*" is preferred.

kind of, sort of. Use *kind of* and *kinds of* to refer to definite things and commodities. *Sort of* and *sorts of* should be saved for indefinite, imprecise types and categories: "The *kind of* speaker who says he's *kind of* sorry will not be taken seriously." (Note: never use *kind of a* or *sort of a* in formal discourse.)

lay, lie. These are among the most misused verbs in the language. *Lay (laid, lain)* is a transitive verb; it takes an object. *Lie (lay, lain)* is an intransitive verb; it does not take an object: "Are you tired? Why not *lay* down your suitcase." "Thanks, but I need to *lie* down for a while."

learn, teach. *Learn* is intransitive, *teach* is transitive: "I *learned* so much French in a year abroad that I ended up *teaching* it to my classmates this year."

less, few. *Less* refers to amounts measured, and *few* refers to things counted: "We have *less* gas than I thought we had, but just a *few* more miles to go."

like, as. *Like* is a preposition, used for comparisons, and *as* is a conjunction, used to link phrases: "We picked up the suspect just *as* he left the premises. We're sticking to him *like* glue."

slow, slowly. *Slow* is an adjective, *slowly* an adverb: "Can you believe it? Danny ran *slowly* again. I'm afraid he's just a *slow* runner."

Improving Your Speech

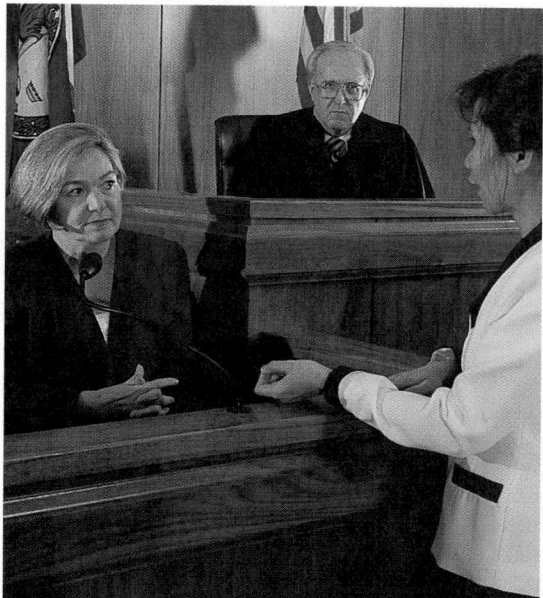

Word choice is especially important in formal or legal situations, such as when giving testimony in court. Try to use words that convey your meaning exactly, and avoid those whose definitions you do not know.

Word choice.

The best advice to inexperienced speakers is also the oldest: be yourself. Only a trained actor should stand in front of people he does not know and pretend to be Mark Twain, or Emily Dickinson, or Clarence Darrow. Most likely you will be speaking words that you wrote, so you had better use ones that you are comfortable with. Think about the way you would normally use persuasion on another person, or marshal your forces for an argument with that person. Those words are precisely the kind you should choose for a talk before a group. Only this time, your argument will be unopposed. Public speakers have that luxury.

A great deal of specialized jargon has crept into American speech, thanks to television, the press, and rock music. Public speakers who use this jargon—often in an attempt to sound "in"—usually end up sounding phony, presumptuous, or condescending.

Anyone can aspire to be a plain speaker. The chief requirements are telling the truth as you see and know it, telling it simply, and treating your audience as intellectual equals. All of these are healthy underpinnings for any public speaking appearance.

Choosing the right words is often complicated by changing times and fashions. Yesterday's "in" word or phrase is today's cliche. At the right is a list of overworked words. Many of them may remind you of others that you may have fallen into the habit of using. Get rid of them, too.

Choosing the right word

Fad words and phrases. Coming from politics, business, and the social sciences, these words sound pretentious in conversational speech. Some examples are:

bottom line, in context, time frame, viable

Pet words. Most of these words are legacies from adolescence. They say (vaguely) what you feel, but never what you think. They make *you* sound dated. A small sampling:

fabulous, cute, far out, right on, awesome

Extra words. More eloquent than *um* or *uh* (but no more meaningful), these extra words are creatures of habit. A thoughtful pause would be more eloquent than:

you know, frankly, so to speak, well

Slang words. Formal language is always acceptable, colloquial language is generally permissible, but slang usage is risky. When in doubt, use your dictionary. Misused slang sounds vulgar or tasteless.

Exaggeration. Most superlatives should be avoided; they are so overused that they have lost their meaning. Personalize your feelings and value judgments with, I think . . . , In my opinion . . . , etc. Meaningless superlatives include:

great, fantastic, terrific, incredible, the most

Pejorative words. Racial slurs and epithets—you know them all. Avoid them.

Adding -wise. Adding *-wise* to nouns is as unnecessary as it is ill-advised. Try the constructions *as to* or *speaking of*.

Profanity. Despite what you see in current movies, read in novels, and hear from comedians, profanity still has no place at all in formal speech or polite society. Swearing is generally offensive to people who know better ways to express themselves.

Overworked words to avoid

alienated	operative
articulate *(as a verb)*	oppressed
awesome	overreact
concept	paranoid
credibility	posture *(for attitude)*
depersonalization	prioritize
dynamic	rhetoric
elegant	ripoff
enrichment	scenario
holistic	structure *(as a verb)*
involved	substantive
manic	superlative
obscene	veritable

Clichés to avoid

When you say . . .	Do you mean?	When you say . . .	Do you mean?
advance planning	planning	game plan	strategy
as far as	as for; as to	guesstimate	rough guess
as you know	as you may know; let me remind you	head tripping	thinking
		impact (as a verb)	affect
at this/that point in time	now or then	in my opinion	I think
beautiful	good, kind, cooperative	in point of fact	in fact
be that as it may	nonetheless; but	insightful	perceptive
bleep out	censor	learning experience	experience
by the same token	also	love	like; approve; admire
charisma	appeal	meaningful dialogue	discussion
confrontation	meeting	meaningful experience	experience
consciousness-raising	educational	more unique	singular
consensus of opinion	consensus; agreement	my personal opinion	my opinion
curiously enough	curiously	needless to say	obviously
dialogue	conversation; meeting	out of sight	impressive
disadvantaged	poor	out of this world	impressive
due to the fact	because	personal friend	friend
encounter	meet	presently	now
escalate	rise; raise	prior to	before
expertise	knowledge; skill	relationship	friendship; acquaintance
fabulous/ fantastic/ far out	good; excellent; acceptable	underprivileged	poor
		valid	true; genuine
for free	free	validate	confirm
frame of reference	background	with reference to	as to; about

Body language

Your eyes are the most obvious indicator of your attitudes and emotions, but your facial expressions, posture, and gestures—singly or together—can just as surely cue an attentive observer to your state of mind. Your most eloquent words cannot dispel the mistrust that is invited by negative body language.

Just as you can train your eyes to make contact with a single listener as well as an entire audience, you can learn to control the attentiveness of the rest of your body—if you become aware of your body language.

Facial expression. Variety is important. If you smile all the time, you may be considered insincere, perhaps even frivolous. By contrast, an unvarying solemn expression may be interpreted as insensitive, even dangerous. Look at photographs of yourself. Are you characteristically gloomy, grinning, frowning, close-mouthed? Are you noticeably out of step with the occasion? An appropriate variety of facial expressions will encourage an audience to trust you.

Posture. Sitting or standing, you want to look poised. Whether you are sitting behind a table or not, sit up straight. If you are on your feet, do not stand at military attention; it is clearly uncomfortable for most speakers. At the same time, slouching is uncomfortable for most audiences—it signals the speaker's lack of interest or his disrespect. Try to find an intermediate posture, with both feet balanced on the floor, in which you lean slightly *toward* your audience. That alone will focus the audience's attention on your eyes and mouth, which is where you want it.

Gestures. The best advice for novice speakers is to do nothing with your hands—rest them on the podium or clasp them behind your back. Do not fold your arms across your chest; that means, in body language, that you are challenging the audience. Hand gestures to emphasize your words can be highly effective, but they must be learned, usually in performance and often in response to the mood of the moment. Furthermore, hand language must be nearly perfectly synchronized to your spoken words or it will look foolish. Practice before a mirror may be helpful here, but audience feedback—time and time again—is the only sure test.

Improving Your Speech

Body language checklist

Here are some suggestions about silent communication for public and nonpublic speaking occasions:

1. Hands held in a relaxed and nonintrusive manner help put a listener at ease.
2. Arms folded across the chest indicate you do not accept what others are saying; open hands extended indicate frustration at not getting your point across.
3. Relaxed posture tells others that you are comfortable with them and with what you are talking about.
4. A stiff stance and hands held together express unease.
5. Upright posture and a pleasant facial expression express self-confidence.
6. Physical contact, such as a pat on the shoulder, expresses friendship, agreement, or concern.

1.

2.

3.

4.

5.

6.

Personal appearance.

A speaker needs more than voice plus message to make a good impression. There are silent factors, too, that contribute to your listeners' acceptance or rejection of what you have to say. Your good looks or lack of them are *not* a factor, but your clothes and grooming definitely are. Before you speak a word, they show your opinion of yourself and affect other people's opinion of you—for good or ill.

Department store salespeople know this well. They do significantly more business when they dress up fully for work, even if the weather is hot and the air conditioning inadequate. Customers, they find, are reluctant to buy from salesmen in shirtsleeves or saleswomen in pants. Experienced job seekers know this, too. Applicants who show up for an interview in business clothes increase their chances of being hired, even for blue collar jobs.

For public speaking or for important personal engagements, the rules are the same: Dress to show yourself to best advantage. For men, this usually means a pressed suit, shined shoes, a tasteful tie, and a freshly pressed shirt with an unfrayed collar. Good grooming is important, too. The absence of a shave will reflect poorly on any speaker, as will unruly hair or a long-overdue haircut.

Women speakers should take care to avoid being too elaborately dressed, coiffed, or made up. A simple, becoming dress or suit, neatly styled hair, and carefully applied tasteful makeup will increase the speaker's confidence and prevent her audience from being distracted by her appearance. As for accessories, leave attention-drawing jewelry, scarves, etc., at home, and make sure that the shoes you choose are shined or cleaned and not run down at the heels.

If you know the audience you will be addressing, then you can predict with reasonable accuracy how they will be dressed and then dress yourself accordingly. You probably own at least one outfit that you know looks good on you. Wear it. You will feel most comfortable in the clothes you like best—which, with very few exceptions, are your best choice for a speaking engagement.

You want to look like your best self, not like someone else. After all, *you* are the one who has been invited to speak. If you pay careful attention to clothes and grooming, you will increase the audience's confidence in you right along with your confidence in yourself.

The form of dress chosen by a public speaker is determined in part by the image the speaker wishes to present to the audience. During the 1996 Republican Presidential primary, Lamar Alexander of Tennessee presented himself at less formal campaign events as a man of the people by wearing a flannel shirt (left), and at more formal events as a polished, competent political leader by wearing a well-tailored dark blue suit (right).

Improving Your Speech

Preparing to speak

Know your audience. For example, the manner in which you would address a group of graduates (left) is quite different from the way in which you would address a political convention (right).

Why do people make speeches? There are three reasons for speechmaking that will probably never change: the speaker has something special to say; he believes he has an audience receptive to his ideas; and he is confident he can make his case in the allotted time and place. With those reasons in mind, here is a speaker's three-part blueprint for a talk:

1. A receptive audience.
2. A central idea.
3. A beginning, middle, and end.

Unless all three of these fundamentals are present, a speaker probably cannot deliver a successful speech. Why?

—Without a receptive audience, one's points cannot be made.

—Without a central idea, a speech is pointless.

—Without a beginning-to-end structure, very few in the audience will get the point.

These basics of public speaking have not been improved upon in the 2400 years since Aristotle explained them in his great book, *Rhetoric*. Every successful speech, from a three-minute talk to a thirty-minute oration, will adhere to the time-tested formula that states, before you say anything, know your audience and organize your thoughts.

A receptive audience.
Who will be in the audience? In most cases, you will know your listeners or at least be known to them (fellow students, townspeople, club or union members, kindred political spirits, etc.). If this is not the case, find out who will be there, or check with someone likely to know. If you find that your listeners will be older or younger than you expected, better educated or less well informed, all male or all female, then tailor your remarks accordingly. A clear idea of who your audience will be gives you the best possible chance of getting through to them in your speech.

A central idea.
Ask yourself why you are motivated to speak in the first place. What is your point? A central idea is easier to arrive at than you might think. The problem is to distill it, to break it down to *one or two sentences* at the most. That brevity is what will make your central idea memorable. Whenever you can make your point memorably, you know you have succeeded.

A beginning, middle, and end.
Briefly, the *beginning* of your talk should do two things: get your listeners' attention and introduce your central idea. The *middle* portion (the longest by far) will support your central idea and expand on it, with examples or evidence, in some depth. The *end* will restate the central idea, summing up with supporting evidence. Ideally, you will come up with a quotable line, perhaps the central idea itself, that members of the audience can take home with them.

When composing your talk, *begin in the middle.* The bulk of your research and the meat of your argument will be found in the middle portion. No doubt your best ideas will stem from there, too. Try to hold off on composing the beginning of your speech—setting forth your central idea—until you have explored the fertile territory in the middle ground.

Because so many professional speakers do it, you may be tempted to begin or end your talk with a humorous anecdote, a topical or local joke. Resist the temptation. The pros know how to get laughs because they do it all the time. A novice speaker should not risk

Improving Your Speech

FORGET the jokes.
FORGET the big fancy words.

not getting a laugh, which can undermine the effectiveness of a speech at the very beginning.

If you stick to the three basics and honor the beginning–middle–end framework, you will not embarrass yourself—even if you are a first-time speaker. The rest of your preparation will consist of researching your subject matter, writing out your speech (one draft is not enough), and reading it aloud.

The best written speech does not always translate from the page to the podium, just as certain great novels do not read well aloud. Plan to read your text aloud before giving it the final touches. You are likely to make minor alterations that will significantly improve the way your speech "plays."

As in most things, skill is achieved through experience. The first time is the worst by far. Because novice speakers are so apprehensive, they tend to remember, vividly, all their mistakes. Knowing those mistakes, they usually do not repeat them. Members of such organizations as Toastmasters, or Dale Carnegie, or the self-help anonymous groups usually find, after they speak the first time, that they enjoy talking in public. It was only that first time that frightened them, like a plunge into cold water.

You will soon be ready to take that plunge.

Writing a speech. Speechwriting differs
from ordinary prose writing in one crucial respect: speeches are read aloud. Prose is meant to be read silently; it is designed solely for transfer from the printed page directly into the reader's mind. Speechwriting is consciously designed to be transferred by a speaker to a listener; the effect of the spoken word must be emotional as well as intellectual.

Even though you take great pains to write it, a good speech should sound as much like normal conversation as possible, using unadorned language that people can understand. A speech that you write should also conform to the way you normally talk—your tone of voice, choice of words, and cadence. Here is how to begin:

1. Using just one page of a yellow legal pad, outline your talk vertically under the three-part basic framework:

    appeal to audience
    central idea
    beginning–middle–end

(Allow 80 percent of the page for the last grouping, and most of that for the middle.)

2. Make short notes to "set" each of the three themes above: your informed appeal to a particular audience; a short statement of your central idea; and your beginning–middle–end structure (starting with the middle).

So far your written preparations for speaking will not have taken up more than a page. But you may already have saved hours in wasted time. You now have a clear idea of whom to convince, your intention, and how to hold your argument together.

A first draft of a speech should be written in longhand or typed quickly. Many writers need to use a typewriter or word processor because they need execution that keeps up with their thoughts. It is helpful to get your spontaneous thoughts down, before you start writing like a writer rather than a talker. Here are some time-tested ingredients of an effective speech that should be of help whatever your subject matter:

- **Beginning.** Start by thanking your host or your sponsoring organization. Then introduce your central idea.
- **Middle.** Drawing on your knowledge of the audience, compliment your listeners. If appropriate, suggest ways in which your central idea coincides with certain goals they have or values they believe in.
- **End.** Work toward what salesmen call the *close,* in which the audience becomes persuaded that your central idea, once a hypothesis, is now a given.

When you write your final draft, remember that a typewritten page takes considerably longer to read aloud than you may think. A ten-minute talk translates to five typewritten pages or less. Try to retain most of the unrehearsed scribbled or hastily typed language of your first draft: that is how you really talk. *Given a choice between a big fancy word and a short plain one, take the little one.* Keep your sentences short, too. Long sentences may be artful on paper, but they are deadly when read aloud. Last of all, *never fail to thank the audience* for their attention.

To illustrate a well-written speech, it might be useful to study one of the very best: Lincoln's Gettysburg Address.

For all its deserved fame, for all its renowned eloquence, Lincoln's address was only 280 words long and required only three minutes to deliver. As an accomplished speaker he knew intuitively the appropriate message to deliver at Gettysburg. How would Lincoln have sketched out the Gettysburg Address?

Abraham Lincoln, when he wrote out the Gettysburg Address (supposedly on the back of an envelope), came up with some phrases that will live forever in American prose. He may have memorized the whole speech; he may have read it. But what if he had restricted himself to one small index card for prompting purposes? The card on the next page shows what it might have looked like.

Lincoln's Gettysburg Address

Fourscore and seven years ago our fathers brought forth on this continent a new nation, conceived in liberty, and dedicated to the proposition that all men are created equal. Now we are engaged in a great civil war, testing whether that nation, or any nation so conceived and so dedicated, can long endure. We are met on a great battlefield of that war. We have come to dedicate a portion of that field, as a final resting place for those who here gave their lives that that nation might live. It is altogether fitting and proper that we should do this. But, in a larger sense, we cannot dedicate—we cannot consecrate—we cannot hallow—this ground. The brave men, living and dead, who struggled here, have consecrated it, far above our poor power to add or detract. The world will little note, nor long remember, what we say here, but it can never forget what they did here. It is for us the living, rather, to be dedicated here to the unfinished work which they who fought here have thus far so nobly advanced. It is rather for us to be here dedicated to the great task remaining before us—that from these honored dead we take increased devotion to that cause for which they gave the last full measure of devotion—that we here highly resolve that these dead shall not have died in vain—that this nation, under God, shall have a new birth of freedom—and that government of the people, by the people, for the people, shall not perish from the earth.

How the speech was planned

1. **Audience**—survivors and mourners of the casualties of Gettysburg. (The occasion is the consecration of the battlefield.)
2. **Central idea**—Civil war is a dreadful, wasteful undertaking, but in the course of history a noble ideal—an indissoluble union—must on occasion be tested by fire.
3. **Rhetorical structure**
   a. *Beginning*—the framers of the Constitution foresaw a nation conceived in liberty, in which all men are created equal.
   b. *Middle*—thousands of Americans, from North and South, died at Gettysburg to test the proposition that the nation can endure, at whatever price.
   c. *End*—everyone here today must now profit from the awful witness of Gettysburg: none of these soldiers shall have died in vain; a new nation shall rise from these ashes; the spirit of the Founding Fathers shall somehow transcend the tragic waste and sacrifice of this battlefield.

A card Lincoln might have used

(beginning)	Fourscore and seven years ago...
	nation conceived in liberty...
	all men equal
(middle)	world will forget us...
	but not men who died here
(end)	new birth of freedom...
	government of, by, for people shall not perish

Reading a speech. Mark Twain once said, "It usually takes me more than three weeks to prepare a good impromptu speech." He meant it, too. The best speakers, like the best actors, have to practice hard in order to appear natural.

There are three methods for speaking in public: (1) from a written text; (2) extemporaneously (from minimal notes); and (3) impromptu (from no notes at all). At first the alternatives may seem progressively less difficult. But in fact, number three is always the riskiest and often the hardest. A novice speaker should never consider "winging it" in front of a group until he is thoroughly familiar with his own voice, his own style, and his own words—written out. In order, here is how each method works:

Delivery from a written text. Written, as used here, refers to remarks or to a speech that you have written yourself. The first rule is not to read your speech at all —that is, never appear to be reading it word for word. This would necessitate your staring at your text, as if it were an unfamiliar book, and rarely coming up for air. Your audience might conclude that their presence does not matter at all. It would also appear that you have no familiarity with your own words. The only situation in which it is not a mistake to read aloud to a live audience is when broadcasting on the radio. And people who read scripts on the radio are usually professional actors or newscasters. In person you must do more than read; you must communicate.

Never forget that your listeners crave eye contact. You cannot begin to establish whole-room eye contact if your head is buried in your text most of the time. The remedy is twofold. First, practice reading your speech over and over again until the beginning of each section or paragraph is a memory cue to the rest. When you know your material well enough, type your final draft in capital letters, with extra space between words so that you can make it out easily from a distance. Next, underline the crucial first words and phrases of paragraphs and sections—or highlight them in yellow, or type them in red—so that you can be a glancer, not a reader. Glancing is a natural thing to do while speaking; reading is patronizing.

Extemporaneous delivery. When you become sufficiently adept at cuing yourself from first words and phrases, you are but a short step away from making seemingly offhand talks—with careful preparation, but no written-out text. For this method it is best to compose a single-page *master note* (see the Lincoln sample on the previous page). This will include, in digest form, the same information as an outline for a written address: appeal to audience, central idea, and beginning–middle–end linkage.

Impromptu delivery. This method is appropriate for speakers who address audiences frequently and are

---

NEVER read your entire speech.

---

very sure of themselves and their subject matter. Impromptu speaking, in fact, requires more expertise and self-confidence than many experienced speakers are likely to possess. Nonprofessionals are well advised to opt for delivery from a written text, or for extemporaneous delivery.

If proper preparation for speaking involves so much rehearsal and homework, why not simply memorize your remarks? Unless you are a trained actor, this method almost never works. At some time you may have been compelled to memorize stanzas of poetry, or lines from plays, or famous historical orations. Were you pleased with the way you sounded in recitation? Most likely, your version of those great words sounded monotonous, or painfully self-conscious, or both. An entire speech, minus an actor's intonation and dramatic embroidery, would probably sound more awkward still. The moment you memorize something, your delivery stops being spontaneous and genuine. Without spontaneity and sincerity, you cannot persuade anyone of anything.

Practicing a speech. Most of your speech preparation can be done all by yourself. One crucial part, however, will require the cooperation of another person and the use of a tape recorder, as discussed earlier.

Record a normal conversation with your cooperating friend. When you play the conversation back, note how he or she reacts to whatever you say. Pay even closer attention to your own "performance." Can you be clearly understood? Is your speaking tone monotonous, tired-sounding, markedly accented, or too excitable? Imagine yourself listening to this voice on the tape for the first time. Does the tone make you feel anxious? Bored? Angry?

Practicing for a specific talk, try to simulate difficult conditions for yourself. Turn on a portable fan or a noisy air conditioner; play a radio in the background; train a lamp or two on your face—whatever might disturb your concentration, because something probably will when you actually speak in front of an audience. As you start the tape recorder, make note of the time; however quickly you get through your trial run, your actual speech will almost surely run longer. Do not talk too loudly—only loud enough to overcome your distractions. Wherever you think an audience reaction (laughter, murmurs, applause) is likely or appropriate, pause until the floor is yours again.

Practice under noisy conditions can help you deal with distractions that occur when giving a talk.

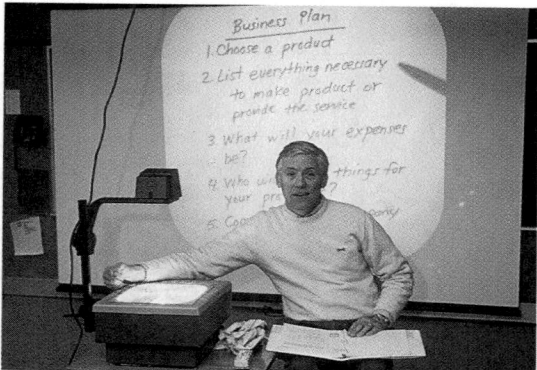

Practicing an illustrated talk before giving it can iron out difficulties with visual aids.

If you have a full-length mirror, use it to practice eye contact. Practice your most comfortable speaking stance as well—standing still or shifting slightly, weight on the balls of your feet or on one foot at a time. (Behind a solid lectern, of course, your feet will not be a problem.) If you feel you must use hand gestures, try to limit them to the few that come most naturally to you.

The whole idea here is to get thoroughly comfortable with your text, voice, pace, stance, etc. If you take the care to go through with this rehearsal as many times as seems necessary, there can be few things that will surprise or unnerve you when you are in front of an audience.

Visual aids help. Some rehearsal is essential in situations where visual aids—slides, blackboards, flip charts, etc.—are to be used. Unfamiliarity with blackboard techniques can produce the high, screeching noise that causes most people to shudder. (You might bring your own soft chalk with you.) Botched slide presentations can turn a lecture into an unintended comedy routine. (Insert the slides yourself and run through each of them beforehand.) And someone else's flip chart can too often fall over. Any of these mishaps can become the most memorable aspect of your well-intentioned presentation. But routine rehearsal and practice should forestall all of them.

Most public speakers find that they can quickly remedy their shortcomings. That worst shortcoming of all —dread of the first time out—is largely self-imposed, and all of these tips are designed to do away with it entirely. A well-organized and well-researched speech, thoroughly rehearsed, can actually inspire anticipation rather than dread. All that preparation means that you are ready, that you have every reason to be confident. Look yourself in the mirror one more time, then go out and let the audience know *you* know what you are talking about.

Everyday uses of speech

Telephone speaking. Have you ever tried to determine how much time you spend on the phone each day? The average time is one hour. You may spend more, or less, but telephone conversation is likely to be a significant part of your daily routine. It makes little sense to undermine your phone communications with discourtesy, incoherence, or impatience.

Most people jump to answer the phone when it rings. Perhaps nothing else in your daily or business life commands such instant obedience. Following such a response, it is curious that so many people answer their phone with an ill-tempered snarl. Whoever is calling will not be likely to call again soon. It is, however, remarkably simple to change your telephone etiquette, starting with the way you answer the phone. The best way is the simplest: "Hello? This is [your name]."

Common courtesy and a positive attitude, practiced and maintained, will serve you well in any conceivable at-home telephone conversation. Business calls, however, frequently require another ingredient: patience. When you place a business call, be organized. Know precisely whom you want to reach (or his or her department or assistant), and state that intention.

Telephone pointers

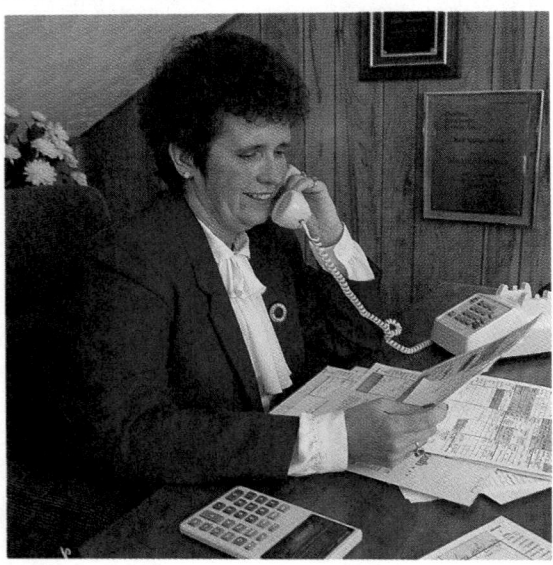

- **Voice.** Unless someone happens to tell you, you may have no idea of how you sound on the phone—too loud perhaps, or too soft, or too fast. Find out. Ask a friend about it or record yourself on tape.

- **Attitude.** When a nervous, inexperienced salesman or fund-raiser calls you, you can tell almost instantly what the call is about. To counteract a bad first impression, try to start every phone conversation as if you really care, as if this call is just the one you were expecting. If it is not, it will not take long to end the conversation.

- **Courtesy.** Before you dial, ask yourself a few questions. Is this an inconvenient time? Is the other person likely to be too busy to talk? Should you call back later? Most of these questions can be answered early in your conversation, before inconsideration sets in. If you reach an answering machine, either hang up or leave a short, straightforward message.

If your quarry is "in conference," it means he or she cannot or will not talk to you now. No matter. Leave your number and call back an hour later if your call is not returned. Call back a second time, even a third, if necessary. Your man or woman's secretary will have dropped the conference excuse by this time, and your courteous persistence cannot fail to make an impression. Your name will go to the top of the call-back list. Courtesy, persistence, and patience all have an important place in telephone business transactions.

Every time you talk to a stranger on the phone you are practicing the same arts of persuasion that you use when speaking in public. On-the-phone training is a daily refresher course. Make the most of it, and try your best to be pleasant.

Salesmanship. The art of salesmanship is primarily a one-to-one test of wits between you, the seller, and your listener, the buyer. (See the *Careers* chapter for a discussion of speaking in a job interview.) Before the buyer orders anything, he must be convinced that the salesman means what he says, that his word is his bond regardless of his product. Effective public speaking operates on the same principle. The listener must be persuaded that you, the speaker, are worthy of belief and trust. Persuasiveness, in both selling and speaking, rests on four fundamental precepts:

1. **Knowledge.** Speakers, like salesmen, must know their subjects—particularly their central ideas or selling points—better than their listeners. You may need to anticipate tricky (even mean-spirited) questions and have a ready answer for anything, which is where research and practice come in. The best salesmen always have tailor-made reasons why *anybody* can use their product. The best speakers, especially debaters, always seem capable of summoning a convincing argument on the spot.

2. **Empathy.** Not to be confused with sympathy (feeling *for* the other person), empathy is the ability to step into the other person's shoes, to feel *with* him or her. In terms of public speaking, empathy is the learned talent for saying the right thing in the right words to markedly different listeners. A skilled speaker delivers the same basic message time and time again, simply altering his tone and his style so as not to offend his present audience, and even to flatter them a bit. Top salesmen must do this constantly, of course, trying to convince a housewife, a teenager, and a grandfather that the same car is the right choice for each of them.

3. **Sincerity.** Presumably, you would not choose to talk, publicly, about something you did not believe in. But the moment you decide to stand up and sound off about a subject, your own faith and belief in it is not enough. You must demonstrate, through your delivery technique, that you truly mean what you say. If anything undermines that sincerity—a monotonous tone of voice, shifty eyes, sloppy posture—your credibility will be damaged and may even disappear.

Improving Your Speech

4. Enthusiasm. You may not be able to define enthusiasm, but you know it when you see it: excitement, energy, contagious self-confidence. Those who know how to transfer that feeling to others are usually outstanding in their field: successful coaches, teachers, businesspeople, politicians, and religious leaders. Such a talent is too easily passed off as speaking ability. What it really is, when practiced and sustained, is inspirational leadership.

Knowledge, empathy, sincerity, and enthusiasm. All are essential to both selling and speaking in public. Knowledge and enthusiasm are largely a matter of thorough preparation and vigorous delivery; empathy and sincerity are largely determined by your listener's perception of your intentions. Salesmen have a harder time with listeners' misconceptions than speakers do—but not much harder.

Another technique shared by salesmen and speakers is the use of the "grabber" in the first paragraph. In sales, the grabber is the unique selling point; in speaking it is the central idea. Whichever form it takes, it should be mentioned early and often. As a public speaker you must never forget that you are selling *yourself* to whomever you address, just as a politician sells himself in painstakingly crafted 30-second spots on television. You, however, will be "live," not taped. Your only product is yourself. It is important to mean what you say about that product—with your words, your eyes, your body language, and your attitude.

Parliamentary procedure.
There are thousands of community organizations and service groups in the United States. Very few of them would accomplish much of anything unless they depended on *Robert's Rules* for order, decorum, and proper parlia-

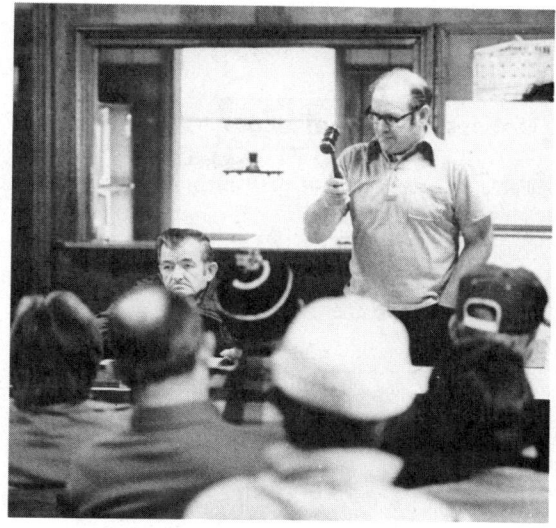

Even in an informal meeting, a chairman has the responsibility of conducting proceedings fairly.

mentary procedure. Although every conceivable point of order is covered in *Robert's*, the group chairman is responsible for invoking, enforcing, and interpreting each parliamentary dispute. (A condensed table of *Robert's Rules* may be found on pages 264-265.)

If you know your rules of procedure, local meetings can provide excellent on-the-floor training for self-assertiveness and for making your points aloud and under pressure. If you become disruptive or obstructionist, the chairperson of the meeting will let you know soon enough. When you learn such a lesson in a crowd, you tend to remember it. Here are some examples of ways—within *Robert's Rules*—to influence the course of a public meeting:

Important procedural rules

Adjournment	The chairperson can hold off a hurry-up vote on adjournment until proper consideration is given to the entire scheduled agenda.
Obstructionism	A chairperson is empowered to tell a troublemaker that he will not be recognized to speak —that he is out of order—until he agrees to behave in accordance with the rules.
Recess	As in a courtroom, the chairperson may declare a short recess at a time when feelings are running too high—or when it looks as if an ill-advised vote is in the offing.
Brokering	The chairperson is entitled to interrupt debate and propose a vote whenever he pleases, or to advise postponement of a vote if he does not like the probable outcome.
Quorum	Organizations establish the requirements for a quorum, the minimum number of people that must be present at a meeting before its proceedings can be regarded as valid. If the quorum criterion is not met, the meeting is invalid.

Robert's Rules of order

Table of precedence of parliamentary motions, points of order, and procedural questions

Type of motion		May be debated	May be amended
Privileged category	Fix time of next meeting	yes[1]	yes
	Adjourn	no	no
	Take a recess	yes[1]	no[2]
	Point of privilege (e.g., group comfort)	no	no
	Point of order (refer, agenda)	no	no
Incidental category	Point of order (refer, ruling)	no	no
	Appeal ruling of the chair	yes[4]	no
	Parliamentary inquiry	no	no
	Withdraw motion[6]	no	no
	Suspend the rules (temporary)	no	no
	Object to consideration	no	no
Subsidiary category	Lay on the table (postpone)	no	no
	Close debate (vote previous question)	no	no
	Limit debate	no	yes
	Postpone (to specific time)	yes	yes
	Refer to committee	yes	yes
	Make amendment	no[8]	yes
	Postpone indefinitely	yes	no
Main or unclassified category	Primary motion	yes	yes
	Take up from the table	no	no
	Reconsider[9]	no[8]	no
	Rescind	yes	yes

Improving Your Speech

Type of vote	Needs second	May interrupt speaker
majority	yes	no
majority	yes	no
majority	yes	no
majority[3]	no	yes
no vote	no	yes
majority[3]	no	yes
majority[5]	yes	yes
no vote	no	yes
no vote[7]	no	no
2/3	yes	no
2/3	no	yes
majority	yes	no
2/3	yes	no
2/3	yes	no
majority	yes	no
majority	yes	no
majority	yes	no
majority	yes	no
majority	yes	no
majority	yes	no
majority	yes	yes
2/3[10]	yes	no

Explanatory footnotes

[1] May be debated *except* when another motion is already on the table.

[2] Only the length of the recess may be amended.

[3] The chair decides—but a majority may overrule.

[4] May be debated *except* when it pertains to a rules violation or to indecorum.

[5] A tie vote upholds the chair's ruling.

[6] Only the person who made the motion may withdraw it.

[7] No objection, no vote. If there is an objection, a majority vote is required.

[8] May be debated *only* if the original motion was ruled debatable.

[9] This is complicated. Only a person who voted on the prevailing side may move to reconsider—and that only on the same day that the original vote was taken (or the next day of the same session). The following motions may *not* be reconsidered: adjourn, point of order (agenda), lay on the table (postpone), point of order (ruling), point of privilege, recess, refer to committee, suspend the rules, and take up from the table.

[10] If notice was given at a previous meeting that a vote to rescind would take place, then a majority vote would suffice. Without such notice, a two-thirds vote is required.

For further reference

Braden, Waldo Warder
 Public Speaking: The Essentials
 Harper & Row
Ehrlich, Eugene and Hawes, Gene R.
 Speak for Success
 Bantam Books
Newman, Edwin
 Strictly Speaking
 Bobbs Merrill
Prochnow, Herbert V. and Herbert V., Jr.
 The Toastmaster's Treasure Chest
 Harper & Row

Rogers, Natalie
 Talk-Power
 Dodd, Mead
Stedman, Raymond William
 A Guide to Public Speaking
 Prentice-Hall
Strunk, William, Jr., and White, E.B.
 The Elements of Style
 Macmillan

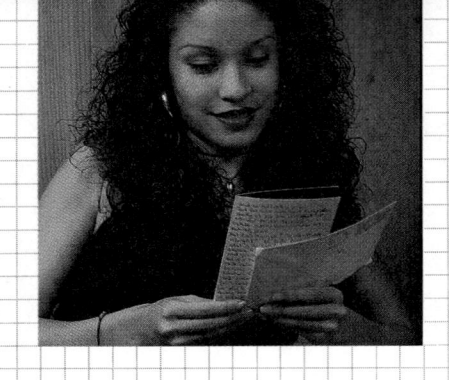

Writing Effective Letters

Letters are an important part of life. They can bring you closer to friends and family. They can bring comfort and cheer and inspire affection and love. The right letter can get you a job, sell your products or services, influence others, initiate action, and build goodwill. Knowing how to write the right letter for the right occasion can be a powerful asset in your social and business life, and it is a skill that anyone can learn.

The secret of writing a successful letter is knowing what you want to say and how to say it. Although neither is necessarily difficult, when confronted by a blank piece of paper, *you* may go blank—because, you think, you do not know what to say. In fact, this is rarely the case. You always have at least one reason for writing a letter and need only ask yourself what it is.

More often, the problem is that you do not know *how* to express yourself. The solution to this problem lies in knowing the kind of letter that you wish to write, whether it is a social or a business letter, and, if it is social, whether it is formal or informal and personal. There are specific techniques for each type of letter. Formal letters, such as announcements, invitations, and responses, have a standard form and wording that are simple to follow. Informal or personal letters to friends and relations are like a "visit" on paper; the trick in writing them is to write as you ordinarily talk. Business letters are written with a specific goal in mind, and usually require some advance preparation. You must decide on your goal and organize your supporting material, facts, arguments, requests, or questions *before* you start writing. In this chapter you will find the ways and means of doing this—techniques for organizing your thoughts, correct forms, and samples that you can use as models for the many occasions in your social and business life when you want to say the right thing in the right way.

Social letters

Your personal letters to friends and family can be relaxed and original in form and content. This is not the case, however, for the "letters of etiquette," the communications of social life that have a specific purpose (invitations, announcements, acceptances and re-grets, thank yous, notes of congratulation or condolence). For these, it is important to be correct, to follow the standard social conventions in appearance and content. This section gives valuable help on writing both informal and formal social letters.

Parts of a letter.

This five-part form is standard for all informal letters:

Heading. This is simply your address and the date or, if you have a printed letterhead, just the date. It goes at least an inch from the top, with at least a ¾-inch margin (larger, if you have a short letter) on the right. Cities and street names should be spelled out, but you can abbreviate the states. *You will notice that the date and return address have been omitted from most of the sample letters in this chapter. This was done to save space, but you should always include them in your letters.*

Salutation. This is the greeting. It goes on the left, at least half an inch below the heading, with the left margin equal to the right margin. The standard form is "Dear Sally" or "Dear Mrs. Thomson," depending on how well you know the person you are writing to. In the United States, "My Dear Mr. Jones" is considered more formal, but in England it is less formal. Salutations such as "Dear Friend," "Dear Sir," or "Dear Madam" are impolite for social letters.

Body. This is the message and there is no special form.

Complimentary closing. How you say "goodby" depends on how well you know the person you are writing to. In the past, closings were elaborate, but today's style is short and simple, such as "Yours sincerely" "Sincerely yours." Closing with just "Yours" sounds abrupt; but "Cordially" and "Sincerely" do not. "Respectfully" is usually reserved for writing to employers or customers.

Signature. This goes below the closing, a little to the right, in ink. The social convention is that you never use a title, such as Dr., Mr., Miss, or Mrs. when signing. A married woman would sign Betty Jordan, but she could, and *would* for business correspondence, add Mrs. Donald Jordan underneath her signature in parentheses. A divorced woman, but not a widow, would add Mrs. Betty Jordan.

Addressing the envelope. Use either the block form or indented form. The return address goes in the upper left. The convention is that women use Miss, Mrs., or Ms., but men do not use Mr. A boy under twelve is addressed as Master (that is, Master John Smith). Boys are not addressed as Mister until they are 18 or girls as Miss until they are 16. Use just the boy's full name when he is between the ages of 13 and 17, and the girl's full name when she is under 16. When addressing a husband and wife, the man's name comes first. You may write Mr. and Mrs. John Smith or John and Mary Smith. The address should be complete. Do not abbreviate people's names (unless *they* always do) or words like Street, Road, or Parkway, and do not forget the zip code. This can go on the same line as the town or city and state or on a separate line after the state.

You may add in the lower left corner:

PERSONAL—when you are sending a purely social and confidential letter to someone's office.

PLEASE FORWARD—when you know only the former address.

OPENED BY MISTAKE—when you mistakenly receive and open another person's mail. If you reseal the envelope, write "Opened by Mistake," sign your name, and mail it for the post office to redeliver, you will not be legally liable if the letter is lost.

Heading

63 Glover Street
Pleasantville, CT zip code
March 29, 1995

Salutation

Dear Sally,

Body

   Thank you so much for the lovely weekend. It was wonderful to see you and Jerry again and such a treat for Tom and me to get out of the city. We loved meeting Betty and Jim Henderson. It is always a pleasure to meet fellow sailors. I think it would be wonderful for us all to go sailing together this summer, but I hope you and Jerry will come for a visit way before then. You are such marvelous hosts and I only hope we can show you as good a time.

Closing Affectionately,
Signature Betty
             Betty

Stationery.
Choose the best quality paper you can afford. Paper comes in different weights: the heavier the weight, the better the quality. A good choice is a 20-pound rag bond.

For formal correspondence (see page 270) that is not printed, the rule is to use plain white paper, a double sheet that folds once into its matching envelope.

For general informal correspondence (everything but personal letters), you have a wide choice, but you will always be in good taste if you stay with subdued shades. The rule used to be, a large sheet of paper, 8 × 10 or 7½ × 10, with matching envelopes in white, cream, or gray for men; and a folded sheet of blue, 5½ × 6½ or 6 × 8, that folds once again into a matching envelope, for women. Today, the larger sizes and a variety of colors are considered suitable for both men and women. For personal letters bright colors are popular and correct now for men and women.

Monograms and letterheads. Stationery printed with your monogram or letterhead costs more but it makes an excellent impression. A monogram is fine for personal letters, but a letterhead (including your telephone number, if you wish) is better for general-purpose letters.

Women have traditionally used the "informal," a folded card of white or off-white with the name engraved in black on the front (Mrs. John Jones, or Harriet Jones if unmarried) for social notes. While this is still correct, today informals can have both the husband's and wife's names, include the address, and be in any color, with printing or engraving in a contrasting color.

Typing vs. writing.
It was once considered bad taste to type personal letters, but this is no longer true. Go ahead and type them, especially if your handwriting is hard to read, but remember to always sign your letters by hand, in ink. Formal invitations and replies, however, are never typed. Although there is no firm rule, it is usually considered more polite, more personal, and more sincere to write short thank-you notes or notes of congratulation or sympathy by hand. (When you type, use larger sheets and do not type on the back of the page.)

Page sequence and folding.
For folded sheets, social notes should be short enough to go on the first page. Longer personal notes are written on pages one and three. A long letter simply follows the natural sequence.

The main point in having matching envelopes is to have as few folds as possible. A double sheet is folded once and put in the envelope fold first, as is a small single sheet. A larger single sheet is folded in three equal sections and inserted with the closed end first in such a way that the letter will be opened right side up.

How to be yourself
- **Visualize the person you are writing to.** Imagine you are face to face. What would you say? What questions would you ask? What questions would the person ask you?
- **Ask, "What would I say to *this* person?"** You would not talk the same way to your dearest friend as you would to a casual acquaintance, your child's school principal, or your boss.
- **Write the way you speak.** Keep thinking about *what* you want to say and do not edit. Your first thought is usually your best. Use the words you normally would in speaking. Most people use contractions (I can't, rather than I cannot) and short, simple words (I *went* to a movie, not I *attended* a movie). Try not to make a special effort to be correct; the result may sound forced and insincere.
- **Use conversational techniques.** You emphasize certain words in conversation by changing your inflection or tone; you can do the same in writing by underlining (Your dinner was *terrific!*), but do not overdo it. You can also occasionally mention the name of the person you are writing to (I wish I could see you, Betty).

Personal letters.
These letters to friends and family can be the most fun to write because they are like a friendly visit. Their purpose is to share experiences and feelings and to give pleasure. Of all the different kinds of letters you write, personal letters give you the best chance to be yourself—which is also the key to writing them well.

Lord Chesterfield, the 18th-century English essayist and social critic, put it very well in this advice to his son: "Write as you speak! Write as though you were seated in a room with me, talking in plain, simple language about the things you have seen and done and thought and experienced since you wrote to me last."

Being yourself or finding your own "voice" is something all good writers must learn. You can tell when you have found your voice because your writing will sound relaxed and easy. Your thoughts and words flow, though this is not always easy to achieve. "Writer's block" can be experienced by letter writers, too. You become tongue-tied, freeze, and feel as though you have nothing to say. That blank piece of paper is intimidating you. The trick to overcoming this, as Lord Chesterfield knew, is to relax and imagine that you are having a conversation with the person you are writing to. Some hints to help you do that are above.

Letters to friends and relatives
Get well

> Dear Uncle Bob,
>   I spoke to Margaret last night and she told me about your kidney stone and that you were much better and would be home from the hospital today. Hurrah! I'm sure you'll be just fine again in no time. In the meantime, here's a new book by our favorite, Guy Murtchie, that I hope you'll like. Get well soon!
>   Cordially,
>   Hank

Travel

Dearest Sandy,

I'm in Fez at the famous Hotel Jamai, where I stayed 40 years ago when it was about one-sixth the size. In a week I'll be home and eager to see you. I know you'd love Morocco. I'm traveling with Gloria French. Gloria knows a lot about rugs, and we intend to visit all the museums.

There are really impressive Roman ruins of temples, much destroyed, but many stones are standing, one 10 feet high.

As for painting, I've been working—produced three pictures and I've done a lot of work on the book. I'm really on the last lap now. I think of you all the time, for your dear friendship and all of your help on my book.

Much love,
Anne

Christmas letter to a sister

Dearest Sis,

It's so good to be back in Jerome and to have all the children with us after the past few years of being all over the map. It has made it a wonderful Christmas, though we miss you and Jim and wish you could be here with us. Maybe next year!

Of course, there's lots of news. Wes has been working on the pipeline, as you know, and Mike has joined him. Mike is in love with a lovely girl. Her name is Tessie and it looks as though they will get married this summer and settle down in Alaska. Caroline took a job with an engineering firm in Nome—so except for Hank, we're all together again. Hank came up from San Diego in the most incredible van (about a block long). He's joined forces with a friend who manufactures water skis and they're going to promote them on a grand tour of European spas—thus, the van. But you'll see for yourself, as he's coming east in March to ship the van to France and, of course, he'll come and see you.

You can imagine what fun it's been in Jerome. We're staying in the hotel (our house is rented for another year yet). We've been spending lots of time downstairs in the Spirit Room, where Wes threw a gigantic party for our anniversary. Lots of people remember you and Jim from your visit three years ago. Tom and Shirley, Dr. Joe and Margaret, and Burt send their best regards, as do Wes and the kids. Let me hear form you! My love to you and Jim.

With love,
Sarah

When you do not know what to say

If, in spite of everything, you still draw a blank, you can simply say, "I don't know what to say," but say *why*. That's what Michael Faraday, the English physicist famous for his work on electricity, did in this letter written to Sarah Bernard in 1820. Sarah Bernard and Michael Faraday were married soon after this letter was written and had a long and happy life together, a tribute in part, perhaps, to the power of the written word.

My Dear Sarah,

It is astonishing how much the state of the body influences the powers of the mind. I have been thinking all the morning of the very delightful and interesting letter I would send you this evening, and now I am so tired, and yet have so much to do, that my thoughts are quite giddy and run round your image without any power of themselves to stop and admire it. I want to say a thousand kind and, believe me, heartfelt things to you, but am not master of words fit for the purpose; and still, as I ponder and think on you, chlorides, trials, oil, steel, miscellanea, mercury, and fifty other professional fancies swim before and drive me further and further into the quandry of stupidness.

From your affectionate
Michael

Invitations

Formal vs. informal. A formal event, such as a large church wedding or dinner-dance, requires a formal invitation. An informal invitation can be used for an informal event such as a small at-home wedding or country weekend. Informal invitations are simply handwritten notes in the first person. Formal invitations can be engraved or handwritten, but they have a specific form. They are written in the third person and are centered on the first page of folded white paper.

Acceptances and regrets. Any invitation should be answered right away. Formal invitations require a handwritten reply that follows the exact form of the invitation.

R.S.V.P. This means "Répondez s'il vous plaît," French for "answer please." It can also be written R.s.v.p. and goes in the lower left with an address beneath on formal invitations, or with a phone number, if you wish, on informal ones. For informal events such as cocktail parties, where you need to know how many people are coming and also want to speed replies, you can write "Regrets only" and your phone number.

Please come to a party to celebrate the publication of Sam Jones's new mystery, A Death in the Afternoon, *at the Little Tor Bookshop, 100 River Road, Grandview, NY.*

Regrets only
555-1212

Formal dinner

> John Gordon and Mary Gordon Green
> the children of
> Henry and Elizabeth Gordon
> request the pleasure of your company
> at a dinner in honor of their parents'
> Golden Wedding Anniversary
> on Saturday, the sixteenth of June
> at eight o'clock
> Tumblebrook Country Club
>
> R.S.V.P.
> Mrs. Robert Green
> 140 Old Mountain Road
> West Hartford, CT zip code

Formal acceptance

> Mr. and Mrs. Harold Smith
> accept with pleasure
> the kind invitation of
> John Gordon and Mary Gordon Green
> to a dinner in honor of
> the Golden Wedding Anniversary
> of their parents
> Henry and Elizabeth Gordon
> on Saturday, the sixteenth of June
> at eight o'clock
> at the Tumblebrook Country Club

Formal regret

> Mr. and Mrs. Harold Smith
> regret that they are unable to accept
> the kind invitation of
> John Gordon and Mary Gordon Green
> to a dinner in the honor of
> the Golden Wedding Anniversary
> of their parents
> Henry and Elizabeth Gordon
> on Saturday, the sixteenth of June
> at eight o'clock
> at the Tumblebrook Country Club

Informal dinner

> Dear Edith,
> My brother John and I are giving a small dinner in honor of our parents' Golden Wedding Anniversary on Saturday, June 16th at eight o'clock at the Tumblebrook Country Club. The celebration wouldn't be complete without you and Harry. I do hope you can come.
> Cordially,
> Mary Green

Informal acceptance

> Dear Mary,
> Harry and I will be delighted to come on Saturday at eight to celebrate your parents' Golden Wedding Anniversary. What a wonderful occasion! Thank you so much for asking us.
> Yours sincerely,
> Edith Smith

Informal regret

> Dear Mary,
> I'm so sorry, but we can't come to what I know will be a wonderful party. We will be away that whole week in Montreal to meet Joe's fiancee and her family, but thank you so much for asking us. Harry and I both wish we could be there.
> Yours sincerely,
> Edith Smith

Writing Effective Letters

Formal wedding. An invitation to a formal church wedding may include another invitation to the reception afterward. If the reception is held before one o'clock, it is called a breakfast; after one, a reception. If space is limited in the church, guests are also sent an admission card or a card for reserved seating "within the ribbon." Invitations are enclosed in *two* envelopes. The inside envelope is not sealed. It holds the invitation and enclosures and is addressed with only the names of the guests.

Formal reply. Formal wedding invitations do not require a reply, but an invitation to the reception does. You can use the shorter form shown at right, or you can repeat the exact wording of the invitation.

Formal wedding invitation

> *Mr. and Mrs. Richard Cameron*
> *request the honor of your presence*
> *at the marriage of their daughter*
> *Nancy Susan*
> *to*
> *Mr. Henry McQuiston*
> *on Saturday morning, the second of June*
> *at ten o'clock*
> *Grace Unitarian Church*
> *Pleasantville, NY*

> *Mr. and Mrs. Richard Cameron*
> *request the pleasure of your company*
> *at breakfast*
> *Saturday, the second of June*
> *at twelve o'clock*
> *Forty-five Riversville Road*
> *Pleasantville, NY*

> *The favor of a reply*
> *is requested*

> *Please present this card*
> *at Grace Unitarian Church*
> *Saturday, June second*

> *Mr. and Mrs. Thomas Putnam*
> *accept with pleasure*
> *Mr. and Mrs. Richard Cameron's*
> *kind invitation for*
> *Saturday, the second of June*
> *at twelve o'clock*

If a husband and wife receive an invitation and only one can attend, the acceptance is stated first, then the regret.

> *Mrs. Thomas Putnam*
> *accepts with pleasure etc.*
> *Mr. Thomas Putnam*
> *regrets exceedingly etc.*

Informal wedding invitation

Dear Sally,

Marlene is being married here at home to Ted Smith on Friday, May 25, at four o'clock. We do hope that you and Jack can come and that you will be able to stay for tea after the ceremony.

> *Love,*
> *Helen*

Informal reply

Dear Helen,

We are so happy about Marlene's forthcoming marriage and are delighted to be included. We look forward to seeing you on May 25, at four.

> *Love,*
> *Sally*

Formal acceptance

> *Mr. and Mrs. Thomas Putnam*
> *accept with pleasure*
> *Mr. and Mrs. Richard Cameron's*
> *kind invitation to be present*
> *at the marriage of their daughter*
> *Nancy Susan*
> *to*
> *Mr. Henry McQuiston*
> *on Saturday, the second of June*
> *at twelve o'clock*
> *and afterward at the wedding breakfast*

Recalling invitations. When a wedding must be postponed or canceled, guests can be notified by telephone, telegram, or, if there is time, by printed cards. The wording is formal, but the style does not have to be indented. Reasons are given for a postponement, but not for a cancellation.

Mr. and Mrs. Raymond Brown regret that owing to their daughter's illness they are obliged to recall the invitations to her wedding on Sunday, the third of June.

> *Mr. and Mrs. Raymond Brown*
> *announce that the marriage of their daughter*
> *Suzanne to Mr. Henry Harrison*
> *will not take place*

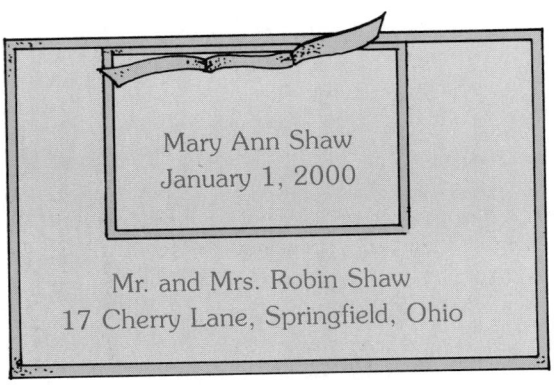

Mary Ann Shaw
January 1, 2000

Mr. and Mrs. Robin Shaw
17 Cherry Lane, Springfield, Ohio

Announcements

Wedding. A wedding is usually announced by calling the society editor of your local paper, but when a wedding is small and private (or when the couple has eloped), formal announcements can be sent out as soon as possible after the event.

> Mr. and Mrs. Anthony Jerome
> announce the marriage of their daughter
> Charlotte
> to
> Mr. Peter Gates
> Captain United States Army
> on Friday, the fifteenth of June
> Saratoga, New York

NOTE: When the bride or groom is an officer, it is customary to give the military title, but the title can be omitted for a noncommissioned officer or an enlisted person.

Birth. A traditional and formal way to announce a baby's birth is shown above. The baby's card is attached to the parents' joint card with a pink, blue, or white ribbon, or, an engraved card can be sent.

> Mr. and Mrs. Robin Shaw
> announce with joy
> the birth of their daughter
> Mary Ann
> on the first of January, 2000

Requests and responses

Excuse for absence from school

Dear Mrs. Shepard,

Please excuse Peter's absence from school this past Monday, Tuesday, and Wednesday. He had a bad cold and I thought it would be best (and best for the other children) to keep him home. Could you please tell Peter, or send me a note, if there is any work to be made up?

Thank you.

> Yours sincerely,
> Ruth Jones

Excuse for lateness

Dear Mrs. Shepard,

Please excuse Peter's lateness this morning. During the storm last night, our electricity must have been off for an hour, as all our clocks and alarms were an hour off, and he missed the school bus. I'm driving him in myself and hope you will forgive his unavoidable lateness.

> Sincerely,
> Ruth Jones

Excuse for future absence

Dear Miss Costanza,

Sally will be absent from school next Thursday and Friday, October 4th and 5th, as this is an important religious holiday (Yom Kippur) and she will be attending services.

If it's possible to give Sally assignments to make up the class work she will miss, she'll do that over the weekend. Thank you.

> Very truly yours,
> Mary Green

Apologetic answer to a complaint about a child

Dear Mr. Johnson,

I can certainly understand your being upset about Tommy's hitting a baseball through your windshield. We've told the boys not to play baseball in the street and now they know why.

K & R Auto informed me of the replacement cost. I've enclosed a check for that amount, which Tommy will make up out of his allowance and paper-route money. He is very sorry about what happened and will be over soon to tell you so himself. I am so sorry about the trouble this has caused you.

> Yours sincerely,
> Sally Smith

Nonapologetic answer to a complaint about a child

Dear Mrs. Henderson,

Billy has told us how upset you were about the noise the children made playing in the vacant lot next to your house over the weekend. I'm sorry that you were disturbed and Billy is, too.

As he explained it, he and his friends have been playing softball in that lot for several years now. The people who used to live in your house, the Jenkins, never objected and it didn't occur to any of the children that you would mind.

He's told me that he and his friends have talked it over and will play future games on the baseball diamond over at the grammar school.

> Yours very truly,
> Hattie Brown

Writing Effective Letters

Thank you notes.

You are expected to send thank-you notes for wedding and shower gifts and for being entertained for the weekend, but there are many other times when they are appropriate—such as for birthday or Christmas presents or when someone has done you a favor or shown you or your family some particular kindness. Thank-you notes can be quite short, but they should be specific and personal. It is easier, and more polite, to write them right away, while the pleasure of receiving a present, or of having a lovely time, is still fresh in your mind.

Dear John,

This is just to tell you how much I have enjoyed working with you over the years, and also to thank you for your part in that fine farewell gift. I have always wanted a matched set of golf clubs and these are superb. Thanks again for making my last day at Acme so memorable.

> *Sincerely,*
> *Henry Maxwell*

When a couple is entertained for the weekend, the "bread and butter" letter is usually written by the wife to the hostess.

Dear Mary Ann,

Thank you so much for an absolutely wonderful weekend. It was such a treat to spend time with you and Jim. Tom hasn't stopped talking about your chocolate soufflé and what a fantastic cook you are. We were especially thrilled with the whale-watching boat trip. How thoughtful of you to know that would be just what we'd love and to arrange it! Thank you again for everything.

> *Love,*
> *Sarah*

Dear Larry,

Thank you so much for the beautiful lamp. It is truly just what I needed. I've clipped it to my drawing board and it not only looks terrific (I love the red color), but it also eliminates the shadows, which is a big help in my work. I feel lucky to have such a wonderful, thoughtful cousin.

> *Much love,*
> *Sally,*

Dear Aunt Sarah,

Tom and I are thrilled with your wonderful wedding present. We have always admired Grace Steven's work, and to have an entire dinner set of her beautiful pottery is just fantastic!

I know it will look spendid on our table and I want you and uncle Joe to come for dinner and see for yourselves as soon as we get back from Bermuda. I will call you then to set a date.

> *Love,*
> *Polly*

Dear Sally,

Angelo doesn't have any words yet, but if he did I know he would thank you for your beautiful present. The baby sack is just what he needed—just the right weight—and the rose and blue stripes make him look so handsome! Thank you so much.

> *Cordially,*
> *Bianca*

Thank you notes from children

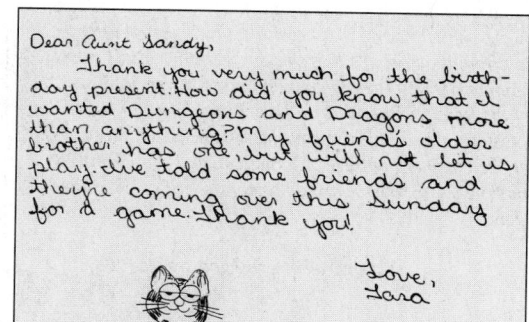

Dear Aunt Sandy,
Thank you very much for the birthday present. How did you know that I wanted Dungeons and Dragons more than anything? My friend's older brother has one, but will not let us play. I've told some friends and they're coming over this Sunday for a game. Thank you!
Love,
Tara

Dear Margie,

Thank you very much for a wonderful time. Your birthday party was great. I loved the treasure hunt (and winning the prize) and I loved staying with you. It was just like old times.

Please thank your Mom for me and ask her to send my Mom her recipe for spaghetti. It's the best I ever tasted. Thanks for everything.

> *Love,*
> *Tina*

Sympathy and condolence.

Writing to someone on the death of a spouse, relative, or friend is difficult for most people and yet there is probably no time when a letter can mean so much and be so deeply appreciated. Your natural feeling of sympathy for someone's loss is what matters here. Your letter can be short, but it should be tactful—not dwelling on the circumstances of the death—and it should be sincere and simple.

To a neighbor

Dear Rose,

I cannot tell you how shocked and sorry I am to learn of Bob's sudden death. He was such a wonderful man and I have such warm memories of his many kindnesses. I know that I will miss him very much and can only imagine what a terrible loss this is to you. Please accept my deepest sympathy.

> *Most sincerely,*
> *Harriet Jones*

To a friend

Dear Margaret,

I have just heard the very sad news that you lost your father and I want you to know how sorry I am. I know how much you loved him and how painful this loss must be for you and your mother.

I wish that words could help, but I know that only time does that. Please know that my loving thoughts and deepest sympathy are with you both.

> *Love,*
> *Sarah*

To an employee

Dear Harry,

I was sorry to hear of your wife's death and can only imagine how terrible this loss must be for you. Although words can do so little, I want you to know that you have my deepest sympathy.

If there is anything that I can do to help in any way, please do not hesitate to call on me.

> *Yours sincerely,*
> *Franklin Rogers*

Acknowledgments.

It is considered correct to send a short thank-you note to everyone who sends a condolence letter. This does not have to be written as promptly as an ordinary thank-you letter, but it should, if possible, be sent within six weeks.

Dear Carol,

I cannot tell you how much your thoughtfulness when my father died meant to me. You are a true and dear friend and I thank you for all your kindness.

> *Love,*
> *Nancy*

Dear Mr. Brown,

Thank you for your very kind and thoughtful letter. It is wonderful to know how well thought of John was among the people he worked with, and I very much appreciate your telling me.

> *Yours sincerely,*
> *Jane Smith*

Lincoln's letter to Mrs. Bixby

One of the most famous letters in American history is Abraham Lincoln's to Mrs. Lydia Bixby after being told by the governor of Massachusetts that she had lost her five sons in the Civil War. That the information turned out to be wrong —that one son survived as a prisoner of war, one went to sea, and one deserted to the Confederate Army—changed the facts upon which the letter was based, but not its substance or its eloquence.

Executive Mansion
Washington, Nov. 21, 1864

To Mrs. Bixby, Boston, Mass.

Dear Madam,

I have been shown in the files of the War Department a statement of the Adjutant General of Massachusetts that you are the mother of five sons who have died gloriously on the field of battle. I feel how weak and fruitless must be any word of mine which should attempt to beguile you from the grief of a loss so overwhelming. But I cannot refrain from tendering you the consolation that may be found in the thanks of the Republic they died to save. I pray that our heavenly Father may assuage the anguish of your bereavement, and leave you only the cherished memory of the loved and lost, and the solemn pride that must be yours to have laid so costly a sacrifice upon the altar of freedom.

> *Yours very sincerely and respectfully,*
> *A. Lincoln*

Writing Effective Letters

Announcing a death.

Often a member of the family of someone who has died will have to tell other family members or friends the sad news that someone close to them has died. This should be done as gently as possible, with an attempt to lessen the shock. It is hard to find a better example of this kind of letter than the one that Charles Dickens wrote to his wife, who was ill and away from home, to prepare her for finding out that their infant daughter had died. (See below.)

To a relative

Dear Uncle Ben,

I'm so sorry to be writing with some very sad news that I know will be a great shock to you: Uncle Harry passed away last night after having had a stroke two days ago. The funeral will be held at St. Agnes Church on Elm Street in New London, Thursday at two o'clock, and afterward family and friends will go to Aunt Mary's.

Affectionately,
Betty

To a friend of the deceased

Dear Mr. Jones,

I am writing to let you know that my father, Timothy Johnson, died in his sleep last night after a short illness. Father spoke of you so often as a friend that I felt you would want to know.

Yours sincerely,
Fred Johnson

Death and funeral notices

These are prepared by the person in charge of the funeral and are then phoned into the newspaper, either as news or as a paid advertisement. The paper will need the following information:

1. Name of deceased (and maiden name of a married woman)
2. Address
3. Date of death
4. Age
5. Names and relationships of survivors
6. Time and place of funeral and burial
7. Whether services are private or open to the public
8. Whether the family wishes no flowers to be sent or the organization and its address to which a memorial contribution can be sent.

Death notice

HENDERSON, MARY (née Bronson), of 27 Pine Street, Harrison, New York, died suddenly on May 12, in her 55th year, beloved wife of John Henderson. She is also survived by their son Howard Henderson, daughters Alice (Mrs. John Lagrange) and Mary (Mrs. Robert Johnson), and grandchildren Ramond and Susan Lagrange. Funeral services at Community Church, corner of Central and Lafayette Avenues, Harrison, NY, 11 AM Monday, May 14. Interment is private. In lieu of flowers, contributions may be made to the Community Care Society, Box 4000, Harrison, NY zip code.

Dickens's letter to his wife

Often family members or friends will have to be told that someone close to them has died. This should be done as gently as possible. It is hard to find a better example than this letter Charles Dickens wrote to his wife to prepare her for the news that their daughter had died.

Devonshire-terrace
Tuesday morning, 15th April, 1851

My dearest Kate,

Now observe you must read this letter very slowly and carefully. If you have hurried on thus without quite understanding (apprehending some bad news) I rely on your turning back and reading again.

Little Dora, without being in the least pain, is suddenly stricken ill. There is nothing in her appearance but perfect rest—you would suppose her quietly asleep, but I am sure she is very ill, and I cannot encourage myself with much hope of her recovery. I do not (and why should I say I do to you, my dear?) I do not think her recovery at all likely.

I do not like to leave home, I can do no good here, but I think it right to stay. You will not like to be away, I know, and I cannot reconcile it to myself to keep you away. Foster, with his usual affection for us, comes down to bring you this letter and to bring you home, but I cannot close it without putting the strongest entreaty and injunction upon you to come with perfect composure—To remember what I have often told you, that we never can expect to be exempt, as to our many children, from the afflictions of other parents, and that if—if when you come I should even have to say to you, "Our little baby is dead," you are to do your duty to the rest, and to show yourself worthy of the great trust you hold in them.

If you will only read this steadily I have a perfect confidence in your doing what is right.

Ever affectionately,
Charles Dickens

Business letters

A successful business letter is not only grammatically correct and neat, it is also friendly and courteous. It is simple, brief, easy to read, and gets right to the point. Such a letter creates a good impression. It makes your reader feel that you are the kind of person or firm that it is good to do business with. In short, a successful business letter looks good and sounds good. Here are some helpful hints.

Looking good.
Business letters are almost always typed on a standard 8½″ × 11″ good quality paper. Most businesses use a letterhead with their name, address, and phone number. The standard formats are shown below. Although some businesses prefer the block form because it saves time for the typist, most use either the modified block or modified semiblock forms.

Basic rules for spacing.
Follow these rules no matter which format you use.
1. Place the address two lines below the date, which is two lines below the heading.
2. Place the salutation two lines below the address.
3. Begin the opening sentence or paragraph two lines below the salutation.
4. Single space for the heading, address, and within paragraphs.
5. Double space between paragraphs.
6. Place the complimentary closing two lines below the last paragraph.
7. Place the typed signature four lines below the complimentary closing.
8. Put any additional data (such as enclosures or initials of the writer and typist) two lines below the typed signature, beginning at the left margin.

Styles

Block

ABC Company
100 Main Street
Anytown, Florida zip code
January 1, 2000

Mr. John Smith
12 Broadway
Apple City, New York zip code

Dear Mr. Smith:

This is an example of the block form of business letter. You will notice that the heading, inside address, closing, and signature all line up at the left and the paragraphs are not indented.

Yours sincerely,

Thomas Rider

Thomas Rider

Modified semiblock

ABC Company
100 Main Street
Anytown, Florida zip code
January 1, 2000

Mr. John Smith
12 Broadway
Apple City, New York zip code

Dear Mr. Smith:

Here is an example of the modified semiblock form. You will notice that the heading, closing, and signature are aligned near the center of the page and the paragraphs are indented. This last point is the only difference between this and the modified block form shown at the right.

Yours sincerely,

Thomas Rider
Thomas Rider

Parts of a business letter

Modified block format

Heading ————

Warner Widget Company
100 Marvin Gardens
Centerville, New Jersey zip code
March 10, 20—

Inside address ————

Mr. Mark Harris
M & H Manufacturing Company
Paradise, Rhode Island zip code

Salutation ———— Dear Mr. Harris:

Body ————

Thank you for your letter of February 24 and for your interest in our products. I am sending you our latest brochure describing our entire selection of widgets and particularly refer you to pages 8 and 9, where you will find some widgets well-suited to your needs.

Jack Armstrong, our New England sales representative, will be calling on you soon and will be happy to answer any further questions you may have. I hope that we may soon count you among our many satisfied customers.

Closing ———— Yours sincerely,

Signature ————

Frank Jones

Frank Jones, Manager
Production Information

Additional data ————

FJ/ms
Enclosure

Writing Effective Letters

Sounding good. You will be able to write successful business letters by following five basic rules:

1. **Be friendly.** Your letter will build goodwill and be more likely to accomplish its purpose if you maintain a friendly tone. Even if you are angry, avoid sarcasm or insults.

2. **Be specific.** Tell the reader exactly what he or she needs to know. If you have a complaint, say precisely what is wrong and what you want done about it. If you need information, note clearly what you need to know.

3. **Be positive.** Even a letter that must say no can do it in a positive way. Compare, for example, "We regret to inform you that the postal strike makes it impossible to ship your order until . . ." with "Thank you for your order. The merchandise will be shipped to you immediately after the postal strike is settled."

4. **Keep your reader's point of view in mind.** Try to see things from his or her vantage point, not yours. One way to tell whether you have done this is to count the "I's" and the "you's." You want lots of you's and few I's. You can usually get the right effect by rephrasing. Compare these examples:

   I: *I* want to express *my* sincere thanks for the kind words *I* received today from . . .
   You: Thank *you* for *your* very kind words.
   Or:
   I: *We* make four styles in all sizes.
   You: *You* may have *your* choice of four styles in all sizes.

5. **Remember the golden rule.** Write the kind of letter you would like to get if you were in the reader's position.

Anatomy of a letter.
You will find it easier to write a clear, well-organized letter if you think of it as having a basic structure—a beginning, a middle, and an end.

The beginning. The purpose of the first sentence is to get the reader's attention and interest. This can often be done by asking a question. An insurance sales letter might ask: "Do you want to save 40 percent on your auto insurance?" Keep the first sentence short. The rest of the opening paragraph explains it.

The emphasis should be on what the *reader* needs, not what *you* need. This holds true even for a letter of complaint. You might, for example, begin such a letter with, "I know you want to maintain good relationships with your customers, but . . ."

The middle. This is where you state and explain *your* purpose. It is important to present your supporting facts or arguments in order of their importance.

It helps to make notes or an outline (see volume 1, page 56) before you start to write.

Often, you are trying to motivate your reader to take some action, or you may be explaining why you will or will not take some action. Give the facts first and then the conclusion. A tenant might say to an uncooperative landlord, "I have talked to my lawyer about your failure to have my water pipes repaired after my repeated requests and was told that under this jurisdiction I may withhold my rent until repairs are made. I plan to do so unless repairs are made this month."

The end. If the purpose of your letter is to get the reader to take some action, sum up at the end with a direct and positive statement. Sounding tentative or doubtful invites rejection. It is better to say, "Your cooperation in sending a check by return mail will be greatly appreciated," than to say, "We hope you will pay as soon as possible." "Our representative will call for an appointment next week" is better than, "May we send our representative to see you soon?" You should be clear (if you want some action taken), courteous (avoid a cold, curt ending), and complete (the reader should feel you have said everything you have to say).

What's wrong with this letter?

The letter below is a good example of what *not to do* in business writing.

> Dear Sir:
>
> We have the latest edition of your Readers' Complete Bookshelf. After reviewing it very thoroughly with my wife and children, the very best we can find to say about it is that we are completely disgusted with it. We have, however, found that it is very useful in teaching our children how the art of misinformation is being used to deceive Americans. We have found many examples in your book.
>
> Please do not send Volume Three.
>
> *Howard Case*
> Howard Case

The tone of this letter could be improved, but the real problem is that the letter is vague. The writer does not give any concrete examples. A better letter would read,

I have gone over the latest volume of your Readers' Complete Bookshelf and am deeply disappointed with it—particularly in the chapter on the War Between the States. I felt you were unjustly critical of the South and not critical enough of what the North did during Reconstruction. There were also several historical inaccuracies. You have the wrong Confederate commander for the Battle. . .

Job applications. A letter written to apply for a job is really a sales letter. You are selling your own qualifications as a prospective employee. As in any sales letter, you want to get your reader's interest, stress what you can do for the reader, and persuade him or her to take an action—in this case, give you an interview. You would also include a résumé that lists your educational and work experience, but the letter of application has the advantage of being written for *this particular job,* as most résumés do not, and allows you to select and emphasize the experience and abilities that qualify you for that job. (For information on choosing a career and finding the job you want, see Advancing Your Career, page 22.)

A famous letter, written to the Duke of Milan in 1482, is hard to beat as an example of super-salesmanship, but then it was written by an extraordinary man who could do everything he said he could do and more. His name was Leonardo Da Vinci. Below are some excerpts from that letter. Leonardo got the job and he kept it for 16 years, until the French Army marched into Milan and took the Duke prisoner.

"Having, most illustrious lord, seen and considered the experiments of all those who pose as masters in the art of inventing instruments of war, and finding that their inventions differ in no way from those in common use, I am emboldened, without prejudice to anyone, to solicit an appointment of acquainting your Excellency with certain of my secrets.

1. I can construct bridges which are very light and strong and very portable, with which to pursue and defeat the enemy; and others more solid, which resist fire and assault, yet are easily removed and placed in position; and I can also burn and destroy those of the enemy.

2. In case of siege I can cut off water from the trenches and make pontoons and scaling ladders and other similar contrivances. . . .

4. I can also make a kind of cannon which is light and easy of transport, with which to hurl small stones like hail, and of which the smoke causes great terror to the enemy, so that they suffer heavy loss and confusion. . . .

10. In time of peace, I believe that I can give you as complete satisfaction as anyone else in the construction of buildings both public and private, and in conducting water from one place to another.

I can further execute sculpture in marble, bronze or clay, also in painting I can do as much as anyone else, whoever he may be.

And if any of the aforesaid things should seem to anyone impossible or impracticable, I offer myself as ready to make trial of them in your park or in whatever place shall please your Excellency. . . .

If you are looking for your first full-time job, you probably do not have much work experience, but you do have some "life experience." Your letter should emphasize your personal qualities and any relevant work, school, or extracurricular activities:

Letter from a college graduate

354 Hardscrabble Road
Anytown, NY zip code
May 4, 2000

Dear Mr. Johnson:

With my college degree in Business and my strong interest in sales, I believe I could do an excellent job as a management trainee with your company. I have achieved high grades in marketing courses and am sure I could learn to market a product successfully.

I know how valuable successful communication is in business, and feel that being editor of our college newspaper has helped me develop communication skills. You will find a complete résumé of my educational experience and extracurricular activities enclosed. I will call on Monday, May 8th, to arrange an interview so that we may discuss my qualifications for your management-trainee program.

Yours sincerely,
Nancy Graham
Nancy Graham

From prospective high-school graduate

Mr. Harold Long
Personnel Director
Carter Paper Company
52 Broadway
Apple City, New York zip code

Dear Mr. Long:

I will graduate from Centerville High School this June and my guidance counselor, Mr. Herbert Jones, suggested that I write to you about a sales position with your company.

I have worked part-time as an ad salesman for the Centerville Bulletin for the past two years. As advertising manager of our high-school yearbook, I produced a $1500 profit—a first for Centerville High. I've also been manager of the track team for the past two years and organized the successful fund-raising campaign that sent the team to the national meet in Washington this year.

I like sales, think I am good at it and want to make it my career—if possible, with the Carter Paper Company. I will call next Monday for an appointment.

Yours sincerely,
Jack Hudson

Writing Effective Letters

Putting it the right way. Helpful sentences:

Salary

I would be happy to discuss salary with you when we meet. My range is—, — to —, —.

I will be glad to discuss the matter of salary with you at a personal interview.

Salary considerations are not as important as the career opportunity this position offers. I am sure we can arrive at a satisfactory arrangement.

References

The following people can tell you about my work from several different points of view:

I refer you specifically to the following people with whom I have worked over the past few years.

My former employers and clients will vouch for my integrity and good reputation in the trade. I refer you to the following:

Selling yourself

I would be happy to show you my proposal for increasing your next year's sales by at least 25 percent.

I would like to show you how I can save you money on your company's liability insurance and will call on Monday for an appointment.

I shall phone your secretary next week to arrange for a meeting at your convenience.

I would very much like to discuss my qualifications for your buyer–training program and will call on Monday to set up an appointment.

Experienced worker answering an advertisement

Box 000, Times
Centerville, NY zip code

Dear Sir:

In response to your advertisement in this morning's Times for an experienced secretary, I would like to apply for that position. I have been a secretary for the past ten years for three prominent executives who will vouch for my efficiency and dependability. They are:

Mr. Harry Ricer, ABC Company, Centerville, NY (Hospital Supplies) 19-- to 19--

Mr. John Kramer, Consolidated Products, Newton, NY (Building Materials) 19-- to 19--

Mr. Peter Kent, Hawkins, Smith & Barnes, Inc., Centerville, NY (Management Consultants) 19-- to 19--

I have worked for Mr. Kent for the past five years. He is being transferred to Minneapolis, and so I am looking for another position.

I would like to come in and talk to you personally, and have enclosed a self-addressed card for you to let me know the most convenient time for you. You can also call me at work. The number is Hudson 5-1212, extension 400.

Sincerely yours,

Susan Graham

Susan Graham

Follow-up letter. It is a very good idea to write again *after* an interview to thank the interviewer and remind him or her of your interest and abilities.

Dear Mr. Smith:

I very much enjoyed talking with you and meeting the members of your staff yesterday afternoon.

I am glad you mentioned the importance of budget constraints and feel that my record of cost-effectiveness as a project manager under government contracts would be a definite asset to your organization. I would be happy to discuss this further and will call again in a few days.

Yours sincerely,

Gerald Simms

Thank-you letter. After you get the job, it is a good idea to write thank-you notes to the people who helped you.

Dear Mr. Jones:

I am very happy to be able to tell you that I am now a project manager at Consolidated Technologies. Mr. Smith told me about the fine letter of recommendation you sent and I am sure that that had a lot to do with my getting the job. Thank you very much for your encouragement and help.

Yours sincerely,

Gerald Simms

Getting help.
Asking for information or services, particularly from the government or corporate bureaucracy, can be frustrating and time-consuming. Yet you can do it easily by writing the right kind of letter. Here are some hints.

State your reason for writing in the first sentence. This saves your reader time and energy.

Include all reference numbers and dates. If you are writing about a bill, an order, or a missing shipment, you will need to include such things as the invoice number or date of purchase. If a company gives you a reference number to use in writing to them, be sure to use it.

Confine your inquiry or request to one point. Do not confuse your reader by covering several subjects. Write a different letter for each. Be short and specific.

Gentlemen:

Could you give me an explanation of line 30 of Commerce Department Form 638: Employer Liability. Specifically, does line 30 refer only to office workers or does it cover field representatives?

When you want action, request it clearly. Do this at the end of your letter. Some examples are:

Please send me a refund.
Please send me a corrected bill.

Be brief. Keep your letter to one page if possible. Write a draft first, put it aside for a while, then see what you can eliminate.

Write to an individual whenever possible. This will speed a reply. Although you can use just the person's title, a name—which you can usually find out by calling the company—is better. When in doubt, write to the president or department head, who will see that the right person gets it. (For help in finding the right person, see box at top right.)

To a drug company

Mr. Frank Jones, President
ABC Vitamin Company
Deercrossing, Colorado zip code

Dear Mr. Jones:

I am writing to ask about the safety of your special Vitamin x compound, Wondervite. I have been taking this vitamin for some time and have just read in the Health and Science section of the Portland Times *that it does* not *lower cholesterol and that it can cause serious side effects.*

I would appreciate your sending me a summary of your laboratory reports on the action and side effects of this vitamin as soon as possible.

Yours sincerely,

Angela Black

Finding the person to write to

Consumer affairs. A pamphlet listing state, city, and county consumer protection offices, Better Business Bureaus, and names and addresses of corporate consumer contacts is available without charge by writing to:

    Consumer Resource Handbook
    Consumer Information Center
    Pueblo, Colorado 81009

U.S. government officials. *The United States Government Manual* is updated regularly to tell you who's who in Congress and all government agencies. You can buy it from the Superintendent of Documents, U.S. Government Printing Office, Washington, D.C. 20402, *but* you must write first for the price (which changes) and the correct order form. You may find it at the public library. *Congressional Staff Directory* is published by Congressional Staff Director, Ltd., Mt. Vernon, Va. 22121. It, too, may be found at the library.

To a company

John Smith, Sales Manager
Acme Office Supplies
Newton, Illinois zip code

Dear Mr. Smith:

Please send me samples and a price quotation for 100 metal paper clips, Product Number 2000 on page 36 of your catalog. I would also like to know the price for an order of 1 million clips.

I would appreciate your sending this information by the end of the week.

Yours sincerely,

Frank Davis

To the Food and Drug Administration

Gentlemen:

I need to know whether it is safe to use the anti-inflammatory drug, Cureall. The drug is produced by Universal Drug Company, Weaver, Illinois. The code number on the label is Y-8000.

I bought the drug about six months ago from my local druggist, Robert Morley, 200 Main Street, Centerville, New York. I have since heard that the drug has been declared unsafe. Could you let me know the current status of this product?

Yours sincerely,

Helen Smith

     Writing Effective Letters

A request for aid

The Reverend Frank E. Roberts
Christ Church
Centerville, New York zip code

Dear Dr. Roberts:

Some of the employees at Consolidated
Industries are repairing broken toys to
be given as Christmas presents to
children in the county. We hoped you
might help us with this project by
setting up a collection depot at the
church and asking parishioners to
contribute broken toys.

I have asked Sandra Smith, an employee
who is one of your parishioners, to speak
to you further about this. Let me just
say that your help would be much
appreciated.

Yours sincerely,

Thomas Brown

Thomas Brown

To a dress company

Manager, Customer Services
Jennie de Woolfe, Inc.
New York, NY zip code

Dear Sir or Madam:

I saw an advertisement for your silk shirtwaist dress on page 35 of the April Vogue magazine and would very much like to buy it.

Could you please tell me if any stores in Marblehead carry the dress or, if not, where I could buy it in Boston?

Yours sincerely,

Barbara Ann Blake

To the Department of Veterans Affairs

Dear Mr. (look up proper person):

Please tell me if you offer educational benefits to children of soldiers killed in action. My husband, Henry Greene, serial number 000-000, died in Saudi Arabia in 1996. He was a sergeant in the Army. My son Henry will be ready for college next year and I need to know whether he is eligible for benefits.

Please let me know as soon as possible.

Yours sincerely,

Ruth Greene

Letter of inquiry.

The following letter follows the formula for a letter of inquiry: it gets the reader's attention; states what is wanted, who wants it, and why; motivates action; and expresses appreciation.

Dear Alumna or Alumnus,

Exciting news! The first Address Register of the Alumnae and Alumni of Evergreen College in ten years will be published in 2000. This new volume will contain an alphabetical listing of alumnae/i names and addresses, cross-referenced with name in college, plus class and geographical listings.

We need your help in completing the register. Please check your listing for accuracy and return the questionnaire in the enclosed envelope by June 1. Please note that the register will be available only to alumnae/i, faculty, and officers of Evergreen College. Your address will not be given out for noncollege use.

An order blank for your copy of the 2000 AAEC Register is attached to the questionnaire. The register is available at the prepublication price of $35. (It will be $40 after June, 2000.)

We hope you will take the time to fill out all of the enclosed questionnaire. If you are one of the 8000 alumnae/i who have joined AAEC's ranks since 1990, do not miss your first chance to tell us about your activities since graduation. If you are one of the 31,000 who were listed in the 1990 directory, this is your chance to bring your record up to date. Information about your current interests and accomplishments helps us in developing our many programs—including our guided travel tours and summer seminars.

Many thanks for your cooperation in filling out this questionnaire. We hope to be flooded by completed answers from all of you!

Yours sincerely,

Annabel Kemp Smith
President, AAEC

Enclosures

Notification of address change

Dear Sir:

Please send all future compensation checks to my new address:

1400 Wharton Avenue
Centerville, New York zip code.

My former address was:

10 Henry Street
Hartsdale, New Jersey zip code.

Yours truly,

Frank Dean

Complaints that get action.

People often have a hard time writing an effective letter of complaint because they are angry and they let their anger take over. The anger becomes the important thing. However, what really matters is getting some action that will remedy the situation. This is much more likely if your tone is reasonable and calm. In some situations, it helps to use humor; in others, just to present the facts clearly and briefly. Sometimes it helps to go ahead and write your enraged letter *and put it away*. Then, with you mind clear, you can write the letter you will actually mail. Here are some hints to help you:

Write to the right person. Think carefully about who will be most likely to take action or get action on your complaint. If you are having a problem with the credit department of a store, for example, you will be more likely to get action if you write directly to the store's president, *not* to the credit department. In general, it is always best to write to the boss—you would be surprised how few people do this.

Keep copies of your letters. Knowing when you said what to whom and when may be important to solving the problem.

Letters of complaint written in anger are often counterproductive. You may need to write several drafts to find the right approach.

Do not get personal. Do not be sarcastic or insulting to your reader. You may be angry about the situation, but remember that the person and the situation are different. Try to put yourself in the other person's place and enlist his or her cooperation.

Organize your ideas. It is important to be clear about what you want, why you want it, and how you think you can get it *before* you start to write. A good way to do this is to make a list of your major points. A general list, with examples for a specific case, is given below.

Sending enclosures. You may want to support your complaint or argument by enclosing such items as bills, receipts, canceled checks, previous correspondence, invoices, and newspaper or magazine articles. If you do, be sure to keep the originals for your records and send a copy to the person you are writing to.

How to get organized

Here is how the master list of major points is applied to the specific case of writing a letter of complaint to a state senator about his position on the death penalty. The final letter appears at the right.

Major points	Examples
1. What you want the reader to do in order to remedy what you are complaining about.	**1.** I want Senator Green to change his mind regarding the death penalty.
2. Your reasons for wanting a remedy—that is, why it is important to *you*.	**2.** I believe it is morally wrong to take a life and that the government has no right to do this.
3. What information your reader needs in order to act.	**3.** There is a lot of evidence that the death penalty is not a deterrent to violent crime. Various presidential commissions on crime and violence have found that the real deterrents are social (doing something about such factors as poverty, unemployment, and family disorganization) and legal (having the court system react quickly so that criminals are tried, convicted, and sent to jail in a relatively short time).
4. What is likely to motivate your reader to take action. This includes appealing to your reader's self-interest and any pressure you can bring to bear.	**4.** I will not vote for Senator Green again unless he changes his position. I will support any opponent of his who is against the death penalty.

Complaint about fraud. The following letter could be sent to the Better Business Bureau and/or the Federal Trade Commission (note that the writer encloses a copy of his receipt, not the original).

Gentlemen:

I am making a complaint about fraudulent pricing. On December 10, I went to Snazzy Sam's Audio Outlet at 81 Spruce Street in Centerville, New York, to buy a CB radio. The salesman claimed that the Star Monitor CB, which he showed me and which I subsequently purchased, was being offered at a special discount price of $89—half the normal retail price. I have enclosed a copy of my receipt. A few days later, at Janes' Department Store in Centerville, I saw the same radio being sold for $69 and was told that this was its normal retail price.

I can only conclude that the salesman at Snazzy Sam's deliberately misrepresented the price of the radio. I am sure you will agree that this store should be investigated and am turning the matter over to you as it involves interstate commerce. Please let me know what action you plan to take.

> *Yours sincerely,*
>
> *Arnold Smart*

Letter to state senator

> 63 Sunnyside Avenue
> Anytown, NY zip code
> May 15, 2000
>
> Dear Senator Green:
>
> I strongly oppose your position on the death penalty. I do not believe, as you do, that the death penalty is a deterrent to violent crime. I support your strong stand against crime, but I think your remedy is wrong.
>
> There is a great deal of evidence that the deterrents to violent crime are social and legal, that violent crime decreases where there are opportunities for work, health care, and education, and a court system that functions efficiently and quickly so that criminals are invariably sentenced and sent to jail. I refer you to various presidential commissions on crime and violence—beginning with President Johnson's—all of which have come to the same conclusions.
>
> I think your emphasis on the death penalty as a deterrent is not only useless, it also diverts attention from the real remedies. I urge you to change your position. If you do not, I will not be able to support your bid for reelection to the State Senate.
>
> Yours very truly,
>
> *Lucy Fuller*
>
> Lucy Fuller
> (Mrs. David Fuller)

Complaint about billing error

Gentlemen:

I have just received my July bill from Universal Utilities and feel that you must have made a mistake. The bill was not only much higher than usual for that month (I have enclosed copies of this and last year's July and August bills), but also our family was away for the entire month.

I always pay my bills promptly and shall continue to do so—as soon as I receive a corrected statement or an explanation of this discrepancy.

> *Yours sincerely,*
>
> *Alice Jones*
> *(Mrs. Sidney Jones)*

Complaint about a warranty (note that the writer refers to a previous letter and gives the company's file number).

> *File #6000-B*

Dear Mr. Brandt:

I believe you are wrong about the term of my warranty on the Gallactic Food Processor that I bought from your company in June of 1982. Your letter of March 1 says that my warranty expired last year. In fact, it is a five-year warranty and will not expire until 1987. I am therefore sending the Gallactic Food Processor back to you C.O.D., and trust that you will have it repaired and returned postage-paid as your warranty promises.

> *Yours sincerely,*
>
> *Ruth Green*

Letters to the editor. If you confine your letter to one issue, it will be more forceful.

To the Editor of the Centerville Times:

I strongly disagree with your March 1st editorial recommending that the north end of Wadsworth Park along Central Avenue be used as the site for the new middle school.

Your editorial quotes Mayor Barnes as saying that this use of the land will save the taxpayers' hard-earned money, which it will. But you do not say what this loss of parkland will mean to the citizens of Centerville.

The 40 acres of Wadsworth Park is the last remaining open, green space in Centerville, providing a retreat from our ever-encroaching urban area, a place for relaxation and quiet walks, and a sanctuary for birds and many small wild animals.

Removing even 10 acres of the park would represent a major loss to the city and would set a dangerous precedent. In the long run, it would be uneconomical to lose even a small part of our precious, irreplaceable parkland.

> *Yours sincerely,*
>
> *Tom Jones*

Answering inquiries.
Whether you are answering a personal inquiry or are answering on behalf of your company, your letter should include the following:

- An acknowledgment of the inquiry, mentioning the date and general subject of the letter to you.
- A detailed response to the questions, or an explanation of why you have to refuse.
- Additional information that may be helpful.
- An offer of further help where appropriate.

To an insurance company

Dear Mr. Smith:

Your letter of March 1 asks me to itemize our losses in the flood last month.

As the damage to furniture, carpets, and appliances was extensive, I have prepared the enclosed list with the approximate cost or value of each item. I hope this will be sufficient for your purposes. Please let me know if you need any further information.

Sincerely yours,

Jim Kiley

enc.

To a prospective customer

Dear Mrs. Blake:

In response to your inquiry about the Jennie deWoolfe dress shown in the advertisement in the April Vogue, *you can buy it in Marblehead at Design Research or, in Boston, at Kemp & Co., Market Fair, or Woman's Haberdasher. All these stories regularly carry our line.*

Many thanks for your interest.

Yours sincerely,

Harry Ross
Customer Service

To a mail order company

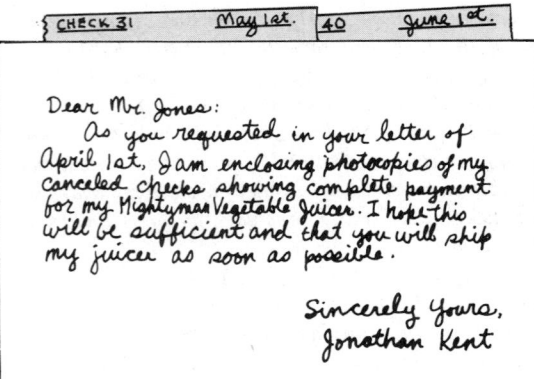

CHECK 31   May 1st.   40   June 1st.

Dear Mr. Jones:
As you requested in your letter of April 1st, I am enclosing photocopies of my canceled checks showing complete payment for my Mightyman Vegetable Juicer. I hope this will be sufficient and that you will ship my juicer as soon as possible.

Sincerely Yours,
Jonathan Kent

Turning inquiries into sales.
Answering an inquiry provides a golden opportunity for a company to create goodwill and promote sales. A courteous and helpful reply can be and will be very good for business. See how this works in the following letter to a potential customer:

Dear Mr. Smith:

Many thanks for your inquiry, just received, about our Miracle Re-Circulating Wood Stoves.

As a builder, you know the importance of first-rate equipment. As heating suppliers, we welcome the chance to tell you more about our fine product.

First, it uses a revolutionary design. The curved ducts and chimney fan capture the heat ordinarily lost up the chimney and blow warm air out at floor level, which improves air circulation.

Second, it is efficient. It burns less wood because its airtight construction causes wood to burn slowly.

Third, it is practical. Its small size allows it to fit easily in most existing fireplaces. For new-home construction, it is unobtrusive and easily installed.

Finally, and perhaps most important, it is safe. Our Teflon-coated stovepipe reduces dangerous creosote build-up and does not need to be cleaned as frequently as ordinary stovepipes.

I have enclosed a brochure showing our complete line of stoves and direct your attention particularly to pages 6 and 7, showing models suitable for small summer homes. I would be happy to answer any further questions and arrange for a demonstration. Just call our toll-free number as soon as you are ready.

Yours sincerely,

Ted Jones

enc.

Answering complaints.
What if you need to *respond* to a complaint. How you respond depends on the particular situation and on whether or not you feel that you (or your company) is at fault. Whatever the case, it is best to be reasonable and courteous. It will help if you do the following things *before you begin to write:*

Organize your response
- Determine the real nature of the complaint. It is important to know exactly what the complainant thinks is wrong.
- Determine your position. Decide on what you want to accomplish with your letter—that is, if you want to apologize, defend your actions without an apology, or something in between.

How to get organized

Major points

As in writing most other kinds of letters, setting down the points you want to make in a clear and logical sequence is important in answering complaints effectively.

1. Summarize the complaint in your first sentence or your first paragraph.
2. Make your position clear in your next paragraph. Say whether you are sorry or think the person complaining has made a mistake.
3. Explain your position. Give the information that justifies or at least explains your actions.
4. State what action you plan to take or want your reader to take in your last paragraph.

Example

The following response includes the major points and has a cooperative tone that should gain time until the facts have been determined.

Dear Mr. Jones:

1. *You believe that we have put our driveway across your property line.*
2. *We are having our lawyer check the deed, since we thought we put in the driveway entirely within our own property.*
3. *We realize that many of the old markers are unclear, so we would like to do more research before we come to any conclusions.*
4. *We know you are concerned about this and will be in touch with you as soon as we hear from our lawyer.*

Yours truly,

Harry Green

Responding to customer complaints. In answering complaints, particularly when you have to refuse a request for an adjustment, a company or an individual businessperson wants to keep the goodwill of the customer without acting against the best interests of his or her business. The best way to do this is to avoid an accusatory tone and to present your facts courteously, simply, and clearly so that the customer will find it hard to argue with your conclusion. This is the case in the following letter, in which the service manager refuses to honor his company's warantee because the damage to the company's product was caused by the owner's misuse.

Dear Mr. Jones:

We do agree with you that your new Easywriter should not have broken down after three months and we were concerned to find out why it did.

That is why we sent it to our laboratory for a thorough examination as soon as we received it. It appears that the machine had been dropped several times and that it must have been left uncovered—a great deal of dust was found inside the motor. Unfortunately, no typewriter can withstand such treatment. If you think it over, we are sure you will agree and will understand why we cannot repair or replace it under the terms of our warranty.

If you have any questions please do not hesitate to call me.

Yours truly,

Howard Smith
Service Manager

When to apologize. This depends on whether you think the complaint has merit. Here are two different responses to slightly different situations:

Apologetic

Dear Mrs. Ashley:

I am very sorry to learn that you are unhappy about the work I did on your house. I want you to be completely satisfied with the job.

I would be glad to come back and touch up the woodwork and window frames as soon as I am available—which should be in about a week. I will call you then to arrange for my completing the work.

Yours truly,

Bob Adams

Nonapologetic

Dear Mrs. Ashley:

I am very sorry that you are unhappy about the completed paint job on your house, particularly the color of the living room and hall.

I would be happy to make any changes you would like, but will have to charge you for the additional time and paint to redo the living room and hall. Under our original agreement, my payment constituted your acceptance of the job.

If you would call me, I would be glad to give you an estimate and arrange for doing the additional work.

Yours truly,

Bob Adams

Collection letters.
Letters asking for money owed are sent after the first bill has not been paid. They include the following points:
- How much is owed (a bill may be enclosed).
- Arguments for payment, including any action you plan (where appropriate).
- Request for payment by a certain date.

A delicate situation. Requests for overdue payments may put you in a somewhat delicate position. You want to get the money owed without antagonizing and losing your customer. You want to convey understanding and tact while remaining firm. Here are some techniques to help you do that.

1. **Put yourself in the other person's place.** Try to see that in most cases the person who owes you money would like to be able to pay on time and is sensitive about being unable. You can make this sensitivity work for you by appealing to his or her self-interest and sense of pride.

2. **Avoid unwarranted threats.** Be careful, you can be held legally liable for threats or insults. Do not accuse your debtor of dishonest behavior or intentions and do not threaten legal action without consulting a lawyer.

3. **Fit the letter to the situation.** Try to think why the payment may be late and use an appropriate approach. It is possible, for example, that the bill was lost or mislaid, that your customer did not understand the terms of sale or credit, or that he or she normally lets small bills accumulate. In such cases, all that is usually needed is a gentle reminder. Here are some examples:

When you opened this letter, I am sure it reminded you of something you meant to do, but forgot—to send us your check. Why not do it now? The amount due is $22.30. Please accept our apologies and thanks if you have already paid.

Perhaps we did not make it clear that our policy is to extend credit for a two-week period only, following the date of purchase.

Your payment of $135.62 was due last week on May 7. We would very much appreciate your sending us your check by return mail.

You may not have noticed that your past-due account with us now totals $236.14. We are trying to clear our books before December 31 and would appreciate your settling your account within the next few days.

Letters in a series. Often collection letters are written in a series, each successive letter getting stronger in tone. It is wise to make sure that your last collection letter reaches the person who owes you money. Send it certified mail, return receipt.

1.

Dear Mrs. Kent:

We find in checking our accounts that you have an unpaid balance for September of $62.42.

I thought that you would want us to bring it to your attention. If your check is already in the mail, just disregard this letter.

Yours truly,

2.

Dear Mrs. Kent:

As you usually pay your bills on time, we wonder why you have overlooked your September bill. The amount, $62.42, is now more than three months overdue.

If there is some reason why you are not paying it, I trust you will let us know. If I do not hear from you, I will look forward to getting your check within a few days.

Yours truly,

3.

Dear Mrs. Kent:

As you know, we do not usually extend credit for more than a month unless some agreement for partial payment has been made. Your bill for $62.42 is now four months overdue.

I urge you, therefore, to send us your check right away. If you cannot pay right now or can make only a partial payment, I am sure we could come to some arrangement. Do let me hear from you about this right away.

Yours truly,

4.

Dear Mrs. Kent:

I am extremely sorry that you have not responded to any of my letters about your overdue bill of $62.42.

I am afraid that unless I get your check in a few days, I will have to turn the matter over to our lawyers, Smith, French, and Block, for legal action.

Yours truly,

Family business.

Opening charge accounts, ordering merchandise, paying bills, planning vacations, contracting for work done to the house or yard—there are many occasions in a family's day-to-day life that require the writing of business letters. It is better to write than to telephone because you will not only have a record of your request, but the recipient will have a constant reminder before him. Here are a few examples:

Request for a delay in paying bills

Gentlemen:

Thank you for your recent letter reminding me that my account is long past due and inquiring as to when you can expect to receive payment.

I am enclosing a check for $50 toward the sum of $250, which is currently owed on my account.

Please accept my apologies for being in arrears. Recent medical expenses have placed a severe financial burden on me that I did not expect when I made the purchases at your store last spring.

I can manage to pay you $50 a month and if I do not hear otherwise from you, I will assume that this schedule is satisfactory. Thank you for your patience about this.

Yours truly,

Mary Snow
(Mrs. Richard Snow)

enc.

To report a lost credit card

> 10 Overlook Drive
> Essex, CT zip code
> May 5, 2000
>
> Galaxy Gas, USA
> Credit Card Center
> P.O. Box 1000
> Houston, TX zip code
>
> Gentlemen:
>
> I wish to make a formal report of the loss of my Galaxy Credit Card, Number 6000-2000-0007-0004, on May 4 in New York City. I called your 800 number immediately to report its loss and understand that I am not liable for any amount over $50 charged to my card.
>
> Please send me a new card with a new charge number. Thank you.
>
> Yours truly,
>
> *Robert Brown*
> Robert Brown

Opening a charge account

Gentlemen:

I would like to open a charge account at your store. I currently have charge accounts at Lord & Taylor, B. Altman, and Saks Fifth Avenue.

If you require further information or references, please let me know.

Yours truly,

Alice McCoy
(Mrs. Robert McCoy)

Making a hotel reservation

Gentlemen:

Please reserve a double room with bath for my husband and myself for the week of July 9th through July 15th. We would prefer a room overlooking the lake and, if possible, twin beds.

We will be arriving by train about noon on the 9th and will take a taxi directly to the hotel. Since we will rent a car during our stay, please send us a list of rental fees.

Please confirm and send your rate schedule.

Yours sincerely,

Harriet Brownly
(Mrs. John Brownly)

Contract in a letter

> Dr. Raymond Brown
> 1 Rolls Plaza
> Centerville, New York zip code
>
> Dear Dr. Brown:
>
> This is to confirm our financial arrangement for Nancy's orthodontic treatment as explained by you in your office last week.
>
> The cost of the treatment is $2080. I agree to make an initial payment of $400 at the beginning of the treatment and to pay the balance of $1680 in 24 monthly payments of $70 each. I understand that there is no finance charge or interest on the balance due.
>
> I also understand that the treatment does not include x-rays, but does include any necessary fillings or extractions.
>
> If these arrangements are agreeable to you, please sign the enclosed copies of this letter and return one to me.
>
> I am very pleased that you are going to treat Nancy and am sure the treatment will be successful.
>
> Yours truly,
> *Henry Graham*
> Henry Graham
>
> enc.

Letters that sell

The basic formula. The formula for a successful sales letter, according to an expert on direct mail, is:

INTEREST — DESIRE — CONVICTION — ACTION.

If you can stimulate each of these in your reader, you have made your sale.

An important point that all good salesmen know is this: people are more interested in the "secondary gains" of *what the product or service will do for them* than they are in the product or service itself. As one advertising professional puts it, "You don't sell the steak, you sell the sizzle."

What people want. Experts have compiled lists of the basic reasons why people buy anything from a magazine subscription to a car. The main ones are:

1. Better Health
2. To make money
3. To save money
4. Popularity
5. To look better
6. Security in old age
7. Praise from others
8. Sexual attractiveness
9. Comfort
10. Increased enjoyment
11. Leisure
12. Business advancement
13. Social advancement
14. Cleanliness
15. To escape physical pain
16. To save time

These basic human desires are the "sizzle."

Seven steps that sell the sizzle

Sample sales letter using the 7 steps

Dear Mr. Jones:

1. Capture attention. Pique your reader's interest and get his or her attention with your first sentence. This is the first thing a good business letter does — often by asking a question, such as, "Do you want to improve your memory 100 percent?"

   1. How would you like to improve your reading speed by 400 percent and remember everything you have read? How would you like to give your children the chance to improve their reading skills and comprehension in the vital early years?

2. Make an offer. Promise something important that your product can do for the reader and make him or her want to find out more about it.

   2. We have developed a foolproof programmed course of instruction that will enable the entire Jones family to develop and perfect these essential skills in only four short months.

3. Appeal to some human need (see checklist).

   3. There is no better investment you could make in your own career or your wife's, or in your children's future.

4. Find at least one way that your product is different from similar ones and show how this difference is important.

   4. Easyreader is different from any other speed-reading program you may have read or heard about because we give you two complete programs — one for adults and one for children. The children's program goes from grades 1 through 12. The adults' begins with short stories and ends with market analyses and international relations.

5. Back up claims with facts. Prove the value of what you are selling. Make your reader agree.

   5. The Howard Smith family of Brocton, Illinois, wrote us that the Easyreader Program was responsible for their son Tom's getting all A's in his last year of high school. Tom Green from Hanover, New Hampshire, said, "My performance on the job was so improved that I got two raises in one year."

6. Persuade your reader to take advantage of the opportunity you are offering.

   6. Do not deprive yourself or your family of this wonderful opportunity to increase your learning and earning power and to enrich your lives. The cost is only $15 a month.

7. Close with a request for action. Give your reader something specific to do right away, such as telephoning or filling out an enclosed order form.

   7. So act now. Phone us toll-free (800-100-1000) or fill out the enclosed form. It will be one of the best and most rewarding decisions you ever made!

   Yours truly,

   Fred Little

enc.

Writing Effective Letters

Magazine subscription renewal. Humor can be an important ingredient in a sales letter. It is a good way to get attention and build goodwill, especially when it is likely that a routine letter would be ignored. This is a common problem for the people who write letters soliciting magazine subscriptions and renewals. The following letter uses humor for a "soft sell" approach.

Dear Reader:

This is to tell you that your future issues of Motor Boat Monthly *are being held captive in the guts of a computer.*

You will never know about the incredible new designs for speed and power, or get a chance to win a family vacation on the Inland Waterway, or read about the amazing race down the Mississippi—unless you send us your check or money order at our special $10 renewal rate, now!

This is no time to hesitate. Act now or you will never see your beloved Motor Boat Monthly *again.*

Yours anonymously,

MBM Subscription Gang

Letter to boss. Here the writer has a new idea that he thinks would be good for business and he wants to "sell" his boss on it. He uses a slightly different approach and does not specifically include steps 3, 4, or 6. But step 5 is particularly important: he backs up his proposal with facts based on a recognized authority.

Milkman's letter for holiday products

Dear Customer:

The holiday season is coming and I'm sure you won't want to run out of all the things you'll need for entertaining friends and family.

Neilson's Dairy is offering two new holiday products this season, which I'm sure you'll enjoy—frozen strawberry cream and frozen lemon soufflé.

Why not use the enclosed form and order everything you'll need in advance?

With best wishes for the holiday season,

George Wilson

Letter promoting winterizing service

Dear Prospective Winter Driver:

Winter is coming. There's a chill in the air that could spell future trouble for your car. Don't wait for signs of trouble. Come in and give your car the attention and cold-weather servicing it needs—right now!

We have the expert mechanics and up-to-date equipment to give your car a thorough inspection and locate any possible difficulties, and repair them. And we are having early-bird specials on replacing coolant, changing oil and oil filters, and putting on snow tires.

Don't put winterizing off and be sorry later. Come in now. You and your car will be glad you did!

Yours truly,

enc.

Tom Benton

TO: Mr. Thomas Grant
FROM: Tony Newman
DATE: August 1, 20—
SUBJECT: Establishing Hang-gliding Training Programs

MEMO

I believe Grant's Glorious Gliders could take advantage of the current surge of interest in hang-gliding to promote our product and build goodwill among a growing group of prospective buyers.

I propose that we initiate a series of hang-gliding training programs and charge an appropriate fee to those who enroll. This would teach many of the inexperienced people who are buying hang-gliders how to use them safely and responsibly, and would enhance our reputation as a company that cares about its products and its customers.

Our expenses in setting up the course would, I believe, represent a sound financial investment in view of the rate at which the sport is growing. Our own sales, as you know, are up 25 percent over the last three months. According to this month's Hang-gliding News, not only is the sport growing nationwide, but enthusiasts are spending up to $2000 on the average for first-time purchases and from $300 to $1000 per year on maintenance and replacement parts. The article goes on to say that enthusiasts are becoming more aware and concerned about good procedure and safety.

If you approve of this proposal, I would like to discuss with you my ideas for putting it into practice. I can meet with you whenever it is convenient.

T. N.
Tony Newman

Clubs and organizations

Letters from clubs and organizations can include anything from announcing a meeting to thanking a speaker.

Announcement of meetings.
Include the names, time, date, and place. For a regular meeting, a simple postcard will be quicker and less expensive than a letter.

Monthly Meeting
South Hampton Garden Club
Saturday, May 26
10:00 A.M.
at the home of Mrs. John Jones
32 Job Lane, South Hampton

Judy Greer, Sec.
Tel. 555-1212

A special business meeting would require a letter:

Notice of the 25th Annual Meeting
of the John and Marian Macy Charity Fund

The annual meeting of the trustees of the John and Marian Macy Charity Fund will be held in the Palisades Community Center on March 1, 2000, at 2:00 P.M. for the purpose of considering and acting on the following:

1. Report of the Secretary
2. Report of the Treasurer
3. Report of the Committee on Disbursements
4. Distribution of Income
5. Election of Trustees

Harriet Drew
Secretary

January 10, 2000

Saving money on postage

```
_____  Nonprofit Org
_____  U.S. POSTAGE
_____  PAID
_____  Anytown, State, zip code
        PERMIT No. 1
```

Your club or organization may be able to save money by applying to the post office for a third-class mailing permit. If yours is a nonprofit organization, the savings compared with first-class postage can be 75 percent. Even a commercial third-class bulk rate saves about 50 percent. Though there are fees for a permit, the savings can be large on frequent mailings.

Announcement of a special event

Dear Parents:

"Bloomsday" is coming and it's only six weeks away!
That is the all-new magic show and musical review being presented by the Bloomfield High School Dramatic Club and Marching Band.
Some of the treats in store for you are:
• A mini-musical comedy with songs, dancing, and lots of laughs in one splendid act.
• Astounding feats of magic by that master magician, School Superintendent Jim Rawson.
It should be a marvelous evening, but that's not all. Proceeds will go to the Bloomfield High School College Scholarship Fund, so the cost of your tickets is tax deductible.
This extraordinary event will take place Friday, June 8, at 8:00 P.M. in the Bloomfield High School Auditorium on North Main Street.
Tickets are $4 each. Just fill out the coupon below and send it to us along with your check and we'll send you your tickets right away—or, for $4.50 each, you may buy them at the door. Come and bring your friends and family. You'll be glad you did.

Yours very truly,

Gertrude Troy

Gertrude Troy
Chairman, Scholarship Fund

Yes, I want to have a wonderful time! Send my tickets at once! Here is my check for $_____
Name _____
Address _____
Phone _____

Note the selling techniques of this letter. Its purpose is to convince the reader to buy a product, which is the ticket, and further, to spend money for the good cause of the scholarship fund. The letter accomplishes its purpose by using the following specific techniques:
• It gets attention and creates interest by giving the event an intriguing name.
• It describes a part of the event to develop the interest further.
• It gives two reasons for buying tickets: the event itself and the scholarship fund, and says that the ticket money is *tax deductible.*
• It does not give the date, time, and place until near the end, *after* the event has been described in an exciting way.
• It suggests an action the reader can take (buying tickets). It provides an easy way to do it (the coupon

Writing Effective Letters

at the bottom) and an incentive for doing it (lower price).
- It ends with a final encouragement to come.

Fund raising.
In today's tight economy, many clubs and organizations have to raise funds, either for their own needs or for civic purposes. The following letters might be part of an annual drive.

Fund drive letter to the editor

To the Editor:

Centerville Memorial Hospital needs your help. Some 25,000 new people have come to our town in the past ten years and our hospital has to grow to keep up. We urgently need a new wing with at least 50 beds, additional operating rooms, and diagnostic equipment. This will cost some $3 million and the Centerville Chamber of Commerce is sponsoring a drive for funds.

Very soon you will be receiving letters asking for pledges and contributions. You will see announcements of special sporting events, concerts, and dinners—all to help us reach our $3 million goal. But you can help us get off to a flying start right now by sending your check made out to "Centerville Memorial Hospital Fund." Send it to me today, at the Centerville Chamber of Commerce, 100 Main Street, Centerville, Ohio, zip code. No contribution is too small. All contributions are tax deductible.

Yours sincerely,

Frank Ross, President
Centerville Chamber
of Commerce

To the general public

Dear _____ (to be filled in):

Did you know that the population of Centerville has grown by some 25,000 over the past ten years? The people at Centerville Memorial Hospital know this only too well, because the hospital must grow to keep up. An additional 50 beds are badly needed, as are more operating rooms and diagnostic facilities.

This is why the Chamber of Commerce is sponsoring a campaign to raise $3 million for a new wing. Only your dollars will make this possible. Your contribution of $100 or more can buy bricks or a bed or a new piece of equipment. It can be dedicated to whomever you wish, and a memorial plaque will be placed in the lobby upon your request. So please send your check or pledge today in the enclosed return envelope. No amount is too small (or too large) and all contributions are tax deductible.

Yours sincerely,

Frank Ross, President
Centerville Chamber
of Commerce

Thanks to a company for their contribution

Dear Mr. Smith:

Your company's generous contribution to the Centerville Memorial Hospital Fund has enabled the hospital to purchase a CAT scanner, which will give it the most modern diagnostic facilities of any hospital in the area. We are deeply grateful.

Yours sincerely,

Frank Ross, President
Centerville Chamber

Invitation to speak

Dear Mr. Hunt:

The American Association of Railroads is going to hold its annual convention this year at the Palmer House in Minneapolis from Monday, May 8 through Friday, May 11. We would very much like to have you speak at the May 10 session.

This session is devoted to safety problems in freight handling, an area in which your own contributions are well known throughout the industry. I have enclosed our tentative schedule of speakers and a short list of suggested topics.

The association will, of course, pay your travel expenses to Minneapolis and hotel expenses for two nights. We are happy we can also offer you an honorarium.

I hope you will be able to accept, as your views on solving current safety problems would be of great interest to our membership.

Very truly yours,

George Brant, Chairman
Organizing Committee

Acceptance

Dear Mr. Brant:

I would be happy to speak at the May 10 session of the American Association of Railroads' annual convention. Your list of speakers is impressive and I am honored to be included. The suggested topic—the application of systems engineering—is fine. I will send you an outline next week.

Yours sincerely,

Robert Hunt

Thanking a speaker

Dear Mr. Hunt:

This year's convention was a big success, due in no small part to your contribution. Many of the people who attended your session told me what a fine and interesting presentation you made. Thank you very much.

Yours sincerely,

George Brant

Tips for retired people

Power in numbers. Today more than 26 million Americans are over 65 years old. This group has grown by 31 percent since the 1970 census and was expected to reach 29 million by the year 2000.

This means that older Americans are an important interest group as consumers and as voters, and a group whose importance can only increase as their numbers grow. So if you have an opinion or complaint, if you need information or assistance—it matters. There are people out there ready to hear from you and ready to help: write to them.

Government agencies. Almost every department of the federal government has policies that affect older people. Special programs on state and local levels were set up by the Older Americans Act and the Older Americans Comprehensive Services Amendments, in such areas as employment, nutrition, recreation, health care, and care of the frail elderly (75 and over).

Finding one's way through the bureaucratic welter can be difficult, but there is a central clearinghouse for information—The Office for the Aging—which also acts as an advocate and mediator between the elderly and various government agencies. There is at least one office in every state. These offices are an invaluable source of information.

Organizations. The number of voluntary organizations of older people who address themselves to a variety of issues on both national and local levels is also growing rapidly. A list of national organizations appears at the end of this section.

You are entitled. If you need help or information in such areas as housing, finance, health, education, travel, recreation, or employment—you are entitled to it. Do not hesitate to ask for it. You can use the telephone, but it is usually better to write a letter. In this section we give you some hints and sample letters to help you do that.

Housing

To a state office for the aging about tax relief

Dear Sir or Madam:

My wife and I are both over 65 and own our own home. I would like to know whether we are eligible for tax abatements, and if so, how we apply.

Yours truly,

John Harris

About eligibility for rent subsidy

```
New York State Office for the Aging
Empire State Plaza
Albany, NY 12230

Gentlemen:

    I would like to know whether I am
eligible for a rent subsidy under any
federal, state, or local program.

    My wife and I are both over 65 and have
been renting the same apartment for 25 years.
We are now living on my pension as a retired
postman and on my wife's Social Security
benefits.  It is sometimes very hard to make
ends meet.  Accordingly, I am eager to know
whether any financial aid is available to
us.  I would appreciate your answer as
soon as possible.

                    Yours truly,

                    Frank Smith
                    Frank Smith
```

About moving to another state

South Carolina Commission on Aging
915 Main Street
Columbia, SC 29201

Dear Sir or Madam:

I plan to retire next year and am very interested in South Carolina as a possible place to live. I need some general information to help me focus on specific towns. I would like to know about the locations of available housing, cost of living and taxes, health care, and special facilities for seniors, including tax exemptions.

My wife and I anticipate a joint income from pensions and Social Security of about $15,000 per year. We plan to sell our house and purchase a small, easily maintained house or apartment for retirement.

I would appreciate any information you can send me on the suitability of South Carolina for retirement, including a list of local Chambers of Commerce to which I can write for more detailed information. Thank you very much.

Yours sincerely,

Henry Crawford

Writing Effective Letters

Finances. Finances are of concern to everyone, but never more than to people who are living, or who are about to begin living, on the reduced income that is a fact of life for so many retirees. If you are planning to retire, finding out before you retire about what is likely to be your future financial situation is an excellent idea. The best way to get started is by writing letters.

Some people will be enrolled in private or company pension plans. Some will be entitled to veterans' benefits or survivor benefits. Some will be eligible for food stamps; most for Social Security benefits. Find out about these as soon as possible. There are several ways to go about it:

Send for the Social Security Handbook. You get it without charge by writing to:

Social Security Handbook
U.S. Government Printing Office
Washington, DC 20402

Visit or write to your local Social Security office. Make an appointment to come in and discuss your situation and options.

Get an accounting. There is a credit system for Social Security benefits measured in quarter years, which do not have to be consecutive. What you get depends on your average wages, when you start to collect, and how much you are earning when you put in a claim. If you want to find out where you stand, you can get an accounting of your Social Security earnings at any age, at any time, by writing to:

The Social Security Administration
P.O. Box 57
Baltimore, MD 21203

To make an appointment

Social Security Administration
410 Nanuet Mall
Anytown, N Y zip code

Dear Sir or Madam:

I am 64 years old and plan to retire next year. I want to plan for my retirement and need to know what my benefits will be. May I come in and discuss this with you? I can take time off from work any morning, provided I give advance notice. Please let me know when I can come in. I'd appreciate your answer as soon as possible.

Yours truly,

Margaret Green

To request an accounting. Requests should be made on either of two forms which you can get from the Social Security Administration. They are (1) Social Security Request for Detailed Earnings Information, which will provide a year-by-year breakdown, and (2) Request for Statement of Earnings, which will cover a

group of years. You should sign your form exactly as you signed your original card. See page 128 for more information.

The Social Security Administration
P.O. Box 57
Baltimore, Md. 21203

Dear Sir or Madam:
Would you please send me your form, Social Security Request for Detailed Earnings Information, as soon as possible? Thank you.

Yours truly,
Robert Stone

To a local utility

Town Gas and Electric Co.
Town, State zip code

Dear Sir or Madam:

I am writing to inquire about your special rates for senior citizens, and want to know what your eligibility requirements are. I am also interested in any help you could give me on energy conservation and weatherization. I am 70 years old, a widow, and live on a small pension.

Yours truly,

Harriet James

To inquire about food stamps

Department of Social Services
County, State zip code

Dear Sir or Madam:

I would like to find out if my husband and I are eligible for food stamps. I am 65 and my husband is 72. As it is very hard for us to get to your offices, I wonder if it is possible to conduct an interview in our home or over the telephone. Also, please tell me what material you will need from us to decide whether we are eligible.

Sincerely yours,
Jane Duffy
Jane Duffy
(Mrs. Thomas Duffy)

Health

Health insurance. Information on *Medicare,* the health insurance program that covers everyone over 65, and on *Medicaid,* the financial assistance program for needy people of all ages who meet their state's requirements, is available from any Social Security office.

Assistance. Your state or county Office for the Aging can also tell you how to arrange for home care, day care, home meals, and medical transportation.

To request information

Office for the Aging
Rockland County Health Center
Pomona, NY zip code

Dear Sir or Madam:

I need transportation from my home to my doctor's office in Pearl River every other month. I am 75 years old and am confined to a wheelchair. Can you provide this service for me on a regular basis?

Yours truly,

Ruth Daley

To apply for Medicaid. You must apply in person, or send a representative if you are unable to come yourself. When you make an appointment, be sure to ask for an application form with its checklist of required information and documents.

```
        Department of Social Services
        Medicaid Unit
        Sanatorium Road
        Pomona, NY zip code

        Dear Sir or Madam:

          I wish an interview in order
        to apply for Medicaid. Please
        send me an application form
        and a list of what I will need
        to prove eligibility. I can
        come in any morning.

                        Yours truly,

                        Ruth Daley
                        Ruth Daley
```

Education.

One of the wonderful things you can do with more time is go back to school. You can finish or further your education and explore new interests, taking courses for credit toward a degree.

Write for information about the many programs available for adult and continuing education from your local school district or community college and from state and private colleges. For summer studies in the United States, Canada, and abroad, investigate ELDERHOSTEL. This program also offers limited fall/winter and winter/spring courses. Write for a catalog (see address on sample letter below).

To a community college

The Institution for Senior Education
Rockland County Community College
Suffern, NY zip code

Dear Sir or Madam:

I have recently retired and would now very much like to finish my college education. Please send me information about your program and about how to apply. I would like to enroll this fall as a sophomore, if that is possible. Please let me hear from you as soon as possible.

Sincerely,

Jane Baker

To inquire about a summer program. There are many special programs open only to retired or elderly people. Here is an example of one:

```
        ELDERHOSTEL
        100 Boyston Street
        Boston, MA 02116

        Dear Sir or Madam:

          I am very interested in finding out about
        the ELDERHOSTEL program. Please send
        me your summer catalog and any other
        information you have about the program.

          I do have some special questions:
        1) Are there are facilities for the
        hearing-impaired?
        2) Can you provide any financial
        assistance? If so, can you send me the
        necessary application forms?
        3) Must students make their own travel
        arrangements?

          I look forward to hearing from you in
        regard to these questions and to receiving
        your catalog.

                        Yours truly,
                        Harry Smith
                        Harry Smith
```

Travel and transportation

Special services. Many municipalities offer transportation to senior centers, doctors and dentists, and grocery stores, but appointments must usually be made well in advance. For information, contact your state or county Office for the Aging.

To request transportation

County Office for the Aging
County Road
City, State zip code

Dear Sir or Madam:

Can you provide transportation from my home to my local senior center and back on Mondays, Thursdays, and Fridays for the next three months? A recent hip operation has confined me to a wheelchair for that period. Thank you.

Yours truly,

John Rudd

To obtain a senior I.D. pass

Rockland County Office for the Aging
Rockland County Health Center
Sanatorium Road
Pomona, NY zip code

Dear Sir or Madam:

I obtained my senior I.D. pass from your office last year and have found it very helpful for my half-fare bus service, and many other discounts. However, I have lost it. Can you send me another or is it necessary for me to come in to your office? Please let me know about this as soon as possible.

Yours truly,

Alice Jones

To a travel agency

Dear Sir or Madam:

I am interested in finding out about group tours on behalf of my Senior Citizens Club. We are interested in spending a week in the White Mountains in New Hampshire. We would need a congenial place that is wheel-chair accessible, with interesting walks (we have quite a few bird watchers), swimming, and golf. There are ten women and eight men in our group.

Could you recommend some hotels that would be appropriate for our needs and send me brochures and rate schedules? We would like to go by chartered bus and would need information on this, as well. I look forward to hearing from you. Thank you.

Yours truly,

Albert Mills

A Guide to U.S. Government Publications, listing many "subject bibliographies" of publications of interest to senior citizens, is available from
U.S. Government Printing Office
Superintendent of Documents
Washington, DC 20402

Recreation.
One of the pleasures retired people have is more leisure time. They also have the pleasure of figuring out what to do with it. Local senior centers, which you can find out about from the State or County Office for the Aging, are a valuable source of information.

Inquiry about a senior center

New York State Office for the Aging
Empire State Plaza
Albany, NY 12230

Dear Sir or Madam:

I would like to know which senior center is nearest to my home. Also, please tell me whether noon meals are available at this center, what special programs they offer, and whether transportation is available.

Yours truly,

Frank Parker

To get a recreational pass

National Park Service
Room 1013
U.S. Department of the Interior
18th & C Streets, NW
Washington, DC 20240

Dear Sir or Madam:

Please send me your list of the federal recreational areas where I can obtain a Golden Age Pass. I understand this will provide me with free entrance and a 50 percent discount on fees for all park facilities. Thank you.

Yours truly,

Roger Williams

Requesting a catalog

Sam's Art Supplies
10 Main Street
Centerville, New York zip code

Dear Sir or Madam:

I see from your advertisement that you offer a 10 percent senior citizens discount. Could you please send me your catalog of art supplies? It would be a great convenience to me to be able to order through the mail.

Yours truly,

Harriet Jackson

Employment

Finding work again. The Age Discrimination in Employment Act of 1969 prohibits discrimination against people between the ages of 40 and 65. Nonetheless, finding employment can be difficult for older people.

Remember that you have a lot to offer a prospective employer—the invaluable experience and skills learned over the years, plus the generally excellent record in terms of productivity and dependability that older people have on the job. You need to tell people what you can do, and a very good way to do this is through letters. It usually takes a lot of letters to get a response, but do not get discouraged. You have nothing to lose by trying.

Start a letter campaign. Select a number of companies in the field where you have experience and write directly to them. Explain the type of job you want and that you are not interested in joining a pension plan.

People starting service businesses, such as landscaping and lawn care, catering or real estate, can also use a letter campaign to good advantage. In addition, you can investigate the various government-funded employment programs by writing to the appropriate agency (see table below).

Write to friends and former business associates. Many jobs are found through personal contacts and here, as someone who has been in the business world for many years, you have a definite advantage. Use it.

To a former business associate

15 India Street
Scotch Plains, NJ zip code
April 3, 2000

Mr. James Morris
Morris and Burgess, Inc.
120 Main Street
Pleasant Valley, NJ zip code

Dear Jim:

As you know, I retired from McKinsey and Otis last spring when Janet and I moved to Scotch Plains. I find now that I really miss my work as an architectural draftsman (Janet and I miss the income, too) and would very much like to go back to work.

I wondered whether you need drafting services in your office—either full-time or on a free-lance basis. If you don't need anyone now, do you know of any openings with other firms in our area?

I know you were pleased with my work at McKinsey and Otis and I would appreciate any suggestions you can give me about job possibilities. I would like to work full-time, but would be happy to take free-lance assignments until I can find something permanent.

I hope to hear from you soon.

Yours truly,
Henry Scott
Henry Scott

Write to people that you think might know, or know someone who knows, about job possibilities.

Government employment programs

Peace Corps. This international program has no upper age limit. Thousands of Peace Corps volunteers work and live for two years in communities in some 90 countries, using their skills and training to help the people with whom they live. For more information, write to Peace Corps, Office of Human Resource Management, Washington, DC 20526, or call (202) 606-3950.

AmeriCorps. This national service program provides opportunities for citizens of all ages to work to solve national and community problems in the areas of public safety, environment, education, and human needs. The term of service is one or two years. In return for their service, AmeriCorps volunteers receive education awards of up to $4725 for each year of service to pay for college education or vocational training or to pay back student loans. For more information write to the Corporation for National and Community Service, 1201 New York Avenue, NW, Washington, DC 20505, or call (202) 606-5000.

Foster Grandparent Program. Also administered by the Corporation for National and Community Service, this program hires low-income persons over 60 to care part-time for children with special needs, including those with physical and developmental disabilities and those living in conditions of poverty. A modest stipend is paid and meals, transportation, and medical examinations are provided.

Senior Companion Program. This program is similar to the Foster Grandparent program, but serves adults with special needs. It is also administered by the Corporation for National and Community Service.

Green Thumb. This program is sponsored by the National Farmers Union and financed primarily by the U.S. Department of Labor. It serves low-income persons over 55, providing job placement, training, and part-time community service jobs. For more information write to Green Thumb, Inc., 2000 North 14th Street, Arlington, VA 22201.

Writing Effective Letters

National organizations

Senior citizens

American Association of Retired Persons (AARP)
601 E Street, NW
Washington, DC 20049

Open to anyone over 55, AARP offers world tours, bimonthly news bulletins, a hospitality house, out-of-hospital major medical insurance (for members 65 and over), life insurance, reduced prices on prescription and nonprescription drugs, a nursing home in California, and Institutes of Lifetime Learning in Long Beach, California, and Washington, D.C. There are almost 500 local chapters.

National Association of Retired Federal Employees (NARFE)
1533 New Hampshire Avenue, NW
Washington, DC 20036

Organized in 1921, NARFE has more than a thousand chapters in the 50 states. NARFE is active in promoting needed legislation and also has separately administered subsidiaries that provide favorable rates in life, casualty, hospital, fire, and automobile insurance. The annual dues include the monthly magazine *Retirement Life*.

National Council of Senior Citizens (NCSC)
1331 F Street, NW
Washington, DC 20004

Established in 1961, NCSC reports a membership of more than 5 million with more than 2000 affiliated clubs in all the states. NCSC is primarily concerned with promoting the general welfare of older people through public understanding and legislation. It also provides low-cost travel, medical, and other services for its members. Its monthly publication is *Senior Citizen News*.

National Council on the Aging (NCOA)
409 3rd Street, SW
Washington, DC 20024

NCOA is a central, national resource. General services include professional consultation, gathering and dissemination of information, a special lending library (largest of its kind), conferences, institutes and seminars, special studies and projects, general liaison with government, and the development and design of funded demonstrations.

National Retired Teachers Association (NRTA)
NRTA was founded in 1947 as a separate organization, but now functions as part of AARP, sharing headquarters, staff, and executive director. It has over 2600 local associations in all the states. Annual membership dues include the bimonthly NRTA edition of *Modern Maturity*.

Retired Officers Association (ROA)
201 North Washington Street
Alexandria, VA 22314

ROA was established in 1929 and reports a membership of more than 380,000 officers from all the services. It encourages legislation that benefits retired military personnel, and provides employment, travel, insurance, and other services for its members. Annual dues include the magazine *The Retired Officer*.

Gray Panthers
P.O. Box 21477
Washington, DC 20009

This group was originally called the Coalition of Older and Younger Adults—which is what it is, a loosely knit network of social activists working to eliminate all forms of age discrimination facing younger and older persons alike.

Minority groups

National Association for the Hispanic Elderly
3325 Wilshire Boulevard, Suite 800
Los Angeles, CA 90010

National Caucus and Center on Black Aged, Inc.
1424 K Street, NW
Washington, DC 20005

National Hispanic Council on Aging
2713 Ontario Road, NW
Washington, DC 20009

National Indian Council on Aging
6400 Uptown Boulevard, NW
City Centre, Suite 510-W
Albuquerque, NM 87110

You and your post office

The U.S. Postal Service has a lot more to offer than stamps, including many special products and services they would like you to know about. Ask for information at your local post office, or write to:

Consumer Advocate
U.S. Postal Service
475 L'Enfant Plaza SW, Room 5821
Washington, DC 20260-2200

Information about U.S. Postal Service products and services may also be found on the Postal Service's World Wide Web site at: http://www.usps.gov

Classes of mail

Designation	Type of mail	Restrictions	Delivery	Rates
1st class	Letters, documents, postcards	Rate is 43 cents for mailings 1 oz. or less <u>and</u> over any of these dimensions: 11 1/2" long, 6 1/8" high, 1/4" thick, or ratio of length to height less than 1 to 3 or more than 2 to 5; over 11 oz., use Priority mail	Usually 2 days but depends on destination; delivery by third day for outlying areas	33 cents for 1st oz., 22 cents each additional oz., 20 cents for single postcards
Priority mail	Letters, documents, etc.	Maximum weight of 70 lbs., maximum size of 108 inches length and girth combined	Usually 2 days	$3.20 up to 2 lbs. or for flat rate envelope; $1.10 additional for each lb. up to 5 lbs.; over 5 lbs., check with post office
Standard mail (A)	Catalogs, advertisements	Maximum weight 16 oz; minimum mailing for bulk rates 200 pieces or 50 lbs.	Varies	Single-piece and bulk rates; single-piece rates are the same as for 1st class up to 11 oz.; 13 oz. $2.90; over 13 but under 16 oz. $2.95
Standard mail (B) (Parcels over 1 lb.)	Parcels, catalogs, books	Same as Priority mail	2 to 9 days	Rates priced by distance and weight; check with post office

Mailing valuables

Registered mail	Anything of value to you (jewelry, documents, etc.)	Certain kinds of wrapping and envelopes are not accepted	Delivery is according to 1st-class mail; may be insured for up to $25,000 against loss or damage; return receipt available	$4.85 and up without postal insurance; $4.95 and up with postal insurance (up to $100 included in lowest rate)
Insured mail	Same as above	Up to $5000	Coverage against loss or damage	85 cents to $50; $1.80 for $50.01 to $100; 95 cents additional for each $100 up to $5000
Money orders	Alternative to sending cash	Up to $700	1st class	80 cents
Express mail	See "For fast delivery" section on page 299 for insurance coverage			

Writing Effective Letters

For fast delivery

Designation	Type of mail	Restrictions	Delivery	Rates
Express mail	Letters, letter packages	Check with post office for areas serviced and for daily deadline; weight up to 70 lbs. and size up to 108 inches length and girth combined	Overnight to areas serviced (most zip codes and some foreign countries); guaranteed (money back) and insured (up to $500 reimbursement for merchandise; additional coverage up to $5000 for 95 cents per $100); service includes weekends and holidays	$11.75 up to 8 oz.; $15.75 up to 2 lbs.; $18.50 up to 3 lbs.; $21.25 up to 4 lbs.; $24.00 up to 5 lbs.; $26.75 up to 6 lbs.; $29.40 up to 7 lbs.; consult post office for weights over 7 lbs. up to 70 lb. limit
Airmail	Letters, packages, postcards	Up to 4 lbs.; mark "Airmail" or "Par Avion"; check with post office for rates and restrictions for parcels and other articles	Depends on destination; check with post office	International: 60 cents for half oz., $1.00 for 1 oz. for all foreign countries other than Canada and Mexico (check with post office for complete rate scale)
Aerogram	Lightweight self-mailer	Must have an overseas destination; self-mailer is single sheet	Depends on destination; check with post office	50 cents to all destinations

Proof of mailing

Designation	Type of mail	Restrictions	Delivery	Rates
Certificate of mailing	Letters, parcels	Items of no intrinsic value	According to class of mail; sender gets a mailing receipt, but post office keeps no record	60-cent fee plus postage according to weight and class of mail
Certified mail	Letters, parcels	1st-class mail only, for items of no intrinsic value	Sender gets a mailing receipt, and post office keeps a record	$1.40 plus postage
Return receipt	Letters, parcels	Given for Certified, Registered, C.O.D., and Express mail, and for any mail insured over $50	According to class/designation of mail; receipt, returned to sender, constitutes proof of delivery	$1.25 plus postage

Among the many services and products available from the United States Postal Service are (1) registered mail, (2) certified mail, (3) return receipt, (4) stamped postal cards, (5) insured mail, (6) stamped envelopes, and (7) Global Priority Mail flat rate envelopes.

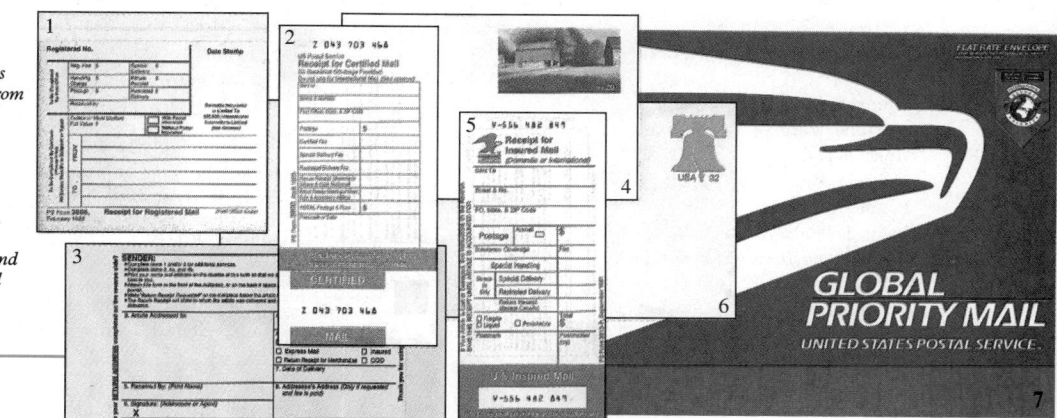

Writing Effective Letters

Correct forms of address

Government officials

Person	Address	Salutation
The President	The President The White House Washington, DC 20510	Dear Mr. President or Madam President
The Vice President	The Vice President United States Senate Washington, DC 20510	Dear Mr. Vice President or Madam Vice President
Cabinet Officers	The Honorable John Smith Secretary of the Interior Washington, DC zip code	Dear Mr. Secretary or Madam Secretary
The Attorney General	The Honorable John Smith Attorney General Washington, DC zip code	Dear Mr. Attorney General or Madam Attorney General
Chief Justice of the United States (same applies for a State Supreme Court)	The Chief Justice of the United States The Supreme Court Washington, DC 20543	Dear Mr. Chief Justice or Madam Chief Justice
Associate Justice	Mr. Justice Smith The Supreme Court Washington, DC 20543	Dear Mr. Justice or Madam Justice
U.S. Senator	The Honorable John Smith United States Senate Washington, DC 20510	Dear Senator Smith
U.S. Representative	The Honorable John Smith The United States House of Representatives Washington, DC zip code	Dear Mr. Smith
Governor	The Honorable John Smith Governor of (State) State Capital	Dear Governor Smith
Lieutenant Governor	The Honorable John Smith Lt. Governor of (State) State Capital	Dear Mr. Smith
State Senator	The Honorable John Smith The State Senate State Capital	Dear Senator Smith
State Assemblyman or Representative	The Honorable John Smith State House of Representatives (or Assembly) State Capital	Dear Mr. Smith
Mayors	The Honorable Jane Smith Mayor of (City or Town) Address	Dear Mayor Smith or Dear Madam Mayor
Lawyers	John Smith, Esq. Address	Dear Mr. Smith
Federal Judge	The Honorable John Smith United States District Judge	Dear Judge Smith

For further reference

Adler, Joan
The Retirement Book
William Morrow
Amy Vanderbilt's Etiquette
Doubleday and Company
Blumenthal, Lassor A.
The Art of Letter Writing
Grosset & Dunlap
Buckley, Earle C.
How to Write Better Business Letters
McGraw-Hill
Mager, N.H. and S.K.
The Complete Letter Writer
Pocket Books
Paxson, William C.
The Business Writing Handbook
Bantam Books
Schuster, M. Lincoln (ed.)
A Treasury of the World's Great Letters
Simon & Schuster
Silverstone, Barbara and Hyman, Helen Kandel
You and Your Aging Parent
Pantheon Books
Watson, Lilian Eichler
The Bantam Book of Correct Letter Writing
Bantam Books

Person	Address	Salutation
Catholic clergy		
The Pope	His Holiness, the Pope Vatican City Rome, Italy	Your Holiness
Cardinals	His Eminence, John Cardinal Smith	Dear Cardinal Smith
Archbishops and Bishops	The Most Reverend John Smith	Dear Archbishop (Bishop)
Abbot	The Right Reverend John Smith Abbot of (abbey)	Dear Father Abbot
Canon	The Very Reverend Canon John Smith	Dear Canon Smith
Monsignors	The Right (Very or Most)* Reverend Msgr. John Smith	Dear Monsignor Smith
Priest	The Reverend John Smith	Dear Father Smith
Brothers	Brother John Smith Name of Community	Dear Brother John
Sisters	Sister (full religious name) Name of Convent	Dear Sister

*The form of address depends on rank. When in doubt, consult the Official Catholic Directory.

Person	Address	Salutation
Protestant clergy		
Presiding Bishop of the Episcopal Church, U.S.A.	The Most Reverend John Smith, D.D.	Dear Bishop Smith
Episcopal Bishops	The Right Reverend John Smith, D.D. Bishop of (area)	Dear Bishop Smith
Dean	The Very Reverend John Smith Dean of (cathedral or seminary)	Dear Dean Smith
Minister or Priest	The Reverend John Smith	Dear Mr. Smith (or, if the person has a doctorate, Dear Dr. Smith)
Jewish clergy		
Rabbi	Rabbi John Smith	Dear Rabbi Smith (or, as above, Dear Dr. Smith)
Cantor	Cantor John Smith	Dear Cantor Smith

Members of the armed forces

The convention for addressing Army, Navy, Air Force, Coast Guard, and Marine officers and enlisted personnel is: full rank followed by the full name, a comma, and the abbreviation for the branch of service.

The abbreviations for the branches of service are: Army—U.S.A.; Army Reserve—U.S.A.R.; Air Force—U.S.A.F.; Air Force Reserve—U.S.A.F.R.; Navy—U.S.N.; Navy Reserve—U.S.N.R.; Coast Guard—U.S.C.G.; Coast Guard Reserve—U.S.C.G.R.; Marine Corps—U.S.M.C.; Marine Corps Reserve—U.S.M.C.R.

Retired generals and admirals keep their military titles in civilian life. The abbreviation (Ret.) is added after the service initials. Inactive reserve officers or retired officers of lower rank do not keep their titles. A retired brigadier general in the Army Reserve would be addressed as Brigadier General John Smith, U.S.A.R. (Ret.). The salutation would be Dear General Smith. Ensigns, petty officers, and warrant officers would be addressed according to the formula, but the salutation would be written Dear Mr. Smith.

Improving Your Reading

In the world we live in, our everyday actions depend to a great extent on our ability to read. We are always reading, often without even being aware of it: we read traffic signs, recipes, words on a television screen, and billboard advertisements. Surrounded by the printed word, many of us often take reading for granted. We come to think of our reading habits and skills as fixed, unchangeable parts of ourselves.

But good readers have one thing in common—they have *made* themselves good readers, often at a late age. One of the most famous books on reading is Mortimer Adler's *How to Read a Book;* in it he wrote: "I did not discover I could not read until after I had left college." Of course he could read newspapers, magazines, and books. But he discovered that he was not a good reader because he was not getting everything possible out of the things he read, nor was he reading with speed, pleasure, and satisfaction.

This chapter will help any reader become a better one, and it will help make reading more enjoyable. Here you will learn how to improve your reading skills through an effective reading improvement program. You will also learn of the many benefits of good reading skills, which will help you get the most out of the sections How to Study in Volume 1, and Literature and *The Young Reader's Companion* in Volume 2.

Enjoying the benefits of reading

The best reason for improving your reading is one of the most neglected. Reading gives pleasure. Good reading skills make reading even more pleasurable. Most of the books offered by a library or bookstore are for leisure reading, because reading is one of the most stimulating ways people can spend free time. Yet many people avoid reading because they think of it as a kind of chore or a kind of homework that they outgrew when they left school. But think of this: as a reader you have a world of entertainment at your fingertips. You can enjoy reading wherever you find yourself and whenever you wish, without depending on others or on the schedules that control movies and television.

The pleasures of reading are not limited to novels or stories. Good readers enjoy the personal satisfaction of learning more about their fields of interest, such as history or biography or sports, and also the satisfaction of developing new interests. People who enjoy reading usually become engrossed in current events. This gives them the satisfaction of understanding in depth the news of the day that is only skimmed by radio or television. Reading does not prevent activity. It makes people more active. Good readers of all ages use "how to" books on home improvement or hobbies for ideas on improving and broadening their leisure activities. Readers do not dislike parties or sports. In fact, they have more enthusiasm for these activities because they are stimulated by reading to seek more exciting ways to live.

In addition to these personal benefits, good reading skills help promote career advancement. Reading lists of required and recommended books are the heart of any formal education, and the ability to master these books fully and quickly is essential for the success of those planning for college, now in college, or returning to college. Independent reading can also open the doors to occupational advancement or to career changes. Because good readers enjoy reading and do more of it, they are more likely to find the books that will help them to obtain promotions or inspire new job ideas. Reading skills are also closely related to important occupational skills, such as writing and public speaking.

Finally, the benefits of good reading habits are felt by the entire family. Children are more likely to read well if they come from homes where books are valued. Reading is not necessarily a solitary activity. It lends itself to group activities, such as reading aloud or discussing the contents of mutually shared books. Children brought up by people who care about reading benefit from the ideas and discussions stimulated by books. Adults, in turn, can better understand their own reading habits by observing their children and by becoming involved with required school reading. Good reading habits can be learned and relearned by all members of the family together.

Evaluating your reading. To improve your reading, you should first find out where you now stand as a reader. This self-evaluation will enable you to concentrate on areas that need attention. It will also make it possible for you to judge your overall improvement as you work on your reading.

Thus, to benefit from the program in reading improvement described in this chapter, your first task is

"He that loves reading, has everything within his reach. He has but to desire, and he may possess himself of every species of wisdom to judge and power to perform."

—*William Godwin*

to examine your reading performance for symptoms of a possible problem. Then you will examine individual habits to isolate the ones that can hold you back. Even if your reading performance is acceptable, you can set new, higher goals and achieve them by continuing to work on fundamental habits with the techniques described here.

The most obvious symptom of a reading problem is boredom. No author tries to bore a reader. Rather, most authors spend considerable effort trying to interest their readers. Without knowing it, people who find

Reading helps increase the enjoyment of a wide variety of activities, such as gardening or how-to projects.

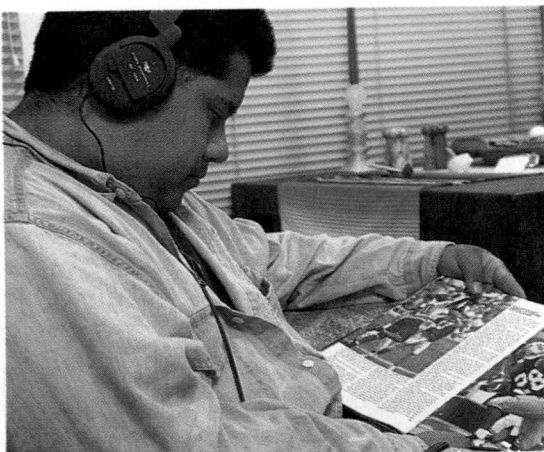

Reading for pleasure helps improve your reading skills while providing relaxation and enabling you to keep up with your interests.

to keep up with reading as a purposeful activity. They need to renew their sense of reading for specific information, whether to pass a school course, secure a job promotion, or obtain a personal benefit.

Finally, the family benefits of reading are lost by people who make no attempt to master what they read. People who find it difficult to retain what they read can regain this ability by discussing their reading with friends, family members, people who are familiar with the same book, or people who may be interested in hearing about a book.

Boredom, failure to comprehend material, and failure to retain information are only the most general symptoms of reading problems. But these symptoms can help you identify specific reading habits that should be corrected or improved in order to better your overall reading performance. The checklist provided here will help you analyze specific reading habits. These habits are discussed later in this chapter.

themselves bored with books and magazines are working against the benefits of reading. In adults, this is usually because their reading habits have deteriorated since their school years.

The personal benefits of reading for pleasure and information are easily undone by neglecting to keep up with reading as a regular activity. People who pick up a book only when they are bored can hardly hope to be anything but bored while reading it. Good readers plan to read regularly, and they keep material at hand that they look forward to reading.

Similarly, the professional and educational benefits of reading are undone by reading without a purpose. People who have trouble getting started in reading, and who find themselves with only a vague understanding of isolated facts when they have finished, have failed

Essential steps to good reading.

If you are dissatisfied with your present reading ability, if you are unsure of how to improve your reading skills, or if you wish to enjoy reading more, this chapter will give you the practical advice you need. You, in turn, must have the willingness to follow a program of regular practice in special reading skills. You may be asked to break habits caused by years of little or no contact with books. You may also find yourself asked to develop new habits, many of which may seem difficult to adopt. But if you accept the fact that reading is an acquired skill rather than a natural talent, and if you agree that all skills can be sharpened by practice, then you are in an excellent position to begin your own program for reading improvement.

Checklist of reading habits

Answer all questions in this checklist for an inventory of your reading habits.

1. Do you suffer from eyestrain or headaches as you read?
2. Do you find yourself distracted as you read?
3. Do you point at words as you read?
4. Do you audibly or silently say words as you read?
5. Do you frequently reread words or phrases?
6. Do you read everything at a single speed?
7. Do you skip over new words without understanding them?
8. Do you quickly forget what you have read?
9. Do you lack a sense of purpose before you begin reading?
10. Do you find certain kinds of reading especially difficult?
11. Do you go many days without reading at all?
12. Do you read only a single kind of book?
13. Do you lack ideas on what new things you might read?

The questions that you answer "yes" identify your reading habits that need improvement. This chapter provides advice on each of them. Questions 1 through 4 are discussed in the section "What is good reading?"; questions 5 through 8 in the sections on "Reading for speed" and "Reading for comprehension"; 9 and 10 in "Special types of reading"; and 11 through 13 in "Continuing to improve."

Setting realistic goals. We all know of highly advertised schemes for miraculous accomplishments in reading improvement. Most of them concentrate only on reading speed. They advertise success as the ability to skim a novel such as Leo Tolstoy's massive *War and Peace* in a few hours. Such schemes may indeed be able to teach people to turn all 1200 pages of that novel in a short amount of time. But the schemes are flawed on two counts: first, no one can understand that novel in a few hours; second, no one can enjoy that novel in a few hours. A further problem with such promises is the proven fact that superspeed reading ability does not last.

The primary goals of this program are to help you enjoy reading more; to allow you to learn the satisfactions of reading well; and to encourage you to want to read more often for pleasure and self-improvement. You will certainly enjoy reading more if you read faster; this program will help you to double your normal reading speed and beyond. But to increase your enjoyment of books, you must also read better; this program will help you to improve your comprehension so you can enjoy stimulating and challenging books. Both of these goals can be achieved by most people in about eight weeks of daily reading practice for about one hour at a time. This is not an overnight key to superspeed reading. It is a responsible program for achieving long-lasting benefits in reading with only 50 to 60 hours of practice.

To begin, *read every day* for about one hour. If possible, this reading session should be scheduled at the same time each day, but make certain that you avoid a time when you are too tired or too distracted to concentrate. For the first two weeks, read any easy material you find enjoyable. Read at your present natural reading speed. As the days go by, work to improve that reading speed by following the advice on "Reading for speed" given in this chapter. Your goal is to double your natural reading speed within two weeks. Then you will be prepared to develop a repertoire of reading speeds for material of different levels of difficulty. This skill is described in the section of this chapter called "Developing three speeds." From week three to week eight, vary the difficulty of your reading material each day. In this stage you will be taking advantage of the advice in the section on "Reading for comprehension." You will also concentrate on special reading skills, and on reading for special purposes. In this way, you will be developing your ability to read different sorts of books and articles with proficiency. At the end of eight weeks of these daily one-hour reading sessions, compare your initial speed and comprehension with your final speeds and comprehension.

Charting your progress. You will need a record of your daily reading to chart your progress through the eight weeks. The best record is a diary of brief entries recorded after each day's reading. You can keep such a diary in any pad or notebook. The box on this page shows the items of information to record as you complete the program. In the first two weeks, you will be concerned only with the first five items. In later weeks, as you work on special skills, you will want to keep track of all ten questions for a thorough evaluation of your improving skills.

Your reading program

This outline of a good program for reading improvement requires only a single hour each day for a period of eight weeks.

Weeks 1–2: Measure beginning reading speed.
　　　　　Read one hour a day.
　　　　　Read easy material.
　　　　　Check reading speed daily.
　　　　　Work to double beginning reading speed.

Weeks 3–8: Measure three reading speeds:
　　　　　rapid, normal, and *study.*
　　　　　Read one hour a day.
　　　　　Alternate readings of easy, average,
　　　　　　and difficult levels of complexity.
　　　　　Check one reading speed daily.
　　　　　Review what has been read.
　　　　　Keep notes on aspects of reading
　　　　　　that need work.

A reader's diary

To keep track of your reading, make brief, daily notes in a diary or notebook. The diary sample shown here supplies all the important questions affecting reading plus answers given by one reader.

When you start your diary, only the first questions will be answered in the first weeks. In later weeks, you will answer all these questions.

Date: 4-6
Words read: 5500
Reading speed: 360 wpm
Level of difficulty: average
Level of speed: normal
Summary completed: clear presentation of personnel evaluation process
Special difficulties: none

What is good reading?

Being a competent reader means having a sufficient knowledge of the fundamental habits necessary for success. Poor readers never examine their habits, so they never discover the wasted movements or persistent distractions that prevent them from increasing their speed and comprehension. Good readers scrutinize their basic habits to find ways to improve. Thus, moving toward competent reading begins with self-examination.

Before you read.
The eyes are the most important physical tools for reading. Schools regularly check the vision of children, so many minor eye problems are identified early in life. The most common of these are *nearsightedness,* which is clear focus only on close objects, and *farsightedness,* which is clear focus only on more distant ones. Another common problem is *astigmatism,* a blurred perception in one eye that causes eyestrain. All these problems are easily corrected by prescription eyeglasses.

After youth, however, the eyes continue to change, and so adults have as much need as children for regular eye examinations. Because of natural changes in the way the eyes focus, adults may require prescription lenses for the first time or new prescriptions to replace old ones. Adults must also be concerned with diseases of the eyes associated with aging. These include *cataracts,* which cause a clouding of the lens of the eye, and *glaucoma,* which is an increase in the pressure within the eye.

Any weakness in eyesight can lead to eyestrain, headaches, fatigue, and restlessness. But correctly prescribed lenses can correct vision, insuring that reading is both more effective and more pleasant. It is a good habit to have your eyes examined at least once every two years.

Congenial surroundings are another fundamental consideration. Good readers make a habit of reading in an environment conducive to concentration. Poor readers often complain of boredom with books when improper surroundings have made concentration impossible.

First, reading requires proper light. Poor lighting can strain the best of eyes. Reading lamps should throw sufficient light on the printed page without causing glare. Ideally, the light should come from behind the reader—usually over the left shoulder—and be shaded from the reader's eyes. Single bright lights in otherwise dark rooms also cause eyestrain, so make certain that your reading room is also lit by a background lamp.

Second, reading requires the quiet essential for concentration. Many people find some background noise, such as a radio, more conducive to concentration than complete silence. That is because the noise remains in the background, is unobtrusive, and has a soothing effect. Other kinds of noise, however, are specifically designed to attract attention. Television commercials, for example, are designed to draw attention from whatever anyone is doing, including reading. It is important, therefore, to test your tolerance for noise while reading. No one needs a private study or library in order to read well, but readers must control their surroundings in order to eliminate distractions that make concentration difficult.

Finally, reading requires an appropriate seating arrangement. This, too, is largely a matter of personal preference. It may seem too obvious a point to bear repeating, but reading in bed is more conducive to sleeping than to reading effectiveness. Everyone enjoys reading as relaxation, but good readers are aware of their physical posture and choose the one best for a particular reading purpose. A comfortable armchair is best for becoming absorbed in a favorite novel or magazine, but a chair and desk or table are necessary for study. While seated before a desk or table, good readers are able to take notes or reach for a handy dictionary or other reference work without the distraction of moving elsewhere to find the necessary book. Your daily reading for this program should be done at a well lighted desk or table in a quiet room. This promotes alertness and concentration on the reading material itself and the particular reading skill you may be practicing that day.

The act of reading.
Reading is primarily a mental activity, requiring only turning pages and moving the eyes. Any other actions are distractions and impediments to understanding. By indulging in bad habits, poor readers often make reading hard for themselves, but good readers free their minds for speedy absorption of written material. To improve your reading, it is important to identify and eliminate physical habits that slow you down while reading.

Eye movements. In reading, the eyes make small, split-second movements across the lines of the page. Only when the eyes stop is vision possible. Thus, only when the eyes stop can reading taking place.

The first person to connect this physical fact with the reading process was the French ophthalmologist Emile Javal. In 1878 he gave the name *saccades* to the jerky jumps of the eye moving across the printed page

Observing eye movements

Most people are unaware of the physical eye movements of reading. Observe the eye movements of another person while reading in order to better understand your own.

1. Have a friend sit in a straight-backed chair.
2. Have the friend hold a book at eye level about 12 inches from the face.
3. As the friend reads, look just over the top of the book at the eyes in motion.
4. Note the movements and pauses of the eyes while reading. Look for regressions and for return eye sweeps from the end of one line to the beginning of the next.

from left to right. He called the pauses between the jumps *fixations*. We are not aware of it as we read, but each line of print is crossed by the eye in a series of these jumps and pauses. For obvious reasons, we cannot observe our own eye movements. But we can observe the eye movements of other people who are reading, and this is a helpful exercise because it demonstrates how our own eyes behave as we read.

During reading, most people fixate on the beginning of a word because their eyes are drawn by the spaces between words. Everyone's reading is a sequence of these fixations. Good readers are able to keep the time of fixation to a minimum, thus speeding the eye along the printed line and on to the next. This increases their interest in the material and their mastery of ideas. Good readers are also able to eliminate *regressions,* the name given to backtracking to words already read. This ensures that they encounter the author's ideas as written and not as a confusing jumble of rearranged and reread words and phrases. As you observe the eye movements of other readers, you can expect to see different numbers of fixations and regressions.

It is important to observe and understand reading eye movement because you can control it. Among the most common bad habits of poor readers are slow or sloppy eye movements and frequent regressions. Both make it harder, not easier, to understand an author's ideas. Both are unnecessary, and both are easy to correct. Prove this to yourself by reading a single page at a slightly faster than normal rate and without any regressions at all. Move your eyes rapidly along the line and do not regress. It takes time to make this a habit, but you will soon notice that the effort increases reading speed and efficiency without any loss in comprehension. (More information on eye movements is provided in the section on "Reading for speed.")

Hand movements. Many young children are instructed to point at words while they are learning to read. Usually these words are in a list, and the exercise is designed to increase vocabulary. Unfortunately, many adult readers are held back because they fail to shed this habit. They read by pointing at words with a finger or a pencil, or even at a whole line of words with a ruler.

The problem with using hand movements is that they not only limit but actually distort reading. Fingers, pencils, and rulers introduce an unnecessary physical act into the reading process—complicating it, slowing it down, and distracting the eye. Habitual hand motions are usually performed at a single speed, making it difficult to achieve the flexibility of speed necessary for efficient reading. Finally, pointers distort reading comprehension because they locate *places on a page* rather than *ideas in a sentence.*

Good readers concentrate on ideas by eliminating the physical distraction of pointing.

Hand movements are a bad reading habit that is easy to correct. Simply refuse to let yourself touch the page when you read. Unless you are taking notes or underlining, place your book on a reading stand or hold it with both hands. A single hour of reading like this will demonstrate that pointing is simply unnecessary. Because a physical hindrance to understanding has been removed, later practice sessions will show improved comprehension.

Lip movements. Although reading is a mental process, many poor readers limit themselves by pronouncing the words they read. This habit is known to specialists as *vocalization,* and it can take several forms. Some people may actually read aloud. Others murmur to themselves. Most vocalizers silently mouth words as they read. These physical actions are the simplest

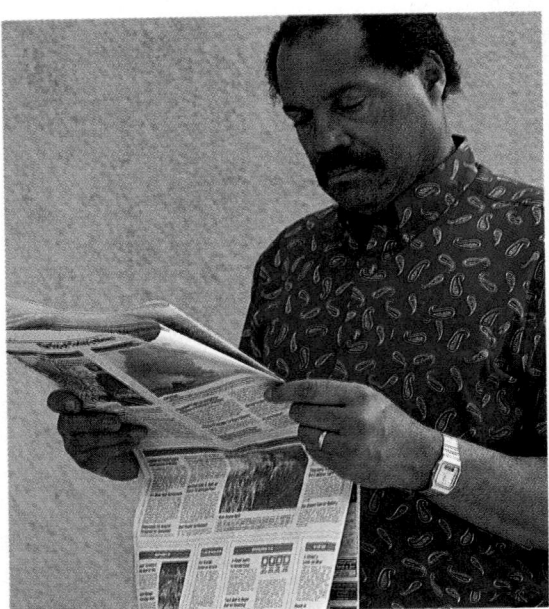
You can tell that this reader is reading efficiently. He does not distract himself by pointing at the words as he reads; nor does he move his lips. The silent reading he practices is truly silent. His attention is on the ideas and information he seeks, not on individual words.

forms of vocalization. More often, people have the habit of *subvocalization,* or mentally reproducing the sound of written words without any apparent physical action. These readers are listening to an interior voice rather than seeing words on a page.

Vocalization and subvocalization are not found among good readers because these habits interfere with both comprehension and speed. As in the case of hand movements, these physical or mental actions are a distraction from the ideas of a written work. These habits also substitute sound for meaning, causing a delay or even a loss in understanding. Since good readers focus on ideas, they are not hindered by vocal distractions.

It is easy to prove to yourself how seriously vocalization and subvocalization can slow your reading. Most speakers are able to read a passage aloud at about 125 words per minute. Mentally listening to the sound of printed words produces a reading rate only insignificantly faster. But even slow readers free from vocalizing habits proceed at close to twice this speed. Open any book or magazine you have handy and select two pages with approximately the same number of words. Time yourself while reading the first page aloud. Then time yourself while reading the second page as quickly as you can without any vocalization at all. Do not be surprised if you find you have read the second page a hundred words a minute faster than the first.

Many good readers have cured themselves of the habit of vocalizing. Some have done this merely by

resisting the temptation to speak or hear the words they read; they insist, "I will *not* vocalize," and overcome the habit by willpower. But there is another method. You used it already if you did the exercise just described. *Simply force yourself to read faster.* If you work at reading fast, your vocal or subvocal voice will not be able to keep up with your eyes. Continued practice at reading faster with your eyes alone will break the vocalization habit and also improve your ability to read for speed.

How we read. One of the most frequent complaints of poor readers is that they get lost when they begin to read. They get a few pages or paragraphs into a book or article and then find themselves confused. The author seems to be saying something they cannot understand, or the author does not seem to be saying anything at all. The result? Boredom and frustration.

These readers have the bad habit of beginning with the first word of a book or article and treating all the words as if they were of equal importance. These readers have failed to use the signposts provided by writers to help guide readers to the points being made. Good readers make a habit of using these pointers to focus on key ideas.

Prereading. You can preview anything you wish to read, thus locating these pointers before you begin to work your way carefully through the text. This is often called *skimming* or *scanning* the written work. It is a good habit because it helps you to read faster and with better understanding. But it is no substitute for careful reading, and so it is useful to think of this process as *prereading.* You will not want to preread casual leisure reading; few readers of mystery novels, for example, enjoy knowing the outcome of the story in advance. But for all difficult or scholarly reading, you will want to preread the text as a technique that will help you understand the text more completely and more quickly.

Published books and articles include many signposts to help the reader. Some of these signposts are part of the format of the work, for example, chapter titles and subheadings within chapters. Others are part of the organization of the work, such as introductory and summary paragraphs. All are intended to help you get a sense of an author's ideas before you begin to read. Good readers take advantage of these signposts and are not likely to get lost while reading. They already know where they are going.

The first step in prereading is to study titles. Books and magazine articles usually have main titles and subtitles. These indicate both the general subject and the author's special approach to it. When you are reading a book, study the chapter titles in the table of contents. Chapter titles can give you an idea of what to expect in the book. If you are reading a magazine, look for subheadings within articles. These break up the text just as chapter titles in longer works do. Subheadings provide clues to the ideas in sections of the article and an outline of the contents of each article.

Depending on the kind of material you are reading, you may be given other signposts. Textbooks often include study questions. They should be consulted *before* you read so you know in advance what to look for and concentrate on. Many books also include important illustrations, diagrams, charts, or graphs. These are visual aids to be consulted in prereading for a quick hint about important concepts. Finally, many books and magazines use boxes to set off important quotations, definitions, and key ideas.

In the second stage of prereading, skim the text itself to understand its organization. This can be done with an entire magazine article, but in books you will want to skim each chapter as you come to it. First, examine the opening and closing paragraphs. Opening paragraphs often introduce you to the material, arouse interest, or identify important ideas. Closing paragraphs often restate conclusions or recapitulate the information presented. Then briefly check the interior paragraphs. This can be done by reading only the opening sentences of the paragraphs. These are called topic sentences when they announce the point of the paragraph.

What to preread

Reading material is full of signposts to check *before* you read. These are the kinds of places you can find pointers to the main ideas in any work.

Full titles	Main titles on opening page
Chapter titles	Found in table of contents
Subheadings	Breaks in text
Study questions	At the ends of some chapters
Illustrations	Visual examples with captions
Boxed text	Words in enlarged type
Opening paragraphs	Introduction for all readers
Closing paragraphs	Conclusion in its plainest form
Topic sentences	Informative openings of paragraphs

Prereading, of course, will not answer all of your questions about a work. That can be done only by careful reading according to the principles described later in this chapter. But prereading is a good reading habit because it shows you what writers call the *shape* of the material. This will help you decide what to read, how fast to read it, and what to look for in it.

Prereading

Prereading alerts you to signposts directing attention to important points. Among these signposts are the topic sentences of paragraphs. Scan the passage below by reading only topic sentences, which are printed in boldface. Then read the passage from beginning to end. You will see that your first prereading scan gives you an excellent preliminary idea of the content of the entire passage.

THE SAN FRANCISCO EARTHQUAKE
by Jack London

Within an hour after the earthquake shock, the smoke of San Francisco's burning was a lurid tower visible a hundred miles away. And for three days and nights this lurid tower swayed in the sky, reddening the sun, darkening the day, and filling the land with smoke. **On Wednesday morning at quarter past five came the earthquake.** A minute later the flames were leaping upward. In a dozen different quarters south of Market Street, in the working class ghetto and in the factories, fires started. There was no opposing the flames. There was no organization, no communication. All the cunning adjustments of a twentieth-century city had been smashed by the earthquake. The streets were humped into ridges and depressions, and piled with the debris of fallen walls. The steel rails were twisted into perpendicular and horizontal angles. The telephone and telegraph systems were disrupted. And the great water mains had burst. All the shrewd contrivances and safeguards of man had been thrown out of gear by thirty seconds' twitching of the earth-crust.

By Wednesday afternoon, inside of twelve hours, half the heart of the city was gone. At that time I watched the vast conflagration from out on the bay. It was dead calm. Not a flicker of wind stirred. Yet from every side wind was pouring in upon the city. East, west, north, and south, strong winds were blowing upon the doomed city. The heated air rising made an enormous suck. Thus did the fire of itself build its own colossal chimney through the atmosphere. Day and night this dead calm continued, and yet, near to the flames, the wind was often half a gale, so mighty was the suck.

Wednesday night saw the destruction of the very heart of the city. Dynamite was lavishly used, and many of San Francisco's proudest structures were crumbled by man himself into ruins, but there was no withstanding the onrush of the flames.

Efficient reading

Efficiency in any operation is getting the best results with minimum effort. An efficient machine produces quality work quickly. Should it be too slow, goods cannot be produced economically. But should it be too fast, the loss of quality offsets any gain by speed.

The same can be said of reading, an operation that should produce maximum understanding with minimum time and effort. Read too fast, and you will not understand what you read. Read too slowly, and you risk losing interest.

Good readers are efficient because they balance these dual concerns of speed and comprehension. In this section you will be given instructions on how to read for speed and how to read for comprehension. First you will concentrate on speed, learning how you can double your reading speed with only a few days of practice. Then you will work on comprehension, learning special skills to help you master even difficult study material.

Reading for speed.
Most poor readers proceed at about 150 to 200 words a minute. Average readers read about 250 to 300 words a minute. Good readers read from 400 to 500 and even more words a minute. But the most important skill of good readers is that they read at more than a single speed. They have a *repertoire of speeds*, an assortment of speeds for easy, average, and difficult material. Like the physical mannerisms discussed earlier, reading speeds are habits that can be corrected and improved. With a little practice, you can increase your average reading speed and develop a repertoire for special occasions

Measure your reading speed. The first step in your program for improvement is to measure your present reading speed. This establishes your beginning point; later, you can check your improvement against this original speed.

For this self-assessment you will need a quiet place, a book you consider easy to read, a watch or clock with a second hand, and paper and pencil. Make sure you will be free from interruptions or distractions. Also make sure you choose reading material you like, so you get an accurate measurement of your speed. Time yourself with the watch, and keep a permanent record of the results on paper.

Reading speed is always measured in words per minute. So the first step is to calculate the words on an average page of the book you will use for the test. The simplest way to do this is to count the words on single lines of text. Count the words in each of five full lines of text. Add the total number of words and divide by five. Now you know the average number of words in each line. You can now count the number of lines on a page. All full pages of text in your book will have

---

How to measure your reading speed

To find your average reading speed, first calculate the words on a page of the book you are going to use. When doing this, count both parts of hyphenated words as separate words. Then calculate your reading speed in words per minute (WPM) on a test. To arrive at an accurate figure, you should complete at least five brief tests and combine the results of each to reach your personal average reading speed.

Calculating words per page

	Words in first line = ____	
	Words in second line = ____	
	Words in third line = ____	
	Words in fourth line = ____	
+	Words in fifth line = ____	
	Total = ____	
	Divided by	5
	Average words per line = ____	
	Multiplied by lines per page × ____	
	Average words per page = ____	

Calculating words per minute (WPM)

$$\frac{\text{Total words read} = \underline{\quad}}{\text{Time in seconds} = \quad} \times 60 = \underline{\quad}\text{WPM}$$

Calculating average reading speed

First test WPM = ____		
Second test WPM = ____		
Third test WPM = ____		
Fourth test WPM = ____		
Fifth test WPM = ____		
Total = ____		
Divided by	5	
Average WPM = ____		

about the same number of lines. You can now multiply the average number of words in a line by the number of lines on a page, thereby obtaining a quick estimate of words per page. Make notes on these counts for later reference. What is the average number of words in a line? What is the average number of lines on a page? What is the average number of words on a page?

Using the same book, test your reading speed. After noting the time, read five pages. Read at your normal speed, making sure you understand the material. Do not rush; you are testing yourself. After five pages, stop and note the elapsed time. You can now calculate your reading speed in words per minute by following the directions in the box on this page.

In this test it is important that you understand what you have read. Rushing to beat the clock is pointless: it makes reading unpleasant and comprehension impossible, and it produces a false estimate of your normal reading speed. After you have finished reading, take a moment to review the main ideas or facts in the pages you have read. If your recall seems poor, you may have read too fast. Another good test is to try to describe what you have read to a family member or friend. If he or she cannot understand the passage from your description of it, then you may not have understood it either. If you do not understand the material, slow down in the next tests and read more carefully.

You will need to conduct five tests in all, for each reading five pages, in order to have an accurate measurement of your average reading speed. After each test, carefully record your speed in words per minute. Relax for a few minutes between tests. It is not necessary to complete all five tests in a single sitting.

After five tests on passages you have understood, average your reading rates for a reliable estimate of your normal reading speed. This is the beginning point for your program to improve your reading speed.

Increasing your reading speed. Your beginning reading speed reflects habits you have developed over a period of years. This means that you cannot expect to increase it dramatically overnight. But it also means that reading speed can be improved by developing new habits.

First, you must focus on the problem of regressions, the backtracking habit you observed while watching the eye movements of another reader. *Regression* is going back to reread a word or, more often, a group of words. For example, suppose a 200-word-per-minute reader regressed five times in a minute to reread five groups of ten words each. In a minute this reader reread 50 words. This reader is actually reading at least 250 words per minute, but all the eye motion is not forward. Eliminating regressions would immediately improve this reader's speed at least 25 percent.

Of course, not all regressions can or even should be eliminated instantly. There are two types of regressions, and it is helpful to distinguish between them. *Voluntary regressions* are necessary searches for key ideas. To read with good comprehension, you must be prepared to reverse occasionally to review information, even at a loss of speed. Remember that speed itself is worthless if it means rushing blindly forward without full understanding. Good readers read for ideas, even if it means some backtracking. If you concentrate and control possible distractions, these voluntary regressions should be infrequent. *Involuntary regressions* are unnecessary. Many poor readers have the bad habit of regressing many times on a page without even being aware that they are doing so.

To correct habitual, unnecessary regressions, do your best to read with concentration and *read forward*. If you feel you are about to go back, ask yourself if it is absolutely necessary. If you have been concentrating, the answer most often will be "no," and you can proceed forward without loss of comprehension. After a few sessions of this exercise, you will find yourself regressing much less often, and so increasing your reading speed.

Another consideration is the *eye return,* the movement of the eye from the end of one line to the beginning of the next. Any typist knows that carriage returns, or the return of the paper for a new line, occupy a surprisingly large portion of typing time. Similarly, eye returns can occupy a large portion of reading time. Lazy eye returns are a bad reading habit, because they also invite distraction and loss of concentration.

To increase your reading speed, you should concentrate on eye returns. Force yourself to move quickly from one line to the next in a swift sweep from right to left without any opportunity for distracting thoughts or daydreams. This is an easily learned good reading habit, one that simultaneously improves both speed and comprehension. Work on eye returns by sweeping from the ends to the beginnings of lines on a page without reading the page at all. Make sure you always sweep to the next line. Readers who do not concentrate may often sweep to the wrong line. Practice demonstrates how fast the return can be if you are conscious of it and its importance.

The key to improved reading speed is practice. Set aside one hour each day. Practice on reading material that is easy and pleasant. Be sure to practice at a well-lit desk in a room free of distractions. As you read, concentrate on eliminating regressions and on speedy return sweeps. This is the way to increase reading speed permanently: practice and force yourself to go faster. Set your goals at a level higher than your present reading speed, and work at achieving them. Push yourself to read faster, eliminate regressions, and concentrate on speedy eye returns. As you achieve one

Regressions

Regressions make reading slower and harder to understand. The two passages printed here are identical except that one shows what a reader sees in making five regressions. You can see that these regressions make the passage longer and far more confusing.

If put to guess his calling and livelihood, I should have taken him for a country schoolmaster as soon as taken him for a country schoolmaster as soon as anything else. He was dressed in a rusty black frock coat and pantaloons, unbrushed, and worn so faithfully that the suit had faithfully that the suit had adapted itself to the curves and angularities of his figure and angularities of his figure, and had grown to be an outer skin of the man. His hair was black, still unmixed with gray, stiff, somewhat bushy, and had apparently been acquainted had apparently been acquainted with neither brush nor comb that morning, after neither brush nor comb that morning, after the disarrangement of the pillow; and as to a nightcap, Uncle Abe probably knows nothing of such effeminacies.

    —Nathaniel Hawthorne, "Abraham Lincoln"

If put to guess his calling and livelihood, I should have taken him for a country schoolmaster as soon as anything else. He was dressed in a rusty black frock coat and pantaloons, unbrushed, and worn so faithfully that the suit had adapted itself to the curves and angularities of his figure, and had grown to be an outer skin of the man. His hair was black, still unmixed with gray, stiff, somewhat bushy, and had apparently been acquainted with neither brush nor comb that morning, after the disarrangement of the pillow; and as to a nightcap, Uncle Abe probably knows nothing of such effeminacies.

    —Nathaniel Hawthorne, "Abraham Lincoln"

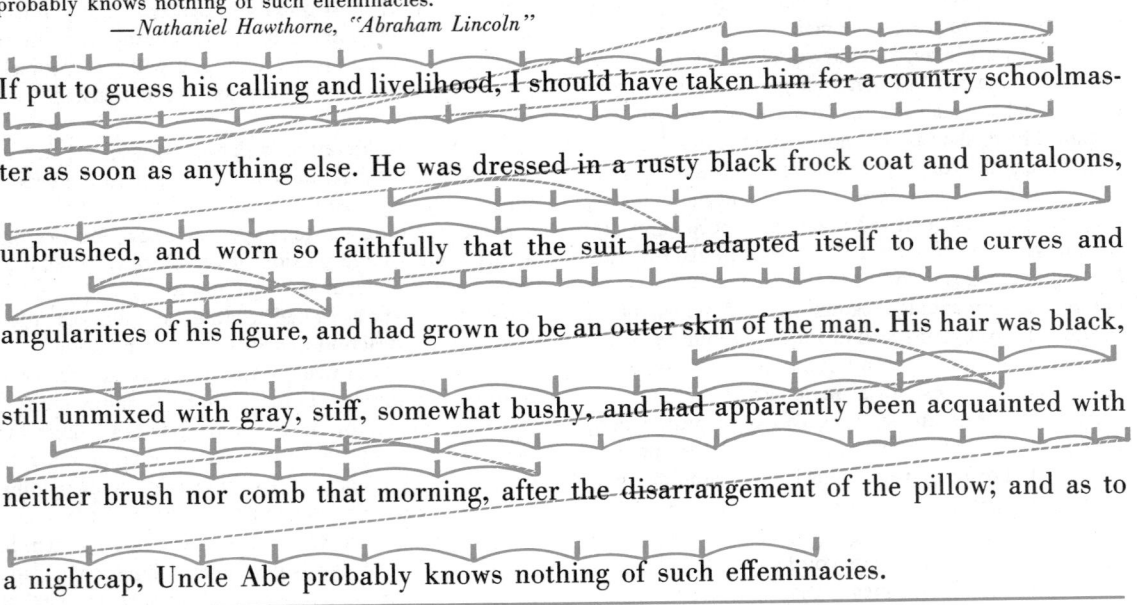

If put to guess his calling and livelihood, I should have taken him for a country schoolmaster as soon as anything else. He was dressed in a rusty black frock coat and pantaloons, unbrushed, and worn so faithfully that the suit had adapted itself to the curves and angularities of his figure, and had grown to be an outer skin of the man. His hair was black, still unmixed with gray, stiff, somewhat bushy, and had apparently been acquainted with neither brush nor comb that morning, after the disarrangement of the pillow; and as to a nightcap, Uncle Abe probably knows nothing of such effeminacies.

WPM (words per minute) goal, it becomes your natural speed. Then you may work on achieving still greater speed.

No matter what your beginning reading speed, you can double it, at least, in only a few days. Continue this daily practice for two weeks. Record your reading speed for each day in your reading diary. Small dips in your reading speed are inevitable because of outside forces such as interruptions or fatigue. With regular practice over two weeks, however, you will soon be reading at your new, faster speed without any special effort or need to slow down.

Developing three reading speeds. As you have already learned, one characteristic of good readers is that they have more than one reading speed. They can shift reading speeds much as a car shifts gears. A car needs different gears for going uphill, downhill, or cruising. Good readers use different speeds for similar reasons. You can prove this to yourself by reading a few pages in a favorite novel and then trying to read a legal document, for example, a mortgage or a lease. One is much less difficult and complex than the other, and so it is neither possible nor desirable to read both at the same speed.

For efficient reading, you should have three speeds. Such a repertoire enables you to get the most out of any material you read and to do so with minimum time and effort. No matter what you read, shifting gears will keep you from reading so slowly that you become bored or reading so quickly that you lose comprehension. The three speeds are *study reading, normal reading,* and *rapid reading.*

Study reading is the slowest speed. It is used, for example, for textbooks and work manuals, which require you to retain facts and master concepts. Naturally, this takes care and concentration, and it would be foolish to rush headlong through such material. In studying, therefore, you should slow down so that you absorb the material in a single reading. For that reason, good readers study at a rate of about 200 words per minute, or even less.

Normal reading is the middle speed for works of average complexity. It is used for books and magazine articles that require close attention, but not intense study. This speed is suitable for books and articles that present facts without demanding an analysis of concepts, and for novels and general nonfiction read for relaxation. Normal reading speed can also be useful for reviewing difficult material that has already been studied once. Most good readers have a normal reading speed close to twice as fast as their study speed. A good normal reading speed would be anywhere from 300 to 400 words per minute.

Rapid reading is used for easy reading material or for sampling material to find out whether you want to read it completely. Rapid reading is used for magazines, newspapers, and other quick reading for general information. The rapid reading speed is the one you will find it easiest to improve quickly. Good rapid reading proceeds at speeds up to 500 words per minute and sometimes even beyond. The maximum reading speed attainable in easy reading without skipping is about 800 words per minute.

Two considerations will help you choose the speed for any reading material. First ask yourself, what is the level of difficulty? Using your prereading skills, check the material for vocabulary, subject matter, amount of important facts, and complexity of important concepts. Grade the work on a scale from difficult to easy and choose the appropriate reading speed. Then ask yourself, why are you reading it? Decide if your purpose is to study, to be generally informed, or to relax. The answers to these questions usually point to a choice of study, normal, or rapid reading.

After working on your average reading speed for at least two weeks, begin to practice the three reading speeds by varying the kind of material you read. Your first practice was on easy material, at a speed closest to your rapid rate. But in your third week of daily reading, begin to practice with difficult and average as well as easy reading matter. You will quickly find your own beginning speed for each; then work to improve it.

You can now begin to add the level of difficulty to your reading diary and to keep track of three reading speeds. Once you have calculated your beginning speed at all three paces, set personal goals for all three speeds. As always, push yourself to go faster, to eliminate regressions, and to make speedy eye returns. After reading, record your speed and review the passage in your mind to check for comprehension. If you have not understood what you have read, you will have to slow down. But if you continue to practice and to vary your reading material, you will find your words per minute scores at all three speeds beginning to improve.

Reading speeds

Good readers have three reading speeds. They are efficient readers because they choose the proper speed for any kind of reading material. Here is the basic repertoire of a good reader, illustrating the uses of each speed and the rates attainable with practice. The young person shown here is reading an entry in an encyclopedia. Because her purpose is careful analysis, she reads at a slow rate.

Speed	Materials	Purposes	Complexity	WPM
Study	Textbooks Work manuals	Careful analysis Memorization Test preparation	Difficult	200 or less
Normal	Novels Nonfiction	Leisure reading General information	Average	300–400
Rapid	Newspapers Magazines	Locating facts Prereading Sampling	Easy	500 or more

Test your speed and comprehension

Time yourself on this passage. Read at your normal speed. When finished, calculate your reading speed using the information provided at the end of the passage. Then test your comprehension with the questions provided. If you cannot answer most of the questions, you need to slow down and work on comprehension. If you can answer most of them, you are ready to practice reading faster.

Most of us have grown up with unfair stereotypes of those Puritan forefathers we heard so much about in high school. We imagine very joyless people, dressed in black, with little taste for experimentation in life.

In fact, the Puritans were among the most innovative people of all times, and certainly among the most adventurous and daring of any people who came to America in the early days of its colonial history. The very name "Puritan" was once synonymous with experimentation, and those who came to Massachusetts in the 17th century were as contentious a bunch as ever sat in the bistros popularized by the poets of Paris. The origins of the movement can be located in the Protestant Reformation launched in England by Henry VIII, who differed from the Pope on matters of divorce law. Henry founded the Church of England, but some thought that his own church needed to be purified even further of some old traditions, and that is why they became known as Puritans.

The first group to land in the new world were bound, aboard the *Mayflower,* for a place around New York bay. But blown off course, they landed in Massachusetts on December 21, 1620, according to tradition, at Plymouth Rock, near Boston. A group of 103 had left on the voyage that took 64 days; by the time they landed at Plymouth in a snowstorm, two had died and one had been born. Unsure of how to govern themselves, they invented a method: it was called the Mayflower Compact, and it is considered one of the forerunners of the United States Constitution.

Landing in winter was a dreadful mistake. By April of 1621 only 50 of the landing 102 had survived "the great sickness," a combination of scurvy contracted aboard ship and starvation through the winter. As their leader, William Bradford, described it, they arrived in a "howling wilderness" of previously unimaginable proportions. Actually, one key problem on Bradford's mind was the extent of the jungle before him. He imagined a "hideous and desolate wilderness" extending forever, or perhaps to some theoretical "South Sea," or Pacific Ocean, limit, populated only by "savage barbarians ready to fill our sides full of arrows." The Puritans knew this as they huddled in their tents—not log cabins—through that first winter. But when the *Mayflower,* with its shipload of skeptical sailors, left North America for home on April 5, 1621, not one of the surviving Puritans chose to return with the ship.

The Puritans, whom we still think of as rigid and impersonal, made the best of their situation. Three thousand miles by sailing ship from any civilized place, they made what friends they could. They met with Indians—the very people the popular stereotype suggests would most horrify the straight-laced Puritans. Miles Standish, Priscilla Mullins, and the rest of these true pioneers readily sat down and ate with visitors whose names have been recorded, no doubt inaccurately, as Samoset and Squanto. Their Thanksgiving probably never happened on November 24, but the Puritans were open-minded and adventurous enough to celebrate, in the fall of 1621, their own survival with a people completely opposite in culture and personal habit. It was this flexibility, this ability to deal honestly with people whose beliefs were light-years away from their own, that enabled the Puritans, in Bradford's words: "To fit up their houses and dwellings against winter, being all well recovered in health and strength and with all things."

$$\frac{\text{Total words} = 580}{\text{Reading time in seconds} =} \times 60 = \underline{\quad} \text{ WPM}$$

1. The author's major point is:
   a. The Puritans have little to do with modern life.
   b. The Puritans are poorly understood by us.
   c. The Puritans should have emigrated to Virginia.

2. The author appreciates the Puritans for their:
   a. Ability to relate to strangers.
   b. Religious piety.
   c. Political activism.

3. Puritans got their name because they:
   a. Hoped to purify the Church of England.
   b. Hoped to purify the Roman Catholic Church.
   c. Hoped to purify the Presbyterian Church.

4. The Puritans came to Massachusetts in the:
   a. 16th century.
   b. 17th century.
   c. 18th century.

5. This passage to tells us:
   a. Whom the Puritan fought against.
   b. The importance of enduring hardship.
   c. Why the Puritans deserve attention.

Answers: 1 (b); 2 (a); 3 (a); 4 (b); 5 (c).
Being able to answer *most* of these questions means correct responses to 3 or more. If you answered 2 or less correctly, you may have read too fast.

Reading for comprehension.

Reading faster is a physical skill. For the most efficient reading, this physical skill must be matched by an intellectual one. Thus, speed must be based on the ability to comprehend written material quickly. Complete comprehension is easier to manage at slow reading speeds, but efficient readers are able to absorb ideas even when pushing to move through a book at rapid reading speed.

Four basic habits are essential to good comprehension: locating key ideas, marking a book while reading, using reference books, and reviewing what has been read.

Locating key ideas. As you have already learned, prereading is possible because all words on a page are not of equal importance. Prereading establishes this fact. The process of prereading is one of locating key ideas embodied in important words and phrases. Even in difficult material, many words may be read quickly—think of "as," "an," and "the," for example. The important words, however, are crucial terms. They carry specific definitions in any written work, such as the term "prereading" in this chapter. Important words also include words or phrases of transition. They signal the direction of ideas. The word "however" is a good example. Efficient readers are able to comprehend material as they read quickly because they are alert to such important words as they push ahead.

Crucial terms are the heart of any written work, because they contain in single words the focused ideas of the author. For example, government spokesmen in both China and the United States are likely to use the word "propaganda" as a crucial term in their statements. One accepted meaning of propaganda is "promotion of ideas," and the spokesmen of both countries mean this when they use the word in reference to political policies. But by this term the spokesman of one country may mean "important and necessary ideas," while the spokesman from the other may mean "false and misleading ideas." For this reason, recognizing uses of this crucial term is essential to comprehending fully the statements made by spokesmen from competing nations.

Good readers spot a crucial term when they read at any speed, and if necessary they pause to consider the term, to locate its definition in the work, or to check its accepted definition in a dictionary. A crucial term can be located by its frequent recurrence in a work. The appearance of a crucial term may be signaled to the reader through the use of italics or the use of the word in chapter titles or subheadings. Any book on American history, for example, can be expected to use the word "Reconstruction" to refer to the post-Civil War era. Good readers recognize this as a crucial term that the author must define. Having met it for the first

Transition words and phrases

Good readers identify relationships between ideas by spotting transition words and phrases. Pivotal terms, such as those listed here, indicate similarity, difference, or sequence. Paying attention to them helps comprehension at any reading speed.

Similarity	*Difference*	*Sequence*
and	but	then
as well as	although	first, second
also	however	earlier
furthermore	nevertheless	later
likewise	despite	before
similarly	yet	after
in addition	on the other hand	last
another	on the contrary	finally
moreover	instead	as a result
so	though	next

time in a chapter title or important topic sentence to a paragraph, they then look for the definition the author will attach to it—what years are included in "Reconstruction" and what gives the era its significance. This may take a moment, but the pause helps both comprehension and speed because the term can be read confidently and quickly when met again.

Transition words and phrases are another class of important words that indicate key ideas. Transition words and phrases indicate directions and relationships. We are all familiar with the basics of this concept. We all know that the word "and" signals a second action, idea, or fact similar in kind to a first one: "Ulysses S. Grant was a Civil War general *and* a United States President." We know that the word "but" signals a second action or idea different from a first one: "Ulysses S. Grant was an effective Civil War general *but* an ineffective United States President." We also know that the word "then" signals a sequence of ideas or actions: "Ulysses S. Grant was a Civil War general and *then* a United States President." We all know these word indicators of direction, but good readers use this knowledge to their advantage as they read for speed. Good readers look for transition words and phrases that show relationships of ideas.

The transition words and phrases you can look for in your reading all fall into three groups. Some, such as "and," signal *similarity*. Others, such as "but," signal *difference*. The last group, such as "then," signals *sequence*. The table of transition terms shown here provides further examples of the words and phrases that fall into each of these three groups. By looking for transition terms, you can more easily and completely comprehend the relationships between key ideas in your reading.

Marking books. By consciously searching for crucial terms and for transition words or phrases, good readers keep themselves alert and so improve both their speed and comprehension. Another habit they use to make reading an active, conscious process is annotating, or *marking*, their books. Obviously, you cannot mark up a book that does not belong to you, whether it comes from a library or from a friend. Nor will you want to bother with careful annotations on easy material intended to be read at your rapid speed. But for all difficult material that is read at your study speed, and some average material that is read at your normal speed, you will find your comprehension improved if you pause to mark the key ideas in the book. Some people are reluctant to mark up a book because they mistakenly believe that this destroys it. But most books, usually relatively inexpensive, easily replaceable, and salable after use even if marked, are not often heirloom possessions to be preserved in mint condition. Rather, they are objects to be used to acquire knowledge, and good use implies some wear and tear. By marking a book, you make it your own.

Marking books is a good reading habit because it increases concentration and alertness. It also improves your reading ability by reminding you that you are searching for the key ideas that deserve annotation. Marking books also improves your ability to retain what you have read because the physical act of under-lining or circling words or phrases on a page impresses them on your memory. Finally, having the marks on the page makes it easier to review books later on for study purposes or for personal interest.

Many adults still own books they marked up in school. A quick examination of one of them will prove how useful annotations are when studying or reviewing reading material. Many people who mark up their books limit themselves to underlining or coloring over lines of text with a soft-tipped marker. Because good reading distinguishes between ideas, and because you are free to mark books in any way you wish, do not limit yourself to a single kind of marking. Good readers develop a variety of markings to use for different purposes when studying difficult material. While working to improve your reading, develop your own markings, remembering that it is essential to have various marks for a variety of purposes. A typical system might mix circles for crucial terms with underlining for their definitions. It could also use marginal numbers for ideas in a sequence, and stars for important facts.

Using reference books. Good readers often are ambitious. They read for pleasure and relaxation, but they also read to broaden their understanding of various fields of knowledge. In books they discover new interests, and they pursue these new interests in other books. Like any rewarding enterprise, this sort of ambitious reading is a challenge. In pursuing interests through books, you will inevitably encounter works that present challenges in ideas and vocabulary.

No one should make reading an unpleasant chore. If

How to mark a book

Marking your books can help you to understand and review what you are reading. It is helpful, therefore, to develop a system of marking you find useful. The passage below shows how one reader marked it, using circles for crucial terms, underlining for definitions, using numbers for ideas in a sequence and stars for important facts.

Historians undertake to arrange sequences—called stories, or histories—assuming in silence a relation of cause and effect. These assumptions, hidden in the depths of dusty libraries, have been astounding, but commonly unconscious and childlike; so much so, that if any captious critic were to drag them to light, historians would probably reply, with one voice, that they had never supposed themselves required to know what they were talking about. Adams, for one, had toiled in vain to find out what he meant. He had even published a dozen volumes of American history for no other purpose than to satisfy himself whether, by the severest process of stating, with the least possible comment, such facts as seemed sure, in such order as seemed rigorously consequent, he could fix for a familiar moment a necessary sequence of human movement. The result had satisfied him as little as at Harvard College. Where he saw sequence, other men saw something quite different, and no one saw the same unit of measure. He cared little about his experiments and less about his statesmen, who seemed to him quite as ignorant as himself and, as a rule, no more honest; but he insisted on a relation of sequence, and if he could not reach it by one method, he would try as many methods as science knew. Satisfied that the sequence of men led to nothing and that the sequence of their society could lead no further, while the mere sequence of time was artificial, and the sequence of thought was chaos, he turned at last to the sequence of force; and thus it happened that, after ten years' pursuit, he found himself lying in the Gallery of Machines at the Great Exposition of 1900, with his historical neck broken by the sudden eruption of forces totally new.

a book seems impenetrable, feel free to abandon it. Choose another on the same subject, or switch to another of your interests. However, many good readers get special satisfaction from mastering difficult works. This is because they have the good reading habit of using *reference books,* most often dictionaries and encyclopedias. Many of the advertised methods to quadruple your reading speed overnight actually advise against using reference books. They do this because they are interested only in how *fast* something is read, not in how *well* it is read. Speed is part of good reading, as this section on efficient reading has stressed, but to read something well at any speed, to gain the satisfaction of mastering demanding works, you will surely have to pause occasionally to consult dictionaries and encyclopedias.

Reference works are used because different authors envision different audiences for their books. For example, authors of high-school textbooks on economics write for an audience that is different from that intended by authors of advanced books on United States economy. The difference is that authors of the advanced books assume that the reader will be familiar with certain words and concepts, so there are fewer explanations in advanced books than in textbooks. The authors of textbooks will, for example, provide a complete definition of "capitalism," while authors of advanced works will assume that their readers already understand the definition.

The meanings of words are the domain of the dictionary. Many people mistakenly think that using a dictionary is childish. In fact, most scholars work with a dictionary close at hand. They do this because the dictionary provides precise definitions of its terms. In addition, dictionaries provide information on the pronunciation, derivation, and multiple meanings of a word. With this knowledge, the precise meaning of a word as it is used in context becomes clear.

Facts and ideas are the domain of the encyclopedia. Most encyclopedia entries open with a brief, precise identification of a person, place, or idea, and then move into more detailed explanation. Thus, a quick look at the opening of an encyclopedia entry may be all you need to return to your book confident that you understand a general concept. Also, many encyclopedia entries are pleasurable and informative reading. If you understand a concept mentioned in your reading but want to go deeper into it, you might make a note to consult an encyclopedia when you have finished reading or before you resume again. A final great advantage of consulting an encyclopedia is that it can lead you to other books of interest on the same subject. Many attach bibliographies to their substantial entries.

There are two sorts of reference works. The most common are general encyclopedias and dictionaries.

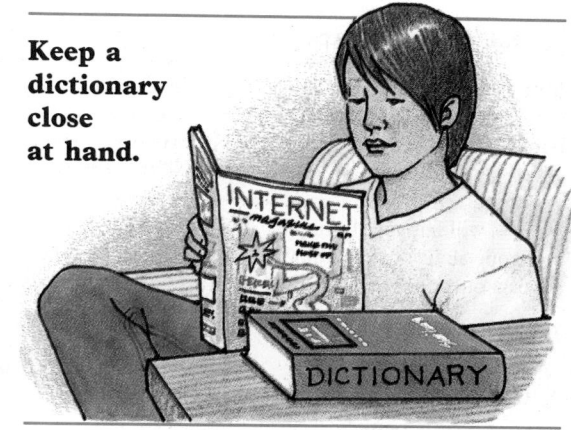

Keep a dictionary close at hand.

These are all-purpose reference works that cover all fields of knowledge. Southwestern's *Volume Library* and the dictionaries in its *Student Handbooks* are general reference works. The second type of reference works comprises specialized dictionaries and encyclopedias. These cover single fields of knowledge, such as medicine, art, literature, or history. All homes should have general reference works available for use by readers of all ages. Specialized reference works, which are consulted less often, can be used in any local library.

Reviewing what you read. A final consideration in reading for comprehension is the ability to retain information obtained from books. Reading and understanding are not the same thing as memorization. No one is expected to retain everything read in a book. In fact, because reading is a process of understanding and assimilating information, no one should even desire complete recall. Good readers concentrate on ideas, intending to retain the main concepts and facts from whatever they are reading. They help themselves retain this information by developing the habit of reviewing what they have read before going on to another activity. In reviewing material that is difficult, average, or easy, repeat the key ideas to yourself and create a double impression of them in your memory, once in reading and once in reviewing. You should be able to review mentally all reading you do, even leisure reading of easy material. However, reviewing is most important for material that is complex enough to require your normal or study speeds. Reviewing is an important part of any overall program to improve your reading speed and comprehension. If your review suggests lack of comprehension, you will have to slow down and read more carefully.

Good readers review material immediately on finishing their reading. In this way they create that double impression on their memory before the information can slip away.

Questions and sample answers for reviewing what you read

Many readers have only a vague recollection of books they have read. Your comprehension and retention of books and articles can be improved by briefly reviewing what you read soon after finishing it. With a series of general questions, you can focus your reactions. This process will improve both your understanding of books and your ability to remember their content. These five general questions can be asked of any reading material:

The general questions for review can help you to form a memorable impression of the ideas in your reading. Here is the way a reader might answer those questions, mentally or on paper, for the reading about the Puritans given as a speed test on page 314.

1. What was the author's general point?	**1.** The author's general point was to make us interested in what we have to learn from the Puritans.
2. What individual ideas did the author use to support his point?	**2.** The individual idea used to suggest this was the way the Puritans made friends with the Indians.
3. What were the crucial terms discussed by the author?	**3.** The name "Puritan" reflects the fact that Puritans hoped to purify their church even more than the English Protestants had already done.
4. What important facts were cited by the author?	**4.** The Puritans came to America in 1620. They landed in Massachusetts even though they intended to go to New York.
5. What did you like or dislike in this work?	**5.** The Puritans may be more interesting than I had thought. I think I will read more about them.

The first step in reviewing is to ask yourself fundamental questions about what you have read. What were the important ideas? What were the important facts? If you have concentrated on locating key ideas by spotting crucial terms and transitions, you should be able to remember these in their proper sequence. If you have taken the time to mark your book, you can use this brief review period to leaf back over the pages you have read, glancing at the key ideas identified by your markings.

The second step in the review process is to summarize the key ideas in your own words. For easy reading material, this can be done mentally. But for difficult material, especially if you have read for study purposes, take the time to summarize on paper what you have read. This can be done in the form of brief notes.

You will find such notes handy for later reference.

Now begin to add this consideration to your reading diary. As described early in this chapter, the diary has space for these new notes on review. First, note whether you have summarized your reading in your mind or on paper. Summarizing readings is always a good habit, but you need not always do so, especially on days when you practice easy reading. Then honestly describe your own sense of your level of comprehension simply by describing your effort at summary as *excellent*, *mediocre*, or *poor*. As your reading diary grows, you will be able to correlate this information on comprehension against your entries on reading speed. Then you can determine whether you are achieving a balance between speed and comprehension; that is, whether you are progressing toward efficient reading.

Special types of reading

To become a proficient reader, you must learn to vary your reading speed to suit different sorts of reading material. But complete proficiency requires the additional skill of learning how to suit reading methods to reading purposes. If an adult seeking relaxation picks up a classic modern novel, for example, that reader has

a reading purpose different from that of a college student reading the same novel for a course in literature.

You should formulate your purposes and expectations before beginning to read. The checklist on this page provides some key questions that can help you do so.

Reading for self-improvement.

Reading for self-improvement requires interest in accumulating general knowledge about a subject. Once you have begun to pursue this interest, your reading purpose should be to add to your fund of knowledge by testing the persuasiveness of different opinions on the subject. An interest in British history, for example, logically begins with some general surveys of events in that long history. But from that point on, you will encounter contradictory accounts and interpretations of the significant movements and periods in British history. Thus, in reading for self-improvement, you should eventually begin to read against your fund of background knowledge, to consider new ideas in the light of older ones.

Reading for this purpose requires regular contact with your chosen subject and careful reading at normal reading speed. Reading for self-improvement also demands the frequent consultation of reference works, which can be counted on to provide relatively objective overviews and impartial summaries of long-standing disputes and differences of opinion. Because this sort of reading constitutes an informal course of study, you probably will not feel it necessary to keep notes on what you read. Another aid to interest and understanding in reading for self-improvement comes from sharing and debating books. That can be done in a reading discussion group, described in the "Continuing to improve" part of this chapter.

Reading for advancement.

No kind of reading provokes a clearer sense of interest and purpose than reading that is intended to develop occupational skills needed for career promotion or change. Here you have a personal interest more intensely felt than that generally found in purely intellectual or leisure pursuits.

Your interest in reading for professional advancement is especially well focused—you want to know what special skill any book or article can teach you. Your purpose in reading is twofold: to determine the relevance of the advice to your position and to master it completely for application to your job or career plans. These two purposes imply two reading strategies. The first demands especially careful prereading so you do not waste your time with irrelevant advice. Most occupational guides are designed to facilitate prereading. Pay close attention to the chapter titles, subtitles, summaries, and questions for review (these are standard features of this sort of reading material). Your second purpose demands that you closely read material of proven relevance at your study speed.

Occupational guides attach special importance to a vocabulary of crucial terms, and mastery of these terms is important in achieving a better job. For that reason, careful note-taking is essential to reading for professional advancement. Be sure to mark your books for later review, and be sure to keep written summaries of especially valuable information. For any occupation, there are likely to be a number of useful guides to advancement. Note-taking can be especially helpful because it makes it possible for you to gather notes on practical advice from many sources.

Reading for pleasure.

Reading for pleasure is the least formal sort of reading endeavor. Your interest in the material might derive from any of the full range of literary pleasures: enjoyment of stories, identification with dynamic characters, or delight in a particular narrative style. Your purpose in reading is a desire for the stimulating and unpredictable entertainment that only books can offer.

But even in reading for pleasure, your repertoire of reading skills is essential for preserving and continually satisfying your desire to read. Reading for enjoyment is best pursued with attention to consciously formulating your interest in the material. Your interest may stem from a particular author's style, the presence of the same interesting character in several novels, or the suspense of a particular kind of plot. Whatever the reason for your interest, you will be led logically to other, similar works that can provide the same enjoyment.

The method of reading for pleasure is as unstructured as the purpose. You should feel free to shift from normal to rapid reading speeds and back again as your interest dictates. Slowing down unnecessarily, however, invites the risk of flagging interest. Brisk reading of works chosen for no interest other than enjoyment can, in fact, intensify delight in them by more quickly and more frequently bringing to the reader the individual features cherished most. No note-taking should intrude on pleasure reading, but you will find it useful to keep some sort of record of your favorite works, either on a shelf that holds your personal library or in a diary of authors and titles.

Study or pleasure? Tailor your approach to your purpose.

Special kinds of reading. Different purposes can change your reading strategy, but differences in reading materials may require special strategies. Technical journals, for example, may rely on complicated charts, graphs, and diagrams to explain ideas discussed in the text or to introduce supplementary ideas. Literary magazines, on the other hand, are rarely broken by any such illustrative material. In the first case, your beginning strategy should be to master the charts, graphs, and diagrams. In the second case, you might begin by prereading titles, subtitles, and topic sentences.

Visual contrasts among kinds of reading materials represent differences of format, both in page arrangements and layouts. But format is indicative of fundamental differences in organization as well. Because a technical journal uses charts, graphs, and diagrams, it may adopt a particular kind of organization.

Kinds of reading

Newspapers. It has been said that no one *reads* newspapers, people just peruse them. There is some truth to this exaggeration. The sheer bulk of your daily newspaper may prohibit careful reading.

Most people read newspapers for quick information on recent events. Newspaper editors know this, and so their news stories feature essential information in the opening paragraphs. There is a journalism school maxim for how to open a news story: Who? What? Where? When? Why? and How? You can see how these important facts find their way into the opening of the sample newspaper story shown on this page. By concentrating only on the opening paragraphs of the news story, you can easily and quickly determine if your are interested enough to read further.

This is true only of news stories. Other parts of the newspaper, such as features and editorials, are organized more along the lines of a magazine article.

Where?
When?
Who?
What?

Why?

How?

MORRISON ELECTION VICTOR

New York City, March 18—Jennifer Morrison was elected president of the new American Federation of Teachers today in a stunning upset over the incumbent, Michael A. Conroy. The vote ended the union's national congress at the convention center here and convincingly demonstrated Ms. Morrison's ability to control the votes of union members disenchanted with the union's pension policies.

The new president made her acceptance speech after midnight from a dais strewn with confetti and streamers. Mr. Conroy, despite losing by a clear margin of 2 to 1, had issued no concession speech.

Magazines. Magazine articles, newspaper editorials, and newspaper features may differ from news stories in at least one important respect: they may be based on opinion rather than fact. For this reason, they are always signed by authors, or, in the case of editorials, they appear on the newspaper's editorial page. Because such articles are not primarily concerned with facts, they open with no recitation of who, what, where, when, why, and how.

Magazines, in particular, tend to pile up as they arrive in the mail. To keep abreast of your magazine reading, you can take advantage of this knowledge of their organization. Preread the table of contents to get an overview of the magazine's contents. Check the full titles and subheadings of individual articles for indications of their special focus. Then go through the opening paragraphs to reach the announcement of the article's purpose and content. If you are interested enough to want to read the entire article, go on. Few good readers ever bother to read all of a magazine.

Mid-Life Career Change:
One Man's Story
by Robert Miller

His job had been "obsoleted," as the supervisor said, by new automation that churned out the product faster, better, and cheaper. His daughters, already enrolled in college by then, had been forced to withdraw in mid-semester. His home, carefully reworked for his family's needs over twenty years of amateur handyman projects, had been repossessed by the bank and shown to strangers. Then, hitting rock bottom, William Jameson found himself on an endless line in an overcrowded office filing for welfare benefits.

Last week Congress opened debate on the nation's chronic unemployment problem. The discussion in Washington has to do with hundreds of thousands of workers, but unemployment is also a personal catastrophe. . . .

Recognizing a format and understanding the organization it implies is a matter of knowing facts about the organization of different sorts of publications and of practicing the reading strategy best suited to each. The following pages give you practical facts about several kinds of reading material.

The reading diary you prepared included a final notation for "special difficulties." At this point in your program for reading improvement, you are ready to begin using that notation. Keep track of the single kinds of written material that seem most confusing. Because you are also already varying daily the difficulty of your reading, you should begin to see a pattern emerging. You will be able to recognize potential stumbling blocks in news articles, magazine stories, reference book entries, or visual aids. Then you can consult or review the relevant information given on these pages.

Reference books.

Reference books are concise compilations of essential knowledge on a wide variety of subjects. They make this knowledge available in individual entries, organized topically or alphabetically. Each entry begins with a broad statement of the subject's significance. Only then does it proceed to a discussion of individual aspects of the subject.

In the sample biographical entry shown, you can see how a reference book gives easy access to essential information, such as dates and nationality.

In reference books you will also find keys to related articles, such as the cross-reference here to a separate entry on "stream of consciousness." If you were only interested in finding out who James Joyce was, you could have stopped reading this entry after the second paragraph. But if your interest went further, you would have continued to the end, where you would likely have found a bibliography.

> JOYCE, JAMES A. (1882–1941). Irish novelist. Although he wrote some poetry (*Chamber Music*, 1907) and one play (*Exiles*, 1918), James Joyce's most important contributions to modern literature were the stories collected in *Dubliners* (1907) and the novels *Portrait of the Artist as a Young Man* (1916), *Ulysses* (1922), and *Finnegans Wake* (1939).
>
> By almost any evaluation, James Joyce ranks as one of the most difficult and most important novelists of the twentieth century. His works have had enormous influence on all subsequent writers because they developed a technique of STREAM OF CONSCIOUSNESS for presentation of the disorganized flow of frequently commonplace thoughts through the minds of their characters.
>
> James Joyce was born in Dublin on. . . .

Tables and graphs.

Tables require close study. You should first note the title and the column and row identifications. In this table, for example, it is important to note that the figures are for five-year periods. Notes and explanations attached to tables are crucial. (Here the notes tell you that all figures except the first row are in billions of dollars; they also tell that the statistics have been obtained from the federal government). After acquainting yourself with a table, analyze the figures for trends.

A line graph like the one shown here is read like a grid. To interpret any point on the lines you must move from it to the vertical or horizontal reference points that explain its value. This graph clearly indicates the overall trend of increase in both liabilities and assets of savings and loan associations. It also shows how closely liabilities follow assets, a fact not as obvious in the table on the same subject. Graphs are limited, however, because they can provide only approximate values.

Balance sheet of savings and loan associations 1970–1989

All figures in billions of dollars except number of associations

	1970	1975	1980	1985	1989
Number of associations	5,669	4,931	4,594	3,535	3,011
Total assets	$176.2	$338.2	$632.8	$1,080.1	$1,253.6
Cash	16.5	30.9	58.6	145.3	167.4
Mortgages	150.3	278.6	503.9	652.4	712.1
Other	9.3	28.7	70.3	282.4	374.1
Liabilities	163.8	318.5	599.4	1,032.9	1,229.6
Net worth	$ 12.4	$ 19.7	$ 33.4	$ 47.2	$ 24.0

Source: U.S. Federal Home Loan Bank Board

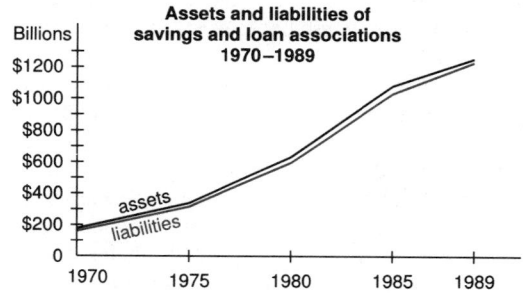

Assets and liabilities of savings and loan associations 1970–1989

Continuing to improve

At the end of eight weeks of daily practice of the principles of good reading, as described in this chapter, you will see a marked improvement in your reading speed and comprehension. Even more important, you will have acquired a new set of reading habits that will make you a better reader and make your reading more enjoyable. You can verify your improvements in speed and comprehension over the eight weeks by comparing the first and the last entries in your reading diary. You can also verify your improvements in reading habits over the same period by answering once again the questions on the "Checklist of reading habits" on page 304.

These improvements will have made you a competent, efficient, and proficient reader by giving you a mastery of important particular skills. But once acquired, the skills must be maintained. People improve their golf or swimming abilities, for example, through a series of lessons. When the lessons are complete, they must practice continually to protect their new abilities at these sports. In the same way, you must practice to protect your new reading skills. This is easier and more enjoyable than learning new habits, because your improved ability will make the practice itself more satisfying and pleasurable.

The checklist for continued improvement shown on this page itemizes the key considerations for maintaining an ongoing reading program of your own. You should periodically review the entire list to protect your new reading skills.

Practice reading.
Daily practice is essential for preserving reading speed and comprehension. You can help yourself with short readings for speed during work breaks. You can mentally summarize your recent reading at virtually any time. Ideally, though, you will continue to set aside a regular reading time each day. Most people find that in addition to keeping their reading skills sharp, regular reading periods become a positive influence on their daily lives, particularly when they choose books of inspirational value or intellectual interest.

Your interest in daily reading can be maintained by varying what you read. There is no need to alternate easy, average, and difficult reading material as rigorously as you did over the eight-week program, but switching from novels to occupational journals or from history books to popular magazines introduces a pleasant variety into your reading and also helps reinforce your repertoire of speeds and your comprehension skills. Even though you may stop thinking about study,

My checklist for continuing to improve

1. I read daily.
2. I vary the kinds of things I read.
3. I vary my reading speeds.
4. I test my speed and comprehension regularly.
5. I follow the principles of good reading.
6. I am always conscious of my purpose in reading.
7. I keep interesting things to read at home.
8. I pursue my reading interests.
9. I visit bookstores and libraries.
10. I share my reading with friends and family.

normal, and rapid reading speeds, you will find yourself shifting automatically into these speeds if you vary the kinds of things you read.

As a final check on maintaining your new reading speeds and strategies, test yourself periodically. A quick calculation of your reading speed on different sorts of materials every few weeks will remind you of the need to continue to work on your new speeds. Periodic tests will also indicate particular aspects of your reading ability that may still require special attention, such as your high speed reading. A brief review of the advice in this chapter, on any aspect of your reading, along with a few refresher practice sessions, will ensure that you preserve your complete repertoire of reading skills.

Group reading.
One of the best ways to continue your reading improvement is to read as a social activity. Sharing reading with friends has two good effects. It increases your interest in reading, because comments from others force you to think about what you have read and give you ideas for what you might read in the future. Sharing reading with others also helps keep you on a continuing program for improvement by encouraging you to finish books so that you can discuss them intelligently with others.

Reading as a family activity. Many people have fond memories of being read to in their childhood. But family reading is not just a memory from the past. Many families continue to read aloud regularly, and reading is often their only group recreational activity. Reading aloud to others is not just for parents with young children. Sharing readings with one's entire family is a gratifying experience; once introduced, such reading quickly proves its value. Family reading offers a refreshing alternative to television, so anyone seri-

Reading is a family activity with lifelong benefits for all members, from the youngest to the most senior. Ideas for books on a wide variety of subjects can often be obtained from book reviews that appear in your local newspaper and in magazines you read.

ously interested in reading should begin to share this activity with the family.

Reading as a social activity. Reading discussion groups are a contagious kind of social activity that can become a regular part of one's life. These discussion groups offer an alternative means of getting together with friends for an evening. Many reading groups thrive for years. Often there is a revolving membership of people of many backgrounds who find that they have much to offer as well as much to learn.

To start a reading group, all you need are a few friends interested in reading the same book. Arrange a time to meet together after everyone has had a chance to finish the book. Most discussions of the book will begin by chatting casually about what the book says and what members of the group have found good or bad about it. Reactions will differ, of course, but different opinions of a book, an author, or a character's worth will enhance the discussion. There is no need to focus on purely intellectual problems, although these may finally become the focus of the discussion.

Reading groups generally vote on the next book to be read. They may also invite additional friends to join the next discussion. Whether the meetings are weekly or monthly, a large membership is useful because it ensures stimulating discussion despite the occasional absence of some regular members.

Keeping in touch with books.

Your reading will be helped by making certain you have an ample supply of books you want to read. More than 40,000 new titles are published in the United States every year. Despite this abundance, many people do not value books highly. While the skill of reading can be acquired through conscious effort, the love of books develops through contact with them.

Bookstores stimulate reading through attractive displays of current books and standard titles that continue to attract readers. Bookstore managers know the books people enjoy reading at any time as well as other works that might match your current reading interests. In comparison with other ages, books in our time are relatively inexpensive. New, hardbound best-sellers may seem difficult to afford, but their worth should be considered in terms of the hours of pleasure or the practical benefits they offer. Almost any reading interest can also be served well by reliance on paperbacks.

Booksellers—often students working their way through college—who come to your door may also offer books of lasting value. Many families fill their bookshelves in this way, establishing reading resources that serve more than a single generation.

Local libraries acquire books they think may be of interest to the taxpayers who support them. A single visit to a library can produce a reading list that will serve for months, and the books may be borrowed at no cost. Libraries, even more than bookstores, keep on hand a variety of books for readers of all ages. Often their books are shelved by age group, so the reading interests of children, young adults, or adults can be fueled simply by browsing along the shelves. All libraries also stock extensive collections of books printed in oversized, especially legible typefaces. These are intended for readers who suffer from poor eyesight. In this way, books become accessible to those who might otherwise be denied.

With bookstores, booksellers, and libraries, you can always keep your home well stocked with books enjoyable to you and all members of your family. Well chosen books, plus attention to the principles of reading discussed in this chapter, can help anyone become and remain a better reader.

Cactus Country
Edward Abbey

Reading lists

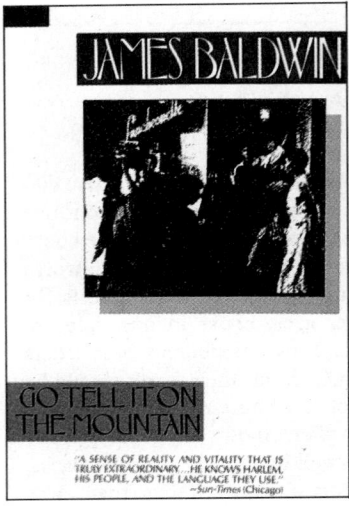

Go Tell It On the Mountain
James Baldwin

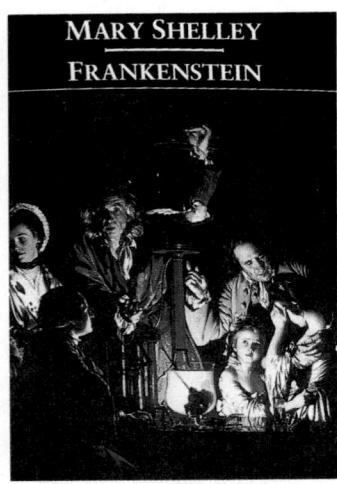

Frankenstein
Mary Shelley

Making reading a lifelong activity. Books lead to books. This means that one book is likely to lead you to another on the same subject or by the same author. The connections are made in the books themselves, in the topical groupings of library shelves, or in shared displays in bookstores.

What follows is a list of worthwhile books in general fields of interest. Any one of these books can serve as the beginning point in a reading hobby that may travel far from these selections or subject areas, but part of the charm of regular reading is that it takes off in unpredictable directions.

Take full advantage of all available sources of interesting titles: friends who read, your local library, bookstores and booksellers, and the book review columns of magazines and newspapers.

Science and nature

Attenborough, David. *Life on Earth* (1981). Attractively illustrated introduction to natural history.

Bell, Eric. *The Magic of Numbers* (1946). Fascinating demonstrations of the power and allure of mathematics.

Bronowski, Jacob. *The Ascent of Man* (1974). The history of scientific advancement since primitive times.

Carson, Rachel. *Silent Spring* (1962). A classic and harrowing account of the dangers of pollution.

Crick, Francis. *Of Molecules and Men* (1966). Narrative account of the Nobelist's achievements in biology.

Eisley, Loren. *The Immense Journey* (1957). Philosophical thoughts on the history of human development.

Freud, Sigmund. *General Introduction to Psychoanalysis* (1920). A general overview of the subject.

Geertz, Clifford. *The Interpretation of Cultures* (1973). Academic introduction to social anthropology.

Hawking, Stephen W. *Black Holes and Baby Universes and Other Essays* (1993). Essays both personal and scientific.

Jastrow, Robert. *Red Giants and White Dwarfs* (1979). A popular guide to new knowledge of astronomy.

Kidder, Tracy. *The Soul of a New Machine* (1981). Exciting story of the construction of a computer.

McPhee, John. *Basin and Range* (1981). An account of learning geology in the field.

Milgram, Stanley. *Obedience to Authority* (1974). Controversial experiment on our will to obey overwhelming our moral precepts.

Sagan, Carl and Richard Turco. *A Path Where No Man Thought* (1990). A scientific discourse on nuclear winter.

Sears, Paul B. *The Living Landscape* (1967). Elegantly written summation of ecological issues.

Thomas, Lewis. *Lives of a Cell* (1974). Enjoyable essays on the lessons drawn from biology.

Turnbull, Colin. *The Mountain People* (1972). A description of a field anthropologist's work.

Ulam, Stanislaw. *Adventures of a Mathematician* (1976). A scientist's story of his work on the atom bomb.

Watson, James D. *The Double Helix* (1967). Exciting narrative of the discovery of DNA.

Wiener, Norbert. *Cybernetics* (1961). A demanding, groundbreaking discussion of the computer age.

Wilson, Edmund O. *Sociobiology* (1975). Challenging behavioral theory of the dominance of genes over will.

History

Allen, Frederick L. *Only Yesterday* (1931). Engaging, novelistic portrait of the years after World War I.

Boorstin, Daniel. *The Americans* (1958-73). Three-volume popular epic by the librarian of Congress.

Carlyle, Thomas. *The French Revolution* (1832). Dramatic saga of heroes and villains of the revolution.

Catton, Bruce. *The Centennial History of the Civil War* (1961-63). Three eminently readable volumes.

Durant, Will and Ariel. *The Story of Civilization* (1935-75). Eleven volumes of enthusiastic history of ideas.

Fitzgerald, Frances. *Fire on the Lake* (1972). Early prize-winning account of the Vietnam War.

Fussell, Paul. *The Great War and Modern Memory* (1975). Literate and surprising discussion of the special significance of World War I.

Gibbon, Edward. *The Decline and Fall of the Roman Empire* (1776-78). The work that created our image of Rome.

Grant, Michael. *The Visible Past* (1990). How modern archaeology has increased our knowledge of the ancient world.

Halberstam, David. *The Best and the Brightest* (1972). How the Kennedy administration slipped toward war in Southeast Asia.

Hamilton, Edith. *The Greek Way* (1930). A persuasive and lucid paean to the merits of ancient Greece.

Hersey, John. *Hiroshima* (1946). The effects of the atomic bomb, focused on the stories of six survivors.

Litvinoff, Barnet. *Fourteen Ninety-Two* (1991). A study of Europe during a year of revolutionary change.

Morison, Samuel Eliot. *The Great Explorers* (1978). A sailor's history of early global navigation.

Plumb, J.H. *The Italian Renaissance* (1965). A beautifully written history of the great flowering.

Shirer, William. *The Rise and Fall of the Third Reich* (1960). A journalist's account of the Hitler years.

Stratton, Joanna L. *Pioneer Women* (1981). Edited diaries of frontier women on the American prairies.

Thomas, Hugh. *A History of the World* (1978). A contemporary overview for background.

Toynbee, Arnold. *A Study of History* (1934-61). A twelve-volume analysis for knowledgeable readers.

Tuchman, Barbara. *A Distant Mirror* (1978). The story of the Middle Ages told through the life of one man.

Tuchman, Barbara. *The March of Folly: From Troy to Vietnam* (1984). Exposé of four historical blunders.

Wills, Gary. *Inventing America* (1978). A journalist's investigation of the Declaration of Independence.

Wood, Gordon S. *The Creation of the American Republic* (1965). A sophisticated political analysis.

Woodham-Smith, Cecil. *The Great Hunger* (1962). Graphic description of the Irish potato famine in 1848.

Places

Abbey, Edward. *Cactus Country* (1973). A naturalist's appreciation of the Sonora Desert, with photographs.

Barzini, Luigi. *The Italians* (1964). Native's discursive reflections on the distinctive features of his culture.

Belloc, Hillaire. *The Path to Rome* (1902). A literary critic travels on foot to the Italian capital.

Bellow, Saul. *To Jerusalem and Back* (1976). an American novelist's portrait of Israel.

Benedict, Ruth. *The Chrysanthemum and the Sword* (1946). Noted anthropologist's visit to Japan.

Dos Passos, John. *Brazil on the Move* (1963). Novelist's journalistic account of the South American nation.

Douglas, William O. *My Wilderness* (1960). A distinguished jurist's salute to the Pacific Northwest.

Fisher, M.F.K. *Map of Another Town* (1964). A noted writer on food describes southern France.

Frady, Marshall. *Southerners* (1980). Magazine writer's irreverant look at his native region.

Gornick, Vivian. *In Search of Ali Mahmoud* (1973). Jewish-American feminist meets modern Egypt.

Hoagland, Edward. *Notes of a Century Before* (1969). Compelling journal of frontier British Columbia.

Krutch, Joseph Wood. *The Forgotten Peninsula* (1961). A scholar and naturalist on the Mexican Baja.

Lavender, David. *The Rocky Mountains* (1980). History and lore tied to the modern state of the region.

McGinniss, Joe. *Going to Extremes* (1980). Desperate lives in the magnificent environment of Alaska.

McPhee, John. *Coming Into the Country* (1977). author describes Alaska and Alaskans.

Mehta, Ved. *Portrait of India* (1970). By an Indian blind since childhood.

Naipaul, V.S. *Among the Believers* (1981). Prominent novelist's exploration of Islamic nations.

Pritchett, V.S. *The Spanish Temper* (1955). An affectionate analysis by a noted English writer and critic.

Smith, Hedrick. *The Russians* (1976). A *New York Times* reporter reflects on his years in Moscow.

Snow, Edgar. *Red Star over China* (1968). One of the first American accounts of life in Communist China.

Steinbeck, John. *Travels with Charley* (1962). The novelist's celebrated cross-country drive, with dog.

Thoreau, Henry David. *The Maine Woods* (1865). Early explorations by the author of *Walden*.

Warner, William W. *Beautiful Swimmers* (1976). Natural history of the Chesapeake.

West, Rebecca. *Black Lamb and Grey Falcon* (1941). A tour of the Balkans in the company of H.G. Wells.

People

Adams, Henry. *The Education of Henry Adams* (1906). Autobiography of a troubled member of a famous family.

Boswell, James. *The Life of Samuel Johnson* (1791). One of the first and finest detailed records of a life.

Caro, Robert. *Means of Ascent* (1990). Biography of Lyndon Johnson's political life.

Curie, Eve. *Madame Curie* (1937). The life of the famous scientist, as told by her daughter.

Ellmann, Richard. *James Joyce* (1982). Revised edition of a great modern biography.

Erikson, Erik H. *Gandhi's Truth* (1969). Theory of identity crisis; portrait of a remarkable man.

Flexner, James Thomas. *Washington: The Indispensable Man* (1979). The author's own condensation of a longer work.

Franklin, Benjamin. *The Autobiography of Benjamin Franklin* (1791). Common sense and humor, for his son.

Fraser, Antonia. *Cromwell: The Lord Protector* (1973). Best of the author's works on British leaders.

Jones, Ernest. *The Life and Work of Sigmund Freud* (1961). Abridgment of a remarkable life, told by a disciple.

Josephson, Matthew. *Edison* (1963). The inventor's deeds made all the more fascinating by demystification.

Kaplan, Justin. *Walt Whitman: A Life* (1980). The poet in the context of 19th-century American society.

Mabee, Carlton T. *The American Leonardo* (1943). the life of Samuel Morse, painter and inventor.

Malcolm X. *The Autobiography of Malcolm X* (1964). Searing story of ghetto and political life.

Manchester, William. *American Caesar: Douglas MacArthur* (1978). Sumptuous life of the general.

McCullough, David. *Truman* (1992). The life of Harry S. Truman by a highly acclaimed historian and biographer.

Mizener, Arthur. *The Far Side of Paradise* (1951). The tragic career of F. Scott Fitzgerald.

Muir, John. *Story of My Boyhood* (1913). The naturalist's youth in Scotland and in America.

Murray, K.M. *Elizabeth. Caught in the Web of Words* (1977). Life of the editor of the *Oxford English Dictionary*.

Pais, Abraham. *Subtle Is the Lord* (1982). Portrait of Albert Einstein, physicist and humanist.

Sandburg, Carl. *Abraham Lincoln* (1926). a stately study of the man and President.

Schoenbaum, Samuel. *Shakespeare's Lives* (1970). The facts and the fiction about the life of the bard.

Strachey, Lytton. *Queen Victoria* (1921). Portrait of the matriarch, by a noted biographer.

Sullivan, J.W.N. *Beethoven* (1927). Convincing links between the man's emotions and the composer's music.

Thurber, James. *The Years with Ross* (1959). Endearing, hilarious life of the first editor of *The New Yorker*.

Literature

Amis, Kingsley. *Lucky Jim* (1954). The most famous of comic novels about professors.

Anderson, Sherwood. *Winesburg, Ohio* (1919). Famous stories of small-town life in the Midwest.

Austen, Jane. *Pride and Prejudice* (1813). Among the wittiest of novels about marriageable ladies.

Baldwin, James. *Go Tell It on the Mountain* (1953). Tense story of black adolescent.

Bellow, Saul. *Henderson the Rain King* (1959). A tragicomedy; traces a man's quest for wisdom.

Bronte, Emily. *Wuthering Heights* (1847). The tempestuous romance of Cathy and Heathcliff.

Burgess, Anthony. *A Clockwork Orange* (1962). Horrific vision of violence in the future.

Caldwell, Erskine. *God's Little Acre* (1933). Folksy story of Georgia mountain families.

Camus, Albert. *The Stranger* (1946). Plainly written novel of modern man's disorientation and loss of self.

Chandler, Raymond. *The Big Sleep* (1939). Philip Marlowe, the archetype of hardboiled detectives.

Cheever, John. *The Stories of John Cheever* (1979). Suburban settings, unpredictable doings, comic tone.

Conrad, Joseph. *Heart of Darkness* (1902). Intricate, enigmatic tale of horrors of African colonization.

Crane, Stephen. *The Red Badge of Courage* (1895). The first, perhaps the best novel of inglorious war.

Dickens, Charles. *David Copperfield* (1850). Poverty and the journey to adulthood in Victorian England.

Dostoevski, Feodor. *The Brothers Karamazov* (1880). Murder, false accusations, moral implications.

Elkin, Stanley. *The Dick Gibson Show* (1971). Almost surreal tale of late-night radio host.

Ellison, Ralph. *Invisible Man* (1952). To many, the best novel ever of black American experience.

Farrell, James T. *Studs Lonigan* (1935). Best of a trilogy of novels about the Irish in Chicago.

Fitzgerald, F. Scott. *The Great Gatsby* (1925). Tragic undoing of a gloriously romantic hero.

Flaubert, Gustave. *Madame Bovary* (1857). Important modern novel of restless wife's petty ambitions.

Garcia-Marquez, Gabriel. *Love in the Time of Cholera* (1988). Love in all its guises during the 20th-century cholera epidemic.

Greene, Graham. *Brighton Rock* (1938). Suspenseful story of gang wars at a British resort.

Hammett, Dashiell. *The Thin Man* (1934). Classic American detective fiction.

Hardy, Thomas. *The Mayor of Casterbridge* (1886). A man doomed by fate and accident.

Heller, Joseph. *Catch-22* (1961). Bleakly humorous novel of combat and red tape in World War II.

Hemingway, Ernest. *A Farewell to Arms* (1929). Terse story of World War I desertion.

Huxley, Aldous. *Brave New World* (1932). Science fiction vision of an impersonal future.

James, Henry. *The Ambassadors* (1902). Complexly told story of American experience in Europe.

Jones, James. *From Here to Eternity* (1951). Novel of military life in Hawaii at the time of the Japanese attack on Pearl Harbor.

Joyce, James. *Dubliners* (1914). Subtle, deceptive short stories, useful as introduction to his novels.

Kafka, Franz. *The Castle* (1926). Nightmarish vision of personal alienation and social bureaucracy.

London, Jack. *The Call of the Wild* (1903). The classic animal story, set in the Yukon, good reading for all ages.

McCarthy, Cormac. *All the Pretty Horses* (1992). Acclaimed novel of a Texas teenager's coming of age.

Melville, Herman. *Moby Dick* (1851). The author's most important work, an epic sea story, with modernistic digressions on good and evil.

Morrison, Toni. *Beloved* (1988). A spiritual landscape chronicling slavery's legacy in America.

O'Connor, Flannery. *A Good Man Is Hard to Find* (1955). Short stories about the South.

O'Flaherty, Liam. *The Informer* (1926). Study of accidental betrayal during the Irish uprising.

Pasternak, Boris. *Dr. Zhivago* (1958). A man's struggle to preserve personal goals and ideals in the midst of the Russian Revolution.

Percy, Walker. *The Moviegoer* (1961). Complicated story of film overwhelming reality in the South.

Poe, Edgar Allan. *Tales of the Grotesque* (1840). Unsurpassed stories of Gothic horror and suspense.

Shelley, Mary. *Frankenstein* (1818). The original tale, more chilling than the movies or imitations.

Tolstoy, Leo. *War and Peace* (1866). Expansive panorama of Russian lives disrupted by Napoleonic invasions.

Twain, Mark. *The Adventures of Huckleberry Finn* (1885). Social satire from a boy's perspective in the years before the Civil War..

Walker, Alice. *The Color Purple* (1982). An unusual, moving exchange between two sisters.

Wolfe, Thomas. *Look Homeward, Angel* (1929). An American epic of families and coming of age.

Woolf, Virginia. *To the Lighthouse* (1927). Modern novel told in stream-of-consciousness technique.

For further reference

Adams, W. Royce
Increasing Reading Speed
Macmillan

Agardy, Franklin J.
How to Read Faster and Better
Simon & Schuster

Berger, Gilda
Learning Disabilities and Handicaps
Watts

Cohn, Marvin
Helping Your Teen-age Student: What Parents Can Do to Improve Reading and Study Skills
Dutton & Co.

Ervin, Jane
Your Child Can Read and You Can Help
Doubleday

Lewis, Norman
How to Read Better and Faster
Harper & Row

Miller, William M.
Reading Faster and Understanding More
Little, Brown

Osman, Betty B.
Learning Disabilities: A Family Affair
Random House

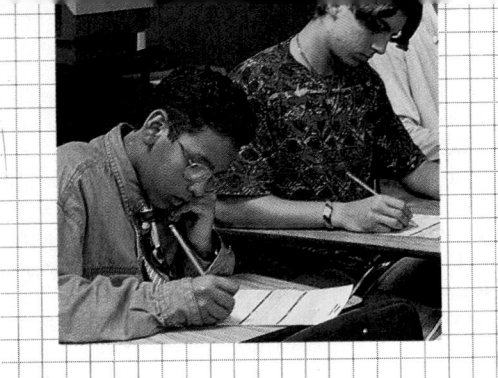

Taking Major Tests

Nearly all people who want to advance their educations or careers must at some time take at least one of the major tests. These tests are designed to evaluate general knowledge, aptitude for college, or qualifications for graduate school. All of these tests are developed by nonprofit organizations, and their scores are generally accepted by employers and educators across the United States.

The achievement test called General Educational Development, or GED, is designed to assess whether a person knows as much as a typical high-school graduate. It is administered to people who dropped out of high school or who never entered high school. A passing grade on the GED is accepted by most employers and colleges as the equivalent of a high-school diploma.

Most colleges, however, want students who are better than the typical high-school graduate. They also want to be able to evaluate the best student in a poor high school against an ordinary student in a good high school. While the best students in poor high schools may be at least as good as ordinary students in good schools, they may actually be much better or much worse. By giving the same aptitude test to everyone who applies for admission, college administrators hope to obtain an objective evaluation. Of course, colleges do not rely on tests alone, but the scores provided by standardized tests may indicate whether a student with poor grades in school may have unrealized potential for academic achievement.

Colleges use one of two aptitude tests to acquire the information they need. (Some colleges will accept scores from either.) The test used most in the eastern United States is the Scholastic Assessment Test, or SAT, prepared by the College Entrance Examination Board. The SAT is the grandfather of all the major aptitude tests and many tests have imitated it. Elsewhere in the United States, the American College Testing Program, or ACT, is used more than the SAT. It is important to remember, though, that around the country individual colleges have different requirements. The admissions offices of the colleges to which you are applying should be consulted as to whether you need to take an aptitude test and, if so, which test.

These tests are called *aptitude tests* because they are intended to measure ability, not knowledge. Some colleges also require *achievement tests*, which measure a student's knowledge of specific subjects, such as French or calculus, rather than his or her ability.

Just as college admissions offices want to have standards to judge applicants from different high schools, administrators of graduate schools want to have similar objective standards for college graduates. The Graduate Record Examination, or GRE, is designed to test the kinds of skills needed in graduate school. Not every graduate school requires the GRE, especially where there are programs that lead directly from a college into a specific course of graduate study. Nevertheless, the GRE is frequently required, and failure to pass it can keep a person out of a graduate program.

Improve your test-taking

Though everyone wants to do as well as possible on tests, some students know more than they are ever able to show because they are test-shy. These students often perform more poorly than students who know less than they do. Thus, good test-takers have an advantage over classmates who do not test well. For this reason, you should learn about various tests and try to become "test-wise," that is, comfortable when taking tests and capable of figuring out correct answers even when you do not have firm knowledge to guide you.

Most good test-takers follow a few simple rules that help them get better scores. Some of these rules apply to all tests. Others are specific for multiple-choice tests, or even more specific for a single test, such as the SAT. The first and most important rule, however, is that the better prepared you are, the easier you will find the test and the better your score will be.

Attitude.
Perhaps the most important rule to help you improve your test-taking is to adopt the right attitude. You cannot do well on a test if your mind is blocked by worry. Remember, tests are designed to measure your mastery of a skill or your knowledge of a subject. They are not designed to embarrass you, fool you, or terrify you. In a sense, taking a test should be no harder for you than taking your temperature.

Forget about the students around you—what they do is of no concern. Forget about the teacher, about the plans you have for after the test, and about anything else that may be on your mind. Until the test is over, the only two things that matter are you and the test. With this single-minded attitude, you are ready to concentrate and do your very best. You may feel keyed up, like an athlete before a game. Being keyed up can make you more alert and ready, but you should not feel agitated or worried.

Preparation.
Not less important than attitude is preparation for a test. There are two kinds of preparation for any test, whether it is an end-of-course achieve- ment test or a general aptitude test. The first is study of the subject matter. Even in taking an aptitude test, knowing the subject matter will help you get a high score. If you do not know the subject matter, only your test-wiseness can help you.

Some students study hard but do not master the material. They may read a chapter over and over, desperately trying to memorize hundreds of facts, or they may run in circles, trying over and over again to master a new problem without first understanding it.

If the test is on subject matter from a book, try this approach. Instead of reading the material over and over, read it once. Then spend some time organizing it on paper. What are the major facts or themes of the material? What are the important names or dates or other facts—those necessary to understand the whole? Many of the names and dates may be less important—in fact, some of them can safely be forgotten.

If you are learning a skill, go back to an example, either in the book or in your notes, and follow it step by step, making sure that you see how the right answer was reached. Then take a new problem and follow exactly the same steps. If you still do not understand, ask for help from a classmate or teacher.

There are many aids available to you in preparing for any of these major tests. The box on page 330 lists some things to consider, including taking a practice test.

If you are having trouble, it is important that you begin preparing for the test early. Otherwise, there will not be time to ask for help. An early start is a good idea in any case, especially when learning the vocabulary of a foreign language or such basic facts as the multiplication table. The mind needs lots of time and much repetition to fix the information firmly. No amount of cramming on the night before the test is likely to make up for work not done ahead of time. Even if you do manage to remember part of the material for the test, you probably will forget it soon afterward; in that case, you will have to do extra studying for the next test.

Ten ways to improve your test scores

Though the various tests may require differing techniques, here are a few tips that apply to all of them:

1. **Take a course** that will prepare you if you are unsure about your ability to deal with a test. Courses are offered in most major cities and are available by mail or on computer programs. The courses are particularly useful for achievement tests. Although some test-makers believe these courses cannot improve aptitude test scores, other experts disagree. Most bookstores carry books with sample questions and the testing organizations also publish their own booklets with sample questions and helpful information.

2. **Take at least one sample test.** This book supplies a few sample questions for the GED but you should obtain a complete sample test for whichever test you plan to take. These are often available from your school library or local bookstore. Try to take the test in the same time limit set for the official test. The experience should not only prepare you but will relax you for the actual test. It also might reveal weak areas that require more study.

3. **Be prepared.** Make sure you have whatever is required when you arrive at the testing place. Some tests require an admission ticket, personal identification (such as a driver's license or birth certificate), and Number 2 pencils. Be sure you know what is needed for your test so you do not forfeit your place.

4. **Relax.** Test-takers foul up more often because they are too tense than because they are too calm. The time to stay up nights studying for a test is in the weeks preceding it, when you can use that excess energy for studying. You should be well-rested by the time the test starts. A good night's sleep is better than staying up late and cramming.

5. **Take a moment to look through the whole test** (if allowed) before answering any questions. Read the directions especially carefully. If you do not know exactly what is wanted, you may make mistakes that reduce your score.

6. **Estimate how much time you have** for answering each question. Count quickly how many questions there are altogether, and estimate the time needed for each. If the test has several parts, jot down a rough timetable for handling each part.

7. **Read each question carefully.** If you misunderstand the question, you will probably answer it incorrectly, no matter how much you know about the subject. Some tests have questions with tricky wording just to test your understanding. Especially when a question is complicated, read it a second time to be sure you have it right.

8. **Answer all the easy questions first** and skip questions you are not sure about. Use the remaining time to consider carefully the hard-to-answer questions. Answering easy questions will warm you up and help prevent a mental block, a temporary inability to remember something that you really know. Answering easy questions first also will ensure that you have answered everything you know best before time runs out.

9. **Answer questions first from parts of the test that carry higher scores.** Obviously, if you know which parts count most and have the correct answers, tackling those questions first will help you get the highest possible score.

10. **If you have time left,** use it to read through all the questions and answers. You may find, for example, that you have failed to answer some items whose answers you know. In multiple choice tests with separate answer sheets, take the time to make sure your answers are in the right spaces or columns. Take a moment to determine that each answer seems reasonable, especially in a mathematics test; if an answer is wrong, do not be too lazy to do your calculations again.

Taking Major Tests

The second kind of preparation for any test consists of making sure that you are physically and mentally ready. One important factor is a good night's sleep. The day before a test, take a few minutes now and then to relax. Finish your studying early so that you can be ready for sleep at your regular bedtime. In the morning, eat a good breakfast. Put aside any worries or excitement for a few hours, until the test is over. You need all your powers of concentration for the test.

During the test. Arrive early and have with you the pencils or any other tools you will need. When the test is handed out, read it through quickly before you answer any of the questions. Be sure you understand *how* you are to provide the answers. Do not, for example, write on the test booklet if a separate answer sheet is required. In fact, it is a good idea to read all the instructions twice. Once you have read through the whole test, do the easy items first. In that way, even if you are short of time, you will make sure you get credit for what you know.

If you do not know the correct answer to a test item, you still have ways to improve your score. Skip over the item temporarily—the answer may pop into your mind later. In addition, if you weed out answers that you know are wrong, you have a better chance of guessing the correct answer. For example, if you can eliminate two of four possible answers, you have a fifty-fifty chance of getting the right answer from the remaining two.

If you are really in trouble, there are other rules you can use for guessing. Be warned, however, that the people who write the tests know these rules also. For example, correct answers often have to be qualified extensively, which means that the right answer is likely to be one of the two longest choices. Similarly, absolute qualifiers, such as *always*, *never*, or *none*, generally apply to incorrect answers, since few things are ever absolute. But sometimes test-makers add absolute qualifiers to correct answers in order to trap the unwary. Finally, the test-makers want there to be about equal numbers of answers labeled A, B, C, D, and E. They know that students might exploit this to improve their test scores, but most test-makers are reluctant to let one answer predominate over the others. Thus, you can use the number of answers for each letter among the items you are sure of as a rough guide to guessing the items of which you are not sure.

Scoring multiple-choice tests.
Multiple-choice exams often test mastery of facts. Read each question and its possible answers carefully. Sometimes, more than one answer may seem correct; choose the one that you think is most accurate.

Short multiple-choice tests usually are graded on the number of right answers. This means that if you do not know the answer to a question, you can guess at answers without being penalized.

Tips on calculators

For certain tests, like the SAT I, you are encouraged to use a handheld calculator when figuring answers to mathematics questions. The calculator is not required, and you can take the test without it. But it is a good idea to take advantage of the calculator's speed and accuracy whenever it is allowed. The extra time it saves may help you answer more questions and so get a better score. Below are some tips on using calculators:

- Find out beforehand if calculators are allowed for the test you are taking.

- Find out exactly which type can be used. For the SAT I mathematics section, you can use most four-function scientific or graphing calculators. But laptop computers, pocket organizers, electronic writing pads, noise-making calculators, and certain others are prohibited. Check to see if your calculator is acceptable before arriving at the test center.

- Bring a calculator you are familiar with. The test is not the time to learn how to use a fancy new device.

- Check to make sure your calculator is working properly and that the batteries are fresh before you enter the testing area. If your calculator stops working during the test, you will have to finish without it.

- Relying on your calculator too much can waste valuable time. Read the question and decide if you actually need the calculator to get the answer before pressing any buttons.

- Take a practice test with your calculator so that you will be comfortable with it during the actual test.

On long multiple-choice tests, such as standardized reading and mathematics tests, you are penalized for guessing. For this kind of test you should not guess at an answer if you have no idea what the answer is. You should guess only if you can eliminate one or more of the possible answers as surely wrong.

Sample test questions. Sample questions for the GED test begin on the following page. For further information and practice questions for other major standardized tests, including the SAT, ACT, and TOEFL (Test of English as a Foreign Language), see College Entrance Exams in Volume IV of the *Student Handbook, College and University Edition*.

You will notice that each question below for the GED is accompanied by a short explanation of why one of the answers is correct. Study these explanations carefully; they will reveal thinking techniques you can use over and over again.

GED

The General Educational Development examination has been developed by the American Council on Education to qualify students who have not finished high school or the equivalent of a secondary school diploma. The GED consists of five parts: writing skills, social studies, science, literature and the arts, and mathematics. The writing skills section is a test of written English, including spelling, capitalization, punctuation, usage, sentence structure, and organization. An essay question (not included in the samples here) also appears on the test. There is no penalty for guessing. Use of a calculator is not allowed.

Writing skills

Directions: Choose the <u>one best answer</u> to each item. <u>The questions</u> refer to the following paragraphs.

(1)When you are in school, almost any Subject seems a potential area for a good job. (2)But when you are out on your own, you may find it difficult to land a job. (3)When you are told time after time that there are no jobs. (4)And it is time for some creative thinking and acting.

(5)Do your homework before applying for any job. (6)First, you should study the openings posted in the local newspapers—subscribe to all of them if possible, or read it at the public library. (7)Familiarize oneself with the types of jobs most often available, with the various employment offices, and with the skills most in demand.

Sentence 1: **When you are in school, almost any Subject seems a potential area for a good job.**

What correction should be made to this sentence?

(1) replace <u>you are</u> with <u>one is</u>
(2) remove the comma after <u>school</u>
(3) change <u>Subject</u> to <u>subject</u>
(4) insert a comma after <u>area</u>
(5) no correction is necessary

Choice (3) is correct. The word *subject* is not a proper noun or the first word of a sentence, so it must not be capitalized.

Sentences 3 and 4: **When you are told time after time that there are no <u>jobs. And it</u> is time for some creative thinking and acting.**

Which of the following is the best way to write the underlined portion of these sentences? If you think the original is the best way, choose option (1).

(1) jobs. And it
(2) jobs, or it
(3) jobs, it
(4) jobs, if it
(5) jobs, and it

Choice (3) is correct. In this form the sentence now has a dependent clause and an independent clause, separated by a comma.

Sentence 5: **Do your homework before applying for any job.**

If you rewrote sentence 5 beginning with <u>Be sure that you</u> the next words should be

(1) got done your homework
(2) got your homework done
(3) had done your homework
(4) did your homework
(5) have done your homework

Choice (5) is correct. the verb *have done* is in the present perfect tense, so it agrees with the verb *Be*, which is in the present tense.

Sentence 6: **First, you should study the openings posted in the local newspapers—subscribe to all of them if possible, or read it at the public library.**

What correction should be made to this sentence?

(1) replace <u>you</u> with <u>one</u>
(2) replace <u>you</u> with <u>they</u>
(3) insert a comma after <u>openings</u>
(4) replace <u>it</u> with <u>them</u>
(5) no correction is necessary

Choice (4) is correct. The pronoun has a plural antecedent, *newspapers*. The pronoun must, therefore, also be plural, *them* not *it*.

Sentence 7: **Familiarize oneself with the types of jobs most often available, with the various employment offices, and with the skills most in demand.**

What correction should be made to this sentence?

(1) change <u>Familiarize</u> to <u>Familiarized</u>
(2) replace <u>oneself</u> with <u>yourself</u>
(3) insert a comma after <u>various</u>
(4) change <u>offices</u> to <u>office</u>
(5) change <u>demand</u> to <u>demanding</u>

Choice (2) is correct. The subject of the verb *Familiarize* does not appear, but it is understood to be the pronoun *you*. The pronoun *yourself* corresponds to the understood subject *you*.

Taking Major Tests

Questions refer to the following passage:

(1)For many people, the movies provided a much needed daversion during the troubled years of the 1930's and 1940's. (2)World War II had followed on the heels of the 1930's depression, and you could scarcely blame people for wanting to escape there cares. (3)In the movies, people had been powerful, rich, happy, and funny, and dark clouds rarely passed over the lens. (4)Where private life was dull or hopeless, they provided easy satisfaction.

Sentence 1: **For many people, the movies provided a much needed daversion during the troubled years of the 1930's and 1940's.**

Which correction should be made to this sentence?

(1) change For many people to For most people
(2) replace troubled years with trouble years
(3) change the movies to movies
(4) replace daversion with diversion
(5) replace 1930's with the thirties

Choice (4) is correct. Diversion is misspelled.

Sentence 2: **World War II had followed on the heels of the 1930's depression, and you could scarcely blame people for wanting to escape there cares.**

What correction should be made to this sentence?

(1) change had followed to followed
(2) change scarcely blame to hardly blame
(3) change heels to heals
(4) change people to them
(5) change there to their

Choice (5) is correct. *There* is sometimes mistakenly used for the possessive pronoun *their* because they sound alike.

Sentence 3: **In the movies, people had been powerful, rich, happy, and funny and dark clouds rarely passed over the lens.**

What change should be made to this sentence?

(1) change movies, people to movies people
(2) change had been to were
(3) replace people with actors
(4) replace happy with smart
(5) no change necessary

Choice (2) is correct. It changes the incorrect past perfect tense to a simple past tense. Past perfect is used to indicate a past action completed before some other past action, but in this case there is no need for that distinction. The simple past tense alone is called for here.

Social studies

Directions: Choose the one best answer to each question.

The next three questions refer to the following information.

Perception plays an important part in marketing products. For example, researchers have learned that the greater the number of colors in a print advertisement, the greater its readership; other tests have shown that women respond to color more readily than men.

Visual cues also do much to create a mood in packaging. There is a world of difference between the stark, no-nonsense black and white of generic products and the lavish, lively color illustrations on cereal boxes designed to appeal to children.

Perception may have subtle ramifications. Because people perceive the smell of lemon to be fresh and clean, its scent is added to such products as dishwashing detergent, furniture wax, and oven cleaner. The fragrance has no functional benefit, but it does sell goods.

Marketing is also concerned with the phenomenon known as perceptual screening. In the modern world of mass communications, we are subjected to a barrage of commercial messages—some 150 a day according to one estimate. Through the process called perceptual screening, we tune out the vast majority of these messages.

Advertisers concluded that their messages must either be intriguing enough to break the "boredom barrier" or be repeated very often. Repetition may be maddening, but there is little doubt that it works.

According to the passage, colorful print advertisements

(1) appeal only to children
(2) are more expensive to produce
(3) get more attention
(4) may dampen product sales
(5) break the boredom barrier

Colorful cereal box illustrations do appeal to children, but we can eliminate choice (1) because people of all ages are attracted by bright colors. Print ads using lavish color are more expensive to produce (2), but the passage makes no mention of this. Choice (4) is wrong based on the information presented, and while a colorful ad may also be intriguing, color was not mentioned specifically as a way to break the boredom barrier (5). The best possible choice is (3), which follows from the second sentence, on colors and readership of print ads.

Answer every question on the GED. There is no penalty for guessing.

One way to DECREASE the sales appeal of a product might be to

(1) add a pleasant scent
(2) advertise it over and over
(3) give it a clever ad campaign
(4) make the packaging more colorful
(5) use plain black and white packaging

Choice (1) is more likely to increase the product's appeal than decrease it. The passage also mentions both clever (3) and repetitive ad campaigns (2) as effective ways to market products. Colorful packaging (4) is mentioned as a marketing tool, particularly in relation to the stark black and white packaging of generic products. From that you can rightly infer that (5) might actually decrease sales appeal.

When people "tune out" most of the advertisements they see, they are

(1) busy with other things
(2) interested only in ads for things they need
(3) waiting for a better ad
(4) engaging in perceptual screening
(5) reacting against the product's shape

In fact, people are sometimes busy with other things (1) or just looking for things they need (2), but these points were not discussed in the passage and so can be eliminated. Choice (5) may apply to a single product, but not to many, and while (3) may be true at times, it does not account for tuning out most ads. That leaves choice (4), engaging in perceptual screening, which the passage discussed as the cause for people blocking out ads.

Which of the following is NOT a continent?

(1) South America
(2) Antarctica
(3) Australia
(4) North America
(5) Arctic

You should surely know to eliminate North America (4) and South America (1). Australia (3) and Antarctica (2) might give you some trouble, but they are also continents. The remaining choice (5), the Arctic, is not a landmass, so (5) is the correct answer.

For the past few decades Japan has exported considerably more to the United States than it has imported. Which of the following measures would likely reduce Japan's trade surplus with the United States?

(1) increase import taxes on U.S. goods
(2) encourage increased American tourism in Japan
(3) encourage Japanese to buy Japanese-made products
(4) increase exports to the United States
(5) increase imports of U.S. goods

Increasing import taxes (1) would only increase the price of American goods in Japan. This would dampen sales and increase Japan's trade surplus. Choice (3) would also reduce sales of American goods. Bringing more American tourists to Japan (2) would mean Americans would be spending still more money in Japan, increasing the trade surplus. Choice (4) created the trade surplus in the first place. The only correct answer then is choice (5), increase imports of U.S. goods.

Among other rights, the First Amendment guarantees Americans the right to

(1) a speedy trial
(2) counsel in criminal cases
(3) free speech
(4) due process of law
(5) bear arms

All five choices are rights guaranteed by the Bill of Rights, which is made up of the first ten amendments to the Constitution. Only choice (3) is one of the freedoms enumerated in the First Amendment, however.

In the United States, a governor of a state has the power to do all of the following EXCEPT

(1) prepare a budget for the next year
(2) veto a law passed by the state legislature
(3) send an ambassador to a foreign country
(4) campaign for the members of his or her political party
(5) suggest laws he or she would like to see passed

Choices (1), (2), and (5) describe activities that might be performed by the governor of a state. Choice (4) describes an activity common to most elected officials. The correct answer is choice (3). Only the federal government of the United States—the President with the advice and consent of the Senate—can send ambassadors to other countries.

DISTRIBUTION OF POPULATION
IN THE UNITED STATES

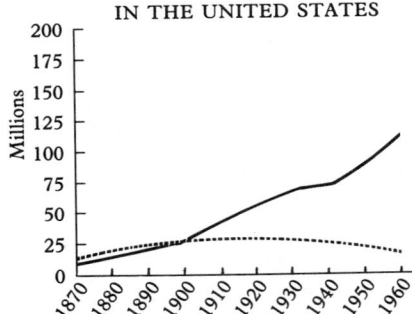

Urban Dwellers—— Farm Dwellers······

According to the graph above, the year the population was evenly distributed between urban and rural areas was approximately

(1) 1880 (2) 1900 (3) 1920
(4) 1940 (5) 1960

First, it is important to understand that "evenly distributed between urban and rural areas" means that the two populations are equal. In a line graph such as the one given here, two quantities are equal when the lines for both quantities cross; that is, because the height of the line above the base represents the quantity, the lines will cross when the heights are the same. The lines for the urban and rural areas cross just once, above the time 1900. Therefore, the correct choice is (2).

Do your scratch work right on the test paper.

Taking Major Tests

The <u>next two questions</u> refer to the following map.

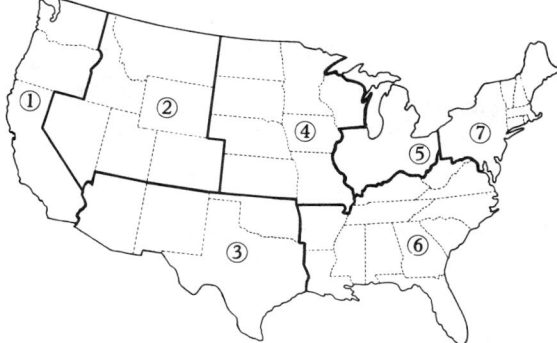

Which area is associated with the Gold Rush of 1849?

(1)   1   (2)   2   (3)   3   (4)   4   (5)   5

Many GED items rely on knowledge that the person taking the test is supposed to have. This is one of them, but you can also eliminate some choices even if you do not remember that the Gold Rush of 1849 brought many people to California. For example, the region east of the Mississippi was filled with people in the 1800's, so choice (5) (region 5) can be ruled out. With only four choices left, you have a better chance of guessing the correct choice, which is (1).

In the middle of the 19th century, American industry was most heavily concentrated in which area?

(1)   1   (2)   3   (3)   4   (4)   6   (5)   7

Make sure that you remember that the 19th century is the same as the 1800's, so this question centers about the years around 1850. As in the previous item, you can eliminate choices (1), (2), and (3) (regions 1, 3, and 4) because these regions did not have enough people to support heavy industry at that time. If you do not remember that heavy industry was concentrated mostly in New England at that time, which is choice (5) (region 7), you still have a fifty-fifty chance of guessing the correct choice.

All of the following are undesirable results of man's efforts to improve his standard of living EXCEPT

(1)   erosion of soils
(2)   desalination of seawater
(3)   destruction of wildlife habitats
(4)   exhaustion of mines
(5)   pollution of air and water

In this kind of a question, there is a "hidden double negative" that can confuse the person taking the test. The "EXCEPT" in the stem means that you want to find a choice that is not undesirable. "Not undesirable" is not necessarily the same as desirable. It means that you need to reject four choices that *are* undesirable. Choices (1), (3), (4), and (5) all describe results that are undesirable. Choice (2) describes something that can be desirable, so it is correct.

Read each question carefully before you try to answer it.

Interpreting Literature and the Arts

<u>Directions:</u> Choose the <u>best</u> answer to each question.

WHAT IS POETRY?

What is poetry? Who knows?
Not the rose, but the scent of the rose;
Not the sky, but the light of the sky;
Not the fly, but the gleam of the fly;
Not the sea, but the sound of the sea;
Not myself, but what makes me
See, hear, feel something that prose
Cannot, and what it is, who knows?

Reprinted by permission of Harold Ober Associates Inc. © 1938 by Eleanor Farjeon, renewed. Copyright 1938, Eleanor Farjeon. Reprinted by permission of J.B. Lippincott Company.

According to the poem, poetry, unlike prose, does which of the following?

(1)   relates to feelings rather than to objects
(2)   explains things fully and logically
(3)   deals with everyday life
(4)   concerns itself with things, not people
(5)   describes things in simple words

Choice (2) is not generally thought of as relating to poetry, so it can be rejected. The poem does not refer to everyday life (3) or simple words (5), so they can be eliminated. Choice (1) fits better than choice (4) because *scent, light, gleam,* and *sound* involve human *feelings* about objects.

In a recent survey, three out of four people interviewed said that they liked Soothies better than the other leading pain reliever. Here's what some of those people had to say:

Ms. R. Jones: "Soothies really make me feel better fast. I've told my friends about them."
Mr. L. Smith: "Soothies taste better than the other leading brand. My children chew Soothies like candy. And for the same price, you get more."
Dr. Q. Brown: "I recommend Soothies for fast relief. They work best for me."

Soothies cost less than the other leading pain reliever. So get the best for less! Try Soothies.

Dr. Brown recommends Soothies because they

(1)   taste good to him   (2)   help most people
(3)   are inexpensive   (4)   bring him relief
(5)   are the leading brand

When asked for a specific detail in a reading passage, focus only on the part that contains the information asked for. In this case, you can go directly to what Dr. Brown has said. Choice (4) is the only one with this idea, so it is correct.

Questions refer to the following excerpt.

WHAT IS MODERN ART?

Painting remained representational to the end of the 1800's, despite tendencies of major painters toward more abstract, nonrepresentational works. Between 1901 and 1906, there were several large exhibitions in Paris of the works of Gauguin, van Gogh, and Cézanne, the three painters who most strongly influenced the painting of the 20th century.

The later works of Cézanne, in particular, show a concern with form and color for their own sake, even though he painted images of the real, perceived world. It was the abstract, nonrepresentational aspects of his painting that impressed younger artists and helped set the direction toward modern art.

Modern art emerged from this movement toward nonrepresentational and abstract art; painters after 1900 completely cut their ties with the real world, leaving behind the idea of pictorial representation in art. Instead, they sought to create visual art using the abstract elements of form, color, and design.

In a sense, artists have always done this. Greek sculpture portrayed ideal rather than real human form. Renaissance paintings exaggerated perspective in the interests of illusion. The liberties 20th-century painters took with the appearance of their subjects were only more extreme than those of earlier times.

According to the excerpt, who among the following had the most influence on the transition to modern art?

(1) Titian
(2) van Gogh
(3) Picasso
(4) Cézanne
(5) Gauguin

The second paragraph identifies Cézanne as a particularly important influence, making (4) the correct choice.

Based on the passage, modern art is

(1) representational art
(2) concerned with presenting real-life objects
(3) an idealized view of the world
(4) based on the use of color and form to create visual art
(5) loosely connected with the real world

The passage clearly indicates modern art is *nonrepresentational*, not representational, eliminating (1) and (2). The notion of idealized art is covered at the end of the passage in connection with Greek sculpture, eliminating (3). Choice (5) relates to the discussion of Cézanne, but he is not a modern artist. He was important in the transition to modern art. Color and form are mentioned as elements of modern art (in the last sentence of the third paragraph), however, making choice (4) the correct one.

Science

Directions: Each of the questions or incomplete statements below is followed by five suggested answers or completions. Select the one that is best in each case and then blacken the corresponding space on the answer sheet.

The next four questions refer to the following information.

The blood circulating through the human body is about 55 percent plasma, a straw-colored liquid that is about 92 percent water. The remaining 8 percent of plasma contains nutrients, hormones, antibodies, proteins, and special inorganic materials. The other 45 percent of blood is composed of three kinds of cells: erythrocytes (red blood cells), leukocytes (white blood cells), and thrombocytes (platelets). All these cellular components, except for one kind of white blood cell, are manufactured in bone marrow.

The disk-shaped red cells outnumber white cells 700 to 1. They carry oxygen from the lungs to all parts of the body, and carry off waste carbon dioxide. White cells protect the body against toxic organisms by engulfing and destroying them. Platelets are vital for blood clotting.

What is the largest component of blood?

(1) platelets
(2) plasma
(3) red blood cells
(4) water
(5) bone marrow

This question requires some thought to arrive at the one best answer. Platelets (1) are one of the three blood cells that make up 45 percent of blood, but the passage gives no indication of their relative numbers. As for red blood cells (3), we know that they greatly outnumber white blood cells, but the passage groups them with other components that make up just 45 percent of blood. Plasma forms the bulk of human blood (55 percent), but is itself a mixture of water and other components. Water (4), which makes up 92 percent of plasma, is blood's largest component and the correct choice. Bone marrow (5) produces blood; it is not a blood component.

Based on the passage, which of the following materials would leukocytes be most likely to engulf?

(1) soot
(2) food particles
(3) bacteria
(4) ozone
(5) oxygen molecules

A careful reading of the appropriate part of the passage is needed here. One sentence clearly states that white blood cells engulf and destroy toxic *organisms*—living things—eliminating all the choices but bacteria (3). The other choices include toxic or nontoxic substances, only some of which are likely to be found in the bloodstream.

Taking Major Tests

Which blood cells become important when you cut your finger?

(1) green cells
(2) thrombocytes
(3) yellow cells
(4) erythrocytes
(5) red cells

You can eliminate choices (1) and (3) immediately. Blood contains no such thing as green or yellow cells, although plasma is yellowish or straw-colored. The blood oozing from a cut finger will appear red because of the red blood cells (erythrocytes), but choices (4) and (5) are not the best answer here. The correct choice, (2), is easy if you remember that the last sentence said that platelets (thrombocytes) are important for blood clotting. Clotting stops the blood from oozing from a cut and so is important in healing a wound.

Based on the passage, which one of the following is most important for the survival of tissue cells served by the bloodstream?

(1) platelets
(2) carbon dioxide
(3) erythrocytes
(4) hormones
(5) oxygen

You probably already know that cells need oxygen and nutrients to survive, but you could deduce that oxygen (5) is the best choice from the sentence on red blood cells carrying it to all parts of the body. Choice (2), carbon dioxide, is something the blood carries off, so that it is not needed by cells. Erythrocytes (3) carry the oxygen, but are not themselves used by the cells. Platelets (1) help clot the blood and so are not as important to the immediate survival of tissue cells. Hormones (4) also have a more indirect effect on the cells' survival.

The next three questions refer to the following information.

   Water, essential to life, is stored for the most part in oceans. Transferred to the atmosphere mainly through evaporation, it reaches vegetation and soil as rainwater, but not all of it becomes available to living things. Some water accumulates on the ground surface and evaporates back into the atmosphere. Much of it moves through the soil and runs into underground channels. In heavy rains, or when the soil is soaked, water may run off the surface and again be lost.
   Some water that enters the soil becomes bound to soil compounds and so is unavailable to plants. The available water held in the soil not only provides plants with life-sustaining water, but also the dissolved chemicals they need. Only part of the solution that enters plant roots is taken into plant cells. The rest is lost through the leaves in the process called transpiration. When animals eat plants, water in the plants is transferred to the animals. Eventually, all of the water used by plants and animals returns to the soil or goes directly into the atmosphere to begin another cycle.

How does most water get into the atmosphere?

(1) thrown skyward as sea spray
(2) transpiration
(3) combustion
(4) evaporation
(5) respiration

Some water indeed gets into the atmosphere as sea spray, but the passage does not even mention this option (1), and so it can be eliminated. The same is true of (5) and (3). Choice (2), transpiration, in which plants give off moisture, is mentioned in the passage, but only part of the water taken up by a plant is released into the atmosphere. The primary means is evaporation (4), as is clearly stated in the second sentence of the passage.

Aside from drinking water, what is another important way animals can get this life-sustaining substance?

(1) standing out in the rain
(2) respiration
(3) eating plants
(4) perspiration
(5) going for a swim

Choices (1) and (5) imply that water can be absorbed through the skin, but this is incorrect. Respiration (2) and perspiration (4) both involve giving off moisture, not taking it in. Thus, the only correct choice is (3), eating plants, which is discussed toward the end of the passage.

Most of the earth's water is stored in

(1) the soil
(2) oceans
(3) the air
(4) plants
(5) animals

While plants (4) and animals (5) contain considerable amounts of water, they are not the primary storage areas for earth's water. The same is true of the air (3), which holds water vapor in varying amounts, and the soil (1), which may be rain-soaked or merely damp. The correct answer is oceans (2), which the passage identifies as the main storage area for water.

Atomic reactors for generating electric power get their energy from the splitting of atoms; this energy is harnessed to produce large amounts of electricity. The atomic reactor's energy is commonly called

(1) electrical energy
(2) fusion energy
(3) thermal energy
(4) chemical energy
(5) nuclear energy

Both chemical energy (4) and fusion energy (2) can be eliminated immediately. They are incorrect when referring to today's nuclear reactors, which produce energy by nuclear fission, not fusion or chemical processes. The energy produced by an atomic chain reaction is in the form of heat, or thermal energy (3), and it is used to produce electrical energy (1), but conventional, non-nuclear power plants also produce thermal and electric energy. The correct choice is the more specific term (5), nuclear energy.

EARTH

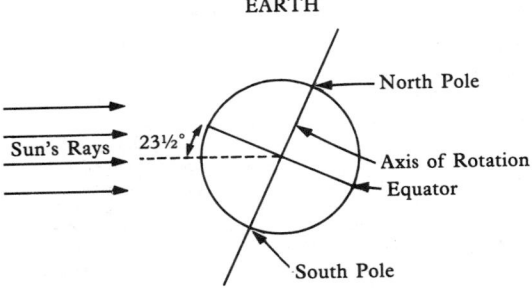

In the diagram above, the sun's rays and the axis of rotation of Earth are both in the plane of the page. The diagram best represents the position of Earth nearest to

(1)   March 21
(2)   June 21
(3)   July 1
(4)   September 23
(5)   December 21

This is the kind of question that asks you to see something in your mind's eye. As you look at the diagram, picture the time of the year when the northern hemisphere is tilted away from the warming rays of the sun: wintertime. This corresponds to choice (5), which is correct.

Evidence indicates that cigarette smoking results in

(1)   cardiovascular stress
(2)   hepatitis
(3)   whooping cough
(4)   pneumonia
(5)   pleurisy

Most people think of lung cancer when they think of the effects of cigarette smoking, but lung cancer is not among the choices. Emphysema, another common disease associated with smoking, also is not present. You might think that choices (3), (4), or (5)—all associated with the lungs—might be correct, but this is one of those cases in which the testmaker has been deliberately misleading. If you recognize that choices (2), (3), (4), and (5) all are infectious diseases, then none of them can be caused by cigarette smoking. Therefore, the correct choice must be (1), cardiovascular stress. It is also helpful to know that *cardiovascular* relates to the heart and blood vessels, and smoking is often thought of as being damaging to the heart.

For further information on the GED, contact your provincial or state department of education, or:

**American Council on Education
One Dupont Circle NW
Washington, DC 20036**

Mathematics

Directions: For all problems choose the <u>one best answer</u>.

The perimeter of a brick patio is 220 feet. If the patio is square in shape, what expression below shows the length, in feet, of the side nearest the house?

(1)   220×4
(2)   220/4²
(3)   220/4
(4)   220/2
(5)   4/220

The answer here is easy if you remember that all sides of a square are equal in length. Since the perimeter of a square is the sum of the lengths of its four sides, and since all sides are equal, dividing the perimeter by four produces the correct figure. Choice (3), 220/4, represents the correct way of showing this. The answer, of course, applies to all four sides, not just the side nearest the house.

Sally earns $12.50 an hour for a 40-hour work week. She gets paid 1½ times that whenever she puts in more than 40 hours. How much did she earn by working 42 hours in one week?

(1) $550
(2) $512.50
(3) $537.50
(4) $500
(5) $496

The first step is to find out how much Sally makes in a normal week. A quick way to calculate that is to break $12.50 down into numbers that are easy to multiply in your head. For example: 40 x $10 (= $400). Write that figure down on your scratch paper.
   The remainder ($2.50 x 40) must be added to that, but if you realize that 40 x $2.50 is the same as 4 x $2.50 (which equals $10) multiplied by 10, you can do that in your head too. Take the total ($100) and add it to the $400 to get Sally's base pay of $500 a week.
   Now figure what she makes for overtime. Since Sally gets half again her normal wage, just add half of $12.50 (which is $6.25) to $12.50 for an overtime hourly wage of $18.75. Multiply $18.75 by the two extra hours she worked to get her total overtime pay for the week, $37.50.
   Her total earnings for the week then were $537.50, which is choice (3).

At Bob's office, 3 out of every 5 employees have computers. If there are 300 people in the office, how many computers are there?

(1)   180
(2)   200
(3)   150
(4)   250
(5)   300

The conventional way to solve this type of problem is to write it out as an equation (3/5 = X/300) and solve for X. Thus X = 3/5 x 300, or X = 180. Thus, choice (1) is correct.

During the month of July the Herbert family spent $32.28, $27.39, $37.54, $54.80, and $52.20 for food. How much did they spend on food for the month?

(1) $184.21   (2) $193.11   (3) $193.21
(4) $203.19   (5) $204.21

Speed helps in getting through a test. While this item can be answered by actually adding the amounts, you should notice at once that three of the choices end in 21 cents. Add just the cents: 0.28 + 0.39 + 0.54 + 0.80 + 0.20 = 2.21, so (as could be suspected) the correct choice has to be (1), (3), or (5). Now look at the dollars. Both (2) and (3) have $193. Since (3) is on the possible correct list and (2) is not, the correct answer is most likely (3). Check by estimating the sum (round off the numbers to whole dollars): $32 + $27 + $38 + $55 + $52 = $204. The correct choice must be (5), not (3). The test-maker was trying to mislead you.

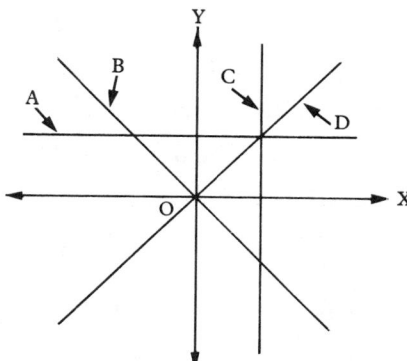

Which of the lines shown in the figure above has zero slope?

(1) A   (2) B   (3) C   (4) D
(5) None of the above

If you have studied slope, it is essential to remember the difference between a slope of zero and no slope. Line A has a slope of zero, while line C has no slope (its slope is undefined). If you have not studied slope, you can still guess that slope refers to the degree of slantedness or steepness of a line. The line that is not slanted, or has zero steepness, is line A. The correct choice is (1).

One statute mile is equal to 5280 feet. If one nautical mile is approximately 1.15 statute miles, then one nautical mile is equal to approximately how many feet?

(1) 4590   (2) 5165   (3) 5395   (4) 5545
(5) 6070

With a question such as this one, you may find it easy to perform the indicated multiplication: 1.15×5280 = 6072. If multiplication is not easy for you, approach the problem the following way.

The statement that a nautical mile is 1.15 statute miles means that a nautical mile is 15 percent larger than a statute mile. Since a nautical mile is larger than a statute mile, you can eliminate choices (1) and (2) automatically. You also can note that 15 percent is halfway between 10 and 20 percent. It is easy to calculate that 10 percent of 5280 is 528 and that twice 528 is 1056, 20 percent of 5280. Therefore, a nautical mile must be about 700 or 800 feet larger than a statute mile. Only choice (5) is anywhere near correct. The method of estimation is especially good, since the actual product of 1.15 and 5280 is 6072, not 6070.

On the number line above, which lettered point could represent the number -9/8?

(1) A   (2) B   (3) C   (4) D   (5) E

From the labels below the number line, it is clear that all the negative numbers are to the left, so you can eliminate points D and E easily. It may help then to think of -9/8 as -1 1/8. Just as +1 1/8 is a number between +1 and +2, -1 1/8 is between -1 and -2, so only A or B could be correct choices. Since -1 1/8 must be closer to -1 than it is to -2, the correct choice is (2) (point B).

If x + y = 36 and x = 2y, then x =

(1) 9   (2) 12   (3) 18   (4) 24
(5) 27

This problem can be solved by a formal method, but it is probably easier, faster, and just as accurate to treat this as a problem in reasoning, not a problem in algebra. Since x = 2y, the value of x must be twice the value of y, or y must be one half of x. This rules out odd numbers for x, since the sum of x and y would then contain a fraction. Of the remaining choices (2), (3), and (4), choices (2) and (3) are easily seen to be too small, so the correct choice must be (4). Always check problems if you can. If x = 24, then y = 12, and 24 + 12 = 36. (Another approach is to use substitution. Since x = 2y, substitute 2y for x in x + y = 36. This produces 2y + y = 36, or 3y = 36. Therefore, y = 36/3, or 12. Now go back to x = 2y to see that x is twice 12, or 24.)

Find out well before your exam what type of calculator, if any, you are permitted to use. Learn thoroughly how to use its functions.

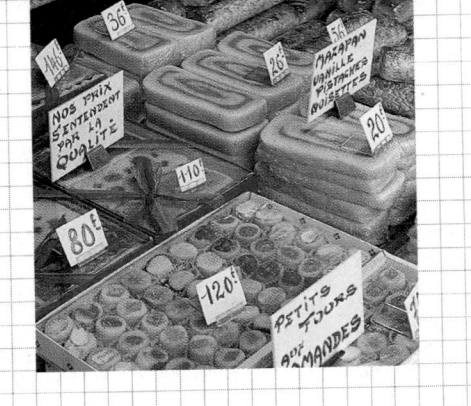

Review of French Grammar

French grammar shares certain characteristics with English grammar, as you may recall from the time when you first studied these languages. For the most part, the names of the parts of speech and the terms used to show how words function in a sentence are the same. Read carefully the sections presented here and be sure to consult the French-English and English-French dictionaries that appear at the end of this review. No matter how long you have been away from the formal study of French, you will quickly find yourself recalling what you once knew.

Articles

Definite articles

Nouns normally are preceded by a definite or indefinite article or by another introductory word. The uses of the definite article *(le, la, les, l')* are shown in the following examples.

Before a noun used in a general or abstract sense.

L'argent ne fait pas le bonheur.

Money does not make for happiness.

Articles

	Singular		Plural
	Masc.	Fem.	Both genders
Definite	le, l'	la, l'	les
Indefinite	un, de	une, de	des

With a title of office or profession followed by a name, except in direct address.

Le président Mitterrand. President Mitterrand.

With proper nouns that are modified.

La pauvre Louise. Poor Louise.

With the name of a language, except immediately after *parler* and after *en.*

Il apprend l'italien. He is learning Italian.

Il parle italien. He speaks Italian.

en italien in Italian

In the singular, with days of the week, to show regularly repeated action.

Il vient ici le mardi et le jeudi.

He comes here on Tuesdays and Thursdays.

With names of seasons and colors.

L'été est la plus chaude des saisons.

Summer is the hottest of the seasons.

Le rose ne vous va pas bien.
Pink does not suit you.
To express "in" with a part of the day.
Le matin je me lève de bonne heure.
In the morning I get up early.
With nouns of weight and measure to express "a," "an," or "per."

trente-cinq francs le kilo
thirty-five francs a kilo

quinze francs la bouteille
fifteen francs a bottle

Cette soie coûte cent francs le mètre.
This silk costs one hundred francs a meter.
To express frequency of occurrence, *par* is used.
deux fois par an twice a year
With place names, except names of cities.
le Japon, l'Amérique, l'Asie Japan, America, Asia
To express "in," "to," and "from" with names of countries and continents.
For all European countries (except Portugal, Luxembourg, and the Netherlands) and all countries and continents whose names are feminine singular.
For "to" and "in," use *en* and omit the article.
For "from," use *de* and omit the article.
J'ai voyagé en Espagne. I have traveled in Spain.
Je reviens d'Espagne. I am returning from Spain.
With countries whose names are plural and all countries outside of Europe whose names are masculine singular.
For "to" and "in," use *à* and the article (*à le = au*).
For "from," use *de* and the article (*de le = du*).
Nous allons au Canada, au Mexique, au Japon.
We are going to Canada, Mexico, and Japan.

Nous revenons du Canada, du Mexique, du Japon.
We are coming back from Canada, Mexico, and Japan.

With names of parts of the body, and often with articles of clothing, when the possessor is clear.
Elle m'a donné la main.
She gave me her hand.

Il avait le chapeau sur la tête.
He had his hat on his head.

Indefinite articles
The indefinite article *(un, une, de, des)* is omitted before an unmodified noun denoting nationality, profession, religion, etc.
Nationality.
Est-il américain? Is he an American?
Profession.
Il est étudiant et il voudrait devenir acteur.
He is a student and would like to become an actor.
Religion.
Etes-vous protestant? Are you a Protestant?
Before nouns in apposition.
M. Durand, professeur de français
Mr. Durand, a French teacher
Before the numbers *cent* and *mille.*
cent fois a hundred times
mille baisers a thousand kisses
After an exclamatory adjective (*quel, quelle,* etc.).
Quelle fraise délicieuse!
What a delicious strawberry!
In numerical titles of monarchs.
Henri Quatre Henry the Fourth
If a noun is modified, the article must be used.
C'est un acteur célèbre.
He is a famous actor.

Partitives
A partitive *(de, de la, de l', du, des)* corresponds to "some" or "any," whether expressed or not. *Des* may express either the partitive plural or indefinite plural.
Singular.
Il a un crayon. He has a pencil.
La carotte est un légume. The carrot is a vegetable.
Plural.
Il a des crayons.
He has pencils.

On cultive des légumes de toutes sortes en France.
They grow vegetables of all kinds in France.
Partitive.
Donnez-lui du pain. Give him some bread.
Avez-vous du sucre? Do you have any sugar?
Il a acheté des légumes. He bought vegetables.

Uses of *de*

Without the article after a negative expression.

Elle ne fait pas de fautes.

She does not make mistakes.

When an adjective precedes the noun.

J'ai vu de beaux papillons.

I saw some beautiful butterflies.

After expressions of quantity.

Il a beaucoup de cousins. He has many cousins.

With adverbs of quantity

The following adverbs of quantity, with certain exceptions, take only *de*.

assez	enough
autant	as much, as many
beaucoup	much, many, a lot
combien	how much, how many
moins	less
peu	little, few
plus	more
tant	so much, so many
trop	too much, too many

The partitive is omitted after *sans* and *ni . . . ni.*

Il n'y a pas de rose sans épines.

There are no roses without thorns.

Il n'a ni frères ni soeurs.

He has neither brothers nor sisters.

The partitive is omitted after expressions that normally take *de: avoir besoin de* "to need," *se passer de* "to get along without," *se servir de* "to use," *se souvenir de* "to remember," *s'approcher de* "to approach," *remplir de* "to fill with," *couvrir de* "to cover with."

Elle ne peut pas se passer de sucre.

She cannot get along without sugar.

Elle a besoin de secours.

She needs help.

If the noun is omitted, the idea of "some" or "any" is expressed by the pronoun *en*.

Avez-vous des amis? Oui, j'en ai.

Have you any friends? Yes, I have some.

Avez-vous besoin de votre voiture? Oui, j'en ai besoin.

Do you need your car? Yes, I need it.

Pronouns and adjectives

Personal pronouns

Pronoun-verb order

Personal object pronouns directly precede the verb, except in affirmative commands. In the *affirmative imperative*, object pronouns are placed directly after the verb and are linked to it by hyphens. The pronouns *me* and *te* become *moi* and *toi* after the verb, but when followed by *en*, they become *m'* and *t'*.

Me réveillez-vous? Are you waking me up?

Ne les a-t-il pas réveillés? Didn't he wake them up?

Ne les réveillez pas. Do not wake them up.

Réveillons-la. Let's wake her up.

Réveillez-moi. Wake me up.

Double object pronouns, like single object pronouns, as well as *y* and *en*, directly precede the verb, except in the case of the affirmative imperative where they follow the verb.

Je compte la lui raconter. I propose to tell it to him.

Tu me la prêtes. You lend it to me.

Il les y a trouvés. He found them there.

Forms of personal pronouns

	Conjunctive			Disjunctive
Subject	**Direct object**	**Indirect object**	**Reflexive**	
je (j')	*me (m')*	*me (m')*	*me (m')*	*moi*
tu	*te (t')*	*te (t')*	*te (t')*	*toi*
il	*le (l')*	*lui*	*se (s')*	*lui*
elle	*la (l')*	*lui*	*se (s')*	*elle*
nous	*nous*	*nous*	*nous*	*nous*
vous	*vous*	*vous*	*vous*	*vous*
ils	*les*	*leur*	*se (s')*	*eux*
elles	*les*	*leur*	*se (s')*	*elles*

Order of personal pronouns

me	before	*le*	before	*lui*	before *y* before *en*
te		*la*		*leur*	before verb
se		*les*			
nous					
vous					

Tu me le prêtes.

Il n'en a pas besoin. He does not need any.
Il nous les a donnés. He gave them to us.
Donnez-le-moi. Give it to me.
Donnez-m'en. Give me some.

Uses of disjunctive pronouns

After a preposition.
avant toi before you
sans lui without him
derrière eux behind them
pour elle for her

When there is no verb.
pas moi not I

Qui l'a dérangé? Elle.
Who disturbed him? She.

Il a plus d'argent qu'eux.
He has more money than they.

As a complement after *être.*
C'est lui. It is he.   *C'est moi.* It is I.
C'est elle. It is she.   *Ce sont eux.* It is they.

For emphasis.
Lui, il l'a fait. He did it.
Elles ne l'aiment pas, lui. They don't like him.

When a subject or object is separated from its verb.
Lui seul peut le dire. He alone can say it.
Il n'a vu ni lui ni elle. He saw neither him nor her.

With two subjects, objects, or indirect objects.
Lui et moi nous sommes partis hier.
He and I left yesterday.

Je vous ai vus, vous et elle.
I saw you and her.

With *même* or *mêmes* for emphasis.
Je l'ai fait moi-même.
I did it myself.

Ils y sont allés eux-mêmes.
They went there themselves.

Forms of relative pronouns

qui	as subject of the verb: who or which
que	as direct object of the verb: whom, which, or that
lequel, laquelle lesquels, lesquelles	as object of a preposition: whom or which
qui quoi dont	whose, of whom, of which

Relative pronouns

Qui is used as subject of the verb of a relative clause.
C'est l'enfant qui a fait cela.
It is the child that did that.

C'est le livre qui est sur la table.
It is the book that is on the table.

Que is used as direct object of the verb of a relative clause.
C'est la femme que vous connaissez.
It is the woman you know.

Ce sont les livres que vous m'avez donnés.
These are the books you gave me.

Lequel, laquelle, lesquels, and *lesquelles* agree in gender and number with their antecedents. *Lequel, lesquels,* and *lesquelles* contract with the preposition *à* into *auquel, auxquels,* and *auxquelles;* with the preposition *de* into *duquel, desquels,* and *desquelles. Laquelle* does not combine.

For persons, *qui* is generally preferred to *lequel, laquelle,* etc.
Où sont les messieurs avec qui vous parliez?
Where are the gentlemen with whom you were talking?

For things, a form of *lequel* has to be used.
La voiture auprès de laquelle il était lui appartient.
The car he was near belongs to him.

The invariable *dont* combines the sense of *de* plus a relative pronoun *(qui, lequel, quoi).*
le garçon dont le père est médecin
the boy whose father is a doctor

le crayon dont je me sers
the pencil I am using

The order of words in a relative clause is *dont* (or *duquel, de laquelle,* etc.) + subject + verb + object. To avoid mistakes in translation of sentences with the relative "whose," replace "whose" with "of whom," "of which," "from which," "in which."
un livre dont j'ai oublié le titre
a book whose title I have forgotten

Où may serve as an adverb replacing *à, en, dans, sur,* plus *lequel,* when the antecedent is a noun of place.
la maison où j'habite
the house in which I live

le trottoir où la neige tombait
the sidewalk on which the snow was falling

le village d'où je viens
the village from which I come

The words "which," "what," and "that" (= a thing *which,* the thing *which,* that *which*) may be translated as follows:
ce qui, subject of a verb
Ce qui est sur la table est à moi.
What is on the table belongs to me.

ce que, direct object of a verb
> *Ce que tu m'as dit est un secret.*
> What you told me is a secret.

ce dont, used with expressions taking *de*
> *Comprends-tu ce dont il parle?*
> Do you understand what he is talking about?

ce à quoi, used with expressions taking *à*
> *Personne ne pouvait deviner ce à quoi je pensais.*
> No one could guess what I was thinking of.

Interrogatives

> *Qui a cassé la tasse?*
> *Qui est-ce qui a cassé la tasse?*
> Who broke the cup?

> *Qui regardez-vous?*
> *Qui est-ce que vous regardez?*
> Whom are you looking at?

> *Avec qui parle-t-il?*
> *Avec qui est-ce qu'il parle?*
> With whom is he talking?

> *De quoi est-ce qu'il parle?*
> *A quoi pensez-vous?*
> What is he talking about?
> What are you thinking of?

When *à* and *de* are used with forms of *lequel,* the usual contractions take place.

> *Laquelle de ces filles est la vôtre?*
> Which of these girls is yours?

> *Auquel de ces garçons avez-vous parlé?*
> To which one of these boys did you speak?

Quel (quelle, quels, quelles) is the interrogative adjective "which" or "what."

> *Quelle robe as-tu choisie?*
> Which dress did you choose?

> *Quel livre lisez-vous?*
> What book are you reading?

Possessives

Adjectives and pronouns agree in gender and number with the object possessed.

> *Il a pris mon livre et le sien.*
> He took his book and mine.

> *Il emmène sa fille et la mienne.*
> He is taking his daughter and mine.

> *Son père est plus sévère que le nôtre.*
> Her father is stricter than ours.

With parts of the body, the possessive adjective is often replaced by the definite article if the identity of the possessor is clear.

> *Elle s'est coupé le doigt.*
> She cut her finger.

> *Elles se sont lavé les mains.*
> They washed their hands.

The definite article preceding the possessive pronoun contracts after *à* and *de.*

> *Cette valise est-elle aux* (not *à les*) *enfants?*
> Is this suitcase the children's?

> *Non, elle est aux filles.*
> No, it's the girls'.

Idiomatic expressions with possessives.

> *un de mes voisins*
> a neighbor of mine

> *bonjour ma tante*
> good morning, aunt

> *une de ses soeurs*
> one of his sisters

> *Dites-leur bonjour de ma part.*
> Say hello to them for me.

> *Serez-vous des nôtres?*
> Will you join us?

The word "own" is expressed by *propre.*

> *Il l'a écrit de sa propre main.*
> He wrote it with his own hand.

Forms of interrogative pronouns

	Subject	Direct object	Object of preposition
persons	*qui* who *qui est-ce qui* who	*qui* whom *qui est-ce que* whom	*qui* whom
things	*qu'est-ce qui* what	*que* what *qu'est-ce que* what	*quoi* what
persons and things	*lequel,* etc. which *and* which one	*lequel,* etc. which *and* which one	*lequel,* etc. which *and* which one
after prepositions	*qui*	*quoi*	

Review of French Grammar

Demonstratives

The following examples illustrate the uses of demonstrative adjectives.

cet avion	this or that	airplane
ce livre		book
cette robe		dress
ces avions	these or those	airplanes
ces livres		books
ces robes		dresses

Uses of *-ci*, *-là*, etc.

In principle *-ci* refers to the nearest object, *-là* to the farthest, but this distinction is not strictly observed unless objects are contrasted.

Comment trouvez-vous ces maisons?
How do you like these (those) houses?

Je préfère cette maison-ci, celle-là est trop grande.
I like this house better; that one is too big.

With demonstrative pronouns, *-ci* or *-là* must be added when the pronoun is not followed by a relative clause or by a prepositional complement. *Celui, celle, ceux,* and *celles* cannot be used alone.

Quelle route faut-il prendre?
What road must we take?

Celle-ci ou celle-là?
This one or that one?

Prenons celle de droite.
Let's take the one on the right.

Ceci, cela, ça, and *ce* are invariable demonstrative pronouns.

ceci	this, it	*ça*	this, that, it
cela	that, it	*ce*	it

Ne prenez pas ceci, prenez cela.
Do not take this; take that.

Ça ne fait rien.
It does not matter.

Ceci or *cela* must be used instead of *ce* when emphasis is desired and when "this" and "that" are contrasted

Forms of demonstratives

	Adjectives Singular	Adjectives Plural	Pronouns Singular	Pronouns Plural
Masc.	*ce* (before a consonant) *cet* (before a vowel)	*ces*	*celui*	*ceux*
Fem.	*cette*	*ces*	*celle*	*celles*

and the pronoun is separated from the verb by any word other than *ne*.

Ceci est correct, cela ne l'est pas.
This is correct; that is not.

Cela n'est pas vrai.
That is not true.

The neuter demonstrative *ce* is used as the subject of *être* (or *devoir* or *pouvoir être*) only in four instances.

1. When *être* is followed by an adjective, *ce* designates something not previously named, or refers to a thought expressed or understood, or refers to a statement.
   Paris est une grande ville; c'est la plus belle du monde.
   Paris is a beautiful city; it is the most beautiful in the world.
   Ce devait être intéressant.
   It must have been interesting.
2. When a noun or pronoun follows *être*.
   Ce doit être celle de mon frère.
   It must be my brother's.
3. When an antecedent is *ceci* or *cela*.
   Goûtez ceci. C'est très bon.
   Taste this. It is very good.
4. When *être* is followed by an adverb or complement.
   Ce n'est pas assez. It is not enough.

Forms of possessive adjectives

	Singular Masc.	Singular Fem.	Plural
my	*mon*	*ma*	*mes*
your	*ton*	*ta*	*tes*
his, her, its	*son*	*sa*	*ses*
our	*notre*	*notre*	*nos*
your	*votre*	*votre*	*vos*
their	*leur*	*leur*	*leurs*

Note: Use *mon, ton, son* instead of *ma, ta, sa* before a word beginning with a vowel or a silent *h*.

Forms of possessive pronouns

	Singular Masc.	Singular Fem.	Plural Masc.	Plural Fem.
mine	*le mien*	*la mienne*	*les miens*	*les miennes*
yours	*le tien*	*la tienne*	*les tiens*	*les miennes*
his, hers, its	*le sien*	*la sienne*	*les siens*	*les siennes*
ours	*le nôtre*	*la nôtre*	*les nôtres*	*les nôtres*
yours	*le vôtre*	*la vôtre*	*les vôtres*	*les vôtres*
theirs	*le leur*	*la leur*	*les leurs*	*les leurs*

Le mien...

Indefinites

Uses of *on*

To translate the indefinite "one," "we," "you," "they," or "people" when there is no definite antecedent.

On n'est pas toujours heureux.
One is not always happy.

On ne sait jamais.
You never know.

On ne fait pas cela ici.
People don't do that here.

If faut qu'on se dépêche.
We must hurry.

On ne doit pas toujours parler de soi.
One must not speak always about himself.

On répare notre voiture.
Our car is being repaired.

Ici on ne sera pas dérangés.
Here we will not be disturbed.

Uses of *quelque*

Quelque and *quelques* are adjectives. In using these words there is no agreement in gender or elision of the final -*e* in the singular. *Quelque* and *quelques* are slightly more specific than the partitive.

On va acheter quelques pommes.
We are going to buy some apples.

Quelqu'un, quelqu'une, quelques uns, and *quelques unes* are the corresponding pronouns.

Quelqu'un l'a cassé.
Someone broke it.

Donnez-moi quelques unes de vos fleurs.
Give me some of your flowers.

Quelque chose, a pronoun meaning "something" or "anything," is followed by *de* before an adjective. It does not require agreement in gender.

Y a-t-il quelque chose qui manque?
Is anything missing?

Oui, il y a quelque chose qui manque.
Yes, something is missing.

Similarly with *pas grand'chose* "little," *autre chose* "something else," and *peu de chose* "little," or "not much."

Common indefinite adjectives and pronouns

Plusieurs, plural adjective and pronoun meaning "several." It shows no agreement for gender.

Nous y sommes allés plusieurs fois.
We went there several times.

J'en ai vu plusieurs.
I saw several of them.

Chaque, singular pronoun meaning "each" or "every." It shows no agreement for gender, no elision.

Chaque artiste est orgueilleux de son oeuvre.
Every artist is proud of his work.

Chacun and *chacune,* singular pronouns meaning "each" or "each one."

Chacun a ses propres traditions.
Each one has its own traditions.

Tout, toute, tous, and *toutes,* pronouns and adjectives meaning "all," "entire," and "every." In the singular (*tout, toute*) without an article, these words mean "every"; with the article, "the whole." In the plural (*tous, toutes*), these words are always accompanied by an article or similar word. As adjectives they precede the noun and the article. These words are never followed by *de.*

Tout chemin mène à Rome.
Every road leads to Rome.

Toutes les bêtes s'étaient sauvées.
All the animals had escaped.

Tous les hommes avaient embarqué.
All the men had embarked.

Tous avaient embarqué.
All had embarked.

Tel, telle, tels, telles, adjectives and pronouns meaning "such," "similar," and "the like." *Tel* as an adjective agrees in gender and number with the noun it modifies. It is preceded by an indefinite article or partitive (*un, une, de*) when *tel* does not introduce a comparison.

Il ne s'attendait pas à une telle chance.
He did not expect such luck.

Tel père tel fils.
Like father like son.

Un and *une* are pronouns only in two constructions:
1. When followed by *de* as one of the objects or persons indicated.
   Une de ces tasses est cassée.
   One of these cups is broken.
2. In contrast with *autre: l'un, l'autre; les uns, les autres.*
   Nous avons besoin l'un de l'autre.
   We need each other.

Même and *mêmes* are used as adjectives meaning "same" before a noun, or "very" or "itself" after a noun; as an adverb meaning "even."

à l'heure même il arrivait à Paris
at the very hour he was arriving in Paris

Ce n'est pas la même chose.
It is not the same thing.

Ce n'est même pas vrai.
It is not even true.

Quiconque, a pronoun meaning "anyone who" or "whoever."

Quiconque le fera sera récompensé.
Whoever does it will be rewarded.

Quelconque, an adjective meaning "any," "of whatever sort," and "no matter what," as an attributive or predicate adjective, meaning "ordinary."

Cette femme est quelconque.
This woman is common.

Donnez-moi un crayon quelconque.
Give me any pencil at all.

Qui que, quoi que, quel que, relative pronouns and adjectives combined with *que* and followed by the subjunctive have an all inclusive sense, and are translated as follows: *qui que ce soit* "whoever it may be," *quoi que ce soit* "whatever it may be," *quel que soit* "whatever," as in *quel que soit l'heure,* "whatever the time." These expressions are the most emphatic forms of *quelque chose* and *quelqu'un.*

Si vous dîtes quoi que ce soit à qui que ce soit, vous le regretterez.

If you say anything at all (whatever it may be) to anyone (without exception, whoever it may be), you will regret it.

Negation

Negation is expressed by *ne* before the verb plus the second part of a negative expression after it. The principal negative expressions are shown here in two groups.

Group A

ne . . . que	only, none but
ne . . . ni . . . ni	neither . . . nor
ne . . . personne	nobody
ne . . . aucun	no, none, not any

Group B

ne . . . pas	not
ne . . . point	not (less common than *ne . . . pas*)
ne . . . guère	hardly, scarcely
ne . . . plus	no more, no longer
ne . . . jamais	never
ne . . . rien	nothing

Placement of the negative expression

In a declarative sentence with a verb in a simple tense, the two parts of the negative are placed before and after the verb.

Elle ne mange pas. She does not eat.
Il n'est pas ici. He is not here.

With compound tenses, the two parts of the negative of Group A expressions are placed before and after the auxiliary verb *(avoir* or *être).*

Je n'ai jamais fait cela. I have never done that.
Il n'a guère mangé. He scarcely ate.

With compound tenses, the two parts of the negative of Group B expressions are placed before and after the complete verb.

Il n'a lu aucun de ces livres.
He read none of these books.

Il n'a vu personne.
He saw no one.

Additional rules of negation

Only conjunctive and reflexive object pronouns *(me, te, le, lui, nous, vous, les, leur, se, y, en)* can come between *ne* and the verb.

Il ne lui parle pas. He does not speak to him.
Elle ne les a pas vus. She did not see them.

Ne . . . aucun!
Ne . . . jamais!

When the negative is used with an infinitive, both parts come before the infinitive and its pronoun objects, if any.

Il a promis de ne plus la voir.
He promised not to see her again.

The *que* of *ne . . . que* immediately precedes the word it modifies.

Je n'ai acheté que deux livres.
I bought only two books.

Je n'ai parlé qu'à lui seul.
I spoke only to him.

Personne, rien, and *aucun* may be used as subjects and as objects of verbs as well as objects of prepositions. *Ne* must not be omitted.

Personne ne peut faire cela. No one can do that.
Aucun n'est venu. No one came.
Je n'ai rien entendu. I heard nothing.

Ne may sometimes be used without *pas* with the verbs *cesser, oser, savoir,* and *pouvoir,* especially when followed by an infinitive and in some expressions that imply hesitancy rather than definite negation.

Je n'ose le dire. I hardly dare say it.
Je ne saurais vous le dire. I couldn't tell you.
Elle ne cesse de parler. She does not stop talking.

Si must be used instead of *oui* in answering a negative question affirmatively.

Ne l'avez-vous pas vu? Haven't you seen it?
Si, je l'ai vu. Yes, I have.

Jamais used without *ne* means "ever."

A-t-on jamais vu pareille chose?
Has anyone ever seen such a thing?

Rien used without *ne* means "anything."

Y a-t-il rien de plus beau?
Is there anything lovelier?

Verbs

Regular verbs

The infinitives of regular verbs end in *-er, -ir,* or *-re.*
The examples shown here are *donner, finir,* and *rompre.*

Formation of tenses

The simple tenses of all regular verbs and most irregular verbs derive from four forms of the verb.

Conjugation of regular verbs

Formation of tenses

Use the *infinitive* to form:

Future
Infinitive plus -ai, -as, -a, -ons, -ez, -ont.
Example: *donner* ai

Conditional
Infinitive plus -ais, -ais, -ait, -ions, -iez, -aient.
Example: *donner* ais
In the third conjugation the final *e* is dropped.
Example: *rompr* ai

Use the *present participle* to form:

Imperfect indicative
Change *-ant* to -ais, -ais, ait, -ions, -iez, -aient.
Example: *donn* ais

Present subjunctive
Change *-ant* to -e, -es, -e, -ions, -iez, -ent.
Example: *donn* e

Moods

Indicative

	Present			*Imperfect*		
	I give, finish, break			I was giving, finishing, breaking		
	I do give, finish, break					
je	donne	finis	romps	donnais	finissais	rompais
tu	donnes	finis	romps	donnais	finissais	rompais
il	donne	finit	romp	donnait	finissait	rompait
nous	donnons	finissons	rompons	donnions	finissions	rompions
vous	donnez	finissez	rompez	donniez	finissiez	rompiez
ils	donnent	finissent	rompent	donnaient	finissaient	rompaient

Conditional

	Present		
	I should give, finish, break		
je	donnerais	finirais	romprais
tu	donnerais	finirais	romprais
il	donnerait	finirait	romprait
nous	donnerions	finirions	romprions
vous	donneriez	finiriez	rompriez
ils	donneraient	finiraient	rompraient

Subjunctive

	Present		
	that I give, finish, break		
que je	donne	finisse	rompe
que tu	donnes	finisses	rompes
qu'il	donne	finisse	rompe
que nous	donnions	finissions	rompions
que vous	donniez	finissiez	rompiez
qu'ils	donnent	finissent	rompent

Don't forget to write

le 5 mai 2000.

Mon cher George,

J'avais promis de vous mettre au courant de tout ce qui m'arriverait pendant mon séjour à New York. Je ne sais que trop bien que j'ai manqué de parole, car je serai de retour à Paris bientôt. Cependant, je vous prie de ne pas me tenir rigueur de ma négligence. J'ai été tellement occupé que c'est à peine si j'ai eu le temps d'écrire à mes parents.

À bientôt.

Votre ami,
Robert

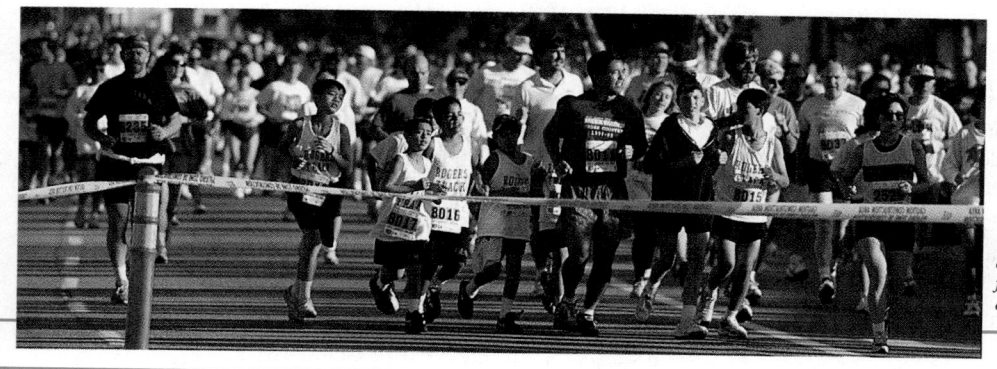

The verb finir, *to finish*, is a good one to use at the end of a long, hard footrace. As you complete your run, exclaim "J'ai fini," *I have finished*.

Use the *present indicative* to form:
Imperative
The pronoun subject is dropped from the second person singular and from the first and second person plural. The -s of the first conjugation is dropped except before *y* and *en*.
Example: *donne, donnons, donnez*

Use the *past definite* to form:
Imperfect subjunctive
Change the final -*i* or -*s* of the first person singular form to -*sse*, -*sses*, -*t*, -*ssions*, -*ssiez*, -*ssent*. A circumflex accent is placed over the last vowel of the third person singular.
Example: *donnât*

Infinitive	-er	-ir	-re
	donner	*finir*	*rompre*
	to give	to finish	to break
Participles			
Present	giving	finishing	breaking
	donnant	*finissant*	*rompant*
Past	given	finished	broken
	donné	*fini*	*rompu*
Imperative			
Singular	give	finish	break
	donne	*finis*	*romps*
Plural	let's give	let's finish	let's break
	donnons	*finissons*	*rompons*
	give	finish	break
	donnez	*finissez*	*rompez*

Past definite			*Future*		
I gave, finished, broke			I shall give, finish, break		
donnai	*finis*	*rompis*	*donnerai*	*finirai*	*romprai*
donnas	*finis*	*rompis*	*donneras*	*finiras*	*rompras*
donna	*finit*	*rompit*	*donnera*	*finira*	*rompra*
donnâmes	*finîmes*	*rompîmes*	*donnerons*	*finirons*	*romprons*
donnâtes	*finîtes*	*rompîtes*	*donnerez*	*finirez*	*romprez*
donnèrent	*finirent*	*rompirent*	*donneront*	*finiront*	*rompront*

May 5, 2000

Dear George,

I had promised to tell you all the things that happened to me during my visit to New York. I know too well that I have broken my promise, but I shall be back in Paris soon. However, I hope you will not hold this against me. I have been so busy that I have not had time even to write to my parents.

See you soon.

Your friend,
Robert

Arriver (*to arrive*) and demander (*to ask*) are two examples of frequently used French regular verbs.

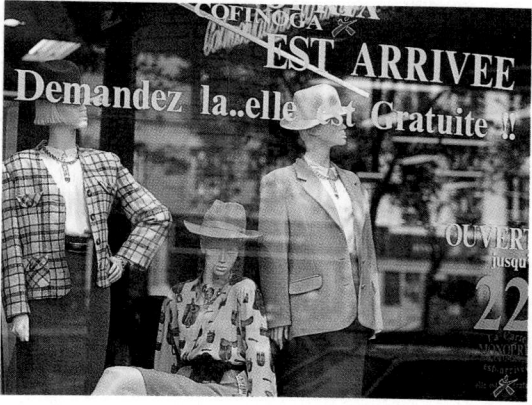

Verbal spelling irregularities

Spelling changes often occur in regular verbs. These changes appear to be needed to retain the original sounds within the infinitive forms. As you will shortly see, for example, by adding a cedilla to *c*, the soft *c* of verbs ending in *cer* is retained before vowels that normally would make the *c* hard.

Spelling irregularities of regular verbs

Verb ending	Change	Example *Present participle*	*Present indicative*	*Imperfect indicative*	*Past definite*	*Imperfect subjunctive*
-cer *avancer* to advance	requires the soft *c* sound throughout the conjugation.	*avançant*	*avance* *avançons*	*avançais* *avancions*	*avançai* *avançâmes*	*avançasse* *avançassions*
-ger *manger* to eat	requires the soft *g*, so *g* followed by *a* or *o* becomes *ge*.	*mangeant*	*mange* *mangeons*	*mangeais* *mangions*	*mangeai* *mangeâmes*	*mangeasse* *mangeassions*

		Present indicative	*Future*	*Conditional*	*Present subjunctive*
-oyer **-uyer** *netoyer* to clean	*y* changes to *i* before *e* in conjugation, but not elsewhere.	*nettoie*, etc.	*nettoierai*	*nettoierais*	*nettoie*, etc.
-ayer **-eyer** *payer* to pay	may either retain *y* throughout, or change to *i* before *e*.	*paye* *paie*	*payerai* *paierai*	*payerais* *paierais*	*paye* *paie*

Verb ending	Change	*Present indicative*	*Future*	*Conditional*	*Present subjunctive*
-er when unaccented and followed by a single consonant *mener* to lead	*e* changes to *è* when the ending begins with an unstressed *e*.	*mène* *mènes* *mène* *menons* *menez* *mènent*	*mènerai* *mèneras* *mènera* *mènerons* *mènerez* *mèneront*	*mènerais* *mènerais* *mènerait* *mènerions* *mèneriez* *mèneraient*	*mène* *mènes* *mène* *menions* *meniez* *mènent*
-eter **-eler** (most verbs) *appeler* to call	the *l* or *t* is doubled to cause the first *e* to be stressed.	*appelle* *appelles* *appelle* *appelons* *appelez* *appellent*	*appellerai* *appelleras* *appellera* *appellerons* *appellerez* *appelleront*	*appellerais* *appellerais* *appellerait* *appellerions* *appelleriez* *appelleraient*	*appelle* *appelles* *appelle* *appelions* *appeliez* *appellent*
jeter to throw		*jette*	*jetterai*	*jetterais*	*jette*
-eter **-eler** (some verbs) *acheter* to buy	follows the rule for unaccented *e*, as in *mener* above.	*achète*	*achèterai*	*achèterais*	*achète*

Review of French Grammar

The auxiliary verbs

Avoir combines with the past participle to form the compound tenses of all transitive verbs and most intransitive verbs. Both *avoir* and *être* themselves are conjugated with *avoir*.

Il a eu besoin d'argent. He needed money.
Il a été malade. He was sick.
Il a acheté des fleurs. He bought some flowers.

Etre is used as the auxiliary to form

1. The compound tenses of all reflexive verbs.
   Elle s'est levée. She got up.
   Elles se sont assises. They sat down.
2. The passive voice.
   Elle est admirée de tous. She is admired by all.
3. The compound tenses of intransitive verbs and their derivatives that indicate motion or change of state:

aller	to go	*venir*	to come
arriver	to arrive	*partir*	to leave
entrer	to go in	*sortir*	to go out
monter	to go up	*descendre*	to go down
naître	to be born	*mourir*	to die
rester	to remain	*retourner*	to go back
tomber	to fall	*devenir*	to become

Certain normally instransitive verbs may also be used transitively, with a corresponding change in meaning. They are conjugated with *avoir* when used transitively.

J'ai descendu ma valise. I took down my suitcase.
Il a sorti les chaises. He took out the chairs.
Il a rentré les chaises. He took in the chairs.

When a verb that is not reflexive is conjugated with *être,* the participle agrees in gender and number with the subject.

Elle est partie ce soir. She left tonight.

When a verb is conjugated with *avoir,* the past participle agrees in gender and number with the direct object, if the direct object precedes the verb.

Il a acheté des fleurs et il les a données à sa mère.
He bought some flowers and gave them to his mother.

Les fleurs qu'il a achetées sont belles.
The flowers he bought are beautiful.

All reflexive verbs are conjugated with *être.* It sometimes is hard to determine whether the reflexive pronoun is the direct object or the indirect object of the verb. In the sentence, *Elle s'est coupée* (she cut herself) the reflexive pronoun, *se,* representing "herself" is the direct object. For this reason there is agreement of the past participle with the direct object. But if the sentence reads *Elle s'est coupé le doigt* (she cut her finger) the direct object is *doigt.* The reflexive pronoun is indirect, merely indicating the possessor. The verb may have but one direct object, so the past participle will not agree with *se.*

As another example, consider the following:

Les chemises qu'il s'est achetées sont belles.
The shirts he bought for himself are pretty.

In this case the preceding direct object is *que* (referring to *chemises,* feminine plural) and *se* is an indirect object. The agreement is with *que: achetées.*

Reflexive verbs may express reciprocal action, that is action which the individuals that are the subject of the verb perform upon each other.

Ils se sont parlé. They spoke to each other.

Auxiliary verbs

Infinitives		*avoir* to have	*être* to be
Participles	*Present*	*ayant* having	*étant* being
	Past	*eu* had	*été* been
Indicative	*Present*	*j'ai*	*je suis*
		tu as	*tu es*
		il a	*il est*
		nous avons	*nous sommes*
		vous avez	*vous êtes*
		ils ont	*ils sont*
	Imperfect	*j'avais*	*j'étais*
		tu avais	*tu étais*
		il avait	*il était*
		nous avions	*nous étions*
		vous aviez	*vous étiez*
		ils avaient	*ils étaient*
	Past definite	*j'eus*	*je fus*
		tu eus	*tu fus*
		il eut	*il fut*
		nous eûmes	*nous fûmes*
		vous eûtes	*vous fûtes*
		ils eurent	*ils furent*
	Future	*j'aurai*	*je serai*
		tu auras	*tu seras*
		il aura	*il sera*
		nous aurons	*nous serons*
		vous aurez	*vous serez*
		ils auront	*ils seront*

Uses of verb tenses

Use the past indefinite when expressing simple past tense and when the verb expresses successive actions.

J'ai frappé à la porte et il me l'a ouverte.

I knocked at the door and he opened it for me.

Use the imperfect for past time only when the verb expresses:

1. A mental state.

    Je savais bien que tu connaissais la vie.

    I knew well that you understood life.

2. A condition, continuing action, or an action occurring while another action occurred.

    Je déjeunais quand il est entré.

    I was having lunch when he came in.

3. A repeated or habitual action.

    Je faisais les courses tous les matins.

    I used to do errands every morning.

4. A permanent characteristic.

    Le jardin était plein de fleurs.

    The garden was full of flowers.

The imperfect is used with *depuis* when the verb conveys an action begun in the past and continuing into a later time.

J'étais là depuis trois jours quand il est arrivé.

I had been there for three days when he arrived. When an action begun in the past is described as continuing up to the present, the present is used with *depuis*.

Elle est ici depuis deux jours.

She has been here for two days.

Conditional sentences

A conditional sentence consists of two parts: a clause expressing a condition, and a clause expressing a result. When the result clause is in the future, the condition clause is in the present.

Si j'étudie, je réussirai à mon examen.

If I study, I will pass my exam.

When the result clause is in the conditional, the condition clause is in the imperfect.

Important irregular verbs

aller　Present: *vais, vas, va, allons, allez, vont*
Imperfect: *allais, allais, allait, allions, alliez, allaient*
Present participle: *allant*
Past participle: *allé*

Infinitive	Present indicative	Future	Present participle	Past participle
asseoir	assieds	assierai	asseyant	assis
battre	bats	battrai	battant	battu
conduire	conduis	conduirai	conduisant	conduit
courir	cours	courrai	courant	couru
couvrir	couvre	couvrirai	couvrant	couvert
craindre	crains	craindrai	craignant	craignis
devoir	dois	devrai	devant	dû
dormir	dors	dormirai	dormant	dormi
écrire	écris	écrirai	écrivant	écrit
mentir	mens	mentirai	mentant	menti
mettre	mets	mettrai	mettant	mis
mourir	meurs	mourrai	mourant	mort
offrir	offre	offrirai	offrant	offert
partir	pars	partirai	partant	parti
recevoir	reçois	recevrai	recevant	reçu
sentir	sens	sentirai	sentant	senti
sortir	sors	sortirai	sortant	sorti
souffrir	souffre	souffrirai	souffrant	souffert
venir	viens	viendrai	venant	venu
vêtir	vets	vêtirai	vêtant	vêtu

Conduis ma mère à sa place.

Si j'étais riche, je voyagerais beaucoup.

If I were rich, I would travel a lot.

The same rule applies to the auxiliaries of compound tenses.

Si je n'étais pas sorti,
je n'aurais pas manqué mes amis.

If I had not gone out,
I would not have missed my friends.

Clauses with *quand* etc.

The future is used after *quand, lorsque, dès que, aussitôt que,* and *tant que* if the action takes place at a future time.

Dès que j'aurai écrit cette lettre, je l'enverrai.

As soon as I have written this letter, I will send it.

Quand je parlerai français, j'irai en France.

When I speak French, I will go to France.

Uses of the infinitive

The infinitive may be used as the subject of a verb.

Réussir est très important.

To succeed is very important.

The infinitive may be used as a complement.

Tu n'arriveras pas à faire ce problème.

You will not succeed in working this problem.

The infinitive may be used after many prepositions to express the English present participle.

Il a passé deux jours sans dormir.

He spent two days without sleeping.

The preposition *après* is followed by a past infinitive. The past infinitive has two parts: an auxiliary *(avoir* or *être)* and the past participle of the verb.

Après avoir dîné, je suis allé au cinéma.

After eating, I went to the movies.

Most adjectives and nouns are followed by *de* before an infinitive, but a few common adjectives are followed by *à* before the infinitive: *habile, lent, prêt, premier, dernier,* and *seul.*

Il est prêt à partir.

He is ready to leave.

Elle est toujours la première à finir.

She is always the first one to finish.

When an infinitive is passive in meaning, it is preceded by *à*.

Elle avait encore tout son travail à faire.

She still had all her work to do.

Some verbs are followed directly by the infinitive without a preposition.

aimer mieux	to prefer	*oser*	to dare
aller	to go	*paraître*	to appear
compter	to intend	*pouvoir*	to be able to
croire	to believe	*préférer*	to prefer
désirer	to wish, want	*regarder*	to watch
devoir	to have to	*savoir*	to know
entendre	to hear	*sembler*	to seem
espérer	to hope	*souhaiter*	to wish
faire	to do	*venir*	to come
laisser	to allow, let	*voir*	to see

Some verbs require *à* before the infinitive, as in *apprendre à conduire,* learn to drive.

aider	to help	*renoncer*	to give up
apprendre	to learn	*réussir*	to succeed
arriver	to succeed	*s'amuser*	to enjoy
avoir	to have	*s'attendre*	to expect
chercher	to seek	*se décider*	to decide
commencer	to begin	*se mettre*	to start
enseigner	to teach	*tarder*	to delay
hésiter	to hesitate	*tenir*	to insist on
inviter	to invite	*venir*	to happen

The infinitive preceded by *à* is used with certain nouns to express function or purpose.

une salle à manger a dining room
une machine à laver a washing machine

Subjunctive

The subjunctive mood is used after certain verbs or expressions that indicate desire, doubt, emotion, necessity, or uncertainty. Verbs in the subjunctive are almost always used in dependent clauses. Such clauses are introduced usually by *que* but sometimes by a relative pronoun.

The present subjunctive is formed by dropping the *-ent* of the third person present indicative form and adding *-e, -es, -e, -ions, -iez, -ent*. These endings are the same for all verbs except *avoir* and *être*.

avoir j'aie, tu aies, il ait,
nous ayons, vous ayez, ils aient

être je sois, tu sois, il soit,
nous soyons, vous soyez, ils soient

A few irregular verbs use only one irregular stem for all forms.

faire: je fasse . . . *pouvoir:* je puisse . . .
falloir: il faille . . . *savoir:* je sache . . .

Nous cherchons quelqu'un qui puisse faire le travail.

We are looking for someone who can do the work.

Some irregular verbs form the present subjunctive by using one stem for the *nous* and *vous* forms (from the imperfect indicative) and one for the other forms. The most common verbs of this type are as follows.

aller que j'aille, tu ailles, il aille,
nous allions, vous alliez, ils aillent

boire que je boive, tu boives, il boive,
nous buvions, vous buviez, ils boivent

croire que je croie, tu croies, il croie,
nous croyions, vous croyiez, ils croient

devoir que je doive, tu doives, il doive,
nous devions, vous deviez, ils doivent

prendre que je prenne, tu prennes, il prenne,
nous prenions, vous preniez, ils prennent

venir *que je vienne, tu viennes, il vienne,*
nous venions, vous veniez, ils viennent

vouloir *que je veuille, tu veuilles, il veuille,*
nous voulions, vous vouliez, ils veuillent

The subjunctive is used in a dependent clause when the subject of the dependent clause is different from the subject of the main clause.

Je veux qu'elle fasse sa chambre.
I want her to clean her room.

Je veux faire ma chambre.
I want to clean my room.

The subjunctive is used after certain expressions. Emotion.

avoir peur	to be afraid
craindre	to fear
être content	to be happy
être désolé	to be sorry
être enchanté	to be delighted
être fâché	to be angry
être heureux	to be happy
être surpris	to be surprised
regretter	to be sorry
s'étonner	to be surprised

Il est fâché qu'elle ne soit pas rentrée.

He is angry that she has not returned.

Verbs of wishing, asking, commanding, permitting, or prohibiting.

aimer mieux	to prefer	*permettre*	to permit
défendre	to forbid	*préférer*	to prefer
demander	to ask	*souhaiter*	to wish
exiger	to demand	*vouloir*	to want
ordonner	to demand		

J'aime mieux qu'il fasse ses devoirs maintenant.
I prefer that he do his homework now.

Je ne crois pas qu'il puisse partir.
I do not think he can leave.

The subjunctive is used when the antecedent is modified by a superlative or by *premier, dernier,* or *seul.*

C'est le premier livre que nous ayons lu.
It is the first book we have read.

The subjunctive is used after certain conjunctions.

afin que	in order that
à moins que	unless
avant que	before
bien que	although
jusqu'à ce que	until
pour que	in order that
pourvu que	provided that
quoique	although

The subjunctive is also used with all conjunctions of condition except *si.*

Pourvu qu'il soit là à temps, c'est tout ce que je veux.
All I want is for him to be on time.
(As long as he is on time, that is all I want.)

Interrogation

There are several ways of changing a declarative sentence to an interrogative sentence.

By prefixing *est-ce que.* No change in word order is needed.

Ce livre est intéressant.
This book is interesting.

Est-ce que ce livre est intéressant?
Is this book interesting?

By inversion of subject and verb.

When the subject is a personal pronoun or *ce* or *on,* it follows the verb and is joined to it by a hyphen.

Est-il chez lui?
Is he at home?

Est-ce vrai?
Is it true?

Parle-t-on toujours d'elle?
Do people still speak of her?

When the subject is a noun, demonstrative pronoun, possessive pronoun, or indefinite pronoun, the subject precedes the verb and is repeated after it in the form of a pronoun.

Votre ami est-il parti? Has your friend left?
Les vôtres sont-ils ici? Are yours here?
Cela est-il vrai? Is that true?
Quel livre choisit-il? What book does he choose?

The noun subject need not be repeated in pronoun form when three conditions are met: (1) the sentence must be introduced by an interrogative adverb *(combien, comment, où, quand)*; (2) the verb must be in a simple tense: present, imperfect, future, conditional, or past definite; and (3) the verb must have neither an object nor a modifying phrase.

Combien coûte ce livre?
How much does this book cost?

Comment va votre soeur?
How is your sister?

When the verb is not a simple tense or has an object or adverbial phrase, subject and verb are inverted or *est-ce que* is used.

Pourquoi votre mère a-t-elle acheté ces fruits?
Why did your mother buy this fruit?

A quelle heure votre ami arrivera-t-il à la gare?
When will your friend arrive at the station?

For the traveler

l'avion

AIR FRANCE

le douanier

la valise

How to travel	Comment voyager
by plane	*en avion*
by train	*en train*
by boat	*en bateau*
by car	*en voiture*
by bus	*en autocar/ autobus*

At the airport — A l'aéroport

The plane is late/ early.	*L'avion est en retard/en avance*

Customs — La douane

Passport, please. Anything to declare?	*Votre passeport, s'il vous plaît?*
No, nothing to declare.	*Non, rien à déclarer.*
Please, open your suitcase.	*Ouvrez votre valise, s'il vous plaît.*
Thank you, Sir.	*Merci, Monsieur.*

From the airport to Paris — De l'aéroport à Paris

I would like to take the bus to Paris..	*Je voudrais prendre l'autobus pour Paris.*
Taxi. Are you free? I would like to go to the train station.	*Taxi. Vous êtes libre?* *Je voudrais aller à la gare.*
I would like to rent a car.	*Je voudrais louer une voiture.*
How much for two weeks?	*C'est combien pour deux semaines?*
Two hundred francs a week.	*Deux cents francs la semaine.*
Which road do I take to go to Paris?	*Quelle route est-ce que je prends pour aller à Paris?*
Take AI, the "Autoroute du Nord," toward Paris.	*Prenez AI, " l'Autoroute du Nord," vers Paris.*
Be careful if you take the opposite direction; it is the road to London via the Eurotunnel.	*Attention Si vous prenez la direction opposée c'est la route qui va à Londres via le Tunnel sous la Manche.*
Watch for the road signs.	*Regardez bien les panneaux.*
I want to take a fast train to London.	*Je veux prendre le Train à Grande Vitesse pour Londres.*
How long is the trip, taking the TGV?	*Combien de temps entre Paris et Londres avec le TGV?*
Three hours between the two cities.	*Trois heures entre les deux villes.*

Road signs *Les panneaux*

autoroute à péage (toll)

AUVERS SUR-OISE

entering the city

AUVERS SUR-OISE

leaving the city

D. departmental
secondary road

N. national
main road

France is a leader in developing high-speed interurban rail service with its celebrated TGV train.

Looking for a hotel   *Chercher un hôtel*

Pardon me, Sir, where is the tourist office?	*Pardon, Monsieur, òu est le bureau de tourisme?*
It is over there, to the right.	*Il est là-bas, à droite.*
It is in the next street, to the left.	*Il est dans la prochaine rue, à gauche.*
Thank you, Sir. Good-bye.	*Merci, Monsieur. Au revoir.*
Good morning, Miss. Could you please tell me if there is a good hotel, not too expensive, near here?	*Bonjour Mademoiselle, pourriez-vous m'indiquer un bon hôtel, pas trop cher, et près d'ici, s'il vous plaît?*
Yes, Sir. When you leave, turn left and it is straight ahead.	*Oui Monsieur. Quand vous sortez, tournez à gauche et c'est tout droit.*
Do you speak English? I do not speak French.	*Parlez-vous anglais? Je ne parle pas français.*
I do not understand.	*Je ne comprends pas.*
Speak more slowly, please.	*Parlez plus lentement s'il vous plaît.*
What does that mean?	*Qu'est-ce que ça veut dire?*
A room for two, with bath	*Une chambre pour deux personnes, avec salle de bains*
It is expensive.	*C'est très cher.*
Is there a phone?	*Y a-t-il un téléphone?*
What time is breakfast?	*A quelle heure est le petit déjeuner?*
From 6:30 to 9:00 in your room.	*De six heures et demie à neuf heures dans votre chambre.*
What do you serve for breakfast?	*Qu'est-ce que vous servez pour le petit déjeuner?*
We have, tea, coffee, or hot chocolate with bread, butter and jam, or croissants.	*Nous avons du thé, du café ou du chocolat avec du pain du beurre et de la confiture ou des croissants.*
At what time do you want your breakfast tomorrow morning?	*A quelle heure voulez-vous votre petit déjeuner demain matin?*

Shopping   *Faire des courses*

Stores   *Les magasins*

jewelry shop	*la bijouterie*
butcher shop	*la boucherie*
bakery	*la boulangerie*
tobacco shop	*le bureau de tabac*
delicatessen	*la charcuterie*
beauty parlor	*le coiffeur pour dames*
department store	*le grand magasin*
bookstore	*la librairie*
pastry shop	*la pâtisserie*

No holiday in France is complete without a visit to at least one pâtisserie, or pastry shop, for a sampling of its wares.

Is there a department store near here?	*Y a-t-il un grand magasin près d'ici?*
Yes, Sir. You will pass by many little shops. Follow this street.	*Oui, Monsieur. Vous passerez devant beaucoup de petits magasins. Suivez cette rue.*
Can I help you, Miss?	*Vous désirez, Mademoiselle?*
I would like to buy a summer dress.	*Je voudrais acheter une robe d'été.*
White, pink, or light blue.	*Blanche, rose, ou bleue claire.*
What is your size, miss?	*Quelle taille faîtes-vous, Mademoiselle?*
I think 12 or 14. I am not sure.	*Je crois 44 or 46 . Je ne suis pas sûre.*
I would like shoes, please. Size 7 or perhaps 8.	*Je voudrais des chaussures s'il vous plaît. pointure 38 ou 39.*
How much does it cost?	*Ça coûte combien?*
May I show you something else?	*Puis-je vous montrer quelque chose d'autre?*
Perhaps, a skirt and a blouse.	*Peut-être une jupe et une blouse.*
I have a matching linen skirt and a silk blouse in different colors.	*J'ai une jupe en lin et une blouse en soie dans des couleurs différentes.*
I would like a man's short sleeve shirt, size 16, and shoes, size 10 or 11.	*Je voudrais une chemise pour homme, taille 40, et des chaussures, pointure 44 ou 45.*
I will take this tie also.	*Je prendrai aussi cette cravate.*
And now, let's have lunch.	*Et maintenant, allons déjeuner.*

At the restaurant   *Au restaurant*

Le menu

Alose à la provençale
shad baked with garlic, onions, tomatoes
black olives, spinach, and parsley

Blanquette de veau
a stew made of veal and a white sauce and
garnished with onions, mushrooms, and parsley

Boeuf bourguignon
a beef dish made with red wine plus
braised onions and mushrooms

Bouillabaisse
a fish stew made with fish available in season, and
flavored with thyme, rosemary, fennel seeds, saffron,
onions, fresh tomatoes, orange rind, and olive oil

Choucroute garnie
a combination of two or more types of sausages
plus shredded white cabbage fermented in salt
and flavored with caraway and juniper berries,
all cooked with smoked pork, lean bacon, goose fat,
white wine, and boiled potatoes

Moules marinières
mussels cooked in a large kettle
with a sauce made of butter, shallots,
pepper, parsley, and white wine

The waiter	*Le garçon*
Good afternoon.	*Bonjour, Madame, Monsieur.*
A table for two near the window please.	*Une table pour deux, près de la fenêtre, s'il vous plaît.*
Follow me.	*Suivez-moi.*
Is this table all right?	*Est-ce que cette table vous convient?*
Yes, very good, thank you.	*Oui, très bien, merci.*
Yes, Sir. Can I help you?	*Oui, Monsieur. Vous désirez?*
The menu, please.	*La carte, s'il vous plaît.*
To start, I will have moules marinières.	*Pour commencer, je prendrai des moules marinières.*
Then, I will have boeuf bourguignon.	*Ensuite, je prendrai du boeuf bourguignon.*
And the lady?	*Et Madame?*
I will have antipasto, veal stew, and French fries.	*Je prendrai des hors d'oeuvre variés et ensuite une blanquette de veau et des pommes frites.*
A bottle of the local wine, please.	*Une bouteille de vin du pays, s'il vous plaît.*
Bread and butter, and we will order dessert and coffee later.	*Du pain et du beurre, et nous commanderons du dessert et du café plus tard.*
The check, please.	*L'addition, s'il vous plaît.*
It is already dark and it is nice out.	*Il fait déjà nuit et il fait bon dehors.*
Let's go see the lights. Let's take the subway.	*Allons voir les lumières. Prenons le métro.*
The subway goes faster and it is easier.	*Le métro va plus vite, et c'est plus facile.*
Then we can walk back to the hotel.	*Après nous pouvons rentrer à pied à l'hôtel.*

The telephone

I would like to call the United States.	*Je voudrais téléphoner aux Etats Unis.*
You need a card.	*Vous avez besoin d'une télécarte.*
How does it work and where do you find them?	*Comment est-ce que ça marche et où les trouve-t-on?*
You can buy the cards at the post office.	*Vous pouvez acheter les télécartes à la poste.*
Let's go; we can buy stamps at the same time.	*Allons-y et nous pouvons acheter des timbres en même temps.*
To call the United States from France, dial 19 then the country code, 1, and your number.	*Pour téléphoner aux Etats-Unis de la France, faites le 19, puis le 1 et votre numéro.*

Au téléphone

French pay telephones accept electronic phone cards, or telecartes. The cards are inserted directly into the telephone. A small screen on the phone displays the units of credit remaining on the card during your call.

Where can you speak French?
Où parle-t-on le français?

Algeria	*Algérie*	Mali	*Mali*
Belgium	*Belgique*	Martinique	*Martinique*
Benin	*Bénin*	Mauritius	*Maurice*
Burkina Faso	*Burkina Faso*	Mauritania	*Mauritanie*
Burundi	*Burundi*	Mayotte	*Mayotte*
Canada	*Canada*	Monaco	*Monaco*
Central African Republic	*Centrafricaine*	Morroco	*Maroc*
Chad	*Tchad*	Niger	*Niger*
Comoros	*Comores*	New Caledonia	*Nouvelle Calédonie*
Republic of Congo	*Congo*	Quebec	*Québec*
Djibouti	*Djibouti*	Reúnion	*Réunion*
France	*France*	Rwanda	*Rwanda*
Guyana	*Guyane*	Senegal	*Sénégal*
French Polynesia	*Polynésie française*	Seychelles	*Seychelles*
Gabon	*Gabon*	Saint Pierre et Miquelon	*St Pierre et Miquelon*
Guadeloupe	*Guadeloupe*	Switzerland	*Suisse*
Guinea	*Guinée*	Togo	*Togo*
Haiti	*Haïti*	Tunisia	*Tunisie*
Ivory Coast	*Côte d'Ivoire*	Vanuatu	*Vanuatu*
Louisiana	*Louisiane*	Wallis et Futuna	*Wallis et Futuna*
Luxembourg	*Lucembourg*	Zaire	*Zaïre*
Madagascar	*Madagascar*		

Numbers

Cardinal numbers

The word *et* is used in numbers only in 21, 31, 41, 51, 61, and 71. In all other compound numbers through 99, the hyphen is used.

Vingt and *cent* are made plural when multiplied and when modifying a noun, but the *s* is droppd before another number.

quatre-vingts-garçons eighty boys
quatre vingt deux garçons eighty-two boys
quatre cents mots four hundred words
quatre cent cinquante mots four hundred fifty words

Cent and *mille* are not preceded by the indefinite article
Numbers, except *un* and *une*, do not show a gender.

cent bateaux a hundred boats
six cents bateaux six hundred boats
mille fois a thousand times
six mille plantes six thousand plants

Periods, not commas, are used with numbers.

2.000.000 2,000, 000

Cardinal numbers

0	*zéro*	45	*quarante-cinq*
1	*un, une*	50	*cinquante*
2	*deux*	51	*cinquante et un*
3	*trois*	53	*cinquante-trois*
4	*quatre*	60	*soixante*
5	*cinq*	61	*soixante et un*
6	*six*	64	*soixante-quatre*
7	*sept*	70	*soixante-dix*
8	*huit*	71	*soixante et onze*
9	*neuf*	75	*soixante-quinze*
10	*dix*	78	*soixante-dix-huit*
11	*onze*	80	*quatre-vingts*
12	*douze*	81	*quatre-vingt-un*
13	*treize*	87	*quatre-vingt-sept*
14	*quatorze*	90	*quatre-vingt-dix*
15	*quinze*	91	*quatre-vingt-onze*
16	*seize*	100	*cent*
17	*dix-sept*	101	*cent-un*
18	*dix-huit*	122	*cent vingt-deux*
19	*dix-neuf*	200	*deux cents*
20	*vingt*	206	*deux cent-six*
21	*vingt et un*	1,000	*mille*
22	*vingt-deux*	1,001	*mille un*
30	*trente*	1,100	*mille cent/ onze cents*
33	*trente-trois*	3,000	*trois mille*
40	*quarante*	1,000,000	*un million*

Ordinal numbers

Ordinal numbers are formed from cardinals by adding *-ième*. Silent *e* is dropped before *-ième*.

deuxième second
quatrième fourth

Exeptions to this rule:

premier, première first
second, seconde second
cinquième (*u* inserted) fifth
neuvième (f changes to *v*) ninth
quatre-vingtième (*s* is omitted) eightieth

Fractions are formed by combining cardinal and ordinal numbers. *Quart, moitié,* and *tiers* are irregular. *Moitié* is a noun and must have an article. *Demi,* generally used as an adjective, is connected by a hyphen when it precedes the noun and is invariable. When *demi* follows a noun that it modifies, it agrees with it in gender.

half the bottle *la moitié de la bouteille*
half an hour *une demi-heure*
an hour and a half *une heure et demie*

Currency

Currency   L'argent

The money used in France is *le franc français. Les billets de banques* have the following values:

500, 200, 100, 50, 20, and 10 *francs.*

Each *billet de banque* bears a portrait of a famous artist, musician, or author. Pascal appears on a 500F bill. Eugène Delacroix appears on a 100F bill. The Banque de France issues the bills.

Les pièces (coins) are 5, 10, 20, 50 *centimes* and 1, 2, 5, and 10 *francs.* On each coin is written *"Liberté Egalité Fraternité."*

There are six different denominations of French banknotes, or billets de banques. Each is a different size and printed in a different color.

Arrival and departure times at French stations use the 24-hour system, rather than the 12-hour, a.m./p.m. system.

The departure board shows:

destination	départ	vol
LE MANS	12 59	2
LE CROISIC	13 45	
NANTES	13 45	
NANTES	13 50	
BORDEAUX	13 55	
TARBES VIA BORDEAUX	14 00	
TARBES VIA BORDEAUX	14 00	
BORDEAUX	14 00	
BREST	14 20	
NANTES	14 50	
LE MANS	15 05	

Time

To express time, *heure* (hour) is used for "o'clock." To alter the hour, the number of minutes is added. The word *et* is used only with *quart* and *demie*. *Moins* is used to express time before the hour.

In public schedules, such as timetables, the 24-hour system is used. Starting at midnight: *9 heures* = 9 a.m. *14 heures* = 2 p.m.

What time is it?	*Quelle heure est-il?*
It is one o'clock.	*Il est une heure.*
It is two o'clock.	*Il est deux heures.*
It is ten past ten.	*Il est dix heures dix.*
It is quarter past eight.	*Il est huit heures et quart.*
It is half past nine.	*Il est neuf heures et demie.*
It is quarter of ten.	*Il est dix heures moins le quart.*
It is ten to eleven.	*Il est onze heures moins dix.*
It is noon.	*Il est midi.*
It is midnight.	*Il est minuit.*

Countries

Germany	*l'Allemagne*
England	*l'Angleterre*
Austria	*l'Autriche*
Belgium	*la Belgique*
Spain	*l'Espagne*
Hungary	*la Hongrie*
Ireland	*l'Irlande*
Italy	*l'Italie*
Netherlands	*les Pays-Bas*
Poland	*la Pologne*
Portugal	*le Portugal*
Switzerland	*la Suisse*

Months, days, seasons

The cardinal numbers are used to express dates, except for the first day of the month, week, etc. The masculine definite article always precedes the date.

April first	*le premier avril*
December 25th	*le vingt-cinq décembre*
1928	*dix-neuf cent vingt-huit*
in 1789	*en dix-sept cent quatre-vingt-neuf*

January	*janvier*
February	*février*
March	*mars*
April	*avril*
May	*mai*
June	*juin*
July	*juillet*
August	*août*
September	*septembre*
October	*octobre*
November	*novembre*
December	*décembre*

Monday	*lundi*
Tuesday	*mardi*
Wednesday	*mercredi*
Thursday	*jeudi*
Friday	*vendredi*
Saturday	*samedi*
Sunday	*dimanche*

spring	*le printemps*
summer	*l'été*
autumn	*l'automne*
winter	*l'hiver*

Mercredi le cinq JUILLET

les Etats-Unis d'Amérique

les cheveux hair
les yeux eyes
les oreilles ears
le nez nose
les joues cheeks
la bouche mouth
le menton chin

La figure The face

Dictionary

Le corps humain The human body

la tête head
le cou neck
l'épaule shoulder
la poitrine chest
le bras arm
le ventre stomach
la main hand
les doigts fingers
la jambe leg
le pied foot

les doigts de pied toes

Dictionary abbreviations. Nouns are identified as masculine *(m)* or feminine *(f)*. Adjectives are identified as *adj*, adverbs as *adv*, conjunctions as *conj*, interjections as *interj*, prepositions as *prep*, pronouns as *pron*, and verbs as *v*. Plurals are identified as *pl*.

French-English

A

à *prep* at, in, to
absence *f* absence
accepter *v* accept
accident *m* accident
accourir *v* run up
accueillir *v* welcome
acheter *v* buy
acquérir *v* acquire, get
activité *f* activity
affaire *f* matter, business
afin de *prep* in order to
afin que *conj* in order that
agent *m* agent
agréable *adj* pleasing
aider *v* help
aimable *adj* friendly, pleasant
aimer *v* love, like
aimer mieux *v* prefer
aller *v* go
amener *v* bring
Américain *adj and noun m* American
Amérique *f* America
ami *m* friend
amie *f* friend
amuser *v* entertain
an *m* year
ancien *adj* old, ancient, former
année *f* year
appartenir *v* belong, pertain
appeler *v* call
apporter *v* bring
apprendre *v* learn, teach
approcher *v* bring near
approuver *v* approve
après *adv* afterward
après *prep* after
après que *conj* after
arbre *m* tree
argent *m* money, silver
arrêter *v* stop
arriver *v* arrive, happen
asseoir *v* seat, **s'asseoir** sit down
assez *adv* enough, **assez de** enough of

attendre *v* wait for, expect
aucun *adj and pron* none, no one, not one, not any
auprès de *prep* near, beside
aussi *adv* also, as, and so
aussitôt *adv* immediately
aussitôt que *conj* as soon as
autant *adv* as much
autant que *conj* as much as
autre *adj* other
autrefois *adv* formerly
avancer *v* move, go forward
avant *adv and prep* before
avertir *v* warn, give notice
avertissement *m* warning
avion *m* plane
avis *m* notice, opinion
avocat *m* lawyer
avoir *v* have

B

bain *m* bath
baiser *m* kiss
bataille *f* battle
bateau *m* boat
battre *v* beat, **se battre** fight
beau, bel *adj m*, **belle** *f* beautiful, handsome, fine, fair
beaucoup *adv* much, many
bénéfice *m* profit
besoin *m* need, **avoir besoin** *v* need
bête *f* animal, beast, brute, fool
beurre *m* butter
bien *adv* well
bien que *conj* although
bière *f* beer
billet *m* ticket
blesser *v* wound, hurt
boire *v* drink
bois *m* wood, forest
boisson *f* drink, beverage
bon *adj m*, **bonne** *f* good
bonheur *m* happiness
bouteille *f* bottle
bruit *m* noise, rumor

Review of French Grammar

brun *adj* brown, brunette
bureau *m* desk, office
but *m* purpose, aim, goal

C

cadeau *m* gift, present
café *m* coffee
carte *f* card, map, chart
casser *v* break
causer *v* chat, cause
céder *v* yield, give in
célèbre *adj* famous
cesser *v* stop, cease
chaise *f* chair
chance *f* luck
chanson *f* song
chanter *v* sing
chapeau *m* hat
chaque *adj* each
charpentier *m* carpenter
chaud *adj* hot
chemin *m* road, path
chemise *f* shirt
chercher *v* seek, look for
chez *prep* at (the home, shop, etc. of . . .)
choisir *v* choose
chose *f* thing, object
clef, clé *f* key
client *m* customer
colère *f* anger, **en colère** angry
colis *m* package
combien *adv* how much, how many
comme *adv* as, how, *conj* as, like
commencer *v* begin, start
comment *adv* how
comprendre *v* understand
compter *v* count, **compter sur** count on
conduire *v* lead, take, drive
conférence *f* lecture, conference
connaissance *f* acquaintance, knowledge
connaître *v* be acquainted with, know
consentir *v* consent
construire *v* build
contenir *v* contain, restrain
content *adj* content, glad
corriger *v* correct
costume *m* suit, costume
coucher *v* put to bed, **se coucher** lie down

coupable *adj* guilty
couper *v* cut
courage *m* courage
courir *v* run
course *f* race, errand
couteau *m* knife
coûter *v* cost
couvrir *v* cover
craindre *v* fear
crainte *f* fear
crayon *m* pencil
croire *v* believe
cueillir *v* gather
cuire *v* cook
cultiver *v* cultivate

D

dame *f* lady
décider *v* decide
déclarer *v* declare, affirm
découvrir *v* discover
décrire *v* describe
défendre *v* defend, forbid
déjeuner *m* lunch, **petit déjeuner** breakfast
délicieux *adj m*, **délicieuse** *f* delicious
demain *adv* tomorrow
demander *v* ask for
demeurer *v* dwell
demi *adj and noun m* half
départ *m* departure
dépit *m* spite, **en dépit de** in spite of
depuis *adv and prep* since
déranger *v* disturb
dernier *adj m* last
dès *prep* since, **dès que** *conj* as soon as
descendre *v* go down, come down
désirer *v* desire, wish
désoler *v* grieve
dessous *m* underside, **au-dessous de,** beneath
dessus *adv* above
devenir *v* become
deviner *v* guess
devoir *m* duty, homework
devoir *v* owe, have to, ought
difficile *adj* difficult, hard
dire *v* say, tell
doigt *m* finger
domestique *m and f* servant

dommage *m* damage, **c'est dommage** that's too bad
donner *v* give
dormir *v* sleep
douter *v* doubt
droit *m* right, law
droit *adj and adv* right, fair
droite *f* right, **à droite** to the right

E

eau *f* water
éblouir *v* dazzle
écarter *v* put aside
échouer *v* fail
écouter *v* listen
écrire *v* write
église *f* church
élève *m or f* pupil
embarquer *v* embark
emmener *v* take away, lead away
empêcher *v* prevent, hinder
encore *adv* again, still, yet
encre *f* ink
endroit *m* place
enfant *m or f* child
enfin *adv* at last, finally
enseigner *v* teach
entendre *v* hear
entrer *v* enter, come in
envie *f* envy, desire, **avoir envie de** feel like
envoyer *v* send, **envoyer chercher** send for
épine *f* thorn, spine
éprouver *v* experience, feel
erreur *f* error, mistake
escalier *m* stairway
espérer *v* hope, await
essuyer *v* wipe
et *conj* and
été *m* summer
éteindre *v* extinguish
étendre *v* extend, stretch out
étonner *v* surprise
étrange *adj* strange, curious
étudiant *m* student
étudier *v* study
évident *adj* evident, obvious
éviter *v* avoid, spare
examen *m* examination, test
exiger *v* require, demand
exprimer *v* express

F

fable _f_ fable, story
fabriquer _v_ manufacture
fâcher _v_ anger, **se fâcher** become angry
facile _adj_ easy
faim _f_ hunger
faire _v_ do, make
falloir _v_ be necessary
famille _f_ family
fatigué _adj_ tired
faute _f_ fault, mistake
femme _f_ woman, wife
fermer _v_ close
fête _f_ celebration, holiday, party
feuille _f_ leaf, sheet
fier _adj_ proud
figure _f_ face
fille _f_ daughter, girl
fils _m_ son
fin _f_ end
finir _v_ finish
fleur _f_ flower
fois _f_ instance, time
forcer _v_ compel, force
fraise _f_ strawberry
franc _m_ franc, **franc** _adj m_ frank, open
franche _adj f_ frank, open
frapper _v_ knock, strike
frère _m_ brother
froid _m and adj_ cold
fuir _v_ flee, shun

G

gagner _v_ acquire, gain, win
gant _m_ glove
garçon _m_ boy, waiter
garder _v_ keep, guard
gare _f_ station
gêner _v_ hinder, bother
goûter _v_ taste
grand _adj_ large, tall, great
grange _f_ barn
guère _adv_ hardly
guerre _f_ war

H

habile _adj_ able, clever
habiller _v_ dress, **s'habiller** put on one's clothing
habit _m_ clothes, coat
habiter _v_ inhabit, dwell in
habituer _v_ accustom, familiarize
haut _adj_ high, **à haute voix** aloud, **en haut** upstairs
hésiter _v_ hesitate
heure _f_ hour, time, **de bonne heure** early
heureux _adj m_, **heureuse** _f_ happy, lucky
hier _adv_ yesterday
histoire _f_ history, story
homme _m_ man
honnête _adj_ honest, upright
horloge _f_ clock
hôte _m_ host, guest

I

ici _adv_ here
informer _v_ inform, **s'informer** make inquiries
ingénieur _m_ engineer
intelligent _adj_ bright, clever
intéresser _v_ interest, concern
interrompre _v_ interrupt
inutile _adj_ useless, unnecessary
inviter _v_ invite

J

jamais _adv_ ever, never, **à jamais** forever
jardin _m_ garden
jaune _adj_ yellow
jeter _v_ throw, cast
jeune _adj_ young
joli _adj_ pretty
jouet _m_ toy
jour _m_ day
jus _m_ juice
jusqu'à _prep_ up to, as far as, until
juste _adj_ just, right, exact
juste _adv_ just, exactly

K

kilo _m_ kilogram

L

lac _m_ lake
lacet _m_ shoelace
laisser _v_ allow
lancer _v_ throw
langage _m_ language
langue _f_ tongue, language
larme _f_ tear
laver _v_ wash, **se laver** wash oneself
leçon _f_ lesson
légume _m_ vegetable
lent _adj_ slow
lettre _f_ letter
lever _v_ raise
ligne _f_ line
lire _v_ read
lit _m_ bed
livre _m_ book, **livre** _f_ pound
longtemps _adv_ longtime
lorsque _conj_ when
louer _v_ rent
loyer _m_ rent
luire _v_ gleam

M

magasin _m_ store
main _f_ hand
maintenant _adv_ now
mais _conj_ but
maison _f_ house
malade _adj_ ill
malle _f_ trunk
manger _v_ eat
manière _f_ manner
manquer _v_ miss, fail, lack
marchand _m_ merchant
marier _v_ marry
matin _m_ morning
mauvais _adj_ bad
médecin _m_ physician, doctor
méfier _v_ **se méfier** mistrust
meilleur _adj_ better, **le meilleur** the best
même _adj_ same
mener _v_ lead
mentir _v_ lie
mère _f_ mother
métier _m_ trade, craft, loom
mètre _m_ meter
mettre _v_ put, set
meuble _m_ furniture
midi _m_ noon, midday
mieux _adv_ better, best
mille _m_ mile, _adj and noun m_ thousand
minuit _m_ midnight
moins _adv_ less, least
mois _m_ month

moitié *f* half
monde *m* world, society
monter *v* go up, take up
moquer *v* **se moquer de** make fun of, mock
mourir *v* die

N

nager *v* swim, float
naissance *f* birth
naître *v* be born
négliger *v* neglect
neige *f* snow
nettoyer *v* clean
neuf *adj and noun m* nine
neuf *adj m*, **neuve** *f* new
ni *conj* nor, **ni . . . ni** neither . . . nor
nier *v* deny
nom *m* name, noun
note *f* grade, note
nouvelle *f* news
nuire *v* harm
nuit *f* night

O

obéir *v* obey
observer *v* observe, notice
oeil *m* eye, *pl* **yeux**
oeuvre *f* work, labor
offrir *v* offer, present
or *m* gold
orage *m* storm
ordonner *v* order, command
ordre *m* order
orgueilleux *adj m*, **orgueilleuse** *f* proud, haughty
oser *v* dare
ou *conj* or
où *adv* where, at, on
oublier *v* forget
oui *adv* yes
ouvrir *v* open

P

page *m* pageboy
page *f* page
pain *m* bread
paix *f* peace
pâlir *v* become pale, fade
panne *f* accident, lard
papier *m* paper

papillon *m* butterfly
paraître *v* appear, seem
pardessus *m* overcoat
pardonner *v* pardon
pareil *adj* like
parier *v* bet
parler *v* speak, talk
parmi *prep* among
partager *v* divide, share
partie *f* part, party
partir *v* leave, go away
passer *v* pass, go by
patiner *v* skate
pauvre *adj* poor
pavé *m* pavement
payer *v* pay
pays *m* country
peine *f* pain, penalty
pendant *prep* during
pendant que *conj* while
penser *v* think, **penser à** think of
perdre *v* lose
père *m* father
péril *m* danger
périr *v* perish
permettre *v* allow, permit
personne *f* person
personne *pron* no one, nobody
petit *adj* small, little, petty
peu *m* little, few
peur *f* fear
pièce *f* piece, coin, play
pied *m* foot
pierre *f* stone
plaindre *v* pity
plaire *v* please
plante *f* plant
plein *adj* full
pleurer *v* weep, cry, mourn
pleuvoir *v* rain
plier *v* fold
pluie *f* rain
plume *f* pen, feather
plupart *f* majority, most
plus *adv* more, most
plusieurs *adj and pron* several
poche *f* pocket
pomme *f* apple, **pomme de terre** potato
porte *f* door
porter *v* carry, bear
pourquoi *adv* why
pourvu que *conj* provided that
pouvoir *v* be able, can

préférer *v* prefer
premier *adj* first
prendre *v* take
près *adv* near, **près de** *prep* near
présenter *v* introduce, present
prêt *adj* ready
prêter *v* lend
projet *m* project, plan
promener *v* take out walking
promettre *v* promise
propos *m* talk, subject, **à propos de** with regard to
propre *adj* own, very, same, clean
propriétaire *m* proprietor
protester *v* protest
provoquer *v* provoke
puis *adv* then

Q

qualifier *v* qualify
qualité *f* quality, nature
quand *conj* when
quart *m* quarter, fourth
quelque *adj* some, any, **quelque chose** something
quelquefois *adv* sometimes
quelqu'un *pron* someone, anyone
quitter *v* leave
quoique *conj* although
quotidien *adj* daily

R

raconter *v* tell, narrate
rafraîchir *v* cool, refresh
raison *f* reason, **avoir raison** be right
ralentir *v* slow down, slacken
ramasser *v* pick up
ramener *v* bring back, take back
rapide *adj* swift
rappeler *v* remember
ravi *adj* delighted
recevoir *v* receive
récompense *f* reward
reconnaissance *f* gratitude, recognition
reconnaître *v* recognize
reculer *v* fall back, go back
réfléchir *v* reflect, think
regarder *v* look
règle *f* rule
regretter *v* regret, be sorry for

rejoindre *v* join
relier *v* bind, connect
remarquer *v* notice
remplir *v* fill
remuer *v* move, stir
rencontrer *v* meet
rendre *v* give back
renoncer *v* renounce, give up
rentrer *v* go home, go back
repas *m* meal
répondre *v* reply, answer
reposer *v* rest
résoudre *v* resolve
rester *v* remain, stay
retard *m* delay, **en retard** late
retourner *v* return, turn around
retrouver *v* find again
réussir *v* succeed
rêve *m* dream
réveiller *v* waken
révéler *v* reveal
revenir *v* come back, return
riche *adj* rich
rien *pron* nothing
rire *v* laugh
robe *f* dress
roman *m* novel
rompre *v* break
rond *adj* round
route *f* road, **en route** under way
rue *f* street

S

sable *m* sand
sage *adj* wise
saisir *v* seize
saison *f* season
sale *adj* dirty
salon *m* parlor
sans *prep* without
sauf *prep* except
sauter *v* leap, jump
sauver *v* save, **se sauver** run away
savoir *v* know, know how
savon *m* soap
secours *m* help
selon *prep* according to
semaine *f* week
sembler *v* seem
sentir *v* feel, smell
serviette *f* napkin, towel
servir *v* serve, **se servir de** use

seul *adj* alone, only, single
sévère *adj* strict, severe
si *conj* if, whether
si *adv* so, yes
soeur *f* sister
soie *f* silk
soif *f* thirst
soigner *v* care for
soir *m* evening
soleil *m* sun
sommeil *m* sleep
sonner *v* sound, ring, strike
sorte *f* kind
sortir *v* go out, get out
souffrir *v* suffer, bear
souhaiter *v* wish
soulager *v* relieve
soulever *v* raise, lift up, arouse
sourire *v and n m* smile
souvenir *m* remembrance, **se souvenir de** remember
souvent *adv* often
sucre *m* sugar
suffire *v* suffice
suivre *v* follow
sur *prep* on, upon, over, about
sûr *adj* sure
surtout *adv* above all, especially

T

table *f* table
tableau *m* picture, blackboard
taire *v* keep quiet, **se taire** be silent
tandis que *conj* while, whereas
tant *adv* so many, so much, **tant que** as long as
tante *f* aunt
tard *adv* late
tarder *v* delay, put off
tasse *f* cup
tel *adj* such
temps *m* time, weather
tenir *v* hold, possess
tenter *v* attempt
terre *f* earth, ground, land
tête *f* head
timbre *m* stamp
tirer *v* draw, pull
tomber *v* fall
tort *m* wrong, **avoir tort** be wrong
tôt *adv* soon, early
toucher *v* touch

toujours *adv* always, yet
tourner *v* turn
tout *adj* all, each, every
tout *pron* everything
tranquille *adj* quiet
travailler *v* work
traverser *v* cross
très *adv* very
tromper *v* deceive, **se tromper** make a mistake, be wrong
trop *adv* too much, too
trottoir *m* sidewalk
trouver *v* find

U

usage *m* use
utile *adj* useful
utiliser *v* use

V

vacances *f pl* vacation
vague *f* wave
vaincre *v* conquer
vaisselle *f* dishes
valise *f* suitcase
valoir *v* be worth
vendre *v* sell
verre *m* glass
vêtir *v* dress
viande *f* meat
vide *adj* empty
vie *f* life
vieillard *m* old man
vieille *adj f* old, *noun f* old woman
vieux *adj m* old
village *m* village
ville *f* city, town
vin *m* wine
vite *adv* quick
vivre *v* live
voici *v* here is, here are
voilà *v* there is, there are
voir *v* see
voisin *m* neighbor
voiture *f* car, automobile
voix *f* voice
vouloir *v* wish, want
voyager *v* travel
vrai *adj* true, real

Y

y *adv* there, in it, to it

Review of French Grammar

Dictionary abbreviations. Nouns are identified as masculine (*nm*) or feminine (*nf*). Adjectives are identified as *adj*, adverbs as *adv*, conjunctions as *conj*, interjections as *interj*, prepositions as *prep*, pronouns as *pron*, and verbs as *v*. Plurals are identified as *pl*.

English-French

A

able *adj* capable, **be able** *v* pouvoir

about *prep* environ, à peu près

above *adv* dessus, au dessus, par dessus

absence *n* absence *f*

accept *v* accepter

accident *n* accident *m*

according to *prep* selon, d'après

accustom *v* habituer

acquaintance *n* connaissance *f*

acquire *v* acquérir

act *v* agir

activity *n* activité *f*

add *v* ajouter, additionner

advise *v* conseiller

afraid *adj* éffrayé

after *adv* après

after *conj* après que

afternoon *n* après-midi *m or f*

afterward *adv* après, ensuite, plus tard

again *adv* encore

agent *n* agent, représentant *m*

ago *adv* il y a, **two days ago** il y a deux jours

agreement *n* accord *m*

aim *n* but *m*

airplane *n* avion *m*

all *adj* tout, tous, toute, toutes

allow *v* laisser, permettre

alone *adj* seul

aloud *adv* à haute voix

already *adv* déjà

also *adv* aussi

although *conj* bien que, quoique

always *adv* toujours

among *prep* parmi, entre

amuse *v* amuser

ancient *adj* ancien, antique

and *conj* et

anger *n* colère *f*

anger *v* fâcher, mettre en colère

animal *n* bête *f*

answer *v* répondre

any *pron* en

anything *pron* quelque chose, **not anything** ne . . . rien, **anything at all** n'importe quoi

anyone *pron* quelqu'un, **not . . .** personne

anywhere *adv* quelque part, **not . . . nulle part**

appear *v* paraître, sembler

apple *n* pomme *f*

approach *v* s'approcher

approve *v* approuver

arrest *v* arrêter

arrive *v* arriver

as *adv* comme, aussi, que

as *conj* comme, en tant que, tel que, **as . . . as** aussi . . . que

ask *v* demander, **ask a question** poser une question

at *prep* à

attain *v* atteindre

aunt *n* tante *f*

automobile *n* automobile *f*, voiture *f*

avoid *v* éviter

await *v* attendre, espérer

away *adv* absent, loin, au loin

B

bachelor *n* célibataire *m*

back *n* dos *m*, dossier *m*, derrière *m*

back up *v* reculer

bad *adj* mauvais

badly *adv* mal

barely *adv* guère, à peine

barn *n* grange *f*

bath *v* bain *m*

battle *n* bataille *f*

be *v* être

bear *v* porter

beast *n* bête *f*

beat *v* battre, vaincre, frapper

beautiful *adj* beau *and* bel *m*, belle *f*

because *conj* parce que

become *v* devenir

bed *n* lit *m*

beer *n* bière *f*

before *adv* avant, devant

begin *v* commencer, se mettre à

behind *adv* derrière

believe *v* croire

belong *v* appartenir

below *prep* sous, dessous, en bas

bend *v* plier

beside *prep* à côté de, auprès de

besides *adv* d'ailleurs

best *adv* mieux, *adj* le meilleur

bet *v* parier, *n* pari *m*

better *adj* meilleur, *adv* mieux

between *prep* entre

big *adj* grand, gros

bird *n* oiseau *m*

birth *n* naissance *f*

bite *v* mordre

blanket *n* couverture *f*

body *n* corps *m*

book *n* livre *m*

born (be) *v* naître

borrow *v* emprunter

both *adj and pron* les deux

bother *v* déranger, gêner

bottle *n* bouteille *f*

box *n* boîte *f*

bread *n* pain *m*

break *v* casser, rompre, briser

breakfast *n* petit déjeuner *m*

bright *adj* brillant, clair, intelligent

bring *v* amener, apporter

bring back *v* ramener

broad *adj* large

brother *n* frère *m*

build *v* construire

business *n* affaires *f pl*

busy *adj* occupé

but *conj* mais

butter *n* beurre *m*

butterfly *n* papillon *m*

buy *v* acheter

by *prep* par, de, à, près de

C

café *n* café *m*

call *v* appeler

can *v* pouvoir

car *n* voiture *f*

carpenter *n* charpentier *m*
carry *v* porter
cast *v* jeter
cat *n* chat *m*
cause *n* cause *f*
cease *v* cesser, discontinuer
celebration *n* fête *f*
certain *adj* certain
chair *n* chaise *f*
chance *n* chance *f*, hasard *m*
chart *n* carte marine *f*
chat *n* causerie *f*, entretien *m*
cheap *adj* bon marché
child *n* enfant *m or f*
choose *v* choisir
church *n* église *f*
city *n* ville *f*
class *n* classe *f*
clean *adj* propre, *v* nettoyer
clear *adj* clair
clever *adj* habile
climb *v* grimper, monter
clock *n* horloge *f*, pendule *f*
close *v* fermer
clothe *v* habiller, vêtir
clothes *n* habits *m pl*, vêtements *m pl*
cloud *n* nuage *m*
coat *n* habit *m*, manteau *m*
coffee *n* café *m*
cold *adj* froid
come *v* venir
command *v* commander, ordonner
company *n* compagnie *f*
compare *v* comparer
compel *v* forcer
complain *v* se plaindre
complaint *n* plainte *f*
concern *v* interesser
conquer *v* vaincre
consent *v* consentir
consider *v* considérer
consist *v* consister
construct *v* construire, fabriquer
contain *v* contenir
contents *n* contenu *m*
continue *v* continuer
convince *v* convaincre
cook *v* cuire
cool *adj* frais *m*, fraîche *f*
cool *v* rafraîchir
correct *v* corriger
cost *v* coûter
costs *n* frais *m pl*

count *v* compter
country *n* pays (nation) *m*, patrie (native country) *f*, campagne (rural area) *f*
courage *n* courage *m*
course *n* cours *m*
cover *v* couvrir
cross *n* croix *f*
cry *v* pleurer
cultivate *v* cultiver
cup *n* tasse *f*
customer *n* client *m*
cut *v* couper

D

daily *adj* quotidien, tous les jours
damage *n* dommage *m*, *v* endommager
dance *n* danse *f*
dance *v* danser
danger *n* danger *m*, péril *m*
dangerous *adj* dangereux
dare *v* oser
date *n* date *f*
daughter *n* fille *f*
day *n* jour *m*, journée *f*
dazzle *v* éblouir
dealer *n* marchant *m*
deceive *v* tromper
decide *v* décider
declare *v* déclarer
defeat *v* vaincre
delay *v* tarder
delicious *adj* délicieux
delight *n* joie *f*, plaisir *m*
delight *v* ravir
delighted *adj* joyeux, ravi
deny *v* nier
depart *v* s'en aller, partir
descend *v* descendre
describe *v* décrire
deserve *v* mériter
desire *v* désirer, vouloir
desk *n* bureau *m*
despair *v* désespérer
destroy *v* détruire
die *v* mourir
difficult *adj* difficile
dine *v* dîner
dining room *n* salle à manger *f*
direct *v* diriger
dirty *adj* sale
dishes *n* vaisselle *f*
displease *v* déplaire

disturb *v* déranger, troubler
dive *v* plonger
divide *v* diviser, partager
do *v* faire
dog *n* chien *m*
door *n* porte *f*
doubt *n* doute *m*
doubt *v* douter
draw *v* tirer (pull), dessiner (sketch)
drawer *n* tiroir *m*
drawing room *n* salon *m*
dress *n* robe *f*
dress *v* vêtir, habiller
drink *n* boisson *f*
drink *v* boire
drive *v* conduire
during *prep* pendant
dust *n* poussière *f*
duty *n* devoir *m*
dwell *v* demeurer, habiter

E

each *adj* chaque, tout
each one *pron* chacun
ear *n* oreille *f*
early *adv* de bonne heure, tôt
earn *v* gagner, mériter
earth *n* terre *f*
easy *adj* facile
eat *v* manger
effort *n* effort *m*
egg *n* oeuf *m*
either *adv* ou
else *adv* autrement, ou bien
elsewhere *adv* ailleurs, autre part
embark *v* embarquer
employ *v* employer
empty *adj* vide
encourage *v* encourager
end *n* fin *f*
end *v* finir, terminer
engineer *n* ingénieur *m*
enjoy *v* jouir
enough *adv* assez
enter *v* entrer
entire *adj* entier, complet
evening *n* soir *m*
equal *adj* égal
error *n* erreur *f*, faute *f*
especially *adv* surtout
even *adv* même

Review of French Grammar

event *n* événement *m*
ever *adv* jamais
every *adj* tout, chaque
everybody *pron* tout le monde
everything *pron* tout
everywhere *adv* partout
evident *adj* évident, clair
exactly *adv* exactement
examination *n* examen *m*
example *n* exemple *m*
except *prep* excepté, sauf
expect *v* attendre, espérer
expensive *adj* cher, coûteux
experience *v* éprouver
explain *v* expliquer
express *v* exprimer, **express** *adj* exprès
extend *v* étendre
extinguish *v* éteindre
eye *n* oeil *m*, yeux *m pl*

F

fable *n* fable *f*
face *n* figure *f*, face *f*
face *v* faire face à, affronter, donner sur
fail *v* échouer, manquer
fair *adj* juste
fairly *adv* assez, pas mal, honnêtement
faithful *adj* fidèle
fall *v* tomber
false *adj* faux *m*, fausse *f*
familiar *adj* familier
family *n* famille *f*
far *adv* loin
fast *adv* vite
father *n* père *m*
fault *n* faute *f*
fear *n* crainte *f*, peur *f*
fear *v* craindre, avoir peur
feed *v* nourrir
feel *v* sentir, tâter (touch)
feel like *v* avoir envie de
few *adj* peu de, quelques, *pron* peu, quelques-uns
fill *v* remplir
fight *v* se battre
finally *adv* enfin, à la fin
find *v* trouver
find out *v* découvrir
finger *n* doigt *m*
finish *v* finir
fire *n* feu *m*

first *adj* premier, *adv* d'abord
fish *n* poisson *m*
fish *v* pêcher
fit *v* aller à, *adj* convenable, capable
flee *v* se sauver, s'enfuir
flower *n* fleur *f*
fly *v* voler
fold *v* plier
follow *v* suivre
food *n* nourriture *f*
foot *n* pied *m*
for *prep* pour, *conj* car
forbid *v* défendre
force *n* force *f*, puissance *f*
force *v* force, obliger
forget *v* oublier
former *adj* ancien
free *adj* libre
freeze *v* geler
friend *n* ami *m*, amie *f*
from *prep* de, depuis (since)
full *adj* plein
fun *n* amusement, plaisanterie, **make fun** se moquer
furniture *n* meubles *m pl*
future *n* avenir *m*

G

gain *n* profit *m*, gain *m*, avantage *m*
gain *v* gagner
game *n* jeu *m*, gibier (hunting) *m*
garden *n* jardin *m*
gate *n* porte *f*, portail *m*, barrière *f*
gather *v* cueillir, ramasser, se réunir
get *v* prendre, avoir, obtenir, gagner, **go and get** aller chercher
gift *n* cadeau *m*, présent *m*
girl *n* fille *f*
give *v* donner
give up *v* renoncer à
glad *adj* content
glass *n* verre *m*
glove *n* gant *m*
go *v* aller, se rendre, **go out** sortir, **go down** descendre
goal *n* but *m*
gold *n* or *m*

good *adj* bon *m*, bonne *f*, **for good** pour de bon
great *adj* grand, gros, **a great deal** beaucoup
greet *v* saluer
ground *n* terre *f*, **on the ground** par terre
grow *v* grandir, pousser
guard *v* garder
guess *v* deviner
guilty *adj* coupable

H

habit *n* habitude *f*
hair *n* cheveux *m pl*
half *adj* demi, *n* moitié *f*
hall *n* vestibule (entrance) *m*, salle (large room) *f*
hand *n* main *m*
happen *v* arriver, se passer
happy *adj* heureux, content
hard *adj* dur
hardly *adv* à peine, ne . . . guère
harm *v* nuire
hat *n* chapeau *m*
hate *v* détester, haïr
haughty *adj* orgueilleux
have *v* avoir
hear *v* entendre
help *n* aide *f*, secours *m*, *interj* au secours!
help *v* aider
here *adv* ici
hesitate *v* hésiter
high *adj* haut
hinder *v* gêner, empêcher
history *n* histoire
hit *v* frapper, battre
hold *v* tenir
holiday *n* fête
home *n* foyer *m*, maison *f*, chez soi, à la maison
homework *n* devoir *m*
honest *adj* honnête
hope *v* espérer
hot *adj* chaud
hour *n* heure *f*
house *n* maison *f*
how *adv* comment, comme (in exclamation), **how much** combien
however *adv* cependant
hunger *n* faim *f*
hurt *v* blesser, faire mal
husband *n* mari *m*, époux *m*

I

ice *n* glace *f*
idea *n* idée *f*
ill *adv* mal, *adj* malade
in *prep* dans, à, en
incite *v* encourager, provoquer
inform *v* informer, renseigner
inhabitant *n* habitant *m*
ink *n* encre *f*
insist *v* insister, tenir à
instance *n* fois *f*
instead of *prep* au lieu de
intend *v* avoir l'intention de
interest *v* intéresser
interrupt *v* interrompre
introduce *v* introduire, présenter
invite *v* inviter

J

join *v* relier, joindre
joke *v* plaisanter
journey *n* voyage *m*
jump *v* sauter
just *adj* juste, précis
just *adv* justement, donc, **to
  have just** venir de

K

keep *v* garder, tenir, **keep from**
  empêcher
key *n* clef *f*
kill *v* tuer
kilogram *n* kilo *m*
kind *adj* aimable, *n* genre
  m, sorte *f*
knife *n* couteau *m*, **pocketknife**
  canif *m*
knock *v* frapper
know *v* savoir, connaître
knowledge *n* science *f*,
  connaissances *f pl*

L

lace *n* dentelle *f*, **shoelace** *n*
  lacet *m*
land *n* terre *f*
land *v* débarquer (ship), atterrir
  (airplane)
language *n* langage *m*, langue *f*
large *adj* grand, gros
last *adj* dernier, **last night** hier
  soir

last *v* durer
late *adj* tard, en retard
later *adj* plus tard
laugh *v* rire, **laugh at** se moquer
law *n* droit *m*
lawyer *n* avocat *m*, avoué *m*
lead *n* plomb *m*
lead *v* mener, conduire
leaf *n* feuille *f*
leap *v* sauter
learn *v* apprendre
least *adv, adj, n m* moins
leave *v* quitter, partir, laisser
lecture *n* conférence *f*
leg *n* jambe *f*
lend *v* prêter
less *adv* moins, *adj* moindre,
  moins de
lesson *n* leçon *f*
let *v* laisser, permettre
letter *n* lettre *f*
lie *v* se coucher
lie *n* mensonge *f*, *v* mentir
life *n* vie *f*, existence *f*
light *n* lumière *f*
light *adj* léger
like *v* aimer
like *adj* comme, pareil, semblable
line *n* ligne *f*
listen *v* écouter
little *adj* petit, *adv* peu
live *v* demeurer, vivre, habiter
living room *n* salon *m*
long *adj* long *m*, longue *f*,
  adv longtemps
look *n* regard *n*
look *v* regarder
look for *v* chercher
look like *v* avoir l'air de
lose *v* perdre
loud *adv* fort, haut
love *v* aimer
luck *n* chance *f*, fortune *f*
lunch *v* déjeuner, *n*
  déjeuner *m*

M

machine *n* machine *f*
maid *n* bonne à tout faire *f*
main *adj* principal
majority *n* la plupart *f*
make *v* faire, fabriquer
man *n* homme *m*
manner *n* manière *f*

many *adv* beaucoup de
map *n* carte *f*
market *n* marchè *m*
marry *v* se marier, épouser
matter *n* matière *f*, sujet *m*
meal *n* repas *m*
mean *v* vouloir dire, signifier
mean *adj* méchant
meat *n* viande *f*
meet *v* rencontrer, rejoindre
midday *n* midi *m*
midnight *n* minuit *m*
mind *n* esprit *m*, intelligence *f*
mirror *n* miroir *m*
miss *v* manquer
mistake *n* erreur *f*, faute *f*
mistrust *v* se méfier
money *n* argent *m*
month *n* mois *m*
more *pron* en . . . davantage, *adj
  and adv* plus, encore
morning *n* matin *m*
most *adv* très, bien, *adj* la
  plupart, *n* le plus *m*
mother *n* mère *f*
mountain *n* montagne *f*
move *v* remuer, avancer
much *adv* beaucoup, **as much**
  autant
must *v* falloir, devoir

N

name *n* nom *m*
name *v* appeler
napkin *n* serviette *f*
narrate *v* raconter
narrow *adj* étroit
near *adj* proche, *adv* près,
  prep près de
necessary *adj* nécessaire
need *n* besoin *m*
need *v* avoir besoin
neglect *v* négliger
neighbor *n* voisin *m*
never *adv* jamais
new *adj* neuf *m*, nouveau *m*,
  neuve *f*, nouvelle *f*
news *n* nouvelles *f pl*
newspaper *n* journal *m*
next *adj* prochain
noise *n* bruit *m*
noon *n* midi *m*
note *v* noter, remarquer
nothing *pron* rien

Review of French Grammar

notice *n* avis *m*
notice *v* remarquer
novel *n* roman *m*
novel *adj* nouveau *m*, nouvelle *f*
now *adv* maintenant, à present

O

obey *v* obéir
observe *v* observer
obvious *adj* évident, clair
offend *v* offenser
offer *v* offrir
office *n* bureau *m*
often *adv* souvent
old *adj* vieux *m*, vieil *m*, vieille *f*
once *adv* une fois, autrefois
only *adj* seulement, seul
open *v* ouvrir
opinion *n* avis *m*
or *conj* ou
order *v* commander, ordonner
order *n* ordre *m*
other *adj* autre
out *adv* dehors
outside *adv* au dehors
overcoat *n* pardessus *m*
owe *v* devoir
own *v* posséder

P

package *n* colis *m*
pageboy *n* page *m*
pail *n* seau *m*
pain *n* peine *f*
paper *n* papier *m*
pardon *v* pardonner, faire grâce
part *n* partie *f*
part *v* se séparer
pass *v* passer, réussir
past *adj* passé
path *n* chemin *m*
pay *v* payer
peace *n* paix *f*
pen *n* plume *f*, stylo *m*
pencil *n* crayon *m*
people *n* gens *m*, monde *m*
perish *v* périr
permit *v* permettre
person *n* personne *f*
physician *n* médecin *m*, docteur *m*
pick *v* ceuillir
pick out *v* choisir

picture *n* tableau *m*
pity *v* plaindre
place endroit *m*, lieu *m*
place *v* placer, mettre
plane *n* avion *m*
play *n* pièce *f*, comédie *f*
play *v* jouer
pleasant *adj* agréable
please *v* plaire
pleasure *n* plaisir *m*
pocket *n* poche *f*
pocketknife *n* canif *m*
pond *n* étang *m*
poor *adj* pauvre, mauvais
possess *v* posséder
potato *n* pomme de terre *f*
pound *n* livre *f*
predict *v* deviner
prefer *v* préférer, aimer mieux
prepare *v* préparer
pretty *adj* joli
prevent *v* empêcher
professor *n* professeur *m*
profit *n* bénéfice *m*, profit *m*
project *n* projet *m*
promise *v* promettre
proud *adj* fier
provided that *conj* pourvu que
pull *v* tirer
punish *v* punir
pupil *n* élève *m and f*
put *v* mettre, poser, **put out** éteindre

Q

qualify *v* qualifier
quality *n* qualité *f*
quantity *n* quantité *f*
quarter *n* quart *m*
question *v* questionner, interroger
quick *adj* rapide, vite
quiet *adj* tranquille, calme
quit *v* quitter
quite *adv* tout à fait, complètement
quiz *n* petit examen *m*

R

race *n* course *f*
rain *v* pleuvoir
rain *n* pluie *f*, **rain** *v* pleuvoir
raise *v* lever, soulever

reach *v* atteindre
read *v* lire
ready *adj* prêt
real *adj* vrai
realize *v* se rendre compte
really *adv* réellement
reason *n* raison *f*
receive *v* recevoir
recognize *v* reconnaître
reflect *v* réfléchir
refresh *v* rafraîchir
regard *v* considérer
regret *v* regretter
relative *n* parent *m*, *adj* relatif
remain *v* rester
remark *n* remarque *f*, propos *m*
remember *v* se rappeler, se souvenir
renounce *v* renoncer
rent *n* loyer *m*
rent *v* louer
repair *v* réparer
reply *v* répondre, répliquer
require *v* exiger, demander
resolve *v* résoudre
rest *n* repos *m*
rest *v* se reposer
retain *v* garder, retenir
return *v* revenir
reward *n* récompense *f*
rich *adj* riche
right *adj* juste, correct, **be right** avoir raison
ring *v* sonner
road *n* route *f*
room *n* place *f*, chambre *f*, salle *f*
round *adj* rond
rule *n* règlement *m*, règle *f*
rumor *n* bruit *m*
run *v* courir

S

sadden *v* désoler, attrister
safe *adj* sûr, en sûreté
salary *n* salaire *m*
same *adj* même, pareil
sand *n* sable *m*
satisfied *adj* satisfait, content
save *v* sauver (rescue), épargner (economize)
say *v* dire
scarcely *adv* à peine, guère

school *n* école *f*
season *n* saison *f*
seat *v* asseoir
see *v* voir
seek *v* chercher
seem *v* paraître, sembler
sell *v* vendre
send *v* envoyer, **send for** envoyer chercher
sentence *n* phrase *f*
servant *n* servante *f*, valet *m*, domestique *m and f*, bonne *f*
serve *v* servir
set *n* serie *f*
set *v* mettre, **set up** monter, dresser
several *adj* plusieurs
share *v* partager
shine *v* briller, luire
shirt *n* chemise *f*
show *n* spectacle *m*
show *v* montrer, faire voir
sidewalk *n* trottoir *m*
sign *v* signer
silk *n* soie *f*
silver *n* argent *m*
similar *adj* pareil, semblable
since *conj* depuis que, puisque, **since** *adv and prep* depuis
sing *v* chanter
sister *n* soeur *f*
sit *v* s'asseoir, **be seated** être assis
skate *v* patiner
slacken *v* ralentir
sleep *n* sommeil *m*
sleep *v* dormir
slow *adj* lent, tardif, en retard
slow down *v* ralentir
small *adj* petit
smell *v* sentir
smile *n* sourire *m*, *v* sourire
smoke *v* fumer
so *adv* si, de telle manière, ainsi
some *adj* quelque, quelques-uns
someone *pron* quelqu'un
something *n* quelque chose *m*
sometimes *adv* quelque fois, parfois
somewhere *adv* quelque part
son *n* fils *m*
song *n* chanson *f*
soon *adv* bientôt
sorrow *n* peine *f*

sorry *adj* fâché, **be sorry** être fâché, regretter
sound *v* sonner
spare *v* épargner, ménager, céder, éviter
speak *v* parler
speech *n* discours *m*
speed *n* vitesse *f*, rapidité *f*
spend *v* dépenser (money), passer (time)
stairs *n* escalier *m*
stamp *n* timbre *m*
start *v* partir, se mettre en route, commencer
station *n* gare *f*, station *f*
stay *n* séjour *m*
stay *v* demeurer, rester
still *adv* encore, toujours, *adj* tranquille, *conj* cependant
stir *v* remuer
stone *n* pierre *f*
stop *v* arrêter, cesser
store *n* magasin *m*, boutique *f*
storm *n* orage *m*
story *n* histoire *f*, récit *m*, conte *m*, étage (floor) *m*
straight *adj* droit
strange *adj* étrange
strawberry *n* fraise *f*
street *n* rue *f*
stretch *v* tendre, étendre
strict *adj* sévère, étroit, strict
strike *v* frapper, sonner
study *n* étude *f*
study *v* étudier
succeed *v* réussir
such *adj* tel pareil, semblable
suffer *v* souffrir, subir, endurer
suffice *v* suffire, satisfaire
sugar *n* sucre *m*
suit *n* complet *m*, procès (law) *m*
suitcase *n* valise *f*
summer *n* été *m*
sun *n* soleil *m*
sure *adj* sûr
surprise *v* surprendre, étonner
swift *adj* rapide
swim *v* nager

T

table *n* table *f*
take *v* prendre, porter, emporter, conduire

tale *n* conte *m*
talk *v* parler, causer
tall *adj* grand, haut
task *n* tâche *f*, besogne *f*
taste *n* goût *m*
tea *n* thé *m*
teach *v* enseigner, apprendre
teacher *n* professeur *m*, maître *m*, instituteur *m*
tear *n* larme *f*
tear *v* déchirer
tell *v* raconter, dire, annoncer
test *n* épreuve *f*, examen *m*
thank *v* remercier
then *adv* alors, ensuite, puis
there *adv* là, **there is** il y a, voilà
thing *n* chose *f*, affaire *f*
think *v* penser, croire
thirst *n* soif *f*
thorn *n* épine *f*
throw *v* jeter
ticket *n* billet *m*
tie *v* lier, attacher
till *v* cultiver
time *n* temps *m*, fois *f*, époque *f*
tired *adj* fatigué
today *adv* aujourd'hui
together *adv* ensemble
tomorrow *adv* demain
tongue *n* langue *f*
touch *v* toucher
toward *prep* vers, envers
towel *n* serviette *f*
town *n* ville *f*
trade *n* marché *m*, commerce *m*
travel *v* voyager
tree *n* arbre *m*
trouble *v* déranger, gêner
true *adj* vrai
trunk *n* malle *f*
trust *v* avoir confiance, se fier à
truth *n* vérité *f*
try *v* tâcher, essayer
turn *n* tour *m*
turn *v* tourner
twice *adv* deux fois

U

under *prep* sous, *adv* au-dessous
underneath *adv* en dessous
understand *v* comprendre
unless *conj* à moins que
unnecessary *adj* inutile

Review of French Grammar

unpleasant *adj* désagréable
until *prep* jusqu'à, *conj* jusqu'à
  ce que
up *adj* en haut, **go up** *v* monter
up to *prep* jusqu'à
use *n* emploi *m*
use *v* se servir de, employer
useful *adj* utile
useless *adj* inutile
usually *adv* ordinairement
utensil *n* ustensile *m*
utilize *v* utiliser

V

vacation *n* vacances *f pl*
vaccinate *v* vacciner
vaccine *n* vaccin *m*
valiant *adj* vaillant
valley *n* vallée *f*
vanilla *n* vanille *f*
vanish *v* s'évanouir
variety *n* variété *f*
various *adj* divers
vary *v* varier
vault *n* voûte *f*
vegetable *n* légume *m*
vehicle *n* véhicule *m*
veil *n* voile *m*
vein *n* veine *f*
very *adv* très, bien, fort,
  beaucoup
village *n* village *m*
visit *n* visite *f*
visit *v* faire visite à
voice *n* voix *f*

W

wager *v* parier
wait *v* attendre
waiter *n* garçon *m*
walk *n* promenade *f*, **walk** *v*
  marcher, se promener
wall *n* mur *m*
want *v* vouloir, avoir envie de
war *n* guerre *f*
warm *adj* chaud
warm *v* chauffer
warn *v* avertir
wash *v* laver
watch *n* montre *f*
watch *v* regarder, surveiller
water *n* eau *f*
way *n* route *f*, voie *f*, chemin *m*,
  moyen (means) *m*

wear *v* porter
weather *n* temps *m*
week *n* semaine *f*
weep *v* pleurer
welcome *v* accueillir
well *adv* bien, **as well as** aussi
  bien que
when *conj* quand
where *adv* où
whether *conj* si
while *conj* pendant que, tandis
  que
whole *adj* tout, entier
wide *adj* large
will *v* vouloir
win *v* gagner
wine *n* vin *m*
wipe *v* essuyer
wise *adj* sage
wish *v* vouloir, désirer, souhaiter
with *prep* avec
withdraw *v* se retirer
within *prep* dedans
without *prep* sans

woman *n* femme *f*
wonder *v* se demander
wood *n* bois *m*
word *n* mot *m*, parole *f*
work *n* travail *m*, besogne *f*,
  ouvrage *m*, tâche *f* oeuvre
work *v* travailler, marcher
world *n* monde *m*
worry *n* ennui *m*, souci *m*,
  v préoccuper
worst *adj* pire, *adv* pis
worth *n* valeur *m*, prix *m*
write *v* écrire
wrong *adj* faux, **be wrong** *v*
  avoir tort

Y

year *n* an *m*, année *f*
yellow *adj* jaune
yesterday *adv* hier
yet *conj* pourtant, cependant,
  adv encore, déjà
yield *v* céder
young *adj* jeune

For further reference

Grammars

Barson, John
  La Grammaire à l'oeuvre
  Holt, Rinehart and Winston
Comeau, Raymond F., Bustin
  Normand, Francine L., and
  Lamoureux, L.
  Ensemble: Grammaire
  Holt, Rinehart and Winston
Daudon, René
  French in Review
  Harcourt Brace Jovanovich
Dubois, J., Jouannon, G., and
  Lagane, R.
  La Grammaire Française
  Librairie Larousse

Fraser, Ian Forbes
  French Reviewed
  Holt, Rinehart and Winston
Grevisse, Maurice
  Grammaire Française
  Librairie A. Hatier
Grevisse, Maurice
  Précis de Grammaire Française
  Editions J. Duculot
Jenkins, E. S.
  French Grammar
  David McKay Company

Dictionaries

Deak, Etienne
  Dictionnaire d'américanismes
  Edition du Dauphin
Hanse, Joseph
  *Dictionnaire des difficultés
    grammaticales et lexicologiques*
  Les Editions Scientifiques et
    Littéraires
Levieux, Michel and Eleanor
  Beyond the Dictionary in French
  Cassell

Mansion, J.E.
  *Harrap's New Standard French and
    English Dictionary*
  Charles Scribner's Sons
Micro Robert
  Le Robert
Thomas, Adolphe V. and Toro,
  Michel de
  Dictionnaire de Poche des difficultés
  Librairie Larousse

POSTBRIEFKASTEN

Review of German Grammar

The grammar of German is closely related to the grammar of English. This is because English, to a large extent, is Germanic in origin, as is obvious from the large number of English words that derive from Germanic sources. Consider *Vater* and father, *Mutter* and mother, *Sohn* and son, to name just a few examples of the many cognates the two languages exhibit.

As you can expect, therefore, German phrases, clauses, and sentences are constructed in somewhat the same way in both languages. The greatest exceptions appear in the relative absence of gender in English nouns, compared with the German noun genders. Another aspect of gender that is missing in English, in contrast with German, is the agreement of adjectives with the gender of the nouns they modify.

To cite an additional difference, German nouns (as well as the adjectives used to modify them) are declined to show their functions in sentences. This means that a noun will change in form to show that it is being used, for example, as the subject of a verb, the object of a verb, or the indirect object of a verb. Yet another form of this linguistic process of declension is the genitive, which we know as the possessive. In English, nouns rarely decline to show function. Instead we show subject, object, and indirect object by placement of the noun within the phrase, clause, or sentence. We do, however, use an apostrophe and the letter *s* to show possession with certain nouns.

Articles

Definite articles

Definite articles agree in gender and number with the nouns they modify: *der* for the masculine singular, *die* for the feminine singular, and *das* for the neuter singular. All three genders have *die* in the plural.

der Mann	the man	*die Männer*	the men
die Frau	the woman	*die Frauen*	the women
das Kind	the child	*die Kinder*	the children

The case of the noun determines the case of the article:
Das Kind sieht den Mann. The child sees the man.
die Frau des Mannes the man's wife
Der Mann geht nach Hause. The man goes home.
The dative and the accusative singular of the definite article are often contracted with a preposition. For example, *am* is used instead of *an dem,* at the. Other

Declension of articles: Definite · Indefinite

Case	Definite Singular Masc.	Fem.	Neuter	Plural	Indefinite Singular Masc.	Fem.	Neuter	Plural
Nominative	der	die	das	die	ein	eine	ein	einige
Genitive	des	der	des	der	eines	einer	eines	einiger
Dative	dem	der	dem	den	einem	einer	einem	einigen
Accusative	den	die	das	die	einen	eine	ein	einige

contractions for prepositions with articles are:

ans = an das beside the
beim = bei dem at the
im = in dem in the
ins = in das into the
zum = zu dem to the

The definite article is used before abstract nouns.

Es lebe die Demokratie! Long live democracy!

Diminutives formed with the endings *chen* and *lein* are always neuter:

das Mädchen the girl
das Fräulein the miss
das Kindchen the little child

Indefinite articles

Indefinite articles agree in gender with the nouns they modify: *ein* for the masculine singular, *eine* for the feminine singular, and *ein* for the neuter singular. There is no plural for the indefinite article. The word *einige*, some, is used for more than one person or thing.

ein Vater a father   *einige Väter* some fathers
eine Mutter a mother *einige Mütter* some mothers
ein Kind a child   *einige Kinder* some children

The case of the noun determines the case of the indefinite article:

ein Kind eines Vaters
a child of a father

einer Mutter Kinder
children of a mother

Eine Mutter hat einige Kinder.
A mother has some children.

die Kinder eines Mannes
a man's children

Nouns

Declining singular nouns

Nouns are either masculine, feminine, or neuter. Nouns are declined. In the genitive singular form, for example, most masculine and neuter nouns add *s* to the nominative singular form.

Nominative   *der Bruder* the brother
Genitive   *des Bruders* of the brother

Nominative   *das Wetter* the weather
Genitive   *des Wetters* of the weather

If a noun is monosyllabic, *es* is added in the genitive singular.

Nominative   *der Sohn* the son
Genitive   *des Sohnes* of the son

Nominative   *das Haus* the house
Genitive   *des Hauses* of the house

Some nouns ending in *e* add *n* in the genitive singular.

Nominative   *der Verwandte* the relative
Genitive   *des Verwandten* of the relative

Der Sohn des Bruders ist der Neffe.
The brother's son is the nephew.

Der Vater des Kindes ist alt.
The child's father is old.

The dative and accusative forms of a masculine or neuter singular noun are usually the same as those of the nominative. If the nominative ends in *e*, however, *n* is added.

Dative	*dem Bruder*	to the brother
Accusative	*den Bruder*	the brother
Dative	*dem Haus*	to the house
Accusative	*das Haus*	the house

Feminine singular nouns remain unchanged in all cases.

Die Tochter der Mutter ist schön.
The mother's daughter is beautiful.

Die Frau gibt der Tochter die Birne.
The woman gives the daughter the pear.

Declining plural nouns

The plural of all genders is formed in four ways. Adding an umlaut to the singular form.

der Bruder the brother *die Brüder* the brothers
Adding *er* plus an umlaut to the singular form.

der Mann the man   *die Männer* the men
Adding *e* plus an umlaut to the singular form.

die Nacht the night   *die Nächte* the nights
Adding *en* to the singular form.

die Frau the woman   *die Frauen* the women

The nominative, genitive, and accusative of plural nouns are all spelled identically. The dative adds *n* to all plural forms, with the exception of plurals formed by adding *en* to the singular.

	men	brothers	women
Nominative	*die Männer*	*die Brüder*	*die Frauen*
Genitive	*der Männer*	*der Brüder*	*der Frauen*
Dative	*den Männern*	*den Brüdern*	*den Frauen*
Accusative	*die Männer*	*die Brüder*	*die Frauen*

All nouns are capitalized.

Forms of the noun

Certain nouns have two forms, one for masculine gender, the other for feminine gender. For such nouns, the feminine form adds *in* to the masculine form.

Masc.	*Fem.*	
der Anwalt	*die Anwältin*	the lawyer
der Arzt	*die Ärztin*	the physician
der Künstler	*die Künstlerin*	the artist
der Lehrer	*die Lehrerin*	the teacher
der Wirt	*die Wirtin*	the host, the hostess

Compound nouns take the gender and declension of the last noun.

das Haus + *die Tür* = *die Haustür*
the house + the door = the door to the house

der Schlaf + *das Zimmer* = *das Schlafzimmer*
the sleep + the room = the bedroom

die Tasche + *das Tuch* = *das Taschentuch*
the pocket + the cloth = the handkerchief

Pronouns

Personal pronouns

Personal pronouns agree in number and gender with their antecedents.

	Nominative singular	*Nominative plural*
1st *person*	*ich* I	*wir* we
2nd *person*	*du* you (informal)	*ihr* you (informal)
3rd *person*	*er, sie, es* he, she, it	*sie* they
		Sie you (formal)

The pronoun *ich* is capitalized only when it is the first word of a sentence. The formal pronoun *Sie* is always capitalized.

Ich sehe dich.
I see you.

Der Tisch ist gross; er ist braun.
The table is big; it is brown.

Die Kinder spielen in dem Haus; sie singen in ihm.
The children play in the house; they sing in it.

Er gibt uns das Brot; er gibt es uns.
He gives us the bread; he gives it to us.

Reflexive pronouns

A reflexive pronoun functions as a direct or indirect object referring to the subject of a verb. It agrees in number and gender with the subject of the verb.

Dieter zieht sich an. Dieter dresses himself.

Wir waschen uns. We wash ourselves.

Ich wasche mir die Hände. I wash my hands.

Ihr ärgert euch. You are angry.

Some verbs that are reflexive in German are not reflexive in English.

sich anziehen to dress
sich erinnern to remember
sich freuen to be glad
sich fürchten to be afraid
sich hüten to be careful
sich trennen to separate
sich verbergen to hide
sich verlassen to rely
sich vorsehen to be careful

Declension of pronouns

Personal pronouns

	Singular			Plural		
	First person	Second person	Third person	First person	Second person	Third person
Nominative	*ich* I	*du* you	*er* he, *sie* she, *es* it	*wir* we	*ihr* you	*sie* they
Genitive	*meiner* of me	*deiner* of you	*seiner* his, *ihrer* her, *seiner* its	*unser* of us	*euer* of you	*ihrer* of them
Dative	*mir* to me	*dir* to you	*ihm* to him, *ihr* to her, *ihm* to it	*uns* to us	*euch* to you	*ihnen* to them
Accusative	*mich* me	*dich* you	*ihn* him, *sie* her, *es* it	*uns* us	*euch* you	*sie* them, *Sie* you (formal)

Reflexive pronouns

Subject	Direct object	Indirect object
ich I	*mich* myself	*mir* (to) myself
du you	*dich* yourself	*dir* (to) yourself
er, sie, es he, she, it	*sich* himself, herself, itself	*sich* (to) himself etc.
wir we	*uns* ourselves	*uns* (to) ourselves
ihr you	*euch* yourselves	*euch* (to) yourselves
sie they	*sich* themselves	*sich* (to) themselves
Sie you (formal)	*sich* yourselves	sich (to) yourselves

Relative pronouns
der who, which, that

	Singular			Plural
	Masc.	Fem.	Neuter	All genders
Nominative	*der*	*die*	*das*	*die*
Genitive	*dessen*	*deren*	*dessen*	*deren*
Dative	*dem*	*der*	*dem*	*denen*
Accusative	*den*	*die*	*das*	*die*

welcher who, which, that

Nominative	*welcher*	*welche*	*welches*	*welche*
Genitive	*dessen*	*deren*	*dessen*	*deren*
Dative	*welchem*	*welcher*	*welchem*	*welchem*
Accusative	*welchen*	*welche*	*welches*	*welche*

Demonstrative pronouns
dieser this

	Singular			Plural
	Masc.	Fem.	Neuter	All genders
Nominative	*dieser*	*diese*	*dieses*	*diese*
Genitive	*dieses*	*dieser*	*dieses*	*dieser*
Dative	*diesem*	*dieser*	*diesem*	*diesen*
Accusative	*diesen*	*diese*	*dieses*	*diese*

jener that

Nominative	*jener*	*jene*	*jenes*	*jene*
Genitive	*jenes*	*jener*	*jenes*	*jener*
Dative	*jenem*	*jener*	*jenem*	*jenen*
Accusative	*jenen*	*jene*	*jedes*	*jede*

Interrogative pronouns
wer who **was** what

Nominative	*wer*	*was*
Genitive	*wessen*	(no form)
Dative	*wem*	(no form)
Accusative	*wen*	*was*

Wer bist du?

Demonstrative pronouns

Demonstrative pronouns agree in number and gender with their antecedents. The demonstrative pronouns are *dieser* this, and *jener* that.

Dieses Buch ist besser als jenes.
This book is better than that.

Relative pronouns

Relative pronouns agree with their antecedents in number and gender. The masculine is *der*, who, that, or which; the feminine is *die*, who, that, or which; and the neuter is *das*, who, that, or which.

Der Eimer, der in der Küche ist, ist voll.
The pail that is in the kitchen is full.

Die Tante, die im Garten arbeitet, ist hübsch.
The aunt who is working in the garden is pretty.

Welcher, welche, welches are relative pronouns, with the same meanings as *der, die,* and *das.* They are usually found in the written language.

Dem Schüler, welchem ich das Buch gab, traue ich.
I trust the student to whom I gave the book.

Interrogative pronouns

The interrogative pronouns are *wer* for persons; *was* for things. *Welcher, welche,* and *welches* are used for "which one." There is no plural for *wer* or *was.*

Wer ist das? Who is this?

Was gebt ihr? What are you giving?

English questions introduced by "with what," "from what," etc. are expressed in German by *wo* "where," plus a preposition.

Wovon spricht er? What is he talking about?

Womit schreibt ihr? What do you write with?

Wofür gibt er Geld? What is he giving money for?

Wo becomes *wor* before a vowel.

Woran denkst du?
What do you think about?

Worin liegt die Tugend?
Where is the virtue?

Worüber unterhalten Sie sich?
What are you talking about?

Possessive pronouns

Possessive pronouns are formed in the following ways. By adding *er, e,* or *es* to the possessive adjective. For example, *meiner, meine, meines.*

Wessen Tasse ist das? Es ist meine.
Whose cup is this? It is mine.

By adding *e* to the possessive adjective and employing the definite article. For example, *der deine, die deine, das deine.*

Wessen Glas ist das? Es ist das deine.
Whose glass is this? It is yours.

By adding *ige* to the possessive adjective and employing the definite article. For example, *der seinige, die seinige, das seinige.*

Ist das dein Papier? Nein, es ist das seinige.
Is this your paper? No, it is his.

Prepositions

Prepositions are followed by words in the genitive, dative, or accusative case.

Prepositions taking the genitive

anstatt instead of	*trotz* in spite of
ausserhalb outside of	*während* during
innerhalb inside of	*wegen* on account of
oberhalb above	

wegen des Wetters because of the weather
trotz der Musik in spite of the music

Prepositions taking the dative

aus out of	*nach* after
ausser besides	*seit* since
bei at	*von* from, of
gegenüber opposite of	*zu* at, to
mit with	

Bei mir zu Hause spricht man deutsch.
At my house everyone speaks German.

Nach der Schule gehe ich nach Hause.
After school I go home.

Prepositions taking the accusative

durch through	*ohne* without
für for	*um* around, about
gegen against, toward	

Ich stimme für den Kandidaten.
I vote for the candidate.

Prepositions taking the dative or the accusative

The following prepositions take the dative case when they answer the question Where? They take the accusative when they answer the question Where to?

an on	*über* over, above
auf on, upon	*unter* under, among
hinter behind	*vor* before
in in, into	*zwischen* between
neben near, beside	

Ich stehe vor der Tür.
I am standing in front of the door.

Ich lege das Buch auf den Tisch.
I put the book on the table.

Adjectives and adverbs

Forms of adjectives

Predicative adjectives never change form.

Der Tiger ist zahm. The tiger is tame.

Das Kind ist frech. The child is impudent.

Attributive adjectives add *e* when they modify a noun preceded by a definite article. They add *er* for the masculine, *e* for the feminine, and *es* for the neuter when they modify a noun preceded by an indefinite article.

der grosse Baum the big tree

das kleine Brot the small bread

ein kleiner Baum a small tree

ein kleines Brot a small bread

The plural adds *en* in all genders and cases.

die schweren Bücher the heavy books

There is no plural form for adjectives used with indefinite articles.

Possessive adjectives

Possessive adjectives agree in number and gender with the nouns they modify and are declined like them.

meine Katze my cat

seines Hundes of his dog

The plural here refers to the number of the noun modified.

deine Bücher your books

ihre Brüder her brothers

Declension of adjectives

with definite article

	Masc.	Singular Fem.	Neuter
Nominative	grosse the big	grosse	grosse
Genitive	grossen of the big	grossen	grossen
Dative	grossen to the big	grossen	grossen
Accusative	grossen the big	grosse	grosse

with indefinite article

	Masc.	Fem.	Neuter
Nominative	grosser a big	grosse	grosses
Genitive	grossen of a big	grossen	grossen
Dative	grossen to a big	grossen	grossen
Accusative	grossen a big	grosse	grosses

der grosse Baum

Forms of possessive adjectives

	Masc.	Singular Fem.	Neuter	Plural All genders
my	mein	meine	mein	meine
your	dein	deine	dein	deine
his	sein	seine	sein	seine
her	ihr	ihre	ihr	ihre
its	sein	seine	sein	seine
our	unser	unsere	unser	unsere
your	euer	eure	euer	eure
their	ihr	ihre	ihr	ihre

Declension of possessive adjectives

	Masc.	Fem.	Neuter	Plural
Nominative	mein	meine	mein	meine
Genitive	meines	meiner	meines	meiner
Dative	meinem	meiner	meinem	meinen
Accusative	meinen	meine	mein	meine
Nominative	dein	deine	dein	deine
Genitive	deines	deiner	deines	deiner
Dative	deinem	deiner	deinem	deinen
Accusative	deinen	deine	dein	deine
Nominative	sein	seine	sein	seine
Genitive	seines	seiner	seines	seiner
Dative	seinem	seiner	seinem	seinen
Accusative	seinen	seine	sein	seine
Nominative	ihr	ihre	ihr	ihre
Genitive	ihres	ihrer	ihres	ihrer
Dative	ihrem	ihrer	ihrem	ihren
Accusative	ihren	ihre	ihr	ihre
Nominative	sein	seine	sein	seine
Genitive	seines	seiner	seines	seiner
Dative	seinem	seiner	seinem	seinen
Accusative	seinen	seine	sein	seine
Nominative	unser	unsere	unser	unsere
Genitive	unseres	unserer	unseres	unserer
Dative	unserem	unserer	unserem	unseren
Accusative	unseren	unsere	unser	unsere
Nominative	euer	eure	euer	eure
Genitive	eures	eurer	eures	eurer
Dative	eurem	eurer	eurem	euren
Accusative	euren	eure	euer	eure
Nominative	ihr	ihre	ihr	ihre
Genitive	ihres	ihrer	ihres	ihrer
Dative	ihrem	ihrer	ihrem	ihren
Accusative	ihren	ihre	ihr	ihre

Adverbs

Adverbs are identical with adjectives but are not declined.

Er geht langsam. He walks slowly.

Comparative forms

The comparative form usually adds *er* to the adjective.

schnell fast *schneller* faster

Sometimes an umlaut is added before the *er*.

arm poor *ärmer* poorer

The comparatives of certain adjectives and adverbs are not formed in the conventional way.

gut good *besser* better
viel much *mehr* more
gern gladly *lieber* rather

Ich lese viel aber er liest mehr.
I read much but he reads more.

Superlatives

The superlative is formed by adding *ste* or *este* to the adjective. An umlaut is sometimes added to the vowel preceding the *ste* or *este*.

der ärmste the poorest
die kleinste the smallest
das dümmste the dumbest
der älteste the oldest

Adjectives with irregular comparative forms also have irregular superlatives.

viel, mehr, am meisten much, more, most
gut, besser, am besten good, better, best

Verbs

Conjugation of auxiliary verbs

The verbs *sein* to be, *haben* to have, and *werden* to become, are used in the compound tenses of other verbs.

Rules for using verbs

There is only one present tense, but it translates in three ways into English.

Ich gehe zur Schule.
I go to school. I am going to school.
I do go to school.

To form a question, subject and verb are reversed.

Du spielst. You are playing.
Spielst du? Are you playing?

In a negative sentence *nicht* is placed after the verb:
Wir lesen nicht. We do not read.

Conjugation of auxiliary verbs

Infinitive	*sein* to be	*haben* to have	*werden* to become			
Indicative	*Present*			*Imperfect*		
ich	*bin*	*habe*	*werde*	*war*	*hatte*	*wurde*
du	*bist*	*hast*	*wirst*	*warst*	*hattest*	*wurdest*
er, sie, es	*ist*	*hat*	*wird*	*war*	*hatte*	*wurde*
wir	*sind*	*haben*	*werden*	*waren*	*hatten*	*wurden*
ihr	*seid*	*habt*	*werdet*	*wart*	*hattet*	*wurdet*
sie	*sind*	*haben*	*werden*	*waren*	*hatten*	*wurden*
(formal) *Sie*	*sind*	*haben*	*werden*	*waren*	*hatten*	*wurden*
	Perfect			*Future*		
ich	*bin gewesen*	*habe gehabt*	*bin geworden*	*werde sein*	*werde haben*	*werde werden*
du	*bist gewesen*	*hast gehabt*	*bist geworden*	*wirst sein*	*wirst haben*	*wirst werden*
er, sie, es	*ist gewesen*	*hat gehabt*	*ist geworden*	*wird sein*	*wird haben*	*wird werden*
wir	*sind gewesen*	*haben gehabt*	*sind geworden*	*werden sein*	*werden haben*	*werden werden*
ihr	*seid gewesen*	*habt gehabt*	*seid geworden*	*werdet sein*	*werdet haben*	*werdet werden*
sie	*sind gewesen*	*haben gehabt*	*sind geworden*	*werden sein*	*werden haben*	*werden werden*
(formal) *Sie*	*sind gewesen*	*haben gehabt*	*sind geworden*	*werden sein*	*werden haben*	*werden werden*

Review of German Grammar

Formation of tenses

To form the perfect tense of any verb, the present tense of *haben* or *sein* is used together with the past participle of the verb.

> *Er hat gehabt.* He has had.
>
> *Sie sind gewesen.* They have been.

To form the future tense of any verb, the present tense of *werden* is used with the infinitive of the verb.

> *Du wirst essen.* You will eat.
>
> *Wir werden tanzen.* We shall dance.

Weak and strong verbs

Weak verbs are known in English as regular verbs. The infinitive, past tense, and past participle are shown here for the weak verb *zahlen*.

> *zahlen, zahlte, gezahlt* (to) pay, paid, paid

Strong verbs are known in English as irregular verbs. The infinitive, past tense, and past participle are shown here for the strong verb *singen*.

> *singen, sang, gesungen* (to) sing, sang, sung

Whether weak or strong, all infinitives end in *en*.

> *machen* (to) make   *gehen* (to) go

Dropping the *en* yields the stem of the verb, for example, *mach* for *machen*, *geh* for *gehen*. The endings for the various tenses can then be added to the stem.

Present tense

To form the present tense, the same endings are used for weak verbs and strong verbs: *e, st, t, en, t, en, en.*

Imperfect tense of weak verbs

The imperfect tense of weak verbs is formed by adding the endings *te, test, te, ten, tet, ten* to the stem of the verb.

If the infinitive stem of a verb ends in *d* or *t*, an *e* precedes the endings. In the verb *warten*, for example, the stem is *wart*. The imperfect of *warten*, therefore, is as follows.

> *ich wartete* I waited   *wir warteten* we waited
>
> *du wartetest* you waited   *ihr wartetet* you waited
>
> *er wartete* he waited   *sie warteten* they waited

Past participle of weak verbs

The past participle of weak verbs is formed by putting *ge* before the third person singular of the present tense of the verb.

> *(er) spielt* he plays, *gespielt* played
>
> *(er) dankt* he thanks, *gedankt* thanked

Conjugation of weak and strong verbs

Infinitive	weak	strong
	machen	*gehen*
	to make	to go

Indicative		*Present*		*Imperfect*		Imperative	
		I make	I go	I made	I went	(fam. sing.)	*mache*
		I do make	I do go	I did make	I did go	(fam. pl.)	*macht*
		I am making	I am going	I was making	I was going	(formal)	*machen Sie*
	ich	*mache*	*gehe*	*machte*	*ging*		
	du	*machst*	*gehst*	*machtest*	*gingst*	(fam. sing.)	*gehe*
er, sie, es		*macht*	*geht*	*machte*	*ging*	(fam. pl.)	*geht*
	wir	*machen*	*gehen*	*machten*	*gingen*	(formal)	*gehen Sie*
	ihr	*macht*	*geht*	*machtet*	*gingt*		
	sie	*machen*	*gehen*	*machten*	*gingen*		
(formal)	*Sie*	*machen*	*gehen*	*machten*	*gingen*		

		Perfect		*Future*		Participles	
		I have made	I have gone	I shall make	I shall go	*Past*	*gemacht*
	ich	*habe gemacht*	*bin gegangen*	*werde machen*	*werde gehen*	*Present*	*machend*
	du	*hast gemacht*	*bist gegangen*	*wirst machen*	*wirst gehen*		
er, sie, es		*hat gemacht*	*ist gegangen*	*wird machen*	*wird gehen*	*Past*	*ist gegangen*
	wir	*haben gemacht*	*sind gegangen*	*werden machen*	*werden gehen*	*Present*	*gehend*
	ihr	*habt gemacht*	*seid gegangen*	*werdet machen*	*werdet gehen*		
	sie	*haben gemacht*	*sind gegangen*	*werden machen*	*werden gehen*		
(formal)	*Sie*	*haben gemacht*	*sind gegangen*	*werden machen*	*werden gehen*		

Perfect tense of weak verbs

The perfect tense of weak verbs is formed by conjugating *sein* to be, or *haben* to have, plus the past participle. Among the verbs forming the perfect with *sein* are verbs of motion.

Ich bin gegangen. I have gone.

Er ist ihm gefolgt. He has followed him.

All reflexive verbs form the perfect with *haben* and the past participle. This is true both for weak and strong verbs.

Sie hat sich gewaschen. She has washed herself.

Wir haben uns gestritten. We have quarreled.

Er hat sich gefreut. He was glad.

Note that past participles are placed at the end of the sentence or independent clause.

Du hast das Buch gelesen. You have read the book.

Imperfect and past participle of strong verbs

Strong verbs form their own imperfect and past participle. Some examples of strong verbs are shown here.

Infinitive	Imperfect	Past participle
fliegen (to) fly	*flog*	*geflogen*
kommen (to) come	*kam*	*gekommen*
lassen (to) let	*liess*	*gelassen*
leiden (to) suffer	*litt*	*gelitten*
rufen (to) call	*rief*	*gerufen*
schlafen (to) sleep	*schlief*	*geschlafen*

Future tense

The future tense of all verbs, whether weak or strong, is formed by conjugating *werden* in the present tense plus the infinitive of the verb.

ich werde halten I shall hold

du wirst halten you will hold

er wird halten he will hold

wir werden halten we will hold

ihr werdet halten you will hold

sie werden halten they will hold

Imperative mood

The imperative with the polite *Sie* is formed by using the infinitive of a verb, followed by *Sie*. To be very polite, the word *bitte* (please) may be added:

Schreiben Sie bitte. Please write.

Gehen Sie bitte. Please go.

The imperative with the *du* form is expressed by deleting the *en* of the infinitive.

Infinitive	Imperative
spielen (to) play	*spiel* play
singen (to) sing	*sing* sing

The imperative for the *ihr,* you plural, form uses the present tense *ihr* form of the verb without the pronoun *ihr*.

ihr geht you go	*geht*	go
ihr nehmt you take	*nehmt*	take

The imperative of the first person plural is expressed by the infinitive followed by *wir* we.

helfen wir let us help   *geben wir* let us give

Sie wird getragen.

Forming the passive voice

To form the passive, the auxiliary verb *werden* (to become) is conjugated and followed by the past participle of the main verb:

Sie wird getragen.

She is being carried.

Er wurde gehört.

He was heard.

Wir werden gelobt werden.

We are going to be praised.

Impersonal verbs

Many verbs are used only in the third person singular with the pronoun *es* it. They are used in all tenses. Some examples follow.

es regnet it is raining

es schneit it is snowing

es klopft there is a knock

es gelingt mir I succeed

es gibt there is, there are

wie geht es dir? how are you?

es geht mir gut I am fine

es tut mir leid I am sorry

Verbal prefixes

There are two types of verbal prefixes: inseparable and separable. Although these prefixes may change the meaning of a verb, they do not affect conjugation. Some examples of inseparable verbal prefixes follow.

be as in *besuchen* (to) visit

ent as in *entspannen* (to) relax

er as in *erlangen* (to) get

ge as in *gelingen* (to) succeed

miss as in *misstrauen* (to) mistrust

ver as in *vertrauen* (to) trust

zer as in *zerbrechen* (to) break

Separable verbal prefixes are prefixes that also function as prepositions. Some examples follow.

anhören (to) listen	*an* at, on, to
aufstehen (to) get up	*auf* on, onto
untergehen (to) perish	*unter* under, among
vorstellen (to) introduce	*vor* before

In the simple tenses, the verbal prefix separates from the verb and is placed at the end of the sentence. Consider this example, which uses the verb *untergehen*.

Die Sonne geht unter. The sun sets.

In compound tenses, the verbal prefix does not separate. The *ge* of the past participle appears between the prefix and the verb.

Er hat zugehört. He has listened.

Wir wurden angestellt. We were hired.

Modal auxiliary verbs

Six verbs expressing certain modes of action have a conjugation of their own.

dürfen (to) be allowed to, expressing permission
können (to) be able to, expressing ability
mögen (to) like to, expressing desire
müssen (to) have to, expressing obligation
sollen (to) be obliged to *or* to be said to, expressing obligation
wollen (to) want, expressing intent

The principal forms of the modal auxiliaries follow.

Infinitive	Imperfect	Past participle
dürfen	durfte	gedurft
können	konnte	gekonnt
mögen	mochte	gemocht
müssen	musste	gemusst
sollen	sollte	gesollt
wollen	wollte	gewollt

The following sentences show typical uses of the modal auxiliary verbs. (Modal auxiliaries are used frequently, since they express thoughts commonly needed in situations that arise in the everyday lives of people of all types.)

Willst du nach Hause gehen?
Do you want to go home?

Er darf nicht spielen.
He is not allowed to play.

Wir konnten rennen.
We were able to run.

Sie mag keine Milch.
She does not like milk.

Er konnte sprechen.
He was able to speak.

Sie muss üben.
She must exercise.

Present tense of modal auxiliary verbs

	dürfen I may	können I can	mögen I may, I like	müssen I must	sollen I should	wollen I want
ich	darf	kann	mag	muss	soll	will
du	darfst	kannst	magst	musst	sollst	willst
er, sie, es	darf	kann	mag	muss	soll	will
wir	dürfen	können	mögen	müssen	sollen	wollen
ihr	dürft	könnt	mögt	müsst	sollt	wollt
sie	dürfen	können	mögen	müssen	sollen	wollen

Conjunctions

There are two types of conjunctions: coordinating conjunctions and subordinating conjunctions.

Coordinating conjunctions

Coordinating conjunctions connect principal clauses and do not affect word order.

Ich trinke Wein, aber Dieter trinkt Bier.
I drink wine but Dieter drinks beer.

Er liest nicht, sondern schläft.
He does not read but sleeps.

Common coordinating conjunctions follow.

aber but
denn for
entweder . . . oder either . . . or
oder or
sondern but (on the contrary)
und and

Subordinating conjunctions

Subordinating conjunctions introduce a dependent clause. Subordinating conjunctions affect the word order.

Er geht langsam, weil er müde ist.
He goes slowly because he is tired.

Sie spielte, obgleich sie müde war.
She was playing although she was tired.

In sentences containing an independent clause and a dependent clause, the auxiliary verb comes last and is preceded by the past participle or an infinitive.

Ich schrieb, nachdem ich angekommen war.
I wrote after I had arrived.

Er trank, weil er durstig gewesen ist.
He drank because he was thirsty.

Common subordinating conjunctions follow.

als when, then
als ob as if
bevor before
bis until
da since, when
damit in order that

dass so that
obgleich although
seit, seitdem since
sobald as soon as
weil because

Word order

Normal word order
As a rule the word order within a sentence is subject, verb, object.

Der Bruder liest das Buch.
The brother reads the book.

If a sentence contains a direct and an indirect object, the indirect object precedes the direct object.

Der Bruder gibt dem Vater das Buch.
The brother gives the father the book.

If the direct object is a pronoun, the direct object precedes the indirect object.

Der Bruder gibt es ihm.
The brother gives it to him.

Der Bruder gibt's dem Vater.
The brother gives it to the father.

Inverted word order
Inverted word order is used in forming questions.

Kann er lesen? Does he know how to read?

Inverted word order is used in expressing commands.

Kommen Sie her! Come here!

Inverted word order is used in sentences beginning with expressions of time or place.

Heute schlafe ich nicht.
Today I do not sleep.

In der Stadt gibt es viele Theater.
There are many theaters in the city.

In the future tense and with a modal auxiliary verb, an infinitive is placed at the end of the sentence.

Sie werden heute spielen. They will play today.
Sie können heute spielen. They can play today.

A past participle is placed at the end of a sentence.

Sie sind angekommen. They have arrived.

Testen Sie Ihre Gesundheit! *is, literally, test you your health. In English the word* you *comes first but is not used.*

Participles
A separable prefix becomes inseparable in the past participle.

A past participle precedes the auxiliary verb in sentences containing an independent clause and a dependent clause.

Wir wissen, dass er gehört hat.
We know that he has heard.

Writing letters

Date
14. August 2000 August 14, 2000

Inside address
Herrn Max Schulz	Mr. Max Schulz
Hauptstrasse 8	8 Hauptstrasse
Düsseldorf	Düsseldorf

Salutation
(informal)
Lieber Herr Schulz Dear Mr. Schulz

(formal)
Sehr geehrter Herr Schulz Dear Mr. Schulz

Complimentary close
(informal)
Mitt freundlichen Grüssen With kindest regards

(formal)
Hochachtungsvoll Very truly yours

A letter to friends or family may close in three ways.

Mit vielen Grüssen
With many regards

Mit den besten Grüssen
With best regards

Viele Grüsse und Küsse
With many regards and kisses

For the traveler

das Flugzeug

Lufthansa

der Zollbeamte

der Koffer

How to travel	Wie man reist
by plane	*mit dem Flugzeug*
by train	*mit dem Zug*
by boat	*mit dem Schiff*
by car	*mit dem Auto*
by bus	*mit dem Bus*

At the airport   *Am Flughafen*

The plane is late/early.	*Das Flugzeug ist verspätet/frühzeitig angekommen.*

Customs   *Der Zoll*

Passport, please. Anything to declare?	*Ihren Paß, bitte. Haben Sie etwas zu verzollen?*
No, nothing to declare.	*Nein, ich habe nichts zu verzollen.*
Please, open your suitcase.	*Bitte öffnen Sie Ihren Koffer.*
Thank you, Sir.	*Danke schön.*

From the airport to Frankfurt center   *Vom Flughafen zur Innenstadt Frankfurt*

I would like to take the bus to Frankfurt.	*Ich möchte gerne den Bus nach Frankfurt nehmen.*
Taxi. Are you free? I would like to go to the train station.	*Taxi. Sind Sie frei?* *Würden Sie mich bitte zum Bahnhof fahren?*
I would like to rent a car.	*Ich möchte ein Auto mieten.*
How much for two weeks?	*Wieviel kostet es für zwei Wochen?*
Four hundred Deutschmark a week.	*Vierhundert Mark pro Woche.*
Which road do I take to Frankfurt?	*Welche Straße kann ich nach Frankfurt nehmen?*
Can you show me on a map?	*Könnten Sie es mir auf einer Straßenkarte zeigen?*
Is the road well marked?	*Ist die Strecke/Straße gut ausgeschildert?*
Watch for the road signs.	*Beachten Sie die Straßenschilder.*

Road signs   *Straßenschilder*

 danger

 intersection

 railroad gate

 state road

 one way

 customs

 European road

 autobahn

 no motorized vehicles

 no autos

 no entry

Road signs along autobahns, or highways, in Germany are well designed and easy to read even at high travel speeds.

Looking for a hotel

Auf der Suche nach einem Hotel

Pardon me, where is the tourist office?	*Entschuldigung, können Sie mir sagen, wo das Fremdenverkehrsamt ist?*
It is over there, to the right.	*Es ist dort drüben, rechts.*
It is in the next street, to the left.	*Es liegt in der nächsten Straße, links.*
Thank you. Good-bye.	*Vielen Dank. Auf Wiedersehen.*
Good morning. Could you please tell me if there is a good hotel, not too expensive, near here?	*Guten Morgen. Gibt es hier in der Nähe ein gutes Hotel, das nicht zu teuer ist?*
Yes, when you walk up this street, turn left at the intersection and it is straight ahead.	*Ja, gehen Sie diese Straße hinauf, biegen Sie an der Kreuzung links ab, dann sehen Sie es schon geradeaus.*
Do you speak English? I do not speak German.	*Sprechen Sie Englisch? Ich spreche leider kein Deutsch.*
I do not understand.	*Ich verstehe es nicht.*
Speak more slowly, please.	*Bitte sprechen Sie etwas langsamer.*
What does that mean?	*Was bedeutet das, bitte?*
A room for two, with bath.	*Ein Doppelzimmer bitte, mit Bad.*
It is expensive.	*Das ist teuer.*
Is there a phone?	*Gibt es hier ein Telefon?*
What time is breakfast?	*Wann servieren Sie Frühstück?*
From 6:00 to 9:00 in the breakfast room.	*Zwischen 6:00 und 9:00 Uhr im Frühstückszimmer.*
What do you serve for breakfast?	*Was bieten Sie zum Frühstück an?*
We have tea, coffee, or hot chocolate, fresh rolls, butter, jam, and honey.	*Als Getränke haben wir Tee, Kaffee, oder heißen Kakao, dann frische Brötchen, Marmelade und Honig.*
At what time to you want your breakfast tomorrow morning?	*Um wieviel Uhr möchten Sie morgen früh frühstücken?*

Shopping　　*Einkaufen*

Stores　　*Geschäfte*

jewelry shop	*Juweliergeschäft*
butcher shop	*Fleischerei*
bakery	*Bäckerei*
tobacco shop	*Tabakladen*
beauty parlor	*Friseur Salon*
department store	*Kaufhaus*
bookstore	*Buchhandlung*
pastry shop	*Konditorei*
drugstore	*Drogerie/Apotheke* (for prescriptions)

Advertising signs abound at this modern German shopping center. If you cannot find what you want here, you probably don't need it.

Is there a department store near here?	*Ist hier ein Kaufhaus in der Nähe?*
Yes, you will pass by many little shops.	*Ja, Sie werden an vielen kleineren Geschäften vorbeikommen.*
Follow this street.	*Gehen Sie diese Straße entlang.*
Can I help you?	*Kann ich Ihnen behilflich sein?*
I would like to buy a summer dress.	*Ich möchte ein Sommerkleid kaufen.*
What is your size?	*Welche Größe tragen Sie?*
I think 12 or 14. I am not sure.	*Ich glaube 44 oder 46. Ich bin nicht ganz sicher.*
I would like shoes, please. Size 7 or perhaps 8.	*Ich möchte Schuhe kaufen, bitte. Größe 38 oder vielleicht 39.*
How much does it cost?	*Wieviel kostet es?*
May I show you something else?	*Darf ich Ihnen noch etwas anderes zeigen?*
Perhaps, a skirt and a blouse. Thank you.	*Ja, vielleicht einen Rock und eine Bluse. Danke.*
I have a matching linen skirt and a silk blouse in different colors.	*Ich kann Ihnen einen Leinenrock mit passender Seidenbluse zeigen. Wir führen sie in verschiedenen Farben.*
I would like a man's shortsleeve shirt, size 16, and shoes, size 10 or 11.	*Ich möchte gerne ein kurzärmeliges Herrenhemd, Größe 44 oder 45.*
I will take this tie also.	*Ich nehme auch diese Krawatte/diesen Schlips.*
And now, let's have lunch.	*Laß uns jetzt zu Mittag essen.*

At the restaurant   Im Restaurant

Speisekarte

Ochsenmaulsalat
(appetizer)
thinly sliced pickled beef tongue, seasoned with
onions, horseradish, vinegar, and oil

Kalbsbraten
roast veal, gravy, fresh vegetables,
boiled potatoes, mixed salad

Jägerschnitzel
breaded veal cutlet (or pork cutlet)
with mushroom sauce,
(mashed) potatoes or dumplings

Kasseler Rippenspeer
smoked pork chops on a bed of sauerkraut,
seasoned with caraway seeds,
served with dumplings or potatoes

Brathähnchen
roasted chicken,
french fries (in German "pommes frites"),
mixed salad

Ungarisches Gulasch
beef stew seasoned with Hungarian paprika,
red cabbage, and potato dumplings

Forelle "Blau"/Forelle "Müllerin Art"
trout poached or panfried
with fresh lemon and Worcestershire sauce
both served with boiled potatoes, wedges of lemon

The waiter	*Der Kellner*
The waitress	*Das Fräulein*
Good afternoon.	*Guten Tag.*
A table for two near the window, please.	*Einen Tisch für zwei Personen, am Fenster, bitte.*
Follow me.	*Bitte, kommen Sie mit.*
Is this table alright?	*Möchten Sie hier sitzen?*
Yes, very good, thank you.	*Ja, danke, das ist gut.*
Yes, Sir. Can I help you?	*Kann ich Ihnen etwas anbieten?*
The menu, please.	*Die Speisekarte, bitte.*
To start, I will have the noodle soup.	*Ich werde mit einer Nudelsuppe anfangen.*
Then, I will have the Jägerschnitzel.	*Danach möchte ich ein Jägerschnitzel.*
And the lady?	*Und die Dame?*
I will have Ochsenmaulsalat, and then Forelle Blau with mixed salad.	*Ich möchte gerne Ochsenmaulsalat, und danach Forelle Blau, mit gemischtem Salat.*
A bottle of the local wine, please.	*Eine Flasche des hiesigen Weines, bitte.*
Bread and butter, and we will order dessert and coffee later.	*Brot und Butter, bitte; den Nachtisch und Kaffee werden wir später bestellen.*
The check, please.	*Die Rechnung, bitte.*
It is already dark outside, but quite warm.	*Es ist schon dunkel draußen, aber noch recht warm.*
Let's go for a stroll.	*Laß uns einen Stadtbummel machen.*
Let's take the subway.	*Laß uns die U-Bahn nehmen.*
The subway goes faster and it is easier.	*Die U-Bahn ist viel schneller und einfacher zu benutzen.*
Then we can walk back to the hotel.	*Danach können wir zum Hotel zurücklaufen.*

The telephone

In der Telefonzelle

I would like to call the United States.	*Ich möchte die Vereinigten Staaten anrufen.*
You need a card.	*Sie brauchen eine Telefonkarte.*
How does it work and where can I buy one?	*Wie benutzt man sie, und wo kann ich eine Karte kaufen?*
You can buy the cards at any post office.	*Sie können die Karte in jedem Postamt kaufen.*
Let's go. We can buy stamps at the same time.	*Laß uns zum Postamt gehen, dann können wir auch gleich dort Briefmarken kaufen.*
To call the United States from Germany, dial 001, then your area code and calling number.	*Wenn Sie die Vereinigten Staaten von Deutschland aus anrufen, wählen Sie 001, dann die Vorwahl und die Telefonnummer.*
Emergency number for police: 110	*Notruf für die Polizei: 110*
Ambulance: 110/Eastern Germany: 115	*Unfallrettung: 110/Deutschland Ost: 115*
Fire department: 112	*Feuerwehr: 112*
U.S. Embassy in Bonn: 0228-3 39-1	*U.S. Botschaft in Bonn: 0228-3 39-1*

German police, fire, and emergency services can be summoned by telephone by dialing a three-digit number, much like the American 911 system.

Where can you speak German?
Wo wird Deutsch gesprochen?

Belgium	*Belgien*
Bulgaria	*Bulgarien*
Denmark	*Dänemark*
Germany	*Deutschland*
Italy	*Italien*
Liechtenstein	*Liechtenstein*
Luxembourg	*Luxemburg*
the Netherlands	*die Niederlande*
Holland	*Holland*
Norway	*Norwegen*
Austria	*Österreich*
Poland	*Polen*
Sweden	*Schweden*
Switzerland	*die Schweiz*
Czechoslovakia	*Tschechoslowakei*
Hungary	*Ungarn*

Some countries have large German ethnic groups:

Argentina	*Argentinien*
Bolivia	*Bolivien*
Brazil	*Brasilien*
Peru	*Peru*
Uruguay	*Uruguay*
Venezuela	*Venezuela*
United States of America	*Vereinigte Staaten von Amerika*

In Africa, some of the former colonial states still speak German:

Tanzania	*Tanganjika (Deutsch Ost-Afrika)*
Cameroon	*Kamerun*
Namibia	*Deutsch Süd-West Afrika*

Numbers

Cardinal numbers

Cardinal numbers are not declined. *Zehn* is added to the numbers three to nine to form thirteen to nineteen. Note the difference in spelling:

sechs 6; *sechzehn* 16; *sieben* 7, *siebzehn* 17.

Zig is added to the numbers three to nine to form thirty, etc. Note the differences in spelling:

zwei 2, *zwanzig* 20;
drei 3, *dreißig* 30;
sechs 6, *sechzig* 60;
sieben 7, *siebzig* 70.

The numbers from 20 to 30 and so on up to 99 are formed by using the single numbers first and adding *und*.

Cardinal numbers

1	*eins*	20	*zwanzig*
2	*zwei*	21	*einundzwanzig*
3	*drei*	22	*zweiundzwanzig*
4	*vier*	30	*dreißig*
5	*fünf*	40	*vierzig*
6	*sechs*	50	*fünfzig*
7	*sieben*	60	*sechzig*
8	*acht*	70	*siebzig*
9	*neun*	80	*achtzig*
10	*zehn*	90	*neunzig*
11	*elf*	100	*hundert*
12	*zwölf*	101	*hunderteins*
13	*dreizehn*	200	*zweihundert*
14	*vierzehn*	1000	*tausend*
15	*fünfzehn*	2000	*zweitausend*
16	*sechzehn*	2300	*zweitausenddreihundert*
17	*siebzehn*	4002	*viertausendzwei*
18	*achtzehn*	10900	*zehntausendneunhundert*
19	*neunzehn*	1000000	*eine Million*

Ordinal numbers

Ordinal numbers are declined as adjectives. They are usually formed by adding *te* to the cardinal numbers. With ordinal numbers beginning with *zwanzig* (20), add *ste* to form the cardinal number. (*der, die, das*)

Ordinal numbers

first	*erste*	eighth	*achte*
second	*zweite*	ninth	*neunte*
third	*dritte*	tenth	*zehnte*
fourth	*vierte*	hundredth	*hundertste*
fifth	*fünfte*	thousandth	*tausendste*
sixth	*sechste*	millionth	*millionste*
seventh	*siebente*		

Arithmetic expressions

Vier und vier ist acht. Four and four are eight. Instead of *und*, *plus* can be used.

Acht weniger sechs ist zwei.

Eight minus six is two.

Instead of *weniger*, *minus* can be used.

Drei mal sieben ist einundzwanzig.

Three times seven is twenty-one.

Zehn geteilt durch zwei ist fünf.

Ten divided by two is five.

To indicate a fraction, *tel* is added to the cardinal number.

viertel 1/4   *fünftel* 1/5   *sechstel* 1/6

An exception is *ein halb* 1/2, which is an adjective and is declined.

Er ißt einen halben Kuchen. He eats half a cake.

Another exception is *ein Drittel,* which derives from *drei* three.

Indefinite numbers and amounts are not declined.

a little	*ein bißchen*
some	*etwas*
a few	*ein paar*
enough	*genug*
a little	*ein wenig*
more	*mehr*

Note that *ein Paar* means a pair.

Currency

1 German Mark (DM) = 100 Pfennig (Pf)

Coins: 1, 2, 5, 10 and 50 Pf
1, 2 and 5 DM

Bills: 5, 10, 20, 50, 100, 200, 500 and 1,000 DM

Banks: Open Monday - Friday 9 a.m. - 12:30 p.m. and from 2:30 p.m. - 4 p.m. (Thursdays to 5:30 p.m.) Closed Saturday, Sunday and holidays.

German banknotes are elegantly engraved, giving them the appearance of small works of art.

Time

The time of day is expressed in two ways.

Es ist drei Uhr.   It is three o'clock.

um drei Uhr   at three o'clock

The progression of time is expressed in two ways. For example, ten-fifteen can be expressed as follows:

Viertel nach zehn   a quarter after ten

Viertel elf   a quarter past ten

Ten-thirty is *halb elf*. Ten-forty-five is *drei viertel elf*. The progression of time can also be expressed by employing minutes.

zehn Minuten vor sieben   ten minutes before seven

zehn Minuten nach sieben   ten minutes after seven

In timetables time is expressed on a 24- hour basis. From 12 noon to midnight, the hours are 13 to 24 o'clock.

acht Uhr fünfundzwanzig   8:25 a.m.

zwanzig Uhr zehn   8:10 p.m.

This electronic Zugfahrplan *(also called a* Bahnfahrplan*), or train schedule, lists departure times for trains to a number of cities in Europe.*

Dates

When numbers are used in expressing dates, they generally are not written out. Instead, a numeral is used and followed by a period.

am 18. Dezember 2000   December 18, 2000

der 19. Mai   May 19th

Months, days, seasons

January	*Januar*
February	*Februar*
March	*März*
April	*April*
May	*Mai*
June	*Juni*
July	*Juli*
August	*August*
September	*September*
October	*Oktober*
November	*November*
December	*Dezember*

Monday	*Montag*
Tuesday	*Dienstag*
Wednesday	*Mittwoch*
Thursday	*Donnerstag*
Friday	*Freitag*
Saturday	*Sonnabend/Samstag*
Sunday	*Sonntag*

spring	*Frühling*
summer	*Sommer*
autumn	*Herbst*
winter	*Winter*

Countries

With few exceptions, the names of countries are not preceded by an article. The exceptions follow.

the Netherlands   *die Niederlande*

Switzerland   *die Schweiz*

Turkey   *die Türkei*

Adjectives describing a country or its people are not capitalized.

der deutsche Wein

German wine

die amerikanische Bevölkerung

the American population

Germany	*Deutschland*
England	*England*
Austria	*Österreich*
Belgium	*Belgien*
Spain	*Spanien*
Hungary	*Ungarn*
Ireland	*Irland*
Italy	*Italien*
the Netherlands	*die Niederlande/Holland*
Poland	*Polen*
Portugal	*Portugal*
Switzerland	*die Schweiz*

die Haare hair
die Ohren ears
die Wangen cheeks
das Kinn chin
die Augen eyes
die Nase nose
der Mund mouth

das Gesicht The face

Dictionary

der Körper The human body

der Kopf head
der Hals neck
die Schulter shoulder
die Brust chest
der Arm arm
der Magen stomach
die Hand hand
die Finger fingers
das Bein leg
der Fuss foot
die Zehen toes

Dictionary abbreviations. Nouns are identified as masculine *(m)*, feminine *(f)*, or neuter *(nt)*. Adjectives are identified as *adj*, adverbs as *adv*, conjunctions as *conj*, interjections as *interj*, prepositions as *prep*, pronouns as *pron*, and verbs as *v*. Plurals are identified as *pl*.

German-English

A

Abend *m* evening
Abenteur *nt* adventure
aber *conj* but
ablehnen *v* decline
ähnlich *adj* similar
also *conj* therefore, so
alt *adj* old
alt werden *v* age
Angina *f* sore throat
Angst *f* fear
Anleihe *f* loan
Ansprache *f* speech
anständig *adj* decent
Antwort *f* reply, answer
antworten *v* answer
Anzug *m* suit
Arbeit *f* work
arbeiten *v* work
Arm *m* arm
arm *adj* poor
Armbanduhr *f* wristwatch
Arzt *m* medical doctor
atmen *v* breathe
auch *conj* also
Aufgabe *f* task
aufpassen *v* watch
aufstehen *v* get up, rise
aufwachen *v* wake up
auf Wiedersehen *interj* goodbye
aufziehen *v* (watch) wind
Auge *nt* eye
Ausflug *m* excursion, outing
Ausgang *m* exit
ausrotten *v* eradicate
ausser *prep* except
Autobahn *f* highway
Autofahrer *m* driver

B

backen *v* bake
Bahnhof *m* station
bald *adv* soon
Ball *m* ball
Bank *f* bench

Bart *m* beard
bauen *v* build, construct
Baum *m* tree
bedeuten *v* mean
beeindrucken *v* impress
behalten *v* keep
Bein *nt* leg
beinahe *adv* almost
bekannt werden *v* become acquainted
Belagerung *f* siege
belasten *v* burden
bellen *v* bark
Belohnung *f* reward
benutzen *v* use
beobachten *v* observe
bequem *adj* comfortable
bereit *adj* ready, prepared
berühmt *adj* famous
bescheiden *adj* modest
Bescheidenheit *f* modesty
beschreiben *v* describe
Beschwerde *f* complaint, burden
Besen *m* broom
besonders *adv* particularly
bestechen *v* bribe
Bestechung *f* bribery, graft
bestimmen *v* determine
bestrafen *v* punish
Besuch *m* visit
besuchen *v* visit
beten *v* pray
Bett *nt* bed
Bevölkerung *f* population
bezahlen *v* pay
billig *adj* cheap
bitte *adv* please
blass *adj* pale
blau *adj* blue
bleiben *v* stay
Bleistift *m* pencil
blind *adj* blind
Blinddarm *m* appendix
Blitz *m* lightning
Blume *f* flower
borgen *v* borrow
Brandstiftung *f* arson

Review of German Grammar

brauchen *v* need
braun *adj* brown
Braut *f* bride
Bräutigam *m* bridegroom
Bremse *f* brake
Brief *m* letter
Briefmarke *f* stamp
Briefumschlag *m* envelope
Brot *nt* bread
Brücke *f* bridge
Bruder *m* brother
Buch *nt* book
Bürger *m* citizen

C

Charakter *m* character
Chef *m* boss
Chemie *f* chemistry
Chirurg *m* surgeon
christlich *adj* Christian

D

Dame *f* lady
Dampf *m* steam
Dank *m* gratitude, thanks
danken *v* thank
Daumen *m* thumb
denken *v* think
deswegen *conj* therefore
dichten *v* write poetry
Dichter *m* poet
dick *adj* thick
Dieb *m* thief
Ding *nt* thing
diskutieren *v* discuss
Donner *m* thunder
Draht *m* wire
draussen *adv* outside
dringend *adj* urgent
Druck *m* pressure
dumm *adj* stupid
dunkel *adj* dark
Durst *m* thirst
durstig *adj* thirsty

E

Ecke *f* corner
Efeu *m* ivy
Egoismus *m* egotism
Ehefrau *f* wife
Ehemann *m* husband
Ei *nt* egg

Eid *m* oath
Eigentum *nt* property
einbrechen *v* burglarize
Einbrecher *m* burglar
Eindruck *m* impression
Einfuhr *f* import
einführen *v* introduce
Eingang *m* entrance
Einkommen *nt* income
einladen *v* invite
Einladung *f* invitation
Einschnitt *m* incision
Einwanderer *m* immigrant
Ellbogen *m* elbow
Eltern *pl* parents
Ende *nt* end
endlich *adv* finally
Engel *m* angel
Enkel *m* grandchild
entlassen *v* dismiss
Entlassung *f* dismissal
entwickeln *v* develop
erbärmlich *adj* miserable
erforderlich *adj* necessary
Ergebnis *nt* result
erhalten *v* receive
erinnern *v* remind
erklären *v* explain
erleichtern *v* facilitate, lighten
ernst *adj* earnest
erschöpfen *v* exhaust
ertragen *v* tolerate
essen *v* eat
Europa *nt* Europe
exponieren *v* expose

F

fähig *adj* capable, able
fahren *v* drive, ride
Fahrer *m* driver
Fahrplan *m* timetable
falsch *adj* wrong, false
Familie *f* family
Farbaufnahme *f* color photo
Farbe *f* color
fegen *v* sweep
Fehler *m* mistake
feiern *v* celebrate
Feiertag *m* holiday
Feind *m* enemy
Ferien *pl* vacation
Ferne *f* distance
feucht *adj* damp
Feuchtigkeit *f* dampness

Feuer *nt* fire
finden *v* find
Finger *m* finger
Flasche *f* bottle, flask
fleissig *adj* diligent
Flugzeug *nt* airplane
fordern *v* request
Forderung *f* request
fortfahren *v* continue
Frage *f* question
Frankreich *nt* France
französisch *adj* French
Frau *f* woman, wife
Fräulein *nt* miss
Freiheit *f* liberty
Freund *m* friend
freundlich *adj* kind, friendly
frieren *v* freeze
fröhlich *adj* merry, cheerful
Frucht *f* fruit
früh *adv* early
Frühling *m* spring
Frühstück *nt* breakfast
Fuchs *m* fox
Führerschein *m* driver's license
Funke *m* spark
funkeln *v* spark
funktionieren *v* function, work
für *prep* for
fürchten *v* fear
Fuss *m* foot
Fussboden *m* floor

G

Gabel *f* fork
Gans *f* goose
garantieren *v* vouch for
garnieren *v* adorn
Gast *m* guest
Gastarbeiter *m* foreign worker
Gastgeber *m* host
geben *v* give
Gebirge *nt* mountain range
Gebühr *f* fee
Geburt *f* birth
Geburtstag *m* birthday
Gedächtnis *nt* memory
Gedanke *m* thought, idea
Gedicht *nt* poem
Geduld *f* patience
geduldig *adj* patient
Gefahr *f* danger
gefährlich *adj* dangerous
gegen *prep* against, toward

Gegend *f* area
Gegenwart *f* presence
Gegner *m* adversary
geheim *adj* secret
Geheimnis *nt* secret
gehen *v* go, walk
gehören *v* belong
gehorsam *adj* obedient
Gehorsamkeit *f* obedience
gelb *adj* yellow
Geld *nt* money
Gelegenheit *f* occasion
genau *adv* precisely
genug *adj* enough
geräumig *adj* spacious
Geräusch *nt* noise
Gerüst *nt* scaffolding
Geschenk *nt* present
Gesetz *nt* law
Gesicht *nt* face
Gespenst *nt* ghost
Geständnis *nt* confession
gestehen *v* confess
gestern *adv* yesterday
gesund *adj* healthy
gewaltsam *adj* violent
Gewalttätigkeit *f* violence
gewiss *adv* certainly
Gewissen *nt* conscience
Gewissensbisse *m* remorse
gewissenhaft *adj* conscientious
gewissermassen *adv* so to speak
Gewitter *nt* thunderstorm
Glas *nt* glass
glatt *adj* slippery
Glatze *f* baldness
gleichzeitig *adv* simultaneously
Glocke *f* bell
Glück *nt* luck
Gott *m* god
göttlich *adj* divine
gottlos *adj* godless
Grab *nt* tomb
Graben *m* ditch
graben *v* dig
gratulieren *v* congratulate
Grippe *f* flu
gross *adj* big, tall
grün *adj* green
Grundlage *f* basis
gründlich *adj* profound
Gruppe *f* group
grüssen *v* greet
gültig *adj* valid
gut *adj* good

H

Haar *nt* hair
Hafen *m* harbor
Hagel *m* hail
Hals *m* neck
Hand *f* hand
Handlung *f* action
Handschuh *m* glove
Handtuch *nt* towel
hauptsächlich *adv* chiefly, *adj* principal
Hauptstadt *f* capital
Hauptstrasse *f* main street
Haus *nt* house
Hauswirt *m* landlord
Haut *f* skin
Heide *f* heath
heilen *v* cure, heal
Heiligabend *m* Christmas eve
heiraten *v* marry
helfen *v* help, assist
Hemd *nt* shirt
Herausgeber *m* publisher
Herbst *m* fall, autumn
herrlich *adj* splendid
Herz *nt* heart
herzlich *adj* affectionate
heute *adv* today
heute abend *adv* tonight
hier *adv* here
Hilfe *f* help
hilflos *adj* helpless
Himmel *m* sky, heaven
hinter *prep* behind, beyond
Hintergrund *m* background
hinzufügen *v* add
hoch *adj* high, tall
Hochzeit *f* wedding
hoffen *v* hope
hoffentlich *adv* I hope
Hoffnung *f* hope
höflich *adj* polite
Hölle *f* hell
Holz *nt* wood
hören *v* hear
Hose *f* pants
hübsch *adj* pretty, handsome
Hunger *m* hunger
hungern *v* starve
hungrig *adj* hungry
Husten *m* cough
husten *v* cough
Hut *m* hat
Hütte *f* cabin

I

immer *adv* always
impfen *v* inoculate
Ingenieur *m* engineer
Inhaltsverzeichnis *nt* table of contents
interessant *adj* interesting
Irrtum *m* error

J

Jagd *f* chase
jagen *v* chase
jedoch *conj* nevertheless
jemand *pron* somebody
jenseits *adv* beyond
jetzt *adv* now
Jugend *f* youth
jugendlich *adj* youthful
jung *adj* young

K

kahl *adj* bold
kalt *adj* cold
Kammermusik *f* chamber music
Kampf *m* fight
kämpfen *v* fight
Kapitel *nt* chapter
Karfreitag *m* Good Friday
Kartoffel *f* potato
Käse *m* cheese
Kassier *m* bank teller
kauen *v* chew
kaufen *v* buy
kaum *adv* hardly
Kehle *f* throat
Keim *m* germ
kennenlernen *v* get acquainted, meet
Kern *m* pit
Kind *nt* child
Kirche *f* church
Kissen *nt* pillow
Klasse *f* class
Klatsch *m* gossip
Klavier *nt* piano
Kleid *nt* dress
klein *adj* little, small
klingeln *v* ring
klug *adj* clever
Knie *nt* knee
kochen *v* cook, boil
Koffer *m* suitcase

kommen *v* come
Konditorei *f* coffee shop
Konkurs *m* bankruptcy
Konzept *nt* plan, draft
Kopf *m* head
Kopfschmerz *m* headache
krank *adj* sick, ill
Krankenhaus *n* hospital
Krebs *m* cancer
Krieg *m* war
krumm *adj* crooked
Krüppel *m* cripple
Küche *f* kitchen
Kuchen *m* cake
Kunde *m* customer
Kunst *f* art
Künstler *m* artist
künstlich *adj* artificial
kürzlich *adv* recently
Kusine *f* female cousin
Kuss *m* kiss

L

lächeln *v* smile
lachen *v* laugh
Lachs *m* salmon
Laken *nt* sheet
langsam *adj* slow
Last *f* burden
lästig *adj* burdensome
Leben *nt* life
leben *v* live
ledig *adj* unmarried
leer *adj* empty
Lehrer *m* teacher
Lehrling *m* apprentice
leicht *adj* easy
leider *adv* unfortunately
leihen *v* lend
leise *adv* softly, *adj* soft
lernen *v* learn
lesen *v* read
Leute *pl* people
Licht *nt* light
Liebe *f* love
lieben *v* love
lieber *adv* rather
lieber haben *v* prefer
Literatur *f* literature
Locke *f* curl
Löffel *m* spoon
Luft *f* air
lügen *v* lie
Lust haben *v* like to

M

machen *v* make
Mädchen *nt* girl
Mahlzeit *f* meal
manchmal *adv* sometimes
Mann *m* man, husband
Mantel *m* overcoat
Märchen *nt* fairy tale
Markt *m* market
Maschine *f* machine
Maus *f* mouse
Mehl *nt* flour
mehrere *adj* several
Mensch *m* human being
merken *v* notice
Merkmal *nt* identification mark
messen *v* measure
Messer *nt* knife
Milch *f* milk
mit *prep* with
Mitglied *nt* member
Mittag *m* noon
Mitte *f* middle
Mitternacht *f* midnight
möglich *adj* possible
Monat *m* month
Mord *m* murder
Mörder *m* murderer
morgen *adv* tomorrow
Morgen *m* morning
Motor *m* engine, motor
Muschel *f* shell
Musik *f* music
Mutter *f* mother

N

Nachfolge *f* succession
Nachname *m* last name
Nachricht *f* news
Nacht *f* night
Nachteil *m* disadvantage
Nachtisch *m* dessert
Nadel *f* needle
nahe *adj* near, close
nähren *v* nurse
Nahrung *f* food
Name *m* name
Nase *f* nose
nass *adj* wet
Nässe *f* wetness
Natur *f* nature
natürlich *adj* natural, *adv* of course

neben *prep* next to, beside
Neffe *m* nephew
nehmen *v* take
Neid *m* envy
neiden *v* envy
Nichte *f* niece
nichts *pron* nothing
nieder *prep* down
Niedergang *m* decline
niedrig *adj* low
niemand *pron* nobody
Nummer *f* number

O

ob *prep* whether
Ober *m* waiter
obgleich *conj* although
oder *conj* or
Ofen *m* stove
öffnen *v* open
oft *adv* often
ohne *prep* without
ohnegleichen *adv* unequaled
ohnehin *adv* in any case
Ohr *nt* ear
Ohrfeige *f* slap in the face
Onkel *m* uncle
Oper *f* opera
Opfer *nt* sacrifice, victim
Ort *m* spot

P

packen *v* pack
Paket *nt* package
Panne *f* breakdown
Papagei *m* parrot
Papier *nt* paper
Papierkorb *m* wastepaper basket
Park *m* park
Pass *m* passport
Passagier *m* passenger
passieren *v* happen
Person *f* person
Pfeife *f* pipe
Pferd *nt* horse
Platz *m* place
Polizei *f* police
Polizeiwache *f* police station
Priester *m* priest
Programm *nt* program
prüfen *v* examine
Prüfung *f* examination
pünktlich *adj* punctual

Q

Qual *f* torture
quälen *v* torture
Qualität *f* quality

R

Rabe *m* raven
Rad *nt* wheel
Rauch *m* smoke
rauchen *v* smoke
rechnen *v* calculate, count
Recht *nt* right
recht *adj* right
recht haben *v* be right
rechtzeitig *adv* on time
Regen *m* rain
Regenmantel *m* raincoat
Regenschirm *m* umbrella
Regierung *f* government
regnen *v* rain
Reifen *m* tire
reinigen *v* clean
reisen *v* travel
reissen *v* tear
rennen *v* run
Reservereifen *m* spare tire
Rock *m* skirt
Roman *m* novel
rot *adj* red
Rücken *m* back
Rucksack *m* knapsack
Ruderboot *nt* rowboat
rufen *v* call
ruhig *adj* quiet, calm

S

sammeln *v* collect
Sammlung *f* collection
Sand *m* sand
Satz *m* sentence
schaffen *v* create
Schaffner *m* conductor
Schaffung *f* creation
scharf *adj* sharp
Scheibenwischer *m* windshield wiper
Schere *f* scissors
Schiff *nt* ship
Schinken *m* ham
schlafen *v* sleep
Schlagsahne *f* whipped cream
schlecht *adj* bad

schliessen *v* close
Schlips *m* necktie
Schloss *nt* castle
schmeicheln *v* flatter
schmutzig *adj* dirty
Schnee *m* snow
schneiden *v* cut
schnell *adj* fast, quick
Schokolade *f* chocolate
schön *adj* beautiful
Schornstein *m* chimney
schreiben *v* write
Schuh *m* shoe
Schule *f* school
Schurke *m* villain
schwach *adj* feeble, weak
schwarz *adj* black
Schwein *nt* pig
schwer *adj* heavy
Schwester *f* sister
Schwiegermutter *f* mother-in-law
Schwiegervater *m* father-in-law
sehen *v* to see
sehr *adv* much
seit *prep* since
Seite *f* page
seltsam *adj* strange
senden *v* send
Serviette *f* napkin
sich sorgen *v* worry
sich setzen *v* sit down
singen *v* sing
sitzen *v* sit
sogar *adv* even
Sohn *m* son
Sommer *m* summer
Sonne *f* sun
Sorge *f* worry
sparen *v* save
Speisekarte *f* menu
Spiegel *m* mirror
Spinne *f* spider
spinnen *v* spin
Sprache *f* language
sprechen *v* speak
Sprecher *m* speaker
Stadt *f* city, town
stark *adj* strong
Staub *m* dust
Stein *m* stone
sterben *v* die
steuern *v* conduct, steer
Steuerrad *nt* steering wheel
Stimme *f* voice, vote

Strand *m* beach
Strasse *f* street
streiten *v* quarrel, fight
studieren *v* study
Studium *nt* study
Stuhl *m* chair
Stunde *f* hour
suchen *v* seek, look for
Suppe *f* soup
surren *v* buzz
suspendieren *v* suspend
Szene *f* scene

T

Tag *m* day
Tankstelle *f* gas station
Tante *f* aunt
Tanz *m* dance
tanzen *v* dance
Tasse *f* cup
taub *adj* deaf
Tee *m* tea
teilnehmen *v* take part, participate
Telefon *nt* telephone
telefonieren *v* telephone
telegraphieren *v* telegraph
Teller *m* plate
teuer *adj* expensive
Theater *nt* theater
tief *adj* deep, low
Tier *nt* animal
Tierarzt *m* veterinarian
Tinte *f* ink
Tisch *m* table
Tochter *f* daughter
Topf *m* pot
Torte *f* fancy cake
tot *adj* dead, *n* **Tot** *m*
totmüde *adj* dead tired
tragen *v* carry
trauern *v* mourn
Traum *m* dream
träumen *v* dream
traurig *adj* sad
Treppe *f* staircase
treu *adj* faithful
trinken *v* drink
Trinkgeld *nt* tip
trocken *adj* dry
Trost *m* consolation
trösten *v* comfort
Tür *f* door
Turm *m* tower

U

über *prep* above, over
überraschen *v* surprise
Überraschung *f* surprise
übertreiben *v* exaggerate
Übertreibung *f* exaggeration
Übung *f* exercise
Uhr *f* clock, watch
ungeduldig *adj* impatient
ungefähr *adv* approximately
ungesund *adj* unhealthy
ungewöhnlich *adj* uncommon
unglücklich *adj* unhappy
Universität *f* university
unter *prep* underneath
unterbrechen *v* interrupt
Unterbrechung *f* interruption
Unterhaltung *f* conversation
Unterricht *m* instruction
unterschreiben *v* sign
unverschämt *adj* impudent
unvollendet *adj* unfinished
unzufrieden *adj* dissatisfied
Ursache *f* cause
ursprünglich *adv* originally

V

Vater *m* father
verbessern *v* improve
verbrennen *v* burn
vereinen *v* unite
vergessen *v* forget
verkaufen *v* sell
Verkehr *m* traffic
Verkehrsampel *f* traffic light
verlangen *v* demand
verlieren *v* lose
vermehren *v* increase
veröffentlichen *v* publish
verrückt *adj* crazy
verschwinden *v* disappear
versenden *v* ship
Versicherung *f* insurance
Verspätung *f* delay
verstehen *v* understand
Versuch *m* attempt
verteidigen *v* defend
vertraut *adj* familiar
verwunden *v* wound
verzeihen *v* pardon, forgive
Vetter *m* cousin
viel *adv* much
Vogel *m* bird

Volkslied *nt* folk song
Volksstamm *m* tribe
voll *adj* full
Vorbereitung *f* preparation
vorgestern *adv* day before yesterday
vorhaben *v* plan
vorher *adv* before
Vorhersage *f* prediction
vorhersagen *v* predict
vorhersehen *v* anticipate
Vorname *m* first name
Vorschlag *m* proposal
vorschlagen *v* propose
vorsichtig *adj* careful
Vorstadt *f* suburb
Vorstellung *f* performance
Vorteil *m* advantage

W

Waage *f* scale
wachsen *v* grow
wagen *v* risk
Wahl *f* election
wählen *v* choose
während *prep* during
Wahrheit *f* truth
wandern *v* wander
warm *adj* warm
warnen *v* warn
Warnung *f* warning
warten *v* wait
warum *adv and conj* why
Wasser *nt* water
wechseln *v* change
Weg *m* path
weich *adj* soft
weil *conj* because
weinen *v* cry
weiss *adj* white
weit *adj* far
weitergehen *v* go on
Welt *f* world
wenig *adj* little
wetten *v* bet
Wetter *nt* weather
wichtig *adj* important
wieder *adv* again
wiederholen *v* repeat
wiegen *v* weigh
wild *adj* wild
Windel *f* diaper
windig *adj* windy
Windschutzscheibe *f* windshield

Winter *m* winter
Winterfrische *f* winter resort
Wintergarten *m* conservatory
winterlich *adj* wintry
winzig *adj* tiny
wir *pron* we
wirbeln *v* whirl
wirken *v* work
wirklich *adj* actual, real
Wirtshaus *nt* inn
wissen *v* know
Wissenschaft *f* science, learning
Woche *f* week
wöchentlich *adv* weekly
Wolkenkratzer *m* skyscraper
Wörterbuch *n* dictionary
Wunder *nt* miracle
wunderbar *adj* wonderful
Wunderkind *n* prodigy
Wunsch *m* desire, wish
wünschen *v* want

Z

zahlen *v* pay
Zahn *m* tooth
Zahnarzt *m* dentist
Zahnbürste *f* toothbrush
zährtlich *adj* tender
Zehe *f* toe
zeigen *v* show
Zeitalter *nt* age
Zeitung *f* newspaper
Zentrum *nt* center
zerbrechen *v* break
ziehen *v* pull
Ziel *nt* aim
ziemlich *adv* rather
Zimmer *nt* room
zittern *v* tremble
zögernd *adv* reluctantly
Zorn *m* anger
Zucker *m* sugar
Zufall *m* accident
Zug *m* train
zuhören *v* listen
zumachen *v* close
Zündung *f* ignition
Zunge *f* tongue
zurück *adv* back, behind
zurückkommen *v* return
zusammen *adj* together
zwingen *v* force
Zwinger *m* kennel
zwischen *prep* between

Dictionary abbreviations. Nouns are identified as masculine *(nm)*, feminine *(nf)*, or neuter *(nt)*. Adjectives are identified as *adj*, adverbs as *adv*, conjunctions as *conj*, interjections as *interj*, prepositions as *prep*, pronouns as *pron*, and verbs as *v*. Plurals are identified as *pl*.

English-German

A

above *prep* über
action *n* Handlung *f*
add *v* hinzufügen
adorn *v* garnieren
advantage *n* Vorteil *m*
adventure *n* Abenteuer *nt*
adversary *n* Gegner *m*
again *adv* wieder
against *prep* gegen
age *n* Zeitalter *nt*
age *v* altern
air *n* Luft *f*
airplane *n* Flugzeug *nt*
alleviate *v* erleichtern
almost *adv* fast
already *adv* schon
although *conj* obgleich
always *adv* immer
angel *n* Engel *m*
animal *n* Tier *nt*
answer *n* Antwort *f*, *v* antworten
anticipate *v* vorhersehen
appendix *n* (medical)
    Blinddarm *m*
apprentice *n* Lehrling *m*
approximately *adv* ungefähr
arm *n* Arm *m*
arrive *v* ankommen
arson *n* Brandstiftung *f*
art *n* Kunst *f*
artist *n* Künstler *m*
attempt *n* Versuch *m*
attempt *v* versuchen
aunt *n* Tante *f*
autumn *n* Herbst *m*
award *n* Belohnung *f*

B

back *adv* zurück
background *n* Hintergrund *m*
bad *adj* schlecht
bake *v* backen
ball *n* Ball *m*
ban *v* verbannen

bark *v* bellen
beach *n* Strand *m*
beard *n* Bart *m*
beautiful *adj* schön
because *adv* weil
bed *n* Bett *nt*
before *adv* vorher
behind *prep* hinter
bell *n* Glocke *f*
belong *v* gehören
beside *prep* neben
bet *v* wetten
between *prep* zwischen
beyond *adv* jenseits
big *adj* gross
birth *n* Geburt *f*
birthday *n* Geburtstag *m*
bite *v* beissen
black *adj* schwarz
blind *adj* blind
bloom *v* blühen
blue *adj* blau
book *n* Buch *nt*
borrow *v* borgen
boss *n* Chef *m*
bottle *n* Flasche *f*
brake *n* Bremse *f*
bread *n* Brot *nt*
breakdown *n* Panne *f*
breakfast *n* Frühstück *nt*
breath *n* Atem *m*
breathe *v* atmen
bribe *n* Bestechung *f*
bribe *v* bestechen
bride *n* Braut *f*
bridegroom *n* Bräutigam *m*
bridge *n* Brücke *f*
broom *n* Besen *m*
brother *n* Bruder *m*
brown *adj* braun
build *v* bauen
burden *n* Last *f*
burden *v* belasten
burglar *n* Einbrecher *m*
burn *v* brennen
but *conj* aber
buy *v* kaufen

C

cabin *n* Hütte *f*
cake *n* Kuchen *m*
cancer *n* Krebs *m*
capable *adj* fähig
capital *n* Hauptstadt *f*
careful *adj* vorsichtig
carry *v* tragen
castle *n* Schloss *nt*
cause *n* Ursache *f*
cautious *adj* vorsichtig
certainly *adv* gewiss
chair *n* Stuhl *m*
chamber music *n*
    Kammermusik *f*
change *v* wechseln, *n*
    Kleingeld *nt*
character *n* Charakter *m*
chase *v* jagen
cheese *n* Käse *m*
chemistry *n* Chemie *f*
chew *v* kauen
chiefly *adv* hauptsächlich
child *n* Kind *nt*
chimney *n* Schornstein *m*
chocolate *n* Schokolade *f*
choose *v* wählen
Christian *adj* christlich
Christmas eve *n* Heiligabend *m*
church *n* Kirche *f*
citizen *n* Bürger *m*
city *n* Stadt *f*
class *n* Klasse *f*
clean *v* reinigen
clever *adj* klug
close *v* schliessen
coat *n* Mantel *m*
coffee shop *n* Konditorei *f*
cold *adj* kalt
collect *v* sammeln
collection *n* Sammlung *f*
color *n* Farbe *f*
color picture *n* Farbaufnahme *f*
come *v* kommen
comfortable *adj* bequem
compassion *n* Mitleid *nt*
compassionate *adj* mitleidig
complain *v* sich beschweren
complaint *n* Beschwerde *f*
conductor *n* (train) Schaffner *m*
confess *v* gestehen
confession *n* Geständnis *nt*
congratulate *v* gratulieren
conscience *n* Gewissen *m*

Review of German Grammar

consolation *n* Trost *m*
contents *n* Inhalt *m*
continuation *n* Fortsetzung *f*
continue *v* fortfahren
cook *n* Koch *m, v* kochen
corner *n* Ecke *f*
cough *v* husten
courage *n* Mut *m*
cousin *n* Vetter *m*, Kusine *f*
create *v* schaffen
creation *n* Schaffung *f*
cup *n* Tasse *f*
customer *n* Kunde *m*
cut *v* schneiden

D

daily *adj.* täglich
damp *adj* feucht
danger *n* Gefahr *f*
dangerous *adj* gefährlich
dark *adj* dunkel
daughter *n* Tochter *f*
day *n* Tag *m*
dead *adj* tot
dead tired *adj* todmüde
deaf *adj* taub
death *n* Tod *m*
decent *adj* anständig
decline *n* Niedergang *m*
decline *v* ablehnen
deep *adj* tief
defend *v* verteidigen
defense *n* Verteidigung *f*
delay *n* Verzögerung *f*
describe *v* beschreiben
description *n* Beschreibung *f*
desire *n* Wunsch *m*
determine *v* bestimmen
develop *v* entwickeln
dictionary *n* Wörterbuch *nt*
die *v* sterben
difficult *adj* schwierig
dig *v* graben
diligent *adj* fleissig
disadvantage *n* Nachteil *m*
dismiss *v* entlassen
dismissal *n* Entlassung
dissatisfied *adj* unzufrieden
distinguish *v* unterscheiden
ditch *n* Graben *m*
divine *adj* göttlich
doctor *n* Arzt *m*
dog *n* Hund *m*
donkey *n* Esel *m*

door *n* Tür *f*
dream *n* Traum *m*
dress *n* Kleid *n*
drink *v* trinken
driver *n* Fahrer *m*
driver's license *n*
  Führerschein *m*
drugstore *n* Drogerie *f*
dry *adj* trocken
during *prep* während
dust *n* Staub *m*

E

eagle *n* Adler *m*
ear *n* Ohr *nt*
early *adv* früh
easy *adj* leicht
eat *v* essen
egg *n* Ei *nt*
egotism *n* Egoismus *m*
elbow *n* Ellbogen *m*
elect *v* auserwählen
election *n* Wahl *f*
emigrant *n* Auswanderer *m*
empty *adj* leer
end *n* Ende *nt*
enemy *n* Feind *m*
engine *n* Motor *m*
enough *adv* genug
enrich *v* bereichern
entrance *n* Eingang *m*
envelope *n* Umschlag *m*
envoy *n* Gesandte *m*
envy *n* Neid *m*
envy *v* neiden
eradicate *v* ausrotten
error *n* Fehler *m*
Europe *n* Europa *nt*
even *adv* sogar
evening *n* Abend *m*
exaggerate *v* übertreiben
exaggeration *n* Übertreibung *f*
except *prep* ausser
excess *n* Übermass *nt*
excursion *n* Ausflug *m*
exhaust *n* Auspuff *m*
exhaust *v* erschöpfen
exhausted *adj* erschöpft
exhibit *n* Austellung *m*
exhibit *v* ausstellen
exit *n* Ausgang *m*
expensive *adj* teuer
explain *v* erklären
eye *n* Auge *nt*

F

face *n* Gesicht *nt*
facilitate *v* erleichtern
fairy tale *n* Märchen *nt*
faithful *adj* treu
false *adj* falsch
familiar *adj* vertraut
family *n* Familie *f*
famous *adj* berühmt
far *adj* weit
fast *adj* schnell
father *n* Vater *m*
father-in-law *n*
  Schwiegervater *m*
fear *n* Furcht *f, v* fürchten
fee *n* Gebühr *f*
fight *n* Kampf *m, v* kämpfen
finally *adv* endlich
find *v* finden
finger *n* Finger *m*
fire *n* Feuer *nt*
first name *n* Vorname *m*
fish *n* Fisch *m*
fish *v* fischen
flatter *v* schmeicheln
flour *n* Mehl *nt*
flower *n* Blume *f*
flue *n* Grippe *f*
food *n* Nahrung *f*
foot *n* Fuss *m*
for *prep* für
force *v* zwingen
foreign worker *n* Gastarbeiter *m*
forget *v* vergessen
forgive *v* vergeben
fox *n* Fuchs *m*
France *n* Frankreich *nt*
freeze *v* frieren
French *adj* französisch
friend *n* Freund *m*, Freundin *f*
friendly *adj* freundlich
fright *n* Furcht *f*
frog *n* Frosch *m*

G

gas station *n* Tankstelle *f*
get up *v* aufstehen
girl *n* Mädchen *nt*
give *v* geben
glass *n* Glas *nt*
glove *n* Handschuh *m*
go *v* gehen
God *n* Gott *m*

good *adj* gut
goodby *interj* auf Wiedersehen
gossip *n* Klatsch *m*
government *n* Regierung *f*
grandchild *n* Enkel *m*, Enkelin *f*
gratitude *n* Dankbarkeit *f*
green *adj* grün
greet *v* grüssen
greeting *n* Gruss *m*
group *n* Gruppe *f*
grow *v* wachsen
guest *n* Gast *m*

H

hail *n* Hagel *m*, *v* hageln
hair *n* Haar *nt*
ham *n* Schinken *m*
hand *n* Hand *f*
happen *v* passieren
harbor *n* Hafen *m*
hardly *adv* kaum
hat *n* Hut *m*
hay *n* Heu *nt*
head *n* Kopf *m*
headache *n* Kopfschmerz *m*
heal *v* heilen
healthy *adj* gesund
hear *v* hören
heart *n* Herz *nt*
heartily *adv* herzlich
heath *n* Heide *f*
heavy *adj* schwer
hell *n* Hölle *f*
help *n* Hilfe *f*, *v* helfen
helpless *adj* hilflos
here *adv* hier
high *adj* hoch
highlight *n* Höhepunkt *m*
highly *adv* höchst
hilarious *adj* ausgelassen
holiday *n* Feiertag *m*
hope *n* Hoffnung *f*
hope *v* hoffen
horse *n* Pferd *nt*
hospital *n* Krankenhaus *nt*
host *n* Gastgeber *m*
hour *n* Stunde *f*
house *n* Haus *nt*
human being *n* Mensch *m*
hunger *n* Hunger *m*
hungry *adj* hungrig
hunt *n* Jagd *f*
hunt *v* jagen
husband *n* Mann *m*

I

idea *n* Gedanke *m*
ignition *n* Zündung *f*
ill *adj* krank
immigrant *n* Einwanderer *m*
impatient *adj* ungeduldig
import *n* Einfuhr *f*
import *v* einführen
important *adj* wichtig
impress *v* beeindrucken
impression *n* Eindruck *m*
improve *v* verbessern
impudent *adj* unverschämt
incision *n* Einschnitt *m*
income *n* Einkommen *nt*
increase *v* vermehren
inexpensive *adj* billig
ink *n* Tinte *f*
inn *n* Wirtshaus *nt*, Gasthaus *nt*
instead of *conj* anstatt
instruction *n* Unterricht *m*
insurance *n* Versicherung *f*
interesting *adj* interessant
interrupt *v* unterbrechen
interruption *n* Unterbrechung *f*
introduce *v* bekannt machen,
   einführen
invent *v* erfinden
invention *n* Erfindung *f*
invite *v* einladen
ivy *n* Efeu *m*

K

kennel *n* Zwinger *m*
kind *adj* freundlich, *n* Art *f*
kiss *n* Kuss *m*
kitchen *n* Küche *nt*
knee *n* Knie *nt*
knife *n* Messer *nt*
know *v* wissen

L

lady *n* Dame *f*
landlord *n* Hauswirt *m*
last name *n* Nachname *m*
laugh *n* Lachen *nt*, *v* lachen
law *n* Gesetz *nt*
lazy *adj* faul
learn *v* lernen
leg *n* Bein *nt*
lend *v* leihen
letter *n* Brief *m*

liberty *n* Freiheit *f*
lie *v* (recline) liegen, (tell
   untruth) lügen, *n* (untruth)
   Lüge *f*
light *adj* (color) hell, (weight)
   leicht
lightning *n* Blitz *m*
like to *v* gern
listen *v* zuhören
literature *n* Literatur *f*
little *adj* klein
live *v* leben
living room *n* Wohnzimmer *nt*
loan *n* Anleihe *f*
lock *v* zuschliessen
lose *v* verlieren
loud *adj* laut
love *n* Liebe *f*, *v* lieben
low *adj* niedrig
luck *n* Glück

M

machine *n* Maschine *f*
Main Street *n* Hauptstrasse *f*
majority *n* Mehrheit *f*
make *v* machen
man *n* Mann *m*
many *adj* viel
market *n* Markt *m*
meal *n* Mahlzeit *f*
mean *v* meinen
measure *n* Mass *nt*
measure *v* messen
meet *v* treffen
member *n* Mitglied *nt*
memory *n* Gedächtnis *nt*
menu *n* Speisekarte *f*
merry *adj* fröhlich
middle *n* Mitte *f*
midnight *n* Mitternacht *f*
milk *n* Milch *f*
minority *n* Minderhait *f*
miracle *n* Wunder *n*
mirror *n* Spiegel *m*
miserable *adj* erbärmlich
mistake *n* Fehler *m*
modest *adj* bescheiden
modesty *n* Bescheidenheit *f*
money *n* Geld *nt*
month *n* Monat *m*
mother *n* Mutter *f*
mother-in-law *n*
   Schwiegermutter *f*
mountain *n* Berg *m*

mourning *n* Trauer *f*
mouse *n* Maus *f*
murder *n* Mord *m*
murderer *n* Mörder *m*
muscle *n* Muskel *m*
music *n* Musik *f*

N

name *n* Name *m*
name *v* ernennen
napkin *n* Serviette *f*
naturally *adv* natürlich
near *adv* nahe
necessary *adj* nötig
neck *n* Nacken *m*
necktie *n* Krawatte *f*, Schlips *m*
needle *n* Nadel *f*
nephew *n* Neffe *m*
never *adv* nie
news *n* Nachricht *f*
next to *prep* neben
niece *n* Nichte *f*
night *n* Nacht *f*
noise *n* Lärm *m*
noon *n* Mittag *m*
no one *pron* niemand
nose *n* Nase *f*
notebook *n* Heft *nt*
nothing *pron* nichts
notice *v* merken
nurse *n* Krankenschwester *f*
nurse *v* nähren

O

oath *n* Eid *m*
obedience *n* Gehorsam *m*
obedient *adj* gehorsam
observation *n* Beobachtung *f*
observe *v* beobachten
occasion *n* Gelegenheit *f*
often *adv* oft
old *adj* alt
on time *adv* rechtzeitig
open *v* öffnen, *adj* offen
opera *n* Oper *f*
or *conj* oder
originally *adv* ursprünglich
otherwise *adv* sonst
outside *adv* draussen

P

pack *v* packen
package *n* Paket *nt*

page *n* Seite *f*
pale *adj* blass
paper *n* Papier *nt*
parents *n* Eltern *pl*
park *n* Park *m*
parrot *n* Papagei *m*
passenger *n* Passagier *m*
passport *n* Pass *m*
patience *n* Geduld *f*
patiently *adv* geduldig
pay *v* zahlen
peculiar *adj* besonders
pea *n* Erbse *f*
peace *n* Friede *m*
pencil *n* Bleistift *m*
people *n* Leute *pl*
person *n* Person *f*
piano *n* Klavier *nt*
pig *n* Schwein *nt*
pillow *n* Kissen *nt*
pipe *n* Pfeife *f*
place *n* Platz *m*
plate *n* Teller *m*
please *interj* bitte, *v* gefallen
poem *n* Gedicht *m*
poet *n* Dichter *m*
police *n* Polizei *f*
police station *n* Polizeiwache *f*
polite *adj* höflich
poor *adj* arm
population *n* Bevölkerung *f*
possible *adj* möglich
pot *n* Topf *m*
potato *n* Kartoffel *f*
pray *v* beten
precisely *adv* genau
predict *v* vorhersagen
prediction *n* Vorhersage *f*
prefer *v* vorziehen
presence *n* Gegenwart *f*
present *n* (gift) Geschenk *nt*
pressure *n* Druck *m*
pretty *adj* hübsch
priest *n* Priester *m*
prison *n* Gefängnis *nt*
profound *adv* gründlich
program *n* Programm *nt*
property *n* Eigentum *nt*
proposal *n* Vorschlag *m*
propose *v* vorschlagen
publish *v* veröffentlichen
publisher *n* Herausgeber *m*
punctual *adj* pünktlich
punish *v* bestrafen
purchase *v* kaufen

Q

quarrel *v* streiten
question *n* Frage *f*
quick *adj* schnell
quiet *adj* ruhig

R

rain *n* Regen *m*, *v* regnen
raincoat *n* Regenmantel *m*
read *v* lesen
ready *adj* bereit
receive *v* erhalten
recently *adv* kürzlich
red *adj* rot
relative *n* Verwandte *m*
reluctant *adj* zögernd
remember *v* sich erinnern an
remorse *n* Gewissensbisse *pl*
request *n* Forderung *f*
request *v* fordern
responsible *adj* verantwortlich
result *n* Ergebnis *nt*
retain *v* zurückbehalten
ride *v* fahren
ring *v* klingeln
rob *v* rauben
robbery *n* Raub *m*
room *n* Zimmer *nt*
runner *n* Läufer *m*

S

sad *adj* traurig
sand *n* Sand *m*
save *v* sparen
scarce *adj* selten
scarcely *adv* kaum
school *n* Schule *f*
science *n* Wissenschaft *f*
scientist *n* Wissenschaftler *m*
scissors *n* Schere *f*
secret *n* Geheimnis *m*
secret *adj* geheim
see *v* sehen
seek *v* suchen
sell *v* verkaufen
send *v* schicken
sentence *n* (grammar) Satz *m*, (judgment) Urteil *nt*
serious *adj* ernst
several *adj* mehrere
share *n* Anteil *m*
share *v* teilen

sharp *adj* scharf
sheet *n* Laken *nt*
shell *n* Muschel *f*
ship *n* Schiff *nt*
ship *v* versenden
shirt *n* Hemd *nt*
shoe *n* Schuh *m*
show *v* zeigen
shut *v* schliessen
sick *adj* krank
siege *n* Belagerung *f*
sign *n* Zeichen *nt*,
   v unterschreiben
similar *adj* ähnlich
simultaneously *adv* gleichzeitig
since *prep* seit
sing *v* singen
sit down *v* sich setzen
skin *n* Haut *f*
skirt *n* Rock *m*
sky *n* Himmel *m*
skyscraper *n* Wolkenkratzer *m*
slaughter *v* schlachten
sleep *v* schlafen
slippery *adj* glatt
slow *adj* langsam
smile *n* Lächeln *nt*, *v* lächeln
smoke *n* Rauch *m*, *v* rauchen
snow *n* Schnee *m*
soft *adj* weich
softly *adv* leise
soiled *adj* schmutzig
somebody *pron* jemand
sometimes *adv* manchmal
son *n* Sohn *m*
soon *adv* bald
soup *n* Suppe *f*
spacious *adj* geräumig
spare tire *n* Ersatzreifen *m*
spark *n* Funke *m*
spark *v* funkeln
speak *v* sprechen
speaker *n* Sprecher *m*
spider *n* Spinne *f*
splendid *adj* herrlich
spoon *n* Löffel *m*
spring *n* Frühling *m*
stamp *n* Briefmarke *f*
staircase *n* Treppe *f*
starve *v* hungern
station *n* (train) Bahnhof *m*
steam *n* Dampf *m*
steer *v* steuern
steering wheel *n* Steuerrad *nt*
stone *n* Stein *m*

stove *n* Ofen *m*
strange *adj* seltsam
street *n* Strasse *f*
strong *adj* stark
study *n* Studium *nt*, *v* studieren
succession *n* Nachfolge *f*
suddenly *adv* plötzlich
sugar *n* Zucker *m*
suit *n* Anzug *m*
suitcase *n* Koffer *m*
summer *n* Sommer *m*
sun *n* Sonne *f*
surgeon *n* Chirurg *m*
swallow *n* Schwalbe *f*
swallow *v* schlucken
sweep *v* fegen

T

table *n* Tisch *m*
table of contents *n*
   Inhaltsverzeichnis *nt*
take *v* nehmen
take part *v* teilnehmen
tale *n* Erzählung *f*
tall *adj* gross
task *n* Aufgabe *f*
tea *n* Tee *m*
teacher *n* Lehrer *m*, Lehrerin *f*
telephone *n* Telefon *nt*
telephone *v* telefonieren
tell *v* erzählen
teller *n* (bank) Kassier *m*
temporary *adj* vorübergehend
thank *v* danken
theater *n* Theater *nt*
therefore *adv* also
thick *adj* dick
thief *n* Dieb *m*
thing *n* Ding *nt*
think *v* denken
thirst *n* Durst *m*
thought *n* Gedanke *m*
thumb *n* Daumen *m*
thunder *n* Donner *m*
thunderstorm *n* Gewitter *nt*
time *n* Zeit *f*
timetable *n* Fahrplan *m*
tip *n* Trinkgeld *nt*
tire *n* Reifen *m*
today *adv* heute
together *adv* zusammen
tolerate *v* ertragen
tomorrow *adv* morgen
tongue *n* Zunge *f*

torture *n* Qual *f*
torture *v* quälen
towel *n* Handtuch *nt*
town *n* Stadt *f*
trade *n* Handel *m*
traffic *n* Verkehr *m*
traffic light *n* Verkehrsampel *f*
train *n* Zug *m*
transmission *n* Übertragung *f*
transmit *v* übertragen
travel *v* reisen
tree *n* Baum *m*
tribe *n* Volksstamm *m*
true *adj* wahr
truth *n* Wahrheit *f*

U

umbrella *n* Regenschirm *m*
uncle *n* Onkel *m*
uncommon *adj* ungewöhnlich
under *prep* unter
understand *v* verstehen
unfinished *adj* unvollendet
unfortunately *adv* leider
unhappy *adj* unglücklich
unhealthy *adj* ungesund
university *n* Universität *f*
unmarried *adj* ledig
unusual *adj* ungewöhnlich
urgent *adj* dringend
use *v* benutzen

V

vacation *n* Ferien *pl*
valid *adj* gültig
very *adv* sehr
veterinarian *n* Tierarzt *m*
victim *n* Opfer *nt*
villain *n* Schurke *m*
violence *n* Gewalttätigkeit *f*
violent *adj* heftig
visit *n* Besuch *m*, *v* besuchen
voice *n* Stimme *f*
vote *v* wählen
voter *n* Wähler *m*
vouch for *v* garantieren

W

wait *v* warten
waiter *n* Ober *m*
war *n* Krieg *m*
wash *v* waschen

waste basket *n* Papierkorb *m*
watch *v* aufpassen
water *n* Wasser *nt*
waterfall *n* Wasserfall *m*
waterproof *adj* wasserdicht
wave *n* Welle *f*
waver *v* schwanken
wavy *adj* wellig
wax *n* Wachs *nt*
way *n* Weg *m*
we *pron* wir
weak *adj* schwach
weaken *v* schwächen, **feel weak**
  v schwach werden
weakness *n* Schwäche *f*
wealth *n* Reichtum *m*
wealthy *adj* reich
weapon *n* Waffe *f*
wear *v* tragen
wear out *v* abtragen
weary *adj* müde
weather *n* Wetter *nt*
wedding *n* Hochzeit *f*
week *n* Woche *f*
weekly *adv and adj* wöchentlich
weep *v* weinen
weigh *v* wiegen
weight *n* Gewicht *nt*
weird *adj* unheimlich
welcome *n* Willkommen *nt*
welcome *v* bewillkommnen
welfare *n* Wohlergehen *nt*
well *adv* gut, (health) gesund
well *n* Brunnen *m*
well-known *adj* bekannt
west *n* Westen *m*
western *adj* westlich
wet *adj* nass
wetness *n* Nässe *f*
wheel *n* Rad *nt*
when *conj* als, *adv* wann
whether *conj* ob
which *adj and pron* welcher
whichever *adj and pron* welcher
while *conj* während
while *n* Weile *f*
whim *n* Laune *f*
whip *n* Peitsche *f*
whip *v* schlagen
whipped cream *n* Schlagsahne *f*
whirl *v* wirbeln
whirlpool *n* Strudel *m*
whirlwind *n* Wirbelwind *m*
whisker *n* Barthaar *nt*
whiskey *n* Whisky *m*

whisper *v* flüstern
whistle *n* Flöte *f*
whistle *v* flöten
white *adj* weiss
wife *n* Frau *f*
wig *n* Perücke *f*
wild *adj* wild
wilderness *n* Wildnis *f*
will *n* Wille *m*
will *v* (future) werden,
  (bequeath) vermachen, (want
  to) wollen
willful *adj* eigensinnig
willow *n* Weide *f*
wilt *v* welken
wilted *adj* welk
win *v* gewinnen
wind *n* Wind *m*
wind *v* aufziehen
windshield *n*
  Windschutzscheibe *f*
windshield wiper *n*
  Scheibenwischer *m*
windy *adj* windig
winter *n* Winter *m*
wire *n* Draht *m*
wire *v* drahten
wish *n* Wunsch *m, v* wünschen
with *prep* mit
within *prep* innerhalb
without *prep* ohne
witness *n* Zeuge *m*
witty *adj* witzig
woe *n* Leid *nt*
wolf *n* Wolf *m*
woman *n* Frau *f*
wood *n* Holz *nt*
woods *n* Wald *m*

word *n* Wort *nt*
work *n* Arbeit *f, v* arbeiten
world *n* Welt *f*
worldly *adj* weltlich
worm *n* Wurm *m*
worn-out *adj* abgenutzt
worry *n* Sorge *f*
worry *v* sich sorgen
worse *adj* schlechter
worship *n* Verehrung *f*
worship *v* verehren
worst *adj* schlechtest
worth *n* Wert *m*
worthless *adj* wertlos
worthy *adj* würdig
wound *n* Wunde *f*
wound *v* verwunden
wrap *n* Umhang *m*
wrap *v* wickeln
wrath *n* Zorn *m*
wreath *n* Kranz *m*
wreck *n* Wrack *nt*
wreck *v* demolieren
wrist *n* Handgelenk *nt*
wristwatch *n* Armbanduhr *f*
write *v* schreiben
write poetry *v* dichten

Y

year *n* Jahr *nt*
yell *v* schreien
yellow *adj* gelb
yesterday *adv* gestern
young *adj* jung
youth *n* Jugend *f*
youthful *adj* jugendlich

For further reference

Texts
Huebener, Theodore, and Newmark,
Maxim
A First Course in German
D.C. Heath and Company
Lange, Eva C.
German in 20 Lessons
R.D. Cortina

Steinhauer, Harry
Read, Write, Speak German
Bantam Books
Steinhauer, Harry, and Sundermeyer,
William
Introduction to German
Macmillan

Dictionaries
Cassell
German/English; English/German
Macmillan

Wehrle, Hugo
Deutscher Wortschatz
Ernst Klett Verlag.

Review of Spanish Grammar

Spanish grammar shares certain characteristics with English grammar, as you may recall from the time when you first studied these languages. For the most part, the names of the parts of speech and the terms used to show how words function in a sentence are the same. Read carefully the sections presented here and consult the Spanish-English and English-Spanish dictionaries at the end of this review. No matter how long you have been away from the formal study of Spanish, you will quickly find yourself recalling what you once learned.

Spanish in Spain and Spanish America

Pronunciation. The *z, ce,* and *ci* are pronounced alike. In southern Spain and Spanish America, they are pronounced like the *s* in *sin.* In central and northern Spain, they are pronounced like the *th* in *thin* and *fifth.*

azúcar sugar
ah-soo-kahr   (Spanish America, southern Spain)
ah-thoo-kahr   (central and northern Spain)

quince fifteen
keen-say   (Spanish America, southern Spain)
keen-thay   (central and northern Spain)

hacienda farm
ah-see-en-dah (Spanish America, southern Spain)
ah-thee-en-dah (central and northern Spain)

The *ll* in southern Spain and Spanish America is pronounced like the *y* in *yes.* In central and north-ern Spain, the *ll* is pronounced like the *ly* sound in the second syllable of *million.*

gallo rooster
gah-yoh   (Spanish America, southern Spain)
gah-lyoh   (central and northern Spain)

Vocabulary. Certain words and expressions differ in Spain and Spanish America, but the differences are minor. A native of one Spanish-speaking country is easily understood by natives of other Spanish-speaking countries.

to drive	*conducir*	(Spain)
	manejar	(Spanish America)
bus	*autobus*	(Spain)
	camión	(Mexico)
peas	*guisantes*	(Spain)
	chícharos	(Spanish America)

The *tortilla* in Spain is an omelet; in Mexico and Guatemala it is a flat corn cake.

Articles

Definite and indefinite articles

	Singular		Plural	
	Masc.	*Fem.*	*Masc.*	*Fem.*
Definite: the	*el*	*la*	*los*	*las*
Indefinite: a, an	*un*	*una*		
some, a few			*unos*	*unas*

The neuter article *lo* is used with adjectives and past participles when they are used as nouns.

    lo bueno y lo malo the good and the bad

Agreement

Articles agree in number and gender with the nouns they modify.

    el niño the boy   *una niña* a girl

El is used instead of *la* before a feminine singular noun that begins with a stressed *a* or *ha*.

    el hacha the ax

Contractions of *el*

The prepositions *de* and *a* combine with the masculine article *el* to form *del* and *al*.

    Voy al cine. I am going to the movies.

Uses of the definite article

Before each noun in a series.

    El padre y el hijo van al centro.

    The father and son are going downtown.

Before the names of languages except directly after *hablar, en,* or *de.*

    El español es importante hoy.

    Spanish is important today.

    Mi padre habla alemán.

    My father speaks German.

Before titles such as *señor, doctor,* and *profesor,* except in direct address.

    El señor López llegó ayer.

    Mr. Lopez arrived yesterday.

    ¿Cómo está usted, señora Gómez?

    How are you, Mrs. Gomez?

Instead of the possessive with clothing and parts of the body.

    Me lavo las manos. I wash my hands.

To express "o'clock."

    Son las ocho. It is eight o'clock.

Before nouns used in a general or abstract sense.

    La medicina es una profesión noble.

    Medicine is a noble profession.

Before an infinitive used as a noun.

    El comer es necesario. Eating is necessary.

With the names of seasons.

    La primavera empieza en marzo.

    Spring begins in March.

With days of the week, except after *ser.*

    Voy de compras el sábado.

    I'm going shopping on Saturday.

    Hoy es jueves.

    Today is Thursday.

Before certain geographic names such as:

    la Argentina Argentina

    el Brasil Brazil

    los Estados Unidos United States

To express *a* or *an* with weights or measures.

    dos pesos el metro two pesos a meter

Omission of the definite article

Before nouns in apposition.

    Antonio, criado de los García, llegó tarde.

    Anthony, the Garcias' servant, arrived late.

Before numerals expressing numerical order of rulers.

    Carlos Quinto Charles the Fifth

Omission of the indefinite article

Before unmodified predicate nouns indicating occupation, profession, or nationality.

    Su hermano es médico. His brother is a physician.

Before *cien, cierto, mil, otro,* and *tal.*

    cien dólares a hundred dollars

    cierto libro a certain book

    mil estudiantes a thousand students

    otro amigo another friend

    tal padre such a father

After the exclamatory *¡que!*

    ¡Qué mujer! What a woman!

Nouns

Gender
Nouns referring to males and nouns ending in *o* are generally masculine.

> *el cuaderno* the notebook
> *el abuelo* the grandfather

Nouns referring to females and nouns ending in *-a,
-ión, -dad, -tad, -tud,* or *-umbre* are generally feminine.

> *la nación* the nation *la madre* the mother

Exceptions
Feminine nouns ending in *o*.

> *la mano* the hand *la radio* the radio

Masculine nouns ending in *a*.

> *el drama* the drama
> *el clima* the climate
> *el poeta* the poet
> *el problema* the problem
> *el tranvía* the streetcar
> *el idioma* the language
> *el mapa* the map

Plurals
For nouns ending in a vowel, add *s;* for nouns ending in a consonant, add *es*.

> *el libro, los libros* the book, the books
> *la pared, las paredes* the wall, the walls

For nouns ending in *z*, change *z* to *c* before adding *es*.

> *la luz, las luces* the light, the lights

Nouns ending in an unaccented syllable with final *s* remain unchanged in the plural.

> *el cumpleaños, los cumpleaños*
> the birthday, the birthdays

For nouns ending in an accented syllable with final *n* or *s*, drop the written accent in the plural.

> *el jardín, los jardines* the garden, the gardens

Nouns indicating rank or relationship may be used in the masculine plural to designate individuals of either sex.

> *los reyes* the kings, or the king and queen

Adjectives and adverbs

Adjectives
Adjectives whose masculine singular forms end in *o* and adjectives of nationality have two singular, two plural forms. All others have one singular, one plural.

Agreement
An adjective agrees in gender and number with the noun modified. An adjective modifying nouns of different genders is generally masculine plural.

> *Los lápices y las plumas son caros.*
> The pencils and pens are expensive.

Position
A descriptive adjective usually follows the noun it modifies.

> *el papel blanco* the white paper

A limiting adjective such as a possessive, a demonstrative, or a number, and an adjective of quantity usually precede the noun.

> *ese vaso* that glass

The following adjectives drop the final *o* before a masculine singular noun: *bueno, malo, uno, primero, tercero, alguno, ninguno*.

> *el primer día* the first day

Grande becomes *gran* before a singular noun of either gender.

> *un gran pintor* a great painter

Ciento becomes *cien* immediately before a noun of either gender.

> *cien vacas* one hundred cows

Forms of adjectives

| | Singular | | Plural | |
	Masc.	Fem.	Masc.	Fem.
tall	*alto*	*alta*	*altos*	*altas*
English	*inglés*	*inglesa*	*ingleses*	*inglesas*
poor	*pobre*	*pobre*	*pobres*	*pobres*
easy	*fácil*	*fácil*	*fáciles*	*fáciles*

Common adjectives that change meaning with a change in position

	AFTER *the noun*	BEFORE *the noun*
antiguo	old (ancient)	old (former), old-time
cierto	sure, reliable	a certain
grande	large, big	great, famous
nuevo	new	another, different
pobre	poor	unfortunate
simple	silly, simple-minded	simple, mere

406

Demonstrative adjectives

	Masc.	*Fem.*
this	este	esta
these	estos	estas
that	ese	esa
those	esos	esas
that	aquel	aquella
those	aquellos	aquellas

(speech bubble: aquellos libros)

Demonstrative adjectives

Demonstrative adjectives precede the nouns they modify and agree with them in number and gender.

esas manzanas those apples

Este refers to what is near the speaker. *Ese* refers to what is near the person addressed.

Aquel refers to what is remote from both the speaker and the person addressed.

Juan, déme Vd. aquellos libros que están en la sala.
John, give me those books that are in the living room.

Adverbs

Many adverbs are formed by adding the suffix *-mente* to the feminine singular form of the adjective.

un hombre ricamente vestido
a richly dressed man

La tortuga anda lentamente.
The turtle walks slowly.

¡Habla claramente!
Speak clearly!

Maneja cuidadosamente.
He drives carefully.

In a series of two or more adverbs normally formed with *-mente,* the suffix is used only with the last adverb.

Arturo escribió clara y facilmente.
Arthur wrote clearly, and easily.

Comparison

Comparison with adjectives

Superiority	*Juan es más rico que María.*
	John is richer than Mary.
Equality	*Juan es tan rico como María.*
	John is as rich as Mary.
Inferiority	*Juan es menos rico que María.*
	John is not as rich as Mary.

The superlative of an adjective is formed by placing the definite article or possessive adjective before the comparative form.

Miguel es el estudiante más inteligente de la clase.
Michael is the most intelligent student in the class.

Comparison with adverbs

Adverbs are compared as shown in this example.

rápidamente quickly
más (menos) rápidamente more (less) quickly
lo más (menos) rápidamente the most (least) quickly

The article *lo* is used with the superlative form.

The superlative form of the adverb is followed by *de.*
The English word "than" is usually translated as *que.*

Tiene más dinero que Ana.
He has more money than Anna.

Before a number, "than" is translated as *de* if the sentence is affirmative and by *que* if negative.

Recibió más de cien dólares.
He received more than one hundred dollars.

Comparisons of equality are expressed by *tan* plus an adjective or adverb plus *como.*

Manuel es tan alto como Andrés.
Manuel is as tall as Andrew.

Tanto (-a, -os, -as) plus a noun plus *como* is used to express as much (as many) as.

Tengo tantas llaves como tú.
I have as many keys as you.

Tanto (-a, -os, -as) plus *como* is used to express as much (as many) as.

Antonio trabaja tanto como su hermano.
Anthony works as much as his brother.

Irregular comparative forms of adjectives

Positive	*Comparative*	*Superlative*
bueno good	*mejor* better	*el mejor* the best
malo bad	*peor* worse	*el peor* the worst
grande great, big	*mayor* greater, older	*el mayor* the greatest, the oldest
	más grande larger	*el más grande* the largest
	menos grande not as large	*el menos grande* the least large
pequeño small	*menor* minor, lesser, younger	*el menor* the least, the youngest
	más pequeño smaller	*el más pequeño* the smallest
	menos pequeño less, small	*el menos pequeño* the least small

Possession

Possession is expressed by *de* + the possessor.

la cama de mi hermano my brother's bed

Possessive adjectives

The short form always precedes the noun; the long form always follows the noun. Both forms agree in gender and number with the person or thing possessed.

nuestros amigos our friends

las maletas tuyas your suitcases

Possessive pronouns

A possessive pronoun is formed by the definite article plus the long form of the possessive adjective.

el tuyo yours

A possessive pronoun agrees in number and gender with the noun it replaces.

mi pelota y la tuya my ball and yours

Possessive adjectives

	Short form Singular Masc.	Plural Fem.	Long form Singular Masc.	Fem.	Plural Masc.	Fem.
my	mi	mis	mío	mía	míos	mías
your (familiar singular)	tu	tus	tuyo	tuya	tuyos	tuyas
your, his, her, its, their	su	sus	suyo	suya	suyos	suyas
our	nuestro nuestra	nuestros nuestras	nuestro	nuestra	nuestros	nuestras
your (familiar plural)	vuestro vuestra	vuestros vuestras	vuestro	vuestra	vuestros	vuestras

Possessive pronouns

	Singular Masc.	Fem.	Plural Masc.	Fem.
mine	el mío	la mía	los míos	las mías
yours (familiar singular)	el tuyo	la tuya	los tuyos	las tuyas
your, his, hers, its, theirs	el suyo	la suya	los suyos	las suyas
ours	el nuestro	la nuestra	los nuestros	las nuestras
yours (familiar plural)	el vuestro	la vuestra	los vuestros	las vuestras

Pronouns

Subject pronouns

Subject pronouns are used for clarity, emphasis, or politeness. The English word "it" is not expressed as a subject.

Es difícil hacer. It is difficult to do.

The plural form *vosotros* is used in Spain. In Spanish America, *ustedes* is preferred.

Object pronouns

A pronoun used as the object of a preposition always follows the preposition.

The pronouns *mí, ti* and *sí* combine with the preposition *con* as follows:

conmigo with me

contigo with you (familiar)

consigo with yourself, himself, herself, themselves

These pronoun forms do not change in gender or number.

An object pronoun, whether direct or indirect, is usually placed immediately before the verb. In an affirmative command, infinitive, or present participle, the object pronoun follows and is joined to the verb. In a negative command, the object pronoun precedes the verb. When the object pronoun is joined to an affirmative command or present participle, an accent mark is needed over the vowel of the accented syllable.

Double object pronouns

When a verb has two object pronouns, the indirect object pronoun precedes the direct object pronoun.

Me los entregan. They deliver them to me.

When both object pronouns are in the third person, the indirect object is written as *se*.

Se lo digo. I tell it to her.

The various meanings of *se* may be clarified by adding *a Vd., a Vds., a él, a ella, a ellos, a ellas.*

No se la enseñamos a ellos.

We don't show it to them.

Forms of pronouns (see also Possession on page 408)

Subject pronouns

Singular		Plural	
yo	I	nosotros, -as	we
tú	you (familiar)	vosotros, -as	you (familiar)
usted (Vd. or Ud.)	you	ustedes (Vds. or Uds.)	you
él	he	ellos	they
ella	she	ellas	they

Pronouns used as objects of prepositions

Singular		Plural	
mí	me	nosotros, -as	us
ti	you (familiar)	vosotros, -as	you (familiar)
usted (Vd. or Ud.)	you	ustedes (Vds. or Uds.)	you
él	him, it	ellos	them (masc.)
ella	her, it	ellas	them (fem.)
sí	yourself, himself, herself, itself	sí	yourselves, themselves

Object pronouns

Indirect		Direct		Reflexive	
Singular		*Singular*		*Singular*	
me	to me	me	me	me	myself
te	to you (familiar)	te	you (familiar)	te	yourself (familiar)
le	to you, to him, to her, to it	le	you (masc.), him	se	yourself, himself, herself, itself
		lo	him, it (masc.)		
		la	you (fem.), her, it (fem.)		
Plural		*Plural*		*Plural*	
nos	to us	nos	us	nos	ourselves
os	to you (familiar)	os	you (familiar)	os	yourselves (familiar)
les	to you, to them	los	you, them (masc.)	se	yourselves, themselves
		las	you, them (fem.)		

Position of object pronouns

Finite verb	Les doy el regalo.	I give them the gift.
Infinitive	Quieren verlo.	They want to see it.
	Lo quieren ver.	
Present participle	Estoy esperándolo.	I am waiting for it.
	Lo estoy esperando.	
Affirmative command	Envíelo Vd.	Send it.
Negative command	No lo envíe Vd.	Don't send it.

Relative pronouns and adjectives

que that, which, who

quien (-es) who

el (la, los, las) cual (-es) which, who

lo cual which

el (la) que (the one) which, (the one) who, he (she) who

los (las) que (the ones) which, (the ones) who, those who

lo que what, which

cuyo (-a, -os, -as) whose (as relative adjective)

Demonstrative pronouns

	Masc.	Fem.	Neut.
this (one)	éste	ésta	esto
these	éstos	éstas	
that (one)	ése	ésa	eso
those	ésos	ésas	
that (one)	aquél	aquélla	aquello
those	aquéllos	aquéllas	

The placement of double object pronouns is the same as that given above for single object pronouns. Double object pronouns are always kept together.

When both object pronouns are attached to the verb, a written accent mark is used to keep the original stress.

Va a servírselo. He is going to serve it to him.

Demonstrative pronouns

Demonstrative pronouns agree in number and gender with the nouns they represent.

Me gustan estas faldas y aquéllas.

I like these skirts and those (distant).

Neuter forms of demonstrative pronouns indicate things indefinitely referred to, or general ideas and situations.

No haré esto. I shall not do this.

Relative pronouns and adjectives

Relative pronouns and adjectives are never omitted in Spanish.

La revista que compraste es interesante.

The magazine you bought is interesting.

Que refers to both persons and things. After a preposition, however, *que* refers only to things; *quien (-es)* refers to persons.

| el chico que jugó | el chico con quien jugué |
| the boy who played | the boy with whom I played |

Negation, interrogatives, and exclamations

Negative words and their opposites

¡NO!
¡NUNCA!

¡SI!
¡SIEMPRE!

Negative	*Affirmative*
no no, not	*sí* yes
nadie no one, nobody, not anyone	*alguien* someone, somebody
nada nothing, not anything	*algo* something
nunca, jamás never, not ever	*siempre* always
tampoco neither, not either	*también* also
ninguno (-a) no, none, not any	*alguno (-a)* some, any
ni . . . ni neither . . . nor, not . . . nor	*o . . . o* either . . . or
sin without	*con* with

The negative word *no* precedes the verb.

¿No encontró usted el reloj?

Didn't you find the watch?

If an object pronoun precedes the verb, the negative word precedes the object pronoun.

No lo recibió. He didn't receive it.

All negative sentences must have a negative word preceding the verb. If the negative word follows the verb, then *no* must precede the verb.

Nunca lo haré. I shall never do it.

No lo haré nunca. I shall never do it.

When *nadie* is the object of the verb, it is preceded by the personal *a*.

No veo a nadie. I don't see anyone.

But is expressed as *sino* when the first element is negative and the second is in direct contrast.

No llevaba abrigo negro, sino azul.

He wasn't wearing a black coat, but a blue one.

Interrogative expressions

¿qué? what?
¿quién (-es)? who?
¿cuál (-es)? which, which one(s)?
¿dónde? where?
¿adónde? where? to where? (with verbs of motion)
¿cuándo? when?
¿cuánto (-a)? how much?
¿cuántos (-as)? how many?
¿cómo? how?
¿por qué? why?

Note that all interrogative expressions carry an accent mark.

Exclamations

All exclamatory words carry written accent marks. The most common are:

¡Qué . . . ! What . . . ! What a . . . ! How . . . !
¡Cuánto (a) . . . ! How much . . . !
¡Cuántos (as) . . . ! How many . . . !

Exclamatory sentences have an inverted exclamation point (¡) at the beginning and a regular exclamation point at the end.

¡Qué día! What a day!

Prepositions

Prepositions with infinitives

The infinitive is the only verb form that may follow a preposition.

Después de vestirse, salió.

After getting dressed, he went out.

The infinitive is used after many verbs. In many cases it follows the verb directly.

Quiere salir temprano. He wants to leave early.

In other cases the infinitive is preceded by a preposition. The following common verbs do not require a preposition before an infinitive.

creer	to believe	*necesitar*	to need
deber	ought to, should	*poder*	to be able, can
desear	to wish, desire	*querer*	to wish, want
esperar	to hope	*saber*	to know how to

Verbs expressing beginning, motion, teaching, or learning and several other verbs require the preposition *a* before a following infinitive.

beginning	*comenzar*	motion	*correr* to run
	empezar		*ir* to go
	ponerse		*llegar* to arrive
	principiar		*salir* to go out to
teaching	*enseñar*	other	*invitar* to invite
learning	*aprender*	verbs	*ayudar* to help
			llamar to call

Los niños empezaron a llorar.

The children began to cry.

The following verbs require the preposition *de* before an infinitive.

acabar	to have just	*dejar*	to cease, stop, fail
acordarse	to remember	*olvidarse*	to forget
alegrarse	to be glad to	*tratar*	to try
cesar	to cease, stop		

Trató de esconderse. He tried to hide.

Uses of the personal *a*

The personal *a* is used before direct objects that denote persons or personified things. The personal *a* is not translated.

Visitan a su abuelo They visit their grandfather.

The personal *a* is used before pronouns referring to persons, even when used in a negative sense.

No veo a nadie. I see no one.

The personal *a* is omitted after the verb *tener* with the meaning "to have."

Tiene muchos amigos. He has many friends.

The personal *a* is used with *querer* when it means "to love" and omitted when it means "to want."

El niño quiere su madre.

The child wants his mother.

El niño quiere a su madre.

The child loves his mother.

This sign announces that the 1992 World's Fair in Seville, Spain, is en marcha, *that is, setting out, or under construction.*

Uses of *para*

Purpose:

Como para vivir. I eat in order to live.

Destination:

Saldrá para España. He will leave for Spain.

Use:

Es una caja para dulces. It is a candy box.

Future time:

Estará listo para el sábado.

It will be ready by Saturday.

"Considering the fact that":

Para estudiante, toca muy bien.

For a student, he plays very well.

"Be about to" after *estar*:

Estoy para salir. I am about to leave.

Uses of *por*

"For the sake of":

Lo hizo por su hermano. He did it for his brother.

Price or exchange:

Compró la revista por un peso.

He bought the magazine for a peso.

Length of time:

Quedó en Perú por dos semanas.

He stayed in Peru for two weeks.

"In the morning, afternoon, or night":

Trabajo por la tarde. I work in the afternoon.

"By, through, along":

Dan un paseo por el parque.

They take a walk through the park.

"For" after the verbs *ir, enviar, luchar, llamar,* or *preguntar*:

Fue por el médico. He went for the doctor.

The following verbs are not followed by *para* or *por,* since "for" is part of the meaning of the verb:

buscar to look for,

esperar to wait for,

pedir to ask for.

Buscaron una mesa. They looked for a table.

Verbs

Conjugation of regular verbs

The three conjugations are distinguished by the infinitive endings: *-ar, -er,* and *-ir.*

Conjugation of regular verbs

Simple tenses
Indicative

		Present I take, eat, live I do take, eat, live			*Imperfect* I was taking, eating, living I used to take, eat, live		
yo		tomo	como	vivo	tomaba	comía	vivía
tú		tomas	comes	vives	tomabas	comías	vivías
Vd., él, ella		toma	come	vive	tomaba	comía	vivía
nosotros, nosotras		tomamos	comemos	vivimos	tomábamos	comíamos	vivíamos
vosotros, vosotras		tomáis	coméis	vivís	tomabais	comíais	vivíais
Vds., ellos, ellas		toman	comen	viven	tomaban	comían	vivían

Subjunctive

	Present that I may take, eat, live			*Imperfect* that I might take, eat, live that I should take, eat, live		
yo	tome	coma	viva	tomara or tomase	comiera or comiese	viviera or viviese
tú	tomes	comas	vivas	tomaras or tomases	comieras or comieses	vivieras or vivieses
Vd., él, ella	tome	coma	viva	tomara or tomase	comiera or comiese	viviera or viviese
nosotros, nosotras	tomemos	comamos	vivamos	tomáramos or tomásemos	comiéramos or comiésemos	viviéramos or viviésemos
vosotros, vosotras	toméis	comáis	viváis	tomarais or tomaseis	comierais or comieseis	vivierais or vivieseis
Vds., ellos, ellas	tomen	coman	vivan	tomaran or tomasen	comieran or comiesen	vivieran or viviesen

Compound tenses
Indicative

Present perfect
Present of *haber* plus past participle

I have taken	I have eaten	I have lived
he tomado	*he comido*	*he vivido*

Pluperfect
Imperfect of *haber* plus past participle

I had taken	I had eaten	I had lived
había tomado	*había comido*	*había vivido*

Subjunctive

Present perfect
Present subjunctive of *haber* plus the past participle

that I may have taken	that I may have eaten	that I may have lived
haya tomado	*haya comido*	*haya vivido*

Progressive

The present participle is used with *estar* to denote continuing action.

I am taking	I am eating	I am living
estoy tomando	*estoy comiendo*	*estoy viviendo*

Review of Spanish Grammar

In all but the future and conditional tenses, the inflexional endings are added to the stem of the verb, for example: *tom*, *com*, and *viv* for *tomar*, *comer*, and *vivir*. Future and conditional endings are added to the infinitive. These endings are the same for all verbs.

Preterite

I took, ate, lived
I did take, eat, live

tomé	comí	viví
tomaste	comiste	viviste
tomó	comió	vivió
tomamos	comimos	vivimos
tomasteis	comisteis	vivisteis
tomaron	comieron	vivieron

Future

I shall take, eat, live
I will take, eat, live

tomaré	comeré	viviré
tomarás	comerás	vivirás
tomará	comerá	vivirá
tomaremos	comeremos	viviremos
tomaréis	comeréis	viviréis
tomarán	comerán	vivirán

Conditional

I should take, eat, live
I would take, eat, live

tomaría	comería	viviría
tomarías	comerías	vivirías
tomaría	comería	viviría
tomaríamos	comeríamos	viviríamos
tomaríais	comeríais	viviríais
tomarían	comerían	vivirían

Infinitives

	-*ar* verb	-*er* verb	-*ir* verb
	tomar	comer	vivir
	to take	to eat	to live

Participles

Present	taking	eating	living
	tomando	comiendo	viviendo
Past	taken	eaten	lived
	tomado	comido	vivido

Imperative

	take	eat	live
Familiar s.	toma	come	vive
Familiar pl.	tomad	comed	vivid
Polite s.	tome Vd.	coma Vd.	viva Vd.
Polite pl.	tomen Vds.	coman Vds.	vivan Vds.

Preterite perfect

Preterite of *haber* plus past participle

I had taken	I had eaten	I had lived
hube tomado	hube comido	hube vivido

Future perfect

Future of *haber* plus past participle

I shall have taken	I shall have eaten	I shall have lived
habré tomado	habré comido	habré vivido

Pluperfect

Either form of the imperfect subjunctive of *haber* plus past participle

that I might have taken	that I might have eaten	that I might have lived
hubiera (hubiese) tomado	hubiera (hubiese) comido	hubiera (hubiese) vivido

Conditional *perfect*

Conditional of *haber* plus past participle

I should have taken	I should have eaten	I should have lived
habría tomado	habría comido	habría vivido

Stem changing verbs

In conjugating Spanish verbs, we are accustomed to changes in the verb endings, but certain verbs also change the spelling of their stems.

Stem changes are not uncommon in English. Consider the way the verb "eat" changes in English: I eat, I ate. Consider the verb "go": I go, I went. Finally, consider the verb "be": I am, I was.

Conjugation of stem-changing verbs

First class

Certain verbs of the first and second conjugations with stem vowels *e* or *o* change *e* to *ie*, *o* to *ue* when stressed. Note that *jugar*, to play, is conjugated as if it were a first class stem-changing verb with stem vowel *o*.

Examples:

pensar	volver
to think	to return

Present participle
pensando volviendo

Review:
First class verbs
e → ie + o → ue
when stressed.

Present indicative		**Present subjunctive**		**Imperative**	
pienso	vuelvo	piense	vuelva		
piensas	vuelves	pienses	vuelvas	piensa	vuelve
piensa	vuelve	piense	vuelva	piense	vuelva
pensamos	volvemos	pensemos	volvamos	pensemos	volvamos
pensáis	volvéis	penséis	volváis	pensad	volved
piensan	vuelven	piensen	vuelvan	piensen	vuelvan

Second class

Certain verbs of the third conjugation with stem vowels of *e* or *o* change *e* to *ie*, *o* to *ue* when stressed. Changes are the same as those listed above with the addition of *e* changing to *i*, and *o* to *u*, when the following syllable contains a stressed *a*, *ie*, or *io*.

Examples:

(ie) sentir	(ue) dormir
to feel	to sleep

Present participle
sintiendo durmiendo

Present indicative		**Present subjunctive**		**Preterite**		**Imperfect subjunctive**		**Imperative**	
siento	duermo	sienta	duerma	sentí	dormí	sintiera	durmiera		
sientes	duermes	sientas	duermas	sentiste	dormiste	sintieras	durmieras	siente	duerme
siente	duerme	sienta	duerma	sintió	durmió	sintiera	durmiera	sienta	duerma
sentimos	dormimos	sintamos	durmamos	sentimos	dormimos	sintiéramos	durmiéramos	sintamos	durmamos
sentís	dormís	sintáis	durmáis	sentisteis	dormisteis	sintierais	durmierais	sentid	dormid
sienten	duermen	sientan	duerman	sintieron	durmieron	sintieran	durmieran	sientan	duerman

Third class

Certain verbs of the third conjugation with stem vowel *e* change *e* to *i* in all forms affected in the first and second classes of stem-changing verbs.

Example:

(i) pedir
to ask for

Present participle
pidiendo

Present indicative	**Present subjunctive**	**Preterite**	**Imperfect subjunctive**	**Imperative**
pido	pida	pedí	pidiera	
pides	pidas	pediste	pidieras	pide
pide	pida	pidió	pidiera	pida
pedimos	pidamos	pedimos	pidiéramos	pidamos
pedís	pidáis	pedisteis	pidierais	pedid
piden	pidan	pidieron	pidieran	pidan

Spelling change verbs

This class of verbs undergoes changes in spelling during conjugation, with the effect of preserving the sound of the consonant found in the infinitive.

The chart below supplies examples of changes in the verbs *buscar* search, *jugar* play, *averiguar* find out, *vencer* conquer, *conocer* know, *escoger* choose, *leer* read, and *seguir* follow.

Spelling change verbs

Verb ending	Spelling change	Examples
in verbs ending in *car*	*c* changes to *qu* before an *e*	*buscar* → *busqué*
in verbs ending in *gar*	insert *u* before an *e*	*jugar* → *jugué*
in verbs ending in *guar*	put dieresis over *u* before an *e*	*averiguar* → *averigüé*
in verbs ending in *cer* or *cir* preceded by a consonant	replace the *c* by *z* before an *a* or *o*	*vencer* → *venzo*
in verbs ending in *cer* or *cir* preceded by a vowel	insert *z* before *c* when followed by an *a* or *o*	*conocer* → *conozco*
in verbs ending in *ger* or *gir*	replace the *g* with *j* before an *a* or *o*	*escoger* → *escojo*
in verbs ending in *er* or *ir*	change the *i* of the endings *ie* and *io* to *y*	*leer* → *leyó*
in verbs ending in *guir* when the *u* is silent	drop the *u* before an *a* or *o*	*seguir* → *sigo*

Correspondencia Correspondence

La carta comercial A business letter

ciudad, fecha city, date	*Miami, 8 de mayo de 19___* Miami, May 8, 19___
destinatario, dirección inside address	*Sr. Juan Encina* *Avenida de las Américas 20* *Lima, Perú*
el saludo salutation	*Estimado (a) señor (a):* Dear Sir (Madam):
despedida closing	*Atentamente,* Attentively, *Sinceramente,* Sincerely,
firma signature	José Antonio Rivera

Carta personal A friendly letter

ciudad, fecha city, date	*Nueva York, 20 de julio de 19___* New York, July 20, 19___
saludo salutation	*Querido (a) amigo (a),* Dear friend,
despedida closing	*Cariñosamente,* Lovingly, *Recuerdos,* Regards,
firma signature	José

Irregular verbs

Irregular verbs are the most difficult verbs to learn. Yet, perhaps unfortunately, they describe actions and states of being that are most frequently needed in speaking and writing Spanish. The verb forms given in the chart below and continuing for two more pages take nineteen irregular verbs through nine tenses. As you will see, the verb endings for certain tenses are the same as those you will encounter in conjugating regular verbs.

Conjugation of irregular verbs

Infinitive	Indicative				Conditional	Subjunctive			Imperative
	Present	*Imperfect*	*Preterite*	*Future*	*Present*	*Present*	*Imperfect (1st form)*	*(2nd form)*	
andar to go, walk	ando	andaba	anduve	andaré	andaría	ande	anduviera	anduviese	
	andas	andabas	anduviste	andarás	andarías	andes	anduvieras	anduvieses	anda
	anda	andaba	anduvo	andará	andaría	ande	anduviera	anduviese	ande
	andamos	andábamos	anduvimos	andaremos	andaríamos	andemos	anduviéramos	anduviésemos	andemos
	andáis	andabais	anduvisteis	andaréis	andaríais	andéis	anduvierais	anduvieseis	andad
	andan	andaban	anduvieron	andarán	andarían	anden	anduvieran	anduviesen	anden
dar to give	doy	daba	di	daré	daría	dé	diera	diese	
	das	dabas	diste	darás	darías	des	dieras	dieses	da
	da	daba	dio	dará	daría	dé	diera	diese	dé
	damos	dábamos	dimos	daremos	daríamos	demos	diéramos	diésemos	demos
	dais	dabais	disteis	daréis	daríais	deis	dierais	dieseis	dad
	dan	daban	dieron	darán	darían	den	dieran	diesen	den
decir to say, tell	digo	decía	dije	diré	diría	diga	dijera	dijese	
	dices	decías	dijiste	dirás	dirías	digas	dijeras	dijeses	di
	dice	decía	dijo	dirá	diría	diga	dijera	dijese	diga
	decimos	decíamos	dijimos	diremos	diríamos	digamos	dijéramos	dijésemos	digamos
	decís	decíais	dijisteis	diréis	diríais	digáis	dijerais	dijeseis	decid
	dicen	decían	dijeron	dirán	dirían	digan	dijeran	dijesen	digan
estar to be	estoy	estaba	estuve	estaré	estaría	esté	estuviera	estuviese	
	estás	estabas	estuviste	estarás	estarías	estés	estuvieras	estuvieses	está
	está	estaba	estuvo	estará	estaría	esté	estuviera	estuviese	esté
	estamos	estábamos	estuvimos	estaremos	estaríamos	estemos	estuviéramos	estuviésemos	estemos
	estáis	estabais	estuvisteis	estaréis	estaríais	estéis	estuvierais	estuvieseis	estad
	están	estaban	estuvieron	estarán	estarían	estén	estuvieran	estuviesen	estén
haber to have	he	había	hube	habré	habría	haya	hubiera	hubiese	
	has	habías	hubiste	habrás	habrías	hayas	hubieras	hubieses	he
	ha	había	hubo	habrá	habría	haya	hubiera	hubiese	haya
	hemos	habíamos	hubimos	habremos	habríamos	hayamos	hubiéramos	hubiésemos	hayamos
	habéis	habíais	hubisteis	habréis	habríais	hayáis	hubierais	hubieseis	habed
	han	habían	hubieron	habrán	habrían	hayan	hubieran	hubiesen	hayan
hacer to make, do	hago	hacía	hice	haré	haría	haga	hiciera	hiciese	
	haces	hacías	hiciste	harás	harías	hagas	hicieras	hicieses	haz
	hace	hacía	hizo	hará	haría	haga	hiciera	hiciese	haga
	hacemos	hacíamos	hicimos	haremos	haríamos	hagamos	hiciéramos	hiciésemos	hagamos
	hacéis	hacíais	hicisteis	haréis	haríais	hagáis	hicierais	hicieseis	haced
	hacen	hacían	hicieron	harán	harían	hagan	hicieran	hiciesen	hagan

416   **Review of Spanish Grammar**

Conjugation of irregular verbs (continued)

Infinitive	Indicative				Conditional	Subjunctive			Imperative
	Present	*Imperfect*	*Preterite*	*Future*	*Present*	*Present*	*Imperfect (1st form)*	*(2nd form)*	
ir to go	voy	iba	fui	iré	iría	vaya	fuera	fuese	
	vas	ibas	fuiste	irás	irías	vayas	fueras	fueses	ve
	va	iba	fue	irá	iría	vaya	fuera	fuese	vaya
	vamos	íbamos	fuimos	iremos	iríamos	vayamos	fuéramos	fuésemos	vamos
	vais	ibais	fuisteis	iréis	iríais	vayáis	fuerais	fueseis	id
	van	iban	fueron	irán	irían	vayan	fueran	fuesen	vayan
oír to hear	oigo	oía	oí	oiré	oiría	oiga	oyera	oyese	
	oyes	oías	oíste	oirás	oirías	oigas	oyeras	oyeses	oye
	oye	oía	oyó	oirá	oiría	oiga	oyera	oyese	oiga
	oímos	oíamos	oímos	oiremos	oiríamos	oigamos	oyéramos	oyésemos	oigamos
	oís	oíais	oísteis	oiréis	oiríais	oigáis	oyerais	oyeseis	oíd
	oyen	oían	oyeron	oirán	oirían	oigan	oyeran	oyesen	oigan
poder to be able	puedo	podía	pude	podré	podría	pueda	pudiera	pudiese	
	puedes	podías	pudiste	podrás	podrías	puedas	pudieras	pudieses	puede
	puede	podía	pudo	podrá	podría	pueda	pudiera	pudiese	pueda
	podemos	podíamos	pudimos	podremos	podríamos	podamos	pudiéramos	pudiésemos	podamos
	podéis	podíais	pudisteis	podréis	podríais	podáis	pudierais	pudieseis	poded
	pueden	podían	pudieron	podrán	podrían	puedan	pudieran	pudiesen	puedan
poner to put	pongo	ponía	puse	pondré	pondría	ponga	pusiera	pusiese	
	pones	ponías	pusiste	pondrás	pondrías	pongas	pusieras	pusieses	pon
	pone	ponía	puso	pondrá	pondría	ponga	pusiera	pusiese	ponga
	ponemos	poníamos	pusimos	pondremos	pondríamos	pongamos	pusiéramos	pusiésemos	pongamos
	ponéis	poníais	pusisteis	pondréis	pondríais	pongáis	pusierais	pusieseis	poned
	ponen	ponían	pusieron	pondrán	pondrían	pongan	pusieran	pusiesen	pongan
querer to want, love	quiero	quería	quise	querré	querría	quiera	quisiera	quisiese	
	quieres	querías	quisiste	querrás	querrías	quieras	quisieras	quisieses	quiere
	quiere	quería	quiso	querrá	querría	quiera	quisiera	quisiese	quiera
	queremos	queríamos	quisimos	querremos	querríamos	queramos	quisiéramos	quisiésemos	queramos
	queréis	queríais	quisisteis	querréis	querríais	queráis	quisierais	quisieseis	quered
	quieren	querían	quisieron	querrán	querrían	quieran	quisieran	quisiesen	quieran
saber to know	sé	sabía	supe	sabré	sabría	sepa	supiera	supiese	
	sabes	sabías	supiste	sabrás	sabrías	sepas	supieras	supieses	sabe
	sabe	sabía	supo	sabrá	sabría	sepa	supiera	supiese	sepa
	sabemos	sabíamos	supimos	sabremos	sabríamos	sepamos	supiéramos	supiésemos	sepamos
	sabéis	sabíais	supisteis	sabréis	sabríais	sepáis	supierais	supieseis	sabed
	saben	sabían	supieron	sabrán	sabrían	sepan	supieran	supiesen	sepan

Conjugation of irregular verbs (continued)

Infinitive	Indicative				Conditional	Subjunctive			Imperative
	Present	Imperfect	Preterite	Future	Present	Present	Imperfect (1st form)	(2nd form)	
salir to go out	salgo	salía	salí	saldré	saldría	salga	saliera	saliese	
	sales	salías	saliste	saldrás	saldrías	salgas	salieras	salieses	sal
	sale	salía	salió	saldrá	saldría	salga	saliera	saliese	salga
	salimos	salíamos	salimos	saldremos	saldríamos	salgamos	saliéramos	saliésemos	salgamos
	salís	salíais	salisteis	saldréis	saldríais	salgáis	salierais	salieseis	salid
	salen	salían	salieron	saldrán	saldrían	salgan	salieran	saliesen	salgan
ser to be	soy	era	fui	seré	sería	sea	fuera	fuese	
	eres	eras	fuiste	serás	serías	seas	fueras	fueses	sé
	es	era	fue	será	sería	sea	fuera	fuese	sea
	somos	éramos	fuimos	seremos	seríamos	seamos	fuéramos	fuésemos	seamos
	sois	erais	fuisteis	seréis	seríais	seáis	fuerais	fueseis	sed
	son	eran	fueron	serán	serían	sean	fueran	fuesen	sean
tener to have	tengo	tenía	tuve	tendré	tendría	tenga	tuviera	tuviese	
	tienes	tenías	tuviste	tendrás	tendrías	tengas	tuvieras	tuvieses	ten
	tiene	tenía	tuvo	tendrá	tendría	tenga	tuviera	tuviese	tenga
	tenemos	teníamos	tuvimos	tendremos	tendríamos	tengamos	tuviéramos	tuviésemos	tengamos
	tenéis	teníais	tuvisteis	tendréis	tendríais	tengáis	tuvierais	tuvieseis	tened
	tienen	tenían	tuvieron	tendrán	tendrían	tengan	tuvieran	tuviesen	tengan
traer to bring	traigo	traía	traje	traeré	traería	traiga	trajera	trajese	
	traes	traías	trajiste	traerás	traerías	traigas	trajeras	trajeses	trae
	trae	traía	trajo	traerá	traería	traiga	trajera	trajese	traiga
	traemos	traíamos	trajimos	traeremos	traeríamos	traigamos	trajéramos	trajésemos	traigamos
	traéis	traíais	trajisteis	traeréis	traeríais	traigáis	trajerais	trajeseis	traed
	traen	traían	trajeron	traerán	traerían	traigan	trajeran	trajesen	traigan
valer to be worth	valgo	valía	valí	valdré	valdría	valga	valiera	valiese	
	vales	valías	valiste	valdrás	valdrías	valgas	valieras	valieses	val
	vale	valía	valió	valdrá	valdría	valga	valiera	valiese	valga
	valemos	valíamos	valimos	valdremos	valdríamos	valgamos	valiéramos	valiésemos	valgamos
	valéis	valíais	valisteis	valdréis	valdríais	valgáis	valierais	valieseis	valed
	valen	valían	valieron	valdrán	valdrían	valgan	valieran	valiesen	valgan
venir to come	vengo	venía	vine	vendré	vendría	venga	viniera	viniese	
	vienes	venías	viniste	vendrás	vendrías	vengas	vinieras	vinieses	ven
	viene	venía	vino	vendrá	vendría	venga	viniera	viniese	venga
	venimos	veníamos	vinimos	vendremos	vendríamos	vengamos	viniéramos	viniésemos	vengamos
	venís	veníais	vinisteis	vendréis	vendríais	vengáis	vinierais	vinieseis	venid
	vienen	venían	vinieron	vendrán	vendrían	vengan	vinieran	viniesen	vengan
ver to see	veo	veía	vi	veré	vería	vea	viera	viese	
	ves	veías	viste	verás	verías	veas	vieras	vieses	ve
	ve	veía	vio	verá	vería	vea	viera	viese	vea
	vemos	veíamos	vimos	veremos	veríamos	veamos	viéramos	viésemos	veamos
	veis	veíais	visteis	veréis	veríais	veáis	vierais	vieseis	ved
	ven	veían	vieron	verán	verían	vean	vieran	viesen	vean

Review of Spanish Grammar

Uses of *ser* and *estar*

Both *ser* and *estar* mean *to be*. They are used in the following ways:

ser

With adjectives to express an inherent or permanent quality, such as age, characteristic, color, possession, shape, size, and wealth.

La casa es blanca. The house is white.

With the preposition *de* to express ownership, material, or origin.

La pulsera es de oro. The bracelet is gold.

With a predicate noun or pronoun.

Él es médico. He is a doctor.

With the past participle in a passive construction.

El libro fue escrito por él.

The book was written by him.

In impersonal expressions

Es mejor hacerlo ahora. It is better to do it now.

estar

With adjectives to express an accidental or temporary condition.

La chica está ausente. The girl is absent.

In expressions of location

Barcelona está en España. Barcelona is in Spain.

In expressions of health.

Estaban enfermos. They were sick.

With the past participle used as an adjective to express a condition.

Las ventanas están cerradas.

The windows are closed.

With the present participle to form the present progressive tense.

Estaba durmiendo. He was sleeping.

Gustar

Gustar, which literally means to be pleasing, is used to translate the verb "to like." For example, in the sentence *Me gustan las revistas,* I like the magazines, the subject becomes the indirect object, *me,* and the direct object *revistas,* becomes the subject of the verb *gustar.*

Reflexive verbs

Reflexive verbs are designated by *se* attached to the infinitive so *lavarse* means to wash oneself. Reflexive pronouns are used with reflexive verbs in any tense, so *se lavaron* means they washed themselves.

Uses of the subjunctive mood

The subjunctive is used mainly in certain types of subordinate clauses introduced by *que.* In general, a verb in the subjunctive expresses a feeling or thought in the mind of the speaker rather than an established fact.

After verbs of volition (with a subject change).

Quiero que lo hagas. I want you to do it.

After verbs of emotion (with a subject change).

Se alegra de que venga.

He is happy that I am coming.

After impersonal expressions followd by a definite subject in the subordinate clause.

Es probable que me escriba.

It is likely that he will write to me.

After verbs of doubt and denial in the affirmative.

Dudo que lo sepa. I doubt that he knows it.

After verbs of thinking and believing used in the interrogative or negative.

No creo que tenga razón. I don't think he is right.

In a relative clause modifying a negative or an indefinite antecedent.

No conozco a nadie que hable alemán.

I don't know anyone who speaks German.

After conjunctions of time, purpose, restriction, or result.

Iré con tal que volvamos temprano.

I shall go provided that we return early.

After certain indefinite expressions, such as *dondequiera que* and *cualquier cosa que.*

Dondequiera que viva será feliz.

Wherever she lives, she will be happy.

Idioms

a tiempo on time
Vuelve a tiempo si quieres ver la película.
Return on time if you want to see the movie.

darse prisa to hurry
Date prisa! Ya son las seis.
Hurry up! It's six o'clock.

de repente suddenly
De repente abrió la puerta.
Suddenly he opened the door.

en seguida immediately
Pagó la cuenta y salió en seguida.
He paid the check and left immediately.

estar de vuelta to be back (in a place)
Mi hijo está de vuelta en Nueva York.
My son is back in New York.

hacer frío (calor) of weather: to be cold (warm)
Hace frío hoy.
It is cold today.

hacer un viaje to take a trip
Hice un viaje a España.
I took a trip to Spain.

tener hambre (sed) to be hungry (thirsty)
Tengo mucha hambre.
I am very hungry.

tratar de to try to
Trata de terminar el trabajo.
He tries to finish the work.

¡Hace frío! **¡Date prisa!**

For the traveler

el avión

el aduanero

la maleta

How to travel — *Como viajar*

by plane	*en avión*
by train	*en tren*
by car	*en carro/ en coche*
by bus	*en autobús/ en camión (México)*

At the airport — *En el aeropuerto*

The plane is late/ early.	*El avión llega con retraso/ temprano.*

Customs — *En la aduana*

Passport, please.	*Pasaporte, por favor.*
Anything to declare?	*¿ Tiene algo que declarar?*
No, nothing to declare.	*No, nada que declarar.*
Please, open your suitcase.	*Por favor, abra su maleta.*
Thank you, Sir.	*Gracias, Señor.*

From the airport to Madrid — *Del aeropuerto a Madrid*

I would like to take the bus to Madrid.	*Quisiera tomar el autobús para Madrid.*
Taxi. Are you free? I would like to go to the train station.	*Taxi. ¿Está libre? Quiero ir a la estación.*
I would like to rent a car.	*Quiero alquilar un carro/ un coche.*
How much for two weeks?	*¿Cuánto cuesta para dos semanas?*
48,000.00 pesetas.	*48.000,00 pesetas.*
Which road do I take to Madrid?	*¿Qué carretera puedo tomar para Madrid?*
Can you show me on a map?	*¿Puede enseñarme en un mapa?*
Is the road well marked?	*¿Está bien señalada la carrtera?*
Watch out for the road signs.	*Fíjese en los señales.*

Review of Spanish Grammar

Road signs *Los señales*

100 kilometers

stop

one hour parking

no passing on left

PEATONES

pedestrian crossing

Spanish hotels vary widely in architectural style. This beautiful example is the Alfonso Hotel, in Seville.

Looking for a hotel   ## *Buscando un hotel*

Looking for a hotel	*Buscando un hotel*
Pardon me, Sir, where is the tourist office?	*Perdóneme, Señor. ¿Dónde está la oficina de turismo?*
It is over there, to the right.	*Está allá, a la derecha.*
It is in the next street, to the left.	*Está en la proxima calle a la izquierda.*
Thank you, Sir. Good-bye.	*Gracias, Señor. Adiós.*
Good morning, Miss. Could you please tell me if there is a good hotel, not too expensive, near here?	*Buenos días, Señorita. ¿Por favor, puede decirme si hay un buen hotel, no muy caro, cerca de aquí?*
Yes, Sir. When you leave, turn left and it is straight ahead.	*Sí, Señor. Cuando sale, doble a la izquierda y está derecho.*
Do you speak English?	*¿Habla Ud, inglés?*
I do not speak Spanish.	*No hablo español.*
I do not understand.	*No comprendo.*
Speak more slowly, please.	*Por favor, hable Ud. mas despacio.*
What does that mean?	*¿Qué quiere decir?*
A room for two, with bath.	*Un cuarto para dos, con baño.*
It is expensive.	*Es muy caro.*
Is there a telephone?	*¿Hay un teléfono?*
What time is breakfast?	*¿A qué hora es el desayuno?*
From 6:30 to 9:00 in your room.	*De las seis y media hasta las nueve en su cuarto.*
What do you serve for breakfast?	*¿Qué hay para el desayuno?*
We have, tea, coffee with bread and butter, and also hot chocolate with churros.	*Tenemos té, café con pan y mantequilla, y también churros y chocolate.*
At what time do you want your breakfast ?	*¿A qué hora desea el desayuno?*

Review of Spanish Grammar   421

Shopping   *De compras*

Stores   *Las tiendas*

jewelry shop	*la joyería*
butcher shop	*la carnicería*
bakery	*la panadería*
tobacco shop	*el estanco*
beauty parlor	*la peluquería*
department store	*el gran almacén*
bookstore	*la librería*
drugstore	*la farmacia*

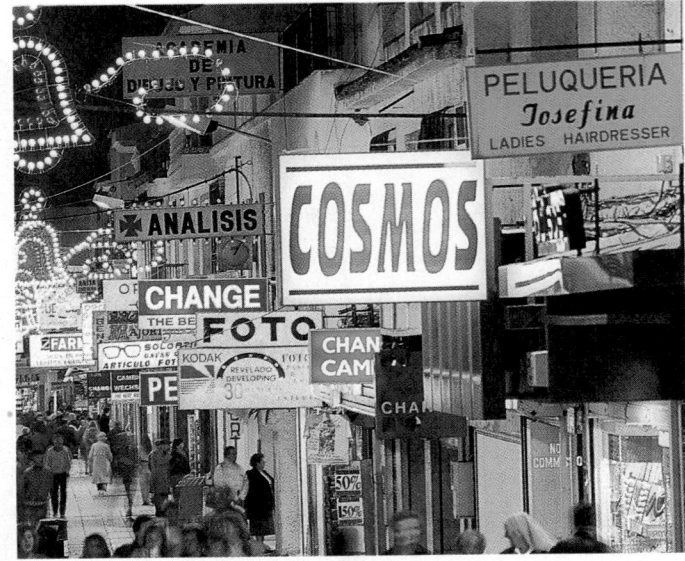

Advertising signs illuminate this night scene in Torremolinos, in southern Spain near Málaga. Note the sign for a peluquería, *or beauty parlor.*

Is there a department store near here?	*¿Hay un gran almacén cerca de aquí?*
Yes, Sir. You will pass by many little stores. Follow this street.	*Sí, Señor. Va a pasar por muchas tiendas pequeñas. Siga esta calle.*
Can I help you?	*¿Qué desea, Señorita?*
I would like to buy a summer dress.	*Quisiera un vestido para el verano.*
White, pink or light blue.	*Blanco, rosado, o azul claro.*
What is your size, Miss?	*¿Cuál es su talla, Señorita?*
I think 12 or 14, I am not sure.	*Creo que es 40 o 42. No estoy segura.*
I would like shoes, please. Size 7 or 8.	*Quisiera un par de zapatos, por favor. Número 38 o 39.*
How much does it cost?	*¿Cuánto cuesta?*
The shoes are not expensive. They are on sale.	*Los zapatos no son caros. Están rebajados.*
May I show you something else?	*¿Puedo enseñarle algo más?*
Perhaps, a skirt and a blouse.	*Tal vez, una falda y una blusa.*
I have a matching linen skirt and silk blouse in different colors.	*Tengo una una falda de lino y una blusa de seda en colores diferentes.*
I would like a man's shortsleeve shirt.	*Quiseria una camisa con mangas cortas.para hombre.*
Also shoes size 10 or 11.	*Y también zapatos número 44 o 45.*
I will take this tie also.	*Me llevo también esta corbata.*
And now, let's have lunch.	*Y ahora vamos a comer*

At the restaurant   *En el restaurante*

El menú

Arroz con pollo
saffron-flavored rice and chicken

Bistec a la parrilla
grilled steak

Churrasco
barbecued steak (South America)

Churro
a twist of batter deep fried,
often eaten as a snack
with hot chocolate in Spain

enchilada
a corn cake stuffed with meat or chicken
rolled and baked with tomato sauce
flavored with chili (Mexico and Guatemala)

Flan
custard

Horchata
a cold drink made of almonds

Paella
saffron-flavored rice, chicken, seafood, and peas

Tortilla omelet
cornmeal cake (in Mexico and Guatemala)

The waiter	*El camarero*
Good afternoon.	*Buenas tardes.*
A table for two near the window, please.	*Una mesa para dos cerca de la ventana, por favor.*
Follow me.	*Sígame.*
Is this table alright?	*¿Esta mesa está buena?*
Yes, very good, thank you	*Sí, está bien, gracias.*
Yes, Sir. Can I help you?	*Sí, Señor. ¿Qué desea Ud?*
The menu, please.	*El menú por favor.*
To start, I will have an omelet.	*Primero, quiero una tortilla.*
Then, I will have paella.	*Después, quiero la paella.*
And the lady?	*¿Y la señora?*
I will have tortilla also and the chicken and rice.	*Quiero una tortilla también y arroz con pollo.*
A bottle of local wine, please.	*Una botella de vino del país, por favor.*
Bread and butter, and we will order dessert and coffee later.	*Pan y mantequilla, y pedimos postre y cafe más tarde.*
The check, please.	*La cuenta, por favor.*
It is already dark but it is nice out.	*Ya está de noche, pero hace buen tiempo afuera.*
Let's go for a stroll.	*Vamos a caminar.*
Let's take the bus.	*Tomemos el autobús*
Then we can walk back to the hotel.	*Luego podemos regresar a pie al hotel.*

The telephone

I would like to call.	*Quisiera hacer una llamada.*
Could you tell me what I have to do?	*¿Puede decirme qué tengo que hacer?*
What number do you want?	*¿Qué número quiere?*
Number 34-27-50.	*El treinta y cuatro-veinte y siete-cincuenta.*
I need to send postcards. Where can I buy stamps?	*Necesito enviar unas tarjetas postales. ¿Dónde puedo comprar sellos?*
At the post office.	*En la oficina de correos.*

El teléfono

(See above — heading repeated as translation of "The telephone")

Currency

The unit of currency in Spain is the *pesata. Los billetes de banco* have the following values:

   10,000, 5,000, 2,000, and 1,000 pesetas

Each *billete* bears a portrait of a famous artist or of *Juan Carlos.*

Numbers

Cardinal numbers

The numbers 16 to 19 and 21 may be written as single words. Note that as single words, 16, 22, 23, and 26 carry accent marks on the final syllable.

   16 *dieciséis,* 22 *veintidós*

The only numbers that change with gender are uno and the compounds of *ciento* from 200 to 900.

   quinientas dos escuelas five hundred and two schools

Ciento becomes *cien* before nouns and before the numbers *mil* and *milliones.* In all other numbers, the full form, *ciento* is used.

   cien soldados one hundred soldiers

Millón requires the preposition *de* before the noun it multiplies.

   tres millones de pesos three million pesos

Un is not used before *ciento* or *mil*. It is used before *millón.*

   ciento doce sillas one hundred and twelve chairs

   un millón de pesos a million pesos

Ordinal numbers

first	*primero*	sixth	*sexto*
second	*segundo*	seventh	*séptimo*
third	*tercero*	eighth	*octavo*
fourth	*cuarto*	ninth	*noveno*
fifth	*quinto*	tenth	*décimo*

Ordinal numbers are generally used only through tenth; beyond that, the cardinal numbers are used. An ordinal number agrees in gender and number with the noun it modifies.

   la quinta avenida Fifth Avenue

The ordinal numbers *primero* and *tercero* drop the final *o* before a masculine singular noun.

   el tercer edificio the third building

Cardinal numbers

0	*cero*	30	*treinta*
1	*uno, una*	31	*treinta y uno*
2	*dos*	32	*treinta y dos*
3	*tres*	40	*cuarenta*
4	*cuatro*	41	*cuarenta y uno*
5	*cinco*	50	*cincuenta*
6	*seis*	51	*cincuenta y uno*
7	*siete*	60	*sesenta*
8	*ocho*	61	*sesenta y uno*
9	*nueve*	70	*setenta*
10	*diez*	71	*setenta y uno*
11	*once*	80	*ochenta*
12	*doce*	81	*ochenta y uno*
13	*trece*	90	*noventa*
14	*catorce*	91	*noventa y uno*
15	*quince*	100	*ciento (cien)*
16	*diez y seis (dieciséis)*	101	*ciento uno*
		102	*ciento dos*
17	*diez y siete (diecisiete)*	200	*doscientos (-as)*
		201	*doscientos uno*
18	*diez y ocho (dieciocho)*	300	*trescientos (-as)*
		400	*cuatrocientos (-as)*
19	*diez y nueve*	500	*quinientos (-as)*
20	*veinte*	600	*seiscientos (-as)*
21	*veinte y uno (veintiuno)*	700	*setecientos (-as)*
		800	*ochocientos (-as)*
22	*veinte y dos (veintidós)*	1,000	*mil*
		2,000	*dos mil*
23	*veinte y tres (veintitrés)*	100,000	*cien mil*
		500,000	*quinientos mil*
		1,000,000	*un millón*

Time

The article *la* is used when expressing *one o'-clock*, *las* when expressing the other hours. *After* or *past* is expressed by *y*; *to* or **of**, by *menos*. After half past the hour, time is expressed by the following hour minus (*menos*) the minutes

What time is it?	*¿Qué hora es?*
It is one o'clock.	*Es la una.*
It is two o'clock.	*Son las dos.*
It is three-thirty.	*Son las tres y media.*
It is a quarter past four.	*Son las cuatro y cuarto.*
It is a quarter to five.	*Son las cinco menos cuarto.*
It is ten minutes past eleven.	*Son las once y diez.*
It is five minutes to eight.	*Son las ocho menos cinco.*
It is exactly seven o'clock.	*Son las siete en punto.*
It is noon (midnight).	*Es mediodía (medianoche)*
At what time?	*¿A qué hora?*
Nine in the morning.	*Las nueve de la mañana.*

Months, days, seasons

The names of the months, days of the week, and the seasons are written with small letters.

enero	January	*el lunes*	Monday
febrero	February	*el martes*	Tuesday
marzo	March	*el miércoles*	Wednesday
abril	April	*el jueves*	Thursday
mayo	May	*el viernes*	Friday
junio	June	*el sábado*	Saturday
julio	July	*el domingo*	Sunday
agosto	August		
septiembre	September	*la primavera*	spring
octubre	October	*el verano*	summer
noviembre	November	*el otoño*	autumn
diciembre	December	*el invierno*	winter

The English word "on" before a day of the week or a date is expressed by the definite article.

Los sábados voy de compras.

On Saturday I go shopping.

The years are expressed in thousands and hundreds.

Nació en mil novecientos setenta.

He was born in nineteen seventy.

Dates

What is today's date?	*¿Cuál es la fecha de hoy?*
	¿A cuántos estamos hoy?
It is March 1.	*Es el primero de marzo.*.
He arrived June 2,1950.	*Llegó el dos de junio de mil novecientos cincuenta.*
He left on May 4.	*Salió el cuatro de mayo.*

Cardinal numbers are used for all dates except primero (first).

Age

Age is expressed with the verb tener.

¿Cuántos años tienes tú? How old are you?

Tengo once años. I am eleven.

Countries

Germany	*Alemania*
Austria	*Austria*
Belgium	*Bélgica*
Canada	*Canadá*
Denmark	*Dinamarca*
Spain	*España*
England	*Inglaterra*
Italy	*Italia*
Peru	*Perú*
Russia	*Rusia*
Sweden	*Suecia*
Switzerland	*Suiza*

Countries where Spanish is spoken

Argentina	*Argentina*
Bolivia	*Bolivia*
Chile	*Chile*
Colombia	*Colombia*
Costa Rica	*Costa Rica*
Cuba	*Cuba*
Ecuador	*Ecuador*
El Salvador	*El Salvador*
Spain	*España*
Guatemala	*Guatemala*
Honduras	*Honduras*
Mexico	*México*
Nicaragua	*Nicaragua*
Panama	*Panamá*
Paraguay	*Paraguay*
Peru	*Perú*
Puerto Rico	*Puerto Rico*
Dominican Republic	*República Dominicana*
Uruguay	*Uruguay*
Venezuela	*Venezuela*

el pelo hair
las orejas ears
las mejillas cheeks
la barba chin
los ojos eyes
la nariz nose
la boca mouth

La cara The face

Dictionary

El cuerpo humano The human body

la cabeza head
el cuello neck
el hombro shoulder
el pecho chest
el brazo arm
el estómago stomach
la mano hand
los dedos fingers
la pierna leg
el pie foot
los dedos del pie toes

Dictionary abbreviations. Nouns are identified as masculine *(m)* or feminine *(f)*. Adjectives are identified as *adj*, adverbs as *adv*, conjunctions as *conj*, interjections as *interj*, prepositions as *prep*, pronouns as *pron*, and verbs as *v*. Plurals are identified as *pl*.

Spanish-English

A

a *prep* at, to
abajo *adv* below, down
abeja *f* bee
abierto *adj* open
abogado *m* lawyer
abrigo *m* overcoat
abrir *v* open
acá *adv* here
acabar *v* finish, **acabar de** to have just . . .
aceite *m* oil
acento *m* accent
aceptar *v* accept
acera *f* sidewalk
acerca de *prep* about, concerning
acercarse *v* approach
acero *m* steel
acompañar *v* accompany
aconsejar *v* advise
acordarse *v* remember
acostarse *v* go to bed
acto *m* act
actual *adj* present
acuerdo *m* agreement
adelante *adv* forward
además *adv* besides
adentro *adv* inside
adiós *interj and m* goodbye
admirar *v* admire
adónde *adv* where
aduana *f* custom house
aeropuerto *m* airport
afecto *m* affection
afilado *adj* sharp
afuera *adv* out, outside
agradable *adj* pleasant, agreeable
agradecer *v* be grateful for
agua *f* water
aguardar *v* wait for
agudo *adj* sharp
águila *f* eagle
aguja *f* needle
ahí *adv* there
ahora *adv* now
aire *m* air

al *prep* to the, at the
albóndiga *f* meatball
alcalde *m* mayor
alcanzar *v* reach, catch
alcoba *f* bedroom
aldea *f* village
alegrarse *v* be glad
alegre *adj* happy
alegría *f* joy
alfiler *m* pin
alfombra *f* carpet, rug
algo *pron* something
algodón *m* cotton
alguien *pron* someone
alguno *adj* some
alimento *m* food
allá *adv* there
allí *adv* there
alma *f* soul
almacén *m* department store
almohada *f* pillow
almorzar *v* lunch
almuerzo *m* lunch
alrededor *adv* around
alto *adj* tall, high
altura *f* height
alumbrar *v* illuminate, light
alumno, -a *n* pupil, student
alzar *v* raise, lift
amable *adj* amiable, kind, pleasant
amar *v* love
amargo *adj* bitter
amarillo *adj* yellow
ambos *adj and pron* both
americano *adj and n* American
amigo, -a, *n* friend
amistad *f* friendship
amor *m* love
ancho *adj* wide
anciano *adj* old
andar *v* walk
ángel *m* angel
anillo *m* ring
anoche *adv* last night
antes *adv* before, formerly
antiguo *adj* former

Review of Spanish Grammar

añadir *v* add
año *m* year
apagar *v* extinguish
aparecer *v* appear, show up
apenas *adv* hardly
aplicado *adj* diligent
aprender *v* learn
aquí *adv* here
árbol *m* tree
arena *f* sand, arena
armario *m* closet
arreglar *v* arrange, fix, repair
arriba *adv* above, up
asar *v* roast
así *adv* so, thus
asiento *m* seat
asistir *v* attend
asustar *v* frighten
atar *v* tie
atrás *adv* behind
avenida *f* avenue
averiguar *v* find out
avisar *v* inform, notify
ayer *adv* yesterday
ayudar *v* help
azul *adj* blue

B

bailar *v* dance
bajar *v* descend, lower
banco *m* bank, bench
bandera *f* flag
baño *m* bath, bathroom
barato *adj* cheap
barba *f* beard, chin
barbero *m* barber
barco *m* ship
barrio *m* district
bastante *adv and adj* enough
beber *v* drink
bello *adj* beautiful
beso *m* kiss
biblioteca *f* library
bien *adv* well
billete *m* ticket
bizcocho *m* cake, biscuit
blanco *adj* white
bolígrafo *m* ballpoint pen
bolsa *f* purse, bag
bolsillo *m* pocket
bonito *adj* pretty
bosque *m* forest
botella *f* bottle
bueno *adj* good

burro *m* donkey
buscar *v* look for
butaca *f* armchair

C

caballero *m* gentleman
caballo *m* horse
cabello *m* hair
cabeza *f* head
cada *adj* each, every
cadena *f* chain
caer *v* fall
café *m* coffee, café
caja *f* box
calentar *v* heat, warm
caliente *adj* hot
calle *f* street
calor *m* heat
cama *f* bed
cambio *m* change, exchange
caminar *v* walk
camino *m* road
campo *m* country
canción *f* song
cansado *adj* tired
cantar *v* sing
cara *f* face
cariño *m* affection
caro *adj* expensive
carro *m* car
carta *f* letter
casa *f* house
casarse *v* get married
casi *adv* almost
cena *f* supper
cepillo *m* brush
cerca *adv* near
cerdo *m* pig, hog
cerrar *v* close
cerveza *f* beer
cielo *m* sky, heaven
cita *f* appointment
ciudad *f* city
clavel *m* carnation
coche *m* car
cocina *f* kitchen
cocinar *v* cook
colina *f* hill
comedia *f* comedy, play
comedor *m* dining room
comenzar *v* begin
comer *v* eat
comercio *m* commerce
comida *f* food, meal, dinner

como *adv and conj* as, like
¿cómo? *interj* how
cómoda *f* dresser
comprar *v* buy
comprender *v* understand
con *prep* with
conocer *v* know
conseguir *v* obtain
contar *v* count, tell
contento *adj* happy
contestar *v* answer
continuar *v* continue
contra *prep* against
copa *f* goblet
correo *m* mail, post office
correr *v* run
corrida *f* race, **corrida de toros**
  bullfight
cortina *f* curtain
corto *adj* short
cosa *f* thing
costar *v* cost
creer *v* believe
criada *f* maid
cristiano *m and adj* Christian
cuadro *m* picture
¿cuál? *interj* which
¿cuándo? *interj* when
¿cuánto? *interj* how much?
¿cuántos? *interj* how many?
cuarto *m* room, quarter
cuchara *f* spoon
cuchillo *m* knife
cuenta *f* bill
cuero *m* leather
cuidado *m* care, caution
cumpleaños *m* birthday

CH

charla *f* chat
cheque *m* check
chico, -a *n* boy, girl
chiste *m* joke
choque *m* collision

D

dama *f* lady
daño *m* damage
dar *v* give
de *prep* of, from
debajo *adv* beneath
deber *v* ought, should, owe
débil *adj* weak

decir *v* say, tell
dejar *v* leave
delante de *prep* in front of
delgado *adj* thin
demasiado *adv and adj* too much, too many, too
dentista *m* dentist
dentro *adv* within
derecho *adj and adv* straight
desastre *m* disaster
desayunarse *v* breakfast
desayuno *m* breakfast
descansar *v* rest
descubrir *v* discover
desear *v* wish, desire
despacio *adv* slowly
despertar *v* wake
después de *prep* after
detrás de *prep* in back of
devolver *v* return
día *m* day
difícil *adj* difficult
dinero *m* money
Dios *m* God
dolor *m* pain
don, doña *n* titles given to gentlemen and ladies. Used with first names.
dónde *conj and adv* where
dormir *v* sleep
dormitorio *m* bedroom, dormitory
duda *f* doubt
dueño *m* master, owner
dulce *adj* sweet
duro *adj* hard

E

e *conj* and (before *i* or *hi*)
echar *v* throw
edad *f* age
edificio *m* building
ejemplo *m* example
ejército *m* army
empleado *m* employee
empresa *f* enterprise
empujar *v* push
en *prep* in, on, at
encantador *adj* charming
encontrar *v* find, meet
enfermo *adj* sick
enfrente de *prep* facing
enojado *adj* angry
enseñar *v* teach

entender *v* understand
entero *adj* entire, whole
entonces *adv* then
entrada *f* entrance
entre *prep* between, among
enviar *v* send, ship
equivocado *adj* mistaken
escalera *f* staircase
escoba *f* broom
escoger *v* choose
escribir *v* write
escuchar *v* listen to
escuela *f* school
español *m and adj* Spanish
espejo *m* mirror
esperar *v* hope, wait
esposa *f* wife
esposo *m* husband
esquina *f* corner
estación *f* station, season
estado *m* state, condition
estar *v* be
este *m* east, *adj* this
estrecho *adj* narrow
estrella *f* star
estudiar *v* study
evitar *v* avoid
éxito *m* success
extranjero *m* foreigner

F

fábrica *f* factory
fácil *adj* easy
factura *f* invoice, bill
falda *f* skirt
falta *f* lack, mistake, fault
familia *f* family
fecha *f* date
feliz *adj* happy
feo *adj* ugly
ferrocarril *m* railroad
fiebre *f* fever
fiesta *f* holiday, festival
figurarse *v* imagine
fin *m* end, purpose
fino *adj* fine
firmar *v* sign
flan *m* custard
flor *f* flower
fonda *f* inn
fondo *m* bottom
francés *m and adj* Frenchman, French
frase *f* sentence

frazada *f* blanket
fresco *adj* cool, fresh
frío *m* cold, tener frío *v* feel cold
fuego *m* fire
fuente *f* fountain
fuera *adv* outside
fuerte *adj* strong, loud
fumar *v* smoke

G

gallina *f* hen
gallo *m* rooster
ganar *v* earn, win
ganga *f* bargain
gastar *v* spend
gato *m* cat
gemelos *m pl* cufflinks, twins
gente *f* people
golpe *m* blow
gordo *adj* fat
gozar *v* enjoy
gracia *f* grace, wit
gracias *f pl* thanks, thank you
grande *adj* large, great
gritar *v* shout
guapo *adj* handsome
guardar *v* keep, guard
guerra *f* war
gustar *v* please
gusto *m* pleasure, taste

H

haber *v* have
habitación *f* room
hablar *v* speak
hacer *v* do, make
hacia *prep* toward
hallar *v* find
hambre *f* hunger, tener hambre be hungry
hasta *prep* until, hasta luego until later
hay *v* there is, there are
hecho *m* fact
hermoso *adj* beautiful
hielo *m* ice
hierba *f* grass
hija *f* daughter
hijo *m* son
hilo *m* thread
hoja *f* leaf
hombre *m* man

Review of Spanish Grammar

hora *f* hour, time
hoy *adv* today
hueso *m* bone
huevo *m* egg

I

idioma *m* language
iglesia *f* church
igualmente *adv* equally
inglés *m and adj* Englishman, English
inquieto *adj* anxious, worried
ir *v* go
isla *f* island
izquierdo *adj* left

J

jabón *m* soap
jamás *adv* never
jardín *m* garden
jefe *m* chief, boss
joven *adj* young
joya *f* jewel, gem
judío *m and adj* Jew, Jewish
juego *m* game
jugar *v* play
jugo *m* juice
junto *adj* together

L

labio *m* lip
lado *m* side
ladrón *m* thief
lago *m* lake
lágrima *f* tear
lana *f* wool
lápiz *m* pencil
largo *adj* long
lástima *f* pity
lata *f* tin, tin can
lavandería *f* laundry
lavar *v* wash
lectura *f* reading
leer *v* to read
legumbres *f pl* vegetables
lejos *adv* far
lento *adj* slow
levantar *v* raise, lift, **levantarse** *v* get up, rise
ley *f* law
libra *f* pound
libre *adj* free

libro *m* book
ligero *adj* light
limpiar *v* clean, wash
lindo *adj* pretty
listo *adj* clever, ready
lobo *m* wolf
loco *adj* crazy
lograr *v* achieve
lucha *f* fight
luego *adv* then
lugar *m* place
luna *f* moon
luz *f* light

LL

llamar *v* call
llamarse *v* be named
llave *f* key
llegar *v* arrive
lleno *adj* full
llevar *v* carry, wear
llorar *v* cry
llover *v* rain
lluvia *f* rain

M

madera *f* wood
madre *f* mother
maestro *m* teacher
maíz *m* corn
mal *adv* badly
maleta *f* suitcase
malo *adj* bad, sick
mandar *v* send
manga *f* sleeve
mano *f* hand
manta *f* blanket
mantel *m* tablecloth
mar *m and f* sea
marido *m* husband
martillo *m* hammer
más *adj and adv* more
matador *m* bullfighter
matar *v* to kill
mayor *adj* greater, older
medianoche *f* midnight
médico *m* doctor
medio *m* half
mejor *adj* better
menor *adj* smaller, younger
mentira *f* lie
mercado *m* market
mes *m* month

mesa *f* table
metro *m* meter, subway
miedo *m* fear
mientras *conj* while
milla *f* mile
mirar *v* look at
mismo *adj* same
modo *m* manner
molestar *v* trouble, disturb
moneda *f* coin
mono *m* monkey
montar *v* mount, climb
moreno *adj* dark, brunette
morir *v* die
mozo *m* waiter, porter, lad
muchacho, -a *n* boy, girl
mucho *adj* much
mueble *m* furniture
muerte *f* death
mujer *f* woman, wife
mundo *m* world
museo *m* museum
muy *adv* very

N

nacer *v* be born
nada *pron* nothing
nadar *v* swim
nadie *pron* nobody
nariz *f* nose
Navidad *f* Christmas
necesitar *v* need
negar *v* deny
negocio *m* business
negro *adj* black
nevar *v* snow
nieta *f* granddaughter
nieto *m* grandson
nieve *f* snow
niña *f* girl
niño *m* boy
no *interj and adv* no, not
noche *f* night
nombre *m* name, noun
norte *m* north
noticia *f* news
novia *f* sweetheart
novio *m* sweetheart, groom
nube *f* cloud
nubile *adj* marriageable
nublado *adj* cloudy
nuevo *adj* new
número *m* number
nunca *adv* never

O

o *conj* or
obra *f* work
océano *m* ocean
ocupado *adj* busy, occupied
oeste *m* west
oído *m* ear (inner)
oír *v* hear
olor *m* odor
olvidar *v* forget
orar *v* pray
orgulloso *adj* proud
orilla *f* shore
oro *m* gold
oso *m* bear
otro *adj* another, other, **otra vez** *adv* again
oveja *f* sheep

P

pagar *v* pay
país *m* country
pájaro *m* bird
palabra *f* word
paloma *f* dove
pañuelo *m* handkerchief
papel *m* paper
paquete *m* package
par *m* pair, equal
para *prep* for
paraguas *m* umbrella
pardo *adj* brown
parecer *v* seem
pariente *m* relative
parque *m* park
partida *f* departure
pasajero *m* passenger
paseo *m* walk
paso *m* step
paz *f* peace
pedir *v* ask (for)
peinarse *v* comb one's hair
pelota *f* ball
peluquero *m* hairdresser
pena *f* pain, grief, trouble
pensar *v* think
peor *adj* worse
pequeño *adj* small
perder *v* lose
perezoso *adj* lazy
periódico *m* newspaper
pero *conj* but
perro *m* dog

pesado *adj* heavy
piedra *f* stone
pintor *m* painter
pintura *f* painting
piso *m* floor
plata *f* silver
plátano *m* banana
playa *f* beach
pluma *f* pen
pobre *adj* poor
poco *adj and adv* little
poder *v* be able
poner *v* put
por *prep* for, by, through
por favor *adv* please
porque *conj* because
¿por qué? *pron* why
precio *m* price
pregunta *f* question
preguntar *v* ask
prestar *v* lend
primero *adj and adv* first
prisa *f* hurry
probar *v* prove
pronto *adv* soon
propina *f* tip
propio *adj* own, proper
pueblo *m* town, people
puerta *f* door
pulsera *f* bracelet

Q

que *pron* that, than
¿que? *pron* what
quedar *v* remain
queja *f* complaint
quemar *v* burn
querer *v* want, love
querido *adj* dear, beloved
quien *pron* who
¿quién? *pron* who
quitar *v* remove
quizá *adv* perhaps

R

raíz *f* root
rana *f* frog
rápido *adj* fast
rato *m* while
raya *f* dash, stripe
razón *f* reason
realizar *v* accomplish
recibir *v* receive

recibo *m* receipt
recoger *v* gather
recordar *v* remember
recuerdo *m* remembrance, memory
redondo *adj* round
regalo *m* gift
regla *f* rule
regresar *v* return
reina *f* queen
reír *v* laugh
reloj *m* watch, clock
repetir *v* repeat
resfriado *m* cold (illness)
respirar *v* breathe
responder *v* answer
respuesta *f* answer
resto *m* remainder
resultado *m* result
retrete *m* toilet
reunión *f* meeting
revista *f* magazine
rey *m* king
rezar *v* pray
rico *adj* rich
rincón *m* corner
río *m* river
robar *v* steal
rogar *v* beg
rojo *adj* red
romper *v* break
rubio *adj* blond
rueda *f* wheel
ruido *m* noise

S

sábana *f* sheet
saber *v* know
sabio *adj* wise
sabor *m* flavor
sacar *v* take out
sacerdote *m* priest
sal *f* salt
sala *f* livingroom
salida *f* exit, departure
salir *v* leave
saltar *v* jump
salud *f* health
saludar *v* greet
sandía *f* watermelon
sangre *f* blood
sano *adj* healthy, sane
sastre *m* tailor
satisfecho *adj* satisfied

Review of Spanish Grammar

seco *adj* dry
sed *f* thirst
seda *f* silk
seguida *f* succession, **en seguida** immediately
seguir *v* follow
seguro *adj* sure
sello *m* stamp
semana *f* week
semejante *adj* similar
señal *f* signal
señor *m* sir, Mr., gentleman
señora *f* madam, Mrs., lady
señorita *f* young lady, Miss
sentarse *v* sit down
sentido *m* meaning, sense
sentir *v* regret, feel, sense
ser *v* be
servicio *m* service
servilleta *f* napkin
servir *v* serve
si *conj* if
sí *interj* yes
siempre *adv* always
sierra *f* mountain range
siglo *m* century
significar *v* mean, signify
siguiente *adj* following
silla *f* chair
simpático *adj* congenial, nice
sin *prep* without
sobre *m* envelope
sobre *prep* on
socio *m* associate, partner
sol *m* sun
solamente *adv* only
solo *adj* alone
sombra *f* shadow
sonar *v* sound
sordo *adj* deaf
sorpresa *f* surprise
subir *v* ascend
suceder *v* happen
sucio *adj* dirty
suelo *m* floor, ground
sueño *m* dream
suerte *f* luck
sur *m* south
susto *m* fright

T

tal *adj* such
tamaño *m* size
también *adv* also

tampoco *adv* neither, either
tan *adv* so
tanto *adj* so much
tarde *f* afternoon
tarjeta *f* card
taza *f* cup
teatro *m* theater
techo *m* ceiling, roof
teléfono *m* telephone
temprano *adv and adj* early
tenedor *m* fork
tener *v* have
terminar *v* end, terminate
tesoro *m* treasure
tiempo *m* time, weather
tienda *f* store
tierra *f* earth, land
tirar *v* throw
tiza *f* chalk
tocar *v* touch, play (instrument)
todo *adj* all
tomar *v* take, drink
tonto *m and adj* fool, foolish
torero *m* bullfighter
toro *m* bull
trabajar *v* work
traducir *v* translate
traer *v* bring
tranvía *m* streetcar
trapo *m* floor, ground
tratar de *v* try to
tren *m* train
trigo *m* wheat
triste *adj* sad
tronco *m* trunk

U

u *conj* or (before *o* or *ho*)
último *adj* last
único *adj* only
unir *v* unite
usar *v* wear, use
útil *adj* useful
uva *f* grape

V

vaca *f* cow
vacaciones *f pl* vacation
vacío *adj* empty
valer *v* be worth
valle *m* valley
vapor *m* steam
varios *adj* several

vaso *m* glass
vecino *m* neighbor
vender *v* sell
venir *v* come
venta *f* sale
ventana *f* window
ver *v* see
veras, de *adv* really
veraz *adj* truthful
verbo *m* verb
verboso *adj* talkative
verdad *f* truth
verde *adj* green
verede *f* path
veredicto *m* verdict
vergonzoso *adj* shameful, shy
vergüenza *f* shame
verificar *v* verify
verja *f* grating
verosímil *adj* likely
vestir *v* dress
vez *f* time, turn
viajar *v* travel
viaje *m* trip
vida *f* life
viejo *adj* old
viento *m* wind
vino *m* wine
visita *f* visit
visitar *v* visit
vista *f* view
viudo, -a *n* widower, widow
vivir *v* live
vivo *adj* living, alive
volar *v* fly
voz *f* voice
vuelta *f* return, turn

Y

y *conj* and
ya *adv* already
yacer *v* lie
yema *f* egg yolk
yerba *f* grass
yerro *m* error

Z

zapatería *f* shoe store
zapato *m* shoe
zarzuela *f* musical comedy
zona *f* zone
zorra *f* vixen
zorro *m* fox

Dictionary abbreviations. Nouns are identified as masculine (*n m*) or feminine (*n f*). Adjectives are identified as *adj*, adverbs as *adv*, conjunctions as *conj*, interjections as *interj*, prepositions as *prep*, pronouns as *pron*, and verbs as *v*. Plurals are identified as *pl*.

English-Spanish

A

a, an *adj* un, una
able *adj* capaz, **be able** *v* poder
abode *n* residencia *f*
about *prep* acerca de
above *adv* arriba
absent *adj* ausente
accent *n* acento *m*
accept *v* aceptar
accompany *v* acompañar
accomplish *v* realizar
ache *n* dolor *m*
achieve *v* lograr
act *n* acto *m*
add *v* añadir
admire *v* admirar
advantage *n* ventaja *f*
advise *v* aconsejar
affection *n* afecto *m*, cariño *m*
after *prep* después de
afternoon *n* tarde *f*
again *adv* otra vez
age *n* edad *f*
agreement *n* acuerdo *m*
air *n* aire *m*
airport *n* aeropuerto *m*
all *adj* todo
almost *adv* casi
alone *adv* solo
already *adv* ya
also *adv* también
always *adv* siempre
American *adj and nm* americano
among *prep* entre
and *conj* y, e
angel *n* ángel *m*
angry *adj* enojado
answer *v* responder, contestar
anxious *adj* inquieto
appear *v* aparecer
appointment *n* cita *f*, nombramiento *m*
approach *v* acercarse a
apron *n* delantal *m*
armchair *n* butaca *f*

army *n* ejército *m*
around *adv* alrededor
arrange *v* arreglar
arrive *v* llegar
as *adv and conj* como
ascend *v* subir
ask *v* preguntar
ask for *v* pedir
associate *n* socio *m*
at *prep* a, **at the** al
attend *v* asistir a
aunt *n* tía *f*
author *n* autor *m*
avenue *n* avenida *f*
avoid *v* evitar
awful *adj* horrible, terrible

B

back *adv* atrás, **in back of** detrás de
backward *adj* atrasado
bad *adj* malo
badly *adv* mal
ball *n* pelota *f*
ballpoint pen *n* bolígrafo *m*
banana *n* plátano *m*
bank *n* banco *m*
barber *n* barbero *m*
bargain *n* ganga *f*
bath *n* baño *m*
bathroom *n* cuarto de baño *m*
be *v* ser, estar
beach *n* playa *f*
bear *n* oso *m*
beard *n* barba *f*
beautiful *adj* bello, hermoso
because *conj* porque
bed *n* cama *f*, **go to bed** acostarse
bedroom *n* alcoba *f*, dormitorio *m*
bee *n* abeja *f*
beer *n* cerveza *f*
before *adv* antes
beg *v* rogar

begin *v* comenzar, empezar
behind *adv* detrás, *prep* detrás de
believe *v* creer
bell *n* campana *f*
below *adv* abajo
bench *n* banco *m*
beneath *adv* debajo
besides *adv* además
better *adj and adv* mejor
between *prep* entre
bill *n* cuenta *f*, factura *f*
bird *n* pájaro *f*
birthday *n* cumpleaños *m*
bitter *adj* amargo
black *adj* negro
blanket *n* manta *f*, frazada *f*
blind *adj* ciego
blond *adj* rubio
blood *n* sangre *f*
blow *n* golpe *m*
blue *adj* azul
boat *n* barco *m*
bone *n* hueso *m*
book *n* libro *m*
born, be *v* nacer
both *adj and pron* ambos
bottle *n* botella *f*
bottom *n* fondo *m*
box *n* caja *f*
boy *n* niño *m*, chico *m*, muchacho *m*
bracelet *n* pulsera *f*
break *v* romper
breakfast *n* desayuno *m*, *v* desayunar
breathe *v* respirar
bring *v* traer
broom *n* escoba *f*
brother *n* hermano *m*
brown *adj* pardo
brunette *adj and nm* moreno
brush *n* cepillo *m*
building *n* edificio *m*
bull *n* toro *m*
bullfight *n* corrida de toros *f*
bullfighter *n* torero *m*, matador *m*
burn *v* quemar
bus *n* autobús *m*
business *n* negocios *m pl*, comercio *m*
busy *adj* ocupado
butter *n* mantequilla *f*
buy *v* comprar

Review of Spanish Grammar

C

cabin *n* cabaña *f*
cage *n* jaula *f*
cake *n* bizcocho *m*
call *v* llamar
car *n* carro *m,* coche *m*
care *n* cuidado *m*
carnation *n* clavel *m*
carpet *n* alfombra *f*
carry *v* llevar
castle *n* castillo *m*
cat *n* gato *m*
ceiling *n* techo *m*
century *n* siglo *m*
chain *n* cadena *f*
chair *n* silla *f*
chalk *n* tiza *f*
change *n* cambio *m*
charming *adj* encantador
chat *n* charla *f*
cheap *adj* barato
check *n* (banking) cheque *m*
chief *n* jefe *m*
chin *n* barba *f*
choose *v* escoger
Christmas *n* Navidad *f*
church *n* iglesia *f*
city *n* ciudad *f*
clean *v* limpiar
clever *adj* listo
clock *n* reloj *m*
close *v* cerrar
closet *n* armario *m*
cloud *n* nube *f*
coffee *n* café *m*
coin *n* moneda *f*
cold *n* frío *m,*
  (illness) resfriado *m*
collar *n* cuello *m*
collision *n* choque *m*
comb (one's hair) *v* peinarse
come *v* venir
comedy *n* comedia *f*
commerce *n* comercio *m*
concerning *prep* acerca de
congenial *adj* simpático
continue *v* continuar
cool *adj* fresco
corn *n* maíz *m*
corner *n* esquina *f,* rincón *m*
cost *v* costar
cotton *n* algodón *m*
count *v* contar
country *n* campo *m,* país *m*

cow *n* vaca *f*
crash *n* choque *m*
crazy *adj* loco
cry *v* llorar
cufflinks *n* gemelos *m pl*
cup *n* taza *f*
custard *n* flan *m*
custom *n* costumbre *f*
customhouse *n* aduana *f*
cut *v* cortar

D

daily *adj* diario
damage *n* daño *m*
dance *v* bailar
dark *adj* moreno, oscuro
dash *n* raya *f*
date *n* fecha *f*
daughter *n* hija *f*
day *n* día *m*
dead *adj* muerto
deaf *adj* sordo
dear *adj* querido
death *n* muerte *f*
decide *v* decidir
deep *adj* hondo
dentist *n* dentista *m, f*
deny *v* negar
department store *n* almacén *m*
departure *n* partida *f,* salida *f*
descend *v* bajar
dew *n* rocío *m*
difficult *adj* difícil
diligent *adj* aplicado
dining room *n* comedor *m*
dinner *n* comida *f*
dirty *adj* sucio
disaster *n* desastre *m*
discover *v* descubrir
dish *n* plato *m*
district *n* barrio *m*
disturb *v* molestar
do *v* hacer
doctor *n* médico *m*
dog *n* perro *m*
donkey *n* burro *m*
door *n* puerta *f*
doubt *n* duda *f*
dove *n* paloma *f*
down *adv* abajo
dozen *n* docena *f*
dream *n* sueño *m, v* soñar
dress *n* vestido *m, v* vestir
dresser *n* cómoda *f*

drink *v* beber
dry *adj* seco
during *prep* durante

E

each cada *adj*
eagle *n* águila *f*
ear *n* (inner) oído *m,* (outer) oreja *f*
early *adv and adj* temprano
earn *v* ganar
east *n* este *m*
Easter *n* Pascua Florida *f*
easy *adj* fácil
eat *v* comer
egg *n* huevo *m*
employee *n* empleado *m*
empty *adj* vacío
end *n* fin *m, v* terminar
enjoy *v* gozar
enough *adj and adv* bastante
enterprise *n* empresa *f*
entire *adj* entero
entrance *n* entrada *f*
envelope *n* sobre *m*
equally *adv* igualmente
even *adj* igual, *adv* hasta
example *n* ejemplo *m*
exchange *n* cambio *m*
exit *n* salida *f*
expensive *adj* caro
extinguish *v* apagar

F

face *n* cara *f*
facing *prep* enfrente de
fact *n* hecho *m*
factory *n* fábrica *f*
fall *v* caer
false *adj* falso
family *n* familia *f*
far *adv* lejos
farm *n* granja, hacienda *f*
fat *adj* gordo
fear *n* miedo *m, v* temer
feel *v* sentir
festival *n* fiesta *f*
fever *n* fiebre *f*
fight *n* lucha *f*
find *v* encontrar, hallar
find out *v* averiguar
fine *adj* fino, *adv* muy bien
finish *v* acabar, terminar

fire *n* fuego *m*
first *adj and adv* primero
flavor *n* sabor *m*
floor *n* piso *m*, suelo *m*
flower *n* flor *f*
fly *v* volar, *n* mosca *f*
follow *v* seguir
following *adj* siguiente
food *n* comida *f*
fool *n* tonto *m*
for *prep* por, para
foreigner *n* extranjero *m*
forest *n* bosque *m*
forget *n* olvidar *v*
fork *n* tenedor *m*
former antiguo *adj*
forward adelante *adv*
fountain *n* fuente *f*
frankly *adv* francamente
free libre *adj*
French *adj and nm* francés
fresh fresco *adj*
friend *n* amigo *m*
friendship *n* amistad *f*
fright *n* susto *m*
frighten asustar *v*
frog *n* rana *f*
from *prep* de
front *n* frente *m*, **in front of** delante de
full *adj* lleno
furniture *n* mueble *m*

G

gaiety *n* alegría *f*
game *n* juego *m*
garbage *n* basura *f*
garden *n* jardín *m*
garlic *n* ajo *m*
gasoline *n* gasolina *f*
gather *v* recoger
gem *n* joya *f*
gentleman *n* caballero *m*, señor *m*
gift *n* regalo *m*
girl *n* chica *f*, muchacha *f*, niña *f*
give *v* dar
glad *adj* contento, **be glad** *v* alegrarse
glass *n* vaso *m*
glove *n* guante *m*
go *v* ir
go out *v* salir
goblet *n* copa *f*

God *n* Dios *m*
gold *n* oro *m*
goodbye *interj* adiós
grace *n* gracia *f*
granddaughter *n* nieta *f*
grandson *n* nieto *m*
grape *n* uva *f*
grass *n* hierba *f*
grateful *adj* agradecido, **be grateful for** *v* agradecer
great *adj* gran, grande
greater *adj* mayor
green *adj* verde
greet *v* saludar
grief *n* pena *f*
ground *n* suelo *m*
guess *v* advinar

H

hair *n* cabello *m*, pelo *m*
hairdresser *n* peluquero *m*
hammer *n* martillo *m*
hand *n* mano *f*
handkerchief *n* pañuelo *m*
handsome *adj* guapo
happen *v* suceder
happy *adj* alegre, feliz, contento
hard *adj* duro
hardly *adv* apenas
have *v* tener, haber
head *n* cabeza *f*
health *n* salud *f*
healthy *adj* sano
hear *v* oír
heat *n* calor *m*, *v* calentar
heavy *adj* pesado
height *n* altura *f*
help *v* ayudar
hen *n* gallina *f*
here *adv* aquí, acá
hill *n* colina *f*
holiday *n* fiesta *f*
honest *adj* honesto
hope *v* esperar
horse *n* caballo *m*
hot *adj* caliente
hour *n* hora *f*
house *n* casa *f*
how *interj* ¿como?
how much, how many *interj* cuánto, cuántos
hunger *n* hambre *f*
hurry *n* prisa *f*
husband *n* esposo, marido *m*

I

ice *n* hielo *m*
if *conj* si
illuminate *v* alumbrar
imagine *v* figurarse
immediately *adv* en seguida
in *prep* en
inform *v* avisar
inn *n* fonda *f*
inside *adv* adentro, *adj and nm* interior
invoice *n* factura *f*
island *n* isla *f*

J

Jew *n* judio *m*, **Jewish** *adj* judio
jewel *n* joya *f*
joke *n* chiste *m*, *v* bromear
joy *n* alegría *f*
juice *n* jugo *m*
jump *v* saltar

K

keep *v* guardar
key *n* llave *f*
kill *v* matar
kind *adj* amable
king *n* rey *m*
kitchen *n* cocina *f*
knife *n* cuchillo *m*
know *v* saber, conocer

L

lack *n* falta *f*, *v* faltar
lady *n* dama *f*, señora *f*, **young lady** señorita *f*
lake *n* lago *m*
land *n* tierra *f*
language *n* idioma *m*
large *adj* grande
last *adj* último
last night *adv* anoche
later, see you hasta luego
laugh *v* reír
laundry *n* lavandería *f*
law *n* ley *f*
lawyer *n* abogado *m*
lazy *adj* perezoso
leaf *n* hoja *f*
learn *v* aprender
leather *n* cuero *m*

leave *v* dejar, salir
left *adj* izquierdo
lend *v* prestar
let *v* dejar
letter *n* carta *f*
library *n* biblioteca *f*
lie *n* mentira *f, v* mentir
life *n* vida *f*
light *adj* ligero, *nf* luz
lip *n* labio *m*
listen (to) *v* escuchar
little *adj* poco
live *v* vivir
living *adj* vivo
livingroom *n* sala *f*
look *n* mirada *f,* **look at** *v* mirar,
   look for buscar
lose *v* perder
love *n* amor *m, v* amar, querer
luck *n* suerte *f*
lunch *n* almuerzo *m, v* almorzar

M

madam *n* señora *f*
magazine *n* revista *f*
maid *n* criada *f*
mail *n* correo *m*
make *v* hacer
man *n* hombre *m*
manner *n* modo *m*
market *n* mercado *m*
marry *v* casarse con
master *n* dueño *m*
mayor *n* alcalde *m*
meal *n* comida *f*
mean *v* significar
meaning *n* sentido *m*
meatball *n* albóndiga *f*
meet *v* encontrar
meeting *n* reunión *f*
meter *n* metro *m*
midnight *n* medianoche *f*
mile *n* milla *f*
mirror *n* espejo *m*
miss *n* señorita *f*
mistake *n* falta *f*
mistaken *adj* equivocado
money *n* dinero *m*
month *n* mes *m*
moon *n* luna *f*
mother *n* madre *f*
mount *v* montar
mountain range *n* sierra *f*
Mr. *n* señor *m*

Mrs. *n* señora *f*
much *adj* mucho, **so much**
   tanto, **too much** demasiado
museum *n* museo *m*

N

name *n* nombre *m*
napkin *n* servilleta *f*
narrow *adj* estrecho
near *adv* cerca
need *v* necesitar
needle *n* aguja *f*
neighbor *n* vecino *m*
neither *adv* tampoco
never *adv* jamás, nunca
new *adj* nuevo
news *n* noticias *f pl*
newspaper *n* periódico *m*
night *n* noche *f*
no *adv* no
nobody *pron* nadie
noise *n* ruido *m*
north *n* norte *m*
nose *n* nariz *f*
not *adv* no
nothing nada *pron*
now *adv* ahora
number *n* número *m*

O

obtain *v* conseguir
ocean *n* océano *m*
odor *n* olor *m*
of *prep* de
oil *n* aceite *m*
old *adj* anciano, viejo
older *adj* mayor
on *prep* en, sobre
only *adv* solamente
open *adj* abierto, *v* abrir
or *conj* o, u
other *adj* otro
ought *v* deber
out *adv* fuera
outside *adv* fuera
overcoat *n* abrigo *m*
own *adj* propio
owner *n* dueño *m*

P

package *n* paquete *m*
pain *n* dolor *m*, pena *f*

painter *n* pintor *m*
painting *n* pintura *f,* cuadro *m*
pair *n* par *m*
paper *n* papel *m*
park *n* parque *m, v* estacionar
partner *n* socio *m*
passenger *n* pasajero *m*
pay *v* pagar, *n* pago, salario *m*
pen *n* pluma *f*
pencil *n* lápiz *m*
people *n* gente *f,* pueblo *m*
perhaps *adv* quizá
picture *n* cuadro *m*
pig *n* cerdo *m*
pillow *n* almohada *f*
pin *n* alfiler *m*
place *n* lugar *m*
play *n* comedia *f, v* jugar
pleasant *adj* agradable
please *v* gustar, *adv* por favor
pleasure *n* gusto *m*
pocket *n* bolsillo *m*
poor *adj* pobre
porter *n* mozo *m*
post office *n* correo *m*
pound *n* libra *f*
pray *v* rezar, orar
present *adj* actual, presente, *n*
   regalo *m*
pretty *adj* bonito, lindo
price *n* precio *m*
priest *n* sacerdote *m*
proud *adj* orgulloso
prove *v* probar
pupil *n* alumno, -a
purse *n* bolsa *f*
push *v* empujar
put *v* poner

Q

quarter *n* cuarto *m*
queen *n* reina *f*
question *n* pregunta *f*

R

rag *n* trapo *m*
railroad *n* ferrocarril *m*
rain *v* llover, *n* lluvia *f*
raise *v* alzar
reach *v* alcanzar
read *v* leer
reading *n* lectura *f*
ready *adj* listo

reason *n* razón *f*
receipt *n* recibo *m*
receive *v* recibir
red *adj* rojo
regret *v* sentir, *n* pena *f*
relative *n* pariente *m*
remain *v* quedar
remainder *n* resto *m*
remember *v* acordarse, recordar
remembrance *n* recuerdo *m*
remove *v* quitar
repeat *v* repetir
rest *v* descansar, *n* descanso *m*
result resultado *m*
return *v* volver, devolver,
  regresar, *n* vuelta *f*
rich *adj* rico
right *adj and n* derecho *m*
ring *n* anillo *m*
rise *v* levantarse
river *n* río *m*
road *n* camino *m*
roast *v* asar
roof *n* techo *m*
room *n* cuarto *m*, habitación *f*
rooster *n* gallo *m*
root *n* raíz *f*
round *adj* redondo
rule *n* regla *f*
run *v* correr

S

sad *adj* triste
sale *n* venta *f*
salt *n* sal *f*, *v* salar
same *adj and pron* mismo
sand *n* arena *f*
satisfied *adj* satisfecho
say *v* decir
school *n* escuela *f*
sea *n* mar *m and f*
season *n* estación *f*
seat *n* asiento *m*
see *v* ver
seem *v* parecer
sell *v* vender
send *v* enviar, mandar
sentence *n* frase *f*
serve *v* servir
service *n* servicio *m*
shadow *n* sombra *f*
shame *n* vergüenza *f*
sharp *adj* afilado, agudo
sheep *n* oveja *f*

sheet *n* sábana *f*
ship *n* barco *m*
shoe *n* zapato *m*
shoe store *n* zapatería *f*
shore *n* orilla *f*
short *adj* corto
should *v* deber
shout *v* gritar
sick *adj* enfermo, malo
side *n* lado *m*
sidewalk *n* acera *f*
sign *v* firmar
signal *n* señal *f*
silk *n* seda *f*
silver *n* plata *f*
similar *adj* semejante, parecido
sing *v* cantar
sir *title* señor
sit down *v* sentarse
size *n* tamaño *m*
skirt *n* falda *f*
sky *n* cielo *m*
sleep *v* dormir
sleeve *n* manga *f*
slow *adj* lento
slowly *adv* despacio
small *adj* pequeño
smaller *adj* menor
smile *v* sonreír, *n* sonrisa *f*
smoke *v* fumar
snow *v* nevar, *n* nieve *f*
so *adv* tan, así
so much *adj* tanto
soap *n* jabón *m*
some *adj and pron* alguno
someone *pron* alguien
something *pron* algo
song *n* canción *f*
soon *adv* pronto
soul *n* alma *f*
sound *v* sonar, *n* sonido *m*
south *n* sur *m*
Spanish *adj and n m* español
speak *v* hablar
spend *v* gastar
spoon *n* cuchara *f*
staircase *n* escalera *f*
stamp *n* sello *m*
star *n* estrella *f*
state *n* estado *m*
station *n* estación *f*
steal *v* robar
steam *n* vapor *m*
steel *n* acero *m*
step *n* paso *m*

stone *n* piedra *f*
store *n* tienda *f*
straight *adj* derecho
street *n* calle *f*
streetcar *n* tranvía *m*
stripe *n* raya *f*
strong *adj* fuerte
study *v* estudiar
subway *n* metro *m*
success *n* éxito *m*
such *adj* tal
suitcase *n* maleta *f*
sun *n* sol *m*
supper *n* cena *f*
sure *adj* seguro
surprise *n* sorpresa *f*
sweet *adj* dulce
sweetheart *n* novio, -a
swim *v* nadar

T

table *n* mesa *f*
tablecloth *n* mantel *m*
tailor *n* sastre *m*
take *v* tomar
take out *v* sacar
tall *adj* alto
teach *v* enseñar
teacher *n* maestro, -a
tear *n* lágrima *f*
telephone *n* teléfono *m*
tell *v* decir
than *conj* que
that *pron* que
then *adv* entonces, luego
there *adv* ahí, allá, allí
there are hay
there is hay
thief *n* ladrón *m*
thin *adj* delgado
thing *n* cosa *f*
think *v* pensar
thirst *n* sed *f*
thread *n* hilo *m*
throw *v* tirar, echar
thus *adv* así
ticket *n* billete *m*
tie *v* atar
time *n* hora *f*, tiempo *m*, vez *f*
tin *n* lata *f*
tin can *n* lata *f*
tip *n* propina *f*
tired *adj* cansado
to *prep* a

today *adv* hoy
together *adj* junto
toilet *n* retrete *m*
too *adv* demasiado, también
touch *v* tocar
toward *prep* hacia
town *n* pueblo *m*
train *n* tren *m*
translate *v* traducir
travel *v* viajar
treasure *n* tesoro *m*
tree *n* árbol *m*
trip *n* viaje *m*
trouble *v* molestar, *n* apuro *m*, pena *f*
trunk *n* tronco *m*
truth *n* verdad *f*
try to *v* tratar de

U

ugly *adj* feo
umbrella *n* paraguas *m*
understand *v* comprender, entender
unite *v* unir
use *v* usar
useful *adj* útil

V

vacation *n* vacaciones *f pl*
valley *n* valle *m*
view *n* vista *f*
village *n* aldea *f*
visit *n* visita *f*, *v* visitar
voice *n* voz *f*

W

wait for *v* aguardar, esperar
waiter *n* mozo *m*, camarero *m*
wake *v* despertar
walk *v* andar, caminar
want *v* querer
war *n* guerra *f*
wash *v* lavar
watch *n* reloj *m*
water *n* agua *f*
watermelon *n* sandía *f*
weak *adj* débil
weather *n* tiempo *m*
week *n* semana *f*
well *adv* bien, *adj* bueno
west *n* oeste *m*

what *interj pron* ¿qué?
wheat *n* trigo *m*
wheel *n* rueda *f*
when *adv* ¿cuándo?, *conj* cuando
where *adv* ¿adónde?, ¿dónde?, *conj* donde
which *pron* ¿cuál?
while *conj* mientras, *n* rato *m*
white *adj* blanco
who *pron* ¿quién?, quien
whole *adj* entero
why *adv* ¿por qué?
wide *adj* ancho
widow *n* viuda *f*
widower *n* viudo *m*
wife *n* esposa *f*, mujer *f*
wild *adj* bárbaro
wilderness *n* desierto *m*
wilt *v* marchitar
win *v* ganar
wind *n* viento *m*
window *n* ventana *f*
wine *n* vino *m*
wing *n* ala *f*
winner *n* ganador *m*
winter *n* invierno *m*
wipe *v* limpiar

wise *adj* sabio
wish *v* desear, *n* deseo *m*
wit *n* gracia *f*
with *prep* con
within *adv* dentro
without *prep* sin
wolf *n* lobo *m*
woman *n* mujer *f*
wood *n* madera *f*
wool *n* lana *f*
word *n* palabra *f*
work *n* obra *f*, *v* trabajar
world *n* mundo *m*
worried *adj* inquieto
worse *adv* peor
worth *n* valor *m*, **be worth** *v* valer
write *v* escribir

Y

year *n* año *m*
yellow *adj* amarillo
yes *adv* sí
yesterday *adv* ayer
young *adj* joven
younger *adj* menor

For further reference

Grammars

Greenfield, Eric V.
  Spanish Grammar
  Barnes and Noble
Jarvis, Ana C., Lebredo, Raquel, and
  Mena, Francisco
  Basic Spanish Grammar
  D. C. Heath and Company

Kendris, Christopher
  301 Spanish Verbs
  Barron's

Dictionaries

Castillo, Carlos and Bond, Otto
  *The University of Chicago
    Spanish-English, English-Spanish
    Dictionary*
  Pocket Books
Cuyás, Arturo
  *Appleton's New Cuyás
    English-Spanish, Spanish-English
    Dictionary*
  Prentice-Hall
Dutton, Brian, Harvey, L.P., and
  Walker, Roger M.
  *Cassell's Compact Spanish-English,
    English-Spanish Dictionary*
  Dell Publishing

Velázquez de la Cadena, Mariano,
  Gray, Edward, and Iribas, Juan R.
  *New Revised Velázquez
    Spanish-English, Diccionario
    Inglés-Español*
  New Century Publishers
Williams, Edwin B.
  *The Bantam New College Spanish
    and English Dictionary*
  Bantam Books

Index

How to use the index. The index to the *Student Handbook* is arranged alphabetically according to a letter-by-letter system. All entries, regardless of punctuation or spaces between words, are in precise alphabetical order; there are no exceptions:

> **Marshall Islands**
> **Marshall, John**
> **Marshall Plan**
> **Mars (planet)**

Names beginning with Mac or Mc are also arranged in strict alphabetical order. The abbreviation St. is indexed as if it were spelled out as Saint.

Each entry ends with a period. Following the period is the number 1, 2, 3, or 4 followed by a colon. These bold-faced numbers indicate the volume in which each page can be found. The page number follows the colon.

A semicolon separates the volumes, when applicable:

> **Lincoln, Abraham. 1:** 119, 121; **2:** 29, 36-37, 52, 56, 59, 99; **3:** 258-259, 274, 312

Most main entries are indexed under the main element of the name, e.g., Sinai, Mount (not Mount Sinai); Marathon, Battle of (not Battle of Marathon); Verdun, Treaty of (not Treaty of Verdun). Handy cross references are provided when a listing may be ambiguous or confusing.

Few abbreviations are used in the index, and those that are used are so standard as to eliminate the need for an abbreviations list.

Books, plays, and other titles are not indexed, but authors, artists, composers, etc., are, and the great works will almost invariably be found on the pages listed under their creators' names. Anonymous works, e.g., *Beowulf*, have their own listings.

The Latin Language

The Latin language began as one of many dialects of a language spoken around Rome and eventually became established as the second language of educated people in the whole of the Mediterranean basin and in large portions of Europe. Though technically a "dead" language, insofar as it no longer produces native speakers, Latin lives on through many descendant languages, such as Italian, Spanish, French, and, indirectly, English. Even if Latin were not the language of rich literary, scientific, and historical traditions, it would still be worthy of close study for what it reveals about the nature and vocabulary of modern European languages.

Pronunciation

We know two things about how ancient Latin was pronounced: (1) it could not have been pronounced like modern Italian or Church Latin, and (2) no one knows *exactly* how it was pronounced, though some reconstructions are better than others. Most consonants were pronounced much like their modern equivalents. Differences are noted in Table 1 on page 3. Long marks were not used in classical Latin, but are included as aids to students in modern elementary and intermediate texts.

Nouns

In a sentence, a noun will have number (singular or plural), gender (masculine, feminine, or neuter), and case (explained below). Gender is a fixed quality of a noun, but number and case can change depending on how the noun is being used.

Case

Endings attached to nouns indicate differing grammatical roles, called "cases." For the most part, Latin recognizes six such roles with discrete endings. See Table 2 on page 3.

Declensions

A declension is a pattern of case endings. There are five declensions, and a noun may belong to only one. See Table 3 on page 3. Notes: (1) One of the characteristics of the third declension is the large variety of nominative forms. They are not infinite, but too numerous to list conveniently in a table; (2) The second and fourth declensions have a subset of neuter endings; (3) The nominative and vocative endings differ only in the singular of the second declension.

To work with a noun, you need to know its meaning, gender, and the declension to which it belongs. A dictionary gives you this information by adopting a convention for the entry. You are first given the nominative case, secondly an abbreviation for the genitive case, which is an unambiguous indicator of the declension and the true stem (if it is not apparent in the nominative), and thirdly the gender. See Table 4 on page 3.

Articles

Latin does not have a definite article (*the*) or an indefinite article (*a, an*), but they are easily supplied in translation. **Hĕrculēs magnam partem diēī frūstrā cōnsūmpsit,** *Hercules spent a great part of the day in vain.* **Iāsŏn, dux Argonautārum, nǎvem dēdǔxit,** *Jason, the leader of the Argonauts, launched the ship.*

Word Order

Because the case endings reveal the function a noun has in its sentence, Latin word order is much more flexible than English, where word order is critical to the syntax. Each of these sentences means, *This girl saw my friend in the road,* although with different rhetorical emphases:

> **Haec puella amícum meum in viā vĭdit; Amĭcum meum in viā haec puella vĭdit; In viā haec puella meum amĭcum vĭdit,** etc.

Adjectives

An adjective is a word that modifies a noun. In Latin, an adjective will acquire some of the characteristics of the noun it is modifying: its number, gender, and case. The modification in form of one word to match another is called "agreement." There are two classes of adjectives: those which derive their endings from the 1st and 2nd declensions, and those which use the endings of the 3rd declension.

Adjectives of the 1st and 2nd declension use 1st declension endings to modify feminine nouns, 2nd declension endings to modify masculine nouns, and 2nd declension -**um** type to modify neuter nouns. See Table 5 on page 5.

Adjectives of the third declension are slightly more complicated. There are three types. The first type has only one form for all three genders in the nominative singular. The second type has two nominative singular forms, one for the masculine and feminine, and one for the neuter. The third has different nominative forms for all three genders.

But after the nominative singular, all third declen-

1

Table 1

Vowels	Sound	Diphthong	Sound
a / ā	dyn<u>a</u>mite / f<u>a</u>ther	ae	<u>ai</u>sle
e / ē	s<u>e</u>t / d<u>a</u>te	au	<u>ou</u>ch
i / ī	t<u>i</u>n / s<u>ee</u>n	ei	cl<u>ai</u>m
o / ō	<u>o</u>ff / r<u>o</u>de	eu	f<u>eu</u>d
u / ū	p<u>u</u>t / t<u>u</u>ne	oe	b<u>oy</u>
y	French t<u>u</u>	ui	g<u>ooey</u>
Consonants			
c	always hard : <u>c</u>at	g	always hard : <u>g</u>et
i	between vowels : <u>y</u>ellow	t	always hard : <u>t</u>on
qu	As in English : <u>qu</u>ick	v	<u>w</u>here

Table 2

Case	Major Grammatical Role
Nominative	Subject of a verb
Genitive	Possession
Dative	Indirect Object
Accusative	Direct Object / Object of a Preposition
Ablative	Adverbial Use / Object of a Preposition
Vocative	Direct Address

Table 3

The Five Declensions

Case	1st	2nd	3rd	4th	5th
Singular					
Nominative	-a	-us (-er) -um	—	-us -ū	-ēs
Genitive	-ae	-ī	-is	-ūs	-ēī
Dative	-ae	-ō	-ī	-uī -ū	-ēī
Accusative	-am	-um	-em —	-um -ū	-em
Ablative	-ā	-ō	-e or -ī	-ū	-ē
Vocative	-a	-e -um	—	-us -ū	-ēs
Plural					
Nom. / Voc.	-ae	-ī -a	-ēs -(i)a	-ūs -ua	-ēs
Genitive	-ārum	-ōrum	-(i)um	-uum	-ērum
Dative	-īs	-īs	-ibus	-ibus	-ēbus
Accusative	-ās	-ōs -a	-ēs (-īs) -(i)a	-ūs -ua	-ēs
Ablative	-īs	-īs	-ibus	-ibus	-ēbus

Table 4

Nouns of Each Declension

Dictionary Entry	Gender	Stem	Declension
puella, -ae, *f., girl*	feminine	puell-	1st
ager, -grī, *m., field*	masculine	agr-	2nd
alacritās, -tātis, *f., eagerness*	masculine	alacritāt-	3rd
manus, -ūs *f., hand, band*	feminine	man-	4th
diēs, diēī, *f., day*	feminine	diē-	5th

Status quo, semper fidelis, nonsequitur magna cum laude, et cetera, ad infinitum...

sion adjectives use the standard third declension endings. Two rules that are always observed, though, are that neuter accusative forms are always the same as the neuter nominative form, and that the neuter plural nominative ending is -ia. Hence it follows that the accusative plural neuter ending will also be -ia. See Table 6 on page 5.

It is very important to note that agreement does not require endings which look alike, but endings which are equivalent in number, gender, and case. Study how the third declension adjective **brevis, -e**, *brief*, modifies the first declension noun **vĭta, -ae, f., life**. See Table 7 on page 5.

Comparative degree

The comparative degree of adjectives is formed by adding a suffix with case endings, similar to the English method of adding *-er* or *-est* to the root of an adjective. The comparative suffix is a third declension **-ior, -ius**. Hence the adjective **certus, -a, -um**, *sure*, in the comparative degree becomes **certior, certius**, *surer*, and declines in the third declension. <u>Singular:</u> *Nom.* **certior / certius;** *Gen.* **certiōris;** *Dat.* **certiōri;** *Acc. m./f.* **certiōrem /** *neuter*, **certius;** *Abl.* **certiōri**, etc. Similarly, **brevis, -e**, *brief*, becomes *briefer*, **brevior, brevius; potēns, -ntis**, *powerful*, becomes **potentior, potentius**, *more powerful*.

The items being compared may be linked with the word **quam**, or the ablative of degree of difference may be used.

> **Vĭta mea brevior erat quam vĭta eius** or . . . **erat vĭtā eius**, *my life was briefer than his life.*

Superlative degree

The superlative degree regularly adds the suffix **-issim-** plus the first and second declension case endings. Hence **certissimus, -a, -um** from **certus, -a, -um**. If the stem of the adjective ends in -r- or -l-, some variation on this rule can be expected: **ācerrimus, -a, -um** from **ācer, ācris, ācre**, *harsh*, and **facillimus, -a, -um** from **facilis, -e**, *easy*.

As in English, some very common adjectives form their degrees irregularly by using different stems. Some Latin examples are *good, better, best:* **bonus, -a, -um; melior, melius; optimus, -a, -um;** *bad, worse, worst:* **malus, -a, -um; pêior, pêius; pessimus, -a, -um;** *big, bigger, biggest:* **magnus, -a, -um; māior, māius; maximus, -a, -um.**

> **Pompeius in** <u>**sānctissimam partem**</u> **templĭ ingressus est**, *Pompey entered the holiest part of the temple;* **Hĕrculēs** <u>**summĭs cum vĭribus**</u> **collum monstri compressit**, *Hercules squeezed the neck of the monster with all his might (with greatest strength).*

Adjectives as Nouns

Consider: *the rich, the poor, the good, the bad, and the ugly.* These are simply adjectives, and an English speaker is easily able to understand the noun that each implies. As in English, Latin adjectives can be used without nouns. **Multĭ tē laudant,** *many <u>people</u> praise you;* <u>**Omnia**</u> **parāta sunt,** *all <u>things</u> were prepared.* **Caesar cum** <u>**suĭs**</u> **profectus est,** *Caesar set out with his own <u>men.</u>*

Adverbs from Adjectives

A common way of deriving adverbs is to attach indeclinable endings to the stem of an adjective: *Positive Degree:* **-ē** for first and second declension adjectives, **-(i)ter** for third declension adjectives; *Comparative Degree:* **-ius** (the neuter accusative adjectival ending); *Superlative:* **-ē** to the superlative (**-issim-**) stem.

Hence from the adjectives **longus, -a, -um,** *long,* and **ācer, ācris, ācre,** *harsh:* <u>Positive:</u> **longē,** *at length;* **ācriter,** *harshly;* <u>Comparative:</u> **longius,** *longer, at greater length;* **ācrius,** *more harshly;* <u>Superlative:</u> **longissimē,** *longest, at greatest length;* **ācerrimē,** *most harshly.*

As may be expected, irregular adjectives will exhibit some slight deviations from these rules: **bene,** *well;* **melius,** *better;* **optimē,** *best;* **magnopere,** *very much; greatly;* **magis,** *more;* **maximē,** *most.*

A very common idiom uses **quam** with the superlative degrees of adjectives and adverbs: **Perseus** <u>**quam ācerrimē**</u> **in mōnstrum impetum fēcit,** *Perseus attacked the monster <u>as fiercely as possible.</u>*

Questions

Latin poses a simple question by attaching **-ne** to the end of the first word of the sentence.

> **Amāsne mē?** *do you love me.*

Other interrogatives can anticipate the response.

> **Num mē amās,** *you don't love me, do you?*
> **Nōnne mē amās,** *you love me, don't you?*

Latin has many interrogative adverbs that are used to form questions: **cūr,** *why;* **quandō,** *when;* **ubi,** *where;* **quōmodo,** *how;* **quō,** *to where;* **unde,** *from where,* etc. There are also a number of interrogative pronouns, which will be discussed below.

The Ablative Case

The ablative case has a variety of special uses, which must be learned. Some of the more common are shown in Table 8 on page 5.

Other Uses of Cases

Showing motion toward and away from named cities and small islands does not require prepositions such as **ad** and **ab**. The accusative case itself indicates motion toward; the ablative case alone indicates motion from. The locative case, which indicates position, is identical in

Table 5

First- and Second-Declension Adjectives

	Feminine	Masculine	Neuter
Nom.	magna	magnus	magnum
Gen.	magnae	magnī	magnī
Dat.	magnae	magnō	magnō
Acc.	magnam	magnum	magnum
Abl.	magnā	magnō	magnō
Voc.	magna	magne	magnum

Etc.

Table 6

Third-Declension Adjectives

One
M./F./N.

Nom.	potēns
Gen.	potentis
Dat.	potentī
Acc.	potentem ‗potēns
Abl.	potentī

Two
M./F.   N.

Nom.	facilis	facile
Gen.	facilis	
Dat.	facilī	
Acc.	facilem	facile
Abl.	facilī	

Three
M.   F.   N.

Nom.	ācer	ācris	ācre
Gen.	ācris		
Dat.	ācrī		
Acc.	ācrem		ācre
Abl.	ācrī		

Table 7

Adjectives

Nom.	vīta brevis
Gen.	vītae brevis
Dat.	vītae brevī
Acc.	vītam brevem
Abl.	vītā brevī

Etc.

Table 8

The Ablative Case

Means	Eum <u>baculō</u> percussit, *he hit him <u>with a cane</u>.*
Manner	<u>Magnā cum celeritāte</u> vēnit, *he came <u>with great speed</u>.*
Personal Agent	<u>Ab Caesare</u> servātī sumus, *we were saved <u>by Caesar</u>.*
Cause	<u>Stultitiā</u> ducis urbs dēlēta est, *the city was destroyed <u>because of the stupidity</u> of the leader.*
Degree of Difference	Puella celerius <u>puerō</u> cucurrit, *the girl ran faster <u>than the boy</u>.*
Separation	Augustus nōs <u>metū</u> līberāvit, *Augustus freed us <u>from fear</u>.*
Time	<u>Illō tempore</u> Rōmae paucī erant, *<u>at that time</u> there were few people in Rome.*
Description	Erat mōnstrum <u>speciē horribilī</u>, *there was a <u>horrible looking</u> monster.*
Specification	Perseus statūrā prōcērus erat, *Perseus was a tall man <u>in height</u>.*

form to the genitive case in first and second declension nouns, and to the ablative case in third declension nouns.

> **Rōmae multī mīlitēs erant,** *there were many soldiers at Rome;* **Mīlitēs Rōmam venient,** *the soldiers will come to Rome,* **Mīlitēs Rōmā profectī sunt,** *the soldiers set out from Rome.*

The dative case can show possession:

> **Mihi** nōmen est Brūtus, *my name is Brutus.*

The accusative case can be used to show the duration of time during which an event occurred:

> **Pugnātum est multās hōrās,** *there was fighting for many hours.*

A common use of the genitive is description:

> **Scipiō magnae virtūtis erat,** *Scipio was a man of great courage.*

The genitive case is often used after neuter pronouns:

> **Quid novī?** *What's new* (literally, *what of new?*); **Satis pecūniae nēmō umquam habēbit,** *no one will ever have enough money.*

Prepositions

Prepositions are words that show literal or figurative spatial relations between words: *in, from, to, with,* etc. In Latin, the objects of prepositions are mostly in the accusative or ablative case. A few prepositions can take either the accusative or ablative case, with a slight change in meaning. In such instances, the accusative will signify motion and the ablative will indicate position. The dictionary lists which case the preposition governs. Accusative Only: **ad,** *to, toward, near;* **circum,** *around;* **iuxtā,** *next to;* Ablative Only: **ab,** *from;* **dē,** *down from;* **ex,** *out of;* Accusative or Ablative: **in,** *into* or *in;* **sub,** *under;* **super,** *over* or *on top of.*

> **Rōmulus lēgātōs in vīcīnās urbēs mīsit,** *Romulus sent representatives into the neighboring cities;* **Castra sub montibus celeriter mūniērunt,** *they quickly fortified a camp beneath the mountains;* **Gladiātōrēs in arēnā relictī erant,** *the gladiators had been left in the sand.*

Numbers

Latin has cardinal numbers, *one, two, three,* etc., ordinal numbers, *first, second, third,* etc., and its own symbolic system known as Roman numerals, I, II, III, etc. A few cardinal numbers act as adjectives and change their termination to agree with nouns: **ūnus, duo,** and **trēs,** for example. You can tell which are adjectives if the dictionary entry lists more than one form in the nominative. All cardinal numbers are adjectives. See Table 9 on page 7.

> **Novem annīs Caesar Galliam in prōvinciae formam redēgit,** *In nine years, Caesar reduced Gaul to a province.* **Ad tertiam vigiliam crepitus immānis audītus est in silvā,** *towards the third watch, a dreadful noise was heard in the forest.* **Oppidum ā castrīs circiter MCC passuum distābat,** *the fort lay about 1200 paces from the camp.*

Verbs

Like nouns, verbs consist of a stem that contains the core meaning of the verb, and endings that indicate variations in the way the action is enacted. Latin verbs can indicate the following syntactical features with endings and infixes: **Person,** 1st, 2nd, 3rd; **Number,** singular, plural; **Voice,** active, passive; **Tense,** present, future, imperfect, perfect, pluperfect, future perfect; **Mood,** indicative, imperative, subjunctive, participial, infinitive.

One of the great challenges to beginning students is to memorize the seemingly limitless number of interchangeable endings and infixes that verbs can use. But with a little effort, patterns and rules can be discerned, which make the challenge, while still formidable, a little less daunting.

Verbs: Present System

Like English verbs, Latin verbs have more than one stem. Each stem is used as the root of a different tense system. For example, the complete dictionary entry for the verb *to love* is **amō, amāre, amāvī, amātus.** These are called the principal parts of the verb. The first two principal parts of all verbs—in this case **amō, amāre**—give you the information you need to form the present system of tenses: the present, future, and imperfect. We will start by examining this system and the first two principal parts.

Latin verbs are divided into four classes, called conjugations, depending on what vowel appears at the end of the present stem. The third conjugation is further divided into i-stem and non i-stem verbs, but this is not related to its stem vowel, which for both is -e-. The final -re is dropped from the second principal part to reveal the stem and the stem vowel. See Table 10 on page 7.

To the stem are added tense signs and personal endings. The personal endings for the present system are: Active: -ō (-m) -s, -t, -mus, -tis, -nt; Passive: -or, -ris (-re), -tur, -mur, -minī, -ntur.

There is no tense sign for the present tense, so the personal endings are added directly to the stem. The short **e** of the third conjugation changes with the addition of the personal endings. But the long stem vowel of the other three conjugations is nearly always visible.

Table 9

Cardinal Numbers	Ordinal Numbers	Roman Numerals
1. ūnus, ūna, ūnum	1. prīmus, -a, -um	1. I
2. duo, duae, duo	2. secundus	2. II
3. trēs, tria	3. tertius	3. III
4. quattuor	4. quārtus	4. IIII or IX
5. quīnque	5. quīntus	5. V
6. sex	6. sextus	6. VI
7. septem	7. septimus	7. VII
8. octō	8. octāvus	8. VIII
9. novem	9. nōnus	9. VIIII or VIX
10. decem	10. decimus	10. X
11. ūndecim	11. ūndecimus	11. XI
12. duodecim	12. duodecimus	12. XII
13. tredecim	13. tertius decimus	13. XIII
14. quattuordecim	14. quārtus decimus	14. XIIII or XIV
15. quīndecim	15. quīntus decimus	15. XV
16. sēdecim	16. sextus decimus	16. XVI
17. septendecim	17. septimus decimus	17. XVII
18. duodēvīginti	18. duodēvicēnsimus	18. XVIII
19. ūndēvīginti	19. ūndēvicēnsimus	19. XVIIII or XIX
20. vīginti	20. vicēnsimus	20. XX

Table 10

Verbs: Present System

Principal Parts	Stem	Stem Vowel	Conjugation
amō, amāre, amāvī, amātus, *love*	amā-	-ā	1st
dēbeō, -ēre, dēbuī, dēbitus, *owe*	dēbē-	-ē	2nd
dūcō, -ere, dūxī, ductus, *lead*	dūce-	-e	3rd
capiō, -ere, cēpī, captus, *take*	cape-	-e	3rd i-stem
audiō, -ire, audivī, auditus, *hear*	audi-	-i	4th

Table 11

The Verb "to be" in the Present System

Person	Present	Future	Imperfect
1st	sum	erō	eram
2nd	es	eris	erās
3rd	est	erit	erat
1st	sumus	erimus	erāmus
2nd	estis	eritis	erātis
3rd	sunt	erunt	erant

amō, *I love;* **dēbētis,** *you (pl.) owe;* **dūcuntur,** *they are led;* **capiunt,** *they take;* **audiris,** *you are heard.*

The tense sign for the future of first and second conjugation verbs is **-be-**. (The short **-e-** changes as personal endings are added.) <u>Active</u>: **-bō, -bis, -bit, -bimus, -bitis, -bunt;** <u>Passive</u>: **-bor, beris, -bitur, -bimur, -biniminí, -buntur.** In the future of third and fourth conjugation verbs, the tense sign is **-ē-**, with the one exception of the first person singular, where it is **-a-**: <u>Active</u>: **-am, -ēs, -et, -ēmus, -ētis, -ent;** <u>Passive</u>: **-ar, -ēris, -ētur, -ēmur, -ēmini, -entur.**

(pl.) will owe; **dūcentur,** *they will be led;* **capient,** *they will take;* **audiēris,** *you will be heard.*

The tense sign for the imperfect is **-bā-** for all four conjugations. It is completely regular. The addition of the personal endings never alters the final vowel.

amābam, *I used to love;* **dēbēbātis,** *you were owing;* **dūcēbantur,** *they were being led;* **capiēbant,** *they were taking;* **audiēbāris,** *you were being heard.*

The Verb "to be" in the Present System

Aside from its inherent importance, the forms of the irregular verb "to be" in the present system must be thoroughly mastered because they are used to build the perfect tense system. The dictionary entry is **sum, esse, fui, futūrus.** See Table 11 on page 7.

Perfect System Active

The tenses of the perfect system are the perfect, pluperfect, future perfect. In the active voice, these tenses are formed from the third principal part of the verb.

amō, amāre, <u>amāvi</u>, amātus
dēbeō, dēbēre, <u>dēbui</u>, dēbitus etc.

The passive voice of the perfect system, discussed later, uses the fourth.

The perfect system active has its own set personal endings, which, unlike in the personal endings of the present system, also indicate tense. Hence there is no tense sign inserted between the stem and the personal endings in the perfect system.

The <u>perfect personal endings</u> are: **-í, -istí, -it, -imus, -istis, -ērunt;** The <u>pluperfect endings</u> are the forms of the imperfect tense of the verb **sum.** The <u>future perfect endings</u> are the forms of the future of the verb **sum** with the exception of the third person plural, which is **-erint** instead of **-erunt.**

amāvi, *I loved*
amāveram, *I had loved*

amāverō, *I will have loved*
dēbuerātis, *you (pl.) had owed*
dūxerint, *they will have led*
cēpērunt, *they took*
audivisti, *you heard*

Participial Mood

A participle is a verbal adjective. As such, it will have features of the verb it comes from—tense and voice—and features that are necessary for its role as an adjective—number, gender, and case. Therefore, a participle will have both a verbal root and adjectival endings that can be altered to agree with its object. Latin has present, future, and perfect participles, though only the future tense has both active and passive participles.

The formulae for the participles are:

> <u>Present Active</u>: present stem + the third declension adjectival endings, **-ns, -ntis;**
> <u>Perfect Passive</u>: fourth principal part with **-ūs, -a, -um** adjectival endings;
> <u>Future Active</u>: fourth principal part + **ur** + adjectival endings **-us, -a, -um;**
> <u>Future Passive</u>: first principal part + **nd** + **-us, -a, -um.**

The complete set of participles from one of our paradigm verbs should illustrate these rules. See Table 13 on page 9.

Translating a participle requires attention to the context: **Trōiāni equum in urbem <u>tractum</u> vidēbant,** *the Trojans were looking at the horse, <u>which had been brought</u> into the city* (literally, <u>*having been brought*</u> *into the city*); **Cīvēs ōrātōri <u>discessūrō</u> dōnum dedērunt,** *the citizens gave the speaker a gift <u>as he was about to depart</u>* (literally, <u>*going to depart*</u>).

The future passive participle is generally used to express a sense of duty or necessity, not simply something that is going to be done. This commonly used construction is called the "passive periphrastic," and the participle is called the "gerundive." The agent in this construction is expressed in the dative case: **Haec verba ōrātōri <u>dicenda erant</u>,** *these words <u>had to be said</u> by the orator.*

Perfect System Passive

The voice of the perfect system of tenses—the perfect, pluperfect, and future perfect—is formed by using the fourth principal part of the verb (also called the perfect passive participle) linked to the subject with a form of the verb **sum.** The present tense of **sum** is used for the perfect tense, the imperfect is used for the pluperfect, and the future is used for the future perfect.

Note that the case ending of the participle must agree with the subject. **Haec mulier laudāta est (erat, erit),** *this woman was (had been, will have been) praised.*

7

Table 12

Demonstratives

	Masc.	Fem.	Neuter
Nom.	hic	haec	hoc
Gen.	huius	huius	huius
Dat.	huic	huic	huic
Acc.	hunc	hanc	hoc
Abl.	hōc	hāc	hōc
Nom.	hae	hī	haec

Etc.

Table 13

Participial Mood

	Active	Passive
Present	amāns, amantis, *loving*	—
Future	amātūrus, *going to love*	amandus, *going to be loved*
Perfect	—	amātus, *having been loved*

Table 14

Infinitive Mood

	Active	Passive
Present	amāre, *to love*	amārī, *to be loved* capī, *to be taken*
Future	amātūrum esse, *to be going to love*	amātum irī, *to be going to be loved*
Perfect	amāvisse, *to have loved*	amātum esse, *to have been loved*

Table 15

Personal Pronouns

	Masc.	Fem.	Neuter
Nom.	is	ea	id
Gen.	eius	eius	eius
Dat.	ei	ei	ei
Acc.	eum	eam	id
Abl.	eō	eā	eō

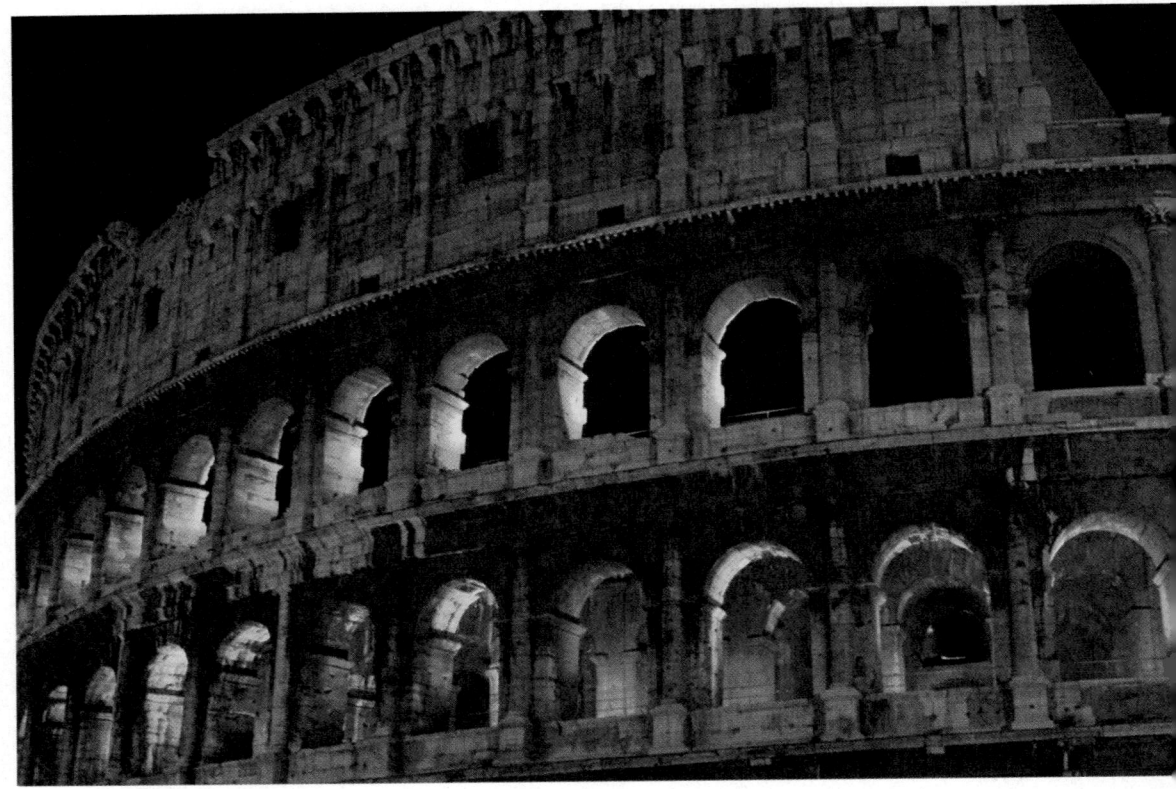

Infinitive Mood

Verbs have three tenses and two voices of the infinitive.

Present Active: present stem + **re;**
Present Passive: present stem + **ri** for 1st , 2nd, and 4th conjugation verbs, or **-i** for the 3rd;
Future Active: future active participle and **esse;**
Future Passive (very rare): supine in **-um** and **iri;**
Perfect Active: 3rd principal part + **isse;**
Perfect Passive: perfect passive participle and **esse.**

Study the infinitives of **amō.** The verb **capiō** is given in the present passive form to show how the third conjugation differs from the other three conjugations. See Table 14 on page 9.

Imperative Mood

To give a direct command, Latin uses the present stem of the verb without an ending for the singular, and the stem + **te** for the plural: **adiuvā mē,** *help me;* **adiuvāte mē,** *help me;* **hoc age,** *do this;* **audi mē,** *hear me.*

Gerund

The nominative verbal noun in Latin is the infinitive; e.g. **esse quam vidērī,** *being rather than seeming* (literally, *to be rather than to seem*). For the other cases, the form is identical to the future passive participle: *Nom.* **gerere,** *to conduct or conducting; Gen.* **gerendi,** *of conducting; Dat.* **gerendō,** *to or for conducting; Acc.* **gerendum,** *conducting; Abl.* **gerendō,** *by conducting.*

Personal Pronouns

The personal pronouns decline through the full case system. Table 16 on page 11 shows **ego,** *I;* **tū,** *you;* **nōs,** *we;* **vōs,** *you (pl.).*

Latin uses the demonstrative **is, ea, id** (*he, she, it*) for its third person pronoun. Its stem is simply **e-,** to which 1st and 2nd declension case endings are added. There are some exceptions, though, in the singular as shown in Table 15 on page 9.

Since the personal ending of the verb already implies the subject, the nominative case of the personal pronouns is used only for extra emphasis.

> **Ego sapientiam amō, at tū amās pecūniam,** *I love wisdom, but* you *love money.*

The genitive case of the 1st and 2nd person pronouns is not used to show possession. Latin prefers the possessive adjectives **meus, -a, -um,** *my;* **noster, -tra, -trum,** *our;* **tuus, -a, -um,** *your,* **vester, -tra, -trum,** *your (pl.)*

> **Equus** meus **in agrō visus est,** *my horse was seen in the field.*

The genitive case of the pronoun is used as the object of certain verbs that require the genitive case, and in the partitive genitive construction.

> **Tuī semper meminerō,** *I will always remember you;* **Pars meī vōbiscum** (= *cum vōbīs*) **post mortem meam nōn remanēbit,** *part of me will not remain with you after my death.*

A reflexive pronoun signifies that the subject both performs and receives the action of the verb; the pronoun points back to the subject: *She helped* herself, *They saw* themselves. Latin uses the forms of the 1st and 2nd pronouns for reflexive pronouns. The third person reflexive pronoun is: *Gen.* **sui;** *Dat.* **sibi;** *Acc.* **sē;** *Abl.* **sē.** There is no distinct plural form. There is also a third person reflexive possessive adjective **suus, -a, -um,** *he/her/its/their own.*

> **Eius amicus nōs vidit,** *his/her friend saw us;* **date id ei,** *give it to him/her.* **In speculō sē vidit,** *he/she saw himself/herself in the mirror.* **Pompeius suōs amīcōs adiūvit,** *Pompey helped his (own) friends.*

Demonstratives

Two very common demonstratives are **hic, haec, hoc,** *this,* and **ille, illa, illud,** *that.* They have the same alternative genitive and dative endings in the singular: *Gen.* **-ius;** *Dat.* **-i. Hic, haec, hoc,** is further complicated by the **-c** suffix attached to most of the case endings in the singular and in the nominative and accusative neuter plural. The **-c** causes the final **-m** of the case endings to change to **-n.** Lastly the normal stem **h-** lengthens to **hu-** in the genitive and dative singular. In the singular it declines as shown in Table 12 on page 9.

The demonstratives can be used to modify nouns, in which case they would be properly called demonstrative adjectives, or without nouns, in which case they would be properly called demonstrative pronouns.

> **Illae fēminae haec verba ad vōs mittent,** *those women will send these words to you;* **amici illius in hāc urbe pācem nōn invenient,** *friends of that (man or woman) will not find peace in this city;* **date illa huic,** *give those (things) to this (man).*

Subjunctive Mood

In the present tense, the subjunctive mood in the 2nd, 3rd, and 4th conjugations is formed by inserting an **-ā-** between the stem vowel and the personal endings. In the 1st conjugation, where the stem vowel is already **-ā-,** the stem vowel is in effect replaced with **-ē-.** Also, in non-i stem third conjugation, the stem vowel **-e-** is lost entirely with the addition of the **-ā-.**

First Conjugation: **amem, amēs, amet, amēmus, amētis, ament;**

9

Table 16

Personal Pronouns

	Singular		Plural	
	1st	**2nd**	**1st**	**2nd**
Nom.	ego	tū	nōs	vōs
Gen.	mei	tui	nostrum	vestrum
			nostri	vestri
Dat.	mihi	tibi	nōbis	vōbis
Acc.	mē	tē	nōs	vōs
Abl.	mē	tē	nōbis	vōbis

Table 17

Main Uses of the Subjunctive

Jussive:	Nunc incipiant, *let them begin now.*
Purpose Clause:	Pontem rescindī iussit nē hostibus usuī esset, *he ordered the bridge to be broken down so it would be useless to the enemy.*
Result Clause:	Tantum erat fulgur, ut tōtum caelum vidērētur ūrī, *the lightning was so great that the whole sky seemed to burn.*
Indirect Question:	Volō scīre ubi hoc plaustrum invēneris, *I want to know where you found this cart.*
Some Conditional Sentences:	Sī modo prius hās litterās accēpissem, iam vīveret, *if only I had received this letter beforehand, he would still be alive.*
Relative Clause of Characteristic:	Est nēmō quī tāle crīmen mōliātur, *there is no one who would engineer such a crime.*
Relative Clause of Purpose:	Nuntium mīsit quī victoriam renuntiāret, *he sent a messenger to report the victory.*
Factitive Clause:	Nōn forte accidit ut Caesar tam grātus esset plēbī, *it did not happen by chance that Caesar was so beloved by the plebeians.*
Indirect Command:	Eum adhortātus est ut Medūsam expeteret, *he urged him to seek out Medusa.*
After Verbs of Fearing:	Timeō nē correptus sit febrī, *I am afraid he is taken with fever.*
Cum Clause:	Cum nihil esset relictum, omnēs Rōman rediērunt, *since nothing was left, they returned to Rome.*
Quīn Clause:	Haud dubium erat quīn brevī advenīret cum auxiliō, *It was hardly doubtful that he would soon arrive with aid.*

Table 18

Subjunctive Mood

Tense	Active	Passive
Imperfect	caperet	caperētur
Perfect	cēperit	captus sit
Pluperfect	cēpisset	captus esset

Second Conjugation: **dēbeam, dēbeās, dēbeat, dēbeāmus, dēbeātis, dēbeant;**
Third Conjugation: **dūcam, dūcās, dūcat, dūcāmus, dūcātis, dūcant;**
Third i-stem Conjugation: **capiam, capiās, capiat, capiāmus, capiātis, capiant;**
Fourth Conjugation: **veniam, veniās, veniat, veniāmus, veniātis, veniant.**

The subjunctive of the verb **sum** is:

Present: **sim, sis, sit, simus, sitis, sint;**
Imperfect: **essem, essēs, esset, essēmus, essētis, essent.**

The remaining three tenses of the subjunctive (the future and future perfect do not have the subjunctive mood) are quite simple. The imperfect subjunctive is, in effect, the present active infinitive plus personal endings, either active or passive. The perfect subjunctive active is the third principal part + **eri** + personal endings of the present system. The perfect subjunctive passive is the perfect passive participle with the present subjunctive of **sum**. The pluperfect subjunctive active is the perfect infinitive + personal endings of the present system. The pluperfect subjunctive passive is the perfect passive participle with the imperfect subjunctive of **sum**. Study the synopsis of the verb **capiō** in the third person singular, shown in Table 18 on page 11.

The main uses of the subjunctive are shown in Table 17 on page 11.

Common Irregular Verbs

Like the English verb, *go, went, gone,* some Latin verbs have irregular principal parts: **ferō, ferre, tulī, lātus,** *to carry.* Such verbs are called *suppletive* because one or more of their principal parts is being *supplied* from another verb.

Another kind of irregular verb will lack one or two of the principal parts altogether: ——, ——, **coepī, coeptus,** *began;* **bibō, bibere, bibī,** ——, *to drink.* Some others will lack some forms which are found in the conjugations of other verbs. The verb **aiō,** *to say,* for example, has no infinitive, nor does it ever appear in the 1st and 2nd persons plural. Such verbs are called *defective.*

Suppletive and defective verbs will nevertheless follow the regular rules of conjugations. The most irregular verbs are those which deviate from the normal rules of conjugation. But in these verbs the irregularities are nearly always limited to the present system of tenses, and even then the exceptions are few. A quick glance at Table 19 on page 13 will reveal most of the normal rules at work.

Three Common Constructions

Indirect statement—reported speech—is formed by changing the original subject nominative of the direct statement to the accusative and the original conjugated form of the verb to the infinitive. If there is a subordinate clause in the original statement, it becomes subjunctive. Direct statement: **Amīcus meus trans agrum currit,** *my friend is running through the field.* As Indirect Statement: **Putō amīcum meum trans argrum currere,** *I think that my friend is running across the field.* Direct statement: **Rōma ab Gallīs oppugnāta est,** *Rome was attacked by the Gauls.* As indirect statement: **Dīxit Rōmam ab Gallīs oppugnātam esse,** *he said that Rome had been attacked by the Gauls.*

The ablative absolute construction allows Latin to state generally an attendant circumstance of the main action of the sentence without specifying the exact nature of the relationship. It is similar to the English nominative absolute: *All things being equal . . . , That said. . . .*

The ablative absolute consists of a noun or pronoun in the ablative case and a participle agreeing with it. **His verbis iūcundis ab ōrātōre dictīs, omnēs civēs ridēre coepērunt,** *when these pleasant words had been said by the orator, all the citizens began to laugh.* **Cīvibus rīdentibus, ōrātor alia verba iūcunda dīxit,** *while the citizens were laughing, the orator said other pleasant words.* Although the verb **sum** has no present participle, Latin can imply one in the ablative absolute as follows: **Per iocum Iuliō et Caesare consulibus actum scriberent,** *as a joke, they would write that it had been done when Julius and Caesar were consuls.*

One way of showing purpose is **ad** plus the gerund or **ad** plus the gerundive agreeing with a noun. **Ad nāvigandum (ad gerendum bellum) omnia parāta sunt,** *everything for sailing (for conducting the war) was made ready.*

Deponent Verbs

Many verbs lack nearly all of their active forms, and their passive forms are translated as if they were active. It is tempting to think that deponent verbs are entirely exempt from the standard rules of conjugation, but this is not so. They follow all the rules that normal verbs do inasmuch as they are able. It is easy to tell from the dictionary entry that a verb is deponent, for it will have no active forms listed. The entry will also lack a principal part for the perfect system active. See Table 20 on page 13.

A regular deponent verb will have present and future active participles, and the future passive participle is translated passively.

Other Pronouns

The relative pronoun is used as the root of several other pronouns. Accordingly, becoming thoroughly

Table 19

Common Irregular Verbs

Two Irregular Verbs in the Present System

Principal Parts		Present			Imperfect				Future	
		Indicative		Subjunctive	Indicative		Subjunctive		Indicative	
eō, īre, iī itus, *to go*	eō īs it	īmus ītis eunt	eam eās eat	eāmus eātis eant	ībam ībās ībat	ībāmus ībātis ībant	īrem īrēs īret	īrēmus īrētis īrent	ībō ībis ībit	ībimus ībitis ībunt
volō, velle, voluī, *to wish*	volō vīs vult	volumus vultis volunt	velim velīs velit	velīmus velītis velint	volēbam volēbās volēbat	volēbāmus volēbātis volēbant	vellem vellēs vellet	vellēmus vellētis vellent	volam volēs volet	volēmus volētis volent

Table 20

Deponent Verbs

1st conjugation	hortor, -ārī, hortātus sum, *to encourage*
2nd conjugation	vereor, -ērī, veritus sum, *to fear*
3rd conjugation	proficiscor, -ī, profectus sum, *to set out*
3rd i-stem conjugation	morior, -ī, mortuus sum, *to die*
4th conjugation	exorior, -īrī, exortus sum, *to come forth*

Table 21

Other Pronouns

Case	Masc.	Fem.	Neuter
Singular			
Nom.	quī	quae	quod
Gen.	cuius	cuius	cuius
Dat.	cui	cui	cui
Acc.	quem	quam	quod
Abl.	quō	quā	quō
Plural			
Nom.	quī	quae	quae
Gen.	quōrum	quārum	quōrum
Dat.	quibus	quibus	quibus
Acc.	quōs	quās	quae
Abl.	quibus	quibus	quibus

acquainted with its inflection is extremely useful. For the most part, it uses 1st and 2nd declension case endings. See Table 21 on page 13.

The most common pronouns that use the forms of the relative pronoun are listed here.

> **Dixit ea quae dīcenda erant,** *he said the things which had to be said.* **Ubi est liber quem legē-bās?** *where is the book which you were reading?*

The interrogative pronoun is identical in form, with the certain exceptions in the singular. (1) The neuter nominative and accusative is **quid.** (2) The masculine and feminine are identical in form throughout all the cases of the singular, and use **quis** instead of **qui** or **quae** for the nominative.

> **Quis est tuus pater?** *who is your father?* **Quid loquēbāris?** *what were you saying?*

The interrogative adjective is the same as the relative pronoun.

> **Cui puerō librum tuum dedit?** *to which boy did he give your book?* **Ē quā urbe ēgressus est?** *from which city did he depart?*

The pronoun meaning "somebody, something" is **ali** + the forms of the interrogative pronoun. After the words **sī, nisī, num** and **nē,** the **ali-** prefix is dropped.

> **Dabunt pecūniam alicui,** *they will give money to someone;* **Sī quem in viā videās, dīc mihi,** *if you should see someone on the road, tell me.*

The pronoun meaning "anybody, anything" is the interrogative pronoun plus the indeclinable suffix **quam: quisquam, quidquam** or **quicquam.**

> **Quisquam poterat frūmentum metere,** *anyone could harvest the grain;* **Nec pānem cuiquam dedit?** *and he didn't give bread to anyone?*

The pronoun meaning "some" or "a certain" is the relative pronoun plus the indeclinable suffix **-dam: quīdam, quaedam, quoddam,** or **quiddam.** A final **-m** of a case ending becomes **-n.** Hence, for example, **quendam** instead of **quemdam.** It can also be used as an adjective in a way that approaches our indefinite article.

> **In nāve erat fīlius quīdam rēgis Aeētae,** *there was in the ship a (certain) son of the king Aeetes;* **Herculēs dēlēgit quōs-dam ex suīs,** *Hercules picked out some of his (men).*

The pronoun meaning "the same" is the third person demonstrative **is, ea, id** + the indeclinable suffix **-dem: īdem, eadem, idem.** As with the suffix **-dam** (see column one), a final **-m** of a case ending becomes **-n: eandem** instead of **eamdem.** As with **quīdam** above, it can be used as an adjective.

> **Quīdam ex Argonautīs ad eandem īnsulam pervēnērunt,** *some of the Argonauts arrived at the same island;* **Ōrātor eadem dīxit,** *the orator said the same (things).*

The intensive adjective/pronoun, **ipse, ipsa, ipsum,** is declined like **is, ea, id,** with the irregular genitive and dative endings.

> **In illā viā vidimus rēgem ipsum,** *we saw the king himself on that road;* **Vīdistī ipsa,** *you saw these very (things).*

Reading Latin

There is no secret key to learning to read Latin comfortably. It takes some talent, but mostly just lots of patience and practice. As you begin, you should make sure you understand every letter of every word—what the source and meaning of all the forms are, what the syntax of each subjunctive is, etc. If you do, you will progress smoothly from the elementary and intermediate school texts into real Latin.

The preceding digest represents probably 90% of the grammar you will need to know for controlled, beginning Latin texts, and 80% for real Latin. Read slowly through the following passage from Caesar's *Gallic Wars* (1.41), and try to see how the translation, which is deliberately left very literal, comes out of the grammar of each word.

> **Hāc ōrātiōne habitā, mīrum in modum conversae sunt omnium mentēs summaque alacritās et cupiditās bellī gerendī innāta est, princepsque decima legiō per tribūnōs mīlitum Caesarī grātiās ēgit, quod dē sē optimum iūdicium fēcisset, sēque esse ad bellum gerendum parātissimam cōnfirmāvit.**

> *When this speech was made, in a wondrous way the minds of all were changed around, and a very great eagerness and desire of waging the war was engendered, and the tenth legion first sent greetings to Caesar through the tribunes of the soldiers, because he had the highest opinion of it, and it assured him that it was entirely ready for waging war.*

—Dale Grote
—John Dillon

13

Some Everyday Latin

A.D.	in annō dominī, *in the year of the Lord*
A.M.	ante merīdiem, *before midday*
etc.	et cētera, *and the other things*
et al.	et āliī, *and other people*
ad infinitum	*and on without limit*
Bona fide(s)	(with the -s-) *good faith;* (without the -s-) *in good faith*
c.	circā, *about, approximately*
E pluribus unum	*one from many*
e.g.	exemplī grātiā, *for the sake of example*
Ergo	*therefore*
gravitas	*seriousness, dignity*
i.e.	id est, *that is, namely*
ipso facto	*by that very fact*
NB	Nōtā bene, *take careful note*
non sequitur	*it doesn't follow*
quid pro quo	aliquid prō aliquō, *something for something*
passim	*throughout*
per se	*through* or *in and of itself*
post mortem	*after death*
P.M.	post merīdiem, *after midday*
pro tem	prō tempore, *for the time being*
PS	post scriptum, *after (it was) written*
rigor mortis	*the stiffness of death*
Semper Fi	semper fidēlēs, *always loyal*
sic	*thus* (indicates that an error in a quotation was in the original source)

arbor, -oris, f.

malleus, -ī, m.

via, -ae, f.

vir, -ī, m.

fēmina, -ae, f.

herba, -ae, f.

puer, -ī, m.

domus, -us, f.

scālae, -ārum, f.

cānis, -is m. and f.

puella, -ae, f.

rastrum, -ī, n.

brācae, -ārum, f.

calceus, -ī, m.

folia, -ōrum, n.

14

Part 2

Roget's University Thesaurus

Edited by
Eugene Ehrlich

This work was originally published under the title
Roget's International Thesaurus of English Words and Phrases.

Preface

This edition of *Roget's University Thesaurus* remains true to the original formulation of Peter Mark Roget, followed by all his distinguished successors, including the late C. O. Sylvester Mawson, who edited the first *University Thesaurus*. The distinguishing feature of the present edition is that it responds to the particular needs of all family members, young and old, who are students. The day does not go by when writing or when preparing a speech that an appropriate word or phrase is difficult to recall. It is at those times that the *University Thesaurus* proves invaluable.

The *University Thesaurus* offers its users

1. a large list of synonyms and antonyms;
2. a special grouping of comparisons and related terms;
3. systematic treatment of specialized terminology;
4. a grouping of synonyms in individual paragraphs supplying words more or less related and interchangeable;
5. characterization of all obsolete, obsolescent, rare, archaic, colloquial, dialectal, and slang words, as well as British, foreign, and special terms;
6. plural forms in all cases of unusual difficulty;
7. numerous phrases and idioms;
8. citations from modern authors.

The words new in the *University Thesaurus* run well into the thousands and embrace all aspects of knowledge, particularly in the sciences and social sciences. The aim has been to suggest ideas and turns of thought. The arrangement of synonyms and antonyms peculiar to the Roget scheme adds to the usefulness of the work: Roget gives *goodness* and *badness,* for example, in sequential entries. There is no need to refer to another part of the book.

Another distinguishing feature of Roget is the inclusion of phrases. Not only does the use of phrases enlarge the group of synonyms for any particular word, but in many instances the phrase furnishes the only possible synonym. Improvement of this feature in the *University Thesaurus* has received painstaking attention.

Our language marches with no frontiers; English is a world possession. Every race and country is reflected in its vocabulary. The *University Thesaurus* is alive to this universality, and, in order to assist writers and speakers in giving local color, the birthplace of every imported word is duly recorded.

Attention must be drawn to the need for using any thesaurus in tandem with a dictionary. Synonyms are often only related words. The dictionary provides precise definitions of individual words, so it must be consulted before using a word or phrase new to the reader.

Eugene Ehrlich

Table of Contents

Abbreviations

abbr. abbreviated, abbreviation
adj. adjective, adjectival expression
adv. adverb, adverbial expression
Afr. Africa
Am. *or* **Amer.** America, American
Am. hist. American history
anat. anatomy
anc. ancient
Anglo-Ind. Anglo-Indian
anon. anonymous
antiq. antiquities
Ar. Arabic
arch. architecture
archaeol. archaeology
arith. arithmetic
A.-S. Anglo-Saxon
astrol. astrology
astron. astronomy
Austral. Australian
Bib. Biblical
biol. biology
bot. botany
Brit. British
Can. Canada, Canadian
Can. F. Canadian French
Celt. Celtic
chem. chemistry
Chin. Chinese
Ch. of Eng. Church of England
class. classical
colloq. colloquial
com. commerce, commercial
conj. conjunction

Du. Dutch
Dan. Danish
derog. derogatory
dial. dialect, dialectal
dim. diminutive
E. East
eccl. ecclesiastical
econ. economics
elec. electricity
Eng. English, England
erron. erroneous, erroneously
esp. especially
exc. except
F. French
fem. feminine
fig. figurative, figuratively
G. *or* **Ger.** German
Gr. Greek
gram. grammar
Gr. Brit. Great Britain
Heb. Hebrew
her. heraldry
Hind. Hindustani
hist. history, historical
Icel. Icelandic
Ind. Indian
Ir. Irish, Ireland
int. interjection
It. Italian
Jap. Japanese
Jew. Jewish
joc. jocular
L. Latin

l.c. lower case
masc. masculine
math. mathematics
Meth. Methodist
Mex. Mexico, Mexican
mil. military
Moham. Mohammedan
myth. mythology
N. North
n. noun
N. Am. North American
naut. nautical
N. E. *or* **New Eng.** New England
neut. neuter
Nfld. Newfoundland
NL. New Latin
Norw. Norwegian
N. W. Northwest, Northwestern
N. Z. New Zealand
obs. obsolete
obsoles. obsolescent
OE. Old English
opp. opposed
orig. original, originally
parl. parliamentary
path. pathology
Per. Persian
Pg. Portuguese
pharm. pharmacy
philos. philosophy
physiol. physiology
P. I. Philippine Islands
pl. plural

Dashes and hyphens are used to avoid the repetition of a term common to each word or phrase in the same group. For example:

"over-, above- the mark;"	=	"over the mark," "above the mark"
"on the -verge, -brink, -skirts of;"	=	"on the verge of," "on the brink of," "on the skirts of"
"brush-, whisk-, turn-, send- -off, -away;"	=	"brush off," "brush away," "whisk off," "whisk away," "turn off," "turn away," "send off," "send away"
"quick-, keen-, clear-, sharp- -eyed, -sighted, -witted;"	=	"quick-eyed," "quick-sighted," "quick-witted," "keen-eyed," "keen-sighted," "keen-witted," "clear-eyed," "clear-sighted," "clear-witted," "sharp-eyed," "sharp-sighted," "sharp-witted"
"away from-, foreign to-, beside- the -purpose, -question, -transaction, -point;"	=	"away from the purpose," "away from the question," "away from the transaction," "away from the point," "foreign to the purpose," etc., "beside the purpose," etc.
"fall, -to the ground;"	=	"fall," "fall to the ground"
"shortness etc. *adj.;*" "shortly etc. *adj.;*" "shortening etc. *v.;*"	=	in a similar manner form other words from the groups of *adjectives* or *verbs* in the same category

How to Use the Thesaurus

1. To find a synonym or antonym for any given WORD:

Turn to the Index Guide and find the particular word or any term of kindred meaning; then refer to the category indicated. Under the part of speech sought for [*n., v., adj., adv.*] will be found a wide choice of synonymous and related terms, with their antonyms in the following category or in the preceding category. For example, suppose a synonym is wanted for the word "rare" in the sense of "choice." Turn to the Index Guide, where the following references will be found:

> **rare** *unique* 20
> *exceptional* 83
> *few* 103
> *infrequent* 137
> *underdone* 298
> *tenuous* 322
> *neologic* 563
> *choice* 648

The italicized words denote the general sense of the related terms in the respective categories. Turning to No. 648 (the sense required), we select the most appropriate expression from the comprehensive list presented. To widen the selection, suggested references are given to allied lists; while in No. 649 are grouped the corresponding antonyms. The groups are arranged, not merely to supply synonyms for some special word, but to suggest new lines of thought and to stimulate the imagination.

The writer at a loss for some archaism, colloquialism, or even slang, will find the *University Thesaurus* a veritable mine, such terms being clearly indicated in the text.

2. To find suitable words to express a given IDEA:

Find in the Index Guide some word relating to the idea, and the categories referred to will supply the need. Thus, suppose a writer wishes to use some less hackneyed phrase than "shuffle off this mortal coil," let him look up "die" or even the phrase itself, and reference to No. 360 will immediately furnish a generous list of synonymous phrases.

3. To find appropriate words or new ideas on any given SUBJECT:

Turn to the subject or any branch of it. The Index Guide itself will frequently suggest various lines of thought, while reference to the indicated groups will provide many words and phrases that should prove helpful.

Thus, suppose "philosophy" is the theme, No. 451 will be found most suggestive. Or again, the subject may be "the drama" (599), "music" (415), "zoology" (368), "psychical research" (992a), or "mythology" (979). Writers may perhaps be hazy about the titles of the ruling chiefs of India. The Thesaurus (875) will prevent applying a Hindu title to a Mohammedan prince. The subject may be such an everyday one as "food" (298), "automobiles" (272), "aviation" (267 and 269a), or various kinds of "amusements" (840); whatever it is, the Thesaurus will prove profitable as regards ideas. Writers and speakers who have acquired the Roget habit do not need to be reminded of this valuable aid.

N.B. To grasp the underlying principle of the classification, study the *Tabular Synopsis of Categories,* which begins on the next page. Reference may be made direct from this Synopsis to the body of the work; but it is usually found more convenient to consult the Index Guide first.

The Guide numbers always refer to the *section numbers* in the text and *not* to pages.

Tabular Synopsis of Categories

Class 1. Abstract Relations
Section 1. Existence

1. ABSTRACT	1. Existence	2. Nonexistence
2. CONCRETE	3. Substantiality	4. Unsubstantiality
3. FORMAL	*Internal* 5. Intrinsicality	*External* 6. Extrinsicality
4. MODAL	*Absolute* 7. State	*Relative* 8. Circumstance

Section 2. Relation

1. ABSOLUTE	9. Relation 11. Consanguinity 12. Correlation 13. Identity	10. Irrelation 14. Contrariety 15. Difference
2. CONTINUOUS	16. Uniformity	16a. Nonuniformity
3. PARTIAL	17. Similarity 19. Imitation 21. Copy	18. Dissimilarity 20. Nonimitation 20a. Variation 22. Prototype
4. GENERAL	23. Agreement	24. Disagreement

Section 3. Quantity

1. SIMPLE	*Absolute* 25. Quantity	*Relative* 26. Degree
2. COMPARATIVE	27. Equality *By Comparison with a Standard* 31. Greatness *By Comparison with a Similar Object* 33. Superiority *Changes in Quantity* 35. Increase	28. Inequality 29. Mean 30. Compensation 32. Smallness 34. Inferiority 36. Decrease
3. CONJUNCTIVE	37. Addition 39. Adjunct 41. Mixture 43. Junction 45. Vinculum 46. Coherence 48. Combination	38. Nonaddition Deduction 40. Remainder 40a. Decrement 42. Simpleness 44. Disjunction 47. Incoherence 49. Decomposition
4. CONCRETE	50. Whole 52. Completeness 54. Composition 56. Component	51. Part 53. Incompleteness 55. Exclusion 57. Extraneous

Section 4. Order

1. GENERAL	58. Order 60. Arrangement	59. Disorder 61. Derangement

x

XV

xvi

Class 1. Abstract Relations

Section 1. Existence

1. Existence

n. **existence**, being, entity, *ens* [*L.*], *esse* [*L.*], subsistence; quid, hypaxis [*rare*], automaton.

reality, actuality; positiveness etc. *adj.;* fact, matter of fact, sober reality; truth etc. 494; actual existence.

presence etc. (*existence in space*) 186; coexistence etc. 120.

stubborn fact; not a dream etc. 515; no joke.

essence, inmost nature, center of life, inner reality, vital principle.

[science of existence] ontology.

v. **exist**, be; having being etc. *n.;* subsist, live, breathe, stand, obtain, be the case; occur etc. (*event*) 151; have place, rank, prevail; find oneself, pass the time, vegetate.

come into existence etc. *n.;* arise etc. (*begin*) 66; come forth etc. (*appear*) 446.

become etc. (*be converted*) 144; bring into existence etc. 161; coexist, postexist [*rare*], preëxist [*rare*].

consist in, lie in; be comprised in, be contained in, be constituted by.

abide, continue, endure, last, remain.

adj. **existing** etc. *v.;* existent, subsistent, under the sun; in existence etc. *n.;* extant; afloat, on foot, current, prevalent; undestroyed.

real, actual, positive, absolute; factual, veritable, true etc. 494; substantial, substantive; self-existing, self-existent; essential.

well-founded, well-grounded; unideal, unimagined; not potential etc. 2; authentic.

adv. **actually** etc. *adj.;* in fact, in point of fact, in reality; indeed; *de facto* [*L.*], *ipso facto* [*L.*].

2. Nonexistence

n. **nonexistence**, nonsubsistence; inexistence; nonentity, *nil* [*L.*]; negativeness etc. *adj.;* nullity; nihility, nihilism; *tabula rasa* [*L.*], blank; abeyance; absence etc. 187; no such thing etc. 4; nonbeing, nothingness, oblivion, *non esse* [*L.*].

annihilation; extinction etc. (*destruction*) 162; extinguishment, extirpation, Nirvana, obliteration.

v. **not exist** etc. 1; have no existence etc. 1; be null and void; cease to exist etc. 1; pass away, perish; be *or* become extinct etc. *adj.;* die out; disappear etc. 449; melt away, dissolve, leave not a rack behind; go, be no more; die etc. 360.

annihilate, render null, nullify; abrogate etc. 756; destroy etc. 162; take away; remove etc. (*displace*) 185; obliterate, extirpate, deracinate [*rare*].

adj. **inexistent**, nonexistent etc. 1; negative, blank; null, minus, missing, omitted; absent etc. 187; insubstantial, shadowy, spectral, visionary.

unreal, potential, virtual; baseless, *in nubibus* [*L.*]; unsubstantial etc. 4; vain.

unborn, uncreated, unbegotten, unconceived, unproduced, unmade.

perished, annihilated etc. *v.;* extinct, exhausted, gone, lost, departed; defunct etc. (*dead*) 360.

fabulous, ideal etc. (*imaginary*) 515; supposititious etc. 514.

adv. negatively, virtually etc. *adj.*

3. Substantiality

n. **substantiality**, hypostasis; person, thing, object, article; something, a being, an existence; creature, body, substance, flesh and blood, stuff, substratum; matter etc. 316; corporeity, element, essential nature, groundwork, materiality, substantialness, vital part.

[totality of existences] world etc. 318; *plenum* [*L.*].

adj. **substantive**, substantial; hypostatic *or* hypostatical; personal, bodily, practical, effective; tangible etc. (*material*) 316; corporeal; right, sober.

adv. **substantially** etc. *adj.;* bodily, essentially.

4. Unsubstantiality

n. **unsubstantiality**, insubstantiality; nothingness, nihility; no degree, no part, no quantity, no thing.

nothing, naught, *nil* [*L.*], nullity, zero, cipher, no one, nobody; never a one, ne'er a one; no such thing, none in the world; nothing whatever, nothing at all, nothing on earth; not a particle etc. (*smallness*) 32; all talk, all moonshine, all stuff and nonsense; matter of no importance, matter of no consequence.

thing of naught, man of straw, John Doe and Richard Roe, fagot (*or* faggot) voter [*polit. cant, Eng.*]; *nominis umbra* [*L.*], nonentity, cipher, nought, nothing, obscurity, lay figure; flash in the pan, *vox et praeterea nihil* [*L.*].

phantom etc. (*fallacy of vision*) 443; shadow; dream etc. (*imagination*) 515; *ignis fatuus*

[*L.*] etc. (*luminary*) 423; "such stuff as dreams are made on" [*Tempest*]; air, thin air; bubble etc. 353; mockery.

blank; void etc. (*absence*) 187; hollowness.

inanity, fatuity, fool's paradise.

v. **vanish**, evaporate, fade, fleet, sink, fly, dissolve, melt away; die, die away, die out; disappear etc. 449.

adj. **unsubstantial**; baseless, groundless; ungrounded; without foundation, having no foundation.

visionary etc. (*imaginary*) 515; immaterial etc. 317; spectral etc. 980; dreamy; shadowy; ethereal, airy, gaseous, imponderable, tenuous, vague, vaporous, dreamlike, mushroom; cloud-built, cloud-formed; gossamery, illusory, insubstantial, unreal, unsolid [*rare*], slight, bodiless.

vacant, vacuous; empty etc. 187; eviscerated; blank, hollow; nominal; null; inane [*rare*].

5. Intrinsicality

n. **intrinsicality**, intrinsicalness, inbeing, inherence, inhesion, immanence, indwelling; subjectiveness; ego; egohood; essence, quintessence, elixir; essentialness etc. *adj.;* essential part, incarnation, quiddity, gist, pith, core, kernel, marrow, sap, lifeblood, backbone, heart, soul, life, substance, flower; important part etc. (*importance*) 642.

principle, nature, constitution, character, type, quality, crasis, diathesis.

temper, temperament; spirit, humor, grain, nature, vein, mood, frame, cue; disposition; habit.

capacity, endowment; capability etc. (*power*) 157.

aspects, moods, declensions, features; peculiarities etc. (*specialty*) 79; idiosyncrasy; idiocrasy etc. (*tendency*) 176; diagnostics.

v. be in the blood, run in the blood; be born so; be intrinsic etc. *adj.*

adj. **intrinsic**, intrinsical; derived from within, subjective; idiocratic *or* idiocratical, idiosyncratic *or* idiosyncratical; fundamental, normal; implanted, inherent, essential, natural; innate, inborn, inbred, ingrained, indwelling, inwrought; coeval with birth, genetic, genetous, haematobious, syngenic; radical, incarnate, thoroughbred, hereditary, inherited, immanent; congenital, congenite [*obs.*]; connate, running in the blood; ingenerate, ingenit *or* ingenite [*obs.*], ingenita [*obs.*], indigenous; in the grain etc. *n.;* bred in the bone, instinctive; inward, internal etc. 221; to the manner born; virtual.

characteristic etc. (*special*) 79, (*indicative*) 550; invariable, incurable, ineradicable, fixed.

adv. **intrinsically** etc. *adj.;* at bottom, in the main, in effect, practically, virtually, substantially, *au fond* [*F.*]; fairly.

6. Extrinsicality

n. **extrinsicality**, objectiveness, *non ego* [*L.*]; extraneousness etc. 57; accident.

adj. **extrinsic**, extrinsical; derived from without; objective; extraneous etc. (*foreign*) 57; modal, adventitious; ascititious, adscititious; incidental, accidental, nonessential, unessential, accessory; contingent, fortuitous, casual, subsidiary.

implanted, ingrafted; inculcated, infused.

outward etc. (*external*) 220.

adv. **extrinsically** etc. *adj.*

7. State

n. **state**, condition, category, estate, lot, case, trim, mood, temper; aspect etc. (*appearance*) 448.

dilemma, pass, predicament, quandary, corner, hole, *impasse* [*F.*], fix, pickle, plight.

frame, fabric etc. 329; stamp, set, fit, mold *or* mould; constitution, habitude, diathesis.

form, fettle, shape, kilter *or* kelter; tone, tenor, turn; trim, guise, fashion, light, complexion, style, character; build etc. 240; mode, modality, schesis [*obs.*]

v. be in–, possess–, enjoy- a state etc. *n.;* be on a footing, do, fare; come to pass.

adj. **conditional**, modal, formal; structural, organic.

adv. **conditionally** etc. *adj.;* as the matter stands, as things are; such being the case etc. 8; *quae cum ita sint* [*L.*].

8. Circumstance

n. **circumstance**, situation, phase, position, posture, attitude, place, point; terms; *régime* [*F.*]; footing, standing, status.

occasion, juncture, conjuncture; contingency etc. (*event*) 151.

predicament; emergency; exigency, crisis, pinch, pass, plight, push; occurrence; turning point.

bearings, how the land lies.

adj. **circumstantial**; given, conditional, provisional; critical; modal; contingent, incidental; adventitious etc. (*extrinsic*) 6; limitative.

detailed, minute, full, fussy.

adv. **thus**, in such wise; in *or* under the circumstances etc. *n.;* in *or* under the conditions etc. 7.

accordingly; that being the case; such being the case; that being so; since, seeing that.

as matters stand; as things go, as times go.

conditionally, provided, if, in case; if so, if so be, if it be so; if it so happen, if it so turn out; in the event of; in such a contingency, in such a case, in such an event; provisionally, unless, without.

according to circumstances, according to the occasion; as it may happen, as it may turn out, as it may be; as the case may be, as the wind blows.

Section 2. Relation

9. Relation

n. **relation**, bearing, reference, connection, concern, cognation, applicability, apposition, appositeness; correlation etc. 12; analogy; similarity etc. 17; affinity, homology, alliance, nearness, rapport, homogeneity, association; approximation etc. (*nearness*) 197; filiation etc. (*consanguinity*) 11; interest; relevancy etc. 23; dependency, relationship, relative position; correlation, interrelation, interconnection.

ratio, proportion; comparison etc. 464.

link, tie, bond of union, privity [*law*].

v. **be related** etc. *adj.;* have a relation etc. *n.;* relate to, refer to; bear upon, regard, concern, touch, affect, have to do with; pertain to, belong to, appertain to; answer to; interest.

associate, connect; bring into relation with, bring to bear upon; draw a parallel; link etc. 43.

adj. **relative**; correlative etc. 12; relating to etc. *v.;* relative to, in relation with, referrable *or* referable *or* referrible to; belonging to etc. *v.;* appurtenant to, in common with.

related, connected; implicated, associated, affiliated; allied, allied to; collateral, connate [*rare*], cognate, congenerous, connatural, affinitive, paronymous; *en rapport* [*F.*], in touch with.

approximative, approximating; proportional, proportionate, proportionable; allusive, comparable, equiparable [*obs. or rare*].

relevant etc. (*apt*) 23; applicable, equiparant; in the same category etc. 75; like etc. 17.

adv. **relatively** etc. *adj.;* pertinently etc. 23.

thereof; as to, as for, as respects, as regards; about; concerning etc. *v.;* anent; relating to, as relates to; with relation to, with reference to, with respect to, with regard to; in respect of; speaking of, *à propos* [*F.*] of; in connection with; by the way, by the by; whereas; for as much as, in as much as; in point of, as far as;

on the part of, on the score of; under the head of etc. (*class*) 75; in the matter of, *in re* [*L.*].

10. Irrelation
[want or absence of relation]

n. **irrelation**, dissociation; misrelation; inapplicability; inconnection; multifariousness; disconnection etc. (*disjunction*) 44; inconsequence, independence; incommensurability; irreconcilableness etc. (*disagreement*) 24; heterogeneity; unconformity etc. 83; irrelevancy, impertinence, *nihil ad rem* [*L.*]; intrusion etc. 24; nonpertinence.

v. **not concern** etc. 9; have no relation to etc. 9; have no bearing upon, have no concern with etc. 9; have no business with; have nothing to do with, have no business there; intrude etc. 24.

bring-, drag-, lug- in by the head and shoulders.

adj. **irrelative**, irrespective, unrelated, disrelated, irrelate [*rare*]; arbitrary; independent, unallied; disconnected, unconnected, adrift, isolated, insular; extraneous, strange, alien, foreign, outlandish, exotic.

not comparable, incommensurable, heterogeneous; unconformable etc. 83.

irrelevant, inapplicable; not pertinent, not to the purpose; impertinent [*legal*], unessential, inessential, accidental, inapposite, beside the mark; aside from-, away from-, foreign to-, beside the -purpose, -question, -transaction, -point; misplaced etc. (*intrusive*) 24; traveling out of the record.

remote, far-fetched, out-of-the-way, forced, neither here nor there, quite another thing; detached, apart, segregated, segregate; disquiparant.

multifarious; discordant etc. 24.

incidental, parenthetical, *obiter dictum* [*L.*], episodic.

adv. **parenthetically** etc. *adj.;* by the way, by the by; *en passant* [*F.*], incidentally, *obiter* [*L.*]; irrespectively etc. *adj.;* without reference to, without regard to; in the abstract etc. 87; *a se* [*L.*].

11. Consanguinity
[relations of kindred]

n. **consanguinity**, relationship, kindred, blood; parentage etc. (*paternity*) 166; filiation, affiliation; lineage, agnation, connation [*obs.*], cognation, connection, alliance; people [as, my *people*], family, family connection, family tie; ties of blood, blood relation; nepotism.

kinsman, kinsfolk; kith and kin; relation, relative; connection; sib [rare]; next of kin; uncle, aunt, nephew, niece; cousin, cousin-german; first cousin, second cousin; cousin once removed, cousin twice removed etc.; near relation, distant relation; brother, sister, one's own flesh and blood.

family, fraternity; brotherhood, sisterhood, cousinhood.

race, stock, generation; sept etc. 166; stirps, side; strain; breed, clan, tribe.

v. be related to etc. *adj.;* claim relationship with etc. *n.*

adj. related, akin, sib [Scot. or archaic], consanguineous, of the blood, family, allied, collateral; cognate, agnate, connate [rare]; kindred; affiliated; fraternal.

intimately related, nearly related, closely related, remotely related, distantly related; intimately allied, nearly allied, closely allied, remotely allied, distantly allied; affinal, german.

12. Correlation
[double or reciprocal relation]

n. reciprocalness etc. *adj.;* reciprocity, reciprocality, reciprocation; mutuality, correspondence, correlation, interrelation, interconnection, interdependence; interchange etc. 148; exchange, barter, *quid pro quo* [L.].

alternation, seesaw, shuttle [rare], to-and-fro. reciprocitist.

v. reciprocate, alternate, interact; interchange etc. 148; exchange; counterchange.

adj. reciprocal, mutual, commutual [rare], correlative; correspondent, corresponding; alternate; interchangeable; international; complemental, complementary; equivalent.

adv. mutatis mutandis [L.]; *vice versa* [L.]; each other; by turns etc. 148; reciprocally etc. *adj.*

13. Identity

n. identity, sameness, identicalness, unity, self-sameness, coincidence, coalescence; convertibility; equality etc. 27; selfness, self, oneself; identification.

connaturality, connature, connaturalness, homogeneity.

monotony; tautology etc. (repetition) 104.

facsimile etc. (copy) 21; homoousia; *alter ego* [L.] etc. (similar) 17; *ipsissima verba* [L.] etc. (exactness) 494; same; self-same, very same, one and the same; counterpart; very thing, actual thing; no other.

v. be identical etc. *adj.;* coincide, coalesce.

treat as the same, render the same; treat as identical; render identical; identify; recognize the identity of.

adj. identical; self, ilk [archaic]; the identical same etc. *n.;* selfsame, homoousian, one and the same; ditto.

coincident, coinciding, coalescing, coalescent, indistinguishable; one; equivalent etc. (equal) 27; much the same, much of a muchness; unaltered.

adv. identically etc. *adj.;* on all fours with; *ibidem* [L.], *ibid.*

14. Contrariety
[noncoincidence]

n. contrariety, contrast, foil, antithesis, antipode, counterpole, counterpoint; counterpart; complement; *vis-à-vis* [F.], oppositeness; contradiction; antagonism etc. (opposition) 708; clashing, repugnance, antipathy.

inversion etc. 218; the opposite, the reverse, the inverse, the converse, the antipodes, the other extreme.

v. be contrary etc. *adj.;* contrast with, oppose, antithesize [rare]; differ *toto coelo* [L.].

invert, reverse, turn the tables; turn topsy-turvy, turn end for end, turn upside down; retrograde, transpose, invaginate, intussuscept.

contradict, contravene; antagonize etc. 708.

adj. contrary, contrarious [archaic], contrariant [rare], opposite, counter, dead against; adverse, averse, converse, reverse; opposed, antithetical, contrasted, antipodean, antagonistic, opposing; conflicting, inconsistent, contradictory, at cross purposes; negative; hostile, inimical etc. 703.

differing *toto coelo* [L.]; diametrically opposite; as opposite as black and white, as opposite as light and darkness, as opposite as fire and water, as opposite as the poles; "Hyperion to a satyr" [Hamlet]; quite the contrary, quite the reverse; no such thing, just the other way, *tout au contraire* [F.].

adv. contrarily etc. *adj.;* contra, contrariwise, *per contra* [L.], on the contrary, nay rather; *vice versa* [L.]; on the other hand etc. (in compensation) 30.

15. Difference

n. difference; variance, variation, variety; diversity, divergence, heterogeneity, discongruity, contrast, inconformity, incompatibility, antithesis, antitheticalness, discrepation [rare], dissimilarity etc. 18; disagreement etc. 24; disparity etc. (inequality) 28; distinction, dissimilitude [*rare*], distinctness, contradiction, contradictoriness, contrariety, contradistinction; alteration.

nice distinction, fine distinction, delicate distinction, subtle distinction; shade of difference, nuance; discrimination etc. 465; differentia.

different thing, something else, apple off another tree, another pair of shoes; this, that, or the other.

modification, commutation [*rare*], moods and tenses.

v. **be different** etc. *adj.;* differ, vary, ablude [*obs.*], mismatch, contrast; diverge from, depart from, deviate from, disaccord with, discrepate [*rare*]; divaricate; differ *toto coelo* [*L.*], differ *longo intervallo* [*L.*].

vary, modify etc. (*change*) 140.

discriminate etc. 465.

adj. **differing** etc. *v.;* different, diverse, heterogeneous; distinguishable; varied, variant, divergent, contrastive, incongruous, discrepant, dissonant, inharmonious, disparate, inconformable, differential, modified; diversified, various, divers [*archaic*], all manner of; variform etc. 81.

other, another, not the same; unequal etc. 28; unmatched; widely apart.

distinctive, characteristic; discriminative, differentiative, distinguishing; diacritic, diacritical; diagnostic.

adv. **differently** etc. *adj.*

16.   Uniformity

n. **uniformity**; homogeneity, homogeneousness; stability, continuity, permanence, consistency; connature [*rare*], connaturality [*rare*], connaturalness; homology; accordance; conformity etc. 82; agreement etc. 23; consonance, uniformness.

regularity, constancy, evenness, sameness, unity, even tenor, routine; monotony.

v. **be uniform** etc. *adj.;* accord with etc. 23; run through.

become uniform etc. *adj.;* conform to etc. 82.

render uniform etc. *adj.;* assimilate, level, smooth, dress.

adj. **uniform**; homogeneous, homologous; of a piece, consistent, connatural; singsong, drear [*rare*], drearisome, dreary, monotonous, even, equable, constant, level; invariable; regular, unchanged, undeviating, unvaried, undiversified, unvarying; jog-trot.

adv. **uniformly** etc. *adj.;* uniformly with etc. (*conformably*) 82; in harmony with etc. (*agreeing*) 23; in a rut.

always, ever, evermore, perpetually, forever, everlastingly, invariably, without exception, never otherwise; by clockwork.

16a.   Nonuniformity
[absence or want of uniformity]

n. **diversity**, irregularity, unevenness; multiformity etc. 81; unconformity etc. 83; roughness etc. 256; dissimilarity, dissimilitude, divarication, divergence, heteromorphism, heterogeneity.

adj. **diversified**, varied, irregular, checkered, daedal, uneven, rough etc. 256; multifarious; multiform etc. 81; of various kinds; all manner of, all sorts of, all kinds of.

adv. in all manner of ways; here, there, and everywhere.

17.   Similarity

n. **similarity**, resemblance, likeness, similitude [*rare*], semblance, consimilarity [*rare*]; affinity, approximation, parallelism; agreement etc. 23; analogy, analogicalness; correspondence, homoiousia, parity.

connaturalness, connature [*rare*], connaturality [*rare*]; brotherhood, family likeness.

alliteration, rime *or* rhyme, pun.

repetition etc. 104; sameness etc. (*identity*) 13; uniformity etc. 16; isogamy.

analogue; the like; match, pendant, fellow, companion, pair, mate, twin, double, congener, counterpart, brother, sister; one's second self, *alter ego* [*L.*], chip of the old block, *par nobile fratrum* [*L.*], *Arcades ambo* [*L.*], birds of a feather, *et hoc genus omne* [*L.*]; *gens de même famille* [*F.*].

simile; parallel; type etc. (*metaphor*) 521; image etc. (*representation*) 554; photograph; close–, striking–, speaking–, faithful etc. *adj.* —likeness, –resemblance.

v. **be similar** etc. *adj.;* look like, resemble, favor [*colloq.*], follow, echo, reproduce, bear resemblance; savor of, smack of; approximate; parallel, match, rime *or* rhyme with; take after; imitate etc. 19; span; hunt in couples, run in couples.

render similar etc. *adj.;* assimilate, approximate, bring near; connaturalize, make alike; rime *or* rhyme, pun.

adj. **similar**; resembling etc. *v.;* like, alike; twin.

analogous, analogical; parallel, of a piece; such as, so; homoiousian.

connatural, correlative, corresponding, cognate, congeneric, congenerous, allied to; akin to etc. (*consanguineous*) 11.

approximate, much the same, near, close, something like, near- [as *near*-silk, *colloq.*], such like; a show of; mock, pseudo, simulating, representing.

exact etc. (*true*) 494; lifelike, faithful; true to nature, true to life; the very image of, the very picture of; for all the world like, *comme deux gouttes d'eau* [F.], as like as two peas, as like as it can stare; *instar omnium* [L.], cast in the same mold, ridiculously like.

adv. **as if**, so to speak; as it were, as if it were; *quasi* [L.], just as.

18. Dissimilarity

n. **dissimilarity**, dissimilitude; unlikeness, diversity, disparity, dissemblance; divergence, variation; difference etc. 15; novelty, originality; creativeness; oögamy.

v. **be unlike** etc. *adj.;* vary etc. (*differ*) 15; bear no resemblance to, differ *toto coelo* [L.].
render unlike etc. *adj.;* vary etc. (*diversify*) 140.

adj. **dissimilar**, unlike, disparate; divergent, nonidentical, unidentical; of a different kind etc. (*class*) 75; unmatched, unique; new, novel; unprecedented etc. 83; original.
nothing of the kind; no such thing, quite another thing; far from it, other than, cast in a different mold, *tertium quid* [L.], as like a dock as a daisy, "very like a whale" [*Hamlet*]; as different as chalk from cheese, as different as Macedon and Monmouth; *lucus a non lucendo* [L.].
diversified etc. 16*a.*

adv. **otherwise**, elsewise; alias.

19. Imitation

n. **imitation**; copying etc. *v.;* transcription; repetition, duplication, reduplication; quotation; reproduction; mimeography.
mockery, apery, mimicking, mimicry.
simulation, personation; parrotism, parrotry; representation etc. 554; semblance, pretense; copy etc. 21; assimilation.
paraphrase, parody etc. 21.
plagiarism; forgery etc. (*falsehood*) 544.
imitator, echo, cuckoo, parrot, ape, monkey, mocking bird, mimic; copyist.

v. **imitate**, copy, mirror, reflect, reproduce, repeat; do like, echo, reëcho, catch; transcribe; match, parallel.
mock, take off, borrow, mimic, ape, simulate, personate; act etc. (*drama*) 599; represent etc. 554; counterfeit, forge, parody, travesty, caricature, burlesque.

follow in the steps of, follow in the footsteps of; follow in the wake of; tread in the steps of, tread in the footsteps of; take pattern by; follow suit [*colloq.*], follow the example of; walk in the shoes of, take a leaf out of another's book, strike in with; take after, model after; emulate.

adj. **imitated** etc. *v.;* mock, mimic; modeled after, molded on.
paraphrastic; literal; imitative; secondhand; imitable; aping, apish, mimicking, borrowed, counterfeit, imitation, false, pseudo, near- [as, *near*-silk, *colloq.*].

adv. **literally**, to the letter, verbatim, *literatim* [L.], *sic* [L.], *totidem verbis* [L.], word for word, *mot à mot* [F.], *verbatim et literatim* [L.]; exactly, precisely.

20. Nonimitation

n. **nonimitation**, no imitation; originality; creativeness.

adj. **unimitated**, uncopied; unmatched, unparalleled; inimitable etc. 33; unique, original, archetypal, prototypal, prototypical, primordial, creative, untranslated; exceptional, rare, *sui generis* [L.], uncommon, unexampled, out-of-the-way, insitate [*rare*], unwonted, *recherché* [F.], unordinary [*rare*], supernormal.

20a. Variation

n. **variation**; alteration etc. (*change*) 140.
modification, moods and tenses; discrepance, discrepancy.
divergency etc. 291; deviation etc. 279; aberration; innovation.

v. **vary** etc. (*change*) 140; deviate etc. 279; diverge etc. 291; alternate, swerve.

adj. **varied** etc. *v.;* modified; diversified etc. 16*a;* dissimilar etc. 18.

21. Copy
[result of imitation]

n. **copy**, facsimile, counterpart, *effigies* [L.], effigy, form, likeness, similitude, semblance, cast, tracing, ectype, electrotype; imitation etc. 19; model, representation, adumbration, study; "counterfeit presentment" [*Hamlet*]; portrait etc. (*representment*) 554; resemblance.
duplicate; transcript, transcription; counterscript; reflex, reflexion; shadow, echo; chip off the old block; reprint, replica, offprint, transfer, reproduction; second edition etc. (*repetition*) 104; *réchauffé* [F.]; apograph, fair copy, revise, rewriting.

matter; manuscript, typescript, flimsy [*cant*].
parody, caricature, burlesque, travesty, *travestie* [*F.*], paraphrase; cartoon.
servile copy, servile imitation; counterfeit etc. (*deception*) 545; *pasticcio* [*It.*].

adj. **faithful**; lifelike etc. (*similar*) 17; close, exact, strict, conscientious.

22. Prototype
[thing copied]

n. **prototype**, original, model, pattern, precedent, standard, scantling [*rare*], type; archetype, antitype; protoplast, protoplasm, plasm [*obs.*], proplasm [*rare*], module, exemplar, example, ensample [*archaic*], paradigm; lay-figure; fugleman, guide.
copy, text, design; keynote.
die, mold; matrix, last, mint, seal, punch, intaglio, negative; stamp.

v. be an example, set an example; set a copy.

23. Agreement

n. **agreement**, accord, accordance; unison, harmony; concord etc. 714; concordance, concert; understanding, mutual understanding; gentleman's agreement, *entente cordiale* [*F.*], consortium; unanimity, consension [*rare*], consentaneity.
conformity etc. 82; conformance; uniformity etc. 16; assonance, consonance, consentaneousness, consistency; congruity, congruence *or* congruency; keeping; congeniality; correspondence, concinnity, parallelism, apposition, union.
fitness, aptness etc. *adj.*; relevancy; pertinence *or* pertinency; sortance [*obs.*]; case in point; aptitude, coaptation, propriety, applicability, admissibility, commensurability, compatibility; cognation etc. (*relation*) 9.
adaptation, adaption, adjustment, graduation, accommodation; reconciliation, reconcilement; assimilation.
consent etc. (*assent*) 488; concurrence etc. 178; consensus, *rapport* [*F.*], meeting of minds, coöperation etc. 709.
right man in the right place, very thing; quite the thing, just the thing.

v. **be accordant** etc. *adj.*; agree, accord, harmonize; correspond, tally, respond; meet, suit, fit, befit, do, adapt itself to; fall in with, chime in with, square with, quadrate with, consort with, comport with; dovetail, assimilate; fit like a glove; fit to a tittle, fit to a T; match etc. 17; become one; homologate.

consent etc. (*assent*) 488.
render accordant etc. *adj.*; fit, suit, adapt, accommodate; graduate; adjust etc. (*render equal*) 27; dress, regulate, readjust; accord, harmonize, reconcile; fadge, dovetail, square.

adj. **agreeing**, suiting etc. *v.*; in accord, accordant, concordant, consonant, congruous, consentaneous [*archaic*], answerable, correspondent, congenial; coherent; becoming; harmonious, reconcilable, conformable; in accordance with, in harmony with, in keeping with, in unison with etc. *n.*; at one with, of one mind, of a piece; consistent, compatible, proportionate; commensurate; on all fours with.
apt, apposite, pertinent, pat; to the point, to the purpose; happy, felicitous, germane, *ad rem* [*L.*], in point, bearing upon, applicable, relevant, admissible.
fit, adapted, *in loco* [*L.*], *à propos* [*F.*], appropriate, seasonable, sortable, suitable, idoneous [*rare*], deft; meet etc. (*expedient*) 646.
at home, in one's proper element.

adv. *à propos* of; pertinently etc. *adj.*

24. Disagreement

n. **disagreement**; discord, discordance, discordancy; dissonance, dissidence, disunity, disunion, discrepancy; unconformity etc. 83; incongruity, incongruence; discongruity, *mésalliance* [*F.*]; jarring etc. *v.*; dissension etc. 713; conflict etc. (*opposition*) 708; bickering, clashing, misunderstanding, wrangle.
disparity, mismatch, disproportion, dissimilitude, inequality; disproportionateness etc. *adj.*; variance, divergence, repugnance.
unfitness etc. *adj.*; inaptitude, impropriety; inapplicability etc. *adj.*; inconsistency, inconcinnity; irrelevancy etc. (*irrelation*) 10.
misjoining, misjoinder; syncretism, intrusion, interference.
fish out of water.

v. **disagree**; clash, conflict, dispute, quarrel, jar etc. (*discord*) 713; interfere, intrude, come amiss; not concern etc. 10; mismatch; *humano capiti cervicem jungere equinam* [*L.*]

adj. **disagreeing** etc. *v.*; discordant, discrepant; at variance, at war; hostile, antagonistic, repugnant, inaccordant, clashing, jarring, factious, dissentient, dissentious, dissident, inacquiescent, incompatible, irreconcilable, inconsistent with; unconformable, exceptional etc. 83; intrusive, incongruent, incongruous; disproportionate, disproportioned; unharmonious, unconsonant; divergent, repugnant to.

inapt, unapt, inappropriate, malappropriate [*rare*], improper; unsuited, unsuitable; inapplicable; unfit, unfitting, unbefitting; unbecoming; ill-timed, ill-adapted, dissuitable [*rare*], infelicitous, unseasonable, *mal à propos* [*F.*], inadmissible; inapposite etc. (*irrelevant*) 10.

uncongenial; ill-assorted, ill-sorted; mismatched, misjoined, misplaced; unaccommodating, irreducible, uncommensurable; unsympathetic.

out of character, out of keeping, out of proportion, out of joint, out of tune, out of place, out of season, out of its element; at odds, at variance with.

adv. in defiance of, in contempt of, in spite of; discordantly etc. *adj.; à tort et à travers* [*F.*].

Section 3. Quantity

25. Quantity

[absolute quantity]

n. **quantity**, magnitude; size etc. (*dimensions*) 192; amplitude, mass, amount, quantum, measure, measurement, substance, strength.

[science of quantity] mathematics, mathesis [*rare*].

[logic] category, general conception, universal predicament.

[definite or finite quantity] armful, handful, mouthful, spoonful, capful; stock, batch, lot, dose; quota, quotiety [*rare*], quotum, pittance, driblet, grist.

v. **quantify**, rate.

adj. **quantitative**, some, any, more or less.

adv. to the tune of.

26. Degree

[relative quantity]

n. **degree**, grade, step, extent, measure, amount, ratio, stint *or* stent, standard, height, pitch; reach, amplitude, range, scope, caliber; gradation, shade; tenor, compass; sphere, station, rank, standing; rate, way, sort.

point, mark, stage etc. (*term*) 71; interval, line [*music*], space [*music*]; intensity, strength etc. (*greatness*) 31.

v. **graduate**, calibrate, measure; rectify.

adj. **comparative**; gradual, gradational, gradatory [*rare*], shading off; within the bounds etc. (*limit*) 233.

adv. **by degrees**, gradually, inasmuch, *pro tanto* [*L.*]; however, howsoever; step by step, bit by bit, little by little, inch by inch, drop by drop;

by inches, by slow degrees, by little and little; in some degree, in some measure; to some extent; *di grado in grado* [*It.*].

27. Equality

[sameness of quantity or degree]

n. **equality**, parity, coextension, symmetry, balance, poise; evenness, monotony, level.

equivalence; equipollence, equipoise, equilibrium, equiponderance; par, quits; not a pin to choose; distinction without a difference, six of one and half a dozen of the other; identity etc. 13; similarity. etc. 17; coequality, coevality [*rare*], isonomy, isopolity, isotropy, parallelism.

equalization, equation; equilibration, coördination, adjustment, readjustment.

tie, dead heat; drawn game, drawn battle; neck-and-neck race.

match, peer, compeer, equal, mate, fellow, brother; equivalent.

v. **be equal** etc. *adj.;* equal, match, reach, keep pace with, run abreast; come to, amount to, come up to; be on a level with, lie on a level with; balance; cope with; come to the same thing, even off.

render equal etc. *adj.;* equalize, level, dress, balance, equate, handicap, give points, trim, adjust, poise; fit, accommodate; adapt etc. (*render accordant*) 23; strike a balance; establish equality, restore equality, establish equilibrium, restore equilibrium; readjust; stretch on the bed of Procrustes.

adj. **equal**, even, level, monotonous, coequal, symmetrical, coördinate; on a par with, on a level with, on a footing with; up to the mark; equiparant, equiparate [*rare*].

equivalent, tantamount; quits; homologous; synonymous etc. 522; resolvable into, convertible; much at one, as broad as long, neither more nor less; much the same as, the same thing as, as good as; all one, all the same; equipollent, equiponderant, equiponderous, equibalanced; equalized etc. *v.;* drawn; half and half; isochronal, isochronous; isoperimetric *or* isoperimetrical; isobath, isobathic.

adv. **equally** etc. *adj.; pari passu* [*L.*], *ad eundem* [*L.*], *caeteris paribus* [*L.*], *in equilibrio* [*L.*]; to all intents and purposes.

28. Inequality

[difference of quantity or degree]

n. **inequality**, inequalness [*rare*]; disparity, imparity [*rare*]; odds; difference etc. 15; unevenness; inclination of the balance, partiality;

shortcoming; casting weight, makeweight; superiority etc. 33; inferiority etc. 34; inequation, inadequation [*archaic*], inadequacy.

v. **be unequal** etc. *adj.;* countervail; have the advantage, give the advantage; turn the scale; kick the beam; topple, topple over; overmatch etc. 33; not come up to etc. 34.

adj. **unequal,** inequal [*rare*], uneven, disparate, partial, inadequate; overbalanced, unbalanced; top-heavy, lopsided; disquiparant; unequaled, unparalleled, fellowless [*rare*], unmatched [*rare*], unrivaled, unique, unapproached, matchless, inimitable, transcendent, peerless, nonpareil, unexampled, unpatterned [*rare*], unpeered [*rare*].

adv. **unequally** etc. *adj.*

29. Mean

n. **mean,** medium, intermedium [*obsoles.*], average, balance, normal, rule, run; mediocrity, generality; golden mean etc. (*mid-course*) 628; middle etc. 68; compromise etc. 774; middle course, middle state; neutrality.

v. **average,** split the difference; take the average etc. *n.;* reduce to a mean etc. *n.;* strike a balance, pair off.

adj. **mean,** intermediate; medial, middle etc. 68; average, normal, standard; neutral.

mediocre, middle-class, *bourgeois* [*F.*], commonplace etc. (*unimportant*) 643.

adv. **on an average,** in the long run; taking one with another, taking all things together, taking it for all in all; *communibus annis* [*L.*], in round numbers.

in the middle, *in medias res* [*L.*].

30. Compensation

n. **compensation,** equation; commutation; indemnification; compromise etc. 774; neutralization, nullification; counteraction etc. 179; reaction; measure for measure; retaliation etc. 718; equalization etc. 27; redemption, recoupment.

set-off, offset; makeweight, casting weight; counterpoise, ballast; indemnity, equivalent, *quid pro quo* [*L.*]; bribe, hush money; gift, donation etc. 784; amends etc. (*atonement*) 952; counterbalance, counterclaim, countervailing; cross debt, cross demand.

pay, payment, reward etc. 973.

v. **compensate,** compense [*obs.*], make compensation, indemnify; counteract, countervail, counterpoise; balance; counterbalance, offset, outbalance, overbalance, set off; hedge, square, give and take; make up for, make leeway; cover,

fill up, neutralize, nullify; equalize etc. 27; make good; recoup, redeem etc. (*atone*) 952; pay, reward etc. 973.

adj. **compensating,** compensatory, compensative, amendatory, indemnificatory, reparative; countervailing etc. *v.;* in the opposite scale; equivalent etc. (*equal*) 27.

adv. **for a consideration,** in return, in consideration.

notwithstanding, but, however, yet, still, nevertheless; although, though; howbeit, albeit; at all events, in spite of, in despite of, despite, at any rate; be that as it may, for all that, even so, on the other hand, at the same time, *quand même* [*F.*], however that may be; after all, after all is said and done; taking one thing with another etc. (*average*) 29.

31. Greatness

n. **greatness** etc. *adj.;* magnitude; size etc. (*dimensions*) 192; multitude etc. (*number*) 102; immensity, enormity, muchness; infinity etc. 105; might, strength, intensity, fullness.

great quantity, quantity, deal [*colloq.*], power [*colloq.*], sight [*colloq.*], pot [*colloq.*], volume, world; mass, heap etc. (*assemblage*) 72; stock etc. (*store*) 636; peck, bushel, load, cargo; cartload, wagonload, shipload; flood, spring tide; abundance etc. (*sufficiency*) 639.

principal part, chief part, main part, greater part, better part, major part, best part, essential part; bulk, mass etc. (*whole*) 50.

fame, distinction, grandeur, dignity; importance etc. 642; generosity.

v. **be great** etc. *adj.;* run high, soar, tower, loom, tower above, rise above, transcend; rise to a great height, carry to a great height; bulk, bulk large; know no bounds; ascend, mount.

enlarge etc. (*increase*) 35, (*expand*) 194.

adj. **great;** greater etc. 33; large, considerable, fair, above par; big, bulky, huge etc. (*large in size*) 192; titanic, Atlantean, Herculean, cyclopean, voluminous; ample; abundant etc. (*enough*) 639; wholesale; many etc. 102; full, intense, strong, sound, passing [*archaic*], heavy, plenary, deep, high; signal, at its height, in the zenith.

worldwide, widespread, far-famed, extensive.

goodly, noble, precious, mighty; sad, grave, serious; far gone, arrant, downright; uttermost; crass, gross, tall, mickle [*archaic*], arch, profound, intense, consummate; rank, unmitigated, red-hot desperate; glaring, flagrant, stark staring; thorough-paced, thorough-going; roaring, whacking [*colloq.*], magnitudinous [*rare*], thumping; extraordinary; important etc. 642; unsurpassed etc. (*supreme*) 33; complete etc. 52.

august, grand dignified, sublime, majestic etc. (*repute*) 873.

vast, immense, enormous, extreme; inordinate, excessive, extravagant, exorbitant, outrageous, preposterous, unconscionable, swinging, monstrous, overgrown; towering, stupendous, prodigious, astonishing, incredible, pronounced, fearful [*colloq.*], thundering [*slang*], terrible [*colloq.*], dreadful [*colloq.*], terrific [*colloq.*]; marvelous etc. (*wonder*) 870.

unlimited etc. (*infinite*) 105; unapproachable, unutterable, indescribable, ineffable, unspeakable, inexpressible, beyond expression, fabulous.

undiminished, unabated, unreduced, unrestricted.

absolute, positive, stark, decided, unequivocal, essential, perfect, finished.

remarkable, of mark, marked, pointed, veriest; notable, noticeable, noteworthy; renowned.

adv. **[in a positive degree]** truly etc. (*truth*) 494; decidedly, unequivocally, purely, absolutely, seriously, essentially, fundamentally, radically, downright, in all conscience; for the most part, in the main.

[in a complete degree] entirely etc. (*completely*) 52; abundantly etc. (*sufficiently*) 639; widely, far and wide.

[in a great or high degree] greatly etc. *adj.;* much, muckle [*archaic*], well, indeed, very, very much, a deal, no end of, most, not a little; pretty, pretty well; enough, in a great measure, no end, passing, richly; to a large extent, to a great extent, to a gigantic extent; on a large scale; so; never so, ever so; ever so much; by wholesale, mighty [*colloq.*], mightily, powerfully; ultra, in the extreme, extremely, exceedingly, intensely, exquisitely, acutely, indefinitely, immeasurably; beyond compare, beyond comparison, beyond measure, beyond all bounds; out of sight [*colloq.*]; incalculably, infinitely.

[in a supreme degree] preëminently, superlatively etc. (*superiority*) 33.

[in a too great degree] immoderately, monstrously, preposterously, inordinately, exorbitantly, excessively, enormously, out of all proportion, with a vengeance.

[in a marked degree] particularly, remarkably, singularly, curiously, uncommonly, unusually, peculiarly, notably, signally, strikingly, pointedly, mainly, chiefly; famously, egregiously, prominently, glaringly, emphatically, strangely, wonderfully, amazingly, surprisingly, astonishingly, incredibly, marvelously, awfully, stupendously.

[in an exceptional degree] peculiarly etc. (*unconformity*) 83.

[in a violent degree] furiously etc. (*violence*) 173; severely, desperately, tremendously, extravagantly, confoundedly, deucedly [*slang*], devilishly [*colloq.*], with a vengeance, à outrance [*F.*], à toute outrance [*F.*].

[in a painful degree] painfully, sadly, grossly, sorely, bitterly, piteously, grievously, miserably, cruelly, woefully, lamentably, shockingly, frightfully, dreadfully, fearfully, terribly, horribly, distressingly, balefully, dolorously.

32. Smallness

n. **smallness** etc. *adj.;* littleness etc. (*small size*) 193; tenuity; paucity; fewness etc. (*small number*) 103; meanness, insignificance etc. (*unimportance*) 643; mediocrity, moderation.

small quantity, modicum, minimum; vanishing point; material point, atom, particle, electron, molecule, muon, photon, quark, corpuscle, point, speck, dot, mote, jot, iota, ace; minutiae, details; look, thought, idea, soupçon [*F.*], dab, dight [*dial.*], whit, tittle, shade, shadow; spark, scintilla, gleam; touch, cast; grain, scruple, granule, globule, minim, sup, sip, sop, spice, drop, droplet, sprinkling, dash, morceau [*F.*], screed [*Scot.*], smack, tinge, tincture; inch, patch, scantling, tatter, cantle, cantlet, flitter, gobbet, dole, mite, bit, morsel, crumb; scrap, shred, tag, splinter, rag; seed, fritter, shive; snip, snippet; snick, snack [*dial.*], snatch, slip; chip, chipping; shiver, sliver, driblet, clipping, paring, shaving, hair.

nutshell; thimbleful, spoonful, handful, capful, mouthful; fragment; fraction etc. (*part*) 51; drop in the ocean.

animalcule etc. 193.

trifle etc. (*unimportant thing*) 643; mere nothing, next to nothing; hardly anything; just enough to swear by; the shadow of a shade.

finiteness, finite quantity.

v. **be small** etc. *adj.;* lie in a nutshell.

diminish etc. (*decrease*) 36, (*contract*) 195.

adj. **small**, little; diminutive etc. (*small in size*) 193; minute, miniature, minikin; fine; inconsiderable, dribbling, paltry etc. (*unimportant*) 643; faint etc. (*weak*) 160; slender, light, slight, scanty, scant, limited; meager etc. (*insufficient*) 640; sparing; few etc. 103; low; soso *or* so-so *or* so so [*colloq.*], middling, tolerable, no great shakes [*slang*]; below par, under par, below the mark, under the mark; at a low ebb; halfway; moderate, modest; tender, subtle.

inappreciable, evanescent, infinitesimal, homeopathic, very small; atomic, corpuscular, microscopic, molecular; skin-deep.

mere, simple, sheer, stark, bare; near run.

dull, petty, shallow, stolid, phlegmatic, unintelligent; Boeotian, ungifted etc. 499.

adv. [in a small degree] to a small extent, on a small scale; a little, a wee bit; slightly etc. *adj.;* imperceptibly; miserably, wretchedly; insufficiently etc. 640; imperfectly; faintly etc. 160; passably, pretty well, well enough.

[in a certain or limited degree] partially, in part; in a certain degree, to a certain degree; to a certain extent; comparatively; some, rather, middling [*colloq.*]; in some degree, in some measure; something, somewhat; simply, only, purely, merely; at least, at the least, at most, at the most; ever so little, as little as may be, *tant soit peu* [*F.*], in ever so small a degree; thus far, *pro tanto* [*L.*], within bounds, in a manner, after a fashion.

almost, nearly, well-nigh, short of, not quite, all but; near upon, close upon; *peu s'en faut* [*F.*], near the mark; within an ace of, within an inch of; on the brink of; scarcely, hardly, barely, only just, no more than.

[in an uncertain degree] about, thereabouts, somewhere about, nearly, say; be the same more or less, be the same little more or less.

[in no degree] noway *or* noways, nowise, not at all, not in the least, not a bit, not a bit of it, not a whit, not a jot, not a shadow; in no wise, in no respect; by no means, by no manner of means; on no account, at no hand.

33. Superiority

[supremacy]

n. **superiority**, majority, plurality; greatness etc. 31; advantage; pull [*slang*]; preponderance, preponderation; vantage ground, prevalence, partiality; personal superiority; scepter, sovereignty, sovranty [*poetic*]; nobility etc. (*rank*) 875; Triton among the minnows, *primus inter pares* [*L.*], *nulli secundus* [*L.*]; superman, overman; captain; crackerjack [*slang*].

supremacy, supremeness, supremity [*rare*], primacy, paramountcy, preëminence; lead; maximum, record; crest, climax; culmination etc. (*summit*) 210; transcendence; *ne plus ultra* [*L.*]; lion's share, Benjamin's mess; excess, surplus etc. (*remainder*) 40; redundance etc. 641.

v. **be superior** etc. *adj.;* exceed, excel, transcend; outdo, outbalance, outweigh, outrank, outrival, out-Herod Herod; pass, surpass, get ahead of; overtop, override, overpass, overbalance, overweigh, overmatch; top, o'ertop, cap, beat, cut out [*colloq.*]; beat hollow [*colloq.*]; outstrip etc. 303; eclipse, throw into the shade, take the shine out of [*colloq.*], put one's nose out of joint [*colloq.*]; have the upper hand, have the whip hand of, have the advantage; turn the scale; play first fiddle etc. (*importance*) 642; preponderate, predominate, prevail; precede, take precedence, come first; come to a head, culminate; beat etc. all others, bear the palm; break the record; take the cake [*slang*].

become *or* render larger etc. (*increase*) 35, (*expand*) 194.

adj. **superior**, greater, major, higher; exceeding etc. *v.;* great etc. 31; distinguished, ultra; vaulting; more than a match for.

supreme, greatest, maximal, maximum, utmost, paramount, preëminent, foremost, crowning, hegemonic [*rare*]; first-rate etc. (*important*) 642, (*excellent*) 648; unrivaled; peerless, matchless; second to none, *sans pareil* [*F.*]; unparagoned, unparalleled, unequaled, unapproached, unsurpassed; superlative, inimitable, *facile princeps* [*L.*], incomparable, sovereign, without parallel, *nulli secundus* [*L.*], *ne plus ultra* [*L.*]; beyond compare, beyond comparison; culminating etc (*topmost*) 210; transcendent, transcendental; *plus royaliste que le Roi* [*F.*].

increased etc. (*added to*) 35; enlarged etc. (*expanded*) 194.

adv. **beyond**, more, over; over the mark, above the mark; above par; upwards of, in advance of; over and above; at the top of the scale, at its height.

[in a superior or supreme degree] eminently, egregiously, preëminently, surpassing, prominently, superlatively, supremely, above all, of all things, the most, to crown all, *par excellence* [*F.*], principally, especially, particularly, peculiarly, *a fortiori* [*L.*], even, yea, still more.

34. Inferiority

n. **inferiority**, minority, subordinacy [*obs.*], subordinance [*obs.*]; shortcoming, deficiency; minimum; smallness etc. 32; imperfection; subjacency [*rare*]; lower quality, lower worth; meanness, poorness, baseness, shabbiness.

[personal inferiority] commonalty etc. 876; juniority, subordinacy; subaltern, sub [*colloq.*].

13

v. **be inferior** etc. *adj.;* fall short of, come short of; not pass, not come up to; want.

become smaller, render smaller etc. (*decrease*), 36, (*contract*) 195; hide its diminished head, retire into the shade, yield the palm, play second fiddle, take a back seat [*colloq.*], kick the beam.

adj. **inferior**, deterior [*rare*], smaller; small etc. 32; minor, less, lesser, deficient, minus, lower, subordinate, secondary, junior, humble; secondrate etc. (*imperfect*) 651; sub-, subaltern.

least, smallest etc. (*see* little, small etc. 193); lowest.

diminished etc. (*decreased*) 36; reduced etc. (*contracted*) 195; unimportant etc. 643.

adv. **less**; under the mark, below the mark, under par, below par; at the bottom of the scale, at a low ebb, at a disadvantage; short of, under.

35. Increase

n. **increase**, augmentation, increasement [*rare*], addition, enlargement, extension; dilatation etc. (*expansion*) 194; increment, accretion; accession etc. 37; development, growth; aggrandizement, accumulation, reënforcement, redoubling, intensification, inflation, enhancement, aggravation; rise; ascent etc. 305; exaggeration, exacerbation; spread etc. (*dispersion*) 73; flood tide, spring tide.

gain, produce, product, profit, gettings [*archaic*], advantage, booty, plunder, superlucration [*rare*], clean-up.

v. **increase**, augment, add to, enlarge; dilate etc. (*expand*) 194; grow, wax, get ahead, gain strength; advance; run up, shoot up; rise; swell, mount, ascend etc. 305; sprout etc. 194.

aggrandize; raise, exalt; deepen, heighten, lengthen, greaten [*archaic*], thicken; eke [*archaic*], inflate; strengthen, intensify, enhance, magnify, redouble, double, triple, etc.; aggravate, exaggerate; exasperate, exacerbate; add fuel to the flame, *oleum addere camino* [*L.*]; superadd etc. (*add*) 37; spread etc. (*disperse*) 73.

adj. **increased** etc. *v.;* on the increase, undiminished; additional etc. (*added*) 37.

increasing, growing, crescent, crescive [*rare*], lengthening, multiplying, intensifying, intensive, intensitive [*rare*], incretionary [*rare*]; crescendo.

adv. crescendo, increasingly.

36. Nonincrease, Decrease

n. **decrease**, diminution, decrescence, decrement, diminishment, lessening etc. *v.;* subtraction etc. 38, reduction, rebatement [*rare*], abatement, declension; shrinkage etc. (*contraction*) 195; coarctation [*obs.*]; curtailment, abridgment etc. (*shortening*) 201; extenuation.

subsidence, wane, ebb, decline; ebb tide, neap tide, ebbing; descent etc. 306; reflux, depreciation, wear and tear, erosion, consumption; deterioration etc. 659; anticlimax; mitigation etc. (*moderation*) 174; catabasis [*med.*].

v. **decrease**, diminish, lessen; abridge etc. (*shorten*) 201; shrink etc. (*contract*) 195; drop off, fall off, tail off; fall away, waste, wear; wane, ebb, decline; descend etc. 306; subside; melt away, die away; retire into the shade, hide its diminished head, fall to a low ebb, run low, languish, decay, crumble, erode, consume away.

bate, abate [*archaic*], dequantitate [*obs.*]; discount, belittle, minify [*rare*], minimize, minish [*rare*], depreciate; extenuate, lower, weaken, attenuate, fritter away; mitigate etc. (*moderate*) 174; dwarf, throw into the shade; reduce etc. 195; shorten etc. 201; subtract etc. 38; deliquesce, ease, remit [*rare*].

adj. **unincreased** etc. (*see* increase etc. 35); decreased, decreasing etc. *v.;* decrescent, reductive; deliquescent, contractive; decrescendo; on the wane etc. *n.*

adv. decrescendo, decreasingly.

37. Addition

n. **addition**, annexation, adjection [*rare*], junction etc. 43; superposition, superaddition, superjunction, superfetation; accession, reënforcement; increase etc. 35; increment.

affix, codicil, subscript, tag, rider, appendage, continuation, equation, postscript, adjunct, etc. 39; supplement; accompaniment etc. 88; interlineation, interposition etc. 228; insertion etc. 300.

computation, footing, totaling, casting, summation.

v. **add**, annex, affix, superadd, subjoin, superpose; clap on, saddle on; tack to, append, tag, adject [*rare*], attach, postfix, adjoin [*rare*], ingraft; saddle with; sprinkle; introduce etc. (*interpose*) 228; insert etc. 300.

compute, foot up, total, cast, sum, count up.

become added, accrue; supervene, advene.

reënforce or reinforce, restrengthen; strengthen, swell the ranks of; augment etc. 35.

adj. **added** etc. *v.;* additional; supplement, supplemental, supplementary; suppletive [*rare*], supervenient [*rare*], suppletory, subjunctive;

adjectitious, adscititious, ascititious; additive, extra, further, fresh, more, new, ulterior, other, remanent [rare]; auxiliary, contributory, accessory; spare.

adv. au reste [F.]; in addition, more, plus, extra; and, also, likewise, too, furthermore, further, item; and also, and eke [archaic]; else, besides, to boot; et cetera, etc.; and so on, and so forth; into the bargain, cum multis aliis [L.], over and above, moreover.

with, withal; including, inclusive, as well as, not to mention, let alone; together with, along with, coupled with, in conjunction with; conjointly; jointly etc. 43.

38. Nonaddition, Deduction

n. **deduction**, subtraction, subduction; retrenchment; removal; sublation [rare], ablation; abstraction etc. (*taking*) 789; garbling etc. *v.;* mutilation, detruncation; amputation; recision, abscision, excision; abrasion; curtailment etc. 201.

rebate etc. (*decrement*) 40a; minuend, subtrahend; decrease etc. 36.

v. **subduct**, subtract, deduct, deduce; bate, retrench; remove, withdraw; take from, take away; detract; garble.

mutilate, amputate, detruncate; cut off, cut away, cut out; abscind, excise.

pare, thin, prune, decimate, eliminate, rebate; bant [colloq.], reduce; abrade, scrape, file.

geld, castrate, envirate [rare], cut, spay (*female*), capon *or* caponize (*a cock*), eunuchize [rare], unman, emasculate.

diminish etc. 36; curtail etc. (*shorten*) 201; deprive of etc. (*take*) 789; weaken.

adj. **subtracted** etc. *v.;* subtractive.

tailless, acaudal, acaudate.

adv. **in deduction** etc. *n.;* less; short of; minus, without, except, excepting, with the exception of, barring, bar, save, exclusive of, save and except, with a reservation, ablatitious [rare].

39. Adjunct

[thing added]

n. **adjunct**; addition, additament; additum [L.], affix, appendage, annex; augment, augmentation; increment, reënforcement, supernumerary, accessory, item; garnish, sauce; accompaniment etc. 88; adjective, addendum (*pl.* addenda); complement, supplement; continuation.

rider, offshoot, episode, side issue, corollary, codicil etc. (*addition*) 37.

flap, lug, lapel, apron, tab, fly, tuck, lap, piece, lappet, skirt, embroidery, trappings, cortege *or* cortège [F.]; tail, suffix etc. (*sequel*) 65; wing.

v. **add**, annex etc. 37.

adj. **additional** etc. 37.

winged, alate *or* alated.

adv. in addition etc. 37.

40. Remainder

[thing remaining]

n. **remainder**, residue; remains, remanet [rare], relict [rare], remanence [rare], remnant, rest, relic; leavings, heeltap, odds and ends, cheeseparings, candle ends, orts; residuum; dregs etc. (*dirt*) 653; refuse etc. (*useless*) 645; stubble, result, educt; fag-end; ruins, wreck, skeleton, stump, rump; alluvium.

surplus, overplus, excess; balance [commercial slang], complement; surplusage; superfluity etc. (*redundance*) 641; survival, survivance [rare]; fossil, shadow, caput mortuum [L.].

v. **remain**; be left etc. *adj.;* exceed, survive; leave.

adj. **remaining**, left; left behind, left over; residual, residuary; over, odd; unconsumed, sedimentary; surviving; net; exceeding, over and above; outlying, outstanding; cast off etc. 782; superfluous etc. (*redundant*) 641.

40a. Decrement

[thing deducted]

n. **decrement**, discount, rebate, rebatement, tare, offtake, drawback, draft, reprise; defect, loss, deduction; afterglow; eduction; waste.

41. Mixture

[forming a whole without coherence]

n. **mixture**, admixture, mixtion [obs.], admixtion, commixture, commixtion *or* commixion [obs.], intermixture, immixture, minglement, eucrasy [med.], interfusion, intertanglement, interlacement, interlacery, intertexture, levigation, alloyage; matrimony; junction etc. 43; combination etc. 48; miscegenation.

impregnation; infusion, diffusion, suffusion, transfusion; infiltration; seasoning, sprinkling, interlarding; interpolation etc. 228; adulteration, sophistication.

[thing mixed] tinge, tincture, touch, dash, smack, sprinkling, spice, seasoning, infusion, soupçon [F.].

[compound resulting from mixture] alloy, amalgam; brass, chowchow, pewter; magma, half-and-half, mélange [F.], tertium quid [L.], miscellany, medley, mess, hash, hodgepodge, hotchpotch, hotchpot, *pasticcio* [*It.*], patch-work, odds and ends, all sorts; jumble etc. (*disorder*) 59; salad, sauce, mash, omnium-gatherum [*colloq.*], gallimaufry, olla-podrida, olio, salmagundi, potpourri, Noah's ark; texture; mingled yarn; mosaic etc. (*variegation*) 440.

half-blood, half-breed, half-caste; mulatto; quarteron *or* quarteroon [*rare*], quintroon *or* quinteron, quadroon, octoroon, sambo *or* zambo; cafuzo; Eurasian; fustee *or* fustie [*W. Ind.*], mestee [*W. Ind.*], mestizo (*fem.* mestiza), griffe, ladino, marabou, sacatra; zebrule; catalo; mule; cross, hybrid, mongrel; cross-breed etc. (*unconformity*) 83.

v. **mix**; join etc. 43; combine etc. 48; commix, immix, intermix; levigate, mix up with, mingle; commingle, intermingle, bemingle; shuffle etc. (*derange*) 61; pound together; hash up, stir up; knead, brew; impregnate with; interlard etc. (*interpolate*) 228; intertwine, interweave etc. 219; associate with; miscegenate.

be mixed etc.; get among, be entangled with.

imbue; infuse, suffuse, transfuse, instill *or* instil, infiltrate, dash, tinge, tincture, season, sprinkle, besprinkle, attemper, medicate, blend, cross; alloy, amalgamate, compound, adulterate, sophisticate, infect.

adj. **mixed** etc. *v.;* implex [*rare*], composite, half-and-half, linsey-woolsey, medley, chowchow, hybrid, mongrel, heterogeneous; motley etc. (*variegated*) 440; miscellaneous, promiscuous, indiscriminate; miscible.

adv. **among**, amongst, amid, amidst; with; in the midst of, in the crowd.

42. Simpleness
[freedom from mixture]

n. **simpleness** etc. *adj.;* purity, homogeneity.

elimination; sifting etc. *v.;* purification etc. (*cleanness*) 652.

v. **render simple** etc. *adj.;* simplify.

sift, winnow, bolt, eliminate; exclude, get rid of; clear; purify etc. (*clean*) 652; disentangle etc. (*disjoin*, 44).

adj. **simple**, uniform, of a piece, homogeneous, Attic, homespun, single, pure, clear, sheer, neat.

unmixed, unmingled, unblended, uncombined, uncompounded; elemental, elementary, undecomposed; unadulterated, unsophisticated, unalloyed, untinged, unfortified; *pur et simple* [*F.*]; incomplex, incomposite [*rare*].

free from, exempt from; exclusive.

adv. **simply** etc. *adj.;* only.

43. Junction

n. **junction**; joining etc. *v.;* joinder, union; connection, conjunction, conjugation; annexion, annexation, annexment [*rare*]; astriction, attachment, compagination [*rare*], subjunction, vincture [*obs.*], ligation, alligation; accouplement; marriage etc. (*wedlock*) 903; infibulation, inosculation, symphysis, anastomosis, confluence, communication, concatenation; meeting, reunion; assemblage etc. 72.

coition, copulation; sexual congress, sexual conjunction, sexual intercourse.

joint, joining, juncture, chiasm, osculature, pivot, hinge, articulation, commissure, seam, gore, gusset, suture, stitch; link etc. 45; miter, mortise.

contingency, emergency, predicament, crisis, concurrence.

closeness, tightness etc. *adj.;* coherence etc. 46; combination etc. 48.

annexationist.

v. **join**, unite; conjoin, connect; associate; put together, lay together, clap together, hang together, lump together, hold together, piece together, tack together, fix together, bind up together; embody, reëmbody; roll into one.

attach, fix, affix, immobilize, saddle on, fasten, bind, secure, clinch, twist, make fast etc. *adj.;* tie, pinion, string, strap, sew, lace, stitch, tack, knit, button, buckle, hitch, lash, truss, bandage, braid, splice, swathe, gird, tether, moor, picket, harness, chain; fetter etc. (*restrain*) 751; lock, latch, belay, brace, hook, grapple, leash, couple, accouple, link, yoke, bracket; marry etc. (*wed*) 903; bridge over, span.

pin, nail, bolt, hasp, clasp, clamp, screw, rivet; impact, solder, braze; cement, set; weld together, fuse together; tighten, trice up, screw up; wedge, rabbet, mortise, miter, jam, dovetail, enchase; graft, ingraft, inosculate.

entwine *or* intwine; interlink, interlace, intertwine, intertwist, interweave; entangle; twine round, belay.

be joined etc.; hang together, hold together; cohere etc. 46.

adj. **joined** etc. *v.;* joint; conjoint, conjunct; corporate, compact; hand in hand.

firm, fast, close, tight, taut *or* taught, secure, set, intervolved [*obs.*]; inseparable, indissoluble, insecable [*obs.*], inseverable.

adv. **jointly** etc. *adj.;* in conjunction with etc. (*in addition to*) 37; fast, firmly, etc. *adj.;* intimately.

44. Disjunction

n. **disjunction**, disconnection, disunity, disunion, disassociation, disengagement, dissociation, disjointure; discontinuity etc. 70; abjunction [*obs.*]; cataclasm; inconnection [*obs.*]; abstraction, abstractedness; isolation; insularity, insulation; oasis; island; separateness etc. *adj.;* severalty; *disjecta membra* [*L.*]; dispersion etc. 73; apportionment etc. 786.

separation; parting etc. *v.;* circumcision, detachment, segregation; divorce, sejunction [*obs.*], seposition [*obs.*], diduction [*rare*], diremption [*rare*], discerption; elision; caesura, division, subdivision, break, fracture, rupture; compartition [*obs.*]; dismemberment, disintegration, dislocation; luxation; severance, disseverance; scission; rescission, abscission; laceration, dilaceration; disruption, abruption; avulsion, divulsion; section, resection, cleavage; fission; partibility, separability, separatism.

fissure, breach, rent, split, rift, crack, slit, incision.

dissection, anatomy; decomposition etc. 49; cutting instrument etc. (*sharpness*) 253; buzz saw, circular saw.

separatist.

v. **be disjoined** etc.; come off, come to pieces, fall off, fall to pieces; peel off; get loose.

disjoin, disconnect, disengage, disunite, dissociate, dispair [*obs.*]; divorce, part, dispart, detach, separate, cut off, rescind, segregate; set apart, keep apart; insulate, isolate; throw out of gear; cut adrift; loose; unloose, undo, unbind, unchain, unlock etc. (*fix*) 43, unpack, unravel; disentangle; set free etc. (*liberate*) 750.

sunder, divide, subdivide, sever, section, sectionize [*rare*], segment, dissever, abscind; circumcise; cut; incide [*obs.*], incise; saw, snip, nib [*obs.*], nip, cleave, rive, rend, slit, split, splinter, chip, crack, snap, break, tear, burst; rend etc., asunder, rend in twain; wrench, rupture, shatter, shiver, crunch, craunch *or* cranch, chop; cut up, rip up; hack, hew, slash; whittle; haggle, hackle, discind [*obs.*], lacerate, scamble [*obs.*], mangle, gash, hash, slice; cut up, carve, quarter, dissect, anatomize; dislimb; take to pieces, pull to pieces, pick to pieces, tear to pieces; tear to tatters, tear piecemeal; divellicate; skin etc. 226.

disintegrate, dismember, disbranch, disband; disperse etc. 73; dislocate, disjoint; break up; mince; comminute etc. (*pulverize*) 330; apportion etc. 786.

partition, parcel, demarcate [*rare*], graduate, district, chapter, canton.

part, part company; separate, leave; alienate, estrange.

adj. **disjoined** etc. *v.;* discontinuous etc. 70; bipartite, biparted [*rare*], multipartite, abstract; disjunctive; secant; isolated etc. *v.;* insular, separate, disparate, discrete, apart, asunder, far between, loose, free; lobate, lobulate, lobulated, lobulose, digitate; unattached, unannexed, unassociated, unconnected; distinct; adrift; straggling; rift, reft, cleft.

[capable of being cut] scissile, divisible, discerptible [*rare*], partible, separable, severable, dividuous [*rare*].

adv. **separately** etc. *adj.;* one by one, severally, apart; adrift, asunder, in twain; in the abstract, abstractedly.

45. Vinculum

[connecting medium]

n. **vinculum**, link; connective, connection; junction etc. 43; bond of union, copula, intermedium, hyphen; bracket; bridge, stepping-stone, isthmus.

bond, tendon, tendril; fiber; cord, cordage; riband, ribbon, rope, guy, cable, line, halser [*obs.*], hawser, painter, moorings, wire, chain; string etc. (*filament*) 205.

fastening, tie; ligament, ligature; strap; tackle, rigging; standing rigging; running rigging; traces, harness; yoke; band, bandage; brace, roller, fillet; inkle; with, withe, withy; thong, braid; girder, tiebeam; girth, girdle, cestus, garter, halter, noose, lasso, surcingle, knot, running knot; *cabestro* [*Sp. Amer.*], cinch, lariat, *legadero* [*Sp. Amer.*], oxreim [*S. Africa*]; suspenders.

pin, corking pin, nail, brad, tack, skewer, staple, clamp; cramp, cramp iron, detent, *larigo* [*Sp. Amer.*], pawl, terret, screw, button, buckle, clasp, hasp, bar, hinge, hank, catch, latch, bolt, latchet, tag; tooth; hook, hook and eye; lock, holdfast, padlock, rivet, couple, coupler, ring; anchor, grappling iron, treenail *or* trennel, stake, post; prop etc. (*support*) 215.

cement, glue, gum, paste, size, wafer, solder, lute, putty, birdlime, mortar, stucco, plaster, grout; viscum.

shackle, rein etc. (*means of restraint*) 752.

v. **bridge over**, span; connect etc. 43; hang etc. 214.

46. Coherence

n. **coherence**, cohesion, cohesiveness, adherence, adhesion, adhesiveness; concretion, accretion;

conglutination, conglomeration, agglutination, agglomeration; aggregation; consolidation, set, cementation; sticking, soldering etc. *v.;* connection; dependence.

tenacity, toughness; stickiness etc. 352; inseparability, inseparableness; bur *or* burr, remora.

conglomerate, concrete etc. *(density)* 321.

v. **cohere,** adhere, coagulate, stick, cling, cleave, hold, take hold of, hold fast, close with, clasp, hug; grow together, hang together; twine round etc. *(join)* 43.

stick like a leech, stick like wax, stick like the paper on the wall; stick closer than a brother; stick close; cling like ivy, cling like a bur; adhere like a remora, adhere like Dejanira's shirt.

glue; agglutinate, conglutinate; cement, lute, belute [*rare*], paste, gum; solder, weld; ferruminate [*archaic*]; cake, consolidate etc. *(solidify)* 321; agglomerate.

adj. **adhesive,** cohesive, adhering, cohering etc. *v.;* tenacious, tough; sticky etc. 352.

united, unseparated, sessile, inseparable, inextricable, infrangible; compact etc. *(dense)* 321.

47. Incoherence
[nonadhesion, immiscibility]

n. **incoherence,** nonadhesion; immiscibility; looseness etc. *adj.;* laxity; relaxation; loosening etc. *v.;* freedom; disjunction etc. 44; rope of sand.

v. **make loose** etc. *adj.;* loosen, slacken, relax; unglue etc. 46; detach etc. *(disjoin)* 44.

adj. **nonadhesive,** immiscible; incoherent, detached, loose, baggy, slack, lax, relaxed, flapping, streaming; disheveled; segregated, like grains of sand; unconsolidated etc. 231; uncombined etc. 48; noncohesive.

48. Combination

n. **combination;** mixture etc. 41; junction etc. 43; union, unification, synthesis, synizesis, syneresis, incorporation, amalgamation, embodiment, coalescence, crasis, fusion, coalescing, blend, blendure [*rare*], blending, absorption, centralization.

alloy, compound, amalgam, composition, *tertium quid* [*L.*]; resultant, impregnation.

v. **combine,** unite, incorporate, inosculate, consubstantiate, alloy, intermix, interfuse, interlard, syncretize, interlace, agglutinate, amalgamate, embody, absorb, reëmbody, blend, merge, fuse, melt into one, consolidate, coalesce, solidify, commix [*archaic*], contemper, centralize, impregnate; put together, lump together.

league, interleague [*rare*], federate, confederate, fraternize, club, associate, amalgamate, cement a union, marry, couple, pair, ally.

adj. **combined** etc. *v.;* wedded; indiscrete, conjunctive, conjugate, conjoint; impregnated with, ingrained; imbued, inoculated.

allied, amalgamated, federate, confederate, corporate, leagued.

49. Decomposition

n. **decomposition,** analysis, dieresis, dissection, resolution, catalysis, dissolution, break-up; dispersion etc. 73; disjunction etc. 44; disintegration.

decay, rot, putrefaction, putrescence, putridity, caries; corruption etc. *(uncleanness)* 653.

electrolysis, electrolyzation, hydrolysis, proteolysis, thermolysis, catalysis.

v. **decompose,** decompound [*rare*]; analyze, disembody, dissolve; resolve into its elements, separate into its elements; dissect, decentralize, break up; disintegrate, disperse etc. 73; unravel etc. *(unroll)* 313; crumble into dust.

corrupt [*archaic*], rot, decay, consume; putrefy, putresce.

electrolyze, hydrolyze, thermolyze, catalyze.

adj. **decomposed** etc. *v.;* catalytic, analytical; resolvent, separative, solvent.

50. Whole
[principal part]

n. **whole,** totality, integrity; totalness etc. *adj.;* entirety, entire [*rare*], *ensemble* [*F.*], collectiveness; unity etc. 87; completeness etc. 52; indivisibility, indiscerptibility; integration, embodiment; integer, integral.

all, general [*archaic*], the whole, total, aggregate, one and all, gross amount, sum, sum total, the altogether [*humorous*], *tout ensemble* [*F.*], length and breadth of, Alpha and Omega, "be all and end all"; complex, *complexus* [*L.*]; lock, stock, and barrel.

bulk, mass, lump, tissue, staple, body, compages; trunk, torso, bole, hull, hulk, skeleton; greater part, major part, best part, principal part, main part; essential part etc. *(importance)* 642; lion's share, Benjamin's mess; the long and the short; nearly all, almost all.

v. **form a whole,** constitute a whole; integrate, embody, amass; aggregate etc. *(assemble)* 72; amount to, come to.

adj. **whole,** total, integral [*rare*], integrate [*rare*], entire; complete etc. 52; one, individual.

unbroken, uncut, undivided, unsevered, unclipped, uncropped, unshorn; seamless; undiminished; undemolished, undissolved, undestroyed, unbruised.

indivisible, indissoluble, indissolvable, indiscerptible.

wholesale, sweeping; comprehensive.

adv. **wholly**, altogether; as a whole, one and indivisible; totally etc. (*completely*) 52; entirely, all, all in all, wholesale, in a body, collectively, all put together; in the aggregate, in the lump, in the mass, in the gross, in the main, in the long run; *en masse* [*F.*], on the whole, bodily, *en bloc* [*F.*], *in extenso* [*L.*], throughout, every inch; substantially.

51. Part

n. **part**, portion; dose, item, particular; aught, any; division; ward, parcel [*law or archaic*], count; sector, segment; fraction, fragment; cantle, cantlet; frustum [*rare*]; detachment, subdivision.

section, chapter, verse; article, clause, phrase, paragraph, passage, number, book, fascicle, fascicule *or* fasciculus, *livraison* [*F.*].

piece, lump, bit, snatch; cut, cutting; chip, chunk, collop, slice, scrap, crumb, scale; lamina etc. 204; small part; morsel, moiety, particle etc. (*smallness*) 32; installment, dividend; share etc. (*allotment*) 786.

oddments, *débris* [*F.*], odds and ends, detritus; *excerpta* [*L.*], excerpt.

member, limb, lobe, lobule, arm, wing, scion, branch, bough, joint, link, offshoot, ramification, twig, bush, spray, sprig; runner, tendril; leaf, leaflet; stump; component part etc. 56; sarmentum.

cue, role, cast; lines, pageant [*archaic*].

compartment; department etc. (*class*) 75; county etc. (*region*) 181.

v. **part**, divide, break etc. (*disjoin*) 44; partition etc. (*apportion*) 786.

adj. **fractional**, fragmentary, portional [*rare*]; sectional, aliquot; divided etc. *v.;* in compartments, multifid; disconnected; incomplete, partial.

divided, broken, cut, severed, clipped, cropped, shorn; seamed.

divisible, dissoluble, dissolvable, discerptible.

adv. **partly**, in part, partially; piecemeal, part by part; by installments, by snatches, by inches, by driblets; bit by bit, inch by inch, foot by foot, drop by drop; in detail, in lots.

52. Completeness

n. **completeness** etc. *adj.;* completion etc. 729; integration; allness [*rare*], totality, integralness, totalness, integrality [*rare*], integrity.

entirety; perfection etc. 650; solidity, solidarity; unity; all; *ne plus ultra* [*L.*], ideal, limit; undividedness, intactness, universality.

complement, supplement, make-weight; filling up etc. *v.*

fill; impletion; saturation, saturity [*obs.*]; high water; high tide, flood tide, springtide; load, bumper, bellyful; brimmer; sufficiency etc. 639.

v. **be complete** etc. *adj.;* come to a head.

render complete etc. *adj.;* complete etc. (*accomplish*) 729; fill, charge, load, stevedore, replenish; make up, make good; piece out, eke out; supply deficiencies; fill up, fill in, fill to the brim, fill the measure of; satiate; saturate.

go the whole hog [*colloq.*], go the whole length; go all lengths; go the limit [*colloq.*].

adj. **complete**, entire; whole etc. 50; perfect etc. 650; full, good, absolute, thorough, plenary; solid, undivided; with all its parts; all-sided.

exhaustive, radical, sweeping, thorough-going; dead.

regular, consummate, unmitigated, sheer, unqualified, unconditional, free; abundant etc. (*sufficient*) 639.

brimming; brimful, topful; chock-full, choke-full; saturated, crammed; replete etc. (*redundant*) 641; fraught, laden; full-laden, full-fraught, full-charged; heavy laden.

completing etc. *v.;* supplemental, supplementary; ascititious.

adv. **completely** etc. *adj.;* altogether, outright, wholly, totally, *in toto* [*L.*], quite; all out; over head and ears; effectually, for good and all, nicely, fully, through thick and thin, head and shoulders, out of sight [*slang*]; neck and heel, neck and crop; in all respects, in every respect; at all points, out and out, to all intents and purposes; *toto coelo* [*L.*]; utterly; clean, clean as a whistle; to the full, to the utmost, to the limit, to the backbone; hollow, stark; heart and soul, root and branch, down to the ground.

to the top of one's bent, as far as possible, *à outrance* [*F.*].

throughout; from first to last, from beginning to end, from end to end, from one end to the other, from Dan to Beersheba, from head to foot, from top to toe, from top to bottom; *de fond en comble* [*F.*]; *à fond* [*F.*]; *a capite ad* *calcem* [*L.*]; *ab ovo usque ad mala* [*L.*]; fore and aft; every whit, every inch; *cap-à-pie* [*F.*], to the end of the chapter; up to the brim, up to the ears, up to the eyes; as . . . as can be.

on all accounts; *sous tous les rapports* [*F.*]; with a vengeance.

53. Incompleteness

n. **incompleteness** etc. *adj.;* deficience [*rare*], deficiency, short weight, short measure; shortcoming etc. 304; want, lack, insufficiency etc. 640; imperfection etc. 651; immaturity etc. (*non-preparation*) 674; half measures.

[part wanting] defect, deficit, defalcation, omission; caret; wantage [*rare*], ullage, shortage; interval etc. 198; break etc. (*discontinuity*) 70; noncompletion etc. 730; missing link.

v. **be incomplete** etc. *adj.;* fall short of etc. 304; lack etc. (*be insufficient*) 640; neglect etc. 460.

adj. **incomplete**; imperfect etc. 651; unfinished; uncompleted etc. (*see* complete etc. 729); defective, deficient, wanting, failing; bobtailed; in default, in arrear; short, short of; hollow, meager, jejune, poor, scarce, lame, half-and-half, perfunctory, sketchy; crude etc. (*unprepared*) 674.

mutilated, garbled, hashed, mangled, butchered, docked, lopped, truncated.

in progress, in hand; going on, proceeding.

adv. **incompletely** etc. *adj.;* by halves.

54. Composition

n. **composition**, constitution; crasis, synizesis, syneresis; confection [*rare*], synthesis, compaction [*rare*], make, make-up; combination etc. 48; inclusion, admission, comprehension, reception; embodiment; formation.

authorship, compilation, composition, *recueil* [*F.*], production, inditing *or* inditement, conflation, invention; writing etc. 590.

hymnody, hymnology, instrumentation; opus, aria etc. (*music*) 415.

painting, scenography, etching, design etc. (*painting*) 556; relief, relievo etc. (*sculpture*) 557.

typesetting, typography etc. (*printing*) 591.

v. **be composed of**, be made of, be formed of, be made up of; consist of, be resolved into.

include etc. (*in a class*) 76; contain, hold, comprehend take in, admit, embrace, embody; involve, implicate; drag into; synthesize.

compose, constitute, form, make; make up, fill up, build up; fabricate, weave, construct; compile, redact, collate, dash off, address, indite, score, scribble, draw, write; set (*in printing*); enter into the composition of etc. (*be a component*) 56.

adj. containing, constituting etc. *v.*

55. Exclusion

n. **exclusion**, nonadmission, omission, exception, rejection, repudiation; exile etc. (*seclusion*) 893; noninclusion, preclusion, debarrance [*rare*], debarment, lock-out, disfellowship [*rare*], ostracism, prohibition.

separation, segregation, seposition [*obs.*], elimination, expulsion; cofferdam.

v. be excluded from etc.

exclude, bar; leave out, shut out, bar out; reject, repudiate, blackball, ostracize; lay apart, lay aside, put apart, put aside, set apart, set aside; relegate, segregate; throw overboard; strike off, strike out; neglect etc. 460; banish etc. (*seclude*) 893; separate etc. (*disjoin*) 44.

pass over, omit; garble; eliminate, weed, winnow.

adj. **excluding** etc. *v.;* exclusive, exclusory; excluded etc. *v.;* unrecounted, not included in; inadmissible, preclusive, preventive, prohibitive.

adv. exclusive of, barring; except; with the exception of; save; bating.

56. Component

n. **component**, integrant; component part, integral part, integrant part; element, constituent, ingredient, leaven; part and parcel; contents; appurtenance; feature; member etc. (*part*) 51; personnel.

v. **enter into**, enter into the composition of; be a component etc. *n.;* be *or* form part of etc. 51; merge in, be merged in; be implicated in; share in etc. (*participate*) 778; belong to, appertain to; combine, inhere in, unite.

form, make, constitute, compose, precompose, recompose; sonnetize [*rare*]; fabricate etc. 54.

adj. **forming** etc. *v.;* inherent, intrinsic, essential.

inclusive, all-embracing, compendious, comprehensive, inclusory.

57. Extraneousness

n. **extraneousness** etc. *adj.;* extrinsicality etc. 6; exteriority etc. 220; alienage, alienism.

foreign body, foreign substance, foreign element.

alien, stranger, intruder, interloper, foreigner, *novus homo* [*L.*], newcomer, jackaroo [*Australia*], griffin [*Anglo-Ind.*]; recruit, immigrant, emigrant; creole, Africander; outsider, outlander [*archaic*], barbarian, extern [*rare*], tramontane [*rare*], ultramontane; tenderfoot.

adj. **extraneous**, foreign, alien, ulterior, exterior, external, outlandish, outside, outland [*archaic*]; barbaric, barbarian, metic, oversea, tramontane [*rare*], ultramontane.

excluded etc. 55; inadmissible; exceptional.

adv. **abroad**, in foreign parts, in foreign lands; beyond seas; oversea, overseas; on one's travels.

Section 4. Order

58. Order

n. **order**, regularity, uniformity, symmetry, *lucidus ordo* [*L.*]; harmony, music of the spheres.

gradation, progression; series etc. (*continuity*) 69.

course, even tenor, routine; method, disposition, arrangement, array, system, economy, discipline; orderliness etc. *adj.;* subordination.

rank, place etc. (*term*) 71.

v. **form**; be *or* become in order etc. *adj.;* fall in, draw up; arrange itself, range itself, place itself; fall into one's place, fall into rank, take one's place, take rank; rally round.

adjust, methodize, regulate, systematize, standardize, normalize; time, police.

adj. **orderly**, regular; in order, in trim, in apple-pie order, in its proper place; neat, tidy, *en règle* [*F.*], well regulated, correct, methodical, uniform, symmetrical, shipshape, businesslike, systematic, systematical, normal, habitual; unconfused etc. (*see* confuse etc. 61); arranged etc. 60.

adv. **in order**; methodically etc. *adj.;* in turn, in its turn; step by step; by regular steps, by regular gradations, by regular stages, by regular intervals; *seriatim* [*NL.*], systematically, by clockwork, gradatim; at stated periods etc. (*periodically*) 138.

59. Disorder

[absence or want of order, etc.]

n. **disorder**; derangement etc. 61; irregularity; deray [*archaic*], deordination [*rare*]; anomaly etc. (*unconformity*) 83; anarchy, anarchism; want of method; untidiness etc. *adj.;* disunion; discord etc. 24.

confusion; confusedness etc. *adj.;* mishmash, mix; disarray, jumble, topsy-turvy, botch, huddle, litter, lumber; *cahotage* [*F.*]; farrago; mess, mash, muddle, muss, hash, hodgepodge, hotchpotch, hotchpot; what the cat brought in [*colloq.*]; imbroglio, chaos, omnium-gatherum [*colloq.*], medley; mere mixture etc. 41; fortuitous concourse of atoms, *disjecta membra* [*L.*].

complexity; complexness etc. *adj.;* complexus, complication, implication; intricacy, intrication [*rare*]; perplexity; network, maze, labyrinth; wilderness, jungle; involution, raveling, entanglement, dishevelment; coil etc. (*convolution*) 248; sleave, tangled skein, knot, Gordian knot, wheels within wheels; kink, gnarl *or* knarl [*obs.*]; webwork.

turmoil; ferment etc. (*agitation*) 315; to-do [*colloq.*], trouble, pudder [*obs. or dial.*], pother, row [*colloq.*], disturbance, convulsion, tumult, uproar, riot, rumpus [*colloq.*], stour [*archaic*], scramble, fracas, embroilment, *mêlée* [*F.*], spill and pelt, rough and tumble; whirlwind etc. 349; bear garden, pandemonium, Babel, Saturnalia, Donnybrook, confusion worse confounded, most admired disorder, *concordia discors* [*L.*]; Bedlam broke loose, hell broke loose; bull in a china shop; all the fat in the fire, *diable à quatre* [*F.*], Devil to pay; pretty kettle of fish; pretty piece of work.

slattern, slut, drab, dowdy, trollop, sloven, draggle-tail [*colloq.*].

v. **be disorderly** etc. *adj.;* ferment, play at cross-purposes.

put out of order; botch, derange etc. 61; drag from under the bed [*colloq.*]; ravel etc. 219; ruffle, rumple.

adj. **disorderly**, orderless; out of order, out of place, out of gear, out of kilter [*colloq.*]; irregular, desultory; anomalous etc. (*unconformable*) 83; acephalous; aimless; disorganized; straggling; unmethodical, immethodical; unsymmetric, unsystematic; untidy, slovenly, messy [*colloq.*], hugger-mugger, dislocated; out of sorts; promiscuous, indiscriminate; chaotic, anarchic, anarchical; unarranged etc. (*see* arrange etc. 60); confused; deranged etc. 61; topsy-turvy etc. (*inverted*) 218; shapeless etc. 241; disjointed, out of joint; gnarled *or* knarled [*obs.*].

complex, complexed; intricate, complicated, perplexed, involved, raveled, entangled, knotted, tangled, inextricable; irreducible.

troublous, tumultuous, turbulent; riotous etc. (*violent*) 173.

adv. **irregularly** etc. *adj.;* by fits, by fits and snatches, by fits and starts; pellmell; higgledy-piggledy; helter-skelter [*colloq.*], harum-scarum [*colloq.*]; in a ferment; at sixes and sevens, at cross-purposes; upside down etc. 218.

60. Arrangement

[reduction to order]

n. **arrangement**; plan etc. 626; preparation etc. 673; disposal, disposition, disposure; collocation, allocation; distribution; sorting etc. *v.;* assortment, allotment, apportionment, taxis, taxonomy, syntaxis, graduation, organization, ordination, grouping, groupage.

analysis, classification, division, systematization, categorization, codification, digestion.

[result of arrangement] orderliness, form, lay, array, digest; synopsis etc. (*compendium*) 596, syntagma, table, atlas; register etc. (*record*) 551; cosmos, schematism, organism, architecture; instrumentation, orchestration, score etc. (*music*) 415; stipulation, settlement, *bandobast* or *bundobust* [*Anglo-Ind.*].

[instrument for sorting] sieve, riddle, screen, bolter, colander, grate, grating.

file, card index.

v. **reduce to order**, bring into order; introduce order into; rally.

arrange, dispose, place, form; put in order, set in order, place in order; set out, collocate, allocate, compose, space, range, pack, marshal, array, size, rank, group, parcel out, allot, distribute, deal; cast the parts, assign the parts; dispose of, assign places to; assort, sort; sift, riddle; put to rights, put into shape, put in trim, put in array, set to rights, set into shape, set in trim, set in array; tidy; apportion.

class, classify; divide; file, list, string together; thread; register etc. (*record*) 551; catalogue, tabulate, index, alphabetize, graduate, digest, grade, codify; orchestrate, score, harmonize.

methodize, regulate, systematize, coördinate, organize, brigade, echelon, seriate [*rare*], settle, fix.

unravel, disentangle, unweave, ravel, card; disembroil; feaze.

adj. **arrange** etc. *v.;* embattled, in battle array; cut and dried; methodical, orderly, regular, systematic, on file; tabular, tabulate.

61. Derangement

[subversion of order; bringing into disorder]

n. **derangement** etc. *v.;* muss, mess, disorder etc. 59; evection, discomposure, disturbance; disorganization, deorganization; dislocation; perturbation, interruption; shuffling etc. *v.;* inversion etc. 218; corrugation etc. (*fold*) 258; involvement; insanity etc. 503.

v. **derange**; misarrange, disarrange, displace, misplace; mislay, discompose, disorder; disorganize; embroil, unsettle, disturb, confuse, trouble, perturb, jumble, tumble; huddle, shuffle, muddle, toss, hustle, fumble, riot; bring into disorder, put into disorder, throw into disorder etc. 59; muss, mess; break the ranks, disconcert, convulse; break in upon.

unhinge, dislocate, put out of joint, throw out of gear.

turn topsy-turvy etc. (*invert*) 218; bedevil; complicate, involve, perplex, confound; embrangle *or* imbrangle, tangle, entangle, ravel, tousle, dishevel, ruffle; rumple etc. (*fold*) 258; dement, become insane etc. 503.

litter, scatter; mix etc. 41.

adj. **deranged** etc. *v.;* syncretic, syncretistic; mussy.

62. Precedence

n. **precedence**; predecession [*rare*]; coming before etc. *v.;* the lead, le pas [*F.*]; superiority etc. 33; importance etc. 642; premise *or* premiss; antecedence *or* antecedency; anteriority etc. (*front*) 234; precursor etc. 64; priority etc. 116; precession [*rare*] etc. 280; anteposition; epacme; preference.

prefix, prefixture [*rare*], prelude, affix, preamble, overture, ritornel, *ritornello* [*It.*], voluntary.

v. **precede**, forerun, forego [*archaic*], prevene [*rare*]; come before, come first; head, lead, take the lead; lead the way, lead the dance; introduce, prologize [*rare*], usher in; have the pas [*F.*]; set the fashion etc. (*influence*) 175; open the ball, lead the cotillion, lead the german; rank, outrank; take precedence, have precedence; have the start etc. (*get before*) 280.

place before; prefix; premise, prelude, preface; affix.

adj. **preceding** etc. *v.;* precedent, antecedent; anterior; prior etc. 116; before; former, foregoing; before mentioned, above mentioned, aforementioned; aforesaid, said; precursory, precursive; prevenient, preliminary, prefatory, introductory; prelusive, prelusory; proemial, preparatory.

adv. **before**; in advance etc. (*precession*) 280.

63. Sequence

n. **sequence**, train, coming after; pursuance, going after etc. (*following*) 281; consecution, succession; posteriority etc. 117.

continuation, prolongation; mantle of Elijah; order of succession; successiveness; paracme.

secondariness; subordinancy [*obs.*], subordinacy etc. (*inferiority*) 34.

afterbirth, afterburden, afterclap, aftercrop, afterglow, aftergrass, aftermath, afterpain, afterpiece, aftertaste; placenta, secundines; sequelae.

v. **succeed**; come after, come on, come next; follow, ensue, step into the shoes of; alternate.

follow, tag [*colloq.*], heel, dog, dodge, shadow, hound, bedog, hunt; trace, retrace.

place after, suffix, append, subjoin.

adj. **succeeding** etc. *v.;* sequent; subsequent, consequent; sequacious, proximate, next; consecutive etc. (*con*tinuity) 69; alternate, amoebean.

latter; posterior etc. 117.

adv. **after**, subsequently; behind etc. (*rear*) 235.

64. Precursor

n. **precursor**, antecedent, precedent, predecessor; forerunner, apparitor, vancourier [*obs.*]; pioneer, prodrome [*obs.*], prodromos [*Gr.*], prodromus [*rare*], outrider; leader, bellwether; herald, harbinger; dawn; bellmare, *avant-coureur* [*F.*], avant-courier, *avant-courrier* [*F.*], forelooper *or* foreloper *or* forelouper [*S. Afr.*], voorlooper [*Dutch*], voortrekker [*Dutch*].

prelude, preamble, preface, prologue, foreword, *avant-propos* [*F.*], protasis, proemium, prolusion [*rare*], proem, prolepsis, prolegomena, prefix, exordium, introduction; heading, frontispiece, groundwork; preparation etc. 673; overture, voluntary, ritornel, *ritornello* [*It.*], descant, symphony; premises.

prefigurement etc. 511; omen etc. 512.

adj. **precursory**; prelusive, prelusory, preludious; proemial [*rare*], introductory, preludial, prefatory, prodromous [*rare*], inaugural, preliminary; precedent etc. (*prior*) 116.

65. Sequel

n. **sequel**, suffix, successor; tail, queue, train, wake, trail, rear; retinue, suite; appendix, postscript, subscript, postlude, conclusion, epilogue; peroration; codicil; continuation, sequela [*pl.* sequelae]; appendage; tailpiece, heelpiece, tag, more last words; colophon.

follower, successor, sectary, heeler [*slang*], pursuer, adherent, partisan, disciple, client; sycophant, parasite.

aftercome [*Scot.*], aftergrowth, afterpart, afterpiece, after course, aftergame, afterthought; *arrière pensée* [*F.*], second thoughts; outgrowth.

66. Beginning

n. **beginning**, incunabula [*pl.*], commencement, opening, outset, incipience, incipiency, inception, inchoation, inchoacy [*rare*]; introduction etc. (*precursor*) 64; alpha, initial; inauguration, ingress, *début* [*F.*], *le premier pas* [*F.*], embarkation, rising of the curtain; curtain-raiser, maiden speech; exordium; outbreak, onset, brunt; initiative, move, first move; prelude, prime, proem, gambit; narrow *or* thin end of the wedge, fresh start, new departure.

first stage, first blush, first glance, first impression, first sight.

origin etc. (*cause*) 153; source, rise; bud, germ etc. 153; egg, embryo, rudiment; genesis, birth, nativity, cradle, infancy; forefront, outstart, start, starting point etc. 293; dawn etc. (*morning*) 125.

head, heading; title-page; van etc. (*front*) 234; caption, *fatihah* [*Ar.*].

entrance, entry; inlet, orifice, mouth, chops, lips, porch, portal, portico, propylon, door; gate, gateway; postern, wicket, threshold, vestibule; propylaeum; skirts, border etc. (*edge*) 231; tee.

rudiments, elements, principia, outlines, grammar, protasis, alphabet, ABC.

v. **begin**, commence, inchoate, rise, arise, originate, conceive, initiate, open, start, gin [*archaic*], dawn, set in, take its rise, enter upon, enter; set out etc. (*depart*) 293; embark in; incept [*rare*], institute.

usher in; lead off, lead the way, take the lead, take the initiative; inaugurate, auspicate, head; stand at the head, stand first, stand for; lay the foundations etc. (*prepare*) 673; found etc. (*cause*) 153; set up, set on foot, set agoing, set abroach, set the ball in motion; apply the match to a train; launch, broach; open up, open the door to; set about, set to work; make a beginning, make a start; handsel; take the first step, lay the first stone, cut the first turf; break ground, break the ice, break cover; pass the Rubicon, cross the Rubicon; open fire, open the ball; ventilate, air; undertake etc. 676.

come into existence, come into the world; make one's *début* [*F.*], take birth; burst forth, break out; spring up, crop up.

recommence; begin at the beginning, begin *ab ovo* [*L.*], begin again, begin *de novo* [*L.*]; start afresh, make a fresh start, shuffle the cards, resume.

adj. **beginning** etc. *v.;* initial, initiatory, initiative; inceptive, introductory, incipient; proemial [*rare*], inaugural, inauguratory; inchoate, inchoative [*rare*]; embryonic, rudimentary, rudimental; primal, primary, prime, premier [*rare*]; primigenial, primigenious *or* primigenous, primogenial; primeval etc. (*old*) 124; aboriginal; natal, nascent.

first, foremost, front, head, leading; maiden.

begun etc. *v.;* just begun etc. *v.*

adv. at *or* in the beginning etc. *n.;* first, in the first place, *imprimis* [*L.*], first and foremost; *in limine* [*L.*]; in the bud, in embryo, in its infancy; from the beginning, from its birth; *ab initio* [*L.*], *ab ovo* [*L.*], *ab incunabilis* [*L.*], *ab origine* [*L.*]; formerly, erst [*archaic*].

67. End

n. **end**, close, termination; desinence [*rare*], conclusion, finis, finale, period, term, terminus, last, omega; extreme, extremity; gable end, butt end, fag-end; tip, nib, point; tail etc. (*rear*) 235; verge etc. (*edge*) 231; tag, peroration, appendix, epilogue; bottom dollar [*colloq.*], bitter end, tail end [*colloq.*], terminal, apodosis.

consummation, *dénouement* [*F.*]; finish etc. (*completion*) 729; fate; doom, doomsday; crack of doom, day of Judgment, fall of the curtain; goal, destination; limit, stoppage, end-all, wind-up [*colloq.*]; determination; expiration, expiry; dissolution, death etc. 360; end of all things; finality; eschatology.

break up, *commencement de la fin* [*F.*], last stage, evening (*of life*); turning point; *coup de grâce* [*F.*], deathblow; knock-out, knock-out blow; sockdolager [*slang*], K. O. [*slang*].

v. **end**, close, finish, terminate, conclude, be all over; expire; die etc. 360; come to a close, draw to a close etc. *n.;* perorate; have run its course; run out, pass away.

bring to an end etc. *n.;* put an end to, make an end of; determine; get through; achieve etc. (*complete*) 729; stop etc. (*make to cease*) 142; shut up shop; hang up the fiddle [*colloq.*], hang up the gloves [*colloq.*].

adj. **ending** etc. *v.;* final, terminal, terminative [*rare*], conclusive, conclusory, determinative, definitive; crowning etc. (*completing*) 729; last, ultimate; hindermost; rear etc. 235; caudal; vergent [*rare*].

conterminate [*obs.*], conterminous, conterminable [*rare*].

ended etc. *v.;* at an end; settled, decided, over, played out, set at rest; conclusive.

penultimate; last but one, last but two, etc.

adv. **finally** etc. *adj.;* in fine; at the last; once for all.

68. Middle

n. **middle**, midst, mid [*rare*], thick, midmost, middlemost [*rare*], mediety [*obs.*]; mean etc. 29; medium, middle term; center etc. 222, midcourse etc. 628; *mezzo termine* [*It.*], *mezzo cammin* [*It.*]; *juste milieu* [*F.*] etc. 628; halfway house, nave, navel, omphalos; nucleus, nucleolus.

equidistance, bisection, half distance; equator, diaphragm, midriff; interjacence etc. 228.

adj. **middle**, medial, mesial, mesian, mean, mid, middlemost, midmost, midway [*rare*], midship, mediate [*rare*]; intermediate etc. (*interjacent*) 228; equidistant; central etc. 222; mediterranean, equatorial; homocentric.

adv. **midway**, halfway; in the middle; midships, amidships, *in medias res* [*L.*] *meden agan* [*Gr.*].

69. Continuity
[uninterrupted sequence]

n. **continuity**, continuousness, unbrokenness; consecution, consecutiveness etc. *adj.;* succession, round, suite, progression, series, train, catena, chain; catenation, concatenation; scale; gradation, course; ceaselessness, constant flow, unbroken extent; perpetuity.

procession, column; retinue, *cortège* [*F.*], cavalcade, parade; funeral, ovation, triumph; rank and file, line of battle, array.

pedigree, genealogy, lineage, history, tree, race; ancestry, descent, family, house; line, line of ancestors; strain.

rank, file, line, row, range, tier, string, thread, team; suit; colonnade.

v. **form a series** etc. *n.;* fall in; follow in a series etc. *n.*

arrange in a series etc. *n.;* string together, file, list, thread, graduate, tabulate.

adj. **continuous**, continued; consecutive; progressive, gradual; serial, successive; immediate, unbroken, entire; linear; in a line, in a row etc. *n.;* uninterrupted, unintermitting; unremitting; perennial, evergreen; constant.

adv. **continuously** etc. *adj.; seriatim* [*NL.*]; in a line etc. *n.;* in succession, in turn; running, gradually, step by step, *gradatim*, at a stretch; in file, in column, in single file, in Indian file.

70. Discontinuity
[interrupted sequence]

n. **discontinuity**, discontinuousness, discreteness, disconnectedness; disjunction [*rare*] etc. 44; anacoluthon; interruption, break, fracture, flaw, fault, crack, cut; gap etc. (*interval*) 198;

solution of continuity, caesura; broken thread; parenthesis, episode, rhapsody, crazy quilt [*colloq.*], patchwork; intermission; alternation etc. (*periodicity*) 138; dropping fire.

v. **be discontinuous** etc. *adj.;* alternate, intermit.

discontinue, pause, interrupt; intervene; break, break in upon, break off; interpose etc. 228; break the thread, snap the thread; disconnect etc. (*disjoin*) 44; dissever.

adj. **discontinuous**, unsuccessive, disconnected, broken, interrupted, *décousu* [*F.*]; disconnected, unconnected; discrete, disjunct [*rare*], disjunctive; fitful etc. (*irregular*) 139; spasmodic, desultory; intermitting etc. *v.*, intermittent; alternate; recurrent etc. (*periodic*) 138.

adv. **at intervals**; by snatches, by jerks, by skips, by catches, by fits and starts; skippingly, *per saltum* [*L.*]; *longo intervallo* [*L.*].

71. Term

n. **term**, rank, station, stage, step; degree etc. 26; scale, remove, grade, link, peg, round of the ladder, status, state, position, place, point, mark, *pas* [*F.*], period, pitch; stand, standing; footing, range.

v. hold a place, occupy a place, find a place, fall into a place etc. *n.;* rank.

72. Assemblage

n. **assemblage**; collection, collocation, colligation; compilation, levy, gathering, ingathering, mobilization, meet, forgathering, muster, *attroupement* [*F.*]; team; concourse, conflux, congregation, contesseration [*obs.*], convergence etc. 290.

meeting, levee, reunion, drawing room, at home; *conversazione* [*It.*] etc. (*social gathering*) 892; assembly, congress, house, senate, legislature, convocation; caucus, séance, eisteddfod, gemot *or* gemote; convention, conventicle; conclave etc. (*council*) 696; Noah's ark.

company, platoon, faction, caravan, claque, posse, *posse comitatus* [*L.*]; watch, squad, corps, troop, troupe; army, regiment etc. (*combatants*) 726; host etc. (*multitude*) 102; populousness.

miscellany, *collectanea* [*L.*]; museum, menagerie etc. (*store*) 636; museology.

crowd, throng; flood, rush, deluge; rabble, mob, rout, press, crush, *cohue* [*F.*], horde, body, tribe; crew, gang, knot, squad, band, party; swarm, shoal, school, covey, flock, herd, drove; kennel; *atajo* [*Sp. Amer.*]; bunch, drive, force, *mulada; remuda* [*Sp.*]; round-up; array, bevy, galaxy.

clan, brotherhood, association etc. (*party*) 712.

group, cluster, Pleiades, clump, pencil; set, batch, lot, pack; budget, assortment, bunch; parcel; packet, package; bundle, fascine, bale, *seron* [*Sp.*], fagot, wisp, truss, tuft; grove, thicket, plump [*archaic*]; shock, rick, fardel, stack, sheaf, haycock, swath; fascicle, fascicule, fasciculus, gavel, hattock [*dial. Eng.*], stook [*dial.*].

volley, shower, storm, cloud.

accumulation etc. (*store*) 636; congeries, heap, lump, pile, rouleau, tissue, mass, pyramid; bing [*obs.*]; drift; snowball, snowdrift; acervation [*rare*], cumulation, amassment; glomeration, agglomeration; conglobation; conglomeration, conglomerate; coacervation [*rare*], coagmentation [*obs.*], aggregation, concentration, congestion, omnium-gatherum [*colloq.*], spicilegium [*L.*], Black Hole of Calcutta; quantity etc. (*greatness*) 31.

collector, gatherer; whip, whipper-in.

v. [be or come together] assemble, collect, muster; meet, unite, join, rejoin; cluster, flock, swarm, surge, stream, herd, crowd, throng, associate; congregate, conglomerate, concentrate; center round, rendezvous, resort; come together, flock together, get together, pig together; forgather *or* foregather; huddle; reassemble.

[get or bring together] assemble, muster; bring together, get together, put together, draw together, scrape together, lump together; collect, collocate, colligate; get in, whip in; gather; hold a meeting; convene, convoke, convocate; rake up, dredge, heap, mass, pile; pack, put up, truss, cram; acervate [*rare*]; agglomerate, aggregate; compile; group, aggroup, concentrate, unite; collect into a focus, bring into a focus; amass, accumulate etc. (*store*) 636; collect in a dragnet; heap Ossa upon Pelion.

adj. **assembled** etc. *v.*, closely packed, dense, serried, crowded to suffocation, teeming, swarming, populous; as thick as hops; swarming like maggots; all of a heap, fasciculated; cumulative.

73. Nonassemblage. Dispersion

n. **dispersion**; disjunction etc. 44; divergence etc. 291; aspersion; scattering etc. *v.;* dissemination, diffusion, dissipation, distribution; apportionment etc. 786; spread, respersion [*obs.*], circumfusion, interspersion, spargefaction [*obs.*], affusion.

waifs and estrays, flotsam and jetsam, *disjecta membra;* waveson.

v. **disperse**, scatter, sow, disseminate, diffuse, radiate, shed, spread, bestrew, overspread, dispense, disband, disembody, dismember, distribute; apportion etc. 786; blow off, let out, dispel, cast forth, draft (*or* draught) off; strew, straw [*obs.*], strow [*archaic*]; ted; spurtle *or* spirtle [*obs.*], cast, sprinkle; issue, deal out, retail, utter; intersperse, resperse [*obs.*]; set abroach, circumfuse.

spread like wildfire, disperse themselves.

turn adrift, cast adrift; scatter to the winds; sow broadcast.

adj. **unassembled** etc. (*see* assemble etc. 72); diffuse, disseminated scattered, strown, strewn, dispersed etc. *v.*, dispersive, dissipative, diffusive, dispellent [*rare*]; sparse, dispread, broadcast, sporadic, widespread; epidemic etc. (*general*) 78; adrift, stray; disheveled, streaming resolvent, discutient [*med.*].

adv. *sparsim* [*L.*], here and there, *passim* [*L.*].

74. Focus

[place of meeting]

n. **focus**; point of convergence etc. 290; corradiation [*rare*]; center etc. 222; gathering place, resort; haunt; retreat; venue; rendezvous; rallying point, headquarters, home, club; depot etc. (*store*) 636; tryst, trysting place; place of meeting, place of resort, place of assignation; *point de réunion* [*F.*] issue

v. bring to a point, bring to a focus, bring to an issue, focus, corradiate [*rare*].

75. Class

n. **class**, division, subdivision, category, head, order, section; department, province, domain, sphere.

kind, sort, estate, genus, species, variety, family, race, tribe, caste, sept, phylum, clan, breed; clique, coterie; type, kit, sect, set; assortment; feather [*rare*], kidney; suit; range; gender, sex, kin.

manner, description, denomination, persuasion, connection, designation, character, stamp; predicament; indication, particularization, selection, specification.

similarity etc. 17.

76. Inclusion

[comprehension under, or reference to, a class]

n. **inclusion**, admission, incorporation, comprisal, comprehension, reception.

composition etc. (*inclusion in a compound*) 54.

v. **be included** in etc.; come under, fall under, range under; belong to, pertain to; range with; merge in.

include, comprise, comprehend, contain, admit, embrace, subsume, receive, inclose etc. (*circumscribe*) 229; incorporate, cover, embody, encircle.

reckon among, enumerate among, number among; refer to; place under, place with, arrange under, arrange with; take into account.

adj. **inclusive**, inclusory; included, including etc. *v.*; congener [*rare*], congenerous; of the same class etc. 75; comprehensive, sweeping, all-embracing, liberal, unexclusive [*rare*].

77. Exclusion[1]

n. **exclusion** etc. 55.

[1]The same set of words is used to express *Exclusion from a class* and *Exclusion from a compound*. Reference is therefore made to the former at 55. This identity does not occur with regard to *Inclusion*, which therefore constitutes a separate category.

78. Generality

n. **generality**, generalization; universality; catholicity, catholicism; miscellany, miscellaneousness; dragnet; common run; worldwideness.

Pan-Americanism, Pan-Anglicanism, Pan-Hellenism, Pan-Germanism, Pan-slavism *or* Pansclavism.

everyone, everybody, *tout le monde* [*F.*]; all hands [*colloq.*], all the world and his wife [*humorous*]; anybody, N or M, all sorts.

prevalence, rifeness, run.

v. **be general** etc. *adj.*; prevail, be going about, stalk abroad.

render general etc. *adj.*; spread, broaden, universalize, generalize.

adj. **general**, generic, collective; current, wide, broad, comprehensive, sweeping; encyclopedic *or* encyclopedical, panoramic; widespread etc. (*dispersed*) 73.

universal; catholic, catholical; common, worldwide, nationwide, statewide, heavenwide, ecumenical; prevalent, prevailing, rife, epidemic, besetting; all over [*colloq.*], covered with.

Pan-American, Pan-Anglican, Pan-Hellenic, Pan-Germanic, Panslavic *or* Pansclavic, Panslavonic, Panslavonian; panharmonic.

every, all; unspecified, impersonal, indefinite.

customary etc. (*habitual*) 613.

adv. whatever, whatsoever; to a man, one and all.

generally etc. *adj.*; always, for better for worse; in general, generally speaking; speaking generally; for the most part; in the long run etc. (*on an average*) 29; by and large, roughly speaking.

79. Specialty

n. **specialty,** *spécialité* [*F.*]; individuality, individuity [*obs.*]; particularity, peculiarity; *je ne sais quoi* [*F.*], *nescio quid* [*L.*]; idiocrasy etc. (*tendency*) 176; personality, characteristic, mannerism, idiosyncrasy, physiognomic [*rare*], diagnostic; specificness etc. *adj.;* singularity etc. (*unconformity*) 83; reading, version, lection; state; trait; distinctive feature; technicality; differentia.

particulars, details, items, counts; minutiae.

I, self, I myself; myself, himself, herself, itself.

v. **specify,** particularize, individualize, realize, specialize, designate, determine; denote, indicate, point out, select, differentiate, come to the point.

itemize, detail, descend to particulars, enter into detail.

adj. **special,** particular, individual, specific, proper, personal, original, private, respective, definite, determinate, minute, especial, certain, esoteric, endemic, partial, party, peculiar, marked, intimate, appropriate, several, characteristic, diagnostic, exclusive, restricted; singular etc. (*exceptional*) 83; idiomatic; typical, representative.

this, that; yon, yonder.

adv. **specially** etc. *adj.;* in particular, *in propria persona* [*L.*]; *ad hominem* [*L.*]; for my part.

each, apiece, one by one; severally, respectively, each to each; *seriatim* [*NL.*], in detail, bit by bit; *pro hac vice* [*L.*], *pro re nata* [*L.*].

namely, that is to say, *videlicet* [*L.*], viz.; to wit.

80. Rule

n. **regularity,** uniformity, constancy, clockwork precision; punctuality etc. (*exactness*) 494; even tenor, rut; system; routine etc. (*custom*) 613; formula; canon, convention, maxim, rule etc. (*form, regulation*) 697; keynote, standard, model; precedent etc. (*prototype*) 22; conformity etc. 82.

law, capitular *or* capitulary, gnomology [*rare*], *règlement* [*F.*], order of things; normality, normalcy; normal state, normal condition, natural state, natural condition, ordinary state, ordinary condition, model state, model condition; standing dish, standing order; Procrustean law; law of the Medes and Persians; hard and fast rule; nature, principle.

adj. **regular,** uniform, symmetrical, constant, steady; according to rule etc. (*conformable*) 82; normal, habitual, customary etc. 613; methodical, orderly, systematic, systematical.

81. Multiformity

n. **multiformity,** omniformity; variety, diversity; multifariousness etc. *adj.;* varied assortment.

adj. **multiform,** multifold, multifarious, multigenerous, multiplex; variform [*rare*], diversiform, amoebiform, manifold, many-sided; omniform, omnigenous, omnifarious; polymorphic, polymorphous, multiphase, metamorphotic, protean, proteiform, heterogeneous, motley, mosaic; epicene.

indiscriminate, desultory, irregular, diversified, different, divers; all manner of; of every description, of all sorts and kinds; *et hoc genus omne* [*L.*]; and what not?

82. Conformity

n. **conformity,** conformance; observance; habituation; naturalization; conventionality etc. (*custom*) 613; agreement etc. 23.

example, instance, specimen, sample, quotation; exemplification, illustration, case in point; object lesson; elucidation.

pattern etc. (*prototype*) 22.

conventionalist, formalist, bromide [*slang*], Philistine.

v. **conform to,** conform to rule; accommodate oneself to, adapt oneself to; rub off corners.

be regular etc. *adj.;* move in a groove, move in a rut, travel in a rut; follow–, observe–, go by–, bend to–, obey- -rules, –precedents; agree with, comply with, tally with, chime in with, fall in with; be guided by, be regulated by; fall into a custom, fall into a usage; follow the fashion, follow the multitude; assimilate to, shape, harmonize, conventionalize, pass muster, do as others do, *hurler avec les loups* [*F.*]; do in Rome as the Romans do; go with the -stream, –current, –tide; swim with the -stream, –current, –tide; pass current; tread the beaten track etc. (*habit*) 613; keep one in countenance.

exemplify, illustrate, example, sample, type [*rare*], cite, quote, put a case; produce an instance etc. *n.;* elucidate, explain.

adj. **conformable to rule;** adaptable, consistent, agreeable, compliant; regular etc. 80; according to regulation, according to rule, according to Cocker, according to Gunter, according to Hoyle [*all colloq.*]; *en règle* [*F.*], *selon les règles* [*F.*], well regulated, orderly; symmetric etc. 242.

conventional etc. (*customary*) 613; of daily occurrence, of everyday occurrence; in the natural order of things; ordinary, common, habitual, usual, commonplace, prosaic, bromidic, Philistine.

in the order of the day; naturalized.

typical, normal, formal; canonical, orthodox, sound, strict, rigid, positive, uncompromising, Procrustean.

secundum artem [*L.*], shipshape, point-device [*archaic*], technical.

exemplary, illustrative, in point.

adv. **conformably** etc. *adj.;* by rule; agreeably to; in conformity with, in accordance with, in keeping with; according to; consistently with; as usual, *ad instar* [*L.*], *instar omnium* [*L.*]; *more solito* [*L.*], *more majorum* [*L.*].

for the sake of conformity; of course, as a matter of course; *pro forma* [*L.*], for form's sake, by the card.

invariably etc. (*uniformly*) 16.

for example, for instance; *exempli gratia* [*L.*]; *e. g.; inter alia* [*L.*].

83. Unconformity

n. **nonconformity** etc. 82; unconformity, disconformity; unconventionality, informality, abnormity, anomaly; anomalousness etc. *adj.;* exception, peculiarity; infraction–, breach–, violation–, infringement- of -law, –custom, –usage; teratism, eccentricity, *bizarrerie* [*F.*], oddity, *je ne sais quoi* [*F.*], monstrosity, rarity; freak of nature.

individuality, idiosyncrasy, singularity, selfness [*rare*], originality, mannerism.

aberration; irregularity; variety; singularity; exemption; salvo [*rare*] etc. (*qualification*) 469.

nonconformist, bohemian, nondescript, character [*colloq.*], original, nonesuch [*rare*], freak, crank [*colloq.*], prodigy, wonder, miracle, curiosity, missing link, flying fish, black swan, monster, white blackbird, basilisk, salamander, *lusus naturae* [*L.*], *rara avis* [*L.*], queer fish [*slang*].

mongrel; half-caste, half-blood, half-breed etc. 41; metis, crossbreed, hybrid, mule, mulatto; *tertium quid* [*L.*], hermaphrodite.

monster, phoenix, chimera, hydra, sphinx, minotaur; griffin *or* griffon; centaur; xiphopagus; hippogriff, hippocentaur; sagittary; kraken, cockatrice, wivern *or* wyvern [*obs.*], roc, dragon, sea serpent; mermaid; unicorn; Cyclops, "men whose heads do grow beneath their shoulders" [*Othello*]; teratology.

fish out of water; neither one thing nor another; neither fish, flesh, fowl, nor good red herring; one in a way, one in a thousand.

outcast, outlaw, Ishmael, pariah.

v. **be uncomformable** etc. *adj.;* abnormalize; leave the beaten track, leave the beaten path; infringe–, break–, violate - a -law, –habit, –usage, –custom; stretch a point; have no business there; baffle all description, beggar all description.

adj. **uncomformable**, exceptional; abnormal, abnormous; anomalous, anomalistic; out of order, out of place, out of keeping, out of tune, out of one's element; irregular, arbitrary; teratogenic, teratogenetic; lawless, informal, aberrant, stray, wandering, wanton; peculiar, exclusive, unnatural, eccentric, egregious; out of the beaten track, out of the common, out of the common run, out of the pale of; misplaced; funny [*colloq.*].

unusual, unaccustomed, uncustomary, unordinary, unwonted, uncommon; rare, singular, unique, curious, odd, extraordinary, strange, monstrous; wonderful etc. 870; unexpected, unaccountable; *outré* [*F.*], out of the way, remarkable, noteworthy, *recherché* [*F.*], queer, quaint, nondescript, *sui generis* [*L.*]; original, unconventional, supernormal [*rare*], bohemian, sulphitic [*slang*], unfashionable; undescribed, unprecedented, unparalleled, unexampled, unheard of, unfamiliar; fantastic, newfangled, grotesque, bizarre; outlandish, exotic, *tombé des nues* [*F.*], preternatural; denaturalized.

heterogeneous, heteroclite, amorphous, mongrel, amphibious, epicene, half blood, hybrid; androgynous, androgynal; unsymmetric etc. 243; adelomorphic *or* adelomorphous, gynandrous, bisexual, hermaphrodite, androgynic, androgynous, monoclinous.

adv. **unconformably** etc. *adj.;* except, unless, save, barring, beside, without, save and except, let alone.

however, yet, but.

int. what on earth! what in the world!

Section 5. Number

84. Number

n. **number**, symbol, numeral, figure, cipher, digit, integer; counter; round number; formula; function; series.

sum, difference, complement, subtrahend; product, total, aggregate; multiplicand, multiplier, multiplicator; coefficient, multiple; dividend, divisor, factor, quotient, submultiple, fraction; mixed number; numerator, denominator; decimal, circulating decimal, repetend; common measure, aliquot part; reciprocal; prime number; totient; quota, quotum [*rare*].

figurate numbers, pyramidal numbers, polygonal numbers.

permutation, combination, variation; election.

ratio, proportion; progression; arithmetical progression, geometrical progression, harmonical progression; percentage.

power, root, radix, exponent, index, logarithm, antilogarithm; modulus. differential, integral, fluxion, fluent.

adj. **numeral**, complementary, divisible, aliquot, reciprocal, prime, fractional, decimal, figurate, incommensurable.

proportional, exponential, logarithmic, logometric, differential, fluxional, integral, totitive.

positive, negative; rational, irrational; surd, radical, real, imaginary, impossible.

85. Numeration

n. **numeration**; numbering etc. *v.;* pagination; tale, tally, telling [*archaic*], recension, enumeration, summation, reckoning, computation, supputation [*obs.*]; calculation, calculus; algorithm, rhabdology, dactylonomy; measurement etc. 466; statistics, logistics.

arithmetic, analysis, algebra, fluxions; differential calculus, integral calculus, infinitesimal calculus; calculus of differences.

[statistics] dead reckoning, muster, poll, census, capitation, roll call, recapitulation; account etc. (*list*) 86.

[operations] notation, addition, subtraction, multiplication, division, proportion, rule of three, practice, equations, extraction of roots, reduction, involution, evolution, approximation, interpolation, differentiation, integration, indigitation [*rare*].

[instruments] abacus, calculator, computer, suan pan, logometer, slide rule, tallies, Napier's bones, calculating machine, difference engine; adding machine; cash register.

arithmetician, calculator, geodesist, abacist; algebraist, geometrician, trigonometrician, mathematician, actuary, statistician.

v. **number**, count, tell; call over, run over; take an account of, enumerate, call the roll, muster, poll, recite, recapitulate; sum; sum up, cast up; tell off, score, cipher, reckon, reckon up, tally estimate, make an estimate, furnish an estimate, make up accounts, compute, calculate, suppute [*obs.*], add, subtract, divide, divide, extract roots, algebraize.

check, prove, demonstrate, balance, audit, overhaul, take stock.

page, affix numbers to, foliate, paginate.

amount to, come to, total.

adj. **numeral**, numerical; arithmetical, analytic, algebraic, statistical, countable, reckonable, numberable, computable, calculable, rhabdological; commensurable, commensurate; incommensurable, incommensurate.

86. List

n. **list**, catalogue *or* catalog, inventory, schedule, calends [*rare*]; register etc. (*record*) 551; account; bill, bill of costs; syllabus; terrier, tally, file; calendar, index, table, atlas, contents; book, ledger; synopsis, *catalogue raisonné* [*F.*]; scroll, brief [*obs.*], screed, manifest, invoice, bill of lading; prospectus, program; bill of fare, menu, carte; score, bulletin, *tableau* [*F.*], census, statistics, returns; Red Book, Blue Book, Domesday Book; directory, gazetteer.

almanac; army list, clergy list, civil service list, navy list; Statesman's Yearbook, Whitaker's Almanack, *Almanach de Gotha*, cadastre *or* cadaster, *cadre* [*F.*], card index; Lloyd's Register, Nautical Almanac, Who's Who.

dictionary, lexicon, glossary, word-book, thesaurus, gloss [*rare*], gradus.

roll; check roll, checker roll, bead roll; muster roll, muster book; roll of honor; roster, slate, rota, poll, panel; chartulary *or* cartulary, diptych.

v. **list**, enroll, schedule, inventorize [*rare*], inventory, register, catalogue *or* catalog, invoice, bill, book, indent, slate, post, manifest, docket; matriculate, empanel, calendar, tally, file, index, tabulate, enter, score, keep score; census.

adj. inventorial, cadastral; listed etc.*v.*

87. Unity

n. **unity**; oneness etc. *adj.;* individuality; solitude etc. (*seclusion*) 893; isolation etc. (*disjunction*) 44; unification etc. 48; completeness etc. 52.

one, unit, ace, monad; individual; none else, no other, nought beside.

integer, item, point, module.

v. **be one**, be alone etc. *adj.*

isolate etc. (*disjoin*) 44.

render one; unite etc. (*join*) 43, (*combine*) 48.

adj. **one**, sole, only-begotten, single, solitary, companionless; individual, apart, alone; kithless.

unaccompanied, unattended; *solus* (*fem., sola*) [*L.*], single-handed; singular, odd, unique,

29

unrepeated, azygous, first and last; isolated etc. (*disjoined*); insular.

monadic, monadical; unific, uniflorous, unilobed, uniglobular, unifoliolate, unigenital, uniliteral, unilocular, unimodular, unitary; monospermous.

inseverable, indiscerptible; compact, irresolvable.

lone, lonely, lonesome; desolate, dreary.

adv. **singly** etc. *adj.;* alone, by itself, *per se* [*L.*], only [*rare*], apart, in the singular number, in the abstract; one by one, one at a time; simply; one and a half, *sesqui-*.

88. Accompaniment

n. **accompaniment**; adjunct etc. 39; context; appendage, appurtenance.

company, association, companionship; coexistence, concomitance; partnership, copartnership; coefficiency.

concomitant, accessory, coefficient; companion, attendant, fellow, associate, *fidus Achates* [*L.*], consort, spouse, colleague; partner, copartner; satellite, hanger-on, shadow; escort, *cortège* [*F.*], suite, train, convoy, follower etc. 65; attribute.

v. **accompany**, coexist, attend, company [*archaic*], convoy, chaperon; hang on, wait on; go hand in hand with; synchronize etc. 120; bear company, keep company; row in the same boat; bring in its train; associate with, couple with.

adj. **accompanying** etc. *v.;* concomitant, fellow, twin, joint; associated with, coupled with; accessory, attendant, comitant [*rare*], obbligato.

adv. **with**, withal; together with, along with, in company with; hand in hand, side by side; cheek by jowl; arm in arm; therewith, herewith; and etc. (*addition*) 37.

together, in a body, collectively, in conjunction.

89. Duality

n. **duality**, dualism; duplicity; biplicity [*rare*], biformity; polarity.

two, deuce, couple, couplet, both, twain, brace, pair, cheeks, twins, Castor and Pollux, gemini, Siamese twins; fellows; yoke, conjugation; dispermy, doublets, dyad, duad, twosome [*rare*], distich, span.

v. [unite in pairs] pair, couple, bracket, yoke; conduplicate; mate, span [*U.S.*]

adj. **two**, twain; dual, dualistic; binary, binomial; twin, biparous; dyadic; conduplicate; duplex etc. 90; biduous, binate, binary, binal [*rare*], diphyletic, dispermic, paired, unijugate; *tête-à-tête* [*F.*].

coupled etc. *v.;* conjugate.

both, both the one and the other.

90. Duplication

n. **duplication**; doubling etc. *v.;* gemination, ingemination; reduplication; iteration etc. (*repetition*) 104; renewal.

duplicate, facsimile, copy, replica, counterpart etc. (*copy*) 21.

v. **double**; redouble, reduplicate; geminate [*rare*]; repeat etc. 104; renew etc. 660.

adj. **double**; doubled etc. *v.;* bicipital, bicephalous, bidental, bilabiate, bivalve, bivalvular, bifold, biform, bilateral, bifarious, bifacial; twofold, twosided; disomatous; duple [*rare*], duplex; double-faced, double-headed; twin, duplicate, geminous [*rare*], geminate, ingeminate; second: dual etc. 89.

adv. **twice**, once more; over again etc. (*repeatedly*) 104; as much again, twofold.

secondly, in the second place, again.

91. Bisection

[division into two parts]

n. **bisection**, bipartition; dichotomy, subdichotomy [*rare*]; halving etc. *v.;* dimidiation.

bifurcation, furcation, forking, branching, ramification, divarication; fork, crotch, furculum, prong; fold.

half, moiety.

v. **bisect**, halve, hemisect [*rare*], divide, split, cut in two, cleave, dimidiate, dichotomize.

go halves, divide with.

separate, fork, bifurcate, furcate, divaricate; branch off *or* out; ramify.

adj. **bisected** etc. *v.;* cloven, cleft; bipartite, dimidiate, divaricate, biconjugate, bicuspid, bifid; bifurcous [*rare*], bifurcate, bifurcated; bigeminate, distichous, distichal, dichotomous, furcular, furcate, lituate [*rare*]; semi-, demi-, hemi-.

92. Triality

n. **triality** [*rare*], trinity, triunity, Trimurti [*Hindu*], triplicity, trialism [*rare*].

three, triad, triplet, ternion, ternary, trine [*rare*], trey, trio, leash; shamrock, tierce, delta, trefoil; triangle, trident, triennium, trigon [*rare*], trinomial, trionym, triplopia *or* triplopy, tripod, trireme, triseme, triskelion *or* triskele, trisul *or* trisula, triumvirate.

third power, cube.

adj. **three**; triform, trinal, trinomial; tertiary; triune; triarch, triadic.

93. Triplication

n. **triplication**, triplicity; trebleness, terza, trine; trilogy.

v. **treble**, triple, triplicate, cube.

adj. **treble**, triple; tern, ternary, ternate, tertiary; triplicate, threefold, trilogistic; triplasic; third; trinal, trine [*rare*].

adv. **three times**, thrice, in the third place, thirdly, threefold, triply, trebly etc. *adj.*

94. Trisection

[division into three parts]

n. **trisection**, tripartition, trichotomy; third, third part.

v. **trisect**, divide into three parts, third.

adj. **trifid**; trisected etc. *v.;* tripartite, trichotomous, trisulcate; ternal, trident, tridental.

triadelphous, triangular, trichotomic, tricuspid, tricapsular, tridental, tridentate *or* tridentated, tridentiferous, trifoliolate, trifurcate *or* trifurcated, trigonoid, trigonous, trigonal, trigrammic *or* trigrammatic, tripedal, trilateral, tripetalous, tripodal, tripodic, triquetral, triquetrous.

95. Quaternity

n. **quaternity** [*rare*], four, tetrad, quartet *or* quartette, quatre [*rare*], quadruplet, quaternion, square, quadrilateral, quadrinomial, biquadrate, quarter, quarto, tetract, tetragon.

quadrangle, quadrature, quadruplet; quatrefoil; tetragram, tetragrammaton; tetrahedron, tetrapody, tetrology, quatrefoil *or* quadrefoil.

v. **square**, biquadrate, reduce to a square.

adj. **four**; quaternary, quaternal; quadratic; quartile, quartic, quadrifid, quadriform, quadric, biquadratic; tetract, tetractine, tetractinal [*zool.*], four-rayed; tetrad, quadrivalent; quadrangular, tetragonal, quadrilateral, tetrahedral.

96. Quadruplication

n. **quadruplication**.

v. **quadruplicate**, biquadrate, multiply by four.

adj. **fourfold**; quadrable, quadruple, quadruplex, quadruplicate, quadrible; fourth.

adv. **four times**; in the fourth place, fourthly.

97. Quadrisection

[division into four parts]

n. **quadrisection**, quadripartition; quartering etc. *v.;* fourth; quart, quarter, quartern; farthing.

v. **quarter**, divide into four parts, quadrisect.

adj. **quartered** etc. *v.;* quadrifid, quadripartite [*rare*]; quadrifoliate, quadrigeminal, quad-

rigeminous, quadrigeminate, quadripennate, quadriplanar, quadriserial, quadrivial, quadrifurcate, quadrumanal, quadrumane, quadrumous.

98. Five, etc.

n. **five**, cinque, quint, quincunx, quintet *or* quintette, quintuple, quintuplet, quinary [*rare*], pentad; pentagon, pentagram, pentameter, pentapody, pentarchy, pentastich, Pentateuch.

six, sise *or* size [*rare*], hexad, sextuplet, hexagon, hexahedron, hexagram, hexameter, hexapod, hexapody, hexastich, Hexateuch, sextet, half-a-dozen.

seven, heptad, septenary [*rare*], heptagon, heptahedron, heptameter, heptarchy, Heptateuch.

eight, octave, octonary, octad, ogdoad, octagon, octahedron, octameter, octastyle, octavo, octet.

nine, novenary [*rare*], ennead, nonary [*rare*]; nonagon, three times three; *novena* [*R. C. Ch.*].

ten, decad [*rare*], decade, dicker; decagon, decagram, decahedron, decapod, decare, decastere, decastyle, decasyllable, decemvir, decemvirate, decennium.

eleven; twelve, dozen; thirteen; long dozen, baker's dozen; twenty, score; twenty-four, four and twenty, two dozen; twenty-five, five and twenty, quarter of a hundred; forty, twoscore; fifty, half a hundred; sixty, sexagenary, threescore; seventy, threescore and ten; eighty, fourscore; ninety, fourscore and ten.

hundred, centenary, hecatomb, century, bicentenary, tercentenary; hundredweight, cwt.; one hundred and forty-four, gross.

thousand, chiliad, milliad [*rare*], millenary [*rare*], millennium; myriad, ten thousand; one hundred thousand, lac *or* lakh [*India*], plum [*obs.*], million; ten million, crore [*India*]; thousand million, billion, milliard.

billion, trillion etc.

v. quintuplicate, sextuple, centuplicate, centuriate [*obs.*].

adj. **five**, fifth, quinary, quintuple; quintuplicate, pentangular, pentagonal, pentastyle.

sixth, senary [*rare*], sextuple, hexagonal, hexangular, hexastyle, hexahedral, sextan.

seventh, septuple, septenary, septimal [*rare*]; heptagonal, heptahedral, heptamerous, heptangular.

eighth, octuple, octonary; octagonal, octahedral, octan, octangular, octastyle.

ninth, ninefold, novenary [*rare*], nonary [*rare*], enneahedral, enneastyle.

tenth, tenfold, decimal, denary, decuple, deca-gonal, decahedral, decasyllabic.

eleventh, undecennial, undecennary.

twelfth, duodenary, duodenal.

in one's teens, thirteenth, etc.

twentieth, vicenary, vicennial, vigesimal, vicesi-mal.

sixtieth, sexagesimal, sexagenary.

seventieth, septuagesimal, septuagenary.

centuple, centuplicate, centennial, centenary, centurial; secular, hundredth; thousandth, millenary, millennial etc.

99. Quinquesection, etc.

n. quinquesection etc.; division by five etc. 98; decimation; fifth etc.

v. decimate; quinquesect; decimalize.

adj. quinquefid, quinqueliteral, quinquepartite.

sexpartite; octofid; decimal, tenth, tithe; duodeci-mal, twelfth; sexagesimal, sexagenary; hun-dredth, centesimal; millesimal etc.

100. Plurality

[more than one]

n. plurality; a number, a certain number; one or two, two or three etc.; a few, several; multitude etc. 102; majority.

adj. plural, more than one, upwards of, some, certain; not, not alone etc. 87.

adv. et cetera, etc.

100a. Fraction

[less than one]

n. fraction, fractional part; part etc. 51.

adj. fractional, fragmentary, inconsiderable, partial, portional.

101. Zero

n. zero, nothing; naught, nought; cipher, none, no-body; *nichts* [*Ger.*], goose egg, nix [*slang*]; not a soul; absence etc. 187; unsubstantiality etc. 4.

adj. no, not one, not any.

102. Multitude

n. multitude; multitudinousness, numerousness etc. *adj.;* numerosity, numerality [*obs.*]; multi-plicity; profusion etc. (*plenty*) 639; legion, host; great number, large number, round number, enormous number; a quantity, numbers, array, sight, army, sea, galaxy; scores, peck, bushel, shoal, oodles [*colloq.*], pile [*colloq.*], heap [*colloq.*], power [*colloq.*], sight [*colloq.*], lot [*colloq.*], lots [*colloq.*], swarm, bevy, cloud, flock, herd, drove, flight, covey, hive, brood, litter, farrow, fry, nest; mob, crowd etc.

(*assemblage*) 72; all the world and his wife [*humorous*].

[increase of number] greater number, majority; multiplication, multiple.

v. be numerous etc. *adj.;* swarm with, teem with, be alive with, creep with; crowd, swarm, come thick upon; outnumber, multiply; people; swarm like locusts, swarm like bees.

adj. many, several, sundry, divers, various, not a few; Briarean; a hundred, a thousand, a myriad, a million, a billion, a quadrillion, a nonillion, a thousand and one; some ten or a dozen, some forty or fifty etc.; half a dozen, half a hundred etc.; alive with; very many, full many, ever so many; numerous; profuse, in profusion; mani-fold, multifold, multiplied, multitudinous, mul-tiple, multinomial, teeming, populous, peopled, outnumbering, crowded, thick, studded; galore [*colloq.*].

thick coming, many more, more than one can tell, a world of; no end of, no end to; *cum multis aliis* [*L.*], thick as hops, thick as hail; plenty as blackberries; numerous as the stars in the firmament, numerous as the sands on the sea-shore, numerous as the hairs on the head; and what not, and heaven knows what; endless etc. (*infinite*) 105.

103. Fewness

n. fewness etc. *adj.;* paucity, scarcity, sparseness, sparsity, small number; only a few; small quan-tity etc. 32; rarity; infrequency etc. 137; hand-ful; minority; exiguity.

[diminution of number] reduction; weeding etc. *v.;* elimination, sarculation [*obs.*], decimation; eradication.

v. be few etc. *adj.*

render few etc. *adj.;* reduce, diminish, diminish the number, weed, eliminate, thin, decimate.

adj. few; scant, scanty; thin, rare, scarce, sparse, thinly scattered, few and far between; exiguous; infre-quent etc. 137; *rari nantes* [*L.*]; hardly any, scarcely any; to be counted on one's fingers, to be counted on the fingers of one hand; reduced etc. *v.;* unrepeated.

adv. here and there.

104. Repetition

n. repetition, iteration, reiteration, iterance [*rare*], reiterance [*rare*], alliteration, duplication, reduplication, monotone, harping, recurrence, succession, run; battology, tautology; monot-ony, tautophony; rhythm etc. 138; diffuseness, pleonasm, redundancy.

chimes, repetend, echo, reëcho, encore, dilogy [*rare*], *ritornello* [*It.*], burden of a song, refrain, undersong; rehearsal; *réchauffé* [*F.*], *rifacimento* [*It.*], recapitulation.

cuckoo etc. (*imitation*) 19; reverberation etc. 408; drumming etc. (*roll*) 407; renewal etc. (*restoration*) 660.

twice-told tale, chestnut [*slang*], old stuff [*slang*], old story, old song; second edition, new edition; reappearance, reproduction; periodicity etc. 138.

v. **repeat**, iterate, reiterate, reproduce, echo, reëcho, drum, harp upon, battologize, tautologize, hammer, redouble.

recur, revert, return, reappear; renew etc. (*restore*) 660.

rehearse; do over again, say over again; ring the changes on; harp on the same string; din in the ear, drum in the ear; conjugate in all its moods, tenses and inflexions; begin again, go over the same ground, go the same round, duplicate, reduplicate, never hear the last of; resume, return to, recapitulate, reword.

adj. **repeated** etc. *v.;* warmed up, warmed over, repetitional, repetitionary, repetitive, repetitious, reduplicatory [*rare*], reduplicative, recurrent, recurring; ever recurring, thick coming; frequent, incessant; redundant, pleonastic, tautological, tautologous, tautophonical; inexhaustible, unplumbed.

monotonous, harping, iterative, unvaried; mocking, chiming; retold; habitual etc. 613; another.

aforesaid, aforenamed; above-mentioned, said.

adv. **repeatedly**, often, again, anew, over again, afresh, once more; ditto, encore, *de novo* [*L.*], bis, *da capo* [*It.*].

again and again; over and over, over and over again; many times over; time and again, time after time; times without number; year after year; day by day etc.; many times, several times, a number of times; many a time, full many a time; frequently etc. 136; inexhaustibly, depth beyond depth.

105. Infinity

n. **infinity**, infinitude, infiniteness etc. *adj.;* perpetuity etc. 112; inexhaustibility, immensity, boundlessness.

v. **be infinite** etc. *adj.;* know no limits, know no bounds, have no limits, have no bounds; go on forever.

adj. **infinite**; immense; numberless, countless, sumless, measureless, innumerable, immeasurable, incalculable, illimitable, interminable, unfathomable, unapproachable; exhaustless, indefinite; without number, without measure, without limit, without end; incomprehensible; limitless, endless, boundless, termless; untold, unnumbered, unmeasured, unbounded, unlimited, illimited; perpetual etc. 112.

adv. **infinitely** etc. *adj.; ad infinitum* [*L.*].

Section 6. Time

106. Time

n. **time**, duration; period, term, stage, space, tide [*archaic*], span, spell, season; the whole time, the whole period; course etc. 109; snap.

intermediate time, while, bit, breathing, interim, interval, pendency; intervention, intermission, intermittence, interregnum, interlude; respite.

era, epoch, Kalpa, eon, cycle; time of life, age, year, date; decade etc. (*period*) 108; point, bell, moment etc. (*instant*) 113; reign etc. 737.

glass of time, ravages of time, whirligig of time, noiseless foot of Time; scythe of Time.

v. **continue**, last, endure, stay, go on, remain, persist, subsist, abide, run, stand, dure [*archaic*], perdure [*rare*], perennate [*rare*], stick [*colloq.*]; intervene; elapse etc. 109; hold out.

take time, take up time, fill time, occupy time.

pass time; pass away time, spend time, while away time, consume time, talk against time; tide over; use time, employ time; seize an opportunity etc. 134; linger on, drag on, drag along, tarry etc. 110; waste time etc. (*be inactive*) 683; procrastinate etc. 133.

adj. **continuing** etc. *v.;* on foot; permanent etc. (*durable*) 110; timely etc. (*opportune*) 134.

adv. **while**, whilst, during, pending; during the time, during the interval; in the course of; for the time being, day by day; in the time of, when; meantime, meanwhile; in the meantime, in the interim; *ad interim* [*L.*], *pendente lite* [*L.*]; *de die in diem* [*L.*]; from day to day, from hour to hour etc.; hourly, always; for a time, for a season; till, until, up to, yet; the whole time, all the time; all along; throughout etc. (*completely*) 52; for good etc. (*diuturnity*) 110.

then, hereupon, thereupon, whereupon; *anno Domini* [*L.*], A.D.; *ante Christum* [*L.*], A.C.; before Christ, B.C.; *anno urbis conditae* [*L.*], A.U.C.; *anno regni* [*L.*], A.R.; once upon a time, one fine morning.

33

107. Neverness

n. **"neverness"**; absence of time, no time; *dies non* [*L.*]; St. Tib's eve; Greek Calends (*or* Kalends).

adv. **never**, ne'er; at no time, at no period; on *or* at the Greek Calends (*or* Kalends); on no occasion, never in all one's born days [*colloq.*], *jamais de ma vie* [*F.*], nevermore, *sine die* [*L.*], in no degree.

108. Period
[definite duration, or portion of time]

n. **period**; second, minute, hour, day, week, month, octave, *novena* [*L.*], semester, quarter, year, decade, decennium, luster *or* lustrum, indication; cycle–, era- of indiction (*or* indictions); quinquennium, lifetime, generation; epoch, era, epact, ghurry *or* ghari [*India*], lunation, moon. century, age, millennium; *annus magnus* [*L.*], *annus mirabilis* [*L.*].

adj. horary; hourly, annual, epochal etc. (*periodical*) 13 ; *ante bellum* [*L.*].

108a. Contingent Duration

adv. during pleasure, during good behavior; *quandiu se bene gesserit* [*L.*].

109. Course
[indefinite duration]

n. corridors of time, sweep of time, vista of time, halls of time, course of time, progress of time, process of time, succession of time, lapse of time, flow of time, flux of time, stream of time, tract of time, current of time, tide of time, march of time, step of time, flight of time; duration etc. 106.

[indefinite time] aeon *or* eon, age, Kalpa; aorist.

v. **elapse**, lapse, flow, run, proceed, advance, pass; roll on, wear on, press on; flit, fly, slip, slide, glide; crawl, drag; run its course, run out; expire; go by, pass by; be past etc. 122.

adj. **elapsing** etc. *v.;* aoristic; transient etc. 111; progressive.

adv. **in time**; in due time, in due season, in due course; in course of time, in process of time, in the fullness of time.

110. Diuturnity
[long duration]

n. **diuturnity** [*rare*]; a long time, length of time; an age, aeon *or* eon, a century, an eternity; slowness etc. 275; coeternity, sempiternity, perpetuity etc. 112; blue moon [*colloq.*], coon's age [*colloq.*], dog's age [*colloq.*].

durableness, durability; persistence, eternalness, lastingness etc. *adj.;* continuance, standing; permanence etc. (*stability*) 150; survival, survivance; longevity etc. (*age*) 128; distance of time.

protraction of time, prolongation of time, extension of time; delay etc. (*lateness*) 133.

v. **last**, endure, stand, remain, abide, continue etc. 106; brave a thousand years.

tarry etc. (*be late*) 133; drag on, drag its slow length along, drag a lengthening chain; protract, prolong; spin out, eke out, draw out; lengthen out; temporize; gain time, make time, talk against time.

outlast, outlive; survive; live to fight again.

adj. **durable**, endurable [*rare*]; lasting etc. *v.;* of long duration, of long standing; permanent, chronic, longstanding; diuturnal [*rare*]; intransient, intransitive; intransmutable, persistent; lifelong, livelong; longeval [*rare*], longevous, endless, fixed, immortal, perdurant [*rare*], perdurable, long-lived, macrobiotic, evergreen, perennial; sempervirent [*rare*], sempervirid; unintermitting, unremitting; perpetual etc. 112.

lingering, protracted, prolonged, spun out etc. *v.;* long-pending, long-winded; slow etc. 275.

adv. **long**; for a long time, for an age, for ages, for ever so long, for many a long day; long ago etc. (*in a past time*) 122; *longo intervallo* [*L.*].

all the day long, all the year round; the livelong day, as the day is long, morning, noon and night; hour after hour, day after day etc.; for good, for good and all; permanently etc. *adj.;* *semper et ubique* [*L.*].

111. Transience
[short duration]

n. **transience**, transiency, ephemerality, transientness [*rare*] etc. *adj.;* evanescence, impermanence *or* impermanency, preterience [*rare*], volatility, fugacity, caducity [*rare*], mortality, span; nine days' wonder, bubble, Mayfly; spurt; temporary arrangement, interregnum, interim.

velocity etc. 274; suddenness etc. 113; changeableness etc. 149.

ephemeron; transient, transient boarder, transient guest, transient rates.

v. **be transient** etc. *adj.;* flit, pass away, fly, gallop, vanish, fleet, sink, melt, fade, evaporate; pass away like a -cloud, –summer cloud, –shadow, –dream.

adj. **transient**, transitory, transitive; passing, evanescent, fleeting; flying etc. *v.;* fugacious, fugitive; transeunt, interim, shifting, slippery; spasmodic.

temporal, temporary; provisional, provisory; cursory, short-lived, ephemeral, ephemerous [*rare*], preterient [*rare*], caducous [*rare*], deciduous; perishable, mortal, precarious; impermanent.

brief, quick, brisk, fleet, cometary, meteoric, volatile, extemporaneous, summary; pressed for time etc. (*haste*) 684; sudden, momentary etc. (*instantaneous*) 113.

adv. **temporarily** etc. *adj.;* pro tempore [*L.*]; for the moment, for a time; awhile, *en passant* [*F.*], *in transitu* [*L.*]; in a short time; soon etc. (*early*) 132; briefly etc. *adj.;* at short notice; on the point of, on the eve of; *in articulo mortis* [*L.*]; between cup and lip.

112. Perpetuity
[endless duration]

n. **perpetuity**, eternity, everness,[1] aye, sempiternity, perenniality [*rare*], coeternity, immortality, athanasy, athanasia; everlastingness etc. *adj.;* perpetuation; continued existence, uninterrupted existence; perennity [*obs.*].

v. **have no end**; last forever, endure forever, go on forever.

eternize, immortalize, eternalize, monumentalize, perpetuate.

adj. **perpetual**, eternal; everduring, everlasting, everliving, everflowing; continual, sempiternal, sempiternous [*rare*], eviternal [*rare*]; coeternal; endless, unending; ceaseless, incessant, uninterrupted, indesinent [*obs.*], unceasing; interminable, eterne [*poetic*], having no end; unfading, evergreen, amaranthine; never-ending, never-dying, never-fading; deathless, immortal, undying, imperishable.

adv. **perpetually** etc. *adj.;* always, ever, evermore [*archaic*], aye; forever, for aye, forevermore, forever and a day, forever and ever; forever and aye, in all ages, from age to age; without end; world without end, time without end; *in secula seculorum* [*L.*]; to the end of time, to the crack of doom, to the "last syllable of recorded time" [*Macbeth*]; till doomsday; constantly etc. (*very frequently*) 136.

113. Instantaneity
[point of time]

n. **instantaneity**, instantaneousness; suddenness, abruptness.

moment, instant, second, minute; twinkling, flash, breath, crack, jiffy [*colloq.*], *coup* [*F.*], burst, flash of lightning, stroke of time.

time; epoch, time of day, time of night; hour, minute; very minute etc., very time, very hour; present time, right time, true time, exact time, correct time.

v. **be instantaneous** etc. *adj.;* twinkle, flash.

adj. **instantaneous**, momentary, extempore, sudden, instant, abrupt; subitaneous [*obs.*], hasty; quick as thought, quick as lightning; rapid as electricity.

adv. **instantaneously** etc. *adj.;* in no time, in less than no time; presto, *subito* [*It. and L.*], instanter, forthright [*archaic*], eftsoon *or* eftsoons [*archaic*], in a trice, in a jiffy [*colloq.*], suddenly, at a stroke, like a shot; in a moment etc. *n.;* in the twinkling of an eye; in one's tracts; right away; *toute à l'heure* [*F.*]; at one jump, in the same breath, *per saltum* [*L.*], *uno saltu* [*L.*]; at once, all at once; plump, slap [*colloq.*]; "at one fell swoop" [*Macbeth*]; at the same instant etc. *n.;* immediately etc. (*early*) 132; extempore, on the moment, on the spot, on the dot [*colloq.*], on the spur of the moment; just then; slapdash etc. (*haste*) 684.

114. Chronometry
[estimation, measurement, and record of time]

n. **chronometry**, horometry, chronology, horology; date, epoch; style, era, age.

almanac, calendar, ephemeris; standard time, daylight-saving time; register, registry; chronicle, annals, journal, diary, chronogram, isochronon.

[instruments for the measurement of time] clock, watch; chronometer, chronoscope, chronograph; repeater; timekeeper, timepiece; dial, sundial, gnomon, horologe, horologium [*rare*], hydroscope, *pendule* [*F.*], hourglass, clepsydra; ghurry *or* ghari [*Hind.*].

chronographer, chronologer, chronologist, horologer; annalist.

v. **fix the time**, mark the time; date, register, chronicle, chronologize; measure time, beat time, mark time; bear date.

adj. **chronologic** *or* chronological, chronometric *or* chronometrical, chronogrammatical; data [*rare*], temporal, isochronous, isochronal, cinquecento, quattrocento, trecento.

adv. o'clock.

115. Anachronism
[false estimate of time]

n. **anachronism**, metachronism, parachronism, prochronism; prolepsis, misdate; anticipation, antichronism [*rare*].

35

disregard of time, neglect of time, oblivion of time.

intempestivity [*rare*] etc. 135.

v. **misdate**, antedate, postdate, overdate; anticipate; take no note of time; anachronize [*rare*].

adj. **misdated** etc. *v.;* undated; overdue; out of date, anachronous, anachronistic, intempestive, behind time.

116. Priority

n. **priority**, antecedence, anteriority, precedence, preëxistence; precession etc. 280; precursor etc. 64; the past etc. 122; premises.

v. **precede**, come before; forerun; prevent [*rare*], antecede; go before etc. (*lead*) 280; preëxist; dawn; presage etc. 511; herald, usher in, announce.

be beforehand etc. (*be early*) 132; steal a march upon, anticipate, forestall; have the start, gain the start.

adj. **prior**, previous; preceding, precedent [*rare*]; anterior, antecedent; preëxistent; former, aforegoing, aforesighted, aforementioned, aforethought, fore [*obs.*], foregoing; beforementioned, above-mentioned; aforesaid, said; introductory etc. (*precursory*) 64; prodromal.

adv. **before**, prior to; earlier; previously etc. *adj.;* afore [*obs.*], aforehand [*archaic*], ere, theretofore, erewhile; ere then, ere now, before then, before now; already, yet, beforehand; or ever, aforetime; on the eve of.

117. Posteriority

n. **posteriority**; succession, sequence; following etc. 281; subsequence, subsequency, supervention; continuance, prolongation; futurity etc. 121; successor; sequel etc. 65; remainder, reversion.

v. **follow after** etc. 281, come after, go after; succeed, supervene; ensue, attend, emanate [*rare*], occur, result; step into the shoes of.

adj. **subsequent**, posterior, following, after, later, succeeding, sequacious [*rare*], successive, sequential [*rare*], ensuing, consecutive, attendant, sequent, postliminary [*rare*], postnate [*obs.*]; postdiluvial, postdiluvian; posthumous; future etc. 121; after-dinner, postprandial.

adv. **subsequently**, after, afterwards, since, later; at a subsequent period, at a later period; next, in the sequel, close upon, thereafter, thereupon, upon which, eftsoon *or* eftsoons [*archaic*]; from that time, from that moment; after a while, after a time; in process of time.

118. Present Time

n. **the present time**, the present day, the present moment, the present juncture, the present occasion; the times, existing time, time being; twentieth century; crisis, epoch, day, hour.

age, time of life.

adj. **present**, actual, instant, current, nonce, latest, existing, that is.

adv. **at this time**, at this moment etc. 113; at the present time etc. *n.;* now, at present; at hand.

at this time of day, to-day, now-a-days; already; even now, but now, just now; on the present occasion; for the time being, for the nonce; on the nail, on the spot; on the spur of the moment, on the spur of the occasion.

until now; to this day, to the present day.

119. Different Time

[time different from the present]

n. different time, other time.

[indefinite time] aorist.

adj. aoristic; indefinite.

adv. **then**, at that time, at that moment, at that instant; at which time, at which moment, at which instant; on that occasion, upon.

when; whenever, whensoever; whereupon, upon which, on which occasion; at another time, at a different time, at some other time, at any time; at various times; some of these days, one of these days, some fine morning, one fine morning; some fine day, on divers occasions, sooner or later; some time or other.

once, formerly, once upon a time.

120. Synchronism

n. **synchronism**; coexistence, coincidence; simultaneousness etc. *adj.;* concurrence, concomitance, unity of time, interim.

[having equal times] isochronism.

contemporary, coeval, coetanian [*obs.*].

v. **coexist**, concur, accompany, go hand in hand, keep pace with; synchronize, isochronize.

adj. **synchronous**, synchronal, synchronic *or* synchronical, synchronistic *or* synchronistical, simultaneous, coexisting, coincident, concomitant, concurrent; coeval, coevous [*obs.*]; contemporary, contemporaneous; coetaneous [*rare*], coinstantaneous, coterminous, collateral, coeternal; isochronous.

adv. **at the same time**; simultaneously etc. *adj.;* together, in concert, during the same time; in the same breath; *pari passu* [*L.*]; in the interim.

at the very moment etc. 113; just as, as soon as; meanwhile etc. (*while*) 106.

121. Futurity

[prospective time]

n. **futurity,** futurition [*rare*]; future, hereafter, time to come; approaching—, coming—, subsequent—, after- -time, —age, —days, —hours, —years, —ages, —life; morrow, to-morrow, by and by, the yet [*rare*]; millennium, chiliad [*rare*], millenary, doomsday, day of judgment, crack of doom, remote future.

approach of time, advent, time drawing on, womb of time; destiny etc. 152; eventuality.

heritage, heirs, posterity, descendants.

prospect, anticipation etc. (*expectation*) 507; foresight etc. 510.

v. **look forward;** anticipate etc. (*expect*) 507, (*foresee*) 510; forestall etc. (*be early*) 132.

approach, await, threaten; impend etc. (*be destined*) 152; come on, draw on; draw near.

adj. **future,** to come; coming etc. (*impending*) 152; next, near; near at hand, close at hand; eventual, ulterior; anticipant, expectant, prospective, in prospect etc. (*expectation*) 507; millenary, millennial.

adv. **prospectively,** hereafter, in future; on the knees of the gods; *kal* [*Hind.*], to-morrow, the day after tomorrow; in course of time, in process of time, in the fullness of time; eventually, ultimately, sooner or later; proximo; *paulo post futurum* [*L.*]; in after time; one of these days; after a time, after a while.

from this time; henceforth, henceforwards; thence; thenceforth, thenceforward; whereupon, upon which.

soon etc. (*early*) 132; on the eve of, on the point of, on the brink of; about to; close upon.

122. Preterition

[retrospective time]

n. **preterition;** priority etc. 116; the past, past time; heretofore [*rare*]; days of yore, days of old, days past, days gone by; times of yore, times of old, times past, times gone by; bygone days; old **times,** ancient times, former times; foretime [*rare*]; yesterday, the olden time, good old time; langsyne; eld [*obs. or poetic*].

antiquity, antiqueness, ancientness, *status quo* [*L.*]; time immemorial, distance of time; history, remote age, remote time; remote past; rust of antiquity.

paleontology, paleography, paleology; palaetiology, archaeology; archaism, antiquarianism, medievalism, Pre-Raphaelitism.

retrospection, looking back; memory etc. 505.

antiquary, antiquarian; paleologist, archaeologist etc.; Oldbuck, Dryasdust; *laudator temporis acti* [*L.*]; medievalist, Pre-Raphaelite.

ancestry etc. (*paternity*) 166.

v. **be past** etc. *adj.;* have expired etc. *adj.,* have run its course, have had its day; pass; pass by, pass away, pass off; go by, go away, go off; lapse, blow over.

look back, trace back, cast the eyes back; exhume.

adj. **past,** gone, gone by, over, passed away, bygone, foregone [*archaic*]; elapsed, lapsed, preterlapsed [*rare*], expired, no more, run out, blown over, that has been, bypast, agone [*archaic*], whilom [*archaic*], extinct, never to return, exploded, forgotten, irrecoverable; obsolete etc. (*old*) 124.

former, pristine, quondam, *ci-devant* [*F.*], late; ancestral.

foregoing; last, latter; recent, overnight, preterit *or* preterite, past, plu-perfect, past perfect.

looking back etc. *v.;* retrospective, retroactive; archaeological etc. *n.*

adv. **formerly;** of old, of yore; erst [*archaic or poetic*], erstwhile [*archaic*], whilom [*archaic*], erewhile [*archaic*], time was, ago, over; in the olden time etc. *n.;* anciently, long ago, long since; a long while ago, a long time ago; years ago, ages ago; some time ago, some time since, some time back.

yesterday, the day before yesterday; last year, last season, last month etc.; *ultimo* [*L.*]; lately etc. (*newly*) 123.

retrospectively; ere now, before now, till now; hitherto, heretofore; no longer; once, once upon a time; from time immemorial; in the memory of man; time out of mind; already, yet, up to this time; *ex post facto* [*L.*].

123. Newness

n. **newness** etc. *adj.;* novelty, recency; neology, neologism; immaturity; youth etc. 127; gloss of novelty.

innovation; renovation etc. (*restoration*) 660.

modernist, neoteric; neologist.

upstart, *narikin* [*Jap.*], start-up [*rare*], *nouveau riche* [*F.*], parvenu.

modernism, modernness, modernity; modernization; *dernier cri* [*F.*]; latest fashion; mushroom.

v. **renew** etc. (*restore*) 660; modernize.

adj. **new,** novel, recent, fresh, green; young etc. 127; evergreen; raw, immature; virgin; untried, unhandseled, unheard-of, untrodden, unbeaten; fire-new, span-new.

modern, late, neoteric, neoterical; new-born, new-fashioned, newfangled, newfledged; of yesterday; just out [*colloq.*], brand-new, up-to-date [*colloq.*]; *fin-de-siècle* [*F.*], vernal, renovated; sempervirent [*rare*], sempervirid [*rare*].

fresh as a rose, fresh as a daisy, fresh as paint [*colloq.*]; spick-and-span, spick-and-span-new, unhandled.

adv. **newly** etc. *adj.;* afresh, anew, lately, just now, only yesterday, the other day; latterly, of late.

not long ago, a short time ago.

124. Oldness

n. **oldness** etc. *adj.;* age, antiquity, eld [*obs. or poetic*]; cobwebs of antiquity.

maturity, matureness, ripeness.

decline, decay; senility etc. 128.

seniority, eldership, primogeniture.

archaism etc. (*the past*) 122; thing of the past, relic of the past; megatherium; Babylonian, Assyrian, Sanskrit.

tradition, prescription, custom, immemorial usage, common law; folklore.

v. **be old** etc. *adj.;* have had its day, have seen its day.

become old etc. *adj.;* age, fade.

adj. **old**, ancient, olden [*archaic*], eldern [*archaic*], antique; of long standing, time-honored, venerable, hoary, vetust [*obs.*]; elder, eldest; firstborn.

primitive, prime, primeval, primigenous, primigenial, primigenious; paleoanthropic; primordial, primordiate [*rare*]; aboriginal etc. (*beginning*) 66; diluvian, antediluvian, protohistoric, prehistoric, dateless, patriarchal, preadamite; palaeocrystic; fossil, paleozoic, preglacial, antemundane; archaic, Vedic, classic, medieval, Pre-Raphaelite, ancestral; blackletter.

immemorial, traditional, traditive, traditionary [*rare*], prescriptive, customary, unwritten, whereof the memory of man runneth not to the contrary; inveterate, rooted.

antiquated, of other times, old as the hills, of the old school, after-age, obsolete; out-of-date, out-of-fashion; stale, old-fashioned, old-fangled [*rare*], fusty, outworn, moth-eaten [*humorous*], behind the age; old-world; exploded; gone out, gone by, *passé* [*F.*], extinct, dead, disused, past, run out; senile etc. 128; timeworn; crumbling etc. (*deteriorated*) 659; secondhand.

old as the hills, old as Methuselah, old as Adam, old as history.

adv. since the world was made, since the year one, since the days of Methuselah.

125. Morning

[noon]

n. **morning**, morn, matins [*eccl.*], morningtide [*rare or poetic*], forenoon, *a.m.*, prime, dawn, daybreak; dayspring, foreday [*chiefly Scot.*], sun-up, peep of day, break of day; aurora; first blush of the morning, first flush of the morning, prime of the morning; twilight, crepuscle *or* crepuscule, sunrise; daylight, daypeep, cockcrow, cockcrowing; the small hours, the wee sma' hours [*Scot.*].

noon, midday, noonday, noontide, meridian, prime; nooning, noontime.

spring, springtide, springtime, seedtime; vernal equinox.

summer, summertide, summertime, midsummer.

adj. **matin**, matutinal, matinal, matutinary [*rare*]; crepuscular.

noon, noonday, midday, meridional [*rare in this sense*].

spring, vernal, vernant [*obs.*].

summer, aestival *or* estival.

adv. **at sunrise** etc. *n.;* with the lark, when the morning dawns.

126. Evening

[midnight]

n. **evening**, eve; decline of day, fall of day, close of day; candlelight, candlelighting; eventide, evensong [*eccl. or archaic*], vespers [*eccl.*], nighttide [*archaic*], nightfall, curfew, dusk, twilight, eleventh hour; sunset, sundown; going down of the sun, cockshut [*obs.*], dewy eve, gloaming, bedtime.

afternoon, *post meridiem* [*L.*], *p.m.*

midnight; dead of night, witching hour of night, witching time of night, killing-time.

autumn; fall, fall of the leaf; harvest, autumnal equinox; Indian summer, St. Luke's summer, St. Martin's summer.

winter, *hiems* [*L.*].

adj. **vesper**, vespertine, nocturnal; autumnal.

wintry, winterly, brumous, brumal.

127. Youth

n. **youth**; juvenility, juvenescence [*rare*]; juniority; infancy; babyhood, childhood, boyhood, girlhood, youthhood [*archaic*]; incunabula; minority, boyage [*rare*], immaturity, nonage, teens, tender age, bloom.

cradle, nursery, leading strings, puberty, pucelage.

flower of life, springtide of life, seedtime of life, prime of life, golden season of life; heyday of youth, school days; rising generation.

adj. **young**, youthful, juvenile, juvenescent, green, callow, budding, sappy, puisne [*law*], beardless, under age, in one's teens, *in statu pupillari* [*L.*]; younger, junior; hebetic, unfledged, unripe.

128. Age

n. **age**; oldness etc. *adj.* old age, advanced age; senility, senescence; years, anility, gray hairs, climacteric, grand climacteric, declining years, decrepitude, hoary age, caducity [*rare*], eld [*archaic*], superannuation; second childhood, childishness; dotage; vale of years, decline of life, senectitude [*rare*], "sear and yellow leaf" [*Macbeth*]; threescore years and ten; green old age, ripe age; longevity; time of life.

seniority, eldership; elders etc. (*veteran*) 130; firstling; *doyen* [*F.*], dean, father; primogeniture.

[science of old age] nostology; geriatrics *and* gerontology *and* gerocomy [*med.*].

v. **be aged** etc. *adj.;* grow old, get old etc. *adj.;* age; decline, wane, senesce [*rare*].

adj. **aged**; old etc. 124; elderly, eldern [*archaic*], senile; matronly, anile; in years; ripe, mellow, run to seed, declining, waning, past one's prime; gray, grayheaded; hoar, hoary; venerable, time-worn, antiquated, *passé* [*F.*], effete, decrepit, superannuated; advanced in life, advanced in years; stricken in years; wrinkled, marked with the crow's foot; having one foot in the grave; doting etc. (*imbecile*) 499; like the last of pea time.

years old; of a certain age, no chicken [*colloq.*], old as Methuselah; ancestral; patriarchal etc. (*ancient*) 124; gerontic.

older, elder, oldest, eldest; senior; firstborn.

129. Infant

n. **infant**, babe, baby; nursling, suckling, yearling, weanling; papoose, *bambino* [*It.*]; vagitus.

child, bairn [*Scot.*], tot, mite, scrap, chick, kid [*slang*], *butcha* or *bacha* [*Hind.*]; little one, brat, chit, pickaninny, urchin; bantling, bratling elf.

youth, boy, lad, laddie, slip, sprig, stripling, youngster, younker [*colloq.*], whipster [*rare*], youngling [*rare*], damoiseau [*archaic*], cub, callant [*Scot.*], whippersnapper [*colloq.*], school-

boy, hobbledehoy, hopeful, cadet, minor, master.

scion, sapling, seedling; tendril, olivebranch, nestling, chicken, duckling, larva, chrysalis, tadpole, whelp, cub, pullet, fry, callow [*obs.*], codling *or* codlin; fetus, calf, colt, pup, puppy, foal, kitten; lamb, lambkin; aurelia, caterpillar, cocoon, nymph, nympha, pupa, staddle.

girl, lass, lassie; wench [*dial.*], miss, damsel; damoiselle, damosel *or* damozel [*archaic*]; demoiselle; maid, maiden; virgin; nymph, colleen, girleen, flapper [*slang*], girly [*colloq.*], minx, missy, baggage, hussy; schoolgirl; hoyden, tomboy, romp.

adj. **infantine**, infantile; puerile; boyish, girlish, childish, babyish, kittenish; childly [*rare*], boylike, girllike, kiddish [*colloq.*], dollish [*colloq.*]; youngling, infant, baby; newborn, unfledged, newfledged, callow.

in the cradle, in swaddling clothes, in long clothes, in arms, in leading strings; at the breast; in one's teens; young etc. 127.

130. Veteran

n. **veteran**, old man, reverend sir, seer, patriarch, graybeard; grandfather, grandsire [*archaic*], grisard [*rare*], oldster [*colloq.*], pantaloon [*obs.*]; gaffer, sexagenarian, octogenarian, nonagenarian, centenarian; *doyen* [*F.*], old stager; dotard etc. 501.

granny, grandam *or* grandame [*archaic*], gammer [*dial. Eng.*], crone, hag, oldwife, beldam *or* beldame.

preadamite, Methuselah, Nestor, old Parr; elders; forefathers etc. (*paternity*) 166; Darby and Joan, Philemon and Baucis, "John Anderson, my jo" [*Burns*].

adj. **veteran**; aged etc. 128.

131. Adolescence

n. **adolescence**, pubescence, majority; adultism; adulthood, adultness etc. *adj.;* manhood, virility; flower of age; full bloom; spring of life.

man etc. 373; woman etc. 374; adult, pubescent, no chicken [*colloq.*].

middle age, *mezzo cammin* [*It.*], maturity, full age, ripe age, prime of life, meridian of life.

v. **come of age**, come to man's estate, come to years of discretion; attain majority, put on long trousers, assume the *toga virilis* [*L.*]; have cut one's eyeteeth [*colloq.*], settle down, have sown one's wild oats.

adj. **adolescent**, pubescent, of age; of full age, of ripe age; out of one's teens, grown up, full-blown, in full bloom, full-grown, manly, manlike, virile, adult; womanly, matronly; marriageable, marriable, nubile.

middle-aged, mature, in one's prime; matronly.

132. Earliness

n.   **earliness** etc. *adj.;* morning etc. 125.

punctuality; promptitude etc. (*activity*) 682; haste etc. (*velocity*) 274; suddenness etc. (*instantaneity*) 113.

prematurity, precocity, precipitation, anticipation, prevenience; a stitch in time.

v.   **be early** etc. *adj.;* be beforehand etc. *adv.;* keep time, take time by the forelock, anticipate, forestall; have the start, gain the start; steal a march upon; gain time, draw on futurity; bespeak, secure, engage, preëngage.

accelerate; expedite etc. (*quicken*) 274; make haste etc. (*hurry*) 684.

adj.   **early,** prime, timely, seasonable, in time, punctual, forward, prompt etc. (*active*) 682; summary.

premature, precipitate, precocious; prevenient, anticipatory; rath *or* rathe [*obs. or poetic*].

sudden etc. (*instantaneous*) 113; unexpected etc. 508; imminent, impending, near, near at hand; immediate.

adv.   **early,** soon, anon, betimes, rath *or* rathe [*poetic*]; eftsoon *or* eftsoons [*archaic*]; ere long, before long; punctually etc. *adj.;* to the minute; in time; in good time, in military time, in pudding time [*obs.*], in due time; time enough, on time, on the dot [*slang*].

beforehand; prematurely etc. *adj.;* precipitately etc. (*hastily*) 684; too soon; before its time, before one's time; in anticipation; unexpectedly etc. 508.

suddenly etc. (*instantaneously*) 113; before one can say "Jack Robinson," at short notice, extempore; on the spur of the moment, on the spur of the occasion [Bacon]; at once; on the spot, on the instant; at sight; off hand, out of hand; *à vue d'oeil* [*F.*]; straight, straightway, straightforth; forthwith, incontinently, summarily, instanter, forthright [*archaic*], immediately, briefly, shortly, erewhile [*archaic*], quickly, speedily, apace, before the ink is dry, almost immediately, presently, at the first opportunity, in no long time, by and by, in a while, directly.

133. Lateness

n.   **lateness** etc. *adj.;* tardiness etc. (*slowness*) 275.

delay, cunctation [*rare*] tarriance, moration [*rare*], delation [*archaic*], procrastination; def-

erring etc. *v.;* postponement, adjournment, prorogation, retardation, respite; protraction, prolongation; after-time; circumlocution office [*ridicule*], "circumlocution court" [Dickens], chancery suit, Fabian policy, *médecine expectante* [*F.*], moratorium; leeway; high time; truce, reprieve, demurrage; stop, stay, suspension, remand.

v.   **be late** etc. *adj.;* tarry, wait, stay, bide, take time; dawdle etc. (*be inactive*) 683; linger, loiter; bide one's time, take one's time; gain time; hang fire; stand over, lie over; hang, hang around *or* about [*colloq.*], hang back [*colloq.*], hang in the balance, hang in the hedge, hang up [*colloq.*], sit up for, stay up for.

put off, defer, delay, lay over, suspend; shift off, stave off; waive, retard, remand, postpone, adjourn; procrastinate; dally; prolong, protract; spin out, draw out, lengthen out; prorogue; keep back; tide over; push to the last, drive to the last; let the matter stand over; table, lay on the table, shelve; respite [*rare*], perendinate [*rare*]; reserve etc. (*store*) 636; temporize, filibuster, stall [*slang*]; consult one's pillow, sleep upon it.

be kept waiting, dance attendance; kick one's heels [*colloq.*], cool one's heels [*colloq.*]; *faire antichambre* [*F.*]; wait impatiently; await etc. (*expect*) 507; sit up, sit up at night; lose an opportunity etc. 135.

adj.   **late,** tardy, slow, cunctatious *or* cunctative [*rare*], behindhand, serotine [*rare*], belated, postliminary [*rare*], posthumous, backward, unpunctual, impunctual [*rare*], overdue, moratory; dilatory etc. (*slow*) 275; delayed etc. *v.;* in abeyance.

adv.   **late;** backward, lateward [*obs.*], late in the day; at sunset, at the eleventh hour, at length, at last; ultimately; after time, behind time; too late; too late for etc. 135.

slowly, leisurely, deliberately, at one's leisure; *ex post facto* [*L.*]; *sine die* [*L.*].

134. Occasion

n.   **occasion,** opportunity, opening, room, scope, space, place, liberty, show [*colloq., U. S.*]; suitable time, suitable season, proper time, proper season; high time; opportuneness etc. *adj.;* tempestivity [*obs.*].

nick of time; golden opportunity, well-timed opportunity, fine opportunity, favorable opportunity; clear stage, fair field; *mollia tempora* [*L.*]; spare time etc. (*leisure*) 685.

crisis, turn, emergency, juncture, conjuncture; turning point, given time.

v. **improve the occasion**; seize etc. (789) an opportunity *or* an occasion; use etc. (677) an opportunity *or* an occasion; give etc. (784) an opportunity *or* an occasion.

suit the occasion etc. (*be expedient*) 646.

strike the iron while it is hot, *battre le fer sur l'enclume* [*F.*], make hay while the sun shines, seize the present hour, take time by the forelock, *prendre la balle au bond* [*F.*].

adj. **opportune**, timely, well-timed, timeful [*obs.*], seasonable, tempestive [*archaic*], timeous [*rare*].

lucky, providential, fortunate, happy, favorable, propitious, auspicious, critical; suitable etc. 23; *obiter dicta* [*L.*].

occasional, accidental, extemporaneous, extemporary; contingent etc. (*uncertain*) 475.

adv. **opportunely** etc. *adj.;* in proper time, in proper course, in proper season; in due time, in due course, in due season; for the nonce; in the nick of time, in the fullness of time; all in good time; just in time, at the eleventh hour, now or never.

by the way, by the by; *en passant* [*F.*], *à propos* [*F.*]; *pro hac vice* [*L.*]; *par parenthèse* [*F.*], parenthetically, by way of parenthesis; while on this subject, speaking of; *par exemple* [*F.*]; extempore; on the spur of the moment, on the spur of the occasion; on the spot etc. (*early*) 132.

135. Intempestivity

n. **intempestivity** [*rare*]; unsuitable time, improper time; unreasonableness etc. *adj.;* evil hour; *contretemps* [*F.*], misventure [*archaic*], misadventure; intrusion; anachronism etc. 115.

v. **be ill-timed** etc. *adj.;* mistime, intrude, come amiss, break in upon; have other fish to fry; be busy, be occupied, be engaged.

lose an opportunity; throw away an opportunity, waste an opportunity, neglect etc. (460) an opportunity; allow *or* suffer the opportunity *or* occasion to -pass, –slip, –go by, –escape, –lapse; waste time etc. (*be inactive*) 683; let slip through the fingers, lock the stable door when the steed is stolen.

adj. **ill-timed**, mistimed; ill-fated, ill-omened, ill-starred; untimely, intrusive, unseasonable; out of date, out of season; inopportune, timeless [*archaic*], inconvenient, intempestive [*rare*], untoward, *mal à propos* [*F.*], unlucky, inauspicious, unpropitious, unfortunate, unfavorable; unsuited etc. 24; inexpedient etc. 647.

unpunctual etc. (*late*) 133; too late for; premature etc. (*early*) 132; too soon for; wise after the event.

adv. **inopportunely** etc. *adj.;* as ill luck would have it, in an evil hour, the time having gone by, a day after the fair.

136. Frequency

n. **frequency**, frequence, oftness [*rare*], oftenness [*rare*], quotiety [*rare*]; repetition etc. 104.

v. **keep**, keep on; recur etc. 104; do nothing but.

adj. **frequent**, often [*archaic*], many, many times, not rare, thickcoming, incessant, perpetual, continual, constant, repeated etc. 104; habitual etc. 613; hourly etc. 138.

adv. **often**, oft, ofttime [*archaic*], ofttimes, oftentimes; oftentime [*rare*], oftentide [*obs.*], not seldom, frequently; repeatedly etc. 104; unseldom, not unfrequently; in quick succession, in rapid succession; many a time and oft; oftly [*rare*], daily, hourly etc.; every day, every hour, every moment etc.

perpetually, continually, constantly, incessantly, unchangingly, steadfastly, without ceasing, at all times, daily and hourly, night and day, day and night, day after day, morning noon and night, ever and anon.

commonly etc. (*habitually*) 613; most often.

sometimes, occasionally, at times, now and then, from time to time, there being times when, *toties quoties* [*L.*], often enough, again and again.

137. Infrequency

n. **infrequency**, infrequence, unfrequency [*rare*], rareness, rarity; sparseness, fewness etc. 103; seldomness; uncommonness.

v. **be rare** etc. *adj.*

adj. **infrequent**, unfrequent [*rare*], seldseen [*archaic*], uncommon, sporadic; rare, rare as a blue diamond; few etc. 103; scarce; almost unheard of, scarce as hen's teeth [*colloq.*], unprecedented, which has not occurred within the memory of the oldest inhabitant, not within one's previous experience.

adv. **seldom**, rarely, scarcely, hardly; not often, unfrequently, infrequently, uncommonly, sparsely, unoften; scarcely ever, hardly ever; once in a blue moon [*colloq.*].

once; once for all, once in a way; *pro hac vice* [*L.*].

138. Regularity of recurrence. Periodicity

n. **periodicity**, intermittence; beat; oscillation etc. 314; pulse, pulsation; systole and diastole; rhythm; alternation, alternateness, alternacy [*rare*], alternativeness, alternity [*rare*].

round, revolution, rotation, bout, turn, say.

anniversary, biennial, triennial, quadrennial, quinquennial, sextennial, septennial, octennial, decennial; tricennial, jubilee, centennial, centenary, bicentennial, bicentenary, tercentenary; birthday, birthright, natal day, fête day, saint's day.

catamenia, courses, menses, menstrual flux.

[regularity of return] rota, cycle, period, stated time, routine; days of the week; Sunday, Monday etc.; months of the year; January etc.; feast, festival, fast etc.; Christmas, Yuletide, New Year's day, Ash Wednesday, Maundy Thursday, Good Friday, Easter; Allhallows, Allhallowmas, All Saints' Day; All Souls' Day; Candlemas, Dewali [*Hindu*], Holi *or* Hoolee [*Hindu*], Memorial *or* Decoration Day, Independence Day, Labor Day, Thanksgiving, ground-hog day, woodchuck day [*U. S.*], Halloween, Hallowmas, Lady Day; leap year, bissextile; Bairam, Ramadan, Muharram [*Mohammedan*]; St. Swithin's Day; Midsummer Day; May Day etc. (*holiday*) 840; year-book.

punctuality, regularity, steadiness.

v. **return**, revolve; recur in regular -order, -succession; come again, come in its turn; come round, –again; beat, pulsate; alternate; intermit.

adj. **periodic**, periodical; serial, recurrent, cyclic, cyclical, rhythmic *or* rhythmical; recurring etc.*v.;* intermittent, remittent; alternate, every other; every.

hourly; diurnal, daily, quotidian [*rare*]; tertian, weekly; hebdomadal, hebdomadary; biweekly, fortnightly; bimonthly; monthly, catamenial, menstrual; yearly, annual; biennial, triennial etc.; centennial, secular; paschal, lenten etc.

regular, steady, constant, methodical, punctual, regular as clockwork.

adv. **periodically** etc. *adj.;* at regular intervals, at stated times; at fixed periods, at established periods; punctually etc. *adj.; de die in diem* [*L.*]; from day to day, day by day.

by turns; in turn, in rotation; alternately, every other day, off and on, ride and tie, round and round.

139. Irregularity of recurrence

n. **irregularity**, uncertainty, unpunctuality; fitfulness etc. *adj.;* capriciousness, ecrhythmus; acatastasia [*med.*].

adj. **irregular**, uncertain, unpunctual, capricious, erratic, heteroclite, ecrhythmic, ecrhythmous, desultory, fitful, flickering; rambling, rhapsodi-

cal; spasmodic; immethodical, unsystematic, unequal, uneven, variable.

adv. **irregularly** etc. *adj.;* by fits and starts etc. (*discontinuously*) 70.

Section 7. Change

---

140. Change
[difference at different times]

n. **change**, alteration, mutation, permutation, variation, novation [*rare*], modification, modulation, inflection *or* inflexion, mood, qualification, innovation, eversion, deviation, shift, turn; diversion; break.

transformation, transfiguration, transfigurement; metamorphosis; metabola *or* metabole [*med.*], transmorphism [*rare*], transmutation; deoxidization, deoxidation; transubstantiation; metagenesis, transanimation, transmigration, metempsychosis, version [*rare*]; metasomatism *or* metasomatosis, metathesis; metabolism, metastasis; transmogrification [*colloq.*]; avatar; alterative.

resolution, conversion etc. (*gradual change*) 144; revolution etc. (*sudden or radical change*) 146; inversion etc. (*reversal*) 218; displacement etc. 185; transference etc. 270.

changeableness etc. 149; tergiversation etc. (*change of mind*) 607.

v. **change**, alter, vary, wax and wane; modulate, diversify, qualify, tamper with; turn, shift, veer, gybe *or* jibe, jib, tack, chop, shuffle, swerve, warp, deviate, dodge, tergiversate, turn aside, evert, intervert [*obs.*]; pass to, take a turn, turn the corner, resume.

work a change, modify, vamp, patch, piece, vamp up, superinduce; transform, transfigure, transmute, transmogrify [*colloq.*], transume [*rare*], transverse [*rare*], transshape [*rare*], metabolize, convert, transubstantiate, resolve, revolutionize; chop and change; metamorphose, ring the changes.

innovate, introduce new blood, shuffle the cards; give a turn to, give a color to; influence, turn the scale; shift the scene, turn over a new leaf.

recast etc. 146; reverse etc. 218; disturb etc. 61; convert into etc. 144.

adj. **changed** etc. *v.;* newfangled; eversible; changeable etc. 149; transitional; modifiable; metagenetic; alterative.

adv. mutatis mutandis [*L.*].

int. quantum mutatus! [*L.*].

141. Permanence
[absence of change]

n. **permanence**, permanency, fixity, persistence, endurance; durableness, durability, lastingness; standing, *status quo* [*L.*]; maintenance, preservation, conservation; conservatism; *laisser faire* [*F.*], *laisser aller* [*F.*]; law of the Medes and Persians; standing dish.

stability etc. 150; quiescence etc. 265; obstinacy etc. 606.

v. **let alone**, let be; persist, remain, stay, tarry, rest; hold, hold on; last, endure, bide, abide, aby *or* abye [*archaic*], dwell, maintain, keep; stand, –still, –fast, –pat [*colloq.*]; subsist, live, outlive, survive; hold–, keep- one's -ground, –footing; hold good.

adj. **permanent**; stable etc. 150; persisting etc. *v.*; established; fixed, irremovable, durable; pucka *or* pukka *or* pakka [*Hind.*]; unchanged etc. (change etc. 140); renewed; intact, inviolate; persistent; monotonous, uncheckered; unfailing, unfading.

undestroyed, unrepealed, unsuppressed; conservative, *qualis ab incepto* [*L.*]; prescriptive etc. (*old*) 124; stationary etc. 265.

adv. **finally**; *in statu quo* [*L.*]; for good, at a stand, at a standstill, *uti possidetis* [*L.*]; without a shadow of turning; as you were!

142. Cessation
[change from action to rest]

n. **cessation**, discontinuance, desistance, desinence. intermission, remission; suspense, suspension; interruption; stop; hitch [*colloq.*]; stopping etc. *v.*; stoppage, halt; arrival etc. 292.

pause, rest, lull, respite, truce, truce of God, armistice, stay, drop; interregnum, abeyance. [in debate] closure, cloture, *clôture* [*F.*].

deadlock, checkmate, backwater, dead water, dead stand, dead stop; end etc. 67; death etc. 360.

punctuation, comma, semicolon, colon, period, full stop, caesura.

v. **cease**, discontinue, desist, stay; break off, leave off; hold, stop, pull up, stop short; check, check in full career, deadlock; stick, hang fire; halt; pause, rest.

come to a -stand, –standstill, –deadlock, –full stop; arrive etc. 292; go out, die away; wear away, wear off; pass away etc. (*be past*) 122; be at an end.

have done with, give over, surcease, shut up shop; give up etc. (*relinquish*) 624.

hold–, stay- one's hand; rest on one's oars, repose on one's laurels.

interrupt, suspend, interpel [*obs.*]; intermit, remit; put an end to, put a stop to, put a period to; derail; bring to a -stand, –standstill; stop, stall, cut short, arrest, stem the -tide, –torrent; pull the check-string.

int. **stop!** hold! enough! avast! [*naut.*], have done! a truce to! soft! leave off! *tenez!* [*F.*], fade away! [*slang*], let up! [*slang*], cut it out! [*slang*].

143. Continuance in action
n. **continuance**, continuation; run, pursuance, maintenance, extension, perpetuation, prolongation; persistence etc. (*perseverance*) 604a; repetition etc. 104.

v. **continue**, persist; go on, jog on, keep on, run on, hold on; abide, keep, pursue, stick to; take–, maintain- its course; carry on, keep up, drag on, stick [*colloq.*], persevere, endure, carry on.

sustain, uphold, hold up, keep on foot; follow up, perpetuate, prolong, maintain; preserve etc. 604a; harp upon etc. (*repeat*) 104.

keep going, keep alive, keep the pot boiling [*colloq.*], keep up the ball [*colloq.*]; die in harness; plug at it *or* along [*slang*]; keep the field, keep the ball rolling, keep at it, keep up; hold on–, pursue -the even tenor of one's way.

let be; *stare super antiquas vias* [*L.*]; *quieta non movere* [*L.*]; let things take their course.

adj. **continuing** etc. *v.*; uninterrupted, unintermitting, unvarying, persistent, unceasing, unremitting, unshifting; unreversed, unstopped, unrevoked, unvaried; sustained; chronic; undying etc. (*perpetual*) 112; inconvertible.

int. carry on! stand fast!

144. Conversion
[gradual change to something different]

n. **conversion**, reduction, transmutation, resolution, assimilation; chemistry, alchemy; lapse, assumption, growth, progress; naturalization; transportation.

proselytization, regeneration, Catholicization, Protestantization.

passage, transit, transition, transmigration; shifting etc. *v.*; flux; phase; conjugation; convertibility.

laboratory etc. 691; crucible, alembic, caldron, retort, mortar; potter's wheel, anvil, lathe, blowpipe.

convert, neophyte, catechumen, proselyte; pervert, renegade, apostate, turncoat.

v. **be converted into**; become, get, wax; come-, turn- -to, -into; turn out, lapse, shift; run-, fall-, pass-, slide-, glide-, grow-, ripen-, open-, resolve itself-, settle-, merge- into; melt, grow, come round to, mature, mellow; assume the - form, -shape, -state, -nature, character- of; illapse [*rare*]; assume a new phase, undergo a change.

convert into, resolve into; make, render; mold, form etc. 240; remodel, new-model, refound, reform, reorganize; assimilate to, bring to, reduce to.

adj. **converted into** etc. *v.;* convertible, resolvable into; conversible [*rare*], chemical, transitional; naturalized.

adv. gradually etc. (*slowly*) 275; *in transitu* [*L.*] etc. (*transference*) 270.

145. Reversion

n. **reversion**, return; revulsion.

turning point, turn of the tide; *status quo ante bellum* [*L.*]; calm before a storm.

alternation etc. (*periodicity*) 138; inversion etc. 219; recoil etc. 277; retrocession, retrospection, regression etc. 283; restoration etc. 660; relapse etc. 661; atavism, throwback; vicinism; escheat.

v. **revert**, reverse, return, turn back; relapse etc. 661; invert etc. 219; recoil etc. 277; retreat etc. 283; restore etc. 660; undo, unmake; turn the tide, turn the scale; escheat.

adj. **reverting** etc. *v.;* revulsive, reactionary; retrorse.

adv. **revulsively**, retrorsely, on the rebound, *à rebours* [*F.*].

146. Revolution
[sudden or violent change]

n. **revolution**, revolt, *bouleversement* [*F.*], subversion, breakup; destruction etc. 162; sudden-, radical-, sweeping-, organic- change; clean sweep, debacle, *débâcle* [*F.*], overturn, overthrow, *coup d'état* [*F.*], rebellion, rising, uprising, mutiny, sansculottism, bolshevism, counter-revolution.

spasm, convulsion, throe, revulsion; storm, earthquake, eruption, upheaval, cataclysm, transilience *or* transiliency [*rare*], jump, leap, plunge, jerk, start, dash; explosion.

legerdemain etc. (*trick*) 545.

v. **revolutionize**, revolt, rebel, insurrect, rise; new-model, remodel, recast; strike out something new, break with the past; change the face of, unsex.

adj. **unrecognizable**; transilient.

revolutionary, catastrophic, cataclysmic, cataclysmal, convulsionary, insurgent, Red, insurrectional, insurrectionary, mutinous, rebellious, sansculottic, bolshevist *or* bolshevik.

147. Substitution
[change of one thing for another]

n. **substitution**, commutation, subrogation [*law*], surrogation [*rare*]; supplanting etc. *v.,* supersession, supersedence, supersedure; metonymy etc. (*figure of speech*) 521.

[thing substituted] substitute, succedaneum, makeshift, temporary expedient; shift, apology, *pis aller* [*F.*], stopgap, jury mast, *locum tenens* [*L.*], alternate, warming pan [*colloq.*], dummy, scapegoat; double; changeling; *quid pro quo* [*L.*], alternative; representative etc. (*deputy*) 759; palimpsest.

price, purchase money, consideration, equivalent.

v. **substitute**, put in the place of, change for; make way for, give place to; supply-, take- the place of; surrogate [*rare*], subrogate [*law*], supplant, supersede, replace, cut out [*colloq.*], serve as a substitute; step into the shoes of, stand in the shoes of; make a shift with, put up with; borrow of Peter to pay Paul; commute, redeem, compound for.

adj. **substituted** etc. *v.;* vicarious, vicarial, substitutional, substitutious [*rare*].

adv. **instead**; by proxy; in place of, in lieu of, in the stead of, in the room of; *faute de mieux* [*F.*].

148. Interchange
[double or mutual change]

n. **interchange**, exchange; commutation, permutation, intermutation; reciprocation, transposition, transposal, shuffle, shuffling; alternation, reciprocity; castling [at chess]; hocus-pocus; swap [*colloq.*].

barter etc. 794; a Roland for his Oliver; tit for tat etc. (*retaliation*) 718; cross fire, battledore and shuttlecock; *quid pro quo* [*L.*].

interchangeableness, interchangeability.

v. **interchange**, exchange, counterchange; bandy, barter, transpose, shuffle, change hands, swap [*colloq.*], permute, reciprocate, commute; interwork, give and take, return the compliment; play at -puss in the corner, -battledore and shuttlecock; take in one another's washing; retaliate etc. 718; requite.

adj. **reciprocal**, interactive, mutual, commutative, interchangeable; interchanged etc. *v.;* intercurrent [*rare*].

international, interstate, interurban, intercollegiate, intertribal, interdenominational, interscholastic.

adv. **in exchange**, *vice versa* [*L.*], conversely, *mutatis mutandis* [*L.*], backwards and forwards, forward and back, to and fro, back and forth, by turns, turn about, contrariwise, commutatively, turn and turn about; each in his turn, every one in his turn.

149. Changeableness

n. **changeableness** etc. *adj.;* mutability, inconstancy; versatility, mobility; instability, unstable equilibrium; vacillation etc. (*irresolution*) 605; fluctuation, vicissitude; dysphoria; alternation etc. (*oscillation*) 314; transientness etc. 111.

[comparisons] moon, Proteus, kaleidoscope, chameleon, quicksilver, shifting sands, weathercock, vane, weathervane, harlequin, turncoat, Vicar of Bray, Cynthia of the minute, April showers; wheel of Fortune.

restlessness etc. *adj.;* fidgets, disquiet; disquietude, inquietude; unrest; agitation etc. 315.

v. **fluctuate**, vary, waver, flounder, flicker, flitter [*archaic*], flit, flutter, shift, shuffle, shake, totter, tremble, vacillate, wamble [*dial.*], turn and turn about, ring the changes; sway–, shift- to and fro; change and change about; oscillate etc. 314; vibrate–, oscillate- between two extremes; alternate; have as many phases as the moon.

adj. **changeable**, changeful; changing etc. 140; mutable, variable, checkered, ever changing, kaleidoscopic; protean, proteiform; versatile.

inconstant, unstaid, unsteady, unstable, unfixed, unsettled; fluctuating etc. *v.;* restless, uneasy; agitated etc. 315; erratic, fickle; mercurial, irresolute etc. 605; capricious etc. 608; touch and go; inconsonant, fitful, spasmodic; vibratory; vagrant, feathery [*rare*], lightheaded, wayward; desultory; afloat; alternating; alterable, plastic, mobile; transient etc. 111; wavering.

adv. **seesaw** etc. (*oscillation*) 314; off and on.

150. Stability

n. **stability**; immutability etc. *adj.;* unchangeableness etc. *adj.;* constancy; stable equilibrium, immobility, soundness, vitality, stabiliment [*rare*], stabilization; stiffness, ankylosis, solidity, *aplomb* [*F.*]; coherence.

permanence etc. 141; obstinacy etc. 606.

fixture, establishment; rock, pillar, tower, foundation, leopard's spots, Ethiopian's skin; law of the Medes and Persians.

standpatter [*politics*].

v. **be firm** etc. *adj.;* stick fast; stand firm, keep firm, remain firm; stand pat; weather the storm.

establish, settle, stablish [*archaic*], ascertain, fix, set, stabilitate [*obs.*], stabilize; stet [*printing*],

retain, keep hold; make good, make sure; fasten etc. (*join*) 43; set on its legs [*colloq.*], set on its feet; float; perpetuate.

settle down; strike root, take root; take up one's abode etc. 184; build one's house on a rock.

adj. **unchangeable**, immutable; unaltered, unalterable; not to be changed, constant; permanent etc. 141; invariable, unyielding, undeviating; stable, durable; perennial etc. (*diuturnal*) 110.

fixed, steadfast, firm, firm as Gibraltar, firm as a rock, on a rock; tethered, anchored, moored, at anchor, firmly -seated, –established etc. *v.;* deep-rooted, ineradicable; fast, steady, balanced; confirmed, inveterate, valid; fiducial; immovable, irremovable, reveted, rooted; stated, settled, stereotyped, established etc. *v.;* obstinate etc. 606; vested; incontrovertible, indeclinable.

stuck fast, transfixed, aground, high and dry, stranded.

incommutable, indefeasible, irretrievable, intransmutable, irresoluble, irrevocable, irreversible, reverseless, inextinguishable, irreducible; indissoluble, indissolvable; indestructible, undying, imperishable, indelible, indeciduous; insusceptible, –of change.

int. stet [*L., printing*].

151. Eventuality

n. **eventuality**, eventuation, event, occurrence, supervention, incident, affair, transaction, proceeding, fact; matter of fact, naked fact; phenomenon: advent.

circumstance, particular, casualty, accident, happening, adventure, passage, crisis, pass, emergency, contingency; concern, business.

consequence, issue, result, termination, conclusion.

affairs, matters; the world, life, things, doings; things–, affairs- in general; the times, state of affairs, order of the day; course–, tide–, stream–, current–, run–, march-of-things, –events; ups and downs of life; chapter of accidents etc. (*chance*) 156; situation etc. (*circumstances*) 8; memorabilia.

v. **happen**, occur; take place, take effect; come, become of; come -off, –about, –round, –into existence, –forth, –to pass, –on; pass, present itself; fall; fall out, turn out; run, be on foot, fall in; befall, betide, bechance; prove, eventuate, draw on; turn up, crop up, spring up, cast up; supervene, survene, [*obs.*] issue, arrive, ensue, result, eventuate, arise, start, hold, take its course; pass off etc. (*be past*) 122.

experience; meet with; fall to the lot of; be one's -chance, –fortune, –lot; find; encounter, undergo; pass through, go through; endure etc. (*feel*) 821.

adj. **happening** etc. *v.;* going on, doing, current; in the wind, afloat; on foot, on the carpet, on the tapis; at issue, in question; incidental.

eventful, stirring, bustling, full of incident; memorable, momentous, signal.

adv. **eventually**, ultimately, finally; in the event of, in case; in the course of things; in the natural *or* ordinary course of things; as things go, as times go; as the world -goes, –wags; as the tree falls, as the cat jumps [*colloq.*]; as it may -turn out, –happen.

152. Destiny

n. **destiny** etc. (*necessity*) 601; future existence, post-existence; hereafter; foredoom, future state, next world, world to come, after life; futurity etc. 121; everlasting life, everlasting death; life beyond the grave, life to come, world beyond the grave; prospect etc. (*expectation*) 507.

v. **impend**; hang over, lie over; threaten, loom, await, hover, come on, approach, stare one in the face; foreordain, preordain; predestine, doom, foredoom, have in store for.

adj. **impending** etc. *v.;* destined; about to be, about to happen; coming, in store, to come, going to happen, instant, at hand, near; near at hand, close at hand; overhanging, hanging over one's head, imminent; brewing, preparing, forthcoming; in the wind, in the cards [*colloq.*], in reserve; that will be, that is to be; in prospect etc. (*expected*) 507; looming in the -distance, –horizon, –future; postexistent, unborn, in embryo; in the womb of -time, futurity; on the knees of the gods, in the future; pregnant etc. (*producing*) 161.

adv. **in time**, in the long run; all in good time; eventually etc. 151; whatever may happen etc. (*certainly*) 474; as chance etc. (156) would have it.

Section 8. Causation

153. Cause

[constant antecedent]

n. **cause**, origin, source, principle, element; prime mover, *primum mobile* [*L.*], primordium [*rare*]; *vera causa* [*L.*], ultimate cause, Great First Cause; author etc. (*producer*) 164; mainspring, agent; leaven; groundwork, foundation etc. (*support*) 215.

spring, fountain, well, font; fountainhead, springhead, reservoir, headspring, wellspring,

wellhead; *fons et origo* [*L.*], genesis; descent etc. (*paternity*) 166; remote cause; influence.

pivot, hinge, turning point, lever; key; heart, nucleus, hub, focus; proximate cause, *causa causans* [*L.*]; the straw that breaks the camel's back.

reason, reason why; ground; why and wherefore [*colloq.*], rationale, occasion, derivation; final cause etc. (*intention*) 620; *les dessous des cartes* [*F.*]; undercurrents.

rudiment, egg, germ, embryo, fetus, bud, root, radix, radical, radication [*rare*], etymon, nucleus, seed, stem, stock, stirps, trunk, taproot, gemma, gemmule, radicle, semen, sperm.

nest, cradle, nursery, womb, nidus, birthplace, breeding-place, hotbed.

causality, causation; origination; causative; production etc. 161.

v. **be the cause of** etc. *n.;* originate; give origin to, give rise to, give occasion to; cause, occasion, sow the seeds of, kindle, suscitate [*obs.*]; bring on, bring to pass, bring about; produce; create etc. 161; set up, set afloat, set on foot; found, broach, institute, lay the foundation of; lie at the root of.

procure, induce, draw down, open the door to, superinduce, evoke, entail, operate; elicit, provoke.

contribute; conduce to etc. (*tend to*) 176; have a hand in; have a finger in the pie [*colloq.*]; determine, decide, turn the scale, have the deciding vote, have the final word; have a common origin; derive its origin etc. (*effect*) 154.

adj. **caused** etc. *v.;* causal, aetiological *or* etiological, original; primary, primitive, primordial; aboriginal; originative, generative, inceptive, productive, creative, constitutive, procreative, formative, demiurgic, protogenic, protogenal; radical; in embryo, embryonic, embryotic; *in ovo* [*L.*]; seminal, germinal; at the bottom of; connate, having a common origin.

adv. **from the beginning**, in the first place, before everything; because etc. 155; behind the scenes.

154. Effect

[constant sequent]

n. **effect**, consequence; aftercome [*Scot.*], aftergrowth, afterclap, aftermath, aftercrop, derivative, derivation; result; resultant; upshot, issue, outcome, resultance [*rare*], *dénouement* [*F.*], conclusion; falling action, catastrophe, end etc. 67; impress, impression; development, outgrowth; blossom, bud, ear, fruit, crop, harvest, product.

production, produce, work, handiwork, fabric, performance; creature, creation; offspring, off-shoot; first fruits, firstlings; heredity, telegony; premices [*obs.*], primices [*obs.*].

v. **be the effect of** etc. *n.;* be due to, be owing to; originate in *or* from; rise from, arise from, take its rise from, spring from, proceed from, emanate from, come from, grow from, bud from, sprout from, germinate from, issue from, flow from, result from, follow from, derive its origin from, accrue from; come to, come of, come out of; depend upon, hang upon, hinge upon, turn upon.

take the consequences, reap where one has sown, make one's bed and lie on it, sow the wind and reap the whirlwind.

adj. **owing to**; resulting from etc. *v.;* resultant, firstling; derivable from; due to; caused by etc. 153; dependent upon; derived from, evolved from; derivative; hereditary; telegonous.

adv. **consequently**, of course, it follows that, naturally; as a consequence, in consequence; through, necessarily, eventually.

155.   Attribution
[assignment of cause]

n.   **attribution**, theory, ascription, assignment, reference to, rationale; accounting for etc. *v.;* etiology, imputation, derivation from.
   filiation, affiliation; filiality; pedigree etc. (*paternity*) 166.
   explanation etc. (*interpretation*) 522; reason why etc. (*cause*) 153.

v.   **attribute to**, ascribe to, impute to, refer to, lay to, point to, trace to, bring home to; put down to, set down to; blame; blame upon [*colloq.*]; charge on, ground on; invest with, assign as cause, lay at the door of, father upon, saddle, filiate, affiliate; account for, derive from, point out the reason etc. 153; theorize; tell how it comes; put the saddle on the right horse; find the real culprit.

adj.   **attributed** etc. *v.;* attributable etc. *v.;* referable *or* referrible; due to, derivable from; affiliate, derivate [*rare*]; owing to etc. (*effect*) 154; putative; ecbatic.

adv.   **hence**, thence, therefore, for, since, on account of, because, owing to; on that account; from this cause, from that cause; thanks to, forasmuch as; whence, *propter hoc* [*L.*].
   why? wherefore? whence? how comes it? how is it? how happens it? how come? [*colloq.*] how does it happen? how so?

in some way, in some such way; somehow, somehow or other.

156.   Chance[1]
[absence of assignable cause]

n.   **chance**, indetermination, accident, fortune, hazard, hap [*rare*], haphazard, chance-medley, random, luck, *raccroc* [*F.*], fluke [*cant*], casualty, fortuity, contingence, adventure, hit; fate etc. (*necessity*) 601; equal chance; lottery; tombola; lotto; toss-up [*colloq.*] etc. 621; turn of the -table, −cards; hazard of the die, chapter of accidents; cast-, throw- of the dice; heads or tails, wheel of Fortune; *sortes* [*L.*], *sortes Virgilianoe* [*L.*].
   probability, possibility, contingency, odds, long odds, run of luck; accidentalness, accidentalism, accidentality; main chance.
   theory of -probabilities, −chances; bookmaking; assurance; gamble, speculation, gaming etc. 621.

v.   **chance**, hap, turn up; fall to one's lot; be one's fate etc. 601; stumble on, light upon; blunder upon, hit, hit upon; take one's chance etc. 621.

adj.   **casual**, fortuitous, accidental, chance, chanceable [*archaic*], chanceful [*archaic*], haphazard, random, casual, adventive, adventitious, causeless, incidental, contingent, uncaused, undetermined, indeterminate; possible etc. 470; unintentional etc. 621.

adv.   **by chance**, by accident; at random, casually; perchance etc. (*possibly*), 470; for aught one knows; as -good, −bad, −ill-luck etc. *n.*- would have it; as it may -be, −chance, −turn up, − happen; as the case may be.

[1]The word *Chance* has two distinct meanings: the first, the absence of assignable *cause*, as above; and the second, the absence of *design*—for the latter see 621.

157.   Power

n.   **power**; potency, potentiality; jiva [*theos.*]; puissance, might, force; energy etc. 171; dint; right hand, right arm; ascendancy, sway, control; prepotency, prepollence *or* prepollency [*rare*]; almightiness, omnipotence; *carte blanche* [*F.*], authority etc. 737; strength etc. 159; predominance.
   ability; ableness etc. *adj.;* competency; efficiency, efficacy; validity, cogency; enablement; vantage ground; influence etc. 175.
   pressure, electromotive force, high pressure; conductivity; elasticity; gravity, electricity, magnetism, magneto-electricity, galvanism, voltaic electricity, voltaism, electromagnetism,

electrostatics, electrokinetics, electrodynamics; electromotion, electrification; magnetization, galvanization; attraction, pull; *vis inertiae* [*L.*], *vis mortua* [*L.*], *vis viva* [*L.*]; potential–, dynamic- energy; friction, suction; live-circuit, –rail, –wire; volt, voltage.

[instruments] galvanometer, rheometer; variometer, magnetometer, magnetoscope, electrometer, electroscope, galvanoscope, electrophorus, electrodynamometer, voltameter, ammeter, voltammeter, voltmeter, wattmeter.

capability, capacity; *quid valeant humeri quid ferre recusent* [*L.*]; faculty, quality, attribute, endowment, virtue, gift, property, qualification, susceptibility.

v. **be powerful** etc. *adj.;* gain power etc. *n.*

belong to, pertain to; lie–, be- in one's power; can.

empower; give–, confer–, exercise-power etc. *n.;* enable, invest; indue, endue; endow, arm; strengthen etc. 159; compel etc. 744.

electrify, magnetize, energize, galvanize, attract.

adj. **powerful**, puissant; potent, potential [*rare*]; capable, able; equal to, up to; cogent, valid; effective, effectual; efficient, efficacious, adequate, competent; multipotent [*rare*], plenipotent [*rare*], prepollent [*rare*], predominant; mighty, ascendent, prepotent, omnipotent, armipotent, mightful [*archaic*]; almighty.

forcible etc. *adj.* (*energetic*) 171; influential etc. 175; productive etc. 168.

electric, electrodynamic, electrokinetic, electromagnetic, electrometric, electrometrical, electromotive, electronegative, electropositive, electroscopic; magnetic, magneto-electric *or* magneto-electrical, magnetomotive; voltametric, voltaic; galvanic, galvanometric, galvanoscopic, dynamo-electric *or* dynamo-electrical; dynamic, static, potential.

adv. **powerfully** etc. *adj.;* by virtue of, by dint of.

158. Impotence

n. **impotence**; inability, disability; disablement, impuissance [*rare*], caducity, imbecility; incapacity, incapability; inaptitude, ineptitude; indocility; invalidity, inefficiency, incompetence, disqualification.

telum imbelle [*L.*], *brutum fulmen* [*L.*], blank cartridge, flash in the pan, *vox et praeterea nihil* [*L.*], dead letter, bit of waste paper, dummy; Quaker gun; cripple.

inefficacy etc. (*inutility*) 645; failure etc. 732.

helplessness etc. *adj.;* prostration, paralysis, palsy, apoplexy, syncope, sideration [*obs.*], vincibility, vincibleness, deliquium, collapse, exhaustion, softening of the brain, senility, superannuation, atony, decrepitude, imbecility, neurasthenia, invertebracy, inanition; emasculation, orchotomy; eunuch.

mollycoddle, old woman, muff [*colloq.*], tenderling [*rare*], milksop, molly [*colloq.*], sissy [*colloq.*], mother's darling.

v. **be impotent** etc. *adj.;* not have a leg to stand on. *vouloir rompre l'anguille au genou* [*F.*], *vouloir prendre la lune avec les dents* [*F.*].

collapse, faint, swoon, fall into a swoon, drop; go by the board; end in smoke etc. (*fail*) 732.

render powerless etc. *adj.;* depotentiate [*rare*], deprive of power; disable, disenable; disarm, incapacitate, disqualify, unfit, invalidate, disinvigorate [*rare*], undermine, deaden, cramp, tie the hands; double up, prostrate, paralyze, muzzle, cripple, becripple, maim, lame, hamstring, unsinew [*rare*], draw the teeth of; throttle, strangle, garrote *or* garrotte, ratten [*trade-union cant*], silence, sprain, clip the wings of, put *hors de combat* [*F.*], spike the guns; take the wind out of one's sails, scotch the snake, put a spoke in one's wheel; break the -neck, –back; unhinge, unfit; put out of gear.

unman, unnerve, devitalize, effeminize, attenuate, enervate; emasculate, evirate [*rare*], spay, eunuchize [*rare*], caponize, castrate, geld, alter.

shatter, exhaust; weaken etc. 160.

adj. **powerless**, impotent, unable, incapable, incompetent; inefficient, ineffective; inept; unfit, unfitted; unqualified, disqualified; unendowed; doddering [*colloq.*], wambly [*Scot. and dial. Eng.*], inapt, unapt; crippled, disabled etc. *v.;* armless; senile, decrepit, superannuated.

harmless, unarmed, weaponless, defenseless, *sine ictu* [*L.*], unfortified, mightless [*archaic*], indefensible, vincible, pregnable, untenable.

paralytic, paralyzed; palsied, imbecile; nerveless, sinewless, marrowless, pithless, lustless; emasculate, disjointed; out of joint, out of gear; unnerved, unhinged; waterlogged, on one's beam ends, rudderless; laid on one's back; done up [*colloq.*], done for [*colloq.*], done brown [*colloq.*], done [*colloq.*], dead-beat [*colloq.*], exhausted, shattered, atonic, demoralized; graveled [*colloq.*] etc. (*in difficulty*) 704; helpless, unfriended, fatherless; without a leg to stand on, *hors de combat* [*F.*], laid on the shelf.

nugatory, null and void, inoperative, good for nothing, invertebrate, ineffectual etc. (*failing*) 732; inadequate etc. 640; inefficacious etc. (*useless*) 645.

159. Strength

[degree of power]

n. **strength**; power etc. 157; energy etc. 171; vigor, force; main–, physical–, brute- force; spring, elasticity, tone, tension, tonicity.

[comparisons] adamant, steel, iron, oak, heart of oak; iron grip; bone.

virility, vitality; stoutness etc. *adj.;* lustihood, stamina, nerve, muscle, sinew *or* sinews, thews and sinews, physique; grit, pith, pithiness.

athletics, athleticism; gymnastics, acrobatism, agonistics, feats of strength.

athlete, gymnast, pancratiast, acrobat; Atlas, Hercules, Antaeus, Samson, Cyclops, Briareus, Colossus, Polyphemus, Titan, Brobdingnagian, Goliath; tower of strength; giant refreshed

strengthening etc. *v.;* invigoration, refreshment, refocillation [*obs.*].

[science of forces] dynamics, statics.

v. **be strong** etc. *adj.,* be stronger; overmatch.

render strong etc. *adj.;* give strength etc. *n.;* strengthen, invigorate, potentiate [*rare*], brace, nerve, fortify, buttress, sustain, harden, case-harden, steel, gird; screw up, wind up, set up; gird–, brace-up one's loins; recruit, set on one's legs [*colloq.*]; vivify; refresh etc. 689; refect [*archaic*], reinforce *or* reënforce etc. (*restore*) 660.

adj. **strong**, mighty, vigorous, forcible, hard, adamantine, stout, robust, sturdy, husky, doughty, hardy, powerful, potent, puissant, valid.

resistless, irresistible, invincible, proof against, impregnable, unconquerable, indomitable, inextinguishable, unquenchable; incontestable; more than a match for; overpowering, overwhelming; all-powerful, all-sufficient; sovereign.

able-bodied; athletic, gymnastic, carobatic, agonistic, palaestral [*rare*]; Herculean, Briarean, Brobdingnagian, Titanic, Cyclopean, Atlantean; muscular, brawny, wiry, well-knit, broad-shouldered, sinewy, sinewous [*rare*], strapping, stalwart, gigantic.

manly, manlike, manful; masculine, male, virile, in the prime of manhood.

unweakened, unallayed, unwithered, unshaken, unworn, unexhausted; in full force, in full swing; in the plentitude of power.

sound; stubborn, thick-ribbed, made of iron, deep-rooted; strong as a -lion, –an ox, –a horse -brandy; sound as a roach; in fine feather, in high feather [*both colloq.*]; like a giant refreshed.

adv. **strongly** etc. *adj.;* by force etc. *n.;* by main force etc. (*by compulsion*) 744.

160. Weakness

n. **weakness** etc. *adj.;* debility, atony, relaxation, languor, enervation; impotence etc. 158; infirmity, effeminacy, feminality; fragility, flaccidity; inactivity etc. 683.

[comparisons] reed, thread, rope of sand, house of cards, house built on sand.

anemia, bloodlessness, deficiency of blood, poverty of blood.

invalidation; declension–, loss–, failure- of strength; delicacy, decrepitude, asthenia, adynamy [*rare*], cachexia *or* cachexy, sprain, strain.

weakling; softling [*obs.*]; infant etc. 129; youth etc. 127.

v. **be weak** etc. *adj.;* drop, crumble, give way, totter, dodder, tremble, shake, halt, limp, fade, languish, decline, flag, fail, have one foot in the grave.

render weak etc. *adj.;* weaken, enfeeble, debilitate, invalidate, shake, deprive of strength, relax, enervate; unbrace, unnerve; cripple, unman etc. (*render powerless*) 158; cramp, reduce, sprain, strain, blunt the edge of; dilute, impoverish; decimate; extenuate; reduce in strength, reduce the strength of; *mettre de l'eau dans son vin* [*F.*].

adj. **weak**, feeble, debile [*obs.*]; impotent etc. 158; relaxed, unnerved etc. *v.;* sapless, strengthless, powerless; weakly, unstrung, flaccid, adynamic, asthenic; nervous.

soft, effeminate, feminate [*obs.*], womanish.

frail, fragile, shattery; flimsy, sleazy, gossamery, papery, unsubstantial, gimcrack, gingerbread; rickety, jerry-built, *kucha or kachcha* [*Hind.*], cranky; craichy [*dial. Eng.*], drooping, tottering, doddering [*colloq.*] etc. *v.;* broken, lame, withered, shattered, shaken, crazy, shaky, tumbledown; palsied etc. 158; decrepit.

unsound, poor, infirm; faint, faintish; sickly etc. (*disease*) 655; dull, slack, evanid [*obs.*], languid; spent, short-winded, effete; weather-beaten; decayed, rotten, forworn [*archaic*], worn, seedy, languishing, wasted, washy, wishy-washy [*colloq.*], laid low, pulled down, the worse for wear.

unstrengthened etc. 159, unsupported, unaided, unassisted; aidless, defenseless etc. 158.

on its last legs; weak as a -child, –baby, –chicken, –cat, –rat, –rag; weak as -water, –water gruel, –gingerbread, –milk and water; colorless etc. 429.

161. Production

n. **production**, creation, construction, formation, fabrication, manufacture; building, architecture, erection, edification; coinage; disaster; organization; *nisus formativus* [*L.*]; putting together etc. *v.;* establishment; workmanship, performance; achievement etc. (*completion*) 729.

flowering, fructification, fruition; inflorescence.

bringing forth etc. *v.;* parturition, birth, birth throe, childbirth, delivery, confinement, *accouchement* [*F.*], travail, labor, midwifery, obstetrics; geniture [*obs.*]; gestation etc. (*maturation*) 673; assimilation; evolution, development, growth; entelechy; fertilization, gemination, germination, heterogamy, genesis, generation, histogenesis, breeding, begetting, isogamy, epigenesis, procreation, progeneration, propagation; fecundation, impregnation; albumen etc. 357.

spontaneous generation; archigenesis, archebiosis, abiogenesis, biogenesis, biogeny, dysmerogenesis, eumerogenesis, heterogenesis, oögenesis, merogenesis, metogenesis, monogenesis, parthenogenesis, homogenesis, xenogenesis.

dissogeny, digenesis, physiogeny, phylogeny, ontogeny, ontogenesis, mitosis, xenogeny; theogony, tocogony, tocology, vacuolation, vacuolization.

publication; works, *oeuvres* [*F.*], opus (*pl.* opera) [*L.*]; authorship

structure, building, edifice, fabric, erection, pile, tower; flower, fruit, blossom.

v. **produce**, perform, operate, do, make, gar [*obs.*], form, construct, fabricate, frame, contrive, manufacture; weave, forge, coin, carve, chisel; build, raise, edify, rear, erect, put together; set up, run up; establish, constitute, compose, organize, institute; achieve, accomplish etc. (*complete*) 729.

flower, burgeon, blossom, bear fruit, fructify, teem, ean [*obs.*], yean, farrow, drop, pup, whelp, kitten, kindle [*obs.*], spawn, spat; bear, lay, bring forth, give birth to, lie in, be brought to bed of, evolve, pullulate, usher into the world.

make productive etc. 168; create; beget, get, generate, fecundate, impregnate; procreate, progenerate, propagate; engender; bring–, call-into -being, –existence; breed, hatch, develop, bring up.

induce, superinduce; suscitate [*obs.*]; cause etc. 153; acquire etc. 775.

adj. **produced, producing** etc. *v.*, productive of; prolific etc. 168; creative; formative; procreant, generative, genitive, genetic, genial [*rare*], genital; pregnant; *enceinte* [*F.*], big with, fraught with; in the family way [*colloq.*], teeming, parturient, in the straw [*colloq.*], brought to bed of; lying-in; puerperal, puerperous [*rare*].

digenetic, heterogenetic, oögenetic, xenogenetic; ectogenous, gamic, hematobious, sporogenous, sporophorous.

architectonic *or* architectonical, constructive.

162. Destruction
[nonproduction]

n. **destruction**; waste, dissolution, breaking up; disruption; diruption [*obs.*], consumption; disorganization.

fall, downfall, ruin, perdition, debacle, *débâcle* [*F.*], crash, *éboulement* [*F.*], smash [*colloq.*], havoc, *délabrement* [*F.*], breakdown, break-up; prostration, cave-in [*colloq.*]; desolation, *bouleversement* [*F.*], wreck, wrack [*archaic*], shipwreck, cataclysm; washout.

extinction, annihilation; destruction of life etc. 361; knock-out, K. O. [*slang*], knock-out blow, knock-down blow; doom, crack of doom.

destroying etc. *v.;* demolition, demolishment [*rare*], overthrow, subversion, suppression; abolition etc. (*abrogation*) 756; biblioclasm; sacrifice; ravage, devastation, razzia; incendiarism; revolution etc. 146; extirpation etc. (*extraction*) 301; *commencement de la fin* [*F.*], road to ruin; dilapidation etc. (*deterioration*) 659; *sabotage* [*F.*].

v. **be destroyed** etc.; perish; fall, fall to the ground; tumble, topple; go–, fall- to pieces; break up; crumble, –to dust; go to -the dogs, –the wall, –smash, –shivers, –wreck, –pot [*colloq.*], –wrack and ruin; go by the board, go down the drain [*colloq.*]; be all over with, be all up with [*colloq.*], go to glory [*colloq.*], go to pieces, go under, go up the spout [*colloq.*], totter to its fall.

destroy; do–, make- away with nullify; annul etc. 756; sacrifice, demolish; tear up; overturn, overthrow, overwhelm; upset, subvert, put an end to seal the doom of, do for [*colloq.*], dish [*slang*], undo; break up, cut up; break down, cut down, pull down, mow down, blow down, beat down; suppress, quash, put down; cut short, take off, blot out; efface, obliterate, cancel, erase, strike out, expunge, delete, dele; dispel, dissipate, dissolve; consume.

smash, crash, quell, squash [*colloq.*], squelch [*colloq.*], crumple up, shatter, shiver; batter;

tear–, crush–, cut–, shake–, pull–, pick -to pieces; laniate [*rare*]; nip; tear to -rags, –tatters; crush–, knock- to atoms; ruin; strike out; throw down, throw over, knock down, knock over, lay out [*slang*], lay by the heels, fell, sink, swamp, scuttle, wreck, shipwreck, engulf *or* ingulf, submerge; lay in ashes, lay in ruins; sweep away, raze; level, –with the -ground, –dust.

deal destruction, lay waste, ravage, gut; disorganize; dismantle etc. (*render useless*) 645; devour, swallow up, desolate, devastate, sap, mine, blast, confound; exterminate, extinguish, quench, annihilate; snuff out, put out, stamp out, trample out; lay–, trample- in the dust; prostrate; tread–, crush–, trample- under foot; lay the ax to the root of; make short work of, make a clean sweep of, make mincemeat of; cut up root and branch; fling–, scatter- to the winds; throw overboard; strike at the root of, sap the foundations of, spring a mine, blow up; ravage with fire and sword; cast to the dogs; eradicate etc. 301.

adj. **destroyed** etc. *v.;* perishing etc. *v.;* trembling–, nodding–, tottering- to its fall; in course of destruction etc. *n.;* extinct; all-destroying, all-devouring, all-engulfing.

destructive, subversive, ruinous, incendiary, deletory [*obs.*]; destroying etc. *n.;* suicidal; deadly etc. (*killing*) 361.

adv. with crushing effect, with a sledge hammer.

163. Reproduction

n. **reproduction,** renovation; restoration etc. 660; renewal; new edition, reprint etc. (*copy*) 21; revival, regeneration, palingenesis, revivification; apotheosis; resuscitation, reanimation, resurrection, resurgence, reappearance; regrowth; Phoenix.

generation etc. (*production*) 161; multiplication.

v. **reproduce;** restore etc. 660; revive, renovate, renew, regenerate, revivify, resuscitate, reanimate, refashion, stir the embers, put into the crucible; multiply, repeat; resurge.

crop up, crop out, spring up like mushrooms.

adj. **reproduced** etc. *v.;* renascent, resurgent, reappearing; reproductive, proligerous [*rare*], progenitive, proliferous, gametal; hydra-headed; suigenetic.

164. Producer

n. **producer,** originator, inventor, author, founder, generator, mover, architect, grower, raiser, introducer, deviser, constructor, begetter, creator; maker etc. (*agent*) 690; prime mover.

165. Destroyer

n. **destroyer** etc. (*destroy* etc. 162); cankerworm etc. (*bane*) 663; assassin etc. (*killer*) 361; executioner etc. (*punish*) 975; biblioclast; eidoloclast, iconoclast, idoloclast; vandal, destructor [*rare*], Hun, nihilist.

166. Paternity

n. **paternity;** parentage; consanguínity etc. 11.

parent, father, sire, dad, papa, governor [*Engl. slang*], pater [*Engl. colloq.*], daddy [*colloq.*], paterfamilias, abba; genitor [*rare*], progenitor, procreator, begetter; ancestor; grandsire, grandfather; great-grandfather; fathership, fatherhood; *mabap* [*Hind.*].

motherhood, maternity, motherhead [*rare*], mothership; mother, dam, mamma *or* mama, mammy, mam [*colloq.*], motherkin, matriarch, materfamilias; grandmother.

stem, trunk, tree, stock, stirps, pedigree, house, lineage, line, family, tribe, sept, race, clan; genealogy, family tree, descent, extraction, birth, ancestry; forefathers, forbears, patriarchs.

adj. **parental;** paternal; maternal; family, ancestral, linear, patriarchal; racial, phyletic.

167. Posterity

n. **posterity,** progeny, breed, issue, offspring, brood, litter, seed, farrow, spawn, spat; family, children, grandchildren, heirs; great-grandchildren.

child, son, daughter, bairn, baby, kid [*colloq.*], papoose [*Am. Ind.*], imp, brat, moppet [*archaic*], lambkin, cub, cherub, nestling, tot, innocent, urchin, chit [*colloq.*]; infant etc. 129; *butcha or bacha* [*Hind.*]; bantling, scion; acrospire, plumule, shoot, sprout, olive-branch, sprit, branch; offshoot, offset; ramification; descendant; heir, heiress; heir-apparent, heir-presumptive; chip of the old block; heredity; rising generation.

lineage, straight descent, sonship, line, filiation, primogeniture.

adj. **filial;** diphyletic.

168. Productiveness

n. **productiveness** etc. *adj.;* fecundity, fertilization, fertility, luxuriance, uberty [*obs.*].

[comparisons] milch cow, rabbit, hydra, warren, seed plot, land flowing with milk and honey.

aftermath, second crop, aftercrop, aftergrowth, arrish [*dial. Eng.*], eddish [*dial. Eng.*], rowen.

multiplication, multiparity, propagation, procreation; superfetation, pregnancy, pullulation [*rare*], fructification.

v. **make productive** etc. *adj.;* fructify; procreate, pullulate, generate, fertilize, spermatize, impregnate; fecundate, fecundify; teem, spawn, multiply; produce etc. 161; conceive.

adj. **productive**, prolific, copious; teeming, teemful [*dial.*]; fertile, fruitful, frugiferous [*obs.*], fructuous [*rare*], plenteous, proliferous, fructiferous, fruitbearing; fecund, luxuriant; pregnant, uberous.

procreant, procreative; generative, life-giving, spermatic, inceptive, originative; multiparous; omnific; propagable.

parturient etc. (*producing*) 161; profitable etc. (*useful*) 644.

169. Unproductiveness

n. **unproductiveness** etc. *adj.;* infertility, sterility, infecundity; impotence etc. 158; unprofitableness etc. (*inutility*) 645.

waste, desert, Sahara, wild, karoo, wilderness, howling wilderness.

v. **be unproductive** etc. *adj.;* hang fire, flash in the pan, come to nothing.

adj. **unproductive**, acarpous, inoperative, barren, addle, unfertile, unprolific, arid, sterile, unfruitful, infecund, [*rare*], jejune, infertile; useless, otiose; *sine prole* [*L.*]; fallow; teemless, issueless, fruitless, infructuose [*rare*]; unprofitable etc. (*useless*) 645; null and void, of no effect.

170. Agency

n. **agency**, operation, force, working, strain, function, office, maintenance, exercise, work, swing, play; interworking, interaction; procuration procurement.

causation etc. 153; mediation, intermediation, instrumentality etc. 631; conation, influence etc. 175; action etc. (*voluntary*) 680; *modus operandi* [*L.*] etc. 627.

quickening–, maintaining–, sustaining- power; home stroke.

v. **be in action** etc. *adj.;* operate, work; act, act upon; perform, play, support, sustain, strain, maintain, take effect, quicken, strike.

come–, bring- into -operation, –play; have play, have free play; bring to bear upon.

adj. **operative**, operant [*rare*], efficient, efficacious, practical, exertive, conative, effectual.

at work, on foot; acting etc. (*doing*) 680; in operation, in force, in action, in play, in exercise; acted upon, wrought upon.

adv. **by the agency of** etc. *n.;* through etc. (*instrumentality*) 631; by means of etc. 632.

171. Energy

n. **energy**, physical energy, force; keenness etc. *adj.;* intensity, vigor, backbone [*colloq.*], vim [*colloq.*], mettle, *vis viva* [*L.*], *vis vitae* [*L.*], pep [*slang*], ginger [*slang*], go [*colloq.*]; strength, elasticity; high pressure; fire; rush; human dynamo.

activity, agitation, effervescence; ferment, fermentation; ebullition, splutter, perturbation, stir, bustle; voluntary energy etc. 682; quicksilver.

exertion etc. (*effort*) 686; excitation etc. (*mental*) 824; resolution etc. (*mental energy*) 604.

acrimony, acridity, acritude [*obs.*]; causticity, virulence, poignancy; harshness etc. *adj.;* severity, edge, point; pungency etc. 392.

excitant, stimulant; Spanish fly, cantharides; seasoning etc. (*condiment*) 393.

v. **give energy** etc. *n.;* energize, stimulate, kindle, excite, exert; activate, potentialize [*rare*], dynamize, doubleshot; sharpen, intensify; inflame etc. (*render violent*) 173; wind up etc. (*strengthen*) 159.

strike, –into, –hard, –home; make an impression.

adj. **energetic**, strong, forcible, active, strenuous, forceful, mettlesome, enterprising; go-ahead [*colloq.*]; intense, deep-dyed, severe, keen, vivid, sharp, acute, incisive, trenchant, brisk.

rousing, irritating; poignant; virulent, caustic, corrosive, mordant, harsh, stringent; double-edged, double-shotted, double-distilled; drastic, escharotic; racy etc. (*pungent*) 392; excitant, excitative, excitatory.

potent etc. (*powerful*) 157; radioactive.

adv. **strongly** etc. *adj.; fortiter in re* [*L.*]; with telling effect.

172. Inertness

n. **inertness**, physical inertness, inertia, *vis inertiae* [*L.*], inertion, inactivity, torpor, languor; dormancy, *fainéance* [*F.*], quiescence etc. 265; latency, inaction; passivity; stagnation; dullness etc. *adj.*

mental inertness; sloth etc. (*inactivity*) 683; inexcitability etc. 826; irresolution etc. 605; obstinacy etc. 606; permanence etc. 141.

v. **be inert** etc. *adj.;* hang fire, smolder *or* smoulder.

adj. **inert**, inactive, passive; torpid etc. 683; sluggish, stagnant, *fainéant* [*F.*], dull, heavy, flat, slack, tame, slow, blunt; lifeless, dead, uninfluential.

latent, dormant, smoldering *or* smouldering, unexerted.

adv. **inactively** etc. *adj.;* in suspense, in abeyance.

173. Violence

n. **violence,** inclemency, vehemence, might, impetuosity, furiosity [*rare*]; boisterousness etc. *adj.;* effervescence, ebullition; turbulence, bluster; uproar, callithump, riot, row [*colloq.*], rumpus, *le diable à quatre* [*F.*], devil to pay [*colloq.*], the fat in the fire [*colloq.*].

ferocity, rage, fury; exacerbation, exasperation, malignity; severity etc. 739.

force, brute force; outrage, *coup de main* [*F.*]; strain, shock, shog [*rare*].

fit, paroxysm, spasm, convulsion, throe; hysterics, passion etc. (*state of excitability*) 825; orgasm, aphrodisia.

outbreak, outburst; debacle; burst, bounce, dissilience [*rare*], discharge, volley, explosion, blow-up, blast, detonation, rush, eruption, displosion [*obs.*], torrent.

turmoil etc. (*disorder*) 59; ferment etc. (*agitation*) 315; storm, tempest, rough weather; squall etc. (*wind*) 349; earthquake, volcano, thunderstorm.

fury, berserk, dragon, demon, tiger, beldam *or* beldame, madcap, wild beast; fire eater [*colloq.*] etc. (*blusterer*) 887; Erinys (*pl.* Erinyes), Eumenides, Tisiphone, Megaera, Alecto.

v. **be violent** etc. *adj.;* run high; ferment, effervesce; romp, rampage; run wild, run riot; break the peace; rush, tear; rush headlong, rush headforemost; run amuck, raise a storm, make a riot; make–, kick up– a row [*colloq.*]; rough-house [*slang*]; bluster, rage, roar, riot, storm; boil, boil over; fume, foam, come in like a lion, wreak, bear down, ride roughshod, out-Herod Herod; spread like wildfire.

explode, go off, displode [*obs.*], detonate, detonize, fulminate, let off, let fly, discharge, thunder, blow up, flash, flare, burst; shock, strain.

break open, force open, prize open, pry open; break out, fly out, burst out.

render violent etc. *adj.;* sharpen, stir up, quicken, excite, incite, urge, lash, stimulate; irritate, inflame, kindle, suscitate [*obs.*], foment; accelerate, aggravate, exasperate, exacerbate, convulse, infuriate, madden, lash into fury; fan the flame, add fuel to the flame; *oleum addere camino* [*L.*].

adj. **violent,** vehement; warm; acute, sharp; rough, tough [*colloq.*], vicious [*colloq.*], rude, ungentle, bluff, boisterous, wild; brusque, abrupt, waspish; impetuous; rampant.

turbulent; disorderly; blustering, towering, raging etc. *v.;* troublous, riotous; tumultuary, tumultuous; obstreperous, uproarious; extravagant; unmitigated, immitigable; ravening, tameless; frenzied etc. (*insane*) 503; desperate etc. (*rash*) 863; infuriate, furious, outrageous, frantic, hysteric, in hysterics.

fiery, flaming, scorching, hot, red-hot, ebullient.

savage, fierce, ferocious, fierce as a tiger.

excited etc. *v.;* unquelled, unquenched, unextinguished, unrepressed, unbridled, unruly; headstrong; ungovernable, unappeasable, unmitigable; uncontrollable, incontrollable; insuppressible, irrepressible; orgastic.

spasmodic, convulsive, explosive; detonating etc. *v.;* volcanic, meteoric; stormy etc. (*wind*) 349.

adv. **violently** etc. *adj.;* amain; by storm, by force, by main force; with might and main; tooth and nail, *vi et armis* [*L.*], at the point of the -sword, –bayonet; at one fell swoop; with a high hand, through thick and thin; in desperation, with a vengeance; *à outrance* [*F.*], *à toute outrance* [*F.*]; headlong, headfirst, headforemost.

aphrodisiac, aphrodisiacal, aphroditous.

174. Moderation

n. **moderation;** lenity etc. 740; temperateness, temperance, passability, passableness, gentleness etc. *adj.;* sobriety; quiet; mental calmness etc. (*inexcitability*) 826.

moderating etc. *v.;* anaphrodisia; relaxation, remission, mitigation, tranquilization, assuagement, alleviation, contemperation [*obs.*], pacification.

mean, measure, *juste milieu* [*F.*], golden mean, *meden agan* [*Gr.*], *ariston metron* [*Gr.*].

moderator; lullaby, sedative, calmative, lenitive, palliative, demulcent, antispasmodic, carminative; laudanum; rose water, balm, poppy, chloroform, opium: soothing sirup, opiate, anodyne, milk.

v. **be moderate** etc. *adj.;* keep within -bounds, –compass; sober down, settle down; keep the peace, remit, relent; take in sail.

moderate, soften, mitigate, temper, accoy [*obs.*]; attemper, contemper [*obs.*], mollify, lenify [*rare*], dulcify, dull, take off the edge, blunt, obtund, sheathe, subdue, chasten; sober down, tone down, smooth down, slow down; weaken etc. 160; lessen etc. (*decrease*) 36; check; palliate.

tranquilize, assuage, appease, suage *or* swage [*dial.*], lull, soothe, compose, still, calm, cool, quiet, hush, quell, sober, pacify, tame, damp, lay, allay, rebate [*archaic*], slacken, smooth, alleviate, rock to sleep, deaden, smother; throw cold water on, throw a wet blanket over; slake; curb etc. (*restrain*) 751; tame etc. (*subjugate*) 749; smooth over; pour oil on the -waves, –troubled waters; pour balm into; *mettre de l'eau dans son vin* [*F.*].

go out like a lamb, "roar you as gently as any sucking dove" [*Midsummer Night's Dream*].

adj. **moderate**; lenient etc. 740; gentle, mild; cool, sober, temperate, reasonable, measured; tempered etc. *v.;* calm, laid back [*slang*], unruffled, quiet, tranquil, still; slow, smooth, untroubled; tame; peaceful, peaceable; pacific, halcyon.

unexciting, unirritating; soft, bland, oily, demulcent, lenitive, anodyne; hypnotic etc. 683; sedative, calmative, assuaging, assuasive, calmant; antiorgastic, anaphrodisiac.

mild as mother's milk, mild as milk, milk and water, gentle as a lamb.

adv. **moderately** etc. *adj.;* gingerly; piano; under easy sail, at half speed, in moderation; within bounds, within compass; in reason.

175. Influence

n. **influence**; importance etc. 642; weight, pressure, preponderance, prevalence, sway; predominance, predominancy; ascendancy; dominance, reign; control, domination, pull [*colloq.*]; authority etc. 737; power, potency, capability etc. (*power*) 157; interest; spell, magic, magnetism.

footing; purchase etc. (*support*) 215; play, leverage, vantage ground, advantage.

tower of strength, host in himself; protection, patronage, auspices; patron etc. (*auxiliary*) 711.

v. **have influence** etc. *n.;* be influential etc. *adj.;* carry weight, sway, bias, actuate, weigh, tell; have a hold upon, magnetize, bear upon, gain a footing, work upon; take root, take hold; strike root in.

pervade, run through; spread like wildfire, be rife etc. *adj.;* rage, gain head.

dominate, subject, predominate; outweigh, overweigh; override, overbear; have–, get–, gain--the upper hand, –full play; prevail.

be recognized, be listened to; make one's voice heard, gain a hearing; play a -part, –leading part- in; lead, control, rule, manage, master, get the mastery of, get control of, make one's influence felt; take the lead, pull strings; wind round one's finger; turn–, throw one's weight into- the scale; set the fashion, lead the dance.

adj. **influential**, effective, effectual [*rare*], potent; important etc. 642; weighty; prevailing etc. *v.;*

prevalent, rife, rampant, dominant, regnant, predominant, in the ascendant, hegemonical; authoritative, recognized, telling.

adv. with telling effect, with authority.

175a. Absence of Influence

n. **impotence** etc. 158; powerlessness; inertness etc. 172; irrelevancy etc. 10.

v. have no influence etc. 175.

adj. **uninfluential**; unconducing [*rare*], nonconductive, unconductive; forceless, powerless etc. 158; irrelevant etc. 10.

176. Tendency

n. **tendency**; aptness, aptitude; proneness, proclivity, bent, turn, tone, bias, set, warp, leaning (*with* to *or* towards), predisposition, inclination, tendence [*rare*], propensity, susceptibility; conatus, conation [*obs.*], nisus; liability etc. 177; quality, nature, temperament; idiocrasy, idiosyncrasy; cast, vein, grain; humor, mood; trend; drift etc. (*direction*) 278; conduciveness, conducement; applicability etc. (*utility*) 644; subservience etc. (*instrumentality*) 631.

v. **tend**, contribute, conduce, lead, influence, dispose, incline, verge, bend to, warp, turn, work towards, trend, affect, carry, redound to, bid fair to, gravitate towards; promote etc. (*aid*) 707.

adj. **tending** etc. *v.;* conative, conducent [*obs.*], conducive, working towards, in a fair way to, likely to, calculated to; liable etc. 177; subservient etc. (*instrumental*) 631; useful etc. 644; subsidiary etc. (*helping*) 707; idiocratic, indiosyncratic, idiosyncratical.

adv. for, whither; for the purpose of.

177. Liability

n. **liability**, liableness; possibility, contingency; susceptivity, susceptiveness, susceptibility.

v. **be liable** etc. *adj.;* incur, lay oneself open to, be subjected to, run the chance, stand a chance; lie under, expose oneself to, open a door to.

adj. **liable**, subject, susceptive; in danger etc. 665; open to, exposed to, obnoxious to; answerable, responsible, accountable, amenable; unexempt from; apt to; dependent on; incident to.

contingent, incidental, possible, on the cards, within range of, at the mercy of.

178. Concurrence

n. **concurrence**, coöperation, coagency; union; coadunation, coaction [*rare*], coworking [*rare*], synergy, collaboration, conformity, conformableness, agreement etc. 23; consilience;

consent etc. (*assent*) 488; alliance; concert etc. 709; partnership etc. 712.

v. **concur**, conduce, conspire, contribute; agree, unite, harmonize, jibe [*colloq.*], coadunate, combine; hang–, pull- together etc. (*coöperate*) 709; help to etc. (*aid*) 707.

keep pace with, run parallel; go with, go along with, go hand in hand with.

adj. **concurring** etc. *v.;* concurrent, conformable, corresponsive [*rare*], joint, coöperative, concomitant, coincident, concordant, harmonious, consentaneous [*archaic*]; coadunate, coadunative, consilient, in alliance with, banded together, of one mind, at one with.

adv. with one consent.

179. Counteraction

n. **counteraction**, opposition; contrariety etc. 14; antagonism, polarity; clashing etc. *v.;* collision, interference, resistance, renitency, friction;

reaction; retroaction etc. (*recoil*) 277; counterblast; neutralization etc. (*compensation*) 30; *vis inertiae* [*L.*]; check etc. (*hindrance*) 706.

voluntary opposition etc. 708; voluntary resistance etc. 719; repression etc. (*restraint*) 751.

v. **counteract**; run counter, clash, cross; interfere with, conflict with; contravene; jostle; go–, run–, beat–, militate- against; stultify; antagonize, frustrate, oppose etc. 708; traverse; overcome, overpower, withstand etc. (*resist*) 719; impede, hinder etc. 706; repress etc. (*restrain*) 751; react etc. (*recoil*) 277.

undo, neutralize, offset, cancel; counterpoise etc. (*compensate*) 30; overpoise.

adj. **counteracting** etc. *v.;* antagonistic, conflicting, retroactive, renitent, reactionary; contrary etc. 14.

adv. **although** etc. 30; against; mauger, malgre [*obs.*], malgrado [*obs.*], notwithstanding; in spite of etc. 708.

Class 2. Space

Section 1. Space in General

180. Space
[indefinite space]

n. **space**, extension, extent, superficial extent, expanse, stretch; room, accommodation, capacity, scope, range, latitude, field, way, expansion, compass, sweep, play, swing, spread.

spare room, elbowroom, houseroom; leeway, seaway, headway, stowage, roomage [*obs.*], tankage, margin; opening, sphere, arena.

open space, free space; void etc. (*absence*) 187; waste, desert, wild; wildness [*obs.*], wilderness; moor, down, downs, upland, moorland; prairie, steppe, llano [*Sp. Amer.*], campagna.

unlimited space; heavens, ether, plenum, infinity etc. 105; world, wide world; ubiquity etc. (*presence*) 186; length and breadth of the land; abyss etc. (*interval*) 198.

proportions, acreage; acres, –roods and perches; square -inches, –yards etc.; ares, arpents.

adj. **spacious**, roomy, extensive, expansive, capacious, ample; widespread, vast, world-wide, wide, far-flung, vasty [*rare*], uncircumscribed; boundless etc. (*infinite*) 105; shoreless, trackless, pathless; extended; beyond the verge, far as the eye can see.

adv. **extensively** etc. *adj.;* wherever; everywhere; far and -near, –wide; right and left, all over, all the world over; throughout the world, –length and breadth of the land; under the sun, in every quarter; in all -quarters, –lands; here, there, and everywhere; from pole to pole, from China to Peru [Johnson], from Indus to the pole [Pope], from Dan to Beersheba, from end to end; on the face of the earth, in the wide world, on the face of the waters, "from the four corners of the earth" [*Merchant of Venice*], from all points of the compass; to the four winds, to the uttermost parts of the earth.

180a. Inextension
n. **inextension**, nonextension, point, dot, speck, spot, pinprick, tittle; atom etc. (*small, ness*) 32.

181. Region
[definite space]

n. **region**, sphere, ground, soil, area, realm, hemisphere, quarter, orb, circuit, circle; pale etc. (*limit*) 233; compartment, department; clearing; domain, tract, terrain, dominion, colony, commonwealth, territory, country, fatherland, motherland.

canton, county, shire, province, *arrondissement* [*F.*], mofussil [*India*], parish, diocese, township, commune, ward, wapentake [*hist.*], hundred, riding, soke [*hist.*], tithing, bailiwick; principality, duchy, palatinate, archduchy, dukedom, kingdom, empire.

precinct, arena, *enceinte* [*F.*], walk, march, district, beat; patch, plot, inclosure, close, enclave, field, garth, court; street etc. (*abode*) 189; paddock etc. (*inclosure*) 232.

clime, climate, zone, meridian, latitude.

adj. **territorial**, local, parochial, provincial, regional, insular.

ins and outs; every hole and corner.

adv. **somewhere**, in some place, wherever it may be, here and there, in various places, *passim* [*L.*].

182. Place
[limited space]

n. **place**, lieu, spot, whereabouts, point, dot; niche, nook etc. (*corner*) 244; hole; pigeonhole etc. (*receptacle*) 191; compartment; confine, premises, precinct, station; area, courtyard, square, *place* [*F.*], *piazza* [*It.*], *plaza* [*Sp.*], forum [*L.*], agora [*Gr.*], hamlet, village etc. (*abode*) 189; pen etc. (*inclosure*) 232; countryside, location, site, locality etc. (*situation*) 183.

183. Situation

n. **situation**, position, locality, locale (*properly, local*), status, latitude and longitude; footing, standing, standpoint, post; stage, aspect, attitude, posture, set [*colloq.*], pose.

place, site, situs, station, seat, venue, whereabouts, environment, ground; bearings etc. (*direction*) 278; spot etc. (*limited space*) 182.

topography, geography, chorography; map etc. 554.

v. **be situated**, be situate, be located; lie; have its seat in.

adj. **situate**, situated; local, topical, topographical etc. *n.*

adv. *in situ* [*L.*], *in loco* [*L.*]; here and there, *passim* [*L.*]; hereabouts, thereabouts, whereabouts; in place, here, there.

in–, amidst- such and such- -surroundings, –environs, -*entourage* [*F.*].

184. Location

n. **location**, localization; lodgment; deposition; reposition; stowage; collocation; packing, lad-

ing; establishment, settlement, installation; fixation; insertion etc. 300.

anchorage, roadstead, mooring, encampment.

settlement, plantation, colony, cantonment; situation; quarters, barracks; habitation etc. (*abode*) 189; "a local habitation and a name" [*Midsummer Night's Dream*].

domestication, cohabitation, colonization; endenization [*obs.*], naturalization.

v. **place**, situate, locate, localize, make a place for, put, lay, set, seat, station, lodge, quarter, post, install; house, stow; establish, fix, pin, root; graft; plant etc. (*insert*) 300; shelve, pitch, camp, lay down, deposit, reposit, store, store away, cradle; moor, tether, picket; pack, tuck in; embed, imbed; vest, invest in.

billet on, quarter upon, saddle with.

load, lade, stevedore, freight; pocket, put up, bag.

inhabit etc. (*be present*) 186; domesticate, colonize, found, people; take root, strike root; anchor; cast–, come to an- anchor; sit down, settle down; settle; take up one's -abode, –quarters; plant–, establish–, locate- oneself; have one's legal residence at; hang out one's shingle [*colloq.*]; squat, perch, hive, *se nicher* [*F.*], bivouac, burrow, get a footing; encamp, pitch one's tent; put up -at; –one's horses at; keep house.

naturalize, endenizen [*rare*], adopt.

put back, replace etc. (*restore*) 660.

adj. **placed** etc. *v.*; situate, posited, ensconced, imbedded, embosomed, rooted; domesticated; vested in, unremoved.

moored etc. *v.*; at anchor.

185. Displacement

n. **displacement**, elocation [*obs.*], heterotopy, transposition.

ejectment etc. 297; exile etc. (*banishment*) 893.

removal etc. (*transference*) 270; unshipment, transshipment *or* transhipment, unplacement [*rare*], moving, shift.

misplacement, dislocation etc. 61; fish out of water.

v. **displace**, displant, dislodge, disestablish; misplace, unplace [*rare*], translocate [*rare*], unseat, disturb, disniche; exile etc. (*seclude*) 893; ablegate [*obs.*], set aside, remove; take away, cart away; take off, draft off; lade etc. 184.

unload, empty etc. (*eject*) 297; transfer etc. 270; dispel.

vacate; depart etc. 293.

adj. **displaced** etc. *v.*; unplaced, unhoused, unharbored, unestablished, unsettled; houseless, homeless, harborless [*archaic*]; out of place, out of a situation.

misplaced, out of its element.

186. Presence

n. **presence**, presentness, occupancy, occupation; attendance.

permeation, pervasion; diffusion etc. (*dispersion*) 73.

whereness, ubiety, ubiquity, ubiquitariness; omnipresence.

bystander etc. (*spectator*) 444.

v. **be present** etc. *adj.; assister* [*F.*]; make one -of, –at; look on, attend, remain; find–, present-oneself; show one's face; fall in the way of, occur in a place; exist in space, lie, stand; occupy.

inhabit, dwell, reside, stay, sojourn, live, abide, lodge, bunk, room, nestle, roost [*colloq.*], perch; take up one's abode etc. (*be located*) 184; tenant; people.

frequent, resort to, haunt; revisit.

pervade, permeate; be diffused through, be disseminated through; overspread, overrun; fill, run through; meet one at every turn.

adj. **present**; occupying, inhabiting etc. *v.;* moored etc. 184; resiant [*obs.*], resident, residential, residentiary; domiciled.

ubiquitous, ubiquitary; omnipresent; universally present.

peopled, populous, full of people, inhabited.

adv. here, there, where, everywhere, aboard, on board, at home, afield; on the spot; here there and everywhere etc. (*space*) 180; in presence of, before; under the eyes of, under the nose of; in the face of; *in propria persona* [*L.*].

187. Absence

[nullibicity]

n. **nullibicity**, nullibiety [*rare*], absence; awayness [*rare*], cut [*colloq.*]; inexistence etc. 2; nonresidence, absenteeism; nonattendance, alibi.

emptiness etc. *adj.;* void, vacuum; vacuity [*rare*], vacancy, voidness [*rare*], *tabula rasa* [*L.*]; exemption; hiatus etc. (*interval*) 198; lipotype.

truant, absentee.

nobody; nobody -present, –on earth; not a soul; no man, nix [*slang*].

v. **be absent** etc. *adj.;* keep away, keep out of the way; play truant, absent oneself, stay away; slip off, slip out, slip away; keep–, hold- aloof.

withdraw, make oneself scarce [*colloq.*], retreat, retire, vacate; go away etc. 293.

adj. **absent**, not present, away, nonresident, gone, from home; missing; lost; wanting; omitted; nowhere to be found; inexistent etc. 2.

empty, void; vacant, vacuous; blank, null; untenanted, unoccupied, uninhabited; tenantless; desert, deserted; devoid; unhabitable, uninhabitable.

exempt from, not having.

adv. **without**, minus, nowhere; elsewhere; neither here nor there; in default of; sans; behind one's back.

188. Inhabitant

n. **inhabitant**; resident, residentiary; dweller, indweller, habitant [*rare*]; addressee; occupier, occupant; householder, lodger, roomer, inmate, tenant, incumbent, sojourner, *locum tenens* [*L.*], commorant; settler, squatter, backwoodsman, colonist; islander; denizen, citizen; burgher, oppidan, cockney, cit [*colloq.*], townsman, burgess; villager; cottager, cottier, cotter; compatriot; backsettler, boarder; hotel keeper, innkeeper; habitant; paying guest; planter.

native, indigene [*rare*], aborigines, autochthon (*pl.* autochthones), aboriginal; newcomer etc. (*stranger*) 57.

American; Briton, Englishman, Britisher, John Bull; Canadian, Canuck [*slang*]; downeaster; Scot, Scotchman, Scotsman, Caledonian; Hibernian, Irishman, Paddywhack, Paddy, Mick, Teague, Greek *or* Grecian [*slang*]; Welshman, Cambrian, Taffy; Frenchman, Parleyvoo, Frog *or* Froggy [*slang*]; Chinaman, Celestial; Uncle Sam, Yankee, Brother Jonathan.

people etc. (*mankind*) 372; colony, settlement; household; mir [*Russia*]; garrison, crew; population.

v. **inhabit** etc. (*be present*) 186; endenizen [*rare*] etc. (*locate oneself*) 184.

adj. **indigenous**; native, natal; autochthonal, autochthonous; British, English; American; Canadian; Irish, Hibernian; Scotch, Scottish; Welsh, Cambrian; French, Gallic; Chinese, Celestial, Sinaean, Sinaic *or* Sinic [*rare*]; domestic; domiciliated, domiciled; naturalized, vernacular, domesticated; domiciliary; colonial.

occupied by, in the occupation of; garrisoned by.

189. Abode

[place of habitation, or resort]

n. **abode**, dwelling, lodging, domicile, residence, address, habitation, where one's lot is cast, local habitation, berth, diggings [*colloq.*], seat, lap, sojourn, housing, pad [*slang*], quarters, headquarters, resiance [*obs.*], tabernacle, throne, ark.

home, fatherland, motherland, country; homestead, home stall [*Eng.*], fireside; hearth, hearthstone; chimney corner, ingleside; harem, seraglio, zenana; household gods, *lares et penates* [*L.*], roof, household, housing, *dulce domum* [*L.*], paternal domicile; native soil, native land, "God's country," down home [*colloq.*]

quarter, parish etc. (*region*) 181.

retreat, haunt, resort; nest, nidus, snuggery [*colloq.*], arbor, bower etc. 191; lair, den, cave, hole, hiding place, cell, sanctum sanctorum, aerie, eyrie *or* eyry, rookery, hive; habitat, covert, perch, roost; nidification; *kala jagah* [*Hind.*].

camp, bivouac, encampment, cantonment; castrametation; barrack, casemate, casern *or* caserne; tent etc. 223.

tenement, messuage, farm, farmhouse, grange, hacienda [*Sp. Amer.*], toft [*Scot., and dial. Eng.*].

cot, cabin, hut, chalet *or chalet* [*F.*], croft, shed, booth, stall, hovel, bothy *or* boothy, shanty, dugout [*U.S.*], wigwam; pen etc. (*inclosure*) 232; barn, bawn [*obs.*], kennel, sty, doghole, cote, coop, hutch; byre, cowhouse, cowshed, cowbyre; stable, dovecote, columbary, columbarium; shippen [*dial.*]; igloo *or* iglu [*Eskimo*], jacal; lacustrine–, lake–, pile- dwelling; log cabin, log house; shack [*colloq.*], shebang [*slang*], tepee, topek.

house, mansion, place, villa, cottage, box, lodge, hermitage, *rus in urbe* [*L.*], folly, rotunda, tower, *château* [*F.*], castle, pavilion, hotel, court, manor-house, messuage, hall, palace; kiosk, brownstone, bungalow, chummery [*esp. Anglo-Indian*], *casa* [*Sp., Pg. and It.*], country seat; apartment–, frame–, ranch–, shingle- house; duplex, flat, high-rise, tenement; building etc. (*construction*) 161; room, chamber etc. (*receptacle*) 191; buildings, mews.

hamlet, village, bustee *or* basti [*Hind.*], thorp *or* thrope, dorp, kraal [*S. Africa*], rancho [*Sp. Amer.*].

town, borough, burgh, ham [*now used only in compounds*], city, capital, metropolis; suburb; provincial town, county town, county seat; courthouse; ghetto.

street, place, terrace, parade, esplanade, *alameda* [*Sp.*], board walk, embankment, road, row, lane, alley, court, quadrangle, quad [*colloq.*], wynd [*dial.*], close, yard, passage.

square, polygon, circus, crescent, mall, piazza, arcade, colonnade, peristyle, cloister; gardens, grove, residences; block of buildings, market place, *place* [*F.*], plaza.

anchorage, roadstead, roads; dock, basin, wharf, quay, port, harbor.

assembly room, auditorium, concert hall, armory, gymnasium; cathedral, church, chapel, meetinghouse etc. (*temple*) 1000; parliament etc. (*council*) 696.

inn, hostel [*archaic*], hostelry [*archaic*], hotel, tavern, caravansary *or* caravanserai, xenodochium, dak bungalow [*India*], khan, hospice; public house, alehouse, pothouse, mughouse; gin palace; bar, barroom cocktail lounge; cabaret, chophouse; club, clubhouse; cookshop, dive; grill room, saloon, shebeen [*Irish and Scot.*]; coffee-house, eating-house; canteen, restaurant, buffet, café, *estaminet* [*F.*], *posada* [*Sp.*]

almshouse, flophouse, poorhouse, townhouse.

garden, park, pleasure ground, pleasance *or* plaisance [*archaic*], demesne.

sanatorium. health resort, Hill station *or* the Hills [*India*], health retreat, sanitarium, spa, watering-place, pump room.

v.   **inhabit** etc. (*be present*) 186; take up one's abode etc. (*locate oneself*) 184.

adj.   **urban**, oppidan [*rare*], metropolitan; suburban; provincial, rural, rustic, agrestic, country, countrified, regional; domestic; cosmopolitan; palatial.

190.   Contents

[things contained]

n.   **contents**; cargo, lading, freight, shipment, load, bale, burden, jag [*Engl. colloq.*]; cartload, shipload; cup of, basket of etc. (*receptacle*) 191; inside etc. 221; stuffing.

v.   **load**, lade, ship, charge, weight, pile, fill, stuff.

191.   Receptacle

n.   **receptacle**, container; inclosure etc. 232; recipient, receiver, reservatory [*obs.*].

compartment; cell, cellule; follicle; hole, corner, niche, recess, nook; crypt, stall, pigeonhole, cove, oriel; cave etc. (*concavity*) 252; mouth.

capsule, vesicle, cyst, pod, calyx, cancelli, utricle, bladder; pericarp, udder.

stomach, paunch, belly, venter, ventricle, ingluvies, crop, craw, maw, gizzard, breadbasket [*slang*], Little Mary [*slang*]; omasum, manyplies, abomasum, rumen, reticulum.

bag, sac, sack, saccule, wallet, pocket, pouch, fob, sheath, scabbard, socket, cardcase, scrip [*archaic*], poke [*chiefly dial.*], knapsack, haversack, satchel, reticule, budget [*dial.*], net; dittybag, –box; housewife *or* hussif; saddlebags; portfolio; quiver etc. (*magazine*) 636.

case, chest, box, coffer, caddy, casket; pyx *or* pix, monstrance [*R. C. Ch.*]; caisson; desk, bureau, reliquary, shrine; trunk, portmanteau, bandbox, valise, grip *or* gripsack [*colloq.*], suitcase, handbag, Boston bag, school bag, brief case, travelingbag, Gladstone *or* Gladstone bag; skippet, vasculum; boot, imperial [*now rare*]; *vache* [*F.*]; cage, manger, rack.

vessel, vase, bushel, barrel; canister, jar; pottle, basket, pannier; buck basket, clothes basket, hopper, maund [*obs.*], creel, cran *or* crane [*Scot.*], crate, cradle, bassinet, whisket *or* wisket [*dial. Eng.*]; *jardinière* [*F.*], *corbeille* [*F.*], hamper, dosser *or* dorser, tray, hod, scuttle, utensil; brazier; cuspidor, spittoon.

[for liquids] cistern etc. (*store*) 636; vat, caldron *or* cauldron, barrel, cask, puncheon, keg, rundlet, tun, butt, firkin, kilderkin, carboy, amphora, bottle, jar, decanter, ewer, cruse, carafe, crock, kit [*dial. Eng.*], canteen, flagon; demijohn; flask, flasket; stoup *or* stoop, noggin, vial, phial, cruet, caster; urn, epergne, salver, patella, *tazza* [*It.*], patera; piggin; biggin, percolator, coffeepot, coffee urn, teapot, tea urn, samovar; tig *or* tyg [*dial. Eng.*], nipperkin [*now rare*], pocket pistol [*slang*], tub, bucket, pail, skeel [*dial.*], pot, tankard, jug, pitcher, mug, pipkin; gallipot; matrass *or* mattrass, receiver, retort, alembic, bolthead, capsule, can, kettle; bowl, basin, jorum [*colloq.*], punch bowl, cup, goblet, chalice, tumbler, glass, rummer, horn, saucepan, skillet, posnet [*obs.*], tureen, stein.

bail, beaker, billy [*Australia*], cannikin *or* canakin; catch basin, catch drain; chatti *or* chatty [*India*], lota *or* lotah [*India*], mussuk *or* mussuck [*India*]; schooner, spider, terrine, toby, *urceus* [*L.*].

plate, platter, dish, trencher, calabash, porringer, potager [*obs.*], saucer, pan, crucible; glassware, tableware; vitrics.

ladle, dipper, tablespoon, spoon; shovel, trowel, spatula.

cupboard, closet, commode, cellaret, chiffonier *or* chiffonnier, *chiffonnière* [*F.*], locker, bin, bunker, buffet, press, clothespress, safe, sideboard, drawer, chest of drawers, till, escritoire, scrutoire [*obs.*], secretary, *secrétaire* [*F.*], dav-

enport, bookcase, cabinet, canterbury; *étagère* [*F.*], vargueno, vitrine.

chamber, apartment, room, cabin; office, court, hall, atrium; suite of rooms, apartment, flat, story; saloon, *salon* [*F.*], parlor; by-room, cubicle; presence chamber; living–, sitting–, drawing–, reception–, state-room; best room [*colloq.*], keeping room [*dial. Eng.*]; gallery, cabinet, closet; pew, box; boudoir; adytum, sanctum; bedroom, dormitory; refectory, dining room, *salle-à-manger* [*F.*]; nursery, schoolroom; library, study; studio; billiard room, bathroom, lavatory, toilet, powder room, smoking room; den; state room, tablinum, tenement.

attic, loft, garret, cockloft, clerestory; cellar, vault, hold, cockpit; cubbyhole; cook house; *entre-sol* [*F.*]; mezzanine *or* mezzanine floor; ground floor, *rez-de-chaussée* [*F.*], basement, kitchen, pantry, *bawarchi-khana* [*Hind.*], scullery, offices; storeroom etc. (*depository*) 636; lumber room; dairy, laundry, coach house; garage; hangar; outhouse, penthouse; lean-to.

portico, porch, stoop [*U.S.*], veranda, lobby, court, hall, vestibule, corridor, passage; anteroom, antechamber; lounge; piazza [= veranda, *U.S.*].

bower, arbor, summerhouse, alcove, grotto, hermitage; conservatory, greenhouse.

lodging etc. (*abode*) 189; bed etc. (*support*) 215.

carriage etc. (*vehicle*) 272.

adj. capsular; saccular, sacculated; recipient; ventricular, cystic, vascular, vesicular, cellular, camerated, locular, multilocular, polygastric; gastric, stomachic, gasteral [*rare*]; marsupial; siliquose, siliquous.

Section 2. Dimensions

192. Size

n. **size**, magnitude, dimension, bulk, volume; largeness etc. *adj.;* greatness etc. (*of quantity*) 31; expanse etc. (*space*) 180; amplitude, mass; proportions.

capacity; tonnage *or* tunnage; cordage; caliber *or* calibre; scantling [*obs.*].

corpulence, obesity; plumpness etc. *adj.; embonpoint* [*F.*], corporation [*colloq.*], flesh and blood, lustihood; turgidity etc. (*expansion*) 194.

hugeness etc. *adj.;* enormity, immensity; monstrosity.

giant, Brobdingnagian, Antaeus, Goliath, Polyphemus, Colossus, Titan, Titaness, Briareus,

Norn, Hercules, Cyclops, Gog and Magog, Gargantua, King Kong; monster, mammoth, cachalot, whale, porpoise, behemoth, leviathan, elephant, jumbo, hippopotamus; colossus.

lump, bulk, block, loaf, mass, swad [*slang*], clod, nugget, tun, cord, bushel; thumper [*slang*], whopper *or* whapper [*colloq.*], spanker [*slang*], strapper [*slang*]; "Triton among the minnows" [*Coriolanus*].

mountain, mound; heap etc. (*assemblage*) 72.

full-size, life-size; largest portion etc. 50.

v. **be large** etc. *adj.;* become large etc. (*expand*) 194.

adj. **large,** big; great etc. (*in quantity*) 31; considerable, bulky, voluminous, ample, massive, massy; capacious, comprehensive, spacious etc. 180; mighty, towering, fine, magnificent.

stout, corpulent, fat, plump, squab, full, lusty, strapping [*colloq.*], bouncing; portly, burly, well-fed, full-grown; corn-fed, gram-fed [*Anglo-Ind.*]; stalwart, brawny, fleshy; goodly; in good -case, –condition; in condition, in shape; chopping, jolly; club-faced [*obs.*], chubby-faced.

large as life; plump as a -dumpling, –partridge; fat as -a pig, –a quail, –butter, –brawn, –bacon [*all colloq.*].

hulky, hulking, unwieldy, lumpish, lubberly, gaunt, spanking [*slang.*], whacking [*colloq.*], whopping [*colloq.*], thumping [*colloq.*], thundering [*colloq.*], overgrown; puffy etc. (*swollen*) 194.

huge, immense, enormous, titanic, mighty; vast, vasty [*archaic*]; stupendous; monster, monstrous; gigantic; elephantine; giant, giantlike; colossal, Cyclopean, Brobdingnagian, Gargantuan; infinite etc. 105.

193. Littleness

n. **littleness** etc. *adj.;* smallness etc. (*of quantity*) 32; exiguity, inextension; parvitude [*rare*], parvity [*obs.*]; duodecimo; epitome; microcosm; rudiment; vanishing point; thinness etc. 203.

dwarf, pygmy *or* pigmy, Liliputian, Negrito, Negrillo; chit, fingerling [*rare*], Pigwiggen, pigwidgeon [*rare*], urchin, elf; atomy, dandiprat [*archaic*], doll, puppet; Tom Thumb, hop-o'-my-thumb; manikin *or* mannikin; micromorph [*rare*], homunculus, dapperling.

mite, insect, arthropod, ephemerid, ephemera, bug [*pop.*], larva, emmet, fly, midge, gnat, shrimp, minnow, worm, maggot, grub; tit, tomtit, runt, mouse, small fry; millet seed, mustard seed; barleycorn; pebble, grain of sand; molehill, button, bubble.

atom, monad, animalcule, animalculum (*pl.* animalcula), diatom, dyad, triad, tetrad, pentad, hexad, heptad, octad, molecule, microbe, germ, microörganism, bacterium (*pl.* bacteria), microphyte, microzyme, amoeba, microzoa, entozoön (*pl.* entozoa), phytozoaria, infusoria.

particle etc. (*small quantity*) 32; point, micron; scintilla; fragment etc. (*small part*) 51; powder etc. 330; point of a pin, mathematical point; minutiae etc. (*unimportance*) 643.

micrography; micrometer, microscope, interferometer, vernier; scale.

v. **be little** etc. *adj.;* lie in a nutshell; become small etc. (*decrease*) 36, (*contract*) 195.

adj. **little;** small etc. (*in quantity*) 32; minute, diminutive, microscopic; inconsiderable etc. (*unimportant*) 643; exiguous, puny, runty, tiny, wee [*colloq.*], petty, minikin [*obs.*], miniature, pygmy *or* pigmy, elfin; undersized; dwarf, dwarfed, dwarfish; spare, stunted, limited; cramp, cramped; pollard, Liliputian, Negritic, dapper, pocket; portative, portable; duodecimo; dumpy, squat; short etc. 201.

impalpable, intangible, evanescent, imperceptible, invisible, inappreciable, infinitesimal, homeopathic; rudimentary, rudimental; embryonic, vestigial.

animalcular, amoebic, amoeboid, diatomaceous, diatomic, microzoal, microbial, microbic, molecular, atomic, corpuscular.

scant, weazen [*obs.*], scraggy, scrubby; thin etc. (*narrow*) 203; granular etc. (*powdery*) 330; shrunk etc. 195; brevipennate.

adv. in a small compass, in a nutshell; on a small scale.

194. Expansion

n. **expansion,** dilation, expansibleness; increase etc. 35 -of size; enlargement, extension, augmentation; amplification, ampliation; aggrandizement, spread, increment, growth, development, pullulation [*rare*], swell, dilatation, rarefaction; turgescence *or* turgescency, turgidness, turgidity; dispansion [*obs.*]; obesity etc. (*size*) 192; hydrocephalus, hydrophthalmus; dropsy, tumefaction, intumescence, swelling, tumor, diastole, distension; puffing, puffiness; inflation; pandiculation.

dilatability, expansibility.

growth, upgrowth; accretion etc. 35; germination, budding, gemmation.

bulb etc. (*convexity*) 250; plumper; superiority of size.

overgrowth, overdistension; hypertrophy, tympany.

v. **become larger** etc. (large etc. 192); expand, widen, enlarge, extend, grow, increase, incrassate, swell, gather; fill out; deploy, take open order, dilate, stretch, spread; mantle, wax; grow up, spring up; bud, burgeon *or* bourgeon, shoot, sprout, germinate, put forth, vegetate, pullulate, open, burst forth; gain flesh, gather flesh; outgrow; spread like wildfire, overrun.

be larger than; surpass etc. (*be superior*) 33.

render larger etc. (large etc. 192); expand, spread, extend, aggrandize, distend, develop, amplify, spread out, widen, magnify, rarefy, inflate, puff, blow up, stuff, pad, cram, bloat; exaggerate; fatten.

adj. **expanded** etc. *v.;* larger etc. (large etc. 192); swollen; expansive; wide open, widespread; fan-shaped, flabelliform; overgrown, exaggerated, bloated, fat, turgid, tumid, hypertrophied, dropsical; pot-bellied, swagbellied [*obs.*]; edematous, corpulent, obese, puffy, pursy, blowzy, distended; patulous; bulbous etc. (*convex*) 250; full-blown, full-grown, full-formed; big etc. 192; abdominous, enchymatous, rhipidate; tumefacient, tumefying.

195. Contraction

n. **contraction**, reduction, diminution; decrease etc. 36 -of size; defalcation, decrement; lessening, shrinking etc. *v.;* compaction [*rare*], tabes, collapse, emaciation, attenuation, tabefaction [*rare*], consumption, marasmus, atrophy; systole, syncopation, syncope; neck, hourglass.

compression, condensation, constraint, astriction [*rare*], compactness; compendium etc. 596; squeezing etc. *v.;* strangulation; corrugation; constringency, astringency; astringents, sclerotics; contractibility, contractibleness, contractility, compressibility, compressibleness, coarctation.

inferiority in size.

v. **become small**, become smaller; lessen, decrease etc. 36; grow less, dwindle, shrink, contract, narrow, shrivel, syncopate, collapse, wither, lose flesh, wizen [*dial.*], fall away, waste, wane, ebb; decay etc. (*deteriorate*) 659.

be smaller than, fall short of; not come up to etc. (*be inferior*) 34.

render smaller, lessen, diminish, contract, draw in, narrow, pucker, cockle, coarct *or* coarctate [*rare*]; boil down; deflate, exhaust, empty; constrict, constringe; condense, compress, squeeze, corrugate, crush, crumple up, warp, purse, purse up, pack, stow; pinch, tighten, strangle;

cramp; dwarf, bedwarf; shorten etc. 201; circumscribe etc. 229; restrain etc. 751.

pare, reduce, attenuate, rub down, scrape, file, grind, chip, shave, shear.

adj. **contracting** etc. *v.;* astringent, constringent, shrunk, shrunken, tabescent, tabetic, contractible, contracted etc. *v.;* strangulated, tabid, wizened, weazen, weazeny [*colloq.*], corky, stunted; waning etc. *v.;* neap, compact, compacted.

unexpanded etc. (expand etc. 194); contractile; compressible; smaller etc. (small etc. 193).

196. Distance

n. **distance**; space etc. 180; remoteness, farness; far cry to; longinquity [*rare*], elongation; easting, westing, drift, offing, background; remote region; removedness; parallax; reach, span, stride.

outpost, outskirt; horizon, sky line; aphelion; foreign parts, *ultima Thule* [*L.*], *ne plus ultra* [*L.*], antipodes; jumping-off place [*colloq.*], long range, giant's stride.

dispersion etc. 73.

v. **be distant** etc. *adj.;* extend to, stretch to, reach to, spread to, go to, get to, stretch away to; range, outreach, outlie [*rare*].

remain at a distance; keep−, stand--away, −off, −aloof, −clear of.

adj. **distant**; far off, far away; remote, telescopic, distal, wide of; stretching to etc. *v.;* yon, yonder; ulterior; transmarine, transpontine, transatlantic, transpacific, transoceanic, transalpine; tramontane; ultramontane, ultramundane; hyperborean, antipodean; inaccessible, out-of-the-way, God-forsaken [*colloq.*]; unapproached, unapproachable; incontiguous [*obs.*].

adv. **far off**, far away; afar, −off; off; away; a -long, −great, −good- way off; wide away, beyond range, aloof; wide of, clear of; out of -the way, −reach; abroad, yonder, farther, further, beyond; *outre mer* [*F.*], over the border, far and wide, "over the hills and far away" [Gay]; from pole to pole etc. (*over great space*) 180; to the -uttermost parts, −ends- of the earth; out of range, out of hearing, nobody knows where, *à perte de vue* [*F.*], out of the sphere of, wide of the mark; a far cry to.

apart, asunder; wide apart, wide asunder; *longo intervallo* [*L.*]; at arm's length.

197. Nearness

n. **nearness** etc. *adj.;* proximity, propinquity; vicinity, vicinage; neighborhood, adjacency, nigh-ness [archaic], appropinquity [rare]; contiguity etc. 199.

short -distance, −step, −cut; earshot, close quarters, range, stone's throw; bowshot, gunshot, pistol shot; hair's breadth, span.

purlieus, neighborhood, vicinage, environs, *alentours* [F.], suburbs, *faubourg* [F.], confines, *banlieue* [F.], borderland; whereabouts.

bystander, spectator; neighbor *or* neighbour, borderer.

approach etc. 286; convergence etc. 290; perihelion.

v. **be near** etc. *adj.;* adjoin, abut, neighbor, hang about, trench on; border upon, verge upon; stand by, approximate, tread on the heels of, cling to, clasp, hug; huddle; hang upon the skirts of, hover over; burn [colloq.].

bring *or* draw near etc. 286; converge etc. 290; crowd etc. 72; place side by side etc.

adv.

adj. **near**, nigh; close−, near- at hand; close, neighboring, vicinal, propinquent [rare]; bordering upon, contiguous, adjacent, adjoining; proximate, proximal; at hand, warm [colloq.], handy; near the mark, near run; home, intimate.

adv. **near**, nigh; hard by, fast by; close to, close upon; hard upon; at the point of; next door to; within -reach, - call, −hearing, −earshot, −range; within an ace of; but a step, not far from, at no great distance; on the -verge, −brink, −skirts- of; in the environs etc. *n.;* at one's -door, −feet, −elbow, −finger's end, −side; on the tip of one's tongue; under one's nose; within a stone's throw etc. *n.;* in sight of, in presence of; at close quarters; cheek by jowl, cheek to cheek, shoulder to shoulder; beside, alongside, side by side, *tête-à-tête* [F.]; in juxtaposition etc. (touching) 199; yardarm to yardarm; at the heels of; on the confines of, at the threshold, bordering upon, verging to; in the way.

about; hereabout *or* hereabouts, thereabout *or* thereabouts; roughly, in round numbers; approximately, approximatively; as good as, wellnigh.

198. Interval

n. **interval**, interspace; separation etc. 44; hiatus, caesura; interruption, interregnum; interstice, intersection, lacuna.

parenthesis etc. (interjacence) 228; void etc. (absence) 187; incompleteness etc. 53.

cleft, break, gap, opening; hole etc. 260; chasm, mesh, crevice, chink, rime [rare], creek, cranny, crack, chap, slit, fissure, scissure, rift, fault,

flaw, breach, fracture, rent, gash, cut, leak, dike, ha-ha.

gorge, defile, ravine, cañon, crevasse, abyss, abysm; gulf; inlet, frith, strait, gully, nullah [India]; pass; furrow etc. 259; *abra* [Sp. Amer.], *barranco* [Sp.], clove, gulch, notch, yawning gulf; *hiatus maxime deflendus* [L.], *hiatus valde deflendus* [L.].

v. **gape** etc. (open) 260; separate etc. 44.

adj. with an interval, far between; breachy, rimose, rimous, rimulose.

adv. **at intervals** etc. (discontinuously) 70; *longo intervallo* [L.].

199. Contiguity

n. **contiguity**, contiguousness, contact, proximity, apposition, abuttal, juxtaposition, touching etc. *v.;* abutment, osculation; meeting, appulse, appulsion, *rencontre* [F.], rencounter, syzygy, conjunction, conjugation, coincidence, coexistence; adhesion etc. 46.

borderland; frontier etc. (limit) 233; tangent; abutter.

v. **be contiguous** etc. *adj.;* join, adjoin, abut on, neighbor, border, march with; graze, touch, meet, osculate, come in contact, coincide; coexist; adhere etc. 46.

adj. **contiguous**; touching etc. *v.;* in contact etc. *n.;* conterminous, end to end, osculatory; pertingent [obs.]; tangential.

hand to hand; close to etc. (near) 197; with no interval etc. 198.

200. Length

n. **length**, longitude, longness [rare], extent, span; mileage.

line, bar, rule, stripe, streak, spoke, radius.

lengthening etc. *v.;* prolongation, production, protraction; tension, tensure [obs.]; extension.

[measures of length] line, nail, inch, hand, palm, foot, cubit, yard, ell, fathom, rood, pole, furlong, mile, knot, league; chain; arpent, handbreadth, *jornada* [Sp. Amer.], kos [Hind.], vara [Sp. & Pg.]; meter, kilometer, centimeter etc.

pedometer, odometer, odograph, viameter, viatometer, log [naut.], speedometer, telemeter, perambulator; scale etc. (measurement) 466.

v. **be long** etc. *adj.;* stretch out, sprawl; extend to, reach to, stretch to; make a long arm, "drag its slow length along" [Pope].

render long etc. *adj.;* lengthen, extend, elongate; stretch; prolong, produce [rare], protract; let out, draw out, spin out; drawl.

enfilade, look along, view in perspective.

adj. **long**, longsome [*archaic*]; elongate *or* elongated, longish, lengthy, wiredrawn, outstretched, extended; lengthened etc. *v.;* sesquipedalian etc. (*words*) 577; interminable, no end of [*colloq.*].

linear, lineal; longitudinal, oblong.

lanky, lank, slabsided [*slang*], rangy; tall etc. 206; macrocolous, long-limbed.

as long as -my arm, –to-day and to-morrow; unshortened etc. (shorten etc. 201).

adv. **lengthwise**, at length, longitudinally, endlong [*archaic*], endways, endwise, along; tandem; in a line etc. (*continuously*) 69; in perspective.

from end to end, from stem to stern, from head to foot, from the crown of the head to the sole of the foot, from tip to toe, from top to toe; fore and aft; over all.

201. Shortness

n. **shortness** etc. *adj.;* brevity littleness etc. 193; a span.

shortening etc. *v.;* abbreviation, abbreviature [*obs.*], abridgment, concision, retrenchment, curtailment, decurtation [*obs.*], epitomization, obtruncation [*rare*], condensation; reduction etc. (*contraction*) 195; epitome etc. (*compendium*) 596.

elision, ellipsis; conciseness etc. (*in style*) 572.

abridger, epitomist, epitomizer, obtruncator [*rare*].

v. **be short** etc. *adj.;* **render short** etc. *adj.;* shorten, curtail, abridge, abbreviate, take in, reduce; compress etc. (*contract*) 195; epitomize etc. 596.

cut short, retrench, obtruncate [*rare*], scrimp, cut, chop up, hack, hew; cut down, pare down; clip, dock, lop, prune, shear, shave, mow, reap, crop; snub; truncate, pollard, stunt, nip, check the growth of; foreshorten [*drawing*].

adj. **short**, brief, curt; compendious, compact; stubby, pudgy, tubby [*colloq.*], squatty, squidgy [*rare*], scrimp; shorn, stubbed; stumpy [*colloq.*], thickset, pug; chunky, curtate, curtal [*archaic*], decurtate; *retroussé* [*F.*], turned up; scrub, stocky; squab, squabby, squat, squattish, dumpy; little etc. 193; curtailed of its fair proportions; short by; oblate; abbreviatory; concise etc. 572; summary.

adv. **shortly** etc. *adj.;* in short etc. (*concisely*) 572.

202. Breadth, Thickness

n. **breadth**, width, latitude, amplitude; diameter, bore, caliber, radius; superficial extent etc. (*space*) 180.

thickness, crassitude [*obs.*]; corpulence etc. (*size*) 192; dilatation etc. (*expansion*) 194.

v. **be broad** etc. *adj.;* become *or* render broad etc. *adj.;* expand etc. 194; thicken, widen, calibrate.

adj. **broad**, wide, ample, extended; discous, discoid; fanlike; outspread, outstretched; "wide as a church-door" [*Romeo and Juliet*]; latifoliate [*rare*], latifolious [*rare*].

thick, dumpy, squab, squat, thickset, stubby etc. 201; thick as a rope.

203. Narrowness, Thinness

n. **narrowness** etc. *adj.;* closeness, exility [*rare*]; exiguity etc. (*little*) 193.

line; hair's-, finger's- breadth; strip, streak, vein.

thinness etc. *adj.;* tenuity; emaciation, marcor [*obs.*], macilence *or* macilency [*rare*].

shaving, slip etc. (*filament*) 205; thread paper, skeleton, shadow, scrag, atomy [*obs. or joc.*], anatomy, [*archaic*], study in anatomy [*humorous*], spindle-shanks [*humorous or contemptuous*], bare-bone, lantern jaws, mere skin and bone.

middle constriction, stricture, coarctation [*med.*]; neck, waist, isthmus, wasp, hourglass; ridge, ghat *or* ghaut [*India*], pass; ravine etc. 198.

narrowing, angustation, tapering; contraction etc. 195.

v. be narrow etc. *adj.;* narrow, taper, contract, etc. 195; render narrow etc. *adj.*

adj. **narrow**, close; slender, gracile, thin, fine; threadlike etc. (*filament*) 205; finespun, taper, slim, slight-made; scant, scanty; spare, delicate, incapacious; contracted etc. 195; unexpanded etc. (*expand* etc. 194); slender as a thread.

lean, emaciated, meager *or* meagre, gaunt, macilent; lank, lanky; weedy [*colloq.*], skinny; scrawny, slinky [*dial.*]; starved, starveling; attenuated, shriveled, pinched, poor, peaked [*colloq.*], lathy [*colloq.*], skeletal, flatsided [*colloq.*], slabsided [*slang*]; spindle-legged, spindle-shanked, spindling; coarctate, angustate, tabic, tabelic, tabid, extenuated, marcid [*obs.*], rawboned; herring-gutted [*colloq.*]; worn to a shadow, "lean as a rake" [*Chaucer*]; thin as a -lath, –whipping post, –wafer; hatchet-faced; lantern-jawed.

204. Layer

n. **layer**, stratum, course, bed, couch, coping, zone, substratum, floor, flag, stage, story, tier, slab, escarpment; table, tablet; dess [*Scot. & dial. Eng.*]; flagstone; board, plank; trencher, platter.

leaf, lamina, lamella, sheet, flake, foil, wafer, scale, coat, peel, pellicle, membrane, film, lap, ply, slice, shive, cut, rasher, shaving, plate; overlay, integument etc. (*covering*) 223; eschar.

stratification, lamination, delamination, foliation; scaliness, nest of boxes, coats of an onion.

v. slice, shave, pare, peel, skive; delaminate; plate, coat, veneer; cover etc. 223.

adj. lamellar, lamelliferous, lamellate *or* lamellated, lamelliform; laminate *or* laminated, laminiferous; micaceous; schistose, schistous; scaly, filmy, membranous, membranaceous, flaky, squamous; foliated, foliaceous; stratified, stratiform; tabular, discoid; spathic, spathose.

205. Filament

n. filament, line; fiber, fibril; funicle, vein, hair, cobweb, capillary, ciliolum, capillament [*rare*], cilium, cirrus, barbel, strand, tendril, gossamer; hair stroke; veinlet, venula, venule.
beard etc. (*roughness*) 256; ramification.

thread, threadlet, harl, yarn, pack-thread, cotton, sewing silk.

string, twine, twist, whipcord, cord, rope, hemp, oakum, jute; tape, ribbon, wire.

strip, shred, slip, spill, list, taenia *or* tenia, band, fillet, fascia; ribbon, ribband *or* riband [*archaic*], roll, lath, splinter, shiver, shaving; ligule *or* ligula.

adj. filamentous, filamentiferous, filaceous [*rare*], filiform; fibrous, fibrillous, fibrilliform, fibrilliferous; thread-like, wiry, stringy, ropy; capillary, capilliform; funicular, wire-drawn; anguilliform; flagelliform; barbate, hairy etc. (*rough*) 256; taeniate, taeniform, taenioid; venose, venous; ligulate *or* ligulated.

206. Height

n. height, altitude, elevation; eminence, pitch; loftiness etc. *adj.;* sublimity, celsitude [*rare*].

tallness etc. *adj.;* stature, procerity [*rare*]; prominence etc. 250; apex, zenith, culmination.

colossus etc. (*size*) 192; giant, grenadier; giraffe, camelopard.

height, mount, mountain; hill, *alto* [*Sp.*], butte, monticule, monticle [*obs.*], fell [*obs. exc. in proper names*], knap; cape; headland, foreland; promontory; ridge, hogback *or* hog's-back, dune, rising–, vantage- ground; down; moor, moorland; Alp; uplands, highlands; heights etc. (*summit*), 210; knob, *loma, pena, picacho* [*Sp.*], tump [*dial.*]; knoll, hummock, hillock, barrow, mound; steeps, bluff, cliff, craig

[*Scot.*], tor, peak, pike [*dial.*], clough [*obs.*]; escarpment, edge, ledge, brae [*Scot. & dial. Eng.*]; dizzy height.

tower, pillar, column, obelisk, monument, belfry, steeple, spire, minaret, campanile, turret, dome, cupola; pylon, *tourelle* [*F.*], barbican, martello tower; pyramid, pagoda, mole [*Rom. antiq.*],
ceiling etc. (*covering*) 223; upstairs.

pole, pikestaff, maypole, flagstaff; mast, mainmast, topmast, topgallant mast.

high water; high–, flood–, spring-tide.

hypsography, hypsometry, hypsometer, altimeter, altimetry etc. (*angle*) 244; hypsophobia.

v. be high etc. *adj.;* tower, soar, command; hover; cap, culminate; overhang, hang over, impend, beetle; bestride, ride, mount; perch, surmount; cover etc. 223; rise above, overtop etc. (*be superior*) 33; stand on tiptoe.

become high etc. *adj.;* grow, grow higher, grow taller; upgrow; rise etc. (*ascend*) 305.

render high etc. *adj.;* heighten etc. (*elevate*) 307.

adj. high, elevated, eminent, exalted, lofty; tall; gigantic etc. (*big*) 192; Patagonian; towering, beetling, soaring, mountained, hanging [gardens]; elevated etc. 307; higher, superior, upper, supernal; highest etc. (*topmost*) 210; high-reaching, insessorial, perching; hill-dwelling, monticoline, monticolous.

tall as a -maypole, –popular, –steeple; lanky etc. (*thin*) 203.

upland, moorland; hilly, knobby; mountainous, alpine, subalpine, heaven-kissing; cloud-topt, cloud-capt, cloud-touching; aërial.

overhanging etc. *v.;* incumbent; overlying; superincumbent, supernatant, superimposed; prominent etc. 250.

hypsographic, hypsographical, hypsometric, hypsometrical.

adv. on high, high up, aloft, up, above, aloof, overhead; airward; upstairs, above stairs; in the clouds; on tiptoe, on stilts, on the shoulders of; over head and ears; breast high.

over, upwards; from top to bottom etc. (*completely*) 52.

207. Lowness

n. lowness etc. *adj.;* debasement; prostration etc. (*horizontal*) 213; depression etc. (*concave*) 252; subjacency; lowlands.

ground floor; *rez de chaussée* [*F.*]; street floor.

basement, basement floor, cellar; hold; base etc. 211.

[comparison] feet, heels; molehill.

low water; low–, ebb–, neap- tide.

v.   **be low** etc. *adj.;* lie low, lie flat; underlie; crouch, slouch, wallow, grovel; lower etc. (*depress*) 308.

adj.   **low**, neap, debased; lower, inferior, under, nether; lowest, nether-most, lowermost; flat, level with the ground; lying low etc. *v.;* crouched, subjacent, squat, prostrate etc. (*horizontal*) 213; depressed.

adv.   **under**; beneath, underneath; below; down, downwards; adown, at the foot of; underfoot, underground; downstairs, belowstairs; at a low ebb; below par.

208.   Depth

n.   **depth**; deepness etc. *adj.;* profundity, depression etc. (*concavity*) 252.

   pit, shaft, hollow, well, crater; gulf etc. 198; deep, abyss, bowels of the earth, bottomless pit, hell.

   soundings, depth of water, water, draft *or* draught, submersion; plummet, sound, probe; sounding-rod, –line; lead; bathometer, bathymeter, bathymetry; benthos; submarine, sub [*colloq.*], U-boat; depth bomb.

v.   **be deep** etc. *adj.;* render deep etc. *adj.;* deepen.

   sound, heave the lead, take soundings; dig etc. (*excavate*) 252; plunge etc. 310.

adj.   **deep**, deep-seated, deep-bosomed; profound, sunk, buried; submerged etc. 310; subaqueous, submarine, subterranean, subterrene [*obs.*], subterraneous; underground.

   knee-deep, ankle-deep.

   bottomless, soundless, fathomless; unfathomed, unfathomable; abysmal; deep as a well; bathycolpian *or* bathukolpic *or* bathukolpian; deep-sea, benthal, benthopelagic; bathymetric, bathymetrical; bathypelagic, bathysmal; downreaching, yawning.

adv.   **out of one's depth**; beyond one's depth; over head and ears.

209.   Shallowness

n.   **shallowness** etc. *adj.;* shoals; mere scratch.

adj.   **shallow**, slight, superficial; skin–, ankle–, knee-deep; depthless, just enough to wet one's feet; shoal, shoaly.

210.   Summit

n.   **summit**, top, vertex, apex, summit [*obs.*], zenith, pinnacle, acme, culmination, meridian, utmost height, *ne plus ultra* [*L.*], height, pitch, maximum, climax; culminating–, crowning–, turning- point; turn of the tide, fountainhead; watershed, water parting; sky, pole.

   tip, tiptoe; crest, crow's nest, cap, truck, peak, nib; end etc. 67; crown, brow; head, nob [*slang*], noddle [*colloq.*], pate [*humorous*]; capsheaf.

   high places, heights.

   topgallant mast, skyscraper; quarter deck, hurricane deck.

   architrave, frieze, cornice, corona, coping, coping stone, zoöphorus, capital, headpiece, capstone, fastigium, larmier, epistyle, sconce, pediment, entablature; tympanum; ceiling etc. (*covering*) 223.

   attic, loft, garret, housetop, upper story, roof.

v.   **crown**, top, cap, crest, surmount; overtop etc. (*be superior to*) 33; culminate.

adj.   **highest** etc. (high etc. 206); top; topmost, overmost, uppermost; tiptop; culminating etc. *v.;* meridian, meridional; capital, head, polar, supreme, supernal, apical, culminate [*rare*], culminal [*rare*], topgallant, skyward.

adv.   **atop**, at the top of the tree; *en flûte* [*F.*]; *à fleur d'eau* [*F.*].

211.   Base

n.   **base**, basement; plinth, dado, wainscot; baseboard, mopboard; bedrock, hardpan; foundation etc. (*support*) 215; substructure, substratum, ground, earth, pavement, floor, paving, flag, carpet, ground floor, deck; footing, ground work, basis; hold, bilge, sump; cullet.

   bed, basin, channel, coulee [*Western N. Amer.*], cañon etc. (*interval*) 198.

   bottom, nadir, foot, sole, toe, hoof, keel, root; centerboard.

adj.   **bottom**, undermost, nethermost; fundamental; founded on, based on, grounded on, built on.

212.   Verticality

n.   **verticality**; erectness etc. *adj.;* perpendicularity, aplomb; right angle, normal; azimuth circle.

   cliff, steep, crag, bluff, palisades; wall, precipice.

   elevation, erection; square, plumb line, plummet.

v.   **be vertical** etc. *adj.;* stand -up, –on end, –erect, –upright; stick up, cock up.

   render vertical etc. *adj.;* set up, stick up, raise up, cock up; erect, rear, raise, pitch, raise on its legs.

adj.   **vertical**, upright, erect, perpendicular, unrecumbent [*rare*], plumb, normal, straight, bolt upright; rampant; straight up; standing up etc. *v.;* rectangular orthogonal.

adv.   **vertically** etc. *adj.;* up, on end; up–, right- on end; *à plomb* [*F.*], endwise; on one's legs; at right angles.

213. Horizontality

n. **horizontality**; flatness; level, plane; stratum etc. 204; dead level, dead flat; level plane.

recumbency; lying down etc. *v.;* reclination, decumbence *or* decumbency, discumbency [*obs.*]; proneness etc. *adj.;* accubation, supination, resupination, prostration; azimuth.

[level surfaces] plain, floor, platform, bowling green; cricket ground; croquet -ground, -lawn; billiard table, pool table; terrace, estrade [*rare*], esplanade, parterre, table-land, plateau, ledge.

v. **be horizontal** etc. *adj.;* lie, recline, couch; lie -down, -flat, -prostrate; sprawl, loll; sit down.

render horizontal etc. *adj.;* lay, lay down, lay out; level, flatten, even, raze, equalize, smooth, align.

prostrate, knock down, floor, fell, ground, drop, grass [*slang*]; cut-, hew-, mow- down.

adj. **horizontal**, level, even, plane, flush; flat etc. 251; flat as a -billiard table, -bowling green, -pool table, -pancake; alluvial; calm, -as a mill pond; smooth, -as glass.

recumbent, procumbent, accumbent, decumbent [*bot.*]; lying etc. *v.;* prone, supine, couchant, jacent [*rare*], prostrate, recubant [*rare*], resupinate.

adv. **horizontally** etc. *adj.;* on one's back, on all fours, on its beam ends.

214. Pendency

n. **pendency**, dependency; suspension, hanging etc. *v.*

pendant, drop, eardrop, tassel, tippet, lobe, tail, train, flap, skirt, queue, pigtail, pendulum; hangnail.

peg, knob, button, hook, nail, stud, ring, staple, tenterhook; fastening etc. 45; spar, horse.

chandelier, gaselier, electrolier.

v. **be pendent** etc. *adj.;* hang, depend, swing, dangle, lower, droop: swag [*dial.*]; daggle, flap, trail, flow; beetle, jut, overhang.

suspend, hang, sling, hook up, hitch, fasten to, append.

adj. **pendent**, pendulous, pendulant [*rare*], decumbent, penduline [*rare*], pensile; hanging etc. *v.;* beetle; beetling, jutting over, overhanging, projecting; dependent; lowering; suspended etc. *v.;* loose, flowing.

having a pendant etc. *n.;* tailed, caudate.

215. Support

n. **support**, ground, foundation, base, basis; *terra firma* [*L.*], bearing, fulcrum, bait, caudex, crib;

point d'appui [*F.*], *pou sto* [*Gr.*], purchase, footing, hold, *locusstandi* [*L.*]; landing, -stage, -place; stage, platform; block; rest, resting place; groundwork, substratum, riprap, sustentation [*now rare*], sustention [*rare*], subvention; floor etc. (*basement*) 211.

supporter; aid etc. 707; prop, stand, anvil, fulciment [*obs.*]; cue rest, jigger [*slang*], monkey [*builders' slang*], hod; stay, shore, skid, rib, truss, bandage; sleeper; stirrup, stilts, shoe, sole, heel, splint, lap; bar, rod, boom, spirit, outrigger; ratline *or* ratlin *or* ratling.

pedicle, pedicel *or* pedicellus *or* pediculus, peduncle [*all bot.*], stalk.

board, ledge, shelf, hob, bracket, trivet, arbor, rack; mantel, mantelpiece, mantelshelf; slab, console; counter, dresser; flange, corbel; table, trestle; shoulder; perch; horse, easel, desk; clotheshorse, hatrack; retable, predella, teapoy.

staff, stick, crutch, alpenstock, baton, crosier, cross, crook, lituus [*Rom. antiq.*], caduceus, thyrsus, staddle; bourdon, cowlstaff [*archaic*], *lathi* [*Hind.*], maulstick *or* mahlstick.

post, pillar, shaft, thill, column, pilaster; pediment, pedestal; plinth, shank, leg, socle *or* zocle; buttress, jamb, mullion, stile, abutment; baluster, banister, stanchion; balustrade; headstone.

frame, framework; scaffold, skeleton, beam, rafter, girder, lintel, joist, travis *or* traviss [*dial. Eng.*], trave, corner stone, summer, breastsummer *or* bressomer, summertree, transom; rung, round, step, sill; angle-rafter, hiprafter; cantilever, modillion; crown-post, king-post; vertebra, modiolus.

columella, backbone; keystone; axle, axletree; axis; arch, mainstay.

trunnion, pivot, rowlock; peg etc. (*pendency*) 214; tiebeam etc. (*fastening*) 45; thole pin.

seat, throne, dais; divan, musnud *or* masnad [*Ar.*], guddee *or* gaddi [*Hind.*]; chair, bench, form, sofa, davenport, couch, day-bed, settee, stall; wingchair, armchair, easychair, elbowchair, rocking-chair; *fauteuil* [*F.*], woolsack, ottoman, settle, squab, bench; long chair, long-sleeve chair [*Anglo-Ind.*], *chaise longue* [*F.*], morris chair; *lamba chauki or lamba kursi* [*Hind.*]; saddle, aparejo, panel *or* pannel, pillion; sidesaddle, packsaddle; pommel, horn.

stool, foldstool, *prie-dieu* [*F.*], hassock, footstool; tabouret; tripod.

bed, berth, pallet, tester-bed, crib, cot, hammock, shakedown, truckle-bed, trundle-bed, cradle, litter, stretcher, bedstead; four-poster, French bed; bunk, kip [*dial.*], *palang* [*Hind.*]; roost [*slang*]; bedding, *bichhana* [*Hind.*], mattress, paillasse; pillow, bolster; mat, rug, cushion.

Atlas, Herakles *or* Hercules; tortoise that supports the earth.

[in architecture] atlas (*pl.* atlantes), telamon (*pl.* telamones), caryatid (*pl.* caryatids *or* caryatides).

v. **be supported** etc.; lie–, sit–, recline–, lean–, loll–, rest–, stand–, step–, repose–, abut–, bear–, be based etc.-on; have at one's back; bestride, bestraddle.

support, bear, carry, hold, sustain, shoulder; hold up, back up, bolster up, shore up; uphold, upbear; brace, truss, cradle, pillow, prop; underprop, underpin, underset; riprap; bandage etc. 43.

give–, furnish–, afford–, supply–, lend- -support, –foundations; bottom, found, base, ground, embed, imbed.

maintain, keep on foot; aid etc. 707.

adj. **supporting,** supported, etc. *v.;* Atlantean, columellar, columelliform; sustentative, sustentational; fundamental; dorsigerous.

having a pedicle etc. *n.;* pedunculate, pedicellate.

adv. **straddle,** astride on.

216. Parallelism

n. **parallelism,** coextension, equidistance, concentricity; collimation.

v. **be parallel** etc. *adj.;* parallel, equal; collimate.

adj. **parallel,** coextensive, equidistant, collateral, concentric, concurrent; abreast, aligned, equal, even, alongside.

adv. alongside etc. (*laterally*) 236.

217. Obliquity

n. **obliquity,** inclination, incline, slope, slant, skew, thrawnness [*Scott. & dial. Eng.*]; crookedness etc. *adj.;* slopeness; leaning etc. *v.;* bevel, ramp, pitch, bezel, tilt; bias, list, twist, swag [*prov. Eng.*], sag, cant, lurch; distortion etc. 243; bend etc. (*curve*) 245; tower of Pisa.

acclivity, rise, ascent, gradient [*chiefly Brit.*], grade [*U. S.*], *khudd* [*Hind.*], glacis, rising ground, hill, bank, declivity, downhill, dip, fall, devexity [*obs.*]; gentle–, rapid- slope; easy -ascent, –descent; shelving beach; talus; *montagne Russe* [*F.*]; *facilis descensus Averni* [*L.*].

steepness etc. *adj.;* cliff, precipice etc. (*vertical*) 212; escarpment, scarp; chevron.

[measure of inclination] clinometer; sine, cosine, cotangent, angle, hypothenuse.

diagonal; zigzag.

v. **be oblique** etc. *adj.;* slope, slant, skew, lean, incline, shelve, stoop, decline, descend, bend, keel, careen, sag, swag [*dial.*], seel [*obs.*], slouch, cant, sidle.

render oblique etc. *adj.;* sway, bias; slope, slant; incline, bend, crook; cant, tilt; distort etc. 243.

adj. **oblique,** inclined; sloping etc. *v.;* tilted etc. *v.;* recubant [*rare*], recumbent, clinical, skew, askew, slant, bias, aslant, plagihedral, indirect, wry, awry; agee *or* ajee, thrawn [*both Scot. & dial. Eng.*], crooked; sinuous, zigzag, zigzaggy, chevrony; knock-kneed etc. (*distorted*) 243; bevel, out of the perpendicular; aslope; asquint, backhand *or* backhanded.

uphill, rising, ascending, acclivous.

downhill, falling, descending; hanging (as, *hanging* gardens), declining, declivitous, proclivous [*rare*], declivous, devex [*obs.*], synclinal, anticlinal.

steep, abrupt, precipitous, breakneck.

diagonal; transverse, transversal; athwart, antiparallel; curved etc. 245; loxic, loxotic, loxodromic.

adv. **obliquely** etc. *adj.;* on one side, all on one side; askew, askance *or* askant, awry, skew, skewed, edgewise, at an angle; sidelong, sideways; slopewise, slantwise; by a side wind.

218. Inversion

n. **inversion,** eversion, subversion, reversion, retroversion, introversion; retroflexion; contraposition etc. 237; contrariety etc. 14; reversal; turn of the tide etc. (*reversion*) 145.

overturn; somersault *or* summersault, somerset *or* summerset; *culbute* [*F.*] eversion [*archaic*]; revulsion; pirouette.

transposition, transposal, anastrophy, metastasis, hyperbaton, anastrophe; hysterology, hysteron proteron; hypallage, synchysis, tmesis, parenthesis; metathesis; palindrome; ectropion [*path.*]; invagination, intussusception.

pronation and supination.

v. **be inverted** etc.; turn–, go–, wheel- -round, –about, –to the right-about [*colloq.*]; turn–, go–, tilt–, topple- over; capsize, turn turtle.

invert, subvert, retrovert, introvert; reverse; turn the cat in the pan [*obs*]; upturn, overturn, upset, overset, *bouleverser* [*F.*], evert [*archaic*]; turn topsy-turvy etc. *adj.; culbuter* [*F.*]; transpose, put the cart before the horse, turn the tables; invaginate, intussuscept.

adj. **inverted** etc. v.; wrong side -out, –up; inside out, upside down; bottom–, keel- upwards; supine, on one's head, topsy-turvy, *sens dessus dessous* [F.]; ectropic.

inverse; reverse etc. (*contrary*) 14; opposite etc. 237; palindromic *or* palindromical.

topheavy, unstable.

adv. **inversely** etc. adj.; heels over head, head over heels.

219. Crossing

n. **crossing** etc. v.; intersection, interdigitation; decussation, transversion; chiasm *or* chiasma; convolution etc. 248; level crossing [Eng.], grade crossing.

network, reticulation, cancellation; inosculation, anastomosis, intertexture, mortise.

net, plexus, plexure, web, mesh, twill, skein, Hippocrates' sleeve, sleave [*archaic*]; sieve, sifter, riddle rocker, screen, cradle; felt, lace; wicker; mat, matting; plait, trellis, wattle, lattice, grating, grille, gridiron, tracery, fretwork, filigree, reticle [*obs.*]; tissue, netting, moke [*dial. Eng.*]; rivulation.

cross, chain, wreath, braid, cat's cradle, knot; entanglement etc. (*disorder*) 59.

crucifix, cross, rood, crisscross, christcross, tau; crux.

[woven fabrics] cloth, linen, muslin, cambric, *toile* [F.], drill, homespun, silk, satin, broadcloth, tweed etc.

v. **cross**, decussate; intersect, interlace, intertwine, intertwist, interweave, interdigitate, interlink, intercross [*rare*], crisscross, crossbar.

twine, entwine, weave, inweave, twist, wreathe; anastomose, inosculate, dovetail, splice, link.

mat, plait, pleat, plat, braid, felt, twill; tangle, entangle, ravel; net, knot; dishevel, raddle.

adj. **crossing** etc. v.; crossed, matted etc. v.; transverse; intersected, decussate *or* decussated; chiasmal.

cross, cross-shaped cruciform, crucial; netlike, retiform, reticular, reticulate; areolar, cancellate *or* cancellated, cancellous, latticed, grated, barred, streaked; textile; crossbarred, cruciate, secant; cruciferous; plexal, plexiform; anastomotic; web-footed, palmiped.

adv. **cross**, thwart, athwart, transversely; at grade; crosswise, thwartwise [*rare*].

220. Exteriority

n. **exteriority**; outside, exterior; surface, superficies; skin etc. (*covering*) 223; superstratum; disk *or* disc; face, facet; extrados.

eccentricity; circumjacence etc. 227.

v. **be exterior** etc. adj.; lie around etc. 227.

place exteriorly, place outwardly, place outside; put out, turn out.

externalize, objectize [*rare*], objectify, visualize, envisage, actualize.

adj. **exterior**, external, extraneous; outer, outermost; outward, outlying, outside, outdoor, *alfresco* [*It.*]; round about etc. 227; extramural; extralimitary, extramundane, extraterrene, extraterrestrial, extraterritorial, exterritorial; extern [*rare*].

extraregarding; eccentric *or* eccentrical; outstanding; extrinsic etc. 6; ecdemic, exomorphic.

superficial, skin-deep; frontal, discoid.

adv. **externally** etc. adj.; out, without, over, outwards, *ab extra* [L.], out of doors; *extra muros* [L.].

in the open air; *sub Jove* [L.], *sub dio* [L.]; *à la belle étoile* [F.], *alfresco* [It.].

221. Interiority

n. **interiority**; inside, interior; interspace, subsoil, substratum; intrados.

contents etc. 190; substance, pith, marrow; backbone etc. (*center*) 222; heart, bosom, breast; abdomen.

vitals, viscera, entrails, bowels, belly, intestines, guts [*vulgar or tech.*], chitterlings, chitlings *or* chitlins, womb, lap [*obs.*], rectum, cecum *or* caecum, ileum, duodenum, jejunum.

gland, glandule [*rare*], gland cell; thyroid, parotid, prostate; liver, kidney.

penetralia, recesses, innermost recesses; cave etc. (*concavity*) 252.

enterology, enterotomy, enteropathy, enteritis, splanchnology; peristalsis, vermiculation.

inmate, intern, inhabitant etc. 188.

v. **be inside** etc. adj.; be within etc. adv.

inclose etc. (*circumscribe*) 229; intern embed *or* imbed etc. (*insert*) 300; place within, keep within.

adj. **interior**, internal; inner, intern [*archaic*], intraneous [*rare*], intimate, inside, inward, intraregarding; inmost, innermost; deep-seated; intestine, intestinal, visceral, rectal, duodenal, splanchnic; subcutaneous; abdominal, celiac *or* coeliac, endomorphic.

intracanal, intracellular, intralobular, intramarginal, intramolecular, intramundane, intraocular, intraseptal, intratelluric, intrauterine, intravascular, intravenous, intraventricular.

interstitial etc. (*interjacent*) 228; inwrought etc. (*intrinsic*) 5; inclosed etc. v.

home, inland, domestic, family, indoor, intramural, vernacular; endemic.

adv. **internally** etc. *adj.;* inwards, within, in, inly; herein, therein, wherein, *ab intra* [*L.*]; indoors, within doors; at home, in the bosom of one's family.

222. Centrality

n. **centrality**, centricalness, centricality, center *or* centre; middle etc. 68; focus etc. 74.

center of -gravity, –pressure, –percussion, –oscillation, –buoyancy etc.; metacenter.

core, kernel; nucleus, nucleolus; heart, pole, axis, bull's-eye, nave, hub, navel, umbilicus; marrow, pith; backbone; vertebra, vertebral column; hotbed.

concentration etc. (*convergence*) 290; centralization; symmetry; metropolis.

v. **be central** etc. *adj.;* converge etc. 290.

render central, centralize, concentrate; bring to a focus.

adj. **central**, centrical; middle etc. 68; axial, pivotal, nuclear, nucleate, centric, focal, umbilical, concentric; middlemost; rachial, rachidial *or* rachidian; spinal, vertebral; metropolitan.

adv. **middle**; midst; centrally etc. *adj.*

223. Covering

n. **covering**, cover, baldachin *or* baldaquin; canopy, *shamianah* [*Hind.*], tilt, awning, tent, marquee, marquise, wigwam, tepee, *tente d'abri* [*F.*], umbrella, parasol, sunshade; veil (*shade*) 424; shield etc. (*defense*) 717.

roof, ceiling, thatch, tile, pantile, tiling, slates, slating, leads, shingles; dome, cupola, mansard, hip roof; barrack, *plafond* [*F.*], planchment, tiling, shed etc. (*abode*) 189.

top, lid, covercle [*obs.*], door, operculum; bulkhead.

wrapping, bandage, dressing, plaster, lint, dossil, pledget, finger stall.

coverlet, counterpane, sheet, quilt, blanket, rug, drugget; housing; tidy, antimacassar, eiderdown quilt *or* eiderdown; comforter *or* comfortable *or* comfort, numdah [*Hind.*], pillowcase, pillowslip; linoleum, oilcloth; tarpaulin; saddle blanket, saddlecloth; tilpah, apishamore, poncho.

tegmen (*pl.* tegmina), integument, tegument; skin, pellicle, fleece, fell, fur, leather, lambskin, sable, miniver, beaver, ermine, shagreen, hide, coat, buff, pelt, peltry [*collective noun*]; cordwain [*archaic*]; robe, buffalo robe.

cuticle, cutis, dermis, corium, scarfskin, epidermis, derm [*rare*], derma; ectoderm, epithelium, ecderon, ecteron, enderon.

exuviae, desquamation, slough, cast, cast-off skin.

clothing etc. 225; mask etc. (*concealment*) 530.

peel, crust, bark, rind. cortex, husk, shell, epicarp, testa; eggshell, glume.

capsule; sheath, sheathing; pod, cod [*dial.*], casing, case, theca; elytron; elytrum; involucrum; wrapping, wrapper; envelope, vesicle; cornhusk, cornshuck.

dermatography, dermatology, dermatogen, dermoplasty, dermatopathy, dermatophyte; conchology; testaceology.

veneer, facing; pavement; imbrication, scale etc. (*layer*) 204; anointing etc. *v.;* ointment etc. (*grease*) 356; inunction; incrustation, superposition, obduction [*obs.*]; coating, paint, stain, engobe; varnish etc. (*resin*) 356a; ground, enamel, whitewash, plaster, stucco, roughcast, plasterwork, scagliola, compo; cerement; cerecloth, shroud.

v. **cover**; superpose, superimpose; overlay, overspread; wrap etc. 225; incase, encase, enchase, face, case, veneer, pave, paper; tip, cap, bind; bulkhead, bulkhead in; clapboard, shingle; imbricate.

overlie, overarch; endome [*rare*]; conceal etc. 528.

coat, paint, stain, varnish, flat, incrust, encrust, crust, cement, roughcast, stucco, dab, plaster, tar; wash; besmear; bedaub; anoint, do over; gild, plate, japan, lacquer, lacker, enamel, whitewash; parget; lay it on thick.

adj. **covering** etc. *v.;* cutaneous, dermal, cortical, cuticular, tegumentary, tegumental, tegmental, integumentary, integumental, epidermal *or* epidermic, endermic, epicarpal, testaceous, dermatopathic, dermatological, dermoplastic, dermatophytic, subcutaneous, hypodermic.

scaly, squamate, squamiferous, squamous; covered etc. *v.;* imbricate, imbricated, loricate, loricated, armored, encuirassed, armor-plated, ironclad, under cover.

hooded, cowled, cucullate *or* cuculated, tectiform, rooflike; vaginate.

skinlike, dermic, dermoid, dermatoid, epidermoid, skinny.

224. Lining

n. **lining**, inner coating; coating etc. (*covering*) 223; stalactite, stalagmite.

filling, stuffing, wadding, padding, facing; bushing.

    wainscot, parietes, wall, brattice, sheathing.

v.   **line**, stuff, incrust, wad, pad, fill, face, ceil, bush, wainscot, sheathe.

adj.   **lined** etc. *v.*

225. Investment

n.   **investment**; covering etc. 223; dress, clothing, raiment, drapery, costume, attire, guise, toilet, toilette, trim; habiliment; vesture, vestment; garment, garb, palliament [*obs.*], apparel, wardrobe, wearing apparel, clothes, things.

    array; tailoring, millinery; best bib and tucker [*colloq.*]; finery etc. (*ornament*) 847; full dress etc. (*show*) 882; garniture; theatrical properties.

    outfit, equipment, trousseau; uniform, khaki, olive-drab, regimentals; continentals [*Am. hist.*]; canonicals etc. 999; livery, gear, harness, turnout, accouterment, caparison, suit, rigging, trappings, traps [*colloq.*], slops, togs [*colloq.*], toggery [*colloq.*]; masquerade.

    dishabille *or* deshabille, morning dress, tea gown, wrapper, negligee *or négligé* [*F.*], dressing gown, undress; kimono; shooting coat; smoking jacket; mufti [*chiefly Eng.*]; rags, tatters, old clothes; mourning, weeds; duds [*colloq.*]; slippers.

    robe, tunic, paletot, habit, gown, coat, frock, blouse, middy blouse *or* middy, jumper, shirt waist, suit; one-piece -, two-piece- suit; toga, smock, frock; Prince Albert coat [*colloq.*]; frock–, sack–, tail- coat.

    dress suit, dress clothes, evening dress, swallow-tailed coat [*colloq.*], claw-hammer coat [*colloq.*]; dinner -coat, –jacket; tuxedo, soup-and-fish [*colloq.*]; glad rags [*slang*].

    cloak, pall [*archaic*], mantle, mantua, mantelet *or* mantlet, sagum, shawl, pelisse, wrapper; veil; cape, kirtle [*archaic*], plaid [*Scot.*], tippet, muffler, comforter, balaklava helmet, haik, huke [*obs.*], chlamys, mantilla, tabard, housing, horse cloth, burnoose *or* burnous, roquelaure; houpland [*hist.*]; surcoat, overcoat, greatcoat, surtout, spencer; oilskins, slicker, mackintosh, waterproof, ulster, dreadnaught *or* dreadnought, wraprascal, poncho; pea-coat, pea-jacket; cardinal, pelerine; chuddar *or* chadar [*Hind.*], jubbah [*Hind.*], pullover, pyjamas *or* pajamas, pilot jacket, sweater, blazer, coatee, cardigan *or* cardigan jacket; Mackinaw coat *or* Mackinaw; talma.

    jacket, vest, jerkin [*hist. or dial.*], *chaqueta* [*Sp.*], sontag, waistcoat, doublet, gaberdine; stays, corsage, corset, bra, *brassière* [*F.*], camisole, corselet, bodice; stomacher.

    skirt, petticoat, farthingale, kilt, filibeg *or* philibeg, jupe, crinoline, bustle, panier, apron, pinafore; bloomer, bloomers; *tablier* [*F.*].

    loin cloth, dhoti [*Hindu*], lungi [*Burmese*]; G string.

    trousers, breeches, pantaloons, inexpressibles [*humorous*], trews [*Scot.*], innominables [*humorous*], unmentionables [*humorous*], continuations [*slang*], kicks [*slang*]; overalls, smalls [*colloq. or archaic*], smallclothes [*archaic*]; pants [*colloq.*]; shintiyan; shorts; tights, drawers; knickerbockers, knickers [*Engl. colloq.*].

    headdress, headgear, coiffure [*F.*], head, headcloths, *chignon* [*F.*]; *chapeau* [*F.*], crush hat, opera hat; kaffiyeh [*Ar.*]; taj, tam-o'-shanter, topee *or* topi [*India*], sola topi [*India*], puggree *or* pagri [*Hind.*]; sombrero, sundown, cap, hat, beaver, castor, bonnet, tile [*slang*], wide-awake, panama, leghorn; derby, bowler [*Eng.*], billycock [*Eng.*]; wimple; nightcap, skullcap; mobcap, boudoir cap, Dutch cap; Salvation-Army bonnet; hood, coif, capote, calash, kerchief, snood; crown etc. (*circle*) 247; pelt, wig, front, peruke, periwig; caftan, turban, fez, tarboosh, shako, busby; kepi, forage cap, campaign hat, overseas cap, bearskin; helmet etc. 717; mask, domino.

    body clothes; linen; hickory shirt [*U. S.*]; shirt, O.-D. (olive-drab) shirt; sark [*archaic or dial.*], smock, shift, chemise; nightgown, nightshirt; bed-gown, *sac de nuit* [*F.*]; jersey; underclothing, underwaistcoat, undershirt, undervest, chemisette, guimpe.

    tie, neckerchief, neckcloth; ruff, collar, cravat, stock, handkerchief, scarf; bib, tucker; boa; girdle etc. (*circle*) 247; cummerbund [*India*], *rumal* [*Hind.*], *rabat* [*F.*], rabato.

    shoe, pump, sneakers, boot, slipper, sandal, galosh *or* galoshe, patten, clog; high-low; Blucher–, Wellington–, Hessian–, jack–, top- boot; Oxford -shoe, –tie; Balmoral; arctics, bootee, bootikin, brogan, brogue, *chaparajos* [*Mex. Sp.*], chaps [*colloq.*], *chivarras or chivarros* [*Sp. Amer.*]; gums [*U. S.*], larrigan [*N. Amer.*], rubbers; snowshoe, ski; stogy, *veldtschoen* [*Dutch*], legging, puttee *or* putty, buskin, greave, galligaskin [*dial.*], moccasin, gambado, gaiter, spatterdashes, spats, gamashes [*archaic or dial. Eng.*], *gamache* [*F.*]; antigropelos.

    stocking, hose, gaskins [*obs.*], trunk hose, sock; hosiery.

    glove, gauntlet, mitten, mitt.

    cuff, wristband; sleeve.

    baby linen, swaddling clothes, diaper, layette.

[suppliers] clothier, tailor, snip [*slang*], tailoress, milliner, costumer, costumier, seamstress *or* sempstress, dressmaker, *modiste* [*F.*], habit-maker; breeches-maker; shoemaker, Crispin cordwainer, cobbler; hosier, hatter, glover, draper, linen draper, haberdasher, mercer; hairdresser, *friseur* [*F.*].

v. **invest**; cover etc. 223; envelop, lap, involve; inwrap *or* enwrap; wrap; fold up, wrap up, lap up, muffle up; overlap; sheathe, swathe, swaddle, roll up in, shroud, circumvest [*obs.*].

clothe, vest [*rare*], array, dress, dight [*archaic*], bedight [*archaic*], drape, robe, enrobe, attire, apparel, tire [*archaic*], habilitate [*rare*], garb, enclothe, breech, coat, jacket, gown, accouter, rig, fit out; dizen, bedizen, deck etc. (*ornament*) 847; perk, equip, harness, caparison.

wear; don; put on, huddle on, slip on; mantle.

adj. **invested** etc. *v.;* habited; dight, dighted; barbed, barded; clad, *costumé* [*F.*], shod, *chaussé* [*F.*]; *en grande tenue* [*F.*] etc. (*show*) 882; *décolletée* [*F.*].

sartorial, sartorian [*rare*].

226. Divestment

n. **divestment**; taking off etc. *v.*

nudity; bareness etc. *adj.;* undress; dishabille etc. 225; altogether; *tout ensemble* [*F.*]; nudation [*rare*], denudation; decortication, depilation, excoriation, desquamation, slough etc. 223; molting *or* moulting, exuviation; exfoliation; trichosis.

baldness, hairlessness, alopecia.

v. **divest**; uncover etc. (cover etc. 223); denude, bare, strip; disfurnish; undress, disrobe etc. (dress, enrobe etc. 225); uncoif; dismantle; put off, take off, cast off; doff.

peel, pare, decorticate, desquamate, slough, excoriate, skin, scalp, flay, bark, husk, rind; expose, lay open; exfoliate, molt *or* moult, exuviate, mew [*archaic*]; cast the skin.

adj. **divested** etc. *v.;* bare, naked, nude; undressed, undraped, unclad, ungarmented, unclothed, unapparelled, unarrayed; exposed; in dishabille.

in a state of nature, in nature's garb, in the buff, in native buff, in birthday suit; *in puris naturalibus* [*L.*]; with nothing on, stark-naked; bare as the back of one's hand.

out at elbows; threadbare, ragged, callow, roofless; barefoot; bareback, barebacked; leafless, napless, hairless.

bald, hairless, depilous [*rare*], glabrous, glabrate, tonsured, beardless, bald as a coot.

exuvial, sloughy, desquamative, desquamatory.

227. Circumjacence

n. **circumjacence** or circumjacency, circumfluence [*rare*], circumambience environment, encompassment; atmosphere, medium; surroundings, *entourage* [*F.*].

outpost; border etc. (*edge*) 231; girdle etc. (*circumference*) 230; outskirts, boulevards, suburbs, purlieus, precincts, *faubourgs* [*F.*], environs, environment, entourage, *banlieue* [*F.*], neighborhood, vicinage, vicinity.

v. **lie around** etc. *adv.;* surround, beset, compass, encompass, environ, inclose *or* enclose, encircle, encincture [*rare*], circle, girdle, ensphere, hedge, embrace, circumvent, lap, gird; belt; begird, engird; skirt, twine round; hem in etc. (*circumscribe*) 229; beleaguer, invest, besiege, beset, blockade.

adj. **circumjacent**, circumambient, circumfluent; ambient; surrounding etc. *v.;* circumferential, suburban.

adv. **around**, about; without; on every side, on all sides; right and left, all round, roundabout.

228. Interjacence

n. **interjacence** or interjacency, intercurrence, intervenience *or* inteveniency [*rare*], interlocation, interdigitation, interpenetration; permeation.

interjection, interpolation, interlineation, interspersion, intercalation; embolism.

intervention, interference, interposition, intromission, intrusion, obtrusion; insinuation; insertion etc. 300; dovetailing; infiltration.

intermedium, intermediary; go-between, interagent, middleman, intervener, mean, medium, bodkin [*colloq.*], intruder, interloper; parenthesis, episode, flyleaf.

partition, septum, interseptum, phragma, septulum, mediastinum, diaphragm, midriff; dissepiment; party wall, panel, bulkhead, brattice, *cloison* [*F.*], perpend, halfway house.

v. **lie between**, come between, get between; intervene, slide in, interpenetrate, permeate.

put between, introduce, import; throw in, wedge in, edge in, jam in, worm in, foist in, run in, plow in, work in; interpose, interject, intercalate, interpolate, interline, interleave, intersperse, interweave, interlard, interdigitate; let in, dovetail, splice, mortise; insinuate, smuggle; infiltrate, ingrain.

interfere, put in an oar, stick one's nose in; intrude, obtrude; have a finger in the pie; introduce the thin end of the wedge; thrust in etc. (*insert*) 300.

adj. **interjacent**, intervenient [*rare*], intervening etc.
v.; intercalary, intercolumnar, intercostal, intercurrent, interfacial, intergrowth, interlineal, interlobular, interlocular, intermedial, intermediary, intermediate, intermaxillary, intermolecular, intermundane, internasal, interneural, internodal, interoceanic, interosseal, interosseous, interplanetary, interpolar, interradial, interrenal, interscapular, interseptal, interstellar, interstitial, intervalvular, intervascular, interventricular, intervertebral; septal, embolismal.

parenthetical, episodic; mediterranean; intrusive; embosomed; merged.

mean, medium, mesne, middle, median.

adv. **between**, betwixt; 'twixt; among *or* amongst; amid, amidst; 'mid, 'midst; in the thick of; betwixt and between [*colloq.*]; sandwich-wise; parenthetically, *obiter dictum* [*L.*].

229. Circumscription

n. **circumscription**, limitation, inclosure; confinement etc. (*restraint*) 751; circumvallation; encincture; envelope etc. 232.

v. **circumscribe**, limit, bound, confine, inclose *or* enclose; surround etc. 227; compass about; imprison etc. (*restrain*) 751; hedge in, wall in, rail in; fence round, hedge round; picket; corral.

enfold, bury, incase, pack up, enshrine, inclasp *or* enclasp; wrap up etc. (*invest*) 225; embay, embosom.

adj. **circumscribed** etc. *v.;* begirt, circumambient, girt, cinct [*rare*], circumcinct [*rare*], lapt; buried in, immersed in; embosomed, in the bosom of, imbedded, encysted, mewed up; imprisoned etc. 751; landlocked, in a ring fence.

230. Outline

n. **outline**, circumference; perimeter, periphery; ambit, circuit, lines, *tournure* [*F.*], contour, profile, silhouette, relief, lineaments; bounds; coast line.

zone, belt, girth, band, baldric, zodiac, girdle, tire, cingle [*rare*], clasp, girt, girth; cordon etc. (*inclosure*) 232; circlet etc. 247.

v. **outline**, contour, delineate, silhouette, block, sketch, profile; circumscribe etc. 229.

adj. **outlined** etc. *v.;* circumferential, perimetric, perimetrical, peripheral.

231. Edge

n. **edge**, verge, brink, brow, brim, margin, border, confine, skirt, rim, flange, side, mouth; jaws, chops, chaps, fauces, lip, muzzle.

shore, coast, strand, bank; bunder, bund [*both Oriental*], quay, wharf, dock, mole, landing.

fringe, flounce, frill, list, trimming, edging, skirting, hem, selvage *or* selvedge, welt; furbelow, valance; frame; exergue.

threshold, door, porch; portal etc. (*opening*) 260.

v. **edge**, border, skirt, fringe, marginate.

adj. **border**, marginal, skirting; labial, labiated, marginated.

232. Inclosure

n. **inclosure** *or* enclosure, envelope; case etc. (*receptacle*) 191; wrapper; girdle etc. 230.

pen, fold; sty, penfold, sheepfold; paddock, croft, pasture, wood lot; pound; corral; yard, compound; net, seine net.

fence etc. (*defense*) 717; pale, paling, balustrade, rail, railing, quickset hedge, park paling, circumvallation, *enceinte* [*F.*]; ring fence; wall; hedge, hedgerow; espalier.

barrier, barricade; gate, gateway; weir; bent, dingle; door, hatch, cordon; prison etc. 752.

dike, ditch, fosse, trench, drain, dugout, *tranchée* [*F.*], *coupure* [*F.*], moat.

v. **inclose** *or* enclose; circumscribe etc. 229.

233. Limit

n. **limit**, boundary, bounds, confine, enclave, term, bourn *or* bourne, verge, curbstone, but [*Scot.*], pale; termination, terminus, terminal; stint, stent; frontier, precinct, marches; backwoods.

boundary line, landmark; line of -demarcation, -circumvallation; pillars of Hercules; Rubicon, turning point; *ne plus ultra* [*L.*]; sluice, floodgate.

v. **limit**, bound, compass, confine, define, circumscribe, demarcate, delimit.

adj. **definite**; conterminate [*obs.*], conterminable; terminable, limitable; terminal, frontier, bordering, border, limitary, boundary, limital [*rare*].

adv. **thus far**, -and no further.

234. Front

n. **front**; fore, fore part *or* forepart; foreground, forefront; face, disk *or* disc, frontage, façade, proscenium, facia, frontispiece; priority, anteriority; obverse (*of a medal*).

van, vanguard; advanced guard; forerank, front rank; outpost; first line; scout.

brow, forehead, visage, physiognomy, phiz [*colloq.*], features, countenance, mug [*slang*]; metoposcopy; chin, mentum; rostrum, beak, bow, stem, prow, prore, jib, bowsprit.

pioneer etc. (*precursor*) 64; metoposcopist, physiognomist

v. **front,** face, confront, breast, buck [*slang*], brave, dare, defy oppose, outbrazen; bend forwards; come to the front, come to the fore; be *or* stand in front etc. *adj.*

adj. **fore,** forward, anterior, front, frontal; metopic

adv. **before** in front, in the van, in advance; ahead right ahead; foremost, headmost in the foreground, in the lee of; before one's -face, −eyes: face to face, *vis-à-vis* [*F.*]; *front à front* [*F.*].

235. Rear

n. **rear,** back, posteriority; rear rank, rear guard, rearward [*archaic*]; background, hinterland. occiput, nape; heels.
spine, backbone, rachis, spinal column, chine.
tail, scut, brush, appendage [*humorous*].
rump, croup, buttock, posteriors, fundament, bottom [*colloq.*], stern [*colloq.*], seat, backside [*vulgar*], breech, dorsum, tergum, loin; dorsal−, lumbar-region; hind quarters; aitchbone.
stern, poop, counter, mizzenmast, postern door, tailpiece, after-part, heel-piece, crupper.
wake; train etc. (*sequence*) 281.
reverse; other side of the shield.

v. **be behind** etc. *adv.;* fall astern; bend backwards; bring up the rear; heel, tag, shadow, follow etc. (*pursue*) 622.

adj. **back,** rear; hind, hinder, hindmost, hindermost; sternmost; postern, posterior; dorsal, after; caudal, tergal, neural, spinal, vertebral, lumbar; mizzen.

adv. **behind;** in the -rear, −background; behind one's back; at the -heels, −tail, −back- of; back to back.
after, aft, abaft, baft, astern, aback, rearward, hindward, backward.

236. Laterality

n. **laterality** [*rare*]; side, flank, quarter, lee; hand; cheek, jowl *or* jole, wing; profile; temple, paries (*pl.* parietes), loin, haunch, hip; beam.
gable, gable-end; broadside; lee side.
points of the compass; East, sunrise, Orient, Levant; West, Occident, sunset; orientation.

v. **flank,** outflank; sidle; skirt, border, wing; orientate; be on one side etc. *adv.*

adj. **lateral,** sidelong; collateral; parietal, flanking, skirting; flanked; sideling.
many-sided; multilateral, bilateral, trilateral, quadrilateral.
eastern, eastward, east, orient, oriental, auroral *or* aurorean; Levantine.

western, west, westerly, westward, occidental, Hesperian.

adv. **sideways** *or* sideway, sidewise, sideling, sidelong; broadside on; on one side, abreast, alongside, beside, aside; by, by the side of; side by side; cheek by jowl etc. (*near*) 197; to windward, to leeward; laterally etc. *adj.;* right and left; on her beam ends.

237. Contraposition

n. **contraposition,** opposition; polarity; inversion etc. 218; opposite side; reverse, inverse; counterpart; antithesis.
antipodes, opposite poles, North and South.

v. **be opposite** etc. *adj.;* subtend.

adj. **opposite;** reverse, inverse; converse; antipodal, diametrical, antithetic, counter, subcontrary; fronting, facing, diametrically opposite.
northern, north, northerly, northward, hyperborean, septentrional, boreal, polar, arctic.
southern, south, southerly, meridional, southward, Austral, antarctic.

adv. **over,** over the way, over against; against; face to face, *vis-à-vis* [*F.*]; as poles asunder.

238. Dextrality

n. **dextrality;** right, right hand; dexter, offside, starboard.

adj. **dextral,** dexterous *or* dextrous, right-handed; dexter, dextrorsal, dextrorse.
ambidexter, ambidextrous, ambidextral.

adv. **dextrad,** dextrally; ambidextrously.

239. Sinistrality

n. **sinistrality,** sinistration; left, left hand, southpaw; *sinistra or sinistra mano* [*music, It.*]; nearside, larboard, port.

adj. **left-handed,** sinister-handed [*obs.*], sinister, sinistral, sinistrorsal, sinistrorse, sinistrous, ambilevous [*rare*]; sinistrogyrate, sinistrogyric.

adv. **sinistrad,** sinistrally, sinistrously.

Section 3. Form

240. Form

n. **form,** figure, shape; conformation, configuration; make, formation, frame, construction, cut, set, build, *tournure* [*F.*], outline, get-up [*colloq.*], trim, cut of one's jib [*colloq.*]; stamp, type, cast, mold *or* mould; fashion; contour etc. (*outline*) 230; structure etc. 329; plasmature [*obs.*].

feature, lineament, turn; phase etc. (*aspect*) 448; posture, attitude, pose.

[science of form] morphology.

[similarity of form] isomorphism; isomorph.

formation, figuration, efformation [*rare*]; forming etc. *v.;* sculpture; plasmation [*rare*].

v. form, shape, figure, fashion, efform [*rare*], carve, cut, chisel, hew, cast; roughhew, roughcast; sketch; block out, hammer out; trim; lick–, put-into shape; model, knead, work up into, set, mold, sculpture; cast, stamp; build etc. (*construct*) 161.

adj. formed etc. *v.;* structural, morphologic *or* morphological.

shapely, well-proportioned, symmetrical, well-made, well-formed, comely, trim, neat.

[receiving form] plastic, fictile; formative, impressible, creative.

[giving form] plasmatic, plasmic; protoplasmic.

[similar in form] isomorphic, isomorphous.

241. Amorphism
[absence of form]

n. amorphism, misproportion, informity [*rare*]; uncouthness; rough diamond; unlicked cub; *rudis indigestaque moles* [*L.*]; disorder etc. 59; deformity etc. 243.

disfigurement, defacement; mutilation; deforming.

v. [destroy form] deface, disfigure, deform, mutilate, truncate; derange etc. 61; blemish, mar.

adj. shapeless, amorphous, formless; unshapely, misshapen, unsymmetrical, malformed, unformed, unhewn, unfashioned, unshapen; anomalous.

rough, rude, Gothic, barbarous, rugged, scraggy, vandalic; in the rough.

242. Symmetry
[regularity of form]

n. symmetry, shapeliness, finish; beauty etc. 845; proportion, eurythmy *or* eurhythmy, eurythmics *or* eurhythmics, uniformity, parallelism; bilateral–, trilateral–, multilateral-symmetry; centrality etc. 222; radiation, regularity, evenness.

arborescence, branching, ramification; arbor vitae; peloria.

adj. symmetrical, shapely, well set, finished; beautiful etc. 845; classic, chaste, severe.

regular, uniform, radiate, radiated, balanced; equal etc. 27; parallel, coextensive.

arborescent, arboriform; dendriform, dendroid *or* dendroidal; branching; ramous, ramose; fern-shaped, filiciform, filicoid; subarborescent; papilionaceous.

243. Distortion
[irregularity of form]

n. distortion, detortion [*rare*], contortion, contortuosity, knot, warp, buckle, screw, twist; crookedness etc. (*obliquity*) 217; grimace; deformity; malformation, malconformation; harelip; monstrosity, misproportion, want of symmetry, anamorphosy, anamorphosis; ugliness etc. 846; talipes, club-foot; teratology.

v. distort, contort, twist, warp, buckle, screw, wrench, writhe, gnarl, wrest, writhe, make faces, deform, misshape.

adj. distorted etc. *v.;* out of shape, irregular, unsymmetric, anamorphous, awry, wry, askew, crooked; not true, not straight; on one side, crump [*obs.*], deformed; harelipped; misshapen, misbegotten; misproportioned, ill-proportioned; ill-made; grotesque, crooked as a ram's horn; camelbacked, humpbacked, hunchbacked, bunchbacked, crook-backed, bandy; bandylegged, bowlegged; bowkneed, knock-kneed; splayfooted, taliped *or* talipedic, club-footed; round-shouldered; snub-nosed; curtailed of one's fair proportions; stumpy etc. (*short*) 201; gaunt (*thin*) etc. 203; bloated etc. 194; scalene; simous.

adv. all manner of ways.

244. Angularity

n. angularity, angularness; aduncity; angle, cusp, bend; fold etc. 258; notch etc. 257; fork, furculum, bifurcation.

elbow, knee, knuckle, ankle, groin, crotch, crutch; crane, fluke, scythe, sickle; zigzag.

corner, nook, recess, niche, oriel, coign (*as in* "coign of vantage").

right angle etc. (*perpendicular*) 212; obliquity etc. 217; angle of 45 degrees, miter; acute–, obtuse–, salient–, reëntering -, spherical-angle.

angular -measurement, –elevation, –distance, –velocity; trigonometry, goniometry; altimeter, pantometer, altimetry; clinometer, graphometer, goniometer; theodolite; transit *or* transit theodolite, sextant, quadrant; dichotomy.

triangle, trigon, wedge; rectangle, square, lozenge, diamond; rhomb, rhombus, rhomboid, rhombohedron, quadrangle, quadrilateral; parallelo-gram; quadrature; polygon, pentagon, hexagon, heptagon, octagon, oxygon, decagon.

Platonic bodies; cube, rhomboid; tetrahedron, pentahedron, hexahedron, octahedron, dode-cahedron, icosahedron; prism, pyramid; parallelepiped *or* parallelepipedon; curb–, gambrel–, French–, mansard- roof.

v. **fork**, furcate, divaricate, branch, ramify, bifur-cate, bend, crinkle.

adj. **angular**, bent, crooked, aduncous, adunc *or* aduncal, aduncate *or* aduncated, uncinated, aquiline, jagged, serrated; falciform, falcated; furcal, furcate, furcated, forked, bifurcate, crotched, zigzag, furcular, hooked; dove-tailed; knockkneed, crinkled, akimbo, kimbo [*obs.*], geniculated; oblique etc. 217.

wedge-shaped, cuneiform; cuneate, multangular, oxygonal; triangular, trigonal, trilateral; quad-rangular, quadrilateral, foursquare, rectangu-lar, square; multilateral; polygonal etc. *n.;* cubical, rhombic *or* rhombical, rhomboidal, pyramidal.

245. Curvature

n. **curvature**, curvity [*rare*], curvation; incurvature, incurvity [*obs.*], incurvation; bend; flexure, flexion; conflexure [*obs.*]; crook, hook, bought [*obs.*], bending; deflexion, inflexion; concamer-ation; arcuation, devexity [*obs.*], turn; devia-tion, detour *or* détour [*F.*], sweep; curl, curling; bough; recurvity [*rare*], recurvation [*rare*]; sinuosity etc. 248; aduncity.

curve, arc, arch, arcade, vault, bow, crescent, meniscus, half-moon, lunule, horseshoe, loop, crane neck; parabola, hyperbola; catacaustic, diacaustic; geanticline, geosyncline; catenarian, catenary, festoon; conchoid, cardioid; caustic; tracery; arched- ceiling, –roof; bay window, bow window.

v. **be curved** etc. *adj.;* sweep, swag [*obs. or dial.*], sag; deviate etc. 279; turn; reënter.

render curved etc. *adj.;* bend, curve, incurvate; deflect, inflect; crook; turn, round, arch, arcu-ate, arch over, embow, recurvate [*rare*], con-camerate [*rare*]; bow, coil, curl, recurve, frizzle, friz *or* frizz.

adj. **curved** etc. *v.;* curvate *or* curvated, lobiform; curviform, curvilineal *or* curvilinear; devex [*obs.*], devious; recurved, recurvous; crump [*obs.*]; bowed etc. *v.;* vaulted; geanticlinal, geo-synclinal; bow-legged etc. (*distorted*) 243; oblique etc. 217; circular etc. 247.

beak-shaped, beaked, rostrate, rostriform, rostr-oid, rhamphoid.

bell-shaped, campaniform, campanular, cam-panulous, campanulate.

boat-shaped, navicular, cymbiform, naviform, scaphoid.

bow-shaped, arcuate *or* arcuated, arcual; ar-ciform, arclike, embowed.

crescent-shaped, crescent, crescentiform, cre-scentic, convexo-concave, sigmoid, semilunar, horned, meniscal, bicorn, bicornute *or* bicornu-ate, bicornuous [*rare*], bicorned *or* bicornous, semicircular.

heart-shaped, cordiform, cardioid, cordate.

helmet-shaped, galeiform, galeate, galeated, cassidiform.

hook-shaped, hooked, hooklike, unciform, un-cate, uncinal, uncinate, hamulate, hamate, hamiform, hamose *or* hamous [*both rare*]; un-guiform, unguiculate *or* unguiculated; cur-vated, aduncate, aduncous, adunc.

kidney-shaped, reniform.

lens-shaped, lenticular, lentoid, lentiform, me-niscal, meniscoid.

moon-shaped, lunar, lunate *or* lunated, luni-form, lunular, lunulate *or* lunulated, crescent-shaped (*q. v.*); Cynthian.

oar-shaped, remiform [*rare*].

pear-shaped, pyriform; obconic.

shell-shaped, conchate, conchiform, conchyla-ceous [*rare*], conchoidal [*min.*].

shield-shaped, scutate, scutiform, peltate, clypeate *or* clypeated, clypeiform.

sickle-shaped, falcate, falciform, falculate [*rare*].

tongue-shaped, linguiform, lingulate, ligulate.

turnip-shaped, napiform.

246. Straightness

n. **straightness**, rectilinearity, rectilinearness; di-rectness; inflexibility etc. (*stiffness*) 323; straight–, bee–, right–, direct- line; short cut.

v. **be straight** etc. *adj.;* have no turning; not -incline, –bend, –turn, –deviate- to either side; go straight; steer for etc. (*direction*) 278.

render straight, straighten, rectify; set–, put-straight; unbend, unfold, uncurl etc. 248; un-ravel etc. 219, unwrap.

adj. **straight**; rectilinear, rectilineal; direct, even, right, true, in a line; virgate, unbent etc. *v.;* undeviating, unturned, undistorted, unswerv-ing; straight-lined, straight as an arrow etc. (*direct*) 278; inflexible etc. 323.

perpendicular, plumb, vertical, upright, erect.

247. Circularity
[simple circularity]

n. **circularity**, roundness; rotundity etc. 249.

circle, circlet, ring, areola, hoop, roundlet, annulus, annulet, bracelet, armlet; ringlet; eye, loop, wheel; cycle, orb, orbit, rundle, zone, belt, cordon, band; contrate–, crown- wheel; hub, nave; sash, girdle, cestus, cest *or* ceste, cincture, baldric, fillet, fascia, wreath, garland; crown, corona, coronet, chaplet, snood, necklace, collar; noose, lasso.

ellipse, oval, ovule; ellipsoid, cycloid, epicycloid, epicycle.

semicircle; quadrant, sextant, sector.

v. **make round** etc. *adj.;* round.

go round; encircle etc. 227; describe a circle etc. 311.

adj. **round**, rounded, circular, annular, orbicular, orbiculate *or* orbiculated; oval, ovate, obovate, ovoid, ovoidal [*rare*], elliptic, elliptical, egg-shaped; pear-shaped etc. 245; cycloidal etc. *n.;* spherical etc. 249; fasciate *or* fasciated.

248. Convolution
[complex circularity]

n. **convolution**, involution, circumvolution; winding etc. *v.;* wave, undulation, tortuosity, anfractuosity; sinuosity, sinuation, sinuousness, flexuosity, tortility; meandering, circuit, circumbendibus [*humorous*], twist, twirl, windings and turnings, ambagiousness, ambages; torsion; inosculation; reticulation etc. (*crossing*) 219; rivulation.

coil, roll, curl, buckle, spiral, helix, corkscrew, worm, volute, whorl, rundle; tendril; scollop, scallop, escalop *or* escallop; kink; ammonite, snakestone.

serpent, snake, eel; maze, labyrinth.

v. **be convoluted** etc. *adj.;* wind, twine, turn and twist, twirl; wave, undulate, meander; inosculate; entwine *or* intwine; twist, coil, roll; wrinkle, curl, crisp, twill; frizz, frizzle; crimp, crape, indent, scollop, scallop; wring, intort; contort; wreathe etc. (*cross*) 219.

adj. **convoluted**; winding, twisted etc. *v.;* tortile, tortive [*obs.*]; wavy; undate *or* undated [*rare*], undulatory; circling, snaky, snakelike, serpentine, serpentiform, anguilliform, anguiform, anguilloid, anguillous, vermiform, vermicular; mazy, tortuous, sinuose, sinuous, sinuate, flexuous; undulating, undulated, wavy; anfractuous, reclivate [*rare*], rivulose, scolecoid; sigmoid, sigmoidal; spiriferous, spiroid.

wreathy, frizzly, *crêpé* [*F.*], buckled; raveled etc. (*in disorder*) 59.

involved, intricate, complicated, perplexed; labyrinthic, labyrinthian, labyrinthine; circuitous, ambagious; peristaltic; Daedalian; kinky, curly.

spiral, coiled, helical; cochlear, cochleate, cochleous [*rare*]; screw-shaped; turbinated, turbiniform, turbinoid, turbinal.

adv. in and out, round and round.

249. Rotundity

n. **rotundity**; roundness etc. *adj.;* cylindricity; sphericality, sphericity, spheroidicity *or* spheroidity, globoseness, globosity, globularity, annularity, orotundity, orbiculation.

cylinder, cylindroid; barrel, drum; roll, roller; rouleau, column, rolling-pin, rundle.

cone, conoid; pear-shape, egg-shape, bell-shape.

sphere, globe, ball, bowlder *or* boulder; spheroid, geoid, globoid, ellipsoid; oblong–, oblate- spheroid; drop, spherule, globule, vesicle, bulb, bullet, pellet, clew, pill, marble, pea, knob, pommel, horn, knot; oval etc. 247.

v. **render spherical** etc. *adj.;* form into a sphere, sphere, roll into a ball; give rotundity etc. *n.;* round.

adj. **rotund**; round etc. (*circular*) 247; cylindric *or* cylindrical, cylindroid *or* cylindroidal, columnar, vermiform, lumbriciform; conic, conical; spherical, spheroidal; globular, globous, globose; gibbous; fungiform, bulbous; *teres atque rotundus* [*L.*]; round as -an orange, –an apple, –a ball, –a billiard ball, –a cannon ball.

bead-shaped, beadlike, moniliform, monilated.

bell-shaped, campaniform, campanulate, campanulous, campanular.

egg-shaped, ovoid, oviform, ovoidal, ovate, globoid, globate *or* globated; obovate, obovoid [*both bot.*].

pear-shaped, pyriform.

rice-shaped, riziform.

250. Convexity

n. **convexity**, prominence, projection, swelling, gibbosity, bilge, bulge, protuberance, protrusion, excrescency; camber, swell.

intumescence, tumidity; tumor *or* tumour; tubercle, tuberousness, tuberosity, carunculation, bubo.

excrescence, hump, hunch, bunch; knob, knur, knurl, gnarl, knot; bow, boss, embossment, bump, mamelon, clump; bulb, node, nodule, nodosity.

tooth, molar; lip, flange; tongue; withers, shoulder, back, dorsum; elbow.

process, apophysis, condyle.

wheel, hub, hubble.

peg; button, stud; ridge, rib, trunnion, snag; sugar loaf etc. (*sharpness*) 253.

pimple, wen, whelk, papula, papule, pustule, pock, proud flesh, growth, sarcoma, caruncle, corn, wart, verruca, furuncle, polypus, fungus, fungosity, exostosis, bleb, blister, bulla, blain; boil etc. (*disease*) 655; air bubble, blob.

papilla, nipple, teat, pap, breast, dug, mammilla.

proboscis, nose, olfactory organ, neb, beak, snout, nozzle.

belly, corporation [*colloq.*], paunch, epigastrium, abdomen.

arch, cupola, dome, vault, beehive; balcony; eaves.

relief, relievo, cameo; low relief, bas-relief, basso-relievo *or* basso-rilievo [*It.*]; half relief, mezzo-relievo *or* mezzo-rilievo [*It.*]; high relief, alto-relievo *or* alto-rilievo [*It.*]; pilaster.

point of land, hill etc. (*height*) 206; cape, promontory, mull; foreland, headland; hummock, ledge, spur; naze, ness; mole, jetty, jutty.

v. **be prominent** etc. *adj.;* project, bulge, protrude, bag, belly, caruncto, pout, bouge [*obs.*], bunch; jut out, stand out, stick out, poke out; stick up, bristle up, start up, cock up, shoot up; swell over, hang over, bend over; beetle.

render prominent etc. *adj.;* raise 307; emboss, chase.

adj. **prominent**, protuberant, protrusile, protrusive; undershot, underhung; projecting etc. *v.;* bossed, bossy, nodular, convex, bunchy; clavate, clavated, claviform; hummocky, *moutonné* [*F.*]; caruncular *or* carunculous, carunculate *or* carunculated; furuncular, furunculous, furunculoid; mammiform; papulous, papulose; hemispheric, bulbous; bowed, arched; bold; bellied; tuberous, tuberculous; tumorous; cornute, odontoid; lentiform, lenticular; gibbous; club-shaped, hubby, hubbly, knobby, papillose; saddle-shaped, selliform; subclavate, torose, ventricose, verrucose; excrescential.

salient, in relief, raised, *repoussé* [*F.*]; bloated etc. (*expanded*) 194.

251. Flatness

n. **flatness** etc. *adj.;* smoothness etc. 255.

plane; level etc. 213; plate, platter, table, tablet, slab.

v. **flatten**; render flat; squelch, squash, fell; level etc. 213.

adj. **flat**, plane, even, flush, scutiform, discoid; complanate, flattish, homaloid; level etc. (*horizontal*) 213; flat as -a pancake, −a fluke, −a flounder, −a board, −my hand; smooth.

adv. **flat**, flatly [*rare*], flatways, flatwise, lengthwise, horizontally.

252. Concavity

n. **concavity**, depression, dip; hollow, hollowness; indentation, intaglio, cavity, vug *or* vugg *or* vugh, dent, dint, dimple, follicle, pit, sinus, antrum, alveolus, lacuna; honeycomb.

excavation, pit, sap, mine, shaft, colliery; caisson, *fougasse* [*F.*], countermine; trough etc. (*furrow*) 259; bay etc. (*of the sea*) 343.

cup, basin, crater, punch bowl; cell etc. (*receptacle*) 191; socket.

valley, vale, dale, dell, dingle, coomb *or* combe, bottom, slade [*obs.*], strath [*Scot.*], gill *or* ghyll [*Scot. & dial. Eng.*], glade, grove, glen, donga [*S. Africa*], nullah [*India*], park.

cave, subterrane, cavern, cove; grot, grotto; alcove, blind alley, *cul-de-sac* [*F.*], hole, burrow, kennel, tunnel; gully etc. 198; arch etc. (*curve*) 245.

excavator, sapper, miner.

v. **be concave** etc. *adj.;* retire, cave in.

render concave etc. *adj.;* depress, dish, hollow; scoop, scoop out; gouge, dig, delve, excavate, dent, dint, mine, sap, undermine, burrow, tunnel, stave in.

adj. **depressed** etc. *v.;* alveolate, alveolar, calathiform, cup-shaped, dishing; favaginous, faveolate, favose; scyphiform, scyphose; concave, hollow, vuggy, stove in; retiring; retreating; cavernous; porous etc. (*with holes*) 260; cellular, spongy, spongious; honey-combed; infundibular, infundibuliform, funnel-shaped, bell-shaped, campani-form, capsular; vaulted, arched.

253. Sharpness

n. **sharpness** etc. *adj.;* acuity, acumination, mucronation; spinosity.

point, spike, spine, spiculum; needle, pin; prick, prickle; spur, rowel, barb; spit, cusp; horn, antler; snag; tag; thorn, bristle; Adam's needle, bear grass, tine, yucca.

nib, tooth, tusk; spoke, cog, ratchet.

beard, cheval-de-frise (*pl.* chevaux-de-frise), porcupine, hedgehog, brier, bramble, thistle; comb; awn, beggar's lice, bur *or* burr, catchweed, cleavers *or* clivers, goose grass, hairif or hariff [*dial. Eng.*], flax comb, hatchel *or* hackle *or* heckle.

peak, crag, crest, *arête* [*F.*], cone, sugar loaf, pike, aiguille; spire, pyramid, steeple.

cutting-edge, knife-edge, blade, edge tool, cutlery, knife, penknife, whittle, razor; scalpel, bistoury, lancet; plowshare, colter; hatchet, ax *or* axe, pickax, mattock, pick, adz *or* adze, bill; billhook, cleaver, cutter; scythe, sickle, scissors, shears; sword etc. (*arms*) 727; wedge; bodkin etc. (*perforator*) 262; *belduque* [*F.*], bowie knife, paring knife; bushwhacker; drawing knife *or* drawknife, drawshave.

sharpener, hone, strop; grindstone, whetstone; novaculite; steel, emery.

v. **be sharp** etc. *adj.;* taper to a point; bristle with, acuminate.

render sharp etc. *adj.;* sharpen, point, aculeate, acuminate, whet, barb, spiculate, set, strop, grind.

cut etc. (*sunder*) 44.

adj. **sharp**, keen; acute; acicular, aciform; aculeate *or* aculeated, acuminate *or* acuminated, pointed; tapering; mucronate *or* mucronated, mucronulate; spiked, spiky, peaked, salient; cusped, cuspidate *or* cuspidated; prickly, echinate *or* echinated, acanaceous, acanthophorous, spiny, spinous, spinulose, spinulescent, spinuliferous; apiculate *or* apiculated; thorny, bristling, muricate *or* muricated, corniculate, pectinate *or* pectinated, studded, thistly, briery; craggy etc. (*rough*) 256; snaggy, digitate *or* digitated, two-edged.

arrow-shaped, arrowheaded, arrowy, sagittal, sagittate, sagittated, sagittiform.

barbed, glochidiate, spurred, aristate, awned, awny, bearded, barbate, crestate, setarious, subulate, tetrahedral.

cone-shaped, conic, conical, coniform [*rare*], pyramidal.

horn-shaped, corniform, cornute *or* cornuted; crescent-shaped; horned, corniculate.

lance-shaped, lanceolate, lanciform.

reed-shaped, calamiform [*rare*], arundinaceous, reedy.

scimitar-shaped, acinaciform.

spear-shaped, hastate, hastiform [*rare*], lance-shaped (*q.v.*).

spindle-shaped, fusiform.

star-shaped, stellate *or* stellated, stelliform, stellular, starlike, starry.

sword-shaped, gladiate, ensate, ensiform, xiphoid.

tooth-shaped, dentiform, toothlike, odontoid, dentoid.

keen-edged, cutting; sharp-edged, knife-edged; sharp–, keen- as a razor; sharp as a needle; sharpened etc. *v.;* set.

254. Bluntness

n. **bluntness** etc. *adj.*

v. **be** *or* **render blunt** etc. *adj.;* obtund, dull; take off the -point, –edge; unedge [*rare*], turn.

adj. **blunt**, obtuse, dull, dullish, pointless, unpointed; unsharpened, bluff; edentate, toothless.

255. Smoothness

n. **smoothness** etc. *adj.;* polish, gloss; lubricity, lubrication.

[smooth surfaces] bowling green etc. (*level*) 213; glass, ice, slide; asphalt, granolithic pavement, wood pavement, flags; down, velvet, silk, taffeta, satin, velveteen, velumen.

smoother; roller, steam roller; sandpaper, emery paper; flatiron, sadiron; burnisher, chamois *or* shammy, turpentine and beeswax.

v. **smooth**, smoothen [*rare*]; plane; file; mow, shave; level, roll; macadamize; polish, burnish, sleek, planish, levigate, calendar, glaze; iron, hot-press, mangle; lubricate etc. (*oil*) 332.

adj. **smooth**; polished etc. *v.;* leiodermatous, slick [*colloq.*], velutinous; even; level etc. 213; plane etc. (*flat*) 251; sleek, glossy, silken, silky; lanate, downy, velvety; glabrous, slippery, glassy, lubricious *or* lubricous, oily, soft; unwrinkled; smooth as -glass, –ice, –monumental alabaster, –ivory, –satin, –velvet, –oil; slippery as an eel; woolly etc. (*feathery*) 256.

256. Roughness

n. **roughness** etc. *adj.;* tooth, grain, texture, ripple; asperity, rugosity, salebrosity [*obs.*], corrugation, nodosity, nodulation; arborescence etc. 242; pilosity.

hair, brush, beard, shag, mane, whiskers, moustache, imperial, trees, lock, curl, ringlet, fimbria, eyelashes, lashes, cilia, villi; lovelock; beaucatcher; curl paper; goatee; papillote; scalp lock, scolding locks [*colloq.*], elf locks, mop, mat, thatch; fringe, toupee; hair shirt.

plumage, plumosity; plume, panache, crest; feather, tuft.

nap, pile, floss, velvet, plush, fur, down, wool, fluff; byssus, moss, bur *or* burr.

v. **be rough** etc. *adj.;* go against the grain.

render rough etc. *adj.;* roughen, knurl, crinkle, ruffle, crisp, crumple, corrugate, engrail;

roughcast; set on edge, stroke the wrong way, rub the fur the wrong way, rumple.

adj. **rough**, uneven; scabrous, knotted; rugged, rugose, rugous, rugulose; nodose, nodular, nodulated; knurled, cross-grained, knurly; asperous [*obs.*], crisp, salebrous [*obs.*], gnarled, gnarly, scraggly, scragged, scraggy; jagged; unkempt, unpolished, unsmooth, rough-hewn; craggy, cragged; crankling [*obs.*]; prickly etc. (*sharp*) 253; arborescent etc. 242; leafy, well-wooded.

feathery, plumose, plumigerous.

hairy, bristly, hirsute, hispid, pappous *or* pappose, pileous, pilose, pilous; trichogenous, trichoid; tufted, ciliated, filamentous; crinose, crinite; bushy; villous, nappy; bearded, shaggy, shagged; setous [*obs.*], setose, setaceous, setiferous, setigerous, setiform; "like quills upon the fretful porcupine" [*Hamlet*]; rough as a -nutmeg grater, —bear.

downy, velvety, flocculent, woolly, lanate, lanated, lanuginous, lanuginose; tomentose; fluffy.

fringed, befringed, fimbriate, fimbriated, fimbricate, laciniate *or* laciniated, laciniform, laciniose.

adv. **against the grain**; the wrong way of the goods; in the rough; on edge.

257. Notch

n. **notch**, dent, nick, cut; dimple; scotch, indent, indentation, denticulation, serration, serrature.
saw, tooth, crenel *or* crenelle, scallop *or* scollop; rickrack, picot edge, vandyke; depression, jag.
embrasure, battlement, machicolation.

v. **notch**, nick, pink, mill, score, cut, dent, indent, jag, scarify, scotch, crimp, scallop *or* scollop, crenulate, crenelate *or* crenellate, vandyke.

adj. **notched** etc. *v.;* crenate *or* crenated; dentate *or* dentated, denticulate *or* denticulated, crenelated *or* crenellated, toothed, palmate *or* palmated, serriform, serrate *or* serrated, serrulate.

258. Fold

n. **fold**, plicature, plication, pleat, plait, ply, crease; knife-pleat, knife-plait, box-pleat, box-plait; accordion pleat, accordion plait; tuck, gather; flexion, flexure, joint, elbow, double, doubling, duplicature, gather, wrinkle, rimple, crinkle, crankle, crumple, rumple, rivel [*archaic*], ruck, ruffle, dog's-ear, corrugation, frounce [*obs.*], flounce, lapel; pucker, crow's-feet.

v. **fold**, double, plicate, pleat, plait, crease, wrinkle, crinkle, crankle, curl, smock, shrivel, cockle up, cocker [*dial.*], rimple, rumple, frizzle, frounce [*archaic*], rivel [*archaic*], twill, corrugate, ruffle, crimple [*obs.*], crumple, pucker; turn–, double- -down, –under; dog's-ear, tuck, ruck, hem, gather.

adj. **folded** etc. *v.*

259. Furrow

n. **furrow**, groove, rut, sulcus, scratch, streak, striae, crack, score, incision, slit; chamfer, fluting; corduroy road, cradle hole [*sleighing*].
trench, ditch, dike *or* dyke, moat, fosse, trough, channel, gutter, ravine etc. (*interval*) 198; depression, tajo.

v. **furrow** etc. *n.;* flute, groove, chamfer, carve, corrugate, cut, chisel, plow; incise, engrave, etch, enchase, mezzotint, crosshatch, hatch, grave, bite in.

adj. **furrowed** etc. *v.;* ribbed, striated, sulcated, fluted, canaliculate *or* canaliculated; bisulcous *or* bisulcate *or* bisulcated; canaliferous; unisulcate; trisulcate; corduroy; costate, rimiform [*rare*].

260. Opening

n. **opening**, aperture, apertness [*archaic*]; hiation [*rare*], yawning, oscitance *or* oscitancy, dehiscence, patefaction [*obs.*], pandiculation; chasm etc. (*interval*) 198.
outlet, inlet; vent, venthole, blow-hole, airhole, spiracle; vomitory [*Rom. arch.*]; embouchure; orifice, mouth, sucker, muzzle, throat, gullet, weasand, wizen [*dial.*], nozzle; placket.

window, casement; embrasure, *abatjour* [*F.*]; light; skylight, fanlight; lattice; bay window, bow window, oriel, dormer; lantern.

portal, porch, gate, ostiary [*obs.*], postern, wicket, trapdoor, hatch, door; arcade; cellarway, driveway, gateway, doorway, hatchway, gangway; lich gate *or* lych gate [*archaic*].

way, path etc. 627; thoroughfare; channel, gully; passage, passageway.

tube, pipe, main; water pipe etc. 350; air pipe etc. 351; vessel, tubule, canal, gut, fistula; ajutage *or* adjutage; ostium; smokestack; chimney, flue, tap, funnel.

tunnel, mine, pit, adit, drift, shaft; gallery.

alley, lane, mall, aisle, glade, vista.

bore, caliber *or* calibre; pore; blind orifice; fulgurite, thunder tube.

hole, foramen; puncture, perforation; fontane *or* fontanelle; transforation; pinhole, keyhole, loophole, porthole, peephole, mousehole, pigeonhole; eye, eye of a needle; eyelet; slot.

porousness, porosity; sieve, strainer, colander *or* cullender; cribble, riddle, screen; honeycomb.

performation, apertion [*archaic*]; piercing etc. *v.;* terebration, empalement, pertusion [*obs.*], puncture, acupuncture, penetration.

opener, key, master key, *passepartout* [*F.*], clavis, open-sesame.

v.　**open**, ope [*poetic*], gape, yawn, hiate [*rare*], dehisce, bilge; fly open.

perforate, pierce, empierce [*obs.*], tap, bore, drill; mine etc. (*scoop out*) 252; tunnel; transpierce, transfix; enfilade, impale, spike, spear, gore, spit, stab, pink, puncture, lance; trepan, trephine; stick, prick, riddle, punch; stave in.

cut a passage through; make way for, make room for.

uncover, unclose, unrip, rip; lay–, cut–, rip–, throw- open.

adj.　**open**; perforated etc. *v.;* perforate; wide open, patulous, agape, dehiscent, ringent; ajar, unclosed, unstopped; oscitant, gaping, yawning; patent.

tubular, cannular, fistulous; pervious, permeable; foraminous; vesicular, vascular; porous, follicular, cribriform, honeycombed, infundibular *or* infundibulate, riddled; tubulose *or* tubulous, tubulate *or* tubulated; piped, tubate, tubiform.

opening etc. *v.;* aperient.

int.　open sesame! gangway! passageway!

261.　Closure

n.　**closure**, occlusion, blockade; shutting up etc. *v.;* obstruction etc. (*hindrance*) 706; embolism, embolus; contraction etc. 195; infarct, infarction; constipation, obstipation; blind -alley, –corner; keddah [*India*], cul-de-sac [*F.*]; cecum *or* caecum; imperforation, imperviousness etc. *adj.;* impermeability; stopper etc. 263; operculum.

v.　**close**, occlude, plug; block up, stop up, fill up; bung up, cork up, button up, stuff up, shut up, dam up; blockade; obstruct etc. (*hinder*) 706; bar, bolt, stop, seal, plumb; choke, throttle; ram down, dam, cram; trap, clinch; put to–, shut-the door; slam, clap, snap.

adj.　**closed** etc. *v.;* shut, operculated; unopened, blank.

unpierced, imporous, caecal; embolic; infarcted, imperforate, impervious, impermeable; impenetrable; impassable, unpassable, invious [*obs.*]; pathless, wayless; untrodden.

tight, unventilated, air-tight, water-tight, hermetically sealed; snug.

262.　Perforator

n.　**performator**, piercer, borer, auger, chisel, gimlet, drill, wimble, awl, bradawl, scoop, terrier [*obs.*], corkscrew, dibble, trocar, trepan, trephine, probe, bodkin, needle, stylet, stiletto, broach, reamer, rimer, lancet; punch, puncheon; spikebit, gouge; spear etc. (*weapon*) 727; puncher; punching machine, punching press; punch pliers.

263.　Stopper

n.　**stopper**, stopple; plug, cork, bung, spike, spill, spile, stopcock, tap, faucet; rammer; ram, ramrod; piston; stop-gap; wadding, stuffing, padding, stopping, dossil, pledget, sponge [*surg.*], tampion *or* tompion, tourniquet.

valve, vent peg, spigot, slide valve, cover etc. 223.

doorkeeper, gatekeeper, janitor, janitress [*fem.*], janitrix [*fem.*], *concierge* [*F.*], porter, portress [*fem.*], warder, beadle, tiler *or* tyler [*Freemasonry*], durwaun [*Hind.*], usher, guard, sentinel; beefeater, yeoman of the guard [*Eng.*]; Cerberus, watch dog, ostiary.

Section 4.　Motion

264.　Motion

[successive change of place]

n.　**motion**, movement, motility, motivity; move; going etc. *v.;* mobility; movableness, motive power, motorium; laws of motion; mobilization. stream, flow, flux, run, course, stir; conduction; evolution; kinematics; telekinesis.

rate, pace, tread, step, stride, gait, port, footfall, cadence, carriage, velocity, angular velocity; clip [*colloq.*], progress, locomotion; journey etc. 266; voyage etc. 267; transit etc. 270.

restlessness etc. (*changeableness*) 149; unrest.

v.　**be in motion** etc. *adj.;* move, go, hie, gang [*Scot. & dial. Eng.*], budge, stir, pass, slit; hover -round, –about; shift, slide, glide; roll, roll on; flow, stream, run, drift, sweep along; wander etc. (*deviate*) 279; walk etc. 266; change–, shift-one's -place, –quarters; dodge; keep going, keep moving.

put in motion, set in motion; move; impel etc. 276; propel etc. 284; render movable, mobilize.

adj. **moving** etc. *v.;* in motion; traveling, transitional, metabatic; motory [*rare*], motive; shifting, movable, mobile, motiferous, motile, motific [*rare*], motor, motorial, quicksilver, mercurial, unquiet; restless etc. (*changeable*) 149; nomadic etc. 266; erratic etc. 279.

telekinetic, kinematic *or* kinematical, evolutionary.

adv. **under way**; on the -move, —wing, —fly, —tramp, —march.

265. Quiescence

n. **rest**; stillness etc. *adj.;* quiescence; stagnation, stagnancy; fixity, immobility, catalepsy; indisturbance [*rare*]; quietism.

quiet, tranquillity, calm; repose etc. 687; peace; dead calm, anticyclone; statue-like repose; silence etc. 403; not a breath of air, not a mouse stirring; not a leaf stirring; sleep etc. (*inactivity*) 683.

pause, lull etc. (*cessation*) 142; stand, standstill; standing still etc. *v.;* lock; deadlock, dead stop, dead stand; full stop; fix; embargo.

resting place; *gîte* [*F.*]; bivouac; home etc. (*abode*) 189; pillow etc. (*support*) 215; haven etc. (*refuge*) 666; goal etc. (*arrival*) 292.

v. **be quiescent** etc. *adj.;* stand still, stand fast, stand firm, lie still; keep quiet, repose, rest one's bonnet on a chair [*dial.*], rest one's face and hands [*dial.*], hold the breath.

remain, stay; stand, lie to, ride at anchor, remain *in situ*, tarry, mark time; bring to, heave to, lay to; pull up, draw up; hold, halt; stop, stop short; rest, pause, anchor; cast anchor, come to anchor; rest on one's oars; repose—, rest- on one's laurels; lie back on one's record; take breath; stop etc. (*discontinue*) 142.

vegetate, stagnate; *quieta non movere* [*L.*]; let alone, let well enough alone; abide, rest and be thankful; keep within doors, stay at home, go to bed, live the life of a claim.

dwell etc. (*be present*) 186; settle etc. (*be located*) 184; alight etc. (*arrive*) 292; stick, stick fast; stand, stand like a post; not stir a -peg, —step; stand like a stuck pig [*colloq.*]; be at a stand etc. *n.*

quell, becalm, hush, calm, still, stay, lull to sleep, lay an embargo on, put the brakes on.

adj. **quiescent**, still; motionless, moveless; fixed; stationary; immotile; at rest, at a stand, at a standstill, at anchor; stock-still; standing still etc.

v.; sedentary, untraveled, stay-at-home; becalmed, stagnant, quiet; unmoved, undisturbed, unruffled; calm, restful; cataleptic; immovable etc. (*stable*) 150; sleeping etc. (*inactive*) 683; silent etc. 403; still as - a statue, —a post, —a stone, —a mouse, —death.

adv. **at a stand** etc. *adj.; tout court* [*F.*]; at the halt.

int. **stop!** stay! avast! [*naut.*], halt! hold hard! whoa! hold! *sabr karo!* [*Hind.*], *arrêtez!* [*F.*], *halte!* [*F.*].

266. Journey
[locomotion by land]

n. **travel**; traveling etc. *v.;* wayfaring, campaigning, nomadization.

excursion, journey, expedition, tour, trip, grand tour, *Wanderjahr* [*Ger.*], circuit, peregrination, discursion [*obs.*], ramble, pilgrimage, hadj *or* hajj [*Ar.*], trek [*S. Africa*], course, ambulation, march, walk, promenade, constitutional [*colloq.*], stroll, saunter, hike [*colloq.*], tramp, jog trot, turn, stalk, perambulation; outing, ride, drive, airing, jaunt.

nightwalking, noctambulation, noctambulism; somnambulism, sleep walking, somnambulation.

riding, equitation, horsemanship, manège, manage [*archaic*], ride and tie.

roving, vagrancy, pereration [*obs.*]; marching and countermarching; nomadism; vagabondism, vagabondage; hoboism; gadding; flit, flitting; migration; emigration, immigration, demigration [*obs.*], intermigration; *Wanderlust* [*Ger.*].

itinerary, plan, guide; handbook, travel guide, roadbook; Baedeker, Bradshaw, Michelin, Murray.

procession, parade, cavalcade, caravan, file, *cortège* [*F.*], column.

organs and instruments of locomotion] cycle, automobile, motor car etc. (*vehicle*) 272; trolley, locomotive; palanquin *or* palankeen, litter, dandy *or* dandi [*India*], jinrikisha *or* jinricksha; roller skates, skates, skis, snowshoes; legs, shanks, feet; pegs, pins, trotters [*colloq.*].

traveler etc. 268.

station, stop, stopping place, terminal, terminus, depot, railway station, *gare* [*F.*].

v. **travel**, journey, course; take—, go- a journey; railroad [*U. S.*]; flit, take wing; migrate, emigrate, immigrate; trek [*S. Africa*]; scour—, traverse- the country; peragrate [*obs.*]; perambulate, circumambulate; tour, peregrinate, itinerate [*rare*], nomadize.

motor, motorcycle, bicycle, cycle, spin, speed, burn up the road; trolley; go by -car, -trolley, -automobile, -rail, -train etc.

motorize, electrify.

wander, roam, range, prowl, rove, jaunt, ramble, stroll, saunter, hover, go one's rounds, straggle; gad, gad about; expatiate [*rare*]; patrol, pace up and down, traverse; take a walk etc. *n.;* go out for a walk etc. *n.;* have a run, take the air; noctambulate; somnambulate.

take horse, ride, drive, trot, amble, canter, prance, fisk [*obs.*], frisk, *caracoler* [*F.*], caracole; gallop etc. (*move quickly*) 274.

walk, march, step, tread, pace, plod, wend [*archaic*]; promenade; trudge, track, hoof it [*slang*], hike [*colloq.*], tramp; stalk, stride, straddle, strut, foot it, stump, bundle, bowl along, toddle; paddle; tread-, follow-, pursue- a path.

peg on, jog on, wag on, shuffle on; stir one's stumps [*colloq.*]; bend one's -steps, -course; make-, find-, wend-, pick-, thread-, plow- one's way.

glide, slide, coast, skim, skate.

file off, march in procession, defile.

go to, repair to, resort to, hie to, betake oneself to.

adj. **traveling** etc. *v.;* ambulatory, itinerant, peripatetic, perambulatory, mundivagant [*rare*], roving, rambling, gadding, discursive, vagrant, migratory, nomadic; circumforanean [*obs.*], circumforaneous.

night-wandering, noctivagant [*rare*], noctambulistic, noctivagous, somnambulistic *or* somnambular, somnambulant.

self-moving, automobile, automotive, locomotive, locomobile, automatic.

wayfaring, wayworn; travel-stained.

adv. on foot, on horseback, on shanks' mare; by the Marrowbone stage; *in transitu* etc. 270; *en route* etc. 282.

Int. come along! step on it!

267. Navigation
[locomotion by water or air]

n. **navigation**; volatility; aquatics; boating, yachting, cruising; ship etc. 273.

oar, scull, sweep, pole; paddle, screw, turbine; sail, canvas.

nation, swimming; fin, flipper, fish's tail.

aeronautics, aerostatics, aerostation, aerodonetics, aerial navigation, aeronautism; aeromechanics, aerodynamics, balloonery; balloon etc. 273; ballooning; aviation, airmanship; flying, flight, volitation; volplaning, planing [*colloq.*], hydroplaning, volplane, glide, dive, nose-dive, spin, looping the loop; wing' pinion, aileron.

voyage, sail, cruise, passage, circumnavigation, periplus; headway, sternway, leeway; fairway.

mariner etc. 269; **aeronaut** etc. 269a.

v. **sail**; put to sea etc. (*depart*) 293; take ship, weigh anchor, get under way; spread -sail, -canvas; gather way, have way on; make-, carry- sail; plow the -waves, -deep, -main, -ocean; ride the waves, ride the storm, buffet the waves, walk the waters.

navigate, warp, luff, scud, boom, kedge; drift, course, cruise, steam, coast; hug the -shore, -land; circumnavigate.

row, paddle, ply the oar, pull, scull, punt.

float, swim, skim, *effleurer* [*F.*], dive, wade.

[in aeronautics] fly, soar, drift, hover, be wafted, aviate, volplane, plane [*colloq.*], glide, dive, fly over, nose-dive, spin, loop the loop, land; take wing, take a flight; wing one's flight, wing one's way.

adj. **sailing** etc. *v.;* seafaring, nautical, maritime, naval; seagoing, coasting; afloat; navigable; grallatorial *or* grallatory.

aeronautic, aeronautical, aerostatic, *or* aerostatical, aeromechanic *or* aeromechanical, aerodynamic, aerial, volant, volitant, volatile, volitational.

aquatic, natatory, natatorial, natational.

adv. **under -way**, -sail, -canvas, -steam; on the wing.

268. Traveler

n. **traveler**, wayfarer, voyager, itinerant, passenger, transient, commuter, straphanger [*colloq.*].

tourist, excursionist, explorer, adventurer, mountaineer, Alpine Club; peregrinator, wanderer, rover, straggler, rambler; landsman, landlubber, horse marine; bird of passage; gadabout [*colloq.*], gadling [*obs.*]; vagrant, scattering [*obs.*], landlouper *or* landloper, waifs and estrays, wastrel, stray; loafer, swagman *or* swagsman [*Australia*], tramp, vagabond, nomad, Bohemian, gypsy, Arab, Wandering Jew, hadji *or* hajji [*Ar.*], pilgrim, palmer; peripatetic; comers and goers, immigrant; *émigré* [*F.*], emigrant; runagate, runaway, renegade, fugitive, refugee; beachcomber; booly [*Irish hist.*]; globe-girdler, globetrotter [*colloq.*]; hobo [*U. S.*], runabout, trekker [*S. Africa*], camper, *zingaro (pl. zingari)* [*It.*].

sleepwalker, somnambulist, somnambulator [*rare*], nightwalker, noctambulist.

courier, messenger, express, *estafette* [*F.*], runner; Mercury, Iris, Ariel; comet.

pedestrian, walker, foot passenger, hiker [*colloq.*], perigrinator [*rare*], tramper.

rider, horseman, horsewoman [*fem.*], equestrian, equestrienne [*fem.*], cavalier, jockey, rough-rider, trainer, breaker, huntsman, whip, postilion *or* postillion, postboy.

driver, coachman, Jehu [*humorous*], charioteer, carter, wagoner, drayman; cabman, cabdriver; *voiturier* [*F.*], *vetturino* [*It.*], *condottiere* [*It.*], gharry-wallah *or* gari-wala [*Hind.*], hackman, syce [*India*], truckman.

[railroad] engine driver [*Brit.*], engineer, fireman, stoker, conductor, guard [*Brit.*], motorman.

[automobile] driver, chauffeur, chauffeuse [*fem.*], automobilist, motorist, truck driver, mechanician; scorcher [*slang*], speed maniac, road hog [*slang*].

269. Mariner

n. **mariner,** sailor, navigator; seaman, seafarer, seafaring man, sea dog [*colloq.*], hand, water dog [*colloq.*], shellback [*slang*]; Ancient Mariner, Flying Dutchman; dock walloper [*slang*]; Jack, Jack Tar *or* jack-tar, tar, jacky (*pl.* jackies) [*landsman's term*], shipman [*obs. or poet.*], gob [*slang*]; salt, able seaman, A. B.; man-of-war's man, bluejacket, galiongee *or* galionji, marine, devil-dog [*slang*], jolly [*slang*]; midshipman, middy [*colloq.*]; lascar, *mangee or manjhi* [*Hind.*], *matelot* [*F.*], captain, commander, master mariner, skipper; mate; boatman, ferryman, waterman, lighterman, bargeman, longshoreman; bargee, gondolier; oar, oarsman; rower; boatswain.

steersman, coxswain *or* cockswain, cox [*colloq.*], helmsman, wheelman, pilot, *patron* [*F.*]; crew.

269a. Aeronaut

n. **aeronaut,** aviator, aeroplanist, airman, airwoman, flyer, birdman [*colloq.*], birdwoman [*colloq.*], aviatress *or* aviatrix, navigator, manbird [*colloq.*], wizard of the air, monoplanist; pilot, observer, spotter, scout, bombardier *or* bomber, ace; balloonist, Icarus.

270. Transference

n. **transfer,** transference; translocation, elocation [*obs.*]; displacement; metastasis, metathesis; removal; remotion; amotion; relegation; deportation, asportation, extradition, conveyance, draft; carrying, carriage; convection, conduc-

tion, contagion, infection; transfusion; transfer etc. (*of property*) 783.

transit, transition; passage, ferry, gestation; portage, porterage, freightage, carting, cartage; shoveling etc. *v.;* vection [*obs.*], vecture [*obs.*], vectitation [*obs.*]; shipment, freight, waftage; transmission, transport, transporation, transumption [*rare*], transplantation, translation; shifting, dodging; dispersion etc. 73; transposition etc. (*interchange*) 148; traction etc. 285; *portamento* [*music, It.*].

[thing transferred] drift, alluvion, alluvium, detritus, deposit, moraine; deed, gift, bequest, legacy, lease; quitclaim; freight, cargo, mail, baggage, luggage, goods.

transferee, grantee, assignee; donee, legatee, consignee, indorsee, devisee.

v. **transfer,** transmit, transport, transplace, transplant, transfuse; convey, carry, bear, fetch and carry; carry over, ferry over; hand, pass, forward; shift; conduct, convoy, bring, fetch, reach; tote.

send, delegate, consign, relegate, turn over to, deliver; ship, freight, embark; waft; shunt; transpose etc. (*interchange*) 148; displace etc. 185; throw etc. 284; drag etc. 285; mail, post.

ladle, bail *or* bale, bucket, lade, dip, drip; shovel, decant, draft off.

adj. **transferred** etc. *v.;* drifted, movable; portable, portative; conductive, contagious, infectious; metastatic, metathetic *or* metathetical; transumptive [*rare*].

transferable, assignable, conveyable, devisable, bequeathable, negotiable, transmittible, transmissible; mailable.

adv. from hand to hand, from pillar to post; by freight, by rail, by steamer, by aeroplane, by trolley, by motor truck, by express, by mail, by special delivery.

on the way, by the way; on the road, on the wing; as one goes; *in transitu* [*L.*], *en route* [*F.*], *chemin faisant* [*F.*], *en passant* [*F.*], in mid-progress.

271. Carrier

n. **carrier,** porter, red cap, bearer, tranter [*obs.*], conveyer; *cargador* [*P.I.*], freighter, express, expressman; stevedore, coolie; conductor, chauffeur, truck driver; letter carrier, postman, man of letters [*humorous*], aerial mail-carrier.

beast of burden, beast, cattle, horse, steed, nag, palfrey, Arab, blood horse, thoroughbred, galloway, charger, courser, racer, hunter, jument [*obs.*], pony; Shetland, —pony; filly, colt, foal, barb, roan, jade, hack, bidet, pad, cob, tit [*dial.*], punch [*dial.*], roadster, goer; race–, pack–, draft–, cart–, dray–, post- horse; shelty *or* sheltie; garran *or* garron [*Brit.*], jennet *or* genet, bayard, mare, stallion, gelding; broncho *or* bronco, cayuse; creature, critter; cow pony, mustang, Narragansett, waler; stud.

ass, donkey, jackass, burro, cuddy [*Scot. & dial. Eng.*], moke [*slang*]; wild ass, onager.

mule, hinny; sumpter -horse, –mule; ladino.

reindeer; camel, dromedary, llama, elephant; carrier pigeon.

Pegasus, Bucephalus, Rosinante *or* Rocinante, Alborak, Bayard, Incitatus, Kantaha, Veillantif, Vindictive, Black Bess, Kelpie *or* Kelpy.

[means of transport] locomotive, motor, trolley, carriage etc. (*vehicle*) 272; ship etc. 273.

adj. equine, asinine; electric, motor, express.

272. Vehicle

n. **Vehicle**, conveyance, carriage, caravan, car, van; wagon *or* waggon, wain [*archaic*], dray, cart, lorry.

cariole *or* carriole; truck, tram; limber, tumbrel *or* tumbril, pontoon; barrow; wheelbarrow, handbarrow; perambulator; Bath–, wheelchair; chaise; police van, patrol wagon, black Maria [*colloq.*]; conestoga wagon *or* wain; jinrikisha *or* jinricksha, ricksha [*colloq.*], dearborn, dump cart, hack, jigger, horse car; kitereen, mail stage, manumotor, rig, rockaway, prairie schooner, shay [*colloq.*], sloven [*Can.*], team, tonga [*India*], Cape cart [*S. Africa*], hackery [*India*], ekka [*India*]; gharri *or* gharry *or* gari [*India*]; gocart.

equipage, turnout [*colloq.*]; coach, chariot, phaeton, mail phaeton, wagonette, break *or* brake, drag, curricle, tilbury, whiskey [*obs.*], landau, barouche, victoria, brougham, clarence, calash, *calèche* [*F.*], britzka, araba [*Oriental*], kibitka; berlin; sulky, *désobligeant* [*F.*], sociable, *vis-à-vis* [*F.*], *dormeuse* [*F.*], jaunting–, outside- car; runabout; *vettura* [*It.*].

post chaise; diligence [*F.*], stage, stagecoach; mail–, hackney–, glasscoach; stage wagon; car, omnibus, bus [*colloq.*]; fly [*Eng.*], cabriolet, cab, hansom, four-wheeler, growler [*slang, Eng.*], droshki *or* drosky.

dogcart, trap [*colloq.*], whitechapel, buggy, *char-à-bancs* (*pl. chars-à-bancs*) [*F.*], shandrydan *or* shandradan [*Scot., Ir., & dial. Eng.*].

team, pair, span, tandem, randem; spike team *or* spike, unicorn; four-in-hand.

litter, palanquin *or* palankeen, sedan *or* sedan chair; palki, jampan, dandy *or* dandi, dooly *or* doolie, munchil [*all India*]; *cacolet* [*F.*]; tonjon [*Ceylon*], brancard, horse litter; stretcher, hurdle; ambulance.

sled, bob, bobsled *or* bobsleigh; cutter; doubleripper, doublerunner; jumper [*U. S. & Can.*], sledge, sleigh, toboggan, cariole *or* carriole [*Can.*], pung; ski (*pl.* ski *or* skis), snowshoes, skates, roller skates.

cycle, monocycle, bicycle, bicycle built for two, tricycle, quadricycle, hydrocycle, tandem; machine [*colloq.*], wheel [*colloq.*], bike [*slang*], safety bicycle *or* safety [*colloq.*], motor cycle *or* motorcycle; velocipede, hobbyhorse, draisine *or* draisene.

automobile, motor car *or* motorcar, limousine, sedan, touring car, roadster, coupé, motor, machine, car, auto, locomobile, autocar, steamer, electric, runabout, couplet, racer, torpedo; truck, tractor; taxicab, taxi, taxicoach, bus, motor bus *or* motorbus; flivver [*slang*], jitney [*colloq.*], *tacot* [*F. mil. slang*].

[allied automobile terms] tonneau, trunk, chassis, hood, top, ignition, spark plug, trunk, generator, distributor, magneto, self-starter, gear, gear box, differential, cylinder, manifold, intake, exhaust, carburetor; four–, six–, eight–, twelve-cylinder; twin six, ammeter, speedometer, oil gauge, primer, clutch, universal joint, crank shaft, transmission, tire, rim; gasoline, petrol [*Brit.*]; trailer; garage; chauffeur etc. 268.

train; express, mail; accommodation–, passenger–, express–, special–, limited–, mail–, corridor–, parliamentary–, luggage [*Brit.*] -, freight–, train; 1st-, 2d-, 3d-class- -train, –carriage, –compartment; rolling stock; cattle truck; car, coach, carriage [*Brit.*]; baggage–, freight–, chair–, drawing- room–, parlor–, Pullman–, sleeping-car; surface–, tram- car; trolley *or* trolley car [*U. S. & Can.*], electric car, electric [*colloq.*]; trollibus, trackless trolley; box car, box wagon; horse box [*Brit.*], horse car; lightning express; mail car, mail van [*Brit.*]; baggage car, luggage van [*Brit.*].

hand car, trolley *or* trolley.

[utensils & implements] spoon, spatula, ladle, hod, hoe; spade, shovel, spaddle [*obs.*], boy [*Ir.*]; spud; pitchfork.

adj. **vehicular**, curricular [*rare*], vehiculatory [*rare*]; ambulatory etc. (*traveling*) 266.

273. Ship

n. **ship**, vessel, sail; craft, bottom.

navy, marine, fleet, flotilla.

shipping, man-of-war etc. (*combatant*) 726; transport, tender, storeship; merchant ship, merchantman; packet, liner; whaler, slaver, collier, coaster, freight-steamer, freighter, lighter; fishing–, pilot- boat; trawler, hulk; yacht; baggala; floating -hotel, –palace; ocean greyhound [colloq.].

ship, bark or barque; shipentine, four-masted bark or barque; brig, snow, hermaphrodite brig; brigantine, barkentine or barquentine, schooner; topsail–, fore-and-aft- schooner; fore-and-after [colloq.]; three–, four–, five–, six- masted schooner; chasse-marée [F.], sloop, cutter, corvet or corvette, clipper, foist [obs.], yawl, dandy, ketch, smack, lugger, barge, hoy, cat, catboat, buss; sailer, sailing vessel; windjammer; steamer, steamboat, steamship; mail–, paddle–, turbine–, screw- steamer; tug; line of steamers etc.

boat, pinnace, launch; lifeboat, long-boat, jollyboat, bumboat, flyboat, cockboat, ferry-boat, canal boat; ark, bully [N fld.], bateau [Can.], broadhorn, dory, drogher, dugout, Durham boat, galiot or galliot, flatboat, shallop, gig, funny [Eng.], skiff, dinghy or dingey or dingy, scow, cockleshell, wherry, coble, punt, cog, lerret [dial. Eng.]; eight–, four–, pair- oar; randan; outrigger; float, raft, pontoon; ice-boat, ice-canoe, ice-yacht.

catamaran, coracle, gondola, caravel or carvel, felucca, caique, canoe; galley, bilander, dogger, hooker or howker [obs.]; argosy, carack or carrack [hist.], galleass or galliass, galleon; polacre or polacca, corsair, piragua, bunderboat [India], tartane, junk, lorcha, praam, proa or prahu, saic, sampan, xebec, dhow; dahabeah; nuggar; kayak, keel boat, canoe, pirogue; quadrireme, trireme; stern-wheeler; wanigan or wangan, wharf boat; derelict.

[aeronautics] balloon; airship, aeroplane, airplane, monoplane, biplane, triplane; avion [F.], aeronat, dirigible, zeppelin, zepp [colloq.]; air cruiser, battle–, bombing–, combat-plane; two-seater, biplace [F.]; single-seater, monoplace [F.], aeroboat, aerobus, aero-hydroplane, aeroyacht, flying boat; aircraft; hydroplane, aerodrome [obsoles.], air–, pilot–, captive–, fire-balloon; aerostat, Montgolfier; kite, parachute.

[allied aeronautical terms] fuselage, gondola, wings, ailes [F.], controls, aileron, lifting power, camouflage, rudder; tail, empennage [F.]; cabane, hangar; aeronaut etc. 269a.

adj. **marine**, maritime, naval, nautical, seafaring, ocean-going; A1, A1 at Lloyd's; seaworthy.

aeronautic or aeronautical, aerial; airworthy; volant etc. 267.

adv. **afloat**, aboard; on board, on ship board; hard-a -lee, –port, –starboard, –weather.

274. Velocity

n. **velocity**, speed, celerity; swiftness etc. adj.; rapidity, eagle speed, lightning speed; expedition etc. (activity) 682; pernicity [obs.], acceleration; haste etc. 684.

spurt, sprint, rush, dash, race, steeple chase; automobile race; Marathon race or Marathon; smart–, lively–, swift etc. adj. -, rattling [colloq.] -, spanking [slang] -, strapping [colloq.]- -rate, –pace; round pace; flying, flight.

pace, gallop, canter, trot, round trot, run, scamper; hand–, full- gallop; swoop.

[comparisons] lightning, light, electricity, wind; cannon ball, rocket, arrow, dart, hydrargyrum, quicksilver, Mercury; wireless, telegraph, express train; swallow flight; torrent.

eagle, antelope, courser, race horse, barb, gazelle, greyhound, hare, doe, squirrel, camel bird, swallow, chickaree, chipmunk, hackee, ostrich.

scorcher [slang], joy rider, speedster, speed maniac.

Mercury, Ariel, Puck, Camilla, Harlequin.

[measurement of velocity] velocimeter, speedometer, patent log, log, log line.

v. **move quickly**, trip, fisk [obs.]; speed, hie, hasten, spurt, sprint, post, spank, scuttle; scud, scuddle [obs. or Scot.], scurry, whiz; thunder -by, –on; scour, scour the plain; scamper; run, run like mad [colloq.], fly, race, run a race, cut away, shoot, tear, whisk, sweep, skim, brush; skedaddle [colloq.], cut and run [colloq.], cut along [colloq.], bowl along; scorch [colloq.]; rush etc. (be violent) 173; dash on, dash off, dash forward; bolt; trot, gallop, bound, flit, spring, dart, boom; march in -quick, –double- time; ride hard, get over the ground; give her the gas, step on her tail, run wide open.

hurry etc. (hasten) 684; bundle, bundle along; bundle on; accelerate, put on; quicken; quicken–, mend -one's pace; clap spurs to one's horse; make haste, make rapid strides, make forced marches, wing one's way, set off at a score; carry sail, crowd sail; go off like a shot, go ahead, gain ground; outstrip the wind, fly on the wings of the wind.

keep up with, keep pace with.

outstrip etc. 303; outmarch.

adj. **fast**, speedy, swift, rapid, quick, fleet; nimble, agile, expeditious; express; active etc. 682; flying, galloping etc. v.; light-footed, nimble-footed; winged, eagle-winged, mercurial, electric, telegraphic; light-legged, light of heel;

swift as an arrow etc. *n.;* quick as lightning etc. *n.;* quick as thought.

adv. **swiftly** etc. *adj.;* with speed etc.*n.;* apace; at a great rate, at full speed, at railway speed; full drive, full gallop; posthaste, in full sail, tantivy; like a shot [*colloq.*], like greased lightning [*colloq.*]; trippingly; instantaneously etc. 113.

under press of -sail, −canvas, −sail and steam; *velis et remis* [*L.*], on eagle's wing, in double-quick time; with rapid strides, with giant strides, *à pas de géant* [*F.*], in seven-league boots; whip and spur; *ventre à terre* [*F.*]; as fast as one's -legs, −heels- will carry one; as fast as one can lay feet to the ground, at the top of one's speed; by leaps and bounds; with haste etc. 684; in high (gear *or* speed).

275. Slowness

n. **slowness** etc. *adj.;* languor etc. (*inactivity*) 683; drawl; creeping etc. *v.,* lentor [*rare*].

jog-trot, dog-trot; amble, rack, pace, single-foot, walk; mincing steps; dead march, slow march, slow time.

retardation; slackening etc. *v.;* delay etc. (*lateness*) 133; claudication [*obs.*].

slow goer, slow coach [*colloq.*]; lingerer, loiterer, sluggard, tortoise, snail; slow poke [*slang*]; dawdle etc. (*inactive*) 683.

v. **move slowly** etc. *adv.;* creep, crawl, lag, slug [*dial.*], walk, drawl, linger, loiter, saunter; plod, trudge, stump along, lumber; trail, drag; dawdle etc. (*be inactive*) 683; grovel, worm one's way, inch, inch along, steal along; jog on, rub on, toddle, waddle, wabble *or* wobble, wamble, traipse [*dial. or colloq.*], slouch, shuffle, halt, hobble, limp, claudicate [*obs.*], shamble: flag, falter, totter, stagger; mince, step short; march in slow time, march in funeral procession; take one's time; hang fire etc. (*be late*) 133.

retard, relax, slacken, check, moderate, rein in, curb; reef; strike-, shorten−, take in- sail; put on the drag, brake, apply the brake; clip the wings; reduce the speed; slacken speed, slacken one's pace, backwater, back pedal, throttle down, lose ground.

adj. **slow,** slack; tardy; dilatory etc. (*inactive*) 683; gentle, easy; leisurely; deliberate, gradual; insensible, imperceptible; languid, sluggish, apathetic, phlegmatic, lymphatic; moderate, slowpaced, tardigrade [*rare*], snail-like; creeping etc. *v.;* reptatorial *or* reptatory.

dull, slow [*colloq.*], prosaic, unentertaining, boresome, wearisome, uninteresting etc. (*dull*) 843.

adv. **slowly** etc. *adj.;* leisurely; *piano* [*It.*], *adagio* [*It.*], *largo* [*It.*], *larghetto* [*It.*], at half speed, under easy sail; at a -foot's, −snail's, −funeral-pace; dead slow [*colloq.*]; slower than- death, −cold molasses [*colloq.*], −a funeral; in slow time; with mincing steps, with clipped wings; in low (gear *or* speed).

gradually etc. *adj.;* gradatim; by degrees, by slow degrees, by inches, by little and little; step by step; inch by inch, bit by bit, little by little, *seriatim* [*L.*], consecutively.

276. Impulse

n. **impulse,** impulsion, impetus; momentum; push, pulsion, thrust, shove, jog, jolt, brunt, boom, booming, boost, throw; explosion etc. (*violence*) 173; propulsion etc. 284.

clash, collision, occursion [*obs.*], encounter, appulsion, appulse, shock, crash, bump; impact; *élan* [*F.*]; charge etc. (*attack*) 716; percussion, concussion; beating etc. (*punishment*) 972.

blow, dint, stroke, knock, tap, rap, slap, smack, pat, dab; fillip; slam, bang; hit, whack, thwack; cuff etc. 972; squash, douse *or* dowse, whap [*dial.*], swap [*obs.*], punch, thump, pelt, kick, punce [*obs.*], calcitration; *ruade* [*F.*]; arietation [*obs.*]; cut, thrust, lunge, yerk [*obs.*]; carom *or* carrom, clip [*slang*], jab, plug [*slang*], sidewinder [*slang*], sidewipe [*slang*].

hammer, sledge hammer, mall, maul, mallet, flail; ram, rammer; ramrod; battering-ram, monkey, tamper, tamping iron, pile driver, pile-driving engine, punch, bat; cant hook; cudgel etc. (*weapon*) 727; ax etc. (*sharp*) 253.

[science of mechanical forces] mechanics, dynamics; kinematics, kinetics; dynamograph, dynamometer; seismometer.

v. **impel,** give an impetus etc. *n.;* push; start, give a start to, set going; drive, urge, boom; thrust, prod, foin [*archaic*]; cant; elbow, shoulder, jostle *or* justle, hustle, hurtle, shove, jog, jolt, encounter; run−, bump−, butt- against; knock−, run- one's head against; impinge; boost; bunt, carom *or* carrom, clip [*slang*]; fan, −out; jab, plug [*slang*].

strike, knock, hit, tap, rap, slap, flap, dab, pat, thump, beat, bang, slam, dash; punch, thwack, whack; hit−, strike- hard; swap [*obs.*], batter, douse *or* dowse, tamp, baste, paste [*slang*], pelt, patter, buffet, belabor; fetch one a blow; poke at, pink, lunge, yerk [*obs.*]; kick, calcitrate; butt, strike at etc. (*attack*) 716; whip etc. (*punish*) 972.

collide; come−, enter- into collision; foul; fall−, run- foul of; telescope, throw etc. (*propel*) 284.

adj. **impulsive,** impellent, propulsive, pulsive [*rare*], booming; dynamic, dynamical; kinetic, kinematic *or* kinematical; impelled etc. *v.;* impelling etc. *v.*

277. Recoil

n. **recoil**; reaction, retroaction; revulsion; rebound, ricochet, backlash, repercussion, recalcitration: kick, *contrecoup* [*F.*]; springing back etc. *v.;* elasticity etc. 325; reflexion, reflex, reflux; reverberation etc. (*resonance*) 408; rebuff, repulse; return.

ducks and drakes; boomerang; spring.

reactionary, reactionist, recalcitrant.

v. **recoil**, react; balk, jib; spring–, fly–, bound-back; rebound, reverberate, repercuss, recalcitrate; echo, ricochet.

adj. **recoiling** etc. *v.;* refluent, repercussive, recalcitrant, reactionary, revulsive, retroactive.

adv. on the recoil etc. *n.*

278. Direction

n. **direction**, bearing, course, set, trend, run, drift, tenor; tendency etc. 176; incidence; bending, trending etc. *v.;* dip, tack, aim, collimation; steering, steerage.

points of the compass, cardinal points; north, east, south, west; NNE, NE, ENE, E, etc.

rhumb, azimuth, line of collimation.

line, path, road, range, quarter, line of march; alignment; air line, bee line; straight shot.

v. **tend toward**, bend toward, point toward; conduct to, go to; point -to, –at; bend, trend, verge, incline, dip, determine.

steer for, steer towards, make for, make toward; aim at, level at; take aim; keep–, hold- a course; be bound for; bend one's steps toward; direct–, steer–, bend–, shape- one's course; align one's march; go straight, –to the point; make a bee line; march -on, –on a point.

ascertain one's direction etc. *n.; s'orienter* [*F.*], see which way the wind blows; box the compass; take the air line.

adj. **directed** etc. *v.,* - toward; pointing toward etc. *v.;* bound for; aligned with; direct, straight; undeviating, unswerving; straightforward; north, northern, northerly, etc. *n.*

directable, steerable, leadable, dirigible, guidable, aimable, determinable.

adv. **towards**; on the -road, –high road- to; *en avant* [*F.*]; *versus* [*L.*], to; hither, thither, whither; directly; straight, –forwards, –as an arrow; point-blank; in a -bee, –direct, –straight- line -to, –for, –with; in a line with; full tilt at, as the crow flies.

before–, near–, close to–, against-the wind; windward, in the wind's eye.

through, *via* [*L.*], by way of; in all -directions, –manner of ways; *quaqua-versum* [*L.*], from the four winds.

279. Deviation

n. **deviation**; swerving etc. *v.;* obliquation [*obs.*], warp, refraction; flection *or* flexion; sweep; deflection, deflexure; declination.

diversion, digression, departure from, aberration, drift, sheer, divergence etc. 291; zigzag; detour etc. (*circuit*) 629; divagation, disorientation, exorbitation [*rare*].

[desultory motion] wandering etc. *v.;* vagrancy, evagation [*obs.*]; bypaths and crooked ways; byroad.

[motion sideways, oblique motion] sidling etc. *v.;* jibe, tack, yaw [*all naut.*]; passage, right passage, left passage [*manège*]; echelon [*mil.*]; knight's move at chess.

v. **deviate**, alter one's course, depart from, turn, trend; bend, curve etc. 245; swerve, heel, bear off; jibe, break, yaw, wear, sheer, tack [*all naut.*].

deflect; intervert [*obs.*]; divert, divert from its course; put on a new scent; shift, shunt, switch, draw aside, crook, warp.

stray, straggle; sidle, edge; diverge etc. 291; tralineate [*obs.*], digress, wander; wind, twist, meander; veer, divagate; go astray, go adrift; lose one's way; ramble, rove, drift.

sidetrack; turn aside, turn a corner, turn away from; wheel, steer clear of; dodge; step aside, ease off, make way for, shy, jib.

glance off, fly off at a tangent; wheel about, face about; turn–, face-to the right-about; echelon [*mil.*]; waddle etc. (*oscillate*) 314; go out of one's way etc. (*perform a circuit*) 629.

adj. **deviating** etc. *v.;* aberrant, errant; excursive, discursive; devious, desultory, loose; rambling; stray, erratic, vagrant, undirected; circuitous, round-about, crooked, sidelong, indirect, zigzag; crab-like.

adv. **astray from**, round about, wide of the mark; to the right about; all manner of ways; circuitously etc. 629.

obliquely, sideling, sidelong, like the knight's move [*chess*].

280. Precession

[going before]

n. **precession**, leading, heading; precedence etc. 62; priority etc. 116; the lead, *le pas* [*F.*]; van etc. (*front*) 234; precursor etc. 64.

v. **precede**, go before, go ahead, go in the van, go in advance; forerun, forego [*archaic*]; usher in,

87

introduce, herald, head, take the lead; lead, lead the way, lead the dance; get–, have- a start; steal a march; get before, get ahead, get in front of; outstrip etc. 303; take precedence etc. (*first in order*) 62.

adj. **leading**, precedent etc. *v.;* first, foremost.

adv. **in advance**, before, ahead, in the van; foremost, headmost; in front.

281. Sequence
[going after]

n. **sequence**; sequel; coming after etc. (*order*) 63, (*time*) 117; following; pursuit etc. 622; run [*cards*].

follower, attendant, satellite, pursuer, shadow, dangler, train.

v. **follow**; pursue etc. 622; go after, fly after.

attend, beset, dance attendance on, dog; tread in the steps of, tread close upon; be–, go–, follow- in the -wake, –trail, –rear- of; follow as a shadow, hang on the skirts of; tread–, follow- on the heels of; camp on the trail.

lag, loiter, linger, get behind.

adj. following etc. *v.*

adv. **behind**; in the rear etc. 235, in the train of, in the wake of; after etc. (*order*) 63, (*time*) 117.

282. Progression
[motion forward; progressive motion]

n. **progression**, progress, progressiveness; advancing etc. *v.;* advance, advancement; ongoing; flood tide, headway; march etc. 266; rise; improvement etc. 658.

v. **advance**; proceed, progress; get on, get along, get over the ground; gain ground; forge ahead; jog on, rub on, wag on [*obs.*], go with the stream; keep–, hold on- one's course; go–, move–, come–, get–, pass–, push–, press- -on, –forward, –forwards, –ahead; press onward *or* onwards, step forward; make–, work–, carve–, push–, force–, edge–, elbow- one's way; make -progress, –head, –way, –headway, –advances, –strides, –rapid strides etc. (*velocity*) 274; go ahead, shoot ahead; drive -on, –ahead; go full steam ahead; distance; make up leeway.

adj. **advancing** etc. *v.;* ongoing; progressive, profluent; advanced.

adv. **forward**, onward; forth, on, ahead, under way, *en route* for, on -one's way, –the way, –the road, –the high road- to; in progress, in mid-progress; *in transitu* [*L.*] etc. 270.

283. Regression
[motion backward]

n. **regression**, regress, retrocession, retrogression, retrogradation, retroaction; *reculade* [*F.*], retreat, withdrawal, retirement, remigration; recession etc. (*motion from*) 287; recess [*obs.*]; crab-like motion.

reflux, refluence, backwater, regurgitation, ebb, return; resilience, resiliency; reflexion (*recoil*) 277; *volte-face* [*F.*].

countermotion, countermovement, countermarch; veering, tergiversation, recidivation [*obs. exc. in criminology*], backsliding, fall; deterioration etc. 659; recidivism *or* recidivity, relapse.

turning point etc. (*reversion*) 145; climax.

v. **recede**, regrade, return, revert, retreat, remigrate, retire; retrograde, retrocede; back, back out [*colloq.*], back down [*colloq.*], balk; crawfish [*slang*], crawl [*slang*]; withdraw; rebound etc. 277; go–, come–, turn–, hark–, draw–, fall–, break–, get–, put–, run- back; lose ground; fall astern, drop astern; backwater, put about [*naut.*], take the back track; veer, veer round; double, wheel, countermarch; ebb, regurgitate; jib, shrink, shy.

turn tail, turn round, turn upon one's heel, turn one's back upon; retrace one's steps, dance the back step; sound–, beat- a retreat; go home.

adj. **receding** etc. *v.;* retrograde, retrogressive; regressive, refluent, reflex, recidivous, resilient; crab-like; contraclockwise, counterclockwise; balky; reactionary etc. 277.

adv. **back**, backward; reflexively, to the right-about; *à reculons* [*F.*], *à rebours* [*F.*].

284. Propulsion
[motion given to an object situated in front]

n. **propulsion**, projection; propelment; *vis a tergo* [*L.*], push etc. (*impulse*) 276; jaculation, ejaculation; ejection etc. 297; throw, fling, toss, shot, discharge, shy.

[science of propulsion] gunnery, ballistics, archery.

propeller, screw, twin-screws, turbine.

missile, projectile, ball, shot; spear, arrow; gun etc. (*arms*) 727; discus, quoit; brickbat.

shooter, shot; archer, toxophilite; bowman, rifleman, marksman, gun [*cant*], gunner, good shot, dead shot, crack shot; sharpshooter etc. (*combatant*) 726.

v. **propel**, project, throw, fling, cast, pitch, chuck, toss, jerk, heave, shy, hurl; flirt, fillip.

dart, lance, tilt; ejaculate, jaculate [*rare*], fulminate, bolt, drive, sling, pitchfork.

send; send off, let off, fire off; discharge, shoot; launch, send forth, let fly; dash.

start; put–, set– in motion; set agoing, give a start to, give an impulse to; bundle, bundle off; impel etc. 276; trundle etc. (*set in rotation*) 312; expel etc. 297.

carry one off one's legs; put to flight.

adj. propelled etc. *v.;* propelling etc. *v.;* propulsive, projectile, ballistic.

285. Traction

[motion given to an object situated behind]

n. **traction**; drawing etc. *v.;* draft *or* draught, pull, haul; rake; "a long pull, a strong pull, and a pull all together"; towage, haulage.

v. **draw**, pull, haul, lug, rake, snake [*slang*], trawl, draggle, drag, tug, tow, trail, train; take in tow.

wrench, jerk, twitch; yank [*U.S.*].

adj. **drawing** etc. *v.;* tractile, tractive, tractional, ductile.

286. Approach

[motion toward]

n. **approach**, approximation, approximateness, appropinquation; access; appulse, appulsion; afflux, affluxion; advent etc. (*approach of time*) 121; pursuit etc. 622.

v. **approach**, approximate [*archaic*], appropinquate [*rare*]; near; get–, go–, draw– near; come, –near, –to close quarters; move towards, set in towards; drift; make up to [*dial. or slang*]; gain upon; pursue etc. 622; tread on the heels of; bear up; make land; hug the shore, hug the land.

adj. **approaching** etc. *v.;* approximate, approximative; affluent; converging, connivent, convergent; impending, imminent etc. (*destined*) 152.

adv. on the road.

int. **approach**! come hither! here! come! come near! forward!

287. Recession

[motion from]

n. **recession**, retirement, withdrawal; retreat; regression, regress, retrogradation, retrocession etc. 283; departure, etc. 293; recoil etc. 277; flight etc. (*avoidance*) 623.

switch, by-pass, shunt.

v. **recede**, go, move back, move from, retire, withdraw, retrograde, retrogress, regress, ebb; shrink; come–, move–, go–, get–, drift- away; depart etc. 293; retreat etc. 283; move off, stand off, sheer off, swerve from; fall back, stand aside; run away etc. (*avoid*) 623.

switch, shunt, sidetrack, turn, remove.

adj. **receding** etc. *v.;* recessive, retrogressive, regressive.

288. Attraction

[motion toward, actively]

n. **attraction**, attractiveness; attractivity; pull, drawing to, pulling towards, attrahent, adduction, magnetism, gravity, attraction of gravitation.

loadstone *or* lodestone, lodestar *or* loadstar, polestar, lode [*archaic*]; magnet, magnetite, siderite.

lure, bait, charm, decoy.

v. **attract**, adduct; draw–, pull–, drag- towards; pull, draw, magnetize, bait, trap, decoy, charm; adduce.

adj. **attracting** etc. *v.;* attrahent, attractive, adducent, adductive.

289. Repulsion

[motion from, actively]

n. **repulsion**; driving from etc. *v.;* repulse, abduction, retrusion [*rare*].

v. **repel**; push from, drive from etc. 276; chase, dispel; retrude [*rare*]; abduce [*obs.*], abduct; send away; repulse; repercuss.

keep at arm's length, turn one's back upon, give the cold shoulder; send -off, –away- with a flea in one's ear [*colloq.*]; send about one's business; send packing.

adj. **repellent**, repulsive; repelling etc. *v.;* abducent, abductive, repercussive.

290. Convergence

[motion nearer to]

n. **convergence** *or* convergency, confluence, concourse, conflux, congress, concurrence, concentration; appulse, meeting; corradiation [*rare*].

assemblage etc. 72; resort etc. (*focus*) 74; asymptote.

v. **converge**, concur; come together, unite, meet, fall in with; close with, close in upon; center *or* centre, center round, center in; enter in; pour in.

89

concentrate, bring into a focus; gather together, unite.

adj. **converging** etc. *v.;* convergent, confluent, concurrent; centripetal; asymptotic *or* asymptotical; confluxible [*rare*].

291. Divergence
[motion further off]

n. **divergence** *or* divergency, divarication, ramification, forking; radiation; separation etc. (*disjunction*) 44; dispersion etc. 73; deviation etc. 279; aberration, declination.

v. **diverge**, divaricate, radiate; ramify; branch off, glance off, file off; fly off, fly off at a tangent; spread, scatter, disperse etc. 73; deviate etc. 279; part etc. (*separate*) 44.

adj. **diverging** etc. *v.;* divergent, divaricate, radiant, radial, centrifugal; aberrant; broadcast.

adv. broadcast; *passim* [*L.*].

292. Arrival
[terminal motion at]

n. **arrival**, advent; landing; debarkation, disembarkation.

reception, welcome; *vin d'honneur* [*F.*].

destination, bourn *or* bourne, goal; landing -place, −stage; bunder *or* bandar [*Pers. & India*]; resting place; harbor, haven, port; terminus, terminal; halting -place, −ground; home, journey's end; anchorage etc. (*refuge*) 666; completion etc. 729.

return, recursion [*obs.*], remigration, reëntry.

meeting, joining, recounter, encounter, rejoining.

v. **arrive**; get to, come to; come; reach, attain; come up, −with, −to; overtake; make, fetch; come from, hail from; complete etc. 729; join, rejoin.

visit, pitch one's tent; sit down etc. (*be located*) 184; get to one's journey's end; be in at the death; come−, get- -back, −home; return; come in etc. (*ingress*) 294; make one's appearance etc. (*appear*) 446; drop in; detrain; out-span, offsaddle [*both S. Africa*].

light, alight, dismount.

land, make land, cast anchor, put in, put into; go ashore, debark, disbark [*rare*], disembark.

meet; encounter, rencounter [*rare*], come in contact; come to hand; come at, come across; hit; come−, light−, pop [*colloq.*] -, bounce [*colloq.*] -, plump [*colloq.*]-, burst−, pitch- upon.

adj. **arriving** etc. *v.;* homeward bound, terminal.

adv. **here**, hither.

int. **welcome**! hail! all hail! good-day! good-morrow! come in and rest your bonnet on a chair! [*Southern U. S.*], bienvenu! [*F.*].

293. Departure
[initial motion from]

n. **departure**, decession [*rare*], decampment; embarkation; outset, start, headway, inspan [*S. Africa*], debouchment, debouch *or* débouché [*F.*]; removal; exit etc. (*egress*) 295; congé [*F.*], exodus, hegira, flight.

leave-taking, valediction, adieu, farewell, good-by *or* good-bye, Godspeed, stirrup cup; valedictorian.

starting point, starting post; point−, place- of -departure, −embarkation; port of embarkation.

v. **depart**; go, go away, part [*archaic*], take one's departure, set out; set−, march−, put−, start−, be−, move−, get−, whip−, pack−, go−, take oneself-off; start, boun [*archaic*], issue, march out, debouch; go forth, sally forth; sally, set forward; be gone.

leave a place, quit, vacate, evacuate, abandon; go off the stage, make one's exit; retire, withdraw, remove; "use your legs" [*Merchant of Venice*]; vamose *or* vamoose [*slang, U. S.*], mizzle [*slang*], skip [*slang*], cut [*colloq. or slang*], go one's way, go along, go from home; take flight, take wing; spring, fly, flit, wing one's flight; fly away, whip away; strike tents, decamp; break camp, break away, break ground, walk one's chalks [*slang*], cut one's stick *or* cut stick [*slang*], cut and run [*colloq.*]; take leave; say−, bid- good-by etc. *n.;* disappear etc. 449; abscond etc. (*avoid*) 623; entrain; saddle, bridle, harness up, hitch up [*colloq.*], inspan [*S. Africa*]; "speed the parting guest" [*Pope*].

embark; go on board, go aboard; set sail; put to sea, go to sea; sail, take ship; hoist the blue Peter; get under way, weigh anchor.

adj. **departing** etc. *v.;* valedictory; outward bound.

adv. **hence**, whence, thence; with a foot in the stirrup; on the wing, on the move.

int. **begone**! etc. (*ejection*) 297; cut! cut away! cut off! [*all colloq.*], away! to horse! boot! saddle! all aboard! busk and boun ye! [*archaic*].

farewell! adieu! good-by *or* goodbye! good-day! *au revoir!* [*F.*], *vale!* [*L.*], fare you well! God bless you! Godspeed! *auf Wiedersehen!* [*G.*], *au plaisir de vous revoir!* [*F.*], *bon voyage!* [*F.*], *glückliche Reise!* [*G.*], *vive valeque!* [*L.*], bye-bye! [*colloq.*], be good! [*slang*], so long! [*slang*], come again!

294. Ingress
[motion into]

n. **ingress**; entrance, entry; introgression, ingressiveness, influx, intrusion, inroad, incursion, invasion, irruption; ingression; penetration, interpenetration; illapse [*rare*], infiltration; insinuation etc. (*interjacence*) 228; insertion etc. 300.

immigration, incoming, foreign influx; admission etc. (*reception*) 296.

import, importation; imports.

immigrant, visitor, incomer, newcomer, comeling [*archaic*], colonist, Buttinsky [*humorous*].

inlet; way in; mouth, door, etc. (*opening*) 260; barway; path etc. (*way*) 627; conduit etc. 350.

v. **enter**; go–, come–, pour–, flow–, creep–, slip–, pop–, break–, burst- -into, –in; have the entrée; set foot on; ingress [*obs.*]; burst–, break-in upon; invade, insinuate itself; interpenetrate, penetrate; infiltrate; find one's way–, wriggle–, worm oneself- into; intrude, butt in [*slang*] horn in [*slang, U. S.*].

give entrance to etc. (*receive*) 296, insert etc. 300

adj. **incoming**, inbound, ingressive, inward, entrant [*rare*]; entering etc. *v.*

295. Egress
[motion out of]

n. **egress**, exit, issue; emersion, emergence; outbreak, outburst, proruption [*rare*], eruption; emanation; egression; evacuation, disemboguement, exudation, transudation; extravasation, perspiration, sweating, leakage, percolation, lixiviation, leaching, distillation, seep, oozing; gush etc. (*water in motion*) 348; outpour, outpouring; effluence, effusion; efflux, effluxion; drain; dribbling etc. *v.;* defluxion; drainage; outcome, output; outflow, discharge etc. (*excretion*) 299.

export, exportation; exports, shipments.

emigration, exodus etc. (*departure*) 293; expatriation, remigration.

emigrant, migrant, redemptioner, colonist, *émigré* [*F.*].

outlet, vent, spout, tap, sluice, flood-gate; vomitory, outgate, sallyport; debouch [*mil.*], *débouché* [*F.*]; way out; mouth, door etc. (*opening*) 260; path etc. (*way*) 627; conduit etc. 350; airpipe etc. 351; pore, emunctory.

v. **emerge**, emanate, issue; egress; go–, come–, move–, pass–, pour–, flow-out of; pass off, evacuate.

exude, transude; leak; run, –out, –through; lixiviate, leach, percolate, transcolate [*obs.*]; egur-

gitate [*rare*]; strain, distill; perspire, sweat, drain, seep, ooze; filter, infiltrate, filtrate; dribble, gush, spout, flow out; well, –out; pour, trickle, etc. (*water in motion*) 348; effuse, extravasate, disembogue, discharge itself, debouch; come–, break forth; burst -out, –through; find vent; escape etc. 671.

adj. **emergent**, emerging, erumpent, eruptive, emanant, emanational, emanative, exudative, porous, pervious, leaky, sweaty, transudatory; effused etc. *v.;* outgoing, outbound, outward-bound.

percolative, oozing, gushing, transuding etc. *v.;* effluent, emunctory, effusive, excretory.

296. Reception
[motion into, actively]

n. **reception**; admission, admittance, entrée, importation; initiation, introduction, intromission; immission, ingestion, imbibition, introception, absorption, resorbence, engorgement, ingurgitation, inhalation; suction, sucking; eating, drinking etc. (*food*) 298; insertion etc. 300; interjection etc. 228; introit.

v. **give entrance to**, give admittance to, give the entrée; introduce, usher, admit, initiate, intromit [*rare*], receive, import, bring in, immit [*rare*], open the door to, throw open, ingest, absorb, imbibe, instill, implant, infiltrate, induct, inhale; let in, take in, suck in; readmit, resorb, reabsorb; snuff up.

swallow, ingurgitate; engulf, engorge; gulp; eat, drink etc. (*food*) 298.

adj. **introductory**, introductive, initiatory, initiary [*rare*], preliminary, ingestive; imbibitory, introceptive, intromittent, intromissive; admissible; absorbent, resorbent; admitting etc. *v.,* admitted etc. *v.*

297. Ejection
[motion out of, actively]

n. **ejection**, emission, effusion, rejection, expulsion, eviction, extrusion, detrusion, trajection; discharge.

egestion, evacuation, vomition; emesis, eruption, eruptiveness, eruptivity, voidance, disgorgement; ructation, eructation; bloodletting, venesection, phlebotomy, extravasation, paracentesis; expuition [*rare*], exspuition [*rare*]; tapping, drainage; emetic; vomiting, excretion etc. 299; clearance, clearage.

dislodgment; deportation; banishment etc. (*punishment*) 972; rogue's march; relegation; extradition.

ejector, bouncer [*slang, U. S.*], chucker-out [*slang*].

v. **eject**, reject; expel, discard; cut [*colloq.*], ostracize, send to Coventry, boycott; *chasser* [*F.*], banish etc. (*punish*) 972; bounce [*slang*]; fire [*slang*]; throw etc. (284) -out, –up, –off, –away, –aside; push etc. (276) -out, –off, –away, –aside; shovel–, sweep- -out, –away; brush–, whisk–, turn–, send- -off, –away; discharge; send–, turn–, cast- adrift; turn out, bundle out; throw overboard; give the sack to [*slang*]; send packing, send about one's business, send to the right-about; strike off the roll etc. (*abrogate*) 756; turn out -neck and heels [*colloq.*], –head and shoulders, –neck and crop [*colloq.*]; pack off; send away with a flea in the ear [*colloq.*]; send to Jericho [*colloq.*]; bow out, show the door to.

evict, oust, dislodge; turn out of -doors, –house and home; unhouse, unkennel; unpeople, dispeople; depopulate; relegate, deport.

let out, give out, pour out, send out; dispatch *or* despatch, exhale, excern [*obs.*], excrete; embogue [*obs.*], disembogue; extravasate, shed, void, egest, evacuate; emit; open the -sluices, –floodgates; turn on the tap; give exit to, give vent to; extrude, detrude; effuse, spend, expend; pour forth; squirt, spurt *or* spirt, spill, slop; perspire etc. (*exude*) 295; breathe, blow etc. (*wind*) 349.

tap, draw off; bale out, lade out; let blood, broach.

empty; drain, –to the dregs; sweep off; clear, –off, –out, –away; suck, draw off; clean out, make a clean sweep of, clear decks, purge.

disembowel, embowel [*rare*], disbowel [*rare*], eviscerate, gut.

root out, root up, unearth; eradicate, averruncate [*obs.*]; weed out, get out; eliminate, get rid of, do away with, shake off; exenterate [*rare*].

vomit, spew, puke]*vulgar*], keck, retch, upchuck [*colloq.*]; cast up, bring up; disgorge.

salivate, ptyalize, expectorate, clear the throat, hawk, spit, sputter, splutter, slobber, drivel, slaver, slabber, drool.

belch, eruct, eructate.

unpack, unlade, unload, unship; break bulk; dump.

emerge, ooze etc. 295; be let out.

adj. **ejective**, emissive, extrusive; egestive; salivant; vomitive, vomitory; emitting, emitted etc. *v.*

int. **begone**! get you gone! get–, go- -away, –along, –along with you! go your way! away, –with! off with you! go! go about your business! be off! avaunt! aroint *or* aroynt! [*archaic*], allez-vous-en! [*F.*], jao! [*Hind.*], va-t'en! [*F.*], scoot! [*colloq.*], shoo! "get thee behind me, Satan!" [*Bible*].

298. Food
[eating]

n. **eating** etc. *v.;* deglutition, gulp, epulation [*rare*], mastication, manducation [*rare*], rumination; gastronomy, gastrology, pantophagy, hippophagy, carnivorism, carnivorousness, herbivority [*rare*], vegetarianism, ichthyophagy; gluttony etc. 957.

carnivore; herbivore, vegetarian.

mouth, jaws, gob [*slang*], mandible, mazard, chaps, chops.

drinking etc. *v.;* potation, draft *or* draught, libation; compotation, symposium; carousal etc. (*amusement*) 840; drunkenness etc. 959.

food, pabulum; aliment, nourishment, nutriment; sustenance, sustentation; nurture, subsistence, provender, corn, feed, fodder, provision, ration, keep, commons, board; commissariat etc. (*provisions*) 637; prey, forage, pasture, pasturage; fare, cheer; diet, dietary; regimen; belly timber [*facetious, dial.*], staff of life; bread, –and cheese; liquid diet, spoon victuals.

eatables, comestibles, victuals, edibles, ingesta; grub [*slang*], prog [*slang*], meat; bread, breadstuffs; cereals, viands, cates [*obs.*], delicacy, dainty, creature comforts, creature, contents of the larder, fleshpots; festal board; ambrosia; good cheer, good living.

[breadstuffs and desserts] biscuit, cracker, bun, cooky *or* cookie, doughnut, cruller, hard-tack, pilot bread, sea biscuit, pilot biscuit, ship biscuit, hoecake, ashcake, corncake, corndodgers, corndabs, shortbread, scone, rusk, matzo [*Jewish*], chupatty [*India*], damper [*Australia*], flapjack, waffle, pancake, griddlecake, pastry, *pâtisserie* [*F.*], pie, *pâté* [*F.*], pasty, patty, turnover, *vol-au-vent* [*F.*], apple dumpling, apple slump, apple dowdy, pandowdy, mince pie, pudding, supawn, apple pie, blueberry pie, custard pie, lemon pie, pumpkin pie, squash pie, charlotte russe, plum pudding, tart, compote, apple fritters, *beignets de pommes* [*F.*], banana fritters, macaroon, meringue, marchpane *or* marzipan, *massepain* [*F.*], whipped cream, *crème fouettée* [*F.*], cake, *gâteau* [*F.*], stewed prunes, *pruneaux* [*F.*], stewed apples, *compote de pommes* [*F.*], blancmange, cornstarch, jam, *confiture* [*F.*], Bar-le-Duc, red currant jelly, *gelée de groseilles* [*F.*], ice cream, *crème glacée* [*F.*], ice, sundae; vanilla–, strawberry–, chocolate–, coffee–, Neapolitan–, country club-ice cream; banana royal, water ice, sherbet; sweets etc. 396; see **fruit.**

[cereals] hominy, oatmeal, mush, hasty pudding, porridge, gruel, crowdie *or* crowdy [*Scot. & dial. Eng.*], atole [*Mex. Sp.*], samp, hulled corn, frumenty.

[soups] *potage* [*F.*], pottage, broth, *bouillon* [*F.*], gravy soup, *consommé* [*F.*], thick soup, *purée* [*F.*], bisque, mulligatawny, turtle soup, mock-turtle soup, oyster stew, oyster chowder, clam chowder, fish chowder, *julienne* [*F.*], *potage à la julienne* [*F.*], vermicelli soup, *potage au vermicelle* [*F.*], chowder, spoon-meat, trepang, ox-tail soup, gumbo, okra soup, stock, *bouillabaisse* [*F.*].

[fish] *poisson* [*F.*], salmon, *saumon* [*F.*], sole, fried sole, *sole frite* [*F.*], shad, plaice, bluefish, whiting, *merlan* [*F.*], trout, *truite* [*F.*], mackerel, *maquereau* [*F.*], herring, *hareng* [*F.*], bloater, kipper, kippered herring, cod, *morue* [*F.*], sturgeon ("Albany beef"), sardines, haddock, *aiglefin* [*F.*], finnan haddie *or* haddock, scrod, sturgeon roe, caviar *or* caviare, shad roe, tarpon, tuna, lobster, *homard* [*F.*], lobster à la King, lobster Newburg, periwinkles, prawns, shrimps, *crevettes* [*F.*], oysters, *huitres* [*F.*], oyster stew, blue points, sea slug, *bêche de mer* [*F.*], clams, eel, *anguille* [*F.*], crab, crab meat, soft-shell crab, crawfish *or* crayfish, *écrevisse* [*F.*].

[meats] *rôti* [*F.*], joint, *pièce de résistance* [*F.*], *relevé* [*F.*], hash, *réchauffé* [*F.*], stew, ragout, fricassee, mince, chow mein, chop suey, salmis, fatling, barbecue, kickshaws, mincemeat, forcemeat, meat balls, croquettes, goulash *or* Hungarian goulash; condiment etc. 393; haggis [*Scot.*], bubble and squeak, pilau *or* pilaw [*India*], curry, aspic jelly; turtle, terrapin, diamond-back terrapin.

beef, *boeuf* [*F.*], porterhouse steak, boiled beef, bouilli, beef à la mode, beefsteak, roast beef, *rosbif* [*F.*], *bifteck* [*F.*], sirloin, rump, chuck.

veal, *veau* [*F.*], fricandeau, calf's head, *tête de veau* [*F.*], tongue, *langue* [*F.*], fried brains, *cervelle frite* [*F.*], sweetbread, *ris de veau* [*F.*], calf's liver, *foie de veau* [*F.*].

mutton, *mouton* [*F.*], mutton chop, *côtelette de mouton* [*F.*], plain chop, *côtelette au naturel* [*F.*], *côtelette à la maître d'hôtel* [*F.*], *côtellette à la jardinière* [*F.*], broiled kidneys, *rognons à la brochette* [*F.*], lamb, *agneau* [*F.*], saddle, *selle* [*F.*]

pork, *porc* [*F.*], pork chop, *côtelette de porc frais* [*F.*], sausage, *saucisson* [*F.*], frankfurter, hot dog [*slang, U. S.*], bacon, ham, *jambon* [*F.*], sucking pig, *cochon de lait* [*F.*], pig's knuckles, pig's feet, trotters, *pieds de cochon* [*F.*], crackling.

poultry, *volaille* [*F.*], capon, *chapon* [*F.*], *poularde* [*F.*], pigeon, fowl, broiler, chicken, *poulet* [*F.*], duck, *canard* [*F.*], muscovy duck, roast duck, *canard rôti* [*F.*], goose, *oie* [*F.*], turkey, *dinde (masc. dindon)* [*F.*], wing, *aile* [*F.*], leg, *cuisse* [*F.*], breast, *filet (of a goose)* [*F.*], *blanc (of a fowl)* [*F.*], drumstick.

game, venison, *chevreuil* [*F.*], hare, *lièvre* [*F.*], jugged hare, *civet* [*F.*], rabbit, *lapin* [*F.*], pheasant, *faisan* [*F.*], partridge, *perdrix* [*F.*], snipe, *bécasse* [*F.*], quail, *caille* [*F.*], wild duck, *canard sauvage* [*F.*], canvasback, teal, *sarcelle* [*F.*], grouse, ricebird [*Southern U. S.*], pigeon, squab.

[eggs] *oeufs* [*F.*], boiled eggs, *oeufs à la coque* [*F.*], fried eggs, *oeufs sur le plat* [*F.*], poached eggs, *oeufs pochés* [*F.*], scrambled eggs, *oeufs brouillés* [*F.*], new-laid eggs, *oeufs frais* [*F.*], buttered eggs, dropped eggs, shirred eggs, stuffed eggs, omelet, *omelette* [*F.*], soufflé *or* *soufflée* [*F.*].

[cheese dishes] cheese, *fromage* [*F.*], cheesecake, *talmouse* [*F.*], cheese-mold, *moule à fromage* [*F.*], Welsh rabbit *or* Welsh rarebit [*an erroneous form*], *rôtie au fromage* [*F.*], golden buck, cheese straws, cheese fondue; cream–, cottage–, Neuchatel–, Swiss (*Schweizerkäse or Schweitzerkäse or Schweitzer*) –, Gruyère –, Emmenthaler–, Dutch–, Edam–, Roquefort–, Brie–, Limburg *or* Limburger–, Wensleydale-cheese.

[vegetables] *légumes* [*F.*], greens, asparagus, *asperge* [*F.*], green peas, *petits pois* [*F.*], artichoke, *artichaut* [*F.*], cabbage, *chou* [*F.*], coleslaw, Brussels sprouts, *choux de Bruxelles* [*F.*], cauliflower, *chou-fleur (pl. choux-fleurs)* [*F.*], lettuce, *laitue* [*F.*], romaine, cos lettuce, *laitue romaine* [*F.*], lima beans, string beans, French beans, *haricots verts* [*F.*], kidney beans, *haricots blancs* [*F.*], baked beans, potatoes, *pommes de terre* [*F.*], yams, sweet potatoes, *patates* [*F.*], spinach, *épinards* [*F.*], endive, *chicorée* [*F.*], pumpkin, squash, sauerkraut, *choucroute* [*F.*], eggplant, oyster plant, salsify, *salsifis* [*F.*], tomato, *tomate* [*F.*], celery, *céleri* [*F.*], cress, *cresson* [*F.*], watercress, *cresson de fontaine* [*F.*], beets, beetroot [*Brit.*], *betterave* [*F.*], parsnips, *panais* [*F.*], turnip, *navet*

[F.], radish, *radis* or *rave* [F.], horse radish, *raifort* [F.], onion, *oignon* [F.], scallion, shalot, *échalote* [F.], cucumber, *concombre* [F.], mushrooms, *champignons* [F.], rhubarb, truffles, succotash.

[fruit] figs, *figues* [F.], raisins, nuts, *noisettes* [F.], almonds: *les quatres mendiants* [F.]; apple, *pomme* [F.], pear, *poire* [F.], alligator pear, avocado, apricot, *abricot* [F.], peach, *pêche* [F.], plantain, banana, breadfruit, grapefruit, mango, mangosteen, grapes, pineapple, *ananas* [F.], walnuts, *noix* [F.], orange, lemon, lime, cherries, *cerises* [F.], watermelon, currants, cranberry, loganberry, blueberry, blackberry, gooseberry, whortleberry, huckleberry, raspberry, strawberry.

table, *cuisine*, bill of fare, menu, *table d'hôte* [F.], ordinary, *à la carte* [F.], cover, *couvert* [F.]; American plan, European plan.

meal, repast, feed [*archaic or colloq.*], spread [*colloq.*]; mess; dish, plate, course; side dish, *hors-d'oeuvre* [F.], entrée, *entremets* [F.], remove, dessert [*in U. S., often includes pastry or pudding*]; regale; regalement, refreshment, entertainment; refection, collation, picnic, feast, banquet, junket; breakfast; lunch, luncheon; *déjeuner* [F.], *déjeuner à la fourchette* [F.]; bever [*dial.*], tiffin, dinner, supper, snack [*colloq.*], whet, bait [*dial.*]; potluck; hearty–, square–, substantial–, full- meal; blowout [*slang*]; light refreshment; *chota hazri, bara hazri, bara khana* [*all Hind.*].

mouthful, bolus, gobbet [*archaic*], tidbit, kickshaw, morsel, sop, sippet.

drink, beverage, liquor, broth, soup; potion, dram, draft *or* draught, drench, swill [*slang*]; nip, sip, sup, gulp.

[beverages] wine, spirits, liqueur, beer, ale, malt liquor, (Sir) John Barleycorn, stingo [*old slang*]; heavy wet [*slang, Eng.*]; grog, toddy, flip, purl, punch, negus, cup, bishop, wassail; hooch [*slang*], whisky *or* whiskey, the creature [*humorous*]; gin etc. (*intoxicating liquor*) 959; coffee, chocolate, cocoa, tea, "the cup that cheers but not inebriates"; bock–, lager–, Pilsener–, schenk–, near- beer; Brazil tea, cider, claret, ice water, maté, mint julep.

restaurant, eating house etc. 189.

v. **eat**, feed, fare, devour, swallow, take; gulp, bolt, snap; fall to; dispatch *or* despatch, discuss [*colloq.*]; take–, get–, gulp- down; lay in, lick, pick, peck; tuck in [*slang*], gormandize etc. 957; bite, champ, munch, craunch *or* cranch, crunch, chew, masticate, nibble, gnaw, mumble.

live on; feed–, batten–, fatten–, feast- upon; browse, graze, crop, regale; carouse etc. (*make merry*) 840; lick one's chops [*colloq.*], make one's mouth water; eat heartily, do justice to, play a good knife and fork [*dial. Eng.*], banquet.

break bread, break one's fast; breakfast, lunch, dine, take tea, sup.

drink, –in, –up, –one's fill; quaff, sip, sup; suck, –up; lap; swig [*dial. or colloq.*], swill [*slang*], tipple etc. (*be drunken*) 959; empty one's glass, drain the cup; toss off, toss one's glass; wash down, crack a bottle [*colloq.*], wet one's whistle [*colloq.*].

cater, purvey etc. 637.

adj. **eatable**, edible, esculent, comestible, gustable, alimentary; cereal, cibarious [*rare*]; dietetic; culinary; nutritive, nutritious; gastric; succulent.

underdone, rare, *saignant* [F.]; well-done, *bien cuit* [F.]; overdone; with gravy, *au jus* [F.]; high [*of game*]; ripe [*of cheese*].

drinkable, potable, potulent [*obs.*]; bibulous.

omnivorous, carnivorous, herbivorous, granivorous, graminivorous, phytivorous, phytophagous, ichthyophagous; omophagic, omophagous; pantophagous, xylophagous.

299. Excretion

n. **excretion**, discharge, emanation, ejection; exhalation, exudation, extrusion, secretion, effusion, extravasation, ecchymosis, evacuation, dejection, feces, defecation, cacation, excrement; bloody flux; celiac *or* coeliac, flux; dysentery; perspiration, sweat; subation [*obs.*], exudation; diaphoresis; sewage; eccrinology.

hemorrhage, bleeding; outpouring etc. (*egress*) 295; menses, menstrual discharge, menstrual flow, catamenial discharge; leucorrhea *or* leucorrhoea, the whites.

ejecta (*pl.*), saliva, spittle, sputum (*pl.* sputa); spit, rheum; ptyalism, salivation, catarrh; diarrhea *or* diarrhoea; egesta (*pl.*), excreta; lava; exuviae etc. (*uncleanness*) 653.

v. **excrete** etc. (*eject*) 297; secrete, secern; emanate etc. (*come out*) 295.

adj. **excretory**, fecal, feculent, secretory.

ejective, eliminative, eliminant.

300. Insertion

[forcible ingress]

n. **insertion**, infixion, implantation, introduction; embolism, interpolation, intercalation, interlineation, insinuation etc. (*intervention*) 228; planting etc. *v.;* injection, inoculation, importation, infusion; forcible ingress etc. 294; immersion; submersion, submergence, dip, plunge; bath etc. (*water*) 337; interment etc. 363.

enema, clyster, glyster, lavage, lavement.

v. **insert**, introduce, intromit, put into, run into; import; inject; imbed, inlay, inweave; interject etc. 228; infuse, instill *or* instil, inoculate, impregnate, imbue, imbrue.

insert etc. itself; plunge *in medias res* [*L.*].

graft, ingraft, engraft, bud, plant, implant; dovetail.

obtrude; thrust in, stick in, ram in, stuff in, tuck in, press in, drive in, pop in, whip in, drop in, put in: impact; pierce etc. (*make a hole*) 260.

immerse, immerge, merge; bathe, soak etc. (*water*) 337; dip, plunge etc. 310.

bury etc. (*inter*) 363.

adj. **inserted** etc. *v.*

301. Extraction
[forcible egress]

n. **extraction**; extracting etc. *v.;* removal, elimination, extrication, eradication, evulsion, extirpation, extermination; ejection etc. 297; export etc. (*egress*) 295; avulsion, wrench, forcible separation.

expression, squeezing; distillation.

extractor, corkscrew, forceps, pliers.

v. **extract**, draw; take out, draw out, pull out, tear out, pluck out, pick out, get out; wring from, wrench; extort; root-, weed-, grub-, rake-up, -out; eradicate; pull-, pluck- up by the roots; averruncate [*obs.*]; unroot; uproot, pull up, extirpate, dredge.

educe, elicit, evolve, bring forth, draw forth; extricate.

eliminate etc. (*eject*) 297; eviscerate etc. 297; remove.

express, squeeze out, press out, distill *or* distil.

adj. **extracted** etc. *v.*

302. Passage
[motion through]

n. **passage**, transmission; permeation; penetration, interpenetration; transudation, infiltration; exosmosis *or* exosmose; osmosis *or* osmose, endosmosis, endosmose; intercurrence; ingress etc. 294; egress etc. 295; path etc. 627; conduit etc. 350; opening etc. 260; journey etc. 266; voyage etc. 267.

v. **pass**, pass through; perforate etc. (*hole*) 260; penetrate, permeate, thread, thrid [*archaic or dial.*], enfilade; go through, go across; go over, pass over; cut across; ford, cross; pass and repass, work; make-, thread-, worm-, force-

one's way; make-, force- a passage; cut one's way through; find its -way, -vent; transmit, make way, clear the course; traverse, go over the ground.

adj. **passing** etc. *v.;* intercurrent; endosmosmic, endosmotic, exosmotic *or* exosmic, osmotic.

adv. **en passant** [*F.*] etc. (*transit*) 270.

303. Overrun
[motion beyond]

n. **overrun**, transcursion [*obs.*], transilience *or* transiliency [*rare*], transgression; trespass; inroad, advancement, intrusion, infraction, encroachment, infringement; extravagation [*obs.*], transcendence; redundance etc. 641.

v. **surpass**, transgress, pass; go beyond, go by; show in front, come to the front; shoot ahead of; steal a march upon, gain upon.

overstep, overpass, overreach, overgo, override, overleap, overjump, overskip, overlap, overshoot the mark; outstrip, outleap, outjump, outgo, outstep, outrun, outride, outrival, outdo; beat, beat hollow [*colloq.*]; distance; leave in the -lurch, -rear; throw into the shade; exceed, transcend, surmount; soar etc. (*rise*) 305.

encroach, trespass, infringe, intrude, invade, accroach [*rare*], advance upon, trench upon, intrench on; strain; stretch-, strain- a point; pass the Rubicon.

adj. **surpassing** etc. *v.*

adv. **ahead**, beyond the mark.

304. Shortcoming
[motion short of]

n. **shortcoming**, failure; falling short etc. *v.;* default, defalcation, delinquency; leeway; labor in vain, no go [*colloq.*]; fizzle [*colloq.*], dud [*slang*], slump [*colloq.*]; flash in the pan.

incompleteness etc. 53; imperfection etc. 651; insufficiency etc. 640; noncompletion etc. 730; failure etc. 732.

v. **fall short**, -of; come short, -of; stop short, -of; not reach; want; keep within -bounds, -the mark, -compass.

collapse, fail, break down, stick in the mud, flat out, come to nothing; fall down, slump, fizzle out [*all colloq.*]; fall through, fall to the ground; cave in [*colloq.*], end in smoke, miss the mark; lose ground; miss stays [*naut.*]; miss one's moorings.

adj. **unreached**; deficient; short, short of; minus; out of depth; perfunctory etc. (*neglect*) 460.

adv. **within the mark**, within compass, within bounds; behindhand; *re infecta* [*L.*]; to no purpose; far from it.

305.　Ascent

[motion upwards]

n.　**ascent**, ascension; rising etc. *v.;* rise, upgrowth, upward flight, upgrade; leap etc. 309; grade, gradient [*Eng.*], ramp, acclivity, hill etc. 217.

　　stairway, staircase, stair [*esp. in Scot.*], stairs; flight of -steps, −stairs; ladder, scaling ladder; Jacob's ladder, companionway, companion, companion ladder [*all naut.*]; escalator, elevator etc. 307.

　　[comparisons] rocket, skyrocket, lark, skylark; Alpine Club.

v.　**ascend**, rise, mount, arise, uprise; go up, get up, work one's way up, start up, spring up, shoot up; aspire, aim high.

　　plane, swim, float.

　　climb, shin [*colloq.*], swarm [*colloq.*], clamber, ramp [*rare*], scramble, escalade, surmount; wind upward; scale, −the heights.

　　tower, soar, hover, spire, go−, fly- aloft; surge; leap etc. 309.

adj.　**rising** etc. *v.;* upcast; scandent, buoyant; supernatant, superfluitant; excelsior.

adv.　**up**, upward *or* upwards, skyward. heavenward, toward the empyrean; upturned; uphill.

306.　Descent

[motion downwards]

n.　**descent**, descension [*rare*], inclination, declension, declination; decurrence [*rare*], downcome, comedown, downcast, setback, fall; falling etc. *v.;* slump [*colloq.*], drop, cadence; subsidence, lapse; downfall, tumble, slip, tilt, trip, lurch; *culbute* [*F.*], titubation, stumble; fate of -Icarus, −Phaëthon, −Lucifer.

　　avalanche, debacle, *débâcle* [*F.*], landslip [*Eng.*], landslide, slide, snowslip, snowslide, glissade.

　　declivity, dip, decline, pitch, drop, down-grade.

　　elevator etc. 307.

　　stairway etc. 305.

v.　**descend**; go−, drop−, come- down; fall, gravitate. drop, slip, slide, settle; decline, set, sink, droop, come down a peg [*colloq.*], slump [*colloq.*].

　　get down, dismount, alight, light; swoop, souse; stoop etc. 308; fall prostrate, precipitate oneself; let fall etc. 308.

　　tumble, trip, stumble, titubate [*rare*], lurch, pitch, swag, topple; topple−, tumble- -down, −over; tilt, sprawl, plump, plump down; come−, fall−, get- a cropper [*colloq. or slang*].

adj.　**steep**, sloping, declivitous, declivous; beetling etc. (*high*) 206; bottomless etc. (*deep*) 208.

　　descending etc. *v.;* down, downcast; descendent; decurrent, decursive; labent [*rare*], deciduous; nodding to its fall.

adv.　**downward** *or* downwards, downhill.

307.　Elevation

n.　**elevation**; raising etc. *v.;* erection, lift; sublevation, upheaval; sublimation, exaltation; prominence etc. (*convexity*) 250.

　　lever etc. 633; crane, derrick, windlass, capstan, winch; dredge, dredger, dredging machine.

　　elevator, *ascenseur* [*F.*], lift [*chiefly Eng.*], dumbwaiter, escalator.

v.　**elevate**, raise, heighten, lift, erect; set up, stick up, perch up, perk up, tilt up; rear, hoist, heave; uplift, upraise, uprear, upbear, upcast, uphoist, upheave; buoy, weigh, mount, give a lift; exalt; sublimate; place−, set- on a pedestal.

　　take up, drag up, fish up; dredge.

　　stand up, rise up, get up, jump up; spring to one's feet; hold oneself up, hold one's head up; draw oneself up to his full height.

adj.　**elevated** etc. *v.;* upturned, *retroussé* [*F.*]; stilted, attollent, rampant.

adv.　on stilts, on the shoulders of, on one's legs, on one's hind legs [*colloq.*].

308.　Depression

n.　**depression**; lowering etc. *v.;* dip etc. (*concavity*) 252; abasement; detrusion; reduction.

　　overthrow, overset, overturn; upset; prostration, subversion, precipitation.

　　bow; curtsy *or* curtsey, dip [*colloq.*], bob, obedience [*archaic*], duck, genuflexion, kotow *or* kowtow [*Chinese*]. obeisance, salaam *or* salam.

v.　**depress**, lower; let−, take- -down, −down a peg [*colloq.*]; cast; let drop, let fall; sink, debase, bring low, abase, reduce, detrude, pitch, precipitate.

　　overthrow, overturn, overset; upset, subvert, prostrate, level, fell; down [*archaic or colloq.*], cast down, take down, throw down, fling down, dash down, pull down, cut down, knock down, hew down; raze, raze to the ground; trample in the dust, pull about one's ears; come off−, pull off- one's high horse [*slang*]; come off−, get off- one's perch [*slang*].

　　sit, sit down, couch, squat; recline etc. 213.

　　crouch, stoop, bend, cower.

　　bow; curtsy *or* curtsey, genuflect, kotow [*Chinese*], duck, bob, dip, kneel; bend−, bow- the

-head, −knee; incline, make obeisance, salaam *or* salam, prostrate oneself, bow down.

adj. **depressed** etc. *v.;* at a low ebb; prostrate etc. (*horizontal*) 213; detrusive.

309. Leap

n. **leap**, jump, hop, spring, bound, vault, pole vault, leaping, saltation [*rare*].

caper; dance, curvet, caracole *or* caracol; gambade, gambado, gambol, frisk, prance, dido, capriole, demivolt; buck, −jump; hop skip and jump; falcade.

[comparisons] kangaroo, jerboa, chamois, goat, frog, grasshopper, flea; buckjumper; wallaby.

v. **leap**; jump -up, −over the moon; hop, spring, bound, vault, negotiate [*cant*], clear, ramp, trip, skip.

prance, dance, caper; buck, buck-jump; curvet, caracole *or* caracol; foot it, bob, bounce, flounce, start; frisk etc. (*amusement*) 840; jump about etc. (*agitation*) 315; cut capers [*colloq.*], cut a dido [*colloq.*]; trip it on the light fantastic toe, dance oneself off one's legs, dance the soles off one's feet.

adj. **leaping** etc. *v.;* saltatorial, saltatoric *or* saltatory; frisky, lively.

adv. on the light fantastic toe.

310. Plunge

n. **plunge**, dip, dive, nose dive [*aviation*], header [*colloq.*]; ducking etc. *v.*

submergence, submersion, immersion, engulfment [*rare*].

diver; diving bird, loon, auk, penguin, grebe, sea duck etc.

v. **plunge**, dip, souse, duck; dive, plump; take a -plunge, −header [*colloq.*]; make a plunge; bathe etc. (*water*) 337; pitch.

submerge, submerse; immerse; douse *or* dowse, sink, engulf, send to the bottom; send to -Davy Jones's locker, −feed the fishes.

founder, welter, wallow; get out of one's depth; go to the bottom, go down like a stone.

adj. **plunging** etc. *v.;* submergible, submersible; soundable.

311. Circuition

[curvilinear motion]

n. **circuition** [*archaic*], circulation, volutation; turn, curvet; excursion; circumvention, circumnavigation, circumambulation, circumambience *or* circumambiency, circumflexion, circumfluence [*rare*], circummigration, circumvolation [*rare*]; Northwest Passage; wheel, gyre, ambit, compass, lap, circuit etc. 629.

turning etc. *v.;* wrench; evolution; coil, spiral, corkscrew.

v. **turn**, bend, wheel; go about, put about [*both naut.*]; heel; go-, turn- -round, −to the right-about; turn on one's heel.

circle, encircle, circumscribe; circuit; make-, describe- a -circle, −complete circle; go-, pass-through -180°, - 360°; circumnavigate, circumambulate, circumvent; "put a girdle round about the earth" [*Midsummer Night's Dream*]; go the round, make the round of, circumvolate [*rare*], circumflex.

round; turn-, round- a corner; double a point [*naut.*]; make a detour etc. (*circuit*) 629.

wind, circulate, meander; whisk, twirl; twist etc. (*convolution*) 248.

wallow, welter, roll, volutate.

adj. **circuitous**; turning etc. *v.;* circumforaneous, circumfluent, roundabout; devious, deviatory; circumambient, circumflex, circumfluent, circumfluous, circumvolant, circumnavigable.

adv. round about.

312. Rotation

[motion in a continued circle]

n. **rotation**, revolution, gyration, circulation, roll; circumrotation, circumvolution [*rare*], circumgyration; circumfusion, circination [*obs.*], turbination, pirouette, convolution.

eddy, vortex, whirlpool, swirl, gurge [*rare*]; verticity [*obs.*]; vertiginousness; whir, whirl; countercurrent; cyclone, tornado; surge; vertigo, dizzy round; maelstrom, Charybdis.

Ixion; Wheel of Fortune.

[comparisons] wheel, screw, propeller, turbine, whirligig, rolling stone, windmill; treadmill, top, teetotum; roller; cogwheel, gear, gearwheel, flywheel; jack, smokejack, turnspit; gyroplane, gyroscope, gyrostat, gyrocar; caster.

axis, axle, spindle, pivot, pin, hinge, pole, swivel, gimbals, arbor, bobbin, spool, reel, mandrel.

[science of rotatory motion] trochilics, gyrostatics.

v. **rotate**; roll, roll along; revolve, spin; turn, turn round; circumvolve [*rare*], circumgyrate [*rare*], circumvolute, circumfuse, turbinate [*rare*], encircle; circulate, gurge [*rare*], swirl, gyre, gyrate, wheel, whirl, twirl, trundle, troll, bowl, roll up, furl.

box the compass; spin like a -top, −teetotum.

adj. **rotating** etc. *v.;* rotatory, rotary; circumrotatory, trochilic, vertiginous, gyral, circumgyratory, circumvolutory, gyratory, gulfy; vorticular, vortical, vorticose; gyrostatic, gyroscopic.

adv. **round and round,** head over heels, like a horse in a mill, in circles, clockwise.

313. Evolution
[motion in a reverse circle]

n. **evolution,** unfolding, development; evolvement; unfoldment; eversion etc. (*inversion*) 218.

v. **evolve;** unfold, unroll, unwind, uncoil, untwist, unfurl, untwine, unravel; disentangle; develop.

adj. **evolutional,** evolutionary; evolving etc. *v.;* evolved etc. *v.*

314. Oscillation
[reciprocating motion, motion to and fro]

n. **oscillation;** vibration, vibratility, libration; motion of a pendulum; nutation, circumnutation; undulation; pulsation; pulse, beat, throb; seismicity, seismism, seismology.

alternation; coming and going etc. *v.;* ebb and flow, flux and reflux, systole and diastole; libration -of the moon, –in latitude; ups and downs; crossruff [*in cards*].

fluctuation; vacillation etc. (*irresolution*) 605.

swing, wave, vibratiuncle [*rare*], beat, shake, wag, seesaw, teeter; dance, lurch, dodge.

rocking stone, logan (*or* loggan) stone.

[instruments] vibroscope, vibrograph; seismograph, seismoscope.

v. **oscillate;** nutate, vibrate, librate; undulate, wave; rock, sway, swing; pulsate, beat; wag, waggle; nod, bob, curtsy *or* curtsey, tick; play; wamble, wabble; dangle, swag [*obs. or dial.*].

fluctuate, dance, curvet, reel, quake; quiver, quaver; shake, flicker; wriggle; roll, toss, pitch; flounder, stagger, totter; move–, bob- up and down etc. *adv.*

alternate, pass and repass, shuttle, ebb and flow, come and go; vacillate etc. 605.

brandish, shake, flourish; agitate etc. 315.

adj. **oscillating** etc. *v.;* oscillatory, undulatory, pulsatory, libratory; vibratory, vibrative, vibratile; seismic *or* seismical, seismal, seismographic, seismological; pendulous; shuttlewise.

adv. **to and fro,** up and down, backwards and forwards, back and forth, in and out, seesaw, zigzag, wibble-wabble [*colloq.*], in and out, from side to side, like buckets in a well.

315. Agitation
[irregular motion]

n. **agitation,** stir, tremor, shake, ripple, jog, jolt, jar, jerk, shock, succussion, trepidation, quiver, quaver, dance, tarantella, tarantism; vellication, jactation, jactitation, quassation [*rare*]; shuffling etc. *v.;* twitter, flicker, flutter.

disquiet, perturbation, commotion, turmoil, turbulence; tumult, tumultuation [*obs.*]; hubbub, rout, bustle, fuss, racket.

twitching, subsultus, floccillation, carphology *or* carphologia; staggers, megrims, epilepsy, fits; chorea, the jerks [*colloq.*], St. Vitus's dance, tilmus.

spasm, throe, throb, palpitation, pitapatation [*humorous*], convulsion, paroxysm, seizure, grip, cramp.

disturbance etc. (*disorder*) 59; restlessness etc. (*changeableness*) 149.

ferment, fermentation; ebullition, effervescence, hurly-burly, *cahotage* or *cahotement* [*F.*], cahot [*Can.*]; tempest, storm, ground swell, heavy sea, whirlpool, vortex etc. 312; whirlwind etc. (*wind*) 349.

v. **be agitated** etc.; shake; tremble, –like an aspen leaf; shake like a jelly, quiver, quaver, quake, shiver, twitter, twire [*obs.*], writhe, toss, jactitate [*rare*], shuffle, tumble, stagger, bob, reel, sway; wag, waggle; wriggle, –like an eel; dance, stumble, shamble, flounder, totter, flounce, flop, curvet, prance, cavort; squirm; bustle.

toss about, jump about; jump like a parched pea; shake like an aspen leaf; shake to its -center, –foundations; be the sport of the winds and waves; reel to and fro like a drunken man; move–, drive- from post to pillar and from pillar to post; keep between hawk and buzzard.

throb, pulsate, beat, palpitate, go pitapat.

flutter, flitter [*archaic*], flicker, bicker; twitch, vellicate.

ferment, effervesce, foam; boil, boil over; bubble, bubble up; simmer.

agitate, shake, convulse, toss, tumble, bandy, wield, brandish, flap, flourish, whisk, jerk, hitch, jolt; jog, joggle; jostle, buffet, hustle, disturb, stir, shake up, churn, jounce, wallop [*dial.*], whip.

adj. **agitated,** tremulous; subsultory [*obs.*], desultory, successive, saltatorial, saltant, saltatoric *or* saltatory; quassative [*rare*]; shambling; giddy-paced, convulsive, jerky; effervescent, effervescive, vellicative, unquiet, restless, all of a twitter [*colloq.*], all of a flutter; shaking etc. *v.*

adv. by fits and starts; subsultorily [*obs.*] etc. *adj.; per saltum* [*L.*]; hop, skip, and jump; in convulsions, in fits, in a flutter.

Class 3. Matter

Section 1. Matter in General

316. Materiality

n. **materiality**, materialness; corporeity, corporality; substantiality, substantialness, materialization, material existence, incarnation, flesh and blood, plenum; physical condition.

matter, body, substance, brute matter, protoplasm, plasma, stuff, element, principle, parenchyma, material, substratum, hyle, *corpus* [*L.*], pabulum; frame.

object, article, thing, something; still life; stocks and stones; *matériel* [*F.*]; materials etc. 635.

[science of matter] physics; somatology, somatics; natural−, experimental- philosophy; physicism; physical science, *philosophie positive* [*F.*], materialism, hylism, hylicism, hylotheism, somatism, substantialism.

materialist; physicist; somatologist, somatist, corporealist [*rare*], hylicist, hylotheist, substantialist.

v. **materialize**, incorporate, substantiate, substantialize, insubstantiate [*rare*], incorporate, embody, incarnate, corporify [*obs.*].

adj. **material**, bodily; corporeal, corporal; physical; somatic, somatoscopic; mundane etc. (*terrestrial*) 318; sensible, tangible, ponderable, palpable, substantial, somatologic *or* somatological; embodied, fleshy.

neuter, unspiritual, materialistic *or* materialistical, hylic, hylotheistic *or* hylotheistical, parenchymatous.

objective, impersonal, nonsubjective.

317. Immateriality

n. **immateriality**, immaterialness; incorporeity, dematerialization, insubstantiality, incorporality, decarnation [*obs.*], unsubstantiation, unsubstantiality, spirituality; inextension; astral plane.

personality; I, myself, me.

ego, spirit etc. (*soul*) 450; astral body, etheric double, subliminal self, subconscious self, higher self.

immaterialism; spiritualism, spiritism, animism, Platonism; Platonic -Idea, −Ideal.

immaterialist, spiritualist, spiritist, animist, Platonist.

v. **immaterialize**, dematerialize, unsubstantialize [*rare*]; disembody, spiritualize.

adj. **immaterial**, immateriate, incorporeal, incorporal, incorporate, unsubstantial, insubstantial, immateriate [*obs.*], spiritistic, animistic; unfleshly; supersensible; asomatous, unextended; unembodied, discarnate, bodiless, decarnate *or* decarnated, disembodied; extramundane, unearthly; pneumatoscopic; spiritual etc. (*psychical*) 450; Platonistic.

subjective, personal, nonobjective.

318. World

n. **world**, creation, nature, universe; earth, globe, wide world; cosmos; Midgard; terraqueous globe, sphere; macrocosm, megacosm; music of the spheres.

heavens, sky, welkin [*archaic*], empyrean; starry -cope, −heaven, −host; firmament, *caelum* [*L.*], hyaline, supersensible regions; *varuna* [*Skr.*]; vault−, canopy- of heaven; celestial spaces.

heavenly bodies, luminaries, stars, asteroids; nebulae; galaxy, Milky Way, galactic circle, *via lactea* [*L.*].

sun, orb of day, day-star [*poetic*], Helios, Apollo, Phoebus etc. (*sun god*) 423; photosphere, chromosphere; solar system; planet, planetoid; Venus, Aphrodite Urania, Hyades; comet; satellite; moon, orb of night, Diana, Luna, Phoebe, Cynthia, Selene, "glimpses of the moon" [*Hamlet*], silver-footed queen; aerolite, meteor; falling−, shooting-star; meteorite, uranolite.

constellation, zodiac, signs of the zodiac; Charles's Wain, The Dipper; Great Bear, Ursa Major; Little Bear, Ursa Minor; Southern Cross, Orion's Belt, Cassiopeia's Chair, Pleiades.

colures, equator, ecliptic, orbit.

[science of heavenly bodies] astronomy; uranography, uranology; uranometry, cosmology, cosmography, cosmogony; eidouranion, orrery; geodesy etc. (*measurement*) 466; star-gazing; observatory; planetarium.

cosmologist, cosmographer, cosmogonist, geodesist, geographer; astronomer, star-gazer.

adj. **cosmic** *or* cosmical, mundane; terrestrial, terrestrious [*obs.*], terraqueous, terrene, terrenous, [*obs.*]; fluvioterrestrial, geodesic *or* geodesical, geodetic *or* geodetical, cosmogonal, cosmogonic, cosmographic *or* cosmographical; telluric, earthly, under the sun; sublunary, subastral.

solar, heliacal; lunar; empyreal, celestial, heavenly, sphery; starry, stellar, stellary, bespangled, sidereal; sideral, astral; nebular; uranic.

adv. in all creation, on the face of the globe, here below, under the sun.

319. Gravity

n. **gravity**, gravitation; weight; heft, heaviness etc. *adj.;* specific gravity; ponderation [*rare*], ponderousness, ponderance [*rare*], ponderosity, pressure, load; burden *or* burthen; ballast, counterpoise; mass; lump–, mass–, weight-of.
[comparisons] lead, millstone, mountain; Ossa on Pelion.

weighing, ponderation, trutination [*obs.*]; weights; avoirdupois–, troy–, apothecaries'-weight; grain, scruple, drachma, dram *or* drachm, ounce, pound, lb., arroba, load, stone, hundred-weight, cwt., ton, quintal, carat, penny-weight, tod; gram *or* gramme, decagram, hectogram, kilogram *or* kilo, myriagram, decigram, centigram, milligram.
[weighing instrument] balance, scales steelyard, beam, weighbridge, spring balance.
[science of gravity] statics.

v. **be heavy** etc. *adj.;* gravitate, weigh, press, cumber, load.
[measure the weight of] weigh, counterweigh, scale [*rare*], poise.

adj. **weighty**; weighing etc. *v.;* heavy, –as lead; ponderous, ponderable; lumpish, lumpy, cumbersome, burdensome; cumbrous, unwieldy, massive; static *or* statical.
incumbent, superincumbent.

320. Levity

n. **levity**; lightness etc. *adj.;* imponderability, buoyancy, volatility; imponderables [*tech.*].
[comparisons] feather, dust, mote, down, thistledown, flue, fluff, cobweb, gossamer, straw, cork, bubble; float, buoy; ether, air.
ferment, leaven, barm, yeast, zyme, enzyme, pepsin, diastase.

v. **be light** etc. *adj.;* float, swim, be buoyed up.
render light etc. *adj.;* lighten.
ferment, work, raise, leaven.

adj. **light**, subtile, subtle, airy; imponderous, imponderable; astatic, weightless, ethereal, sublimated; gossamery; suberose *or* suberous, subereous; uncompressed, volatile; buoyant, floating etc. *v.;* foamy, frothy; portable.
light as -a feather, –thistledown, –air.
fermenting, fermentative, zymogenic, zymologic *or* zymological, diastatic, yeasty.

Section 2. Inorganic Matter

321. Density

n. **density**, solidity; solidness etc. *adj.;* impenetrability, impermeability; incompressibility; imporosity; cohesion etc. 46; costiveness, constipation, consistence, spissitude.
specific gravity; hydrometer, areometer.
condensation; caseation; solidation [*obs.*], solidification, consolidation, concretion, coagulation; petrification etc. (*hardening*) 323; crystallinity, crystallizability, crystallization, precipitation; deposit, precipitate; inspissation; incrassation, crassitude; thickening etc. *v.*
indivisibility, indiscerptibility, indissolvableness [*rare*], infrangibility, infrangibleness, indissolubility, indissolubleness.
solid body, mass, block, knot, lump; concretion, concrete, conglomerate; cake, stone, bone, gristle, cartilage.
clot, coagulum, casein, crassament [*obs.*], crassamentum, legumin, curd; clabber, bonnyclabber, clotted cream, Devonshire cream, grume.
sediment, lees, dregs, settlings.

v. **be dense** etc. *adj.;* become *or* render solid etc. *adj.;* solidify, solidate; concrete, set, take a set, consolidate, congeal, coagulate; curd, curdle, cruddle [*dial.*], lopper; fix, clot, cake, candy, precipitate, deposit, cohere, crystallize; petrify etc. (*harden*) 323.
condense, thicken, inspissate, incrassate.
compress, squeeze, ram down, constipate [*rare*].

adj. **dense**, solid; solidified etc. *v.;* caseate, caseous; pucka *or* pakka [*Hind.*], coherent, cohesive etc. 46; compact, close, serried, thickset; substantial, massive, lumpish; impenetrable, impermeable; imporous; incompressible; constipated, costive; crass, spiss [*obs.*], clabber, kern [*chiefly dial.*]; concrete etc. (*hard*) 323; knotted, knotty; gnarled; crystallitic, crystalline, crystallizable; thick, grumose, grumous, stuffy.
undissolved, unmelted, unliquefied, unthawed.
indivisible, indiscerptible, infrangible, indissolvable [*rare*], indissoluble, insoluble, infusible.

322. Rarity

n. **rarity**; tenuity; absence of solidity etc. 321; subtility; subtilty; sponginess, compressibility.
rarefaction, rarefication [*rare*], expansion, dilatation, inflation, subtilization.
ether etc. (*gas*) 334.

v. **rarefy**, expand, dilate, subtilize [*rare*], attenuate, thin.

adj. **rare**, subtile [*now rare*], subtle, thin, fine, tenuous, compressible, flimsy, slight; light etc. 320; cavernous, porous, spongy etc. (*hollow*) 252.

rarefied etc. v.; unsubstantial; uncompact, uncompressed; rarefiable, rarefactive, rarefactional.

323. Hardness

n. **hardness** etc. *adj.;* rigidity; renitency *or* renitence; inflexibility, temper, callosity, durity [*obs.*].

induration, petrifactioon; lapidification, lapidescence [*rare*]; cornification, chondrification, vitrification, vitrescence, ossification; crystallization.

[comparisons] stone, pebble, flint, marble, rock, fossil, crag, crystal, quartz, granite, adamant; bone, cartilage; calculus; hardware; heart of oak, block, board, deal board; iron, steel; cast-, decarbonized-, wrought- iron; nail; brick, concrete; cement; osmiridium, iridosmine *or* iridosmium.

v. **harden**; render hard etc. *adj.;* stiffen, indurate, petrify, temper, ossify, vitrify, lithify, lapidify, cement.

adj. **hard**, rigid, stubborn, stiff, firm; starch, starched; stark, unbending, unlimber, renitent, unyielding; inflexible, tense; indurate, indurated; gritty, proof.

adamantine, adamantean; concrete, stony, rocky, granitic, calculous, lithic, vitrescent, vitrifiable, vitrescible, vitreous; horny, cornified, callous, corneous; bony, ossipid, osseous, ossific; cartilaginous; lapideous, lapidific *or* lapidifical [*rare*]; crystallized, crystalloid; hard as a -stone etc. *n.;* stiff as -buckram, -a poker.

324. Softness

n. **softness**, pliableness etc. *adj.;* flexibility; pliancy, pliability; sequacity [*obs. in this sense*], malleability, ductility, ductibility, tractability, tractility, extensibility, extendibility; plasticity; inelasticity, flaccidity, laxity, flabbiness, flocculence; mollescence, mollification; softening etc. *v.*

[comparisons] clay, alumina, argil; wax, putty, butter, dough, pudding; cushion, pillow, feather bed, down, eider down, padding, wadding.

v. **soften**; render soft etc. *adj.;* mollify, mellow, milden, tender [*rare*], gentle [*rare*], dulcify; relax, temper; mash, knead, massage, squash [*colloq.*].

bend, yield, relent, relax, give.

adj. **soft**, tender, supple; pliant, pliable; flexible, flexile; lithe, lithesome; lissom, limber, plastic; ductile, ductible [*rare*], tractile, tractable; malleable, extensile, extensible, lax, sequacious [*obs. in this sense*], inelastic; aluminous; remollient [*obs.*], mollient, mollescent, mollitious, mollified.

yielding etc. v.; flabby, limp, flimsy.

flaccid, flocculent, downy; spongy, oedematous *or* edematous, medullary, doughy, clayey, argillaceous, mellow.

soft as -butter, -down, -silk, -putty, -a feather bed; yielding as wax; tender as a chicken.

325. Elasticity

n. **elasticity**, springiness, spring, resilience *or* resiliency, renitency, buoyancy, tensibility, tensibleness, tensility, extensibility; recoil, rebound, reflex.

[comparisons] India rubber *or* india-rubber, caoutchouc, gum elastic, whalebone, baleen; turf, moss; balloon, battledore.

v. **be elastic** etc. *adj.;* spring back etc. (*recoil*) 277.

adj. **elastic**, tensile, tensible, springy, resilient, renitent, ductile, extensible, buoyant.

326. Inelasticity

n. **inelasticity** etc. (*softness*) 324; want of-, absence of- elasticity etc. 325; irresilience.

adj. **inelastic** etc. (*soft*) 324; irresilient.

327. Tenacity

n. **tenacity**, toughness, strength; cohesiveness, cohesion etc. 46; sequacity, sequaciousness [*both obs. in this sense*]; stubbornness etc. (*obstinacy*) 606; gumminess, glutinousness, viscidity etc. 352.

[comparisons] leather; white leather *or* whitleather, tawed leather; gristle, cartilage.

claw, talon, pincers, nippers, vise; bulldog.

v. **be tenacious** etc. *adj.;* resist fracture.

adj. **tenacious**, cohesive, tough, strong, resisting, adhesive, stringy, viscid, gummy, glutinous, gristly, cartilaginous, leathery, coriaceous, tough as whitleather; stubborn etc. (*obstinate*) 606.

328. Brittleness

n. **brittleness** etc. *adj.;* fragility, friability, frangibility, fissility [*rare*], frailty, cold-shortness; house of -cards, -glass.

v. **be brittle** etc. *adj.;* live in a glass house.

break, crack, snap, split, shiver, splinter, crumble, crash, crush, break short, burst, fly, give way; fall to pieces; fall to dust; crumble -to, -into- dust.

adj. **brittle**, brash, frangible, breakable, friable, delicate, shattery [*rare*], fragile, frail, gimcrack, shivery, fissile; splitting etc. *v.;* lacerable, splintery, crisp, crimp, short, brittle as glass, cold-short; crisp as celery.

329. Texture

[structure]

n. **structure**, organization, anatomy, frame, mold *or* mould, fabric, construction; framework, carcass, architecture; stratification, cleavage.

substance, stuff, compages, parenchyma; constitution, staple, organism.

[science of structures] organology, osteology, myology, splanchnology, neurology, angiology, adenology; angiography, adenography, organography.

texture, intertexture, contexture; tissue, grain, web, surface; warp and -woof, −weft; gossamer, homespun, linsey-woolsey, frieze, fustian; satin, velvet; tooth, nap etc. (*roughness*) 256; fineness−, coarseness- of grain; dry goods.

[science of textures] histology.

adj. **structural**, organic; anatomic *or* anatomical; splanchnic, splanchnological, visceral, adenological.

textural, textile; fine-grained, coarse-grained, ingrained, ingrain; fine, delicate, subtle, subtle, gossamer, gossamery, filmy; coarse; homespun, linsey-woolsey.

330. Pulverulence

n. [**state of powder**] **pulverulence**; sandiness etc. *adj.;* efflorescence; friability, friableness, arenosity, sabulosity.

particle etc. (*smallness*) 32; powder, dust, sand, shingle; sawdust; grit; meal, bran, flour, farina, rice, paddy, spore, sporule; crumb, seed, grain; limature [*obs.*], filings, *débris* [*F.*], detritus, scobs, magistery, fine powder; flocculi.

smoke; cloud of -dust, −sand, −smoke; puff−, volume- of smoke; sand storm, dust storm.

[reduction to powder] pulverization, comminution, attenuation, granulation, disintegration, subaction, contusion, trituration, levigation, abrasion, detrition, multure limitation; tripsis; filing etc. *v.*

[instruments for pulverization] mill, arrastra, gristmill, grater, rasp, file, pestle and mortar, nutmeg grater, teeth, grinder, grindstone, kern [*dial.*], quern, quernstone, millstone.

[science] koniology.

v. **come to dust**; be disintegrated, be reduced to powder etc.

pulverize, comminute, granulate, triturate, levigate; reduce *or* grind to powder; scrape, file, abrade, rub down, grind, grate, rasp, pound, bray, bruise, contuse, contund [*rare*]; beat, crush, craunch *or* cranch, crunch, scranch [*colloq.*], crumble, disintegrate; attenuate etc. 195.

adj. **powdery**, pulverulent, granular, mealy, floury, farinaceous, branny, furfuraceous, flocculent, dusty, sandy, sabulous, psammous; detrital, arenaceous, arenose, arenarious, gritty; efflorescent, impalpable; lentiginous, lepidote, sabuline; sporaceous, sporous.

pulverable *or* pulverizable; friable, crumbly, shivery; pulverized etc. *v.;* attrite; in pieces.

331. Friction

n. **friction**, attrition; rubbing etc. *v.;* attriteness, attritus, erasure; confrication [*obs.*], contrition [*obs.*]; affriction [*obs.*], abrasion, arrosion [*obs.*], limature [*obs.*], anatripsis, anatripsology, frication, rub; elbow grease [*colloq.*]; rosin; massage.

masseur (*fem. masseuse*) [*F.*], massagist, rubber.

v. **rub**, abrade, scratch, scrape, scrub, fray, rasp, graze, curry, scour, polish, rub out, raze, erase, gnaw; file, grind etc. (*reduce to powder*) 330; rosin; massage.

set one's teeth on edge.

adj. **abrasive**, anatriptic; attrite [*rare*], attritive [*obs.*].

332. Lubrication

[absence of friction. prevention of friction]

n. **lubrication**, lubrification [*rare*], lubricity; anointment; oiling etc. *v.*

smoothness etc. 255; unctuousness etc. 355.

lubricant, lubricator, synovia; glycerin, oil etc. 356; saliva; lather; ointment, salve, balm, unguent, unguentum [*pharm.*], lenitive, unction.

v. **lubricate**, lubricitate [*obs.*]; oil, grease, lather, soap; wax; anoint; salivate.

adj. **lubricated** etc. *v.;* lubricous, lubricant, lubric [*rare*]; lenitive, synovial.

333. Fluidity

n. **fluidity**, liquidity, liquefaction; liquidness etc. *adj.;* gaseity etc. 334; solution, chylifaction, serosity.

fluid, inelastic fluid; liquid, liquor; lymph, humor, juice, sap, serum, blood, gravy, rheum, ichor, sanies; chyle.

solubility, solubleness.

[science of liquids at rest] hydrology, hydrostatics, hydrodynamics, hydrometry, hydrokinetics.

hydrometer, hydrophone, hydrostat, meter.

v. **be fluid** etc. *adj.;* flow etc. (*water in motion*) 348; liquefy etc. 335.

adj. **liquid**, fluid, serous, juicy, succulent, sappy; ichorous; rheumy, chylous, sanious, lymphatic; fluent etc. (*flowing*) 348.

liquefied etc. 335; uncongealed; soluble.

hydrological, hydrostatic *or* hydrostatical, hydrodynamic *or* hydrodynamical, hydrometric *or* hydrometrical.

334. Gaseity

n. **gaseity**, gaseousness, vaporousness etc. *adj.;* flatulence *or* flatulency; volatility; aeration, aerification; gasification.

elastic fluid, gas, air, vapor *or* vapour, ether, steam, fume, reek, effluvium, flatus; cloud etc. 353; ammonia, ammoniacal gas; volatile alkali.

[science of elastic fluids] pneumatics, pneumatology, pneumatonomy, pneumatostatics; aerostatics, aerodynamics, aeroscopy, aerography, aerology, aeromechanics.

pneumatoscope, pneumatometer, gasometer, gas meter; air–, swimming-bladder, sound (*of a fish*).

v. **gasify**, aërify, aërate; emit vapor etc. 336.

adj. **gaseous**, gasiform, aeriferous, aëriform, ethereal, aery, aerial, airy, vaporous, volatile, evaporable, flatulent.

pneumatolytic, aerostatic *or* aerostatical, aerodynamic, aeromechanic.

335. Liquefaction

n. **liquefaction**; liquescence, liquescency; deliquescence; melting etc. (*heat*) 384; colliquation [*obs.*], colliquefaction [*obs.*]; thaw; solubleness, deliquation [*obs.*], liquation; lixiviation, dissolution.

solution, decoction, apozem [*rare*], infusion, flux; alloy; lixivium.

solvent, diluent, resolvent, dissolvent, menstruum, alkahest.

v. **render liquid** etc. 333; liquefy, run; deliquesce; melt etc. (*heat*) 384; solve; dissolve, resolve; liquate; hold in solution.

leach, lixiviate, percolate.

adj. **liquefied** etc. *v.*, liquescent, liquefiable; deliquescent, soluble, dissoluble, dissolvable, colliquative; leachy, porous.

solvent, diluent, resolutive, resolvent, dissolvent.

336. Vaporization

n. **vaporization**, volatilization; gasification; evaporation, vaporation [*rare*], vaporishness, vaporosity, atomization, distillation, cupellation, cohobation, sublimation, exhalation; volatility.

fumigation, steaming.

vaporizer, atomizer, spray, evaporator, cohobator, finestill, still, retort.

bay salt, chloride of sodium.

v. **render gaseous** etc. 334; vaporize, volatilize, atomize. spray; distill, sublime, sublimate, evaporate, exhale, smoke, transpire, emit vapor, fume, reek, steam, fumigate; cohobate; finestill.

adj. **volatile**, evaporable, vaporizable, vaporific, vapory, vaporous, gaseous; volatilized etc. *v.;* reeking etc. *v.*

337. Water

n. **water**, lymph; *aqua* [*L.*], *eau* [*F.*], flood, crystal [*poetic*], Adam's ale [*humorous*], *agua* [*Sp.*], *pani* [*Hind.*]; diluent, serum etc. 333.

washing etc. *v.;* immersion, mersion [*obs.*]; dilution, maceration, lotion; humectation, infiltration, spargefaction [*obs.*], affusion, irrigation, seepage, balneation, bath.

deluge etc. (*water in motion*) 348; high water, flood tide, springtide.

sprinkler, sparger, aspergillum *or* aspergill, shower *or* shower bath, douche, enema; nozzle; atomizer etc. 336.

v. **be watery** etc. *adj.;* reek.

water, wet; moisten etc. 339; dilute, add water, dip, immerse; merge; soak, drouk [*Scot.*]; affuse [*rare*], immerge, douse *or* dowse, submerge; plunge, souse, duck, drown; steep, macerate, wash, sprinkle, sparge, humect *or* humectate [*rare*], lave, bathe, splash, swash, drench; dabble, slop, slobber, irrigate, inundate, deluge; infiltrate, percolate, seep; slosh; marinate *or* marinade, pickle.

inject, gargle; syringe, douche.

adj. **watery**, aqueous, aquatic, hydrous, lymphatic; balneal; diluent, solvent, hydrotic *or* hydrotical; infiltrative, seepy; drenching etc. *v.;* diluted etc. *v.;* weak; wet etc. (*moist*) 339.

338. Air

n. **air** etc. (*gas*) 334; common–, atmospheric- air; atmosphere; aerosphere [*rare*].

the open, –air; sky, lift [*archaic*], welkin [*archaic*], the blue, blue serene, blue sky; cloud etc. 353.

weather, climate; rise and fall of the -barometer, –mercury.

isopiestic line, isobar.

exposure to the -air, –weather; ventilation.

[science of air] aerology, aerometry, aeroscopy, aerography; meteorology, climatology; pneumatics; aeronautics; eudiometry; eudiometer, barometer, vacuometer, climatometer, aerometer, aeroscope; aneroid, baroscope, weatherglass, weathergauge, barograph.

aerostation etc. (*aeronautics*) 267; aeronaut etc. 269a.

weathervane, weathercock, vane, cock.

v. **air,** ventilate, perflate [*rare*]; fan etc. (*wind*) 349.

fly, soar, drift, hover; aviate etc. (*aeronautics*) 267.

adj. **containing air,** flatulent, effervescent; windy etc. 349.

atmospheric, airy; aerial, aeriform; aery, pneumatic.

meteorologic *or* meteorological, aerological, aerometric, eudiometric *or* eudiometrical, barometric *or* barometrical, barographic, baroscopic *or* baroscopical; isobaric, isopiestic; aerographic *or* aerographical; weatherwise.

adv. **in the open air,** *à la belle étoile* [*F.*], in the open, out of the blue, under the stars, out of doors, outdoors; *al fresco* [*It.*]; *sub Jove* [*L.*], *sub dio* [*L.*].

339. Moisture

n. **moisture;** moistness etc. *adj.;* humidity, humectation; madefaction [*obs.*], dew; *serein* [*F.*]; marsh etc. 345.

hygrometry, hygrometer.

v. **moisten,** wet; humect *or* humectate [*rare*]; sponge, damp, bedew; imbue, imbrue, infiltrate, saturate; soak, sodden, seethe, sop, dampen; drench etc. (*water*) 337.

be moist etc. *adj.;* not have a dry thread; perspire etc. (*exude*) 295.

adj. **moist,** damp; watery etc. 337; madid [*now rare*], undried, humid, wet, dank, muggy, dewy; roric; roriferous, rorifluent [*both rare*], roral [*obs.*], rorid [*obs.*]; roscid [*rare*]; juicy.

saturated etc. *v.;* wringing wet; wet through, wet to the skin.

sodden, swashy [*dial.*], soppy, soggy, dabbled; reeking, dripping, soaking, droukit [*Scot.*], soft, sloppy, muddy; swampy etc. (*marshy*) 345; irriguous.

340. Dryness

n. **dryness** etc. *adj.;* siccity [*rare*], siccation, aridness, aridity, drought *or* drouth.

ebb tide, low water.

desiccation, exsiccation [*rare*], dehydration, insolation, anhydration, anhydromyelia [*med.*], evaporation, arefaction [*rare*], dephlegmation, drainage.

drier, desiccative, desiccator.

v. **be** *or* **render dry** etc. *adj.;* dry; dry up, soak up; sponge, swab, wipe. drain, parch, sear.

be fine, hold up; be bright and fair.

desiccate, exsiccate, dehydrate, anhydrate, evaporate, insolate, infumate, torrefy, siccate [*rare*], arefy.

adj. **dry,** arid; droughty, waterless, siccaneous [*rare*], siccate [*obs.*], aneroid, sear *or* sere, siccant [*rare*], siccific, desiccatory; adjust, arescent; dried etc. *v.;* undamped; dephlegmatory; juiceless, sapless; corky; husky; rainless, without rain, fine; dry as -a bone, –dust, –a stick, –a mummy, –a biscuit; waterproof, watertight.

anhydrous, desiccated, desiccate, anhydric, dehydrated, insolated.

341. Ocean

n. **ocean,** sea, main, deep, blue, brine, salt water, waters, waves, billows, high seas, offing, great waters, watery waste, "vasty deep" "briny deep," "swan-bath" [*A.-S.*], "swan-road" [*A.-S.*], "whale-path" [*A.-S.*], mere [*archaic*], herring pond *or* pond [*humorous for Atlantic*], hyaline, the Seven Seas, *kala pani* [*Hind.*]; wave, tide etc. (*water in motion*) 348; ocean basin; ocean lane, steamer track.

Neptune, Poseidon, Oceanus, Thetis, Triton, Naiad, Nereid; sea nymph, Siren, mermaid, merman; trident, dolphin.

oceanography, hydrography; oceanographer, hydrographer.

adj. **oceanic,** marine, maritime; pelagic; seaworthy, seagoing; hydrographic *or* hydrographical, oceanographic *or* oceanographical; bathybic, cotidal.

adv. at sea, on sea; afloat; oversea *or* overseas, oceanward *or* oceanwards.

342. Land

n. **land,** earth, ground, soil, dry land, *terra firma* [*L.*].

continent, mainland, main, peninsula, chersonese, delta; tongue–, neck- of land; isthmus, oasis; promontory etc. (*projection*) 250; highland etc. (*height*) 206.

realty, real estate etc. (*property*) 780; acres.

coast, shore, scar *or* scaur, strand, beach; *playa* [*Sp.*]; bank, lea; seaboard, seaside, sea bank, seacoast, seabeach; seashore, rock-bound coast, iron-bound coast; loom of the land; derelict; innings; reclamation, made land, alluvium, alluvion; *ancon* [*S. W. U. S.*].

    region etc. 181; home, fatherland etc. (*abode*) 189.

    soil, glebe, clay, loam, marl, cledge [*dial. Eng.*], chalk, gravel, mold *or* mould, subsoil, clod, clot [*dial.*].

    rock, crag, cliff.

    geography, geodesy, geology, geognosy, geogony, agriculture, agronomics, agronomy, geoponics, georgics.

    geographer, geodesist, geologist, geognost.

    landsman, landlubber, tiller of the soil; agriculturist etc. 371.

v. **land**, disembark, debark, come to land; set foot on -the soil, −dry land; come−, go- ashore.

adj. **earthy**; continental, midland; terrene etc. (*world*) 318.

    littoral, riparian, riparial, riparious, ripicolous, ripuarian; alluvial.

    landed, predial, territorial; geophilous.

    geographic *or* geographical, geodesic *or* geodesical, geodetic *or* geodetical, geognostic *or* geognostical, geologic *or* geological, geoponic; agricultural etc. 371.

adv. **ashore**; on shore, on land, on dry land, on *terra firma* [*L.*].

343. Gulf. Lake

n. **gulf**, gulph, bay, inlet, bight, estuary, arm of the sea, bayou, fiord, armlet; frith *or* firth, ostiary [*obs.*], mouth; lagoon *or* lagune; indraft *or* indraught [*obs.*], cove, creek; natural harbor; roads; strait; narrows; euripus; sound, belt, gut, kyle [*Scot.*].

    lake, loch [*Scot.*], lough, [*Ir.*], mere, tarn, plash, broad [*Eng.*], pond, pool, sump [*Scot. or dial. Eng.*], slab [*dial.*], linn *or* lin [*Scot.*], tank, puddle, well, artesian well; standing−, dead−, sheet of- water; fish−, mill- pond; ditch, dike *or* dyke, dam, race, mill race; reservoir etc. (*store*) 636; *alberca* [*Sp. Amer.*], hog wallow, buffalo wallow.

adj. **lacustrine**, lacustral.

344. Plain

n. **plain**, tableland, face of the country; open−, champaign-country; basin, downs, waste, weary waste, desert, wild, steppe, tundra, peneplain, pampas, savanna, prairie etc. (*grassland*) 367; heath, common, wold, veldt *or* veld, moor, moorland; bush, plateau etc. (*level*) 213;

campagna [*obs. as Eng.*], champaign, uplands, fell [*Brit.*]; reach, stretch, expanse; alkali flat, llano; mesa, mesilla, *playa* [*Sp.*]; shaking−, trembling- prairie; *vega* [*Sp. Amer.*].

    meadow, mead, haugh [*Scot. & dial. Eng.*], pasture, lea, ley *or* lay [*dial.*], pasturage, field.

    lawn, green, plat, plot, grassplat.

    greensward, sward, turf, sod, grass; heather.

    grounds; *maidan* [*India*], park, common, campus, *agostadero* [*Sp.*].

adj. **champaign**, campestral, campestrial [*obs.*], campestrian, campestrine.

    alluvial, fluvio-marine.

adv. in the bush.

345. Marsh

n. **marsh**, swamp, morass, marish [*archaic*], peat bog, moss, fen, bog, quagmire, slough, sump [*Scot. or dial. Eng.*], bottoms, holm [*Eng.*], wash; mud, squash, slush; baygall, *ciénaga* [*Sp.*], *jhil* [*India*], *vlei* [*S. Africa*].

adj. **marsh**, marshy, swampy, boggy, plashy, poachy, quaggy, soft; muddy, sloppy, squashy, spongy; paludal; moorish, moory; fenny, marish [*archaic*].

346. Island

n. **island**, isle, islet, ait *or* eyot, holm, reef, atoll; archipelago; islander.

v. **insulate**, island, enisle [*rare*], isle [*rare*].

adj. **insular**, insulary [*rare*], seagirt; archipelagic.

347. Stream
[fluid in motion]

n. **stream** etc. (*of water*) 348, (*of air*) 349.

v. **flow** etc. 348; **blow** etc. 349.

348. River
[water in motion]

n. running water.

    jet, swash, spurt *or* spirt, squirt, spout, splash, rush, gush, *jet d'eau* [*F.*]; sluice.

    waterspout, waterfall; fall, cascade, force *or* foss [*dial. Eng.*], linn *or* lin [*Scot.*], gill *or* ghyll; Niagara; cataract, catadupe [*obs.*], cataclysm; debacle, inundation, deluge; chute, washout.

    rain, rainfall; *serein* [*F.*]; plash, shower, scud [*dial.*]; downpour; downflow, pour, cloudburst, drencher; driving−, drenching- rain; predominance of Aquarius, reign of St. Swithin; drisk, brash [*dial.*], mizzle [*dial.*], drizzle, stillicidium, dropping etc. *v.*; rains, rainy season, monsoon, *bursat or barsat* [*Hind.*]; falling weather [*colloq.*].

    hyetology, hyetography; hyetograph, rain chart.

stream, course, flux, flow, profluence; effluence etc. (*egress*) 295; defluxion; flowing etc. *v.;* current, tide, race, mill race, tide race.

spring; fount, fountain; rill, rivulet, rillet; streamlet, brooklet; branch; runnel, runlet; sike, burn [*both dial. Eng. & Scot.*], beck [*Eng.*], brook, river; reach; tributary.

body of water, torrent, rapids, flush, flood, swash; spring–, high–, flood–, full- tide; bore, eagre *or* hygre; fresh, freshet; indraft *or* indraught; ebb, refluence, reflux, undercurrent, undertow, eddy, vortex, gurge [*rare*], whirlpool, Charybdis, Maelstrom (*also* maelstrom), regurgitation, overflow, alluvion; confluence, corrivation [*obs.*].

wave, billow, surge, swell, ripple, *anerithmon gelasma* [*Gr.*]; beachcomber, riffle, tidal wave, comber, chop, choppiness, roll, rollers, ground swell, surf, breakers, white horses; rough–, heavy–, cross–, long–, short–, choppy–, chopping- sea.

[science of fluids in motion] hydrodynamics; hydraulics, hydrostatics, hydrokinetics, hydromechanics, pegology, pluviometry.

[measures] hyetometer, hyetometrograph, hydrodynamometer, nilometer, fluviometer, fluviograph, marigraph, hydrometer, hydrometrograph, udometer, ombrometer, rain gauge *or* gage, pluviometer, pluviograph.

irrigation etc. (*water*) 337; pump; watering- pot, –cart; hydrant, standpipe, syringe, siphon, *mussuk* [*Hind.*].

water carrier, bheesty *or* bheestie [*India*], Water Bearer, Aquarius.

v. **flow**, run; meander; gush, pour, spout, roll, jet, well, issue; drop, drip, dribble, plash, spirtle, trill, trickle, distill, percolate; stream, gurge [*rare*], surge, swirl, overflow, inundate, deluge, flow over, splash, swash; guggle, murmur, babble, bubble, purl, gurgle, sputter, spurt, regurgitate; ooze, flow out etc. (*egress*) 295.

flow into, fall into, open into, drain into; discharge itself, disembogue.

[cause a flow] pour; pour out etc. (*discharge*) 297; shower down; irrigate, drench etc. (*wet*) 337; spill, splash.

[stop a flow] stanch *or* staunch; dam, dam up etc. (*close*) 261; obstruct etc. 706.

rain, –hard, –in torrents, –cats and dogs, –pitchforks [*both colloq.*]; pour, shower, sprinkle, pour with rain, drizzle, spit [*colloq.*], set in; mizzle.

adj. **fluent**, deliquescent, defluent, profluent [*rare*], diffluent, affluent; tidal; flowing etc. *v.;* mean-

dering, meandrous, meandry [*obs.*], flexuous, fluvial, fluviatile; streamy, streamful; choppy, rolling; stillicidious [*obs.*], stillatitious [*rare*]; hydragogue [*med.*].

rainy, showery, pluvial [*rare*], pluvious, pluviose [*rare*], drizzly, drizzling, mizzly, wet; pluviometric *or* pluviometrical.

349. Wind

[air in motion]

n. **wind**, draught, flatus, afflatus, sufflation [*rare*], insufflation, perflation, inflation, afflation, indraft *or* indraught, efflation; air; breath, –of air; puff, whiff, whiffet, zephyr, blow, drift; aura; stream, current; undercurrent.

Aeolus *or* Eolus, Boreas, Euroclydon, Eurus, Notus [*rare*], Zephyr *or* Zephyrus, Favonius; cave of Aeolus *or* Eolus; Wabun (east wind), Kabibonokka (north wind), Shawondasee (south wind), Mudjekeewis (west wind) [*all four from Hiawatha*].

gust, blast, breeze, capful of wind, fresh breeze, stiff breeze, keen blast, squall, half a gale, gale.

trade wind, trades, monsoon.

storm, tempest, hurricane, whirlwind, tornado, samiel, cyclone, typhoon, simoom *or* simoon, harmattan, sirocco, mistral, *bise* [*F.*], *tramontana* [*It.*], tramontane, levant, levanter; blizzard, barber [*Can.*], *candelia* [*Sp. Am.*], chinook, foehn, khamsin, norther, northeaster, northeast gale, *vendaval* [*Sp.*], wuther [*dial.*], willy-willy [*Austral.*].

windiness etc. *adj.;* ventosity [*obs.*]; rough–, dirty–, ugly–, wicked–, foul–, stress of-weather; dirty sky, mare's-tail, mackerel sky; cloud etc. 353; thick–, black–, white- squall.

anemography, anemology, anemometry, aerology, aerography, aerodynamics.

wind-gauge, anemometer, anemoscope, anemograph, anemometrograph; weathercock, weathervane, vane.

breathing, respiration, inspiration, inhalation, expiration, exhalation; blowing, fanning, etc. *v.;* ventilation; sneezing etc. *v.;* errhine; sternutation; hiccup *or* hiccough, eructation, catching of the breath; inspirator, respirator, ejector.

air pump, lungs, bellows, pulmotor, blowpipe; branchiae, gills.

fan, punkah *or* punka [*India*], flabellum, thermantidote, electric fan; *ventilabrum* [*L.*].

ventilator, louver, aerator [*rare*], transom; air-pipe etc. 351; hygrometer, psychrometer.

v. **blow**, waft; blow -hard, –great guns, –a hurricane etc. *n.;* storm; wuther [*dial.*], stream, issue.

respire, breathe, inhale, exhale; inspire, expire; puff; whiff, whiffle; gasp, wheeze; snuff, snuffle; sniff, sniffle; sneeze, cough, hiccup *or* hiccough; belch, eruct [*rare*].

fan, ventilate; inflate, pump, perflate [*obs.*]; blow up.

whistle, scream, roar, howl, sing, sing in the shrouds, growl.

adj. **windy**, airy, aeolian *or* eolian, borean, favonian; ventilative; blowing etc. *v.;* breezy, gusty, squally.

stormy, tempestuous, blustering, cyclonic, typhonic; boisterous etc. (*violent*) 173.

anemographic, anemological, anemometric *or* anemometrical, aerologic *or* aerological, aerographic *or* aerographical, aerodynamic.

pulmonic, pulmonary, pulmonate.

nasal, errhine; sternutative, sternutatory.

flatulent, gassy, windy, ventose.

350. Conduit
[channel for the passage of water]

n. **conduit**, channel, duct, watercourse, cañon *or* canyon, coulee *or* coulée [*geol.*], water gap, gorge, ravine, chasm; race; head–, tail- race; abito [*F. Amer.*], aboideau *or* aboiteau [*local Can.*], bito [*dial., U. S.*]; acequia [*Sp. Amer.*], acequiador [*Sp. Amer.*], arroyo; adit, aqueduct, canal, trough, gutter, pantile; flume, dike, main; gully, gullet [*rare*], gulch, moat, ditch, drain, sewer, culvert, cloaca, sough [*dial. Eng.*], kennel, siphon; piscine, piscina; pipe etc. (*tube*) 260; funnel; tunnel etc. (*passage*) 627; water–, waste- pipe; emunctory, gully hole, spout, scupper; ajutage; hose; gargoyle *or* gurgoyle; penstock, pentrough, weir, lock weir, floodgate, water gate, sluice, lock, valve; rose, rosehead; waterworks.

[for metal] ingate, runner, tedge.

[anatomy] artery, vein, *vena* [*L.*], blood vessel, lymphatic, pore; aorta; intestines, bowels; small intestine, duodenum, jejunum, ileum; large intestine, cecum *or* caecum, colon, rectum; esophagus, gullet; throat.

adj. **vascular** etc. (*with holes*) 260.
excretory, eliminative.

351. Air Pipe
[channel for the passage of air]

n. **air pipe**, air tube, air hole, blowhole, breathing hole, spiracle, touchhole, vent hole, spile hole, bung, bunghole; shaft, airway, air shaft, smoke-shaft, flue, chimney, funnel, vent, ventage; ventiduct, ventilator; pipe etc. (*tube*) 260; blowpipe etc. (*wind*) 349.

nostril, nozzle, throat, weasand, bronchus (*pl.* bronchi), larynx, tonsils, windpipe, trachea.

louver, Venetian blind, Venetian shutter, *jalousie* [*F.*], *jhilmil* [*India*].

352. Semiliquidity

n. **semiliquidity**; stickiness etc. *adj.;* viscidity, viscosity, mucidness, gummosis, emulsification, jellification; gummosity [*rare*], glutinosity [*rare*], mucosity; crassitude, spissitude; lentor [*now rare*]; pastiness; adhesiveness etc. (*cohesion*) 46; succulence *or* succulency; lactescence.

inspissation, incrassation, crassamentum, coagulum; thickening.

[comparisons] jelly, gelatin, carlock, ichthyocol, ichthyocolla, isinglass; mucus, pus, phlegm, pituite; lava; paste; library–, flour- paste; glair, starch, gluten, albumen, milk, cream, protein; treacle, rob, syrup, molasses; gum, size, glue, varnish, mastic, mucilage, fish glue; wax, beeswax; emulsion; gruel, porridge; *purée* [*F.*], soup.

squash, mud, slush, slime, ooze; moisture etc. 339; marsh etc. 345.

v. **inspissate**, incrassate; coagulate, gelatinate, gelatinize; jellify, jelly, jell; emulsify, thicken; mash, squash, churn, beat up.

adj. **semifluid**, semiliquid; half-melted, half-frozen; milky, muddy etc. *n.;* lacteal, lactean [*rare*], lacteous, lactescent, lactiferous; emulsive, curdled, thick, succulent, uliginose *or* uliginous.

gelatinous, albuminous, mucilaginous, glutinous; gummous, spissated [*rare*], crass, tremelloid, tremellose, amylaceous, ropy, clammy, clotted; viscid, viscous; sticky, tacky; slab [*dial.*], slabby; lentous [*obs.*], pituitous; mucid, muculent, mucous.

353. Bubble. Cloud
[mixture of air and water]

n. **bubble**; foam, froth, head, spume, scum, fume, lather, suds, spray, surf, yeast, barm, spoondrift *or* spindrift.

effervescence, fermentation; bubbling etc. *v.;* evaporation, exhalation, emanation.

cloudiness etc. (*opacity*) 426; nebulosity etc. (*dimness*) 422.

cloud, vapor, fog, mist, haze, steam; scud, rack, nimbus; cumulus, nebula, meteor, woolpack, cirrus, curl cloud, thunderhead, stratus; cirrostratus, cumulo-stratus; cirro-cumulus; mackerel sky, mare's-tail, colt's-tail, cat's-tail, cocktail, dirty sky; frost smoke.

[science of clouds] nephology, nephelognosy, meteorology; nephoscope, nephelometer, nephograph.

v. **bubble**, boil, foam, spume, froth, mantle, sparkle, guggle, gurgle; effervesce, pop, ferment, fizzle; aerate.

cloud, overcast, overcloud, befog, becloud, adumbrate [*rare*], mist, fog, overshadow, shadow.

adj. **bubbling** etc. *v.;* frothy, nappy [*obs.*], effervescent, sparkling, *mousseux* [*F.*], fizzy, heady, with a head on, with a collar on [*slang*], up [*colloq.*].

cloudy etc. *n.;* cirrous, cirrose; nubiferous, cumulous, thunderheaded; vaporous, nebulous, overcast.

nephological, nepheloscopic, nephelometric, meteorologic *or* meteorological.

354. Pulpiness

n. **pulpiness** etc. *adj.;* pulp, paste, dough, sponge, batter, clotted cream, curd, pap, jam, pudding, poultice, grume.

v. **pulp**, pulpify [*rare*], mash, squash [*colloq.*], masticate, macerate; coagulate etc. 352.

adj. **pulpy** etc. *n.;* pultaceous, grumous; baccate; [*of fruit*] fleshy, succulent.

355. Unctuousness

n. **unctuousness** etc. *adj.;* unctiousness [*rare*], unguent, unctuosity, lubricity; salve, cerate; ointment etc. (*oil*) 356; anointment; lubrication etc. 332.

v. **oil**, anoint, lubricate etc. 332; smear, salve, grease, lard, pinguefy.

adj. **unctuous**, unctious [*rare*], unguentary, unguentous, oily, oleaginous, adipose, sebaceous, unguinous, fat, fatty, greasy; waxy, butyraceous, soapy, saponaceous, pinguid, lardaceous; slippery.

356. Oil

n. **oil**, fat, butter, cream, grease, tallow, suet, lard, dripping, exunge [*obs.*], blubber; glycerin *or* glycerine, stearin, elain *or* elaine, olein, oleagine; coconut butter; soap; soft soap, wax, cerement; paraffin, benzine, gasoline, petrol, spermaceti, adipocere; petroleum, mineral–, rock–, crystal- oil; vegetable–, colza–, olive–, salad–, linseed–, cottonseed–, coconut–, palm–, nut- oil; animal–, neat's-foot–, train-

oil; ointment, pomade, pomatum, unguent, liniment; amole, Barbados tar; fusel–, grain–, rape–, seneca-oil; hydrate of amyl, ghee *or* ghi [*India*], kerosene, naphtha.

356a. Resin

n. **resin**, rosin, colophony, gum; lac, shellac, sealing wax; amber, ambergris; bitumen, pitch, tar; asphalt *or* asphaltum; camphor; varnish, copal, mastic, megilp *or* magilp, lacquer, japan, Brunswick black.

v. **varnish** etc. (*overlay*) 223; rosin, resin.

adj. **resinous**, resiny, rosinous [*rare*], lacquered, japanned, camphorated, tarred, tarry, pitched, pitchy, gummed, gummy, gummous, waxed; bituminous, asphaltic, asphaltite.

Section 3. Organic Matter

357. Organization

n. **organization**, organized world, organized nature, living nature, animated nature; living beings; organic remains; organism, bion [*physiological individual*]; morphon [*morphological individual*]; biota, animal and plant life, fauna and flora.

fossils, fossilization, lapidification, petrification, petrifaction, paleontology *or* palaeontology, paleozoölogy *or* paleozoölogy; paleontologist.

[science of living beings] biology, natural history; zoölogy etc. 368; botany etc. 369; physiology, anatomy, cytology, embryology, organic chemistry, morphology; promorphology, tectology; cell theory *or* cellular theory, evolution, metabolism; abiogenesis, spontaneous generation; archigenesis etc. (*production*) 161; biotaxy, ecology, ontogeny, phylogeny, polymorphism, oxidation, invagination, vertebration.

Darwinism, Lamarckism, neo-Lamarckism, Weismannism.

naturalist, biologist, zoölogist, botanist, bacteriologist, embryologist, Darwinian.

protoplasm, plasma *or* plasm, cytoplasm, metaplasm, karyoplasm, bioplasm, trophoplasm, idioplasm; cell, proteid, protein, albumen, albumin, albuminoid; structure etc. 329; chromatin; centrosome, nucleolus, karyosome, vacuole, chromosome; protoplast, protozoan, amoeba; karyaster, erythroblast, dysmeromorph, antherozoid.

ovum, oösperm, zygote, oösphere, oöcyte, ooecium, ovicell, oögonium; oöphyte, oöspore, oögamy, heterogamy, isogamy, oögenesis; gamete, gametophore, gametophyte, sporophyte, sporocyte, sporocyst, sporocarp, cystocarp, sporogonium, sporozoite, gametangium, antheridium *or* antherid; macrospore, megasporangium; microspore, microsporangium; biophore; spermatozoid, zoöspore, macrogamete, microgamete, spermatozoön, spermatium, spermatia, spermatocyte, spermatogenesis, spermatophore, spermatozoid, spermatozooid; spermogonium, spermary, sperm gland, testis, testicle, ovary; germ cell, blastoderm, mesoblast *or* mesoplast, meroblast (*opp. to* holoblast); germinal matter, biogenesis *or* biogeny, germ plasm, zooid.

v. **organize**, systematize, form, arrange, construct.
fossilize, petrify, lapidify, mummify.

adj. **organic**, organized; biotic, zooid, zooidal.
fossilized, petrified, petrifactive, lapidined; paleontologic, paleontological *or* palaeontological, paleozoölogical *or* palaeozoölogical.
protoplasmic, plasmatic *or* plasmic, cytoplasmic, metaplasmic, karyoplasmic, bioplasmic, trophoplasmic, idioplasmic; cellular, cellulous; proteid, proteinaceous, albuminous *or* albuminose, albuminoidal, structural; nuclear, nucleate, nucleolar, nucleolate *or* nucleolated; vacuolar, protoplastic, protozoan, amoebic, amoeboid.
ovarian, oviferous, oviparous (*opp. to* viviparous), ovicular; oöphytic, oösporic, oösporous, oögamous, heterogamous (*opp. to* autogamous *or* isogamous); gamic, sporogenous; spermatic, spermatogenetic, spermatoid, spermatophoral, spermatozoal; blastodermic, mesoblastic (*opp. to* holoblastic), biogenetic, germinal; zoögleic, zoögleoid; unsegmentic, dioecious *or* diecious (*opp. to* monoecious *or* monecious).

358. Inorganization

n. **mineral kingdom**, mineral world; unorganized–, inorganic–, brute–, inanimate- matter.
[science of the mineral kingdom] mineralogy, geology, geognosy, geoscopy, metallurgy, metallography, lithology, petrology, oryctology [*obs.*], oryctography [*obs.*].

v. **mineralize**; pulverize, turn to dust.

adj. **inorganic**, inanimate, unorganized *or* inorganized, lithoid, *or* lithoidal; azoic; mineral.

359. Life

n. **life**; vitality, viableness, viability; animation.
vital spark, vital flame, Promethean spark, lifeblood; respiration, wind; breath of life, breath of one's nostrils; Archeus *or* Archaeus; *anima* [*L.*], *anima bruta* [*L.*], *anima divina* [*L.*], *anima mundi* [*L.*]; world -soul, −spirit, −principle; existence etc. 1.
vivification; oxygen; vital -air, −force; life force; vitalization; revival; revivification etc. 163; Prometheus; Deucalion and Pyrrha; life to come etc. (*destiny*) 152.
"a short summer" [Johnson]; "a bubble" [Browne]; "a battle" [Aurelius]; "one dem'd horrid grind" [Dickens].
[science of life] physiology, biology, etiology, embryology; animal economy.
nourishment, staff of life etc. (*food*) 298.

v. **live**; be alive etc. *adj.;* breathe, respire, suspire; subsist etc. (*exist*) 1; walk the earth; (a poor player that) "struts and frets his hour upon the stage" [*Macbeth*]; be spared.
be born, see the light, come into the world; fetch–, draw- -breath, −the breath of life; breathe the vital air; quicken; revive; come to, −life.
give birth to etc. (*produce*) 161; bring to life, put into life, vitalize; vivify, vivificate [*rare*]; reanimate etc. (*restore*) 660.
keep alive, keep body and soul together, keep the wolf from the door; support life.
have nine lives like a cat.

adj. **living**, alive; in life, in the flesh, in the land of the living; on this side of the grave, above ground, breathing, quick, animated; animative; lively etc. (*active*) 682; alive and kicking [*colloq.*]; tenacious of life.
vital, vitalic; vivifying, vivified etc. *v.;* viable, zoëtic; Promethean.

adv. *vivendi causa* [*L.*].

360. Death

n. **death**; decease, demise; mortality; dying; passing -away, −of the soul; dissolution, departure, obit, release, rest, eternal rest, quietus, fall; loss, bereavement.
end etc. 67–, cessation etc. 142–, loss–, extinction–, ebb- of life etc. 359.
death-warrant, deathwatch, death rattle, deathbed; stroke–, agonies–, shades–, valley of the shadow–, summons–, jaws–, hand–, bridge–, river- of death; Jordan, Jordan's bank, "one more river to cross"; last -breath, −gasp, −agonies; dying -day, −breath. −agonies; swan song, *chant du cygne* [*F.*]; *rigor mortis* [*L.*]; Stygian shore; "crossing the bar" [Tennyson]; the great adventure.
euthanasia, euthanasy [*rare*]; happy release, *bona mors* [*L.*]; break-up of the system; natural -death, −decay; sudden–, violent- death; un-

timely end, taking off [*colloq.*], watery grave; debt of nature; mortification, heart failure, suffocation, asphyxia; fatal disease etc. (*disease*) 655; deathblow etc. (*killing*) 361.

angel of death, death's bright angel, Azrael; King -of terrors, −Death; Death, doom etc. (*necessity*) 601; "Hell's grim Tyrant" [*Pope*].

necrology, bills of mortality, obituary.

death song etc. (*lamentation*) 839.

v. **die**, expire, perish; meet one's -death, −end; pass away, pass over, be taken; yield−, resign- one's breath; resign one's -being, −life; end one's -days, −life, −earthly career; breathe one's last; cease to -live, −breathe; depart this life; be no more etc. *adj.;* go off [*colloq.*], drop off [*colloq.*], pop off [*slang*]; lose−, lay down−, relinquish−, surrender- one's life; drop−, sink- into the grave; close one's eyes; fall−, drop- -dead, −down dead; break one's neck; give−, yield- up the ghost; be all over with one.

pay the debt to nature, shuffle off this mortal coil, take one's last sleep; go the way of all flesh; hand−, pass- -in one's checks, −in one's chips [*all slang*]; go over to the−, join the- -greater number, −majority, −great majority; join the choir invisible; awake to life immortal; come−, turn- to dust; give an obolus to Charon; cross the Stygian ferry; go to one's long account, go to one's last home, go to Davy Jones's locker, go to glory [*colloq.*]; receive one's death warrant, make one's will, step out [*colloq.*], die a natural death, go out like the snuff of a candle; come to an untimely end; catch one's death; go off the hooks, kick the bucket, hop the twig, turn up one's toes [*all slang*]; die a violent death etc. (*be killed*) 361.

die for one's country, make the supreme sacrifice, go West [*World War I euphemism*].

adj. **dead**, lifeless; deceased, demised, departed, defunct; late, gone, no more; exanimate [*rare*], inanimate; out of the world, taken off, released; bereft of life; stone dead; departed this life etc. *v.;* dead and gone; dead as -a doornail, −a doorpost, −mutton, −a herring, −nits [*all slang or colloq.*]; launched into eternity, gathered to one's fathers, numbered with the dead; born into a better world, born into the next world; gone to a better land; dying−, dead- in the Lord; asleep in Jesus; with the saints.

stillborn; mortuary; deadly etc. (*killing*) 361.

dying etc. *v.;* moribund, morient [*obs.*]; Hippocratic; *in articulo* [*L.*], *in extremis* [*L.*]; in the -jaws, −agony- of death; going, −off; *aux abois* [*F.*]; on one's -last legs [*colloq.*], −death-

bed; at the point of death, at death's door, at the last gasp; near one's end, given up, given over, booked [*slang*]; with one foot in−, tottering on the brink of- the grave.

adv. post obit [*L.*], post mortem [*L.*].

361. Killing

[destruction of life; violent death]

n. **killing** etc. *v.;* homicide, manslaughter, murder, assassination, trucidation [*obs.*], occision [*obs.*]; effusion of blood; blood, bloodshed; gore, slaughter, carnage, butchery; *battue* [*F.*]; bomb explosion, electrocution, shipwreck; gladiatorial combat; lapidation.

massacre; fusillade, *noyade* [*F.*]; thuggism, thuggee, thuggery; saturnalia of blood, sacrifice to Moloch; organized massacre, *pogrom* [*Russia*].

war, warfare, "organized murder," *horrida bella* [*L.*], crusade, jihad *or* jehad [*Moham.*]; battle; war to the death etc. (*warfare*) 722; Armageddon; gigantomachy; deadly weapon etc. (*arms*) 727.

deathblow, finishing stroke, *coup de grâce* [*F.*], quietus; execution etc. (*capital punishment*) 972; judicial murder; martyrdom.

suffocation, strangulation, garrote *or* garrotte; hanging etc. *v.*

slayer, butcher, murderer, Cain, assassin, cutthroat, garroter *or* garrotter, bravo, Thug *or* thug, Moloch, matador, *sabreur* [*F.*]; *guetapens* [*F.*]; gallows, executioner etc. (*punishment*) 975; man-eater, Apache, hatchet man, highbinder, gunman, bandit, lapidator [*rare*].

regicide, parricide, fratricide, infanticide; feticide, aborticide; uxoricide, vaticide [*these words ending in* -cide *refer to both doer and deed*].

suicide, self-murder, self-destruction, *felo-de-se* (*pl. felos-de-se*), seppuku [*Jap.*], hara-kiri [*Jap.*], suttee, sutteeism, car of Jagannath *or* Juggernaut [*an erroneous assumption*]; immolation, holocaust.

fatal accident, violent death, casualty, disaster, calamity.

Aceldama (*often l.c.*), potter's field, field of blood.

[destruction of animals] slaughtering; phthiozoics; sport, sporting; the chase, venery; hunting, coursing, shooting, fishing; pig-sticking.

sportsman, huntsman, fisherman; hunter, Nimrod.

shambles, slaughterhouse, *abattoir* [*F.*].

v. **kill**, put to death, slay, shed blood; murder, assassinate, butcher, slaughter, victimize, immolate; massacre; take away−, deprive of- life; make away with, put an end to; dispatch *or* despatch; burke, settle [*colloq.*], do to death, do for [*colloq.*]; hunt.

shoot, –dead; blow one's brains out; brain, knock on the head, blackjack; drop in one's tracks; stone, lapidate; give–, deal- a deathblow; give the -quietus, –*coup de grâce* [*F.*].

strangle, garrote *or* garrotte, hang, throttle, choke, stifle, suffocate, stop the breath, smother, asphyxiate, drown.

saber *or* sabre; cut -down, –to pieces, –the throat; jugulate; stab, run through the body, bayonet; put to the -sword, –edge of the sword.

execute, behead, guillotine, hang, electrocute; bowstring etc. (*execute*) 972.

cut off, nip in the bud, launch into eternity, send to one's last account, sign one's death warrant, strike the death knell of.

give no quarter, pour out blood like water; decimate; run amuck *or* amok; wade knee-deep in blood; dye–, imbrue- one's hands in blood.

die a violent death, welter in one's blood; dash–, blow- out one's brains; commit suicide; kill–, make away with–, put an end to- oneself; suicide [*colloq.*]; disembowel, commit hara-kiri.

adj. **murderous**, slaughterous, sanguinary, sanguinolent, blood-stained, blood-thirsty; killing etc. *v.*; homicidal, red-handed; bloody, bloody-minded; ensanguined, gory, sanguineous.

mortal, fatal, lethal; deadly, deathly; mortiferous [*obs.*], lethiferous; unhealthy etc. 657; mutually destructive, internecine; suicidal.

sporting; piscatorial, piscatory.

int. thumbs down! *habet! hoc habet!* [*L.*], let him have it!

362. Corpse

n. **corpse**, corse [*archaic*], carcass, cadaver, bones, skeleton, dry bones; defunct, relics, reliquiae, remains, mortal remains, dust, ashes, earth, clay; mummy; carrion; food for -worms, –fishes; tenement of clay, "this mortal coil" [*Hamlet*]; "this too, too solid flesh" [*Hamlet*].

ghost, shade, manes, phantom, specter *or* spectre, apparition, spirit, revenant, sprite [*archaic*], spook [*colloq.*].

organic remains, fossils.

adj. **cadaverous**, cadaveric, corpse-like; unburied etc. 363.

363. Interment

n. **interment**, burial, sepulture, entombment *or* intombment, inhumation, humation [*obs.*]; obsequies, exequies; funeral, wake.

cremation, burning; pyre, funeral pile.

funeral rite, funeral solemnity; knell, passing bell, death bell, funeral ring, tolling; dirge etc. (*lamentation*) 839; cypress; obit, dead march, muffled drum; elegy; funeral -oration, –sermon.

undertaker, mortician, funeral director.

mourner, mute, keener [*Ireland*], lamenter; pall-bearer, bearer.

graveclothes, shroud, winding sheet, cerecloth; cerements.

coffin, casket, shell, sarcophagus.

urn, cinerary urn; pall, bier, litter, hearse, catafalque.

burial place, grave, pit, sepulcher *or* sepulchre, tomb, vault, crypt, catacomb, mausoleum, cenotaph, golgotha, house of death, narrow house, low green tent, low house, long home, last home; cemetery, necropolis; burial ground; graveyard, churchyard; God's acre; potter's field; cromlech, barrow, tumulus, cairn; ossuary; bonehouse, charnel-house, deadhouse; morgue, mortuary; lich gate; burning ghât *or* ghaut [*India*]; crematorium, crematory; mastaba *or* mastabah [*Egypt*], tope *or* stupa [*Buddhist*]; dokhma, Tower of Silence [*Parsee*].

gravedigger, sexton, *fossoyeur* [*F.*].

monument, cenotaph, shrine; gravestone, headstone, tombstone; *memento mori* [*L.*]; hatchment, stone, marker, cross; epitaph, inscription.

necropsy, necroscopy, autopsy, *post mortem* examination *or post mortem* [*L.*].

exhumation, disinterment.

v. **inter**, bury; lay in–, consign to- the -grave, –tomb; entomb *or* intomb; inhume; hold–, conduct- a funeral; put to bed with a shovel [*colloq.*]; inurn; cremate.

lay out; embalm, mummify; toll the knell.

exhume, disinter, unearth.

adj. **funereal**, funebrial [*now rare*], funeral, funerary, mortuary, sepulchral, cinerary; buried etc. *v.*; burial; elegiac; necroscopic *or* necroscopical.

adv. hic jacet [*L.*], *ci-gît* [*F.*], *R. I. P.*; in memoriam [*L.*]; *post obit* [*L.*], *post mortem* [*L.*]; beneath the sod, under the sod, underground; at rest.

364. Animality

n. **animality**, animalism, animal life; animation, animalization, animalness.

corporeal nature, human system; breath; flesh, flesh and blood; physique; strength etc. 159.

v. **animalize**; incarnate, incarn [*rare*], incorporate.

adj. **fleshly**, carnal, human, corporeal.

365. Vegetation

n. **vegetation**, vegetable life, vegetability [*obs.*], vegetativeness, vegetism, vegetality [*rare*]; herbage, flowerage.

v. **vegetate**, germinate, sprout, grow, shoot up, luxuriate, fungate; grow -rank, –lush, –like a weed; flourish etc. 367; cultivate.

adj. **vegetative**, vegetal, vegetable; leguminous etc. 367.

luxuriant, rank, dense, lush, wild, jungly.

366. Animal

n. **animal kingdom**, fauna, brute creation.

animal, creature, created being; creeping thing, living thing; dumb animal, dumb friend, dumb creature; brute, beast.

mammal, quadruped, bird, reptile, fish, crustacean, shellfish, mollusk, worm, insect, zoöphyte; plankton, nekton, benthos; animalcule etc. 193.

beasts of the field, fowls of the air, denizens of the day; flocks and herds, live stock, domestic animals; wild animals, *ferae naturae* [*L.*], game.

[domestic animals] horse etc. (*beast of burden*) 271; cattle, kine, ox; bull, bullock; cow, milch cow, Alderney, Guernsey, Holstein, Jersey, calf, heifer, shorthorn, yearling, steer, stot [*prov. Eng.*]; sheep; lamb, lambkin, ewe lamb, pet lamb; ewe, ram, tup, wether, tag [*prov. Eng.*], teg [*prov. Eng.*]; pig, swine, boar, hog, sow; yak, zebu, Indian buffalo.

dog, hound, canine; pup, puppy; whelp, cur [*contemptuous*].

house–, watch–, sheep–, shepherd's–, sporting–, hunting–, fancy–, lap–, toy- dog; collie; mastiff; bulldog, English bulldog, Boston bull, bull terrier, French bull; police dog, bloodhound, greyhound, staghound, deerhound, foxhound, coach dog, bandog, lurcher, Russian *or* Siberian wolfhound, boarhound, St. Bernard, husky *or* Eskimo dog; otter-hound; harrier, beagle, spaniel, pointer, setter, retriever, Newfoundland; water -dog, –spaniel; pug, poodle; turnspit; terrier; fox–, Airedale–, Yorkshire–, Irish–, Skye–, toy-terrier; Dandie Dinmont; dachshund, badger dog; brindle; Pomeranian, cocker spaniel, King Charles spaniel, toy spaniel, spitz dog; chow *or* chow-dog, Japanese poodle.

pariah dog, pye-dog *or* pie-dog [*India*]; mongrel, mutt [*slang*].

female, bitch, slut, brach, brachet, lady [*euphemistic*].

cat, feline, puss, pussy, grimalkin, tomcat *or* tom, gib [*rare*], Angora, Persian, Maltese, tortoise-shell, mouser; tabby; kitten, kit, catling, kitling [*dial.*].

[wild animals] deer, buck, doe, fawn, stag, hart, hind, roe, roebuck, caribou, elk, moose, reindeer, sambar, wapiti *or* American elk, mule deer, black-tailed deer *or* Virginia deer, fallow deer, red deer.

antelope, gazelle, nilghau, eland, gnu, hartebeest, springbok *or* springbuck, oryx, steinbok, ibex; American antelope *or* pronghorn, chamois, koodoo *or* kudu.

armadillo, peba, poyou, tatouay; wild ass, kiang, dziggetai, onager; bear, polar bear, grizzly bear, brown bear; beaver; bison, buffalo; musk ox, giraffe, okapi, tapir; wild boar; babiroussa *or* babirussa; ape, monkey, gorilla, marmoset, chimpanzee, lemur, baboon, orang-utan *or* orang-outang; kangaroo, opossum; wild horse, zebra; elephant, *hathi* [*Hind.*]; fox, reynard, Reynard, vixen [*fem.*], varmin *or* varmint [*dial.*], prairie fox, gray fox, red fox, arctic fox; dingo, coyote; wildcat, lynx, bobcat; skunk; hippopotamus, rhinoceros, lion, tiger etc. (*wild beast*) 913; squirrel, chipmunk, gopher, prairie dog, ferret, stoat, weasel, mongoose, raccoon *or* coon, bandicoot, rat, mouse; bat, flying mouse, flying phalanger, flying squirrel; flying fox, flying lemur, colugo.

lizard, saurian, iguana, eft, newt, chameleon, gecko, Gila monster, dragon, horned toad, horned lizard.

crocodilian, crocodile, mugger *or* magar [*India*], gavial [*India*], alligator, cayman, American crocodile.

whale, sperm whale, baleen whale; shark, porpoise, walrus, seal, octopus, devilfish; swordfish; pike; salmon etc. (*food*) 298.

[birds] feathered tribes, feathered songster, singing bird, warbler, dickybird [*colloq.*].

canary, vireo, linnet, finch, goldfinch, brown thrasher, siskin, crossbill, aberdevine, chewink, peewee, lapwing [*Scot.*], titmouse *or* chickadee, nightingale, lark; magpie, cuckoo, mocking bird, catbird, laughing jackass, starling, myna *or* mina; bobolink, reedbird, ricebird, cardinal, cowbird, crow, rook, jackdaw, raven; pigeon, dove, cushat, ringdove, wood pigeon; swan, cygnet, goose, gander, duck, drake, wild duck, mallard; flamingo, heron, crane, stork, eagle, kingfisher, sandpiper, lyre bird, robin, thrush, hermit thrush, veery, mavis, missel thrush, ouzel *or* ousel, blackbird, red-winged blackbird; kingbird, fly-catcher; woodpecker, flicker; sparrow, song sparrow, chipping sparrow, vesper sparrow; swallow, swift, martin, sand martin, oriole, bluebird, meadow lark; bird of paradise, parrot, parrakeet *or* parakeet; penguin, pelican; gull, sea gull, albatross, petrel, stormy petrel *or* Mother Carey's chicken, fulmar *or* Mother Carey's goose; ostrich, emu; owl, bird of night; hawk, vulture, buzzard, turkey buzzard; eagle, bird of freedom, bird of Jove.

game, black game, black grouse, ruffed grouse, grouse, blackcock, duck, plover, rail, snipe; pheasant etc. 298.

poultry, fowl, cock, rooster, chanticleer, dunghill fowl, barndoor fowl, barnyard fowl, hen, Partlet, chicken, chick, chickabiddy; guinea fowl, guinea hen; peafowl, peacock, bird of Minerva, peahen.

[insects] ant, bee, honeybee, queen bee, drone; ant, white ant, termite; wasp, sawfly, locust, grasshopper, cicada, cicala, cricket; dragon fly, June fly, caddis fly; beetle; butterfly, moth; fly, May fly, thrips, aphid, bug; ant lion, hellgramite *or* hellgamite, earwig; springtail, podura, lepisma; buffalo bug, buffalo carpet beetle etc. (*injurious insects*) 913.

vermin, lice, cooties [*slang*], flies, fleas, cockroaches *or* roaches, water bugs *or* Croton bugs, bugs, bedbugs, Norfolk Howards [*slang*], mosquitoes; rats, mice, weasels.

snake, serpent, viper; asp, adder, copperhead, coral snake *or* harlequin snake, sidewinder, krait [*India*], viper, cobra, cobra de capello, king cobra, rattlesnake *or* rattler, copperhead, constrictor, boa constrictor, boa, python, Kaa [*Kipling*], ophidian.

[mythological] dipsas (*pl.* dipsades), basilisk, cockatrice, amphiobaena, Python, Hydra.

salamander; griffin *or* griffon *or* gryfon; chimaera; Cerberus.

adj. **animal**, zoic, zooid *or* zooidal, zoölogical.

equine; bovine, vaccine; canine; feline; fishy, piscatory, piscatorial; molluscous, vermicular; gallinaceous, rasorial, solidungulate, soliped; planktonic, nekteric, benthonic.

ophidian, ophiologic, ophiomorphous, reptilian, anguine, ophic [*rare*], snakelike, serpentiform [*rare*], viperine, colubrine.

367. Vegetable

n. **vegetable**, vegetable kingdom; flora.

organism, plant, tree, shrub, bush, creeper, vine; herb, seedling, plantlet, exotic, annual, perennial, biennial, triennial; legume, pulse, vetch, greens; asparagus etc. (*vegetables*) 298.

foliage, leafage, verdure, foliation, frondescence [*rare*]; prefoliation, vernation; branch, bough, ramage, stem, tigella *or* tigelle *or* tigellum *or* tigellus; leaf, spray, leaflet, frond, foliole, bract, bractlet, bracteole, cotyledon, pad, flag, petal, needle, sepal; spray etc. 51; petiole, petiolule, bine; shoot, tendril.

flower, blossom, bud, burgeon, blow, blowth [*rare*]; floweret, floret, floscule, flowering plant; inflorescence, flowerage.

tree, sapling, seedling, stand, pollard, dryad [*fig.*]; oak, elm, beech, birch, timber tree, pine, palm, spruce, fir, hemlock, yew, larch, cedar, savin *or* savine, juniper, chestnut, maple, alder, ash, myrtle, magnolia, walnut, olive, poplar, willow, linden, lime; apple etc. (*fruit trees*) 298; arboretum etc. 371.

banyan, teak, acacia, deodar, pipal *or* pipal tree; fig tree, eucalyptus, gum tree.

woodlands, virgin forest, forest primeval, forest, wood, timberland, timber, wood lot; hurst, frith, holt [*poetic or dial.*], weald, wold [*obs.*], park, chase [*Eng.*], greenwood, grove, copse, coppice, *bocage* [*F.*], tope [*India*], clump of trees, thicket, spinet [*obs.*], spinney [*Eng.*], bosk, chaparral, *ceja* [*Texas*], motte [*local, U. S.*]; jungle, bush.

undergrowth, underwood, brushwood, brake, "the mid-forest brake" [*Keats*], boscage, scrub, palmetto barrens, bosch [*Dutch*]; heath, heather, fern, bracken, furze, gorse, whin, broom, genista, sedge, rush, bulrush, bamboo; weed, moss, foggage [*Scot.*], lichen, Iceland moss, mushroom, toadstool, fungus; turf, turbary, mold *or* mould.

grass, fog, second growth, second crop; herbage.

alfalfa, lucern *or* lucerne, alfilaria, clover, bent *or* bent grass, timothy, redtop *or* English grass, switch grass *or* black bent, blue grass, Kentucky blue grass, ribbon grass, meadow grass, spear grass, wire grass, blue joint, crab grass, bunch grass, meadow fescue, meadow foxtail, grama *or* mesquite grass, gama *or* sesame grass, sheep's fescue; cereal, wheat, barley, buckwheat, maize *or* Indian corn, oats, rice, rye.

grassland, greensward, green, lawn, sward, common, maidan [*India*], mead, meadow, pasture, pasturage, prairie, pampas, steppe, llano, savanna, campo, plain, field, campus.

seaweed, alga (*pl.* algae), fucus, fucoid, conferva (*pl.* confervae), confervoid, wrack, dulse, kelp, rockweed, sea lettuce, gulfweed, sargasso, sargassum; plankton, benthos; Sargasso Sea.

v. **vegetate**, grow, flourish, bloom, flower, blossom; bud etc. (*expand*) 194; timber, retimber, coppice, copse; bush, plant, trim, cut.

adj. **vegetable**, vegetal, vegetive [*obs.*], vegetative, vegetarian; leguminous, herbaceous, herbal, botanic *or* botanical; arborary, arboreous, arborescent, arborical [*obs.*], arboreal, arboral; silvan *or* sylvan; treelike, dendriform, dendritic *or* dendritical, dendroid; grassy, verdant, verdurous; floral, floreal [*rare*], lignose *or* lignous [*rare*], ligneous, lignescent, wooden, woody; bosky, cespitose, copsy; mossy, turfy, turf-like; fungous, fungiform, fungoid; tigellate, radiculose, radicular, radiciform, radiciflorous, rhizanthous, radicated; endogenous, exogenous; deciduous, evergreen.

native, domestic, indigenous, native-grown, home-grown.

algal, fucoid, confervoid; planktonic, benthonic.

368. Zoology
[science of animals]

n. **zoology**, zoonomy, zoography, zootomy; morphology, anatomy, histology, embryology; comparative anatomy, animal physiology, comparative physiology; mammalogy.

anthropology, anthropotomy, ornithology, ornithotomy, ichthyology, ichthyotomy, herpetology, herpetotomy, ophiology, malaeology, helminthology, entomology, entomotomy; oryctology [*obs.*], paleontology *or* palaeontology; mastology, vermeology; taxidermy.

zoologist, zoographer, zoographist, zootomist, anatomist, anthropotomist, morphologist, promorphologist, anthropologist, ornithologist, ornithotomist, ichthyologist, ichthyotomist, herpetologist, herpetotomist, ophiliologist, malacologist, helminthologist, entomologist, entomotomist; oryctologist [*obs.*], paleontologist *or* palaeontologist; vermeologist, taxidermist.

[principal groups] **protozoa** (the simplest animals): Rhizopoda, rhizopod; Foraminifera, foraminifer; Radiolaria, radiolarian; Flagellata, Flagellata; Infusoria, infusorian; Gregarinae, gregarine.

coelentera *or* **coelenterata** (sponges, corals, jellyfishes): Porifera, poriferan; Cnidaria, cnida; Spongiae *or* Spongiaria *or* Spongiozoa, sponge, calcareous sponges, siliceous sponges; Anthozoa, anthozoan, coral polyps; Hydrozoa, hydrozoön, hydroid, medusa.

echinodermata (crinoids, starfishes, and sea urchins): Pelmatozoa, Asterozoa, Echinozoa; Cystidea *or* Cystoidea, cystid, cystidean; Crinoidea, stone lilies, crinoidean; Blastoidea, blastoid; Ophiuroidea *or* Ophiurioidea, brittle stars, ophiuroid *or* ophiurid; Asterioidea *or* Asteridea, starfishes, asteridian; Echinoidea, sea urchins, echinoid; Holothurioidea, sea cucumbers, holothurian, holothure.

vermes (worms): Platyhelminthes *or* Plathelminthes, flatworms, platyhelminth; Rotifera, rotifer; Nemathelminthes *or* Nematelminthes, roundworms; Gephyrea, marine annelids, gephyrean, gephyreoid; Annelida, annelid, annelidan, annelloid.

molluscoidea (mollusk-like animals): Bryozoa *or* Polyzoa, sea mosses, bryozoan; Brachiopoda, lamp shells, brachiopod.

mollusca (mollusks): Pelecypoda *or* Lamellibranchia, bivalves, lamellibranch; Scaphopoda, tooth-shells *or* tusk-shells, scaphopod; Amphineura, chitons; Gastropoda, univalves, snails, gastropod; Cephalopoda, nautilus, cuttlefish, squid, octopus, cephalopod *or* cephalopode.

arthropoda (articulates): Branchiata, Tracheata; Crustacea, crustacean; Trilobita, trilobite; Limuloidea *or* Xiphosura, horseshoe crab, limulus; Entomostraca, ostracoids, barnacles, entomostracan; Malacostraca, lobsters, crabs, malacostracan; Myriapoda, centipedes, galleyworms, millipeds, myriapod; Arachnida *or* Arachnoidea, spiders, scorpions, mites, ticks, arachnid, arachnidan; Insecta, insects.

vertebrata (vertebrate animals): Cyclostomata *or* Cyclostoma, lampreys; Pisces, fishes; Selachii, sharks, rays, selachian; Holocephali *or* Holocephala, chimaeras, spooks; Dipnoi, lungfishes; Teleostomi, ordinary fishes, ganoids, teleost, teleostean; Amphibia, amphibians, batrachians; Reptilia, reptiles; Aves, birds; Mammalia, mammals; Monotremata *or* Prototheria, monotremes; Marsupialia, marsupials, marsupialian *or* marsupian; Placentalia, placentals.

adj. **zoological**, zoologic; zoonomic; zoographical etc.
n.

114

protozoan, rhizopodous; foraminiferous, foraminous, foraminated; radiolarian; flagellate; infusorial, infusory; gregarine.

coelenterate, poriferan, spongiose *or* spongious, spongoid, spongiform; anthozoan, anthozoic, corallaceous, coralliferous, coralliform, coralligenous, coralligerous, coralloid, coralloidal; polyparous, polypean; hydrozoal, hydroid; medusiform, medusoid.

echinodermatous, echinodermal; pelmatozoan; crinoidal, crinoid; ophiuran, ophiuroid; asteridian; echinoid, holothurian.

vermicious, vermicular, vermiculate, vermiculose *or* vermiculous, vermiform; gephyrean, gephyreoid; annelid *or* annelidan, annelidous.

molluscoid, molluscoidal; bryozoan; brachiopod.

molluscan, molluscoid, molluscous; lamellibranch, lamellibranchiate, bivalvular, bivalvous, bivalved; gastropodous, univalve *or* univalved, univalvular; cephalopodic, cephalopodous, nautiloid.

arthropodal, articulate; branchial, branchiate, branchiferous; tracheate; crustacean, crustaceous; arachnoid, arachnoidal, arachnidan, arachnidial; insectile, insected.

vertebrate, vertebrated, vertebral; cyclostome, cyclostomous; piscatorial *or* piscatory, pisciform, piscine; amphibian, amphibial [*rare*], amphibious; batrachian, batrachoid; reptilian; avicular; mammalian, mammiferous.

369. Botany
[science of plants]

n. **botany**; physiological–, structural–, systematic-botany; phytography, phytology, phytotomy, phytobiology, phytogenesis *or* phytogeny, phytonomy, phytopathology; phytochemistry, phytochimy [*obsoles.*], vegetable chemistry; pomology; vegetable physiology, herborization, dendrology, mycology, fungology, algology; flora, Flora, Pomona; botanic garden etc. (*garden*) 371; *hortus siccus* [*L.*]; herbarium, herbal [*obs.*].

phyton, phytomer *or* phytomeron.

[principal groups] **thallogens** *or* **thallophytes** (thallus plants): algae and algoid forms: Cyanophyceae, blue-green algae; Chlorophyceae, green algae; Phaeophyceae, brown algae; Rhodophyceae, red algae.

fungi and fungoid forms: Schizomycetes, fission fungi, bacteria; Myxomycetes, slime molds; Phycomycetes, algae fungi, water molds; Ascomycetes, sac fungi, lichen fungi; Basidiomycetes, basidium fungi, rusts, mushrooms.

bryophytes (moss plants): Hepaticae, liverworts; Musci, mosses.

pteridophytes (fern plants): Lycopodiales: Sigillaria, Stigmaria, Lepidodendra, fossil trees, lepidodendrid, lepidodendroid; Lycopodiaceae; club mosses: Equisetales, calamites, Equisetacae, horsetails, equisetum; Filicales: Cycadofilices, cycad ferns; Filices, ferns, filicoid.

spermatophytes (seed plants): Gymnospermae (naked-seeded plants): gymnosperm. Cycadales, cycads; Gnetales, gnetums; Ginkgoales, ginkgo (*pl.* ginkgoes); Coniferae, conebearing evergreens, conifer.

Angiospermae (covered-seeded plants): angiosperm; Monocotyledones, monocotyledon, cereals, palms, lilies, orchids, banana, pineapple etc., endogens; Dicotyledones: oak, apple, sunflower, pea, dicotyledon.

botanist, phytologist, phytotomist, phytobiologist, dendrologist; mycologist, fungologist; phytopathologist, horticulturist etc. 371; herbalist, herbist, herbarist [*obs.*], herborist, herbarian; pomologist.

v. **botanize,** herborize.

adj. **botanic** *or* botanical, phytoid, dendroid *or* dendroidal, herbose *or* herbous, dendriform, dendritic *or* dendritical, dendrologous, herby, herbal; fungoid, fungous, mycologic *or* mycological, mycetoid, phytobiological, phytochemical, phytogenetic *or* phytogenous, pomological, horticultural.

thalloid, thalline; hepatic, musciform, muscoid, lycopodiaceous, lepidodendroid, equisetaceous, equisetiform, filicoid, filiciform, gymnospermous, cycadaceous, coniferous, angiospermous, angiospermatous, monocotyledonous, endogenous, dicotyledonous.

370. Cicuration
[economy or management of animals]

n. **cicuration** [*obs.*], taming etc. *v.;* zoohygiantics; domestication, domesticity; manège *or* manege, veterinary art; farriery; breeding; pisciculture; apiculture.

menagerie, vivarium, zoological garden, zoo [*colloq.*]; bear pit; aviary; apiary, alvearium, alveary, beehive, hive; aquarium, fishery, fish hatchery, fish pond; swan pond, duck pond; incubator.

[destruction of animals] phthisozoics etc. (*killing*) 361.

[keeper] herder, oxherd, neatherd (*obs.*), cowherd, grazier, drover, cowkeeper; shepherd, shepherdess; keeper, gamekeeper; trainer, breeder; bull whacker, cowboy, cow puncher, *vaquero* [*Sp. Amer.*]; horse trainer, bronchobuster [*slang*]; apiarian [*rare*], apiarist, apiculturist.

veterinarian, veterinary surgeon, vet [*colloq.*], horse doctor, horse leech [*rare*]; farrier [*obsoles. as veterinarian*], horseshoer.

inclosure, stable, barn, byre; cage etc. (*prison*) 752; hencoop, bird cage, coif, cauf; sheepfold etc. 232.

v. **tame**, domesticate, domesticize, acclimatize, breed, tend, corral, round up, break in, gentle, cicurate [*obs.*], break, bust [*slang*], break to harness, train; ride, drive etc. (*take horse*) 266; cage, bridle, etc. (*restrain*) 751; guide, spur, prick, lash, goad, whip; trot, gallop etc. (*move quickly*) 274; bolt; yoke, harness, harness up [*colloq.*], hitch, hitch up [*colloq.*], cinch.

groom, rub down, brush, currycomb; water, feed, fodder; bed, bed down, litter; drench, embrocate.

tend stock, milk, shear; water etc. (*groom*) *v.;* herd; raise, bring up, bring up by hand.

hatch, incubate, sit, brood, cover.

swarm, hive.

adj. **pastoral**, bucolic, rural; agricultural etc. 371.

tame, domestic, domesticated, broken, gentle, docile.

371. Agriculture

[economy or management of plants]

n. **agriculture**, cultivation, husbandry, farming; georgics, geoponics; agronomy, agronomics, tillage, tilth, gardening, spade husbandry, vintage; horticulture, arboriculture, silviculture, forestry; floriculture; landscape gardening; viticulture.

husbandman, horticulturist, gardener, florist; agricultor [*rare*], agriculturist, agronomist, yeoman, farmer, cultivator, tiller of the soil, plowman *or* ploughman, reaper, sower; logger, lumberman, lumberjack, forester, woodcutter, pioneer, backwoodsman; granger, habitant, *vigneron* [*F.*], viniculturist, vine-grower, vintager, viticulturist; Triptolemus.

garden; botanic–, winter–, ornamental–, flower–, kitchen–, market–, truck–, hop- garden; nursery; greenhouse, hothouse; conservatory, forcing house, cold-frame; bed, border,

seed plot; grassplot *or* grassplat, lawn; parterre; shrubbery, plantation, avenue, arboretum, pinery, pinetum, orchard; vineyard, vinery, orangery.

field, meadow, mead, green, common, maidan [*India*]; park etc. (*pleasure ground*) 840; farm etc. (*abode*) 189.

v. **cultivate**, till, till the soil, farm, garden, sow, plant; reap, mow, cut; manure, dress the ground, dig, spade, delve, dibble, hoe, plow *or* plough, harrow, rake, weed, lop and top; backset; force, seed, turf, transplant, thin out, bed, prune, graft.

adj. **agricultural**, agronomic, geoponic, georgic, agrestical [*obs.*], agrestian, praedial *or* predial; horticultural, viticultural.

arable, plowable *or* ploughable, tillable.

rural, rustic, country, agrarian, pastoral, bucolic, Arcadian.

372. Mankind

n. **mankind**, man; human -race, –species, –kind, –nature; humanity, mortality, flesh, generation.

[science of man] anthropology, anthropogeny, anthropography, anthroposophy; ethnology, ethnography; anthropotomy, androtomy; humanitarianism.

human being; person, personage; individual, creature, fellow creature, mortal, body, somebody, one; such a one, some one; soul, living soul; earthling; party, head, hand; member, members of the cast, *dramatis personae* [*L.*]; *quidam* [*L.*].

people, persons, folk, public, society, world; community, –at large; general public; nation, nationality; state, realm; commonweal, commonwealth; republic, body politic; million etc. (*commonalty*) 876; population etc. (*inhabitant*) 188.

cosmopolite; lords of creation; ourselves.

adj. **human**, mortal, personal, individual, national, civic, public, social; cosmopolitan; anthropoid.

372a. Anthropology

n. **anthropology**; physical anthropology, anthropometry, human evolution, human paleontology; cultural anthropology *or* social anthropology, ethnology, ethnography, archaeology, linguistics.

[eras of recent life] Cenezoic era; Tertiary period *or* Age of Mammals (Paleocene epoch, Eocene epoch, Oligocene epoch, Miocene epoch, Pliocene epoch), Quaternary period *or* Age of Man (Pleistocene epoch, Holocene epoch).

[fossil primates] Parapithecus; Propliopithecus; Dryopithecus, Dryopithecus fontani, Dryopithecus rhenanus, Dryopithecus darwini; Proconsul africanus; Pliopithecus; Australopithecus africanus, Paranthropus robustus, Plesianthropus transvaalensis.

[fossil races of man] Gigantanthropus *or* Gigantopithecus blacki, Meganthropus paleojavanicus; Pithecanthropus robustus, Pithecanthropus erectus, Pithecanthropus modjokertensis; Sinanthropus pekinensis *or* Peking man; Homo soloensis *or* Solo man; Homo Africanthropus; Homo heidelbergensis *or* Heidelberg man; Homo neanderthalensis *or* Neanderthal man, Rhodesian group, Mousterian group, Ehringsdorf group (Ehringsdorf forms, Tabun Mt. Carmel forms, Steinheim forms), Skhul Mt. Carmel forms, Galilee forms; Homo Sapiens, Galley Hill man, London man, Swanscombe man, Fontechevade man; Cro-Magnon man, Grimaldi man, Predmost man, Brünn man, Chancelade man, Ofnet man; Wadjak man, Keilor man, Talgai man; Oldoway man, Boskop man, Springbok man, Fish Hoek man; Eoanthropus dawsoni *or* Piltdown "man."

[prehistoric cultural eras] Eolithic *or* Dawn Stone Age; Paleolithic *or* Old Stone Age, Lower Paleolithic Age (pre-Chellean stage, Chellean stage, Acheulean stage), Middle Paleolithic Age *or* Mousterian stage, Upper Paleolithic Age (Aurignacian stage, Solutrean stage, Magdalenian stage); Epipaleolithic *or* Mesolithic Age *or* Azilian-Tardenoisian stage; Neolithic or New Stone Age; Metal Age; Bronze Age, Early Bronze Age, Middle Bronze Age, Late Bronze Age; Iron Age.

[races] Caucasoid (Ainu, Australoid, Dravidian, Vedda; Alpine, Armenoid, Mediterranean, Nordic; Dinaric, East Baltic, Polynesian); Mongoloid (Asiatic, Indonesian-Malay, American Indian); Negroid (Forest Negro, Negrito; Hottentot-Bushman, Nilote *or* Nilotic Negro, Oceanic Negro).

index; acrocranic index, acromiocristal index, bodily fullness index, brachial index, cephalic index (dolichocephalic index, mesocephalic index, brachycephalic index), cranial index, cranial breadth-height index, cranial length-height index, crural index, facial index (euryprosopic index, mesoprosopic index, leptoprosopic index), femorohumeral index, forearm-hand index, gnathic index, hand index, intermembral index, ischium-pubis index, length-breadth sacral index, lower leg-foot index, maxillo-alveolar index, morphological *or* Naccarati's index, nasal index (platyrrhine index, mesorrhine index, leptorrhine index), orbital index, palatal index, pelvic breadth-height index, pelvic inlet index, pilastric index, platycnemic index, platymeric index, sicklemia index, stem-leg length *or* Manouvrier's skelic index, thoracic index, tibio-femoral index, tibio-radial index, total facial index, transverse fronto-parietal index, trunk index, upper facial index, vertical lumbar index; Frankfort line *or* Frankfort plane; Mongoloid eye; epicanthic *or* Mongoloid fold, external epicanthic fold, internal epicanthic fold; Negroid lip; prognathism; peppercorn hair; steatopygy *or* steatopygia; genotype, phenotype; blood type *or* group; constitutional type, pyknic type, leptosome type, athletic type; ectomorphy, mesomorphy, endomorphy.

culture; culture pattern, ideal pattern, behavioral pattern; integration of culture; function, theme, configuration, drive, postulate, affirmation; Apollonian configuration, Dionysian configuration; culture trait *or* element; trait complex *or* culture complex; age area, culture area, culture center *or* nucleus, marginal area; cultural evolution, savagery, barbarism, civilization; invention, discovery; convergence, parallelism; cultural transmission *or* borrowing; diffusion, stimulus diffusion; assimilation; acculturation, antagonistic acculturation, marginal acculturation, planitational acculturation; evolutionism, diffusionism (heliolithic diffusionism, culture-historical diffusionism), Kulturkreis, functionalism.

folkway; custom; mos; moral; law, collective responsibility; tort *or* private wrong crime *or* public wrong; sanction, legal *or* organized sanction; oath, compurgation; ordeal.

kinship; kin group; consanguine kinship, affinal kinship; unilateral kinship *or* descent, bilateral kinship *or* descent, mixed kinship *or* descent; patrilineal *or* agnatic kinship, matrilineal *or* uterine kinship; sibling; cross-cousin, parallel cousin *or* ortho-cousin; family; nuclear family, stem family, elementary family, composite family, extended family, joint family (patrilocal joint family, matrilocal joint family); conjugal *or* biological *or* small family, consanguineal family; patriarchal family; paternal family, maternal family; sib; clan; complex *or* genealogical clan, equalitarian clan; patrilineal clan, matrilineal clan; gens; lineage, unilocal lineage, multilocal lineage; phratry; moiety, simple moiety, compound moiety; tribe; familiarity *or* privileged familiarity, kin familiarity (avunculate, amitate), joking relationship; kin avoidance.

373. Man

n. **man**, male, he; manhood etc. (*adolescence*) 131; gentleman, sir, master, dan [*archaic*], don, huzur [*India*], sahib [*India*]; yeoman, chap [*colloq.*], wight [*now chiefly jocose*], swain, fellow, blade, beau, gaffer [*dial. Eng.*], goodman [*archaic*]; husband etc. (*married man*) 903; boy etc. (*youth*) 129.

mister, Mr., *monsieur* (abbr. M., *pl.* MM. *or* Messrs.) [*F.*], Herr [*Ger.*], signor [*It., used before name*], signore [*It.*], signorino [*It., dim. of signore*], signior [*Eng. form*], seignior, señor [*Sp.*], senhor [*Pg.*].

[*male animal*] cock, drake, gander, dog, boar, stag, hart, buck, horse, entire horse, stallion; gib [*rare*], tom, tomcat; he-goat, billy-goat [*colloq.*]; ram, tup; bull, bullock; capon; ox, gelding; steer, stot [*prov. Eng.*].

adj. **male**, he, masculine; manly, virile; unwomanly, unfeminine.

374. Woman

n. **woman**, she, female, petticoat; skirt, jane [*both slang*].

feminality, femininity, femineity, feminacy, feminity, muliebrity; gynics.

womankind; womanhood etc. (*adolescence*) 131; the sex, the fair; fair sex, softer sex; weaker vessel.

dame [*archaic except as an elderly woman*], madam, mastress [Chaucer, *obs.*], lady, Donna, belle, matron, dowager, goody, grammer [*dial. Eng.*], memsahib [*Anglo-Ind.*], sahiba [*Hind.*], bibi [*Hind.*], frow, vrouw [*Du.*], good woman, good wife [*archaic*]; squaw; wife etc. (*marriage*) 903; matronage, matronhood.

bachelor girl, new woman, feminist, suffragist, suffragette; spinster, old maid.

nymph, houri, wench, grisette; girl etc. (*youth*) 129.

mistress, Mrs., *madame* (*pl.* mesdames) [*F.*], Frau [*Ger.*], signora [*It.*], señora [*Sp.*], senhora [*Pg.*]; Ms.; miss, *mademoiselle* (*pl.* mesdemoiselles*) [*F.*], Fräulein [*Ger.*], signorina [*It.*], señorita [*Sp.*], senhorita [*Pg.*].

[*effeminacy*] betty, cot betty, cotquean, henhussy, molly, mollycoddle, muff, old woman, tame cat [*all contemptuous*].

[*female animal*] hen; bitch, slut, brach, brachet; sow, doe, roe, mare; she-goat, nanny-goat [*colloq.*], nanny [*colloq.*]; ewe, cow; lioness, tigress; vixen.

harem, gynaeceum *or* gynaecium, seraglio, zenana [*India*], purdah [*India*].

adj. **female**, she; feminine, womanly, ladylike, matronly, girlish, maidenly; womanish, effeminate, unmanly; gynecic *or* gynaecic.

375. Physical Sensibility

n. **sensibility**; sensitiveness etc. *adj.;* physical sensibility, feeling, impressibility, perceptivity, susceptibility, aesthetics *or* esthetics; moral sensibility etc. 822.

sensation, impression; consciousness etc. (*knowledge*) 490.

external senses.

v. **be sensible of** etc. *adj.;* feel, perceive; feel keenly, -exquisitely.

render sensible etc. *adj.;* sharpen, refine, excite, stir, cultivate, tutor.

impress, cause sensation; excite-, produce- an impression.

adj. **sensible**, sensitive, sensuous; aesthetic *or* esthetic, perceptive, sentient; conscious etc. (*aware*) 490; alive, alive to impressions, answering quickly to, impressionable, responsive, easily affected, quick in response.

acute, sharp, keen, vivid, lively, impressive, thin-skinned.

adv. **to the quick**; on the raw [*slang*].

376. Physical Insensibility

n. **insensibility**, physical insensibility; obtuseness etc. *adj.;* palsy, paralysis, anaesthesia *or* anesthesia, narcosis, narcotization, hypnosis, stupor, coma; twilight sleep, *Dämmerschlaf* [*Ger.*]; sleep etc. (*inactivity*) 683; moral insensibility etc. 823; hemiplegia, motor paralysis.

anaesthetic *or* anesthetic, anaesthetic agent; local-, general- anaesthetic; opium, ether, chloroform, chloral; nitrous oxide, laughing gas; exhilarating gas, protoxide of nitrogen; cocaine, novocain; refrigeration.

v. **be insensible** etc. *adj.;* have a -thick skin, -rhinoceros hide.

render insensible etc. *adj.;* blunt, cloy, satiate, pall, obtund, benumb, numb, deaden, freeze, paralyze; anaesthetize *or* anesthetize, put under the influence of chloroform etc. *n.;* put to sleep, hypnotize, stupefy, stun.

adj. **insensible**, unfeeling, senseless, imperceptient, callous, thick-skinned, pachydermatous; hard, hardened; case-hardened; proof; obtuse, dull; anaesthetic *or* anesthetic; paralytic, palsied, numb, dead.

377. Physical Pleasure

n. **pleasure**; physical–, sensual–, sensuous - pleasure; bodily enjoyment, animal gratification, delight, sensual delight, hedonism, sensuality; luxuriousness etc. *adj.;* dissipation, round of pleasure; titillation, gusto, creature comforts, comfort, ease; pillow etc. (*support*) 215; luxury, lap of luxury; purple and fine linen; bed of -down. –roses; velvet, clover; cup of Circe etc. (*intemperance*) 954.

treat; diversion, entertainment, banquet, regalement, refreshment, regale; feast; delice [*obs.*]; dainty etc. 394; *bonne bouche* [*F.*].

source of pleasure etc. 829; happiness, felicity, bliss, beatitude etc. (*mental enjoyment*) 827.

v. **enjoy**, pleasure [*rare*]; feel–, experience–, receive- pleasure; relish; luxuriate–, revel–, riot–, bask–, swim–, wallow- in; feast on; gloat -over, –on; smack the lips; roll under the tongue.

live on the fat of the land, live in comfort etc. *adv.;* bask in the sunshine, *faire ses choux gras* [*F.*].

give pleasure etc. 829; charm, delight, enchant.

adj. **enjoying** etc. *v.;* luxurious, voluptuous, sensual, comfortable, cosy, snug, in comfort, at ease, in clover [*colloq.*].

agreeable etc. 829; grateful, refreshing, comforting, cordial, genial; gratifying, titillative, sensous; apolaustic, hedonic, hedonistic, palatable etc. 394; sweet etc. (*sugar*) 396; fragrant etc. 400; melodious etc. 413; lovely etc. (*beautiful*) 845.

adv. **in comfort** etc. *n.;* on a bed of roses etc. *n.;* at one's ease; on flowery beds of ease.

378. Physical Pain

n. **pain**; suffering, sufferance [*rare*]; bodily–, physical- -pain, –suffering; mental suffering etc. 828; dolor *or* dolour, ache; aching etc. *v.;* smart; shoot, shooting; twinge, twitch, gripe, hurt, cut; sore, soreness; discomfort; headache, *malaise* [*F.*], megrim, migraine, cephalalgy, cephalalgia; otalgia, earache, ischiagra, lumbago, arthritis, neuritis, gout, podagra, rheumatism, sciatica, ischialgia, neuralgia, tic douloureux, toothache, odontalgia; stiffneck, torticollis.

spasm, cramp; nightmare, ephialtes; kink, crick, stitch; convulsion, throe; throb etc. (*agitation*) 315; pang; colic; tormina, gripes.

sharp–, piercing–, throbbing–, grinding–, stabbing–, shooting–, gnawing–, burning- pain.

torment, torture, agony, anguish, lancination, rack, cruciation, crucifixion, martyrdom; vivisection.

martyr, sufferer; toad under a harrow.

v. **suffer**; feel–, experience–, suffer–, undergo- pain etc. *n.;* ache, smart, bleed; tingle, shoot; twinge, twitch, lancinate; writhe, wince, make a wry face; sit on -thorns, –pins and needles.

pain, give pain, inflict pain; lacerate; hurt, chafe, sting, bite, gnaw, stab, grind, gripe, pinch, tweak; grate, gall, fret, prick, pierce, wring, convulse; torment, torture; rack, agonize; crucify; cruciate [*obs.*], excruciate, break on the wheel, put to the rack; flog etc. (*punish*) 972; grate on the ear etc. (*harsh sound*) 410.

adj. **in pain** etc. *n.,* in a state of pain; under the harrow; pained etc. *v.;* gouty, podagric, torminous, torminal.

painful; aching etc. *v.;* poignant, pungent, torturous, baleful [*rare*], biting; with exposed nerves, sore, raw.

379. Touch

[sensation of pressure]

n. **touch**; tact, taction, tactility; contact, tangency, tangence [*rare*], impact, attain [*archaic*]; feeling, kiss, osculation, graze, glance, brush; lick, licking, lambency, palpation, palpability; contrectation [*rare*]; manipulation, palmation [*obs.*], contaction [*obs.*]; stereognosis; rubbing, kneading, massage.

[organ of touch] hand, palm, finger, forefinger, thumb, paw, feeler, antenna; tongue, palpus.

v. **touch**, feel, handle, finger, thumb, paw, fumble, grope, grabble; twiddle, tweedle [*obs. or dial.*]; pass–, run- the fingers over; stroke, palpate, palm, massage, rub, knead, manipulate, wield; throw out a feeler.

adj. **tactual**, tactile; tangible, palpable, tangent, contactual [*rare*], lambent; touching etc. *v.;* stereognostic.

380. Sensations of Touch

n. **itching** etc. *v.;* formication; aura [*med.*].
tickling, titillation.
itch, scabies, psora, pruritus, prurigo [*all med.*]; mange.

v. **itch**, tingle, creep, thrill, sting; prick, prickle.
tickle, titillate.

adj. **itching**, tingling etc. *v.*
ticklish, titillative.

119

itchy, psoric, scabious, mangy; creepy, crawly; prurient.

381. Numbness
[insensibility to touch]

n. **numbness** etc. (*physical insensibility*) 376; anaesthesia *or* anesthesia, narcosis, narcotization; pins and needles [*colloq.*].

v. **benumb** etc. 376; stupefy, narcotize, drug, deaden, paralyze.

adj. **numb**; benumbed etc. *v.*; insensible, unfeeling, anaesthetic *or* anesthetic, deadened; intangible, impalpable; dazed, dazy [*rare*], comatose, torporific, narcotic, carotic.

382. Heat

n. **heat**, caloric; temperature, warmth, fervor, calidity [*obs.*], torridity; incalescence *or* incalescency [*rare*], incandescence; recalescence, decalescence; adiathermancy, athermancy, diathermacy, diathermance *or* diathermancy *or* diathermaneity; phlogiston [*old chem.*], phlogisis; thermogenesis; liquation.

summer, dog days, canicule, canicular days; baking etc. 384–, white–, tropical–, Afric–, Indian–, Bengal–, summer–, blood- heat; sirocco, simoom *or* simoon, hot wave, sun at noon, "the bloody Sun, at noon" [Coleridge], vertical rays, broiling sun; insolation; warming etc. 384.

flush, glow, blush, bloom, redness; rubicundity; fever, hectic; febricity, pyrexia.

fire, spark, scintillation, flash, flame, blaze; bonfire; firework, pyrotechny; wildfire; sheet of fire, lambent flame; devouring element; pyrotechnics.

sun etc. (*luminary*) 423.

hot springs, geysers; thermae, hot baths; sauna, hot tub; Turkish–, electric–, Russian-bath; steam.

fire worship, pyrolatry, sun worship, heliolatry, Sabaeanism *or* Sabeanism *or* Sabeism, Parsiism *or* Parseeism, Zoroastrianism; pyrolator, heliolator, Sabaean *or* Saban, Parsi *or* Parsee, Zoroastrian.

[science of heat] pyrology; thermology, thermotics; thermometer etc. 389.

v. **be hot** etc. *adj.*; glow, flush, sweat, swelter, bask, smoke, reek, stew, simmer, seethe, boil, burn, singe, scorch, scald, grill, broil, blaze, flame; smolder *or* smoulder; parch, fume, pant.

heat etc. (*make hot*) 384; insolate, incandesce, recalesce.

thaw, fuse, melt, liquate, liquefy; give.

adj. **warm**, mild, genial, tepid, lukewarm, unfrozen; calid; warm as -toast, –wool.

hot, heated, fervid, fervent; roasting, sweltry; reeking etc. *v.*; ardent, aglow; baking etc. 384; sunny, sunshiny, aestival *or* estival, canicular, torrid, tropical; thermal, thermic; calorific.

red–, white–, smoking–, burning etc. *v.* –, piping- hot; like -a furnace, –an oven; hot as -fire, –pepper; hot enough to roast an ox.

close, sultry, stifling, stuffy, suffocating, oppressive.

fiery; incandescent, incalescent [*rare*]; candent, ebullient, glowing, smoking; live; on fire; blazing etc. *v.*; in flames, in a blaze; alight, afire, ablaze; unquenched; unextinguished; smoldering *or* smouldering; in a -heat, –glow, –perspiration, –sweat; sudorific; sweltering, sweltered; blood-hot, blood-warm; recalescent, decalescent, thermogenic, thermogenous, thermogenetic, thermotic *or* thermotical; pyrotechnic *or* pyrotechnical; phlogotic *or* phlogistic; pyrological.

[transmitting radiant heat] diathermic, diathermal, diathermanous.

[not transmitting radiant heat] athermanous, adiathermal, adiathermanous, adiathermic.

volcanic, plutonic, igneous.

isothermal, isothermic, isothermical.

feverish, febrile, febricose [*rare*], febrific, febrifacient, pyretic, pyrexic [*rare*], inflamed, burning; in a fever.

383. Cold

n. **cold**, coldness etc. *adj.*; frigidity, gelidity, algidity, glaciation, gelidness [*rare*], frore [*poetic*], inclemency, fresco [*obs.*]; "a hard, dull bitterness of cold" [Whittier].

winter; depth of–, hard- winter; Siberia, Nova Zembla; Arctic, North Pole; Antarctic, South Pole.

ice; sleet; hail, hailstone; frost, rime, hoarfrost; rime–, white–, hard–, black–, sharp-frost; *barf* [*Hind.*], glaze, lolly [*N. Amer.*]; icicle, thick-ribbed ice; iceberg, floe, berg, ice field, ice float *or* ice floe, ice pack, glacier; *nevé* [*F.*], *sérac* [*F.*]; *pruina* [*L. & It.*]; icequake.

snow, snowflake, snowdrift, fall of snow, snowstorm, heavy fall; snowball, snowslide, snowslip, snow avalanche.

[sensation of cold] chilliness etc. *adj.*; chill; shivering etc. *v.*; goose flesh, goose skin, rigor, horripilation, aching, ache, chilblains, frostbite, chattering of teeth.

v. **be cold** etc. *adj.;* shiver, starve [*rare in U. S.*], quake, shake, tremble, shudder, didder, quiver; perish with cold; chill etc. (*render cold*) 385; horripilate, glaciate [*obs.*].

adj. **cold**, cool; chill, chilly; gelid, frigid, frore [*poet.*], algid; fresh, keen, bleak, raw, inclement, bitter, biting, cutting, nipping, piercing, pinching; clay-cold; starved etc. (*made cold*) 385; shivering etc. *v.;* aguish, *transi de froid* [*F.*], frostbitten, frost-bound, frost-nipped.

cold as - a stone, −marble, −lead, −iron, −a frog, −charity, −Christmas; cool as -a cucumber, −custard.

icy, glacial, ice-built, frosty, freezing, wintry, brumal, hibernal, boreal, arctic, Siberian, hiemal *or* hyemal; hyperborean, hyperboreal [*rare*]; snow-bound, ice-bound; frozen out.

unwarmed, unheated; unthawed.

lukewarm, tepid; warm etc. *adj.* 382.

isocheimal, isocheimenal, isocheimic.

adv. **coldly**, bitterly etc. *adj.; à pierre fendre* [*F.*]; with chattering teeth.

384. Calefaction

n. **calefaction**, tepefaction, torrefaction; increase of temperature; heating etc. *v.;* melting, fusion; liquefaction etc. 335; burning etc. *v.;* combustion; incension [*obs.*], accension [*archaic*]; concremation, cremation; scorification; cautery, cauterization; ustulation [*rare*], calcination; incineration; carbonization; cupellation.

ignition, kindling, inflammation, adustion [*rare*], flagration [*obs.*], deflagration, conflagration; empyrosis, incendiarism; arson; *auto-da-fé* [*Pg.*], *auto-de-fe* [*Sp.*], the stake, burning at the stake; suttee.

incendiary, arsonist, arsonite, *pétroleur (fem. pétroleuse)* [*F.*], pyromaniac, fire bug, macher [*slang*].

boiling etc. *v.;* coction, ebullition, ebullience *or* ebulliency, aestuation *or* estuation, elixation [*obs.*], decoction; ebullioscope, ebulliometer; hot spring, geyser.

crematory, crematorium, burning ghat [*India*], incinerator, calcinatory; cupel; furnace etc. 386.

wrap, blanket, flannel, wool, fur; muff, mittens, wristers; muffler, fascinator, comforter, comfortable; ear-muffs, ear-flaps; shawl; wadding etc. (*lining*) 224; clothing etc. 225.

cauterant, scorifier; match etc. (*fuel*) 388; caustic, lunar caustic, apozem, moxa; aqua fortis, aqua regia; catheretic, nitric acid, nitro-chlorohydric acid, nitromuriatic acid, radium.

sunstroke, *coup de soleil* [*F.*]; insolation [*rare*], siriasis, [*med.*]; sunburn, burn, tan, suntan, ambustion [*rare*].

pottery, ceramics, crockery, porcelain, china; earthenware, stoneware; pot, mug, terra cotta, brick.

[products of combustion] cinder, ash, scoriae; embers, slag, cinders, clinker, coke, carbon, charcoal.

inflammability, combustibility, accendibility.

[transmission of heat] diathermance *or* diathermancy etc. 382; transcalency.

v. **heat**, warm, chafe, foment; make hot etc. 382; sun oneself, bask in the sun.

fire, set fire to, set on fire; kindle, enkindle, light, ignite, strike a light; apply the -match, −torch-to; rekindle, relume; fan−, add fuel to- the flame; poke−, stir−, blow- the fire; make a bonfire of; build a campfire.

melt, thaw, fuse; liquefy etc. 335.

burn, inflame, roast, toast, fry, grill, incinerate, singe, parch, bake, torch [*slang*], torrefy, scorch; brand, cauterize, sear, burn in; corrode, char, carbonize, calcine, incinerate, calefy, calcinate [*rare*], tepefy, cupel, cupellate [*rare*], deflagrate [*chem.*]; smelt, scorify; reduce to ashes; burn to a cinder; commit−, consign- to the flames.

take−, catch- fire; blaze etc. (*flame*) 382.

boil, digest, stew, cook, seethe, ebullate [*rare*], scald, parboil, simmer; do to rags [*colloq.*].

adj. **heated** etc. *v.;* molten, sodden; *réchauffé* [*F.*]; heating etc. *v.;* adust; ambustial [*rare*], calefactive, deflagrable [*chem.*], ustulate; calcinatory, cauterant; aestuous [*rare*]; apozemial, scoriaceous; transcalent; burnt etc. *v.;* volcanic.

inflammable, burnable, inflammatory, accendible, combustible.

diathermic, diathermal, diathermanous.

radioactive; salamandrine.

385. Refrigeration

n. **refrigeration**, infrigidation, reduction of temperature; cooling etc. *v.;* congelation, conglaciation [*obs.*], glaciation, regelation; ice etc. 383; solidification etc. (*density*), 321; ice box, cooler, ice chest; refrigerator, freezer, etc. 387.

fire-extinguisher, *extincteur* [*F.*]; fire annihilator; amianthus, amianth, earth flax, mountain flax; asbestos, flexible asbestos; fireman, fire brigade, fire department, fire engine.

incombustibility, incombustibleness etc. *adj.*

v. **cool**, fan, refrigerate, infrigidate, refresh, ice; congeal, freeze, glaciate; benumb, starve [*rare in U. S.*], pinch, chill, petrify, chill to the marrow, regelate, nip, cut, pierce, bite, make one's teeth chatter.

damp, slack; quench; put out, stamp out; extinguish.

go out, burn out, die.

adj. **cooled** etc. *v.;* frozen out; cooling etc. *v.;* frigorific, infrigidative [*rare*], refrigerative [*rare*].

incombustible, asbestic, nonflammable, unflammable, uninflammable; fireproof; amianthine, amianthoid *or* amianthoidal.

386. Furnace

n. **furnace**, stove; air-tight–, Franklin–, Dutch–, gas–, oil–, electric- stove; cookstove, cooker, oven, brick oven, tin oven, Dutch oven, range, kitchener [*Eng.*]; fireless- heater, –cooker; forge, fiery furnace; kiln, brickkiln, limekiln; tuyère, brasier, salamander, heater, warming pan, foot-stove, foot-warmer; radiator, register, coil; boiler, caldron *or* cauldron, seething caldron, pot; urn, kettle, frying pan, stew pan, spider, broiler, skillet, tripod, chafing dish; retort, crucible, alembic, still; waffle irons; flatiron, sadiron; curling tongs; toasting fork, toaster.

galley, caboose *or* camboose; hothouse, conservatory, bakehouse, washhouse, laundry; athanor, hypocaust, reverberatory; volcano.

fireplace, hearth, grate, firebox, andiron, firedog, fire-irons; poker, tongs, shovel, hob, trivet; damper, crane, pothooks, chains, turnspit, spit, gridiron.

hot bath; thermae, calidarium, tepidarium, vaporarium, sudatorium [*all L.*]; sudatory; Turkish–, Russian –vapor–, electric–, sitz–, hip–, shower–, warm - bath; tub, hot tub, sauna; lavatory.

387. Refrigeratory

n. **refrigeratory**, refrigerator; frigidarium; cold storage; ice–, freezing–, refrigerating- machine; refrigerating plant; icehouse, ice pail, ice bag, ice box, ice chest, ice pack, cold pack; cooler, wine cooler.

refrigerant, freezing mixture, ice, ammonia.

388. Fuel

n. **fuel**, firing, combustible, coal, wallsend [*Eng.*], anthracite, blind coal, glance coal; bituminous–, egg–, stove–, nut–, pea- coal; culm, coke, carbon, briquette, slack, cannel coal *or* cannel, lignite, charcoal; turf, peat; oil, gas, natural gas, electricity; ember, cinder etc. (*products of combustion*) 384; ingle; port-fire; fire-barrel, fireball, firebrand.

log, backlog, yule log *or* yule clog, firewood, fagot *or* faggot, kindling wood, kindlings, brushwood, bavin [*dial. Eng.*].

tinder, touchwood; punk, German tinder, amadou; smudge [*U. S. & Can.*], pyrotechnic sponge.

fumigator, incense, joss-stick; sulphur, brimstone, disinfectant.

[illuminants] candle etc. (*luminary*) 423; oil etc. (*grease*) 356.

brand, torch, fuse *or* fuze, wick; spill, match, safety match, lights [*chiefly Eng.*], light, lucifer, congreve, vesuvian, vesta, fusee *or* fuzee, locofoco [*obs.*], linstock [*obs. or hist.*].

v. coal, stoke; feed, fire etc. 384.

adj. carbonaceous; combustible, inflammable; slow-burning, free-burning.

389. Thermometer

n. **thermometer**, thermocouple, thermometrograph, thermopile, thermostat, thermoscope; differential thermometer, telethermometer, pyrometer, calorimeter, radiomicrometer.

390. Taste

n. **taste**, flavor, gust [*archaic*], gusto, savor; goût [*F.*], relish; sapor [*obs.*], sapidity; twang [*dial. Eng.*], smack, smatch [*dial. Eng.*]; aftertaste, tang.

tasting; degustation, gustation.

palate; tongue; tooth; stomach.

v. **taste**, savor, smatch [*dial. Eng.*], smack, flavor; tickle the palate etc. (*savory*) 394; smack the lips.

adj. **sapid**, saporific, gustable, gustatory, gustative, tastable, savory, gustful, tasty; strong; flavored, spiced, tanged [*obs.*]; palatable etc. 394.

391. Insipidity

n. **insipidity**; tastelessness etc. *adj.;* jejuneness.

v. **be tasteless** etc. *adj.*

adj. **insipid**; void of taste etc. 390; tasteless, gustless [*obs.*], unsavory, unflavored, jejune, savorless; ingustible [*obs.*], mawkish, milk and water, weak, stale, flat, vapid, *fade* [*F.*], wishy-washy [*colloq.*], mild; untasted.

392. Pungency

n. **pungency**, piquancy, poignancy, *haut-goût* [*F.*], acrity [*obs.*], strong taste, twang [*dial. Eng.*], race, tang, nip, kick [*slang*].

sharpness etc. *adj.;* acrimony, acridity; roughness etc. (*sour*) 392; unsavoriness etc. 395.

[pungent articles] niter, saltpeter; mustard, cayenne, caviare; seasoning etc. (*condiment*) 393; brine; carbonate of ammonia; sal-ammoniac, sal-volatile; smelling salts; hartshorn.

dram, cordial, nip, toothful [*colloq.*], tickler [*colloq.*], bracer [*colloq.*], pick-me-up [*colloq.*], potion, liqueur, *pousse-café* [*F.*].

tobacco, Lady Nicotine, Nicotiana, nicotian [*rare*], nicotine; snuff, quid; cigar *or* segar, cigarette, fag [*slang*], cheroot, Trichinopoli cheroot, Trichi [*colloq.*], Havana *or* Habana [*Sp.*], Cuban tobacco; weed [*colloq.*]; fragrant-, Indianweed; Cavendish, fid [*dial.*], rappee, stogy, old soldier [*slang*].

v. **be pungent** etc. *adj.;* bite the tongue.

render pungent etc. *adj.;* season, spice, bespice, salt, pepper, pickle, brine, devil, curry.

use tobacco, smoke, chew, inhale, take snuff.

adj. **pungent**, strong; high-flavored, full-flavored; high-tasted, high-seasoned; gamy, high; sharp, stinging, rough, piquant, racy; biting, mordant; spicy; seasoned etc. *v.;* hot, -as pepper; peppery, vellicative, vellicating, escharotic, meracious [*obs.*]; acrid, acrimonious, bitter; rough etc. (*sour*) 397; unsavory etc. 395.

salt, saline, brackish, briny; salt as -brine, -a herring, -Lot's wife.

393. Condiment

n. **condiment**, flavoring, salt, ketchup *or* catsup, mustard, pepper, cayenne, cinnamon, nutmeg, curry, seasoning, sauce, spice, relish, *sauce piquante* [*F.*], *sauce tartare* [*F.*], caviare, pot herbs, onion, sauce-alone, hedge garlic, garlic, pickle; achar [*Hind.*], allspice, appetizer; bell-, Jamaica-, red- pepper; horseradish, capsicum, chutney, tabasco; cubeb, pimento.

v. **season** etc. (*render pungent*) 392.

394. Savoriness

n. **savoriness** etc. *adj.;* nectareousness; relish, zest.

appetizer, *apéritif* [*F.*], *hors d'oeuvre* [*F.*]

delicacy, titbit, dainty, ambrosia, nectar, delice [*obs.*], *bonne-bouche* [*F.*]; game, turtle, venison; delicatessen.

v. **be savory** etc. *adj.;* tickle the -palate, -appetite; tempt the appetite, taste good, taste of something; flatter the palate.

render palatable etc. *adj.*

relish, like, smack the lips.

adj. **savory**, to one's taste, tasty, good, palatable, good-tasting, pleasing, nice, dainty, delectable; toothful [*obs.*], toothsome; gustful, appetizing, lickerish *or* liquorish [*rare*], delicate, delicious,

exquisite, rich, luscious, ambrosial, ambrosian, nectareous, distinctive.

adv. per amusare la bocca [*It.*].

395. Unsavoriness

n. **unsavoriness** etc. *adj.;* amaritude [*rare*], acrimony, acritude [*obs.*], acridity, acridness, roughness etc. (*sour*) 397; acerbity, austerity.

gall and wormwood, rue, quassia, aloes, asafetida *or* asafoetida; hemlock; sickener; Marah.

v. **be unpalatable** etc. *adj.;* sicken, disgust, nauseate, pall, turn the stomach.

adj. **unsavory**, unpalatable, unsweet; ill-flavored; bitter, bitter as gall; amarulent [*obs.*], acrid, acrimonious; rough.

offensive, repulsive, nasty; sickening etc. *v.;* nauseous; loathsome, fulsome; unpleasant etc. 830.

396. Sweetness

n. **sweetness**, dulcitude, saccharinity.

sugar, saccharin *or* saccharine, saccharose, crystallose; cane-, beet-, loaf-, lump-, granulated- sugar.

preserve, conserve, confiture [*obs.*], jam, julep; sugar candy, sugarplum; marmalade.

sweets, confectionery, caramel, lolly [*colloq.*], lollipop, bonbon, licorice, jujube, comfit, sweetmeat, confection, confectionery; honey, manna; apple butter, glucose, sucrose, dulcin [*chem.*], dulcite [*chem.*]; sirup *or* syrup, treacle, molasses, maple sirup *or* syrup, maple sugar; *mithai* [*India*], sorghum, taffy, butterscotch.

[sweet beverages] nectar; hydromel, mead, metheglin, liqueur, sweet wine, *eau sucrée* [*F.*].

pastry, cake, pie, tart, puff, pudding.

dulcification, dulcoration [*obs.*], saccharification, saccharization, edulcoration.

v. **be sweet** etc. *adj.*

render sweet etc. *adj.;* sweeten, sugar, saccharize, saccharify, sugar off [*local, U. S. & Can.*]; edulcorate; dulcorate [*obs.*], dulcify [*obs.*]; candy; mull.

adj. **sweet**, sugary, saccharine, sacchariferous, saccharoid *or* saccharoidal; dulcet, candied, honied, luscious, cloying, honey-sweet, nectarious [*rare*], nectareous, nectareal, nectarous, nectarean, nectarian; melliferous; sweetened etc. *v.*

sweet as -sugar, -honey.

397. Sourness

n. **sourness** etc., *adj.;* acid, acetosity, acerbity, acidity, subacidity; acescence *or* acescency; acetous fermentation.

[sour articles] vinegar, acetum, tartar, verjuice, crab, alum; acetic acid; lime, lemon, crab apple, chokeberry, chokecherry; unripe–, green fruit.

v. **be sour,** turn sour etc. *adj.;* set the teeth on edge.

render sour etc. *adj.;* acidify, acidulate, acetify, acetize [*are*], tartarize, ferment.

adj. **sour;** acid, acidulous, acidulated; tart, crab, crabbed; acetous, acetose, acerb, acetic; sour as vinegar, sourish; acescent, subacid; hard, rough, unripe, green; astringent, styptic.

398. Odor

n. **odor** *or* odour, smell, odorament [*obs.*], scent, effluvium; emanation, exhalation; fume, essence, trail, nidor [*obs.*], redolence.

scent; sense of smell; act of smelling etc. *v.;* olfaction, olfactories.

v. **have an odor** etc. *n.;* smell, –of, –strong of; exhale, effluviate [*rare*]; give out a smell etc. *n.;* scent.

smell, scent; snuff, –up; sniff, nose, inhale.

adj. **odorous,** odorant [*rare*], odoriferous; smelling, strong-scented, effluvious, redolent, nidorous, pungent.

[relating to the sense of smell] olfactory, olfactive, olfactible *or* olfactable; quick-scented.

399. Inodorousness

n. **inodorousness;** absence–, want- of smell. deodorization; deodorizer, deodorant.

v. **be inodorous** etc. *adj.;* not smell. deodorize.

adj. **inodorous,** inodorate [*obs.*], scentless; without–, wanting- smell etc. 398. deodorized, deodorizing.

400. Fragrance

n. **fragrance,** aroma, redolence, incensation, thurification [*rare*], perfume, bouquet; sweet smell, sweet odor *or* odour, aromatic perfume, scent.

[comparisons] agalloch *or* agallochum, agalwood, eaglewood, aloes wood, sandalwood, cedar, champak, calambac *or* calambour, lignaloes, linaloa; bayberry, bay leaf, balsam, fir balsam; wild clove, wild cinnamon, Jamaica bayberry, oil of myrcia, bay rum; horehound, Marrubium, mint, musk root, muskrat, napha water, olibanum.

perfumery; incense, frankincense; musk, pastil *or* pastille; myrrh, perfumes of Arabia; attar *or* ottar *or* otto; bergamot, balm, civet, potpourri, pulvil [*obs.*]; tuberose, hyacinth, heliotrope, rose, jasmine, lily, lily of the valley, violet, arbutus, carnation, sweet pea, sweet grass, new-mown hay, lilac; pomade, pomatum, pomander, toilet water; *eau de cologne* [*F.*], cologne, cologne water.

bouquet, nosegay, posy [*archaic or colloq.*], boughpot *or* bowpot; *boutonnière* [*F.*], buttonhole [*colloq.*].

spray; wreath, garland, chaplet.

[scent containers] smelling bottle, scent bottle, vinaigrette; scent bag, sachet; thurible, censer, incense burner, incensorium, incensory; atomizer, spray.

perfumer, *parfumeur* [*F.*]; thurifer.

v. **be fragrant** etc. *adj.;* have a perfume etc. *n.;* smell sweet, scent, perfume; embalm.

incense, cense, thurificate, thurify [*rare*]; aromatize.

adj. **fragrant,** aromatic, redolent, spicy, balmy, scented; sweet-smelling, sweet-scented; perfumed, perfumatory [*rare*], perfumy, incense-breathing, thuriferous; fragrant–, sweet- as a rose, muscadine, ambrosial.

401. Fetor

n. **fetor** *or* foetor; bad etc. *adj.* -smell, –odor *or* odour; stench, stink; foul odor, malodor *or* malodour, fetidness, mephitis, empyreuma; fustiness, mustiness etc. *adj.;* rancidity, reastiness *or* reasiness [*dial. Eng.*]; foulness etc. (*uncleanness*) 653.

[comparisons] stoat, polecat, skunk, zoril; foumart *or* foulmart, fitchew, fitchet, peccary; asafetida *or* assafoetida; fungus, garlic, onion, leek, skunk cabbage; stinkpot, stinkball, stinker, stinkhorn, stinkbush, stinkstone, stinkweed, stinkwood.

v. **have a bad smell** etc. *n.;* smell, empyreumatize; stink, –in the nostrils, –like a polecat; smell strong etc. *adj.,* smell to heaven, stench [*obs.*], smell offensively.

adj. **fetid;** strong-smelling; high, bad, strong, fulsome, offensive, graveolent, noisome, rank, rancid, reasty *or* reasy [*dial. Eng.*], moldy *or* mouldy, tainted, musty, frowsty [*dial. Eng.*], fusty, frowsy *or* frouzy; olid, olidous [*obs.*]; nidorous [*rare*], smelling, stinking; putrid etc. 653; suffocating, mephitic; empyreumatic *or* empyreumatical.

402. Sound

n. **sound,** noise; sonority, sonorosity [*obs.*], sonification, strain; accent, twang, intonation, tune, cadence; sonorescence, sonorousness etc. *adj.;* audibility; resonance etc. 408; voice etc. 580; phonation; aspirate; phonogram, ideophone; rough breathing.

[science of sound] acoustics, acoumetry, diacoustics, catacoustics, diaphonics, cataphonics, polycoustics, phonics, phonetics, phonology, phonography; telephony, radiophony, photophony; polyphony, homophony; phonetism; acoustician.

v. **produce sound**; sound, make a noise; give out sound, emit sound; phonate, consonate [*rare*], resound etc. 408.

phoneticize, phonetize [*rare*].

adj. **sounding**; soniferous; sonorous, sonorescent; sonorific [*rare*]; sonorant, sonoric; resonant, audible, distinct; auditory, acoustic, acoustical, diacoustic, polycoustic; stertorous, ear-splitting.

phonic, phonetic; homophonic *or* homophonous (*opp. to* polyphonic), monodic, monophonic; sonant; ideophonous; phonocamptic [*rare*].

403. Silence

n. **silence**; stillness etc. (*quiet*) 265; peace, hush, lull; rest [*music*]; muteness etc. 581; solemn–, awful–, dead–, deathlike- silence; silence of the -tomb, -grave.

v. **be silent** etc. *adj.;* hold one's tongue etc. (*not speak*) 585; whist [*dial. Eng.*].

render silent etc. *adj.;* silence, still, hush; stifle, muffle, gag, stop; muzzle, put to silence etc. (*render mute*) 581.

adj. **silent**; still, stilly; noiseless, quiet, calm, hush [*archaic*], echoless, speechless, soundless; hushed etc. *v.;* aphonic, surd, mute etc. 581.

solemn, soft, awful, deathlike; silent as the -tomb, -grave; inaudible etc. (*faint*) 405.

adv. **silently** etc. *adj.; sub silentio* [*L.*]; in–, in dead–, in perfect- silence.

int. **hush!** silence! soft! whist! mum! sh! chut! tut! *pax!* [*L.*], *tais-toi!* [*F.*], hold your tongue! shut up! [*colloq.*], be quiet! be silent! be still! *chup!* [*Hind.*], *chup rao!* [*Hind.*], *tace!* [*L.*].

404. Loudness

n. **loudness**, power; vociferation, uproariousness.

din, loud noise, clang, clangor, clatter, noise, bombilation, roar, uproar, racket, clutter, hullabaloo, pandemonium, hell let loose; outcry etc. 411; hubbub; explosion, detonation; bobbery, fracas, charivari.

blare, trumpet blast, flourish of trumpets, fanfare, tintamarre [*archaic*]; blast; peal, swell, larum [*archaic*], alarum, boom; resonance etc. 408.

lungs; stentor; megaphone; calliope, steam siren, steam whistle; watchman's rattle.

[comparisons] artillery, cannon, guns, bombs, shells, barrage; thunder.

v. **be loud** etc. *adj.;* peal, swell, clang, boom, thunder, fulminate, bombilate [*rare*], roar; resound etc. 408; speak up, shout etc. (*vociferate*) 411; bellow etc. (*cry as an animal*) 412.

clatter, clutter, racket, uproar [*rare*].

rend the air, rend the skies; fill the air; din–, ring–, thunder- in the ear; pierce–, split–, rend-the-ears, –head; deafen, stun; *faire le diable à quatre* [*F.*]; make one's windows shake; awake the echoes, startle the echoes; give tongue.

adj. **loud**, sonorous; high-sounding, big-sounding; deep, full, powerful, noisy, blatant, clangorous, multisonous; thundering, deafening etc. *v.;* trumpet-tongued; ear-splitting, ear-rending, ear-deafening; piercing; shrill etc. 410; obstreperous, rackety, uproarious; enough to wake the -dead, –seven sleepers; clamorous etc. (*vociferous*) 411; stentorian, stentorophonic [*obs.*].

adv. **loudly** etc. *adj.;* aloud; with one wild yell; at the top of one's -lungs, –voice; lustily, in full cry.

405. Faintness

n. **faintness** etc. *adj.;* faint sound, whisper, breath; undertone, underbreath; murmur, hum, buzz, purr, lap [*of waves*], plash; sough, moan, rustle, susurration [*rare*], tinkle; "still small voice."

hoarseness etc. *adj.*

silencer, muffler; soft pedal, damper, mute, *sordino* [*It.*], sordine [*all music*].

v. **whisper**, breathe; mutter etc. (*speak imperfectly*) 583; susurrate [*rare*].

murmur, purl, hum, gurgle, ripple, babble, flow; rustle, tinkle.

steal on the ear, melt in the air, float on the air.

muffle, deaden, mute, subdue.

adj. **faint**, scarcely–, barely–, just-audible; low, dull; stifled, muffled; inaudible; hoarse, husky; gentle, soft; floating; purling, flowing etc. *v.;* muttered; whispered etc. *v.;* liquid; soothing; dulcet etc. (*melodious*) 413; susurrant [*rare*], susurrous [*rare*].

adv. **in a whisper**, with bated breath, *sotto voce* [*It.*], between the teeth, aside; piano, pianissimo [*both music*], *sordamente* [*It.*], *sordo* [*It.*], *à la sourdine* [*F.*]; out of earshot; inaudibly etc. *adj.*

406. Snap

[sudden and violent sounds]

n. **snap** etc. *v.;* toot, shout, yell, yap [*dial.*], yelp, bark; rapping etc. *v.*

125

report, decrepitation, crepitation; thump, knock, clap, thud; burst, thunderclap, thunderburst, eruption, blowout [*tire*], explosion, discharge, detonation, firing, salvo, volley.

detonator, bomb, gun, rifle; torpedo, squib, cracker, firecracker, popgun, rattle.

v. **snap**, rap, tap, knock; click; clash; crack, crackle; crash; pop; slam, bang, clap; thump, toot, yap [*dial.*], yelp, bark, fire, explode, rattle, burst on the ear; crepitate, flump.

adj. rapping etc. *v.;* crepitant.

adv. **slap-bang** or slam-bang [*colloq.*], bang [*colloq.*].

int. **bang**! crash!

407. Roll
[repeated and protracted sounds]

n. **roll** etc. *v.;* drumming etc. *v.; berloque* [*F.*], ululation, howl, bombilation, bombination, rumbling; dingdong; tantara, rataplan, ratatat, rubadub, tattoo; pitapat; quaver, clutter, brustle [*dial.*], charivari, racket; cuckoo; repetition etc. 104; peal of bells, devil's tattoo; drum fire, barrage; whirr, rattle, drone; reverberation etc. 408.

v. **roll**, drum, rataplan, boom; whirr, rustle, tootle, clutter, roar, drone, rumble, rattle, clatter, patter, clack; bombinate, bombilate [*rare*].

hum, trill, shake; chime, peal, toll; tick, beat.

drum in the ear, din in the ear.

adj. **rolling**, etc. *v.;* monotonous etc. (*repeated*) 104; like a bee in a bottle.

408. Resonance

n. **resonance**; ring etc. *v.;* ringing etc. *v.;* reflection or reflexion; clangor, bell-note, tintinnabulation, vibration, reverberation.

low–, base–, bass–, flat–, grave–, deep- note; bass; *basso* [*It.*], *basso profondo* [*It.*]; barytone or baritone, contralto; pedal point, organ point.

v. **resound**, reverberate, reëcho; ring, sound, jingle or gingle, chink, clink; tink, tinkle; chime; gurgle etc. 405; plash, guggle, echo, ring in the ear.

adj. **resonant**, reverberant, resounding etc. *v.;* tinnient [*obs.*], tintinnabula or tintinnabulary; deep -toned, –sounding, –mouthed; hollow, sepulchral; gruff etc. (*harsh*) 410.

408a. Nonresonance

n. **nonresonance**; mutescence; thud, thump, dead sound; muffled drums, cracked bell; damper, *sordino* [*It.*], sordine, mute; muffler, silencer.

v. **muffle**, deaden, mute; sound dead; stop–, damp–, deaden–, the -sound, –reverberations; use or employ the *sordino* [*It.*] etc. *n.*

adj. **nonresonant**, dead, mute; muffled etc. *v.*

409. Sibilation
[hissing sounds]

n. **sibilation**; zip; hiss etc. *v.;* sternutation; high note etc. 410.

goose, serpent, snake.

v. **hiss**, buzz, whiz, rustle; fizz, fizzle; wheeze, whistle, snuffle; squash; sneeze; sizz [*colloq.*], sizzle, swish.

adj. **sibilant**; hissing etc. *v.;* wheezy; sternutative.

410. Stridor
[harsh or high sounds]

n. **stridor**, harshness, roughness, sharpness etc. *adj.;* raucousness, raucity; creak etc. *v.;* creaking etc. *v.;* discord, etc. 414; cacophony; cacoëpy.

high note, acute note; soprano, treble, tenor, alto, falsetto; *voce di testa* [*It.*], head voice, head tone; shriek, yell; cry etc. 411.

penny trumpet, piccolo, fife, whistle; penny–, willow- whistle; Panpipes, syrinx; pipes, bagpipes, doodlesack [*Scot.*].

v. **grate**, creak, saw, snore, jar, burr, pipe, twang, jangle, clank, clink; scream etc. (*cry*) 411; yelp etc. (*animal sound*) 412; buzz etc. (*hiss*) 409.

set the teeth on edge, *écorcher les oreilles* [*F.*]; pierce–, split- the -ears, –head; offend–, grate upon–, jar upon- the ear.

adj. **grating**, creaking etc. *v.;* stridulous, strident, harsh, coarse, hoarse, horrisonant [*obs.*], raucous, metallic, horrisonous [*obs.*], rough, rude, jangly [*rare*], gruff, grum, sepulchral, hollow.

high, sharp, acute, shrill; trumpet-toned; piercing, ear-piercing, high-pitched, high-toned; cracked; discordant etc. 414; cacophonous.

411. Cry

n. **cry** etc. *v.;* voice etc. (*human*) 580; view halloo, yoicks [*both hunting*]; hubbub; bark etc. (*animal*) 412.

outcry, vociferation, hullabaloo, chorus, clamor or clamour, hue and cry, plaint; lungs; Stentor, stentor.

v. **cry**, roar, shout, bawl, brawl, halloo, halloa, yo-ho, yoick, whoop or hoop [*rare*], yell, bellow, howl, scream, screech, screak, shriek, shrill, squeak, squeal, squall, whine, pule, pipe, yap, yaup or yawp.

cheer, huzza, hurrah; hoot.

moan, grumble, groan.

snort, snore; grunt etc. (*animal sounds*) 412.

vociferate; raise–, lift up- the voice; yell out, call out, sing out, cry out; exclaim; rend the air;

make the welkin ring; split the -throat, –lungs; thunder–, shout- at the -top of one's voice, –pitch of one's breath; *s'égosiller* [*F.*]; strain the -throat, –voice, –lungs; give cry; give a cry etc.; clamor *or* clamour.

adj. **clamant,** clamorous; crying etc. *v.;* vociferous; stentorian etc. (*loud*) 404; open-mouthed; full-mouthed.

412. Ululation

[animal sounds]

n. **ululation,** howling, mugiency [*obs.*], reboation [*rare*]; cry etc. *v.;* crying etc. *v.;* call, note, howl, bark, yelp, bow-wow, latration, belling; woodnote; insect cry, twittering, fritiniancy [*obs.*], drone; cuckoo.

v. **ululate,** howl, cry, roar, bellow, blare, rebellow, latrate, bark, yelp; bay, bay the moon; yap, growl, yarr [*obs.*], yawl [*dial.*], yaup *or* yawp, snarl, howl; grunt, gruntle; snort, squeak; neigh, bray; mew, mewl, purr, caterwaul, miaow; bleat, low, moo; troat [*rare*], croak, crow, screech, caw, coo, gobble, quack, cackle, gaggle, guggle; chuck, chuckle; cluck, clack; chirp, cheep, chirrup, chirk [*obs.*], peep, sing, pule, twitter, chatter, hoot, wail, cuckoo; hum, buzz; hiss, blatter, blat [*colloq.*].

adj. **ululant,** crying etc. *v.;* blatant, latrant, remugient [*obs.*], mugient; deep-mouthed, full-mouthed; rebellowing, reboant [*rare*].

adv. in full cry.

413. Melody. Concord

n. **melody,** rhythm, measure; rime *or* rhyme etc. (*poetry*) 597.

[musical terms] pitch, timbre, intonation, tone, overtone.

orchestration, harmonization, modulation, phrasing, temperament, syncope, syncopation, preparation, suspension, solution, resolution.

staff *or* stave, line, space, brace; bar, rest; *appoggiato* [*It.*], *appoggiatura* [*It.*]; *acciaccatura* [*It.*], trill *or* shake, turn, *arpeggio* [*It.*].

note, musical note, notes of a scale; sharp, flat, natural; high note etc. (*shrillness*) 410; low note etc. 408; interval; semitone; second, third, fourth etc.; diatessaron [*ancient music*].

breve, semibreve *or* whole note, minim *or* half note, crotchet *or* quarter note, quaver *or* eighth note, semiquaver *or* sixteenth note, demisemiquaver *or* thirty-second note, hemidemisemiquaver *or* sixty-fourth note; sustained note, drone, bourdon, burden.

scale, gamut; diapason; diatonic-, chromatic-, enharmonic- scale; key, clef, chords.

tonic; key-, leading-, fundamental- note; supertonic, mediant, dominant; pedal point, organ point; submediant, subdominant; octave, tetrachord; Dorian *or* Doric - mode, –tetrachord; major-, minor- -mode, –scale, –key; passage, phrase.

harmony, concord, emmeleia; euphony, euphonism; tonality; consonance; concent [*archaic*], concentus; part.

unison, unisonance; chime, homophony.

[science of harmony] harmony, harmonics; thorough bass, fundamental bass; counterpoint; faburden [*medieval music*].

opus (*pl.* opera) [*L.*], piece of music etc. 415.

composer, harmonist, contrapuntist.

v. **harmonize,** chime, symphonize, transpose, orchestrate; blend, put in tune, tune, accord, string; be harmonious etc. *adj.*

adj. **harmonious,** harmonic, harmonical; in concord etc. *n.,* in tune, in concert, in unison; unisonant, concentual *or* concentuous [*rare*], symphonizing, isotonic, homophonous, assonant; ariose, consonant.

measured, rhythmic *or* rhythmical, diatonic, chromatic, enharmonic.

melodious, musical; melic; tuneful, tunable; sweet, dulcet, canorous; mellow, mellifluous; soft; clear, –as a bell; silvery; euphonious, euphonic *or* euphonical, symphonious; enchanting etc. (*pleasure-giving*) 829; fine-toned, silver-toned, full-toned, deep-toned.

adv. **harmoniously** etc. *adj.*

414. Discord

n. **discord,** discordance; dissonance, cacophony, want of harmony, caterwauling; harshness etc. 410; charivari, shivaree [*dial., U. S.*], racket; consecutive fifths.

[confused sounds] Babel, pandemonium; Dutch concert, cat's concert, marrowbones and cleavers [*all colloq.*].

v. **be discordant** etc. *adj.;* jar etc. (*sound harshly*) 410; shivaree [*dial., U. S.*].

adj. **discordant,** dissonant, absonant; out of tune, tuneless; unmusical, untunable; immelodious, unmelodious, unharmonious, inharmonious, unsweet [*rare*], singsong; cacophonous; harsh etc. 410; jarring.

415. Music

n. **music;** strain, tune, air; melody etc. 413; piece of music, *morceau* [*F.*], rondo, rondeau, *pas-*

torale [*It.*], pastoral, cavatina, fantasia, *toccata* [*It.*], *toccatella* [*It.*], *toccatina* [*It.*], *capriccio* [*It.*], fugue, canon; potpourri, medley, incidental music; variations, roulade, cadenza, cadence, trill; serenade, *notturno* [*It.*], nocturne; *passamezzo* [*It.*]; staff *or* stave etc. 413.

instrumental music; orchestral score, full score; minstrelsy, tweedledum and tweedledee [*applied by John Byrom to the feuds between Handel and Bononcini*]; band, orchestra etc. 416; composition, *opus* (*pl. opera*) [*L.*], movement, concert piece, concerted piece, symphony, *concerto* [*It.*], sonata, symphonic poem, tone poem; chamber music; overture, prelude, voluntary, *Vorspiel* [*Ger.*]; string quartet *or* quartette.

lively music, polka, reel etc. (*dance*) 848; ragtime, disco, reggae, rock, hard rock, acid rock, punk rock, jazz; syncopation; *allegro* etc. *adv.*

slow music, slow movement, Lydian measures; *adagio* etc. *adv.;* minuet; siren strains, soft music; lullaby, cradle song, *berceuse* [*F.*]; dump [*obs.*]; dirge etc. (*lament*) 839; pibroch, coronach [*Scot. & Ir.*], dead march, martial music, march; waltz etc. (*dance*) 840.

vocal music, vocalism; chaunt [*archaic*], chant; psalm, psalmody, hymnology; hymn; song etc. (*poem*) 597; oratorio, opera, operetta; canticle, cantata, lay, ballad, ditty, carol, pastoral, recitative *or* recitativo, *aria parlante* [*It.*], aria, arietta *or* ariette, canzonet; bravura, *coloratura* [*It.*], colorature; virtuoso music, cantabile.

solo, duet, *duo* [*It.*], trio, terzetto, quartet *or* quartette, quintet *or* quintette, sestet *or* sextet, septet, double quartet, chorus; part song, descant, glee, madrigal, catch, round, chorale; antiphon, antiphony; accompaniment; inside part, second, alto, tenor, bass; score, piano score, vocal score; burden, bourdon, drone.

concert, musicale, musical [*colloq.*], recital, chamber concert, popular concert *or* pop [*colloq.*], open-air concert, rock concert, serenade, *aubade* [*F.*]; community singing, singsong [*colloq.*].

method, *solfeggio* [*It.*], tonic sol-fa, solmization; sight -singing, -reading; reading at sight.

composer etc. 413; **musician** etc. 416.

v. **compose**, write, set to music, arrange etc. 416; attune.

perform, execute, play etc. 416.

adj. **musical**; instrumental, vocal, choral, lyric, melodic, pure, operatic; classic, modern, orchestral, symphonic, contrapuntal, program;

imitative, falsetto; harmonious etc. 413; Wagnerian.

adv. adagio; *largo, larghetto, andante, andantino; alla cappella; maestoso, moderato; allegro, allegretto; spiritoso, vivace, veloce; presto, prestissimo; con brio; capriccioso; scherzo, scherzando; legato, staccato, crescendo, diminuendo, rallentando, affettuoso; arioso, parlante, cantabile; obbligato; pizzicato; desto* [*all It.*].

416. Musician

[performance of music]

n. **musician**, *artiste* [*F.*], virtuoso, performer, player, minstrel; bard etc. (*poet*) 597; accompanist, instrumentalist, organist, pianist, violinist, tweedledee [*Scot.*], fiddler, catgut scraper [*slang*]; flutist *or* flautist; harpist *or* harper, fifer, trumpeter, cornetist, piper, drummer; accordionist.

orchestra; string -orchestra, -quartet; strings, woodwind, brass; band, brass band, military band, German band, jazz band; street musicians, waits.

vocalist, melodist, singer, warbler; songster, chanter *or* chaunter [*archaic*]; *cantatore* [*It.*], *cantatrice* [*F.*], improvisator, *improvvisatore or improvisatore* [*It.*]; *improvvisatrice or improvisatrice* [*It.*], songstress, chantress *or* chauntress [*archaic*]; chorister; chorus singer.

choir *or* quire [*archaic*]; chorus; *Liedertafel* [*Ger.*], *Liederkranz* [*Ger.*], choral -club, -society; singing -club, -society; festival chorus, eisteddfod [*Welsh*].

song bird, nightingale, philomel, lark, ringdove, bulbul, cuckoo, thrush, mavis.

[patrons] Orpheus, Apollo, Apollo Musagetes, the Muses, Polyhymnia, Erato, Euterpe, Terpsichore; Pierides, sacred nine, tuneful nine, tuneful quire [*archaic*]; Siren.

composer etc. 413.

conductor, choirmaster, bandmaster, concert master *or Konzertmeister* [*Ger.*], drum major, song leader, precentor.

performance, execution, touch, expression.

v. **play**, tune, tune up, pipe, pipe up, strike up, sweep the chords, fiddle, scrape [*derog.*], strike the lyre, beat the drum; blow-, sound-, wind- the horn; doodle [*Scot. or colloq.*]; toot, tootle, grind the organ; touch the guitar etc. (*instruments*) 417; twang, pluck, pick, paw the ivories [*slang*]; pound, thump; drum, thrum, strum, beat time.

execute, perform; accompany; sing-, play- a second.

compose, set to music, arrange, harmonize, orchestrate.

sing, chant *or* chaunt [*archaic*], intone, hum, warble, carol, yodel, chirp, chirrup, lilt, purl, quaver, trill, shake, twitter, whistle; sol-fa; do-re-mi.

have an ear for music, have a musical ear, have a correct ear, have absolute pitch.

adj. **musical**; lyric, dramatic; *coloratura* [*It.*], bravura, florid, brilliant; playing etc. *v.*

adv. adagio [*It.*], andante [*It.*] etc. (*music*) 415.

417. Musical Instruments

n. **musical instruments**; orchestra, band; string band, military band, brass band; orchestrion, orchestrina.

[stringed instruments] polychord, harp, lyre, lute, archlute, theorbo, cithara, cither, cittern *or* cithern, gittern, zither, psaltery, guitar, banjo, banjo-zither; rebec *or* rebeck, mandola, mandolin *or* mandoline, ukulele [*Hawaii*]; *bandurria* [*It.*], samisen [*Jap.*]; bina, vina [*India*].

violin, Cremona, Stradivarius; fiddle, kit; viol, vielle; viola, *–d'amore, –di gamba;* tenor, violoncello, bass viol *or* base viol; double bass, *contrabasso* [*It.*], *violone* [*It.*]; bow, fiddlestick, strings, catgut.

piano *or* pianoforte; grand–, concert-grand–, baby-grand–, square–, upright - piano; harpsichord, monochord [*hist.*], clavichord, clarichord, manichord *or* manichordon, clavier, spinet, virginals, dulcimer; hurdy-gurdy, street piano, piano organ; pianette, pianino, piano player, player piano, player; Aeolian (*or* Eolian) harp.

[wind instruments] organ; church–, pipe–, reed-organ; seraphine *or* seraphina, harmonium, cabinet organ, American organ; harmoniphon [*obs.*], barrel organ, hand organ, melodeon, accordion, concertina; humming top.

flute, fife, piccolo, flageolet, clarinet *or* clarionet, bass clarinet, basset horn, *corno di bassetto* [*It.*], musette, oboe *or* hautboy, *cor anglais* [*F.*], English horn, *corno inglese* [*It.*], bassoon, double bassoon, *contrafagotto* [*It.*], serpent, bag-pipes, union pipes, doodlesack [*Scot.*]; ocarina, Panpipes *or* Pandean pipes; reed instrument; pipe, pitch-pipe, whistle; willow–, penny- whistle; calliope, siren *or* sirene; cat-call.

horn, bugle, cornet, cornet-à-pistons, cornopean [*obs.*], clarion [*now chiefly poetic*], trumpet, trombone, tuba, bombardon, bass tuba, ophicleide; French horn, bugle horn, post horn, sax-horn, *Flügelhorn* [*Ger.*], alt horn *or* althorn, tenor horn, sackbut, euphonium.

[vibrating surfaces] cymbals, bell, gong; drum, tambour, snare drum, side drum, tabor *or* tabour, taboret *or* tabouret, kettle drum, timpano (*pl.* timpani), timbal *or* tymbal, tom-tom *or* tam-tam, timbrel, tambourine, castanet, bones; musical glasses, musical stones; mouth organ, harmonica; sounding-board, *abatvoix* [*F.*]; rattle, watchman's rattle; phonograph, graphophone, gramophone, stereo, victrola [*trade-mark name*]; *zambomba* [*Sp.*].

[vibrating bars] reed, tuning fork, triangle, jew's-harp, music box *or* musical box, harmonicon, xylophone.

mute, sourdine, *sordino* [*It.*], sordine, sordet, sourdet.

418. Hearing
[sense of sound]

n. **hearing** etc. *v.;* audition, auscultation; audibility; acoustics etc. 402; eavesdropping.

acute–, nice–, delicate–, quick–, sharp–, correct–, musical- ear; ear for music.

ear, auricle, pinna, concha, labyrinth, lug [*Scot.*], lobule *or* lobe, acoustic organs, auditory apparatus, eardrum, tympanum; malleus, incus, stapes, vestibule, cochlea, auditory nerve, Eustachian tube.

ear trumpet, speaking trumpet; telephone, phonograph, microphone; gramophone, phonograph, victrola [*trademark name*], megaphone, phonorganon; dictagraph *or* dictograph [*trademark name*], dictophone [*trade-mark name*], audiphone, dentiphone; stethoscope; telephone etc. 527.

hearer, auditor, auditory, audience, listener, eavesdropper.

otology, otoscopy, auriscopy; otoscope, auriscope; otopathy, otography, otoplasty; otorrhea, tympanitis; otologist, aurist.

v. **hear**, overhear; hark, hearken *or* harken; list, listen; give–, lend–, bend- an ear; strain one's ears, attend to, give attention, catch a sound, prick up one's ears; give ear, give a hearing to, give audience to.

hang upon the lips of, be all ear, listen with both ears.

become audible; meet–, fall upon–, catch–, reach- the ear; be heard; ring in the ear etc. (*resound*) 408.

adj. **hearing** etc. *v.;* auditory, otic, aural, acoustic, acoustical, phonic; auriculate, auricular; auricled, eared; auditive.

adv. arrectis auribus [*L.*]; all ears.

int. **hark**! hark ye! hear! list! listen! oyez *or* oyes! attend! attention! lend me your ears!

419. Deafness

n. **deafness**, hardness of hearing, surdity [*obs.*], deaf ears; inaudibility, inaudibleness.

adder, beetle, slowworm, blindworm; deaf-mute.

dactylology, deaf-and-dumb alphabet.

v. **be deaf** etc. *adj.;* have no ear; shut–, stop–, close- one's ears; turn a deaf ear to.

render deaf, stun, deafen; split the -ears, –eardrum.

adj. **deaf**, earless, surd; hard–, dull- of hearing; deaf-mute; stunned, deafened; stone deaf; deaf as -a post, –an adder, –a beetle, –a trunkmaker; inattentive etc. 458.

inaudible, out of -earshot, –hearing.

420. Light

n. **light**, ray, beam, stream, gleam, streak, pencil; sunbeam, moonbeam; aurora, dawn.

day; sunshine; light of -day, –heaven; sun etc. (*luminary*) 423, daylight, broad daylight, noontide light; noontide, noonday.

glow etc. *v.;* afterglow, sunset glow; glimmering etc. *v.;* glint; glare; play–, glare–, flood- of light; phosphorescence, lambent flame.

halo, glory, nimbus, aureola, aureole, gloriole [*rare*], aura.

spark, scintilla; facula; sparkling etc. *v.;* emication [*obs.*], scintillation, flash, blaze, coruscation, fulguration [*now rare*]; flame etc. (*fire*) 382; lightning, levin; *ignis fatuus* [*L.*] etc. (*luminary*) 423.

luster *or* lustre, sheen, shimmer, reflection *or* reflexion; gloss, tinsel, spangle, brightness, brilliancy, splendor *or* splendour, effulgence, refulgence; fulgor, fulgidity [*rare*]; dazzlement, resplendence *or* resplendency, transplendency [*rare*], luminousness etc. *adj.;* luminosity; lucidity; nitency [*rare*]; radiance, radiation; irradiation, illumination.

[science of light] optics; photology, photics; actinology, actinometry, radiology, heliology, radiometry, radioscopy, photometry, dioptrics, catoptrics; photography, photolithography, photomicography, phototelegraphy, radiotelegraphy; phototherapy, heliotherapy, radiotherapy; heliometry, heliography.

actinic rays, actinism; radioactivity, radium emanation, exradio; Röntgen *or* Roentgen rays, X-rays, ultra-violet rays; photometer etc. 445; heliometer, refractometer.

[distribution of light] *chiaroscuro* or *chiarooscuro* [*It.*], clair-obscure, *clair-obscure* [*F.*], mezzotint, mezzotinto, half tone *or* half-tone, demitint, half tint; breadth, light and shade, black and white, tonality.

reflection, refraction, dispersion; refractivity.

illuminant, artificial light; gas etc. 423.

v. **shine**, glow, beam, glitter; glister, glisten; twinkle, gleam; flare, flare up; glare, shimmer, glimmer, flicker, sparkle, scintillate, coruscate, flash, blaze; be bright etc. *adj.;* reflect light, daze, dazzle, bedazzle, radiate, shoot out beams; fulgurate, phosphoresce.

clear up, brighten.

lighten, enlighten; levin; light, light up; irradiate, shine upon; give–, hang out a - light; cast–, throw–, shed-luster, –light- upon; illume, illumine, illuminate; relume, strike a light; kindle etc. (*set fire to*) 384.

adj. **luminous**, luminiferous; shining etc. *v.;* lucid, lucent, luculent, luciferous [*rare*], lucific [*rare*]; illuminate [*archaic*], illuminant, light, lightsome; bright, vivid, splendent, nitid, lustrous, shiny, beamy, scintillant, fulgurant, radiant, lambent; sheen, sheeny; glossy, burnished, glassy, sunny, orient, meridian; noonday, noontide; cloudless, clear; unclouded, unobscured.

garish; resplendent, transplendent [*rare*]; refulgent, effulgent, fulgid, fulgent, relucent, splendorous *or* splendrous, splendid, blazing, in a blaze, ablaze, rutilant, meteoric, phosphorescent; aglow.

bright as silver; light–, bright- as -day, –noonday, –the sun at noonday.

[scientific] actinic, radioactive; optic, optical, photologic *or* photological, heliological; photogenic, photographic; heliographic; heliophagous.

421. Darkness

n. **darkness** etc. *adj.;* tenebrosity, umbrageousness, dunness [*rare*], caliginousness, lightlessness, sootiness; blackness etc. (*dark color*) 431; obscurity, gloom, murk *or* mirk, murkiness *or* mirkiness, darksomeness; dusk etc. (*dimness*) 422.

Cimmerian–, Stygian–, Egyptian-darkness; night; midnight; dead of–, witching hour of–, witching time of- night; darkness visible; "darkness which may be felt" [*Bible*]; "the palpable obscure" [Milton]; "embalmèd darkness" [Keats]; Erebus; "the jaws of darkness" [*Midsummer Night's Dream*]; "sable-vested Night" [Milton].

shadow, shade, umbra, penumbra; skiagraphy *or* sciagraphy; skiagram *or* sciagram, skiagraph *or* sciagraph; radiograph.

obscuration; obumbration [*rare*]; obtenebration [*rare*], offuscation [*obs.*], caligation [*obs.*], adumbration; extinction; eclipse, total eclipse; gathering of the clouds.

shading; distribution of shade; *chiaroscuro* [*It.*] etc. (*light*) 420.

v. be dark etc. *adj.;* be in darkness etc. *n.*

darken, obscure, shade; dim; tone down, lower; overcast, overshadow; cloud, cloud over, darken over, murk *or* mirk; eclipse; offuscate [*obs.*], obumbrate, obtenebrate [*rare*], obfuscate; adumbrate; cast into the shade; becloud, bedim, bedarken; cast-, throw-, spread- a -shade, -shadow, -gloom; "walk in darkness and in the shadow of death" [*Book of Common Prayer*].

extinguish, put out, blow out, snuff out, dout [*obs. or dial. Eng.*]

adj. dark, darksome, darkling; obscure, tenebrious, tenebrous, sombrous, pitch dark, pitchy; caliginous [*archaic*]; black etc. (*in color*) 431.

dark as -pitch, -the pit, -Erebus.

sunless, lightless etc. (*see* sun, light, etc. 423); somber, dusky; unilluminated etc. (*see* illuminate etc. 420); nocturnal; dingy, lurid, gloomy; murky *or* mirky, murksome *or* mirksome, sooty, shady, umbrageous; overcast etc. (*dim*) 422; cloudy etc. (*opaque*) 426; darkened etc. *v.*

benighted; noctivagant, noctivagous.

adv. in the -dark, -shade; at night, by night, through the night; darkling, darklings [*rare*].

422. Dimness

n. dimness etc. *adj.;* darkness etc. 421; paleness etc. (*light color*) 429.

half light, *demi-jour* [*F.*]; partial shadow, partial eclipse; "shadow of a shade" [Aeschylus]; "shadows numberless" [Keats]; glimmer, glimmering; nebulosity, nebulousness, obnubilation [*rare*]; cloud etc. 353; eclipse.

twilight, aurora, dusk, nightfall, gloaming, gloam [*rare*], blind man's holiday, *entre chien et loup* [*F.*], *inter canem et lupem* [*L.*], shades of evening, crepuscule, cockshut time [*obs.*]; break of day, daybreak, dawn.

moonlight, moonbeam, moonglade, moonshine; owl's-light, starlight, candlelight, rushlight, firelight; farthing candle.

v. be *or* grow dim etc. *adj.;* gloom; cloud over; flicker, twinkle, glimmer, loom, lower; fade; pale, "pale his uneffectual fire" [*Hamlet*].

render dim etc. *adj.;* dim, bedim, obscure, shade, shadow; encompass with -gloom, -shadow; darken, dark [*archaic*], cloud, becloud, darkle.

adj. dim, dull, lackluster, dingy, darkish, dusky, shorn of its beams; dark etc. 421.

faint, shadowed forth; glassy; cloudy; misty etc. (*opaque*) 426; blear; fuliginous; nebulous, nebular, obnubilated [*rare*], obnubilous [*obs.*].

lurid, leaden, dun, dirty; overcast, muddy; looming etc. *v.*

twilight, crepuscular, crepusculous [*rare*], crepusculine [*rare*].

pale etc. (*colorless*) 429; confused etc. (*invisible*) 447.

423. Luminary
[source of light]

n. luminary; light etc. 420; flame etc. (*fire*) 382. spark, scintilla; phosphorescence.

[heavenly bodies] sun, orb of day, day-star [*poetic*], Aurora; star, orb, meteor; falling star, shooting star; blazing star, dog star, canicula, Sirius, Aldebaran; constellation, galaxy, Milky Way; pole star, Polaris; Cynosure; anthelion; morning star, Lucifer, Phosphor, Phosphorus; Venus, Hesperus, evening star; mock sun, parhelion, sun dog *or* sundog, moon etc. 318.

sun god, Helios, Titan, Phaëthon, Phoebus, Apollo, Hyperion, Ra *or* Re [*Egypt*], Shamash [*Babylon & Assyria*].

lightning, levin; chain-, fork-, sheet-, summer-lightning.

phosphorus; *ignis fatuus* [*L.*]; Jack o'-, Friar's-lantern; will-o'-the-wisp, firedrake, Fata Morgana, St. Elmo's fire, Castor and Pollux [*naut.*], corposant.

glowworm, firefly.

polar lights, northern lights, *aurora borealis* [*L.*], *aurora australis* [*L.*]; aurora; zodiacal light.

[artificial light] gas, gaslight, electric light; headlight, searchlight, spotlight, flashlight, limelight, calcium light, lamplight, lamp; lantern, lanthorn [*archaic*]; electric torch, dark lantern, bull's-eye; candle; wax-, tallow-, bayberry-candle; farthing dip, tallow dip [*colloq.*]; bougie, taper, rushlight; oil etc. (*grease*) 356; wick, burner; Argand, moderator, duplex; torch, flambeau, link, brand; gaselier, chandelier, electrolier; candelabrum, girandole, sconce, luster *or* lustre, candlestick.

firework, Catherine wheel, Roman candle, fizgig; pyrotechnics.

signal light, rocket, balefire, beacon fire; light-house etc. (*signal*) 550.

pyre, funeral pyre; death fire; corpse candle.

v. **illuminate** etc. (*light*) 420.

adj. **self-luminous;** phosphoric, phosphorescent; radiant etc. (*light*) 420.

424. Shade

n. **shade;** awning etc. (*cover*) 223; parasol, sunshade, umbrella.

screen, curtain, chick [*India*], purdah [*India*], *portière* [*F.*]; shutter, blind, Venetian blind, *jalousie* [*F.*].

gauze, veil, mantle, mask, yashmak [*Turk.*].

cloud, mist; gathering of clouds; smoke screen [*mil.*].

umbrage [*archaic*], glade; shadow etc. 421; ambush, covert.

blinkers, blinders; smoked glasses, colored spectacles.

v. **veil** etc. *v.;* draw a curtain; put up–, close– a shutter; cast a shadow etc. (*darken*) 421.

adj. **shady,** umbrageous, shadowy, bowery.

425. Transparency

n. **transparency,** transparence, translucence, translucency, diaphaneity, diaphanousness; lucidity, pellucidity, limpidity; fluorescence; transillumination, translumination.

transparent medium, glass, crystal, lymph, water, hyalite, hyaline.

v. **be transparent** etc. *adj.;* transmit light.

adj. **transparent,** pellucid, lucid, diaphanous; translucent, traluncent [*obs.*], limpid, clear, serene, crystalline, clear as crystal, pervious [*rare*], vitreous, transpicuous [*rare*], glassy, hyaline, hyaloid [*rare*], vitreform.

426. Opacity

n. **opacity;** opaqueness etc. *adj.;* obfuscation, fuliginosity, nubilation.

film; cloud etc. 353.

v. **be opaque** etc. *adj.;* obstruct the passage of light; obfuscate, offuscate [*obs.*].

adj. **opaque,** impervious to light; adiaphanous; dim etc. 422; turbid, thick, muddy, opacous [*obs.*], obfuscated, fuliginous, cloudy, nubilous, nubilose [*obs.*], foggy, vaporous, nubiferous.

smoky, fumid [*obs.*], murky *or* mirky, smeared, dirty.

427. Semitransparency

n. **semitransparency,** opalescence, milkiness, pearliness.

[comparisons] gauze, muslin, cypress *or* cyprus [*hist.*], bombyx, thin silk; film; mica, mother-of-pearl, nacre, opal glass, opaline, frosted glass; mist etc. (*cloud*) 353.

adj. **semitransparent,** semipellucid, semidiaphanous, semiopacous [*obs.*], semiopaque; opalescent, opaline; pearly, milky, frosted, nacreous; hazy, misty.

v. **cloud,** frost, cloud over, frost over; become -pearly, –milky, –misty.

be opalescent etc. *adj.;* opalesce.

428. Color

n. **color** *or* colour, hue, tint, tinct [*archaic*], tinction, tinge, dye, complexion, shade, tincture, cast, livery, coloration, chromatism *or* chromism, glow, flush; tone, key.

pure–, positive–, primary–, primitive–, complementary- color; three primaries; spectrum, chromatic dispersion; broken–, secondary–, tertiary- color.

local color, coloring, keeping, tone, value, aerial perspective.

[science of color] chromatics, spectrum analysis; chromatography, chromatology, chromatoscopy; chromatograph, chromatometer, chromatoscope, chromoscope, chromatrope, chromometer, colorimeter; prism, spectroscope, kaleidoscope.

pigment, coloring matter, paint, dye, wash, distemper, stain, chromogen; medium; mordant; oil paint etc. (*painting*) 556.

v. **color** *or* colour, dye, tinge, stain, tint, tinct [*archaic*], hue, tone, complexion [*rare*]; paint, wash, distemper, ingrain, grain, illuminate, emblazon, imbue; paint etc. (*fine art*) 556.

adj. **colored** etc. *v.;* colorific, tingent [*rare*], tinctorial; chromatic, prismatic; full–, high–, rich–, deep- colored; double-dyed; polychromatic; chromatogenous; chromatophoric, chromatophorous; tingible.

bright, vivid, intense, deep; fresh, unfaded; rich, gorgeous; bright-colored, gay.

gaudy, florid; garish; showy, flaunting; flashy; many-colored, party-colored *or* parti-colored, variegated; raw, crude; glaring, flaring; discordant, inharmonious.

mellow, harmonious, pearly, sweet, delicate, subtle, tender.

dull, sad, somber *or* sombre, sad-colored, grave, gray, dark.

429. Achromatism
[absence of color]

n. **achromatism,** achromatization; decoloration, decolorization, discoloration; pallor, pallidity; paleness etc. *adj.;* etiolation.

neutral tint, monochrome, black and white.

v. **lose color** etc. 428; fade, fly, go, become colorless etc. *adj.;* turn pale; pale, fade out, bleach out; wan; fly, go.

deprive of color, decolor *or* decolour, decolorize *or* decolourize, whiten, bleach, tarnish, achromatize, blanch, etiolate, wash out, tone down.

adj. **colorless**; achromatic; uncolored etc. (*see* color etc. 428); etiolated; hueless, pale, pallid; pale-faced, anemic, tallow-faced; faint, dull, cold, muddy, leaden, dun, wan, sallow, dead, dingy, ashy, ashen, ghastly, cadaverous, glassy, lackluster; discolored etc. *v.*

pale as -death, –ashes, –a witch, –a ghost, –a corpse.

light-colored, fair, blond, ash-blond; white etc. 430; tow-headed, tow-haired.

430. Whiteness

n. **whiteness** etc. *adj.;* whitishness, canescence; argent, argentine.

albification, albication, albinism, albinoism; leucopathy, leucoderma *or* leucodermia [*med.*], dealbation, albescence, etiolation; lactescence.

[comparisons] snow, paper, chalk, milk, lily, ivory, silver, alabaster; albata, eburin *or* eburine *or* eburite, German silver, white metal, barium sulphate, *blanc fixe* [*F.*], pearl white; white lead, ceruse, carbonate of lead, Paris white, zinc white, flake white, Chinese white.

whitewash, whiting, whitening, calcimine.

v. **be white** etc. *adj.*

render white etc. *adj.;* whiten, bleach, blanch, etiolate, silver, besnow, dealbate [*obs.*], albify [*rare*], frost.

whitewash, calcimine, white.

adj. **white**; snow-white; snowy, niveous; candent, candid [*archaic*], frosted, hoar, hoary; silvery, silver, argent, argentine; canescent, chalky, cretaceous; lactescent, milk-white, milky, marmoreal *or* marmorean; albificative, albicant, albescent; albinistic.

white as -a sheet, –driven snow, –a lily, –silver; like ivory etc. *n.*

whitish, creamy, pearly, ivory, fair, blond, ash-blond; blanched etc. *v.;* high in tone, light.

431. Blackness

n. **blackness** etc. *adj.;* darkness etc. (*want of light*) 421; swarthiness, swartness; lividity; dark -color, –tone; *chiaroscuro* [*It.*] etc. 420.

nigrification [*rare*], nigrefaction [*obs.*], nigrescence, denigration, infuscation [*rare*].

[comparisons] jet, ink, ebony, ebon [*now poetic*], coal, pitch, soot, charcoal, sloe; smut, smutch, smudge, smirch; raven, crow.

negro, negress, blackamoor, man of color, colored man, colored woman, black, Black, Ethiop, Ethiopian, buck [*colloq.*], kala admi [*Hind.*], Melanesian, Hottentot, Pygmy, Bushman, Negrillo [*African Pygmy*], Negrito [*Asiatic Pygmy*], African, Mandingo, Senegambian, Sudanese, Papuan, blackfellow, Australian aborigine.

[pigments] lamp–, ivory–, blue-black; writing–, printing–, printer's–, Indian- ink.

v. **be black** etc. *adj.*

render black etc. *adj.;* black, blacken, infuscate [*rare*], denigrate, nigrify; blot, blotch, smut, smudge, smutch, smirch; darken etc. 421.

adj. **black**, sable, somber *or* sombre, livid, dark, inky, ebon, atramentous, jetty; coal-black, jet-black; fuliginous, pitchy, sooty; dhu [*Ir. & Gaelic*], swart, swarthy, dusky, dingy, murky *or* mirky; blotchy, smudgy, smutty; nigrine [*rare*], nigricant, nigrescent, Ethiopian, Ethiopic; low-toned, low in tone; of the deepest dye.

black as -jet etc. *n.*, - my hat, –a shoe, –a tinker's pot, –November, –the ace of spades, –thunder, –midnight; nocturnal etc. (*dark*) 421; gray etc. 432; obscure etc. 421.

adv. in mourning.

432. Gray

n. **gray** *or* grey etc. *adj.;* neutral tint, silver, dove-color, pepper and salt, *chiaroscuro* [*It.*], grisaille.

grayness *or* greyness etc. *adj.*

[pigments] Payne's gray; black etc. 431.

v. **render gray** etc. *adj.;* gray *or* grey.

adj. **gray** *or* grey; iron-gray, dun, drab, dingy, leaden, livid, somber, sad, pearly, calcareous, limy, silver, silvery, silvered; French–, steel–, Quaker–, dapple- gray; dappled; dove-colored, *gorge-de-pigeon* [*F.*]; ashen, ashy, favillous; cinereous, cineritious; grizzly, grizzled; slate-colored, stone-colored, mouse-colored, ash-colored; cool.

433. Brown

n. **brown** etc. *adj.;* brownness.

[pigments] bister *or* bistre, brown ocher *or* ochre, mummy, sepia, Vandyke brown.

v. **render brown** etc. *adj.;* brown, tan, embrown, imbrown, bronze.

adj. **brown**, adust [*rare*], castaneous, toast-brown, nut-brown, seal-brown, cinnamon, hazel, fawn, puce, musteline, musteloid, écru, *feuille-morte* [*F.*], tawny, fuscous, chocolate, maroon, tan, brunette, whitey-brown; fawn-colored, snuff-colored, liver-colored; brown as -a berry, –mahogany, –oak leaves; khaki.

reddish-brown, terra cotta, rufous, russet, russety, russetish, ferruginous, rust, foxy, bronze, coppery, copperish, copper-colored; bay, bayard, roan, sorrel, henna, auburn, chestnut, mahogany; rubiginous, rubiginose, rust-colored; lurid.

sun-burnt; tanned etc. *v.*

434. Redness

n. **red**, scarlet, cardinal, cardinal red, vermilion, carmine, crimson, pink, rose, cerise, cherry, rouge, coquelicot, salmon, lake, maroon, carnation, *couleur de rose* [*F.*], *rose du Barry* [*F.*]; magenta, solferino, damask, flesh -color, –tint; color; fresh–, high-color; warmth; gules [*her.*].

redness etc. *adj.;* rubescence, rubicundity, ruddiness, rubefaction, rubrication, rubification; erubescence, blush.

[comparisons] ruby, *grenat* [*F.*], garnet, carbuncle; rust, iron mold *or* mould; rose, cardinal flower, lobelia; cardinal-bird, –grosbeak; red-start.

[dyes and pigments] cinnabar, cochineal, red ocher *or* ochre, stammel, fuchsine *or* fuchsin, vermilion; ruddle, madder; Indian red, palladium red, light red, Venetian red; red ink, annatto *or* annotto, realgar, minium, red lead.

v. **be** *or* **become red** etc. *adj.;* blush, flush, color, color up, mantle, redden.

render red etc. *adj.;* redden, rouge, crimson, encrimson [*rare*], empurple; rubify [*rare*], rubricate; incarnadine; ruddle, rust.

adj. **red** etc. *n.,* reddish; incarnadine, sanguine, sanguineous, bloody, gory; coral, coralline, rosy, roseate; stammel, blood-red, laky, wine-red, wine-colored, vinaceous; incarmined [*rare*], rubiform [*rare*], rufous, rufulous, murrey, bricky, lateritious [*rare*]; rubineous, rubious, rubricate, rubricose; Pompeiian red; reddish-brown etc. 433.

rose–, ruby–, cherry–, claret–, flame–, flesh–, peach–, salmon–, brick–, rust-colored.

red as -fire, –blood, –scarlet, –a turkey cock, –a lobster; warm, hot.

red-complexioned, red-faced, florid, burnt, rubicund, ruddy, red, blowzed, blowzy, glowing, sanguine, blooming, rosy, hectic, flushed, inflamed; blushing etc. *v.;* erubescent, rubescent; reddened etc. *v.*

[of hair] sandy, carroty, brick-red, Titian red, auburn, chestnut.

435. Greenness

n. **green** etc. *adj.;* blue and yellow; vert [*her.*].

greenness, verdancy, verdure, viridescence, viridity.

[comparisons] emerald, malachite, chrysoprase, jasper, chrysolite *or* olivine, beryl; verd antique, verdigris, aquamarine; reseda, mignonette, absinthe, *crême de menthe* [*F.*].

[pigments] *terre verte* [*F.*], viridian, bice, verditer, verdine, celadon.

v. **render green** etc. *adj.;* green.

adj. **green**, verdant; glaucous, olive; green as grass; verdurous, citrine *or* citrinous, porraceous, olivaceous, smaragdine [*rare*].

emerald–, pea–, grass–, apple–, sea–, olive–, cucumber–, leaf–, Irish–, Nile–, Kelly–, bottle- green.

greenish, virent [*rare*], virescent, viridescent [*rare*], chlorine; aquamarine, blue-green.

436. Yellowness

n. **yellow** etc. *adj.;* or [*her.*]; yellowness etc. *adj.;* xanthocyanopia *or* xanthocyanopsia, xanthochroia.

[comparisons] crocus, jonquil, saffron, topaz; xanthite; gold, gilding, gilt; yolk; jaundice, icterus; London fog.

[pigments] gamboge, fustic, massicot; cadmium–, chrome–, Indian–, king's–, lemon-yellow; orpiment, yellow ocher, Claude tint, aureolin; xanthein, xanthin; xanthophyll.

v. **render yellow** etc. *adj.;* yellow, gild; jaundice.

adj. **yellow**, aureate, golden, gold, gilt, gilded, flavous [*obs.*], citrine, citreous, lemon, fallow; fulvous, fulvescent, fulvid [*rare*]; sallow, lutescent, luteolous, luteous, tawny, cream, creamy, sandy; xanthic, xanthous; jaundiced; auricomous, ocherous *or* ochreous, ochery *or* ochry, flaxen, yellowish, buff, écru; icterine, icteritious *or* icteritous, icteroid; xanthochroid, yellow complexioned.

gold–, saffron–, citron–, lemon–, sulphur–, amber–, straw–, primrose–, cream-colored; xanthocarpous, xanthopous [*bot., rare*].

yellow as a -quincy, –crow's foot; yellow as saffron.

437. Purple

n. **purple** etc. *adj.;* blue and red, bishop's purple; gridelin, amethyst; damson, heliotrope; purpure [*her.*].

lividness, lividity.

v.   **render purple** etc. *adj.;* purple, empurple.

adj.   **purple**, violet, plum-colored, lavender, lilac, puce, mauve, purplish, purpurate [*archaic*], violaceous, hyacinthine, amethystine, magenta, solferino, heliotrope; livid.

438. Blueness

n.   **blue** etc. *adj.;* garter-blue; watchet [*obs.*]; blueness, bluishness; bloom.

[comparisons] *lapis lazuli* [*L.*], sapphire, turquoise; indicolite.

[pigments] ultramarine, smalt, cobalt, cyanogen; Prussian–, syenite- blue; bice, indigo; zaffer.

v.   **render blue** etc. *adj.;* blue.

adj.   **blue**, azure, cerulean, cyanic; sky-blue, sky-colored, sky-dyed; navy blue, midnight blue, cadet blue, robin's-egg blue, baby blue, ultramarine, aquamarine, electric blue *or* electric, steel blue *or* steel; cerulescent; bluish; atmospheric, retiring; cold.

439. Orange

n.   **orange**, red and yellow; old gold; gold color etc. *adj.*

[pigments] ocher *or* ochre, Mars orange, cadmium.

v.   **gild**, engild, deaurate [*rare*], warm.

adj.   **orange**; ocherous *or* ochreous, ochery *or* ochry; henna, burnt orange; orange–, gold–, brass–, apricot- colored; warm, hot, glowing, flame-colored.

440. Variegation

n.   **variegation**; dichroism, trichroism; iridescence, irisation, play of colors, polychrome, maculation, spottiness, striae.

[comparisons] spectrum, rainbow, iris, tulip, peacock, chameleon, butterfly, zebra, leopard, jaguar, panther, cheetah, ocelot, ophite, nacre, mother-of-pearl, tortoise shell; opal, cymophane, marble; mackerel, mackerel sky; harlequin; Joseph's coat; tricolor.

check, plaid, tartan, patchwork; marquetry, parquet, parquetry, mosaic, tesserae, tessellation, checkerwork; chessboard, checkers *or* chequers.

v.   **variegate**, stripe, streak, checker *or* chequer, fleck, bespeckle, speckle, besprinkle, sprinkle; stipple, maculate, dot, bespot; tattoo, inlay, tessellate. damascene; embroider, braid, quilt. be variegated etc. *adj.*

adj.   **variegated** etc. *v.;* many-colored, many-hued; divers-colored, party-colored *or* parti-colored,

dichromatic, polychromatic; bicolor, tricolor, versi-color; of all the colors of the rainbow, of all manner of colors; kaleidoscopic, naevose *or* nevose, daedal.

iridescent, opaline, opalescent, prismatic, nacreous, pearly, shot, *gorge-de-pigeon* [*F.*], chatoyant; irised, irisated, pavonine; tortoise-shell.

mottled, pied, piebald, skewbald; motley, marbled, pepper-and-salt, paned, dappled, clouded, cymophanous.

checkered *or* chequered, mosaic, tessellated, plaid.

spotted, spotty; punctate *or* punctuated [*rare*], powdered; speckled etc. *v.;* freckled, flea-bitten, studded; flecked, fleckered.

striated, barred, veined; brinded, brindled, tabby; watered; strigose, strigillose, strigate, striolate; listed; embroidered etc. *v.*

441. Vision

n.   **vision**, sight, optics, eyesight.

view, look, espial, glance, ken, *coup d'oeil* [*F.*]; glimpse, glint, peep, peek; gaze, stare, leer; perlustration [*rare*], contemplation; conspection [*obs.*], conspectuity [*obs.*]; regard, survey; inspection, introspection; reconnoissance, reconnaissance, speculation, watch, espionage, *espionnage* [*F.*]; autopsy; ocular -inspection, –demonstration; sight-seeing, globe-trotting.

viewpoint, standpoint, point of view; gazebo, loophole, belvedere, watchtower.

field of view; theater *or* theatre, amphitheater *or* amphitheatre, arena, vista, horizon; commanding view, bird's-eye view, panoramic view.

visual organ, organ of vision; eye; naked eye, unassisted eye; retina, pupil, iris, cornea, white; optics, orbs; saucer–, goggle–, gooseberry- eyes.

short sight etc. 443; clear–, sharp–, quick–, eagle–, piercing–, penetrating-sight, –glance, –eye; perspicacity, discernment; catopsis.

[comparison] eagle, hawk; cat, lynx, weasel; Argus.

evil eye, blighting glance; basilisk, cockatrice.

[optical devices] spectacles, eyeglass, lorgnette, monocle, reading glass, field glass, opera glass; telescope etc. 445; microscope, periscope.

v.   **see**, behold, discern, perceive, have in sight, descry, sight, make out, discover, distinguish, recognize, spy, espy, ken [*archaic*]; get–, have–, catch- a -sight, –glimpse -of; command a view of; witness, contemplate, speculate; cast–, set- the eyes on; be a spectator of etc. 444; look on etc. (*be present*) 186; see sights etc. 455; see at a glance etc. 498.

look, view, eye; lift up the eyes, open one's eye; look -at, –on, –upon, –over, –about one, –round; survey, scan, inspect; run the eye -over, –through; reconnoiter *or* reconnoitre, glance- round, –on, –over; turn–, bend- one's looks upon; direct the eyes to, turn the eyes on, cast a glance.

observe etc. (*attend to*) 457; watch etc. (*care*) 459; see with one's own eyes; watch for etc. (*expect*) 507; peep, peek, peer, pry, take a peep; play at bopeep.

look full in the face, look hard at, look intently; strain one's eyes; fix–, rivet- the eyes upon; stare, gaze; pore over, gloat on, gloat over; leer, ogle, glare; goggle; cock the eye, squint, gloat, look askance *or* askant.

adj. **ocular**; seeing etc. *v.;* visual, optic *or* optical; ophthalmic.

clear-sighted etc. *n.;* clear-eyed, far-sighted; eagle–, hawk–, lynx–, keen–, Argus-eyed.

visible etc. 446.

adv. **visibly** etc. 446; in sight of, with one's eyes open.

at sight, at first sight, at a glance, at the first blush; *prima facie* [*L.*].

int. **look!** etc. (*attention*) 457.

442. Blindness

n. **blindness**, sightlessness, benightedness, anopsia *or* anopsy, cecity, excecation [*obs.*], cataract, ablepsia *or* ablepsy [*rare*], prestriction [*obs.*]; dim-sightedness etc. 443; amaurosis, *gutta serena* ["drop serene" *of Milton*], teichopsia.

[type for the blind] Braille *or* Braille type, New York point, Gall's serrated type, Howe's American type *or* Boston type, Moon's type; Alston's Glasgow type, Lucas's type, Frere's type; string alphabet, writing stamps, noctograph.

v. **be blind** etc. *adj.;* not see; lose sight of; have the eyes bandaged; grope in the dark.

not look; close–, shut–, turn away–, avert- the eyes; look another way; wink etc. (*limited vision*) 443; shut the eyes to, be blind to; wink at, blink at.

render blind etc. *adj.;* excecate [*obs.*], blind, blindfold; hoodwink, dazzle; put one's eyes out; throw dust into one's eyes; *jeter de la poudre aux yeux* [*F.*]; screen from sight etc. (*hide*) 528.

adj. **blind**; eyeless, sightless, visionless; dark; stoneblind, stark-blind, sand-blind [*archaic*]; undiscerning; dimsighted etc. 443.

blind as -a bat, –a buzzard, –a beetle, –a mole, –an owl; wall-eyed.

blinded etc. *v.*

adv. **blindly**, blindfold; darkly.

443. Dim-sightedness
[imperfect vision]

n. dim–, dull–, half–, short–, near–, long–, double–, astigmatic–, failing- sight; dim etc. -sightedness; purblindness, monocularity, blearedness, lippitude; myopia, presbyopia; confusion of vision; astigmatism; color blindness, chromato-pseudoblepsis, Daltonism; day blindness, hemeralopia; snow blindness; xanthocyanopia *or* xanthocyanopsia; ophthalmia; cataract; nyctalopia, moon blindness.

squint, cross-eye, strabismus, strabism, nystagmus; cast in the eye, swivel eye, cockeye, goggle-eyes; obliquity of vision.

winking etc. *v.;* nictitation, nictation; blinkard, albino.

dizziness, swimming, scotomy *or* scotoma [*med.*].

[limitation of vision] blinker, blinder; screen etc. (*hider*) 530.

[fallacies of vision] *deceptio visus* [*L.*]; refraction, distortion, illusion, false light, anamorphosis, virtual image, spectrum, mirage, looming, phasma [*obs.*]; phantasm, phantasma, phantom; vision; specter *or* spectre, apparition, ghost; *ignis fatuus* [*L.*] etc. (*luminary*) 423; specter of the Brocken; magic mirror; magic lantern etc. (*show*) 448; mirror, lens etc. (*instrument*) 445.

v. **be dim-sighted** etc. *n.;* see double; "see men as trees walking" [*Bible*]; have a mote in the eye, have a mist before the eyes, have a film over the eyes; see through a -prism, –glass darkly; wink, blink, nictitate, nictate; squint; look askance *or* askant, screw up the eyes, glare, glower.

dazzle, glare, swim, blur, loom.

adj. **dim-sighted** etc., myopic, nearsighted, shortsighted; presbyopic; astigmatic; moon–, blear–, goggle–, gooseberry–, one- eyed; blind of one eye, monoculous *or* monocular *or* monoculate; half-blind, purblind; cockeyed [*colloq.*], dim-eyed, mole-eyed, mope-eyed [*obs.*]; dichroic.

blind as a bat etc. (*blind*) 442; winking etc. *v.*

444. Spectator

n. **spectator**, beholder, observer, looker-on, onlooker, *assistant* [*F.*], viewer, gazer, witness, eye-witness, bystander, passer-by; sightseer; rubberneck.

spy, scout; sentinel etc. (*warning*) 668.

grandstand [*fig.*], bleachers, gallery, the gods [*slang*].

v. **witness,** behold etc. (*see*) 441; look on etc. (*be present*) 186; rubber *or* rubberneck.

445. Optical Instruments

n. **optical instruments**; lens, meniscus, magnifier; microscope, simple microscope *or* single microscope, compound microscope, projecting microscope, ultramicroscope; spectacles, glasses, barnacles [*colloq., Eng.*], gig lamps [*slang*], goggles, eyeglass, *pince-nez* [*F.*]; periscopic lens; telescope, glass, teinoscope, prism telescope; lorgnette, binocular; spyglass, opera glass, field glass; burning glass, convex lens.

prism; camera, hand camera, kodak [*trade name*], moving-picture machine; camera-lucida, camera-obscura; magic lantern etc. (*show*) 448; megascope; stereopticon; chromatrope, thaumatrope; stereoscope, pseudoscope, polyscope, kaleidoscope, kaleidophon *or* kaleidophone.

photometer, optometer, eriometer, actinometer, lucimeter, radiometer; abdominoscope, gastroscope, helioscope, polariscope, polemoscope, spectroscope, spectrometer.

mirror, reflector, speculum; looking-glass, pier-glass, cheval-glass; hand mirror.

optics, optician; photography, photographer; optometry, optometrist; abdominoscopy; gastroscopy; microscopy, microscopist.

446. Visibility

n. **visibility,** perceptibility, perceivability; conspicuousness, distinctness etc. *adj.;* conspicuity [*rare*]; appearance etc. 448; basset [*geol.*]; exposure; manifestation etc. 525; ocular-proof, –evidence, –demonstration; field of view etc. (*vision*) 441; periscopism.

v. **be** *or* **become visible** etc. *adj.;* appear, open to the view; meet–, catch-the eye; basset [*geol.*], crop out; present–, show–, manifest–, produce–, discover–, reveal–, expose–, betray-itself; stand forth, stand out; materialize; show; arise; peep out, peer out; start up, spring up, show up [*colloq.*], turn up, crop up; glimmer, gleam, glitter, glow, loom; glare; burst forth; burst upon the -view, –sight; heave in sight [*naut. or colloq.*]; come in sight, come into view, come out, come forth, come forward; see the light of day; break through the clouds; make its appearance, show its face, appear to one's eyes,

come upon the stage, float before the eyes, speak for itself etc. (*manifest*) 525; attract the attention etc. 457; reappear; live in a glass house.

expose to view etc. 525.

adj. **visible,** perceptible, perceivable, discernible, apparent; in view, in full view, in sight; exposed to view, *en évidence* [*F.*]; unclouded.

distinct, plain, clear, definite; obvious etc. (*manifest*) 525; well-defined, well-marked; in focus; recognizable, palpable, autoptic *or* autoptical; glaring, staring, conspicuous; stereoscopic *or* stereoscopical; in bold relief, in strong relief, in high relief.

periscopic *or* periscopical, panoramic.

adv. **before one;** under one's -nose, –very eyes; before–, under- one's eyes; *à vue d'oeil* [*F.*], in one's eye, *oculis subjecta fidelibus* [*L.*]; visibly etc. *adj.;* in sight of; *veluti in speculum* [*L.*].

447. Invisibility

n. **invisibility,** invisibleness, nonappearance, imperceptibility; indistinctness etc. *adj.;* mystery, delitescence *or* delitescency.

concealment etc. 528; latency etc. 526.

v. **be invisible** etc. *adj.;* be hidden etc. (*hide*) 528; lurk etc. (*lie hidden*) 526; escape notice.

render invisible etc. *adj.;* conceal etc. 528; put out of sight.

not see etc. (*be blind*) 442; lose sight of.

adj. **invisible,** imperceptible; undiscernible, indiscernible; unapparent, nonapparent; out of sight, not in sight; *à perte de vue* [*F.*], behind the -scenes, –curtain; viewless, sightless, unconspicuous, inconspicuous; unseen etc. (*see* see etc. 441); covert etc. (*latent*) 526; eclipsed, under an eclipse.

indistinct; dim etc. (*faint*) 422; mysterious, dark, obscure, confused; indistinguishable, undiscernible *or* undiscernable, shadowy, indefinite; undefined; ill-defined, ill-marked; blurred, blurry, fuzzy, out of focus; misty etc. (*opaque*) 426; veiled etc. (*concealed*) 528; delitescent.

448. Appearance

n. **appearance,** phenomenon, sight, spectacle, show, premonstration [*obs.*], scene, species, view, *coup d'oeil* [*F.*]; lookout, outlook, prospect, vista, perspective, bird's-eye view, scenery, landscape, seascape, picture, tableau; display, exposure, *mise en scène* [*F.*], rising of the curtain.

phantasm, phantom etc. (*fallacy of vision*) 443.

spectacle, pageant; peep show, raree-show, galanty (*or* gallanty) show; *ombres chinoises* [*F.*]; magic lantern, phantasmagoria, dissolving views; biograph, cinematograph, cinema, moving pictures, movies, photoplay, photodrama; panorama, diorama, cosmorama, georama; *coup de théâtre* [*F.*], *jeu de théâtre* [*F.*]; pageantry etc. (*ostentation*) 882; insignia etc. (*indication*) 550.

aspect, angle, phase, phasis, seeming; shape etc. (*form*) 240; guise, look, complexion, color, image, mien, air, cast, carriage, port, demeanor; presence, expression, first blush, face of the thing; point of view, light.

lineament, feature, trait, lines; outline, outside; contour, silhouette, face, countenance, visage, phiz [*colloq.*], cast of countenance, profile, *tournure* [*F.*], cut of one's jib [*colloq.*], outside etc. 220.

physiognomy, metoposcopy, phrenology; physiognomist, metoposcopist, phrenologist.

v. **appear**; be *or* become visible etc., 446; seem, look, show; present–, wear–, carry–, have–, bear–, exhibit–, take–, take on–, assume- the -appearance, –semblance- of; look like; cut a

figure, figure; present to the view; show etc. (*make manifest*) 525.

adj. **apparent**, seeming, ostensible; on view.

adv. **apparently**; to all seeming, to all appearance; ostensibly, seemingly, as it seems, on the face of it, *prima facie* [*L.*]; at the first blush, at first sight; in the eyes of; to the eye.

449. Disappearance

n. **disappearance**, evanescence, eclipse, occultation; insubstantiality.

departure etc. 293; exit; vanishing, vanishment, vanishing point; dissolving views.

v. **disappear**, vanish, dissolve, fade, melt away, pass, go, avaunt [*obs.*]; be gone etc. *adj.*; leave no trace, "leave not a rack behind" [*Tempest*]; go off the stage etc. (*depart*) 293; suffer–, undergo-an eclipse; retire from sight; be lost to view, be lost to sight, see no longer, fade away [*slang*], pass out of sight.

lose sight of.

efface etc. 552.

adj. **disappearing** etc. *v.;* evanescent; missing, lost; lost to sight, lost to view; gone.

int. **vanish**! disappear! fade! [*slang*], beat it! [*slang*], avaunt! etc. (*ejection*) 297.

Class 4. Intellect

Division 1. Formation of Ideas

Section 1. Operations of Intellect in General

450. Intellect

n. **intellect**, mind, understanding, reason, thinking principle; rationality; cogitative–, cognitive–, discursive–, reasoning–, intellectual-faculties; faculties, senses, consciousness, observation, percipience *or* percipiency, apperception, mentality, intelligence, intellection [*obs.*], intuition, association of ideas, instinct, conception, judgment, wits, parts, capacity, intellectuality, genius; brains, cognitive–, intellectual-powers; wit etc. 498; ability etc. (*skill*) 698; wisdom etc. 498; *Vernunft* [*Ger.*], *Verstand* [*Ger.*].

ego, soul, spirit, ghost [*archaic*], inner man, heart, breast, bosom, *penetralia mentis* [*L.*], *divina particula aurae* [*L.*], *anima divina* [*L.*], heart's

core; psyche, pneuma, subconscious self, subliminal consciousness, supreme principle, the Absolute.

seat of thought, organ of thought, sensorium, sensory, brain; head, headpiece; pate [*colloq.*], noodle [*colloq.*], noddle [*slang*], skull, pericranium, cerebrum, cranium, brain pan, brain box, brain case, sconce [*colloq.*], upper story [*colloq.*].

[science of mind] metaphysics; philosophy etc. 451; psychics; pneumatology, psychology, psychogenesis; noölogy, noöscopics, ideology; mental–, moral-philosophy; philosophy of the mind.

phrenology; craniology, cranioscopy; psychometry, psychophysics, psycho-analysis.

ideality, idealism; transcendentalism, immateriality etc. 317; universal -concept, –conception; mahat [*theos.*].

psychical research; telepathy, thought transference, thought reading; clairaudience; clairvoyance, mediumship; spiritualism etc. 992a.

metaphysician, philosopher, psychiatrist, psychologist, psychometer, psychopath, psychophysicist psychotherapist; psychic, medium, spiritist; adept, mahatma, yogi [*Hinduism*].

v. **reason**, understand, think, reflect, cogitate, excogitate, conceive. judge, contemplate, meditate; ruminate etc. (*think*) 451.

note, notice, mark; take -notice, –cognizance- of; be aware of, be conscious of; realize; appreciate; fancy etc. (*imagine*) 515.

adj. [**relating to intellect**] intellectual, mental, rational, endowed with reason; subjective, noöscopic, psychological; cerebral; percipient, appercipient, animastic; brainy [*colloq.*].

hyperphysical, superphysical; subconscious, subliminal; telepathic, clairaudient, clairvoyant; psychic *or* psychical, spiritual, ghostly; metaphysical, transcendental.

immaterial etc. 317.

450a.   Absence or want of Intellect

n. **absence of intellect**, want of intellect etc. 450; apartments to let [*slang*], nobody home [*slang*], nobody home upstairs [*slang*], *non compos mentis* [*L.*], unintellectuality; imbecility etc. 499; brutality, brute instinct, brute force.

adj. unendowed with-, void of- reason; unintelligent etc. (*imbecile*) 499.

451.   Thought

n. **thought**; exercitation–, exercise- of the intellect; intellection; reflection, cogitation, consideration, meditation, study, lucubration, speculation, deliberation, pondering; head work, brainwork; cerebration; mentation, deep reflection; close study, application etc. (*attention*) 457.

association–, succession–, flow–, train–, current- of -thought, –ideas.

mature thought; afterthought, reconsideration, second thoughts; retrospection etc. (*memory*) 505; excogitation; examination etc. (*inquiry*) 461; invention etc. (*imagination*) 515.

thoughtfulness etc. *adj.*

abstraction, abstract thought, contemplation, musing; brown study etc. (*inattention*) 458; reverie *or* revery, depth of thought, workings of the mind, thoughts, inmost thoughts; self-counsel, self-communing, self-consultation.

[philosophy] philosophical -opinions, –systems, –schools; the handmaid of theology, *ancilla theologioe* [*L.*].

oriental philosophy: Vedânta *or* Uttara-Mîmâmsâ ["later investigation"]; Pûrva-Mîmâmsâ ["prior investigation"]; Sâmkhyas–, Yoga–, Nyâya–, Vaisheshika- philosophy.

greek and greco-roman philosophy: Ionian–, Pythagorean–, Eleatic- school; Atomism; Sophism *or* Sophistic philosophy.

Socratic–, Megarian *or* Eristic–, Elean- school; Cynic philosophy; Cyrenaic *or* Hedonistic school, Hedonism; Platonism; philosophy of the -Absolute, –Academy; Aristotelianism, philosophy of the Lyceum; Peripatetic school [historical formula: *concept, Idea, essence*].

Stoic philosophy, Stoicism, philosophy of the Porch; Epicureanism, philosophy of the Garden; Scepticism; Eclecticism.

Neo-Phythagoreanism; Neo-Platonism.

patristic philosophy: Gnosticism, Manicheism; Alexandrian school; philosophy of the Ante-Nicene Fathers, philosophy of the Post-Nicene Fathers.

scholastic philosophy: Scholasticism; Eclecticism; Mysticism, Mystic philosophy; Pantheistic school, pantheism; Thomism, Scotism, voluntarism; Averroism.

modern philosophy: Post-Reformation philosophy; Humanism, rationalism, political philosophy; Cartesianism; Spinozism; empiricism, moralism; idealistic philosophy, idealism; Leibnitzianism *or* Leibnizianism, Berkeleian philosophy, Berkeleyism; pan-phenomenalism.

modern German philosophy: Kantianism, Fichteanism, Schelling's philosophy, Hegelianism, Herbartianism, Schopenhauer's philosophy; neocriticism; Freudianism, Freudian theory; Einstein theory, relativism.

modern French philosophy: traditionalism; psychologico-spiritualistic school; Positivism; sociological school; Bergsonism.

modern English philosophy: associational psychology, utilitarianism, Darwinism, evolutionistic ethics; Spencerian philosophy; agnosticism, idealism, Neo-Hegelianism.

modern Italian philosophy: Vicoism, sensism, empiricism, criticism, idealism, ontologism, Neo-Scholasticism.

American philosophy: Transcendentalism, pragmatism, neo-voluntarism, new ethical movement; Neo-Hegelianism, Neo-Hegelian movement.

v. **think**, reflect, cogitate, excogitate, consider, reason, deliberate; bestow -thought, –consideration -upon; speculate, contemplate, meditate, ponder, muse, dream, ruminate; brood over, con over, study; mouse over, mull over, sweat over [*colloq.*]; bend–, apply- the mind etc. (*attend*) 457; digest, discuss, hammer at, hammer out, weigh, perpend [*archaic*]; realize, appreciate; fancy etc. (*imagine*) 515; trow [*archaic*].

rack–, ransack–, crack–, beat–, cudgel- one's brains; set one's -brain, –wits- to work; cerebrate, mentalize [*rare*].

harbor–, entertain–, cherish–, nurture- an idea etc. 453, take into one's head; bear in mind; reconsider.

take into consideration; take counsel etc. (*be advised*) 695; commune with oneself, bethink oneself; collect one's thoughts; revolve–, turn over–, run over-in the mind; chew the cud upon [*colloq.*], sleep upon; take counsel of–, advise with- one's pillow.

suggest itself, present itself, occur; come–, get- into one's head; strike one, flit across the view, come uppermost, run in one's head; enter–, pass in–, cross, –, flash on–, flash across–, float in–, fasten itself on–, be uppermost in–, occupy- the mind; have in one's mind.

make an impression; sink–, penetrate- into the mind; engross the thoughts.

adj. **thoughtful**, pensive, meditative, reflective, cogitative, excogitative, museful, wistful, contemplative, speculative, deliberative, studious, sedate, introspective, Platonic, philosophical; thinking etc. *v.*

under consideration, in contemplation, under advisement.

absorbed, rapt; lost in thought etc. (*inattentive*) 458; engrossed in etc. (*intent*) 457.

adv. all things considered, taking everything into -account, –consideration.

452. Incogitance
[absence or want of thought]

n. **incogitance** *or* incogitancy, vacancy, inunderstanding, vacancy of mind, poverty of intellect etc. 499; thoughtlessness etc. (*inattention*) 458; inanity, fatuity, vacuity.

v. **not think** etc. 451; not think of; dismiss from the -mind, –thoughts etc. 451.

indulge in reverie etc. (*be inattentive*) 458.

put away thought; unbend–, relax–, divert- the mind; make the mind a blank, let the mind lie fallow.

adj. **vacant**, inane, unintellectual, nonunderstanding, unideal, unoccupied, unthinking, incogitant, incogitative, unreasoning, inconsiderate, thoughtless; absent etc. (*inattentive*) 458; diverted; irrational etc. 499; narrow-minded etc. 481.

unthought of, undreamt of, unconsidered; off one's mind; incogitable, inconceivable, not to be thought of.

453. Idea
[object of thought]

n. **idea**, notion, conception, thought, apprehension, impression, perception, image, eidolon, sentiment, reflection, observation, consideration; abstract idea; archetype, formative notion; guiding–, organizing- conception; image in the mind, regulative principle.

view etc. (*opinion*) 484; theory etc. 514; conceit, fancy; phantasy etc. (*imagination*) 515.

viewpoint, point of view; aspect etc. 448; field of view.

454. Topic
[subject of thought]

n. **subject of thought**, material for thought; food for the mind, mental pabulum.

subject, subject matter; matter, *motif* [*F.*], theme, *noemata* [*Gr.*], topic, what it is about, thesis, text, business, affair, matter in hand, argument; motion, resolution; head, chapter; case, point; proposition, theorem; field of inquiry; moot point, debatable point, point at issue, point in question; problem etc. (*question*) 461.

v. float–, pass- in the mind etc. 451.

adj. **thought of**; uppermost in the mind; *in petto* [*It.*].

adv. **under consideration**, under advisement; in question, in the mind; at issue, up for discussion, before the house, on foot, on the docket, on the carpet, on the tapis, *sur le tapis* [*F.*]; relative to etc. 9.

Section 2. Precursory Conditions and Operations

455. Curiosity
[desire of knowledge]

n. **curiosity**, curiousness; interest, thirst for knowledge, mental acquisitiveness; newsmongery, inquiring mind; inquisitiveness.

questioner, *enfant terrible* [*F.*], walking question mark [*humorous*], quidnunc.

busybody, newsmonger; Peeping Tom, Paul Pry, eavesdropper; gossip etc. (*news*) 532.

sight-seer, rubberneck.

v. **be curious** etc. *adj.;* take an interest in, stare, gape; prick up the ears, see sights, lionize; rubber *or* rubberneck.

pry, nose, search, ferret out, poke one's nose into.

adj. **curious,** inquisitive, burning with curiosity, over-curious, nosey [*colloq.*]; inquiring etc. 461; prying; inquisitorial; agape etc. (*expectant*) 507.

456. Incuriosity
[absence of curiosity]

n. **incuriosity;** incuriousness etc. *adj.;* apathy, insouciance etc. 866; indifference.

v. **be incurious** etc. *adj.;* have no curiosity etc. 455; be bored by, take no interest in etc. 823; mind one's own business, pursue the even tenor of one's way, glance neither to the right hand nor to the left.

adj. **incurious,** uninquisitive, indifferent; impassive etc. 823; uninterested, bored.

457. Attention

n. **attention;** mindfulness etc. *adj.;* intentness, intentiveness [*rare*]; alertness; thought etc. 451; advertence *or* advertency; observance, observation; consideration, reflection, perpension [*obs.*]; heed; heedfulness; particularity; notice, regard etc. *v.;* circumspection etc. (*care*) 459; study, scrutiny; inspection, introspection; revision, revisal.

active–, diligent–, exclusive–, minute–, close–, intense–, deep–, profound–, abstract–, labored–, deliberate- -thought, –attention, –application, –study.

absorption of mind etc. (*abstraction*) 458.

minuteness, meticulosity, meticulousness, finicality, finicalness; circumstantiality, attention to detail.

indication, calling attention to etc. *v.*

v. **be attentive** etc. *adj.;* attend, advert to, observe, look, see, view, remark, notice, regard, take notice, mark; give–, pay- -attention, –heed- to; know what time it is [*colloq.*], know the time of day [*colloq.*]; incline–, lend- an ear to; trouble one's head about; give a thought to, animadvert; occupy oneself with; contemplate etc. (*think of*) 451; look -at, –to, –after, –into, –over; see to; turn–, bend–, apply–, direct–, give- the -mind, –eye, –attention -to; have an eye to, have in one's eye; bear in mind; take into -account, –consideration; keep in -sight, –view; have regard to, heed, mind, take cogni-

zance of, entertain, recognize; make–, take- note of; note.

examine, –closely, –intently; scan, scrutinize, consider; give–, bend- one's mind to; overhaul, revise, pore over; inspect, review, pass under review; take stock of; get the gist of; fix–, rivet–, devote- the -eye, –mind, –thoughts, –attention- on *or* to; hear out, think out; mind one's business, attend to one's business.

examine cursorily; glance -at, –upon, –over; cast–, pass- the eyes over; run over, turn over the leaves, dip into, perstringe [*obs.*]; skim etc. (*neglect*) 460; take a cursory view of.

revert to, hark back to; watch etc. (*expect*) 507, (*take care of*) 459; hearken *or* harken to, listen to; prick up the ears; have–, keep- the eyes open; come to the point.

meet with attention; fall under one's -notice, –observation; be under consideration etc. (*topic*) 454.

catch–, strike- the eye; attract notice; catch–, awaken–, wake–, invite–, solicit–, attract–, claim–, excite–, engage–, occupy–, strike–, arrest–, fix–, engross–, absorb–, rivet- the -attention, –mind, –thoughts; be present to the mind, be uppermost in the mind.

call attention to, bring under one's notice; point -out, –to, –at, –the finger at; lay the finger on, indigitate [*obs.*], indicate; direct attention to; show; put a mark upon etc. (*sign*) 550; call soldiers to "attention"; bring forward etc. (*make manifest*) 525.

adj. **attentive,** mindful, heedful, intentive [*rare*], advertent, all eyes and ears, observant, regardful; alive to, awake to; on the job [*colloq.*]; there with the goods [*colloq.*], with it [*slang*]; observing etc. *v.;* alert; taken up with, occupied with; engaged in, engrossed in, wrapped in; absorbed, rapt; breathless; preoccupied etc. (*inattentive*) 458; watchful etc. (*careful*) 459; intent on, all eyes [*colloq.*], open-eyed; breathless, undistracted, upon the stretch; on the watch etc. (*expectant*) 507.

steadfast etc. (*persevering*) 604a.

int. **see!** look! look you! look to it! mark! lo! behold! soho! hark! hark ye! mind! look out! look alive! [*colloq.*]; look here! [*colloq.*]; halloo! observe! lo and behold! attention! *nota bene* [*L.*]; **n.b.;** *, †; I'd have you know! notice! O yes! Oyez! *dekko!* [*Hind.*], *ecco!* [*It.*], yo-ho! ho!

458. Inattention

n. **inattention,** inconsideration, want of consideration; inconsiderateness etc. *adj.;* oversight; inadvertence *or* inadvertency, nonobservance, disregard.

supineness etc. (*inactivity*) 683; *étourderie* [*F.*]; want of thought; heedlessness etc. (*neglect*) 460; insouciance etc. (*indifference*) 866.

abstraction; absence of mind, absorption of mind; preoccupation, distraction, reverie *or* revery, brown study [*colloq.*], woolgathering, moonraking [*dial. Eng.*], pipe dream [*colloq.*], castle in the air, *château en Espagne* [*F.*], fancy, deep musing, fit of abstraction.

v. **be inattentive** etc. *adj.*; overlook, disregard; pass by etc. (*neglect*) 460; not observe etc. 457; think little of.

close–, shut- one's eyes to; pay no attention to; dismiss–, discard–, discharge- from one's -thoughts, –mind; drop the subject, think no more of; set–, turn–, put- aside: turn away from, turn one's attention from, turn a deaf ear to, turn one's back upon.

abstract oneself, dream, be somewhere else, be absent, be woolgathering, indulge in reverie *or* revery.

escape notice, escape attention; come in at one ear and go out at the other; forget etc. (*have no remembrance*) 506.

call off–, draw off–, call away–, divert–, distract- the -attention, –thoughts, –mind; put out of one's head.

confuse, disconcert, discompose, put out, perplex, bewilder, moider [*dial. Eng.*], fluster, flurry, rattle [*colloq.*], muddle, dazzle.

adj. **inattentive**; unobservant, unmindful, unheeding, undiscerning; inadvertent; mindless, regardless, respectless; listless etc. (*indifferent*) 866; blind, deaf; hen-headed [*colloq.*], flighty, giddy-pated, giddy-headed, bird-witted; hand over head [*rare*]; cursory, percursory [*rare*], volatile, scatter-brained, hare-brained; unreflecting, *écervelé* [*F.*], inconsiderate, offhand, thoughtless, dizzy, muzzy [*colloq.*], brainsick; giddy, –as a goose; wild, harum-scarum [*colloq.*], rantipole, heedless, careless etc. (*neglectful*) 460.

abstracted, absent, *distrait* [*F.*], woolgathering, moonraking [*dial. Eng.*], dazed, absent-minded, lost; lost–, wrapped- in thought; rapt, in the clouds, bemused, day-dreaming; dreaming of–, musing on- other things; preoccupied, engrossed etc. (*attentive*) 457; in a reverie etc. *n.*; off one's guard etc. (*inexpectant*) 508; napping; dreamy; caught napping.

disconcerted, put out etc. *v.*; rattled [*colloq.*].

adv. **inattentively**, inadvertently etc. *adj.*; *per incuriam* [*L.*], *sub silentio* [*L.*].

459. Care

[vigilance]

n. **care**, solicitude, heed, concern, reck [*poetic*], heedfulness etc. *adj.*; scruple etc. (*conscientiousness*) 939.

vigilance; watchfulness etc. *adj.*; surveillance, eyes of a lynx, eyes of Argus, watch, vigil, lookout, watch and ward, *l'oeil du maître* [*F.*].

espionage etc. (*reconnoitering*) 461; invigilation, watching.

alertness etc. (*activity*) 682; attention etc. 457; prudence etc., circumspection etc. (*caution*) 864; anxiety; forethought etc. 510; precaution etc. (*preparation*) 673; tidiness etc. (*order*) 58, (*cleanliness*) 652; accuracy etc. (*exactness*) 494; minuteness, meticulousness, meticulosity, circumstantiality, attention to detail.

watcher, watchdog etc. 664.

v. **be careful** etc. *adj.*; reck [*archaic*]; take care etc. (*be cautious*) 864; pay attention to etc. 457; take care of; look–, see- to, –after; keep an eye upon, keep a sharp eye upon; chaperon, matronize, play gooseberry; keep watch, keep watch and ward; mount guard, set watch, watch; keep in -sight, –view; mind, mind one's business.

look sharp, look about one; look with one's own eyes; keep a -good, –sharp-lookout; have all one's -wits, –eyes-about one; watch for etc. (*expect*) 507; keep one's eyes open, have the eyes open, sleep with one eye open; catch a weasel asleep.

do one's best etc. 682; mind one's Ps and Qs [*colloq.*], speak by the card, pick one's steps.

take precautions etc. 673; protect etc. (*render safe*) 664.

adj. **careful**, regardful, heedful; taking care etc. *v.*; particular; prudent etc. (*cautious*) 864; considerate; thoughtful etc. (*deliberative*) 451; provident etc. (*prepared*) 673; alert etc. (*active*) 682; sure-footed.

guarded, on one's guard; on the -*qui vive* [*F.*], –alert, –watch, –lookout; awake, broad awake, vigilant; watchful, wakeful, Argus-eyed, lynx-eyed; wide awake etc. (*intelligent*) 498; on the watch for etc. (*expectant*) 507.

scrupulous etc. (*conscientious*) 939; tidy etc. (*orderly*) 58, (*clean*) 652; accurate etc. (*exact*) 494; *cavendo tutus* [*L.*] etc. (*safe*) 664.

adv. **carefully** etc. *adj.*; with care, gingerly.

460. Neglect

n. **neglect**; carelessness etc. *adj.*; trifling etc. *v.*; negligence; omission, laches [*obs.*], deferment, cunctation, procrastination, default; supineness etc. (*inactivity*) 683; conspiracy of silence; inattention etc. 458; nonchalance etc. (*insensibility*) 823; imprudence, recklessness etc. 863; slovenliness etc. (*disorder*) 59, (*dirt*) 653; improvidence etc. 674; noncompletion etc. 730; inexactness etc. (*error*) 495.

paraleipsis *or* paralipsis *or* paralepsis [*rhet.*].

trifler, waiter on Providence; Micawber; waster [*colloq.*], wastrel [*dial. Eng.*], drifter [*colloq.*], bum [*slang*], hobo, tramp, Knight of the Road [*humorous*], down-and-outer [*colloq.*], deadbeat, dead one [*slang*], stiff [*slang*], roustabout, sundowner [*Australia*]; slacker.

v. **be negligent** etc. *adj.*; take no care of etc. (take care of etc. 459); neglect; let slip, let go; lay–, set–, cast–, put- aside; keep–, leave- out of sight; lose sight of.

delay, defer, procrastinate, postpone, adjourn, pigeonhole, tie up with red tape, shelve, stay, suspend, table, lay on the table.

overlook, disregard; pass over, pass by; let pass; blink; wink at, connive at; gloss over; take no -note, –notice, –thought, –account- of; pay no regard to; *laisser aller* [*F.*].

scamp; trifle, fribble; do by halves; slight etc. (*despise*) 930; play with, trifle with; slur; skimp [*dial. & colloq.*]; skim, –the surface; *effleurer* [*F.*]; take a cursory view of etc. 457; slur–, slip–, skip–, jump- over; pretermit, miss, skip, jump, cut [*colloq.*], omit, push aside, throw into the background, sink.

ignore, refuse to notice, shut one's eyes to, refuse to hear, turn a deaf ear to, leave out of one's calculation; not attend to etc. 457, not mind; not trouble -oneself, –one's head- with, –about: forget etc. 506.

be caught napping etc. (*not expect*) 508; leave a loose thread; let the grass grow under one's feet.

render neglectful etc. *adj.*; put *or* throw off one's guard.

adj. **neglecting** etc. *v.*; unmindful, negligent, neglectful; heedless, careless, thoughtless, inconsiderate; perfunctory, remiss.

unwary, unwatchful, unguarded, incircumspect [*rare*], uncircumspect, off one's guard, offhand.

supine etc. (*inactive*) 683; inattentive etc. 458; insouciant etc. (*indifferent*) 823; imprudent,

reckless etc. 863; slovenly etc. (*disorderly*) 59, (*dirty*) 653; inexact etc. (*erroneous*) 495; improvident etc. 674.

neglected etc. *v.*; unheeded, uncared for, unperceived, unseen, unobserved, unnoticed, unnoted, unmarked, unattended to, unthought of, unregarded, unremarked, unmissed; shunted, shelved.

unexamined, unstudied, unsearched, unscanned, unweighed, unsifted, unexplored.

abandoned; buried in a napkin; hid under a bushel.

adv. **negligently** etc. *adj.*; hand over head [*obs.*], in any old way [*colloq.*], anyhow; in an unguarded moment etc. (*unexpectedly*) 508; *per incuriam* [*L.*]; when the cat is away.

int. **never mind**, no matter, let it pass; it will be all the same a hundred from now; *mañana* [*Sp.*].

461. Inquiry

[subject of inquiry. question]

n. **inquiry**; request etc. 765; search, research, quest; pursuit etc. 622.

examination, review, scrutiny, investigation, indagation [*obs.*]; perquisition, perscrutation [*rare*], pervestigation [*obs.*]; inquest, inquisition; exploration; exploitation, ventilation.

sifting; calculation, analysis, dissection, resolution, induction; Baconian method.

strict–, close–, searching–, exhaustive- inquiry; narrow–, strict-search; study etc. (*consideration*) 451.

scire facias [*L.*], *ad referendum* [*L.*]; trial.

questioning etc. *v.*; interrogation, interrogatory; interpellation; challenge, examination, third degree [*colloq.*], cross-examination, catechism, catechesis; feeler, Socratic method, zetetic philosophy; leading question; discussion etc. (*reasoning*) 476.

reconnoitering, reconnaissance *or* reconnoissance, prying etc. *v.*; espionage, *espionage* [*F.*]; domiciliary visit, peep behind the curtain; lantern of Diogenes.

question, query, problem, poser, desideratum, point to be solved, porism; subject–, field- of -inquiry, –controversy; point–, matter- in dispute; moot point; issue, question at issue; bone of contention etc. (*discord*) 713; plain–, fair–, open- question; enigma etc. (*secret*) 533; knotty point etc. (*difficulty*) 704; *quodlibet* [*L.*]; threshold of an inquiry.

inquirer, investigator, inquisitor, inspector, querist, examiner, probator, catechist; scrutator, scrutineer, scrutinizer; analyst; quidnunc etc. (*curiosity*) 455.

v. **inquire**, seek, search; make inquiry etc. *n.;* look -for, –about for, –out for; scan, reconnoiter *or* reconnoitre, explore, sound, rummage, ransack, pry, peer, look round; look–, go- -over, –through; give the once-over [*slang*]; spy, overhaul.

scratch the head, slap the forehead.

look–, peer–, pry- into every hole and corner; visit–, look- behind the scenes; nose, nose out, trace up; hunt out, fish out, ferret out; unearth; leave no stone unturned.

track, seek a clew *or* clue; hunt, trail, shadow, mouse, dodge, trace; follow the -trail, –scent; pursue etc. 662; beat up one's quarters; fish for; feel for etc. (*experiment*) 463.

investigate; take up–, institute–, pursue–, follow up–, conduct–, carry on–, prosecute- an inquiry etc. *n.;* look at, look into; pre-examine; discuss, canvass, agitate.

examine, mouse over, study, consider, calculate; dip–, dive–, delve–, go deep- into; make sure of, probe, sound, fathom; probe to the -bottom, –quick; scrutinize, analyze, anatomize, dissect, parse, resolve, sift, winnow; view–, try- in all its phases; thresh out.

bring in question, subject to examination, pose; put to the proof etc. (*experiment*) 463; audit, tax, pass in review; take into consideration etc. (*think over*) 451; take counsel etc. 695.

question, ask, demand; put–, propose–, propound–, moot–, start–, raise–, stir–, suggest–, put forth–, ventilate–, grapple with–, go into- a question.

interrogate, put to the question, catechize, pump; cross-question, cross-examine; roast [*colloq.*], grill [*colloq.*], put through the third degree [*colloq.*]; dodge; require an answer; pick–, suck- the brains of; feel the pulse.

be in question etc. *adj.;* undergo examination.

adj. **inquiring** etc. *v.;* inquisitive etc. (*curious*) 455; requisitive [*obs.*], requisitory; catechetical, inquisitorial, analytic; in search of, in quest of; on the lookout for, interrogative, zetetic; all-searching.

undetermined, untried, undecided, tentative; in question, in dispute, in issue, in course of inquiry; under -discussion, –consideration, –investigation etc. *n.;* sub judice [*L.*], moot, proposed; doubtful etc. (*uncertain*) 475.

adv. **what?** why? wherefore? *pourquoi?* [*F.*], *warum?* [*Ger.*], whence? whither? where? *quoere?* [*L.*]; how comes it? how does it happen? how is it? what is the reason? what's the matter? what's in the wind? what's afoot? what's up? what's in the air? what is it all about? what on earth? when? who? *nicht wahr?* [*Ger.*].

462. Answer

n. **answer**, response, reply, replication, riposte *or* ripost, subjoinder, rejoinder, retort, repartee; rescript, rescription [*archaic*]; antiphon, antiphony; acknowledgment; password; echo; counterstatement, counterblast, countercharge, contradiction.

[law] defense, plea, surrebutter, surrejoinder, reply, rejoinder, rebutter.

solution etc. (*explanation*) 522; discovery etc. 480a; rationale etc. (*cause*) 153; clew *or* clue etc. (*indication*) 550.

Oedipus; oracle etc. 513; return etc. (*record*) 551.

v. **answer**, respond, reply, rebut, riposte *or* ripost, retort, rejoin; give answer, return for answer; acknowledge, echo.

[law] defend, plead, surrebut, surrejoin, rebut, reply.

explain etc. (*interpret*) 522; solve etc. (*unriddle*) 522; discover etc. 480a; fathom, hunt out etc. (*inquire*) 461; satisfy, set at rest, determine.

adj. **answering** etc. *v.;* responsive, respondent; antiphonal; Oedipean, oracular; conclusive.

adv. **for this reason**; because etc. (*cause*) 153; on the scent, on the right scent.

int. eureka.

463. Experiment

n. **experiment**; essay etc. (*attempt*) 675; analysis etc. (*investigation*) 461; docimasy, trial, tentative method, *tâtonnement* [*F.*].

verification, probation, *experimentum crucis* [*L.*], proof, criterion, diagnostic, test, crucial test; assay, ordeal.

reagent, crucible, check, touchstone, pyx *or* pix [*Brit. mint*], curcuma paper, turmeric paper.

empiricism, rule of thumb.

feeler; pilot–, messenger- balloon; pilot engine; scout; straw to show the wind.

speculation, random shot, leap in the dark.

experimenter, experimentist, experimentalist, assayer, analyst, analyzer; prospector *or* prospector, Forty-Niner, adventurer; speculator, gambler, stock gambler, plunger [*slang*].

v. **experiment**; essay etc. (*endeavor*) 675; try, assay; make an experiment, make trial of; give a trial to; put upon–, subject to- trial; experiment upon; rehearse; put–, bring–, submit- to the

-test, –proof; prove, verify, test, touch, practice upon, try one's strength.

grope; feel–, grope- -for, –one's way; fumble, *tâtonner* [*F.*], *aller à tâtons* [*F.*]; put–, throw-out a feeler; send up a pilot balloon; see how the -land lies, –wind blows; consult the barometer; feel the pulse; fish for, bob for; cast–, beat-about for; angle, trawl, cast one's net, beat the bushes.

venture; try one's fortune etc. (*adventure*) 675; explore etc. (*inquire*) 461.

adj. **experimental**, probative, probatory, probationary; analytic, docimastic *or* docimastical, speculative, tentative; empirical.

tried, tested, proved.

on trial, on examination, on *or* under probation, "on suspicion," under suspicion; on one's trial.

464. Comparison

n. **comparison**, collation, contrast, parallelism, balance; identification; comparative–, relative- estimate.

simile, similitude, parallelization [*rare*]; allegory etc. (*metaphor*) 521.

v. **compare**, –to, –with; collate, confront; place side by side etc. (*near*) 197; set–, pit- against one another; contrast, balance.

compare notes; institute a comparison; *parva componere magnis* [*L.*].

parallel, parallelize; draw a parallel.

adj. **comparative**, relative, contrastive; metaphorical etc. 521.

compared with etc. *v.;* comparable; judged by comparison.

adv. **relatively** etc. (*relation*) 9; as compared with etc. *v.*

465. Discrimination

n. **discrimination**, distinction, differentiation, diagnosis, diorism; nice perception; perception–, appreciation- of difference; estimation etc. 466; nicety, refinement; taste etc. 850; critique, judgment; tact; discernment etc. (*intelligence*) 498; acuteness, penetration; *nuances* [*F.*].

tip, pointer, dope [*slang*]; past performances, record.

v. **discriminate**, distinguish, severalize [*obs.*]; separate; draw the line, sift; separate–, winnow- the chaff from the wheat; separate the wheat from the tares; separate the sheep from the goats; split hairs.

estimate etc. (*measure*) 466; tip, tip off, sum up, criticize; know which is which, know what's what [*colloq.*], know one's way about, know a thing or two, know what o'clock it is, know the time of day, have cut one's eyeteeth, know the ways of the world [*all colloq.*]; "know a hawk from a handsaw" [*Hamlet*].

take into -account, –consideration; give–, allow-due weight to; weigh carefully.

adj. **discriminating** etc. *v.;* dioristic *or* dioristical [*obs.*], critical, diagnostic, perceptive, discriminative, distinctive; nice, acute.

465a. Indiscrimination

n. **indiscrimination**; indistinctness, indistinction; want of distinction, want of discernment, inability to discriminate; uncertainty etc. (*doubt*) 475.

v. **not discriminate** etc. 465; overlook etc. (*neglect*) 460- a distinction; confound, confuse, jumble, jumble together, heap indiscriminately; swallow whole, judge in a lump, use loosely.

adj. **indiscriminate**, indistinguishable, lacking distinction, undistinguished, undistinguishable; unmeasured; promiscuous, undiscriminating.

466. Measurement

n. **measurement**, admeasurement, mensuration, metage, survey, valuation, appraisement, assessment, assize; estimate, estimation; dead reckoning [*naut.*]; reckoning etc. (*numeration*) 85; gauging etc. *v.;* horse power, candle power, candle foot, foot candle, volt ampere, kilowatt; foot pound, foot poundal, foot ton.

metrology, weights and measures, compound arithmetic.

measure, yard measure, standard, rule, foot rule, spirit level, plumb line; square, T-square, steel square, compass, dividers, calipers; gauge *or* gage, standard gauge, broad *or* wide gauge, narrow gauge; log, log-line, patent log [*naut.*]; meter, line, rod, check.

flood mark, high-water mark, load-line mark, Plimsoll mark; index etc. 550.

scale; graduation, graduated scale; nonius; vernier etc. (*minuteness*) 193; quadrant, theodolite, transit *or* transit theodolite, viagraph; scale, beam, steelyard, weighing machine, balance etc. (*weight*) 319; anemometer etc. (*wind*) 349; barometer etc. (*air*) 338; bathometer etc. (*depth*) 208; dynamometer etc. (*force*) 276; galvanometer etc. (*power*) 157; goniometer etc. (*angle*) 244; hyetometer etc. (*fluids in motion*) 348; landmark etc. (*limit*) 233; pedometer etc. (*length*) 200; photometer etc. (*optical instruments*) 445; radiometer etc. (*light*) 420; stethoscope etc. (*medical*) 662; thermometer etc. 389.

coordinates, ordinate and abscissa, polar coordinates, latitude and longitude, declination and right ascension, altitude and azimuth.

geometry, stereometry, planimetry, hypsometry, altimetry, hypsography, chorometry, chorography, topography, cartography; surveying, land surveying, geodesy, geodetics, geodaesia *or* geodesia, orthometry; cadastre *or* cadaster; cadastral survey, cadastration.

astrolabe, armillary sphere.

surveyor, land surveyor; geometer, chorographer, topographer, cartographer.

v. **measure**, meter, mete; value, assess, rate, appraise, estimate, form an estimate, set a value on; appreciate; standardize.

span, pace, step, inch, dial; caliper, divide, apply the compass etc. *n.;* gauge *or* gage; balance, poise, hold the scales, place in the beam, kick the beam; plumb, probe, sound, fathom; heave the -log, -lead; survey, plot, block in, block out, rule, draw to scale.

take an average etc. 29; graduate, calibrate.

adj. **measuring** etc. *v.;* metric, metrical; measurable; geodetical, cadastral, hypsographic *or* hypsographical, hypsometric *or* hypsometrical, chorographic *or* chorographical, topographic *or* topographical, cartographic *or* cartographical.

Section 3. Materials for Reasoning

467. Evidence

[on one side]

n. **evidence**; facts, premises, data, praecognitum (*pl.* praecognita), grounds; indication etc. 550; criterion etc. (*test*) 463.

testimony, testification; attestation; affirmation, declaration; deposition etc. 535; examination.

authority, warrant, credential, diploma, voucher, certificate, docket; *testamur* [*L.*]; record etc. 551; muniments; document; *pièce justificative* [*F.*]; deed, warranty etc. (*security*) 771; autograph, handwriting, signature, seal etc. (*identification*) 550; exhibit; citation, reference, quotation; admission etc. (*assent*) 488.

witness, indicator, eyewitness, earwitness, deponent; sponsor; cojuror, oath-helper [*hist.*], compurgator [*hist.*].

evidence in chief; oral-, documentary-, hearsay-, external-, extrinsic-, internal-, intrin-sic-, circumstantial-, cumulative-, *ex parte* [*L.*]-, presumptive-, collateral-, constructive- evidence; proof etc. (*demonstration*) 478; finger print, thumb print.

secondary evidence; confirmation, corroboration, support; ratification etc. (*assent*) 488; authentication; compurgation [*hist.*], wager of law [*hist.*], comprobation [*obs.*].

writ, summons etc. (*lawsuit*) 696.

v. **be evidence** etc. *n.;* evince, show, betoken, tell of; indicate etc. (*denote*) 550; imply, involve, argue, bespeak, breathe.

have weight, carry weight; tell, speak volumes; speak for itself etc. (*manifest*) 525.

rest upon, depend upon; repose on.

bear witness etc. *n.;* give evidence etc. *n.;* testify, depose, witness, vouch for; sign, seal, undersign, set one's hand and seal, sign and seal, deliver as one's act and deed, certify, attest; acknowledge etc. (*assent*) 488.

confirm, make absolute, ratify, corroborate, indorse *or* endorse, countersign, support, bear out, vindicate, uphold, warrant.

adduce, attest, evidence, cite, quote; refer to, appeal to; call, call to witness; bring forward, bring on, bring into court; allege, plead; produce-, confront- witnesses; collect-, bring together-, rake up- evidence.

establish; have-, make out- a case; authenticate, circumstantiate, substantiate, verify, make good, quote chapter and verse; bring home to, bring to book, bring off.

adj. **evidential**; showing etc. *v.;* indicative, indicatory; deducible etc. 478; grounded on, founded on, based on; first-hand, authentic, verificative, verifiable, veridical, cumulative, corroborative, confirmatory; significant, weighty, overwhelming, damning, conclusive.

oral, documentary, hearsay etc. (*evidence in chief*) *n.*

adv. **by inference**; according to, witness, *a fortiori* [*L.*]; still more, still less; *raison de plus* [*F.*]; in corroboration of etc. *n.;* *valeat quantum* [*L.*]; under seal, under one's hand and seal; at first hand, at second hand.

468. Counterevidence

[evidence on the other side]

n. **counterevidence**; evidence on the other -side, -hand; disproof; refutation etc. 479; negation etc. 536; conflicting evidence.

plea etc. 617; vindication etc. 937; counter-protest; *tu quoque* [*L.*] argument; other side-, reverse- of the shield; *reductio ad absurdum* [*L.*].

v. **countervail**, oppose; rebut etc. (*refute*) 479; subvert etc. (*destroy*) 162; check, weaken; contravene; run counter; contradict etc. (*deny*) 536; tell another story, turn the scale, alter the case; turn the tables; cut both ways; prove a negative. *audire alteram partem* [*L.*].

adj. **countervailing** etc. *v.;* contradictory, in rebuttal.

unattested, unauthenticated, unsupported by evidence; supposititious, trumped up.

adv. **conversely**, on the other hand, on the other side, in opposition; *per contra* [*L.*].

469. Qualification

n. **qualification**, limitation, modification, coloring.
allowance, grains of allowance, consideration, extenuating circumstances; mitigation.
condition, proviso, exception; exemption; salvo [*rare*], saving clause; discount etc. 813; restriction.

v. **qualify**, limit, modify, affect, leaven, take color from, give a color to, introduce new conditions, narrow, temper.
allow for, make allowance for; admit exceptions, take into account; modulate.
take exception, file exceptions, object, raise objections, rise to a point of order.

adj. **qualifying** etc. *v.;* modificatory, extenuatory, mitigatory, lenitive, palliative; conditional; exceptional etc. (*unconformable*) 83.
hypothetical etc. (*supposed*) 514; contingent etc. (*uncertain*) 475.

adv. **provided**, –always; if, unless, but, yet; according as; conditionally, admitting, supposing; on the supposition of etc. (*theoretically*) 514; with the understanding, even, although, though, for all that, after all, at all events.
if possible etc. 470; with grains of allowance, *cum grano salis* [*L.*]; *exceptis excipiendis* [*L.*], wind and weather permitting.
subject to; with this proviso etc. *n.*

470. Possibility

n. **possibility**, potentiality, potency; what may be, what is possible etc. *adj.;* compatibility etc. (*agreement*) 23.
practicability, feasibility, workability, workableness; practicableness etc. *adj.*
contingency, chance etc. 156.

v. **be possible** etc. *adj.;* stand a chance; have a leg to stand on; admit of, bear.

render possible etc. *adj.;* put in the way of, bring to bear, bring together.

adj. **possible**; on the -cards, –dice; *in posse* [*L.*], within the bounds of possibility, conceivable, imaginable, credible; compatible etc. 23; likely.
practicable, feasible, workable, performable, achievable; within -reach, –measurable distance; accessible, superable, surmountable; attainable, obtainable; contingent etc. (*doubtful*) 475.

adv. **possibly**, by any possibility; perhaps, perchance, peradventure; may be, it may be, haply, mayhap.
if possible, wind and weather permitting, God willing, *Deo volente* [*L.*], D. V.; as luck may have it.

471. Impossibility

n. **impossibility** etc. *adj.;* what cannot be, what can never be; sour grapes; hopelessness etc. 859; infeasibility, infeasibleness, impracticality; discrepancy etc. (*disagreement*) 241.
[comparisons] Canute (commanding the tide), Mrs. Partington (and her mop).

v. **be impossible** etc. *adj.;* have no chance whatever.
attempt impossibilities; square the circle, find the elixir of life, discover the philosopher's stone, discover the grand panacea, find the fountain of youth, discover the secret of perpetual motion; wash a blackamoor white; skin a flint; make a silk purse out of a sow's ear, make bricks without straw; have nothing to go upon; weave a rope of sand, build castles in the air, *prendre la lune avec les dents* [*F.*], extract sunbeams from cucumbers, milk a he-goat into a sieve, catch a weasel asleep, *rompre l'anguille au genou* [*F.*], be in two places at once; gather grapes from thorns, fetch water in a sieve, catch wind in cabbage nets, fling eels by the tail, make cheese of chalk.

adj. **impossible**; not possible etc. 470; absurd, contrary to reason; at variance with the facts; unlikely; unreasonable etc. 477; incredible etc. 485; beyond the bounds of -reason, –possibility; from which reason recoils; visionary; inconceivable etc. (*improbable*) 473; prodigious etc. (*wonderful*) 870; unimaginable, inimaginable [*obs.*], not to be thought of, unthinkable.
impracticable, unachievable; unfeasible, infeasible; insuperable; insurmountable *or* unsurmountable, unattainable, unobtainable; out of reach, out of the question; not to be had; be-

yond control; desperate etc. (*hopeless*) 859; in-compatible etc. 24; inaccessible, uncomeatable [*colloq.*], impassable, impervious, innavigable, inextricable; self-contradictory.

out of–, beyond- one's -power, –depth, –reach, –grasp; too much for; *ultra crepidam* [*L.*].

472. Probability

n. **probability**, likelihood; credibleness; likeliness etc. *adj.*; *vraisemblance* [*F.*], verisimilitude, plausibility; color, semblance, show of; presumption; presumptive–, circumstantial- evidence; credibility.

reasonable–, fair–, good–, favorable- -chance, –prospect; prospect, well-grounded hope; chance etc. 156.

v. **be probable** etc. *adj.*; give–, lend- color to; point to; imply etc. (*evidence*) 467; bid fair etc. (*promise*) 511; stand fair for; stand a chance; stand–, run- a good chance; stand–, run- an even chance.

presume, infer, venture, suppose, take for granted, think likely, dare say, flatter oneself; expect etc. 507; count upon etc. (*believe*) 484.

adj. **probable**, likely, hopeful, to be expected, in a fair way.

plausible, specious, ostensible, colorable, *ben trovato* [*It.*], well-founded, reasonable, credible, easy of belief, presumable, presumptive, apparent.

adv. **probably** etc. *adj.*; belike [*archaic*]; in all probability, in all likelihood; very–, most- likely; like enough; very like; ten etc. to one; apparently, seemingly, to all seeming, as like as not [*colloq.*], according to every reasonable expectation; *prima facie* [*L.*]; to all appearance etc. (*to the eye*) 448.

473. Improbability

n. **improbability**, unlikelihood; unfavorable–, bad–, ghost of a–, little–, small–, poor–, scarcely any–, no- chance; bare possibility; long odds; incredibility etc. 485.

v. **be improbable** etc. *adj.*; violate–, stretch- the probabilities; go beyond reason, strain one's credulity; run counter to the laws of nature; have a small chance etc. *n.*; stand a poor show [*colloq.*].

adj. **improbable**, unlikely, contrary to all reasonable expectation; contrary to -fact, –experience; implausible, rare etc. (*infrequent*) 137; unheard of, inconceivable; unimaginable, inimaginable [*obs.*]; incredible etc. 485; more than doubtful.

int. **not likely**! no fear! [*chiefly Eng.*]; I ask you! [*slang*]; catch me! [*slang*].

474. Certainty

n. **certainty**; necessity etc. 601; certitude, sureness, surety, assurance; dead–, moral- certainty; infallibleness etc. *adj.*; infallibility, reliability, reliableness; indubitableness, inevitableness, unquestionableness.

gospel, scripture, church, pope, court of final appeal; *res adjudicata*, [*L.*], *res judicata* [*L.*]; ultimatum.

fact; positive fact, matter of fact; *fait accompli* [*F.*].

bigotry, positiveness, dogmatism, dogmatization; fanaticism.

dogmatist, dogmatizer, doctrinaire, bigot, opinionist, Sir Oracle; dogmatic theorist; zealot, fanatic; *ipse dixit* [*L.*].

v. **be certain** etc. *adj.*; stand to reason.

render certain etc. *adj.*; insure *or* ensure, assure; clinch, make sure; determine, find out once for all, decide, set at rest, "make assurance double sure" [*Macbeth*]; know etc. (*believe*) 484; dismiss all doubt, admit of no doubt.

dogmatize, lay down the law.

adj. **certain**, sure; assured etc. *v.*; solid, well-founded.

unqualified, absolute, positive, determinate, definite, clear, unequivocal, categorical, unmistakable, decisive, decided, ascertained.

inevitable, unavoidable, avoidless; ineluctable.

conclusive, unimpeachable, undeniable, unquestionable; indefeasible, indisputable, incontestable, incontrovertible, indubitable; irrefutable etc. (*proven*) 478; without power of appeal, inappealable, final.

indubious; without–, beyond a–, without a shade or shadow of- -doubt, –question; past dispute; clear as day; beyond all -question, –dispute; undoubted, uncontested, unquestioned, undisputed; questionless, doubtless.

authoritative, authentic, official, governmental, curule.

sure as -fate, –death and taxes, –a gun [*colloq.*].

evident, self-evident, axiomatic; clear, –as day, –as the sun at noonday; apparent etc. (*manifest*) 525.

infallible, unerring; unchangeable etc. 150; to be depended on, trustworthy, reliable, bound.

dogmatic, opinionative, opinionated, dictatorial, doctrinaire; fanatical, bigoted.

adv. **certainly** etc. *adj.*; for certain, certes [*archaic*], sure, no doubt, doubtless, and no mistake [*colloq.*], *flagrante delicto* [*L.*]; sure enough, to be sure, of course, as a matter of course, *a coup sûr* [*F.*], *sans doute* [*F.*], questionless [*rare*], for a certainty, of a certainty, to a certainty; in truth etc. (*truly*) 494; at any rate, at all events; without fail; *coûte que coûte* [*F.*], *coûte qu'il coûte* [*F.*]; whatever may happen, if the worse come to the worst; come what may, come what will, happen what may, happen what will; sink or swim; rain or shine, live or die.

475. Uncertainty

n. **uncertainty**, incertitude, doubt; doubtfulness etc. *adj.*; dubiety, dubitation, dubitancy [*obs.*], dubiosity, dubiousness.

hesitation, suspense, state of suspense; perplexity, embarrassment, dilemma, Morton's fork [*hist.*], bewilderment; botheration [*colloq.*]; puzzle, quandary; timidity etc. (*fear*) 860; vacillation etc. 605; aporia, diaporesis, indetermination; sealed orders.

vagueness etc. *adj.*; haze, fog; obscurity etc. (*darkness*) 421; ambiguity etc. (*double meaning*) 520; contingency, double contingency, possibility upon a possibility; open question etc. (*question*) 461; *onus probandi* [*L.*], blind bargain, pig in a poke, leap in the dark, something or other; needle in a haystack; roving commission.

fallibility; unreliability, unreliableness, untrustworthiness; precariousness etc. *adj.*

v. **be uncertain** etc. *adj.*; wonder whether.

lose the -clew *or* clue, -scent; miss one's way, wander aimlessly, beat about, hang around.

not know -what to make of etc. (*unintelligibility*) 519, -which way to turn, -whether one stands on one's head or one's heels; float in a sea of doubt, hesitate, flounder; lose oneself, lose one's head; muddle one's brains.

render uncertain etc. *adj.*; put out, pose, puzzle, perplex, embarrass; muddle, confuse, confound, fluster; bewilder, bother, moider [*dial.*], rattle [*colloq.*], nonplus, addle the wits, throw off the scent, keep in suspense, keep one guessing.

doubt, etc. (*disbelieve*) 485; hang in the balance, tremble in the balance; depend.

adj. **uncertain**, unsure; casual; random etc. (*aimless*) 621; changeable, changeful etc. 149.

doubtful, dubious; dazed; insecure, unstable, indecisive; unsettled, undecided, undetermined; in suspense, open to discussion; controvertible; in question etc. (*inquiry*) 461.

vague; indeterminate, indefinite; ambiguous, equivocal; undefined, undefinable, confused etc. (*indistinct*) 447; mysterious, cryptic, veiled, obscure, oracular.

perplexing etc. *v.*; enigmatic, paradoxical, apocryphal, problematical, hypothetical; experimental etc. 463.

fallible, questionable, precarious, slippery, ticklish, debatable, disputable; unreliable, untrustworthy.

unauthentic, unauthenticated, unauthoritative; unascertained, unconfirmed; undemonstrated; untold, uncounted.

contingent, contingent on, dependent on; subject to; dependent on circumstances; occasional; provisional.

in a state of uncertainty, on the horns of a dilemma, in a cloud, in a maze; bushed, off the track; derailed; ignorant etc. 491; afraid to say; out of one's reckoning, out of one's bearings, astray, adrift; at sea, at fault, at a loss, at one's wit's end, at a non-plus; puzzled etc. *v.*; lost, abroad, *désorienté* [*F.*]; distrait, distracted, distraught.

adv. **uncertainly** etc. *adj.*; at random, until things straighten out, while things are so uncertain, in this state of suspense; *pendente lite* [*L.*]; *sub spe rati* [*L.*].

Section 4. Reasoning Processes

476. Reasoning

n. **reasoning**; ratiocination, rationalism; dialectics, dialecticism, induction, generalization.

discussion, comment; ventilation; inquiry etc. 461.

argumentation, controversy, debate; polemics, wrangling; contention etc. 720; logomachy, disputation, disceptation [*archaic*]; paper war.

logic, art of reasoning.

process-, train-, chain- of reasoning; deduction, induction; synthesis, analysis.

argument; case, plea, *plaidoyer* [*F.*], opening; premise *or* premiss; lemma, proposition, terms, premises; postulate, data, starting point, principle; inference etc. (*judgment*) 480.

prosyllogism, syllogism; enthymeme, sorites, dilemma, *a fortiori* reasoning, *a priori* reasoning, *reductio ad absurdum* [*L.*], horns of a dilemma, *argumentum ad hominem* [*L.*], comprehensive argument; empirema, epagoge.

logical sequence; good case; correct–, just–, sound–, valid–, cogent–, irrefutable–, logical–, forcible–, persuasive–, persuasory [*rare*]–, consectary [*obs.*]–, conclusive etc. 478–, subtle- reasoning; force of argument; strong -point, –argument.

arguments, reasons, pros and cons.

reasoner, logician, dialectician; disputant; controversialist, controvertist; wrangler, arguer, debater, devil's disciple, polemic, casuist, rationalist; scientist; eristic.

v. **reason**, argue, discuss, debate, dispute, wrangle; argufy *or* argify [*dial.*], bandy -words, –arguments; chop logic; hold–, carry on- an argument; controvert etc. (*deny*) 536; canvass; comment–, moralize- upon; consider etc. (*examine*) 461.

try conclusions; open a -discussion, –case; join–, be at- issue; moot; come to the point; stir–, agitate–, ventilate–, torture- a question; take up a -side, –case.

contend, take one's stand upon, insist, lay stress on; infer etc. 480.

follow from etc. (*demonstration*) 478.

adj. **reasoning** etc. *v.;* rational, ratiocinative, rationalistic; argumentative, controversial, dialectic, polemical; discursory, discursive; disputatious; logomachic *or* logomachical; Aristotelian, eristic *or* eristical.

debatable, controvertible.

logical; syllogistic, soritical, epagogic, inductive, deductive, synthetic *or* synthetical, analytic *or* analytical; relevant etc. 23.

adv. **for**, because, hence, whence, seeing that, since, sith [*archaic*], then, thence, so; for -that, –this, –which- reason; for as much as *or* forasmuch as, in as much as *or* inasmuch as; whereas, *ex concesso* [*L.*], considering, in consideration of; therefore, argal [*archaic*], wherefore; consequently, *ergo* [*L.*], thus, accordingly; *a priori* [*L.*]; *a fortiori* [*L.*].

finally, in conclusion, in fine; after all, *au bout du compte* [*F.*], on the whole, taking one thing with another; pro and con; rationally etc. *adj.*

477. Intuition
[absence of reasoning]

Sophistry
[specious reasoning]

n. **intuition**, instinct, association; presentiment; rule of thumb.

sophistry, paralogy, perversion, casuistry, jesuitry, equivocation, evasion, mental reserva-tion; chicane, chicanery; quiddit [*obs.*], quiddity; mystification; special pleading; speciousness etc. *adj.;* nonsense etc. 497; word fence, tongue fence; overrefinement, hairsplitting, quibbling etc. *v.*

false–, fallacious–, specious–, vicious- reasoning; begging of the question, *petitio principii* [*L.*], *ignoratio elenchi* [*L.*]; *post hoc ergo propter hoc* [*L.*]; *non sequitur* [*L.*], *ignotum per ignotius* [*L.*].

misjudgment etc. 481; false teaching etc. 538.

sophism, solecism, paralogism; quibble, quirk, elench, elenchus, fallacy, *quodlibet* [*L.*], subterfuge, shift, subtlety, quillet [*archaic*]; inconsistency, antilogy; claptrap, mere words; "lame and impotent conclusion" [*Othello*].

meshes–, cobwebs- of sophistry; flaw in an argument; weak point, bad case.

sophist, casuist, paralogist.

v. **judge intuitively**, judge by intuition; hazard a proposition, talk at random.

pervert, quibble; equivocate, mystify, evade, elude; gloss over, varnish; misteach etc. 538; mislead etc. (*error*) 495; cavil, refine, subtilize, split hairs; misrepresent etc. (*lie*) 544.

reason ill, reason falsely etc. *adj.;* misjudge etc. 481; paralogize.

beg the question, reason in a circle, cut blocks with a razor, beat about the bush, play fast and loose, blow hot and cold, prove that black is white and white black, travel out of the record, *parler à tort et à travers* [*F.*], put oneself out of court, not have a leg to stand on.

adj. **intuitive**, instinctive, impulsive; independent of–, anterior to- reason; gratuitous, hazarded; unconnected.

illogical, unreasonable, false, unsound, invalid; unwarranted, not following, incongruous, inconsequent, inconsequential; inconsistent; absonous [*obs.*], absonant, unscientific; untenable, inconclusive, incorrect; fallacious, fallible; groundless, unproved.

specious, sophistic *or* sophistical, jesuitic *or* jesuitical, casuistic *or* casuistical, paralogistic, paralogical; deceptive, illusive, illusory; hollow, plausible, *ad captandum* [*L.*], evasive; irrelevant etc. 10.

weak, feeble, poor, flimsy, loose, vague, irrational; nonsensical etc. (*absurd*) 497; foolish etc. (*imbecile*) 499; frivolous, pettifogging, quibbling; finespun, overrefined.

at the end of one's tether, *au bout de son latin* [*F.*].

adv. **intuitively** etc. *adj.;* by intuition.

illogically etc. *adj.*

478. Demonstration

n. **demonstration**, proof, irrefragability; conclusiveness etc. *adj.;* apodeixis *or* apodixis, probation, comprobation [*obs.*].

logic of facts etc. (*evidence*) 467; *experimentum crucis* [*L.*] etc. (*test*) 463; argument etc. 476; rigorous–, absolute- establishment.

v. **demonstrate**, prove, establish, make good; show, evince etc. (*be evidence of*) 467; verify etc. 467; settle the question, reduce to demonstration, set the question at rest.

make out, –a case; prove one's point, have the best of the argument; draw a conclusion etc. (*judge*) 480.

follow, –of course; stand to reason; hold good, hold water [*colloq.*].

adj. **demonstrating** etc. *v.;* demonstrative, demonstrable; probative, unanswerable, conclusive, convincing; apodeictic *or* apodictic, apodeictical *or* apodictical; irresistible, irrefutable, irrefragable, undeniable.

categorical, decisive, crucial.

demonstrated etc. *v.;* proven; unconfuted, unanswered, unrefuted; evident etc. 474.

deducible, consequential, consectary [*obs.*], inferential, following.

adv. **of course**, in consequence, consequently, as a matter of course.

479. Confutation

n. **confutation**, refutation; answer, complete answer; disproof, conviction, redargution, invalidation; exposure, exposition, *exposé* [*F.*], clincher [*colloq.*], retort, *reductio ad absurdum* [*L.*]; knock-down-; *tu quoque*- argument; sockdolager [*slang*].

v. **confute**, refute; parry, negative, disprove, redargue, expose, show up, show the fallacy of, rebut, defeat; demolish etc. (*destroy*) 162; overthrow, overturn; scatter to the winds, explode, invalidate; silence; put–, reduce- to silence; clinch -an argument, –a question; stop the mouth, shut up; have, have on the hip, have the better of; confound, convince.

not leave a leg to stand on, cut the ground from under one's feet; smash all opposition; knock the bottom out of an argument [*colloq.*].

be confuted etc.; fail; expose–, show- one's weak point.

adj. **confutable**, confutative, refutable; confuting, confuted, etc. *v.;* capable of refutation.

condemned -on one's own showing, –out of one's own mouth; "hoist with his own petar" [*Hamlet*].

Section 5. Results of Reasoning

480. Judgment
[conclusion]

n. **judgment**, decision, determination, finding, verdict, sentence, decree; *res adjudicata* [*L.*], *res judicata* [*L.*]; opinion etc. (*belief*) 484; good judgment etc. (*wisdom*) 498.

result, conclusion, upshot; deduction, inference, ergotism [*obs.*], illation; corollary, porism; moral.

estimation, valuation, appreciation, judication; dijudication, adjudication; arbitrament, arbitrement, arbitration; assessment, ponderation [*rare*]; valorization.

estimate, award; review, criticism, critique, notice, report.

plebiscite, plebiscitum, voice, casting vote; vote etc. (*choice*) 609.

arbiter, arbitrator; judge, umpire; assessor, referee; inspector, inspecting officer; censor.

reviewer, critic; connoisseur; commentator etc. 524.

v. **judge**, conclude, opine; come to–, draw–, arrive at- a conclusion; ascertain, determine, make up one's mind.

deduce, derive, gather, collect, infer, draw an inference, make a deduction, weet [*obs.*], ween [*archaic*].

estimate, form an estimate, appreciate, value, count, assess, rate, rank, account; regard, consider, think of; look upon etc. (*believe*) 484; review; size up [*colloq.*].

decide, settle; pass–, give- an opinion; try, pronounce, rule; pass -judgment, –sentence; sentence, doom, decree; find; give–, deliver- judgment; adjudge, adjudicate, judicate [*rare*]; arbitrate, award, report; bring in a verdict; make absolute, set a question at rest; confirm etc. (*assent*) 488.

hold the scales, sit in judgment; try a cause, hear a cause.

review, comment, criticize; pass under review etc. (*examine*) 457; investigate etc. (*inquire*) 461.

adj. **judging** etc. *v.;* judicious etc. (*wise*) 498; determinate, conclusive, confirmatory.

critical, hypercritical, hairsplitting, censorious.

adv. **on the whole**, all things considered, taking all this into consideration, this being so, *quae cum ita sint* [*L.*], therefore, wherefore.

480a. Discovery

[result of search or inquiry]

n. **discovery**, detection, disenchantment; ascertainment, disclosure, find, revelation.

trover etc. 775.

v. **discover**, find, determine, evolve; fix upon; find–, trace–, make–, hunt–, fish–, worm–, ferret–, dig–, root- out; fathom; bring out, draw out; educe, elicit, bring to light; dig up, grub up, fish up; unearth, disinter.

solve, resolve; unriddle, unravel, ravel, ravel out, unlock; pick–, open- the lock; find a clew *or* clue to; interpret etc. 522; disclose etc. 529.

trace, get at; hit it, have it; lay one's -finger, –hands- upon; spot [*colloq.*], see through a millstone [*colloq.*]; get–, arrive- at the -truth etc. 494; put the saddle on the right horse, hit the right nail on the head.

scent, be near the truth, be warm [*colloq.*], burn [*colloq.*]; smoke, sniff, smell out, smell a rat [*colloq.*].

see through, see daylight, see in its true colors, see the cloven foot; open the eyes to; detect; catch, catch tripping.

meet with; pitch–, fall–, light–, hit–, stumble–, pop- upon; come across; fall in with.

recognize, realize, verify, make certain of, identify.

int. eureka! I have it! at last!

481. Misjudgment

n. **misjudgment**, obliquity of judgment, warped judgment; miscalculation, miscomputation, misconception etc. (*error*) 495, hasty conclusion.

preconception, prejudgment, prejudication [*rare*], prejudice; foregone conclusion; prenotion, prevention [*Gallicism*], predilection, prepossession, preapprehension, presumption, presentiment, foreboding; fixed idea; *idée fixe* [*F.*], obsession, preconceived idea, *mentis gratissimus error* [*L.*]; fool's paradise.

partisanship, *esprit de corps* [*F.*], party spirit, mob spirit, class prejudice, class consciousness, race prejudice, provincialism, clannishness, prestige.

quirk, shift, quibble, equivocation, evasion, subterfuge.

bias, warp, twist; hobby, whim, craze, fad, crotchet, partiality, infatuation, blind side, blind spot, mote in the eye.

one-sided–, partial–, narrow–, confined–, superficial- -views, –ideas, –conceptions, –no-

tions; purblindness, *entêtement* [*F.*]; narrow mind; bigotry etc. (*obstinacy*) 606; *odium theologicum* [*L.*]; pedantry; hypercriticism.

doctrinaire etc. (*positive*) 474.

v. **misjudge**, misestimate, misesteem, misthink, misconjecture, misconceive etc. (*error*) 495; fly in the face of facts; miscalculate, misreckon, miscompute.

overestimate etc. 482; underestimate etc. 483.

prejudge, forejudge; presuppose, presume, prejudicate [*rare*], dogmatize; have a bias etc. *n.;* have only one idea; *jurare in verba magistri* [*L.*], run away with the notion; jump–, rush- to a conclusion; go off half-cocked [*colloq.*]; look only at one side of the shield; view with jaundiced eye, view through distorting spectacles; not see beyond one's nose; *dare pondus fumo* [*L.*]; get the wrong sow by the ear etc. (*blunder*) 699.

bias, warp, twist; give a -bias, –twist; prejudice, prepossess.

adj. **misjudging** etc. *v.;* ill-judging, wrong-headed; prejudiced, prepossessed; jaundiced; short-sighted, purblind; partial, one-sided, superficial.

narrow, narrow-minded, narrow-souled; provincial, parochial, insular; mean-spirited; confined, illiberal, intolerant, besotted, infatuated, fanatical, *entêté* [*F.*], positive, dogmatic, dictatorial; pragmatic *or* pragmatical, egotistical, conceited; opinioned, opinionated, opinionate [*rare*], opinionative [*rare*], opinative [*obs.*], opiniative [*obs.*]; self-opinionated; self-opinioned, wedded to an opinion, *opiniâtre* [*F.*]; bigoted etc. (*obstinate*) 606; crotchety, fussy, impracticable; unreasonable, stupid etc. 499; credulous etc. 486; warped.

misjudged etc. *v.*

adv. *ex parte* [*L.*].

482. Overestimation

n. **overestimation** etc. *v.;* exaggeration etc. 549; vanity etc. 880; optimism, pessimism.

much cry and little wool, much ado about nothing; storm in a teacup; fine talking; fine writing, rodomontade, gush [*colloq.*], hot air [*slang*].

egoism, egotism, bombast, conceit, swelled head [*slang*], megalomania.

egoist, egotist, megalomaniac; optimist, booster, pessimist; Rodomont, Braggadochio, braggart, boaster, braggadocio, swaggerer; hot-air artist [*slang*], gas-bag [*slang*], wind-bag [*slang*].

v. **overestimate**, overrate, overvalue, overprize, overweigh, overreckon, overstrain, overpraise;

estimate too highly, attach too much importance to, make mountains of molehills, catch at straws; strain, magnify; exaggerate etc. 549; set too high a value upon; think-, make- -much, -too much- of; out-reckon.

have too high an opinion of oneself etc. (*vanity*) 880.

eulogize, panegyrize, optimize, gush [*colloq.*], gush over [*colloq.*], boost; puff *or* puff up [*colloq.*]; extol, -to the skies; make the -most, -best, -worst- of; make two bites of a cherry.

adj. overestimated etc. *v.;* oversensitive etc. (*sensibility*) 822.

inflated, puffed up; grandiose, stilted, pompous, pretentious, megalomaniacal, braggart, bombastic.

483. Underestimation

n. **underestimation**; depreciation etc. (*detraction*) 934; pessimism; self-detraction, self-depreciation; undervaluation, miosis, litotes [*rhet.*]; undervaluing etc. *v.;* modesty etc. 881.

pessimist, depreciator, knocker [*slang*], crapehanger [*slang*].

v. **underrate**, underestimate, undervalue, underreckon; depreciate; disparage etc. (*detract*) 934; not do justice to; misprize, disprize; ridicule etc. 856; pessimize; slight etc. (*despise*) 930; neglect etc. 460; slur over.

make -light, -little, -nothing, -no account- of; belittle, knock [*slang*], slam [*slang*], run down [*colloq.*], minimize, think nothing of; set no store by, set at naught; shake off like water from a duck's back, shake off as dewdrops from the lion's mane.

adj. **depreciating** etc. *v.;* depreciative, depreciatory.

depreciated etc. *v.;* unappreciated, unvalued, unprized.

484. Belief

n. **belief**; credence; credit; assurance; faith, trust, troth, confidence, presumption, sanguine expectation etc. (*hope*) 858; dependence on, reliance on.

conviction, persuasion, convincement, plerophory [*rare*], self-conviction; certainty etc. 474; opinion, mind, view; conception, thinking; impression etc. (*idea*) 453; surmise etc. 514; conclusion etc. (*judgment*) 480.

tenet, dogma, principle, persuasion, views, way of thinking; popular belief etc. (*assent*) 488.

firm-, implicit-, settled-, fixed-, rooted-, deep-rooted-, staunch-, unshaken-, stead-

fast-, inveterate-, calm-, sober-, dispassionate-, impartial-, well-founded- -belief, -opinion etc.; *uberrima fides* [*L.*].

doctrine, system of opinions, school, articles, canons; article-, declaration-, profession- of faith; tenets, credenda, creed, credo, thirty-nine articles etc. (*orthodoxy*) 983a; gospel, gospel truth; catechism; assent etc. 488; propaganda etc. (*teaching*) 537.

credibility etc. (*probability*) 472.

v. **believe**, credit; give -faith, -credit, -credence- to; see, realize; assume, receive; set down for, take for; have it, take it; consider, esteem, presume.

count-, depend-, calculate-, pin one's faith-, reckon-, lean-, build-, rely-, rest- upon; cast one's bread upon the waters; lay one's account for; make sure of.

make oneself easy -about, -on that score; take on -trust, -credit; take for -granted, -gospel; allow-, attach- some weight to.

know, -for certain; be in the know [*slang*]; have-, make- no doubt; doubt not; be-, rest- -assured etc. *adj.*; persuade-, assure-, satisfy- oneself; make up one's mind.

confide in, believe in, put one's trust in; give one credit for; place-, repose- implicit confidence in; take one's word for, take at one's word; place reliance on, rely upon, swear by, regard to.

think, hold; take, take it; opine, be of opinion, conceive, trow [*archaic*], ween [*archaic*], fancy, apprehend; have-, hold-, possess-, entertain-, adopt-, imbibe-, embrace-, get hold of-, hazard-, foster-, nurture-, cherish- -a belief, -an opinion etc. *n.*

view as, consider as, take as, hold as, conceive as, regard as, esteem as, deem as, look upon as, account as, set down as; surmise etc. 514.

get-, take- it into one's head; come round to an opinion; swallow etc. (*credulity*) 486.

persuade; cause to be believed etc. *v.;* satisfy, bring to reason, have the ear of, gain the confidence of, assure; convince, convict, convert; wean, bring round; bring-, win- over; indoctrinate etc. (*teach*) 537; cram down the throat; produce-, carry- conviction; bring-, drive- home to.

find credence, go down, pass current; be received etc. *v.*, be current etc. *adj.*; possess-, take hold of-, take possession of- the mind.

adj. **believing** etc. *v.;* certain, sure, assured, positive, cocksure [*colloq.*], satisfied, confident, unhesitating, convinced, secure.

under the impression; impressed–, imbued–, penetrated- with.

confiding, trustful, suspectless [*obs.*], unsuspecting, unsuspicious, void of suspicion; credulous etc. 486; wedded to.

believed etc. *v.;* accredited, putative; unsuspected, trusted, undoubted.

worthy of–, deserving of–, commanding- -belief, –confidence; credible, reliable, trustworthy, to be depended on; satisfactory; probable etc. 472; fiducial, fiduciary; persuasive, impressive.

doctrinal, relating to belief.

adv. **in the opinion of,** in the eyes of; *me judice* [*L.*]; meseems [*archaic*], methinks [*archaic*]; to the best of one's belief; in my opinion, in my judgment, according to my belief; I dare say, I doubt not, I have no doubt, I am sure; cocksure, sure enough etc. (*certainty*) 474; depend–, rely- upon it; be–, rest-assured; I'll warrant you etc. (*affirmation*) 535.

485. Unbelief. Doubt

n. **unbelief,** disbelief, misbelief; discredit, miscreance *or* miscreancy [*archaic*]; infidelity etc. (*irreligion*) 989; wrangling, ergotism [*rare*]; dissent etc. 489; change of opinion etc. 484; retractation etc. 607.

doubt etc. (*uncertainty*) 475; skepticism *or* scepticism, misgiving, demur; distrust, mistrust; misdoubt, suspicion, jealousy, scruple, qualm; *onus probandi* [*L.*].

incredibility, incredibleness, incredulity, unbelievability.

agnostic, skeptic *or* sceptic; unbeliever etc. 487.

v. **disbelieve,** discredit; not believe etc. 484; misbelieve; refuse to admit etc. (*dissent*) 489; refuse to believe etc. (*incredulity*) 487.

doubt; be doubtful etc. (*uncertain*) 475; doubt the truth of; be skeptical as to etc. *adj.;* diffide [*obs.*], distrust, mistrust; suspect, smoke, scent, smell, smell a rat [*colloq.*], have–, harbor–, entertain- -doubts, –suspicions; have one's doubts.

throw doubt upon, raise a question; bring–, call- in question; question, challenge; dispute; deny etc. 536; cause–, raise–, start–, suggest–, awake- a -doubt, –suspicion; cavil, wrangle, ergotize [*rare*].

demur, stick at, pause, hesitate, shy at, scruple; stop to consider, waver.

hang in suspense, hang in doubt.

stagger, startle; shake–, stagger- one's -faith, –belief.

adj. **unbelieving;** skeptical *or* sceptical, incredulous–, skeptical- as to; distrustful of, shy of, suspicious of; doubting etc. *v.*

doubtful etc. (*uncertain*) 475; disputable; unworthy–, undeserving- of -belief etc. 484; questionable; suspect [*archaic*], suspicious; open to -suspicion -doubt; staggering, hard to believe, incredible, unbelievable, not to be believed, inconceivable.

fallible etc. (*uncertain*) 475; undemonstrable; controvertible etc. (*untrue*) 495.

adv. **with caution,** *cum grano salis* [*L.*]; with grains of allowance.

486. Credulity

n. **credulity,** credulousness etc. *adj.*; gullibility, cullibility [*obs.*]; gross credulity, infatuation; self-delusion, self-deception; superstition; one's blind side; bigotry etc. (*obstinacy*) 606; hyperorthodoxy etc. 984; misjudgment etc. 481.

credulous person etc. (*dupe*) 547.

v. **be credulous** etc. *adj.;* *jurare in verba magistri* [*L.*]; follow implicitly; swallow, swallow whole, gulp down; take on trust; take for -granted, –gospel; take on faith; run away with -a notion, –an idea; jump–, rush- to a conclusion; think the moon is made of green cheese; take–, grasp- the shadow for the substance; catch at straws.

impose upon etc. (*deceive*) 545.

adj. **credulous,** gullible; easily deceived etc. 545; simple, green, soft, childish, silly, stupid; easily convinced; overcredulous, overconfident, overtrustful; infatuated, superstitious; confiding etc. (*believing*) 484.

487. Incredulity

n. **incredulity.** incredulousness; skepticism, free thought, Pyrrhonism; want of faith etc. (*irreligion*) 989; minimifidianism; unbelief etc. 485.

suspiciousness etc. *adj.*; scrupulosity; suspicion etc. (*unbelief*) 485; inconvincibility.

unbeliever, skeptic *or* sceptic, miscreant [*archaic*], doubting Thomas, disbeliever, agnostic, infidel, misbeliever, nullifidian, minimifidian, zendik [*Oriental*], freethinker, Pyrrhonist etc. (*irreligion*) 989; heretic etc. (*heterodox*) 984.

v. **be incredulous** etc. *adj.;* distrust etc. (*disbelieve*) 485; refuse to believe; shut one's eyes to, shut one's ears to; turn a deaf ear to; hold aloof; ignore, *nullius jurare in verba magistri* [*L.*].

adj. **incredulous**, skeptical *or* sceptical, dissenting, unbelieving, inconvincible; hard of belief, shy of belief; suspicious, scrupulous, distrustful, disposed to doubt, indisposed to believe; heterodox.

488. Assent

n. **assent**, assentment [*archaic*]; acquiescence, admission; nod; accord, concord, concordance; agreement etc. 23; affirmance, affirmation; recognition, acknowledgment, avowal, recognizance [*rare*], confession, confession of faith.

unanimity, common consent, consensus, acclamation, chorus, *vox populi* [*L.*]; popular-, current- -belief, -opinion; public opinion; concurrence etc. (*of causes*) 178; cooperation etc. (*voluntary*) 709.

ratification, confirmation, corroboration, approval, acceptance, visa, *visé* [*F.*]; indorsement etc. (*record*) 551.

consent etc. (*compliance*) 762.

affirmant, assentant [*obs.*], professor [*esp. in relig.*], confirmist, consenter, covenantor, subscriber, indorser *or* endorser; upholder etc. (*auxiliary*) 711.

v. **assent**; give-, yield-, nod- assent; acquiesce; agree etc. 23; receive, accept, accede, accord, concur, lend oneself to, consent, coincide, reciprocate, go with; be at one with etc. *adj.;* go along with, chime in with, strike in with, close with; echo, enter into one's views, agree in opinion; vote for, give one's voice for; recognize; subscribe-, conform-, defer- to; say -yes, -ditto, -amen, -aye- to.

go-, float-, swim- with the stream; float with the current; get on the band wagon [*slang*]; be in the fashion, join in the chorus; be in every mouth.

arrive at-, come to- -an understanding, -terms, -an agreement.

acknowledge, own, admit, allow, avow, confess; concede etc. (*yield*) 762; come round to; abide by; permit etc. 760.

confirm, affirm; ratify, approve, indorse, visa, *visé* [*F.*], countersign; corroborate etc. 467.

adj. **assenting** etc. *v.;* of one -accord, -mind; of the same mind, affirmant, assentaneous [*rare*], assentant [*obs.*], at one with, agreed, acquiescent, content; willing etc. 602.

uncontradicted, unchallenged, unquestioned, uncontroverted.

carried-, agreed- -*nem. con.* [*L.*] etc. *adv.;* unanimous; agreed on all hands, carried by acclamation.

affirmative etc. 535.

adv. **yes**, yea, aye *or* ay, true; good; well; how true, very -well, -true; well and good; granted; even so, just so; to be sure, as you say, sure, surely, assuredly, "thou hast said"; truly, exactly, precisely, that's just it, indeed, certainly, certes [*archaic*], *ex concesso* [*L.*], of course, unquestionably, no doubt, doubtless.

be it so; so be it, so let it be; so mote it be, with all one's heart; amen; willingly etc. 602.

affirmatively, in the affirmative.

unanimously, *unâ voce* [*L.*], by common consent, in chorus, to a man; with one -consent, -voice, -accord; *nem. con.* [*L.*]; *nemine contradicente* [*L.*], *nemine dissentiente* [*L.*], without a dissentient voice; as one man, one and all, on all hands.

489. Dissent

n. **dissent**, nonconsent, discordance etc. (*disagreement*) 24; difference-, diversity- of opinion.

nonconformity etc. (*heterodoxy*) 984; protestantism, recusancy, schism; disaffection; secession etc. 624; recantation etc. 607.

dissension etc. (*discord*) 713; discontent etc. 832; caviling, wrangling, ergotism [*rare*].

protest; contradiction etc. (*denial*) 536; noncompliance etc. (*rejection*) 764.

dissentient, dissenter, nonconformist; sectary, separatist, recusant, schismatic, protestant; heretic etc. (*heterodoxy*) 984.

v. **dissent**, nonconsent, demur; call in question etc. (*doubt*) 485; differ in opinion, disagree, agree to differ; say no etc. 536; refuse -assent, -to admit; cavil, wrangle, ergotize [*rare*], protest, raise one's voice against, repudiate; contradict etc. (*deny*) 536.

have no notion of, differ *toto coelo* [*L.*], revolt at, revolt from the idea.

shake the head, shrug the shoulders; look askance *or* askant.

secede; recant etc. 607.

adj. **dissenting** etc. *v.;* negative etc. 536; dissident, dissentient; unconsenting etc. (*refusing*) 764; noncontent, nonjuring; protestant, recusant; unconvinced, unconverted.

unavowed, unacknowledged; out of the question.

unwilling etc. 603; extorted; discontented etc. 832.

sectarian, sectary [*rare*], denominational, schismatic; heterodox; intolerant.

adv. **no** etc. 536; at variance with, at issue with; under protest.

int. **God forbid**! not for the world! I'll be hanged if! [*colloq.*]; not another word! no, sirree!; not if I know it! I beg to differ; never tell me! pardon me.

490. Knowledge

n. **knowledge**; cognizance, cognition, cognoscence [*obs.*]; acquaintance, experience, ken, privity, insight, familiarity; comprehension, apprehension; recognition; appreciation etc. (*judgment*) 480; intuition; conscience, consciousness; perception, apperception, precognition; acroamatics.

system-, body- of knowledge; science, philosophy, pansophism, pansophy; acroama; theory, aetiology *or* etiology; circle of the sciences; pandect, doctrine, body of doctrine; cyclopedia *or* cyclopaedia, encyclopedia *or* encyclopaedia, circle of knowledge; school etc. (*system of opinions*) 484.

tree of knowledge; republic of letters etc. (*language*) 560.

enlightenment, light; glimpse, inkling, glimmer, glimmering, dawn; scent, suspicion; impression etc. (*idea*) 453; discovery etc. 480a.

learning, erudition, lore, scholarship, reading, letters; literature; book madness; book learning, bookishness; bibliomania, bibliolatry; information, general information; store of knowledge etc.; education etc. (*teaching*) 537; culture, *Kultur* [*Ger.*], cultivation, menticulture, attainments; acquirements, mental acquisitions; accomplishments; proficiency; practical knowledge etc. (*skill*) 698; liberal education, higher education; dilettantism; rudiments etc. (*beginning*) 66.

deep-, profound-, solid-, accurate-, acroatic-, acroamatic-, vast-, extensive-, encyclopedic- -knowledge, -learning; omniscience, pantology.

march of intellect; progress-, advance- of -science, -learning; schoolmaster abroad.

v. **know**, ken [*dial.*], scan, wot [*archaic*]; wot of [*archaic*], be aware of etc. *adj.*; ween [*archaic*], weet [*obs.*], trow [*archaic*]; have, possess.

conceive; apprehend, comprehend; take, realize, understand, savvy [*slang*], be wise to [*slang*], appreciate; fathom, make out; recognize, discern, perceive, see, get a sight of, experience.

know full well; have-, possess- some knowledge of; be *au courant* [*F.*] etc. *adj.*; have in one's head, have at one's fingers' ends; know by -heart, -rote; be master of; *connaître le dessous*

des cartes [*F.*], know what's what [*colloq.*] etc. 698.

discover etc. 480a; see one's way.

learn, come to one's knowledge etc. (*information*) 527.

adj. **knowing** etc. *v.*; cognitive; acroamatic *or* acroamatical, apperceptive, appercipient.

aware of, cognizant of, conscious of; acquainted with, made acquainted with; privy to, no stranger to; *au fait* [*F.*], *au courant* [*F.*]; in the secret; up to [*colloq.*], alive to; behind the -scenes, -curtain; let into; apprised of, informed of; undeceived.

proficient in, versed in, read in, forward in, strong in, at home in; conversant with, familiar with.

educated, erudite, instructed, learned, lettered; well-informed, well-versed, well-read, well-grounded, well-educated; enlightened, shrewd, *savant* [*F.*], bluestocking, high-brow [*slang*], bookish, scholastic, solid, profound, deep-read, book-learned, aetiological *or* etiological, pansophic *or* pansophical; accomplished etc. (*skillful*) 698; omniscient; self-taught, self-educated, autodidactic; self-made.

known etc. *v.*; ascertained, well-known, recognized, received, notorious, noted; proverbial; familiar, -as household words, -to every schoolboy; hackneyed, trite, commonplace.

knowable, cognizable, cognoscible.

adv. to-, to the best of- one's knowledge; as every schoolboy knows.

490a. Astronomy

n. **astronomy**, cosmogony, interpretational astronomy, observational astronomy, descriptive astronomy, astrometry, geometrical astronomy, celestial mechanics; astrophysics, astrionics, radio astronomy, solar radio astronomy; astrobiology; planetology, heliography, actinometry, areography, cometography, astrography; celestial navigation, astrogation, nautical astronomy.

Ptolemaic system; Copernican system; evolutionary theory of the universe, expanding universe hypothesis, nebular hypothesis, collision hypothesis; planetismal hypothesis, protoplanet hypothesis; Lorentz-Fitzgerald contraction theory; infinity of the universe; Newton's universal laws of motion; Bode's law; Kepler's laws; Fechner's law; fission theory.

universe, cosmos, metagalaxy; firmament, space, deep space, interplanetary space, intergalactic space, interstellar space; lunar space, solar space.

solar system; planet; inner planets, outer planets; minor planets, major planets; inferior planets, superior planets; Mercury, Venus, Earth, Mars, Jupiter, Saturn, Uranus, Neptune, Pluto; evening star, morning star; satellite; asteroid, planetoid; comet (nucleus, coma, tail), periodic comets (Encke, Giacobini-Zinner, Pons-Winnecke, Biela, Faye, Arend, Westphal, Olbers, Halley, Herschel-Rigollet), comet group, comet family.

meteor, fire ball, bolide; meteor shower, Aquarids, Arietids, Draconids, Geminids, Leonids, Perseids; micrometeorite; meteorite, aerolite, achrondite, siderite, ataxite, siderolite.

sun; photosphere, sunspots, granules, faculae, plages, maculae; M regions; reversing layer; chromosphere, flocculi, spicules; corona, K corona, F corona; prominences, jets; limb; aureole; halo; Zeeman effect.

moon, new moon, first quarter, crescent moon, half-moon, last quarter gibbous moon, full moon; harvest moon, hunter's moon; lunar plains *or* maria *or* seas (Mare Foecunditatis, Mare Nectaris, Mare Crisium, Mare Tranquillitatis, Mare Serenitatis, Mare Imbrium, Oceanus Procellarum, Mare Nubium, Mare Humorum), lunar mountain ranges, lunar rays, lunar rills, lunar craters (Alphonsus, Archimedes, Aristarchus, Aristoteles, Arzachel, Bullialdus, Catharina, Clavius, Copernicus, Cyrillus, Eratosthenes, Furnerius, Gassendi, Grimaldi, Kepler, Langrenus, Maginus, Maurolycus, Petavius, Plato, Proclus, Ptolemaeus, Schickard, Theophilus, Tycho).

star, circumpolar star, double star, binary star, lucid star, lucida, faint companion star, astrometric companion, multiple star, nova, supernova, Kepler's star; Population I stars, Population II stars; main sequence stars; dwarf, subdwarf, white dwarf, subgiant, giant, red giant, blue giant, supergiant; variable star, Cepheid variables, RR Lyrae variables, irregular variables, eclipsing variables, Mira-type stars; high velocity stars; star cluster, galactic cluster, globular cluster, moving cluster; Hertzsprung-Russell diagram, color-magnitude diagram, color index; magnitude, apparent magnitude, absolute magnitude, bolometric magnitude; absolute luminosity, period-luminosity relation; Messier number.

[stars] Achernar, Acrux, Adhara, Albireo, Alcor, Aldebaran, Algol, Alioth, Alkaid, Alphard, Alphecca, Alpheratz, Altair, Antares, Arcturus, Bellatrix, Benetnasch, Betelgeuse, Canopus, Capella, Caph, Castor, Cor Caroli, Deneb,

Deneb Kaitos, Denebola, Dubhe, Fomalhaut, Hamal, Kaus Australis, Kochab, Marfak, Markab, Megrez, Merak, Mira, Mizar, Phad, Polaris, Pollux, Procyon, Rasalhague, Regulus, Rigel, Rigil Kentaurus, Saiph, Shaula, Sirius, Spica, Thuban, Vega; (constellations) Andromeda, Aquarius, Aquila, Ara, Aries, Auriga, Boötes, Canes Venatici, Canis Major, Canis Minor, Capricornus, Carina, Cassiopeia, Centaurus, Cepheus, Cetus, Columba, Corona Borealis, Corvus, Crux, Cygnus, Delphinus, Draco, Eridanus, Gemini, Grus, Hercules, Hydra, Hydrus, Leo, Lepus, Libra, Lupus, Lyra, Musca, Ophiuchus, Orion, Pavo, Pegasus, Perseus, Phoenix, Puppis, Sagitta, Sagittarius, Scorpius, Serpens, Taurus, Triangulum, Triangulum Australe, Tucana, Ursa Major, Ursa Minor, Vela, Virgo.

nebulae, galactic nebulae, bright nebulae, dark nebulae, planetary nebulae, diffuse nebulae; Orion Nebula, Coal Sack Nebula, Loop Nebula; extragalactic nebulae, external galaxy, galaxy, spiral galaxy, barred spiral galaxy, elliptical galaxy, irregular galaxy; galactic cluster; galactic window; Milky Way; Magellanic Clouds, Andromeda Nebula.

celestial sphere; celestial equator, celestial poles, celestial meridian, antimeridian, zenith, nadir, vertical circle, diurnal circle, horizon, azimuth; hour angle, hour circle; amplitude; altitude, altitude circle, altitude difference; declination; apex, antapex; culmination; astronomical latitude, celestial latitude, astronomical longitude, celestial longitude; ecliptic; right ascension; equinox, autumnal equinox, vernal equinox; solstice, summer solstice, winter solstice.

celestial motion; proper motion; rotation; revolution; orbit, perihelion, aphelion, apogee, perigee; inclination, perturbation; libration; precession, nutation; acceleration, deceleration; antecedence; arc of progression, arc of retrogression; anomaly; inequality; daily aberration, annual aberration.

transit; occultation; immersion; eclipse, annular eclipse, partial eclipse, total eclipse, umbra, penumbra; conjunction, inferior conjunction, synodic period, sidereal period.

gravity; acceleration of gravity, g; antigravity; barycenter; galactic center; atmospheric tides.

[instruments] accelerometer; astrolabe; astronomical triangle; barograph, barometer; chronometer, chronograph, astronomical clock; helioscope, spectrohelioscope, spectroheliograph, coronagraph, heliometer, magnetograph; illuminometer; sextant; thermocouple;

157

spectroscope, spectrograph, spectrobolometer, micrometer; telescope, astronomical telescope, meridian circle telescope, equatorial telescope; reflecting telescope, Newtonian telescope, coelostat; refracting telescope; radio telescope; astronomical observatory; planetarium.

490b. Chemistry

n. **chemistry**, general chemistry, inorganic chemistry, organic chemistry, analytical chemistry (qualitative analysis, quantitative analysis), biological chemistry *or* biochemistry, radiochemistry *or* nuclear chemistry, theoretical chemistry *or* physical chemistry.

matter, organic matter, inorganic matter; homogeneous matter, substance, stable substance, unstable substance, volatile substance, amorphous substance, crystalline substance; element, active element, inactive element, nonmetal, metal, alkali metal, alkaline earth metal, amphoteric element; free state, combined state; allotropic forms, allotropy.

[chemical notation] symbol, coefficient, subscript, radical; formula, equation, word equation, skeleton equation, balanced equation, ionic equation; molecular weight, formula weight; valence, negative valence, positive valence, zero valence.

mixture; compound, binary compound, ternary compound, electrovalent compound, ionic compound, chain compound, covalent compound; covalent linkage; law of definite proportions; heat of formation, heat of neutralization.

chemical change, chemical reaction, chemical combination, decomposition, displacement, double decomposition; irreversible reaction, completion, reversible reaction, complete reaction, incomplete reaction; endothermic reaction, exothermic reaction, photochemical reaction; dynamic equilibrium, equilibrium constant, ionization constant, solubility product constant; common ion effect; catalyst *or* catalytic agent; law of conservation of matter, law of mass action.

ionization *or* dissociation, nonionization, electrolytic dissociation; electrolyte, nonelectrolyte; electrolysis; ion, positive ion *or* cation, negative ion *or* anion; positive electrode *or* anode, negative electrode *or* cathode; Ionization Theory *or* Theory of Electrolytic Dissociation; activity coefficient.

acid, binary acid, ternary acid, monobasic acid, dibasic acid, tribasic acid; weak acid (*or* base), strong acid (*or* base); base, alkali, monoacid

base, diacid base, triacid base; salt, binary salt, ternary salt, acid salt, basic salt, normal salt, double salt, complex salt; neutralization, hydrolysis, titration; indicators, litmus, phenolphthalein, methyl orange, methyl violet, alizarin yellow; hydrogen ion concentration *or* pH.

ascorbic acid, benzoic acid, boric acid, butyric acid, carbolic acid, citric acid, formic acid, gallic acid, hydrochloric acid, hydrofluoric acid, lactic acid, malic acid, nitric acid, oleic acid, oxalic acid, phosphoric acid, picric acid, prussic acid, salicylic acid, stearic acid, sulfuric acid, tannic acid, tartaric acid; (bases) ammonium hydroxide, calcium hydroxide, magnesium hydroxide, potassium hydroxide, sodium hydroxide; (salts) ammonium chloride, bismuth subnitrate, calcium carbonate, potassium chloride, potassium nitrate, sodium acetate, sodium acid phosphate, sodium bicarbonate, sodium bisulfite, sodium chloride.

solution, gaseous solution, liquid solution, solid solution, dilute solution, concentrated solution, unsaturated solution, supersaturated solution; molar solution, molal solution, normal solution, standard solution; solute, solvent; seeding, precipitate, filtration; suspension.

crystal, ionic crystal, atom crystal, molecule crystal; crystal symmetry, isometric crystal (cube), hexagonal crystal, tetragonal crystal, orthorhombic crystal, monoclinic crystal, triclinic crystal; water of crystallization *or* water of hydration; hydrate, anhydrous compound; decrepitation, sublimation; deliquescent substance, hygroscopic substance, efflorescent substance.

oxide, metallic oxide *or* basic anhydride, nonmetallic oxide *or* acid anhydride, amphoteric oxide, neutral oxide, suboxide, saline oxide, peroxide; oxidation, rapid oxidation, combustion, spontaneous combustion, slow oxidation, organic oxidation, inorganic oxidation; oxidizing agent; reduction, reducing agent; kindling temperature, temperature of combustion, heat of combustion.

hydrocarbons; aliphatic hydrocarbons, saturated *or* methane series (methane, ethane, propane), unsaturated series, ethylene series (ethylene, propylene, butylene), acetylene series (acetylene, allylene); aromatic hydrocarbons, benzene series (benzene, toluene, xylene), naphthalene series (naphthalene), anthracene series (anthracene).

[hydrocarbon derivatives] halogen substitution products (chloroform *or* trichloromethane); alcohols, monohydroxy alcohols, dihydroxy alcohols (methyl alcohol, ethyl alcohol); aldehydes (formaldehyde, acetaldehyde); ketones (acetone, butanone); organic acids; ethers (diethyl ether); esters (methyl acetate); carbohydrates (sugars, starches, cellulose); proteins (albumin, globulin, glutelin).

colloid, natural colloid, lyophobic colloid, hydrophobic colloidal system, lyophilic colloid, hydrophilic colloidal system; sol, gel; dispersed medium, dispersing medium; condensation *or* coagulation method, dispersion method (mechanical disintegration, peptization, emulsification); emulsion, temporary emulsion, permanent emulsion; emulsifying agent *or* protective colloid; miscible liquids, nonmiscible liquids; dialysis, adsorption, flotation process, Cottrell process, cataphoresis, electroendosmosis.

[apparatus] aspirator, blowpipe, Büchner funnel, Bunsen burner, burette *or* buret, crucible, disiccator, distiller, etna, Kipp apparatus, matrass, mortar, pestle, reagent bottle, receiver, retort, ring, ring stand, still, test tube.

490c. Geology

n. **geology**, mineralogy, petrology, stratigraphy, paleontology, structural geology, glacial geology, geomorphology, oceanography, meteorology, geophysics, terrestrial magnetism, seismology, geodesy, geochemistry, petroleum geology, economic geology, engineering geology, hydrology.

crystal, crystallization; euhedral crystal, subhedral crystal, anhedral crystal; crystal symmetry, isometric system, hexagonal system, tetragonal system, orthorhombic system, monoclinic system, triclinic system.

minerals, amphibole group, feldspar group, mica group, pyroxene group; hornblende, apatite, azurite, bauxite, bornite, calcite, carnotite, cassiterite, chalcopyrite, chert, chlorite, chromite, copper, corundum, diamond, dolomite, epidote, microcline, orthoclase, albite, labradorite, anorthite, fluorite, galena, garnet, gold, graphite, gypsum, halite, hematite, kyanite, limonite, magnetite, malachite, biotite, lepidolite, muscovite, olivine, pyrite, augite, pyrrhotite, quartz, serpentine, sillimanite, sphalerite, staurolite, sulfur, talc, tourmaline.

[properties of minerals], specific gravity, cleavage, hardness, fracture, luster (adamantine luster, vitreous luster, resinous luster, greasy luster, pearly luster, silky luster), color, streak, taste, radio-activity, magnetism, opalescence, fluorescence; twinning.

[gross features of earth's crust] continent, continental shield, young folded mountain belt; zone of transition, continental margin, continental shelf, continental slope, continental rise; island arcs; ocean basin, deep oceanic crust, mid-ocean ridges; ocean currents; drift, tide, tidal current, wave, breaker, surf, sea, ground swell.

earthquake, shallow earthquake, intermediate earthquake, deep earthquake, volcanic earthquake; seismism; elastic rebound, foreshock, aftershock; shock wave, P wave *or* dilational wave *or* compressional wave *or* longitudinal wave, S wave *or* shear wave *or* transverse wave; Rayleigh wave; seismograph, seismometer, seismogram, accelerograph.

[deformation of earth's crust] isostasy; epeirogeny, uplifting, downwarping; orogeny, mountain building; diastrophism, confining pressure, stress, strain; fold, anticline, sycline, dome, basin, monocline; fault, fault plane, slickensides, hanging-wall side, foot-wall side, strike-slip movement, dip-slip movement, oblique-slip movement, normal fault, reverse fault, scissors fault, transverse fault, thrust fault, fault scarp, graben, horst, klippe, nappe *or* decke; fracture, tension fracture, shear fracture, rock cleavage; unconformity.

metamorphism, rock flowage; granulation, recrystallization, recombination; contact metamorphism, dynamic metamorphism; foliated metamorphic rock, nonfoliated metamorphic rock; slates, schists, gneisses, phyllites, marble, quartzite, hornfels, amphiboles.

volcano, cinder cone, lava cone, composite cone; shield volcano, flood basalt; vent, fumarole, solfatara, spatter cone, caldera; volcanism, eruption, explosion, expulsion, lava flow; (pyroclastic materials) blocks, bombs, lapilli, ash, volcanic dust; gases; lava, basalt lavas, rhyolite lavas, andesite lavas.

igneous rock, magmas, basaltic magma, granitic magma; (discordant igneous intrusions) batholith, stock, dike; (concordant igneous intrusions) sill, laccolith, lopolith; aphanitic rock, phaneritic rock, porphyritic rock, glassy rock; granite, graphic granite, granite pegmatite, orbicular granite, syenite, diorite, gabbro, peridotite, dunite, pyroxene, hornblendite, felsite, basalt, dolerite, obsidian, pitchstone, pumice, scoria; pyroclastic debris, tuff, agglomerate, volcanic breccia.

sedimentary rock; marine environment, transitional environment, continental environment; residual deposits, transported deposits; mechanical deposition, chemical deposition, organic deposition; rudaceous rocks, arenaceous rocks, silty rocks, argillaceous rocks, chemically deposited siliceous rocks, carbonate rocks, chemically deposited ferruginous rocks, salt rocks, organically deposited siliceous rocks, calcareous rocks, phosphatic rocks, organically deposited ferruginous rocks, carbonaceous rocks; conglomerate, breccia; sandstone, arkose, graywacke; siltstone, loess; mudstone, shale; sinter, chert-flint; tufa, travertine, oölitic limestone, dolostone, lithographic limestone; ironstone, caliche, gypsum, anhydrite, halite; radiolarian ooze, diatom ooze; fossiliferous limestone, chalk, marl; rock phosphates, guano; bog iron ore; coal.

erosion, weathering; mechanical weathering, thermal contraction *and* expansion, unloading, crystal growth, freezing; chemical weathering, oxidation, hydration, carbonation; (specialized erosion) deflation, corrasion, abrasion, impact, corrosion, hydraulicking, quarrying, plucking, solution, slump, rolling, sliding, dislodgement, falling; transportation; deposition.

[wind erosion] undercut hill, cave rock, table, mushroom rock, ventifact, desert pavement, lag gravel; (running water erosion) river valley, pediment, peneplain, river terrace, wadi, pothole; (glacial erosion) striation, groove, drumlin, crescentic mark, u-shaped valley, truncated spur, hanging valley, cirque, fiord, col, arête, horn; (ground water erosion) cave, sinkhole, karst topography; (mass movement erosion) slide scar, surface subsidence; (ocean erosion) cliff, terrace, guyot, stack, arch, sea cave, notch.

geologic time, era, period, epoch, age; rock system, rock series, rock stage; Precambrian Era; Paleozoic Era, Cambrian Period, Ordovician Period, Silurian Period, Devonian Period, Mississippian Period, Pennsylvanian Period, Permian Period; Mesozoic Era, Triassic Period, Jurassic Period, Cretaceous Period; Cenozoic Era, Paleogene Period, Paleocene Epoch, Eocene Epoch, Oligocene Epoch, Neogene Period, Miocene Epoch, Pliocene Epoch, Pleistocene Epoch.

490d. Physics

n. **physics**, classical physics, modern physics; mechanics (kinematics, dynamics, statics, hydrostatics, hydrodynamics, hydraulics), heat (thermometry, calorimetry, thermodynamics), sound, acoustics, light, optics, spectroscopy, electricity (electrostatics, electronics), magnetism; high-energy physics *or* elementary-particle physics, nuclear physics, atomic physics, molecular physics, solid-state physics, physics of liquids, physics of gases, plasma physics, biophysics, low-temperature physics, mathematical physics, theoretical physics, space physics.

atom, neutral atom, ion, nucleus, atomic number, atomic weight, mass number, isobar, isotope; elementary particles *or* subatomic particles; hyperons, nucleons, mesons, leptons, photons; proton, neutron, electron, positron; element; molecule; chemical change, nuclear change, physical change.

matter; solid, liquid, gas, extension *or* volume, mass, weight, density, fluid; specific gravity, impenetrability; elasticity, stress, strain, elastic limit; malleability, ductility; adhesion, cohesion, surface tension, capillarity, diffusion, osmosis, Brownian movement, buoyancy, viscosity; pressure, atmospheric pressure, air pressure; Hooke's law, kinetic theory of matter *or* molecular theory of matter, Pascal's law, Archimedes' principle, Bernoulli's principle; pycnometer, hydrometer, barometer, aneroid barometer, barograph, altimeter, manometer.

fusion, heat of fusion, melting, melting point; freezing, freezing point; regelation; vaporization, heat of vaporization; boiling, boiling point; evaporation, dew point, humidity, absolute humidity, relative humidity; sublimation, volatile liquid *or* solid; condensation *or* liquefaction, critical temperature, critical pressure, vapor; distillation, fractional distillation, distillate.

motion, rectilinear motion, curvilinear motion, circular motion, projectile motion, rotation *or* rotary motion, precession, revolution; velocity, terminal velocity, acceleration, speed, momentum, impulse, inertia; Newton's laws of motion; projectile, trajectory; pendulum, simple pendulum, compound pendulum, compensation pendulum, seconds pendulum; center of percussion; oscillation *or* vibration, amplitude, period, frequency.

force, centrifugal force, centripetal force, parallel forces, couple, component forces, effective component, ineffective component, resultant force; friction, coefficient of friction; equilibrant, equilibrium; resolution of forces, composition of forces, moment of force *or* torque; vector, vector quantity, scalar quantity; dyne, poundal, slug, newton; gravitation, gravity; free fall; Newton's law of universal gravitation.

work; foot-pound, foot-poundal; gram-centimeter, kilogram-meter; erg, joule; power, horsepower; energy, potential energy, kinetic energy; law of conservation of energy.

machines, simple machine, compound machine; inclined plane, screw, wedge, lever and fulcrum, wheel and axle, pulley; mechanical advantage, ideal mechanical advantage, actual mechanical advantage; efficiency, input, output.

[heat] conduction, conductor, conductometer; insulator, convection; radiation; law of heat exchange, Newton's law of cooling; expansion, linear expansion, coefficient of linear expansion, differential expansion; bimetallic bar, compound bar, thermostat; pressure coefficient of gases, general gas law, Boyle's law, Charles's law, Gay-Lussac's law; standard conditions, standard pressure, standard temperature; absolute zero; heat engine, internal-combustion engine, external-combustion engine, turbine; Joule's equivalent; temperature, degree; thermometer, absolute scale, Kelvin scale, Fahrenheit scale, centigrade scale; foot-pound-second system, centimeter-gram-second system; British thermal unit, btu; calorie, kilogram-caloric; specific heat.

[sound] wave, wavelength, sound wave, longitudinal wave (condensation, rarefaction); transverse wave (crest, trough); pitch, intensity, loudness; bel, decibel; beat, echo, reverberation; interference, resonance; frequency, audio frequency, ultrasonic frequency, infrasonic frequency.

[musical sound] tone, fundamental tone, overtone, quality, major chord, musical interval; consonance, dissonance; noise; musical scale, chromatic scale or tempered scale, diatonic scale; standing wave, node, antinode, loop, segment.

[light] luminosity, incandescence, fluorescence, illuminated body; opaque body, translucent body, transparent body; shadow, umbra, penumbra; photometry, photometer; luminous intensity, candle power, candle, foot-candle, lumen, illumination; quantum, quantum theory; Einstein's special theory of relativity, Einstein's general theory of relativity; Doppler effect.

reflection, diffusion, angle of reflection, angle of incidence; image, real image, virtual image; magnification; mirror, concave mirror, convex mirror; center of curvature, radius of curvature, principal axis; focus, virtual focus, focal length, principal focus, focal plane; spherical aberration.

refraction, angle of refraction, index of refraction, critical angle; diffraction; convex lens or positive lens, concave lens or negative lens; optical center, optical density; achromatic lens, chromatic aberration; diopter.

color, primary colors, complementary colors; pigments, primary pigments; complementary pigments; monochromatic light, polychromatic light, polarized light, polarization; polarizer, analyzer.

spectrum; dispersion; electromagnetic spectrum, electromagnetic radiations (infrared rays, ultraviolet rays, X-rays, gamma rays); angstrom; continuous spectrum, absorption spectrum (Fraunhofer lines); bright-line spectrum, dark-line spectrum; spectroscope.

[magnetism], induced magnetism, residual magnetism; magnet, saturated magnet, temporary magnet, permanent magnet; lodestone, magnetic compass, dipping needle; magnetic retentivity; magnetic poles, south-seeking pole, north-seeking pole; magnetic line of force, magnetic field, magnetic flux, magnetic permeability, magnetic transparency; magnetic delination, isogonic line, agonic line; magnetic inclination, isoclinic line, magnetic equator, aclinic line.

[electricity], static electricity; electric current, direct current, D.C., alternating current, A.C.; induced current; eddy current; electromagnetism; electric field; circuit, parallel circuit, series circuit; electromotive force or e.m.f.; resistance, specific resistance or resistivity; reactance, inductive reactance, capacitive reactance; impedance; conduction, conductance, conductor; induction, electromagnetic induction, inductance; self-inductance; capacitance; electrolysis; dissociation; electroplating; electrolyte, nonelectrolyte, Ohm's law, Coulomb's law, inverse-square law, Lenz's law.

generator, motor; armature or keeper, commutator, brush, slip rings; electrophorus; capacitor or condenser; insulator or dielectric; transformer; primary coil, secondary coil; rectifier; rheostat, galvanoscope; oscillator, relay; shunt; electrode, anode or plate, cathode; electrolytic cell; Leyden jar, voltaic cell, storage cell.

coulomb, ohm, ampere, volt, henry, farad, watt; watt-hour, kilowatt-hour; electroscope, ammeter, galvanometer, voltmeter.

diode, triode, vacuum tube; cathode-ray tube, cathode rays; photoelectric cell, photoelectric effect; transistor.

[radioactivity], alpha particle, beta particle, gamma rays, cosmic rays; isotope, radioactive isotope; transmutation of elements; particle accelerator *or* atom smasher, betatron, cyclotron, synchrotron; nuclear reactor, uranium-graphite pile; atomic energy, nuclear energy; fission, chain reaction, critical mass; fusion, thermonuclear reaction.

491. Ignorance

n. **ignorance**, nescience, *tabula rasa* [*L.*], illiteracy, unlearnedness, crass ignorance, *ignorance crasse* [*F.*]; unacquaintance; unconsciousness etc. *adj.;* darkness, blindness; incomprehension; inexperience, simplicity.

sealed book, *terra incognita* [*L.*], virgin soil, unexplored ground; dark ages.

unknown quantities; *x, y, z.*

[imperfect knowledge] smattering, superficiality, half-learning, shallowness, sciolism, glimmering; bewilderment etc. (*uncertainty*) 475; incapacity.

[affectation of knowledge] pedantry, charlatanry, charlatanism; Philistine, *Philister* [*Ger.*].

v. **be ignorant** etc. *adj.;* not know etc. 490; know -not, -not what, -nothing of; have no -idea, -notion, -conception; not have the remotest idea.

ignore, be blind to; keep in ignorance etc. (*conceal*) 528.

see through a glass darkly; have a film over the eyes, have a glimmering etc. *n.;* wonder whether; not know what to make of etc. (*unintelligibility*) 519; not pretend to say, not take upon oneself to say.

adj. **ignorant**; nescient; unknowing, unaware, unacquainted, unapprised, unwitting, unweeting [*obs.*], unconscious; witless, weetless [*obs.*]; a stranger to; unconversant.

uninformed, uncultivated, unversed, uninstructed, untaught, uninitiated, untutored, unschooled, unscholarly, unguided, unenlightened; Philistine; behind the age.

shallow, superficial, green, rude, empty, half-learned, half-baked [*colloq.*], low-brow [*slang*]; illiterate; unread, uninformed, uneducated, unlearned, unlettered, unbookish; empty-headed; pedantic.

in the dark; benighted, belated; blinded, blindfold; hoodwinked; misinformed; *au bout de son latin* [*F.*], at the end of his tether, at fault; at

sea etc. (*uncertain*) 475; caught tripping, caught napping.

unknown, unapprehended, unexplained, unascertained, uninvestigated, unexplored, unheard of, unperceived; concealed etc. 528; novel.

adv. **ignorantly** etc. *adj.;* unawares; for anything one knows, for aught one knows; not that one knows.

int. God-, Heaven-, the Lord-, nobody- knows!

492. Scholar

n. **scholar**, savant [*F.*], pundit *or* pandit [*India*], schoolman, professor, graduate, wrangler [*Cambridge Univ., Eng.*], academician, academist [*obs.*], doctor, fellow, don [*Eng. Univ. cant*], graduate, postgraduate, clerk [*archaic*]; *Artium Magister* [*L.*], A.M. *or* M.A., master of arts; *Artium Baccalaureus*, A.B. *or* B.A., bachelor of arts; bookman [*rare*], classicist, licentiate, gownsman; philosopher, philomath; scientist, connoisseur, sophist, sophister; linguist; etymologist, philologist; philologer [*now rare*]; lexicographer, glossographer, glossologist, lexicologist, scholiast, commentator, annotator; grammarian; *littérateur* [*F.*], *literati* [*L.*], *dilettanti* [*It.*], illuminati; mayven [*Jew.*], munshi *or* moonshee [*India*], mullah [*Moslem*], moolvi [*India*], guru [*India*]; Hebraist, Hellenist, Graecist, Sanskritist; sinologist, sinologue.

bookworm, *helluo librorum* [*L.*], bibliophile, bibliophilist, bibliomaniac, blue-stocking [*colloq.*], *bas-bleu* [*F.*], high-brow [*slang*].

Admirable Crichton, Mezzofanti, "learned Theban" [*King Lear*], Dominie Sampson [*Guy Mannering*], Socrates.

learned man, literary man; *homo multarum literarum* [*L.*]; man of -learning, -letters, -education, -genius; giant of learning, colossus of knowledge, prodigy.

antiquarian, antiquary, archaeologist, Assyriologist, Egyptologist, sage etc. (*wise man*) 500.

pedant, doctrinaire; pedagogue, Dr. Pangloss; pantologist; instructor etc. (*teacher*) 540.

student, learner, classman, senior, junior, sophomore, freshman, pupil, schoolboy etc. (*learner*) 541.

adj. **learned** etc. 490; brought up at the feet of Gamaliel.

493. Ignoramus

n. **ignoramus**, illiterate, dunce, duffer, woodenhead [*colloq.*], bonehead [*slang*], solid ivory [*slang*], numskull [*colloq.*], wooden spoon [*Cambridge Univ., Eng., cant*]; no scholar.

sciolist, smatterer, dabbler, half scholar; charlatan; wiseacre.

novice, tenderfoot; greenhorn etc. (*dupe*) 547; plebe *or* pleb [*cant, U. S.*]; tyro etc. (*learner*) 541; lubber etc. (*bungler*) 701; fool etc. 501.

adj. **bookless,** shallow, simple, lumpish, dull, dumb [*colloq.*], dense, crass, imbecile; wise in his own conceit; ignorant etc. 491.

494. Truth

[object of knowledge]

n. **truth,** verity; fact, reality etc. (*existence*) 1; plain matter of fact; nature etc. (*principle*) 5; gospel; orthodoxy etc. 983*a*; authenticity; veracity etc. 543.

plain-, honest-, sober-, naked-, unalloyed-, unvarnished-, unqualified-, stern-, exact-, intrinsic- truth; *nuda veritas* [*L.*]; the very thing; not an illusion etc. 495; real Simon Pure; unvarnished tale; the truth, the whole truth and nothing but the truth; just the thing.

accuracy, exactitude; exactness, preciseness etc. *adj.;* precision, delicacy; rigor, mathematical precision, fidelity; clockwork precision etc. (*regularity*) 80; conformity to rule; nicety.

orthology; *ipsissima verba* [*L.*], the very words; realism.

v. **be true** etc. *adj.,* be the case; stand the test; have the true ring; hold good, hold true, hold water.

render true, prove true etc. *adj.;* substantiate etc. (*evidence*) 467.

get at the truth etc. (*discover*) 480*a*.

adj. **true,** real, actual etc. (*existing*) 1; veritable; certain etc.; 474; substantially-, categorically-true etc.; true -to the letter, -as gospel, -as steel, -to life, -to the facts; unimpeachable; veracious etc. 543; unrefuted, unconfuted; unideal, unimagined; realistic.

exact, accurate, definite, precise, well-defined, just, right, correct, strict, severe; close etc. (*similar*) 17; orthological, literal; rigid, rigorous; scrupulous etc. (*conscientious*) 939; religiously exact, punctual, punctilious, mathematical, scientific; faithful, constant, unerring; curious, particular, nice, meticulous, delicate, fine; clean-cut, clear-cut.

authentic, genuine, legitimate; orthodox etc. 983*a*; official, *ex officio* [*L.*].

pure, natural, sound, sterling, true-blue; unsophisticated, unadulterated, Simon-Pure [*colloq.*], unvarnished, uncolored; in its true colors.

valid, well-grounded, well-founded; solid, substantial, pukka *or* pucca *or* pakka [*Hind.*], tan-

gible; undistorted, undisguised; unaffected, unexaggerated, unromantic, unflattering.

adv. **truly** etc. *adj.;* verily, indeed, in reality; in very truth, in fact, as a matter of fact, to state the facts; beyond -doubt, -question; with truth etc. (*veracity*) 543; certainly etc. (*certain*) 474; actually etc. (*existence*) 1; in effect etc. (*intrinsically*) 5.

exactly etc. *adj.; ad amussim or adamussim* [*L*], verbatim, *verbatim et literatim* [*L.*]; word for word, literally, *literatim* [*L.*], *totidem verbis* [*L.*], *sic* [*L.*], to the letter, chapter and verse, *ipsissimis verbis* [*L.*]; *ad unguem* [*L.*]; to an inch; to a -nicety, -hair, -tittle, -turn, -T; *au pied de la lettre* [*F.*]; neither more nor less; in every respect, in all respects; *sous tous les rapports* [*F.*]; at any rate, at all events; strictly speaking.

495. Error

n. **error,** fallacy; misconception, misapprehension, misunderstanding; aberration, aberrance *or* aberrancy; inexactness etc. *adj.;* laxity; misconstruction etc. (*misinterpretation*) 523; anachronism; miscomputation etc. (*misjudgment*) 481; *non sequitur* [*L.*] etc. 477; misstatement, misreport; mumpsimus.

mistake; miss, fault, blunder, cross-purposes, oversight, misprint, erratum, corrigendum, slip, blot, flaw, loose thread; trip, stumble etc. (*failure*) 732; botchery etc. (*want of skill*) 699; slip of the tongue, *lapsus linguae* [*L.*]; slip of the pen, *lapsus calami* [*L.*], clerical error; bull etc. (*absurdity*) 497; Spoonerism, Malapropism, Leiterism [*U. S.*], Mrs. Partington; haplography.

delusion, illusion; false-, warped-, distorted-impression, -idea; bubble; self-deceit, self-deception; mists of error; exploded -notion, -idea, -superstition.

heresy etc. (*heterodoxy*) 984; hallucination etc. (*insanity*) 503; false light etc. (*fallacy of vision*) 443; dream etc. (*fancy*) 515; fable etc. (*untruth*) 546; bias etc. (*misjudgment*) 481; misleading etc. *v.*

v. **be erroneous** etc. *adj.*

mislead, misguide; lead astray, lead into error; cause error; beguile, misinform etc. (*misteach*) 538; delude; give a false -impression, -idea; falsify, misstate; deceive etc. 545; lie etc. 544.

err; be in error etc. *adj.,* be mistaken etc. *v.;* be deceived etc. (*duped*) 547; mistake, receive a false impression, deceive oneself; fall into-, lie under–, labor under- an error etc. *n.;* be in the wrong, blunder; misapprehend, misconceive, misunderstand, misreckon, miscount, miscalculate etc. (*misjudge*) 481.

play–, be- at cross purposes etc. (*misinterpret*) 523.

trip, stumble; lose oneself etc. (*uncertainty*) 475; go astray; fail etc. 732; be in the wrong box; take the wrong sow by the ear etc. (*misman-age*) 699; put the saddle on the wrong horse; reckon without one's host; take the shadow for the substance etc. (*credulity*) 486; dream etc. (*imagine*) 515.

adj. **erroneous**, untrue, false, devoid of truth, faulty, erring, fallacious, apocryphal, unreal, ungrounded, groundless; unsubstantial etc. 4; heretical etc. (*heterodox*) 984; unsound; illogical etc. 477.

inexact, unexact, inaccurate, incorrect; indefinite etc. (*uncertain*) 475.

illusive, illusory, delusive; mock, ideal etc. (*imaginary*) 515; spurious etc. 545; deceitful etc. 544; perverted.

controvertible, unsustainable, unsustained, unauthentic, unauthenticated, untrustworthy.

exploded, refuted, discarded.

mistaken etc. *v.;* in error, under an error etc. *n.;* tripping etc. *v.;* out, out in one's reckoning; aberrant; beside–, wide of- -the mark, –the truth; astray etc. (*at fault*) 475; on -a false, –the wrong- -scent, –trail; in the wrong box; at cross-purposes, all in the wrong; at sea, bewildered.

adv. more or less.

496. Maxim

n. **maxim**, aphorism; apothegm *or* apophthegm; dictum, saying, adage, saw, proverb, epigram, gnomic saying, gnome, sentence, mot [*Gallicism*], motto, word, byword, bromide, bromidium [*slang*], commonplace, moral, phylactery, protasis [*rare*].

wise–, sage–, received–, admitted–, recognized- maxim etc.; true–, common–, hackneyed–, trite–, commonplace- saying etc.

axiom, theorem, scholium, truism, postulate.

principle, principia; profession of faith etc. (*belief*) 484; settled principle, formula; reflection etc. (*idea*) 453; conclusion etc. (*judgment*) 480; golden rule etc. (*precept*) 697.

adj. **aphoristic**, aphorismic, aphorismatic, proverbial, phylacteric; axiomatic *or* axiomatical, gnomic *or* gnomical.

adv. as the saying is, as they say, as it was said by them of old.

497. Absurdity

n. **absurdity**, absurdness etc. *adj.;* imbecility etc. 499; alogy [*obs.*], comicality, nonsense, paradox, inconsistency; stultiloquy [*rare*], stultiloquence [*rare*], stultification, futility, nugacity.

blunder, muddle, bull; Irishism, Hibernicism; anticlimax, bathos; sophism etc. 477.

farce, galimatias, burlesque, parody, fiddle-faddle [*colloq.*], amphigory *or* amphigouri, rhapsody; farrago etc. (*disorder*) 59; *bêtise* [*F.*]; extravagance, romance; sciamachy.

pun, sell [*colloq.*], catch [*colloq.*], verbal quibble, macaronic composition, limerick, joke.

jargon, slipslop [*colloq.*], gibberish, balderdash, bombast, claptrap, fustian, twaddle etc. (*no meaning*) 517; exaggeration etc. 549; moonshine, stuff; mare's-nest, quibble, self-delusion.

tomfoolery, vagary, mummery, monkeyshine, monkey trick, *boutade* [*F.*], frisk, practical joke, escapade.

v. **play the fool** etc. 499; stultify, blunder, muddle; employ absurdity etc. *n.;* rhapsodize; romance, sell [*slang*], fiddle-faddle [*colloq.*]; talk nonsense, *parler à tort et à travers* [*F.*]; *battre la campagne* [*F.*]; *anemolia bazein* [*Gr.*]; be absurd etc. *adj.;* frisk, caper, joke, play practical jokes.

be the fool, be the goat [*colloq.*], bite [*colloq.*].

adj. **absurd**, nonsensical, farcical, preposterous, egregious, senseless, inconsistent, stultiloquent [*rare*], stulty [*obs.*], ridiculous, extravagant, quibbling; self-annulling, self-contradictory; paradoxical, macaronic *or* maccaronic, punning.

burlesque, foolish etc. 499; sophistical etc. 477; unmeaning etc. 517; amphigoric; without rhyme or reason; fantastic *or* fantastical, rhapsodic *or* rhapsodical, bombastic, high-flown.

int. fiddledeedee! pish! pooh! pooh-pooh! bah! stuff and nonsense! fiddle-faddle! bosh! come off! [*slang*].

498. Intelligence. Wisdom

n. **intelligence**, capacity, comprehension, understanding; cuteness [*colloq.*], sabe [*slang*], savvy [*slang*]; intellect etc. 450; nous [*colloq.*], docity [*dial.*], parts, sagacity, mother wit, wit, *esprit* [*F.*], gumption [*colloq.*], quick parts, grasp of intellect; acuteness etc. *adj.;* acumen, longheadedness, arguteness, subtility, subtlety, penetration, perspicacy [*obs.*], perspicacity, discernment, due sense of, good judgment; discrimination etc. 465; cunning etc. 702; refinement etc. (*taste*) 850.

head, brains, gray matter [*colloq.*], brain-stuff [*colloq.*], headpiece, upper story [*colloq.*], long head.

eagle -eye, –glance; eye of a lynx, eye of a hawk.

wisdom, sapience, sense; good–, common–, horse - [*colloq.*], plainsense; clear thinking, rationality, reason; reasonableness etc. *adj.*; judgment, solidity, depth, profundity, caliber *or* calibre; enlarged views; reach–, compass- of thought; enlargement of mind.

genius, lambent flame of intellect, inspiration, *Geist* [*Ger.*], fire of genius, heaven-born genius, soul; talent etc. (*aptitude*) 698.

[wisdom in action] prudence etc. 864; vigilance etc. 459; tact etc. 698; foresight etc. 510; sobriety, self-possession, *aplomb* [*F.*], ballast, mental poise, balance.

a bright thought, an inspiration, not a bad idea.

v. **be intelligent** etc. *adj.*; have all one's wits about one; be brilliant, be witty, scintillate, coruscate; understand etc. (*intelligible*) 518; catch–, take in- an idea; take a -joke, –hint.

penetrate; see through, see at a glance, see with half an eye, see far into, see through a millstone [*colloq.*]; discern etc. (*descry*) 441; foresee etc. 510.

discriminate etc. 465; know what's what [*colloq.*] etc. 698; listen to reason.

adj. **[applied to persons] intelligent**, quick of apprehension, keen, acute, alive, brainy [*colloq.*], awake, bright, quick, sharp; quick–, keen–, clear–, sharp- -eyed, –sighted, –witted; wide-awake; canny, sly, pawky [*dial.*], shrewd, astute; clear-headed; farsighted etc. 510; discerning, perspicacious, penetrating, piercing; argute; nimble-witted, needle-witted; sharp as a tack; alive to etc. (*cognizant*) 490; clever etc. (*apt*) 698; arch etc. (*cunning*) 702; *pas is bête* [*F.*]; acute etc. 682.

wise, sage, sapient [*often in irony*], sagacious, reasonable, rational, sound, in one's right mind, sensible, *abnormis sapiens* [*L.*], judicious, strong-minded.

impartial, unprejudiced, unbiased, unbigoted, unprepossessed; undazzled, unperplexed; of unwarped judgment, equitable, fair.

cool; cool–, long–, hard–, strong-headed; long-sighted, calculating, thoughtful, reflecting; solid, deep, profound.

prudent etc. (*cautious*) 864; sober, staid, solid; considerate, politic, wise in one's generation; watchful etc. 459; provident etc. (*prepared*) 673; in advance of one's age; wise as -a serpent, –Solomon, –Solon, –Nestor, –Mentor.

oracular; heaven-directed, heaven-born.

[applied to actions] **wise**, sensible, reasonable, judicious; well-judged, well-advised; prudent, politic; expedient etc. 646.

499. Imbecility. Folly

n. **imbecility**; want of intelligence etc. 498, want of intellect etc. 450; shallowness, unwisdom, silliness, foolishness etc. *adj.*; morosis, incapacity, vacancy of mind, poverty of intellect, clouded perception, poor head; apartments–, rooms–, space- to let [*all slang*]; nobody home [*slang*]; stupidity, insulsity [*rare*], stolidity; hebetude, dull understanding, meanest capacity, short-sightedness; incompetence etc. (*unskillfulness*) 699.

bias etc. 481; infatuation etc. (*insanity*) 503; one's weak side.

simplicity, puerility, babyhood; senility, dotage, anility, second childishness, fatuousness, fatuity; idiocy, idiotism, jobbernowlism [*colloq., Eng.*], driveling, driveling idiocy; senile dementia.

folly, frivolity, irrationality, trifling, ineptitude, nugacity, futility, inconsistency, lip wisdom, conceit; sophistry etc. 477; giddiness etc. (*inattention*) 458; eccentricity etc. 503; extravagance etc. (*absurdity*) 497; rashness etc. 863.

act of folly etc. 699.

v. **be imbecile** etc. *adj.*; have no -brains, –sense etc. 498; have a screw loose [*colloq.*].

trifle, drivel, *radoter* [*F.*], dote, ramble etc. (*madness*) 503; play the -fool, –monkey; take leave of one's senses; not see an inch beyond one's nose; stultify oneself etc. 699; talk nonsense etc. 497.

adj. **[applied to persons] unintelligent**, unintellectual, unreasoning; mindless, witless, reasonless, brainless; half-baked [*colloq.*], having no head etc. 498; not bright etc. 498; inapprehensive, thick [*colloq.*].

blockish, unteachable; Boeotian, Boeotic; bovine; ungifted, undiscerning, unenlightened, unwise, unphilosophical; apish, simious, simian.

weak–, addle–, puzzle–, blunder–, muddle- [*colloq.*], jolter–, jolt–, chowder–, pig–, beetle–, buffle- [*obs.*], chuckle–, mutton–, gross-headed; maggot-pated [*obs.*], beef-headed, beef-witted, fat-headed, fat-witted.

weak-minded, feeble-minded; dull–, shallow–, lack- brained; rattle- brained, –headed; saphead [*colloq.*], muddy-brained, addle-brained; half–, lean–, short–, shallow–, dull–, blunt-witted; shallow–, clod–, addle- pated; dim–, short- sighted; thick-skulled; thick-headed;

weak in the upper story [*colloq.*], inapprehensible, nutty [*slang*], batty [*slang*], loony [*slang*].

shallow, *borné* [*F.*], weak, wanting, soft [*colloq.*], sappy, spoony *or* spooney [*slang*]; dull, —as a beetle.

stupid, heavy, insulse [*rare*], obtuse, blunt, stolid, doltish; asinine; inapt etc. 699; prosaic etc. 843; hebetudinous, hebetate, hebete [*rare*].

childish, childlike; infantine, infantile, babyish, babish; puerile, senile, anile; simple etc. (*credulous*) 486; old-womanish.

imbecile, fatuous, idiotic, driveling; blatant, babbling; vacant; sottish; bewildered etc. 475.

foolish, silly, senseless, irrational, insensate, nonsensical, inept; maudlin.

narrow-minded etc. 481; bigoted etc. (*obstinate*) 606; giddy etc. (*thoughtless*) 458; rash etc. 863; eccentric etc. (*crazed*) 503.

[applied to actions] **foolish**, unwise, injudicious, improper, unreasonable, without reason, ridiculous, silly, stupid, asinine; ill-imagined, ill-advised, ill-judged, ill-devised; *mal entendu* [*F.*]; inconsistent, irrational, unphilosophical; extravagant etc. (*nonsensical*) 497; sleeveless [*obs.*], idle; useless etc. 645; inexpedient etc. 647; frivolous etc. (*trivial*) 643.

500. Sage

n. **sage**, wise man; master mind, master spirit of the age; longhead, thinker, philosopher.

authority, oracle, mentor, luminary, shining light, *esprit fort* [*F.*], *magnus Apollo* [*L.*], Solon, Solomon, Buddha, Confucius, Mentor, Nestor, the Magi; Seven Wise Men of Greece, Seven Sages, Philosophical Pleiad; "second Daniel."

savant [*F.*], pundit etc. (*scholar*) 492; wiseacre [*archaic or ironical*]; expert etc. 700; wizard etc. 994.

adj. **venerable**, venerated, reverenced, revered, honored, looked up to; authoritative, wise, oracular; erudite etc. (*knowledge*) 490; *emeritus* [*L.*].

501. Fool

n. **fool**, idiot, tomfool, wiseacre, simpleton, Simple Simon, moron, gaby [*colloq.*], witling, dizzard [*obs.*], donkey, ass; ninny, ninny hammer, chowderhead [*dial.*], jolterhead *or* jolthead, chucklehead [*colloq.*], dolt, booby, tomnoddy, loony [*slang*], looby, hoddy-doddy [*obs.*], noddy, nonny [*dial.*], noodle, nizy [*obs.*], owl, goose, imbecile; *radoteur* [*F.*], nincompoop [*colloq.*], *badaud* [*F.*], zany; trifler, babbler; pretty fellow; natural, *niais* [*F.*].

child, baby, infant, innocent, milksop, sop.

oaf, lout, loon *or* lown [*dial.*]; bullhead, blunderhead, addle-pate, addlebrain, addlehead [*all colloq.*]; blockhead, dullhead, bonehead [*slang*], rattlepate, dullard, doodle [*obs.*], calf [*colloq.*], colt, buzzard [*obs.*], block, put, stick [*colloq.*], stock, numps [*obs.*], tony [*obs.*]; logerhead, beetlehead, grosshead [*obs.*], muttonhead [*colloq.*], noodlehead, giddyhead [*colloq.*], numskull [*colloq.*], thickhead [*colloq.*], thick skull; lackbrain, shallowbrain; half-wit, lackwit; dunderpate; lunkhead.

sawney [*dial. Eng.*], clod, clodhopper; clodpoll, clodpate, clotpole *or* clotpoll [*obs.*], clotpate [*obs.*], soft *or* softy [*colloq. or slang*], saphead [*slang*], bull calf [*colloq.*], spoony *or* spooney [*slang*], gawk, gawky, gowk, Gothamite, lummox [*dial.*], rube; men of Boeotia, wise men of Gotham.

un sot à triple étage [*F.*], sot [*Scot.*], jobbernowl [*colloq., Eng.*], changeling [*archaic*], mooncalf, *gobe-mouches* [*F.*].

greenhorn etc. (*dupe*) 547; dunce etc. (*ignoramus*) 493; lubber etc. (*bungler*) 701; madman etc. 504; solid ivory.

one who -will not set the Thames on fire, —did not invent gunpowder, —does not exactly scintillate; *qui n'a pas inventé la poudre* [*F.*]; no conjurer; no Solomon.

dotard, driveler; old fogy *or* fogey [*colloq.*], old woman; crone, grandmother; cotquean [*archaic*], henhussy, betty [*contempt*].

502. Sanity

n. **sanity**; soundness etc. *adj.*; rationality, normalcy, normality, sobriety, lucidity, lucid interval; senses, sober senses, common sense, horse sense [*colloq.*], sound mind, *mens sana* [*L.*].

v. **be sane** etc. *adj.*; retain one's senses, —reason.

become sane etc. *adj.*; come to one's senses, sober down, cool down, get things into proportion, see things in proper perspective.

render sane etc. *adj.*; bring to one's senses, sober, bring to reason.

adj. **sane**, rational, normal, wholesome, right-minded, reasonable, *compos mentis* [*L.*], of sound mind; sound, sound-minded; lucid.

self-possessed; sober, sober-minded.

in one's -sober senses, —right mind; in possession of one's faculties.

adv. **sanely** etc. *adj.*; in reason, within reason, within bounds; according to the dictates of -reason, —common sense; in the name of common sense.

503. Insanity

n. **insanity**, lunacy; madness etc. *adj.*, mania, rabies, furor, mental alienation, aberration, amentia, paranoia; dementation, dementia, demency [*rare*], morosis, idiocy; *dementia a potu* [*L.*], delirium tremens, d.t.'s, the horrors [*colloq.*]; phrenitis, frenzy, raving, incoherence, wandering, delirium, calenture of the brain, delusion, hallucination; lycanthropy.

derangement; disordered -reason, -intellect; diseased-, unsound-, abnormal- mind; unsoundness.

vertigo, dizziness, swimming, sunstroke, *coup de soleil* [*F.*], siriasis.

oddity, eccentricity, twist, monomania; fanaticism, infatuation, craze; kleptomania, dipsomania; hypochondriasis etc. (*low spirits*) 837; melancholia, hysteria.

screw-, tile-, slate-loose; bee in one's bonnet, rats in the upper story, bats in the belfry, bee in the head [*all colloq.*].

dotage etc. (*imbecility*) 499.

v. **be** *or* **become insane** etc. *adj.*; lose one's senses, -reason, -faculties, -wits; go mad, run mad; rave, dote, ramble, wander; drivel etc. (*be imbecile*) 499; have a screw loose etc. *n.*, have a devil; *avoir le diable au corps* [*F.*]; lose one's head etc. (*be uncertain*) 475.

derange; render *or* drive mad etc. *adj.*; madden, dementate [*rare*], addle the wits, derange the head, infatuate, befool; turn the brain, turn one's head.

adj. **insane**, mad, lunatic; crazy, crazed, *aliéné* [*F.*], *non compos mentis* [*L.*], not right, dement [*rare*], dementate, cracked [*colloq.*], touched; bereft of reason; all-possessed, unhinged, unsettled in one's mind; insensate, reasonless, beside oneself, demented, maniacal, daft; frenzied, frenetic *or* frenetical; possessed, -with a devil; deranged, far gone, maddened, moonstruck; shatterpated, shatterbrained; madbrained, scatterbrained, crack-brained; off one's head.

Corybantic, dithyrambic; rabid, giddy, vertiginous, wild; haggard, mazed; flighty; distracted, distraught; bewildered etc. (*uncertain*) 475.

mad as a -March hare, -hatter; of unsound mind etc. *n.*; touched-, wrong-, not right- in one's -head, -mind, -wits, -upper story [*colloq.*]; out of one's -mind, -senses, -wits; not in one's right mind; nutty [*slang*].

odd, fanatical, infatuated, eccentric; hypochondriac, hyppish [*rare*], hipped *or* hypped [*colloq.*], hippish [*colloq.*].

delirious, light-headed, incoherent, rambling, doting, wandering; frantic, raving, stark mad, stark staring mad.

imbecile, silly, etc. 499.

adv. like one possessed.

504. Madman

n. **madman**, lunatic, maniac, bedlamite, candidate for Bedlam, raver, phrenetic, madcap; energumen [*eccl. antiq.*]; automaniac, monomaniac, dipsomaniac, kleptomaniac, paranoiac; hypochondriac etc. (*low spirits*) 837; crank, Tom o' Bedlam; nut [*slang*].

dreamer etc. 515; rhapsodist, seer, highflier *or* highflier [*obs.*], enthusiast, fanatic, *fanatico* [*It.*], *exalté* [*F.*], Don Quixote, Ophelia, Madge Wildfire.

idiot etc. 501.

Section 6. Extension of Thought

505. Memory

n. **memory**, remembrance; retentivity, retention, retentiveness; tenacity; tablets of the memory; readiness.

retentive-, tenacious-, trustworthy-, capacious-, faithful-, correct-, exact-, ready-, prompt- memory; Memory's halls, Memory's pictures.

recollection, reminiscence, recognition, recurrence, rememoration [*rare*], rememorance [*rare*]; retrospect, retrospection; "that inward eye" [Wordsworth]; afterthought.

reminder; suggestion etc. (*information*) 527; prompting etc. *v.*; hint, token of remembrance, memento, souvenir, keepsake, relic, memorandum (*pl.* memoranda); remembrancer, flapper; memorial etc. (*record*) 551; commemoration etc. (*celebration*) 883.

things to be remembered, memorabilia.

mnemonics; art of-, artificial- memory; *memoria technica* [*L.*]; mnemotechnics, mnemotechny; Mnemosyne.

aids to memory, jogger [*colloq.*], memorandum book, notebook, promptbook, engagement book.

fame, celebrity, renown, reputation etc. (*repute*) 873.

v. **remember**, mind [*obsoles.*], rememorate [*rare*]; retain the -memory, -remembrance- of; keep in view.

have-, hold-, bear-, carry-, keep-, retain- in *or* in the -thoughts, -mind, -memory,

–remembrance; be in–, live in–, remain in–, dwell in–, haunt–, impress- one's -memory, –thoughts, –mind.

sink in the mind; run in the head; not be able to get it out of one's head; be deeply impressed with; rankle etc. (*revenge*) 919.

recognize, bethink oneself, recall, call up, conjure up, retrace; look–, trace- -back, –backwards; think upon, look back upon; review; call–, recall–, bring- to -mind, –remembrance; carry one's thoughts back; rake up the past.

redeem from oblivion; keep the -memory alive, –wound green; *tangere ulcus* [*L.*]; keep the memory green, keep up the memory of; commemorate etc. (*celebrate*) 883.

recollect, recur to the mind; flash on the mind, flash across the memory.

remind; suggest etc. (*inform*) 527; prompt; put–, keep- in mind; fan the embers; call up, summon up; renew; *infandum renovare dolorem* [*L.*]; task–, tax–, jog–, flap–, refresh–, rub up–, awaken- the memory; pull by the sleeve; bring back to the memory, put in remembrance, memorialize.

memorize, commit to memory; con, –over; fix–, rivet–, imprint–, impress–, stamp–, grave–, engrave–, store–, treasure up–, bottle up–, embalm–, bury–, enshrine- in the memory; load–, store–, stuff–, burden- the memory with; get–, have–, learn–, know–, say–, repeat- by -heart, –rote; get–, drive- into one's head; bury in the mind; say one's lesson; repeat, –like a parrot; have at one's fingers' ends.

make a note of etc. (*record*) 551.

adj. **remembering**, remembered etc. *v.;* mindful, reminiscential; alive in memory; retained in the memory etc. *v.;* pent up in one's memory; fresh; green, –in remembrance; still vivid, rememorant [*rare*]; not–, never -to be erased, –to be forgotten; unforgettable *or* unforgetable; enduring, –in memory; unforgotten, present to the mind; within one's memory etc. *n.;* indelible; uppermost in one's thoughts; memorable etc. (*important*) 642; suggestive.

adv. **by heart**, *par coeur* [*F.*], by rote; without book, *memoriter* [*L.*].

in memory of; *in memoriam* [*L.*]; *memoria in aeterna* [*L.*].

506. Oblivion

n. **oblivion**; forgetfulness etc. *adj.;* obliteration etc. (552) of–, insensibility etc. (823) to- the past.

short–, treacherous–, loose–, slippery–, failing- memory; decay–, failure–, lapse- of memory;

mind–, memory- like a sieve; untrustworthy memory; waters of -Lethe, -oblivion; amnesia.

amnesty, general pardon.

v. **forget**; be forgetful etc. *adj.;* fall–, sink- into oblivion; have a short memory etc. *n.,* have no head.

forget one's own name, have on the tip of one's tongue, come in one ear and go out the other.

slip–, escape–, fade from–, die away from- the memory; lose, lose sight of.

efface etc. (552)–, discharge- from the memory; unlearn; consign to -oblivion, –the tomb of the Capulets; think no more of etc. (*turn the attention from*) 458; cast behind one's back, wean one's thoughts from; let bygones be bygones etc. (*forgive*) 918.

adj. **forgotten** etc. *v.;* unremembered, past recollection, bygone, out of mind; buried–, sunk- in oblivion; clean forgotten; gone out of one's -head, –recollection.

forgetful, oblivious, mindless, Lethean; insensible etc. (823) to the past; heedless.

507. Expectation

n. **expectation**, expectance, expectancy; anticipation, contingency, contingent, reckoning, calculation; foresight etc. 510; contemplation, prospection.

prospect, lookout [*chiefly Eng.*], perspective, horizon, vista; destiny etc. 152; futures [*stock exchange*].

suspense, waiting, abeyance; curiosity etc. 455; anxious–, ardent–, eager–, breathless–, sanguine- expectation; torment of Tantalus.

assurance, confidence, presumption, reliance; hope etc. 858; trust etc. (*belief*) 484; prognosis [*med.*], prognostic, prognostication; auspices etc. (*prediction*) 511.

v. **expect**; look -for, –out for, –forward to; hope for, anticipate; have in -prospect, –contemplation; keep in view; contemplate, promise oneself; not wonder at *or* if etc. 870.

wait for, tarry for, lie in wait for, watch for, bargain for; keep a -good, –sharp -lookout for; await; stand at "attention," abide, mark time, bide one's time, watch.

prick up one's ears, hold one's breath.

foresee etc. 510; prepare for etc. 673; forestall etc. (*be early*) 132; count upon etc. (*believe in*) 484; think likely etc. (*probability*) 472; bargain for; make one's mouth water.

predict, prognosticate, forecast; lead one to expect etc. (*predict*) 511; have in store for etc. (*destiny*) 152.

adj. **expectant**; expecting etc. *v.*; in expectation etc. *n.*; on the watch etc. (*vigilant*) 459; open-eyed, open-mouthed; agape, gaping, all agog; on tenterhooks, on tiptoe, on the tiptoe of expectation; *aux aguets* [*F.*]; ready, prepared, provided for, provisional, provident; curious etc. 455; looking forward to; on the rack.

expected etc. *v.*; long expected, foreseen; in prospect etc. *n.*; prospective, future, coming; in one's eye, in view, on the horizon; impending etc. (*destiny*) 152.

adv. **expectantly**; on the watch etc. *adj.*; in the event of; as a possible contingency; with muscles tense, on edge [*colloq.*]; with eyes–, with ears -strained; with ears pricked forward; *arrectis auribus* [*L.*]; with breathless expectation etc. *n.*, with bated breath.

soon, shortly, forthwith, anon [*archaic*], presently; prospectively etc. 121.

508. Inexpectation

n. **inexpectation** [*rare*], nonexpectation; unforeseen contingency, the unforeseen; false expectation etc. (*disappointment*) 509; miscalculation etc. 481.

surprise, sudden burst, thunderclap, blow, shock; bolt out of the blue; astoundment [*rare*], astonishment, mazement [*rare*], amazement; wonder etc. 870; eye opener.

v. **not expect** etc. 507; be taken by surprise; start; miscalculate etc. 481; not bargain for; come–, fall- upon.

be unexpected etc. *adj.*; come unawares etc. *adv.*; turn up, pop [*colloq.*], drop from the clouds; come–, burst–, flash–, bounce–, steal–, creep- upon one; come–, burst- like a -thunderclap, –thunderbolt; take–, catch- -by surprise, –unawares; catch napping, catch off one's guard; yach [*S. Africa*].

surprise, startle, take aback [*colloq.*], electrify, stun, stagger, take away one's breath, throw off one's guard; pounce upon, spring, spring upon, spring a mine upon; stound [*archaic*], astound; astonish etc. (*strike with wonder*) 870.

adj. **nonexpectant**, inexpectant; surprised etc. *v.*; unwarned, unaware; off one's guard; inattentive etc. 458.

unexpected, unanticipated, unlooked for, unforeseen, unhoped for; dropped from the clouds; beyond–, contrary to–, against- expectation; out of one's reckoning; unheard of etc. (*exceptional*) 83, startling; sudden etc. (*instantaneous*) 113.

adv. **unexpectedly**, abruptly, plump, pop, *à l'improviste* [*F.*], unawares; without -notice, –warning, –saying "by your leave"; like a thief in the night, like a thunderbolt; like a lightning flash; in an unguarded moment; suddenly etc. (*instantaneously*) 113.

int. heydey! etc. (*wonder*) 870; do tell!

509. Disappointment
[failure of expectation]

n. **disappointment**; blighted hope, disillusion, balk; blow; slip 'twixt cup and lip; nonfulfillment of one's hopes; sad–, bitter- disappointment; trick of fortune; afterclap; false–, vain- expectation; miscalculation etc. 481; fool's paradise; much cry and little wool.

v. **be disappointed**; look blank, look blue [*colloq.*]; look *or* stand aghast etc. (*wonder*) 870; find to one's cost; laugh on the wrong side of one's mouth [*colloq.*], laugh out of the other corner of the mouth [*colloq.*]; find one a false prophet.

disappoint; crush–, dash–, balk–, disappoint–, blight–, falsify–, defeat- not realize- one's -hope, –expectation; balk, jilt, bilk; play one -false, –a trick; dash the cup from the lips; tantalize; dumfounder *or* dumbfounder, dumfound *or* dumbfound, disillusion, disillusionize; come short of; dissatisfy, make dissatisfied, disgruntle.

adj. **disappointed** etc. *v.*; disconcerted, aghast; disgruntled; out of one's reckoning; short of expectations.

510. Foresight

n. **foresight**, prospicience, prevision, long-sightedness, farsightedness; anticipation; providence etc. (*preparation*) 673.

forethought, forecast; predeliberation, presurmise; foregone conclusion etc. (*prejudgment*) 481; prudence etc. (*caution*) 864.

foreknowledge, precognition, prescience, prenotion, presentiment; second sight; sagacity etc. (*intelligence*) 498; antepast, prelibation; prophasis [*med.*], prognosis [*med.*].

prospect etc. (*expectation*) 507; foretaste; prospectus etc. (*plan*) 626.

v. **foresee**; look -forward to, –ahead, –beyond; scent from afar; feel it in one's bones [*colloq.*]; look–, pry–, peep- into the future.

see one's way; see how the -land lies, –wind blows, –cat jumps [*colloq.*].

anticipate; expect etc. 507; be beforehand etc. (*early*) 132; predict etc. 511; foreknow, forejudge, forecast; surmise; have an eye to the -future, −main chance; *respicere finem* [*L.*]; keep a sharp lookout etc. (*vigilance*) 459; forewarn etc. 668.

adj. **foreseeing** etc. *v.;* prescient, anticipatory; farseeing, farsighted, long-sighted; sagacious etc. (*intelligent*) 498; weatherwise; provident etc. (*prepared*) 673; on the lookout, −for; prospective etc. 507.

adv. against the time when; for a rainy day.

511. Prediction

n. **prediction**, announcement; program *or* programme etc. (*plan*) 626; premonition etc. (*warning*) 668; prognosis, prognostic, presage, presagement, precurse [*obs.*], prophecy, vaticination, mantology [*rare*], prognostication, premonstration [*obs.*]; augury, auguration [*obs.*], ariolation [*obs.*], hariolation [*obs.*], foreboding, aboding [*obs.*], abode [*obs.*], bode [*obs.*], bodement, abodement; omniation [*obs.*], auspice (*pl.* auspices), forecast; omen etc. 512; horoscope, nativity; sooth [*obs.*], soothsaying, fortune-telling; divination.

adytum, oak of Dodona; cave of the Cumaean Sibyl, Sibylline leaves, Sibylline books; tripod of the Pythia.

prefiguration, prefigurement; prototype, type.

[divination by the stars] astrology, astromancy, horoscopy, genethlialogy, judicial *or* mundane astrology.

oracle, prophet, seer etc. 513.

[means of divination] crystal, ink, tea leaves, cards; Hallowe'en -nuts, mirror; divining-rod, witch-hazel; hand of glory; wax image; teraphim; shadows etc. [*see footnote*]; spell, charm etc. 993.

sorcery, magic, necromancy etc. 992; heteroscopic divination.[1]

v. **predict**, prognosticate, prophesy, vaticinate, divine, foretell, soothsay, augurate, tell fortunes; cast a horoscope, cast a nativity; advise; forewarn, prewarn etc. 668.

presage, augur, bode, abode [*obs.*], forebode; foretoken, betoken; prefigure, prefigurate, augurate [*rare*], ariolate [*rare*], figure [*obs.*], forecast, precurse, portend; preshow, foreshow, foreshadow; shadow forth, typify, pretypify, ominate [*obs.*], signify, point to.

hold out−, raise−, excite- -expectation, −hope; bid fair, promise, lead one to expect; be the precursor etc. 64.

herald, usher in, premise, announce; lower.

adj. **predicting** etc. *v.;* predictive, prophetic, fatidic *or* fatidical, precursal, precurrent, presageful, vaticinal, oracular, fatiloquent [*rare*], haruspical; Sibylline; weatherwise.

ominous, portentous; augurous, augurial, augural, precursive, precursory, auspicial, auspicious; prescious [*rare*], prescient, monitory, extispicious [*obs.*], premonitory, significant of, pregnant with, big with the fate of.

[1]The following terms, expressive of different forms of divination, have been collected from various sources, and are here given as a curious illustration of bygone superstitions:

Divination *by oracles,* theomancy; *by the Bible,* Bibliomancy; *by ghosts,* psychomancy; *by crystal gazing,* crystallomancy; *by shadows or manes,* sciomancy; *by appearances in the air,* aeromancy, chaomancy; *by the stars at birth,* genethliacs; *by meteors,* meteoromancy; *by winds,* austromancy; *by sacrificial appearances,* aruspicy (*or* haruspicy), hieromancy, hieroscopy; *by the entrails of animals sacrificed,* extispicy, hieromancy; *by the entrails of a human sacrifice,* anthropomancy; *by the entrails of fishes,* ichthyomancy; *by sacrificial fire,* pyromancy; *by redhot iron,* sideromancy; *by the smoke from the altar,* capnomancy; *by mice,* myomancy; *by birds,* orniscopy, ornithomancy; *by a cock picking up grains,* alectryomancy (*or* alectoromancy); *by snakes,* ophiomancy; *by herbs,* botanomancy; *by water,* hydromancy; *by fountains,* pegomancy; *by a wand,* rhabdomancy; *by dough of cakes,* crithomancy; *by meal,* aleuromancy, alphitomancy; *by salt,* halomancy; *by lead,* molybdomancy; *by dice,* cleromancy; *by arrows,* belomancy; *by a balanced hatchet,* axinomancy; *by a balanced sieve,* coscinomancy; *by a suspended ring,* dactyliomancy; *by dots made at random on paper,* geomancy; *by precious stones,* lithomancy; *by pebbles,* pessomancy; *by pebbles drawn from a heap,* psephomancy; *by mirrors,* catoptromancy; *by writings in ashes,* tephramancy; *by dreams,* oneiromancy; *by the hand,* palmistry, chiromancy; *by nails reflecting the sun's rays,* onychomancy; *by finger rings,* dactylomancy; *by numbers,* arithmancy; *by drawing lots,* sortilege; *by passages in books,* stichomancy; *by the letters forming the name of the person,* onomancy, nomancy; *by the features,* anthroposcopy; *by the mode of laughing,* geloscopy; *by ventriloquism,* gastromancy; *by walking in a circle,* gyromancy; *by dropping melted wax into water,* ceromancy; *by currents,* bletonism; *by the color and peculiarities of wine,* oenomancy; *by the shoulder blade,* scapulimancy *or* scapulomancy, omoplatoscopy.

512. Omen

n. **omen**, portent, presage, prognostic, augury, auspice; sign etc. (*indication*) 550; harbinger etc. (*precursor*) 64; yule candle, yule log *or* clog.

bird of ill omen; halcyon birds; signs of the times; gathering clouds, thunder, lightning, rainbow, comet, shooting star; rain of blood, warning etc. 668.

prefigurement etc. 511; adytum etc. 511.

adj. **ill-boding,** ill-omened, inauspicious.

513. Oracle

n. **oracle**; prophet, seer, soothsayer, augur, medium, clairvoyant, palmist, fortune teller, prophetess, sibyl, witch, geomancer, haruspice *or* aruspice, haruspex *or* aruspex; Sibyl, python, pythoness, Pythia; Pythian oracle, Delphian (*or* Delphic) oracle; Monitor, Sphinx, Tiresias, Cassandra, Sibylline leaves; oak–, oracle– of Dodona; sorcerer etc. 994; interpreter etc. 524.

weather prophet, weather sharp [*slang*], weather bureau, Old Probabilities *or* Old Prob. [*humorous nickname for U. S. weather bureau*]; Old Moore, Zadkiel.

Section 7. Creative Thought

514. Supposition

n. **supposition,** assumption, supposal, supposableness [*rare*], suppositality [*obs.*], postulation [*rare*], condition, presupposition, hypothesis, postulate, postulatum, theory, data; proposition, position; thesis, theorem; proposal etc. (*plan*) 626; assumed position.

bare–, vague–, loose- -supposition, –suggestion; conceit; conjecture; guess, guesswork; rough guess, shot [*colloq.*]; conjecturality [*rare*], suggestiveness, presurmise, surmise, suspicion, inkling, suggestion, association of ideas, hint; presumption etc. (*belief*) 484; divination, speculation, shot in the dark.

theorist, theorizer, speculatist [*rare*], speculator, notionalist, hypothesist, hypothetist [*rare*], doctrinaire, doctrinarian.

v. **suppose,** conjecture, surmise, suspect, guess, divine; theorize; presume, presuppose; assume, fancy, wis [*archaic*], take it; give a guess, speculate, believe, dare say, take it into one's head, take for granted.

propound, propose, put forth; start, put a case, submit, move, make a motion; hazard–, venture–, throw out–, put forward- a -suggestion, –conjecture, –supposition; hypothesize.

suggest, allude to, hint, put it into one's head.

suggest itself etc. (*thought*) 451; run in the head etc. (*memory*) 505; marvel - wonder- -if, –whether.

adj. **supposing** etc. *v.;* given, mooted, postulatory [*now rare*]; assumed etc. *v.;* suppositive, supposititious; gratuitous, speculative, conjectural, conjecturable, hypothetical, theoretical, academic, supposable, presumptive, putative; suppositional, suppositionary.

suggestive, allusive, stimulating.

adv. **if,** if so be; an [*archaic*]; on the supposition etc. *n.; ex hypothesi* [*L.*], in case, in the event of; if that [*archaic*], so that, whether; quasi, as if, provided; perhaps etc. (*by possibility*) 470; for aught one knows.

515. Imagination

n. **imagination,** originality, invention; fancy; inspiration; verve.

warm–, heated–, excited–, sanguine–, ardent–, fiery–, boiling–, wild–, bold–, daring–, playful–, lively–, fertile- -imagination, –fancy.

"mind's eye" [*Hamlet*]; "the mind's internal heaven" [*Wordsworth*]; "such stuff as dreams are made on" [*Tempest*].

ideality, idealism; romanticism, utopianism, castle-building; dreaming; frenzy, ecstasy; calenture etc. (*delirium*) 503; reverie *or* revery, brown study, pipe dream, daydream, trance; somnambulism.

conception, *Vorstellung* [*Ger.*], excogitation, "a fine frenzy" [*Midsummer Night's Dream*]; cloudland, dreamland; flight–, fumes- of fancy; "thick-coming fancies" [*Macbeth*]; creation–, coinage- of the brain; imagery; word painting.

fantasy, conceit, figment, myth, dream, vision, shadow, chimera; phantasm, phantasy, fancy; maggot, whim, whimwham, whimsey *or* whimsy, vagary, rhapsody, romance, gest *or* geste, extravaganza; "air-drawn dagger" [*Macbeth*], bugbear, nightmare; flying Dutchman, great sea serpent, man in the moon, castle in the air, castle in Spain, *château en Espagne* [*F.*], pleasure dome of Kubla Khan, Utopia; Heavenly City, New Jerusalem; Atlantis, Happy Valley [*Johnson*], millennium, fairyland; land of Prester John, kingdom of Micomicon; Estotiland *or* Estotilandia [*Milton*]; Laputa; Cockagne, Lubberland; Arabian nights; *le pot au lait* [*F.*]; pot of gold at the end of the rainbow; dream of Alnaschar etc. (*hope*) 858; golden dream.

[creative works] work of fiction etc. (*novel*) 594; poetry etc. 597; play, tragedy, comedy etc. (*drama*) 599; sonata etc. (*music*) 415.

illusion etc. (*error*) 495; phantom etc. (*fallacy of vision*) 443; *Fata Morgana* [*L.*] etc. (*ignis* *fatuus*) 423; vapor etc. (*cloud*) 353; stretch of the imagination etc. (*exaggeration*) 549; mythogenesis.

idealist, romanticist, visionary; mopus [*slang*], romancer, daydreamer, dreamer; somnambulist; rhapsodist etc. (*fanatic*) 504; castle-builder, fanciful projector; "sweetest Shakespeare, Fancy's child" [Milton].

v. **imagine**, fancy, conceive; idealize, realize; dream, −of; "gives to airy nothing a local habitation and a name" [*Midsummer Night's Dream*].

set one's wits to work; strain−, crack- one's invention; rack−, ransack−, cudgel- one's brains; excogitate.

give -play, −the reins, −a loose [*obs.*]- to the--imagination, −fancy; tilt at windmills; indulge in reverie.

conjure up a vision; fancy−, represent−, picture−, figure- to oneself; *vorstellen* [*Ger.*]; "see visions and dream dreams" [*Bible*].

float in the mind; suggest itself etc. (*thought*) 451.

create, originate, devise, invent, make up, coin, fabricate; improvise, strike out something new.

adj. **imagined** etc. *v.;* *ben trovato* [*It.*]; air-drawn, air-built.

imaginative; imagining etc. *v.;* original, inventive, creative, fertile, productive, ingenious.

extravagant, romantic, high-flown, flighty, preposterous; rhapsodic *or* rhapsodical; fanatic, enthusiastic, Utopian, Quixotic.

ideal, unreal; in the clouds, *in nubibus* [*L.*]; unsubstantial etc. 4; illusory etc. (*fallacious*) 495; fictitious, theoretical, hypothetical.

fanciful; fabulous, legendary, mythic *or* mythical, mythological, chimerical; imaginary, visionary; dream-beset, dream-ridden, dreamy, entranced, notional, fancy, fantastical, high-fantastical, fantasied, maggoty, made of empty air, vaporous, whimsical; fairy, fairylike.

Division 2. Communication of Ideas

Section 1. Nature of Ideas Communicated

516. Meaning

[idea to be conveyed]
[thing signified]

n. **meaning**; signification, significance; sense, expression; import, purport; implication, connotation, essence, force; drift, tenor, spirit, bearing, coloring; scope.

allusion etc. (*latency*) 526; suggestion etc. (*information*) 527; interpretation, acceptation etc. 522; acceptance [*rare*].

general−, broad−, substantial−, colloquial−, literal−, primary−, accepted−, essential−, plain−, simple−, natural−, unstrained−, true etc. (*exact*) 494−, honest etc. 543−, *prima facie* [*L.*] etc. (*manifest*) 525- meaning.

literality; literal−, obvious−, real- -meaning, −sense, −interpretation.

equivalent meaning; interchangeable word, figure of speech etc. 521; equivalent, synonym etc. 522.

thing signified, matter, subject, subject matter, substance, sum and substance; gist etc. 5; argument, text.

v. **mean**, signify, connote, denote, express; import, purport; convey, imply, breathe, indicate, bespeak, bear a meaning, bear a sense; tell of, speak of; touch on; point to, allude to; drive at; involve etc. (*latency*) 526; declare etc. (*affirm*) 535.

understand by etc. (*interpret*) 522.

synonymize, express by a synonym; paraphrase, state differently.

adj. **meaning** etc. *v.;* expressive, suggestive, allusive; significant, significative, significatory; pithy; meaningful; full of−, pregnant with- meaning; explicit etc. 525.

declaratory etc. 535; intelligible etc. 518.

literal, metaphrastic *or* metaphrastical, word-for-word, verbatim; exact, real.

synonymous; tantamount etc. (*equivalent*) 27.

implied etc. (*latent*) 526; understood, tacit.

adv. **to that effect**; that is to say etc. (*being interpreted*) 522.

verbatim, literally; evidently, apparently, from the context.

517. Unmeaningness

[absence of meaning]

n. **unmeaningness** etc. *adj.;* scrabble, scribble, scrawl, pothooks.

empty sound, dead letter, *vox et praeterea nihil* [*L.*]; "a tale told by an idiot, full of sound and fury, signifying nothing" [*Macbeth*]; "weasel words" [Roosevelt]; "sounding brass or a tinkling cymbal" [*Bible*].

nonsense, jargon, gibberish, jabber, mere words, hocus-pocus, fustian, rant, bombast, balderdash, palaver, patter, flummery, verbiage, babble, *bavardage* [*F.*], *baragouin* [*F.*], platitude, *niaiserie* [*F.*]; inanity; flapdoodle [*colloq.*]; rigmarole, rodomontade; truism; twaddle, twattle, fudge, trash; poppy-cock; stuff, –and nonsense; bosh [*colloq.*], rubbish, moonshine, wish-wash [*slang*], fiddle-faddle [*colloq.*]; absurdity etc. 497; imbecility, folly etc. 499; unintelligibleness, ambiguity, vagueness etc. (*unintelligibility*) 519.

v. **mean nothing**; be unmeaning etc. *adj.;* twaddle, quibble, jabber, rant, rodomontade, palaver, babble, fiddle-faddle [*colloq.*].

scribble, scrawl, scrabble, scratch.

adj. **unmeaning**; meaningless, senseless; nonsensical etc. 497; void of sense etc. 516.

inexpressive, unexpressive; vacant; not significant etc. 516; insignificant.

trashy, washy, wishy-washy [*colloq.*], inane, wash [*obs.*], rubbishy, vague, trumpery, trivial, fiddle-faddle [*colloq.*], twaddling, quibbling.

unmeant, not expressed; tacit etc. (*latent*) 526.

inexpressible, undefinable, ineffable, unutterable, incommunicable.

int. **fudge!** stuff! stuff and nonsense! bosh! fiddle-faddle! [*colloq.*]; poppycock! *oh! la-la!* [*F.*]; rubbish! fiddledee-dee! etc. 497.

518. Intelligibility

n. **intelligibility**; clearness, clarity, explicitness etc. *adj.;* lucidity, comprehensibility, perspicuity; legibility, plain speaking etc. (*manifestation*) 525; precision etc. 494; *phonanta sunetoisi* [*Gr.*], a word to the wise.

v. **be intelligible** etc. *adj.;* speak for itself, speak volumes; tell its own tale, lie on the surface.

render intelligible etc. *adj.;* popularize, simplify, clear up; elucidate etc. (*explain*) 522.

understand, comprehend; take, –in; catch, grasp, follow, collect, master, make out; see with half an eye, see daylight, see one's way [*all colloq.*]; enter into the ideas of; come to an understanding.

adj. **intelligible**; clear, clear as -day, –noonday, –crystal; lucid; perspicuous, transpicuous; luminous, transparent.

easily understood, easy to understand, for the million, intelligible to the meanest capacity, popularized.

plain, distinct, clear-cut, hard-hitting, to the point, explicit; positive; definite etc. (*precise*) 494.

unambiguous, unequivocal, unmistakable etc. (*manifest*) 525, unconfused; legible, recognizable; obvious etc. 525.

graphic, telling, vivid; expressive etc. (*meaning*) 516; illustrative etc. (*explanatory*) 522.

adv. in plain -terms, –words, –English; hitting the nail on the head.

519. Unintelligibility

n. **unintelligibility**, incomprehensibility, imperspicuity [*rare*]; inconceivableness, unknowability, unknowableness, vagueness etc. *adj.;* obscurity; ambiguity etc. 520; doubtful meaning; uncertainty etc. 475; perplexity etc. (*confusion*) 59; spinosity; *obscurum per obscurius* [*L.*]; mystification etc. (*concealment*) 528; latency etc. 526; transcendentalism.

pons asinorum [*L.*], asses' bridge; double Dutch, high Dutch [*slang*], Greek, Hebrew, Choctaw; jargon etc. (*unmeaning*) 517.

enigma, riddle etc. (*secret*) 533; paradox; *dignus vindice nodus* [*L.*]; sealed book; steganography, cryptography, freemasonry.

v. **be unintelligible** etc. *adj.;* require explanation etc. 522; have a doubtful meaning, pass comprehension.

render unintelligible etc. *adj.;* conceal etc. 528; darken etc. 421; confuse etc. (*derange*) 61; mystify, perplex etc. (*bewilder*) 475.

not understand etc. 518; lose, –the clew; miss; not know what to make of, be able to make nothing of, give it up; not be able to -account for, –make head or tail of; be at sea etc. (*uncertain*) 475; wonder etc. 870; see through a glass darkly etc. (*ignorance*) 491.

not understand one another; play at cross-purposes etc. (*misinterpret*) 523.

adj. **unintelligible**, unaccountable, undecipherable, undiscoverable, unknowable, unfathomable; incognizable, inexplicable, inscrutable; inapprehensible, incomprehensible; insolvable, insoluble; impenetrable.

puzzling, as Greek to one, unexplained, paradoxical, enigmatic *or* enigmatical, indecipherable, illegible.

obscure, crabbed, imperspicuous [*rare*], dark, muddy, clear as mud [*colloq.*], seen through a mist, dim, nebulous, shrouded in mystery; undiscernible etc. (*invisible*) 447; misty etc. (*opaque*) 426; hidden etc. 528; latent etc. 526; mysterious; mystic, mystical, acroamatic *or* acroamatical, metempiric *or* metempirical; transcendental; occult, esoteric, recondite, abstruse.

indefinite etc. (*indistinct*) 447; perplexed etc. (*confused*) 59; undetermined, vague, loose, ambiguous.

inconceivable, inconceptible [*obs.*]; searchless; above–, beyond–, past-comprehension; beyond one's depth; unconceived.

inexpressible, unutterable, ineffable, undefinable, incommunicable.

520. Equivocalness
[having a double sense]

n. **equivocalness** etc. *adj.*; equivocation; double meaning etc. 516; ambiguity, *double entente* [*F.*], double-entendre, pun, paragram [*rare*], *calembour* [*F.*], quibble, equivoque *or* equivoke, anagram; conundrum etc. (*riddle*) 533; word play etc. (*wit*) 842; homonym, homonymy; amphiboly, amphibologism, amphilogism *or* amphilogy [*rare*], anagrammatism, ambilogy, ambiloquy [*obs.*].

Sphinx, Delphic oracle.

equivocation etc. (*duplicity*) 544; white lie, mental reservation etc. (*concealment*) 528; paltering.

v. **equivocate** etc. (*palter*) 544; anagrammatize; be equivocal etc. *adj.*; have two meanings etc. 516.

adj. **equivocal**, ambiguous, amphibolous [*obs.*], doubtful, amphibolic, ambiloquent [*obs.*], ambiloquous, homonymic, homonymous; double-tongued etc. (*lying*) 544; enigmatical, indeterminate.

521. Metaphor

n. **figure of speech**; *façon de parler* [*F.*], way of speaking, colloquialism.

phrase etc. 566; figure, trope, metaphor, tralatition, metonymy, enallage, catachresis, synecdoche, antonomasia; satire, irony, figurativeness etc. *adj.*; image, imagery, metathesis, metalepsis, type, anagoge, simile.

personification, prosopopoeia, allegory, allegorization, apologue, parable, fable.

inference, implication, deduction, allusion, adumbration; euphemism, euphuism, application.

v. **employ metaphor** etc. *n.*; personify, allegorize, fable, adumbrate, shadow forth, apply, allude to.

adj. **metaphorical**, tropical, tralatitious, figurative, catachrestic *or* catachrestical, antonomastic *or* antonomastical, typical, parabolic *or* parabolical, allegoric *or* allegorical, allusive, referential, anagogic *or* anagogical; euphuistic *or* euphuistical, euphemistic *or* euphemistical, ironic, ironical; colloquial.

adv. **as it were**, so to -speak, –say, –express oneself; in a manner of speaking [*colloq.*].

522. Interpretation

n. **interpretation**, definition; explanation, explication; solution, answer; rationale; plain–, simple–, strict- interpretation; meaning etc. 516; *mot d'énigme* [*F.*]; clew etc. (*indication*) 550.

symptomatology, semeiology *or* semiology, diagnosis, prognosis; metoposcopy, physiognomy; paleography etc. (*philology*) 560; oneirology.

translation; rendering, rendition; reddition; literal–, free- translation; key; secret; *clavis* [*L.*], crib, pony, trot [*Eng.*].

comment, commentary; exegesis; expounding, exposition; hermeneutics; inference etc. (*deduction*) 480; illustration, exemplification; gloss, annotation, scholium, note; enucleation, elucidation, dilucidation [*obs.*]; *éclaircissement* [*F.*].

acception [*obs.*], acceptation, acceptance; light, reading, lection, construction, version.

equivalent, –meaning etc. 516; synonym, pœcilonym, polyonym [*rare*]; paraphrase, metaphrase; convertible terms, apposition.

dictionary etc. 562; polyglot.

prediction etc. 511; chiromancy *or* cheiromancy, palmistry; astrology.

v. **interpret**, explain, define, construe, translate, render; do into, turn into; transfuse the sense of.

find out etc. (480*a*)- -the meaning of etc. 516; read; spell out, make out; decipher, unravel, disentangle; find the key of, enucleate, resolve, solve; consignify [*rare*]; read between the lines, read into.

elucidate, account for; find–, tell- the cause of etc. 153; throw–, shed- -light, –new light, –fresh light- upon; clear up.

illustrate, exemplify; unfold, expound, comment upon, annotate; popularize etc. (*render intelligible*) 518.

understand by; take–, understand–, receive–, accept- in a particular sense; put a construction on, be given to understand.

adj. **explanatory**, expository; explicative, explicatory; exegetical; construable; hermeneutic *or*

174

hermeneutical, interpretive, interpretative, commentarial, commentatorial, inferential, illustrative, exemplificative, exemplificational, annotative, scholiastic, elucidative; symptomatological; paleographic *or* paleographical.

equivalent etc. 27; paraphrastic, consignificative [*rare*], consignificant, synonymous, poecilonymic, polyonymal [*rare*], polyonymic [*rare*]. metaphrastic, literal etc. 516; polyglot.

adv. **in explanation** etc. *n.;* that is to say, *id est* [*L.*], *videlicet* [*L.*], to wit, namely, in other words.

literally, strictly speaking: in -plain, –plainer- -terms, –words, –English; more simply.

523. Misinterpretation

n. **misinterpretation**, misapprehension, misdoubt, misconception, misunderstanding, misacceptation [*obs.*], misconstruction, misapplication; catachresis; eisegesis; cross-reading, cross-purposes; mistake etc. 495.

misrepresentation, perversion, misstatement, exaggeration etc. 549; false -coloring, –construction; abuse of terms; play upon words, *jeu de mots* [*F.*], pun, parody, travesty; double-talk; falsification etc. (*lying*) 544.

v. **misinterpret**, misapprehend, misunderstand, misconceive, misjudge, misdeem, misdoubt, misspell, mistranslate, misconstrue, misapply; mistake etc. 495.

misrepresent, pervert; explain wrongly, misstate; garble etc. (*falsify*) 544; distort, detort [*obs.*]; travesty, play upon words; stretch–, strain–, twist–, wrench–, wring–, wrest- the -sense, –meaning; explain away; put a -bad, –wrong, –erroneous, –false- construction on; give a false coloring; look through dark–, rose-colored- spectacles.

be out; be–, play- at cross-purposes; be off [*slang*], be 'way off [*slang*], be off base [*slang*].

adj. **misinterpreted** etc. *v.;* eisegetical, catachrestic *or* catachrestical; untranslated, untranslatable.

confused, tangled, snarled, mixed, dazed, perplexed, bewildered, rattled [*slang*], benighted.

adv. **at cross-purposes**, at sixes and sevens [*colloq.*]; *à tort et à travers* [*F.*]; all balled up [*colloq.*], in a maze, all fouled up [*slang*].

524. Interpreter

n. **interpreter** (*fem.* interpretress), translator, expositor, expounder, exponent, explainer; demonstrator.

commentator, scholiast, annotator; metaphrast, paraphrast; glossarist, prolocutor.

spokesman, speaker, mouthpiece, foreman of the jury; mediator, delegate, exponent, representative, diplomatic agent, ambassador, plenipotentiary; advocate, judge, Supreme Court.

guide, dragoman, courier, *valet de place* [*F.*], cicerone, showman, barker [*colloq.*], oneirocritic; Oedipus, Joseph; oracle etc. 513.

Section 2. Modes of Communication

525. Manifestation

n. **manifestation**, unfoldment, unfolding; plainness etc. *adj.;* plain speaking; expression; showing etc. *v.;* exposition, demonstration, séance, materialization; exhibition, production; display, show-down [*slang*], show, showing off [*colloq.*]; premonstration [*obs.*].

[thing shown] exhibit, exhibition, exposition, show [*colloq.*], performance.

indication etc. (*calling attention to*) 457; publicity etc. 531; disclosure etc. 529; openness etc. (*honesty*) 543, (*artlessness*) 703; *épanchement* [*F.*]; saliency, prominence.

v. **make** *or* **render manifest** etc. *adj.;* materialize; bring -forth, –forward, –to the front, –into view; give notice; express; represent, set forth, evidence, exhibit; show, –up; expose; produce; hold up–, expose- to view; set–, place–, lay-before -one, –one's eyes; tell to one's face; trot out [*colloq.*], put through one's paces [*colloq.*], show one's paces, show off [*colloq.*]; show forth, unveil, bring to light, display, demonstrate, unroll; lay open; draw out, bring out; bring out in strong relief; call–, bring- into notice; hold up the mirror to; wear one's heart upon his sleeve; show one's -face, –colors; manifest oneself; speak out; make no -mystery, –secret- of; unfurl the flag; proclaim etc. (*publish*) 531.

indicate etc. (*direct attention to*) 457; disclose etc. 529; translate, transcribe, decipher, decode; elicit etc. 480a.

be manifest etc. *adj.;* appear etc. (*be visible*) 446; transpire etc. (*be disclosed*) 529; speak for itself, stand to reason; stare one in the face, loom large, appear on the horizon, rear its head; give -token, –sign, –indication of; tell its own tale etc. (*intelligible*) 518; go without saying, be self-evident.

adj. **manifest**, apparent; salient, striking, demonstrative, prominent, in the foreground, notable, pronounced.

flagrant; notorious etc. (*public*) 531; arrant; stark-staring; unshaded, glaring.

plain, clear, defined, definite, distinct, conspicuous etc. (*visible*) 446; obvious, evident, unmistakable, conclusive, indubitable, not to be mistaken, palpable, self-evident, autoptic *or* autoptical; intelligible etc. 518; clear as -day, –daylight, –noonday; plain as -a pikestaff [*colloq.*], –the sun at noonday, –the nose on one's face [*colloq.*], –way to parish church [*colloq.*].

ostensible; open, –as day; overt, patent, express, explicit; naked, bare, literal, downright, undisguised, exoteric.

unreserved; frank, plain-spoken etc. (*artless*) 703.

barefaced, brazen, bold, shameless, daring, flaunting, *risqué* [*F.*], loud.

manifested etc. *v.;* disclosed etc. 529; capable of being shown, producible; unconcealable.

adv. **manifestly**, openly etc. *adj.;* before one's eyes, under one's nose [*colloq.*], under one's very eyes, to one's face, face to face, above board, cards on the table, *cartes sur table* [*F.*], on the stage, in open court, in the open streets, in plain sight, in the open, at the cross-roads, in the market place, in market overt; in the face of -day; –heaven; in- broad–, open- daylight; without reserve; at first blush, *prima facie* [*L.*], on the face of; in set terms.

526. Latency

n. **latency**, inexpression; hidden–, occult- meaning; obscurity etc. (*unintelligibility*) 519; occultness, mystery, cabala *or* cabbala, cabalism, occultism, mysticism, symbolism, anagoge; silence etc. (*taciturnity*) 585; concealment etc. 528; more than meets the -eye, –ear; Delphic oracle; *le dessous des cartes* [*F.*], undercurrent; "something rotten in the state of Denmark" [*Hamlet*].

snake in the grass etc. (*pitfall*) 667; secret etc. 533. darkness, invisibility, imperceptibility.

allusion, insinuation, inference, implication; innuendo etc. 527; adumbration.

latent influence, invisible government, power behind the throne, friend at court, wire-puller [*colloq.*], king-maker; "a destiny that shapes our ends" [*Hamlet*].

v. **be latent** etc. *adj.;* lurk, smolder *or* smoulder, underlie, make no sign; escape -observation, –detection, –recognition; lie hid etc. 528.

laugh up one's sleeve; keep back etc. (*conceal*) 528.

involve, imply, implicate, connote, import, understand, allude to, infer, leave an inference; mysticize [*rare*], symbolize; whisper etc. (*conceal*) 528.

adj. **latent**; lurking etc. *v.;* secret, occult, anagogic *or* anagogical, cabalistic *or* cabalistical, symbolic, esoteric, recondite, veiled, symbolic, cryptic *or* cryptical; mystic, mystical; implied etc. *v.;* dormant; abeyant.

unapparent, unknown, unseen etc. 441; in the background; invisible etc. 447; indiscoverable, dark; impenetrable etc. (*unintelligible*) 519; unspied, unsuspected.

undeveloped, unsolved, unexplained, untraced, undiscovered etc. 480*a*, untracked, unexplored, uninvented.

unexpressed, unmentioned, unpronounced, unsaid, unwritten, unpublished, unbreathed, untalked of, untold etc. 527, unsung, unexposed, unproclaimed, undisclosed etc. 529, not expressed, tacit.

indirect, crooked, inferential; by inference, by implication; implicit; constructive; allusive, covert, muffled, steganographic; understood, underhand, underground; concealed; under cover etc. 528; delitescent.

adv. **secretly** etc. 528; by a side wind; *sub silentio* [*L.*]; in the background; behind the scenes, behind one's back; on the tip of one's tongue; between the lines; by a mutual understanding; *sub rosa* [*L.*]; below the surface.

527. Information

n. **information**, advisement [*archaic*], enlightenment, acquaintance, knowledge etc. 490; publicity etc. 531.

mention; acquainting etc. *v.;* instruction etc. (*teaching*) 537; outpouring; intercommunication, communicativeness.

intimation, communication, notice, notification, enunciation, annunciation, announcement, *communiqué* [*F.*]; representation, round robin, presentment.

report, advice, monition; news etc. 532; return etc. (*record*) 551; account etc. (*description*) 594; statement etc. (*affirmation*) 535; case, estimate, specification.

dispatch *or* despatch, message, wire [*colloq.*], cable, telegram, telex etc. (*news*) 532; telephone, phone [*colloq.*], radiophone, wireless telephone, telegraphone.

informant, authority, teller, annunciator, harbinger, herald, intelligencer [*now rare*], reporter, exponent, mouthpiece; spokesman etc. (*interpreter*) 524; informer, eavesdropper, delator, detective, bull [*slang, U. S.*], sleuth [*colloq.*]; *mouchard* [*F.*], spy, newsmonger; messenger etc. 534; *amicus curiae* [*L.*].

guide, *valet de place* [*F.*], cicerone, pilot, guidebook, handbook; *vade mecum* [*L.*], manual; map, plan, chart, gazetteer; itinerary etc. (*journey*) 266.

hint, suggestion, innuendo, inkling, whisper, passing word, word in the ear, subaudition, subauditur, cue, byplay; gesture etc. (*indication*) 550; gentle-, broad- hint; *verbum sapienti* [*L.*]; word to the wise; insinuation etc. (*latency*) 526.

v. **tell**; inform, –of; acquaint, –with; impart, –to; make acquainted with, apprise, advise, enlighten, awaken.

let fall, mention, express, intimate, represent, communicate, make known; publish etc. 531; notify, signify, specify, convey the knowledge of; retail, render an account; give an account etc. (*describe*) 594; state etc. (*affirm*) 535.

let one know, have one know; give one to understand; give notice; set-, lay-, put- before; point out, put into one's head; put one in possession of; instruct etc. (*teach*) 537; direct the attention to etc. 457.

announce, annunciate; report, –progress; bring-, send-, leave-, write- word; telegraph, wire [*colloq.*], telephone, telex, phone [*colloq.*].

disclose etc. 529; show cause; explain etc. (*interpret*) 522.

hint; give an inkling of; give-, drop-, throw out- a hint; insinuate; allude to, make allusion to; glance at; tip off [*slang*], give one a tip [*colloq.*]; tip the wink [*slang*] etc. (*indicate*) 550; suggest, prompt, give the cue, breathe; whisper, –in the ear.

berate, scold, chide, strafe [*colloq.*], score [*colloq.*], dress down [*colloq.*], reprove, trim [*slang*], rate; give one a -bit, –piece- of one's mind; tell one -plainly, –once for all; speak volumes.

undeceive, unbeguile; set right, correct, open the eyes of, disabuse.

be informed of etc.; know etc. 490; learn etc. 539; get scent of, gather from; sleuth [*colloq.*]; awaken to, open one's eyes to; become -alive, –awake- to; hear, understand; come to one's -ears, –knowledge; reach one's ears; overhear etc. (*hear*) 418; get wise to [*slang*].

adj. **informed** etc. *v.*; *communiqué* [*F.*]; informational, advisory, intelligential; reported etc. *v.*; published etc. 531.

expressive etc. 516; explicit etc. (*open*) 525, (*clear*) 518; plain-spoken etc. (*artless*) 703.

declaratory, declarative, enunciative, nunciative [*rare*], annunciative [*rare*], enunciatory, insinuant [*rare*]; oral, nuncupative [*said of oral wills*], nuncupative [*said of oral wills*], nuncupatory [*obs.*]; expository; communicative, communicatory.

adv. **from information received**; according to -reports, –suggestion, –rumor; from notice given; by the underground route; as a matter of -general information, –common report; in the air; according to-, from- what one can gather.

528. Concealment

n. **concealment**; hiding etc. *v.;* occultation, mystification.

reticence, reserve, reservation; mental reservation, aside; *arrière pensée* [*F.*], suppression, evasion, white lie, misprision; silence etc. (*taciturnity*) 585; suppression of truth etc. 544; underhand dealing; closeness, secretiveness etc. *adj.;* mystery.

seal of secrecy; freemansonry; screen etc. 530; disguise etc. 530; masquerade; masked battery; hiding place etc. 530.

cryptography, steganography; cipher, code, cable code; sympathetic ink, palimpsest.

stalking, still-hunt, hunt.

stealth, stealthiness; obreption [*obs.*]; slyness etc. (*cunning*) 702.

secrecy, latitancy [*rare*], latitation [*obs.*]; seclusion etc. 893; privacy, secretness, hugger-mugger [*archaic*]; disguise, incognito (*fem.* incognita).

mysticism, occultism, supernaturalism; esotericism, esoterics, esotery.

latency etc. 526; snake in the grass; secret etc. 533; stowaway; blind baggage [*slang*].

masquerader, masker, mask, domino.

v. **conceal**, hide, secrete, put out of sight; lock up, seal up, bottle up.

cover, screen, cloak, veil, shroud; cover up one's tracks; screen from -sight, –observation; draw the veil; draw-, close- the curtain; curtain, shade, eclipse, throw a veil over; becloud, bemask; mask, camouflage, disguise, ensconce, muffle; befog; whisper.

keep- from, –back, –to oneself; keep -snug, –close, –secret, –dark; bury; sink, suppress; keep -from, –out of- -view, –sight; keep in-, throw into- the -shade, –background; stifle, hush up, smother, withhold, reserve; fence with a question; ignore etc. 460.

code, codify; use a -code, –cipher.

keep a secret, keep one's own counsel; hold one's tongue etc. (*silence*) 585; make no sign, not let it go further; not breathe a -word, —syllable- about; not let the right hand know what the left is doing; hide one's light under a bushel, bury one's talent in a napkin.

hoodwink; keep–, leave- in -the dark, —igno- rance; blind, —the eyes; blindfold, mystify; puz- zle etc. (*render uncertain*) 475; bamboozle etc. (*deceive*) 545.

be concealed etc. *v.;* suffer an eclipse; occult, retire from sight, couch; hide oneself; lie -hid, —in ambush, —perdu, —snug, —low [*colloq.*], —close; latitate [*obs.*]; seclude oneself etc. 893; lurk, sneak, skulk, slink, prowl, gumshoe [*slang*]; steal -into, —out of, —by, —along; play at -bopeep, —hide and seek; hide in holes and corners; still-hunt.

adj. **concealed** etc. *v.;* hidden; secret, latitant [*rare*], recondite, mystic, mystical, cabalistic *or* caba- listical, occult, dark; cryptic *or* cyptical, pri- vate, privy, *in petto* [*It.*], auricular, clandestine, close, close-mouthed, inviolate; tortuous.

behind a screen etc. 530; under -cover, —an eclipse; in ambush, in hiding, in disguise; in a -cloud, —fog, —mist, —haze, —dark corner; in the -shade, —dark; clouded, wrapt in clouds; invisible etc. 447; buried, underground, perdu; secluded etc. 893.

undisclosed etc. 529, untold etc. 527; covert etc. (*latent*) 526; mysterious etc. (*unintelligi- ble*) 519.

inviolable, irrevealable, confidential; esoteric; not to be spoken of.

furtive, obreptitious, stealthy, feline; skulking etc. *v.;* surreptitious, underhand, hole and cor- ner [*colloq.*]; sly etc. (*cunning*) 702; secretive, clandestine, evasive; reserved, reticent, uncom- municative, buttoned up; close, —as wax; taci- turn etc. 585.

adv. **secretly** etc. *adj.;* in secret, in private, in one's sleeve, in holes and corners [*colloq.*]; in the dark etc. *adj.*

januis clausis [*L.*], with closed doors, *à huis clos* [*F.*]; hugger-mugger, in hugger-mugger [*archaic*], *à la dérobée* [*F.*], under the -cloak of, —rose, —table; *sub rosa* [*L.*], *en tapinois* [*F.*], in the background, aside, on the sly [*colloq.*], with bated breath, sotto voce, in a whisper, without beat of drum, *à la sourdine* [*F.*].

behind the veil; beyond -mortal ken, —the grave, —the veil; hid from mortal vision; into the -eternal secret, —realms supersensible, —su- preme mystery.

confidentially etc. *adj.;* in–, in strict- confi- dence; between -ourselves, —you and me; *entre nous* [*F.*], *inter nos* [*L.*], under the seal of se- crecy; *à couvert* [*F.*].

underhand, by stealth, like a thief in the night; stealthily etc. *adj.;* behind -the scenes, —the curtain, —one's back, —a screen etc. 530; incog- nito; *in camera* [*L.*].

529. Disclosure

n. **disclosure**; retection [*obs.*]; unveiling etc. *v.;* deterration [*obs.*], revealment, revelation; di- vulgement, divulgation [*rare*], divulgence, ex- position, exposure, publication, *exposé* [*F.*], whole truth; telltale etc. (*news*) 532.

bursting of a bubble; *dénouement* [*F.*].

acknowledgment, avowance, avowal; confes- sion, confessional; shrift.

narrator etc. 594; talebearer etc. 532.

v. **disclose**, discover, dismask [*obs.*]; draw–, draw aside–, lift–, raise–, lift up–, remove–, tear- the -veil, —curtain; unmask, unveil, unfold, un- cover, unseal, unkennel; take off–, break- the seal; lay open, lay bare; expose; open, —up; bare, bring to light; evidence; make -clear, —evident, —manifest; evince.

raise–, drop–, lift–, remove–, throw off- the mask; expose; lay open; undeceive, unbeguile; disabuse, set right, correct, open the eyes of; *désillusionner* [*F.*].

divulge, reveal, break [*obs.*]; let into the secret; reveal the secrets of the prison house; tell etc. (*inform*) 527; rat [*slang*], squeal [*slang*]; breathe, utter, blab, peach [*slang*]; let -out, —fall, —drop, —slip, —the cat out of the bag [*colloq.*], come out with it [*colloq.*], come it [*slang*], betray; tell tales, —out of school; come out with; give vent to, give utterance to; open the lips, blurt out, vent, whisper about; speak out etc. (*make manifest*) 525; break the news; make public etc. 531; unriddle etc. (*find out*) 480a; split.

acknowledge, allow, concede, grant, admit, own, confess, avow, throw off all disguise, turn inside out, make a clean breast; show one's -hand, —cards; unburden–, disburden- one's mind, —conscience, —heart; open–, lay bare–, give one a piece of [*colloq.*]- one's mind; unbosom oneself, "own the soft impeachment" [Sheri- dan]; say–, speak- the truth; turn informer; turn -King's, —Queen's, —State's- evidence.

be disclosed etc.; transpire, come to light; come in sight etc. (*be visible*) 446; become known, escape the lips; come out, ooze out, creep out, leak out, peep out, crop out, crop forth, crop up; show its -face, —colors; discover etc. itself; break through the clouds, flash on the mind; come to one's ears etc. 527.

adj. **disclosed** etc. *v.;* revelative, revelatory, revelational, expository, confessional, confessionary, confessory.

int. out with it! 'fess up! [*slang*]; open up! [*colloq*].

530. Ambush
[means of concealment]

n. **ambush**, ambuscade; stalking-horse; lurking-hole, —place; secret path, back stairs; retreat etc. (*refuge*) 666.

hiding place, hidlings [*Scot. & dial. Eng.*]; secret -place, —drawer; recess, hole, cubbyhole, hidie-hole [*Scot.*], holes and corners; closet, crypt, adytum, abditory [*rare*], *oubliette* [*F.*]; safe, safe-deposit box, safety-deposit box.

screen, cover, shade, blinker; veil, curtain, blind, purdah [*India*], cloak, cloud.

mask, visor *or* vizor, vizard [*archaic*], disguise, masquerade dress, domino.

pitfall etc. (*source of danger*) 667; trap etc. (*snare*) 545.

v. **ambush**, ambuscade; lie in ambush etc. (*hide oneself*) 528; lie in wait for; set a trap for etc. (*deceive*) 545.

adv. aux aguets [*F.*]; *janius clausis* [*L.*] etc. 528.

531. Publication

n. **publication**; public announcement etc. 527; promulgation, propagation, proclamation, pronouncement, *pronunciamiento* [*Sp.*], pronunciamento, edict, encyclical; circulation, indiction [*rare*], edition, impression, imprint.

publicity, notoriety, currency, flagrancy, cry, hue and cry, *bruit* [*F.*]; bruit, oyez *or* oyes, *vox populi* [*L.*]; report etc. (*news*) 532; telegram, cable [*colloq.*] etc. 532; telegraphy; publisher etc. *v.*

the press, the Fourth Estate, public press, newspaper, tabloid, journal, gazette, daily, weekly, monthly, quarterly, annual; magazine.

advertisement, ad., placard, bill, flyer [*cant*], leaflet, handbill, *affiche* [*F.*], broadside, broadsheet, poster; circular, —letter; manifesto; notice etc. 527; program *or* programme.

v. **publish**; make -public, —known etc. (*information*) 527; speak of, talk of; broach, utter; put forward; circulate, propagate, promulgate; spread, —abroad; rumor, diffuse, disseminate, evulgate [*obs.*]; put-, give-, send- forth; emit, edit, get out; issue; bring-, lay-, drag- before

the public; give -out, —to the world; report, cover [*newspaper cant*]; put-, bandy-, hawk-, buzz-, whisper-, bruit-, blaze- about; drag into the -open day, —limelight [*colloq.*], throw the spotlight on [*colloq.*]; voice, bruit.

proclaim, herald, blazon; blaze-, noise- abroad; sound a trumpet; trumpet-, thunder- forth; give tongue; announce with -beat of drum, —flourish of trumpets; proclaim -from the housetops, —at Charing Cross, —at the crossroads, —at the market cross.

raise a -cry, —hue and cry, —report; set news afloat.

telegraph, cable, wireless [*colloq.*], broadcast, telecast, televise, wire [*colloq.*].

advertise, placard; post, —up; *afficher* [*F.*], publish in the Gazette, send round the crier, cry abroad.

be published etc.; be *or* become public etc. *adj.;* come out; go-, fly-, buzz-, blow- about; get -about, —abroad, —afloat, —wind; find vent; see the light; go forth, take air, acquire currency, pass current; go the rounds, go the round of the newspapers, go through the length and breadth of the land; *virum volitare per ora* [*L.*]; pass from mouth to mouth; spread; run-, spread- like wildfire.

adj. **published** etc. *v.;* current etc. (*news*) 532; in circulation, public; notorious; flagrant, arrant; open etc. 525; trumpet-tongued; encyclic *or* encyclical, proclamatory, annunciatory, promulgatory; exoteric.

telegraphic, cabled, radiotelegraphic, telegraphed, wireless; radiophonic.

adv. **publicly** etc. *adj.;* in public, in open court, with open doors; in the -limelight, —spotlight [*both colloq.*]; for publication.

int. Oyez! Oyes! notice! flash!

532. News

n. **news**; information etc. 527; piece-, budget- of -news, —information; intelligence, tidings; beat *or* scoop [*newspaper cant*], story, copy [*cant*], print, letterpress.

fresh-, stirring-, old-, stale- news; glad tidings; old-, stale- story; chestnut [*slang*].

message, word, advice, aviso, dispatch *or* despatch; telegram, cable [*colloq.*], wire [*colloq.*], radio [*colloq.*], radiogram, wireless telegram, wireless [*colloq.*], marconigram, pneumatogram, communication, errand, embassy; bulletin; broadcast.

report, rumor, hearsay, on-dit, flying rumor, news stirring, cry, buzz, bruit, fame; talk, *ouï-dire* [*F.*], scandal, eavesdropping; town–, table- -talk, –gossip; tittle-tattle; canard, topic of the day, idea afloat.

narrator etc. (*describe*) 594; newsmonger, scandalmonger; busybody, talebearer, telltale, gossip, tattler, blab, babbler, tattletale, chatterer; informer, squealer [*slang*].

v. **transpire** etc. (*be disclosed*) 529; rumor etc. (*publish*) 531.

adj. **rumored**; publicly–, currently- -rumored, –reported; many-tongued; rife, current, floating, afloat, going about, in circulation, in every one's mouth, all over the town.

having news value, newsy [*colloq.*], snappy [*slang*].

adv. **as they say**; as the story -goes, –runs; it is said.

by telegraph, by cable, by radio [*colloq.*], by television, by wireless [*colloq.*].

533. Secret

n. **secret**; dead–, profound- secret; arcanum, mystery; latency etc. 526; Asian mystery; sealed book, secrets of the prison house; *le dessous des cartes* [*F.*].

enigma, riddle, puzzle, nut to crack, conundrum, charade, rebus, logogriph; monogram, anagram, anagrammatism; Sphinx; *crux criticorum* [*L.*].

maze, labyrinth, meander [*usually in pl.*], Hyrcynian wood; intricacy.

problem etc. (*question*) 461; paradox etc. (*difficulty*) 704; unintelligibility etc. 519; *terra incognita* [*L.*] etc. (*ignorance*) 491.

adj. **secret** etc. (*concealed*) 528; involved etc. 248; labyrinthian, labyrinthine, labyrinthic *or* labyrinthical, mazy, meandrous.

enigmatic *or* enigmatical, anagrammatic *or* anagrammatical, monogrammatic, logogriphic, cryptic *or* cryptical.

534. Messenger

n. **messenger,** angel, envoy, emissary, legate, delegate, nuncio, internuncio, intermediary, go-between; ambassador etc. (*diplomatist*) 758. Gabriel, Hermes, Mercury, Iris, Ariel. marshal, flag bearer, herald, crier, trumpeter, bellman, pursuivant, *parlementaire* [*F.*], apparitor.

courier, runner, dak *or* dawk [*India*], estafette *or* estafet, commissionaire; errand boy, chore boy, newsboy.

mail; post, post office; letter bag, mail bag; postman, mail-man, letter carrier; mail train, mail boat, mailer; aërial mail; carrier pigeon.

telegraph, cable [*colloq.*], wire [*colloq.*], radiotelegraph, wireless telegraph, wireless [*colloq.*], radio [*colloq.*], television [*colloq.*].

telephone, phone [*colloq.*], radio-telephone, radiophone, wireless telephone.

reporter, newspaperman, journalist; gentleman–, representative- of the Press; penny-a-liner; hack writer, special–, war–, own-correspondent; spy, scout; informer etc. 527.

535. Affirmation

n. **affirmation,** affirmance, statement, allegation, assertion, predication, predicate [*logic*], declaration, word, averment; confirmation.

asseveration, adjuration, swearing, oath, affidavit; deposition etc. (*record*) 551; avouchment, avouch [*rare*], assurance; protest, protestation; profession; acknowledgment etc. (*assent*) 488; legal pledge, pronouncement; solemn -averment, -avowal, -declaration.

vote, voice; ballot, suffrage; *vox populi* [*L.*].

remark, observation; position etc. (*proposition*) 514; saying, dictum, sentence, *ipse dixit* [*L.*].

positiveness, emphasis, peremptoriness; dogmatism etc. (*certainty*) 474; weight.

dogmatist etc. 887.

v. **assert**; make an assertion etc. *n.*; have one's say; say, affirm, predicate, declare, state; protest, profess; acknowledge etc. (*assent*) 488.

put forth, put forward; advance, allege, propose, propound; announce etc. 527; enunciate, broach, set forth, hold out, maintain, contend, pronounce, pretend.

depose, depone, aver, avow, avouch, asseverate, swear, rap [*archaic slang*], affirm; make–, take one's- oath; make–, swear–, put in- an affidavit; take one's Bible oath, kiss the book, vow, *vitam impendere vero* [*L.*]; swear till -one is black in the face, -all's blue [*both colloq.*]; be sworn, call Heaven to witness; vouch, warrant, certify, assure; swear by bell, book, and candle; attest etc. (*evidence*) 467; adjure etc. (*put to one's oath*) 768.

emphasize; swear by etc. (*believe*) 484; insist upon, take one's stand upon; lay stress on; assert -roundly, -positively; lay down, -the law; raise one's voice, dogmatize, have the last word; rap out; repeat; reassert, reaffirm.

adj. **affirmative**; asserting etc. *v.*; declaratory, predicatory, predicative, predicational, pronunciatory, pronunciative, *soi-disant* [*F.*]; positive; unmistakable, clear; certain etc. 474; express, explicit etc. (*patent*) 525; absolute, emphatic, flat, broad, round, pointed, marked, distinct, decided, assertive, insistent, confident, trenchant, dogmatic, definitive, formal, solemn, categorical, peremptory; unretracted.

predicable, affirmable, attributable.

adv. **affirmatively** etc. *adj.;* in the affirmative.

with emphasis, ex-cathedra, without fear of contradiction.

I must say, indeed, i' faith, let me tell you, why, give me leave to say, marry [*archaic*], you may be sure, I'd have you know; upon my -word, –honor; by my troth, egad [*euphemism*], I assure you; by jingo, by Jove, by George etc. [*all colloq.*]; troth, seriously, sadly [*obs.*]; in –, in sober- -sadness, –truth, –earnest; of a truth, truly, pardie *or* perdy [*archaic*]; in all conscience, upon oath; be assured etc. (*belief*) 484; yes etc. (*assent*) 488; I'll -warrant, –warrant you, –engage, –answer for it, –be bound, –venture to say, –take my oath; in fact, forsooth, joking -aside, –apart; in all -soberness, –seriousness; so help me God; not to mince the matter.

536. Negation

n. **negation**, abnegation; denial; disavowal, disclaimer; abjuration; contradiction, contravention; recusation, protest; recusancy etc. (*dissent*) 489; flat-, emphatic- -contradiction, –denial; *démenti* [*F.*].

qualification etc. 469; repudiation etc. 610; recantation, revocation; retractation etc. 607; rebuttal; confutation etc. 479; refusal etc. 764; prohibition etc. 761.

v. **deny**; contradict, contravene; controvert, give denial to, gainsay, negative, shake the head; take the Fifth [*slang*].

deny -flatly, –peremptorily, –emphatically, –absolutely, –wholly, –entirely; give the lie to, belie.

disclaim, disown, disaffirm, disavow, abjure, forswear, abnegate, renounce; recant etc. 607; revoke etc. (*abrogate*) 756.

dispute, impugn, traverse, rebut, join issue upon; bring *or* call in question etc. (*doubt*) 485; give (one) the lie in his throat.

repudiate etc. 610; set aside, ignore etc. 460; rebut etc. (*confute*) 479; qualify etc. 469; refuse etc. 764.

adj. **denying** etc. *v.;* denied etc. *v.;* revocatory, abjuratory, abnegative [*rare*], contradictory; negative, negatory; recusant etc. (*dissenting*) 489; at issue upon.

adv. **no**, nay, not, nowise, no way [*colloq.*], noways; not a -bit, –whit, –jot; not at all, not in the least,

not so; no such thing; nothing of the -kind, –sort; quite the contrary, *tout au contraire* [*F.*], far from it; *tant s'en faut* [*F.*]; on no account, in no respect; by no means, by no manner of means; negatively.

537. Teaching

n. **teaching** etc. *v.;* pedagogics, pedagogy; instruction; edification; education; tuition; tutorship, tutorage, tutelage; direction, guidance; opsimathy [*rare*].

preparation, qualification, training, schooling etc. *v.;* discipline; exercise, exercitation, drill, practice.

persuasion, proselytism, propagandism, propaganda; indoctrination, inculcation, inoculation, initiation.

lesson, lecture, sermon, homily, harangue, disquisition; apologue, parable; discourse, prelection, preachment; explanation etc. (*interpretation*) 522; chalk talk [*colloq.*].

Chautauqua -system, –course; lyceum.

exercise, task; curriculum; course, –of study; grammar, three R's; A. B. C. etc. (*beginning*) 66.

[*education*] elementary–, primary–, grammar school–, common school–, high school–, secondary–, technical–, college–, collegiate–, military–, university–, liberal–, classical–, academic–, religious–, denominational–, moral–, secular- education; propaedeutics, moral tuition; the humanities, humanism, humane studies.

normal–, kindergarten- -course, –training; vocational -training, –therapeutics; Montessori system.

physical education, physical drill, gymnastics, calisthenics, eurythmics *or* eurhythmics; sloyd.

v. **teach**, instruct, edify, school, tutor; cram [*colloq.*], grind [*colloq.*], prime, coach; enlighten etc. (*inform*) 527.

inculcate, indoctrinate, inoculate, infuse, instill, infix, ingraft *or* engraft, infiltrate; imbue, impregnate, implant; graft, sow the seeds of, disseminate, propagate.

give an idea of; put up to [*slang*]; put in the way of; set right.

sharpen the wits, enlarge the mind; give new ideas, open the eyes, bring forward, "teach the young idea how to shoot" [Thomson]; improve etc. 658.

direct, guide; direct attention to etc. (*attention*) 457; impress upon the -mind, –memory; beat into, –the head; convince etc. (*belief*) 484.

expound etc. (*interpret*) 522; lecture; read–, give- a -lesson, –lecture, –sermon, –discourse; incept [*Cambridge Univ., Eng.*]; hold forth, preach; prelect, sermonize, moralize; point a moral.

train, discipline; bring up, –to; educate, form, ground, prepare, qualify, drill, exercise, practice, habituate, familiarize with, nurture, dry-nurse, breed, rear, take in hand; break, –in; tame; preinstruct; initiate, graduate; inure etc. (*habituate*) 613.

put to nurse, send to school.

adj. **educational**; scholastic, academic, doctrinal; disciplinal, disciplinary, instructive, instructional, hortatory, homiletic *or* homiletical, pedagogic *or* pedagogical, didactic; teaching etc. *v.*; taught etc. *v.*; propaedeutic *or* propaedeutical; propagative; cultural, humanistic, humane; pragmatic *or* pragmatical, practical, utilitarian; naturalistic, psychological, scientific, sociological, eclectic, coeducational.

538. Misteaching

n. **misteaching**, misinformation, misintelligence, misguidance, misdirection, mispersuasion [*archaic*], misinstruction, misleading etc. *v.*; perversion; false–, dangerous- teaching; sophistry etc. 477; college of Laputa; the blind leading the blind.

v. **misinform**, misteach, misdescribe, misdirect, misguide, misinstruct, miscorrect; pervert; put on a false–, throw off the- scent; deceive etc. 545; mislead etc. (*error*) 495; misrepresent; lie etc. 544; *spargere voces in vulgum ambiguas* [Virgil], preach to the wise, teach one's grandmother to suck eggs [*colloq.*].

render unintelligible etc. 519; bewilder etc. (*uncertainty*) 475; mystify etc. (*conceal*) 528; unteach [*archaic*].

adj. **misteaching** etc. *v.*; unedifying.

539. Learning

n. **learning**; acquisition of -knowledge etc. 490, –skill etc. 698; acquirement, attainment; mental cultivation, edification, scholarship, erudition; acquired knowledge, lore; wide–, general-information; wide reading; self-instruction; study, grind [*colloq.*], reading, perusal; inquiry etc. 461.

docility etc. (*willingness*) 602; aptitude etc. 698.

apprenticeship, prenticeship [*obs. or colloq.*], pupilage, tutelage, novitiate.

examination, matriculation; responsions *or* smalls [*Oxford Univ.*], previous examination or little go [*Cambridge Univ., Eng.*], moderations *or* mods. [*Oxford Univ.*], final examination, finals, greats [*Oxford Univ.*], great go, tripos [*both Cambridge Univ., Eng.*].

translation, crib [*student cant*]; pony, trot, horse [*all student slang*].

v. **learn**; acquire–, gain–, receive–, take in–, drink in–, imbibe–, pick up–, gather–, get–, obtain–, collect–, glean- -knowledge, –information, –learning.

acquaint oneself with, master; make oneself -master of, –acquainted with; grind [*college slang*], cram *or* cram up [*colloq.*], get up, coach up [*colloq.*]; learn by -heart, –rote.

read, spell, peruse; con; run–, pore–, thumb-over; wade through, run through, plunge into, dip into; glance–, run the eye- -over, –through; turn over the leaves.

study; be studious etc. *adj.*; consume–, burn- -the midnight oil; mind one's book, bury oneself in.

go to -school, –college, –the university; serve an (*or* one's) apprenticeship, serve one's time; learn one's trade; be informed etc. 527; be taught etc. 537.

adj. **studious**; industrious etc. 682; scholastic, scholarly, well read, widely read, well posted [*colloq.*], erudite, learned; full of -information, –learning, –lore.

teachable; docile etc. (*willing*) 602; apt etc. 698.

adv. at one's books; *in statu pupillari* [*L.*] etc. (*learner*) 541.

540. Teacher

n. **teacher**, trainer, perceptor, instructor, institutor [*obs.*], master, tutor, director, coryphaeus [*Oxford Univ.*], dry nurse [*slang*], coach [*colloq.*], crammer [*colloq.*], grinder [*college slang, Eng.*], don [*Univ. cant*]; governor [*obs.*], bear leader [*humorous*]; governess, duenna; disciplinarian.

professor, lecturer, reader, prelector *or* praelector, prolocutor, preacher; chalk talker, *khoja* [*Turk.*], munshi *or* moonshee [*Moham.*]; pastor etc. (*clergy*) 996; schoolmaster, dominie, usher [*Brit.*], pedagogue, abecedarian; schoolmistress, dame [*rare*], kindergartner, monitor, pupil teacher.

guide; docent, coach, expositor etc. 524; guru [*Hindu*]; mentor etc. (*adviser*) 695; pioneer, apostle, missionary, propagandist; example etc. 22.

professorship etc. (*school*) 542.

tutelage etc. (*teaching*) 537.

adj. **pedagogic** *or* pedagogical, preceptorial, tutorial, professorial; scholastic etc. 537.

541. Learner

n. **learner**, scholar, student, alumnus (*fem.* alumna, *pl.* alumni), *élève* [*F.*], pupil, schoolboy, schoolgirl; questionist, questioner, inquirer; monitor, prefect; beginner, tyro, abecedarian, alphabetarian.

    undergraduate, undergrad. [*colloq.*], freshman, fresh *or* freshie *or* frosh [*slang*], plebe [*West Point cant*], sophomore, soph [*colloq.*], junior, senior; commoner; pensioner, sizar [*both Cambridge Univ., Eng.*]; exhibitioner, scholar [*winner of a scholarship*], fellow commoner [*Eng. Univ.*], demy [*Magdalene Coll., Oxford*]; junior, sophister *or* soph, senior sophister *or* soph, sophister, questionist [*all Eng. Univ.*].

    graduate student, post-graduate student, post-doctoral fellow.

    class, form, grade, room; promotion, graduation, remove; pupilage etc. (*learning*) 539.

    disciple, chela [*India*], follower, apostle, proselyte.

    fellow student, *condiscipulus* [*L.*], condisciple, classmate, schoolmate, schoolfellow, fellow pupil.

    novice, recruit, tenderfoot [*slang*], neophyte, inceptor, *débutant* [*F.*], catechumen, probationer; apprentice, prentice [*obs. or colloq.*], articled clerk.

adj. *in statu pupillari* [*L.*], in leading strings, pupillary, monitorial; abecedarian, rudimentary; probationary, probatory, probational; sophomoric *or* sophomoral.

542. School

n. **school**, academy, lyceum, *Gymnasium* [*Ger.*], *lycée* [*F.*], palaestra *or* palestra, seminary, college, educational institution, institute; university, 'varsity [*colloq.*], *Alma Mater* [*L.*].

    [general] day–, boarding–, preparatory *or* prep [*colloq.*], –, elementary–, common–, denominational–, secondary–, endowed–, free–, continuation–, convent–, art–, music–, military–, naval–, technical–, library–, secretarial–, business–, correspondence- school; kindergarten, nursery, day nursery, nursery school, *crèche* [*F.*]; Sunday–, Sabbath–, Bible-school; reform school, reformatory; teachers' training college; university extension -lectures, –course.

    [british] primary–, infant–, dame [*hist.*]–, voluntary–, government–, Board–, higher grade–, National–, mission–, missionary–, British and Foreign–, state-aided–, grant-in-aid–, middle-class–, County Council–, training–, normal–, grammar–, collegiate–, high–, upper–, modern–, lower–, County–, County high–, Cathedral–, municipal secondary–, municipal technical–, Friends'–, coeducational *or* dual–, Polytechnic–, King Henry VIII's–, King Edward's–, Queen Elizabeth's–, Queen Mary's–, merchant guild–, Blue-Coat- school; Christ's Hospital; public school (*as* Eton, Harrow, Rugby etc.); school of art, school of arts and crafts, trade school; Royal Naval College, Royal Military Academy (Woolwich), Royal Military College (Sandhurst); training ship for -royal navy, –mercantile marine; College of Preceptors; Royal Academy–, London College–, Trinity College- of Music; Royal College of Organists.

    [united states] district–, grade–, parochial–, public–, primary–, grammar–, junior high–, high–, Latin- school; private–, technological–, normal–, kindergarten training- school; summer school; military academy (West Point); naval academy (Annapolis); college, freshwater college [*slang*], jerk water college [*slang*], State university; graduate school, post-graduate school.

    class, division, form etc. 541; seminar *or* seminary.

    class room, room, school room, recitation room, lecture room, lecture hall, theater *or* theatre, amphitheater *or* amphitheatre.

    desk, reading desk, ambo, pulpit, forum, stage, rostrum, platform, hustings, tribune.

    schoolbook, textbook, hornbook; grammar, primer, abecedary [*rare*], abecedarium, New England Primer, rudiments, manual, *vade mecum* [*L.*]; encyclopedia *or* encyclopaedia; cyclopedia *or* cyclopaedia; Lindley Murray, Cocker; dictionary, lexicon, thesaurus.

    professorship, associate professorship, lectureship, readership, fellowship, preceptorship, tutorship, instructorship; chair.

    directorate, board, syndicate; College Board, Board of Regents (N. Y.), School Board, Council of Education; Board of Education; Board–, Prefect- of Studies; Textbook Committee; propaganda.

adj. **scholastic**, academic, collegiate; educational, palaestral *or* palestral, cultural; gymnastic, athletic, physical, eurythmic.

adv. ex-cathedra.

543. Veracity

n. **veracity**; truthfulness, frankness etc. *adj.;* truth, soothfastness [*archaic*], smooth [*archaic*], veridicality, sincerity, candor, honesty, fidelity; plain dealing, *bona fides* [*L.*]; love of truth; probity etc. 939; ingenuousness etc. (*artlessness*) 703.

the truth the whole truth and nothing but the truth; honest–, unvarnished–, sober- truth etc. (*fact*) 494; unvarnished tale; light of truth.

v. **speak the truth**, tell the truth; speak on oath; speak without -equivocation, –mental reservation; speak by the card; paint in its–, show oneself in one's- true colors; make a clean breast, let it all hang out [*slang*] etc. (*disclose*) 529; speak one's mind etc. (*be blunt*) 703; not lie etc. 544, not deceive etc. 545.

adj. **truthful**, true; veracious, veridical; scrupulous etc. (*honorable*) 939; sincere, candid, frank, open, straightforward, unreserved; open–, frank–, true–, simple- hearted; soothfast [*archaic*], truth-telling, honest, trustworthy; undissembling etc. (dissemble etc. 544); guileless, pure; truth-loving; unperjured; true-blue, as good as one's word; one's word one's bond; unaffected, unfeigned, *bona fide* [*L.*]; outspoken, ingenuous etc. (*artless*) 703; undisguised etc. (*real*) 494.

adv. **truly** etc. (*really*) 494; in plain words etc. 703; in–, with–, of a–, in good- truth; as the dial to the sun, as the needle to the pole; honor bright [*colloq.*]; troth; in good -sooth, –earnest; soothfast [*archaic*], unfeignedly, with no nonsense, in sooth, sooth to say, *bona fide* [*L.*], *in foro conscientiae* [*L.*]; without equivocation; *cartes sur table* [*F.*], from the bottom of one's heart; by my troth etc. (*affirmation*) 535.

544. Falsehood

n. **falsehood**, falseness; falsity, falsification; deception etc. 545; untruthfulness; untruth etc. 546; guile; lying etc. *v.*, misrepresentation; mendacity, perjury, false swearing; forgery, invention, fabrication; subreption; covin [*archaic*].

perversion–, suppression- of truth; *suppressio veri* [*L.*]; perversion, distortion, false coloring; exaggeration etc. 549; prevarication, equivocation, shuffling, fencing, evasion, fraud; *suggestio falsi* [*L.*] etc. (*lie*) 546; mystification etc. (*concealment*) 528; simulation etc. (*imitation*) 19; dissimulation, dissembling; deceit; *blague* [*F.*].

sham, pretense, scam [*slang*], pretending, malingering.

duplicity, double dealing, insincerity, tartufism *or* tartuffism, hypocrisy, cant, humbug, fake [*slang*]; casuistry, jesuitism, jesuitry; pharisaism; Machiavelism, "organized hypocrisy"; lip -homage, –service; mouth honor; hollowness; mere -show, –outside; crocodile tears, mealymouthedness, quackery; charlatanism, charlatanry; gammon [*Eng. colloq.*], buncombe *or* bunkum *or* bunk, flam: bam [*slang*], flimflam, cajolery, flattery; Judas kiss; perfidy etc. (*bad faith*) 940; *il volto sciolto i pensieri stretti* [*It.*].

unfairness etc. (*dishonesty*) 940; artfulness etc. (*cunning*) 702; misstatement etc. (*error*) 495.

v. **be false** etc. *adj.,* be a liar etc. 548; speak falsely etc. *adv.;* tell a lie etc. 546; lie, fib; lie like a trooper; swear falsely, forswear, perjure oneself, bear false witness.

falsify, misstate, misquote, miscite, misreport, misrepresent; belie, pervert, distort; put a false construction upon etc. (*misinterpret*) 523.

prevaricate, equivocate, quibble; palter, –to the understanding; *répondre en Normand* [*F.*]; trim, shuffle, fence, mince the truth, beat about the bush, blow hot and cold [*colloq.*], play fast and loose.

garble, gloss over, disguise, give a color to; give–, put- a -gloss, –false coloring- upon; color, varnish, cook [*colloq.*], doctor [*colloq.*], dress up, embroider; exaggerate etc. 549; *blague* [*F.*].

fabricate, invent, trump up, get up; forge, fake [*slang*], hatch, concoct; romance etc. (*imagine*) 515; cry "wolf!"

dissemble, dissimulate; feign, assume, put on, pretend, make believe; act the old soldier [*colloq.*], play possum; play -false, –a double game; coquet; act–, play- a part; affect etc. 855; simulate, pass off for; counterfeit, sham, make a show of; malinger; say the grapes are sour.

cant [*dial. Eng.*], play the hypocrite, sham Abram *or* Abraham, *faire pattes de velours* [*F.*], put on the mask, clean the outside of the platter, lie like a thief, lie through one's teeth; hand out–, hold out–, sail under- false colors; "commend the poisoned chalice to the lips" [*Macbeth*]; *spargere voces in vulgum ambiguas* [*Virgil*]; deceive etc. 545.

adj. **false**, deceitful, mendacious, unveracious, fraudulent, dishonest; faithless, truthless, untruthful, trothless [*archaic*]; unfair, uncandid; hollowhearted; evasive; uningenuous, disingenuous; hollow, insincere, *Parthis mendacior* [*L.*]; forsworn.

collusive, collusory [obs.]; artful etc. (cunning) 702; perfidious etc. 940; spurious etc. (deceptive) 545; untrue etc. 546; falsified etc. v.; covinous.

hypocritical, canting, jesuitical, pharisaical; tartufish or tartuffish; Machiavellic, Machiavellian or Machiavelian; double, –tongued, –handed, –minded, –hearted, –dealing; two-faced, double-faced; Janus-faced; smooth-faced, –spoken, –tongued; plausible; mealy-mouthed; affected etc. 855.

adv. **falsely** etc. *adj.;* à la Tartufe [F.], with a double tongue; slily etc. (cunning) 702.

545. Deception

n. **deception**; falseness etc. 544; untruth etc. 546; imposition, imposture; fraud, deceit, guile; fraudulence, fraudulency; covin [archaic]; knavery etc. (cunning) 702; misrepresentation etc. (falsehood) 544; bluff; straw-bail, straw-bid; spoof [slang]; hocus-pocus, escamoterie [F.], jockeyship; trickery, coggery [obs.], pettifoggery, sharp practice, chicanery; supercherie [F.], cozenage, circumvention, ingannation [obs.], collusiveness, collusion; treachery etc. 940; practical joke.

delusion, gullery [archaic]; juggling, jugglery; sleight of hand, legerdemain; prestigiation [obs.], prestidigitation; magic etc. 992; conjuring, conjuration.

trick, cheat, wile, blind, feint, plant [slang], bubble, fetch, catch [dial.], chicane, artifice, reach [obs.], bite [obs., colloq.], juggle, hocus [archaic]; thimble-rig, card sharping, artful dodge, swindle; tricks upon travelers; trapan or trepan [archaic]; stratagem etc. (artifice) 702; fake [colloq. or slang], hoax; theft etc. 791; ballot-box stuffing, barney [slang], bunko or bunco, bunko game; confidence -trick, -game; brace–, drop–, gum–, panel–, shell–, skin- game [all slang]; gold brick [colloq.].

snare, trap, pitfall, Cornish hug, decoy, gin; springe, springle [obs.]; noose, hook; bait, decoy duck, stool pigeon, tub to the whale, baited trap, guet-apens [F.]; cobweb, net, meshes, toils, mouse trap, birdlime; Dionaea, Venus's flytrap; ambush etc. 530; trapdoor, sliding panel, false bottom; spring net, spring gun; mask, masked battery; mine; flytrap; green goods; panel house.

disguise, disguisement; false colors, masquerade, mummery, borrowed plumes; wolf in sheep's clothing etc. (deceiver) 548; pattes de velours [F.].

sham; mockery etc. (imitation) 19; copy etc. 21; counterfeit, make-believe, forgery, fraud; lie etc. 546; "a delusion, a mockery, and a snare" [Denman], hollow mockery; whited–, painted-sepulcher; jerry-building, jerryism [builders' cant]; man of straw.

tinsel, paste, false jewelry, scagliola, ormolu, mosaic gold, brummagem, German silver, albata, paktong, white metal, Britannia metal, paint.

illusion etc. (error) 495; ignis fatuus [L.] etc. 423; mirage etc. 443.

v. **deceive**, take in, Machiavellize; defraud, cheat, jockey, do [slang], escamoter [F.], cozen, diddle [dial.], nab [slang], chouse [colloq.], bite [colloq.], play one false, bilk, cully, jilt [obs.], pluck [rare], swindle, victimize; abuse; mystify; blind, –one's eyes; blindfold, hoodwink; throw dust into the eyes, "keep the word of promise to the ear and break it to the hope" [Macbeth].

impose–, practice–, play–, put–, palm–, foist- upon; snatch a verdict; bluff, –off; bunko or bunco, four-flush [slang]; gum [slang], spoof [slang], stuff (a ballot box) [U. S.].

circumvent, overreach; outreach, outwit, outmaneuver or outmanoeuvre, steal a march upon, give the go-by to [slang], leave in the lurch.

insnare, ensnare; set–, lay- a -trap, –snare- for; bait the hook, forelay [obs.], spread the toils, lime; decoy, waylay, lure, beguile, delude, inveigle; trapan or trepan [archaic]; kidnap; let in, hook in; trick; entrap or intrap, nick, springe [rare], nousel or nousle [obs.]; blind a trail, enmesh or immesh; shanghai, crimp; catch, –in a trap; sniggle, entangle, illaqueate [rare], balk, trip up; throw a tub to a whale, hocus.

fool, befool, practice on one's credulity, dupe, gull, hoax, bamboozle [colloq.]; hum [slang or colloq.], humbug, gammon [Eng. colloq.], stuff up [slang], stuff [slang], sell [slang]; play a -trick, –practical joke- upon one; fool to the top of one's bent, send on a fool's errand; make -game, –a fool, –an April fool, –an ass- of; trifle with, cajole, flatter; come over etc. (influence) 615; gild the pill, make things pleasant, divert, put a good face upon; dissemble etc. 544.

live by one's wits; cog [rare], cog the dice; play at hide and seek; obtain money under false pretenses etc. (steal) 791; conjure, juggle, practice chicanery; deacon; jerry-build; pass by trickery, play off, palm off, foist off, fob off [archaic].

185

mislead etc. (*error*) 495; lie etc. 544; misinform etc. 538; betray etc. 940.

be deceived etc. 547.

adj. **deceptive**, decepious [*rare*], deceitful, covinous [*law*]; delusive, delusory; illusive, illusory; deceived etc. *v.;* deceiving etc. *v.;* cunning etc. 702; prestigious [*obs.*], prestigiatory [*obs.*]; elusive, insidious, *ad captandum vulgus* [*L.*].

make-believe; untrue etc. 546; mock, sham, counterfeit, snide [*slang*], pseudo, spurious, so-called, pretended, feigned, trumped-up, bogus [*colloq.*], scamped, fraudulent, tricky, factitious, artificial, bastard; surreptitious, illegitimate, contraband, adulterated, sophisticated; unsound, rotten at the core; colorable; disguised; meretricious; jerry-built, jerry [*builders' cant*]; tinsel, pinchbeck, plated; catchpenny; brummagem; simulated etc. 544.

adv. under -false colors, –the garb of, –cover of; over the left [*slang*].

546. Untruth

n. **untruth**, falsehood, lie, story, thing that is not, fib, bounce, crammer [*slang*], tarradiddle *or* taradiddle [*colloq.*], whopper *or* whapper [*colloq.*], *jhuth* [*Hind.*].

fabrication, forgery, invention; misstatement, misrepresentation, perversion, falsification, gloss, *suggestio falsi* [*L.*]; exaggeration etc. 549.

fiction; fable, nursery tale; romance etc. (*imagination*) 515; absurd–, untrue–, false–, trumped up- -story, –statement; thing devised by the enemy; canard; shave [*slang, Eng.*], sell [*colloq.*], hum, [*slang*], whopper [*colloq.*], yarn [*colloq.*], fish story [*colloq.*], tall tale, traveler's tale, Canterbury tale, cock-and-bull story, fairy tale, fake, press-agent's yarn [*colloq.*], hot air [*slang*], claptrap.

myth, moonshine, bosh [*colloq.*], all my eye and Betty Martin [*colloq.*], all my eye [*colloq.*], mare's-nest, farce.

half truth, white lie, pious fraud; mental reservation etc. (*concealment*) 528; irony.

pretense, pretext; false plea etc. 617; subterfuge, evasion, shift, shuffle, make-believe; sham etc. (*deception*) 545; profession, empty words; Judas kiss etc. (*hypocrisy*) 544; disguise etc. (*mask*) 530.

v. **ring untrue**; have a -false meaning, –hidden meaning, –false appearance; be an untruth etc. *n.;* lie etc. 544.

feign, pretend, sham, counterfeit, gammon [*Eng. colloq.*], make-believe.

adj. **untrue**, false, trumped up; void of–, without-foundation; fictive, far from the truth, false as dicer's oaths; unfounded, *ben trovato* [*It.*], invented, fabulous, fabricated, fraudulent, forged; fictitious, factitious, supposititious, surreptitious; illusory, elusory; evasive, satiric *or* satirical, ironical; *soi-disant* [*F.*] etc. (*misnamed*) 565.

547. Dupe

n. **dupe**, gull, gudgeon, *gobemouche* [*F.*], cully, victim, April fool; jay, sucker, pigeon, cull [*all slang*]; laughingstock etc. 857; simple Simon, flat [*colloq.*], greenhorn; fool etc. 501; puppet, cat's-paw.

v. **be deceived** etc. 545, be the dupe of; fall into a trap; swallow–, nibble at- the bait; bite; catch a Tartar.

adj. **credulous** etc. 486.

mistaken etc. (*error*) 495.

548. Deceiver

n. **deceiver** etc. (deceive etc. 545); dissembler, hypocrite; sophist, Pharisee, Jesuit, Mawworm, Pecksniff, Joseph Surface, Tartufe *or* Tartuffe, Janus; serpent, snake in the grass, cockatrice, Judas, wolf in sheep's clothing; jilt; shuffler.

liar etc. (*lie* etc. 544); Tom Pepper, Machiavel, Machiavelist; story-teller, perjurer, false witness, *menteur à triple étage* [*F.*], Scapin; bunko artist, bunko steerer, carpetbagger, capper [*all slang, U. S.*], faker [*slang*], fraud, four-flusher [*slang*], confidence man, grifter, horse coper [*Eng.*], ringer [*slang*], spieler [*colloq.*]; straw bidder; crimp; decoy duck, stool pigeon; rogue, knave, cheat; swindler etc. (*thief*) 792; jobber, gypsy.

impostor, pretender, malingerer, humbug; adventurer, adventuress; Cagliostro, Fernam Mendex Pinto; ass in lion's skin etc. (*bungler*) 701; actor etc. (*stage player*) 599.

quack, charlatan, mountebank, saltimbanco [*obs.*], *saltimbanque* [*F.*], *blagueur* [*F.*], empiric, quacksalver [*now rare*], medicaster.

conjuror, juggler, trickster, prestidigitator, necromancer, sorcerer, magician, wizard, mage [*archaic*], medicine man, shaman.

549. Exaggeration

n. **exaggeration**; expansion etc. 194; hyperbole, stretch, strain, coloring; high coloring, caricature, *caricatura* [*It.*]; extravagance etc. (*nonsense*) 497; Baron Munchausen; Munchausenism; men in buckram, big one, yarn [*colloq.*], fringe, embroidery, tall tale, traveler's tale; fish story [*colloq.*], gooseberry [*slang*].

storm–, tempest- in a teacup; much ado about nothing etc. (*overestimation*) 482; puffery etc. (*boasting*) 884; rant etc. (*turgescence*) 577.

false coloring etc. (*falsehood*) 544; aggravation etc. 835.

figure of speech, *façon de parler* [*F.*]; stretch of -fancy, –the imagination; flight of fancy etc. (*imagination*) 515.

v. **exaggerate**, magnify, pile up, aggravate; amplify etc. (*expand*) 194; optimize; overestimate etc. 482; hyperbolize; overcharge, overstate, overdraw, overlay, overshoot the mark, overpraise; make much of, make the most of; strain, –a point; stretch, –a point; go great lengths; spin a long yarn [*colloq.*]; draw–, pull–, use–, shoot with- a (*or* the) longbow [*colloq.*]; deal in the marvelous.

out-Herod Herod, run riot, talk at random.

overcolor, heighten; color -highly, –too highly; *broder* [*F.*], embroider, be flowery; flourish; color etc. (*misrepresent*) 544; puff etc. (*boast*) 884.

underrate, pessimize, underestimate etc. 483.

adj. **exaggerated** etc. *v.*; overwrought; bombastic etc. (*magniloquent*) 577; hyperbolical, on stilts; fabulous, extravagant, preposterous, egregious, *outré* [*F.*], highflying.

Section 3. Means of Communication

550. Indication

n. **indication**; symbolism, symbolization; symptomatology, semeiology *or* semiology, semeiotics *or* semiotics, pathognomy; *Zeitgeist* [*Ger.*], sign of the times.

means of recognition; lineament, feature, trait, trick, carmark, characteristic, diagnostic; diving rod; cloven hoof; footfall.

sign, symbol; index, indice [*obs.*], indicator, point, pointer; exponent, note, token, symptom; dollar mark; type, figure, emblem, cipher, device; representation etc. 554.

motto, epigraph, epitaph, posy [*archaic*].

gesture, gesticulation; pantomime; wink, glance, leer; nod, shrug, beck; touch, cudge; grip, freemasonry; telegraphy, byplay, dumb show; cue; hint etc. 527.

track, spoor, trail, footprint, scent; clew *or* clue, key.

dactylology, dactylography, dactylonomy, dactyliomancy, chirology [*rare*], chiromancy, palmistry; finger print, Bertillon system.

signal, signal post, rocket, blue light, red light; watch fire, watchtower; telegraph, semaphore, flagstaff; fiery cross; calumet, peace pipe; heliograph; guidon; headlight, searchlight, flashlight, spotlight.

mark, line, stroke, score, stripe, streak, scratch, tick, dot, point, notch, nick, blaze; red letter, sublineation, underlining, jotting; print; imprint, impress, impression; note, annotation.

[map drawing] hachure, contour line; isobar, isopiestic line, isobaric line; isotherm, isothermal line; latitude, longitude, meridian, equator.

[typography] dash, hyphen, parentheses, brackets *or* crotchets, apostrophe, question mark, exclamation *or* exclamation point; acute–, grave-accent; long *or* macron, short *or* breve, dieresis, caret, brace, ellipsis, leaders, asterisk, dagger *or* obelisk, double dagger, section, parallels, paragraph, index, asterism, cedilla, guillemets [*rare*], quotation marks *or* quotes [*colloq.*], tilde, circumflex.

[for identification] badge, criterion; countercheck, countermark, countersign, counterfoil, stub, duplicate, tally; label, ticket, billet, letter, counter, check, chip, chop [*Oriental*], dib [*slang*]; broad arrow; government mark; totem; tessera, card, bill; witness, voucher; stamp; *cachet* [*F.*]; trade–, hall- mark; signature; address–, visiting- card; *carte de visite* [*F.*]; credentials etc. (*evidence*) 467; attestation; hand, handwriting, sign manual; cipher; monogram; seal, sigil, signet; autograph, autography; finger print; paraph, brand; superscription; indorsement *or* endorsement; title, heading, docket; tonsure, scalp lock; mortar board [*colloq.*], cap and gown, hood; caste mark; *mot de passe* [*F.*], *mot du guet* [*F.*]; passeparole *or* passparole [*obs.*], shibboleth; watchword, catchword, password; sign, countersign, pass, dueguard, grip; open-sesame; timbrology [*rare*].

insignia; banner, banneret; banderole, bandrol *or* bannerol; flag, colors, streamer, standard, eagle, vexillum, labarum, oriflamme *or* oriflamb; figurehead; ensign; pennant, whip *or* coach-whip, pennon, burgee, blue peter, jack, ancient [*rare*], gonfalon, union jack; "Old Glory" [*colloq.*], quarantine flag; yellow flag, yellow jack; tricolor, *drapeau tricolore* [*F.*], stars and stripes; stars and bars; half-masted flag, union down; red flag; bunting.

heraldry, crest; arms, coat of arms; armorial bearings, hatchment; escutcheon *or* scutcheon, achievement, shield, supporters; livery, uniform; cockade, brassard, epaulet, chevron; garland, chaplet, fillet [*antiq.*], love knot, favor.

[of locality] beacon, beacon fire, cresset, cairn, post, staff, flagstaff, hand, pointer, vane, cock, weathercock, weathervane; guide-, hand-, finger-, directing-, sign- post; pillars of Hercules, pharos; balefire, signal fire; *l'Etoile du Nord* [*F.*], North Star, polestar, Polaris; landmark, seamark; lighthouse, balize [*rare*], lodestar *or* loadstar; cynosure, guide; address, direction, name; sign, signboard.

[of the future] warning etc. 668; omen etc. 512; prefigurement etc. 511.

[of the past] trace, record etc. 551.

[of danger] warning etc. 668; fire alarm, burglar alarm; alarm etc. 669.

[of authority] scepter etc. 747.

[of triumph] trophy etc. 733.

[of quantity] gauge etc. 466.

[of distance] milestone, milepost; mileage ticket; milliary [*Rom. antiq.*].

[of disgrace] brand, fool's cap, mark of Cain, stigma, stripes, broad arrow.

[for detection] check, time clock, telltale; test etc. (*experiment*) 463.

notification etc. (*information*) 527; advertisement etc. (*publication*) 531.

call, word of command; bugle call, trumpet call; bell, alarum, cry; battle-, rallying- cry; reveille, taps, last post; sacring bell, Sanctus bell, angelus; pibroch, keen [*Ir.*], coronach [*Scot. & Ir.*], dirge.

v. **indicate**; be the sign of etc. *n.;* denote, betoken; argue, testify etc. (*evidence*) 467; bear the impress of etc. *n.;* connote, connotate, signify.

represent, stand for; typify etc. (*prefigure*) 511; symbolize.

mark; put an indication, put a mark etc. *n.;* note, tick, stamp, nick, earmark; blaze; label, ticket, docket; dot, spot, score, dash, trace, chalk.

print, imprint, impress; engrave, stereotype, electrotype, lithograph; prove, pull, reprint.

make a sign etc. *n.;* signalize; give-, hang out- a signal; beck [*archaic*], beckon; nod; wink, glance, leer, nudge, shrug, tip the wink [*slang*]; gesture, gesticulate; raise-, hold up- the -finger, -hand; saw the air, "suit the action to the word" [*Hamlet*].

wave-, unfurl-, hoist-, hang out- a banner etc. *n.;* wave -the hand, -a kerchief; give the cue etc. (*inform*) 527; show one's colors; give-,

sound- an alarm; beat the drum, sound the trumpets, raise a cry.

sign, seal, attest etc. (*evidence*) 467; underscore, underline etc. (*give importance to*) 642; call attention to etc. (*attention*) 457; give notice etc. (*inform*) 527.

adj. **indicative**, indicatory; indicating etc. *v.* connotative, denotative; diacritical, representative, typical, symbolic *or* symbolical, pantomimic, pathognomonic *or* pathognomonical, symptomatic, semeiotic *or* semiotic, sematic, ominous, characteristic, significant, significative, demonstrative, diagnostic, exponential, emblematic, armorial; individual etc. (*special*) 79.

known by, recognizable by; indicated etc. *v.;* pointed, marked.

[capable of being denoted] denotable; indelible.

adv. **symbolically** etc. *adj.;* in token of; in dumb show, in pantomime.

551. Record

n. **trace**, vestige, relic, remains; scar, cicatrix; footstep, footmark, footprint; pug [*India*], track, mark, wake, trail, scent, *piste* [*F.*].

monument, hatchment, achievement; escutcheon *or* scutcheon; slab, tablet, trophy, obelisk, pillar, column, monolith; memorial; memento etc. (*memory*) 505; testimonial, medal, Congressional medal; cross, Victoria cross *or* V. C., iron cross [*Ger.*]; ribbon, garter; commemoration etc. (*celebration*) 883.

record, note, minute; register, registry; roll etc. (*list*) 86; chartulary *or* cartulary, diptych, Domesday book; *catalogue raisonné* [*F.*]; entry, memorandum, indorsement *or* endorsement, inscription, copy, duplicate, docket; notch etc. (*mark*) 550; muniments; deed etc. (*security*) 771; document; deposition, *procés verbal* [*F.*]; affidavit; certificate etc. (*evidence*) 467.

notebook, memorandum book, pocketbook, commonplace book, portfolio; bulletin, bulletin board, score board, score sheet, totalizator [*racing*] tote board [*colloq.*]; card index, file, letter file, pigeonholes; *excerpta* [*L.*], excerpt, extract, adversaria, jottings, dottings.

newspaper, daily, gazette etc. (*publication*) 531; magazine.

calendar, ephemeris, diary, log, log book *or* logbook, journal, daybook, ledger, cashbook, petty cashbook.

archive, scroll, state paper, return, bluebook *or* blue book; almanac *or* almanack, gazetteer, Almanach de Gotha, Statesman's Year-book, Whitaker's Almanack; census report; statistics etc. 86; *compte rendu* [*F.*]; Acts–, Transactions–, Proceedings- of; Hansard's Debates; Congressional Records; minutes, chronicle, annals; legend; history, biography etc. 594.

registration; registry, enrollment *or* enrolment, tabulation; entry, booking; signature etc. (*identification*) 550; recorder etc. 553; journalism.

mechanical record, recording instrument; gramophone, phonograph etc. 418; seismograph, seismometer; speedometer, pedometer, patent log [*naut.*]; ticker, tape; time clock; anemometer etc. (*measurement*) 466; turnstile; cash register; votograph.

v. **record**; put–, place- upon record; chronicle, calendar, excerpt, hand down to posterity; keep up the memory etc. (*remember*) 505; commemorate etc. (*celebrate*) 883; report etc. (*inform*) 527; commit to–, reduce to- writing; put–, set down- -in writing, –in black and white; put–, jot–, take–, write–, note–, set-down; note, minute, put on paper; take–, make- a -note, –minute, –memorandum; summarize, make a return; mark etc. (*indicate*) 550; sign etc. (*attest*) 467.

enter, book; post, post up; insert, make an entry of; mark off, tick off; register, list, docket, enroll, inscroll; file etc. (*store*) 636.

adv. **on record**, on file; in one's -good books, –bad books.

552. Obliteration
[suppression of sign]

n. **obliteration**, erasure, rasure [*rare*]; cancel, cancellation; circumduction [*rare*], deletion, blot; *tabula rasa* [*L.*]; effacement, extinction.

v. **efface**, obliterate, erase, rase [*rare*], expunge, cancel, dele; blot–, take–, rub–, scratch–, strike–, wipe–, wash–, sponge- out; wipe off, rub off; wipe away; deface, render illegible; draw the pen through, rule out, apply the sponge.

be effaced etc.; leave no trace etc. 550; "leave not a rack behind" [*Tempest*].

adj. **obliterated** etc. *v.;* leaving no trace; intestate; unrecorded, unregistered, unwritten; printless, out of print.

int. dele; out with it!

553. Recorder

n. **recorder**, notary, clerk; registrar, registrary [*obs.*], register; prothonotary; amanuensis, secretary, recording secretary, stenographer, scribe, babu [*India*], remembrancer, book-

keeper, *custos rotulorum* [*L.*], Master of the Rolls.

annalist, historian, historiographer, chronicler; biographer etc. (*narrator*) 594; antiquary etc. (*antiquity*) 122; memorialist.

journalist, newspaperman, reporter, interviewer, pressman, publicist, author, editor.

554. Representation

n. **representation**, depiction, depicture; imitation etc. 19; illustration, delineation, depictment; imagery, portraiture, iconography; design, designing; art, fine arts; painting etc. 556; sculpture etc. 557; engraving etc. 558.

photography; radiography, X-ray photography, skiagraphy; spectroheliography, photospectroheliography.

personation, personification; impersonation; drama etc. 599.

drawing, picture, sketch, draft *or* draught; tracing; copy etc. 21.

photograph, photo [*colloq.*], daguerreotype, talbotype, calotype; heliotype, heliograph; print, cabinet, *carte de visite* (*pl. cartes de visite*) [*F.*], ping-pong [*cant*], snapshot.

image, likeness, icon, portrait; striking likeness, speaking likeness; spitting image [*colloq.*]; very image; effigy, facsimile.

figure, figurehead; puppet, doll, figurine, aglet *or* aiglet, manikin, mannequin, lay figure, model, marionette, fantoccini, waxwork, bust; statue, statuette, hieroglyph.

hieroglyphic, anaglyph, diagram, monogram.

map, plan, chart; ground plan, projection, elevation; atlas; outline, scheme; view etc. (*painting*) 556; ichnography, cartography.

radiograph, radiogram, scotograph, skiagraph *or* sciagraph, skiagram *or* sciagram, CAT scan, ultrasound image, X-ray photograph, X-ray [*colloq.*]; spectrogram, spectroheliogram, photospectroheliogram.

delineator, draftsman *or* draughtsman; artist etc. 559; photographer, radiographer, X-ray photographer, skiagrapher, daguerreotypist.

v. **represent**, delineate, depict, depicture, portray, picture, limn, take–, catch- a likeness etc. *n.;* hit off, photograph, daguerreotype; snapshot; figure; shadow -forth, –out; adumbrate; body forth; describe etc. 594; trace, copy; mold *or* mould.

illustrate, symbolize; paint etc. 556; carve etc. 557; engrave etc. 558.

personate, personify, impersonate, dress up [*colloq.*], assume a character, pose as, act; play etc. (*drama*) 599; mimic etc. (*imitate*) 19; hold the mirror up to nature.

adj. **representing** etc. *v.*, representative; illustrative; represented etc. *v.;* imitative, figurative; iconic, like etc. 17; graphic etc. (*descriptive*) 594. Renaissance, trecento, quattrocento, cinquecento, Directoire, Moyen Age.

555. Misrepresentation

n. **misrepresentation**, misstatement, falsification, caricatura [*obs.*], exaggeration; daubing etc. *v.;* bad likeness, daub, scratch; imitation, effigy.

distortion, anamorphosis, anamorphoscope; Claude Lorrain–, concave–, convex- mirror.

burlesque, travesty, parody, takeoff, caricature, extravaganza.

v. **misrepresent**, distort, overdraw, exaggerate, daub; falsify, understate, overstate, stretch.

burlesque, travesty, parody, caricature.

adj. **misrepresented** etc. *v.;* bluesky.

556. Painting and Black and White

n. **painting**; depicting; drawing etc. *v.;* design; perspective; *chiaroscuro* etc. (*light*) 420; composition; treatment; arrangement, values, atmosphere, tone, technique.

historical–, portrait–, miniature–, landscape–, marine–, flower–, poster–, interior–, scene-painting; scenography.

pallet, palette; easel; brush, pencil, stump; black lead, charcoal, crayons, chalk, pastel; paint etc. (*coloring matter*) 428; water–, body–, oil- color; oils, oil paint; varnish etc. 356a; priming; *gouache* [*F.*], tempera, distemper, fresco, water glass; enamel; encaustic painting; mosaic; tapestry, batik; sun painting.

style, school; the grand style, high art, *genre* [*F.*], portraiture; futurist, cubist, vorticist; ornamental art etc. 847; monochrome, polychrome; grisaille.

[schools of painting] Italian–, Bolognese–, Florentine–, Milanese–, Modena–, Parma–, Neapolitan–, Paduan–, Roman–, Umbrian–, Venetian–, British–, Dutch–, Flemish–, French–, German–, Spanish- School; School of Raphael etc.

picture, painting, piece, tableau, canvas; oil painting etc.; fresco, cartoon; easel–, cabinet-picture; drawing, draft *or* draught; pencil etc. drawing, water-color drawing; still life; sketch, outline, study.

portrait etc. (*representation*) 554; whole–, full–, half- length; three-quarters profile; head; miniature; shade, silhouette; profile.

view, landscape, seascape, sea view, seapiece; scene, prospect; interior; panorama, bird's-eye view, diorama.

picture gallery, art gallery, art museum, pinacotheca; studio, *atelier* [*F.*].

photography, skiagraphy, radiography etc. 554; photograph, radiograph etc. 554; scenograph.

v. **paint**, design, limn, draw, sketch, pencil, scratch, shade, stipple, hatch, dash off, chalk out, square up; color, dead color, wash, varnish; draw in pencil etc. *n.;* paint in oils etc. *n.;* stencil; depict etc. (*represent*) 554.

adj. **pictorial**, graphic; painted etc. *v.;* picturesque, genre; historical etc. *n.;* monochrome, polychrome; scenographic; futurist, cubist, vorticist; in the grand style; painty, pastose.

pencil, oil etc. *n.*

adv. in pencil etc. *n.*

557. Sculpture

n. **sculpture**, insculpture [*obs.*]; carving etc. *v.;* statuary, anaglyptics, cermaics.

marble, bronze, terra cotta; ceramic ware, pottery, porcelain, china, earthenware; cloisonné, enamel, faïence, satsuma.

relief, relievo; basso-relievo *or bassorilievo* [*It.*], low relief, bas-relief; alto-relievo *or alto-rilievo* [*It.*], high relief; mezzo-relievo *or mezzo-rilievo* [*It.*]; glyph, intaglio, anaglyph; medal, medallion; cameo.

[schools of sculpture] Aeginetan–, Attic–, Chian–, Pergamene–, Rhodian–, Samian–, Sicyonian- School.

statute etc. (*image*) 554; cast etc. (*copy*) 21; glyptotheca.

[statues] Apollo Belvedere, Venus of Melos *or* Milo, Cnidian Aphrodite, Venus de' Medici, Dying Gaul, Farnese Hercules, Laocoön, Niobe, Silenus and Infant Bacchus, Theseus, Centaur and Eros, Niké *or* Winged Victory of Samothrace, The Wrestlers, Michelangelo's David, Mercury taking Flight, Rodin's The Thinker.

v. **sculpture**, carve, cut, chisel, model, mold; cast.

adj. **sculptured** etc. *v.;* in relief, glyptic, anaglyphic, anaglyptic, ceroplastic. ceramic; Parian; marble etc. *n.;* xanthian.

558. Engraving

n. **engraving**, chalcography, glyptography; line–, mezzotint–, stipple–, chalk- engraving; dry point, bur; etching, aquatint *or* aquatinta; chiseling; plate–, copperplate–, steel–, halftone–, process–, wood- engraving; xylography, lignography, glyptography, cerography, lithography, chromolithography, photolithography, zincography, glyphography, xerography.

graver, burin, etching point, style; plate, stone, wood block, negative; die, punch, stamp.

printing; plate–, copperplate–, anastatic–, color–, lithographic- printing; type printing etc. 591; three-color process.

impression, print, engraving, plate; steel-plate, copperplate; etching; aquatint, mezzotint, lithotint; cut, woodcut; stereotype, graphotype, autotype, heliotype; xylograph, lignograph, glyptograph, cerograph, lithograph, chromolithograph, photolithograph, zincograph, glyphograph; process.

illustration, illumination; half tone; photogravure; rotogravure [*trade name*]; vignette, initial letter, *cul de lampe* [*F.*], tailpiece.

v. **engrave**, grave, insculp [*rare*], stipple, scrape, etch; bite, bite in; lithograph etc. *n.;* print.

adj. **engraved** etc. *v.;* insculptured, glyptographic; "insculp'd upon" [*Merchant of Venice*].

559. Artist

n. **artist**; painter, limner, drawer, sketcher, designer, engraver, chalcographer, glyptographer, graver, line engraver, draftsman *or* draughtsman copyist; enameler *or* enameller, enamelist *or* enamellist; cartoonist, caricaturist.

historical–, landscape–, marine–, flower–, portrait–, genre–, miniature–, scene- painter; carver, chaser, modeler, *figuriste* [*F.*], statuary, sculptor.

Phidias, Praxiteles, Apelles, Raphael, Michelangelo, Titian; Royal Academician.

560. Language

n. **language**; phraseology etc. 569; speech etc. 582; tongue, lingo [*chiefly humorous*], vernacular; mother–, vulgar–, native- tongue; household words; King's *or* Queen's English; dialect, brogue, gobbledegook, patois etc. 563; idiom, idiotism.

confusion of tongues, Babel; *pasigraphie* [*F.*], pasigraphy; universal language, Volapük, Esperanto, Ido; pantomime etc. (*signs*) 550.

linguistics, lexicology, philology, glossology, glottology, comparative philology; Grimm's law, Verner's law; comparative grammar, phonetics; chrestomathy; paleology *or* palaeology, paleography *or* palaeography.

onomatopoeia, betacism, mimmation, myatism, nunnation.

literature, letters, polite literature, *belles lettres* [*F.*], muses, humanities, *litterae humaniores* [*L.*], republic of letters, dead languages,

classics; genius–, spirit–, idiom- of a language; scholarship etc. (*knowledge*) 490.

linguist etc. (*scholar*) 492.

v. **express**, say, express by words etc. 566.

adj. **lingual**, linguistic; dialectic; vernacular, current; bilingual; diglot, hexaglot, polyglot; literary; colloquial, slangy.

561. Letter

n. **letter**; character; hieroglyphic etc. (*writing*) 590; type etc. (*printing*) 591; capitals; digraph, trigraph; ideogram, ideograph; majuscule, *majusculoe* [*L.*]; minuscule, *minusculae* [*L.*]; alphabet, ABC, abecedary, christcrossrow *or* crisscross-row [*obs. or dial. Eng.*].

consonant, vowel; diphthong, triphthong; mute, surd, sonant, liquid, labial, palatal, cerebral, dental, guttural; guna, vriddhi [*Skr. gram.*].

syllable; monosyllable, dissyllable, polysyllable; affix, prefix, suffix.

spelling, orthography; phonography, phonetic spelling, phonetics; anagrammatism, metagrammatism.

cipher, monogram, anagram; acrostic, double acrostic, double crostic.

v. spell, orthographize [*rare*]; gunate; transliterate.

cipher, decipher; code, decode; make–, construct- acrostics; design monograms; play anagrams; use–, invent- ciphers.

adj. **literal**; alphabetical, abecedarian; syllabic; majuscular, minuscular; uncial etc. (*writing*) 590.

phonetic, voiced, tonic, sonant; voiceless, surd; mute, labial, palatal, cerebral, dental, guttural, liquid.

562. Word

n. **word**, term, vocable; name etc. 564; phrase etc. 566; root, etymon; derivative; part of speech etc. (*grammar*) 567; ideophone, ideogram, ideograph.

dictionary, lexicon, vocabulary, word book, index, glossary, thesaurus, gradus, delectus, concordance; Rosetta stone.

[science of language] etymology, derivation, glottology *or* glossology, semantics, linguistics; terminology, orismology; translation; pronunciation, orthoëpy; paleology etc. (*philology*) 560; lexicography.

lexicographer, lexicologist, etymologist, linguist, orthoëpist, verbarian; semanticist, glossographer etc. (*scholar*) 492.

verbosity, verbiage, wordiness; loquacity etc. 584.

v. vocalize; etymologize, derive, philologize; index; translate.

191

adj. **verbal**, literal; titular, nominal.
  [similarly derived] conjugate, paronymous; derivative.
  verbose, wordy etc. 573; loquacious etc. 584.
adv. **verbally** etc. *adj.; verbatim* [*L.*] etc. (*exactly*) 494.

563. Neology

n. **neology**, neologism; newfangled expression; caconym; barbarism; archaism, black letter, monkish Latin; corruption, missaying, antiphrasis; pseudology; idioticon.
  play upon words, paronomasia; word play etc. (*wit*) 842; *double-entente* [*F.*] etc. (*ambiguity*) 520; palindrome, paragram, clinch [*now rare*], double entendre pun; abuse of -language, -terms.
  dialect, brogue, patois, provincialism, broken English, Anglicism, Briticism, Gallicism, Scotticism, Hibernicism, Americanism; Gypsy lingo, Romany.
  lingua franca, pidgin *or* pigeon English; Chinook, Hindustani, kitchen Kaffir, Swahili, Haussa, Volapük, Esperanto, Ido.
  jargon, dog Latin, gibberish; confusion of tongues, Babel; babu English, chi-chi [*Anglo-India*].
  colloquialism etc. (*figure of speech*) 521; byword; technicality, lingo, slang, cant, argot, *bat* [*Hind.*], macaronics, rhyming slang, St. Giles's Greek, thieves' Latin, peddler's French, flash tongue, Billingsgate, Franglais.
  pseudonym etc. (*misnomer*) 565; Mr. So-and-so; "Sergeant What-is-name" [*Kipling*]; what d'ye call 'em, what's his name, thingummy, thingamabob, thingummybob [*all colloq.*]; *je ne sais quoi* [*F.*].
  neologist, coiner of words.
v. coin words; Americanize, Anglicize, Gallicize; sling the bat [*slang, Anglo-Ind.*].
adj. neologic, neological; archaic, rare, obsolescent; obsolete etc. (*old*) 124; colloquial, dialectal, dialectic *or* dialectical; slang, cant, flash, barbarous; *Anglice* [*NL.*].

564. Nomenclature

n. **nomenclature**; naming etc. *v.;* nuncupation [*obs.*], nomination [*obs.*], baptism; orismology; onomatopoeia; antonomasia.
  name; appellation, appellative; designation; title; head, heading; caption; denomination; byname; nickname etc. 565; epithet; what one may -well, -fairly, -properly, -fitly- call.
  style, proper name; praenomen, agnomen, cognomen; patronymic, surname; cognomination;

eponym; compellation, description, synonym, antonym; empty -title, -name; title, handle to one's name; namesake.
  term, expression, noun; byword; convertible terms etc. 522; technical term; cant etc. 563.
v. **name**, call, term, denominate, designate, style, entitle, clepe [*archaic*], dub [*colloq. or humorous*], christen, baptize, nickname, characterize, specify, define, distinguish by the name of; label etc. (*mark*) 550.
  be called etc. *v.;* take-, bear-, go (*or* be known) by-, go (*or* pass) under-, rejoice in- the name of; hight [*archaic*], yclept *or* ycleped [*archaic or humorous*].
adj. **named** etc. *v.;* known as; nuncupatory [*obs.*], nuncupative [*obs.*]; cognominal, titular, nominal, orismological.

565. Misnomer

n. **misnomer**; *lucus a non lucendo* [*L.*]; Mrs. Malaprop; what d'ye call 'em etc. (*neologism*) 563.
  nickname, *sobriquet* [*F.*] *or* soubriquet, pet name, little name, by-name; assumed -name, -title; alias; *nom de course* [*F.*], *nom de théâtre* [*F.*], stage name; *nom de guerre* [*F.*], *nom de plume* [*English formation*], pen name, pseudonym; pseudonymity, pseudonymousness.
v. **misname**, miscall, misterm; call out of one's name [*colloq.*], nickname; assume -a name, -an alias; take an -alias, -assumed name.
adj. **misnamed** etc. *v.;* pseudonymous; *soi-disant* [*F.*]; self-called, self-styled, self-christened; so-called, quasi.
  nameless, anonymous; without a-, having no-name; innominate, unnamed; unacknowledged; pseudo, bastard.
adv. in no sense; by whatever name, under any name.

566. Phrase

n. **phrase**, expression, locution, set phrase; sentence, paragraph; figure of speech etc. 521; idiom, idiotism; turn of expression; style.
  paraphrase etc. (*synonym*) 522; euphemism; euphuism; periphrase etc. (*circumlocution*) 573; motto etc. (*proverb*) 496; phraseology etc. 569.
v. **express**, phrase; word, word it; give -words, -expression -to; voice; arrange in-, clothe in-, put into-, express by- words; couch in terms; find words to express; speak by the card; call, denominate, designate, dub.
adj. expressed etc. *v.;* idiomatic; stylistic.
adv. in -round, -set, -good set- terms; in set phrases; by the card.

567. Grammar

n. **grammar**, accidence, syntax, analysis, praxis, punctuation; parts of speech; jussive; syllabication *or* syllabification, paradigm, syllepsis, synopsis; inflection, case, declension, conjugation; *jus et norma loquendi* [*L.*]; Lindley Murray etc. (*schoolbook*) 542; correct style, philology etc. (*language*) 560.

v. parse, analyze *or* analyse, conjugate, decline; punctuate, syllabicate, syllabize.

adj. grammatical, syntactic *or* syntactical, inflectional; synoptic.

568. Solecism

n. **solecism**; bad–, false–, faulty-grammar; grammatical blunder; *faux pas* [*F.*], error, slip; slip of the pen, *lapsus calami* [*L.*]; slip of the tongue, *lapsus linguae* [*L.*]; slipslop; bull, Hibernianism; barbarism, impropriety.

v. **solecize** *or* solecise, commit a solecism; use -bad, –faulty- grammar; murder the King's (*or* Queen's) English; speak–, write-out of the idiom; break Priscian's head.

adj. **ungrammatical**; incorrect, inaccurate, faulty; improper, incongruous; solecistic *or* solecistical; slipslop.

569. Style

n. **style**, diction, phraseology, wording; manner, strain; composition; mode of expression, idiom, choice of words; mode of speech, literary power, ready pen, pen of a ready writer; grand style, grand manner; command of language etc. (*eloquence*) 582; authorship, artistry; *la morgue littéraire* [*F.*].

v. **word**; express by words etc. 566; write; apply–, employ- the file.

570. Perspicuity

n. **perspicuity** etc. (*intelligibility*) 518; plain speaking etc. (*manifestation*) 525; definiteness, definition; exactness etc. 494; explicitness, lucidness, lucidity, limpidity, clearness.

adj. **lucid** etc. (*intelligible*) 518; limpid, pellucid, clear; explicit etc. (*manifest*) 525; exact etc. 494.

571. Obscurity

n. **obscurity** etc. (*unintelligibility*) 519; involution, crabbedness, confusion; hard words; ambiguity etc. 520; unintelligibility, unintelligibleness; vagueness etc. 475, inexactness etc. 495; what d'ye call 'em etc. (*neologism*) 563; darkness of meaning.

adj. **obscure** etc. *n.;* crabbed; involved, confused.

572. Conciseness

n. **conciseness** etc. *adj.;* brevity, "the soul of wit," laconicism *or* laconism; ellipsis; syncope; abridgment etc. (*shortening*) 201; compression etc. 195; epitome etc. 596; monostich; Spartans; Tacitus.

portmanteau-word [Lewis Carroll]; brunch [breakfast+lunch], squarson [squire+parson]; slithy, *adj.* [slimy+lithe], torrible, *adj.* [torrid +horrible], crowzy, *adj.* [crowded+cozy], motel, *n.* [motor+hotel].

v. **be concise** etc. *adj.;* telescope, laconize; condense etc. 195; abridge etc. 201; abstract etc. 596; come to the point.

adj. **concise**, brief, short, terse, close; to the point, exact; neat, compact; compressed, condensed, pointed; laconic, curt, pithy, trenchant, summary; pregnant; compendious etc. (*compendium*) 596; succinct; elliptical, epigrammatic, crisp; sententious.

adv. **concisely** etc. *adj.;* briefly, summarily; in brief, in short, in a word, in few words; for the sake of brevity, for shortness' sake; to come to the point, to make a long story short, to cut the matter short, to be brief; it comes to this, the long and short of it is, the gist is.

573. Diffuseness

n. **diffuseness** etc. *adj.;* amplification etc. *v.;* dilating etc. *v.;* verbosity, wordiness; verbiage, cloud of words, *copia verborum* [*L.*]; flow of words etc. (*loquacity*) 584; looseness.

tautology, battology, polylogy [*obs.*], perissology [*obs.*]; pleonasm, exuberance, redundance; thrice-told tale; prolixity, longiloquence, longsomeness, circumlocution, ambages [*rare*], periphrase, periphrasis, roundabout phrases; episode; expletive; penny-a-lining; richness etc. 577; padding; drivel, twaddle, drool.

v. **be diffuse** etc. *adj.;* run out on, descant, expatiate, enlarge, dilate, amplify, expand, inflate, pad [*editor's cant*], launch out, branch out; rant.

maunder, prose; harp upon etc. (*repeat*) 104; dwell on, insist upon.

digress, ramble, *battre la campagne* [*F.*], beat about the bush, perorate, spin a long yarn, protract; spin–, swell–, draw- out; battologize *or* battalogize; drivel, twaddle, drool.

adj. **diffuse**, profuse; wordy, verbose, largiloquent [*obs.*], copious, exuberant, pleonastic, lengthy; long, longsome, long-winded, longspun, long drawn out; spun out, protracted, prolix, diffusive, prosing, maundering; circumlocutory, periphrastic, ambagious *or* ambaguious, ambagitory, roundabout; digressive; discursive, excursive; loose; rambling, episodic; flatulent, frothy.

adv. **diffusely** etc. *adj.;* at large, *in extenso* [*L.*]; about it and about.

574. Vigor

n. **vigor**, power, force; boldness, raciness etc. *adj.;* intellectual force; spirit, punch [*slang*], point, piquancy; verve, ardor, enthusiasm, glow, fire, warmth; strong language; gravity, weight, sententiousness.

loftiness, elevation, sublimity, grandeur.

eloquence; command of words, command of language.

adj. **vigorous**, nervous, powerful, forcible, forceful, mordant, biting, trenchant, incisive, graphic, impressive; sensational.

spirited, lively, glowing, sparkling, racy, bold, slashing, crushing; pungent, piquant, full of beans [*slang*], full of pep [*slang*], having punch [*slang*], full of point, pointed, pithy; sententious.

lofty, elevated, sublime, poetic, grand, weighty, ponderous; eloquent.

vehement, petulant, passionate, burning, impassioned.

adv. in -glowing, −good set, −no measured- terms; with his heart on fire; like a ton of bricks [*colloq.*].

575. Feebleness

n. **feebleness** etc. *adj.;* enervation, flaccidity, vapidity, poverty, frigidity.

adj. **feeble**, bald, tame, meager *or* meagre, insipid, watery, nerveless, jejune, vapid, trashy, cold, frigid, poor, dull, dry, languid; colorless, enervated; prosing, prosy, prosaic, unvaried, monotonous, weak, washy, wishy-washy [*colloq.*], sloppy, sketchy, slight; careless, slovenly, loose, disjointed, disconnected, lax; slipshod, slipslop; inexact; puerile, childish; flatulent; rambling etc. (*diffuse*) 573.

576. Plainness

n. **plainness** etc. *adj.;* simplicity, *simplex munditiis* [Hor.], lack of ornamentation, severity; plain talk; plain -terms, −English; Saxon English; household words.

v. **speak plainly**, waste no words, call a spade a spade; plunge *in medias res* [*L.*]; come to the point.

adj. **plain**, simple; unornamented, unadorned, unvarnished; homely, homespun; neat; severe, chaste, pure, Saxon; commonplace, matter-of-fact, natural, prosaic, sober, unimaginative.

dry, unvaried, monotonous etc. 575.

adv. **point-blank**; in plain -terms, words, −English; in common parlance.

577. Ornament

n. **ornament**; floridness etc. *adj.;* turgidity, turgescence *or* turgescency; altiloquence [*obs.*], grandiloquence, magniloquence, declamation, teratology [*obs.*]; well-rounded periods; elegance etc. 578; orotundity.

inversion, antithesis, alliteration, paronomasia; trope; figurativeness etc. (*metaphor*) 521.

flourish; flowers of -speech, −rhetoric; frills, −of style; euphuism, euphemism.

bombast, big-sounding words, high-sounding words; macrology, *sesquipedalia verba* [*L.*], sesquipedalian words, sesquipedality, sesquipedalianism, Alexandrine; inflation, pretension; rant, fustian, highfalutin' [*slang*], buncombe *or* bunkum *or* bunk, balderdash; prose run mad; fine writing; purple patches; Minerva press.

phrasemonger, euphuist, euphemist; word coiner.

v. **ornament**, overlay with ornament, overcharge, overload; euphuize, euphemize; buncomize [*colloq.*]; smell of the lamp.

adj. **ornate**; ornamented etc. *v.;* beautified etc. 847; florid, rich, flowery; euphuistic, euphemistic; sonorous; high- big- sounding; inflated, swelling, tumid; turgid, turgescent; pedantic, pompous, stilted; orotund; high-flown, high-flowing, highfalutin' [*slang*]; sententious, rhetorical, declamatory; grandiose; grandiloquent; magniloquent; altiloquent [*obs.*]; sesquipedal, sesquipedalian; Johnsonian, mouthy; bombastic; fustian; frothy, flashy, flamboyant.

antithetical, alliterative; figurative etc. 521; artificial etc. (*inelegant*) 579.

adv. *ore rotundo* [*L.*], with rounded phrase.

578. Elegance

n. **elegance**, distinction, clarity, purity, grace, felicity, ease; gracefulness, readiness etc. *adj.;* concinnity, concination [*rare*], euphony; balance, rhythm, symmetry, proportion, taste, good taste, restraint, nice discrimination, propriety, correctness; Attic salt, Atticism, classicalism, classicism.

well-rounded–, well-turned–, flowing- periods; the right word in the right place; antithesis etc. 577.

purist, classicist, stylist.

v. **flow -smoothly**, –with ease; discriminate nicely, display elegance etc. *n.;* point an antithesis, round a period.

adj. **elegant**, polished, classic *or* classical, classicistic, concinnous [*rare*], correct, Attic, Ciceronian, artistic; chaste, pure, Saxon, academic *or* academical.

graceful, easy, readable, fluent, flowing, tripping; unaffected, natural, unlabored; mellifluous, euphonious; euphemistic; symmetrical, balanced, restrained; rhythmic *or* rhythmical.

felicitous, happy, neat; well–, neatly- -put, –expressed.

579. Inelegance

n. **inelegance**, impurity, vulgarity; want of–, poor–, bad- taste; stiffness etc. *adj.;* "unlettered Muse" [Gray]; cacology, cacography, poor diction, poor choice of words; loose–, slipshod- construction; want of balance, ill-balanced sentences; barbarism; slang etc. 563; solecism etc. 568; mannerism etc. (*affectation*) 855; euphuism, Marinism, Gongorism; fustian etc. 577; cacophony; words that -break the teeth, –dislocate the jaw.

cacographer, barbarian; euphuist, Marinist, Gongorist.

v. **be inelegant** etc. *adj.;* employ inelegance etc. *n.*

adj. **inelegant**, graceless, ungraceful; harsh, abrupt; dry, stiff, cramped, formal, *guindé* [*F.*]; forced, labored; artificial, mannered, ponderous; awkward, uncourtly, unpolished; turgid etc. 577; affected, euphuistic; barbarous, uncouth, grotesque, rude, crude, halting, cacographic *or* cacographical; offensive to ears polite; vulgar, tasteless.

580. Voice

n. **voice**; vocality; organ, lungs, bellows; good–, fine–, powerful etc. (*loud*) 404–, musical etc. 413- voice; intonation; tone etc. (*sound*) 402- of voice.

utterance; vocalization; cry etc. 411; strain, prolation [*archaic*]; exclamation, ejaculation, vociferation, ecphonesis; enunciation, articulation; articulate sound, distinctness; clearness, –of articulation; stage whisper; delivery, attack.

accent, accentuation; emphasis, stress; broad–, strong–, pure–, native–, foreign- accent; pronunciation; orthoëpy; euphony etc. (*melody*) 413; polyphonism, polyphony.

[words similarly pronounced] homonyms.

ventriloquism *or* ventriloquy, ventrilocution, gastriloquism *or* gastriloquy [*rare*]; ventriloquist, gastriloquist [*rare*].

[science of voice], phonology; etc. (*sound*) 402.

v. **speak**, utter, breathe; give utterance, give tongue; cry etc. (*shout*) 411; ejaculate, rap out; vocalize, prolate [*obs.*], articulate, enunciate, pronounce, accentuate, aspirate, deliver, emit; whisper, murmur, whisper in the ear; ventriloquize.

adj. **vocal**, phonetic, oral; ejaculatory, articulate, articulated, distinct, enunciative, accentuated, aspirated; euphonious etc. (*melodious*) 413; whispered.

ventriloquous, ventriloquistic, gastriloquial [*rare*], gastriloquous [*rare*].

581. Aphonia

n. **aphonia** *or* aphony; dumbness etc. *adj.;* obmutescence [*rare*]; absence–, want- of voice; dysphonia *or* dysphony; silence etc. (*taciturnity*) 585; raucity; harsh voice etc. 410, unmusical voice etc. 414; quaver, quavering; falsetto, "childish treble"; deaf-mutism, deaf-muteness, deaf-dumbness, mute, dummy, deaf-mute.

v. **speak low**, speak softly; whisper etc. (*faintness*) 405; keep silence etc. 585.

silence; render -mute, –silent; muzzle, muffle, suppress, smother, gag, strike dumb, dumfound *or* dumbfound dumfounder *or* dumbfounder, mum [*obs.*], drown the voice, put to silence, stop one's mouth, cut one short.

stick in the throat.

adj. **aphonous**, nonvocal, aphonic, dumb, mute, deaf and dumb, deaf-dumb; mum; obmutescent [*rare*], tongue-tied; breathless, tongueless, voiceless, speechless, wordless; mute as a -fish, –stockfish, –mackerel; silent etc. (*taciturn*) 585; muzzled; inarticulate, inaudible.

croaking, raucous, hoarse, husky, dry, hollow, sepulchral, hoarse as a raven; rough.

adv. **with bated breath**, with the finger on the lips; *sotto voce* [*It.*]; in a -low tone, –cracked voice, –broken voice; in broken tones, aside, in an aside.

int. **mum**! hush! sh! silence! whist! whisht! [*dial.*]; *chut!* etc. (*silence*) 403.

582. Speech

n. **speech,** faculty of speech; locution, talk, parlance, verbal intercourse, prolation [*archaic*], oral communication, word of mouth, parole, palaver, prattle.

oration, recitation, delivery, say [*colloq.*], speech, lecture, prelection *or* praelection, harangue, sermon, tirade, formal speech, peroration; speechifying; soliloquy etc. 589; allocution etc. 586; interlocution etc. 588; salutatory [*U. S.*]; screed; valedictory [*U. S.*].

oratory, elocution, eloquence, rhetoric, declamation; grandiloquence, multiloquence, talkativeness; burst of eloquence; facundity [*obs.*]; flow–, command- of -words, –language; *copia verborum* [*L.*]; power of speech, gift of gab [*colloq.*]; *usus loquendi* [*L.*].

speaker etc. *v.;* spokesman; prolocutor, interlocutor; mouthpiece, Hermes; orator, oratrix, oratress; Demosthenes, Cicero; rhetorician, lecturer, preacher, prelector *or* praelector; elocutionist, reciter, reader; spellbinder; stump–, platform- orator; speechmaker, patterer, monologist, monologuist, improvisator, *improvvisatore or improvisatore* [*It.*], *improvvisatrice or improvisatrice* [*It.*].

v. **speak,** –of; say, utter, pronounce, deliver, give utterance to; utter–, pour- forth; breathe, let fall, come out with; rap out, blurt out; have on one's lips; have at the -end, –tip-of one's tongue.

soliloquize etc. 589; tell etc. (*inform*) 527; speak to etc. 586; talk together etc. 588.

break silence; open one's -lips, –mouth; lift–, raise- one's voice; give tongue, wag the tongue [*colloq.*]; talk, outspeak; put in a word or two.

declaim, hold forth; make–, deliver- a speech etc. *n.;* speechify [*derisive or humorous*], harangue, stump [*colloq.*], flourish, spout, rant, recite, lecture, prelect *or* praelect, sermonize, discourse, be on one's legs; have–, say- one's say; expatiate etc. (*speak at length*) 573; speak one's mind, go on the–, take the-stump [*U. S.*].

be eloquent etc. *adj.;* have a tongue in one's head, have the gift of gab [*colloq.*] etc. *n.*

pass one's lips, escape one's lips; fall from the -lips, –mouth.

adj. **oral,** lingual, phonetic, not written, nuncupative [*of wills*], unwritten; speaking etc., spoken etc. *v.;* outspoken, facund [*archaic*].

eloquent, oratorical, rhetorical, elocutionary, declamatory; grandiloquent etc. 577; talkative etc. 584; Ciceronian, Tullian.

adv. **orally** etc. *adj.;* by word of mouth, *viva voce* [*L.*], from the lips of; from his own mouth.

583. Stammering
[imperfect speech]

n. **inarticulateness;** stammering etc. *v.;* hesitation etc. *v.;* impediment in one's speech; titubancy [*obs.*], traulism [*obs.*]; whisper etc. (*faint sound*) 405; lisp, drawl, tardiloquence [*rare*]; nasal -tone, –accent; twang; falsetto etc. (*want of voice*) 581; cacology, cacoëpy; broken -voice, –accents, –sentences; brogue etc. 563.

slip of the tongue, *lapsus linguae* [*L.*].

v. **stammer,** stutter, hesitate, falter, hammer [*obs. or dial. Eng.*], balbutiate [*obs.*], balbucinate [*obs.*], haw, hem and haw, be unable to put two words together.

mumble, mutter, maund [*obs.*], maunder; whisper etc. 405; mince, lisp; jabber, gabble, gibber; splutter, sputter; muffle, mump; drawl, mouth; croak; speak thick, speak through the nose; talk incoherently, quaver, snuffle, clip one's words.

murder the language, murder the King's (*or* Queen's) English; mispronounce, missay [*rare*].

adj. **inarticulate;** stammering etc. *v.;* guttural, throaty, nasal; tremulous; affected; stertorous; cacoëpistic.

adv. **sotto voce** etc. (*faintly*) 405.

584. Loquacity

n. **loquacity,** loquaciousness, effusion; talkativeness etc. *adj.;* garrulity; multiloquence, much speaking.

gabble, gab [*colloq.*], jaw [*colloq.*], hot air [*slang*]; jabber, chatter; prate, prattle, cackle, clack; twaddle, twattle, rattle, *caquet* [*F.*], *caqueterie* [*F.*], blabber, *bavardage* [*F.*], bibble-babble, gibble-gabble; small talk etc. (*converse*) 588; Babel.

fluency, flippancy, volubility, flowing tongue; flow, –of words; *flux de -bouche, –mots* [*F.*]; *copia verborum* [*L.*], *cacoëthes loquendi* [*L.*]; *furor loquendi* [*L.*]; verbosity etc. (*diffuseness*) 573; gift of the gab etc. (*eloquence*) 582.

talker; chatterer, chatterbox; babbler etc. *v.;* rattle; "agreeable rattle" [Goldsmith]; ranter; sermonizer, proser, driveler *or* driveller, blatherskite [*colloq.*], blab, jaw-box [*slang*], gas-bag [*slang*], wind-bag [*slang*], hot-air artist [*slang*]; gossip etc. (*converse*) 588; magpie, jay, parrot, poll *or* polly; *moulin à paroles* [*F.*].

v. **be loquacious** etc. *adj.;* talk glibly, pour forth, patter; prate, palaver, prose, maunder, chatter, blab, gush, prattle, clack, jabber, jaw [*low*], shoot one's mouth off [*slang*]; blather, blatter, blether; rattle, –on; twaddle, twattle; babble, gabble; outtalk; talk oneself -out of breath, –hoarse; talk–, run on- like a mill race; have one's tongue hanging in the middle and wagging at both ends; talk the hind legs off a mule, talk one deaf and dumb, clack like a hen, go on forever; expatiate etc. (*speak at length*) 573; gossip etc. (*converse*) 588; din in the ears etc. (*repeat*) 104; talk at random, talk nonsense etc. 497; be hoarse with talking.

adj. **loquacious**, talkative, garrulous, linguacious [*obs.*], multiloquent *or* multiloquous; chattering etc. *v.;* chatty etc. (*sociable*) 892; declamatory etc. 582; open-mouthed.
  fluent, voluble, glib, flippant; long-tongued, long-winded etc. (*diffuse*) 573.

adv. **glibly** etc. *adj.;* trippingly on the tongue.

585. Taciturnity

n. **silence**, muteness, obmutescence [*rare*], laconism, laconicism, taciturnity, pauciloquy, costiveness [*obs.*], curtness; reserve, reticence etc. (*concealment*) 528.
  man of few words; Spartan, Laconian.

v. **be silent** etc. *adj.;* keep silence; hold one's -tongue, –peace; not speak etc. 582; say nothing; seal–, close–, put a padlock on- the -lips, –mouth; put a bridle on one's tongue; keep one's tongue between one's teeth; make no sign, not let a word escape one; keep a secret etc. 528; have not a word to throw at a dog, not have a word to say; lay–, place- the finger on the lips; render mute etc. 581.
  stick in one's throat.

adj. **silent**, mute, mum; silent as a -post, –stone, –the grave etc. (*still*) 403; dumb etc. 581; unconversable.
  taciturn, laconic, pauciloquent, concise, sententious, sparing of words; close, close-mouthed, close-tongued; costive [*obs.*], inconversable [*obs.*], curt; reserved; reticent etc. (*concealing*) 528.

int. **silence!** tush! mum! hush! *chut!* [*F.*], hist! tut! not another word! shut up! stop right there! be still! *chup!* [*Hind.*].

586. Allocution

n. **allocution**, alloquy [*obs.*], address; smoke talk, chalk talk [*both colloq.*]; speech etc. 582; apostrophe, interpellation, appeal, invocation, salutation, salutatory; word in the ear.
  platform etc. 542; plank [*politics*].
  audience etc. (*interview*) 588.
  [feigned dialogue] dialogism.

v. **address**, speak to, accost, make up to [*colloq.*], apostrophize, appeal to, invoke; hail, salute; call to, halloo.
  lecture etc. (*make a speech*) 582; preach, sermonize, harangue, spellbind.
  take aside, take by the button; talk to in private.

int. soho! halloo! hey! hist! hi!

587. Response

etc. *see* ANSWER 462.

588. Interlocution

n. **interlocution**; collocution, colloquy, converse, conversation, confabulation, confab [*colloq.*], chin-music [*slang*], talk, discourse, verbal intercourse; oral communication, commerce; dialogue, duologue, trialogue.
  "the feast of reason and the flow of soul" [Pope]; *mollia tempora fandi* [*L.*].
  chat, causerie [*F.*], chitchat; small–, table–, tea-table–, town–, village–, idle-talk; tattle, gossip, tittle-tattle; babble, babblement; *tripotage* [*F.*], cackle, prittle-prattle, *on dit* [*F.*]; talk of the -town, –village.
  conference, parley, interview, audience, *pourparler* [*F.*]; *tête-à-tête* [*F.*]; reception, *conversazione* [*It.*]; congress etc. (*council*) 696; powwow.
  hall of audience, durbar [*India*], auditorium, assembly room.
  debate, palaver, logomachy, war of words, controversy, newspaper war.
  talker, gossip, tattler; Paul Pry; tabby [*colloq.*], chatterer etc. (*loquacity*) 584; interlocutor etc. (*spokesman*) 582; conversationist, conversationalist, dialogist.

v. **converse**, talk together, confabulate; dialogue, dialogize; hold–, carry on–, join in–, engage in- a conversation; put in a word; shine in conversation; bandy words; parley; palaver; chat, gossip, tattle; prate etc. (*loquacity*) 584; powwow.
  confer with, discourse with, commune with, commerce with; hold -converse, –conference,

–intercourse; talk it over; be closeted with; talk with one in private, talk with one *tête-à-tête* [*F.*].

adj. **conversing** etc. *v.;* interlocutory; conversational, conversable; discursive *or* discoursive [*obs.*]; chatty etc. (*sociable*) 892; colloquial, confabulatory, *tête-à-tête* [*F.*].

589. Soliloquy

n. **soliloquy**, monology, monologue, apostrophe; monology.

soliloquist, monologist, monologuist, monologian, soliloquizer; speaker etc. 582; Dr. Johnson, Coleridge.

v. **soliloquize**, monologize, monologuize, say–, talk- to oneself; rehearse a speech, address an imaginary audience; address the four walls; say aside, think aloud, apostrophize.

adj. **soliloquizing** etc. *v.;* monologic *or* monological; apostrophic, apostrophal [*rare*].

adv. **aside**, apart.

590. Writing

n. **writing** etc. *v.;* chirography, stelography [*rare*], monography, stylography, cerography, graphology; pencraft, penmanship; quill driving [*humorous*]; typewriting.

stroke–, dash- of the pen; *coup de plume* [*F.*]; line; headline; pen and ink.

manuscript, MS., writing, *litterae scriptae* [*L.*]; these presents [*law*].

character, letter etc. 561; uncial writing, cuneiform character, arrowhead, contraction; Ogham, runes; hieroglyphic, hieratic, demotic, Hebrew, Greek, Cyrillic, Roman; Arabic, Persian, Naskhi *or* Neskhi, Shikasta, Nasta'lik *or* Ta'lik; Brahmi, Devanagari, Nagari; Chinese; script.

shorthand; stenography, brachygraphy, tachygraphy; secret writing, writing in cipher; cryptography, steganography; phonography, pasigraphy, polygraphy [*rare*], logography.

copy; transcript, rescript; rough–, fair- copy; rough draft.

handwriting; signature, sign manual, mark, autograph, monograph, holograph; hand, fist [*colloq.*].

calligraphy; good–, running–, flowing–, cursive–, Italian–, slanting–, perpendicular–, round–, copybook–, fine–, legible–, boldhand.

cacography, *griffonage* [*F.*], *barbouillage* [*F.*]; bad–, cramped–, crabbed–, illegible- hand;

scribble etc. *v.; pattes de mouche* [*F.*], fly tracks; ill-formed letters; pothooks and hangers.

stationery; pen, reed, quill, goose quill; pencil, style, stylograph, stylographic pen, fountain pen; paper, foolscap, parchment, vellum, papyrus, tablet, block, pad, notebook, memorandum book, copybook, commonplace-book; slate, marble, pillar, table; blackboard; ink-bottle, inkhorn, inkpot, inkstand, inkwell; typewriter.

composition, authorship; *cacoëthes scribendi* [*L.*]; graphomania; lucubration, production, work, preparation; screed, article, paper, pamphlet; book etc. 593; essay, theme, thesis; novel, textbook, poem, book of poems, book of verse; compilation, anthology; piece of music, *morceau* [*F.*] etc. (*musical composition*) 415.

transcription etc. (*copy*) 21; inscription etc. (*record*) 551; superscription etc. (*indication*) 550.

writer, scribe, amanuensis, scrivener, secretary, clerk, penman, copyist, transcriber, quill driver [*humorous*]; stenographer, brachygrapher, tachygrapher, phonographer, logographer, cipherer, cryptographer *or* cryptographist, steganographist; typewriter, typist; writer for the press etc. (*author*) 593; chirographer, cerographist; monographist, graphomaniac; calligraphist, calligrapher; cacographer; graphologist.

v. **write**, pen, typewrite, type [*colloq.*]; copy, engross; write out, –fair; transcribe; scribble, scrawl, scrabble, scratch; interline; take down in -shorthand, –longhand; spoil–, stain- paper [*humorous*]; note down; write down etc. (*record*) 551; sign etc. (*attest*) 467; enface.

compose, indite, draw up, draft, formulate; dictate; inscribe, throw on paper, dash off; manifold.

take up the pen, take pen in hand; shed–, spill–, dip one's pen in- ink.

adj. writing etc. *v.;* written etc. *v.;* in writing, in black and white; under one's hand.

uncial, runic, cuneiform, hieroglyphic *or* hieroglyphical, arrowhead etc. *n.*

stenographic, phonographic, brachygraphic, cryptographic, pasigraphic, logographic, tachygraphic; stenographical etc.

adv. currente calamo [*L.*]; pen in hand; with the pen of a ready writer; that "the wayfaring men, though fools, shall not err therein" [*Bible*].

591. Printing

n. **printing**; block–, type- printing; linotype, monotype; plate printing etc. (*engraving*) 558; the press etc. (*publication*) 531; composition.

print, letterpress, text, matter; live–, standing–, dead- matter; copy; context, page, column, note, section; catch-word; running head, running title; signature; justification; dummy.

folio etc. (*book*) 593; copy, impression. pull, proof, revise, advance sheets; author's–, galley–, page–, plate–, press- proof; press revise.

typography; stereotype, electrotype; matrix; font *or* fount; pi *or* pie; roman, italics; capitals etc. (*letters*) 561, caps., small caps., upper case, lower case; logotype; type-bar, type-slug; type-body; em; en; type measure, type scale; type casting, type metal, type mold, typograph; type foundry, letter foundry; composing stick, stick; composing -frame. -rule, –stand; foot stick; chase, form, galley, measure, scale, case, boxes; gauge, gauge pin, feed gauge, guide, dabber, gutter, gutter stick; brayer, boss, batter, bank; bearer, guard; bed, blanket, tympan, turtle, platen, bevel, burr, frame, frisket, gripper; quadrat, quad; quoin, slug, slur, ratchet, reglet; guillotine, rounce, cylinder; overlay, underlay, sinkage, macule; platen press, perfecting machine; printing-press, printing-machine; press-work; sheet work; off-cut, off-print; set-off; off-set, smut; turn, turned letter; bookplate, bookstamp, colophon; composing room, press room.

space, 3-em, thick space; 4-em, 5-em, thin space; 6-em, hair space; patent space.

metal type, body, shank, face, shoulder, counter, serif *or* ceriph, stem, beard, groove, feet.

styles of type: Old English, Black Letter, German Text, Gothic, Antique, Clarendon, Bold-face *or* Full-face, French Elzevir, Caslon Old Style, Ionic, Script, Typewriter.

point system: 4½ point (diamond), 5 pt. (pearl), 5½ pt. (agate *or* ruby), 6 pt. (nonpareil), 7 pt. (minion), 8 pt. (brevier), 9 pt. (bourgeois), 10 pt. (long primer), 11 pt. (small pica), 12 pt. (pica), 14 pt. (English), 16 pt. (Columbian), 18 pt. (great primer).

printer, compositor, reader, proof reader;- printer's devil; copyholder.

v. **print**; compose; put–, go- to press; pass–, see-through the press; publish etc. 531; bring out; appear in–, rush into- print; set up, stick, make-up, impose, justify, macule *or* mackle, mortise, offset, overrun, rout.

distribute, pi *or* pie, pi a form.

adj. **typographical** etc. *n.;* printed etc. *v.;* in type; solid in galleys; kerned, deckle-edged; bold-faced *or* full-faced; pied.

592. Correspondence

n. **correspondence**, letter, epistle, note, billet, written communication, post card *or* postcard, postal, postal card; missive, circular, favor, *billet-doux* [*F.*]; chit *or* chitty [*India*], letter card [*Brit.*], picture post card; dispatch *or* despatch; bulletin, these presents [*law*]; rescript, rescription [*archaic*]; post etc. (*messenger*) 534.

letter writer, epistolarian, correspondent, writer, communicator; author, contributor.

v. **correspond**, –with; write to, send a letter to; drop a line to [*colloq.*]; start–, begin–, keep up- a correspondence; deluge with -letters, –post cards; communicate by -writing, –letter; let one know by -post, –mail; dispatch *or* despatch, circularize, follow up, bombard; reply, reply by return mail, communicate.

adj. **epistolary**, epistolarian.

593. Book

n. **book**, booklet; writing, work, volume, tome, opuscule *or* opuscle, opusculum; tract, tractate, treatise, *livret* [*F.*], brochure, monograph, pamphlet, codex, libretto; handbook, manual, enchiridion; novel etc. (*composition*) 590; circular, publication; the press etc. 531; chapbook.

part, issue, number, *livraison* [*F.*]; album, portfolio; periodical, serial, magazine, ephemeris, annual, journal.

paper, bill, sheet, broadsheet; leaf, leaflet; fly leaf, page; quire, ream.

pasteboard, cardboard, strawboard, millboard, binder's board; carton.

make-up, bastard title, title, printer's imprint, subtitles, dedication, preface, contents, list of plates *or* illustrations, errata, introduction, text; chapter, section, head, article, paragraph, passage, clause; recto, verso *or* reverso; supplement, appendix, index.

[sizes] folio, quarto (4to *or* 4°); octavo (8vo), cap 8vo, demy 8vo, imperial 8vo, medium 8vo, royal 8vo, post 8vo, pott 8vo, crown 8vo, foolscap 8vo; duodecimo, twelvemo *or* 12mo; sextodecimo, sixteenmo *or* 16mo; octodecimo, eighteenmo *or* 18mo.

bookbinding, bibliopegy; folding, stitching, wire-stitching; tooling; blind–, gold- tooling; binder's title; case, cover; quarter–, half–, three-quarters- bound book; full leather.

[binding materials] paper, paper boards, buckram, cloth, skiver, roan, pigskin, Russia, Turkey morocco, levant morocco, seal, parchment, vellum.

work of reference, encyclopedia *or* encyclopaedia, cyclopedia *or* cyclopaedia, dictionary, thesaurus, concordance, anthology; compilation.

writer, author, *littérateur* [*F.*], essayist; pen, scribbler, the scribbling race; free lance; literary hack, Grub-street writer; adjective jerker [*slang*], hack writer, hack, ghost [*cant.*], ghost writer, ink slinger [*slang*]; journalist, publicist, writer for–, gentleman of–, representative of–the press; reporter, correspondent; war–, special- correspondent; knight of the -plume, –pen, –quill [*all humorous*]; penny-a-liner; editor, subeditor, reviser, diaskeuast; scribe etc. 590; playwright etc. 599; poet etc. 597.

the trade, publisher, bookseller; book -salesman, –agent, –canvasser, –solicitor.

bibliopole, bibliopolist, book collector; bookbinder, bibliopegist; bookworm etc. 492; bibliologist, bibliographer, bibliophile, bibliognost, librarian, bibliothec.

bookstore, bookshop, bookseller's shop, *librairie* [*F.*], publishing house.

library, bibliotheca, public library, lending library.

knowledge of books, bibliography, bibliology; book learning etc. (*knowledge*) 490; bookselling, bibliopolism.

594. Description

n. **description**, account, statement, report; *exposé* [*F.*] etc. (*disclosure*) 529; specification, particulars; summary of facts; brief etc. (*abstract*) 596; return etc. (*record*) 551; *catalogue raisonné* [*F.*] etc. (*list*) 86; guidebook etc. (*information*) 527.

delineation etc. (*representation*) 554; sketch, pastel, vignette, monograph; minute–, detailed–, particular–, circumstantial–, graphic- account; narration, recital, rehearsal, relation.

narrative, history; memoir, memorials; annals etc. (*chronicle*) 551; saga; tradition, legend, story, tale, historiette; personal narrative, journal, letters, biography, autobiography, life; obituary, orbit [*cant.*], necrology; adventures, fortunes, experiences, confessions; anecdote, ana.

historiography, chronography; historic Muse, Clio.

work of fiction, novel, romance, short story; detective -story, –yarn; "grue" [Stevenson]; fairy–, nursery- tale; fable, parable, apologue, allegory; dime novel, penny dreadful, shilling shocker [*slang*].

relator etc. *v.; raconteur* [*F.*]; historiographer, chronographer, historian etc. (*recorder*) 553; biographer, fabulist, novelist, story-teller, romancer, spinner of yarns, teller of tales, anecdotist, word-painter; writer etc. 593.

v. **describe**; set forth etc. (*state*) 535; draw a picture, picture; portray etc. (*represent*) 554; characterize, analyze, give words to, narrate, relate, recite, recount, sum up, run over, recapitulate, rehearse, fight one's battles over again; harrow up the soul, hold one breathless, novelize, romance.

unfold etc. (*disclose*) 529- a tale; tell; give–, render-' an account of; report, make a report, draw up a statement; throw into -essay form, –book form; stick to the facts, show life as it is; historicize.

detail, particularize, itemize; enter into–, descend to- -particulars, –details.

adj. **descriptive**, graphic, narrative, epic, suggestive, well-drawn; historic *or* historical, historiographical, chronographic *or* chronographical, biographic *or* biographical, autobiographical; traditive [*esp., from ancestors to descendants*], traditional, traditionary; legendary, mythical, fabulous; anecdotic, storied; described etc. *v.;* romantic, idealistic; realistic, true to life; expository.

595. Dissertation

n. **dissertation**, treatise, essay; thesis, theme; tract, tractate, tractation [*obs.*]; discourse, memoir, disquisition, lecture, sermon, homily, pandect, digest; excursus.

investigation etc. (*inquiry*) 461; study etc. (*consideration*) 451; discussion etc. (*reasoning*) 476; exposition etc. (*explanation*) 522.

commentary, commentation, review, critique, criticism, article; leader, leading article; editorial; running commentary.

commentator, critic, essayist, pamphleteer, publicist, reviewer, leader writer, editor, annotator.

v. **comment**, explain, interpret, criticize, illuminate; dissert [*rare*]–, descant–, write–, touch-upon a subject; treat of–, take up–, ventilate–, discuss–, deal with–, go into–, canvass–, handle–, do justice to- a subject; show the true inwardness of.

adj. **disquisitional**, disquisitive, disquisitionary [*rare*]; expository, commentarial, commentatorial, critical.

discursive, discoursive, digressive, desultory.

596. Compendium

n. **compendium**, compend, abstract, *précis* [*F.*], epitome, *multum in parvo* [*L.*], analysis, pandect, digest, sum and substance, brief, abridgment, *abrégé* [*F.*], summary, *aperçu* [*F.*], draft, minute, note; excerpt, extract; synopsis, textbook, conspectus, outlines, syllabus, contents, heads, prospectus.

album; scrap–, note–, memorandum–, commonplace- book.

fragments, ana, extracts, *excerpta* [*L.*], cuttings; fugitive -pieces, –writings; *spicilegium* [*L.*], flowers, anthology, miscellany, collectanea, analects *or* analecta; compilation.

recapitulation, *résumé* [*F.*], review.

abbreviation, abbreviature; contraction; shortening etc. 201; compression etc. 195.

v. **abridge**, abstract, epitomize, summarize; make–, prepare–, draw–, compile- an abstract etc. *n.;* abbreviate etc. (*shorten*) 201; condense etc. (*compress*) 195.

compile etc. (*collect*) 72; note down, collect, edit.

recapitulate, review, skim, run over, sum up.

adj. **compendious**, synoptic, analectic; *abrégé* [*F.*], abridged etc. *v.;* abbreviatory; analytic *or* analytical; variorum.

adv. **in short**, in epitome, in substance, in few words.

597. Poetry

n. **poetry**, poetics, poesy, Muse, tuneful Nine, Apollo, Apollo Musagetes, Calliope, Parnassus, Helicon, Pierides, Pierian spring; inspiration, fire of genius, coal from off the altar.

poem; epic, epic poem; epopee *or* epopoeia, epos, ode, epode, idyl *or* idyll, lyric, eclogue, pastoral, bucolic, georgic, dithyramb *or* dithyrambus, anacreontic, sonnet, roundelay, rondeau, rondel, roundel, rondelet; triolet, sestina, virelay, ballade, cento, ghazal *or* ghazel, madrigal, monody, elegy; amoebaeum, palinode.

dramatic–, didactic–, narrative–, lyric–, satirical- poetry; satire, opera.

anthology, posy [*archaic*], garland, miscellany, *disjecta membra poetae* [*L.*].

song, ballad, lay; love–, drinking–, war–, seasong; lullaby, *aubade* [*F.*]; music etc. 415; nursery rhymes.

[bad poetry] doggerel, Hudibrastic verse; macaronics, macaronic verse; "not poetry, but prose run mad" [Pope].

versification, riming *or* rhyming, making verses; prosody; scansion, scanning, orthometry [*rare*].

canto, stanza, distich, verse, line, couplet, triplet, quatrain; strophe, antistrophe; refrain, chorus, burden; octave, sextet.

verse, rime *or* rhyme, assonance, crambo [*contemptuous*], meter, measure, foot, numbers, strain, rhythm; ictus, beat, accent; accentuation etc. (*voice*) 580; iambus, iambic, iamb; dactyl, spondee, trochee, anapest etc.; hexameter, pentameter; Alexandrine; anacrusis, antispast, blank verse, Leonine verse, runes, alliteration; *bout-rimé* [*F.*].

elegiacs etc. *adj.;* elegiac etc. *adj.* -verse, –meter *or* metre, –poetry.

poet, minor poet; genius, maker [*obs.*], creator; poet laureate; laureate; bard, lyrist, scald *or* skald, scop [*hist.*], idylist *or* idyllist, sonneteer, rhapsodist, epic [*obs.*], epic poet, dithyrambic, satirist, troubadour, trouvère; minstrel; minnesinger, Meistersinger; jongleur, improvisator *or* improvvisatore [*It.*] *or* improvisatore; versifier, rimer *or* rhymer, rimester *or* rhymester; ballad monger, runer; poetaster; *genus irritabile vatum* [*L.*].

v. **poetize**, sing, "lisp in numbers" [Pope], build the stately rime, sing deathless songs, make immortal by verse; satirize; compose epic etc. *adj.* -poetry; string verses together, cap rimes, poeticize, versify, make verses, rime *or* rhyme, scan.

produce -lame verses, –limping meters, –halting rime.

adj. **poetic** *or* poetical; lyric *or* lyrical; tuneful; epic; dithyrambic etc. *n.;* metrical; acatalectic, catalectic; elegiac, iambic, dactylic, spondaic *or* spondaical, trochaic, anapestic; amoebaeic, Melibean, scaldic *or* skaldic; Ionic, Sapphic, Alcaic, Pindaric, Pierian.

598. Prose

n. **prose**, prosaism, prosaicness, prosaicism [*rare*]; poetic prose; history etc. (*description*) 594.

prose writer, essayist, monographer, monographist, novelist; *raconteur* [*F.*] etc. 594.

v. **prose**; write -prose, –in prose.

adj. **prosaic**, prosy, prosal [*obs.*]; unpoetical. rimeless *or* rhymeless, unrimed *or* unrhymed, in prose, not in verse.

599. The Drama

n. **the drama**, the stage, the theater *or* theatre, the play; theatricals, dramaturgy, histrionic art, mimography, buskin, sock, cothurnus, Melpomene and Thalia, Thespis.

play, drama, stageplay, piece, five-act play, tragedy, comedy, opera, vaudeville, comedietta, *lever de rideau* [*F.*], curtain raiser, interlude, afterpiece, exode [*Rom. antiq.*], farce, *divertissement* [*F.*], extravaganza, burletta, harlequinade, pantomime, burlesque, *opéra bouffe* [*F.*], ballet, spectacle, masque, *drame* [*F.*], *comédie drame* [*F.*]; melodrama; *comédie larmoyante* [*F.*]; emotional -drama, –play; sensation drama; tragi-comedy; light–, genteel–, low–, farce- comedy, comedy of manners, farcical-comedy; monodrama, monodram *or* monodrame, monologue, duologue, dialogue; trilogy; charade, *proverbe* [*F.*]; mystery, miracle play, morality play.

act, scene, tableau, curtain; introduction, induction [*archaic*], exposition, expository scenes; prologue, epilogue; libretto, book, text, prompter's copy.

performance, representation, show [*colloq.*], *mise en scène* [*F.*], stage setting, stagery [*obs.*], stagecraft, *jeu de théâtre* [*F.*]; acting; gesture etc. 550; impersonation etc. 554; stage business, gag, patter, slap-stick [*slang*], buffoonery.

theater *or* theatre, playhouse, opera house; music hall; amphitheater *or* amphitheatre, circus, hippodrome; moving-picture theater, moving pictures, movies [*colloq.*], films, cinematograph *or* cinema [*colloq., Brit.*]; puppet show, fantoccini; marionettes. Punch and Judy.

auditory, auditorium, front of the house, front [*colloq. and professional*], stalls [*chiefly Eng.*], orchestra seats *or* orchestra, pit [*chiefly Eng.*], parquet, orchestra circle, boxes, balcony, gallery, peanut gallery [*slang*]; dressing rooms, greenroom.

scenery; back scene, flat; drop, drop scene; wing, screen, coulisse, side scene, transformation scene, curtain, act drop; proscenium; fire curtain, asbestos curtain.

stage, movable stage, scene, the boards; trap, mezzanine floor; flies; floats, footlights; limelight, spotlight, colored light; klieg light; orchestra.

theatrical costume, theatrical properties, props [*theat. cant*].

cast, *dramatis personae* [*L.*], persons in the play; role, part, character; repertoire, repertory, *répertoire* [*F.*].

actor, player; stage–, strolling- player; barnstormer, stager [*rare*], old stager; masker, masquer [*rare*], mime, mimer, mimic, mimester [*rare*]; *artiste* [*F.*], performer, star, headliner; comedian, tragedian, *tragédienne* [*F.*], Thespian, Roscius, ham [*slang*], hamfatter [*slang*]; utility, general utility, utility man.

buffoon, pantomimist, clown, *farceur* [*F.*], *buffo* (*pl. buffi*) [*It.*], grimacer, pantaloon, harlequin, columbine; punch, punchinello, *pulcinella* [*It.*].

mummer, guiser [*Eng. & Scot.*], guisard [*Scot.*], gysart [*obs.*], masque [*obs.*], mask.

mountebank, Jack Pudding; tumbler, posture master, acrobat; contortionist; ballet dancer, ballet girl; *coryphée* [*F.*], *danseuse* [*F.*]; chorus girl, chorus singer.

company; first tragedian, prima donna, leading lady; lead; leading man, protagonist; *jeune premier* [*F.*], *débutant* (*fem. débutante*) [*F.*]; light–, genteel–, low- comedian; walking gentleman *or* lady [*obsoles.*], *amoroso* [*It.*], juvenile lead, juvenile; heavy lead, heavy; heavy father, ingenue, *ingénue* [*F.*], *jeune veuve* [*F.*], soubrette, *farceur* (*fem. farceuse*) [*F.*].

mute, figurant, figurante, walking part, supernumerary, super [*theat. cant*], supe [*theat. cant*].

manager; stage–, actor–, acting- manager; *entrepreneur* [*F.*], impresario; angel [*slang*].

[theater staff] property man, prop [*theat. cant*]; costumer, costumier, wig-maker, make-up artist; sceneshifter, grip, stage hand, stage carpenter, machinist, electrician, chief electrician; prompter, call boy; advance agent, publicity agent.

dramatist, playwright, playwriter; dramatic -author, –writer; mimographer, mimist [*obs.*]; dramatic critic.

audience, auditory, house; orchestra etc. *n.*; gallery, the gods [*colloq.*], gallery gods [*collow.*].

v. **act**, play, perform; put on the stage, dramatize, stage, produce, set; personate etc. 554; mimic etc. (*imitate*) 19; enact; play–, act–, go through–, perform-a part; rehearse, spout, gag [*slang*], patter [*slang*], rant; strut and fret one's hour upon the stage; tread the -stage, –boards; make one's début, take a part, come out; star; supe [*slang*].

adj. **dramatic**; theatric *or* theatrical; scenic, histrionic, comic, tragic, buskined, cothurned; farcical, tragi-comic, melodramatic, operatic; stagy *or* stagey; spectacular, stellar, all-star [*cant*]; stagestruck.

adv. **on the stage**, on the boards; in the limelight, in the spotlight; before the floats, before the footlights, before the curtain, before an audience; behind the scenes.

Class 5. Volition

Division 1. Individual Volition

Section 1. Volition in General

600. Will

n. **will**, volition, conation, volitiency, velleity; *liberum arbitrium* [*L.*]; will and pleasure, free will; freedom etc. 748; discretion; choice, inclination, intent, purpose, voluntarism; option etc. (*choice*) 609; voluntariness; spontaneity, spontaneousness; originality.

wish, desire, pleasure, mind, frame of mind etc. (*inclination*) 602; intention etc. 620; predetermination etc. 611; self-control etc. determination etc. (*resolution*) 604; force of will, will power, autocracy, bossiness [*colloq.*].

v. **will**, list [*archaic*]; see fit, think fit; determine etc. (*resolve*) 604; enjoin; settle etc. (*choose*) 609; volunteer.

have a will of one's own; do what one chooses etc. (*freedom*) 748; have it all one's own way; have one's will, have one's own way; use-, exercise- one's discretion; take -upon oneself, —one's own course, —the law into one's own hands; do of one's own accord, do upon one's own authority, do upon one's own responsibility; take responsibility, boss [*colloq.*], take the bit between one's teeth; originate etc. (*cause*) 153.

adj. **voluntary**, volitional, willful *or* wilful; free etc. 748; optional; discretional, discretionary; volitient, volitive; volunteer, voluntaristic; dictatorial, bossy [*colloq.*].

minded etc. (*willing*) 602; prepense etc. (*predetermined*) 611; intended etc. 620; autocratic; unbidden etc. (bid etc. 741); spontaneous; original etc. (*causal*) 153; unconstrained.

adv. **voluntarily** etc. *adj.;* at will, at pleasure; *à volonté* [*F.*], *à discrétion* [*F.*]; *al piacere* [*It.*]; *ad libitum* [*L.*], *ad arbitrium* [*L.*]; as one thinks proper, as it seems good to; *a beneplacito* [*It*].

of one's own -accord, —free will; on one's own responsibility; *proprio-, suo-, ex mero- motu* [*L.*]; out of one's own head; by choice etc. 609; purposely etc. (*intentionally*) 620; deliberately etc. 611.

601. Necessity

n. **involuntariness**; instinct, blind impulse; inborn-, innate- proclivity; native-, natural- tendency; natural impulse, predetermination.

necessity, necessitation, necessitarianism, obligation; compulsion etc. 744; subjection etc. 749; stern-, hard-, dire-, imperious-, inexorable-, iron-, adverse- -necessity, —fate; *anagke* [*Gr.*], what must be.

destiny, destination; fatality, fate, kismet, doom, foredoom, election, predestination; preordination, foreordination; lot, fortune; fatalism; inevitableness etc. *adj.;* spell etc. 993.

fates, Parcae, Sisters three, book of fate; God's will, Heaven, will of Heaven; star, stars; planet, planets; astral influence; wheel of Fortune, Ides of March, Hobson's choice.

last shift, last resort; *dernier ressort* [*F.*]; *pis aller* etc. (*substitute*) 147; necessaries etc. (*requirement*) 630.

necessarian, necessitarian; fatalist; automaton, pawn.

v. **lie under a necessity**; be fated, be doomed, be destined etc., be in for, be under the necessity of; be obliged, be forced, be driven; have no -choice, —alternative; be one's fate to etc. *n.;* be pushed to the wall, be driven into a corner, be unable to help, be swept on, be drawn irresistibly.

destine, doom, foredoom, devote; predestine, preordain; cast a spell etc. 992; necessitate; compel etc. 744.

be decreed, be determined, be destined etc., be written; be written in the -book of fate, —stars.

adj. **necessary**, necessarian, necessitarian; needful etc. (*requisite*) 630.

fated; destined etc. *v.;* fateful, big with fate; set apart, devoted, elect.

compulsory etc. (*compel*) 744; uncontrollable, inevitable, unavoidable, indefeasible, irresistible, irrevocable, inexorable, binding; avoidless, resistless.

involuntary, instinctive, automatic, blind, mechanical; unconscious, unwitting, unthinking; unintentional etc. (*undesigned*) 621; spellbound; impulsive etc. 612.

adv. **necessarily** etc. *adj.;* of necessity, of course; *ex necessitate rei* [*L.*]; needs must; perforce etc. 744; *nolens volens* [*L.*]; will he nil he, will I nill I, willy-nilly, *bon gré mal gré* [*F.*]; willing or unwilling, *coûte que coûte* [*F.*]; compulsorily, by compulsion, by force.

faute de mieux [*F.*]; by stress of; if need be; *que faire?* [*F.*].

602. Willingness

n. **willingness**, voluntariness etc. *adj.;* willing mind, heart.

disposition, inclination, liking, turn, propensity, propension, propenseness, leaning, animus; frame of mind, humor, mood, vein; bent etc. (*turn of mind*) 820; *penchant* [*F.*] etc. (*desire*) 865; aptitude etc. 698.

docility, docibleness [*rare*], docibility [*rare*], appetency, tractability, tractableness, persuadability, persuadableness, persuasibleness, persuasibility; pliability etc. (*softness*) 324.

geniality, cordiality; goodwill; alacrity, readiness, zeal, enthusiasm, earnestness, forwardness; eagerness etc. (*desire*) 865.

assent etc. 488; compliance etc. 762; pleasure etc. (*will*) 600.

labor of love, self-appointed task, volunteering; gratuitous service; social service, welfare work.

volunteer, unpaid worker, amateur, voluntary [*rare*]; social worker, welfare worker.

v. **be willing** etc. *adj.;* incline, lean to, mind, propend [*rare*], had as lief, would as lief; lend–, give–, turn– a willing ear; have -a, –half a, –a great- mind to; hold to, cling to; desire etc. 865.

acquiesce etc. (*assent*) 488; see think- -good, –fit, –proper; comply with etc. 762.

swallow–, nibble at- the bait; swallow bait, hook, and sinker; swallow bait and all; gorge the hook; have–, make- no scruple of; make no bones of [*colloq.*]; jump at, catch at; go in for, go in at [*both colloq.*]; take up, plunge into, have a go at [*colloq.*]; meet halfway.

volunteer, offer, proffer; offer oneself etc. 763.

adj. **willing**, minded, fain, disposed, inclined, favorable; favorably -minded, –inclined, –disposed; well-disposed, lief [*archaic*], nothing loth; in the -vein, –mood, –humor, –mind.

ready, forward, earnest, eager, zealous, enthusiastic; bent upon etc. (*desirous*) 865; predisposed, desirous, propense.

docile; persuadable, persuasible; suasible, amenable, easily persuaded, facile, easy-going; tractable etc. (*pliant*) 324; genial, gracious, cordial, cheering, hearty; content etc. (*assenting*) 488.

voluntary, gratuitous, spontaneous; unasked etc. (ask etc. 765); unforced etc. (*free*) 748.

adv. **willingly** etc. *adj.;* fain, freely, as lief, heart and soul; with pleasure, with all one's heart, with open arms; with good will, with right good will; *de bonne volonté* [*F.*], *ex animo* [*L.*], *con amore* [*It.*], heart in hand, nothing loath, without reluctance, of one's own accord, graciously, with a good grace; without demur.

à la bonne heure [*F.*]; by all means, by all manner of means; to one's heart's content; yes etc. (*assent*) 488.

int. **surely**! sure! with pleasure! of course! delighted!

603. Unwillingness

n. **unwillingness** etc. *adj.;* indisposition, indisposedness, disinclination, aversation [*rare*], aversion; averseness etc. (*dislike*) 867; nolleity [*rare*], nolition [*rare*]; renitence *or* renitency; reluctance; indifference etc. 866; backwardness etc. *adj.;* slowness etc. 275; want of -alacrity, –readiness; indocility etc. (*obstinacy*) 606.

scrupulousness, scrupulosity; qualms–, twinge- of conscience; delicacy, demur, scruple, qualm, shrinking, recoil; hesitation etc. (*irresolution*) 605; fastidiousness etc. 868.

dissent etc. 489; refusal etc. 764.

forced labor, unwilling service, peonage; compulsion etc. 744; slacker.

v. **be unwilling** etc. *adj.;* nill [*archaic*]; dislike etc. 867; grudge, begrudge; not find it in one's heart to, not have the stomach to.

demur, stick at, scruple, stickle; hang fire, run rusty [*colloq.*], go stale; give up, let down [*slang*]; pull back, be a dead weight, be a passenger in the boat, not pull fair, shirk, slack, shy [*dial. Eng.*], fight shy of, get by [*slang*], duck [*slang*]; recoil, shrink, swerve; hesitate etc. 605; avoid etc. 623.

oppose etc. 708; dissent etc. 489; refuse etc. 764.

adj. **unwilling**; not in the vein, loath *or* loth, shy of, disinclined, indisposed, averse, reluctant, not content; renitent, opposed; adverse etc. (*opposed*) 708; laggard, backward, remiss, slack, slow to; indifferent etc. 866; scrupulous; squeamish etc. (*fastidious*) 868; repugnant etc. (*dislike*) 867; restiff [*obs.*], restive; demurring etc. *v.;* unconsenting etc. (*refusing*) 764; involuntary etc. 601; grudging, forced; irreconcilable.

adv. **unwillingly** etc. *adj.;* grudgingly, with a heavy heart; with -a bad, –an ill- grace; against–, sore against- -one's wishes, –one's will, –the grain;

invita Minerva [*L.*]; *à contre coeur* [*F.*]; *malgré soi* [*F.*]; in spite of -one's teeth, −oneself; *nolens volens* [*L.*] etc. (*necessity*) 601; perforce etc. 744; under protest; no etc. 536; if I must I must; not if one can help it; not for the world; far be it from me.

604. Resolution

n. **determination**, will; iron will, unconquerable will; will of one's own, decision, resolution; backbone; clear grit, grit [*U. S. & Can.*]; sand [*slang*]; strength of -mind, −will; resolve etc. (*intent*) 620; intransigence *or* intransigency, *intransigeance* [*F.*]; firmness etc. (*stability*) 150; energy, manliness, vigor; resoluteness etc. (*courage*) 861; zeal etc. 682; desperation; devotion, devotedness.

self-control, *aplomb* [*F.*], mastery over self, self-mastery, self-command, self-possession, self-reliance, self-government, self-restraint, self-conquest, self-denial; moral -courage, −fiber, −strength.

tenacity, perseverance etc. 604*a;* obstinacy etc. 606; game, pluck; fighting cock, game cock; bulldog; British lion.

irreconcilable, intransigent, *intransigeant* [*F.*], bitter-ender [*colloq.*]; fighting minority, militant remnant.

v. **have determination** etc. *n.;* know one's own mind; be resolved etc. *adj.;* make up one's mind; will, resolve, determine; decide etc. (*judgment*) 480; form−, come to- a -determination, −resolution, −resolve; conclude, fix, seal, determine once for all, bring to a crisis, drive matters to an extremity; take a decisive step etc. (*choice*) 609; take upon oneself etc. (*undertake*) 676.

steel oneself, devote oneself to, give oneself up to; throw away the scabbard, kick down the ladder, nail one's colors to the mast, set one's back against the wall, burn one's bridges, grit one's teeth, set one's teeth, set one's jaw, take the bit in one's mouth, put one's foot down, take one's stand, stand firm etc. (*stability*) 150; stand no nonsense, not listen to the voice of the charmer; insist upon, make a point of; set one's heart upon, set one's mind upon.

buckle to; buckle oneself; put−, lay−, set- one's shoulder to the wheel; put one's heart into; run the gauntlet, make a dash at, take the bull by the horns; rush−, plunge- *in medias res* [*L.*]; go in for [*colloq.*].

stick at nothing; make short work of etc. (*activity*) 682; not stick at trifles; go all lengths,

go the limit [*slang*], go the whole hog [*slang*], go it blind [*slang*]; go down with one's colors flying; die game; persist etc. (*persevere*) 604 *a;* go through fire and water, "ride in the whirlwind and direct the storm" [Addison].

adj. **resolved** etc. *v.;* determined; strong-willed, strong-minded; resolute etc. (*brave*) 861; self-possessed, earnest, serious; decided, definitive, peremptory, unhesitating, unflinching, unshrinking; firm, iron, game, plucky, tenacious, gritty, indomitable, game to the backbone, game to the last; inexorable, relentless, not to be -shaken, −put down; *tenax propositi* [*L.*]; obstinate etc. 606; steady etc. (*persevering*) 604*a.*

unbending, unyielding; set−, bent−, intent- upon; grim, stern; inflexible etc. (*hard*) 323; cast-iron, irrevocable, irreversible; not to be deflected; firm as Gibraltar.

steeled−, proof- against; *in utrumque paratus* [*L.*].

adv. **resolutely** etc. *adj.;* in earnest, in good earnest; seriously, joking apart, earnestly, heart and soul; on one's mettle; manfully, like a man; with a high -heart, −courage, −hand; with a strong hand etc. (*exertion*) 686.

at all risks, at all hazards, at all events; at any -rate, −risk, −hazard, −price, −cost, −sacrifice; *à bis ou à blanc* [*F.*], cost what it may; *coûte que coûte* [*F.*]; *à tort et à travers* [*F.*]; once for all; neck or nothing; survive or perish, live or die; rain or shine.

604a. Perseverance

n. **perseverance**; continuance etc. (*inaction*) 143; permanence etc. (*absence of change*) 141; firmness etc. (*stability*) 150.

constancy, steadiness; singleness−, tenacity- of purpose; persistence, plodding, patience; sedulity [*rare*] etc. (*industry*) 682; pertinacy [*obs.*], pertinacity, pertinaciousness; iteration etc. 104.

grit, bottom, game, pluck, stamina, backbone, sand [*slang*]; indefatigability, indefatigableness; tenacity, staying power, endurance; bulldog courage.

v. **persevere**, persist; hold -on, −out; die in the last ditch, be in at the death; stick to, cling to, adhere to; stick to one's text; keep on, carry on, hold on; keep to−, maintain- one's -course, −ground; go all lengths, go through fire and water; bear up, keep up, hold up; plod; stick to work etc. (*work*) 686; continue etc. 143; follow up; die in harness, die at one's post.

adj. **persevering**, constant; steady, steadfast; undeviating, unwavering, unfaltering, unswerving, unflinching, unsleeping, unflagging, undrooping; steady as time; unintermitting, unremitting; plodding; industrious etc. 682; strenuous etc. 686; pertinacious; persisting, persistent.

solid, sturdy, stanch *or* staunch, true to oneself; unchangeable etc. 150; unconquerable etc. (*strong*) 159; indomitable, game to the last, indefatigable, untiring, unwearied, never tiring.

adv. **without fail**; through evil report and good report, through thick and thin, through fire and water; *per fas et nefas* [*L.*]; sink or swim, at any price, *vogue la galère* [*F.*]; rain or shine, fair or foul, in sickness and in health.

605. Irresolution

n. **irresolution**, infirmity of purpose, indecision, indetermination, undetermination [*rare*], instability; loss of will power, abulia, abulomania; unsettlement; uncertainty etc. 475; demur, suspense; hesitating etc. *v.*, hesitation, hesitancy; wabble *or* wobble; revocability, vacillation; changeableness etc. 149; fluctuation; alternation etc. (*oscillation*) 314; caprice etc. 608; lukewarmness, Laodiceanism.

fickleness, levity, *légèreté* [*F.*]; pliancy etc. (*softness*) 324; weakness; timidity etc. 860; cowardice etc. 862; half measures.

waverer, shilly-shally, ass between two bundles of hay; shuttlecock, butterfly, feather, piece of thistledown; house built on sand; doughface; turncoat, opportunist, Vicar of Bray, Dite Deuchars; Laodicean; timeserver etc. 607.

v. **be irresolute** etc. *adj.*; hang-, keep- in suspense; leave *ad referendum;* think twice about, pause; dawdle etc. (*inactivity*) 683; remain neuter; dilly-dally, hesitate, boggle, hover, dacker *or* daiker [*dial. Eng. & Scot.*], wabble *or* wobble [*colloq.*], shilly-shally, hem and haw, demur, not know one's own mind; debate, balance; dally with, coquet with; will and will not, *chasser-balancer* [*F.*]; go halfway, compromise, make a compromise; be thrown off one's balance, stagger like a drunken man; be afraid etc. 860; let "I dare not" wait upon "I would" [*Macbeth*]; falter, waver.

vacillate etc. 149; change etc. 140; retract etc. 607; fluctuate; pendulate; alternate etc. (*oscillate*) 314; keep off and on, play fast and loose; blow hot and cold etc. (*caprice*) 608; turn one's coat.

shuffle, palter, blink, shirk, trim.

adj. **irresolute**, infirm of purpose, palsied, drifting, double-minded, half-hearted; undecided, unresolved, undetermined; shilly-shally, wabbly *or* wobbly; fidgety, tremulous; hesitating etc. *v.;* off one's balance; abulic; at a loss etc. (*uncertain*) 475.

vacillating etc. *v.;* unsteady etc. (*changeable*) 149; unsteadfast, fickle, unreliable, irresponsible, unstable, unstable as water, without ballast; capricious etc. 608; volatile, frothy; light, lightsome, lightminded; giddy; fast and loose.

weak, feeble-minded, frail; timid etc. 860; cowardly etc. 862; dough-faced; facile; pliant etc. (*soft*) 324; unable to say "no," easy-going.

revocable, reversible.

adv. **irresolutely** etc. *adj.;* irresolvedly; in faltering accents; off and on; on the sands; from pillar to post; seesaw etc. 314.

606. Obstinacy

n. **obstinateness** etc. *adj.;* obstinacy, tenacity; cussedness; perseverance etc. 604a; immovability; old school; inflexibility etc. (*hardness*) 323; obduracy, obduration [*rare*], obdurateness, doggedness, dogged resolution; resolution etc. 604; ruling passion; blind side.

self-will, contumacy, perversity; pervicaciousness [*rare*], pervicacy [*obs.*], pervicacity [*obs.*]; indocility [*obs.*].

bigotry, intolerance, dogmatism; opiniatry [*obs.*], opiniativeness [*rare*]; impersuasibility, impersuadableness; intractableness, incorrigibility; fixed idea etc. (*prejudgment*) 481; fanaticism, zealotry, infatuation, monomania; opinionatedness, opinionativeness.

bigot, opinionist [*obs.*], opinionatist [*obs.*], opiniator [*obs.*], opinator [*obs.*]; stickler, dogmatist, zealot, enthusiast, fanatic, bitter-ender [*colloq.*]; mule.

v. **be obstinate** etc. *adj.;* stickle, take no denial, fly in the face of facts; opinionate [*rare*], be wedded to an opinion, hug a belief; have one's own way etc. (*will*) 600; persist etc. (*persevere*) 604a; have-, insist on having- the last word.

die hard, die fighting, fight to the last ditch, fight against destiny, not yield an inch, stand out.

adj. obstinate, tenacious, stubborn, obdurate, case-hardened; inflexible etc. (*hard*) 323; balky; immovable, not to be moved; inert etc. 172; unchangeable etc. 150; inexorable etc. (*determined*) 604; mulish, obstinate as a mule, pigheaded.

dogged; sullen, sulky; unmoved, uninfluenced, unaffected.

willful or wilful, self-willed, perverse; resty [*dial. Eng.*], restive, pervicacious [*rare*], ungovernable, wayward, refractory, unruly; heady, headstrong; *entêté* [*F.*]; contumacious; cross-grained.

arbitrary, dogmatic, positive, bigoted, opinionated, opinionative, opinionate [*obs.*], opinioned, opiniative [*rare*]; prejudiced etc. 481; creed-bound; prepossessed, infatuated; stiff-backed, stiff-necked, stiff-hearted; hard-mouthed, hidebound; unyielding; impervious, impracticable, impersuasible, impersuadable, unpersuadable; untractable, intractable; incorrigible, deaf to advice, impervious to reason; crotchety etc. 608.

adv. obstinately etc. *adj.;* with set jaw, with sullen mouth; no surrender.

607. Tergiversation

n. **tergiversation**, tergiversating, recantation; palinode, palinody [*rare*]; renunciation; abjuration, abjurement; defection etc. (*relinquishment*) 624; going over etc. *v.;* apostasy; retraction, retractation; withdrawal; disavowal etc. (*negation*) 536; revocation, revokement [*rare*], reversal; repentance etc. 950; *redintegratio amoris* [*L.*].

change of -mind, -intention, -purpose; afterthought.

coquetry, flirtation; vacillation etc. 605.

recidivism, recidivation, backsliding; *volte-face* [*F.*].

turncoat, turn-tippet [*obs.*]; rat [*cant*], apostate, renegade, pervert, deserter, backslider; recidivist; crawfish [*slang*], mugwump; blackleg, scab [*slang*]; proselyte, convert.

timeserver, time-pleaser; timist [*obs.*], Vicar of Bray, trimmer, ambidexter; double dealer; weathercock etc. (*changeable*) 149; Janus; co-quet, flirt.

v. **tergiversate**, veer round, wheel round, turn round; change one's- mind, -intention, -purpose, -note; abjure, renounce; withdraw from etc. (*relinquish*) 624; turn a pirouette; go over-, pass-, change-, skip- from one side to another; go to the right-about; box the compass, shift one's ground, go upon another tack.

apostatize, change sides, go over, rat [*cant*], *tourner casaque* [*F.*], recant, retract; revoke; rescind etc. (*abrogate*) 756; recall; forswear, unsay; come -over, -round- to an opinion.

back down, draw in one's horns, eat one's words; eat-, swallow- the leek; swerve, flinch, back out of, retrace one's steps, crawfish, crawl

[*both slang*]; think better of it; come back-, return- to one's first love; turn over a new leaf etc. (*repent*) 950.

trim, shuffle, play fast and loose, blow hot and cold, coquet, flirt, be on the fence, straddle, hold with the hare but run with the hounds; *nager entre deux eaux* [*F.*], wait to see how the -cat jumps, -wind blows.

adj. **changeful** etc. 149; irresolute etc. 605; ductile, slippery as an eel, trimming, ambidextrous, timeserving; coquetting etc. *v.*

revocatory, reactionary.

608. Caprice

n. **caprice**, fancy, humor; whim, whimsey or whimsy, whim-wham, crotchet, *capriccio* [*It.*], quirk, freak, maggot, fad, vagary, prank, fit, flimflam, escapade, boutade [*obs.*], wild-goose chase; capriciousness etc. *adj.;* kink.

v. **be capricious** etc. *adj.;* have a maggot in the brain; take it into one's head, take the bit in one's teeth; strain at a gnat and swallow a camel; blow hot and cold; play fast and loose, play fantastic tricks; *tourner casaque* [*F.*].

adj. **capricious**; erratic, eccentric, fitful, hysterical; full of whims etc. *n.;* maggoty; inconsistent, fanciful, fantastic, whimsical, crotchety, kinky, particular, humorsome, freakish, skittish, wanton, wayward; contrary; captious; unreasonable, unrestrained, undisciplined, not amenable to reason, arbitrary; unconformable etc. 83; penny wise and pound foolish; fickle etc. (*irresolute*) 605; frivolous, sleeveless [*obs.*], giddy, volatile.

adv. **by fits**, by fits and starts, without rime or reason, at one's own sweet will; without counting the cost.

609. Choice

n. **choice**, option; discretion etc. (*volition*) 600; preoption; alternative; dilemma, *embarras de choix* [*F.*]; adoption, coöptation; novation [*law*]; decision etc. (*judgment*) 480.

election, poll, ballot, vote, division, voice, suffrage, cumulative vote; plebiscitum, plebiscite, *vox populi* [*L.*], popular decision, referendum; electioneering; voting etc. *v.;* elective franchise; straight ticket, ticket; ballot box.

selection, excerption, gleaning, eclecticism; *excerpta* [*L.*]; gleanings, cuttings, scissors and paste; pick etc. (*best*) 650.

preference, prelation [*rare*]; predilection etc. (*desire*) 865; Apple of Discord; choice of Hercules; Scylla and Charybdis; good and evil.

v. **offer for one's choice,** set before; hold out–, present–, offer- the alternative; put to the vote.

choose, elect; coöpt, coöptate [*rare*]; take–, make- one's choice; make choice of, fix upon; use–, exercise–, one's- -discretion, –option; adopt, take up, embrace, espouse.

settle; decide etc. (*adjudge*) 480; list etc. (*will*) 600; make up one's mind etc. (*resolve*) 604.

vote, poll, hold up one's hand, give a (*or* the) voting sign; divide.

select; pick, –and choose; pick–, single- out; excerpt, cull, glean, winnow; sift–, separate–, winnow- the chaff from the wheat; pick up, pitch upon; pick one's way; indulge one's fancy.

set apart, mark out for; mark etc. 550.

prefer; have rather, had (*or* would) as lief; fancy etc. (*desire*) 865; reserve, set one's seal upon; be persuaded etc. 615.

take a decided step, take a decisive step; commit oneself to a course; pass–, cross- the Rubicon; cast in one's lot with; take for better or for worse.

adj. **optional;** coöptative; discretional etc. (*voluntary*) 600; at choice, on approval.

choosing etc. *v.;* eclectic; preferential.

chosen etc. *v.;* choice etc. (*good*) 648; elect, select, popular.

adv. **optionally** etc. *adj.;* at pleasure etc. (*will*) 600; either, –the one or the other; or; at the option of; whether or not; once for all; for one's money.

by choice, by preference; in preference; rather, before.

609a. Absence of Choice

n. **no choice,** Hobson's choice; first come first served; necessity etc. 601; not a pin to choose etc. (*equality*) 27; any, the first that comes; that or nothing.

neutrality, indifference; indecision etc. (*irresolution*) 605.

v. **be neutral** etc. *adj.;* have no -preference, –choice; waive, not vote; abstain–, refrain, –from voting; leave undecided; "make a virtue of necessity" [*Two Gentlemen from Verona*].

adj. **neutral,** neuter; indifferent; undecided etc. (*irresolute*) 605.

adv. **either** etc. (*choice*) 609.

610. Rejection

n. **rejection,** repudiation, exclusion; refusal etc. 764; declination, declinature, withdrawal; averseness.

v. **reject;** set–, lay- aside; give up; decline etc. (*refuse*) 764; exclude, except; pluck up, spurn, cast out.

repudiate, scout, set at naught; fling–, cast–, throw–, toss- -to the winds, –to the dogs, –overboard, –away; send to the right-about; disclaim etc. (*deny*) 536; discard etc. (*eject*) 297, (*have done with*) 678.

adj. **rejected** etc. *v.;* rejectaneous [*obs.*], rejectitious [*obs.*], declinatory; not chosen etc. 609, not to be thought of; out of the question; "declined with thanks."

adv. **neither,** neither the one nor the other; no etc. 536.

611. Predetermination

n. **predetermination,** predestination, preordination, premeditation, predeliberation; foregone conclusion; *parti pris* [*F.*]; resolve, propendency [*obs.*]; intention etc. 620; project etc. 626; fate, foredoom, necessity.

schedule, list, calendar, docket, slate, register, roster, poll, muster, draft, *cadre* [*F.*], panel.

v. **predetermine,** predestine, preordain, premeditate, preresolve, preconcert; resolve beforehand.

list, schedule, docket, slate, register, poll, empanel, draft.

adj. **premeditated** etc. *v.;* predesigned; prepense, advised, studied, designed, calculated; aforethought; intended etc. 620; foregone.

well-laid, well-devised, well-weighed; maturely considered; cut-and-dried, slated; cunning.

adv. **advisedly** etc. *adj.;* with premeditation, deliberately, all things considered, with eyes open, in cold blood; intentionally etc. 620.

612. Impulse

n. **impulse,** sudden thought; impromptu, improvisation; inspiration, flash, spurt.

improvisor, extemporizer, *improvvisatore* or *improvisatore* [*It.*]; creature of impulse.

v. flash on the mind.

improvise, extemporize; say what comes uppermost, say what comes first into one's head; act on the spur of the moment, rise to the occasion; spurt.

adj. **extemporaneous,** impulsive, indeliberate [*rare*]; snap; improvised, improvisate, improviso, improvisatory; unpremeditated; unmeditated, improvisatorial, improvisatory, *improvisé* [*F.*]; unprompted, unguided; natural, unguarded; spontaneous etc. (*voluntary*) 600; instinctive etc. 601.

adv. **extempore**, extemporaneously; offhand, impromptu, *a l'improviste* [*F.*]; on the spur of the -moment, −occasion.

613. Habit

n. **habit**, habitude, habituation, assuetude [*obs.*], assuefaction [*obs.*]; wont; run, way; habitual attitude, habitual state of mind, habitual course.

common−, general−, natural−, ordinary- -course, −run, −state- of things; matter of course; beaten -path, −track, −ground.

cacoëthes; bad−, confirmed−, inveterate−, intrinsic etc. (5)- habit; addictedness, addiction, trick.

custom, use, usage, prescription, immemorial usage, practice; prevalence, observance; conventionalism, conventionality; mode, fashion, vogue; etiquette etc. (*gentility*) 852; order of the day, cry; conformity etc. 82; consuetude, dastur *or* dustoor [*India*].

one's old way, old school, *veteris vestigia flammae* [*L.*]; *laudator temporis acti* [*L.*].

rule, standing order, precedent, routine; red tape, red-tapism; pipe clay; rut, groove.

addict, habitué, habitual [*colloq.*], frequenter, case [*slang*], hard case [*slang*], the limit [*slang*].

inurement; training etc. (*education*) 537; seasoning, hardening; radication; second nature, acclimatization; knack etc. (*skill*) 698.

v. **be wont** etc. *adj.*

fall into a custom etc. (*conform to*) 82; tread−, follow- the beaten -track, −path; *stare super antiquas vias* [*L.*]; move in a rut, run on in a groove, go round like a horse in a mill, go on in the old jog-trot way; get wound up in red tape.

habituate, inure, harden, season, caseharden; accustom, familiarize; naturalize, acclimatize; keep one's hand in; train etc. (*educate*) 537.

get into the -way, −knack- of; learn etc. 539; cling to, adhere to; repeat etc. 104; acquire−, contract−, fall into- a -habit, −trick; addict oneself to, take to, accustom oneself to.

be habitual etc. *adj.;* prevail; come into use, become a habit, take root; gain upon one, grow upon one.

adj. **habitual**; accustomary, customary; prescriptive; accustomed etc. *v.;* of -daily, −everyday- occurrence; consuetudinary; wonted, usual, general, ordinary, common, frequent, every day, household, jog-trot; well-trodden, well-known; familiar, vernacular, trite, commonplace, conventional, regular, set, stock, established, stereotyped; prevailing, prevalent; current, received, acknowledged, recognized, accredited; of course, admitted, understood.

conformable etc. 82; according to -use, −custom, −routine; in vogue, in fashion; fashionable etc. (*genteel*) 852.

wont; used to, given to, addicted to, attuned to, habituated to etc. *v.;* in the habit of; *habitué* [*F.*]; at home in etc. (*skillful*) 698; seasoned; imbued with, soaked in, permeated with, never free from; devoted to, wedded to.

hackneyed, fixed, rooted, deep-rooted, ingrafted *or* engrafted, permanent, inveterate, besetting, naturalized; ingrained etc. (*intrinsic*) 5.

adv. **habitually** etc. *adj.;* always etc. (*uniformly*) 16.

as usual, as is one's wont, as things go, as the world goes, as the sparks fly upwards; as you were [*mil.*]; *more suo* [*L.*], *more solito* [*L.*]; *ex more* [*L.*].

as a rule, for the most part; generally etc. *adj.;* most -often, −frequently.

614. Desuetude

n. **desuetude**, disusage; obsolescence, disuse etc. 678; want of -habit, −use, −practice; inusitation [*rare*]; newness to; new brooms.

nonprevalence; infraction of usage etc. (*unconformity*) 83; "a custom more honored in the breach than the observance" [*Hamlet*].

v. **be unaccustomed** etc. *adj.;* leave off−, cast off−, break off−, cure oneself of−, wean oneself from−, shake off−, violate−, break through−, infringe- a habit, −a custom, −a usage; break one's -chains, −fetters; do old things in a new way, give an original touch, give a new dress to old ideas; disuse etc. 678; wear off.

adj. **unaccustomed**, unused, unwonted, unseasoned, uninured, unhabituated, untrained; new, fresh, original; impulsive etc. *adj.* 612; green etc. (*unskilled*) 699; unhackneyed.

unconventional, unfashionable; dissident, protestant; unusual etc. (*unconformable*) 83; nonobservant; disused etc. 678.

adv. **contrary to -custom**, --usage, −convention; for once, just once; "this time doesn't count."

615. Motive

n. **motive**, springs of action.

reason, ground, call, principle; by-end, by-purpose; mainspring, *primum mobile* [*L.*], keystone; the why and the wherefore; *pro* and *con*, reason why; secret motive, ulterior motive; *arrière pensée* [*F.*]; intention etc. 620.

inducement, consideration; attraction; loadstone; magnet, magnetism, magnetic force; allectation [*obs.*], allective [*obs.*], temptation, enticement, *agacerie* [*F.*], allurement, witchery; bewitchment, bewitchery; charm; spell etc. 993; fascination, blandishment, cajolery; seduction, seducement; honeyed words, voice of the tempter, song of the Sirens; forbidden fruit, golden apple.

persuasibility, persuasibleness, persuadability, persuadableness; attractability; impressibility, susceptibility; softness; persuasiveness, attractiveness; tantalization.

influence, prompting, dictate, instance; impulse, impulsion; incitement, incitation; press, insistence, urge [*rare*], instigation; provocation etc. (*excitation of feeling*) 824; inspiration; persuasion, suasion; encouragement, advocacy; exhortation, hortation; advice etc. 695; solicitation etc. (*request*) 765; lobbyism; pull [*slang*].

incentive, stimulus, spur, fillip, whip, goad, ankus [*India*], rowel, provocative, whet, dram.

bribe, lure; decoy, decoy duck; bait, trail of a red herring; bribery and corruption; sop, sop to Cerberus.

tempter, seducer, seductor, seductress; prompter, suggester, coaxer, wheedler, Siren, Circe, vampire [*colloq.*], vamp [*slang*]; instigator, *agent provocateur* [*F.*]; lobbyist; firebrand, incendiary.

v. induce, move; draw, draw on; bring in its train, give an impulse to etc. *n.;* inspire; put up to [*slang*], prompt, call up; attract, beckon.

stimulate etc. (*excite*) 824; spirit, spirit up, inspirit; rouse, arouse, animate, incite, provoke, instigate, set on, actuate; act upon, work upon, operate upon; encourage; pat-, clap- on the -back, -shoulder.

set an example, set the fashion; keep in countenance, back up.

influence, weigh with, bias, sway, incline, dispose, predispose, turn the scale, inoculate; lead, -by the nose; have-, exercise-, influence- -with, -over, -upon; go-, come- round one [*colloq.*]; turn the head, magnetize; lobby [*chiefly U. S.*].

persuade; prevail -with, -upon; overcome, carry; bring round, bring to one's senses; draw-, win-, gain-, talk- over; come over [*colloq.*]; procure, enlist, engage; invite, court.

tempt, seduce, overpersuade, entice, allure, captivate, fascinate, bewitch, carry away, charm, conciliate, wheedle, coax, lure, vamp [*slang*]; inveigle; tantalize; cajole etc. (*deceive*) 545.

bribe, tamper with, suborn, grease the palm, bait with a silver hook, gild the pill, make things pleasant, put a sop into the pan, throw a sop to, bait the hook.

enforce, force; impel etc. (*push*) 276; propel etc. 284; whip, lash, goad, spur, prick, urge; egg on, hound on, hurry on; drag etc. 285; exhort; advise etc. 695; call upon etc., press etc. (*request*) 765; advocate.

be persuaded etc.; yield to temptation, come round [*colloq.*]; concede etc. (*consent*) 762; obey a call; follow -advice, -the bent, -the dictates of; act on principle.

adj. impulsive, motive; persuasive, persuasory [*rare*], hortative, hortatory; protreptical [*obs.*]; inviting, tempting, etc. *v.;* suasive, suasory [*obs.*], irresistible, seductive, attractive; fascinating etc. (*pleasing*) 829; provocative etc. (*exciting*) 824.

induced etc. *v.;* disposed; persuadable etc. (*docile*) 602; spellbound; instinct-, taken-, smitten- with; inspired by etc. *v.*

adv. because, therefore etc. (*cause*) 155; from this motive, from that motive; for this reason, for that reason; for; by reason of, for the sake of, on the score of, on account of; out of, from, as, forasmuch as.

for all the world; on principle.

615a. Absence of Motive

n. absence of motive; caprice etc. 608; chance etc. (*absence of design*) 621.

v. scruple etc. (*be unwilling*) 603; have no motive.

adj. aimless etc. (*chance*) 621; without rhyme or reason.

adv. capriciously, out of mere caprice.

616. Dissuasion

n. dissuasion, dehortation [*rare*], expostulation, remonstrance; deprecation etc. 766.

discouragement, dehortative [*rare*], monitory, damper, wet blanket; contraindicant.

curb etc. (*means of restraint*) 752; constraint etc. (*restraint*) 751; check etc. (*hindrance*) 706.

reluctance etc. (*unwillingness*) 603; contraindication.

v. dissuade, dehort [*rare*], cry out against, remonstrate, expostulate, warn, contraindicate.

disincline, indispose, shake, stagger; dispirit; discourage, dishearten, disenchant; deter; hold back, keep back etc. (*restrain*) 751; render averse etc. 603; repel; turn aside etc. (*deviation*) 279; wean from; act as a drag etc. (*hinder*) 706; throw cold water on, damp, cool, chill, blunt, calm, quiet, quench; deprecate etc. 766.

adj. **dissuading** etc. *v.;* dissuasive; dehortatory [*rare*], dehortative [*rare*], expostulatory; monitive [*obs.*], monitory, monitorial.

dissuaded etc. *v.;* admonitory; uninduced etc. (induce etc. 615); unpersuadable etc. (*obstinate*) 606; averse etc. (*unwilling*) 603; repugnant etc. (*dislike*) 867.

617. Plea

[ostensible motive, ground, or reason]

n. **plea**, pretext; allegation, advocation [*archaic*]; ostensible -motive, −ground, −reason etc. (*vindication*) 937; color; gloss; guise.

handle, peg to hang on; room, *locus standi* [*L.*]; stalking-horse, *cheval de bataille* [*F.*], cue.

loophole, starting-hole [*obs.*]; hole to creep out of, come-off [*colloq.*], way of escape.

pretense etc. (*untruth*) 546; put-off, subterfuge, dust thrown in the eye; blind; moonshine; mere−, shallow- pretext; lame -excuse, −apology; tub to a whale; false plea, sour grapes; makeshift, shift, white lie; special pleading etc. (*sophistry*) 477; soft sawder [*slang*] etc. (*flattery*) 933.

v. **plead**, allege; shelter oneself under the plea of; creep out of; tell a white lie; excuse etc. (*vindicate*) 937; color, gloss over, lend a color to; furnish a handle etc. *n.;* make a pretext of, make a handle of; use as a plea etc. *n.;* take one's stand upon, make capital out of; pretend etc. (*lie*) 544.

adj. **advocatory** [*rare*], excusing; **ostensible** etc. (*manifest*) 525; alleged, apologetic; pretended etc. 545.

adv. **ostensibly**; under the plea of, under the pretense of.

618. Good

n. **good**, benefit, advantage; improvement etc. 658; greatest−, supreme- good; interest, service, behoof, behalf; weal [*archaic*]; main chance, *summum bonum* [*L.*]; commonwealth [*now rare*], commonweal *or* common weal; "consummation devoutly to be wished" [*Hamlet*]; gain, boot [*archaic*]; profit, harvest.

boon etc. (*gift*) 784; good turn; blessing, benison; world of good; piece of good -luck, −fortune; nuts [*now Eng. slang*], prize, windfall, godsend, waif, treasure-trove.

good fortune etc. (*prosperity*) 734; happiness etc. 827.

[source of good] goodness etc. 648; utility etc. 644; remedy etc. 662; pleasure giving etc. 829.

v. **benefit**, profit, advantage, serve, help, avail, boot [*archaic*], good [*obs.*], do good to.

gain, prosper, flourish, thrive etc. 734.

adj. **commendable** etc. 931; useful etc. 644; good etc., beneficial etc. 648.

adv. **well**, aright, satisfactorily, favorably, not amiss; all for the best; to one's advantage etc. *n.;* in one's favor, in one's interest etc. *n.*

619. Evil

n. **evil**, ill, harm, hurt, mischief, nuisance; machinations of the devil, Pandora's box, ills that flesh is heir to; mental suffering etc. (*pain*) 828.

[evil spirit] demon etc. 980.

[cause of evil] bane etc. 663.

[production of evil] badness etc. 649; painfulness etc. 830; evildoer etc. 913.

blow, buffet, stroke, scratch, bruise, wound, gash, mutilation; mortal -blow, −wound; *immedicabile vulnus* [*L.*]; damage, loss etc. (*deterioration*) 659.

disadvantage, prejudice, drawback.

disaster, accident, casualty; mishap etc. (*misfortune*) 735; bad job [*colloq.*], devil to pay [*colloq.*]; calamity, bale [*chiefly poetic*], woe, fatal mischief, catastrophe, tragedy; ruin etc. (*destruction*) 162; adversity etc. 735.

outrage, wrong, injury, foul play; bad turn, ill turn; disservice; spoliation etc. 791; grievance, crying evil.

v. **disserve**, do disservice to, harm, injure, hurt.

be in trouble etc. (*adversity*) 735.

adj. **disastrous**, bad etc. 649; awry, out of joint; disadvantageous; disserviceable, injurious, harmful.

adv. **amiss**, wrong, ill, to one's cost.

Section 2. Prospective Volition

620. Intention

n. **intention**, intent, intentionality; purpose; *quo animo* [*L.*]; project etc. 626; undertaking etc. 676; predetermination etc. 611; design, ambition.

contemplation, mind, animus, view, purview [*law*], proposal; study; lookout.

object, aim, end; final cause; *raisòn d'être* [*F.*]; *cui bono* [*L.*]; "the be-all and the end-all" [*Macbeth*]; drift etc. (*meaning*) 516; tendency etc. 176; destination, mark, point, butt, goal, target, bull's-eye, quintain; prey, quarry, game.

decision, determination, resolve; fixed–, set–, settled- purpose; ultimatum; resolution etc. 604; wish etc. 865; *arrière pensée* [*F.*]; motive etc. 615.

[study of final causes] teleology.

v. **intend**, purpose, design, mean; have to; propose to oneself; harbor a design; have in -view, –contemplation, –one's eye; have *in petto* [*It.*]; have an eye to.

bid for, labor for; be after, aspire to *or* after, endeavor after; be at, aim at, drive at, point at, level at; take aim; set before oneself; study to.

contemplate, meditate; take upon oneself etc. (*undertake*) 676; take into one's head; think of, dream of, talk of; premeditate etc. 611; compass [*legal*], calculate; destine, destinate; propose.

project etc. (*plan*) 626; have a mind to etc. (*be willing*) 602; desire etc. 865; pursue etc. 622.

adj. **intended** etc. *v.*; intentional, advised, express, determinate; prepense etc. 611; bound for; intending etc. *v.*; disposed, inclined, minded; bent upon etc. (*earnest*) 604; at stake; on the -anvil, –tapis; in view, in prospect, in the breast of; *in petto* [*It.*]; teleological.

adv. **intentionally** etc. *adj.*; advisedly, wittingly, knowingly, designedly, purposely, on purpose, by design, studiously, pointedly; with intent etc. *n.*; deliberately etc. (*with premeditation*) 611; with one's eyes open, in cold blood.

for; with a view to, with an eye to; in order -to, –that; to the end that, with the intent that; for the purpose of, with the view of, in contemplation of, on account of.

in pursuance of, pursuant to; *quo animo* [*L.*]; to all intents and purposes.

621. Chance

[absence of purpose]

n. **chance** etc. 156; lot, fate etc. (*necessity*) 601; luck; good luck etc. (*good*) 618; hoodoo, jinx [*slang*], jadoo *or* jadu [*Hind.*]; voodoo, voodooism; swastika *or* swastica, fylfot, gammadion; wheel of chance, Fortune's wheel; mascot.

speculation, venture, mere–, random- shot; blind bargain, leap in the dark; pig in a poke etc. (*uncertainty*) 475; fluke [*sporting cant*], potluck, flyer [*slang*], flutter [*Eng. slang*]; futures.

gambling, game of chance; drawing lots; sortilegy, sortition [*obs.*]; *rouge et noir* [*F.*], hazard, ante, chuck-a-luck *or* chuck-luck, crack-loo, craps; faro, faro bank; roulette, pitch and toss, chuck-farthing, cup tossing, heads or tails, cross and pile [*archaic*], dice, dice box, poker-dice; fan-tan [*Chinese*].

wager; gamble, risk, stake, pyramid, plunge; bet, betting; gambling; the turf.

gambling house, gaming house, gambling den, pool room, betting-house; bucket shop; joint [*slang*]; parimutuel, totalizator, totalizer tote board; hell; betting ring; Wall Street, Stock Exchange, curb, curb market.

gambler, gamester, dicer, sport [*cant*], punter, plunger, speculator, hazarder, sucker, bookmaker, bookie [*colloq.*], man of the turf; pool shark [*colloq.*], shark, adventurer.

v. **chance** etc. (*hap*) 156; stand a chance etc. (*be possible*) 470.

toss up; cast–, draw- lots; leave–, trust- -to chance, –to the chapter of accidents; tempt fortune; chance it, take one's chance; run–, incur–, encounter- the -risk, –chance; stand the hazard of the die.

speculate, try one's luck, set on a cast, raffle, put into a lottery, buy a pig in a poke, shuffle the cards.

risk, venture, hazard, stake; ante; lay, –a wager; make a bet, wager, bet, gamble, game, play for; play at chuck-farthing; play the ponies, play the bangtails [*both slang*]; play–, shoot- craps etc.

adj. **fortuitous** etc. 156; unintentional, unintended; accidental; not meant; undesigned, unpurposed; unpremeditated etc. 612; never thought of.

indiscriminate, promiscuous; undirected, random; aimless, driftless, designless, purposeless, causeless; without purpose.

possible etc. 470.

adv. **casually** etc. 156; unintentionally etc. *adj.*; unwittingly.

incidentally, *en passant* [*F.*], by the way.

at random, at a venture, at haphazard; as luck would have it; in luck; out of luck; by chance, by good fortune; as it may happen.

int. what luck! better luck next time!

622. Pursuit

[purpose in action]

n. **pursuit**; pursuing etc. *v.*; prosecution; pursuance; enterprise etc. (*un*dertaking) 676; business etc. 625; adventure etc. (*essay*) 675; quest etc. (*search*) 461; scramble, hue and cry, game; hobby; still-hunt.

chase, hunt, *battue* [*F.*], race, steeplechase, hunting, coursing; venation [*obs.*], venery; fox chase, fox hunting; sport, sporting; shooting, angling, fishing, hawking; shikar [*India*].

pursuer; hunter, huntsman, the field; shikari [*India*], sportman, Nimrod; hound etc. 366.

v. **pursue**, prosecute, follow; run–, make–, be–, hunt–, prowl- after; shadow; carry on etc. (*do*) 680; be absorbed in; engage in etc. (*undertake*) 676; set about etc. (*begin*) 66; endeavor etc. 675; court etc. (*request*) 765; seek etc. (*search*) 461; aim at etc. (*intention*) 620; follow the trail etc. (*trace*) 461; fish for etc. (*experiment*) 463; press on etc. (*haste*) 684; run a race etc. (*velocity*) 274.

tread a path; take–, hold- a course; shape–, direct–, bend- one's -steps, –course; play a game; fight–, elbow- one's way; follow up; take to, take up; go in for; ride one's hobby.

chase, give chase, still-hunt, stalk, shikar [*India*], course, dog, hunt, hound; tread–, follow- on the heels of, etc. (*sequence*) 281; start game.

rush upon; rush headlong etc. (*violence*) 173; ride at, run full tilt at; make a leap at, jump at, snatch at; run down.

adj. **pursuing** etc. *v.;* in quest of etc. (*inquiry*) 461; in pursuit, in full cry, in hot pursuit; on the scent.

adv. **after**; in pursuance of etc. (*intention*) 620.

int. tallyho! yoicks! soho!

623. Avoidance

[absence of pursuit]

n. **avoidance**, evasion, elusion; seclusion etc. 893. avolation [*obs.*], flight; escape etc. 671; retreat etc. 287; recoil etc. 277; departure etc. 293; rejection etc. 610.

abstention, abstinence; forbearance; refraining etc. *v.;* inaction etc. 681; neutrality.

shirker etc. *v.;* slacker, shirk, quitter, eye servant, truant; fugitive, refugee, runaway, runagate, deserter, renegade, backslider; maroon.

v. **abstain**, refrain, spare, not attempt; not do etc. 681; maintain the even tenor of one's way.

eschew, keep from, let alone, have nothing to do with; keep–, stand–, hold- -aloof, –off; take no part in, have no hand in.

avoid, shun; steer–, keep- clear of; fight shy of; keep one's distance, keep at a respectful distance; keep–, get- out of the way; evade, elude, turn away from; set one's face against etc. (*oppose*) 708; deny oneself.

shrink; hang–, hold–, draw- back; recoil etc. 277; retire etc. (*recede*) 287; flinch, blink, blench, shy, shirk, dodge, parry, make way for, give place to.

beat a retreat; turn tail, turn one's back; take to one's heels; run, run away, run for one's life; maroon; cut and run [*colloq.*]; be off, –like a shot; fly, flee, fly–, flee–, run away- from; take flight, take to flight; desert, elope; make off,

scamper off, sneak off, shuffle off, sheer off; break–, burst–, tear oneself–, slip–, slink–, steal- -away, –away from; slip cable, part company, turn on one's heel; sneak out of, play truant, give one the go-by [*slang*], give leg bail [*slang*], take French leave, slope [*slang*], decamp, flit, bolt, abscond, levant [*slang, Eng.*], skedaddle [*dial.*], absquatulate, cut one's stick [*slang*], walk one's chalks [*slang*], show the heels, show a clean (*or* light) pair of heels, make oneself scarce [*slang*]; escape etc. 671; go away etc. (*depart*) 293; abandon etc. 624; reject etc. 610.

lead one a dance, lead one a pretty dance; throw off the scent, play at hide and seek.

adj. **avoiding** etc. *v.;* neutral; unsought, unattempted; shy of etc. (*unwilling*) 603; elusive, evasive; fugitive, runaway; shy, wild.

adv. **lest**, in order to avoid.

int. forbear! keep off! hands off! *sauve qui peut!* [*F.*], devil take the hindmost!

624. Relinquishment

n. **relinquishment**, abandonment; desertion, defection, secession, withdrawal; cave of Adullam; *nolle prosequi* [*L.*].

discontinuance etc. (*cessation*) 142; renunciation etc. (*recantation*) 607; abrogation etc. 756; resignation etc. (*retirement*) 757; desuetude etc. 614; cession etc. (*of property*) 782.

v. **relinquish**, give up, abandon, desert, forsake, leave in the lurch; go back on [*colloq.*]; depart–, secede - withdraw- from; back out of [*colloq.*], back down from [*colloq.*]; leave, quit, take leave of, bid a long farewell; vacate etc. (*resign*) 757.

renounce etc. (*abjure*) 607; forego, have done with, drop; nol-pros [*law*]; disuse etc. 678; discard etc. 782; wash one's hands of; drop all idea of.

break off, leave off; desist; stop etc. (*cease*) 142; hold one's hand, stay one's hand; quit one's hold; give over, shut up shop; throw up the -game, –cards.

give up the -point, –argument; pass to the order of the day, move the previous question, table, table the motion.

adj. **unpursued**; relinquished etc. *v.;* relinquishing etc. *v.*

int. avast! etc. (*stop*) 142.

625. Business

n. **business**, occupation, employment, undertaking; pursuit etc. 622; what one is doing, what one is about; affair, concern, matter, case.

task, matter in hand, irons in the fire; thing to do, agendum (*pl.* agenda), work, job, chore, errand, commission, mission, charge, care; duty etc. 926.

exercise; work etc. (*action*) 680; avocation, hobby; press of business etc. (*activity*) 682.

function, part, role, cue; province, lookout [*colloq.*], department, capacity, sphere, orb [*now rare*], field, line; walk, –of life; beat, round, routine; race, career.

office, place, post, chargeship, incumbency, living; situation, berth, billet, appointment, employ [*rare*], service etc. (*servitude*) 749; engagement; undertaking etc. 676.

vocation, calling, profession, cloth, faculty; industry, art; industrial arts; craft, mystery [*obs.*], handicraft; trade etc. (*commerce*) 794.

v. **occupy oneself with**; pass–, employ–, spend- one's time in; employ oneself -in, –upon; concern oneself with; make it one's business etc. *n.;* undertake etc. 676; enter a profession; betake oneself to, turn one's hand to; have to do with etc. (*do*) 680.

be about, be doing, be engaged in, be employed in, be occupied with, be at work on; have one's hands in, have in hand; have on one's -hands, –shoulders; bear the burden; have one's hands full etc. (*activity*) 682.

ply one's task, ply one's trade; drive a trade; carry on–, do–, transact- -business, –a trade etc. *n.;* keep a shop; labor in one's vocation; pursue the even tenor of one's way; attend to business, attend to one's work.

officiate, serve, act; act one's part, play one's part; do duty; serve–, discharge–, perform- the -office, –duties, –functions- of; hold–, fill- -an office, –a place, –a situation; hold a portfolio.

be in the hands of, be on the stocks, be on the anvil; pass through one's hands.

adj. **businesslike**; workaday; professional, vocational; official, functional; humming, busy etc. (*actively employed*) 682.

in hand, on hand; on *or* in one's hands; afoot; on foot, on the anvil; going on; acting.

adv. **in the course of business**, all in the day's work; professionally etc. *adj.*

626. Plan

n. **plan**, scheme, design, project, proposal, proposition, suggestion; resolution, motion; precaution etc. (*provision*) 673; deep-laid etc. (*premeditated*) 611- plan etc.; germ etc. (*cause*) 153.

system etc. (*order*) 58; organization etc. (*arrangement*) 60.

outline, sketch, skeleton, draft *or* draught, ébauche [*F.*], brouillon [*F.*]; rough -cast, –draft *or* draught, –copy; copy; proof, revise.

forecast, program *or* programme, prospectus; carte du pays [*F.*]; card; bill, protocol; order of the day, memoranda, list of agenda; bill of fare etc. (*food*) 298; base of operations; platform, plank, slate, ticket.

role; policy etc. (*line of conduct*) 692.

contrivance, invention, expedient, receipt, nostrum, artifice, device; pipelaying; stratagem etc. (*cunning*) 702; trick etc. (*deception*) 545; alternative, loop-hole; shift etc. (*substitute*) 147; last shift etc. (*necessity*) 601, gadget.

measure, step; stroke, –of policy; masterstroke; trump, trump card, courtcard; cheval de bataille [*F.*], great gun; coup, - d'état [*F.*]; clever–, bold–, good- -move, –hit, –stroke; bright -thought, –idea; great idea.

intrigue, cabal, plot, conspiracy, complot, machination; underplot, counterplot; mine, countermine.

schemer, schemist [*rare*], schematist [*obs.*]; strategist, machinator; Machiavellian, Machiavellist, conspirator; intrigant etc. (*cunning*) 702.

projector, promoter, designer etc. *v.;* organizer, founder (*fem.* foundress), author, artist, builder.

v. **plan**, scheme, design, frame, contrive, project, forecast, sketch; devise, invent etc. (*imagine*) 515; set one's wits to work etc. 515; spring a project; fall upon, hit upon; strike–, chalk–, cut–, lay–, map- out; lay down a plan; shape–, mark-out a course; predetermine etc. 611; concert, preconcert, preëstablish; prepare etc. 673; hatch, –a plot; concoct; take -steps, –measures.

systematize, organize; cast, recast, arrange etc. 60; digest, mature.

plot; counterplot, mine, countermine, dig a mine; lay a train; intrigue etc. (*cunning*) 702.

adj. **planned** etc. *v.;* strategic *or* strategical.

planning etc. *v.;* in course of preparation etc. 673; under consideration, on the tapis, on the carpet, on the table.

627. Method

[path]

n. **method**, way, manner, wise [*rare, exc. in phrases*], gait, form, mode, fashion, tone, guise; modus operandi [*L.*]; procedure etc. (*line of conduct*) 692.

path, road, route, course; line of way, line of road; trajectory, orbit, track, beat, tack.

steps; stair, staircase; flight of -steps, —stairs; ladder, stile; perron.

bridge, footbridge, viaduct, pontoon, stepping-stone, plank, gangway; draw-bridge.

pass, ford, ferry, tunnel; pipe etc. 260.

means of access, adit, entrance, approach, passage, cloister, covered way, lobby, corridor, aisle; alley, lane, vennel [*Scot. & dial. Eng.*], avenue, artery, channel; gateway etc. (*opening*) 260; door, backdoor, backstairs; secret passage; covert way.

roadway, express; thoroughfare; highway, macadam, parkway, boulevard; turnpike-, royal-, state-, coach- road; broad-, King's-, Queen's- highway; beaten -track, —path; horse-, bridle- -road, —track, —path; walk, *trottoir* [*F.*], footpath, pathway, pavement, flags, sidewalk, by-road, crossroad; by-, cross--path, —way; cut; short cut & (*mid-course*) 628; *carrefour* [*F.*]; private-, occupation- road; highways and byways; railroad, railway, trolley track, tramroad, tramway; towpath; causeway; street etc. (*abode*) 189; stairway, gangway; speedway; canal etc. (*conduit*) 350.

adv. **how**; in what way, in what manner; by what mode; so, thus, in this way, after this fashion.

one way or another, anyhow; somehow or other etc. (*instrumentality*) 631; by way of; *via* [*L.*]; *in transitu* [*L.*] etc. 270; on the high road to, on the way to.

628. Mid-course

n. **mid-course**, midway [*rare*], middle way, middle course; moderation; mean etc. 29; middle etc. 68; *juste milieu* [*F.*], *mezzo termine* [*L.*], golden mean, *ariston metron* [*Gr.*], *aurea mediocritas* [*L.*]; fifty-fifty [*colloq.*].

shortcut, crosscut; straight etc. (*direct*) 278 -course, —path; great-circle sailing.

compromise, half measures, half-and-half measures; neutrality.

v. **keep the golden mean**; keep in-, steer-, preserve- -a middle, —an even- course; avoid both Scylla and Charybdis; go straight etc. (*direct*) 278.

compromise, make a compromise, go fifty-fifty [*colloq.*], concede half, go half-way.

adj. **neutral**, average, even, evenly balanced; impartial, moderate; straight etc. (*direct*) 278.

adv. **midway**, in the mean; in moderation.

629. Circuit

n **circuit**, round-about way, digression, detour, circumbendibus [*humorous*], circumambience, circumambiency, circumambulation, ambages,

loop; winding etc. (*circuition*) 311; zigzag etc. (*deviation*) 279.

v. **go round about**, circumambulate, perform a circuit, make a circuit, go out of one's way; make a detour; meander etc. (*deviate*) 279.

lead a pretty dance; beat about, —the bush; make two bites of a cherry.

adj. **circuitous**, circumambient, circumambulatory, indirect, roundabout; zigzag etc. (*deviating*) 279; backhanded.

adv. **in a roundabout way**; by a side wind, by an indirect course; from pillar to post.

630. Requirement

n. **requirement**, need, wants, necessities; necessaries, —of life; stress, exigency, pinch, *sine qua non* [*L.*], matter of necessity; case of need, case of life or death.

desideratum etc. (*desire*) 865; want etc. (*deficiency*) 640.

needfulness, essentiality, necessity, indispensability, urgency, prerequisite; the least one can -do, —require.

requisition etc. (*request*) 765 (*exaction*) 741; run; demand for, call for.

charge, claim, command, injunction, mandate, order, precept, ultimatum.

v. **require**, need, want, have occasion for; not be able to do without, not able to dispense with; prerequire.

be necessary etc. *adj.;* stand in need of; lack etc. 640; desiderate; desire etc. 865.

render necessary, necessitate, create a necessity for, call for, put in requisition; make a requisition etc. (*ask for*) 765, (*demand*) 741.

adj. **necessary**; required etc. *v.;* requisite, needful, imperative, essential, indispensable, prerequisite; called for; in demand, in request.

in want of; destitute of etc. 640.

urgent, exigent, pressing, instant, crying, absorbing.

adv. **of necessity**; *ex necessitate rei* [*L.*] etc. (*necessarily*) 601; out of -stern necessity, —bitter need; in a pinch.

631. Instrumentality

n. **instrumentality**; aid etc. 707; subservience *or* subserviency, intermediacy, intermediation, mediation, intervention, medium, intermedium, intermediary, interagent, intermediate, mediating agency, vehicle, hand; agency etc. 170.

minister, handmaid; midwife, *accoucheur* [*F.*], *accoucheuse* [*fem., F.*], obstetrician; servant, slave, maid, valet; friend at court; go-between; cat's-paw; stepping-stone.

key, master–, pass–, latch- key; "open sesame"; passport, *passe-partout* [*F.*], safe-conduct; pull [*slang*], influence.

instrument etc. 633; expedient etc. (*plan*) 626; means etc. 632.

v. **subserve**, minister, mediate, intervene, intermediate, come–, go- between; interpose; pull the -strings, –wires; use one's influence; be instrumental etc. *adj.*; pander to; officiate; tend.

adj. **instrumental**; useful etc. 644; ministerial, subservient, serviceable; mediatorial, intermedial, intermediary, intermediate, intervening; conducive.

adv. **through**, by, *per* [*L.*]; whereby, thereby, hereby; by the agency of etc. 170; by dint of; by *or* in virtue of; through the medium of etc. *n.*; along with; on the shoulders of; by means of etc. 632; by *or* with the aid of etc. (*assistance*) 707.

somehow; *per fas et nefas* [*L.*]; by fair means or foul; somehow or other; by hook or by crook.

632. Means

n. **means**, resources, wherewithal, ways and means; capital etc. (*money*) 800; revenue, income; stock in trade etc. 636; provision etc. 637; reserve, remnant, last resource, a shot in the locker [*colloq.*]; appliances etc. (*machinery*) 633; means and appliances; conveniences; cards to play; expedients etc. (*measures*) 626; two strings to one's bow; wheels within wheels; sheet anchor etc. (*safety*) 666; aid etc. 707; medium etc. 631.

v. **provide the wherewithal**; find–, have–, possess- means etc. *n.*; have something laid by, –for a rainy day; have powerful friends, have friends at court; have something to draw on; beg, borrow, or steal.

adj. **instrumental** etc. 631; **mechanical** etc. 633. **reliable**, trustworthy, efficient; honorable etc. (*upright*) 939.

adv. **by means of**, with; by -what, –all, –any, –some- means; wherewith, herewith, therewith; wherewithal.

how etc. (*in what manner*) 627; through etc. (*by the instrumentality of*) 631; with *or* by the aid of etc. (*assistance*) 707; by the agency of etc. 170.

633. Instrument

n. **machinery**, mechanism, engineering.

instrument, organ, tool, implement, utensil, machine, engine, lathe, gin, mill; air–, caloric–,

heat–, steam–, internal-combustion- engine; motor.

equipment, gear, tackle, tackling; rigging, apparatus, appliances; plant, *matériel* [*F.*]; harness, trappings, fittings, accouterments *or* accoutrements, impedimenta; equipment, equipage; appointments, furniture, upholstery; chattels; paraphernalia etc. (*belongings*) 780.

mechanical powers; mechanical -advantage, –movements, –contrivances; leverage; fulcrum lever, crow, crowbar, gavelock [*Scot. & dial. Eng.*], jemmy, jimmy, marline spike *or* marlinspike, handspike, arm, limb, wing; oar, paddle etc. (*navigation*) 267.

wheel and axle; wheelwork, clockwork; rolling contact; epicyclic train; revolving lever; wheels within wheels; pinion, crank, winch; cam; capstan etc. (*lift*) 307; wheel etc. (*rotation*) 312; bevel gearing, spur gearing, universal joint; fly wheel, governor, turbine, water wheel; pump, lift-pump, force-pump, hydraulic ram.

pulley, crane, derrick; belt, open belt, crossed belt; cone pulley, stepped speed pulley.

inclined plane; wedge; screw; jack; spring, mainspring; can hook, glut, heald, heddle, loom, shuttle, jenny, parbuckle, sprag.

[tools etc.] hammer etc. (*impulse*) 276; edge tool etc. (*cut*) 253; turnscrew, screw driver *or* screwdriver; borer etc. 262; vise, teeth, etc. (*hold*) 781; nail, rope etc. (*join*) 45; peg etc. (*hang*) 214; support etc. 215; spoon etc. (*vehicle*) 272; arms etc. 727.

handle, hilt, haft *or* heft, shaft, shank, blade, trigger, tiller, rudder, helm, treadle, pedal, key; knocker.

adj. **instrumental** etc. 631.

mechanical, machinal [*rare*]; brachial; propulsive, driving, hoisting, elevating, lifting.

useful, labor-saving, ingenious; simple; complicated; well made, well fitted, sharp, in good order, well equipped.

634. Substitute

n. **substitute** etc. 147; proxy, alternate, stand-in [*colloq.*], understudy; deputy etc. 759; *badli* [*Hind.*].

635. Materials

n. **material**, raw material, stuff, stock, staple; ore. [building material] marble, granite, limestone, freestone, sandstone, brown stone; stone, metal, brick, bricks and mortar; chinking, mortar, lime, chunam [*India*], clay, plaster, daubing, concrete, cement, reinforced concrete; un-burnt brick, adobe; composition, compo; slates, tiles; whitewash etc. 223.

wood, timber, clapboard, shingle, shake, puncheon, log, rafter, beam, joist; two-by-four, four-by-four; post, upright, stud, lath; wall board.

materials; supplies, munition, fuel, grist, house-hold stuff; crockery etc. 384; pabulum etc. (*food*) 298; oilcloth, linoleum; ammunition etc. (*arms*) 727; contingents; relay, reënforcement; baggage etc. (*personal property*) 780; means etc. 632.

fabrics, calico, cambric, cashmere, linen, cotton, wool, silk; muslin, lawn, voile, gingham, dimity, broadcloth, homespun, serge, tweed, crêpe de chine, chiffon, satin, velvet.

adj. raw etc. (*unprepared*) 674; finished; wooden etc. *n.;* adobe.

636. Store

n. **stock**, fund, mine, vein, lode, quarry; spring; fount, fountain; well, wellspring [*obs. exc. fig.*]; orchard, garden, farm; milch cow; hen.

stock in trade, supply; heap etc. (*collection*) 72; treasure; reserve, *corps de réserve* [*F.*], reserve fund, nest egg, savings, *bonne bouche* [*F.*].

crop, harvest, vintage, yield, product, gleaning.

store, accumulation, hoard; mow, rick, stack; lumber; relay etc. (*provision*) 637.

storehouse, storeroom, store closet; depository, depot, cache, repository, reservatory [*obs.*], repertory; repertorium [*rare*]; promptuary, warehouse, godown [*Oriental*], entrepôt [*F.*], magazine; buttery, larder, spence [*dial. Eng.*]; garner, granary, grain elevator, silo; cannery, safe-deposit vault, stillroom, bank etc. (*treasury*) 802; armory; arsenal; dock; freight yard, train shed, carbarn, power station; stable, barn, byre, cowhouse; piggery; hen house; fish hatchery; hothouse, conservatory.

quiver, bandolier *or* bandoleer; coffer etc. (*receptable*) 191.

reservoir, cistern, *aljibar* [*Sp. Am.*], tank, pond, mill pond; gasometer.

[collections] library, public library, library of Congress, British Museum, Bodleian, Bibliothek; gallery, art gallery, picture gallery, Louvre, museum, Madame Tussaud's, zoölogical garden, zoo [*colloq.*], aquarium, menagerie.

work of reference, dictionary, lexicon, encyclopedia *or* encyclopaedia, cyclopedia *or* cyclopaedia, thesaurus, atlas, concordance, anthology.

conservation; storing etc. *v.;* storage.

file, letter file, card index, portfolio, budget; photographic -plate, −film; memory.

v. **store**; put by, lay by, set by; stow away; set apart, lay apart; store up, hoard up, treasure up, lay up, heap up, put up, garner up, save up; bank; cache; accumulate, amass, hoard, fund, garner, save.

reserve; keep back, hold back; husband, −one's resources.

deposit; stow, stack, load; harvest; heap, collect etc. 72; lay in store etc. *adj.;* keep, file [papers]; lay in etc. (*provide*) 637; preserve etc. 670.

adj. **stored** etc. *v.;* in store, in reserve, in ordinary; spare, supernumerary.

adv. for a rainy day, for a nest egg, to fall back upon; on deposit.

637. Provision

n. **provision**, supply; grist, −to the mill; subvention etc. (*aid*) 707; resources etc. (*means*) 632; groceries, grocery.

providing etc. *v.;* purveyance; reenforcement; commissariat.

provender etc. (*food*) 298; ensilage; viaticum; ration; emergency−, iron-ration.

caterer, purveyor, provider, commissary, quartermaster, steward, purser, housekeeper, manciple, feeder, batman, victualer *or* victualler, comprador *or* compradore [*China*]; innkeeper, landlord, innholder, mine host, khansamah [*India*], *restaurateur* [*F.*]; grocer, green grocer, huckster, fishmonger, provision merchant; sutler etc. (*merchant*) 797.

provision shop, provision store, meat shop, fish store; market, supermarket, public market; grocery, grocery store.

v. **provide**; make -provision, −due provision for; lay in, −a stock, −a store.

supply, suppeditate [*obs.*]; furnish; find, find one in; arm.

cater, victual, provision, purvey, forage; beat up for; stock, −with; make good, replenish; fill, −up; recruit, feed.

store, have in -store, −reserve; keep, keep by one; have to fall back upon; store etc. 636; provide against a rainy day etc. (*economy*) 817; conserve, keep, preserve, lay by, gather into barns.

638. Waste

n. **consumption**, expenditure, exhaustion; dispersion etc. 73; ebb; leakage etc. (*exudation*) 295; loss etc. 776; wear and tear; waste; prodigality etc. 818; misuse etc. 679; wasting etc. *v.;* rubbish etc. (*useless*) 645.

v. **consume**, spend, expend, use, swallow up; exhaust; impoverish; spill, drain, empty, deplete; disperse etc. 73.

cast–, fool–, muddle–, throw–, fling–, fritter-away; burn the candle at both ends, waste; squander etc. 818.

labor in vain etc. (*useless*) 645; "waste its sweetness on the desert air" [Gray]; cast pearls before swine; employ a steam engine to crack a nut, waste powder and shot, break a butterfly on a wheel; cut blocks with a razor, pour water into a sieve, tilt at windmills.

run to waste; ebb; leak etc. (*run out*) 295; melt away, run dry, dry up; spoil.

adj. **wasted** etc. *v.;* gone to waste, useless, rendered useless, made unavailable; run to seed; dried up; at a low ebb.

wasteful etc. (*prodigal*) 818; penny wise and pound foolish.

639. Sufficiency

n. **sufficiency**, adequacy, enough, wherewithal, *quantum sufficit* [L.], satisfaction, competence; no less.

mediocrity etc. (*average*) 29.

fill; fullness etc. (*completeness*) 52; plenitude, plenty; abundance; copiousness etc. *adj.;* amplitude, galore [*rare*], lots [*colloq.*], profusion; full measure; "good measure, pressed down, and shaken together, and running over" [*Bible*].

luxuriance etc. (*fertility*) 168; affluence etc. (*wealth*) 803; fat of the land; "a land flowing with milk and honey" [*Bible*]; cornucopia; horn of -plenty, –Amalthaea; mine etc. (*stock*) 636.

outpouring; flood etc. (*great quantity*) 31; tide etc. (*river*) 348; repletion etc. (*redundance*) 641; satiety etc. 869.

rich man etc. (*wealth*) 803; financier, banker, creditor etc. 805; plutocrat.

v. **be sufficient** etc. *adj.;* suffice; do, just do [*both colloq.*], satisfy, pass muster; have enough etc. *n.;* eat–, drink–, have- one's fill; roll in, swim in; wallow in etc. (*superabundance*) 641; wanton.

abound, exuberate, teem, flow, stream, rain, shower down; pour, pour in; swarm; bristle with; superabound.

render sufficient etc. *adj.;* replenish etc. (*fill*) 52.

adj. **sufficient**, enough, adequate, up to the mark, commensurate, competent, satisfactory, valid, tangible.

moderate etc. (*temperate*) 953; measured.

ample; full etc. (*complete*) 52; plenty, plentiful, plenteous; plenty as blackberries; copious, abundant; abounding etc. *v.;* replete, enough and to spare, flush; chock-full *or* choke-full; well-stocked, well-provided; liberal; unstinted, unstinting; stintless; without stint; unsparing, unmeasured; lavish etc. 641; wholesale.

unexhausted, unwasted; exhaustless, inexhaustible.

rich; luxuriant etc. (*fertile*) 168; affluent etc. (*wealthy*) 803; wantless; big with etc. (*pregnant*) 161.

adv. **sufficiently**, amply etc. *adj.;* full; in abundance etc. *n.;* with no sparing hand; to one's heart's content, *ad libitum* [L.], without stint; to the good.

640. Insufficiency

n. **insufficiency**, inadequacy, inadequateness; incompetence etc. (*impotence*) 158; deficiency etc. (*incompleteness*) 53; imperfection etc. 651; shortcoming etc. 304; paucity; stint; scantiness etc. (*smallness*) 32; none to spare; bare subsistence.

scarcity, dearth; want, need, lack, poverty, exigency; inanition, starvation, famine, drought *or* drouth.

dole, mite, pittance; short -allowance, –commons; half rations; banyan day; fast day, Lent.

depletion, emptiness, poorness etc. *adj.;* vacancy, flaccidity; ebb tide; low water; "a beggarly account of empty boxes" [*Romeo and Juliet*]; indigence etc. 804; insolvency etc. (*nonpayment*) 808.

poor man, pauper etc. 804; bankrupt etc. (*nonpayment*) 808.

miser, niggard etc. (*parsimony*) 819.

v. **be insufficient** etc. *adj.;* not suffice etc. 639; kick the beam; come short of etc. 304; run dry.

want, lack, need, require; *caret* [L.]; be in want etc. (*poor*) 804; live from hand to mouth.

render insufficient etc. *adj.;* drain of resources; impoverish etc. (*waste*) 638; stint etc. (*begrudge*) 819; put on short -allowance, –commons.

do insufficiently etc. *adv.;* scotch the snake.

adj. **insufficient**, inadequate; too little etc. 32; not enough etc. 639; unequal to; incompetent etc. (*impotent*) 158; perfunctory etc. (*neglect*) 460; deficient etc. (*incomplete*) 53; wanting etc. *v.;* imperfect etc. 651; ill-furnished, ill-provided, ill-stored, ill-off.

short of, out of, destitute of, devoid of, bereft of etc. 789, denuded of; slack, at a low ebb; empty, vacant, bare; dry, drained.

unprovided, unsupplied, unfurnished; unreplenished, unfed; unstored, untreasured; empty-handed.

meager *or* meagre, poor, thin, scrimp, sparing, stunted, spare, stinted; starved, starveling, emaciated, undernourished, underfed, half-starved, famine-stricken, famished; jejune.

scarce; not to be had, –for love or money, –at any price; scurvy; stingy etc. 819; at the end of one's tether; without resources etc. 632; in want etc. (*poor*) 804; in debt etc. 806; scant etc. (*small*) 32.

adv. insufficiently etc. *adj.;* in default of, for want of; failing.

641. Redundance

n.   **redundance**; too much, too many; superabundance, superfluity, superfluence [*obs.*], supersaturation; nimiety [*rare*], transcendency, exuberance, profuseness; profusion etc. (*plenty*) 639; repletion, enough in all conscience, *satis superque* [*L.*], lion's share; more than enough etc. 639; plethora, engorgement, congestion, load, surfeit, sickener; turgescence etc. (*expansion*) 194; overdose, overmeasure, oversupply, overflow; inundation etc. (*water*) 348; avalanche, deluge.

pleonasm etc. (*diffuseness*) 573; too many irons in the fire; *embarras de richesses* [*F.*]; embarrassment of riches; money to burn [*colloq.*].

accumulation etc. (*store*) 636; heap etc. 72; drug, –in the market; glut; crowd; burden.

excess, surplus, overplus; epact; margin; remainder etc. 40; duplicate; surplusage, expletive; work of supererogation; bonus, bonanza.

luxury; extravagance etc. (*prodigality*) 818; exorbitance, lavishment; intemperance etc. 954.

v.   **superabound**, overabound; know no bounds, swarm; meet one at every turn; creep with, bristle with; overflow; run–, flow–, well–, brim-over; run riot; overrun, overstock, overlay, overcharge, overdose, overfeed, overburden, overload, overdo, overwhelm, overshoot the mark etc. (*go beyond*) 303; surcharge, supersaturate, gorge, glut, load, drench, whelm, inundate, deluge, flood; drug, –the market; hepatize.

send–, carry- -coals to Newcastle, –owls to Athens; teach one's grandmother to suck eggs [*colloq.*]; *pisces natare docere* [*L.*]; kill the slain,

butter one's bread on both sides, put butter upon bacon; employ a steam engine to crack a nut etc. (*waste*) 638.

wallow in; roll in etc. (*plenty*) 639; remain on one's hands, hang heavy on hand, go a-begging *or* go begging; exaggerate etc. 549.

cloy, choke, accloy [*archaic*], suffocate; pile up, lay on thick; lay it on, –with a trowel; impregnate with; lavish etc. (*squander*) 818.

adj.   **redundant**; too much, too many; exuberant, inordinate, superabundant, excess, overmuch, replete, profuse, lavish; prodigal etc. 818; exorbitant; overweening; extravagant; overcharged etc. *v.;* supersaturated, drenched, overflowing; running -over, –to waste, –down.

crammed–, filled- to overflowing; gorged, stuffed, smothered, ready to burst; dropsical, turgid, plethoric; full-blooded, haematose *or* hematose; obese etc. 194.

superfluous, unnecessary, needless, supervacaneous [*obs.*], uncalled for, to spare, in excess; over and above etc. (*remainder*) 40; *de trop* [*F.*]; adscititious etc. (*additional*) 37; supernumerary etc. (*reserve*) 636; on one's hands, spare, duplicate, supererogatory, expletory, expletive; *un peu fort* [*F.*].

adv.   **over and above**; over much, too much; too far; over, too; without–, beyond–, out of- measure; with . . . to spare; over head and ears; over one's head; up to one's -eyes, –ears; extra; beyond the mark etc. (*overrun*) 303; *acervatim* [*L.*].

642. Importance

n.   **importance**, consequence, moment, prominence, consideration, mark, materialness, materiality.

greatness etc. 31; superiority etc. 33; notability etc. (*repute*) 873; weight etc. (*influence*) 175; value etc. (*goodness*) 648; usefulness etc. 644.

import, significance, concern; emphasis, interest.

gravity, seriousness, solemnity; no joke, no laughing matter; pressure, urgency, stress; matter of life and death.

memorabilia, notabilia, great doings; red-letter day.

salient point, outstanding feature; great -thing, –point; main chance, "the be-all and the end-all" [*Macbeth*]; cardinal point; substance, gist etc. (*essence*) 5; sum and substance, gravamen, head and front; important-, principal-, prominent-, essential- part; half the battle; *sine qua non* [*L.*]; breath of one's nostrils etc. (*life*) 359; cream, salt, core, kernel, heart, nucleus; key, keynote; keystone; corner stone; trump card etc. (*device*) 626.

chief, top sawyer, first fiddle, top banana [*cant*], prima donna, triton among the minnows; "it"; the only pebble on the beach; burra (*or* bara) sahib [*India*]; bigwig etc. 875.

v. **be important** etc. *adj.;* be somebody, be something; import, signify, matter, be an object; carry weight etc. (*influence*) 175; make a figure etc. (*repute*) 873; be in the ascendant, come to the front, lead the way, take the lead, play first fiddle, throw all else into the shade; lie at the root of; deserve–, merit–, be worthy of– –notice, –regard, –consideration.

value; attach–, ascribe–, give– importance etc. *n.*- to; care for; set store -upon, –by; mark etc. 550; mark with a white stone, underline; write–, put–, print- in -italics, –capitals, –large letters, –large type, –bold-faced type, -letters of gold; accentuate, emphasize, lay stress on.

make much of; make -a fuss, –a stir, –a piece of work, –much ado- about.

adj. **important**; of importance etc. *n.;* momentous, material; to the point; not to be -overlooked, –despised, –sneezed at [*colloq.*]; egregious; weighty etc. (*influential*) 175; of note etc. (*repute*) 873; notable, prominent, salient, signal; memorable, remarkable; worthy of -remark, –notice; never to be forgotten; stirring, eventful.

in the front rank, first-rate, A1 *or* A number 1 [*colloq.*], first chop [*Anglo-Ind. & colloq.*]; superior etc. 33; considerable etc. (*great*) 31; marked etc. *v.;* rare etc. 137.

grave, serious, earnest, noble, grand, solemn, impressive, commanding, imposing.

urgent, pressing, critical, instant.

paramount, essential, vital, all-absorbing, radical, cardinal, chief, main, prime, primary, principal, leading, capital, foremost, overruling; of vital etc. importance.

significant, telling, trenchant, emphatic, pregnant; *tanti* [*L.*].

adv. **in the main**; materially etc. *adj.;* above all, in the first place, before everything else; *kat' exochen* [*Gr.*], *par excellence* [*F.*], to crown all.

643. Unimportance

n. **unimportance,** insignificance, nothingness, immateriality.

triviality, levity, frivolity, fribble; paltriness etc. *adj.;* poverty; smallness etc. 32; vanity etc. (*uselessness*) 645; matter of indifference etc. 866; no object.

nothing, –to signify, –worth speaking of, –particular, –to boast of, –to speak of; small–, no great–, trifling etc. *adj.*- matter; mere joke, mere nothing; hardly–, scarcely- anything; nonentity, small beer, cipher; no great shakes [*colloq.*], *peu de chose* [*F.*]; child's play.

toy, plaything, popgun, paper pellet, gimcrack, gewgaw, bauble, trinket, bagatelle, kickshaw, knickknack, whimwham, trifle, "trifles light as air" [*Othello*].

trumpery, trash, rubbish, stuff, *fatras* [*F.*], frippery; "leather or prunello" [*Pope*]; fiddle-faddle [*colloq.*], fingle-fangle; chaff, drug, froth, bubble, smoke, cobweb; weed; refuse etc. (*inutility*) 645; scum etc. (*dirt*) 653.

joke, jest, snap of the fingers, snap of one's thumb; fudge etc. (*unmeaning*) 517; fiddlestick, pack of nonsense, mere farce.

trifle, straw, pin, fig, fico [*archaic*], button, rush; bulrush, feather, half-penny, farthing, brass farthing, doit, peppercorn, iota, tinker's dam (*or* damn), continental, jot, mote, rap, pinch of snuff, old song; cent, mill, picayune; pai, pice [*both India*]; pistareen, red cent.

nine days' wonder, *ridiculus mus* [*L.*]; flash in the pan etc. (*impotence*) 158; much ado about nothing etc. (*overestimation*) 482; tempest–, storm- in a teapot.

minutiae, details, minor details, small fry; dust in the balance, feather in the scale, drop in the ocean, fleabite, pin prick, molehill.

v. **be unimportant** etc. *adj.;* not matter etc. 642; go for–, matter–, signify- -little, –nothing, –little or nothing; not matter a straw etc. *n.*

make light of etc. (*underestimate*) 483; catch at straws etc. (*overestimate*) 482; tumble–, stumble- over one's shadow; make mountains out of molehills, make much ado about nothing.

adj. **unimportant**; of -little, –small, –no- -account, –importance etc. 642; immaterial; nonessential, unessential, irrelevant, not vital, uninteresting; indifferent, amateurish.

subordinate etc. (*inferior*) 34; mediocre etc. (*average*) 29; passable, fair, respectable, tolerable, commonplace; uneventful, mere, common; ordinary etc. (*habitual*) 613; inconsiderable, soso *or* so-so, insignificant, nugatory, inappreciable.

trifling, trivial; slight, slender, light, flimsy, frothy, idle; puerile etc. (*fool*-ish) 499; airy, shallow; weak etc. 160; powerless etc. 158; frivolous, petty, niggling; peddling, piddling, fribbling, fribble, inane, ridiculous, farcical; finical, finicking *or* finicky *or* finikin, mincing, fiddle-faddle [*colloq.*], namby-pamby, wishy-washy [*colloq.*], milk and water, insipid.

paltry, poor, pitiful; contemptible etc. (*contempt*) 930; sorry, mean, meager *or* meagre, shabby, miserable, wretched, vile, scrubby, scrannel [*archaic*], weedy, niggardly, scurvy, beggarly, worthless, twopenny-halfpenny, two-for-a-cent, two-bit, two-by-four, cheap, trashy, catchpenny, gimcrack, trumpery; one-horse.

not worth -the pains, −while, −mentioning, −speaking of, −a thought, −a curse, −a cent, −a rap, −a hair, −a straw etc. *n.;* beneath contempt, below par; not up to -sample, −specification; beneath-, unworthy of- -notice, −regard - consideration; *de lana caprina* [*L.*]; vain etc. (*useless*) 645.

adv. **slightly** etc. *adj.;* rather, somewhat, pretty well, fairly, fairly well, tolerably.

for aught one cares; it matters not, it does not signify; it is of no -consequence, −importance.

int. **no matter**! pish! tush! tut! pshaw! pugh! pooh, −pooh! fudge! bosh! humbug! fiddlestick, −end! fiddledeedee! never mind! *n'importe!* [*F.*]; what signifies! what matter! what boots it! what of that! what's the odds! a fig for! stuff! nonsense! stuff and nonsense!

644. Utility

n. **utility**; usefulness etc. *adj.;* efficacy, efficiency, adequacy; service, use, stead, avail, boot [*archaic*]; help etc. (*aid*) 707; applicability etc. *adj.;* subservience etc. (*instrumentality*) 631; function etc. (*business*) 625; value; worth etc. (*goodness*) 648; money's worth; productiveness etc. 168; *cui bono* etc. (*intention*) 620; utilization etc. (*use*) 677; step in the right direction.

commonweal *or* common weal; commonwealth; public -good, −service, −interest; utilitarianism etc. (*philanthropy*) 910; public servant.

v. **be useful** etc. *adj.;* avail, serve; subserve [*rare*] etc. (*be instrumental to*) 631; conduce etc. (*tend*) 176; answer−, serve- -one's turn, −a purpose.

act a part etc. (*action*) 680; perform−, discharge -a function etc. 625; do−, render- -a service, −good service, −yeoman's service; bestead, stand one in good stead; be the making of; help etc. 707.

benefit etc. (*do good*) 648; bear fruit etc. (*produce*) 161; bring grist to the mill; profit, remunerate.

find one's -account, −advantage- in; reap the benefit of etc. (*be better for*) 658.

render useful etc. (*use*) 677.

adj. **useful**; of use etc. *n.;* serviceable, proficuous [*obs.*], good for; subservient etc. (*instrumental*) 631; conducive etc. (*tending*) 176; subsidiary etc. (*helping*) 707.

advantageous etc. (*beneficial*) 648; profitable, gainful, remunerative, worth one's salt; valuable; invaluable, beyond price, of general utility; prolific etc. (*productive*) 168.

adequate; efficient, efficacious; effective, effectual; expedient etc. 646.

applicable, usable, available, ready, handy, at hand, tangible; commodious, adaptable; of all work.

adv. **usefully** etc. *adj.*

for use, for service; in the public service; for the good of the -people, −public, −service; *pro bono publico* [*L.*].

645. Inutility

n. **inutility**; uselessness etc. *adj.;* inefficacy, futility; ineptitude, inaptitude; inadequacy etc. (*insufficiency*) 640; unfitness; inefficiency etc. (*incompetence*) 158; unskillfulness etc. 699; disservice; unfruitfulness etc. (*unproductiveness*) 169; labor -in vain, −lost, −of Sisyphus; lost -trouble, −labor; work of Penelope; Penelope's web; sleeveless [*obs.*]-, bootless- errand; wild-goose chase, mere farce.

redundance, supererogation etc. 641; tautology etc. (*repetition*) 104.

worthlessness; vanity, *vanitas vanitatum* [*L.*], inanity, nugacity; triviality etc. (*unimportance*) 643.

worthless residue, *caput mortuum* [*L., old chem.*]; waste paper, dead letter; blunt tool.

rubbish, junk, lumber, litter, odds and ends, cast-off clothes; button top; shoddy; rags, orts [*archaic*], leavings, dross, trash, refuse, sweepings, scourings, offscourings, waste, rubble, *débris* [*F.*]; chaff, stubble, broken meat; dregs etc. (*dirt*) 653; weeds, tares; rubbish heap, dust hole; *rudera* [*L.*], deads, slag.

idler; *fruges consumere natus* [Horace] etc. (*drone*) 683.

v. **be useless** etc. *adj.;* go a-begging etc. (*redundant*) 641; fail etc. 732.

labor in vain; seek−, strive- after impossibilities; use vain efforts, roll the stone of Sisyphus, beat the air, lash the waves, *battre l'eau avec un bâton* [*F.*], *donner un coup d'épée dans l'eau* [*F.*], fish in the air, milk the ram, drop a bucket into an empty well, pour water into a sieve, sow the sand; bay the moon; preach−, speak- to the winds; whistle jigs to a milestone; kick against the pricks, *se battre contre des moulins* [*F.*]; lock the stable door when the steed is stolen etc. (*too late*) 135; hold a farthing candle to the sun; cast pearls before swine etc. (*waste*) 638; carry coals to Newcastle etc. (*redundance*) 641; wash a blackamoor white etc. (*impossible*) 471.

render useless etc. *adj.;* dismantle, dismast, dismount, disqualify, disable; unrig [*chiefly naut.*]; hamstring, hock *or* hough, cripple, lame etc. (*injure*) 659; spike guns, clip the wings; put out of gear; throw a wrench in the machinery, throw a monkey-wrench into the works.

adj. **useless**, inutile, nugatory, inefficacious, futile, unavailing, bootless; inoperative etc. 158; inadequate etc. (*insufficient*) 640; inservient [*obs.*], inept, inefficient etc. (*impotent*) 158; of no avail etc. (*use*) 644; ineffectual etc. (*failure*) 732; incompetent etc. (*unskillful*) 699; "weary, stale, flat, and unprofitable" [*Hamlet*]; superfluous etc. (*redundant*) 641; dispensable; thrown away etc. (*wasted*) 638; abortive etc. (*immature*) 674.

worthless, valueless, unsalable; not worth a straw etc. (*trifling*) 643; dear at any price.

vain, empty, inane; gainless, profitless, fruitless; unserviceable, unprofitable; ill-spent; effete, barren, sterile, impotent, worn out; unproductive etc. 169; *hors de combat* [*F.*], past work etc. (*impaired*) 659; obsolete etc. (*old*) 124; fit for the dust hole; good for nothing; of no earthly use; not worth -having, –powder and shot; leading to no end, uncalled for; unnecessary, unneeded, superfluous.

adv. **uselessly** etc. *adj.;* to -little, –no, –little or no-purpose.

int. *cui bono?* [*L.*]; what's the good! what's the use!

646. Expedience

[specific subservience]

n. **expedience** *or* expediency, desirability, desirableness etc. *adj.;* fitness etc. (*agreement*) 23; utility etc. 644; propriety; opportunism; advantage, opportunity; pragmatism, pragmaticism; a working proposition.

high time etc. (*occasion*) 134; suitable time *or* season, tempestivity [*obs.*].

v. **be expedient** etc. *adj.;* suit etc. (*agree*) 23; befit; suit-, befit- the -time, –season, –occasion; produce the goods [*colloq.*].

conform etc. 82.

adj. **expedient**; desirable, advisable, acceptable; convenient; worth while, meet; fit, fitting; due, proper, eligible, seemly, becoming; befitting etc. *v.;* opportune etc. (*in season*) 134; in

loco [*L.*]; suitable etc. (*accordant*) 23; applicable etc. (*useful*) 644.

practical, practicable, effective, pragmatic, pragmatical.

adv. **conveniently** etc. *adj.;* in the nick of time; in the right place.

647. Inexpedience

n. **inexpedience** *or* inexpediency, undesirability, undesirableness etc. *adj.;* discommodity, impropriety; unfitness etc. (*disagreement*) 24; inutility etc. 645; disadvantage, disadvantageousness, inconvenience, inadvisability.

v. **be inexpedient** etc. *adj.;* come amiss etc. (*disagree*) 24; embarrass etc. (*hinder*) 706; put to inconvenience.

adj. **inexpedient**, undesirable; unadvisable [*rare*], inadvisable, unsuitable, troublesome, objectionable; inapt, ineligible, inadmissible, inconvenient; incommodious, discommodious; disadvantageous; inappropriate, unfit etc. (*inconsonant*) 24.

ill-contrived, ill-advised; unsatisfactory; unprofitable etc., inept etc. (*useless*) 645; inopportune etc. (*unseasonable*) 135; out of-, in the wrong- place; improper, unseemly.

clumsy, awkward; cumbrous, cumbersome; lumbering, unwieldy, hulky; unmanageable etc. (*impracticable*) 704; impedient etc. (*in the way*) 706.

unnecessary etc. (*redundant*) 641.

648. Goodness

[capability of producing good, good qualities]

n. **goodness** etc. *adj.;* excellence, merit; virtue etc. 944; value, worth, price.

superexcellence, supereminence, quintessence; superiority etc. 33; perfection etc. 650; *coup de maître* [*F.*]; masterpiece, *chef d'oeuvre* [*F.*], prime, flower, cream, *élite* [*F.*], pick, nonesuch [*now rare*], A1 *or* A number 1 [*colloq.*], *nonpareil* [*F.*], *crème de la crème* [*F.*], flower of the flock, cock of the walk, salt of the earth; champion; prodigy, wonder, best ever [*colloq.*].

gem, –of the first water; *bijou* [*F.*], precious stone, jewel, pearl, diamond, ruby, brilliant, treasure; tidbit, good thing; *rara avis* [*L.*], one in a thousand.

beneficence etc. 906.

good man etc. 948.

v. **be beneficial** etc. *adj.;* produce *or* do good etc. 618; profit etc. (*be of use*) 644; benefit; confer a benefit etc. 618.

222

produce a good effect; be the making of, do a world of good, make a man of; do a good turn, confer an obligation; improve etc. 658.

do no harm, break no bones.

be good etc. *adj.*; be pure gold, be all wool; be the real -thing, −article; look good to [*colloq.*]; excel, transcend etc. (*be superior*) 33; bear away the bell.

stand the -proof, −test; pass muster, pass an examination.

vie, challenge comparison, emulate, rival.

adj. **beneficial**, valuable, of value; serviceable etc. (*useful*) 644; advantageous, profitable, edifying; salutary etc. (*healthful*) 656.

harmless, hurtless; unobnoxious; innocuous, innocent, inoffensive.

favorable; propitious etc. (*hopegiving*) 858; fair.

good, good as gold; excellent; better; superior etc. 33; above par; nice, fine; genuine etc. (*true*) 494.

choice, best, select, picked, elect, *recherché* [*F.*], rare, priceless; unparagoned [*rare*], matchless, peerless, unequaled *or* unequalled, unparalleled etc. (*supreme*) 33; superlatively etc. (33)- good; bully [*slang*], crackerjack [*slang*], gilt-edge *or* gilt-edged [*colloq.*]; superfine, superexcellent; of the first water; first-rate, first-class; high-wrought, exquisite, very best, crack [*colloq.*], prime, tip-top [*colloq.*], capital, cardinal; standard etc. (*perfect*) 650; inimitable.

admirable, estimable; praiseworthy etc. (*approve*) 931; pleasing etc. 829; *couleur de rose* [*F.*], precious, of great price; costly etc. (*dear*) 814; worth -its weight in gold, −a king's ransom; priceless, invaluable, inestimable, precious as the apple of the eye.

satisfactory, up to the mark, unexceptionable, unobjectionable; tidy [*colloq.*].

in -good, −fair- condition; unspoiled, fresh; sound etc. (*perfect*) 650.

adv. **beneficially** etc. *adj.*; well etc. 618; for one's benefit.

649. Badness

[capability of producing evil, bad qualities]

n. **hurtfulness** etc. *adj.*; virulence.

bane etc. 663; plague spot etc. (*insalubrity*) 657; evil star, ill wind; hoodoo [*colloq.*], jinx [*slang*], *jadu* [*Hind.*], Jonah; snake in the grass, skeleton in the closet; *amari aliquid* [*L.*]; thorn in the -side, −flesh.

malignity, damnability, damnification, damnifying; malevolence etc. 907; tender mercies [*irony*].

ill-treatment, annoyance, molestation, abuse, oppression, persecution, outrage; misusage etc. 679; *damnum* [*L.*], scathe; injury etc. (*damage*) 659; Mickey, Mickey Finn [*both slang*], knockout drops.

badness etc. *adj.*; peccancy, abomination; painfulness etc. 830; pestilence etc. (*disease*) 655; guilt etc. 947; depravity etc. 945.

bad man etc. 949; evildoer etc. 913.

v. **be hurtful** etc. *adj.*; cause-, produce−, inflict−, work−, do- evil etc. 619; damnify, endamage, hurt, harm, scathe; injure etc. (*damage*) 659; pain etc. 830.

wrong, aggrieve, oppress, persecute; trample-, tread−, bear hard−, put-upon; overburden; weigh -down, −heavy on; victimize; run down, run hard; thwart; molest etc. 830.

maltreat, abuse; ill-use, illtreat; buffet, bruise, scratch, maul; smite etc. (*scourge*) 972; do violence, do a mischief; stab, pierce, outrage.

do mischief, do harm, make mischief, bring−, lead−, get- into trouble; hex, hoodoo [*colloq.*].

destroy etc. 162.

adj. **hurtful**, harmful, scathful [*obs. or dial.*], scatheful, baneful, baleful, injurious, deleterious, detrimental, noxious, pernicious, mischievous, full of mischief, mischief-making, malefic, malignant, nocuous, noisome; prejudicial; disserviceable, disadvantageous; wide-wasting.

unlucky, sinister; obnoxious; untoward, disastrous.

oppressive, burdensome, onerous; malign etc. (*malevolent*) 907.

corrupting etc. (*corrupt* etc. 659); virulent, venomous, envenomed, corrosive; poisonous etc. (*morbific*) 657; deadly etc. (*killing*) 361; destructive etc. (*destroying*) 162; inauspicious etc. 859.

bad, ill, arrant, as bad as bad can be, dreadful; horrid, horrible; dire; rank, peccant, foul, fulsome; rotten, rotten at the core.

unsatisfactory, indifferent; injured etc. deteriorated etc. 659; exceptionable, below par etc. (*imperfect*) 651; ill-contrived, ill-disposed, ill-conditioned.

deplorable, wretched, sad, grievous, lamentable, pitiful, pitiable, woeful etc. (*painful*) 830; mean etc. (*paltry*) 643.

evil, wrong; depraved etc. 945; shocking; reprehensible etc. (*disapproved*) 932.

hateful, −as a toad; abominable, vile, base, villainous, detestable, execrable, cursed, accursed, confounded; damned, damnable, damnatory, damnific [*rare*]; infernal; diabolic etc. (*malevolent*) 907.

inadvisable, unadvisable [*rare*] etc. (*inexpedient*) 647; unprofitable etc. (*useless*) 645; incompetent etc. (*unskillful*) 699; irremediable etc. (*hopeless*) 859.

adv. **badly** etc. *adj.;* wrong, ill; to one's cost; where the shoe pinches; with malignity etc. *n.*

650. Perfection

n. **perfection**; perfectness etc. *adj.;* indefectibility; impeccancy, impeccability.

paragon, pink, *beau ideal* [*F.*]; pink–, acme- of perfection; *ne plus ultra* [*L.*]; summit etc. 210.

[comparisons] *cygne noir* [*F.*]; Phoenix *or* Phenix; black tulip, *tulipe noir* [*F.*]; philosopher's stone; Koh-i-noor.

model, standard, pattern, mirror, Admirable Crichton; trump, brick, corker, caution, humdinger [*all slang*]; "the observed of all observers" [*Hamlet*], very prince of.

Bayard, *chevalier sans peur et sans reproche* [*F.*]; Roland, Sidney.

masterpiece, masterstroke, prize-winner, prize; superexcellence etc. (*goodness*) 648; transcendence etc. (*superiority*) 33.

v. **be perfect** etc. *adj.;* transcend etc. (*be supreme*) 33.

perfect, bring to perfection, ripen, mature; consummate, crown, put the finishing touch to (*or* upon); complete etc. 729; put in trim etc. (*prepare*) 673; maturate [*rare*].

adj. **perfect**, faultless; indefective [*rare*], indeficient [*rare*], indefectible; immaculate, spotless, impeccable; free from imperfection etc. 651; unblemished, uninjured etc. 659; sound, –as a roach; in perfect condition; scathless [*obs.* or *dial.*], scatheless, intact, harmless; seaworthy etc. (*safe*) 644; right as a trivet; *in se ipso totus teres atque rotundus* [Hor.]; consummate etc. (*complete*) 52; finished etc. 729; complete in itself; well-rounded.

best etc. (*good*) 648; model, standard; inimitable, unparagoned [*rare*], unparalleled etc. (*supreme*) 33; superhuman, divine; beyond all praise etc. (*approbation*) 931; *sans peur et sans reproche* [*F.*].

adv. **to perfection**; perfectly etc. *adj.;* *ad unguem* [*L.*]; clean, –as a whistle; with a finish; to the limit.

651. Imperfection

n. **imperfection**; imperfectness etc. *adj.;* deficiency; inadequacy etc. (*insufficiency*) 640; peccability, defection, peccancy etc. (*badness*) 649; immaturity etc. 674.

fault, defect, "little rift within the lute" [Tennyson], weak point; screw loose; flaw etc. (*break*) 70; gap etc. 198; twist etc. 243; taint, attainder; *mésalliance* [*F.*], bar sinister; hole in one's coat; blemish etc. 848; weakness etc. 160; shortcoming etc. 304; drawback; seamy side.

half blood, drop of black blood, touch of the tar-brush [*colloq.*].

mediocrity; no great -shakes, –catch [*both colloq.*]; not much to boast of; one-horse shay; one-horse town; peanut -politics, –policy.

v. **be imperfect** etc. *adj.;* rot before it ripens, bear within it the seeds of decay; have a defect etc. *n.;* lie under a disadvantage; spring a leak.

not pass muster, barely pass muster; fall short etc. 304.

adj. **imperfect**; not perfect etc. 650; deficient, defective; faulty, unsound, tainted, specked; mutilated; out of order; out of tune, cracked; leaky; sprung; warped etc. (*distort*) 243; lame; injured etc. (*deteriorated*) 659; peccant etc. (*bad*) 649; frail etc. (*weak*) 160; inadequate etc. (*insufficient*) 640; crude etc. (*unprepared*) 674; incomplete etc. 53; found wanting; below par; short-handed; below–, under- its full -strength, –complement.

indifferent, middling, ordinary, mediocre; average etc. 29; soso *or* so-so; *couci-couci* [*F.*], milk-and-water; tolerable, fair, passable; pretty -well, –good; rather–, moderately- good; good–, well- enough; decent; not bad, not amiss; unobjectionable, admissible, bearable, better than nothing.

secondary, inferior; second-rate, second best; one-horse; two-bit, two-by-four.

adv. **almost** etc.; to a limited extent, rather etc. 32; pretty, moderately; only, considering, all things considered, enough; might be worse.

652. Cleanness

n. **cleanness** etc. *adj.;* purity; cleaning etc. *v.;* purification, defecation etc. *v.;* purgation, lustration; abstersion [*rare*], detersion; aspersion, asperges [*R. C. Ch.*]; epuration [*rare*], mundation [*obs.*], ablution, lavation, colature [*obs.*]; disinfection etc. *v.;* drainage, sewerage.

bath, bathroom, swimming pool, natatorium, swimming bath, public bath, baths, bathhouse, hot bath, sauna etc. 386; lavatory; laundry, washhouse.

cleaner, washerwoman, laundress, dhobi [*India*], laundryman, washerman; scavenger, sweeper; mehtar (*fem.* mehtrani), bhangi [*all India*]; mud lark [*slang*]; sanitation worker, crossing–, street- sweeper, white wings; dustman; sweep.

brush; broom, besom, vacuum cleaner, carpet sweeper; mop, swab, hose; scraper; rake, shovel; sieve, riddle, screen, filter; blotter.

napkin, serviette, cloth, maukin [*obs.*], malkin [*obs.*], handkerchief, towel, sudary, sudarium, face cloth, wash cloth; doily *or* doyley, bib; carving cloth, tablecloth; duster, sponge.

mat, doormat, rug, drugget, cover.

[cleansing agents] wash, lotion, detergent, soap, purifier etc. *v.;* disinfectant; benzene, benzine, benzol, benzolin; bleaching powder, chloride of lime; lye, buck.

dentifrice, tooth paste, tooth powder; mouth wash.

cathartic, purgative, aperient, deobstruent, laxative.

v. **be** *or* **render clean** etc. *adj.*

clean, cleanse; mundify [*obs.*], rinse, wring, flush, full, wipe, mop, sponge, scour, swab, scrub.

wash, lave etc. (*water*) 337; launder, buck; absterge [*rare*], deterge; decrassify; clear, purify; depurate, spurate [*rare*], despumate, defecate; purge, expurgate, elutriate, lixiviate, edulcorate, clarify, refine, rack; percolate, separate, strain, filter, filtrate, drain.

sift, winnow, sieve, bolt, screen, riddle; pick, weed.

comb, rake, scrape, rasp; hackle, heckle, card.

sweep, brush, brush up, whisk, broom, vacuum [*colloq.*].

rout–, clear–, sweep etc.- out; make a clean sweep of, clean house, spruce up [*colloq.*].

disinfect, fumigate, ventilate, deodorize; whitewash.

adj. **clean**, cleanly; pure; immaculate; spotless, stainless, taintless, trig [*dial.*], without a stain, unstained, unspotted, unsoiled, unsullied, untainted, uninfected; sweet, –as a nut.

neat, spruce, tidy, trim, jimp *or* gimp [*Scot. & dial. Eng.*], clean as a new penny, like a cat in pattens; cleaned etc. *v.;* kempt [*archaic*].

abstergent, detergent, depurative, abstersive [*rare*], cathartic, cleansing, purifying.

adv. **neatly** etc. *adj.;* clean as a whistle.

653. Uncleanness

n. **uncleanness** etc. *adj.;* impurity; immundity [*rare*], immundicity [*rare*], mucidness, impurity etc. (of mind) 961.

defilement, contamination etc. *v.;* defoedation [*obs.*]; soilure, soiliness [*obs.*]; abomination; taint, tainture [*obs.*]; fetor etc. 401.

lousiness, pediculosis, pediculation, phthiriasis [*med.*].

decay; putrescence, putrefaction; corruption; mold *or* mould, must, mildew, dry rot, mucor [*rare*], caries [*med.*], rubigo [*obs.*].

slovenry; slovenliness etc. *adj.;* squalor.

dowdy, drab, slut, malkin *or* mawkin [*obs. or dial. Eng.*], slattern, sloven, slammerkin [*obs.*], slammock *or* slummock [*dial.*], drabble-tail, draggle-tail, mud lark [*slang*], dustman, sweep; beast, pig.

dirt, filth, soil, slop; dust, cobweb, flue; smoke, soot, smudge, smut, grime, raff [*dial.*], riffraff; sossle *or* sozzle [*dial.*].

dregs, sordes, grounds, lees; argol; sediment, settlement; heeltap; dross, drossiness; mother [*obs.*], precipitate, *scoriae* [*L.*], ashes, cinders, recrement, slag; scum, froth.

useless refuse, hogwash [*colloq.*], swill, garbage, ditch water, dishwater, bilge-water; rinsings, cheeseparings; sweepings etc. 645; outscourings, offscourings, offscum; *caput mortuum* [*L.*], residuum, sprue, dross, clinker, draff; scurf, scurfiness; exuviae; furfur, dandruff; tartar, fur.

spawn, offal, gurry; carrion; slough, peccant humor, pus, matter, suppuration.

dung, ordure, lienteria; feces *or* faeces, excrement, feculence; excreta etc. 299; sewage, sewerage [*rare in this sense*]; fertilizer, muck; coprolite; guano, manure, compost.

[receptacles] dunghill, colluvies [*med.*]; mixen, midden [*both archaic or dial. Eng.*], bog, laystall [*obs.*]; cesspool; sump [*Scot. & dial. Eng.*], sough [*dial. Eng.*], cloaca, Cloaca Maxima; sink, drain, sewer, common sewer; Cloacina; dust hole; glory hole [*colloq.*].

water-closet, w. c., toilet [*colloq.*], *cabinet d'aisance* [*F.*], latrine, backhouse, necessary, privy, jakes [*rare*], Mrs. Jones; head [*naval slang*].

sty, pigsty, lair, den, Augean stable, sink of corruption; slum, rookery.

mud, mire, quagmire, alluvium, silt, sludge, slime, slush, slosh [*dial.*], sposh.

vermin, louse, flea, nit, bug, chinch; lice etc. 366.

v. **be** *or* **become unclean** etc. *adj.;* rot, putrefy, fester, rankle, reek; stink etc. 401; mold *or* mould, molder *or* moulder; go bad etc. *adj.*

wallow in the mire; slobber, slabber.

render unclean etc. *adj.;* dirt, dirty; soil, smoke, tarnish, slaver, spot, smear; daub, blot, blur, smudge, smutch, smirch; begrease; drabble, dabble, daggle, spatter, slubber [*dial.*]; besmear etc., bemire, beslime, begrime, befoul; splash, stain, distain [*archaic*], maculate, sully, pollute, defile, debase, contaminate, taint, leaven; corrupt etc. (*injure*) 659; cover with dust etc. *n.;* drabble in the mud; roil.

adj. **unclean**, dirty, filthy, grimy; soiled etc. *v.;* not to be handled -without gloves, −with kid gloves; dusty, snuffy, smutty, sooty, smoky; thick, turbid, dreggy; slimy; mussy.

lousy, pedicular, pediculous.

uncleanly, slovenly, slatternly, untidy, sluttish, dowdy, draggle-tailed, drabble-tailed; uncombed, unkempt, unscoured, unswept, unwiped, unwashed, unstrained, unpurified; squalid; lutose, slammocky *or* slummocky [*dial.*], sossly *or* sozzly [*dial.*], sloppy [*colloq.*].

offensive, nasty, coarse, foul, impure, abominable, beastly, reeky, reechy [*dial. Eng.*]; fetid etc. 401.

moldy *or* mouldy, musty, fusty, mildewed, rusty, moth-eaten, mucid, rancid, bad, gone bad, lentiginous *or* lentiginose, touched, reasty [*dial. Eng.*], rotten, corrupt, tainted, high, flyblown, maggoty; putrid, putrefactive, putrescent, putrefied; saprogenic *or* saprogenous; purulent, carious, peccant; fecal, feculent; stercoraceous, excrementitious; scurfy, impetiginous; gory, bloody; rotting etc. *v.;* rotten as -a pear, −cheese.

crapulous etc. (*intemperate*) 954; beastlike; gross etc. (*impure in mind*) 961; fimetarious, fimicolous.

int. pah! faugh! ugh!

654. Health

n. **health**, sanity; soundness etc. *adj.;* vigor; good−, perfect−, excellent−, rude−, robust-health; bloom, *mens sana in corpore sano* [*L.*]; Hygeia; incorruption, incorruptibility; valetude [*obs.*]; good state−, clean bill- of health; eupepsia *or* eupepsy, euphoria *or* euphory; convalescence, upgrade; strength, poise.

v. **be in health** etc. *adj.;* be bursting with -vigor, −pep [*slang*]; never feel better; bloom, flourish. keep body and soul together, keep on one's legs; enjoy -good, −a good state of- health; have a clean bill of health.

return to health; recover etc. 660; get better etc. (*improve*) 658; take a -new, −fresh- lease of life; convalesce, be convalescent; add years to one's life; recruit; restore to health; cure etc. (*restore*) 660.

adj. **healthy**, healthful; in health etc. *n.;* well, sound, whole, strong, blooming, hearty, hale, fresh, green, florid, flush, hardy, stanch *or* staunch, brave, robust, vigorous, weatherproof.

on one's legs; sound as a -roach, −bell; fresh as -a daisy, −a rose, −April; walking on air; hearty as a buck; in -fine, −high- feather; in good case, in full bloom; pretty bobbish [*Eng. dial. or slang*]; bursting with -health, −vigor; in fine fettle; chipper [*colloq.*]; tolerably well, as well as can be expected.

unscathed, uninjured, unmaimed, unmarred, untainted; sound of wind and limb, without a scratch, safe and sound.

sanitary etc. (*health-giving*) 656; sanatory etc. (*remedial*) 662.

655. Disease

n. **disease**; illness, sickness etc. *adj.;* ailing etc. *v.;* "the thousand natural shocks That flesh is heir to" [*Hamlet*]; "all ills that men endure" [Cowley]; morbidity, morbosity [*obs.*]; infirmity, ailment, indisposition; complaint, disorder, malady, distemperature [*archaic*]; valetudinarianism; loss of health, delicacy, delicate health, invalidity, invalidism, invalescence [*rare*]; malnutrition, want of nourishment, cachexia *or* cachexy; prostration, decline, collapse; decay etc. 659.

visitation, attack, seizure, stroke, fit, epilepsy, apoplexy, bloodstroke; palsy, paralysis, motor paralysis, sensory paralysis, hemiplegia, paraplegia *or* paraplegy; *paralysis agitans* [*L.*], shaking palsy, Parkinson's disease; shock; shellshock [*World War I*].

taint, virus, pollution, infection, contagion; septicaemia *or* septicemia, blood poisoning, pyaemia *or* pyemia, septicity; epidemic; sporadic, endemic; plague, pestilence.

fever, calenture; inflammation; ague; intermittent−, remittent−, congestive−, pernicious-fever; malaria, malarial fever; dengue *or* dandy fever, breakbone fever; yellow fever, yellow jack; typhoid *or* typhoid fever, enteric fever; typhus; eruptive fever; scarlet fever, scarlatina; smallpox, variola; varioloid; vaccinia, cow pox; varicella, chicken pox; rubeola, measles.

eruption, rash, brash, breaking out; canker rash; dartre, exanthema *or* exanthem; scabies, itch, psora; pox; eczema, tetter, psoriasis; lichen, papular rash; lichen tropicus, prickly heat; impetigo; erythema; erysipelas, St. Anthony's fire; urticaria, hives, nettlerash; herpes; herpes zoster, shingles; herpes simplex *and* circinatus, ringworm; miliaria, pemphigus, rupia.

sore, canker, ulcer, fester, boil, gumboil; pimple etc. (*swelling*) 250; carbuncle; gathering; abscess, impostume *or* imposthume [*obsoles.*], aposteme; Rigg's disease, pyorrhea *or* pyorrhoea; chancre; peccant humor; proud flesh; corruption; enanthem *or* enanthema, gangrene; mortification, sphacelus, sphacelation; slough, caries, necrosis; cancer, carcinoma; tumor, leprosy.

heart disease, carditis, pericarditis, endocarditis, valvular lesion; hypertrophy–, dilatation–, atrophy–, fatty degeneration- of the heart; angina pectoris.

wasting disease, marasmus, emaciation, atrophy; consumption, white plague, tuberculosis, T.B. [*med. cant*], phthisis; pulmonary–, galloping- consumption; pulmonary phthisis, phthisipneumonia, pneumonia; chlorosis, green sickness; anaemia *or* anemia; leucocythaenia *or* leucocythenia.

throat disease, laryngitis, tonsillitis, quinsy, cynanche; bronchitis, diphtheria, whooping cough, pertussis; thrush, canker.

cold, cough; rheum; catarrh, hay fever; influenza, grippe *or* grip; rose cold.

indigestion, dyspepsia, poor digestion, pyrosis, water qualm; cardialgia, heartburn; seasickness, *mal de mer* [*F.*]; nausea; giddiness, vertigo; constipation, autointoxication.

eye disease, trachoma, conjunctivitis, pink eye; cataract, caligo, pin-and-web, *gutta serena* [*L.*].

veneral disease, pox, syphilis; gonorrhea *or* gonorrhoea, blennorrhea *or* blennorrhoea, blennorrhagia.

[various diseases] headache etc. (*physical pain*) 378; goiter *or* goitre, bronchocele, struma, tracheocele; lockjaw, tetanus, trismus; diarrhea *or* diarrhoea, dysentery, bloody flux, flux, issue, hemorrhage; hemorrhoids, piles; cholera, cholera morbus, Asiatic cholera, cholera infantum, summer complaint; colic; jaundice, icterus; apnea; asthma; king's evil, scrofula; rickets, rachitis; appendicitis; gall-stones, biliary calculus, stone; hernia, rupture; varicosis, varicose veins; arteriosclerosis, hardening of the arteries; neuritis; nervous prostration; St. Vitus's dance, chorea; neurasthenia; sciatica; rheumatism, arthritis, lumbago; dropsy, edema; elephantiasis; beriberi; locomotor ataxia; paresis, softening of the brain; bubonic plague; black death; leprosy, elephantiasis; sleeping sickness.

fatal etc. (*hopeless*) 859 -disease etc.; dangerous illness, churchyard cough; general breaking up, break-up of the system.

[disease of mind] idiocy etc. 499; insanity etc. 503.

martyr to disease; cripple; "the halt, the lame, and the blind"; valetudinary, valetudinarian; invalid, patient, case.

sick-room, sick-chamber; hospital etc. 662.

[science of disease] pathology, pathogeny, etiology, nosology, nosography, nosogeny, therapeutics; diagnostics, symptomatology, semeiology, semeiography, prognosis, diagnosis; clinic, polyclinic.

[veterinary] anthrax, splenic fever, woolsorter's disease, charbon, milzbrand, malignant pustule, quarter evil, quarter ill, Texas fever, blackwater, murrain, bighead; blackleg, black quarter; cattle plague, glanders, milk sickness; rinderpest, foot-and-mouth disease, hog cholera; epizoötic; heaves, rot, sheep rot; scabies, mange, distemper.

v. **be** *or* **feel ill** etc. *adj.;* ail, suffer, labor under, be affected with, complain of; droop, flag, languish, halt; sicken, peak, pine, dwindle; gasp; drop down in one's tracks; waste away, fail, lose strength, lose one's grip.

keep one's bed; lay by, lay up; be laid by the heels; lie helpless, –on one's back.

fall a victim to–, be stricken by–, take–, catch- -a disease etc. *n.,* - an infection; break out.

malinger, feign sickness etc. (*falsehood*) 544.

adj. **ailing** etc. *v.;* ill, ill of; taken ill, seized with; indisposed, unwell, sick, squeamish, poorly, seedy [*colloq.*]; affected–, afflicted- with illness; laid up, confined, bedridden, invalided, in hospital, on the sick list; out of health, out of sorts [*colloq.*], under the weather; valetudinary.

unsound, unhealthy; morbose [*obs.*], healthless, infirm, chlorotic, unbraced, cranky [*dial. Eng.*], sickly, weakly, weakened etc. (*weak*) 160; drooping, flagging; lame, halt, crippled, halting; *hors de combat* [*F.*] etc. (*useless*) 645.

touched in the wind, broken-winded, spavined, gasping.

diseased, morbid, tainted, vitiated, peccant, contaminated, poisoned, septic, septical, tabetic, tabid, mangy, leprous, cankered; rotten, –to, –at- the core; withered; palsied, paralytic; dyspeptic; luetic, pneumonic, pulmonic, phthisic *or* phthisical, consumptive, tubercular, tuberculous, rachitic; syntectic *or* syntectical, varicose.

decrepit; decayed etc. (*deteriorated*) 659; incurable etc. (*hopeless*) 859; in declining health; in a bad way, in danger, prostrate; moribund etc. (*death*) 360.

epidemic, epizoötic [*of animals*]; zymotic, contagious; morbific etc. 657.

227

656. Salubrity

n. **salubrity,** salubriousness, wholesomeness, healthfulness; healthiness etc. *adj.;* Hygeia, Aesculapius.

fine -air, −climate; eudiometer.

[preservation of health] hygiene; valetudinarianism; pure air, exercise, nourishment, tonic; immunity; sanitarium, sanatorium; valetudinarian, sanitarian.

v. **be salubrious** etc. *adj.;* make for health, conduce to health; be good for, agree with; assimilate etc. 23.

adj. **salubrious,** salutary, salutiferous [*rare*]; wholesome; healthy, healthful; sanitary, prophylactic; benign, bracing, tonic, invigorating, good for, nutritious; hygeian, hygienic; Hygeian.

sanative etc. (*remedial*) 662; restorative etc. (*reinstate*) 660; useful etc. 644.

innoxious, innocuous, innocent; harmless, uninjurious, uninfectious; immune.

657. Insalubrity

n. **insalubrity,** insalubriousness; unhealthiness etc. *adj.;* plague spot; malaria etc. (*poison*) 663; death in the pot, contagion; poisonousness, toxicity.

v. **be insalubrious** etc. *adj.;* disagree with; shorten one's days.

adj. **insalubrious;** unhealthy, unwholesome; noxious, noisome; morbific *or* morbifical, morbiferous; mephitic, septic, azotic, deleterious; pestilent, pestiferous, pestilential; virulent, venomous; envenomed, poisonous, toxic, toxiferous, narcotic; deadly etc. (*killing*) 361.

innutritious, unnutritious [*rare*], undigestible [*rare*], indigestible, ungenial; uncongenial etc. (*disagreeing*) 24.

contagious, infectious, catching, taking, communicable, inoculable, epidemic, zymotic, sporadic, endemic, pandemic; epizoötic [*of animals*].

658. Improvement

n. **improvement,** amelioration, melioration, betterment; mend, amendment, emendation; mending etc. *v.;* advancement; advance etc. (*progress*) 282; ascent etc. 305; promotion, preferment; elevation etc. 307; increase etc. 35.

cultivation, culture, march of intellect, menticulture; race-culture, acculturation, civilization; culture zone; eugenics.

reform, reformation; revision, radical reform; second thoughts, correction, refinement, elaboration; purification etc. 652; repair etc. (*restoration*) 660; recovery etc. 660.

revise, revised edition, new edition, new issue.

reformer, reformist, progressive, radical.

v. **improve;** be−, become−, get- better; mend, amend.

advance etc. (*progress*) 282; ascend etc. 305; increase etc. 35; fructify, ripen, mature; pick up, come about, rally, take a favorable turn; turn over a new leaf, turn the corner; raise one's head, have sown one's wild oats; recover etc. 660.

profit by; be better etc. *adj.,* be improved by; turn to -right, −good, −best- account; reap the benefit of; make good use of, make capital out of; place to good account.

render better, improve, mend, amend, better; ameliorate, meliorate, relieve; correct; repair etc. (*restore*) 660; doctor etc. (*remedy*) 662; purify etc. 652; decrassify.

improve−, refine- upon; rectify; enrich, mellow, elaborate, fatten.

refresh, revive; put−, infuse- new blood into; invigorate etc. (*strengthen*) 159; reinvigorate, recruit, renew, make over, revivify, freshen.

promote, cultivate, advance, forward, enhance; bring forward, bring on; foster etc. 707.

touch up, rub up, brush up, furbish up, bolster up, vamp up, brighten up, warm up; polish, cook, make the most of, set off to advantage; prune; put in order etc. (*arrange*) 60.

revise, edit, redact, digest, review, make corrections, make improvements etc. *n.*

reform, remodel, reorganize; build -afresh, −anew; reclaim, civilize; lift, uplift, inspire; new-model.

view in a new light, think better of, appeal from Philip drunk to Philip sober.

palliate, mitigate; lessen etc. (36) an evil.

adj. **better,** -off, -for; all the better for; better advised; improving etc. *v.;* progressive, improved etc. *v.*

reformatory, emendatory; reparatory etc. (*restorative*) 660; remedial etc. 662.

corrigible, improvable, curable; accultural.

adv. **on consideration,** on reconsideration, on second thoughts, on better advice; on the mend, on the upgrade; *ad melius inquirendum* [*L.*].

659. Deterioration

n. **deterioration,** debasement; wane, ebb; recession etc. 287; retrogradation etc. 283; decrease etc. 36.

degeneracy, degeneration, degenerateness; degradation; depravation, depravement [*rare*], depravedness; devolution; depravity etc. 945; demoralization, retrogression; masochism.

impairment, inquination [*obs.*], injury, damage, loss, detriment, delaceration [*obs.*], outrage, havoc, inroad, ravage, scathe, scath [*dial.*], perversion, prostitution, vitiation, discoloration, pollution, defoedation, poisoning, venenation [*rare*], leaven, contamination, canker, corruption, adulteration, alloy.

decline, declension, declination; decadence *or* decadency; falling off etc. *v.;* caducity [*rare*], senility, decrepitude.

decay, dilapidation, ravages of time, wear and tear; erosion, corrosion, moldiness *or* mouldiness; rottenness; moth and rust, dry rot, blight, marcescence, marasmus, atrophy, collapse; disorganization; *délabrement* [*F.*] etc. (*destruction*) 162; aphid, aphis (*pl.* aphides), plant louse; vine fretter, vine grub; gypsy (*or* gipsy) moth; buffalo carpet beetle etc. (*injurious insects*) 913.

wreck, mere wreck, honeycomb, *magni nominis umbra* [*L.*], jade, rackabones, skate; tacky *or* tackey, plug [*slang*].

v. **deteriorate**; be-, become- -worse, -deteriorated etc. *adj.;* have seen better days, degenerate, fall off; wane etc. (*decrease*) 36; ebb; retrograde etc. 283; decline, droop; go down etc. (*sink*) 306; go downhill, go on from bad to worse, go farther and fare worse; jump out of the frying pan into the fire; avoid Scylla and fall into Charybdis.

run to -seed, -waste; swale [*obs.*], sweal [*obs.*]; lapse, be the worse for; sphacelate; break, break down; spring a leak, crack, start; shrivel etc. (*contract*) 195; fade, go off, wither, molder *or* moulder, rot, rankle, decay, go bad; go to-, fall into- decay; fall "into the sere, the yellow leaf" [*Macbeth*]; rust, crumble, shake; totter, -to its fall; perish etc. 162; die etc. 360.

[render less good] deteriorate; weaken etc. 160; put back; taint, infect, contaminate, poison, empoison, envenom, canker, corrupt, exulcerate [*obs.*], pollute, vitiate, inquinate [*obs.*], debase, embase [*obs.*]; denaturalize, leaven; deflower, debauch, defile, deprave, degrade; ulcerate; stain etc. (*dirt*) 653; discolor; alloy, adulterate, sophisticate, tamper with, prejudice.

pervert, prostitute, demoralize, brutalize; render vicious etc. 945.

embitter, acerbate, exacerbate, aggravate.

injure, impair, labefy [*rare*], damage, harm, hurt, shend, scath [*dial.*], scathe, spoil, mar, despoil, dilapidate, waste; overrun; ravage; pillage etc. 791.

wound, stab, pierce, maim, lame, surbate [*obs.*], cripple, hock *or* hough, hamstring, hit between wind and water, scotch, mangle, mutilate, disfigure, blemish, deface, warp.

blight, rot; corrode, erode; wear away, wear out; gnaw, — at the root of; sap, mine, undermine, shake, sap the foundations of, break up; disorganize, dismantle, dismast; destroy etc. 162.

damnify etc. (*aggrieve*) 649; do one's worst; knock down; deal a blow to; play -havoc, — sad havoc, -the mischief [*colloq.*], -the deuce [*colloq.*], — the very devil [*colloq.*]- -with, — among; decimate.

adj. **deteriorated** etc. *v.;* altered, — for the worse; unimproved etc. (improve etc. 658); injured etc. *v.;* sprung; withering, spoiling etc. *v.;* on the -wane, -decline; tabid; degenerate; worse; the —, all the- worse for; out of -repair, — tune; imperfect etc. 651; the worse for wear; battered; weathered, weather-beaten; stale, *passé* [*F.*], shaken, dilapidated, frayed, faded, wilted, shabby, secondhand, threadbare; worn, -to- -a thread, — a shadow, — the stump, — rags; reduced, — to a skeleton; far-gone; tacky.

decayed etc. *v.;* moth-eaten, worm-eaten; mildewed, rusty, moldy *or* mouldy, spotted, seedy, time-worn, moss-grown; discolored; effete, wasted, crumbling, moldering *or* mouldering, rotten, cankered, blighted, marcescent, tainted; depraved etc. (*vicious*) 945; decrepit; broken-down; done, — for, — up [*all colloq.*]; worn-out, used up [*colloq.*]; fit for the -dust hole, — waste-paper basket; past work etc. (*useless*) 645.

at a low ebb, in a bad way, on one's last legs; undermined, deciduous; nodding to its fall etc. (*destruction*) 162; tottering etc. (*dangerous*) 665; past cure etc. (*hopeless*) 859; washed out, run down; fatigued etc. 688; unprogressive, improgressive [*rare*], backward, stagnant, behind the times; retrograde etc. (*retrogressive*) 283; deleterious etc. 649.

adv. **on the down grade**, on the downward track; beyond hope.

660. Restoration

n. **restoration**, restoral [*rare*], restorance [*obs.*]; reinstatement, replacement, rehabilitation, reëstablishment, reconstitution, reconstruction; reproduction etc. 163; renovation, renewal; revival, revivement [*rare*], revivescence *or* revivescence; refreshment etc. 689; resuscitation, reanimation, revivification, reviction [*obs.*]; reorganization.

reaction; redemption etc. (*deliverance*) 672; restitution etc. 790; relief etc. 834.

recurrence etc. (*repetition*) 104; *réchauffé* [*F.*], *rifacimento* [*It.*].

renaissance, renascence, rebirth, second youth, rejuvenescence, rejuvenation, new birth; regeneration, regeneracy, regenerateness, regenesis, palingenesis, reconversion; resurgence, resurrection.

redress, retrieval, reclamation, recovery; convalescence; resumption, *résumption* [*F.*]; sanativeness.

cure, recure [*obs.*], sanation [*obs.*]; healing etc. *v.;* redintegration; rectification; instauration; cicatrization; disinfection; delousing, delousement.

repair, repairing, reparation, mending; recruiting etc. *v.;* tinkering.

mender, doctor, physician, surgeon; priest, clergyman, pastor; carpenter, joiner, plumber, tinker, cobbler; reviver, revivor [*rare*], renewer, *vis medicatrix* [*L.*] etc. (remedy) 662.

curableness, curability, reparability, restorableness, retrievability, recoverability, recoverableness.

v. **return to the original state**; recover, rally, revive; come to, come round, come to oneself; pull through, weather the storm, be oneself again; get -well, — round, — the better of, — over —, up, — about; rise from -one's ashes, — the grave; resurge, resurrect; survive etc. (*outlive*) 110; resume, reappear; come to, — life again; live again, rise again.

heal, heal over, skin over, cicatrize; right itself, heal itself.

restore, put back, place *in statu quo* [*L.*]; reinstate, replace, reseat, rehabilitate, reëstablish, reëstate, reinstall.

reconstruct, rebuild, reorganize, reconstitute; convert, reconvert; recondition, renew, renovate; regenerate; rejuvenate.

redeem, reclaim, recover, retrieve; rescue etc. (*deliver*) 672.

cure, heal, remedy, doctor, physic, medicate; redress, recure; break of; bring round, set on one's legs.

resuscitate, revive, reanimate, revivify, recall to life; reproduce etc. 163; warm up; reinvigorate, refresh etc. 689.

redintegrate, make whole; recoup etc. 790; make good, make all square; rectify; put —, set--right, — to rights, — straight; set up, correct; put in order etc. (*arrange*) 60; refit, recruit; fill up, — the ranks; reinforce.

repair, mend; put in repair, put in thorough repair; retouch, botch, vamp, tinker, cobble; do up, patch up, plaster up, vamp up; darn, finedraw, heelpiece; stop a gap, stanch *or* staunch, calk *or* caulk, careen, splice, bind up wounds.

adj. **restored** etc. *v.;* redivivus, redivivous [*rare*], reviviscible, convalescent; in a fair way; none the worse; rejuvenated; renascent.

restoring etc. *v.;* restorative, recuperative; sanative, sanatory; reparative, reparatory; curative, remedial.

restorable, recoverable, remediable, retrievable, curable, sanable [*rare*].

adv. *in statu quo* [*L.*]; as you were.

661. Relapse

n. **relapse**, lapse; falling back etc. *v.;* retrogradation etc. (*retrogression*) 283; deterioration etc. 659. [return to, or recurrence of, a bad state] backsliding, recidivation [*obs.*]; recidivism, recidivity; recrudescence.

v. **relapse**, lapse; fall —, slide —, slip —, sinkback; have a relapse, be overcome, be overtaken, yield again to, fall again into; return; retrograde etc. 283; recidivate [*rare*]; fall off etc. 659- again.

adj. **backsliding**, relapsing etc. *v.;* recidivous, recidivistic, recrudescent, retrograde.

662. Remedy

n. **remedy**, help, redress; anthelmintic, vermifuge, helminthagogue; antifebrile, febrifuge; antipoison, antidote, mithridate [*old pharm.*], theriaca *or* theriac, counterpoison; antispasmodic; lithagogue; bracer, pick-me-up [*colloq.*], stimulant, tonic; abirritant, prophylactic, antiseptic, germicide, bactericide, corrective, restorative; alterant, alterative; cathartic etc. 652; specific; emetic, carminative.

materia medica, pharmacy, pharmacology, pharmaceutics, acology, posology, dosology [*rare*]; pathology etc. 655; pharmacopoeia.

narcotic, nepenthe *or* nepenthes, opium, morphine, cocaine, hashish, methadone, bhang, ganja; dope, speed, grass, crystal, angel dust, acid, horse, coke [*all slang*]; sedative etc. 174.

cure; partial —, attempted —, radical —, perfect —, certain- cure; sovereign remedy, panacea, cure-all, catholicon.

physic, medicine, simples, drug, potion, draft *or* draught, dose, pill, bolus, electuary; lincture *or* linctus; medicament; pharmacon.

nostrum, recipe, receipt, prescription; elixir, *elixir vitae* [*L.*], balm, balsam, cordial, tisane, ptisan.

agueweed, boneset; arnica, benzoin, cream of tartar, bitartrate of potash, calomel, mercurous chloride; catnip, catmint; Epsom salts; fever-root *or* feverwort, feverweed, friar's balsam, Indian sage; ipecac *or* ipecacuanha; Peruvian bark, Jesuits' bark, cinchona, quinine *or* quinin, sassafras, yarrow.

salve, ointment, cerate, oil, lenitive, palliative, lotion, embrocation, liniment.

harquebusade *or* arquebusade, traumatic, vulnerary, pepastic, maturative, maturant, suppurative; eyewater, collyrium; cosmetic; depilatory.

poultice, cataplasm, vesicatory, plaster, *emplastrum* [*L.*], epithem, sinapism.

compress, pledget; bandage etc. (*support*) 215.

treatment, medical treatment, regimen, diet; dietary, dietetics; *vis medicatrix* [*L.*]; *vis naturae* [*L.*]; *médecine expectante* [*F.*]; bloodletting, bleeding, venesection, phlebotomy, cupping, sanguisuge, leeches; operation, the knife [*colloq.*], surgical operation; major operation; electrolysis, electrolyzation.

healing art, leechcraft [*archaic*], practice of medicine, therapeutics; allopathy, homeopathy, osteopathy, eclecticism, heteropathy; gynecology, gyniatrics, gynecological therapeutics; pediatrics; surgery, chirurgery [*archaic*]; orthopedics, orthopedia *or* orthopaedia, orthopraxy, orthopraxis, orthopedic surgery; sarcology, organotherapy; hydrotherapy, hydropathy, cold-water cure; faith cure, faith healing, mind cure, psychotherapy, psychotherapeutics; Christian Science, Eddyism; radiotherapy, heliotherapy, serotherapy, serum therapy; aerotherapy, pneumatotherapy; occupational *or* vocational therapy; dentistry, surgical dentistry; midwifery, obstetrics, tocology.

hospital, infirmary, clinic, *hôpital* [*F.*], general hospital, *hotel-Dieu* [*F.*]; special hospital (cancer, children's, dental, fever, maternity *or* lying-in, ophthalmic etc); pesthouse, lazarhouse, lazaretto, lazaret; lock hospital [*Eng.*]; *maison de santé* [*F.*]; *Hôtel des Invalides* [*F.*]; sanatarium, sanitarium, sanatorium, springs, baths, spa, pump room, well; hospice; asylum, home; Red Cross; ambulance.

dispensary, dispensatory, drug store, chemist's shop [*Brit.*].

doctor, physician, leech [*archaic*], medical man, disciple of Aesculapius; medical —, general-practitioner; medical attendant, specialist; surgeon, chirurgeon [*archaic*].

consultant, operator; resident, interne; anaesthetist *or* anesthetist; aurist, oculist, dentist, dental surgeon; osteopath, osteopathist, orthopedist; gynecologist, obstetrician; Christian Science

practitioner, faith healer; medical student, medic [*colloq.*]; *accoucheur* (*fem. accoucheuse*) [*F.*], midwife; nurse; registered —, graduate —, trained —, district —, practical —, monthly-, visiting —, nurse; sister, nursing sister; dresser, bonesetter, apothecary, druggist, chemist [*Brit.*], pharmacopolist, pharmaceutist, pharmacist, pharmaceutical chemist, pharmacologist; Aesculapius, Hippocrates, Galen; *masseur* (*fem. masseuse*) [*F.*], massagist, rubber.

[instruments] stethoscope, stethometer, stethograph, respirometer, spirometer, pneumometer, spirograph, pneumatograph, pneumatometer, pulmotor.

v. **apply a remedy** etc. *n.;* doctor [*colloq.*], dose, physic, nurse, minister to, attend, dress the wounds, plaster, poultice; strap, splint, bandage; prevent etc. 706; relieve etc. 834; palliate etc. 658; heal, cure, "kill or cure," work a cure, remedy, stay (disease), snatch from the jaws of death; restore etc. 660; drench with physic; consult, specialize, operate, anaesthetize *or* anesthetize; straighten, mold *or* mould; deliver; extract, fill, stop; transfuse, bleed, cup, let blood; electrolyze.

manicure; pedicure; shampoo; massage, rub.

adj. **remedial**; restorative etc. 660; corrective, palliative, healing; sanatory, sanative; prophylactic; salutiferous etc. (*salutary*) 656; medical, medicinal; therapeutic, hypnotic, neurotic, chirurgical [*archaic*], surgical, epulotic [*obs.*], paregoric, tonic, corroborant, roborant; analeptic, balsamic, anodyne, narcotic, sedative, lenitive, demulcent, emollient; detersive, detergent; abstersive, disinfectant; febrifugal, antifebrile; alternative; traumatic, vulnerary.

allopathic, homeopathic, eclectic, hydropathic, heteropathic; aperient, laxative, cathartic, purgative; septic, aseptic, antiseptic; antiluetic, antisyphilitic; anthelmintic, vermifugal; chalybeate, deobstruent; purifying, cleansing, depurative, depuratory; electrolytic *or* electrolytical.

dietetic, dietary, alimentary; nutritious, nutritive; digestive, digestible, peptic.

remediable, curable; antidotal, alexipharmic, alexiteric.

663. Bane

n. **bane**, curse, hereditary evil, thorn in the flesh; *bête noir* [*F.*], bugbear; evil etc. 619; hurtfulness etc. (*badness*) 649; painfulness etc. (*cause of pain*) 830; scourge etc. (*punishment*) 975; *damnosa hereditas* [*L.*]; white elephant.

rust, worm, helminth, moth, "moth and rust" [*Bible*], fungus, mildew; dry rot; canker, cankerworm; cancer; viper etc. (*evildoer*) 913; demon etc. 980.

sting, fang, thorn, tang [*dial. Eng.*], bramble, brier *or* briar, nettle.

poison, leaven, virus, venom; arsenic, Prussic acid, antimony, tartar emetic, strychnine, tannin *or* tannic acid, nicotine; miasma *or* miasm, effluvium, mephitis, stench; fetor etc. 401; malaria, azote [*rare*], nitrogen, coal gas, illuminating gas, natural gas, gas, poison gas, mustard gas, chlorine, tear gas, lachrymose gas; sewer gas; pest.

Albany hemp, arsenious -oxide, — acid; bichloride of mercury; carbonic acid, — gas; choke damp, black damp, fire damp, afterdamp, marsh gas, methane; cyanide of potassium, carbolic acid, corrosive sublimate; hydrocyanic acid, hydrocyanide; nux vomica, ratsbane.

toxicant, intoxicant, deliriant, delirifacient, hemlock, hellebore, nightshade, deadly nightshade, belladonna, henbane, aconite; banewort, opium, bhang [*India*], ganja [*India*], hemp, cannabin, cannabis, marijuana, hashish; Upas tree.

[science of poisons] toxicology.

adj. **baneful** etc. (*bad*) 649; poisonous etc. (*unwholesome*) 657.

664. Safety

n. **safety**, security, surety, impregnability; invulnerability, invulnerableness etc. *adj.*; danger -past, — over; storm blown over; coast clear; escape etc. 671; means of escape; blow-, safety-, snifting- valve; safeguard, palladium; sheet anchor; rock, tower.

guardianship, wardship, wardenship; tutelage, custody, safe-keeping; preservation etc. 670; guardship [*obs.*], protection, auspices.

protector, guardian; warden, warder; preserver, life saver, custodian, duenna, chaperon, third person.

safe-conduct, escort, convoy; guard, shield etc. (*defense*) 717; guardian angel; tutelary -god, — deity, — saint; *genius loci* [*L.*].

watchdog, bandog; Cerberus.

watchman, patrolman, policeman, police officer, officer, "the finest"; cop, copper, peeler, bobby [*all slang*], blue coat [*colloq.*], constable, roundsman, *gendarme* [*F.*], military police; detective, tec [*slang*], bull [*slang*], spotter [*slang*]; sheriff, deputy; sentinel, sentry, scout etc. (*warning*) 668.

armed force, garrison, life guard, State guard, militia, regular army, navy; volunteer; marine etc. 726; battleship, man-of-war etc. 726.

[means of safety] refuge etc., anchor etc. 666; precaution etc. (*preparation*) 673; guard, guard rail, hand rail; bulkhead, watertight compartment, safety appliance; bolt, hasp etc. (*pin*) 45; cyclone cellar, dugout, bombproof dug-out; quarantine, *cordon sanitaire* [*F.*].

[sense of security] confidence etc. 858.

judge, justice, judiciary, magistrate, beak [*slang, Eng.*], justice of the peace, J. P.; deemster [*Isle of Man*], hakim [*Oriental*]; chancellor etc. 967.

v. **be safe** etc. *adj.*; keep one's head above water, tide over, save one's bacon [*colloq.*]; ride out —, weather- the storm; light upon one's feet; bear a charmed life; escape etc. 671; possess nine lives.

protect, watch over; make *or* render safe etc. *adj.*; take care of etc. (*care*) 459; preserve etc. 670; cover, screen, shelter, shroud, flank, ward; take charge of; guard etc. (*defend*) 717; garrison; man the -garrison, — lifeboat; secure etc. (*restrain*) 751; intrench *or* entrench, mine, countermine; dig in; fence round etc. (*circumscribe*) 229; house, nestle, ensconce.

escort, support, accompany, convoy.

watch, mount guard, patrol, go on one's beat; do —, perform- sentry go; scout, spy.

take precautions etc. (*prepare for*) 673; "make assurance double sure" [*Macbeth*] etc. (*caution*) 864; take up a loose thread; reef, take in a reef, make all snug, have an anchor to windward, double reef topsails.

seek safety; take —, find- shelter etc. 666; run into port.

adj. **safe**, secure, sure; in safety, in security; in shelter, in harbor, in port; in the shadow of a rock; on *terra firma* [*L.*]; on the safe side; under the -shield of, — shade of, — wing of, — shadow of one's wing; under cover, under lock and key; out of -danger, — the meshes, — harm's way; on sure ground, at anchor, high and dry, above water; unthreatened, unmolested; protected etc. *v.*; *cavendo tutus* [*L.*]; panoplied etc. (*defended*) 717.

safe and sound etc. (*preserved*) 670; harmless; scatheless etc. (*perfect*) 650; unhazarded; not dangerous etc. 665.

snug, seaworthy, airworthy; watertight, weathertight, weatherproof, waterproof, fireproof; bombproof, shellproof.

defensible, tenable, proof against, invulnerable; unassailable, unattackable; "founded upon a rock" [*Bible*], impregnable, imperdible [*obs.*]; inexpugnable.

protecting etc. *v.;* guardian, tutelary; preservative etc. 670; trustworthy etc. 939.

adv. *ex abundante cautela* [*L.*]; with impunity.

int. **all's well**! all clear! all serene! [*slang*]; safety first! at rest! at ease!

665. Danger

n. **danger**, peril, insecurity, jeopardy, risk, hazard, venture, precariousness, slipperiness; instability etc. 149; defenselessness etc. *adj.*

exposure etc. (*liability*) 177; vulnerability; vulnerable point, heel of Achilles; forlorn hope etc. (*hopelessness*) 859.

[dangerous course] leap in the dark etc. (*rashness*) 863; road to ruin, *facilis descensus Averni* [Vergil], hairbreadth escape.

[approach of danger] cause for alarm; source of danger etc. 667; rock —, breakers- ahead; storm brewing; clouds -in the horizon, — gathering; warning etc. 668; alarm etc. 669.

[sense of danger] apprehension etc. 860.

v. **be in danger** etc. *adj.;* be exposed to —, run into —, incur —, encounter- danger etc. *n.;* run a risk; lay oneself open to etc. (*liability*) 177; lean on —, trust to- a broken reed; feel the ground sliding from under one, have to run for it; have the -chances, — odds- against one.

hang by a thread, totter; tremble on the verge; totter on the brink; sleep —, stand- on a volcano; sit on a barrel of gunpowder, live in a glass house.

endanger; bring —, place —, put- in -danger etc. *n.;* expose to danger, imperil; be proscribed; have one's name on the danger list; be overdue [*naut.*], be despaired of; be under sentence of death; jeopard, jeopardize; put one's head in the lion's mouth; beard the lion in his den; compromise; sail too near the wind etc. (*rash*) 863.

threaten etc. (909) danger; run one hard; lay a trap for etc. (*deceive*) 545.

adventure, risk, hazard, venture, stake, set at hazard; run the gauntlet etc. (*dare*) 861; engage in a forlorn hope.

adj. **in danger** etc. *n.;* endangered etc. *v.;* fraught with danger; dangerous, hazardous, perilous, periculous [*obs.*], parlous [*archaic*], unsafe, unprotected etc. (safe, protect etc. 664); insecure, untrustworthy, unreliable; built upon sand, on a sandy basis; unsound, speculative, wild-cat.

defenseless, guardless, fenceless [*archaic*], harborless, unsheltered, unshielded; vulnerable, expugnable, exposed; open to etc. (*liable*) 177.

aux abois [*F.*], at bay, with one's back to the wall; on the wrong side of the wall, on a lee shore, on the rocks.

precarious, critical, ticklish; slippery, slippy; hanging by a thread etc. *v.;* with a halter round one's neck; between -the hammer and the anvil, — Scylla and Charybdis, — two fires; on the edge, brink, *or* verge of -a precipice, — a volcano, — an abyss, —a pit; in the lion's den, on slippery ground, under fire; not out of the wood; in the condemned cell, under sentence of death; at stake, in question.

unwarned, unadmonished, unadvised; unprepared etc. 674; off one's guard etc. (*inexpectant*) 508.

tottering, unstable, unsteady; shaky, top-heavy, tumble-down, ramshackle, crumbling, waterlogged; helpless, guideless; in a bad way; reduced to —, at- the last extremity; trembling in the balance; nodding to its fall etc. (*destruction*) 162.

threatening etc. 909; ominous, ill-omened; alarming etc. (*fear*) 860; explosive; poisonous; venomous etc. (*insalubrious*) 657; rotten at the core.

adventurous etc. (*rash*) 863, (*bold*) 861.

int. **stop**! look! listen! look out! watch your step! look alive! look slippy! [*colloq.*]; below there! 'ware heads! beware! take care! *prenez garde!* [*F.*].

666. Refuge

[means of safety]

n. **refuge**, sanctuary, retreat, fastness, stronghold, fortress, castle, acropolis; keep, last resort; ward; prison etc. 752; asylum, ark, home, refuge for the destitute; almshouse; hiding place &. (*ambush*) 530; *sanctum sanctorum* [*L.*] etc. (*privacy*) 893.

anchorage, roadstead; breakwater, mole, port, haven; harbor, — of refuge; seaport; pier, jetty, embankment, quay, wharf, landing place; bund, bunder [*both Oriental*]; water wing [*arch.*].

covert, shelter, screen, lee wall, wing, shield, umbrella; dashboard, dasher, splashboard, mud guard *or* mudguard, wheel guard.

wall etc. (*inclosure*) 232; fort etc. (*defense*) 717.

anchor, sheet anchor, sacred anchor [*Gr. & Rom. antiq.*], kedge *or* kedge anchor; Trotman's —, Martin's —, mushroom- anchor; killick; grapnel, grappling iron; mainstay; support etc. 215; check etc. 706; ballast.

233

means of escape etc. (*escape*) 671; lifeboat, swimming belt, cork jacket, life preserver, buoy, breeches buoy; parachute, plank, stepping-stone.

safeguard etc. (*protection*) 664.

jury mast; vent-peg; safety -valve, — lamp; lightning -rod, — conductor.

v. **seek** *or* **find safety** etc. 664; seek —, take —, find- refuge etc. *n.;* claim sanctuary; head for the hills, take to the high ground; throw oneself into the arms of; break for the tall timber, break for the woods; fly to, reach in time; make port, make the harbor; anchor in the roadstead; crouch in the lee of; reach -shelter, — home, — running water.

bar the gate, let the portcullis down; lock —, bolt —, make fast- the door; raise the drawbridge.

667. Pitfall
[source of danger]

n. rocks, reefs, coral reef, sunken rocks, snags; sands, quicksands; syrt [*rare*], syrtis [*rare*]; Goodwin sands, sandy foundation; slippery ground; breakers, shoals, shallows, bank, shelf, flat, lee shore, ironbound coast, rockbound coast; rock —, breakers- ahead; derelict.

abyss, abysm, pit, void, chasm, crevasse.

whirlpool, eddy, vortex, gurge [*rare*], rapids, undertow; current, tide gate, tide race, maelstrom; eagre, bore, tidal wave.

pitfall; ambush etc. 530; trapdoor; trap etc. (*snare*) 545; mine, masked battery, spring-gun.

pest, ugly customer, dangerous person, *le chat qui dort* [*F.*]; crouching tiger; incendiary, firebug [*slang*]; firebrand; hornet's nest.

sword of Damocles; wolf at the door, snake in the grass, snake in one's bosom, death in the -cup, — pot; latency etc. 526.

668. Warning

n. **warning,** caution, caveat; notice etc. (*information*) 257; premonition, premonishment [*rare*]; prediction etc. 511; symptom, contraindication, lesson, dehortation; admonition, monition; alarm etc. 669.

handwriting on the wall, *tekel upharsin* [*Heb.*], yellow flag; red flag, red light, fog-signal, foghorn; siren; monitor, warning voice, Cassandra, signs of the times, Mother Cary's chickens, stormy petrel, bird of ill omen, gathering clouds, cloud no bigger than a man's hand, clouds in the horizon, death watch, death lights etc. (*premonitions*) 992a.

watchtower, beacon, signal post; lighthouse etc. (*indication of locality*) 550.

sentinel, sentry; watch, watchman; watch and ward, watchdog, bandog, house dog; patrol, vedette, picket, bivouac, scout, spy, spial [*obs.*]; advanced —, rear- guard; lookout, flagman.

cautiousness etc. 864.

v. **warn,** caution; forewarn, prewarn; admonish, forebode, premonish [*rare*]; give -notice, — warning; menace etc. (*threaten*) 909; put on one's guard; sound the alarm etc. 669; croak.

beware, ware [*dial.*]; take -warning, — heed at one's peril; look out, keep one's wits about one; keep watch and ward etc. (*care*) 459.

adj. **warning** etc. *v.;* premonitory, monitory, cautionary, admonitory, admonitive [*rare*]; ominous, threatening, lowering, minatory etc. (*threat*) 909; symptomatic, sematic [*biol.*].

warned etc. *v.;* on one's guard etc. (*careful*) 459, (*cautious*) 864.

adv. with alarm, on guard, after due warning, with one's eyes open; *in terrorem* [*L.*].

int. **beware**! ware! take care! mind —, take care- what you are about! mind! look out! watch your step!

669. Alarm
[indication of danger]

n. **alarm;** alarum, larum [*archaic*], alarm bell, tocsin, *alerte* [*F.*], beat of drum, sound of trumpet, note of alarm, hue and cry, fiery cross; signal of distress; flag at -half-mast, — half-staff; blue lights; war cry, war whoop; warning etc. 668; fog signal, fog bell, fog horn, siren; yellow flag; danger signal; red light, red flag; fire bell, fire alarm, still alarm; burglar alarm; watchman's rattle, police whistle.

false alarm, cry of wolf; bugbear, bugaboo.

v. **alarm;** give —, raise —, sound —, turn in —, beat- the *or* an -alarm etc. *n.;* warn etc. 668; ring the tocsin; *battre la générale* [*F.*]; cry wolf; half-mast.

adj. **alarmed;** warned; alarming etc. *v.*

int. *sauve qui peut!* [*F.*]; *qui vive?* [*F.*]; who goes there?

670. Preservation

n. **preservation;** safe-keeping; conservation etc. (*storage*) 636; maintenance, support, sustentation [*rare*], conservatism; economy; *vis conervatrix* [*L.*]; salvation etc. (*deliverance*) 672.

[means of preservation] prophylaxis; preserver, preservative; hygiastics, hygianics [*both rare*]; hygiene, hygienics; cover, drugget; *cordon sanitaire* [*F.*]; ensilage; dehydration, anhydration, evaporation; drying, putting up, canning, pickling; tinned goods [*chiefly Brit.*], canned goods; hyanization.

[superstitious remedies] charm etc. 993.

v. **preserve**, maintain, keep, sustain, support; keep -up, — alive; not willingly let die; nurse; cure etc. (*restore*) 660; save, rescue; be —, make-safe etc. 664; take care of etc. (*care*) 459; guard etc. (*defend*) 717; bank, bank up, shore up.

embalm, dry, cure, salt, pickle, season, kyanize, bottle, pot, tin [*chiefly Brit.*], can; dehydrate, anhydrate, evaporate; husband etc. (*store*) 636.

hold one's own; *stare super antiquas vias* [Bacon]; hold —, stand- one's ground etc. (*resist*) 719.

adj. **preserving** etc. *v.;* conservative; prophylactic; preservatory, preservative; hygienic.

preserved etc. *v.;* unimpaired, unbroken, uninjured, unhurt, unsinged, unmarred; safe, — and sound; intact, with a whole skin, without a scratch.

671. Escape

n. **escape**, scape [*obs.*]; avolation [*obs.*], elopement, flight; evasion etc. (*avoidance*) 623; retreat; narrow —, hairbreadth- escape; close call [*colloq.*], close shave, near shave [*colloq.*]; come off, impunity.

[means of escape] loophole etc. (*opening*) 260; path etc. 627; secret -chamber, passage; refuge etc. 666; vent, — peg; safety valve; drawbridge, fire escape.

reprieve etc. (*deliverance*) 672; liberation etc. 750.

refugee etc. (*fugitive*) 623.

v. **escape**, scape [*archaic*]; make —, effect —, make good- one's escape; break jail; get off, get clear off, get well out of; *échapper belle* [*F.*], save one's bacon [*colloq.*], make a get-away [*slang*]; weather the storm etc. (*safe*) 664; escape scot-free.

elude etc., make off etc. (*avoid*) 623; march off etc. (*go away*) 293; give one the slip; slip through the -hands, — fingers; slip the collar, wriggle out of; break loose, break from prison; break — slip —, get- away; find vent, find a hole to creep out of.

adj. escaping, escaped etc. *v.;* stolen away, fled; scot-free.

672. Deliverance

n. **deliverance**, extrication, rescue, ransom; reprieve, reprieval [*rare*], respite; armistice, truce; liberation etc. 750; emancipation; redemption, redeemableness, salvation; exemp-

tion; day of grace; riddance; jail (*Brit.* gaol) delivery.

v. **deliver**, extricate, rescue, save, free, liberate, set free, release, emancipate, redeem, ransom; bring -off, — through; *tirer d'affaire* [*F.*], get the wheel out of the rut, snatch from the jaws of death, come to the rescue; rid; retrieve etc. (*restore*) 660; be —, get- rid of.

adj. saved etc. *v.;* extricable, redeemable, rescuable.

int. to the rescue! a rescue! saved!

673. Preparation

n. **preparation**; providing etc. *v.;* provision, providence; anticipation etc. (*foresight*) 510; precaution, preconcertedness, preconcertion, predisposition; forecast etc. (*plan*) 626; rehearsal, note of preparation; dissemination, propaganda.

groundwork, first stone, cradle, stepping-stone; foundation, first rung, scaffold etc. (*support*) 215; scaffolding, *échafaudage* [*F.*].

elaboration; ripening etc. *v.;* maturation, evolution; perfection; concoction, digestion; gestation, hatching, incubation, sitting.

[putting in order] arrangement etc. 60; clearance; adjustment etc. 23; tuning; equipment, outfit, accouterment *or* accoutrement, armament, array.

[preparation of men] training etc. (*education*) 537; inurement etc. (*habit*) 613; novitiate.

[preparation of food] cooking, cookery, culinary art; brewing.

[preparation of the soil] tilling, plowing *or* ploughing, sowing, semination, cultivation.

[state of being prepared] preparedness, readiness, ripeness, mellowness; maturity; *un impromptu fait à loisir* [*F.*].

[preparer] preparer, trainer, coach; teacher etc. 540; pioneer; *avant-courrier* [*F.*], *avant-coureur* [*F.*]; *voortrekker* [*Dutch*]; prophet; forerunner etc. (*precursor*) 64; sappers and miners, pavior, navvy; packer, stevedore, longshoreman; warming pan.

v. **prepare**; get —, make- ready; predispose, address oneself to, get under weigh; make preparations, settle preliminaries, get up, sound the note of preparation.

set *or* put in order etc. (*arrange*) 60; forecast etc. (*plan*) 626; prepare —, plow —, dress- the ground; till —, cultivate- the soil; sow the seed, lay a train, dig a mine; lay —, fix- the -foundations, — basis, — groundwork; dig the foundations, erect the scaffolding; lay the first stone etc. (*begin*) 66.

roughhew; cut out work; block out, hammer out; lick into shape etc. (*form*) 240.

elaborate, mature, ripen, mellow, season, bring to maturity; nurture etc. (*aid*) 707; hatch, cook, brew; temper, anneal, smelt; barbecue; dry, cure, salt, smoke, infumate [*rare*]; maturate.

equip, arm, man; fit out, fit up; furnish, rig, dress, garnish, betrim, accouter *or* accoutre, array, fettle, fledge; dress up, furbish up, brush up, vamp up; refurbish; sharpen one's tools, trim one's -tackle, — foils; set, prime, attune; whet the -knife, — sword; wind up, screw up; adjust etc. (*fit*) 27; put in -trim, — train, — gear, — working order, — tune, — a groove for, — harness; pack, stow away, stow down, stow, load, store.

prepare for etc.; train etc. (*teach*) 537; inure etc. (*habituate*) 613; breed; rehearse; make provision for; take -steps, — measures, — precautions; provide, provide against; beat up for recruits; open the door to etc. (*facilitate*) 705.

set one's house in order, make all snug; clear decks, clear for action; close one's ranks; shuffle the cards.

prepare oneself; serve an apprenticeship etc. (*learn*) 539; lay oneself out for, get into harness, gird up one's loins, buckle on one's armor, *reculer pour mieux sauter* [*F.*], prime and load, shoulder arms, get up steam; put the horses to, harness, harness up [*colloq.*], hitch up [*colloq.*].

guard against, make sure against; forearm, make sure, prepare for the evil day, have a rod in pickle, have a bone to pick, provide against a rainy day, feather one's nest; lay in provisions etc. 637; make investments; keep on foot, keep going.

be prepared, be ready etc. *adj.*; hold oneself in readiness, watch and pray, keep one's powder dry, lie in wait for etc. (*expect*) 507; anticipate etc. (*foresee*) 510; *principiis obstare* [*L.*]; *venienti occurrere morbo* [*L.*].

adj. **preparing** etc. *v.*; in preparation, in course of preparation, in agitation, in embryo, in hand, in train; afoot, afloat; on foot, on the stocks, on the anvil; under consideration etc. (*plan*) 626; in consultation; brewing, hatching, forthcoming, brooding; in store for, in reserve.

precautionary, provident; preparative, preparatory; provisional, inchoate, under revision; under advisement; preliminary etc. (*precedent*) 62.

prepared etc. *v.*; in readiness; ready, — to one's hand, ready made; cut and dried; made to one's hand, ready cut, made to order, at one's elbow, ready for use, all ready; handy, on the table; in gear; running -smoothly, — sweetly; in working -order, — gear; snug; in practice.

in full feather, in best bib and tucker [*colloq.*]; in —, at- harness; in the saddle, in arms, in battle array, in war paint; up in arms; armed -at all points, — to the teeth, — *cap à pie* [*F.*]; sword in hand; booted and spurred.

in utrumque paratus [Virgil], *semper paratus* [*L.*]; on the alert etc. (*vigilant*) 459; at one's post.

ripe, mature, mellow; pucka *or* pukka *or* pakka [*Hind.*]; practiced etc. (*skilled*) 698; labored, elaborate, high-wrought, smelling of the lamp, worked up.

adv. **in preparation**, in anticipation of; afoot, astir, abroad; abroach; in fine fettle.

674. Nonpreparation

n. **nonpreparation**, unpreparedness; absence of —, want of- preparation; inculture [*obs.*], inconcoction [*obs.*], improvidence.

immaturity, crudity; rawness etc. *adj.*; abortion; disqualification.

[absence of art] nature, state of nature; virgin soil, unweeded garden; rough diamond; neglect etc. 460.

rough copy etc. (*plan*) 626; germ etc. 153; raw material etc. 635.

improvisation etc. (*impulse*) 612.

v. **be unprepared** etc. *adj.*; want —, lack- preparation; lie fallow; *s'embarquer sans biscuits* [*F.*]; live from hand to mouth.

[render unprepared] dismantle etc. (*render useless*) 645; undress etc. 226.

extemporize, improvise; cook up, fix up, vamp.

surprise, drop in on [*colloq.*], pay a surprise visit, drop in [*colloq.*], give a surprise party, take potluck with; take —, catch- unawares; take by surprise, call informally.

adj. **unprepared** etc. (prepare etc. 673); without preparation etc. 673; incomplete etc. 53; rudimental, embryonic, abortive; immature, unripe, kutcha *or* kachcha [*Hind.*]; callow, unfledged, unhatched, unnurtured, raw, green, crude; coarse; rough, roughcast, roughhewn; in the rough; rough-edged, unhewn, unformed, unfashioned, unwrought, unlabored, unblown; indigested, undigested; unmellowed, unseasoned, unleavened; uncooked, unboiled, unconcocted; unpolished, uncut, deckle-edged.

untaught, uneducated, untrained, untutored, undrilled, unexercised; unlicked; precocious, premature.

fallow, unsown, untilled, uncultivated.

natural, *in puris naturalibus* [*L.*], in a state of nature; undressed; in dishabille, *en déshabillé* [*F.*], in negligee.

unfitted, disqualified, unqualified, ill-digested; unbegun, unready, unarranged, unorganized, unfurnished, unprovided, unequipped, untrimmed; out of -gear, — kilter *or* kelter [*colloq.*], — order; dismantled etc. *v.*

shiftless, improvident, unthrifty, thriftless, thoughtless, unguarded; happy-go-lucky; slack, remiss; caught napping etc. (*inexpectant*) 508; unpremeditated etc. 612.

adv. **inadvertently**, by surprise, without premeditation; extempore etc. 612.

675. Essay

n. **essay**, trial, endeavor, attempt; aim, struggle, venture, adventure, speculation, *coup d'essai* [*F.*], *début* [*F.*]; probation etc. (*experiment*) 463.

v. **try**, essay; experiment etc. 463; endeavor, strive; tempt, attempt, make an attempt; venture, adventure, speculate, take one's chance, tempt fortune; try one's -fortune, — luck, — hand; use one's endeavor; feel —, grope —, pick- one's way.

try hard, push, make a bold push, use one's best endeavor; do one's best etc. (*exertion*) 686.

adj. **essaying** etc. *v.;* experimental etc. 463; tentative, empirical, problematic *or* problematical, probationary.

adv. **experimentally** etc. *adj.;* on trial, at a venture; by rule of thumb.

if one may be so bold.

676. Undertaking

n. **undertaking**; compact etc. 769; adventure, venture; engagement etc. (*promise*) 768; enterprise, emprise *or* emprize [*archaic*]; pilgrimage; matter in hand etc. (*business*) 625; move; first move etc. (*beginning*) 66.

v. **undertake**; engage —, embark- in; launch —, plunge- into; volunteer; apprentice oneself to; engage etc. (*promise*) 768; contract etc. 769; take upon -oneself, — one's shoulders; devote oneself to etc. (*determination*) 604.

take up, take on, take in hand; tackle [*colloq.*]; set —, go- about; set —, fall- -to, — to work; launch forth; break the ice; set up shop; put in -hand, — execution; set forward; break the neck of a -day's work, — business; be in for [*colloq.*]; put one's hand to; betake oneself to, turn one's hand to, go to do; be in the midst of; begin etc. 66; broach, institute etc. (*originate*) 153; put —, lay- one's -hand to the plow, — shoulder to the wheel.

have in hand etc. (*business*) 625; have many irons in the fire etc. (*activity*) 682.

adj. **undertaking** etc. *v.;* on the anvil etc. 625; available, receptive; full of pep [*colloq.*], peppy [*colloq.*], energetic; adventurous, venturesome.

int. here goes! shoot! [*colloq.*].

677. Use

n. **use**, employ; exercise, exercitation; application, appliance; adhibition, disposal; consumption; agency etc. (*physical*) 170; usufruct; usefulness etc. 644; benefit; recourse, resort, avail; pragmatism, pragmaticism.

[conversion to use] utilization, utility, service, wear.

[way of using] usage, employment, *modus operandi* [*L.*].

user, consumer, purchasing public, buying public; market, public demand, popular demand, demand.

v. **use**, make use of, employ, put to use; apply; put in -action, — operation, — practice; set in motion, set to work.

ply, work, wield, handle, manipulate; play, play off; exert, exercise, practice, avail oneself of, profit by; resort to, lay one's hand to, fall back upon, have recourse to, recur to, take to, take up, betake oneself to; take up with, take advantage of; lay one's hands on, try.

render useful etc. 644; mold *or* mould; turn to -account, — use; convert to use, utilize; administer; work up; call —, bring- into play; put into requisition; call —, draw- forth; press —, enlist- into the service; task, tax, put to task; bring to bear upon, devote, dedicate, consecrate, apply, adhibit, dispose of; make a handle of, make a cat's-paw of.

fall back upon, make a shift with; make the most of, make the best of.

consume, use up, devour, swallow up; absorb, expend; wear, outwear.

adj. **in use**; used etc. *v.;* well-worn, well-trodden.

useful etc. 644; subservient etc. (*instrumental*) 631; utilitarian, pragmatic *or* pragmatical.

678. Disuse

n. **disuse**; forbearance, abstinence; relinquishment etc. 782; desuetude etc. (*want of habit*) 614; disusage.

v. **not use**; do without, dispense with, let alone, not touch, forbear, abstain, spare, waive, neglect; keep back, reserve.

disuse; lay up, lay by, lay on the shelf, lay up in a napkin; shelve; set —, put —, lay- aside;

leave off, have done with; supersede; discard etc. (*eject*) 297; dismiss, give warning.

> **throw aside** etc. (*relinquish*) 782; make away with etc. (*destroy*) 162; cast —, heave —, throw- overboard; cast to the -dogs, — winds; dismantle etc. (*render useless*) 645.
>
> lie —, remain- unemployed etc. *adj.*

adj. **not used** etc. *v.;* unemployed, unapplied, undisposed of, unspent, unexercised, untouched, untrodden, unessayed, ungathered, unculled; uncalled for, not required.

> **disused** etc. *v.;* done with, run down, worn out, not worth saving.

int. no use!

679. Misuse

n. **misuse,** misusage, misemployment, misapplication, misappropriation.

> **abuse,** profanation, prostitution, desecration; waste etc. 638.

v. **misuse,** misemploy, misapply, misappropriate.

> **desecrate,** abuse, profane, prostitute.
>
> **overtask,** overtax, overwork, overdrive; squander etc. 818; waste etc. 638.
>
> cut blocks with a razor, employ a steam engine to crack a nut; catch at a straw.

adj. **misused** etc. *v.*

Section 3. Action

680. Action

n. **action,** performance; doing etc. *v.;* perpetration; exercise, exercitation; movement, operation, evolution, work, employment; labor etc. (*exertion*) 686; *praxis* [*L.*], execution; procedure etc. (*conduct*) 692; handicraft; business etc. 625; agency etc. (*power at work*) 170.

> **deed,** act, overt act, stitch, touch, gest *or* geste; transaction, job, doings, dealings, proceeding, measure, step, maneuver *or* maneuvre, manoeuver *or* manoeuvre, bout, passage, move, stroke, blow; *coup,* — *de main,* — *d'état* [*F.*]; *tour de force* [*F.*] etc. (*display*) 882; feat, exploit; achievement etc. (*completion*) 729; handiwork, craftsmanship, workmanship; manufacture; stroke of policy etc. (*plan*) 626.
>
> **actor** etc. (*doer*) 690.

v. **do,** perform, execute; achieve etc. (*complete*) 729; transact, enact; commit, perpetrate, inflict; exercise, prosecute, carry on, work, practice, play.

> **employ oneself,** ply one's task; officiate, have in hand etc. (*business*) 625; labor etc. 686; be at work; pursue a course; shape one's course etc. (*conduct*) 692.
>
> **act,** operate; take action, take steps; strike a blow, mix it up with [*slang*], lift a finger, stretch forth one's hand; take in hand etc. (*undertake*) 676; put oneself in motion; put in practice; carry into execution etc. (*complete*) 729; act upon.
>
> **be an actor** etc. 690; take —, act —, play —, perform- a part in; participate in; have a -hand in, — finger in the pie; have to do with; be a party to, be a participator in; bear —, lend- a hand; pull an oar, run in a race; mix oneself up with etc. (*meddle*) 682.
>
> **be in action;** come into operation etc. (*power at work*) 170.

adj. **in action;** doing etc. *v.;* acting; in harness; up to one's ears in work; in the midst of things; on duty; at work; operative; in operation etc. 170.

adv. in the -act, — midst of, — thick of; red-handed, *in flagrante delicto* [*L.*]; while one's hand is in; while one is at it.

681. Inaction

n. **inaction,** passiveness, abstinence from action; watchful waiting; noninterference; Fabian —, *laisser-aller* [*F.*] —, *laisser-faire* [*F.*] —, conservative- policy; neglect etc. 460.

> **inactivity** etc. 683; stagnation, vegetation, loafing, loaf; rest etc. (*repose*) 687; quiescence etc. 265; want of occupation, unemployment, inoccupation; idle hours, idle hands, time hanging on one's hands, *dolce far niente* [*It.*]; shore duty; interregnum; sinecure; soft snap, soft thing, soft touch, cinch [*all four slang*].

v. **not do,** not act, not attempt; be inactive etc. 683; abstain from doing, do nothing, hold, spare; not stir —, not move —, not lift- a -finger, — hand, — foot, — peg; fold one's -arms, — hands; leave —, let- alone; let be, let pass, let things take their course, let it have its way, let well alone, let well enough alone; *quieta non movere* [*L.*]; *stare super antiquas vias* [*L.*]; rest and be thankful, live and let live; lie —, rest- upon one's oars; *laisser aller* [*F.*], *laisser faire* [*F.*]; stand aloof; refrain etc. (*avoid*) 623; keep oneself from doing; remit —, relax- one's efforts; desist etc. (*relinquish*) 624; stop etc. (*cease*) 142; pause etc. (*be quiet*) 265.

> **wait,** lie in wait, bide one's time, take time, tide it over.
>
> cool —, kick- one's heels; while away the -time, — tedious hours; pass —, fill up —, beguile- the time; talk against time; waste time etc. (*inactive*) 683.

lie by, lie on the shelf, lie idle, lie to, lie fallow; keep quiet, slug [*obs.*]; have nothing to do, whistle for want of thought; twiddle one's thumbs.

undo, do away with; take down, take to pieces; destroy etc. 162.

adj. **not doing** etc. *v.;* not done etc. *v.;* undone; passive; unoccupied, unemployed; out of -employ, — work, — a job; uncultivated, fallow; *désoeuvré* [*F.*].

adv. **at a stand**, *re infecta* [*L.*], *les bras croisés* [*F.*], with folded arms; with the hands -in the pockets, — behind one's back; *pour passer le temps* [*F.*].

int. **stop!** etc. 142; hands off! so let it be! enough! no more! *bas!* [*Hind.*], *basta!* [*It.*].

682. Activity

n. **activity;** briskness, liveliness etc. *adj.;* animation, life, vivacity, spirit, verve, pep [*slang*], dash, go [*colloq.*], energy; snap, vim.

smartness, nimbleness, agility; quickness etc. *adj.;* velocity etc. 274; alacrity, promptitude; dispatch *or* despatch, expedition; haste etc. 684; punctuality etc. (*early*) 132.

eagerness, zeal, ardor, enthusiasm, *perfervidum ingenium* [*L.*], *empressement* [*F.*], earnestness, intentness; *abandon* [*F.*]; vigor etc. (*physical energy*) 171; devotion etc. (*resolution*) 604; exertion etc. 686.

industry, assiduity; assiduousness etc. *adj.;* sedulity [*rare*], sedulousness; laboriousness; drudgery etc. (*labor*) 686; painstaking, diligence; perseverance etc. 604*a;* indefatigation [*obs.*]; businesslike habits, habits of business.

vigilance etc. 459; wakefulness; sleeplessness, restlessness; insomnia; pervigilium, *insomnium* [*L.*]; racketing.

bustle, hustle [*colloq.*], movement, stir, fuss, ado, bother, fidget, fidgetiness; flurry etc. (*haste*) 684.

officiousness; dabbling, meddling; interference, interposition, intermeddling; butting in [*slang*], horning in [*slang*], intrusiveness, minding others' business, not minding one's own business; tampering with, intrigue.

press of business, no sinecure, plenty to do, a great deal doing [*colloq.*], a lot going on [*colloq.*], many irons in the fire, great doings, busy hum of men, the madding crowd, the thick of things, battle of life, thick of the action.

man of action, busy bee; new broom; sharp fellow, blade; devotee, enthusiast, fanatic, zealot, hummer [*slang*], hustler [*colloq.*], humdinger [*slang*], rustler [*slang*]; live wire, human dynamo [*both colloq.*], live man.

meddler, intermeddler, intriguer, intrigant *or* intriguant, telltale, busybody, pickthank [*archaic*].

v. **be active** etc. *adj.;* busy oneself in; stir, stir about, stir one's stumps [*colloq.*]; bestir —, rouse- oneself; speed, hasten, peg away, lay about one, bustle, fuss; raise —, kick up- a dust; push; make a -fuss, — stir; go ahead, push forward; fight —, elbow- one's way; make progress etc. 282; toil etc. (*labor*) 686; moil, drudge, plod, persist etc. (*persevere*) 604*a;* keep up the ball; keep the pot boiling.

look sharp; have all one's eyes about one etc. (*vigilance*) 459; rise, arouse oneself, hustle [*colloq.*], push [*colloq.*], get up early, be about, keep moving, steal a march, catch a weasel asleep, kill two birds with one stone; seize the opportunity etc. 134; lose no time, not lose a moment, make the most of one's time, not suffer the grass to grow under one's feet, improve the shining hour, make short work of; dash off; make haste etc. 684; do one's best, take pains etc. (*exert oneself*) 686; do —, work- wonders; have a lot of -kick [*colloq.*], — pep [*slang*].

have many irons in the fire, have one's hands full, have much on one's hands; have other -things to do, — fish to fry; be busy; not have a moment -to spare, — that one can call one's own.

have one's fling, run the round of; go all lengths, stick at nothing, run riot.

outdo; overdo, overact, overlay, weigh down, overshoot the mark; make a toil of a pleasure.

have a hand in etc. (*act in*) 680; take an active part, put in one's oar, have a finger in the pie, mix oneself up with, trouble one's head about, intrigue; agitate.

meddle, tamper with, intermeddle, interfere, interpose; obtrude; poke —, thrust- one's nose in; butt in, horn in [*both slang*].

adj. **active**, brisk, — as a lark, — as a bee; lively, animated, vivacious; alive, — and kicking [*colloq.*]; frisky, spirited, stirring.

nimble, — as a squirrel; agile; light-footed, nimble-footed; featly tripping.

quick, prompt, yare [*archaic*], instant, ready, alert, spry, sharp, smart; fast etc. (*swift*) 274; capable, smart as a steel trap, no sooner said than done etc. (*early*) 132; quick as a lamplighter, expeditious; awake, broad awake; go-ahead, live, hustling [*colloq.*]; wide-awake etc. (*intelligent*) 498.

forward, eager, ardent, strenuous, zealous, enterprising, in earnest; resolute etc. 604.

industrious, assiduous, diligent, sedulous, notable [*obsoles. in this sense*], painstaking; intent etc. (*attention*) 457; indefatigable etc. (*persevering*) 604a; unwearied, never weary, sleepless, unsleeping, never tired; plodding, hard-working etc. 686; businesslike.

bustling; restless, — as a hyena; fussy, fidgety, pottering; busy as a hen with one chicken.

working, at work, on duty, in harness; up in arms; on one's legs, at call; up and -doing, — stirring; laboring, workday, workaday.

busy, occupied; hard at work, hard at it; up to one's ears in, full of business; busy as a -bee, — housewife.

meddling etc. *v.*; meddlesome, pushing, officious, overofficious, *intrigant* [*F.*].

astir, stirring; agoing, afoot; on foot; in full swing; eventful; on the alert etc. (*vigilant*) 459.

adv. **actively** etc. *adj.*; featly [*archaic*]; with life and spirit, with might and main etc. 686, with haste etc. 684, with wings; full tilt, *in mediis rebus* [*L.*].

int. be —, look- -alive, — sharp! move on! push on! keep moving! go ahead! stir your stumps! [*colloq.*]; *age quod agis!* [*L.*], *jaldi!* [*Hind.*], *jaldi karo!* [*Hind.*], step lively! get a move on!

683. Inactivity

n. **inactivity**; inaction etc. 681; inertness etc. 172; obstinacy etc. 606.

lull etc. (*cessation*) 142; quiescence etc. 265; rust, rustiness.

idleness, remissness etc. *adj.*; sloth, indolence, indiligence [*rare*]; dawdling etc. *v.*; ergophobia, otiosity, hoboism.

dull work; pottering; relaxation etc. (*loosening*) 47; Castle of Indolence.

languor; dullness etc. *adj.*; segnity [*obs.*], segnitude [*obs.*], lentor; sluggishness etc. (*slowness*) 275; procrastination etc. (*delay*) 133; torpor, torpidity, torpescence; stupor etc. (*insensibility*) 823; somnolence; drowsiness etc. *adj.*; nodding etc. *v.*; oscitation, oscitancy; pandiculation, hypnotism, lethargy; statuvolence *or* statuvolism; sand in the eyes, heaviness, heavy eyelids.

sleep, slumber; sound —, heavy —, balmy-sleep; Morpheus; Somnus; coma, trance, catalepsy, hypnosis, ecstasis, dream; hibernation; nap, doze, snooze [*colloq.*], siesta, wink of sleep, forty winks [*colloq.*]; snore; hypnology.

[cause of inactivity] lullaby, *berceuse* [*F.*],

Schlummerlied [*Ger.*]; anaesthesia *or* anesthesia, anaesthetic *or* anesthetic, opiate, sedative etc. 174.

idler, drone, dawdle [*rare*], dawdler; dead head, stiff, dead one [*all slang*], mopus [*obs.*], do-little, *fainéant* [*F.*], dummy, sleeping partner; afternoon farmer; truant etc. (*runaway*) 623; bummer, bum [*slang*], Weary Willie [*colloq.*], tramp, sundowner [*slang, Austral.*], hobo, fakir *or* fakeer [*Moham.*], sunyasi [*Hind.*]; beggar, cadger [*slang*], lounge lizard [*slang*], lounger, lazzarone, loafer; lubber, lubbard [*rare*]; slow coach etc. (*slow*) 275; opium —, lotus- eater; slug; laggard, sluggard; slumberer, the Dustman, the Sandman; the Fat Boy in Pickwick; dormouse, marmot; waiter on Providence, *fruges consumere natus* [*L.*]; Mr. Micawber.

v. **be inactive** etc. *adj.*; do nothing etc. 681; move slowly etc. 275; let the grass grow under one's feet; take one's time, dawdle, drawl, lag, hang back, slouch; loll, lollop [*colloq., Brit.*], lounge, poke, loaf, loiter; go to sleep over; sleep at one's post, *ne battre que d'une aile* [*F.*].

take it easy, take things as they come; lead an easy life, vegetate, swim with the stream, eat the bread of idleness, goof off [*slang*]; loll in the lap of -luxury, — indolence; waste —, consume —, kill —, lose- time; burn daylight, waste the precious hours.

dally, dilly-dally; idle —, trifle —, fritter —, fool- away time; spend —, take- time in; peddle, piddle; potter, putter, dabble, faddle [*dial. Eng.*], fribble, fiddle-faddle.

sleep, slumber, be asleep; hibernate; oversleep; sleep like a -top, — log, — dormouse; sleep -soundly, — heavily; doze, drowse, snooze [*colloq.*], nap; take a nap etc. *n.*; dream; snore; settle —, go —, go off- to sleep; drop off [*colloq.*]; fall asleep, drop asleep; get some shut-eye [*slang*], close —, seal up- -the -eyes, — eyelids; weigh down the eyelids; get sleepy, nod, yawn; go to bed, turn in, hit the hay [*slang*], hit the sack [*slang*], rest in the arms of Morpheus.

languish, expend itself, flag, hang fire; relax.

render idle etc. *adj.*; sluggardize; mitigate etc. 174.

adj. **inactive**; motionless etc. 265; unoccupied etc. (*doing nothing*) 681.

indolent, lazy, slothful, idle, lusk [*obs.*], remiss, slack, inert, torpid, torpescent, sluggish, otiose, languid, supine, heavy, dull, leaden, lumpish; drony, dronish; lazy as Ludlam's dog.

dilatory, laggard; lagging etc. *v.*; slow etc. 275; rusty, flagging; fiddle-faddle; pottering etc. *v.*; shilly-shally etc. (*irresolute*) 605.

exanimate [*now rare*], soulless; listless; lackadaisical, maudlin.

sleeping etc. *v.;* asleep; fast —, dead —, sound-asleep; in a sound sleep; sound as a top, dormant, comatose; in the -arms, — lap- of Morpheus.

sleepy, sleepful [*rare*], full of sleep, oscitant, dozy, drowsy, somnolent, torpescent; lethargic *or* lethargical, somnifacient; statuvolent, statuvolic; heavy, heavy with sleep; nappy, somnific, somniferous; soporose *or* soporous, soporific, soporiferous; hypnotic; balmy, dreamy; unawakened, unwakened.

sedative etc. 174.

adv. **inactively** etc. *adj.;* at leisure etc. 685; with half-shut eyes, half asleep; in dreams, in dreamland.

684. Haste

n. **haste**, urgency, dispatch *or* despatch, acceleration, spurt *or* spirt, forced march, rush, scurry *or* skurry, scuttle, dash; velocity etc. 274; precipitancy, precipitation, precipitousness etc. *adj.;* impetuosity; *brusquerie* [*F.*]; hurry, drive, scramble, bustle, fuss, fidget, flurry, flutter, splutter.

v. **haste**, hasten; make haste, make a dash etc. *n.;* hurry —, dash —, whip —, push —, press- -on, — forward; hurry, scurry *or* skurry, scuttle along, bundle on, dart to and fro, bustle, flutter, scramble; plunge, — headlong; dash off; rush etc. (*violence*) 173; express, railroad [*colloq.*].

bestir oneself etc. (*be active*) 682; lose -no time, — not a moment, — not an instant; make short work of; make the best of one's -time, — way.

be precipitate etc. *adj.;* jump at, be in haste, be in a hurry etc. *n.;* have -no time —, have not a moment- -to lose, — to spare; work against time, work under pressure.

quicken etc. 274; accelerate, expedite, put on, precipitate, urge, whip, spur, flog, goad.

adj. **hasty**, hurried, brusque; scrambling, cursory, precipitate, headlong, furious, boisterous, impetuous, hot-headed; feverish, fussy; pushing.

in haste, in a hurry etc. *n.;* in hot haste, in all haste; breathless, pressed for time, hard pressed, urgent.

adv. **with haste**, with all haste, with breathless speed; in haste etc. *adj.;* apace etc. (*swiftly*) 274; amain; all at once etc. (*instantaneously*) 113; at short notice etc., immediately etc. (*early*) 132; posthaste; by cable, by telegraph, by wireless [*colloq.*], by airmail, by air, by return mail, by steam [*colloq.*], by forced marches.

hastily, precipitately etc. *adj.;* helter-skelter, hurry-skurry, holus-bolus; slap-dash, slap-bang; full-tilt, full-drive; heels over head, head and shoulders, headlong, *à corps perdu* [*F.*].

by fits and starts, by spurts; hop skip and jump.

int. **rush!** immediate! urgent! look alive! *jaldi karo!* [*Hind.*]; get with it [*colloq.*], get a move on! [*colloq.*], get a wiggle on! [*colloq.*]; quickmarch! [*mil.*], double! [*mil.*]; gallop! charge! [*mil.*].

685. Leisure

n. **leisure**; convenience; spare -time, — hours, –moments; vacant hour; time, — to spare, — to burn [*slang*], — on one's hands; holiday etc. (*rest*) 687; *otium cum dignitate;* ease.

v. **have leisure** etc. *n.;* take one's -time, — leisure, — ease; repose etc. 687; move slowly etc. 275; while away the time etc. (*inaction*) 681; be master of one's time, be an idle man; *desipere in loco* [*L.*].

686. Exertion

n. **exertion**, effort, strain, tug, pull, stress, throw, stretch, struggle, spell, spurt *or* spirt; stroke —, stitch- of work.

"a long pull, a strong pull, and a pull all together"; dead lift; heft [*dial.*]; wear and tear; ado; toil and trouble; uphill —, hard —, warm- work; harvest time.

exercise, exercitation, practice, play, gymnastics, field sports; breather [*colloq.*], racing, running, jumping, riding etc.

labor, work, toil, travail [*rare*], manual labor, sweat of one's brow, swink [*obs.*], operoseness, drudgery, slavery, fag [*colloq., Eng.*], faggery, fagging, hammering; *limae labor* [*L.*]; operosity [*obs.*], operoseness.

trouble, pains, duty; resolution etc. 604; energy etc. (*physical*) 171.

worker, plodder, laborer, drudge, fagger, fag [*Eng. schools*], slave; man of action etc. 682; agent etc. 690; Samson, Hercules.

v. **exert oneself**; exert —, tax- one's energies; use exertion.

labor, work, toil, moil, sweat, fag, swink [*archaic*], toil and moil, drudge, slave, drag a lengthened chain, wade through, strive, strain; make —, stretch- a long arm; pull, tug, ply; ply —, tug at- the oar; do the work; take the laboring oar.

bestir oneself (*be active*) 682; take trouble, trouble oneself.

work hard; rough it; put forth -one's strength, — a strong arm; fall to work, bend the bow; buckle to, set one's shoulder to the wheel etc.

(*resolution*) 604; work like a -horse, — cart horse, — dog, — galley slave, — coal heaver, — Briton; labor —, work- day and night; redouble one's efforts; do double duty; work double -hours, — tides; sit up, burn the candle at both ends, burn the midnight oil; stick to etc. (*persevere*) 604a; work —, fight- one's way; lay about one, hammer at.

do one's best, do one's level best, do one's utmost; take pains; do the best one can, do all one can, do all in one's power, do as much as in one lies, do what lies in one's power; use one's -best, — utmost- endeavor; try one's- -best, — utmost; play one's best card; put one's -best, — right- leg foremost; put one's best foot foremost; have one's whole soul in his work, put all one's strength into, strain every nerve; spare no -efforts, —pains; go all lengths; go through fire and water etc. (*resolution*) 604; move heaven and earth, leave no stone unturned.

adj. laboring etc. *v.*

laborious, hefty [*colloq.*], operose, elaborate; strained; toilsome, troublesome, wearisome, burdensome; uphill; herculean, gymnastic, palaestric *or* palestric, athletic.

hardworking, painstaking, strenuous, energetic, never idle.

hard at work, on the stretch, on the move, on the jump, on the dead jump, on the run.

adv. **laboriously** etc. *adj.;* lustily; *pugnis et calcibus* [*L.*]; with might and main, with all one's might, with a strong hand, with sledge hammer, with much ado; to the best of one's abilities, *totis viribus* [*L.*], *vi et armis* [*L.*], *manibus pedibusque* [*L.*], tooth and nail, *unguibus et rostro* [*L.*], hammer and tongs, heart and soul; through thick and thin etc. (*perseverance*) 604a.

by the sweat of one's brow, *suo Marte* [*L.*].

687. Repose

n. **repose**, rest, silken repose; sleep etc. 683.
relaxation, breathing time; halt, stay, pause etc. (*cessation*) 142; respite.

day of rest, *dies non* [*L.*], Sabbath, Lord's day, Sunday, First Day, holiday, red-letter day; gala day etc. (*amusement*) 840; vacation, recess.

v. **repose**; rest, rest and be thankful; take rest, take one's ease.
lie down; recline, recline on a bed of down, recline on an easychair; go to -rest, — bed, — sleep etc. 683.

relax, unbend, slacken; take breath etc. (*refresh*) 689; rest upon one's oars; pause etc. (*cease*) 142; stay one's hand.

take a holiday, shut up shop; lie fallow etc. (*inaction*) 681.

adj. **reposing** etc. *v.;* unstrained.
holiday, festal, ferial [*rare*]; sabbatic *or* sabbatical.

adv. at rest.

688. Fatigue

n. **fatigue**; weariness etc. 841; yawning, drowsiness etc. 683; lassitude, tiredness, fatigation [*obs.*], sweat.

shortness of breath; anhelation [*rare*], dyspnea, panting, labored breathing.

faintness, fainting, swoon, goneness, exhaustion, collapse, prostration, deliquium, syncope, lipothymy.

v. **be fatigued** etc. *adj.;* yawn etc. (*get sleepy*) 683; droop, sink, flag; lose breath, lose wind; gasp, pant, puff, blow, drop, swoon, faint, succumb.

fatigue, tire, bore, weary, irk [*chiefly impersonal, as, it irks me*], flag, jade, harass, exhaust, knock up, wear out, bleed white, prostrate.

tax, task, strain; overtask, overwork, overburden, overtax, overstrain, fag, fag out.

adj. **fatigued** etc. *v.;* weary etc. 841; drowsy etc. 683; drooping etc. *v.;* haggard; toilworn, wayworn; footsore, surbated [*obs.*], weather-beaten; faint; done, done up, knocked up [*all Brit. colloq.*]; bushed [*slang*], done in; exhausted, used up [*colloq.*], prostrate, spent; overtired, overspent, overfatigued; unrefreshed, unrestored.

ready to drop, all in [*slang*], more dead than alive, dog-weary, dog-tired, walked off one's legs, tired to death, on one's last legs, played out, *hors de combat* [*F.*].

worn, worn out; battered, shattered, pulled down, seedy [*colloq.*], enfeebled, altered.

breathless, windless; short of —, out of -breath, — wind; blown, puffing and blowing; short-breathed; anhelose; broken-winded, short-winded; dyspneal, dyspneic.

689. Refreshment

n. **recuperation**; recovery of strength etc. 159; refreshing, bracing etc. *v.;* restoration, revival etc. 660; repair, refection, refocillation [*obs.*], refreshment, regale, regalement, bait; relief etc. 834.

v. **refresh**; brace etc. (*strengthen*) 159; reinvigorate; air, freshen up, recruit; repair etc. (*restore*) 660; fan, refocillate [*obs.*]; refresh the inner man; get better, raise one's head; recover —, regain —, renew- one's strength etc. 159; perk up.

breathe, respire; drink in the ozone; draw —, take —, gather —, take a long —, regain —, recover- breath.

recuperate; come to oneself etc. (*revive*) 660; feel like a giant refreshed.

adj. **refreshing** etc. *v.;* recuperative etc. 660.

refreshed etc. *v.;* untired, unwearied.

690. Agent

n. **agent**, doer, actor, performer, perpetrator, operator; executor, executrix; practitioner, worker, old stager; mediary, medium, reagent.

minister etc. (*instrument*) 631; representative etc. (*commissioner*) 758, (*deputy*) 759; factor, steward.

servant etc. 746; factotum, general, maid-of-all-work, servant-of-all-work, do-all [*colloq.*].

[comparisons] bee, ant, working bee, termite, white ant; laboring oar; shaft horse.

workman, artisan; craftsman, handicraftsman; mechanic, operative; workingman, laboring man; hewers of wood and drawers of water, laborer, navvy [*Eng.*]; hand, man, day laborer, journeyman, hack; mere tool etc. 633; beast of burden, drudge, fag; lumper, stevedore, roustabout.

maker, artificer, *artifex* [*L.*], artist, wright, manufacturer, architect, contractor, builder, mason, bricklayer, smith, forger, Vulcan; carpenter; platelayer; blacksmith, locksmith, sailmaker, tailor, cordwainer, wheelwright.

machinist, mechanician, engineer, electrician, plumber, gasfitter.

workwoman, charwoman, seamstress *or* sempstress, needlewoman, laundress, washerwoman, "Madonna of the tubs" [Phelps].

coworker, associate, fellow worker, cooperator, colleague, *confrère* [*F.*]; party to, participator in, *particeps criminis* [*L.*], *dramatis personae* [*L.*]; *personnel* [*F.*].

691. Workshop

n. **workshop**, workhouse; laboratory, manufactory, armory, arsenal, mill, factory, *usine* [*F.*], mint, loom; cabinet, bureau, studio, *atelier* [*F.*]; hive, hive of industry; plant; hothouse, hotbed; kitchen; alveary, beehive, bindery, forcing pit, nailery, dock, dockyard, slip, yard, wharf; foundry *or* foundery, forge, furnace; vineyard, orchard, nursery, truck garden, truck farm, farm.

melting pot, crucible, caldron *or* cauldron, mortar, alembic; matrix.

692. Conduct

n. **conduct**, behavior; deportment, comportment; carriage, *maintien* [*F.*], demeanor, guise, bearing, manner, observance.

course —, line- of -conduct, — action, — proceeding; role; process, ways, practice, procedure, *modus operandi* [*L.*]; method etc., path etc. 627.

dealing, transaction etc. (*action*) 680; business etc. 625.

policy, polity; tactics, game, generalship, statesmanship, seamanship; strategy, strategics; plan etc. 626.

management; government etc. (*direction*) 693; stewardship, husbandry; housekeeping, housewifery; ménage *or* menage; régime *or* regime, regimen, economy, economics; political economy.

career, life, course, walk, province, race, record; execution, manipulation, treatment; campaign.

v. **transact**, execute; dispatch *or* despatch, proceed with, discharge; carry -on, — through, — out, — into effect; work out; go through, get through; enact; put into practice; officiate etc. 625.

bear —, behave —, comport —, demean —, carry —, conduct —, acquit- oneself.

run a race, lead a life, play a game; take —, adopt- a course; steer —, shape- one's course; play one's part, play one's cards; shift for oneself; paddle one's own canoe; bail one's own boat.

conduct; manage etc. (*direct*) 693.

deal with, have to do with; treat, handle a case; take -steps, — measures.

adj. **conducting** etc. *v.;* directive, strategic *or* strategical, methodical, business-like, practical, executive; economic.

693. Direction

n. **direction**; management, managery [*obs.*]; government, gubernation [*obs.*], conduct, legislation, regulation, guidance; bossism; legislature; steerage, pilotage; reins, — of government; helm, rudder, needle, compass; guiding star, lodestar *or* loadstar, polestar; cynosure.

ministry, ministration; administration; stewardship, proctorship; chair; agency.

supervision, superintendence; surveillance, oversight; eye of the master; control, charge; auspices; board of control etc. (*council*) 696; command etc. (*authority*) 737.

statesmanship; statecraft, kingcraft, queencraft; premiership, senatorship; director etc. 694; seat, portfolio.

v. **direct**, manage, govern, conduct; order, prescribe, cut out work for; head, lead; lead the way, show the way; take the lead, lead on; regulate, guide, steer, pilot; take the helm, be at the helm; have —, handle —, hold —, take- the reins; drive, tool [*cant*], tackle.

superintend, supervise; overlook, oversee, control, keep in order, look after, see to, legislate for; administer, ministrate [*obs.*]; matronize; patronize; have the -care, — charge- of; have —, take- the direction; pull the -strings, — wires; rule etc. (*command*) 737; be the guiding force; have —, hold- -office, — the portfolio; preside, — at the board; take —, occupy —, be in- the chair; pull the stroke oar.

adj. **directing** etc. *v.;* executive, gubernatorial, supervisory; hegemonic *or* hegemonical, predominant; statesmanlike.

adv. **in charge of**, under the guidance of, under the auspices of; in control of, at the helm, at the head of.

694. Director

n. **director**, manager, governor, rector [*rare*], controller, comptroller; superintendent, supervisor; intendant; overseer, overlooker; supercargo, husband [*archaic*], inspector, foreman, ganger [*Eng.*], visitor, ranger, surveyor, aedile *or* edile [*Rom. hist.*], moderator, monitor, taskmaster; master etc. 745; leader, ringleader, agitator, demagogue, corypheus, conductor, fugleman, precentor, bellwether; *caporal* [*F.*], choregus, collector, file leader, flugelman, linkboy.

guiding star etc. (*guidance*) 693; adviser etc. 695; guide etc. (*information*) 527; pilot; helmsman; steersman, steersmate [*obs.*]; wire-puller.

driver, whip, jehu [*humorous*], charioteer; coachman, carman, cabman; postilion, *vetturino* [*It.*], muleteer, *arriero* [*Sp.*], teamster; whipper-in; chauffeur, motorman, engine-driver.

head, headman, chief, principal, president, speaker; chair, chairman; captain etc. (*master*) 745; superior; mayor etc. (*civil authority*) 745; vice-president, prime minister, premier, vizier *or* vizir, grand vizier, eparch.

officer, functionary, minister, official, red-tape, red-tapist, bureaucrat; Jack in office; office bearer, office holder; person in authority etc. 745.

statesman, strategist, legislator, lawgiver, politician, statist [*rare*], statemonger; Minos, Draco; arbiter etc. (*judge*) 967; boss, political dictator, dictator, power behind the throne, kingmaker;

secretary, — of state; Reis Effendi; vicar etc. (*deputy*) 759; board etc. (*council*) 696.

steward, factor; agent etc. 758; bailiff, middleman; clerk of works; landreeve; factotum, major-domo, seneschal, housekeeper, shepherd; croupier; proctor, procurator, curator, librarian.

adv. *ex officio.*

695. Advice

n. **advice**, counsel, adhortation [*obs.*]; word to the wise; suggestion, submonition [*obs.*], recommendation, advocacy; advisement [*archaic*]; consultation.

exhortation etc. (*persuasion*) 615; expostulation etc. (*dissuasion*) 616; admonition etc. (*warning*) 668; guidance etc. (*direction*) 693.

instruction, charge, injunction; Governor's —, President's- message; King's —, Queen's- speech; message, speech from the throne.

adviser, prompter; counsel, counselor; monitor, mentor, Nestor, sage, wise man, wise woman; *magnus Apollo* [*L.*], senator; teacher etc. 540; yogi *or* yogin; physician, leech [*archaic*]; archiater; arbiter etc. (*judge*) 967.

guide, manual, chart etc. (*information*) 527.

consultation, conference, *pourparler* [*F.*], parley, powwow; reference, referment.

v. **advise**, counsel; give -advice, — counsel, — a piece of advice; suggest, prompt, submonish [*obs.*], recommend, prescribe, advocate; exhort etc. (*persuade*) 615.

enjoin, enforce, charge, instruct, call; call upon etc. (*request*) 765; dictate.

expostulate etc. (*dissuade*) 616; admonish etc. (*warn*) 668.

advise with; lay heads —, consult- together; compare notes; hold a council, deliberate, be closeted with.

confer, consult, refer to, call in; follow, follow implicitly; take —, follow- advice; be advised by, have at one's elbow, take one's cue from.

adj. **recommendatory**; hortative etc. (*persuasive*) 615; dehortatory etc. (*dissuasive*) 616; admonitory etc. (*warning*) 668; consultative; dictatory, dictatorial; didactic.

int. go to!

696. Council

n. **council**, committee, subcommittee, comitia [*Rom. hist.*], privy council, court, chamber, cabinet, board, bench, staff.

junta, divan, musnud, sanhedrin *or* sanhedrim [*Jewish antiq.*], amphictyonic council [*Gr.*

hist.]; syndicate; court of appeal etc. (*tribunal*) 966; board of -control, — works; county council, local board, parish council, common council, town meeting; board of overseers; *zemstvo* [*Russ.*].

[ecclesiastical] convocation, synod, congregation, church, chapter, directory, vestry, consistory, conventicle, conclave, convention, classis.

legislature, parliament, congress, national council, states-general, diet.

Duma [*Russia*], Storthing *or* Storting [*Norway*], Rigsdag [*Denmark*], Riksdag [*Sweden*], Knesset [*Israel*], Cortes [*Spain*], Reichsrath *or* Reichsrat [*Austria*], Volksraad [*Dutch*]; Dail Eireann [*Ireland*]; witan, witenagemot *or* witenagemote [*Anglo-Saxon hist.*].

upper house, upper chamber, first chamber, senate, *senatus* [*Rom. hist.*], legislative council, House of Lords, House of Peers; Bundesrath *or* Bundesrat [*Ger.*], federal council, Lagting [*Nor.*], Landsthing [*Den.*].

lower house, lower chamber, second chamber, house of representatives, House of Commons, the house, legislative assembly, chamber of deputies; Odelsting [*Nor.*], Folkething [*Den.*], Reichstag [*Ger.*].

assembly, plenum, caucus, clique; meeting, sitting, séance, *camarilla* [*Sp.*], conference, hearing, session, palaver, *pourparler* [*F.*], durbar [*India*]; quorum; council fire [*N. Am.*], pow-wow.

[representatives] congressman, M. C., senator, representative; member, — of parliament, M. P.; representative of the people; assemblyman, councilor.

adj. curule, congressional, senatorial, parliamentary; synodic *or* synodical.

697. Precept

n. **precept**, direction, instruction, charge; prescript, prescription; recipe, receipt; golden rule; maxim etc. 496.

rule, canon, law, code, *corpus juris* [*L.*], *lex scripta* [*L.*], convention; unwritten law; canon law; act, statute, rubric, stage direction, regulation; model, form, formula, formulary; technicality; nice point, fine point, norm.

order etc. (*command*) 741.

698. Skill

n. **skill**, skillfulness *or* skilfulness, address; dexterity, dexterousness *or* dextrousness, adroitness, expertness etc. *adj.*; proficiency, competence, craft; callidity [*rare*], callidness, facility, knack,

trick, sleight; mastery, mastership; excellence, panurgy [*rare*]; ambidexterity, ambidextrousness; sleight of hand etc. (*deception*) 545.

seamanship, airmanship, marksmanship, horsemanship; rope-dancing; tight-rope —, slack-rope- walking.

accomplishment, acquirement, attainment; art, science; finish, finished execution, technique, technique, practical —, technical- knowledge; technology.

world wisdom, knowledge of the world, *savoir faire* [*F.*]; tact; mother wit etc. (*sagacity*) 498; discretion etc. (*caution*) 864; finesse; craftiness etc. (*cunning*) 702; management etc. (*conduct*) 692; self-help.

cleverness, talent, ability, ingenuity, capacity, parts, talents, faculty, endowment, forte, turn, gift, genius; intelligence etc. 498; sharpness, readiness etc. (*activity*) 682; invention etc. 515; aptness, aptitude; turn for, capacity for, genius for; felicity, capability, *curiosa felicitas* [*L.*], qualification, habilitation.

proficient, expert, adept etc. 700.

masterpiece, masterwork, *coup de maître* [*F.,*] *chef d'oeuvre* [*F.*], *tour de force* [*F.*]; good stroke etc. (*plan*) 626.

v. **be skillful** etc. *adj.*; excel in, be master of; have a turn for etc. *n.*

know what's what, know- a hawk from a handsaw, — what one is about, — on which side one's bread is buttered, — what's o'clock, — what o'clock it is, — what's up, — the time of day, — a thing or two, — the ropes; have cut one's -eyeteeth, — wisdom teeth; see through a millstone; be up to [*all colloq.*]

see one's way, see where the wind lies, see which way the wind blows; have all one's wits about one, have one's hand in; *savoir vivre* [*F.*]; *scire quid valeant humeri quid ferre recusent* [*L*].

look after the main chance; cut one's coat according to one's cloth; live by one's wits; exercise one's discretion, feather the oar, sail near the wind; stoop to conquer etc. (*cunning*) 702; play one's cards well, play one's best card; hit the nail on the head, put the saddle on the right horse.

take advantage of, make the most of; profit by etc. (*use*) 677; make a hit etc. (*succeed*) 731; make a virtue of necessity; make hay while the sun shines etc. (*occasion*) 134.

adj. **skillful** *or* skilful, dexterous *or* dextrous, adroit, expert, apt, handy, quick, deft, ready, slick [*slang*], smart etc. (*active*) 682; proficient, good at, up to, at home in, master of, a good hand at, *au fait* [*F.*], thoroughbred, masterly, crack [*colloq.*], crackerjack [*slang*], accomplished; conversant etc. (*knowing*) 490.

experienced, practiced, skilled; up in, well up in; in practice; competent, efficient, qualified, capable, fitted, fit for, up to the mark, up and coming, trained, initiated, prepared, primed, finished.

clever, cute [*colloq.*], able, ingenious, felicitous, gifted, talented, endowed; inventive etc. 515; shrewd, sharp etc. (*intelligent*) 498; cunning etc. 702; alive to, up to snuff [*slang*], not to be caught with chaff; discreet.

neat-handed, fine-fingered, nimble-fingered, ambidextrous, sure-footed; cut out for [*colloq.*], fitted for.

technical, artistic, scientific, daedalian, shipshapelike, workmanlike, businesslike, statesmanlike.

adv. **skillfully** *or* skilfully etc. *adj.;* well etc. 618; artistically; with skill, with fine technique, with consummate skill; *secundum artem* [*L.*], *suo Marte* [*L.*]; to the best of one's abilities etc. (*exertion*) 686; like a machine.

699. Unskillfulness

n. **unskillfulness** *or* unskilfulness etc. *adj.;* want of skill etc. 698; incompetence *or* incompetency, inability, infelicity, indexterity [*rare*], clumsiness, inaptitude etc. *adj.;* inexperience; disqualification, unproficiency; quackery.

folly, stupidity etc. 499; indiscretion etc. (*rashness*) 863; thoughtlessness etc. (*inattention*) 458, (*neglect*) 460; sabotage [*F.*].

mismanagement, misconduct, misfeasance; inexpedience, bad policy, impolicy; maladministration; misrule, misgovernment, misapplication, misdirection.

absence of rule, rule of thumb; bungling etc. *v.;* failure etc. 732; screw loose; too many cooks.

blunder etc. (*mistake*) 495; *étourderie* [*F.*], *gaucherie* [*F.*], act of folly, *balourdise* [*F.*], bungle, botch, botchery; bad job, sad work.

sprat sent out to catch a whale, butterfly broken on a wheel, tempest in a teacup, storm in a teacup, much ado about nothing, wild-goose chase.

bungler etc. 701; fool etc. 501; hen with its head cut off [*colloq.*].

v. **be unskillful** *or* unskilful, etc. *adj.;* not see an inch beyond one's nose; blunder, bungle, muff [*esp., baseball*], boggle, fumble, botch, mar, spoil, bitch [*obs.*], flounder, stumble, trip; hob-

ble etc. 275; put one's foot in it [*colloq.*]; make a -mess, — hash, — sad work- of [*all colloq.*]; overshoot the mark.

play tricks with, play Puck; mismanage, misconduct, misdirect, misapply, missend.

act foolishly; stultify —, make a fool of —, commit- oneself; play the fool; put oneself out of court; lose one's -head, — senses, — cunning; begin at the wrong end; do things by halves etc. (*not complete*) 730; make two bites of a cherry; play at cross-purposes; strain at a gnat and swallow a camel etc. (*caprice*) 608; put the cart before the horse; lock the stable door when the horse is stolen etc. (*too late*) 135.

not know what one is about, not know one's own interest, not know on which side one's bread is buttered; stand in one's own light, quarrel with one's bread and butter, throw a stone in one's own garden, kill the goose which lays the golden eggs, pay dear for one's whistle, cut one's own throat, burn one's fingers; knock —, run- one's head against a stone wall; bring the house about one's ears; have too many -eggs in one basket (*imprudent*) 863, — irons in the fire.

cut blocks with a razor; hold a farthing candle to the sun etc. (*useless*) 645; fight with —, grasp at- a shadow; catch at straws, lean on a broken reed, reckon without one's host, go on a wildgoose chase; go on a fool's errand, go on a sleeveless errand [*obs.*]; go further and fare worse; fail etc. 732.

mistake etc. 495; take the shadow for the substance etc. (*credulity*) 486; bark up the wrong tree; be in the wrong box, aim at a pigeon and kill a crow; take —, get- -the wrong pig by the tail, — the wrong sow by the ear, — the dirty end of the stick [*all colloq.*]; put the saddle on the wrong horse, put a square thing into a round hole, put new wine into old bottles; lose one's way, miss one's way; fall into a trap, catch a Tartar.

adj. **unskillful** *or* unskilful etc. 698; unskilled, inexpert; bungling etc. *v.;* awkward, clumsy, unhandy, lubberly, *gauche* [*F.*], maladroit; left-handed, heavy-handed; slovenly, slatternly; gawky.

adrift, at fault.

inapt, unapt; inhabile [*obs.*]; untractable, unteachable; giddy etc. (*inattentive*) 458; inconsiderate etc. (*neglectful*) 460; stupid etc. 499; inactive etc. 683; incompetent; unqualified, disqualified, ill-qualified; unfit; quackish; raw, green, inexperienced, rusty, out of practice.

unaccustomed, unused, untrained etc. 537, uninitiated, unconversant etc. (*ignorant*) 491; unbusinesslike, unpractical, shiftless; unstatesmanlike.

ill-advised, unadvised, misadvised; ill-devised, ill-imagined, ill-judged, ill-contrived, ill-conducted; unguided, misguided; misconducted, foolish, wild; infelicitous; penny wise and pound foolish etc. (*inconsistent*) 608.

700. Proficient

n. proficient, expert, adept; dab, dabster [*both colloq. or dial.*], connoisseur etc. (*scholar*) 492; master, — hand; top sawyer, top banana [*cant*], prima donna, *première danseuse* [*F.*], first fiddle, *chef de cuisine* [*F.*]; protagonist; past master; mahatma.

nice —, good —, clean- hand; practiced —, experienced- -eye, — hand; marksman; good —, dead —, crack- shot [*colloq.*]; ropedancer, ropewalker, funambulist; contortionist, acrobat; conjuror etc. (*deceiver*) 548; wizard etc. 994.

picked man; medallist, prizeman, honorsman.

veteran; old -stager, — campaigner, — soldier, — file, — hand; man of business, man of the world.

genius; master -mind, — head, — spirit.

pantologist, Admirable Crichton, Jack of all trades; prodigy of learning, quiz kid [*colloq.*], walking encyclopedia, mine of information.

man of cunning; cunning —, sharp- -blade, — fellow; diplomatist, diplomat, Machiavellian; politician, jobber; tactician, strategist.

peculator, forger, coiner; cracksman etc. 792.

701. Bungler

n. bungler; blunderer, blunderhead; marplot, fumbler, lubber, clown, lout, duffer [*colloq.*]; stick, poor stick, odd stick [*all colloq.*]; bad —, poor- -hand, — shot; butterfingers [*colloq.*], fumble-fist [*colloq.*].

no conjuror; flat, muff, muffer, slow coach [*all colloq.*]; looby, swab [*slang & dial.*], doit, yokel [*Eng.*], clod; awkward squad, novice, greenhorn, *blanc-bec* [*F.*], galoot [*slang*].

fish out of water, ass in lion's skin, jackdaw in peacock's feathers; quack etc. (*deceiver*) 548; Lord of Misrule, Abbot of Unreason [*both obs. or hist.*].

landlubber, fresh-water sailor, fair-weather sailor, horse marine.

sloven, slattern, traipse *or* trapes [*obs. or dial. Eng.*], slut.

702. Cunning

n. cunning, craft; cunningness, craftiness etc. *adj.;* subtlety, subtilty, subtility [*rare*]; the cunning of the -serpent, — Old Boy [*slang*]; artificiality; maneuvering *or* manoeuvring etc. *v.;* temporization; circumvention.

chicane, chicanery; sharp practice, knavery, jugglery; concealment etc. 528; guile [*colloq.*], doubling, duplicity etc. (*falsehood*) 544; foul play.

diplomacy, politics; Machiavellianism *or* Machiavellism; gerrymander, jobbery, back-stairs influence.

artifice, art, device, machination; plot etc. (*plan*) 626; maneuver, stratagem, dodge, artful dodge, wile; trick, trickery etc. (*deception*) 545; ruse, *ruse de guerre* [*F.*]; finesse, side blow, thin end of the wedge, shift, go-by [*colloq.*], subterfuge, evasion; white lie etc. (*untruth*) 546; juggle, *tour de force* [*F.*]; tricks -of the trade, — upon travelers; gold brick [*colloq.*], imposture, deception; *espièglerie* [*F.*]; net, trap etc. 545.

schemer, trickster, keener [*Western U. S.*], Philadelphia lawyer [*colloq.*]; sly boots [*humorous*], fox, reynard; intriguer, intrigant; repeater, floater; man of cunning etc. 700; horse trader; Indian giver [*colloq.*].

Ulysses, Machiavelli *or* Machiavel.

v. be cunning etc. *adj.;* have cut one's eyeteeth; contrive etc. (*plan*) 626; live by one's wits; maneuver *or* manoeuvre; intrigue, gerrymander, finesse, double, temporize, stoop to conquer, *reculer pour mieux sauter* [*F.*], circumvent, steal a march upon; outdo, get the better of, snatch a thing from under one's nose; overreach etc. 545; throw off one's guard; surprise etc. 508; snatch a verdict; waylay, undermine, introduce the thin end of the wedge; be too much for, be too deep for, sell a gold brick to [*colloq.*], give the go-by to [*slang*]; play a deep game, play tricks with; flatter, make things pleasant; have an ax to grind.

adj. cunning, crafty, artful; skillful *or* skilful etc. 698; subtle, subtile, feline, vulpine; cunning as a -fox, — serpent; deep, — laid; profound; designing, contriving; intriguing etc. *v.;* strategic, diplomatic, politic, Machiavellian *or* Machiavelian, timeserving; artificial; tricky, tricksy [*rare*], wily, sly, slim [*S. Africa*], insidious, stealthy; underhand etc. (*hidden*) 528; subdolous [*obs.*], double-faced, double-tongued, shifty, deceptive; deceitful etc. 545; crooked; arch, pawky [*Scot. & dial. Eng.*], shrewd, acute; sharp, — as a needle; canny *or* cannie, astute, leery [*slang*], knowing, up to snuff [*slang*], too clever by half, not to be caught with chaff.

adv. **cunningly** etc. *adj.;* slily, on the sly [*colloq.*], by a side wind.

703. Artlessness

n. **artlessness** etc. *adj.;* inartificiality, unsophistication; nature, simplicity; innocence etc. 946; *bonhomie* [*F.*], *naïveté* [*F.*], *abandon* [*F.*], candor, sincerity; singleness of -purpose, –heart; honesty etc. 939; plain speaking; *épanchement* [*F.*].

rough diamond, matter-of-fact man; *le palais de vérité* [*F.*]; *enfant terrible* [*F.*].

v. **be artless** etc. *adj.;* be round with one [Shakespeare]; look one in the face; wear one's heart upon one's sleeve for daws to peck at; think aloud; speak -out, –one's mind; be free with one, call a spade a spade; tell the truth, the whole truth, and nothing but the truth.

adj. **artless**, natural, pure, native, confiding, simple, plain, inartificial, untutored, unsophisticated, *ingénu* [*F.*], unaffected, naïve; sincere, frank; open, –as day; candid, ingenuous, guileless; unsuspicious, honest etc. 939; childlike; innocent etc. 946; Arcadian; undesigning, straightforward, unreserved, above-board; simple-minded, single-minded; frank–, open–, single–, simple- hearted.

matter-of-fact, free-spoken, plainspoken, outspoken; blunt, downright, direct, unpoetical; unflattering, untrimmed, unvarnished.

adv. **in plain -words**, –English; without mincing the matter; not to mince the matter etc. (*affirmation*) 535.

Section 4. Antagonism

704. Difficulty

n. **difficulty**; hardness etc. *adj.;* impracticability etc. (*impossibility*) 471; tough–, hard–, uphill- work; hard–, Herculean–, Augean- task; task of Sisyphus, Sisyphean labor, tough job [*colloq.*], tough proposition [*colloq.*], teaser [*colloq.*], rasper [*slang*], dead weight, dead lift.

dilemma, embarrassment; deadlock; perplexity etc. (*uncertainty*) 475; intricacy; entanglement etc. 59; cross fire; awkwardness, delicacy; delicate ground, thin ice, ticklish card to play, knot, Gordian knot, *dignus vindice nodus* [*L.*], net, meshes, maze; coil etc. (*convolution*) 248; crooked path; involvement; hard road to travel.

vexed question, *vexata quoestio* [*L.*], poser; puzzle etc. (*riddle*) 533; nice–, delicate–, subtle–, knotty- point; paradox; hard–, nut to crack; bone to pick, crux, *pons asinorum* [*L.*], where the shoe pinches.

quandary, nonplus, strait, pass, pinch, rub, pretty pass, stress, brunt; critical situation, crisis; trial, emergency, exigency, scramble.

scrape, hobble, slough, quagmire, hot water [*colloq.*], hornet's nest; sea–, peck- of troubles; pretty kettle of fish [*colloq.*]; pickle, stew, imbroglio, mess, muddle, botch, fuss, bustle, ado; false position; stand; deadlock, dead set; fix, horns of a dilemma, *cul de sac* [*F.*], blind alley; hitch; stumblingblock etc. (*hindrance*) 706.

v. **be difficult** etc. *adj.;* run one hard, go against the grain, try one's patience, put one out; put to one's -shifts, –wit's end; go hard with one, try one; pose, perplex etc. (*uncertain*) 475; pother, bother, nonplus, gravel [*colloq.*], bring to a deadlock; be impossible etc. 471; be in the way of etc. (*hinder*) 706.

be in difficulty etc. *n.;* meet with–, labor under–, get into–, plunge into–, struggle with–, contend with–, grapple with- difficulties; labor under a disadvantage; fish in troubled waters, buffet the waves; swim against the -current, –stream; scud under bare poles; have much ado with, have a hard time of it; come to the -push, –pinch; bear the brunt; grope in the dark, lose one's way, weave a tangled web, walk on eggshells, walk among eggs.

get into a scrape etc. *n.;* bring a hornet's nest about one's ears; be put to one's shifts; flounder, boggle, struggle; not know which way to turn etc. (*uncertain*) 475; *perdre son latin* [*F.*]; stick -at, –in the mud, –fast; come to a -stand, –deadlock; get all -balled up [*slang*], –snarled up, –tangled up, –wound up; hold the wolf by the ears.

render difficult etc. *adj.;* enmesh, encumber, embarrass, ravel, entangle; put a spoke in the wheel etc. (*hinder*) 706; spike one's guns; lead a wild-goose chase, lead a pretty dance.

adj. **difficult**, not easy, hard, tough [*colloq.*]; troublesome, toilsome, irksome; operose, laborious, onerous, arduous, Herculean, formidable; sooner–, more easily- said than done; difficult–, hard- to deal with; ill-conditioned, crabbed; not to be handled with kid gloves, not made with rose water.

awkward, unwieldy, unmanageable; intractable, stubborn etc. (*obstinate*) 606; perverse, refractory, plaguy [*colloq.*], trying, thorny, rugged;

knotted, knotty; invious [*obs.*]; pathless, track-less; labyrinthine etc. (*convoluted*) 248; intri-cate, complicated etc. (*tangled*) 59; imprac-ticable etc. (*impossible*) 471; not feasible etc. 470; desperate etc. (*hopeless*) 859.

embarrassing, perplexing etc. (*uncertain*) 475; delicate, ticklish, critical, uncertain, thorny, set with thorns; beset with–, full of–, surrounded by–, entangled by–, encompassed with- diffi-culties.

under a difficulty; in a box; in difficulty, in hot water [*colloq.*], in the suds [*colloq.*], in the soup [*slang*], in a cleft stick, in a fix [*colloq.*], in the wrong box, in a scrape etc. *n.*, in deep water, in a fine pickle [*colloq.*], *in extremis* [*L.*]; be-tween -two stools, –Scylla and Charybdis; on the horns of a dilemma; on the rocks; sur-rounded by -shoals, –breakers, –quicksands; at cross-purposes; not out of the wood.

reduced to straits; hard–, sorely- pressed; run hard; pinched, put to it, straightened; hard up [*slang*]; hard put to it, hard set [*both colloq.*]; put to one's shifts; puzzled, at a loss, etc. (*uncer-tain*) 475; at the end of one's tether, at one's wits' end, at a nonplus, at a standstill; graveled, nonplused *or* nonplussed, stranded, aground; stuck–, set- fast; out, put out, out in one's reck-oning; up a tree, at bay, *aux abois* [*F.*], driven -into a corner, –from post to pillar, –to ex-tremity, –to one's wit's end, –to the wall; *au bout de son Latin* [*F.*]; out of one's depth; thrown out.

accomplished with difficulty; hard-fought, hard-earned.

adv. **with difficulty**, with much ado; hardly etc. *adj.*; uphill; upstream; against the -stream, –grain; *à rebours* [*F.*]; *invita Minerva* [*L.*]; in the teeth of; at a pinch, upon a pinch; at long odds.

705. Facility

n. **facility**, ease; easiness etc. *adj.*; capability; feasi-bility etc. (*practicability*) 470; flexibility, pli-ancy etc. 324; smoothness etc. 255; disencum-brance, disentanglement; deoppilation [*obs.*]; permission etc. 760.

plain–, smooth–, straight- sailing; mere child's play, holiday task; cinch, snap [*both slang*].

all clear, smooth water, fair wind; smooth–, roy-al- road; clear -coast, –stage, –course; straight course; *tabula rasa* [*L.*]; full play etc. (*free-dom*) 748.

v. **be easy** etc. *adj.*; go on–, run- smoothly; have full play etc. *n.*; go–, run- on all fours [*colloq.*]; hit

on all -four, –six, –eight, –twelve (cylinders) [*automobile cant*]; obey the helm, work well, work smoothly, work like a machine.

flow–, swim–, drift–, go- with the- -stream, –tide; see one's way; have it all one's own way, have the game in one's own hands; walk over the course, win at a canter, win at a walk, win hands down [*colloq.*]; make little of, make light of, make nothing of; be at home in etc. (*skill-ful*) 698.

render easy etc. *adj.*; facilitate, smooth, ease, popularize; lighten, –the labor; free, clear; disencumber, disembarrass, disentangle, disen-gage; deobstruct, unclog, extricate, unravel, unknot, get the kinks out of; untie–, cut- the knot; disburden, unload, exonerate, emanci-pate, free from, deoppilate [*obs.*]; humor etc. (*aid*) 707; lubricate etc. 332; relieve etc. 834.

leave a hole to creep out of, leave a loophole, leave a way out, leave the matter open; give the reins to, give full play, give full swing; make way for; open the -door to, –way; prepare–, smooth–, clear- the -ground, –way, –path, –road; make all clear for, pave the way, bridge over; permit etc. 760.

adj. **easy**, facile; feasible etc. (*practicable*) 470; easily -managed, –accomplished; within reach, ac-cessible, easy of access, for the million, open to.

manageable, wieldy [*rare*], toward, towardly, tractable; submissive; yielding, ductile; suant *or* suent [*local U. S. & prov. Eng.*]; tractable etc. (*docile*) 602, pliant etc. (*soft*) 324; glib [*obs.*], slippery; smooth etc. 255; on friction wheels, on velvet.

unburdened, disburdened, disencumbered, disembarrassed; exonerated; unloaded, unob-structed, untrammeled; unrestrained etc. (*free*) 748; at ease, light.

at home, quite at home; in one's element, in smooth water.

adv. **easily** etc. *adj.*; readily, smoothly, swimmingly, with no effort, on easy terms, single-handed, with one hand tied behind one's back.

706. Hindrance

n. **prevention**, preclusion, obstruction, stoppage; embolus, clot, embolism; interruption, inter-ception, interclusion [*obs.*], hindrance, im-pedition [*obs.*]; retardment, retardation; embarrassment, oppilation [*obs.*], striction, constriction, coarctation, stricture, restriction; infarct, infarction; restraint etc. 751; inhibition etc. 761; blockade etc. (*closure*) 261.

interference, interposition; obtrusion; discouragement, discountenance; disapproval, disapprobation, opposition.

impediment, let [archaic], obstacle, obstruction, knot, knag; check, hitch, contretemps [F.], screw loose, grit in the oil; stumbling-block, stumbling-stone; lion in the path; snag; snags and sawyers, sawyer, planter [local, U. S.]

bar, stile, barrier; turnstile, turnpike; gate, portcullis; beaver dam; barricade etc. (defense) 717; wall, dead wall, breakwater, groin or groyne; bulkhead, block, buffer; stopper etc. 263; boom, dam, weir.

check; encumbrance or incumbrance; clog, skid, shoe, spoke, brake; drag anchor, drag sail, drag sheet, drift sail, sea anchor, floating anchor; anchor; mushroom-, sheet-, kedge- anchor; kedge, bower; checkrein, bearing rein; bit, snaffle, curb, curb bit; drag, -chain, -weight; load, burden, fardel [obs.], onus, millstone round one's neck, impedimenta; dead weight; lumber, pack; nightmare, ephialtes, incubus, old man of the sea; remora [surg.]; stay, stop; preventive, prophylactic.

drawback, objection; difficulty etc. 704; insuperable etc. (471) obstacle; trail of a red herring; estoppel [law]; ill wind; head wind etc. (opposition) 708; trammel, tether etc. (means of restraint) 752; holdback, counterpoise.

damper, wet blanket, hinderer, marplot, kill-joy, crape-hanger [slang], dog in the manger, Nosy Parker [colloq.], buttinsky [humorous]; usurper, interloper; opponent etc. 710; filibusterer.

v. hinder, impede, filibuster [U. S.], impedite [obs.], embarrass.

avert, keep off, stave off, ward off; obviate; antevert [obs.]; turn aside, draw off, prevent, forfend or forefend [archaic], nip in the bud; retard, slacken, check, let [archaic]; counteract, countercheck; preclude, debar, foreclose, estop [law]; inhibit etc. 761; shackle etc. (restrain) 751; restrict.

obstruct, stop, stay, bar, bolt, lock; block, -up; choke off; belay, barricade; block-, stop- the way; forlay or forelay [obs.], dam up etc. (close) 261; put on the brake etc. n.; scotch-, lock-, put a spoke in- the wheel; put a stop to etc. 142; traverse, contravene; interrupt, intercept; oppose etc. 708; hedge -in, -round; cut off; interclude [obs.].

interfere, interpose, intermeddle etc. 682.

encumber or incumber; cramp, hamper; clog, -the wheels; cumber; handicap; choke; saddle with, load with; overload, overlay, overwhelm; lumber, trammel, tie one's hands, put to inconvenience; incommode, discommode; discompose; hustle [colloq.], corner, drive into a corner.

run foul of, fall foul of; cross the path of, break in upon.

thwart, frustrate, disconcert, balk, foil; faze, feeze or feaze; baffle, snub, override, circumvent; defeat etc. 731; spike guns etc. (render useless) 645; spoil, mar, clip the wings of; cripple etc. (injure) 659; put an extinguisher on; damp; dishearten etc. (dissuade) 616; discountenance, throw cold water on, spoil sport; lay-, throw- a wet blanket on; steal one's thunder; cut the ground from under one, take the wind out of one's sails, undermine; be-, stand- in the way of; act as a drag; hang like a millstone round one's neck.

adj. hindering etc. v.; obstructive, obstruent; intrusive, meddlesome; impeditive, impedient; intercipient [obs.]; prophylactic etc. (remedial) 662; impedimentary, impedimental.

in the way of, unfavorable; onerous, burdensome; cumbrous, cumbersome; obtrusive.

hindered etc. v.; windbound, water-logged, heavy laden; hard pressed.

unassisted etc. (see assist etc. 707); single-handed, alone; deserted etc. 624; unseconded.

adv. in the way, with everything against one, with one's wheels clogged, through all obstacles; with many difficulties, under many difficulties.

707. Aid

n. aid, aidance, assistance, help, opitulation [obs.], succor; support, lift, advance, furtherance, promotion; coadjuvancy etc. (cooperation) 709.

patronage, auspices, championship, countenance, favor, interest, advocacy.

sustenance, sustentation [rare], maintenance, alimentation, nutrition, nourishment; eutrophy; manna in the wilderness; food etc. 298; means etc. 632; subsidy, bounty, subvention.

ministry, ministration; subministration [obs.], accommodation.

relief, rescue; help at a dead lift; supernatural aid; deus ex machina [L.].

supplies, reënforcements, succors, contingents, recruits; support etc. (physical) 215; adjunct, ally etc. (helper) 711.

v. aid, assist, help, succor, lend one's aid; come to the aid of etc. n.; contribute, subscribe to; bring-, give-, furnish-, afford-, supply aid etc. n.; give-, stretch-, lend-, bear-, hold out- a -hand, -helping hand; give one a -lift,

250

−cast, −turn; take by the hand, take in tow; help a lame dog over a stile, lend wings to.

relieve, rescue; set up, set agoing, set on one's legs; bear−, pull- through; give new life to, be the making of; reënforce, recruit; set−, put−, push- forward; give -a lift, −a shove, −an impulse- to; promote, further, forward, advance; speed, expedite, quicken, hasten.

support, sustain, uphold, prop, hold up, bolster.

nourish, nurture, nurse, cradle, dry nurse, suckle, foster, cherish, put out to nurse; manure, cultivate, force; foment; feed−, fan- the flame.

serve; do service to, tender to, pander to; administer to, subminister to [*obs.*], minister to; tend, attend, wait on; take care of etc. 459; entertain; smooth the bed of sickness.

oblige, accommodate, consult the wishes of; humor, cheer, encourage.

second, stand by; back, −up; pay the piper, abet; work for, make interest for, stick up for [*colloq.*], stick by, take up the cudgels for; take up−, espouse−, adopt- the cause of; advocate, beat up for recruits, press into the service; squire [*colloq.*], give moral support to, keep in countenance, countenance, patronize, take up; lend one's name to; lend oneself to, lend one's countenance to; smile upon, shine upon; favor, befriend, take in hand, enlist under the banners of; side with etc. (*cooperate*) 709.

be of use to; subserve etc. (*instrument*) 631; benefit etc. 648; render a service etc. (*utility*) 644; conduce etc. (*tend*) 176.

adj. **aiding** etc. *v.;* auxiliary, adjuvant, helpful; coadjuvant etc. 709; subservient, ministrant, ancillary, accessary, accessory, subsidiary.

friendly, amicable, favorable, propitious, well-disposed; neighborly; obliging etc. (*benevolent*) 906; at one's beck.

adv. **with** *or* **by the aid of** etc. *n.;* on−, in- behalf of; in aid of, in the service of, in favor of, in the name of, in furtherance of; on account of; **for** the sake of, on the part of; *non obstante* [*L.*].

int. **help**! save us! to the rescue! this way! *à moi!* [*F.*].

708. Opposition

n. **opposition**, antagonism; oppugnancy, oppugnation [*rare*]; impugnation, impugnment, contrariousness [*rare*], contrariness, contrariety; contravention; counteraction etc. 179; counterplot.

resistance etc. 719; restraint etc. 751; hindrance etc. 706; absence of aid etc. 707.

cross fire, cross current, undercurrent, head wind.

clashing, collision, conflict, discord, want of harmony; filibuster, filibusterism.

competition, two of a trade, rivalry, emulation, race, contest; tug of war.

v. **oppose**, counteract, run counter to; withstand etc. (*resist*) 719; control etc. (*restrain*) 751; hinder etc. 706; antagonize, oppugn, fly in the face of, go dead against, kick against, cross, kick at, fall out with, fall foul of; set−, pit-against; face, confront, cope with; make a -stand, −dead set- against; set -oneself, −one's face- against; protest−, vote−, raise one's voice- against; disfavor, turn one's back upon; set at naught, slap in the face, slam the door in one's face.

thwart, be−, play- at cross-purposes; counterwork, countermine; over-thwart.

encounter, stem, breast; stem−, breast- the -tide, −current, −flood; buffet the waves; beat up against, make head against; grapple with; kick against the pricks etc. (*resist*) 719; contend with *or* against etc. 720; do battle with *or* against etc. (*warfare*) 722.

contradict, contravene; belie; go−, run−, beat−, militate- against; come in conflict with.

compete, emulate etc., 720; rival, spoil one's trade, force out, drive one out of business.

adj. **opposing**, opposed etc. *v.;* adverse, antagonistic, oppugnant, overthwart; contrary etc. 14; at variance etc. 24; at issue, at war with, in controversy with, in opposition; "agin' the government."

in hostile array, front to front, with crossed bayonets, at daggers drawn; up in arms; resistant etc. 719.

unfavorable, unpropitious, unfriendly, hostile, inimical, cross; filibusterous.

competitive, emulous, cut-throat; in rivalry with, in friendly rivalry.

adv. **against**, *versus* [*L.*], counter to, in conflict with, at cross-purposes, cross, contrariwise, unfavorably.

against the -grain, −current, −stream, −wind, −tide; with a head-wind; with the wind -ahead, −in one's teeth.

in spite, in despite, in defiance; in the -way, −teeth, −face- of; across; athwart, overthwart; where the shoe pinches; in one's teeth.

though etc. 30; even; *quand même* [*F.*]; *per contra* [*L.*].

709. Cooperation

n. **cooperation**; coadjuvancy, coadjutorship, coadjument [*rare*], coagency, coefficiency; concert, concurrence, complicity, coadministration, coaction; participation; union etc. 43; coefficacy; combination etc. 48; collusion, collusiveness.

   association, alliance, colleagueship, joint stock, copartnership, pool, gentleman's agreement; cartel; confederation etc. (*party*) 712; coalition, federation, fusion; a long pull a strong pull and a pull all together; logrolling, *quid pro quo* [*L.*], freemasonry.

   unanimity etc. (*assent*) 488; *esprit de corps* [*F.*], party spirit; clanship, partisanship; concord etc. 714; synergy, synergism.

v. **cooperate**, concur; conduce etc. 178; combine, coadjute, coadjuvate, coact [*rare*], unite one's efforts; keep–, draw–, pull–, club–, hand–, hold–, league–, band– be banded- together; pool; stand–, put- shoulder to shoulder; act in concert, join forces, fraternize, cling to one another; vote solidly, vote in blocks; conspire, concert, lay one's heads together; confederate, make an agreement with, be in league with; collude, understand one another, play into the hands of, hunt in couples.

   side with, take sides with, go along with, go hand in hand with, join hands with, make common cause with, strike in with, unite with, join with, mix oneself up with, take part with, cast in one's lot with; join–, enter into- partnership with; rally round, flock to, follow the lead of; come to, pass over to, come into the views of; be–, row–, sail- in the same boat; sail on the same tack.

   participate, be a party to, lend oneself to; chip in [*colloq.*], have a -hand in, –finger in the pie; take–, bear- part in; second etc. (*aid*) 707; take the part of, play the game of; espouse a -cause, –quarrel.

adj. **cooperating** etc. *v.*; in cooperation etc. *n.*, in league etc. (*party*) 712; coadjuvant, coadjutant, coadjutive, coactive, coalitional, hand in glove with; dyed in the wool; synergetic, synergistic.

   favorable to etc. 707; unopposed etc. 708.

adv. **unanimously**, as one man etc. 488; shoulder to shoulder, in cooperation with.

710. Opponent

n. **opponent**, antagonist, adversary, oppugnant [*rare*]; adverse party, opposition; enemy etc. 891; assailant.

   oppositionist, obstructive; brawler, wrangler, brangler [*rare*], disputant; filibuster, filibusterer, extremist, bitter-ender, irreconcilable, obstructionist, "willful men."

   malcontent; demagogue, reactionist; anarchist, anarch; Jacobin, Fenian, Sinn Feiner, Red; Industrial Workers of the World, I. W. W.

   rival, competitor, contestant, entrant; the field.

711. Auxiliary

n. **auxiliary**; recruit; assistant; adjuvant, adjutant; *ayudante* [*Sp. Amer.*], co-aid; adjunct; help, helper, helpmate, helping hand; colleague, partner, mate, confrère, cooperator; coadjuvant, coadjutant, coadjutator [*rare*], coadjutor, coadjutrix, collaborator.

   ally; friend etc. 890; confidant (*fem.* confidante), *fidus Achates* [*L.*], *alter ego* [*L.*], pal [*slang*], chum [*colloq.*], mate, comate.

   aide-de-camp [*F.*], secretary, clerk, associate, marshal; right-hand, right-hand man; candleholder, bottle-holder [*colloq.*]; handmaid; servant etc. 746.

   puppet, cat's-paw, creature, jack-straw, tool; jackal; *âme damnée* [*F.*]; satellite, adherent; parasite, dependent, client [*Rom. hist.*].

   confederate; complice [*archaic*], accomplice; accessory, –after the fact; *particeps criminis* [*L.*]; *socius criminis* [*L.*].

   upholder; votary; sectarian, sectary; seconder, backer, supporter, abettor, advocate, partisan, champion, patron, friend at court, mediator; angel [*slang*].

   friend in need, jack at a pinch, special providence, *deus ex machina* [*L.*], guardian angel, fairy godmother, tutelary genius.

712. Party

n. **party**, faction, denomination, class, communion, side, crew, team; band, horde, posse, phalanx; caste, family, gens [*Rom. hist.*], clan etc. 166. Confederates, Conservatives, Democrats, Federalists, Federals, Liberals, Libertarians, Radicals, Republicans, Socialists, Tories, Whigs etc.

   community, body, fellowship, solidarity; freemasonry; party spirit etc. (*cooperation*) 709; fraternity, sodality, confraternity, sorority; *familistère* [*F.*], familistery; brotherhood, sisterhood.

   fraternal order, Elks, Freemasons, Knights Templars, Odd Fellows, Knights of Pythias; Royal Arcanum etc.

   gang, tong [*Chin.*]; Camorra, Kuklux, Kuklux Klan, Molly Maguires, Fenians, Sinn Feiners,

Bolsheviki, Bolshevists, Industrial Workers of the World, I. W. W., Luddites; ring, machine; Tammany, –Hall; junto, cabal, camarilla, brigue [*obs.*].

clique, knot, circle, set, coterie; club, casino.

corporation, corporate body, guild; establishment, company, copartnership, partnership, cahoot [*slang*]; firm, house; joint concern, joint-stock company; cartel, combine [*colloq.*], trust; holding company, consortium, merger.

society, association; institute, institution; union; trades union; league, syndicate, alliance; *Verein, Bund, Zollverein* [*all Ger.*]; combination; *Turnverein* [*Ger.*]; *Liedertafel* etc. (*singing societies*) 416; league–, alliance- offensive and defensive; coalition; federation; confederation, confederacy.

staff; cast, *dramatis personae* [*L.*].

v. **unite**, join; band together; club together etc. (*cooperate*) 709; found a -firm, –house; cement-, form- a party etc. *n.;* associate etc. (*assemble*) 72; federate, federalize, go cahoots [*slang*], go fifty-fifty [*slang*].

adj. **in league**, in partnership, in alliance etc. *n.* bonded–, banded–, linked etc. (*joined*) 43- together; embattled; confederated, federative, joint, corporate, organized, enleagued, leagued, syndicated; clubbable *or* clubable, fraternal, Masonic, institutional, denominational; cliquish, cliquy *or* cliquey; union-made.

adv. **side by side**, hand in hand, shoulder to shoulder, *en masse* [*F.*], in the same boat.

713. Discord

n. **discord**, disaccord, dissidence, dissonance; disagreement etc. 24; jar, clash, break, shock; jarring, jostling etc. *v.;* screw loose.

variance, difference, dissension, misunderstanding, cross-purposes, odds, *brouillerie* [*F.*]; division, split, rupture, disruption, division in the camp, house divided against itself, "rift within the lute" [*Tennyson*], disunion, breach; schism etc. (*dissent*) 489; feud, faction.

polemics; litigation; strife etc. (*contention*) 720; warfare etc. 722; outbreak, open rupture, breaking off of negotiations, recall of ambassadors, declaration of war.

quarrel, dispute, tiff, bicker, *tracasserie* [*F.*], squabble, altercation, barney [*slang*], *démêlé* [*F.*], snarl, spat [*colloq. or dial.*], towrow [*Scot. & dial Eng.*], words, high words; wrangling etc. *v.;* jangle, brabble [*archaic*], brabblement [*archaic*], cross questions and crooked answers, snip-snap [*rare*]; family jars.

broil, brawl, row [*colloq.*], racket, hubbub, rixation [*obs.*]; embroilment, embranglement, imbroglio, fracas, breach of the peace, piece of work, scrimmage, rumpus [*colloq.*]; breeze [*colloq.*], squall; riot, disturbance etc. (*disorder*) 59; commotion etc. (*agitation*) 315; bear garden, Donnybrook.

subject of dispute, ground of quarrel, battle ground, disputed point; bone -of contention, –to pick; apple of discord, *casus belli* [*L.*]; question at issue etc. (*subject of inquiry*) 461; vexed question, *vexata quaestio* [*L.*], brand of discord.

contentiousness etc. *adj.;* enmity etc. 889; hate etc. 898; troublous times; cat-and-dog life; Kilkenny cats; disputant etc. 710; strange bedfellows.

v. **disagree**; be discordant etc. *adj.;* disaccord, come amiss etc. 24; clash, jar, jostle, pull different ways, conflict, have no measures with, misunderstand one another; live like cat and dog; differ; dissent etc. 489; have a bone to pick with, have a crow to pluck with.

quarrel, fall out, dispute; litigate; controvert etc. (*deny*) 536; squabble, tiff, spat, altercate, row [*colloq.*], brabble, wrangle, jangle, brangle, bicker, nag; spar etc. (*contend*) 720; have words with etc. *n.;* fall foul of.

split; break–, break squares–, part company- with; declare war, try conclusions; join-, put in- issue; pick a quarrel, fasten a quarrel on; sow-, stir up- dissension etc. *n.;* embroil, entangle, disunite, widen the breach; rub one's fur the wrong way; get one all het up [*dial.*]; get one hot under the collar [*colloq.*]; set at odds, set together by the ears; set-, pit- against.

get into hot water, fish in troubled waters, brawl; kick up a -row, –dust [*colloq.*]; turn the house out of window.

adj. **discordant**, dissident; disagreeing etc. *v.;* out of tune, dissonant, harsh, grating, jangling, unmelodious, inharmonious, ajar; on bad terms, dissentient etc. 489; unreconciled, unpacified; inconsistent, contradictory, incongruous, discrepant.

quarrelsome, unpacific; gladiatorial, controversial, polemic, disputatious; factious; litigious, litigant.

at strife, at odds, at loggerheads, at daggers drawn, at variance, at issue, at cross-purposes, at sixes and sevens, at feud, at high words; up in arms, heated, het up [*dial.*], hot under the collar [*colloq.*], together by the ears, in hot water, embroiled; torn, disunited.

714. Concord

n. **concord**, accord, harmony, symphony; homologue, homology, correspondence; agreement etc. 23; sympathy etc. (*love*) 897; response; union, unison, unity; bonds of harmony; peace etc. 721; unanimity etc. (*assent*) 488; league etc. 712; happy family.

rapprochement [*F.*], reunion; amity etc. (*friendship*) 888; alliance, *entente cordiale* [*F.*], good understanding, conciliation, arbitration.

peacemaker, intercessor, interceder, propitiator, mediator.

v. **agree** etc. 23; accord, harmonize with, blend in with; fraternize; be concordant etc. *adj.;* go hand in hand; run parallel etc. (*concur*) 178; understand one another; pull together etc. (*cooperate*) 709; put up one's horses together, sing in chorus.

side with, sympathize with, go with, chime in with, fall in with; come round [*colloq.*]; be pacified etc. 723; assent etc. 488; enter into the -ideas, -feelings- of; reciprocate.

hurler avec les loups [*F.*]; go-, swim- with the stream; get on the band wagon [*slang*].

smooth, pour oil on the troubled waters; keep in good humor, render accordant, put in tune; come to an understanding, meet halfway; keep the peace, remain at peace; mediate, intercede.

adj. **concordant**, congenial; agreeing etc. *v.;* in accord etc. *n.;* harmonious, united, cemented; banded together etc. 712; allied; friendly etc. 888; fraternal; conciliatory; at one with; of one mind etc. (*assent*) 488.

at peace, in still water; tranquil etc. (*pacific*) 721.

adv. **unanimously**, without a dissentient voice; with one voice etc. (*assent*) 488; in concert with, hand in hand; on one's side.

int. make it unanimous! are you with us?

715. Defiance

n. **defiance**; daring etc. *v.;* dare, defial, defi [*slang*]; "dare, dare, and double-dare" [*child's challenge*]; challenge, cartel; threat etc. 909; war cry, war whoop.

v. **defy**, dare, beard; brave etc. (*courage*) 861; bid defiance to; bite the thumb at; set at defiance, set at naught; hurl defiance at; dance the war dance; snap the fingers at, laugh to scorn; disobey etc. 742.

show -fight, -one's teeth, -a bold front; bluster, look big, stand with arms akimbo; double-, shake- the fist; threaten etc. 909.

challenge, call out; throw-, fling- down the -gauntlet, -gage, -glove.

adj. **defiant**; defying etc. *v.;* with arms akimbo; rebellious, bold, insolent, reckless, contemptuous, greatly daring, regardless of consequences.

adv. **in defiance of**, in the teeth of; under one's very nose; in open rebellion.

int. do your worst! come if you dare! come on! just try it! marry come up! [*archaic or dial.*], hoity toity!

716. Attack

n. **attack**; assault, -and battery; onset, onslaught, charge.

base of operations, point of attack; echelon; open order; close formation.

aggression, offense; incursion, inroad, invasion; irruption; outbreak; bucking, estapade [*manège*], ruade [*F.*], kicking, kick; punch etc. (*impulse*) 276; coup de main [*F.*]; sally, sortie, camisade *or* camisado [*archaic*], raid, foray; run at, run against; dead set at.

storm, storming; boarding, escalade; siege, investment, obsession [*obs.*], bombardment, cannonade, barrage; zero hour.

battue [*F.*], razzia, dragonnade *or* dragoonade; devastation etc. 162; éboulement [*F.*].

fire, volley; direct-, ricochet-, plunging-, rolling-, horizontal-, vertical-, platoon-, file-fire; fusilade; fire of demolition, percussion fire; sharpshooting, broadside; raking-, cross-fire; volley of grapeshot, feu d'enfer [*F.*].

cut, thrust, lunge, pass, passado [*obs.*], stoccado *or* stoccata [*archaic*], carte (*or* quarte) and tierce, home thrust; coup de bec [*F.*].

assailant, aggressor, invader; sharpshooter, dead shot, fusilier, dragoon, Uhlan.

v. **attack**, assault, assail; set upon, fall upon; charge, impugn, break a lance with, enter the lists.

show fight, come on; assume-, take- the offensive; be-, become- the aggressor; strike the first blow, throw the first stone at, fire the first shot; lift a hand-, draw the sword- against; take up the cudgels; advance-, march- against; march upon, invade, harry.

strike at, poke at, thrust at; aim-, deal- a blow at; give-, fetch- one a -blow, -kick; have a -cut, -shot, -fling, -shy- at; be down upon, pounce upon; fall foul of, light into [*colloq.*], pitch into [*colloq.*], launch out against; bait, slap on the face; make a -thrust, -pass, -set, -dead set- at; bear down upon.

close with, come to close quarters, bring to bay, come to blows.

ride full tilt against; let fly at, dash at, run a tilt at, rush at, tilt at, run at, fly at, hawk at, have at, let out at; make a -dash, -rush at; attack tooth and nail; strike home; drive–, press- one hard; be hard upon, run down, strike at the root of.

lay about one, run amuck.

fire upon, fire at, fire a shot at; draw a bead on; shoot at, pop at, level at, let off a gun at; open fire, pepper, bombard, shell, pour a broadside into; fire a volley, fire red-hot shot; spring a mine.

stone, lapidate, pelt; throw - a stone, –stones - at; hurl -at, –against, –at the head of; rock.

beset, besiege, beleaguer; lay siege to, invest, open the trenches, plant a battery, sap, mine; storm, board, scale the walls, go over the top.

cut and thrust, bayonet, give one the bayonet; butt; kick, strike etc. (*impulse*) 276; horsewhip, whip etc. (*punish*) 972.

adj. **attacking** etc. *v.;* aggressive, offensive, incursive, invasive, irruptive, obsidional.

up in arms.

adv. **on the offensive**, on the warpath, amuck, amok. over the top; at bay.

int. "up and at them!"

717. Defense

n. **defense** *or* defence, protection, guard, ward; shielding etc. *v.;* propugnation [*obs.*]; preservation etc. 670; guardianship.

self-defense, self-preservation; resistance etc. 719.

safeguard etc. (*safety*) 664; screen etc. (*shelter*) 666, (*concealment*) 350; fortification; munition, muniment; bulwark, fosse, trench, mine, countermine, dugout; moat, ditch, intrenchment *or* entrenchment, vallation, rampart, scarp, escarp, counterscarp, vanfoss; dike *or* dyke; parapet, sunk fence, haha, embankment, mound, mole, bank; earthwork, fieldwork; fence, wall, dead wall, contravallation *or* countervallation; paling etc. (*inclosure*) 232; palisade, stockade, stoccado [*obs.*], laager [*S. Africa*], sangar [*India*]; barrier, barricade; boom; portcullis, *chevaux de frise* [*F.*]; abatis *or* abattis, barbed wire entanglements, vallum [*Rom. antiq.*], circumvallation, merlon, battlement, glacis; casemate; buttress, abutment; shore etc. (*support*) 215.

breastwork, banquette, mantelet *or* mantlet, tenaille *or* tenail, ravelin, curtain, demilune, half-moon; bastion, demibastion, redan; vauntmure [*rare*], faussebraie *or* faussebraye, advanced work, hornwork, lunette, outwork; barbican, redoubt, sconce, fortalice; lines.

machicolation, bartizan, loophole, balistraria [*ancient fortification*]; postern gate, sally port.

stronghold, hold, fastness; asylum etc. (*refuge*) 666; keep, donjon, citadel, capitol, castle; tower, –of strength; fortress, propugnaculum, fort, kila [*India*]; barracoon, barrack; pah *or* pa [*N. Z.*]; peel, peel tower, peelhouse; rath [*Ir. antiq.*]; martello tower, blockhouse, wooden walls.

[protective devices] buffer, fender, cowcatcher; apron, mask, gauntlet, thimble; armor *or* armour, shield, buckler, scutum [*Rom. antiq.*], target, targe [*archaic*], aegis, breastplate, cuirass, backplate, habergeon, mail, coat of mail, brigandine, hauberk, lorica, helm [*archaic*], armet, basinet *or* bassinet, sallet *or* salade, greave, jambe, heaume, morion, cabasset, beaver, visor *or* vizor; face guard, helmet, casque, casquetel, siege cap, headpiece; steel helmet, tin -helmet, –hat [*soldiers' cant*]; camail, neckguard; *Pickelhaube* [*Ger.*]; spiked helmet, shako etc. (*dress*) 225; bearskin; vambrace, rerebrace, cubitière; sollerets, pédieux; panoply, caparison, housings; chamfron *or* chamfrain; truncheon etc. (*weapon*) 727; carapace, shell; spines, needles.

defender, protector; Defender of the Faith, *fidei defensor* [*L.*], guardian etc. (*safety*) 664; bodyguard, champion; knight-errant, Paladin; propugnator *or* propugner *or* propugnor [*obs.*]; picket; garrison.

v. **defend**, forfend *or* forefend [*archaic*], fend; shield, screen, shroud; engarrison, garrison, man; fence round etc. (*circumscribe*) 229; fence, intrench *or* entrench; arm, harness [*archaic*], accouter *or* accoutre; guard etc. (*keep safe*) 664; guard against; take care of etc. (*vigilance*) 459; bear harmless; fend–, keep–, ward–, beat- off; hinder etc. 706.

repel, parry, propugn [*obs.*], put to flight; give a warm reception to [*ironical*]; hold - keep- at -bay, –arm's length.

resist invasion, stand siege; be–, stand–, act- on the defensive; show fight; maintain–, stand- one's ground; stand by; hold one's own; bear–, stand- the brunt; fall back upon, hold, stand in the gap.

adj. **defending** etc. *v.;* defensive; mural; armed, –at all points, –cap-a-pie, –to the teeth; panoplied; accoutered *or* accoutred, harnessed [*archaic*], "in complete steel" [*Hamlet*]; iron-plated, iron-clad; loopholed, castellated, machicolated, casemated; defended etc. *v.;* proof against, ball-proof, bullet-proof; protective.

adv. **defensively**; on the defensive; in defense; in self-defense; at bay, *pro aris et focis* [*L.*].

int. **no surrender**! *"ils ne passeront pas!"* "they shall not pass!" [*the French at Verdun*].

718. Retaliation

n. **retaliation**, reprisal, talion [*rare*], retort; counterstroke, counterblast, counterplot, counterproject; retribution, *lex talionis* [*L.*]; reciprocation etc. (*reciprocity*) 12.

requital, desert; tit for tat, give and take, blow for blow, *quid pro quo* [*L.*], a Roland for an Oliver, measure for measure, diamond cut diamond, an eye for an eye, boomerang, the biter bit, a game at which two can play; reproof valiant, retort courteous.

recrimination etc. (*accusation*) 938; revenge etc. 919; compensation etc. 30; reaction etc. (*recoil*) 277.

v. **retaliate**, retort, turn upon; pay, pay off, pay back; pay in -one's own, –the same- coin; cap, match; reciprocate etc. 148; turn the tables upon, return the compliment; give a *quid pro quo* etc. *n.,* give as much as one takes; give as good as was sent; exchange blows; give and take, exchange fisticuffs; be quits, be even with; pay off old scores.

serve one right, be hoist on one's own petard, throw a stone in one's own garden, catch a Tartar.

adj. **retaliating** etc. *v.;* retaliatory, retaliative, retributive, recriminatory, reciprocal; talionic [*rare*].

adv. **in retaliation**; *en revanche* [*F.*].

719. Resistance

n. **resistance**, stand, front, oppugnation [*rare*], oppugnance, oppugnancy; opposition etc. 708; renitency, renitence, reluctance [*archaic*], reluctation [*rare*], recalcitrance *or* recalcitrancy, recalcitration; repugnance, repulsion; kicking etc. *v.*

repulse, rebuff, snub.

insurrection etc. (*disobedience*) 742; strike; turn-out [*colloq.*], lockout; barring-out; *levée en masse* [*F.*], *Jacquerie* [*F. hist.*]; rebellion; boycott; riot etc. (*disorder*) 59.

v. **resist**; not submit etc. 725; repugn [*obs.*], reluctate [*rare*], oppugn, withstand; stand up-, strive-, bear up-, be proof-, make head-against; stand, –firm, –fast, –one's ground, –the brunt of, –out; hold -one's ground, –one's own, –out; stick it out [*colloq.*].

face, confront, breast the -wave, –current; stem the -tide, –torrent; grapple with; show a bold

front etc. (*courage*) 861; present a front, make a stand, take one's stand.

oppose etc. 708; kick, –against; recalcitrate, kick against the pricks; fly in the face of; lift the hand against etc. (*attack*) 716; withstand -an attack, –a siege, –the onset; rise up in arms etc. (*war*) 722; strike, turn out; draw up a round robin etc. (*remonstrate*) 932; put one's foot down; boycott; revolt etc. (*disobey*) 742; make a riot.

prendre le mors aux dents [*F.*], take the bit between the teeth; sell one's life dearly, die hard, keep at bay; repel, repulse.

adj. **resisting** etc. *v.;* oppugnant, resistive, resistant; refractory etc. (*disobedient*) 742; repugnant; recalcitrant, renitent, repulsive, repellent; up in arms.

proof against; unconquerable etc. (*strong*) 159; stubborn, unconquered; indomitable etc. (*persevering*) 604a; unyielding etc. (*obstinate*) 606.

int. **hands off**! keep off!

never say die! stick it! [*colloq.*]; show what you're made of! give 'em hell! [*colloq.*]; "up, Guards, and at them!" [Wellington—*at Waterloo, as alleged*].

720. Contention

n. **contention**, strife; contest, contestation; struggle; belligerency; opposition etc. 708.

controversy, polemics; debate etc. (*discussion*) 476; war of words, logomachy, litigation; paper war; high words etc. (*quarrel*) 713; sparring etc. *v.*

competition, rivalry; corrivalry, corrivalship; agonism [*obs.*], *concours* [*F.*], match, race, tug of war, horse racing, heat, dash, steeple chase, point-to-point race, handicap; regatta; field day; sham fight, Derby day; turf, sporting, bullfight, tauromachy [*rare*], gymkhana [*orig. Anglo-Indian*]; boat race, torpids [*Oxford Univ.*].

pugilism, boxing, fisticuffs, spar, mill [*cant*], set-to [*colloq.*], round, bout, event; prize fighting; quarterstaff, single stick; gladiatorship, gymnastics; wrestling; catch-as-catch-can–, Greco-Roman (or Graeco-Roman)–, Cornish–, Westmorland and Cumberland- style [of wrestling]; jujutsu (*also* jujitsu, jiujutsu, jiujitsu), *samo* [*Jap.*], *kooshti* [*Hind.*]; karate; athletics, athletic sports; games of skill etc. 840.

fracas etc. (*discord*) 713; clash of arms; tussle, scuffle, broil, fray; affray, affrayment [*obs.*]; velitation [*obs.*]; luctation [*rare*], colluctation [*obs.*], shindy [Brit. *colloq.*], brigue [*obs.*], brabble, scramble, *mêlée* [*F.*], scrimmage, stramash [*dial. or slang*], free-for-all [*cant*]; free–, stand up–, hand to hand–, running- fight.

conflict, skirmish; encounter, rencounter, rencontre, collision, affair, brush, fight; sharp contest, hard knocks; battle, –royal; combat, action, engagement, just *or* joust, tournament; tilt, tilting; tourney, lists; pitched battle; guerrilla (*or* guerilla)–, irregular- warfare; bush-fighting.

deeds–, feats- of arms; pugnacity; combativeness etc. *adj.*; bone of contention etc. 713.

death struggle, struggle for life or death, Armageddon.

naval engagement, naumachia *or* naumachy, sea fight.

duel, duello [*rare*], single combat, *monomachia* [*L.*] *or* monomachy, satisfaction, *passage d'armes* [*F.*], passage of arms, affair of honor; triangular duel; hostile meeting, digladiation [*archaic*]; appeal to arms etc. (*warfare*) 722.

v. **contend**; contest, strive, struggle, scramble, wrestle; spar, square [*colloq.*]; exchange -blows, –fisticuffs; fib [*slang, Eng.*], jostle *or* justle, tussle, tilt, box, stave [*obs. or dial.*], fence; skirmish; pickeer [*obs.*]; fight etc. (*war*) 722; wrangle etc. (*quarrel*) 713.

contend etc. with; grapple–, engage–, close–, buckle [*obs.*]–, bandy–, try conclusions–, have a brush etc. *n.* –, tilt- with; encounter, fall foul of, pitch into [*colloq.*], clapperclaw [*archaic or dial.*], run a tilt at; oppose etc. 708; reluct.

compete–, cope–, vie–, race- with; outvie, emulate, rival; run a race.

contend etc. for, stipulate for, stickle for; insist upon, make a point of.

join issue, come to blows; be at–, fall to–, go to- loggerheads; set to, come to the scratch, pull a gun [*slang*], exchange shots, measure swords, meet hand to hand; take up the -cudgels, –glove, –gauntlet; tourney, just *or* joust, enter the lists; couch one's lance; give satisfaction; appeal to arms etc. (*warfare*) 722.

lay about one; break the peace.

adj. **contending** etc. *v.*; at loggerheads, at war, at issue.

contentious, combative, bellicose, belligerent, unpeaceful; warlike etc. 722; quarrelsome etc. 901; pugnacious, pugilistic; tauromachian *or* tauromachic [*rare*]; gladiatorial.

athletic, gymnastic, palaestral *or* palestral, palaestric *or* palestric [*rare*]; competitive, rival.

721. Peace

n. **peace**; amity etc. (*friendship*) 888; pacifism; harmony etc. (*concord*) 714; tranquility etc. (*quiescence*) 265; truce etc. (*pacification*) 723; pipe of peace, calumet.

piping time of peace, quiet life; neutrality.

v. **be at peace**; keep the peace etc. (*concord*) 714; make peace etc. 723; pacify; be a pacifist.

adj. **pacific**; peaceable, peaceful; calm, tranquil, untroubled, halcyon; bloodless; neutral, pacifistic, "too proud to fight" [Woodrow Wilson].

722. Warfare

n. **warfare**; fighting etc. *v.*; hostilities; war, arms, the sword; Mars, Bellona, grim-visaged war, *horrida bella* [*L.*]; bloodshed.

appeal to -arms, –the sword; ordeal–, wager- of battle; *ultima ratio regum* [*L.*], arbitrament of the sword, declaration of war.

battle array, campaign, crusade, expedition; mobilization; state of siege; battlefield etc. (*arena*) 728; warpath.

art of war, rules of war, the war game, tactics, strategy, castrametation; generalship, soldiership; military evolutions, ballistics, gunnery; aviation; chivalry; gunpowder, shot, shell, poison gas.

battle, conflict etc. (*contention*) 720; service, campaigning, active service, tented field; kriegspiel *or* Kriegsspiel [*Ger.*], fiery cross, trumpet, clarion, bugle, pibroch, slogan; war cry, war whoop; battle cry, beat of drum, *rappel* [*F.*], tom-tom; word of command; password, watchword; *passage d'armes* [*F.*].

war to the -death, –knife; *guerre à -mort, –outrance* [*F.*]; open–, trench–, guerrilla (*or* guerilla)–, internecine–, civil- war (*or* warfare).

war medal, military medal, Congressional medal, Victoria Cross, V. C., *croix de guerre* [*F.*], *médaille militaire* [*F.*], iron cross [*Ger.*].

war news, war bulletin, war extra; war correspondent.

v. **arm**; prepare for war; raise–, mobilize- troops; raise up in arms; take up the udgels etc. 720; take up–, fly to–, appeal to- -arms, –the sword; draw–, unsheathe- the sword; dig up the -hatchet, –tomahawk.

war, make war, go to war, declare war, wage war, "let slip the dogs of war" [*Julius Caesar*]; cry havoc; kindle–, light- the torch of war; raise one's banner, send round the fiery cross, hoist the black flag; throw–, fling- away the scabbard; take the field; take the law into one's own hands; do–, give–, join–, engage in–, go to-battle; flesh one's sword; set to, fall to, engage, measure swords with, draw the trigger, cross swords; come to -blows, –close quarters; fight; combat; contend etc. 720; battle with, break a lance with.

serve; enroll, enlist; see–, be on- -service, –active service; campaign; wield the sword, shoulder a musket, smell powder, be under fire; spill blood, imbrue the hands in blood; be on the warpath.

carry on -war, –hostilities; keep the field; fight the good fight; take by storm; go over the top [*World War I*]; fight -it out, –like devils, –one's way, –hand to hand; cut one's way -out, –through; sell one's life dearly.

adj. **armed**, –to the teeth, –cap-a-pie; sword in hand; contending, contentious etc. 720; in–, under–, up in- arms; at war with; bristling with arms; in battle array, in open arms, in the field; embattled; battled.

warlike, belligerent, combative, armigerous, bellicose, martial, unpacific, unpeaceful; military, militant; soldier like, soldierly, chivalrous; strategical, civil, internecine; irregular, guerrilla *or* guerilla.

adv. *flagrante bello* [*L.*], in the thick of the fray, in the cannon's mouth; at the sword's point, at the point of the bayonet.

int. **to arms**! *vae victis!* [*L.*] to your tents O Israel! *c'est la guerre!* [*F.*].

723. Pacification

n. **pacification**, conciliation; reconciliation, reconcilement, shaking of hands, calumet, peace pipe; accommodation, arrangement, adjustment; terms, compromise; amnesty, deed of release.

peace offering; olive branch; calumet, –of peace; overture, preliminaries of peace.

truce, armistice; suspension of -arms, –hostilities; truce of God; breathing time; convention; *modus vivendi* [*L.*]; flag of truce, white flag, *parlementaire* [*F.*], cartel.

hollow truce, *pax in bello* [*L.*]; drawn battle.

v. **pacify**, tranquilize, compose; allay etc. (*moderate*) 174; reconcile, propitiate, placate, conciliate, meet halfway, hold out the olive branch, heal the breach, make peace, restore harmony, bring to terms.

make up a quarrel; settle–, arrange–, accommodate- -matters, –differences; set straight; *tantas componere lites* [*L.*]; come to -an understanding, –terms; bridge over, hush up; make it up, make matters up; shake hands; mend one's fences.

raise a siege; put up–, sheathe- the sword; bury the hatchet, lay down one's arms, turn swords into plowshares; smoke the calumet, close the temple of Janus; keep the peace etc. (*concord*) 714; be pacified etc.; come round.

adj. **conciliatory**, pacificatory; composing etc. *v.*; pacified etc. *v.*; accommodative.

724. Mediation

n. **mediation**, mediatorship, mediatization, mediatorialism; intervention, interposition, interference, intermeddling, intercession; parley, negotiation, arbitration; flag of truce etc. 723; good offices, peace offering; diplomatics [*rare*], diplomacy; compromise etc. 774.

mediator, intercessor, peacemaker, make-peace, negotiator, go-between; diplomatist etc. (*consignee*) 758; moderator; propitiator; umpire, arbitrator, referee.

v. **mediate**, mediatize; intercede, interpose, interfere, intervene; step in, negotiate; meet halfway; arbitrate, propitiate; agree to arbitration; submit; *componere lites* [*L.*].

adj. **mediatory**, mediatorial, negotiable; mediating etc. *v.*; propitiatory, diplomatic.

725. Submission

n. **submission**, yielding, acquiescence, compliance, submittal, submissiveness, deference, nonresistance; obedience etc. 743.

surrender, cession, capitulation, resignation, backdown [*colloq.*]; passing under the yoke, laying down one's arms, delivering up the keys (of the city etc.), handing over one's sword.

obeisance, homage, kneeling, genuflexion, curtsy *or* curtsey, kotow *or* kowtow [*Chinese*], salaam *or* salam [*Oriental*], prostration.

v. **submit**, succumb, yield, bend, stoop, accede, relent, resign, defer to.

surrender, –at discretion; cede, capitulate, come to terms, retreat, beat a retreat; lay down–, deliver up- one's arms; lower–, haul down–, strike- one's -flag, –colors; draw in one's horns etc. (*humility*) 879; give -way, –ground, –in, –up; cave in [*colloq.*]; suffer judgment by default; bend, –to one's yoke, –before the storm; reel back; bend–, knuckle- -down, –to, –under; knock under.

humble oneself; eat -dirt, –crow, –the leek, –humble pie; bite–, lick- the dust; be–, fall- at one's feet; crouch before, throw oneself at the feet of; swallow the -leek, –pill; kiss the rod; turn the other cheek; *avaler les couleuvres* [*F.*], gulp down.

pocket the affront; make the best of, make a virtue of necessity; grin and abide, grin and bear it, shrug the shoulders, resign oneself; submit with a good grace etc. (*bear with*) 826.

yield obeisance; obey etc. 743; kneel to, bow to, pay homage to, cringe to, truckle to; bend the -neck, –knee; kneel, fall on one's knees, bow submission, curtsy *or* curtsey, kotow *or* kowtow [*Chinese*].

adj. **submissive**, resigned, crouching, prostrate; downtrodden; surrendering etc. *v.;* down on one's marrowbones [*slang*]; on one's bended knee; nonresisting, unresisting; pliant etc. (*soft*) 324; humble etc. 879; undefended.

untenable, indefensible, insupportable, unsupportable.

726. Combatant

n. **combatant**; disputant, controversialist, polemic, litigant, belligerent; competitor, rival, corrival; fighter, assailant; champion, Paladin; moss-trooper, swashbuckler, fire eater, duelist, swordsman, *sabreur* [*F.*], *beau sabreur* [*F.*]; athlete, wrestler, boxer.

bully, bludgeon man, rough, rowdy, ruffian, tough [*colloq., U. S.*], gunman [*colloq.*], Thug *or* thug; terrorist etc. 887; fighting man, prize fighter, pugilist, bruiser, the fancy [*now rare*], gladiator, fighting-cock, gamecock.

soldier, warrior, brave, man at arms, guardsman, *gendarme* [*F.*]; campaigner, veteran; redcoat, military man, Rajput; armiger, esquire, knight; Amazon.

Janizary *or* Janissary; myrmidon; Mameluke *or* Mamaluke, spahi *or* spahee, bashi-bazouk [*Turk.*], Cossack, Croat, Pandor; irregular, free lance, franc-tireur, tirailleur, guerrilla *or* guerilla, *condottiere* [*It.*], mercenary; bushwhacker, companion; Hessian.

private, –soldier; Tommy Atkins [*Brit.*], doughboy [*slang*], grunt [*slang*], G.I. [*slang*], rank and file, peon, sepoy [*India*], *légionnaire* [*F.*], legionary, food for powder, fodder for cannon, cannon fodder, *Kannonenfutter* [*Ger.*]; spearman, pikeman; archer, bowman; halberdier; musketeer, carabineer, rifleman, sharpshooter, jäger *or* yager, skirmisher; grenadier, fusileer, infantryman, foot soldier, footman [*rare*], light infantryman, chasseur, zouave; artilleryman, gunner, cannoneer, bombardier [*hist.*], matross [*obs.*]; engineer; sapper, –and miner; cavalryman, trooper, sowar [*India*], dragoon; light–, heavy- dragoon; heavy, cuirassier, hussar, lancer; recruit, rookie [*slang*], conscript, drafted man, enlisted man.

officer etc. (*commander*) 745; subaltern, ensign, standard bearer.

horse and foot; cavalry, horse, light horse, mounted rifles; infantry, foot, light infantry, rifles; artillery, horse artillery, field artillery, gunners; military train.

armed force, troops, soldiery, military, forces, Sabaoth, host, the army, standing army, regulars, the line, troops of the line, militia, national guard, state guard, bodyguard, yeomanry, volunteers, trainband, fencibles [*hist.*]; auxiliary, *bersagliere* [*It.*]; garde -nationale, –royale [*F.*]; minuteman [*Am. hist.*]; auxiliary–, reserve- forces; reserves, *posse comitatus* [*L.*], posse; guards, yeomen of the guard, beefeaters [*Eng.*], life guards, household troops, Horse Guards, Foot Guards; Swiss guards.

levy, draft *or* draught; raw levies, awkward squad; Landwehr, Landsturm.

army, *crops d'armée* [*F.*], army corps; host, division, battalia [*rare*], sotnia [*Russ.*], column, wing, detachment, garrison, flying column, brigade, regiment, corps, battalion, squadron, company, battery, subdivision, section, platoon, squad; picket, guard, rank, file; legion, phalanx, cohort, maniple, manipulus [*Rom. hist.*]; cloud of skirmishers.

war horse, charger, destrer *or* destrier [*archaic*].

navy, first line of defense, wooden walls, naval forces, fleet, flotilla, armada, squadron; man-of-war's man etc. (*sailor*) 269; marines.

man-of-war, line-of-battle ship, ship of the line, battleship, warship, ironclad, war vessel, war castle, H.M.S., U.S.S.; superdreadnought, dreadnought, cruiser; armored–, protected-cruiser; torpedo-boat, –destroyer; destroyer, torpedo-catcher, gunboat; submarine, submersible, U-boat; submarine chaser; mine layer, sweeper; turret ship, ram, monitor, floating battery; first-rate, frigate, sloop of war, corvet *or* corvette; bomb vessel; flagship, guard ship, privateer; troopship, transport, tender, store-ship, catamaran [*obs.*], fire boat.

aeroplane, airplane, *avion* [*F.*], Fokker, dirigible, blimp; zeppelin etc. (*aeronautics*) 273.

727. Arms

n. **arms**, arm, weapon, deadly weapon; armament, armature; panoply, stand of arms; armor etc. (*defense*) 717; armory etc. (*store*) 636; *apparatus belli* [*L.*]; gunnery; ballistics etc. (*propulsion*) 284.

side arms, *armes blanches* [*F.*], sword; good–, trusty–, naked- sword; cold steel, naked steel,

steel, blade, brand [*archaic*]; broadsword, Toledo, Ferrara, claymore, glaive [*archaic*] *or* glave [*obs.*]; saber *or* sabre, cutlass, hanger, bilbo, falchion, scimitar *or* cimeter [*obs.*], whinyard [*obs.*], rapier, tuck [*hist.*], foil, yataghan (*also* ataghan, attaghan); dagger, poniard, baselard, dirk, stiletto, katar *or* kuttar [*India*], stylet; skean, skean dhu [*Scot.*]; creese *or* kris; dudgeon [*archaic*], bowie knife; bayonet, sword bayonet, sword stick.

ax *or* **axe**, battle ax, Lochaber ax, adaga, poleax *or* poleaxe, halberd *or* halbert, gisarme, tomahawk, bill, black bill, brown bill, partisan.

spear, lance, pike, spontoon, assagai *or* assegai, javelin, jereed *or* jerid, dart, shaft, bolt, reed, arrow; harpoon, gaff, eelspear; weet-weet, womerah, throwing stick, throw stick, boomerang; oxgoad, ankus.

club, war club, waddy [*Austral.*], mace, truncheon, staff, bludgeon, cudgel, shillalah *or* shillelagh, handstaff, quarterstaff; bat, cane, stick, walking-stick, knuckle duster; billy, life-preserver, blackjack, sandbag.

bow, crossbow, arbalest, ballista *or* balista, balister [*obs.*], trebuchet *or* trebucket, catapult, sling; battering-ram etc. (*impulse*) 276.

firearms; gun, piece; artillery, ordnance; siege–, battering- train; park, battery; cannon, gun of position, heavy gun, fieldpiece, field gun, mountain gun, siege gun, seacoast gun; mortar, howitzer, carronade, culverin, basilisk [*obs.*]; falconet, jingal swivel, swivel gun, pedrero *or* pederero, *bouche à feu* [*F.*], smooth bore, rifled cannon; Armstrong–, Lancaster–, Paixhans–, Whitworth–, Parrott–, Krupp–, Vickers–, Benet-Mercié–, Gatling–, Maxim–, machine- gun; pompom, *mitrailleuse* [*F.*]; "seventy-five" [*French rapid-fire 75 mm. field gun*]; Lewis gun; auto-rifle, ten-pounder; bazooka; flame-thrower, *Flammenwerfer* [*Ger.*], *lance-flamme* [*F.*].

small arms; musketry; musket, firelock, fowling piece, rifle, fusil [*obs. or hist.*], escopette *or* escopet, carbine, blunderbuss, musketoon, Brown Bess, matchlock, harquebus *or* arquebus, caliver, hackbut *or* hagbut, shotgun, petronel [*hist.*]; small bore; breechloader, muzzle-loader; gunflint, gunlock; Minié–, Enfield–, Flobert–, Westley Richards–, Snider–, Martini-Henry–, Lee-Metford–, Lee-Enfield–, Mauser–, Mannlicher–, Springfield–, magazine- rifle; needle gun, *chassepot* [*F.*]; wind gun, air gun; automatic -gun, –pistol; automatic; revolver, repeater; shooting iron [*slang*],

shooter [*colloq.*], six-shooter, gun, pistol, pistolet [*obs.*].

missile, bolt, projectile, shot, ball; grape; grape–, canister–, bar–, cannon–, langrage *or* langrel–, round–, chain- shot; slung shot; shrapnel, *mitraille* [*F.*], grenade, hand grenade, rifle grenade; shell, high-explosive shell, *obus explosif* [*F.*], bomb, depth bomb, smoke bomb, gas bomb; bullet; dumdum–, man-stopping–, explosive–, expanding- bullet; petard; infernal machine, torpedo; carcass, rocket; congreve, –rocket; slug, stone, rock, brickbat.

thunderbolt, levin- -bolt, –brand; stroke, stroke of lightning, thunderstone [*obs. or dial. Eng.*].

ammunition; powder, –and shot; explosive; gunpowder, "villanous saltpetre" (*villainous saltpeter*) [*Henry IV.*]; guncotton, pyroxylin *or* pyroxyline, dynamite, melinite, cordite, gelignite, lyddite, nitroglycerin *or* nitroglycerine, trinitrotoluol, trinitrotoluene, T.N.T.; cartridge; ball cartridge, cartouche, fireball; poison gas, mustard gas, chlorine gas, tear gas etc.

728. Arena

n. **arena**, field, platform; scene of action, theater *or* theatre, walk, course; hustings; stage, boards etc. (*playhouse*) 599; amphitheater *or* amphitheatre, Coliseum, Colosseum; Flavian amphitheater, hippodrome, circus, race course, *corso* [*It.*], turf, cockpit, bear garden, gymnasium, palaestra *or* palestra, ring, lists; tilt-yard, tilting ground; *Campus Martius* [*L.*], *Champ de Mars* [*F.*]; campus, playing field, playground.

battle field, battle ground; field of -battle, –slaughter; No Man's Land [*World War I*]; "over there" [*used in America, esp. of the Western Front in World War I*], "out there" [*corresponding term in Eng.*]; theater–, seat- of war; Aceldama, camp; the enemy's camp.

trysting place etc. (*place of meeting*) 74.

Section 5. Results of Action

729. Completion

n. **completion**; accomplishment, achievement, fulfillment *or* fulfilment; performance, execution; dispatch *or* despatch, consummation, culmination; finish, conclusion; limit, effectuation; close etc. (*end*) 67; terminus etc. (*arrival*) 292; winding up; *finale* [*It.*], *dénouement* [*F.*], catastrophe, issue, upshot, result; final–, last–, crowning–, finishing- -touch, –stroke; last finish, *coup de grâce* [*F.*]; crowning of the

260

edifice; coping stone, copestone, keystone; missing link etc. 53; superstructure, *ne plus ultra* [*L.*], work done, *fait accompli* [*F.*]. elaboration; finality; completeness etc. 52.

v. **complete**, perfect; effect, effectuate; accomplish, achieve, compass, consummate, hammer out; bring to -maturity, –perfection; elaborate.

do, execute, make; go–, get- through; work out, enact; bring -about, –to bear, –to pass, –through, –to a head.

dispatch *or* despatch, knock off [*colloq.*], finish off, polish off; make short work of; dispose of, set at rest; perform, discharge fulfill *or* fulfil, realize; put in -practice, –force; carry -out, –into effect, –into execution; make good; be as good as one's word.

do thoroughly, not do by halves, go the whole hog [*colloq.*]; drive home, be in at the death etc. (*persevere*) 604a; carry through, deliver the goods [*colloq.*], play out, exhaust; fill the bill [*colloq.*].

finish, bring to a close etc. (*end*) 67; wind up, stamp, clinch, seal, set the seal on, put the seal to; give the final touch etc. *n.* to; put the -last, –finishing- touch to; crown, crown all; cap.

ripen, culminate; come to a -head, –crisis; come to its end; die a natural death, die of old age; run its course, run one's race; touch–, reach–, attain- the goal; reach etc. (*arrive*) 292; get in the harvest.

adj. **completing**, final; concluding, conclusive; crowning etc. *v.;* exhaustive, elaborate, complete, mature, perfect, consummate, thorough.

done, completed etc. *v.;* done for [*colloq.*], sped, wrought out; highly wrought etc. (*preparation*) 673; thorough etc. 52; ripe etc. (*ready*) 673.

adv. **completely** etc. (*thoroughly*) 52; to crown all, out of hand; with absolute -perfection, –finish; as a last stroke; as a fitting climax.

730. Noncompletion

n. **noncompletion**, nonfulfillment *or* nonfulfilment, shortcoming etc. 304; incompleteness etc. 53; drawn -battle, –game; work of Penelope; Sisyphean -labor, –toil, –task.

nonperformance, inexecution; neglect of execution; neglect etc. 460.

v. **not complete** etc. 729; leave unfinished etc. *adj.,* leave undone; neglect etc. 460; let alone, let slip; lose sight of.

fall short of etc. 304; do things by halves, scotch the snake not kill it; hang fire; be slow to; collapse etc. 304.

adj. **incomplete** etc. 53; not completed etc. *v.;* uncompleted, unfinished, unaccomplished, unperformed, unexecuted; sketchy; addle, muddled, sterile.

in progress, in hand, on the stocks, in preparation, moving, getting along, going on, proceeding; on one's hands; on the anvil.

adv. **re infecta** [*L.*]; without–, lacking- -the final touches, –the finishing stroke.

731. Success

n. **success**, successfulness; speed; advance etc. (*progress*) 282.

trump card; hit, stroke; lucky–, fortunate–, good- -hit, –stroke; bold stroke, masterstroke; ten-strike [*colloq.*]; *coup de maître* [*F.*], checkmate; half the battle, prize; profit etc. (*acquisition*) 775.

continued success; good fortune etc. (*prosperity*) 734; time well spent.

mastery, advantage over; upper hand, whip hand; ascendancy, expugnation [*obs.*], conquest, victory, walkover [*colloq.*], subdual; subjugation etc. (*subjection*) 749; triumph etc. (*exultation*) 884; proficiency etc. (*skill*) 698; a feather in one's cap [*colloq.*].

victor, victress [*rare*], victrix [*rare*], conqueror, master, champion, winner; master of the -situation, –position.

v. **succeed**; be successful etc. *adj.;* gain one's -end, –ends; crown with success.

gain–, attain–, carry–, secure–, win- a point, –an object; get there [*colloq.*]; manage to, contrive to; accomplish etc. (*effect, complete*) 729; do–, work- wonders; make a go of it [*colloq.*].

come off -well, –successfully, –with flying colors; make short work of; take–, carry- by storm; bear away the bell; win one's spurs, win the battle; win–, carry–, gain- the -day, –prize, –palm; have the best of it, have it all one's own way, have the game in one's own hands, have the ball at one's feet, have one on the hip; walk over the course; carry all before one, remain in possession of the field; socre a success, strike it rich, hit pay dirt.

make progress etc. (*advance*) 282; win–, make–, work–, find- one's way; speed; strive to some purpose; prosper etc. 734; drive a roaring trade; make profit etc. (*acquire*) 775; reap–, gather- the -fruits, –benefit of, –harvest; strike oil [*slang*], make one's fortune, get in the harvest, turn to good account; turn to account etc. (*use*) 677.

triumph, be triumphant; gain–, obtain- -a victory, –an advantage; chain victory to one's car. surmount–, overcome–, get over- -a difficulty, –an obstacle etc. 706; *se tirer d'affaire* [*F.*]; make head against; stem the -torrent, –tide, –current; weather -the storm, –a point; turn a corner, keep one's head above water, tide over; master; get–, have–, gain- the -better of, –best of, –upper hand, –ascendancy, –whip hand, –start of; distance; surpass etc. (*superiority*) 33.

defeat, conquer, vanquish, discomfit; euchre [*slang*]; overcome, overthrow, overpower, overmaster, overmatch, overset, override, overreach; outwit, outdo, outflank, outmaneuver *or* outmanoeuvre, outgeneral, outvote; take the wind out of one's adversary's sails; beat, beat hollow [*colloq.*], lick [*colloq.*], rout, drub, floor, worst, lick to a frazzle [*colloq.*]; put -down, –to flight, –to the rout, –*hors de combat* [*F.*], –out of court.

settle [*colloq.*], do for [*colloq.*], break the -neck of, –back of; capsize, sink, shipwreck, drown, swamp; subdue; subjugate etc. (*subject*) 749; reduce; make the enemy bite the dust; victimize, roll in the dust, trample under foot, put an extinguisher upon.

checkmate, silence, quell, nonsuit, upset, confound, nonplus, stalemate, trump; baffle etc. (*hinder*) 706; circumvent, elude; trip up, –the heels of; drive -into a corner, –to the wall; run hard, put one's nose out of joint [*colloq.*].

avail; answer, –the purpose; prevail, take effect, do, turn out well, work well, take [*colloq.*], tell, bear fruit; hit it, hit the mark, hit the nail on the head; nick it; turn up trumps, make a hit; find one's account in.

adj. **successful**; prosperous etc. 734; succeeding etc. *v.;* triumphant; flushed–, crowned- with success; victorious; set up [*colloq.*]; in the ascendant; unbeaten etc. (*see* beat etc. *v.*); well-spent; felicitous, effective, in full swing.

adv. **successfully** etc. *adj.;* with flying colors, in triumph, swimmingly; *à merveille* [*F.*], beyond all hope; to some–, to good- purpose; to one's heart's content.

732. Failure

n. **failure**, unsuccess, nonsuccess, nonfulfillment *or* nonfulfilment; dead failure, successlessness; abortion, miscarriage; *brutum fulmen* [*L.*] etc. 158; labor in vain etc. (*inutility*) 645; no go [*colloq.*]; inefficacy; inefficaciousness etc. *adj.;* vain–, ineffectual–, abortive- -attempt, –efforts, flash in the pan, "lame and impotent conclusion" [*Othello*]; frustration; slip 'twixt cup and lip etc. (*disappointment*) 509.

blunder etc. (*mistake*) 495; fault, omission, miss, oversight, slip, trip, stumble, claudication [*obs.*] footfall; false–, wrong- step; *faux pas* [*F.*], titubation, *bévue* [*F.*], *faute* [*F.*], lurch; botchery etc. (*want of skill*) 699; scrape, mess, muddle, botch, fiasco, breakdown; flunk [*colloq.*].

mishap etc. (*misfortune*) 735; split, collapse, smash, blow, explosion.

repulse, rebuff, defeat, rout, overthrow, discomfiture; beating, drubbing; quietus, nonsuit, subjugation; checkmate, stalemate, fool's mate. losing game, *affaire flambée* [*F.*]

fall, downfall, ruin, perdition; wreck etc. (*destruction*) 162; deathblow; bankruptcy etc. (*nonpayment*) 808.

victim, prey; bankrupt; flunker [*colloq.*], flunky *or* flunkey [*cant*].

v. **fail**; be unsuccessful etc. *adj.;* not succeed etc. 731; make vain efforts etc. *n.;* do–, labor–, toil- in vain; flunk [*colloq.*]; lose one's labor, take nothing by one's motion; bring to naught, make nothing of; wash a black-amoor white etc. (*impossible*) 471; roll the stone of Sisyphus etc. (*useless*) 645; do by halves etc. (*not complete*) 730; lose ground etc. (*recede*) 283; fall short of etc. 304; go to -the wall, –the dogs, –pot [*colloq.*], lick–, bite- the dust; be defeated etc. 731; have the worst of it, lose the day, come off second best, lose; not have a leg to stand on; fall a prey to; succumb etc. (*submit*) 725.

miss, –one's aim, –the mark, –one's footing, –stays [*naut.*]; slip, trip, stumble; make a slip etc., *n.;* make a blunder etc. 495, make a mess of, make a botch of; bitch it [*obs.*], miscarry, abort, go up like a rocket and come down like the stick, reckon without one's host; get the wrong -pig by the tail, –sow by the ear [*colloq.*] etc. (*blunder, mismanage*) 699.

flounder, falter; limp, halt, hobble, titubate; fall, tumble; lose one's balance; fall to the ground, fall between two stools; stick in the mud, run aground, split upon a rock; run–, knock–, dash- one's head against a stone wall; break one's back; break down, sink, drown, founder, have the ground cut from under one; get into -trouble, –a mess, –a scrape; come to grief etc. (*adversity*) 735.

come to nothing, end in smoke; flat out [*colloq.*]; fall -to the ground, –through, –dead, –stillborn, –flat; slip through one's fingers; hang fire, misfire, flash in the pan, collapse;

topple down etc. (*descent*) 305; go to wrack and ruin etc. (*destruction*) 162.

go amiss, go wrong, go cross, go hard with, go on a wrong tack; go on-, come off-, turn out-, work- ill; take a wrong turn, take an ugly turn, be all over with, be all up with; explode; dash one's hopes etc. (*disappoint*) 509; defeat the purpose; sow the wind and reap the whirlwind, jump out of the frying pan into the fire.

adj. **unsuccessful**, successless, stick-it [*Scot.*]; failing, tripping etc. *v.;* at fault; unfortunate etc. 735.

abortive, sterile, impotent, addle, stillborn; fruitless, bootless; ineffectual, ineffective; inefficient etc. (*impotent*) 158; inefficacious; lame, hobbling, *décousu* [*F.*]; insufficient etc. 640; unavailing etc. (*useless*) 645; of no effect.

stranded, aground, grounded, swamped, cast away, wrecked, foundered, capsized, shipwrecked, nonsuited; foiled; defeated etc. 731; struck-, borne-, broken- down; downtrodden; overborne, overwhelmed; all up with [*colloq.*]; plowed *or* ploughed [*Eng. Univ. cant*], plucked [*college cant*].

undone, lost, ruined, broken; bankrupt etc. (*not paying*) 808; played out; done up, done for [*both colloq.*]; deadbeat [*colloq.*], ruined root and branch, *flambé* [*F.*], knocked on the head; destroyed etc. 162.

frustrated, thwarted, crossed, unhinged, disconcerted, dashed; thrown -off one's balance, -on one's back, -on one's beam ends; unhorsed, in a sorry plight; hard hit; stultified, befooled, dished [*colloq.*], hoist on one's own petard; victimized, sacrificed.

wide of the mark etc. (*error*) 495; out of one's reckoning etc. (*inexpectation*) 508; left in the lurch; thrown away etc. (*wasted*) 638; unattained; uncompleted etc. 730.

adv. **unsuccessfully** etc. *adj.;* to little or no purpose, in vain, *re infecta* [*L.*].

733. Trophy

n. **trophy**; medal, prize, palm, laurel, laurels, bays, crown, chaplet, wreath, civic crown; insignia etc. 550; eulogy, citation; fellowship, scholarship; feather in one's cap etc. (*honor*) 873; garland; triumphal arch; Victoria Cross, Congressional medal, *croix de guerre* [*F.*], *médaille militaire* [*F.*], Iron Cross; Pulitzer Prize, Oscar, Emmy; Carnegie medal, Nobel prize; blue ribbon; red ribbon of the Legion of Honor; decoration etc. 877.

triumph etc. (*celebration*) 883; flying colors etc. (*show*) 882.

734. Prosperity

n. **prosperity**, welfare, well-being; affluence etc. (*wealth*) 803; success etc. 731; thrift, roaring trade; good-, smiles of - fortune; blessings; godsend; bed of roses; fat of the land, milk and honey, loaves and fishes, fleshpots of Egypt.

luck; good-, run of- luck; sunshine; fair -weather, -wind; fair wind and no favor; palmy-, bright-, halcyon-days; piping times, tide, flood, high tide.

golden age, golden time, *Saturnia regna* [*L.*], Saturnian age.

man of substance, made man, lucky dog, *enfant gâté* [*F.*], spoiled child of fortune.

upstart, parvenu, *nouveau riche* [*F.*], *narikin* [*Jap.*], skipjack [*dial. Eng.*], mushroom.

v. **prosper**, thrive, flourish; be prosperous etc. *adj.;* drive a roaring trade; go on -well, -smoothly, -swimmingly; sail before the wind, swim with the tide; run -smooth, -smoothly, -on all fours [*colloq.*].

rise-, get on- in the world; work-, make- one's way; look up; lift-, raise-one's head, make one's fortune, feather one's nest, make one's pile [*slang*].

flower, blow, blossom, bloom, fructify, bear fruit, fatten, batten.

keep oneself afloat; keep-, hold-one's head above water; light-, fall-on one's -legs, -feet; drop into a good thing; bear a charmed life; bask in the sunshine; have a good (*or* fine) time of it; have a run, -of luck; have the good fortune etc. *n.* to; take a favorable turn; live -on the fat of the land, -in clover, -on velvet.

adj. **prosperous**; thriving etc. *v.;* in a fair way, buoyant; well off, well to do, well to live [*archaic*], set up [*colloq.*], well to do in the world; at one's ease; rich etc. 803; in good case; in full feather, in high feather; fortunate, lucky, in luck; born with a silver spoon in one's mouth, born under a lucky star; on the sunny side of the hedge.

palmy, halcyon; agreeable etc. 829; *couleur de rose* [*F.*].

auspicious, propitious, providential.

adv. **prosperously** etc. *adj.;* swimmingly; as good luck would have it; beyond all -expectation, -hope; beyond one's deserts; beyond the dreams of avarice.

735. Adversity

n. **adversity**, evil etc. 619; failure etc. 732; bad -ill-, evil-, adverse-, hard- -fortune, -hap, -luck, -lot; frowns of fortune; evil -dispensation, −star, −genius; ups and downs of life; the sport of fortune; broken fortunes; hard -case, −lines, −life; sea−, peck- of troubles; hell upon earth; slough of despond.

pressure of the times, iron age, evil day, time out of joint; hard−, bad−, sad- times; rainy day, cloud, dark cloud, gathering clouds, ill wind; affliction etc. (*painfulness*) 830; bitter -pill, −draft (*or* draught), −cup; care.

trouble, hardship, curse, blight, blast, load, pressure, humiliation.

misfortune, misventure [*archaic*], mishap, mischance, misadventure, disaster, calamity, catastrophe; accident, casualty, cross, blow, trial, sorrow, visitation, infliction, reverse, check, *contretemps* [*F.*], pinch, rub; backset, comedown, setback.

downfall, fall; losing game; falling etc. *v.;* ruination, ruinousness, undoing; extremity; ruin etc. (*destruction*) 162.

v.   **be ill of** etc. *adj.;* go hard with; fall on evil, −days; go on ill; not prosper etc. 734.

come to grief, go downhill, go to rack and ruin etc. (*destruction*) 162, go to the dogs [*colloq.*]; fall, −from one's high estate; decay, sink, decline, go down in the world; have seen better days; bring down one's gray hairs with sorrow to the grave; be all over with, be all up with [*colloq.*]; bring a wasp's (*or* hornet's) nest about one's ears.

adj.   **unfortunate,** unblest, unhappy, unlucky, unprosperous, improsperous [*obs.*]; hoodooed [*colloq.*], Jonahed [*slang*], jinxed [*slang*], luck-less, hapless; out of luck; in trouble, in a bad way, in an evil plight; under a cloud; clouded; ill off, badly off; in adverse circumstances; poor etc. 804; behindhand, down in the world, decayed, undone; on the road to ruin, on its last legs, on the wane; in one's utmost need; up the creek without a paddle [*colloq.*].

ill-fated, ill-starred, ill-omened; planet-struck, devoted, doomed; inauspicious, unauspicious [*rare*], ominous, sinister, unpropitious; unfavorable; born -under an evil star, −with a wooden ladle in one's mouth.

adverse, untoward; disastrous, calamitous, ruinous, dire, deplorable.

adv.   if the worst come to the worst, as ill luck would have it, from bad to worse, out of the frying pan into the fire.

736. Mediocrity

n.   **mediocrity;** golden mean etc. (*mid-course*) 628, (*moderation*) 174; moderate−, average- circumstances; respectability.

middle classes, *bourgeoisie* [*F.*].

v.   strike the golden mean; preserve a middle course etc. 628.

jog on, get along [*colloq.*], get by [*slang*]; go−, get on- -fairly, −quietly, −peaceably, −tolerably, −respectably.

adj.   **middling,** *comme ci comme ça* [*F.*], so-so, fair, fair to middling [*colloq.*], medium, moderate, mediocre, ordinary; second−, third−, fourth-rate.

adv.   with nothing to brag about.

Division 2. Intersocial Volition

Section 1. General

737. Authority

n.   **authority;** influence, patronage, power, preponderance, credit, prestige, prerogative, jurisdiction; right etc. (*title*) 924.

divine right, dynastic rights, authoritativeness; royalty, regality, imperiality [*rare*]; absoluteness, absolutism, despotism, tyranny; *jus nocendi* [*L.*]; *jus divinum* [*L.*].

command, empire, sway, rule; dominion, domination; sovereignty, supremacy, suzerainty; kinghood, kingship; lordship, headship; chiefdom; patriarchy, patriarchate; leadership, hegemony; seigniory; mastery, mastership, masterdom; government etc. (*direction*) 693; dictation, control.

hold, grasp; grip, gripe; reach; iron sway etc. (*severity*) 739; fangs, clutches, talons; rod of empire etc. (*scepter*) 747.

reign, *régime* [*F.*], dynasty; directorship, dictatorship; protectorate, protectorship; caliphate, pashalic, electorate; presidency, presidentship; administration; consulship, proconsulship; prefecture; seneschalship; magistrature, magistracy.

[governments] empire; monarchy; limited−, constitutional- monarchy; aristarchy, aristocracy; oligarchy, democracy, demagogy; heteronomy;

republic; thearchy; diarchy, duarchy, duumvirate; triarchy, triumvirate; heterarchy [*obs.*]; autocracy, monocracy.

representative government, constitutional government, *vox populi* [*L.*], home rule, dominion rule [*Brit.*], colonial government; self-government, autonomy, self-determination; republicanism, federalism; socialism; collectivism; pantisocracy; *imperium in imperio* [*L.*]; bureaucracy; beadledom, Bumbledom; stratocracy [*rare*], martial law; military -power, –government; feodality, feodatory, feudal system, feudalism.

gynocracy, gynarchy, gynecocracy, matriarchy, matriarchate, metrocracy; petticoat government.

[vicarious authority] commission etc. 755; deputy etc. 759; permission etc. 760.

state, realm, commonwealth, country, power, polity, body politic, *posse comitatus* [*L.*]; toparchy.

ruler; person in authority etc. (*master*) 745; judicature etc. 965; cabinet etc. (*council*) 696; seat of -government, –authority; headquarters.
usurper, tyrant, jack-in-office.

[acquisition of authority] accession; installation etc. 755; usurpation.

v. **authorize** etc. (*permit*) 760; warrant etc. (*right*) 924; dictate etc. (*order*) 741; have–, hold–, possess–, exercise–, exert–, grasp–, seize–, wrest–, wield- -authority etc. *n.*

rule, sway, command, control, administer; govern etc. (*direct*) 693; lead, preside over, reign; possess–, be seated on–, occupy–, seize- the throne; sway–, wield- the scepter *or* sceptre; wear the crown.

be at the head of etc. *adj.;* hold–, be in–, fill an-office; hold–, occupy- a post; be master etc. 745.

dominate; have–, get- the -upper, –whip-hand; gain a hold upon, preponderate, dominate, rule the roast; boss [*colloq.*]; override, overrule, overawe; lord it over, hold in hand, keep under, make a puppet of, lead by the nose, turn round one's little finger, bend to one's will, hold one's own, wear the breeches [*colloq.*]; have the ball at one's feet, have it all one's own way, have the game in one's own hand, have on the hip, have under one's thumb; be master of the situation; take the lead, play first fiddle, set the fashion; give the law to; carry with a high hand; lay down the law; "ride in the whirlwind and direct the

storm" [*adapted from* Addison]; rule with a rod of iron etc. (*severity*) 739.

assume authority etc. *n.;* ascend–, mount- the throne; take the reins, –into one's hand; assume the reins of government; take–, assume the- command.

be governed by, be in the power of; be under the -rule of, –dominion of.

adj. **ruling** etc. *v.;* regnant, at the head, dominant, paramount, supreme, predominant, preponderant, in the ascendant, influential; gubernatorial; imperious; authoritative, executive, administrative, clothed with authority, official, bureaucratic, departmental, *ex officio* [*L.*], imperative, peremptory, overruling, absolute; hegemonic *or* hegemonical; arbitrary; compulsory etc. 744; stringent.

at one's command; in one's power, in one's grasp; under control; authorized etc. (*due*) 924.

sovereign; regal, royal, royalist, monarchical, kingly; dynastic, imperial, imperialistic; princely; feudal; aristocratic, autocratic; oligarchic etc. *n.;* democratic, republican.

adv. in the name of, by the authority of, at one's command, *de par le Roi* [*F.*], in virtue of; under the auspices of, in the hands of.

at one's pleasure; by a dash (*or* stroke) of the pen; at one's nod; by lifting one's finger; *ex mero motu* [*L.*]; *ex cathedra* [*L.*].

738. Laxity
[absence of authority]

n. **laxity**; laxness, looseness, slackness; toleration etc. (*lenity*) 740; freedom etc. 748.

anarchy, interregnum; relaxation; loosening etc. *v.;* remission; dead letter, *brutum fulmen* [*L.*], misrule; license, licentiousness; insubordination etc. (*disobedience*) 742; mob rule, mob law, mobocracy, ochlocracy; lynch law etc. (*illegality*) 964, nihilism, reign of violence.

[deprivation of power] dethronement, impeachment, deposition, abdication; usurpation.

v. **be lax** etc. *adj.; laisser faire* [*F.*], *laisser aller* [*F.*]; hold a loose rein; give the reins to, give rope enough, give a loose to [*obs.*], give a free course to, give free rein to; tolerate; relax; misrule.

go beyond the length of one's tether; have one's -swing, –fling; act without -instructions, –authority; act on one's own responsibility, usurp authority, undermine the authority of.

dethrone, depose; abdicate.

adj. **lax**, loose; slack; remiss etc. (*careless*) 460; weak.

relaxed; licensed; reinless, unbridled; anarchic *or* anarchical, nihilistic; "agin the government"; unauthorized etc. (*unwarranted*) 925; adespotic, undespotic; not imperious etc. (*ruling*) 737.

739. Severity

n. **severity**; strictness, harshness etc. *adj.;* rigor, stringency, austerity; inclemency etc. (*pitilessness*) 914*a*; arrogance etc. 885; precisianism, formalism.

arbitrary power; absolutism, despotism; dictatorship, autocracy, tyranny, domineering, domination, oppression; assumption, usurpation; inquisition, reign of terror, martial law; iron -heel, –rule, –hand, –sway; tight grasp; brute -force, –strength; coercion etc. 744; strong–, tight- hand.

bureaucracy, red-tapism, pipe-clay, officialism; hard -lines, –measure; tender mercies [*ironical*]; sharp practice.

tyrant, disciplinarian, precisian, martinet, stickler, bashaw, despot, the Grand Panjandrum himself, hard master, Draco, oppressor, inquisitor, extortioner, harpy, vulture; Accipitres, Raptores, raptors [*obs.*], birds of prey.

v. **be severe** etc. *adj.*

arrogate, assume, usurp, take liberties; domineer, bully etc. 885; tyrannize; wrest the law to one's advantage; inflict, wreak, stretch a point, put on the screw; be hard upon; bear–, lay- a heavy hand on; be down upon [*slang*], come down upon [*colloq.*]; illtreat; deal hardly with, deal hard measure to; rule with a rod of iron, chastise with scorpions; dye with blood; oppress, override; trample–, tread- -down, –upon, –under foot; crush under an iron heel, ride roughshod over; rivet the yoke; hold–, keep- a tight hand; force down the throat; coerce etc. 744; give no quarter etc. (*pitiless*) 914*a*.

adj. **severe**; strict, hard, harsh, dour [*Scot.*], rigid, stiff, stern, rigorous, uncompromising, exacting, exigent, *exigeant* [*F.*], inexorable, inflexible, obdurate, austere, hard-headed, hard-shell [*colloq.*], relentless, Spartan, Draconian, stringent, strict, prudish, precise, puritanical, strait-laced, searching, unsparing, iron-handed, peremptory, absolute, positive, arbitrary, imperative; coercive etc. 744; tyrannical, extortionate, grinding, withering, oppressive, inquisitorial; inclement etc. (*ruthless*) 914*a;* cruel etc. (*malevolent*) 907; haughty, arrogant etc. 885; precisian, formal, punctilious.

adv. **severely** etc. *adj.;* with a -high, –strong, –tight, –heavy- hand.

at the point of the -sword, –bayonet.

740. Lenity

n. **lenity**, lenitence, lenitency; moderation etc. 174; tolerance, toleration; mildness, gentleness; favor; indulgence, indulgency [*rare*], clemence [*obs.*], clemency, mercy, forbearance, quarter; compassion etc. 914.

v. **be lenient** etc. *adj.;* tolerate, bear with; *parcere subjectis* [*L.*], spare the vanquished, give quarter.

indulge; allow one to -go his own gait, –have his own way, spoil.

adj. **lenient**; mild, –as milk; gentle, soft; tolerant, indulgent, easy, moderate, complaisant, unconcerned, easy-going; clement etc. (*compassionate*) 914; forbearing; long-suffering.

741. Command

n. **command**, order, ordinance, act, fiat, *hukm* [*Hind.*], bidding, dictum, hest, behest, call, beck, nod.

dispatch *or* despatch, message, direction, injunction, charge, instructions; appointment, fixture.

demand, exaction, imposition, requisition, claim, reclamation, revendication [*rare*]; ultimatum etc. (*terms*) 770; request etc. 765; requirement.

decree, dictate, dictation, mandate, caveat, *senatus consultum* [*L.*]; precept; prescript, rescript, writ, ordination, bull, edict, decretal, dispensation, prescription, brevet, placet, *placitum* [*L.*], ukase, firman, hatti-sherif, hatti-humayoun (*or* humayun), warrant, passport, mittimus, mandamus, summons, subpoena, *nisi prius* [*L.*], interpellation, citation; word, –of command; *mot d'ordre* [*F.*]; bugle-, trumpet-call; beat of drum, tattoo; order of the day; enactment etc. (*law*) 963; plebiscite etc. (*choice*) 609.

v. **command**, order, decree, enact, ordain, dictate, direct, give orders.

issue a command; make–, issue–, promulgate- -a requisition, –a decree, –an order etc. *n.;* give the -word of command, –word, –signal; call to order; give–, lay down- the law; assume the command etc. (*authority*) 737; remand.

prescribe, set, appoint, mark out; set–, prescribe–, impose- a task; set to work, put in requisition.

bid, enjoin, charge, call upon, instruct; require, –at the hands of; exact, impose, tax, task; demand; insist on etc. (*compel*) 744.

claim, lay claim to, revendicate [*rare*], reclaim.
cite, summon, avoke; call for, send for; subpoena; beckon.
be ordered etc.; receive an order etc. *n.*

adj. **commanding** etc. *v.;* authoritative etc. 737; decretory, decretive, decretal; callable; imperative, jussive; decisive, final, without appeal; interpellative, demanded, commanded etc. *v.*

adv. in a commanding tone; by a -stroke, −dash- of the pen; by order, at beat of drum, on the first summons, to order, at the word of command; by -command, −order, −decree- of; as required, as requested, as ordered, as commanded.

742. Disobedience

n. **disobedience,** insubordination, contumacy; infraction, infringement; violation, noncompliance; nonobservance etc. 773.

revolt, rebellion, mutiny, outbreak, rising, uprising, insurrection, *émeute* [*F.*], riot, tumult etc. (*disorder*) 59; strike etc. (*resistance*) 719; barring out; defiance etc. 715.

mutinousness etc. *adj.;* mutineering; sedition, treason; high−, petty−, misprison of- treason; praemunire *or* premunire; *lèse-majesté* [*F.*]; violation of law etc. 964; defection, secession, Sinn Fein; revolution; overthrow−, overturn- of -government, −authority; *sabotage* [*F.*], sansculottism, bolshevism.

insurgent, mutineer, rebel, revolter, rioter, traitor, *Carbonaro* [*It.*], sansculotte, red republican, *bonnet rouge* [*F.*], communist, Fenian, Sinn Feiner, Red, Bolshevist, *frondeur* [*F.*], seceder, Secessionist [*esp., U. S. hist.*] *or* Secesh [*colloq. or slang*]; apostate, renegade, runaway, runagate; brawler, anarchist, demagogue; Spartacus, Masaniello, Wat Tyler, Jack Cade; ringleader.

v. **disobey,** violate, infringe; shirk, slide out of, slack; set at defiance etc. (*defy*) 715; set authority at naught, run riot, fly in the face of; take the law into one's own hands; kick over the traces; refuse to support, bolt.

turn−, run- restive; champ the bit; strike etc. (*resist*) 719; rise, −in arms; secede; mutiny, rebel.

adj. **disobedient;** uncomplying, uncompliant; unsubmissive, unruly, ungovernable; breachy, insubordinate, impatient of control; restive, restiff [*obs.*], refractory, contumacious; recusant etc. (*refuse*) 764; recalcitrant; resisting etc. 719; lawless, riotous, mutinous, seditious, insurgent, revolutionary, sansculottic, secessionist.

unobeyed, disobeyed; unbidden.

743. Obedience

n. **obedience;** observance etc. 772; compliance; submission etc. 725; subjection etc. 749; nonresistance; passiveness, passivity, resignation.

allegiance, loyalty, fealty, homage, deference, devotion; constancy, fidelity.

submissiveness, submissness [*obs.*]; ductility etc. (*softness*) 324; obsequiousness etc. (*servility*) 886.

v. **be obedient** etc. *adj.;* obey, bear obedience to; submit etc. 725; comply, answer the helm, come at one's call; do one's bidding, do what one is told, do suit and service; attend to orders; serve -faithfully, −loyally, −devotedly, −without question; give -loyal, −devoted-service; be resigned to, be submissive to.

follow, −the lead of, −to the world's end; serve etc. 746; play second fiddle.

adj. **obedient,** law-abiding, complying, compliant; loyal, faithful, devoted; at one's -call, −command, −orders, −beck and call; under beck and call, under control.

restrainable; resigned, passive; submissive etc. 725; henpecked; pliant etc. (*soft*) 324.

unresisted, unresisting.

adv. **obediently** etc. *adj.;* as you please, if you please; in compliance with, in obedience to; at your -command, −orders, −service.

744. Compulsion

n. **compulsion,** coercion, coaction, constraint; restraint etc. 751; duress, enforcement, press, conscription; eminent domain.

force; brute−, main−, physical- force; the sword, *ultima ratio* [*L.*]; club−, lynch−, mob- law, *argumentum baculinum* [*L.*], *le droit du plus fort* [*F.*]; the force of -might, −right; martial law.

necessity etc. 601; *force majeure* [*F.*], spur of necessity, Hobson's choice.

v. **compel,** force, make, drive, coerce, constrain, enforce, necessitate, oblige.

force upon, press; cram−, thrust−, force- down the throat; say it must be done, make a point of, insist upon, take no denial; put down, dragoon.

extort, wring from; put−, turn- on the screw; drag into; bind, −over; pin−, tie- down; require, tax, put in force; commandeer; restrain etc. 751.

adj. **compelling** etc. *v.;* coercive, coactive; inexorable etc. 739; compulsory, compulsatory; obligatory, stringent, peremptory, binding.

forcible, not to be trifled with; irresistible etc. 601; compelled etc. *v.;* fain to.

adv. **forcibly**; by force etc. *n.,* by force of arms; on compulsion, perforce; *vi et armis* [*L.*], under the lash; at the point of the -sword, –bayonet; by a strong arm.

under protest, in spite of, in one's teeth; against one's will etc. 603; *nolens volens* [*L.*] etc. (*of necessity*) 601; by stress of -circumstances, –weather; under press of; *de rigueur* [*F.*].

745. Master

n. **master**, *padrone* [*It.*], lord, –paramount; commander, commandant, captain, chief, chieftain; paterfamilias [*Rom. law*], patriarch; sahib [*India*], bara (*or* burra) sahib [*India*], sirdar, sheik; head, senior, governor, ruler, dictator; leader etc. (*director*) 694; boss, baas [*Dutch*]; cockarouse [*obs.*], sachem, sagamore, werowance.

lord of the ascendant; cock of the -walk, –loft, –midden [*archaic*], –roost; gray mare; mistress.

potentate; liege, –lord; suzerain, overlord, overking, sovereign, monarch, autocrat, despot, tyrant, oligarch; boss of bosses [*slang*], godfather [*slang*].

crowned head, emperor, king, anointed king, majesty, imperator, protector, president, stadholder *or* stadtholder, judge.

caesar, kaiser, czar *or* tsar, sultan, soldan [*obs.*], grand Turk, caliph, imam *or* imaum, shah, padishah, sophi, mogul, great mogul, khan, lama, pendragon, tycoon, mikado, inca, cazique; voivode *or* waywode, hospodar, landamman; sayid *or* sayyid, cacique, czarevitch, grand seignior.

prince, duke etc. (*nobility*) 875; archduke, doge, elector; seignior; landgrave, margrave; maharajah, rajah, emir, nizam, nawab etc. (*Indian ruling chiefs*) 875.

empress, queen, sultana, czarina *or* tsarina, princess, infanta, duchess, margravine; czarevna *or* tsarevna, czarina; maharani, rani [*both Hindu*], begum [*Moham.*]; rectoress *or* rectress, rectrix.

regent, viceroy, exarch, palatine, khedive, beglerbeg *or* beylerbey, three-tailed bashaw, pasha *or* bashaw, bey *or* beg, dey, shereef *or* sherif, tetrarch, satrap, mandarin, nabob, burgrave; laird etc. (*proprietor*) 779; commissioner, deputy commissioner, collector, woon *or* wun [*Burmese*].

the authorities, the powers that be, the government, "them above" [Eliot]; staff, *état major* [*F.*], aga, official, man in office, person in authority; sirkar *or* sircar; Sublime Porte.

[military authorities] marshal, field marshal, *maréchal* [*F.*], generalissimo; commander-in-chief, seraskier [*Turk.*], hetman [*Cossack*]; general, brigadier general, brigadier, lieutenant general, major general, colonel, lieutenant colonel, major, captain, ressaldar *or* risaldar [*India*], subahdar *or* subadar [*India*]; centurion, lieutenant, jemadar [*India*], sublieutenant, officer, staff officer, aide-de-camp, brigade major, adjutant, ensign, cornet, cadet, subaltern; non-commissioned officer; sergeant, –major; color sergeant; top-sergeant [*U.S.*], havildar [*India*]; corporal, –major; lance corporal, acting corporal; naik [*India*]; drum major; captain general, knight marshal.

[civil authorities] mayor, mayoralty; *maire* [*F.*], prefect, chancellor, archon [*Gr.*], provost, magistrate, syndic; alcalde [*Sp.*], alcaide *or* alcaid; burgomaster, *corregidor* [*Sp.*], seneschal, alderman, warden, constable, portreeve; lord mayor; officer etc. (*executive*) 965; diwan *or* dewan [*India*]; hakim; *fonctionnaire* [*F.*].

[naval authorities] admiral, admiralty; rear–, vice–, port- admiral; commodore, captain, commander, lieutenant; skipper, master, mate, navarch [*Gr. antiq.*].

746. Servant

n. **servant**, retainer, follower, henchman, servitor, domestic, menial, help, lady help [*Brit.*], employee *or* employé; *attaché* [*F.*], official.

subject, liege, liegeman; people, "my people."

retinue, suite, *cortège* [*F.*], staff, court; office force, clerical staff, clerical force, workers, associate workers, employees, the help.

attendant, squire, usher, donzel [*obs.*], apprentice, prentice [*colloq. or dial.*]; page, buttons [*colloq.*], footboy; trainbearer, cupbearer; waiter, tapster, butler, livery servant, lackey, footman, flunky *or* flunkey [*colloq.*]; bearer [*Anglo-Ind.*], boy; hamal [*India*], scout [*Oxford Univ.*], gyp [*Camb. Univ.*], valet, *valet de chambre* [*F.*]; equerry, groom; jockey, hostler *or* ostler, orderly, messenger, gillie *or* gilly, caddie *or* caddy, herdsman, swineherd; barkeeper, bartender, barkeep; boots [*Brit.*]; cad [*Eng. Univ. cant*], bell boy, bellhop [*slang*], tiger, chokra [*India*], boy; counterjumper [*colloq.*]; khansamah *or* khansaman [*India*], khitmutgar [*India*]; yardman, journeyman.

bailiff, castellan *or* castellain, seneschal, chamberlain, major-domo, groom of the chambers.

secretary; under–, assistant- secretary; stenographer, clerk; subsidiary; agent etc. 758; subaltern; underling, understrapper; man.

maid, maidservant; girl, help, handmaid; confidant (*fem.* confidante), *confident (fem. confidente)* [*F.*]; lady's maid, abigail, soubrette, amah [*Oriental*], biddy [*colloq.*], *bonne* [*F.*], ayah [*India*]; nurse–, nursery–, house–, parlor–, waiting–, chamber–, kitchen–, scullery-maid; *femme –, fille- de chambre* [*F.*]; *chef de cuisine* [*F.*], *cordon bleu* [*F.*], chef, cook, scullion, Cinderella; pot-walloper; maid–, servant-of all work; slavey [*slang, Eng.*], general servant [*Brit.*], general housework maid, general [*colloq.*]; washerwoman, laundress, bedmaker; charwoman etc. (*worker*) 690.

dependent *or* dependant, hanger-on, led friend [*obs.*], satellite; parasite etc. (*servility*) 886; led captain; *protégé* [*F.*], ward, hireling, mercenary, puppet, man of straw, creature; serf, vassal, slave, negro, helot; bondsman, bondswoman; bondslave, *âme damnée* [*F.*], odalisque *or* odalisk, ryot, *adscriptus gleboe* [*L.*], villein *or* villain [*hist.*], churl *or* ceorl [*hist.*]; beadsman *or* bedesman; sizar *or* sizer [*Camb. & Dublin Univs.*], pensioner, pensionary; client.

badge of slavery; bonds etc. 752.

v. **serve,** minister to, help, coöperate; wait–, attend–, dance attendance–, fasten oneself–, pin oneself- upon; squire, valet, tend, hang on the sleeve of; chore [*dial.*], do the chores [*colloq.*], char [*dial. Eng.*], do for [*colloq.*], fag.

adj. **serviceable,** useful, helpful; cooperative.

serving etc. *v.*; in the train of; in one's -pay, –employ; at one's call etc. (*obedient*) 743; in bonds.

servile, slavish, vernile [*rare*]; subject, thrall, bond; subservient, obsequious, base, fawning, truckling, sycophantic *or* sycophantical, sycophantish [*rare*], parasitic, cringing.

747. Scepter

[insignia of authority]

n. [**regal**] scepter *or* sceptre, rod of empire; orb; pall; robes of -state, –royalty; ermine, purple; crown, coronet, diadem, cap of maintenance; triple plume, Prince of Wales's feathers; uraeus, flail [*both Egyptian*]; signet, seal.

[ecclesiastical] tiara, triple crown; ring, keys; miter *or* mitre, crozier, crook, staff; cardinal's hat; bishop's -apron, –sleeves, –lawn, –gaiters, –shovel hat; fillet.

[military] epaulet *or* epaulette, star, bar, eagle, crown [*Brit.*], oak leaf, Sam Browne belt; chevron, stripe.

caduceus; Mercury's -staff, –rod, –wand; mace, fasces, ax *or* axe, truncheon, staff, baton, wand, rod; staff–, rod- -of office, –of authority; in-

signia–, ensign–, emblem–, badge- of authority; flag etc. (*insignia*) 550; regalia; toga, mantle, decoration; title etc. 877; portfolio.

throne, Peacock throne [*Chinese*], musnud *or* masnad [*Ar.*]; raj-gaddi, gaddi *or* guddee [*India*], divan; wool-sack, chair; dais etc. (*seat*) 215.

talisman, amulet, charm, sign.

helm; reins etc. (*means of restraint*) 752.

748. Freedom

n. **freedom,** liberty, independence; license etc. (*permission*) 760; eleutherism [*rare*]; facility etc. 705.

scope, range, latitude, play; free–, full- -play, -scope; free field and no favor; swing, full swing, elbowroom, margin, rope, wide berth; Liberty Hall.

franchise, denization; prerogative etc. (*dueness*) 924.

freeman, freedman, liveryman [*London guilds*], citizen, denizen.

immunity, exemption; emancipation etc. (*liberation*) 750; affranchisement, enfranchisement; right, privilege.

autonomy, self-government, liberalism, free trade; self-determination; noninterference etc. 706; Monroe Doctrine.

free land, freehold; alod *or* allod, alodium *or* allodium; frankalmoign *or* frankalmoigne [*Eng. law*], tenure in (*or* by) free alms [*Eng. law*]; dead hand, mortmain [*law*].

independent, free lance, freethinker, free trader *or* freetrader; bushwhacker.

v. **be free** etc. *adj.*; have -scope etc. *n.*, - the run of, –one's own way, –a will of one's own, –one's fling; do what one -likes, –wishes, –pleases, –chooses; go at large, feel at home, paddle one's own canoe; stand on one's rights; stand on one's own legs; shift for oneself.

take a liberty; make free with, make oneself quite at home; use a freedom; take leave, take French leave.

free, liberate, set free etc. 750; give the reins to etc. (*permit*) 760; allow–, give -scope etc. *n.* to; give a horse his head.

make free of; give the -freedom of, –franchise; enfranchise, affranchise.

laisser faire [*F.*], *laisser aller* [*F.*]; live and let live; leave to oneself; leave *or* let alone, mind one's own business.

adj. **free,** -as air; out of harness, independent, at large, loose, scot-free; left -alone, –to oneself.

unconstrained, unbuttoned, unconfined, unrestrained, unchecked, unprevented, unhindered, unobstructed, unbound, uncontrolled, untrammeled, uncaught; in full swing.

unsubject, ungoverned, unenslaved, unenthralled, unchained, unshackled, unfettered, unreined, unbridled, uncurbed, unmuzzled, unvanquished.

unrestricted, unlimited, unconditional; absolute; with unlimited -power, −opportunity; discretionary etc. (*optional*) 600.

unassailed, unforced, uncompelled.

unbiased, unprejudiced, uninfluenced; spontaneous.

free and easy; at−, at one's- ease; *dégagé* [*F.*], quite at home; beyond all bounds; wanton, rampant, irrepressible.

exempt; freed etc. 750; freeborn; autonomous, freehold, alodial *or* allodial; eleutherian [*rare*].

gratuitous, gratis etc. 815; for nothing, for love.

unclaimed, going a-begging.

adv. freely etc. *adj.*; ad libitum [*L.*] etc. (*at will*) 600; with no restraint etc. 751.

749. Subjection

n. **subjection**; dependence, dependency; subordination; thrall, thralldom *or* thraldom, enthrallment *or* enthralment, subjugation, bondage, serfdom; feudalism, feudality; vassalage, villenage *or* villeinage, slavery, enslavement, involuntary servitude; conquest.

service; servitude, servitorship; tendence, employ, tutelage, clientship; liability etc. 177; constraint etc. 751; oppression etc. (*severity*) 739; yoke etc. (*means of restraint*) 752; submission etc. 725; obedience etc. 743.

v. **be subject** etc. *adj.*; be *or* lie at the mercy of; depend−, lean−, hang- upon; fall a prey to, fall under; play second fiddle.

be a -mere machine, −puppet, −doormat, −football; not dare to say one's soul is his own; drag a chain.

serve etc. 746; obey etc. 743; submit etc. 725.

subjugate, subject, tame, break in; master etc. 731; tread -down, −under foot; weigh down; drag at one's chariot wheel; reduce to -subjection, −slavery; enthrall *or* enthral, inthrall *or* inthral, bethrall, enslave, lead captive; take into custody etc. (*restrain*) 751; rule etc. 737; drive into a corner, hold at the sword's point; keep under; hold in -bondage, −leading strings, −swaddling clothes; have at one's -apron strings, −beck and call; have in one's pocket.

adj. **subject**, dependent, subordinate; feudal, feudatory; in subjection to, servitorial [*rare*], under

control; in leading strings, in harness; subjected, thrall [*archaic*]; servile, slavish etc. 746; enslaved etc. *v.*; constrained etc. 751; downtrodden; overborne, overwhelmed; under the lash, on the hip, led by the nose, henpecked; the -puppet, −sport, −plaything- of; under one's -orders, −command, −thumb; used as a doormat, treated like dirt under one's feet; a slave to; at the mercy of; in the -power, −hands, −clutches- of; at the feet of; in one's pocket; tied to one's apron strings; uxorious; at one's beck and call etc. (*obedient*) 743; liable etc. 177; parasitical; stipendiary.

adv. **under**; under -orders, −the heel, −command; at one's orders; with no -mind, −will, −soul- of one's own.

750. Liberation

n. **liberation**, disengagement, release, enlargement, emancipation, disenthrallment *or* disenthralment, Emancipation Proclamation; affranchisement, enfranchisement; manumission; discharge, dismissal.

deliverance etc. 672; redemption, extrication, acquittance, absolution; acquittal etc. 970; escape etc. 671.

v. **liberate**, free; set free, set at liberty; render free, emancipate, release; enfranchise, affranchise; manumit; enlarge; demobilize, disband, discharge, disenthrall *or* disenthral, disinthrall *or* disinthral, dismiss; let go, let loose, let out, let slip; cast−, turn- adrift; deliver etc. 672; absolve etc. (*acquit*) 970.

unfetter etc. 751, untie etc. 43; loose etc. (*disjoin*) 44; loosen, relax; unbolt, unbar, unclose, uncork, unclog, unhand, unbind, unchain, unharness; disengage, disentangle; clear, extricate, unloose; reprieve.

become free; gain−, obtain−, acquire- one's -liberty etc. 748; get rid of, get clear of; deliver oneself from; shake off the yoke, slip the collar; break loose, break prison; tear asunder one's bonds, cast off trammels; escape etc. 671.

adj. **liberated** etc. *v.*; out of harness etc. (*free*) 748; foot-loose; breathing free air again; one's own master again.

adv. **at large**, at liberty; adrift.

int. unhand me! let me go! reprieve! go in peace! free!

751. Restraint

n. **restraint**; hindrance etc. 706; coercion etc. (*compulsion*) 744; cohibition [*rare*], constraint, repression; discipline, control.

limitation, restriction, protection, monopoly; prohibition etc. 761; economic pressure.

confinement, restringency [*obs.*], durance, duress; imprisonment; incarceration, coarctation [*obs.*], entombment, mancipation [*obs.*], thrall; thralldom etc. (*subjection*) 749; durance vile, limbo, captivity; blockade; detention camp; quarantine station.

arrest, arrestation [*rare*], arrestment, custody.

keep, care, charge, ward.

curb etc. (*means of restraint*) 752; *lettres de cachet* [*F.*].

repressionist, monopolist, protectionist.

prisoner etc. 754.

v. **restrain,** check; put–, lay- under restraint, put under arrest; enthrall *or* enthral, inthrall *or* inthral, bethrall *or* bethral; restrict; debar etc. (*hinder*) 706; constrain; coerce etc. (*compel*) 744; curb, control; hold–, keep- -back, –from, –in, –in check, –within bounds; hold in -leash, –leading strings; withhold.

repress, suppress; keep under; smother; pull in, rein in; hold, –fast; keep a tight hand on; prohibit etc. 761; inhibit, cohibit.

fasten etc. (*join*) 43; enchain, fetter, shackle; entrammel, trammel; bridle, muzzle, hopple, gag, pinion, manacle, handcuff, tie one's hands, hobble, bind, bind hand and foot; swathe, swaddle; pin down, tether; picket; tie, –up, –down; peg -out, –down; keep [*archaic*], secure; forge fetters.

confine; shut -up, –in; clap up, lock up, box up, mew up, bottle up, cork up, seal up, button up; hem in, bolt in, wall in, rail in; impound, pen, coop; inclose etc. (*circumscribe*) 229; cage; incage *or* encage; close the door upon, cloister; imprison, jug [*slang*], immure; incarcerate, entomb; clap–, lay- under hatches; put in -irons, –a strait-waistcoat; throw–, cast- into prison; put into bilboes.

arrest; take -up, –charge of, –into custody; restringe [*rare*], cohibit [*rare*]; take–, make- -prisoner, –captive; captivate [*rare*]; lead -captive; –into captivity; send–, commit- to prison; commit; give in -charge, –custody; subjugate etc. 749.

adj. **restrained,** constrained; imprisoned etc. *v.*; pent up; jammed in, packed in, wedged in; under -restraint, –lock and key, –hatches; in swaddling clothes; on parole; serving–, doing- time [*colloq. or slang*]; in irons, in the guardhouse; in custody etc. (*prisoner*) 754; cohibitive [*rare*]; mancipatory [*Rom. law*]; coactive etc. (*compulsory*) 744.

icebound, windbound, weatherbound; "cabined, cribbed, confined" [*Macbeth*]; in lob's pound, laid by the heels.

stiff, restringent [*obs.*], narrow, prudish, straitlaced, hidebound, barkbound.

adv. **under restraint,** under discipline; in prison, in jail, in durance vile, in confinement; behind bars; in captivity, during captivity; under arrest; under prohibition; within limits, within bounds.

752. Prison
[means of restraint]

n. **prison,** prisonhouse; jail *or* gaol, cage, coop, den, cell; stronghold, fortress, keep, donjon, dungeon, Bastille, *oubliette* [*F.*], bridewell [*Eng.*], jug [*slang*], house of correction, hulks, tollbooth, panopticon, penitentiary, state prison, guardroom, lockup, roundhouse [*archaic*], watch-house [*obs. or Scot.*], station house, station [*colloq.*], sponging house; house of detention, poky [*slang*], black hole, pen [*also slang for penitentiary*], fold, pinfold *or* penfold, pound; inclosure etc. 232; penal settlement; bilboes, stocks, limbo *or* limbus, quod [*slang*], hoosegow [*slang*], calaboose [*local*], choky *or* chokey [*Anglo-Ind. or slang, Eng.*]; chauki, thana [*both India*]; workhouse [*U.S.; in England, a workhouse is a poorhouse*], reformatory, reform school; debtor's prison, college [*slang, Eng.*].

Tower, Newgate, Fleet, Marshalsea; King's (*or* Queen's) Bench; Alcatraz, Sing Sing, the Tombs.

[restraining devices] shackle, bond, gyve, fetter, trammel, irons, pinion, manacle, handcuff, strait-waistcoat, hopples; vise *or* vice; bandage, splint, strap.

yoke, collar, halter, harness; muzzle, gag, bit, curb, snaffle, bridle; rein, reins; bearing rein; martingale; leading string; tether, picket, band, guy, chain; cord etc. (*fastening*) 45; cavesson, hackamore [*Western U.S.*], jaquima [*S. W. U. S.*], headstall, lines [*U.S. & dial. Eng.*], ribbons [*colloq.*]; brake.

bar, bolt, lock, padlock; rail, paling, palisade; wall, fence, barrier, barricade.

drag etc. (*hindrance*) 706.

adj. imprisoned etc. (*restrained*) 751.

753. Keeper

n. **keeper,** custodian, *custos* [*L.*], ranger, gamekeeper, warder, jailer *or* gaoler, turnkey, castellan, guard; watch, watchdog, watchman, night watchman, Charley *or* Charlie [*Brit.*]; chokidar

[*Anglo-Ind.*], durwan [*Anglo-Ind.*], hayward; sentry, sentinel, watch and ward; *concierge* [*F.*], coastguard.

escort, bodyguard; convoy.

guardian, protector, governor, duenna; governess etc. (*teacher*) 540; nurse, *bonne* [*F.*], amah [*Oriental*], ayah [*India*].

754. Prisoner

n. **prisoner**, convict, captive, *détenu* [*F.*], collegian [*slang*], close prisoner.

jailbird or gaolbird, ticket-of-leave man [*Brit.*], *chevronné* [*F.*].

v. stand committed, be imprisoned etc. 751.

adj. **imprisoned** etc. 751; in prison, in quod [*slang*], in durance vile, in limbo, in custody, in charge, in chains; behind bars; under lock and key, under hatches.

on parole.

755. Commission

[vicarious authority]

n. **commission**, delegation; consignment, assignment; proxy, power of attorney, procuration; deputation, legation, mission, embassy; agency, agentship; clerkship.

errand, charge, brevet, diploma, exequatur, permit etc. (*permission*) 760.

appointment, nomination, return; charter; ordination; installation, inauguration, investiture; accession, coronation, enthronement.

regency, regentship; vicegerency.

viceroy etc. 745; consignee etc. 758; deputy etc. 759.

v. **commission**, delegate, depute; consign, assign; charge; intrust *or* entrust; commit, —to the hands of; authorize etc. (*permit*) 760.

put in commission, accredit, engage, hire, bespeak, appoint, name, nominate, return, ordain; install, induct, inaugurate, invest, crown; enroll, enlist; give power of attorney to; employ, empower; set—, place- over; send out.

be commissioned, be accredited; represent, stand for; stand in the -stead, -place, -shoes- of.

adj. commissioned etc. *v.*

adv. **instead of**; in one's -stead, —place; as proxy for; *per procurationem* [*L.*], *in loco parentis* [*L.*].

756. Abrogation

n. **abrogation**, annulment, nullification; *vacatur* [*L.*]; *nolle prosequi* [*L., law*]; canceling etc. *v.*; cancel; revocation, revokement; repeal, rescission, defeasance.

dismissal, *congé* [*F.*], demission [*obs.*]; bounce [*slang*]; deposal, deposition; dethronement;

disestablishment, disendowment; secularization, deconsecration; sack [*slang*], walking-papers, walking-ticket [*both colloq.*], yellow cover [*slang*].

abolition, abolishment; dissolution.

counterorder, countermand; repudiation, retractation; recantation etc. (*tergiversation*) 607.

abolitionist, prohibitionist.

v. **abrogate**, annul, cancel; destroy etc. 162; abolish; revoke, repeal, rescind, reverse, retract, recall; overrule, override; set aside; disannul, dissolve, quash, nullify, make void, nol-pros [*law*], declare null and void; disestablish, disendow; deconsecrate.

countermand, counterorder; do away with; sweep—, brush- away; throw overboard, throw to the dogs; scatter to the winds, cast behind.

disclaim etc. (*deny*) 536; ignore, repudiate; recant etc. 607; divest oneself, break off.

dismiss, discard; cast—, turn- -off, —out, —adrift, —out of doors, —aside, —away; send off, send away, send about one's business; discharge, get rid of etc. (*eject*) 297; bounce [*slang*]; fire, fire out, sack [*all slang*].

cashier; break; oust; unseat, unsaddle; unthrone, dethrone, disenthrone, depose, uncrown; unfrock, strike off the roll; disbar, disbench.

be abrogated etc.; receive its quietus.

adj. **abrogated** etc. *v.; functus officio* [*L.*].

int. get along with you! begone! go about your business! away with!

757. Resignation

n. **resignation**, retirement, abdication; renunciation, retractation, retraction, renunciance [*rare*], disclamation, disclaimer, abjuration; abandonment, relinquishment.

v. **resign**; give up, throw up; lay down, throw up the cards, wash one's hands of, abjure, renounce, forego, disclaim, retract; deny etc. 536.

abrogate etc. 756; desert etc. (*relinquish*) 624; get rid of etc. 782.

vacate, —one's seat; abdicate; accept the stewardship of the Chiltern Hundreds [*Eng.*]; retire; tender—, pass in—, hand in- one's resignation.

adj. **abdicant**; resigning etc. *v.;* renunciatory, renunciant [*rare*], abjuratory, disclamatory [*rare*], retractive.

758. Consignee

n. **consignee**, trustee, nominee; committee.

functionary, placeman, curator; treasurer etc. 801; agent, factor, reeve [*Eng. hist.*], steward, gomashta [*India*], bailiff, clerk, secretary, attorney, solicitor, proctor, broker, dalal

[*India*], dubash [*India*]; insurer, underwriter, commission agent, auctioneer, one's man of business; factotum etc. (*director*) 694; caretaker; garnishee; under agent, employé; servant etc. 746.

negotiator, go-between; middleman; shop steward *and* walking delegate [*labor unions*].

delegate; commissary, commissioner; emissary, envoy, commissionaire; messenger etc. 534.

diplomatist, diplomat *or* diplomate, *corps diplomatique* [*F.*], embassy; ambassador *or* embassador, diplomatic agent, representative, resident, consul, legate, nuncio, internuncio, *chargé d'affaires* [*F.*], *attaché* [*F.*]; vicegerent etc. (*deputy*) 759; plenipotentiary.

salesman, traveler, bagman, *commis voyageur* [*F.*], traveling salesman, commercial traveler, drummer [*U. S.*], traveling man; agent for (firm *or* commodity); touter [*colloq.*], barker [*colloq*].

reporter; newspaper–, own–, foreign–, war–, special- correspondent.

759. Deputy

n. **deputy**, substitute, proxy, *locum tenens* [*L.*], *badli* [*Hind.*], delegate, representative, next friend [*law*], pinch hitter [*cant*], *prochein ami* [*F. law*], surrogate, secondary; vice-president, vice-chairman, vice [*colloq.*].

regent, vicegerent, vizier, minister, vicar; premier etc. (*director*) 694; chancellor, prefect, provost, warden, lieutenant, archon [*antiq.*], consul, proconsul [*Rom. antiq.*]; viceroy etc. (*governor*) 745; ambassador; commissioner etc. 758; plenipotentiary, plenipotent; *alter ego* [*L.*].

team, eight, nine, eleven; captain, champion.

v. **be deputy** etc. *n.;* stand–, appear–, hold a brief–, answer- for; represent; stand–, walk- in the shoes of; stand in the stead of.

delegate, depute, empower, commission, substitute, ablegate [*R. C. Ch.*], accredit.

adj. **acting**; vice, viceregal; accredited to; delegated etc. *v.;* representative, plenipotent [*rare*], consular, proconsular.

adv. **in behalf of**, in the place of, as representing, by proxy.

Section 2. Special

760. Permission

n. **permission**, leave; allowance, sufferance; tolerance, toleration; liberty, law, license, concession, grace; indulgence etc. (*lenity*) 740; favor, dispensation, exemption, release; connivance; vouchsafement.

authorization, warranty [*law*], accordance, admission.

permit, warrant, brevet, precept, sanction, authority, firman; *hukm* [*Hind.*]; pass, passport; furlough, license, *carte blanche* [*F.*], ticket of leave; grant, charter, patent.

v. **permit**; give permission etc. *n.*, give power; let, allow, admit; suffer, bear with, tolerate, recognize; concede etc. 762; accord, vouchsafe, favor, humor, gratify, indulge, stretch a point; wink at, connive at; shut one's eyes to.

grant, empower, charter, enfranchise, privilege, confer a privilege, license, authorize, warrant; sanction; intrust etc. (*commission*) 755.

give *carte blanche* [*F.*], give the reins to, give scope to etc. (*freedom*) 748; leave -alone, –it to one, –the door open; open the -door to, –floodgates; give a loose to [*obs.*].

ask–, beg–, crave–, request- -leave, –permission.

let off; absolve etc. (*acquit*) 970; release, exonerate, dispense with.

adj. **permitting** etc. *v.;* permissive, indulgent.

permitted etc. *v.;* patent, chartered, permissible, allowable, lawful, legitimate, legal; legalized etc. (*law*) 963; licit; unforbid [*archaic*], unforbidden; unconditional.

adv. **permissibly**, licitly; by–, with–, on- leave etc. *n.; speciali gratia* [*L.*]; under favor of; *pace* [*L.*]; *ad libitum* [*L.*] etc. (*freely*) 748, (*at will*) 600; by all means etc. (*willingly*) 602; yes etc. (*assent*) 488.

761. Prohibition

n. **prohibition**, inhibition; veto, disallowance; interdict, interdiction; injunction; embargo, ban, taboo *or* tabu, proscription; *index expurgatorius* [*L.*], restriction etc. (*restraint*) 751; hindrance etc. 706; forbidden fruit; Maine law, Volstead Act, 18th amendment.

v. prohibit, inhibit; forbid, put one's veto upon, disallow; bar; debar etc. (*hinder*) 706, forfend *or* forefend [*archaic*].

restrain etc. 751; keep -in, –within bounds; cohibit [*rare*], withhold, limit, circumscribe, clip the wings of, restrict; interdict, taboo *or* tabu; put–, place- under -an interdiction, –the ban; proscribe; exclude, shut out; shut–, bolt–, show- the door; warn off; dash the cup from one's lips; forbid the banns.

adj. **prohibitive**, prohibitory; proscriptive; restrictive, exclusive; forbidding etc. *v.*

prohibited etc. *v.;* not permitted etc. 760; unlicensed, contraband, under the ban of, taboo *or* tabu; illegal etc. 964; unauthorized, not to be thought of.

adv. on no account etc. (*no*) 536.

int. forbid it heaven! heaven forbid! etc. (*deprecation*) 766.

hands off! keep off! hold! stop! avast!

762. Consent

n. **consent**; assent etc. 488; acquiescence; approval etc. 931; compliance, agreement, concession; yieldance [*obs.*], yieldingness; accession, acknowledgment, acceptance, agnition [*obs.*].

settlement, adjustment, ratification, confirmation.

permit etc. (*permission*) 760; promise etc. 768.

v. **consent**; assent etc. 488; yield assent, admit, allow, concede, grant, yield; come over, come round; give into, acknowledge, agnize [*archaic*], give consent, comply with, acquiesce, agree to, fall in with, accede, accept, embrace an offer, close with, take at one's word, have no objection.

satisfy, meet one's wishes, settle, come to terms etc. 488; not refuse etc. 764; turn a willing ear etc. (*willingness*) 602; jump at; deign, vouchsafe; promise etc. 768.

adj. **consenting** etc. *v.;* complaint, agreeable [*colloq.*], willing, eager; agreed etc. (*assent*) 488; unconditional.

adv. **yes** etc. (*assent*) 488; by all means etc. (*willingly*) 602; if you please, as you please; be it so, so be it, well and good, of course.

763. Offer

n. **offer**, proffer, presentation, tender, bid, overture; proposal, proposition; motion, invitation; candidature, candidacy; offering etc. (*gift*) 784.

v. **offer**, proffer, present, tender; bid; propose, move; make a motion, make advances; start; invite, hold out, place in one's way; put–, place- at one's disposal; put in one's power, make possible, put forward.

hawk about; offer for sale etc. 796; press etc. (*request*) 765; go a-begging; lay at one's feet.

volunteer, come forward, be a candidate; offer–, present- oneself; stand for, bid for; seek; be at one's service.

bribe etc. (*give*) 784; grease the palm [*slang*].

adj. **offering**, offered etc. *v.;* in the market, for sale, to let, disengaged, on hire; at one's disposal.

764. Refusal

n. **refusal**, rejection; noncompliance, incompliance; denial; declining etc. *v.;* declension; declinature; peremptory–, flat–, point blank- refusal;

repulse, rebuff; discountenance, disapprobation.

negation, recusancy, abnegation, protest, disclamation, renunciation, disclaimer; dissent etc. 489; revocation etc. 756.

v. **refuse**, reject, deny, decline; nill [*archaic*], turn down [*slang*], abnegate, negate, negative; refuse–, withhold- one's assent; shake the head; close the -hand, –purse; grudge, begrudge, be slow to, hang fire; pass [*at cards*].

stand aloof, be deaf to; turn a deaf ear to, turn one's back upon; set one's face against, discountenance, not hear of, have nothing to do with, wash one's hands of, forswear, set aside, cast behind one; not yield an inch etc. (*obstinacy*) 606.

resist, cross; not grant etc. 762; repel, repulse; shut–, slam- the door in one's face; rebuff; send -back, –to the right about, –away with a flea in the ear [*colloq.*]; deny oneself, not be at home to; discard etc. (*repudiate*) 610; rescind etc. (*revoke*) 756; disclaim, protest; dissent etc. 489.

adj. **refusing** etc. *v.;* restive, restiff [*obs.*]; recusant; uncomplying, noncompliant, incompliant, unconsenting; declinatory, uncomplaisant, disclamatory [*rare*], negatory, protestant; not willing to hear of, deaf to.

refused etc. *v.;* ungranted, out of the question, not to be thought of, impossible.

adv. **no** etc. 536; on no account, not for the world; no thank you; your humble servant [*ironically*], *bien obligé* [*F.*], not on your life!

765. Request

n. **request**, requisition; claim etc. (*demand*) 741; petition, suit, prayer; begging letter, round robin.

motion, overture, application, canvass, address, appeal, apostrophe; imprecation; rogation [*eccl.*]; proposal, proposition.

orison etc. (*worship*) 990; incantation etc. (*spell*) 993.

mendicancy, mendication [*rare*]; asking, begging etc. *v.;* postulation, solicitation, invitation, entreaty, importunity, supplication, instance, impetration, imploration, obsecration, obtestation, invocation, interpellation.

v. **request**, ask, beg, crave, sue, pray, petition, solicit, invite, pop the question [*colloq.*], make bold to ask; beg leave, beg a boon; apply to, call to, put to; call upon, call for; make–, address–, prefer–, put up- a -request, –prayer, –petition; make -application, –a requisition; ask–, trouble- one for; claim etc. (*demand*) 741;

offer up prayers etc. (*worship*) 990; whistle for [*colloq.*].

bespeak, canvass, tout [*cant, Eng.*], make interest, court; seek, bid for etc. (*offer*) 763; publish the banns.

entreat, beseech, plead, supplicate, beg hard, implore; conjure, adjure; obsecrate [*rare*], apostrophize, obtest [*rare*]; cry to, kneel to, appeal to; invoke, evoke; impetrate, imprecate, ply, press, urge, beset, importune, dun, tax, clamor for; cry aloud, cry for help; fall on one's knees; throw oneself at the feet of; come down on one's marrowbones [*slang or humorous*].

beg from door to door, send the hat round, go a-begging; mendicate [*rare*], mump, cadge [*dial. or slang, Eng.*], beg one's bread.

dance attendance on, besiege, knock at the door.

adj. **requesting** etc. *v.,* precatory, supplant, supplicant, supplicatory, invocative, invocatory, invitatory, imprecatory, rogatory; postulatory [*rare*], postulant; obsecratory [*rare*], obsecrationary [*rare*]; imploratory [*rare*], mendicant, mendicatory [*obs.*].

importunate, clamorous, urgent, solicitous; cap in hand; on one's -knees, -bended knees, -marrowbones [*slang or humorous*].

adv. **please**, prithee, do, pray; be so good as, be good enough; have the goodness, vouchsafe, will you, I pray thee, if you please.

int. for- God's, -heaven's - goodness', -mercy's- sake! we beseech thee to hear us! help! save me!

766. Deprecation
[negative request]

n. **deprecation**, expostulation; intercession, mediation, protest, remonstrance.

v. **deprecate**, protest, expostulate, enter a protest, intercede for; remonstrate.

adj. **deprecatory**, expostulatory, intercessory, mediatorial.

deprecated, protested.

unsought, unbesought; unasked etc. (*see* ask etc. 765).

Int. **God forbid**! cry you mercy! forbid it Heaven! Heaven forfend (*or* forefend)! Heaven forbid! far be it from! hands off! etc. (*prohibition*) 761.

767. Petitioner

n. **petitioner**, solicitor, applicant, suppliant, supplicant, suitor, candidate, claimant, postulant, aspirant, competitor, bidder; place hunter, pothunter, prizer [*archaic*].

salesman, drummer [*archaic*]; bagman etc. 758; canvasser.

beggar, mendicant, mumper, sturdy beggar, panhandler [*slang*], cadger.

hotel runner [*cant*] touter [*colloq.*], runner [*cant*], steerer, tout [*cant, Eng.*]; barker [*colloq.*].

sycophant, parasite etc. (servility) 886.

Section 3. Conditional

768. Promise

n. **promise**, undertaking, word, troth, plight, pledge, parole, word of honor, vow; oath etc. (*affirmation*) 535; profession, assurance, warranty, guarantee, insurance, obligation; contract etc. 769; stipulation.

engagement, preengagement; affiance; betrothal, betrothment; marriage -contract, -vow; plighted faith, troth-plight [*Scot. or dial.*], gage d'amour [*F.*].

v. **promise**; give a promise etc. *n.;* undertake, engage; make-, form- an engagement; enter into *or* on an engagement; bind-, tie-, pledge-, commit-, take upon- oneself; vow; swear etc. (*affirm*) 535, give-, pass-, pledge-, plight- one's -word, -honor, -credit, -troth; betroth, plight faith, take the vows, trothplight [*Scot. or dial.*].

assure, warrant, guarantee; covenant etc. 769; avouch, vouch for; attest etc. (*bear witness*) 467.

hold out an expectation; contract an obligation; become bound to, become sponsor for; answer for, be answerable for; secure; give security etc. 771; underwrite.

adjure, administer an oath, put to one's oath, swear a witness.

adj. **promising** etc. *v.;* promissory; votive; under hand and seal, upon oath, upon the Book; upon-, on- affirmation.

promised etc. *v.;* affianced, pledged, bound; committed, compromised; in for it [*colloq.*].

adv. as true as I live; in all soberness; upon my honor; my word for it; my head upon it; I call God to witness; as one's head shall answer for; *ex voto* [*L.*].

768a. Release from engagement

n. **release** etc. (*liberation*) 750.

adj. **absolute**; unconditional etc. (*free*) 748.

769. Compact

n. **compact**, contract, specialty, bundobast [*India*], deal [*colloq.*], agreement, bargain; affidation [*rare*], pact, paction [*chiefly Scot.*], bond, covenant, indenture [*law*].

stipulation, settlement, convention; compromise, cartel.

negotiation etc. (*bargaining*) 794; diplomacy etc. (*mediation*) 724; negotiator etc. (*agent*) 758.

treaty, protocol, concordat, *Zollverein* [*Ger.*], *Sonderbund* [*Ger.*], charter, Magna Charta *or* Magna Carta, pragmatic sanction.

ratification, completion, signature, seal, sigil, signet, bond.

v. **contract**, covenant, agree for; engage etc. (*promise*) 768; indent.

negotiate, treat, stipulate, make terms; bargain etc. (*barter*) 794.

conclude, close, close with, complete; make-, strike- a bargain; come to -terms, -an understanding; compromise etc. 774; set at rest; settle; confirm, ratify, clinch *or* clench, subscribe, underwrite; indorse, endorse, put the seal to; sign on the dotted line; sign, seal etc. (*attest*) 467; take one at one's word, bargain by inch of candle.

adj. **contractual**, complete; agreed etc. *v.;* conventional; under hand and seal; signed, sealed, and delivered.

adv. **as agreed upon**, as promised, as contracted for; according to the -contract, -bargain, -agreement, on the dotted line [*slang*].

770. Conditions

n. **conditions**, terms; articles, -of agreement; memorandum; clauses, provisions; proviso etc. (*qualification*) 469; covenant, stipulation, obligation, ultimatum, *sine qua non* [*L.*]; *casus foederis* [*L.*].

v. **condition**, make it a condition, stipulate, insist upon, make a point of; bind, tie up; fence in, hedge in, have a string to it [*colloq.*]; make-, come to- -terms etc. (*contract*) 769.

adj. **conditional**, provisional, guarded, fenced, hedged in.

adv. **conditionally** etc. (*with qualification*) 469; provisionally, *pro re nata* [*L.*], on condition; with a string to it [*colloq.*], with strings attached [*colloq.*], with a reservation.

771. Security

n. **security**; guaranty, guarantee; gage, warranty, bond, tie, pledge, *vadium vivum* [*L.*], plight [*rare*], mortgage, *vadium mortuum* [*L.*], debenture, hypothec [*Rom. & civil law*], hypothecation, bill of sale, lien, pawn, pignoration; real security; vadium, collateral, bail; parole etc. (*promise*) 768.

stake, deposit, earnest, handsel *or* hansel, handsale, caution [*Scot. law*].

promissory note; bill, -of exchange; I.O.U.; personal security, covenant.

acceptance, indorsement *or* endorsement, signature, execution, stamp, seal.

sponsor, surety, bail, replevin; mainpernor, mainprise *or* mainprize [*hist. law*]; hostage; godchild, godfather, godmother; sponsion, sponsorship.

recognizance; deed-, covenant- of indemnity.

authentication, verification, warrant, certificate, voucher, docket *or* doquet [*obs.*]; record etc. 551; probate, attested copy.

acquittance, quittance; discharge, release; receipt.

muniments, title deed, instrument; deed, deed poll, indenture; specialty; insurance; charter etc. (*compact*) 769; charter poll; paper, parchment, settlement, will, testament, last will and testament, codicil.

v. **give security**, give bail, give substantial bail; go bail; handsel *or* hansel, pawn, put in pawn, pledge, put up the spout [*slang*], hock [*slang*], impawn *or* empawn [*obs.*], spout [*slang*], impignorate, mortgage, hypothecate.

guarantee, warrant, assure; accept, indorse *or* endorse, underwrite, insure.

execute, stamp; sign, seal etc. (*evidence*) 467.

let, set *or* sett [*Scot. law*]; grant-, take-, hold- a lease; hold in pledge; lend on security etc. 787.

adj. **pledged**, pawned etc. *v.;* secure; impignorate, pignorative [*rare*], in pawn, up the spout [*slang*]; at stake, on deposit, as earnest.

sponsorial, sponsional [*rare*]; as sponsor etc. *n.*

let, leased; held in pledge.

772. Observance

n. **observance**, performance, compliance, acquiescence, concurrence; obedience etc. 743; fulfillment *or* fulfilment, satisfaction, discharge; acquittance, acquittal.

adhesion, acknowledgment; fidelity etc. (*probity*) 939; exact etc. 494- observance; unserving fidelity to.

v. **observe**, comply with, respect, acknowledge, abide by; cling to, adhere to, be faithful to, act up to; meet, fulfill *or* fulfil; carry out, carry into execution; execute, perform, keep, satisfy, discharge; do one's office.

keep faith with; perform-, fulfill-, discharge-, acquit oneself of- an obligation; make good; make good-, keep- one's -word, -promise; redeem one's pledge; stand to one's engagement.

adj. **observant**, faithful, true, loyal; honorable etc. 939; true as the dial to the sun, true as the needle to the pole; punctual, punctilious, scrupulous, meticulous; literal etc. (*exact*) 494; as good as one's word.

adv. **faithfully** etc. *adj.;* to the letter.

773. Nonobservance

n. **nonobservance** etc. 772; evasion, inobservance, failure, omission, neglect, laches [*law*], casualness, slackness, laxness, laxity, informality.

lawlessness; disobedience etc. 742; bad faith etc. 940.

infringement, infraction; violation, transgression; piracy.

retractation, repudiation, nullification; protest; forfeiture.

v. **evade**, fail, neglect, omit, elude, give the go-by to [*slang*], cut [*colloq.*], set aside, ignore; shut–, close- one's eyes to.

infringe, transgress, violate, pirate, break, trample under foot, do violence to, drive a coach and four (*or* six) through.

discard, protest, repudiate, fling to the winds, set at naught, nullify, declare null and void; cancel etc. (*wipe off*) 552.

retract, go back from, be off, forfeit, go from one's word, palter; stretch a point, strain a point.

adj. **violating** etc. *v.;* lawless, transgressive; elusive, evasive, slack, lax, casual, slippery; nonobservant.

unfulfilled etc. (*see* fulfill etc. 772).

774. Compromise

n. **compromise**, commutation, composition; middle term, *mezzo termine* [*It.*]; compensation etc. 30; abatement of differences, adjustment, mutual concession.

v. **compromise**, commute, compound; take the mean; split the difference, meet one halfway, give and take; come to terms etc. (*contact*) 769; submit to arbitration, abide by arbitration; patch up, bridge over, arrange; straighten out, adjust, adjust differences; agree; cut a deal [*slang*]; make the best of, make a virtue of necessity; take the will for the deed.

Section 4. Possessive Relations

775. Acquisition

n. **acquisition**; gaining etc. *v.;* obtainment, procuration, procurement; purchase, descent, inheritance; gift etc. 784.

recovery, retrieval, revendication [*rare*], replevin; redemption, salvage, trover; find, *trouvaille* [*F.*], foundling.

gain, thrift; money-making, money-grubbing; lucre, filthy lucre, loaves and fishes, fleshpots of Egypt, the main chance, pelf; emolument etc. (*remuneration*) 973.

profit, earnings, winnings, innings, pickings, perquisite, accruement [*obs.*], net profit; avails; income etc. (*receipt*) 810; proceeds, produce, product; outcome, output; return, fruit, crop, harvest; second crop, aftermath; benefit etc. (*good*) 618.

prize, sweepstakes, trick, pool; kitty, jackpot, pot; wealth etc. 803.

[fraudulent acquisition] subreption; obreption; stealing etc. 791.

v. **acquire**, get, gain, win, earn, obtain, procure, gather; collect etc. (*assemble*) 72; pick, pick up; glean.

find; come–, pitch–, light- upon; come across, come at; scrape -up, –together; get in, reap and carry, net, bag, sack, bring home, secure; derive, draw, get in the harvest.

get hold of, get between one's finger and thumb, get into one's hand, get at; take–, come into–, enter into- possession.

profit; make–, draw- profit; turn to -profit, –account; make capital out of, make money by; obtain a return, reap the fruits of; reap–, gain- an advantage; turn -a penny, –an honest penny; hit the jackpot [*colloq.*], strike it rich; make the pot boil, bring grist to the mill; make–, coin–, raise- money; raise funds, raise the wind [*slang*]; fill one's pocket etc. (*wealth*) 803.

realize, clear; treasure up etc. (*store*) 636; produce etc. 161; take etc. 789.

receive etc. 785; come by, come in for; inherit; step into, –a fortune, –the shoes of; succeed to.

recover, get back, regain, retrieve, revendicate [*rare*], replevin, replevy, redeem, come by one's own.

be profitable etc. *adj.;* pay, answer.

accrue etc. (*be received*) 785.

adj. **acquisitive**, productive, profitable, advantageous, gainful, remunerative, paying, lucrative, acquiring, acquired etc. *v.*

adv. in the way of gain; for money; at interest.

776. Loss

n. **loss**, perdition, deperdition [*archaic*]; forfeiture, lapse.

privation, bereavement; deprivation etc. (*dispossession*) 789; riddance; damage, squandering, waste.

v. **lose**; incur–, experience–, meet with- a loss; miss; mislay, let slip, allow to slip through the fingers; be deprived of; be without etc. (*exempt*) 777*a*; forfeit, pay with.

squander; get rid of etc. 782; waste etc. 638.

be lost, lapse.

adj. **losing** etc. *v.;* not having etc. 777*a*.

deprived of; shorn of, deperdite [*rare*], denuded, bereaved, bereft, minus [*colloq., exc. in math.*], cut off; dispossessed etc. 789; rid of, quit of; out of pocket.

lost etc. *v.;* long lost; irretrievable etc. (*hopeless*) 859; off one's hands.

int. **farewell to!** adieu to! good riddance.

777. Possession

n. **possession**, seizin *or* seisin; ownership etc. 780; occupancy; hold, holding; tenure, tenancy, feodality, feodatory, feud *or* feod, fief, fee, fee tail, fee simple; dependency; villenage *or* villeinage; socage, chivalry, knight service.

bird in hand, *uti possidetis* [*L.*], chose in possession [*rare*].

exclusive possession, impropriation, monopoly, retention etc. 781; prepossession, preoccupancy; nine points of the law; corner, usucapion *or* usucaption [*Rom. law*], prescription.

future possession, heritage, inheritance, heirship, reversion, fee; primogeniture, ultimogeniture.

v. **possess**, have, hold, occupy, enjoy; be possessed of etc. *adj.;* have in hand etc. *adj.;* own etc. 780; command.

inherit; come to, come in for.

monopolize, engross, forestall, regrate, impropriate, appropriate, usucapt [*Rom. law*], have all to oneself; corner; have a firm hold of etc. (*retain*) 781; get into one's hand etc. (*acquire*) 775.

belong to, appertain to, pertain to; be in one's possession etc. *adj.;* vest in.

adj. **possessing** etc. *v.;* worth; possessed of, seized of, master of, usucapient [*Rom. law*]; in possession of; endowed–, blest–, instinct–, fraught–, laden–, charged- with.

possessed etc. *v.;* on hand, by one; in hand, in store, in stock; unsold, unshared; in one's -hands, –grasp, –possession; at one's command, at one's disposal; one's own etc. (*property*) 780.

777a. Exemption

n. **exemption**; absence etc. 187; exception, immunity, privilege, release.

v. **not have** etc. 777; be without etc. *adj.;* excuse.

adj. **devoid of**, exempt from, without, unpossessed of, unblest with; immune from.

not having etc. 777; unpossessed; untenuated etc. (*vacant*) 187; without an owner.

unobtained, unacquired.

778. Participation

[joint possession]

n. **participation**; condominium, cotenancy, joint tenancy; occupancy–, possession–, tenancy- in common; joint–, common- stock; limited partnership, copartnership, partnership; communion; community of -possessions, –goods; communication, communalization; communism, communalism, collectivism, socialism; cooperation etc. 709.

snacks [*obs.*], coportion [*obs.*], picnic, hotchpot *or* hotchpotch, hodgepodge; coheirship, coparcenary *or* coparceny; gavelkind.

participator, sharer, copartner, partner; shareholder; cotenant, joint tenant; tenants in common; coheir, coparcener.

communist, communitarian, communalist, collectivist, socialist.

v. **participate**, partake; share, share in; come in for a share; go shares, go snacks [*obs.*], go cahoots [*slang*], halve; share and share alike.

join in; have a hand in etc. (*coöperate*) 709.

communize, communalize; have–, possess–, be seized- -in common, –as joint tenants etc. *n.*

adj. **partaking** etc. *v.*

communistic, communalistic, socialistic; cooperative, profit-sharing.

adv. **in common**, share and share alike; on shares; in cahoots [*slang*].

779. Possessor

n. **possessor**, holder; occupant, occupier; tenant; person *or* man in possession etc. 777; renter, lodger, lessee, underlessee; zamindar *or* zemindar [*India*]; ryot [*India*]; tenant -on sufferance, –at will, –from year to year, –for years, –for life.

owner; proprietor, proprietress, proprietary; impropriator, master, mistress, lord.

landholder, landowner, landlord, landlady; lord -of the manor, –paramount; heritor [*Scots law*], laird [*Scot.*], vavasor *or* vavasour [*feud. law*]; landed gentry, mesne lord; planter.

beneficiary, *cestui que* (or *qui*) *trust* [*law*], mortgagor.

grantee, feoffee, feoffee in trust, releasee, devisee; legatee, legatary [*rare*].

trustee; holder etc. of the legal estate; mortgagee. right owner, rightful owner.

[future possessor] heir, −apparent, −presumptive; inheritor, reversioner; remainder-man; heiress, inheritress, inheritrix.

780. Property

n. **property**, possession, seizin *or* seisin; tenure etc. (*possession*) 777; *suum cuique* [*L.*], *meum et tuum* [*L.*].

ownership, proprietorship, lordship; seigniory *or* seignory *or* seigneury, seignoralty; empire etc. (*dominion*) 737.

estate, interest, stake, right, title, claim, demand, holding; vested−, contingent−, beneficial−, equitable- interest; use, trust, benefit; legal−, equitable- estate.

absolute interest, paramount estate, freehold; fee, −simple, −tail; estate -in fee, −in tail, −tail; estate in tail -male, −female, −general.

term, limitation, lease, settlement, strict settlement, particular estate; estate -for life, −for years, −*pur autre vie* [*F.*]; remainder, reversion, expectancy, possibility.

dower, dowry, jointure, appanage *or* apanage, inheritance, heritage, patrimony, alimony; legacy etc. (*gift*) 784; Falcidian law, paternal estate, thirds.

assets, belongings, means, resources, circumstances; wealth etc. 803; money etc. 800; what one -is worth, −will cut up for [*colloq.*]; estate and effects.

realty, land, lands; landed−, real- -estate, −property; tenements; hereditaments; corporeal−, incorporeal- hereditaments; acres; ground etc. (*earth*) 342; acquest, mesestead [*archaic*], messuage, toft [*Scot. & dial. Eng.*].

manor, honor [*Eng. feudal law*], domain, demesne; farm, plantation, hacienda [*Sp. Am.*]; alodium *or* allodium etc. (*free*) 748; feoff, fief, feud *or* feod, zamindari *or* zemindari [*India*], arado [*S. W. U. S.*], rancho [*S. W. U. S.*], ranch, spread.

freeholds, copyholds, leaseholds; folkland [*O. Eng. law*].

chattels real; fixtures, plant, heirloom; easement; right of -common, −user.

territory, state, kingdom, principality, realm, empire, protectorate, dependency, sphere of influence, mandate.

personalty; personal -property, −estate, −effects; chattels, goods, effects, movables; stock, −in trade; things, traps [*colloq.*], chattels

personal, rattletraps, paraphernalia; equipage etc. 633; parcels [*Eng.*], appurtenances.

impedimenta; luggage, baggage; bag and baggage; pelf; cargo, lading.

income etc. (*receipts*) 810; rent roll; maul and wedges [*U. S.*].

patent, copyright; chose in action; credit etc. 805; debt etc. 806.

v. **possess** etc. 777; be the possessor of etc. 779; own; have for one's -own, −very own; come in for, inherit; enfeoff.

savor of the realty.

belong to; be one's property etc. *n.;* pertain to, appertain to.

adj. **one's own**; landed, praedial *or* predial, manorial, alodial *or* allodial; seigniorial *or* seigneurial; freehold, copyhold, leasehold; feudal *or* feodal; hereditary, entailed, real, personal.

adv. **to one's credit**, to one's account; to the good.

to one and -his heirs for ever, −the heirs of his body, −his heirs and assigns, −his executors, administrators and assigns.

781. Retention

n. **retention**; retaining etc. *v.;* keep [*archaic*], detention, custody; tenacity, firm hold, grasp, gripe, grip, iron grip; bond etc. (*vinculum*) 45.

clutches, tongs, forceps, tenaculum, pincers, nippers, pliers, vise, hook.

fangs, teeth, claws, talons, nail, unguis, tentacle.

paw, hand, finger, wrist, fist, nieve *or* nief [*archaic or dial.*].

captive etc. 754; bird in hand.

v. **retain**, keep; hold, −fast, −tight, −one's own, −one's ground; clinch, clench, clutch, grasp, gripe, hug, have a firm hold of.

secure, withhold, detain; hold−, keep- back; keep close; husband etc. (*store*) 636; reserve; have−, keep- in stock etc. (*possess*) 777; entail, tie up, settle.

adj. **retentive**, tenacious; retaining etc. *v.*

unforfeited, undeprived, undisposed, uncommunicated.

incommunicable, inalienable; in mortmain; in strict settlement.

782. Relinquishment

n. **relinquishment**, abandonment etc. (*of a course*) 624; renunciation, expropriation, dereliction; cession, surrender, dispensation; resignation etc. 757; riddance.

derelict etc. *adj.;* jetsam *or* jettison; abandoned farm; waif, foundling.

v. **relinquish**, give up, surrender, yield, cede; let go, let slip; spare, drop, resign, forego, renounce, abandon, expropriate, give away, dispose of, part with; lay -aside, –apart, –down, –on the shelf & (disuse) 678; set aside, put aside; make away with, cast behind; discard, cast off, dismiss; maroon.

cast–, throw–, pitch–, fling- -away, –aside, –overboard, –to the dogs; cast–, throw–, sweep- to the winds; put–, turn–, sweep- away; jettison.

quit one's hold.

supersede, give notice to quit, give warning; be or get rid of; be or get quit of; eject etc. 297.

rid–, disburden–, divest–, dispossess- oneself of; wash one's hands of.

divorce, unmarry [rare]; cut off, desert, disinherit; separate.

adj. **relinquished** etc. v.; cast off, derelict; unowned, disowned, disinherited, divorced; unappropriated, unculled; left etc. (residuary) 40.

int. away with!

783. Transfer

n. **transfer**, conveyance, assignment, alienation, abalienation; demise, limitation; conveyancing; transmission etc. (transference) 270; enfeoffment, bargain and sale, lease and release; exchange etc. (interchange) 148; barter etc. 794; substitution etc. 147.

succession, reversion; shifting use, shifting trust; devolution.

v. **transfer**, convey; alien, alienate; assign; enfeoff; grant etc. (confer) 784; consign; make over, hand over; pass, hand, transmit, negotiate; hand down; exchange etc. (interchange) 148.

change hands, change from one to another; devolve, revert, succeed; come into possession etc. (acquire) 775.

disinherit; abalienate [rare]; dispossess etc. 789; substitute etc. 147.

adj. **alienable**, negotiable, transferable, reversional, transmissive; inherited.

adv. **by transfer** etc. n.; on lease.

784 Giving

n. **giving** etc. v.; bestowal, bestowment, donation; presentation, presentment; accordance; concession, cession; delivery, consignment, dispensation, communication, endowment; investment, investiture; award.

charity, almsgiving, liberality, generosity.

[thing given] gift, donation, present, cadeau [F.]; fairing; free gift, boon, favor, benefaction, grant, offering, oblation, sacrifice, immolation.

grace, act of grace, bonus.

allowance, contribution, subscription, subsidy, tribute, subvention.

bequest, legacy, devise, will, dotation, dot, appanage or apanage, dowry, dower; voluntary -settlement, –conveyance etc. 783; amortization.

gratuity, lagniappe or lagnappe [Louisiana], pilon [S. W. U. S.]; alms, largess, bounty, dole, sportule [obs.], donative, help, oblation, offertory, honorarium, Peter pence, sportula, Christmas box, Easter offering, vails [rare], douceur [F.], drink money, tip, hand out [slang], pourboire [F.], Trinkgeld [G], baksheesh or bakshish, cumshaw [China], dash or dashee [Africa]; fee etc. (recompense) 973; consideration.

bribe, bait, ground bait; peace offering; handsel or hansel; boodle [slang], graft [colloq.], grease [slang].

giver, grantor etc. v.; donor, almoner, testator, feoffer, settlor [law]; investor, subscriber, contributor; Fairy Godmother [or l. c.].

v. **deliver**, hand, pass, put into the hands of; hand–, make–, deliver–, pass–, turn- over; assign dower.

present, give away, dispense, dispose of; give–, deal–, dole–, mete–, squeeze-out; fork over, fork out, shell out [all slang].

make a present; allow, contribute, subscribe, furnish its quota.

pay etc. 807; render, impart, communicate.

concede, cede, yield, part with, shed, cast; spend etc. 809; sacrifice, immolate.

give, bestow, donate, confer, grant, accord, award, assign; offer etc. 763.

intrust, consign, vest in.

invest, endow, settle upon; bequeath, leave, devise.

furnish, supply, help; administer to, minister to; afford, spare; accommodate with, indulge with, favor with; shower down upon; lavish, pour on, thrust upon.

bribe, tip; tickle–, grease- the palm [slang].

adj. **giving** etc. v.; given etc. v.; allowed, allowable; concessional; communicable.

charitable, eleemosynary, sportulary [obs.], tributary; gratis etc. 815; donative.

adv. **as a free gift** etc. n.; in charity; toward the endowment fund.

int. don't mention it! not another word! glad to do it!

785. Receiving

n. **receiving** etc. *v.;* acquisition etc. 775; reception etc. (*introduction*) 296; suscipiency [*rare*], acceptance, admission.

recipient, receiver, suscipient [*rare*], accipient; assignee, devisee; legatee, legatary; grantee, feoffee, donee, relessee, lessee.

beneficiary, sportulary [*obs.*], stipendiary; pensioner, pensionary; almsman.

income etc. (*receipt*) 810.

v. **receive**; take etc. 789; acquire etc. 775; admit.

pocket; take in, catch, touch; put into one's -pocket, –purse; accept; take off one's hands.

be received; come in, come to hand; pass-, fall- into one's hand; go into one's pocket; fall to one's -lot, –share; come-, fall- to one; accrue; have given etc. (784) to one.

adj. **receiving** etc. *v.;* recipient, suscipient [*rare*]; stipendiary, stipendarian, pensionary.

received etc. *v.;* given etc. 784; secondhand.

not given, unbestowed etc. (*see* give, bestow etc. 784).

786. Apportionment

n. **apportionment**, allotment, consignment, assignment, allocation, appointment; appropriation; dispensation, distribution; division, deal; partition, repartition, administration.

portion, dividend, contingent, share, allotment, lot, measure, dose; dole, meed, pittance; *quantum* [*L.*], ration; ratio, proportion, quota, modicum, mess, allowance.

v. **apportion**, divide; distribute, administer, dispense; billet, allot, allocate, detail, cast, share, mete; portion-, parcel-, dole- out; deal, carve.

partition, assign, appropriate, appoint.

participate, come in for one's share etc. 778.

adj. apportioning etc. *v.;* apportioned etc. *v.;* respective.

adv. respectively, each to each; by lot; in equal shares.

787. Lending

n. **lending** etc. *v.;* loan, advance, accommodation, feneration [*obs.*]; mortgage etc. (*security*) 771; investment.

pawnshop, spout [*slang*], *mont de piété* [*F.*], my uncle's [*slang*].

lender, pawnbroker, money lender, usurer, Shylock.

v. **lend**, advance, accommodate with; lend on security; loan; pawn etc. (*security*) 771.

invest; intrust; place-, put- out to interest; place, put; embark, risk, venture, sink, fund.

let, lease, set *or* sett [*Scot. law*], sublet, sublease, underlet; demise.

adj. **lending** etc. *v.;* lent etc. *v.;* come across (*or* down) with the needful [*slang*].

adv. in advance; on loan, on security.

788. Borrowing

n. **borrowing**, pledging, pawning, putting up the spout [*slang*].

borrowed plumes; plagiarism etc. (*thieving*) 791.

v. **borrow**, desume [*obs.*]; pawn, put up the spout [*slang*], patronize my uncle [*slang*].

raise-, take up- money; raise the wind [*slang*]; get the -dough, –needful [*both slang*]; fly a kite, borrow from Peter to pay Paul; run into debt etc. (*debt*) 806.

hire, rent, farm; take a -lease, –demise; take-, hire- by the -hour, –mile, –year etc.

appropriate, adopt, apply, imitate, make use of, take; plagiarize, pirate.

replevy.

adj. borrowed etc. *v.*

789. Taking

n. **taking** etc. *v.;* reception etc. (*taking in*) 296; deglutition etc. (*taking food*) 298; appropriation, prehension [*chiefly zoöl.*], prensation [*obs.*]; capture, caption; apprehension, deprehension [*obs.*]; abreption [*obs.*], seizure; abduction, ablation; subtraction etc. (*subduction*) 38; abstraction, ademption; androlepsia *or* androlepsy.

dispossession; deprivation, deprivement; bereavement; divestment; disinheritance, dishersion; distraint, distress, attachment, execution; sequestration, confiscation; eviction etc. 297.

rapacity, rapaciousness, extortion, predacity; bloodsucking, vampirism; theft etc. 791.

resumption; reprises [*law*], reprisal; recovery etc. 775.

clutch, swoop, wrench; grip etc. (*retention*) 781; haul, take, catch; scramble.

taker, captor, capturer; extortioner *or* extortionist; vampire.

v. **take**, catch, hook, nab [*slang*], bag, sack, pocket, put into one's pocket; receive; accept.

reap, crop, cull, pluck; gather etc. (*get*) 775; draw.

appropriate, impropriate [*Eng. eccl. law*]; assume, possess oneself of; take possession of; commandeer [*colloq.*]; lay–, clap- one's hands on [*colloq.*]; help oneself to; make free with, dip one's hands into, lay under contribution; intercept; scramble for; deprive of.

seize, abstract; take–, carry–, bear- -away, –off; adeem [*law*]; hurry off–, run away- with; abduct; steal etc. 791; ravish; pounce–, spring- upon; swoop to, swoop down upon; take by -storm, –assault; snatch, reave [*archaic*].

snap up, nip up, whip up, catch up; kidnap, crimp, capture, lay violent hands on.

get–, lay–, take–, catch–, lay fast–, take firm- hold of; lay by the heels, take prisoner; fasten upon, grapple, embrace, grip, gripe, clasp, grab [*colloq.*], make away with, clutch, collar, throttle, take by the throat, claw, clinch, clench, make sure of.

catch at, jump at, make a grab at, snap at, snatch at; reach, make a long arm [*colloq.*], stretch forth one's hand.

disseize *or* disseise; take from, take away from; deduct etc. 38; retrench etc. (*curtail*) 201; dispossess, ease one of, snatch from one's grasp; tear–, tear away–, wrench–, wrest–, wring- from; extort; deprive of, bereave; disinherit, cut off with a shilling; oust etc. (*eject*) 297; divest; levy, distrain, confiscate; sequester, sequestrate; accroach; usurp; despoil, strip, fleece, shear, displume.

absorb etc. (*suck in*) 296; draw off; suck, –like a leach, –the blood of; impoverish, eat out of house and home; drain, –to the dregs; gut, dry, exhaust, swallow up.

retake, resume; recover etc. 775.

adj. **taking** etc. *v.;* privative, prehensile; predacious *or* predaceous, predal [*obs.*], predatory, wolfish, lupine, rapacious, raptorial; ravening, ravenous; parasitic; all-devouring, all-engulfing. bereft etc. 776.

adv. at one fell swoop.

790. Restitution

n. **restitution**, return; rendition, reddition; restoration, reinstatement, reinvestment, recuperation; rehabilitation etc. (*reconstruction*) 660; reparation, atonement; compensation, indemnification.

recovery etc. (*getting back*) 775; release, replevin, replevy, redemption; reversion; remitter.

v. **restore**, return; give–, carry–, bring- back; render, –up; give up; let go, unclutch; disgorge, regorge; regurgitate; recoup, reimburse, com-

pensate, indemnify, reinvest, reinstate, remit, rehabilitate; repair etc. (*make good*) 660.

recover etc. (*get back*) 775; redeem; take back again; revest, revert.

adj. **restoring** etc. *v.;* recuperative etc. 660; compensatory, indemnificatory; reversionary, redemptive, revertible.

adv. in full restitution; as partial compensation; to atone for.

791. Stealing

n. **stealing** etc. *v.;* theft, thievery, robbery, direption [*rare*]; abstraction, appropriation; plagiary [*rare*], plagiarism, autoplagiarism; rape, depredation; kidnaping *or* kidnapping.

pillage, spoliation, plunder, sack, sackage [*rare*], rapine, brigandage, latrociny [*obs.*], latrocinium [*Rom. law*], highway robbery, holdup [*slang*]; raid, foray, razzia; piracy, privateering, buccaneering; filibustering, filibusterism; burglary, housebreaking; abaction, cattle stealing, cattle lifting [*colloq.*], cattle rustling horse stealing; automobile–, car- stealing.

blackmail, badger game [*cant*], Black Hand [*U. S.*].

peculation, embezzlement; fraud etc. 545; larceny, petty larceny, pilfering, shoplifting.

thievishness, rapacity, predacity, predaciousness; kleptomania.

Alsatia; Whitefriars; den of Cacus, den of thieves.

license to plunder, letters of marque.

v. **steal**, thieve, rob, purloin, pilfer, filch, prig [*Brit. cant*], bag, nim [*obs.*], crib [*colloq.*], cabbage, palm; abstract; appropriate, plagiarize.

disregard the distinction between *meum* and *tuum*.

abduct, convey away, carry off, kidnap, crimp, impress, press [*rare*]; make–, walk–, run- off with; run away with; spirit away, seize etc. (*lay violent hands on*) 789.

plunder, pillage, rifle, sack, loot, ransack, spoil, spoliate, despoil, strip, sweep, gut, forage, levy blackmail, pirate, pickeer [*obs.*], maraud, lift cattle [*colloq.*], poach, rustle, smuggle, run; badger [*cant*], bunko *or* bunco; hold up; bail up, stick up [*both colloq. or slang, Austral.*], filibuster.

swindle, peculate, embezzle; sponge, mulct, rook, bilk, pluck, pigeon [*slang*], thimblerig; diddle [*colloq. or dial.*], fleece; defraud etc. 545; obtain under false pretenses; live by one's wits.

rob–, borrow from- Peter to pay Paul; set a thief to catch a thief.

adj. **thieving** etc. *v.;* thievish, light-fingered, furacious [*rare*]; furtive; piratical; predacious *or* predaceous, predal [*obs.*], predatory; raptorial etc. (*rapacious*) 789.

stolen etc. *v.*

792. Thief

n. **thief**, robber, *homo trium literarum* [*L.*], spoiler, depredator, pillager, marauder; pilferer, rifler, filcher, plagiarist; harpy, shark [*slang*], land rat [*cant*], land pirate, land shark, falcon; smuggler, poacher; abductor, badger [*cant*], kidnaper *or* kidnapper; *chor* [*Hind.*], crook [*slang*], lifter, skin [*slang*], contrabandist, hawk; hold-up, jackleg, rustler [*all three slang*]; spieler [*colloq., Austral.*], sandbagger, sneak thief, strong-arm man.

pirate, corsair, viking, sea king, buccaneer, privateer; Paul Jones.

brigand, bandit, freebooter, thug, dacoit [*India*]; rover, ranger, pickeerer [*obs.*], picaroon, filibuster, rapparee [*Ir.*]; cattle thief, abactor; bushranger, mosstrooper [*hist.*], Bedouin; wrecker; highwayman, footpad, sturdy beggar, knight of the road.

Dick Turpin, Claude Duval, Jonathan Wild, Macheath, Nevison, Jesse James.

pickpocket, dip [*slang*], cutpurse, pickpurse [*rare*], light-fingered gentry; sharper; card sharper, card cheat, Greek; thimblerigger; bunkoman *or* buncoman, rook [*slang*], welsher [*slang*], blackleg [*colloq.*], leg [*slang, Eng.*], diddler [*colloq. or slang*], defaulter; Autolycus, Jeremy Diddler, Robert Macaire, Artful Dodger, trickster; swell mob [*slang*], *chevalier d'industrie* [*F.*]; shoplifter.

swindler, duffer [*Eng.*], peculator; forger, coiner, smasher [*cant, Eng.*], counterfeiter; fence, receiver of stolen goods.

burglar, housebreaker, yeggman *or* yegg [*slang*], cracksman [*slang*], magsman [*slang*], sneak thief; second-story -thief, -man; Bill Sikes, Jack Sheppard.

793. Booty

n. **booty**, spoil, plunder, prize, loot, swag [*cant*]; perquisite, boodle [*polit. cant*], graft [*colloq.*], pork barrel [*polit. cant*], pickings; *spolia opima* [*L.*], prey; blackmail; stolen goods.

adj. **looting**, plundering, spoliative, manubial [*obs.*].

794. Barter

n. **barter**, exchange, scorse [*obs.*], truck system; interchange etc. 148.

a Roland for an Oliver, *quid pro quo* [*L.*], commutation, composition; Indian gift [*colloq.*].

trade, commerce, mercature [*obs.*], buying and selling, bargain and sale; traffic, business, nundination [*obs.*], custom, shopping; commercial enterprise, speculation, jobbing, stockjobbing, agiotage, brokery.

dealing, transaction, negotiation, bargain.

free trade [*opp. to* protection].

v. **barter**, exchange, truck, scorse [*obs.*], swap *or* swop [*colloq. & dial.*]; interchange etc. 148; commutate etc. (*sub titute*) 147; compound for.

trade, traffic, buy and sell, give and take, nundinate [*obs.*]; carry on-, ply-, drive- a trade; be in -business, -the city; keep a shop, deal in, employ one's capital in.

trade-, deal-, have dealings- with; put through a deal with; have truck with; transact-, do- business with; open-, have-, keep- an account with.

bargain; drive-, make- a bargain; negotiate, bid for; haggle, stickle, -for; higgle, dicker, chaffer, huckster, cheapen, beat down; underbid; outbid; ask, charge; strike a bargain etc. (*contract*) 769.

speculate; give-, bait with- a sprat to catch a -herring, -mackerel; buy low and sell high, buy in the cheapest and sell in the dearest market; stag the market [*London Stock Exchange*], rig the market [*Exchange cant*].

adj. **commercial**, mercantile, trading; interchangeable, marketable, staple, in the market, for sale; at a bargain, marked down.

wholesale, retail.

adv. over the counter; in the marts of trade; on the Rialto, on 'change.

795. Purchase

n. **purchase**, emption [*rare*]; buying, purchasing, shopping; preëmption, refusal.

coemption [*Rom. law*]; bribery; slave trade.

buyer, purchaser, emptor [*law*], coemptor, vendee; client, customer, clientele, clientage; patron, employer.

v. **buy**, purchase, invest in, regrate, procure; rent etc. (*hire*) 788; repurchase, buy in.

make-, complete- a purchase; buy over the counter; pay cash for; charge, -to one's account.

shop, market, go a-shopping.

keep in one's pay, bribe, suborn; pay etc. 807; spend etc. 809.

adj. purchased etc. *v.;* emptorial, coemptional, coemptive; cliental.

796. Sale

n. **sale**, vent [*rare*], vend [*Eng.*], disposal; auction, roup [*Scot.*], outcry, vendue, Dutch auction; custom etc. (*traffic*) 794.

salableness, salability, marketability, vendibility, vendibleness.

seller, vender, vendor; consigner; *institor* [*L.*]; rouping wife [*Scot.*]; merchant etc. 797; auctioneer.

salesmanship, selling ability.

v. **sell**, vend, dispose of, make a sale, effect a sale; sell over the counter, sell at auction, sell by [*esp. Brit.*] auction, auction, roup [*Scot.*], outcry; put up to (*or* at) auction; bring to (*or* under) the hammer; offer–, put up– for sale; hawk, bring to market; wholesale; dump, unload, place; offer etc. 763; undersell; dispense, retail; deal in etc. 794; sell -off, –out; turn into money, realize.

let; mortgage etc. (*security*) 771.

adj. **for sale**, under the hammer, in the market.

salable, marketable, vendible, staple, merchantable; in demand, popular.

unsalable etc., unpurchased, unbought; on the shelves, shelved, on one's hands.

797. Merchant

n. **merchant**, trader, dealer, monger, chandler, salesman; money changer, changer [*archaic*]; regrater; shopkeeper, shopman; tradesman, tradespeople, tradesfolk.

retailer; chapman, hawker, huckster, higgler; peddler *or* pedlar, colporteur, cadger, Autolycus; sutler, vivandière; costerman, costermonger; tallyman [*rare*], canvasser, solicitor; cheap Jack, *camelot* [*F.*]; faker [*slang*]; vintner; greengrocer, groceryman, haberdasher.

money-lender, cambist, usurer, moneyer [*obs.*], banker; money-changer, money-broker.

jobber; broker etc. (*agent*) 758; buyer etc. 795; seller etc. 796; bear, bull [*Stock Exchange*].

concern, house, corporation; firm etc. (*partnership*) 712.

798. Merchandise

n. **merchandise**, ware, commodity, effects, goods, article, stock, produce, staple commodity; stock in trade etc. (*store*) 636; cargo etc. (*contents*) 190.

799. Mart

n. **mart**, market, marketplace; fair, bazaar, staple, exchange, stock exchange, Wheat Pit [*Chi-*

cago]; 'change, bourse, curb, hall, guildhall; tollbooth [*Scot. & dial. Eng.*], customhouse; Tattersall's.

shop, stall, booth; wharf; office, chambers, countinghouse, bureau; counter *or* compter [*obs.*].

store etc. 636; department store, finding store [*U. S.*], grindery warehouse, warehouse, wareroom; depot, interposit [*rare*], entrepôt [*F.*], emporium, establishment.

market overt, open market.

800. Money

n. **money**, finance; money -matters, –market; accounts etc. 811; funds, treasure; capital, stock; assets etc. (*property*) 780; wealth etc. 803; supplies, ways and means, wherewithal *or* wherewith, sinews of war, almighty dollar, cash.

solvency, responsibility, reliability, solidity, soundness.

sum, amount; balance, balance sheet; sum total; proceeds etc. (*receipts*) 810.

currency, circulating medium, specie, coin, piece, hard cash; dollar, sterling; pounds, shillings, and pence, £ s. d.; guinea; gold mohur [*India*]; eagle, double eagle; pocket, breeches pocket [*colloq.*], wallet, roll, purse; money in hand; *argent comptant* [*F.*], ready [*colloq.*], ready money; Federal–, fractional–, postal-currency; bottom dollar [*colloq.*]; checks, chips.

[*slang terms*] the needful, rhino, brass, blunt, dust, mopus, tin, salt, chink, dough, jack, moss, rock, dibs, slug [*Calif.* 1849]; buzzard dollar, spondulics, long green; barrel, pile, wad; dough, bread, long green.

precious metals, gold, silver, copper, bullion, ingot, bar, nugget.

petty cash, pocket money, pin money, spending money, change, small coin; long bit, short bit, two bits, quarter [*all U. S.*]; dime, nickel, cent, red cent [*colloq., U.S.*]; doit, stiver, rap, mite, farthing, sou, penny, shilling, tester, groat, rouleau.

wampum, wampumpeag, seawan *or* seawant, roanoke, cowrie.

great wealth, money to burn [*colloq.*]; power–, mint–, barrel–, raft- of money [*all colloq.*]; good–, round–, lump- sum; plum (=£100,-000) [*rare slang*]; million, millions, thousands; crore (= ten million rupees, written *Rs.* 1,00,00,000) [*India*]; lac *or* lakh, lac of rupees (= 100,000 rupees, written *Rs.* 1,00,000) [*India*].

[*science of coins*] numismatics, numismatology, chrysology.

paper money; money–, postal–, post office-order; note, –of hand; bank–, promissory-note; I O U, bond; bill, –of exchange; draft, check [*esp. U.S.*] or cheque [*esp. Brit.*], hundi [*India*], order, warrant, coupon, debenture, exchequer bill, assignat, greenback; blueback, shinplaster [*slang*].

remittance etc. (*payment*) 807; credit etc. 805; liability etc. 806.

drawer, drawee; obligor, obligee.

counterfeit–, false–, bad- money; queer [*slang*], base coin, flash note, slip [*obs.*], kite [*slang*]; fancy stocks; Bank of Elegance.

counterfeiter, coiner, moneyer, forger.

v. **total**, amount to, come to, mount up to.

touch the pocket; draw, draw upon; back; indorse etc. (*security*) 771; discount etc. 813.

issue, utter, circulate; fiscalize, monetize, remonetize.

demonetize, deprive of standard value; cease to issue.

coin, counterfeit, forge; circulate bad money, shove the queer [*slang*].

adj. **monetary**, pecuniary, crumenal [*obs.*], fiscal, financial, sumptuary, numismatical; sterling; nummary.

solvent, sound, substantial, good, reliable, responsible, solid, having a good rating; able to pay -20 shillings to the pound, -100 cents on the dollar.

801. Treasurer

n. **treasurer**; bursar, purser, purse bearer; cash keeper, banker; depositary; questor or quaestor [*Rom.*], receiver, liquidator, steward, trustee, accountant, expert accountant, Accountant General, almoner or almner, paymaster, cashier, teller; cambist; money changer etc. (*merchant*) 797.

financier, Chancellor of the Exchequer, Secretary of the Treasury, minister of finance.

802. Treasury

n. **treasury**, bank, exchequer, almonry, fisc or fiscus, hanaper; kutchery or cutcherry or kachahri [*India*], bursary; strong box, stronghold, strong room; coffer; chest etc. (*receptacle*) 191; safe; depository etc. 636; cash register, cash box, money-box, till, tiller.

purse, moneybag, portemonnaie, pocketbook, wallet; purse strings; pocket, breeches pocket.

sinking fund; stocks; public–, parliamentary--stocks, –funds, –securities; Consols, *crédit mobilier* [*F.*]; bonds, government bonds, Lib-

erty bonds, savings bonds, three per cents; gilt-edged securities.

803. Wealth

n. **wealth**, riches, fortune, handsome fortune, opulence, affluence; good–, easy- circumstances; independence; competence etc. (*sufficiency*) 639; solvency etc. 800.

capital, money; round sum; great wealth etc. (*treasure*) 800; mint of money, mine of wealth, bonanza, El Dorado, Pactolus, Golconda, Potosi, Philosopher's Stone; the Golden Touch.

long–, full–, well lined–, heavy- purse; purse of Fortunatus; *embarras de richesses* [*F.*].

pelf, Mammon, lucre, filthy lucre; loaves and fishes, fleshpots of Egypt.

means, resources, substance, command of money; property etc. 780; income etc. 810.

provision, maintenance, livelihood; dowry, alimony.

rich man, moneyed man, warm man [*old slang*], man of substance; capitalist, millionaire, tippybob [*slang*], Nabob, Croesus, Midas, Plutus, Dives, Timon of Athens; Danaë.

timocracy, plutocracy.

v. **be rich** etc. *adj.;* roll–, wallow- in -wealth, –riches; have money to burn [*colloq.*].

afford, well afford; command -money, –a sum; make both ends meet, hold one's head above water.

become rich etc. *adj.;* fill one's pocket etc. (*treasury*) 802; feather one's nest, make a fortune; make money etc. (*acquire*) 775.

enrich, imburse [*rare*].

worship Mammon, worship the golden calf.

adj. **wealthy**, rich, affluent, opulent, moneyed, worth a great deal; well-to-do, well off; warm [*old slang*]; well–, provided for.

made of money; rich as - Croesus; rolling in -riches, –wealth; having a power of money etc. (*great wealth*) 800.

flush, –of -cash, –money, –tin [*slang*]; in funds, in cash, in full feather.

solvent etc., 800; pecunious [*rare*], out of debt, all straight.

804. Poverty

n. **poverty**, indigence, penury, pauperism, destitution, want; need, neediness; lack, necessity, privation, distress, difficulties, wolf at the door.

straits; bad–, poor–, needy–, embarrassed–, reduced–, straightened- circumstances; slender–, narrow- means; hand-to-mouth existence, *res angusta domi* [*L.*], low water [*slang*], impecuniosity.

mendicity, beggary, mendicancy; broken–, loss of– fortune; insolvency etc. (*nonpayment*) 808.

empty -purse, –pocket; light purse; "a beggarly account of empty boxes" [*Romeo and Juliet*].

poor man, pauper, mumper, mendicant, beggar, starveling; *pauvre diable* [*F.*], fakir *or* fakeer [*India*], sunyasi [*India*], schnorrer [*Yiddish*].

v. **be poor** etc. *adj.;* want, lack, starve, live from hand to mouth, have seen better days, go down in the world, come upon the parish; go to -the dogs, –the almshouse, –the poorhouse, –rack and ruin; not have a -penny etc. (*money*) 800, –shot in one's locker; beg one's bread, –from door to door; *tirer le diable par la queue* [*F.*]; run into debt etc. (*debt*) 806.

render poor etc. *adj.;* impoverish; reduce, –to poverty; pauperize, fleece, ruin, bring on the parish.

adj. **poor**, indigent; poverty-stricken; badly–, poorly–, ill- off; poor as -a rat, –a church mouse, –Job, –Job's turkey [*colloq.*]; fortuneless, dowerless, moneyless, penniless; unportioned, unmoneyed; impecunious; out–, short- of -money, –cash; without–, not- worth- a rap etc. (*money*) 800; *qui n'a pas le sou* [*F.*], out of pocket, hard up; out at -elbows, –heels; seedy [*colloq.*], in rags, barefooted; beggarly, beggared, destitute; fleeced, stripped; bereft, bereaved; reduced.

in want etc. *n.;* needy, necessitous, distressed, pinched, straitened; put to one's -shifts, –last shifts; unable to -keep the wolf from the door, –make both ends meet; embarrassed, under hatches; involved etc. (*in debt*) 806; insolvent etc. (*not paying*) 808.

adv. in forma pauperis [*L.*].

805. Credit

n. **credit**, trust, tick [*colloq.*], strap [*slang*], score, tally, account.

paper credit, letter of credit, circular note; duplicate; mortgage, lien, debenture, floating capital; draft, *lettre de créance* [*F.*], securities.

creditor, lender, lessor, mortgagee; dun, dunner; usurer.

v. **credit**, accredit, intrust *or* entrust; keep–, run up- an account with.

place to one's -credit, –account; give–, take- credit; fly a kite [*com. slang*]; have one's credit good for.

adj. **accredited**; of good credit, of unlimited credit; well rated; credited, crediting.

adv. on credit etc. *n.;* to the account of, to the credit of; *à compte* [*F.*].

806. Debt

n. **debt**, obligation, liability, indebtment, debit, score.

arrears, deferred payment, deficit, default; insolvency etc. (*nonpayment*) 808; bad debt.

interest; premium; usance [*obs.*], usury; floating -debt, –capital.

debtor, debitor [*obs.*], mortgagor; defaulter etc. 808; borrower.

v. **be in debt** etc. *adj.;* owe; incur–, contract- a debt etc. *n.;* run up -a bill, –a score, –an account; go on tick [*colloq.*]; borrow etc. 788; run–, get- into debt; be over head and ears in debt; be in difficulties; outrun the constable.

answer for, go bail for; back one's note.

adj. **liable**, chargeable, answerable for.

indebted, in debt, in embarrassed circumstances, in difficulties; encumbered *or* incumbered, involved; involved–, plunged–, deep–, over head and ears- in debt; deeply involved; fast tied up; insolvent etc. (*not paying*) 808; minus [*colloq.*], out of pocket.

unpaid; unrequited, unrewarded; owing, due, in arrear, outstanding.

807. Payment

n. **payment**, defrayment; discharge; acquittance, quittance; settlement, clearance, liquidation, satisfaction, reckoning, arrangement.

acknowledgment, release; receipt, –in full, –in full of all demands; voucher.

repayment, reimbursement, retribution; pay etc. (*reward*) 973; money paid etc. (*expenditure*) 809.

ready money etc. (*cash*) 800; stake, remittance, installment *or* instalment.

payer, liquidator etc. 801.

v. **pay**, defray, make payment; pay -down, –on the nail [*slang*], –ready money, –at sight, –in advance; cash, honor a bill, acknowledge; redeem; pay in kind.

pay one's -way, –shot, –footing; pay -the piper, –sauce for all [*both colloq.*], –costs; come down with the needful [*slang*]; shell–, fork- out [*both slang*]; come down with, –the dust [*both slang*]; tickle–, grease- the palm [*both colloq.*]; expend etc. 809; put down, lay down.

discharge, settle, quit [*archaic*], acquit oneself of; foot the bill [*colloq.*]; account with, reckon with, settle with, be even with, be quits with; strike a balance; settle–, balance–, square- accounts with; quit scores [*archaic*]; wipe-, clear- off old scores; satisfy; pay in full; satisfy-, pay in full- all demands; clear, liquidate; pay -up, —old debts.

repay, refund, reimburse, retribute [*obs.*]; make compensation etc. 30; disgorge, make repayment.

adj. **paying** etc. paid etc. *v.;* owing nothing, out of debt, all straight, all clear, clear of encumbrance, clear of debt, above water; unowed, never indebted; solvent etc. 800.

adv. to the tune of [*colloq.*]; on the nail [*slang*], money down, cash down, cash on delivery, C.O.D.

808. Nonpayment

n. **nonpayment**; default, defalcation; protest, repudiation; application of the sponge; whitewashing.

insolvency, bankruptcy, failure; insufficiency etc. 640; run upon a bank; overdrawn account.

waste paper bonds; dishonored-, protested- bills; bogus check *or* cheque, rubber check [*colloq.*].

defaulter, bankrupt, insolvent debtor, lame duck [*slang*], man of straw; welsher *or* welcher, stag [*obs.*], levanter, absconder.

v. **not pay** etc. 807; fail, break, stop payment; become -insolvent, —bankrupt; be gazetted; have one's check -dishonored, —protested.

pay under protest; button up one's pockets, draw the purse strings; apply the sponge; pay over the left shoulder [*colloq.*], get whitewashed; swindle etc. 791; run up bills, fly kites [*com. slang*].

protest, dishonor, repudiate, nullify.

adj. **not paying**; in debt etc. 806; behindhand, in arrear; beggared etc., (*poor*) 804; unable to make both ends meet, minus [*colloq.*], worse than nothing.

insolvent, bankrupt, in the gazette, gazetted, ruined.

unpaid etc. (*outstanding*) 806; gratis etc. 815; unremunerated.

809. Expenditure

n. **expenditure**, money going out; outgoings, outlay; expenses, disbursement; prime cost etc. (*price*) 812; circulation; run upon a bank.

[money paid] payment etc. 807; pay etc. (*remuneration*) 973; bribe etc. 973; fee, footing, garnish [*obs.*]; subsidy; tribute; contingent, quota; donation, gift etc. 784.

investment; purchase etc. 795.

deposit, pay in advance, earnest, handsel *or* hansel, installment *or* instalment.

v. **expend**, spend; run-, get- through; pay, disburse; ante, ante up [*both poker*]; pony up [*slang*]; open-, loose-, untie- the purse strings, lay out, shell out [*slang*], fork out [*slang*]; bleed; make up a sum, invest, sink money.

fee etc. (*reward*) 973; pay one's way etc. (*pay*) 807; subscribe etc. (*give*) 784; subsidize; bribe.

adj. **expending**, expended etc. *v.;* sumptuary, lavish, free, free with one's money, liberal; beyond one's income.

expensive, costly, dear, high-priced, precious, high.

810. Receipt

n. **receipt**, value received, money coming in; income, incomings [*rare*], revenue, return, proceeds; gross receipts, net profit; earnings etc. (*gain*) 775; *accepta* [*L.*], avails.

rent, rent roll; rental, rentage [*obs.*], rack-rent.

premium, bonus; sweepstakes, tontine, prize, drawings, hand-out [*slang*].

pension, annuity; jointure etc. (*property*) 780; alimony, pittance; emolument etc. (*remuneration*) 973.

v. **receive** etc. 785; get, have an income of, be in receipt of, have coming in; take money; draw from, derive from; acquire etc. 775; take etc. 789; have in prospect.

yield, bring in, afford, pay, return; accrue etc. (*be received from*) 785.

adj. **receiving**, received etc. *v.;* well-paying, remunerative, interest-bearing; well-, profitably-invested; profitable etc. (*gainful*) 775.

adv. at interest; within one's income.

811. Accounts

n. **accounts**, accompts [*archaic*]; business-, commercial-, monetary- arithmetic; statistics etc. (*numeration*) 85; money matters, finance, budget, bill, score, reckoning, account.

bookkeeping, audit, single entry, double entry; computation, calculation, casting up.

account book, books, ledger; day-, cash-, petty-cash-, pass- book; journal; debtor and creditor-, cash-, running- account; account current; balance, —sheet; *compte rendu* [*F.*], account settled; *acquit* [*F.*], assets, expenditure, liabilities, outstanding accounts; profit and loss -account, —statement; receipts; receipt -in full, —in part, —on account; spread sheet.

accountant, auditor, actuary, bookkeeper; financier etc. 801; accounting party; chartered accountant [*Eng.*], certified public accountant [*U. S.*], C.P.A., bank examiner, bank auditor.

v. **keep accounts**, enter, post, post up, book, credit, debit, carry over; take stock; tot up [*colloq.*], add, add up; balance–, make up–, square–, settle–, wind up–, cast up- accounts; make accounts square.

bring to book, audit, examine the books, tax.

falsify, surcharge; falsify–, garble- an account; cook–, doctor- an account [*both colloq.*]; cook–, doctor- the books [*both colloq.*].

adj. monetary etc. 800; accountable, accounting; statistical; entered etc. *v.*

812. Price

n. **price**, amount, cost, expense, prime cost, charge, figure, demand, damage [*colloq.*], fare, hire; wages etc. (*remuneration*) 973.

dues, duty, toll, tax, impost, tariff, cess, sess [*obs.*], tallage *or* tailage [*Old Eng. law*], levy; *abkari* [*India*], capitation, capitation tax, poll tax; doomage, *likin* [*Chinese*], gabel *or* gabelle, salt tax; gavel [*Old Eng. law*], octroi [*F.*], custom, excise, assessment, taxation, benevolence [*hist.*], forced loan; tenths [*hist.*], tithe, exactment, ransom, salvage, towage; brokerage, wharfage, freightage.

worth, rate, value, par value, valuation, appraisement, money's worth; penny etc. -worth; price current, market price, quotation, current quotation; what it will fetch etc. *v.*

bill etc. (*account*) 811; shot, scot, scot and lot.

v. **price**; bear–, set–, fix- a price; appraise, assess, doom, charge, demand, ask, require, exact, run up; distrain; run up a bill etc. (*debt*) 806; have one's price; liquidate.

amount to, come to, mount up to; stand one in [*colloq.*], put one back [*slang*].

fetch, sell for, cost, bring in, yield, afford.

adj. **priced** etc. *v.;* to the tune of, *ad valorem* [*L.*]; dutiable, taxable, assessable; mercenary, venal.

813. Discount

n. **discount**, abatement, concession, reduction, depreciation, allowance, qualification, set-off, drawback, poundage, agio, percentage; rebate, rebatement, backwardization [*Eng.*], backwardation [*Eng.*], contango [*Eng. Stock Exchange*]; salvage; tare [*com.*], tare and tret.

v. **discount**, bate, rebate, abate, deduct, strike off, mark down, reduce, take off, allow, give, make allowance; depreciate.

adj. **discounting** etc. *v.;* concessional; marked down; depreciative.

adv. **at a discount**, at a bargain, below par, on sale.

814. Dearness

n. **dearness** etc. *adj.;* high–, famine–, fancy- price; overcharge; extravagance; exorbitance, extortion; heavy pull upon the purse.

v. **be dear** etc. *adj.;* cost much, cost a pretty penny [*colloq.*]; rise in price, look up.

overcharge, bleed [*colloq.*], skin [*slang*], fleece, extort.

pay too much, pay through the nose [*colloq.*], pay too dear for one's whistle [*colloq.*].

adj. **dear**; high, –priced; of great price, expensive, costly, precious, dear bought; unreasonable, extravagant, exorbitant, extortionate.

at a premium; not to be had, –for love or money; beyond price, above price; priceless, of priceless value.

adv. **dear**, dearly; at great cost, at heavy cost, at a high price, *à grands frais* [*F.*].

815. Cheapness

n. **cheapness**, low price; depreciation; bargain, *bon marché* [*F.*]; good penny etc. -worth; drug in the market.

[absence of charge] gratuity; free -quarters, –seats, –admission; free lunch; run of one's teeth [*slang*]; nominal price, peppercorn rent; labor of love.

deadhead [*colloq.*], dead beat [*slang*], beat [*slang*], sponger.

v. **be cheap** etc. *adj.;* cost little; come down–, fall-in price; be marked down.

buy for a mere nothing, buy at a bargain, buy dirt-cheap, buy for an old song; have one's money's worth; beat down, cheapen.

adj. **cheap**; low, –priced; moderate, reasonable; inexpensive *or* unexpensive; well–, worth the money; *magnifique et pas cher* [*F.*]; good–, cheap- at the price; dirt-cheap, dog-cheap; cheap as dirt, cheap and nasty [*colloq.*]; peppercorn; catchpenny.

reduced, half-price, depreciated, shopworn, marked down, unsalable.

gratuitous, gratis, free, for nothing; costless, expenseless; without charge, not charged, untaxed; scot-free, shot-free, rent-free; free of -cost, –expense; complimentary, honorary, unbought, unpaid for.

adv. **at a bargain**, for a mere song; at cost price, at prime cost, at a reduction; on the cheap [*colloq., Eng.*]; *bon marché or à bon marché* [*F.*].

816. Liberality

n. **liberality**, generosity, munificence; bounty, bounteousness, bountifulness; hospitableness, hospitality; charity etc. (*beneficence*) 906; open–, free- hand; open–, large–, free- heart; enough and to spare.

cheerful giver, free giver, patron; benefactor etc. 912.

v. **be liberal** etc. *adj.;* spend–, bleed- freely; shower down upon; open one's purse strings etc. (*disburse*) 809; spare no expense, give *carte blanche* [*F.*]; give with both hands; give the coat off one's back; keep open house, fill one's house with guests.

adj. **liberal**, free, generous; charitable etc. (*beneficent*) 906; hospitable; bountiful, bounteous, ample, handsome; unsparing, ungrudging; unselfish; open–, free–, full- handed; open–, large–, free-hearted; munificent, princely.

adv. **liberally** etc. *adj.;* ungrudgingly; with open hands, with both hands.

817. Economy

n. **economy**, frugality; thrift, thriftiness; care, husbandry, good housewifery, savingness, retrenchment.

savings; prevention of waste, save-all; parsimony etc. 819.

v. **be economical** etc. *adj.;* practice economy, economize, save; retrench, cut down expenses; cut one's coat according to one's cloth, make both ends meet, keep within compass, meet one's expenses, keep one's head above water, pay one's way; husband etc. (*lay by*) 636; save–, invest- money; put out to interest; provide–, save- -for, –against- a rainy day; feather one's nest; look after the main chance [*colloq.*].

adj. **economical**, frugal, careful, thrifty, saving, chary, spare, sparing; parsimonious etc. 819; sufficient; plain.

adv. **sparingly** etc. *adj.; ne quid nimis* [*L.*].

818. Prodigality

n. **prodigality**, prodigence [*obs.*], wastefulness, wastry *or* wastrie [*Scot.*], unthriftiness, waste; profusion, profuseness; extravagance; squandering etc. *v.;* lavishness.

pound-foolishness, pound-folly, penny wisdom.

prodigal, spendthrift, wastethrift, wastrel [*dial. Eng.*], waster, high roller [*slang*], squanderer, spender, spendall, scattergood [*archaic*]; locust; Prodigal Son; Timon of Athens.

v. **be prodigal** etc. *adj.;* squander, lavish, sow broadcast; blow in [*slang*]; pay through the nose etc. (*dear*) 814; spill, waste, dissipate, ex-

haust, drain, eat out of house and home, overdraw, outrun the constable; run out, run through; misspend; throw good money after bad, throw the helve after the hatchet; burn the candle at both ends; make ducks and drakes of one's money; fool–, potter–, muddle–, fritter–, throw- away one's money; squander one's substance in riotous living; spend money like water; pour water into a sieve, kill the goose that lays the golden eggs; *manger son blé en herbe* [*F.*].

adj. **prodigal**, profuse, thriftless, unthrifty, improvident, wasteful, losel, extravagant, lavish, dissipated, over-liberal; full-handed etc. (*liberal*) 816; overpaid.

penny-wise and pound-foolish.

adv. with an unsparing hand; money burning one's pocket.

int. keep the change! hang the expense!

819. Parsimony

n. **parsimony**, parcity [*obs.*]; parsimoniousness, stinginess etc. *adj.;* stint; illiberality, avarice, tenacity, avidity, rapacity, extortion, malversation, venality, cupidity; lack of prodigality etc. 818; selfishness etc. 943; *auri sacra fames* [*L.*]; cheeseparings and candle ends.

miser, niggard, churl, screw, skin-flint, skin [*slang*], codger [*dial. Eng.*], money-grub [*slang*], muckworm, scrimp [*colloq.*], pinchgut [*obs. or vulgar*], lick-penny, hunks [*colloq.*], curmudgeon, harpy, extortioner, usurer, Hessian [*U.S.*]; pinchfist, pinchpenny [*obs.*].

Harpagon, Euclio, Silas Marner, Daniel Dancer.

v. **be parsimonious** etc. *adj.;* grudge, begrudge, stint, pinch, gripe, screw, dole out, hold back, withhold, starve, famish, live upon nothing, skin a flint [*colloq.*], pinch a sixpence till it squeaks.

drive a bargain, cheapen, beat down; stop one hole in a sieve; have an itching palm, grasp, grab.

adj. **parsimonious**, penurious, stingy, miserly, mean, shabby, peddling, penny wise, near, near as the bark on a tree, niggardly, close; close-handed, close-fisted, fast-handed [*obs.*], hard-fisted, straithanded [*obs.*], tight-fisted; tight [*colloq.*], sparing; chary; grudging, gripping etc. *v.;* illiberal, ungenerous, churlish, hidebound, sordid, mercenary, venal, covetous, usurious, avaricious; greedy, extortionate, rapacious; underpaid.

adv. with a sparing hand.

289

Class 6. Affections

Section 1. Affections in General

820. Affections

n. **character**, qualities, disposition, affections, nature, spirit, tone; temper, temperament; diathesis, idiosyncrasy; cast–, habit–, frame- of -mind, –soul; predilection, turn; natural–, turn of mind; bent, bias, predisposition, proneness, proclivity, propensity, propenseness, propension, propendency [*obs.*]; vein, humor, mood, grain, mettle, backbone; sympathy etc. (*love*) 897.

soul, heart, breast, bosom, inner man; heart's -core, –strings, –blood; heart of hearts, *penetralia mentis* [*L.*]; secret and inmost recesses of the heart, cockles of one's heart; inmost- heart, –soul.

passion, pervading spirit; ruling–, master- passion; *furore* [*It.*], furor; fullness of the heart, heyday of the blood, flesh and blood, flow of soul.

energy, fervor, fire, verve, force.

v. have *or* possess character etc. *n.;* be of a character etc. *n.;* be affected etc. *adj.;* breathe energy etc. *n.*

adj. **characterized**, affected, formed, molded *or* moulded, cast; attemperate, attempered, tempered; framed.

prone, predisposed, disposed, inclined; having a bias etc. *n.;* tinctured–, imbued–, penetrated–, eaten up- with.

inborn, inbred, ingrained; deep-rooted, ineffaceable, inveterate; congenital, dyed in the wool, implanted by nature, inherent, in the grain.

adv. in one's heart etc. *n.;* at heart; heart and soul etc. 821; in the vein, in the mood.

821. Feeling

n. **feeling**; suffering etc. *v.;* endurance, tolerance, sufferance, experience, response; sympathy etc. (*love*) 897; impression, inspiration, affection, sensation, emotion, pathos, deep sense.

warmth, glow, unction, gusto, vehemence, fervor, fervency; heartiness, cordiality; earnestness, eagerness; *empressement* [*F.*], gush [*colloq.*], ardor, zeal, passion, enthusiasm, verve, *furore* [*It.*], furor, fanaticism; excitation of feeling etc. 824; fullness of the heart etc.

(*disposition*) 820; passion etc. (*state of excitability*) 825; ecstasy etc. (*pleasure*) 827.

state of excitement; blush, suffusion, flush; hectic, hectic fever, hectic flush; tingling, thrill, turn, shock; agitation etc. (*irregular motion*) 315; quiver, heaving, flutter, flurry, fluster, twitter, tremor; throb, throbbing; pulsation, palpitation, panting; trepidation, perturbation, ruffle, hurry of spirits, pother, stew [*colloq.*], ferment.

v. **feel**; receive an impression etc. *n.;* be impressed with etc. *adj.;* entertain–, harbor–, cherish- -feeling etc. *n.*

respond; catch the -flame, –infection; enter into the spirit of.

bear, suffer, support, sustain, endure, thole [*obs. or dial.*], aby *or* abye; brook; abide etc. (*be composed*) 826; experience etc. (*meet with*) 151; taste, prove; labor–, smart- under; bear the brunt of, brave, stand.

be agitated, be excited etc, 824; swell, glow, warm, flush, blush, crimson, change color, mantle; darken, whiten, pale; turn -color, –pale, –red, –black in the face; tingle, thrill, heave, pant, throb, palpitate, go pitapat, tremble, quiver, flutter, twitter; shake etc. 315; blench, stagger, reel; look -blue, –black; wince, draw a deep breath.

impress etc. (*excite the feelings*) 824.

adj. **feeling** etc. *v.;* sentient; sensuous, sensorial, sensory; emotive, emotional; of *or* with feeling etc. *n.*

lively, quick, smart, strong, sharp, acute, cutting, piercing, incisive; keen, –as a razor; trenchant, pungent, racy, piquant, poignant, caustic.

impressive, deep, profound, indelible; deep-felt, homefelt, heartfelt; swelling, soul-stirring, heart-expanding, electric, thrilling, rapturous, ecstatic; pervading, penetrating, absorbing.

earnest, wistful, eager, breathless; fervent, fervid, gushing [*colloq.*], warm, passionate, warm-hearted, hearty, cordial, sincere, zealous, enthusiastic, glowing, ardent, burning, red-hot, fiery, flaming; boiling, –over.

rabid, raving, feverish, fanatical, hysterical; impetuous etc. (*excitable*) 825; overmastering.

impressed–, moved–, touched–, affected–, penetrated–, seized–, imbued etc. 820- with; devoured by; wrought up etc. (*excited*) 824; struck all of a heap [*colloq.*]; rapt; in a quiver etc. *n.;* enraptured etc. 829.

the heart -big, –full, –swelling, –beating, –pulsating, –throbbing, –thumping, –beating high, –melting, –overflowing, –bursting, –breaking.

adv. **heartily**, heart and soul, from the bottom of one's heart, *ab imo pectore* [*L.*], *de profundis* [*L.*]; at heart, *con amore* [*It.*], devoutly, over head and ears.

821a. Psychology and Psychotherapy

n. **psychology**, psychonomics, abnormal psychology, applied psychology, animal psychology, child psychology, clinical psychology, comparative psychology, differential psychology, dynamic psychology, experimental psychology, existential psychology, faculty psychology, functional psychology, genetic psychology, individual psychology, industrial psychology, parapsychology, rational psychology, self-psychology, structural psychology; physiological psychology, psychobiochemistry, psychobiology, psychophysics; psychoasthenics, psychostatics, psychogenetics; psychotechnics, psychotechnology.

[systems] Freudian psychology; Gestalt psychology *or* configurationism; behavior psychology *or* Watson's psychology; association psychology, mental chemistry.

psychiatry, psychiatrics, neuropsychiatry; prophylactic psychiatry, mental hygiene; psychosomatic medicine; psychosocial medicine.

psychotherapy; group therapy; occupational therapy; recreational therapy; narcotherapy, narcoanalysis, amytal *or* pentothal interview; hypnotherapy, hypnoanalysis; psychosurgery; suggestion therapy; hypnotic suggestion, post-hypnotic suggestion; autosuggestion; sleep treatment; shock therapy, electroshock therapy, protein shock therapy, metrazol shock therapy, hypoglycemic shock therapy, insulin shock therapy, insulin coma therapy, convulsive shock therapy; psychoanalysis, depth interview; psychoanalytic therapy, depth psychology; psychognosis; dream analysis, interpretation of dreams, dream symbolism.

psychological test; aptitude test, Oseretsky test, Stanford scientific aptitude test; personality test, Bernreuter personality inventory, Minnesota multiplastic personality inventory; association test, controlled association test, free association test; apperception test, card test; Rorschach test, ink-blot test; intelligence test, I.Q. test; alpha test, beta test, Babcock-Levy test, Binet-Simon test, Goldstein-Sheerer test,

Kent mental test, aussage test; Wechsler-Bellevue intelligence scale, Gesell's development schedule, Minnesota preschool scale, Cattell's infant intelligence scale.

psyche, mind; preconscious, foreconscious, coconscious; subconscious, unconscious, submerged mind; libido, libidinal energy, libidinal object; id, ego, superego; ego-ideal, ego-id conflict.

[pathological personality types] neurotic, psychoneurotic, neuropath; maladjusted personality, hostile personality; antisocial personality, sociopath; escapist; psychotic personality; mental defective, ament; hypochondriac; alcoholic.

neurosis, psychoneurosis, functional nervous disorder; pathoneurosis, actual neurosis, anxiety neurosis, blast neurosis, fright neurosis, traumatic neurosis, transference neurosis; compulsion neurosis, obsessional neurosis, obsessive-compulsion neurosis; occupational neurosis, professional neurasthenia; combat *or* war neurosis, battle fatigue, shell-shock; nervous breakdown.

psychosis, psychopathy, psychopathic condition; schizophrenia, functional disintegration, dissociation of personality, split personality, multiple personality; dementia praecox, paranoia, catatonia; hebephrenia, paraphrenia, schizophasia, schizothymia; melancholia, manic-depressive insanity, affective psychosis, cyclothymia; Korsakoff's psychosis, polyneuritic psychosis; amentia, fugue; dementia paralytica; senile dementia, senile psychosis, degenerative psychosis; presenile dementia; psychopathia sexualis, psychosexuality; pharmacopsychosis; arteriosclerotic psychosis, climacteric psychosis, exhaustive psychosis, gestational psychosis, involuntary psychosis, involutional psychosis, metabolic psychosis, organic psychosis, postinfectious psychosis, psychasthenia, psycholepsy, psychokinesia, psychorhythmia, toxic psychosis; moral insanity, psychopathic personality; rabies, hydrophobia.

[neurotic symptoms] anxiety, precordial anxiety, free-floating anxiety; asthenia; hysteria, conversion hysteria, anxiety hysteria; dissociation, emotional instability, flight reaction, immaturity; depression; detachment; passive aggression, passive dependence; phobia, morbid fear, astraphobia (lightning and thunder), acrophobia (heights), agoraphobia (open places), ailurophobia (cats), claustrophobia (confined places), hematophobia (blood), hydrophobia (water), pyrophobia (fire), scotophobia (darkness), toxiphobia (being poisoned), xenophobia (strangers); unresponsiveness, apathy; stupor, catatonic stupor, euphoria, elation.

mania, obsession, compulsion; megalomania, monomania, kleptomania, pyromania, erotomania, dipsomania.

complex, inferiority complex, superiority complex, Oedipus *or* nuclear complex, Electra complex, persecution complex, castration complex; fixation, libido fixation, arrested development; infantile fixation, pregenital fixation; regression.

defense mechanism, psychological *or* sociological adjustive reaction; negativism; escape mechanism; withdrawal; isolation, emotional insulation; autistic thinking; compensation, overcompensation, decompensation; substitution; sublimation; projection; displacement; rationalization; suppression, repression, inhibition, reaction formation.

822. Sensibility

n. **sensibility**, sensibleness, sensitiveness; moral sensibility; impressibility, affectibility; susceptibleness, susceptibility, susceptivity; mobility; vivacity, vivaciousness; tenderness, softness; sentimentality, sentimentalism.

excitability etc. 825; fastidiousness etc. 868; physical sensibility etc. 375; sensitive plant.

sore point, sore place; quick, raw; where the shoe pinches.

v. **be sensible** etc. *adj.;* have a tender, –warm, –sensitive- heart; be all heart.

take to heart, treasure up in the heart; shrink, wince, blench, quiver.

"die of a rose in aromatic pain" [Pope]; touch to the quick; touch–, flick one- on the raw.

adj. **sensible**, sensitive; impressible, impressionable; susceptive, susceptible; alive to, impassionable, gushing [*colloq.*]; warm-hearted, tender-hearted, soft-hearted; tender, soft, maudlin, sentimental, romantic; enthusiastic, impassioned, highflying, spirited, mettlesome, vivacious, lively, expressive, mobile, tremblingly alive; excitable etc. 825; oversensitive, without skin, thin-skinned; fastidious etc. 868.

adv. **sensibly** etc. *adj.;* to the quick, on the raw, to the inmost core.

823. Insensibility

n. **insensibility**, insensibleness; want of sensibility etc. 823; moral insensibility; inertness, inertia, *vis inertiae* [*L.*]; impassibility, impassibleness;

inappetency, apathy, phlegm, dullness, hebetude, supineness, insusceptibility, unimpressibility, luke-warmness.

coldness; cold -fit, –blood, –heart; coolness; frigidity, *sang-froid* [*F.*], stoicism, imperturbation etc. (*inexcitability*) 826; nonchalance, unconcern, dry eyes; insouciance etc. (*indifference*) 866; recklessness etc. 863; callousness, callosity, obtundity, brutification; heart of stone, blood and iron, stock and stone, marble, deadness.

neutrality; quietism, vegetation.

torpor, torpidity; obstupefaction [*obs.*], lethargy, coma, trance; sleep etc. 683; inanimation [*rare*], suspended animation; stupor, stupefaction; paralysis, palsy; numbness etc. (*physical insensibility*) 376; analgesia.

stoic, Indian, man of iron, pococurante, pococurantist; the Fat Boy in Pickwick.

trifler, dabbler, dilettante, sciolist etc. 493.

v. **be insensible** etc. *adj.;* have a rhinoceros hide; show insensibility etc. *n.;* not mind, not care, not be affected by; have no desire for etc. 866; have–, feel–, take- no interest in; *nil admirari* [*L.*]; not care a straw etc. (*unimportance*) 643 for; disregard etc. (*neglect*) 460; set at naught etc. (*make light of*) 483; turn a deaf ear to etc. (*inattention*) 458; vegetate.

render insensible, render callous; blunt, obtund, numb, benumb, paralyze, chloroform, deaden, hebetate, stun, stupefy; brutify, brutalize.

insure; harden, harden the heart; steel, case-harden, sear.

adj. **insensible**, unconscious; impassive, impassible; blind to, deaf to, dead to; obtundent, insusceptible *or* unsusceptible, unimpressionable, unimpressible; passionless, spiritless, heartless, soulless, unfeeling; unmoral.

apathetic, unemotional, leucophlegmatic [*obs.*], phlegmatic; dull, frigid; cold cold-blooded, cold-hearted; cold as charity; flat, obtuse, inert, supine, sluggish, torpid, torpedinous [*rare*], torporific; sleepy etc. (*inactive*) 683; languid, half-hearted, tame; numb, numbed; comatose; anaesthetic etc. 376; stupefied, chloroformed, palsy-stricken.

indifferent, lukewarm, Laodicean, careless, mindless, regardless; inattentive etc. 458; neglectful etc. 460; disregarding.

unconcerned, nonchalant, pococurante, insouciant, *sans souci* [*F.*]; unambitious etc. 866.

unaffected, unruffled, unimpressed, uninspired, unexcited, unmoved, unstirred, untouched, unshocked, unstruck; unblushing etc. (*shameless*) 885; unanimated; vegetative.

callous, thick-skinned, pachydermatous, impervious; hard, hardened; inured, casehardened; steeled-, proof- against; imperturbable etc. (*inexcitable*) 826; unfelt.

adv. **insensibly** etc. *adj.; aequo animo* [*L.*], without being -moved, -touched, -impressed; in cold blood; with dry eyes, with withers unwrung.

int. never mind! it is of no consequence etc. (*unimportant*) 642; it cannot be helped! it is all the same!

824. Excitation

n. **excitation of feeling**; mental-, excitement; suscitation [*obs.*], suscitability [*obs.*], galvanism, high pressure, stimulation, piquancy, provocation, inspiration, calling forth, infection; animation, agitation, perturbation; subjugation, fascination, intoxication, enravishment, ravishment, entrancement; unction, impressiveness etc. *adj.*

trial of temper, *casus belli* [*L.*], irritation etc. (*anger*) 900; passion etc. (*state of excitability*) 825; thrill etc. (*feeling*) 821; repression of feeling etc. 826.

emotional appeal, melodrama; great moment, crisis; sensationalism, yellow journalism.

v. **excite**, affect, touch, move, impress, strike, interest, animate, inspire, impassion, smite, infect; stir-, fire-, warm- the blood; set astir; awake, wake; awaken, waken; call forth; evoke, provoke; raise up, summon up, call up, wake up, blow up, get up, light up; raise; get up the steam, rouse, arouse, stir, fire, kindle, enkindle, illumine, illuminate, apply the torch, set on fire, inflame.

stimulate; exuscitate *or* exsuscitate [*both obs.*], suscitate [*obs.*]; inspirit; spirit up, stir up, work up; infuse life into, give new life to; bring-, introduce- new blood; quicken; sharpen, whet; work upon etc. (*incite*) 615; hurry on, give a fillip, fillip, put on one's mettle.

fan the -fire, -flame; blow the coals, stir the embers; fan, fan into a flame; foster, heat, warm, foment, raise to a fever heat; keep up, keep the pot boiling; revive, rekindle, rake up, rip up.

intoxicate, overwhelm, overpower, *bouleverser* [*F.*], upset, turn one's head; send [*slang*], fascinate; enrapture etc. (*give pleasure*) 829.

penetrate, pierce; stir-, play on-, come home to- the feelings; touch -a string, -a chord, -the soul, -the heart; go to one's heart, go through one, open the wound, turn the knife in the wound; touch to the quick; possess-, pervade-, imbue-, penetrate-, imbrue [*obs.*]-, absorb-, affect-, disturb- the soul; rivet the attention; sink into the -mind, -heart; absorb; prey on the mind.

agitate, perturb, ruffle, fluster, flutter, flurry, shake, disturb, startle, shock, stagger; give one a -shock, -turn; strike all of a heap [*colloq.*], strike dumb, stun, astound, electrify, galvanize, petrify.

irritate, sting; cut; cut to the -heart, -quick; try one's temper; fool to the top of one's bent, pique; infuriate, madden, make one's blood boil; lash into fury etc. (*wrath*) 900.

be excited etc. *adj.;* flash up, flare up; catch the infection; thrill etc. (*feel*) 821; mantle; work oneself up; seethe, boil, simmer, foam, fume, flame, rage, rave; run mad etc. (*passion*) 825; run amuck *or* amok.

adj. **excited** etc. *v.;* wrought up, on the *qui vive,* astir, sparkling; in a -quiver etc. 821, -fever, -ferment, -blaze, -state of excitement; in hysterics; black in the face, overwrought; hot, red-hot, flushed, feverish; all of a -flutter, -twitter; all in a pucker [*colloq.*]; with quivering lips, with trembling lips, with twitching lips, with tears in one's eyes.

raging, flaming; boiling, -over; ebullient, seething; foaming, -at the mouth; fuming; stung to the quick; on one's high ropes; on one's high horse; carried away by passion, wild, raving, frantic, mad, amuck, distracted, beside oneself, out of one's wits, ready to burst, *bouleversé* [*F.*], demoniacal.

lost, *éperdu* [*F.*], tempest-tossed; haggard; ready to sink.

exciting etc. *v.;* impressive, warm, glowing, fervid, swelling, imposing, spirit-stirring, thrilling; high-wrought; soul-stirring, soul-subduing; heart-stirring, heart-swelling, heart-thrilling; agonizing etc. (*painful*) 830; telling, sensational, melodramatic, hysterical; overpowering, overwhelming; more than flesh and blood can bear; yellow.

piquant etc. (*pungent*) 392; spicy, appetizing, stinging, provocative, *provoquant* [*F.*], tantalizing.

adv. at a critical -moment, -period, -point; under a sudden strain; with heart-interest [*cant*]; with plenty of pep [*slang*], with a punch [*slang*]; till one is blue in the face.

825. Excitability

[excess of sensitiveness]

n. **excitability**, impetuosity, vehemence; boisterousness etc. *adj.;* turbulence; impatience, intolerance, non-endurance; irritability etc. (*irascibility*) 901; itching etc. (*desire*) 865; wincing; disquiet, disquietude; restlessness; fidgets, fidgetiness; agitation etc. (*irregular motion*) 315.

trepidation, perturbation, ruffle, hurry, fuss, flurry, fluster, flutter; pother, stew [*colloq.*], ferment; whirl; buck fever [*colloq.*]; stage fright; hurry-scurry *or* hurry-skurry; thrill etc. (*feeling*) 821; state-, fever- of excitement; transport.

passion, excitement, flush, heat; fever, fever-heat; fire, flame, fume, blood boiling; tumult; effervescence, ebullition; boiling, -over; whiff, gust, storm, tempest; scene, breaking out, burst, fit, paroxysm, explosion, outbreak, outburst; agony.

fury; violence etc. 173; fierceness etc. *adj.;* rage, furor, *furore* [*It.*], desperation, madness, distraction, raving, delirium; frenzy *or* phrensy, hysterics; intoxication; tearing-, raging- passion; towering rage; anger etc. 900.

fixed idea, *l'idée fixe* [*F.*], monomania; fascination, infatuation, fanaticism; Quixotism, Quixotry; *tête montée* [*F.*].

v. **be impatient** etc. *adj.;* not be able to bear etc. 826; bear ill, wince, chafe, champ the bit; be in a stew [*colloq.*] etc. *n.;* be out of all patience, fidget, fuss, not have a wink of sleep; toss, -on one's pillow.

fume, rage, foam; lose one's temper etc. 900; break out, burst out, fly out, go-, fly- -off, -off at a tangent; explode; flare up, flame up, fire up, burst into a flame, take fire, fire, burn; stew [*colloq.*]; boil, -over; rave, rant, tear; go-, run- -wild, -mad; go into hysterics; run riot, run amuck *or* amok; *battre la campagne* [*F.*], *faire le diable à quatre* [*F.*]; play the deuce [*slang*]; raise -Cain, -the mischief, -the devil [*all slang*].

adj. **excitable**, easily excited, in an excitable state; startlish, mettlesome, high-mettled, skittish; high-strung; irritable etc. (*irascible*) 901; impatient, intolerant; moody, maggoty-headed.

feverish, febrile, hysterical; delirious, mad.

unquiet, mercurial, electric, galvanic, hasty, hurried, restless, fidgety, fussy; chafing etc. *v.*

vehement, demonstrative, violent, wild, furious, fierce, fiery, hot-headed, madcap.

overzealous, enthusiastic, impassioned, fanatical; rabid etc. (*eager*) 865.

rampant, clamorous, uproarious, turbulent, tempestuous, tumultuary, boisterous.

impulsive, impetuous, passionate, uncontrolled, uncontrollable, ungovernable, irrepressible, stanchless *or* staunchless, inextinguishable, burning, simmering, volcanic, ready to burst forth.

excited, exciting etc. 824.

adv. in confusion, pell-mell; in trepidation etc. *n.*

int. pish! pshaw! horrors!

826. Inexcitability

n. **inexcitability**, imperturbability, inirritability; even temper, tranquil mind, dispassion; toleration, tolerance, patience.

passiveness etc. (*physical inertness*) 172; hebetude, hebetation; impassibility etc. (*insensibility*) 823; stupefaction.

calmness etc. *adj.;* composure, placidity, indisturbance, imperturbation, *sang-froid* [*F.*], coolness, tranquillity, serenity; quiet, quietude; peace of mind, mental calmness.

equanimity, poise, staidness etc. *adj.;* gravity, sobriety, quietism, Quakerism; philosophy, stoicism, command of temper; self-possession, self-control, self-command, self-restraint; presence of mind.

resignation, submission etc. 725; sufferance, supportance, endurance, longsufferance, forbearance, longanimity, fortitude; patience of Job, "patience on a monument" [*Twelfth Night*], "patience sovereign o'er transmuted ill" [*Johnson*]; moderation; repression-, subjugation- of feeling; restraint etc. 751; tranquilization etc. (*moderation*) 174.

v. **be composed** etc. *adj.*

laisser faire [*F.*], *laisser aller* [*F.*]; take things -easily, -as they come; take it easy, rub on [*colloq.*], live and let live; take -easily, -coolly, -in good part; *aequam servare mentem* [*L.*].

endure; bear, -well, -the brunt; go through, support, brave, disregard; tolerate, suffer, stand, bide; abide, aby *or* abye; bear with, put up with, take up with, abide with; acquiesce; submit etc. (*yield*) 725; submit with a good grace; resign-, reconcile- oneself to; brook, digest, eat, swallow, pocket, stomach; carry on, carry through; make light of, make the best of, make "a virtue of necessity" [*Chaucer*]; put a good face on, keep one's countenance; check etc. 751- oneself.

compose, appease etc. (*moderate*) 174; propitiate; repress etc. (*restrain*) 751; render insensible etc. 823; overcome-, allay-, repress- one's excitability etc. 825; master one's feelings; make -one-self, -one's mind- easy; set one's mind at -ease, -rest; calm-, cool- down; gentle, tame, thaw, grow cool.

be borne, be endured, be swallowed; go down.

adj. **inexcitable**, imperturbable; unsusceptible etc. (*insensible*) 823; dispassionate, unpassionate, cold-blooded, unirritable, inirritable; enduring etc. v.; stoical, Platonic, philosophic, staid, stayed [obs.], sober, –minded; grave; sober–, grave- as a judge; sedate, demure, cool-headed, level-headed.

easy-going, peaceful, placid, calm; quiet, –as a mouse; tranquil, serene; cool, –as -a cucumber, –custard [both colloq.]; undemonstrative.

composed, collected; temperate etc. (moderate) 174; unexcited, unstirred, unruffled, undisturbed, unperturbed, unimpassioned.

meek, tolerant; patient, –as Job; unoffended; unresisting; submissive etc. 725; tame; content, resigned, chastened, subdued, lamblike; gentle, –as a lamb; suaviter in modo [L.]; mild, –as mother's milk; soft as peppermint; armed with patience, bearing with, clement, long-suffering, forbearant, longanimous.

adv. "like patience on a monument smiling at grief" [Twelfth Night]; aequo animo [L.], in cold blood etc. 823; more in sorrow than in anger.

int. patience! and shuffle the cards.

Section 2. Personal

827. Pleasure

n. **pleasure**, gratification, enjoyment, fruition, delectation, oblectation [rare]; relish, zest; gusto etc. (physical pleasure) 377; satisfaction etc. (content) 831; complacency.

well-being; good etc. 618; snugness, comfort, ease; cushion etc. 215; sans souci [F.], mind at ease.

joy, gladness, delight, glee, cheer, sunshine; cheerfulness etc. 836.

treat, refreshment; amusement etc. 840; luxury etc. 377.

happiness, felicity, bliss; beatitude, beatification; enchantment, transport, rapture, ravishment, ecstasy; summum bonum [L.]; paradise, elysium etc. (heaven) 981; third–, seventh- heaven; unalloyed happiness etc.; hedonics, hedonism.

mens sana in corpore sano [Juvenal].

honeymoon; palmy–, halcyon- days; golden -age, –time; Eden, Paradise; Dixie, Dixie land or Dixie's land; Saturnia regna [L.], Arcadia, Cockaigne, happy valley, Agapemone.

v. **be pleased** etc. 829; oblectate [rare]; feel–, experience- pleasure etc. n.; joy; enjoy–, hug- oneself; be in clover [colloq.] etc. 377, be in elysium etc. 981; tread on enchanted ground; fall–, go- into raptures.

feel at home, breathe freely, bask in the sunshine.

enjoy, like, relish; be pleased with etc. 829; receive–, derive- pleasure etc. n.- from; take pleasure etc. n.- in; delight in, rejoice in, indulge in, luxuriate in; gloat over etc. (physical pleasure) 377; love etc. 897; fall for [slang]; take to, take a fancy to [both colloq.]; have a liking for; enter into the spirit of; take in good part; treat oneself to, solace oneself with.

adj. **pleased** etc. 829; not sorry; glad, gladsome; pleased as Punch; pleased as a child with a new toy.

happy, blest, blessed, blissful, beatified; happy as -a clam at high water [U. S.], –a king, –the day is long; thrice happy, ter quaterque beatus [L.]; enjoying etc. v.; joyful etc. (in spirits) 836; hedonic.

in a blissful state, in paradise etc. 981, in raptures, in ecstasies, in a transport of delight.

comfortable etc. (physical pleasure) 377; at ease; in clover [colloq.]; content etc. 831; sans souci [F.].

overjoyed, entranced, enchanted; raptured, enraptured, enravished, ravished, transported; fascinated, captivated.

with a joyful face, with sparkling eyes.

pleasing etc. 829; ecstatic, beatific or beaitifical; painless, unalloyed, without alloy, cloudless.

adv. **happily** etc. adj.; with pleasure etc. (willingly) 602; with glee etc. n.

828. Pain

n. **pain**, mental suffering, dolor, suffering, sufferance [rare], ache; smart etc. (physical pain) 378; passion.

displeasure, dissatisfaction, discomfort, discomposure, disquiet; malaise [F.], inquietude, uneasiness, vexation of spirit; taking [colloq.]; discontent etc. 832.

dejection etc. 837; weariness etc. 841; anhedonia.

annoyance, irritation, worry, infliction, visitation; plague, bore; bother, botheration [colloq.], stew [colloq.], vexation, mortification, chagrin, esclandre [F.]; mauvais quart d'heure [F.].

care, anxiety, solicitude, trouble, trial, ordeal, fiery ordeal, shock, blow, cark [archaic], dole [archaic], fret, burden, load.

grief, sorrow, distress, affliction, woe, bitterness, heartache; carking cares [archaic]; concern; heavy–, aching–, bleeding–, broken- heart; heavy affliction, gnawing grief.

misery, unhappiness, infelicity, tribulation, wretchedness, desolation; despair etc. 859; extremity, prostration, depth of misery; slough of despond etc. (*adversity*) 735; peck–, sea- of troubles; "the thousand natural shocks that flesh is heir to" [*Hamlet*] etc. (*evil*) 616; miseries of human life; the iron entering the soul; "unkindest cut of all' [*Julius Caesar*].

nightmare, ephialtes, incubus.

anguish, pang, agony, torture, torment; crucifixion, martyrdom, rack; purgatory etc. (*hell*) 982; hell upon earth; iron age, reign of terror.

sufferer, victim, prey, martyr, object of compassion, wretch, shorn lamb.

v. **suffer**, ail; feel–, suffer–, experience–, undergo–, bear–, endure- pain etc. *n.,* smart, ache etc. (*physical pain*) 378; bleed; be the victim of.

labor under afflictions; bear–, stagger under–, take up- the cross; quaff the bitter cup, have a bad time of it; fall on evil days etc. (*adversity*) 735; go hard with, come to grief, fall a sacrifice to, drain the cup of misery to the dregs, "sup full of horrors" [*Macbeth*].

fret, chafe, sit on thorns, be on pins and needles, wince, worry oneself, be in a taking [*colloq.*], fret and fume; take on [*colloq.*], take to heart; cark [*archaic*].

grieve; mourn etc. (*lament*) 839; yearn, repine, pine, droop, languish, sink; give way; despair etc. 859; heart-scald [*dial. Eng.*]; break one's heart; weigh upon the heart etc. (*inflict pain*) 830.

adj. **pained**, afflicted; in–, in a state of–, full of- pain etc. *n.;* suffering etc. *v.;* worried, displeased etc. 830; aching, griped, sore etc. (*physical pain*) 378; on the rack, in limbo; between hawk and buzzard.

uneasy, uncomfortable, ill at ease; in a taking, in a way [*both colloq.*]; disturbed; discontented etc. 832; out of humor etc. 901a; weary etc. 841.

unfortunate etc. (*hapless*) 735; to be pitied, doomed, devoted, accursed, undone, lost, stranded; fey [*obs.*]; victimized, a prey to, ill-used.

unhappy, infelicitous, poor, wretched, miserable, woe-begone; cheerless etc. (*dejected*) 837; careworn; heavy laden, stricken, crushed.

concerned, sorry; sorrowing, sorrowful; cut up [*colloq.*], chagrined, horrified, horror-stricken; in–, plunged in–, a prey to- grief etc. *n.;* in tears etc. (*lamenting*) 839; steeped to the lips in misery; heartstricken, heartbroken, heart-scalded [*dial. Eng.*]; broken-hearted; in despair etc. 859.

829. Pleasurableness
[capability of giving pleasure]

n. **pleasurableness**, pleasantness, agreeableness etc. *adj.;* pleasure giving, jucundity [*rare*], jocundity, delectability; amusement etc. 840; goodness etc. 648; manna in the wilderness, land flowing with milk and honey, "the shadow of a great rock in a weary land" [*Bible*]; flowery beds of ease; fair weather.

treat; regale etc. (*physical pleasure*) 377; sweets etc. (*sugar*) 396; dainty, *bonne bouche* [*F.*], titbit *or* tidbit; sweets, sweetmeats, nuts, *sauce piquante* [*F.*], salt, savor; a sight for sore eyes [*colloq.*].

attraction etc. (*motive*) 615; attractiveness, attractability [*rare*], attractableness; invitingness etc. *adj.;* charm, fascination, captivation, enchantment, witchery, seduction, winning ways, amenity, amiability; winsomeness; loveliness etc. (*beauty*) 845; sunny side, bright side.

v. **delight**, charm, becharm, imparadise; gladden etc. (*make cheerful*) 836; win–, gladden–, rejoice–, warm the cockles of- the heart; do one's heart good; bless, beatify; take, captivate, fascinate; enchant, entrance, enrapture, transport, bewitch, ravish, enravish.

cause–, produce–, create–, give–, afford–, procure–, offer–, present–, yield- pleasure etc. 827.

please, satisfy, gratify, –desire etc. 865; slake, satiate, quench; indulge, humor, flatter, tickle; tickle the palate etc. (*savory*) 394; regale, refresh; enliven; treat; amuse etc. 840; take–, tickle–, hit- one's fancy; meet one's wishes.

attract, allure etc. (*move*) 615; stimulate etc. (*excite*) 824; interest.

make things pleasant, make everyone feel happy, popularize, gild the pill, sweeten; smooth–, pour oil upon- the troubled waters.

adj. **pleasurable**, causing pleasure etc. *v.;* laetificant; pleasure-giving; pleasing, pleasant, amiable, agreeable, grateful, gratifying; lief *or* leef [*obs.*], acceptable; dear, beloved; welcome, –as the roses in May; welcomed; favorite; to one's taste, –mind, –liking; satisfactory etc. (*good*) 648.

refreshing; comfortable; cordial; genial; glad, gladsome; sweet, delectable, nice, dainty; delicate, delicious; dulcet; luscious etc. 396; palatable etc. 394.

luxurious, voluptuous; sensual etc. 377.

attractive etc. 615; inviting, prepossessing, engaging; winning, winsome; taking, fascinating, captivating, killing [*colloq.*]; seducing, seductive; heart-robbing; alluring, enticing, appetizing etc. (*exciting*) 824; cheering etc. 836; bewitching; enchanting, entrancing, enravishing.

delightful, charming, felicitous, exquisite; lovely etc. (*beautiful* 845; ravishing, rapturous; heartfelt, thrilling, ecstatic, beatific *or* beatifical, seraphic; empyrean; paradisaic *or* paradisaical; elysian etc. (*heavenly*) 981.

palmy, halcyon, Saturnian.

adv. **to one's delight**, to one's heart's content, in utter satisfaction; at one's ease; in clover; in heaven, in paradise, in elysium; from a full heart.

830. Painfulness
[*capability of giving pain*]

n. **painfulness** etc. *adj.;* trouble, care etc. (*pain*) 828; trial, affliction, infliction; cross, blow, stroke, burden, load, curse; bitter -pill, -draft *or* draught, -cup; cup-, waters- of bitterness.

annoyance, grievance, nuisance, vexation, mortification, sickener [*rare*], worry, bore, bother, pother, hot water, "sea of troubles" [*Hamlet*], hornet's nest, plague, pest.

source of -irritation, -annoyance; wound, sore subject, skeleton in the closet; thorn in -the flesh, -one's side; where the shoe pinches, gall and wormwood; fly in the ointment; worm at the heart of the rose; crumpled rose-leaf; pea in the shoe.

cancer, ulcer, sting, thorn; canker etc. (*bane*) 663; scorpion etc. (*evildoer*) 913; dagger etc. (*arms*) 727; scourge etc. (*instrument of punishment*) 975; carking care [*archaic*], canker worm of care.

mishap, misfortune etc. (*adversity*) 735; désagrément [*F.*], esclandre [*F.*], rub.

sorry sight, heavy news, provocation; affront etc. 929; "head and front of one's offending" [*Othello*].

infestation, molestation; malignity etc. (*malevolence*) 907.

v. **pain**, hurt, wound; cause-, occasion-, give-, bring-, induce-, produce-, create-, inflict- pain etc. 828.

pinch, prick, gripe etc. (*physical pain*) 378; pierce, lancinate, cut.

hurt-, wound-, grate upon-, jar upon- the feelings; wring-, pierce-, lacerate-, break-, rend- the heart; make the heart bleed; tear-, rend- the heartstrings; draw tears from the eyes; add a nail to one's coffin.

sadden; make unhappy etc. 828; plunge into sorrow, grieve, fash [*Scot.*], afflict, distress; cut up [*colloq.*], cut to the heart.

annoy, incommode, displease, discompose, trouble, disquiet; faze [*U. S.*], feeze *or* feaze [*colloq., U. S. & dial. Eng.*], disturb, cross, thwart, perplex, molest; tease, tire, irk, vex, mortify, wherret [*obs.*], worry, plague, bother, pester, bore, pother, harass, harry, badger, heckle, bait, beset, infest, persecute, importune.

torment, wring, harrow, torture; bullyrag; put to the -rack, -question; break on the wheel, rack, scarify; cruciate [*obs.*], crucify; convulse, agonize; barb the dart; plant a - dagger in the breast, -thorn in one's side.

irritate, provoke, sting, nettle, try the patience, pique, fret, roil rile [*colloq. & dial.*], tweak the nose, chafe, gall; sting-, wound-, cut- to the quick; aggrieve, affront, enchafe [*obs.*], enrage, ruffle, sour the temper; give offense etc. (*resentment*) 900.

maltreat, bite, snap at, assail; smite etc. (*punish*) 972; bite the hand that feeds one.

repel, revolt; sicken, disgust, nauseate; disenchant, offend, shock, stink in the nostrils; go against-, turn- the stomach; make one sick, set the teeth on edge, go against the grain, grate on the ear; stick in one's -throat, -gizzard [*colloq.*]; rankle, gnaw, corrode, horrify, appal, freeze the blood; make the flesh creep, make the hair stand on end; make the blood -curdle, -run cold; make one shudder.

haunt, haunt the memory; weigh-, prey- on the -heart, -mind, -spirits; bring one's gray hairs with sorrow to the grave.

adj. **painful**, causing pain, hurting etc. *v.;* hurtful etc. (*bad*) 649; dolorific *or* dolorifical, dolorous.

unpleasant, unpleasing, displeasing, disagreeable, unpalatable, bitter, distasteful, unpleasing, uninviting, unwelcome, undesirable, undesired; obnoxious; unacceptable, unpopular, thankless.

untoward, unsatisfactory, unlucky, inauspicious, ill-starred, uncomfortable.

distressing; afflicting, afflictive; joyless, cheerless, comfortless, dismal, disheartening; depressing, depressive; dreary, melancholy, grievous, piteous, woeful, rueful, mournful; deplorable, pitiable, lamentable, sad, affecting, touching, pathetic.

irritating, provoking, stinging, annoying, aggravating [*colloq.*], exasperating, mortifying, galling; unaccommodating, invidious, vexatious; troublesome, tiresome, irksome, weari-

297

some; plaguing, plaguesome, plaguy [*colloq.*]; awkward.

importunate; teasing, pestering, bothering, harassing, worrying, tormenting, carking [*archaic*].

insufferable, intolerable, insupportable, unbearable, unendurable; past bearing; not to be -borne, —endured; more than flesh and blood can bear; enough to -drive one mad, —provoke a saint, —make a parson swear [*colloq.*], —try the patience of Job.

shocking, terrific, grim, appalling, crushing; dreadful, fearful, frightful; thrilling, tremendous, dire; heartbreaking, heart-rending, heart-wounding, heart-corroding, heart-sickening; harrowing, rending.

odious, hateful, execrable, repulsive, repellent, abhorrent; horrid, horrible, horrific, horrifying; offensive; nauseous, nauseating; disgusting, sickening, revolting; nasty; loathsome, loathful; fulsome; vile etc. (*bad*) 649; hideous etc. 846.

acute, sharp, sore, severe, grave, hard, harsh, cruel, biting, caustic; cutting, corroding, consuming, racking, excruciating, searching, searing, grinding, grating, agonizing; envenomed; catheretic, pyrotic.

cumbrous, cumbersome, burdensome, onerous, oppressive.

desolating, withering, tragical, disastrous, calamitous, ruinous.

adv. **painfully** etc. *adj.;* with pain etc. 828; deuced *or* deucedly [*slang*]; under torture, in agony, out of the depths.

int. woe's me! alas! that I had ever been born! *hinc illae lacrimae!* [Terence].

831. Content

n. **content**, contentment, contentedness; complacency, satisfaction, entire satisfaction, ease, heart's ease, peace of mind; serenity etc. 826; cheerfulness etc. 836; ray of comfort; comfort etc. (*well-being*) 827.

patience, moderation, endurance; conciliation, reconciliation; resignation etc. (*patience*) 826; quietism.

waiter on Providence; quietist.

v. **be content** etc. *adj.;* rest satisfied, rest and be thankful; take the good the gods provide, let well enough alone, feel oneself at home, hug oneself, lay the flattering unction to one's soul.

take up with, take in good part; assent etc. 488; be reconciled to, make one's peace with; get over it; take heart, take comfort; put up with etc. (*bear*) 826.

render content etc. *adj.;* set at ease, comfort; set one's -heart, —mind- at -ease, —rest; speak peace; conciliate, reconcile, win over, propitiate, disarm, beguile; content, satisfy; gratify etc. 829.

be tolerated etc. 826; go down, go down with [*colloq.*], do.

adj. **content**, contented; satisfied etc. *v.;* at ease, at one's ease, at home; with the mind at ease, *sans souci* [*F.*], *sine curâ* [*L.*], easy-going, not particular; conciliatory; unrepining, of good comfort; resigned etc. (*patient*) 826; cheerful etc. 836.

serene etc. 826; unafflicted, unvexed, unmolested, unplagued; at rest; snug, comfortable; in one's element; not easily perturbed; imperturbable.

satisfactory, adequate, commensurate, sufficient, ample, equal to; satisfying.

adv. to one's heart's content; à la bonne heure [*F.*]; all for the best.

int. amen etc. (*assent*) 488; very well! all the better! so much the better! well and good! it will do! that will do! it cannot be helped! done! content! i' faith! [*archaic*]; better and better! good! good for you! put it thar, pard! [*colloq.*].

832. Discontent

n. **discontent**, discontentment; dissatisfaction; "the winter of our discontent" [*Henry VI*]; dissent etc. 489; querulousness etc. (*lamentation*) 839; hypercriticism.

disappointment, mortification; cold comfort; regret etc. 833; repining, taking on [*colloq.*] etc. *v.;* inquietude, vexation of spirit, soreness; heartburning, heart-grief.

malcontent, grumbler, growler, grouch [*slang*], croaker, *laudator temporis acti* [*L.*]; censurer, complainer, faultfinder, murmurer.

The Opposition; Bitter-Enders [*U. S. politics*], Die-Hards; cave of Adullam; indignation meeting.

v. **be discontented** etc. *adj.;* quarrel with one's bread and butter; repine; regret etc. 833; wish one to Jericho, wish one at the bottom of the Red Sea; take on [*colloq.*], take to heart; shrug the shoulders; make a wry face, pull a long face; knit one's brows; look blue, look black, look black as thunder, look blank, look glum.

grumble, take ill, take in bad part; fret, chafe, make a piece of work [*colloq.*], croak; lament etc. 839.

cause discontent etc. *n.;* dissatisfy, disappoint, mortify, put out [*colloq.*], disconcert; cut up; dishearten.

adj. **discontented**; dissatisfied etc. *v.;* unsatisfied, ungratified; dissident; dissentient etc. 489; malcontent, exigent, exacting, hypercritical.

repining etc. *v.;* regretful etc. 833; down in the mouth etc. (*dejected*) 837.

glum, sulky; in high dudgeon, in a fume, in the sulks, in the dumps, in bad humor; sour, sour as a crab; sore as a crab [*colloq.*]; soured, sore; out of humor, out of temper.

disappointing etc. *v.;* unsatisfactory.

adv. **from bad to worse**, out of the frying pan into the fire, in the depths of despair.

int. so much the worse! that's bad! couldn't be worse! worse and worse!

833. Regret

n. **regret**, repining; homesickness, nostalgia; *mal du pays* [*F.*], *maladie du pays* [*F.*]; lamentation etc. 839; penitence etc. 950.

bitterness, heartburning.

laudator temporis acti [*L.*] etc. (*discontent*) 832.

v. **regret**, deplore; bewail etc. (*lament*) 839; repine, cast a longing lingering look behind; rue, rue the day; repent etc. 950; *infandum renovare dolorem* [*L.*].

prey–, weigh–, have a weight- on the mind; leave an aching void.

adj. **regretting** etc. *v.;* regretful; homesick.

regretted etc. *v.;* much to be regretted, regrettable; lamentable etc. (*bad*) 649.

int. what a pity! hang it *or* hang it all! [*colloq.*].

834. Relief

n. **relief**; deliverance; refreshment etc. 689; easement, softening, alleviation, mitigation, palliation, soothing; lullaby, cradle-song, *berceuse* [*F.*].

solace, consolation, comfort, encouragement; crumb of comfort, balm in Gilead.

lenitive, palliative, restorative etc. (*remedy*) 662; stupe, poultice, fomentation, assuasive; cushion etc. 215.

v. **relieve**, ease, alleviate, mitigate, palliate, soothe; salve; soften, –down; forment, stupe, poultice; assuage, allay, abirritate.

remedy; cure etc. (*restore*) 660; refresh; pour balm into, pour oil on.

smooth the ruffled brow of care, temper the wind to the shorn lamb, lay the flattering unction to one's soul.

cheer, comfort, console; enliven; encourage, bear up, pat on the back, give comfort, set at ease; gladden–, cheer- the heart; inspirit, invigorate.

disburden etc. (*free*) 705; take off a load of care.

be relieved; breathe more freely, draw a long breath; take comfort; dry the eyes, dry the tears, wipe the eyes, wipe away the tears; pull oneself together.

adj. **relieving** etc. *v.;* consolatory, soothing; assuaging, assuasive; balmy, balsamic; lenitive, palliative; anodyne etc. (*remedial*) 662; curative etc. 660.

835. Aggravation

n. **aggravation**, heightening; exacerbation; exasperation; overestimation etc. 482; exaggeration etc. 549.

v. **aggravate**, render worse, heighten, embitter, sour; exacerbate, acerbate, exasperate, envenom; enrage, provoke, tease.

add fuel to the -fire, –flame; fan the flame etc. (*excite*) 824; go from bad to worse etc. (*deteriorate*) 659.

adj. **aggravated** etc. *v.;* worse, unrelieved; aggravable [*obs.*], aggravative, aggravating etc. *v.*

adv. out of the frying pan into the fire, from bad to worse, worse and worse.

int. so much the worse! *tant pis!* [*F.*].

836. Cheerfulness

n. **cheerfulness** etc. *adj.;* geniality, gayety, *L'Allegro* [*It.*], cheer, good humor, spirits; high spirits, animal spirits, flow of spirits; glee, high glee, light heart; sunshine of the -mind, –breast; *gaieté de coeur* [*F.*], *bon naturel* [*F.*].

liveliness etc. *adj.;* life, alacrity, vivacity, animation, *allégresse* [*F.*]; jocundity, joviality, jollity; levity; jocularity etc. (*wit*) 842.

mirth, merriment, hilarity, exhilaration; laughter etc. 838; merrymaking etc. (*amusement*) 840; heyday, rejoicing etc. 838; marriage bell.

nepenthe *or* nepenthes, lotus; Euphrosyne.

optimism etc. (*hopefulness*) 858; self-complacency; hedonics, hedonism.

v. **be cheerful** etc. *adj.;* have the mind at ease, smile, put a good face upon, keep up one's spirits; view the bright side of the picture, view things *en couleur de rose* [*F.*]; look through rose-colored spectacles; *ridentem dicere verum* [*L.*], cheer up, brighten up, light up, bear up; take heart, cast away care, drive dull care away, perk up; keep a stiff upper lip [*slang*].

rejoice etc.; 838; carol, chirp, chirrup, lilt; frisk, rollic, give a loose to mirth [*obs.*].

cheer, enliven, elate, exhilarate, gladden, inspirit, animate, raise the spirits, inspire; put in good humor; cheer–, rejoice- the heart; delight etc. (*give pleasure*) 829.

adj. **cheerful**; happy etc. 827; cheery, of good cheer, smiling; blithe; in spirits, in good spirits; breezy, bully [*slang*], chipper [*colloq.*]; in high -spirits, –feather; happy as -the day is long, –a king; gay, gay as a lark; *allegro* [*It.*]; debonair *or* debonaire, light, lightsome, lighthearted; buoyant, bright, free and easy, airy; jaunty *or* janty, rollicky [*colloq.*], canty [*Scot. & dial. Eng.*], "crouse an' canty" [Burns]; hedonic; riant; sprightly, sprightful; spry; spirited, spiritful [*rare*], lively, animated, vivacious; brisk, –as a bee; sparkling; sportive; full of -play, –spirit; all alive.

sunny, palmy; hopeful etc. 858.

merry, –as a -cricket, –grig, –marriage bell; joyful, joyous, jocund, jovial; jolly, –as a thrush, –as a sand-boy; blithesome; gleeful, gleesome; hilarious, rattling [*colloq.*].

winsome, bonny, hearty, buxom.

playful, playsome; *folâtre* [*F.*], playful as a kitten, tricksy, frisky, frolicsome; gamesome; jocose, jocular, waggish; mirth-loving, laughter-loving, abderian; mirthful, rollicking.

elate, elated; exulting, jubilant, flushed; rejoicing etc. 838; cock-a-hoop.

cheering, inspiriting, exhilarating; cardiac *or* cardiacal; pleasing etc. 829; palmy, flourishing, halcyon.

adv. **cheerfully** etc. *adj.*; cheerily, with good cheer; with a cheerful etc. heart; with relish, with zest; on the crest of the wave.

int. **never say die**! come! cheer up! hurrah! etc. 838; "hence loathed melancholy!" begone dull care! away with melancholy!

837. Dejection

n. **dejection**; dejectedness etc. *adj.*; depression, prosternation [*obs.*], mopishness, damp; lowness–, depression- of spirits; weight–, oppression–, damp- on the spirits; low–, bad–, drooping–, depressed- spirits; heart sinking; heaviness–, failure- of heart.

heaviness etc. *adj.*; infestivity, gloom; weariness etc. 841; *taedium vitae* [*L.*], disgust of life; *mal du pays* [*F.*] etc. (*regret*) 833; anhedonia.

melancholy; sadness etc. *adj.*; *Il Penseroso* [*Old It.*], melancholia, dismals, blue devils [*colloq.*], blues [*colloq.*], mopes, lachrymals *or* lacrimals, mumps, dumps [*chiefly humorous*], doldrums, vapors [*archaic*], megrims, spleen [*obsoles.*], horros, hypochondriasis, hypochondria, jawfall [*rare*], pessimism; *la maladie sans maladie* [*F.*], despondency, slough of Despond; disconsolateness etc. *adj.*; hope deferred, blank despondency; voiceless woe.

prostration, prostration of soul; broken heart; despair etc. 859; cave of despair, cave of Trophonius.

gravity; demureness etc. *adj.*; solemnity; long face, grave face.

hypochondriac, seek-sorrow, self-tormentor, *heautontimorumenos* [*Gr.*], *malade imaginaire* [*F.*], *médecin tant pis* [*F.*]; croaker, pessimist; mope, mopus [*dial. Eng. & slang*], damper, wet blanket crape-hanger [*slang*], Job's comforter.

[cause of dejection] affliction etc. 830; sorry sight; *memento mori* [*L.*]; deathwatch, death's-head, skeleton at the feast.

v. **be dejected** etc. *adj.*; grieve; mourn etc. (*lament*) 839; take on [*colloq.*], give way, lose heart, despond, droop, sink.

lower, look downcast, frown, pout; hang down the head; pull–, make- a long face; laugh on the wrong side of the mouth; grin a ghastly smile; look blue, look like a drowned man; lay to heart, take to heart.

mope, brood over; fret; sulk; pine, pine away; yearn; repine etc. (*regret*) 833; despair etc. 859.

refrain from laughter, keep one's countenance; be *or* look grave etc. *adj.*; repress a smile, keep a straight face.

depress, discourage, dishearten, dispirit; damp, dull, deject, lower, sink, dash, knock down, unman, prostrate, break one's heart; frown upon; cast a gloom on, cast a shade on; sadden; damp–, dash–, wither- one's hopes; weight–, lie heavy–, prey- on the -mind, –spirits; damp–, dampen–, depress- the spirits.

adj. **cheerless**, joyless, spiritless, uncheerful, uncheery, unlively; unhappy etc. 828; melancholy, dismal, somber, dark, gloomy, *triste* [*F.*], clouded, murky, lowering, frowning, lugubrious, funereal, mournful, lamentable, dreadful.

dreary, flat; dull, –as -a beetle, –ditchwater; depressing etc. *v.*; damp [*archaic*].

downcast, downhearted, mopy [*colloq.*], "melancholy as a gib cat" [*Henry IV Part I*]; a prey to melancholy; "besieged with sable-coloured melancholy" [*Love's Labour Lost*]; down in the mouth [*colloq.*], down on one's luck [*colloq.*]; heavy-hearted; in the -dumps, –suds [*colloq.*], –sulks, –doldrums; in doleful dumps, in bad humor; sullen; mumpish, dumpish, mopish, moping; moody, glum; sulky etc. (*discontented*) 832; out of -sorts, –humor, –heart, –spirits; ill at ease, low-spirited, in low spirits, a cup too low; weary etc. 841; discouraged, disheartened, desponding, chapfallen *or* chopfallen, jawfallen [*rare*]; crestfallen.

sad, pensive, *pensieroso* [*It.*], tristful; dolesome, doleful; woe-begone, lachry-mose, in tears, melancholic, hypochondriacal, bilious, jaundiced, atrabilious, saturnine, splenetic; lackadaisical.

serious, sedate, staid, earnest; grave, –as -a judge, –an undertaker, –a mustard pot [*colloq.*]; sober, solemn, demure; grim, grim-faced, grim-visaged; rueful, wan, long-faced.

disconsolate, inconsolable, forlorn, comfortless, desolate, *désolé* [*F.*], sick at heart; soul-sick, heartsick; *au désespoir* [*F.*]; in despair etc. 859; lost.

overcome; broken-down, borne-down, bowed-down; heartstricken etc. (*mental suffering*) 828; cut up [*colloq.*], dashed, sunk; unnerved, unmanned; downfallen, downtrodden; broken-hearted; careworn.

adv. **sadly** etc. *adj.;* with a long face, with tears in one's eyes.

838. Rejoicing
[expression of pleasure]

n. **rejoicing**, exultation, triumph, jubilation, heyday, flush, reveling *or* revelling; merrymaking etc. (*amusement*) 840; jubilee etc. (*celebration*) 883; paean, *Te Deum* [*L.*] etc. (*thanksgiving*) 990; congratulation etc. 896.

smile, simper, smirk, grin; broad grin, sardonic grin.

laughter, giggle, titter, snicker, snigger, crow, cheer, chuckle, shout; Homeric laughter; horse–, hearty- laugh; guffaw; burst–, fit–, shout–, roar–, peal- of laughter; cachinnation; Kentish fire.

risibility; derision etc. 856; "sport that wrinkled Care derides" [Milton].

Momus; Democritus the Abderite; rollicker.

cheer, huzza, hurrah *or* hurra, cheering; shout, yell, college yell; tiger [*colloq.*].

v. **rejoice**; thank–, bless- one's stars; congratulate oneself, hug oneself; rub–, clap- one's hands; smack the lips, fling up one's cap; dance, skip; sing, carol, chirrup, chirp; hurrah *or* hurra; cry for joy, leap with joy, skip for joy; exult etc. (*boast*) 884; triumph; hold jubilee etc. (*celebrate*) 883; sing a *Te Deum,* sing a paean of triumph; make merry etc. (*sport*) 840.

smile, simper, smirk; grin, –like a Cheshire cat [*colloq.*]; mock, laugh in one's sleeve.

laugh, –outright; giggle, titter, snigger, snicker, crow, smicker [*obs.*], chuckle, cackle; burst out; burst into a roar of laughter, burst into a fit of laughter; shout, split [*colloq.*], roar.

shake–, split–, hold both- one's sides; roar–, shake–, nearly die–, die- with laughter.

raise laughter etc. (*amuse*) 840.

adj. **rejoicing** etc. *v.;* jubilant, exultant, triumphant; flushed, elated; laughing etc. *v.;* risible; ready to -burst, –split, –die with laughter [*all colloq.*]; convulsed with laughter; shaking like a jelly with -laughter, –suppressed merriment [*both colloq.*].

laughable etc. (*ludicrous*) 853.

adv. **laughingly**; on a broad grin, in fits of laughter, amid peals of laughter; in triumph; in mockery; with a -roar, –peal, –outburst- of laughter.

int. **hurrah**! huzza! three cheers! right on! hip, hip, hurrah! aha! hail! tolderolloll! Heaven be praised! *tant mieux!* [*F.*], so much the better! good enough! tra-la-la!

839. Lamentation
[expression of pain]

n. **lamentation**, lament, wail, complaint, plaint, murmur, mutter, grumble, groan, moan, whine, whimper, sob, sigh, suspiration, deep sigh; frown, scowl.

cry etc. (*vociferation*) 411; scream, howl; outcry, wail, wail of woe.

weeping etc. *v.;* tear; flood of tears, fit of crying, lachrymation [*rare*], crying; melting mood; "weeping and gnashing of teeth" [*Bible*].

plaintiveness etc. *adj.;* languishment; condolence etc. 915.

mourning, weeds [*colloq.*], widow's weeds, willow, cypress, crape, deep mourning; sackcloth and ashes; lachrymatory, tear bottle, lachrymals *or* lacrimals; knell etc. 363; dump [*obs.*], death song, dirge, coronach [*Scot. & Ir.*], nenia, requiem, elegy, epicedium; threne [*rare*], menody, threnody; jeremiad *or* jeremiade, ululation, keen [*Ir.*], ullalulla [*Ir.*].

mourner, keener [*Ir.*]; grumbler etc. (*discontent*) 832; Niobe; Heraclitus, Jeremiah, Mrs. Gummidge.

v. **lament**, mourn, deplore, grieve, keen [*Ir.*], weep over; bewail, bemoan; condole with etc. 915; fret etc. (*suffer*) 828; wear–, go into–, put on- mourning; wear -the willow, –sackcloth and ashes; *infandum renovare dolorem* [Virgil] etc. (*regret*) 833; give sorrow words.

sigh; give–, heave–, fetch- a sigh; "waft a sigh from Indus to the pole" [Pope]; sigh "like furnace" [*As You Like It*]; wail.

cry, weep, sob, greet [*archaic or Scot.*], blubber, snivel, bibber, whimper, pule; pipe, pipe one's eye [*both slang, orig. naut.*]; drop–, shed- -tears,

–a tear; melt–, burst- into tears; *fondre en larmes* [*F.*], cry oneself blind, cry one's eyes out; yammer [*dial.*].

scream etc. (*cry out*) 411; mew etc. (*animal sounds*) 412; groan, moan, whine, yelp, howl, yell, ululate; roar; roar–, bellow- like a bull; cry out lustily, rend the air.

show signs of grief; frown, scowl, make a wry face, gnash one's teeth, wring one's hands, tear one's hair, beat one's breast, roll on the ground, burst with grief.

complain, murmur, mutter, grumble, growl, clamor, make a fuss about, croak, grunt, maunder [*obs.*]; deprecate etc. (*disapprove*) 932.

cry out before one is hurt, complain without cause.

adj. **lamenting** etc. *v.;* in mourning, in sackcloth and ashes; ululant, ululative [*obs.*], clamorous; crying–, lamenting- to high heaven, sorrowing, sorrowful etc. (*unhappy*) 828; mournful, tearful; lachrymose, lachrymal *or* lacrimal, lachrymatory, plaintive, plaintful; querulous, querimonious; in the melting mood.

in tears, with tears in one's eyes; with moistened eyes, with watery eyes; bathed–, dissolved- in tears; "like Niobe, all tears" [*Hamlet*].

elegiac, epicedial, threnetic *or* threnetical.

adv. de profundis [*L.*], les larmes aux yeux [*F.*].

int. **alas**! alack! heigh-ho! O dear! ah me! woe is me! lackadaisy! well a day! lack a day! alack a day! wellaway! alas the day! *O tempora, O mores!* [*L.*]; what a pity! *miserabile dictu!* [*L.*]; too true!

840. Amusement

n. **amusement**, entertainment, diversion, divertisement, *divertissement* [*F.*]; reaction, relaxation, solace; pastime, *passe-temps* [*F.*], sport; labor of love; pleasure etc. 827.

fun, frolic, merriment, jollity, joviality, jovialness; heyday; laughter etc. 838; jocosity, jocoseness; drollery, buffoonery, tomfoolery; mummery, mumming, masquing, pageant; pleasantry; wit etc. 842; quip, quirk.

play; game, game of romps; gambol, romp, prank, antic, frisk, rig [*obs. or dial.*], lark [*colloq.*], spree, skylarking, vagary, monkey trick, *fredaine* [*F.*], escapade, *échappée* [*F.*], bout, *espièglerie* [*F.*]; practical joke etc. (*ridicule*) 856.

[dance steps] *gambade* [*F.*], gambado, *pas* [*F.*]; pigeonwing, heel-and-toe, buck-and-wing, shuffle, double shuffle; *chassé* [*F.*], *coupé* [*F.*], grapevine, etc.

[dances] dance, hop [*colloq.*], stag dance, shindig [*slang*]; ball; *bal, bal masqué, bal costumé*

[*all F.*], masquerade, masquerade ball, cornwallis [*U. S.*]; mistletoe-bough dance; Dance of Death, *danse macabre* [*F.*]; interpretative dance, step dance, sand dance, *pas seul* [*F.*], skirt dance, folk dance; Morisco *or* morice [*obs.*], morris dance, saraband, fandango, bolero, tarantella, boutade, gavot *or* gavotte, minuet, *allemande* [*F.*], rigadoon, fling, Highland fling, Highland schottische, strathspey, reel, jig, hornpipe, sword dance, breakdown, cakewalk; kantikoy, snake dance; country dance, Scotch reel, Virginia reel, Sir Roger de Coverley, Portland fancy; ballet etc. (*drama*) 599; ragtime [*colloq.*] etc. (*music*) 415; jazz [*slang*]; nautch [*India*].

square dance, quadrille, Lancers, cotillion *or* cotillon [*F.*], German.

round dance, waltz, *valse* [*F.*], polka, mazurka, galop, gallopade *or* galopade, schottische, one-step, two-step, fox-trot, turkey-trot; shimmy.

danse du ventre [*F.*], belly dance, break dance, *chonchina* [*Jap.*], cancan.

dancer, *danseur* (*fem. danseuse*) [*F.*], *première danseuse* [*F.*], ballet dancer; geisha [*Jap.*]; nautch girl, bayadere [*both India*]; clog–, step–, skirt–, figure-dancer; figurant (*fem. figurante*), Morisco [*obs.*], morris dancer; terpsichorean [*colloq.*]; Terpsichore.

festivity, merrymaking; party etc. (*social gathering*) 892; revels, revelry, reveling *or* revelling, carnival, Saturnalia, jollification [*colloq.*], junket, picnic.

fête champêtre [*F.*], lawn party, garden party, regatta, field day, *fête* [*F.*], festival, gala, gala day; feast, banquet etc. (*food*) 298; regale, symposium, high jinks [*colloq.*], carouse, carousal, brawl; wassail; wake; bust [*slang*], tear [*slang*]; *Turnerfest* [*Ger.*]; gymkhana [*orig. Anglo-Ind.*]; treat; *ridotto* [*It.*], drum [*obs. or hist.*], kettledrum [*colloq.*], rout [*archaic*]; tea party, tea, tea fight [*slang*]; *Kaffee-Klatsch* [*Ger.*]; concert etc. (*music*) 415; show [*colloq.*]; play etc. (*drama*) 599; randy [*dial.*]; clambake, fish fry, beefsteak fry, squantum, donation party [*all U. S.*]; bat, bum [*both slang*], jamboree [*slang*].

round of pleasure, dissipation, a short life and a merry one, racketing, holiday making.

rejoicing etc. 838; jubilee etc. (*celebration*) 883.

fireworks, *feu-de-joie* [*F.*], firecrackers, bonfire.

holiday; red-letter day, play day; high days and holidays; high holiday, Bank holiday [*Eng.*]; May day, Derby day [*Eng.*]; Easter Monday, Whitmonday, Twelfth Night, Halloween;

Christmas etc. 138; Dewali [*Hindu*], Holi *or* Hoolee [*Hindu*]; Bairam, Muharram [*both Moham.*]; wayzgoose [*Printers*], beanfeast [*Eng.*]; Arbor–, Declaration–, Independence–, Labor–, Memorial *or* Decoration–, Thanksgiving- Day; Washington's–, Lincoln's–, King's- birthday; Empire Day [*Brit.*]; Mardi gras, *mi-carême* [*F.*], *feria* [*S. W. U. S.*], *fiesta* [*Sp.*].

place of amusement, theater *or* theatre; concert -hall, –room; ballroom, dance hall, assembly room; moving-picture–, cinema- theater; movies [*colloq.*]; music hall; vaudeville -theater, –show; circus, hippodrome.

park, pleasance *or* plaisance [*archaic*]; arbor; garden etc. (*horticulture*) 371; pleasure–, play–, cricket–, croquet- archery–, polo–, hunting-ground; tennis–, racket–, squash–, badminton-court; bowling- green, –alley; croquet lawn, rink, glaciarium, ice rink, skating rink; golf links, race course, athletic field, stadium; gymnasium, swimming -pool, –bath; billiard room, pool room, casino, shooting gallery; flying horses, roundabout, merry-go-round; swing; *montagne Russe* [*F.*]; aërial railway, scenic railway, roller coaster, chutes, flying boats, etc.

Vauxhall, Ranelagh, Hurlingham; Lord's, Epsom, Newmarket, Doncaster, Sandown Park, Henley, Cowes, Mortlake [*all in Eng.*]; Coney Island; Brooklands, Sheepshead Bay, Belmont Park, Saratoga; New London, Forest Hills, Longwood [*all in U. S.*]; Monte Carlo; Longchamps [*France*]; Flemington [*Melbourne, Australia*].

[sports and games] athletic sports, track events, gymnastics; archery, rifle shooting; tournament, pugilis m etc. (*contention*) 720; sporting etc. 622; horse racing, the turf; water polo; aquatics etc. 267.

skating, ice skating, roller skating, sliding; cricket, tennis, lawn tennis, pallone, rackets, squash, fives, trap bat and ball, badminton, battledore and shuttlecock, pall-mall, croquet, golf, curling, hockey, shinny *or* shinney; polo, football, Rugby, rugger [*colloq.*]; association, soccer [*colloq.*]; tent pegging, tilting at the ring, quintain, greasy pole; knur (*or* knurr) and spell [*Eng.*]; quoits, discus; hammer–, horseshoe-throwing; putting the -weight, –shot; hurdling; leapfrog; sack–, potato–, obstacle–, three-legged- race; hop skip and jump; French and English, tug of war; rounders, baseball, basket ball, pushball, captain ball; lacrosse; tobogganing.

blind-man's buff, hunt the slipper, hide and seek, kiss in the ring; snapdragon; cross questions and crooked answers, twenty questions, what's my thought? charades, crambo, dumb crambo, crisscross, proverbs, *bouts rimés* [*F.*]; hopscotch, jackstones, mumble-the-peg *or* mumblety-peg; ping-pong, tiddledywinks, tipcat.

billiards, pool, pyramids, bagatelle; bowls, skittles, ninepins, American bowls; tenpins, bowling, tivoli.

chess, draughts, checkers *or* chequers, backgammon, dominoes, halma, dice, craps, crap shooting, crap game, "negro golf," "indoor golf" [*both humorous*]; merelles, nine men's morris, gobang, "the royal game of goose" [Goldsmith]; fox and geese; lotto *or* loto etc.

cards; whist, rubber; round game; loo, cribbage, *bésique* [*F.*], euchre, cutthroat euchre, railroad euchre; drole, *écarté*, picquet, all fours, quadrille, omber *or* ombre, reverse, Pope Joan, commit; boston, *vingt et un* [*F.*], quinze, thirty-one, put, speculation, connections, brag, cassino, lottery, commerce, snip-snap-snorem, lift smoke, blind hookey, Polish bank, Earl of Coventry, napoleon *or* nap [*colloq.*]; banker, penny-ante, poker, jack pot; blind–, draw–, straight–, stud–, poker; bluff; bridge, –whist; auction; monte, reversis, squeezers, old maid, fan-tan, fright, beggar-my-neighbor, goat, hearts, patience, solitaire, pairs.

court cards; ace, king, queen, knave, jack, joker; bower; right–, left- bower; dummy; hand; trump; face cards, diamonds, hearts, clubs, spades; pack, deck; flush, full-house, straight, three of a kind, pair, *misère* [*F.*] etc.

toy, plaything, bauble; doll etc. (*puppet*) 554; teetotum; knickknack etc. (*trifle*) 643; magic lantern etc. (*show*) 448; peep–, puppet–, raree–, galanty *or* gallanty–, Punch-and-Judy-show; marionettes; toy-shop; "quips and cranks and wanton wiles, nods and becks and wreathed smiles" [Milton].

sportsman (*fem.* sportswoman), hunter, Nimrod. archer, toxophilite; cricketer, footballer, ball-players etc.

gamester (*fem.* gamestress), sport, gambler; dicer, punter, plunger.

reveler *or* reveller, carouser; master of the -ceremonies, –revels; *arbiter elegantiarum* [*L.*]; *arbiter bibendi* [*L.*].

devotee, enthusiast, follower, fan [*slang*], rooter [*slang*]; turfman.

v. **amuse,** entertain, divert, enliven; tickle, -the fancy; titillate, raise a smile, put in good humor;

cause–, create–, occasion–, raise–, excite–, produce–, convulse with– laughter; set the table in a roar, be the death of one.

cheer, rejoice; recreate, solace; please etc. 829; interest; treat, regale.

amuse oneself; game; play, –a game, –pranks, –tricks; sport, disport, toy, wanton, revel, junket, feast, carouse, banquet, make merry, drown care; drive dull care away; frolic, gambol, frisk, romp; caper; dance etc. (*leap*) 309; keep up the ball; run a rig, sow one's wild oats, have one's fling, take one's pleasure; paint the town red [*slang*]; see life; *desipere in loco* [Horace], play the fool.

make–, keep– holiday; go a-Maying.

while away–, beguile– the time; kill time, dally.

adj. **amusing**, entertaining, diverting etc. *v.;* recreative, lusory; pleasant etc. (*pleasing*) 829; laughable etc. (*ludicrous*) 853; witty etc. 842; festive, festal; jovial, jolly, jocund, roguish, rompish; playful, –as a kitten; sportive, ludibrious [*obs.*].

amused etc. *v.;* "pleased with a rattle, tickled with a straw" [Pope].

adv. "on the light fantastic toe" [Milton], at play, in sport.

int. *vive la bagatelle!* [*F.*], *vogue la galère!* [*F.*], come on fellows! "hail, hail, the gang's all here!" some party! [*slang*].

841. Weariness

n. **weariness**, defatigation [*obs.*], ennui, boredom; lassitude etc. (*fatigue*) 688; drowsiness etc. 683.

disgust, nausea, loathing, sickness; satiety etc. 869; *taedium vitae* [*L.*] etc. (*dejection*) 837.

tedium, wearisomeness, tediousness etc. *adj.;* heavy hours, dull work, monotony, twice-told tale; "the enemy" [time].

bore, buttonholer, proser, dry-as-dust, fossil [*colloq.*], wet blanket; pill, stiff [*both slang*].

v. **weary**; tire etc. (*fatigue*) 688; bore–, weary–, tire– -to death, –out of one's life, –out of all patience; set–, send- to sleep; buttonhole.

pall, sicken, nauseate, disgust; harp on the same string; drag its -slow, –weary- length along.

never hear the last of; be tired etc. *adj.* of *or* with; yawn; die with *ennui*.

adj. **wearying** etc. *v.;* wearing; wearisome, tiresome, irksome; uninteresting, stupid, bald, devoid of interest, jejune, dry, monotonous, dull, arid, tedious, humdrum, mortal [*colloq.*], flat; prosy, prosing; slow; soporific, somniferous, dormitive, opiate.

disgusting etc. *v.;* unenjoyed.

weary; tired etc. *v.;* drowsy etc. (*sleepy*) 683; uninterested, flagging, used up, worn out, *blasé* [*F.*], life-weary, weary of life; sick of.

adv. **wearily** etc. *adj.; usque ad nauseam* [*L.*].

842. Wit

n. **wit**, wittiness; Attic -wit, –salt; Atticism; salt, *esprit* [*F.*], point, fancy, whim, humor *or* humour, drollery, pleasantry.

buffoonery, fooling, farce, tom-foolery; shenanigan [*slang*], harlequinade etc. 599; broad -farce, –humor; fun, *espiéglerie* [*F.*]; *vis comica* [*L.*].

jocularity; jocosity, jocoseness; facetiousness; waggery, waggishness; whimsicality; comicality etc. 853.

smartness, ready wit, banter, persiflage, *badinage* [*F.*], retort, repartee, *quid pro quo* [*L.*]; ridicule etc. 856.

facetlae, quips and cranks; jest, joke, capital joke; *canorae nugae* [*L.*]; standing -jest, –joke; conceit, quip, quirk, crank, quiddity [*rare*], *concetto* [*It.*], *plaisanterie* [*F.*], brilliant idea; merry–, bright–, happy- thought; sally; flash, –of wit, –of merriment; scintillation; *mot*, –*pour rire* [*F.*]; witticism, smart saying, *bon mot* [*F.*], *jeu d'esprit* [*F.*], epigram; jest book; dry joke, *quodlibet* [*L.*], cream of the jest.

word-play, *jeu de mots* [*F.*], play upon words; pun, punning; *double entente* [*F.*] etc. (*ambiguity*) 520; quibble, verbal quibble; conundrum etc. (*riddle*) 533; anagram, acrostic, double acrostic, trifling, idle conceit, turlupinade [*obs.*].

old joke, Joe Miller, chestnut [*slang*]; hoary-headed -joke, –jest; joke–, jest- with whiskers [*humorous*].

v. **joke**, jest, cut jokes; crack a joke, get off a joke; pun; perpetrate a -joke, –pun; make fun of, make merry with; set the table in a roar etc. (*amuse*) 840; tell a good -story, –yarn.

retort, flash back, flash, scintillate; banter etc. (*ridicule*) 856; *ridentem dicere verum* [*L.*]; joke at one's expense.

adj. **witty**, Attic; clever, keen, keen-witted, brilliant, pungent; quick-witted, nimble-witted; smart; jocular, jocose, funny, waggish, facetious, whimsical, humorous; playful etc. 840; merry and wise; pleasant, sprightly, cute [*colloq.*], *spirituel* [*F.*], sparkling, epigrammatic, full of point, *ben trovato* [*It.*]; comic etc. 853.

adv. in joke, in jest, for the jest's sake, in sport, in play.

843. Dullness

n. **dullness** *or* dulness, heaviness, flatness; infestivity etc. 837, stupidity etc. 499; want of originality; dearth of ideas.

prose, matter of fact; heavy book, *conte à dormir debout* [*F.*]; commonplace, platitude.

v. **be dull** etc. *adj.;* hang fire, fall flat; platitudinize, prose, take *au sérieux* [*F.*], be caught napping.

render dull etc. *adj.;* damp, depress, throw cold water on, lay a wet blanket on; fall flat upon the ear.

adj. **dull,** −as ditch water; jejune, dry, unentertaining, uninteresting, unlively, heavy-footed, elephantine; slow of comprehension; insipid, tasteless, slow as molasses [*colloq.*], logy; unimaginative; insulse; dry as dust; prosy, prosing, prosaic; matter-of-fact, commonplace, platitudinous, pointless; "weary, stale, flat, and unprofitable" [*Hamlet*].

stupid, slow, flat, humdrum, monotonous; melancholic etc. 837; stolid etc. 499; plodding.

844. Humorist

n. **humorist,** wag, wit, reparteeist, epigrammatist, punster; *bel esprit* [*F.*], life of the party; joker, jester, Joe Miller, *drôle de corps* [*F.*], galliard *or* gaillard [*archaic*], spark; *bon diable* [*F.*]; *persifleur* [*F.*], banterer, "Agreeable Rattle" [Goldsmith].

buffoon, *farceur* [*F.*], merry-andrew, mime, tumbler, acrobat, mountebank, charlatan, posture master, harlequin, punch, punchinello, *pulcinella* [*It.*], Scaramouch, clown; wearer of the -cap and bells, −motley; motley fool; pantaloon, gypsy; jack-pudding [*archaic*], Jack-in-the-green; jack-a-dandy; zany; madcap, pickle-herring, witling, caricaturist, grimacer, grimacier.

845. Beauty

n. **beauty,** beautifulness, pulchritude; the beautiful, *to kalon* [*Gr.*].

beauty unadorned; form, elegance, grace, *belle tournure* [*F.*]; symmetry etc. 242; concinnity, delicacy, refinement, charm, *je ne sais quoi* [*F.*], *nescio quid* [*L.*], style.

comeliness, fairness etc. *adj.;* polish, gloss; good effect, good looks; trigness.

bloom, brilliancy, radiance, splendor *or* splendour, gorgeousness, magnificence; sublimity, sublimification [*obs.*].

beau ideal, *le beau idéal* [*F.*]; Venus, Aphrodite, Hebe, the Graces, Peri, Houri, Cupid, Apollo, Hyperion, Adonis, Antinous, Narcissus, Astarte; Helen of Troy, Cleopatra; Venus of Milo, Apollo Belvedere.

[comparisons] butterfly; flower, flow'ret gay; garden, anemone, asphodel, buttercup, crane's-bill, daffodil, lily, lily of the valley, ranunculus, rose, rhododendron, windflower.

the flower of, the pink of; *bijou* [*F.*]; jewel etc. (*ornament*) 847; work of art.

loveliness, pleasurableness etc. 829.

beautifying, beautification [*rare*]; landscape gardening; decoration etc. etc. 847; calisthenics, physical culture.

[science of the perception of beauty] callaesthetics.

v. **be beautiful** etc. *adj.;* shine, beam, bloom; become one etc. (*accord*) 23; set off, become, grace.

render beautiful etc. *adj.;* beautify; polish, burnish; gild etc. (*decorate*) 847; set out.

"snatch a grace beyond the reach of art" [Pope].

adj. **beautiful,** beauteous, handsome; pretty; lovely, graceful, elegant, exquisite, flowerlike, delicate, dainty, refined.

comely, fair, personable, seemly [*obs.*], decent [*archaic*], proper, bonny, good-looking; well-favored, well-made, well-formed, well-proportioned, shapely, zaftig [*colloq.*]; symmetrical etc. (*regular*) 242; harmonious etc. (*color*) 428; sightly, fit to be seen.

bright, bright-eyed; rosy-cheeked, cherry-cheeked; rosy, ruddy; blooming, in full bloom.

goodly, dapper, tight, jimp *or* gimp [*Scot. & dial. Eng.*], jaunty *or* janty, trig, natty [*orig. slang*], quaint [*archaic*], trim, tidy, neat, spruce, smart, tricksy [*rare*].

brilliant, shining; beamy, beaming; sparkling, radiant, splendid, resplendent, dazzling, glowing; glossy, sleek; rich, gorgeous, superb, magnificent, grand, fine, sublime.

artistic *or* artistical, aesthetic; picturesque, pictorial; *fait à peindre* [*F.*], paintable, well-composed, well-grouped, well-varied; curious.

enchanting etc. (*pleasure-giving*) 829; attractive etc. (*inviting*) 615; becoming etc. (*accordant*) 23; ornamental etc. 847; of consummate art.

perfect, unspotted, spotless etc. 650; immaculate; undeformed, undefaced.

passable, presentable, tolerable, not amiss.

846. Ugliness

n. **ugliness** etc. *adj.;* deformity, inelegance; acomia, baldness, alopecia; disfigurement etc. (*blemish*) 848; want of symmetry, inconcinnity

[rare], "uglification" [Carroll]; distortion etc. 243; squalor etc. (uncleanness) 653.

forbidding countenance, vinegar aspect, hanging look, wry face, face that would stop a clock [colloq.]; spretae injuria formae [Virgil].

eyesore, object, figure, sight [colloq.], fright, octopus. specter or spectre. scarecrow, hag, harridan, satyr, witch, toad, baboon, monster, Caliban, Aesop; monstrum horrendum informe ingens cui lumen ademptum [Virgil].

v. **be ugly** etc. adj.; look ill, grin horribly a ghastly smile, grin through a horse collar [colloq.], make faces.

render ugly etc. adj.; deface; disfigure, defigure [obs.], deform, uglify [rare], spoil; distort etc. 243; blemish etc. (injure) 659; soil etc. (render unclean) 653.

adj. **ugly,** −as -sin, −a toad, −a scarecrow, −a dead monkey; plain, coarse; homely etc. (unadorned) 849; ordinary, unornamental, inartistic; unsightly, unseemly, uncomely, unshapely, unlovely; sightless [obs.], seemless [obs.], not fit to be seen; unbeauteous, unbeautiful, beautiless.

bald, bald-headed, acomous, hairless, chauve [F.], depilous [rare], glabrous [bot.]; smooth-faced, beardless, whiskerless, clean-shaven.

misshapen, misproportioned; shapeless etc. (amorphous) 241; monstrous; gaunt etc. (thin) 203; dumpy etc. (short) 201; curtailed of its fair proportions; ill-made, ill-shaped, ill-proportioned; crooked etc. (distorted) 243.

unprepossessing, hard-featured, hard-visaged; ill-favored, hard-favored, evil-favored; ill-looking; squalid, haggard; grim, grim-faced, grim-visaged; grisly, ghastly; ghostlike, death-like; cadaverous, gruesome or grewsome.

uncouth, ungainly, graceless, inelegant; ungraceful, stiff; rugged, rough, gross, rude, awkward, clumsy, slouching, rickety, gawky, lumping, lumpish, lumbering, hulking or hulky, unwieldy.

repellent, forbidding, frightful, hideous, odious, uncanny, repulsive; horrid, horrible; shocking etc. (painful) 830.

foul etc. (dirty) 653; dingy etc. (colorless) 429; gaudy etc. (color) 428; tarnished, smeared, besmeared, bedaubed; disfigured etc. v.; discolored, spotted, spotty.

showy, specious, pretentious, garish etc. (ostentatious) 882.

847. Ornament

n. **ornament,** ornamentation, ornamental art; ornature [rare], ornateness, ornation [rare], adornment, decoration, embellishment; architecture.

garnish, polish, varnish, French polish, gilding, japanning, lacquer, ormolu, enamel; champlevé ware, cloisonné ware; cosmetics.

[ornamentation] pattern, diaper, powdering, paneling, graining, inlaid work, pargeting; detail; texture etc. 329; richness; tracery, molding or moulding, fillet, listel, strapwork, coquillage [F.], flourish, fleur-de-lis [F.], arabesque, fret, anthemion; egg and -tongue, −dart; astragal, zigzag, acanthus, cartouche; pilaster etc. (projection) 250; bead, beading; frostwork, tooling; Moresque, Morisco.

embroidery, broidery [archaic], needlework, brocade, brocatel or brocatelle, bugles, beads, galloon, lace, fringe, border, insertion, motif [F.], edging, trimming; trappings; drapery, over-drapery, hanging, tapestry, arras; millinery, ermine; drap d'or [F.].

wreath, festoon, garland, chaplet, flower, nosegay, bouquet, posy; "daisies pied and violets blue" [Love's Labour Lost].

tassel, knot; shoulder knot, epaulet or epaulette, aglet or aiglet, aigulet [rare], frog; star, rosette, bow; feather, plume, panache, aigret or aigrette; fillet, snood.

jewelry or jewellery, bijouterie [F.] or bijoutry; tiara, crown, coronet, diadem; jewel, bijou [F.], trinket, locket, necklace, bracelet, bangle; armlet, anklet, earring, nose-ring, carcanet [archaic], chain, chatelaine, brooch, torque.

gem, precious stone; diamond, brilliant; pearl; sapphire, Oriental topaz, lapis lazuli; ruby, balas or balais or balas ruby; emerald, beryl, aquamarine, alexandrite; opal, fire opal, girasol or girasole; garnet, carbuncle; amethyst, plasma; turquoise or turquois; topaz; coral; chalcedony, agate, onyx, sard, sardonyx, chrysoprase, carnelian, cat's-eye, jasper; heliotrope, bloodstone; hyacinth, jacinth, zircon, jargon or jargoon; chrysolite, peridot; spinel or spinelle, spinel ruby; moonstone, sunstone.

frippery, finery, gewgaw, knickknack, gimcrack, tinsel, spangle, clinquant, pinchbeck, paste; excess of ornament etc. (vulgarity) 851; gaud, pride, show, ostentation.

illustration, illumination, vignette; fleuron [F.]; headpiece, tailpiece, cul-de-lampe [F.]; purple patches, flowers of rhetoric etc. 577.

virtu, article of virtu, piece of virtu, work of art, bric-a-brac, curio; rarity, a find.

v. **ornament,** embellish, enrich, decorate, adorn, beautify; adonize [rare], dandify.

garnish, furbish, polish, gild, varnish, whitewash, enamel, japan, lacquer, paint, grain.

spangle, bespangle, bead, embroider, work; chase, tool, emboss, fret; emblazon, blazon, illuminate; illustrate.

smarten, trim, dizen, bedizen, prink, prank; trick up, trick out, fig out; deck, bedeck, dight [*archaic*], bedight [*archaic*], array; titivate *or* tittivate [*colloq.*], spruce up [*colloq.*]; smarten up, dress, dress up; powder.

become etc. (*accord with*) 23.

adj. **ornamented**, beautified etc. *v.;* ornate, rich, gilt, begilt, tessellated, inlaid, festooned; *champlevé* [*F.*], *cloisonné* [*F.*], topiary [*rare*].

smart, gay, tricksy [*rare*], flowery, glittering; new-gilt, new-spangled; fine; fine as -a Mayday queen, –fivepence, –a carrot fresh scraped, –a fiddle [*all colloq.*]; pranked out, bedight [*archaic*], well-groomed.

in full dress etc. (*fashion*) 852; *en grande -tenue, –toilette* [*F.*]; in one's best bib and tucker, in Sunday best, *endimanché* [*F.*]; dressed to advantage.

showy, flashy; gaudy etc. (*vulgar*) 851; garish *or* gairish, splendiferous [*humorous*], gorgeous.

ornamental, decorative; becoming etc. (*accordant*) 23.

848. Blemish

n. **blemish**, disfigurement, deformity; adactylism; defect etc. (*imperfection*) 651; flaw, maculation; injury etc. (*deterioration*) 659; spots on the sun; eyesore.

stain, blot, spot, spottiness; speck, speckle, blur, freckle, mole, macula, macule, patch, blotch, birthmark; blobber lip, blubber lip, harelip; blain, tarnish, smudge; dirt etc. 653; scar, wem [*obs.*], wen; pustule; whelk; excrescence, pimple etc. (*protuberance*) 250; burn, blister, roughness.

v. **disfigure** etc. (*injure*) 659; uglify [*rare*]; render ugly etc. 846.

adj. **disfigured**; discolored; imperfect etc. 651; blobber-lipped *or* blubber-lipped, harelipped; chapped, specked, speckled, freckled, pitted, bloodshot, bruised; injured etc. (*deteriorated*) 659.

849. Simplicity

n. **simplicity**; plainness, homeliness; undress, nudity, beauty unadorned; chasteness, chastity, restraint, severity, naturalness, unaffectedness.

v. **be simple** etc. *adj.*

render simple etc. *adj.;* simplify, reduce to simplicity, strip of ornament, chasten, restrain.

adj. **simple**, plain, homelike, homish, homely, homespun [*fig.*], ordinary, household.

unaffected, natural, native; inartificial etc. (*artless*) 703; free from -affectation, –ornament; *simplex munditiis* [Horace]; *sans façon* [*F.*], *en déshabillé* [*F.*].

chaste, inornate, severe.

unadorned, unornamented, undecked, ungarnished, unarranged, untrimmed, unvarnished.

bald, flat, blank, dull.

simple-minded, childish, credulous etc. 486.

850. Taste

[good taste]

n. **taste**; good–, refined–, cultivated- taste; delicacy, refinement, fine feeling, gust, gusto, tact, finesse; nicety etc. (*discrimination*) 465; *to prepon* [*Gr.*], polish, elegance, grace.

artistic quality, virtu; dilettanteism, virtuosity, connoisseurship, fine art of living; fine art; culture, cultivation.

"caviare to the general" [*Hamlet*].

[science of taste] aesthetics.

man of taste etc.; connoisseur, judge, critic, conoscente, virtuoso, amateur, dilettant; Aristarchus, Corinthian; Aristotle, Stagirite; Petronius, *arbiter elegantiae* [*L.*], *arbiter elegantiarum* [*L.*].

euphemist, purist, precisian.

v. **display taste** etc. *n.;* appreciate, judge, criticize, discriminate etc. 465.

adj. **in good taste**, tasteful, unaffected, pure, chaste, classical, Attic, cultivated; attractive, charming, dainty; aesthetic, artistic.

refined, tasty [*colloq.*]; prim, precise, formal, prudish; elegant etc. 578; euphemistic.

to one's taste, to one's mind; after one's fancy; *comme il faut* [*F.*]; *tiré à quatre épingles* [*F.*].

adv. **elegantly** etc. *adj.;* with quiet elegance; with elegant simplicity; without ostentation.

851. Vulgarity

[bad taste]

n. **vulgarity**, vulgarism; barbarism, Vandalism, Gothicism; *mauvais goût* [*F.*], bad taste; want of tact; ungentlemanliness, ungentlemanlikeness; ill-breeding etc. (*discourtesy*) 895.

coarseness etc. *adj.*; indecorum, loud behavior [*colloq.*], misbehavior; *gaucherie* [*F.*], awkwardness; boorishness etc. *adj.;* homeliness, rusticity.

lowness, low life, *mauvais ton* [*F.*]; brutality; blackguardism, rowdyism, ruffianism; ribaldry; slang etc. (*neology*) 563.

bad joke, *mauvaise plaisanterie* [*F.*], poor joke, joke in bad taste; practical joke.

[excess of ornament] gaudiness, tawdriness, gingerbread, false ornament, cheap jewelry; flashy -clothes, −dress; finery, frippery, trickery, tinsel, gewgaw, clinquant.

vulgarian, rough diamond; clown etc. (*commonalty*) 876; Goth, Vandal, Boeotian; snob, cad [*colloq.*], gent [*humorous*]; parvenu etc. 876; frump [*colloq.*], dowdy; slut, slattern etc. 653; tomboy, hoyden, cub, unlicked cub.

v. be vulgar etc. *adj.;* misbehave; talk−, smell of the-shop; show a want of -tact, −consideration; be a vulgarian etc. *n.*

adj. **in bad taste**, vulgar, unrefined, coarse, indecorous, ribald, gross; unseemly, unbeseeming, unpresentable; *contra bonos mores* [*L.*]; ungraceful etc. (*ugly*) 846; dowdy; slovenly etc. (*dirty*) 653; ungenteel, shabby genteel; low etc. (*plebeian*) 876.

extravagant, monstrous, horrid; shocking etc. (*painful*) 830.

ill-mannered, ill-bred, underbred, snobbish, uncourtly; uncivil etc. (*discourteous* 895; ungentlemanly, ungentlemanlike; unladylike, unfeminine; wild, wild as a hawk, wild as an unbacked colt.

uncouth, unkempt, uncombed, untamed, unlicked, unpolished, plebeian; incondite [*rare*]; heavy, rude, awkward; homely, homespun, homebred; provincial, countrified, rustic; boorish, clownish; savage, brutish, blackguard, blackguardly, rowdyish, rowdy.

barbarous, barbaric, Gothic, heathenish, tramontane, outlandish; uncultivated; Bohemian; unclassical, doggerel *or* doggrel.

obsolete etc. (*antiquated*) 124; out of fashion, old-fashioned, out of date, unfashionable.

newfangled etc. (*unfamiliar*) 83; fantastic, fantastical, odd etc. (*ridiculous*) 853; particular; affected etc. 855.

tawdry, gaudy, meretricious, brummagem [*slang*], bedizened, tricked out; obtrusive, flaunting, loud, crass, showy, flashy, garish.

852. Fashion

n. **fashion**, style, *ton* [*F.*], *bon ton* [*F.*], society; good−, polite- society; *monde* [*F.*]; drawing-room, civilized life, civilization, town, *beau monde* [*F.*], high life, court; world; fashionable−, gay- world; height−, pink−, star−, glass- of fashion; "the glass of fashion and the mould of form" [*Hamlet*]; Vanity Fair; Mayfair; show etc. (*ostentation*) 822.

manners, breeding etc. (*politeness*) 894; air, demeanor etc. (*appearance*) 448; *savoir faire* [*F.*]; gentlemanliness, gentility, decorum, propriety, *bienséance* [*F.*]; conventions of society; Mrs. Grundy; dictates of -Society, −Mrs. Grundy; convention, conventionality, the proprieties; punctiliousness, punctilio, form, formality; etiquette, point of etiquette.

mode, vogue, style, the latest thing, *dernier cri* [*F.*], the go [*colloq.*], the rage etc. (*desire*) 865; prevailing taste; dress etc. 225; custom etc. 613.

leader of fashion; *arbiter elegantiarum* [*L.*] etc. (*taste*) 850; man−, woman- of -fashion, −the world; clubman, clubwoman; upper ten thousand etc. (*nobility*) 875; upper ten [*colloq.*]; *élite* [*F.*] etc. (*distinction*) 873; smart set [*colloq.*]; the four hundred.

v. **be fashionable** etc. *adj.,* be the rage etc. *n.;* have a run, pass current.

follow−, keep up with−, conform to−, fall in with- the fashion etc. *n.;* go with the stream etc. (*conform*) 82; be on (*or* get on) the band wagon [*slang*], be in the swim [*colloq.*]; *savoir -vivre, −faire* [*F.*]; keep up appearances, behave oneself.

set the fashion, bring into fashion; give a tone to society, cut a figure in society [*colloq.*]; brush shoulders with -the nobility, −royalty; appear−, be presented- at court.

keep one's -automobile, −car, −carriage, −yacht, −house in town [*Eng.*], −cottage at Newport; be a member of the best clubs.

adj. **fashionable**; in fashion etc. *n.;* *à la mode* [*F.*], *comme il faut* [*F.*]; admitted−, admissible- in society etc. *n.;* presentable; punctilious, decorous, conventional etc. (*customary*) 613; genteel; well-bred, well-mannered, well-behaved, well-spoken; gentlemanlike, gentlemanly; ladylike; civil, polite etc. (*courteous*) 894.

dashing, jaunty *or* janty, showy, spirited, fast.

polished, refined, thoroughbred, gently bred, courtly; *distingué* [*F.*], distinguished, aristocratic *or* aristocratical; unselfconscious, self-possessed, poised, easy, frank, unconstrained, unembarrassed, *dégagé* [*F.*].

modish, stylish, swell [*slang*], recherché, *récherché* [*F.*]; newfangled etc. (*unfamiliar*) 83; all the rage, all the go [*colloq.*].

in -court, −full, −evening- dress; *en grande tenue* [*F.*] etc. (*ornament*) 847.

adv. **fashionably** etc. *adj.;* for fashion's sake; in fear of Mrs. Grundy; in the latest -style, −mode.

int. it isn't done!

853. Ridiculousness

n. **ridiculousness** etc. *adj.;* comicality, oddity etc. *adj.;* drollery; farce, comedy; burlesque etc. (*ridicule*) 856; buffoonery etc. (*fun*) 840; frippery; amphigory *or* amphigouri, doggerel (*or* doggrel) verses; bull, Irish bull, Hibernicism, Hibernianism, Spoonerism; absurdity etc. 497.

fustian, extravagance, bombast etc. (*unmeaning*) 517; anticlimax, bathos; monstrosity etc. (*unconformity*) 83; laughingstock etc. 857; screamer *or* scream [*slang*].

v. **be ridiculous** etc. *adj.;* pass from the sublime to the ridiculous; make one laugh; play the fool, make a fool of oneself, commit an absurdity; ride–, play– the goat [*colloq.*].

make ridiculous, make a goat of [*colloq.*], make a fool of, play a joke on.

adj. **ridiculous**, ludicrous, comic *or* comical, drollish, waggish, quizzical, droll, funny, laughable, risible, farcical, screaming; serio-comic, serio-comical; tragi-comic, tragi-comical; *pour rire* [*F.*].

odd, grotesque; whimsical, –as a dancing bear; fanciful, fantastic, queer, rum [*slang*], quaint, bizarre; eccentric etc. (*unconformable*) 83; strange, outlandish, out-of-the-way, baroque, rococo; awkward etc. (*ugly*) 846.

extravagant, *outré* [*F.*], monstrous, preposterous, absurd, bombastic, inflated, stilted, burlesque, mock heroic.

trivial, doggerel *or* doggrel, gimcrack, contemptible etc. (*unimportant*) 643.

derisive, ironical etc. 856.

854. Fop

n. **fine gentleman**, fop, swell [*colloq.*], dandy, exquisite, coxcomb, beau, macaroni [*hist.*]; blade, blood, buck [*archaic*], man about town, fast man, *roué* [*F.*]; fribble, jemmy [*obs.*], spark, popinjay, puppy [*contemptuous*], prig, *petit maître* [*F.*]; jackanapes, jack-a-dandy, jessamy [*obs.*], man milliner; carpet knight; masher [*slang*], dude [*colloq.*].

fine lady, belle, flirt, coquette, toast.

855. Affectation

n. **affectation**; affectedness etc. *adj.;* acting a part etc. *v.;* pretense etc. (*falsehood*) 544, (*ostentation*) 882; boasting etc. 884; charlatanism, quackery, shallow profundity.

pretension, airs, pedantry, pedantism, purism, precisianism, stiffness, formality, buckram; prunes and prisms; euphuism; teratology etc. (*altiloquence*) 577.

prudery, demureness, mock modesty, *minauderie* [*F.*], sentimentalism; *mauvaise honte* [*F.*], false shame.

mannerism, *simagrée* [*F.*], grimace.

foppery, dandyism, man millinery, coxcombry, coquetry, puppyism, conceit.

affecter *or* affector, performer, actor; pedant, pedagogue, doctrinaire, purist, euphuist, mannerist; grimacier [*rare*]; lump of affectation, *précieuse ridicule* [*F.*], *bas bleu* [*F.*], blue stocking, poetaster; prig; charlatan etc. (*deceiver*) 548; *petit maître* [*F.*] etc. (*fop*) 854; flatterer etc. 935; coquette, prude, puritan, precisian, formalist.

v. **affect**, act a part, put on; give oneself airs etc. (*arrogance*) 885; boast etc. 884; coquet; simper, mince, attitudinize, pose; flirt a fan; languish; euphuize; overact, overdo.

adj. **affected**, full of affectation, pretentious, pedantic, stilted, stagy, theatrical, big-sounding, *ad captandum* [*L.*]; canting, insincere; not natural, unnatural; self-conscious; mannered, *maniéré* [*F.*]; artificial; overwrought, overdone, overacted; euphuistic etc. 577.

stiff, starch, formal, prim, smug, demure, *tiré à quatre épingles* [*F.*], quakerish, puritanical, prudish, pragmatical.

priggish, conceited, coxcomical, foppish, dandified, finical, finicking *or* finicky *or* finikin; mincing, simpering, namby-pamby, sentimental, languishing.

856. Ridicule

n. **ridicule**, derision; sardonic -smile, –grin; irrision [*obs.*], snicker *or* snigger, grin, twit [*rare*]; scoffing etc. (*disrespect*) 929; mockery, quiz, banter, irony, persiflage, raillery, chaff, *badinage* [*F.*]; quizzing etc. *v.;* asteism.

squib, satire, skit, quip, quib [*obs.*].

burlesque, parody, travesty, *travestie* [*F.*]; farce etc. (*drama*) 599; caricature.

buffoonery etc. (*fun*) 840; practical joke, horseplay, roughhouse [*slang*].

v. **ridicule**, deride; laugh at, grin at, smile at; snicker *or* snigger; laugh in one's sleeve; banter, rally, chaff, joke, twit, quiz, poke fun at, roast [*slang*], guy [*colloq.*], jolly [*colloq.*], rag [*slang, Eng.*]; haze; tehee *or* teehee; fleer; play upon, play tricks upon; get the laugh on [*slang*]; fool, –to the top of one's bent; show up.

turn into ridicule; make merry with; make -fun, –game, –a fool, –an April fool- of; rally; scoff etc. (*disrespect*) 929.

burlesque, satirize, parody, caricature, travesty.

be ridiculous etc. 853; raise a laugh etc. (*amuse*) 840; play the fool, make a fool of one-self.

adj. derisive, derisory, mock; sarcastic, ironical, quizzical, burlesque, Hudibrastic, Rabelaisian; scurrilous etc. (*disrespectful*) 929.

adv. in ridicule etc. *n.;* as a joke, to raise a laugh.

int. "What fools these mortals be!" [*Midsummer Night's Dream*].

857. Laughingstock
[object and cause of ridicule]

n. laughingstock, jesting-stock, gazing-stock; butt, game, fair game; April fool etc. (*dupe*) 547, original, oddity; queer-, odd- fish [*colloq.*], figure of fun [*colloq.*]; quiz, square toes; old fogy *or* fogey [*colloq.*].

monkey; buffoon etc. (*jester*) 844; pantomimist etc. (*actor*) 599.

jest etc. (*wit*) 842.

858. Hope

n. hope, hopes; desire etc. 865; fervent hope, sanguine expectation, trust, confidence, reliance; faith etc. (*belief*) 484; affiance, assurance; secureness, security; reassurance.

good -omen, -auspices; promise, well-grounded hopes; good-, bright-prospect; clear sky.

hopefulness, buoyancy, optimism, enthusiasm, heart of grace, aspiration; assumption, presumption; anticipation etc. (*expectation*) 507.

optimist, utopist [*rare*], utopian.

daydream, castles in the air, castles in Spain, *châteaux en Espagne* [*F.*], *le pot au lait* [*F.*], Utopia, millennium; golden dream; dream of Alnaschar; airy hopes, fool's paradise; mirage etc. (*fallacies of vision*) 443; fond hope.

ray of hope; beam-, gleam-, glimmer-, dawn-, flash-, star- of hope; cheer; bit of blue sky, silver lining of the cloud, bottom of Pandora's box, balm in Gilead.

mainstay, anchor, sheet anchor; staff etc. (*support*) 215; heaven etc. 981.

v. hope, trust, confide, rely on, put one's trust in, lean upon; pin one's hope upon, pin one's faith upon etc. (*believe*) 484.

feel-, entertain-, harbor-, indulge-, cherish-, feed-, foster-, nourish-, encourage-, cling to-, live in- hope etc. *n.;* see land; feel-, rest-assured, -confident etc. *adj.*

hope for etc. (*desire*) 865; anticipate; presume; promise oneself; expect etc. (*look forward to*) 507.

be hopeful etc. *adj.;* look on the bright side of, view on the sunny side, *voir en couleur de rose* [*F.*], make the best of it, hope for the best; hope against hope; put -a good, -a bold, -the best- face upon; keep one's spirits up; take heart, -of grace; be of good -heart, -cheer; flatter oneself, "lay the flattering unction to one's soul" [*Hamlet*].

catch at a straw, hope against hope, count one's chickens before they are hatched.

encourage, hearten, inspirit; give-, inspire-, raise-, hold out- hope etc. *n.;* raise expectations; encourage, cheer, assure, reassure, buoy up, embolden; promise, bid fair, augur well, be in a fair way, look up, flatter, tell a flattering tale.

adj. hopeful, confident; hoping etc. *v.;* in hopes etc. *n.;* secure etc. (*certain*) 484; sanguine, in good heart, buoyed up, buoyant, elated, flushed, exultant, enthusiastic; heartsome [*chiefly Scot.*]; utopian.

fearless; free from-, exempt from- fear, -suspicion, -distrust, -despair; unsuspecting, unsuspicious, undespairing, self-reliant; dauntless etc. (*courageous*) 861.

propitious, promising; probable, on the high road to; within sight of -shore, -land; of-, full of- promise; of good omen; auspicious, *de bon augure* [*F.*]; reassuring; encouraging, cheering, inspiriting, looking up, bright, roseate, *couleur de rose* [*F.*], rose-colored.

adv. hopefully etc. *adj.*

int. God speed! good luck!

859. Hopelessness
[absence, want, or loss of hope]

n. hopelessness etc. *adj.;* despair, desperation; despondency etc. (*dejection*) 837; pessimism.

hope deferred, dashed hopes; vain expectation etc. (*disappointment*) 509.

airy hopes etc. 858; bad -job, -business; gloomy-, clouds on the-, black spots in the- horizon; dark future; slough of Despond, cave of Despair; *immedicabile vulnus* [*L.*].

forlorn hope, *enfant perdu* (*pl. enfants perdus*) [*F.*]; goner [*slang*]; gone -case, -coon [*slang*].

pessimist, Job's comforter; hypochondriac etc. 837; bird of bad omen, bird of ill omen.

v. despair; lose-, give up-, abandon-, relinquish- -all hope, -the hope of; give up, give over; yield to despair; falter; despond etc. (*be dejected*) 837; *jeter le manche après la cognée* [*F.*].

shatter one's hopes; inspire-, drive to- despair etc. *n.;* disconcert; dash-, crush-, destroy-one's hopes; dash the cup from one's lips; undermine one's foundation; take away one's last hope.

adj. **hopeless**, desperate, despairing, gone, in despair, *au désespoir* [*F.*], forlorn; inconsolable etc. (*dejected*) 837; broken-hearted.

out of the question, not to be thought of; impracticable etc. 471; past -hope, −cure, −mending, −recall; at one's last gasp etc. (*death*) 360; given up, given over.

undone, ruined; incurable, cureless, immedicable, remediless, beyond remedy; incorrigible; irreparable, irremediable, irrecoverable, irreversible, irretrievable, irreclaimable, irredeemable, irrevocable, immitigable.

unpropitious, unpromising, inauspicious, ill-omened, threatening, clouded over, lowering, ominous.

860. Fear

n. **fear**, timidity, diffidence, want of confidence; apprehensiveness, fearfulness etc. *adj.;* solicitude, anxiety, care, apprehension, misgiving; feeze [*colloq., U. S.*]; mistrust etc. (*doubt*) 485; suspicion, qualm; hesitation etc. (*irresolution*) 605.

trepidation, flutter, fear and trembling, perturbation, tremor, quivering, shaking, trembling, throbbing heart, palpitation, ague fit, cold sweat; nervousness, restlessness etc. *adj.;* inquietude, disquietude, heartquake; abject fear etc. (*cowardice*) 862; mortal funk [*colloq.*], heartsinking, despondency; despair etc. 859.

batophobia, hypsophobia; claustrophobia; agoraphobia.

fright, affright [*archaic*], affrightment [*archaic*], boof [*slang*], alarm, dread, awe, terror, horror, dismay, consternation, panic, scare, panic fear, panic terror; "terror by night" [*Bible*]; chute [*N. U. S.*], stampede [*of horses*].

intimidation, terrorism, reign of terror; terrorist.

[object of fear] bugbear, bugaboo, scarecrow; hobgoblin etc. (*demon*) 980; nightmare, Gorgon, mormo [*obs.*], ogre, Hurlothrumbo, raw head and bloody bones, fee-faw-fum, *bête noire* [*F.*], *enfant terrible* [*F.*].

alarmist etc. (*coward*) 862.

v. **fear**, stand in awe of; be afraid etc. *adj.;* have qualms etc. *n.;* apprehend, sit upon thorns, eye askance; distrust etc. (*disbelieve*) 485.

hesitate etc. (*be irresolute*) 605; falter, funk [*colloq.*], cower, crouch; skulk etc. (*cowardice*) 862; take fright, take alarm; start, wince, flinch, shy, shrink, blench; fly etc. (*avoid*) 623.

grow pale, turn pale, stand aghast; be in a daze; not dare to say one's soul is one's own.

tremble, shake; shiver, −in one's shoes; shudder, flutter; shake−, tremble- -like an aspen leaf, −all over; quake, quaver, quiver, quail.

frighten, fright, affright, terrify; inspire−, excite- -fear, −awe; raise apprehensions; bulldoze [*colloq.*], faze [*colloq.*], feeze *or* feaze [*colloq.*]; give−, raise−, sound- an alarm; alarm, startle, scare, cry "wolf," disquiet, dismay, astound; frighten from one's propriety; frighten out of one's -wits, −senses, −seven senses; awe; strike all of a heap [*colloq.*], strike an awe into, strike terror; harrow up the soul, appall *or* appal, unman, petrify, horrify; pile on the agony.

make one's -flesh creep, −hair stand on end, −blood run cold, −teeth chatter; take away−, stop- one's breath; make one tremble etc.

daunt, put in fear, intimidate, cow, daunt, overawe, abash, deter, discourage; browbeat, bully; threaten etc. 909; terrorize, put in bodily fear.

haunt, obsess, beset, besiege; prey−, weigh- on the mind.

adj. **afraid**, fearful, timid, timorous, nervous, diffident, coy, faint-hearted, tremulous, shaky, afraid of one's shadow, apprehensive, restless, fidgety; more frightened than hurt.

fearing etc. *v.;* frightened etc. *v.;* in fear, in a fright etc. *n.;* haunted with the fear of etc. *n.;* afeard [*dial.*].

aghast; awe-struck, awe-stricken; horror-struck, horror-stricken; terror-struck, terror-stricken; panic-struck, panic-stricken; frightened to death, white as a sheet; pale, -as -death, −ashes, −a ghost; breathless, in hysterics.

inspiring fear etc. *v.;* alarming; formidable, redoubtable; perilous etc. (*danger*) 665; portentous; fearful, dread, dreadful, fell, dire, direful, shocking, frightful, terrible, terrific, tremendous; horrid, horrible, horrific, ghastly, awful, awe-inspiring; revolting etc. (*painful*) 830; Gorgonian, Gorgon-like.

adv. in terrorem [*L.*].

int. "angels and ministers of grace defend us!" [*Hamlet*].

861. Courage

[absence of fear]

n. **courage**, bravery, valor *or* valour; resoluteness, boldness etc. *adj.;* spirit, daring, gallantry, intrepidity, prowess, heroism, chivalry; contempt−, defiance- of danger; derring-do [*pseudo-archaic*]; audacity; rashness etc. 863; dash; defiance etc. 715; confidence, self-reliance.

manhood, manliness, nerve, pluck, mettle, game; heart, −of grace; spunk [*colloq.*], grit, virtue, hardihood, fortitude; firmness etc. (*stability*) 150; heart of oak; bottom, backbone etc. (*perseverance*) 604*a;* resolution etc. (*determination*) 604; tenacity, bulldog courage.

exploit, feat, deed, act, achievement; heroic, −deed, −act; bold stroke.

brave man, man of courage, man of mettle; a man; hero, demigod, paladin; Hercules, Theseus, Perseus, Achilles, Hector; Bayard, *chevalier sans peur et sans reproche;* Lancelot, Sir Galahad.

brave woman, heroine, Amazon, Joan of Arc.

[comparisons] lion, tiger, panther, bulldog; gamecock, fighting-cock.

dare-devil, fire eater etc. 863.

v. **be courageous** etc. *adj.;* dare, venture, make bold; face−, front−, affront−, confront−, brave−, defy−, despise−, mock- danger; look in the face; look -full, −boldly, −danger- in the face; face; meet, meet in front; brave, beard; defy etc. 715.

bell the cat, take the bull by the horns, beard the lion in his den, march up to the cannon's mouth, go through fire and water, run the gantlet *or* gauntlet.

nerve oneself; take−, muster−, summon up−, pluck up- courage; take heart; take−, pluck up- heart of grace; hold up one's head, screw one's courage to the sticking place; come -to, −up to- the scratch; stand, −to one's guns, −fire, −against; bear up, −against; hold out etc. (*persevere*) 604*a.*

put a bold face upon; show−, present- a bold front; show fight; face the music.

hearten; give−, infuse−, inspire- courage; reassure, encourage, embolden, inspirit, cheer, nerve, put upon one's mettle, rally, raise a rallying cry; pat on the back, make a man of, keep in countenance.

adj. **courageous**, brave, valiant, valorous, gallant, intrepid, spirited, spiritful; high-spirited, high-mettled, mettlesome, plucky; manly, manful, resolute, stout, stout-hearted; iron-hearted; lion-hearted; heart of oak; Penthesilean.

bold, bold-spirited; daring, audacious; fearless, dauntless, aweless, dreadless [*obs.*]; undaunted, unappalled, undismayed, unawed, unblenched, unabashed, unalarmed, unflinching, unshrinking, unblenching, unapprehensive; confident, self-reliant; bold as -a lion, −brass [*colloq.*].

enterprising, adventurous, venturous, venturesome, dashing, chivalrous; soldierly etc. (*warlike*) 722; heroic.

fierce, savage; pugnacious etc. (*bellicose*) 720.

strong-minded, strong-willed, hardy, doughty [*archaic or humorous*]; firm etc. (*stable*) 150; determined etc. (*resolved*) 604; dogged, indomitable etc. (*persevering*) 604*a.*

upon one's mettle; up to the scratch; reassured etc. *v.;* unfeared, undreaded.

862. Cowardice

[excess of fear]

n. **cowardice**, pusillanimity; cowardliness etc. *adj.;* timidity, effeminacy.

poltroonery, baseness, dastardness, dastardy, abject fear, funk [*colloq.*]; Dutch courage [*colloq.*]; fear etc. 860; white feather, faint heart; cold feet [*slang*], yellow streak [*slang*].

coward, poltroon, dastard, sneak, recreant; shy−, dunghill- cock; coistrel *or* coistril [*archaic*], milksop, white-liver [*colloq.*], nidget [*obs.*]; slink [*Scot. & dial. Eng.*], cur [*contemptuous*], craven, caitiff; Bob Acres, Jerry Sneak.

alarmist, terrorist, pessimist; sheep in wolf's clothing.

shirker, slacker; runagate etc. (*fugitive*) 623.

v. **quail** etc. (*fear*) 860; be cowardly etc. *adj.,* be a coward etc. *n.;* funk [*colloq.*], cower, skulk, sneak; flinch, shy, fight shy, slink, turn tail; run away etc. (*avoid*) 623; show the white feather.

adj. **cowardly**, coward, fearful, shy, timid, timorous, skittish; poor-spirited, spiritless, soft, effeminate; weak-minded; infirm of purpose etc. 605; weak−, faint−, chicken−, hen−, pigeon-hearted; white−, lily−, milk- livered; smock-faced.

dastard, dastardly, base, craven, sneaking, dunghill, recreant; unwarlike, unsoldierlike; "in face a lion but in heart a deer"; "more like a rabbit than a robber."

unmanned; frightened etc. 860.

adv. with fear and trembling, in fear of one's life, in a blue funk [*colloq.*]; "with groanings that cannot be uttered" [*Bible*].

int. *sauve qui peut!* [*F.*], devil take the hindmost!

863. Rashness

n. **rashness** etc. *adj.;* temerity, want of caution, imprudence, indiscretion; overconfidence, presumption, audacity; precipitancy, precipitation, impetuosity; levity; foolhardihood, foolhardiness; heedlessness, thoughtlessness etc. (*inattention*) 458; carelessness etc. (*neglect*) 460; desperation; Quixotism, knight-errantry; fire eating.

gaming, gambling; blind bargain, leap in the dark, fool's paradise; too many eggs in one basket.

desperado, rashling [*obs.*], madcap, daredevil, Hotspur, Hector; scapegrace, *enfant perdu* [*F.*]; Don Quixote, knight-errant, Icarus; adventurer; dynamiter *or* dynamitard; fire eater, bully, bravo.

gambler, gamester etc. (*chance*) 621.

v. **be rash** etc. *adj.;* stick at nothing, play a desperate game; run into danger etc. 665; play with -fire, –edge tools; *donner tête baissée* [*F.*]; knock one's head against a wall etc. (*be unskillful*) 699; kick against the pricks; rush on destruction; tempt Providence, go on a forlorn hope.

carry too much sail, sail too near the wind, ride at single anchor, go out of one's depth; go to sea in a sieve.

take a leap in the dark; buy a pig in a poke; bet against a dead certainty.

count one's chickens before they are hatched; reckon without one's host; catch at straws; trust to–, lean on- a broken reed.

adj. **rash,** incautious, indiscreet, injudicious, imprudent, improvident, temerarious; uncalculating, impulsive; heedless; careless etc. (*neglectful*) 460; without ballast, head over heels, heels over head; giddy etc. (*inattentive*) 458.

reckless, wanton, wild, madcap, desperate, devil-may-care, death-defying; hot-blooded, hot-headed, hot-brained; headlong, headstrong; breakneck, foolhardy, harebrained, precipitate.

overconfident, overweening; venturesome, venturous, adventurous, Quixotic; fire-eating.

unexpected; off one's guard etc. (*inexpectant*) 508.

adv. posthaste, *à corps perdu* [*F.*], hand over head [*rare*], *tête baissée* [*F.*], headforemost; happen what may.

864. Caution

n. **caution;** cautiousness etc. *adj.;* discretion, prudence, cautel [*obs.*], heed, circumspection, calculation, deliberation.

foresight etc. 510; vigilance etc. 459; warning etc. 668.

worldly wisdom; "safety first," Fabian policy, "watchful waiting."

coolness etc. *adj.;* self-possession, self-command; presence of mind, *sang-froid* [*F.*], well-regulated mind.

v. **be cautious** etc. *adj.;* take -care, –heed, –good care; have a care; mind, mind what one is about; be on one's guard etc. (*keep watch*) 459; "make assurance double sure" [*Macbeth*].

think twice, look before one leaps, keep one's eye peeled [*slang*], keep one's weather eye open [*colloq.*]; count the cost, look to the main chance; cut one's coat according to one's cloth; feel one's -ground, –way; see how the land lies etc. (*foresight*) 510; pussy-foot; wait to see how the cat jumps; bridle one's tongue; *reculer pour mieux sauter* [*F.*] etc. (*prepare*) 673; let well enough alone, *ne pas reveiller le chat qui dort* [*F.*]; let sleeping dogs lie.

keep out of -harm's way, –troubled waters; keep at a respectful distance, stand aloof; keep–, be-on the safe side.

anticipate; bespeak etc. (*be early*) 132.

lay by; husband one's resources etc. 636.

warn, caution etc. 668.

adj. **cautious,** wary, guarded, guardful [*rare*]; on one's guard etc. (*watchful*) 459; gingerly, precautious [*rare*], suspicious, leery [*slang*]; *cavendo tutus* [*L.*]; *in medio tutissimus* [*L.*]; vigilant; careful, heedful, cautelous [*obs.*], stealthy, chary, shy of, circumspect, prudent, canny [*Scot.*], safe, noncommittal, discreet, politic; sure-footed etc. (*skillful*) 698.

unenterprising, unadventurous, cool, steady, self-possessed; overcautious.

adv. cautiously etc. *adj.*

int. have a care! look out! danger! mind your eye! [*colloq.*]; stop! look! listen! *cave canem!* [*L.*].

865. Desire

n. **desire,** wish, fancy, fantasy; inclination, leaning, bent, mind, animus, partiality, *penchant* [*F.*], predilection; propensity etc. 820; willingness etc. 602; liking, love, fondness, relish.

longing, hankering, yearning, coveting; aspiration, ambition, vaulting ambition; eagerness, zeal, ardor, *empressement* [*F.*], breathless impatience, solicitude, anxiety, overanxiety; impetuosity etc. 825.

need, want, exigency, urgency, necessity.

appetite, appetition, appetence, appetency; sharp appetite, keenness, hunger, stomach, twist; thirst, thirstiness; drought *or* drouth, mouth-watering.

edge of -appetite, –hunger; torment of Tantalus; sweet tooth [*colloq.*], lickerish (*or* liquorish) tooth; longing–, wistful–, sheep's- eyes.

avidity, greed, greediness, covetousness, ravenousness etc. *adj.;* grasping, craving, canine appetite, rapacity; voracity etc. (*gluttony*) 957.

passion, rage, furor, frenzy, mania, manie [*obs.*]; itching palm; inextinguishable desire; itch, itching, prurience, cacoëthes, cupidity, lust, concupiscence; kleptomania, dipsomania; monomania, *idée fixe* [F.].

[of animals] heat, rut, oestrus.

[person desiring] lover, amateur, votary, devotee, aspirant, solicitant, candidate; cormorant etc. 957; parasite, sycophant.

[object of desire] desideratum, desideration; want etc. (*requirement*) 630; "a consummation devoutly to be wish'd" [*Hamlet*]; attraction, magnet, loadstone, lure, allurement, fancy, temptation, seduction, fascination, prestige, height of one's ambition, idol; whim, whimsey *or* whimsy, whim-wham; maggot; hobby, hobbyhorse [*rare*].

Fortunatus's cap; wishing -cap, –stone, –well; love potion; aphrodisiac.

v. **desire**; wish, wish for; be desirous etc. *adj.;* have a longing etc. *n.;* hope etc. 858.

care for, affect, like, list [*archaic*]; take to, cling to, take a fancy to; fancy; prefer etc. (*choose*) 609; have an eye to, have a mind to; find it in one's heart etc. (*be willing*) 602; have a fancy for, set one's eyes upon; cast sheep's eyes upon, look sweet on [*colloq.*]; take into one's head, have at heart, be bent upon; set one's cap at [*colloq.*], set one's heart upon, set one's mind upon; covet.

hunger–, thirst–, crave–, lust–, itch–, hanker–, run mad- after; raven for, die for; burn to; sigh–, cry–, gape–, gasp–, pine–, pant–, languish–, yearn–, long–, be on thorns–, hope- for; aspire after; catch at, grasp at, jump at.

woo, court, ogle, solicit; fish for, whistle for, put up for [*slang*].

want, miss, need, lack, desiderate, feel the want of; would fain -have, –do; would be glad of.

hunger; be hungry etc. *adj.;* have a good appetite, play a good knife and fork [*colloq.*].

attract, allure; cause–, create–, raise–, excite–, provoke- desire; whet the appetite; appetize, titillate, take one's fancy, tempt; hold out -temptation, –allurement; tantalize, make one's mouth water, *faire venir l'eau à la bouche* [F.].

gratify desire etc. (*give pleasure*) 829.

adj. **desirous**; desiring etc. *v.;* orectic, appetitive; inclined etc. (*willing*) 602; partial to [*colloq.*]; fain, wishful, longing, wistful; optative; anxious, curious; at a loss for, sedulous, solicitous.

eager, avid, keen; burning, fervent, ardent; agog; all agog; breathless; impatient etc. (*impetu-*

ous) 825; bent–, intent–, set- -on, –upon; mad after, *enragé* [F.], rabid, dying for, devoured by desire.

aspiring, ambitious, vaulting, sky-aspiring, high-reaching.

craving, hungry, sharp-set, peckish [*colloq.*], ravening, with an empty stomach, esurient, lickerish, thirsty, athirst, parched with thirst, pinched with hunger, famished, dry, droughty *or* drouthy; hungry as a -hunter, –hawk, –horse, –church mouse.

greedy, –as a hog; overeager, voracious; ravenous, –as a wolf; open-mouthed, covetous, rapacious, grasping, extortionate, exacting, sordid, *alieni appetens* [L.]; insatiable, insatiate, unquenchable, quenchless; omnivorous.

unsatisfied, unsated, unslaked.

desirable; desired etc. *v.;* in demand, popular; pleasing etc. (*giving pleasure*) 829; appetizing, appetible; tantalizing.

adv. **fain**; with eager appetite; wistfully etc. *adj.*

int. would that! would it were! O for! if only! *esto perpetua!* [L.].

866. Indifference

n. **indifference**, neutrality; unconcern, insouciance, nonchalance; want of -interest, –earnestness; anorexia *or* anorexy, inappetence *or* inappetency; apathy etc. (*insensibility*) 823; supineness etc. (*inactivity*) 683; disdain etc. 930; recklessness etc. 863; inattention etc. 458; coldness etc. *adj.;* anaphrodisia.

anaphrodisiac *or* antaphrodisiac; lust-quencher, passion-queller.

v. **be indifferent** etc. *adj.;* stand neuter; take no interest in etc. (*insensibility*) 823; have no desire for etc. 865, have no taste for, have no relish for; not care for; care nothing -for, –about; not care a -straw etc. (*unimportance*) 643 -about, –for; not mind.

set at naught etc. (*make light of*) 483; spurn etc. (*disdain*) 930.

adj. **indifferent**, cold, frigid, luke-warm; cool, –as a cucumber; neutral, unconcerned, insouciant, phlegmatic, pococurantish, pococurante, easy-going, devil-may-care, careless, listless, lackadaisical; half-hearted, unambitious, unaspiring, undesirous, unsolicitous, unattracted, inappetent, all one to.

unattractive, unalluring, undesired, undesirable, uncared for, unwished, unvalued.

insipid etc. 391.

adv. for aught one cares; with utter indifference.

int. **never mind!** who cares! it's all one to me!

867. Dislike

n. **dislike**, distaste, disrelish, disinclination, displacency [*rare*].

reluctance; backwardness etc. (*unwillingness*) 603.

repugnance, disgust, queasiness, nausea, loathing, loathfulness [*rare*], aversion, averseness, aversation [*obs.*], abomination, antipathy, abhorrence, horror; mortal-, rooted- -antipathy, -horror; hatred, detestation; hate etc. 898; animosity etc. 900.

hydrophobia, canine madness; xenophobia, batophobia etc. (*nervousness*) 860; Anglophobia, Germanophobia, Slavophobia etc.

sickener; gall and wormwood etc. (*unsavory*) 395; shuddering, cold sweat.

v. **dislike**, mislike, disrelish; mind, object to; would rather not, not care for; have-, conceive-, entertain-, take- -a dislike, -an aversion- to; have no -taste, -stomach- for; shrug the shoulders at, shudder at, turn up the nose at, look askance at; make a -mouth, -wry face, -grimace; make faces.

shun, avoid etc. 623; eschew; withdraw-, shrink-, recoil - from; not be able to -bear, -abide, -endure.

loathe, nauseate, wamble [*obs. or dial. Eng.*], abominate, detest, abhor; hate etc. 898; take amiss etc. 900; have enough of etc. (*be satiated*) 869.

cause dislike, excite dislike; disincline, repel, sicken; make sick, render sick; turn one's stomach, nauseate, disgust, shock, stink in the nostrils; go against the -grain, -stomach; stick in the throat; make one's blood run cold etc. (*give pain*) 830; pall.

adj. **disliking** etc. *v.;* averse to, loath *or* loth, adverse; shy of, sick of, out of conceit with; disinclined; heartsick, dogsick; queasy.

disliked etc. *v.;* uncared for, unpopular, out of favor; repulsive, repugnant, repellent; abhorrent, insufferable, fulsome, nauseous, loathsome, loathful [*rare*], offensive; disgusting etc. *v.;* disagreeable etc. (*painful*) 830.

uneatable, inedible, inesculent [*rare*], unappetizing, unsavory.

adv. **to satiety**, to one's disgust; *usque ad nauseam* [*L.*].

int. faugh! foh! ugh!

868. Fastidiousness

n. **fastidiousness** etc. *adj.;* nicety, meticulosity, hypercriticism, difficulty in being pleased; *friandise* [*F.*], epicurism, *omnia suspendens naso* [*L.*].

discrimination, discernment, perspicacity, perspicaciousness [*rare*], keenness, sharpness, insight.

epicure, gourmet.

[excess of delicacy] prudery, prudishness, primness.

v. **be fastidious** etc. *adj.;* split hairs; hunt for the crumpled rose-leaf.

mince the matter; turn up one's nose at etc. (*disdain*) 930; look a gift horse in the mouth, see spots on the sun; see the mote in one's brother's eye.

discriminate, have nice discrimination; have exquisite taste; be discriminative etc. *adj.*

adj. **fastidious**, nice, delicate, *délicat* [*F.*]; meticulous, finicking *or* finicky *or* finikin, exacting, finical; difficult, dainty, lickerish, squeamish, thin-skinned; queasy; hard-, difficult- to please; querulous; particular, scrupulous; censorious etc. 932; hypercritical; overcritical.

prudish, strait-laced, prim.

discriminative, discriminating, discerning, discriminant [*rare*], judicious, keen, sharp, perspicacious.

869. Satiety

n. **satiety**, satisfaction, saturation, repletion, glut, surfeit; cloyment [*obs.*], satiation; weariness etc. 841.

spoiled child; *enfant gâté* [*F.*]; too much of a good thing, *toujours perdrix* [*F.*]; a diet of cake; *crambe repetita* [Juvenal].

v. **sate**, satiate, satisfy, saturate; cloy, quench, slake, pall, glut, gorge, surfeit; bore etc. (*weary*) 841; tire etc. (*fatigue*) 688; spoil.

have enough of, have quite enough of, have one's fill, have too much of; be satiated etc. *adj.*

adj. **satiated** etc. *v.;* overgorged; gorged with plenty, overfed; *blasé* [*F.*], used up [*colloq.*], sick of, heartsick.

int. **enough!** hold! *eheu jam satis!* [*L.*].

870. Wonder

n. **wonder**, marvel; astonishment, amazement, wonderment, bewilderment; amazedness etc. *adj.;* admiration, awe; stupor, stupefaction, stound [*obs.*], fascination; sensation; surprise etc. (*inexpectation*) 508.

note of admiration; thaumaturgy etc. (*sorcery*) 992.

v. **wonder**, marvel, admire; be surprised etc. *adj.;* start; stare; open-, rub-, turn up- one's eyes; gloar [*obs.*]; gape, open one's mouth, hold one's breath; look-, stand- -aghast, -agog;

315

look blank etc. (*disappointment*) 509; *tomber des nues* [*F.*]; not believe one's -eyes, –ears, –senses; not be able to account for etc. (*unintelligible*) 519; not know whether one stands on one's head or one's heels.

astonish, surprise, amaze, astound; dumfound *or* dumbfound, dumfounder *or* dumbfounder, startle, dazzle; daze; strike, –with - wonder, –awe; electrify; stun, stupefy, petrify, confound, bewilder, flabbergast [*colloq.*]; stagger, throw on one's beam ends, fascinate, turn the head, take away one's breath, strike dumb; make one's -hair stand on end, –tongue cleave to the roof of one's mouth; make one stare.

take by surprise, take unawares etc. (*be unexpected*) 508.

be wonderful etc. *adj.;* beggar–, baffle- description; stagger belief.

adj. **astonished**, surprised etc. *v.;* aghast, all agog, breathless, agape; open-mouthed; awe–, thunder–, moon–, planet- struck; spellbound; lost in -amazement, –wonder, –astonishment; struck all of a heap [*colloq.*], unable to believe one's senses; like a duck in -a fit, –thunder [*both colloq.*].

wonderful, wondrous; surprising etc. *v.;* unexpected etc. 508; unheard of; mysterious etc. (*inexplicable*) 519; miraculous.

monstrous, prodigious, stupendous, marvelous; inconceivable, incredible, inimaginable [*obs.*], unimaginable; strange etc. (*uncommon*) 83; passing strange.

striking etc. *v.;* overwhelming; wonder-working.

indescribable, inexpressible, ineffable; unutterable, unspeakable.

adv. **wonderfully** etc. *adj.;* fearfully; for a wonder, in the name of wonder; strange to say; *mirabile dictu* [*L.*], *mirabile visu* [*L.*]; to one's great surprise.

with wonder etc. *n.,* with gaping mouth, with open eyes, with upturned eyes; with the eyes starting out of one's head.

int. **lo!** lo and behold! O! heyday! halloo! what! indeed! really! surely! humph! hem! good -lack, –heavens, –gracious! gad so! welladay! dear me! only think! lackadaisy! my stars! my goodness! gracious goodness! goodness gracious! mercy on us! heavens and earth! God bless me! bless us! bless my heart! odzookens! *O gemini!* adzooks! hoity-toity! strong! Heaven save–, bless- the mark! can such things be! zounds! 'sdeath! what on earth! what in the world! who would have thought it! etc. (*inexpectation*) 508; you don't say so! what do you

say to that! *nous verrons!* [*F.*], how now! where am I? fancy! do tell! *Ciel!* [*F.*]; what do you know! [*slang*]; what do you know about that! [*slang*], well, I'll be jiggered! [*colloq.*].

871. Expectance
[absence of wonder]

n. **expectance**, expectancy etc. (*expectation*) 507.

imperturbability. imperturbableness, imperturbation, *sang-froid* [*F.*], calmness, unruffled calm, coolness, coldbloodedness, hardheadedness, steadiness, lack of nerves, want of imagination, practicality.

nothing out of the ordinary.

v. **expect** etc. 507; not be surprised, not wonder etc. 870; *nil admirari* [*L.*], make nothing of; take it coolly; be unamazed etc. *adj.;* display imperturbability etc. *n.*

adj. **expecting** etc. *v.;* unamazed, astonished at nothing; *blasé* [*F.*] etc. (*weary*) 841; expected etc. *v.;* foreseen.

imperturbable, nerveless, cool, cool-headed, unruffled, calm, steady, hard-headed, practical, unimaginative.

common, ordinary etc. (*habitual*) 613.

int. no wonder! of course! why not?

872. Prodigy

n. **prodigy**, phenomenon, wonder, wonderment, marvel, miracle; freak, freak of nature, *lusus naturae* [*L.*], monstrosity; monster etc. (*unconformity*) 83; curiosity, infant prodigy, lion, sight, spectacle; *jeu–, coup- de théâtre* [*F.*]; gazingstock; sign; St. Elmo's -fire, –light; portent etc. 512.

what no words can paint; wonders of the world; *annus mirabilis* [*L.*]; *dignus vindice nodus* [*L.*].

detonation; bursting of a -shell, –bomb, –mine; volcanic eruption, peal of thunder; thunderclap, thunderbolt, thunderstone [*obs. or dial. Eng.*].

873. Repute

n. **repute**, reputation; distinction, mark, name, figure; good–, high- repute; note, notability, notoriety, éclat, "the bubble reputation" [*As You Like It*], vogue, celebrity; fame, famousness; renown; popularity, *aura popularis* [*L.*]; approbation etc. 931; credit, *succès d'estime* [*F.*], prestige, talk of the town; name to conjure with.

account, regard, respect; reputability [*rare*], reputableness etc. *adj.;* respectability etc. (*probity*) 939; good -name, –report; fair name.

dignity; stateliness etc. *adj.;* solemnity, grandeur, splendor, nobility, majesty, sublimity; glory, honor; luster etc. (*light*) 420; illustriousness etc. *adj.*

rank, standing, brevet rank, precedence, *pas* [*F.*], station, place, status; position, -in society; order, degree, *locus standi* [*L.*], caste, condition.

graduation, university degree, baccalaureate, doctorate, doctorship; scholarship, fellowship.

eminence; greatness etc. *adj.;* height etc. 206; importance etc. 642; preëminence, supereminence; high mightiness, primacy; top of the -ladder, -tree; elevation; ascent etc. 305; superexaltation, exaltation, dignification [*rare*], aggrandizement; dedication, consecration, enthronement.

celebrity, worthy, hero, man of mark, great card, lion, *rara avis* [*L.*], notability, somebody; "the observed of all observers" [*Hamlet*]; classman; man of rank etc. (*nobleman*) 875; pillar of the -state, -church; "a mother in Israel" [*Bible*].

chief etc. (*master*) 745; first fiddle etc. (*proficient*) 700; scholar, *savant* [*F.*] etc. 492; cynosure, mirror; flower, pink, pearl; paragon etc. (*perfection*) 650; "the choice and master spirits of this age" [*Julius Caesar*]; *élite* [*F.*]; star, sun, constellation, galaxy.

ornament, honor, feather in one's cap, halo, aureole, nimbus; halo-, blaze- of glory; "blushing honors" [*Henry VIII*]; laurels etc. (*trophy*) 733.

posthumous fame, memory, niche in the temple of fame; celebration, canonization, enshrinement, glorification; immortality, immortal name; *magni nominis umbra* [Lucan].

v. **glory in**; be conscious of glory; be proud of etc. (*pride*) 878; exult etc. (*boast*) 884; be vain of etc. (*vanity*) 880.

be distinguished etc. *adj.;* shine etc. (*light*) 420; shine forth, figure; cut a figure, cut a dash [*colloq.*], make a splash [*colloq.*].

surpass, outshine, outrival, outvie, outjump, eclipse; throw-, cast- into the shade; overshadow.

rival, emulate, vie with.

gain *or* **acquire honor** etc. *n.;* live, flourish, glitter; flaunt; play first fiddle etc. (*be of importance*) 642; bear the -palm, -bell; lead the way, take precedence, take the wall of [*obs.*]; gain-, win- -laurels, -spurs, -golden opinions etc. (*approbation*) 931; graduate, take one's degree, pass one's examination; win a -scholarship, -fellowship.

make -a, -some- -noise, -noise in the world; leave one's mark, exalt one's horn, star, have a run, be run after; be lionized, come into vogue, come to the front; raise one's head.

honor; give-, do-, pay-, render- honor to; accredit, pay regard to, dignify, glorify; sing praises to etc. (*approve*) 931; look up to; exalt, aggrandize, elevate, nobilitate [*archaic*]; enthrone, signalize, immortalize, deify, exalt to the skies; hand one's name down to posterity.

consecrate; dedicate to, devote to; enshrine, inscribe, blazon, lionize, blow the trumpet, crown with laurel.

confer *or* reflect honor on etc. *n.;* shed a luster on; redound to one's honor, ennoble.

adj. **distinguished,** *distingué* [*F.*], noted; of note etc. *n.;* honored etc. *v.;* popular; fashionable etc. 852; remarkable etc. (*important*) 642; notable, notorious; celebrated, renowned, in every one's mouth, talked of, famous, famed, far-famed; conspicuous, to the front; foremost; in the -front rank, -ascendant.

in good odor; in favor, in high favor; reputable, respectable, creditable.

imperishable, deathless, immortal, never fading, fadeless, *aere perennius* [*L.*], time-honored.

illustrious, glorious, splendid, brilliant, radiant; bright etc. 420; full-blown; honorific.

eminent, prominent; high etc. 206; in the zenith; at the -head of, -top of the tree; peerless, of the first water; superior etc. 33; supereminent, preëminent.

great, dignified, proud, noble, honorable, worshipful, lordly, grand, stately, august, princely, imposing, solemn, transcendent, majestic, sacred, sublime, heaven-born, heroic, *sans peur et sans reproche* [*F.*]; sacrosanct.

int. **hail!** all hail! ave! [*L.*], viva! [*It.*], vive! [*F.*], long life to! glory-, honor- be to!

874. Disrepute

n. **disrepute,** discredit; ill-, bad- -repute, -name, -odor, -favor; disapprobation etc. 932; ingloriousness, derogation, abasement, debasement; abjectness etc. *adj.;* degradation, dedecoration [*rare*]; "a long farewell to all my greatness" [*Henry VIII*]; odium, obloquy, opprobrium, ignominy.

dishonor, disgrace, shame, crying-, burning-shame; humiliation; scandal, baseness, vileness; turpitude etc. (*improbity*) 940; infamy.

stigma, brand, reproach, imputation, slur, stain, blot, spot, blur; *scandalum magnatum* [*L.*], badge of infamy, blot in one's escutcheon; bend sinister, bar sinister, champain, point champain [*her.*]; byword of reproach; object of scorn, hissing [*archaic*]; Ichabod.

tarnish, taint, defilement, pollution.

argumentum ad verecundiam [*L.*]; sense of shame etc. 879.

v. **be inglorious** etc. *adj.*; incur disgrace etc. *n.*; have–, earn- a bad name; put–, wear- a halter round one's neck; disgrace–, expose- oneself.

play second fiddle; lose caste; "pale his uneffectual fire" [*Hamlet*]; recede into the shade; fall from one's high estate; keep in the background etc. (*modesty*) 881; be conscious of disgrace etc. (*humility*) 879; look -blue, –foolish, –like a fool; cut a -poor, –sorry- figure; laugh on the wrong side of the mouth [*colloq.*]; make a sorry face, go away with a flea in one's ear [*colloq.*], slink away.

cause shame etc. *n.*; shame, disgrace, put to shame, dishonor; throw–, cast–, fling–, reflect- dishonor etc. *n.* upon; be a reproach to etc. *n.*; derogate from.

tarnish, stain, blot, sully, taint; discredit; degrade, debase, defile; beggar; expel etc. (*punish*) 972.

stigmatize, vilify, defame, slur, cast a slur upon, impute shame to, brand, post, hold up to shame, send to Coventry; tread–, trample- under foot; show up [*colloq.*], drag through the mud, drag through the mire, heap dirt upon; reprehend etc. 932.

bring low, put down, snub; take down; take down a peg, –lower, –or two [*colloq.*].

obscure, eclipse, outshine, take the shine out of [*colloq.*]; throw–, cast- into the shade; overshadow; leave–, put- in the background; push into a corner, put one's nose out of joint [*colloq.*]; put out, put out of countenance.

disconcert, upset, throw off one's center, discompose; put to the blush etc. (*humble*) 879.

adj. **disgraced** etc. *v.*; blown upon; "shorn of its beams" [*Milton*], shorn of one's glory; overcome, downtrodden; loaded with shame etc. *n.*; in bad repute etc. *n.*; out of -repute, –favor, –fashion, –countenance; at a discount; under -a cloud, –an eclipse; unable to show one's face; in the -shade, –background; out at elbows, down in the world, down on one's uppers [*colloq.*], down and out.

inglorious, nameless, renownless, obscure, unknown to fame, unnoticed, unnoted, unhonored, unglorified.

discreditable, shameful, disgraceful, disreputable, despicable; questionable; unbecoming, unworthy, derogatory; degrading, humiliating,

infra dignitatem [*L.*], dedecorous [*rare*]; scandalous, infamous, too bad, unmentionable, ribald, opprobrious; arrant, shocking, outrageous, notorious.

ignominious, scrubby, dirty, abject, vile, beggarly, pitiful, low, mean, petty, shabby; base etc. (*dishonorable*) 940.

adv. to one's shame be it spoken.

int. **shame**! fie! for shame! *proh pudor!* [*L.*]; O tempora! O mores! [*L.*]; ough! *sic transit gloria mundi!* [*L.*].

875. Nobility

n. **nobility**, rank, condition, distinction, optimacy [*rare*], blood, *pur sang* [*F.*], birth, high descent, order; quality, gentility; blue blood of Castile; "all the blood of all the Howards" [Pope]; caste of "Vere de Vere" [Tennyson]; *ancien régime* [*F.*].

high life, *haut monde* [*F.*]; upper classes, upper ten [*colloq.*], upper ten thousand; the four hundred; *élite* [*F.*], aristocracy, great folks; fashionable world etc. (*fashion*) 852.

personage–, man- of -distinction, –mark, –rank; notables, notabilities; celebrity, bigwig [*humorous*], magnate, great man, star; big bug, big gun, great gun [*colloq.*]; gilded rooster [*slang*]; *magni nominis umbra* [Lucan]; "every inch a king" [*Lear*].

[the nobility] peerage, baronage; house of -lords, –peers; lords, –temporal and spiritual; noblesse; knightage.

peer, noble, nobleman; lord, lording [*archaic*], lordling; grandee, magnifico, hidalgo; daimio, samurai, *shizoku* [*Jap.*]; don; aristocrat, swell [*colloq.*], three-tailed bashaw; gentleman, squire, squireen [*humorous, Eng.*], patrician; laureate.

gentry, gentlefolk; squirarchy *or* squirearchy, better sort, magnates, primates, optimates; pantisocracy.

king etc. (*master*) 745; atheling [*hist.*]; prince, duke, marquis, earl, viscount, baron, thane [*hist.*], banneret, baronet, knight, chevalier, count, armiger, esquire, laird [*Scot.*]; signior, seignior; *signor* [*It.*], *señor* [*Sp.*], *senhor* [*Pg.*]; boyar *or* boyard [*Russ.*]; effendi, sheik *or* sheikh, emir, shereef *or* sherif, pasha, sahib; palsgrave [*Ger. hist.*], waldgrave, margrave; vavasor [*feudal law*].

empress, queen, princess, duchess, marchioness, viscountess, countess; lady, *doña* [*Sp.*], *dona* [*Pg.*]; *signora* [*It.*], *señora* [*Sp.*], *senhora* [*Pg.*]; dame; memsahib.

[indian ruling chiefs] raja, rana, rao, rawal, rawat, rai, raikwar, raikbar, raikat; maharaja, maharana, maharao etc.; Gackwar [*lit.* co-wherd; *Baroda*]; maharaja bahadur, raja bahadur, rai (*or* rao) bahadur; rai (*or* rao) sahib; jám, thakur [*all Hindu titles*].

nawab, wali, sultan, ameer *or* amir, mir, mirza, mian, khan; Nizam, nawab bahadur, khan bahadur, khan sahib [*all Moham. titles*].

sirdar *or* sardar, diwan *or* dewan [*both Hindu and Moham. titles*].

[honorifics] shahzada ["King's son"], kumar *or* kunwar ["prince"]; mirza [*when appended it signifies* "prince"; *when prefixed,* "Mr."]; arbab ["lord"]; malik ["master"]; khanzada ["son of a khan"]; huzur *or* huzoor ["the presence"].

[female titles] rani, maharani [*Hindu*]; sultana, malikah, begum *or* begam [*Moham.*].

shahzadi, kumari *or* kunwari, raj-kumari, malikzadi, khanam [*all equivalent to* "princess"].

[rank or office] kingship, dukedom, marquisate, earldom; viscountship, viscounty, viscountcy; lordship, baronetcy, knighthood, donship.

v. be noble etc. *adj.*

adj. **noble**, exalted; of rank etc. *n.;* princely, titled, patrician, aristocratic; highborn, well-born; of gentle blood; genteel, *comme il faut* [*F.*], gentlemanlike, courtly etc. (*fashionable*) 852; highly respectable.

adv. in high quarters.

876. Commonalty

n. **commonalty**, democracy; obscurity; low -condition, −life, −society, −company; *bourgeoisie* [*F.*]; mass of -the people, −society; Brown, Jones, and Robinson; Tom, Dick, and Harry; "the four million" [O. Henry]; the peepul [*humorous*]; lower−, humbler- -classes, −orders; vulgar−, common- herd; rank and file, *hoc genus omne* [*L.*]; the -many, −general, −crowd, −people, −populace, −multitude, −million, −masses, −mobility [*humorous*], −other half, −peasantry; king Mob; proletariat; *fruges consumere nati* [*L.*], *demos* [*Gr.*], *hoi polloi* [*Gr.*], great unwashed; man in the street.

rabble, −rout; chaff, rout, horde, canaille; scum−, residuum−, dregs- of -the people, −society; mob, swinish multitude, *foex populi* [*L.*]; trash; *profanum−, ignobile- vulgus* [*L.*]; vermin, raff, riffraff, rag-tag and bobtail; small fry.

commoner, one of the people, democrat, plebeian, republican, proletary, proletarian, proletaire, *roturier* [*F.*], John Smith, Mr.

Snooks, *bourgeois* [*F.*], *épicier* [*F.*], Philistine, cockney; grisette, demimonde, demimondaine.

peasant, countryman, boor, carl *or* carle [*Scot. or archaic*], churl; villain *or* villein [*obs. or rare*], serf; *terrae filius* [*L.*], kern *or* kerne [*Ir.*], gossoon [*Anglo-Ir.*]; tike *or* tyke [*archaic or dial.*], ryot [*India*], fellah [*Ar. pl.* fellahin *or* fellaheen]; docker, stevedore, longshoreman; swain, clown, hind [*Eng.*], clod, clodhopper, hobnail, yokel, bogtrotter, bumpkin; plowman *or* ploughman, plowboy *or* ploughboy; chuff, hayseed [*slang*], rustic, lunkhead [*colloq.*], loon [*archaic*], rube [*slang*], chaw-bacon [*slang*], tiller of the soil; hewers of wood and drawers of water; sons of Martha; groundling [*obs.*], gaffer, put, cub, Tony Lumpkin [Goldsmith], looby, lout, underling; gamin, street Arab, mudlark.

rough, rowdy, roughneck [*slang*], ruffian, tough [*colloq.*], pot-walloper [*slang*], scullion, slubberdegullion [*obs.*], vulgar−, low- fellow; cad.

upstart, parvenu, skipjack [*dial. Eng.*]; nobody, −one knows; *hesterni quirites* [*L.*], *pessoribus orti* [*L.*]; *bourgeois gentilhomme* [*F.*]; *novus homo* [*L.*], snob, gent [*vulgar or humorous*], mushroom, no one knows who, adventurer; *nouveau riche* (*pl.* nouveaux riches; *fem.* nouvelles riches) [*F.*].

vagabond, beggar, gaberlunzie [*Scot.*], beadsman *or* bedesman [*Scot.*], muckworm, *sans-culotte* [*F.*], tatterdemalion, caitiff, ragamuffin, pariah, outcast of society, tramp, bezonian [Shakespeare], panhandler [*slang*], sundowner [*Austral.*], bum [*slang*], hobo; chiffonier *or* chiffonnier [*rare*], ragman, ragpicker, sweeper, sweep, scrub.

wench, slut, quean, Cinderella.

barbarian, Goth, Vandal, Hottentot, Zulu, savage, Yahoo; unlicked cub, rough diamond.

barbarousness, barbarism, savagery; Boeotia; Philistinism; parvenuism, parvenudom.

v. **be ignoble** etc. *adj.,* be nobody etc. *n.;* be of (*or* belong to) the common herd etc. *n.*

adj. **ignoble**, common, mean, low, base, vile, sorry, scrubby, beggarly; below par; no great shakes etc. (*unimportant*) 643; homely, homespun, vulgar, low-minded; snobbish, parvenu, low bred; menial, underling, servile.

plebeian, proletarian; of -low, −mean- -parentage, −origin, −extraction; lowborn, baseborn, earthborn; mushroom, dunghill, risen from the ranks; unknown to fame, obscure, untitled.

rustic, country, uncivilized; loutish, boorish, clownish, churlish, brutish, raffish; rude, unpolished, unlicked.

barbarous, barbarian, barbaric, barbaresque [De Quincey].

cockney, born within sound of Bow bells.

adv. below the salt.

877. Title

n. **title**, honor; knighthood etc. (*nobility*) 875.

highness, excellency, grace, lordship, worship; reverence; reverend; esquire, sir, master, Mr., *signor* [*It.*], *señor* [*Sp.*], etc. 373; *Mein Herr* [*Ger.*], mynheer; your–, his- honor; serene highness.

madam, *madame* [*F.*] etc. (*mistress*) 374; empress, queen etc. 875.

decoration, laurel, palm, wreath, garland, bays, medal, ribbon, riband, blue ribbon, red ribbon, cordon, cross, crown, coronet, star, garter, fleece; feather, –in one's cap; epaulet *or* epaulette, chevron, *fourragère* [*F.*], colors, cockade; livery; order, arms, coat of arms, shield, escutcheon *or* scutcheon, crest; reward etc. 973; handle to one's name.

878. Pride

n. **pride**; haughtiness etc. *adj.;* high notions, hauteur; vainglory, crest; arrogance etc. (*assumption*) 885; self-importance, pomposity, pompousness; side [*slang*], swank, swagger, toploftiness [*colloq.*].

proud man, highflyer *or* highflier; fine gentleman; fine lady, *grande dame* [*F.*].

dignity, self-respect, *mens sibi conscia recti* [Virgil].

v. **be proud** etc. *adj.;* put a good face on; look one in the face; stalk abroad, perk, perk up, perk oneself up; think no small beer of oneself [*colloq.*]; think no small potatoes of oneself [*colloq.*]; presume, swagger, strut; rear–, lift up–, hold up- one's head; hold one's head high, look big, take the wall; "bear like the Turk no rival near the throne" [Pope]; carry with a high hand; ride the–, mount on one's- high horse; set one's back up, bridle, toss the head; give oneself airs etc. (*assume*) 885; boast etc. 884.

pride oneself on; glory in, take a pride in; pique–, plume–, hug- oneself; stand upon, be proud of; not hide one's light under a bushel, not put one's talent in a napkin; not think small beer of oneself [*colloq.*] etc. (*vanity*) 880.

adj. **dignified**; stately, proud-crested, lordly, baronial; lofty-minded, high-souled, high-minded, high-mettled, high-plumed, high-flown, high-toned.

proud, haughty, lofty, high, mighty, swollen, puffed up, flushed, blown; vainglorious; purse-proud, fine; proud as -a peacock, –Lucifer; bloated with pride.

supercilious, disdainful, bumptious, magisterial, imperious, high-handed, high and mighty, overweening, consequential; pompous, toplofty [*colloq.*]; arrogant etc. 885; unblushing etc. 880.

stiff, stiff-necked; starched, perked up, stuck up [*colloq.*]; in buckram, strait-laced; prim etc. (*affected*) 855.

on one's dignity; on one's -high horse, –tight ropes, –high ropes; on stilts; *en grand seigneur* [*F.*].

adv. with head erect; *de haut en bas* [*F.*]; with nose in air, with nose turned up; with a sneer, with curling lip.

879. Humility

n. **humility**, humbleness, meekness, lowness, lowliness, lowlihood; abasement, self-abasement; submission etc. 725; resignation.

modesty, timidity etc. 881; verecundity [*obs.*], blush, suffusion, confusion; sense of -shame, –disgrace; humiliation, mortification; letdown, setdown.

condescension; affability etc. (*courtesy*) 894.

v. **be humble** etc. *adj.;* deign, vouchsafe, condescend; humble oneself, demean oneself [*colloq.*]; stoop, –to conquer; carry coals; submit etc. 725; submit with a good grace etc. (*brook*) 826; yield the palm.

lower one's -tone, –note; sing small [*colloq.*], draw in one's horns [*colloq.*], sober down; hide one's -face, –diminished head; not dare to show one's face, take shame to oneself, not have a word to say for oneself; feel–, be conscious of- -shame, –disgrace; be humiliated, be put out of countenance, be shamed, be put to the blush etc. *v.;* receive a snub; eat humble pie, eat crow, eat dirt; drink the cup of humiliation to the dregs.

blush for, blush up to the eyes; redden, change color; color up; hang one's head, look foolish, feel small.

render humble; humble, humiliate; let–, set–, take–, tread–, frown-down; snub, abash, abase, make one sing small [*colloq.*], strike dumb; teach one his distance; take down a peg, –lower; throw–, cast- into the shade etc. 874; stare–, put- out of countenance; put to the blush; confuse, ashame [*rare*], shame, mortify,

320

disgrace, crush; send away with a flea in one's ear [*colloq.*].

get a setdown.

adj. **humble**, lowly, meek; modest etc. 881; humble-minded, sober-minded; unoffended; submissive etc. 725; servile etc. 886.

condescending; affable etc. (*courteous*) 894.

humbled etc. *v.;* bowed down, resigned; abashed, ashamed, dashed; out of countenance; down in the mouth; down on one's -knees, –marrow-bones [*colloq.*], –uppers [*colloq.*]; humbled in the dust, brow-beaten; chapfallen, crestfallen; dumfoundered *or* dumbfoundered, flabbergasted [*colloq.*], struck all of a heap [*colloq.*]; shorn of one's glory etc. (*disrepute*) 874.

adv. **humbly**; with downcast eyes, with bated breath, on bended knee; on all fours; with one's tail between one's legs.

under correction, with due deference.

880. Vanity

n. **vanity**; conceit, conceitedness; self-conceit, self-complacency, self-confidence, self-sufficiency, self-esteem, self-love, self-approbation, self-praise, self-glorification, self-laudation, self-gratulation, self-applause, self-admiration; *amour propre* [*F.*]; selfishness etc. 943.

pretensions, airs, affected manner, mannerism; egoism, egotism, priggism, priggishness; coxcombery, gaudery, vain-glory, elation; pride etc. 878; ostentation etc. 882; assurance etc. 885.

vox et praeterea nihil [*L.*].

egoist, egotist; peacock; coxcomb etc. 854; Sir Oracle etc. 887.

v. **be vain** etc. *adj.;* be vain of; pique oneself etc. (*pride*) 878; lay the flattering unction to one's soul.

have -too high, –an overweening- opinion of -oneself, –one's talents; blind oneself as to one's own merit; not think small beer of oneself [*colloq.*]; strut; put oneself forward; fish for compliments; give oneself airs etc. (*assume*) 885; boast etc. 884.

render vain etc. *adj.;* inspire with vanity etc. *n.;* inflate, puff up, turn one's head.

adj. **vain**, –as a peacock; conceited, overweening, pert, forward; vainglorious, high-flown; ostentatious etc. 882; puffed up, inflated, flushed.

self-satisfied, self-confident, self-sufficient, self-flattering, self-admiring, self-applauding, self-glorious, self-opinioned; *entêté* [*F.*] etc. (*wrong-headed*) 481; wise in one's own conceit, pragmatical [*rare*], overwise, pretentious, prig-

gish; egotistic *or* egotistical; *soidisant* [*F.*] etc. (*boastful*) 884; arrogant etc. 885; assured.

unabashed, unblushing, unconstrained, unceremonious; free and easy.

adv. **vainly** etc. *adj.*

881. Modesty

n. **modesty**; humility etc. 879; diffidence, timidity; retiring disposition; unobtrusiveness; bashfulness etc. *adj.;* *mauvaise honte* [*F.*]; blush, blushing; verecundity [*obs.*]; self-knowledge.

reserve, constraint; demureness etc. *adj.;* "blushing honors" [*Henry VIII*].

[comparison] violet.

v. **be modest** etc. *adj.;* retire, reserve oneself; give way to; draw in one's horns etc. 879; hide one's face.

keep private, keep in the background, keep one's distance; pursue the noiseless tenor of one's way, "do good by stealth and blush to find it fame" [Pope], hide one's light under a bushel; cast sheep's eyes.

adj. **modest**, diffident; humble etc. 879; timid, timorous, bashful; shy, nervous, skittish, coy, sheepish, shame-faced, blushing, overmodest.

unpretending, unpretentious; unobtrusive, unassuming, unostentatious, unboastful, unaspiring; poor in spirit; deprecative, deprecatory.

reserved, constrained, demure.

abashed, ashamed; out of countenance etc. (*humbled*) 879.

adv. **modestly** etc. *adj.;* quietly, privately; without -ceremony, –beat of drum; *sans façon* [*F.*].

882. Ostentation

n. **ostentation**, display, show, *coup d'oeil* [*F.*], flourish, parade, *étalage* [*F.*], pomp, magnificence, splendor, pageantry, array, state, solemnity; dash [*colloq.*], splash [*colloq.*], splurge [*colloq.*], glitter, strut, pomposity, pompousness; pretense, pretensions, showing off; fuss; grand doings.

demonstration, flying colors; flourish of trumpets etc. (*celebration*) 883; pageant, spectacle, exhibition, exposition, procession, turnout [*colloq.*], set out; grand function; fête, gala, field day, review, march past, promenade, "insubstantial pageant" [*Tempest*].

coup de théâtre [*F.*], stage effect, stage trick; claptrap; *mise en scène* [*F.*], *tour de force* [*F.*], chic [*colloq., F.*].

dress; court-, full-, evening–, ball–, fancy-dress; tailoring, millinery, man millinery, frippery; foppery, equipage.

ceremony, ceremonial, ritual, form, formality, etiquette, puncto [*obs.*], punctilio, punctiliousness, starchedness, stateliness.

mummery, solemn mockery, mouth honor; tomfoolery; attitudinarianism.

attitudinarian; fop etc. 854; no modest violet.

v. **be ostentatious** etc. *adj.;* come forward, put oneself forward, attract attention, star; make−, cut- a -figure, −dash, −splash, −splurge [*all colloq.*]; strut; blow one's own trumpet; have no false modesty; figure; make a show, −display; glitter.

show off, show one's paces; parade, march past; display, exhibit, put forward, hold up; trot out [*slang*], hand out; sport [*colloq.*], brandish, blazon forth; dangle, −before the eyes; cry up etc. (*praise*) 931; *prôner* [*F.*], flaunt, emblazon, prink, set off, mount, have framed and glazed.

put on the mask; put a -good, −smiling- face upon; clean the outside of the platter etc. (*disguise*) 544.

adj. **ostentatious**, showy, dashing, pretentious, jaunty *or* janty, grand, pompous, high-sounding; turgid etc. (*big-sounding*) 577; garish *or* gairish; gaudy, −as a -peacock, −butterfly, −tulip; flaunting, flashing, flaming, glittering; gay etc. (*ornate*) 847.

splendid, magnificent, sumptuous, palatial.

theatrical, theatric, dramatic, spectacular, scenic, scenical; dramaturgic *or* dramaturgical.

ceremonial, ritual, ritualistic; solemn, stately, majestic, formal, stiff, ceremonious, punctilious, starched, starchy.

en grande tenue [*F.*], in one's best bib and tucker [*colloq.*], in one's Sunday best, *endimanché* [*F.*], *chic* [*colloq., F.*].

adv. with flourish of trumpet, with beat of drum, with flying colors, with a brass band; at the head of the procession; with no false modesty.

endimanché ad captandum vulgus [*L.*].

883. Celebration

n. **celebration**, solemnization, commemoration, ovation, triumph; lionization.

inauguration, installation, presentation; coronation; *début* [*F.*], coming out [*colloq.*]; Lord Mayor's show [*London, Eng.*]; harvest-home, husking bee, quilting bee; birthday, anniversary, biennial, triennial etc.; centenary, centennial; bicentenary, bicentennial; tercentenary, tercentennial etc.; "the day we celebrate"; red-letter day; trophy etc. 733; jubilation, laudation, paean *or* pean; *Te Deum* etc. (*thanksgiving*) 990; festivity, festival; fête etc.

882; Forefathers' Day [*U. S.*], Independence Day, "the Glorious Fourth"; holiday etc. 840.

triumphal arch, bonfire; salute, salvo, salvo of artillery; *feu de joie* [*F.*], flourish of trumpets, fanfare, colors flying, illuminations.

[wedding anniversaries] *wooden* wedding [5th], *tin* wedding [10th], *crystal* wedding [15th], *china* wedding [20th], *silver* wedding [25th], *golden* wedding [50th], *diamond* wedding [60th].

jubilee, 50th anniversary; diamond jubilee, 60th anniversary.

v. **celebrate**, keep, signalize, do honor to, commemorate, solemnize, hallow; keep high festival, keep holiday; mark with a red letter.

pledge, drink to, toast; hob and nob, hobnob with; present.

inaugurate, install, instate, induct, chair.

rejoice etc. 838; kill the fatted calf, hold jubilee; roast an ox, serve up the Thanksgiving turkey, serve up the Christmas goose; fire a salute, dip the colors, present arms; paint the town red [*colloq.*]; maffick [*colloq., Eng.*].

adj. **celebrating** etc. *v.;* commemorative, celebrated, immortal; solemn; jubilant; kept, kept in remembrance.

adv. **in honor of**, in commemoration of, in celebration of, in memory of; as a toast.

int. **hail**! all hail! "see the conquering hero comes!" "Hail! hail! the gang's all here!"

884. Boasting

n. **boasting** etc. *v.;* boast, vaunt, crake [*obs.*], pretense, pretensions, cock-a-hoopness, braggadocio, braggadocianism, puff [*colloq.*], puffery; flourish, fanfaronade; gasconade, bluff, highfaluting *or* highfalutin, *blague* [*F.*]; side [*slang, Eng.*], swagger, jingoism, spread-eagleism; brag, braggartism *or* braggardism, braggartry, bounce, rant, bluster, bravado, bunk *or* buncombe *or* bunkum; jactation, jactitation, jactancy; vendition [*obs.*], vaporing, rodomontade, bombast, gas [*slang*], hot air [*slang*], fine talking, tall talk, tall story [*both colloq.*], fish story [*humorous*]; magniloquence, teratology [*obs.*], heroics; chauvinism; exaggeration etc. 549; vanity etc. 880; *vox et praeterea nihil* [*L.*]; much cry and little wool, *brutum fulmen* [*L.*].

exultation, gloriation [*obs.*], glorification; flourish of trumpets; triumph etc. 883.

boaster, braggart, braggadocio, fanfaron, pretender, bluffer, blower [*slang*], blower of his own trumpet, windbag [*slang*], hot-air artist [*slang*], Fourth of July orator; Thraso, Gascon; chauvinist, jingo, jingoist; blusterer, swaggerer etc. 887; charlatan, trumpeter; puppy etc. (*fop*) 854.

v. **boast**, make a boast of, brag, vaunt, puff, show off, flourish, crake [*obs.*], crack, trumpet, strut, swagger, *blague* [*F.*], gasconade, vapor; blow [*slang*], four-flush [*slang*], bluff; talk big, draw the long bow, speak for Buncombe; *faire claquer son fouet* [*F.*], blow one's own trumpet; put on side [*slang, Eng.*], swank [*dial. Eng.*]; let the American eagle scream, sing "Rule, Britannia," indulge in jingoism; *se faire valoir* [*F.*], take merit to oneself, make a merit of; holloa before one is out of the wood.

exult; crow, crow over [*both colloq.*], triumph, glory, jubilate, rejoice, maffick [*colloq., Eng.*], throw up one's cap, yell oneself hoarse, cheer.

gloat, gloat over; chuckle; neigh.

adj. **boasting** etc. *v.;* magniloquent, flaming, thrasonic [*rare*], thrasonical, stilted, gasconading, braggart, boastful, pretentious; vainglorious etc. (*conceited*) 880; highfaluting *or* highfalutin; spread-eagle [*colloq. & humorous*].

elate, elated, jubilant, triumphant, exultant; in high feather; flushed, —with victory; cock-a-hoop, cock-a-hoopish; on stilts [*colloq.*].

vaunted etc. *v.*

adv. **vauntingly** etc. *adj.;* in triumph; with a blare of trumpets.

885. Insolence
[undue assumption of superiority]

n. **insolence**, brashness, brazenness, malapertness; haughtiness etc. *adj.;* arrogance, airs; bumptiousness, toploftiness [*colloq.*], assumption, presumption; assumption of infallibility; contumely, disdain, insult; overbearance, domineering etc. *v.;* bluster, swagger, swaggering etc. *v.;* bounce; terrorism; tyranny etc. 739; beggar on horseback; usurpation.

impertinence, cheek [*colloq. or slang*], nerve [*slang*], nerviness [*slang*], sauce [*colloq.*], abuse; sauciness etc. *adj.;* flippancy, dicacity [*obs.*], petulance [*rare in this sense*], procacity [*rare*].

impudence, self-assertion, assurance, audacity, hardihood; front, face, brass, gall [*slang*]; shamelessness etc. *adj.;* effrontery, hardened front, face of brass.

jingoism, chauvinism; *Kultur* [*Ger.*], "might is right," *Macht ist Recht* [*Ger.*].

malapert, saucebox etc. (*blusterer*) 887.

jingo, jingoist, chauvinist; fire eater [*colloq.*]; boaster etc. 884.

v. **be insolent** etc. *adj.;* bluster, vapor, swagger, swell, give oneself airs, snap one's fingers, kick up a dust [*colloq.*]; swear etc. (*affirm*) 535; rap out oaths; roister.

arrogate, assume, presume; make bold, make free; take a liberty, give an inch and take an ell.

outface, outlook, outstare, outbrazen, outbrave; stare out of countenance; brazen out; lay down the law; teach one's grandmother to suck eggs [*colloq.*]; assume a lofty bearing; talk big, look big, put on big looks, act the *grand seigneur;* mount-, ride- the high horse; toss the head, carry with a high hand; tempt Providence; want snuffing [*colloq.*].

domineer, bully, dictate, hector; lord it over; *traiter-, regarder- de haut en bas* [*F.*]; exact; snub, huff, beard, fly in the face of; put to the blush; bear-, beat- down; browbeat, intimidate; trample-, tread- -down, -under foot; dragoon, ride roughshod over; bulldoze [*colloq.*], terrorize.

adj. **insolent**, haughty, arrogant, imperious, magisterial, dictatorial, arbitrary; high-handed, high and mighty; contumelious, supercilious, overbearing, toplofty [*colloq.*], toploftical [*rare*], intolerant, domineering, overweening, high-flown; precocious, assuming, would-be, bumptious.

pert, flippant, fresh [*slang*], brash, cavalier, saucy, forward, impertinent, malapert; impudent, audacious, presumptuous.

brazen, bluff, shameless, aweless, unblushing, unabashed; bold-faced, bare-faced, brazen-faced; dead-, lost- to shame.

blustering, swaggering, hectoring, rollicking, roistering, vaporing, free and easy, devil-may-care, jaunty *or* janty; thrasonic [*rare*], thrasonical, fire-eating [*colloq.*]; "full of sound and fury" [*Macbeth*].

jingo, jingoistic, chauvinistic.

adv. **insolently** etc. *adj.;* with nose in air; with arms akimbo; *de haut en bas* [*F.*]; with a high hand; *ex cathedra* [*L.*].

886. Servility

n. **servility**; slavery etc. (*subjection*) 749; obsequiousness etc. *adj.;* subserviency; abasement, prostration, prosternation [*obs.*]; genuflection etc. (*worship*) 990; toadeating; fawning etc. *v.;* tufthunting, timeserving, flunkyism *or* flunkeyism; sycophancy etc. (*flattery*) 933; humility etc. 879.

sycophant, parasite; toad, toady, toadeater, tuft-hunter; snob, flunky *or* flunkey, lapdog, spaniel, lick-spit, lick-spittle, smell-feast, *Graeculus esuriens* [*L.*], hanger on, *cavalier (or cavaliere) servente* [*It.*], led captain, carpet knight; timeserver, fortune hunter, Vicar of Bray, Sir Pertinax MacSycophant, pickthank; flatterer etc. 935; doer of dirty work; *âme damnée* [*F.*], tool; reptile; slave etc. (*servant*) 746; *homme de cour* [*F.*], courtier; beat [*slang*], dead beat [*slang*], doughface [*slang*]; heeler, ward heeler [*both polit. cant*]; jackal, sponge, sponger, sucker [*slang*], tagtail, truckler.

v. **cringe**, bow, stoop, kneel, bend the knee; fall on one's knees, prostrate oneself; worship etc. 990.

fawn, crouch, cower, sneak, crawl, sponge, truckle, toady, truckle to, grovel, lick the feet of, lick one's shoes, make a doormat of oneself, kiss the hem of one's garment; be servile etc. *adj.*

pay court to; feed on, fatten on, batten on, dance attendance on, follow at heel, pin oneself upon, hang on the sleeve of, *avaler les couleuvres* [*F.*], keep time to, fetch and carry, do the dirty work of.

go with the stream, follow the crowd, worship the rising sun, hold with the hare and run with the hounds; get on the band wagon; be a timeserver etc. *n.*

adj. **servile**, obsequious; supple, —as a glove; soapy [*slang*], oily, pliant, cringing, abased, dough-faced [*colloq.*], fawning, slavish, groveling, reptilian, sniveling, mealy-mouthed; beggarly, sycophantic, parasitical; abject, prostrate, down on one's marrowbones [*jocular or slang*]; base, mean, sneaking; crouching etc. *v.;* timeserving.

adv. **with servility** etc. *n.;* hat—, cap- in hand; "in a bondman's key" [*Merchant of Venice*]; "with bated breath and whispering humbleness" [*ibid.*].

int. so please you! as my lord wills! don't mind me!

887. Blusterer

n. **blusterer**, swaggerer, vaporer, roisterer, brawler; fanfaron; braggart etc. (*boaster*) 884; bully, terrorist, rough, ruffian, rough-neck [*slang*], tough [*colloq.*], rowdy, bulldozer [*colloq.*], roarer [*slang, obs.*], slang-whanger [*slang*], larrikin [*Austral. & Eng.*]; hoodlum [*colloq.*], hooligan [*slang*], Mohock, Mohawk [*rare*], Drawcansir, swashbuckler, Captain Bobadil, Sir Lucius O'-Trigger, Thraso, Pistol, Parolles, Bombastes Furioso, Hector, Chrononhotonthologos; jingo; desperado, dare-devil, fire eater [*colloq.*]; fury etc. (*violent person*) 173.

puppy etc. (*fop*) 854, jackanapes, bantam-cock; malapert, saucebox [*colloq.*]; minx, hussy.

dogmatist, doctrinaire, Sir Oracle, stump orator etc. 582; prig, Jack-in-office.

Section 3. Sympathetic

888. Friendship

n. **friendship**, amity; friendliness etc. *adj.;* brotherhood, fraternity, sodality, confraternity; sorority, sorosis, sisterhood; harmony etc. (*concord*) 714; peace etc. 721.

firm—, staunch—, intimate—, familiar—, bosom—, cordial—, tried—, devoted—, lasting—, fast—, sincere—, warm—, ardent- friendship.

cordiality, fraternization, association, *entente cordiale* [*F.*], good understanding, *rapprochement* [*F.*], sympathy, fellow-feeling, response, welcomeness; affection etc. (*love*) 897; partiality, favoritism; good will etc. (*benevolence*) 906.

acquaintance, introduction, familiarity, intimacy, intercourse, fellowship, knowledge of.

v. **be friendly** etc. *adj.,* be friends etc. 890, be acquainted with etc. *adj.;* know; have the ear of; keep company with etc. (*sociality*) 892; hold communication with, have dealings with, sympathize with; have a leaning to; bear good will etc. (*benevolent*) 906; love etc. 897; make much of; befriend etc. (*aid*) 707; introduce to.

set one's horses together; have the latchstring out; hold out—, extend- the right hand of -friendship, —fellowship; become friendly etc. *adj.;* make friends etc. (890) with; break the ice, be introduced to; pick up acquaintance; make—, scrape- acquaintance with; get into favor, gain the friendship of.

shake hands with, strike hands with, fraternize, sororize [*rare*], embrace; receive with open arms, throw oneself into the arms of; meet halfway, take in good part.

adj. **friendly**, amicable, amical; well-affected, unhostile, neighborly; brotherly, fraternal, sisterly, sororal [*rare*]; ardent, devoted, sympathetic, harmonious, hearty, cordial, warm-hearted.

friends with, at home with, hand in hand with; on -good, —friendly, —amicable, —cordial, —familiar, —intimate- terms, —footing; on speaking terms, on visiting terms, on one's visiting list; in one's good -graces, —books.

acquainted, familiar, intimate, thick, hand and glove, hail fellow well met, free and easy; welcome.

adv. **amicably** etc. *adj.;* with open arms, *à bras ouverts* [*F.*]; *sans cérémonie* [*F.*]; arm in arm.

889. Enmity

n. **enmity,** hostility, antagonism; unfriendliness etc. *adj.;* discord etc. 713; bitterness, rancor; heartburning; animosity etc. 900; malevolence etc. 907.

alienation, estrangement; dislike etc. 867; aversion, hate etc. 898.

v. **be unfriendly** etc. *adj.;* keep-, hold- at arm's length; be at loggerheads; bear malice etc. 907; fall out; take umbrage etc. 900; harden the heart, alienate, estrange.

adj. **unfriendly,** inimical, hostile; at enmity, at variance, at daggers drawn, at open war with; up in arms against; in bad odor with.

on bad terms, not on speaking terms; cool, cold, cold-hearted; estranged, alienated, disaffected, irreconcilable.

890. Friend

n. **friend,** -of one's bosom; *alter ego* [*L.*], other self; intimate, confidant (*masc.*), confidante (*fem.*), confident; best-, bosom-, fast-friend; *amicus usque ad aras* [*L.*], *fidus Achates* [*L.*]; *persona grata* [*L.*]; well-wisher; neighbor *or* neighbour, acquaintance.

favorer, fautor [*rare*], patron, backer, Maecenas; tutelary saint, good genius, advocate, partisan, sympathizer; ally; friend in need etc. (*auxiliary*) 711.

associate, consociate, compeer, comrade, mate, companion, *camarade* [*F.*], *confrère* [*F.*], colleague, comate, copemate *or* copesmate [*obs.*]; partner; side-partner, copartner, consort; old-, crony; chum [*colloq.*], pal [*slang*], buddy [*slang*]; playfellow, playmate, schoolfellow; bedfellow, bunkie [*colloq.*], bedmate, chamberfellow; classfellow, classman, classmate; roommate, shopmate, shipmate, messmate; fellow-, boon-, pot- companion; fellow-man, stable companion; best man, bridesmaid, maid of honor.

[famous friendships] Pylades and Orestes, Castor and Pollux, Achilles and Patroclus, Diomedes and Sthenalus, Hercules and Iolaus, Theseus and Pirithoüs, Epaminondas and Pelopidas, Nisus and Euryalus, Damon and Pythias, David and Jonathan, Christ and the beloved disciple; Soldiers Three, the Three Musketeers.

par nobile fratrum [*L., often ironical*]; *Arcades ambo* [*L.*].

host, hostess (*fem.*), Amphitryon, Boniface.
guest, visitor, frequenter, habitué, *protégé* [*F.*].
compatriot; fellow-, countryman; fellow townsman, townie [*slang*].

int. "Thank God for a trusty chum!" [Kipling].

891. Enemy

n. **enemy;** antagonist; foe, foeman; open-, bitterenemy; opponent etc. 710; backfriend [*obs.*], copemate *or* copesmate [*obs.*], "dearest foe"; mortal -aversion, -antipathy; snake in the grass.

public enemy, enemy to society; anarchist, seditionist, traitor, traitress (*fem.*).

892. Sociality

n. **sociality,** sociability, sociableness etc. *adj.;* social intercourse, consociation, intercourse, intercommunion; consortship, companionship, comradeship, fellowship; urbanity etc. (*courtesy*) 894; intimacy, familiarity; clubbability *or* clubability [*colloq.*], clubbism; *esprit de corps* [*F.*]; *morale* [*F.*].

conviviality; good- fellowship, -company; joviality, jollity, *savoir vivre* [*F.*], *joie de vivre* [*F.*], festivity, festive board, walnuts and wine, merrymaking; loving cup; hospitality, heartiness; cheer; "the feast of reason and the flow of soul" [Pope].

welcome, welcomeness, greeting; hearty-, warm-, welcome- reception; hearty welcome; hearty-, warm- greeting; the glad hand [*slang*].

boon companion; good-, jolly-fellow; *bon enfant* [*F.*], bawcock [*archaic*], crony, *bon vivant* [*F.*]; a good mixer [*colloq.*].

social-, family- circle; family hearth; circle of acquaintance, coterie, society, company; club etc. (*association*) 712.

social gathering, social reunion; assembly etc. (*assemblage*) 72; barbecue; bee; corn-husking, corn-shucking; husking, husking-bee; hen party [*colloq.*]; house raising, house-warming, hanging of the crane; infare *or* infair [*Scot. & dial., U. S.*]; smoker, -party [*both colloq.*]; Dutch treat [*colloq.*]; stag, -party [*both colloq.*]; sociable, tamasha [*Hind.*], party, entertainment, reception, levee, at home, *conversazione* [*It.*], soirée [*F.*], matinée; evening-, morning-, afternoon-, garden-, coming-out-, surprise- party; *partie carrée* [*F.*]; kettledrum, drum, drum major, rout [*archaic*], tempest, hurricane; *ridotto* [*It.*]; ball, hunt ball, dance, dinner dance, festival etc. (*amusement*) 840.

[social meals] breakfast, wedding breakfast, hunt breakfast; luncheon, lunch; picnic lunch, basket lunch, picnic; tea, afternoon tea, five o'clock tea, cup of tea, dish of tea [*esp. Brit.*], *thé dansant* [*F.*], coming-out tea [*colloq.*]; tea party, tea fight [*slang*]; dinner, potluck, bachelor dinner, stag dinner [*colloq.*], hunt dinner; church supper, high tea; banquet etc. 298.

visit, visiting; round of visits; call, morning call; interview etc. (*interlocution*) 588; assignation; tryst, trysting place; appointment.

v. be sociable etc. *adj.;* know; be acquainted etc. *adj.;* associate with, sort with, consort with, keep company with, walk hand in hand with; eat off the same trencher, club together, consort, bear one company, join; consociate [*rare*], intercommunicate, intercommune [*rare*], make acquaintance with etc. (*friendship*) 888; make advances, fraternize, embrace.

visit, pay a visit; interchange -visits, -cards; call at, call upon; leave a card; drop in, look in, look one up, beat up one's quarters [*colloq.*].

receive hospitality; be−, feel−, make oneself- at home with; make free with; crack a bottle with; take potluck with; live at free quarters; find the latchstring out.

entertain; give a party etc. *n.;* be at home, see one's friends, keep open house, do the honors; receive, −with open arms; welcome; give a warm reception etc. *n.* to; kill the fatted calf.

adj. **sociable**, companionable, clubbable *or* clubable [*colloq.*], clubbish; conversable, cozy *or* cosy *or* cosey, chatty, conversational; convivial, festive, festal, jovial, jolly, hospitable.

welcome, −as roses in May; fêted, entertained.

free and easy, hail fellow well met, familiar, intimate, consociate, consociated; associated with etc. *v.;* on visiting terms, acquainted; social, neighborly.

international, cosmopolitan; gregarious.

adv. **sociably** etc. *adj.;* *en famille* [*F.*], in the family circle; on terms of intimacy; in the social whirl; *sans -façon,* −*cérémonie* [*F.*], arm in arm.

893. Seclusion. Exclusion

n. **seclusion**, privacy, retirement, eremitism, anchoretism, anchoritism, reclusion, recess; suspension; snugness etc. *adj.;* concealment, delitescence; rustication, *rus in urbe* [*L.*], ruralism, rurality [*rare*], solitude; solitariness etc. (*singleness*) 87; isolation; "splendid isolation"; loneliness etc. *adj.;* estrangement from the world, voluntary exile; aloofness.

depopulation, desertion, desolation; wilderness etc. (*unproductive*) 169; howling wilderness; rotten borough, Old Sarum [*Eng.*].

retreat, cell, hermitage, cloister; convent etc. 1000; *sanctum sanctorum* [*L.*], study, library, den [*colloq.*].

exclusion, excommunication, banishment, exile, ostracism, proscription; economic pressure; cut, cut direct; dead cut.

unsociability, unsociableness, dissociability, dissociality; inhospitality, inhospitableness etc. *adj.;* domesticity, self-sufficiency, Darby and Joan.

recluse, hermit, eremite, anchoret *or* anchorite, anchorist [*obs.*]; santon; stylite, pillarist, pillarsaint [*all Ch. hist.*]; St. Simeon Stylites; caveman, cave-dweller, troglodyte, Timon of Athens, solitarian [*obs.*], solitaire, ruralist [*obs.*], disciple of Zimmermann, closet cynic, cynic, Diogenes.

outcast, pariah, leper; outsider, rank outsider; castaway, pilgarlic [*low*], wastrel [*dial. Eng.*], losel, foundling; wilding.

v. **be** *or* **live secluded** etc. *adj.;* keep−, stand−, hold oneself- -aloof, −in the background; keep snug; shut oneself up; deny oneself, seclude oneself; creep into a corner, rusticate, dissocialize; retire, −from the world; hermitize; take the veil; abandon etc. 624; sport one's oak [*Univ. slang, Eng.*].

exclude, repel; cut, −dead; refuse to -associate with, −acknowledge; send to Coventry, look cool−, turn one's back−, shut the door- upon; blackball, excommunicate, exile, expatriate; banish, outlaw, maroon, ostracize, proscribe, cut off from, keep at arm's length, draw a cordon round, boycott, embargo, blockade, isolate.

depopulate, dispeople, unpeople; desolate, devastate.

adj. **secluded**, sequestered, retired, delitescent, private, by; in a backwater; out of the world, out of the way; "the world forgetting by the world forgot" [Pope].

unsociable, unsocial, dissocial, inhospitable, cynical, inconversable [*obs.*], unclubbable *or* unclubable [*colloq.*], *sauvage* [*F.*]; hermitical, eremitic *or* eremitical, anchoretic *or* anchoretical, anchoritic *or* anchoritical, anchoretish, anchoritish, troglodytic.

snug, domestic, stay-at-home.

excluded etc. *v.;* unfrequented, unvisited, unintroduced, uninvited, unwelcome; on the fringe of society; under a cloud, left to shift for oneself; deserted, −in one's utmost need; unfriended, friendless, kithless, homeless, desolate, lorn, forlorn; solitary, lonely, lonesome, isolated, single, estranged; derelict, outcast, outside the gates, "yammering at the bars"; banished etc. *v.;* under an embargo.

uninhabited, unoccupied, untenanted, tenantless, abandoned; uninhabitable.

894. Courtesy

n. **courtesy**; respect etc. 928; good- manners, –behavior, –breeding; manners; politeness etc. *adj.; bienséance* [*F.*], urbanity, comity, gentility, breeding, gentle breeding, cultivation, culture, polish, presence; civility, civilization; amenity, suavity; good temper, good humor, amiability, easy temper, complacency, soft tongue, mansuetude [*archaic*]; condescension etc. (*humility*) 879; affability, complaisance, compliance, *prévenance* [*F.*], amiability, gallantry, chivalry; fine flower of -courtesy, –chivalry.

pink of courtesy, pink of politeness; flower of knighthood, *chevalier sans peur et sans reproche,* Bayard, Sidney, "a verray parfit gentil knight" [Chaucer], Chesterfield; Launcelot, Gawaine, Colonel Newcome; "gentle Shakespeare" [Ben Jonson].

compliment; fair–, soft–, sweet- words; honeyed phrases, ceremonial; salutation, reception, presentation, introduction, *accueil* [*F.*], greeting, recognition; welcome, abord [*obs.*], respects, *devoir* [*F.*], duty [*archaic*], regards, remembrances; kind -regards, –remembrances; deference, love, best love, empty encomium, flattering remark, hollow commendation; salaams.

[forms of greeting] obeisance etc. (*reverence*) 928; bow, curtsy *or* curtsey, scrape, salaam, kotow *or* kowtow [*China*], bowing and scraping; kneeling; genuflection etc. (*worship*) 990; obsequiousness etc. 886; capping, pulling the forelock, making a leg [*colloq.*], shaking hands, etc. *v.;* grip of the hand; embrace, hug, squeeze, kiss, buss, smack; salute, accolade; loving cup, *vin d'honneur* [*F.*], pledge; love token etc. (*endearment*) 902.

mark of recognition, nod; "nods and becks and wreathed smiles" [Milton]; valediction etc. 293; condolence etc. 915.

v. **be courteous** etc. *adj.;* show courtesy etc. *n.*

mind one's P's and Q's [*colloq.*], behave oneself, be all things to all men, conciliate, speak one fair, take in good part, do the amiable [*colloq.*]; look as if butter would not melt in one's mouth; mend–, mind- one's manners.

do the honors, usher, usher in, receive, greet, hail, bid welcome; welcome, –with open arms; shake hands; hold out–, press–, squeeze- the hand; bid Godspeed; speed the parting guest; cheer, serenade.

visit, wait upon, present oneself, pay one's respects, pay a visit etc. (*sociability*) 892; dance attendance on etc. (*servility*) 886; pay attentions to; do homage to etc. (*respect*) 928; give *or* send one's regards to etc. *n.*

salute; embrace etc. (*endearment*) 902; kiss, –hands; drink to, pledge, hob and nob; move to [*colloq.*], nod to; smile upon.

uncover, cap; touch–, raise–, lift–, take off- the hat; doff the cap; tip the hat to [*slang*]; pull the forelock; present arms; make way for; bow, make one's bow, make a leg scrape, curtsy *or* curtsey, bow and scrape, bob a curtsy, kneel; bow–, bend- the knee; salaam, kotow *or* kowtow [*China*]; prostrate oneself etc. (*worship*) 990.

render polite etc. *adj.;* polish, rub off the -corners, –rough edges; cultivate, civilize, humanize.

adj. **courteous**, polite, civil, mannerly, urbane; well-behaved, well-mannered, well-bred, well-brought up; gently bred; of gentle -manners, –breeding; good-mannered, polished, civilized, cultivated; refined etc. (*taste*) 850; gentlemanlike etc. (*fashion*) 852; gallant, chivalrous, chivalric; on one's good (*or* best) behavior.

ingratiating, winning, gentle, mild; good-humored, cordial, gracious, amiable, tactful, affable, familiar; neighborly; obliging, complaisant, complacent, conciliatory.

bland, suave; fine–, fair–, soft- spoken; honey-mouthed, honey-tongued; oily, oily-tongued; unctuous; obsequious etc. 886.

adv. **courteously** etc. *adj.;* with a good grace; with open arms, with outstretched arms, *à bras ouverts* [*F.*]; *suaviter in modo* [*L.*], with perfect courtesy, in good humor.

int. **hail**! welcome! well met! ave! [*L.*]; all hail! good -day, –morrow, –morning, –evening, –afternoon, –night! sweet dreams! Godspeed! *pax vobiscum!* [*L.*]; all good go with you! may your shadow never be less!

895. Discourtesy

n. **discourtesy**; ill-breeding; ill–, bad–, ungainly- manners; tactlessness; uncourteousness etc. *adj.;* rusticity, inurbanity; illiberality, incivility, displacency [*obs.*]; lack *or* want of courtesy etc. 894; disrespect etc. 929; procacity [*obs.*], impudence, misbehavior, barbarism, barbarity; brutality, brutishness, brutification, blackguardism, conduct unbecoming a gentleman, *grossièreté* [*F.*], *brusquerie* [*F.*], vulgarity etc. 851.

bad temper, ill temper; peevishness, surliness; churlishness etc. *adj.;* spinosity, perversity; moroseness etc. (*sullenness*) 901a.

sternness etc. *adj.;* austerity; moodishness, captiousness etc. 901; cynicism; tartness etc. *adj.;* acrimony, acerbity, virulence, asperity.

scowl, black looks, frown; sulks, short answer, rebuff; hard words, contumely; unparliamentary language, personality.

bear, bruin, grizzly, grizzly bear; brute, blackguard, beast; unlicked cub; frump [*colloq.*], crosspatch [*colloq.*]; grouch, old grouch; saucebox etc. 887; crooked stick.

v. **be rude** etc. *adj.;* insult etc. 929; treat with discourtesy; take a name in vain; make bold with, make free with; take a liberty; stare out of countenance, ogle, point at, put to the blush.

cut; turn one's back upon, turn on one's heel; give the cold shoulder; keep at -a distance, −arm's length; look -cool, −coldly, −black- upon; show the door to, send away with a flea in the ear [*colloq.*].

lose one's temper etc. (*resentment*) 900; mump [*dial.*], sulk etc. 901a; frown, scowl, glower, pout; snap, snarl, growl.

render rude etc. *adj.;* brutalize, brutify.

adj. **discourteous,** uncourteous, uncourtly; ill-bred, ill-mannered, ill-behaved, ill-conditioned, unbred; unmannerly, unmannered, impolite, unpolite, uncivil, ungracious, unceremonious, cool; unpolished, uncivilized, ungenteel, ungentlemanlike, ungentlemanly; unladylike; blackguard; vulgar etc. 851; dedecorous [*obs.*]; foul-mouthed, foul-spoken; abusive.

pert, forward, obtrusive, impudent, rude, saucy, procacious [*archaic*], brash; flippant etc. (*insolent*) 885.

repulsive; uncomplaisant, unaccommodating, unneighborly, ungallant; inaffable; ungentle, ungainly, rough, rugged, bluff, blunt, gruff; churlish, boorish, bearish; brutal, brusque, stern, harsh, austere; cavalier.

bad-tempered, ill-tempered, ill-humored; out of -temper, −humor; crusty, tart, sour, crabbed, sharp, short, trenchant, sarcastic, biting, doggish, currish, caustic, virulent, bitter, acrimonious; venomous, contumelious; snarling etc. *v.;* surly, -as a bear; perverse; grim, sullen etc. 901a; peevish etc. (*irascible*) 901; bristling, thorny, spinose, spinous.

adv. **discourteously** etc. *adj.;* with discourtesy etc. *n.,* with a bad grace.

896. Congratulation

n. **congratulation,** gratulation, felicitation; salute etc. 894; condolence etc. 915; compliments of the season; good wishes, best wishes.

v. **congratulate,** gratulate, felicitate; give joy, wish one joy; compliment; tender−, offer- one's congratulations; wish many happy returns of the day, wish a merry Christmas and a happy new year.

congratulate oneself etc. (*rejoice*) 838.

adj. **congratulatory,** gratulatory.

897. Love

n. **love,** affection, sympathy, fellow-feeling; tenderness etc. *adj.;* heart, brotherly love; charity, good will; benevolence etc. 906; attachment; fondness etc. *adj.;* liking; inclination etc. (*desire*) 865; regard, dilection [*obs.*], admiration, fancy.

yearning, *eros* [*Gr.*], tender passion, amour; gyneolatry; gallantry, passion, flame, devotion, fervor, enthusiasm, transport of love, rapture, enchantment, infatuation, adoration, idolatry.

mother love, maternal love, natural affection, *storge* [*Gr.*].

attractiveness, charm; popularity; idol, favorite etc. 899.

god of love, Cupid, Venus, Eros, Kama [*Hindu*]; myrtle; turtle dove, sparrow; cupid amoretto; true lover's knot; love -token, −suit, −affair, −tale, −story; the old story, plighted love; courtship etc. 902; amourette; free-love.

lover, suitor, *fiancé* [*F.*], follower [*colloq.*], admirer, adorer, wooer, amoret [*obs.*], amorist, beau, sweetheart, inamorato, swain, young man [*colloq.*], flame [*colloq.*], love, truelove; leman [*archaic*], Lothario, gallant, paramour, captive; *amoroso, cavaliere servente, cicisbeo, caro sposo* [*all It.*].

ladylove, sweetheart, mistress, inamorata, idol, darling, duck, Dulcinea, angel, goddess, *cara sposa* [*It.*]; betrothed, affianced, *fiancée* [*F.*].

flirt, coquette, amorette.

pair of turtledoves; abode of love; Agapemone [*Ch. hist.*].

v. **love,** like, affect, fancy, care for, take an interest in, be partial to, sympathize with; affection; be in love with etc. *adj.;* have−, entertain−, harbor−, cherish- a love for etc. *n.;* regard, revere; take to, bear love to, be wedded to; set one's affections on; burn; adore, idolize, love to distraction, *aimer éperdument* [*F.*]; dote- on, −upon.

make much of, feast one's eyes on; hold dear, prize; hug, cling to, cherish, caress, fondle, pet.

take a fancy to, look sweet upon [*colloq.*]; become enamored etc. *adj.;* fall in love with, lose one's heart; desire etc. 865.

excite love; win-, gain-, secure-, engage- the -love, -affections, -heart; take the fancy of; have a place in-, wind round- the heart; attract, attach, endear, charm, fascinate, captivate, bewitch, seduce, enamor, enrapture, turn the head.

get into favor; ingratiate-, insinuate-, worm- oneself; propitiate, curry favor with, pay one's court to, *faire l'aimable* [*F.*], set one's cap at [*colloq.*], coquet, flirt.

adj. **loving** etc. *v.;* fond of; taken with [*colloq.*], struck with [*colloq.*], smitten, bitten [*colloq.*]; attached to, wedded to; enamored; charmed etc. *v.;* in love; love-sick; over head and ears in love.

affectionate, tender, sweet upon [*colloq.*], sympathetic, amorous, amatory; fond, erotic, uxorious, ardent, passionate, rapturous, devoted, motherly.

loved etc. *v.;* beloved, well beloved, dearly beloved; dear as the apple of one's eye, nearest to one's heart; dear, precious, darling, pet, little; favorite, popular.

congenial; to-, after- one's -mind, -taste, -fancy, -own heart; in one's good graces etc. (*friendly*) 888.

lovable, adorable, lovely, sweet, attractive, seductive, winning, winsome, charming, engaging, interesting, enchanting, captivating, fascinating, bewitching, amiable; seraphic *or* seraphical, angelic, like an angel.

898. Hate

n. **hate**, hatred, vials of hate; "Hymn of Hate."

disaffection, disfavor; alienation, estrangement, coolness; enmity etc. 889; animosity etc. 900; malice etc. 907; implacability etc. (*revenge*) 919.

umbrage, pique, grudge, dudgeon, spleen, bitterness, bitterness of feeling; ill blood, bad blood; acrimony.

repugnance etc. (*dislike*) 867; odium, unpopularity; detestation, abhorrence, loathing, execration, abomination, aversion, antipathy; demonophobia, gynephobia, negrophobia; Anglophobia etc. 867.

object of hatred, an abomination, an aversion, *bête noire* [*F.*]; enemy etc. 891; bitter pill; source of annoyance etc. 830.

v. **hate**, detest, abominate, abhor, loathe; recoil at, shudder at; shrink from, view with horror, hold

in abomination, revolt against, execrate; scowl etc. 895; disrelish etc. (*dislike*) 867.

owe a grudge; bear spleen, bear a grudge, bear malice etc. (*malevolence*) 907; conceive an aversion to.

excite hatred, provoke hatred etc. *n.;* be hateful etc. *adj.;* stink in the nostrils; estrange, alienate, repel, set against, sow dissension, set by the ears, envenom, incense, irritate, rile [*dial. or colloq.*], ruffle, vex, roil; horrify etc. 830.

adj. **hating** etc. *v.;* abhorrent; averse from etc. (*disliking*) 867; set against; bitter etc. (*acrimonious*) 895; implacable etc. (*revengeful*) 919.

unloved, unbeloved, unlamented, undeplored, unmourned, uncared for, unendeared, unvalued; disliked etc. 867.

crossed in love, forsaken, rejected, lovelorn, jilted.

hateful, obnoxious, odious, abominable, repulsive, offensive, shocking; disgusting etc. (*disagreeable*) 830; reprehensible.

invidious, spiteful; malicious etc. 907.

insulting, irritating, provoking.

[mutual hate] at daggers drawn; not on speaking terms etc. (*enmity*) 889; at loggerheads.

899. Favorite

n. **favorite**, pet, fondling, cosset, minion [*rare*], idol, jewel, spoiled child, *enfant gâté* [*F.*]; led captain; crony; apple of one's eye, man after one's own heart; *persona grata* [*L.*].

love, dear, darling, duck, honey, jewel; mopsy *or* mopsey, moppet; sweetheart etc. (*love*) 897.

general-, universal- favorite; idol of the people; matinée idol.

900. Resentment

n. **resentment**, displeasure, animosity, anger, wrath, ire, indignation; exasperation, vexation, bitter resentment, wrathful indignation.

pique, umbrage, huff, miff [*colloq.*], soreness, dudgeon, acerbity, virulence, bitterness, acrimony, asperity, spleen, gall; heartburning, heartswelling; rankling.

ill-, bad- -humor, -temper; irascibility etc. 901; scowl etc. 895; sulks etc. 901*a;* ill blood etc. (*hate*) 898; revenge etc. 919.

irritation; warmth, bile, choler, fume, pucker [*colloq.*], dander [*colloq.*], ferment, excitement, ebullition; angry mood, taking [*colloq.*], pet, tiff, passion, fit, tantrum.

rage, fury; towering -rage, -passion; *acharnement* [*F.*], desperation, burst, explosion, paroxysm, storm; violence etc. 173; fire and fury; viais of wrath; gnashing of teeth, hot blood, high words.

329

furies, Erinyes (*sing.* Erinys), Eumenides; Alecto, Megaera, Tisiphone.

[cause of umbrage] affront, provocation, offense; indignity etc. (*insult*) 929; grudge; crow to -pluck, –pick, –pull; red rag, last straw, sore subject, *casus belli* [*L.*]; ill turn, outrage.

buffet, blow, slap in the face, box on the ear, rap on the knuckles.

v. **resent**; take -amiss, –ill, –to heart, –offense, –umbrage, –huff, –exception; not take it as a joke; *ne pas entendre raillerie* [*F.*]; take in bad part, take in ill part.

pout, knit the brow, frown, scowl, lower, snarl, growl, gnarl, gnash, snap; redden, color; look black, look black as thunder, look daggers; bite one's thumb; show–, grind- one's teeth; champ the bit.

be angry; fly–, fall–, get- into a -rage, –passion; fly off the handle, fly off at a tangent; let one's angry passions rise; bridle up, bristle up, froth up, fire up, flare up; foam at the mouth; open–, pour out- the vials of one's wrath.

chafe, mantle, fume, kindle, fly out, take fire; boil, –over; boil with- indignation, –rage; rage, storm, foam; hector, bully, bluster; vent one's -rage, spleen; lose one's temper; have a fling at; kick up a -row, –dust, –shindy [*all slang*]; cut up rough [*slang*], stand on one's hind legs, stamp the foot; stamp–, quiver–, swell–, foam- with rage; burst with anger; raise -Cain, –the devil, –Ned, –the mischief, –the roof [*all slang*]; breathe fire and fury; breathe revenge.

bear malice etc. (*revenge*) 919.

cause anger, raise anger; affront, offend; give -offense, –umbrage; anger; hurt the feelings; insult, discompose, fret, ruffle, roil, heckle, nettle, huff, pique; excite etc. 824; irritate, stir the blood, stir up bile; sting, –to the quick; rile, provoke, chafe, wound, incense, inflame, wrath [*obs.*], make one hot under the collar [*slang*], enrage, aggravate, add fuel to the flame, fan into a flame, widen the breach, envenom, embitter, exasperate, infuriate, kindle wrath; stick in one's craw *or* crop *or* gizzard [*colloq.*]; rankle etc. 919; hit–, rub–, sting–, strike- on the raw.

put out of -countenance, –humor; put (*or* get) one's monkey up [*colloq.*], put (*or* get) one's back up; raise one's -gorge, –dander [*colloq.*], –choler; work up into a passion, make one's blood boil, make the ears tingle, throw into a ferment, madden, drive one mad; lash into -fury, –madness; fool to the top of one's bent; set by the ears; bring a hornet's nest about one's ears.

adj. **angry**, wroth, irate, ireful, wrathful; cross etc. (*irascible*) 901; Achillean; sulky etc. 901a; bitter, virulent; acrimonious etc. (*discourteous*) etc. 895; offended etc. *v.;* waxy [*slang, Eng.*], wrought, worked up; indignant, hurt, sore; set against.

warm, burning; boiling, –over; fuming, raging, hot under the collar [*slang*]; *acharné* [*F.*]; foaming, –at the mouth; convulsed with rage; fierce, wild, rageful, furious, mad with rage, fiery, infuriate, rabid, savage; relentless etc. 919; violent etc. 173.

flushed with -anger, –rage; in a- huff, –stew [*colloq.*], –fume, –pucker [*dial. or colloq.*], –wax [*slang*], –passion, –rage, –fury, –taking [*colloq.*]; on one's high ropes [*colloq.*], up in arms; in high dudgeon.

adv. **angrily** etc. *adj.;* in the height of passion; in the heat of -passion, –the moment; in an ecstasy of rage.

int. *tantaene animis caelestibus irae!* [Virgil]; marry come up! zounds! 'sdeath!

901. Irascibility

n. **irascibility**, irascibleness, temper; crossness etc. *adj.;* susceptibility, procacity [*rare*], petulance, irritability, tartness, acerbity, acrimony, asperity, protervity [*rare*]; huff etc. (*resentment*) 900; a word and a blow; pugnacity etc. (*contentiousness*) 720; excitability etc. 825; bad–, fiery–, crooked–, irritable etc. *adj.* - temper; *genus irritabile* [*L.*], hot blood.

ill humor etc. (*sullenness*) 901a; churlishness etc. (*discourtesy*) 895.

Sir Fretful Plagiary; brabbler, Tartar; shrew, vixen, virago, termagant, dragon, scold, Xanthippe *or* Xantippe, Kate the Shrew; porcupine; spitfire; fire eater etc. (*blusterer*) 887; fury etc. (*violent person*) 173.

v. **be irascible** etc. *adj.;* have a temper etc. *n.*, have a devil in one, be possessed of the devil, have the temper of a fiend; brabble [*archaic or dial.*]; fire up etc. (*be angry*) 900.

adj. **irascible**, bad-tempered, ill-tempered, irritable, susceptible; excitable etc. 825; thin-skinned etc. (*sensitive*) 822; fretful, fidgety; on the fret.

hasty, overhasty, quick, warm, hot, testy, touchy, techy *or* tetchy; like -touch- wood, –tinder, –a barrel of gunpowder; huffy, pettish, petulant, querulous, captious, moody, moodish; fractious, peevish, *acariâtre* [*F.*].

quarrelsome, contentious, disputatious; pugnacious etc. (*bellicose*) 720; cantankerous [*colloq.*], exceptious [*rare*], cross-grained; waspish, snappish, peppery, fiery, passionate, choleric, shrewish, "sudden and quick in quarrel" [*As You Like It*]; restive etc. (*perverse*) 901 *a;* churlish etc. (*discourteous*) 895; cross, −as -crabs, −a bear with a sore head, −a cat, −a dog, −two sticks, −the tongs [*all colloq.*]; sore, sore as a crab [*colloq.*].

in a bad temper; sulky etc. 901*a;* angry etc. 900; resentful, resentive; vindictive etc. 919.

int. pish!

901a. Sullenness

n. **sullenness** etc. *adj.;* morosity, spleen; churlishness etc. (*discourtesy*) 895; irascibility etc. 901; moodiness etc. *adj.;* perversity; obstinacy etc. 606; torvity [*obs.*], thorniness, spinosity; crabbedness etc. *adj.*

ill−, bad- -temper, −humor; sulks, dudgeon, mumps, dumps [*humorous*], doleful dumps [*colloq. or humorous*], vapors [*archaic*], glooming, doldrums, fit of the sulks, bouderie, black looks, scowl; grouch [*slang*]; huff etc. (*resentment*) 900.

v. **be sullen** etc. *adj.;* sulk; frown, scowl, lower, glower, pout, have a hangdog look, glout [*rare or dial.*], grouch, grout.

adj. **sullen,** sulky; ill-tempered, ill-humored, ill-affected, ill-disposed; grouty; in -an ill, −a bad, −a shocking- -temper, −humor; out of - temper, −humor; naggy [*colloq.*], torvous [*obs.*], crusty, crabbed, sour, sore, sore as a crab; surly etc. (*discourteous*) 895.

moody, moodish, spleenish, spleeny, spleenful, splenetic, cankered; cross, cross-grained; perverse, wayward, humorsome; restive, restiff [*rare*], malignant, refractory, ungovernable, cantankerous, intractable, exceptious [*rare*], sinistrous [*obs.*], deaf to reason, unaccommodating, rusty [*dial. Eng.*], froward, cussed [*vulgar*], curst [*archaic or dial.*].

grumpy, glum, grim, grum, morose, frumpish [*obs.*]; in the sulks etc. *n.;* out of sorts; scowling, glowering, growling, grouchy; peevish etc. (*irascible*) 901; dogged etc. (*stubborn*) 606.

902. Endearment
[expression of affection]

n. **endearment,** caress, blandishment, blandiment [*obs.*]; *épanchement* [*F.*], fondling, billing and cooing, dalliance, caressing, embrace, salute, kiss, buss, smack, osculation, deosculation [*obs.*].

courtship, wooing, suit, addresses, the soft impeachment; love-making; calf love [*colloq.*];

amorous glances, ogle, side-glance, sheep's eyes, goo-goo eyes [*slang*]; serenading, caterwauling.

flirting etc. *v.;* flirtation, gallantry; coquetry, spooning [*slang*].

true lover's knot, plighted love, engagement, betrothal; marriage etc. 903; honeymoon; love tale, love token; love letter, *billet-doux* [*F.*]; posy [*archaic*]; valentine.

Strephon and Chloe, 'Arry and 'Arriet.

flirt, coquette; male flirt, philanderer; spoon [*slang*].

v. **caress,** fondle, pet, dandle; pat, −on the -head, −cheek; chuck under the chin, smile upon, coax, wheedle, cosset, coddle, cocker, make much of, cherish, foster, kill with kindness.

clasp, hug, cuddle; fold to the heart, press to the bosom; fold−, strain- in one's arms; take to one's arms; snuggle, nestle, nuzzle; embrace, kiss, buss, smack, blow a kiss; salute etc. (*courtesy*) 894.

make love, bill and coo, spoon [*slang*], toy, dally, flirt, coquet, gallivant *or* galavant; philander; pay one's -court, −addresses, −attentions- to; serenade; court, sweetheart [*colloq. or dial.*], woo; set one's cap at *or* for [*colloq.*]; be *or* look sweet upon [*colloq.*]; ogle, cast sheep's eyes upon, make goo-goo eyes at [*slang*], *faire les yeux doux* [*F.*].

fall in love with, fall over head and ears in love with; win the affections etc. (*love*) 897; die for.

propose; make−, have- an offer; pop the question [*colloq.*]; become engaged, become betrothed; plight one's -troth, −faith.

adj. **caressing** etc. *v.;* "sighing like furnace" [*As You Like It*]; love-sick, spoony *or* spooney [*slang*].

caressed etc. *v.*

903. Marriage

n. **marriage,** matrimony, wedlock, union, intermarriage, miscegenation, marriageability; *vinculum matrimonii* [*L.*], nuptial tie, nuptial knot; match; betrothment etc. (*promise*) 768.

married state, coverture, bed, cohabitation.

wedding, nuptials, Hymen, bridal, espousals, spousals; leading to the altar etc. *v.;* nuptial benediction, epithalamium; sealing.

torch−, temple- of Hymen; saffron -veil, −robe; hymeneal altar; honeymoon.

bridesmaid, maid of honor, matron of honor; usher, best man, bridesman, groomsman; bride, bridegroom.

married man, neogamist [*obs.*], Benedict, partner, spouse, mate, yokemate, husband, man, consort, baron [*old law & her.*], goodman [*archaic or dial.*], old man.

married woman, wife, wife of one's bosom, wedded wife, rib [*dial. & sportive*], helpmeet, helpmate, better half, ball and chain [*slang*], gray mare, goodwife [*archaic or dial.*], old lady or old woman [*vulgar*].

feme, −covert [*law*]; lady [*obs. or uncultivated*]; squaw; matron, matronship, matronage, matronhood.

married couple, man and wife, wedded pair, wedded couple, Darby and Joan, Philemon and Baucis.

affinity, soul-mate; spiritual wife, spiritual husband.

[kinds of marriage] monogamy, monogyny; bigamy, digamy, deuterogamy; trigamy; polygamy, polygyny, polyandry, polyandrism; Mormonism, spiritual wifery (*or* wifeism); levirate.

harem, seraglio; Mormon.

monogamist, monogynist, bigamist etc.; Turk, Bluebeard.

unlawful−, left-handed−, morganatic−, ill-assorted- marriage; *mésalliance* [*F.*], *mariage de convenance* [*F.*].

marriage broker, matchmaker, professional matchmaker, schatchen [*Yiddish*]; matrimonial -agency, −agent, −bureau.

v. **marry**, wive, take to oneself a wife; be married, be spliced [*colloq.*]; go off, go to the world [*obs.*], pair off; wed, espouse, lead to the hymeneal altar, take "for better for worse," give one's hand to, bestow one's hand upon.

marry, join, handfast [*archaic*]; couple etc. (*unite*) 43; be made one; tie the nuptial knot; give away, give in marriage; seal; affy, affiance; betroth etc. (*promise*) 768; publish−, call−, proclaim−, bid- the banns, be asked in church.

remarry, rewed; intermarry, interwed.

adj. **married** etc. *v.;* one, one bone and one flesh.

marriageable, nubile.

engaged, betrothed, affianced.

matrimonial, marital, conjugal, connubial, wedded; nuptial, hymeneal, spousal, bridal; monogamous etc.

904. Celibacy

n. **celibacy**, singleness, single blessedness; bachelorhood, bachelorship; misogamy, misogyny.

virginity, pucelage [*rare*], maidhood [*rare*], maidenhood, maidenhead.

unmarried man, bachelor, Coelebs, agamist, old bachelor; misogamist, misogynist; monk, priest, celibate, religious.

unmarried woman, spinster, maid, maiden; virgin, *feme sole* [*law*], old maid; bachelor-girl, girl-bachelor; nun, sister, vestal, vestal virgin; Diana, St. Agnes.

v. live single, enjoy single blessedness, keep bachelor hall.

adj. **unmarried**, unwedded; wifeless, spouseless; single, celibate, virgin.

905. Divorce. Widowhood

n. **divorce**, divorcement; separation, judicial separation, separate maintenance; *separatio a -mensa et thoro, −vinculo matrimonii* [*L.*].

widowhood, viduity [*rare*], viduage, viduation, weeds; viduate [*eccl.*].

widow, relict, dowager; divorcée; grass widow.

widower; grass widower; cuckold.

v. live separate; separate, divorce, disespouse [*obs.*], put away; cheat on [*slang*]; wear the horns.

906. Benevolence

n. **benevolence**, Christian charity; God's love, God's grace; good will; philanthropy etc. 910; unselfishness etc. 942.

good -nature, −feeling, −wishes; kindness, kindliness etc. *adj.;* loving-kindness, benignity, brotherly love, charity, humanity, kindly feelings, fellow-feeling, sympathy; goodness−, warmth- of heart; warm-heartedness, bonhomie *or* bonhommie, kind-heartedness; amiability, milk of human kindness, tenderness; love etc. 897; friendship etc. 888; toleration, consideration; mercy etc. (*pity*) 914.

charitableness etc. *adj.;* bounty, almsgiving; good works, beneficence, generosity; "the luxury of doing good" [Goldsmith].

acts of kindness, a good turn; good−, kind--offices, −treatment.

philanthropist, "one who loves his fellow-men" [Hunt], salt of the earth; good Samaritan, sympathizer, well-wisher, *bon enfant* [*F.*]; altruist.

v. **be benevolent** etc. *adj.;* have one's heart in the right place, bear good will; wish well, wish Godspeed; view−, regard - with an eye of favor; take in good part; take−, feel - an interest in; be−, feel- interested- in; have a fellow-feeling for, sympathize with, feel for; fraternize etc. (*be friendly*) 888.

enter into the feelings of others, practice the Golden Rule, do as you would be done by, meet halfway.

treat well; give comfort, smooth the bed of death; do good, do a good turn; benefit etc. (*good-*

ness) 648; render a service, render assistance, give one a hand, be of use; aid etc. 707.

adj. **benevolent**, kind, kindly, well-meaning, amiable, cordial; obliging, accommodating, indulgent, gracious, complacent, good-humored; tender, considerate; warm-hearted, kind-hearted, tender-hearted, large-hearted, broad-hearted, soft-hearted; merciful etc. 914.

good-natured, well-natured, spleenless [*rare*]; sympathizing, sympathetic; complaisant etc. (*courteous*) 894; well-meant, well-intentioned, kindly meant.

full of natural affection, fatherly, motherly, brotherly, sisterly; paternal, maternal, fraternal; sororal [*rare*]; friendly etc. 888.

charitable, beneficent, philanthropical, generous, humane, benignant, bounteous, bountiful.

adv. **with good will**, with a good intention [*rare*], with the best intentions; out of deepest sympathy; in a burst of generosity.

int. **godspeed!** good luck! all good luck go with you! count on me!

907. Malevolence

n. **malevolence**, bad intent, bad intention, unkindness, diskindness [*obs.*]; ill-nature, ill-will, ill-blood, bad blood; enmity etc. 889; hate etc. 898; malice, −prepense, −aforethought; malignance, malignancy, malignity; maliciousness etc. *adj.*; spite, despite, resentment etc. 900.

uncharitableness etc. *adj.*; incompassion [*rare*], incompassionateness [*rare*] etc. 914a; gall, venom, rancor, rankling, virulence, mordacity, acerbity; churlishness etc. (*discourtesy*) 895; hardness of heart, heart of stone, obduracy; evil eye, cloven -foot, −hoof.

ill turn, bad turn; affront etc. (*disrespect*) 929; bigotry, intolerance, tender mercies [*ironical*]; "unkindest cut of all" [*Julius Caesar*].

cruelty, cruelness etc. *adj.*; brutality, savagery, ferity, ferocity; outrage, atrocity, ill-usage, persecution; barbarity, inhumanity, immanity [*obs.*], truculence, ruffianism; Inquisition, torture, vivisection.

v. **be malevolent** etc. *adj.*; bear−, harbor- -spleen, −a grudge, −malice; betray−, show- the cloven foot; hurt etc. (*physical pain*) 378; annoy etc. 830; injure, harm, wrong; do harm to, do an ill office to; outrage; disoblige, malign, plant a thorn in the breast; turn and rend one.

molest, worry, harass, haunt, harry, bait, tease; throw stones at; play the devil with; hunt down, dragoon, hound; persecute, oppress, grind; maltreat, ill-treat, ill-use, misuse.

wreak one's malice on, do one's worst, break a butterfly on the wheel; dip−, imbrue- one's hands in blood; show no quarter, have no mercy etc. 914a.

adj. **malevolent**, unbenevolent, unbenign; ill-disposed, ill-intentioned, ill-natured, ill-conditioned, ill-contrived; evil-minded, evil-disposed, black-browed; malicious, malign, malignant; rancorous, spiteful, despiteful, treacherous, mordacious, caustic, bitter, envenomed, acrimonious, virulent; unamiable, uncharitable; maleficent, venomous, grinding, galling.

harsh, disobliging, unkind, unfriendly, ungracious, inofficious [*obs.*], invidious; churlish etc. (*uncourteous*) 895; surly, sullen etc. 901a.

cold-blooded, cold-hearted; black-hearted, hard-hearted, flint-hearted, marble-hearted, stony-hearted, hard of heart, cold, unnatural; ruthless etc. (*unmerciful*) 914a; relentless etc. (*revengeful*) 919.

cruel, brutal, brutish, savage; savage as a -bear, −tiger; ferine, ferocious, feral, inhuman; barbarous, fell, untamed, tameless, truculent, incendiary; blood-thirsty etc. (*murderous*) 361; atrocious; bloody-minded; fiendish, fiendlike; demoniac *or* demoniacal; diabolic *or* diabolical, devilish, infernal, hellish, Tartarean *or* Tartareous, Satanic.

adv. **malevolently** etc. *adj.*; with bad intent etc. *n.*; with the ferocity of a tiger.

908. Malediction

n. **malediction**, malison, curse, imprecation, denunciation, execration; anathema, −maranatha; maranatha [*a misinterpretation*]; ban, proscription, excommunication, commination, thunders of the Vatican, fulmination; aspersion, disparagement, vilification, vituperation.

abuse; foul−, bad−, strong−, unparliamentary-language; billingsgate, sauce [*colloq.*]; blackguardism etc. (*discourtesy*) 895; evil speaking; cursing etc. *v.*; profane swearing, oath; foul invective, ribaldry, rude reproach, scurrility, threat etc. 909; more bark than bite; invective etc. (*disapprobation*) 932.

v. **curse**, accurse, imprecate, damn; curse with bell, book, and candle; invoke−, call down- curses on the head of; call down curses upon one's devoted head; devote to destruction.

execrate, beshrew [*archaic*], scold; anathematize etc. (*censure*) 932; hold up to execration, denounce, proscribe, excommunicate, fulminate,

333

thunder against; curse up hill and down dale; threaten etc. 909.

swear, curse and swear; swear like a trooper; fall a-cursing, rap out an oath, swear at, damn.

adj. **maledictory,** imprecatory; cursing, cursed etc. *v.*

int. woe to! beshrew! [*archaic*], *ruat coelum!* [*L.*], woe betide! ill betide! confusion seize! damn! confound! blast! curse! devil take! hang! out with! a plague upon! out upon! aroynt! *honi soit!* [*F.*], *parbleu!* [*F.*].

909. Threat

n. **threat,** menace; defiance etc. 715; abuse, minacity [*rare*], minaciousness, intimidation; denunciation; fulmination; commination etc. (*curse*) 908; gathering clouds etc. (*warning*) 668.

v. **threaten,** threat, menace; snarl, growl, gnarl, mutter, bark, bully.

defy etc. 715; intimidate etc. 860; keep-, hold up-, hold out- *in terrorem* [*L.*]; shake-, double-, clinch- the fist at; thunder, talk big, fulminate, use big words, bluster, look daggers.

adj. **threatening,** menacing, minatory, minacious, comminatory, abusive; *in terrorem* [*L.*]; ominous etc. (*predicting*) 511; defiant etc. 715; under the ban.

int. *vae victis!* at your peril! do your worst! look out!

910. Philanthropy

n. **philanthropy,** altruism, humanity, humanitarianism, universal benevolence, eudaemonism *or* eudemonism, *deliciae humani generis* [*L.*].

public welfare, commonwealth [*now rare*], commonweal *or* common weal [*now rare*]; socialism, communism; Fourierism, phalansterism *or* phalansterianism, Saint Simonianism; cosmopolitanism, utilitarianism, the greatest happiness of the greatest number, social science, sociology.

public spirit, patriotism, civism, nationality, love of country, *amor patriae* [*L.*].

chivalry, knight errantry; generosity etc. 942.

philanthropist, eudaemonist *or* eudemonist, utilitarian, Benthamite, socialist, communist, cosmopolite, citizen of the world, *amicus humani generis* [*L.*]; altruist etc. 906; "little friend of all the world" [Kipling]; knight errant; patriot.

adj. **philanthropic,** altruistic, humanitarian, utilitarian, cosmopolitan; public-spirited, patriotic; humane, large-hearted etc. (*benevolent*) 906; chivalric, chivalrous; generous etc. 942.

adv. *pro bono publico* [*L.*]; *pro aris et focis* [Cicero].

911. Misanthropy

n. **misanthropy,** incivism; egotism etc. (*selfishness*) 943; moroseness etc. 901a; cynicism; want of patriotism etc. 910.

misanthrope, misanthropist, egotist, cynic, man hater, Timon, Diogenes.

woman hater, misogynist.

adj. **misanthropic,** antisocial, unpatriotic; egotistical etc. (*selfish*) 943; morose etc. 901a.

912. Benefactor

n. **benefactor,** savior, protector, good genius, tutelary saint, guardian angel, good Samaritan; friend in need, "a very present help in time of trouble" [*Bible*]; fairy godmother; *pater patriae* [*L.*]; salt of the earth etc. (*good man*) 948; auxiliary etc. 711.

913. Evildoer

[maleficent being]

n. **evildoer,** evil worker, malfeasor; wrongdoer etc. 949; mischiefmaker, marplot; oppressor, tyrant; firebrand, incendiary, fire bug, macher *or* torch [*slang*], pyromaniac, arsonist etc. 384; anarchist, nihilist, destroyer, Vandal, iconoclast, terrorist; Attila, scourge of the human race.

bane etc. 963; torpedo, bomb, U-boat.

savage, brute, ruffian, barbarian, semibarbarian, caitiff, desperado; Apache, gunman, hoodlum [*colloq.*], plug-ugly [*slang*], Redskin, tough [*colloq.*], Mohock, Mohawk [*rare*], bludgeon man, bully, rough, hooligan [*slang*], larrikin [*Austral. & Eng.*], ugly customer, dangerous classes; thief etc. 792; butcher, hangman; cutthroat etc. (*killer*) 361.

wild beast, tiger, leopard, panther, hyena, catamount, catamountain, lynx, cougar, jaguar, puma; bloodhound, hellhound, sleuth-hound; gorilla; vulture.

cockatrice, adder; snake, -in the grass; serpent, cobra, asp, rattlesnake, anaconda; boa; viper etc. (*snake*) 366; *alacrán* [*Sp. Amer.*], alligator, cayman, crocodile, mugger *or* magar [*Hind.*]; Gila monster; octopus.

[injurious insects] buffalo carpet beetle, cucumber flea beetle, elm-tree beetle, striped cucumber beetle, Japanese beetle, gypsy (*or* gipsy) moth, brown-tail moth, flat-headed apple-tree borer, peach-tree borer, round-headed apple-tree borer, squash vine borer, bedbug, harlequin cabbage bug, potato bug, buffalo bug, rose bug, squash bug, tent caterpillar; curculio, weevil, snout beetle, billbeetle, billbug, plum curculio; horn fly, white grub, San José scale, onion maggot, clover-seed midge, grain weevil, bollworm, cankerworm, cutworm, fall web-worm, tobacco worm, tomato worm, wireworm; white ant, scorpion, hornet, mosquito, locust, Colorado beetle.

hag, hellhag, beldam, Jezebel.

monster; fiend etc. (*demon*) 980; devil incarnate, demon in human shape; Frankenstein's monster; cannibal, anthropophagus, anthropophagist; bloodsucker, vampire, ogre, ghoul.

harpy, siren, vampire [*colloq.*], vamp [*slang*]; Furies, Eumenides.

914. Pity

n. **pity,** compassion, commiseration; bowels, –of compassion; sympathy, fellow-feeling, tenderness, soft-heartedness, yearning, forbearance, humanity, mercy, clemency; leniency etc. (*lenity*) 740; exorability, exorableness; charity, ruth, long-suffering.

melting mood; *argumentum ad misericordiam* [*L.*]; quarter, grace, *locus poenitentiae* [*L.*].

sympathizer; advocate, friend, partisan, patron, wellwisher, defender, champion.

v. **pity;** have–, show–, take- pity etc. *n.;* commiserate, compassionate; condole etc. 915; sympathize; feel for, be sorry for, yearn over; weep, melt, thaw, enter into the feelings of.

forbear, relent, relax, give quarter, wipe the tears, *parcere subjectis* [*L.*]; give a *coup de grâce* [*F.*], put out of one's misery; be cruel to be kind.

raise *or* **excite pity** etc. *n.;* touch, soften, melt, melt the heart; appeal, –to one's better feelings; propitiate, disarm.

supplicate etc. (*request*) 765; ask for mercy etc. *n.;* cry for quarter, beg one's life, kneel; deprecate.

adj. **pitying** etc. *v.;* pitiful, compassionate, sympathetic, touched.

merciful, clement, ruthful; humane; humanitarian etc. (*philanthropic*) 910; tender, tender-hearted; soft, soft-hearted; unhardened; lenient etc. 740; exorable, forbearing; melting etc. *v.;* weak.

int. for pity's sake! mercy! have–, cry you- mercy! God help you! poor -thing, –dear, –fellow! woe betide! *quis talia fando temperet a lachrymis!* [*Virgil*].

914a. Pitilessness

n. **pitilessness** etc. *adj.;* inclemency, inexorability, inflexibility, incompassion [*rare*], hardness of heart; want of pity etc. 914; severity etc. 739; malevolence etc. 907.

v. **be pitiless** etc. *adj.;* turn a deaf ear to; claim one's "pound of flesh" [*Merchant of Venice*]; have no–, shut the gates of- mercy etc. 914; give no quarter.

adj. **pitiless,** merciless, ruthless, bowelless; unpitying, unmerciful, inclement; grim-faced, grim-visaged; uncompassionate, incompassionate [*rare*], uncompassioned; inflexible, relentless, inexorable; unrelenting etc. 919; harsh etc. 739; cruel etc. 907.

915. Condolence

n. **condolence;** lamentation etc. 839; sympathy, consolation.

v. **condole with,** console, sympathize; express–, testify- pity; afford–, supply- consolation; lament with etc. 839; express sympathy for, feel for, send one's condolences; feel -grief, –sorrow- in common with; share one's sorrow.

916. Gratitude

n. **gratitude,** gratefulness, thankfulness; feeling of–, sense of- obligation.

acknowledgment, recognition, thanksgiving, giving thanks; thankful good will.

thanks, praise, benediction; paean; *Te Deum* etc. (*worship*) 990; grace, –before meat, –after meat; thank offering; requital.

v. **be grateful** etc. *adj.;* thank; give–, render–, return–, offer–, tender-thanks etc. *n.;* acknowledge, requite.

feel–, be–, lie- under an obligation; *savoir gré* [*F.*]; not look a gift horse in the mouth; never forget, overflow with gratitude; thank–, bless- one's stars; fall on one's knees.

adj. **grateful,** thankful, obliged, beholden, indebted to, under obligation

int. **thanks!** many thanks! gramercy! much obliged! thank you! thank Heaven! Heaven be praised!

917. Ingratitude

n. **ingratitude,** thanklessness, oblivion of benefits, unthankfulness.

"benefits forgot" [*As You Like It*]; thankless task, thankless office.

v. **be ungrateful** etc. *adj.;* feel no obligation, owe one no thanks, forget benefits; look a gift horse in the mouth.

adj. **ungrateful,** unmindful, unthankful; thankless, ingrate, wanting in gratitude, insensible of benefits.

forgotten; unacknowledged, unthanked, unrequited, unrewarded; ill-requited; ill-rewarded.

int. thank you for nothing! *"et tu Brute!"* [*Julius Caesar*].

918. Forgiveness

n. **forgiveness,** pardon, condonation, grace, remission, absolution, amnesty, oblivion; indulgence; reprieve.

conciliation; reconcilement; reconciliation etc. (*pacification*) 723; propitiation.

longanimity, placability; *amantium iroe* [*L.*]; *locus poenitentiae* [*L.*]; forbearance.

exoneration, excuse, quittance, release, indemnity; bill–, act–, covenant–, deed– of indemnity; exculpation etc. (*acquittal*) 970.

v. **forgive,** –and forget; pardon, condone, think no more of, let bygones be bygones, shake hands; forget an injury; bury the hatchet; drown all unkindness; start afresh, make a new start.

let off [*colloq.*], remit, absolve, give absolution; blot out one's –sins, –offenses, –transgressions, –debts; wipe the slate clean; reprieve; acquit etc. 970.

excuse, pass over, overlook; wink at etc. (*neglect*) 460; bear with; allow for, make allowances for; let one down easily, not be too hard upon, pocket the affront.

conciliate, propitiate, placate; beg–, ask–, implore– pardon etc. *n.;* make up a quarrel etc. (*pacify*) 723; let the wound heal.

adj. **forgiving,** placable, conciliatory.

forgiven etc. *v.;* unresented, unavenged, unrevenged.

int. have mercy! cry you mercy! forgive and forget!

919. Revenge

n. **revenge,** revengement [*rare*], vengeance; avengement, avengeance [*obs.*], sweet revenge, vendetta, death feud, blood for blood; eye for an eye, tooth for a tooth, *lex talionis* [*L.*], retaliation etc. 718; day of reckoning.

rancor, vindictiveness, immitigability; implacability; malevolence etc. 907; ruthlessness etc. 914*a*.

avenger, vindicator [*obs.*], Nemesis, Eumenides.

v. **revenge,** avenge, vindicate [*obs.*]; take revenge, have one's revenge; breathe -revenge, –vengeance; wreak one's - vengeance, –anger; cry quittance; give no quarter, take no prisoners.

have accounts to settle, have a crow to pluck, have a rod in pickle.

keep the wound green; nurse one's revenge, harbor -revenge, –vindictive feeling; bear malice; rankle, rankle in the breast.

have at a disadvantage, have on the hip, have the upper hand, have at one's mercy.

adj. **revengeful,** vengeful, vindictive, rancorous; pitiless etc. 914*a*; ruthless, rigorous, avenging, retaliative, grudgeful [*rare*].

unforgiving, unrelenting; inexorable, stonyhearted, implacable, relentless, remorseless.

rankling, immitigable; *aeternum servans sub pectore vulnus* [*L.*].

920. Jealousy

n. **jealousy,** jealousness; jaundiced eye; distrust, mistrust, misdoubt, heartburn; envy etc. 921; doubt, envious suspicion, suspicion; "green-eyed monster" [*Othello*]; yellows; Juno.

v. **be jealous** etc. *adj.;* view with jealousy, view with a jealous eye, view with a jaundiced eye; grudge, begrudge.

doubt, distrust, mistrust, suspect, misdoubt, heartburn [*obs.*]; jealouse [*obs. or Scot. & dial. Eng.*].

adj. **jealous,** jealous as a Barbary pigeon; jaundiced, yellow-eyed, envious; beside oneself with -jealousy, –envy.

921. Envy

n. **envy;** enviousness etc. *adj.;* rivalry; *jalousie de métier* [*F.*]; ill-will, spite; jealousy etc. 920.

v. **envy,** covet, grudge, begrudge, burst with envy, break the tenth commandment.

adj. **envious,** individious, covetous, grudging, begrudged; belittling; *alieni appetens* [*L.*].

Section 4. Moral

922. Right

n. **right;** what ought to be, what should be; what is fit etc. *adj.;* fitness etc. *adj.;* *summum jus* [*L.*].

justice, equity; equitableness etc. *adj.;* propriety; fair play, square deal [*colloq.*], impartiality, measure for measure, give and take, *lex talionis* [*L.*].

scales of justice, evenhanded justice, karma; *suum cuique* [*L.*]; clear stage–, fair field- and no favor; retributive justice, nemesis.

Astraea, Nemesis, Themis, Rhadamanthus.

morals etc. (*duty*) 926; law etc. 963; honor etc. (*probity*) 939; virtue etc. 944.

v. **be right** etc. *adj.;* stand to reason.

see justice done, see one righted, see fair play; do justice to; recompense etc. (*reward*) 973; hold the scales even, give and take; serve one right, put the saddle on the right horse; give every one his due, give the devil his due; *audire alteram partem* [*L.*].

deserve etc. (*be entitled to*) 924.

adj. **right,** good; just, reasonable; fit etc. 924; equal, equable, equitable; evenhanded, fair, square, fair and square.

legitimate, justifiable, rightful; as it should be, as it ought to be; lawful etc. (*permitted*) 760, (*legal*) 963.

deserved etc. 924.

adv. rightly etc. *adj.; à–, au- bon droit* [*F.*], in justice, in equity, in reason.

without -distinction of, –regard to, –respect to- persons; upon even terms.

int. all right!

923. Wrong

n. wrong; what ought not to be, what should not be *malum in se* [*L.*]; unreasonableness grievance; shame.

injustice; unfairness etc. *adj.;* iniquity, foul play, partiality, leaning, favor, favoritism, nepotism; partisanship, party spirit; undueness etc. 925; unlawfulness etc. 964.

robbing Peter to pay Paul etc. *v.;* the wolf and the lamb; vice etc. 945.

v. be wrong etc. *adj.;* cry to heaven for vengeance.

do wrong etc. *n.;* be inequitable etc. *adj.;* favor, lean towards; encroach; impose upon; reap where one has not sown; give an inch and take an ell; rob Peter to pay Paul.

adj. wrong, wrongful; bad, too bad; unjust, unfair, inequitable, unequitable, unequal, partial, one-sided; injurious.

unjustifiable, unreasonable, unallowable, un-warrantable, objectionable, improper, unfit; unjustified etc. 925; illegal etc. 964; iniquitous; immoral etc. 945.

in the wrong, –box; in bad [*slang*], in wrong [*slang*].

adv. wrongly etc. *adj.*

int. this is too bad! it will not do!

924. Dueness

n. dueness, right, droit [*law*], due, privilege, pre-rogative, prescription, title, claim, pretension, demand, birthright.

immunity, license, liberty, franchise; vested -interest, –right.

sanction, authority, warranty [*law*], charter, lic-itness, warrant etc. (*permission*) 760; constitu-tion etc. (*law*) 963; tenure; bond etc. (*security*) 771.

deserts, merits, dues; all that is coming to one [*colloq.*].

claimant, appellant; plaintiff etc. 938.

v. be due to etc. *adj.;* be the due of etc. *n.;* have -right, –title, –claim- to; be entitled to; have a claim upon; belong to etc. (*property*) 780.

deserve, merit, be worthy of, richly deserve.

demand, claim; call upon one for, come upon one for, appeal to for; revendicate [*rare*], revindi-cate, reclaim; exact; insist -on, –upon; chal-lenge; take one's stand, make a point of, require, lay claim to; assert, assume, arrogate.

make good; substantiate; vindicate a -claim, –right; fit–, qualify- for; make out a case.

use a right, assert, enforce, put in force, lay under contribution.

entitle; give *or* confer a right; authorize etc. 760; sanction, sanctify, legalize, ordain, prescribe, allot.

give every one his due etc. 922; pay one's dues; have one's -due, –rights; stand upon one's rights.

adj. having a right to etc. *v.;* entitled to; claiming; deserving, meriting, worthy of.

privileged, allowed, sanctioned, warranted, au-thorized; ordained, prescribed, constitutional, chartered, enfranchised.

prescriptive, presumptive, absolute, indefeasible, unalienable, inalienable, imprescriptible, invio-lable, unimpeachable, unchallenged; sac-rosanct.

due to, merited, deserved, condign [*archaic, except of punishment*], richly deserved.

right, fit, fitting, correct, proper, meet, befitting, becoming, seemly; decorous; creditable, up to the mark, right as a trivet; just–, quite- the thing; *selon les règles* [*F.*]; square, unexceptiona-ble, equitable etc. 922; due, *en règle* [*F.*].

lawful, licit, legitimate, legal; legalized etc. (*law*) 963; allowable etc. (*permitted*) 760.

adv. duly; as is -right, –fitting, –just; unexceptiona-bly; *ex officio* [*L.*], *de jure* [*L.*]; by right, by divine right; *jure divino* [*L.*], *Dei gratia* [*L.*], in the name of.

925. Undueness
[absence of right]

n. undueness etc. *adj.; malum prohibitum* [*L.*]; im-propriety; illegality etc. 964.

falseness etc. *adj.;* emptiness–, invalidity- of title; illegitimacy.

loss of right, disfranchisement, forfeiture.

assumption, usurpation, tort [*law*], violation, breach, encroachment, presumption, seizure; stretch, exaction, imposition, lion's share.

usurper, pretender, impostor.

v. be undue etc. *adj.;* not be due etc. 924.

infringe, encroach, trench on, exact; arrogate, –to oneself; give an inch and take an ell; stretch–, strain- a point; usurp, violate, do vio-lence to; get under false pretenses, sail under false colors.

337

disentitle, disfranchise, disqualify; invalidate.

relax etc. (be lax) 738; misbehave etc. (vice) 945; misbecome.

adj. **undue**; unlawful etc. (*illegal*) 964; unconstitutional, illicit, unauthorized, unwarranted, unallowed, unsanctioned, unjustified; disentitled, unentitled; disqualified, unqualified; unprivileged, unchartered.

undeserved, unmerited, unearned; unfulfilled. forfeited, disfranchised.

illegitimate, bastard, spurious, false; usurped, tortious [*law*].

improper; unmeet, unfit, unbefitting, unseemly, unbecoming, misbecoming, seemless [*obs.*]; *contra bonos mores* [*L.*]; not the thing, out of the question, not to be thought of; preposterous, pretentious, would-be.

926. Duty

n. **duty**, what ought to be done, moral obligation, accountableness, liability, onus, responsibility; bounden—, imperative- duty; call, -of duty; accountability.

allegiance, fealty, tie; engagement etc. (*promise*) 768; part; function, calling etc. (*business*) 625.

observance, fulfillment, discharge, performance, acquittal, satisfaction, redemption; good behavior.

morality, morals, decalogue; case of conscience; conscientiousness etc. (*probity*) 939; conscience, inward monitor, still small voice within, sense of duty, tender conscience; the hell within [*P.L.*].

propriety, fitness; dueness etc. 924; seemliness, amenableness, amenability, decorum, *to prepon* [*Gr.*]; the thing, the proper thing; the -right, -proper- thing to do.

[science of morals] ethics, ethology [*obs. in this sense*]; deontology, aretology [*obs.*]; moral–, ethical- philosophy; casuistry, polity.

v. **be the duty of**, be incumbent on etc. *adj.;* be responsible etc. *adj.;* behoove, become, befit, beseem; belong to, pertain to; fall to one's lot; devolve on; lie upon, lie on one's head, lie at one's door; rest with, rest on the shoulders of.

take upon oneself etc. (*promise*) 768; be–, become- -bound to, -sponsor for; incur a responsibility etc. *n.;* be–, stand–, lie- under an obligation; stand responsible for; have to answer for; owe it to oneself.

enter upon–, perform–, observe–, fulfill–, discharge–, adhere to–, acquit oneself of–, satisfy- -a duty, –an obligation; act one's part, redeem one's pledge, do justice to, be at one's

post; do duty; do one's duty etc. (*be virtuous*) 944.

be on one's good behavior, mind one's P's and Q's; walk the straight path.

impose a duty etc. *n.;* enjoin, require, exact; bind, –over; saddle with, prescribe, assign, call upon, look to, oblige.

adj. **obligatory**, binding; imperative, peremptory; stringent etc. (*severe*) 739; behooving etc. *v.;* incumbent on, chargeable on; under obligation; obliged by, bound by, tied by; saddled with.

due to, beholden to, bound to, indebted to; tied down; compromised etc. (*promised*) 768; in duty bound.

amenable, liable, accountable, responsible, answerable.

right, meet etc. (*due*) 924; moral, ethical, casuistical, conscientious, ethological.

adv. with a safe conscience, as in duty bound on good behavior, on one's own responsibility, at one's own risk, *suo periculo* [*L.*]; *in foro conscientiae* [*L.*]; *quamdiu se bene gesserit* [*L.*]; at one's post.

927. Dereliction of Duty

n. **dereliction of duty**; fault etc. (*guilt*) 947; sin etc. (*vice*) 945; nonobservance, nonperformance, noncoöperation; indolence, neglect, relaxation, infraction, violation, transgression, failure, evasion; eyeservice; dead letter.

slacker, loafer, time-killer; eyeserver, eyeservant; striker; noncoöperator.

v. **violate**; break, break through; infringe; set aside, set at naught; encroach upon, trench upon; trample -on, –under foot; slight, get by [*slang*], neglect, evade, renounce, forswear, repudiate; wash one's hands of; escape. transgress, fail.

call to account etc. (*disapprobation*) 932.

927a. Exemption

n. **exemption**, freedom, irresponsibility, immunity, liberty, license, release, quitclaim [*law*]; exoneration, excuse, dispensation, absolution, franchise [*obs.*], renunciation, discharge; exculpation etc. 970.

v. **exempt**, release, acquit, discharge, quitclaim [*law*], remise, remit; free, set at liberty, let off [*colloq.*], pass over, spare, excuse, dispense with, give dispensation, license; stretch a point; absolve etc. (*forgive*) 918; exonerate etc. (*exculpate*) 970; save the necessity.

be exempt etc. *adj.*

adj. **exempt**, free, immune, at liberty, scot-free; released etc. *v.;* unbound, unencumbered; irresponsible, not responsible, unaccountable, not answerable; excusable.

928. Respect

n. **respect**, regard, consideration; courtesy etc. 894; attention, deference, reverence, honor, esteem, estimation, veneration, admiration; approbation etc. 931.

homage, fealty, obeisance, genuflection, kneeling, prostration; obsequiousness etc. 886; salaam, kotow *or* kowtow [*Chinese*], bow, presenting arms, salute.

respects, regards, duty, *devoirs* [*F.*], *égards* [*F.*].

devotion etc. (*piety*) 987.

v. **respect**, regard; revere, reverence; hold in reverence, honor, venerate, hallow; esteem etc. (*approve of*) 931; think much of; entertain–, bear– respect for; look up to, defer to; have–, hold– a high opinion of; pay attention to, pay respect to etc. *n.;* do *or* render honor to; do the honors, hail; show courtesy etc. 894; salute, present arms.

do *or* pay homage to; pay tribute to, kneel to, bow to, bend the knee to; fall down before, prostrate oneself, kiss the hem of one's garment; worship etc. 990.

keep one's distance, make room, observe due decorum, stand on ceremony.

command respect, inspire respect; awe, impose, overawe, dazzle.

adj. **respecting** etc. *v.;* respectful, deferential, decorous, reverential, obsequious, ceremonious, bareheaded, cap in hand, on one's knees; prostrate etc. (*servile*) 886.

respected etc. *v.;* in high -esteem, –estimation; time-honored, venerable, *emeritus* [*L.*].

adv. **in deference to**; with all respect, with due respect, with the highest respect; with submission.

excusing the liberty; saving your -grace, –presence; *salva sit reverentia* [*L.*]; *pace tanti nominis* [*L.*].

int. hail! all hail! *hoch!* [*Ger.*]; *esto perpetua!* [*L.*], may your shadow never be less!

929. Disrespect

n. **disrespect**, disesteem, disestimation; disfavor, disrepute, want of esteem, low estimation, disparagement etc. (*dispraise*) 932, (*detraction*) 934; irreverence; slight, neglect; superciliousness etc. (*contempt*) 930.

indignity, vilipendency [*obs.*], contumely, affront, dishonor, insult, outrage, discourtesy etc. 895; practical joking; scurrility, scoffing; sibilation, hiss, hissing, hoot, irrision [*rare*], derision; mockery; irony etc. (*ridicule*) 856; sarcasm.

gibe *or* jibe, flout, jeer, scoff, gleek [*obs.*], fleer, taunt, sneer, quip, fling, twit, wipe [*dial. or slang*], slap in the face.

v. **treat with disrespect** etc. *n.;* hold in disrespect etc. (*despise*) 930; misprize, disregard, slight, undervalue, humiliate, depreciate, trifle with, set at naught, pass by, push aside, overlook, turn one's back upon, laugh in one's sleeve; be disrespectful etc. *adj.;* be discourteous etc. 895; set down, browbeat.

dishonor, desecrate; insult, affront, outrage.

speak slightingly of; disparage etc. (*dispraise*) 932; vilipend, call names; throw–, fling- dirt; throw mud at; make ride the rail, drag through the mud, point at, indulge in personalities; make mouths [*archaic*], make faces; bite the thumb; take–, pluck- by the beard; toss in a blanket, tar and feather.

deride, have *or* hold in derision; scoff, barrack [*dial. Eng. & Austral.*], sneer, laugh at, snigger, ridicule, gibe *or* jibe, mock, jeer, taunt, twit, niggle, gleek [*obs.*], gird, flout, fleer; roast [*colloq.*], guy [*colloq.*], rag [*dial. Eng. & college slang*] smoke [*old slang*]; turn into ridicule; burlesque etc. 856; laugh to scorn etc. (*contempt*) 930; lead one a dance, have a fling at, scout, hiss, hoot, mob.

fool; make game of, make a fool of, make an April fool of; play a practical joke.

adj. **disrespectful**; aweless, irreverent; disparaging etc. 934; insulting etc. *v.;* supercilious etc. (*scornful*) 930; rude, derisive, sarcastic; scurrile, scurrilous, contumelious, contemptuous, insolent, disdainful.

unrespected, unworshiped, unenvied, unsaluted; unregarded, disregarded.

adv. **disrespectfully** etc. *adj.*

930. Contempt

n. **contempt**, disdain, scorn, sovereign contempt; despisal [*rare*], despiciency [*obs.*], despisement [*rare*]; vilipendency [*obs.*], contumely; slight, sneer, spurn, byword; despect [*rare*].

contemptuousness etc. *adj.;* scornful eye; smile of contempt; derision etc. (*disrespect*) 929.

[state of being despised] despisedness.

v. **despise**, contemn, scorn, disdain, feel contempt for, view with a scornful eye; disregard, slight, not mind; pass by etc. (*neglect*) 460; look down upon; hold - cheap, –in contempt, –in disrespect; think nothing of, think small beer of [*colloq.*]; make light of; underestimate etc. 483; esteem slightly, esteem of small or no account; take no account of, care nothing for; set no store by; not care a straw etc. (*unimportance*) 643; set at naught, laugh in one's sleeve, snap one's fingers at, shrug one's shoulders, turn up one's nose at, pooh-pooh, "damn with faint praise" [*Pope*].

sneeze at, whistle at, sneer at; curl up one's lip, toss the head, *traiter de haut en bas* [*F.*]; laugh at etc. (*be disrespectful*) 929; point the finger of–, hold up to–, laugh to- scorn; scout, hoot, flout, hiss, scoff at.

spurn, turn one's back upon, turn a cold shoulder upon; tread–, trample- -upon, –under foot; kick; fling to the winds etc. (*repudiate*) 610; send away with a flea in the ear [*colloq.*].

adj. contemptuous, disdainful, scornful, withering, contumelious, supercilious, cynical, haughty, cavalier; derisive; with the nose in air, *de haut en bas* [*F.*].

contemptible, despicable; pitiable; pitiful etc. (*unimportant*) 643; despised etc. *v.;* downtrodden; unenvied.

adv. contemptuously etc. *adj.*

int. a fig for etc. (*unimportant*) 643; bah! pooh! pshaw! never mind! away with! hang it! fiddledeedee!

931. Approbation

n. approbation, approval, approvement [*obs.*], bepraisement, sanction, advocacy; nod of approbation; esteem, estimation, good opinion, golden opinions, admiration; love etc. 897; appreciation, regard, account, popularity, *kudos* [*Gr.*], credit; repute etc. 873.

commendation, praise, laud, laudation; good word; meed–, tribute- of praise; encomium, eulogy, eulogium, *éloge* [*F.*], panegyric, blurb [*slang*]; homage, hero worship; benediction, blessing, benison.

applause, plaudit, clap; clapping, –of hands; acclaim, acclamation; cheer; paean, hosanna; shout–, peal–, chorus–, thunders- of -applause etc.; prytaneum.

winner, prize winner, best seller, corker [*slang*], peach [*slang*], oner [*slang*], the real thing [*colloq.*], the goods [*slang*].

v. approve, approbate, think good of, think much of, think well of, think highly of; esteem, value, prize; set great store by.

honor, hold in esteem, look up to, admire; like etc. 897; be in favor of, wish Godspeed; hail, hail with satisfaction, do justice to, appreciate.

stand up for, stick up for [*colloq.*], uphold, hold up, countenance, sanction; clap–, pat- on the back; keep in countenance, indorse *or* endorse; give credit, recommend; mark with a white -mark, –stone.

commend, belaud, praise, laud, compliment, pay a tribute, bepraise; clap, –the hands; applaud, cheer, acclaim, acclamate [*rare*], encore; panegyrize, eulogize, boost [*colloq.*], root for [*slang*], cry up, *prôner* [*F.*], puff; extol, –to the skies; magnify, glorify, exalt, swell, make much of; flatter etc. 933; bless, give a blessing to; have–, say- a good word for; speak - well, –highly, –in high terms- of; sing–, sound–, chant–, resound- the praises of; sing praises to; cheer–, applaud- to the -echo, –very echo.

redound to the -honor, –praise, –credit- of; do credit to; deserve -praise etc. *n.;* recommend itself; pass muster.

be praised etc.; receive honorable mention; be in favor with, be in high favor with; ring with the praises of, win golden opinions, gain credit, find favor with, stand well in the opinion of; *laudari a laudato viro* [*L.*].

adj. approving etc. *v.;* in favor of; lost in admiration; commendatory, complimentary, benedictory, laudatory, panegyrical, eulogistic, encomiastic, acclamatory, lavish of praise, uncritical.

approved, praised etc. *v.;* uncensured, unimpeached; popular, in good odor; in high esteem etc. (*respected*) 928; in favor, in high favor.

praiseworthy, commendable, of estimation; deserving–, worthy of- praise etc. *n.;* good etc. 648; meritorious, estimable, creditable, unimpeachable; beyond all praise.

adv. commendably, with credit, to admiration; well etc. 618; with three times three.

int. hear hear! good for you! do it again! bully for you! [*slang*], well done! fine! bravo! *bravissimo!* [*It.*], *euge!* [*Gr. & L.*], *macte virtute!* [*L.*], so far so good! that's right! quite right! one cheer more! may your shadow never be less! *esto perpetua!* [*L.*], long life to! *viva!* [*It.*], *evviva!* [*It.*], Godspeed! *valete et plaudite!* [*L.*], *encore!* [*F.*], *bis!* [*L. & F.*].

932. Disapprobation

n. disapprobation, disapproval, improbation [*obs.*], disesteem, displacency [*rare*]; odium; dislike etc. 867; black list, blackball, ostracism, boycott; index expurgatorius.

disparagement, depreciation, disvaluation, dispraise, discommendation; detraction etc. 934; denunciation; condemnation etc. 971; animadversion, reflection, stricture, objection, exception, criticism; blame, censure, obloquy; sardonic -grin, –laugh; sarcasm, satire, insinuation, innuendo; bad–, poor–, left-handed-compliment.

sneer etc. (*contempt*) 930; taunt etc. (*disrespect*) 929; cavil, carping, censoriousness; hypercriticism etc. (*fastidiousness*) 868.

reprehension, remonstrance, expostulation, reproof, reprobation, admonition, increpation [*archaic*], reproach; rebuke, reprimand, castigation, jobation [*colloq.*], lecture, curtain lecture, blowup [*colloq.*]; blowing up, trimming, wigging, dressing, dressing down [*all colloq.*]; rating, scolding, correction, set down, rap on the knuckles, *coup de bec* [*F.*], rebuff; slap, slap on the face; home thrust, hit; frown, scowl, black look.

diatribe, jeremiad *or* jeremiade, tirade, philippic.

chiding, upbraiding etc. *v.;* exprobration [*rare*], personal remarks, abuse, vituperation, invective, objurgation, contumely; hard–, cutting–, bitter- words; evil-speaking; bad language etc. 908; personality.

clamor, outcry, hue and cry; hiss, hissing, sibilation, catcall; execration etc. 908.

v. **disapprove**; dislike etc. 867; lament etc. 839; object to, take exception to; be scandalized at, think ill of; view with -disfavor, –dark eyes, –jaundiced eyes; *nil admirari* [*L.*], disvalue, improbate [*obs.*].

frown upon, look grave; bend–, knit- the brows; shake the head at, shrug the shoulders; turn up the nose etc. (*contempt*) 930; look askance, look black upon; look with an evil eye; make a wry face at, make a face at, make a mouth at [*archaic*], set one's face against.

blame; lay–, cast- blame upon; censure, *fronder* [*F.*], reproach, pass censure on, reprobate, impugn, impeach; disbar, unfrock.

accuse etc. 938; impeach, denounce; hold up to -reprobation, –execration; expose, brand, gibbet, stigmatize; show up, pull up [*both colloq.*]; take up; cry "shame" upon; be outspoken; raise a hue and cry against.

reprehend, chide, admonish; berate, betongue; bring–, call- -to account, –over the coals [*colloq.*], –to order; take to task, haul over the coals [*colloq.*], reprove, lecture, bring to book; read a -lesson, –lecture- to; rebuke, correct; reprimand, chastise, castigate, lash, trounce; trim, blow up, give it to, give one fits, give it to one, lay out [*all six colloq.*]; *laver la tête* [*F.*], overhaul.

remonstrate, expostulate, recriminate.

execrate etc. 908; exprobate [*rare*], speak daggers, vituperate; abuse, –like a pickpocket; tonguelash [*colloq.*], scold, rate, objurgate, upbraid, fall foul of; jaw [*low*]; rail, –at, –in good set terms; bark at, yelp at, anathematize, call names; call by -hard, –ugly- names; avile [*obs.*], revile, vilify, vilipend, bespatter; clapperclaw [*archaic*]; rave–, thunder–, fulminate- against; load with reproaches.

decry, cry down, run down, frown down; exclaim–, protest–, inveigh–, declaim–, cry out–, raise one's voice- against; clamor, hiss, hoot, –catcall, mob; backbite; ostracize, blacklist, boycott, blackball; draw up–, sign- a round robin.

take down, set down; snub, snap one up, give a rap on the knuckles; throw a stone -at, –in one's garden; have a fling at, have a snap at; have words with, pluck a crow with; give one a wipe [*dial. or slang*]; give one a lick with the rough side of the tongue [*colloq.*].

animadvert upon, reflect upon; glance at; cast -reflection, –reproach - a slur- upon; insinuate, "damn with faint praise" [Pope]; "hint a fault and hesitate dislike" [Pope]; not to be able to say much for.

disparage, depreciate, knock [*colloq.*], dispraise, discommend [*rare*], deprecate, speak ill of, not speak well of; condemn etc. (*find guilty*) 971; scoff at, point at; twit, taunt etc. (*disrespect*) 929; sneer at etc. (*despise*) 230; satirize, lampoon; defame etc. (*detract*) 934; depreciate, find fault with, criticize, cut up; pull–, pick- to pieces; take exception; cavil; peck at, nibble at, carp at; be censorious etc. *adj.;* pick -holes, –a hole, –a hole in one's coat; poke holes in; make a fuss about.

incur blame, excite disapprobation, scandalize, shock, revolt; get a bad name, forfeit one's good opinion, be under a cloud, come under the ferule, bring a hornet's nest about one's ears.

take blame, stand corrected; have to answer for.

adj. **disapproving** etc. *v.;* disparaging, condemnatory, damnatory, denunciatory, reproachful, abusive, objurgatory, clamorous, vituperative; defamatory etc. 934.

satirical, sarcastic, sardonic, cynical, dry, sharp, cutting, biting, severe, withering, trenchant, hard upon; censorious, critical, captious, carping, hypercritical; scandalized; fastidious etc. 868; sparing of–, grudging -praise.

disapproved, chid etc. *v.;* in bad odor, blown upon, unapproved; unblest; at a discount, exploded; weighed in the balance and found wanting.

unlamented, unbewailed, unpitied.

blameworthy, reprehensible etc. (*guilt*) 947; to–, worthy of– blame; answerable, uncommendable, exceptionable, not to be thought of; bad etc. 649; vicious etc. 945.

adv. **reproachfully** etc. *adj.;* with a wry face.

int. it is too bad! it won't do! it will never do! it isn't done! marry come up! [*archaic or dial.*], Oh! come! 'sdeath! [*archaic*].

forbid it Heaven! God forbid! Heaven forbid! out upon it! fie upon it! away with! tut! *O tempora! O mores!* [*L.*]; shame! fie, –for shame! out on you!

tell it not in Gath!

933. Flattery

n. **flattery**, adulation, gloze [*rare*]; blandishment [*rare*], blandiloquence; cajolery; fawning, wheedling etc. *v.;* captation, coquetry, obsequiousness, sycophancy, flunkeyism, toadyism, toadeating, tufthunting; snobbishness.

incense, honeyed words, flummery, buncombe *or* bunkum [*cant or slang*]; blarney, butter, soft soap, soft sawder [*all colloq.*]; rose water.

voice of the charmer, mouth honor; lip homage; euphemism; unctuousness etc. *adj.*

v. **flatter**, praise to the skies, puff; wheedle, cajole, glaver [*obs. or dial.*], coax; fawn, –upon; humor, gloze [*now rare*], soothe, pet, coquet, slaver, butter [*colloq.*], jolly [*colloq.*]; bespatter, beslubber, beplaster, beslaver; lay it on thick, overpraise; cog [*obs.*], collogue [*obs. in this sense*]; truckle to, pander *or* pandar to, pay court to; court; creep into the good graces of, curry favor with, hang on the sleeve of; fool to the top of one's bent; lick the dust.

lay the flattering unction to one's soul, gild the pill, make things pleasant.

overestimate etc. 482; exaggerate etc. 549.

adj. **flattering** etc. *v.;* adulatory; mealy-mouthed, honey-mouthed, honeyed, smooth, smooth-tongued; soapy [*slang*], oily, unctuous, blandiloquous, specious; fine–, fair– spoken; plausible, servile, sycophantic, fulsome; courtierly, courtierlike.

adv. ad captandum.

934. Detraction

n. **detraction**, disparagement, depreciation, vilification, obloquy, scurrility, scandal, defamation, aspersion, traducement [*rare*], slander, calumny, obtrectation [*obs.*], evil-speaking, backbiting, *scandalum magnatum* [*L.*].

sarcasm, cynicism; criticism (*disapprobation*) 932; invective etc. 932; envenomed tongue; *spretae injuria formae* [*L.*].

personality, libel, lampoon, skit [*Scot. & dial.*], squib, pasquil, pasquinade; *chronique scandaleuse* [*F.*], roorback.

detractor etc. 936.

v. **detract**, derogate, decry, depreciate, disparage; run down, cry down; back-cap; belittle; pessimize [*obs.*]; sneer at etc. (*contemn*) 930; criticize, pull to pieces, pick a hole in one's coat, asperse, cast aspersions, blow upon, bespatter, blacken, vilify, vilipend, avile [*obs.*]; give a dog a bad name, brand, malign; backbite, libel, lampoon, traduce, slander, defame, caluminate, bear false witness against; speak ill of behind one's back.

muckrake; fling dirt etc. (*disrespect*) 929; anathematize etc. 932; dip the pen in gall, view in a bad light.

adj. **detracting** etc. *v.;* defamatory, traducent [*rare*], detractory, derogatory, disparaging, libelous; scurrile, scurrilous, abusive; foul-spoken, foul-tongued, foul-mouthed; slanderous, calumnious, calumniatory; sarcastic, sardonic, satirical, cynical.

935. Flatterer

n. **flatterer**, adulator, eulogist, euphemist; optimist, encomiast, laudator, booster [*colloq.*], whitewasher.

today, toadeater, sycophant, courtier, flattercap [*obs. or dial. Eng.*], pickthank [*archaic or dial.*], Damocles, Sir Pertinax MacSycophant; *flatteur* [*F.*], *prôneur* [*F.*]; puffer, claquer [*F.*], claquer; tout, touter [*both colloq.*], clawback [*obs. or dial. Eng.*], slaverer; doer of dirty work; parasite, hanger-on etc. (*servility*) 886.

adj. flattering etc. 933.

936. Detractor

n. **detractor**, reprover; censor, censurer; cynic, critic, caviler, carper, word-catcher, *frondeur* [*F.*], barracker [*dial. Eng. & Austral.*].

defamer, knocker [*colloq.*], backbiter, slanderer, Sir Benjamin Backbite, lampooner, satirist, traducer, libeler, caluminator, dearest foe, Thersites; Zoilus; good-natured friend [*satirical*]; reviler, vituperator, castigator; shrew etc. 901; muckraker.

disapprover, *laudator temporis acti* [Horace].

adj. black-mouthed, abusive etc. 934.

937. Vindication

n. **vindication**, justification, warrant; exoneration, exculpation, disculpation; acquittal etc. 970; whitewashing.

extenuation, palliation, palliative, softening, mitigation.

plea etc. 617; apology, gloss, varnish; salvo [*rare*], excuse, extenuating circumstances; allowance, –to be made; *locus poenitentiae* [*L.*]; reply, defense *or* defence; recrimination etc. 938.

apologist, vindicator, justifier; defendant etc. 938.

true bill, justifiable charge.

v. **justify**, warrant; be an excuse for etc. *n.;* lend a color, furnish a handle; vindicate, exculpate, disculpate [*rare*]; acquit etc. 970; clear, set right, exonerate, whitewash; clear the skirts of.

extenuate, palliate, excuse, soften, apologize, varnish, slur, gloze; put a -gloss, –good face- upon; mince; gloss over, bolster up, help a lame dog over a stile.

advocate, defend, plead one's cause; stand up for, stick up for [*colloq.*], speak up for; contend for, speak for; bear out, keep in countenance, support; plead etc. 617; say in defense; plead ignorance; confess and avoid, propugn [*obs.*], put in a good word for.

take the will for the deed, make allowance for, do justice to; give one his due, give the Devil his due.

make good; prove the truth of, prove one's case; be justified by the event.

adj. **vindicative**, vindicatory, vindicated, vindicating etc. *v.;* palliative; exculpatory, disculpatory, apologetic.

excusable, defensible, pardonable; venial, veniable [*obs.*]; specious, plausible, justifiable.

938. Accusation

n. **accusation**, charge, imputation, slur, inculpation, exprobration [*rare*], delation; crimination, incrimination, accrimination [*obs.*], recrimination; *tu quoque* argument; invective etc. 932.

denunciation, denouncement [*archaic*]; libel, challenge, citation, arraignment, impeachment, appeachment [*obs.*], indictment, bill of indictment, true bill; lawsuit etc. 969; condemnation etc. 971.

gravamen of a charge, head and front of one's offending, *argumentum ad hominem* [*L.*]; scandal etc. (*detraction*) 934; *scandalum magnatum* [*L.*].

accuser, prosecutor, plaintiff, complainant, libelant, delator, informant, informer.

accused, defendant, prisoner, respondent, corespondent; litigant; panel.

v. **accuse**, charge, tax, impute, twit, taunt with, reproach; brand with reproach; stigmatize, slur; cast a stone at, cast a slur on; criminate, incriminate, inculpate, implicate; call to account etc. (*censure*) 932; take to -blame, –task; put in the black book.

inform against, indict, denounce, arraign; impeach, appeach [*obs.*]; have up, show up [*colloq.*], pull up [*colloq.*]; challenge, cite, lodge a complaint; prosecute, bring an action against etc. 969; blow upon [*colloq.*], squeal [*slang*].

charge with, saddle with; lay to one's -door, –charge; lay the blame on, bring home to; cast-, throw- in one's teeth; cast the first stone at.

have–, keep- a rod in pickle for; have a crow to pluck with.

trump up a charge.

adj. **accusing** etc. *v.;* accusatory, accusative, imputative, denunciatory, recriminatory, criminatory.

accused etc. *v.;* suspected; under -suspicion, –a cloud, –surveillance.

in custody, in detention, in the lockup, in the watch-house, in the jug [*slang*], in stir [*slang*], in the house of detention.

accusable, imputable, indefensible, inexcusable, unpardonable, unjustifiable; vicious etc. 845.

int. look at home! *tu quoque* [*L.*] etc. (*retaliation*) 718.

939. Probity

n. **probity**, integrity, rectitude; uprightness etc. *adj.;* honesty, faith; honor; *bonne foi* [*F.*], good faith, *bona fides* [*L.*]; purity, grace; clean hands.

constancy; faithfulness etc. *adj.;* fidelity, loyalty, incorruption [*archaic*], incorruptibility; trustworthiness etc. *adj.;* truth, candor, singleness of heart; veracity etc. 543; tender conscience etc. (*sense of duty*) 926.

fairness etc. *adj.;* fair play, justice, equity, impartiality, principle.

court of honor, a fair field and no favor; *argumentum ad verecundiam* [*L.*].

punctiliousness, punctilio, delicacy, nicety, scrupulosity, scrupulousness etc. *adj.;* scruple; point, –of honor; punctuality [*rare in this sense*].

dignity etc. (*repute*) 873; respectability, respectableness etc. *adj.*

man of honor, man of his word, gentleman, *gentilhomme* [*F.*], *fidus Achates* [*L.*], *preux* *chevalier* [*F.*], *galantuomo* [*It.*]; true-penny, trump [*slang*], brick [*slang or colloq.*], true Briton.

v. **be honorable** etc. *adj.;* deal -honorably, −squarely, −impartially, −fairly; speak the truth etc. (*veracity*) 543; draw a straight furrow; tell the truth and shame the Devil, *vitam impendere vero* [*L.*]; show a proper spirit, make a point of; do one's duty etc. (*virtue*) 944; play the game [*colloq.*].

redeem one's pledge etc. 926; keep−, be as good as- one's -promise, −word; keep faith with, not fail.

give and take, *audire alteram partem* [*L.*], give the Devil his due, put the saddle on the right horse.

redound to one's honor.

adj. **upright**; honest, −as daylight; veracious etc. 543; virtuous etc. 944; noble, honorable, reputable, respectable; fair, right, just, equitable, impartial, evenhanded, square; fair−, open- and aboveboard; white [*slang*].

inviolable, inviolate, unviolated, unbroken, unbetrayed; unbought, unbribed.

constant, −as the northern star; faithful, loyal, staunch; true, −blue, −to one's colors, −to the core, −as the needle to the pole; "marble-constant" [*Antony and Cleopatra*]; true-hearted, trusty, trustworthy; as good as one's word, to be depended on, incorruptible, honest as the day.

manly, straightforward etc. (*ingenuous*) 703; frank, candid, open-hearted.

conscientious, tender-conscienced, right-minded, high-principled, high-minded, scrupulous, religious, strict; nice, punctilious, overscrupulous, correct, punctual.

stainless, unstained, untarnished, unsullied, untainted, unperjured, uncorrupt, uncorrupted; innocent etc. 946; pure, undefiled, undepraved, undebauched; *integer vitae scelerisque purus* [Horace]; *justus et tenax propositi* [Horace]; supramundane, unworldly.

chivalrous, jealous of honor, *sans peur et sans reproche* [*F.*]; high-spirited.

adv. **honorably** etc. *adj.; bona fide* [*L.*]; on the square [*colloq.*], in good faith, in all honor, by fair means, *foro conscientiae* [*L.*], with clean hands.

int. on my honor! honor bright! [*colloq.*]; by my faith!

940. Improbity

n. **improbity**, dishonesty, dishonor; deviation from rectitude; disgrace etc. (*disrepute*) 874; fraud etc. (*deception*) 545; lying etc. 544; mouth honor etc. (*flattery*) 933; bad faith, *mala fides* [*L.*], Punic faith, *Punica fides* [*L.*]; infidelity; faith-

lessness etc. *adj.;* Judas kiss, betrayal; perfidy; perfidiousness etc. *adj.;* treachery, double dealing; unfairness etc. *adj.*

breach of -promise, −trust, −faith; prodition [*obs.*], disloyalty, divided allegiance, hyphenated allegiance [*cant*], treason, high treason; apostasy etc. (*tergiversation*) 607; nonobservance etc. 773.

shabbiness etc. *adj.;* villainy; baseness etc. *adj.;* abjection, debasement, degradation, turpitude, moral turpitude, laxity, trimming, shuffling.

knavery, roguery, rascality, foulplay; jobbing, jobbery, graft [*colloq.*], venality, nepotism; corruption, job, shuffle, fishy transaction; barratry [*law*], sharp practice, heads I win tails you lose.

v. **be dishonest** etc. *adj.;* play false; break one's -word, −faith, −promise; jilt, betray, forswear; shuffle etc. (*lie*) 544; play with marked cards, cheat at cards, live by one's wits, sail near the wind.

disgrace−, dishonor−, lower−, demean−, degrade- oneself; derogate, stoop, grovel, sneak, lose caste; sell oneself, squeal [*slang*], go back on [*colloq.*], go over to the enemy; seal one's infamy.

adj. **dishonest**, dishonorable; unconscientious, unscrupulous; fraudulent etc. 545; knavish; disgraceful etc. (*disreputable*) 974; wicked etc. 945.

false-hearted, disingenuous; unfair, one-sided; double, double-hearted, double-tongued, double-faced; time-serving, crooked, tortuous, insidious, Machiavellian, dark, slippery; fishy [*colloq.*], questionable.

infamous, arrant, foul, base, vile, low, ignominious, blackguard, perfidious, treacherous, perjured; hyphenated [*cant*].

contemptible, abject, mean, shabby, little, paltry, dirty, scurvy, scabby, sneaking, groveling, scrubby, rascally, barratrous [*law*], pettifogging; corrupt, venal; debased, mongrel; beneath one.

low-minded, low-thoughted, base-minded.

derogatory, degrading, undignified, indign [*obs.*], unbecoming, unbeseeming, unbefitting, *infra dignitatem* [*L.*], ungentlemanly, ungentlemanlike; unknightly, unchivalric, unmanly, unhandsome; recreant, inglorious.

faithless, of bad faith, false, unfaithful, disloyal; untrustworthy; trustless, trothless [*archaic*], lost to shame, dead to honor.

adv. **dishonestly** etc. *adj.; mala fide* [*L.*]; like a thief in the night, by crooked paths, by foul means.

int. *O tempora! O mores!* [Cicero].

941. Knave

n. **knave**, rogue, villain; Scapin, rascal; Lazarillo de Tormes; bad man etc. 949; blackguard etc. 949; barrator *or* barrater [*law*], shyster.

traitor, betrayer, archtraitor, conspirator, Judas, Catiline; reptile, serpent, snake in the grass, wolf in sheep's clothing, sneak, Jerry Sneak, squealer [*slang*], telltale, mischief-maker; trimmer, renegade etc. (*tergiversation*) 607; truant, recreant, slacker; sycophant etc. (*servility*) 886.

942. Disinterestedness

n. **disinterestedness** etc. *adj.;* generosity; liberality, liberalism; altruism; benevolence etc. 906; elevation, loftiness of purpose, exaltation, magnanimity; chivalry, chivalrous spirit, heroism, sublimity.

self-denial, self-abnegation, self-sacrifice, self-devotion, self-immolation, self-control etc. (*resolution*) 604; stoicism, devotion; martyrdom, suttee.

labor of love.

[comparisons] Good Shepherd, Good Samaritan, Bishop Bienvenu [Victor Hugo], Great Heart.

v. **be disinterested** etc. *adj.;* make a sacrifice, lay one's head on the block; put oneself in the place of others, do as one would be done by, do unto others as we would men should do unto us.

adj. **disinterested**, unselfish, self-denying, self-sacrificing, self-devotional.

magnanimous, noble-minded, high-minded; princely, handsome, great, high, elevated, lofty, exalted, spirited, stoical, great-hearted, large-hearted; generous, liberal; chivalrous, heroic, sublime.

unbought, unbribed; uncorrupted etc. (*upright*) 939.

943. Selfishness

n. **selfishness** etc. *adj.;* self-love, self-indulgence, self-worship, self-seeking, self-interest; egotism, egoism; *amour propre* [*F.*] etc. (*vanity*) 880; nepotism; charity that begins at home.

worldliness etc. *adj.;* world wisdom.

illiberality; meanness etc. *adj.*

self-seeker, timeserver, time-pleaser, tufthunter, fortune hunter; jobber, worldling; egotist, egoist, monopolist, nepotist; dog in the manger, *canis in praesepi* [*L.*], "foes to nobleness," temporizer, hyphenate [*cant*], trimmer; hog, road-hog, end-seat hog [*colloq.*].

v. **be selfish** etc. *adj.;* please–, indulge–, pamper–, coddle- oneself; consult one's own -wishes, –pleasure; look after one's own interest; feather one's nest; take care of number one, have an eye to the main chance, know on which side one's bread is buttered; give an inch and take an ell.

adj. **selfish**, self-seeking, self-indulgent, self-interested; wrapt up in self, centered in self; egotistic *or* egotistical, egotistic *or* egotistical.

illiberal, mean, ungenerous, narrowminded; mercenary, venal; covetous etc. 819.

worldly, unspiritual, earthly, earthly -minded, mundane, worldly-minded, worldly-wise; timeserving.

interested; *alieni appetens sui profusus* [Sallust].

adv. **ungenerously** etc. *adj.;* to gain some private ends, from selfish motives, from interested motives.

944. Virtue

n. **virtue**; virtuousness etc. *adj.;* morality; moral rectitude; integrity etc. (*probity*) 939; nobleness etc. 873.

merit, worth, desert, excellence, credit; self-control etc. (*resolution*) 604; self-denial etc. (*temperance*) 953.

well-doing; good actions, good behavior; discharge–, fulfillment–, performance- of duty; well-spent life; innocence etc. 946.

morals; ethics etc. (*duty*) 926; cardinal virtues.

[science of virtue] aretaics (*contrasted with* eudemonism); aretology.

v. **be virtuous** etc. *adj.;* practice virtue etc. *n.;* do–, fulfill–, perform–, discharge- one's duty; redeem one's pledge etc. 926; act well, –one's part; fight the good fight; acquit oneself well; command–, master- one's passions; keep in the right path, keep on the straight and narrow way.

set an example, set a good example; be on one's -good, –best- behavior.

adj. **virtuous**, good; innocent etc. 646; meritorious, deserving, worthy, desertful [*rare*], correct; dutiful, duteous; moral, right, righteous, rightminded; well-intentioned, creditable, laudable, commendable, praiseworthy; above praise, beyond all praise; excellent, admirable; sterling, pure, noble; whole-souled.

exemplary; matchless, peerless; saintly, saintlike; heaven-born, angelic, seraphic, godlike.

adv. **virtuously** etc. *adj.;* *e merito* [*L.*].

945. Vice

n. **vice**; evildoing, evil courses; wrongdoing; wickedness, viciousness etc. *adj.;* hardness of heart;

iniquity, peccability, demerit; sin, Adam, old Adam, offending Adam.

immorality, impropriety, indecorum, scandal, laxity, looseness of morals; want of -principle -ballast; knavery, etc. (*improbity*) 940; atrocity, brutality etc. (*malevolence*) 907; obliquity, backsliding, infamy.

depravity, demoralization, pravity, pollution; corruption etc. (*debasement*) 659; profligacy; flagrancy, unnatural desires, unnatural habits, Sadism, Lesbianism, sodomy; lust etc. 961.

lowest dregs of vice, sink of iniquity, Alsatian den; *gusto picaresco* [*L.*].

cannibalism, endocannibalism, endophagy; exocannibalism, exophagy; "long pig" [*humorous*].

weakness etc. *adj.;* infirmity, weakness of the flesh, frailty, imperfection, error; weak side; foible; failing, failure; crying sin, besetting sin; defect, deficiency; cloven foot.

fault, crime; criminality etc. (*guilt*) 947.

reprobate; sinner etc. 949.

[resorts] brothel etc. 961; gambling house etc. 621; joint [*slang*], opium den.

v.   **be vicious** etc. *adj.;* sin, commit sin, do amiss, err, transgress; misdemean–, forget–, misconduct- oneself; misdo [*rare*], misbehave; fall, lapse, slip, trip, offend, trespass; deviate from the -line of duty, –path of virtue etc. 944; take a wrong course, go astray; hug a sin, hug a fault; sow one's wild oats.

render vicious etc. *adj.;* demoralize, brutalize; corrupt etc. (*degrade*) 659.

adj.   **vicious**; sinful; sinning etc. *v.;* wicked, iniquitous, immoral, unrighteous, wrong, criminal; unprincipled, lawless, disorderly, dissolute, profligate, scampish; worthless, desertless [*rare*], disgraceful, recreant, disreputable; demoralizing, degrading.

miscreated, misbegotten; demoralized, corrupt, depraved; Sadistic, degenerate.

evil-minded, evil-disposed; ill-conditioned; malevolent etc. 907; heartless, graceless, shameless, virtueless, abandoned, lost to virtue; unconscionable; sunk–, lost–, deep–, steeped- in iniquity.

base, sinister, scurvy, foul, gross, vile, black, grave, facinorous [*obs.*], felonious, nefarious, shameful, scandalous, infamous, villainous, of a deep dye, heinous; flagrant, flagitious, atrocious, incarnate, accursed.

diabolic *or* diabolical, Mephistophelian, satanic, hellish, infernal, stygian, fiendlike, hellborn, demoniacal, devilish, fiendish.

incorrigible, irreclaimable, obdurate, reprobate, past praying for; culpable, reprehensible etc. (*guilty*) 947.

unjustifiable, indefensible, inexcusable, inexpiable, unpardonable, irremissible.

improper, unseemly, indecorous, indiscreet, *contra bonos mores* [*L.*], unworthy, blameworthy, reprehensible, uncommendable, discreditable; naughty, incorrect, unduteous, undutiful.

weak, frail, lax, infirm, imperfect; spineless, invertebrate [*both fig.*]; dotty [*slang*].

adv.   wrong; sinfully etc. *adj.;* without excuse.

int.   fie upon! it smells to heaven!

946. Innocence

n.   **innocence**; guiltlessness etc. *adj.;* incorruption, impeccability, inerrability, inerrableness.

clean hands, clear conscience, *mens sibi conscia recti* [Virgil].

innocent, new-born babe; lamb, dove.

v.   **be innocent** etc. *adj.; nil conscire sibi nulla pallescere culpa* [Horace].

acquit etc. 970; exculpate etc. (*vindicate*) 937.

adj.   **innocent**, not guilty; unguilty; guiltless, faultless, sinless, stainless, bloodless, spotless; clear, immaculate; *rectus in curia* [*L.*]; unspotted, unblemished, unerring; undefiled etc. 939; unhardened, Saturnian; Arcadian etc. (*artless*) 703; paradisaic *or* paradisaical, paradisiac *or* paradisiacal.

inculpable, unculpable [*rare*], unblamed, unblamable, blameless, unfallen, inerrable, above suspicion, irreproachable, irreprovable [*rare*], irreprehensible; unexceptionable, unobjectionable, unimpeachable; salvable; venial etc. 937.

virtuous etc. 944; unreproved, unimpeached, unreproached.

harmless, inoffensive, innoxious [*obs.*], innocuous; dovelike, lamblike; pure, harmless as doves; innocent as -a lamb, –the babe unborn; "more sinned against than sinning" [*Lear*].

adv.   **innocently** etc. *adj.;* with clean hands; with a -clear, –safe- conscience.

947. Guilt

n.   **guilt**, guiltiness, culpability, criminality, criminousness [*obs.*]; deviation from rectitude etc. (*improbity*) 940; sinfulness etc. (*vice*) 945; peccability.

misconduct, misbehavior, misdoing, misdeed; fault, sin, error, transgression; dereliction, delinquency.

indiscretion, lapse, slip, trip, *faux pas* [*F.*], peccadillo; flaw, blot, omission, failing, failure; blunder, break *or* bad break [*colloq.*].

offense, trespass; misdemeanor, tort [*law*], delict, *delictum* [*L.*]; misfeasance [*law*], misprision, misprision of treason *or* felony [*law*]; malfeasance [*law*], official misconduct, nonfeasance [*law*]; malefaction, malversation, corruption, malpractice; crime, felony, capital crime.

enormity, atrocity, outrage; unpardonable sin, deadly sin, mortal sin; "deed without a name" [*Macbeth*].

corpus delicit [*L.*], body of the crime, substantial facts, fundamental facts, damning evidence.

adj. **guilty**, blamable, culpable, peccable, in fault, censurable, reprehensible, blameworthy.

objectionable, exceptionable, uncommendable, illaudable; weighed in the balance and found wanting.

adv. **in the very act**, *in flagrante delicto* [*L.*], red-handed.

948. Good Man
[good woman]

n. **good man**, worthy.

model, paragon etc. (*perfection*) 650; good example; hero, demigod, seraph, angel; saint etc. (*piety*) 987; benefactor etc. 912; philanthropist etc. 910; Aristides; noble liver, pattern.

salt of the earth; one in ten thousand; a man among men, white man [*slang*]; brick [*slang*], trump [*slang*], rough diamond.

good woman, virgin, innocent; goddess, queen, Madonna, ministering angel, heaven's noblest gift; "a perfect woman, nobly planned" [Wordsworth].

949. Bad Man
[bad woman]

n. **bad man**, wrongdoer, worker of iniquity; evil-doer etc. 913; sinner, transgressor; the wicked etc. 945; bad example.

rascal, scoundrel, villain, miscreant, budmash [*India*], caitiff, wretch, reptile, viper, serpent, cockatrice, basilisk; tiger, monster; devil etc. (*demon*) 980; devil incarnate; demon in human shape, Nana Sahib; hellhound, rakehell.

roué [*F.*], rake; Sadist, one who has sold himself to the devil, fallen angel, *âme damnée* [*F.*], *vaurien* [*F.*], *mauvais sujet* [*F.*], loose fish [*colloq.*], rounder [*slang*]; lost sheep, black sheep; castaway, recreant, defaulter; prodigal etc. 818.

bad woman, jade, Jezebel, hell-cat, quean, wench, slut; adultress etc. 962.

rough, rowdy, ugly customer, ruffian, bully, tough [*colloq.*], hoodlum etc. 886; Jonathan Wild; hangman; incendiary, fire bug; thief etc. 792; murderer etc. 361.

culprit, delinquent, criminal, malefactor, misdemeanant; felon; convict, jailbird *or* gaolbird, ticket-of-leave man [*Brit.*]; outlaw.

riffraff, scum of the earth; blackguard, *polisson* [*F.*], loafer, sneak, rascalion *or* rascallion; cullion, mean wretch, varlet [*archaic*], kern [*obs.*], *âme-de-boue* [*F.*], *drôle* [*F.*]; cur, dog, hound, whelp, mongrel; losel [*archaic or dial.*], loon *or* lown [*obs. or dial. variant*], ronion *or* ronyon *or* runnion [*obs. or rare*]; outcast, vagabond, runagate; rogue etc. (*knave*) 941.

scamp, scapegrace, rip [*colloq.*], ne'er-do-well, good for nothing, reprobate, scalawag *or* scallawag [*colloq.*], sad dog [*colloq.*], limb [*colloq.*], rapscallion [*all the words in this paragraph are commonly applied jocularly or lightly*].

int. sirrah!

950. Penitence

n. **penitence**, contrition, compunction, repentance, remorse; regret etc. 833.

self-reproach, self-reproof, self-accusation, self-condemnation, self-humiliation; stings–, pangs–, qualms–, prickings–, twinge–, twitch–, touch–, voice- of conscience; "compunctious visitings of nature" [*Macbeth*].

acknowledgment, confession etc. (*disclosure*) 529; apology etc. 952; recantation etc. 607; penance etc. 952; resipiscence [*rare*].

awakened conscience, deathbed repentance, *locus poenitentiae* [*L.*], stool of repentance, cutty stool [*Scot.*], mourners' bench [*local*].

penitent, repentant [*rare*], Magdalen, prodigal son, returned prodigal, "a sadder and a wiser man" [Coleridge].

v. **repent**, be sorry for; be penitent etc. *adj.;* rue; regret etc. 833; think better of; recant etc. 607; knock under etc. (*submit*) 725; plead guilty; sing -*miserere*, -*de profundis* [*L.*]; cry *peccavi* [*L.*]; say *culpa mea* [*L.*], own oneself in the wrong; acknowledge, confess etc. (*disclose*) 529; humble oneself; beg pardon etc. (*apologize*) 952; turn over a new leaf, put on the new man, turn from sin; repent in sackcloth and ashes etc. (*do penance*) 952; learn by experience.

reclaim, reform, regenerate, redeem, convert, amend, set straight again, make a new man of, restore self-respect.

adj. **penitent**; repenting etc. *v.;* repentant, contrite, softened, melted, touched; conscience-smitten, conscience-stricken; self-accusing, self-convicted.

penitential, penitentiary; reclaimed; not hardened: unhardened.

adv. mea culpa [*L.*]; *de profundis* [*L.*].

951. Impenitence

n. **impenitence**, irrepentance, recusancy, recusance; lack of contrition.

hardness of heart, heart of stone, seared conscience, induration, obduracy; deaf ears.

v. **be impenitent** etc. *adj.;* steel the heart, harden the heart; turn away from the light; die game, die and make no sign.

adj. **impenitent**, uncontrite, obdurate, hard, hardened, seared, recusant, unrepentant; relentless, remorseless, graceless, shriftless.

lost, incorrigible, irreclaimable.

unreclaimed, unreformed; unrepented, unatoned.

952. Atonement

n. **atonement**, reparation; compromise, composition; compensation etc. 30; quittance, quits [*rare*], expiation, redemption, reclamation, conciliation, propitiation; indemnification, redress.

amends, apology, *amende honorable* [*F.*], satisfaction; peace-, sin-, burnt- offering; scapegoat, sacrifice.

penance, fasting, maceration, sackcloth and ashes, white sheet, shrift, flagellation, lustration; purgation, purgatory.

v. **atone**, atone for; expiate; propitiate; make amends, make good; reclaim, redeem, repair, ransom, absolve, purge, shrive, do penance, stand in a white sheet, repent in sackcloth and ahses.

set one's house in order, wipe off old scores, make matters up; pay the forfeit, pay the penalty.

apologize, express regret, beg pardon, *faire l'amende honorable* [*F.*], give satisfaction; get-, fall- down on one's knees, -marrowbones [*slang or jocular*].

adj. **propitiatory**, expiatory, sacrifice, sacrificial, sacrificatory [*rare*]; piacular, piaculous [*rare*].

953. Temperance

n. **temperance**, moderation, sobriety, soberness.

forbearance, abnegation; self-denial, self-restraint, self-control etc. (*resolution*) 604.

abstinence, abstemiousness, asceticism; Encratism, prohibition; frugality; vegetarianism, teetotalism, total abstinence; system of -Pythagoras, -Cornaro; Pythagorism; Stoicism.

abstainer, Pythagorean, gymnosophist; nephalist, teetotaler etc. 958; Encratite, vegetarian, fruitarian, hydropot [*rare*]; ascetic etc. 995.

v. **be temperate** etc. *adj.*; abstain, forbear, refrain, deny oneself, spare; know when one has had enough; take the pledge; prohibit; control the -old Adam, -carnal man, -fleshly lusts; refrain from indulgence, look not upon the wine when it is red.

adj. **temperate**, moderate, sober, frugal, sparing, abstemious, abstinent; within compass; measured etc. (*sufficient*) 639.

Pythagorean; vegetarian, fruitarian; teetotal.

954. Intemperance

n. **intemperance**, sensuality, rakery [*rare*], animalism, carnality; tragalism; pleasure; effiminacy, silkiness; luxury, luxuriousness; lap of -pleasure, -luxury; free-living.

indulgence; high living, inabstinence, self-indulgence; voluptuousness etc. *adj.;* epicurism, epicureanism, sybaritism.

dissipation; licentiousness etc. *adj.;* debauchery; crapulence.

revel, revels, revelry, orgy; drunkenness etc. 959; debauch, carousal, jollification [*colloq.*], high old time [*colloq.*], drinking bout, wassail, saturnalia, excess, too much.

drug habit; Circean cup; bhang, hashish, opium, hop [*slang*], dope [*slang*], cocaine; drug fiend, dope fiend [*slang*].

v. **be intemperate** etc. *adj.;* indulge, exceed; live -well, -high, -on the fat of the land; eat drink and be merry, look upon the wine when it is red, dine not wisely but too well; give free rein to indulgence etc. *n.;* wallow in voluptuousness etc. *n.;* plunge into dissipation; sensualize, brutify, carnalize.

revel, rake, live hard, run riot, sow one's wild oats; slake one's -appetite, -thirst; swill; pamper.

adj. **intemperate**, inabstinent, excessive; sensual, self-indulgent; voluptuous, licentious, wild, dissolute, rakish, fast, debauched; orgiastic, Corybantic, Paphian.

brutish, crapulous, swinish, piggish, hoggish, beastlike, theroid [*med.*].

luxurious, Epicurean, Sybaritical; bred-, nursed- in the lap of luxury; indulged, pampered; full fed, high fed.

intoxicated, drunk etc. 959.

954a. Sensualist

n. **sensualist,** Sybarite, voluptuary, Sardanapalus, man of pleasure, carpet knight; epicure, epicurean, *gourmet* [*F.*]; gourmand; glutton etc. 957; pig, hog; votary–, swine- of Epicurus; Heliogabalus; free liver, hard liver; libertine etc. 962; hedonist; tragalist.

955. Asceticism

n. **asceticism,** puritanism, sabbatarianism; cynicism, austerity; total abstinence; nephalism; Yoga.

mortification, maceration, sackcloth and ashes, flagellation; penance etc. 952; fasting etc. 956; martyrdom.

ascetic, anchoret *or* anchorite, *Heautontimorumenos* [*Gr.*]; hermit etc. (*recluse*) 893; puritan, sabbatarian, cynic; bhikshu, sannyasi *or* sanyasi, yogi [*all Hindu*]; dervish, fakir [*both Moham.*]; martyr.

adj. **ascetic,** austere, puritanical; cynical; over-religious; acerb, acerbic.

956. Fasting

n. **fasting;** xerophagy; famishment, starvation.

fast, *jour maigre* [*F.*]; fast day, banyan day; Lent, quadragesima; Ramadan *or* Ramazan [*Moham.*]; spare–, meager- diet; lenten -diet, –entertainment; *soupe maigre* [*F.*], short commons, Barmecide feast; short rations; punishment of Tantalus.

v. **fast,** starve, clem [*obs.*], famish, perish with hunger; dine with Duke Humphrey; make two bites of a cherry; "keep the larder lean."

adj. **fasting** etc.*v.;* lenten, quadragesimal; unfed; starved etc. *v.;* half-starved; hungry etc. 865.

957. Gluttony

n. **gluttony;** greed; greediness etc. *adj.;* voracity.

epicurism, gastronomy; good–, high-living; edacity, gulosity [*rare*], crapulence; guttling, guzzle [*rare*], guzzling; pantophagy.

feast etc. (*food*) 298; good cheer, blow out [*slang*]; *batterie de cuisine* [*F.*].

glutton, gormandizer, gourmand, cormorant, pig, hog etc. (*sensualist*) 954a; guttler, pantophagist; belly-god, Apicius, gastronome.

epicure, *bon vivant* [*F.*], gourmand *gourmet* [*F.*], gourmet.

v. **gormandize,** gorge; overgorge oneself, overeat oneself, glut, satiate, engorge, eat one's fill, cram, stuff, guttle, guzzle, bolt, devour, gobble up; overindulge; gulp etc. (*swallow food*) 298; raven, eat out of house and home; have the stomach of an ostrich; play a good knife and fork etc. (*appetite*) 865; have a capacious -gorge, –maw.

pamper [*obs. as glut*], indulge.

adj. **gluttonous,** greedy; gormandizing etc. *v.;* edacious, omnivorous, pantophagic, pantophagous, voracious, devouring, all-devouring, crapulent, swinish.

pampered [*obs. as fed to excess*]; overfed, overgorged, overindulged.

958. Sobriety

n. **sobriety;** teetotalism, nephalism.

water-drinker; hydropot [*rare*], prohibitionist; teetotaler *or* teetotaller, abstainer, nephalist, Good Templar, band of hope, W. C. T. U. (Women's Christian Temperance Union).

v. take the pledge, swear off.

adj. **sober,** –as a judge; temperate, moderate.

959. Drunkenness

n. **drunkenness** etc. *adj.;* intemperance; drinking etc. *v.;* inebriety, inebriation, ebriety [*rare*], ebriosity [*rare*], insobriety, intoxication; temulence [*rare*], bibacity, wine-bibbing; compotation, potation; deep potations, bacchanals, bacchanalia, bacchanalianism, libations; bender [*slang*].

alcoholism, oinomania, dipsomania; delirium tremens, D. T.'s [*colloq.*]; *mania a potu* [*L.*].

drink, alcoholic drinks, alcohol, blue ruin [*slang*], booze *or* bouse [*colloq.*], "the luscious liquor" [Milton]; grog, port wine, punch; punchbowl, cup, rosy wine, flowing bowl; drop, –too much; dram; beer etc. (*beverage*) 298; *aguardiente* [*Sp.*]; apple-brandy, apple-jack; bourbon; brandy, brandy smesh; chain lightning [*slang*], champagne, cocktail; gin, gin-sling; highball, peg [*slang, orig. India*]; burra (*or* bara) peg, chota peg [*both India*]; rum, schnapps, sherry, xeres, sling, usquebaugh, vodka, whisky *or* whiskey, rye; stirrup cup, parting cup, doch-an-dorrach *or* doch-an-dorris [*Scot.*].

illicit distilling; moonshining, moonshine *or* moonshine whisky [*colloq.*], hooch [*slang*], home-brew; white lightning; moonshiner [*colloq.*], bootlegger [*slang*].

drunkard, sot, toper, tippler, bibber, winebibber; hard–, gin–, dram- drinker; soaker [*slang*], sponge [*slang*], tun [*jocose*], love-pot, tosspot, guzzler, guzzle [*rare*], barfly, boozer *or* bouser [*colloq.*], bum [*slang*], tavern haunter, thirsty soul, reveler, carouser, Bacchanal, Bacchanalian; Bacchae, bacchante, maenad; devotee to Bacchus.

v. **get** *or* **be drunk** etc. *adj.;* see double; take a -drop, –glass- too much; get smashed [*slang*]; drink, tipple, tope [*colloq.*], booze *or* bouse [*colloq.*], guzzle, swill [*slang*], soak [*slang*], sot [*rare*], bum [*slang*], besot, have a jag on [*slang*], lush [*slang*], bib [*obs. or dial.*], swig [*dial. or colloq.*], carouse; sacrifice at the shrine of Bacchus; take to drinking; drink -hard, –deep, –like a fish; have one's swill [*slang*], drain the cup, splice the main brace [*slang*], take a hair of the dog that bit you.

liquor, liquor up [*both slang*], wet one's -whistle, –clay, –swallow [*colloq. or humorous*]; wet the red lane [*humorous*]; raise the elbow, raise the little finger, hit the booze [*slang*], take a whet; crack a–, pass the- bottle; toss off etc. (*drink up*) 298; go to the -alehouse, –public house, –saloon.

make one drunk etc. *adj.;* inebriate, fuddle [*colloq.*], befuddle, fuzzle [*obs.*], get into one's head.

sell illicitly, bootleg [*slang*].

adj. **drunk**, tipsy, intoxicated, bibacious, inebrious, inebriate, inebriated; in one's cups; in a state of intoxication etc. *n.;* temulent, temulentive [*both rare*]; fuddled [*colloq.*], mellow, cut [*slang*], boozy *or* bousy [*colloq.*], full [*vulgar*], fou [*Scot.*], lit up [*slang*], glorious [*humorous*], fresh [*slang*], merry, elevated; flush, flushed, flustered, disguised [*archaic*], groggy [*colloq.*], beery; top-heavy; pot-valiant, potulent [*obs.*], squiffy [*slang*]; overcome, overtaken [*obs.*], whittled [*obs.*]; screwed, tight, primed, corned, raddled, smashed, stoned, sewed up, lushy [*all slang*], muzzy [*colloq.*], nappy [*rare*], muddled, obfuscated, maudlin; crapulous, blind drunk, dead drunk.

inter pocula [*L.*], in liquor, the worse for liquor; having had a drop too much, half-seas over [*slang*], three sheets in the wind [*sailors' slang*], under the table.

drunk as -a piper, –a fiddler, –a lord, –Chloe, –an owl, –David's sow, –a wheelbarrow [*all colloq.*].

drunken, bibacious, sottish; given–, addicted- to -drink, –the bottle; toping etc. *v.;* primed, –on the hip; heeled [*slang*].

960. Purity

n. **purity**; decency, decorum, delicacy; continence, chastity, honesty, virtue, modesty, shame; pudicity, pucelage [*rare*], virginity.

virgin, vestal, prude; Lucretia, Diana, Athena Parthenos; Joseph, Hippolytus.

adj. **pure**, undefiled, modest, delicate, decent, decorous; *virginibus puerisque* [*L.*]; chaste, continent, virtuous, honest, Platonic.

961. Impurity

n. **impurity**; uncleanness etc. (*filth*) 653; immodesty; grossness etc. *adj.;* indelicacy, indecency, impudicity, obscenity, ribaldry, smut, bawdry, *double entente, équivoque* [*F.*]; pornography.

incontinence, debauchery, libertinism, libertinage, fornication, wenching, venery, dissipation.

concupiscence, lust, carnality, flesh, salacity; pruriency, lechery, lasciviousness, lewdness, lasciviency [*obs.*], lubricity; Sadism, Sapphism, Lesbianism, nymphomania, aphrodisia, satyriasis.

seduction; defloration, defilement, abuse, violation, stupration, rape; incest.

social evil, harlotry, whoredom, concubinage, cuckoldom, adultery, advoutry [*obs.*], crim. con.; free-love.

intrigue, amour, amourette, *liaison* [*F.*], *faux pas* [*F.*], entanglement; gallantry.

[resorts] brothel, bagnio, stew, bawdyhouse, lupanar, house of ill fame, bordel [*obs.*]; Yoshiwara [*Jap.*], red-light district.

harem, seraglio, zenana [*India*].

v. **be impure** etc. *adj.;* debauch, defile, seduce; prostitute; abuse, violate, rape, stuprate [*rare*], deflower; commit adultery etc. *n.;* intrigue.

adj. **impure**; unclean etc. (*dirty*) 653; not to be mentioned to ears polite; immodest, shameless, indecorous, indelicate, indecent, Fescennine; loose, *risqué* [*F.*], coarse, gross, broad, free, equivocal, smutty, fulsome, ribald, obscene, bawdy, pornographic.

concupiscent, prurient, lickerish, rampant, lustful; carnal, carnal-minded; lewd, lascivious, lecherous, libidinous, erotic, ruttish, must *or* musty [*said of elephants*]; salacious, Paphian, voluptuous; goatish, beastly, bestial, incestuous.

unchaste, light, wanton, licentious, adulterous, debauched, dissolute; of loose character, of easy virtue; frail, gay, riggish [*obs.*], incontinent, meretricious, rakish, gallant, dissipated; no better than she should be; on the town, on the streets, on the *pavé* [*F.*], on the loose [*colloq.*].

962. Libertine

n. **libertine**; voluptuary etc. 954*a;* rake, debauchee, loose fish [*colloq.*], rip [*colloq.*], rakehell, fast man; intrigant, gallant, seducer, fornicator, lecher, satyr, goat, whoremonger, *paillard* [*F.*], advocater [*obs.*], adulterer, gay deceiver, Lothario, Don Juan, Bluebeard; chartered libertine.

adultress, advoutress [*obs.*], courtesan, prostitute, strumpet, harlot, whore, hooker [*slang*], punk [*obsoles.*], *fille de joie* [*F.*], woman, woman of the town, streetwalker, Cyprian, miss [*obs.*], piece [*slang*], demirep, wench, trollop, trull, baggage, hussy, drab, bitch [*low*], jade, skit [*obs.*], rig [*obs.*], quean, mopsy [*dial. Eng.*], slut, minx, harridan; unfortunate, –female, –woman; woman -of easy virtue etc. (*unchaste*) 961; wanton, fornicatress; *lorette* [*F.*], *cocotte* [*F.*], *petite dame* [*F.*], grisette; demimondaine; chippy [*slang*]; Sapphist; white slave.

Jezebel, Messalina, Delilah, Thais, Phryne, Aspasia, Lais.

demimonde, erring sisters, fallen women, frail sisterhood.

mistress, concubine, kept woman, doxy, *chère amie* [*F.*]; *bona roba* [*It.*]; spiritual wife.

procurer, pimp, pander *or* pandar, bawd, *conciliatrix* [*L.*], procuress, mackerel [*archaic*], wittol [*obs.*].

963. Legality

n. **legality**, legitimacy, legitimateness; legitimatization, legitimization.

law, code, *corpus juris* [*L.*], constitution, pandect, charter, act, enactment, statute, rule; canon etc. (*precept*) 697; ordinance, institution, regulation; bylaw *or* bye-law; rescript, decree etc. (*order*) 741; ordonnance; standing order; plebiscite etc. (*choice*) 609; legislature.

legal process; form, formula, formality, rite, arm of the law; *habeas corpus* [*L.*]; *fieri facias* [*L.*].

equity, common law; *lex scripta* [*L.*]; *lex non scripta* [*L.*], unwritten law; law of nations, *droit des gens* [*F.*], international law, *just gentium* [*L.*]; *just civile* [*L.*]; civil–, canon–, crown–, criminal–, statute–, ecclesiastical- law; *lex mercatoria* [*L.*].

constitutionalism, constitutionality; justice etc. 922.

[science of law] jurisprudence, nomology; legislation, codification, nomography.

v. **legalize**, legitimate, legitimize, legitimatize; enact, ordain; decree etc. (*order*) 741; pass a law, legislate; codify, formulate, formalize, regularize, authorize.

adj. **legal**, legitimate; according to law; vested, constitutional, chartered, legalized; lawful etc. (*permitted*) 760; statutable, statutory; legislatorial, legislative; judicial, juridical; nomistic, nomothetical.

adv. **legally** etc. *adj.;* in the eye of the law; *de jure* [*L.*].

964. Illegality

[absence or violation of law]

n. **lawlessness**; illicitness; breach–, violation- of law; disobedience etc. 742; unconformity etc. 83; arbitrariness etc. *adj.;* antinomy, violence, brute force, despotism, tyranny, outlawry.

mob–, lynch–, club–, Lydford–, martial–, drumhead- law; *coup d'état* [*F.*]; *le droit du plus fort* [*F.*]; *argumentum baculinum* [*L.*].

illegality, informality, unlawfulness, illegitimacy, bar sinister.

trover and conversion; smuggling, bootlegging [*slang*], illicit distilling etc. 959; poaching; simony.

v. **violate the law**, offend against the law, set the law at defiance, ride roughshod over, drive a coach and six through a statute; make the law a dead letter, take the law into one's own hands.

smuggle, run, poach, bootleg [*slang*].

adj. **illegal**; prohibited etc. 761; not allowed, unlawful, illegitimate, illicit, contraband, actionable.

unchartered, unconstitutional; unwarranted, unwarrantable, unauthorized; informal, unofficial, injudicial [*rare*], extra-judicial.

lawless, arbitrary, despotic, despotical; summary, irresponsible; unanswerable, unaccountable.

null and void; a dead letter.

adv. **illegally** etc. *adj.;* with a high hand, in violation of law.

965. Jurisdiction

[executive]

n. **jurisdiction**, judicature, administration of justice; soc, soke [*both A. S. & early Eng. law*]; executive, commission of the peace; magistracy etc. (*authority*) 737; judge etc. 967; tribunal etc. 966.

city government, municipal government, commission government, Oregon plan; municipality, corporation, bailiwick, shrievalty; police, police force; constabulary, Bumbledom.

executive officer, officer, commissioner, lord lieutenant [*Brit.*], collector [*India*]; city manager, mayor, alderman, councilor *or* councillor, selectman; bailiff, tipstaff, bumbailiff [*Eng.*], catchpole *or* catchpoll, beadle; sheriff, shrieve [*obs.*], bailie [*Scot.*], constable; policeman, police constable, police sergeant, patrolman etc. 664; sbirro [*It.*], alguazil, *gendarme* [*F.*], kavass [*Turk.*], lictor, mace bearer, *huissier* [*F.*], tithingman; excise man, gauger *or* gager, customhouse officer, *douanier* [*F.*]; press gang *or* pressgang.

coroner, aedile *or* edile; reeve, portreeve [*early Eng. hist.*], paritor [*obs.*], *posse comitatus* [*L.*].

bureau, cutcherry [*India*], department, portfolio, secretariat.

v. **judge**, sit in judgment; have jurisdiction over.

adj. **executive**, administrative, judicative, municipal; inquisitorial, causidical; judicatory, judiciary, judicial, juridical.

adv. *coram judice* [*L.*].

966. Tribunal

n. **tribunal**, court, curia, board, bench, judicature, judicatory; court of -justice, -law, -arbitration; inquisition; guild; durbar [*India*], divan [*Oriental*], Areopagus.

justice-, judgment-, mercy-seat; woolsack; bar, bar of justice; dock; forum, hustings, bureau, drumhead; jury-box; witness box, witness stand.

senate-house, town hall, theater *or* theatre; House of Commons, House of Lords; statehouse, townhouse, courthouse.

[British courts], sessions; petty-, quarter-, special-, general- sessions [*Eng. law*]; assizes; eyre, justices in eyre, wardmote, burghmote, barmote, courtleet, court-baron, court of piepoudre [*all old Eng. law*]; superior courts of Westminster; court of -record, -oyer and terminer, -assize, -appeal, -error; High court of -Judicature, -Appeal; Judicial Committee of the Privy Council; Star Chamber; Court of -Chancery, -King's *or* Queen's Bench, -Exchequer, -Common Pleas, -Probate, -Admiralty; Lords Justices'-, Rolls-, Vice Chancellor's-, Stannary-, Divorce-, Palatine-, county-, police- court; Court of Criminal Appeal; Court of Small Causes [*India*]; court of common council; board of green cloth.

[United States courts] United States -Supreme Court, -District Court, -Circuit Court of Appeal; Federal Court of Claims, Court of Private Land Claims; Supreme Court, court of sessions, criminal court, police court, juvenile court, night court [*colloq.*], municipal court.

court-martial (*pl.* courts-martial), drumhead court-martial.

ecclesiastical court, Rota *or* Rota Romana [*R. C. Ch.*]; Court of Arches [*Eng.*].

Papal Court, Curia.

adj. **judicial** etc. 965; appellate; curial.

967. Judge

n. **judge**, justice; justiciar [*Eng. [Scot. hist.*]; justiciary [*Eng. & Scot. hist.*]; chancellor; justice-, judge- of assize; recorder, common serjeant; puisne-, assistant-, county court- judge; conservator-, justice- of the peace; J.P.; "the Great Unpaid" [*Eng.*]; court etc. (*tribunal*) 966; deemster [*Isle of Man & archaic*], moderator, bencher [*archaic*], jurat, magistrate, police magistrate, beak [*slang*]; his worship, his honor, his lordship; the court.

Lord Chancellor, Lord Justice; Master of the Rolls, Vice Chancellor; Lord Chief -Justice, -Baron; Chief Justice; Mr. Justice; Baron, -of the Exchequer.

assessor; arbiter, arbitrator, doomsman *or* domesman [*obs.*], umpire, referee, referendary [*rare*]; revising barrister [*Eng.*], receiver, official receiver; censor etc. (*critic*) 480; barmaster [*Eng.*].

archon, tribune, praetor, ephor, syndic, podesta [*It.*]; mollah, ulema, hakim, mufti, cadi *or* kadi [*all Moham.*]; alcalde [*Sp.*]; Rhadamanthus, Minos, Solomon.

jury, grand jury, petty jury, inquest, panel, country; twelve men in a box.

juror, juryman, talesman; grand-juror, grand-juryman, recognitor; petty-juror, petty-juryman.

litigant etc. (*accusation*) 938.

v. **adjudge** etc. (*determine*) 480; try a case, try a prisoner.

adj. judicial etc. 965.

968. Lawyer

n. **lawyer**, jurist, legist, pundit [*India*], civilian, publicist, jurisconsult, legal adviser, advocate; barrister, barrister-at-law; counsel, counselor *or* counsellor, King's *or* Queen's counsel; K. C.; Q. C.; silk *or* silk gown; junior counsel, stuff *or* stuff gown; leader, serjeant-at-law, bencher, pleader, special pleader; tubman [*Eng. law*], judge etc. 967.

solicitor, attorney, vakil *or* vakeel [*India*], proctor; equity draftsman, conveyancer, notary, –public; scrivener, cursitor [*Eng. law*]; writer, –to the signet; S.S.C.; limb of the law; pettifogger, shyster.

bar, legal profession, gentlemen of the long robe; junior–, outer–, inner- bar; Inns of Court [*Eng.*].

v. **practice law**; practice at (*or* within) the bar, plead; call to (*or* within) the bar, be called to (*or* within) the bar; admitted to the bar, take silk.

disbar, disbench [*Eng. law*], degrade.

adj. learned in the law; at the bar; forensic.

969. Lawsuit

n. **lawsuit**, suit, action, cause; litigation; suit in law; dispute etc. 713.

writ, summons, subpoena, citation, latitat [*Eng. law*]; *nisi prius, venire, venire facias, habeas corpus* [*all L.*].

arraignment, prosecution, impeachment; accusation etc. 938; presentment, true bill, indictment.

arrest, apprehension, committal, commitment; imprisonment etc. (*restraint*) 751.

pleadings; declaration, bill, claim; *procès-verbal* [*F.*], bill of right, information, *corpus delicti* [*L.*]; affidavit, state of facts, libel; answer, replication, plea, demurrer, rebutter, rejoinder; surrebutter, surrejoinder.

suitor, libelant *or* libellant, party to a suit; litigant etc. 938.

hearing, trial; judgment, sentence, finding, verdict etc. 480; appeal, –motion; writ of error; certiorari.

case, decision, precedent; decided case, reports.

v. **go to law**, appeal to the law; bring to -justice, –trial, –the bar; put on trial, pull up; accuse etc. 938; prefer *or* file a claim etc. *n.;* take the law of [*colloq.*], inform against.

cite, summon, summons, serve with a writ, arraign, sue, prosecute, bring an action against, indict, impeach, attach, distrain, commit; apprehend, arrest; give in charge etc. (*restrain*) 751.

empanel a jury, challenge the jurors; implead, join issue; close the pleadings; set down for hearing.

try, hear a cause; sit in judgment; adjudicate etc. 480.

adj. **litigious** etc. (*quarrelsome*) 713; *qui tam, coram judice, sub judice* [*all L.*].

adv. *pendente lite* [*L.*].

970. Acquittal

n. **acquittal**, acquitment [*obs.*]; exculpation, acquittance, clearance, exoneration; discharge etc. (*release*) 750; *quietus* [*L.*], absolution, compurgation, reprieve, respite; pardon etc. (*forgiveness*) 918.

[exemption from punishment] impunity, immunity.

v. **acquit**, exculpate, exonerate, clear; absolve, whitewash, assoil [*archaic*], assoilzie [*Scot.*]; discharge, release; liberate etc. 750.

reprieve, respite; pardon etc. (*forgive*) 918; let off, let off scot-free.

adj. **acquitted** etc. *v.;* uncondemned, unpunished, unchastised; recommended to mercy.

971. Condemnation

n. **condemnation**, conviction, judgment, penalty, sentence; proscription, damnation; death warrant.

attainder, attainture, attaintment.

v. **condemn**, convict, cast [*obs. or dial.*], bring home to, find guilty, damn, doom, sign the death warrant, sentence, pass sentence on, attaint, confiscate, proscribe, sequestrate; nonsuit.

disapprove etc. 932; accuse etc. 938.

stand condemned, be convicted.

adj. **condemnatory**, damnatory; condemned etc. *v.;* nonsuited etc. (*failure*) 732; self-convicted.

972. Punishment

n. **punishment**, punition, chastisement, chastening, correction, castigation; discipline, infliction, trial; judgment; penalty etc. 974; retribution; thunderbolt, Nemesis, Eumenides, the Furies; requital etc. (*reward*) 973; retributive justice; penology.

[forms of punishment] lash, scaffold etc. (*instrument of punishment*) 975; imprisonment etc. (*restraint*) 751; transportation, banishment, expulsion, exile, involuntary exile, ostracism; penal servitude, hard labor; galleys etc. 975; beating etc. *v.;* flagellation, fustigation, cudgeling, gantlet, strappado, estrapade, bastinado, *argumentum baculinum* [*L.*], stick law, rap on the knuckles, box on the ear; blow etc. (*impulse*) 276; stripe, cuff, kick, buffet, pummel; slap, –in the face; wipe [*dial. or slang*], douse *or* dowse [*rare*]; torture, rack; rail-riding, scarpines; picket [*obs.*], picketing; dragonnade.

capital punishment, execution; hanging, shooting etc. *v.;* electrocution, decapitation, decollation, dismemberment; strangling, strangulation, garrote *or* garrotte; crucifixion, impalement; martyrdom, *auto-da-fé* (*pl. autos-da-fé*) [*Pg.*], *auto-de-fe* [*Sp.*], *noyade* [*F.*], harakiri [*Jap.*], seppuku [*Jap.*], happy dispatch [*jocular*], lethal chamber, hemlock.

v. **punish**, chastise, chasten, castigate, correct, inflict punishment, administer correction, deal retributive justice; tar and feather; masthead, keelhaul.

visit upon, pay; pay out [*colloq.*], serve out [*colloq.*], settle, settle with, do for [*colloq.*], get even with, get one's own back [*slang*], make short work of, give a lesson to, serve one right, make an example of; have a rod in pickle for; give it to, give it one [*both colloq.*].

strike etc. 276; deal a blow to, administer the lash, smite; slap, –the face; smack, cuff, box the ears, spank, thwack, thump, beat, lay on, swinge, buffet; thresh, thrash, pummel, drub, leather [*slang*], trounce, baste, belabor; lace, –one's jacket; dress, dress down, give a dressing, trim [*colloq.*], warm [*dial.*], warm one's jacket [*colloq.*], wipe [*slang*], tund [*obs.*], cob [*dial., Eng.*], bang, strap, comb [*humorous*], lick, larrup [*both colloq.*], wallop [*Scot., dial. Eng. & colloq., U. S*]., cowhide, lambaste [*slang*], lash, whop [*obs.*], flog, scourge, whip, birch, cane, give the stick, switch, flagellate, horsewhip, bastinado, towel [*slang*], rub down with an oaken towel [*slang*], ribroast [*slang*], dust one's jacket [*slang*], fustigate, pitch into [*colloq.*], lay about one, beat black and blue; beat to a -pulp, –mummy, –jelly; give a black eye; hit on the head, crack on the bean [*slang*], sandbag, blackjack, put away [*slang*]; pelt, stone, lapidate.

execute; bring to the -block, –gallows; behead, decapitate, decollate, guillotine; hang, turn off [*slang*], gibbet, bowstring, dismember, hang draw and quarter; shoot; burn; break on the wheel, crucify; impale *or* empale, flay; lynch; electrocute.

torture, agonize, rack, put on (*or* to) the rack, martyr, martyrize, picket [*obs. or hist.*]; prolong the agony, kill by inches.

banish, exile, transport, deport, expel, ostracize; rusticate; drum out; dismiss, disbar, disbench [*Eng. law*]; strike off the roll, unfrock; post.

suffer, suffer for, suffer punishment; be flogged, be hanged etc.; come to the gallows, dance upon nothing [*ironical*], die in one's shoes; be rightly served.

adj. **punishing** etc. *v.*; penal, punitory, punitive, inflictive, castigatory; punished etc. *v.*

int. *à la lanterne!* [*F.*].

973. Reward

n. **reward**, recompense, remuneration, prize, meed, guerdon, reguerdon [*obs.*]; price; indemnity, indemnification; quittance, compensation, reparation, redress, retribution, reckoning, acknowledgment, requital, amends, sop; atonement; consideration, return, *quid pro quo* [*L.*]; salvage.

perquisite, perks [*slang*]; vail etc. (*donation*) 784; *douceur* [*F.*], tip; bribe, bait etc. 784; hushmoney, smart-money, blackmail; carcelage [*obs.*]; solatium.

allowance, salary, stipend, wages; pay, payment; emolument; tribute; batta [*India*], shot, scot; premium, fee, honorarium; hire; dasturi *or* dustoori [*India*]; mileage.

crown etc. (*decoration of honor*) 877.

v. **reward**, recompense, repay, requite; remunerate, munerate [*obs.*]; compensate; fee, tip, bribe; pay one's footing etc. (*pay*) 807; make amends, indemnify, atone; satisfy, acknowledge.

get for one's pains, reap the fruits of.

adj. remunerative, remuneratory [*rare*], munerary [*obs.*], compensatory, retributive, reparatory [*rare*], reparative.

974. Penalty

n. **penalty**; retribution etc. (*punishment*) 972; pain, pains and penalties; wergild *or* weregild [*hist.*], bloodwite *or* bloodwit [*early Eng. law*]; *peine forte et dure* [*F.*]; penance etc. (*atonement*) 952; the devil to pay.

fine, mulct, amercement, sconce [*Oxford Univ., Eng.*], forfeit, forfeiture, escheat, damages, deodand, sequestration, confiscation, praemunire *or* premunire; domage.

v. **penalize**, fine, mulct, amerce, sconce, confiscate, sequestrate, sequester, escheat, estreat, forfeit.

975. Scourge
[instrument of punishment]

n. **scourge**, whip, lash, strap, thong, cowhide, knout, cat, cat-o'-nine-tails; rope's end; *azote* [*Sp. Am.*], black-snake, bullwhack, kurbash [*Turk.*], chabuk [*Hind.*], quirt, rawhide, sjambok [*S. Africa*].

rod, cane, stick, rattan *or* ratan, birch, birch rod; rod in pickle; switch, ferule, cudgetl, truncheon.

[various instruments] pillory, stocks, whipping post; cucking stool, ducking stool, brank, trebuchet *or* trebucket; triangle, wooden horse, maiden; thumbscrew, boot, rack, wheel, iron heel; treadmill, crank, galleys; bed of Procrustes.

scaffold; block, ax, guillotine; stake; cross, gallows, gibbet, tree, drop; noose, rope, halter, bowstring; death chair, electric chair; *mecate* [*Sp.*].

prison, house of correction etc. 752; jailer *or* gaoler.

executioner; electrocutioner; lyncher, garroter *or* garrotter, torturer; headsman, hangman, topsman *or* topping cove [*slang*], Jack Ketch.

malefactor, criminal, culprit, felon, evildoer, misdemeanant; victim, gallows-bird [*slang*], Jack Ketch's pippin [*old slang*].

Section 5. Religious

976. Deity

n. **deity**, Divinity, Godhead, Godship, Omnipotence, Omniscience, Providence.

[quality of being divine] divineness, divinity.

GOD, Lord, Jehovah, The King of Kings, The Lord of Lords, The Almighty, The Supreme Being, The Eternal Being, The Absolute Being, The First Cause; I AM, The All-Father, *Ens Entium* [*L.*], Author of all things, Creator of all things, Author of our being; Cosmoplast, Demiurge; The Infinite, The Eternal; The All-powerful, The Omnipotent, The All-wise, The All-merciful, The All-holy, The All-knowing, The Omniscient.

Deus [*L.*], *Theos* [*Gr.*], *Dieu* [*F.*], *Gott* [*Ger.*], *Dio* [*It.*], *Dios* [*Sp.*], *Deos* [*Pg.*], *Gud* [*Nor., Sw., & Dan.*], *God* [*Du.*], *Bog'* [*Russ.*], *Brahmă* [*Skr.*], *Deva* [*Skr.*], *Khuda* [*Hind.*], *Allah* [*Ar.*], *Kami* [*Jap.*], *Ten-shu* [*Jap., Christian*], *Jahweh* [*Heb.*].

[attributes and perfections] infinite -power, –wisdom, –goodness, –justice, –truth, –love, –mercy; omnipotence, omniscience, omnipresence; unity, immutability, holiness, glory, light, majesty, sovereignty; infinity, eternity etc. (*perpetuity*) 112.

THE TRINITY, The Holy Trinity, The Trinity in Unity, The Triune God, Triunity, Threefold Unity, "Three in One and One in Three."

I. GOD THE FATHER, The Maker, The Creator, The Preserver.

[functions] creation, preservation, divine government, Theocracy, Thearchy; Providence; ways–, dealings–, dispensations–, visitations-of Providence.

II. GOD THE SON, Jesus Christ; The Messiah, The Anointed, The Saviour, The Redeemer, The Mediator, The Intercessor, The Advocate, The Judge; The Son of God, The Son of Man, The Son of David; The Only-Begotten, The Lamb of God, The Word, Logos; The Man of Sorrows, Jesus of Nazareth, King of the Jews, The Son of Mary, The Risen, Immanuel, Emmanuel, The King of Kings and Lord of Lords, The King of Glory, The Prince of Peace, The Good Shepherd, The Way, The Door, The Truth, The Life, The Bread of Life, The Light of the World, The Vine, The True Vine; The Lord our Righteousness, The Sun of Righteousness.

The Incarnation, The Hypostatic Union, The Word made Flesh.

[functions] salvation, redemption, atonement, propitiation, mediation, intercession, judgment; soteriology.

III. GOD THE HOLY GHOST, The Holy Spirit, Paraclete, The Comforter, The Consoler, The Intercessor, The Spirit of God, The Spirit of Truth, The Dove.

[functions] inspiration, unction, regeneration, sanctification, consolation, grace.

[the deity in other religions] **brahmanism** *or* **hinduism**: Brahm *or* Brahmă (*neuter*), the Supreme Soul *or* Essence of the Universe; Trimurti *or* Hindu trinity *or* Hindu triad: (1) Brahmā (*masc.*), the Creator; (2) Vishnu, the Preserver, (3) Siva *or* Shiva, the Destroyer and Regenerator. For other Hindu deities see 979.

buddhism: the Protestantism of the East; Buddha, the Blessed One, the Teacher, the Lord Buddha.

zoroastrianism: Zerâna-Akerana, the Infinite Being; Ahuramazda *or* Ormazd, the Creator, the Lord of Wisdom, the Wise Lord, the Wise One, the King of Light, the Guardian of Mankind (*opposed by* Ahriman, the King of Darkness).

mohammedanism *or* **islam**: Allah.

judaism: Jehovah.

v. **create**, fashion, make, form, mold *or* mould, manifest.

preserve, uphold, keep, perpetuate, immortalize.

atone, redeem, save, propitiate, expiate; intercede, mediate.

predestinate, predestine, foreordain, preordain; elect, call, ordain.

bless, sanctify, hallow, justify, absolve, glorify.

adj. **almighty**, all-powerful, omnipotent; omnipresent, all-wise, all-seeing, all-knowing, omniscient, supreme.

divine, heavenly, celestial; holy, hallowed, sacred, sacrosanct.

supernatural, superhuman, hyperphysical, superphysical, spiritual, ghostly, supramundane, supersensuous, supersensitive, supersensual, supernormal, unearthly.

theistic; theocratic; deistic; anointed; soterial.

adv. **under God**, by God's will, by God's help, *Deo volente* [*L.*], D. V., God willing; in Jesus' name, in His name, in His fear, to His glory; *jure divino* [*L.*], by divine right.

977. Angel
[beneficient spirits]

n. **angel**, archangel, Messenger of God, guardian angel, ministering spirits, invisible helpers, Choir Invisible, heavenly host, host of heaven, sons of God; morning star; saint.

[celestial hierarchy of pseudo-dionysius] (1) Seraphim (*sing.* seraph, *E. pl.* seraphs), Cherubim (*sing.* cherub, *E. pl.* cherubs; cherubim *or* cherubin *are often treated as sing.*), Thrones; (2) Dominions, Virtues, Powers; (3) Principalities, Archangels, Angels.

Michael, Gabriel, Raphael, Uriel, Chamuel, Jophiel, Zadkiel; Abdiel, Azrael.

madonna, Our Lady, *Notre Dame* [*F.*], Holy Mary, The Virgin, The Blessed Virgin, The Virgin Mary; *Dei Mater* [*L.*], Mother of God; *Regina Coeli* [*L.*], Queen of Heaven; *Regina Angelorum* [*L.*], Queen of Angels; *Stella Maris* [*L.*], Star of the Sea; *Mater Dolorosa* [*L.*]; Zion's Lily; *Alma Mater Redemptoris, Virgo Gloriosa, Virgo Sponsa Dei, Virgo Potens, Virgo Veneranda, Virgo Proedicanda, Virgo Clemens, Virgo Sapientissima, Sancta Virgo Virginum* [*all L.*]; *La Vergine Gloriosa* [*It.*]; *La Grande Vierge* [*F.*].

adj. **angelic**, seraphic, cherubic, archangelic.

978. Satan
[maleficent spirits]

n. **satan**, the Devil, Lucifer, Belial, Beëlzebub, Eblis [*Ar.*], Ahriman [*Zoroastrianism*], Mephistopheles, Mephisto, Shaitan [*Hind.*], Samael, Asmodeus, Satanas [*archaic*], Abaddon [*Heb.*], Apollyon, *le Diable* [*F.*], Deil [*Scot.*], *Teufel* [*Ger.*], *Diabolus* [*L.*].

his Satanic Majesty, the Prince of the Devils, the Prince of Darkness, the Prince of this world, the Prince of the power of the air; the Tempter, the Adversary, the Evil One, the Evil Spirit, the Archenemy, the Archfiend, the Foul Fiend, the Devil Incarnate, the Father of Lies, the Author of Evil, the Father of Evil, the Old Serpent, the Wicked One, the Common Enemy, the angel of the bottomless pit; the Deuce, the Dickens, the Old Gentleman, Old Nick, Old Scratch, Old Horny, Old Harry, Old Gooseberry [*all slang*].

fallen angels, unclean spirits, devils; the rulers of darkness, the powers of darkness; inhabitants of Pandemonium; demon etc. 980.

moloch, Mammon, Azazel [*Milton*]; Belial [*P. L.*], Beëlzebub [*in P. L., the fallen angel next to Satan*], Loki [*Norse myth.*]

diabolism, devil worship, devil lore, diablerie *or* diablery, diabolology *or* diabology, Satanism, devilism; devilship; devildom; demonry, demonism, demonology, Manichaeism *or* Manicheism; Black Mass, Black Magic, demonolatry, demonomagy; witchcraft etc. (*sorcery*) 992; the cloven hoof; hoofs and horns; demonomy.

diabolist, demonologist, demonologer, demonolater, demonist, demonographer [*rare*], demonomist; Manichaean *or* Manichean.

v. **diabolize** [*rare*], demonize; bewitch, bedevil etc. (*sorcery*) 992; possess, obsess.

adj. **satanic**, diabolic *or* diabolical, devilish, demoniac *or* demoniacal, infernal, hellborn.

979. Mythic and pagan deities

n. **god**, goddess; *deus* [*L.*], *dea* [*L.*]; *deva* (*fem.* devi) ["the shining ones," *Skr.*]; heathen gods and goddesses; pantheon; theogony.

[Greek and Latin] Zeus, Jupiter *or* Jove (*King*); Apollon, Apollo (*the sun*); Ares, Mars (*war*); Hermes, Mercury (*messenger*); Poseidon, Neptune (*ocean*); Hephaistos, Vulcan (*smith*); Dionysus, Bacchus (*wine*); Pluton *or* Hades [*Gr.*], Pluto *or* Dis [*L.*] (*King of the lower world*); Kronos, Saturn (*time*); Eros, Cupid (*love*); Pan, Faunus (*flocks, herds, forests, and wild life*).

Hera, Juno (*Queen*); Demeter, Ceres (*fruitfulness*); Persephone, Proserpina *or* Proserpine (*Queen of the lower world*); Artemis, Diana (*the moon and hunting*); Athena, Minerva (*wisdom*); Aphrodite, Venus (*love and beauty*); Hestia, Vesta (*the hearth*); Rhea *or* Cybele ("Mother of the gods," *identified with* Ops, *wife of Saturn*); Gaea *or* Ge, Tellus (*earth goddess, mother of the Titans*).

[Norse] Ymir (*primeval giant*), Reimthursen (*frost giants*), Bori (*fashioner of the world*), Bor (*father of Odin*), Odin *or* Woden (*the All-father,*

= *Zeus*); the Aesir *or* Asas; Thor (*the Thunderer*), Balder *or* Baldr (= *Apollo*), Freyr (*fruitfulness*), Tyr *or* Tyrr (*war*), Bragi (*poetry and eloquence*), Höder *or* Hödr (*blind god of the winter*), Heimdall (*warder of Asgard*), Vidar (= *Pan*), Uller *or* Ullr (*the chase*), Forseti (*peacemaker*), Vali (*knowledge and eternal light*), Loki (*evil*).

the Vanir *or* Vans: Njorth *or* Njord (*the winds and the sea*), Frey *or* Freyr (*prosperity and love*), Freya *or* Freyja (*goddess of love and beauty*, = *Venus*).

Frigg *or* Frigga (*wife of Odin*), Hel (*goddess of death*, = *Persephone*), Sif (*wife of Thor*), Nanna (*wife of Balder*), Idun (*goddess of spring, wife of Bragi*), Sigyn (*wife of Loki*).

[Hindu] **vedic gods**: Dyaus (*the Heaven*), Indra (*cloud-compeller*), Varuna (*the sky, also the waters*), Surya (*the sun*, = *Gr.* Helios), Savitar ("*the Inciter,*" *a sun god*), Soma (*the sustainer*), Agni (*fire*), Vavu (*the winds*), the Marutas (*storm gods*), Ushas ("*the Dawn,*" *goddess of wisdom*).

brahmanic gods: Brahmâ, Vishnu, Siva *or* Shiva etc. (*Brahmanism*) 976; avatars of Vishnu: (1) Matsya, the fish; (2) Karma, the turtle; (3) Varah, the boar; (4) Narsinh, man-lion; (5) Vaman, the dwarf; (6) Parshuram, a Brahman; (7) Rama; (8) Krishna; (9) Buddha; (10) Kalki; Jagannath *or* Juggernaut (*Krishna*); Ganesha *or* Ganpati (*wisdom*), Hanuman (*monkey god*), Yama (*judge of the dead*).

Sarasvati (*sakti or wife of Brahmâ; goddess of poetry, wisdom, and fine art*), Lakshmi (*wife of Vishnu; goddess of wealth, and prosperity*), Durga *or* Kali (*wife of Siva, conceived as a malignant deity*); Devi ("*the goddess*") *or* Uma ("*light*") *or* Gauri ("*the brilliant*") *or* Parvati ("*the mountaineer,*" *wife of Siva, conceived as a beneficient deity*).

[Egyptian] Ra *or* Amun-Ra (*the sun god*), Neph *or* Nef (*spirit or breath*), Pthah (*demiurge*), Khem (*reproduction*), Mut *or* Maut (= *Gr.* Demeter), Osiris (*judge of the dead*), Isis (*wife of Osiris*), Horus (*the morning sun; son of Osiris and Isis*), Anubis (*jackal-god, brother of Horus, a conductor of the dead*), Nephthys (*sister of Isis*), Set (*evil deity, brother of Osiris*), Thoth (*clerk of the underworld*), Bast *or* Bubastis (*a goddess with head of a cat*), the Sphinx (*wisdom*).

[various] Baal (*Heb. pl.* Baalim) [*Semitic*]; Astarte *or* Ashtoreth (*goddess of fertility and love*) [*Phoenician*]; Bel *Babylonian*]; The Great Spirit [*N. Amer Indian*]; Mumbo Jumbo [*Sudanese Negroes, an idol or bugaboo*].

nymph, dryad, hamadryad, alseid, wood nymph; naiad, fresh-water nymph; oread, mountain nymph; nereid, sea nymph; limoniad *or* leimoniad, meadow nymph *or* flower nymph; Oceanid, ocean nymph; napaea, glen nymph; potamid, river nymph; Pleiades *or* Atlantides, Hyades, Dodonides.

fairy, fay, sprite *or* spright [*archaic*]; nix (*fem.* nixie), water sprite; the Good Folk, brownie *or* browny, pixy, elf (*pl.* elves), banshee *or* banshie; the Fates *or* Moerae, *Clotho* (Spinner), *Lachesis* (Disposer of Lots), *Atropos* (Inflexible One); gnome, kelpie; faun; peri, nis, kobold, sylph, sylphid; undine, sea maid, sea nymph, mermaid (*masc.* merman); Mab, Oberon, Titania, Ariel; Puck, Robin Goodfellow, Hobgoblin; Leprechaun; denizens of the air; afreet etc. (*bad spirit*) 980.

familiar spirit, familiar, genius, guide, good genius, tutelary genius, daimon, demon *or* daemon, guardian.

mythology, mythical lore, heathen mythology, folklore, fairyism, fairy mythology.

adj. **mythical**, mythic, mythological, fabulous, legendary etc. 515.

fairylike, sylphlike, sylphine, sylphish, sylphidine; elfin, elflike, elfish, nymphlike.

980. Evil Spirits

n. demon, fiend, devil etc. (*Satan*) 978; evil genius, familiar, familiar spirit; bad-, unclean- spirit; cacodaemon *or* cacodemon, incubus, succubus *and* succuba; daeva *or* deev, bad peri, afreet, lamia, barghest *or* barguest; ogre, ogress, ghoul, vampire, harpy; Fury, the Furies, the Erinyes, the Eumenides; Titan; Friar Rush.

imp, bad fairy, sprite, jinni *or* jinnee (*pl.* jin), genius (*pl.* genii), flibberti-gibbet, ouphe, dwarf, troll, urchin, Cluricaune.

changeling, elf-child, auf, oaf; werewolf, *loup-garou* [*F.*]; satyr.

elemental, sylph, gnome, salamander, nymph [*Rosicrucian*].

siren, nixie, undine, Lorelei.

bugbear, bugaboo, bogy *or* bogey *or* bogie, bug [*obs.*], poker [*rare*], goblin, hobgoblin, boggart *or* boggard.

demonology, demonry etc. (*diabolism*) 978.

adj. demoniac, demoniacal, fiendish, fiendlike, evil, ghoulish; pokerish [*colloq.*], bewitched.

980a. Specter

n. **specter** *or* spectre, ghost, revenant, apparition, spirit, sprite, shade, shadow, wraith, spook [*now humorous*], phantom, phantasm, fantasm [*rare*], idolum; materialization [*Spiritualism*], ectoplasmic manifestation; double, etheric body, etheric self, aura, auric egg, astral body, *mayavi rupa*, ego [*all Theos. and Occultism*]; vision, theophany.

banshee, White Lady, the White Ladies of Normandy, the White Lady of Avenel [Scott]; lemures, larva *or* larve [*Roman relig.*].

will-o'-the-wisp, Friar's lantern etc. 423.

adj. **spectral**, ghostly, ghostlike, spiritual, wraithlike, weird, uncanny, eerie *or* eery, spooky *or* spookish [*colloq.*], haunted; unearthly, supernatural.

981. Heaven

n. **heaven**; kingdom of -heaven, –God; heavenly kingdom; heaven of heavens, God's throne, throne of God, presence of God; inheritance of the saints in light.

paradise, Eden, Zion, Holy City, New Jerusalem, Heavenly City, City Celestial, abode of the blessed; celestial bliss, eternal bliss, unending bliss, glory, never-ending day.

[mythological heaven or paradise] Olympus; Elysium, Elysian fields, Islands (*or* Isles) of the Blessed, Happy Isles, Fortunate Isles, Arcadia, bowers of bliss, garden of the Hesperides, third heaven, seventh heaven; Valhalla *or* Walhalla [*Scandinavian*]; Nirvana [*Buddhist*]; happy hunting grounds [*N. Amer. Indian*]; *Alfardaws, Assama; Falak al aflak,* ("the highest heaven") [*Mohammedan*].

future state, life after death, eternal home, resurrection, translation; resuscitation etc. 660; apotheosis, deification.

[theosophy] Devachan *or* Devaloka, the land of the Gods.

adj. **heavenly**, celestial, supernal, unearthly, from on high, paradisaic *or* paradisaical, paradisiac *or* paradisiacal, beatific, elysian, Olympian, Arcadian.

982. Hell

n. **hell**, bottomless pit, place of torment; habitation of fallen angels; Pandemonium, Abaddon, Domdaniel; *jahannan* [*Hind.*], Sheol.

hell fire; everlasting -fire, –torment; lake of fire and brimstone; fire that is never quenched, worm that never dies.

purgatory, limbo, gehenna, abyss, Tophet.

[mythological hell] Tartarus, Hades, Avernus, Styx, Stygian creek, pit of Acheron, Cocytus; infernal regions, inferno, shades below, realms of Pluto.

pluto, Rhadamanthus, Erebus, Charon, Cerberus; Persephone, Proserpina *or* Proserpine; Minos, Osiris.

rivers of hell: Styx, Acheron, Cocytus, Phlegethon, Lethe.

adj. **hellish**, infernal, stygian.

983. Theology

[religious knowledge]

n. **theology** (natural and revealed), theosophy, divine wisdom, divinity, hagiology, hagiography, hierography; Caucasian mystery; monotheism, theism, religion; religious -persuasion, –sect, –denomination, –affiliation; creed etc. (*belief*) 484; articles–, declaration–, profession–, confession- of faith.

theologian, theologue [*now rare*], scholastic, divine, schoolman, canonist, theologist [*now rare*], theologus; monotheist, theist; Homoousian (*opp. to* Homoiousian); the Fathers.

adj. **theological**, religious, divine, canonical; denominational; sectarian etc. 984.

983a. Orthodoxy

n. **orthodoxy**; strictness, soundness, religious, truth, true faith; truth etc. 494; soundness of doctrine.

christianity, Christianism; Catholicism, Catholicity; "the faith once delivered to the saints"; hyperorthodoxy etc. 984.

the church, Holy Church, Church Militant, Church Triumphant; Catholic–, Universal–, Apostolic–, Established- Church; the Bride of the Lamb; temple of the Holy Ghost; Church–, body–, members–, disciples–, followers- of Christ; Christians.

true believer; textualist, textuary; canonist etc. (*theologian*) 983; the Orthodox; Christian community; Christendom, collective body of Christians.

canons etc. (*belief*) 484; thirty-nine articles; Apostles'–, Nicene–, Athanasian- Creed; Church Catechism.

adj. **orthodox**, sound, strict, faithful, catholic, schismless, Christian, evangelical, scriptural, literal, divine, monotheistic, theistic; true etc. 494; true blue.

984. Heterodoxy

[sectarianism]

n. **heterodoxy**; error etc. 495; false doctrine, heresy, schism, schismaticism, schismaticalness; recusancy, backsliding, apostasy; materialism, hylotheism; atheism etc. (*irreligion*) 989.

anthropomorphism, anthropopathism, anthropopathy; idolatry etc. 991; superstition etc. (*credulity*) 486.

bigotry etc. (*obstinacy*) 606; fanaticism, iconoclasm; hyperorthodoxy, precisianism; bibliolatry, hagiolatry; sabbatarianism, puritanism.

sectarianism, sectarism [*obs.*], nonconformity; dissent etc. 489; secularism; syncretism; religious sects, the clash of creeds.

protestantism, Arianism, Adventism, Jansenism, Stundism, Erastianism, Calvinism, Quakerism, Methodism, Anabaptism, Puseyism, tractarianism, ritualism, Origenism, Sabellianism, Socinianism, Gnosticism, Mormonism, Second Adventism, materialism, positivism, latitudinarianism, ethicism, deism, higher pantheism, henotheism; monism, philosophical unitarianism etc.; the isms.

anglicanism, Church of England; High−, Low−, Broad−, Free-Church; ultramontanism; monasticism, monkery; Catholicism, Romanism, popery, papism, papistry, papacy, Maryolatry [*usually opprobrious*], Scarlet Woman, Church of Rome; Greek Church. [*Generally speaking, each sect is* orthodox *to itself and* heterodox *to others.*]

judaism; Mohammedanism, Islam, Islamism.

theosophy, New Thought, ethical culture, mental science, mental healing; Christian Science, Eddyism; Spiritualism, Spiritism, occultism; Swedenborgianism.

paganism, heathenism, heathendom; mythology; animism, polytheism, ditheism, tritheism, pantheism; dualism.

gentilism, Babism, Sufiism, Neoplatonism, Brahmanism, Hinduism, Vedantism, Buddhism, Lamaism; Sikhism, Jainism; Confucianism, Taoism; Shintoism, Sabaeanism *or* Sabeanism *or* Sabeism.

pagan, heathen, paynim; *giaour* [*Turk.*], Gheber *or* Ghebre, kafir, non-Mohammedan; gentile; pantheist, polytheist, animist.

misbeliever, heretic, apostate; backslider; antichrist; idolater; skeptic etc. 989.

bigot etc. (*obstinacy*) 606; fanatic, abdal, dervish, iconoclast.

sectarian, sectary, sectarist [*rare*], schismatic; seceder, separatist, recusant, dissenter, nonconformist, nonjuror.

Huguenot, Protestant, Episcopalian; Trinitarian; latitudinarian; limitarian; orthodox dissenter, Puritan, Unitarian, Congregationalist, Independent; Presbyterian; Lutheran, Ubiquitarian, Calvinist, Methodist, Wesleyan; Anabaptist,

Baptist; Mormon, Latter-day Saint; Irvingite, Sandemanian, Glassite, Erastian, Sublapsarian, Supralapsarian; Gentoo, Antinomian, Swedenborgian; Adventist, Second Adventist, Bible Christian, Bryanite, Brownian, Dunker, Ebionite, Eusebian; Faith Curer, Faith Christ, Faith Healer, Mental Healer, Christian Scientist; Familist, Jovinianist, Libadist, Restitutionist, Quaker, Shaker, Quietist, Stundist, Tunker etc.

catholic, Roman Catholic, Romanist, Papist, ultramontane; Anglican, Oxford School; tractarian, Puseyite, ritualist; High Churchman.

jew, Hebrew, Rabbinist; Mohammedan, Mussulman, Moslem, Islamite, Osmanli, Motazilite, Shiah, Sunni, Wahabi; Brahman *or* Brahmin; Brahmo; Vedantist, Jain *or* Jaina, Sikh, Parsi *or* Parsee, fire worshiper, Zoroastrian [*erron. called fire worshiper*]; Sufi, Babist, Buddhist; Confucianist, Taoist, Shintoist; Magi, Gymnosophist, Sabian, henotheist, Gnostic, Sadducee, Rosicrucian, Mystic, Occultist, Theosophist, Spiritualist, Spiritist etc.

materialist, hylotheist; positivist, deist, agnostic, atheist etc. 989.

adj. **heterodox**, heretical, unorthodox, unscriptural, uncanonical, unchristian, antiscriptural, apocryphal; antichristian; schismatic, recusant, iconoclastic; sectarian, dissenting, dissident [*now rare*]; Protestant etc. *n.;* secular etc. (*lay*) 997; deistic, agnostic, atheistic; skeptical etc. 989.

bigoted etc. (*prejudiced*) 481, (*obstinate*) 606; superstitious etc. (*credulous*) 486; fanatical; idolatrous etc. 991; visionary etc. (*imaginative*) 515.

judaical; Mohammedan, Islamic *or* Islamitic, Moslem; Brahmanic *or* Brahmanical, Brahminic *or* Brahminical; Buddhist etc. *n.*

popish, papish, papistic *or* papistical, Romish.

pagan, heathen, heathenish, ethnic, ethnical; gentile, paynim; polytheistic, pantheistic, animistic.

985. Revelation

[biblical]

n. **revelation**, inspiration, *afflatus* [*L.*]; theophany, theopneusty.

the bible, the Book, the Book of Books, the Good Book, the Word, the Word of God, Scripture, the Scriptures, Holy Writ, Holy Scriptures, inspired writings, Gospel.

old testament, Septuagint, Vulgate, Pentateuch; Octateuch; the Law, the Jewish Law; the Prophets; major−, minor- Prophets; Hagiographa, Hierographa; Apocrypha.

new testament; Gospels, Evangelists, Synoptic Gospels, Acts, Epistles, Apocalypse, Revelation; Good Tidings, Glad Tidings.

[hebrew] Talmud, Torah, Mishna, Gemara; Masora *or* Masorah.

inspired writers, inspired penmen; prophet etc. (*seer*) 513; evangelist, apostle, disciple, saint; the Fathers, the Apostolic Fathers; Holy Men of old.

adj. **scriptural**, biblical, sacred, prophetic; evangelical, evangelistic, apostolic, apostolical; inspired, theopneustic, theopneusted [*rare*], apocalyptic, revealed; ecclesiastical, canonical, textuary; Talmudic.

986. Sacred Writings
[non-biblical]

n. The Vedas (Rig-Veda, Yajur-Veda, Sama-Veda, Atharva-Veda), the Upanishads, the Puranas, Sutras, Sastra *or* Shastra, Tantra, Bhagavad Gita [*all Brahmanic*]; Zenda-vesta, A vesta [*Zoroastrian*]; The Koran *or* Alcoran [*Mohammedan*]; Tripitaka, Dhammapada [*Buddhist*]; Granth, Adigranth [*Sikh*]; the Agamas [*Jain*]; the Kings [*Chinese*]; the Eddas [*Scandinavia*].

arcana Coelestia etc. [*Swedenborgian*]; Book of Mormon; "Science and Health with Key to the Scriptures" [*Christian Science*].

[non-biblical prophets and religious founders] Gautama (Buddha); Zoroaster, Confucius, Lao-tse [*Taoism*], Mohammed, Nanak Shah [*Sikhism*], Vaddhamana, "Maha-vira" [*Jainism*], Mirza Ali Mohammed, "Bab-ud-Din" (*Per.* "Gate of the Faith") [*Babism*], Ram Mohun Roy [*Brahmo-Samaj*].

swedenborg, Joseph Smith [*Mormonism*], Mary Baker Eddy [*Christian Science*].

987. Piety

n. **piety**, religion, theism, faith; religiousness, religiosity, holiness etc. *adj.;* saintship; religionism; sanctimony etc. (*assumed piety*) 988; reverence etc. (*respect*) 928; humility, veneration, devotion; prostration etc. (*worship*) 990; grace, unction, edification; sanctity, sanctitude [*rare*]; consecration.

spiritual existence, odor of sanctity, beauty of holiness.

theopathy, beautification, adoption, regeneration, conversion, justification, theodicy, sanctification, salvation, inspiration, bread of life; Body and Blood of Christ.

believer, convert, theist, Christian, devotee, pietist, Saint.

the -good, -righteous, -just, -believing, -elect; the children of -God, -Our Father, -the kingdom, -light.

v. **be pious** etc. *adj.;* have faith etc. *n.;* believe, receive Christ; venerate, adore, worship, perform the acts of devotion; revere etc. 928; be converted etc.; experience the divine illumination [*Mysticism*]; be at one with God, be on God's side, stand up for Jesus, fight the good fight, keep the faith, let one's light shine.

regenerate, convert, edify, sanctify, hallow, keep holy, beatify, inspire, consecrate, enshrine.

adj. **pious**, religious, devout, devoted, reverent, godly, heavenly-minded, humble, pure, pure in heart, holy, spiritual, pietistic, saintly, saintlike; seraphic, sacred, solemn.

believing, faithful, Christian, Catholic.

regenerated; inspired, born-again, consecrated, converted, unearthly, not of the earth, in the world not of it.

elected, adopted, justified, sanctified.

988. Impiety

n. **impiety**; sin etc. 945; irreverence; profaneness etc. *adj.*, profanity, profanation; blasphemy, desecration, sacrilege; scoffing etc. *v.*

[assumed piety] hypocrisy etc. (*falsehood*) 544; pietism, cant, pious fraud; lip-devotion, lip-service, lip-reverence; misdevotion, formalism, austerity; sanctimony, sanctimoniousness etc. *adj.;* pharisaism, precisianism; sabbatism, sabbatarianism; *odium theologicum* [*L.*], sacerdotalism; bigotry etc. (*obstinacy*) 606, (*prejudice*) 481; blue laws.

apostasy, recusancy, hardening, backsliding, declension, perversion, reprobation.

hypocrite etc. (*dissembler*) 548; "Scribes and Pharisees" [*Bible*]; *Rawana-sannyasi* [*Hind.*]; Tartufe, Mawworm, Holy Willie [*Burns*].

bigot, saint [*ironical*]; Pharisee, sabbatarian, formalist, methodist, puritan, pietist, precisian, religionist, devotee, ranter, fanatic; juramentado [*Moro*].

sinner etc. 949; scoffer, blasphemer, sacrilegist [*rare*], sabbath breaker; worldling.

the wicked, the evil, the unjust, the reprobate; sons of -men, -Belial, -the wicked one; children of -the devil, -darkness.

v. **be impious** etc. *adj.;* profane, desecrate, blaspheme, revile, scoff; swear etc. (*malediction*) 908; commit sacrilege.

dissemble, simulate, play the hypocrite, hypocrify [*obs.*], hypocrize [*rare*], snuffle, talk through the nose, talk nasally, hold up the hands in horror, turn up the whites of the eyes; sing psalms for a pretense, make long prayers.

adj. **impious**; irreligious etc. 989; desecrating etc. *v.;* profane, irreverent, sacrilegious, blasphemous.

unhallowed, unsanctified, unregenerate; hardened, perverted, reprobate.

hypocritical etc. (*false*) 544; canting, pietistical, sanctimonious, unctuous, pharisaical, over-righteous, righteous over much.

bigoted, fanatical, hidebound, narrow, illiberal, prejudiced, little; provincial, parochial, insular; priest-ridden.

adv. under the -mask, –cloak, –pretense, –form, –guise- of religion; in blasphemy.

989. Irreligion

n. **irreligion**, indevotion, impiety; ungodliness etc. *adj.;* laxity, apathy, indifference; quietism, passiveness, passivity.

skepticism, doubt; unbelief, disbelief, incredulity, incredulousness etc. *adj.;* want of -faith, –belief; pyrrhonism; doubt etc. 485; agnosticism, freethinking; deism; hylotheism; materialism, rationalism, positivism; nihilism.

infidelity, antichristianity, antichristianism, atheism.

unbeliever, infidel, atheist, antichristian; *giaour* [*Turk.*], heretic, miscreant [*archaic*], heathen, alien, gentile, Nazarene; *espirit fort* [*F.*], freethinker, skeptic, pyrrhonist, deist, latitudinarian, rationalist; materialist, positivist, nihilist, agnostic, somatist, theophobist.

v. **be irreligious** etc. *adj.;* disbelieve, lack faith; doubt, question etc. 485.

dechristianize, antichristianize [*rare*]; serve Mammon, contend against the light, love darkness rather than light, deny the truth.

adj. **irreligious**; indevout, undevout, devoutless, godless, graceless, ungodly; unholy, unsanctified, unhallowed; atheistic, without God.

skeptical, freethinking, unbelieving, unconverted; incredulous, faithless, lacking faith; deistic, deistical; antichristian, unchristian.

worldly, mundane, earthly, carnal; worldly etc. worldly-minded, unspiritual.

adv. **irreligiously** etc. *adj.*

990. Worship

n. **worship**, adoration, devotion, cult, aspiration, homage, service, humiliation; kneeling, genuflection, prostration; latria, dulia, hyperdulia.

prayer, invocation, supplication, rogation, intercession, orison, holy breathing, petition etc. (*request*) 765; collect, litany, Lord's prayer, paternoster; *Ave Maria* [*L.*]; Hail, Mary; rosary, bead-roll.

revival; anxious–, revival–, camp- meeting.

thanksgiving; giving–, returning- thanks; grace, praise, glorification, paean, benediction, doxology, hosanna, hallelujah *or* halleluiah, alleluia *or* alleluiah; *Te Deum, non nobis Domine, nunc dimittis; O Salutaris* [*all L.*]; Sanctus, *Agnus Dei* [*L.*], *Kyrie Eleison* [*Gr.*], *Gloria* [*L.*], The Annunciation, Tersanctus, Trisagion.

psalm, psalmody; hymn, plain song, chant, chaunt [*archaic*], response, anthem, motet, antiphon, antiphony.

oblation, sacrifice, incense, libation, offering; burnt–, heave–, thank–, votive- offering; offeratory, collection.

discipline, self-discipline, self-examination, self-denial; fasting, penance, confession.

divine service, office, duty; exercises; morning prayer; Mass, matins, nones, complin *or* compline, evensong, vespers, vigils, lauds; undersong, tierce; holyday etc. (*rites*) 998.

prayer book, missal, breviary, Virginal; ritual etc. 998.

worshiper, congregation, communicant, celebrant.

v. **worship**, lift up the heart, aspire; revere etc. 928; adore, do service, pay homage; humble oneself, kneel; bow–, bend- the knee; throw oneself on one's knees, fall down, fall on one's knees; prostrate oneself, bow down and worship; beat the breast.

intone, chant, deacon *or* deacon off [*colloq.*], lead the choir, sing.

pray, invoke, supplicate; put–, offer- up -prayers, –petitions; beseech etc. (*ask*) 765; say one's prayers, tell one's beads, recite the rosary.

give thanks, return thanks, say grace, bless, praise, laud, glorify, magnify, sing praises; give benediction.

propitiate, offer sacrifice, fast, deny oneself; vow, offer vows, give alms.

attend service, attend Mass, go to church, attend divine service; communicate etc. (*rite*) 998; work out one's salvation.

adj. **worshiping** etc. *v.;* devout, devotional, reverent, pure, solemn; fervid etc. (*heartfelt*) 821.

int. **hallelujah** *or* halleluiah! alleluia *or* alleluiah! hosanna! glory be to God! *sursum corda* [*L.*], *Deo gratias* [*L.*].

o Lord! pray God that! God -grant, –bless, –save, –forbid!

991. Idolatry

n. **idolatry**, idolatrousness, idololatry, idolism, idolodoulia, demonism, demonolatry, demonology; idol–, chthonian–, demon–, devil–, fire-worship; zoölatry, fetishism *or* fetichism; ecclesiolatry, heliolatry, bibliolatry, hierolatry [*rare*].

idolization, deification, apotheosis, canonization; hero worship.

sacrifice, idolothyte, hecatomb, holocaust; human sacrifices, immolation, mactation, infanticide, self-immolation, suttee.

idol, golden calf, graven image, fetish *or* fetich, eidolon, *thakur* [*Hind.*], joss [*Chinese*], *lares et penates* [*L.*]; god (*or* goddess) of one's idolatry; Baal, Moloch, Dagon, Juggernaut.

idolater, idolatress, demonolater *or* demonolator, chthonian, fetishist *or* fetichist; idolatrizer, idolizer, idolant [*obs.*], idolaster [*obs.*]; ecclesiolater, heliolater, zoölater, bibliolater.

v. **idolatrize**, idolize; *adorer le veau d'or* [*F.*]; worship -idols, –pictures, –relics; apotheosize, worship, put on a pedestal, prostrate oneself before; make sacrifice to, immolate before; deify, canonize.

adj. **idolatrous**, idololatric [*rare*], idolatric [*rare*], idolistic, chthonian, demonolatrous, fetishic [*rare*], fetishistic *or* fetichistic, idolothyte; worshiping *or* worshipping, prone before, prostrate before, in the dust before, at the feet of; heliolatrous, zoölatrous.

992. Sorcery

n. **sorcery**; occult -art, –sciences; magic, black magic, the black art, necromancy, theurgy, thaumaturgy; demonology, demonomy [*obs.*], demonomancy, demonship; diablerie, bedevilment, witchcraft, witchery; fetishism *or* fetichism; ghost dance, hoodoo, voodoo, voodooism; fire worship, heliolatry; obi *or* obiism, shamanism, vampirism; conjuration, incantation, bewitchment, glamour, enchantment; obsession, possession; exorcism.

divination etc. (*prediction*) 511; sortilege, ordeal, *sortes Vergilianae*; hocuspocus etc. (*deception*) 545.

v. **practice sorcery** etc. *n.*; cast a nativity, cast a horoscope, conjure, exorcise *or* exorcize [*rare in the sense of* conjure], charm, enchant, bewitch, bedevil, overlook, look on with the evil eye, witch, voodoo, hoodoo [*colloq.*]; entrance, fascinate etc. (*influence*) 615; taboo *or* tabu; wave a wand; rub the -ring, –lamp; cast a spell; call up spirits; raise spirits from the dead; raise ghosts, lay ghosts; command jinn *or* genii.

adj. **magic**, magical; witching, weird, cabalistic, talismanic, phylacteric, incantatory; charmed etc. *v.*; Circean; voodoo.

992a. Psychical Research

n. **psychical research**, psychical (*or* psychic) investigation; abnormal psychology; abnormal–, supernormal–, mediumistic-phenomena; mysticism; psychophysics; "psychologist's fallacy" [William James].

the subconscious, the subconscious self, the subliminal self, the higher self; ego etc. 980 *a*; subconsciousness, subliminal consciousness; dual personality, mental duality, secondary consciousness, intuition; multiple personality, mental dissociation, dissociation of personality, functional disintegration; impersonation, obsession, possession.

psychotherapy, psychotherapeutics, psychoanalysis; hysteria, neurasthenia, psychasthenia; over-stimulation; dreams, visions, apparitions, hallucinations, veridical hallucinations; Freud's theory.

mesmerism, animal magnetism; od, odyl *or* odylic force [*obsoles.*], electrobiology; mesmeric trance; hypnotism; hypnosis, hypnoidal state.

[*phenomena*] **telepathy**, thought transference, thought transmission, telepathic transmission; "malicious animal magnetism" *or* "M. A. P."; telepathic dreams; second sight, clairvoyance, clairaudience, psychometry.

premonitions, previsions, telepathic hallucinations; premonitory apparition, fetch, wraith, double; symbolic hallucinations; death lights, ominous dreams, ominous animals.

automatism, automatic writing, planchette, ouija board, trance writing, spirit writing, psychography; trance speaking, inspirational speaking.

crystal gazing, crystallomancy, crystal vision; hydromancy, lecanomancy, catoptromancy, onychomancy.

spiritualism, spiritism, spirit rapping, "Rochester knockings," table-turning, Poltergeist; spirit manifestations; ghost, specter etc. 980*a*; haunted houses; trance, spirit control, spirit possession; mediumistic communications; séance; materialization.

[*theosophy and occultism*] astral body etc. 980*a*, *kamarupa* [*Skr.*], desire body; etheric body, *linga sharira* [*Skr.*]; dense body, *sthula sharira* [*Skr.*]; mental body; causal body; bliss body, Buddhic body.

seven principles of man: (1) spirit *or atma* [*Skr.*], (2) spiritual mind, (3) intellect, (4) instinctive mind, (5) prana *or* vital force, (6) astral body, (7) physical body [*Yogi philosophy*].

medium, ecstatica [*rare*], seer, clairvoyant, clairaudient, telepathist; guide, control; mesmerist, hypnotist.

v. **psychologize**; investigate the -abnormal, –suprarational, –supernormal, –the subconscious, –the subliminal; search beyond the threshold, traverse the borderland, know oneself.

mesmerize, magnetize, hypnotize, place under control, subject to suggestion, place in a trance, induce hypnosis.

hold a séance, call up spirits, summon familiar spirits, "call spirits from the vasty deep" [*I Henry IV*]; hold spirit communications; materialize.

adj. **psychical**, psychic, psychal [*rare*], psychological; spiritistic, spiritualistic, spiritual; subconscious, "coconscious" [Morton Prince], subliminal (*opp. to* supraliminal); supernormal, abnormal, suprarational; mystic *or* mystical.

mediumistic, clairvoyant, clairaudient, telepathic; psychometric; hypnoidal, hypnagogic.

993. Spell

n. **spell**, charm, incantation, exorcism, weird [*obs. or Scot.*], cabala *or* cabbala, exsufflation [*obs.*], cantrip *or* contraip *or* contrap [*chiefly Scot.*], runes, abracadabra, open sesame, *or* open-sesame, hocus-pocus, counter-charm, Ephesian letters, bell book and candle, Mumbo Jumbo, evil eye.

talisman, amulet, madstone, periapt, telesm [*archaic*], phylactery, philter *or* philtre, fetish *or* fetich, manito *or* manitou *or* manitu; furcula, furculum, wishbone, merrythought; mascot *or* mascotte, rabbit's foot, hoodoo [*colloq.*], jinx [*slang*], scarabaeus *or* scarab; Om *or* Aum, *Om mani padme hum* [*Buddhist*]; sudarium, veronica, triskelion; swastika, fylfot, gammadion.

wand, caduceus, rod, divining rod, witch hazel, Aaron's rod.

[magic wish-givers] Aladdin's lamp, Aladdin's casket, magic casket, magic ring, magic belt, magic spectacles, wishing cap, Fortunatus's cap; seven-league boots; cap of darkness, Tarnkappe, Tarnhelm.

[fairy lore] fairy ring, fairy circle, fairy round; fernseed, rowan tree, quicken tree [*dial. Eng.*].

994. Sorcerer

n. **sorcerer**, magician, wizard, warlock, necromancer, conjuror, prestidigitator, *prestidigitateur* [*F.*], charmer, exorcist, voodoo,

thaumaturge, thaumaturgist, theurgist, image [*poetic*], Magi (*sing.* Magus); diviner, dowser.

sorceress, witch, hag.

medicine man *or* medicine, witch doctor, shaman, shamanist.

vampire, lamia, ghoul; siren, harpy; incubus etc. 980.

astrologer, figure caster [*obs.*], figure flinger [*obs.*]; soothsayer etc. 513.

Katerfelto, Cagliostro, Merlin, Comus; Circe, weird sisters, Graeae *or* Graiae, witch of Endor.

995. Churchdom

n. **churchdom**; church, ministry, apostleship, priesthood, prelacy, hierarchy, church government, pale of the church, christendom.

clericalism, sacerdotalism, episcopalianism, ultramontanism; ecclesiology; theocracy; priestcraft, *odium theologicum* [*L.*]; religious sects etc. 984.

monasticism, monkhood, monachism; celibacy.

[ecclesiastical offices and dignities] cardinalate, cardinalship; primacy, archbishopric, archiepiscopacy; prelacy, bishopric, bishopdom, episcopate, episcopacy, see, diocese; deanery, stall; canonry, canonicate; prebend, prebendaryship, prebendal stall; benefice, incumbency, glebe, advowson, living, cure, charge, cure of souls; rectorship, vicariate, vicarship; pastorate, pastorship, pastoral charge; deaconry, deaconship; curacy; chaplaincy, chaplainship, chaplainry *or* chaplanry [*Scot.*]; abbacy, presbytery.

holy orders, ordination, institution, consecration, induction, reading in [*Eng.*], preferment, translation, presentation.

papacy, pontificate, popedom, See of Rome, the Vatican, the apostolic see.

council etc. 696; conclave, college of cardinals, convocation, conference [*Meth.*], session, synod, consistory, chapter, vestry, presbytery, standing committee; sanhedrin, *congé d'élire* [*F.*].

ecclesiastical courts, consistorial court, court of Arches.

v. **call**, ordain, induct, prefer [*rare*], translate, consecrate, present, elect, bestow

take orders, take the veil, take vows.

adj. **ecclesiastical**, ecclesiological; clerical, sacerdotal, priestly, prelatical, pastoral, ministerial, capitular, theocratic; hierarchical, archiepiscopal; episcopal, episcopalian; canonical; monastic, monachal, monkish; abbatial, abbatical; Anglican; Aaronic, levitical, pontifical, papal, apostolic; ultramontane; priestridden.

996. Clergy

n. **clergy**, clericals, ministry, priesthood, presbytery, the cloth, the pulpit, the desk.

clergyman, divine, ecclesiastic, churchman, priest, presbyter, hierophant, pastor, shepherd, minister, clerk in holy orders, parson, sky pilot [*slang*]; father, –in Christ; padre, abbé [*F.*], curé [*F.*]; reverend; black coat; confessor.

[dignitaries of the church] ecclesiarch, sacrist, hierarch; patriarch [*Eastern Ch.*]; Abba Salamah, Abuna [*Abyssinian Ch.*]; eminence, reverence, primate, metropolitan, archbishop, bishop, angel [*as in the Cath. Apostolic Ch.*], prelate, diocesan, suffragan, bishop coadjutor, dean, subdean, archdeacon, prebendary, canon, rural dean, rector, vicar, perpetual curate, residentiary, beneficiary, incumbent, chaplain, curate; elder, deacon, deaconess; preacher, reader, Bible reader, lay reader, lecturer; capitular; missionary, propagandist, Jesuit, revivalist, field preacher, colporteur.

churchwarden, deacon, questman [*hist.*], sidesman; clerk, precentor, choir; almoner, suisse [*F.*], verger, beadle, sexton, sacristan; acolyte, thurifer, censor-bearer; choirster, choir boy, member of the choir; soloist, quartet *or* quartette; organist.

[roman catholic priesthood] Pope, Holy Father, papa [*obs. or rare*], pontiff, high priest, cardinal; archbishop, bishop, bishop coadjutor; canon-regular, canon-secular, confessor, penitentiary, Grand Penitentiary, spiritual director.

religious, monastic, cenobite, conventual, abbot, prior, monk, friar, lay brother, beadsman *or* bedesman, mendicant, pilgrim, palmer; Jesuit, Franciscan, Friars minor, Minorites; Observant, Capuchin, Dominican, Carmelite; Augustinian; Gilbertine; Austin–, Black–, White–, Gray–, Crossed–, Crutched- Friars; Bonhomme, Carthusian, Benedictine, Cistercian, Trappist, Cluniac, Premonstratensian, Maturine; Templar, Hospitaler; Bernardine, Lorettine, pillarist, stylite; caloyer, hieromonach [*both Eastern Ch.*].

nun, sister, religieuse [*F.*]; priestess, abbess, prioress, canoness; mother superior, superioress, the reverend mother; novice, postulant.

[jewish] prophet, priest, high priest, Levite; Rabbi, Rabbin, scribe.

[mohammedan] imam *or* imaum, kahin, kasis, sheik; mullah, murshid, mufti; hadji *or* haji, muezzin [*all Ar.*]; dervish *or* darvesh [*Pers.*], abdal (*pl.* abdali) [*Pers.*], fakir *or* faquir [*Ar.*], beshara [*Hind.*], bashara [*Hind.*], santon [*Turkey*].

[hindu] Brahman *or* Brahmin, pujari, purohit [*family priest*]; pundit *or* pandit, guru; yogi, sannyasi *or* sanyasi; bhikshu, bhikhari, vairagi *or* bairagi, Ramwat, Ramanandi [*all Hind.*].

[buddhist] poonghie *or* poonghee [*Burma*], talapoin [*Ceylon & Indo-China*], bonze; lama, Grand Lama *or* Dalai Lama [*Tibet*].

[various] druid, druidness [*ancient Celts*]; flamen [*Rom. relig. and ancient Britain*]; hierus, hierophant [*Gr. relig.*]; daduchus *or* dadouchos, mystae, epoptae [*Eleusinian Mysteries*].

v. take orders etc. 995.

adj. **ordained**, in orders, in holy orders, called to the ministry; the Reverend, the very Reverend, the Right Reverend.

997. Laity

n. **laity**, flock, fold, congregation, assembly, brethren, people; society; class [*Meth.*], meeting.

layman, civilian [*obs.*], laic, parishioner, catechumen; secularist.

v. **laicize**, secularize.

adj. **secular**, lay, laic *or* laical, congregational, civil, temporal, profane.

998. Rite

n. **rite**, ceremony, ceremonial, ordinance, observance, function, duty; form, formulary; solemnity, sacrament; incantation etc. (*spell*) 993; service, ministry, ministration; liturgics.

sermon, preaching, preachment, predication [*obs. or Scot.*], exhortation, religious harangue, homily, lecture, discourse, pastoral.

[seven sacraments] **baptism**, immersion, christening, chrism; baptismal regeneration; font.

confirmation, imposition of hands, laying on of hands.

eucharist, Lord's supper, communion; the sacrament, the holy sacrament; consecrated elements, bread and wine; intinction; celebration, high celebration; missa cantata [*L.*]; asperges [*L.*]; offertory; introit; consecration; consubstantiation, impanation, subpanation, transubstantiation; real presence; elements; Mass; high–, low–, dry- mass; hunter's (*or* hunting) mass [*obs.*].

penance etc. (*atonement*) 952; flagellation, maceration, fasting, sackcloth and ashes.

extreme unction, last rites, viaticum.

holy orders, ordination etc. (*churchdom*) 995.

matrimony, marriage, wedlock etc. 903.

worship etc. 990; invocation of saints, canonization, transfiguration, auricular confession, the confessional; absolution; reciting the rosary, telling of beads; processional; thurification, incense, holy water, aspersion.

circumcision; purification; visitation of the sick; burial etc. 363.

[sacred articles] relics, rosary, beads, reliquary, host, cross, rood, crucifix; pyx, pix [*obs.*]; pax, *Agnus Dei* [*L.*], censer, thurible, incensory, patera; urceus, urceole; prayer wheel, prayer machine; Sangraal *or* Sangrael, Holy Grail.

ritual, rubric, canon, ordinal, missal, breviary, Mass book, beadroll; farse; liturgy, prayer book, Book of Common Prayer, *Pietà* [*It.*], euchologion *or* euchology [*Eastern Ch.*], litany, lectionary.

psalter, psalm book, hymn book, hymnal; hymnology, psalmody.

ritualism, ceremonialism; sabbatism, sabbatarianism; ritualist, sabbatarian.

holyday, feast, fast; Sabbath, Passover, Pentecost; Advent, Christmas, Epiphany, Lent; Passion Week, Holy Week; Good Friday, Easter; Ascension Day, Holy Thursday; Whitsuntide, Whitsunday *or* Whit-Sunday [*erroneously,* Whitsun Day]; Trinity Sunday, Corpus Christi; All Saints *or* All Saints' Day, All Souls' Day; love feast, agape; Candlemas *or* Candlemas Day; Lammas, Lammas Day, Lammastide; Michaelmas, Martinmas.

v. **perform service**, do duty, minister, officiate; baptize, dip, sprinkle; confirm, lay hands on; give–, administer–, take–, receive–, attend–, partake of- the -sacrament, –communion, –Holy Eucharist; communicate; celebrate Mass, celebrate; administer–, receive- extreme unction; anele [*obs.*], shrive, absolve; administer–, receive- absolution; confess, make confession; do–, perform–, receive–, inflict- penance; tell one's beads; genuflect; make the sign of the Cross.

excommunicate, ban with bell book and candle.

preach, sermonize, predicate, lecture, address the congregation.

adj. **ritual**, ritualistic, ceremonial; liturgic *or* liturgical; baptismal, eucharistical; paschal.

999. Canonicals

n. **canonicals**, vestments; robe, gown, Geneva gown, frock, pallium, surplice, cotta, cassock; communion cloth, eileton [*Eastern Ch.*], corporal [*Western Ch.*]; scapular *or* scapulary, cope, mozetta *or* mozzetta, amice, scarf, fanon *or* fannel, bands, chasuble, tunicle, dalmatic, alb *or* alba, stole; tonsure, cowl, hood, capuche, calotte; vagas *or* vakas *or* vakass; apron, lawn sleeves, pontificals, pall; miter *or* mitre, tiara, triple crown; shovel–, cardinal's-hat; biretta *or* berretta; crosier *or* crozier, cross staff, pastoral staff; Sanctus bell, sacring bell; seven-branched candlestick; monstrance; censer etc. 998; costume etc. 225.

1000. Temple

n. **temple**, place of worship; house of God, house of prayer; cathedral, minister, church, kirk [*Scot. & dial. Eng.*], chapel, meeting-house, bethel, ebenezer [*Eng.*], conventicle, basilica, fane, holy place, chantry, oratory.

synagogue, tabernacle; mosque, masjid [*Moham.*]; dewal, kan-pati [*both Hindu*], girja [*Hind., Christian*]; pagoda, pagod [*archaic*], kiack [*Buddhist*]; Chinese temple, joss house [*colloq.*]; pantheon.

shrine, dagoba [*India*]; tope, stupa [*Buddhist*], Marabout [*Moham.*].

[interior] altar, sanctuary, Holy of Holies, *sanctum sanctorum* [*L.*], sacristy; sacrarium; communion–, holy–, Lord's- table; table of the Lord; pyx; baptistery, font; piscina; stoup; holy-water stoup, holy-water basin; ambry, aumbry [*archaic*]; sedile; reredos; rood screen, rood beam, chapel screen, jube; rood loft.

chancel, apse, choir, quire [*archaic*], nave, triforium, blindstory, aisle, transept, crypt, porch, cloisters; churchyard, golgotha; calvary, Easter sepulcher; stall, pew, seat, seating; pulpit, ambo, lectern, reading desk; confessional; prothesis, table (*or* altar) of prothesis, chapel of prothesis [*Eastern Ch.*]; credence, baldachin *or* baldaquin; belfry; vestry, chapter house; presbytery; diaconicon *or* diaconicum; mourners' bench, mourners' seat; anxious bench, anxious seat, penitent form.

monastery, priory, abbey, friary, convent, nunnery, cloister.

parsonage, rectory, vicarage, manse, deanery, clergy house; glebe; Vatican; bishop's palace; Lambeth.

adj. **churchly**, claustral, cloistered, monastic, monasterial, monachal, conventual; cruciform.

Index Guide

The numbers refer to the headings under which the words or phrases occur. When the same word or phrase can be used in various senses, the several headings under which it, or its synonyms, will be found are indicated by *italics*. These words in italics are not intended to explain the meaning of the word or phrase to which they are annexed, but only to assist in the required reference.

Italicized references within parentheses are merely suggestive, the parentheses indicating that the term itself is not included in the list referred to.

When the word given in the Index Guide is itself the title or heading of a category, the reference number is printed in bold-face type, thus: **abode 189.**

To keep the Index Guide—necessarily very large—from becoming unwieldy, a considerable number of obsolete, rare, foreign, dialectic, and slang terms have been omitted. Such words, while useful in the text, are not the ones for which synonyms would ordinarily be sought.

Derivatives likewise have been sparingly admitted, since the allied or basic term will serve as a key to the various derived forms; thus, *cold* is given, but not *coldness* or *coldly*. By such means, unnecessary duplication is avoided.

IMPORTANT NOTE

The numbers following all references in this Index Guide refer to the *section numbers* in the text, and *not* to pages. Thus "Aaronic 995" refers to *section* 995, under which the citation will be found. For further ease of reference, the *section* numbers will be found at the *top* of every page.

A

A 1 273, 648
  −at Lloyd's 273
Aaronic 995
A. B. 269
abacist 85
aback 235 take−508
abaction 791
abacus 85
Abaddon 978, 982
abaft 235
abalienate 783
abandon
  depart from 293
  −*a purpose* 624
  −*property* 782
  −*hope* 859
  −*society* 893
abandon *lively* 682
  artless 703
abandoned
  neglected 460
  forsaken 893
  vicious 945
  −*farm* 782
abandonment 757
abase *depress* 308
  degrade 879
abased 886
abasement
  disrepute 874
  servility 886
abash *daunt* 860
  humiliate 879

abashed *modest* 881
abate *lessen* 36
  −*a price* 813
abatement 36
  −*of differences* 774
abatjour 260
abattis 717
abattoir 361
abat−voix 417
abba 166
abbacy 995
abbatial 995
abbatis 717
abbess 996
abbey 1000
abbot 996
abbreviation
  shortening 201
  compendium 596
abbreviatory
  short 201
  compendious 596
abbreviature 596
A B C *beginning* 66
  teaching 537
  letters 561
abdal *fanatic* 984
  clergy 996
abderian 836
abdicant 757
abdicate
  −*a throne* 738
  resign 757
abditory 530
abdomen 221, 250
abdominal 221, 250

abdominoscope 445
abdominous 194
abducent 289
abduct *repel* 289
  take 789
  steal 791
abduction 289
abductor 792
abecedarian
  teacher 540
  learner 541
abecedary *school* 542
  letter 561
aberdevine 366
aberrant
  exceptional 83
  deviating 279
  divergent 291
  erroneous 495
aberration
  (*see aberrant*)
  variation 20a
  mental −503
abet 707
abettor 711
abeyance *extinction* 2
  suspense 142
  expectation 507
  in −172
abeyant 526
abhor *dislike* 867
  hate 898
abhorrence
  (*see abhor*)
abhorrent
  painful 830

abide *endure* 1, 106
  remain 110
  continue 141, 143
  dwell 186
  quiet 265
  expect 507
  −*by assent* 488
  observe 772
  −*with*
    be composed 826
    not−867
abigail 746
abilities
  to the best of one's
    −686
ability *power* 157
  skill 698
abiogenesis 161, 357
abirritate 834
abito 350
abject *vile* 874, 940
  servile 886
  −*fear* 862
abjunction 44
abjuratory 536, 757
abjure *deny* 536
  renounce 607
  resign 757
abkari 812
ablation
  subduction 38
  taking 789
ablaze *heat* 382
  light 420
able *capable* 157
  skillful 698

  −*seaman* 269
able−bodied 159
ablegate *displace* 185
  depute 759
ablepsia 442
ablude 15
ablution 652
abnegation
  denial 536
  refusal 764
  forbearance 953
  self−942
abnormal 83
  −*mind* 503
abnormalize 83
aboard *present* 186
  ship 273
  go−293
abode 189 *presage* 511
  take up one's
  −*settle* 150
  locate oneself 184
abodement 511
aboideau 350
abolish (*see abolition*)
abolition *destroy* 162
  abrogate 756
abolitionist 756
abolitionize 756
abomasum 191
abominable *bad* 649
  foul 653
  hateful 898
abominate
  dislike 867
  hate 898

trial 675
undertaking 676
adventurer
traveler 268
experimenter 463
deceiver 548
gambler 621
rash 863
ignoble 876
adventures
history 594
adventuress 548
adventurous
undertaking 676
bold 861
rash 863
adversaria 551
adversary 710
Adversary, the—978
adverse *contrary* 14
opposed 708
unprosperous 735
disliking 867
—*party* 710
adversity 735
advert 457
advertent 457
advertise 531
advice *notice* 527
news 532
counsel **695**
*good—*695
advisable 646
advise *predict* 511
inform 527
counsel 695
—*with one's pillow* 451
advised
predetermined 611
intended 620
*better—*658
advisement
advice 695
(see advise)
*under—*453
adviser *teacher* 540
counselor 695
advisory 527
advocacy
approbation 931
advocate
interpreter 524
prompt 615
recommend 695
aid 707
auxiliary 711
friend 890, 914
vindicate 937
counselor 968
Advocate, the—
Savior 976
advocation *plea* 617
advoutress 962
advoutry 961
advowson 995

adynamic 160
adytum *room* 191
prediction 511
secret place 530
aedile 965
aegis 717
Aeolian 349
—*harp* 417
Aeolus 349
aeon 109, 110
aerate 334, 353
aeration 334
aerial *elevated* 206
navigation 267, 273
gas 334
air 338
—*mail* 534
—*mail-carrier* 271
—*navigator* 269
—*perspective* 428
—*railway* 840
aerie 189
aeriferous 334
aerification 334
aeriform 334
aerify 334
aeroboat 273
aerobus 273
aerodonetics 267
aerodrome 273
aerodynamics
navigation 267
gas 334
wind 349
aerography 334, 349
aero-hydroplane
273
aerolite 318
aerology *gaseity* 334
air 338
wind 349
aeromancy 511
aeromechanic 267,
334
aerometer 338
aerometric 338
aeronat 273
aeronaut 269a
aeronautic 273
(see aeronautics)
aeronautics
navigation 267
air 338
aeroplane 273
combatant 726
*by—*684
aeroplanist 269
aeroscope 338
aeroscopy 334
aerosphere 338
aerostat *balloon* 273
aerostatics 267 334
aerostation 338
aerotherapy 662
aeroyacht 273
aery *gaseous* 334

atmospheric 338
Aesculapius 662
Aesop 846
aesthetic
sensibility 375
beauty 845
taste 850
aestival 125
aestivation 384
aetiology *causes* 155
life 359
knowledge 490
disease 655
afar 196
afeard 860
affable
condescending 879
courteous 894
affair *event* 151
topic 454
business 625
battle 720
—*of honor* 720
affaires, chargé d'—
758
affect *relate to* 9
tend to 176
qualify 469
feign 544
touch 824
desire 865
love 897
affectation 855
affected 583
—*manner* 880
affected with
feeling 821
disease 655
affectibility 822
affecting *pathetic* 830
affection *feeling* 821
love 897
affectionate 821, 897
affections 820
affettuoso *music* 415
affiance *promise* 768
trust 858
affianced *love* 897
marriage 903
affiche 531
affidation 769
affidavit
affirmation 535
record 551
lawsuit 969
affiliation *relation* 9
kindred 11
attribution 155
affinal 11
affinitive 9
affinity *relation* 9
similarity 17
affirmant 488
affirmation
evidence 467
assent 488

assert **535**
affirmative 535
affix *add* 37
sequel 39
fasten 43
precedence 62
letter 561
afflation 349
afflatus *wind* 349
inspiration 985
afflict 830
—*with illness* 655
affliction *pain* 828
infliction 830
adversity 735
affluence
sufficiency 639
prosperity 734
wealth 803
affluent *river* 348
afflux 286
afford *supply* 784
wealth 803
yield 810
sell for 812
—*aid etc.* 707
affranchise
make free of 748
liberate 750
affray 720
affriction 331
affright 860
affront *molest* 830
provocation 900
insult 929
—*danger* 861
affuse 337
affusion 73
afield 186
afire 382
afloat *extant* 1
unstable 149
going on 151
ship 273
navigation 267
ocean 341
news 532
preparing 673
*keep oneself—*734
set—publish 531
afoot *on hand* 625
ready 673
astir 682
afore 116
aforegoing 116
aforehand 116
aforementioned 62,
116
aforesaid
preceding 62
repeated 104
prior 116
aforesighted 116
aforethought 116,
611, 907
aforetime 116

a fortiori
superiority 33
evidence 467
reasoning 476
afraid 860—*to say*
uncertain 4
be—irresolute 605
afreet 980
afresh *repeated* 104
new 123
African 431
Afric heat 382
Afrikander 57
aft 235
after *in order* 63
in time 117
too late 135
rear 235
pursuit 622
—*all for all that* 30
qualification 469
on the whole 476
—*time* 133
be—intention 620
pursuit 622
go—follow 281
after acceptation
516
after-age 124
afterbirth 63
afterburden 63
afterclap 63, 154,
509
aftercome 65, 154
aftercrop 63, 154,
168
afterdamp 663
afterdinner 117
afterglow
decrement 40a
sequence 63
light 420
aftergrass 63
aftergrowth 65, 154
afterlife 152
aftermath
sequence 63
effect 154
fertile 168
profit 775
afternoon 126
—*farmer* 683
afterpain 63
after-part *sequel* 65
rear 235
afterpiece 63, 599
aftertaste 63, 390
afterthought
thought 451
memory 505
change of mind 607
aftertime 121, 133
afterwards 117
aga 745
again *duplicate* 90
repeated 104

altar *marriage* 903
  church 1000
alter 140
  emasculate 158
  —one's course 279
  —the case 468
alterable 149
alterant 662
alteration
  correlation 12
  difference 15
alterative *remedy* 662
altercation 713
altered *worn* 688
  —for the worse 659
alter ego *similar* 17
  auxiliary 711
  deputy 759
  friend 890
alternacy 138
alternate
  reciprocal 12
  vary 20a
  sequence 63
  discontinuous 70
  periodic 138
  substitute 147, 634
  changeable 149
  oscillate 314
alternation 148
alternative
  substitute 147
  choice 609
  plan 626
although
  compensation 30
  counteraction 179
  unless 469
  (*opposition* 708)
altiloquence 577
altimeter 206
altimetry *height* 206
  angle 244
  measurement 466
altitude *height* 206
  —and azimuth 466
alto 410, 415 hill 206
altogether
  collectively 50
  entirely 52
  the—50, 226
alto—rilievo
  convex 250
  sculpture 557
altruism 910, 942
altruist 906
alum 397
alumina 324
alumnus 541
alveary 370, 691
alveolate 252
alveolus 252
always *uniformly* 16
  generally 78
  during 106
  perpetually 112

  habitually 613
a.m. 125
amadou 388
amah 746, 753
amain *violence* 173
  haste 684
amalgam,—ate
  mixture 41
  compound 48
amanuensis
  recorder 553
  secretary 590
amaranthine 112
amaritude 395
amass *whole* 50
  collect 72
  store 636
amassment 72
amateur
  willingness 602
  taste 850
  votary 865
amateurish 643
amatory 897
amaurosis 442
amaze 870
amazement 508
amazingly 31
Amazon *warrior* 726
  courage 861
ambage
  convolution 248
  circumlocution 573
  circuit 629
ambagious
  winding 248
  diffuse 573
ambassador
  interpreter 524
  messenger 534
  representative 758
  deputy 759
amber 356a
  —color 436
ambergris 356a
ambidexter
  right and left 238
  fickle 607
  clever 698
ambient 227
ambiguous
  uncertain 475
  unintelligible 519
  equivocal 520
  obscure 571
ambilevous 239
ambilogy 520
ambiloquy 520
ambit 230, 311
ambition
  intention 620
  desire 865
ambitious
  (*see* ambition)
amble *pace* 266
  slowness 275

ambo *school* 542
  pulpit 1000
  alike 17
  friends 890
  bad men 949
ambrosia 298
ambrosial *savory* 394
  fragrant 400
ambulance
  vehicle 272
  hospital 662
ambulation 266
ambuscade 530
ambush *shade* 424
  hiding **530**
  pitfall 667
  lie in—528
ambustion 384
âme damnée
  catspaw 711
  servant 746
  servile 886
  bad man 949
ameer 875
ameliorate 658
amen *assent* 488
  submission 725
  content 831
amenable *liable* 177
  docile 602
  answerable 926
amend *improve* 658
  repent 950
amendatory 30
amendment 658
  18th—761
amends
  compensation 30
  atonement 952
  reward 973
amenity *pleasing* 829
  courtesy 894
amentia 503
amerce 974
American 188
  —organ 417
  —plan 298
Americanism 563
Americanize 563
amethyst *purple* 437
  jewel 847
amethystine 437
amiable *pleasing* 829
  courteous 894
  loving 897
  kind 906
amianthoid 385
amianthus 385
amicable
  assisting 707
  friendly 888
amice 999
amidships 68
amidst *mixed with* 41
  between 228
amiss 619 come

  —disagree 24
  mistime 135
  inexpedient 647
  do—945
  go—732
  nothing comes—823
  take—dislike 867
  resent 900
amity *concord* 714
  peace 721
  friendship 888
ammeter 157, 272,
  490a
ammonia 334, 387
ammonite 248
ammonium chloride
  490b
ammunition
  materials 635
  war 727
amnesia 506
amnesty
  pacification 723
  forgiveness 506, 918
amoeba 193, 357
amoebaeic 597
amoebean 63
amoebic 193
amoebiform 81
amoeboid 193
amole 356
among *mixed with* 41
  between 228
amorist 897
amoroso 599
amorous 897
  —glances 902
amorphism **241**
amorphous
  irregular 83
  formless 241
amortization 784
amotion 270
amount *quantity* 25
  degree 26
  sum of money 800
  price 812
  —to *equal* 27
  number 85
  gross—50
amour *love* 897
  intrigue 961
  —propre 880
amourette 897
amphibians 368
amphibious 83
amphibology 520
Amphictyonic
  council 696
amphigory 497, 853
amphitheater
  prospect 441
  school 542
  theater 599
  arena 728
Amphitryon 890

amphora 191
ample *much* 31
  spacious 180
  large 192
  broad 202
  copious 639
  content 831
amplify *expand* 194
  exaggerate 549
  diffuse style 573
amplitude
  quantity 25
  degree 26
  size 192
  breadth 202
  enough 639
amputate 38
amuck *run*—kill 361
  attack 716
  excite 825
amulet *talisman* 747
  charm 993
amuse *please* 298
  divert 840
amusement 840
  place of—840
amylaceous 352
an *if* 514
ana 594, 596
Anabaptist 984
anachronism
  false time **115**
  inopportune 135
  error 495
anachronize 115
anacoluthon 70
anaconda 913
anacreontic 597
anacrusis 597
anaemia 160
anaemic 429
anaesthesia
  insensibility 376
  numbness 381
  inactivity 683
anaesthetist 662
anaesthetize 376,
  662
anaglyph
  representation 554
  sculpture 557
anagoge
  metaphor 521
  latency 526
anagram
  double sense 520
  secret 533
  letter 561
  wit 842
  play—561
anagrammatism
  520, 533
anagrammatize 520
analecta 596
analeptic 662
analgesia 823

analogy *relation* 9
  similarity 17
analysis
  decomposition 49
  arrangement 60
  algebra 85
  inquiry 461
  experiment 463
  reasoning 476
  grammar 567
  compendium 596
analyst
  investigator 461
  experimenter 463
analytical
  (*see* analysis)
analyze *grammar* 567
  describe 594
  (*see* analysis)
anamorphoscope 555
anamorphosis
  distortion 243
  optical 443
  misrepresentation 555
anapest 597
anaphrodisia 174, 866
anarch 710
anarchist
  opponent 710
  insurgent 742
  enemy 891
  evil doer 913
anarchy *disorder* 59
  social 738
anastatic printing 558
anastomosis
  junction 43
  crossing 219
anastomotic 219
anastrophe 218
anathema 908
anathematize
  curse 908
  censure 932
  detract 934
anatomize *dissect* 44
  investigate 461
anatomy *dissection* 44
  leanness 203
  texture 329
  science 357
  comparative–368
anatripsis 331
anatriptic 331
ancestor 69, 166
ancestral *bygone* 122
  old 124
  aged 128
ancestry 69, 166
anchor *connection* 45
  stop 265
  safeguard 666
  check 706
  hope 858

at–*fixed* 150
  stationed 184
  safe 664
  cast–*settle* 184
  arrive 292
  sheet–*means* 632
anchorage
  location 184
  roadstead 189
  refuge 666
anchored *fixed* 150
anchoretic 893
anchorite *recluse* 893
  ascetic 955
ancien régime 875
ancient *old* 124
  flag 550
  –*mariner* 269
  –*times* 122
ancientness 122
ancillary 707
ancon 342
and *addition* 37
  accompaniment 88
andante 415
andiron 386
androgynous 83
androlepsia 789
Andromeda 490a
androtomy 372
anecdote 594
anecdotist 594
anele 998
anemograph 349
anemography 349
anemology 349
  anemometer
  wind 349
  measure 466
  record 551
anemometrograph 349
anemometry 349
anemone 845
anemoscope 349
anent 9
aneroid 338, 340
anew *again* 104
  newly 123
anfractuosity 248
angel *messenger* 534
  backer 599, 711
  object of love 897
  good person 948
  supernatural being 977
  bishop 996
 –of death 360
  fallen–*bad man* 949
  devil 978
  guardian–*safety* 664
  auxiliary 711
  benefactor 912
angelic 944
angelus 550
anger 900

angina pectoris 655
angiology 329
angle 244
  point of view 448
  try 463
  at an–217
angle rafter 215
Anglican
  sectarian 984
  ecclesiastical 995
Anglicanism 984
Anglice 563
Anglicism 563
angling 622
Anglophobia 898
angry (*see* anger)
anguiform 248
anguilliform
  filament 205
  serpentine 248
anguilloid 248
anguillous 248
anguine 366
anguish *physical* 378
  moral 828
angular 244
  –*velocity* 264
angularity 244
angustation 203
anhedonia 828, 837
anhelation 688
anhydrate 340, 670
anhydration 340
anhydric 340
anhydrous 340
anility *age* 128
  imbecility 499
anima 359–bruta 359
  –*divina* 359
  –*mundi* 359
animadvert
  attend to 457
  reprehend 932
animal 366–cries 412
  –*economy* 359
  –*gratification* 377
  –*life* 364
  –*magnetism* 992a
  –*physiology* 368
  –*spirits* 836
  female–364
animalcular 193
animalcule
  minute 193
  animal 366
animalism
  animality 364
  sensuality 954
animality 364
animalization 364
animastic 450
animate *induce* 615
  excite 824
  enliven 836
animation *life* 359
  animality 364

activity 682
  vivacity 836
  suspended–823
animative 359
animism 317, 984
animist 317
animosity *dislike* 867
  enmity 889
  hatred 898
  anger 900
animus
  willingness 602
  intention 620
  desire 865
ankle 244–deep
  deep 208
  shallow 209
anklet 847
ankus 615
ankylosis 150
annalist
  chronologist 115
  recorder 553
annals *chronology* 114
  record 551
  account 594
annatto 434
anneal 673
annex *add* 37, 39
  join 43
annexationist 43
annexe 39
annihilate
  extinguish 2
  destroy 162
anniversary 138, 883
anno 106
annotation
  explanation 522
  note 550
annotator *scholar* 492
  interpreter 524
  commentator 595
annotto 434
announce *herald* 116
  predict 511
  inform 527
  publish 531
  assert 535
announcement
  (*see* announce)
annoy *molest* 649, 907
  disquiet 830
annoyance 828
  source of–830
annual *periodic* 138
  plant 367
  book 593
annuity 810
annul *destroy* 162
  abolish 756
annular 247
annularity 249
annulet 247
annunciate
  inform 527

(*publish* 531)
Annunciation, the– 990
annunciative 527
annunciator 527
annunciatory 531
anodyne *lenitive* 174
  remedial 662
  relief 834
anoint *coat* 223
  lubricate 332
  oil 355
Anointed, the 976
anointment
  lubrication 332
  oil 355
anomalous 241
anomaly *disorder* 59
  irregularity 83
anon 132
anonymous 565
anopsia 442
anorexy 866
another *different* 15
  repetition 104
  –*time* 119
answer
  to an inquiry **462**
  confute 479
  solution 522
  succeed 731
  pecuniary profit 775
  pleadings 969
  –*for deputy* 759
  promise 768
  go bail 806
  –*one's turn* 644
  –*the helm* 743
  –*the purpose* 731
  –*to correspond* 9
  require an–461
answerable
  agreeing 23
  liable 177
  bail 806
  duty 926
  censurable 392
ant 366, 690
Antaeus *strength* 159
  size 192
antagonism
  difference 14
  physical 179
  voluntary 708
  enmity 889
antagonist 710
antagonistic 24
antaphrodisiac 866
antarctic 237, 383
ante 621 *expend* 809
  –up 809
antecedence
  in order 62
  in time 116
antecedent 64
antechamber 191

antedate 115
antediluvian 124
antelope 274, 360
antemundane 124
antenna 379
antepast 510
anteposition 62
anterior *in order* 62
   in time 116
   in place 234
   —*to reason* 477
anteroom 191
antevert 706
anthelion 423
anthelmintic 662
anthem 990
anthemion 847
antherozoid 357
anthology
   writing 590
   book 593
   collection 596
   poem 597
   store 636
anthracite 388
anthrax 655
anthropod 193
anthropogeny 372
anthropoid 372
anthropology
   zoology 368
   mankind 372
anthropomancy 511
anthropomorphism 984
anthropophagus 913
anthroposcopy 511
anthroposophy 372
anthropotomy 372
antic 840
antichristian
   heterodox 984
   irreligious 989
antichronism 115
anticipant 120
anticipate
   anachronism 115
   priority 116
   future 121
   early 132
   expect 507
   foresee 510
   prepare 673
   hope 858
   caution 864
anticipation 120
   (*see* anticipate)
anticlimax
   decrease 36
   bathos 497, 853
anticlinal 217
anticyclone 265
antidote 662
antigropelos 225
antifebrile 662
antilogarithm 84

antilogy 477
antiluetic 662
antimacassar 223
antimony 663, 490a
Antinomian 984
antinomy 964
Antinous 845
antiorgastic 174
antiparallel 217
antipathy
   contrariety 14
   dislike 867
   hate 898
antiphon *music* 415
   answer 462
   worship 990
antiphonal 462
antiphrasis 563
antipodes
   difference 14
   distance 196
   contraposition 237
antipoison 662
antiquary
   past times 122
   scholar 492
   historian 553
antiquated *aged* 128
   (*out of fashion* 851)
antique 124
antiquity 122
antiscriptural 984
antiseptic 662
antisocial 911
antispasmodic 174, 662
antispast 597
antistrophe 597
antithesis *contrast* 14
   difference 15
   contraposition 237
   style 577
antithesize 14
antitype 22
antler 253
antonomasia
   metaphor 521
   nomenclature 564
antrum 252
anvil *conversion* 144
   support 215
   on the—
   intended 620
   in hand 625, 730
   preparing 673
anxiety *solicitude* 459
   pain 828
   fear 860
   desire 865
anxious (*see* anxiety)
   —bench 1000
   —expectation 507
   —meeting 1000
   —seat 1000
any *some* 25
   part 51

   no choice 609a
   at—rate *certain* 474
   true 494
   at all hazards 604
anybody 78
anyhow *careless* 460
   in some way 627
aorist 109, 119
aorta 350
apace *early* 132
   swift 274
Apache 913
apache *assassin* 361
aparejo 215
apart *irrelative* 10
   separate 44
   singleness 87
   soliloquy 589
   set—636
   wide—196
apartment 191
   —house 189
   —s to let
   imbecile 450a, 499
apathetic 275
apathy
   incuriosity 456
   insensibility 823
   irreligion 989
ape *monkey* 366
   imitate 19
aperient 652, 662
apéritif 394
aperture 260
apery 19
apex *height* 206
   summit 210
aphelion 196
aphid 366, 659
Aphis 659
aphonic 403, 581
aphonia 581
aphorism 496
aphrodisia 173, 961
aphrodisiac 865
Aphrodite 845
apiarism 370
apiarist 370
apiary 370
apical 210
apiculate 253
apiculture 370
apiece 79
apish 19, 499
apishamore 223
aplomb *stability* 150
   verticality 212
   self-possession 498
   resolution 604
Apocalypse 985
Apocrypha 985
apocryphal
   uncertain 475
   erroneous 495
   heterodox 984
apodeictic 478

apodeixis 478
apodosis 67
apogee 490a
apograph 21
apolaustic 377
Apollo *sun* 318
   music 416
   luminary 423
   beauty 845
   —Musagetes 416
   magnus—*sage* 500
   adviser 695
apologue
   metaphor 521
   teaching 537
   description 594
apology
   substitution 147
   excuse 617
   vindication 937
   penitence 950
   atonement 952
apophysis 250
apoplexy 158
aporia 475
apostasy
   recantation 607
   dishonor 940
   heterodoxy 984
   impiety 988
apostate *convert* 144
   turncoat 607
   seceder 742
   heretic 984
   (*recreant* 941)
apostatize 607
apostle *teacher* 540
   disciple 541
   inspired 985
   —'s creed 983a
apostolic 985
   —church 983a
   —see 995
apostrophe
   typography 550
   address 586
   soliloquy 589
   appeal 765
apostrophize 765
apothecary 662
   —'s weight 319
apothegm 496
apotheosis
   resuscitation 163
   heaven 981
   hero worship 991
apozem *liquefy* 335
   fuse 384
apozemial 384
appal *pain* 830
   terrify 860
appanage
   property 780
   gift 784
apparatus 633
apparel 225

apparent *visible* 446
   appearing 448
   probable 472
   manifest 525
   heir—779
apparition *shade* 362
   fallacy of vision 443
   spirit 980a
   psychical research 992a
   (*appearance* 448)
apparitor
   precursor 64
   messenger 534
appeach 938
appeal *address* 586
   request 765
   —motion 969
   —to
   call to witness 467
   —to arms 722
   —to for (*claim*) 924
   court of—966
appear
   come in sight 446
   show itself 525
   (*come into being* 1)
   —for 759
   —in print 591
appearance 448
   make one's—
   arrive 292
   to all—*to the eye* 448
   probable 472
appearances
   keep up—852
appease 174
appellant
   claimant 924
appellate 966
appellation 564
append *add* 37
   sequence 63
   hang 214
appendage
   addition 37
   adjunct 39
   accompaniment 88
   rear 235
appendicitis 655
appendix 65, 67
apperception 450, 490
appercipient 450
appertain *related to* 9
   component 56
   belong 777
   property 780
appetence 865
appetency 602
appetite 865
   tickle the—
   savory 394
appetitive 865
appetizer 393, 394
appetizing 865

exciting 824
applaud 931
applause 931
apple 298, 369
–brandy 959
–butter 396
–dumpling 298
–fritters 298
–jack 959
–of discord 713
–of one's eye
good 648
love 897
favorite 899
–pie 298
–slump 298
golden–
allurement 615
apple green 435
apple–pie order 58
appliance *use* 677
–s *means* 632
machinery 633
applicable
revelant 9, 23
useful 644
expedient 646
applicant 767
application *study* 457
metaphor 521
use 677
request 765
apply *appropriate* 788
–a match 384
–the mind 457
–a remedy 662
appoggiato 413
appoggiatura 413
appoint *prescribe* 741
assign 786
appointment
business 625
order 741
charge 755
assignment 786
interview 892
appointments
gear 633
apportion *arrange* 60
disperse 73
allot 786
(*portion* 51)
apportionment 786
apposition *relation* 9
relevancy 23
closeness 199
paraphrase 522
appraise *estimate* 466
value 812
appreciate
realize 450, 451
measure 466
judge 480
know 490
taste 850
approve 931

apprehend
believe 484
know 490
fear 860
seize 969
apprehension
idea 453
taking 789
apprehensive 860
apprentice 541
servant 746
–oneself 676
apprenticeship
learning 539
training 673
apprise 527
apprised of 490
approach *of time* 121
impend 152
nearness 197
move **286**
path 627
approbation 931
appropinquation 286
appropinquity 197
appropriate *fit* 23
peculiar 79
possess 777
assign 786
borrow 788
take 789
steal 791
(*expedient* 646)
appropriation
allotment 786
taking 789
stealing 791
approval *assent* 488
commend 931
approve 488, 931
approximate
related to 9
resemble 17
in mathematics 85
nearness 197
approach 286
appulse *meeting* 199
collision 276
approach 286
converge 290
appulsion 199, 276
appurtenance
adjunct 88
component 56
belonging 780
(*part* 51)
appurtenant
relating 9
apraxia 821a
apricot *fruit* 298
color 439
April–fool *dupe* 547
laughingstock 857
–showers 149
make an–fool of
545

a priori reasoning
476
apron
clothing 39, 225
defense 717
canonicals 999
à propos *relative* 9
apt 23
occasion 134
(*expedient* 646)
apse 1000
apt *consonant* 23
tendency 176, 177
docile 539
willing 602
clever 698
(*intelligent* 498)
(*expedient* 646)
aqua 337
–fortis 384
–regia 384
aquamarine 435, 438
aquarium 370, 636
Aquarius *rain* 348
aquatic 267, 337
aquatics 267
aquatinta 558
aquatist 558
aqueduct 350
aqueous 337
aquiline 244
A. R. 106
Arab *wanderer* 268
horse 271
araba 272
arabesque 847
Arabian–nights 515
–perfumes 400
arable 371
arado 780
arbiter *critic* 480
director 694
adviser 695
judge 967
–bibendi 840
–elegantiarum
revels 840
taste 850
fashion 852
arbitrament
judgment 480
(*choice* 609)
–of the sword 722
arbitrary
without relation 10
irregular 83
willful 606
capricious 608
authoritative 737
severe 739
insolent 885
lawless 964
–power 739
arbitrate
adjudicate 480
mediate 724

arbitration
concord 714
compromise 774
court of–966
submit to–774
arbitrator 724
arbor *abode* 189
summerhouse 191
support 215
rotation 312
plaisance 840
Arbor Day 840
arboreal 367
arborescent
ramifying 242
rough 256
trees 367
arboriculture 371
arboriform 242
arc 245
arcade *street* 189
curve 245
gateway 260
Arcadia *pleasure* 827
paradise 981
Arcadian
pastoral 371
artless 703
innocent 946
arcanum 533
arch *great* 31
support 215
curve 245
convex 250
concave 252
clever 498
cunning 702
triumphal–
trophy 733
celebration 883
archaeologist
antiquary 122
scholar 492
archaeology 122
archaic *old* 124
archaism
past times 122
obsolete phrase 563
archangel 977
archbishop 996
archbishopric 995
archdeacon 996
archduchy 181
archduke 745
archdukedom 180
archebiosis 161
arched roof 245
archenemy, the–978
archer 726, 840
archery 840
Arches, court of–
tribunal 966
churchdom 995
archetypal 20
archetype 22, 453
Archeus 359

archfiend 978
archiater 695
archiepiscopal 995
archigenesis 161, 357
archipelago 346
architect
constructor 164
agent 690
architectonic 161
architecture
arrangement 60
construction 161
fabric 329
ornament 847
architrave 210
archive 551
archlute 417
archon *ruler* 745
deputy 759
judge 967
archtraitor 941
arclike 245
arctic *northern* 237
cold 383
arctics 225
arcuation 245
ardent *fiery* 382
eager 682
feeling 821
loving 897
–expectation 507
–imagination 515
ardor *vigor* 574
activity 682
feeling 821
desire 865
arduous 704
area 181, 182
arefaction 340
arefy 340
arena *space* 180
region 181
field of view 441
field of battle **728**
arenaceous 330
arenosity 330
areola 247
areolar 219
areometer 321
Areopagus 966
ares 180
arescent 340
aretaics 944
arête 253
aretology 926, 944
Argand lamp 423
argent 430
argentine 430
argil 324
argillaceous 324
argol 653
argosy 273
argot 563
argue *evidence* 467
reason 476
indicate 550

repute 873
lord of the-745
one's star in the-
prosperity 734
ascension
(see ascend)
calefaction 384
Ascension Day 998
ascent (see ascend)
gradient 217
rise **305**
glory 873
ascertain *fix* 150
determine 480
ascertained
certain 474
known 490
ascertainment 480*a*
ascetic 955
asceticism 953, **955**
ascititious *intrinsic* 6
additional 37
supplementary 52
ascribe 155
ascription
(see ascribe)
aseptic 662
ash 367, 384
-blond 429
-colored 432
ashamed 879, 881
ash cake 298
ashen 429
ashes *corpse* 362
dirt 653
lay in-162
pale as-
colorless 429
fear 860
ashore 342 go
-arrive 292
Ash Wednesday 138
ashy 429
Asian mystery 533
aside *laterally* 236
whisper 405
private 528
-from the purpose
10
say-589
set-*displace* 185
neglect 460
negative 536
reject 610
disuse 678
abrogate 756
discard 782
step-279
asinine *ass* 271
fool 499
ask *inquire* 461
request 765
for sale 794
price 812
(*invoke* 990)
-leave 760

askance 217 eye
-*fear* 860
look
-*vision* 441, 443
dissent 489
dislike 867
disapproval 932
asked in church 903
askew *oblique* 217
distorted 243
asking (see ask)
aslant 217
asleep 683
aslope 217
Asmodeus 978
asomatous 317
asp *animal* 366
evil doer 913
asparagus 298, 367
Aspasia 962
aspect *feature* 5
state 7
situation 183
appearance 448
aspen leaf
shake like an-
motion 315
fear 860
asperges 998
aspergillum 337
asperity
roughness 256
discourtesy 895
anger 900
irascibility 901
asperse 934
aspersion
nonassemblage 73
cleanness 652
malediction 908
rite 998
asphalt *smooth* 255
resin 356*a*
asphodel 845
asphyxia 360
asphyxiate 361
aspirant
candidate 767
desire 865
aspirate 402, 580
aspirated 681
aspire *rise* 305
project 620
hope 858
desire 865
worship 990
asportation 270
asquint 217
ass
beast of burden 271
fool 501
-'s bridge
unintelligible 519
cheat 548
bungler 701
make an-of

delude 545
assafetida 401
assagai 727
assail *attack* 716
pain 830
assailant
opponent 710
attacker 726
assassin,-ate 361
assault 716
take by-789
assay 463
assayer 463
assemblage 72
assembly *council* 696
society 892
religious 997
assemblyman 696
assembly room 189,
588
assent *belief* 484
agree **488**
willing 602
consent 762
content 831
assert *affirm* 535
claim as a right 924
assess *measure* 466
determine 480
tax 812
assessor *judge* 967
assets *property* 780
money 800
accounts 811
asseverate 535
assiduous 682
assign *commission* 755
transfer 783
give 784
allot 786
-a duty 926
-as cause 155
-dower 784
-places 60
assignable 270
assignat 800
assignation *tryst* 892
place of-74
assignee *transfer* 270
donee 785
assignment 155
assimilate *uniform* 16
resemble 17
imitate 19
agree 23
transmute 144
assimilation 161
assist 707
assistant 711
assize *measure* 466
tribunal 966
justice of- 967
associate *mix* 41
unite 43
combine 48
collect 72

accompany 88
colleague 690
auxiliary 711
friend 890
-*professorship* 542
-with *sociality* 892
association
(see associate)
relation 9
cooperation 709
partnership 712
friendship 888
-of ideas *intellect* 450
thought 451
intuition 477
hint 514
**associational
psychology** 457
assoil *acquit* 970
(*liberate* 750)
assoilzie 970
assonance
agreement 23
music 413
poetry 597
assort *arrange* 60
assortment
collection 72
class 75
assuage *moderate* 174
relieve 834
(-*morally* 826)
assuasive 174, 834
assuetude 613
assume *believe* 484
suppose 514
falsehood 544
take 789
insolent 885
right 924
-a character 554
-a form 144
-authority 737
-command 741
-the offensive 716
assumed-name 565
-position 514
assuming
insolent 885
assumption
(see assume)
severity 739
hope 858
insolence 885
seizure 925
assurance
speculation 156
certainty 474
belief 484
confidence 507
assertion 535
promise 768
security 771
hope 858
vanity 880
insolence 885

make-double sure
safe 664
caution 864
assure
render certain 474
believe 484
certify 535
promise 768
secure 771
give hope 858
assured
self-satisfied 880
assuredly *assent* 488
astatic 320
asteism 856
asterisk 550
astern 235 fall-283
asteroid 318
asthenia 160
astigmatism 443
astir *ready* 673
active 682
set-824
astonish 870
astonishing *great* 31
astonishment 508,
870
astound
be unexpected 508
excite 824
fear 860
surprise 870
astraddle 215
astragal 847
astral 318
-body 317, 992*a*
-influence 601
-plane 317
astray *at fault* 475
error 495
go-*deviate* 279
sin 945
astriction 43, 195
astride 215
astringent 195, 397
astrolabe 466, 490*a*
astrology 511, 522
astronomy 490a, 318
astute *wise* 498
cunning 702
asunder *separate* 44
distant 196
as poles-237
asylum *hospital* 662
retreat 666
defense 717
asymptote 290
ataghan 727
atajo 72
atavism 145
atelier *studio* 556
workshop 691
athanasia 112
Athanasian creed
983*a*
athanor 386

music 415, 416, 417
party 712
shackle 752
—of hope 958
—s *canonicals* 999
—together 709
—with 720
bandage *tie* 43
ligature 45
support 215
cover 223
remedy 662
restraint 752
the eyes—d 442
bandbox 191
banded together
concurring 178
party 712
banderole 550
bandit *slayer* 361
brigand 792
bandmaster 416
bandobast
(*see* bundobust)
bandog *animal* 366
safeguard 664
warning 668
bandolier 636
bandrol 550
bandurria 417
bandy *exchange* 148
agitate 315
—about *publish* 531
—legged 243
—words *discuss* 476
converse 588
bane *evil* 619
source of evil 663
baneful 649
banewort 663
bang *impel* 276
sound 406
beat 972
banish *eject* 297
seclude 893
punish 972
(*exclude* 55)
banister 215
banjo 417
bank *acclivity* 217
side of lake 342
store 636
sand 667
fence 717
money 802
—*examiner* 811
—*holiday* 840
—of Elegance 800
—up 670
*sea—*342
banker
man of means 639
merchant 797
treasurer 801
card game 840
bank note 800

bankrupt 640
—of life 683
bankruptcy
failure 732
nonpayment 808
banlieue *near* 197
circumjacent 227
banner 550
enlist under the—s
of 707
raise one's—722
banneret 875
banns forbid the—761
publish the—
ask 765
marriage 903
banquet *meal* 298
pleasure 377
feast 840
banquette 717
banshee 979, 980*a*
bant 38
bantam cock 887
banter *wit* 842
ridicule 856
banterer 844
bantling *child* 129
scion 167
Bantu 372*a*
banyan *tree* 367
stint 640
fast 956
baptize 564, 998
baptism *name* 564
rite 998
Baptist 984
baptistery 1000
bar *except* 38
fastening 45
exclude 55
hotel 189
line 200
support 215
inclosure 232
close 261
music 413
hindrance 706
insignia 747
prison 752
prohibit 761
tribunal 966
legal profession 968
—room 189
—sinister *flaw* 651
disrepute 874
illegal 964
—tender 746
baragouin 517
bara hazri 298
bara khana 298
bara sahib 642, 745
barb *spike* 253
nag 271
velocity 274
—the dart *pain* 830
Barbados tar 356

barbarian *alien* 57
inelegance 579
uncivilized 876
evildoer 913
barbaric
extraneous 57
vulgar 851
rude 876
barbarism
neology 563
solecism 568
bad style 579
vulgarity 851
discourtesy 895
barbarous
unformed 241
neologic 563
plebeian 876
maleficent 907
barbate 205, 253
barbecue
repast 298, 892
cook 673
barbed 225
—wire entanglements
717
barbel 205
barber *wind* 349
barbican 206, 717
barbouillage 590
bard *musician* 416
poet 597
barded 225
bare *mere* 32
nude 226
manifest 525
disclose 529
scanty 640
—possibility 473
—supposition 514
bareback 226
barebone 203
barefaced 885
barefoot 226
poor 804
bareheaded *respect* 928
bargain *compact* 769
barter 794
cheap 815
—and sale
transfer of property
783
—for 507
into the—37
barge 273
bargee 269
barghest 980
barf 383
baritone 408
barium sulphate 430
bark *rind* 223
flay 226
ship 273
yelp 406, 412
—at *threaten* 909
censure 932

—up the wrong tree 699
—worse than bite 885
more—than bite 908
barkbound 751
barkeep 746
barkeeper 746
barkentine 273
barker *guide* 524
tout 758
petitioner 767
barley 367
barleycorn *little* 193
Barleycorn, Sir John
298
barm *leaven* 320
bubbles 353
barmaster 967
Barmecide feast 956
barmote 966
barn 189, 370, 636
barnacles 368, 445
barndoor fowl 366
barney 545, 713
barograph 338, 490*a*
barometer *air* 338
measure 466, 490*a*
consult the—463
baron *peer* 875
husband 903
—of the Exchequer 967
court—966
baronage 875
baronet 875
baronial 878
baroque 853
baroscope 338
barouche 272
barque 273
barrack
encampment 184
abode 189
shed 223
jibe 929
defense 717
barracker 936
barracoon 717
barrage *loudness* 404
drumming 407
attack 716
barranco 198
barrator 941
barratrous 940
barratry 940
barred *crossed* 219
striped 440
barrel *vessel* 191
cylinder 249
—organ 417
barrel house 189
barren 169
barricade *fence* 232
obstacle 706
defense 717
prison 752
barrier
(*see* barricade)

barring *save* 38
excluding 55
except 83
—out *resist* 719
disobey 742
barrister 968
revising—967
barrow *mound* 206
vehicle 272
grave 363
barter *reciprocate* 12
interchange 148
commerce 794
barway 294
basalt 490*c*
bas bleu *scholar* 492
affectation 855
base *low* 207
lowest part 211
support 215
evil 649
menial 746
cowardly 862
shameful 874
servile 886
dishonorable 940
vicious 945
—coin 800
—note 408
—of operations
plan 626
attack 716
baseball 840
baseboard 211
baseborn 876
based on
ground of belief 467
baselard 727
baseless *unreal* 2
unsubstantial 4
basement *cellar* 191
lowest part 207, 211
baseness (*see* base)
inferiority 34
bashaw *tyrant* 739
ruler 745
bashful 881
bashfulness 881
bashi-bazouk 726
basilica 1000
basilisk
unconformity 83
sight 441
cannon 737
serpent 366, 949
basin *dock* 189
vessel 191, 211
hollow 252
plain 344
basis *lowest part* 211
support 215
preparation 673
bask
physical enjoyment
377
warmth 382

−intentions 906	**betrothal** 902	−price 814	**biconjugate** 91	*impious* 988
−man *marriage* 903	(*see* betroth)	−question 474	**bicorn** 245	**bigwig** 875
−part *great* 31	**betrothed** 897	−range 196	**bicuspid** 91	**bijou** *goodness* 648
nearly all 50	**better** *good* 648	−reason 471	**bicycle** 266, 272	*beauty* 845
−room 191	*improve* 658	−remedy 859	**bid** *order* 741	*ornament* 847
−seller 931	−half 903	−seas 57	*offer* 763	**bijouterie** 847
do one's−*care* 459	−sort *beau monde* 875	−the grave 528	−a long farewell 624	**bike** 272
try 675	for−for worse	−the mark	−defiance 715	**bilabiate** 90
activity 682	*choice* 609	*transcursion* 303	−fair *tend* 176	**bilander** 273
exertion 686	*marriage* 903	*redundance* 641	*probable* 472	**bilateral** *two* 90
have the−of it **731**	get−*health* 654	−the veil 528	*promise* 511	*side* 236
make the−of it	*improve* 658	−the verge 180	*hope* 858	**bilbao** 727
overestimate 482	*refreshment* 689	go−303	−for *intend* 620	**bilboes** 752
use 677	*restoration* 660	**bezel** 217	*offer* 763	put into−751
submit 725	get the−of 731	**bezonian** 876	*request* 765	**bile** 900
compromise 774	seen−days	**bhang** 663, 954	*bargain* 794	**bilge** *base* 211
take easily 826	*deteriorate* 659	**bhangi** 652	−the banns 903	*convex* 250
hope 858	*adversity* 735	**bhikshu** 955	**bidder** 767	*yawn* 260
make the−of one's	*poor* 804	**bias** *influence* 175	**bidding** *command* 741	−water 653
time 684	think−of *correct* 658	*tendency* 176	**biddy** 746	**biliary calculus** 655
to the−of one's	*repent* 950	*slope* 217	**bide** *wait* 133	**bilingual** 560
belief 484	**betting house** 621	*prepossession* 481	*remain* 141	**bilious** 837
bestead 644	**betty** 374	*disposition* 820	*take coolly* 826	**bilk** *disappoint* 509
bestial 961	**between** 228	(*motive* 615)	−one's time 133	*cheat* 545
bestir oneself	−cup and lip 111	**bib** *pinafore* 225	*watch* 507	*steal* 791
activity 682	−ourselves 528	*drink* 959	*inactive* 681	**bill** *list* 86
haste 684	−the lines 526	*cleanness* 652	**bidental** 90	*hatchet* 253
exertion 686	−two fires 665	**bibber** *weep* 839	**bidet** 271	*placard* 531
bestow *give* 784	far−198	*tope* 959	**biduous** 89	*ticket* 550
a benefice 995	lie−228	**bibble−babble** 584	**biennial** *periodic* 138	*paper* 593
−one's hand 903	**betwixt** 228	**Bible** 985	*plant* 367	*plan* 626
−thought 451	**bevel** 217	−Christian 984	*celebration* 883	*weapon* 727
bestraddle 215	**bever** 298	−oath 535	**bienséance** *polish* 852	*money order* 800
bestrew 73	**beverage** 298	**biblioclams** 162	*manners* 894	*money account* 811
bestride *mount* 206	**bevue** 732	**biblioclast** 165	**bier** 363	*charge* 812
ride 215	**bevy** *assemblage* 72	**bibliognost** 593	**bifacial** 90	*in law* 969
bet 621	*multitude* 102	**bibliographer** 593	**bifarious** 90	−and coo 902
betacism 560	**bewail** *regret* 833	**bibliography** 593	**bifid** 91	−of exchange
betake oneself to	*lament* 839	**bibliolatry**	**bifold** 90	*security* 771
journey 266	**beware** 668	*learning* 490	**biform** *double* 90	−of fare *food* 298
business 625	**bewilder** *put out* 458	*heterodoxy* 984	(*two* 89)	*plan* 626
use 677	*uncertain* 475	*idolatry* 991	**bifurcate** *bisect* 91	−of indictment 938
betatron 490d	*astonish* 870	**bibliologist** 593	*angle* 244	−of sale 771
bête noire *fear* 860	**bewildered** 495, 523	**bibliomancy** 511	**big** *in degree* 31	−s of mortality 360
hate 898	**bewitch** *fascinate* 615	**bibliomania** 490	*in size* 192	true−969
bethel 1000	*please* 829	**bibliomaniac** 492	*wide* 194	**billet** *locate* 184
bethink *think* 451	*excite love* 897	**bibliopegist** 593	−bug 875	*apportion* 786
remember 505	*diabolize* 978	**bibliophile** 492, 593	−gun 875	**billet** *ticket* 550
bethrall	*hoodoo* 992	**bibliopole** 593	−sounding *loud* 404	*epistle* 592
subjection 749	**bey** 745	**bibliotheca** 593	*words* 577	*business* 625
restraint 751	**beyond** *superior* 33	**bibulous** 298	*affected* 855	−doux 902
betide 151	*distance* 196	**bice** 435, 438	−with 161	**billhook** 253
betimes 132	−compare 31, 33	**bicentenary,** 98, 138,	−with the fate of 511	**billiard−ball**
bêtise 497	−control 471	883	look−*defy* 715	*round* 249
betoken *evidence* 467	−expression 31	**bicentennial** 98, 138,	*proud* 878	−room 191
predict 511	−hope 731, 734	883	*insolent* 885	−table *flat* 213
indicate 550	−measure 641	**bicephalous** 90	talk−885 *threat* 909	**billiards** 840
betongue 932	−mortal ken 528	**bichhona** 215	**bigamist** 903	**billingsgate** *slang* 563
betray *disclose* 529	−one's depth	**bichloride of**	**bigamy** 903	*curse* 908
deceive 545	*deep* 208	**mercury** 663	**biggin** 191	(*censure* 932)
dishonor 940	*unintelligible* 519	**bicipital** 90	**bighead** 655	**billion** 98, 102
−itself *visible* 446	−one's grasp 471	**bicker** *flutter* 315	**bight** 343	**billow** *sea* 348
betrayer 941	−possibility 471	*quarrel* 713	**bigot** *positive* 474	**billows** *ocean* 341
betrim 673	−praise *perfect* 650	(*contend* 720)	*prejudice* 481	**billy** *kettle* 191
betroth *promise* 768	*approbation* 931	**bickering** 24	*obstinate* 606	*club* 727
marriage 903	*virtue* 944	**bicolor** 440	*heterodox* 984	**billycock** 225

bluestocking
pedant 491
scholar 492
affectation 855
bluff *violent* 173
high 206
cliff 212
blunt 254
deceive 545
brag 884
card game 840
insolent 885
discourteous 895
—off 545
bluffer *boaster* 884
blunder *error* 495
absurdity 497
awkward 699
failure 732
indiscretion 947
—upon 156
blunderbuss 727
blunderhead 701
blunderheaded 499
blunt *weaken* 160
inert 172
to moderate 174
obtuse 254
benumb 376
to damp 616
plain—spoken 703
cash 800
deaden feelings 823
discourteous 895
—tool 645
—witted 499
bluntness 254
blur *dim* 443
dirt 653
blemish 848
stigma 874
blurb 931
blurred *invisible* 477
blurt out *disclose* 529
speak 582
blush *heat* 382
redden 434
feel 821
humbled 879
modest 881
at first—see 441
appear 448
manifest 525
put to the—
humble 879
browbeat 885
discourtesy 895
blushing honors
repute 873
modesty 881
bluster *violent* 173
defiant 715
insolent 885
resent 900
threaten 909
blusterer 887

blustering
(*see* bluster)
windy 349
Blut und Eisen 159
boa 225
—constrictor 366
boar *animal* 366
male 373
wild— 366
board *layer* 204
support 215
food 298
hard 323
directorate 542
council 696
attack 716
tribunal 966
—of education 542
—of Regents 542
—of studies 542
—school 542
festive— 892
go by the—
powerless 158
destruction 162
go on— 293
on—present 186
ship 273
preside at the— 693
boarder 188
boards *theater* 599
arena 728
boardwalk 189
boast 884
not much to—of 651
boaster 884 *jingo* 885
boastful 884
boasting 884
boat 273—*race* 720
in the same—
accompany 88
party 712
boating 267
boatman 269
boat—shaped 245
boatswain 269
bob *depress* 308
leap 309
oscillate 314
agitate 315
—a courtesy 894
—for *fish* 463
Bobadil, Captain— 887
bobbery 404
bobbin 312
bobbish 654
bobcat 366
bobsled 272
bobtailed 53
bocage 367
bock beer 298
bode 511
bodice 225
bodiless 317
bodily *substantially* 3

wholly 50
material 316
—enjoyment 377
—fear 860
—pain 378
bodkin
go between 228
perforator 262
body *substance* 3
whole 50
assemblage 72
matter 316
party 712
—and blood of Christ 987
—clothes 225
—color 556
—forth 554
—of doctrine 490
—of knowledge 490
—of water 348
—politic *mankind* 372
authority 737
in a—together 88
keep—and soul together 654
bodyguard
defense 717
combatant 726
keeper 753
Boeotian *small* 32
stupid 499
fool 501
vulgar 851
ignoble 876
bog *swamp* 345
dunghill 653
—trotter 876
boggart 980*a*
boggle *hesitate* 605
awkward 699
difficulty 704
bogie 980
bogle 980
bogus 545—*check* 808
Bohemian
unconformity 83
traveler 268
ungenteel 851
boil *violence* 173
effervesce 315
bubble 353
heat 382, 384
ulceration 655
excitement 824, 825
anger 900
—down 195
boiled (*see* boil)
—beef 298
—eggs 298
boiler 386
boisterous
violent 173
hasty 684
excitable 825
bold *prominent* 250

unreserved 525
vigorous 574
defiant 715
brave 861
—push *essay* 675
—relief *visible* 446
—stroke *plan* 626
success 731
make—with
discourtesy 895
show a—front
defy 715
brave 861
bold face *type* 591
boldfaced
insolent 885
printing 591
bole 50
bolero 840
boldness (*see* bold)
bolshevism 146, 742
bolshevist 146, 712
bolster *support* 215
repair 658
aid 707
—up *vindicate* 937
bolt *sift* 42, 652
fasten 43
fastening 45
close 261
move rapidly 274
propel 284
run away 370, 623
safety 664
escape 671
hindrance 706
shaft 727
shackle 752
—food *swallow* 298
gormandize 957
—in 751
—out of the blue 508
—the door 761
—upright 212
bolthead 191
bolus *mouthful* 298
remedy 662
bomb 404, 406, 727
—explosion 361
—vessel 726
bombard 716
circularize 592
bombardier 726
bombardon 417
bombast
overestimation 482
absurdity 497
unmeaning 517
magniloquence 577
ridiculous 853
boasting 884
(*exaggeration* 549)
bombastic
(*see* bombast)
bomber 269*a*
bombilation 404, 407

bombinate 407
bombing cruiser 273
bombproof 664
bon:—diable 844
—enfant *social* 892
kindly 906
—mot 842
—ton 852
—vivant 957
voyage 267
bona fides
veracity 543
probity 939
bonanza *extra* 641
wealth 803
bonbon 396
bond *tie* 45
servile 746
compact 769
security 771
money 800
right 924
—of union 9, 45
bondage 749
bonded together 712
bonds (*see* bond)
fetters 752
securities 802
—of harmony 714
in—service 746
bondsman 746
bone *dense* 321
hard 323
strength 159
—of contention 713, 720
—to pick
difficulty 704
discord 713
bred in the— 5
one—and one flesh 903
bonehouse 363
bones (*see* bone)
corpse 362
music 417
break no— 648
make no
—*willing* 602
bonesetter 662
bonfire 382
festivity 840
celebration 883
make a—of 384
bonhomie *candor* 703
kindness 906
bonhomme 996
Boniface 890
bonne *servant* 746
nurse 753
—bouche *treat* 377
savory 394
saving 636
pleasant 829
bonnet 225
—rouge 742

bonny *cheerful* 836
　pretty 845
bonnyclabber 321
bonus *extra* 641
　gift 784
　money 810
bony 323
bonze 996
booby 501
boodle 784
boof 860
book *part* 51
　register 86
　record 551
　volume **593**
　libretto 599
　enter accounts 811
　at one's–s 539
　–*collector* 593
　–*learning* 490
　–*madness* 490
　–*of fate* 601
　–*of poems* 590
　bring to–
　evidence 467
　account 811
　reprove 932
　mind one's–539
　school–542
　without–
　by heart 505
bookbinder 593
bookbinding 593
bookcase 191
booked *dying* 360
bookish 490
bookkeeper 553
bookkeeping 811
bookless
　unlearned 493
bookmaker 156
bookmaking 156
bookseller 593
bookshop 593
bookstore 593
bookworm 492, 593
booly 268
boom *support* 215
　sail 267
　rush 274
　impulse 276
　sound 404
　roll 407
　obstacle 706
　defense 717
boomerang *recoil* 277
　weapon 727
boon 784 beg a–765
　–*companion* 890
boor *clown* 876
boorish *ridiculous* 851
　uncourteous 895
boost *impulse* 276
　praise 931
booster 935
boot *box* 191

　dress 225
　advantage 618
　punishment 975
　to–added 37
booted and spurred
　673
bootee 225
booth *stall* 189
　shop 799
bootikin 225
bootleg
　drunkenness 959
bootlegging 964
bootless *useless* 645
　failing 732
boots *dress* 225
　servant 746
　what–it 643
booty 35, **793**
booze 959
bo–peep *peep* 441
　hide 528
bordel 961
border *contiguity* 199
　edge 231
　flank 236
　flower bed 371
　ornament 847
　–*upon* 197, 199
borderer 197
bordering 233
　–*upon* 197
bore *diameter* 202
　hole 260
　tide 348
　tidal wave 667
　trouble 828
　plague 830
　weary 841
Boreal *Northern* 237
　cold 383
borean 349
Boreas 349
boredom 841
borer 262
boresome 275
born 359–so 5
　–*to other things* 865
　–*under a lucky star*
　734
　–*under an evil star*
　735
borne 826–down
　failure 732
　defection 837
borné 499
borough 189
　rotten–893
borrow *imitate* 19
　receive 788
borrowed plumes
　deception 545
borrower 806
borrowing 788
boscage 367
bosh *absurdity* 497

　unmeaning 517
　untrue 546
　trifling 643
bosk 367
bosky 367
bosom *breast* 221
　mind 450
　affections 820
　–*friend* 890
　–*of one's family* 225
　in the–of 229
boss *knob* 250
　will 600
　politician 694
　rule 737
　master 745
bossiness 600
bossism 693
boston 840
Boston bag 191
botanic 369
　–*garden* 369, 371
botanomancy 511
botany 367, **369**
botch *disorder* 59
　mend 660
　unskillful 699
　difficulty 704
　fail 732
both 89
bother
　uncertainty 475
　bustle 682
　difficulty 704
　trouble 828
　harass 830
botheration 828
bothy 189
bottle *receptacle* 191
　preserve 670
　bee in a–407
　–*green* 435
　–*holder auxiliary* 177
　mediator 724
　–*up remember* 505
　hide 528
　restrain 751
　crack a–298
　pass the–959
　smelling–400
bottom
　lowest part 211
　support 215
　rear 235
　combe 252
　ship 273
　pluck 604a
　courage 861
　at–5
　at the–of cause 153
　–*dollar* 67, 800
　–*upwards* 218
　from the–of one's
　heart veracity 543
　feeling 821
　go to the–310

　probe to the–461
bottomless 208
　–*pit* 982
bottoms 345
bouderie 901a
boudoir 191–*cap* 225
bouge 250
bough *part* 51
　curve 245
　tree 367
boughpot 400
bought *flexure* 245
bougie 423
bouilli 298
boulder 249
boulevards 227
bouleversement
　revolution 146
　destruction 162
　excite 824
bounce *eject* 297
　jump 309
　lie 546
　dismiss 756
　boast 884
　insolence 885
　–*upon arrive* 292
　surprise 508
bouncer *ejection* 297
bouncing *large* 192
bound
　circumscribe 229,
　233
　swift 274
　leap 309
　certain 474
　–*back recoil* 277
　–*by* 926
　–*for direction* 278
　destination 620
　–*to promise* 768
　responsible 926
　I'll be–535
boundary 233
bounden duty 926
boundless
　infinite 105
　space 180
bounds 233
　outline 230
　–*of modesty* 881
　–*of possibility* 470
　keep within–
　moderation 174
　shortcoming 304
　restrain 751
　prohibit 761
bountiful *liberal* 816
　benevolent 906
bounty *aid* 707
　gift 784
bouquet *fragrant* 400
　beauty 847
bourdon *staff* 215
　melody 413
　drone 415

bourgeois *medium* 29
　type 591
　commoner 876
bourgeon 161, 194
bourn 233, 292
bourse 799
bouse 959
bout *turn* 138
　job 680
　fight 720
　prank 840
　drinking–954
boutade *absurdity* 497
　caprice 608
boutonnière 400
bovine *ox* 366
　beef–witted 499
bow *fore part* 234
　curve 245
　projection 250
　stoop 308
　fiddlestick 417
　weapon 727
　ornament 847
　servility 886
　reverence 894
　respect 928
　bend the–686
　–*down worship* 990
　–*out* 297
　–*submission* 725
　–*window* 245, 260
Bow bells 876
bowed down
　lament 837
　humble 879
bowelless 914a
bowels *inside* 221
　conduit 350
　–*full of wrath* 722
　–*of compassion* 914
　–*of the earth* 208
bower *abode* 189
　alcove 191
　cards 840
　–*s of bliss* 981
bowery 424
bowie knife 253, 727
bowl *vessel* 191
　rotate 312
　–*along walk* 266
　swift 274
　flowing–959
bow–legged 243
bowler *hat* 225
bowling green
　level 213
bowls 840
bowman 726
bowshot 197
bowsprit 234
bowstring
　execution 972, 975
bowwow 412
box *house* 189
　chest 191

breathe · **broken** index

not a—of air
quiet 265
hot 382
out of—688
shortness of—688
take away one's—
unexpected 508
fear 860
wonder 870
take—*rest* 265
refresh 689
with bated—581
breathe *exist* 1
blow 349
live 359
faint sound 405
evince 467
mean 516
inform 527
disclose 529
utter 580
speak 582
refresh 689
—freely *pleasure* 827
relief 834
—one's last 360
—the vital air 359
not—a word 528
breathing *time* 106
air 349
—time *repose* 687
truce 723
breathing–hole 351
breathless
voiceless 581
out of breath 688
feeling 821
fear 860
eager 865
wonder 870
—attention 457
—expectation 507
—impatience 865
—speed 684
breech *invest* 225
rear 235
breeches 225
—maker 225
—pocket
money 800, 802
wear the—737
breechloader 727
breed *race* 11
kind 75
multiply 161
progeny 167
animals 370
rear 537
(*prepare* 673)
breeding
production 161
style 852
politeness 894
—place 153
breeze *wind* 349
discord 713

breezy 836
brethren 997
breve 413
brevet *warrant* 741
commission 755
permit 760
—rank 873
breviary 990, 998
brevier 591
brevipennate 193
brevity *short* 201
concise 572
brew *mix* 41
prepare 673
brewing
impending 152
Briarean 102, 159
Briareus 159, 192
bribe *equivalent* 30
tempt 615
offer 763
gift 784
buy 795
reward 809, 973
bribery (*see* bribe)
bric–a–brac 847
brick *hard* 323
pottery 384
material 635
trump 939, 948
—color 434
—over 386
—red 434
make—s without
straw 471
brickbat 727
brickkiln 386
bricklayer 690
bricky 434
bridal 903
bride 903
bridegroom 903
bridesmaid 890, 903
bridesman 903
bridewell 752
bridge
intermedium 45
way 627
card game 840
—of death 360
—over *join* 43
facilitate 705
make peace 723
compromise 774
bridle *depart* 293
restrain 751
rein 752
—one's tongue
silent 585
cautious 864
—road 627
—up 900
brief *time* 111
space 201
concise 572
compendium 596

—case 191
hold a—for 759
briefly *anon* 132
brier *sharp* 253
bane 663
brig 273
brigade *arrange* 60
military 726
brigadier 745
brigand 792
brigandage 791
brigandine 717
brigantine 273
bright *shine* 420
color 428
intelligent 498
cheery 836
beauty 845
glory 873
—colored 428
—days 734
—prospect 858
—side 829
—thought *sharp* 498
good stroke 626
wit 842
look at the—side
cheer 836
hope 858
brighten up
furbish 658
bright–eyed 845
brigue *party* 712
contention 720
brilliant *shining* 420
music 416
good 648
witty 842
beautiful 845
gem 847
glorious 873
be—*intellectual* 498
—idea 842
brim 231—over 641
brimful 52
brimstone 388
brindled 440
brine *sea* 341
salt 392
bring 270—about
cause 153
achieve 729
—back 790
—back to the memory
505
—forth *produce* 161
extract 301
—forward
evidence 467
manifest 525
teach 537
improve 658
—gray hairs to the
grave
adversity 735
pain 830

—grist to the mill 644
—home 775
—home to 155
—in *receive* 296
income 810
price 812
—in a verdict 480
—in its train 88
—in question 461
—into being 161
—into play 677
—low 874
—off 672
—out *discover* 480a
manifest 525
publish 591
—over *persuade* 484
—round *persuade* 615
restore 660
—to *convert* 144
halt 265
—to a crisis 604
—to a point 74
—to bear 470
—to bear upon
relation 9
action 170
—together *assemble* 72
—to life 359
—to light 480a
—to maturity
prepare 673
complete 729
—to mind 505
—to perfection 677
—to terms 723
—to trial 969
—under one's notice
457
—up *develop* 161
vomit 297
train 370
educate 537
—up the rear 235
—word 527
brink 231
—of the grave 360
on the—*almost* 32
coming 121
near 197
briny 392—deep 341
brio *music* 415
briquette 388
brisk *prompt* 111
energetic 171
active 682
cheery 836
bristle 253—up
stick up 250
angry 900
—with *plenty* 639
too much 641
—with arms 722
bristling *thorny* 253
discourtesy 895
bristly *rough* 256

Britannia metal 545
Briticism 563
British 188
—courts 966
—lion 604
Britisher 188
Briton 188 true—939
brittle 328
brittleness 328
britzka 272
broach *begin* 66
found 153
perforate 262
tap 297
publish 531
assert 535
broad *general* 78
space 202
lake 343
emphatic 535
indelicate 961
—accent 580
—arrow 550
—awake *vigilant* 459
brisk 682
—daylight *light* 420
manifest 525
—farce 842
—gauge 466
—grin 838
—highway 627
—hint 527
—meaning 516
broadcast
disperse 73, 291
publish 531
news 532
sow—818
broadcloth 219, 635
broaden 78
broadhearted 906
broadhorn 273
broadsheet 531, 593
broad–shouldered
159
broadside *lateral* 236
publication 531
cannonade 716
broadsword 727
Brobdingnagian 159,
192
brocade 847
brocatelle 847
brochure 593
broder 549
brogan 225
brogue *boot* 225
dialect 560, 563
broidery 847
broil *heat* 382
fry 384
fray 713, 720
broiler *fowl* 298
broken *divided* 51
discontinuous 70
weak 160

393

of horses 370
–color 428
–down *decrepit* 659
failing 732
dejected 837
–English 563
–fortune
adversity 735
poverty 804
–heart *pain* 828
dejected 837
hopeless 859
–meat 645
–reed 665
–voice 581, 583
–winded *disease* 655
fatigue 688
broker *agent* 758
merchant 797
brokerage *pay* 812
brokery 794
bromide
conventionalist 82
bromidium 496
bronchia 351
broncho 271
–buster 370
bronchocele 655
bronze *brown* 433
sculpture 557
brooch 847
brood *multitude* 102
family 167
hatch 370
–over *think* 451
mope 837
brooding
preparing 673
brook *stream* 348
bear 826
broom
undergrowth 367
sweep 652
broomstick 491
broth 298
brothel 945, 961
brother *kin* 11
similar 17
equal 27
–Jonathan 188
brotherhood 712
brotherly
friendship 888
love 897
benevolence 906
brougham 272
brought to bed 161
brouillerie 713
brouillon 626
brow *top* 210
edge 231
front 234
browbeat
intimidate 860
swagger 885
disrespect 929

–en *humbled* 879
brown 433–Bess 727
–ocher 433
–stone 635
–stone house 189, 831
–study *thought* 451
inattention 458
imagination 515
Brownian 984
brownie 979
brownness 433
browse 298
bruin 895
bruise *powder* 330
hurt 619
injure 649
bruised *blemished* 848
bruiser 726
bruit 531, 532
brumal 383
brummagem 545
brunch 572
brunette 433
Brünn man 372a
Brunswick black 356a
brunt *beginning* 66
impulse 276
bear the–
difficulty 704
defense 717
endure 821, 826
(*resist* 719)
brush *tail* 235
rough 256
rapid motion 274
groom 370
touch 379
clean 652
fight 720
–away *reject* 297
abrogate 756
–up *clean* 652
furbish 658
prepare 673
paint– 556
brushwood 367, 388
brusque *violent* 173
haste 684
discourtesy 895
Brussels sprouts 298
brustle 407
brutal *vulgar* 851
rude 895
savage 907
brutalize (*see* brutal)
corrupt 659
deaden 823
vice 945
brute *animal* 366
rude 895
maleficent 913
–force *strength* 159
violence 173
animal 450a

severe 739
compulsion 744
lawless 964
–matter *matter* 316
inorganic 358
brutify 954
brutish (*see* brute)
vulgar 851
ignoble 876
intemperate 954
Bryanite 984
bryophites 369
bubble
unsubstantial 4
transient 111
little 193
light 320
water 348
air **353**
error 495
deceit 545
trifle 643
–burst *fall short* 304
disappoint 509
fail 732
–reputation 873
–up *agitation* 315
bubbling 353
bubo 250
bubonic plague 655
buccaneer 791, 792
Bucephalus 271
buck *confront* 234
leap 309
stag 366
male 373
negro 431
wash 652
fop 854
–basket 191
–fever 825
–jump 309
–nigger 431
bucket *receptacle* 191
load 270
–shop 621
kick the– 360
bucking *attack* 716
buckle *tie* 43
fastening 45
distort 243
curl 248
–oneself 604
–on one's armor 673
–to *resolution* 604
exertion 686
–with *grapple* 720
buckler 717
buckram
affectation 855
pride 878
men in– 549
buckwheat 367
bucolic
pastoral 370, 371
poem 597

bud *beginning* 66
germ 153
expand 194
graft 300
blossom 367
–from 154
Buddha 976, 986
Buddhism 976, 984
Buddhist 984
–priests 996
–temple 1000
budding *young* 127
expansion 194
buddy *chum* 890
budge 264
budget *heap* 72
bag 191
store 636
finance 811
–of news 532
budmash 949
buff *skin* 223
color 436
native– 226
buffalo 366–bug 366
–robe 223
–wallow 343
buffer *hindrance* 706
defense 717
buffet *strike* 276
agitate 315
evil 619
bad 649
affront 900
smite 972
–the waves
difficulty 704
opposition 708
buffet *bar* 189
cupboard 191
buffle–headed 499
buffo 599
buffoon *actor* 599
humorist 844
butt 857
buffoonery
amusement 840
humor 842
bug *littleness* 193
insect 366, 653
bugaboo *alarm* 669
fear 860
bugbear
imaginary 515
alarm 669
fear 860, 980
buggy 272
bugle *instrument* 417
war cry 722
–call *sign* 550
command 741
bugles *ornament* 847
build *construct* 161
form 240
–a campfire 384
–up *compose* 54

–upon *belief* 484
–upon a rock 150
builder 626, 690
building material 635
buildings 189
built on *basis* 211
bulb *knob* 249
projection 250
bulbul 416
bulge 250
bulk *be great* 31
whole 50
size 192
bulkhead
covering 223
interjacence 228
safety 664
hindrance 706
bulky 31
bull *animal* 366
male 373
error 495
absurdity 497
solecism 568
detective 664
ordinance 741
stock exchange 797
–in a china shop 59
take the–by the horns
resolution 604
courage 861
Bull, John– 188
bulla 250
bull calf 501
bulldog
animal 327, 366
pluck 604, 604a
courage 861
bulldoze 860, 885
bulldozer 887
bullet *ball* 249
arms 727
(*missile* 284)
–proof 717
bulletin *list* 86
news 532
record 551
letter 592
–board 551
bullfight 720
bullhead 501
bullion 800
bull's–eye *center* 222
lantern 423
aim 620
bullwhack 975
bullwhacker 370
bully *boat* 273
first–rate 648
fighter 726
jovial 836
frighten 860
rashness 863
bluster 885

-up one's pockets
808
take by the-586
buttoned-up
reserved 528
buttonhole *flower* 400
bore 841
buttonholer 841
buttons *page* 746
button-top
useless 645
buttress *strength* 159
support 215
defense 717
butyraceous 355
buxom 836
buy 795-and sell 794
-a pig in a poke 621
buzz *hiss* 409
insect cry 412
publish 531
news 532
-saw 44
buzzard *bird* 366
fool 501
between hawk and-
agitation 315
worry 828
blind as a-442
-dollar 800
by *alongside* 236
instrumental 631
sequestered 893
-and by 121, 132
-itself 87
-means of 632
-my troth etc. 535
-no means 32
-telegraph 532
-the by 134
-the card 82
-the hour etc.
hire 788
-the way *à propos* 9
beside the purpose 10
parenthetical 134
-wireless 532
go-*pass* 303
have-one
provide 637
possess 777
bye *departure* 293
by-end 615
bygone *past* 122
forgotten 506
let-s be bygones
918
bylaw 963
byname 565
by-pass 287
bypast 122
bypath 279
byplay *hint* 527
gesture 550
by-purpose 615
byre 189, 370, 636

byroad 278, 627
by-room 191
byssus 256
bystander *near* 197
spectator 444
byway 627
byword *maxim* 496
cant term 563, 564
reproach 874
contempt 930

C

cab 272
cabal *plan* 626
confederacy 712
cabala *latency* 526
spell 993
cabalism 526
cabalistic *hidden* 528
sorcery 992
cabane 273
cabaret 189
cabasset 717
cabbage 298, 791
cabestro 45
cabin *room* 189
receptacle 191
cabined 751
cabinet *receptacle* 191
workshop 691
council 696
-*picture* 556
cable *link* 45
dispatch 527
news 531, 532
telegraph 534
by-684
-code 528
slip-623
telegraphic-534
cabled *telegraphic* 531
cabman *traveler* 268
director 694
caboose 386
cabriolet 272
cacation 299
cachalot 192
cache 636
cachet 550
lettre de-751
cachexia
weakness 160
disease 655
cachinnation 838
cacique 745
cackle *of geese* 412
chatter 584
talk 588
laugh 838
cacodemon 980
cacoëpy 410, 583
cacoëthes *habit* 613
itch 865
-loquendi 584

-scribendi 590
cacographer 579
cacographic 579
cacography 590
cacology 579, 583
caconym 563
cacophonous
(*see* cacophony)
cacophony
stridor 410
discord 414
style 579
Cacus, den of- 791
cad *servant* 746
vulgar 851
plebeian 876
cadastral survey 466
cadastration 466
cadastre *list* 86
measurement 466
cadaverous
corpse 362
pale 429
hideous 846
caddy 191
cadeau 784
cadence *pace* 264
fall 306
sound 402
music 415
cadenza 415
cadet *junior* 129
soldier 726
officer 745
-blue 438
cadge 765
cadger *beggar* 767
huckster 797
cadi 967
cadmium 439
caduceus *insignia* 747
wand 215, 993
caducity *fugacity* 111
age 128
impotence 158
decay 659
caducous 111
caecal 261
caecum 221, 350
Caesar 745
caesura
disjunction 44
discontinuity 70
cessation 142
interval 198
café 189
caftan 225
cage *receptacle* 191
restrain 751
prison 752
Cagliostro
impostor 548
sorcerer 994
cahoot 712, 778
cahot 250, 315

cahotage *disorder* 59
agitation 315
Cain 361
caique 273
cairn *grave* 363
sign 550
caisson 191, 252
caitiff *churl* 876
ruffian 913
villain 949
cajole *flatter* 933
(*see* cajolery)
cajolery
imposition 544, 545
persuasion 615
flattery 933
cake *stick* 46
pastry 298, 396
consolidate 321
-walk 840
calabash 191
calaboose 752
calambac 400
calambour 400
calamiform 253
calamitous
adverse 935
disastrous 830
calamity *killing* 361
evil 619
adversity 735
suffering 830
calash *cap* 225
vehicle 272
calathiform 252
calcareous 432
calcimine 430
calcinatory 384
calcine 384
calcitrate 276
calcium light 423
calculate *reckon* 85
investigate 461
expect 507
intend 620
-upon 484
calculated
tending 176
premeditated 611
calculating
prudent 498
-machine 85
calculation
(*see* calculate)
accounts 811
caution 864
calculous 323
calculus 85, 323
caldron
(*see* cauldron)
calèche 272
Caledonian 188
calefaction **384**
calefy 384
calembour 520
calendar *list* 86

chronicle 114
record 551
schedule 611
calender 255
calenture
delirium 503
disease 655
calf *young* 129
animals 366
fool 501
-love 902
golden-986, 991
Caliban 846
caliber *degree* 26
size 192
breadth 202
opening 260
intellectual capacity
498
calibrate *degree* 26
breadth 202
measure 466
caliche 490a
calico 635
calid 382
calidarium 386
calidity 382
caliginous 421
calipers 466
caliph 745
caliphate 737
calisthenics
training 537
beauty 845
caliver 727
calk 660
call *signal* 550
name 564
express 566
motive 615
visit 892
sanctify 976
ordain 995
at one's- *alert* 682
obedient 743
-attention to 457
-for *require* 630
order 741
ask 765
-forth *resort to* 677
excite 824
-in *advice* 695
-in question 485
-into being 161
-into notice 525
-into play 677
-names 929, 932
-of duty 926
-off the attention
458
-out *cry* 411
challenge 715
-over *number* 85
-to 586
-to account 932
-to mind 505

steal 791
—on
  (*see below*)
—oneself 692
—out *conduct* 692
  complete 729
—over *transfer* 270
  accounts 811
—through 692, 729
—weight *influence* 175
  evidence 467
  importance 642
—with a high hand
  authority 737
  pride 878
  insolence 885
  reap and—775
carry on
  continue 143
  persevere 604a
  pursue 622
  do 680
  conduct 692
—an argument 476
—an inquiry 461
—a trade 794
—business 625
—war 722
cart 272—away 185
—before the horse
  disorder 59
  inversion 218
  bungling 699
—horse 271
—load *much* 31
  contents 190
cartage 270
carte *list* 86
—and tierce 716
—blanche *power* 157
  permit 760
  liberal 816
—de visite 550, 554
cartel *defiance* 715
  truce 723
  compact 709, 769
carter 268
Cartesianism 451
Carthusian 996
cartilage *dense* 321
  hard 323
  tough 327
cartilaginous
  hard 323
  tenacious 327
cartographer 466
cartography 466, 554
carton 593
cartoon 21, 556
cartoonist 558
cartouche
  ammunition 727
  ornament 847
cartridge 727
cartulary *list* 86
  record 551

caruncle 250
caruncular 250
carunculation 250
carve *cut* 44
  make 161
  form 240
  furrow 259
  sculpture 557
  apportion 786
—one's way 282
carvel 273
carver 559
Caryatides 215
casa 189
cascade 348
case *state* 7
  box 191
  sheath 223
  topic 454
  argument 476
  specification 527
  grammar 567
  affair 625
  patient 655
  lawsuit 969
  be the—*exist* 1
  true 494
—in point *agree* 23
  conform 82
  in—*circumstance* 8
  event 151
  supposition 514
  in good
—*healthy* 654
  prosperous 734
  make out a—
  evidence 467
  right 924
caseate 321
caseation 321
caseharden
  strengthen 159
  habituate 613
casehardened
  callous 376, 823
  obstinate 606
casein 321
casemate *barrack* 189
  defense 717
casement 260
casern 189
cash *money* 800
  pay 807
—account 811
—down 810
—on delivery 810
—register 85, 551, 802
  in—803
cashbook 551, 811
cashbox 802
cashier *dismiss* 756
  treasurer 801
cashmere 635
casing 223
casino 712
cask 191

casket *box* 191
  coffin 363
casque *helmet* 717
casquetel 717
Cassandra
  prophet 513
  warning 668
cassino 840
Cassiopeia's Chair
  318
cassock 999
cast *mold* 21
  small quantity 32
  add 37
  role 51
  spread 73
  tendency 176
  exuvial 223
  form 240
  throw 284
  tinge 428
  aspect 448
  plan 626
  staff 712
  give 784
  allot 786
  condemn 971
—about for 463
—accounts 811
—adrift *disperse* 73
  eject 297
  liberate 750
  dismiss 756
—a gloom 837
—a nativity
  predict 511
  sorcery 992
—anchor *stop* 265
  arrive 292
—a shade 421
—aside 460
—a slur *discredit* 874
  accuse 938
—a spell 992
—aspersions 934
—away *reject* 610
  waste 638
  lost 732
—away care 836
—behind one
  forget 506
  refuse 764
  relinquish 782
—dishonor upon 874
—down 308
  dejected 837
—eyes on 441
—in one's lot with
  609
—in the eye 443
—in the same mold
  17
—in the teeth 938
—iron *metal* 323
  resolute 604
—lots 621

—luster upon 420
—of countenence 448
—of mind 820
—of the dice 156
—off *divest* 226
  dismiss 756
  relinquish 782
—off a habit 614
—off clothes 645
—off skin 223
—off trammels 750
—one's net 463
—out 610
—overboard
  disuse 678
—reflection upon 932
—the eyes back 122
—the eyes over 457
—the parts 60
—the skin 226
—to the dogs 162
—up *add* 85
  happen 151
  eject 297
  give one a—707
  set on a—621
castaneous 433
castanet 417
castaway *exile* 893
  reprobate 949
  (*impious* 988)
caste *class* 75
  party 712
  rank 873
  —mark 550
  lose—940
castellan *servant* 746
  keeper 753
castellated 717
caster *cruet* 191
  wheel 312
castigate *reprove* 932
  punish 972
castigator 936
casting—vote 480
  —weight 28, 30
castle *at chess* 148
  abode 189
  refuge 666
  defense 717
  —builder 515
  —in the air
  inattention 458
  impossible 471
  imagination 515
  hope 858
castor *hat* 225
Castor and Pollux
  twins 89
  luminary 423
  friends 890
castrametation
  building 189
  war 722
castrate *subduct* 38
  impotent 158

casual *incidental* 6
  chance 156
  uncertain 475
  nonobservant 773
casualty *event* 151
  killed 361
  evil 619
  misfortune 735
casuist 476
casuistic 477
casuistry
  sophistry 477
  falsehood 544
  duty 926
casus belli
  quarrel 713
  irritation 824, 900
cat *boat* 273
  nine lives 359
  animal 366
  keen sight 441
  fall on one's feet 734
  cross 901
  as the—jumps
  event 151
—and dog life 713
—in pattens 652
  gib—, tom—*male* 373
  let—out of bag 529
  see how the—jumps
  foresight 510
  fickleness 607
  caution 864
catabasis 36
catacaustic 245
catachresis
  metaphor 521
  misinterpretation
  523
cataclasm 44
cataclysm
  convulsion 146
  destruction 162
  deluge 348
  (*redundance* 641)
catacomb 363
catacoustics 402
catafalque 363
catalectic 597
catalepsy 265, 683,
  821a
catalo 41
catalogue *arrange* 60
  list 86
  —raisonné 551
catalysis 49
catamaran *vessel* 273
  fighter 726
catamenia 138
catamount 913
cataphonics 402
cataplasm 662
catapult
  propulsion 284
  weapon 727
cataract *waterfall* 348

central 68, 222
centrality 222
centralize *combine* 48
centric 222
centricality 222
centrifugal 291
centripetal 290
centrosome 357
centuple 98
centuplicate 98
centuriate 98
centurion 745
century *hundred* 98
  period 108
  long time 110
cephalalgia 378
ceramic 384
  –*ware* 557
ceramics 557
cerate 355, 662
Cerberus *janitor* 263
  custodian 664
  sop for–615
cereal 298, 367
cereals 369
cerebral *phonetic* 561
cerebrate 451
cerebration 451
cerebrum 450
cerecloth 223, 363
cerement
  covering 223
  wax 356
  burial 363
ceremonious 928
ceremony *parade* 882
  courtesy 894
  rite 998
cerise 434
cerograph 558
cerography
  engraving 558
  writing 590
ceromancy 511
ceroplastic 557
certain *special* 79
  indefinite number 100
  sure 474
  belief 484
  true 494
  make–*of* 480a
  of a–*age* 128
  to a–*degree* 32
certainly *yes* 488
certainty **474**
certes *surely* 474
  yes 488
certificate
  evidence 467
  record 551
  security 771
certify *evince* 467
  affirm 535
certiorari 969
certitude 474

cerulean 438
cerulescent 438
ceruse 430
cespitose 367
cess *tax* 812
cessation **142**
cession *surrender* 725
  of property 782
  gift 784
cesspool 653
cest 247
cestus *ligtaure* 45
  girdle 247
Cetus 490a
chabuk 975
chafe
  physical pain 378
  warm 384
  irritate 825
  mental pain 828, 830
  discontent 832
  incense 900
chaff *trash* 643
  rubbish 645
  ridicule 856
  vulgar 876
  not to be caught with– *clever* 698
  cunning 702
  winnow–*from wheat* 609
chaffer 794
chafing dish 386
chagrin 828
chain *fasten* 43
  vinculum 45
  series 69
  measure 200
  interlinking 219
  imprison 752
  ornament 847
  adamantine–*s* 360
  –*lightning* 423
  drink 959
  –*s fireplace* 386
  drag a–749
  drag a lengthened– 686
  in–*s prisoner* 754
chain shot 727
chair *support* 215
  vehicle 272
  professorship 542
  throne 747
  celebration 883
  president 694
  –*car* 272
  in the–693
chairman 694
chaise 272
chalcedony 847
chalcography 558
chalet 189
chalice 191
chalk *earth* 342

  white 430
  mark 550
  drawing 556
  –*out plan* 626
  –*talk* 537, 584
  –*talker* 540
chalky 430
challenge
  question 461
  doubt 485
  claim 924
  defy 715
  accuse 938
  –*comparison* 648
  –*the jurors* 969
chalybeate 662
chamber *room* 191
  council 696
  mart 799
  –*concert* 415
  –*fellow* 890
  –*music* 415
  sick–655
chamberlain 746
chambermaid 746
chameleon *lizard* 366
  changeable 149
  variegated 440
chamfer 259
chamois
  smoothness 255
  leap 306
  animal 366
champ 298–*the bit*
  disobedient 742
  chafe 825
  angry 900
champagne 959
champaign 344
champain 874
champak 400
champion *best* 648
  auxiliary 711
  defense 717
  combatant 726
  victor 731
  representative 759
  pity 914
championship 707
champlevé 847
chance
  absence of cause **156**
  liability 177
  absence of aim **621**
  as–*would have it* 152
  be one's–151
  –*s against one*
  danger 665
  game of–840
  great–472
  small–473
  stand a–*liable* 177
  possible 470
  take one's–675
chanceable 156

chanceful 156
chancel 1000
chancellor
  judge 664, 967
  president 745
  deputy 759
  –*of the exchequer* 801
chancery–*suit*
  delay 133
  court of–966
chandelier 214, 423
chandler 797
change *alteration* **140**
  interchange 148
  mart 799
  small coin 800
  –*about* 149
  –*color* 821
  –*for* 147
  –*hands* 783
  –*of mind* 607
  –*of opinion* 485
  –*of place* 264
  radical–146
  sudden–146
changeable 149
changeableness
  mutable **149**
  irresolute 605
changeful 607
changeling
  substitute 147
  fool 501
changer 797
channel *base* 211
  furrow 259
  opening 260
  conduit 350
  artery 627
chant *song* 415
  sing 416
  worship 990
chanter 416
chanticleer 366
chantress 416
chantry 1000
chaomancy 511
chaos 59
chap *crack* 198
  jaw 231
  fellow 373
chaparajos 225
chaparral 367
chap book 593
chapeau 225
chapel 189, 1000
chaperon
  accompany 88
  guard 459
  safety 664
chapfallen 837, 878
chaplain 996
chaplaincy 995
chaplet *circle* 247
  fragrance 400

  favor 550
  trophy 733
  ornament 847
chapman 797
chaps *chaparajos* 225
chapter *partition* 44
  part 51
  topic 454
  book 593
  council 696
  church 995
  –*and verse*
  evidence 467
  exact 494
  –*of accidents* 156, 621
chapter house 1000
chaqueta 225
char 384
char–à–bancs 272
character *nature* 5
  state 7
  class 75
  oddity 83
  letter 561
  drama 599
  disposition 820
characteristic
  intrinsic 5
  special 79
  mark 550
characterize
  name 564
  describe 594
characterized 820
charade *riddle* 533
  drama 599
charcoal
  fuel 384, 388
  black 431
  drawing 556
charge *fill* 52
  contents 190
  business 625
  mandate 630
  direction 693
  advice 695
  precept 697
  attack 716
  order 741
  custody 751
  commission 755
  bargain for 794
  price 812
  accusation 938
  churchdom 995
  –*d with*
  possessed of 777
  –*on attribute* 155
  in–*prisoner* 754
  justifiable–937
  take–*of safe* 664
  take in–751
chargeable *debt* 806
  –*on duty* 926
chargé d'affaires 758

stability 150
dense 321
coherent 23
cohesion 46
cohesive 46, 327
cohibit *restrain* 751
  prohibit 761
  (*counteract* 179)
cohobation 336
cohort 726
cohue 72
coif 225, 370
coiffure 225
coign 244
coil *disorder* 59
  convolution 248
  circuition 311
  radiator 386
  shuffle off this
    mortal–360
coin *fabricate* 161
  imagine 515
  money 800
  –money 775
  –words 563
coincide
  (*see* coincidence)
coincidence
  identity 13
  in time 120
  in place 199
  in opinion 488
coincident 13, 178
coiner *thief* 792
  counterfeiter 800
coinstantaneous 120
coistril 862
coition 43
cojuror 467
coke 388
colander 60, 260
colature 652
cold *frigid* **383**
  color 429, 438
  style 575
  insensible 823
  indifferent 866
  –comfort 832
  –feet *cowardice* 862
  –shoulder
    discourtesy 895
    contempt 930
  –steel 727
  –storage 387
  –sweat *fear* 860
  dislike 867
  –water cure 662
  in–blood
  premediated 611
  purposely 620
  unfeeling 823
  dispassionate 826
  throw–water on
  dissuade 616
  hinder 706
  dull 843

coldbloodedness 871
cold–frame 371
cold–hearted
  unfeeling 823
  hostile 889
  malevolent 907
cold–short 328
coleslaw 298
colic 378
Coliseum 728
collaboration 178
collaborator 711
collapse
  prostration 158
  contract 195
  shortcoming 304
  disease 655
  deteriorate 659
  fatigue 688
  failure 732
collar *dress* 225
  circlet 247
  shackle 752
  seize 789
  slip the–750
collate 54, 464
collateral *relative* 9
  relation 11
  synchronous 120
  parallel 216
  lateral 236
  –evidence 467
collation *repast* 298
  comparison 464
colleague
  accompany 88
  associate 690
  cooperation 709
  auxiliary 711
  friend 890
collect *assemble* 72
  opine 480
  understand 518
  compile 596
  acquire 775
  prayer 990
  (*take* 789)
  –evidence 467
  –knowledge 539
  –one's thoughts 451
collectanea
  assemblage 72
  compendium 596
collected *calm* 826
collection
  assemblage 72
  store 636
  offertory 990
collective 78
collectively *whole* 50
  generality 78
  together 88
collectivism 737, 778
collectivist 778
collector
  director 694, 745

colleen 129
college 542
  –board 542
  –education 537
  –yell 838
  go to–539
collide 276
collie 366
collier 273
colliery 252
colligate 72
collimate 216
collimation 216, 278
colliquation 335
collision *clash* 179
  percussion 276
  opposition 708
  encounter 720
collocate *arrange* 60
  assemble 72
  place 184
collocution 588
collogue *wheedle* 933
colloid 490b
collop 51
colloquial
  figure of speech 521
  language 560
  neology 563
  conversation 588
  –meaning 516
colluctation 720
collusion *deceit* 545
  conspiring 709
collusive 544
colluvies 653
collyrium 662
cologne 400
colon *punctuation* 142
  intestine 350
colonel 745
colonial 188
colonist 188, 294, 295
colonization 184
colonize 184
colonnade *series* 69
  houses 189
colony
  region 181, 184
  settlement 188
colophon 65
colophony 356a
color *hue* **428**
  tone 431
  redden 434
  appearance 448
  probability 472
  disguise 544
  paint 556
  plead 615
  plea 617
  be angry 900
  all–s 440
  change–
  shame 879
  –too highly 549

–up *redden* 434
  blush 879
  give a–to
  change 140
  qualify 469
  probable 472
  falsehood 544
  lend a–to *plea* 617
  vindicate 937
  man of–431
  show in true–s 543
colorable
  ostensible 472
  deceptive 545
Colorado beetle 913
coloration 428
coloratura 415, 416
color–blindness 443
colored (*see* color)
  –man 431
  –spectacles 424
colorimeter 428
coloring (*see* color)
  meaning 516
  –matter 428
  false–523
colorless *weak* 160
  pale 429
  feeble 575
color–printing 558
colors *ensign* 550
  decoration 877
  false–544, 545
  flying–*display* 882
  celebration 883
  lower one's–735
  nail one's–to the
    mast 604
  show one's–
  manifest 525
  disclose 529
  true to one's–939
color–sergeant 745
colossal 192
Colosseum 728
colossus *strength* 159
  size 192
  height 206
colporteur 797, 996
colt *young* 129
  horse 271
  fool 501
colter 253
colubrine 366
columbarium 189
columbine 599
columella 215
columelliform 215
column *series* 69
  height 206
  support 215
  cylinder 249
  caravan 266
  monument 551
  printing 591
  troop 726

colures 318
coma
  inactive 683
  insensible 376, 823
comate 711, 890
comb *teeth* 253
  clean 652
  punish 972
combat 720, 722
  –plane 273
combatant **726**
combative 720, 722
combe 252
comber *wave* 348
combination **48**
  arithmetical 84
  party 712
  –of fortuitous
    circumstances 621
combine *unite* 48
  component 56
  concur 178
  partnership 712
  cooperate 709
combustible 388
combustion 384
come *happen* 151
  approach 286
  arrive 292
  cheer up! 836
  out upon! 932
  –about 658
  –across *discover* 480a
  –after *sequence* 63
  posterior 117
  –amiss
  disagreeable 24
  ill–timed 135
  –and go 314
  –at one's call 743
  –back 283
  –before 116
  –by 775
  –down with 807
  –first *superior* 33
  precede 62
  –forth *egress* 295
  appear 446
  –forward 763
  –from *follow* 154
  hail from 292
  –in *ingress* 294
  receipt 785
  –in for
  property 778, 780
  –into existence *be* 1
  begin 66
  –into operation 170
  –into the views of
  cooperate 709
  –into the world 359
  –into use 613
  –into view 446
  –near 286
  –of 154
  –of age 131

companionway 305
company *assembly* 72
  actors 599
  party, partnership 712
  troop 726
  sociality 892
  (*merchants* 791)
  bear–88
  in–with 88
comparable 9
comparative
  degree 26
  compare 464
  –anatomy 368
  –estimate 464
comparatively 32
compare 464
  –notes 695
comparison 464
compartition 44
compartment
  part 51
  region 181
  place 182
  cell 191
  carriage 272
compass
  degree 26
  space 180
  surround 227
  circumscribe 233
  circuition 311
  measure 466
  intent 620
  guidance 693
  achieve 729
  box the
  –azimuth 278
  rotation 312
  –about 229
  –of thought 498
  in a small–193
  keep within–
   moderation 174
  fall short 304
  economy 817
  points of the–236
compassion 914
  object of–828
compassionate 914
compatible
  consentaneous 23
  possible 470
compatriot
  inhabitant 188
  friend 890
compeer *equal* 27
  friend 890
compel 744
compellation 564
compelled 744
compendious
  inclusive 56
  short 201
compendium 596

compensate
  make up for 30
  restore 790
  requite 973
compensation 30
compensatory 30, 790
compete 708, 720
competence
  power 157
  sufficiency 639
  skill 698
  wealth 803
competition
  opposition 708
  contention 720
competitor
  opponent 710
  combatant 726
  candidate 767
compilation
  composition 54
  collect 72
  writing 590
  book 593
  compendium 596
compile 54, 72
complacent
  pleased 827
  content 831
  courteous 894
  kind 906
complain 839
  –without cause 839
complainant 938
complainer 832
complaint *illness* 655
  murmur 839
  lodge a–938
complaisant
  lenient 740
  courteous 894
  kind 906
complanate 251
complement
  counterpart 14
  adjunct 39
  remainder 40
  part 52
  arithmetic 84
complemental 12
complete *entire* 52
  accomplish 729
  conclude 769
  –answer 479
  –circle 311
  in a–degree 31
completeness 52
  unity 87
completion 729
complex 59
complexion *state* 7
  color 428
  appearance 448
complexity 59
complexus 50, 59

compliance
  conformity 82
  submission 725
  obedience 743
  consent 762
  observance 772
  courtesy 894
compliant
  (*see* compliance)
complicate
  derange 61
complicated
  disorder 59
  convolution 248
  mechanical 633
complice 711
complicity 709
compliment
  courtesy 894
  congratulate 896
  praise 931
  –s of season 896
  poor–932
complimentary 815
complot 626
comply
  (*see* compliance)
compo *coating* 223
  material 635
component 56
comport–oneself 692
  –with 23
compos 502
compose
  make up 54, 56
  arrange 60
  produce 161
  moderate 174
  music 416
  write 590
  printing 591
  pacify 723
  assuage 826
composed
  self–*possessed* 826
composer *music* 413
composing
  –frame 591
  –room 591
  –rule 591
composite 41
composition 54
  (*see* compose)
  combination 48
  piece of music 415
  picture 556
  style 569
  writing 590
  building material 635
  compromise 774
  barter 794
  atonement 952
compositor 591
compost 653
composure 826

compotation 298, 959
compote 298
compound *mix* 41
  combination 48
  yard 232
  compromise 774
  –arithmetic 466
  –for *substitute* 147
  barter 794
  (*stipulate* 769)
comprador 637
comprehend
  compose 54
  include 76
  know 490
  understand 518
comprehensibility 518
comprehension
  (*see* comprehend)
  intelligence 498
comprehensive
  wholesale 50
  inclusive 56, 76
  general 78
  wide 192
  –argument 476
compress
  contract 195
  curtail 201
  condense 321
  remedy 662
compressed 572
compressible 322
comprise 76
comprised be–in 1
comprobation
  evidence 467
  demonstration 478
compromise
  dally with 605
  mid–course 628
  danger 665
  pacify 723
  compact 769
  compound 774
  atone 952
compromised
  promised 768
compter 799
compte rendu
  record 551
  accounts 811
  (*abstract* 596)
comptroller
  director 694
  (*master* 745)
compulsion 744
  forced labor 603
compulsion neurosis 821a
compulsory 601, 744
compunction 950
compurgation
  evidence 467

acquittal 970
compurgator 467
computable 85
compute 37, 85
computation
  addition 37
  accounts 811
comrade 890
comradeship 892
con *think* 451
  get by heart 505
  learn 539
conation *agency* 170
  tendency 176
  will 600
conative 170, 176
conatus 176
concamerate 245
concatenation
  junction 43
  continuity 69
  –of circumstances 621
concave 252
  –mirror 555
concavity 252
conceal *invisible* 447
  hide 528
  cunning 702
concealment 528
concede *assent* 488
  admit 529
  permit 760
  consent 762
  give 784
conceit *idea* 453
  overestimation 482
  folly 499
  supposition 514
  imagination 515
  wit 842
  affectation 855
  vanity 880
conceited
  dogmatic 481
conceivable 470
conceive *begin* 66
  teem 168
  note 450
  believe 484
  understand 490
  imagine 515
  concent 413
concentrate
  assemble 72
  centrality 222
  converge 290
concentric 216, 222
concentricity 216
conception
  (*see* conceive)
  intellect 450
  idea 453
  guiding–453
concern *relation* 9
  event 151

governor 745
officer 965
constancy 743
constant *uniform* 16
continuous 69
regular 80
frequent 136
periodic 138
immutable 150
exact 494
persevering 604a
faithful 939
–*flow* 69
constellation
stars 318
luminary 423
glory 873
consternation 860
constipate 321
constipation
closure 261
density 321
constituency 609
constituent 56, 609
constitute
compose 54, 56
produce 161
constituted by 1
constitution *nature* 5
state 7
composition 54
structure 329
charter 924
law 963
higher law than–
926
constitutional
walk 266
–*government* 737
constitutive 153
constrain *compel* 744
restrain 751
abash 881
constraint
contraction 195
[*see* constrain]
constrict 195
constriction 706
constringe 195
constringency 195
construct *compose* 54
produce 161
organize 357
construction
production 161
form 240
structure 329
meaning 522
put a false–upon
523
constructive
creative 161
latent 526
–*evidence* 467
constructor 164
construe 522

consubstantiation
998
consuetude 613
consul 758, 759
consular 759
consulship 737
consult *remedy* 662
advise 695
–one's own wishes
943
–one's pillow 133
–the wishes of 707
consultant 662
consultation 695
consume *decay* 49
destroy 162
waste 638
use 677
time *time* 106
inactivity 683
consumer *user* 677
consuming 830
consummate *great* 31
complete 52
be perfect 650
completed 729
–*skill* 698
consummation
end 67
completion 729
–devoutly to be
wished *good* 618
desire 865
consumption
[*see* consume]
decrease 36
shrinking 195
disease 655
consumptive 655
contact *contiguity* 199
touch 379
come in–
arrive 292
contagion
transfer 270
unhealthy 657
contagious 655, 657
contain
be composed of 54
include 76
contained in 1
container
receptacle 191
contaminate *soil* 653
spoil 659
contaminated
diseased 655
contamination 653,
659
contango 813
contemn 930
contemper 48, 174
contemplate
view 441
intellect 450
think 451

expect 507
purpose 620
contemplation
[*see* contemplate]
contemporaneous
120
contemporary 120
contemporation 174
contempt 930
–of danger 861
contemptible
unimportant 643
dishonorable 940
contemptuous
defiant 715
disrespectful 929
disdainful 930
contend *reason* 476
assert 535
fight 720
–for *vindicate* 937
–with difficulties 704
content *assenting* 488
willing 602
calm 826
satisfied 831
to one's heart's–
sufficient 639
success 731
contention 720
contentious 901
contents
ingredients 56
list 86
components 190
book 593
synopsis 596
conterminate *end* 67
limit 233
conterminous 199
contesseration 72
contest 708, 720
contestant 710
context 591
contexture 329
(*state* 7)
contiguity 199
contiguous 197
continence 960
continent 342
continental *trifle* 643
continentals 225
contingency
junction 43
event 151
uncertainty 475
expectation 507
contingent *extrinsic* 6
conditional 8
casual 156
liable 177
possible 470
uncertain 475
supply 635
aid 707
allotted 786

donation 809
–*duration* 108a
–*interest* 780
continual
perpetual 112
frequent 136
continuance 117, 143
continuation *affix* 37
adjunct 39
sequence 63
sequel 65
–*school* 542
continuations
trousers 225
continue *exist* 1
endure 106, 110
persist 143
continued 69
–*existence* 112
–*success* 731
continuing 143
continuity 16, 69
continuous 69
contortion
distortion 243
convolution 248
(*ugliness* 846)
contortionist 599
contortuosity 243
contour *outline* 230
appearance 448
–*line* 550
contra 14 per–708
contraband
deceitful 545
prohibited 761
illicit 964
contrabandist 792
contrabasso 417
contraclockwise 283
contract *shrink* 195
narrow 203
promise 768
bargain 769
(*decrease* 36)
(*curtail* 201)
–a debt 806
–a habit 613
–an obligation 768
contractible 195
contractility 195
(*elasticity* 325)
contraction 195
shorthand 590
compendium 596
contractive 36, 464
contractor 690
contractual 769
contradict
contrary 14
dissent 489
deny 536
oppose 708
contradiction
difference 15
answer 462

contradictoriness 15
contradictory
evidence 468
discordant 713
contradistinction 15
contrafagotto 417
contraindicant 616
contraindicate
dissuade 616
warning 668
contralto 408
contraposition
inversion 218
reversion 237
contrapuntal 415
contrapuntist 413
contrariety 14, 15,
708
contrariness 708
contrariwise 148,
708
contrary *opposite* 14
antagonistic 179
captious 608
opposing 708
–to expectation
improbable 473
unexpected 508
–to reason 471
quite the–536
contrast
contrariety 14
difference 15
comparison 464
contrastive 15
contrate wheel 247
contravallation 717
contravene
contrary 14
counteract 179
counterevidence 468
deny 536
hinder 706
oppose 708
contre–coup 277
contrectation 379
contretemps
ill timed 135
hindrance 706
misfortune 735
contribute *cause* 153
tend 176
concur 178
aid 707
give 784
contribution 784
lay under– *take* 789
due 924
contributor
correspondent 592
giver 784
contributory *extra* 37
contrition
abrasion 331
penitence 950
contrivance 626

contrive *produce* 161
  plan 626
  —to *succeed in* 731
contriving
  cunning 702
control *power* 157
  influence 175
  aviation 273
  regulate 693
  authority 737
  restrain 751
  board of—696
  get—of 175
  under—
  obedience 743
  subjection 749
controller 694
controversial
  discussion 476
  discordant 713
controversialist 476, 726
controversy
  discussion 476
  interlocution 588
  contention 720
controvert *deny* 536
controvertible
  uncertain 475
  debatable 476
  untrue 495
contumacy
  obstinacy 606
  disobedience 742
contumely
  arrogance 885
  rudeness 895
  disrespect 929
  scorn 930
  reproach 932
contund 330
contuse 330
conundrum *pun* 520
  riddle 533
  wit 842
  (*problem* 461)
convalesce 654
convalescence 654, 660
convection 270, 490a
convene 72
convenience 685
conveniences 632
convenient 646
convent 1000
  —school 542
conventicle
  assembly 72
  council 696
  chapel 1000
convention
  assembly 72
  canon 80
  council 696
  law 697
  treaty of peace 723

compact 769
  —of society 852
conventional
  customary 613
conventionalism 613
conventionalist 82
conventionality 613
conventionalize 82
conventual *monk* 996
  convent 1000
converge 290
convergence 290, 372a
convergent 286, 290
conversable *talk* 588
  sociable 892
conversant *know* 490
  skillful 698
conversation 588
conversational 588
  sociable 892
conversationist 588
conversazione
  interlocution 588
  social gathering 892
converse
  reverse 14, 237
  talk 588
  hold high—539
conversely 148, 168
conversible 144
conversion 144
  trover and—964
convert *change* 140
  change to 144
  opinion 484
  tergiversation 607
  penitent 950
  religion 987
  —to use 677
convertible
  identical 13
  equal 27
  —terms 522
convex 250
  —lens 445, 490a
  —mirror 555
convexity 250
convey *transfer* 270
  mean 516
  assign 783
  —away 791
  —the knowledge of 527
conveyable 270
conveyance
  (*see* convey)
  vehicle 272
conveyancer 968
conveyancing 783
convict *convince* 484
  prisoner 754
  condemned 949
  condemn 971
conviction
  confutation 479

belief 484
  prove guilty 971
convince *confute* 479
  belief 484
  teach 537
  easily—d 486
convincing
  conclusive 478
convivial 892
convocate 72
convocation
  assemblage 72
  council 696
  church 995
convoke 72
convolution *coil* **248**
  rotation 312
convoy *transfer* 270
  accompany 88
  guard 664
  escort 753
convulse *derange* 61
  violent 173
  agitate 315
  bodily pain 378
  mental pain 830
convulsed with
  —laughter 838
  —rage 900
convulsion
  (*see* convulse)
  disorder 59
  revolution 146
  in—s 315
convulsive shock therapy 821a
coo 412
cook *heat* 384
  falsify 544
  improve 658
  prepare 673
  servant 746
  —accounts 811
  too many—s 699
cooker *range* 386
cookery 673
cook house 191
cookie 298
cookshop 189
cookstove 386
cool *moderate* 174
  cold 383
  refrigerate 385
  gray 432
  dissuade 616
  inexcitable 826
  cautious 864
  indifferent 866
  :*mperturbable* 871
  unfriendly 889
  discourteous 895
  —down
  become sane 502
  be composed 826
  —one's heels
  kept waiting 133

inaction 681
  look—upon
  unsocial 893
  take—ly 826
cooler 387
cool—headed
  judicious 498
  unexcitable 826
coolie *bearer* 271
cooling 385
coolness (*see* cool)
  insensibility 823
  estrangement 898
coomb 252
coon's age 110
coop *abode* 189
  restrain 751
  prison 752
cooperate 709
cooperation
  physical 178
  voluntary **709**
  participation 778
cooperative
  concurring 178
  cooperating 709
  helpful 746
cooperator 690, 711
cooptative 609
cooptation 609
coordinate *equal* 27
  arrange 60
  measure 466
cop 664
copal 356a
coparcener 778
copartner
  accompanying 88
  participator 778
  associate 890
copartnership
  cooperation 709
  party 712
  participation 778
cope *equal* 27
  oppose 708
  contend 720
  canonicals 999
copemate *enemy* 891
coping 204, 210
  —stone *top* 210
  completion 729
copious
  productive 168
  diffuse style 573
  abundant 639
coportion 778
copper *money* 800
copper—colored 433
copperhead 366
copperish 433
copperplate
  engraving 558
coppery 433
coppice 367
coprolite 653

coprophilia 821a
copse 367
copula 45
copulation 43
copy *imitate* 19
  facsimile 21
  prototype 22
  duplicate 90
  record 561
  represent 554
  write 590
  for the press 591
  plan 626
copyhold 780
copyholder 591
copyist *imitator* 19
  artist 559
  writer 590
copyright 780
coquelicot 434
coquet *lie* 544
  change the mind 607
  affected 855
  love 897
  endearment 902
  flattery 938
  —with *irresolute* 605
coquette
  affected 854, 855
  flirt 897, 902
coquillage 847
coracle 273
coral *animal* 368
  red 434
  ornament 847
  —reef 667
coralline 434
cor Anglais 417
corbeille 191
corbel 215
cord *tie* 45
  size 192
  filament 205
cordage 45, 192
cordate 245
cordial *pleasure* 377
  dram 392
  willing 602
  remedy 662
  feeling 821
  grateful 829
  friendly 888
  courteous 894
  benevolent 906
cordiality
  goodwill 602
  fervor 821
  friendship 888
cordiform 245
cordite 727
cordon *inclosure* 232
  circularity 247
  decoration 877
  —bleu 746
  —sanitaire *safety* 664
  preservation 670

perfect 650
proficient 700
crick *pain* 378
cricket *insect* 366
game 840
–ground *level* 213
cricketer 840
crier 534
send round the–531
crim. con. 961
crime *guilt* 947
criminal *vicious* 945
culprit 949
malefactor 975
(–*conversation* 961)
–*law* 963
criminality 947
criminate 938
crimp *crinkle* 248
notch 257
brittle 328
deception 545
deceiver 548
take 789
steal 791
crimple 258
crimson *color* 434
feeling 821
cringe *submit* 725
servility 886
cringing *servile* 746
crinite 256
crinkle *angle* 244
convolution 248
ruffle 256
fold 258
crinoid 368
crinoline 225
cripple *disable* 158
weaken 160
injure 659
crippled *disease* 655
crisis *conjuncture* 8
contingency 43
present time 118
opportunity 134
event 151
strait 704
bring to a–604
come to a–729
crisp *rumpled* 248
rough 256
brittle 328
style 572
Crispin 225
crisscross 219, 840
criterion *test* 463
evidence 467
indication 550
crithomancy 511
critic *judge* 480
taste 850
detractor 936
and stand a–480
critical *contingent* 8
opportune 134

discriminating 465
judicious 480
important 642
dangerous 665
difficult 704
censorious 932
nothing if not–480
criticism
judgment 480
dissertation 595
disapprobation 932
detraction 934
criticize
discriminate 465
judge 480
disapprove 932
detract 934
critique
(*see* criticism)
discrimination 465
critter 271
croak *cry* 412
hoarseness 581
stammer 583
warning 668
discontent 832
lament 839
croaker 832, 837
Croat 726
crochet *obstinacy* 608
crock 191
crockery 384
crocodile 366, 913
crocodile tears 54
crocus *yellow* 436
Croesus 803
croft 189, 232
cromlech 363
crone *veteran* 130
fool 501
crony *friend* 890
sociality 892
favorite 899
crook *support* 215
curve 245
deviation 279
thief 792
crooked *sloping* 217
distorted 243
angular 244
deviating 279
latent 526
crafty 702
ugly 846
dishonorable 940
–*path* 704
–stick *discourtesy* 895
–*temper* 901
–*ways* 279
croon 405
crop *stomach* 191
harvest 154
shorten 201
eat 298
store 636
gather 775

take 789
–out *reproduce* 163
visible 446
disclose 529
–up *begin* 66
take place 151
reproduction 163
second –*fertile* 168
profit 775
cropped
fragmentary 51
cropper *fall* 306
croquet *game* 840
–ground *level* 213
croquette 298
crore 98
crosier 215, 999
cross *mix* 41
support 215
across 219
pass 302
interment 363
oppose 708
failure 732
disaster 735
refuse 764
vex 830
decoration 877
fretful 901
punishment 975
rites 998
–and pile 621
–*debt* 30
–fire *interchange* 148
difficulty 704
opposition 708
attack 716
–purposes
contrary 14
disorder 59
error 495
misinterpret 523
unskillful 699
difficulty 704
opposition 708
discord 713
–questions
inquiry 461
discord 713
game 840
–sea 348
–swords 722
–the mind 451
–the path of 706
–the Rubicon 609
–fire–722
red–662
crossbar 219
crossbarred 219
crossbow 727
crossbreed 41, 83
crosscut 628
crossed 219
–bayonet 708
–in love 898
cross–examine 461

cross–eye 443
cross–grained
rough 256
obstinate 606
irascible 901
sulky 901a
crosshatch 259
crossing 219–the bar
death 360
crosspatch 895
crossroad 627
crossruff 314
cross–shaped 219
crosswise 219
crotch 91, 244
crotchet *music* 413
misjudgment 481
caprice 608
crouch *lower* 207
stoop 308
fear 860
servile 886
–before 725
croup 235
croupier 694
crow *bird* 366
cry 412
black 431
rejoice 838
boast 884
as the–flies 278
–to pluck *discord* 713
anger 900
accuse 938
pluck a–with 932
crowbar 633
crowd *assemblage* 72
multitude 102
close 197
redundance 641
the masses 876
–is not company 892
–in the–*mixed* 41
the madding–893
crowded 72, 102, 197
(*see* crowd)
crown *top* 210
circle 247
be perfect 650
complete 729
trophy 733
scepter 747
install 755
jewel 847
decoration 877
reward 973
–ed head 745
–law 963
–of sorrow 828
–wheel 247
–with laurel 873
–with success 731
to–all 33, 642
crowning (*see* crown)
superior 33
end 67

–point 210
crown–post 215
crow's–foot *age* 128
crow's nest
nautical 210
crozier 747
crucial *crossing* 219
proof 478
–test 463
cruciate
cruciform 219
physical pain 378
mental pain 830
crucible *dish* 191
conversion 144
furnace 386
experiment 463
laboratory 691
put into the–163
cruciferous 219
crucifix 219, 998
crucifixion
anguish 828
(*see* crucify)
cruciform 219, 1000
crucify
physical torture 378
mental agony 830
execution 972
crude *color* 428
inelegant 579
unprepared 674
cruel *painful* 830
inhuman 907
–as death 907
–only to be kind 830
cruelly *much* 31
cruelty (*see* cruel)
cruet 191
cruise *navigation* 267
cruiser 726
cruller 298
crumb *small* 32
bit 51
powder 330
(*part* 51)
(*little* 193)
–of comfort 834
crumble *decrease* 36
weak 160
destruction 162
brittle 328
pulverize 330
spoil 659
–into dust
decompose 49
–under one's feet 735
crumbling
(*see* crumble)
dangerous 665
crumbly 330
crumenal 800
crump *distorted* 243
curved 245
crumple *ruffle* 256
fold 258

up *destroy* 162
crush 195
crunch *shatter* **44**
chew 298
pulverize 330
crupper 235
crusade 361, 722
cruse 191
crush *crowd* 72
destroy 162
compress 195
shatter 328
pulverize 330
humble 879
(*injure* 649)
–one's hopes
disappoint 509
hopeless 859
–under an iron heel
739
crushed *unhappy* 828
crush hat 225
crushing *vigorous* 574
painful 830
crust 223
crustacean 366, 368
crusty
discourteous 895
sullen 901a
crutch *support* 215
angle 244
crux *cross* 219
difficulty 704
Crux 490a
cry *stridor* 410
human **411**
animal 412
publish 531, 532
call 550
voice 580
vogue 613
weep 839
–aloud *implore* 765
–and little wool
overrate 482
boast 884
disappoint 509
–before hurt 839
–down 932, 934
–for 865
–for joy 838
–for vengeance 923
–out against
dissuade 616
censure 932
–shame 932
–to *beseech* 765
–up 931
–wolf *false* 544
alarm 669
–you mercy
depreciate 766
pity 914
forgive 918
far–to 196
full–*loud* 404

raise a–550
crying (*see* cry)
urgent 630
–evil 619
–shame 874
–sin 945
crypt *cell* 191
grave 363
ambush 530
altar 1000
cryptic *uncertain* 475
concealed 528
secret 533
cryptography
unintelligibility 519
hidden 528
writing 590
crystal *hard* 323
water 337
transparent 425
–gazing 992a
–oil 356
snow–383
crystalline *dense* 321
transparent 425
crystallinity 321
crystallization 321,
323
crystallize 321
crystallomancy 511
crystallose 396
cub *young* 129
offspring 167
vulgar 851
clown 876
unlicked–241
cubby–hole 191, 530
cube
three dimensions 92,
93
form 244
cubeb 393
cubicle 191
cubist 556
cubit 200
cucking stool 975
cuckold 905
cuckoldom 961
cuckoo *imitation* 19
repetition 104
bird 366
sound 407
cry 412
songbird 416
cucullate 223
cucumber 298
–green 435
cuddle 902
cuddy 271
cudgel *beat* 276
weapon 727
punish 975
–one's brains
think 451
imagine 515
take up the–s

aid 707
attack 716
contention 720
cudgeling
punishment 972
cue *humor* 5
role 51, 625
hint 527
watchword 550
plea 617
take one's–from
695
cue rest 215
cuff *sleeve* 225
blow 276
punishment 972
cuirass 717
cuirassier 726
cuisine 298
culbute *inversion* 218
fall 306
cul–de–lampe
engraving 558
ornament 847
cul–de–sac
concave 252
closed 261
difficulty 704
culet 211
culinary 298 –art 673
cull *dupe* 547
choose 609
take 789
cullender 260
cullibility 486
cullion 949
cully *deceive* 545
dupe 547
culm 388
culminate
maximum 33
height 206
top 210
complete 729
culpability *vice* 945
guilt 947
culprit 949, 975
cult 990
cultivate *till* 365, 371
sharpen 375
improve 658
prepare 673
aid 707
courtesy 894
cultivated
courteous 894
–taste 850
cultivation
(*see* cultivate)
knowledge 490
cultivator 371
cultural 537, 542
**cultural
anthropology** 372a
culture *knowledge* 490
improvement 658

taste 850
courtesy 894
culverin 727
culvert 350
cumber *load* 319
obstruct 706
cumbersome
incommodious 647
disagreeable 830
cumbrous 830
cummerbund 225
cumshaw 784
cumulative
assembled 72
evidential 467
–evidence 467
–vote 609
cumulous 353
cumulus 353
cunctation *delay* 133
(*inactivity* 683)
cuneate 244
cuneiform 244, 372a
–character 590
cunning *prepense* 611
sagacious 698
artful 702
–fellow 700
cup *vessel* 191
hollow 252
beverage 298
remedy 662
tipple 959
between–and lip
111
bitter–828
–of humiliation 879
–that cheers etc. 298
–too low 837
–tossing 621
dash the–from
one's lips 509
in one's–s 959
cupbearer 746
cupboard 191
cupel 384
cupellation 336, 384
Cupid *beauty* 845
love 897
cupidity *avarice* 819
desire 865
cupola *height* 206
dome 223, 250
cupping 662
cup–shaped 252
cur *dog* 366
sneak 949
curable 658, 660, 662
curacy 995
curate 996
curative 660
curator 694, 758
curb *moderate* 174
slacken 275
dissuade 616
chance 621

check 706
restrain 751
shackle 752
mart 799
–bit 706
–roof 244
curcuma paper 463
curd *density* 321
pulp 354
(*cohere* 46)
curdle *condense* 321
make the blood–
830
curdled 352
cure *reinstate* 660
remedy 662
preserve 670
benefice 995
curé 996
cure–all 662
cureless 859
curfew 126
curia 966
curio 847
curiosity
unconformity 83
inquiring 455
phenomenon 872
curious *exceptional* 83
inquisitive 455
true 494
beautiful 845
desirous 865
curiously *very* 31
curl *bend* 245
convolution 248
hair 256
cockle up 258
–cloud 353
–paper 256
–up one's lip 930
curling *game* 840
curling tongs 386
curly 248
curmudgeon
miser 819
currants 298
currency
publicity 531
money 800
current *existing* 1
general 78
present 118
happening 151
of water 348
of air 349
rife 531, 532
language 560
habit 613
danger 667
–account 811
against the–708
–belief 488
–of events 151
–of ideas 451
–of time 109

–before yesterday
122
–by day
  repeatedly 104
  time 106
  periodic 138
–of judgment 121
–of rest 686
–one's own 731
–s gone by 122
–s numbered
  transient 111
  death 360
–s of week 138
  decline of– 126
  denizens of the– 366
  happy as the–is
    long 827, 836
  have had its– 124
  open as– 703
  order of the– 613
  red letter– 642
  see the light of– 446
day–bed 215
day–blindness 443
daybook *record* 551
  accounts 811
daybreak
  morning 125
  dim 422
daydream *fancy* 515
  hope 858
daydreamer 515
daydreaming 458
day–laborer 690
daylight *morning* 125
  light 420
  see–*intelligible* 518
daypeep 125
dayspring 125
day–star 318, 423
daze 420, 870
  in a– 860
dazed *inattentive* 458
  uncertain 475
  confused 523
dazzle *light* 420
  blind 422, 443
  put out 458
  astonish 870
  awe 928
dazzling (*see* dazzle)
  beautiful 845
deacon 996 *juggle* 545
  intone 990
deaconry 995
dead *complete* **52**
  obsolete 124
  inert 172
  colorless 429
  lifeless 360
  insensible 376
  –against *contary* 14
  oppose 708
  –asleep 683
  –beat *powerless* 158

sponger 886
–certainty 474
–color 556
–cut 893
–drunk 959
–failure 732
–flat 213
–heat 27
–languages 560
–letter *impotent* 158
  unmeaning 517
  useless 645
  laxity 738
  exempt 927
  illegal 964
–lift *exertion* 686
  difficulty 707
–march 275, 363, 415
–of night
  midnight 126
  dark 421
–one 460
–reckoning
  numeration 85
  measurement 466
–secret 533
–set against 708
–set at *attack* 716
–shot 284, 700, 716
--silence 403
–slow 275
–sound 408a
–stop 142
–to 823
–wall *hindrance* 706
  defense 717
–water 142, 343
–weight 706
  more–than alive
  688
deaden
  weaken 158
  moderate 174
  insensible 376
  muffle 405, 408a
  benumb 823
deadened 381
deadhead 815
deadhouse 363
deadlock *cease* 142
  stoppage 265
  difficulty 704
deadly *killing* 361
  pernicious 649
  unhealthy 657
  –sin 947
  –weapon 361, 727
deads 645
deaf 419
  inattentive 458
  –and dumb 581
  –ears 419
  –to *insensible* 823
  –to advice 606
  –to reason 901a
  turn–ear to

neglect 460
unbelief 487
refuse 764
deafen *loud* 404
deaf–mute 419, 581
deaf–mutism 581
deafness 419
deal *much* 31
  arrange 60
  compact 769
  allot 786
  –a blow *injure* 659
  attack 716
  punish 972
  –board 323
  –in 794
  –out *scatter* 73
  give 784
  –with *treat of* 595
  handle 692
  barter 794
dealbation 430
dealer 797
dealings *action* 680
  have–with
  trade 794
  friendly 888
dean *age* 128
  clergyman 996
deanery *office* 995
  house 1000
dear *expending* 809
  high priced 814
  loved 897
  favorite 899
  –at any price 646
  –me *wonder* 870
  O–! *lament* 839
dearborn 272
dearness 814
dearth 640
  –of ideas 843
death 360
  be the–of one
  amuse 840
  –defying 863
  –in the pot
  unhealthy 657
  hidden danger 667
  do to– 361
  house of– 363
  in at the–*arrive* 292
  persevere 604a
  pale as–*colorless* 429
  fear 860
  put to– 361
  still as– 265
  violent– 361
deathbed 360
  –repentance 950
death bell 363
deathblow *end* 67
  killing 361
  failure 732
death chair 975
death fire 423

deathless
  perpetual 112
  fame 873
deathlike *silent* 403
  hideous 846
death's–head 837
death–song 839
death–struggle 720
death–warrant 971
deathwatch 668, 837
debacle
  revolution 146
  destruction 162
  violence 173
  downfall 306
  torrent 348
debar *hinder* 706
  restrain 751
  prohibit 761
debark 292, 342
debarment 55
debase *depress* 308
  foul 653
  deteriorate 659
  degrade 874
debased *lowered* 207
  dishonored 940
debatable 475
  –point 454
debate *reason* 476
  talk 588
  hesitate 605
  dispute 720
debauch *spoil* 659
  intemperance 954
  impurity 961
debauchee 962
debenture
  security 771
  money 800
  credit 805
debility 160
debit *debt* 806
  accounts 811
debitor 806
debonair 836
debouch 293, 295
debouchment 293
debris *fragments* 51
  crumbled 330
  useless 645
debt 800
  –of nature 360
  get out of– 807
  out of– 803
debtor 806
  –and creditor 811
début *beginning* 66
  essay 675
débutant *learner* 541
  drama 599
decade *ten* 98
  period 108
  celebration 883
decadence 659
decagon 98, 244

decagonal 98
decahedral 98
decalescence 382
decalogue 926
decamp *go away* 293
  run away 623
decant 270
decanter 191
decapitate *kill* 361
  punish 972
decarbonized iron
313
decare 98
decarnate 317
decastyle 98
decasyllable 98
decay *decrease* 36
  decomposition 49
  shrivel 195
  unclean 653
  disease 655
  spoil 659
  adversity 735
  –of memory 506
  natural–360
decayed (*see* decay)
  old 124
  rotten 160
decease 360
deceit *falsehood* 544
  deception 545
  cunning 702
deceitful (*see* deceit)
deceive 545
deceived *in error* 495
  duped 547
deceiver **548** gay–962
decemvir 98
decennial **138**
decennium 108
decent *mediocre* 651
  pure 960
decentralize 49
deception 545, 702
deceptive
  sophistical 477
  deceiving 545
  cunning 702
  –reasoning 477
decession 293
dechristianize 989
decibel 490d
decide
  turn the scale 153
  judge 480
  choose 609
decided *great* 31
  ended 67
  certain 474
  resolved 604
  take a–step 609
deciduous
  transitory 111
  falling 306
  vegetation 367
  spoiled 659

decimal
numeration 84
tenth 98, 99
decimalize 99
decimate *subtract* 38
tenth 99
few 103
weaken 160
kill 361
play havoc 659
decipher 522, 525, 561
decision
judgment 480
resolution 604
intention 620
law case 969
decisive *certain* 474
proof 478
commanding 741
take *a*–*step* 609
deck *floor* 211
cards 840
beautify 847
deckle–edged 674
declaim 582
–*against* 932
declamatory
style 577
speech 582
declaration
evidence 467
affirmation 535
law pleadings 969
–of faith *belief* 484
theology 983
–of war 713, 722
declarative 527
declaratory
meaning 516
inform 527
declare 535
declension
(*see* decline)
grammar 567
backsliding 988
declensions 5
declination
(*see* decline)
deviation 279
divergence 291
measurement 466
rejection 610
declinatory 764
declinature 764
decline *decrease* 36
old 124
weaken 160
descent 306
grammar 567
be unwilling 603
reject 610
disease 655
become worse 659
adversity 735
refuse 764

–of day 126
–of life 128
declivitous 217, 306
declivity *slope* 217
descent 306
declivous 306
decoction 335, 384
decode 525, 561
decollate 972
décolletée 225
decolor 429
decoloration 429
decolorize 429
decompose 49
decomposition 49
decompound 49
deconsecrate 756
decoloration
trophy 733
insignia 747
ornament 847
title 877
Decoration Day 840
decorous
(*see* decorum)
proper 924
respectful 928
decorticate 226
decorum *fashion* 852
duty 926
purity 960
decoy *draw* 288
deceive 545
deceiver 548
entice 615
decrassify 652, 658
decrease *in degree* 36
in size 195
decree *judgment* 480
order 741
law 963, 969
decrement
decrease 36
thing deducted 40a
contraction 195
decrepit *old* 128
impotent 158
weak 160
disease 655
decayed 659
decrepitate 406
decrepitation 490b
decrepitude
(*see* decrepit)
decrescence 36
decrescendo 36
decretal 741
decretive 741
decry *underrate* 483
censure 932
detract 934
decumbent 213, 214
decuple 98
decursive 306
decurtation 201
decussate 219

decussation 219
dedecorous
disreputable 874
discourteous 895
dedicate *use* 677
inscribe 873
dedication *book* 593
(*see* dedicate)
deduce *deduct* 38
infer 480
deducible
evidence 467
proof 478
deduct *retrench* 38
deprive 789
deduction
(*see* deduce)
decrement 40a
reasoning 476
inference 521
deductive 476
deed *transference* 270
evidence 467
record 551
act 680
security 771
–s of arms 720
–*without a name* 947
deem 484
deemster 664, 967
deep *great* 31
profound 208
sea 341
sonorous 404
cunning 702
–*color* 428
–*game* 702
–*in debt* 806
–*knowledge* 490
–*mourning* 839
–*note* 408
–*potations* 959
–*reflection* 451
–*sea* 208
–*sense* 821
–*sigh* 839
–*study* 457
–*toned* 413
in–*water* 704
plough the–267
deep–dyed
intense 171
black 431
vicious 945
deepen *increase* 35
deep–felt 821
deep–laid *plan* 626
deeply (*see* deep)
deep–mouthed
resonant 408
bark 412
deep musing 458
deep–read 490
deep–rooted
stable 150
strong 159

belief 484
habit 613
affections 820
deep–seated 208
interior 221
deer 366
in heart a–862
deev 980
deface
destroy form 241
obliterate 552
injure 659
render ugly 846
defalcation
incomplete 53
contraction 195
shortcoming 304
nonpayment 808
defamation
(*see* defame)
defamatory 932, 934
defame *shame* 874
censure 932
detract 934
defamer 936
defatigation 841
default *incomplete* 53
shortcoming 304
neglect 460
insufficiency 640
debt 806
nonpayment 808
in–*of* 187
judgment by–725
defaulter *thief* 792
nonpayer 808
rogue 949
defeasance 756
defeat *confute* 479
succeed 731
failure 732
–*one's hope* 509
defecate 652
defecation 299
defect *decrement* 40a
incomplete 53
imperfect 651
failing 945
defection
relinquishment 624
imperfection 651
disobedience 742
defective
incomplete 53
insufficient 640
imperfect 651
defend (*see* defense)
defendant 938
defender 914
defense *answer* 462
resist 717
vindication 937
defenseless
impotent 158
weak 160
exposed 665

defense mechanism 821a
defensible *safe* 664
excusable 937
defensive alliance 712
defer *put off* 133
neglect 460
–*to assent* 488
submit 725
respect 928
deference
submission 725
obedience 743
humility 879
courtesy 894
respect 928
deferment 460
defial 715
defiance 715
threat 909
–*of danger* 861
in–*opposition* 708
set at–*disobey* 742
defiant 715
deficiency
(*see* deficient)
vice 945
–*of blood* 160
deficient *inferior* 34
incomplete 53
shortcoming 304
insufficient 640
imperfect 651
deficit
incompleteness 53
debt 806
defigure 846
defile *interval* 198
march 266
dirt 653
spoil 659
shame 874
impure 961
define *limit* 233
explain 522
name 564
definite *special* 79
limited 233
visible 446
certain 474
exact 494
intelligible 518
manifest 525
perspicuous 570
definition
interpretation 521
definitive *final* 67
affirmative 535
decided 604
deflagration 384
deflate 195
deflect *curve* 245
deviate 279
deflower *spoil* 659
violate 961

defluent 348
defluxion *egress* 295
  flowing 348
defoedation 653, 659
deform 241, 846
deformed 243
deforming 241
deformity
  distortion 243
  ugliness 846
  blemish 848
defraud *cheat* 545
  swindle 791
defray 807
defrayment 807
deft *suitable* 23
  clever 698
defunct 360, 362
defy *confront* 234
  set at defiance 715
  disobey 742
  threaten 909
  −*danger* 861
dégagé *free* 748
  fashion 852
degeneracy 659
degenerate
  deteriorate 659
  vice 945
deglutition 298
degradation
  deterioration 659
  shame 874
  dishonor 940
degrade *disbar* 968
  (*see* degradation)
degree 26 *term* 71
  honor 873
  by−s 26
  by slow−s 275
  in no−107
  no−4
degustation 390
dehisce 260
dehiscence 260
dehort *dissuade* 616
  advise 695
dehydrate 340, 670
dehydration 340, 670
deification 981
deify *honor* 873
  idolatry 991
deign *condescend* 762
  consent 879
deism *heterodoxy* 984
  irreligion 989
deistic 976, 989
Deity 976
  tutelary−664
dejection
  excretion 299
  melancholy 837
déjeuner 298
dejudication 480
dekko 457
delaceration 659

delaminate 204
delation 133, 938
delator 527, 938
delay 133, 460
dele 162, 552
delectable *savory* 394
  agreeable 829
delectation 827
delectus 562
delegate *transfer* 270
  interpreter 524
  messenger 534
  commission 755
  consignee 758
  deputy 759
delegated *acting* 759
delegation 755
delete 162
deleterious
  pernicious 649
  unwholesome 657
deletion 552
deletory
  destructive 162
deliberate *slow* 275
  think 451
  attentive 457
  leisure 685
  advise 695
  cautious 864
deliberately
  (*see* deliberate)
  late 133
  with premeditation
    611
deliberation
  (*see* deliberate)
delicacy *weak* 160
  slender 203
  dainty 298
  texture 329
  savory 394
  delicate ear 418
  exact 494
  scruple 603
  ill health 655
  difficult 704
  pleasing 829
  beauty 845
  taste 850
  fastidious 868
  honor 939
  pure 960
delicate (*see* delicacy)
  color 428
  brittle 328
delicatessen 394
délice 377
delicious *taste* 394
  pleasing 829
delict 947
delictum 947
delight
  pleasure 377, 827
  pleasing 829
Delilah 962

delimit 233
delineate *outline* 230
  represent 554
  describe 594
delineavit 556
delinquency 304, 947
delinquent 949
deliquation 335
deliquesce 36, 335
deliquescent 335, 348
deliquium
  paralysis 158
  fatigue 688
deliriant 663
delirifacient 663
delirious 503, 825
delirium *raving* 503
  passion 825
  −*tremens* 959
delitescence
  invisible 447
  latency 526
  seclusion 893
deliver *transfer* 270
  utter 580, 582
  remedy 662
  rescue 672
  liberate 750
  give 784
  relieve 834
  −*as one's act and*
    deed 467
  −*a speech* 582
  −*judgment* 480
  −*the goods* 729
deliverance 672
delivery (*see* deliver)
  bring forth 161
dell 252
Delphic oracle
  prophetic 513
  equivocal 520
  latent 526
Delphinus 490a
delta *triad* 92
  land 342
delude *error* 495
  deceive 545
deluge *crowd* 72
  water 337
  flood 348
  redundance 641
delusion (*see* delude
  insane 503
  self−*credulous* 486
delve *dig* 252
  till 371
  −*into inquire* 461
demagogue
  director 694
  malcontent 710
  rebel 742
demagogy 737
demand *inquire* 461
  user 677
  order 741

  ask 765
  price 812
  claim 924
  in−*require* 630
  salable 795
  desire 865
  public−677
demarcate 233
demarcation 233
dematerialize 317
demean oneself
  conduct 692
  humble 879
  dishonor 940
demeanor *aid* 448
  conduct 692
  fashion 852
demency 503
dement 61
dementate 503
démenti 536
dementia 503
demerit 945
demesne *abode* 189
  property 780
demi- 91
demigod *hero* 861
  angel 948
  −*Authority* 737
demigration 266
demijohn 191
demi−jour 422
demimondaine 876
demimonde
  plebeian 876
  licentious 962
demirep 962
demise *death* 360
  transfer 783
  lease 787
demisemiquaver 413
demission 756
demitint 421
Demiurge 976
demiurgic 153
demivolt 309
demobilize 750
democracy *rule* 737
  commonalty 876
democratic 737
Democrats 712
Democritus 838
demoiselle 129
demolish 479
demolishment 162
demon *violent* 173
  bane 663
  familiar spirit 979
  devil 980
  −*in human shape*
    913, 949
  −*worship* 991
demonetize 800
  wicked 945
demoniacal
  malevolent 907

  furious 824
demonist 978
demonize 978
demonology
  demons 980
  sorcery 992
demonophobia 898
demonry 980
demonstration
  number 85
  proof 478
  manifest 525
  ostentation 882
  ocular−441, 446
demonstrative
  manifest 525
  indicative 550
  vehement 825
demonstrator 524
demoralize
  unnerve 158
  spoil 659
  vicious 945
Demosthenes 582
demulcent *mild* 174
  soothing 662
demur *disbelieve* 485
  dissent 489
  unwilling 603
  hesitate 605
demure *grave* 826
  sad 837
  affected 855
  modest 881
demurrage 133
demurrer 969
den *abode* 189
  study 191
  sty 653
  prison 752
  seclusion 893
  −*of thieves* 791
denary 98
denaturalize
  corrupt 659
denaturalized
  abnormal 83
dendriform 242, 367
dendroid 242
dendrology 369
Deneb 490a
dengue fever 655
denial *negation* 536
  refusal 764
  self−953
denigrate 431
denization 748
denizen
  inhabitant 188
  freeman 748
  −s *of the air* 979
  −s *of the day* 366
denominate 566
denomination
  class 75
  name 564

designate *specify* 79
  call 564
  express 566
designation *kind* 75
designed
  aforethought 611
designer 559, 626
designing
  cunning 702
designless 621
desinence *end* 67
  discontinuance 142
desirability 646
desirable 646
desire 865 *will* 600
  have no–for 866
desirous *ready* 602
  desiring 865
desist *discontinue* 142
  relinquish 624
  inaction 681
desk *box* 91
  support 215
  school 542
  pulpit 1000
  the–996
désobligeant
  carriage 272
desolate *alone* 87
  ravage 162
  afflicted 828
  dejected 837
  secluded 893
desolating
  painful 830
desolation
  (*see* desolate)
despair *grief* 828
  hopeless 859
despatch
  (*see* dispatch)
despect 930
desperado *rash* 863
  blusterer 887
  evil doer 913
desperate *great* 31
  violent 173
  impossible 471
  resolved 604
  difficult 704
  excitable 825
  hopeless 859
  rash 863
  anger 900
despicable
  trifling 643
  shameful 874
  contemptible 930
despise 930
  –*danger* 861
despite 30, 907
  in–708
despoil *injure* 659
  take 789
  rob 791
despond *dejected* 837

fear 860
despot 745
despotism
  authority 737
  severity 739
  arbitrary 964
despumate 652
desquamate 226
desquamation 223,
  226
dess 204
dessert 298
destination *end* 67
  arrival 292
  intention 620
destine 620
destiny *chance* 152
  fate 601
  fight against–606
destitute
  insufficient 640
  poor 804
  refuge for–666
desto 415
destrier 726
destroy *demolish* 162
  injure 659
  –hopes 859
  –life 361
destroyed
  (*see* destroy)
  inexistent 2
  failure 732
destroyer 165
  naval 726
  evil doer 913
destruction
  (*see* destroy)
destructive *bad* 649
  mutually–361
destructor 165
desuetude 614
  disuse 678
desultory
  disordered 59
  fitful 70
  multiform 81
  irregular in time 139
  changeable 149
  deviating 279
  agitated 315
  discursive 595
desume 788
detach 44
detached
  irrelated 10
  loose 47
detachment *part* 51
  army 726
detail *item* 79
  describe 594
  allot 786
  ornament 847
  attention to–457,
    459
  in–51

detailed
  circumstantial 8
details *minutiae* 32
  unimportant 643
detain 781
detect 480a
detective 527, 664
detent 45
detention 781
  –camp 751
  house of–752
  in house of–938
deter *dissuade* 616
  alarm 860
deterge *clean* 652
detergent 652, 662
deteriorate 659
deterioration 659
determinable 278
determinate
  special 79
  exact 494
  conclusive 480
  intended 620
determinative 67
determine *end* 67
  define 79
  cause 153
  direction 278
  satisfy 462
  make sure 474
  judge 480
  discover 480a
  resolve 604
determined
  resolute 604
deterration 529
detersion 652
detersive 662
detest *dislike* 876
  hate 898
detestable 649
dethronement
  anarchy 738
  abrogation 756
detonate *explode* 173
  sound 406
detonation 404, 406,
  872
detortion *form* 243
  meaning 523
detour *curve* 245
  circuit 629
detract *subduct* 38
  underrate 483
  defame 934
  slander 938
detraction 934
detractor 936
detrain 292
detriment *evil* 619
  deterioration 659
detrimental 649
detrital 330
detrition 330
detritus *fragments* 51

transference 270
  powder 330
detrude *cast out* 297
  cut down 308
detruncate 38
detrusion
  (*see* detrude)
detrusive 308
deuce *two* 89
  devil 978
  –is in him 608
  play the–825
deuced *great* 31
  painful 830
deux ex machina
  aid 707
  auxiliary 711
deuterogamy 903
deva 979
Devanagari 590
devastate *destroy* 162
  havoc 659
  depopulate 893
devastation 162
develop *increase* 35
  produce 161
  expand 194
  evolve 313
development 194
devexity *bending* 217
  curvature 245
deviate *vary* 20a
  change 140
  turn 279
  diverge 291
  circuit 629
  –from 15
  –from rectitude 940
  –from virtue 945
deviation 279
deviatory 311
device *motto* 550
  expedient 626
  artifice 702
devil
  seasoned food 392
  evil doer 913
  bad man 949
  Satan 978
  demon 980
  –in one
  headstrong 863
  temper 901
  –may care *rash* 863
  indifferent 866
  insolent 885
  –'s tattoo 407
  –take 908
  –take the hindmost
  run away 623
  haste 684
  cowardice 862
  –to pay *disorder* 59
  violence 173
  evil 619
  failure 732

penalty 974
  –worship 978
  fight like –s 722
  give the–his due
  right 922
  vindicate 937
  fair 939
  have a–503
  machinations of the
    –619
  play the–with
  injure 659
  malevolent 907
  printer's–591
devil–dog 269
devilish *great* 31
  bad 649
  malevolent 907
  vicious 945
devious *curved* 245
  deviating 279
  circuitous 311
devisable 270
devise *imagine* 515
  plan 626
  bequeath 784
  –d by the enemy 546
devisee
  transference 270
  possess 779
  receive 785
deviser 164
devitalize 158
devoid *absent* 187
  empty 640
  not having 777a
devoir *courtesy* 894
  respect 928
devolution 659, 783
devolve 783–on 926
Devonian Period
  490c
Devonshire cream
  321
devote *destine* 601
  employ 677
  consecrate 873
  –oneself to 604
  –the mind to 457
  –to destruction 908
devoted *habit* 613
  ill–fated 735
  obedient 743
  undone 828
  love 897
devotee *zealot* 682
  sports 840
  aspirant 865
  pious 987
  fanatic 988
devotion
  (*see* devotee,
    devoted) *love* 897
  piety 987
  worship 990
  self–942

devour *destroy* 162
  eat 298
  gluttony 957
devoured by
  feeling 821
devouring element
  382
devout 987, 990
devoutless 989
devoutly 821
dew 339
Dewali 138
dewan 745
dewy 339–eve 126
dexter 238
dexterous 238, 698
dextrality 238
dextrorsal 238
dey 745
dhobi 652
dhoti 225
dhow 273
dhu 431
diablerie 992
diabolic *bad* 649
  malevolent 907
  wicked 945
  satanic 978
diabolist 978
diabolology 978
diacaustic 245
diaconicum 1000
diacoustics 402
diacritical 15, 550
diadem 747, 847
diaeresis 49, 550
diagnosis 465, 522,
  655
diagnostic
  distinguishable 15
  special 79
  experiment 463
  discriminative 465
  indication 550
  (*intrinsic* 5)
diagnostics 655
diagonal 217
diagram 554
dial 114 *measure* 466
  as the–to the sun
  veracious 543
  faithful 772
dialect 563
dialectic
  argument 476
  language 56
dialogism 586
dialogue 588, 599
diameter 202
diametrical 237
  –ly opposite
  contrariety 14
  contraposition 237
diamond *lozenge* 244
  goodness 648
  ornament 847

–cut diamond
  cunning 702
  retaliation 718
  –wedding 883
  rough–703
Diana *moon* 318
  chaste 960
diapason 413
diaper 847
diaphanous 425
diaphonics 402
diaphoresis 299
diaphragm *middle* 68
  partition 228
diaporesis 475
diarrhea 290
diary *journal* 114
  record 551
diaskenast 593
diastase 320
diastatic 320
diaster 161
diastole 194
diatessaron 413
diathermancy 384
diathermic 384
diathesis *nature* 5
  state 7
  temperament 820
diatom 193
diatomic 193
diatonic 413
diatribe 932
dib 550
dibasic acid 490a
dibble *perforator* 262
  till 371
dibs 800
dicacity 885
dice *chance* 156, 621
  on the–470
dicer 621, 840
dichotomy *bisect* 91
  angle 244
dichroic 443
dichroism 440
dickens 978
dicker *ten* 98
  haggle 794
dictagraph 418
dictate *write* 590
  enjoin 615
  advise 695
  authority 737
  command 741
dictator 745
dictatorial
  certain 474
  narrow 481
  willful 600
  insolent 885
dictatorship 737, 739
diction 569
dictionary *list* 542
  words 562
  book 593

store 636
dictophone 418
dictum *maxim* 496
  affirmation 535
  command 741
didactic 537
didder 383
diddle 545
dido 309
diduction 44
die *mould* 22
  expire 360
  burn out 385
  engraving 558
  –and make no sign
  951
  –a violent death 361
  –away *dissolve* 4
  decrease 36
  cease 142
  –for *desire* 865
  endearment 902
  –for one's country
  360
  –from the memory
  536
  –game 951
  –hard *obstinate* 606
  resist 719
  –in harness
  continue 143
  persevere 604a
  –in one's shoes 972
  –in the last ditch
  604a
  –of a rose in
  aromatic pain 822
  –out *pass away* 2
  vanish 4
  –with ennui 841
  –with laughter 838
  hazard of the–621
  never say–604a
  not willingly let–
  670
  the–is cast 601
dieresis 49, 550
dies–faustus 731
  –infaustus 732
  –irae 919, 982
  –non never 107
  rest 687
diet *food* 298
  remedy 662
  council 696
  spare–956
dietetics 662
differ 15 *discord* 713
  –in opinion 489
  –toto coelo
  contrary 14
  dissimilar 18
difference 15
  (see **differ**)
  numerical 84
  –engine 85

perception of–465
  split the–774
different 15
  multiform 81
  –time 119
differentia 15
differential
  differing 15
  number 84
  gear 272
  –calculus 85
  –thermometer 389
differentiate 79
differentiation
  calculation 85
  discrimination 465
differentiative 15
difficult 704
  –to please 868
difficulties
  poverty 804
  in–806
difficulty 704
  question 461
diffide 485
diffident *fearful* 860
  modest 881
diffluent 348
diffuse *mix* 41
  disperse 73
  publish 531
  style 573
  (*permeate* 186)
diffuseness 104, **573**
diffusion 73, 372a,
  490a
diffusive *dispersed* 73
  verbose 573
dig *deepen* 208
  excavate 252
  till 371
  –in *intrench* 664
  –the foundations 673
  –up 480a
  –up the tomahawk
  722
digamy 903
digenesis 161
digest *arrange* 60
  boil 384
  think 451
  dissertation 595
  compendium 596
  plan 626
  improve 658
  prepare 673
  brook 826
digestible 662
digestion 673
digestive 662
diggings 189
dight *dress* 225
  ornament 847
digit 84 *morsel* 32
digitated 253
digladiation 720

diglot 560
dignified 31
dignify 873
dignitary *clergy* 996
dignity *greatness* 31
  glory 873
  pride 878
  honor 939
digraph 561
digress *deviate* 279
  style 573
digression *circuit* 629
digressive 595
dijudication 480
dike *gap* 198
  fence 232
  furrow 259
  gulf 343
  conduit 350
  defense 717
dilaceration 44
dilapidation 659
dilation (see **dilate**)
dilate *increase* 35
  swell 194
  widen 202
  rarefy 322
  expatiate 573
dilation 194
dilatory *slow* 275
  inactive 683
dilection 897
dilemma *state* 7
  uncertain 475
  logic 476
  choice 609
  difficulty 704
dilettante
  connoisseur 492
  dabbler 823
  taste 850
dilettantism
  knowledge 490
  taste 850
diligence *coach* 272
diligent *active* 682
  –thought 457
dilly–dally
  irresolution 605
  inactivity 683
dilogy 104
dilucidation 522
diluent 335
dilute *weaken* 160
  water 337
diluvian 124
dim *dark* 421
  faint 422
  invisible 447
  unintelligible 519
  –eyed 443
dime 800–novel 594
dimension 192
dimidiate 91
diminish *lessen* 36
  reduce 103

distrain *take* 789
  appraise 812
  attach 969
distrait 458
distraught 475, 503
distress *distraint* 789
  poverty 804
  affliction 828
  cause pain 830
  signal of—669
distribute *arrange* 60
  disperse 73
  type 591
  allot 786
distribution
  (*see* distribute)
distributor
  electrical 272
district
  to partition 44
  area 181
  —*court* 966
distrust *disbelief* 485
  fear 860
distrustful 487
disturb *derange* 61
  change 140
  displace 185
  agitate 315
  excite 824
  distress 828, 830
disturbance
  disorder 59
disunion
  disagreement 24
  separation 44
  disorder 59
  discord 713
disunite *separate* 44
  break with 713
disunity 24
disuse *desuetude* 614
  relinquish 624
  unemploy **678**
disused 124, 678
disvaluation 932
disvalue 932
ditch *inclosure* 232
  hollow 252
  trench 259
  water 343
  conduit 350
  defense 717
ditch water 653
ditheism 984
dithyramb *poetry* 597
dithyrambic
  wild 503
ditto *identity* 13
  repetition 104
  say—to 488
ditty 415—bag 191
diurnal 138
diuturnal 110
diuturnity 110
divagate 279

divan *sofa* 215
  council 696
  throne 747
  tribunal 966
divaricate *differ* 15
  bifurcate 91
  fork 244
  diverge 291
divarication 16a
dive *resort* 189
  swim 267
  plunge 310
  —into *inquire* 461
divellicate 44
diverge
  (*see* divergence)
divergence
  nonuniformity 16a
  difference 15
  dissimilarity 18
  variation 20a
  disagreement 24
  deviation 279
  separation **291**
divers *different* 15
  multiform 81
  many 102
  —*colored* 440
diverse 15
diversiform 81
diversify
  (*see* diversity)
  vary 20a
  change 140
diversion *change* 140
  deviation 279
  pleasure 377
  amusement 840
diversity *difference* 15
  irregular 16a
  dissimilar 18
  multiform 81
  —*of opinion* 489
divert *turn* 279
  deceive 545
  amuse 840
  —the mind 452, 458
divertissement
  drama 599
  amusement 840
Dives 803
divest *denude* 226
  take 789
  —oneself of
  abrogate 756
  relinquish 782
divestment 226
divide *separate* 44
  part 51
  arrange 60
  arithmetic 85
  bisect 91
  measure 466
  vote 609
  apportion 786
dividend *part* 51

  number 84
  portion 786
dividers 466
divination
  prediction 511
  sorcery 992
divine *predict* 511
  guess 514
  perfect 650
  of God 976, 983,
   983a
  clergyman 996
  —right *authority* 737
  due 924
  —*service* 990
diviner 994
diving 267—bird 310
divining rod *sign* 550
  magic 993
Divinity *God* 976
  theology 983
divisible (*see* divide)
  number 84
division (*see* divide)
  part 51
  class 75
  arithmetic 85
  school 542
  election 609
  discord 713
  military 726
divisor 84
divorce *separation* 44
  relinquish 782
  matrimonial **905**
Divorce Court 966
divorcée 905
divulge 529
divulsion 44
diwan 745
dixi 535
Dixie's land 827
dizen 225, 847
dizzard 501
dizziness (*see* dizzy)
dizzy *dim—sighted* 443
  confused 458
  vertigo 503
  —*height* 206
  —*round* 312
do *fare* 7
  suit 23
  produce 161
  cheat 545
  act 680
  complete 729
  succeed 731
  I beg 765
  all one can—686
  —as done by 906, 942
  —a service *useful* 644
  aid 707
  —as one pleases 748
  —as others do 82
  —away with
  destroy 162

  eject 297
  abrogate 756
  —battle 722
  —business 625
  —for *destroy* 162
  kill 261
  conquer 731
  punish 972
  —good 906
  —harm 907
  —honor 873
  —into *translate* 522
  —justice to 595
  —like 19
  —little 683
  —no harm 648
  —nothing 681
  —nothing but 136
  —one's bidding 743
  —one's office 772
  —over 223
  —tell 508
  —the work 686
  —up 660
  —without 678
  —wrong 923
   have to—with 680,
   692
   plenty to—682
   thing to—625
doch—an—dorrach
959
docile *of horses* 370
  learning 539
  willing 602
docimastic 463
docimasy 463
dock *diminish* 36
  cut off 38
  port 189
  shorten 201
  store 636
  tribunal 966
  —*walloper* 269
docked
  incomplete 53
docket *list* 69, 86
  evidence 467
  note 550
  record 551
  schedule 611
  security 771
  on the—454
dockyard 691
doctor
  learned man 492
  prevaricate 544
  improve 658
  restore 660
  remedy 662
  after death the—135
  —accounts 811
  when —s disagree
   475
doctorate 873
doctorship 873

doctrinaire
  positive 474
  pedant 492
  theorist 514
  affectation 855
  blusterer 887
doctrinal 537
doctrine *tenet* 484
  knowledge 490
document 551
documentary 467
  —*evidence* 467
dodder 160
dodecahedron 244
dodge *follow* 63
  change 140
  shift 264
  deviate 279
  oscillate 314
  pursue 461
  avoid 623
  stratagem 702
  (*deceive* 545)
doe *swift* 274
  deer 366
  female 374
doer *originator* 164
  agent 690
doff 226—the cap 894
dog *follow* 63, 281
  animal 366
  male 373
  pursue 622
  wretch 949
  cast to the—s
  destroy 162
  reject 610
  disuse 678
  abrogate 756
  relinquish 782
  —in manager 943
  —in office 737
  —s of war 722
  go to the—s
  destruction 162
  fail 732
  adversity 735
  poverty 804
  hair of—that bit you
   959
dogcart 272
dog—cheap 815
dog days 382
doge 745
dogged *obstinate* 606
  valor 861
  sullen 901a
doggedness 606
  (*see* dogged)
dogger 273
doggerel *verse* 597
  ridiculous 851, 853
doggish 895
doghole 189
dog Latin 563
dogma *tenet* 484

theology 983
dogmatic *certain* 474
  positive 481
  assertion 535
  obstinate 606
dogmatism
  (*see* dogmatic)
dogmatist 887
dogmatization 474
dog's age 110
dog's-ear 258
dogsick 867
dog star 423
dogtrot 275
dog-weary 688
doily 852
doing up and—682
  what one is—625
doings *events* 151
  actions 680
  conduct 692
doit *trifle* 643
  coin 800
dokhma 363
dolce far niente 681
doldrums
  dejection 837
  sulks 901a
dole *mite* 32
  scant 640
  give 784
  allot 786
  parsimony 819
  grief 828
doleful 837
doll *small* 193
  image 554
dollar 800—mark 550
dollish 129
dolor *physical* 378
  moral 828
dolorous 830
dolphin 341
dolt 501
doltish 499
domain *class* 75
  region 181
  property 780
dome *high* 206
  covering 223
  convex 250
Domesday book
  list 86
  record 551
domesman 967
domestic
  inhabitant 188
  home 189
  interior 221
  servant 746
  secluded 893
  —animals 366
domesticate
  locate 184
  acclimatize 613
  —animals 370

domesticize 370
domicile 189
domiciled
  inhabitating 186
domiciliary 188
  —visit 461
dominant
  influence 175
  note in music 413
dominate
  influence 175
  rule 737
domination 175, 737, 939
domineer
  tyrannize 739
  insolence 885
Dominican 996
Dominie 540
dominion 181, 737
  —rule 737
domino *dress* 225
  mask 530
  concealment 528
  game 840
don *put on* 225
  man 373
  scholar 492
  tutor 540
  noble 875
Do—na 875
donate 784
donation
  compensation 30
  gift 784
  —party 840
donative 784
done *finished* 729
  —for *impotent* 158
  spoilt 659
  failure 732
  —up *impotent* 158
  tired 688
  have—with *cease* 142
  relinquish 624
  disuse 678
  work—729
donee 270, 785
donga 252
donjon *defense* 717
  prison 752
donkey *ass* 271
  fool 501
Donna 374
Donnybrook
  disorder 59
  discord 713
donor 784
donship 875, 877
donzel 746
doodle 501 *music* 416
doodlesack 410, 417
dooly 272
doom *end* 67
  fate 152
  destruction 162

death 360
judgment 480
necessity 601
assess 812
sentence 971
—sealed *death* 360
adversity 735
doomage 812, 974
doomed 735, 828
doomsday *end* 67
  future 121
  till—112
door *entrance* 66
  cover 223
  brink 231
  barrier 232
  opening 260
  passage 627
  at one's—197
  beg from door to—765
  close the—upon 751
  death's—360
  keep within—s 265
  lie at one's—926
  open a—to
  liable 177
  open the—to
  receive 296
  facilitate 705
  permit 760
  show the—to
  eject 297
  discourtesy 895
  (*prohibit* 761)
doorkeeper 263
doormat 652
doorway 260
dope 465, 662
Doppler effect 490d
Dorado, El 803
dormancy 172
dormant *inert* 172
  latent 526
  asleep 683
dormer 260
dormeuse 272
dormitive 841
dormitory 191
dormouse 683
dorp 189
dorsal 235
dorser 191
dorsigerous 215
dorsum *back* 235
  hump 250
dory 273
dose *quantity* 25
  part 51
  medicine 662
  apportion 786
dosser 191
dossil *cover* 223
  stopper 263
dot *small* 32
  point 180a

place 182
little 193
variegate 440
mark 550
dot *dowry* 784
dotage *age* 128
  imbecility 499
dotard *old* 130
  foolish 501
dotation 784
dote *drivel* 499, 503
  —upon 897
dotted 440
douanier 965
double *similar* 17
  increase 35
  duplex 90
  substitute 147
  fold 258
  turn 283
  finesse 702
  specter 980a
  wraith 992a
  —acrostic *letters* 561
  wit 842
  —a point 311
  —eagle 800
  —entry 811
  —meaning 520
  —quartet 415
  —reef topsails 664
  —sure 474
  —the fist 909
  —up
  render powerless 158
  in quick time 274
  march at the—274
  see—*dim sight* 443
  drunk 959
  work—tides 686
double bass 417
double-dealer 607
double-dealing
  lie 544
  cunning 940
double-distilled 171
double-dyed 428
double-edged 171
double entente
  ambiguity 520
  impure 961
double-faced
  lie 544
  cunning 702
  dishonorable 940
double-handed 544
double-headed 90
double-hearted 940
double-minded 605
double-ripper 272
double-runner 272
double-shot 171
double-shotted 171
doublet 225
double-talk 523
doublets 89

double-tongued
  lie 544
  cunning 702, 940
doubling 702
doubt *uncertain* 475
  disbelieve **485**
  skeptic 989
doubtful
  uncertain 475
  equivocal 520
  —meaning
  unintelligible 519
  (*equivocal* 520)
  more than—473
doubtless *certain* 474
  belief 484
  assent 488
douceur *gift* 784
  reward 973
douche 337
dough *inelastic* 324
  pulp 354
  money 800
doughboy 726
doughface 605, 886
doughnut 298
doughty 159, 861
dour 739
douse *blow* 276, 972
  immerse 310
  splash 337
Dove
  Holy Ghost 976
dove *bird* 366
  innocent 946
  roar like sucking—174
dove-color 432
dovecote 189
dovetail *agree* 23
  join 43
  intersect 219
  intervene 228
  angle 244
  insert 300
dowager *lady* 374
  widow 905
dowdy *dirty* 653
  vulgar 851
dower *property* 780
  bequest 784
  wealth 803
dowerless 804
down *upland* 180
  below 207
  sleep 306
  cast down 308
  light 320
  bear—upon 716
  bed of—*pleasure* 377
  repose 687
  be—upon *attack* 716
  severe 739
  come—306
  —in price 815
  —in the mouth 837

hate 898
anger 900
sullenness 901a
duds 225
due expedient 646
  owing 806
  proper 924, 926
  –respect 928
  –sense of 498
  –time soon 132
  –to
    cause and effect 154, 155
    give–weight 465
    give his–to
    right 922
    vindication 937
    fair 939
    in–course 109
    occasion 134
dueguard 550
duel 720
duelist 726
duello 720
dueness 924
duenna teacher 540
  guardian 664
  keeper 753
dues 812
duet 415
duffer ignoramus 493
  bungler 701
  smuggler 792
dug 250
dugout dwelling 189
  tench 232
  boat 273
  safety 664
  defense 717
duke ruler 745
  noble 875
dukedom 877
dulcet sweet 396
  sound 405
  melodious 413
  agreeable 829
dulcify 174, 324, 396
dulcimer 417
dulcin 396
Dulcinea 897
dulcorate 396
dulia 990
dull weak 160
  unintelligent 32, 493
  inert 172
  moderate 174
  blunt 254
  slow 275
  insensible 376
  sound 405
  dim 422
  color 428
  colorless 429
  stolid 499
  style 575
  inactive 683

unapt 699
callous 823
dejected 837
weary 841
prosing 843
simple 849
–of hearing 419
–sight 443
dullard 501
dullish blunt 254
dullness 843
duly 924
dulse 367
duma 696
dumb ignorant 493
  voiceless 581
  –animal 366
  –friend 366
  –show 550
  strike–astonish 870
  humble 879
dumb–waiter 307
dumdum bullet 727
dumfound
  disappoint 509
  silence 581
  astonish 870
  humble 879
dummy substitute 147
  impotent 158
  speechless 581
  printing 591
  inactive 683
  cards 840
dump unload 297
  music 415
  sale 796
  lament 839
  –cart 272
dumps discontent 832
  dejection 837
  sulk 901a
dumpy little 193
  short 201
  thick 202
dun din 422
  colorless 429
  gray 432
  importune 765
  creditor 805
dunce ignoramus 493
  fool 501
dunderhead 501
dune 206
dung 653
dungeon 752
dunghill dirt 653
  cowardly 862
  baseborn 876
  –cock 366
Dunker 984
duo 415
duodecimal 99
duodecimo little 193
  book 593
duodenal 221

duodenary 98
duodenum 221, 350
duologue
  interlocution 588
  drama 599
dupe credulous 486
  deceive 545
  deceived **547**
duplex 90–house 189
duplicate copy 21
  double 90
  repetition 104
  tally 550
  record 551
  redundant 641
  pawn 805
duplication
  imitation 19
  doubling **90**
  repetition 104
duplicature fold 258
duplicity duality 89
  falsehood 544
durability 141
durable long time 110
  permanent 141
  stable 150
durance 751 in–754
duration 106
  contingent–108a
durbar conference 588
  council 696
  tribunal 966
dure 106
duress compulsion 744
  restraint 751
Durga 979
Durham boat 273
during 106
  –pleasure etc. 108a
durity 323
durwan 263, 753
dusk evening 126
  half–light 422
dusky dark 421
  dim 422
  black 431
dust levity 320
  powder 330
  corpse 362
  trash 643
  dirt 653
  money 800
  come to–die 360
–in the balance 643
–one's jacket 972
  humbled in the–879
  kick up a–885
  level with the–162
  lick the–submit 725
  fail 732
  make to bite the – 731
  throw–in the eyes
  blind 442
  deceive 545

plead 617
turn to–
  deorganized 358
  die 360
duster 652
dust hole 519
  fit for the–
  useless 645
  dirty 653
  spoilt 659
dustman cleaner 652
dustoor 613
dustoori 973
dust storm 330
dusty powder 330
  dirt 653
Dutch–auction 796
  –cap 225
  –courage 862
  –oven 386
  –treat 892
  high–519
  it beats the–508
Dutchman 57
  flying–515
dutiable 812
dutiful 944
duty business 625
  work 686
  tax 812
  courtesy 894
  obligation **926**
  respect 928
  worship 990
  rite 998
  do one's–virtue 944
  on–680, 682
duumvirate 737
Duval, Claude–792
D.V. 470
dwarf lessen 36
  small 193
  elf 980
dwell reside 186
  abide 265
  –upon descant 573
dweller 188
dwelling location 184
  abode **189**
dwindle lessen 36
  shrink 195
  droop 655
dyad 193
dyadic 89
dye 428
  –d in the wool 709, 820
dying 360
dyke (see dike)
dynamic 157
  –energy 157
dynamics 276
dynamitard 863
dynamite 727
dynamize 171
dynamo 157

dynamograph 276
dynamometer 276, 466
dynasty 737
dyne 490d
dysentery 299
dysmerogenesis 161
dysmeromorph 357
dyspepsia 655
dyspeptic 655
dysphonia 581
dysphoria 149
dyspnea 688

E

each 79
  –in his turn 148
  –other 12
  –to each 786
eager willing 602
  active 682
  consenting 762
  ardent 821
  desirous 865
  –expectation 507
eagle bird 366
  standard 550
  insignia 747
  coin 800
  –eye sight 441
  intelligence 498
  –winged swift 274
eagre 348, 667
ean 161
ear of corn 154
  hearing 418
  all–418
  come to one's–s 527
  sin in the–loud 404
  drum 407
  –for music 416, 418
  have the–of
  belief 484
  friendship 888
  in at one–out at the other
  inattention 458
  forget 506
  lend an–hear 418
  attend 457
  make the–s tingle
  anger 900
  meet the–418
  nice–418
  no–419
  not for–s polite 961
  offend the–410
  prick up the–s
  attention 457
  expectation 507
  pull about one's–s 308
  quick–418

reach one's–s 527
ring in the–408
set by the–s
  discord 713
  hate 898
  resentment 900
split the–s 404
together by the–s
  discord 713
up to one's–s
  redundance 641
  active 682
  willing–602
  word in the–586
earache 378
eardrop 214
eardrum 418
eared 419
earl 875
earldom 877
earless 419
earliness 132
early 132 get up–682
earmark 550
ear muffs 384
earn 775
earnest *willing* 602
  determined 604
  emphatic 642
  pledge 771
  pay in advance 809
  eager 821
  serious 837
  in–*affirmation* 535
  veracious 543
  strenuous 682
earnings 775
ear–piercing 410
earring 847
earshot 197
  out of–405
ear–splitting 402,
404
earth *ground* 211
  world 318
  land 342
  corpse 362
  –flax 385
  what on
  –*inquiry* 461
  wonder 870
earthenware
  baked 384
  sculpture 557
earthling 372
earthly 318
earthly–minded
  selfish 943
  irreligious 989
earthquake
  revolution 146
  violence 173
earthwork 717
ear–witness 467
ease *abate* 36
  bodily 377

style 578
leisure 685
facility 705
mental 827
content 831
at one's–
  prosperous 734
–off *deviate* 297
–one of *take* 789
mind at–
  cheerful 836
set at–*relief* 834
take one's–687
easel *support* 215
  painting 556
  –picture 556
easement
  property 780
  relief 834
easily (*see easy*)
  –accomplished 705
  –affected 375
  –deceived 486
  –persuaded 602
  let one down–918
east *side* 236
  direction 278
Easter *period* 138
  rite 998
  –Monday
    holiday 840
  –offering *gift* 784
  –sepulcher 1000
eastern 236
Easterner 57
easting 196
eastward 236
easy *gentle* 275
  style 578
  facile 705
  –ascent 217
  –chair *support* 215
  repose 687
  –circumstances 803
  –of belief 472
  –sail *moderate* 174
  slow 275
  –temper 894
  –terms 705
  –to understand 518
  –virtue 961
  make one self–
    about 484
  take it–*inactive* 683
  inexcitable 826
easy–going
  willing 602
  irresolute 605
  lenient 740
  inexcitable 826
  contented 831
  indifferent 866
eat *food* 298
  tolerate 826
  –dirt 725
  –heartily 298

–off the same
  trencher 892
–one's fill *enough* 639
  gorge 957
–one's words 607
–out of house and
  home *take* 789
  prodigal 818
  gluttony 957
eatable 298
eatables 298
eaten up with 820
eating 298
eating house 189
eau de Cologne 400
eau sucrée 396
eaves 250
eavesdropper
  curiosity 455
  informer 527
eavesdropping
  hearing 418
  news 532
ebb *decrease* 36
  contract 195
  regress 283
  recession 287
  tide 348
  waste 638
  spoil 659
  –and flow 314
  low–36 *low* 207
  depression 308
  insufficient 640
ebb tide *decrease* 36
  low 207
  dry 340
ebenezer 1000
Ebionite 984
Eblis 978
ebon 431
ebony 431
éboulement 162, 716
ebriety 959
ebullience
  (*see ebullient*)
  calefaction 384
ebullient *violent* 173
  hot 382
  excited 824
ebulliometer 384
ebullioscope 384
ebullition *energy* 171
  violence 173
  agitation 315
  heating 384
  excitation 825
  anger 900
eburin 430
écarté 840
ecbatic 155
eccentric *irregular* 83
  exterior 220
  foolish 499
  crazed 503

capricious 608
ecchymosis 299
ecclesiarch 996
ecclesiastic
  church 995
  clergy 996
ecclesiastical
  canonical 985
  temple 1000
  –law 963
ecclesiolatry 991
ecco 457
eccrinology 299
ecdemic 220
ecderon 223
échafaudage 673
echelon *arrange* 60
  oblique motion 279
  attack 716
echinate 253
echinodermata 368
echo *similarity* 17
  imitate 19
  copy 21
  repeat 104
  recoil 277
  resonance 408
  answer 462
  assent 488
  applaud to the–931
echoes awaken–404
echolalia 821a
echoless 403
éclat 873
eclectic *teaching* 537
  choice 609
eclecticism 451, 662
eclipse *surpass* 33
  disappearance 449
  hide 528
  outshine 873, 874
  partial–*dim* 422
  total–*dark* 421
  under an
  –*invisible* 447
  out of repute 874
ecliptic 318
eclogue 597
ecology 357
economic 692
  –pressure 751
economical 817
economics 692
economize 817
economy *order* 58
  preservation 670
  conduct 692
  frugality **817**
  (*plan* 626)
  animal–359
ecphonesis 580
ecrhythmic 139
ecrhythmus 139
écru 426, 433
ecstasis 683
ecstasy *frenzy* 515

transport 821
rapture 827
ecstatic 829
ecstatica 992a
ecteron 223
ectoderm 223
ectogenous 161
ectomorphy 372a
ectropic 218
ectype 21
ecumenical 78
edacity 957
Edda 986
eddish 168
Eddy, Mary Baker–
  986
eddy *whirlpool* 348
  current 312, 490a
  danger 667
Eden *heaven* 827
  (*pleasure* 827)
edentate 254
edge *energy* 171
  height 206
  brink **231**
  deviate 279
  cutting–253
  –in 228
  –of hunger 865
  –one's way 282
  set on–256
  take the–off 174
edge tools 253
  play with–863
edgewise 217
edging *obliquity* 217
  border 231
  ornament 847
edible 298
edict 531, 741
edification
  building 161
  teaching 537
  learning 539
  piety 987
edifice 161
edifying *good* 648
edile 965
edit *publication* 531
  compile 596
  revise 658
  (*printing* 591)
edition 531 new–658
editor *recorder* 553
  book 593
  commentator 595
editorial 595
educate *teach* 537
  (*prepare* 673)
educated 490
education
  teaching 537
  knowledge 490
  man of–492
educational 537
  school 542

437

to one's—525
wry—378
face cloth
 cleanness 652
face guard 717
facet 220
facetiae 842
facetious 842
facia 234
facile *willing* 602
 irresolute 605
 easy 705
facile princeps 33
facilitate 705
facility *skill* 698
 easy **705**
facing *covering* 223
 lining 224
facinorous 945
façon de parler
 figure of speech 521
 exaggeration 549
facsimile *copy* 21
 duplication 90
 representation 554
fact *existence* 1
 event 151
 certainty 474
 truth 494
 in—535
faction *company* 72
 party 712
 feud 713
factious 24, 713
factitious 545, 546
factor *numerical* 84
 agent 690
 director 694
 consignee 758
 (*merchant* 797)
factory 691
factotum *agent* 690
 manager 694
 employé 758
facts *evidence* 467
 summary of—594
factual 1
facula 420
faculties 450
 in possession of
  one's—502
faculty *power* 157
 profession 625
 skill 698
facundity 582
fad *bias* 481
 caprice 608
faddle 683
fade *vanish* 4
 transient 111
 become old 124
 droop 160
 grow dim 422
 lose color 429
 disappear 449
 spoil 659

—away *cease* 142
 disappear 449
—from the memory
 506
—out 129
fadeless 873
fadge 23
faeces [*see* feces]
fag *labor* 686
 fatigue 688
 drudge 690
—end *remainder* 40
 end 67
fagot *bundle* 72
 fuel 388
—voter 4
Fahrenheit scale
 490d
faïence 557
fail *droop* 160, 655
 shortcoming 304
 be confuted 479
 not succeed 732
 not observe 773
 not pay 808
 dereliction 927
failing (*see* fail)
 incomplete 53
 insufficient 640
 vice 945
 guilt 947
—heart 837
—luck 735
—memory 506
—sight 443
—strength 160
failure 732
fain *willing* 602
 compulsive 744
 wish 865
fainéant 683
faint
 small in degree 32
 impotent 158
 weak 160
 sound 405
 dim 422
 color 429
 swoon 688
 damn with—*praise*
  930, 932, 934
—heart *fear* 860
 cowardice 862
 wooing 902
faintness *sound* **405**
 (*see* faint)
fair *in degree* 31
 pale 429
 white 430
 wise 498
 important 643
 good 648
 moderate 651
 mart 799
 beautiful 845
 just 922

honorable 939
by—means or foul
 631
—chance 472
—copy *copy* 21
 writing 590
—field *occasion* 134
 freedom 748
—game 857
—name 873
—play 922, 923
—question 461
—sex 374
—weather 734
 pleasurableness 829
—weather sailor 701
—wind 705
—words 894
 in a—way
 tending 176
 probable 472
 convalescent 658
 prosperous 734
 hopeful 858
fairing 784
fairly *intrinsically* 5
 slightly 643
 get on—736
fair-spoken
 courtesy 894
 flattery 933
fairway 267
fairy *fanciful* 515
 fay 979
 imp 980
—lore 993
—tale 594
 fabrication 546
fairyism 979
fairyland 515
fait accompli
 certain 474
 complete 729
faith *belief* 484
 hope 858
 honor 939
 piety 987
 declaration of—983
—cure 662
—curer 984
—healing 662
 i'—535
 keep—with
 observe 772
 plight—*promise* 768
 love 902
 true—*orthodox* 983a
 want of—
 incredulity 487
 irreligious 989
faithful (*see* faith)
 like 17
 copy 21
 exact 494
 obedient 743
—memory 505

—to 772
faithless *false* 544
 dishonorable 940
 skeptical 989
fake *imitation* 19
 concoct 544
 swindle 545
 untruth 546
faker 548, 683, 797
fakir 804, 955, 996
falcade 309
falcate *pointed* 244
 carved 245
falchion 727
Falcidian law 780
falciform (*see* falcate)
falcon 792
falconet 727
faldstool 215
fall *autumn* 126
 happen 151
 perish 162
 slope 217
 regression 283
 descend 306
 die 360
 fail 732
 adversity 735
 vice 945
—a cursing 908
—a prey to
 defeated 732
 subject 749
—asleep 683
—astern *rear* 235
 regress 283
—at one's feet 725
—away 195
—back *return* 283
 recede 287
 relapse 661
—back upon *use* 677
 defense 717
—dead *die* 360
—down *collapse* 304
 worship 990
—down before 928
—flat on the ear 843
—foul of *blow* 276
 hinder 706
 oppose 708
 discord 713
 attack 716
 contention 720
 censure 932
—from one's high
 estate
 adversity 735
 disrepute 874
—from the lips 582
—in *order* 58
 continuity 69
 event 151
—in love with 897
—in price 815
—in the way of 186

—in with *agree* 23
 conform 82
 converge 290
 discover 480a
 concord 714
 consent 762
—into *conversion* 144
 river 348
—into a custom
 conform to 82
—into a habit 613
—into a passion 900
—into a trap 547
—into decay 659
—into oblivion 506
—into raptures 827
—of day 125
—off *decrease* 36
 deteriorate 659
—off again 661
—of snow 383
—of the curtain 67
—of the leaf 126
—of the mercury 338
—on one's knees
 submit 725
 servile 886
 gratitude 916
 worship 990
—out *happen* 151
 quarrel 713
 enmity 889
—short *inferior* 34
 contract 195
 shortcoming 304
—through *fail* 732
—to *eat* 298
 take in hand 676
 do battle 722
—to dust 328
—to one's lot
 event 151
 chance 156
 receive 785
 duty 926
—to pieces
 disjunction 44
 destruction 162
 brittle 328
—to the ground
 be confuted 479
 fail 732
—to work 686
—under *inclusion* 76
 subjection 749
—under one's notice
 457
—upon *discover* 480a
 unexpected 508
 devise 626
 attack 716
—upon the ear 418
 have to—back upon
 provision 637
 let—*lower* 308
 inform 527

water–348
fallacy *sophistry* 477
  error 495
  show the–of 497
fallen angel
  bad man 949
  Satan 978
fallible *uncertain* 475
  sophistical 477
falling–*action* 154
  –*star world* 318
  luminary 423
  –*weather* 348
fallow
  unproductive 169
  yellow 436
  unready 674
  inactive 681
false *sophistry* 477
  error 495
  untrue 544, 546
  spurious 925
  dishonorable 940
  –*alarm* 669
  –*coloring*
    misinterpretation
    523
    falsehood 544
  –*construction* 523,
    544
  –*doctrine* 984
  –*expectation* 509
  –*hearted* 940
  –*impression* 495
  –*light vision* 443
  –*money* 800
  –*ornament* 851
  –*plea untruth* 546
    plea 617
  –*position* 704
  –*pretenses steal* 791
  –*prophet*
    disappoint 509
    (*pseudo–revelation*)
    986
  –*reasoning* 477
  –*scent error* 495
    mislead 538
  –*shame* 855
  –*statement* 546
  –*step* 732
  –*teaching* 538
  –*witness deceiver* 548
    detraction 934
falsehood 544, 546
falsetto *squeak* 410
  music 415
  want of voice 581
falsification 555
falsify *error* 495
  falsehood 544, 546
  misrepresent 555
  –*accounts* 811
  –*one's hope* 509
falsity (*see* false)
falter *slow* 275

stammer 583
  hesitate 605
  slip 732
  hopeless 859
  fear 860
fame *greatness* 31
  memory 505
  renown 873
familiar *known* 490
  habitual 613
  sociable 892
  affable 894
  spirit 979, 980
  on–*terms* 888
familiarity
  (*see* familiar)
familiarize *teach* 537
  habit 613
Familist 984
familistery 712
family *kin* 11
  pedigree 69
  class 75
  ancestors 166
  posterity 167
  domestic 221
  party 712
  –*circle* 892
  –*jars* 713
  –*likeness* 17
  –*tie* 11
  –*tree* 166
  happy–714
  in the bosom of
    one's–221
  in the–*way* 161
famine 640
  –*price* 814
famine–stricken 640
famish *stingy* 819
  fasting 956
famished
  insufficient 640
  hungry 865
famous 873
famously *much* 31
fan *strike* 276
  blow 349
  cool 385
  refresh 689
  stimulate 824
  enthusiast 840
  –into a flame
    anger 900
  –the embers 505
  –the flame
    violence 173
    heat 384
    aid 707
    excite 824
  flirt a–855
fanatic *dogmatist* 474
  madman 504
  imaginative 515
  zealot 682
  religious–988

fanatical
  dogmatic 474
  misjudging 481
  insane 503
  emotional 821
  excitable 825
  heterodox 984
  overrighteous 988
fanaticism
  dogmatism 474
  obstinacy 606
  (*see* fanatical)
fanciful
  imaginative 515
  capricious 608
  ridiculous 853
  –*projector* 515
fancy *think* 451
  idea 453
  believe 484
  suppose 514
  imagine 515
  caprice 608
  choice 609
  pugilism 726
  wit 842
  desire 865
  love 897
  after one's–850
  –*dog* 366
  –*price* 814
  –*stocks* 800
  indulge one's–609
  take a–to
    delight in 827
    desire 865
  take one's
    –*please* 829
fandango 840
fane 1000
fanfare *loudness* 404
  celebration 883
fanfaron 887
fanfaronade 884
fangs *venom* 663
  rule 737
  retention 781
fanlight 260
fanlike 202
fannel 999
fanon 999
fan–shaped 194
fantasia 415
fantastic *odd* 83
  absurd 497
  imaginative 515
  capricious 608
  bad taste 851
  ridiculous 853
fantasy
  imagination 515
  desire 865
fantoccini
  representation 554
  drama 599
faquir (*see* fakir)

far–and near 180
  –and wide 31, 180,
    196
  –as the eye can see
    180
  –away 196
  –be it from
    unwilling 603
    deprecation 766
  –between
    disjunction 44
    few 103
    interval 198
  –from it *unlike* 18
    shortcoming 304
    no 536
  –from the truth 546
  –off 196
farad 490d
farce *absurdity* 497
  untruth 546
  drama 599
  wit 842
  ridiculous 853
  mere–
  unimportant 643
  useless 645
farceur *actor* 599
  humorist 844
farcical *absurd* 497
  ridiculous 853
fardel *bundle* 72
  hindrance 706
fare *state* 7
  food 298
  price 812
  bill of–*list* 86
farewell
  departure 293
  relinquishment 624
  loss 776
  –to greatness 874
far–famed 31, 873
far–fetched 10
far–flung 180
far–gone *much* 31
  insane 503
  spoiled 654
farina 330
farinaceous 330
farm *till* 371
  productiveness 636
  property 780
  rent 788
farmer 371
  afternoon–683
farmhouse 189
faro 621–bank 621
farrago 59
farrier 370
farrow *produce* 161
  litter 167
  multitude 102
farse 998
far–sighted
  vision 441

foresight 510
farther 196
  (*see* further)
farthing *quarter* 97
  worthless 643
  coin 800
  –*candle* 422
farthingale 225
fasces 747
fascia *band* 205
  circle 247
fasciate 247
fascicle 51, 72
fasciculated 72
fascinate
  influence 615
  excite 824
  please 829
  astonish 870
  love 897
  conjure 992
fascinated
  pleased 827
fascination
  (*see* fascinate)
  infatuation 825
  desire 870
  (*spell* 993)
fascinator *wrap* 384
fascine 72
fash 830
fashion *state* 7
  form 240
  custom 613
  method 627
  ton **852**
  create 976
  after a–*middling* 32
  after this–627
  be in the–488
  follow the–82
  for–'s sake 852
  man of–852
  set the
    –*influence* 175
    authority 737
fast *joined* 43
  steadfast 150
  rapid 274
  fashionable 852
  intemperate 954
  not eat 956
  worship 990
  rite 998
  –and loose
    sophistry 477
    falsehood 544
    irresolute 605
    tergiversation 607
    caprice 608
  –*asleep* 683
  –by 197
  –day 640, 956
  –friend 890
  –man *fop* 854
    libertine 962

fellow–companion
890
fellow–countryman
890
fellow–creature 372
fellow–feeling
  friendship 888
  love 897
  benevolence 906
  pity 914
fellowless 28
fellow–man 890
fellowship
  academic 542
  partnership 712
  rank 873
  friendship 888
  good–892
fellow–student 541
felo–de–se 361
felon 949, 975
felonious 945
felony 947
felt *texture* 219
  heart–821
felucca 273
female 374
feme covert 903
feme sole 904
feminality
  weakness 160
  woman 374
feminine 269
feminity 374
femme de chambre
746
fen 345
fence *enclose* 232
  evade 544
  defense 717
  fight 720
  prison 752
  thief 792
  (*safety* 664)
  (*refuge* 666)
  –round 229
  –with a question 528
  on the–607
  word–477
fenced 770
fenceless 665
fencibles 726
feneration 787
fend 717
fender 717
Fenian
  malcontent 710
  party 712
  rebel 742
fenny 345
feodal 780
feodality
  government 737
  possession 777
feoff *property* 780
feoffee *possessor* 779

receiver 785
feoffer 784
ferae naturae 366
feria 840
ferine 907
ferment *disorder* 59
  energy 171
  violence 173
  agitation 315
  lightness 320
  effervesce 353
  sour 397
  emotion 821
  excitement 824, 825
  anger 900
fermentation
  (*see* ferment)
  acetous–397
fern 367–plants 369
fern–shaped 242
ferocity *violence* 173
  brutality 907
Ferrara *sword* 727
ferret 366–out
  be curious 455
  inquire 461
  discover 480a
ferruginous 433
ferry *transfer* 270
  way 627
ferryboat 273
ferryman 269
fertile *productive* 168
  (*abundant* 639)
  –imagination 515
fertilization 161, 168
fertilize 168
fertilizer 653
ferule 975
  come under the–
  932
fervent *hot* 382
  desirous 865
  –hope 858
fervid *hot* 382
  heartfelt 821
  excited 824
fervor *heat* 382
  passion 820
  animation 821
  love 897
Fescennine 961
festal *eating* 298
  holiday 687
  social 892
fester *corrupt* 653
  disease 655
festival *regularity* 138
  celebration 883
  –chorus 416
festivity
  amusement 840
  celebration 883
  sociality 892
festoon *curve* 245
  ornament 847

fetch *bring* 270
  arrive 292
  evasion 545
  sell for 812
  –and carry
  servile 886
  –a sigh 839
  –one a blow
  strike 276
  attack 716
  –water in a sieve 471
fetch *wraith* 992a
fete *amusement* 840
  gala 882
fetich (*see* fetish)
feticide 361
fetid 401
fetish 991, 993
fetishism 992
fetor 663
fetter *restrain* 751
  shackle 752
fettle 7, 673
fetus 129, 153
feu de joie
  amusement 840
  celebration 883
feud *discord* 713
  possession 777
  property 780
  death–919
feudal
  government 737
  tenure 780
feudatory 749
fever *heat* 382
  disease 655
  excitement 825
feverish *hot* 382
  hurry 684
  animated 821
  excited 824
feverwort 662
few 103 a–100
  –and far between 70
  –words *concise* 572
  taciturn 585
  compendium 596
fewness 103
fey 828
fez 225
fiancée 897
fiasco 732
flat 741
flat lux 161
fib *falsehood* 544, 546
  thump 720
fiber *link* 45
  filament 205
  resolution 604
fibrilliferous 205
Fichteanism 451
fickle *changeable* 149
  irresolute 605
fictile 240
fiction *untruth* 546

(*fancy* 515)
  work of–594
fictitious 515, 546
fictive 546
fid 392
fiddle *play* 416
  violin 417
fiddledeedee
  absurd 497
  unimportant 643
  contempt 930
fiddle–faddle
  absurdity 497
  unmeaning 517
  trifle 643
  dawdle 683
fiddler 416
fiddlestick 417
  –end 643
fidei defensor 717
fidelity *truth* 494
  veracity 543
  obedience 743
  observance 772
  honor 939
fidget *changes* 149
  activity 682
  hurry 684
  excitability 825
fidgety *irresolute* 605
  fearful 860
  irascible 901
fiducial 150
fiduciary 484
fidus Achates
  auxiliary 711
  friend 890
fie *disreputable* 874
  –upon it *censure* 932
field *scope* 180
  region 181
  plain 344
  agriculture 367, 371
  business 625
  arena 728
  property 780
  beasts of the–366
  –of blood 361
  –of inquiry *topic* 454
  inquiry 461
  –of view *vista* 441
  idea 453
  the–*competitors* 710
  take the–722
field day
  contention 720
  amusement 840
  display 882
field glass 445
field marshal 745
field piece 727
field preacher 996
field work 717
fiend *ruffian* 913
  demon 980
fiendish 945

fiendlike
  malevolent 907
  wicked 945
  fiend 980
fierce *violent* 173
  passion 825
  daring 861
  angry 900
fieri facias 963
fiery *violent* 173
  hot 382
  strong feeling 821
  excitable 825
  angry 900
  irascible 901
  –cross *indication* 550
  alarm 669
  warfare 722
  –furnace 386
  –imagination 515
  –ordeal 828
fiesta 840
fife 410, 417
fifer 416
fifth 98, 99
fifty 98 go–fifty 628
fig *food* 298
  unimportance 643
  –out 857
  –tree 367
fight *contention* 720
  warfare 722
  –against destiny 606
  –it out 722
  –one's battles again
  594
  –one's way
  –shy *avoid* 623
  coward 862
  pursue 622
  active 682
  exertion 686
  –the good fight 944
  show–*defense* 717
  courage 861
fighter 726
fighting cock
  tenacity 604
  combatant 726
  courage 861
fighting man 726
figment 515
figurante 599
figurate number 84
figuration 240
figurative
  metaphorical 521
  representing 554
  –style 577
figure *number* 84
  form 240
  appearance 448
  metaphor 521
  indicate 550
  represent 554
  price 812

−away money 818
−away time 683
−'s errand
  deceived 545
  unskillful 699
−'s mate 732
−'s paradise
  unsubstantial 4
  misjudgment 481
  disappoint 509
  hope 858
  rash 863
−s rush in 499
−to the top of one's
  bent *excite* 824
  anger 900
  flatter 933
  make a−of oneself
  bungle 699
  ridiculous 853
  motley−844
  play the−*folly* 499
  amusement 840
foolhardy 863
fooling *humor* 842
foolish 499
  act−ly 699
  look−*disrepute* 874
  shame 879
foolscap *sign* 550
  paper 590
foot *length* 200
  stand 211
  meter 579
  at−'s pace 275
  at the−of 207
−by foot 51
−it *journey* 266
  dance 309
−the bill 807
  keep on
−*continue* 143
  support 215
  prepare 673
  not stir a−681
  on−*existing* 1
  during 106
  event 151
  action 170
  journey 266
  topic 454
  business 625
  preparing 673
  active 682
  one−in the grave
  age 128
  death 360
  put one's−down
  resolved 604
  put one's−in
  bungle 699
  set−on land 342
  trample under−930
football
  subjection 749
  game 840

footballer 840
footboy 746
footbridge 627
foot candle 466
footfall *motion* 264
  indication 550
  stumble 732
foot guards 726
footing
  circumstances 8
  addition 37
  rank 71
  influence 175
  situation 183
  foundation 211
  support 215
  payment 809
  be on a−*state* 7
  friendly−888
  get a−*location* 184
  pay one's−807
footlights *stage* 599
foot−loose
  liberated 750
footman 746
footmark 551
footpad 792
foot passenger 268
footpath 627
foot pound 466
footprint 550, 551
foot soldier 726
foot−sore 688
footstep *trace* 551
footstool 215
foot−stove 386
foot ton 466
foot−warmer 386
fop 854
foppery *display* 882
foppish *affected* 855
for *cause* 155
  tendency 176
  reason 476
  motive 615
  intention 620
−all that
  notwithstanding 30
  qualification 469
−a season 106
−a time 111
−aught one knows
  156
−better for worse 78
−ever 16, 112
−example 82
−form's sake 82
−good *complete* 52
  diuturnity 110
  permanence 141
−nothing 815
−the most part
  great 31
  general 78
  special 79
−the nonce 118

−the time being 106
  have−*price* 812
forage *food* 298
  provision 637
  steal 791
forage cap 225
foramen 260
foraminous 260
forasmuch as
  relating to 9
  cause 155
  reason 476
  motive 615
foray *attack* 716
  robbery 791
forbear *avoid* 623
  spare 678
  lenity 740
  sufferance 826
  pity 914
  abstain 953
forbearance 918
forbid 761 God
−*dissent* 489
  deprecation 766
  censure 932
  prayer 990
forbidden fruit
  seduction 615
  prohibition 761
forbidding
  prohibitive 761
  ugly 846
force *assemblage* 72
  power 157
  strength 159
  agency 170
  energy 171
  violence 173
  cascade 348
  agriculture 371
  significance 516
−*of style* 574
  urge 615
  cultivate 707
  compulsion 744
  passion 820
  armed−726
  brute−964
−down the throat
  severe 739
  compel 744
−majeure 744
−of argument 476
−of arms 744
−of will 600
−one's way
  progression 282
  passage 302
−open 173
  put in−924
forced *irrelative* 10
−*style* 579
  unwilling 603
−labor 603
−loan 812

−march 744
forceful 171, 574
forceless 175a
forcemeat 298
forceps *extraction* 301
  grip 781
forces 726
forcible (see force)
−*separation* 301
forcing house 371
forcing pit 691
ford *passage* 302
  way 627
fore 116, 234
fore−and−aft
  complete 52
  lengthwise 200
−schooner 273
fore−and−after 273
forearm 673
forebears 166
forebode 511, 668
forecast *foresight* 510
  prediction 507, 511
  plan 626
  (*prepare* 673)
foreclose 706
foreday 125
foredoom 152, 601,
  611
forefathers
  ancestors 166
  (*veteran* 130)
Forefathers' Day
  883
forefend *prohibit* 761
  (*hinder* 706)
  (*guard* 717)
forefinger 379
forefront 66, 234
forego *relinquish* 624
  renounce 757
  surrender 782
foregoing
  preceding 62
  prior 116
foregone *past* 122
−conclusion
  prejudged 481
  predetermined 611
foreground 234
  in the−*manifest* 525
forehead 234
foreign *alien* 10
  extraneous 57
−accent 580
−parts 196
foreigner 57
forejudge
  prejudge 481
  foresight 510
foreknow 510
foreknowledge 510
foreland *height* 206
  projection 250
forelay 706

forelock
  take time by the−
  early 132
  occasion 134
forelooper 64
foreman 694
foremost *superior* 33
  beginning 66
  front 234
  in advance 280
  important 642
  reputed 873
forenoon 125
forensic 968
foreordain
  destine 152
  predestinate 976
foreordination
  necessity 601
fore part 234
forerun *precede* 62
  prior 116
  go before 280
forerunner
  precursor 64
  preparer 673
  (*omen* 512)
foresee *expect* 507
  foreknow 510
foreseen 871
foreshadow 511
foreshorten 201
foreshow 511
foresight 510
  caution 864
forest 367
−primeval 367
forestall *prior* 116
  early 132
  possession **777**
  (*expect* 507)
  (*prepare* 673)
forester 371
forestry 371
foretaste 510
foretell 511
forethought 510
  vigilance 459
foretoken 511
forever 16, 112
forewarn *predict* 511
  warn 668
foreword 64
forfeit *fail* 773
  lose 776
  penalty 974
−one's good opinion
  932
forfeiture
  disfranchisement 925
forfend *hinder* 706
  defend 717
forgather 72
forge *imitate* 19
  produce 161
  furnace 368

—weed 392
frail *weak* 160
  brittle 328
  irresolute 605
  imperfect 651
  failing 945
  impure 961
  —sisterhood 962
frailty (see frail)
frame *intrinsicality* 5
  condition 7
  make 161
  support 215
  border 231
  form 240
  substance 316
  structure 329
  contrive 626
  —of mind
  inclination 602
  disposition 820
  have—d and glazed
  822
frame house 189
framework
  support 215
  structure 329
franchise *freedom* 748
  right 924
  exemption 927a
Franciscan 996
franc–tireur 726
frangible 328
frank *open* 525
  sincere 543
  artless 703
  honorable 939
  —as rain 703
frankalmoigne 748
Frankenstein 913
Frankfurter 298
frankincense 400
frantic *violent* 173
  delirious 503
  excited 824
fraternal *brother* 11
  leagued 712
  concord 714
  friendly 888
  (*benevolent* 906)
  —order 711
fraternity *brothers* 11
  party 712
  friends 888
fraternize *combine* 48
  cooperate 709
  agree 714
  sympathize 888
  associate 892
fratricide 361
Frau 374
fraud *falsehood* 544
  deception 545
  impostor 548
  dishonor 940
  pious—988

fraudulent
  (see fraud)
  untruth 546
fraught *full* 52
  pregnant 161
  possessing 777
  (*sufficient* 639)
  —with danger 665
fray *rub* 331
  battle 720
  in the thick of the—
  722
frayed *worn* 659
freak 608
  —of nature 83
freckle 848
freckled 440, 848
fredaine 840
free *detached* 44, 47
  unconditional 52
  deliver 672
  unobstructed 705
  liberate 748, 750
  expending 809
  gratis 815
  liberal 816
  insolent 885
  exempt 927a
  impure 961
  —and easy
  cheerful 836
  vain 880
  insolent 885
  friendly 888
  sociable 892
  —companion 726
  —fight 720
  —from *simple* 42
  —from imperfection
  650
  —gift 784
  —giver 816
  —lance 523, 726, 748
  —land 748
  —liver 954a
  —living 954
  —love 897, 961
  —lunch 815
  —play 170, 748
  —quarters *cheap* 815
  hospitality 892
  —space 180
  —stage 748
  —trade *commerce* 794
  —translation 522
  —will 600
  make—of 748
  make—with
  frank 703
  take 789
  sociable 892
  uncourteous 895
freebooter 792
freeborn 748
free–burning 388
freedman 748

freedom 748
free–handed 816
freehold 780
freely *willingly* 602
freeman 748
Freemason 711
freemasonry
  unintelligible 519
  secret 528
  sign 550
  cooperation 709
  party 712
free–spoken 703
freestone 635
freethinker 487, 748,
989
free thought 487
free trader 748
freeze 376, 385
  —the blood 830
freezing 383
  —machine 387
  —mixture 387
freight *lade* 184
  cargo 190
  transfer 270
  —train 272
  —yard 636
freightage 270, 812
freighter *carrier* 271
  vessel 273
French 188
  —beans 298
  —gray 432
  —horn 417
  —leave *avoid* 623
  freedom 748
  —philosophy 451
  —polish 847
  peddler's–563
Frenchman 188
frenetic 503
frenzy *madness* 503
  imagination 515
  excitement 825
frequency 136
frequent
  in number 104
  in time 136
  in space 186
  habitual 613
frequenter 613
fresco *cold* 383
  painting 556
  al—*out of doors* 220
  in the air 338
fresh *extra* 37
  new 123
  flood 348
  cold 383
  color 428
  remembered 505
  novice 541
  unaccustomed 614
  good 648
  healthy 654

  pert 885
  tipsy 959
  —breeze 349
  —color 434
  —news 532
freshen 689
freshet 348
freshman 492, 541
freshness (see fresh)
fresh–water
  —college 542
  —sailor 701
fret *suffer* 378
  grieve 828
  gall 830
  discontent 832
  sad 837
  ornament 847
  irritate 900
  —and fume 828
fretful 901
fretwork 219
Freud's theory 992a
friable *brittle* 328
  pulverulent 330
friandice 868
friar 996 Black—s 996
  —Rush 980
  —'s balsam 662
  —'s lantern 423
friary 1000
fribble *slur over* 460
  trifle 643
  dawdle 683
  fop 854
fricassee 298
frication 331
friction *force* 157
  obstacle 179
  rubbing **331**
  on—wheels 705
fried—brains 298
  —eggs 298
  —sole 298
friend *auxiliary* 711
  wellwisher **890**
  sympathizer 914
  be—s 888
  —at court 631
  next—759
  see one's—s 892
friendless 893
friendliness 888
friendly *amicable* 714
friendship 888
frieze 210, 329
frigate
  man–of–war 726
  (*ship* 273)
fright *cards* 840
  alarm 860
frighten 860
frightful *dreadful* 830
  ugly 846
frightfully *much* 31
frigid *cold* 383

  —style 575
  callous 823
  indifferent 866
frigidarium 387
frigorific 385
frill *border* 231
  convolution 248
frills 577
  —of style 577
fringe *border* 231
  lace 256
  exaggeration 549
  ornament 847
frippery *trifle* 643
  ornament 847
  finery 851
  ridiculous 853
  ostentation 882
  (*dress* 225)
friseur 225
frisk *prance* 266
  leap 309
  absurdity 497
  gay 836
  amusement 840
frisky *brisk* 682
  in spirits 836
frith *chasm* 198
  strait 343
  forest 367
fritiniancy 412
fritter *small* 32
  —away *lessen* 36
  waste 638
  (*misuse* 679)
  —away time 683
frivolity
  (see frivolous)
frivolous
  unreasonable 477
  foolish 499
  capricious 608
  trivial 643
friz *curl* 245, 248
  fold 258
frock *dress* 225
  canonicals 999
  —coat 225
frog *leaper* 309
  ornament 847
frolic 840
frolicsome 836
from *motive* 615
  —day to day 106, 138
  —end to end 52
  —that time 117
  —this cause 155
  —time immemorial
  122
  —time to time 136
frond 367
fronder *censure* 932
frondeur *disobey* 742
  detract 936
front *first* 66
  wig 225

strain at a—etc.
caprice 608
gnaw *eat* 298
rub 331
injure 659
gnawing
—grief 828, 830
—pain 378
gnome 496, 980
gnomic 496
gnomon 114
Gnostic 984
Gnosticism 451
gnu 366
go *cease to exist* 2
energy 171, 682
move 264
recede 287
depart 293
jade 429
disappear 449
fashion 852
as things—613
come and—314
give the—by to
neglect 460
deceive 545
avoid 623
not observe 773
—about
turn round 311
published 531
undertake 676
—about your business
ejection 297
dismissal 756
—across 302
—after *in time* 117
in motion 281
—against 708
—ahead *precede* 280
advance 282
active 682
—all lengths 604a
complete 52
resolve 604
exertion 686
—aloft 305
—astray 495
—away 293
—back 283
—back on 624
—bad 659
—bail 771
—before 280
—beyond 303
—by *conform to* 82
elapse 109
past 122
outrun 303
subterfuge 702
—by the board 158
—by the name of 564
—cahoots 712
—deep into 461
—down *sink* 306

decline 659
—down with
believed 484
tolerated 826
content 831
—farther and fare
worse 659
—for nothing
sophistry 477
unimportant 643
—forth *depart* 293
publish 531
—from one's word
773
—halves 91
—hand in hand
accompany 88
same time 120
—hard 704
—in 294
—in for *resolution* 604
pursuit 622
—into *ingress* 294
inquire 461
dissert 595
—mad 503
—near 286
—no further
keep secret 528
—off *explode* 173
depart 293
die 360
wither 659
marry 903
—on *time* 106
continue 143
advance 282
—on for ever 112
—on ill 735
—on the stump 582
—out *cease* 142
egress 295
extinct 385
—out of one's head
506
—over *passage* 302
explore 461
apostate 607
faithless 940
—round 311
—shares 778
—the limit 52, 604
—through
meet with 151
pass 302
explore 461
perform 599
conduct 692
complete 729
endure 826
—through fire and
water 604a
—to extend 196
travel 266
direction 278
remonstrance 695

—to glory 162, 360
—to pieces 162
—to sleep 683
—to war 722
—under 162
—up 305
—West *die* 360
—with *assent* 488
concord 714
—with the stream
conform 82
servile 886
goad *for oxen* 370
motive 615
quicken 684
go—ahead 171, 682
goal *end* 67
reach 292 *object* 620
reach the—
complete 729
goat *jumper* 309
lecher 962
he—*male* 373
goatee 256
goatish 961
gob *sailor* 269
jaws 298
gobang 840
gobbet *small piece* 32
food 298
gobble *cry* 412
gormandize 957
eat 298
gobemouche *fool* 501
dupe 547
go—between
interjacent 226
instrumental 631
mediate 724
agent 758
goblet 191
goblin 980
(*bugbear* 860)
gocart 272
GOD 976
for—'s sake 765
—bless me! 870
—bless you
farewell 293
—forbid 766
—forsaken 196
—grant 990
—knows 491
—'s acre 363
—'s grace 906
—'s love 906
—'s own country 189
—'s will 601
—willing 470
house of—1000
kingdom of—981
sons of—977
to—be true 772
god 979
household—s 189
the—s

gallery 444, 599
tutelary—664
godchild 771
goddess *love* 897
good woman 948
heathen 979
she moves a—374
godfather 771
Godhead 976
godlike 987
godly 944
godmother 771
godown 636
godsend *good* 618
prosperity 734
Godspeed
farewell 293
hope 858
courtesy 894
benevolence 906
approbation 931
goer *horse* 271
goes (see go)
as one—270
here—676
goggle 441
goggle—eyed 443
goggles 445
going (see go)
general 78
rumor 532
—on
incomplete 53, 730
current 151
transacting 625
—to happen 152
goiter 655
Golconda 803
gold *yellow* 436
orange 439
money 800
all is not—486
—brick 545, 702
—mohur 800
worth its weight in—
648
write in letters of—
642
golden (see gold)
—age *prosperity* 734
pleasure 827
—apple 615
—calf *wealth* 803
idolatry 991
—dream
imagination 515
hope 858
—mean
moderation 174
mid—course 628
—opinions 931
—opportunity 134
—rule *precept* 697
—season of life 127
—wedding 883
music's—tongue 415

golf 840
Golgotha *burial* 363
churchyard 1000
Goliath *strength* 159
size 192
gomashta 758
gondola 273
gondolier 269
gone (see go) *past* 122
absent 187
dead 360
hopeless 859
—bad 653
—by *antiquated* 124
—case 859
—coon 859
—out of one's
recollection 506
—where the woodbine
twineth 771
goneness 688
goner 859
gonfalon 550
gong 417
goniometer *angle* 244
measure 466
gonorrhea 655
good *complete* 52
palatable 394
assent 488
benefit **618**
beneficial 648
right 922
virtuous 944
pious 987
as—as 197
be—enough 765
be so—as 765
do—906
for—*diuturnal* 110
permanent 141
—actions 944
—as one's word
veracity 543
observance 772
probity 939
—at 698
—at the price 815
—auspices 858
—behavior
contingent 108a
duty 926
virtue 944
—bye 293
—chance 472
—cheer *food* 298
cheerful 826
—circumstances 803
—condition 192
—day *arrival* 292
departure 293
courtesy 894
—effect *goodness* 648
beauty 845
—enough
not perfect 651

—fellow 892
—fight *war* 722
  virtue 944
—for *useful* 644
  salubrious 656
—fortune 734
—Friday 138, 998
—genius *friend* 890
  benefactor 912
  god 979
—hand 700
—humor *concord* 714
  cheerfulness 836
  amuse 840
  courtesy 894
  kindly 906
—intention 906
—judgment 498
—lack! 870
—living *food* 298
  gluttony 957
—look out 459
—looks 845
—luck 734
—man *man* 373
  husband 903
  worthy **948**
—manners 894
—morrow 292
—name 873
—nature 906
—offices
  mediation 724
  kind 906
—old time 122
—omen 858
—opinion 931
—pennyworth 815
—repute 873
—sense 498
—society 852
—taste 850
—tasting 394
—temper 894
—thing 648
—time *early* 132
  opportune 134
  prosperous 734
—turn *kindness* 906
—understanding 714
—wife *woman* 374
  spouse 903
—will *willingness* 602
  benevolence 906
—woman 948
—word *approval* 931
  vindication 927
—works 906
  in—case 192
  in—odor *repute* 873
  approbation 931
  in one's—books 888
  in one's—graces 888
  make—*evidence* 467
  provide 637
  restore 660

complete 729
substantiate 924
vindicate 937
atone for 952
put a—face upon
cheerful 836
proud 878
so far so—931
take in—part
pleased 827
courteous 894
kind 906
think—931
to—purpose 731
to the—780
turn to—account 731
what's the—645
good—for—nothing
  impotence 158
  useless 645
good—looking 845
goodly *great* 31
  large 192
  handsome 845
good—natured 906
goodness
  (see good) **648**
  virtue 944
  —gracious! 870
  —of heart 906
  have the
  —*request* 765
goods *effects* 780
  merchandise 798
Goodwin sands 667
goody 374
goose *bird* 298, 366
  hiss 409
  game of—840
  giddy as a—458
  —egg *zero* 101
  —flesh 383
  —grass 253
  kill the—with golden
  eggs *bungler* 699
  prodigal 818
gooseberry *fruit* 298
  yarn 549
  —eyes 441, 443
  old—978
goosecap 501
goosequill 590
goose—skin 383
Gordian knot
  tangled 59
  difficulty 704
  (*problem* 461)
gore *gusset* 43
  stab 260
  blood 361
gorge *ravine* 198, 350
  fill 641
  satiety 869
  gluttony 957
  (*eat* 298)

—the hook 602
raise one's—900
gorge—de—pigeon 432, 440
gorgeous *color* 428
  beauty 845
  ornament 847
Gorgon 860
gorilla 366, 913
gormandize *eat* 298
  gluttony 957
gorse 367
gory *murderous* 361
  red 434
  unclean 653
gospel *certainty* 474
  doctrine 484
  truth 494
  take for—484
Gospels 985
gossamer
  filament 205
  light 320
  texture 329
gossamery
  unsubstantial 4
  weak 160
  light 320
gossip *news* 532
  babbler 584
  conversation 588
gossoon 876
Goth *vulgar* 851
  barbarian 876
gothamite 501
Gotham, wise men of 501
gothic *amorphous* 241
Gothicism 851
gouache 556
gouge *concave* 252
  perforator 262
goulash 298
gourmand
  sensualist 954a
  glutton 957
gourmet
  fastidious 868
  sybarite 954a
gout 378
goût 390
govern *direct* 693
  authority 737
governess 540
government
  (see govern)
  ruling power 745
  divine—976
  —bonds 802
  —mark 550
  —s *authority* 737
  —school 542
  petticoat—699
governor *father* 166
  tutor 540
  director 694

ruler 745
keeper 753
—'s message 695
gowk 501
gown *dress* 225
  canonicals 999
gownsman 492
grab *take* 789
  miser 819
grabble 379
grace *style* 578
  permission 760
  concession 784
  elegance 845
  polish 850
  title 877
  pity 914
  forgiveness 918
  honor 939
  piety 987
  worship 990
  act of—784
  God's—906
—before meat 916
  heart of—861
  in one's good—s 888
  say—990
  submit with a good —826
  with a bad—603
  with a good—
  willing 602
  courteous 894
graceful *elegant* 578
  beautiful 845
  tasteful 850
graceless
  inelegant 579
  ugly 846
  vicious 945
  impenitent 951
  irreligious 989
Graces 845
gracile 203
gracious *willing* 602
  courteous 894
  kind 906
  good—870
gradatim *in order* 58
  continuous 69
  slow 275
gradation *degree* 26
  order 58
  continuity 69
gradatory 26
grade *degree* 26
  classify 60
  term 71
  obliquity 217
  ascent 305
  class 541, (75)
  at—219
  —crossing 219
gradient 217, 305
gradual *degree* 26
  continuous 69

slow 275
graduate *adjust* 23
  degree 26
  divide 44
  arrange 60
  series 69
  measure 466
  scholar 492
  teaching 537
  rank 873
  —school 542
graduated scale 466
graduation *class* 541
  rank 873
gradus 86, 562
Graecist 492
graft *join* 43
  locate 184
  insert 300
  —a *plant* 371
  teach 537
  bribe 784
  improbity 940
grain *essence* 5
  small 32
  tendency 176
  little 193
  rough 256
  weight 319
  texture 329
  powder 330
  paint 428
  temper 820
  ornament 847
  against the—
  rough 256
  unwilling 603
  opposing 708
  —elevator 636
  —oil 356
  —s of allowance
  qualification 469
  doubt 485
  in the—820
  like—s of sand
  incoherent 47
grallatory 267
gramercy 916
gram—fed 192
graminivorous 298
grammar
  beginning 66
  teaching 537
  school 542
  language **567**
  bad—568
  comparative—560
  —school 537
grammarian 492
grammatical 567
  —blunder 568
grammatism 561
gramophone 417, 418, 551
granary 636
grand *august* 31

fearful 860
Hesperian 236
Hesperides
  garden of the–981
Hesperus 423
Hessian 726, 819
Hessian boot 225
hest 741
heterarchy 737
heteroclite 83, 139
heterodox 487, 489
heterodoxy 984
heterogamy 161, 357
heterogeneity 15, 16a
heterogeneous
  unrelated 10
  different 15
  mixed 41
  multiform 81
  exceptional 83
heterogenesis 161
heteromorphism 16a
heteronomy 737
heteropathy 662
heterotopy 185
hetman 745
hew *cut* 44
  shorten 201
  fashion 240
  –down 213, 308
hewers of wood
  workers 690
  commonalty 876
hexad 98, 193
hexaglot 560
hexagon 98, 244
hexahedral 98
hexahedron 98, 244
hexameter 98, 597
hexangular 98
hexastyle 98
heyday
  exultation 836, 838
  festivity 840
  wonder 870
  –of the blood 820
  –of youth 127
hiation 260
hiatus *interval* 198
  (*discontinuity* 70)
hibernal 383
hibernate 683
Hibernian 188
Hibernicism
  absurdity 497
  neology 563
hiccup 349
hickory shirt 225
hid
  –under a bushel 460
hidalgo 875
hidden 528
  –meaning 526
hide *skin* 223

conceal 528
–and seek
  deception 545
  avoid 623
  game 840
–diminished head
  inferior 34
  decrease 36
  humility 879
  –one's face
  modesty 881
hidebound
  strait–laced 751
  stingy 819
  bigoted 988
hideous 846
hiding place
  abode 189
  ambush 530
  refuge 666
hie *go* 264
  speed 274
  –to 266
hiemal 383
hierarch 996
hierarchy 995
hieratic 372a
hieroglyphic
  representation 554
  letter 561
  writing 590
hierographa 985
hierography 983
hierolatry 991
hieromancy 511
hierophant 996
hieroscopy 511
higgle 794
higgledy–piggledy 59
higgler 797
high *much* 31
  lofty 206
  of game 298
  fetid 401
  treble 410
  foul 653
  noted 873
  proud 878
  from on–981
  –and dry *stable* 150
  safe 664
  –and mighty
  pride 878
  insolence 885
  –art 556
  –as heaven 67
  –celebration 998
  –color *color* 428
  red 434
  exaggerate 549
  –days and holidays 840
  –descent 875
  –glee 836
  –hand *violent* 173

resolved 604
  authority 737
  severe 739
  pride 878
  insolence 885
  lawless 964
  –in tone *white* 430
  –life *fashion* 852
  rank 875
  –living
  intemperance 954
  gluttony 957
  –mass 998
  –mightiness 873
  –note 410
  –notions 878
  –places 210
  –pressure *power* 157
  energy 171
  excitation of feeling 824
  –price 814
  –priest 996
  –principled 939
  –repute 873
  –school 542
  –seas 341
  –tide *wave* 348
  prosperity 734
  –time *late* 133
  occasion 134
  –treason
  disobedience 742
  dishonor 940
  –words *quarrel* 713
  anger 900
  in a–degree 31
  in–*automobile* 274
  in–esteem 928
  in–feather
  strong 159
  health 654
  cheerful 836
  boasting 884
  in–quarters 875
  in–spirits 836
  on–206
  on one's–ropes
  excitation 824
  pride 878
  anger 900
  on the–road to
  way 627
  hope 858
  ride the–horse 878
  think–ly of 931
highball 959
highbinder 361
highborn 875
high–brow
  pedantry 491
higher 33, 206
  –education 490
  –pantheism 984
highest 210
  –heaven 981

highfaluting 577, 884
high–fed 954
high–flavored 392
highflier
  madman 504
  proud 878
high–flown
  absurd 497
  imaginative 515
  style 577
  proud 878
  vain 880
  insolent 885
highflyer
  madman 504
highflying
  exaggerated 549
  ostentatious 822
highlands 206
high–low 225
high–mettled
  excitable 825
  brave 861
high–minded
  honorable 939
  magnanimous 942
highness *title* 877
high–pitched 410
high–plumed 878
high–priced 809
high–reaching 206, 865
high–roller 818
high–seasoned 392
high–souled 878
high–sounding
  loud 404
  words 577
  display 882
high–spirited
  brave 861
  honorable 939
high–strung 825
hight 564
high–toned 410, 878
highwater
  completeness 52
  height 206
  crater 337
  –mark *measure* 466
highway 627
  –s and byways 627
highwayman 792
high–wrought
  good 648
  prepared 673
  excited 824
hike 260
hiker 268
hilarity 836
hill *height* 206
  convexity 250
  ascent 305
  –station 189
hill–dwelling 206
hillock 206

hilly 206
hilt 633
hind *back* 235
  deer 366
  clown 876
  on one's–legs
  elevation 307
  anger 900
hinder *impede* 706
  (*counteract* 179)
  (*prohibit* 761)
hindermost *end* 67
  back 235
hind quarters 235
Hindu *deities* 979
  priests 996
  temples 1000
Hinduism 976, 984
Hindustani 563
hindrance 706
hindward 235
hinge *fasten* 43
  fastening 45
  cause 153
  depend upon 154
  rotate 312
hinny 271
hint *reminder* 505
  suppose 514
  inform 527
  –a fault etc. 932
  take a–498
hinterland 235
hip 236 have on the–
  confute 479
  success 731
  authority 737
  subjection 749
hip bath 386
hipped *deranged* 503
hippish 503
hippocentaur 80
Hippocrates 219, 662
hippocratic 360
hippodrome
  drama 599
  arena 728
hippogriff 83
Hippolytus 960
hippophagy 298
hippopotamus 192, 366
hip rafter, 215
hip roof 223
hire *commission* 755
  borrowing 788
  price 812
  reward 973
  (*purchase* 795)
  on–763
hireling 746
hirsute 256
hispid 256
hiss *sound* 409
  animal cry 412
  disrespect 929

implanted
 ingrained 5
 adventitious 6
 −*by nature* 820
implausible 473
implead 969
implement 633
impletion 52
implex 41
implicate
 involve 54, 526
 accuse 938
implicated
 related 9
 component 56
implication
 disorder 59
 meaning 516
 metaphor 521
 latency 526
implicit 526
 −*belief* 484
implied (*see* imply)
implore 765
imply *evidence* 467
 mean 516
 involve 526
 (*metaphor* 521)
impolicy 699
impolite 895
imponderable 4, 320
imporous *closed* 261
 dense 321
import
 put between 228
 ingress 294
 take in 296
 insert 300
 mean 516
 involve 526
 be of consequence
  642
importance
 greatness 31
 consequence **642**
 attach−to 642
 attach too much−to
  482
 of no−643
important 642
importune *ask* 765
 pester 830
impose *print* 591
 order 741
 awe 928
 −*upon credulity* 486
 deceive 545
 be unjust 923
imposing
 important 642
 exciting 824
 glorious 873
imposition
 (*see* impose)
 undue 925
 −*of hands* 998

impossibilities
 seek after−645
impossibility 471
impossible 471
 deception 702
 refusal 764
 (*difficulty* 704)
 −*quantity algebra* 84
impost 812
impostor 548, 925
impostume 655
imposture 545
impotence 158
impotent 732
 −*conclusion* 732
 −*to rise* 158
impound
 imprison 751
 (*inclose* 229)
impoverish
 weaken 160
 waste 638
 despoil 789
 render poor 804
impracticable
 impossible 471
 misjudging 481
 obstinate 606
 difficulty 704
impracticality 471
imprecation
 prayer 765
 curse 908
imprecatory 765, 908
impregnable
 strong 159
 safe 664
impregnate *mix* 41
 combine 48
 fecundate 161, 168
 insert 300
 teach 537
 −*with cloy* 641
impresario 599
imprescriptible 924
impress *effect* 154
 cause sensation 375
 mark 550
 excite feeling 824
 −*upon the mind*
 memory 505
 teach 537
impressed with
 belief 484
 feeling 821
impressibility 375
impressible
 motive 615
 sensibility 822
impression *effect* 154
 sensation 375
 idea 453
 belief 484
 publication 531
 mark 550
 engraving 558

print 591
 emotion 821
 make an *act* 171
 thought 451
impressionable 375,
822
impressive
 language 574
 important 642
 feeling 821, 824
imprimit 558
imprimus 66
imprint *publisher* 531
 indication 550
 −*in the memory* 505
imprison
 circumscribe 229
 restrain 751
 punish 972
improbability 473
improbate 932
improbity 940
impromptu 612
improper
 incongruous 24
 foolish 499
 solecistic 568
 inexpedient 647
 wrong 923
 unmeet 925
 vicious 945
 −*time* 135
impropriate
 possess 777
 take 789
impropriator 779
impropriety
 (*see* improper)
improve 658
 −*the occasion* 134
 −*the shining hour*
  682
 −*upon* 658
improvement 658
improvident
 careless 460
 not preparing 674
 prodigal 818
 rash 863
improvisator 416,
582
improvisatore
 speech 582
 poetry 597
 impulse 612
improvise
 imagination 515
 extemporize 612
 unprepared 674
improviser 612
imprudent
 neglectful 460
 rash 863
 (*unwise* 699)
impudence
 insolence 885

discourtesy 895
impudent
 insolent 885
 discourteous 895
impudicity 961
impugn *deny* 536
 attack 716
 blame 932
impugnation 708
impugnment 708
impuisance 158
impulse *push* **276**
 sudden thought **612**
 motive 615
 blind−601
 creature of−612
 give an−*to*
 propel 284
 aid 707
impulsive
 (*see* impulse)
 intuitive 477
 unaccustomed 604
 excitable 825
 rash 863
impunctual 133
impunity
 escape 671
 acquittal 970
 with−*safely* 664
impurity
 inelegance 579
 foul 653
 licentious **961**
imputation
 ascribe 155
 slur 874
 accuse 938
in 221 *go*−294
 −*a jiffy* 113
 −*and out* 314
 −*a rut* 16
 −*as much as*
  relation 9
  degree 26
 −*for undertake* 676
  promise 768
 −*s and outs* 182
in−*camera* 528
 −*extenso whole* 50
 diffuse 573
 −*loco* 23
 −*medias res* 68
 −*propria persona* 79,
  186
 −*re* 9
 −*statu quo* 141
 −*statu quo ante*
  bellum 140
 −*toto* 52
 −*transitu*
  transient 111
  transfer 270
inability
 want of power 158
 want of skill 699

−*to discriminate*
  465a
inabstinent 954
inaccessible
 distant 196
 impossible 471
inaccordant 24
inaccurate *error* 495
 solecism 568
inacquiescent 24
inaction *inertness* 172
 not doing **681**
inactivity 683
 inertness 172
inadequacy
 (*see* inadequate)
inadequate
 unequal 28
 powerless 158
 insufficient 640
 useless 645
 imperfect 651
 (*weak* 160)
inadmissible
 incongruous 24
 excluded 55
 extraneous 57
 inexpedient 647
inadvertence 458
inadvisable 647, 649
inaffable 895
inalienable
 retention 781
 right 924
inamorata 897
inane *void* 4
 incogitancy 452
 unmeaning 517
 insufficient 640
 trivial 643
 useless 645
inanimate 360
 −*matter* 358
inanition 158
inanity (*see* inane)
inappetency
 insensibility 823
 indifference 866
inapplicable
 irrelation 10
 disagreement 24
inapposite
 irrelation 10
 disagreement 24
inappreciable
 in degree 32
 in size 193
 unimportant 643
inapprehensible
 stolid 499
 unintelligible 519
inappropriate
 unconsonant 24
 inexpedient 647
inapt *incongruous* 24
 impotent 158

useless 645
inexpedient 647
unskillful 699
inarticulate 581, 583
inartificial 703
inartistic 846
inasmuch *whereas* 9
however 26
because 476
inattention 458
inattentive 419, 458
inaudible *silence* 403
faint sound 405
deaf 419
voiceless 581
inaugural
precursor 64
inaugurate *begin* 66
install 755
celebrate 883
inauguratory 66
inauspicious
untimely 135
untoward 649
adverse 735
hopeless 859
inbeing 5
inborn *intrinsic* 5
affections 820
(habit 613)
−proclivity 601
inbound 294
inbred (*see* inborn)
inca 745
incage 751
incalculable *much* 31
infinite 105
incalescence 382
incandescence 382
incantation
invocation 765
spell 993
incantatory 992
incapable
impotent 158
(weak 160)
incapacious 203
incapacitate 158
incapacity
impotence 158
ignorance 491
stupidity 499
(weakness 160)
incarcerate
imprison 751
(surround 229)
incarnadine 434
incarnate *intrinsic* 5
materiality 316
to incorporate 364
vicious 945
devil−bad man 949
Satan 978
incarnation 316, 976
incase *cover* 223
surround 229

incautious *rash* 863
(neglect 460)
incendiary
destroy 162
burn 384
influence 615
pitfall 667
malevolent 907
evildoer 913
bad man 949
incensation 400
incense *fuel* 388
fragrant 400
hate 898
anger 900
flatter 933
worship 990
rite 998
−breathing 400
−burner 400
incension
burning 384
incensorium 400
incentive 615
incept 66, 537
inception 66
inceptive
beginning 66
causal 153
generative 168
inceptor 541
incertitude 475
incessant
repeated 104
ceaseless 112
frequent 136
incest 961
inch *small* 32
length 200
move slowly 275
measure 466
by−es 275
*give an−and take
an ell* 789
−by inch
by degrees 26
in parts 51
slowly 275
*not see an−beyond
one's nose* 699
*not yield an−*606
*to an−*494
inchoation
beginning 66
preparation 673
incide 44
incidence 278
incident 151
*full of−*151
incidental *extrinsic* 6
circumstance 8
irrelative 10
occurring 151
casual 156
liable 177
chance 621

−music 415
incinerate 384
incinerator 384
incipience 66
incircumspect 460
incise *cut* 44
furrow 259
incision *cut* 44
furrow 259
incisive *energy* 171
vigor 574
feeling 821
incite *exasperate* 173
urge 615
incitement
(*see* incite)
incivility 895
incivism 911
inclasp 229
inclement
violent 173
cold 383
severe 739
pitiless 914a
inclination
(*see* incline)
descent 306
will 600
affection 820
desire 865
love 897
incline *tendency* 179
slope 217
direction 278
willing 602
induce 615
−an ear to 457
inclined *oblique* 217
intended 620
−plane 633
inclose
place within 221
surround 227
hem in 229
inclosure *region* 181
envelope **232**
fence 752
include
composition 54
−in a class 76
inclusion 76
inclusive *additive* 37
component 56
class 76
inclusory 56
incogitance 452
incognito 528
incognizable 519
incoherence
physical **47**
mental 503
incombustible 385
income *means* 632
profit 775
property 780
wealth 803

receipt 810
incomer
immigrant 294
incoming *ingress* 294
receipt 810
incommensurable
irrelation 10
(disagreeing 24)
−quantity 84, 85
incommode
hinder 706
(trouble 830)
(incommodious 647)
incommodious 647
incommunicable
unmeaning 517
unintelligible 519
retention 781
incommutable 150
incomparable
superior 33
(good 648)
incompassionate
914*a*
incompatibility 15
incompatible 24
incompetence
inability 158
incapacity 499
unskillful 699
incomplete
fractional 51
not complete 53, 730
incompleteness 53
noncompletion 730
incomplex 42
incompliance 764
incomprehensible
infinite 105
unintelligible 519
incomprehension
491
incompressible 321
inconceivable
unthought of 452
impossible 471
improbable 473
incredible 485
unintelligible 519
wonder 870
inconceptible 519
inconcinnity
disagreement 24
ugliness 846
inconclusive 477
inconcoction 674
incondite 851
inconformity 15
incongruous
differing 15
disagreeing 24
faulty 568
discordant 713
inconnection
irrelation 10
disjunction 44

inconsequence
irrelation 10
inconsequential
illogical 477
inconsiderable
small 32
fractional 100a
unimportant 643
inconsiderate
thoughtless 452
inattentive 458
neglectful 460
foolish 699
inconsistent
contrary 14
disagreeing 24
illogical 477
absurd 497
foolish 499
discordant 713
capricious 608
inconsolable 837
inconsonant
disagreeing 24
fitful 149
inconspicuous 447
inconstant 149
incontestable
strong 159
certain 474
incontiguous 196
incontinent 961
incontinently 132
incontrollable 173
incontrovertible
certain 474
(stable 150)
inconvenience 647
*put to−*706
inconvenient 135,
647
inconversable
taciturn 585
unsociable 893
inconvertible
continuing 143
(stable 150)
inconvincible 487
incorporality 317
incorporate
combine 48
include 76
materialize 316
immaterial 317
animality 364
incorporation
(*see* incorporate)
incorporeal 317
−hereditaments 780
incorrect *illogical* 477
erroneous 495
solecism 568
vicious 945
incorrigible
obstinate 606
hopeless 859

—one's fancy 609
—with *give* 784
indulgence
  (*see* indulge)
  absolution 918
indulgent *kind* 906
induration
  hardening 323
  impenitence 951
industrious
  studious 539
  (*see* industry)
industry *business* 625
  activity 682
  hive of—691
indweller 188
indwelling 5
inebriety 959
inedible 867
ineffable *great* 31
  unmeaning 517
  wonderful 870
ineffaceable 820
ineffectual
  incapable 158
  useless 645
  failing 732
  —*attempt* 732
  pale its—*fire* 422
inefficacious
  incapable 158
  useless 645
  failing 732
inefficient 158
inelastic *soft* 324
  —*fluid* 333
inelasticity 326
inelegance
  in language **579**
  ugly 846
ineluctable 474
inept *incapable* 158
  useless 645
  (*inexpedient* 647)
inequality 24, **28**
inequation 28
inequitable 923
ineradicable
  intrinsic 5
  stable 150
inerrable 946
inert (*see* inertness)
inertia 172
inertness
  physical **172**
  inactive 683
  moral 823
inessential 10
inestimable 648
inevitable *certain* 474
  destiny 601
inexact *erroneous* 495
  feeble 575
inexcitability 826
inexcusable
  accusable 938

vicious 945
inexecution 730
inexhaustibility 105
inexhaustible 104,
  639
inexistence 2
inexorable
  unavoidable 601
  resolved 604
  stern 739
  compelling 744
  pitiless 914a
  revengeful 919
  (*wrathful* 900)
  (*malevolent* 907)
inexpectation 508
inexpedience 647,
  699
inexpensive 815
inexperience
  ignorant 491
  unskillful 699
inexpert 699
inexpiable 945
inexplicable 519
inexpressible
  great 31
  unmeaning 517
  unintelligible 519
  wonderful 870
inexpressibles 225
inexpression
  latency 526
inexpressive 517
inexpugnable 664
inextension 180a
  littleness 193
  immateriality 317
inextinguishable
  stable 150
  strong 159
  excitable 825
  —*desire* 865
inextricable
  coherent 46
  disorder 59
  impossible 471
  (*difficult* 704)
infallibility 474
  assumption of—885
infallible 474
infamy *shame* 874
  dishonor 940
  vice 945
infancy
  beginning 66
  youth 127
infant 129 *fool* 501
Infanta 745
infanticide
  killing 361
  sacrifice 991
infantine 129
  foolish 499
infantry 726
infarct 261, 706

infarction 261, 706
infare 892
infatuation
  misjudgment 481
  credulity 486
  folly 499
  insanity 503
  obstinacy 606
  passion 825
  love 897
infeasible 471
infect *mix with* 41
  contaminate 659
  excite 824
infection
  transference 270
  disease 655
infectious 270, 657
infecund 169
infelicitous 24, 828
infelicity
  inexpertness 699
  misery 828
infer *presume* 472
  deduce 480
  imply 526
inference
  reasoning 476
  judgment 480
  implication 521
  latency 526
  by—467
inferential
  demonstrative 478
  construable 522
  latent 526
inferior
  (*see* inferiority)
  low 207
inferiority
  in degree **34**
  in size 195
  imperfection 651
  personal—34
infernal *bad* 649
  malevolent 907
  wicked 945
  satanic 978
  —*machine* 727
  —*regions* 982
infertility 169
infest 830
infestivity *sad* 837
  dull 843
infibulation 43
infidel 487, 989
infidelity
  dishonor 940
  irreligion 989
infiltrate *mix* 41
  intervene 228
  interpenetrate 294
  ooze 295
  receive 296
  moisten 337, 339
  teach 537

infiltration
  passage 302
  (*see* infiltrate)
infinite 105
  —*goodness* 976
Infinite, the— 976
infinitely *great* 31
infinitesimal
  small 32
  little 193
  —*calculus* 85
infinity 105
infirm *weak* 160
  disease 655
  vicious 945
  —*of purpose* 605
infirmary 662
infirmity (*see* infirm)
infix 537
infixion 300
inflame
  render violent 173
  burn 384
  excite 824
  anger 900
  (*incite* 615)
inflamed *red* 434
  (*see* inflame)
inflammable
  burn 384
  fuel 388
inflammation
  heating 384
  disease 655
inflammatory
  heated 384
  (*see* inflame)
inflate *increase* 35
  expand 194
  blow 349
inflated *style* 573, 577
  ridiculous 853
  vain 880
inflation (*see* inflate)
  rarefaction 322
inflect 245
inflection *change* 140
  curvature 245
  grammar 567
inflectional 567
inflexible *hard* 323
  resolved 604
  obstinate 606
  stern 739
  a will—906
  —*in faith* 159
inflexion
  (*see* inflection)
inflict *act upon* 680
  severity 739
  —*evil* 649
  —*pain bodily pain* 378
    mental pain 830
  —*punishment* 972
infliction
  adversity 735

  mental pain 828,
    830
  punishment 972
inflorescence 161
influence *cause* 153
  change 140
  physical—**175**
  tendency 176
  inducement 615
  instrumentality 631
  authority 737
  (*importance* 642)
  absence of—**175a**
  make one's—*felt* 175
  sphere of—780
influenza 655
influx 294
inform 527—*against*
  accuse 938
  go to law 969
informal *irregular* 83
  lawless 964
informality
  nonobservance 773
informant 527, 938
information
  knowledge 490
  communication **527**
  lawsuit 969
  pick up—539
  wide—539
informed 527
informity 241
infraction
  infringement 303
  disobedience 742
  nonobservance 773
  exemption 927
  —*of usage*
    unconformity 83
    desuetude 614
infrangible
  combined 46
  dense 321
infrequency 137
infrequent 137
infrigidation 385
infringe
  transgress 303
  disobey 742
  not observe 773
  undueness 925
  dereliction 927
  —*a law* 83
infructuose 169
infumate 340, 673
infundibular
  concave 252
  hole 260
infuriate *violent* 173
  excite 824
  anger 900
infuscate 431
infuse *mix* 41
  insert 300
  teach 537

−courage 861
−life into 824
−new blood 658
infused 6
infusible 321
infusion (*see* infuse)
  liquefaction 335
infusoria 193
ingannation 545
ingate 350
ingathering 72
ingemination 90
ingenerate 5
ingenious
  original 515
  instrumental 633
  skillful 698
ingenit 5
ingénu *artless* 703
ingénue *actress* 599
ingenuity 698
ingenuous *artless* 703
  (*sincere* 543)
  (*honorable* 939)
ingesta 298
ingestion 296
ingestive 296
ingle 388
ingle side 189
inglorious
  disreputable 874
  dishonorable 940
ingluvies 191
ingot 800
ingraft *add* 37
  join 43
  insert 300
  teach 537
ingrafted *extrinsic* 6
  habit 613
ingrain *insinuate* 228
  texture 329
  color 428
ingrained *intrinsic* 5
  combined 48
  habit 613
  character 820
ingrate 917
ingratiate 897
ingratiating 894
ingratitude **917**
ingredient 56
ingress **294**
  forcible−300
ingressive 294
ingurgitate 296
ingustible 391
inhabile 699
inhabit 186
inhabitant **188**
inhalation
  (*see* inhale)
inhale *receive* 296
  breathe 349
  smoke 389
  smell 398

inharmonious 15,
  713−*color* 428
  −*sound* 414
inhere in 56
inherence 5
inherent 56, 820
inherit *acquire* 775
  possess 777
inheritance
  property 780
  −*of the saints* 981
inherited *intrinsic* 5
  transfer 783
inheritor 779
inhesion 5
inhibit *hinder* 706
  restrain 751
  prohibit 761
  (*restrain* 615)
inhospitable 893
inhuman 907
inhume 363
inimaginable
  impossible 471
  improbable 473
  wonderful 870
inimical *contrary* 14
  opposition 708
  enmity 889
inimitable
  nonimitation 20
  unequal 28
  supreme 33
  very good 648
  perfect 650
iniquity *wrong* 923
  vice 945
  worker of−949
inirritability 826
initial 66−*letter* 558
initiate *begin* 66
  receive 296
  teach 537
initiated *skillful* 698
initiatory 296
inject 300 *fluid* 337
injudicial 964
injudicious 499, 863
injunction
  command 630
  advice 695
  command 741
  prohibition 761
injure *evil* 619
  damage 659
  spite 907
injurious 619, 923
  −*insects* 913
injury *evil* 619
  badness 649
  damage 659
injustice 923
ink 431
  before the−*is dry*
  132
  pen and−590

ink−blot test 821a
inkhorn 590
inkle 45
inkling *knowledge* 490
  supposition 514
  information 527
inkslinger 593
inkwell 590
inlaid 847−*work* 847
inland 221
inlay 300, 440
inlet *beginning* 66
  interval 198
  opening 260
  ingress 294
  −*of the sea* 343
inly 221
inmate 188, 221
inmost 221−*nature* 1
  −*soul* 820
  −*thoughts* 451
  to the−*core* 822
inn 189
innate 5 (*habit* 613)
  −*proclivity* 601
innavigable 471
inner 221
  −*coating* 224
  −*man intellect* 450
  affections 820
  −*reality* 1
innermost 221
  −*recesses* 221
innings *land* 342
  acquisition 775
innkeeper 188, 637
innocence **946**
innocent *child* 167
  fool 501
  good 648
  healthy 656
  artless 703
  guiltless 946
  good woman 948
innocuous *good* 648
  healthy 656
  innocent 946
innominables 225
innominate 565
innovation
  variation 20a
  new 123
  change 140
innoxious
  salubrious 656
  innocent 946
innuendo *hint* 527
  censure 932
innumerable 105
innutritious 657
inobservance 773
  (*disobedience* 742)
inoccupation 681
inoculate *insert* 300
  teach 537
  influence 615

inoculated 48
inoculation
  (*see* inoculate)
inodorous **399**
inoffensive *good* 648
  innocent 946
inofficious 907
inoperative
  powerless 158
  unproductive 169
  useless 645
inopportune
  untimely 135
  inexpedient 647
inordinate *great* 31
  excessive 641
inorganic 358
inorganic chemistry
  490b
inorganization **358**
inornate 849
inosculate *join* 43
  combined 48
  intersect 219
  convoluted 248
inquest 461, 967
inquietude
  changeable 149
  uneasy 828
  discontent 832
  apprehension 860
  (*motion* 264)
inquinate 659
inquire 461−*into* 595
inquirer 461, 541
inquiring 461
  −*mind* 455
inquiry **461**
inquisition
  inquiry 461
  severity 739
  tribunal 966
inquisitive 455
inquisitorial
  prying 455
  inquiry 461
  severe 739
  jurisdiction 965
inroad *ingress* 294
  trespass 303
  devastation 659
  invasion 716
insalubrity **657**
insanity 61, **503**
insatiable 865
inscribe *write* 590
  blazon 873
inscription
  (*see* inscribe)
  interment 363
  record 551
inscroll 551
inscrutable 519
insculpture 557
insculptured 558
insecable *junction* 43

unity 87
insect 366, 368
  minute 193
  injurious−s 913
  −*cry* 412
insecure *danger* 665
  (*uncertain* 475)
insensate *foolish* 499
  insane 503
insensibility *slow* 275
  physical **376**
  moral **823**
  −*of benefits* 917
  −*to the past* 506
insensible *numb* 381
  (*see* insensibility)
inseparable
  junction 43
  coherence 46
insert *locate* 184
  interpose 228
  enter 294
  put in 300
  record 551
  −*itself* 300
insertion **300**
  ornament 847
inservient 645
insessorial 206
inseverable
  junction 43
  unity 87
inside 221−*out* 218
  −*part music* 415
  turn−*out* 529
insidious
  deceitful 545
  cunning 702
  dishonorable 940
insight 490, 868
insignia 550
  −*of authority* 747
insignificant
  unmeaning 517
  unimportant 643
insincere 544, 855
insinuate
  intervene 228
  ingress 294
  insert 300
  latency 526
  hint 527
  ingratiate 897
  blame 932
  (*suppose* 514)
  (*mean* 516)
insipid *tasteless* 391
  style 575
  trifling 643
insipidity
  tasteless **391**
  indifferent 866
insist *argue* 476
  command 741
  −*upon affirm* 535
  dwell on 573

love 897
take no—in
insensibility 823
indifference 866
want of–866
interested *selfish* 943
interesting
lovable 897
interfacial 228
interfere *disagree* 24
counteract 179
intervene 228
activity 682
thwart 706
mediate 724
interferometer 193
interfuse 48
interfusion 41
intergrowth 228
interim *time* 106
short time 111
interior 221
painting 556
interiority 221
interjacence
middle 68
coming between **228**
interject *interpose* 228
insert 300
interlace *join* 43
combine 48
twine 219
interlacement 41
interlard *mix* 41
combine 48
interpolate 228
interleave 228
interline
interpolate 288
write 590
interlineal 228
interlineation 37,
300
interlink *join* 43
twine 219
interlobular 228
interlocation 228
interlocular 228
interlocution **588**
interlocutor 582
interloper
extraneous 57
intervene 228
obstruct 706
interlude *time* 106
dramatic 599
intermarriage 903
intermarry 903
intermaxillary 228
intermeddle
interfere 682
hinder 706
intermeddling 724
intermedial 228, 631
intermediary 534,
631

intermediate
mean 29
middle 68
intervening 228
ministerial 631
–*time* 106
intermediation
agency 170
intermedium
mean 29
link 45
intervention 228
instrument 631
(*means* 632)
interment **363**
insertion 300
intermigration 266
interminable
infinite 105
eternal 112
long 200
intermingle 41
intermission
time 106
discontinuance 142
intermit *interrupt* 70
recur 138
discontinue 142
intermittence
time 106
periodicity 138
intermittent 138
intermix 41, 48
intermolecular 228
intermundane 228
intermutation 148
intern 221
internal *intrinsic* 5
interior 221
–*evidence* 467
internasal 228
international
reciprocal 12
interchange 148
sociality 892
–*law* 963
interne 662
internecine 361
–*war* 722
interneural 228
internodal 228
internuncio
messenger 534
diplomatist 758
interoceanic 228
interosseal 228
interpel 142
interpellation
inquiry 461
address 586
summons 471
command 741
appeal 765
interpenetration
interjacence 228
ingress 294

passage 302
interplanetary 228
interpolar 228
interpolation
analytical 85
interpose 228
insertion 300
interpose
intervene 228
act 682
hinder 706
mediate 724
interposit 799
interposition
(*see* interpose)
interpret 522, 595
interpretation 516,
522 (*answer* 462)
interpreter **524**
interradial 228
interregnum
intermission 106
transient 111
discontinuance 142
interval 198
inaction 681
laxity 738
(*discontinuity* 70)
interrelation 9, 12
interrenal 228
interrogate 461
interrogation 461
typography 550
interrupt
discontinuity 70
cessation 142
hinder 706
interruption
derangement 61
interval 198
interscapular 228
interscholastic 148
intersect 219
intersection 198, 219
interseptal 228
interspace
interval 198
interior 221
intersperse *diffuse* 73
interpose 228
(*music* 41)
interstate 148
interstellar 228
interstice 198
interstitial
internal 221
interjacent 228
intertanglement 41
intertexture
mixture 41
intersection 219
tissue 329
intertribal 148
intertwine *unite* 43
cross 219
intertwist 43, 219

interurban 148
interval *degree* 26
–*of time* 106
–*of space* **198**
–*in music* 413
at–*s*
discontinuously 70
at regular–*s* 138
intervalvular 228
intervascular 228
intervene
–*in order* 70
–*in time* 106
–*in space* 228
be instrumental 631
mediate 724
(*agent* 758)
intervener 228
interventricular 228
intervert *change* 140
deviate 279
intervertebral 228
interview
conference 588
society 892
interviewer 553, 554
intervolved 43
interweave *join* 43
cross 219
interjacence 228
interwork 148
interworking 170
intestate 552
intestine 221, 350
inthrall
subjection 749
restraint 751
intimacy 888
intimate *special* 79
close 197
tell 527
friendly 888
friend 890
intimately joined 43
intimation 527
intimidate
frighten 860
insolence 885
threat 909
intinction 998
into go–294
put–300
run–300
intolerable 830
intolerance
prejudice 481
obstinacy 606
impatience 825
insolence 885
malevolence 907
intolerant 489
intomb 363
intonation *sound* 402
musical 413
voice 580
intone *sing* 416

worship 990
intort 248
intoxicant *bane* 663
intoxicated 959
intoxication
excitement 824, 825
inebriation 959
intracanal 221
intracellular 221
intractable
obstinate 606
difficult 704
sullen 901a
intrados 221
intralobular 221
intramarginal 221
intramolecular 221
intramundane 221
intramural 221
intransient 110
intransigence 604
intransigent 604
intransitive 110
intransmutable
diuturnal 110
stable 150
intraocular 221
intrap 545
intraregarding 221
intraseptal 221
intratelluric 221
intrauterine 221
intravascular 221
intravenous 221
intraventricular 221
intrench *safety* 664
defend 717
–*on* 303
intrepid 861
intricacy 533
intricate *confused* 59
convoluted 248
difficult 704
intrigant
meddlesome 682
cunning 702
libertine 962
intrigue *plot* 626
activity 682
cunning 702
licentiousness 961
intriguer *activity* 682
cunning 702
intrinsic 5 *forming* 56
–*evidence* 467
–*habit* 613
–*truth* 494
intrinsicality **5**
introception 296
introduce *lead* 62
interpose 228
precede 280
insert 300
–*new blood* 140
–*new conditions* 469
–*to* 888

jerry *deceived* 545	**jingoism** 884, 885	–in 778	**Joseph** 960	*interpreter* 524
jerry–build 545	**jinks, high**–840	–in the chorus 488	–'s coat 440	*justice* 664
jerry–building 545	**jinn** 980	–issue *discuss* 476	**joss** 991	*master* 745
jerry–built 160, 545	**jinrikisha** 266, 272	*deny* 536	**joss–house** 1000	*taste* 850
Jerry Sneak	**jitney** 272	*quarrel* 713	**joss–stick** 388	*magistrate* **967**
coward 862	**jiujitsu** 720	*contend* 720	**jostle** *rush* 276	–in a lump 465a
knave 941	**jiva** 157	*lawsuit* 969	*jog* 315	**Judge** *deity* 976
Jersey *cow* 366	**job** *business* 625	–the choir invisible	*clash* 713	**Judgment, Day of**–
jersey *clothing* 225	*action* 680	360	*contend* 720	67
jessamy	*unfair* 940	–the majority 360	*(disagree* 24)	**judgment**
affectation 855	*tough*–704	–with 709	**jot** *small* 32	*intellect* 450
jest *trifle* 643	**Job**–'s comforter	**joining** *meeting* 292	*unimportant* 643	*discrimination* 465
wit 842	*dejection* 837	**joint** *junction* 43	**jotting** *indication* 550	*decision* **480**
jest book 842	*hopeless* 859	*part* 51	*record* 551	*wisdom* 498
jester 844	*patience of*–826	*accompanying* 88	**joule** 490d	*condemnation* 971
jesting stock 857	*poor as*–804	*concurrent* 178	**jounce** 315	*sentence* 972
Jesuit *deceiver* 548	**jobation** 932	*meat* 298	**journal** *annals* 114	**judgment seat** 966
priest 996	**jobber** *deceiver* 548	*low resort* 621, 945	*newspaper* 531	**judication** 480
jesuitical	*tactician* 700	–concern 712	*record* 551	**judicatory** 965, 966
sophistical 477	*merchant* 797	**joint stock**	*magazine* 593	**judicature** 965, 966
deceitful 544	*trickster* 943	*cooperation* 709	*narrative* 594	**judicial** 965
Jesus 976	**jobbernowl** 501	*participation* 778	*accounts* 811	–astrology 511
jet *stream* 348	**jobbery** *cunning* 702	**joint tenancy** 778	**journalism** 551	–murder 361
–black 431	*improbity* 940	**jointure** 780	**journalist**	–separation 905
jetsam 782	**jobbing** *barter* 794	**joist** 215	*recorder* 553	**judiciary** 664
jettison 782	**jockey** *rider* 268	**joke** *absurdity* 497	*representation* 554	**judicious** 498
jetty *projection* 250	*deceive* 545	*trifle* 643	*author* 593	**jug** 191
harbor 666	*servant* 746	*wit* 842	**journey** 266	**juggernaut** *kill* 361
jeu–de mots 842	**jocose** *gay* 836	*ridicule* 856	–'s end 292	*god* 979
–d'esprit 842	*witty* 842	in–842	**journeyman**	*idolatry* 991
–de theatre 599	**jocoseness** *fun* 840	*mere*–643	*artisan* 690	**juggle** *deceive* 545
jewel *gem* 648	**jocular** *gay* 636	*no–existing* 1	*servant* 746	*cunning* 702
ornament 847	*droll* 842	*important* 642	**joust** 720	**juggler** 548
favorite 899	**jocund** *gay* 836	*practical*–	**Jove** 979 sub	**jugglery** 545
–s five words long	*sportive* 840	*deception* 545	–out of doors 220	**jugulate** 361
648	**Joe Miller** *wit* 842	*ridicule* 856	*air* 338	**juice** **333**
jewelry 847 false–545	*humorist* 844	*disrespect* 929	**jovial** *gay* 836	**juiceless** 340
jew's–harp 417	**jog** *push* 276	take a–498	*amusement* 840	**juicy** 339
Jezebel *wicked* 913	*shake* 315	**joker** 844 *cards* 840	*social* 892	**jujube** 396
wretch 949	–on *continue* 143	**joking apart**	**Jovinianist** 984	**julep** 396
courtesan 962	*trudge* 266	*affirmation* 535	**jowl** 236	**julienne** *soup* 298
jhil 345	*slow* 275	*resolution* 604	**joy** 827 give one–896	**jumble** *mixture* 41
jhilmil 351	*advance* 282	**jole** 236	–rider 274	*confusion* 59
jib *reverse* 140	*mediocrity* 736	**jollification**	**joyful** 836	*derange* 61
front 234	–the memory 505	*amusement* 840	**joyless** *painful* 830	*indiscrimination*
recoil 276	**jogger**	*intemperance* 954	*sad* 837	465a
regression 283	*memory aid* 505	**jollity** *amusement* 840	**J. P.** 967	**Jumbo** 192
cut of one's–	**joggle** 315	*sociality* 892	**Juan, Don**–962	**jument** 271
form 240	**jog–trot**	**jolly** *plump* 192	**jubbah** 225	**jump**
appearance 448	*uniformity* 16	*marine* 269	**jube** 1000	*sudden change* 146
jibe *concur* 178	*trudge* 266	*gay* 836	**jubilant** *gay* 836	*leap* 309
jiffy 113	*slow* 275	*flattery* 933	*rejoicing* 838	*neglect* 460
jig *dance* 840	*habit* 613	–boat 273	*celebrating* 883	at one–113
(music 415)	**John Doe and**	–fellow 892	*boastful* 884	–about 315
jigger 215, 272	**Richard Roe** 4	**jolt** *impulse* 276	**jubilate** 884	–at *willing* 602
jilt *disappoint* 509	**Johnsonian** 577	*agitation* 315	**jubilee**	*pursue* 622
deceive 545	**join** *connect* 43	**jolthead** 501	*anniversary* 138	*hasten* 684
deceiver 548	*assemble* 72	**Jonah** 621, 649	*celebration* 883	*consent* 762
dishonor 940	*contiguous* 199	**Jones**	**jucundity** 829	*seize* 789
jilted 898	*arrive* 272	Davy–'s locker 360	**Judaism** 984	*desire* 865
jimp 845	*party* 712	Paul–792	**Judas** *deceiver* 548	–over 460
jingal 727	*sociality* 892	**jongleur** 597	*knave* 941	–to a conclusion
jingle 408	*marry* 903	**jonquil** 436	–kiss *hypocrisy* 544	*misjudge* 481
jingo *boaster* 884	–battle 722	**Jordan** 360	*base* 940	*credulous* 486
insolence 885	–forces 708	**jornada** 200	**judge** *intellect* 450	–up 307, 309
blusterer 887	–hands 708	**jorum** 191	*decide* 480	**jumper** *clothing* 225

leave *remainder* 40
  part company 44
  relinquish 624
  permission 760
  bequeath 784
  French–623
  give me–to say 535
 –alone *inaction* 681
  freedom 748
  permit 760
 –a loophole 705
 –an inference 526
 –a place 293
 –in the lurch
  pass 303
  decisive 545
 –it to one 760
 –no trace
  disappear 449
  obliterate 552
 –off *cease* 142
  desuetude 614
  relinquish 624
  disuse 678
 –out 55
 –out of one's
  calculation 460
 –the beaten track 83
 –to chance 621
 –to oneself 748
 –undecided 609a
 –undone 730
 –void *regret* 833
 –word 527
  take–*depart* 293
  freedom 748
leaven *component* 56
  cause 153
  lighten 320
  qualify 469
  deterioration 659
  bane 663
leavings *remainder* 40
  useless 645
lecher 962
lechery 961
lectern 1000
lection *special* 79
  interpretation 522
lectionary 998
lecture *teach* 537
  speak 582
  dissertation 595
  censure 932
  sermon 998
 –room 542
lecturer *teacher* 540
  speaker 582
  preacher 996
lectureship 542
led–captain
  follower 746
  servile 886
  favorite 899
 –by the nose 749
ledge *height* 206

  horizontal 213
  shelf 215
  projection 250
ledger *list* 86
  record 551
  accounts 811
lee *front* 234
  side 236
leech *remedy* 662
  physician 695
Lee Enfield rifle 727
leef 829
leek 401 eat the
 –recant 607
  submit 725
Lee–Metford rifle
  727
leer *stare* 441
  dumb show 550
leery 702
lees 321, 653
lee shore
  danger 665, 667
leet, court–966
lee wall 666
leeward 236
leeway *tardy* 133
  space 180
  navigation 267
  progression 282
  shortcoming 304
left *residuary* 40
  sinistral 239
 –alone 748
 –bower 840
 –in the lurch 732
 –to shift for oneself
  893
  over the–545
  pay over the–
   shoulder 808
left–handed
  clumsy 699
 –compliment 932
 –marriage 903
leg *support* 215
  walker 266
  food 298
  thief 792
  best–foremost 686
  fast as–s will carry
   274
  keep on one's–s
   654
  last–s *spoiled* 659
  fatigue 688
 –bail 623
  light on one's–s 734
  make a–894
  not a–to stand on
  illogical 477
  confuted 479
  failure 732
  off one's–s
  propulsion 284
  on one's–s

  upright 212
  elevation 307
  speaking 582
  in health 654
  active 682
  free 748
  set on one's–s 660
legacy
  transference 270
  property 780
  gift 784
legadero 45
legal *permitted* 760
  legitimate 924
  relating to law 963
 –adviser 968
 –estate 780
 –pledge 535
legality 963
legalize 963
legate 534
legatee *transferee* 270
  possessor 779
  receiver 785
legation 755
legato 415
legend *record* 551
  description 594
legendary
  imaginary 515
  mythical 979
legerdemain
  change 146
  trick 545
  (*cunning* 702)
leggings 225
leghorn 225
legible 518–hand 590
legion *multitude* 102
  army 726
legionary 726
legislation
  government 693
  legality 963
legislative
 –assembly 696
legislator 694
legislature 72, 696
legist 968
legitimate *true* 494
  permitted 760
  right 922
  due 924
  legal 963
legume 298, 367
legumin 321
leguminous 365, 367
Leibnitzianism 451
leiodermatous 255
leisure *spare time* **685**
  (*opportunity* 134)
  at one's–*late* 133
leisurely *slowly* 275
leman 897
lemma 476
lemon *fruit* 298

  sour 397
  color 436
 –pie 298
lemures 980
lend 787–a hand 680
 –aid 707
 –countenance 707
 –oneself to
  assent 488
  cooperate 709
 –on security 789
 –wings to 707
lender *creditor* 805
lending 787
 –library 593
length 200 at
 –*in time* 133
  full–*portrait* 556
  go all–s
  resolution 604
  activity 682
  exertion 686
  go great–s 549
 –and breadth of 50
 –and breadth of the
  land *space* 180
  publication 531
 –of time 110
lengthen *increase* 35
  make long 200
 –out *diuturnity* 110
  late 133
lengthwise 200, 251
lengthy *long* 200
  diffuse 573
lenient *moderate* 174
  mild 740
  compassionate 914
lenify 174
lenitive
  moderating 174
  lubricant 332
  qualification 469
  remedy 662
  relieving 834
lenity 740
lens 445
lens–shaped 245
Lent *fasting* 956
  rite 998
lenten 956
lenticular *curved* 245
  convex 250
lentiginous 330, 653
lentor *slowness* 275
  spissitude 352
  inactivity 683
  (*inertness* 172)
lentous 352
Lenz's law 490d
leonine verses 597
leopard
  variegated 440
 –'s spots
  unchanging 150
leper *outcast* 892

  lepidote 330
Leprechaun 979
leprosy 655
lerret 273
Lesbianism 945, 961
lèse–majesté 742
less *inferior* 34
  subduction 38
 –than no time 113
lessee *possessor* 779
  receiver 785
lessen
 –*in quantity or degree*
  36
 –*in size* 195
 –an evil 658
lesson *teaching* 537
  warning 668
  give a–to
  punish 972
  read a–to
  censure 932
  say one's–
  memory 505
lessor 805
lest 623
let *hindrance* 706
  permit 760
  least 771
  lend 787
  sell 796
  apartments to–
  fool 499
 –alone *besides* 37
  permanence 141
  quiescence 265
  avoid 623
  disuse 678
  inaction 681
  not complete 730
  free 748
 –be *permanence* 141
  continuance 143
  inaction 681
 –blood 297
 –down *depress* 308
  humble 879
 –down easily
  forgive 918
 –fall *drop* 308
  inform 527
  speak 582
 –fly *violence* 173
  propel 284
 –fly at 716
 –go *neglect* 460
  liberate 750
  relinquish 782
  restitution 790
 –"I dare not" wait
  upon "I would" 605
 –in *interpose* 228
  admit 296
  trick 545
 –into *inform* 490
  disclose 529

descend 306
levity 320
kindle 384
match, illuminant 388
luminosity **420**
luminary 423
–*in color* 429
white 430
aspect 448
knowledge 490
interpretation 522
unimportant 643
easy 705
gay 836
loose 961
blue–*signal* 550
bring to–
  discover 480a
  manifest 525
disclose 529
children of–987
come to–529
false–s 443
foot–s 599
half–422
in one's own–699
–and shade 420
–comedy 599
–fantastic toe 309
–heart 836
–horse 726
–infantry 726
–of heel 274
–of truth 543
–purse 804
–under a bushel
  hide 528
  not hide 878
  modesty 881
–up *illumine* 420
  excite 824
  cheer 836
–upon one's feet 664
–upon *chance* 156
  arrive at 292
  discover 480a
  acquire 775
  make–of
    underrate 483
  easy 705
  inexcitable 826
  despise 930
  obstruct the–426
  see the–*life* 359
  publication 531
  throw–upon 522
  transmit–425
lighten
  make light 320
  illume 420
  facilitate 705
lighter *boat* 273
lighterman 269
light–fingered 791,
792

light–footed *fleet* 274
  active 682
light–headed 149,
503
lighthouse 550
lightless 421
light–minded 605
lightning *velocity* 274
  flash 420
  spark 423
  omen 512
  brief as the–421
  –express 272
  –speed 274
Light of the World
976
lightsome
  luminous 420
  irresolute 605
  cheerful 836
lign–aloes 400
ligneous 367
lignite 388
lignography 558
ligulate 205, 245
like *similar* 17
  relish 394
  enjoy 827
  wish 865
  love 897
  do what one's 748
  –a shot 274
  –master like man 19
  look–448
likely 470, 472
  think–507
  –to 176
likeness *copy* **21**
  portrait 554
  bad–555
likewise 37
likin 812
liking *willingness* 602
  desire 865
  love 897
  have a–for 827
  to one's–829
lilac *color* 437
Liliputian 193
lilt *cheery* 836
  sing 416
lily *botany* 369
  white 430
  beauty 845
  paint the–641
lily–livered 862
lima beans 298
limae labor
  improve 658
  toil 686
limature
  pulverulence 330
  friction 331
limb *member* 51
  instrument 633
  scamp 949

–of the law 968
limber *fleet* 272
  pliable 324
limbo *prison* 751, 752
  pain 828
  purgatory 982
lime *fruit* 298, 367
  sour 397
  entrap 545
limekiln 386
limelight
  luminary 423
  publicity 531
  theater 599
limerick 497
limestone 635
limine, in–66
limit *complete* 52
  end 67
  circumscribe 229
  boundary 233
  qualify 469
  completion 729
  restrain 751
  prohibit 761
limitarian 984
limitation (*see* limit)
  estate 780, 783
limitative 8
limited
  –*in quantity* 32
  –*in size* 193
  –*train* 272
  to a–extent
  imperfect 651
limitless 105
limn 554, 556
limner 559
limousine 272
limp *weak* 160
  slow 275
  supple 324
  fail 732
limpid 425, 570
limy 432
lin *lake* 343
  river 348
linaloa *fragrance* 400
lincture 662
linden 367
line *fastening* 45
  lineage 69
  continuous 69
  ancestors 166
  descendants 167
  length 200
  no breadth 203
  string 205
  lining 224
  outline 230
  straight 246
  direction 278
  music 26, 413
  appearance 448
  measure 466
  mark 550

writing 590
verse 597
vocation 625
army and navy 726
between the–s 526
boundary–233
draw the–465
in a– *continuous* 69
  straight 246
in a–with 278
–*engraving* 558
–of action 692
–of battle 69
–of battle ship 726
–of march 278
–of road 627
–of steamers 273
–s *cue* 51
  read between the–s
  522
  sounding–208
  straight–246
  troops of the–726
lineage *kindred* 11
  series 69
  ancestry 166
  posterity 167
lineament
  outline 230
  feature 240
  appearance 448
  mark 550
linear *continuity* 69
  pedigree 166
  length 200
linen 225, 635
linen draper 225
liner 273
lines *fortification* 717
  reins 752
  hard–*adversity* 735
  severity 739
linger *protract* 110
  delay 133
  loiter 275, 291
  –on *time* 106
lingo *language* 560
  neology 563
linguacious 584
lingua franca 563
lingual *language* 560
  speech 582
linguiform 245
linguist 492, 562
linguistic families
372a
linguistics 560, 562
lingulate 245
liniment
  ointment 356
  remedy 662
lining 224
link *relation* 9
  connect 43
  connecting–45
  part 51

term 71
crossing 219
torch 423
missing–*wanting* 53
completing 729
linkboy 694
linked together
  party 712
linn 343, 348
linoleum 223, 635
linotype 591
linseed oil 356
linsey–woolsey 41,
329
linstock 388
lint 223
lintel 215
lion *animal* 366
  courage 861
  prodigy 872
  repute 873
  come in like a–173
  heard–s roar 861
  in the–'s den 665
  –in the path 706
  –lies down with the
    lamb 721
  –'s share *more* 33
  chief part 50
  too much 641
  undue 925
lioness 374
lion–hearted 861
lionize *curiosity* 455
  repute 873
lip *beginning* 66
  edge 231
  side 236
  prominence 250
  between cup and–
    111
  finger on the –s
  silent 581
  speechless 585
  hang on the–s of
    418
  –homage *flattery* 933
  –service
    falsehood 544
    hypocrisy 988
  –*wisdom* 499
  open one's–s
    speak 582
  seal the–s 585
  smack the–*taste* 390
    savory 394
lipothymy 688
lipotype 187
lippitude 443
liquation 382
liquefaction 333, **335**
  –*by heat* 384
liquefy 382, 335
liquescence 335
liqueur
  drink 298, 392

-car 272
-coach 272
-steamer 273
-train 534
mailable 270
mailer 534
maim *cripple* 158
  injure 659
main *tunnel* 260
  ocean 341
  land 342
  conduit 350
  principal 642
  in the-
  intrinsically 5
  greatly 31
  on the whole 50
  principally 642
-chance *chance* 156
  good 618
  important 642
  profit 775
  look to the-*chance*
  foresight 510
  skill 698
  economy 817
  caution 864
  selfish 943
-force *strength* 159
  violence 173
  compulsion 744
-part 31, 50
  plow the-267
  with might and-686
Maine law 761
mainland 342
mainmast 206
mainpernor 771
mainprise 771
mainspring
  cause 153
  instrument 633
  (*motive* 615)
mainstay *support* 215
  refuge 666
  hope 858
maintain
  permanence 141
  continue 143
  sustain 170
  support 215
  assert 535
  preserve 670
-one's course
  presevere 604a
-one's ground 717
-the even tenor of
  one's way 623
maintenance
  (*see* maintain)
  wealth 803
maintien 692
maison de santé 662
maize 367
majestic *grand* 31
  glorious 873

stately 882
majesty *king* 745
  rank 873
  deity 976
major *greater* 33
  officer 745
-domo *director* 694
  retainer 746
-general 745
-key 413
-part *great* 31
  all 50
majority
  superiority 33
  plurality 100
  multitude 102
  age 131
  join the-360
majuscalae 561
make *constitute* 54, 56
  render 144
  produce 161
  form 240
  arrive at 292
  complete 729
  compel 744
  create 976
-acquainted with
  inform 527
  learn 539
-after 622
-a fuss
  importance 642
  activity 682
-a go of it 731
-a piece of work 832
-a present 784
-a push 682
-a requisition
  demand 741
  ask for 765
-a speech 582
-a splurge 882
-away with
  destroy 162
  kill 361
-a wry face 867
-believe 544, 545,
  546
-choice of 609
-fast 43
-for 278
-fun of *wit* 842
  ridicule 856
-good
  compensation 30
  complete 52, 729
  establish 150
  evidence 467
  demonstrate 478
  provide 637
  restore 660
-haste 684
-hay while the sun
  shines 134
-interest 765

-its appearance 446
-known 527
-light of
  underestimate 483
  easy 705
-love 902
-money 775
-much of
  exaggerate 549
  importance 642
-no doubt 484
-no secret of 525
-no sign *latent* 526
  hidden 528
-nothing of
  unintelligible 519
  not wonder 871
-off *run away* 623
  escape 671
-off with 791
-oneself master of
  539
-one's escape 671
-one's fortune 734
-one's mouth water
  298
-one's way *go on* 302
  prosper 734
-one's word 772
-out *see* 441
  evidence 467
  demonstrate 478
  discover 480a
  know 490
  intelligible 518
  interpret 522
  due 924
-over *transfer* 783
  give 784
-peace 723, 724
-public 531
-ready 673
-sure *stable* 150
  prepare 673
-terms 769
-the best of 725
-the land 292
-things pleasant 702
-time 110
-towards 278
-up
  (*see below*)
-use of 677, 788
-way *progress* 282
  (*improve* 658)
-way for
  substitution 147
  avoid 623
maker *artificer* 690
  (*producer* 164)
Maker, the-976
makeshift
  substitute 147
  excuse 617
make up *complete* 52
  compose 54

printing 591
-accounts 811
-a quarrel 723
-a sum 809
-for 30
-matters 952
-one's mind
  judgment 480
  belief 484
  resolve 604
-to *approach* 286
  address 586
make-up
  composition 54
  printing 591
  book 593
makeweight
  inequality 28
  compensation 30
  completeness 52
making be the-of
  utility 644
  goodness 648
  aid 707
malachite 435
malacology 368
maladministration
  699
maladroit 699
malady 655
mala fides 940
malaise
  bodily pain 378
  mental pain 828
malapert 885, 887
malappropriate 24
Malaprop, Mrs.-565
Malapropism 495
mal à propos
  discordant 24
  inopportune 135
malaria
  unhealthy 657
  poison 663
malarial fever 655
Malay 372a
malconformation
  243
malcontent
  opposition 710
  discontent 832
male *strong* 159
  man 373
-animal 373
-flirt 902
malediction 908
malefaction 947
malefactor 949, 975
malefic 649
maleficent 907
-being 913
malevolence 907
malfeasance 647
malfeasor 913
malformation
  distortion 243

(*ugliness* 846)
malformed 241
malgre 179
malice *hate* 898
  spite 907
  bear-*revenge* 919
-prepense 907
malign *bad* 649
  malevolent 907
  detract 934
malignant 649, 901a,
  907
malignity 173, 907
malinger 544, 548,
  655
malison 908
malkin *mop* 652
  slattern 653
mall *walk* 189
  opening 260
  club 276
malleable *soft* 324
  (*facile* 705)
mallet 276
malleus 418
malnutrition 655
malodor 401
malpractice 974
malt liquor 298
maltreat
  injure 649
  aggrieve 830
  molest 907
malversation
  rapacious 819
  guilt 947
mamelon 250
Mameluke 726
mamma 166
mammal 366, 368
mammalogy 368
mammiform 250
mammilla 250
Mammon 803
mammoth 192
man *adult* 131
  mankind 372
  male **373**
  prepare 673
  workman 690
  defend 717
  servant 746
  courage 861
  husband 903
  make a-of *good* 648
  brave 861
-among men 948
-and a brother 372
-and wife 903
-at-arms 726
-in office 745
-in the street 876
-of action 682, 686
-of letters 271
-of straw 545, 746
-'s estate 131

501

metastasis
change 140
inversion 218
displacement 270
metathesis
change 140
inversion 218
displacement 270
metaphor 521
mete *measure* 466
distribute 786
−out *give* 784
metempirical 519
metempsychosis 140
meteor
heavenly body 318,
353
luminary 423
meteoric
transient 111
violent 173
light 420
meteorite 318
meteorology 338, 353
meteoromancy 466
meter *length* 200
measure 333, 466
versification 597
methane 663
metheglin 396
methinks 484
method *order* 58
way **627**
want of−59
methodical
arranged 60
regular 80, 138
businesslike 692
Methodist 984
methodist
formalist 988
methodize 58, 60
Methuselah 130
old as−128
since the days of−
124
metic 57
meticulosity 457,
459, 868
meticulous *exact* 494
observant 772
fastidious 868
métis 83
metogenesis 161
metonymy 521
metopic 234
metoposcopist 234,
448
metoposcopy
front 234
appearance 448
interpret 522
metrical
measured 466
verse 597
metrocracy 737

metrology 466
metropolis 189, 222
metropolitan
archbishop 996
mettle *energy* 171
spirit 820
courage 861
man of−861
on one's−
resolved 604
put on one's−
excite 824
encourage 861
mettlesome
energetic 171
sensitive 822
excitable 825
brave 861
meum et tuum 777,
780
disregard distinction
between−791
mew *molt* 226
cry 412
−up 751
mewed up 229
mewl 412
mews 189
mezzanine floor
house 191
theater 599
Mezzofanti 492
mezzo rilievo
convex 250
sculpture 557
mezzotint 259, 421,
558
miasm 663
miasma 663
mica 527
micaceous 204
mi−careme 840
Micawber 460
Michaelmas 998
mickle 31
Micomicon 519
microbe 193
microbic 193
microcosm 193
microgamete 357
micrography 193
micrometer 193
micromorph 193
micron 193
microörganism 193
microphone 418
microphyte 193
microscope *little* 193
vision 441
optics 445
microscopic 32, 193
microspore 357
microzoa 193
microzyme 193
mid 68
Midas 803

mid−course 29, **628**
midday 125
midden 653
middle−*in degree* 29
−*in order* **68**
−*in space* 222
interjacent 228
−age 131
−classes 736
−constriction 203
−course 628
−man *director* 694
agent 758
−state 29
−term 68
compromise 774
middle−aged 131
middleman 328
middlemost 222
middling *small* 32
imperfect 651
mediocre 736
middy 269
−blouse 225
Midgard 318
midge 193
midland 342
midmost 68
midnight
night 126
dark 421
−blue 438
−oil 539
midriff *middle* 68
interjacence 228
midshipman 269
midships 68
midst−*in order* 68
central 222
interjacent 228
in the−of
mixed with 41
doing 680
midsummer 125
−day 138
midway 68, 628
midwife
instrument 631
remedy 662
midwifery
production 161
surgery 662
mien 448
miff 900
might *power* 157
violence 173
energy 686
mightless 158
mighty *much* 31
strong 159
large 192
haughty 878
mignonette 435
migraine 378
migrate 266
mikado 745

milch cow
productive 168
animal 366
store 636
mild *moderate* 174
warm 382
insipid 391
lenient 740
calm 826
courteous 894
milden 324
mildew *dirt* 653
bane 663
mildewed *spoiled* 659
mile 200
mileage 200, 973
−ticket 550
milestone 50
whistle jigs to a−
645
militant 722
military 722 *warfare*
soldiers 726
−authorities 745
−band 416, 417
−education 537
−power 737
−school 542
−time 132
−train 726
militate against 708
militia 664, 726
milk *moderate* 174
semiliquid 352
−cows 370
white 430
mild 740
flow with−and
honey *plenty* 639
prosperity 734
pleasant 829
−a he−goat into a
sieve 471
−and water *weak* 160
insipid 391
unimportant 643
imperfect 651
−of human kindness
906
−sickness 655
−the ram 645
−white 430
milk−livered 862
milksop *impotent* 158
fool 501
coward 862
milky (*see* milk)
semitransparent 427
white 430
become−427
Milky Way 318, 423
mill *indent* 257
pulverize 330
machine 633
unimportance 643
workshop 691

fight 720
like a horse in a−
312
millboard 593
millenary 98, 120
millennium
number 98
period 108
futurity 121
utopia 515
hope 858
millesimal 99
millet seed 193
milliard 98
milliary 550
milliner 225
man−854
millinery *dress* 225
ornament 847
display 882
man−855
million 98
multitude 102
people 372
populace 876
for the−
intelligible 518
easy 705
millionaire 803
mill pond *level* 213
pond 343
store 636
mill race 343, 348
millstone 330
mime *player* 599
buffoon 844
mimeography 19
mimic *imitate* 19
actor 599
mimmation 560
mimography 599
minacity 909
minaret 206
minatory 668
minauderie 855
mince *cut up* 44
slow 275
food 298
stammer 583
affected 855
extenuate 937
−the matter 868
−the truth 544
not−the matter
affirm 525
artless 703
mincemeat 298
make−of 162
mince pie 298
mincing 855
−steps 275
mind *intellect* 450
attend to 457
take care 459
believe 484
remember 505

will 600
willing 602
purpose 620
warning 668
desire 865
dislike 867
bear in–*thought* 451
attention 457
bit of one's–527
food for the–454
give one a piece of
one's–529
give the–to 457
have a–to
willing 602
desire 865
in the–*thought* 451
topic 454
willing 602
make one's–easy
826
make up one's–
opinion 484
resolve 604
–at ease 827
–cure 662
–one's book 539
–one's business
incurious 456
attentive 457
–'s eye 515
–what one is about
864
never–*neglect* 460
unimportant 643
not know one's own
–605
not–866
out of–506
set one's–upon 604
speak one's
–*say* 582
blunt 703
to one's–*taste* 850
love 897
the public–488
willing–602
minded *willing* 602
intending 620
mindful *attentive* 457
memory 505
mindless
inattentive 458
imbecile 499
forgetful 506
insensible 823
mine *sap* 162
hollow 252
open 260
snare 545
intrigue 626
store 636
abundance 639
damage 659
intrench 664
pitfall 667

attack 716
defense 717
dig a–*plan* 626
prepare 673
–layer 726
–of wealth 803
spring a–
unexpected 508
attack 716
miner 252
sapper and–726
mineral 358–oil 356
mineralize 358
mineralogy 358
Minerva invita
unwilling 603
difficult 704
Minerva press
fustian 577
mingle 41
miniature
small 32, 193
portrait 556
–*painter* 559
Minié rifle 727
minikin 32, 193
minim *small* 32
music 413
minimifidian 487
minimize 36, 483
minimum *small* 32
inferior 34
minion 899
minister
instrumentality 631
remedy 662
agent 690
director 694
aid 707
deputy 759
give 784
clergy 996
rites 998
–*to help* 746
ministerial
clerical 995
ministering–angel
948–*spirit* 977
ministration
direction 693
aid 707
rite 998
ministry
direction 693
aid 707
church 995
clergy 996
rite 998
minimum 434
miniver 223
minnesinger 597
minnow 193
minor *inferior* 34
infant 129
–*key* 413
–*poet* 597

Minorites 996
minority *few* 103
youth 127
Minos 694
minotaur 83
minster 1000
minstrel
musician 416
poet 597
minstrelsy 415
mint *mold* 22
fragrance 400
workshop 691
wealth 803
–*julep* 298
minuend 38
minuet *music* 415
dance 840
minus *inexistent* 2
less 34
subtracted 38
absent 187
deficient 304
loss 776
in debt 806
nonpayment 808
minusculae 561
minute
circumstantial 8
–*in degree* 32
special 79
–*of time* 108
instant 113
–*in size* 193
record 551
compendium 596
(*unimportant* 643)
–account 594
–*attention* 457
to the–132
minutemen 726
minuteness *care* 459
minutiae *small* 32
details 79
unimportant 643
minx *girl* 129
malapert 887
wanton 962
miosis 483
mir 188
Mira 490a
miracle
exceptional 83
prodigy 872
–*play* 599
miraculous
wonderful 870
mirage 443
mire 653
mirror *imitate* 19
reflector 445
perfection 650
glory 873
hold the–up to
nature 554
hold up the–525

magic–443
mirth 836
misacceptation 523
misadventure
contretemps 135
adversity 735
(*evil* 619)
(*failure* 732)
misadvised 699
misanthropy 911
misapply
misinterpret 523
misuse 679
mismanage 699
misapprehend
mistake 495
misinterpret 523
misappropriate 679
misarrange 61
misbecome 925
misbegotten
crooked 243
vicious 945
misbehave
vulgar 851
vice 945
misbehavior
discourtesy 895
guilt 947
misbelief 485
misbeliever 487, 984
miscalculate
misjudge 481
err 495
disappoint 509
miscall 565
miscarry 732
miscegenation 41,
903
miscellany
mixture 41
collection 72
generality 78
compendium 596
poetry 597
mischance *evil* 619
misfortune 735
(*failure* 732)
mischief 619 do–649
make–649
mischief–maker
evildoer 913
knave 941
mischievous 649
miscible 41
miscite 544
miscompute
misjudge 481
mistake 495
misconceive
mistake 495
misinterpret 523
misconception 495,
523
misconduct
bungling 699

guilt 947
–oneself 945
misconjecture 481
misconstrue 523
miscorrect 538
miscount 495
miscreance 485
miscreant 487, 949
miscreated 945
misdate 115
misdeed 947
misdemean 945
misdemeanant 949,
975
misdemeanor 947
misdescribe 538
misdevotion 988
misdirect
misteach 538
unskillful 699
misdo 945
misdoing 947
misdoubt 485, 523
mise en scène
appearance 448
drama 599
display 882
misemploy 679
miser 640, 819
miserable *small* 32
contemptible 943
unhappy 828
miserably *very* 31
misère 840
miserere *sing*–950
misericordia
Domini 470
miserly 819
misery 828
put out of one's–
914
misesteem 481
misestimate
misjudge 481
(*mistake* 495)
misfeasance
bungling 699
guilt 947
misfire 732
misfortune
adversity 735
unhappiness 830
(*evil* 619)
(*failure* 732)
misgiving *doubt* 485
fear 860
misgovern 699
misguide *error* 495
misteaching 538
misguided 699
mishap *evil* 619
failure 732
misfortune 735
painful 830
mishmash 59
Mishna 985

virtue 944
morass 345
moration 133
moratorium 133
moratory 133
morbid 655
morbific 657
morceau 32, 415
mordacity 907
mordant *keen* 171
  pungent 392
  color 428
  vigorous 574
more *superior* 33
  extra 37
  –last words 65
  –or less *quantity* 25
  small 32
  inexact 495
  –than a match for
    superior 33
    strong 159
  –than enough 641
  –than flesh and
    blood can bear
    830
  –than meets the eye
    526
  –than one 100
moreover 37
mores, O–932
Moresque 847
morganatic
  marriage 903
morgue 363
  –*littéraire* 569
moribund *dying* 360
  sick 655
morient 360
morion 717
morisco 840
mormo 860
Mormon 984
Mormonism
  polygamy 903
  heterodoxy 984
morning 125
  –dress 225
  –noon and night
  diuturnal 110
  frequent 136
  –star 423, 977
moron 501
morose *rude* 895
  sulky 901a
morosis 499, 503
Morpheus 683
morphine 662
morphological index
  372a
morphology 357
  form 240
  zoölogy 368
morphon 357
morris
  nine men's–840

morris–chair 215
morris dance 840
morrow 121
morsel *small* 32
  portion 51
  food 298
mortal *transient* 111
  fatal 361
  man 372
  wearisome 841
  –antipathy 867
  –blow 619
  –coil 362
  –funk 860
  –remains 362
  –sin 947
mortality
  evanescence 111
  death 360
  mankind 372
  bills of–360
mortar *cement* 45
  conversion 144
  pulverizer 330
  crucible 691
  cannon 727
  –board 550
mortgage *security* 771
  lend 787
  sale 796
  credit 805
mortgagee
  possessor 779
  creditor 805
mortgagor
  possessor 779
  creditor 805
mortgagor
  possessor 779
  debtor 806
mortician 363
mortiferous *fatal* 361
  (*unhealthy* 657)
mortification
  death 360
  disease 655
  pain 828
  vexation 830
  discontent 832
  humilation 879
  asceticism 955
mortise *unite* 43
  intersect 219
  interjacence 228
  printing 591
mortmain 748
  in–781
Morton's fork 475
mortuary *death* 360
  interment 363
mosaic *mixture* 41
  multiform 81
  variegation 440
  painting 556
  –gold *deception* 545
Moslem 984

mosque 1000
mosquito 366, 913
moss *tuft* 256
  elasticity 325
  marsh 345
  vegetation 367, 369
  money 800
moss–grown 659
mosstrooper
  fighter 726
  thief 792
most 31 at–32
  for the–part
  generally 78
  habit 613
  make the–of
  overestimate 482
  exaggerate 549
  improve 658
  use 677
  skill 698
  make the–of one's
    time 682
  –often 136
  the–33
mot 496
Motazilite 984
mote *small* 32
  light 320
  –in the eye
  dim–sighted 443
  misjudging 481
motet 990
moth 366, 663
moth–eaten *old* 124
  unclean 653
  deteriorated 659
mother *parent* 166
  mold 653
  –superior 996
  –tongue 560
  –wit 498
motherhood 166
motherland 166, 181,
  189
motherly *love* 897
  kind 906
mother–of–pearl
  427, 440
motif 454
motiferous 264
motile 264
motion
  change of place **264**
  topic 454
  plan 626
  proposal 763
  request 765
  make a–763
  –downwards 306
  –from *recession* 287
    repulsion 289
  –into *ingress* 294
    reception 296
  –out of 295
  –through 302

  –towards
  approach 286
  attraction 288
  –upwards 305
  put in–284
  put oneself in–680
  set in–677
motionless 265
motive 615
  absence of–**615a**
  –power 264
motivity 264
motley *multiform* 81
  variegated 440
  wearer of the–844
motor *motion* 264
  journey 266
  carrier 271
  vehicle 272
  instrument 633
  –paralysis 376
motor bus 272
motor car 272
motorcycle 266, 272
motorial 264
motorist 268
motorium 264
motorize 266
motorman 268, 694
motory 264
motte 367
mottled 440
motto *maxim* 496
  device 550
  phrase 566
mouchard 527
mould (*see* mold)
mound *large* 192
  hill 206
  defense 717
mount *greatness* 31
  increase 35
  hill 206
  ascend 305
  raise 307
  display 882
  –guard *care* 459
  safety 664
  –up to *money* 800
  price 812
mountain *large* 192
  hill 206
  weight 319
  make–s of molehills
    482
  –brought forth
    mouse
  disappoint 509
  –flax 385
mountaineer 268
mountainous 206
mountebank
  quack 548
  drama 599
  buffoon 844
mounted rifles 726

mourn *grieve* 828
  lament 839
mourner 839
mourners' bench
  1000
mournful
  afflicting 830
  sad 837
  lamentable 839
mourning *dress* 225
  in–*black* 431
  lament 839
mouse *little* 193
  animal 366
  search 461
  mountain brought
    forth–509
  –over 451, 461
  not a–stirring 265
mouse–colored 432
mousehole 260
mouser 366
mouse trap 545
mousseux 353
Mousterian group
  372a
mouth *entrance* 66
  receptacle 191
  brink 231
  opening 260
  eat 298
  estuary 343
  drawl 583
  down in the–879
  make–s 929
  –honor *falsehood* 544
  show 882
  flattery 933, 940
  –wash 652
  –watering 865
  open one's–582
  pass from–to mouth
    531
  stop one's–581
  word of–582
mouthful *quantity* 25
  small 32
  food 298
mouthpiece
  speaker 534
  information 527
  speech 582
mouthy *style* 577
moutonné 250
movable *motion* 26
  transference 270
movables 780
move *begin* 66
  motion 264
  propose 514
  induce 615
  undertake 676
  act 680
  offer 763
  excite 824
  good–626

−object 643
−one 4
−one knows who 876
−other *same* 13
  one 87
−scholar 493
−sooner said than
  done
  instantaneous 113
  early 132
−stranger to 490
−such thing
  nonexistent 2
  unsubstantial 4
  contrary 14
  dissimilar 18
−thank you 764
−wonder 871
  on−account 761
  unable to say−605
  with−interval 199
Noah's ark
  mixture 41
  assemblage 72
nob 210
Nobel prize 733
nobilitate 873
nobility 875
noble *great* 31
  important 642
  rank 873
  peer 875
  upright 939
  disinterested 942
  virtuous 944
−liver 948
−scorn 919
noblesse 875
noblesse oblige 875
nobody
  unsubstantial 4
  zero 101
  absence 187
  lowborn 876
−home
  want of intellect
    450a
−knows
  ignorance 491
−knows where
  distance 196
−present 187
−would think 508
noctambulation 266
noctambulist 268
noctivagant
  travel 266
  dark 421
noctograph 442
nocturnal *night* 126
  dark 421
  black 431
nocturne 415
nocuous 649
nod *wag* 314
  assent 488

signal 550
sleep 683
command 741
bow 894
(*hint* 527)
−of approbation 931
−of assent 488
nodding to its fall
  destruction 162
  descent 306
noddle *summit* 210
  head 450
noddy 501
node 250
nodose 256
nodosity *convex* 250
  rough 256
nodule 87, 250
noggin 191
noise *sound* 402
  loud 404
  make a−in the
    world 873
−abroad 531
noiseless 403
noisome *fetid* 401
  bad 649
  unhealthy 657
noisy 404
nolition 603
nolleity 603
nolle prosequi 624
nomad 268
nomadic 266
nomadization 266
Nomancy 511
nom de guerre 565
nom de plume 565
nomenclature 564
nominal
  unsubstantial 4
  word 562
  name 564
−price 815
nomination
  naming 564
  appointment 755
nominee 758
nomistic 965
nomography 963
nomology 963
nomothetical 965
non−ens 2−esse 2
−sequitur 477
nonaddition 38
nonadmission 55
nonage 127
nonagenarian 130
nonappearance 447
nonary 98
nonassemblage 73
nonattendance 187
nonbeing 2
non−Biblical
−prophets 986
−writings **986**

nonce 118 for the−
  present 118
  occasion 134
nonchalance
  neglect 460
  insensibility 823
  indifference 866
noncohesive 47
noncoincidence 14
**noncommissioned
officer** 745
noncommittal 864
noncompletion 730
noncompliance
  disobedience 742
  refusal 764
nonconductive 175a
nonconformity
  exception 83
  dissent 489
  sectarianism 984
nonconsent 489
noncooperation 927
nondescript 83
none 101−else 87
−in the world 4
−the worse 660
−to spare 640
nonendurance 825
nonentity
  inexistence 2
  unsubstantial 4
  unimportant 643
nonessential
  extrinsic 6
  unimportant 643
nonesuch
  unconformity 83
  goodness 648
nonexistence 2
nonexpectance 508
nonextension 180a
nonfeasance 947
nonfulfillment 730,
  732
−of one's hopes 509
nonidentical 18
nonillion 102
nonimitation 20
noninclusion 55
noninterference
  inaction 681
  freedom 748
nonius 466
nonjuror
  dissent 489
  heterodox 984
nonny 501
nonobjective 317
nonobservance
  inattention 458
  desuetude 614
  infraction **773**
  dereliction 927
nonpareil 28, 648
nonpayment 808

nonperformance
  noncompletion 730
  dereliction 927
nonpertinence 10
nonplus
  uncertain 475
  difficulty 704
  conquer 731
nonpreparation 674
nonprevalence 614
nonresidence 187
nonresistance
  submission 725
  obedience 743
nonresonance 408a
nonsense
  absurdity 497
  unmeaning 517
  trash 643
  talk−*folly* 499
  to varnish−499
nonsubjective 316
nonsubsistence 2
nonsuccess 732
nonsuit *defeat* 731
  fail 732
  condemn 971
nonunderstanding
  452
nonuniformity 16a
nonvocal 581
noodle 501
nook *place* 182
  receptacle 191
  corner 244
noölogy 450
noon *midday* 125
noonday *midday* 125
  light 420
  clear as−
  intelligible 518
  manifest 525
nooning 125
noontide 420
nooscopic 450
noose *ligature* 45
  loop 247
  snare 545
  gallows 975
N or M 78
norm 697
normal *intrinsic* 5
  average 29
  orderly 58
  regular 80, 82
  perpendicular 212
  sane 502
−condition *rule* 80
normalcy 80, 502
normality
  (see normal)
normalize 58
Norse mythology
  979
North 278
−and South 237

−Pole 383
−Star 550
northeaster 349
norther 349
northerly 237
northern 237
−lights 423
−star *constant* 939
northward 237
Northwest passage
  311
nose *prominence* 250
  curiosity 455, 461
  smell 398
  lead by the−
  induce 615
  govern 737
  led by the−749
−out 461
  not see beyond
    one's−
  misjudge 481
  folly 499
  unskillful 699
  put one's−out of
    joint *defeat* 731
  disrepute 874
  (*supplant* 147)
  speak through the−
    583
  thrust one's−in
  interjacence 228
  busy 682
  under one's−
  present 186
  near 197
  manifest 525
  defy 715
nose dive
  aeronautics 267
nosegay *fragrance* 406
  ornament 847
nosey *curious* 455
nosology 655
nostalgia 833
nostology 128
nostril 351
  breath of one's−s
    359
  stink in the−s 401
nostrum
  contrivance 626
  remedy 662
not *negation* 536
  (*dissent* 489)
  it will−do 923
−a bit 536
−a few 102
−a leg to stand on
    158
−a little 31
−allowed 964
−amiss *good* 618
  mediocre 651
  pretty 845
−any 101

–a particle 4
–a pin to choose 27
–a soul 101
–at all 32
–bad 651
–bargain for 508
–come up to 34
–expect 508
–fail 939
–far from 197
–fit to be seen 846
–following 477
–for the world
  unwilling 603
  refusal 764
–grant 764
–guilty 946
–hardened 950
–having *absent* 187
  exempt 777a
–hear of 764
–included 55
–know what to make
  of 519
–matter
  unimportant 643
–mind *insensible* 823
  contempt 930
–often 137
–of the earth 987
–one 101
–on speaking terms
  889
–on your life 764
–particular 831
–pay 808
–quite 32
–reach 304
–right 503
–seldom 136
–sorry 827
–the thing 925
–to be borne 830
–to be despised 642
–to be had
  impossible 471
  insufficient 640
–to mention
  together with 37
–to be put down 604
–to be thought of
  incogitancy 452
  impossible 471
  refusal 764
  hopeless 859
  undue 925
  disapprobation 932
–trouble oneself
  about 460
–understand 519
–vital
  unimportant 643
–vote 609a
–within previous
  experience 137
–wonder 871

–worth *trifling* 643
  useless 645
  what is–546
  what ought–923
nota bene 457
notabilia 642
notabilities 875
notable *great* 31
  manifest 525
  important 642
  active 682
  distinguished 873
notables 875
notably 31
notary *recorder* 553
  lawyer 968
notation 85
notch *gully* 198
  nick 257
  mark 550
note *music* 413
  take cognizance 450
  remark 457
  explanation 522
  sign 550
  record 551
  printing 591
  epistle 592
  minute 596
  money 800
  fame 873
  change one's–607
  make a–of 551
–of admiration 870
–of alarm 669
–of preparation 673
  of–873
  take–of 457
notebook *record* 551
  compendium 569
  writing 590
noted *known* 490
  famous 873
noteworthy *great* 31
  exceptional 83
  important 642
nothing *nihility* 4
  zero 101
  trifle 643
  come to–
  fall short 304
  fail 732
  do–681
  for–815
  go for–643
  good for–646
  make–of
  underestimate 483
  fail 732
–comes amiss 831
–in it 4
–loth 602
–more to be said 478
–of the kind
  unlike 18
  negation 536

–on 226
–to do 681
–to do with 764
–to go upon 471
–to signify 643
  take–by 732
  think of–930
  worse than–808
nothingness 2
notice *intellect* 450
  observe 457
  review 480
  information 527
  warning 668
  bring into–525
  deserve–642
  give–*manifest* 525
  inform 527
  indicate 550
–is hereby given
  publication 531
–to quit 782
  short–111
  take–of 450
  this is to give–457
  worthy of–642
noticeable 31
notification
  information 527
  (*publication* 531)
notion *idea* 453
  (*belief* 484)
  (*knowledge* 490)
  have no–of 489
notional *fanciful* 515
notionalist 514
notoriety
  publication 531
  fame 873
notorious *known* 490
  public 531
  famous 873
  infamous 874
Notre Dame 977
notturno 415
notwithstanding 30,
  179
nought
  unsubstantiality 4
  (*see* naught)
noun 564
nourish 707
nourishment
  food 298
  aid 707
nous 498
nousle 545
nouveau riche 123
novaculite 253
novation 140, 609
Nova Zembla 383
novel *dissimilar* 18
  new 123
  unknown 491
  tale 594
  (*romance* 515)

(*fiction* 546)
novelist 594, 598
novelize 594
novena 98, 108
novenary 98
novice *ignoramus* 493
  learner 541
  bungler 701
  religious 996
novitiate
  learning 539
  training 673
novocain 376
novus homo
  stranger 57
  upstart 876
now 118
–and then 136
–or never 134
noways 32, 536
nowhere 187
nowise *small* 32
  negation 536
noxious *bad* 649
  unhealthy 657
noyade *kill* 361
  punish 972
nozzle *projection* 250
  opening 260
  for water 337
  air pipe 351
nuance *difference* 15
  discrimination 465
nubiferous 353, 426
nubilation 426
nubile *adolescent* 131
  marriage 903
nubilous 426
nuclear 222
nuclear energy 490d
nucleolus 357
nucleus *middle* 68
  cause 153
  center 222
  kernel 642
nudation 226
nude 226
nudge 550
nudity 226, 849
nugacity
  absurdity 497
  folly 499
  inutility 645
nugatory
  powerless 158
  useless 645
nuggar 273
nugget *mass* 192
  money 800
nuisance *evil* 619
  annoyance 830
null *inexistent* 2
  unsubstantial 4
  absent 187
  declare–and void
  abrogation 756

nonobservance 773
–and void
  powerless 158
  unproductive 169
  illegal 964
  (*inexistence* 2)
nullah 198, 252
nullibiety 187
nullicity 187
nullifidian 487
nullify *inexistence* 2
  compensate 30
  destroy 162
  abrogate 756
  not observe 773
  not pay 808
nullity *inexistence* 2
  unsubstantiality 4
numb
  physically insensible
    376, 381
  morally insensible
    823
number *part* 51
  abstract –**84**
  count 85
  plural 100
–of a magazine etc.
    593
–among 76
–of times 104
  take care of–one
    943
numbered, days–
  kill 361
  necessity 601
  hopeless 859
–with the dead 360
numberless 105
numbers *many* 102
  verse 597
numbness 381
numdah 223
numerable 85
numeral 84, 85
numeration 85
numerator 84
numerical 85
numerous 102
numismatics 800
nummary 800
numps 501
numskull 493, 501
nun 904, 996
nunc dimittis 990
nuncio *messenger* 534
  diplomatist 758
nuncupation
  naming 564
nuncupative 527, 582
nuncupatory
  informing 527
nundination 794
nunnation 560
nunnery 1000
nuptial 903–knot 903

overfeed 641
overflow *stream* 348
  redundance 641
  —with gratitude 916
overgo 303
overgorged
  satiety 869
  gluttony 957
overgrown *much* 31
  large 192
  expanded 194
overhang *high* 206
  pendency 214
overhanging
  destiny 152
  pendency 214
overhasty 901
overhaul *count* 85
  attend to 457
  inquire 461
  censure 932
overhead 206
overhear *hear* 418
  be informed 527
overjoyed 827
overjump 303
overlap *inwrap* 225
  go beyond 303
overlay *layer* 204
  cover 223
  exaggerate 549
  excess 641
  overdo 682
  hinder 706
  —with ornament
  writing 577
overleap 303
overliberal 818
overlie 223
overload
  ornament 577
  redundance 641
  hinder 706
overlook *slight* 458
  neglect 460
  superintend 693
  forgive 918
  disparage 929
  bewitch 992
overlooked 642
  *not to be—*642
overlooker 694
overlord 745
overlying 206
overman 33
overmaster 731
overmastering 821
overmatch
  unequal 28
  superior 33
  strength 159
  conquer 731
overmeasure 641
overmodest 881
overmost 210
overmuch 641

overnight 122
overofficious 682
overpaid 816
overpass *exceed* 33
  transgress 303
overpersuade 615
overplus
  remainder 40
  excess 641
overpoise 179
overpower
  counteract 179
  subdue 731
  emotion 824
overpowering
  strong 159
overpraise
  overrate 482
  exaggerate 549
  flatter 933
overprize 482
overrate 482
overreach *pass* 303
  deceive 545
  baffle 545
overreckon 482
overrefinement 477
over-religious 955
override *superior* 33
  influence 175
  pass 303
  hinder 706
  defeat 731
  authority 737
  severity 739
  abrogate 756
overrighteous 988
overrule *control* 737
  cancel 756
overruling
  important 642
overrun *presence* 186
  spread 194
  motion beyond **303**
  printing 591
  redundance 641
  despoil 659
overscrupulous 939
oversea 57, 341
overseas cap 225
oversee 693
overseer 694
oversensitive 822
overset
  invert 218
  level 308
  subvert 731
overshadow
  darken 353, 421
  repute 873
  disrepute 874
overshoot the mark
  go beyond 303
  exaggerate 549
  overdo 682
  clumsy 699

oversight
  inattention 458
  error 495
  superintendence 693
  failure 732
overskip 303
oversleep 683
overspent 688
overspread
  disperse 73
  be present 186
  cover 233
overstate 549, 555
overstep 303
overstock 641
overstrain *extol* 482
  fatigue 688
oversupply 641
overt 525—*act* 680
overtake 292
overtaken *tipsy* 959
overtask *misuse* 679
  fatigue 688
overtax 679, 688
overthrow
  revolution 146
  destroy 162
  level 308
  confute 479
  vanquish 751
overthrown
  vanquished 732
overthwart 708
overtired 688
overtone 413
overtop *surpass* 33
  height 206
  (perfection 650)
overtrustful 486
overture
  precursor 62, 64
  music 415
  offer 763
  request 765
overturn
  revolution 146
  destroy 162
  invert 218
  level 308
  confute 479
overvalue 482
overweening
  excess 641
  rash 863
  pride 878
  conceit 880
  insolence 885
overweigh *exceed* 33
  influence 175
  overrate 482
overwhelm *ruin* 162
  redundant 641
  thwart 706
  affect 824
overwhelmed
  defeated 732

  subjection 749
overwhelming
  strong 159
  wonderful 870
overwise 880
overwork *misuse* 679
  fatigue 688
overwrought
  exaggerated 549
  emotion 824
  affectation 855
overzealous 825
ovicell 357
oviform 249
ovo, in—153
ovoid 247, 249
ovule 247
ovum 357
owe 806
  —it to oneself 926
owelty 27
owing *debt* 806
  attribution 155
owl *bird* 366
  fool 501
  —'s light 422
  —s to Athens 641
  screech—412
own *assent* 488
  divulge 529
  possess 777
  property 780
  act on one's—
    responsibility 738
  after one's—heart
    897
  at one's—risk 926
  come by one's—775
  condemned out of
    one's—mouth 479
  hold one's—737
  look after one's—
    interest 943
  look with one's—
    eyes 459
  out of one's—head
    600
  —flesh and blood
    consanguinity 11
owner
  possessor 779
  without an—777a
ownership
  property 780
ox *animal* 366
  male 373
  hot enough to roast
    an—382
Oxford school 984
Oxford shoe 225
oxgoad 727
oxidation 357
oxreim 45
ox-tail soup 298
oxygen 359
oxygon 244

oyer and terminer,
  court of—966
oyes 531
oyez! *hear* 418
  publication 531
oyster 298—*plant* 298
  —stew 298

P

P mind one's—'s and Q's
  care 459
  polite 894
  duty 926
pabulum *food* 298
  material 316
  mental—454
pace *walk* 264
  journey 266
  measure 466
  keep—with
  concur 178
  velocity 274
  —up and down 266
  put through one's—s
    525
  show one's—s
  ostentation 882
pace *permission* 760
  —tanti nominis 928
pachydermatous
  physically—376
  morally—823
pacific 721
pacification **723**
pacifism 721
pacify *allay* 174
  (compose 823)
  (forgive 918)
pack *arrange* 60
  assemblage 72
  locate 184
  squeeze 195
  prepare 673
  burden 706
  —off *depart* 293
  eject 297
  —of nonsense 643
  —up 229
  send—ing 297
package
  assemblage 72
packer 673
packet
  assemblage 72
  ship 273
pack horse 271
pack saddle 215
pack thread 205
pact 769
Pactolus 803
pad *thicken* 194
  line 224
  horse 271
  diffuseness 573

writing 590
padding *lining* 224
  stopper 263
  soft 324
  diffuseness 573
paddle *walk* 266
  row 267
  oar 633
  −one's own canoe
    conduct 692
    free 748
  −steamer 273
paddock 232
Paddy *Irishman* 188
paddy *rice* 330
padishah 745
padlock *fastening* 45
  fetter 752
  put a−on one's lips
    585
padre 996
padrone 745
paean *rejoicing* 838
  celebration 883
  gratitude 916
  approbation 931
  worship 990
pagan 984
  −deities **979**
paganism 984
page *numeration* 85
  printing 591
  book 593
  attendant 746
pageant *spectacle* 448
  amusement 840
  show 882
pagination 85
pagoda 206, 1000
pagri 225
pah 717
pai 643
pail 191
paillard 962
paillasse 215
pain *physical −***378**
  *moral −***828**
  penalty 974
painfulness 830
painfully *very* 31
painless 827
pains 686
  get for one's−973
  −and penalties 974
  take−686
painstaking
  active 682
  laborious 686
paint *coat* 223
  color 428
  deceive 545
  delineate 556
  ornament 847
  −the lily 641
  −the town red 840
painter *rope* 45

artist 559
painting 54, **556**
painty 556
pair *similar* 17
  combine 48
  couple 89
  −horses 272
  −off *average* 29
  marry 903
pair−oar 273
pairs *cards* 840
pajamas 225
pakka (*see* pucka)
paktong 545
pal *ally* 711
  chum 890
palace 189
  bishop's−1000
  −car 272
Paladin *defense* 717
  combatant 726
palaeocrystic 124
palaeology
  (*see* paleology etc.)
palaestra *school* 542
  arena 728
palaestral
  strength 159
  school 542
  contention 720
palaestric
  exertion 686
  (*see* palaestral)
palang 215
palanquin 266, 272
palatable *savory* 394
  pleasant 829
palatal *phonetic* 561
palate 390
  tickle the−394
palatial *palace* 189
  ostentatious 882
palatinate 181
palatine 745
Palatine Court 966
palaver
  unmeaning 517
  speech 582
  loquacity 584
  colloquy 588
  council 696
pale *region* 181
  inclosure 232
  limit 233
  dim 422
  colorless 429
  frightened 860
  −its ineffectual fire
    dim 422
  out of repute 874
  −of the church 995
  turn−*lose color* 429
  emotion 821
  fear 860
pale−faced 429
paleoanthropic 124

paleography *past* 122
  philology 560
Paleolithic Age 372a
paleology *past* 122
  language 160
paleontology 357,
  368
paleozoic 124, 372a
paleozoology 357
palestra
  (*see* palaestra etc.)
paletot 225
palette 556
palfrey 271
palimpsest 147, 528
palindrome
  inversion 218
  neology 563
paling *fence* 232
  prison 752
palingenesis 163, 660
palinody 607
palisade *defense* 717
  prison 752
  −s *cliff* 212
palki 272
pall *mantle* 225
  funeral 363
  disgust 395
  insignia 747
  weary 841
  dislike 867
  satiety 869
  canonicals 999
  −bearer 363
palladium *safety* 664
  (*defense* 717)
pallet *support* 215
  painter's −556
palliament 225
palliate *moderate* 174
  mind 658
  relieve 834
  extenuate 937
  moderation 174
palliative 174
  qualification 469
  remedy 662
pallid 429
pallium 999
pall−mall 840
pallone 840
pallor 429
palm
  measure of length
    200
  tree 367, 369
  touch 379
  trophy 733
  steal 791
  laurel 877
  bear the−873
  grease the
  −*induce* 615
  give 784
  itching−865

−off 545
−upon 545
  win the−731
palmated 257
palmer *traveler* 268
  clergy 996
palmiped 219
palmist 513
palmistry 500, 511,
  522
palm oil 356
palmy *prosperous* 734
  pleasant 829
  joyous 836
  −days *prosperity* 734
  pleasure 827
palpable *material* 316
  tactile 379
  obvious 446
  manifest 525
  (*intelligible* 518)
  −obscure 421
palpate 379
palpation 379
palpitate *tremble* 315
  emotion 821
  fear 860
palpus 379
palsgrave 875
palsied (*see* palsy)
  irresolute 605
palsy *impotence* 158
  physical insensibility
    376
  disease 655
  mental insensibility
    823
  (*weakness* 160)
palter *falsehood* 544
  shift 605
  elude 773
paltering 520
paltry *small* 32
  unimportant 643
  mean 940
paludal 345
pampas 344, 367
pamper *indulge* 954
  gorge 957
pamphlet 590, 593
pamphleteer 595
pan 191
panacea 662
panache *plume* 256
  ornament 847
panama *hat* 225
Pan−American 78
Pan−Anglican 78
pancake 298
pancratiast 159
pandar (*see* pander)
Pandean pipes 417
pandect
  knowledge 490
  dissertation 595
  compendium 596

code 963
pandemic 657
Pandemonium 982
  inhabitants of−978
pandemonium 59,
  404, 414
pander *pimp* 962
  −to *instrument* 631
  help 707
  flatter 933
pandiculation
  expansion 194
  opening 260
  sleepy 683
Pandoor 726
Pandora's box 619
  bottom of−858
pan−dowdy 298
paned 440
panegyric 931
panegyrize 482
panel *list* 86
  partition 228
  accused 938
  jury 967
  −game 545
  sliding−545
paneling 847
pang *physical* −378
  moral 828
Pan−Germanic 78
Pangloss 492
panhandler 876
panharmonic 78
Pan−Hellenic 78
pani 337
panic 860−*fear* 860
panier 225
pannel 213
pannier 191
panoply 490
  defense 717
  arms 727
panopticon 752
panorama *view* 448
  painting 556
panoramic 78, 446
  −view 441
pan−
  phenomenalism
    451
Panpipes 417
Panslavic 78
pansophism 490
pant *heat* 382
  fatigue 688
  emotion 821
  −for 865
pantaloon
  old man 130
  pantomimist 599
  buffoon 844
pantaloons 225
pantheism 451, 984
Pantheon *gods* 979
  temple 1000

peduncle 215
pedunculate 215
peek 441
peel *layer* 204
  skin 223
  uncover 226
  −off *separate* 44
peeler 664
peelhouse 717
peep *chirp* 412
  look 441
  −behind the curtain 461
  −into the future 510
  −of day 125
  −out *visible* 446
  disclosure 529
peephole 260
Peeping Tom 455
peep show *view* 448
  amusement 840
peer *equal* 27
  pry 441
  inquire 461
  lord 875
  −out 446
peerage 875
peerless *unequaled* 28
  supreme 33
  best 648
  glorious 873
  virtuous 944
  (*perfect* 650)
peevish *cross* 895
  irascible 901
peg *grade* 71
  hang 214
  project 250
  drink 959
  come down a−306
  let down a−308
  not stir a−*quiet* 265
  inaction 681
  −away *activity* 682
  −on *journey* 266
  −to hang on *plea* 617
Pegasus 271, 490a
pegology 348
pegomancy 511
pegs *legs* 266
Peking man 372a
pelagic 341
pelerine 225
pelf *gain* 775
  property 780
  money 803
pelican 366
pelisse 225
pellet 249 paper−643
pellicle *film* 204
  skin 223
pellmell 59, 825
pellucid 425, 570
peloric 242
pelt *skin* 223
  dress 225

throw 276
attack 716
punish 972
peltate 245
peltry 223
pen *inclosure* 232
  write 590
  writer 593
  restrain 751
  imprison 752
  draw the−through 552
  −and ink 590
  −in hand 590
  ready−569
  slip of the
  −*error* 495
  solecism 568
  stroke of the−
  write 590
  authority 737
  command 741
pena 206
penal 972
  −servitude 972
  −settlement 752
penalize 974
penalty 971, 974
penance
  atonement 952
  penalty 974
  worship 990
penchant *willing* 602
  desire 865
  love 897
pencil *bundle* 72
  −*of light* 420
  write 590
pencil drawing 556
pencraft 590
pendant *match* 17
  pendency 214
  −world 318
pendency *time* 106
  hanging 214
pendragon 745
pendulate 605
pendulous
  hanging 214
  oscillating 314
pendulum *hang* 214
  motion of a−314
Penelope, work of−
  useless 645
  incomplete 730
peneplain 344
penetralia 221
penetrate *ingress* 294
  passage 302
  sagacity 498
  −the soul 824
penetrated with
  belief 484
  feeling 821
penetrating
  sagacious 498

feeling 821
−*glance* 441
penetration 465
penguin 310, 366
peninsula 342
penitence 950
penitentiary 752
  confessor 996
penknife 253
penman 590
  inspired−985
penmanship 590
pen name 565
pennant 550
penniless 804
  a−lass 804
pennon 550
penny 800
  cost a pretty−814
  in for a−in for a pound 768
  no−no paternoster 812
  not have a−804
  −ante 840
  −dreadful 594
  −trumpet 410
  −whistle 410, 417
  turn a−775
penny−a−liner
  envoy 534
  writer 593
penny−a−lining
  diffuse style 573
pennyweight 319
penny wise 819
  −and pound foolish
  caprice 608
  waste 638
  prodigal 818
pennyworth 812
penology 972
pensée, arrière−528
penseroso 837
pensile 214
pension *income* 810
pensioner *learner* 541
  servant 746
  receiver 785
pensive
  thoughtful 451
  sad 837
penstock 350
pentad 193
pentagon 98, 244
pentahedron 244
pentameter 98, 597
pentangular 98
pentastyle 98
Pentateuch 985
Pentecost 998
Penthesilean 861
penthouse 191
pent up 751
  −in one's memory 505

penultimate 67
penumbra 421
penurious 819
penury *poverty* 804
  (*scantiness* 640)
peon 726
peonage 603
people
  consanguinity 11
  multitude 102
  location 184
  inhabit 186
  mankind 372
  subjects 746
  commonalty 876
  laity 997
pep 171, 682
  full of−574
pepastic 662
pepper *pungent* 392
  condiment 393
  attack 716
  (*energy* 171)
pepper−and−salt
  gray 432
  variegated 440
peppercorn 643
  cheap 815
  −rent 815
peppery *irascible* 901
pepsin 320
peptic 662
per 631−contra
  contrariety 14
  counterevidence 468
  opposition 708
  −saltum
  discontinuous 70
  instantaneous 113
  −se 87
peradventure 470
peragrate 266
perambulate 266
perambulator
  measure of length 200
  vehicle 272
perambulatory 266
perceivable 446
perceive
  be sensible of 375
  see 441
  know 490
percentage
  number 84
  discount 813
perceptible 446
perception *idea* 453
  knowledge 490
perceptive 375, 465
perch *location* 184
  abide 186
  habitation 189
  height 206
  support 215
  −up 307

perchance
  by chance 156
  possibly 470
perching 206
percipience 450
percolate
  ooze out 295
  liquefaction 335
  water 337
  stream 348
  clean 652
percolator 191
percursory 458
percussion 276
  center of−222
percussive 277
perdition
  destruction 162
  ruin 732
  loss 776
perdu 528 enfant
  −*hopeless* 859
  rash 863
perdure 106
perdy 535
peregrination 266
peregrinator 268
peremptory
  assertion 535
  firm 604
  authoritative 737
  rigorous 739
  compulsory 744
  duty 926
  −denial 536
  −refusal 764
perennate 106
perennial
  continuous 69
  diuturnal 110
  −*plants* 367
perennity 112
pererration 266
perfect *great* 31
  entire 52
  excellent 650
  complete 729
perfection **650**
  bring to−729
  let us go on unto− 650
perfidy 940
perfiate 349
perforate 260
perforator 262
perforce *necessity* 601
  compulsion 744
perform *produce* 161
  do 170
  −*music* 416
  action 680
  achieve 729
  fulfill 772
  −a circuit 629
  −a duty 926
  −a function 644

527

proud 878
prima donna
  actress 599
  important 642
  proficient 700
primacy
  superiority 33
  celebrity 873
  church 995
prima facie *sight* 441
  appearance 448
  probable 472
  —*meaning* 516
  manifest 525
primal 66
primary *initial* 66
  cause 153
  important 642
  —*color* 428
  —*education* 537
primate 996
primates 875
prime *initial* 66
  primeval 124
  early 132
  teach 537
  important 642
  excellent 648
  prepare 673
  in one's—131
  —and load 673
  —cost *price* 812
  cheap 815
  —*minister* 694
  —*mover* 153, 164
  —*number* 84
  —of life *youth* 127
  adolescence 131
  —of the morning 125
primed *skilled* 698
  tipsy 959
primer
  automobile 272
  schoolbook 542
primeval 124
primices 154
primigenous 124
priming 556
primitive *old* 124
  cause 153
primogenial
  beginning 66
primogeniture
  old 124
  age 128
  posterity 167
  heritage 777
primordial
  original 20
  old 124
  cause 153
primordiate 124
primordium 153
primrose—colored
  436
prince *perfection* 650

master 745
  nobility 875
  —of darkness 978
Prince Albert coat
  225
princely
  authoritative 737
  liberal 816
  famous 873
  noble 875
  generous 942
princess 745, 875
principal
  important 642
  director 694
  —*part great* 31
  whole 50
principality
  region 181
  property 780
principally 33
principia 66, 496
principle *intrinsic* 5
  rule 80
  cause 153
  element 316
  reasoning 476
  tenet 484
  maxim 496
  motive 615
  probity 939
  on—615
  want of—945
prink *adorn* 847
  show off 882
print *news* 532
  mark 550
  engraving 558
  letterpress 591
  out of—552
printer 591
printing 591
  —press 591
prior—*in order* 62
  —*in time* 116
  clergy 996
priority 116, 234
priory 1000
prism *angularity* 244
  optical instrument
  445
  see through a—443
prismatic *color* 428
  variegated 440
prison 752
  cast into—751
  in—751, 754
prisoner *restraint* 751
  captive **754**
  accused 938
  take—*restrain* 751
  seize 789
pristine 122
prithee 765
prittle—prattle 588
privacy *conceal* 528

seclude 893
private *special* 79
  hidden 528
  secluded 893
  in—528
  keep—881
  —*road* 627
  —*soldier* 726
  talk to in—586, 588
  to gain some—ends
  943
privateer
  combatant 726
  robber 792
privateering 791
privately 881
privation *loss* 776
  poverty 804
privative 789
privilege *freedom* 748
  permission 760
  exemption 777a
  due 924
privity *relation* 9
  knowledge 490
privy *hidden* 528
  latrines 653
  —to 490
Privy Council
  tribunal 966
prize *good* 618
  masterpiece 650
  palm 733
  gain 775
  booty 793
  love 897
  approve 931
  —*open* 173
  win the—731
prizer 767
prize fighter 726
prize fighting 720
prizeman 700
prizewinner 650, 931
pro—and con
  reasoning 476
  motive 615
  —bono publico
  utility 644
  philanthropy 910
  —formâ 82
  —re natâ
  circumstances 8
  relation 9
  special 79
  occasion 134
  conditions 770
  —*tanto degree* 26
  small 32
  —*tempore* 111
proa 273
probability
  chance 156
  likelihood **472**
probable *hopeful* 858
probate *security* 771

(*evidence* 467)
Probate, Court of—
  966
probation *trial* 463
  demonstration 478
probationary 463
  learner 541
  essay 675
probationer 541
probative 478
probator 461
probe *depth* 208
  perforator 262
  investigate 461
  measure 466
probity 939
problem *topic* 454
  question 461
  enigma 533
problematic 675
problematical
  uncertain 475
  (*hidden* 528)
proboscis 250
procacity
  insolence 885
  rudeness 895
  irascibility 901
procedure
  method 627
  action 680
  conduct 692
proceed *time* 109
  advance 282
  —from 154
  —with 692
proceeding
  incomplete 53
  event 151
  action 680
  not finished 730
  course of—692
  —s *records* 551
proceeds *gain* 775
  money 800
  receipts 810
procerity 206
process *projection* 250
  engraving 558
  conduct 692
  (*action* 680)
  in—of time
  posterior 117
  legal—963
  —of time *course* 109
procession
  continuity 69
  march 266
  ceremony 882
processional *rite* 998
procès verbal
  record 551
  law proceeding 969
prochronism 115
proclaim 531
proclamatory 531

proclivity
  tendency 176
  proneness 820
  (*disposition* 602)
proclivous 217
Proclus 490a
proconsul 759
proconsulship 737
procrastination
  delay 133
  neglect 460
  inactivity 683
procreant 161, 168
procreate
  produce 161
  productive 168
procreative 153, 168
procreator 166
procrustean 82
  —*law* 80
Procrustes
  stretch on the bed
  of—27
proctor *officer* 694
  consignee 758
  lawyer 968
proctorship 693
procumbent 213
procuration 170, 755
procurator 694
procure *cause* 153
  induce 615
  get 775
  buy 795
procurement 170
procuress 962
prod 276
prodigal *lavish* 641
  extravagant 818
prodigality 818
prodigious *much* 31
  wonderful 870
prodigy *exception* 83
  genius 492
  élite 648
  wonderful 872
  —of learning 700
prodition 940
prodromal 116
prodrome 64
produce *increase* 35
  cause 153
  effect 154
  create 161
  prolong 200
  show 525
  stage 599
  fruit 775
  merchandise 798
  —*itself* 446
producer **164**
product *multiple* 84
  effect 154
  gain 775
production 161
  composition 54

writing 590
(*see* produce)
productive *cause* 153
  power 157
  imagination 515
  acquiring 775
productiveness 168
proem 64, 66
proemial
  preceding in order 62
  beginning 66
profane *desecrate* 679
  impious 988
  laical 997
  −*swearing* 908
profess
  (*see* profession)
profession
  assertion 535
  pretense 546
  business 625
  promise 768
  enter a−625
  −*of faith belief* 484
  theology 983
professional
  business 625
  −*matchmaker* 903
professor
  learned man 492
  teacher 540
professorship 542
proffer 602, 763
proficient
  knowledge 490
  skill 698
  adept **700**
proficuous 644
profile *outline* 230
  side 236
  appearance 448
  portraiture 556
profit *increase* 35
  advantage 618
  utility 644
  acquisition 775
  −*and loss account* 811
  −*by use* 677
profitable *useful* 644
  good 648
  gainful 775
  (*receipts* 810)
profitless 646
profligacy 945
profluent
  progressive 282
  stream 348
profound *great* 31
  deep 208
  learned 490
  wise 498
  sagacious 702
  feeling 821
  −*attention* 457

−*knowledge* 490
−*secret* 533
profundity
  (*see* profound)
profuse
  diffuse style 573
  redundant 641
  prodigal 818
profusion
  multitude 102
  plenty 639
prog 298
progenerate 161
progenitive 163
progenitor 166
progeny 167
prognathism 372a
prognosis
  foresight 510
  prediction 511
  interpretation 522
  disease 655
prognostic 507, 511, 512
prognosticate 511
program *catalogue* 86
  music 415
  publication 531
  plan 626
progress *growth* 144
  motion 264
  advance 282
  (*improvement* 658)
  in
  −*incomplete* 53, 730
  in mid−270
  make−282
  −*of science* 490
  −*of time* 109
progression
  gradation 58
  series 69
  numerical−84
  motion **282**
progressive
  continuous 69
  course 109
  advancing 282
  improving 658
prohibition 761
  exclusion 55
  temperance 953
prohibitionist 756, 958
prohibitive 55, 761
project *bulge* 250
  impel 284
  intend 620
  plan 626
projectile 727
projecting 214
projection *map* 554
projector
  promoter 626
prolation *voice* 580
  speech 582

prolegomena 64
prolepsis *precursor* 64
  anachronism 115
proletarian 876
proliferous 163, 168
prolific 168
proligerous 163
prolix 573
prolixity 573
prolocutor
  interpreter 524
  teacher 540
  speaker 582
prologue *precursor* 64
  drama 599
  what's past is−122
prolong *protract* 110
  late 133
  continue 143
  lengthen 200
prolongation
  sequence 63
  protraction 110
  posterity 117
  continuance 143
prolusion 64
promenade *walk* 266
  display 882
Promethean 359
  −*spark* 359
prominence
  (*see* prominent)
prominent
  convex 250
  manifest 525
  important 642
  eminent 873
prominently
  much 31
  more 33
promiscuous
  mixed 41
  irregular 59
  indiscriminate 465a
  casual 621
promise *predict* 511
  engage **768**
  hope 858
  keep one's−939
  keep−*to ear and break to hope* 545
  −*of celestial worth* 511
  −*oneself expect* 507
  hope 858
promissory 768−*note*
  security 771
  money 800
promontory
  height 206
  projection 250
  land 342
promorphology 357
promote *improve* 658
  aid 707

promoter
  planner 626
promotion *class* 541
  improvement 658
prompt *early* 132
  remind 505
  tell 527
  induce 615
  active 682
  advise 695
  (*quick* 274)
  −*book* 505
  −*memory* 505
prompter *theater* 599
  tempter 615
  adviser 695
promptuary 636
promulgate 531
  −*a decree* 741
pronation and supination 218
prone *horizontal* 213
proneness
  tendency 176
  disposition 820
prôner
  ostentation 882
  praise 931
prôneur 935
prong 91
pronounce
  judge 480
  assert 535
  voice 580
  speak 582
pronounced 31, 525
pronouncement 531, 535
pronunciation 562, 580
pronunciative 535
proof *hard* 323
  insensible 376
  test 463
  demonstration 478
  indication 550
  printing 591
  draft 626
  ocular−446
  −*against strong* 159
  resolute 604
  safe 664
  defense 717
  resistance 719
  insensible 823
proof reader 591
prop *support* 215
  help 707
propaedeutic 537
propaedeutics 537
propagable 168
propaganda
  teaching 537
  school 542
  preparation 673
propagandism 537

propagandist
  teacher 540
  priest 996
propagate
  droduce 161
  be productive 168
  publish 531
  teach 537
propel 284
propeller 284, 312
propend 602
propendency
  predetermination 611
  inclination 820
propense 602
propension 820
propensity
  tendency 176
  willingness 602
  inclination 820
proper *special* 79
  expedient 646
  handsome 845
  due 924
  (*right* 922)
  in its−*place* 58
  −*name* 564
  −*time* 134
  show a−*spirit* 939
  the−*thing duty* 926
properties, theatrical−
  costume 225
  drama 599
property *power* 157
  possessions **780**
  wealth 803
property−**man** 599
prophasis 510
prophecy 511
prophet *oracle* 511
  seer 513
  preparer 673
  priest 996
  non−*Biblical*−*s* 986
prophetess 513
prophetic *predict* 511
  revelation 985
Prophets, the−985
prophylactic
  healthful 656
  remedy 662
  preservative 670
  hindrance 706
prophylaxis 670
propinquity 197
propitiate *pacify* 723
  mediate 724
  calm 826
  content 831
  love 897
  pity 914
  forgive 918
  atone 952
  worship 990

propitiator 714, 724
propitious *timely* 134
  beneficial 648
  helping 707
  prosperous 734
  auspicious 858
proplasm 22
proportion *relation* 9
  mathematical 84
  sum 85
  symmetry 242
  elegance 578
  allotment 786
proportionate
  agreeing 23
proportions
  space 180
  size 192
proposal 765
  plan 626
propose *suggest* 514
  broach 535
  intend 620
  offer 763
  offer marriage 902
  –a question 461
proposition
  supposition 454
  reasoning 476
  project 626
  suggestion 514
  offer 763
  request 765
propound *suggest* 514
  broach 535
  –a question 461
proprietary 779
proprietor 779
proprietorship 780
propriety
  agreement 23
  elegance 578
  expedience 646
  fashion 852
  right 922
  duty 926
propugn *resist* 717
  vindicate 937
propugnaculum 717
propulsion 284
propulsive 276, 284, 633
propylon 66
prore 234
prorogue 133
proruption 295
prosaic *usual* 82
  slow 275
  –*style* 575
  dry 576
  dull 843
prosaism *prose* 598
prosal 598
proscenium
  front 234
  theater 599

proscribe
  interdict 761
  banish 893
  curse 908
  condemn 971
  (*exclude* 77)
prose *diffuse style* 573
  prate 584
  not verse **598**
  –run mad *ornate* 577
  poetical 597
  –writer 598
prosecute *pursue* 622
  act 680
  accuse 938
  arraign 969
  –an inquiry 461
prosecutor 938
proselyte
  conversion 144
  learner 541
  convert 607
proselytism 537
proser 841
prosody 597
prosopopoeia 521
prospect *futurity* 121
  view 448
  probability 472
  expectation 507
  landscape painting 556
  good–858
  in–*intended* 620
prospector 463
prospective 121, 507
prospectively 121, 50
prospectus *list* 86
  foresight 510
  compendium 596
  scheme 626
prosper 618, 734
prosperity 734
prospicience 510
prostate 221
prosternation
  dejection 837
  servility 886
prostitute
  corrupt 659
  misuse 679
  impure 961
  courtesan 962
prostrate
  powerless 158
  destroyed 162
  low 207
  horizontal 213
  depress 308
  laid up 655
  exhausted 688
  submissive 725
  dejected 837
  servile 886
  fall–306
  –oneself *servile* 886

obeisance 928
  worship 990
prostration
  (*see* prostrate)
  sickness 655
  submission 725
  pain 828
prosy *feeble style* 575
  weary 841
  dull 843
prosyllogism 476
protagonist *actor* 599
  proficient 700
protasis *precursor* 64
  beginning 66
  maxim 496
protean 81, 149
protect *safe* 664
protected cruiser 726
protection
  influence 175
  defense 717
  restrain 751
protectionist 751
protective 717
  –devices 717
protector 664, 717
  master 745
  keeper 753
protectorate 737
  realm 780
protégé *servant* 746
  friend 890
proteid 357
proteiform 149
protein
  semiliquid 352
  organic 357
proteolysis 49
protervity 901
protest *dissent* 489
  assert 535
  deny 536
  refuse 764
  deprecate 766
  not observe 773
  not pay 808
  counter–468
  enter a–766
  –against *oppose* 708
  disapprove 932
  under
  –*unwilling* 603
  compulsion 744
Protestant 984
protestant
  dissenting 489
  unaccustomed 614
  refusing 764
Protestantization 144
protested bills 808
Proteus 149
prothesis 1000
prothonotary 553

protocol *scheme* 626
  compact 769
  (*record* 551)
  (*warrant* 771)
protogenal 153
protohistoric 124
protoplasm
  prototype 22
  organization 357
protoplasmic 240, 357
protoplast 22, 357
prototypal
  original 20
prototype 22
  prediction 511
protoxide of nitrogen 376
protozoa 357, 368
protract *time* 110
  late 133
  lengthen 200
  diffuse style 573
protreptical 615
protrude 250
protrusile 250
protrusive 250
protuberance 250
protypify 511
proud *dignified* 873
  lofty 878
  –flesh 250
prove *arithmetic* 85
  turn out 151
  try 463
  demonstrate 478
  indicate 550
  affect 821
  –one's case
   vindication 937
  –true 494
provender *food* 298
  provision 637
proverb *maxim* 496
  (*phrase* 566)
proverbial 490
provide *furnish* 637
  –against *prepare* 673
  –against a rainy day 817
provided
  conditionally 8
  qualification 469
  supposition 514
  (*conditions* 770)
  –for 803
  well–639
providence
  foresight 510
  preparation 673
  divine government 976
Providence 976
  waiter on–*idle* 683
  contented 831
provident *careful* 459

wise 498
  prepared 673
providential
  opportune 134
  fortunate 734
provider 637
province
  department 75
  region 181
  office 625
  career 692
  (*duty* 926)
provincial
  (*see* province)
  narrow 481
  vulgar 851
  impiety 988
provincialism
  neology 563
provision *food* 298
  supply **637**
  preparation 673
  wealth 803
  (*materials* 635)
  –shop 637
provisional 475
  circumstances 8
  temporary 111
  uncertain 475
  expectation 507
  preparing 673
provisions
  conditions 770
proviso
  qualification 469
  condition 770
provisory 111
provoke *cause* 153
  incite 615
  excite 824
  vex 830
  aggravate 835
  anger 900
  –desire 865
  –hatred 898
provoquant 824
provost *master* 745
  deputy 759
prow 234
prowess 861
prowl *walk* 266
  lurk 528
  –after 622
proximate *next* 63
  near 197
  –cause 153
proximity *near* 197
  adjacent 199
proximo 121
proxy 634, 755
  by–147, 759
prude *affected* 855
  chaste 960
prudent *careful* 459
  wise 498
  cautious 864

(*skillful* 698)
prudery
  affectation 855
  fastidiousness 868
prudish *severe* 739
  stiff 751
  taste 850
  (*see* prudery)
pruina 383
prune *take away* 38
  lop 201, 371
  repair 658
  –s and prisms 855
prunello
  leather or–643
prurience *desire* 865
  lust 961
prurient 380, 961
Prussian blue 438
Prussic acid 663
pry *look* 441
  curiosity 455
  inquire 461
  –into the future 510
  –open 173
prytaneum 931
psalm *music* 415
  worship 990
psalm book 998
psalmody 415
psalter 998
psaltery 417
psammous 330
psephomancy 511
pseudo *simulated* 17
  imitative 19
  sham 545
  misnomer 565
pseudoblepsis 443
pseudology 563
pseudonym 565
pseudonymity 565
pseudoscope 445
pshaw *trifling* 643
  excitement 825
psora 380, 655
psychasthenia 992*a*
psyche 450, 821*a*
psychic 450
psychical 450
  –research 450, **992a**
psychoanalysis 450
psychogenesis 450
psychological 450, 537
psychologico-spiritualistic school 451
psychologize 992*a*
psychology 821*a*, 450
psychomancy 511
psychometry 450
psychoneurosis 821*a*
psychopath 450
psychophysicist 450
psychophysics 450

psychosis 821*a*
psychotherapy 821*a*, 662, 992*a*
psychrometer 349
pteridophytes 369
ptisan 662
ptyalism 299
ptyalize 297
puberty 127
pubescent 131
public , general–372
  make–531
  –demand 677
  –enemy 891
  –good 644
  –library 593
  –mind 593
  –opinion 488
  –press 531
  –school 542
  –servant 644
  –spirit 910
  –welfare 910
  purchasing–677
publication
  production 161
  disclosure 529
  promulgation **531**
  book 593
public house 189
  go to the–959
publicist 554, 593, 968
publicity 531
publish 531
  –the banns 765
publisher 593
puce 433, 437
pucelage *youth* 127
  celibacy 904
  purity 960
Puck 274, 979
  play–699
pucka *permanent* 141
  solid 321
  valid 494
  ripe 673
pucker *contracted* 195
  fold 258
  anger 900
  in a–*excited* 824
pudder *disorder* 59
pudding *food* 298
  soft 324
  pulpy 354
  sweets 396
  in–*time* 132
puddle 343
pudgy 201
pudicity 960
puerile *boyish* 129
  foolish 499
  feeble 575
  trifling 643
puerperal 161
puff *inflate* 194

  wind 349
  tartlet 396
  pant 688
  boast 884
  praise 931
  flatter 933
  –of smoke 330
  –up *vanity* 880
puffed up
  inflated 482
  pride 878
puffer 935
puffery 884
puffy 194
pug *short* 201
  dog 366
  footprint 551
puggaree 225
pugilism 720
pugilist 726
pugilistic 720
pugnacity
  contentiousness 720
  irascibility 901
puisne *young* 127
puissant *powerful* 157
  strong 159
puke 297
pulchritude 845
pulcinella *actor* 599
  buffoon 844
pule *cry* 411, 412
  weep 839
pull *superiority* 33
  power 157
  influence 175, 615, 631
  row 267
  draw 285
  attraction 288
  indicate 550
  printing 591
  a long and a strong – *cooperate* 709
  –about one's ears 308
  –an oar 680
  –by the sleeve 505
  –different ways 713
  –down *destroy* 162
    lay low 308
  –in 751
  –out 301
  –the check string 142
  –the wires 693
  –through
    restoration 660
    aid 707
  –together 709
  –to pieces
    separate 44
    destroy 162
    censure 932
    detract 934
  –towards *attract* 288
  –up *stop* 142
    rest 265

  root out 301
  reprimand 932
  accuse 969
  –upon the purse 814
  strong–*exertion* 686
pulled down
  weak 160
  fatigued 688
pullet 129
pulley 633
Pullman car 272
pullulate
  produce 161, 168
  multiply 168
  grow 194
pulmonary 349
pulmonate 349
pulmonic 655
pulmotor 349, 662
pulp 354
pulpiness 354
pulpit *rostrum* 542
  clergy 996
  church 1000
pulsate *periodic* 138
  oscillate 314
  agitate 315
pulsation *feeling* 821
pulse (*see* pulsate)
  vegetable 367
  feel the–*inquire* 461
  test 463
pulsion 276
pultaceous 354
pulverable 330
pulverize 330, 358
pulverulence **330**
pulvil 400
puma 913
pummel (*see* pommel)
pump *shoe* 225
  water supply 348
  inflate 349
  inquire 461
  instrument 633
pumpkin 298
pump room
  house 189
  remedy 662
pun *similarity* 17
  absurdity 497
  ambiguity 520
  misinterpretation 523
  neology 563
  wit 842
punce 276
Punch *buffoon* 844
  –and Judy 599
punch *mold* 22
  perforate 260
  perforator 262
  nag 271
  strike 276, 716
  beverage 298
  engrave 558

  vigor 574
punchbowl *vessel* 191
  hollow 252
  tippling 959
puncheon 635
  vessel 191
  perforator 262
puncher 262
punchinello 599, 844
punctated 440
punctilio *fashion* 852
punctilious *exact* 494
  severe 739
  observant 772
  ostentation 882
  scrupulous 939
puncto 882
punctual *early* 132
  periodical 138
  exact 494
  observance 772
  scrupulous 939
punctuation 567
puncture 260
pundit
  learned man 492
  sage 500
  lawyer 968
pung 272
pungency 392
  physical energy 171
  taste 392
pungent *pain* 378
  taste 392
  odor 398
  vigor 574
  feeling 821
punish 972
punishment **972**
punition 972
punitive 972
punk 962 *fuel* 388
punkah 349
punster 844
punt *row* 267
  boat 273
punter 840
puny 193
pup *infant* 129
  give birth 161
  dog 366
pupa 129
pupil–*of the eye* 441
  student 492
  learner 541
pupilage
  youth 127
  learning 539
pupillary 541
puppet *little* 193
  dupe 547
  effigy 554
  auxiliary 711
  tool 746
  be the–of 749
  make a–of 737

pygmy 193
pyknic type 372a
Pylades and Orestes 890
pylon 260
pyramid *heap* 72
  height 206
  point 253
  chance 621
pyramids
  billiards 840
pyre 363, 423
pyretic 383
pyrexia 382
pyriform 245, 249
pyrolator 382
pyrolatry 382
pyrology 282
pyromancy 511
pyromaniac 384, 913
pyrometer 389
pyrosis 655
pyrotechnics 382, 423
pyrotechnic sponge 388
pyrotechny 382
pyrotic 830
pyroxylin 727
pyrrhonism
  incredulity 487
  irreligion 989
Pythagorean 953
  –school 451
Pythia *oracle* 513
Python 366, 513
python *snake* 366
Pythoness *oracle* 513
pyx *vessel* 191
  experiment 463
  rites 998
  temple 1000

Q

Q. C. 968
Q. E. D. 478
quack *cry* 412
  impostor 548
quackery
  falsehood 544
  want of skill 699
  affectation 855
quacksalver 548
quad 189
quadrable 96
quadragesima 956
quadrangle
  quaternity 95
  house 189
  angular 244
quadrant *angle* 244
  circle 247
  measurement 466
quadrate with 23

quadratic 95
quadrature *four* 95
  angle 244
quadrennial 138
quadric 95
quadricycle 272
quadrified 97
quadrifoil 95
quadrifoliate 97
quadriform 95
quadrigeminal 97
quadrilateral
  quaternity 95
  sides 236
  angles 244
quadrille 840
quadrillion 102
quadripartition 97
quadriplanar 97
quadrireme 273
quadrisect 97
quadrisection 97
quadriserial 97
quadroon 41
quadrumanous 97
quadruped 366
quadruplet 95
quadruplication 96
quaff 298
  –the bitter cup 828
quaggy 345
quagmire *marsh* 345
  dirty 653
  difficult 704
quail *bird* 298
  fear 860
  cowardice 862
quaint *odd* 83
  pretty 845
  ridiculous 853
quake *oscillate* 314
  shake 315
  cold 383
  fear 860
Quaker 984–gray 432
  –gun 158
quakerish *prim* 855
  calm 826
Quakerism 984
qualification
  (see *qualify*)
  power 157
  modification 469
  skill 698
  discount 813
qualify *change* 140
  modify 469
  deny 536
  teach 537
  (*prepare* 673)
  –for 924
qualities
  character 820
quality *nature* 5
  power 157
  tendency 176

good taste 850
  nobility 875
qualm *disbelieve* 485
  unwilling 603
  fear 860
  –s of conscience 950
quandary *state* 7
  uncertainty 475
  difficulty 704
quantify 25
quantity 25 *much* 31
  multitude 102
quantum *amount* 25
  allotment 786
quarantine 664
  –flag 550
  –station 751
quark 32
quarrel 24, 713
  –with one's bread
    and butter
    bungling 699
    discontent 832
quarrelsome 901
quarry *object* 620
  mine 636
quart 97
quarter *cut up* 44
  fourth 95
  quadrisection 97
  period 108
  region 181
  locate 184
  abode 189
  side 236
  direction 278
  forbearance 740
  coin 800
  mercy 914
  give–914
  give no–*kill* 361
  severe 739
  pitiless 914a
  –of a hundred 98
  –upon 184
quarter–deck 210
quarter evil 655
quartermaster 637
quartern 95
quarteron 41
quarters *abode* 189
  take up one's–184
quarter sessions 966
quarterstaff
  contention 720
  weapon 727
quartet *four* 95
  music 415
  church 996
quarto 95, 593
quartz 323
quash *destroy* 162
  annul 756
quasi *similar* 17
  supposed 514
quassation 315

quassia 395
quaternity 95
quatrain 597
quatrefoil 95
quattrocento 114, 554
quaver *oscillate* 314
  shake 315
  sound 407
  music 413, 416
  aphony 581
  imperfect speech 583
  fear 860
quay *houses* 189
  harbor 666
quean 876, 962
queasiness *dislike* 867
queasy *fastidious* 868
Quechuan 372a
queen 745 *cards* 840
  title 877
  good woman 948
queencraft 693
Queen's–Bench
  prison 732
  court 966
  –counsel 968
  –English 560
  –evidence 529
  –highway 627
  –speech 695
queer *singular* 83
  ridiculous 853
  –fish 857
quell *destroy* 162
  moderate 174
  quiescence 265
  subdue 731
quench *destroy* 162
  cool 385
  dissuade 616
  gratify 829
  satiate 869
quenchless 865
querimonious 839
querist 461
quern 330
quernstone 330
querulous
  complaining 839
  fastidious 868
  irritable 901
query 461
quest 461
question *inquiry* 461
  doubt 485
  deny 536
  in–*event* 151
  topic 454
  inquiry 461
  danger 665
  pop the–902
  put to the–830
  –at issue 461
questionable
  uncertain 475

doubtful 485
  disreputable 874
  improbity 940
questioner 455
questionist 541
questionless
  certain 541
questor 801
queue 65, 214
quib 856
quibble *sophistry* 477
  quirk 481
  unmeaning 517
  equivocation 520
  falsehood 544
  wit 842
  verbal
  –*absurdity* 497
quick *transient* 111
  rapid 274
  alive 359
  intelligent 498
  active 682
  skillful 698
  feeling 821
  sensibility 822
  irascible 901
  cut to the–824
  probe to the–461
  –as thought 113
  –ear 418
  –eye 441
  –in response 375
  –succession 136
  –time 274
  sting to the–
    pain 830
    anger 900
  to the
  –*physically* 375
    mentally 822
  touch to the–822, 824
quicken *work* 170
  violence 173
  come to life 359
  promote 707
  excite 824
quickening power 170
quickly *soon* 132
quicksand *danger* 667
  difficulty 704
  –of deceit 545
quick–scented 398
quickset hedge 232
quicksilver
  changeable 149
  energy 171
  motion 264
  velocity 274
quick–witted 842
quid *essence* 1
  pungency 392
quid pro quo
  compensation 30

measure 466
estimation 480
berate 527
price, tax 812
abuse 932
at a great–274
rath *early* 132
fort 717
rather *a little* 32
trifling 643
have–609
have–not 867
–good 651
ratification
confirm 467
affirm 488
consent 762
compact 769
ratio *relation* 9
degree 26
proportion 84
apportionment 786
ratiocination 476
ration *food* 298
provision 637
allotment 786
rational–*quantity* 84
intellectual 450
reasoning 476
judicious 498
sane 502
rationale *cause* 153
attribution 155
answer 462
interpretation 522
rationalism
philosophy 451
reasoning 476
irreligion 989
rationalization 821a
ratlings 215
ratsbane 663
rattan 975
ratten 158
rattle *noise* 406, 407
music 417
confuse 458
prattle 584
death–360
–on 584
rattle–brained 499
rattled
inattentive 458
confused 523
rattle–headed 499
rattlesnake 366, 913
rattletraps 780
rattling 836
–pace 274
raucity 410
raucous *strident* 410
hoarse 581
ravage *destroy* 162
despoil 659
–s of time 659
rave *madness* 503

excitement 824, 825
–against 932
ravel *untwist* 60
derange 61
entangle 219
solve 480a
difficulty 704
raveled 59
ravelin 717
raven *bird* 366
black 431
hoarse 581
gorge 957
–for 865
ravening *violent* 173
desire 865
ravenous
grasping 789
desirous 865
raver 504
ravine *interval* 198
narrow 203
dike 259, 350
raving *mad* 503
feeling 821
excitement 824, 825
ravish *seize* 789
please 829
ravished *pleased* 827
ravishment 824
raw *immature* 123
sensitive 378
cold 383
color 428
unprepared 674
unskilled 699
sensibility 822
on the–375
–head and bloody
bones 860
–levies 726
–material 635
rawboned 203
rawhide 975
ray *fish* 368
light 420
–of comfort 831
thou living–450
rayah 745
Rayleigh wave 490c
rayless 421
raze *destroy* 162
level 213
friction 331
–to the ground
lower 308
razor 253
cut blocks with a–
waste 638
misuse 679
unskillful 699
keen as a–821
razzia *destruction* 162
attack 716
plunder 791
reabsorb 296

reach *degree* 26
equal 27
distance 196
fetch 270
arrive at 292
plain 344
river 348
deceive 545
grasp 737
take 789
–of thought 498
–the ear *hearing* 418
information 527
–to *distance* 196
length 200
within–*near* 197
possible 470
reaction
compensation 30
counteraction 179
recoil 277
restoration 660
reactionary
reversion 145
tergiversation 607
reactionist
opponent 710
read *interpret* 522
learn 539
–a lecture 537
well–490
readable 578
reader *teacher* 540
speaker 582
printer 591
clergyman 996
readership 542
readily 705
reading *specialty* 79
knowledge 490
interpretation 522
learning 539
–at sight *music* 415
–in 995
reading desk 1000
readjust *agree* 23
equalize 27
readmit 296
ready *expecting* 507
willing 602
useful 644
prepare 673
active 682
skillful 698
cash 800
get–673
make–673
–made 673
–memory 505
–money 800
–pen 569
–to burst forth 825
–to sink 824
–wit 842
reaffirm 535
reagent 463, 690

real *existing* 1
–*number* 84
true 494
liberal 516
property 780
–estate 780
–property 780
–security 771
realgar 434
realism 494
realistic 494, 594
realize *speciality* 79
intellect 450
think 451
discover 480a
believe 484
conceive 490
imagine 515
accomplish 729
acquire 775
sell 796
really *wonder* 870
(*very* 31)
realm *region* 181
people 372
government 737
property 780
realty 342, 780
ream 593
reamer 262
reanimate
reproduce 163
life 359
resuscitate 660
reap *shorten* 201
agriculture 371
take 789
–and carry 775
–the benefit of
be better for 658
–the fruits
succeed 731
acquire 775
reward 973
–the whirlwind
product 154
failure 732
–where one has not
sown 154, 923
reaper 371
reappear
repetition 104
reproduce 163
visible 446
restore 660
(*frequent* 136)
rear *sequel* 65
end 67
bring up 161
erect 212
back 235
elevate 307
teach 537
in the–281
–its head
manifest 525

–one's head
pride 878
rear admiral 745
reason *cause* 153
intellect 450
thought 451
argue 476
wisdom 498
motive 615
by–of 615
feast of–588
for this–462
in–*moderate* 174
sanity 502
right 922
listen to–498
–in a circle 477
–why *cause* 153
motive 615
stand to
–*certain* 474
proof 478
manifest 525
what's the–? 461
without rime or–
615a
reasonable
moderate 174
probable 472
judicious 498
sane 502
cheap 815
right 922
–prospect 472
reasoner 476
reasoning 476
–faculties 450
reasonless 499
reasons 476
reassemble 72
reassert 535
reassure *hope* 858
courage 861
reasty *fetid* 401
unclean 653
reave 789
rebate *deduction* 38
discount 40a
moderate 174
discount 813
rebatement 36, 813
rebec 417
rebel *revolution* 146
disobedience 742
(*resistance* 719)
rebellion
revolution 146
insurrection 719
revolt 742
rebellious *defiant* 715
(see rebellion)
rebellow 412
rebirth 660
reboation 412
rebound *recoil* 277
regression 283

reversis 840
revert *repeat* 104
  return 145
  turn back 283
  revest 790
  –to 457
revest 790
reviction 660
review *consider* 457
  inquiry 461
  judge 480
  recall 505
  dissertation 595
  compendium 596
  revise 658
  parade 882
reviewer 480, 595
revile *abuse* 932
  blaspheme 988
reviler 936
revise *copy* 21
  consider 457
  printing 591
  plan 626
  edit 658
revising barrister
  967
revision 658
  under–673
revisit 186
revival
  reproduction 163
  life 359
  restoration 660
  worship 990
revivalist 996
revive *reproduce* 163
  refresh 658
  resuscitate 660
  excite 824
revivify *reproduce* 163
  life 359
  resuscitate 660
revocable 605
revocation 536
revoke *recant* 607
  cancel 756
  (*deny* 536)
  (*refuse* 764)
revolt *contrariety* 14
  revolution 146
  resist 719
  disobey 742
  shock 830
  disapproval 932
  –against *hate* 898
  –at the idea
  dissent 489
revolting
  painful 830
revolution
  periodicity 138
  change 146
  rotation 312
revolutionary 146,
  742

revolutionize 140,
  146
revolve
  (*see* revolution)
  –in the mind 451
revolver 727
revulsion
  reversion 145
  revolution 146
  inversion 218
  recoil 277
revulsive 276
revulsively 145
reward 30, **973**
reword 104
rewriting 21
Reynard *animal* 366
  cunning 702
rez de chaussée
  room 191
  low 207
rhabdology 85
rhabdomancy 511
rhadamanthus
  judge 967
  hell 982
rhamphoid 245
rhapsodical
  irregular 139
rhapsodist
  fanatic 504
  poet 597
rhapsodize 497
rhapsody
  discontinuity 70
  nonsense 497
  fancy 515
rheometer 157
rheostat 490d
rhetoric *speech* 582
  flowers of–577
rheum *excretion* 299
  fluidity 333
rheumatism 378
rhino 800
rhinoceros 366–hide
  physically insensible
  376
  morally insensible
  823
rhipidate 194
rhizanthous 367
rhododendron 845
rhomb 244
rhomboid 244
rhubarb 298
rhumb 278
rhyme (*see* rime etc.)
rhythm
  periodicity 138
  melody 413
  elegance 578
  verse 597
rhythmic 413, 578
rhythmical–*style* 578
riant 836

rib *support* 215
  ridge 250
  wife 903
ribald *vulgar* 851
  disreputable 874
  impure 961
ribaldry 908
ribband (*see* ribbon)
ribbed *furrowed* 259
ribbon *tie* 45
  filament 205
  record 551
  decoration 877
ribbons *reins* 752
ribroast 972
rice 330, 367
ricebird 298
rich *savory* 394
  color 428
  language 577
  abundant 639
  wealthy 803
  beautiful 845
  ornament 847
  –gifts wax poor 907
  –man 639, 803
riches 803
richly *much* 31
  –deserve 924
rick *accumulation* 72
  store 636
rickety *weak* 160
  ugly 846
  imperfect 651
rickrack 257
ricksha 272
ricochet 277
rid *deliver* 672
  get–of *eject* 297
  liberation 750
  loose 776
  relinquish 782
riddance 672, 776,
  782
riddle *arrange* 60
  crossing 219
  sieve 260
  secret 533
  sift 652
  (*question* 461)
ride *get above* 206
  move 266
  –a horse 370
  –and tie
  periodicity 138
  journey 266
  –at anchor 265
  –full tilt at
  pursue 622
  attack 716
  –hard 274
  –in the whirlwind
  will 604
  rule 737
  –one's hobby 622
  –out the storm 664

–roughshod
  violence 173
  severity 739
  insolence 885
  illegality 964
  –the waves 267
rider *affix* 37
  appendix 39
  equestrian 268
ridge *narrow* 203
  height 206
  prominence 250
ridicule 856
  disrespect 929
ridiculous *absurd* 497
  foolish 499
  trifling 643
  grotesque 853
ridiculousness 853
riding *district* 181
  journey 266
ridotto *gala* 840
  rout 892
rifacimento
  repetition 104
  resuscitation 660
rife *general* 78
  influence 175
riffle 348
riffraff *dirt* 653
  commonalty 876
  bad folk 949
rifle *musket* 406, 727
  plunder 791
  –grenade 727
rifled cannon 727
rifleman 726
rifler 792
rifles 726
rifle shooting 840
rift *separation* 44
  fissure 198
rig *dress* 225
  vehicle 272
  prepare 673
  frolic 840
  strumpet 962
  –the market 794
  run the–upon 929
rigadoon 840
rigging *ropes* 45
  gear 225
  instrument 633
riggish 961
right *dextral* 238
  straight 246*true* 494
  freedom 748
  property 780
  just **922**
  privilege 924
  duty 926
  honor 939
  virtuous 944
  bill of–969
  by–924
  have a–to 924

hit the–nail on the
  head
  discover 480a
  skill 698
  in one's–mind
  wise 498
  sane 502
  in the–place 646
  keep the–path 944
  –about
  (*see below*)
  –ahead 234
  –and left *space* 180
  circumjacence 227
  lateral 236
  –angle 212
  –as a trevet 650
  –ascension 466
  –away 113, 143
  –bower 840
  divine–of kings 737
  –establishment 478
  –hand
  (*see below*)
  –itself 660
  –line 246
  –man in the right
    place 23
  –owner 779
  –passage 279
  –thing to do 926
  –word in the right
    place 578
  set–*inform* 527
  disclose 529
  step in the–
    direction 644
  that's–931
right–about
  go to the–
  circuit 311
  tergiversation 607
  send to the
  –*eject* 297
  reject 610
  refuse 764
  to the–283
  turn to the–
  inversion 218
  deviation 279
righteous
  virtuous 944
  –overmuch 988
  the–987
Righteousness
  Lord our–976
  Sun of–976
rightful 922
  –owner 779
right hand *power* 157
  dextrality 238
  help 711
  not let the–know
    what the left is
    doing 528
  –of friendship 888

sematic 668
semblance
  similarity 17
  imitation 19
  copy 21
  probability 471
  wear the–of
    appearance 448
semeiology 522, 655
semeiotics 550
semen 153
semester 108
semi–91
semibarbarian 913
semibreve 413
semicircle 247
semicircular 245
semicolon 142
semidiaphanous 427
semifluid 352
semiliquidity 352
semilunar 245
seminal *causing* 153
seminar 542
seminary 542
semination
  preparation 673
semiopaque 427
semipellucid 427
semiquaver 413
Semitic 372*a*
semitone 413
semitransparency
  427
sempervirid 110, 123
sempiternal 112
sempiternity 110,
  112
senary 98
senate 72, 696
senate house 966
senator *counsel* 695
  councillor 696
senatorship 693
send *transfer* 270
  propel 284
  –about one's business
    289
  –adrift 597
  –a letter to 592
  –away *repel* 289
    eject 297
    refuse 764
  –for 741
  –forth *propel* 284
    publish 531
  –off 284
  –out *eject* 297
    commission 755
  –word 527
seneca–oil 356
senectitude 128
senescence 128
seneschal
  director 694
  master 745

servant 746
seneschalship 737
senile 128, 158, 499
  –dementia 499, 821*a*
senior *age* 128
  student 492
  master 745
seniority *oldness* 124
  age 128
señor 877
sensation
  physical sensibility
    375
  emotion 821
  wonder 870
sensational
  language 574
  exciting 824
sensation drama 599
sensations of touch
380
sense *wisdom* 498
  meaning 516
  accept in a
    particular–522
  deep–821
  in no–565
  –of duty 926
senseless
  insensible 376
  absurd 497
  foolish 499
  unmeaning 517
senses *external*–375
  intellect 450
  sanity 502
sensibility
  physical–**375**
  moral **822**
sensible *material* 316
  wise 498
sensitive 375, 822
  –plant 822
sensorial 821
sensorium 450
sensual *pleasure* 377
  intemperate 954
sensualist 954*a*
sensualize 954
sensuous
  sensibility 375
  pleasure 377
  feeling 821
sentence *decision* 480
  maxim 496
  affirmation 535
  phrase 566
  lawsuit 969
  condemnation 971
  my–is for war 722
sententious
  concise 572
  –*language* 574, 577
  taciturn 585
sentiment
  –*physically* 375

  –*morally* 821
sentiment *idea* 453
  (*opinion* 484)
  (*maxim* 496)
sentimental
  sensitive 822
  affected 855
sentinel *guard* 263
  guardian 664
  watch 668
  keeper 753
sentry 664, 668, 753
sepal 367
separable 44
separate *disjoin* 44
  exclude 55
  bisect 91
  diverge 291
  clean 652
  divorce 782, 905
  –into elements 49
  –maintenance 905
  –the chaff from the
    wheat
  discriminate 465
  select 609
separation
  (*see* separate)
separatist 489, 984
  disjunction 44
separative 49
sepia 433
seposition
  disjunction 44
  exclusion 55
sepoy 726
seppuku 972
sept *kin* 11
  class 75
  clan 166
septal 228
septenary 98
septennial 138
Septentrional 237
septet 415
septic 655, 657, 662
septicemia 655
septicity 655
septimal 98
septuagenary 98
septuagesimal 98
Septuagint 985
septulum 228
septum 228
septuple 98
sepulcher 363
  whited–545
sepulchral
  interment 363
  resonance 408
  stridor 410
  hoarse 581
sepulture 363
sequacious 63, 117
sequacity *soft* 324
  tenacity 327

sequel *following* **65**
  –*in time* 117
  sequence 281
  (*addition* 39)
sequela 63, 65
sequence–*in order* **63**
  –*in time* 117
  motion **281**
  logical–476
sequent 63, 117
sequester *take* 789
  confiscate 974
  (*hide* 528)
sequestered
  secluded 893
sequestrate *seize* 789
  condemn 971
  confiscate 974
sérac 383
seraglio *abode* 189
  woman 374
  marriage 903
  impurity 961
seraph *saint* 948
  angel 977
seraphic *blissful* 829
  virtuous 944
  pious 987
Seraphim 977
seraphina 417
seraskier 745
sere (*see* sear)
  –and yellow leaf 128
serein *dew* 339
  rain 348
serenade *music* 415
  compliment 894
  endearment 902
serene *pellucid* 425
  calm 826
  content 831
  –*highness* 877
serf *slave* 746
  clown 876
serfdom 749
serge 635
sergeant 745
serial *continuous* 69
  periodic 138
  book 593
seriatim *in order* 58
  continuously 69
  each to each 79
  slowly 275
series *continuity* 69
  number 84
serif 591
serio–comic 853
serious *great* 31
  resolved 604
  important 642
  dejected 837
seriously 535
serjeant
  common–967
  –at–law 968

sermon *lesson* 537
  speech 582
  dissertation 595
  pastoral 998
  funeral–363
sermonize 586
sermonizer 584
serosity *fluid* 333
serotherapy 662
serotine 133
serpent *tortuous* 248
  snake 366
  hiss 409
  wind instrument 417
  wise 498
  deceiver 548
  cunning 702
  evildoer 913
  knave 941
  demon 949
  great sea–515
  the old–978
serpentine 248
serrated *angular* 244
  notched 257
serried *crowded* 72
  dense 321
serum *lymph* 333
  water 337
servant *minister* 631
  agent 690
  help 711
  retainer **746**
  –of all work 690
serve *benefit* 618
  business 625
  utility 644
  aid 707
  warfare 722
  obey 743
  servant 746
  (*work* 680)
  –an apprenticeship
    539
  –as a substitute 147
  –faithfully 743
  –one right
    retaliation 718
    right 922
    punish 972
  –one's turn 644
  –out 972
  –with a writ 969
service *good* 618
  utility 644
  use 677
  warfare 722
  servitude 749
  worship 990
  rite 998
  at one's–763
  press into the–677
  render a–*utility* 644
  benevolence 906
serviceable
  instrumental 631

snippet 32
snip–snap 713
snivel *weep* 839
sniveling *servile* 886
snob *vulgar* 851
  plebeian 876
  servile 886
snobbishness
  flattery 933
snood *headdress* 225
  circle 247
snooze 683
snore *noise* 441
  sleep 683
snort 411, 412
snorter 83
snout 250
snow *ship* 273
  ice 383
  white 430
snow avalanche 383
snow ball 72, 383
snow blindness 443
snow–bound 383
snowdrift 72
snowshoes 225, 266, 272
snowslide 306, 383
snowslip 306, 383
snowstorm 383
snub *short* 201
  hinder 706
  cast a slur 874
  humiliate 879
  bluster 885
  censure 932
snub–nosed
  distortion 243
  (*ugly* 846)
snuff *blow* 349
  pungent 392
  odor 398
  go out like the–of a candle 360
  –out *destroy* 162
  dark 421
  –up *inhale* 296
  smell 398
  up to–*skillful* 698
  cunning 702
snuff–color 433
snuffle *blow* 349
  hiss 409
  stammer 583
  hypocrisy 988
snuffy 653
snug *closed* 261
  comfortable 377
  safe 664
  prepared 673
  content 831
  secluded 893
  keep–*conceal* 528
  seclude 893
  make all
  –*prepare* 673

snuggery 189
snuggle 902
snugness 827
so *similar* 17
  very 31
  therefore 476
  method 627
  –be it *assent* 488
  consent 762
  –far so good 618
  –let it be 681
  –much the better
  content 831
  rejoicing 838
  –much the worse
  discontent 832
  aggravation 835
  –to speak *similar* 17
  metaphor 521
soak *immerse* 300
  water 337
  moist 339
  drunkenness 959
  –up 340
soap *lubricate* 332
  oil 356
soapy *unctuous* 355
  service 886
  flattery 933
soar *great* 31
  height 206
  fly 267
  rise 305
  air 338
sob 839
sober *substantial* 3
  moderate 174
  wise 498
  sane 502
  plain 576
  grave 837
  temperate 953
  abstinent 958
  in–*sadness*
  affirmation 535
  –down 174, 502
  humility 879
  –senses 502
  –truth *fact* 494
sober–minded 502
  calm 826
  humble 879
soberness 953
sobriety 958
sobriquet 565
soc *jurisdiction* 965
socage 777
so–called
  deception 545
  misnomer 565
sociable *carriage* 272
  sociality 892
social *mankind* 372
  sociable 892
  –circle 892
  –evil 961

–gathering 892
  –science 910
  –service 602
  –smile 906
  –worker 602
socialism
  government 737
  participation 778
  philanthropy 910
Socialists 712
sociality 892
society *mankind* 372
  party 712
  fashion 852
  sociality 892
  laity 997
  position in–873
sociological 537
  –school 451
sociology 910
sociopath 821a
socius criminis 711
sock *hosiery* 225
  drama 599
sockdolager 67, 479
socket *receptacle* 191
  concave 252
socle 215
Socratic method 461
Socratic school 451
sod 344
  beneath the–363
sodality *party* 712
  friendship 888
  (*sociality* 892)
sodden *moist* 339
  boiled 384
sofa 215
soft *stop!* 142
  weak 160
  moderate 174
  smooth 255
  not hard 324
  moist 339
  marsh 345
  silence! 403
  –*sound* 405
  dulcet 413
  credulous 486
  silly 499
  lenient 740
  tender 822
  timid 862
  (*docile* 602)
  (*irresolute* 605)
  own the–
  impeachment 529
  –buzzing slander 934
  –music 415
  –pedal 405
  –sawder *plea* 617
  flattery 933
  –snap 681
  –soap *oil* 356
  flattery 933
  –thing 681

–tongue,–words 894
soften (*see* soft)
  moderate 174
  relieve 834
  pity 914
  palliate 937
  penitent 950
  –down 834
softening 324
  –of the brain 158
softer sex 374
soft–hearted 914
softling 160
softness 324
  persuasibility 615
soft–spoken 894
soggy 339
soho *attention* 457
  parley 586
  hunting 622
soi–distant
  asserting 535
  misnomer 565
  vain 880
soil *region* 181
  land 342
  dirt 653
  deface 846
  (*spoil* 659)
  (*blemish* 848)
  till the–
  agriculture 371
  prepare 673
soilure 653
soirée 892
sojourn *dwell* 186
  abode 189
  (*rest* 265)
sojourner 188
soke 181
solace *relief* 834
  recreation 840
  –oneself with
  pleasure 827
solar 318–system 318
solatium 973
sola topi 225
soldan 745
solder *join* 43
  cement 45
  cohere 46
soldier 726
soldierlike *war* 722
  brave 861
sole *alone* 87
  base 211
  support 215
  fish 298
  feme–904
solecism
  ungrammatical **568**
  (*sophistry* 477)
solemn
  affirmation 535
  important 642
  grave 837

glorious 873
  ostentatious 882
  commemoration 883
  religious 987
  worship 990
  –avowal 535
  –declaration 535
  –mockery 882
  –silence 403
solemnity *rite* 998
solemnization 883
sol–fa 416
solfeggio 415
solferino 434, 437
solicit *induce* 615
  request 765
  desire 865
  –the attention 457
solicitor *agent* 758
  petitioner 767
  merchant 797
  lawyer 968
solicitous 765, 865
solicitude *care* 459
  pain 828
  anxiety 860
  desire 865
solid *complete* 52
  dense 321
  certain 474
  learned 490
  exact 494
  wise 498
  persevering 604a
  –in galleys 591
solidarity *party* 712
solidify 48, 321
solidity (*see* solid)
  solvency 800
solidungulate 366
soliloquist 589
soliloquy 589
soliped 366
solitaire *game* 840
  hermit 893
solitary *alone* 87
  secluded 893
solitude 87, 893
solmization 415
solo 415
soloist 996
Solomon 498, 500
Solon 498, 500
solstice dance 372a
soluble *fluid* 333
  liquefy 335
solus 87
solution *fluid* 333
  liquefaction 335
  music 413
  answer 462
  explanation 522
  –of continuity 70
solve *liquefy* 335
  discover 480a
  unriddle 522

575

synonym
  meaning 516
  interpretation 522
  nomenclature 564
synonymize 516
synopsis
  arrangement 60
  list 86
  grammar 567
  compendium 596
synovia
  lubrication 332
  oil 356
synovial 332
syntactic 567
syntagma 60
syntax 567
syntectic 655
synthesis
  combination 48
  composition 54
  reasoning 476
synthetic 476
syringe *water* 337
  stream 348
syrinx 410
syrt 667
syrup 352, 396
system *order* 58
  rule 80
  plan 626
  –of knowledge 490
  –of opinions 484
systematic *regular* 80
systematize *order* 58
  arrange 60
  organize 357
  plan 626
systole 195
  –and diastole 138, 314
syzygy 199

T

T to a–494
tab 39
tabard 225
tabasco 393
tabby *mottled* 440
  gossip 588
tabefaction 195
tabernacle *house* 189
  temple 1000
tabes 195
tabescent 195
tabetic 195, 203, 655
tabic 203
tabid *shrunk* 195
  thin 203
  disease 655
  deteriorated 659
table *arrangement* 60
  list 86
  defer 133

layer 204
  support 215
  flat 251
  repast 298
  neglect 460
  writing 590
  on the
  –preparing 673
  –of the Lord 1000
  turn the–s 218
  under the
  –hidden 528
  drunk 959
tableau *list* 86
  appearance 448
  painting 556
  theatrical 599
tablecloth 652
table d'hôte 298
table–land
  horizontal 213
  plain 344
tablespoon 191
tablet *layer* 204
  flat 251
  record 551
  writing 590
  –s of the memory
    505
table talk *news* 532
  conversation 588
table–turning 992
tableware 191
tablier 225
tablinum 191
taboo *prohibited* 761
  magic 992
tabor 417
tabouret 215
tabret 417
tabular 60
tabula rasa
  inexistence 2
  absence 187
  ignorance 491
  obliterated 552
  facility 705
tabulate *arrange* 60
  series 69
  list 86
tabulation *record* 551
tace 403
tachygraphy 590
tacit *implied* 516
  latent 526
taciturnity 585
Tacitus
  concise style 572
tack *join* 43
  nails 45
  change course 140
  direction 278
  turn 279
  way 627
  –to *add* 37
  wrong–732

tackle *fastening* 45
  gear 633
  undertake 676
  manage 693
tacky 352 *dowdy* 659
tact *touch* 379
  discrimination 465
  wisdom 498
  skill 698
  taste 850
  want of–851
tactful (*see* tact)
  affable 894
tactician 700
tactics *conduct* 692
  warfare 722
  (*plan* 626)
  (*skill* 698)
tactile 379
taction 379
tactlessness 895
tactual 379
tadpole 129
taenia 205
taeniate 205
taffeta 255
taffy 396
tag *small* 32
  addition 37
  fastening 45
  follow 63, 235
  sequel 65
  end 67
  point 253
  animal 366
  game 840
  (*adjunct* 39)
tagtail 886
tail *sequel* 65
  end 67
  pendent 214
  rear 235
  aeronautics 273
  estate–780
  –off *decrease* 36
  turn–623
tail coat 225
tailless 38
tailor *clothier* 225
  workman 690
tailoress 225
tailoring *clothes* 225
  finery 882
tailpiece
  sequel 65, 235
  engraving 558
  ornament 847
tailrace 350
taint *imperfection* 651
  dirt 653
  decay 659
  disgrace 874
tainted *fetid* 401
  diseased 655
taintless 652
taj 225

tajo 259
take *eat* 298
  believe 484
  know 490
  understand 518
  succeed 731
  receive 785
  appropriate 788, 789
  captivate 829
  give and–718
  –aback
    unexpected 508
    astonish 870
  –a back seat 34
  –a course 692
  –action 680
  –a disease 655
  –advice 695
  –after 17
  –a hint 498
  –a leaf out of
    another's book 19
  –a lease 788
  –a liberty 748
  –a likeness 554
  –an account of
    enumerate 85
  –an ell 885
  –an infection 655
  –a peep 441
  –aside 586
  –a turn 140
  –away *annihilate* 2
    subtract 38
    remove 185
    seize 789
  –away life 361
  –back again 790
  –by
    (*see below*)
  –care *warning* 668
    cautious 864
  –care of 459
  –comfort
    constant 831
    relief 834
  –coolly 826
  –down *swallow* 298
    depress 308
    record 551
    dismantle 681
    humiliate 874
    censure 932
  –easily 826
  –effect *event* 151
    act 170
  –exception 932
  –fire 384
  –flight 623
  –for
    (*see below*)
  –from *subtract* 38
    seize 789
  –heart *contented* 831
    cheerful 836
  –heed 864

–hold of *cohere* 46
    seize 789
  –hold of the mind
    484
  –ill 832
  –in
    (*see below*)
  –it *believe* 484
    suppose 514
  –its course
    continue 143
    event 151
  –its rise *begin* 66
    result 154
  –leave of 624
  –measures 626
  –money 810
  –no care of 460
  –no denial
    obstinate 606
    compel 744
  –no interest in 823
  –no note of 460
  –no note of time 115
  –notice 457
  –off
    (*see below*)
  –on
    (*see below*)
  –one at one's word
    769
  –one's chance
    chance 621
    essay 675
  –one's choice 609
  –oneself off 293
  –one's fancy
    pleasing 829
    desire 865
  –one's oath 535
  –one with another 29
  –on trust 484
  –out *extract* 301
    obliterate 552
  –part with 709
  –pattern by 19
  –pen in hand 590
  –place 151
  –possession of 789
  –precedence
    superior 33
    precede 62
  –root *firm* 150
    located 184
  –ship 267
  –steps *prepare* 673
    act 680
  –stock 85
  –the air line 278
  –the back track 283
  –the cake 33
  –the consequences
    154
  –the field 722
  –the good the gods
    provide 831

589

tripsis 330
Triptolemus 371
triquetral 94
trireme 92, 273
Trisagion 900
triseme 92
trisection **94**
triskelion 92, 993
trismus 655
triste 837
tristful 837
trisula 92
trisulcate *trisected* 94
  furrow 259
trite *known* 490
  conventional 613
  –saying 496
tritheism 984
Triton *sea* 341
  –among the minnows
  superior 33
  huge 192
  important 642
trituration 330
triumph *procession* 69
  success 731
  trophy 733
  exult 838
  celebrate 883
  boast 884
triumvirate 92, 737
triune 93
Triune God 976
triunity 92
trivet *support* 215
  stove 386
  right as a–
  perfect 650
  due 924
trivial *unmeaning* 517
  trifling 643
  useless 645
  ridiculous 853
  (*small* 32)
troat 412
trocar 262
trochaic 597
trochee 597
trochilic 312
trodden down–749
  well–*habitual* 613
  used 677
troglodyte 893
troll *roll* 312
  fairy 980
trolley 266, 271, 273
  –car 272
trollibus 273
trollop 59, 962
trombone 417
troop *assemblage* 72
  soldiers 726
  raise–s 722
trooper 726
  lie like a–544
  swear like a–908

troopship 726
trope 521
Trophonius, cave of
  –837
trophoplasm 357
trophy *record* 551
  palm **733**
tropical 382
  metaphorical 521
trot *run* 266, 370
  velocity 274
  translation 539
  –out *manifest* 525
  display 882
troth *belief* 484
  veracity 543
  promise 768
  by my–535
  plight one's–902
trothless *false* 544
  dishonorable 940
trotters 266, 298
trottoir 627
troubadour 597
trouble *disorder* 59
  derange 61
  exertion 686
  difficulty 704
  adversity 735
  pain 828
  painful 830
  bring into–649
  get into–732
  in–*evil* 619
  adversity 735
  take–686
  –one for 765
  –oneself 686
  –one's head about
  682
troubled (*see* trouble)
  fish in–waters 704
troublesome
  inexpedient 647
  exertion 686
  difficult 704
  painful 830
troublous 59
  violent 173
  –times 713
trough *hollow* 252
  trench 259
  conduit 350
trounce *censure* 932
  punish 972
troupe 72
trousers 225
  put on long–131
trousseau 225
trout 298
trouvaille 775
trouvère 597
trover *acquisition* 775
  unlawful 964
trow *think* 451
  believe 484

know 490
trowel 191
troy weight 319
truant *absent* 187
  runaway 623
  idle 682
  apostate 941
truce *lateness* 133
  cessation 142
  deliverance 672
  peace 721
  pacification 723
  flag of–724
  –of God 142
trucidation 361
truck *summit* 210
  vehicle 272
  barter 794
  –driver 268, 271
  –farm 691
  –garden 371, 691
truckle–bed 215
truckler 886
truckle to *submit* 725
  servile 886
  flatter 933
truckling *servile* 746
truckman 268
truculent 907
trudge *walk* 266
  move slowly 275
true *real* 1
  straight 246
  assent 488
  accurate 494
  veracious 543
  faithful 772
  honorable 939
  orthodox 983a
  see in its–colors
  480a
  –bill *vindicate* 937
  accuse 938
  lawsuit 969
  –faith 983a
  –meaning 516
  –to nature 17
  –to oneself 604a
  –saying 496
true–blue 494
true–hearted 543,
  939
truelove 897
truelover's knot
  love 897
  endearment 902
trueness (*see* true)
true–penny 939
truffles 298
truism *axiom* 496
  unmeaning 517
trull 962
truly *very* 31
  assent 488
  really 494
  indeed 535

trump *perfect* 650
  cards 840
  honorable 939
  good man 948
  –card *device* 626
  success 731
  –up *falsehood* 544
  accuse 938
  turn up–s 731
trumped up
  counterevidence 468
  deception 545
  untruth 546
trumpery
  unmeaning 517
  trifling 643
trumpet *music* 417
  war cry 722
  boast 884
  ear–418
  flourish of–s
  ostentation 882
  celebration 883
  boasting 884
  penny–*skill* 410
  sound of
  –alarm 669
  speaking–418
  –blast 404
  –call *signal* 550
  command 741
  –forth 531
trumpeter
  musician 416
  messenger 534
  boaster 884
trumpet–toned
  shrill 410
trumpet–tongued
  loud 404
  public 531
truncate *shorten* 201
  formless 241
truncated
  incomplete 53
truncheon
  weapon 727
  staff of office 747
  instrument of
  punishment 975
trundle *propel* 284
  roll 312
  –bed 215
trunk *whole* 50
  origin 153
  paternity 166
  box 191
trunk hose 225
trunnion *support* 215
  projection 250
truss *tie* 43
  pack, packet 72
  support 215
trust *belief* 484
  property 780
  credit 805

hope 858
  –to a broken reed
  699
  –to the chapter of
  accidents 621
trusted 484
trustee *consignee* 758
  possessor 779
  treasurer 801
trustful 484
trustless 940
trustworthy
  certain 474
  belief 484
  –*memory* 505
  veracious 543
  reliable 632
  honorable 939
truth *exactness* **494**
  veracity 543
  probity 939
  arrive at the–480a
  in–*certainly* 474
  love of–543
  of a
  –*affirmation* 535
  veraciously 543
  prove the–of 937
  religious–983a
  speak the
  –*disclose* 529
  veracity 543
Truth, Spirit of–976
truthless 544
truth–loving 543
truth–telling 543
trutination 319
try *experiment* 463
  adjudge 480
  endeavor 675
  use 677
  lawsuit 969
  –a case 967
  –a cause 480
  –a prisoner 967
  –conclusions
  discuss 476
  quarrel 713
  contend 720
  –one *difficulty* 704
  –one's hand 675
  –one's luck 621
  –one's temper 824
  –one's utmost 686
  –the patience 830
trying *fatigue* 688
  difficulty 704
tryst 74, 892
trysting place 74
tsar 745
tub 191, 386
  –to a whale
  deception 545
  excuse 617
tuba 417
tubate 260

(*wonderful* 870)
unaccustomed
  unusual 83
  unused 614
  unskillful 699
unachievable 471
unacknowledged
  ignored 489
  nameless 565
  unrequited 917
unacquainted 491
unacquired 777a
unactuated (616)
unadmonished 665
unadorned *style* 576
  simple 849
  beauty–845
unadulterated
  simple 42
  genuine 494
  (*good* 648)
unadventurous 864
unadvisable 647
unadvised
  dangerous 665
  unskillful 699
unaffected
  genuine 494
  sincere 543
  –*style* 578
  obstinate 606
  artless 703
  insensible 823
  simple 849
  taste 850
  (*physically callous* 376)
unafflicted 831
unaided
  weak 160
  (*unsupported* 706)
unalarmed 861
unalienable 924
unallayed 159
unallied 10
unallowable 923
unallowed 925
unalloyed 42
  –*happiness* 827
  –*truth* 494
unalluring 866
unalterable 150
unaltered
  identical 13
  stable 150
  (*unchanged* 141)
unamazed 871
unambiguous 518
unambitious 866
unamiable 907
unanimated 823
unanimity
  agreement 23
  assent 488
  accord 714
unannexed 44

unanswerable
  demonstrative 478
  irresponsible 927a
  arbitrary 964
  (*certain* 474)
unanswered 478
unanticipated 508
unappalled 861
unappareled 226
unapparent
  latent 526
  (*invisible* 447)
unappeasable 173
unappetizing 867
unapplied 678
unappreciated 483
unapprehended 491
unapprehensive 861
unapprised 491
unapproachable
  great 31
  infinite 105
  distant 196
unapproached
  unequal 28
  superior 33
unappropriated 782
unapproved 932
unapt *incongruous* 24
  impotent 158
  unskillful 699
  (*inexpedient* 647)
unarmed 158
unarranged
  disorder 59
  unprepared 674
unarrayed 226, 849
unartificial 849
unascertained
  uncertain 475
  ignorant 491
unasked
  voluntary 602
  not asked 766
unaspiring
  indifferent 866
  modest 881
unassailable 664
unassailed 748
unassembled 73
unassisted *weak* 160
  unaided 706
  –*eye* 441
unassociated 44
unassuming 881
unatoned 951
unattached 44
unattackable 664
unattainable 471
unattained 732
unattempted 623
unattended 87
  –*to* 460
unattested
  not evidence 468
  (*unrecorded* 552)

unattracted
  indifferent 866 (616)
unattractive 866
unauthenticated
  improved 468
  uncertain 475
  inexact 495
unauthoritative
  uncertain 475
unauthorized
  prohibited 761
  undue 925
  lawless 964
unavailing *useless* 645
  failure 732
unavenged 918
unavoidable
  certain 474
  necessary 601
unavowed 489
unawakened 683
unaware *ignorant* 491
  unexpecting 508
unawed 861
unbalanced 28
unbar 750
unbearable 830
unbeaten 123
unbeauteous 846
unbecoming
  incongruous 24
  disreputable 874
  undue 925
  dishonorable 940
  –*a gentleman* 895
unbefitting *inapt* 24
  undue 925
  improbity 940
  (*see unbecoming*)
unbegotten 2
unbeguile *inform* 527
  disclose 529
unbegun
  unprepared 674
unbeheld (447)
unbelief 485
  irreligion 989
  (*incredulity* 487)
unbelievable 485
unbeliever *infidel* 989
unbelieving 485
unbeloved 898
unbend *straighten* 246
  repose 687
  –*the mind* 452
unbending *hard* 323
  resolute 604
unbenevolent 907
unbenign 907
unbent 246
unbeseeming
  vulgar 851
  dishonorable 940
unbesought
  not ask 766
  (*spontaneous* 602)

unbestowed (785)
unbetrayed 939
unbewailed 932
unbiased *wise* 498
  free 748
  (*spontaneous* 602a)
unbidden *willful* 600
  disobedient 742
unbigoted 498
unbind *detach* 44
  release 750
unblamable 946
unblamed 946
unblemished
  perfect 650
  innocent 946
unblenching 861
unblended 42
unblest
  unfortunate 735
  not approved 932
  –*with* 777a
unblown 674
unblushing
  proud 878
  vain 880
  imprudent 885
unboastful 881
unbodied 317
unboiled 674
unbolt *liberate* 750
  (*unfasten* 44)
unbookish 491
unborn *not existing* 2
  destined 152
  (*future* 121)
unbosom oneself 529
unbought
  not bought 796
  honorary 815
  honorable 939
  unselfish 942
unbound *free* 748
  exempt 927a
unbounded
  infinite 105
  (*great* 31)
  (*large* 192)
  (*space* 180)
unbrace *weaken* 160
  relax 655
unbreathed 526
unbred 895
unbribed
  honorable 939
  disinterested 942
unbridled *violent* 173
  lax 738
  free 748
unbroken *entire* 50
  continuous 69
  preserved 670
  unviolated 939
  –*extent* 69
unbruised 50
unbuckle 44

unburden
  –*one's mind* 529
unburdened 705
unburied 362
unbuttoned 748
uncalculating 863
uncalled for
  redundant 641
  useless 645
  not used 678
uncandid
  insincere 544
  morose 907
uncanny *ugly* 846
  spectral 980a
uncanonical 984
uncared for
  neglected 460
  indifferent 866
  disliked 867
  hated 898
uncase (226)
uncate 245
uncaught *free* 748
uncaused 156
unceasing 112, 143
uncensured 931
unceremonious
  vain 880
  discourteous 895
uncertain
  irregular 139
  not certain 475
  doubtful 485
  embarrassing 704
  in an–degree 32
uncertainty 475
unchain *unfasten* 44
  liberate 750
unchained *free* 748
unchallenged
  assent 488
  due 924
unchangeable
  stable 150
  persevering 604a
unchanged 16, 141
unchangingly 136
uncharitable 907
unchartered
  undue 925
  illegal 964
unchaste 961
unchastised 970
unchecked 748
uncheckered 141
uncheerful 837
unchivalric 940
unchristian
  heterodox 984
  irreligious 989
uncial 590
unciform 245
uncinated 244
uncircumscribed 180
uncircumspect 460

uncivil *vulgar* 851
  rude 895
uncivilized *low* 876
  uncourteous 895
unclad 226
unclaimed 748
unclassed (59)
unclassical 851
unclassified (59)
uncle *kin* 11
  my-'s
  pawnshop 787
unclean 653
  -spirit 978, 980
uncleanness 653
Uncle Sam 188
unclipped 50
unclog *facilitate* 705
  liberate 750
unclose *open* 260
  liberate 750
unclothed 226
unclouded *light* 420
  visible 446
  (*joyful* 827)
unclubbable 893
unclutch 790
uncoif 226
uncoil *evolve* 313
  (*straighten* 246)
uncollected (73)
uncolored
  achromatic 429
  true 494
  (*veracious* 543)
uncombed
  dirty 653
  vulgar 851
uncombined
  simple 42
  incoherent 47
uncomeatable 471
uncomely 846
uncomfortable
  annoyed 828
  annoying 830
uncommendable
  blamable 932
  bad 945
  guilt 947
uncommensurable
  24
uncommon
  unimitated 20
  exceptional 83
  infrequent 137
uncommonly 31
uncommonness 137
uncommunicated
  781
uncommunicative
  528
uncompact 322
uncompassionate
  914*a*
uncompelled 748

uncomplaisant 764
  (895)
uncompleted
  incomplete 53
  unfinished 730
  failure 732
uncomplying
  disobedient 742
  refusing 764
uncompounded 42
uncompressed
  light 320
  rare 322
uncompromising
  conformable 82
  severe 739
unconcealable 525
unconceived
  uncreated 12
  unintelligible 519
unconcern
  insensible 823
  indifferent 866
unconcerned
  tolerant 740
  (*see* unconcern)
unconcocted 674
uncondemned 970
unconditional
  complete 52
  free 748
  permission 760
  consent 762
  release 768*a*
unconducive 175*a*
unconfined 748
unconfirmed 475
unconformity
  disagreement 24
  irregularity **83**
unconfused
  methodical 58
  clear 518
unconfuted
  demonstrated 478
  true 494
uncongealed 333
uncongenial
  disagreeing 24
  insalubrious 657
unconnected
  irrelative 10
  disjointed 44
  discontinuous 70
  illogical 477
unconquerable
  strong 159
  persevering 604*a*
  -will 604
unconquered 719
unconscientious 940
unconscionable
  excessive 31
  unprincipled 945
unconscious
  ignorant 491

  insensible 823
unconsenting
  unwilling 603
  refusing 764
unconsidered 452
unconsolidated 47
unconsonant 24
unconspicuous
  invisible 447
  (*latent* 526)
unconstitutional
  undue 925
  illegal 964
unconstrained
  free 748
  fashion 852
  unabashed 880
  will 600
unconsumed
  remaining 40
uncontested 474
uncontradicted 488
uncontrite 951
uncontrollable
  violent 173
  necessity 601
  emotion 825
uncontrolled *free* 748
  excitability 825
uncontroverted 488
unconventional 83,
  614
unconversable 585
unconversant
  ignorant 491
  unskilled 699
unconverted
  dissenting 489
  irreligious 989
unconvinced 489
uncooked 674
uncopied 20
uncork 750
uncorrupted
  upright 939
  (*innocent* 946)
uncounted 475
uncouple (44)
uncourteous 895
uncourtly
  inelegant 579
  vulgar 851
  rude 895
uncouth-*style* 579
  ugly 846
  vulgar 851
  (*ridiculous* 853)
uncouthness
  (*see* uncouth)
  amorphism 241
uncover *denude* 226
  open 260
  disclose 529
  bow 894
uncreated 2
uncritical 931

uncropped 50
uncrown 756
unction
  lubrication 332
  emotion 821, 824
  divine functions 976
  piety 987
  extreme-998
  lay the flattering-to
    one's soul
  relief 834
  hope 858
unctuous *oily* 355
  bland 894
  flattering 933
  hypocritical 988
unctuousness 355
unculled *unused* 678
  relinquished 782
unculpable 946
uncultivated
  ignorant 491
  fallow 674
  vulgarity 851
uncurbed 748
uncurl 246
uncustomary
  exceptional 83
  (*desuetude* 614)
uncut 50, 674
undamaged (648)
undamped 340
undated
  without date 115
  waving 248
undaunted 861
undazzled 498
undebauched
  honorable 939
  (*innocent* 946)
undecayed (648)
undeceive *inform* 527
  disclose 529
undeceived
  knowing 490
undecennary 98
undecided
  inquiring 461
  uncertain 475
  irresolute 605
  leave-609*a*
undecipherable 519
undecked 849
undecomposed 42
undefaced 845, 847
undefended 725
undefiled *honest* 939
  innocent 946
  chaste 960
undefinable
  uncertain 475
  unmeaning 517
  unintelligible 519
undefined
  invisible 447
  uncertain 475

  (*unintelligible* 519)
undeformed 845, 847
undemolished 50
undemonstrable 485
undemonstrated 475
undemonstrative
  826
undeniable 474, 478
undeplored 898
undepraved 939
undeprived 781
under *less* 34
  below 207
  subject to 749
  range-76
  -age 127
  -agent 758
  -breath 405
  -cover covered 223
  hidden 528
  safe 664
  -foot
  (*see below*)
  -full strength 651
  -lock and key 664
  -one's control 743
  -one's eyes 446
  -press of 744
  -protest dissent 489
  compulsion 744
  -restraint 751
  -seal 467
  -subjection 749
  -the circumstances 8
  -the head of 9
  -the mark 34
  -the sun 1
  -way 282
underbid 794
underbreath 405
underbred 851
underclothing 225
undercurrent
  cause 153
  stream 348, 349
  latent 526
  opposing 709
underdone 298
underestimation 483
underfed 640
underfoot 207
  tread-739
undergo 151
  -a change 144
  -pain 828
undergraduate 541
underground *low* 207
  deep 208
  latent 526
  hidden 528
undergrowth 367
underhand *latent* 526
  hidden 528
  -dealing 528
underhung 250
underlay 591

unobtained 777*a*
unobtrusive 881
unoccupied
  vacant 187
  unthinking 452
  doing nothing 681
  inactive 683
  leisured 685
  secluded 893
unoffended
  enduring 826
  humble 879
unofficial 964
unoften 137
unopened 261
unopposed 709
unordinary 20, 83
unorganized 358
  unprepared 674
  −matter 358
unornamental 846
unornamented
  −*style* 576
  simple 849
unorthodox 984
unostentatious 881
unowed 807
unowned 782
unpacific
  discordant 713
  warfare 722
unpacified 713
unpack *unfasten* 44
  take out 297
unpaid *debt* 806
  honorary 815
  −*worker*
  volunteer 602
unpalatable
  unsavory 395
  disagreeable 830
  (*dislike* 867)
unparagoned
  supreme 33
  best 648
  perfect 650
unparalleled
  unimitated 20
  unequaled 28
  supreme 33
  exceptional 83
  best 648
unpardonable
  inexcusable 938
  wicked 945
unparliamentary
language
  discourteous 895
  cursing 908
unpassable 261
unpassionate 826
unpatriotic 911
unpatterned 28
unpeaceful
  contention 720
  war 722

unpeered 28
unpeople
  emigration 297
  banishment 893
  (*displace* 185)
unperceived
  neglected 460
  unknown 491
  (*latent* 526)
unperformed 730
unperjured
  truthful 543
  honorable 939
unperplexed 498
unpersuadable
  obstinate 606
unpersuaded 616
unperturbed 826
unphilosophical 499
unpierced 261
unpin (44)
unpitied 932
unpitying
  pitiless 914*a*
  (*angry* 900)
  (*malevolent* 907)
unplaced 185
unplagued 831
unpleasant 830
unpleasing 830
unplumbed 104
unpoetical *prose* 598
  matter of fact 703
unpointed *blunt* 254
unpolished *rough* 256
  inelegant 579
  unprepared 674
  vulgar 851
  rude 895
unpolite 895
unpolluted *good* 648
  perfect 650
unpopular
  disagreeable 830
  dislike 867
unpopularity
  hatred 898
unportioned 804
unpossessed 777*a*
unpracticed (699)
unprecedented
  exceptional 83
  rare 137
unprejudiced 498,
748
unpremeditated
  impulsive 612
  undesigned 621
  unprepared 674
unprepared 674
unprepossessed 498
unprepossessing 846
unpresentable 851
unpretending 881
unpretentious 881
unprevented 748

unprincipled 945
unprivileged 925
unprized 483
unproclaimed 526
unproduced
  inexistent 2
unproductive
  useless 645
unproductiveness
169
unproficiency 699
unprofitable
  unproductive 169
  useless 645
  inexpedient 647
  bad 649
unprogressive 659
unprolific 169
unpromising 859
unprompted 612
unpronounced
  latent 526
unpropitious
  ill−timed 135
  opposed 708
  adverse 735
  hopeless 859
unproportioned
  (*disagreeing* 24)
unprosperous 735
unprotected 665
unproved 477
unprovided
  scanty 640
  unprepared 674
unprovoked (616)
unpublished 526
unpunctual
  tardy 133
  untimely 135
  irregular 139
unpunished 970
unpurchased 796
unpurified 653
unpurposed 621
unpursued 624
unqualified
  incomplete 52
  impotent 158
  certain 474
  unprepared 674
  inexpert 699
  unentitled 925
  −truth 494
unquelled 173
unquenchable
  strong 159
  desire 865
unquenched
  violence 173
  heat 382
unquestionable
  certain 474
unquestionably
  assent 488
unquestioned 474

agreed upon 488
unquiet *motion* 264
  agitation 315
  excitable 825
unravel *untie* 44
  arrange 60
  straighten 246
  evolve 313
  discover 480*a*
  interpret 522
  disembarrass 705
  (*solve* 462)
unreached 304
unread *ignorant* 491
unready 674
unreal *not existing* 2
  unsubstantial 4
  erroneous 495
  imaginary 515
unreasonable
  impossible 471
  illogical 477
  misjudging 481
  foolish 499
  capricious 608
  exorbitant 814
  unjust 923
  unreasoning 452
unreclaimed 951
unrecognizable 146
unreconciled 713
unrecorded 552
unrecounted 55
unrecumbent 212
unreduced 31
unrefined 851
unreflecting 458
unreformed 951
unrefreshed 688
unrefuted *proved* 478
  true 494
unregarded
  neglected 460
  unrespected 929
unregenerate 988
unregistered 552
unreined 748
unrelated 10
unrelenting
  pitiless 914*a*
  revengeful 919
  (*malevolent* 907)
unreliable
  uncertain 475
  vacillating 605
  insecure 665
unrelieved 835
unremarked 460
unremembered 506
unremitting
  continuous 69, 143
  continuing 110
  persevering 604*a*
  (*industrious* 682)
unremoved 184
unremunerated 808

unrenewed 141
unrepaid (806)
unrepealed 141
unrepeated *single* 87
  few 103
unrepentant 951
unrepining 831
unreplenished 640
unreported (526)
unrepressed 173
unreproached 946
unreproved 946
unrequited
  owing 806
  ingratitude 917
unresented
  forgiven 918
unresenting
  enduring 826
unreserved
  manifest 525
  veracious 543
  artless 703
unresisted 743
unresisting 725
unresolved 605
unrespected 929
unrespited 971
unrest *changeable* 149
  moving 264
unrestored
  fatigue 688
unrestrained
  capricious 608
  unencumbered 705
  free 748
unrestricted
  undiminished 31
  free 748
unretracted 535
unrevealed (528)
unrevenged 918
unreversed 143
unrevoked 143
unrewarded
  unpaid 806
  ingratitude 917
unrhymed 598
unriddle
  find out 480*a*
  disclose 529
  (*interpret* 522)
unrig 645
unrighteous 945
unrip 260
unripe *youth* 127
  sour 397
  unprepared 674
  −*fruit* 397
unrivaled
  unequaled 28
  supreme 33
  (*good* 648)
unrivet (44)
unrobe (226)
unroll *evolve* 313

display 525
(*unravel* 47)
(*straighten* 246)
unromantic 494
unroof (226)
unroot *extract* 301
(*destroy* 162)
unruffled *calm* 174
quiet 265
unaffected 823
placid 826
imperturbable 871
(*in order* 58)
unruly *violent* 173
obstinate 606
disobedient 742
unsaddle 756
unsafe 665
unsaid 526
unsalable *useless* 645
selling 796
cheap 815
unsaluted 929
unsanctified
impiety 988
irreligion 989
unsanctioned 925
unsated 865
unsatisfactory
inexpedient 647
bad 649
displeasing 830
discontent 832
unsatisfied
discontented 832
desirous 865
unsavoriness 395
unsavory *insipid* 391
not savory 395
inedible 867
unsay *recant* 607
(*negation* 536)
unscanned 460
unscathed 654
unscattered (72)
unscholarly 491
unschooled
ignorant 491
(*unskillful* 699)
unscientific
illogical 477
(*erroneous* 495)
unscoured 653
unscreened (665)
unscrew (44)
unscriptural 984
unscrupulous 940
unseal 529
unsearched 460
unseasonable
inappropriate 24
ill–timed 135
(*inexpedient* 647)
unseasoned
unaccustomed 614
unprepared 674

unseat *displace* 185
abrogate 756
unseconded
unassisted 706
unseemly
inexpedient 647
ugly 846
vulgar 851
undue 925
vicious 945
unseen *invisible* 447
neglected 460
latent 526
unsegmentic 357
unseldom 136
unselfconscious 852
unselfish 816, 942
unseparated 46
unserviceable 645
unservient 645
unsettle *derange* 61
unsettled *mutable* 149
displaced 185
uncertain 475
–*in one's mind* 503
unsevered 50
unsex 146
unshackle (*untie* 44)
(*liberate* 750)
unshackled (*free* 748)
unshaded
manifest 525
unshaken *strong* 159
(*resolute* 604)
–*belief* 484
unshapely 241, 846
unshapen
amorphous 241
(*ugly* 846)
unshared 777
unsheathe
(*uncover* 226)
–*the sword war* 722
unsheltered 665
unshielded 665
unshifting 143
unship 297
unshipment 185
unshocked 823
unshorn 50
unshortened 200
unshrinking
determined 604
courageous 861
unsifted 460
unsightly 846
unsinged 670
unskilled 699
unskillfulness 699
unslaked 865
unsleeping
persevering 604a
active 682
unsmooth 256
unsociable 893
unsocial 893

unsoiled 652
unsold 777
unsolder (*disjoin* 44)
(*incoherence* 47)
unsoldierlike 862
unsolicitous 866
unsolved 526
unsophisticated
simple 42
genuine 494
artless 703
(*good* 648)
unsorted 59
unsought *avoided* 623
unrequested 766
unsound *weak* 160
illogical 477
erroneous 495
deceptive 545
imperfect 651
speculative 665
(*unhealthy* 655)
–*mind* 503
unsown 674
unsparing
abundant 639
severe 739
liberal 816
with an–hand 818
unspeakable *great* 31
wonderful 870
unspecified 78
unspent 678
unspied 526
unspiritual 316
unspoiled *good* 648
unspoken (581)
unspotted *clean* 652
beautiful 845
innocent 946
unstable
changeable 149
inverted 218
vacillating 605
precarious 665
–*equilibrium* 149
unstaid 149
unstained *clean* 652
honorable 939
unstatesmanlike 699
unsteadfast 605
unsteady *mutable* 149
irresolute 605
in danger 665
(*fickle* 607)
unstinted 639
unstirred 823, 826
unstopped
continuing 143
open 260
unstored 640
unstrained
turbid 653
relaxed 687
–*meaning* 516
unstrengthened 160

unstruck 823
unstrung 160
unstudied 460
unsubject 748
unsubmissive 742
unsubstantial 4
weak 160
immaterial 317
rare 322
erroneous 495
imaginary 515
unsubstantiality 4
unsuccess 732
unsuccessful 732
unsuccessive 70
unsuitable
incongruous 24
inexpedient 647
–*time* 135
unsullied *clean* 652
honorable 939
(*guiltless* 946)
unsung 526
unsupplied 640
unsupported
weak 160
(*unassisted* 706)
–*by evidence* 468
unsuppressed 141
unsurmountable 471
unsurpassed 33
unsusceptible 823
unsuspected
belief 484
latent 526
unsuspecting
hopeful 858
unsuspicious
belief 484
artless 703
hope 858
unsustainable
erroneous 495
unsustained
error 495
(*weak* 160)
(*unassisted* 706)
unswayed (616)
unsweet 395, 414
unswept 653
unswerving
straight 246
direct 278
persevering 604a
unsymmetric
uncomformable 83
unsymmetrical
irregular 59
shapeless 241
distorted 243
unsympathetic 24
unsystematic 59, 139
untack (44)
untainted *pure* 652
healthy 654
honorable 939

untalked of 526
untamed *rude* 851
ferocious 907
untangled (58)
untarnished
honorable 939
(*innocent* 946)
untasted 391
untaught
ignorant 491
untrained 674
untaxed 815
unteach 538
unteachable
foolish 499
unskillful 699
untempted (616)
untenable
powerless 158
illogical 477
undefended 725
secluded 893
untenanted 187
unthanked 917
unthankful 917
unthankfulness 915
unthawed *solid* 321
cold 383
unthinkable 471
unthinking
unconsidered 452
involuntary 601
unthought of
unconsidered 452
neglected 460
unthreatened 664
unthrifty
unprepared 674
prodigal 818
unthrone 756
untidy *in disorder* 59
slovenly 653
untie *liberate* 750
(*loose* 44)
–*the knot* 705
until 106 (108)
–*now* 118
untilled 674
untimely 135
–*end* 360
untinged *simple* 42
(*uncolored* 429)
untired 689
untiring 604a
untitled 876
untold *countless* 105
uncertain 475
latent 526
secret 528
untouched
disused 678
insensible 823
untoward
ill–timed 135
bad 649
unprosperous 735

607

edge 231
limit 233
direction 278
vergent 67
verger 996
veridical 467, 543
 —*hallucination* 992*a*
veriest 31
verification *test* 463
 warrant 771
verificative 467
verify 463
 evidence 467
 demonstrate 478
 find out 480*a*
verily *truly* 494
 (*positively* 32)
verisimilitude 472
veritable 1, 494
verity 494
verjuice 397
vermeology 368
vermes 368
vermicelli 298
vermicular
 convoluted 248
 worm 366
vermiculation 221
vermiform 248, 249
vermifuge 662
vermilion 434
vermin *animal* 366
 unclean 653
 base 876
vernacular
 native 188
 internal 221
 language 560
 habitual 613
vernal *early* 123
 spring 125
vernier
 minuteness 193
 —*scale* 466
Vernunft 450
veronica 993
verruca 250
versatile
 changeable 149
 (*irresolute* 605)
 (*fickle* 607)
verse *division* 51
 poetry 597
versed in
 knowledge 490
 (*skill* 698)
versicolor 440
versify 597
version *special* 79
 change 140
 interpretation 522
Verstand 450
versus *towards* 278
 against 708
vert 435
vertebra 215, 222

vertebral 222, 235
 —*column* 222
vertebrate 368
vertebration 357
vertex 210
vertical 212, 246
 —*rays* 382
verticality 212
verticity 312
vertigo *rotation* 312
 delirium 503
verve *imagination* 515
 vigorous language
  574
 activity 682
 feeling 821
very 31—*best* 648
 —*image* 554
 —*many* 102
 —*minute* 113
 —*much* 31
 —*picture* 17
 —*small* 32
 —*thing* *identity* 13
 agreement 23
 exact 494
 —*true* *assent* 488
 —*well* *content* 831
vesicatory 662
vesicle *cell* 191
 covering 223
 globe 249
vesicular *cells* 191
 holes 260
vesper 126
vespers 126, 990
vespertine
 evening 126
vessel *receptacle* 191
 tube 260
 ship 273
vest *place* 184
 dress 225
 —*in* *belong to* 777
 give 784
vesta *match* 388
vestal 960—*virgin* 904
vested *fixed* 150
 legal 963
 —*in* *located* 184
 —*interest* *given* 780
 due 924
vestibule *entrance* 66
 room 191
 hearing 418
vestige 551
vestigial 193
vestment *dress* 225
 canonicals 999
vestry *council* 696
 churchdom 995
 church 1000
vesture 225
vesuvian *match* 388
vet *veterinarian* 370
veteran *old* 130

adept 700
 warrior 726
veterinarian 370
veterinary art 370
veto 761
vettura 272
vetturino 694
vetust 124
vex 830, 898
vexation
 pain 828, 830
 —*of spirit* 828
 discontent 832
vexatious 830
vexed question
 difficulty 704
 discord 713
vexillum 550
via *direction* 278
 way 627
viable 359
viaduct 627
viagraph 466
vial 191
 —*s of hate* 898
 —*s of wrath* 900
via lactea 318
viameter 200
viands 298
viaticum
 provision 637
 rite 998
viatometer 200
vibrate 314
 —*between two
  extremes* 149
vibratile 314
vibration 314, 408
vibratiuncle 314
vibrative 314
vibratory
 changeable 149
vibrograph 314
vibroscope 314
vicar *deputy* 759
 clergyman 996
 —*of Bray*
  changeableness 149
 tergiversation 607
 servility 886
vicarage 1000
vicarial 147
vicariate 995
vicarious
 substitute 147
vicarship 995
vice *pinion* 752
 deputy 759
 wickedness 945
vice—admiral 745
vice—chairman 759
Vice—Chancellor 967
 —'s *Court* 966
vicegerency 755
vicegerent 758, 759
vicenary 98

vice—president 694,
 759
vice—regal 759
viceroy *governor* 745
 deputy 759
vicesimal 98
vice versâ
 reciprocal 12
 contrary 14
 interchange 148
vicinage 197, 227
vicinal 197
vicinism 145
vicinity 197, 227
vicious 173, 945
 render—659
 —*reasoning* 477
vicissitude
 changeable 149
 (*change* 140)
victim *dupe* 547
 defeated 732
 sufferer 828
 culprit 975
victimize *kill* 361
 deceive 545
 injure 649
 baffle 731
victimized 828
victor 731
victoria *carriage* 272
Victoria Cross 551,
 722, 733
victory 731
victrola 417, 418
victual *provide* 637
victuals 298
videlicet
 specification 79
 namely 522
 (*example* 82)
viduation 905
viduity 905
vie *good* 648
 —*with* *contend* 720
 (*oppose* 708)
vielle 417
view *sight* 441
 appearance 448
 attend to 457
 opinion 484
 landscape painting
  556
 intention 520
 bring into—525
 come into—446
 commanding—441
 in—*visible* 446
 intended 420
 expected 507
 keep in—457
 on—448
 present to the—448
 —*as* 484
 —*halloo* 411
 —*in a new light* 658

 —s *tenet* 484
 with a—*to* 620
viewer 444
viewless 447
viewpoint 441, 453
vigesimal 98
vigil *care* 459
vigilance *care* 459
 wisdom 498
 activity 682
vigilant 864
vigils *worship* 990
vigneron 371
vignette
 engraving 558
 sketch 594
 embellishment 847
vigor *strength* 159
 energy 171
 style 574
 resolution 604
 health 654
 activity 682
viking 792
vile *valueless* 643
 hateful 649
 painful 830
 disgraceful 874
 plebeian 876
 dishonorable 940
 vicious 945
vilification 908
vilify *shame* 874
 censure 932
 detract 934
 (*disrespect* 929)
 (*contempt* 930)
vilipend
 disrespect 929
 censure 932
 detract 934
vilipendency 930
villa 189
village 189—*talk* 588
villager 188
villain *servant* 746
 serf 876
 rascal 949
villainous *evil* 649
 wicked 945
 —*saltpeter* 727
villainy 940
vellein (*see* villein)
villenage
 subjection 749
 tenure 777
villi 256
villous 256
vim 171, 682
vina 417
vinaceous 434
vinaigrette 400
vincible *impotent* 158
 (*weak* 160)
vincture 43
vinculum 45

vindicate
  evidence 467
  avenge 919
  justify 937
  –a right 924
vindication 937
vindicator
  revenge 919
vindictive
  irascible 901
  revengeful 919
vine 367
vinegar 397
  –aspect 846
vine–grower 371
vinegrub 659
vineyard *tillage* 371
  workshop 691
vingt et un 840
viniculturist 371
vintage
  agriculture 371
  store 636
vintner 797
viol 417
violaceous 437
violate *disobey* 742
  nonobservance 773
  undue 925
  dereliction 927
  ravish 961
  –a law 83
  –a usage 614
  –the law 964
violence 173
  arbitrary 964
  do–to *bad* 649
  nonobservance 773
  undue 925
violent 173
  excitable 825
  in a–degree 31
  lay–hands on 789
  –death *death* 360
  kill 361
violet 437
  modesty 881
violin 417
violinist 416
violoncello 417
violone 417
viper *snake* 366
  bane 663
  evildoer 913
  bad man 949
viperine 366
virago 901
virent 435
virescence 435
virgate 246
virgin *new* 123
  girl 129
  spinster 904
  good woman 948
  pure 960
  –soil *ignorance* 491

untilled 674
virginal 900
virginals 417
Virginia
  crooked as–fence
    243
  –reel 840
viridian 435
viridity 435
virile *adolescent* 131
  strong 159
  manly 373
virtu 847, 850
virtual *inexistent* 2
  unsubstantial 5
  –image 443
virtually 5
  (*truly* 494)
virtue *power* 157
  courage 861
  goodness 944
  purity 960
  by–of *power* 157
  instrumentality 631
  in–of *authority* 737
  make a–of necessity
  no choice 609a
  skill 698
  submit 725
  compromise 774
  bear 826
virtueless 945
virtuosity *taste* 850
virtuoso 415, 416,
  850
virtuous *virtue* 944
  purity 960
virulence *energy* 171
  noxiousness 649
  insalubrity 657
  discourtesy 895
  anger 900
  malevolence 907
virus *disease* 655
  poison 663
vis inertiae
  power 157
  inertness 172
  insensibility 823
visa 488
visage *front* 234
  appearance 448
vis-à-vis
  contrariety 14
  front 234
  opposite 237
  carriage 272
viscera 221
visceral 221, 329
viscid 327, 352
viscidity 327
viscount 875
viscountship 877
viscous 352
viscum 45
vise 327, 752, 781

Vishnu 979
visibility 446
visible 446
  (*intelligible* 518)
  become–448
  be–448
  darkness–421
vision *sight* 441
  phantasm 443
  dream 515
  specter 980a
  psychical research
    992a
  organ of–441
visionary *inexistent* 2
  unsubstantial 4
  impossible 471
  imaginary 515
  heterodox 984
  (*untrue* 495)
visionless 442
visit *arrival* 292
  social 892
  courtesy 894
  –behind the scenes
    461
  –upon 972
visitation *disease* 655
  adversity 735
  suffering 828
  (*evil* 619)
  –of the sick 998
  –s of Providence 976
visiting 892
  on–terms
  friendship 888
  sociality 892
  –card 550
visitor *immigrant* 294
  director 694
  friend 890
visor 530
vista *convergence* 260
  sight 441
  appearance 448
  expectation 507
  –of time 109
visual 441–organ 441
visualize 220
vitability 359
vital *life* 359
  important 642
  –air 359
  –force 359
  –part 3
  –principle 1
vitalic 359
vitality *stability* 150
  strength 159
  life 359
vitalize 359
vitals 221
vitiate *deteriorate* 659
vitiated *diseased* 655
viticulture 371
vitreform 425

vitreous *hard* 323
  transparent 425
vitrescent 323
vitrics 191
vitrify 323
vitrine 191
vituperate 932
vituperation 908
vituperator 936
viva! *glory* 873
  praise 931
vivace *music* 415
vivacious *active* 682
  sensitive 822
  cheerful 836
vivandière 797
vivarium 370
viva voce 582
vive *glory be to* 873
  on the qui–824
vivid *energetic* 171
  sensibility 375
  light 420
  color 428
  graphic 518
  (*powerful* 157)
  still–
  remembering 506
vivify *strength* 159
  life 359
vivisection *pain* 378
  cruelty 907
vixen *fox* 366
  female 374
  shrew 901
viz. (see videlicet)
vizier *director* 694
  deputy 759
vizor *mask* 530
  shield 717
vlei 345
vocable 562
vocabulary 562
vocal *music* 415
  voice 580
  –score 415
vocalist 416
vocalize 562, 580
vocation *business* 625
  (*duty* 926)
vocational 625
  –therapy 662
  –training 537
vociferation *loud* 404
  cry 411
  voice 580
vogue *custom* 613
  fashion 852
  fame 873
voice *sound* 402
  cry 411
  judgment 480
  promulgate 531
  affirmation 535
  express 566
  human–580

choice 609
  (*belief* 484)
  give one's–for 488
  make one's–heard
    175
  raise one's
  –shout 411
  speak 582
  still small–
  faint sound 405
  conscience 926
  want of–581
  warning–668
  –against *dissent* 489
  oppose 708
  –of the charmer 933
  –of the tempter 615
voiceless 561, 581
  –woe 837
void *unsubstantial* 4
  absence 187
  emit 297
  abyss 667
  (*inexistence* 2)
  null and–964
  –of foundation 546
  –of reason 450a
  –of suspicion 484
voidance 297
voile 635
voiturier 268
voivode 745
volant 267
Volapük 560, 563
volatile *transient* 111
  light 320
  gaseous 334
  vaporizable 336
  assent 488
  irresolute 605
  capricious 608
  –alkali 334
vol-au-vent 298
volcanic *violent* 173
  heat 382
  burnt 388
  excitable 825
volcanism 490c
volcano *violence* 173
  furnace 386
  pitfall 667
  on a–*danger* 665
volitation 267
volitient 600
volksraad 696
volley *collection* 72
  violence 173
  report 406
  attack 716
  (*impulse* 276)
volplane 267
volplaning 267
Volstead Act 761
volt 490d
voltaic 157
  –electricity 157

−and found wanting
  inferior 34
  disapproved 932
weighing machine
  466
weight *influence* 175
  contents 190
  gravity 319
  affirmation 535
  vigor 574
  importance 642
  attach−to 484
  carry−175
  drag−706
  have−*evidence* 467
  throw one's−into
    the scale 175
weightless 320
weights and
  measures 466
weighty (*see* weight)
  evidence 467
weir *inclosure* 232
  conduit 350
  hindrance 706
weird *spectral* 980a
  mystic 992
  spell 993
  −sisters 994
Weismannism 357
welcome *arrival* 292
  grateful 829
  friendly 888
  sociality 892
  reception 894
weld *join* 43
  cohere 46
welfare 734
  −work 602
  −worker 602
welkin *worlds* 318
  air 338
  make the−ring **411**
well *much* 31
  origin 153
  deep 208
  exude 295
  pool 343
  flow 348
  assent 488
  good 618
  store 636
  healthy 654
  spa 662
  act−944
  all's−664
  drop a bucket into
    an empty−645
  get−660
  go on−734
  let−alone
  quiescence 265
  inaction 681
  think−of 931
  treat−906
  turn out−731

−and good *assent* 488
  consent 762
  content 831
  −done! 931
  −enough *not much* 32
  imperfect 651
  −out 295
  −over 641
  −up in 698
  −with 888
  work−731
welladay *lament* 839
  wonder 870
well−advised 498
well−affected 888
well−behaved
  genteel 852
  courteous 894
well−being
  prosperous 734
  happy 827
well−beloved 897
well−born 875
well−bred *genteel* 852
  (*courteous* 894)
well−composed 845
well−defined
  visible 446
  exact 494
  predetermined 611
  (*plan* 626)
well−devised 611
well−disposed 602,
  707
well−doing 944
well−done *cooked* 298
well−favored 845
well−formed 240,
  845
well−fed 192
well−founded
  existent 1
  probable 472
  certain 474
  −belief 484
  true 494
well−grounded
  existent 1
  informed 490
  −hope 858
well−grouped 845
wellhead 153
well−informed 490
Wellington boots
  225
well−intentioned
  benevolent 906
  virtuous 944
well−knit *strong* 159
well−known
  knowledge 490
  habitual 613
well−laid 611
well−made *form* 240
  beauty 845
well−mannered 894

well−marked 446
well−meaning 906
well−meant 906
well−met 894
well−natured 906
well−nigh *almost* 32
  near 197
well−off
  prosperous 734
  rich 803
well−proportioned
  240, 845
well−provided 639
well−regulated
  order 58
  conformity 82
  circumspect 864
well−set 242
well−spent
  successful 731
  virtuous 944
wellspring 153, 636
well−timed 134
well−to−do
  prosperous 734
  rich 803
well−turned periods
  578
well−weighed 611
wellwisher 890, 906,
  914
Welsh 188−rabbit 298
welsher *swindler* 792
  nonpayment 808
welt 321
welter *plunge* 310
  roll 311
  −in one's blood 361
wem 848
wen 250, 848
wench *girl* 129
  woman 374
  peasant 876
  impure 962
wenching 961
wend 266
were, as you−660
wergild 974
werewolf 980
werowance 745
Wesleyan 984
west *lateral* 236
  direction 278
westing 196
Westminster
  superior courts of−
  966
westward 236
wet *water* 337, 348
  moist 339
  just enough to−
    one's feet 209
  −blanket *dissuade* 616
  hindrance 706
  sadden 837
  weary 841

  dull 843
  −one's whistle
  drink 298
  tipple 959
wether 366
whack 276
whacking
  large 31, 192
whale *large* 192
  mammal 366
  sprat to catch a−
    699
  tub to a−
  deception 545
  excuse 617
whalebone 325
whaler 273
whap 276
wharf *houses* 189
  refuge 666
  workshop 691
  mart 799
wharfage 812
wharf boat 273
what *inquiry* 461
  wonder 870
  and−not 81
  know−'s what
  discriminate 465
  intelligent 498
  skill 698
  −d'ye call 'em 563
  −in the world
  singular 83
  wonderful 870
  −is the reason? 461
  −next 455
  −on earth *singular* 83
  −'s his name 563
  −signifies 643
whatever 78
  −may happen 474
wheal 250
wheat 367
  winnow the chaff
    from the−609
Wheat Pit *mart* 799
wheedle *coax* 615
  endearment 902
  flatter 933
wheedler 615
wheel *circle* 247
  convexity 250
  bicycle 272
  deviate 279
  turn back 283
  circuition 311
  rotation 312
  rack 975
  break on the−
  pain 478
  punish 972
  get the−out of the
    rut 672
  scotch the−706
  −about 279

  −and axle 633
  −guard 666
  −of Fortune
  changeable 149
  chance 156
  rotation 312
  necessity 601
  −round *inversion* 218
  tergiversation 607
  −s within wheels
  entangled 59
  machinery 633
wheelbarrow 272
wheel chair 272
wheelman 268, 269
wheelwork 633
wheelwright 690
wheeze *blow* 349
  hiss 409
wheezy 409
whelk 250, 848
whelm 641
whelp *infant* 129
  production 161
  dog 366
  rogue 949
when *inquiry* 461
  (*different time* 119)
  in the time−106
whence
  attribution 155
  departure 293
  inquiry 461
  reasoning 476
where *presence* 186
  inquiry 461
  −am I? 870
whereabouts
  place 182
  situation 183
  near 197
whereas *relating to* 9
  because 476
whereby 631
wherefore
  attribution 155
  inquiry 461
  reasoning 476
  judgment 480
  motive 615
wherein 221
whereness 186
whereupon *time* 106
  different time 119
  after 121
wherever 180, 182
wherewith *means* 632
  money 800
wherewithal 639
wherret 830
wherry 273
whet *sharpen* 253
  meal 298
  incite 615
  excite 824
  take a−*tipple* 959